THE
ALL ENGLAND
LAW REPORTS

Incorporating the

**LAW TIMES
REPORTS**

**LAW JOURNAL
REPORTS**

1966
VOLUME 2

Consulting Editor for Taxation Cases
CYRIL KING, Q.C.
Bencher of the Middle Temple

Editor
J. T. EDGERLEY
of the Inner Temple and Lincoln's Inn, Barrister-at-Law

LONDON
BUTTERWORTHS

ENGLAND: BUTTERWORTH & CO. (PUBLISHERS) LTD.
                    LONDON: 88 Kingsway, W.C.2

AUSTRALIA: BUTTERWORTH & CO. (AUSTRALIA) LTD.
                    SYDNEY: 20 Loftus Street
                    MELBOURNE: 473 Bourke Street
                    BRISBANE: 240 Queen Street

CANADA: BUTTERWORTH & CO. (CANADA) LTD.
                    TORONTO: 1367 Danforth Avenue, 6

NEW ZEALAND: BUTTERWORTH & CO. (NEW ZEALAND) LTD.
                    WELLINGTON: 49/51 Ballance Street
                    AUCKLAND: 35 High Street

SOUTH AFRICA: BUTTERWORTH & CO. (SOUTH AFRICA) LTD.
                    DURBAN: 33/35 Beach Grove

U.S.A.:   BUTTERWORTH INC.
                    WASHINGTON, D.C.: 7300 Pearl Street, 20014.

Printed in Great Britain by R. J. Acford, Ltd., Industrial Estate, Chichester, Sussex.

HOUSE OF LORDS

The Lord High Chancellor of Great Britain: The Rt. Hon. Lord Gardiner

Lords of Appeal in Ordinary

The Rt. Hon. Lord Reid
The Rt. Hon. Lord Morris of Borth-y-Gest
The Rt. Hon. Lord Hodson
The Rt. Hon. Lord Guest

The Rt. Hon. Lord Pearce
The Rt. Hon. Lord Upjohn
The Rt. Hon. Lord Donovan
The Rt. Hon. Lord Wilberforce
The Rt. Hon. Lord Pearson

COURT OF APPEAL

The Lord High Chancellor of Great Britain

Lord Chief Justice of England: The Rt. Hon. Lord Parker

Master of the Rolls: The Rt. Hon. Lord Denning

President of the Probate, Divorce and Admiralty Division:
The Rt. Hon. Sir Jocelyn Simon

The Rt. Hon. Lord Justice Sellers
The Rt. Hon. Lord Justice Willmer
The Rt. Hon. Lord Justice Harman
The Rt. Hon. Lord Justice Danckwerts

The Rt. Hon. Lord Justice Davies
The Rt. Hon. Lord Justice Diplock
The Rt. Hon. Lord Justice Russell
The Rt. Hon. Lord Justice Salmon

The Rt. Hon. Lord Justice Winn

CHANCERY DIVISION

The Lord High Chancellor of Great Britain

The Hon. Mr. Justice Lloyd-Jacob
The Hon. Mr. Justice Cross
The Hon. Mr. Justice Buckley
The Hon. Mr. Justice Pennycuick

The Hon. Mr. Justice Plowman
The Hon. Mr. Justice Ungoed-Thomas
The Hon. Mr. Justice Stamp
The Hon. Mr. Justice Goff

QUEEN'S BENCH DIVISION

Lord Chief Justice of England: The Rt. Hon. Lord Parker

The Hon. Mr. Justice Stable
The Hon. Mr. Justice McNair
  (retired July 29, 1966)
The Hon. Mr. Justice Havers
The Hon. Mr. Justice Glyn-Jones
The Hon. Mr. Justice Sachs
The Hon. Mr. Justice Ashworth
The Hon. Mr. Justice Hinchcliffe
The Hon. Mr. Justice Paull
The Hon. Mr. Justice Melford Stevenson
The Hon. Mr. Justice Edmund Davies
The Hon. Mr. Justice Thesiger
The Hon. Mr. Justice Marshall
  (died June 20, 1966)
The Hon. Mr. Justice Phillimore
The Hon. Mr. Justice Fenton Atkinson
The Hon. Mr. Justice Nield
The Hon. Mr. Justice Howard
The Hon. Mr. Justice Veale

The Hon. Mr. Justice Megaw
The Hon. Mr. Justice Lawton
The Hon. Mr. Justice Widgery
The Hon. Mr. Justice MacKenna
The Hon. Mr. Justice Mocatta
The Hon. Mr. Justice Thompson
The Hon. Mr. Justice Brabin
The Hon. Mr. Justice Roskill
The Hon. Mr. Justice Lyell
The Hon. Mr. Justice John Stephenson
The Hon. Mr. Justice Milmo
The Hon. Mr. Justice Cantley
The Hon. Mr. Justice Browne
The Hon. Mr. Justice Waller
The Hon. Mr. Justice Lawrence
The Hon. Mr. Justice James
The Hon. Mr. Justice Blain
The Hon. Mr. Justice Cusack
The Hon. Mr. Justice Chapman
The Hon. Mr. Justice Willis

The Hon. Mr. Justice Swanwick (appointed July 4, 1966)

PROBATE, DIVORCE AND ADMIRALTY DIVISION

President: The Rt. Hon. Sir Jocelyn Simon

The Hon. Mr. Justice Karminski
The Hon. Mr. Justice Wrangham
The Hon. Mr. Justice Hewson
The Hon. Mr. Justice Lloyd-Jones
The Hon. Mr. Justice Cairns
The Hon. Mr. Justice Baker
The Hon. Mr. Justice Ormrod
The Hon. Mr. Justice Rees

The Hon. Mr. Justice Payne
The Hon. Mr. Justice Faulks
The Hon. Mr. Justice Stirling
The Hon. Mr. Justice Cumming-Bruce
The Hon. Mr. Justice Latey
The Hon. Mr. Justice Park
The Hon. Mrs. Justice Lane
The Hon. Mr. Justice Orr

REPORTERS

HOUSE OF LORDS	WENDY SHOCKETT KATHLEEN O'BRIEN	} Barristers-at-Law
PRIVY COUNCIL	KATHLEEN O'BRIEN	Barrister-at-Law
COURT OF APPEAL, No. 1	F. GUTTMAN, ESQ.	Barrister-at-Law
COURT OF APPEAL, No. 2	HENRY SUMMERFIELD, ESQ.	Barrister-at-Law
COURT OF APPEAL, No. 3	F. A. AMIES, ESQ.	Barrister-at-Law
COURT OF APPEAL, No. 4	HENRY SUMMERFIELD, ESQ.	Barrister-at-Law
COURT OF CRIMINAL APPEAL	N. P. METCALFE, ESQ.	Barrister-at-Law
COURTS-MARTIAL APPEALS	N. P. METCALFE, ESQ.	Barrister-at-Law
CHANCERY DIVISION	JENIFER SANDELL JACQUELINE METCALFE	} Barristers-at-Law
QUEEN'S BENCH DIVISION and COURTS OF ASSIZE	M. DENISE CHORLTON MARY COLTON K. B. EDWARDS, ESQ. T. M. EVANS, ESQ. S. A. HATTEEA, ESQ. D. M. HUGHES, ESQ. LAURENCE H. KINGSLEY, ESQ. GWYNEDD LEWIS DEIRDRE McKINNEY K. DIANA PHILLIPS KAUSHALYA PURIE O. K. SAMPSON, ESQ. G. M. SMAILES, ESQ.	} Barristers-at-Law
RATING CASES	F. A. AMIES, ESQ.	Barrister-at-Law
REVENUE CASES	F. A. AMIES, ESQ.	Barrister-at-Law
PROBATE AND DIVORCE	ALICE BLOOMFIELD	Barrister-at-Law
ADMIRALTY	N. P. METCALFE, ESQ.	Barrister-at-Law
RESTRICTIVE PRACTICES COURT	MARY COLTON	Barrister-at-Law

CITATION

These reports are cited thus:

[1966] 2 All E.R.

REFERENCES

These reports contain references, which follow after the headnotes, to the following major works of legal reference described in the manner indicated below—

HALSBURY'S LAWS OF ENGLAND, SIMONDS EDITION

The reference 2 HALSBURY'S LAWS (3rd Edn.) 20, para. 48, refers to paragraph 48 on page 20 of Volume 2 of the third edition of Halsbury's Laws of England, of which Viscount Simonds is Editor-in-Chief.

HALSBURY'S STATUTES OF ENGLAND, SECOND EDITION

The reference 26 HALSBURY'S STATUTES (2nd Edn.) 138, refers to page 138 of Volume 26 of the second edition of Halsbury's Statutes.

ENGLISH AND EMPIRE DIGEST

The reference 41 DIGEST 290, *1492*, refers to case No. 1492 on page 290 of Volume 41 of the Digest.

There are three cumulative supplements to the Digest, described as Digest Supp., 2nd Digest Supp. and 3rd Digest Supp.; of these the first two include cases up to December 31, 1939, and December 31, 1951, respectively.

The reference 31 DIGEST (Repl.) 244, *3794*, refers to case No. 3794 on page 244 of Digest Replacement Volume 31.

The reference DIGEST (Cont. Vol. A) 287, *2666a*, refers to case No. 2666a on page 287 of Digest Continuation Volume A.

HALSBURY'S STATUTORY INSTRUMENTS

The reference 12 HALSBURY'S STATUTORY INSTRUMENTS 124, refers to page 124 of Volume 12 of Halsbury's Statutory Instruments, first edition.

A reference to a volume as " 1st Re-issue " refers to the first re-issue of the appropriate volume of Halsbury's Statutory Instruments.

ENCYCLOPAEDIA OF FORMS AND PRECEDENTS, THIRD EDITION

The reference 15 ENCY. FORMS & PRECEDENTS (3rd Edn.) 938, Form 231, refers to Form 231 on page 938 of Volume 15 of the third edition of the Encyclopaedia of Forms and Precedents.

CASES REPORTED

IN VOLUME 2

INDEX

CASES NOTED

STATUTES, ETC., NOTED

COMMONWEALTH AND DEPENDENCIES

RULES

REGULATIONS

ORDERS

MISCELLANEOUS

WORDS AND PHRASES

CORRIGENDA

[1966] 2 All E.R.

p. 26.   R. v. HERRON.   Counsel for the Crown: read " James Harper " instead of " Norman Harper ".

p. 453.   R. v. AITKEN.   Solicitors for the appellant: substitute " Baldwin, Mellor & Co. for Abbott, Baldwin & Co.

p. 542.   CARL-ZEISS-STIFTUNG v. RAYNER AND KEELER, LTD. (No. 2).   Counsel for the respondents: read " Mark Littman, Q.C., Michael Kerr, Q.C., and T. M. Shelford " instead of as printed.

p. 577.   CARL-ZEISS-STIFTUNG v. RAYNER AND KEELER, LTD. (No. 2).   Line H.5 : for " validity " read " invalidity ".

p. 672.   HALE v. VICTORIA PLUMBING CO., LTD. AND EN-TOUT-CAS CO., LTD.   Line B.2: for " judgment creditor had " read " judgment debtor had ".

THE
ALL ENGLAND
LAW REPORTS

INCORPORATING THE

LAW TIMES REPORTS

AND THE

LAW JOURNAL REPORTS

HANCOCK AND OTHERS v. B. W. BRAZIER (ANERLEY), LTD.

[QUEEN'S BENCH DIVISION (Diplock, L.J., sitting as an additional judge), January 31, February 1, 2, 1966.]

Sale of Land—Warranty—House—Sale by builder of house in course of erection—
D *Express term for completing house in proper manner—Whether warranty of fitness of materials should also be implied—Whether defective work done before contract of sale was within clause for properly completing house—Defects clause not taking away rights under warranty clause.*

A builder sold a house, which he was then erecting, to a purchaser under a contract which provided by cl. 9 that the builder would " prior to com-
E pletion . . . in a proper and workmanlike manner erect build and complete . . . a dwelling-house in accordance with the plan and specification ". The plan showed the floors of the ground floor rooms as " four inch site concrete on hardcore ". The contract further provided, by cl. 11, that " if the purchaser shall discover any structural defects in the said house and works within six months from the date of completion and shall notify the [builder]
F thereof in writing the [builder] shall forthwith make good such structural defects without expense to the purchaser ". The sale was, by cl. 12, made " subject to . . . the National Conditions of Sale (16th Edn.) so far as the same are applicable to a sale by private treaty and are not inconsistent with the aforesaid conditions ". By condition 12 (3) of the National Conditions " the purchaser shall be deemed to buy with full notice in all respects of the
G actual state and condition of the property and shall take the property as it is ".

Before the contract was made the builder had already completed laying the foundations and the ground floors, and had used as the hardcore, underneath the four inches of concrete, material which contained sodium sulphate, and so was wholly unsuitable for use as hardcore beneath concrete. It would
H not have been apparent to the builder, on reasonable examination, that this material was unsuitable for this use, nor was the danger of sodium sulphate in the hardcore generally recognised at the time, so that the builder was not negligent in failing to appreciate either the presence or the danger of the sodium sulphate. More than two years after the contract had been completed by registered transfer and the purchaser had moved in, the sodium sulphate
I caused the floors and walls to crack, causing substantial damage to the house. In an action by the purchaser for damages for breach by the builder of his obligation under cl. 9 of the contract to build " in a proper and workmanlike manner . . . in accordance with the plan and specification ", the builder advanced the following contentions, of which (d) was the principal contention—(a) that the contract had merged in the transfer and so the purchaser could no longer rely on cl. 9; (b) that cl. 9 did not apply to the work which had already been done before the contract was made; (c) that by virtue of National Condition 12 (3) the purchaser was deemed to buy with full

knowledge of the defect, because it already existed at the date of the contract;   **A**
(d) that the only obligation under cl. 9 with respect to the selection of the
hardcore was that the builder should use due skill, care and judgment,
which he had, and (e) that after completion the purchaser could no longer
rely on cl. 9, because his rights were limited to those given him by cl. 11.

Held: the purchaser was entitled to damages for breach by the builder
of implied warranty under cl. 9 because—   **B**

(i) as the contract contained no definite specification of the hardcore
to be used, it was open to the court to imply and the court would imply
in cl. 9 a contractual warranty by the builder that the hardcore put under
the site concrete of the floors should be fit, proper and suitable, for that
purpose; and because, if such a warranty were implied, there was admittedly
a breach of it (see p. 8, letter H, post).   **C**

Principle stated by PARKER, L.J., in *Lynch* v. *Thorne* ([1956] 1 All E.R.
at p. 750) applied.

(ii) cl. 11 of the contract did not take away on completion the rights given
to the purchaser by cl. 9, for cl. 11 was limited to structural defects while
cl. 9, as construed at (i) above, required the house to be completed with
suitable materials in accordance with the plan and specification (see p. 9,   **D**
letter A, post).

Kent v. *Saltdean Estates Co., Ltd.* ((1964), 114 L.Jo. 555) and *Marsden
Urban District Council* v. *Sharp* ((1931), 48 T.L.R. 23) explained and
distinguished.

(iii) moreover, (a) the contract to build had not merged in the transfer   **E**
(see p. 6, letter C, post).

Lawrence v. *Cassell* ([1930] All E.R. Rep. 733) followed.

(b) the fact that the hardcore and concrete floor had been laid before
the date of the contract did not render cl. 9 of the contract inapplicable,
for an undertaking to build erect and complete the house in a proper and
workmanlike manner involved curing defects which existed before the con-   **F**
tract was entered into (see p. 6, letters D and H, post).

Dicta of SCRUTTON, L.J., in *Lawrence* v. *Cassell* ([1930] All E.R. Rep.
at p. 735) and of ROMER, L.J., in *Perry* v. *Sharon Development Co., Ltd.*
([1937] 4 All E.R. at p. 394) followed.

(c) condition 12 (3) of the National Conditions of Sale was, on this matter,
inconsistent with cl. 9 of the contract, and so, by virtue of cl. 12 of the   **G**
contract, was not incorporated in the contract (see p. 7, letter C, post).

Jennings v. *Tavener* ([1955] 2 All E.R. 769) followed.

[As to the implied warranty given by a builder who sells a house in course of
erection, see 34 HALSBURY'S LAWS (3rd Edn.) 213, 214, para. 356, text and notes
(b), (c); as to the right of a purchaser to recover damages after conveyance
in respect of breach of a collateral stipulation, see 34 HALSBURY'S LAWS (3rd   **H**
Edn.) 379, para. 662, text and note (m); and for cases on remedies after completion, see 40 DIGEST (Repl.) 379-387, *3044-3059.*]

Cases referred to:
    Cammell Laird & Co., Ltd. v. *Manganese Bronze and Brass Co.*, [1934] All E.R.
        Rep. 1; [1934] A.C. 402; 103 L.J.K.B. 289; 151 L.T. 142; 39 Digest   **I**
        (Repl.) 544, *784.*
    Jennings v. *Tavener*, [1955] 2 All E.R. 769; [1955] 1 W.L.R. 932; 7 Digest
        (Repl.) 347, *43.*
    Kent v. *Saltdean Estates Co., Ltd.* (1964), 114 L.Jo. 555.
    Lawrence v. *Cassell*, [1930] All E.R. Rep. 733; [1930] 2 K.B. 83; 99 L.J.K.B.
        525; 143 L.T. 291; 40 Digest (Repl.) 380, *3052.*
    Lynch v. *Thorne*, [1956] 1 All E.R. 744; [1956] 1 W.L.R. 303; 7 Digest (Repl.)
        347, *44.*

A *Marsden Urban District Council* v. *Sharp*, (1930), 47 T.L.R. 549; *on appeal*,
      C.A., (1931), 48 T.L.R. 23; 7 Digest (Repl.) 402, *254*.
   Miller v. *Cannon Hill Estates, Ltd.*, [1931] All E.R. Rep. 93; [1931] 2 K.B. 113;
      100 L.J.K.B. 740; 144 L.T. 567; 7 Digest (Repl.) 346, *39*.
   Perry v. *Sharon Development Co., Ltd.*, [1937] 4 All E.R. 390; 7 Digest (Repl.)
      346, *40*.

B **Action.**

   Lawrence Patrick Hancock, Leonard George Hone and his wife Grace Joan
Hone, and Michael George Lovelace Sewell, the purchasers of three houses in
course of erection from B. W. Brazier (Anerley), Ltd., the builders, brought this
action against the builders for damages for breach of the contracts to complete
and sell the houses, and for negligence in building the houses. The facts are
C set out in the judgment.

   The cases noted below* were cited during the argument in addition to those
referred to in the judgment.

   E. H. Laughton-Scott for the purchasers.
   Ian Percival, Q.C., and *J. G. K. Sheldon* for the builders.

D   **DIPLOCK, L.J.:** This is an action brought by three purchasers of houses
from the defendants, who are a firm of builders. In 1959 the defendant builders
were developing an estate known as Haven Close Estate in Swanley, which
consisted of some forty houses or so, and in the spring of that year each of the
plaintiff purchasers respectively entered into a contract with the builders to
buy particular houses. I shall have to look at the terms of that contract in
E detail a little later.

   The purchaser, Mr. Hancock, entered into his agreement on Jan. 6, 1959, in
respect of a house, No. 74, Haven Close. He took a conveyance of it, pursuant
to that contract, on May 1, 1959. The purchasers Mr. and Mrs. Hone entered
into a similar agreement on Mar. 26, 1959, in respect of No. 52, Haven Close
and took their conveyance on June 22, 1959. The purchaser Mr. Sewell entered
F into an agreement on Apr. 14, 1959, in respect of No. 60, Haven Close and took
the transfer on the same day as Mr. and Mrs. Hone, June 22, 1959. The contracts
are in similar terms, so were the conveyances, and I will, for convenience, deal
with the contract entered into by the first-named plaintiff, Mr. Hancock.

   What happened was this. The houses at the time at which these agreements
were entered into, had all been started and the building work had reached some
G stage which varied from house to house, but in each of them the work of the
foundations and of laying the floors was complete at the time that the
purchasers entered into their respective contracts. I shall have to look at the
specifications a little later but, for the purpose of recounting the facts, it is
sufficient if I say that the floors of the rooms on the ground floor of the houses
were of four inch concrete laid on hardcore. What has now emerged from the
H evidence, and is common ground, is that when the hardcore was put in beneath
the floors of the purchasers' three houses it contained some material, sodium
sulphate, which had two qualities which made it wholly unsuitable for use for
that purpose. One of the qualities was that, when exposed to moisture, the
sodium sulphate took up the moisture, the water, and became, if it had originally
been anhydrous, a hydrated sulphate, or, if it were already hydrated, a further
I hydrated sulphate, and in doing so it expanded, and expanded with sufficient
force to break through the concrete itself or to cause it to crack. The other
quality which it had which made it unsuitable for the use to which it was put
was that, being soluble, if it were dissolved by the moisture, the sodium sulphate,
in solution, entered into a chemical reaction with the ordinary constituents of

---

   * *Leggott* v. *Barrett,* [1874-80] All E.R. Rep. 567; (1880), 15 Ch.D. 306; *Joliffe* v.
Baker, (1883), 11 Q.B.D. 255; *Palmer* v. *Johnson,* [1881-85] All E.R. Rep. 719; (1884), 13
Q.B.D. 351; *Cunliffe* v. *Hampton Wick Local Board,* (1893), 9 T.L.R. 378; *Greswolde-
Williams* v. *Barneby,* (1900), 83 L.T. 708.

concrete which caused the concrete itself to expand internally and crack, and **A**
ultimately to disintegrate. That is a process which, on the evidence, may take
considerable time, because it depends on the temperature and on the amount of
moisture which gets to the sodium sulphate; and in the case of each of the
purchasers the deleterious effects of the sodium sulphate beneath their floors did
not manifest themselves until some time—two years at the earliest, and generally
three or four years—after the houses were completed and the purchasers had **B**
taken possession of them.

Although it was originally disputed that the cause of the damage was sodium
sulphate in the hardcore, this was common ground by the time the matter came
before this court. I have not gone into the details of the damage caused because
that is a matter which, if I find for the purchasers, will have to be referred to some
other tribunal to determine the details. Suffice it to say that the damage was **C**
substantial. The floors cracked, the walls cracked, and in the case of one house
which was built on a slope, the evidence was that there was serious danger of
collapse of the house. In the case of the other houses the danger was less serious,
but the details of the damage are not for me.

A good deal of time has been spent in this court seeing to what extent it
would have been possible to identify this deleterious material in the hardcore **D**
at the time it was delivered. I do not propose to go into that evidence in detail.
It is sufficient for me to say that I am not satisfied, on the evidence, that this
material, at the time it was delivered, was recognisably unsuitable for the purpose,
and by " recognisably " I mean I am not satisfied that it would have been
apparent on visual examination. I should also add that the evidence satisfies
me that although it was known in 1959 that soluble sulphates were capable of **E**
attacking hardcore, the danger was not one which was generally recognised as
likely to arise in the ordinary course of building a house and acquiring hardcore
for it. If, therefore, this case depended on a plea of negligence, which is made
in the statement of claim in para. 5, I should myself have held that the purchasers
had not succeeded in establishing common law negligence on the part of the
builders. What I think is quite apparent now is that the source of the hardcore **F**
must have been some demolished factory in which sodium sulphate was produced,
probably as a byproduct in an industrial process; but I cannot say, on the
evidence before me, that the builders showed lack of reasonable care in failing
to appreciate that or to appreciate the presence of this exceedingly dangerous
substance, as it has turned out, in the hardcore used under the purchasers'
houses. **G**

The essence of the purchasers' claim, however, is not based on tort but on
contract, and on a breach of what they allege to be a term, it matters not whether
you call it an express term or an implied term, of the contract entered into
between them and the builders. It is therefore necessary that I should now
turn to the contract, and I take the contract entered into by the purchaser
Mr. Hancock on Jan. 6, 1959. I do not think that I need read many of the **H**
clauses in it. Clause 1 begins:

" The vendor sells and the purchaser buys the freehold land more particularly described in the schedule hereto at the price of £2,750 ",

and then goes on to deal with the deposit. Clauses 2, 3 and 4 deal with the title
to be made and the nature of the conveyance, which was to be a registered
transfer. Clause 5 deals with the date of completion. Clause 6 provides for **I**
vacant possession of the property to be given on completion. Clause 7 provides
for a covenant by the purchaser, to be inserted in the transfer, to maintain the
boundary walls; and cl. 8 excludes the grant of any right of light which might
otherwise have been an automatic result of the transfer. Clause 9 is the vital
clause on which this claim is based. It reads as follows:

" The vendor will prior to completion at its own cost and charge and in a
proper and workmanlike manner erect build and complete on the above

A freehold land a messuage or dwellinghouse in accordance with the plan and specification supplied to the purchaser subject only to such variations as may be ordered by the purchaser."

The house was to be built in accordance with the plan and specification supplied to the purchaser. The specification contains no express provision as to what is to go under the site concrete on the floors. The plan, however, fills that lacuna
B by showing on it, under the four inch site concrete, the following rubric: "4″ site conc. on hardcore ". The plan and specification therefore require that the builders shall put under the concrete floor the material " hardcore ".

I turn back to the terms of the contract. Clause 10 deals with a covenant by the vendor to make up the road and maintain it until taken over by the local authority. Clause 11 and cl. 12 are as follows:
C
" 11. If the purchaser shall discover any structural defects in the said house and works within six months from the date of completion and shall notify the vendor thereof in writing the vendor shall forthwith make good such structural defects without expense to the purchaser.

" 12. The property is sold subject to the aforesaid conditions and to the
D conditions known as the National Conditions of Sale (16th Edn.) so far as the same are applicable to a sale by private treaty and are not inconsistent with the aforesaid conditions."

That is the contract and, in particular, cl. 9 thereof, on which the purchasers bring their action.

Before I come to the points of law in this case I should also refer to the form
E of the transfer, because part of the defence, with which I shall have to deal, is founded on this document. The transfer is an ordinary transfer of registered land, and I will read that little bit of it on which counsel for the builders particularly relied. It provides:

" We [and it sets out the name of the builders] as beneficial owners hereby transfer to [the purchaser] the land more particularly described in the
F Schedule hereto and shown on the plan bound up within being Plot 19 The Grove Estate and known as 74, Haven Close, Swanley, and being part of the land comprised in the Title above mentioned."

In the Schedule there is a description of the land, and it goes on:

" Together with the messuage or dwellinghouse erected or in the course of
G erection thereon or on some part thereof and known as 74, Haven Close, Swanley."

In addition to the clause itself operating the transfer it contained three extra covenants, one by which the transferee undertook to maintain the boundary walls and fences; another in which it was declared he had no right to free passages of light or air; the third by which the transferor covenanted to build
H and maintain the road.

What is said by the purchasers—whose case is put quite simply—is this, that these houses were not built with proper and suitable material so far as the hardcore is concerned; and they would add, I think, that they were not fit for human habitation because they had in them the seeds of the damage which has later manifested itself.

I That is, on the face of it, a simple case, but there are several defences which have been raised and argued before me, some of them raised at the eleventh hour by an amendment, leave to make which I granted at the beginning of this trial. Three of them I can deal with shortly. The first defence I so deal with is the argument that, on the execution of the transfer, the contract in relation to the building of the house merged in the transfer, and since no express provision for liability in relation to the construction of the house was included in the transfer the purchaser can no longer rely on cl. 9 of the contract. Even if I wished to subscribe to such a doctrine of merger—which I certainly do not—I should be bound by the decision of the Court of Appeal in *Lawrence* v. *Cassel* (1). It is, of **A** course, trite law that if one purchases a completed house there is no warranty by the vendor as to the quality of the house or as to the size or description of the land. It is also trite law that in such a case warranties of that kind given before the conveyance are merged in the conveyance; but when the contract is of a dual nature, as is the case with building contracts of this kind, viz., a contract to do two things, one to convey the land and the other to build a house, it is in my **B** view quite clear that there can have been no intention on the part of the parties that the contract to build a house should disappear because the contract to convey the land is merged in the actual conveyance of it. That was said with the greatest clearness by SCRUTTON, L.J., in *Lawrence* v. *Cassel* (1). It has been acted on time and time again since that date, and I have no doubt that the obligation, such as it was, on the builders under cl. 9, as well as cl. 11, of the **C** contract survived the transfer.

The next defence is the contention that cl. 9 does not apply to any work already done before the contract was entered into, and it is shown on the evidence that the insertion of the hardcore and, indeed, the completion of the floors, was already done before any of these contracts were entered into. In my view there is no substance in that contention. In *Lawrence* v. *Cassel* (1), SCRUTTON, L.J., **D** did allude to the point in a dictum, where he said (2):

" There is a good deal to be said for the view that a contract to complete a house in a workmanlike manner is not fulfilled by making a house full of defects, some of which have probably arisen in consequence of work badly done before the contract, and some of which are due to defects which have developed afterwards." **E**

The same point was also referred to by ROMER, L.J., in his judgment in *Perry* v. *Sharon Development Co., Ltd.* (3), where he said:

" Where, however, the contract is for the sale of a house when completed, there is an implied contract on the part of the vendor, in the absence of there being any express contract as to the way in which the house is to be completed, **F** that the house shall be completed in such a way that it is fit for human habitation. In my opinion, in such a case as that, it matters not that the house has already been partly constructed. It was, indeed, argued by counsel for the appellants that, in such a case, although a contract in relation to work thereafter to be done might be implied, there could by implication be thrown on the vendor no obligation to do anything further to work **G** which had already been done. I do not take that view."

That ends the quotation from ROMER, L.J. I now cease to quote him and repeat that *I* do not take that view.

It seems to me that when a vendor undertakes to erect, build and complete a dwellinghouse in a proper and workmanlike manner he does not fulfil that obligation if, at the contractual time, he hands over a house which is not built, **H** erected and completed in a proper and workmanlike manner. If work before the date of the contract had been done improperly then to build, erect and complete that house in a proper and workmanlike manner means curing the defects which already existed, if there were any, before the contract was entered into. I therefore reject that defence.

The third contention was alternative to the one which I have just mentioned. **I** It was said that the effect of condition 12 (3) of the National Conditions of Sale, which were incorporated into the contract by cl. 12 of the original contract, prevented the purchasers from claiming in respect of any defects existing before the date of the contract for sale. Condition 12 (3) of the National Conditions of Sale reads as follows:

(1) [1930] All E.R. Rep. 733; [1930] 2 K.B. 83.
(2) [1930] All E.R. Rep. at p. 735; [1930] 2 K.B. at p. 89.
(3) [1937] 4 All E.R. 390 at pp. 394, 395.

A
" The purchaser shall be deemed to buy with full notice in all respects of the actual state and condition of the property and shall take the property as it is."

Counsel for the builders concedes, as I understand it, and rightly concedes, that " as it is " must mean as it is at the date of the contract. The short answer

B to that contention is that such a clause is wholly inconsistent with the provisions of cl. 9, that the builder, the vendor, must change the property as it is, the dwellinghouse, into something which it is not at the time of the contract before he hands it over on completion, namely, he must change it from an incomplete dwellinghouse to a complete dwellinghouse. Moreover, by cl. 12 of the original contract the National Conditions of Sale are only incorporated insofar as they " are not inconsistent with the aforesaid conditions ". In my judgment

C condition 12 (3) is clearly inconsistent with this condition.

I should have added, in deference to the diligence of counsel, that JONES, J., in *Jennings* v. *Tavener* (4), came to a similar conclusion with a similar apparent lack of hesitation as I have.

That leads me to what I have suggested in the course of argument was the real nub of this case: what is the effect of cl. 9, the express provision in the

D contract as to the completion of the dwellinghouse, together with such implications as arise from the nature of the contract itself? Before I deal with the clause in detail there is a passage in the judgment of PARKER, L.J., in *Lynch* v. *Thorne* (5) which seems to me to put much better and more succinctly than I should do the proper approach to this kind of clause in a building contract of this kind. What he said was this (6):

E
‘ This contract was, at any rate, partly a contract for work and labour. The plaintiff clearly desired the house for habitation, and to some extent relied on the skill and judgment of the defendant, who was a builder of houses. Those facts must be taken to have been known by the defendant. In those circumstances I think that prima facie there is an implied condition

F that the house, when built, shall be fit for human habitation. I say ‘ prima facie ’ because, of course, the express terms of the contract may be such as to show that they are wholly or partly inconsistent with any such implied condition. If they are wholly inconsistent, that will quite clearly negative any reliance which, otherwise, it could be said the buyer placed on the skill and judgment of the seller. If, on the other hand, the express terms

G are only partly inconsistent, there will be room for the implied condition to operate in the area not covered by the express condition."

In saying that, PARKER, L.J., was following the decision of the House of Lords in *Cammell Laird & Co., Ltd.* v. *Manganese Bronze and Brass Co.* (7), where reliance on the skill and judgment of the seller was limited to a very small part of the specification of the work to be done.

H
One other case that I should cite before I come to look at cl. 9 again is the very well known case *Miller* v. *Cannon Hill Estates, Ltd.* (8), a judgment of the Divisional Court and a judgment which, if my memory serves me, at the time was regarded as constituting a milestone in the law relating to the purchase of buildings under construction. I read the judgments for SWIFT, J.'s and MAC-NAGHTEN, J.'s formulation of the implied condition which, in the ordinary way,

I would arise apart from any express term of the contract contradicting it or cutting it down. SWIFT, J., put it this way (9)—he is here referring to *Lawrence* v. *Cassel* (10), a case which he himself decided at first instance:

" I do not think that it was ever disputed in the Court of Appeal that the

(4) [1955] 2 All E.R. 769.   (5) [1956] 1 All E.R. 744.
(6) [1956] 1 All E.R. at p. 750.   (7) [1934] All E.R. Rep. 1; [1934] A.C. 402.
(8) [1931] All E.R. Rep. 93; [1931] 2 K.B. 113.
(9) [1931] All E.R. Rep. at p. 97; [1931] 2 K.B. at p. 122.
(10) [1930] All E.R. Rep. 733; [1930] 2 K.B. 83.

very foundation of the action was that it was implied that the materials **A**
used should be suitable and fit and proper for the purpose, and that the
work should be carried out in a proper, efficient and workmanlike manner."

MACNAGHTEN, J., put it this way (11):

" It can hardly be doubted that the obligation of the builder must have
been an obligation to build properly, to build with proper materials and in a **B**
proper manner, and to provide a house fit for the purpose for which the
house was required, namely, for the habitation of the plaintiff and his wife."

That formulation of the implied warranty, is sometimes varied by the use of the
words " a house fit for human habitation ", but I think that it is fairly clear
from the judgments of the Court of Appeal in *Perry* v. *Sharon Development
Co., Ltd.* (12), which I have already cited, that there is no substantial or significant **C**
difference between the formulation of the warranty that the house should be
built of materials suitable and fit and proper for the purpose and the work should
be carried out in a proper, efficient and workmanlike manner, and the alternative
way of stating it, that the house is habitable and fit for humans to live in.

Therefore following the advice of PARKER, L.J., in *Lynch* v. *Thorne* (13) I
approach cl. 9 to see to what extent there is room for the implied condition to **D**
operate in the area not covered by the express condition. The express condition
I have already read. There is first a reference to the completion of the house
in a proper and workmanlike manner. My inclination would be to regard that
express clause as relating to the way in which the work was carried out rather
than to the materials, and that clause requires that the work shall be carried out
with due skill, care and judgment. Then it goes on: the house is to be erected, **E**
built and completed in accordance with the plan and specification supplied to
the purchaser. It is in the plan and specification that one finds the reference
to materials and, as I have said, the only reference to the hardcore as a material
is to be found in the specification, and the only express term about it is the
description of it, the single word " hardcore ". I put to counsel for the builders
in argument that, it having appeared on the evidence which he called himself that **F**
there is no well-known specification of " hardcore " in the building trade, it
cannot have been intended by the parties that any old hardcore, anything which
could be described as hardcore, however unsuitable for the purpose, could
properly be used in performance of this contract. Counsel for the builders,
I think, was constrained to agree that there must be some obligation as to the
quality of the hardcore. What he sought to say was that the obligation (if **G**
there was one) was an express obligation under cl. 9, that the hardcore should be
selected with reasonable skill and judgment. I do not take that view. It
seems to me that since there was no definite specification of the hardcore to be
used, as there was with regard to the material to be used in that part of *Lynch*
v. *Thorne* (14) which came to the Court of Appeal, there is, in the words of PARKER,
L.J. (13), room for the implied condition that the materials shall be fit, proper **H**
and suitable for the purpose to operate in the area of the hardcore, and I would
read this clause as containing a contractual warranty on the part of the builders
that the hardcore used for the purpose of being put under the site concrete of the
floors should be fit, proper and suitable for that purpose. As I have said, there
is a plain breach—and, indeed, an admitted breach—of that warranty, if that
be the warranty applicable to this case.

There is one other line of defence to which I should refer—that the effect of **I**
cl. 11 and cl. 9 is that cl. 9 deals only with rights prior to completion and that
cl. 11 comes into operation on completion of the sale, and thereafter the only
rights which the purchasers have are rights derived under cl. 11. I have read
cl. 11 and it creates rights by providing that the builders will make good any

(11) [1931] All E.R. Rep. at p. 98; [1931] 2 K.B. at p. 123.
(12) [1937] 4 All E.R. 390.   (13) [1956] 1 All E.R. at p. 750.
                    (14) [1956] 1 All E.R. 744.

A structural defects which are discovered within six months. If that clause is to take away the rights of the purchasers which normally follow at common law in the case of a breach of contract, it must do so in very clear terms if the court is going to give to it that effect. I can see no grounds whatever in this case for giving that effect to cl. 11. It does not cover the same ground as cl. 9, for it is limited to structural defects, and cl. 9, as I have construed it, requires the house

B to be completed with materials fit and suitable for the purpose in a proper and workmanlike manner in accordance with the plan and specification. There are, therefore, all sorts of breaches of cl. 9, as I have construed it, which would not be covered by cl. 11 at all. I can see no reason why, because an alternative remedy is given for a limited number of breaches of a limited kind discovered in a limited period, I should hold that by some implication the purchasers have

C given up all rights which cl. 9 expressly bestows on them. I therefore reject that defence.

I should perhaps add one further word about it, because I was pressed by counsel for the builders with a decision in *Kent* v. *Saltdean Estates Co., Ltd.* (15) which came before His Honour NORMAN RICHARDS, Q.C., as Official Referee, a case which is cited in a footnote to HUDSON'S BUILDING CONTRACTS (16). I

D have been provided with a shorthand note of the judgment. The terms of the contract with which he was dealing were different from the terms of this contract. In particular there was an express provision that the work should be carried out and completed to the reasonable satisfaction of the purchaser or her surveyor; but cl. 10 did contain a discovery of defects clause not, I think, different in principle from cl. 11 in this contract. The Official Referee's decision, having

E regard to the difference in the terms of the contract, would not, I think, in any event be decisive as to the decision on this contract, but I should observe that the foundation of one at least of the arguments which were addressed to me by the builders was that the Official Referee appeared to take the view that on the conveyance there was a merger of the express term of the contract that " the vendors will erect and complete in a good and workmanlike manner the said

F bungalow ". It is unnecessary for me to deal with the matter in detail but I think, as the case has been cited and as it is referred to in a footnote in HUDSON (16), it would be right for me to say that I should require a great deal of persuasion that the learned Official Referee was right in applying the doctrine of merger to that case, although his actual decision may well be right for other reasons. One other comment. The learned Official Referee did appear to rely on *Marsden*

G *Urban District Council* v. *Sharp* (17) as giving support to the proposition that when there is what I may call a discovery of defects clause of this character it takes away any rights which might otherwise arise to remedies for breach of contract. At a cursory reading I think such an impression might be derived from *Marsden Urban District Council* v. *Sharp* (17) if one reads it only in the Court of Appeal. If, however, one turns back and sees the circumstances in which that case came

H before the court at first instance (18), it becomes quite apparent that the only question before the court in that case was: what amounts to discovery of defects? The case came before the court as a Case Stated by an arbitrator. A Case Stated by an arbitrator raises a specific point of law, and the only specific point of law raised was that. It is therefore no sort of authority that a discovery of defects clause has any effect in taking away common law rights of action for

I damages for breaches of the contract. There may be such clauses. There often are in building contracts where there are provisions for final certificates. There may well have been a clause in *Marsden's* case (18) to that effect, for at any rate this is apparent from the judgment, that there were at least thirty-four other clauses which were not relevant to the particular point of law discussed in that case.

---

(15) (1964), 114 L.Jo. 555.
(17) (1931), 48 T.L.R. 23.

(16) (9th Edn.), p. 288, footnote 54a.
(18) (1930), 47 T.L.R. 549.

I therefore take the view that the purchasers here have established the liability **A** of the builders.

As I say, the question of the quantum of damages has not been argued before me. Accordingly I will declare that the builders are liable to each of the purchasers for damages for breach of the warranty contained in cl. 9 of their respective contracts.

Judgment for the purchasers; assessment of damages to be referred to an Official **B** *Referee failing agreement; liberty to apply; leave to appeal.*

Solicitors: *Warren & Warren*, agents for *Chancellor & Ridley*, Dartford (for the purchasers); *Bower, Cotton & Bower* (for the builders).

[*Reported by* HENRY SUMMERFIELD, ESQ., *Barrister-at-Law.*]

C

MALZ v. ROSEN.

[QUEEN'S BENCH DIVISION (Diplock, L.J., sitting as an additional judge), **D** February 9, 10, 11, 1966.]

Malicious Prosecution—Reasonable and probable cause—Advice of apparently responsible police officer to whom prosecutor has given honest and reasonably accurate account of incident.

Malicious Prosecution—Prosecutor—Private citizen who had reported matter to police, signed charge, being invited to do so by police officer—Prosecution **E** *conducted by solicitor and counsel retained by police—Whether private citizen was " prosecutor ".*

If a private citizen goes to the police, gives them an honest and reasonably accurate account of an event which has occurred, is advised by someone appearing to be a responsible police officer that that event constitutes a particular offence, and bona fide believes that advice, and on it prosecutes **F** the person concerned in the event, the private citizen has reasonable and probable grounds for prosecuting and so has a complete defence to an action by the person prosecuted for malicious prosecution (see p. 13, letter H, and p. 14, letter A, post).

Principle stated by VISCOUNT SIMONDS in *Glinski* v. *McIver* ([1962] 1 All E.R. at p. 701) applied to a person acting on the advice of a responsible **G** police officer.

The defendant, having been involved in an altercation with the plaintiff, gave a police sergeant at the local police station an honest and accurate account of what had occurred. The police sergeant said that the plaintiff had committed an offence, and asked the defendant if he would be prepared to prefer a charge and give evidence. The defendant said he would do so, **H** and gave the police a written statement ending " I am willing to attend court to give evidence of this if required ". Subsequently a charge of using insulting behaviour whereby a breach of the peace might have been occasioned was prepared, and read out to the plaintiff, by the police sergeant. The police asked the defendant if he would sign the charge, and he did so. It was intended originally that the prosecution should be conducted by a **I** police officer, but the plaintiff was represented by a solicitor who asked for the hearing to be adjourned, and so the Metropolitan Police instructed solicitor and counsel, who conducted the prosecution, the defendant giving evidence for the prosecution at the trial of the charge. The plaintiff was acquitted, and brought an action against the defendant for malicious prosecution.

Held: (i) the defendant was a prosecutor of the plaintiff (see p. 13, letter G, post).

A   (ii) for the reasons stated at p. 10, letter F, ante, the defendant had reasonable and probable cause for the prosecution, and so the plaintiff's action failed (see p. 14, letter F, post).

Per CURIAM: if a person gives the police an account which he knows to be untrue, that fact in itself would be strong evidence of the ingredient of malice necessary for a successful action for malicious prosecution (see

B   p. 14, letter B, post).

[As to what is reasonable and probable cause for a prosecution, see 25 HALSBURY'S LAWS (3rd Edn.) 358, 359, para. 699; and for cases on the subject, see 33 DIGEST (Repl.) 418-422, *368-404.*

As to who may be liable as a prosecutor, see 25 HALSBURY'S LAWS (3rd Edn.)

C   349, 350, paras. 684, 685; and for cases on the subject, see 33 DIGEST (Repl.) 389-392, *20-39.*]

Case referred to:

Glinski v. *McIver*, [1962] 1 All E.R. 696; [1962] A.C. 726; [1962] 2 W.L.R. 832; 33 Digest (Repl.) 431, *504.*

Action.

D   Moris Henry Malz, the plaintiff, brought this action against David Peter Rosen, the defendant, for damages for malicious prosecution and false imprisonment. The facts are set out in the judgment.

M. Waters for the plaintiff.
John Wilmers, Q.C., for the defendant.

E   **DIPLOCK, L.J.:** This is an action for malicious prosecution and false imprisonment brought by the plaintiff, who was tried at Highgate magistrates' court on June 29, when the matter was adjourned, and on July 16, 1964. He was originally charged jointly with another man called Langdale with using insulting behaviour whereby a breach of the peace might have been occasioned in Tillingbourne Way, London, N.3, on June 24, 1964, contrary to s. 54 (13) of

F   the Metropolitan Police Act, 1839. He was acquitted on that charge. The person who signed the charge sheet, in the circumstances which I shall shortly describe, was the defendant; and in this action the plaintiff claims damages against the defendant for malicious prosecution and for false imprisonment. He claims under the former head, general damages for the damage to his fair name and reputation, and special damages in the sum of £120 costs which he

G   paid to his solicitor, Mr. Sidney Rutter, for his successful defence to the charge. There has been a great conflict of evidence in this case, and the result turns on the view which I take of the reliability of the witnesses, and in particular on the view that I take of the reliability of the plaintiff and of the defendant respectively.

The plaintiff is a dealer in second-hand cars; he may be described as a " kerb dealer ", for he has no premises of his own on which to display his merchandise,

H   but parks them in the Queen's highway or anywhere else where he can get away with it. On June 24, one of the places where he was " getting away with it " was a private road, or at any rate a road not declared a public highway, known as Tillingbourne Way, which runs into the North Circular Road at Finchley from another unadopted highway, Tillingbourne Gardens. Tillingbourne Way runs north and south between a public house called " The Golden Eagle " and

I   a block of flats to the west, called Queensborough Court, where the defendant then lived; there were lock-up garages and the wall of a garden to the east. The plaintiff, in the witness box, told me that he had permission from the manager of the public house to use the road, Tillingbourne Way, for parking vehicles which he had for sale. I have heard the manager of the public house and I am perfectly clear that the plaintiff had not such permission; that he knew that he had no such permission and that he was taking advantage of an answer to a deceptive request which he put to the manager of the public house, namely that he could park a car in the ordinary way, as a customer at the public house.

On June 24, the plaintiff had two of the vehicles which he had for sale parked A
in Tillingbourne Way; one of them, with which I am concerned, a van, was
parked on the west side of the road immediately opposite Queensborough Court,
and on the east side of the road there was another car parked, thus leaving a
fairly narrow but adequate passage for cars to come down Tillingbourne Way.
The plaintiff, having a customer or an enquiry for the van which was parked
there had sent someone connected with him, who had taken the customer down B
to the van, but the van on examination proved to have some defect to the wheel.
I use the description " someone connected with him " advisedly, because the
connexion was by no means clear; he was a man called Langdale, who was
assisting but not employed by the plaintiff.   Attempts were made—maybe
successfully, I know not—to cure the defect to the wheel, and then it was
discovered that, in addition to this, the battery was flat, and a message was C
sent to the plaintiff to come to the rescue.   The plaintiff came in a large Plymouth
car, and, finding that the battery was flat, was anxious to start the van by passing
a lead from the battery of his Plymouth car to the van.   Because there was not
room to park bonnet to bonnet on the east side of the road, he put his Plymouth
car across the road diagonally, so as to get his bonnet as near to the bonnet of
the van as possible, and he thereby blocked the whole of the road.   When his D
car was in that position, a Riley car, driven by a Mr. Levy, a young man who
has been called as a witness, with the defendant as passenger came down Tillingbourne Way with the object of dropping the defendant at the front entrance to
Queensborough Court, where he lived, which was in the North Circular Road.
This was a route which was not uncommonly used by the defendant when Mr.
Levy was driving him, and sometimes with his own car.   The defendant says, E
and I believe him, that he had never been formerly incommoded or blocked
when driving down that way.

When Mr. Levy's car came to the part of the road which was being blocked by
the plaintiff, there ensued an altercation, to which I shall have to return in
greater detail because it lies at the root of this case.   As a result of the altercation
the defendant left the scene and telephoned the local police station, to whom he F
gave, as he says, an accurate account—I do not know whether it was a detailed
one, but it was an accurate account of the incident which had just taken place.
I accept that the account which he gave was substantially the same as that which
he gave later in the evening at the police station, and which he gave in evidence
on oath at the hearing of the charge at Highgate magistrates' court and which
he gave again in the witness box in this court.   As a result of his conversation G
with the police they apparently took the view—rightly or wrongly I do not
know—that as Tillingbourne Way was not an adopted road there was probably
nothing that the police could do about it, but they asked the defendant to find
out what was the registration number of the car blocking the road.   He went,
and he found that by that time the plaintiff's car had disappeared.   The plaintiff
had gone back home to get another lead to see if he could start the van, and the H
defendant inquired from Mr. Langdale who was left there, what the registration
number of the van was.   Mr. Langdale refused the number, and behaved, according to the defendant and Mr. Levy, in a threatening manner.   As a result the
defendant returned to his flat, telephoned the police, and reported what had
just happened; and the police said that they would send an officer round.

Shortly after there arrived at the front entrance to Queensborough Court two I
detective constables in plain clothes.   To them the defendant recounted what he
said had happened, and the four of them, that is the defendant, Mr. Levy and
the two detective constables went over to Tillingbourne Way where they found
that the plaintiff had returned with his car.   The defendant, or perhaps Mr.
Levy, repeated the defendant's account of what had happened in front of the
plaintiff, and the detective constables, or one of them, then said that they had
better go down to the police station.   The plaintiff and Mr. Langdale went in the

A plaintiff's car accompanied by the police officers, and the defendant and Mr. Levy went by themselves, and in fact arrived at the police station sometime before the plaintiff.

When they arrived they recounted again to the police sergeant what they said had occurred, substantially to the same effect as the evidence which they gave in the box yesterday.   There is no doubt about what took place on this occasion,

B for it is verified by the police sergeant, whose evidence I find most reliable. The police sergeant then said to them that, according to their evidence, the plaintiff and Mr. Langdale had committed an offence.   The police sergeant had in fact decided the nature of the offence.   The police sergeant said that the plaintiff and Langdale had committed an offence but that the police could not proceed without the evidence of the defendant and of Mr. Levy.   The police

C sergeant asked them whether they would be prepared to prosecute or prefer charges; he explained the responsibility of preferring a charge and giving evidence because the evidence of the police officers only tended to support it. The defendant said that he was prepared to do so, though I do not doubt that at this stage he was not aware what were the formalities or the precise nature of " preferring a charge ".   He was certainly willing to go and give evidence on

D oath of the facts as he had stated them to the police sergeant.

Thereafter written statements were taken both of the defendant and of Mr. Levy setting out their version of the facts and finishing up, in the case of the defendant, with: " I am willing to attend court to give evidence of this if required ".   While those statements were being taken the plaintiff was brought along to the police station by the detective constables, and on arrival he expressed

E a desire to see his solicitor, to whom a communication had already been made by his wife. Accordingly, and this was at his request, the formality of charging was deferred until his solicitor had come to see him.   The solicitor arrived at about a quarter-to-nine; he very sensibly wished to see his client in private to obtain his client's version of the facts.   When the solicitor had seen the plaintiff privately, the plaintiff was taken into the charge-room.   The charge

F had been prepared by the station sergeant in the terms which I have already read out, and this was read out to him.   The defendant and Mr. Levy were asked whether they would sign the charge, and the defendant signed it.   It was needless to say, never intended or thought by anyone that the defendant would conduct or have the actual conduct of the prosecution at the magistrates' court. The original intention of the police was that one of the police officers would

G conduct it, but on June 29, the day fixed for the hearing, the plaintiff appeared by his solicitor and the matter was adjourned.   In the result at the adjourned hearing the prosecution was represented by a solicitor and counsel who were instructed by the Metropolitan Police.

On those facts I accept that the defendant was in the position of prosecutor and that, therefore, if it can be shown that he brought the accusation without

H reasonable or probable cause and with malice, an action for malicious prosecution will lie against him.   I am, however, quite clear, and this in the result is not disputed by counsel for the plaintiff, that, if an ordinary private citizen such as the defendant goes to the police and having given them an accurate and honest account of circumstances which have occurred, is told by a responsible police officer that according to those facts, an offence has been committed, and is

I asked by the police officer whether he is prepared to prefer a charge, then, if the ordinary citizen accepts that advice, there is no doubt that in law he has reasonable and probable cause for the prosecution.   In saying that, I am adopting what VISCOUNT SIMONDS said in *Glinski* v. *McIver* (1) in relation to a charge brought on the advice of counsel or of a competent legal adviser.   *Glinski* v. *McIver* (2) was a case in which a police officer was the defendant, but in the case

---

(1) [1962] 1 All E.R. 696 at p. 701; [1962] A.C. 726 at p. 745.
(2) [1962] 1 All E.R. 696; [1962] A.C. 726.

of an ordinary citizen the law, I am confident, is that if such a citizen goes to the **A** police, gives them an honest and reasonably accurate account of an event which has occurred and is advised by someone appearing to be a responsible police officer that that constitutes a particular offence, then, if the ordinary citizen bona fide believes that advice, he has a complete defence to an action for malicious prosecution. If on the other hand, he goes to the police with an account which he knows to be untrue, then not only has he no reasonable or **B** possible ground for the prosecution but also that fact in itself would be strong evidence of the ingredient of malice necessary for a successful action for malicious prosecution.

This case, therefore, in my view turns on whether or not I accept the evidence of the defendant, which is in considerable conflict with that of the plaintiff, as to what occurred at the altercation in Tillingbourne Way at about half-past six **C** that evening. I accept the defendant as being a witness of truth in the essential matters in this case. That does not mean that I accept his memory as being necessarily accurate in all the details of what occurred one-and-three-quarter years ago in a fairly short time when tempers were, no doubt, aroused to some extent on either side, but basically I accept his account of what occurred on that occasion. I have seen the plaintiff in the box; I thought him prepared to say **D** anything which he thought would assist his case, and where his evidence conflicts in any material particular with the evidence of any other witness in this case, I reject it. [His LORDSHIP stated the plaintiff's and defendant's accounts of what occurred when the car driven by Mr. Levy came down the road where the plaintiff's van was, and concluded:] I accept that in substance the matter occurred as the defendant and Mr. Levy described. I am satisfied that that **E** was what the defendant reported to the police over the telephone and that was what he told the police sergeant and the detective constables had occurred. It follows therefore that I am satisfied that the defendant gave an honest and accurate account to a police officer of what had occurred on that evening.

I might add that there is no suggestion here of any ulterior motive that the defendant may have had; he did not know the plaintiff before, but I do not **F** think that that would have mattered if I had thought that he had given an intentional lying account to the police. It is a pure question of fact depending on the credibility of the witnesses. I am satisfied that the account which the defendant gave was substantially accurate and honest. It therefore follows that this action fails and there must be judgment for the defendant.

Judgment for the defendant. **G**

Solicitors: *S. Rutter* (for the plaintiff); *Pollards* (for the defendant).

[*Reported by* HENRY SUMMERFIELD, ESQ., *Barrister-at-Law.*]

A

JENKINS *v.* RICHARD THOMAS & BALDWINS, LTD.

[COURT OF APPEAL (Lord Denning, M.R., Danckwerts and Salmon, L.JJ.), January 26, 27, 1966.]

Damages—Assessment—Appeal—Further evidence—Assessment once and for all
B   *—Wrong basis of reckoning loss of future earnings at trial—Assessment*
     reviewed in light of further evidence.

Court of Appeal—Evidence—Further evidence—Damages awarded to workman
     for personal injuries—Basis of assessment of loss of future earnings proved
     wrong after trial—R.S.C., Ord. 58, r. 9 (2).

The plaintiff was employed by the defendants as a pitman earning £19 10s.
C   a week. As a result of an accident to his right eye in 1959 for which the
defendants were held liable, he was employed as a labourer keeping bricklayers' books. At the trial, in March, 1964, the defendants agreed to train
him as a grinder, in which employment he could earn £17 a week. On the
basis of a loss of future earnings of £2 10s. a week at eight years' purchase,
the trial judge awarded him £1,040 under that head. The plaintiff was put
D   onto grinding work shortly after the trial but never obtained a certificate of
proficiency, without which he could not earn the average wage of £17 a week
of a grinder but remained at a labourer's wage of some £11 a week. On appeal
on the ground that the trial judge had underestimated the loss of future
earnings, the Court of Appeal admitted further evidence. The court accepted
the evidence of the medical specialist for the defendants that, so far as any
E   optical injury was concerned, there was no reason from the point of view of
his eyesight why the plaintiff should not be able to do the grinding work but
that there was something in the nature of self-suggestion which was honest
and was itself the result of the original injury which made the plaintiff unable
to do that work,

Held: the amount of damages had been wrongly calculated at the trial,
F   since the trial judge's estimate of £17 a week in the future was too high, and,
having regard to the further evidence, the proper assessment was to increase
the award by £1,000 (see p. 17, letters F and H, and p. 18, letter B, post).

Per SALMON, L.J.: the general rule is that damages in actions for damages
for personal injuries have to be assessed once and for all at the trial. If the
basis on which the damages have been assessed proves to be wrong very
shortly after the trial and the point is promptly taken up with the other
G   side, then, in the exceptional circumstances, there may be good grounds for
the Court of Appeal giving leave to call further evidence (see p. 18, letters
C and D, post).

Appeal allowed.

[As to loss of earnings by personal injury, see 11 HALSBURY'S LAWS (3rd Edn.)
H   258, 259, para. 430; and as to the rule that damages are assessed once and for all
see ibid., p. 227, para. 395.

As to the power of the Court of Appeal to receive further evidence, see 30
HALSBURY'S LAWS (3rd Edn.) 468, 469, para. 884; and for cases on the subject,
see DIGEST (Practice) 776-778, *3398-3420.*]

Case referred to:
I   Curwen v. *James,* [1963] 2 All E.R. 619; [1963] 1 W.L.R. 748; Digest (Cont.
          Vol. A) 1210, *1208b.*

Appeal.
This was an appeal by the plaintiff from a judgment of WINN, J., dated Mar. 17,
1964, awarding him £3,040 damages in an action against his employers, the
defendants, for damages for personal injuries sustained in an accident while at
work. The notice of appeal was dated May 20, 1965. The Court of Appeal
allowed the plaintiff's application to adduce further oral evidence on the appeal,

to show that the basis on which the loss of future earnings was assessed at the **A**
trial was wrong. The facts are set out in the judgment of LORD DENNING, M.R.

E. D. Sutcliffe, Q.C., and *R. E. Hammerton* for the plaintiff.
Tudor Evans, Q.C., and *A. G. Davies* for the defendants.

LORD DENNING, M.R.: This is an unusual case in which we gave leave
to adduce further evidence. Mr. Jenkins, the plaintiff, was a pitman employed **B**
by the defendants, Richard Thomas & Baldwins, Ltd., at their Panteg steelworks.
In 1959, when he had been with them some twenty years, he had an accident at
his work. There was an explosion in which he was injured. Some metal got into
his right eye. He was in hospital for three weeks and received treatment afterwards. In consequence he was not able to go back to his work as a pitman. The
defendants found work for him as a labourer, but of rather a better kind. It was **C**
keeping bricklayers' books. He got about £1 more a week than an ordinary
labourer. He was engaged on that work until the trial of his action for damages
which came on at the Newport Assizes in March, 1964. There was a contest on
liability which WINN, J., decided in favour of the plaintiff. He held that the
accident was due to the fault of the defendants and that there was no contributory
negligence by the plaintiff. He then had to assess damages. He assessed the **D**
general damages (including his loss of earnings up to the date of trial) at £2,000;
but then came the question of the loss of future earnings after the trial. In the
course of the concluding speech for the defendants, WINN, J., asked whether
there was not some better work which the defendants could give him. They
are big employers in the neighbourhood. Counsel took instructions and said
that the defendants were able and willing to offer him employment as a grinder **E**
in which he could wear goggles. Payment would be at the basic rate of some
£12 a week plus an incentive bonus. Altogether he should make £17 a week.
The judge took that into account in assessing the damages. If he had remained
as a pitman, he would have been making some £19 10s. a week. The judge
accepted that that would have been his wages if uninjured. He deducted the
£17 a week as the wages he would get now. Thus the judge took the loss to **F**
be £2 10s. a week—£130 a year. He assessed it at eight years' purchase, making
£1,040. He added the £1,040 on to the £2,000 and awarded him £3,040 damages.

The defendants very shortly afterwards put the plaintiff on to grinding work.
They gave him training. It usually takes one to three weeks to train a man as
a grinder and usually every man becomes proficient. During the training
period, the defendants would pay him ordinary labourer's wages, but after **G**
training as a grinder, when he was proficient and certified by the departmental
foreman as proficient, he would get an additional amount out of the pool. All
proficient workmen employed as grinders put their work into a pool. There is
a lump sum paid to the group of grinders according to the tonnage they produce.
Each receives a share of the amount, thus bringing each man's wages up to
about £17. Unfortunately the plaintiff did not manage to do the work at all **H**
well. He never obtained a certificate of proficiency. So he remained at the
labourer's wage, some £11 a week, instead of the £17 a week which was contemplated when the damages were assessed by WINN, J. The plaintiff said that the
reason he could not do this grinding work was because of the original injury to
his eye. He said that his sight was blurred and that he saw straight lines as
crooked, so he could not see the little faults or seams which had to be removed **I**
in the grinding work. He applied for a new trial on this question of damages so as
to show that this £17 was erroneous. He said that the proof of the pudding
was in the eating. He did not earn £17 a week.

It is very unusual for this court to grant a new trial, but we were urged to do
so here on the authority of *Curwen* v. *James* (1). In that case, a widow had
married after the trial. The expectation (on which damages had been assessed)
had been entirely falsified by the event. So, here, the plaintiff said that he

(1) [1963] 2 All E.R. 619.

A   could show that, immediately after the trial, the judge's estimate had been falsified by the event.   We have had evidence from most distinguished medical men on each side.   We have to make up our minds whether there is any continuing optical injury which prevents the plaintiff doing this grinder's work. The defendants suggested that there was no reason whatever why he should not have done it.   They said that he was not trying to make himself proficient; B   he was deliberately going slow so as to make a claim for further damages.   I must say that the plaintiff struck me as being completely honest; and Mr. Morgan, who worked alongside him, said that he was a conscientious worker, who was doing his best.   On the other hand, the medical specialist for the defendants, Mr. Trevor Roper, impressed me greatly.   I accept his evidence and hold that, so far as any optical injury is concerned, there is no reason from C   the point of view of his eyesight why the plaintiff should not be able to do this grinding work.   The explanation is, I think, what Mr. Trevor Roper indicated. There must be something in the nature of self-suggestion which makes the plaintiff unable to do the work.   He worked himself up into feeling that he could not do it; but this self-suggestion was honest and was itself the result of the original injury.   On this footing, his continuing loss is a result of the D   original injury and, therefore, the loss of wages which he has suffered from the date of the trial until this date is really a consequence of the injury.   That is to say, instead of assessing his potential earnings as £17, we should take them as the £11 or thereabouts which he had been earning during this time as a grinder.

A question arose whether, when he found he could not do grinder's work, he ought to have requested some other work at a higher wage or whether he E   should have been offered it.   In the early days Mr. Millington senior indicated that he did not think there was any other work.   It seems to me that what he has done has been quite reasonable up to the moment, continuing as a grinder as best he could.   Lately he has been doing much better, but Mr. Morgan said that it would be some time before he got proficient as a grinder, if he ever does.   Putting aside the grinder's work, we have to see what he can do.   It F   is quite plain that he can earn more than £11 a week.   He can get £13 a week working forty-five hours a week, as he did as a pitman.   He ought to get more than an ordinary labourer, and that would increase it to £14 10s. or even more a week—say between £14 10s. and £15 for the future.   That would seem to be the fair basis.   In those circumstances for the future the judge's estimate of £17 a week was too high.   One has to consider rather in general terms what G   sum should be assessed so as to correct the under-estimate of the judge.   The estimate of the judge was based on £17 a week from the date of the trial.   It must be re-assessed in the circumstances which I have mentioned, namely, that, although he only earned what he could as a grinder up to today, from today onwards he ought to be able to earn as a reasonable man £14 to £15 a week.   I would like to say, however, that, if he does not earn £14 to £15 a week, H   he cannot come back again.   The general rule is that damages are assessed once and for all.   The estimate of future earnings is made once and for all.   It is only in the very special circumstances of this case that we heard fresh evidence; for here he was in effect told he would get work at £17 a week and only got £11.

On the whole I think that the proper assessment is to increase the judge's award by the sum of £1,000, and I would allow the appeal accordingly.

I

DANCKWERTS, L.J.: I agree.   The position is that, as the result of the unfortunate accident, the plaintiff has been deprived of the chance of returning to his former employment as a pitman in which he was earning £19 10s. a week. That, therefore, is the measure of damages for loss of earnings except in so far as it can be shown that he is still capable of earning a wage of some amount or other which would reduce the amount of the damages.   The suggestion was put forward on behalf of the defendants at the trial that they would be able to employ him as a grinder, which would produce for him a wage of £17 a week.   I am

sure that that was put forward in perfect good faith, but, when it came to the **A**
point, it turned out that the plaintiff was not really fit, or was not adapted,
whatever the reason was, to do the job of a grinder so successfully that he would
get the bonus which could be received and make up his wage to £17 a week. As has
been pointed out, he has been getting less than that amount, and it seems probable
that he will earn a much smaller amount than £17 a week in the future.   Therefore, the amount of the damages at the trial has in fact been wrongly calculated **B**
and it seems to me plain that the position ought to be put right.

I agree with the figure which has been reached by LORD DENNING, M.R.,
and that the matter should be adjusted accordingly.

SALMON, L.J.: I entirely agree.   I wish to add only a word on the admission of fresh evidence in matters of this kind.   The general rule is that damages **C**
in actions of this type have to be assessed once and for all at the trial.   It not
infrequently happens that, when damages are assessed at the trial on the basis
that the plaintiff will in future probably be able to earn such and such a sum,
it turns out that he is actually able to earn, and does earn, either substantially
more or substantially less.   It must not be thought that, whenever this occurs,
one side or the other can come to this court and appeal and ask for leave to call **D**
further evidence with a view to having the damages reduced or increased as the
case may be.   If the basis on which the damages have been assessed proves to
be wrong very shortly after the trial and the point is promptly taken up with the
other side, then, in the exceptional circumstances, there may be good grounds
for this court giving leave, as we have done here, to call further evidence. Another
exceptional circumstance in the present case is that the assumption that the **E**
plaintiff would be able to earn £17 a week as a grinder was largely based on what
had been said on behalf of the defendants—genuinely, but mistakenly—at the
trial.   Save in exceptional circumstances, the rule is that, for better or for
worse, the assessment at the trial is once and for all.   It may well be that that
rule is very much worse.   It would, perhaps, be better, when questions of loss of
earning capacity are being considered, that the amount to be awarded by way of **F**
damages should be assessed by way of an award of an annual or monthly sum,
with liberty to apply to the court should the circumstances change.   This might
well be much fairer from the point of view of both plaintiffs and defendants;
but that is not the law at the moment.   The law is that the damages must be
assessed at the trial once and for all and awarded in a lump sum.   It is a rule
which is very rarely departed from.   This case and *Curwen* v. *James* (2), to **G**
which LORD DENNING, M.R., has referred, are quite exceptional.

I agree that this appeal should be allowed and the order varied as LORD
DENNING has proposed.

Appeal allowed.

Solicitors: *Milners, Curry & Gaskell*, agents for *Granville-West, Chivers &
Morgan*, Newbridge, Mon. (for the plaintiff); *Abbott, Baldwin & Co.*, agents for **H**
Francis Ryan & Co., Cardiff (for the defendants).

[*Reported by* F. GUTTMAN, ESQ., *Barrister-at-Law.*]

I

---

(2) [1963] 2 All E.R. 619.

A INLAND REVENUE COMMISSIONERS v. CLEARY.
INLAND REVENUE COMMISSIONERS v. PERREN.

[COURT OF APPEAL (Lord Denning, M.R., Danckwerts and Salmon, L.JJ.), February 10, 11, March 4, 1966.]

Surtax—Tax advantage—Counteracting—Transaction in connexion with distribution of profits—Phrase including transfer of assets of company—Advantage by receipt of sum as capital instead of dividend—Shareholders' sale of other company's shares to company—Avoidance of surtax—Finance Act, 1960 (8 & 9 Eliz. 2 c. 44), s. 28 (1), (2) (d), s. 43 (4) (g).

The taxpayers who were sisters owned in equal shares the whole of the issued share capital of two companies. Each of the sisters sold to one of the companies, which then had a balance on profit and loss account of £180,000 and £130,000 cash at bank, twenty-two thousand £1 shares in the other company (which had an issued share capital of £50,000) for £60,500 in cash, that being the full value of the shares ascertained on a proper valuation. They were each served by the Commissioners of Inland Revenue with a notice under s. 28 (3) of the Finance Act, 1960, that an adjustment was necessary for counteracting the tax advantage obtained by each taxpayer by the sale, the adjustment comprising the recomputation of the liability of each to surtax on the basis that the £60,500 consideration paid to each taxpayer should be taken into account as if it were the net amount of a dividend paid on the same date. On appeal,

Held: s. 28 of the Finance Act, 1960, applied and liability to surtax was recomputable on the basis mentioned above, for the following reasons—

(i) the taxpayers received the sums of £60,500 " in connexion with the distribution of profits" within the subsection, since that phrase, in view of the definitions of " distribution " and " profits " in s. 28 (2), included transfer of assets and so included the payment of the price of the shares (see p. 22, letter D, p. 23, letter F, and p. 25, letter G, post).

(ii) the taxpayers obtained a tax advantage within s. 43 (4) (g) by avoiding an assessment to surtax which would have resulted if they had received the sums by way of dividend instead of as the purchase price of shares; and that was so notwithstanding that the company could distribute by way of dividend the shares that it had bought or their proceeds, since it was most unlikely that the company would so distribute them, and (per LORD DENNING, M.R.) if the company did so, the court would not allow the taxpayers to be taxed twice (see p. 22, letters E and H, p. 23, letter D, and p. 24, letters E and I, post).

Decision of PENNYCUICK, J. ([1965] 2 All E.R. 603) reversed.

[As to the counteracting of tax advantages, see SUPPLEMENT to 20 HALSBURY'S LAWS (3rd Edn.), para. 276A.

For the Finance Act, 1960, s. 28 (1), (2), and s. 43 (4) (g), see 40 HALSBURY'S STATUTES (3rd Edn.) 447, 448, 465, 466.]

Cases referred to:

Inland Revenue Comrs. v. *Parker,* [1966] 1 All E.R. 399.

Macaura v. *Northern Assurance Co., Ltd.,* [1925] All E.R. Rep. 51; [1925] A.C. 619; 94 L.J.P.C. 154; 133 L.T. 152; 29 Digest (Repl.) 52, 76.

St. Aubyn (L. M.) v. *A.-G. (No. 2),* [1951] 2 All E.R. 473; [1952] A.C. 15; 21 Digest (Repl.) 50, 199.

Thomas v. *Marshall (Inspector of Taxes),* [1953] 1 All E.R. 1102; [1953] A.C. 543; [1952] 2 W.L.R. 944; 34 Tax Cas. 178; 28 Digest (Repl.) 283, 1253.

Appeal.

These were appeals by the Crown from orders of PENNYCUICK, J., dated Apr. 15, 1965, dismissing two appeals by the Crown from the decision of the

Affirmed, H.L. [1967] 2 All E.R. 48.

Special Commissioners of Income Tax that though the payment of £60,500 to A
each taxpayer was a transfer of assets to her within s. 28 (2) of the Finance Act,
1960, yet neither taxpayer obtained from it a " tax advantage " within s. 43 (4)
(g) of the Act.

The first taxpayer, Mrs. K. S. Cleary, had appealed to the Special Commissioners
of Income Tax against a notice dated Nov. 13, 1963, given by the Commissioners
of Inland Revenue to the taxpayer under s. 28 (3) of the Finance Act, 1960. B
The notice was to the effect that certain adjustments were requisite for counteracting the tax advantage obtained or obtainable by the taxpayer by her sale
on or about July 24, 1961, to Gleeson Development Co., Ltd. of twenty-two
thousand ordinary shares of £1 each in M. J. Gleeson, Ltd. The adjustment
referred to was the computation or recomputation of the first taxpayer's liability
to surtax for the year of assessment 1961-62, on the basis that the consideration C
of £60,500 which the first taxpayer received from Gleeson Development Co., Ltd.
should be taken into account as if it were the net amount received in respect
of a dividend payable at the date of its receipt from which deduction of tax was
authorised by s. 184 (1) of the Income Tax Act, 1952, and any assessment or
additional assessment to surtax which might be requisite to give effect to such
computation or recomputation. D

The two companies had carried on property development businesses in pre-war
years but after the war had been holding and not developing property. The
property which the companies held in post-war years consisted mainly of detached
and semi-detached houses built in pre-war years which remained unsold and
were let by the companies to tenants. In 1957 many of the properties ceased to
be rent-controlled. Thereupon the first taxpayer and her sister, Mrs. W. M. Perren, E
the second taxpayer, who were at that time the sole shareholders of the two
companies, wished to adopt different policies of estate management as respects
the properties, and with that in mind took steps to have the properties valued
with a view to their being divided between them and their families. The sisters
wished to arrange, first, for the estates to be split geographically so as to ensure
as far as possible that on any subsequent rise in values in any particular locality F
each family would get an equal share of such potential increase; secondly,
that reversionary interests should be divided as fairly as possible; and, thirdly,
that such of the properties as still remained subject to rent control would be
divided as fairly as possible. The difference between the views which the sisters
took on policy regarding estate management persisted. The re-arrangement of
interests which the sisters envisaged could not be readily achieved by putting the G
two companies into liquidation because Gleeson Development Co., Ltd. had
substantial outstanding liabilities in connexion with estate roads and the amount
of those liabilities could not be readily determined.

On Feb. 13, 1964, the Special Commissioners issued surtax clearance certificates
in respect of the income of Gleeson Development Co., Ltd., for the year ended
Dec. 31, 1962, and in respect of the estate or trading income of M. J. Gleeson, Ltd. H
for that year. At Dec. 31, 1960, and at all material times thereafter, Gleeson
Development Co., Ltd. had an issued capital of two hundred thousand 1s. ordinary
shares of which half were owned by each taxpayer. At Dec. 31, 1960, and at all
material times thereafter, M. J. Gleeson, Ltd. had an issued capital of fifty thous-
and £1 ordinary shares of which, at Dec. 31, 1960, half were owned by each
taxpayer. On or about July 24, 1961, the first and second taxpayer each sold I
twenty-two thousand shares in M. J. Gleeson, Ltd. to Gleeson Development Co.,
Ltd., in consideration for which each of them received from the latter company
£60,500 in cash, that being the full value of the shares as ascertained by valuation.

Arthur Bagnall, Q.C., *J. R. Phillips* and *J. P. Warner* for the Crown.
E. I. Goulding, Q.C., and *N. P. M. Elles* for the respondent taxpayers.

Cur. adv. vult.

Mar. 4. The following judgments were read.

A   LORD DENNING, M.R. (read by DANCKWERTS, L.J.): Two sisters,
Mrs. Cleary and Mrs. Perren, the first and second taxpayers, owned all the shares
in two companies. They had half each. Gleeson Development Co., Ltd., had issued
two hundred thousand shares. Each sister had one hundred thousand. M. J.
Gleeson, Ltd., had issued fifty-thousand shares. Each sister had twenty-five
thousand. At the end of 1960 each company had sold off a good deal of property
B   and had a lot of cash at bank. Gleeson Development Co., Ltd., had
£130,653 0s. 11d. cash at bank. M. J. Gleeson, Ltd., had £80,273 19s. 7d. cash at
bank.

On July 24, 1961, the first and second taxpayers each sold twenty-two thousand
shares in M. J. Gleeson, Ltd., to Gleeson Development Co., Ltd., for £60,500.
Each sister received £60,500 in cash. This was the full value of the shares. The
C   result was that the cash which Gleeson Development Co., Ltd., had at the bank
(over £130,000) was reduced by £121,000; and instead of the cash, Gleeson
Development Co., Ltd., had forty-four thousand shares in M. J. Gleeson, Ltd.
So Gleeson Development Co., Ltd., lost nothing. They had shares instead of cash.
That is all. M. J. Gleeson, Ltd., of course, lost nothing. It still had all its cash and
assets. Only the shareholding was changed. Instead of the two sisters holding all
D   the fifty thousand shares in M. J. Gleeson, Ltd., they only held six thousand, the
remaining forty-four thousand were held by Gleeson Development Co., Ltd.;
but, as the two sisters held all the shares in Gleeson Development Co., Ltd., they
really still owned M. J. Gleeson, Ltd., as effectively as they did before.

If we were at liberty to lift the curtain which conceals the truth, we should see
that the sisters each withdrew £60,500 in cash from Gleeson Development Co., Ltd.,
E   without paying tax on it. It was money which was available for distribution by
way of dividend. If it had been so distributed, the grossed-up figure for each sister
would be £98,777. The Revenue now claim tax on that figure from each sister.
Apart from s. 28 of the Finance Act, 1960, the Revenue could not have claimed
tax on these sums of £60,500. They were sums received as capital as the purchase
price of shares. They were not income at all. The whole question is whether these
F   transactions are caught by s. 28 of the Finance Act, 1960. That section, in the
words of LORD WILBERFORCE (1), "mounted a massive attack against tax
avoidance in many forms ". Bond-washing and dividend-stripping are caught
by sub-s. (2) (a), (b) and (c). Other transactions are caught by sub-s. (2) (d).
An instance of a transaction so caught is *Inland Revenue Comrs.* v. *Parker* (2).
Is the present case another instance?

G   Section 28 (2) (d) applies only to companies under the control of five persons or
less. It is designed so as to catch devices whereby the persons in control of the
company get a tax advantage by manipulating its finances. Previously, when
such a company had money available for distribution by way of dividend, there
were means whereby the money could be taken out in the form of capital so as
not to attract income tax. Now Parliament strikes at those transactions. It
H   enables the commissioners to counteract the tax advantage by making an assessment as if the money were received as income and not capital. We have here a
company to which sub-s. 2 (d) applies, viz., Gleeson Development Co., Ltd. We
have a " transaction in securities ", viz., the sale of shares for cash. We have
moneys received by the sisters which was " available for distribution by way of
dividend ", viz., £60,500 each. They so received the money that they did not pay
I   tax on it. It is not suggested that the transaction was carried out " for bona fide
commercial reasons or in the ordinary course of making or managing investments ". It is, therefore, caught by sub-s. 2 (d) provided: (i) that the sisters
received the moneys " in connexion with the distribution of profits " of Gleeson
Development Co., Ltd., within sub-s. (2) (d); and (ii) that the sisters obtained a
" tax advantage " within s. 43 (4) (g). Those are the only two points in the case.
As the argument proceeded before us, it was agreed that we must not lift the

---

(1) In *Inland Revenue Comrs.* v. *Parker*, [1966] 1 All E.R. 399 at p. 413, letter I.
(2) [1966] 1 All E.R. 399.

curtain and look inside the bodies corporate. We must treat them as legal persons **A** separate and distinct from their shareholders.

1. Did each of the sisters receive her £60,500 " in connexion with the distribution of profits "? If it were not for the definition clause, the answer would be " No ". Gleeson Development Co., Ltd., did not distribute any profits. It only bought shares; but the definition clause says that references to " profits " include references to " income, reserves and other assets ", and that references to " distri- **B** bution " include references to " transfer or realisation ". It seems to me, therefore, that instead of the words " distribution of profits ", we can read " transfer of assets ". Counsel for the taxpayers submitted that that was too naive an approach. He besought us to expand sub-s. (2) (d) in full, after the manner in which LORD GUEST expanded it in *Parker's* case (3) and said that it would then appear that the receipt of these sums of £60,500 by the sisters was not caught by the subsection. **C** I do not accept counsel's argument. My mind is too simple to follow him into these niceties. I think that, if these sums were received by the sisters " in connexion with the transfer of assets ", that is enough. The commissioners thought that there was no transfer of assets here, relying on *St. Aubyn (L.M.)* v. *A.-G. (No. 2)* (4). PENNYCUICK, J., thought (5) that there was a transfer of assets, relying on *Thomas* v. *Marshall (Inspector of Taxes)* (6). I agree with PENNYCUICK, J., on **D** this point. I think that the payment of these two sums of £60,500 was a " transfer of assets " by the company. True the transfer was the purchase price of shares: but it was a transfer of assets all the same. The sums were received by the sisters " in connexion with the transfer of assets ", and were, therefore, " in connexion with the distribution of profits " within sub-s. (2) (d).

2. Did the sisters obtain a " tax advantage" within s. 43 (4) (g)? The **E** relevant words are that " tax advantage " means " the avoidance or reduction of an assessment to income tax, or the avoidance of a possible assessment thereto ". It seems to me that the sisters did obtain a tax advantage. They avoided an assessment to income tax or a possible assessment in this way. If the two sums of £60,500 had been received by the sisters by way of dividend, they would have been assessed to tax; but, as the two sums were received by the sisters as the **F** purchase price for shares, they avoided that assessment. Counsel for the taxpayers says that this view is wrong, because Gleeson Development Co., Ltd., received forty-four thousand shares in exchange for £121,000. The company could have distributed those shares *in specie* by way of dividend, or it could have sold the shares and distributed the proceeds by way of dividend. On any such distribution, the sisters would be liable to be assessed for tax. So they did not **G** avoid an assessment or possible assessment to tax.

This is an attractive argument but I do not think that it should prevail. The suggestion is utterly unreal. Gleeson Development Co., Ltd., would never have dreamt of distributing the shares by way of dividend or of realising them and distributing the proceeds. As there was no possibility of such a distribution, there was no possible assessment; and, therefore, no avoidance of a possible **H** assessment. Counsel for the taxpayer said that, however improbable, it was possible; and it would be most unfair that the sisters should now be caught under sub-s. (2) (d) and afterwards caught on a distribution of dividend. I am sure that the courts are well able to take care of that contingency. They would not allow the sisters to be taxed twice over in that way. In my opinion, therefore, the sisters did obtain a " tax advantage " within s. 43 (4) (g). This means **I** that the Crown succeed. Their massive attack on tax avoidance seems to have reached its objective. I would allow the appeal accordingly.

DANCKWERTS, L.J.: Section 28 of the Finance Act, 1960, is a highly artificial section and not at all easy to follow in its complicated language. Its

(3) [1966] 1 All E.R. at p. 412, letter B.   (4) [1951] 2 All E.R. 473; [1952] A.C. 15.
(5) [1965] 2 All E.R. 603 at p. 609, letter D.
(6) [1953] 1 All E.R. 1102; [1953] A.C. 543; 34 Tax Cas. 178.

A objects are clear: to enable the Commissioners of Inland Revenue to out-manoeuvre the ingenuity of wealthy taxpayers in arranging their business affairs so as to avoid or minimise tax. How delightful it must be to a taxing officer to have the power to counteract " a tax advantage ", which a person is in a position to obtain, or has obtained, by assessment or other adjustments! The section is indeed a tax collector's dream. Gone is the old principle that a citizen

B was entitled to arrange his affairs so as to minimise his liability to tax.

LORD DENNING, M.R., has set out fully the facts and the arguments, and I agree with his conclusion that the transaction in this case is within the words of the section. There is no dispute that the operations carried out involved a transaction in securities. The money which the sisters received in exchange for the shares which they sold was undoubtedly money in the possession of Gleeson

C Development Co., Ltd., which was available to that company for distribution by way of dividend. If it could be transferred to the sisters in the form of capital in such a way that it would avoid payment of income tax, then " a tax advantage" would have been obtained by them. It was not a transaction carried out " for bona fide commercial reasons or in the ordinary course of making or managing investments ". Indeed, it is plain that the transaction was carried out for the

D very natural purpose of avoiding the heavy taxation which would be incurred if the money was distributed as dividends. This brings the transaction at once within the definition of " tax advantage " in s. 43 (4) (*g*) of the Act:

" ' Tax advantage ' means a relief or increased relief from, or repayment or increased repayment of, income tax, or the avoidance or reduction of an assessment to income tax or the avoidance of a possible assessment thereto,

E whether the avoidance or reduction is effected by receipts accruing in such a way that the recipient does not pay or bear tax on them, or by a deduction in computing profits or gains."

That is what the subsection says. The result is that the " tax advantage " can be " counteracted " by the means mentioned in s. 28 (3).

F It also seems to me that it is impossible to say that the transfer of the shares as a result of the sales was not a " transfer of assets " within the wide definitions introduced into s. 28 by the provisions of s. 28 (2) (*d*). Counsel for the taxpayers advanced an ingenious argument, but I did not find it convincing. I sympathise with the two sisters who will suffer such heavy demands for tax. All taxation is confiscation and this is a very severe case. I agree that the appeal must be allowed.

G
SALMON, L.J.: I agree, and, but for the fact that we are differing from the judge (7), I should have been content to add nothing to what has fallen from my lords. The taxpayers would not be caught by s. 28 of the Finance Act, 1960, if they could bring themselves within the exception in sub-s. (1) by showing that the transactions in question were carried out

H ". . . either for bona fide commercial reasons or in the ordinary course of making or managing investments and that none of them has as . . . one of their main objects, to enable tax advantages to be obtained . . ."

This they did not attempt to do, and the natural inference is that they were unable to do so. If the taxpayers did not carry out the transactions in the

I ordinary course of business or in making or managing investments, a strong inference, on the facts of this case, is that they carried out the transactions with the object of gaining a tax advantage. The appeal really depends on whether or not they succeeded in attaining this object.

The accounts of Gleeson Development Co., Ltd., show that immediately prior to the transactions in question there was upwards of a £180,000 favourable balance in the company's profit and loss account and £130,000 in cash at the bank. Clearly, on a most conservative basis, £121,000 could easily have been

(7) [1965] 2 All E.R. 603.

distributed to the shareholders by way of dividend but it would have been liable **A**
to surtax in the hands of the taxpayers who were the only shareholders.   They
held in equal shares all the issued share capital in Gleeson Development Co., Ltd.,
and M. J. Gleeson, Ltd.   Thus they controlled both companies.   Each sold
twenty-two thousand of her shares in M. J. Gleeson, Ltd., to Gleeson Development
Co., Ltd., for £60,500.   As a result of the transactions £121,000 in cash was paid to
the taxpayers out of the coffers of Gleeson Development Co., Ltd., and that com-   **B**
pany, which was wholly owned by the taxpayers, became the registered holder of
forty-four thousand shares in M. J. Gleeson, Ltd.   If tax could thus be successfully
avoided, the door would be wide open.   Imagine two other companies, A and B,
whose shares were wholly owned by the same persons.   Each company had a
flourishing business and large accumulations of undistributed profits represented
by cash at the bank, and also fixed assets worth even more than the cash balances.   **C**
The profits had been left undistributed because the shareholders were large
surtax payers.   This is not uncommon.   The shares in each company were
properly valued at more than the amount of the fixed assets.   If the construction
of s. 28 adopted by the judge is correct, the shareholders could draw out the whole
amount of undistributed profits in each company without incurring any surtax
liability by the simple expedient of selling a block of their shares in company A   **D**
to company B and vice versa.   At the end of the day, all the undistributed
profits in both companies would have found their way out of the coffers of the
companies into the pockets of the shareholders, and the shareholders would for
all practical purposes enjoy the same control over the shares as they had enjoyed
formerly.   It seems to me that, in such circumstances, it would be an affront
to common sense to say that no tax advantage had been obtained.   **E**

I, of course, appreciate that a limited company is an entirely separate entity
from its corporators and that, even if there be only one corporator, he has no
legal or equitable property in the assets of the corporation.   This doctrine is as
well established as it is rigidly applied; indeed, it has been pushed to the length
of holding that such a corporator has no insurable interest in the assets of the
corporation—even though their destruction spells his ruin (*Macaura* v. *Northern*   **F**
Assurance Co., Ltd. (8)).   This seems to me to be a strange result, especially as
the rule that an insurance policy cannot be enforced by the assured unless he has
an insurable interest in the thing insured was evolved only to prevent gambling
and wagering transactions from being enforced in our courts.   It is perhaps time
that the application of the doctrine stated in *Macaura's* case (8) should be
reconsidered.   That authority is, however, binding on this court.   It compels   **G**
me to recognise that the taxpayers have no legal or equitable property in the
forty-four thousand shares in M. J. Gleeson, Ltd., which they sold to Gleeson
Development Co., Ltd.   It does not, in my view, inhibit me from regarding the
realities of the situation when I consider what was the taxpayers' object in
entering into these transactions.   Their object was clearly to obtain £121,000 in
cash, free from surtax, out of the assets of Gleeson Development Co., Ltd., which   **H**
were available for distribution as dividends and to retain control of the forty-four
thousand shares in M. J. Gleeson, Ltd., which were transferred to Gleeson Development Co., Ltd.   I have no doubt that the taxpayers have attained all those
objects and would be able to retain the tax advantage but for s. 28.   They have
received £121,000 which " represents the value of assets " which were " available
for distribution by way of dividend ".   And they have paid no surtax on this sum.   **I**

It seems to me quite unrealistic for the taxpayers to say that this is not a tax
advantage because, if in the future Gleeson Development Co., Ltd., were to sell
the M. J. Gleeson, Ltd., shares and distribute the proceeds by way of dividend
or distribute those shares in specie, the taxpayers might be called on to pay the
tax again.   It is highly unlikely that Gleeson Development Co., Ltd., will
distribute the forty-four thousand M. J. Gleeson, Ltd. shares or their proceeds by
way of a dividend.   In the meantime they have saved the surtax on the grossed-up

(8) [1925] All E.R. Rep. 51; [1925] A.C. 619.

A sum of about £196,000. The amount of interest on this sum, whilst it remained in their hands, would be considerable. It seems to me, obvious therefore, that in any event the taxpayers would in fact obtain a very real tax advantage within the meaning of those words as defined in s. 43 (4) (*g*), and that they cannot lose it except by reason of the present proceedings.

   The judge bases his decision on this proposition (9);

B
   "... it is necessary to compare like with like ... one cannot look at an actual transaction by way of sale, under which a member of a company transfers to the company property equivalent to the amount paid by the company to the member, and compare that transaction with a simple receipt by the member from the company without consideration. That is a
C transaction not only different in form but producing quite a different result."

The judge went on to say that counsel for the Crown sought to overcome the difficulty by contending that the result of the transaction was in substance the same as a simple payment by the company to the taxpayers because they remained at one remove the beneficial owners of the shares in the M. J. Gleeson, Ltd.
D company. The judge observed (10):

   " I do not think that it is legitimate thus to disregard the corporate entity of the G.D. company ... I do not think that I am entitled to treat this sale as being, in substance, the equivalent of a gratuitous disposition by the G.D. company."

E No doubt the corporate entity of the company must be acknowledged and it is impossible to treat this sale as a gratuitous distribution by the company, but in my view this begs the question. As Lord Wilberforce pointed out in *Inland Revenue Comrs.* v. *Parker* (11), s. 28 mounts a massive attack on tax avoidance in many forms. I can see no good reason for concluding that the attack turns aside from all transactions in which the taxpayer is or appears to
F be giving some consideration for what he receives. In the present case it seems plain that the taxpayers obtained a tax advantage, that the transactions in question (i) were transactions in securities, (ii) were not carried out for bona fide commercial reasons or in the ordinary course of making or managing investments, and (iii) had as their main object the obtaining of a tax advantage. Moreover, it is equally plain that the taxpayers received a consideration, viz., £121,000,
G which was or which represented the value of assets available for distribution by way of dividend. The transactions were transactions in connexion with the transfer of assets, and for the purpose of the section, the transfer of assets is deemed to be equivalent to the distribution of profits. The company was under the control of not more than five people. Thus all the relevant requirements of s. 28 (1) (*a*) and (*b*) and (2) (*c*) and (*d*) are met. Accordingly, the transactions
H are caught by the section.

   I too have considerable sympathy for the taxpayers, since, after the amounts they have been paid are grossed up for surtax purposes, there will be very little left for them. It may be that there are other ways in which they could have obtained much of the money locked up in these companies without incurring any surtax liability. Quite apart from a winding-up, they might have interposed
I a buyer between themselves and Gleeson Development Co., Ltd., in which case the consideration which they received might not have been or represented the value of assets available for distribution by way of dividend; they might have taken a simple loan from the company. There are many things which they might have done. I have no doubt, however, that, unfortunately for them,

---

(9) [1965] 2 All E.R. at p. 609, letters H, I.
(10) [1965] 2 All E.R. at p. 610, letters B, D.
(11) [1966] 1 All E.R. at p. 413, letter I.

what they did obtained a tax advantage which s. 28 takes away. I would **A**
accordingly allow the appeal.

     Appeals allowed.   Leave to appeal to the House of Lords granted.

  Solicitors: *Solicitor of Inland Revenue; Trollope & Winckworth* (for the
respondent taxpayers).

         [*Reported by* F. A. AMIES, ESQ., *Barrister-at-Law.*] **B**

R. *v.* HERRON.

[COURT OF CRIMINAL APPEAL (Havers, Veale and MacKenna, JJ.), February 21,
1966.] **C**

*Criminal Law—Evidence—Previous convictions—Receiving stolen property—
Discretion—Court has discretion to exclude such evidence although satisfying
conditions for admissibility—Larceny Act,* 1916 (6 & 7 *Geo.* 5 *c.* 50),
s. 43 (1) (*b*).

  Where the prosecution seek to adduce evidence by virtue of s. 43 (1) (*b*)*
of the Larceny Act, 1916, the trial judge has the overriding duty to secure a **D**
fair trial, and has a discretion for that purpose; accordingly if, even though
certain evidence is strictly admissible in a particular case, yet its prejudicial
effect once admitted will be such as to make it virtually impossible for a
dispassionate view of the crucial facts of the case to be taken thereafter by
the jury, then the trial judge should, in the exercise of his discretion, exclude
that evidence (see p. 30, letter B, post). **E**

  R. v. *List* ([1965] 3 All E.R. 710) approved.

  Appeal allowed.

 [As to proof of guilty knowledge on a charge of receiving stolen property, see
10 HALSBURY'S LAWS (3rd Edn.) 445, para. 820; 814, 815, para. 1576; and for
cases on the subject, see 15 DIGEST (Repl.) 1150-1154, *11,572-11,641.*

  For the Larceny Act, 1916, s. 43, see 5 HALSBURY'S STATUTES (2nd Edn.) 1038.] **F**

Cases referred to:

  R. v. *List,* [1965] 3 All E.R. 710.

  Murdoch v. *Taylor,* [1965] 1 All E.R. 406; [1965] A.C. 574; [1965] 2 W.L.R.
   425; 129 J.P. 208; 49 Cr. App. Rep. 119.

  Appeal. **G**

  This was an appeal by Ronald Robert Herron against his conviction on
Apr. 28, 1965, at Sunderland Quarter Sessions, before the Recorder (R. R.
RAWDEN-SMITH, ESQ.) and a jury of receiving £280, for which he was sentenced
to three years' imprisonment. The facts are set out in the judgment of the court.

  The cases noted below† were cited during the argument in addition to those
referred to in the judgment. **H**

  Myrella Cohen for the appellant.
  Norman Harper for the Crown.

  HAVERS, J., delivered the following judgment of the court: Counsel who
appears for the appellant has taken a number of points on his behalf. First of
all, she contends that there was in fact no case to go to the jury, and that the **I**
learned recorder was in error too in allowing the case to go to the jury. Secondly,
she contends that there was a wrongful admission of evidence of a highly prejudicial character, because the learned recorder allowed evidence of a previous
conviction for receiving and a sentence of three years to be admitted in evidence

----

 * Section 43 (1) is set out at p. 28, letters C to F, post.
 † *R.* v. *Seymour,* (1923), 17 Cr. App. Rep. 128; *R.* v. *Davies,* [1953] 1 All E.R. 341;
[1953] 1 Q.B. 489; *Director of Public Prosecutions* v. *Nieser,* [1958] 3 All E.R. 662;
[1959] 1 Q.B. 254; *Noon* v. *Smith,* [1964] 3 All E.R. 895.

A under s. 43 (1) (*b*) of the Larceny Act, 1916. Thirdly, she contends that the verdict was unreasonable and against the weight of evidence, and fourthly she asks the court to give leave to call additional evidence.

The short facts of the case were that a Mr. McGough, who was a fish merchant dealing largely in the market, on Saturday, Mar. 20, 1965, left his house at about 8.25 p.m. and went to see a friend in a public house about three-quarters of a

B mile away, arriving there about 8.30 p.m. He had at his house at that time in a wardrobe a sum of £2,000 which was made up in four packets of £500, each packet being made up of £5 notes and kept together by a blue elastic band. Mr. McGough returned home about 10.25 p.m., and found that his house had been broken into and the door of the wardrobe forced, and that the £2,000 which had been in the wardrobe had been stolen. It was plain from the evidence that

C the thief or thieves, whoever they were, were not aware of the presence of this money in his house because the house had been thoroughly ransacked in a search for money, and the thieves had not gone straight to this bundle of notes which they would have done if they had known of their presence in the house. There was no positive identification of the money which was subsequently found in the possession of Mrs. Borg, who was a sister of the woman who was living with the

D appellant. Mr. McGough was called, and all that he was able to say was that he had been shown the sum of £280 which had been found in the possession of Mrs. Borg, which was also kept together with a blue elastic band, that they were similar to the £5 notes which had been in his wardrobe that night, and that the elastic band was similar to the elastic band round the notes in the wardrobe. He had not kept a note of the numbers of the £5 notes. There were no marks of any

E distinction on them which were capable of being identified. Consequently, there was no positive identification of the money in the possession of Mrs. Borg as being the moneys of Mr. McGough. This is a matter of considerable importance, because it was the first and main issue which the prosecution had to prove as against the appellant.

The Crown sought to prove its case in this way. A witness, Mrs. Borg, who, as

F I have said, was a sister of Miss Elsie Jarvis who at that time was living with the appellant, was called to say that her sister, Miss Jarvis, called at her house and handed her on the night of Saturday, Mar. 20, 1965, a brown paper bag containing a quantity of £5 notes, kept together by a blue elastic band, and that she had asked Mrs. Borg to keep the money for her, saying that it belonged to the appellant. Mrs. Borg was a witness for the prosecution, and her evidence was that her

G sister arrived some time after 8 o'clock, and in cross-examination she said that it was between 8.0 p.m. and 8.30 p.m. and probably nearer 8.0 p.m. On this issue, time was of vital importance in this case because, if she was right and it was somewhere nearer 8.0 p.m. and before 8.30 p.m., it would have been impossible for the money which Miss Jarvis brought to Mrs. Borg to have been the money of Mr. McGough. The next day Sunday, Mar. 21, 1965, the appellant and another

H man came to Mrs. Borg's flat between 6.0 p.m. and 7.0 p.m. The appellant said that the door of his flat had been forced and he asked if Miss Jarvis had brought the money, and Mrs. Borg told him it was in her wardrobe. As he left, he asked Mrs. Borg to keep the money for him because the door of his flat had not yet been repaired. He said that the flat had been broken into. Later that evening, Mrs. Borg noticed that the wrapping of the packet had been disturbed and that

I the packet appeared smaller as if some of the money had been removed. On Sunday, Mar. 28, 1965, the police went to Mrs. Borg's flat and took possession of £280 all in £5 notes, kept together with an elastic band similar to the one Mr. McGough had put round his money, and the evidence was that this blue elastic band was of a common type which could be found in many places, amongst others in the market place. Eventually the appellant was arrested and charged with stealing this money. The prosecution put in evidence a previous conviction of the appellant at Newcastle Assizes in February, 1963, for receiving £1,004, and

also evidence of the fact that he had been sentenced to three years' imprison- **A**
ment in connexion with that offence. In addition, the prosecution called evidence
with a view to establishing that what the appellant had said, that his flat had
been broken into, was untrue and that, therefore, the reason which he gave for
asking Miss Jarvis to take the money to Mrs. Borg's was untrue. Evidence was
also called by the prosecution from a national assistance officer to show that the
appellant had been in receipt of national assistance for a considerable period and **B**
had made a statement to one of them that he had not any savings.

The first and main issue which the prosecution had to prove was that the money
which was found in Mrs. Borg's possession was in fact the money of Mr. McGough,
and there was, as I have said, no positive evidence of identification at all. In
those circumstances, the prosecution, who clearly had a discretion whether they
took advantage of s. 43 (1) of the Larceny Act, 1916, or not, took advantage of **C**
it, and put in evidence this previous conviction. That subsection reads a
follows:

"Whenever any person is being proceeded against for receiving any
property, knowing it to have been stolen, or for having in his possession
stolen property, for the purpose of proving guilty knowledge there may be
given in evidence at any stage of the proceedings—(*a*) the fact that other **D**
property stolen within the period of twelve months preceding the date of the
offence charged was found or had been in his possession; (*b*) the fact that
within the five years preceding the date of the offence charged he was
convicted of any offence involving fraud or dishonesty . . ."

The subsection goes on to say that this fact
                                                                               E
"may not be proved unless—(i) seven days' notice in writing has been
given to the offender that proof of such previous conviction is intended to be
given; (ii) evidence has been given that the property in respect of which the
offender is being tried was found or had been in his possession."

A notice was duly given under the Act of 1916 and, accordingly, when it was
sought to introduce this evidence into the case before the learned recorder, counsel **F**
for the appellant said that the defence objected to this evidence. She contended
that the learned recorder, notwithstanding the wording of the section, had a
discretion which he could properly have exercised and should properly have
exercised to exclude it. This section introduces what is something of an anomaly
in our practice in regard to criminal proceedings, because, in the circumstances
indicated in the section, it allows evidence of previous convictions to be brought **G**
before a jury which, except in most rare cases, is contrary to our usual practice
in the criminal law. It needs no words to emphasise what a highly prejudicial
effect this may have on a jury; and the effect could be even more highly prejudicial in this case if the jury allowed it to influence their minds on the question
of identity of the money, which was the first and main issue in this case, and not
on the issue of guilty knowledge, which was the only purpose for which evidence **H**
may properly be admitted as the section provides. It was plain in all the circumstances of this case that this money was not only red hot, it was white hot. If it
was once proved that the money which was in Mrs. Borg's house was the money
of Mr. McGough, it became transparently clear that the appellant must have had
guilty knowledge. The interval of time which could have elapsed between the
time when the thief broke into the premises and stole the money and the time **I**
when it found its way to Mrs. Borg's house some mile away would have been
extremely small, and the Crown, therefore, would have had no difficulty whatever, if they proved the identity of the money, in establishing in the circumstances
of this case that the appellant clearly had guilty knowledge. It was in the light
of those circumstances that the prosecution elected to introduce this evidence.

There has never been any decision of this court whether or not the learned
judge presiding over the trial has any discretion to refuse to allow evidence to be
given when it is tendered under s. 43 (1) of the Larceny Act, 1916. At the time

A when counsel was prosecuting there had been no report of the decision of ROSKILL, J., in *R.* v. *List* (1). There, ROSKILL, J., had a very similar case, and he had to make up his mind whether he had under the terms of this section overriding discretion to allow or disallow the admission of evidence if its prejudicial effect would make it virtually impossible to take a dispassionate view of the facts of the case. ROSKILL, J., having considered the arguments of counsel in **B** that case, said this (2):

" Am I then compelled, as a matter of law, to allow this evidence to be given? The Crown say that I am, and that there is a distinction to be drawn between the provisions of this subsection, where the evidence is allowed to be given for a specific purpose, and the provisions of the Criminal Evidence Act, 1898, under which similar problems do from time to time arise. In a **C** case under s. 43 (1), says counsel for the Crown, this type of evidence is allowed to be used for the single purpose of proving guilty knowledge at the time of receipt of the goods: under the Act of 1898, when evidence of previous convictions is allowed to be introduced at all, it is introduced for what counsel called ' the general purpose of attacking the prisoner's credit as a whole '. Thus it is reasonable, he argued, that the court should have an **D** overriding discretion in the latter case though not in the former. That there is force in this submission is without doubt. I drew counsel's attention to the recent decision of the House of Lords in *Murdoch* v. *Taylor* (3), where the House had to consider the position where one prisoner had given evidence against another, and whether or not in those circumstances the second prisoner had a right of counter-attack as of right in respect of which the **E** court had no discretion. The House held that there was no such discretion in any case falling within proviso (*f*) (iii) to s. 1 of the Act of 1898. It is, I think, important to observe that their lordships drew a clear distinction between the position where one prisoner attacks another prisoner, and where the prosecution seeks to adduce evidence of previous bad character."

F Then there is a reference to the speech of LORD DONOVAN, in the course of which he said (4):

" So far as concerns the prosecution, therefore, the matter should be one for the exercise of the judge's discretion, as it is in the case of proviso (*f*) (ii); but when it is the co-accused who seeks to exercise the right conferred by proviso (*f*) (iii) different considerations come into play."

G Then ROSKILL, J., goes on (5):

" Although, as I have already said, that decision of the House of Lords was a decision on the Criminal Evidence Act, 1898, and not on s. 43 of the Larceny Act, 1916, in my judgment the same principles apply. A trial judge always has an overriding duty in every case to secure a fair trial, and if in any particular case he comes to the conclusion that even though certain **H** evidence is strictly admissible, yet its prejudicial effect once admitted is such as to make it virtually impossible for a dispassionate view of the crucial facts of the case to be thereafter taken by the jury, then the trial judge, in my judgment, should exclude that evidence. I have ventured to deal with this at some length, not only in deference to the arguments to which I have listened, but because I am told that this point has never previously arisen for **I** decision at assizes."

He calls attention then to a passage in PROFESSOR CROSS'S book on EVIDENCE (2nd Edn., 1963) which says (at a footnote on p. 328): " The court may have a discretion under s. 43 (1) (*b*) of the Act of 1916." ROSKILL, J., continues (6):

(1) [1965] 3 All E.R. 710.   (2) [1965] 3 All E.R. at p. 711.
(3) [1965] 1 All E.R. 406; [1965] A.C. 574.
(4) [1965] 1 All E.R. at p. 416; [1965] A.C. at p. 593.
(5) [1965] 3 All E.R. at p. 712.   (6) [1965] 3 All E.R. at p. 713.

"I have reached my decision, first, as a matter of construction of the **A** statute, and, second, as a matter of principle, the principle being that a trial judge, as has been repeatedly said, has an overriding discretion to exclude any evidence the prejudicial effect of which hopelessly outweighs its probative value. In my judgment, that is the position here, and I therefore do not propose to allow this evidence to be adduced."

This court, after careful consideration of that case and that decision, is of the **B** opinion that the judgment of ROSKILL, J., is correct and sound in law. We adopt and follow it on the construction of the statute and on the principle that the judge always has the discretion and overriding duty in every case to secure a fair trial, and if, in any particular case, he comes to the conclusion that, even though certain evidence is strictly admissible, yet its prejudicial effect once admitted is such as to make it virtually impossible for a dispassionate view of the **C** crucial facts of the case to be thereafter taken by the jury, then he should exclude that evidence. We think that it is difficult to imagine a case in which that principle could apply more fully and aptly than this case. There was this principal issue that the prosecution had to establish that this money was the money of Mr. McGough, and the introduction of this evidence of a previous conviction for receiving a large sum of money, and a sentence of three years, was bound to have **D** an extremely prejudicial effect and one which, in the opinion of this court, would make it virtually impossible for a dispassionate view of the facts of this case to be taken thereafter by the jury. Counsel for the appellant has said that she contended before the learned recorder that he had a discretion; that the learned recorder did not really want to decide whether he had or not, but he did make it plain that, if he had a discretion, he was disposed to exercise it in favour of the prosecution. **E** If the learned recorder did not exercise his discretion, then, in the opinion of this court, he was wrong in not doing so. If, on the other hand, he did—and it may be that this is what he did—this court is of the opinion that, on the facts of this case, it was a wrong exercise of his discretion. It may well be that he had not in his mind, at the time when he was called on to exercise his discretion, the significant fact that the question of guilty knowledge in the circumstances of this case **F** was not really a live issue and that the real and only issue for the jury to decide was the identity of the money. If, in the circumstances, he did exercise his discretion, this court is of the opinion that he exercised it wrongly, and it must have had a highly prejudicial effect on the jury and made it virtually impossible for them to take a dispassionate view of the crucial facts. There was, therefore, a wrong admission of evidence of a highly prejudicial character in this case and, in **G** the circumstances, therefore, on this ground alone this court thinks that this appeal must be allowed and that the conviction must be quashed, and the appellant is entitled to succeed in this appeal.

Appeal allowed.

Solicitors: *Cohen, Gillis & Co.*, Sunderland (for the appellant); *Gordon & Slater*, Sunderland (for the Crown).   **H**

[*Reported by* N. P. METCALFE, ESQ., *Barrister-at-Law.*]

A   SOLDIERS', SAILORS' AND AIRMEN'S FAMILIES
          ASSOCIATION v. MERTON CORPORATION.

[CHANCERY DIVISION (Buckley, J.), February 3, 4, 1966.]

*Rates—Rateable occupation—Charity—Armed forces dependants—Charity owned
seventy-eight flats in which dependants of deceased officers resided—Whether
flats occupied by dependants or by charity—Charity entitled to rating relief—
Rating and Valuation Act, 1961 (9 & 10 Eliz. 2 c. 45), s. 11 (1) (a).*

The plaintiff association was incorporated by a royal charter. One of its
purposes was declared to be " to aid the families, widows and other dependants of deceased commissioned officers of all branches " of the armed
forces. The plaintiffs owned a property, comprised within which were
seventy-eight flats that were occupied by ladies who were widows or other
dependants of deceased commissioned officers. The plaintiffs gave priority
to those applicants for flats whose incomes were below a certain figure.
On being accepted each applicant entered into a tenancy agreement with the
plaintiffs whereby she agreed, inter alia, to observe the regulations made by
the committee that managed the flats, whether made before or during her
residence. The flats were unfurnished, the residents had their own furniture
and keys, the electricity and gas supply to each flat was separately metered
and the residents arranged their own heating appliances. There were important differences from an ordinary commercial letting, e.g., the flats were
rent free, the residents were obliged to observe the regulations, and the
plaintiffs could turn out a resident for any cause, or without giving a reason,
on one month's notice. Under the regulations the residents were obliged
to have a co-resident if the committee considered it advisable, for reasons of
infirmity, ill-health or senility; there were restrictions on visitors to the
flats, residents were not permitted to leave their flats for more than three
months in any one year and were obliged to give notice of any absence,
however short. The plaintiffs applied to the defendant local authority for rating relief under s. 11 (1) (a)* of the Rating and Valuation Act, 1961, in respect
of the flats on the ground that they were occupied by the plaintiffs, a charity,
and were used for charitable purposes, but the defendant refused the application on the ground that the flats were not occupied by the plaintiffs, but by
the lady residents. The plaintiffs applied to the court for a declaration that
they were entitled to rating relief under s. 11 (1) (a).

Held: looking at the substance of the matter and not the form, the
plaintiffs carried on at the property the charitable activity of making
living accommodation available to needy dependants of deceased officers
and the plaintiffs were, themselves, in rateable occupation of the premises
where those activities were carried on, the occupation by the dependants
being subsidiary to the occupation by the charity; accordingly, on the true
construction of s. 11 (1) (a) the plaintiffs were entitled to rating relief in
respect of the flats (see p. 34, letter H, and p. 37, letters G and H, post).

Test stated by LORD RUSSELL OF KILLOWEN in *Westminster City Council
v. Southern Ry. Co.* ([1936] 2 All E.R. at pp. 326, 329) applied.

[As to limitation on the amount of rates chargeable where hereditaments
occupied by charitable organisations, see 32 HALSBURY'S LAWS (3rd Edn.) 160,
para. 210 and SUPPLEMENT; and for cases on the subject, see 38 DIGEST (Repl.)
531, 532, *326-330*.

For the Rating and Valuation Act, 1961, s. 11, see 41 HALSBURY'S STATUTES
(2nd Edn.) 949.]

---

* Section 11 (1) of the Rating and Valuation Act, 1961, provided, so far as is relevant—
" If notice in writing is given . . . that (a) any hereditament occupied by . . . a charity . . .
is one falling within this subsection, then . . . the amount of any rates . . . shall not exceed
one-half of the amount which would " otherwise be chargeable.

Affirmed. C.A. [1966] 3 All E.R. 780.

Cases referred to: A
   Cory v. *Bristow*, [1874-80] All E.R. Rep. 136; (1877), 2 App. Cas. 262; 46
     L.J.M.C. 273; 36 L.T. 594; 41 J.P. 709; 38 Digest (Repl.) 504, *189*.
   Glasgow City Corpn. v. *Johnstone*, [1965] 1 All E.R. 730; [1965] A.C. 609;
     [1965] 2 W.L.R. 657.
   Westminster City Council v. *Southern Ry. Co.*, [1936] 2 All E.R. 322; [1936]
     A.C. 511; 105 L.J.K.B. 537; sub nom. *Re Southern Ry. Co.'s Appeals*,   B
     155 L.T. 33; 100 J.P. 327; 38 Digest (Repl.) 634, *969*.

Adjourned Summons.

This was an application by originating summons dated June 24, 1964, by the
plaintiffs, the Soldiers', Sailors' and Airmen's Families Association, a body
incorporated by royal charter, claiming a declaration that on the true construction
of s. 11 (1) (*a*) of the Rating and Valuation Act, 1961, the plaintiffs were entitled   C
to rating relief under the section in respect of the property owned by them and
known as Queen Alexandra's Court, Wimbledon, and every part thereof. The
defendant was the corporation of Merton. The facts are set out in the judgment.

   B. J. H. Clauson for the plaintiffs.
   Charles Sparrow for the defendant local authority.
                                                                                      D

     BUCKLEY, J.: The question which I have to decide in this case is whether
the plaintiffs, the Soldiers', Sailors' and Airmen's Families Association, qualify
for rating relief under s. 11 of the Rating and Valuation Act, 1961, which makes
provision for reduction and omission of rates payable by charitable or other
organisations. To succeed in obtaining relief under that section, it is incumbent
on the plaintiffs to show that the premises in respect of which they are claiming   E
relief are occupied by the plaintiffs, who are a charitable body, and are wholly
or mainly used for charitable purposes.

     The plaintiffs were incorporated by royal charter in the year 1926 to continue
activities theretofore carried on as a voluntary unincorporated body, and their
primary purpose is stated in their charter to be: " . . . to aid the wives, families
and widows and other dependants of all ranks (other than commissioned officers)   F
of all branches . . ." of the armed forces. An ancillary purpose is declared to be
". . . to aid the families, widows and other dependants of deceased commissioned
officers of all branches . . ." of the armed forces, by means of funds expressly
earmarked for that purpose.

     The plaintiffs own a property at Wimbledon which is known as the Royal
Homes, comprised within which there are four blocks of flats, called Queen   G
Alexandra's Court, and in those four blocks there are seventy-eight flats, which are
occupied by ladies who are widows or other dependants of deceased commissioned
officers. There are also certain flats in those blocks which are occupied by officials
or employees of the plaintiffs. No question arises with regard to those. I am
only concerned with the flats occupied by widows or other dependants of deceased
officers. The plaintiffs impose no formal means test on applicants for each flat,   H
but any applicant whose income is above a certain figure is informed that her
name will be put on the waiting list but that prior consideration may be given
to later applicants whose income is lower. The accommodation is provided
rent free, as will appear from what I shall say in a moment, but occupants who
are financially able are expected, as a matter of honour, without any legal obligation, to provide some contribution towards the running of the home. Each   I
applicant for a flat whose application is accepted by the plaintiffs enters into an
agreement with the plaintiffs in the following terms:

     " Memorandum of agreement made the . . . day of . . . 19 . . . Between . . .
   for and on behalf of the Soldiers', Sailors' and Airmen's Families Association,
   hereinafter called ' the landlords ', of the one part, and . . . hereinafter
   called ' the lady resident ', of the other part, Whereby the landlords agree
   to let, and the lady resident agrees to take, the suite of apartments, designated

A . . . in Queen Alexandra's Court, Wimbledon, for a term of one calendar month from the . . . day of . . . 19 . . . at the rent of a peppercorn per week if demanded until her tenancy shall be determined in manner hereinafter provided and subject to the terms hereinafter set forth.

" The lady resident hereby agrees with the landlords—(a) That she will pay the rent hereinbefore reserved when demanded at such times, and at

B such place as the committee having the management of the homes may appoint, and will observe, perform and keep the regulations for residents at present in force, or as may from time to time be made by the committee. (b) That at the expiration or sooner determination of the tenancy hereby created she will deliver up the apartments clean and in the same order (fair wear and tear excepted) as when she was admitted, together with all the

C landlord's fixtures and fittings as per schedule. (c) That in case of her death whilst an inmate, unless her friends or representatives shall see to her funeral within four days, the said committee may do so and sell her furniture to provide funds for the expenses.

" 2. The tenancy hereby created shall be determined—(a) Forthwith, in case the lady resident being the daughter of an officer shall marry or being

D a widow shall re-marry, but the lady resident shall be allowed fourteen days to vacate possession. (b) At the expiration of one calendar month after the death of the lady resident.

" 3. The tenancy hereby created may be determined by the lady resident by her giving to the said committee not less than one calendar month's notice in writing of her wish to vacate the apartments, and naming in such

E notice the date when she will give up possession.

" 4. The tenancy hereby created may be determined by the landlords . . . in case the landlords or the said committee having the management of the homes shall be of opinion that the lady resident has not kept, observed and performed the agreements on her part hereinbefore contained, or for any other cause shall deem the lady resident's retention of the apartments

F inadvisable and shall give the lady resident not less than one calendar month's notice in writing of their intention to determine the tenancy, without being called upon to give any reason for the same."

The regulations referred to in that agreement, as at present in force, are fifty-three in number.

The first regulation stipulates that

G

" The suite of apartments is granted free of rates and taxes, but the residents are responsible for charges for any gas and electric light consumed . . ."

and must defray all other expenses. Regulation 2 requires that every lady resident, on Jan. 1 each year, shall make a declaration as to her income and as to the income of her co-resident. The lady residents must at once report to the com-

H mittee any change which has taken place since their last declaration either with regard to their income or the personnel of their co-residents. The reference there to " co-resident " takes one to reg. 18, which states that it is desirable that the lady resident, if she has not a servant, should have a relative or friend to reside permanently with her, and it positively requires that she must have a co-resident when, in the opinion of the committee, a companion is desirable for

I reasons of her infirmity, ill-health or extreme old age.

There are restrictions on keeping pets and, by reg. 13, lady residents are required to make their own arrangements for the proper care of their apartments either by themselves or by a servant. Regulation 14 states that it is their responsibility for sweeping the chimneys in their own apartments and they must notify the superintendant as to what they have done in that respect. Regulation 17 forbids any lady resident to carry on any business or profession or trade in her apartments, and various other matters are also forbidden relating to the user of the flat. Regulation 26 provides that each lady resident will furnish and provide

everything for her own apartments and the committee do not hold themselves A
responsible for the safety of any article of furniture, goods, or chattels, or loss or
damage by fire, burglary or otherwise.

Regulation 34 is in these terms.

" The exercise of the usual powers of entry of the landlords, or their
agents, for inspection or otherwise must always be permitted."
                                                                               B
The duplicate key for the door to each flat must be retained in the superintendent's
office. Regulation 38 provides that the lady resident will not be permitted to
leave her apartment for more than three months in any one year. Notice of her
intention to be absent for any period, however short, with her temporary address,
must be given to the superintendent before her departure, on the form supplied
for this purpose and she must also report her return to the superintendant. C
Regulation 42 states:

" The occupation of the apartments is strictly limited to three persons,
i.e., the lady resident and two others. No male above the age of twelve years is
permitted as a resident. The underletting of apartments is not permitted.
Lady residents must not allow their apartments to be used or occupied by any
persons suffering from any mental trouble, or any infectious or incurable   D
disease."

Re-decoration of the flats is to be carried out at the expense of the association,
although lady residents are permitted to choose the colours, and repairs and
maintenance is also carried out at the expense of the association. By reg. 55,
it is provided:
                                                                               E
" Visitors are allowed temporarily to reside in a lady resident's apartments,
subject to the following conditions: (a) For ladies and children, a notification
must be made to the superintendent, before the date of the visitor's arrival,
on a form provided for the purpose. (b) For male visitors over twelve years of
age, permission must first be obtained in writing from the head office."

Those, I think, are the only regulations to which I need refer.   F
The plaintiffs have applied to the defendant local authority, or, rather, have
applied to its predecessor before the reorganisation of the local government of the
Greater London Area, the then Borough of Wimbledon, which has now been
superseded by the Borough of Merton which is now the defendant in these
proceedings. The plaintiffs applied to that authority for relief under s. 11 (1) (a),
but the defendant local authority refused to grant that relief, on the footing that G
the plaintiffs did not fall within the requirements of s. 11 (1) (a).

In these proceedings the plaintiffs seek a declaration that on the true construction of s. 11 (1) (a) of the Rating and Valuation Act, 1961, the plaintiffs are entitled
to rating relief under the section in respect of these flats. The question whether
the flats ought, in the circumstances, properly to be regarded as being occupied by
the plaintiffs or whether they ought to be regarded as occupied respectively by H
the lady residents, who physically enjoy them, is a question of fact which has to
be answered in the light of all the relevant circumstances which have a bearing
on the proper answer to that question. The occupation that is here in question is
rateable occupation, such occupation as will attract assessment to rates. Mere
physical occupation of a flat by one of these residents is not in itself conclusive
that the resident is the person properly to be regarded as occupying the flat.

I have been referred to two authorities, one of which is a decision on a Scottish I
statute: *Glasgow City Corpn.* v. *Johnstone* (1). That case related to a house which
joined or actually formed part of one structure with a church; it was occupied
by an official of the church, who was referred to as a church officer, but who, I
think, would be called a verger in this country. He occupied the house in question
rent free as resident, being employed the whole time as church officer and being
required as part of the terms of his employment to occupy this particular house

(1) [1965] 1 All E.R. 730; [1965] A.C. 609.

A   on terms that he would vacate it on the termination of his employment. It was held that the house was occupied by the charity, the church, since the church officer's residence was directed to the more efficient performance of his duty and, accordingly, the church was held to be entitled to relief from rates under s. 4 (2) of the Local Government (Financial Provisions, etc.) (Scotland) Act, 1962, which was there under consideration.

B   The other authority to which I was referred was *Westminster City Council* v. *Southern Ry. Co.* (2), in which the question was whether certain bookstalls, chemist's shop, kiosks, and so forth, within Victoria Station, London, were so let out by the railway as to be capable of separate assessment, or whether the railway company itself was assessable in respect of those hereditaments on the footing that they were " railway hereditaments " within the meaning of the

C   Railways (Valuation for Rating) Act, 1930. I need not mention the facts of that case in detail, but there are some passages in the speeches of the learned lords who decided the case which are of assistance in the present case. LORD RUSSELL OF KILLOWEN said this (3):

D   " Subject to special enactments, people are rated as occupiers of land, land being understood as including not only the surface of the earth but all strata above or below. The occupier, not the land, is rateable; but, the occupier is rateable in respect of the land which he occupies. Occupation, however, is not synonymous with legal possession: the owner of an empty house has the legal possession, but he is not in rateable occupation. Rateable occupation, however, must include actual possession, and it must have some degree of permanence: a mere temporary holding of land will not constitute

E   rateable occupation. Where there is no rival claimant to the occupancy, no difficulty can arise; but in certain cases there may be a rival occupancy in some person who, to some extent, may have occupancy rights over the premises. The question in every case must be one of fact, viz., whose position in relation to occupation is paramount, and whose position in relation to occupation is subordinate; but, in my opinion, the question must be considered

F   and answered in regard to the position and rights of the parties in respect of the premises in question, and in regard to the purpose of the occupation of those premises. In other words, in the present case, the question must be, not who is in paramount occupation of the station, within whose confines the premises in question are situate, but who is in paramount occupation of the particular premises in question."

G   Then he went on to refer to the rating of lodging houses. He said (4) that it had been settled that lodgers were not rateable, which decision purported:

" . . . to be based upon the paramountcy of the landlord's occupation, arising from his control of the front door and his general control over and right of access to the lodgers' rooms for the proper conduct of the lodging

H   house . . . On the other hand, the occupation of a person residing in a flat is such that he is (generally speaking) rateable, although as a matter of practice, the owner of the block of flats usually pays the rates charging the tenant an inclusive rent."

LORD RUSSELL then said this (4):

I   " My lords, I cannot but feel that the position of the lodger in relation to rateability is an exceptional one, and is largely the product of practical considerations. But it can I think be justified and explained when we remember that the landlord, who is the person held to be rateable, is occupying the whole premises for the purpose of his business of letting lodgings, that for the purpose of that business he has a continual right of access to the

---

(2) [1936] 2 All E.R. 322; [1936] A.C. 511.
(3) [1936] 2 All E.R. at p. 326; [1936] A.C. at p. 529.
(4) [1936] 2 All E.R. at p. 327; [1936] A.C. at p. 530.

lodgers' rooms, and that he, in fact, retains the control of ingress and egress   A
to and from the lodging house, notwithstanding that the power of ingress
and egress at all hours, is essential to the lodger. The general principle applicable to the cases where persons occupy parts of a larger hereditament seems
to be that if the owner of the hereditament (being also in occupation by
himself or his servants) retains to himself general control over the occupied
parts, the owner will be treated as being in rateable occupation; if he retains   B
to himself no control, the occupiers of the various parts will be treated as in
rateable occupation of those parts."

Later, he pointed out that the question of fact which had to be determined was
not one which turned on the title, whether the title to occupy was attributable
to a lease, a licence, or an easement (5). I do not think that he was there saying
that the formal aspects of the matter were irrelevant, but he was saying that   C
they were certainly not conclusive. He also said (6):

"In truth the effect of the alleged control upon the question of rateable
occupation must depend upon the facts in every case; and in my opinion
in each case the degree of the control must be examined, and the examination
must be directed to the extent to which its exercise would interfere with the
enjoyment by the occupant of the premises in his possession for the purposes   D
for which he occupies them, or would be inconsistent with his enjoyment of
them to the substantial exclusion of all other persons."

LORD WRIGHT, in the course of his speech, also referred to the lodging house
decisions. After quoting some observations of LORD HATHERLEY, recorded in
Cory v. *Bristow* (7), LORD WRIGHT said (8): "In other words the landlord
occupies his premises and uses them for his business of keeping lodgers." He   E
continued (9):

". . . the theory of the lodger does not depend on the fact that the landlord
still lives in the house, but on the fact that he still retains control for purposes
of his business of the whole house . . ."

The principle which underlines the "lodger decisions" is not one which is   F
confined to the relation of landlord to lodger, but has also been accepted as
pertaining to other facts. There is no doubt that the ladies who are residents in
these flats at Queen Alexandra's Court occupy them and no doubt in very much
the same way as a tenant of any flat let on a commercial basis would occupy
his flat. The flats are not let furnished; the lady residents have their own furniture
and keys; the electricity and gas supply to each flat is separately metered and   G
the ladies arrange their own heating appliances, and so on. Each flat is the
subject matter of a separate agreement in the form that I have read, and in many
ways the occupation by these ladies of these flats is not to be distinguished from
the occupation by an ordinary tenant of a flat let on a commercial basis. There
are, however, important differences: for one thing the flats are let at the purely
nominal rent of a peppercorn; there is no monetary rent whatever; in fact and in   H
substance the flats are rent free. The ladies are required to observe regulations
made by the committee, appointed by the plaintiffs for that purpose, that are
in force from time to time. They must observe any regulations that may be
imposed whether they are in force at the time when the lady residents come into
residence, or are imposed afterwards while they are residents. There is very
limited security of tenure: the plaintiffs can turn out any lady resident for any   I
cause or without giving any reason, on one month's notice, and the plaintiffs, by
means of their regulations, impose restrictions on the lady residents of a kind
which would be quite alien to the idea of an ordinary commercial letting. Perhaps the most noticeable examples are: the requirement that a lady resident

(5) [1936] 2 All E.R. at p. 329; [1936] A.C. at p. 533.
(6) [1936] 2 All E.R. at p. 328; [1936] A.C. at p. 532.
(7) [1874-80] All E.R. Rep. 136 at p. 141; (1877), 2 App. Cas. 262 at p. 276.
(8) [1936] 2 All E.R. at p. 345; [1936] A.C. at p. 556.
(9) [1936] 2 All E.R. at p. 349; [1936] A.C. at p. 561.

A must have a co-resident if the committee consider that is desirable, for reasons of her infirmity or ill-health or old age; the restrictions put on visitors to the flats, and the restriction which forbids residents from going away from their flats for more than three months in any one year and the obligation to give notice of any absence from their flats, however short, to the superintendent.

B Counsel for the defendant local authority has urged on me that on the true view of the facts in the present case these ladies are tenants of their flats and that the relationship between the plaintiffs and the lady residents is, in fact, that of landlord and tenant. He has urged on me the facts that they have, in substance at any rate, exclusive use of their flats, and it is not disputed by counsel for the plaintiffs that, as against everyone except the plaintiffs, the ladies are entitled to the exclusive use of their flats. Counsel for the defendant local authority

C points out that the rights of each resident are regulated by a formal agreement, that they are not subject to being moved from one flat to another, as lodgers might be subject to being moved from one room to another by a landlord of a lodging house, that they are free to come and go as they like, that the plaintiffs do not lock the gates or in any way control the ingress or egress to and from the flats, that the ladies are themselves responsible for furnishing and taking care

D of their respective flats, and that those are all important considerations to be taken into account.

On the other hand, counsel for the plaintiffs says that this is a case in which the plaintiffs do retain a substantial control of the use of these flats. They retain the right to make such regulations as they think fit from time to time. They retain the right to remove any resident on one month's notice, it is true, but without

E being under any obligation to give any reason for doing so; and he says that this is a case which is more nearly analagous to the lodging house decisions than to an ordinary commercial letting.

I think that it is clear from what was said in *Westminster City Council* v. *Southern Ry. Co.* (10), that I must have regard to the substance of the matter and not to the form. I have to discover, having regard to all the circumstances, whether, in

F substance, it is the lady residents who are in occupation of their flats or whether it is the charity itself which is in occupation in the course of carrying out its charitable activity.

It seems to me that the latter is the proper view. Although the ladies' rights and privileges are stated in the form of a tenancy agreement, I think that the true view on these facts is that the plaintiffs are carrying on a charitable activity

G at Queen Alexandra's Court, the activity of making living accommodation available to needy ladies who are widows or dependants of deceased officers in the armed forces, and that, although that is not a commercial business in the way that the landlord of a lodging house would be said to be carrying on a commercial business, yet the charity is here carrying on a business or activity, in consequence of which the charity is itself in occupation of the premises where the activity

H is being carried on; and that the occupation by the ladies of their respective flats is not of a kind that is paramount to the occupation by the charity, but is subordinate to it. For that reason, I think that the first requirement of s. 11 (1) (*a*), that the hereditament in respect of which the relief is sought must be occupied by a charity, is established, and it follows from what I have said that, in my judgment, these flats are being used for the charitable purpose which I have mentioned.

I Accordingly I declare that the plaintiffs, on the true construction of s. 11 (1) (*a*), are entitled to relief under the said section in respect of Queen Alexandra's Court.

Declaration accordingly.

Solicitors: *Rider, Heaton, Meredith & Mills* (for the plaintiffs); *Sharpe, Pritchard & Co.*, agents for *Town Clerk*, Wimbledon (for the defendant local authority). [*Reported by* JENIFER SANDELL, *Barrister-at-Law.*]

A

Re BRACE (a debtor), *Ex parte* THE DEBTOR *v.* GABRIEL AND THE OFFICIAL RECEIVER.

[COURT OF APPEAL (Sellers, Russell and Winn, L.JJ.), February 11, 1966.]

Bankruptcy—Adjudication—Appeal—Allegation that petition not served on debtor—Process server cross-examined—Debtor and his witness tendered for cross-examination but not cross-examined—No request by debtor to give oral evidence—Acceptance of process server's evidence and dismissal of appeal by registrar—Whether registrar entitled to accept process server's evidence without cross-examining debtor.

B

On the hearing of an application by a debtor to set aside, on the ground that the bankruptcy petition had not been served on him, a receiving order made against him, there were before the Registrar in Bankruptcy two affidavits, one by the debtor and one by another witness, filed on behalf of the debtor, and one affidavit of service of the petition. Having read these three affidavits the registrar asked to hear the process server, who was then cross-examined by counsel for the debtor. The debtor and his witness, whose affidavits were equivocal, were present, and were tendered for cross-examination, but were not cross-examined and did not ask to give oral evidence on oath. The registrar stated that he believed the process server, and dismissed the debtor's application. On appeal the debtor contended that the registrar should not have dismissed his application without having him and his witness cross-examined.

C

D

Held: the registrar had acted properly, the debtor had not been shut out from leading further evidence, and so the appeal failed.

E

[As to cross-examination on affidavits in bankruptcy proceedings, see 2 HALSBURY'S LAWS (3rd Edn.) 599, para. 1201; and for cases on the subject, see 4 DIGEST (Repl.) 555-557, *4875-4917*.]

Appeal.

F

This was an appeal by the debtor, David Bruce Brace, against the refusal of Mr. Registrar CUNLIFFE, in bankruptcy, on Oct. 26, 1965, to set aside a receiving order made against the debtor, on the petition of Harry Gabriel, a creditor. The facts are stated in the judgment of SELLERS, L.J.

A. L. Figgis for the debtor.
R. P. Ellis for the petitioning creditor.
The Official Receiver appeared in person.

G

SELLERS, L.J.: This appeal in my view is untenable and without foundation. The appellant debtor stated in his affidavit that a receiving order had been made against him of which he knew nothing until it was brought to his notice and that he had no prior knowledge of the proceedings leading up to it. Arrangements were made for him to come before the court on a request that the receiving order should be set aside, and Mr. Registrar CUNLIFFE fixed a day for the matter to be heard. The only question before the learned registrar was whether the bankruptcy petition had been properly served on the appellant debtor.

H

Two affidavits were put in on behalf of the debtor, one by the debtor himself and one by a Mr. Cox, and they were read along with the formal affidavit of Mr. Lowe, who said that he had served the petition on Monday, Aug. 19, 1965. The registrar, having read the affidavits and heard counsel for the debtor, said that he would like to hear Mr. Lowe. That seems to be a fair version of what happened. Mr. Lowe gave his evidence and at the conclusion of that evidence, after what the registrar described as a " searching " cross-examination by learned counsel for the debtor, the registrar said that he believed Mr. Lowe and he dismissed the application for the receiving order to be rescinded.

I

A   It is said before this court that there was some misconduct in those proceedings, based on the remarkable contention that there was no cross-examination on the two affidavits which the debtor had put in. There was no occasion for any cross-examination. The evidence was given by the one witness who was desired to be cross-examined on his affidavit, on oath, and that was convincing evidence which overbore the evidence on oath of the other two deponents, the debtor B and his other witness. I can see no ground whatever for saying that that matter was not perfectly conducted. There was no request on behalf of the debtor that he or his witness should give evidence on oath. All that is said is that the witnesses were there and were offered for cross-examination. I can see no occasion for any cross-examination at all. The affidavits on their face were not very convincing; they were equivocal; and the evidence of Mr. Lowe had C been convincing. That was the simple issue for the registrar, and he decided against the debtor.

This appeal is misconceived and I would dismiss it.

RUSSELL, L.J.: I agree. This is not a case in which the debtor was shut out from leading further or supplementary evidence. The only complaint is D that there was no cross-examination of him and his witness, which it is said might have given them an opportunity (so to speak) to show their paces. The point is hopeless.

WINN, L.J.: I emphatically agree with both the judgments of my lords.

Appeal dismissed.

E   Solicitors: *Balin & Co.* (for the debtor); *Stanley Wise & Co.* (for the petitioning creditor).

[*Reported by* HENRY SUMMERFIELD, ESQ., *Barrister-at-Law.*]

F

_____

G   ## *PRACTICE DIRECTION.*

Divorce—Practice—Documents—Copies—Discretion of registrar.

A registrar has a discretion under the proviso (1) to r. 79 (2) of the Matrimonial Causes Rules, 1957, to allow solicitors, not on the court record, to obtain on behalf of parties copies of documents relating to proceedings.

H   A solicitor applying for copies should be prepared to satisfy the registrar that he is instructed by one of the parties and each case will be considered on its merits.

COMPTON MILLER,
Mar. 21, 1966.   Senior Registrar.

I

_____

_____

(1) The proviso was added by the Matrimonial Causes (Amendment) Rules, 1961, S.I. 1961 No. 1082, r. 9, which gives the registrar power to grant, to persons not parties to the proceedings, leave to take copies of or extracts from such documents.

FREEMAN v. MINISTER OF PENSIONS AND NATIONAL INSURANCE.

[QUEEN'S BENCH DIVISION (Edmund Davies, J.), February 3, 1966.]

War Pension—Attributability—Suicide—Service conditions having played a part in producing conditions that led to suicide—Causation—Widow entitled to award.

In 1941 the appellant's husband suffered permanent disability while on war service. This disability resulted in amputation of both his legs. In 1962 he committed suicide. The Pensions Appeal Tribunal found that "the pain, suffering, and the anxiety resulting from his physical handicap, due to his accepted disability, made a major contribution to the depression which ended in his taking his own life". On appeal against the tribunal's refusal to award the widow a service pension,

Held: if service conditions had in fact played a part in producing the general complex of conditions which ended in a serviceman's taking his own life, his dependants were entitled to an award, for it was not necessary to show that service conditions were the sole cause; accordingly the appellant had established attributability (as, indeed, was conceded) in the present case and was entitled to an award (see p. 43, letter E, post).

Fuller v. Minister of Pensions ((1948), 3 W.P.A.R. 1617) and *Blanchflower v. Minister of Pensions* ((1950), 4 W.P.A.R. 887) distinguished.

Appeal allowed.

[As to whether death is attributable to active service, see 39 HALSBURY'S LAWS (3rd Edn.) 157, para. 151; and for cases on the subject, see 39 DIGEST (Repl.) 416, 417, *323-333.*]

Cases referred to:

Blanchflower v. *Minister of Pensions*, (1950), 4 W.P.A.R. 887.
Duff v. *Minister of Pensions*, 1949 S.C. 63; 39 Digest (Repl.) 418. *85.*
Fuller v. *Minister of Pensions*, (1948), 3 W.P.A.R. 1617.

Appeal.

This was an appeal by Christine Mary Frances Freeman, by notice of motion dated Nov. 23, 1965, pursuant to leave granted by the Pensions Appeal Tribunal on Nov. 10, 1965, from the decision of the tribunal given on Sept. 1, 1965, disallowing her appeal against the decision of the Minister of Pensions and National Insurance that the death of her husband, Frank Walter Freeman, was not directly attributable to a war injury or a war risk injury. The appellant sought an order reversing the tribunal's decision of Sept. 1, and awarding her children's allowances in accordance with the terms of the War Pensions (Mercantile Marine) Scheme* in that behalf, or alternatively remitting her claim to the tribunal for assessment of a pension. The questions of law raised by the appellant were: (i) whether the tribunal erred in law in deciding that the decisions in *Fuller* v. *Minister of Pensions*† and *Blanchflower* v. *Minister of Pensions*‡ precluded a finding in favour of the appellant, or in deciding against the appellant's contention; (ii) whether the decisions in *Fuller*† and *Blanchflower*‡ correctly and fully represented the law in cases where a claim is made consequent on suicide. The grounds of appeal were: (a) that the tribunal erred in law in that they did not hold that the death of Frank Walter Freeman was directly attributable to a war injury, namely, the injury that led to his accepted disability of below-knee amputation of both legs; (b) that the tribunal erred in law in regarding the cases of *Fuller*† and *Blanchflower*‡ as necessarily decisive of the claim. The said cases conflicted with

---

* The current scheme is the War Pensions (Mercantile Marine) Scheme 1964, S.I. 1964 No. 2058, which revoked and replaced the War Pensions (Mercantile Marine) Scheme, 1949, S.I. 1949 No. 1852, as amended by S.I. 1963 No. 1112.
† (1948), 3 W.P.A.R. 1617.
‡ (1950), 4 W.P.A.R. 887.

A   the decisions in *XY* v. *Minister of Pensions**, *Duff* v. *Minister of Pensions*† and *McCrorie* v. *Minister of Pensions*‡, and the tribunal was entitled to follow, and should have adopted the approach of, the latter cases;   (c) that if the tribunal regarded the cases of *Fuller*§ and *Blanchflower*|| as necessarily decisive of the claim before them, and binding on them, and were right to do so, the said cases of *Fuller*§ and *Blanchflower*|| were wrongly decided or should be reconsidered and

B   modified in the light of the decisions in *XY**, *Duff*† and *McCrorie*‡; and (d) that if the tribunal did not regard *Fuller*§ and *Blanchflower*|| as necessarily decisive of the appellant's claim, then having found in relation to her husband

> " that the pain, suffering and the anxiety resulting from his physical handicap, due to his accepted disability, made a major contribution to **Mr.** Freeman's mental depression, which ended in his taking his own life "

C   they should as a matter of law have held that the death of the deceased was directly due to mental depression, which in turn was directly due to his accepted disability, which in turn was directly due to his war injury, and that accordingly his death was directly attributable to his war injury.

D   *P. H. Ripman* for the appellant.
Nigel Bridge for the Ministry.

EDMUND DAVIES, J.:   The appellant is the widow of Frank Walter Freeman, who died on Oct. 31, 1962, at his home in Costa Rica as a result of a self-inflicted gunshot wound.   It is common ground that he committed suicide. At the time of his death Mr. Freeman was in receipt of a disability pension

E   assessed at one hundred per cent. for disability arising from below-knee amputation of both legs.   This resulted from his exposure for nine days in an open boat after the sinking by enemy action of the S.S. Oakcrest on which he was serving. In 1941 the right leg had to be amputated and in 1943 the left leg, for he had had frostbite and ensuing gangrene and obviously suffered a great deal of agony.

In December, 1963, the appellant applied for a service pension on the ground

F   that her husband's death the previous year was directly attributable to a war injury or a war risk injury.   The Minister having rejected her application, she appealed to the tribunal but in September, 1965, they disallowed her appeal, obviously doing so with reluctance but under the misapprehension that, despite the findings of fact at which they had arrived, which were strongly in favour of the appellant, the state of our law compelled them to reject the application.   In

G   that, as will shortly appear, they were wrong.   It would indeed be a remarkable state of affairs if, on the facts of this case as found by the tribunal, the appellant would not be entitled to a pension and it makes the court happy to think that the law does not require a refusal of an award to her.   Regretful that they had found themselves obliged to reject her appeal to them, the tribunal on Nov. 10, 1965, granted the appellant leave to appeal to this court against their decision and in

H   that way the matter comes before me today.

The findings of fact of the tribunal are vitally important and counsel for the ministry has told me that the reason why up to the tribunal's decision the application of the appellant was being resisted was on the issues of fact.   The ministry's advisers obviously were following the line that the deceased's temperament and personality was such that, quite apart from any war injury, his suicide would have

I   occurred and accordingly the death could not be said to be attributable in any way to the injuries and their sequelae (appalling though they were) sustained as a result of and during his war service.

The tribunal felt that no useful purpose could be served by dealing in detail with the degree of pain and suffering which the deceased had sustained as a result of the frostbite and gangrene caused by his exposure;   they found it

---

* [1947] 1 All E.R. 38.   † 1949 S.C. **63.**
‡ (1949), 2 W.P.A.R. 783.   § See footnote †, p. 40, ante.
        || See footnote ‡, p. 40, ante.

sufficient to say that he suffered very considerably and continued to do so in   A
varying degrees right up to the time of his death. They accepted the appellant
as a witness of truth. She testified that before the war her husband had been a
very active man, his chief hobbies being swimming and sailing; that, after his
war injuries were sustained, he was trained in England under a government
scheme and qualified as a physiotherapist; that he went to Costa Rica in 1946
and started a rehabilitation department, of which he became the head; but that   B
as the years passed that profession became more and more competitive and for
about three years before his death he was in continual fear of losing his job
because of his frequent unavoidable absences from work by reason of the trouble
which he was having with the stumps of both legs, particularly on the right side.
They accepted that over the years the deceased's temper became more and more
frayed and, furthermore, that this worsening of his temper was a result of his   C
physical disability. They accepted further that the deterioration in his behaviour
led to violence of such a character that, in order to protect herself and her
children, the appellant had been obliged to obtain a legal separation which had
become effective about six weeks before the deceased terminated his life. They
were satisfied that the medical evidence fully supported the testimony of the
appellant regarding the degree and extent and persistence of the pain and   D
suffering which the deceased had endured. After the last operation to one of his
stumps in 1959, the surgeon had recommended that a wheelchair be utilised
whenever possible in order to avoid further breakdowns in the stumps.

Then comes the crucial finding in this case. It is fatal to the ministry's resistance
to the claim, as they now concede. The tribunal expressed themselves in these
terms: E

" Having considered all the evidence with anxious care, we think it reasonable to conclude that the pain, suffering, and the anxiety resulting from
his physical handicap, due to his accepted disability, made a major contribution to [the deceased's] mental depression, which ended in his taking his
own life."
                                                                                  F
In other words, a major cause of the mental depression which led to suicide was
the disability resulting from the deceased's appalling war injury.

On that finding of fact one is surprised that the tribunal did not make an
award in the appellant's favour by allowing her appeal. Why did they not do so,
as they manifestly wanted to do? Their explanation is this:

" In rejecting the widow's claim for a pension the ministry, basically,   G
relies on the decision in the cases of *Fuller* v. *Minister of Pensions* (1) and
Blanchflower v. *Minister of Pensions* (2), and we have reached the conclusion,
with regret, that the reasons for those decisions also apply to the facts in this
case, and preclude a finding that [the deceased's] death was directly
attributable to a war injury or a war risk injury."
                                                                                  H
Therefore, although they had found all the facts which the applicant sought to
have found in her favour, they held nevertheless that the state of our law as
embodied in those two decisions compelled them to reject her appeal.

I must not refrain from expressing my sympathy with the tribunal in the error
into which they undoubtedly fell. Why did they decide as they did? I think that
they decided as they did because of a major misconception which crept into the   I
Minister's expressed reason for maintaining rejection of the appellant's
application. It is to be found in the Statement of Case and is in these words:

" The attention of the tribunal is drawn to the High Court judgment in
the case of *Fuller* (1) in which it was held that the act of suicide is an act of
which the cause lies in the man's own individuality *and nothing else* [I stress
those last three words] and that the worries, whether they be personal or

---

(1) (1948), 3 W.P.A.R. 1617.   (2) (1950), 4 W.P.A.R. 887.

A whether they be connected with his work, are the conditions in which the cause operates and are not a cause at all. The attention of the tribunal is also drawn to the case of *Blanchflower* (4)."

B The implication of those words is inescapably this, as I think, that in no case where a service man or ex-service man commits suicide can his dependants ever succeed in gaining an award, for the state of the law is such as to compel a finding that the service conditions cannot have played any part in the ensuing suicide. That would be a remarkable state of the law in any civilised society; it certainly never has been the law of England. For *Blanchflower's* case (4) and *Fuller's* case (5) decided no such thing. They are cases which turn on their own facts. The one principle of law which can be extracted from them and the other cases is this C and nothing more than this, that the fact that a person who commits suicide is at the time of his suicide in army or other service, or has previously been in service, does not of itself establish that his suicide is to be attributed to service conditions. In both those cases the facts were clearly against the applicant; in both those cases it would have been inconceivable that there could have been an award in the applicant's favour on the ground that service conditions operated in D any way to lead to the suicide. There are, however, reported cases where an award has been given on the basis of suicide. For example, in *Duff* v. *Minister of Pensions* (6) it was held to be quite wrong in a suicide case to impose the test whether the service conditions would or would not have caused a person of reasonable balance to terminate his life; that is, in considering the question of causation one had to take the service man as one found him and if, being the sort E of person he was, service conditions played a part in producing the general complex of circumstances which led to his ending his life, then his dependants would be entitled to an award. It is not necessary for an applicant to show—and I am here expressing a legal truism—that service conditions were the sole cause of the suicide; it is sufficient if they played a part in bringing it about.

F In the circumstances of this case counsel for the ministry concedes that, the tribunal having arrived at the findings of fact which they did, the ministry cannot resist this appeal. That, if I may say so, is the sort of concession which one would expect from the ministry in the light of those findings. There could be no clearer case than the present. The appellant is entitled to have her claim allowed on the basis of attributability and I accordingly allow this appeal.

Appeal allowed.

G Solicitors: *Vizard, Oldham, Crowder & Cash* (for the appellant); *Solicitor, Ministry of Pensions and National Insurance.*

[*Reported by* MARY COLTON, *Barrister-at-Law.*]

H

I

---

(4) (1950), 4 W.P.A.R. 887.   (5) (1948), 3 W.P.A.R. 1617.
(6) 1949 S.C. 63.

Re E. (*deceased*). E. *v*. E.

[CHANCERY DIVISION (Stamp, J.), February 15, 16, March 2, 1966.]

Family Provision—Deserted wife—Small estate—Deceased left wife and lived
with another woman for over twenty years until his death—He gave a house
and made weekly payments to his wife during the period of his desertion—
Nearly all his small estate was made up of a death benefit earned while living
with the other woman—Four children by her, two of whom were still at school
—Not unreasonable for him to make no provision for wife—Effect of a
claimant's eligibility for national assistance—Inheritance (Family Provision)
Act, 1938 (1 & 2 Geo. 6 c. 45), s. 1, as amended by Intestates' Estates Act,
1952 (15 & 16 Geo. 6 & 1 Eliz. 2 c. 64), s. 7, Sch. 3.

The deceased married the plaintiff in 1925. In 1941 the deceased deserted
the plaintiff and in 1943 he set up house with the defendant. There were
four children of the union. In 1941 the deceased and the plaintiff entered
into a separation agreement under which he was to pay her £2 10s. a week,
she was to live in the matrimonial home rent free, and was to maintain
the inside and to discharge the mortgage payments. He was to maintain
the outside of the premises. In 1946 the deceased entered the service of
Middlesex County Council; he held that appointment until his death, receiving £14 weekly. In 1950, as a result of the compromise of proceedings brought
by the plaintiff, the deed of separation was modified and a new agreement
entered into whereby he agreed to transfer the house to her and pay off
the mortgage and the weekly payment was reduced to £1. In 1953 the
deceased made over to the defendant the house in which they were then
living. In 1956 when the plaintiff, at the age of sixty, retired from her
work in a laundry she brought proceedings against the deceased on the
ground of his neglect to maintain her; the proceedings were dismissed.
In 1959 she transferred the house to herself, her daughter and her daughter's
husband. The two latter agreed to keep the house in repair. The deceased
left all his estate to the defendant; it amounted to about £1,000, of
which £971 was a death benefit from the county council in respect of his
services. The plaintiff applied to the court for reasonable provision to be
made for her out of his estate. At the date of the application the plaintiff's
assets were: the house, which was worth £3,500, her state retirement
pension of £3 7s. 6d. a week, and £300 a year from letting lodgings in the
house, making £475 per annum in all; she put her expenses at £10 a week.
The deceased had provided the defendant with a house, and they had lived
together from 1943 until his death in 1963. The four children were still
living with the defendant, and two of them were still at school.

Held: on a consideration of the facts the court did not find that it was
unreasonable of the deceased to have made no provision for the plaintiff
out of his very small estate, most of which arose from a grant earned by the
deceased during his cohabitation with the defendant; and he was entitled
to regard his estate as something that he could freely give to the woman
who had shared his life for over twenty years (see p. 47, letters E and H,
post).

Dictum of MORTON, J., in *Re Styler* ([1942] 2 All E.R. at p. 204) applied.

Per CURIAM: where a deceased's estate is so small, and the means of the
claimant so exiguous, that the only effect of making provisions for the
claimant would be pro tanto to relieve the national assistance fund, it would
not be unreasonable for the deceased to make no provision for the claimant;
but the fact that people who are very badly off can obtain national
assistance does not justify a deceased in making no provision for a claimant
out of a large estate (see p. 48, letter D, post).

Re Watkins ([1949] 1 All E.R. 695) considered.

A   [As to reasonable provision for a dependant, see 16 HALSBURY'S LAWS (3rd
Edn.) 461, 462, para. 920; and for cases on the subject, see 24 DIGEST (Repl.)
967-973, *9753-9771*.

For the Inheritance (Family Provision) Act, 1938, s. 1, as amended, see 32
HALSBURY'S STATUTES (2nd Edn.) 139.]

B   Cases referred to:

Inns, Re, Inns v. Wallace, [1947] 2 All E.R. 308; [1947] Ch. 576; [1947]
L.J.R. 1207; 177 L.T. 165; 24 Digest (Repl.) 973, *9769*.

Joslin, Re, Joslin v. Murch, [1941] 1 All E.R. 302; [1941] Ch. 200; 110 L.J.Ch.
65; 165 L.T. 171; 24 Digest (Repl.) 973, *9767*.

Styler, Re, Styler v. Griffith, [1942] 2 All E.R. 201; [1942] Ch. 387; 111 L.J.Ch.
263; 167 L.T. 295; 24 Digest (Repl.) 967, *9755*.

C   Watkins, Re, Hayward v. Chatterton, [1949] 1 All E.R. 695; 24 Digest (Repl.)
968, *9758*.

Adjourned Summons.

This was an application by originating summons dated May 15, 1964, by the
plaintiff, E.M.E., under the Inheritance (Family Provision) Act, 1938, that such
reasonable provision as the court should think fit should be made for her main-
D   tenance out of the estate of H.G.E., her deceased husband. The defendant was
S.E.E. who was the sole executrix of the will of the deceased. The facts are
set out in the judgment.

R. A. R. Evans for the plaintiff.

S. Ibbotson for the defendant.

E   *Cur. adv. vult.*

Mar. 2. **STAMP, J.,** read the following judgment: This is an application
by E.M.E., who was born in 1896 and is now the widow of H.G.E., under the
Inheritance (Family Provision) Act, 1938. I reserved judgment in order to
consider the implications, or possible implications, in a case such as the present
one of the decision of ROXBURGH, J., in *Re Watkins, Hayward v. Chatterton* (1).
F   The deceased died on Sept. 3, 1963, aged sixty.

At the time of his marriage to the plaintiff in 1925 he was in the Royal Air
Force, but shortly afterwards he left the Service and became a carpenter, and
after employment in various builders' firms he eventually entered in 1946 the
service of Middlesex County Council as a clerk of the works. He held that
appointment until his death, and received a wage of approximately £14 a week.
G   His net estate is of a value of approximately £1,000, of which no less than £971
represents a death benefit received from Middlesex County Council in respect
of his service with that council. At the date of the marriage the plaintiff had
an illegitimate daughter then aged eight, who was subsequently brought up by
her grandparents until she was eighteen. When she was about eighteen she
was received into the deceased's home, and there she remained until her marriage
H   in 1940. The deceased during that period helped her with money.

In 1935 the deceased for a period had an affair with another woman who was
not the defendant. He, however, returned to the plaintiff, and the plaintiff
asserts that until the defendant, S.E.E., came on the scene the marriage was
happy. There were no children. In May, 1941, the deceased deserted the
plaintiff never to return. In September, 1943, he set up house with the defendant,
I   a married woman. There were three daughters of the union between the deceased
and the defendant born in the years 1943, 1946 and 1949 respectively. The
defendant had also a son, born in 1942.

In the meantime in August, 1941, after his departure from the matrimonial
home, where the plaintiff still resides, and which was then subject to a building
society mortgage, the deceased and the plaintiff entered into a separation deed.
Under it the deceased was to pay the plaintiff £2 10s. a week. She was to live

(1) [1949] 1 All E.R. 695.

at the matrimonial home rent free. He was to keep the outside of the property A
in repair and she was to see to the inside of the property and was to keep down
the outgoings and discharge the building society repayments. Out of the
provision made for her she was to maintain herself and there was the usual
covenant against molestation. The plaintiff had the furniture in the house.

In about 1944 at a magistrates' court the plaintiff was bound over to keep the
peace following acts of molestation against the deceased. She had, it appears, B
written a postcard to the deceased's employers; she had put an advertise-
ment in the local newspaper; she had written to friends of the deceased; she
had written to the deceased's masonic lodge with the result that he had to resign,
and she had written to the allotment association, of which he was a member,
with the same result. In 1950 the plaintiff, claiming that the deceased was in
arrear in his weekly payments and that he had failed to keep the outside of C
the matrimonial home in repair, brought proceedings in a county court. The
proceedings were compromised on the terms that there were to be modifications
of the terms of separation. A new agreement was entered into which provided
that the deceased should transfer the matrimonial home to the plaintiff, and
should pay off the mortgage. It was provided, no doubt as a quid pro quo,
that the weekly payment should be reduced to £1 per week. D

The mortgage was in due course paid off and the house transferred to the
plaintiff, and although there is some slight evidence that at times the payments of
the £1 per week were a little in arrear there is no evidence that the deceased
otherwise failed to perform his obligations fully under the new separation
agreement down to the date of his death.

The plaintiff, prior to her retirement in 1956 at the age of sixty, worked in a E
laundry. Very shortly after her retirement and regardless of the separation
deed, the plaintiff applied for relief to a magistrates' court on the ground of
the deceased's alleged neglect to maintain her. I have had the advantage
of reading notes of the evidence given on that occasion, which are fairly
voluminous. What emerges is that there was no real ground for that application,
and that she hoped by putting pressure on her husband to induce him to increase F
the maintenance payments by an additional £1 per week. Not surprisingly
the application was dismissed with costs. Taxed in cross-examination with the
fact that she had not divorced her husband, she said she was not prepared to
overlook adultery, that she did not believe in divorce and that she had a higher
morality than that of her husband. She conceded that her daughter was the
child of a married man. G

On Mar. 17, 1959, the plaintiff transferred the matrimonial home to herself, her
daughter's husband and her daughter as joint tenants in consideration of a
covenant by the daughter's husband and the daughter to keep the house in
good and substantial repair and decoration, and during the life of the plaintiff
not to reside therein without her consent. The house is now of a value of £3,500.

The plaintiff has a state retirement pension of £3 7s. 6d. a week. Since her H
retirement she has let lodgings in the house and the letting she says produces
£300 a year, giving her a total income of £475 per annum. She put her expenses,
including the cost of feeding her lodgers, at £10 a week. Except for her interest
in the house the plaintiff has no capital.

It is common ground that the fact that the matrimonial home was made over to
the plaintiff by the deceased is one of the facts which are relevant to the question I
which I have to decide. Some of its present value, however, is no doubt attributable to the performance of the covenant to repair and decorate entered into by
the plaintiff's daughter and her husband. It is also said by the plaintiff that
the daughter and her husband had prior to the 1959 transfer put the house in
repair. I cannot, however, in the absence of authority, accept the submission
on the plaintiff's behalf that I ought, in considering whether the deceased acted
reasonably, to treat him as only having given the plaintiff a third of the value of
the house on the ground that I must look at the facts as at the date of the death

A of the deceased. If I were to do so, it would follow that a man who had during his life amply provided for a wife living apart from him by giving her a house and £50,000 which she had spent by extravagant living by the time of his death, could be said to have acted unreasonably in failing to leave her out of his estate of £10,000 a further endowment to support her.

I have to consider the deceased's moral obligations to the partner who is the
B mother of his family. The defendant was forty-three at the time of the death of the deceased, and is a far younger woman than the plaintiff. She was, at the death of the deceased, about the same age as the plaintiff was before the deceased deserted her, but she was divorced by her husband in March, 1947, on account of her adultery with the deceased. It is, no doubt, true that she can far more easily earn her living than the plaintiff can, and, indeed, I understand
C that she is now going out to work. She will not, however, always be forty-three— she is now forty-five in fact—and I cannot assume that she will find it any easier to save money in the years that lie ahead than the plaintiff has done. She, like the plaintiff, has been provided by this £14-per-week man with the house in which she resides with her four children: a house in Surrey which, it is agreed, I should treat as having a value approximately the same as the matrimonial
D home. If loss of income occasioned by the death of the deceased is, in any degree, to be taken into account in considering whether the deceased acted reasonably, the defendant has lost immeasurably more than the plaintiff by the death. All the four children lived and live with the defendant, and the two younger are still at school. Except that there is a Surrey County Council grant of £219 per annum in respect of one of the younger children, and that I am told
E the defendant now goes out to work and that she has this house in Surrey in which to live rent free, I know nothing of the defendant's means. The deceased was entitled I think at the moment prior to his death to have regard to the fact that almost the whole of his small estate of £1,000 was made up of a grant which was earned during the period in which he was living with the defendant and was supporting her and the four children. In fact by his will made as long ago as 1944
F not long after the birth of the eldest daughter, he gave the whole of his estate, in the event which happened of her surviving him, to the defendant and appointed her his sole executrix.

As far as I know the deceased and the defendant lived happily together, and the fact that in 1953 the deceased made over the house in Surrey to the defendant by way of gift supports such a conclusion.

G It would no doubt have been reasonable for the deceased out of his very small estate to have made up to his wife the £1 a week she was to lose by his death, but a judge cannot interfere with the deceased's dispositions merely because he thinks that he would have been inclined, if he had been in the position of the deceased, to make provision for the claimant.

". . . the court has to find that it was unreasonable on the part of the
H [deceased] to make no provision for the [claimant] or that it was unreasonable not to make a larger provision."

See the judgment of Morton, J., in *Re Styler, Styler* v. *Griffith* (2).

Taking into account the facts which I have recounted, I cannot hold that it was unreasonable of the deceased to make no provision for the plaintiff out of this very small estate. He was in my judgment entitled to regard it as an estate
I which he could freely give to a woman who had shared his life and family and home for over twenty years, and that is sufficient to dispose of this case.

Since, however, the decision of Roxburgh, J., in *Re Watkins, Hayward* v. *Chatterton* (3) has been pressed on me I think it right to add something more. In that case the plaintiff, who was the testator's daughter, was detained in a well-known mental hospital and there was, it appeared, no hope of her recovery.

(2) [1942] 2 All E.R. 201 at p. 204; [1942] Ch. 387 at p. 389.
(3) [1949] 1 All E.R. 695.

There was evidence that the testator in that case took the view that since the **A**
duties of the Minister under the National Health Service Act, 1946, which had
become an Act of Parliament but was not in operation before the testator died,
would require the Minister to maintain the daughter in a mental hospital, free
of charge, there was no duty on the deceased to make provision for her out of
his comparatively large estate. ROXBURGH, J., thought that the testator was
entitled, if he was so minded, to distribute his estate on the footing that his **B**
daughter could, as she certainly could and should, take advantage of the provisions
of the National Health Service Act, 1946, and that in doing so he acted reasonably.
Although, today, with experience of the needs, by way of comforts, of patients
in National Health Service hospitals, one might perhaps think that something
might have been provided for comforts, this decision seems to me logical and
sensible; for a man cannot be said to be acting unreasonably in not providing for **C**
something for which the state will provide and the provision of which by him
would only operate to relieve, not the defendant, but the state.

Counsel on behalf of the defendant invited me to apply the ratio decidendi of
that case to one where the plaintiff may be expected to be able to obtain national
assistance, and he called my attention to a passage in THEOBALD ON WILLS (12th
Edn.) at para. 331, where the implications of the judgment of ROXBURGH, J., are **D**
stated to be far-reaching. I accept the submission of counsel for the defendant to
this extent, that where the deceased's estate is so small, and the means of the
claimant so exiguous, that the only effect of making provision for the claimant
will be pro tanto to relieve the national assistance fund it would not be unreasonable for the deceased to take the view that there was no point in making
provision for the claimant, and that it would be reasonable not to do so. In **E**
my view, however, the ratio decidendi of *Re Watkins* (4) reaches no further. The
fact that today the very badly off can obtain national assistance, and will not be
left to starve, would not in my judgment afford any good reason of itself to
justify a deceased from making no provision for a claimant out of a large estate.
The purpose of the Inheritance (Family Provision) Act, 1938, is not to require
a deceased to keep the dependants there specified above the breadline but to **F**
ensure that reasonable provision is made for them having regard to all the circumstances of the case. It is, in my judgment, clear that it would be no answer to a
claim by a poor widow against her rich husband's estate that she can always
get public assistance, and that the deceased was accordingly entitled to make
no provision for her. This is of course a small, and not a large estate, but on the
facts of this case I am not satisfied that the payment out of the estate of £1 per **G**
week, or the provision for the plaintiff of a capital sum of, say, £500 as the equivalent of such a weekly sum, would merely have the effect of relieving the national
assistance fund from the burden of maintaining the plaintiff. There is no evidence
that if the plaintiff applied for national assistance she would get it; but if it
be the fact that she was, at the death of the deceased, in a position to obtain
national assistance, or was likely to be in that position, that would in my judgment **H**
be an additional reason for regarding the deceased as not having failed to make
reasonable provision for her.

The plaintiff is legally aided and I suppose this means that the costs of the
defendant, which are no doubt substantial, will fall on this little estate. If so,
it is a matter to be deplored and I can only hope that the remarks in the latter
part of this judgment will discourage applications under the Inheritance (Family **I**
Provision) Act, 1938, where the estate is pitifully small and the applicant is in
such a position that she is entitled to call on the state for national assistance.
There is judicial authority which, in so far as I know, has never been questioned
that the jurisdiction under the Act of 1938 should be cautiously if not sparingly
used, even where the estate is one of magnitude: see *Re Inns, Inns* v. *Wallace* (5).
It is no doubt true that, often, when proceedings are launched the plaintiff is

---

(4) [1949] 1 All E.R. 695.   (5) [1947] 2 All E.R. 308; [1947] Ch. 576.

A　unaware of the size of the estate, but where that fact has been ascertained the case ought in my judgment to be reconsidered. Where the plaintiff is, as in this case, legally aided I doubt not that this ought to be done.

In this case I would think it right, if I had power to do so, to echo the words of FARWELL, J., in *Re Joslin, Joslin* v. *Murch* (6) to prevent the very small provision made for the defendant from being reduced by these proceedings and B　dismiss the summons with costs.

Application dismissed.

Solicitors: *Cripps, Harries, Willis & Willis*, agents for *Garner & Hancock*, Hounslow (for the plaintiff); *H. R. Hodder & Son* (for the defendant).

[*Reported by* JENIFER SANDELL, *Barrister-at-Law.*]

C

ROGERS (Inspector of Taxes) v. LONGSDON.

[CHANCERY DIVISION (Stamp, J.), December 9, 10, 1965, January 31, 1966.]

Income Tax—Profits—Mining rents and royalties—Minerals recovered from dumps
D　　*of waste materials—Whether dumps had become part of the land—Whether*
　　　dumps were a " mine "—Payments at a rate per ton worked—Whether
　　　rent or payment in respect of an easement—Income Tax Act, 1952 (15 & 16
　　　Geo. 6 & 1 Eliz. 2 c. 10), s. 180 (1), (2), (3), s. 82, Sch. A, para. 1 (b).

During mining operations before 1874 on land for the extraction of lead, waste materials had been " dumped " on part of an area of about thirty-E　five acres of land, of which the taxpayer was tenant for life. About 1874 the dumps were planted with larch and other trees, and they subsequently became covered with willow weed, wild strawberries and coarse grass and for a time were used for grazing. The dumps contained fluorspar which at the time of dumping had no value, but had subsequently acquired a value. By an agreement dated Oct. 24, 1955, the taxpayer, a farmer, sold F　the " mines, veins and beds of fluorspar, calcite and associated minerals " in the dumps to a mineral merchant, who was authorised to work them on making payments which included one of 5s. for every ton of mineral worked. The minerals were not worked underground, but were got by pick and shovel and a tractor-loader. There was no evidence that fluorspar, etc. was normally gotten by mining operations or was a substance ejusdem generis with coal G　and other substances specified in para. 1 (b) of Sch. A to the Income Tax Act, 1952. The workings were not a mine within the Mines and Quarries Act, 1954. The taxpayer was assessed to income tax in respect of the payments on the basis that they were rent or payments in the nature of rent in respect of the dumps as land and were chargeable to tax under s. 180* of the Income Tax Act, 1952. The Commissioners of Income Tax discharged the assess-H　ments, holding that the dumps had not become part of the land, that the payments were not rent and were not payments in respect of an easement. On appeal,

Held: (i) when in 1955 the taxpayer sold the minerals in the dumps, the material dumped, having been originally waste, having lain on the land for some eighty years, having become covered by vegetation and having been I　planted with trees, had become part of the land (see p. 57, letters C and D, post).

Boileau v. *Heath* ([1898] 2 Ch. 301) applied.

Shingler v. *P. Williams & Sons, Ltd.* ((1933), 17 Tax Cas. 574) criticised and not followed.

(ii) the concern worked by the mineral merchant was not a concern referred to in s. 180 (1) (a)* of the Income Tax Act, 1952, because it was not an

----

(6) [1941] 1 All E.R. 302; [1941] Ch. 200.
* Section 180, so far as material, is set out at p. 52, letters E to H, post.

" other mine " within the meaning of para. 1 (*b*) of Sch. A, for the question
whether a concern was such a mine fell to be determined by its condition   A
and what was done there, not by what the mineral merchant agreed to do,
and these minerals were not won (nor was there evidence that they were
normally won) by underground workings; therefore s. 180 did not apply
and the assessments had rightly been discharged (see p. 57, letter E, and
p. 60, letter A, post).
 Jones v. *Cwmorthen Slate Co.* ((1879), 5 Ex.D. 93) followed.   B
 South Staffordshire Mines Drainage Comrs. v. *Grosvenor Colliery Co., Ltd.*
((1961), 125 J.P. 484) considered.
 (iii) moreover, the operations carried out by the mineral merchant were
not mining operations, and the concern was not a mine, because what was
worked was not raw material naturally in and under the surface of land
but was waste deposits artificially created; minerals in such material   C
could not be lying in a " bed ", " seam " or " stratum " and the workings
had no similarity to, e.g., opencast coal mining (see p. 60, letter F, post).
 Dictum of SCOTT, L.J., in *Mosley* v. *George Wimpey & Co., Ltd.* ([1945]
1 All E.R. at p. 678), held to have been rejected by the House of Lords in
Russell (*Inspector of Taxes*) v. *Scott* ([1948] 2 All E.R. 1), not followed.
 Appeal dismissed.   D

[As to the assessment of mining rents and royalties formerly not charged
under Sch. A, see 20 HALSBURY's LAWS (3rd Edn.) 221, 222, para. 395; and for
cases on the subject, see 28 DIGEST (Repl.) 159-161, *624-637*.
 For the Income Tax Act, 1952, s. 180, see 31 HALSBURY's STATUTES (2nd Edn.)
177 and, as amended, SUPPLEMENT, AMENDED TEXTS to Vol. 16, para. [182].]   E

Cases referred to:
 Boileau v. *Heath*, [1898] 2 Ch. 301; 67 L.J.Ch. 529; 33 Digest (Repl.) 730, *69*.
 Jacobs v. *London County Council*, [1950] 1 All E.R. 737; [1950] A.C. 361;
  114 J.P. 204; 30 Digest (Repl.) 212, *545*.
 Jones v. *Cwmorthen Slate Co.*, (1879), 5 Ex.D. 93; 49 L.J.Q.B. 110; 41 L.T.
  575; 1 Tax Cas. 267; 28 Digest (Repl.) 144, *552*.   F
 Mosley v. *George Wimpey & Co., Ltd.*, [1945] 1 All E.R. 674; 173 L.T. 24;
  27 Tax Cas. 315; *revsg. in part* [1944] 1 All E.R. 135; 28 Digest (Repl.)
  161, *637*.
 Russell (*Inspector of Taxes*) v. *Scott*, [1948] 2 All E.R. 1; [1948] A.C. 422;
  [1948] L.J.R. 1265; 30 Tax Cas. 394; 28 Digest (Repl.) 142, *543*.
 Shingler v. *P. Williams & Sons, Ltd.*, (1933), 148 L.T. 474; 17 Tax Cas. 574;   G
  28 Digest (Repl.) 34, *153*.
 South Staffordshire Mines Drainage Comrs. v. *Grosvenor Colliery Co., Ltd.*,
  (1961), 125 J.P. 484; 33 Digest (Repl.) 725, *23*.

Case Stated.
 The respondent taxpayer appealed to the General Commissioners of Income
Tax for the High Peak Division of Derbyshire, against the following assessments   H
to income tax made on him under Case VI of Sch. D to the Income Tax Act, 1952,
in respect of receipts by him in connexion with the disposal of fluorspar located
on land of which he was tenant for life: 1955-56, £207; 1956-57, £670; 1957-58,
£504; 1958-59, £326; 1959-60, £304; 1960-61, £750. The taxpayer was the
tenant for life of land at Longstone, Derbyshire, on which many years before
material from lead workings had been dumped. The material contained quantities   I
of fluorspar, which had been waste material when the lead was worked. The
receipts consisted of sums paid by a Mr. Broadbent to the taxpayer under the
terms of an agreement in respect of the right to remove fluorspar, calcite and
associated minerals from the dumps which had been made before 1874. The
taxpayer contended as follows: (i) that the payments made under the agreement
were not rents within the terms of s. 180 of the Act of 1952 paid in respect of
land which was not separately assessed under Sch. A. The area of the land on

A which the dumps were situate was in fact assessed under Sch. A. (ii) that the
payments made under the agreement were not made "in respect of any easement" within the meaning of s. 180. The payments were made as consideration
for being allowed to take away minerals dumped on the surface of the land and
were accordingly payments for the acquisition of chattels and not for a right to
use or an easement in respect of land (per FINLAY, J., in *Shingler* v. *P. Williams*
B *& Sons, Ltd.**). (iii) that proper tests for determining whether dumps of materials
on land retained their own nature as separate material or had reverted to and
become part of the soil were: (a) whether such dumps had reached such a condition that their contents would require to be excavated in the same way as
though they were virgin soil, (b) whether the land, including the dumps, had
reverted to its former use, and (c) whether the dumps were separately identifiable
C as matter deposited on the land; and that the result of applying such tests
in the taxpayer's case supported the view that the dumps in question had not
become pars soli. (iv) that the receipts in respect of which the assessments under
appeal had been made had already been the subject of a decision within the
meaning of s. 510 of the Act of 1952. The Crown originally sought to tax the
receipts under s. 179 of the Act of 1952 by requiring them to be included as a
D receipt in the taxpayer's farming business. That contention was not accepted
by the taxpayer and an appeal against the limitation of a claim under s. 341
on that ground was listed for hearing by the General Commissioners, but the
inspector of taxes by letter withdrew his contention that the receipts for fluorspar
were within s. 179 of the Act of 1952 and agreed the original claim for losses under
s. 341. Those claims related to the years 1955-56, 1956-57 and 1957-58, and the
E settlement between the taxpayer and the inspector allowing those losses without
deduction of the receipts from fluorspar was a decision within the terms of s. 510
of the Act of 1952 and such receipts could not subsequently be the subject of
assessment under s. 180. (v) that, even if the payments for fluorspar were such as
to fall within s. 180 of the Act of 1952, direct assessments in respect thereof could
only be made on the recipient if the payments were such as to fall within the
F terms of s. 170†. It had been admitted by the Crown that Mr. Broadbent, the
payer, had been allowed to deduct the payments in arriving at his business
profits subject to tax. On the basis that s. 180 applied as claimed by the
Crown, the allowance of such deduction was contrary to s. 137 (*n*). On that
basis, the taxpayer's alternative contention was that, if the correct procedure
had been followed in dealing with the business accounts of Mr. Broadbent, the
G payments would clearly have fallen within s. 169 and as such would not have been
assessable on the taxpayer.

The Crown contended as follows: (i) (a) that the original dumps made on the
land had become part of the land and had ceased to be chattels and accordingly
the payments were rents payable in respect of an easement within the meaning
of s. 180. (b) that the operations carried on by Mr. Broadbent in connexion with
H which the easement was used, occupied or enjoyed, constituted a mine and
accordingly the easement was used, occupied or enjoyed in connexion with one
of the concerns specified in the proviso of para. 1 of Sch. A within the meaning
of s. 180 (1) (*a*). (c) that therefore the payments were chargeable to tax under
Sch. D in accordance with s. 180 (1). (ii) that as the payments to the taxpayer
had been made without deduction of tax and had not been made out of profits
I or gains brought into charge, the assessments under appeal were correctly raised
on the taxpayer by virtue of s. 148 of the Act. (iii) that the letter written by the
inspector of taxes was written before the assessments in question had been raised
and accordingly it could not constitute a basis for invoking in relation to those
assessments the provisions of s. 510.

The commissioners did not accept the taxpayer's contention that the receipts
could not be the subject of assessment under s. 180 because there had been a

---

* (1933), 17 Tax Cas. 574 at pp. 583, 584.   † Sic; query s. 179.

previous decision affecting them under s. 510. However, they held that the A
waste materials had not reverted to and become part of the land but " had
remained as materials lying on the land and no action had been taken to render
the land on which they lay available for any useful purpose "; that insofar as
there was a conflict on that point between *Boileau* v. *Heath** and *Shingler* v.
P. Williams & Sons, Ltd.† they accepted the latter case and adopted the view
of FINLAY, J., that the dumps were not part of the land but " stuff " deposited B
on it. The payments made to the taxpayer were therefore not payments in respect
of an easement within the terms of s. 180 of the Act of 1952. They allowed the
appeals and discharged the assessments. The Crown appealed by way of Case
Stated to the High Court, and gave notice of a further contention that even if the
dumps had not become part of the land the payments were, on the facts and true
construction of the agreement of Oct. 24, 1955, rents payable in respect of an C
easement within s. 180 of the Income Tax Act, 1952.

The cases noted below‡ were cited during the argument in addition to those
referred to in the judgment.

Sir George Honeyman, Q.C., and *J. R. Phillips* for the Crown.
P. M. B. Rowland for the taxpayer.

Cur. adv. vult. D

Jan. 31. **STAMP, J.**, read the following judgment: The question to be
determined in this case is whether certain periodical payments made to a taxpayer
in accordance with the terms of the agreement, to which I shall refer, fall within
s. 180 of the Income Tax Act, 1952. That section contains, so far as is material,
these provisions: E

" (1) Where rent is payable in respect of any land the property in which is
not separately assessed and charged under Sch. A, or in respect of any
easement, and—(*a*) the land or easement is used, occupied or enjoyed
in connexion with any of the concerns specified in the proviso to para. 1
of Sch. A; or [then follows in para. (*b*) an alternative to which I need not
refer] the rent shall be charged to tax under Sch. D and shall, subject to F
the provisions of this section, be subject to deduction of tax under Ch. I
of this Part of this Act as if it were a royalty or other sum paid in respect of
the user of a patent."

Then there is a proviso which is, I think, immaterial for the purposes of this case.
Subsection (2) contains provisions to which I need not refer, and then sub-s. (3) G
provides, inter alia,

" For the purposes of this section—' easement ' includes any right,
privilege or benefit in, over or derived from land; and ' rent ' includes a rent
service, rentcharge, fee farm rent, feu duty or other rent, toll, duty, royalty
or annual or periodical payment in the nature of rent, whether payable in
money or money's worth or otherwise . . ." H

and then there is a provision for exclusion, which I do not think is relevant.
Then the subsection goes on to enlarge references to easements, but nothing

---

* [1898] 2 Ch. 301.
† (1933), 17 Tax Cas. 574.
‡ *R.* v. *Dunsford*, (1835), 2 Ad. & El. 568; *Darvill* v. *Roper*, (1855), 3 Drew. 294; I
Dowager Duchess of Cleveland v. *Meyrick*, (1867), 37 L.J.Ch. 125; *Holland* v. *Hodgson*,
[1861-1873] All E.R. Rep. 237; (1872), L.R. 7 C.P. 328; *Glasgow Corpn.* v. *Fairie*,
[1886-90] All E.R. Rep. 115; (1888), 13 App. Cas. 657; *Midland Ry. Co.* v. *Robinson*,
[1886-90] All E.R. Rep. 742; (1889), 15 App. Cas. 19; *Reynolds* v. *Ashby & Sons*,
[1904-07] All E.R. Rep. 401; [1904] A.C. 466; *Morgan* v. *Russell & Sons*, [1909] 1
K.B. 357; *Golden Horseshoe (New), Ltd.* v. *Thurgood (Inspector of Taxes)*, [1933] All
E.R. Rep. 402; [1934] 1 K.B. 548; *Stratford* v. *Mole and Lea*, (1941), 24 Tax Cas. 20;
Earl Fitzwilliam's Collieries Co. v. *Phillips*, [1943] 2 All E.R. 346; [1943] A.C. 570;
Craigenlow Quarries, Ltd. v. *Inland Revenue Comrs.*, 1952 S.C. 765; 32 Tax Cas. 326;
Inland Revenue Comrs. v. *Broomhouse Brick Co., Ltd.*, 1952 S.C. 407; 34 Tax Cas. 1.

A turns on that enlargement. The concerns specified in the proviso to para. 1 of
Sch. A, which are referred to in para. (a) of s. 180 (1), are these:

" (a) quarries of stone, slate, limestone or chalk; and (b) mines of coal,
tin, lead, copper, mundic, iron and other mines; and (c) ironworks, gasworks,
salt springs or works, alum mines or works, waterworks, streams of water,
canals, inland navigations, docks, drains or levels, fishings, rights of markets
B and fairs, tolls, railways and other ways, bridges, ferries and other concerns
of the like nature having profits from or arising out of any lands, tenements,
hereditaments or heritages."

Before I refer to the facts of the case, I find it convenient to read those parts
of the agreement which appear to me to be relevant for the purposes of this case.
C The agreement is dated Oct. 24, 1955, and was expressly made between the
taxpayer of the one part, who is described as a farmer and the vendor, and Mr.
Willis Joseph Broadbent who is described as of Main Street, Calver, in the
county of Derbyshire, a mineral merchant. The agreement provides by cl. 1
as follows:

" In consideration of the payments mentioned in Sch. 1 hereto and of the
D covenants on the part of the purchaser hereinafter contained the vendor
doth hereby sell and the purchaser doth hereby purchase all the mines
veins and beds of fluorspar calcite and associated minerals therewith including
all such minerals and hillocks and dumps of miners refuse upon the surface
(hereinafter called the said minerals) lying in and upon or under the area of
land (hereinafter called the mineral area) particularly described in Sch. 2
E hereto which shall be gotten or worked by the purchaser during the term
referred to in Sch. 3 hereto or any extension thereof."

Those are the only provisions in what I might describe as the operative part
of the agreement to which I need refer. Schedule 1 contains particulars of the
payments to be made by the purchaser and so far as is material is as follows:

F " (1) Upon signing of this agreement a sum of £400 in respect of the
timber other than elm sycamore and other hardwoods upon the mineral
area which shall thereupon become the absolute property of the purchaser
who shall cut and remove the same during the term of ten years or working
term or any extension thereof and shall remove the roots of all such trees
from the land and burn them together with all loppings and toppings from the
G trees aforesaid leaving no unburnt timber belonging to the purchaser upon
the mineral area or elsewhere on the vendor's property excepting the hardwoods as aforesaid.

" (2) A sum of 5s. for every ton of the said minerals worked or gotten
by the purchaser being the price of the said minerals. And it is hereby
agreed that the purchaser shall during each month of the said term remove
H not less than sixteen tons of the said minerals and even if the said quantity of
sixteen tons shall not be removed shall pay the vendor a payment of £4
for each month which payment shall be deemed to merge with the price of
minerals in every month where more than sixteen tons shall be removed."

Then there is a wayleave payment:

" (3) In respect of minerals (including lead) on in or under the said land,
I which are not the property of the vendor and which the purchaser is duly
authorised to work or remove a wayleave payment of five per centum of the
market value of the quantity of such minerals removed such market value
being the price then ruling for such minerals when offered for sale."

Paragraph 4 of Sch. 1 contains a provision for the making of a deposit as a
security for the purchaser's covenants.

Schedule 2 contains a description of the mineral area, described as " An
enclosure of land situate in the parish of Great Longstone in the county of

Derby ", and there is a reference to the number on the Ordnance sheets, " con- **A** taining 8.3 acres or thereabouts which property is for identification purposes shown on the plan attached " to the agreement. Schedule 3 contains particulars of the purchaser's powers and liberties for working, and paras. (1) and (2) provide:

" (1) At any time during the term of ten years from the date hereof (herein-after called the working term) to enter upon the said land for the purpose of removing the said minerals and to search for work and get thereout the **B** said minerals by usual and proper means and to dispose of the same in and under the said area by either opencast or underground workings or by removal of hillocks or dumps of miners refuse deposited on the surface by former mineral works. (2) During the working term or any extension thereof the right to make and place in and upon the mineral area for the purposes afore-said such sheds buildings drains plant machinery not requiring permanent **C** foundations and other works as are necessary efficiently to carry out the working of the said minerals and to heap waste and rubbish upon the surface thereof temporarily in such reasonable proportions as are necessary in accordance with recognised mining practice,"

and there is a proviso to which I need not refer, and a clause relating to a right **D** of way which is also irrelevant for purposes of anything that I have to decide.

Schedule 4 contains covenants by the purchaser. I need read only those set out in cll. (3) and (4) of that schedule.

" (3) Unless prevented by fire or water or arising from unavoidable accident or by strikes or combination of workmen or owing to any lockout of workmen to work the said minerals vigorously and continuously in the most improved **E** system of working minerals of a like nature adopted in the district. (4) To keep all shafts pits and other workings safely and substantially fenced off and to indemnify the vendor from and against all action proceedings claims demands and expenses arising or alleged to arise out of or in connexion with the working of the said minerals or the exercise of the liberties rights and privileges hereby granted." **F**

Then Sch. 5 contains agreements, including the agreement in cl. (4) of that Schedule, in the following terms:

" (4) There are expressly excepted out of this sale and reserved to the ven-dor (a) the surface of the whole of the mineral area excepting only such as is in occupation by the purchaser in exercise of his rights and liberties herein-before granted (b) all rights of way for the vendor and his other tenants and **G** all persons authorised by him necessary for the full enjoyment by the vendor of his property (c) all minerals and mineral substances of every kind (includ-ing petroleum natural gas and related hydrocarbons) hereinafter referred to as the excepted minerals in or under or which may emanate from the mineral area other than the said minerals and (d) the right to search for work and get **H** the excepted minerals by any means and the right to deposit on the mineral area or any part thereof spoil or refuse produced in working the excepted minerals even though the deposit of such spoil may interfere with the exercise of the rights and liberties hereinbefore granted to the purchaser."

On behalf of the Crown it was accepted that the payments in this case fall within s. 180 of the Act of 1952 only if the following conditions or qualifications are **I** satisfied: (i) that the payments are " rent ", which is defined by s. 180 (3) to include an annual or periodical payment in the nature of rent; (ii) that the rent is payable in respect of an " easement ", which is defined to include any right, privilege or benefit in, over, or derived from, land; (iii) that it is land and not, as is contended by the taxpayer in this case, a chattel or chattels over which the easement is enjoyed; and (iv) that it is in connexion with a " mine " within the meaning of the phrase " other mines " in para. (b) of the proviso to para. 1 of Sch. A that the easement is enjoyed.

A   It was contended on behalf of the taxpayer that the land of the taxpayer in this case was unaffected by the rights conferred by the agreement which I have read, those rights being exercisable not in relation to the taxpayer's land but in relation to artificial deposits or dumps on that land, which were thus chattels and not land, so that the third of the qualifications necessary to satisfy s. 180 (1) is not satisfied. Further, it is contended on behalf of the taxpayer that, whether

B the third qualification is or is not satisfied, there was here no " concern " properly falling within the description " other mines ". The taxpayer concedes that if the third and fourth qualifications are satisfied the payments made under the agreement were rent as defined in s. 180, and that that rent was payable in respect of an easement. The commissioners before whom the matter came, taking the view that the deposit or dumps were not land and so finding in favour of the

C taxpayer, did not make any finding whether there was a concern which was within the description of " other mines ".

    The land described as the mineral area in Sch. 2 to the agreement is part of land of which the taxpayer is the tenant for life—it has been in his family for some hundreds of years. It is at Little Longstone in Derbyshire, and forms part of an area of about thirty-five acres in extent situate at a height of over one thousand

D feet above sea level. The whole thirty-five acres with which the agreement was concerned is, or was, marked off by the remains of a dry stone wall. At some time prior to 1874 materials had been left on the land comprised in the agreement from workings which took place in the land for the extraction of lead. In the Case Stated by the commissioners, the materials so left on the land are described as having been " dumped " on the land, and without prejudice to the question

E whether that is an apt description I will refer to these materials as deposits or dumps. They are described as dumps in the Case Stated. They are described by one of the witnesses, to whose evidence I will have to refer, as tailings or waste from previous mining operations. There is no suggestion that the materials so left were left for any specific purpose, or that they were thought to have any mineral or other value. The materials, however, contain the mineral fluorspar.

F The materials were waste materials when the lead workings took place but are now, because of their fluorspar content, of commercial value. About 1874 larch wood and other trees were planted on the eight acres. During the period between 1874 and the date of the agreement, nature had reasserted herself, and the surface over the dumps had become covered with willow weed, wild strawberries and coarse grass, and with the trees which had been so planted. It will be remembered

G that under the agreement Mr. Broadbent was to pay a sum of £400 in respect of the timber other than elm, sycamore and other hardwoods on the mineral area which were to become his absolute property and he was bound to cut down and remove them and to remove their roots and to burn those roots.

    At the time when the case came before the commissioners in July, 1962, the deciduous trees had been cut down by Mr. Broadbent and sold except for the

H hardwoods, which still remained; but fifty per cent. of the hardwood had fallen, this being due—I quote the words of the findings of the commissioners— " to undermining by Broadbent or the increased exposure to wind as a result of the removal of larches and Scotch firs."

    The evidence of a Mr. Frank Robinson, the general manager and a director of a company called Glebe Mines, Ltd., which was carrying out operations on land

I adjoining that belonging to the taxpayer, and who had thirty-four years' experience of the extraction of minerals in the area and was familiar with the taxpayer's land, was accepted by the commissioners so far as it consisted of statements of fact. He said that the original dumps from the mining area were identifiable on the land and were the result of extensive lead mining which had been carried on in the area during the nineteenth century, and were not part of the natural contour of the land. In his opinion the dumps had not reverted to and become part of the soil, and they still appeared as deposits on the land. He said in effect that some lead had remained causing oxidisation poisonous to cattle, and that the

land was not suitable for agricultural use. Although the dumps had become grassed A
over in places the vegetation was very poor, and of no agricultural value. (In fact,
as the commissioners found, during the period when the mineral area had been used
for grazing a cow had died.) Mr. Robinson was of the opinion that Mr. Broadbent
was not carrying out mining operations either underground or opencast, but was
merely removing materials from the original dumps. In cross-examination he
said that he based the latter opinion on the facts that (i) the workings carried B
out by Mr. Broadbent were not mines within the meaning of the Mines and
Quarries Act, 1954, (1) and were not visited and examined by the inspectors
appointed under the Act, and (ii) the material which was being removed was not
part of the land, but consisted of tailings or waste from previous mining operations. Two photographs of the mining area are exhibited to the Case Stated.
They were taken by the taxpayer in February, 1960. In my view anyone looking C
at those photographs would think that he was looking at land which had been
violently disturbed by man in the past, but was reverting to a natural state.
Apart from hollows which may or may not be where trees have either been
removed or fallen as a result of Mr. Broadbent's operations, the area appears to
be, as the commissioners found it to be, covered with vegetation.

The commissioners in coming to their conclusion held that the materials in D
question had not reverted to and become part of the land; they had, they said,
remained as materials lying on the land and no action had been taken to render
the land on which they lay available for any useful purpose; they said that in
so far as there was a conflict on this point between *Boileau* v. *Heath* (2) and
Shingler v. *P. Williams & Sons, Ltd.* (3), they accepted the latter case and adopted
the view of FINLAY, J., that the dumps were not part of the land but " stuff " E
deposited on it, and that the payments made to the taxpayer were not therefore
payments in respect of an easement within the terms of s. 180. They gave no
other reason for their decision.

In my judgment the commissioners, in so far as they thought it relevant,
as clearly they did, that no action had been taken to render the land on which
the materials lay available for any useful purpose, were misdirecting themselves. F
The question which they had to decide was no doubt a mixed question of fact
and of law, and this court is in my judgment bound to draw its own conclusions
of law on the facts found by the commissioners. Although no doubt assistance
is to be derived from the cases to which the commissioners particularly referred,
neither case is in my view an authority on the question whether the deposits or
dumps in this particular case were at the date of the agreement, or were not, G
part and parcel of the taxpayer's land. It is to be observed that, if the taxpayer
is right that the dumps or deposits had not become part of the land, it would
have followed that if one of his ancestors had died intestate prior to 1925 the
materials would have passed to his next of kin, and not along with the land to his
heir-at-law. That there were differences between the dumps or deposits which
FINLAY, J., in *Shingler* v. *P. Williams & Sons, Ltd.* (3) thought were chattels H
and the deposits or dumps in the present case can hardly be doubted, and any
argument that FINLAY, J., thought that the dumps with which he was concerned
were chattels, and that there was little difference between those dumps and those
in the present case is, I think, fallacious. The difference may well have been one
which FINLAY, J., would have thought made all the difference and constituted
a vital distinction. There was no finding of fact in the case before FINLAY, J., I
that the dumps were covered with willow weed, wild strawberries and coarse
grass, or had been planted with trees.

Nor can I accept FINLAY, J.'s dismissal as mere dicta of a passage in the judgment of BIGHAM, J., in *Boileau* v. *Heath* (2) from which I derive some assistance.
In the latter case BIGHAM, J., said of the waste material which formed the dumps
in that case (4):

(1) See 34 HALSBURY'S STATUTES (2nd Edn.) 639.   (2) [1898] 2 Ch. 301.
(3) (1933), 17 Tax Cas. 574.   (4) [1898] 2 Ch. at p. 305.

A   " They could not sell it and did not want to sell it, and when they piled it on the earth their intention was that it should once more form part of the earth out of which it had been produced, and should no longer be, if ever it was, of the nature of a chattel."

This was admittedly one of the two grounds on which BIGHAM, J., came to his conclusion on that case. It is in my judgment, however, clear law that, when a

B judge gives two grounds for coming to his decision, each of them is as much the ratio decidendi as the other: for if it were not so a case which ex facie decided two things would be authority for nothing (see, e.g., *Jacobs* v. *London County Council* (5)). To the extent that the intention of those who placed or piled the waste material on the earth at some time prior to 1874 is relevant or decisive of the question whether many years later the material formed part of the land,

C I would infer that they did so intending it once more to become part of the land out of which it was produced. It was waste material of no value.

Irrespective of any such intention, however, and even on the assumption that the intention was quite the contrary, I hold that by the time of the agreement the dumps were part and parcel of the land. Having regard to the circumstances in which the materials came to be on the area in question, the fact that they had

D no value as chattels at the time they came to be there, that trees were planted on the materials, that the area had become covered with vegetation and was used for summer grazing, that there is no evidence that the materials can be removed without disturbing the soil on which they stand, that when one observes the area in the photographs it has the appearance which I have described and that the materials had lain there for nearly eighty years, I find that they had at the

E date of the agreement become part and parcel of the land on which they lay.

It is, however, not enough for the Crown to show that the deposits or dumps have become part of the land of the taxpayer; it must also be established that the concern carried on by Mr. Broadbent is within the description " other mines ". As I have said, the commissioners made no finding on this part of the case, but neither party invited me to send it back to them, and I must do the best I can

F on the findings of fact in the Case Stated. The terms of the agreement no doubt assist the Crown on this part of the case. There is nothing in the agreement to confine the operations of Mr. Broadbent to the deposits or dumps, and what he by para. 1 of the agreement was expressed to be buying was " all the mines veins and beds of fluorspar, calcite and associated minerals therewith ", including all such minerals and hillocks and dumps of miners' refuse on the surface lying in

G and on or under the mineral area which should be gotten or worked by Mr. Broadbent during the term of the agreement. He was given liberty to enter on the land for the purpose of removing the minerals and to search for, work and get thereout the said minerals by usual and proper means, and to dispose of the same in and under the said area by either opencast or underground workings or by removing all hillocks or dumps of miners' refuse deposited on the surface

H by former mineral works. He was to work the said minerals vigorously and continuously in the most improved system of working minerals of a like nature adopted in the district.

Nevertheless, in my judgment the question whether the concern was at the material time a mine falls to be ascertained by reference to its condition and what was being done there, and not on what Mr. Broadbent was allowed or agreed

I to do. I observe in this connexion that it was found as a fact that Mr. Broadbent " excavates from the original dumps the minerals to which he is entitled both with pick and shovel and a tractor-loader ".

I have been referred to a number of authorities on the meaning of the word " mine " in different contexts, and it is necessary to call attention to the context in which the word is used in the proviso to para. 1 of Sch. A. Concerns there are described under three heads: first, quarries of stone, slate, limestone or chalk;

---

(5) [1950] 1 All E.R. 737; [1950] A.C. 361.

second, mines of coal, tin, lead, copper, mundic, iron and other mines; and, **A**
third, other concerns which with the exception of " alum mines " are neither
quarries nor mines. The Crown placed considerable reliance on dicta of Scott,
L.J., in *Mosley* v. *George Wimpey & Co., Ltd.* (6). The passage relied on is long
and I will not burden this judgment by reading it. What Scott, L.J., said in
effect was that he did not accept the view of the judge in the court below that
opencast working of a mineral, whether coal, ironstone or gravel, could not be **B**
mining so as to bring a concern within the statutory provision which was the
predecessor of para. (b). He expressed the view that the word " mine " was
habitually used as a synonym of " bed ", " seam " or " stratum " of coal or of
fireclay, that opencast extraction of coal was an ordinary method of coal mining,
and towards the end of the passage he went on to say that he would therefore
be inclined to hold that opencast workings of any mineral falling within the **C**
scope of the rule corresponding to para. (b) (which he pointed out was not limited
to metallic ores) would be a mine. The whole of that passage must, however, be
read with reservations because it was introduced by another passage in the lord
justice's judgment (7) in which he said that each descriptive word contained in
the three lists which then corresponded to the three sub-paragraphs of the proviso
which I am considering should be given as wide a construction as is compatible **D**
with its ordinary sense in order to give effect to what in Scott, L.J.'s opinion
appeared to have been the dominant thought in the mind of Parliament, and
that this conclusion applied to generic as to specific words of description. This
approach to the construction of the list of concerns was, however, in my judgment
clearly and decisively rejected by the House of Lords in *Russell* (*Inspector of
Taxes*) v. *Scott* (8) and, in the absence of some other authority constraining me **E**
to take a contrary view, I am quite unable to place reliance on dicta expressing a
view of the construction of para. (b) when those dicta have been introduced by a
statement of the principle applicable to that construction which has itself been
held to be erroneous in law.

It was submitted on behalf of the Crown that I ought to follow the dicta of
Scott, L.J., on which the Crown relies because they received the approval **F**
of the Court of Appeal in *South Staffordshire Mines Drainage Comrs.* v. *Grosvenor
Colliery Co., Ltd.* (9). In that case the question was whether opencast working
of coal was a mine within the meaning of a private Act of Parliament, and the
only member of the court to refer to the dicta of Scott, L.J., which I am considering was Donovan, L.J. He did so to support the view that there was no decision
to warrant the conclusion that the word " mines " is prima facie exclusive of **G**
opencast workings. For that purpose Donovan, L.J. (10) quoted the following
part of the dicta of Scott, L.J., relied on by the Crown (7):

" ' I think it right to add that I do not accept the view of Macnaghten, J.
(11), that opencast working of a mineral, whether coal, ironstone or gravel,
cannot be mining, because, as he said, the word " mine " must in r. 2 be construed as limited to undertakings where the system of extraction is carried **H**
out by underground workings only. The word " mine " is, in everyday
knowledge, at any rate in Lancashire, with whose coal-mining I have been
familiar since 1892, habitually used throughout the coal-mining industry
of that county as a mere synonym of " bed ", " seam " or " stratum " of
coal (or of fireclay for that matter) and so used by colliers, mine managers,
engineers, land agents and solicitors in daily parlance and in mining leases. **I**
In the second place when coal-mining began in England four or five centuries
ago, it was by opencast extraction at the outcrop, and that method of
extraction has been revived and extended by many coal-mining concerns

---

(6) [1945] 1 All E.R. 674 at p. 678; 27 Tax Cas. 315 at p. 324.
(7) [1945] 1 All E.R. at p. 678; 27 Tax Cas. at p. 324.
(8) [1948] 2 All E.R. 1; 30 Tax Cas. 394.   (9) (1961), 125 J.P. 484.
(10) (1961), 125 J.P. at p. 499.   (11) [1944] 2 All E.R. 135 at p. 137.

A   during the war, in order to increase the national output. It is thus again today an ordinary method of coal mining, though of course the total yield is very much smaller than that from underground working. Thirdly there are many coal mines in the world where the seam is immensely thick and the whole mining is done by opencast method '."

B   DONOVAN, L.J., after reading that passage went on to say (12):

" There is, therefore, in my view, no initial presumption that the word ' mines ' in relation to coal [I underline the words " in relation to coal "] and in the natural and ordinary meaning of the word, excludes opencast workings. If I were to pass a big opencast working in the Midlands and I described it as an opencast mine, I doubt if I should be thought to be mis-
C   describing the place, even by a coal miner."

It is to be observed that the only part of SCOTT, L.J.'s dicta approved by DONO-VAN, L.J., was that relating to coal, and, while accepting that it is the law that an opencast working of coal is prima facie a mine of coal within para. (*b*), the *South Staffordshire Mines* case (13) in my judgment does not go further than that. A mine of coal is specifically mentioned in para. (*b*). It is moreover consistent
D   with the judgment of the Court of Appeal in *Jones* v. *Cwmorthen Slate Co.* (14), to which I refer more fully later in this judgment, to regard a coal mine worked by opencast working as a mine of coal within para. (*b*). It by no means follows, however, that because the fluorspar in this case is worked by opencast working the concern is within the words " other mines " which are found in that para-graph. Nor does it follow that, because the word mine does not prima facie
E   exclude opencast mining, therefore the concern operated by Mr. Broadbent is a " mine ". Counsel for the Crown submitted that the essence of mining is excava-tion for minerals, and that if the expression " mines " covers an opencast mine then there being here evidence of excavation there is here a mine. This seems to me, if I may say so, to approach dangerously near the argument that, as a dog is an animal with four legs and here is an animal with four legs, therefore it is a
F   dog. Slate is extracted by surface excavations, but such a concern is not a mine. In my judgment the dicta of SCOTT, L.J., so far as they were quoted by DONOVAN, L.J., amount to no more than this, that a coal mine which is one of the concerns specified in para. (*b*) is no less a coal mine within that paragraph because it is worked by opencast means, just as, on the authority of *Jones* v. *Cwmorthen Slate Co.* (14) a slate quarry is none the less a slate quarry within the paragraph and
G   not a mine because in a particular case it is worked by underground operations.

I have referred more than once to *Jones* v. *Cwmorthen Slate Co.* (14). It was pointed out by BRAMWELL, L.J., in that case that in view of the reference to alum mines in para. (*c*), " other mines " in para. (*b*) must be construed ejusdem generis with those specifically mentioned in para. (*b*). And, as I read the judg-ments of the Court of Appeal in that case, the genus which binds the particular
H   concerns specified in para. (*b*) together is that they are concerns for the working of substances ejusdem generis with coal, tin, lead, copper, mundic and iron, perhaps because those substances are normally worked and won by mining and not by quarrying operations, the distinction being not between the method of working in a particular case but the substance. This is in my judgment the ratio decidendi of that case, for the Court of Appeal there held that, although the
I   slate, with which the case was concerned, was worked by underground mining operations, it was nevertheless a quarry of slate within para. (*a*) and not a mine within para. (*b*). If this be the correct view, a coal mine would be a mine of coal within para. (*b*) whether worked underground or opencast. In the absence of any finding that fluorspar, calcite and associated minerals are substances ejusdem generis with coal, tin, lead, copper, mundic or iron, or are ordinarily worked by

---

(12) (1961), 125 J.P. at p. 500.   (13) (1961), 125 J.P. 484.
         (14) (1879), 5 Ex.D 93; 1 Tax Cas. 267.

means similar to those ordinarily used in relation to mining coal, tin, lead, copper, **A**
mundic or iron—no one has advanced any ground for suggesting that they are—
I find that the concern here is not a mine within the meaning of para. (*b*). All
I know is that this concern is not worked underground.

In case, however, I have misunderstood the judgment of the Court of Appeal,
or even if there was evidence that fluorspar was ejusdem generis with the substances specified in para. (*b*), or normally won by mining operations similar to **B**
those performed in mining those substances, the operations described by Mr.
Robinson are still in my judgment not mining operations, and the concern is
not a mine within any ordinary meaning of those terms.

I have been referred to a number of other authorities on the meaning of the
word " mine ". I say no more about them than this, that they establish that
the word " mine " may have quite a different significance in different contexts. **C**
I can extract no principle from them which helps me in this case. None of them
in my judgment assists the Crown to establish that the concern in this case is a
mine in any sense in which that word may be legitimately used. The commissioners
found that what Mr. Broadbent was doing was to excavate from the original
dumps the materials to which he was entitled both with pick and shovel and a
tractor-loader. Mr. Frank Robinson said that Mr. Broadbent was not in his **D**
opinion carrying out mining operations either underground or opencast, but was
merely removing materials from the original dumps. In cross-examination he
stated that he based his view that Mr. Broadbent was not carrying out mining
operations on the facts which I have indicated: (i) that the workings carried out by
Mr. Broadbent were not mines within the meaning of the Mines and Quarries Act,
1954, (15) and were not visited and examined by the inspectors appointed under **E**
the Act, and (ii) that the material which was being removed was not part of the land,
but consisted of tailings or waste from previous mining operations. Although the
first reason given by Mr. Robinson is not in my judgment sustainable as a reason
for his conclusion, and although Mr. Robinson has stated that the material
which was being removed was not part of the land, a view which I have held as
erroneous in point of law, this does not vitiate his second reason. What is being **F**
worked, if I may so put it, is not the natural raw material found under the surface
of the earth, but mounds or dumps of artificial deposits described by Mr. Robinson
as tailings or waste from mining operations, and it is in my judgment nothing to
the point that for the reasons which I have mentioned the waste materials and
tailings have as a technical matter ceased to be chattels—if ever they were—and
become part of the land. The minerals to be won from these waste materials and **G**
deposits cannot lie in a " bed ", " seam " or " stratum " such as was mentioned
in the judgment of SCOTT, L.J. (16), and in my judgment the workings have no
similarity at all to the opencast working of a coal or any other mine.

Appeal dismissed.

Solicitors: *Solicitor of Inland Revenue; Guscotte, Fowler & Cox* (for the **H**
taxpayer).

[*Reported by* F. A. AMIES, ESQ., *Barrister-at-Law.*]

I

---

(15) For the definition of " mine " in the Mines and Quarries Act, 1954, see s. 180 (1);
34 HALSBURY'S STATUTES (2nd Edn.) 639.
(16) See p. 58, letter H, ante.

A   SUISSE ATLANTIQUE SOCIÉTÉ D'ARMEMENT MARITIME
S.A. *v.* N.V. ROTTERDAMSCHE KOLEN CENTRALE.

[HOUSE OF LORDS (Viscount Dilhorne, Lord Reid, Lord Hodson, Lord Upjohn
and Lord Wilberforce), January 11, 12, 13, 17, 18, 19, March 31, 1966.]

Contract—Exception clause—Fundamental breach of contract—Effect on exception
B   *clause—Affirmation of contract by party not in breach—Consecutive voyages*
charterparty requiring despatch by charterers—Delay by charterers causing
loss of profitability to owners—Demurrage clause—Whether owners entitled
to general damages over and above demurrage payments.

Shipping—Demurrage—Deliberate delay—Demurrage clause a stipulation for
agreed damages, not an exception clause inserted for the benefit of one party—
C   *Demurrage clause continuing applicable after assumed fundamental breach*
of charterparty by wilful delay.

There is no rule of law that an exceptions clause is nullified by a fundamental breach of contract or breach of a fundamental term, but in each
case the question is one of the construction of the contract whether the
exceptions clause was intended to give exemption from the consequences of
D   fundamental breach; if a breach occurs, entitling the other party to repudiate
the contract, but he elects to affirm it, the exceptions clause continues
unless on the true construction of the contract the exceptions clause is not
intended to apply to and to continue after such a breach, in which case
the party in breach is unable to rely on the exceptions clause (see p. 67,
letter F, p. 71, letter G, p. 76, letter C, p. 78, letter I, p. 79, letter A, and
E   p. 88, letter F, post; cf., p. 92, letter D, and p. 94, letter A, post).

Dictum of PEARSON, L.J., in *U.G.S. Finance, Ltd. v. National Mortgage*
Bank of Greece and National Bank of Greece, S.A. ([1964] 1 Lloyd's Rep. at
p. 453) applied.

Dicta of DEVLIN, J., in *Smeaton Hanscomb & Co., Ltd. v. Sassoon I.*
Setty Son & Co. (No. 1) ([1953] 2 All E.R. at p. 1473) and of DENNING, L.J.,
F   in *Karsales (Harrow), Ltd. v. Wallis* ([1956] 2 All E.R. at p. 868) and in
U.G.S. Finance, Ltd. v. *National Mortgage Bank of Greece and National Bank*
of Greece, S.A. ([1964] 1 Lloyd's Rep. at p. 450) not followed.

By a charterparty dated December, 1956, the respondents agreed to
charter a vessel from the appellants for the carriage of coal from the United
States to Europe. The charter was to remain in force for a total of two
G   years' consecutive voyages. The vessel had with all possible dispatch to sail
and proceed to a port in the United States and, having loaded a cargo of
coal, proceed with all possible dispatch to a port in Europe. She had to be
loaded at a specified rate per running day and, if she was detained beyond the
loading time, the respondents were to pay $1,000 a day demurrage. Similarly,
if she were detained longer than was required to unload her at the stipulated
H   rate per day and that was not due to strikes, etc., or other causes beyond the
control of the respondents, the respondents, who were to discharge the
cargo, were to pay demurrage at the rate of $1,000 a day. In September,
1957, the appellants regarded themselves as entitled to treat the charterparty
as repudiated by reason of the respondents' delays in loading and discharging
the vessel. That was not accepted by the respondents, and, in October,
I   1957, the appellants and respondents agreed, without prejudice to their
dispute, that from thenceforward the charterparty would be carried out.
Between then and the end of the charter the vessel made eight round voyages.
The appellants alleged that, due to delays in loading and unloading for which
the respondents were responsible, the vessel did not make as many voyages
as she should have done, with the result that they were deprived of the
freights they would have earned on the additional voyages and, after giving
credit for the demurrage payments received by them, claimed damages from
the respondents. The appellants contended that, if the delays for which the

Followed in GEORGE MITCHELL LTD
v FINNEY LOCK SEEDS [1983]
1 All ER 108

respondents were responsible were such as to entitle the appellants to treat   A
the charterparty as repudiated, the demurrage provisions did not apply and
they were entitled to recover the full loss that they had suffered.

 Held: the appellants, having elected in October, 1957, to affirm the
charterparty, continued bound by its provisions, including the demurrage
provisions, and on the true construction of the charterparty the demurrage
provisions (cl. 3) were not to be regarded as limiting the respondents' liability   B
but were provisions for payment of agreed damages, and on proof of breach
by detention (within cl. 3) the appellants were entitled only to the agreed
damages, and not to damages for loss of profit, i.e., loss of freight, notwithstanding that the breach was deliberate and that the loss of profit was
wilfully caused, if those were the facts (see p. 69, letters C, E and G, p. 77,
letters A and B, p. 81, letter C, p. 85, letter G, p. 88, letter I, and p. 96,   C
letter A, post).

 Per VISCOUNT DILHORNE and LORD UPJOHN: there is a difference between
a fundamental breach of contract and breach of a fundamental term;
in the case of a fundamental breach the question is whether, having regard
to the character of the breach, performance has become something totally
different from what the contract contemplated, but a breach of a fundamental   D
term goes to the root of the contract and, without regard having to be had
to other circumstances, entitles the party not in breach to repudiate the
contract (see p. 68, letters D and E, and p. 86, letter C, post; cf. p. 78, letter
H, post).

 Appeal dismissed.

[As to prosecution of the voyage, see 35 HALSBURY'S LAWS (3rd Edn.) 268,   E
269, para. 409; p. 412, para. 588; and for cases on the subject, see 41 DIGEST
(Repl.) 375-389, *1666-1781.*

 As to the construction of exceptions clauses (relieving charterer), see 35
HALSBURY'S LAWS (3rd Edn.) 318, 319, para. 460; and (generally) see SUPPLE-
MENT TO 8 HALSBURY'S LAWS (3rd Edn.), para. 215A; and for cases on maritime
negligence clauses, see 41 DIGEST (Repl.) 309-316, *1166-1206.*]   F

Cases referred to:

 Alexander v. *Railway Executive,* [1951] 2 All E.R. 442; [1951] 2 K.B. 882;
  3 Digest (Repl.) 93, *225.*

 Astley Industrial Trust, Ltd. v. *Grimley,* [1963] 2 All E.R. 33; [1963] 1 W.L.R.
  584; Digest (Cont. Vol. A) 645, *36ba.*

 Balian & Sons v. *Joly, Victoria & Co., Ltd.,* (1890), 6 T.L.R. 345; 41 Digest   G
  (Repl.) 384, *1729.*

 Bontex Knitting Works, Ltd. v. *St. John's Garage,* [1943] 2 All E.R. 690; *affd.*
  C.A., [1944] 1 All E.R. 381, n.; 3 Digest (Repl.) 97, *249.*

 Boshali v. *Allied Commercial Exporters, Ltd.,* (1959), unreported.

 Brandt & Co. v. *Liverpool, Brazil & River Plate Steam Navigation Co., Ltd.,*
  [1923] All E.R. Rep. 656; [1924] 1 K.B. 575; 93 L.J.K.B. 646; 130   H
  L.T. 392; 16 Asp. M.L.C. 262; 41 Digest (Repl.) 251, *698.*

 Cap Palos, The, [1921] All E.R. Rep. 249; [1921] P. 458; 91 L.J.P. 11; 126
  L.T. 82; 15 Asp. M.L.C. 403; 42 Digest (Repl.) 783, *5531.*

 Cellulose Acetate Silk Co., Ltd. v. *Widnes Foundry (1925), Ltd.,* [1932] All E.R.
  Rep. 567; [1933] A.C. 20; 101 L.J.K.B. 694; 147 L.T. 401; 17 Digest
  (Repl.) 150, *493.*   I

 Chandris v. *Isbrandsten Moller Co., Inc.,* [1950] 1 All E.R. 768; [1951]
  1 K.B. 240; *rvsd.* C.A., [1950] 2 All E.R. 618; 41 Digest (Repl.) 195, *291.*

 Chanter v. *Hopkins,* (1838), 4 M. & W. 339; 8 L.J.Ex. 14; 150 E.R. 1484;
  17 Digest (Repl.) 318, *1250.*

 Charterhouse Credit Co., Ltd. v. *Tolly,* [1963] 2 All E.R. 432; [1963] 2 Q.B.
  683; [1963] 2 W.L.R. 1168; Digest (Cont. Vol. A) 649, *43b.*

 Cunard S.S. Co., Ltd. v. *Buerger,* [1926] All E.R. Rep. 103; [1927] A.C. 1; 96
  L.J.K.B. 18; 135 L.T. 494; 17 Asp. M.L.C. 92; 41 Digest (Repl.) 385, *1732.*

A   *Davies* v. *Garrett*, (1830), 6 Bing. 716; 8 L.J.O.S.C.P. 253; 130 E.R. 1456; 41 Digest (Repl.) 384, *1728*.

Empress Maritime de Transportes S.A. v. *A. T. Mancy Oil Co.*, [1965] A.M.R. 517.

Ethel Radcliffe S.S. Co., Ltd. v. *Barnett*, (1926), 24 Lloyd L.R. 277; 95 L.J.K.B. 561; 135 L.T. 176; 17 Asp. M.L.C. 55; 41 Digest (Repl.) 418, *2040*.

B   *Gibaud* v. *Great Eastern Ry. Co.*, [1921] All E.R. Rep. 35; [1921] 2 K.B. 426; 90 L.J.K.B. 535; 125 L.T. 76; 8 Digest (Repl.) 141, *906*.

Glynn v. *Margetson*, [1891-94] All E.R. Rep. 693; [1893] A.C. 351; 62 L.J.Q.B. 466; 66 L.T. 1; 7 Asp. M.L.C. 366; 41 Digest (Repl.) 163, *82*.

Gunyon v. *South Eastern & Chatham Ry. Co.'s Managing Committee*, [1915] 2 K.B. 370; 84 L.J.K.B. 1212; 113 L.T. 282; 8 Digest (Repl.) 69, *466*.

C   *Hain S.S. Co., Ltd.* v. *Tate & Lyle, Ltd.*, [1936] 2 All E.R. 597; 155 L.T. 177; 19 Asp. M.L.C. 62; 41 Digest (Repl.) 385, *1737*.

Hardwick Game Farm v. *Suffolk Agricultural and Poultry Producers Association, Ltd.*, [1966] 1 All E.R. 309; [1966] 1 W.L.R. 287.

Hawksley v. *Outram*, [1892] 3 Ch. 359; 62 L.J.Ch. 215; 67 L.T. 804; 44 Digest (Repl.) 94, *763*.

D   *Hong Kong Fir Shipping Co., Ltd.* v. *Kawasaki Kisen Kaisha, Ltd.*, [1962] 1 All E.R. 474; [1964] 2 Q.B. 26; [1962] 2 W.L.R. 474; 41 Digest (Repl.) 363, *1553*.

Inverkip S.S. Co. v. *Bunge & Co.*, [1917] 2 K.B. 193; 86 L.J.K.B. 1042; 117 L.T. 102; 14 Asp. M.L.C. 110; 41 Digest (Repl.) 492, *2649*.

Karsales (Harrow), Ltd. v. *Wallis*, [1956] 2 All E.R. 866; [1956] 1 W.L.R. E   936; 26 Digest (Repl.) 666, *35*.

Leduc & Co. v. *Ward*, [1886-90] All E.R. Rep. 266; (1888), 20 Q.B.D. 475; 57 L.J.Q.B. 379; 58 L.T. 908; 6 Asp. M.L.C. 290; 41 Digest (Repl.) 381, *1709*.

Lilley v. *Doubleday*, (1881), 7 Q.B.D. 510; 51 L.J.Q.B. 310; 44 L.T. 814; 46 J.P. 709; 3 Digest (Repl.) 82, *183*.

F   *London & North Western Ry. Co.* v. *Neilson*, [1922] 2 A.C. 263; 91 L.J.K.B. 680; sub nom. *Neilson* v. *London & North Western Ry. Co.*, [1922] All E.R. Rep. 395; 8 Digest (Repl.) 69, *467*.

Mallet v. *Great Eastern Ry. Co.*, [1899] 1 Q.B. 309; 68 L.J.Q.B. 256; 80 L.T. 53; 8 Digest (Repl.) 47, *283*.

Margaronis Navigation Agency, Ltd. v. *Henry W. Peabody & Co. of London,* G   *Ltd.*, [1964] 2 All E.R. 296; [1965] 1 Q.B. 300; [1964] 3 W.L.R. 111; *affd.* C.A., [1964] 3 All E.R. 333; [1965] 2 Q.B. 430; [1964] 3 W.L.R. 873; 41 Digest (Repl.) 202, *326*.

Morrison (James) & Co., Ltd. v. *Shaw, Savill and Albion Co., Ltd.*, [1916-17] All E.R. Rep. 1068; [1916] 2 K.B. 783; 86 L.J.K.B. 97; 115 L.T. 508; 13 Asp. M.L.C. 504; 41 Digest (Repl.) 381, *1713*.

H   *Pinnock Bros.* v. *Lewis & Peat, Ltd.*, [1923] 1 K.B. 690; 92 L.J.K.B. 695; 129 L.T. 320; 39 Digest (Repl.) 594, *1124*.

Pollock & Co. v. *Macrae*, 1922 S.C. (H.L.) 192; [1922] S.L.T. 510; 39 Digest (Repl.) 578, **566*.

Reidar (Akt.) v. *Arcos, Ltd.*, [1926] 2 K.B. 83; *affd.* C.A., [1926] All E.R. Rep. 140; [1927] 1 K.B. 352; 95 L.J.K.B. 33; 136 L.T. 1; 17 Asp. M.L.C. I   144; 14 Digest (Repl.) 201, *323*.

Scaramanger v. *Stamp*, (1880), 5 C.P.D. 295; 49 L.J.Q.B. 674; 42 L.T. 840; 4 Asp. M.L.C. 295; 41 Digest (Repl.) 379, *1700*.

Shaw v. *Director of Public Prosecutions*, [1961] 2 All E.R. 446; [1962] A.C. 220; [1961] 2 W.L.R. 897; 125 J.P. 437; 45 Cr. App. Rep. 113; Digest (Cont. Vol. A) 339, *919a*.

Smeaton Hanscomb & Co., Ltd. v. *Sassoon I. Setty, Son & Co. (No. 1)*, [1953] 2 All E.R. 1471; [1953] 1 W.L.R. 1468; 39 Digest (Repl.) 582, *1046*.

Stag Line, Ltd. v. *Foscolo, Mango & Co., Ltd.*, [1931] All E.R. Rep. 666; [1932] A
A.C. 328; 101 L.J.K.B. 165; 146 L.T. 305; 18 Asp. M.L.C. 266;
41 Digest (Repl.) 379, *1698.*

Sze Hai Tong Bank, Ltd. v. *Rambler Cycle Co., Ltd.*, [1959] 3 All E.R. 182;
[1959] A.C. 576; [1959] 3 W.L.R. 214; 41 Digest (Repl.) 441, *2226.*

Thorley (Joseph), Ltd. v. *Orchis S.S. Co., Ltd.*, [1907] 1 K.B. 660; 76 L.J.K.B.
595; 96 L.T. 488; 10 Asp. M.L.C. 431; 41 Digest (Repl.) 384, *1725.* B

U.G.S. Finance, Ltd. v. *National Mortgage Bank of Greece and National Bank
of Greece, S.A.*, [1964] 1 Lloyd's Rep. 446.

United States Shipping Board v. *Bunge y Born Limitada Sociedad*, [1925] All
E.R. Rep. 173; 134 L.T. 303; 16 Asp. M.L.C. 577; 41 Digest (Repl.)
382, *1716.*

Wallis, Son & Wells v. *Pratt and Haynes*, [1911-13] All E.R. Rep. 989; [1911] C
A.C. 394; 80 L.J.K.B. 1058; 105 L.T. 146; 39 Digest (Repl.) 588,
1089.

Western S.S. Co. v. *Amaral Sutherland & Co.*, [1913] 3 K.B. 366; 82 L.J.K.B.
1180; 109 L.T. 217; 12 Asp. M.L.C. 358; *on appeal*, C.A., [1914]
3 K.B. 55; 83 L.J.K.B. 1201; 111 L.T. 113; 41 Digest (Repl.) 492,
2648. D

Yeoman Credit, Ltd. v. *Apps*, [1961] 2 All E.R. 281; [1962] 2 Q.B. 508; [1961]
3 W.L.R. 94; Digest (Cont. Vol. A) 648, *43a.*

Appeal.

This was an appeal by the appellants, Suisse Atlantique Société d'Armement
Maritime S.A., the owners of the m.v. General Guisan, chartered to the respon-
dents, N.V. Rotterdamsche Kolen Centrale, under a charterparty dated Dec. 21, E
1956, from an order of the Court of Appeal (SELLERS, HARMAN and DIPLOCK,
L.JJ.), dated Mar. 11, 1965, dismissing the appellants' appeal from an order of
MOCATTA, J., dated Jan. 11, 1965, made on a Consultative Case Stated under
s. 21 (1) (*a*) of the Arbitration Act, 1950. The facts are set out in the opinion of
VISCOUNT DILHORNE.

H. V. Brandon, Q.C., R. A. MacCrindle, Q.C., and *Anthony Evans* for the F
appellants.

J. F. Donaldson, Q.C., and *C. J. Staughton* for the respondents.

Their lordships took time for consideration.

Mar. 31. The following opinions were delivered.

VISCOUNT DILHORNE: My Lords, this appeal is from a decision of the G
Court of Appeal (SELLERS, HARMAN and DIPLOCK, L.JJ.) dismissing an appeal
by the appellants from a decision by MOCATTA, J., on a Consultative Case in
relation to a dispute between the parties which has arisen in connexion with the
charter of a vessel from the appellants.

On Dec. 21, 1956, the respondents agreed to charter a vessel from the appellants
for the carriage of coal from the United States to Europe. That charter was to H
remain in force "for a total of two years' consecutive voyages" (cl. 23 of the
charterparty). The vessel had "with all possible dispatch" to "sail and proceed"
to a port in the United States and there load on each voyage a cargo of coal
"and being so loaded, shall therewith proceed with all possible dispatch" to a
port in Europe (cl. 1). She had to be loaded at a specified rate per running day
and, if she was detained beyond the loading time, the respondents were to pay I
$1,000 a day demurrage. In computing the loading time, detention of the vessel in
consequence of the happening of certain events was to be disregarded (cl. 3).
Similarly, if she was detained longer than was required to unload her at the
stipulated rate per day and that was not due to strikes, etc., or other causes
beyond the control of the respondents, the respondents, who were to discharge
the cargo, were to pay demurrage at the rate of $1,000 a day. On Sept. 16, 1957,
the appellants regarded themselves as entitled to treat the charterparty as
repudiated by reason of the respondents' delays in loading and discharging the

A   vessel.   This was not accepted by the respondents, and on Oct. 8, 1957, it was agreed, without prejudice to this dispute, that from thenceforward the charterparty would be carried out.   Between Oct. 16, 1957, and the end of the charter the vessel made eight round voyages.   The appellants contended that she ought reasonably to have completed each round voyage in thirty or thirty-seven days including loading and unloading.   On this basis, eight voyages would have taken

B   240 or 296 days.   In fact, they took 511 and the difference, the appellants alleged, was due to delays in loading and unloading for which the respondents were responsible.   The result was, so the appellants alleged, that the vessel did not make as many voyages as she should have done, with the result that they were deprived of the freights which they would have earned on nine, or alternatively six, voyages.   On this basis, after giving credit for the demurrage payments received

C   by them, they claimed $772,866.92, and alternatively $476,490.92 from the respondents.

This claim went to arbitration and, at the request of the appellants, the arbitrators stated the following questions in the form of a Consultative Case:

" (A) (i) The [appellants] are entitled to recover (subject to giving credit for the demurrage payments received by them) any damages suffered by

D   them by reason of the respondents having failed to load and discharge the vessel within the laydays whereby the charterparty was (if so proved) rendered less profitable to the [appellants] by consequent loss of voyages or voyage time.   (ii) Upon the assumption that such loss of profitability resulted from the respondents having deliberately (i.e., with the wilful intention of limiting the number of contractual voyages) failed to load and/or

E   discharge the vessel (a) with such ordinary despatch as the circumstances permitted or (b) within the laydays, the [appellants] are entitled to recover any damages suffered by the [appellants] through the charterparty having been rendered less profitable as aforesaid subject to giving credit for the demurrage payments received by them and for any such despatch money as would have been earned by the respondents.

F   " (B) If the answer to any of the questions under (' A ') be ' Yes ', the payment by the respondents and acceptance by the [appellants] of demurrage in respect of those periods when the laydays were exceeded preclude the [appellants] from recovering any damages otherwise recoverable by them in accordance with such answer or answers."

G   Before Mocatta, J., it was agreed that he should confine his decision to answering questions A (i) and (ii), and that the words " or voyage time " at the end of A (i) added nothing.

Counsel for the appellants submitted to your lordships, as he had in the courts below, that the appellants had, under the charterparty, a contractual right to the number of voyages which would be performed if both parties complied with their obligations; and, secondly, that the appellants' claim for the loss of freight

H   on the voyages which should have been performed was not limited to the demurrage payments.   In my opinion, no such contractual right is to be implied either on the construction of the charterparty or by operation of law.   The charterparty might have provided that not less than a certain number of voyages should be accomplished.   It did not do so.   In support of their second contention, the appellants relied on *Akt. Reidan* v. *Arcos, Ltd.* (1) and, in particular, on the

I   judgment of Bankes, L.J.   Although he came to the same conclusion as Atkin, L.J., and Sargant, L.J., he did so on somewhat different grounds.   I do not consider that this decision affords any basis for the contention that, where demurrage provisions apply, it is possible to obtain more than the demurrage payments for the detention of a vessel.   On these issues I agree with, and do not think that it is necessary to add to, the judgments of the Court of Appeal and Mocatta, J.

_____

(1) [1926] All E.R. Rep. 140;   [1927] 1 K.B. 352.

If in this case the appellants had been able to establish a breach of the charter- A
party other than by the detention of the vessel, then *Akt. Reidar* v. *Arcos, Ltd.*
(2) is authority for saying that the damages obtainable would not be limited to
the demurrage payments. In my opinion, they have not done so.

Towards the conclusion of his argument, Mr. MacCrindle sought to put forward
a new argument, not advanced in the courts below nor in the appellants' case,
to the effect that, if the delays for which the respondents were responsible were B
such as to entitle the appellants to treat the charterparty as repudiated, the
demurrage provisions did not apply and they were entitled to recover the full loss
which they had suffered. While ordinarily this would not be premitted, as the
result of refusing to allow it in the present case might be that the question would
come before the courts on another Consultative Case, involving delay and expense,
their lordships decided to allow the argument to be advanced on condition that C
Supplemental Cases should be filed, the hearing adjourned and on the appellants
undertaking to pay the costs involved. At the resumed hearing Mr. Brandon
sought to sustain this contention. He cited a large number of cases in which it
had been held that, where there had been deviation of a vessel, the owners of the
ship were not entitled to rely on provisions in a charterparty or bill of lading
protecting them from liability or limiting their liability for the loss of the kind D
that had occurred. It is not, I think, necessary to refer to all the cases cited.
The principle is well established.

In *Hain S.S. Co., Ltd.* v. *Tate & Lyle, Ltd.* (3), LORD ATKIN, with whose opinions
LORD THANKERTON and LORD MACMILLAN agreed, said:

". . . the effect of a deviation upon a contract of carriage by sea has been
stated in a variety of cases but not in uniform language . . . Occasionally E
language has been used which suggests that the occurrence of a deviation
automatically displaces the contract, as by the now accepted doctrine does
an event which ' frustrates ' a contract. In other cases where the effect of
deviation upon the exceptions in the contract had to be considered language
is used which . . . shows that the sole effect is as it were to expunge the
exceptions clause, as no longer applying to a voyage which from the beginning F
of the deviation has ceased to be the contract voyage. I venture to think
that the true view is that the departure from the voyage contracted to be
made is a breach by the shipowner of his contract, but a breach of such a
serious character that however slight the deviation the other party to the
contract is entitled to treat it as going to the root of the contract, and to
declare himself as no longer bound by any of its terms." G

Later he said (4):

" If this view be correct then the breach by deviation does not automatically cancel the express contract, otherwise the shipowner by his own
wrong can get rid of his own contract. Nor does it affect merely the exceptions
clauses. This would make those clauses alone subject to a condition of no H
deviation, a construction for which I can find no justification. It is quite
inconsistent with the cases which have treated deviation as precluding enforcement of demurrage provisions. The event falls within the ordinary law
of contract. The party who is affected by the breach has the right to say,
I am not now bound by the contract whether it is expressed in charterparty,
bill of lading, or otherwise . . . I am satisfied that once he elects to treat the I
contract as at an end he is not bound by the promise to pay the agreed freight
any more than by his other promises. But on the other hand, as he can elect
to treat the contract as ended, so he can elect to treat the contract as subsisting: and if he does this with knowledge of his rights he must in accordance
with the general law of contract be held bound."

(2) [1926] All E.R. Rep. 140; [1927] 1 K.B. 352.
(3) [1936] 2 All E.R. 597 at p. 600.   (4) [1936] 2 All E.R. at p. 601.

A   LORD WRIGHT, M.R., in the same case said (5): " An unjustified deviation is a
fundamental breach of a contract of affreightment ", and (6):

" But however fundamental is the condition, it may still be waived by
the goods owner. For this purpose the case is like any other breach of a
fundamental condition, which constitutes the repudiation of a contract by
one party; the other party may elect not to treat the repudiation as being
B   final, but to treat the contract as subsisting and to that extent may waive
the breach, any right to damages being reserved."

See also *Chandris* v. *Isbrandsten Moller Co., Inc.* (7), per DEVLIN, J. This House
thus treated the deviation cases as coming within the ordinary law of contract.
Counsel for the appellants also cited *Mallet* v. *Great Eastern Ry. Co.* (8), where
C   goods were sent by a different route from that contracted for and a clause
relieving the company of liability was consequently held not to apply; *Gunyon*
v. *South Eastern & Chatham Ry. Co.'s Managing Committee* (9), where fruit was
carried by goods train when the contract was for it to go by passenger train and
so an exemption clause was held not to apply; and *Lilley* v. *Doubleday* (10),
where goods were destroyed by fire in a warehouse other than that contracted
for and an exemption clause was held not to apply. These are all cases which
D   illustrate the principle that, where there has been a fundamental breach—and
deviation is a fundamental breach—or a breach of a fundamental term, the party
guilty of the breach cannot successfully rely on provisions in the contract
designed for his protection in the performance of the contract. In a number of
cases (e.g., *Smeaton Hanscomb & Co., Ltd.* v. *Sassoon I. Setty, Son & Co. (No. 1)*
E   (11); *Karsales (Harrow), Ltd.* v. *Wallis* (12); *Yeoman Credit, Ltd.* v. *Apps* (13);
Astley Industrial Trust, Ltd. v. *Grimley* (14); *Charterhouse Credit Co., Ltd.* v.
Tolly (15) and *U.G.S. Finance, Ltd.* v. *National Mortgage Bank of Greece and
National Bank of Greece, S.A.* (16)) there are judicial observations to the
effect that exempting clauses, no matter how widely they are drawn, only
avail a party when he is carrying out the contract in its essential respects.
F   In my view, it is not right to say that the law prohibits and nullifies a clause
exempting or limiting liability for a fundamental breach or breach of a fundamental term. Such a rule of law would involve a restriction on freedom of
contract, and in the older cases I can find no trace of it. In each case not only
have the terms and scope of the exempting clause to be considered but also the
contract as a whole. In the cases that I have cited above, I think that, on construction of the contract as a whole, it is apparent that the exempting clauses were not
G   intended to give exemption from the consequences of the fundamental breach.
Any provision that does so must be expressed in clear and unambiguous terms:
see *Cunard S.S. Co., Ltd.* v. *Buerger* (17), per LORD PARMOOR and *London &
North Western Ry. Co.* v. *Neilson* (18), per LORD DUNEDIN. It must be apparent
that such is its purpose and intention. In *Glynn* v. *Margetson* (19), the contract
was for the carriage of oranges from Malaga to Liverpool, and the charterparty
H   contained a provision giving the vessel liberty to go to any port not on the route
from Malaga to Liverpool. As a result of the vessel going to a port not on the
route from Malaga to Liverpool the oranges were damaged. In that case, LORD
HERSCHELL, L.C., said (20) that the main object and intent of the charterparty
was the voyage so agreed on and—

I   (5) [1936] 2 All E.R. at p. 607.   (6) [1936] 2 All E.R. at p. 608.
(7) [1950] 1 All E.R. 768 at pp. 774, 775; [1951] 1 K.B. 240 at pp. 248, 249.
(8) [1899] 1 Q.B. 309.   (9) [1915] 2 K.B. 370.
(10) (1881), 7 Q.B.D. 510.   (11) [1953] 2 All E.R. 1471.
(12) [1956] 2 All E.R. 866.   (13) [1961] 2 All E.R. 281; [1962] 2 Q.B. 508.
(14) [1963] 2 All E.R. 33.   (15) [1963] 2 All E.R. 432; [1963] 2 Q.B. 683.
(16) [1964] 1 Lloyd's Rep. 446.
(17) [1926] All E.R. Rep. 103 at p. 108; [1927] A.C. 1 at p. 13.
(18) [1922] All E.R. Rep. 395 at p. 400; [1922] 2 A.C. 263 at p. 272.
(19) [1891-94] All E.R. Rep. 693; [1893] A.C. 351.
(20) [1891-94] All E.R. Rep. at p. 695; [1893] A.C. at p. 354.

" it would be to defeat what is the manifest object and intention of such a   A
contract to hold that it was entered into with a power to the shipowners to
proceed anywhere . . ."

I think that the legal position was most clearly and accurately stated by
Pearson, L.J., in *U.G.S. Finance, Ltd.* v. *National Mortgage Bank of Greece and
National Bank of Greece, S.A.* (21). He said:

" As to the question of ' fundamental breach ', I think there is a rule of   B
construction that normally an exception or exclusion clause or similar
provision in a contract should be construed as not applying to a situation
created by a fundamental breach of contract. This is not an independent rule
of law imposed by the court on the parties willy-nilly in disregard of their
contractual intention. On the contrary it is a rule of construction based on
the presumed intention of the contracting parties. It involves the implica-   C
tion of a term to give to the contract that business efficacy which the parties
as reasonable men must have intended it to have. This rule of construction
is not new in principle but it has become prominent in recent years in
consequence of the tendency to have standard forms of contract containing
exceptions clauses drawn in extravagantly wide terms, which would produce
absurd results if applied literally."   D

Although the terms are sometimes used as if their meaning was the same, a
fundamental breach differs from a breach of a fundamental term. In *Smeaton
Hanscomb & Co., Ltd.* v. *Sassoon I. Setty, Son & Co. (No. 1)* (22), Devlin, J.,
said that he thought a fundamental term was

" something which underlies the whole contract so that, if it is not complied   E
with, the performance becomes something totally different from that which
the contract contemplates."

In relation to a fundamental breach, one has to have regard to the character of
the breach and determine whether, in consequence of it, the performance of the
contract becomes something totally different from that which the contract
contemplates.   F

The provisions as to demurrage in the charterparty indicate that it was
appreciated that the respondents might be in breach of the charterparty by
detaining the vessel beyond the laydays and yet carry out the charterparty. I
do not think that breach of the charterparty by detention beyond the laydays
can be regarded as a breach of a fundamental term.

Delay in the performance of a charterparty may amount to deviation and so   G
to a fundamental breach. In *The Cap Palos* (23), where the contract was for the
towage of a vessel, Atkin, L.J., said:

" The [towage] figures appear to me to indicate such delay as to make
the purported performance something quite different from that contracted
for, a form of deviation quite familiar in maritime adventures."   H

In *Brandt & Co.* v. *Liverpool, Brazil & River Plate Steam Navigation Co., Ltd.* (24),
delay by the owners of a vessel in dealing with bags of zinc was held by Scrutton,
L.J., and Atkin, L.J., to amount to a deviation. Breach of a charterparty by the
detention of the vessel beyond the laydays by the charterers may, in my view,
take on the character of a fundamental breach. If, for instance, there was a delay
of many weeks in the loading of the vessel, the consequence would be that the   I
voyages, though in fact consecutive, would be totally different from those
contemplated by the contract. Further, if it was established that a breach,
though of itself not of sufficient duration as to lead to the conclusion that the
performance of the contract became totally different from that contemplated,
was committed deliberately and wilfully with the object of reducing the number

(21) [1964] 1 Lloyd's Rep. at p. 453.   (22) [1953] 2 All E.R. at p. 1473.
(23) [1921] All E.R. Rep. 249 at p. 254; [1921] P. 458 at p. 470.
(24) [1923] All E.R. Rep. 656 at pp. 663, 665; [1924] 1 K.B. 575 at pp. 597, 601.

A   of voyages accomplished, the breach might, in my opinion, take on the character of a fundamental breach.   It is only in this connexion, in determining whether there has been repudiatory conduct, that, in my opinion, the wilfulness of the breach has any relevance.

In this case, the appellants contend that the totality of the delays in loading and unloading constituted a fundamental breach entitling them to treat the B   contract as repudiated and the demurrage provisions as not applying.   They do not suggest that, at any particular time between Oct. 16, 1957, and the end of the charter, the delays were such as to constitute a fundamental breach.   If there was a time after Oct. 16, 1957, and before the end of the charterparty when they could have said that it had been repudiated by the respondents, they did not do so.   They had full knowledge of the delays as they occurred, and, if C   there was a time when they could have elected to treat the charterparty as at an end, they must, in my view, be taken to have elected to waive the repudiation and to have affirmed the charterparty.   If they affirmed the charterparty, then they were bound by its provisions in respect of events occurring after the affirmation, but waiver of the breach does not mean waiver of the right to damages for that breach: *Hain S.S. Co., Ltd.* v. *Tate & Lyle, Ltd.* (25); *Chandris* v. *Isbrandtsen* D   *Moller Co., Inc.* (26), per Devlin, J.   In this connexion there are, I think, certain passages in *Charterhouse Credit Co., Ltd.* v. *Tolly* (27) which require reconsideration.   If the appellants were entitled to treat the charterparty as repudiated, the demurrage provisions could be held not to apply only if they were provisions limiting the respondents' liability and, on construction of the contract as a whole, they were held not to apply in relation to the fundamental breach.

E   In my view, the demurrage provisions are not to be regarded as limiting the respondents' liability.   In the circumstances of this case, it may be that the amount of the demurrage payments bears little relation to the loss which the appellants claim to have suffered.   In *Chandris* v. *Isbrandtsen Moller Co., Inc.* (28), Devlin, J., said that the sum produced by demurrage " is generally less than damages for detention " and that a demurrage clause is merely a clause F   providing for liquidated damages for a certain type of breach.   While it may be that a demurrage clause in a particular case is so drawn that, on its proper construction, it is to be treated as imposing a limitation on liability, in this case the demurrage provisions are, in my opinion, clearly provisions for the payment of agreed damages.   If the clauses imposed a limit on liability, then the appellants would have to prove the actual loss they sustained and if it was less than the G   amount stated they would recover only the loss which they proved.   Here the parties agreed that demurrage at a daily rate should be paid in respect of the detention of the vessel and, on proof of breach of the charterparty by detention, the appellants are entitled to the demurrage payments without having to prove the loss which they suffered in consequence.   In my view, the appellants cannot avoid the operation of these provisions and cannot recover more than the agreed H   damages for the detention of their vessel: see *Cellulose Acetate Silk Co., Ltd.* v. *Widnes Foundry (1925), Ltd.* (29).

For these reasons the further contention advanced by the appellants in my view fails and, in my opinion, this appeal should be dismissed.

LORD REID: My Lords, I am satisfied that, for the reasons given by your lordships, this appeal could not succeed on any of the grounds submitted to the I   Court of Appeal and to your lordships at the first hearing of this appeal.   But at the end of his opening address, counsel for the appellants put forward a new contention based on there having been a fundamental breach of contract by the respondents.   Normally this House would not permit a new question of that

---

(25) [1936] 2 All E.R. 597.
(26) [1950] 1 All E.R. at p. 774;   [1951] 1 K.B. at p. 248.
(27) [1963] 2 All E.R. 432;   [1963] 2 Q.B. 683.
(28) [1950] 1 All E.R. at p. 775;   [1951] 1 K.B. at p. 249.
(29) [1932] All E.R. Rep. 567;   [1933] A.C. 20.

character to be argued; but this is a Consultative Case Stated by arbitrators, **A** and the appellants could still raise such a new question before the arbitrators. So, in order to avoid delay and expense, your lordships adjourned the hearing on terms as to costs and ordered the parties to lodge supplementary cases dealing with this new contention. I only intend to deal with the new question argued at the second hearing.

The case arises out of a charterparty for two years' consecutive voyages made **B** on Dec. 21, 1956, between the appellants, the owners, and the respondents, the charterers. After a dispute, the parties made a further agreement on Oct. 8, 1957, to perform the charterparty for the remainder of the two year period. The purpose of the charterparty was that, on each voyage, the vessel should proceed in ballast to an Atlantic port in the United States and there load coal to be carried to a port in the Netherlands. During this remaining part of the two years **C** the vessel made only eight voyages and she spent some 380 days in ports of loading or discharge. There was provision for payment of demurrage with wide exceptions of causes of delay beyond the control of the charterer; but the respondents have admitted liability to pay demurrage for some 150 days. The complaint of the appellants is that, by reason of the failure of the respondents to perform their contractual obligations to load and discharge within the lay days, **D** the appellants have been deprived of the freight which would have been earned on the additional voyages which would have been performed had there not been this delay for which the respondents are responsible. They claim that six or nine more voyages would have been performed within the period if the respondents had fulfilled their obligations, and they estimate their loss from that cause at $875,000, or alternatively $580,000. The respondents' answer is that the appel- **E** lants are only entitled to demurrage at the agreed rate of $1,000 per day and they have paid some $150,000 as demurrage.

The new contention submitted by the appellants is that the breaches of contract which caused these delays amounted to fundamental breach or breach going to the root of the contract, so that, at some time during the currency of the agreement, the appellants would have been entitled to treat the breaches as a **F** repudiation, to terminate or rescind the contract and to claim damages at common law. It is, I think, clear that, if they did have that right, they must be held to have elected not to treat the breaches as repudiatory; but they argue that, nevertheless, the fact that there was a fundamental breach prevents the respondents from relying on the demurrage clause as limiting their responsibility. So the first question must be whether these delays can be regarded as involving **G** fundamental breach. If so, it is for the arbitrators, at least in the first instance, to decide whether there was fundamental breach. The respondents deny that these breaches are capable of being regarded as amounting to fundamental breach. General use of the term " fundamental breach " is of recent origin, and I can find nothing to indicate that it means either more or less than the well known type of breach which entitles the innocent party to treat it as repudiatory and to **H** rescind the contract. The appellants allege that the respondents caused these delays deliberately (i.e., with the wilful intention of limiting the number of contractual voyages). They do not allege fraud or bad faith. This allegation would appear to cover a case where the charterers decided that it would pay them better to delay loading and discharge and pay the resulting demurrage at the relatively low agreed rate, rather than load and discharge more speedily and **I** then have to buy more coal and pay the relatively high agreed freight on the additional voyages which would then be possible. If facts of that kind could be proved, I think that it would be open to the arbitrators to find that the respondents had committed a fundamental or repudiatory breach. One way of looking at the matter would be to ask whether the party in breach has by his breach produced a situation fundamentally different from anything which the parties could as reasonable men have contemplated when the contract was made. Then one would have to ask not only what had already happened but also what was

A likely to happen in future. And there the fact that the breach was deliberate might be of great importance.

If fundamental breach is established, the next question is what effect, if any, that has on the applicability of other terms of the contract. This question has often arisen with regard to clauses excluding liability, in whole or in part, of the party in breach. I do not think that there is generally much difficulty where the

B innocent party has elected to treat the breach as a repudiation, bring the contract to an end and sue for damages. Then the whole contract has ceased to exist, including the exclusion clause, and I do not see how that clause can then be used to exclude an action for loss which will be suffered by the innocent party after it has ceased to exist, such as loss of the profit which would have accrued if the contract had run its full term. But that is not the situation in the present case,

C where, in my view, the appellants elected that the contract should continue in force. Where the contract has been affirmed by the innocent party, at first sight the position is simple. You must either affirm the whole contract or rescind the whole contract; you cannot approbate and reprobate by affirming part of it and disaffirming the rest—that would be making a new contract. So the clause excluding liability must continue to apply. But that is too simple, and there is

D authority for two quite different ways of holding that, in spite of affirmation of the contract as a whole by the innocent party, the guilty party may not be entitled to rely on a clause in it. One way depends on construction of the clause. The other way depends on the existence of a rule of substantive law.

As a matter of construction, it may appear that the terms of the exclusion clause are not wide enough to cover the kind of breach which has been committed.

E Such clauses must be construed strictly and, if ambiguous, the narrower meaning will be taken. Or it may appear that the terms of the clause are so wide that they cannot be applied literally; that may be because this would lead to an absurdity, or because it would defeat the main object of the contract or perhaps for other reasons. And where some limit must be read into the clause, it is generally reasonable to draw the line at fundamental breaches. There is no reason why a

F contract should not make a provision for events which the parties do not have in contemplation or even which are unforeseeable, if sufficiently clear words are used; but if some limitation has to be read in, it seems reasonable to suppose that neither party had in contemplation a breach which goes to the root of the contract. Then the true analysis seems to me to be that the whole contract, including the clause excluding liability, does survive after election to affirm it, but that that

G does not avail the party in breach. The exclusion clause does not change its meaning; as a matter of construction it never did apply and does not after election apply to this type of breach, and, therefore, is no answer to an action brought in respect of this type of breach. But applying a strict construction to these clauses is not sufficient to exclude them in all cases of fundamental breach. It cannot be said as a matter of law that the resources of the English language are

H so limited that it is impossible to devise an exclusion clause which will apply to at least some cases of fundamental breach without being so widely drawn that it can be cut down on any ground by applying ordinary principles of construction. So, if there is to be a universal rule that, no matter how the exclusion clause is expressed, it will not apply to protect a party in fundamental breach, any such rule must be a substantive rule of law nullifying any agreement to the contrary

I and to that extent restricting the general principle of English law that parties are free to contract as they may see fit.

There is recent authority for the existence of such a rule of law, but I cannot find support for it in the older authorities. Most of them arose out of deviation from the contractual voyage or similar breaches of contracts of carriage by land. Any deviation has always been regarded as a breach going to the root of the contract, and it was held in these earlier cases that, if the consignor's goods were lost after there had been a deviation, the shipowner could not rely on clauses excluding or limiting his liability. The reasons given for this varied, but I do

not think that it is useful now to examine them in detail because it was made clear A
in the speeches in this House in *Hain S.S. Co., Ltd.* v. *Tate & Lyle, Ltd.* (30) that
there is no special rule applicable to deviation cases; the ordinary principles of
the law of contract must be applied. The special feature of these cases is that the
consignor's goods were lost before he knew of the deviation and, therefore, before
he had any opportunity to elect whether or not to treat it as bringing the contract
to an end. When he learns of the deviation and of the subsequent loss of his goods, B
there is hardly room for any election, but the fact that he sues for their value could
be treated as an election to terminate the contract by reason of and immediately
after the deviation. Among the reasons given in the earlier cases I do not find
any reliance on any rule of law that a party guilty of a breach going to the root of
the contract can never rely on clauses excluding his liability. And I do not think
that the decision in *Tate & Lyle's* case (30) assists us. There, the owners of the C
goods had known of the deviation and had elected to waive it before the goods
were lost. The breach was not a continuing breach and it did not cause the loss
of the goods. In this case, the breach, if it was a fundamental breach, was a
continuing breach and it did cause the loss of which the appellants complain.
   I think that *Smeaton Hanscomb & Co., Ltd.* v. *Sassoon I. Setty, Son & Co. (No.
1)* (31) can be regarded as the first of the series of recent cases dealing with funda- D
mental breach. There the question was whether a claim by the buyer was barred
by a clause in the contract " Any claim must be made within fourteen days from
the final discharge of the goods . . ." DEVLIN, J., said (32):

     " It is, no doubt, a principle of construction that exceptions are to be
   construed as not being applicable for the protection of those for whose benefit
   they are inserted if the beneficiary has committed a breach of a fundamental E
   term of the contract, and that a clause requiring the claim to be brought
   within a specified period is to be regarded as an exception for this purpose . . .
   I do not think that what is a fundamental term has ever been closely defined.
   It must be something, I think, narrower than a condition of the contract, for
   it would be limiting the exceptions too much to say that they applied only to
   breaches of warranty. It is, I think, something which underlies the whole F
   contract so that, if it is not complied with, the performance becomes
   something totally different from that which the contract contemplates."

It is true that DEVLIN, J., says that he is applying a principle of construction,
but I think that he is really applying a substantive rule of law. He does not
reach his conclusion by construing the clause in its context; there is no statement G
of any reason why the apparently general terms of this particular clause must be
cut down or limited so as to make it only applicable to claims in respect of
breaches which do not go to the root of the contract or which are not breaches of
fundamental terms. And it does not appear to me to be obvious that some canon
of construction would require a limitation of the apparently general terms of this
clause.   H
   The next case is *Karsales (Harrow), Ltd.* v. *Wallis* (33). There the contract
provided that

     " No condition or warranty that the vehicle is roadworthy or as to its age,
   condition or fitness for any purpose is given by the owner or implied herein."

DENNING, L.J., said (34):   I

     " Notwithstanding earlier cases which might suggest the contrary, it is
   now settled that exemption clauses of this kind, no matter how widely they
   are expressed, only avail the party when he is carrying out his contract in
   its essential respects. He is not allowed to use them as a cover for misconduct
   or indifference or to enable him to turn a blind eye to his obligations. They

(30) [1936] 2 All E.R. 597.   (31) [1953] 2 All E.R. 1471.
(32) [1953] 2 All E.R. at p. 1473.   (33) [1956] 2 All E.R. 866.
              (34) [1956] 2 All E.R. at p. 868.

A   do not avail him when he is guilty of a breach which goes to the root of the contract."

And PARKER, L.J., said (35):

" In my judgment, however extensive the exception clause may be, it has no application if there has been a breach of a fundamental term."

B   This is a clear statement of a rule of law. If it is right, it would be irrelevant that, on its true construction, an exempting clause must be held to be intended to apply to the breach in question, and that it is not so wide in its terms that as a matter of construction in its context its applicability must be limited. It must mean that the law does not permit contracting out of common law liability for a fundamental breach. I think that I should go on to examine the rest of the series of recent

C   cases, but, under the present practice of the Court of Appeal with regard to the binding character of any of its own decisions, it was hardly to be expected that this statement of the law would not be followed. I should add that I cannot deduce from the authorities cited in *Karsales (Harrow), Ltd.* v. *Wallis* (36) that the proposition stated in the judgments could be regarded as in any way settled law.

D   In *Sze Hai Tong Bank, Ltd.* v. *Rambler Cycle Co., Ltd.* (37), I think that the ground of decision was (38) that

" The clause must, therefore, be limited and modified to the extent necessary to enable effect to be given to the main object and intent of the contract ",

E   applying *Glynn* v. *Margetson* (39). But in delivering the judgment of the Board, LORD DENNING made some observations about deliberate breach. He said (38):

" And they deliberately disregarded one of the prime obligations of the contract. No court can allow so fundamental a breach to pass unnoticed under the cloak of a general exemption clause ",

and (40):

F   " The self-same distinction runs through all the cases where a fundamental breach has disentitled a party from relying on an exemption clause. In each of them there will be found a breach which evinces a deliberate disregard of his bounden obligations."

Then he cited *Bontex Knitting Works, Ltd.* v. *St. John's Garage* (41); *Alexander*

G   v. *Railway Executive* (42) and *Karsales (Harrow), Ltd.* v. *Wallis* (36), and added (43):

" In each of those cases it could reasonably be inferred that the servant or agent deliberately disregarded one of the prime obligations of the contract. He was entrusted by the principal with the performance of the contract on his behalf; and his action could properly be treated as the action of his

H   principal. In each case it was held that the principal could not take advantage of the exemption clause. It might have been different if the servant or agent had been merely negligent or inadvertent."

In this connexion, I may refer to *The Cap Palos* (44), where ATKIN, L.J., referred to the importance of a breach being deliberate.

Yeoman Credit, Ltd. v. *Apps* (45) was another case of hire-purchase of a car

I
---
(35) [1956] 2 All E.R. at p. 871.   (36) [1956] 2 All E.R. 866.
(37) [1959] 3 All E.R. 182; [1959] A.C. 576.
(38) [1959] 3 All E.R. at p. 185; [1959] A.C. at p. 587.
(39) [1891-94] All E.R. Rep. 693; [1893] A.C. 351.
(40) [1959] 3 All E.R. at p. 186; [1959] A.C. at p. 588.
(41) [1943] 2 All E.R. 690; C.A. [1944] 1 All E.R. 381, n.
(42) [1951] 2 All E.R. 442; [1951] 2 K.B. 882.
(43) [1959] 3 All E.R. at p. 186; [1959] A.C. at p. 589.
(44) [1921] All E.R. Rep. 249; [1921] P. 458.
(45) [1961] 2 All E.R. 281; [1962] 2 Q.B. 508.

with an exemption clause similar to that in *Karsales (Harrow), Ltd.* v. *Wallis* A
(46). HOLROYD PEARCE, L.J., quoted (47) the passages from the judgments in
Karsales (48) to which I have referred, and referred (49) to

" such a non-performance, or repudiation, or breach going to the root of
the contract, as disentitles a party to take refuge behind an exception
clause intended to give protection only in regard to those breaches which are
. not inconsistent with and not destructive of the whole essence of the B
contract."

Charterhouse Credit Co., Ltd. v. *Tolly* (50) was a similar case but with more
complicated facts. It had been argued that the exemption clause was not
sufficiently clear to be given effect. DONOVAN, L.J., said (51):

" I do not find it necessary to determine the true construction of this C
clause, for even if it bears the construction contended for by the finance
company, I am of the opinion that it is of no avail to them in this case. As
has often been said in recent years, a fundamental breach of contract, that is,
one which goes to its very root, disentitles the party in breach from relying
on the provisions of an exempting clause ",

and he gives *Karsales (Harrow), Ltd.* v. *Wallis* (52) as his authority. There was a D
finding that the hirer had elected to treat the contract as still on foot, and it was
argued that, therefore, he must be as much bound by the exemption clause as by
any other clause. On this matter, DONOVAN, L.J., said (53):

" The point is, apparently, free from direct authority, but, on principle,
the election by the hirer of one remedy, ought, as I see it, to make no differ- E
ence to the ineffectiveness of an exempting clause in face of such a breach.
However this may be, two decisions of the House of Lords exist where one
party to a contract elected to treat it as still subsisting despite a fundamental
breach by the other, and succeeded in obtaining damages for such breach
despite the existence in the contract of an exempting clause similar to cl. 5
here. One is *Pollock & Co.* v. *Macrae* (54); and the other *Wallis, Son & Wells* F
v. *Pratt & Haynes* (55). The contention that I am now considering was not
specifically raised in either case, but it is impossible to think that, if valid,
it would have been overlooked not only by the parties sued, but by all the
courts before which the two cases came."

UPJOHN, L.J., said (56):

" The authorities establish that where there is a breach of a fundamental G
term the person in breach cannot rely on clauses of exclusion to protect
him as against the other party; but the finance company said with some force
that that is so, no doubt, when the innocent party treats the contract as
repudiated, yet if he elects to affirm the contract, then he must take the
benefit of the contract subject to all its provisions, including a clause of
exclusion, and he can no longer plead that the other party, though in breach H
of a fundamental term, cannot rely on a clause of exclusion. That is not, I
think, an easy question, and there appears to be no authority, where the
matter has been expressly decided. If I am right in the analysis of this
fundamental term, that it really stems from the fact that the finance company
must lend that which they contract to lend and not something which is

I
_____

(46) [1956] 2 All E.R. 866.
(47) [1961] 2 All E.R. at pp. 287, 288; [1962] 2 Q.B. at p. 517.
(48) [1956] 2 All E.R. at pp. 868, 871.
(49) [1961] 2 All E.R. at pp. 289, 290; [1962] 2 Q.B. at p. 520.
(50) [1963] 2 All E.R. 432; [1963] 2 Q.B. 683.
(51) [1963] 2 All E.R. at p. 438; [1963] 2 Q.B. at p. 702.
(52) [1956] 2 All E.R. at pp. 868 et seq.
(53) [1963] 2 All E.R. at pp. 438, 439; [1963] 2 Q.B. at p. 704.
(54) 1922 S.C. (H.L.) 192.   (55) [1911-13] All E.R. Rep. 989; [1911] A.C. 394.
        (56) [1963] 2 All E.R. at p. 442; [1963] 2 Q.B. at p. 709.

A   essentially different, it seems to me that the principle must apply whether
it is a case of repudiation accepted by the hirer or whether he affirms the
contract and sues for damages."

This was substantially repeated by Upjohn, L.J., in *Astley Industrial Trust, Ltd.*
v. *Grimley* (57).   My noble and learned friend gave (58) the example of a contract
for delivery of a tractor and delivery instead of Suffolk Punch horses.   I would
B   be inclined to think that that was not delivery under the contract at all, but that
it was an offer of a new contract on terms to be implied.

I do not think that either of the two cases to which Donovan, L.J., referred
is of assistance in this connexion.   In each it was held that, on a true construction,
the exempting clause was not wide enough to apply to the breach.   In *Pollock
& Co.* v. *Macrae* (59), Lord Dunedin said:

C   " such condition to be effectual must be most clearly and unambiguously
expressed, as is always necessary when a well known common law liability
is sought to be avoided."

Then he referred to *London & North Western Ry. Co.* v. *Neilson* (60), and
continued:

D   " Reading the clauses in this light I am of opinion that, although they
excuse from damage flowing from the insufficiency of a part or parts of the
machinery, they have no application to damage arising when there has
been total breach of contract by failing to supply the article truly contracted
for."

In *Wallis, Son & Wells* v. *Pratt & Haynes* (61), an inferior variety of seed was
E   delivered but the buyer did not discover this until it was too late to reject the
goods; so he sued for damages. The contract included the clause " Sellers give no
warranty express or implied ", but it was held that this was not wide enough in its
terms to apply to breach of a condition.   In neither case was there any question of
cutting down or limiting the application of a clause apparently wide enough
to apply to the breach. Both really turned on pure construction.
F   In *U.G.S. Finance, Ltd.* v. *National Mortgage Bank of Greece and National
Bank of Greece, S.A.* (62), the question related to a condition to the effect that
interest coupons were forfeited if not presented within six years. Lord Denning,
M.R., repeated in substance what he had said in *Karsales (Harrow), Ltd.* v.
Wallis (63), and added (64):

G   " The doctrine does not depend on the customer electing to disaffirm
the contract.   Usually he has no option open to him.   The contract has
been broken irretrievably before he gets to know of it, and the only course
for him is to sue for the breach. So the point does not very often arise.   But
even if he does get to know of it, in time to affirm or disaffirm, he can still
treat the contract as in being, and sue for the breach (without being defeated
H   by the exemption clause) provided always that the breach itself is continuing
to operate and cause damage to him."

A different view was expressed by Pearson, L.J. (65):

" As to the question of ' fundamental breach ', I think there is a rule
of construction that normally an exception or exclusion clause or similar
provision in a contract should be construed as not applying to a situation
I   created by a fundamental breach of the contract. This is not an independent
rule of law imposed by the court on the parties willy-nilly in disregard of their
contractual intention. On the contrary it is a rule of construction based on the

---

(57) [1963] 2 All E.R. at p. 46.
(58) [1963] 2 All E.R. at p. 442;   [1963] 2 Q.B. at p. 710.
(59) 1922 S.C. (H.L.) at p. 199.   (60) [1922] All E.R. Rep. 395; [1922] 2 A.C. 263.
(61) [1911-13] All E.R. Rep. 989;   [1911] A.C. 394.
(62) [1964] 1 Lloyd's Rep. 446.   (63) [1956] 2 All E.R. at p. 868.
(64) [1964] 1 Lloyd's Rep. at p. 450.   (65) [1964] 1 Lloyd's Rep. at p. 453.

presumed intention of the contracting parties. It involves the implication   A
of a term to give to the contract that business efficacy which the parties as
reasonable men must have intended it to have. This rule of construction is not
new in principle but it has become prominent in recent years in consequence
of the tendency to have standard forms of contract containing exceptions
clauses drawn in extravagantly wide terms, which would produce absurd
results if applied literally."   B

If this new rule of law is to be adopted, how far does it go? In its simplest form it
would be that a party is not permitted to contract out of common law liability
for a fundamental breach. If that were right, then a demurrage clause could
not stand as limiting liability for loss resulting from a fundamental breach;
and the same would apply to any clause providing for liquidated damages. I
do not suppose that anyone has intended that this rule should go quite so far as   C
that; but I would find it difficult to say just where the line would have to be
drawn. In my view, no such rule of law ought to be adopted. I do not take that
view merely because any such rule is new or because it goes beyond what can
be done by developing or adapting existing principles. Courts have often introduced new rules when, in their view, they were required by public policy. In   D
former times, when Parliament seldom amended the common law, that could
hardly have been avoided. There are recent examples although, for reasons
which I gave in *Shaw* v. *Director of Public Prosecutions* (66), I think that this
power ought now to be used sparingly. But my main reason is that this rule
would not be a satisfactory solution of the problem which undoubtedly exists.

Exemption clauses differ greatly in many respects. Probably the most
objectionable are found in the complex standard conditions which are now so   E
common. In the ordinary way the customer has no time to read them, and,
if he did read them, he would probably not understand them. If he did understand and object to any of them, he would generally be told that he could
take it or leave it. If he then went to another supplier, the result would be
the same. Freedom to contract must surely imply some choice or room for
bargaining. At the other extreme is the case where parties are bargaining on terms   F
of equality and a stringent exemption clause is accepted for a quid pro quo or
other good reason; but this rule appears to treat all cases alike. There is no
indication in the recent cases that the courts are to consider whether the exemption is fair in all the circumstances or is harsh and unconscionable, or whether
it was freely agreed by the customer. It does not seem to me to be satisfactory
that the decision must always go one way if, e.g., defects in a car or other goods   G
are just sufficient to make the breach of contract a fundamental breach, but must
always go the other way if the defects fall just short of that. This is a complex
problem which intimately affects millions of people, and it appears to me that its
solution should be left to Parliament. If your lordships reject this new rule, there
will certainly be a need for urgent legislative action but that is not beyond
reasonable expectation.   H

I have no doubt that exemption clauses should be construed strictly, and
I think that this case must be decided by considering whether there is any
ground for adopting any but the natural meaning of the demurrage clause.
Having provided for the calculation of the laydays and for extension of the
laydays when delays are caused by various events for which the charterer is
not responsible, cl. 3 of the charterparty continues: I

" If longer detained, charterer to pay $1,000 U.S. currency payable
in the same manner as the freight per running day (or pro rata for part
thereof) demurrage. If sooner dispatched, vessel to pay charterer or his
agents $500 U.S. currency per day (or pro rata for part thereof) dispatch
money for lay time saved."

---

(66) [1961] 2 All E.R. 446; [1962] A.C. 220.

A It is impossible to hold that these words are not wide enough to apply to the circumstances of the present case, whether or not there was fundamental breach. So the only question is whether there is any reason for limiting their scope. The authorities are against the appellants, but, even putting them aside, I can find no such reason. The appellants chose to agree to what they now say was an inadequate sum for demurrage, but that does not appear to me to affect the

B construction of this clause. Even if one assumes that the $1,000 per day was inadequate and was known to both parties to be inadequate when the contract was made, I do not think that it can be said that giving to the clause its natural meaning could lead to an absurdity or could defeat the main object of the contract or could for any other reason justify cutting down its scope. If there was a fundamental breach, the appellants elected that the contract should continue,

C and they did so in the knowledge that this clause would continue. On the whole matter I am of opinion that this appeal fails, and that the questions should be answered as my noble and learned friend proposes.

LORD HODSON: My Lords, I agree with the judgments given already in the Court of Appeal and at first instance that this contract cannot be held to contain an implied obligation involving payment for the greatest number of

D voyages which could have been made if no delays had been experienced. Further, I do not find that the appellants can find support from the decision in *Akt. Reidar* v. *Arcos, Ltd.* (67). The trial judge, GREER, J., and two of the lords justices, ATKIN and WARRINGTON, L.JJ., were agreed that damages were payable as for dead freight beyond the sum due for demurrage. There, a chartered vessel had been sent to Archangel, a White Sea port, to load a cargo of timber. She went

E there in plenty of time within the laydays to load a full and complete cargo according to the summer marks and summer carrying capacity of the vessel. Delay took place in loading, and the number of laydays was exceeded in order to load the quantity which was loaded. She sailed with 306 standards short of the 850 standards of timber which she could have loaded because, by the time the vessel sailed, she could only load in order to comply with the law down to her

F winter marks. There was a breach separate from although arising from the same circumstances as the delay, and it was in these circumstances that damages were awarded.

The charterparty now under consideration provided for the carriage of coal from the United States (East Coast) to Europe and to return in ballast between each trip and remained in force " for a total of two years consecutive voyages "

G (cl. 23). Fixed periods of laytime were provided within which the respondents were obliged respectively to load and discharge the vessel on each voyage. During the relevant part of the two year period the vessel performed eight voyages, whereas the appellants contend that a further six voyages could have been performed if the loading and discharging had been completed within the laytime, or a further nine voyages if the respondents had loaded and discharged the vessel

H with reasonable despatch. The detention beyond the agreed laytime is admittedly a breach of the charterparty, and the only question is whether, in circumstances such as those which have arisen here, the appellants are entitled to any further sum from the respondents over and above their demurrage for which the appellants give credit in their claim. The matter for your lordships to decide arises on a Consultative Case stated by arbitrators. The only relevant question is

I " Whether upon the facts found and upon the true construction of the charterparty dated Dec. 21, 1956, and the agreement dated Oct. 8, 1957:— (A) (i) the [appellants] are entitled to recover (subject to giving credit for the demurrage payments received by them) any damages suffered by them by reason of the respondents' having failed to load and discharge the vessel within the laydays whereby the charterparty was (if so proved) rendered less profitable to the [appellants] by consequent loss of voyages or voyage time.

---

(67) [1926] All E.R. Rep. 140; [1927] 1 K.B. 352.

(ii) Upon the assumption that such loss of profitability resulted from the   A
respondents having deliberately (i.e., with the wilful intention of limiting the
number of contractual voyages) failed to load and/or discharge the vessel
(a) with such ordinary despatch as the circumstances permitted or (b) within
the laydays, the [appellants] are entitled to recover any damages suffered by
the [appellants] through the charterparty having been rendered less profitable
as aforesaid subject to giving credit for the demurrage payments received   B
by them and for any such despatch money as would have been earned by the
respondents."

It is emphasised on behalf of the appellants that, since their obligation throughout was to perform all parts of the agreed voyages " with all possible despatch ",
subject only to the operation of excepted perils, the respondents, as charterers,
should likewise as a matter of construction of the clauses of the charterparty   C
be held to be bound to load and discharge the vessel on a specific number of voyages only ascertainable and then with some difficulty at the end of the two year
period. This argument was, I think, rightly rejected, but before your lordships
the argument was carried further, in that it was said that, although the demurrage
rate here would be the measure of compensation in the ordinary case for delay
of the vessel, yet where the detention is so long as to frustrate the contract the   D
words of the charterparty " if longer detained " whether or not the detention is
deliberate, i.e., with the wilful intention of limiting the number of contractual
voyages, no longer govern the measure of compensation payable to the owners.
Detention cannot, it is said, cover delay by the charterers of such a kind as to
amount to repudiatory breach of the contract. Often expressions have been used
in various cases such as fundamental breach or breach going to 'the root of a   E
contract to describe those situations which may be brought about through the
fault of one party which have a frustrating effect and make the contract in its
original form at any rate impossible of performance. Sometimes it is said that to
hold the parties to the original contract after the breach would be to make a new
contract for them not to insist on performance of the old. The argument is quite
general in its scope and not confined to cases involving the carriage of goods by   F
sea or by land. Before considering the argument further it is pertinent to remember
that your lordships are not concerned with a case where the appellants have
accepted a repudiation of the contract or purported to do so and sailed away.
The appellants continued to perform the contract and seek damages for delay
over and above the demurrage rate. Thus, if they were to succeed in this appeal
they would be faced with the difficulty of establishing when, if at all, the accumu-   G
lated delay was such as would entitle them to sue for damages at large for the loss
which they have suffered.

As has been recognised at the Bar on both sides, the expression " fundamental
breach " is of comparatively recent origin and has seemed to have attained some
mystical meaning in the law of contract. For my part, I doubt whether anything
is to be gained by analysing the various expressions which have been used to   H
describe breaches of contract so serious as to justify the injured party in throwing
up the contract if he so chooses. Sometimes it has been declared that, where a
fundamental breach of contract had occurred, an exceptions clause could not as
a matter of law be relied on, but the better view on the authorities, and that
accepted by both sides before your lordships, is that, as a matter of construction,
normally an exception or exclusive clause or similar provision in a contract should   I
be construed as not applying to a situation created by a fundamental breach of
contract. I have here quoted the langugage used by PEARSON, L.J., in U.G.S.
Finance, Ltd. v. National Mortgage Bank of Greece and National Bank of Greece,
S.A. (68), which is contained in the passage cited by my noble and learned
friend, LORD REID (69)—see also the judgment of DIPLOCK, L.J., in Hardwick
Game Farm v. Suffolk Agricultural and Poultry Producers Assocn., Ltd. (70), in

(68) [1964] 1 Lloyd's Rep. at p. 453.   (69) See p. 75, letter I, ante.
(70) [1966] 1 All E.R. 309 at p. 346.

A   which judgment was delivered on Dec. 20, 1965—a recent example of the acceptance of the opinion of PEARSON, L.J.

So long as one remembers that one is construing a document and not applying some rule of law superimposed on the law of contract so as to limit the freedom of the parties to enter into any agreement they like within the limits which the law prescribes, one can apply one's mind to each contract as it comes up for

B   consideration. I would adopt the language of ATKIN, L.J., in *The Cap Palos* (71):

> " I am far from saying that a contractor may not make a valid contract that he is not to be liable for any failure to perform his contract, including even wilful default; but he must use very clear words to express that purpose . . ."

C   This passage has the support of LORD PARMOOR in *Cunard S.S. Co., Ltd.* v. *Buerger* (72). I think that it is unnecessary to refer in detail to those cases where the doctrine of fundamental breach has been stated as if it went further than a matter to be dealt with on construction. By way of example, in an unreported case, Privy Council Appeal No. 51 of 1959, *Boshali* v. *Allied Commercial Exporters, Ltd.* (73), the Board stated unequivocally that a breach which goes to the root

D   of a contract disentitles a party from relying on an exemption clause (*Karsales (Harrow), Ltd.* v. *Wallis* (74), per DENNING, L.J.). It is to be noticed, however, that LORD DENNING himself, delivering a judgment of the Board in the year 1959 in the *Sze Hai Tong Bank, Ltd.* v. *Rambler Cycle Co., Ltd.* (75), treated the same matter as one of construction. As in this case, counsel there conceded that finally the question was one of construction, and in the judgment of the Board this

E   phrase appears (76): " . . . as matter of construction, their lordships decline to attribute to it [viz., the clause] the unreasonable effect contended for." Thus, even if the accumulated delays of the chartered ship were such as to justify the finding that the respondents are guilty of a fundamental breach of contract, nevertheless it would not follow as a matter of law that the demurrage clause entitling the amount of compensation for detention would not apply. Even if one

F   were to describe the demurrage clause as an exemption or exclusive clause, which I do not think that it is, this result would not follow, for the contract must still be construed. Moreover, if one drives the argument that " fundamental breach " of contract introduces a rule of law that exemption clauses cannot be relied on far enough, it would no doubt be sufficient to destroy the effect of a clause by which " demurrage " (that is, agreed damages for detention) should be calculated.

G   No case has ever gone so far.

It is convenient to remember that a great number of marine cases have been heard over the years in which " deviation " has been in question, and deviation has always been regarded as a serious matter. As LORD ATKIN said in *Hain S.S. Co., Ltd.* v. *Tate & Lyle, Ltd.* (77):

H   > " I venture to think that the true view is that the departure from the voyage contracted to be made is a breach by the shipowner of his contract, but a breach of such a serious character that however slight the deviation the other party to the contract is entitled to treat it as going to the root of the contract, and to declare himself as no longer bound by any of its terms."

Later, he said (77):

I   > " No doubt the extreme gravity attached to a deviation in contracts of carriage is justified by the fact that the insured cargo owner when the ship has deviated has become uninsured."

---

(71) [1921] All E.R. Rep. at p. 254;   [1921] P. at pp. 471, 472.
(72) [1926] All E.R. Rep. at p. 108;   [1927] A.C. at p. 13.
(73) (1959), unreported.   (74) [1956] 2 All E.R. 866 at p. 869.
(75) [1959] 3 All E.R. 182;   [1959] A.C. 576.
(76) [1959] 3 All E.R. at p. 185;   [1959] A.C. at p. 587.
(77) [1936] 2 All E.R. at p. 601.

Deviation cases are convenient examples for consideration because they involve **A** breaches of a fundamental term of the contract, and there is usually no difficulty in ascertaining whether that term has been breached. If it has been, the breach will be fundamental. The case is more difficult as a rule where, as here, the term involved can hardly be described as fundamental, yet breaches of it may be said in the aggregate to be fundamental. I doubt whether it is helpful to analyse or to sub-divide the cases which are concerned with these serious breaches or to try **B** to give special names to individual clauses of such cases. The leading case of *Glynn* v. *Margetson* (78) is a striking example of a breach of a deviation clause in a contract which has been described as an application of the " main purpose " rule. This was a case of deviation where the main purpose of the contract was the delivery of oranges from Malaga to Liverpool. The ship made in the opposite direction videlicet to Burriana, going further away from Liverpool **C** than she was at Malaga, and the oranges were damaged owing to the delay on the voyage. The shipowner relied on a clause which gave him liberty to proceed to and stay at any port or ports within wide limits staying there as long as he liked for any purpose. Both LORD HERSCHELL, L.C., and LORD HALSBURY, with whom the other members of the House agreed, treated the matter as one of construction of the contract, and on that basis limited the liberty to ports in the course of the **D** voyage.

Other expressions have been used, e.g., " the four corners rule ". Thus, under a contract of carriage or bailment, if the carrier or bailee uses a place other than that agreed on for storing the goods, or otherwise exposes the goods to risks quite different from those contemplated by the contract, he cannot rely on clauses in the contract designed to protect him against liability within the four corners of **E** the contract, and has only such protection as is afforded by the common law. *Lilley* v. *Doubleday* (79) and *Gibaud* v. *Great Eastern Ry. Co.* (80) are examples of such cases, all of which depend on the construction of the contract. Sometimes a position of absurdity is reached by the tacking on to formal words in a printed contract designed for a variety of purposes a specific bargain which cannot be performed if the printed words are to apply. Such a case was *Glynn* v. **F** *Margetson* (78). LORD HERSCHELL, L.C., said (81):

" Where general words are used which are obviously intended to be applicable to the circumstances of the particular contract, which particular contract is to be embodied in or introduced into that printed form, I think you are justified in looking at the main object and intent of the contract and in limiting the general words used, having in view that object and intent." **G**

Treating the matter as one of construction, the case is not affected by the affirmation of the contract. In this case, the appellants, the owners of the ship, did not sail away; they continued to perform the contract to the bitter end and, accordingly, are bound by such of the terms of the contract as are applicable notwithstanding the breach of contract by the respondents, the charterers. I see no **H** reason why the agreement as to the demurrage rate should not apply so long as the contract is being performed, whether the breach is treated as fundamental or not.

I think that the decision of this House in *Pollock & Co.* v. *Macrae* (82) is of some assistance. There, a contract for the building and installation of a set of motor marine engines which bound the builders to replace any parts faulty through bad **I** material or workmanship contained a clause providing that all goods were supplied on the condition that the builders should not be liable for direct or consequential damages arising from the defective material or workmanship. It was held that this clause, while it protected the builders where a part or parts of the engines

(78) [1891-94] All E.R. Rep. 693; [1893] A.C. 351.   (79) (1881), 7 Q.B.D. 510.
(80) [1921] All E.R. Rep. 35; [1921] 2 K.B. 426.
(81) [1891-94] All E.R. Rep. at p. 695; [1893] A.C. at p. 355.
(82) 1922 S.C. (H.L.) 192.

A   were defective, was of no avail where there had been a complete breach of contract owing to a series of defects in the engines which rendered them practically unserviceable. The buyer then had ineffectively elected to reject the goods and treat the contract as repudiated, but was allowed to fall back on his alternative remedy for damages. LORD DUNEDIN said (83):

B   " Now, where there is such a congeries of defects as to destroy the workable character of the machine, I think this amounts to a total breach of contract, and that each defect cannot be taken by itself separately so as to apply the provisions of the conditions of guarantee and make it impossible to claim damages."

C   The case turned on pure construction, but it was decided on the basis that the whole of the contract had to be construed. I think that the same applies to *Wallis, Son & Wells* v. *Pratt and Haynes* (84), another case of breach of contract of a repudiatory quality followed by affirmation.

On the construction of this contract, I am of opinion that the parties have agreed to limit the damages payable for detention at the agreed demurrage rate and that there is no reason for not so limiting them whether or not there was

D   an intention on the part of the respondents wilfully to limit the number of voyages. As has been stated in SCRUTTON ON CHARTERPARTIES (85), and as MOCATTA, J., pointed out: demurrage, in its strict meaning, is a sum agreed by the charterer to be paid as liquidated damages for delay beyond a stipulated or reasonable time for loading or unloading. As a rule some deliberate or negligent conduct on the part of the charterer is involved, for he is protected by a number

E   of exceptions against any risks outside his control. No English authority was cited which assists the appellants. The researches of counsel only discovered one case which raises the point of deliberate delay consisting of detention so long as it suits the charterers' convenience. This was *Ethel Radcliffe S.S. Co.* v. *Barnett* (86). Damages at large at common law were awarded by an arbitrator, but the award was varied by ROWLATT, J., and the Court of Appeal rejected the

F   submission which had at first succeeded. There, the clause to be construed was as follows:

" Orders as to port of discharge are to be given to the master within twenty-four hours after receipt by consignees of master's telegraphic report to consignees . . . of his arrival at the port of call, and for any detention waiting for orders after the aforesaid twenty-four hours, the charterers or their

G   agents shall pay to the steamer 30s. sterling per hour . . ."

The court treated the twenty-four hours as equivalent to laydays and the 30s. per hour as demurrage and applied to the situation the passage at p. 348 of SCRUTTON ON CHARTERPARTIES (12th Edn.) art. 128:

" Stipulations for demurrage may be (1) Exhaustive: as ' ten days for loading and demurrage at £20 per diem afterwards ', which covers all delay.

H   On such a provision the shipowner cannot say that the provision for £20 a day demurrage only applies to a reasonable time, after the lapse of which he can claim damages for detention. After the lapse of a reasonable time he may take his ship away, but if he allows her to stay on he can only claim the agreed rate of demurrage."

I   In the current (17th) edition of this work (87), the last sentence has been rewritten so as to read: " If the contract be not repudiated or frustrated, he can only claim the agreed rate of demurrage." Thus, the question of a frustrating delay is left open, but the general proposition stated in the paragraph is supported by *Inverkip S.S. Co.* v. *Bunge & Co.* (88), as ATKIN, L.J., pointed out.

An American case which was relied on by the appellants should be noticed as

---

(83) 1922 S.C. (H.L.) at p. 200.   (84) [1911-13] All E.R. Rep. 989; [1911] A.C. 394.
(85) (17th Edn.), p. 305, art. 131.
(87) Article 131, p. 306.   (86) (1926), 24 Lloyd L.R. 277.
(88) [1917] 2 K.B. 193 at p. 281.

the language of the judgment lends some support to their submission. This was A
Empress Maritime de Transportes S.A. v. *A.T. Mancy Oil Co.* (89), tried in
the United States District Court Eastern District of Virginia Norfolk Division
in 1963. In that case, damages were claimed for wrongful detention of the
motor vessel " Blue Star " within the lay days, the allegation being that the
defendant coal supplier conspired with the charterer of the vessel intentionally
to delay the " Blue Star " at loading by arranging that the coal would not B
be loaded on the vessel until laytime was about to expire so as to diminish
the number of consecutive voyages the vessel could perform under a two year
consecutive voyage time charter agreement. The charter was also written
on an Americanised Welsh Coal Charter Form. The claim succeeded on the
construction of the charterparty, but the facts were special and in any case, as
the editors of the report point out in a note, there is authority in the courts of this C
country for the proposition that, when a charterparty prescribes a fixed time to
load, there is no basis for implying an obligation on the part of the voyage charterer
to load within a lesser time: see *Margaronis Navigation Agency, Ltd.* v. *Henry
W. Peabody & Co. of London, Ltd.* (90).

For myself, I see no reason to hold that attributing to the respondents a wilful
intention of limiting the number of contractual voyages affects the sums other- D
wise payable by way of demurrage so as to open the way to a claim for damages
at large. I would, accordingly, agree with the learned judge that the question
(A) in the Consultative Case be answered in the negative and dismiss the appeal.

LORD UPJOHN: My Lords, in this appeal, your lordships are concerned
with the rights and obligations of the contracting parties to a consecutive voyage
charterparty dated Dec. 21, 1956, made between the appellants, owners of the E
ship, and the respondents, the charterers. It provided for the carriage of coal
for two years' consecutive voyages terminating in March, 1959, between Hampton
Roads, Baltimore or Philadelphia on one side of the Atlantic and one safe port,
Belgium, Holland or Germany on the other side, returning in ballast to the U.S.A.
for a further cargo. Clause 3 of the charterparty provided for loading at an agreed
rate with a widely drawn provision excluding from loading time (or lay days as F
they are usually called) time lost from a variety of events and causes immaterial
to the matters in issue before your lordships. The clause provided " If longer
detained, charterer to pay $1,000 U.S. currency . . . per running day (or pro
rata for part thereof) demurrage ". There was a similar provision for demurrage
if the time for the agreed rate of discharge was exceeded. Whether because of the
fall in freight rates after the re-opening of the Suez Canal in April, 1957, or for G
some other reason, the ship greatly exceeded the permitted lay time in port, and
your lordships were told that, at one time, the appellants sailed the ship away
treating the contract as repudiated by the respondents and accepting that
repudiation. This led to an arbitration between the parties, not yet determined,
and without prejudice to that arbitration the parties on Oct. 8, 1957, agreed to
perform the charterparty for the remainder of the stipulated term. Thereafter, H
save for the first voyage, the ship always greatly exceeded the lay days in port
both loading and unloading, and in fact during the term of the charterparty the
ship performed only eight voyages. The respondents do not dispute their liability
to pay demurrage for these lost days which amounts to the substantial sum of
approximately $150,000. The appellants, however, allege that, but for the days
lost in port, the ship could have performed some six to nine additional profitable I
voyages during that time and, on that footing, they claim large additional damages
for loss of profit which the ship could have earned by reason of these additional
voyages. This dispute was referred to arbitration and has reached this House on a
Consultative Case by the arbitrators.

(89) [1965] A.M.R. 517.
(90) [1964] 2 All E.R. 296; [1965] 1 Q.B. 300; *affd.* C.A., [1964] 3 All E.R. 333;
[1965] 2 Q.B. 430.

A   When the matter first came before your lordships it was opened, as in the courts below, on the footing that, though the delays (beyond the lay days) in port were considerable, such delays did not amount to repudiatory conduct on the part of the charterers. It is not in doubt that every time the respondents exceeded the lay days in port they committed a breach of contract; a breach, however, for which the parties have agreed damages at the rate of $1,000 a day. But the

B appellants argue that as this is not a single voyage charter but one contract for the performance of a number of consecutive voyages, damages are not to be determined solely by the length of detention of the ship in excess of the lay days in port as it was admitted they would have been in a single voyage charter, but that there was a further obligation on the respondents to load and discharge within the lay time provided by the charterparty so that the ship might perform

C such a number of consecutive voyages each of a duration not exceeding the sea passage plus the permitted lay times in port, as proved to be capable of performance within the term of the charter. In other words, in a consecutive voyage charter there is a larger obligation on the charterers to load and discharge the cargo within the lay days, so that the owners may benefit from the profitable employment of their ship contemplated by the charterparty for the period of the

D charter. This obligation was said to arise either as a matter of construction of the charterparty regarded as a whole, or from an implied term that the respondents would co-operate or concur in doing all things necessary to enable the appellants to perform the maximum possible number of voyages and to earn the maximum possible amount of freight, which could in the ordinary course of events be performed or earned during the term of the charter.

E   My lords, the charterparty, in my opinion, does not bear this construction. It is clear that the respondents have broken no express clause of the charterparty except the provision for detention in the ports of loading or discharge in excess of the lay days. The voyages have been in fact consecutive and I, for my part, can find nothing in the contract which imposes on the respondents as a matter of construction or as a matter of necessary implication an obligation to undertake

F any additional requirement of loading within the lay days for breach of which they will be liable in damages beyond the rate of demurrage specified in the contract for exceeding those days. As both Mocatta, J., and the Court of Appeal held, there was only one breach by the respondents, namely, a breach of the obligation to load and discharge at an agreed rate, and the detention of the ship in a port beyond that date was a breach of contract for which the parties had

G agreed damages. The appellants, however, placed much reliance on *Akt. Reidar* v. *Arcos, Ltd.* (91), but with all respect to the argument that was a very different case. In the view of Greer, J., at first instance (92) and the majority of the Court of Appeal, there were in that case breaches of two quite independent obligations; one was demurrage for detention (as here), the other was a failure to load a full and complete cargo, which had become impossible owing to the onset of winter conditions and, therefore, entirely different considerations applied

H to that case. It is true that Bankes, L.J., reached the same result by a different route on the particular facts of that case, but, as Mocatta, J., and the Court of Appeal, with whose judgments I am in full agreement, pointed out, his ratio decidendi does not assist the owners in this quite different case. Accordingly, in my opinion that case does not help your lordships. My lords, I have dwelt on

I this case at a little length because, in the end, I believe that the considerations which I have already mentioned are very material in deciding this appeal.

  At the conclusion of his main argument, counsel for the appellants endeavoured to take a new point not raised in the courts below, namely, that the respondents had committed a fundamental breach of the contract which amounted to a repudiation and on that footing it was urged that the appellants were entitled to general damages for lack of profitability and were not confined to demurrage. Your lordships, in the special circumstances of this case, permitted the appeal to

---

(91) [1926] All E.R. Rep. 140; [1927] 1 K.B. 352.   (92) [1926] 2 K.B. 83.

be re-argued de novo after Supplemental Cases had been lodged by each side. A
The appellants' basic argument on this new case is that, after the first voyage
after Oct. 8, 1957, there were such delays beyond the lay days each time that
the ship entered port for loading or discharge that the delays, each admittedly a
breach of the charterparty, amounted cumulatively to a repudiation of the
contract which entitled the respondents at their option to accept and to treat
the contract as at an end and sail away. This appeal comes before your lordships B
on a Consultative Case by the arbitrators and the relevant facts have not yet
been found on this point, so for the purposes of this point it is necessary to make
the double assumption in favour of the appellants, first, that it is open to the
arbitrators on the facts to find that there has been a breach of contract by the
respondents which goes to its root and entitled the appellants to treat the contract
as at an end and, secondly, that in fact they will so find. It was submitted by the C
respondents that, on the facts of this case, as a matter of law it was not open to
the arbitrators to find in favour of the appellants for it was said that, out of 511
days which was the term of the charter after the agreement of October, 1957, only
154 days were demurrage days. I cannot agree with this submission. It is a
proper matter of fact for the arbitrators to consider. Accordingly, for the purpose
solely of dealing with the argument I am prepared to make the assumptions D
desired by the appellants.

But what seems to me quite clear, making these assumptions, is that there has
been no acceptance by the appellants of the repudiation which brought the
contract to an end. On the contrary, it seems to me clear that, by their conduct,
the appellants expressly affirmed the contract. The relevant facts were known
at all material times to them for they must have been made currently aware of E
the excessive delays in port; they had already sailed away once—I say nothing
about that for it is still sub judice—but it was for the appellants, knowing of the
delays, to make up their minds whether to sail away again. They did not do so,
and with full knowledge of all the facts elected to treat the contract as on foot
until the expiry of the charterparty by effluxion of time. It is this feature which
gives rise to the whole difficulty in this interesting case. For it is common ground F
that, had the appellants accepted the assumed repudiation and sailed away,
thereby terminating the contract, none of its terms survived, and damages for
breach of contract would have been at large including damages for loss of profitable
employment of the ship for the term of the charterparty.

In general, it cannot be disputed that where a party having an option to treat
a contract at an end nevertheless affirms it, that contract and all its terms must G
remain in full force and effect for the benefit of both parties during the remainder
of the period of performance, for it is not possible even for the innocent party to
make a new contract between the parties without the concurrence of the other.
As LORD ATKIN in *Hain S.S. Co., Ltd.* v. *Tate & Lyle, Ltd.* (93) said:

> ". . . he can elect to treat the contract as subsisting; and if he does this
> with knowledge of his rights he must in accordance with the general law of H
> contract be held bound ",

and as LORD WRIGHT, M.R., said even more clearly (94):

> " In the present case, the charterers elected to waive the breach, with the
> result that the charterparty was not abrogated, but remained in force. The
> appellants were thus entitled to the benefit of the contract conditions and I
> in particular to rely on the exceptions of perils of the sea . . ."

and see *Chandris* v. *Isbrandtsen Moller Co., Inc.* (95), per DEVLIN, J. That is this
case. It is, in my opinion, quite clear that, as a matter of construction of the
charterparty, the demurrage clause, both as to loading and discharging, is
expressed without limitation of time and, therefore, applies throughout the term
of the contract. If authority be wanted for this self-evident proposition, it is to

(93) [1936] 2 All E.R. at p. 601.   (94) [1936] 2 All E.R. at p. 608.
                (95) [1950] 1 All E.R. at p. 774; [1951] 1 K.B. at p. 248.

A be found in *Western S.S. Co.* v. *Amaral Sutherland & Co.* (96), *Inverkip S.S. Co., Ltd.* v. *Bunge & Co.* (97) and *Ethel Radcliffe S.S. Co.* v. *Barnett* (98). Therefore, to succeed in this appeal, the appellants must displace the demurrage clause. They seek to do so in reliance on the well-known doctrine that, in certain circum-stances, a party to a contract cannot rely on an exception or limitation clause inserted solely for his benefit. But before examining this doctrine, the first

B question which logically must be asked is, surely, whether this demurrage clause is a provision of exception or limitation? Whatever the ultimate ambit of the doctrine may be found to be it is, in my opinion, confined to clauses which are truly clauses of exception or limitation, that is to say, clauses essentially inserted for the purpose only of protecting one contracting party from the legal conse-quences of other express terms of the contract or from terms which would other-

C wise be implied by law or from the terms of the contract regarded as a whole; just as a party may waive a clause which is inserted for solely his own benefit (see *Hawksley* v. *Outram* (99)) so, per contra, there are occasions when a party cannot be permitted to rely on such a clause. But if it is inserted for the benefit of both, I know of no authority—and none has been cited—which entitles one party unilaterally to disregard its provisions. In my opinion, the demurrage

D clause with which we are concerned is a clause providing for agreed damages and is different from a clause excluding or limiting liability for damage by breach of contract by one party. An agreed damage clause is for the benefit of both; the party establishing breach by the other need prove no damage in fact; the other must pay that, no less but no more. But where liability for damage is limited by a clause, then the person seeking to claim damages must prove them at least

E up to the limit laid down by the clause; the other party, whatever may be the damage in fact, can refuse to pay more if he can rely on the clause. As GREER, J., said in relation to a demurrage clause in *Akt. Reidar* v. *Arcos, Ltd.* (100): " This clause was put in for my benefit as well as yours; it measures the damages I have to pay . . ." Counsel for the appellants sought to say that the agreed damages of $1,000 a day were much too low to be an estimate of damage, and that it might

F be open to the arbitrators to hold that, in truth, this was in the nature of a penalty clause or a limitation clause limiting liability. I do not think that it is open now to the appellants to make this submission. It is quite clear on the authorities that the parties need not agree on a true estimate of damage. They are perfectly entitled to agree on a low rate: see *Cellulose Acetate Silk Co., Ltd.* v. *Widnes Foundry (1925), Ltd.* (101), and the *Chandris* case (102).

G Accordingly, in my opinion the demurrage clause is a clause which, the contract being affirmed, remains an agreed damages clause for the benefit of both parties, and it is not a clause of exception or limitation inserted for the benefit of one party only to which the doctrine under consideration can properly be applied. That is sufficient to dispose of this appeal.

   But in view of the arguments that have been addressed to your lordships, I

H think that it is right that I should express my views thereon on the footing that the demurrage clause in this case is indeed a clause of exception or limitation of liability inserted solely for the benefit of the charterer, and that it is therefore a clause to which in certain circumstances the doctrine relied on by the appellants applies. That the doctrine exists is not in doubt, but it is necessary to examine the authorities to understand the principle on which it is based. There was much

I discussion during the argument on the phrases " fundamental breach " and " breach of a fundamental term ", and I think that it is true that in some of the cases these terms have been used interchangeably; but in fact they are quite different. I believe that all of your lordships are agreed and, indeed, it has not

---

(96) [1913] 3 K.B. 366.   (97) [1917] 2 K.B. 193.
(98) (1926), 24 Lloyd L.R. 277.   (99) [1892] 3 Ch. 359.
(100) [1926] 2 K.B. at p. 86.   (101) [1932] All E.R. Rep. 567; [1933] A.C. 20.
          (102) [1950] 1 All E.R. at p. 775; [1951] 1 K.B. at p. 249.

seriously been disputed before us that there is no magic in the words " fundamen- A
tal breach " ; this expression is no more than a convenient shorthand expression
for saying that a particular breach or breaches of contract by one party is or
are such as to go to the root of the contract which entitles the other party to treat
such breach or breaches as a repudiation of the whole contract. Whether such
breach or breaches do constitute a fundamental breach depends on the construction of the contract and on all the facts and circumstances of the case. The B
innocent party may accept that breach or those breaches as a repudiation and
treat the whole contract at an end and sue for damages generally, or he may at
his option prefer to affirm the contract and treat it as continuing on foot, in
which case he can sue only for damages for breach or breaches of the particular
stipulation or stipulations in the contract which has or have been broken. But
the expression " fundamental term " has a different meaning. A fundamental C
term of a contract is a stipulation which the parties have agreed either expressly
or by necessary implication or which the general law regards as a condition
which goes to the root of the contract so that *any* breach of that term may at
once and without further reference to the facts and circumstances be regarded
by the innocent party as a fundamental breach and thus is conferred on him
the alternative remedies at his option that I have just mentioned. I discussed D
this matter in the Court of Appeal in *Hong Kong Fir Shipping Co., Ltd.* v. *Kawasaki
Kisen Kaisha, Ltd.* (103).
    With these preliminary observations I must now examine some of the cases
that were cited to your lordships as examples of the principle that, in some circumstances, a party to the contract cannot rely on clauses inserted for his benefit.
The earlier cases were nearly all cases of carriage of goods by sea or by land or E
concerned with the warehousing of goods. The principles on which these cases,
mainly in the last century, were decided were not expressed by the judges to be
related to repudiatory conduct on the part of one party thereto nor to any principle
of frustration, for these conceptions were not so fully developed as they are now.
Thus, in cases of carriage of goods by sea, an unreasonable deviation from the
usual and customary course is, and has always been, considered as precluding F
the shipowner from relying on any clauses inserted for his protection: see, for
example, *Davies* v. *Garrett* (104) and *Scaramanger* v. *Stamp* (105). So strict is
this rule that, although the deviation has not been the cause of any loss to the
plaintiff's goods and was, so to speak, a mere incident in the voyage, nevertheless
having taken place the owner is no longer entitled to rely on clauses of exception
contained in the relevant contract, unless it can be shown that the loss would G
have happened in any event: see *United States Shipping Board* v. *Bunge y
Born Limitada Sociedad* (106); *James Morrison & Co., Ltd.* v. *Shaw, Savill &
Albion Co., Ltd.* (107). It was not, however, until this century that deviation was
finally established as a fundamental breach. This was first suggested, rather
tentatively, by LORD ESHER, M.R., in *Balian & Sons* v. *Joly, Victoria & Co.,
Ltd.* (108), but was accepted as the basis of his decision by the Court of Appeal H
in *Joseph Thorley, Ltd.* v. *Orchis S.S. Co., Ltd.* (109). SIR RICHARD HENN COLLINS,
M.R., pointed out (110) that the deviation goes to the root of the contract and
its performance is a condition precedent to the right of a shipowner to put the
bill of lading in suit. Finally, this House, in *Hain S.S. Co., Ltd.* v. *Tate & Lyle,
Ltd.* (111), established the proposition in relation to carriage of goods by sea in
the words of LORD ATKIN (112) (with which the other lords agreed): I
    " I venture to think that the true view is that the departure from the

---

(103) [1962] 1 All E.R. 474 at p. 483; [1962] 2 Q.B. 26 at p. 63.
(104) (1830), 6 Bing. 716.   (105) (1880), 5 C.P.D. 295.
(106) [1925] All E.R. Rep. 173.
(107) [1916-17] All E.R. Rep. 1068; [1916] 2 K.B. 783.
(108) (1890), 6 T.L.R. 345.   (109) [1907] 1 K.B. 660.
(110) [1907] 1 K.B. at p. 667.   (111) [1936] 2 All E.R. 597.
             (112) [1936] 2 All E.R. at p. 601.

A   voyage contracted to be made is a breach by the shipowner of his contract, but a breach of such a serious character that however slight the deviation the other party to the contract is entitled to treat it as going to the root of the contract, and to declare himself as no longer bound by any of its terms."

B   So the law is now quite clearly established that, unless the parties otherwise agree, the usual and customary course on any voyage described in a charterparty is a fundamental term and, therefore, *any* breach of it (however, for practical purposes, irrelevant) is a fundamental breach: see this stated explicitly by LORD WRIGHT, M.R., in the *Tate & Lyle* case (113).   Moreover, LORD ATKIN made it clear that the rule that the owner cannot rely on an exception clause in such a case is not because of anything special about such a clause but is the result of the application of the ordinary law of contract.   He said (114):

C

"   If this view be correct then the breach by deviation does not automatically cancel the express contract, otherwise the shipowner by his own wrong can get rid of his own contract.   Nor does it affect merely the exceptions clauses.   This would make those clauses alone subject to a condition of no deviation, a construction for which I can find no justification.   It is quite inconsistent with the cases which have treated deviation as precluding enforcement of demurrage provisions.   The event falls within the ordinary law of contract.   The party who is affected by the breach has the right to say, I am not now bound by the contract whether it is expressed in charterparty, bill of lading or otherwise."

D

E   LORD ATKIN then went on to point out that equally the innocent party electing to treat the contract as at an end is not bound by his promise to pay the agreed freight any more than by his other promises.

The warehouse cases and cases of carriage by land have developed on parallel lines.   The principle on which these cases proceeded originally is well stated by SCRUTTON, L.J., in *Gibaud* v. *Great Eastern Ry. Co.* (115), where he said:

F   "   It is a fairly well-known principle and *Lilley* v. *Doubleday* (116) is perhaps the best illustration of it that if you undertake to do a thing in a certain way or to keep a thing in a certain place with certain conditions protecting it, and you have broken the contract by not doing the thing contracted for in the way contracted for or not keeping the article in the place in which you have contracted to keep it, you cannot rely on the conditions which were only intended to protect you if you carried out the contract in the way in which you had contracted to do it."

G

These observations have subsequently been approved in your lordships' House in *London & North Western Ry. Co.* v. *Neilson* (117).   Thus, to give one or two examples from the cases to illustrate the general proposition, in *Lilley* v. *Doubleday* (116) itself the warehouseman contracted to store his goods at A but in fact

H   he stored them at B.   It was held that he could not rely on a clause of exception excusing him from loss without negligence though he could have relied on the clause if they had been warehoused at A.   Again, in *Mallet* v. *Great Eastern Ry. Co.* (118), a consignment of fish contracted to be sent to Jersey by the Weymouth route was sent by the consignor by mistake via the Southampton route and although the steamers were due to arrive at Jersey at about the same time the

I   Southampton steamer, being on a longer sea route, was delayed by bad weather and it was held that the consignor could not rely on the clause of exception for he had done something wholly at variance with the contract.   So, too, in *Gunyon* v. *South Eastern & Chatham Ry. Co.'s Managing Committee* (119), the goods were

---

(113) [1936] 2 All E.R. at p. 607.   (114) [1936] 2 All E.R. at p. 601.
(115) [1921] All E.R. Rep. 35 at p. 39; [1921] 2 K.B. 426 at p. 435.
(116) (1881), 7 Q.B.D. 510.   (117) [1922] All E.R. Rep. 395; [1922] 2 A.C. 263.
(118) [1899] 1 Q.B. 309.   (119) [1915] 2 K.B. 370.

by mistake transferred from a passenger train by which means the consignor had A
contracted to send them on to a goods train, and it was held that the consignor
could not rely on a clause of exception against liability for loss. Just as in the
case of deviation in sea voyages, it is a fundamental term of the relevant contract
that ships shall proceed by the ordinary and customary route and that any
deviation changes the adventure and is at once a fundamental breach, regardless
of the consequences, so in the other cases to which SCRUTTON, L.J., referred in B
Gibaud's case (120) the true ratio decidendi, in my view, is that the law treats
the stipulation that the goods shall be housed in a particular place or that they
shall be consigned by a particular route or on a particular type of train as a
fundamental term, breach of which at once entitles the other side to accept, if
he so desires, as a fundamental breach. In forming this view, I am fortified by
the observations of LORD DUNEDIN in *London & North Western Ry. Co.* v. *Neilson* C
(121) where he treats these observations of SCRUTTON, L.J., as being illustrative
of, or comparable to, a deviation in a shipping contract. I can see no justification
for applying some special rule to those classes of case any more than in the
deviation cases. Both are governed by and *only* by the general law relating to
contracts.

If I am right in drawing this conclusion, then the necessary result, in my D
opinion, is that the principle on which one party to a contract cannot rely on the
clauses of exception or limitation of liability inserted for his sole protection is not
because they are regarded as subject to any special rule of law applicable to such
clauses as being in general opposed to the policy of the law or for some other
reason but, just as in the deviation cases, it is the consequence of the application
of the ordinary rules applicable to all contracts that, if there is a fundamental E
breach accepted by the innocent party, the contract is at an end; the guilty
party cannot rely on any special terms in the contract. If not so accepted, the
clauses of exception or limitation remain in force like all the other clauses of the
contract. Thus, for my part, if in *Karsales (Harrow), Ltd.* v. *Wallis* (122) DENNING,
L.J., or PARKER, L.J., in passages which have already been quoted in the speech
of LORD REID and which, therefore, I shall not repeat, were intending to lay F
down some special rule of law applicable to exclusion or limitation clauses, I find
myself unable to agree. I prefer the view of PEARSON, L.J., in *U.G.S. Finance,
Ltd.* v. *National Mortgage Bank of Greece and National Bank of Greece, S.A.* (123)
that the matter is one of the true construction of the contract. But before considering this question of construction one matter remains to be stated. In very
many of the cases which were cited to your lordships there was no question of G
any election by the innocent party either to affirm or disaffirm the contract when
the other party had committed a fundamental breach. This is because in so many
cases, as LORD DENNING, M.R., pointed out in the *U.G.S. Finance, Ltd.* case (124),
the voyage or journey or warehousing contract has been completed before the
innocent party gets to know of any breaches of it, and the only course open to
him is to sue for breach, and he does so on the footing that he is entitled to treat H
the whole contract as at an end, for the law is clear that, where there has been
a fundamental breach, he can only be taken to affirm the contract if he knows
his full rights. Thus, in the *Bunge y Born* case (125), the whole argument in your
lordships' House turned on the question whether there had been a deviation or
not, and it was assumed that, if deviation was proved, the charterer could
thereupon at the conclusion of the voyage sue as for a fundamental breach. I
Therefore, my lords, as in my opinion the appellants have expressly affirmed the
contract they cannot escape from the consequences of the demurrage clause,
unless, as a matter of construction of that clause, they can show that it has no
application to the events of this case; this they cannot do for the reasons that I

---

(120) [1921] All E.R. Rep. 35; [1921] 2 K.B. 426.
(121) [1922] All E.R. Rep. at p. 400; [1922] 2 A.C. at p. 272.
(122) [1956] 2 All E.R. at pp. 868, 871.   (123) [1964] 1 Lloyd's Rep. 446.
(124) [1964] 1 Lloyd's Rep. at p. 450.   (125) [1925] All E.R. Rep. 173.

A   have already given. Accordingly, on the footing that the demurrage clause is a clause of exclusion or limitation, this does not avail the appellants in this case.

But, my lords, again having regard to the arguments addressed to your lordships, I think that I ought to make one or two observations on the question of construction of exclusion or limitation clauses. It cannot be doubted that, even while the contract continues in force (that is when there has been no fundamental

B   breach but only some lesser breach), exclusion clauses are strictly construed. Why this should be so is largely a matter of history and, I think, probably stems from the facts that in so many cases exceptions clauses are to be found in rather small print sometimes on the back of the main terms of the contract and that the doctrine of " contra proferentes " has been applied. But whatever the reason, that they are strictly construed against the contracting party seeking protection

C   even during the currency of the contract cannot be doubted. I refer only to two examples: the first is to be found in the judgment of LORD STERNDALE, M.R., in *The Cap Palos* (126), where he expressly put his decision on a strict construction of the exclusion clause relied on, and treated the contract as continuing. With all respect to the judgment of ATKIN, L.J., in that case, I think that the reasoning of LORD STERNDALE is to be preferred. A second example is to be found in the

D   observations of LORD SUMNER in *London & North Western Ry. Co.* v. *Neilson* (127), where he (in contrast to the other lords) expressly put his decision on the footing that the contract remained on foot, but he gave a very strict construction to the words " in transit ", and held that it did not apply to goods not actually in transit which had wrongly been delivered to a railway cloakroom.

But where there is a breach of a fundamental term, the law has taken an even

E   firmer line, for there is a strong, though rebuttable, presumption that, in inserting a clause of exclusion or limitation in their contract, the parties are not contemplating breaches of fundamental terms and such clauses do not apply to relieve a party from the consequences of such a breach even where the contract continues in force. This result has been achieved by a robust use of a well-known canon of construction, that wide words which taken in isolation would bear one

F   meaning must be so construed as to give business efficacy to the contract and the presumed intention of the parties, on the footing that both parties are intending to carry out the contract fundamentally. Thus, in *Leduc & Co.* v. *Ward* (128), where the charterparty was for a voyage from Fiume to Dunkirk " with liberty to call at any ports in any order ", it was construed by LORD ESHER, M.R., to mean any ports which would be substantially ports which in the course of the voyage

G   would be passed on the named voyage, so that a call at Glasgow was held to be a deviation and, therefore, a breach of the fundamental term, notwithstanding the wide words of the exception. Again, in your lordships' House, in *Glynn* v. *Margetson* (129), under a bill of lading the ship was to carry oranges from Malaga to Liverpool, but the words of exclusion permitted the ship to visit almost any ports in Europe or Africa. The voyage from Malaga to Liverpool was treated by

H   LORD HERSCHELL, L.C. (130), as the main object and intent of the contract (that is, parenthetically, a fundamental term), and the wide words permitting calls at almost any port must be cut down so as not to defeat that object and intent. LORD HALSBURY said (131):

I   " Looking at the whole of the instrument, and seeing what one must regard, for a reason which I will give in a moment, as its main purpose, one must reject words, indeed whole provisions, if they are inconsistent with what one assumes to be the main purpose of the contract."

---

(126) [1921] All E.R. Rep. at p. 252; [1921] P. at p. 465.
(127) [1922] All E.R. Rep. at p. 403; [1922] 2 A.C. at p. 278.
(128) [1886-90] All E.R. Rep. 266; (1888), 20 Q.B.D. 475.
(129) [1891-94] All E.R. Rep. 693; [1893] A.C. 351.
(130) [1891-94] All E.R. Rep. at p. 695; [1893] A.C. at p. 355.
(131) [1891-94] All E.R. Rep. at p. 696; [1893] A.C. at p. 357.

Cunard S.S. Co., Ltd. v. *Buerger* (132) and the *Neilson* case (133) support the A
same view. In the former case, LORD PARMOOR said (134) of an exception clause:

" [Stipulations limiting liability] do not apply when such loss or damage
has occurred outside the route or voyage contemplated by the parties . . .
unless the intention that such limitations should apply is expressed in clear
and unambiguous language."

In the latter case, LORD DUNEDIN said (135):   B

". . . it is a broad principle of great importance in all contracts of carriage
that when a carrier protects himself by exceptions, *unless they are very clearly
worded* they only apply to his carrying out of the contract, and do not apply
if he is doing something which he has not contracted to do . . ." [The italics
are mine.]   C

Both noble lords were dealing with what we now call fundamental terms and
illustrate both the presumption and its rebuttable character. The appellants
relied strongly on *Charterhouse Credit Co., Ltd.* v. *Tolly* (136). That case affords
no help to them, for it was dealing with breach of a fundamental term and there
is no suggestion of such a breach in this case. That case is open to review by your
lordships and, having had the advantage of much fuller argument than was   D
afforded to us in the Court of Appeal in that case, it is possible that the true
justification of that decision lies in the application of the presumption which
I have mentioned to the relevant clause of exclusion in that case.

My lords, in view of the introduction in the questions posed by the arbitrator of
the impact of an assumed wilful default, for my part, I think that it is only
necessary to say that it seems to me as a matter of general principle that wilful E
default in connexion with the matters we are now considering is relevant, and
relevant only, to one matter, that is to say, whether in fact the appellants can
establish a fundamental breach. In cases such as this, where there has been no
breach of any fundamental term, the question whether there has been a fundamental breach must be a question of fact and degree in all the circumstances of
the case, but one of the elements in reaching a conclusion on that matter is   F
necessarily the question whether there has been a wilful breach, for, as a practical
matter, it cannot be doubted that it is easier to find as a fact, for such it primarily
is, that the respondents are evincing an intention no longer to be bound by the
terms of the contract and are, therefore, guilty of repudiatory conduct if it can be
established that the breaches have been wilful and not innocent. I say no more
on that.   G

My lords, I would dismiss this appeal.

LORD WILBERFORCE: My Lords, I agree that the present appeal, in
so far as it is based on the reasons advanced in the original Case lodged by the
appellants, must fail and I do not find it necessary to add to the reasons for so
finding given by MOCATTA, J., and the Court of Appeal. It is only on the sub- H
missions contained in the appellants' Supplementary Case that I desire to add
some observations, since these involve some issues of general importance in the
law of contract.

The nature of the appellants' contentions can most conveniently be seen
from the answer which they suggest should be given to the questions stated in
the Consultative Case. To the first question (which is whether the appellants can I
recover damages suffered by reason of the respondents having failed to load and
discharge the vessels within the lay days whereby the charterparty was rendered
less profitable to the appellants by consequent loss of voyages or voyage time)

---

(132) [1926] All E.R. Rep. 103; [1927] A.C. 1.
(133) [1922] All E.R. Rep. 395; [1922] 2 A.C. 263.
(134) [1926] All E.R. Rep. at p. 108; [1927] A.C. at p. 13.
(135) [1922] All E.R. Rep. at p. 400; [1922] 2 A.C. at p. 272.
(136) [1963] 2 All E.R. 432; [1963] 2 Q.B. 683.

A the appellants suggest the qualified answer " Yes, if the detention of the vessel was a deviation from or repudiation or fundamental breach of, the charterparty. Otherwise, no ". And they suggest that the same answer should be given to the second question which is based on the assumption that such loss of profitability resulted from the respondents' having deliberately (i.e., with the wilful intention of limiting the number of contractual voyages) failed to load and or discharge the

B vessel within the lay days. In amplification of this, the appellants submit that the qualification appearing in the suggested answer would apply first, if the detention of the vessel caused by the respondents' breaches of contract was in the aggregate so long as to frustrate the commercial purpose of the charterparty, or, secondly, if that detention was deliberate, in the special sense used in the Consultative Case. Whether either of these situations existed would be for the arbitrators to find. I

C am prepared to deal with the submissions of law so made on the assumption that it is open to the arbitrators so to find that they might do so.

The appellants' main argument in law is formulated as follows: First, they say that a breach of contract which goes to the root of the contract or which conflicts with its main purpose is a deviation from, or a repudiation or funda- mental breach of, such contract. Secondly, they contend that exceptions clauses

D do not apply to breaches which are deviations from, or repudiations or funda- mental breaches of, the contract. These propositions contain in themselves implicitly or explicitly several distinct lines of argument. It is necessary to separate the strands before attempting to examine them. It is convenient first to segregate the reference to what is sometimes (and conveniently) described as the main purpose rule. This is a rule of construction, a classic statement of which

E is found in LORD HALSBURY'S speech in *Glynn* v. *Margetson* (137): it can be summed up in his words:

" Looking at the whole of the instrument, and seeing what one must regard . . . as its main purpose, one must reject words, indeed whole provisions, if they are inconsistent with what one assumes to be the main purpose of the contract."

F The decision in that case was that printed words in a document intended to be used in a variety of contracts of affreightment between a variety of ports ought to be restricted so as to be consistent with the purpose of the particular charter- party which was for a voyage from Malaga to Liverpool. There is no difficulty as to this, and I shall consider in due course whether it has any application to the relevant clause (i.e., the demurrage clause) in the contract.

G Next for consideration is the argument based on " fundamental breach " or, which is presumably the same thing, a breach going " to the root of the con- tract ". These expressions are used in the cases to denote two quite different things, namely, (i) a performance totally different from that which the contract contemplates, (ii) a breach of contract more serious than one which would entitle the other party merely to damages and which (at least) would entitle him to

H refuse performance or further performance under the contract. Both of these situations have long been familiar in the English law of contract; and it will have to be considered whether the conception of " fundamental breach " extends beyond them. What is certain is that to use the expression without distinguishing to which of these, or to what other, situations it refers is to invite confusion. The importance of the difference between these meanings lies in this, that they

I relate to two separate questions which may arise in relation to any contract. These are (as to (i)) whether an " exceptions " clause contained in the contract applies as regards a particular breach and (as to (ii)) whether one party is entitled to elect to refuse further performance.

The appellants, in their submission that exceptions clauses do not apply to " fundamental breaches " or " repudiations ", confuse these two questions. There is in fact no necessary coincidence between the two kinds of (so-called

(137) [1891-94] All E.R. Rep. at p. 696; [1893] A.C. 351 at p. 357.

fundamental) breach. For, though it may be true generally, if the contract **A**
contains a wide exceptions clause, that a breach sufficiently serious to take
the case outside that clause will also give the other party the right to refuse
further performance, it is not the case, necessarily, that a breach of the latter
character has the former consequence. An act which, apart from the exceptions
clause, might be a breach sufficiently serious to justify refusal of further performance, may be reduced in effect, or made not a breach at all, by the terms of **B**
the clause. The present case is concerned with the application of what may be
said (with what justice will be later considered) to be an exceptions clause to a
possible type of " fundamental breach ". I treat the words " exceptions clause "
as covering broadly such clauses in a contract as profess to exclude or limit, either
quantitatively or as to the time within which action must be taken, the right of
the injured party to bring an action for damages. Such a clause must, ex hypothesi, **C**
reflect the contemplation of the parties that a breach of contract, or what apart
from the clause would be a breach of contract, may be committed, otherwise the
clause would not be there; but the question remains open in any case whether
there is a limit to the type of breach which they have in mind. One may safely
say that the parties cannot, in a contract, have contemplated that the clause
should have so wide an ambit as in effect to deprive one party's stipulations of all **D**
contractual force; to do so would be to reduce the contract to a mere declaration
of intent. To this extent it may be correct to say that there is a rule of law
against the application of an exceptions clause to a particular type of breach.
But short of this it must be a question of contractual intention whether a particular
breach is covered or not, and the courts are entitled to insist, as they do, that the
more radical the breach the clearer must the language be if it is to be covered. **E**
As LORD PARMOOR said in *Cunard S.S. Co., Ltd.* v. *Buerger* (138) in relation to
exception clauses:

> " [they] do not apply when such loss or damage has occurred outside the
> route or voyage contemplated by the parties . . . unless the intention that
> such limitations should apply is expressed in clear and unambiguous
> language."   **F**

And in *The Cap Palos* (139) ATKIN, L.J., similarly said:

> " I am far from saying that a contractor may not make a valid contract
> that he is not to be liable for any failure to perform his contract, including
> even wilful default; but he must use very clear words to express that
> purpose . . ."   **G**

In application to more radical breaches of contract, the courts have sometimes
stated the principle as being that a " total breach of the contract " disentitles
a party to rely on exceptions clauses. This formulation has its use so long as one
understands it to mean that the clause cannot be taken to refer to such a breach,
but it is not a universal solvent; for it leaves to be decided what is meant by a **H**
" total " breach for this purpose—a departure from the contract? but how great a
departure? a delivery of something or a performance different from that promised?
but how different? No formula will solve this type of question, and one must
look individually at the nature of the contract, the character of the breach and
its effect on future performance and expectation and make a judicial estimation
of the final result.   **I**
A few illustrations from three groups of decided cases may explain how the
courts have dealt with this problem:
(i) *Supply of a different article.* As long ago as 1838, where the contract provided
for the supply of peas, but beans were delivered, LORD ABINGER, C.B., explained
the difference between this case and a breach of " condition ": " the contract

---

(138) [1926] All E.R. Rep. at p. 108; [1927] A.C. at p. 13.
(139) [1921] All E.R. Rep. at p. 254; [1921] P. at pp. 471, 472.

A is to sell peas, and if he sends him anything else in their stead, it is a non-performance of it " *Chanter* v. *Hopkins* (140). This was followed (after the Sale of Goods Act, 1893) in *Pinnock Bros.* v. *Lewis & Peat, Ltd.* (141) (copra cake), and PEARSON, L.J., accepted the principle, while modernising the illustration (chalk for cheese) in *U.G.S. Finance, Ltd.* v. *National Mortgage Bank of Greece and National Bank of Greece, S.A.* (142). Since the contracting parties could
B hardly have been supposed to contemplate such a mis-performance, or to have provided against it without destroying the whole contractual substratum, there is no difficulty here in holding exception clauses to be inapplicable.

(ii) *Hire-purchase cases.* In several recent decisions, the courts have been able to hold wide exception clauses inapplicable by finding that what was delivered was totally different from that promised. Such are *Karsales (Harrow), Ltd.* v.
C *Wallis* (143) and *Charterhouse Credit Co., Ltd.* v. *Tolly* (144). These cases, and others, follow the judgment of DEVLIN, J., in *Smeaton Hanscomb & Co., Ltd.* v. *Sassoon I. Setty, Son & Co. (No. 1)* (145), where he expressed the test as being whether there was a performance totally different from that contemplated by the contract. In some of these cases difficult questions of fact have arisen in deciding whether there is the total difference, or merely a serious breach of
D contract, as can be seen by comparing the *Karsales* case (143) with *Astley Industrial Trust, Ltd.* v. *Grimley* (146), and some doubt may be felt whether the right result on the facts was reached in *Charterhouse Credit Co., Ltd.* v. *Tolly* (144); but the principle is well in line with that of the cases mentioned under (i).

(iii) *Marine cases relating to deviation.* There is a long line of authority, the commencement of which is usually taken from the judgment of TINDAL, C.J.,
E in *Davies* v. *Garrett* (147), which shows that a shipowner, who deviates from an agreed voyage, steps out of the contract, so that clauses in the contract (such as exceptions or limitation clauses) which are designed to apply to the contracted voyage are held to have no application to the deviating voyage. The basis for the rule was explained in *Stag Line, Ltd.* v. *Foscolo Mango & Co., Ltd.* (148) by LORD RUSSELL OF KILLOWEN in these terms:

F " It was well settled before the Act [of 1924] that an unjustifiable deviation deprived a ship of the protection of exceptions. They only applied to the contract voyage."

In *The Cap Palos* (149) ATKIN, L.J., had applied this principle to contracts generally, adopting for this purpose the formulation of SCRUTTON, L.J., in
G *Gibaud* v. *Great Eastern Ry. Co.* (150):

  " It is a fairly well-known principle—and *Lilley* v. *Doubleday* (151) is perhaps the best illustration of it—that if you undertake to do a thing in a certain way, or to keep a thing in a certain place with certain conditions protecting it, and you have broken the contract by not doing the thing contracted for in the way contracted for or not keeping the article in the
H place in which you have contracted to keep it, you cannot rely on the conditions which were only intended to protect you if you carried out the contract in the way in which you had contracted to do it."

The words " intended to protect you " show quite clearly that the rule is based on contractual intention.
I The conception, therefore, of " fundamental breach " as one which, through

---

(140) (1838), 4 M. & W. 339 at p. 404.　　　　(141) [1923] 1 K.B. 690.
(142) [1964] 1 Lloyd's Rep. 446.　　　　　　　(143) [1956] 2 All E.R. 866.
(144) [1963] 2 All E.R. 432; [1963] 2 Q.B. 683.　(145) [1953] 2 All E.R. 1471.
(146) [1963] 2 All E.R. 33.　　　　　　　　　(147) (1830), 6 Bing. 716.
(148) [1931] All E.R. Rep. 666 at p. 675; [1932] A.C. 328 at p. 347.
(149) [1921] All E.R. Rep. at p. 254; [1921] P. at p. 471.
(150) [1921] All E.R. Rep. at p. 39; [1921] 2 K.B. at p. 435.
(151) (1881), 7 Q.B.D. 510.

ascertainment of the parties' contractual intention, falls outside an exceptions   A
clause is well recognised and comprehensible. Is there any need, or authority,
in relation to exceptions clauses, for extension of it beyond this? In my opinion,
there is not. The principle that the contractual intention is to be ascertained—
not just grammatically from words used, but by consideration of those words in
relation to commercial purpose (or other purpose according to the type of contract)—is surely flexible enough, and, though it may be the case that adhesion   B
contracts give rise to particular difficulties in ascertaining or attributing a
contractual intent, which may require a special solution, those difficulties need
not be imported into the general law of contract nor be permitted to deform it.

The only new category of " fundamental breach " which in this context I
understand to have been suggested is one of " deliberate " breaches. This
most clearly appears in the Privy Council case of *Sze Hai Tong Bank, Ltd.* v.   C
Rambler Cycle Co., Ltd. (152). The decision itself presents no difficulty and seems
to have been based on construction; it was that an exceptions clause referring to
" discharge " of the goods did not apply to a discharge wholly outside the contract, a case I would have thought well within the principle of the " deviation "
cases. But the appellants rely on one passage in the judgment of the Board which
seems to suggest that " deliberate " breaches may, of themselves, form a separate   D
category, citing three previous English decisions. Two of them—*Alexander* v.
Railway Executive (153) and *Karsales (Harrow), Ltd.* v. *Wallis* (154) (on which I
have already commented)—are straightforward cases of " total departure "
from what is contractually contemplated and present no difficulty. The third,
Bontex Knitting Works, Ltd. v. *St. John's Garage* (155) does not appear to be based
on the deliberate character of the breach. The decision may be justified on the   E
basis that there was a breach of contract equivalent to a deviation, but if it goes
beyond this I would regard it as of doubtful validity. The " deliberate " character
of a breach cannot, in my opinion, of itself give to a breach of contract a " fundamental " character, in either sense of that word. Some deliberate breaches there
may be of a minor character which can appropriately be sanctioned by damages;
some may be, on construction, within an exceptions clause (for example, a deliber-   F
ate delay for one day in loading). This is not to say that " deliberation " may not
be a relevant factor; depending on what the party in breach " deliberately "
intended to do, it may be possible to say that the parties never contemplated
that such a breach would be excused or limited; and a deliberate breach may
give rise to a right for the innocent party to refuse further performance because
it indicates the other party's attitude towards future performance. All these   G
arguments fit without difficulty into the general principle; to create a special
rule for deliberate acts is unnecessary and may lead astray.

I now come to the facts of the present case. First, it is necessary to decide
what is the legal nature of the demurrage clause; is it a clause by which damages
for breach of the contract are agreed in advance, a liquidated damages clause as
such provisions are commonly called, or is it, as the appellants submit, a clause   H
limiting damages? If it is the latter, the appellants are evidently a step nearer
the point when they can invoke cases in which clauses of exception, or exemption,
do not apply to particular breaches of contract. The appellants' strongest argument here rests on the discrepancy which they assert to exist between the demurrage rate of $1,000 per diem and the freight rate for which the charterparty
provides. The extent of the discrepancy is said to be shown by the difference   I
between the appellants' claim for lost freight (which is of the order of $900,000
on one calculation and $600,000 on another) and the amount which they would
receive under the demurrage provision, which is approximately $150,000. So,

---

(152) [1959] 3 All E.R. 182; [1959] A.C. 576.
(153) [1951] 2 All E.R. 442; [1951] 2 K.B. 882.   (154) [1956] 2 All E.R. 866.
    (155) [1943] 2 All E.R. 690; C.A. [1944] 1 All E.R. 381, n.

A the argument runs, the $1,000 per diem cannot be a pre-estimate of damage; it must be a limit in the respondents' favour. I am unable to accept this. Leaving aside that the figures quoted for lost freight represent merely the appellants' claim, it must be borne in mind that the $1,000 a day figure has to cover a number of possible events. There might have been delay for one day or a few days beyond the laytime, in which case the appellants might, and probably would, lose nothing in the way of freight and only suffer through increased overheads in port. Even

B if a case were to arise where freight was lost, over a period of two years circumstances might well change which would affect adversely the appellants' anticipated rate of profit. So I am far from satisfied that any such discrepancy has been shown between the agreed figure and reality as requires the conclusion that the clause is not what on its face it purports to be—particularly when one bears in mind

C that each side derives an advantage from having the figure fixed and so being assured of payment without the expense and difficulty of proof.

The form of the clause is, of course, not decisive, nor is there any rule of law which requires that demurrage clauses should be construed as clauses of liquidated damages; but it is the fact that the clause is expressed as one agreeing a figure, and not as imposing a limit; and, as a matter of commercial opinion and practice,

D demurrage clauses are normally regarded as liquidated damage clauses. (This has the authority of Scrutton on Charterparties, 10th and following editions and see *Chandris* v. *Isbrandtsen Moller Co., Inc.* (156), per Devlin, J.)

The clause being, then, one which fixes, by mutual agreement, the amount of damages to be paid to the owners of the vessel if " longer detained " than is permitted by the contract, is there any reason why it should not apply in the

E present case in either of the assumed alternatives, i.e., either that the aggregated delays add up to a " frustrating " breach of contract, or that the delays were " deliberate " in the special sense? In answering these questions, it is necessary to have in mind what happened. It appears that there was an initial dispute between the appellants and the respondents in which the appellants claimed that they were entitled to treat the respondents as having repudiated the charterparty.

F This dispute was resolved by an agreement on Oct. 8, 1957, under which the respondents agreed to pay an agreed sum as demurrage, leaving it to arbitration to decide whether the appellants' claim was correct and, if so, what damages they should recover. It was further agreed that the charterparty should be performed for the remainder of the agreed two-year period. The manner in which it was performed is set out in a schedule to the Consultative Case. There were eight

G voyages in all, the last terminating on Mar. 7, 1959, three days before the termination date. It is as regards these eight voyages that it is claimed that the delays in question occurred. During the whole of the period, although the periods spent in port on either side of the Atlantic (in fact at Rotterdam and, in every case but the first, Newport) must have been known to the appellants, who must also have been in a position to ascertain the availability

H of cargo and of loading and discharging facilities, the appellants took no steps which would indicate that they regarded the charterparty as repudiated; they did not sail their vessel away but allowed it to continue with further voyages and took demurrage at the agreed rate for the delays. So there is no question here of any termination of the contract having taken place. Is there, then, any basis on which the appellants can escape from their bargain as regards detention

I of the vessel? In my opinion there is not. The arbitrators can (on the assumptions required) only find that the breach of contract falls within one, or other, or both of the two stated categories, namely, that they " frustrate the commercial purpose of the charterparty ", or that the delays were " deliberate " (in the special sense). In either case, why should not the agreed clause operate? Or what reason is there for limiting its application to such delays as fall short of such as " frustrate

---

(156) [1950] 1 All E.R. at p. 775; [1951] 1 K.B. at p. 249.

the commercial purpose " or such as are not " deliberate "?   I can see no such   A
reason for limiting a plain contractual provision, nor is there here any such
conflict between the demurrage clause and the main purpose of the contract
as to bring into play the doctrine of *Glynn* v. *Margetson* (157).   On a consideration of the nature of this clause, together with the events which took
place, and in particular the fact that the appellants did not during its currency
put an end to the contract, I reach the conclusion that the appellants are clearly   B
bound by it and can recover no more than the appropriate amount of demurrage.

I find support for this conclusion in two decisions of the Court of Appeal.
In *Inverkip S.S. Co., Ltd.* v. *Bunge & Co.* (158), there was a detention of
the ship beyond (as was held) a reasonable time for keeping it on demurrage.
The demurrage clause was in a similar form to that in the present case: "If
detained longer than five days ", and was held to be applicable to the whole   C
period of delay. The Court of Appeal did not decide the question whether the delay
was such as to amount to a " repudiatory breach ", so that the master could
have sailed away, but the implication at least of the judgment of WARRINGTON,
L.J., is that the same result would have followed if this had been so.   Then in
Ethel Radcliffe S.S. Co. v. *Barnett* (159), there was a deliberate detention.   The
arbitrators' actual finding (which it is relevant to compare with the possible   D
finding here) was that " the respondents neglected and refused to give such orders
until Aug. 29, 1924, and did so deliberately as it suited their business arrangements to keep the steamer at St. Vincent ".   It was argued that the charterer
had repudiated the contract and that the demurrage clause did not cover wilful
detention, but the Court of Appeal held to the contrary. Counsel for the appellants
submitted that these cases were wrongly decided, but they seem to me to be   E
entirely in accordance with principle, and I respectfully agree with them.

On the whole case, I would dismiss the appeal.

Appeal dismissed.

Solicitors: *Richards, Butler & Co.* (for the appellants); *William A. Crump
& Son* (for the respondents).   F

[*Reported by* KATHLEEN J. H. O'BRIEN, *Barrister-at-Law.*]

G

H

I

(157) [1891-94] All E.R. Rep. 693; [1893] A.C. 351.   (158) [1917] 2 K.B. 193.
(159) (1926), 24 Lloyd L.R. 277.

A

R. *v.* POLLOCK AND DIVERS.

[COURT OF CRIMINAL APPEAL (Havers, Veale and MacKenna, JJ.), February 22, 24, March 4, 1966.]

Criminal Law—Robbery—Common law robbery—Common law offence still in

B   *existence—Robbery by threat of accusation of sodomitical practices—Necessity of proof of animus furandi at time of threat or accusation.*

Criminal Law—Indictment—Common law offence covered by words of modern statute—Indictment should be framed contra formam statuti.

The offence of robbery by means of threats to accuse of sodomy has existed and exists at common law, the nature of the accusation being limited

C   to buggery, attempted buggery, assault with intent to commit buggery and solicitation or persuasion to commit buggery (see p. 105, letter F, post).

R. v. Egerton ((1819), Russ. & Ry. 375) (approving *R. v. Hickman* ((1784), 1 Leach, 278)) and *R. v. Knewland and Wood* ((1796), 2 Leach, 721) applied.

Dictum of LORD MORRIS OF BORTH-Y-GEST in *Smith v. Desmond* ([1965] 1 All E.R. at p. 979) followed.

D   The common law offence of robbery, in all its forms, involves proof by the prosecution of an animus furandi, and, in cases of robbery by accusation of sodomitical practices, it involves proof of an animus furandi at the time of the threat or accusation (see p. 106, letter E, post).

Dicta of WILLES, J., in *R. v. Donnally* ((1779), 1 Leach at pp. 195, 196) and of BLACKBURN, J., in *R. v. Richards* ((1868), 11 Cox, C.C. 43) applied.

E   Robbery by threat of accusation of sodomitical practices exists at common law alongside the statutory offence of demanding money by menaces in the Larceny Act, 1916, s. 29; but when the elements of an old common law offence are plainly covered by the words of a modern statute, it is preferable that the indictment should be framed contra formam statuti (see p. 105, letters G and H, post).

F   [As to what constitutes robbery, see 10 HALSBURY'S LAWS (3rd Edn.) 794-796, para. 1537; and for cases on the subject, see 15 DIGEST (Repl.) 1117-1120. *11,089-11,163.*

As to setting out particulars of the offence in an indictment, see 10 HALSBURY'S LAWS (3rd Edn.) 386, para. 699.

For the Interpretation Act, 1889, s. 33, see 24 HALSBURY'S STATUTES (2nd Edn.)

G   226.]

Cases referred to:

R. v. Cannon, (1809), Russ. & Ry. 146; 168 E.R. 730; 15 Digest (Repl.) 1120, *11,157.*

R. v. Carlile, (1819), 3 B. & Ald. 161; 106 E.R. 621; 14 Digest (Repl.) 231,

H   *1943.*

R. v. Donnally, (1779), 1 Leach, 193; 2 East, P.C. 713, 715; 168 E.R. 199; 15 Digest (Repl.) 1118, *11,113.*

R. v. Egerton, (1819), Russ. & Ry. 375; 168 E.R. 852; 15 Digest (Repl.) 1120, *11,154.*

R. v. Elmstead, (1802), 2 Russell on Crime (10th Edn.), 1018; 15 Digest (Repl.)

I   1120, *11,153.*

R. v. Gardner, (1824), 1 C. & P. 479; 171 E.R. 1282; 15 Digest (Repl.) 1120, *11,159.*

R. v. Gascoigne, (1783), 1 Leach, 280; 2 East, P.C. 709; 168 E.R. 243; 15 Digest (Repl.) 1119, *11,126.*

R. v. Henry and Taunton, (1840), 2 Mood. C.C. 118; 9 C. & P. 309; 169 E.R. 47; 15 Digest (Repl.) 1120, *11,161.*

R. v. Hickman, (1784), 2 East, P.C. 728; 1 Leach, 278; 168 E.R. 241; 15 Digest (Repl.) 1119, *11,152.*

R. v. *Jones (alias Evans)*, (1776), 2 East, P.C. 714; 1 Leach, 139; 168 E.R.   **A**
171; 15 Digest (Repl.) 1119, *11,150.*

R. v. *Morris*, [1861-73] All E.R. Rep. 484; (1867), L.R. 1 C.C.R. 90; 36
L.J.M.C. 84; 16 L.T. 636; 31 J.P. 516; 14 Digest (Repl.) 383, *3736.*

R. v. *Norton*, (1838), 8 C. & P. 671; 173 E.R. 667; 15 Digest (Repl.) 1120,
11,160.

R. v. *Richards*, (1868), 11 Cox, C.C. 43; 15 Digest (Repl.) 1126, *11,231.*   **B**

R. v. *Stringer and Newstead*, (1842), 1 Car. & Kir. 188; 2 Mood. C.C. 261;
169 E.R. 104; 15 Digest (Repl.) 1120, *11,162.*

R. v. *Wood and Knewland*, (1796), 2 East, P.C. 732; sub nom. *R.* v. *Knewland
and Wood*, 2 Leach, 721; 168 E.R. 461; 15 Digest (Repl.) 1119, *11,149.*

Smith v. *Desmond*, [1965] 1 All E.R. 976; [1965] A.C. 960; [1965] 2 W.L.R.
894; 129 J.P. 331; 49 Cr. App. Rep. 246.   **C**

Appeals.

These were appeals by Thomas Pollock and Gilbert McConnell Divers against
their convictions at the Central Criminal Court on Sept. 30, 1965, before His
Honour JUDGE EDWARD CLARKE, Q.C., and a jury of aggravated robbery, for
which offence they were each sentenced to fifteen months' imprisonment. On
Feb. 11, 1966, the appellants were given leave to appeal against their conviction   **D**
by the Court of Criminal Appeal (HINCHCLIFFE, NIELD and MEGAW, JJ.), the
following questions arising for consideration: (i) Was there ever a form of
robbery at common law that involved no violence or threat of violence, but
only involved a putting in fear by an accusation or threat of accusation of an
unnatural crime? If yes, what sort of unnatural crime was contemplated?
(ii) If there was such an offence at common law, was it affected by any of the   **E**
Acts of Parliament dealing with this matter, and, if so, in what way? (iii) On
the assumption that such an offence remained in existence at common law,
unaffected by statute, at what stage in the offence must the prosecution show
an animus furandi? The facts are set out in the judgment of the court.

The authorities and cases noted below* were cited during the argument in
addition to those referred to in the judgment.   **F**

R. E. Auld for the appellants.

H. J. Leonard for the Crown.

Cur. adv. vult.

Mar. 4.   **VEALE, J.**, read the following judgment of the court at the
invitation of HAVERS, J.: The two appellants, Thomas Pollock and Gilbert   **G**
McConnell Divers, were convicted at the Central Criminal Court on Sept. 30,
1965, of aggravated robbery and were each sentenced to imprisonment for fifteen
months. The indictment against them and a younger man of seventeen called
McDade contained four counts, the first of which alleged robbery with violence,
on which all three were acquitted by the jury. The second count, which was
alternative to the first, and on which the two appellants, but not McDade, were   **H**
convicted, alleged robbery being together. The third count alleged assault,
and to this the appellant Divers pleaded guilty. The fourth count alleged receiving
against McDade alone, and on this he was convicted.

The case against the appellants can be shortly summarised. In June, 1965,
they, together with the youth McDade, came from Scotland to seek work and all
three shared a room in London. On July 8, 1965, one McCann met McDade and   **I**
the appellants in a public house in Acton. McCann, an older man, and McDade
visited another public house together, and McCann offered McDade £2 because

---

* 1 HALE'S PLEAS OF THE CROWN (1736 Edn.), p. 532, " Robbery "; ARCHBOLD'S
CRIMINAL PLEADING, EVIDENCE AND PRACTICE (35th Edn.) paras. 1451, 1452, 1637;
R. v. *Blackburn*, (1787), 2 East, P.C. 711; *R.* v. *McGrath*, (1869), 1 C.C.R. 205;
R. v. *Lovell*, (1881), 8 Q.B.D. 185; *R.* v. *Bryant*, [1955] 2 All E.R. 406; [1956] 1 All E.R.
340 n.; *R.* v. *Caslin*, [1961] 1 All E.R. 246; *R.* v. *Flynn*, [1961] 3 All E.R. 58; [1963]
1 Q.B. 729; *R.* v. *Quinn*, *R.* v. *Bloom*, [1961] 3 All E.R. 88; [1962] 2 Q.B. 245.

A he was hard up. They then met, apparently by chance, the two appellants at a coffee bar, after which McCann and McDade went to the room shared by McDade and the appellants. There McDade took off some clothes and lay on the bed, but nothing indecent occurred. The two appellants then came into the room, shouted " What's this? " or " What's the score? ", attacked McCann, and took his watch and wallet in circumstances which, if true, certainly involved violence

B to the person of McCann. They then took the wallet and watch to a lavatory. The jury, however, acquitted them of robbery with violence. The evidence of the two appellants did not dispute the earlier events of that evening. They agreed that they came into the room, but they said that they found McCann undressed, and they agreed that they did say " What's this? " or " What's the score? " McDade said " He persists in trying to go to bed with me ", and the appellant

C Divers then assaulted McCann but the appellant Pollock restrained him. McCann said, " I know I'm a queer but I can't help it ". Both appellants said that they intended to report McCann to the police. While McCann was dressing, this threat was repeated and McCann said, " Take anything you like but do not report it ". He thrust his wallet into their hands, and three times offered his watch, which eventually the appellant Pollock reluctantly took. Both the appellants then

D went to the lavatory where the watch was hidden in order to teach McCann a lesson. The appellant Divers was minded to keep the £15 which was in the wallet as hush money, but the appellant Pollock said he intended that McCann should eventually get his watch and money back. Both appellants were in substance saying that their threats to report McCann to the police were not uttered with the object of extorting money or goods, but were made with the

E object of scaring McCann, who said that he was a queer, and who offered his money and watch as an inducement not to report him.

The learned judge in his summing-up, having dealt with the evidence, and having dealt with the ingredients of the first count of robbery with violence, went on to deal with the alternative second count of robbery being together as follows:

F   " Members of the jury, I want to direct you in this way. Supposing you came to the conclusion that the evidence of [the appellants] was right, in other words, their defence, what is the position? You have got this position: that they admit themselves that each of them together threatened McCann that they would go to the police and they did it to scare him—and you may think, members of the jury, that whether they intended to or not it had

G the effect of scaring him—and, to put it in legal words, which are also commonsense words, you may think, that that threat put him in fear, the threat of accusing him of a serious criminal offence. As a result of that threat [the appellants] were handed by McCann and eventually accepted three £5 notes and a wrist watch. Members of the jury, if you come to the conclusion that McCann handed that over as a free gift and that he was

H really willing to do it, of course that could not be robbery, but if a man hands money over to somebody who is threatening him with an allegation of going to the police and accusing him of a serious criminal offence and he hands it over having been put in fear by that threat, then, of course, it is not free will. Did [the appellants] intend to keep that property? You have a sentence in [the appellant] Pollock's evidence that, in fact, he intended

I to give it back to him at some time. Members of the jury, if you come to the conclusion that [the appellant] Pollock intended to find out McCann afterwards and go and give it him back you may well think you should acquit him. If you believe that to be quite untrue where are you? Robbery consists in the felonious and forcible taking from the person of another or in his presence against his will of any money. I direct you, members of the jury, that that taking, if you come to that conclusion, from McCann of the watch and of the £5 notes, if it was done as a result of putting him in fear of an

accusation of a criminal offence, would amount to a forcible taking from his   A
person or in his presence against his will. So, members of the jury, you are
left in this position: even if you accept the evidence that [the appellants]
have given in this case concerning the circumstances in which they obtained
possession of the watch and that money, your verdict on the robbery being
together against [the appellants] must be guilty. Of course, if you find
them guilty on the first count, you accept McCann's evidence as being   B
true, you need not worry about the second count. But even if you acquit
them on the first count, on their own evidence on the second count you
would be bound to find them guilty of robbery."

The jury were not told here or elsewhere in the summing-up that they could
not convict the appellants unless they were satisfied that the threats were
made with the intent of extorting money or property from McCann. It was open   C
to the jury on this direction to convict the appellants even though they believed
them to have made the threats from an innocent motive and without any
intention of extortion. The jury, accordingly, having acquitted on the count
for robbery with violence, convicted on the count for robbery being together.
It was in these circumstances that, on Feb. 11, 1966, the appellants were given
leave by this court to appeal against their conviction, and the following questions   D
arise for consideration: (i) Was there ever a form of robbery at common law
that involved no violence or threat of violence, but only involved a putting in
fear by accusation or threat of accusation of an unnatural crime? If yes, what
sort of unnatural crime was contemplated? (ii) If there was such an offence at
common law, was it affected by any of the Acts of Parliament dealing with
this matter, and, if so, in what way? (iii) On the assumption that such an offence   E
remained in existence at common law, unaffected by statute, at what stage in
the offence must the prosecution show an animus furandi?

The main part of counsel's argument for the appellants related to his proposition that the common law never in fact contemplated robbery by accusation
or threats of accusation of an unnatural crime alone. He pointed out, rightly,
that in the early cases, such as R. v. Jones (alias Evans) (1) in 1776, there was a   F
threat of actual violence—in that case " to raise the mob "—coupled with the
threat of accusation. The development of this argument involved asking this
court to decide that cases such as R. v. Hickman (2) and R. v. Egerton (3) were
wrongly decided and that the observations of LORD MORRIS OF BORTH-Y-GEST
in Smith v. Desmond (4) were obiter and should not be followed. In Smith v.
Desmond (5) the House of Lords were considering another aspect of the offence   G
of robbery. In the course of his speech, LORD MORRIS OF BORTH-Y-GEST said (6):

" There is little doubt that the writings and the decisions in regard to
robbery reveal a continuous and progressive process of definition. In
earlier times the offence was probably limited to cases where there was
actual violence to the person and a forcible taking from the person. Gradually
the conceptions as to what constituted robbery were extended. Actual   H
violence was not necessary. There might be a putting in fear of violence
as by a threat of violence. That could be called constructive violence. So
there might be a putting in fear by other means. There could be fear induced
by the threat of a charge of an infamous crime."

The accuracy of this review of the history of the offence is borne out by the
cases. R. v. Jones (alias Evans) (1) in 1776 was followed in 1779 by R. v.   I
Donnally (7). This was a case of a threat to accuse of unnatural crime with
the additional threat " you had better comply or I will take you before a magistrate ". Twelve judges, having heard counsel and having deliberated among

(1) (1776), 1 Leach, 139.   (2) (1784), 1 Leach, 278.
(3) (1819), Russ. & Ry. 375.
(4) [1965] 1 All E.R. 976 at p. 979; [1965] A.C. 960 at p. 979.
(5) [1965] 1 All E.R. 976; [1965] A.C. 960.
(6) [1965] 1 All E.R. at p. 979; [1965] A.C. at p. 979.   (7) (1779), 1 Leach, 193.

A themselves, each gave their reasons for upholding the conviction (8). A judgment
was delivered eventually by WILLES, J. (9).   The case is not altogether satisfactory, since the reasons of the judges by no means coincide, but there is no
doubt that they were unanimous that it was a case of robbery on the particular
facts. In *R.* v. *Hickman* (10), the threat was to accuse of sodomy coupled with
a threat to take before a justice, but the evidence of the prosecutor was that he

B had parted with his money under an idea of preserving his character from
reproach and not from the fear of personal violence.   There was, therefore,
raised the direct issue whether or not threats to accuse of sodomy were alone
sufficient to create the offence of robbery.   In view of this distinction from
Donnally's case (11), the matter was again considered by the judges.   Their
judgment was given by ASHHURST, J.   The judges were of opinion (12) that

C the case

" does not materially differ from the case of *Donnally* (11), for that the true
definition of robbery is the stealing, or taking from the person, or in the
presence of another, property of any amount with such a degree of force or
terror as to induce the party unwillingly to part with his property; and
whether the terror arises from real or expected violence to the person or

D from a sense of injury to the character, the law makes no kind of difference;
for to most men the idea of losing their fame and reputation is equally, if not
more terrific, than the threat of personal injury.   The principle ingredient
in robbery is a man's being forced to part with his property, and the judges
are unanimously of opinion, that upon the principles of law, and the authority
of former decisions, a threat to accuse a man of having committed the

E greatest of all crimes is, as in the present case, a sufficient force to constitute
the crime of robbery by putting in fear."

This case, if the whole judgment is to be taken literally, goes a very long way.
A " sense of injury to the character " might include threats to accuse of any
crime at all, homosexual, sexual, or otherwise. We do not think that this was
intended by ASHHURST, J., and the decision itself is limited to putting in fear

F by an accusation of sodomy " the greatest of all crimes ".   In the same year,
1783, NARES, J., directed a jury:

" So, also, to obtain money by means of a threat to accuse another of
having committed an unnatural crime, is held to be obtaining money by such
a degree of terror as will constitute the crime of robbery."

G See *R.* v. *Gascoigne* (13).

It must be borne in mind that, at this period of our history, the offence of
buggery was viewed with particular horror.   Conviction of the offence carried
sentence of death.   It was the abominable and unmentionable crime, and even in
some Law Reports the word buggery is written b——y. In 4 BLACKSTONE'S
COMMENTARIES (6th Edn.) published in 1774, the offence is not mentioned by
its name at all.   It is said (at p. 215) to be a crime

H
" of a still deeper malignity [than rape] . . . a disgrace to human nature
. . . a crime not fit to be named . . . peccatum illud horribile, inter christianos
non nominandum."

It was a crime which (14) " the voice of nature and of reason and the express
law of God determine to be capital ". It was against this background of opinion

I that the extension of the offence of robbery to include threats to accuse of sodomy
was made, but that this extension was not to be further extended to other
threats was made clear in 1796 in *R.* v. *Knewland and Wood* (15).   Delivering
the opinion of the judges in that case, ASHHURST, J., said (16):

---

(8) (1779), 2 East, P.C. at p. 715.
(9) (1779) 2 East, P.C. at p. 721; 1 Leach at p. 195.
(10) (1784), 1 Leach, 278.   (11) (1779), 1 Leach, 193.
(12) (1784), 1 Leach at p. 280.   (13) (1783), 1 Leach, 280 at p. 284.
(14) See BLACKSTONE'S COMMENTARIES (1774 Edn.) at p. 216.
(15) (1796), 2 Leach, 721.   (16) (1796), 2 Leach at pp. 730, 731.

" Terror is of two kinds; namely, a terror which leads the mind of the   A
party to apprehend an injury to *his person*, or a terror which leads him to
apprehend an injury to *his character*. The first kind of terror is that which
is commonly made use of on the commission of this offence and is always
held sufficient to support an indictment of this description. But the second
species of terror has never been deemed sufficient, except in the particular
case of exciting it by means of insinuations against, or threats to destroy   B
the character of the party pillage, by accusing him of sodomitical practices.
The fears considerably excited by this means have, on several occasions,
been determined by the judges to be sufficient to constitute the crime
of robbery (*R.* v. *Donnally* (17), *R.* v. *Hickman* (18), *R.* v. *Jones* (19));
but it is confined to these cases only. The bare idea of being thought
addicted to so odious and detestable a crime is of itself sufficient to   C
deprive the injured person of all the comforts and advantages of society:
a punishment more terrible, both in apprehension and reality, than even
death itself. The law, therefore, considers the fear of losing character by
such an imputation as equal to the fear of losing life itself, or of sustaining
other personal injury."

To some modern ears, this attitude may sound extraordinary and, by some   D
modern standards, the extension limited to threats of sodomitical practices is
quite illogical. It nevertheless, in our view, did exist as an extension at common
law, although judicial opinion was not always unanimous. Thus, in *R.* v.
Elmstead (20) in 1802, an accusation of sodomy was coupled with the threat
that the prisoner would not leave the prosecutor until he had pulled his house
down, but the money was paid by the victim from fear of losing his reputation   E
and situation. The editor of RUSSELL ON CRIME stated that most of the judges
thought that this case was within *R.* v. *Hickman* (18), nine judges holding *R.*
v. *Hickman* (18) binding, three judges thinking it was not law. Again, in *R.* v.
Cannon (21) there was a threat of accusation of attempted buggery, coupled
with a certain amount of constraint in the calling of a coach and taking the
prosecutor in it. Ten judges held that this was sufficient to constitute robbery,   F
but they were divided equally whether or not the mere apprehension of danger
to character would be sufficient to constitute the offence. The matter was,
however, in our view, settled beyond doubt in 1819 in *R.* v. *Egerton* (22). The
headnote to that case reads:

" Fear of loss of character and service, upon a charge of sodomitical
practices is sufficient to constitute robbery, though the party has no fear   G
of being taken into custody, or of punishment."

Eleven of the judges thought that this case was similar to *R.* v. *Hickman* (18)
and that they would not with propriety depart from that decision. HOLROYD, J.,
BAYLEY, J., and RICHARDS, C.B., expressly stated (23) that, in their opinion,
Hickman's case (18) was rightly decided, because a charge of this description
carried with it such a degree of fear as might be expected to overcome a firm and   H
constant mind. GRAHAM, B., on the other hand, thought (23) *Hickman's* case (18)
was not rightly decided, but he said that he would, on this point, be influenced
in future by what appeared to be the general opinion of the judges. Five years
later, in 1824, the decision was followed by LITTLEDALE, J., at Gloucester Assizes
in *R.* v. *Gardner* (24).

That robbery at common law could be committed by threats to accuse of   I
sodomitical practices is, we think, emphasised by consideration of the statutes.
As was pointed out by LORD PEARCE in *Smith* v. *Desmond* (25) the word " rob "
in the early statutes

---

(17) (1779), 1 Leach, 193.   (18) (1784), 1 Leach, 278.
(19) (1776), 1 Leach, 139.   (20) (1802), 2 RUSSELL ON CRIME (10th Edn.) 1018.
(21) (1809), Russ. & Ry. 146.   (22) (1819), Russ. & Ry. 375.
(23) (1819), Russ. & Ry. at p. 377.   (24) (1824), 1 C. & P. 479.
          (25) [1965] 1 All E.R. at p. 988; [1965] A.C. at p. 993.

A   " is sometimes used without precision, sometimes to describe the robbery
of a person, sometimes the robbery of a house or church,"
and in no statute was any definition of robbery attempted. In 1827, against the
background of dissent by some judges on the question of robbery by threats
to accuse of sodomy, Parliament passed "an act for consolidating and amending
the laws in England relative to larceny and other offences connected therewith ".

B   This statute, 7 & 8 Geo. IV, c. 29, contained seventy-seven sections, each containing the words " be it enacted " as was customary at that time. Section 7
alone begins: " Be it declared and enacted ", and continues:

  " that if any person shall accuse or threaten to accuse any other person
  of any infamous crime, as hereinafter defined, with a view or intent to extort
  or gain from him, and shall by intimidating him by such accusation or threat
C   extort or gain from him any chattel, money, or valuable security, every such
  offender shall be deemed guilty of robbery, and shall be indicted and
  punished accordingly."

The " infamous crime " is defined in s. 9. We do not think that this section had
the effect of creating a new offence; we hold that it was intended to be declara-
D   tory of the common law as decided in R. v. *Hickman* (26) and R. v. *Egerton* (27),
but as limited in R. v. *Knewland and Wood* (28). No doubt the word " deemed "
was used in the section in recognition of the constructive character of this kind
of robbery. Section 7 of the Act of 1827 was repealed by s. 1 and re-enacted
with little alternative by s. 4 of the Act of 1837 (7 Will. IV and 1 Vict. c. 87),
save that the definition of infamous crime was incorporated into the section
E   itself. However, the penalty was no longer to be death but a maximum of
transportation for life and the offence was no longer to be " deemed to be
robbery " as under s. 7 of the Act of 1827, but was to be " felony ". This section,
therefore, created a new statutory offence, but in neither the Act of 1827 nor
in the Act of 1837 are there any words indicating any intention to abolish the
common law offence of robbery. It was said by Best, J., in R. v. *Carlile* (29)
F   in 1819:

  "It has long been a settled maxim, that neither the provisions of the
  common or statute law are abrogated but by the express words of Parliament,
  or by subsequent enactments, so inconsistent with the previous law as to
  raise a necessary implication that the legislature intended it should be
  altered."

G   And Byles, J., in R. v. *Morris* (30), said:

  ". . . it is a sound rule to construe a statute in conformity with the
  common law rather than against it, except where or so far as the statute
  is plainly intended to alter the course of the common law."

It is unnecessary to deal with this part of the case in detail as it has been frankly
H   and rightly conceded by counsel for the appellants that, if there did exist at
common law an offence of robbery by threats to accuse of sodomy, it would
have continued to exist at common law side by side with the statutory offence.
Suffice it to say that the score of this new statutory offence was enlarged by
the Larceny Acts, 1861 and 1916, though neither statute has had the effect
of altering the common law; and by s. 33 of the Interpretation Act, 1889,

I   " Where an act or omission constitutes an offence under two or more Acts,
 or both under an Act and at common law, whether any such Act was passed
 before or after the commencement of this Act, the offender shall, unless the
 contrary intention appears, be liable to be prosecuted and punished under
 either or any of those Acts or at common law, but shall not be liable to be
 punished twice for the same offence."

(26) (1784), 1 Leach, 278.   (27) (1819), Russ. & Ry. 375.
(28) (1796), 2 Leach, 721.   (29) (1819), 3 B. & Ald. 161 at p. 165.
(30) [1861-73] All E.R. Rep. 484 at p. 486; (1867), L.R. 1 C.C.R. 90 at p. 95.

Counsel for the appellants referred us to three cases subsequent to the Act of **A** 1837. The report of *R.* v. *Norton* (31) is not satisfactory. The prisoner was charged before the recorder of London on an indictment containing three counts, namely, (i) threat of accusation of buggery, contrary to s. 4 of the Act of 1837; (ii) robbery on the basis of the threat, coupled with a threat of personal violence, and (iii) demanding with menaces with intent to steal, contrary to s. 7 of the Act of 1837. He was convicted on counts 2 and 3 only, as the threat was only a **B** threat to the effect that the prosecutor had " taken indecent liberties ". The case is of no authority that threats or accusations alone are sufficient, as on the facts these were coupled with a threat of personal violence. The report contains a footnote (32), from which it appears that the recorder consulted PARKE, B. The footnote reads:

". . . they were both of opinion that in those cases where the money was **C** obtained by any of the threats specified in the statute, the indictment must be upon the statute, and not for robbery; but where the money was obtained by threats to accuse, other than those which are specified in the statute, the indictment might be for robbery, if the party was put in fear, and parted with his property in consequence."

If this be an accurate report of the views of PARKE, B., we cannot agree with **D** them. No doubt it was eminently desirable to frame indictments under the statute, but we do not think that this footnote can be taken as any authority for the proposition that an indictment could not be framed in a proper case at common law, and we think it equally wrong to say that robbery at common law could be committed only by threats to accuse of minor indecencies. In 1839 a very different point arose before PARKE, B., in *R.* v. *Henry and Taunton* (33). **E** According to the jury's findings, Taunton was a party to threats to accuse of sodomy made by Henry but was not a party to actual violence used by Henry. Both men were tried on an indictment for robbery " in ordinary form ". No question arose as to the guilt of Henry, but the judge, having directed a verdict of guilty in the case of Taunton, reserved the question to the judges. All save one of the judges present thought that, inasmuch as the Act of 1837 repealed s. 7 **F** of the Act of 1827, the offence intended by Taunton was that of extorting money by accusation under the Act of 1837 and was no longer robbery under the Act of 1827, and that the conviction was, therefore, wrong. The reasoning is not clear. There are, it seems three possibilities: (i) the judges thought that *Hickman's* case (34), and the cases which followed it, were wrongly decided, that the legislature which enacted s. 7 of the Act of 1827 was mistaken in its belief that the **G** section declared the common law, and that, since the repeal of s. 7, there was no longer any authority, statutory or otherwise, for indicting the makers of such threats as robbers, or (ii) the legislature in 1837, by repealing that part of the earlier Act which provided that the making of the threats should be indictable as robbery, and by enacting that it should now be a felony, though nameless, had indicated an intention that it should no longer be indictable as robbery, or **H** (iii) where a statute such as s. 4 of the Act of 1837 describes the elements of a common law felony and expressly provides that they shall constitute a felony, an indictment cannot thereafter charge the offender with the common law offence but must charge him with a breach of the statute. None of these are satisfactory reasons. The first would of course be inconsistent with the view attributed to PARKE, B., in *Norton's* case (35), but we cannot conclude that the judges intended **I** to hold that *Hickman's* case (34) and the cases that followed it had been wrongly decided. The second would be a doubtful piece of statutory construction, and would raise the question for us (if it were right) as to the intention of the legislature in 1861 when it repealed s. 4 of the Act of 1837 and did not re-enact it. The

(31) (1838), 8 C. & P. 671.   (32) (1838), 8 C. & P. at p. 674.
(33) (1840), 2 Mood. C.C. 118.   (34) (1784), 1 Leach, 278.
                    (35) (1838), 8 C. & P. at p. 674.

A third seems hardly consistent with the presuppositions of s. 33 of the Interpretation Act, 1889, which provides that where an act or omission constitutes an offence under an Act of Parliament and at common law, the offender shall be liable to be punished either under the Act or at common law, but not both. This pre-supposes that an offence may continue to exist at common law after it has been enacted as a statutory offence; but if it continues to exist as a common law

B offence, why should it not be indictable as such? In this connexion, we repeat the observations already quoted of BEST, J., in *R.* v. *Carlile* (36). It is not surprising, therefore, that the opinion expressed in *Henry's* case (37) should have been doubted. We share those doubts which were expressed two years later by the judges in *R.* v. *Stringer* (38). The headnote to the report of this latter case reads:

C " Assaulting and threatening to charge with an infamous crime with intent thereby to extort money is assault with intent to rob under 1 Vict., c. 87, s. 3. *Semble*, it is still robbery to extort money by threatening a charge of sodomy, etc."

The indictment in this case was framed under s. 3, not s. 4, of the Act of 1837 and there were threats of accusation of gross indecency, not buggery, coupled

D with actual violence. The decision is not, therefore, directly in point, but the report concludes (39) that the judges

" doubted whether *R.* v. *Henry* (37) was rightly decided on the ground on which it was decided, viz., that it was not robbery to obtain money by threat of a charge of sodomy."

E The use made by counsel for the appellants of these three cases, *R.* v. *Norton* (40), *R.* v. *Taunton and Henry* (37) and *R.* v. *Stringer* (38), subsequent to the legislation of 1827 and 1837, is to point his argument that the common law offence of robbery was always ill-defined, and he submitted that it was open to this court today to decide that no such offence as robbery by means of threats to accuse of sodomy exists or ever did exist. We hold that such a variety of robbery did exist

F at common law, certainly since *R.* v. *Hickman* (41), and though there were subsequent doubts by some of the judges from time to time, by the time of *R.* v. *Egerton* (42), the matter was settled. We further hold, however, that it was not every threat to accuse which amounted to robbery, and the effect of *R.* v. *Knewland and Wood* (43) was to limit the nature of the accusation to " the infamous crime " of buggery, attempted buggery, assault with intent to commit buggery

G and solicitation or persuasion to commit buggery. We further hold that the common law offence of robbery, in all its common law forms, continues to this day, although, of course, the penalties for the differing forms of robbery are governed by statute. In particular, we hold that robbery by threat of accusation of sodomitical practices exists at common law alongside the statutory offence of demanding money by menaces, now contained in s. 29 of the Larceny Act, 1916,

H which section includes threats to accuse of any crime carrying a sentence of seven years' imprisonment. This is not to say that we think that it would be good practice in framing indictments to charge acts as robbery at common law which could be charged as blackmail under s. 29 of the Larceny Act, 1916. When the elements of an old common law offence are plainly covered by the words of a modern statute, it is preferable that the indictment should be framed, to use the

I old expression, contra formam statuti.

The other matter argued before us was the question of animus furandi at the time of making the threat. It is not disputed that a victim who hands over property as a direct result of a threat is not handing over of his own free will; but the important point, in our judgment, is the intention in the mind of the accused

---

(36) (1819), 3 B. & Ald. at p. 165.
(38) (1842), 2 Mood. C.C. 261.
(40) (1838), 8 C. & P. 671.
(42) (1819), Russ. & Ry. 375.

(37) (1840), 2 Mood. C.C. 118.
(39) (1842), 2 Mood. C.C. at p. 263.
(41) (1784), 1 Leach, 278.
(43) (1796), 2 Leach, 721.

at the time of making the threat. We are quite clear that the threat must be **A** made with an intent to extort. If an offence of indecency, of whatever sort, has been committed, or, if a person bona fide believes that such an offence has been committed, he has a duty to report it. To say, in such circumstances, that one is going to report it, without any intention of using the threat of reporting as a means to extort money or goods, is merely saying that one is going to fulfil a public duty and is not a criminal offence. In our view, the intention behind the **B** threat is all-important. We know of no case to the contrary. Indeed, in *R.* v. *Donnally* (44), WILLES, J., stressed the animus furandi at the outset; and in *R.* v. *Richards* (45), BLACKBURN, J., in charging a jury at Devon Assizes in 1868, said:

" Whether the crime charged upon the prosecutor by the prisoner was or was not one in fact is not material in this, that if the prisoner intended to **C** extort money by threatening to make the accusation, he is equally guilty whether it was or was not true; but it is material for you in considering what was the intention of the prisoner in demanding money. If the prisoner believed the statement of his son, and acting on that belief, went to the prosecutor and accused him of the crime but without any purpose, at that time, to extort money by such accusation, he had not been guilty of the **D** offence laid in the indictment; and if, after the accusation is made, with a belief in its truth, the prisoner endeavoured to compromise it by payment of money, he might be guilty of the offence of compounding a felony, but he would not be guilty of obtaining money by threats."

We, therefore, hold that the common law offence of robbery, in all its forms, **E** involves proof by the prosecution of an animus furandi, and, in cases of robbery by accusation of sodomitical practices, it involves proof of an animus furandi at the time of the threat or accusation.

It is, therefore, necessary, in the present case, to consider the effect of the learned judge's direction to the jury that they must convict of robbery on the basis of the evidence given by the two appellants. Had their evidence been that they intended at the outset to extort money, and had the accusation been **F** necessarily one of sodomitical practices, this direction would have been correct. In fact, however, the evidence of the appellants was that they had no intent to extort, that the threat to go to the police was merely to give McCann a fright, and that the wallet and watch were voluntarily handed over; and it was for the jury to say whether the fact that McCann was undressed and described himself as a " queer " necessarily connoted sodomitical practices. In these circumstances, **G** however unlikely it was that the jury would have accepted the evidence of the appellants, it was wrong to direct them that they must, of necessity, convict of robbery. It was for this reason, and for this reason alone, that this court, at the close of the arguments, ordered that the convictions be quashed.

Appeals allowed. **H**

Solicitors: *Registrar, Court of Criminal Appeal* (for the appellants); *Solicitor, Metropolitan Police* (for the Crown).

[*Reported by* N. P. METCALFE, ESQ., *Barrister-at-Law.*]

I

---

(44) (1779), 1 Leach, 193.   (45) (1868), 11 Cox, C.C. 43.

A   CHESWORTH v. FARRAR AND ANOTHER

[QUEEN'S BENCH DIVISION (Edmund Davies, J.), March 3, 15, 1966.]

*Bailment—Duty of bailee to take care of goods—Breach of duty—Cause of action
—Whether in tort—Action commenced more than six months after death of
bailee—Law Reform (Miscellaneous Provisions) Act, 1934 (24 & 25 Geo. 5*
B   *c. 41), s. 1 (3) as amended by Law Reform (Limitation of Actions &c.) Act,
1954 (2 & 3 Eliz. 2 c. 36), s. 4.*

*Money—Money had and received—Cause of action not in tort within Law Reform
(Miscellaneous Provisions) Act, 1934 (24 & 25 Geo. 5 c. 41), s. 1 (3) as
amended by Law Reform (Limitation of Actions &c.) Act, 1954 (2 & 3
Eliz. 2 c. 36), s. 4.*

C   The plaintiff was for many years tenant of an antique shop and dwelling-
house. Latterly she was often absent for long periods. On Aug. 12, 1960,
having obtained an order for possession and for payment of arrears of rent,
the landlord took possession. He thereby became bailee of her goods on
the premises. She was absent at the time. The plaintiff alleged that
antiques which had been on the premises when possession was taken had
D   not been accounted for to her and were lost, and that other of her antiques
had been sold by the landlord realising a sum of which £2,291 17s. 6d.
remained unaccounted for to her. The landlord died on July 19, 1961, and
letters of administration to his estate were granted to the defendants on
Apr. 11, 1962. On Apr. 7, 1964, the plaintiff brought an action against the
defendants claiming (in addition to claims in detinue and conversion) that
E   the landlord became a bailee of the plaintiff's goods and had failed to take
proper care of them, and claiming £2,291 17s. 6d. as money had and received.
If these causes of action lay in tort, they were statute-barred under s. 1 (3)
of the Law Reform (Miscellaneous Provisions) Act, 1934, as amended by
s. 4 of the Law Reform (Limitation of Actions &c.) Act, 1954*. On a
preliminary issue,
F   **Held:** (i) in order to establish her claim for alleged failure to take proper
care as bailee the plaintiff's case rested basically on the simple fact of the
landlord's possession of her goods, independent of the circumstances giving
rise to that possession, and was therefore a cause of action in tort; accordingly the cause of action was statute-barred (see p. 111, letters B and F, and
p. 112, letter G, post).

G   Dicta of BRAMWELL, L.J., in *Bryant* v. *Herbert* ((1878), 3 C.P.D. at p. 390)
and of GREER, L.J., in *Jarvis* v. *Moy, Davies, Smith, Vandervell & Co.*, ([1936]
1 K.B. at p. 405) applied.
Turner v. *Stallibrass* ([1898] 1 Q.B. 56) applied.
(ii) the claim for money had and received was not an action in tort and
was not statute-barred (see p. 113, letter F, post).
H   Dicta of LORD GREENE, M.R., in *Re Diplock's Estate* ([1948] 2 All E.R.
at p. 343) and of LORD WRIGHT in *Fibrosa Spolka Akcyjna* v. *Fairbairn
Lawson Combe Barbour, Ltd.* ([1942] 2 All E.R. at p. 135) applied.

[As to the definition of bailment, see 2 HALSBURY'S LAWS (3rd Edn.) 94,
para. 190; as to the survival of causes of action against the estates of deceased
persons, see 16 HALSBURY'S LAWS (3rd Edn.), 481, 482, para. 981; and as to
I   the meaning of cause of action, and the distinction between causes of action
founded in contract and in tort, see 1 HALSBURY'S LAWS (3rd Edn.) 6, para. 9,
and p. 36, paras. 73, 74; for cases on the obligation of the bailee to account and
on his liability, see 3 DIGEST (Repl.) 111-112, *327-331*, 115, 116, *354-363.*
For the Law Reform (Miscellaneous Provisions) Act, 1934, s. 1 (3), see 9
HALSBURY'S STATUTES (2nd Edn.) 793, and for the Law Reform (Limitation
of Action &c.) Act, 1954, s. 4, see 34 ibid., 466.]

* For s. 1 (3) as amended, so far as material, see p. 109, letter C, post.

Cases referred to:

Bagot v. *Stevens Scanlon & Co.*, [1964] 3 All E.R. 577; [1964] 3 W.L.R. 1162; 3rd Digest Supp.

Ballett v. *Mingay*, [1943] 1 All E.R. 143; [1943] 1 K.B. 281; 112 L.J.K.B. 193; 168 L.T. 34; 28 Digest (Repl.) 526, *421*.

Bryant v. *Herbert*, (1878), 3 C.P.D. 389; 47 L.J.Q.B. 670; 39 L.T. 17; 43 J.P. 52; 45 Digest (Repl.) 277, *13*.

Diplock's Estate, Re, Diplock v. *Wintle*, [1948] 2 All E.R. 318; sub nom. *Re Diplock, Diplock* v. *Wintle*, [1948] Ch. 465; [1948] L.J.R. 1670; affd. H.L. sub nom. *Ministry of Health* v. *Simpson*, [1950] 2 All E.R. 1137; [1951] A.C. 251; 2nd Digest Supp.

Fibrosa Spolka Akcyjna v. *Fairbairn Lawson Combe Barbour, Ltd.*, [1942] 2 All E.R. 122; [1943] A.C. 32; 111 L.J.K.B. 433; 167 L.T. 101; 12 Digest (Repl.) 448, *3383*.

Groom v. *Crocker*, [1938] 2 All E.R. 394; [1939] 1 K.B. 194; 108 L.J.K.B. 296; 158 L.T. 477; 29 Digest (Repl.) 517, *3641*.

Hambly v. *Trott*, (1776), 1 Cowp. 371; 98 E.R. 1136; 2 Digest (Repl.) 141, *1099*.

Jackson v. *Mayfair Window Cleaning Co., Ltd.*, [1952] 1 All E.R. 215; 45 Digest (Repl.) 276, *9*.

Jarvis v. *Moy, Davies, Smith, Vandervell & Co.*, [1936] 1 K.B. 399; 105 L.J.K.B. 309; 154 L.T. 365; 45 Digest (Repl.) 279, *30*.

Matthews v. *Kuwait Bechtel Corpn.*, [1959] 2 All E.R. 345; [1959] 2 Q.B. 57; [1959] 2 W.L.R. 702; Digest (Cont. Vol. A) 304, *5265a*.

Morris v. *C. W. Martin & Sons, Ltd.*, [1965] 2 All E.R. 725; [1965] 3 W.L.R. 276.

Phillips v. *Homfray, Homfray* v. *Phillips*, (1883), 24 Ch.D. 439; 52 L.J.Ch. 833; 49 L.T. 5; on appeal, H.L., sub nom. *Phillips* v. *Fothergill*, (1886), 11 App. Cas. 466; 24 Digest (Repl.) 688, *6731*.

R. v. *Ashwell*, (1885), 16 Q.B.D. 190; 55 L.J.M.C. 65; 53 L.T. 773; 50 J.P. 181, 198; 15 Digest (Repl.) 1048, *10,325*.

R. v. *McDonald*, [1881-85] All E.R. Rep. 1063; (1885), 15 Q.B.D. 323; 52 L.T. 583; 49 J.P. 695; 14 Digest (Repl.) 59, *231*.

Sachs v. *Henderson*, [1902] 1 K.B. 612; 71 L.J.K.B. 392; 86 L.T. 437; 45 Digest (Repl.) 278, *27*.

Taylor v. *Manchester, Sheffield and Lincolnshire Ry. Co.*, [1891-94] All E.R. Rep. 857; [1895] 1 Q.B. 134; 64 L.J.Q.B. 6; 71 L.T. 596; 59 J.P. 100; 45 Digest (Repl.) 278, *22*.

Turner v. *Stallibrass*, [1898] 1 Q.B. 56; 67 L.J.Q.B. 52; 77 L.T. 482; 46 Digest (Repl.) 276, *8*.

Preliminary point of law.

The plaintiff, Clare Elizabeth Chesworth, brought an action by writ dated Apr. 7, 1964, against the defendants, Douglas Bernard Farrar and Ann Elizabeth Trevor-Jones, as administrators of the estate of Bernard Farrar, deceased, claiming damages for the wrongful sale and/or conversion of the plaintiff's goods and chattels and/or loss of the plaintiff's goods and chattels while in the deceased's possession at 77, High Street, East Grinstead, Sussex, and/or repayment of the balance of the proceeds of sale. By para. 14 of their amended defence the defendants pleaded that the causes of action were statute-barred under s. 1 (3) of the Law Reform (Miscellaneous Provisions) Act, 1934, and by a consent order made by Master HARWOOD on Mar. 26, 1965, this issue was ordered to be tried as a preliminary point of law under R.S.C., Ord. 34, r. 2. The material provisions of the agreed statement of facts are set out in the judgment at p. 109, letter E, to p. 110, letter D, post.

D. Taverne, Q.C., and *E. Cotran* for the plaintiff.
Bruce Holroyd Pearce for the defendants.

Cur. adv. vult.

A   Mar. 15.   **EDMUND DAVIES, J.,** read the following judgment: In April, 1964, the plaintiff issued a writ against the defendants, as administrators of the estate of Bernard Farrar, deceased,

" for damages for the wrongful sale and/or conversion of the plaintiff's goods and chattels and/or loss of the plaintiff's goods and chattels whilst in the possession of the late Bernard Farrar at 77, High Street, East

B   Grinstead . . . and for repayment of the balance of proceeds of sale thereof."

The defendants have pleaded (inter alia) that the plaintiff's alleged causes of action are barred by s. 1 (3) of the Law Reform (Miscellaneous Provisions) Act, 1934. As amended by the Law Reform (Limitation of Actions &c.) Act, 1954, s. 1 (3) provides that

C   " No proceedings shall be maintainable in respect of a cause of action in tort which by virtue of this section has survived against the estate of a deceased person, unless either (*a*) proceedings against him in respect of that cause of action were pending at the date of his death; or (*b*) . . . proceedings are taken in respect thereof not later than six months after his personal representative took out representation."

D   Later the master made by consent an order under R.S.C., Ord. 34, r. 2, that this issue be tried as a preliminary point. Pursuant to that order a statement of facts was agreed and the matter was set down as a special paper.

The material parts of the statement of agreed facts are these:

" 1. From about Aug. 22, 1938, until about Aug. 12, 1960, the plaintiff

E   occupied premises at 77, High Street, East Grinstead, Sussex, which premises were partly an antique shop and partly a dwelling house.

" 2. The plaintiff first occupied the said premises under a tenancy agreement dated Aug. 21, 1938, and made between the above-named Bernard Farrar, deceased (hereinafter called the ' deceased ') and Elsie Bertha Farrar as landlords and the plaintiff herself as tenant. At the expiration

F   of the said tenancy in 1941 a further agreement was made between the said parties for a further letting of three years at an annual rent of £95 and thereafter the plaintiff continued as a statutory tenant.

" 3. From about 1956 the plaintiff was absent from the said premises for long periods which absence the plaintiff says was due to an illness.

" 4. On or about July 15, 1960, the deceased obtained judgment against

G   the plaintiff in the East Grinstead county court for possession of the said premises on the grounds of rent being in arrears and also for recovery of the sum of £55 8s. 4d. for the said arrears and £13 16s. costs. The present plaintiff was ordered to give up possession of the said premises unless the sum of £69 4s. 4d. was paid by Aug. 12, 1960. The plaintiff was absent from the said premises throughout 1960 and claims she received no notification

H   of the said proceedings or judgment.

" 5. On or about Aug. 12, 1960, the deceased took possession of the said premises.

" 6. It is alleged by the plaintiff that antiques to the value of £59,848 were on the premises when the deceased took possession thereof, but have not been accounted for to the plaintiff by the deceased or by the defendants

I   and are lost. Further the plaintiff alleges that other antiques belonging to the plaintiff were sold by the deceased for £4,841 17s. 6d. In respect of this sum the plaintiff agrees that £1,500 has been paid to her by the defendants and that the defendants were entitled to retain a further £1,050 as the agreed cost of dilapidations.

" 7. The plaintiff alleges that on taking possession of the premises the deceased became a bailee of the plaintiff's property which was on the premises; that it was an implied term of the contract of bailment, which was implied between the deceased and the plaintiff in all the circumstances, that the

deceased should protect and take good care of such property; that the   A
antiques not accounted for were lost by reason of the deceased's breach of
his duty under the contract of bailment; and that a further breach of duty
was committed by the deceased in selling more goods than he was entitled
to sell. In the alternative the plaintiff claims the value of the goods lost
in an action for detinue and claims that the wrongful sale of the plaintiff's
goods was an act of conversion. In the further alternative the plaintiff   B
claims the sum of £2,291 17s. 6d. (being the sum realised by the deceased
on sale of the plaintiff's goods, less the sums for which the plaintiff gives
credit) as money had and received by the defendants to the use of the
plaintiff.

" 8. The deceased died on July 19, 1961. The defendants were granted
letters of administration in respect of the deceased's estate on Apr. 11, 1962.   C
The writ in the action was issued on Apr. 7, 1964. The defendants have
contended inter alia that the plaintiff's alleged causes of action are barred
by virtue of s. 1 (3) of the Law Reform (Miscellaneous Provisions) Act,
1934.

" 9. It is agreed by the plaintiff that in so far as the plaintiff's action is
based on claims in detinue and conversion it is time-barred by reason of s. 1   D
(3) of the Law Reform (Miscellaneous Provisions) Act, 1934."

The question now falling to be determined is expressed in this way:

" 10. Assuming (which is not admitted by the defendants) (i) that the
deceased failed to protect and take proper care of the plaintiff's property
which was on the premises when the deceased took possession thereof and
further that the plaintiff's goods were lost as a result of such failure; and   E
(ii) that the deceased sold more of the plaintiff's goods than he was entitled
to sell and/or failed to account to the plaintiff for £2,291 17s. 6d. due to the
plaintiff in respect of goods sold by the deceased, the question for the
opinion of this honourable court are 1. whether the plaintiff's claim for
breach of the deceased's alleged duty as bailee; and 2. whether the plaintiff's
claim for £2,291 17s. 6d. as money had and received by the deceased to the   F
use of the plaintiff, is a cause of action in tort for the purposes of the Law
Reform (Miscellaneous Provisions) Act, 1934."

It is clear that two different sets of circumstances call for consideration; but
if the remedy available to the plaintiff in either case can be said to be " a cause
of action in tort " which, further, survives against the estate of a deceased person   G
only by virtue of s. 1 of the Act of 1934 then that remedy is barred.

What is " a cause of action in tort "? Until the County Courts Act, 1959,
s. 47, this question was important as to costs, and it remains important as to
statutes of limitation: see, for example, Bagot v. Stevens Scanlon & Co. (1);
as to the measure of damages Groom v. Crocker (2); as to service out of the
jurisdiction Matthews v. Kuwait Bechtel Corpn. (3); and, as in the present case,   H
in relation to the " Actio personalis moritur cum persona " rule. Some assistance
in answering it can be derived from decisions as to what was an " action founded
on contract ", as opposed to " an action founded on tort ", for the purpose of
the various County Courts Acts. As PROFESSOR WINFIELD pointed out, however
(THE PROVINCE OF THE LAW OF TORT (1931), p. 76),

" . . . the influence of the County Courts Acts on the division between   I
contract and tort, whatever its practical success, has been unfortunate as
a matter of science ",

for such a classification takes no account of the existence of quasi-contract.
The dichotomy has also been judicially criticised, for example, by LINDLEY, L.J.,
in Taylor v. Manchester, Sheffield and Lincolnshire Ry. Co. (4) and by SIR RICHARD

(1) [1964] 3 All E.R. 577.   (2) [1938] 2 All E.R. 394; [1939] 1 K.B. 194.
(3) [1959] 2 All E.R. 345; [1959] 2 Q.B. 57.
(4) [1891-94] All E.R. Rep. 857 at p. 859; [1895] 1 Q.B. 134 at p. 138.

A   HENN COLLINS, M.R., in *Sachs* v. *Henderson* (5). It does not follow that an
action " founded on tort " for the purposes of the County Courts Act, 1959, must
also be " a cause of action in tort " within the meaning of s. 1 (3) of the Act of
1934. In interpreting both expressions, however, the court has to look at the
substance of the matter. A long line of cases, exemplified by the decision of
that great master of the common law, BRAMWELL, L.J., in *Bryant* v. *Herbert* (6),

B   establishes that the foundation of an action consists solely in those facts which
are necessary to be alleged and proved in order to maintain it, that it is those
facts alone which determine the legal nature of the action, and that the form of
the action as stated in the pleadings is immaterial. The test propounded by
GREER, L.J., in *Jarvis* v. *Moy, Davies, Smith, Vandervell & Co.* (7), and now
generally accepted is this:

C   " . . . where the breach of duty alleged arises out of a liability independently of the personal obligation undertaken by contract, it is tort, and it
may be tort even though there may happen to be a contract between the
parties, if the duty in fact arises independently of that contract. Breach
of contract occurs where that which is complained of is a breach of duty
arising out of the obligations undertaken by the contract."

D   The practical application of these principles is usefully illustrated by *Jackson* v.
Mayfair Window Cleaning Co., Ltd. (8). A chandelier having fallen from a ceiling
when being cleaned under a contract made with its owner, an action in negligence
was brought against the cleaning company. Holding that it was an action
" founded on tort ", BARRY, J., said (9):

E   " That there was a contract . . . is, of course, not in dispute. Moreover,
the acts complained of might well have been pleaded as a breach of that
contract. What I have to ask myself, however, is whether, in essence, the
plaintiff must rely on that contract in order to establish her claim or whether
she can properly treat the contract as a mere matter of history, explaining
the presence of the defendants' workman in her flat, and establish a breach

F   of duty independent of any obligations undertaken by the defendants to her
under that contract."

It is by looking in this manner at substance, rather than at form, that I proceed
to deal with the two questions which I am here called on to decide.

Question 1. It is common ground that the deceased became bailee of the
plaintiff's antiques when he took possession of the premises in August, 1960.

G   That relationship imposed a common law duty on the bailee (a) to take reasonable
care to keep the goods safe and (b) not to do any intentional act inconsistent with
the bailor's rights in the goods, e.g., not to convert them (*Morris* v. *C. W.
Martin & Sons, Ltd.* (10)). On the assumption that he thereafter failed to take
proper care of the goods as such bailee and that in consequence they were lost,
does the claim to damages for such failure sound in tort? If so, it is admittedly

H   barred by the Act of 1934.

The court has had submitted to it a wealth of authorities as to the legal nature
of bailment, counsel for the plaintiff seeking to establish (i) that it is a contract
and (ii) that, accordingly, any action for a breach of the bailee's duty of care
must necessarily be in contract and is therefore unaffected by the Act of 1934.
LORD COLERIDGE, C.J., (in *R.* v. *Ashwell* (11)), STORY (LAW OF BAILMENTS

I   (7th Edn., 1863), p. 3), that great pundit MR. RALPH SUTTON, Q.C. (2 HALSBURY'S
LAWS (3rd Edn.) 94, para. 190) and others were cited in support of the proposition
that bailment is a contract. The court was reminded, on the other hand,
that LORD COLERIDGE, C.J., had earlier said (in *R.* v. *McDonald* (12)) that

(5) [1902] 1 K.B. 612 at p. 616.   (6) (1878), 3 C.P.D. 389 at p. 390.
(7) [1936] 1 K.B. 399 at p. 405.   (8) [1952] 1 All E.R. 215.
(9) [1952] 1 All E.R. at p. 217.   (10) [1965] 2 All E.R. 725 at p. 738.
(11) (1885), 16 Q.B.D. 190 at p. 223.
(12) [1881-85] All E.R. Rep. 1063 at p. 1064; (1885), 15 Q.B.D. 323 at p. 326.

there can be a complete bailment without a contract. PROFESSOR WINFIELD A
(THE PROVINCE OF THE LAW OF TORT, p. 100) considered that bailment was more
fittingly regarded as a distinct branch of the law of property (under the title
" Possession ") rather than as belonging to either contract or tort, but added that
it by no means followed that remedies in contract or tort were inapplicable to
breach of bailment. Finding my diffident way as best I can through this thicket,
I respectfully prefer, as DIPLOCK and SALMON, L.JJ., did in *Morris* v. *C. W.* B
Martin & Sons, Ltd. (13), to regard bailment simply as a legal relationship
between the parties which, while frequently arising from contract, can exist
independently thereof.

The circumstances, contractual or otherwise, which give rise to a bailment do
not of themselves determine the legal nature of proceedings brought between the
parties thereto in relation to its subject-matter. *Turner* v. *Stallibrass* (14) is the C
locus classicus on this point. There the plaintiff delivered his horse to the
defendants to be agisted and cared for at an agreed rate of remuneration. He
later sued them for negligently erecting a low wire fence in the field where the
horse was turned out, as a result of which it was injured; and he alternatively
alleged that the defendants in breach of their contract negligently allowed the
horse to be kept in a field which had a concealed fence. Holding that the action D
was one " founded on tort " within the meaning of s. 116 of the County Courts
Act, 1888, A. L. SMITH, L.J., said (15):

"The question is whether upon the facts of the case this was an action
which could be maintained without relying on the contract of agistment.
I think that the plaintiff showed a good cause of action by proving a bailment on which a duty arose at common law on the part of the defendants   E
not to be negligent in respect of the plaintiff's horse, independently of any
contract, and a breach of that duty."

It is to be observed that in that case there was in actuality a contract of bailment, but the proceedings were nevertheless held to be founded on tort. So, too,
in *Ballett* v. *Mingay* (16) where goods had been lent for a weekly sum and the F
bailee wrongfully parted with them to a third party, the action brought for their
return or their value was held, notwithstanding the contract, to be in detinue.

In the present case, what is the substance of the claim for failure to take proper
care of the plaintiff's goods and so to be unable to account for them? If, in the
circumstances which are required to be assumed, it could be said to be equally
poised in contract and in tort, I should have held that the plaintiff could rely G
on that aspect which put her in the more favourable position both under the
statutes of limitation and under the " actio personalis " rule. I find myself,
however, compelled to hold that the claim rests basically on the simple fact of
possession of the plaintiff's goods and is independent of the circumstances which
gave rise to that possession. If this is right, it follows that the claim is one " in
respect of a cause of action in tort " and, further, that as such a cause of action H
survives against the wrongdoer's estate only by virtue of the Act of 1934, it is
statute-barred by reason of non-compliance with s. 1 (3) thereof. In my judgment,
accordingly, the first question raised in the special paper must be answered in the
affirmative, that is to say, in a manner adverse to the plaintiff.

Question 2. Assuming that the deceased sold more of the plaintiff's goods than
he was entitled to sell and/or failed to account to the plaintiff for £2,291 17s. 6d.
due to the plaintiff in respect of goods sold by him, is the claim to recover that   I
sum an action in tort which is likewise barred by the Act of 1934? Or is it an
action analogous to one brought in contract, regarding which the " actio personalis " rule does not apply and which may be instituted within the periods
allowed by the Limitation Act, 1939? In my judgment, the latter answer is the
correct one, and I confess that I should not have held otherwise unless I found

(13) [1965] 2 All E.R. 725.   (14) [1898] 1 Q.B. 56.
(15) [1898] 1 Q.B. at p. 58.   (16) [1943] 1 All E.R. 143; [1943] 1 K.B. 281.

A that the state of the law conclusively compelled me to do so. A person on whom a tort has been committed has at times a choice of alternative remedies, even though it is a sine qua non regarding each that he must establish that a tort has been committed. He may sue to recover damages for the tort, or he may waive the tort and sue in quasi-contract to recover the benefits received by the wrongdoer. It has long been recognised that (as is pointed out in the recently

B published and admirable " LAW OF RESTITUTION " by GOFF and JONES, at p. 427):

> " the advantages of suing in quasi-contract were substantive as well as procedural. In particular, it was a useful method of circumventing short limitation periods and the old common law rule that tortious actions died with the person."

C

Holding in *Hambly* v. *Trott* (17) that trover did not lie against the estate of a wrongdoer, LORD MANSFIELD nevertheless said (18):

> " So far as the tort itself goes, an executor shall not be liable . . . but so far as the act of the offender is beneficial, his assets ought to be answerable, and his executor therefore shall be charged."

D

In *Phillips* v. *Homfray, Homfray* v. *Phillips* (19) BOWEN, L.J., expressed himself to the like effect. No authority was cited for the proposition that an action for money had and received is an action in tort and one which, but for the Act of 1934, would die with the wrongdoer. On the contrary, in *Re Diplock's Estate, Diplock* v. *Wintle* (20) LORD GREENE, M.R., said that it must be assumed that

E such an action was one " founded on simple contract " within the meaning of s. 1 (1) of the Limitation Act, 1939, while in *Fibrosa Spolka Akcyjna* v. *Fairbairn Lawson Combe Barbour, Ltd.* (21) LORD WRIGHT, in dealing with cases of unjust enrichment, said:

> " Such remedies in English law are generically different from remedies in contract or in tort, and are now recognised to fall within a third category

F of the common law which has been called quasi-contract or restitution."

In the light of the foregoing, I hold that question 2 must be answered in the negative. In other words, the plaintiff's claim for £2,291 17s. 6d. as money had and received by the deceased to the use of the plaintiff is not an " action in tort " for the purposes of the Law Reform (Miscellaneous Provisions) Act, 1934, and

G is accordingly not statute-barred by s. 1 (3) thereof.

Decision accordingly.

Solicitors: *Hatchett Jones & Co.* (for the plaintiff); *Johnson, Jecks & Landons,* agents for *Pearless, de Rougemont & Co.,* East Grinstead (for the defendants).

[*Reported by* MARY COLTON, *Barrister-at-Law.*]

H

I

---

(17) (1776), 1 Cowp. 371.   (18) (1776), 1 Cowp. at pp. 376, 377.
(19) (1883), 24 Ch.D. 439 at p. 454.
(20) [1948] 2 All E.R. 318 at p. 343; [1948] Ch. 465 at p. 514.
(21) [1942] 2 All E.R. 122 at p. 135; [1943] A.C. 32 at p. 61.

WEBB v. LEADBETTER.   A

[QUEEN'S BENCH DIVISION (Lord Parker, C.J., Winn, L.J., and Sachs, J.),
January 27, 1966.]

*Magistrates—Procedure—Evidence—Witness called after magistrates had retired
to consider their decision.*

In the absence of some special circumstances it is wrong for justices to   B
allow a witness to be called after they have retired to consider their decision
(see p. 115, letters C and G, post).

[As to the admissibility of fresh evidence after the close of a case for the
defence, see 10 HALSBURY'S LAWS (3rd Edn.) 422, para. 776; and as to the judge's
discretion, see ibid., p. 423, para. 778.]
                                                                                   C
Case referred to:
   Saunders v. *Johns,* (1964), " The Times ", Nov. 19.

Case Stated.

This was a Case Stated by justices for the county of Lancaster (acting in and
for the petty sessional division of Eccles), in respect of their adjudication as a
magistrates' court sitting at Eccles on June 28, 1965.   On Apr. 21, 1965, the   D
respondent, John Leadbetter, preferred an information against the appellant,
George Thomas Webb, that he did on Mar. 2, 1965, in the borough of Eccles,
drive a motor vehicle, namely a motor car, on a road called Parrin Lane without
due care and attention, contrary to s. 3 of the Road Traffic Act, 1960.

At the hearing the prosecution called their only witness, Mr. Landing, who had
been driving behind an articulated lorry and closed the case for the prosecution. E
The defendant then gave evidence denying that the manner of his driving had
caused the articulated lorry to swerve or brake.   After the defence had closed
their case and the justices had retired to consider their decision, they returned into
court and on being informed that a witness, Mr. Robson, had just arrived in court
after a break-down with his car, they allowed the prosecution to call Mr. Robson,
who was the driver of the articulated vehicle and who gave similar evidence to   F
Mr. Landing and was cross-examined by the defence.   It was contended before
the justices by the appellant that (a) at the close of the case for the defence
there was insufficient evidence to support a conviction, (b) that it was wrong in
law to admit the evidence of Mr. Robson after the case for the defence was closed
and the justices had retired to consider their decision.   It was contended before
the justices by the prosecution that Mr. Robson's evidence was admissible and   G
receivable in the case.   The justices were of the opinion that Mr. Robson's
evidence was admissible and allowed his evidence to be given.   The justices
found the appellant guilty of the offence and convicted him accordingly.   The
appellant now appealed.

B. H. Gerrard for the appellant.
The respondent did not appear and was not represented.   H

   LORD PARKER, C.J.:   In this case the prosecution had two witnesses
whom they desired to call, a man called Landing and a man called Robson.   When
the case was called on, Mr. Robson had not so far arrived, and the prosecution
elected, rather than ask for an adjournment, to go on with the case.   Accordingly,
Mr. Landing was the only witness; the prosecution case closed, and the appellant I
went into the witness box and gave evidence, and the defence case closed.   Thereupon the justices retired to consider their decision.   Before they had arrived
at their decision, they were informed that the witness, Mr. Robson, had
just arrived in court after a breakdown with his car, and they then went back
into court and allowed the prosecution to call the witness.   He gave evidence
corroborating Mr. Landing; he was cross-examined by the defence, and I will
assume, although it is not stated, that the defence was given a further opportunity
of addressing the court.

Dictum of LORD PARKER CJ at 115
applied in PHELAN v BACK [1972] 1
All ER 901

A   The question is whether the justices were wrong in law in allowing the witness, Mr. Robson, to give evidence for the prosecution after the defence had closed its case and the justices had retired to consider their decision.

It is, of course, quite clear, under our law that he who affirms must prove; therefore, strictly, once the prosecution have closed their case, there would be no opportunity for them to call further evidence, subject of course, to evidence in

B   rebuttal, with which we are not concerned. Nevertheless, it does seem to me that there must always be some residuary discretion in the court to allow, in particular circumstances, evidence to be called, but the manner in which that discretion is exercised must depend on the stage of the case. If one turns to indictable offences, it is perfectly clear that it has become now an established rule of law that no evidence can be called after the summing-up (1), and a judge who in

C   his discretion sought to exercise his discretion by allowing evidence to be called at that stage would be acting entirely wrongly and the conviction would be quashed.

The same considerations do not wholly apply in magistrates' courts, but, nevertheless, as a general rule and in the absence of some special circumstances, it would certainly be wholly wrong for the justices to purport to exercise a dis-

D   cretion to allow evidence to be called once they had retired, and indeed, probably, after the defence had closed their case.

At an earlier stage it may well be proper to exercise the discretion in favour of allowing a witness to be called, and indeed that was suggested in a decision of this court in *Saunders* v. *Johns* (2). In that case, this court held that it was too late to allow fresh evidence to be heard, since the defence had in fact closed

E   their case, but in giving judgment, I see that I said:

" What might well, and indeed, should have happened in this case, was that as soon as a submission of no case was made, the prosecution themselves, or the court of its motion, could then have recalled the police constable and obtained this evidence, evidence which could show that there was a prima facie case."

F

I only mention that, because certainly the court there envisaged that at that stage of the case it might not be too late, and that in the exercise of its discretion the court might allow a witness to be recalled or to recall the witness themselves.

So far as this case is concerned I am quite satisfied that there was only one way in which any residuary discretion in the magistrates could have been exer-

G   cised, the prosecution having closed their case, the defence having closed their case and they having retired. In those circumstances, I think that there is no option but to quash this conviction.

WINN, L.J.: I agree.

SACHS, J.: I agree; this is not one of those cases in which there were

H   the very special circumstances to which Lord Parker, C.J., has referred.

Appeal allowed.   Conviction quashed.

Solicitors: *Gouldens*, agents for *Kirk, Jackson & Co.*, Swinton (for the appellant).

[*Reported by* Kaushalya Purie, *Barrister-at-Law.*]

I

---

(1) See, e.g., *R.* v. *Owen*, [1952] 1 All E.R. 1040, and *R.* v. *Sanderson*, [1953] 1 All E.R. 485.
(2) (1964), " The Times ", Nov. 19.

HOLDER v. HOLDER AND OTHERS.

A

[CHANCERY DIVISION (Cross, J.), January 18, 19, 20, 21, 24, 26, 27, 28, February 11, 21, 1966.]

Acquiescence—Equitable defence—Knowledge—Rescission of sale sought by plaintiff beneficiary on ground that purchaser's renunciation of executorship was invalidated by prior acts of administration—Plaintiff received payment on account of his share of proceeds of sale—Whether knowledge of right to avoid sale should in the circumstances be imputed to plaintiff.

B

Agriculture—Agricultural holding—Tenancy—Inference of contractual tenancy from owner allowing occupation for an annual payment—Agricultural Holdings Act, 1948 (11 & 12 Geo. 6 c. 63), s. 2 (1).

Executor and Administrator—Purchase by executor of asset of estate—Farms sold by proving executors to son of testator who had purported to renounce probate— Son had acted in administration of estate before renouncing—Beneficiary claimed to have sale rescinded—Tenancy of farms in favour of son disputed by plaintiff—Form of relief—Whether acquiescence by plaintiff.

C

The testator owned two farms, Glebe Farm (157 acres) and Lower Farm (259 acres). By his will he appointed his wife, a daughter, and a son, V., to be executors and trustees and, subject to a legacy to his widow, gave all his estate to his trustees to sell and divide the proceeds between his widow and his ten children (eight daughters and two sons). The plaintiff, a son of the testator, occupied the farm house on Glebe Farm, but the testator farmed the land. In 1952 the testator granted V., and one D., a tenancy of part (153 acres) of Lower Farm at a rent of £250 per annum. V. also helped his father with Glebe Farm and the untenanted part of Lower Farm. In 1957, the testator, who was then seventy-two years of age, arranged orally with V. that V. should take over responsibility for farming Glebe Farm and the untenanted part of Lower Farm and should pay the testator £504 per annum in all (roughly £2 per acre) for this as from Michaelmas, 1957. The testator continued to live at Lower Farm as he had done before, and he paid the rates. On Aug. 7, 1959, the testator died. In October, 1959, an executors' bank account was opened in the names of the executors and moneys were paid into it and cheques, signed by all three executors, were drawn on and paid out of the account. It was conceded that by these and other acts V. acted in the administration of the estate. The testator's widow instructed valuers to value the farms on the basis that V. and D. (as to 153 acres) and V. (as to the rest) were entitled to tenancies. The plaintiff disputed V.'s claim to tenancies. At a meeting of beneficiaries in March, 1960, agreement was not reached. Thereafter V. was separately represented. On Aug. 22, 1960, V. executed a renunciation of the executorship. On Nov. 10, 1960, probate was granted to the widow and the daughter. In July, 1961, the farms were offered by the proving executors for sale by auction subject to the tenancies in favour of V. and D. (153 acres) and V. (the rest), reserve prices of £17,000 for Lower Farm and £14,000 for Glebe Farm being fixed on valuers' advice given on the basis of the rents being increased as from Michaelmas, 1962, since higher rents than those being paid could be obtained at that time. At the auction sale on July 12, 1961, V. bought Lower Farm for £18,250 and Glebe Farm for £14,000. Notices to increase rent were subsequently served on V. He was unable to complete punctually owing to difficulty in obtaining a mortgage. In February, 1962, the plaintiff through his solicitors pressed the executors to forfeit the deposit that V. had paid and to re-sell. Later the plaintiff issued a writ against the executors for an account of their dealings with the estate. In June, 1962, V. completed the purchase, having obtained a mortgage for a sufficient sum bearing interest at 7½ per cent. per annum. In June, 1962, a sum of £2,000 was paid to the plaintiff's solicitors on account of his share of the proceeds of sale. He did not know at this time of the acts of V. in relation to cheques and

D

E

F

G

H

I

Affirmed in part, reversed in part,
C.A. [1968] 1 All E.R. 665.

A   the executors' bank account which constituted acts of administration in the
estate.   The plaintiff, having changed his solicitors, claimed in February,
1963, that the executors had not been entitled to sell to V., and by writ issued
in January, 1964, claimed rescission of the sale and a declaration that the
farms should be sold with vacant possession.   At the trial the tenancy of V.
and D. of 153 acres of Lower Farm was not in issue.   The trial judge found that
B   rents paid for the farms in 1961 were substantially lower than the level prevailing in the district, but that this did not affect the prices realised as a
purchaser would know that the rents could be increased, and that the prices
fetched at the auction sale were, on the footing that V. was entitled to a
tenancy of Glebe Farm and part of Lower Farm, good prices.

   Held: (i) where an owner of land allowed another to occupy the land for
C   an annual payment, the inference was, in the absence of evidence to the contrary, that the owner had granted a contractual tenancy or licence; on the
evidence in the present case there was nothing to displace that inference, and
accordingly it was established that as from Michaelmas 1957, V. had been
granted by the testator an agricultural tenancy (within s. 2 (1)* of the
Agricultural Holdings Act, 1948) of Glebe Farm and of all that was then
D   unlet of Lower Farm, at an aggregate annual rent of £504 (see p. 123, letter I,
p. 125, letter I, and p. 126, letter D, post).

   (ii) when V. bought the farms at the auction sale in July, 1961, he was
within the rule of equity that disentitled a trustee to purchase trust property,
because, prior to his purported renunciation of the executorship, he had
performed acts of administration, and therefore remained executor despite
E   his renunciation, though he had not the legal estate at the time of the sale
as he was not one of the proving executors; the sale to V. was thus voidable
at the instance of a beneficiary, and, since there had not been acquiescence
sufficient to bar the plaintiff's right in equity to avoid the sale (as at the time
when the plaintiff did relevant acts, e.g., receiving money on account of the
proceeds of sale, he neither knew nor was to be deemed himself, or con-
F   structively through his solicitors, to know of his right to avoid the sale), the
plaintiff was entitled to impeach V.'s purchase of the reversion in the farms
(see p. 126, letter I, and p. 128, letters B and F, post).

   Stafford v. *Stafford* ((1857), 1 De G. & J. 193) distinguished.
   Dictum of WILBERFORCE, J., in *Re Pauling's Settlement Trusts* ([1961] 3
All E.R. at p. 730) followed.

G   (iii) (a) without the consent of the other beneficiaries the plaintiff was not
entitled to an order that the reversion in the farms should be re-conveyed
by V. to the trustees of the testator's will, but at the most was entitled to an
order for its re-sale under the directions of the court on the footing that any
surplus over a reserve price fixed by the court would belong to the trust, the
amount of the reserve being equal to the price given by V. together with
H   the value of any improvements made by him subsequently to his purchase
in July, 1961; if the re-sale did not show a profit to the trust, then V. should
be held to his bargain (see p. 128, letters G to I, and p. 129, letter E,
post).

   (b) the value to be attributed to improvements, when computing the
reserve price, would be the difference between the value of the property as
I   improved and its value if the improvements had not been made (see p. 129,
letter H, post).

   Robinson v. *Ridley* ((1821), 6 Madd. 2) followed.
   Dictum of KAY, J., in *Luddy's Trustee* v. *Peard* ([1886-90] All E.R. Rep.
at p. 974) not followed.

   (c) if the reversion were re-sold, V. should be credited in account with
interest at five per cent. on the purchase price that he had paid (although

_____
* The terms of s. 2 (1), so far as relevant, are printed at p. 125, letter A, post.

his mortgage interest ran at 7½ per cent.), and should be debited with a   **A**
notional rent at the rate of £3 10s. per acre since Michaelmas, 1962 (see
p. 130, letters E and G, post).

(d) since the plaintiff objected to V. being allowed to bid on a re-sale, he
would not be allowed to do so (see p. 130, letter I, post).

Tennant v. *Trenchard* ((1869), 4 Ch. App. 537) followed.

[As to disqualification of trustees for acquiring trust property and the setting   **B**
aside of such purchases, see 38 HALSBURY'S LAWS (3rd Edn.) 961-964, paras.
1664-1669; and for cases on these subjects, see 43 DIGEST 778-784, *2189-2245*.

As to renunciation of office of executor, see 16 HALSBURY'S LAWS (3rd Edn.)
131-132, paras. 197-199; and as to the elements of estoppel by acquiescence, see
14 HALSBURY'S LAWS (3rd Edn.) 639, para. 1179.

For s. 2 of the Agricultural Holdings Act, 1948, see 28 HALSBURY'S STATUTES   **C**
(2nd Edn.) 29.]

Cases referred to:

Badenach, In the Goods of, (1864), 3 Sw. & Tr. 465; 33 L.J.P.M. & A. 179; 11
    L.T. 275; 28 J.P. 711; 164 E.R. 1355; 23 Digest (Repl.) 47, *344*.

Boles and British Land Co.'s Contract, Re, [1902] 1 Ch. 244; 71 L.J.Ch. 130;   **D**
    85 L.T. 607; 43 Digest 781, *2214*.

Clark v. *Clark,* (1884), 9 App. Cas. 733; 53 L.J.P.C. 99; 51 L.T. 750; 36
    Digest (Repl.) 573, *1309*.

Cockerell v. *Cholmeley,* (1830), 1 Russ. & M. 418; 39 E.R. 161; 35 Digest
    (Repl.) 97, *20*.

Dumbell, Re, Ex p. Hughes, Ex p. Lyon, (1802), 6 Ves. 617; 31 E.R. 1223;   **E**
    4 Digest (Repl.) 249, *2256*.

Goldsack v. *Shore,* [1950] 1 All E.R. 276; [1950] 1 K.B. 708; 2 Digest (Repl.)
    7, *12*.

Howlett (decd.), Re, Howlett v. *Howlett,* [1949] 2 All E.R. 490; [1949] Ch. 767;
    [1949] L.J.R. 1632; 32 Digest (Repl.) 570, *1605*.

Luddy's Trustee v. *Peard,* [1886-90] All E.R. Rep. 968; (1886), 33 Ch.D. 500;   **F**
    55 L.J.Ch. 884; 55 L.T. 137; 43 Digest (Repl.) 85, *729*.

Pauling's Settlement Trusts, Re, Younghusband v. *Coutts & Co.,* [1961] 3 All E.R.
    713; [1962] 1 W.L.R. 86; *rvsd.* C.A., [1963] 3 All E.R. 1; [1964] Ch.
    303; [1963] 3 W.L.R. 742; 3rd Digest Supp.

Robinson v. *Ridley,* (1821), 6 Madd. 2; 56 E.R. 988; 40 Digest (Repl.) 396, *3168*.

Stafford v. *Stafford,* (1857), 1 De G. & J. 193; 29 L.T.O.S. 368; 44 E.R. 697;   **G**
    20 Digest (Repl.) 560, *2636*.

Stevens, Re, Cooke v. *Stevens,* [1897] 1 Ch. 422; 66 L.J.Ch. 155; 76 L.T. 18;
    affd. C.A., [1898] 1 Ch. 162; 67 L.J.Ch. 118; 77 L.T. 508; 23 Digest
    (Repl.) 45, *317*.

Tennant v. *Trenchard,* (1869), 4 Ch. App. 537; 38 L.J.Ch. 661; 43 Digest
    781, *2213*.   **H**

Action.

This was an action brought by the plaintiff, Frank William Holder, the elder
son of the testator, Frank Holder, by writ issued on Jan. 29, 1964, against three
defendants, Emily Louisa Holder (the testator's widow), Barbara Mary Campbell
(a daughter of the testator) and Victor James Holder (the testator's younger son).
The first and second defendants were executors and trustees of the will of the   **I**
testator, who died on Aug. 7, 1959; probate of the testator's will dated July 11,
1956, was granted to them on Nov. 10, 1960. The third defendant was also
appointed an executor and trustee of the testator's will, but he renounced probate
by writing dated Aug. 22, 1960. It was conceded that prior to that purported
renunciation he had acted in the administration of the testator's estate. The
testator owned two farms, Lower Farm and Glebe Farm. The plaintiff disputed
a tenancy of Glebe Farm and part of Lower Farm, which the third defendant
maintained that the testator had granted to him. On July 12, 1961, the farms

A were offered for sale by auction by the first and second defendants, subject to the tenancy in dispute and another tenancy, and were bought by the third defendant for £32,250.   By his statement of claim dated Apr. 16, 1964, the plaintiff after alleging among other matters that the third defendant continued to be an executor notwithstanding his renunciation and that he was not entitled to the tenancy of Glebe Farm and part of Lower Farm claimed (i) a declaration that

B the sales of the two farms ought to be rescinded and set aside with all necessary accounts and enquiries and a declaration that the farms ought to be sold with vacant possession; (ii) alternatively, as against the first and second defendants, an account of the farms and the rents and profits and the proceeds of sale thereof on the footing of wilful default.

The first two defendants denied by their defence that the third defendant's

C renunciation was ineffective and alleged that his tenancy in fact existed, or alternatively that they had reasonable grounds for thinking that he was tenant and alleged that the plaintiff had acquiesced in the sale of the farms.   The third defendant, in addition to pleading like defences, counterclaimed possession of the farm house on Glebe Farm.

The cases noted below* were cited during the argument in addition to those

D referred to in the judgment.

H. E. Francis, Q.C., and *Paul V. Baker* for the plaintiff.
P. R. Oliver, Q.C., and *J. Maurice Price* for the first and second defendants.
Martin Nourse for the third defendant.

Cur. adv. vult.

E   Feb. 11.   **CROSS, J.**, read the following judgment: The testator, Frank Holder, was a Gloucestershire farmer.   He owned two farms, Lower Farm, Oxenton, and Glebe Farm, Bishop's Cleeve. Lower Farm is of some 259 acres and on it there is a good farmhouse in which the testator lived.   Glebe Farm is of some 157 acres.   The land is better than the Lower Farm land, or at all events most of Lower Farm, but the house on it is small and old-fashioned.

F   The testator, who was married to the first defendant, Emily Louisa Holder, in 1911, had ten children, eight daughters and two sons. The older son, the plaintiff, Frank William Holder, was born in 1920 and the younger son, the third defendant, Victor James Holder, was born in 1931.   When the plaintiff left school in 1934 he continued to live at home on Lower Farm and helped his father, but in fact during the war the farming of the greater part of the land was taken over by the

G war agricultural committee.   In 1952 the plaintiff married and went to live in the house on Glebe Farm as a licensee, or tenant at will, paying no rent.   He was supposed to look after, or help to look after, the stock on Glebe Farm and the testator paid him £2 10s. a week.   The size of that weekly payment suggests that neither side expected that the plaintiff would do very much work on Glebe Farm, and I accept the evidence of the third defendant that in fact the plaintiff

H did very little.   He did not, however, engage in any other employment, but was content to live on what was, in effect, pocket money from the testator and what his wife earned.

The third defendant is a more energetic character.   In 1952 the testator granted him and Alec Denley, who had married one of his daughters, a tenancy of 153 acres of Lower Farm at a rent of £250 a year.   As well as farming that part of

I Lower Farm in partnership with Mr. Denley, the third defendant helped the testator in farming the rest of Lower Farm and Glebe Farm.   In 1953 the third defendant married, but he continued to live with his wife in the Lower Farm farmhouse with the first defendant and the testator.   Shortly before that date he began to buy stock of his own which, with the testator's consent, he reared

---

* *Ex p. Lacey*, (1802), 6 Ves. 625; *Ex p. James*, (1803), 8 Ves. 337; *Stacey* v. *Elph*, (1833), 1 My. & K. 195; *Hill* v. *Curtis*, (1864), L.R. 1 Eq. 90; *De Bussche* v. *Alt*, [1874-80] All E.R. Rep. 1247; (1878), 8 Ch. 286; *Head* v. *Gould*, [1898] 2 Ch. 250; *Wright* v. *Morgan*, [1926] All E.R. Rep. 201; [1926] A.C. 788.

on the testator's land. By 1955, about half the stock on the unlet part of Lower **A** Farm and on Glebe Farm belonged to the third defendant. On July 11, 1956, the testator made his will. By it he appointed as executors and trustees the first defendant, one of his daughters, the second defendant, Barbara Campbell, who was still unmarried and was then at home, and the third defendant. Subject to a legacy of £1,000 to the first defendant, he gave his estate to his trustees on trust to sell and divide the proceeds between the first defendant and his **B** children, that is, in eleven shares. As time passed and his stock increased, and the testator's stock decreased, the third defendant thought that he ought to pay the testator something for the use which he had made of the testator's land. Accordingly, in about April, 1957, he paid the testator £250 which was, I gather, intended to be a payment for the year from Michaelmas 1956 to Michaelmas 1957. Soon after this the testator, who was about seventy-two years old **C** and in bad health, decided that he could no longer continue to farm his land. He, therefore, arranged with the third defendant that he should take over the entire responsibility for the farming of the untenanted portion of Lower Farm and Glebe Farm, and pay him £504 a year as from Michaelmas 1957. One of the issues in this case is whether this arrangement gave the third defendant an agricultural tenancy or tenancies. I will return to this question later in my **D** judgment.

The testator died on Aug. 7, 1959. The chief asset of the estate, apart from the farms, was £4,500 odd on deposit account. Nothing was done about the administration of the estate until the beginning of October when the first defendant instructed Messrs. Griffiths & Lewis, solicitors of Cheltenham, to act for the executors. They obtained the signatures of the executors for the purpose of **E** opening an executors account at the Cheltenham branch of Lloyds Bank and £758 14s. was paid into this account on Oct. 22, being made up almost entirely of rent due from the third defendant, and from the third defendant and Mr. Denley, for the year 1958-1959. Between Oct. 29, 1959, and August, 1960, nine cheques, totalling nearly £600, were drawn on this account, each signed by all three executors, for the purpose of paying funeral expenses, a sum required to **F** redeem land tax and various liabilities of the estate. Soon after the account was opened several insurance policies, standing in the testator's name, were endorsed with the names of the executors. As well as instructing solicitors, the first defendant also instructed Mr. Hone, a local estate agent, to value the farms on the basis that not only had the third defendant and Mr. Denley a tenancy of the part of Lower Farm let to them in 1952, but that the third defendant had a **G** tenancy of the rest of Lower Farm and of Glebe Farm. Mr. Hone valued Lower Farm on this basis at £14,000 and Glebe Farm at £8,000, and agreed their values with the district valuer. When the plaintiff was told by the first defendant that the third defendant claimed these tenancies he disputed this claim and in the middle of November, 1959, he instructed Messrs. Ivens, Thompson & Green, solicitors of Cheltenham, to act for him. **H**

In March, 1960, a meeting was held at the offices of Messrs. Griffiths & Lewis which was attended by Mr. White of that firm and the executors, Mr. Brooks, of Messrs. Ivens, Thompson & Green, and the plaintiff, and all the other members of the family who were in England. Three of the daughters are in fact married to husbands living abroad. Mr. White put before the meeting such evidence as he had as to the existence of the tenancies and that question, and the related **I** question of Mr. Hone's valuation, were discussed. The family were divided; no agreement could be reached; and Mr. White suggested to the third defendant that he had better be separately represented.

A further family meeting, without any solicitors present, was held at Lower Farm in April, but again no agreement could be come to. Soon afterwards, the third defendant instructed Messrs. T. Weldon Thomson & Co., of Tewkesbury, to act for him and on Aug. 22 he executed a renunciation of the executorship in the usual form. On Sept. 8 another meeting was held at the offices of Messrs.

A Griffiths & Lewis which was attended by the same members of the family as attended the March meeting and four solicitors: Mr. White for the first and second defendants; Colonel Hattrell, of Messrs. T. Weldon Thomson & Co., for the third defendant; Mr. Brooks for the plaintiff and another solicitor for Mr. Denley. Mr. White explained to the meeting that the third defendant had renounced probate and that the first and second defendants were applying for a

B grant. The question of the tenancies was again discussed, but again no agreement was reached. The third defendants made an offer of £30,000 for the farms, but this was not acceptable to some of the beneficiaries. It was left that if the third defendant could not make a better offer acceptable to everyone the proving executors would have to offer the farms for sale by auction.

Probate was granted to the first and second defendants on Nov. 10, 1960.

C The third defendant made no further offer, but it was not until July 12, 1961, that the proving executors offered these farms for sale by auction. Part of the reason for this delay was that, although Mr. White and the first defendant were satisfied that the testator had granted tenancies to the third defendant, the second defendant was for a long time not satisfied on this point. A day or two before the auction the first and second defendants and Mr. White attended

D a meeting at Mr. Hone's offices to fix the reserves. The rents payable under the tenancies that is, £250 by the third defendant and Mr. Denley, and £504 by the third defendant, were admittedly substantially lower than could be obtained in 1961. The executors had not themselves served any notice of increase, but any purchaser at the auction would be entitled to serve a notice before the end of September which would result in an increased rent—arrived at in default

E of agreement by arbitration—becoming payable as from Michaelmas, 1962. It was, therefore, necessary to fix the reserves on the basis of the higher rent which would be obtained. On this basis Mr. Hone advised, and the executors agreed to, a reserve of £17,000 on Lower Farm and £14,000 on Glebe Farm. The auction, which was held at the Swan Hotel, Tewkesbury, was attended by most of the members of the family and a fair number of others. The particulars stated that

F the farms were subject to the tenancies, to which I have referred, and that the plaintiff was occupying Glebe Farm house rent-free. It was provided in the conditions that the date for completion was to be Sept. 27.

Before the properties were put up for sale, Mr. Green, of Ivens, Thompson & Green, who was present with the plaintiff, claimed that his client had a tenancy of the Glebe Farm house and not merely a licence. Mr. Lewis, of Messrs. Griffiths

G & Lewis, replied that the executors were satisfied that the position was as stated in the particulars and that the sale must proceed on that footing. Someone then asked whether the notice to increase the rent had been given, to which Mr. Hone replied that no notice had been given, but that the purchaser would have time to serve notices himself before Michaelmas. After some fairly brisk bidding both farms were knocked down to Colonel Hattrell who was bidding on behalf

H of the third defendant. Lower Farm at £18,250 and Glebe Farm at £14,000, a total of £32,250. The third defendant paid a deposit of £3,250, but was unable to complete on Sept. 22, because the credit squeeze interfered with his arrangements to raise the rest of the purchase price on mortgage.

On Sept. 26, 1962, the executors served on him notices to increase the rents and on Oct. 10 a notice calling on him to complete within twenty-one days. His

I solicitors, however, contended that this letter was bad and on Dec. 13, the executors served another twenty-one day notice. On Feb. 23, 1962, the plaintiff's solicitors wrote to the executors' solicitors pressing them to forfeit the third defendant's deposit and to put the farms up for sale again. As the executors took no steps to do this the plaintiff, on May 21, 1962, issued a writ against them for an account of their dealings with the estate. By this time, however, the third defendant had been able to make arrangements to find the balance of the purchase price and the sale was completed on June 5, 1962. Of the balance of purchase price payable, £21,000 was provided by the Agricultural Mortgage

Corpn. on a first charge repayable over sixty years, while the first defendant **A**
and one of his sisters, Mrs. Waller, each lent him £3,000 on a second charge,
that being approximately equal to their shares in the estate. The third defendant
was himself indebted to the estate for £1,500, but there would be approximately
another £1,500 coming to him, so that the sum which he had actually to find
over and above the deposit was quite small.

On June 27, 1962, Messrs. Griffiths & Lewis sent to Messrs. Ivens, Thompson **B**
& Green £2,000 on account of the plaintiff's one-eleventh share in the estate.
It was calculated that the balance of his share would be about £1,000. Disputes
then arose between the third defendant and the plaintiff as to the plaintiff's
position with regard to the Glebe Farm house of which he was then claiming a
tenancy, though it is now conceded that he was never more than a licensee.
On Nov. 14, the third defendant's solicitors gave notice determining this licence **C**
and demanding possession on Nov. 30. The plaintiff was at this time also maintaining a claim against the estate for arrears of wages which prevented the
executors from completing the distribution of the estate. That claim is not raised
in this action.

Some time in the latter part of 1962, the plaintiff changed his solicitors and
his new advisers, Messrs. Rowberry Morris & Co., of Gloucester, suggested, in **D**
February, 1963, that the third defendant might not have been entitled to purchase the properties; a point which had not hitherto occurred to anyone. The
third defendant meanwhile refrained from taking proceedings for possession
against the plaintiff. Throughout the rest of 1963 a desultory correspondence
was maintained between the plaintiff's solicitors and the executors' solicitors
and eventually on Jan. 29, 1964, the writ in this action was issued. **E·**

The statement of claim, after stating the testator's ownership of the farms, his
will and his death, the third defendant's purported renunciation and the grant
of probate, continued as follows:

"Notwithstanding such purported renunciation the third defendant is
and has at all material times been an executor of the estate of the testator
by virtue of the following acts of administration. (a) On or before Oct. 12, **F**
1959, by joining with the first and second defendants to open an executorship account at Lloyds Bank Limited of 130, High Street, Cheltenham, in
the County of Gloucestershire in the names of all three defendants and
thereafter joining as aforesaid to operate the account by signing all cheques
drawn thereon. (b) By allowing insurance policies relating to property of
the testator to be endorsed in the names of all three defendants. (c) In **G**
October, 1959, by joining with the first and second defendants and instructing solicitors to act on his and their behalf in administrating the estate
of the testator and continuing to retain the same solicitors until August,
1960. (d) On or about May 13, 1960, by calling at the Ministry of Agriculture
to negotiate for a grant towards the cost of a Dutch barn for erection on
one of the said farms which barn had been ordered by the testator in **H**
July, 1959. (e) At and from the death of the testator by taking possession
of and using the farming stock of the testator and by occupying and carrying
on a farming business on his said two farms."

At the trial no reliance was placed on sub-paras. (d) and (e). What the third
defendant did in relation to the Dutch barn he appears to have done in his
capacity of tenant, or alleged tenant, rather than as executor and the testator **I**
had no farming stock or business at the date of his death. On the other hand,
the third defendant's counsel conceded at the trial that the facts stated in sub-
paras. (a), (b) and (c) were acts of administration by the third defendant which
rendered his renunciation invalid.

Paragraph 5 of the statement of claim set out the facts with regard to the
auction. The statement of claim continued:

"At the time of his death the testator was in possession of the said two

A farms and no such tenancies as set forth in the said particulars [that is the auction particulars] or any tenancies existed or ever had existed save only the tenancy granted to the third defendant and Alec Denley in or about 1952. At the said auction sale the said farms were knocked down to the third defendant at an aggregate price of £32,250. The said sales were completed on May 31, 1962. [The date was in fact June 5.]

B " 8. The value of the said farms at that time with vacant possession was £50,000 approximately. The market rental value of the said farms at that time was £1,250 for the Lower Farm and £750 for the Glebe Farm.

" 9. Further or alternatively, the plaintiff contends that the first and second defendants were in breach of their duty as executors in offering the said farms for sale subject to the said tenancies and were guilty of wilful

C default. The wilful default relied on is as follows: (a) accepting without any sufficient evidence that the said tenancies existed and (b) failing to take any steps to raise the rent of the said farms to the market rental."

At the trial the plaintiff abandoned any claim against the first two defendants based on their failure to increase the rent of the farms. The prayer is as follows:

D " (1) A declaration that the said sales of the said two farms ought to be rescinded and set aside with all necessary accounts and enquiries and an order accordingly together with the declaration that the said farms ought to be sold with vacant possession subject only to the tenancy originally granted to the third defendant and the said Alec Denley as aforesaid. (2) Alternatively as against the first and second defendants an account of the

E said farms and the rents and profits and the proceeds of sale thereof on the footing of wilful default."

Then there was a prayer for further or other relief and costs.

The defences, so far as relevant in view of the concessions made on either side at the trial, are as follows. The first two defendants say that the third defendant was a tenant of the property in question or alternatively that they had reasonable

F grounds for thinking that he was. The third defendant too says that he was a tenant and he further claims that he was entitled to purchase notwithstanding the admitted invalidity of the renunciation, and that, if he was not so entitled, the plaintiff consented to, or acquiesced in, the sale to him and cannot now complain of it. Further, he counterclaims for possession of the house on Glebe Farm, which claim the plaintiff resists on the ground that the third defendant,

G having no tenancy of the farm, is not entitled to possession against him.

I will at this point state my view of the effect of the evidence as to values.

(i) If the third defendant had no tenancies so that Glebe Farm and so much of the Lower Farm as was not let to the third defendant and Mr. Denley could and should have been sold with vacant possession, the properties would have realised much more than the prices fetched at the auction. Perhaps as much as

H £50,000.

(ii) The rents payable by the third defendant and by the third defendant and Mr. Denley were substantially lower than the levels prevailing in 1961, but that fact did not affect the prices obtained at the auction because the prospective purchasers knew that they could increase them to the proper level.

(iii) The prices fetched at the auction on the footing that the third defendant

I was entitled to the tenancies were good prices.

(iv) The level of rents has increased between 1961 and today and if the farms were resold today, subject to the same tenancies as they were sold subject to in 1961, they would probably fetch appreciably more than they fetched in 1961.

I now turn to the first issue in the case, namely, whether the arrangement come to between the testator and the third defendant in the summer of 1957 gave the third defendant an agricultural tenancy of Glebe Farm and that part of Lower Farm which was not already let to the third defendant and Mr. Denley. The testator executed no document granting a tenancy, but then neither was the tenancy granted to the third defendant and Mr. Denley in writing. The third **A** defendant's evidence-in-chief was to the following effect:

" In 1957 my father was a sick man. He had not been doing much work for some time. He said that he had not much stock left and suggested that I take his land over. He said that he could let it at £2 an acre. I suggested that he let it to me at that figure. He said that I could have Glebe Farm at £2 an acre—making £314 for the 157 acres—and the unlet part of Lower **B** Farm for £190. I do not know why he fixed £190 instead of £212 for the 106 acres. There was no suggestion of excluding any land from the tenancies."

In cross-examination he agreed that he did not become a tenant of any land when he paid the £250 in April, 1957. He further admitted that he could not say whether his father intended to create an agricultural tenancy or even intended the arrangement to be legally binding at all. He impressed me as an honest **C** witness.

When the testator's remaining stock was disposed of in the autumn of 1957, the third defendant bought eighty ewes at £5 each. £200 of this £400 purchase price was set off against certain improvements which he had made to the farmhouse in 1954 and 1955. In October, 1958, the third defendant gave the testator **D** a cheque for £700, being as to £200 the balance of the purchase price of the ewes and as to £500 the payment for Glebe Farm and the rest of Lower Farm for the year 1957-1958.

The first defendant said that when the testator retired from farming in the autumn of 1957 he told the third defendant, in her presence, that he might as well have the rest of the farm and work it. He never told her the terms arranged **E** between him and the third defendant, but he told her in October, 1958, when the cheque for £700 was paid into his bank account, that £500 of it was for rent. The plaintiff said that when the testator in 1957 discontinued the payments of £2 10s. a week which he had been making to him, he did not tell him that he had granted the third defendant a tenancy of the farm. He simply said that the plaintiff had better get the money from the third defendant. One of his **F** sisters, Mrs. Davies, who lived near and used to visit her father regularly, said that he never told her that he had granted a tenancy to the third defendant. Mrs. Campbell, the second defendant, said the same.

In January, 1959, the testator signed an application form for a grant from the Ministry of Agriculture towards the cost of a Dutch barn on Lower Farm which named him as the owner and the third defendant as the tenant; but the reference to the third defendant's tenancy appears to have been filled in by the Ministry **G** on the basis of information supplied by the third defendant, and the testator may well not have read the form carefully. The testator went to see his accountant, Mr. Parker, several times at the time of and after his retirement in connexion with his tax returns. He told Mr. Parker that the third defendant was taking over the farms and was paying an increased rent which was, I think, a reference to the increase from £250, which the third defendant had paid for the year **H** 1956-57, to the £504 which he was paying from Michaelmas, 1957. On the basis of the information which the testator gave, Mr. Parker's firm wrote a letter to the tax inspector on June 30, 1959, which contains the following paragraph:

" Owing to increasing ill-health our client let his lands as follows: Glebe Farm, the whole, to Mr. Victor J. Holder (son), 157 acres at £2 per acre, **I** £314; Lower Farm, top part, to Mr. Victor J. Holder ninety-five acres at £2 per acre, £190 [making £504 in all]. Remainder of Lower Farm, to Mr. Victor J. Holder and Mr. Alec Denley (in partnership as Holder & Denley) 152 acres at £250 per annum: £250."

Mr. Parker said that on more than one occasion he advised the testator to have a document drawn up recording the terms arranged between him and the third defendant, but that the testator " never got round to doing it ". The testator continued to live at Lower Farm after Michaelmas, 1957, just as he had done

A   before.   The third defendant paid for the electricity as from the end of 1958, but the testator continued to pay the rates.

Section 2 (1) of the Agricultural Holdings Act, 1948, so far as is material, is in the following terms:

B   " Subject to the provisions of this section, where under an agreement made on or after Mar. 1, 1948, any land is let to a person for use as agricultural land for an interest less than a tenancy from year to year, or a person is granted a licence to occupy land for use as agricultural land, and the circumstances are such that if his interest were a tenancy from year to year he would in respect of that land be the tenant of an agricultural holding, then, unless the letting or grant was approved by the Minister before the agreement was entered into, the agreement shall take effect, with the necessary modifica-
C   tions, as if it were an agreement for the letting of the land for a tenancy from year to year."

It was held by the Court of Appeal in *Goldsack* v. *Shore* (1), that the word " licence " in the section means a contractual licence and does not cover a voluntary permission to occupy land free of charge. Counsel for the plaintiff submitted, and I
D   accept it, that the section also does not apply to an arrangement which is not intended to create legal rights at all. He further submitted, and again I accept it, that the third defendant's claim to a tenancy, being a claim against the estate of a dead man based on an alleged oral agreement, must be scrutinised carefully and that I must not give effect to it unless I am fully satisfied that he has made it out. He submits that I ought not to be so satisfied because the evidence,
E   read in the light of the surrounding circumstances, is just as consistent, if not more consistent, with a family arrangement not intended to create legal rights as with the creation of a legal tenancy or the grant of a contractual licence. The third defendant did not suggest that any tenancy between him and his father was created when he paid £250 for the use which he had of the land in 1956-1957. Why then should a tenancy have been created when he got whole use of the land as from Michaelmas 1957?   He further submitted that it was most
F   unlikely that the testator intended to give the third defendant a tenancy of the farmhouse, which was his own home, or even of the house on Glebe Farm where the plaintiff was living, and that to give the third defendant a tenancy of this land would inevitably confer an advantage on the third defendant as against his other children when the farms came to be sold on his death, although as his will showed he meant to treat them all equally. Of course, if the arrangement
G   made conferred no legal rights on either party it would follow that the third defendant could not have been compelled to pay the £504 so-called rent in October, 1958, but on the other hand the testator would always be able to turn him out of his farm at a moment's notice, so that his position would remain a very strong one.

As it seems to me, it may very well be that neither the testator nor the third
H   defendant directed their minds to the question of whether or not the arrangement they were making conferred any legal right. After all, they were father and son who had lived together all their lives and were on the best of terms. What I have to consider is whether, in the absence of any positive evidence that they did not intend to create legal rights, there are any circumstances in the case which would, or might, prevent the law from drawing the inference that a legally
I   binding relationship was created. After all, if one man allows another to occupy his land in return for an annual payment the inference, in the absence of evidence to the contrary, must be that he is granting a tenancy or a contractual licence. In my judgment, there is really nothing to displace that inference here. When the testator became unable through ill-health to go on farming his land, he was faced with the necessity of getting an income from somebody for the use of it. If the third defendant was not prepared to pay him an adequate rent for it,

---

(1) [1950] 1 All E.R. 276; [1950] 1 K.B. 708.

he would be forced to let it to an outsider. In these circumstances why should A the third defendant have been expected to provide the testator with an income for the rest of his life without getting any interest in the land in return? I cannot doubt that if this point had been raised at the time the third defendant would have said that the arrangement was to be mutually binding in law and that the testator would have agreed to this. It may be that if the testator had in fact instructed his solicitors to embody it in a document they would have inserted B a clause guaranteeing his right to occupy part of the Lower Farmhouse for the rest of his life; but I do not suppose that the testator would have attached much importance to this. As I said, he and the third defendant were on the best of terms and for practical purposes it made very little difference whether the legal position was that he could turn the third defendant out of the farmhouse or that the third defendant could turn him out. As for the house on Glebe Farm, the C testator was on bad terms with the plaintiff and I do not think that he would have cared in the least whether the right to turn him out belonged to the third defendant or to himself.

In the result, therefore, I am satisfied that the third defendant was granted a tenancy as from Michaelmas, 1957, of all the testator's property which was unlet at that date at the rent of £504 a year, £314 for Glebe Farm and £190 for D the unlet portion of Lower Farm. It follows that the plaintiff's claim against the first two defendants fails and that the third defendant is entitled to judgment on his counterclaim. He is willing that the order on that should be for possession at the expiry of twelve months from today and he is prepared to waive any claim to mesne profits.

I turn now to consider whether the plaintiff is entitled to any relief in respect E of the sale of the farms to the third defendant subject to the tenancies. An executor who renounces before he has done any acts of administration is entitled to buy any part of the testator's property from the proving executors; see *Clark* v. *Clark* (2). In this case, however, it is conceded that the third defendant had performed some acts of administration before he purported to renounce probate and that his renunciation was invalid. The submission made on his behalf F on this part of the case was as follows: "Like a trustee who has been discharged an executor who has acted but has not proved a will and has ceased to act prior to the purchase is not disabled from purchasing the trust property providing he can justify his purchases."

It is true that a trustee who has been discharged from the trust before any question of sale of the property in question has arisen is entitled to purchase; G see *Re Boles and British Land Co.'s Contract* (3). In this case, however, the purported renunciation was made in order to enable the third defendant to purchase these farms, and even if the analogy with a trustee who has been discharged was a true one, I doubt very much whether one could apply it to the facts of this case; but in truth the position of an executor who has made an ineffective renunciation is quite different from that of a trustee who has been discharged, H for he remains an executor. He can be cited to take probate by creditors or beneficiaries and can claim to take it himself; see *In the Goods of Badenach* (4) and *Re Stevens, Cooke* v. *Stevens* (5). It is true that unless and until he takes probate the proving executors have the legal estate in the testator's land vested in them exclusively and can make title without his co-operation, but he has still the duties of an executor and is, in my judgment, within the rule which says I that a trustee who purchases the trust property from his co-trustees cannot obtain an unimpeachable title unless he has the consent of all the beneficiaries or the protection of an order of the court. When, therefore, the third defendant became the purchaser of the farms at the auction held on July 12, 1961, he obtained a title to them which was voidable by any of the beneficiaries.

It is, however, submitted on his behalf that the plaintiff is not now entitled

(2) (1884), 9 App. Cas. 733.   (3) [1902] 1 Ch. 244.
(4) (1864), 3 Sw. & Tr. 465.   (5) [1897] 1 Ch. 422.

A to avoid that title because after the auction, so far from taking any steps to avoid it, he pressed the proving executors to forfeit the third defendant's deposit as he had failed to complete, and after the completion he received a substantial payment on account of his share of the proceeds. To this argument the plaintiff replies that he did not in fact know of his right to avoid the contract until shortly before he issued his writ in this action because he, like everyone else concerned,

B assumed that the third defendant had effectively thrown off any fiduciary character. To this reply the defendants rejoin first, that the plaintiff knew certain facts from which, if he had been a keen-eyed lawyer, he would have seen that the third defendant could not renounce his executorship and, secondly, that even if it would not be right to impute this knowledge of the law to the plaintiff himself, he had at all material times a solicitor acting for him who had

C as great a knowledge of the relevant facts as the plaintiff had. A knowledge of the relevant law should be imputed to him and through him to the plaintiff. It is not suggested that the plaintiff knew that an executors' account had been opened or that the third defendant had joined in signing cheques on it in discharge of liabilities of the estate. The only facts within the plaintiff's knowledge which are relied on are: (i) That the executors had instructed Messrs. Griffiths &

D Lewis to act for them, and (ii), that Mr. Hone had been instructed by the executors to make a valuation of the testator's properties. I am not myself satisfied that if that was all that the third defendant had done he would have been precluded from renouncing probate, but assuming that he would have been so precluded it is clear that the plaintiff was totally unaware of that fact.

The question of how far a plea of acquiescence can be defeated by showing

E that a plaintiff, though he knew certain facts, did not appreciate their legal effect, is one on which the authorities are not entirely consistent. In *Cockerell* v. *Cholmeley* (6), SIR JOHN LEACH, M.R., said:

" In equity it is considered, as good sense requires it should be, that no man can be held by any act of his to confirm a title, unless he was fully aware at the time, not only of the fact upon which the defect of title depends,

F but of the consequence in point of law; and here there is no proof that the defendant, at the time of the acts referred to, was aware of the law on the subject, nor was it even alleged in argument."

On the other hand, in *Stafford* v. *Stafford* (7) KNIGHT BRUCE, L.J., said:

" Generally, when the facts are known from which a right arises, the right

G is presumed to be known; and I am not satisfied that in the present case, upon the materials before us, it would be right to ascribe to the lady any degree of ignorance of her rights."

In *Re Howlett* (decd.), *Howlett* v. *Howlett* (8), DANCKWERTS, J., accepted SIR JOHN LEACH'S statement of the law as correct, but unfortunately in that case the defendant's leading counsel failed to refer the judge to the rival statement

H by KNIGHT BRUCE, L.J. (7).

In *Re Pauling's Settlement Trusts*, *Younghusband* v. *Coutts & Co.* (9), WILBER- FORCE, J., reviewed the authorities on the analogous question of what degree of knowledge the beneficiary must have in order to be held to have concurred in a breach of trust. He expressed his conclusions as follows (10):

I " The result of these authorities appears to me to be that the court has to consider all the circumstances in which the concurrence of the cestui que trust was given with a view to seeing whether it is fair and equitable that, having given his concurrence, he should afterwards turn round and sue the trustees: that, subject to this, it is not necessary that he should know that what he is concurring in is a breach of trust, provided that he fully understands what he

---

(6) (1830), 1 Russ. & M. 418 at p. 425.   (7) (1857), 1 De G. & J. 193 at p. 202.
(8) [1949] 2 All E.R. 490 at p. 493; [1949] Ch. 767 at p. 775.
(9) [1961] 3 All E.R. 713 at pp. 729, 730.   (10) [1961] 3 All E.R. at p. 730.

is concurring in, and that it is not necessary that he should himself have   **A**
directly benefited by the breach of trust."

Equally, in my judgment, in cases of alleged acquiescence one cannot lay down
a hard and fast rule to this effect that knowledge of the legal consequences of
known facts is or is not essential to the success of the plea. It all depends on the
circumstances. On the facts in *Stafford* v. *Stafford* (11) one can well see why the   **B**
lords justices thought that it would be unjust to allow the petitioner to rely on
her ignorance of her rights. However, in this case—and assuming for the moment
that the plaintiff had no legal advice—it would, to my mind, be altogether unjust
to impute to him knowledge of the legal consequences, or what I am assuming
to be the legal consequences, of the facts which he did know.

Is the position altered by the fact that he had a solicitor acting for him?   **C**
I think not. If the plaintiff had been a prospective purchaser of the property
from the third defendant, who had instructed his solicitor to examine the third
defendant's title before entering into a contract to buy, and subsequently wished
to get out of his contract on the ground that the renunciation was invalid, it
may be that the court would hold that the plaintiff had contracted with constructive notice of the invalidity. However, the plaintiff did not employ his   **D**
solicitor to advise him whether the third defendant would get a good title to the
property if he bought it. He employed him to safeguard his interests as one of
the residuary legatees and as the occupant of the house on Glebe Farm. The
solicitor's duty was to investigate and if possible defeat the third defendant's
claim to the tenancies—which would reduce the values of the farms—and to
try to arrive at some arrangement which would safeguard his client's occupation
of his home; but he was not concerned to prevent the third defendant's buying   **E**
the properties provided he paid a proper price for them. It was, indeed, suggested
that his duty to the plaintiff included putting every possible " spoke " in the
third defendant's " wheel " and that, as it might weaken the third defendant's
position if he could not purchase the farms, the plaintiff's solicitor was under
a duty to enquire into the validity of the renunciation, and that consequently
he had constructive notice of its invalidity which could be imputed to the plaintiff.   **F**
To my mind, so to hold would be to extend the doctrine of constructive notice
beyond all reasonable limits. In the result, I hold that the plaintiff can impeach
the third defendant's title to the reversion in the farms.

It remains to consider the form of the relief to which the plaintiff is entitled
against the third defendant. It is sometimes said that the beneficiary may elect
either to have the property in question reconveyed to him or to have it resold   **G**
under the direction of the court; see LEWIN ON TRUSTS (16th Edn.), pp. 701, 703,
and 38 HALSBURY'S LAWS (3rd Edn.), pp. 693, 694, para. 1668. In my judgment,
however, when the plaintiff is one of several beneficiaries he has no right to insist
on the property being reconveyed by the purchasing trustee to the vendor trustees
without the consent of the other beneficiaries. On a reconveyance the purchasing
trustee would be relieved of his bargain and if the vendor trustees were unable to   **H**
resell the property at a higher price the beneficiaries would be worse off than if
the claim had never been made. The most that the plaintiff can be entitled to
is an order that the third defendant resells the property under the directions of
the court on the footing that if it realises more than the reserve fixed by the
court the surplus belongs to the trust, whereas if it realises less the third defendant will be held to his bargain. Obviously there is a number of matters to be   **I**
determined before any such resale can take place. First, there is the question
of the appropriate reserve which must be equal at least to what the third defendant gave, together with the value of any capital improvements made by him.
Then there is the question of whether the third defendant should be allowed to
bid. Again there is the question of the costs of the resale. If the property is
sold at a price substantially above the reserve the costs would no doubt be

---

(11) (1857), 1 De G. & J. 193.

A payable by the trust, but if the reserve is not reached, or only just exceeded, it may be that it would be right that the plaintiff, who has claimed a resale, should bear these costs himself. I will hear further argument on these points and also on the question of the costs of this action down to date.

[His Lordship then heard argument on the form of the order to be made and on the liability for costs. The cases noted below* were cited during the argument

B in addition to those referred to in the judgment.]

Feb. 21. CROSS, J., read the following judgment as to the relief to be awarded: When one of a number of beneficiaries establishes, as the plaintiff here has done, a right to have property purchased by a trustee put up for sale again, the matter ceases to be one simply between the plaintiff and the purchasing

C trustee and becomes one in which all the beneficiaries have a right to be heard. It would, for example, be wrong that the third defendant and the plaintiff should be in a position to enter into a bargain compromising the plaintiff's claim while leaving the possible claims of other beneficiaries outstanding. I propose, therefore, to make an order for the resale of the farms subject to the tenancies by the court and to direct that the eight beneficiaries who are not at present before the court shall be given notice of the order so that they will have

D an opportunity of being heard and will be bound by what is done. I cannot foresee all the questions which may arise in connexion with the resale, but one or two points were argued after I had given my main judgment on which I shall state my views now.

First as to the reserve price, unless the resale shows a profit to the trust, the third defendant must be held to his bargain and the reserve must therefore be

E the sum which, if there was a resale, the third defendant would be entitled to receive out of the proceeds. It is common ground that that must include, as well as the purchase price which the third defendant paid and which would be refunded to him or his mortgagees, something also in respect of improvements made by the third defendant since his purchase. Should that something be the actual cost of the improvements, however, or the value of the improvements,

F i.e., the difference between the value of the property to be sold as it is, and what its value would be if the improvements in question had not been made? In a case like this where the property is sold subject to tenancies of indefinite duration in favour of the third defendant it may make a considerable difference which yardstick one adopts. The authorities on this subject are old and conflicting.

G In *Re Dumbell, Ex p. Hughes, Ex p. Lyon,* (12), the master was asked to certify what sum the purchasing trustee had expended in improvements (13) and the same view seems to have been taken by Kay, J., in *Luddy's Trustee v. Peard* (14), where he said that the purchasing trustee was entitled to receive as a condition of reconveying the property (inter alia) " all outlay by him in improvement, with interest at four per cent.". On the other hand in *Robinson v. Ridley* (15), Sir John Leach, V.-C., ordered that the improvements should be valued and

H the estate put up for resale at the improved value. In my judgment that is the proper course. It would be inequitable that the beneficiaries should get the benefit of any expenditure made in good faith by the third defendant which he would not have made if he had not thought that he owned the land and which has enhanced its value and will be reflected in the purchase price. On the other hand, there is no reason in equity why the trustee should be given credit for

I expenditure which did not increase the value of the land or the value of which is exhausted before the resale or reconveyance which may not take place until many years after the original conveyance to him.

---

* *Ex p. Lacey,* (1802), 6 Ves. 625; *Lister v. Lister,* (1802), 6 Ves. 631; *Ex p. James* (1803), 8 Ves. 337; *Ex p. Bennett,* (1805), 10 Ves. 381; *Baker v. Carter,* (1835), 1 Y. & C. Ex. 250.

(12) (1802), 6 Ves. 617.   (13) (1802), 6 Ves. at pp. 624, 625.
(14) [1886-90] All E.R. Rep. 968 at p. 974; (1886), 33 Ch.D. 500 at p. 522.
(15) (1821), 6 Madd. 2.

Another point which was argued was whether any balance on income account   A
should be added to or deducted from the reserve. Obviously, if the property is
resold there will have to be taken at some time an income account, crediting
the third defendant with interest on the purchase price and the improvements
and debiting him with a proper rent. Should the result of that account, however,
be reflected in the reserve or should the reserve contain only items of a capital
nature? The cases of resales under the order of the court, which are all over one   B
hundred years old, do not lend any support to the former alternative. Nevertheless, I think that the analogy of what is done in cases of reconveyance shows
that it must be right in principle. The purchasing trustee cannot be obliged to
reconvey except on being paid, not only the purchase price, but also, if there is
such an excess, the excess of interest on the purchase price at the appropriate
rate over the rents actually or notionally received by him. The property stands   C
as security for that composite sum. Similarly the reserve fixed ought to be equal
to the total of what the purchasing trustee would be entitled to receive out of
the purchase price on a resale before anything goes to the trust and that must
include any excess of interest over rents if there is such an excess. Conversely,
if the rents for which he is accountable exceed the interest which is due to him
the reserve price ought to be reduced accordingly.   D
   On the income account itself two questions were argued, first, the rate of
interest with which the third defendant should be credited, and secondly, the
amount of the rent with which he should be debited. The third defendant raised
nearly all the purchase price on mortgage and it was suggested that in respect of
that part of the purchase price he should be credited with interest at the rate which
he had to pay, which in the case of the first mortgage to the Agricultural Mortgage   E
Corporation is 7½ per cent. I cannot accept that argument. How the third
defendant raised the purchase price is no concern of the beneficiaries. On the
other hand, I think that in present-day conditions to credit him with interest
at four per cent. only would be unfair. He ought, I think, to be allowed five
per cent. If the property is resold the third defendant will, in fact, have been
occupying it from the date of his purchase until the date of the resale as a tenant   F
at a rent of £504 per annum. That is, in fact, substantially less than the rent
which a purchaser other than the third defendant would have obtained from
the third defendant as from Michaelmas, 1962, under the operation of the notices
served by the executors in September, 1961. Ought the third defendant to be
debited with a rent of more than £504? I think that equity requires that he
should be as from Michaelmas, 1962, and I shall fix that rent on the basis of   G
£3 10s. an acre which in the light of the evidence of the valuers is perhaps slightly
favourable to him.
   Next comes the question whether the third defendant should be allowed to
bid at the auction. He wishes to do so but the plaintiff objects. Apart from
authority I would have thought that that ought to be a matter to be decided
by the court in the interests of the trust as a whole, if the beneficiaries were not   H
in agreement. If, for example, it was clear—I do not say that it is clear here—
that no outside purchaser would be likely to give as much as the trustee, it would
seem wrong that a single beneficiary should be entitled to prevent the trust
receiving the best price. The point was fully argued, however, before LORD
HATHERLEY, L.C., sitting as the Court of Appeal in Chancery in *Tennant* v.
Trenchard (16) and he decided that the court had no power to allow the trustee   I
to bid if any adult beneficiary objected to his doing so. That decision is binding
on me.
   It was common ground that the costs of the resale must be reserved. If the
property fetches substantially more than the reserve so that after all costs are
paid there is a benefit for the trust, then it would presumably be right for the
costs to come out of the estate. If, on the other hand, the reserve is not reached
or only exceeded by an amount which would not cover the costs of resale, there
_____
(16) (1869), 4 Ch. App. 537.

A would be a strong argument for ordering the plaintiff to pay the costs, or some
   of them, so far as an order to that effect can be made having regard to the fact
   that he is legally aided. In view of this possibility it was suggested that
   the plaintiff should be ordered to give security for the resale costs. I have no
   doubt that the court has power to make such an order, if it thinks that an impecunious beneficiary is insisting on a resale which is unlikely to result in any
B benefit to the trust simply in order to spite the purchasing trustee or to put himself
   in a strong bargaining position. On the other hand if the evidence showed that
   the resale was likely to result in an appreciable profit to the trust the court would
   be unwilling to prevent an impecunious beneficiary from getting his share of
   that profit simply because other beneficiaries were likely to acquiesce in the
   original sale. In this case the evidence indicated that a substantial profit was
C likely to be realised, but I do not propose to decide the point now. The order will
   expressly reserve liberty to any beneficiary to apply within a reasonable time
   for an order that the plaintiff give security for the costs of the resale.

   Finally I come to the costs of the action to date. As the plaintiff is legally
   aided I cannot, in any event, make any enforceable order for costs against him
   without conducting an enquiry into his financial position. I think, however, that
D it is desirable that I should state what order I should have made if the plaintiff
   were not legally aided. The question whether any order should, in fact, be made,
   and whether any order under the Legal Aid Act 1964 should be made, may have
   to be debated at an adjourned hearing. On the pleadings there were several
   distinct issues. There was the claim that the testator had not granted the third
   defendant tenancies of the farms. This affected both the executors and the third
E defendant and the plaintiff failed on it. There was the claim that the executors
   ought to have raised the rent payable if there was a tenancy. This affected the
   executors and the plaintiff abandoned the claim at the trial. Then there was the
   claim that, tenancy or no tenancy, the third defendant's title to the freehold was
   voidable at the instance of the plaintiff. This affected the third defendant but
   not the executors and the third defendant lost on it. To direct separate taxations
F of the costs of different issues is generally unsatisfactory and the parties agreed
   that it would be better for me to fix what I consider to be the fractions of the
   various sets of costs in question attributable to the different issues. On the
   whole I think it would be fair to attribute half of the costs to the issues as to
   the tenancies and the rent and half to the issue as to the third defendant's title.
   In considering the position as between the plaintiff and the executors, one
G must bear in mind that although the executors would have been necessary parties
   to the action even if the plaintiff had limited his claims to the issue on which
   he succeeded, they need not have taken an active part in the case and would
   have incurred far less costs. In these circumstances, if the plaintiff were not
   legally aided I would have ordered him to pay three-quarters of the executors'
   costs. In so far as the executors' costs are not recovered from the plaintiff or
H from the State they will come out of the estate.

Order accordingly.

The order, dated Feb. 21, 1966, read as follows:

" THIS COURT DOTH DECLARE that if the properties known as Lower Farm . . .
and Glebe Farm . . . can be resold (subject as hereinafter mentioned) at a price
I equal to or exceeding the reserve price hereinafter specified then the sales thereof
to the third defendant on July 21, 1961, ought to be set aside and the said
properties ought to be resold accordingly AND IT IS ORDERED that subject to the
said reserve price being reached the said properties be resold as aforesaid with
the approbation of the judge free from the incumbrances (if any) of such of the
incumbrancers as shall consent to a resale and subject to the incumbrances of
such of them as shall not consent and subject also to a tenancy of . . . Lower Farm
to the third defendant at a rent of £440 per annum and to a tenancy of Glebe
Farm to the said defendant at a rent of £314 per annum AND THAT the money to

arise from the resale be lodged in court to the credit of this action ' Re . . . Pro- A
ceeds of sale of real estate ' AND if such money or any part thereof shall arise
from property sold with the consent of incumbrancers the money so arising is to
be applied in the first place in payment of what shall appear to be due to such
incumbrancers according to their priorities.

" AND IT IS ORDERED that the first and second defendants do cause notice of this
order to be given to such of the persons beneficially interested under the will of B
the testator . . . as are not parties to this action.

" AND IT IS ORDERED that the following accounts and inquiries be taken and
made that is to say:—(1) An account of interest at the rate of five per cent. per
annum on the sum of £32,250 (being the purchase money paid by the third
defendant in respect of the said sales of the said properties to him on July 12,
1961) from the date or dates on which the same was paid until the date which C
shall be appointed for resale; (2) An inquiry what capital improvements to the
said properties (being improvements of the nature specified in Sch. 3 to the
Agricultural Holdings Act, 1948) have been made by the third defendant since
July 12, 1961, and of the value of such improvements as at the date of this
order such value to be ascertained by taking the difference between the value
of the said properties in their existing state as at the date of this order and D
the value which the said properties would have had at such date if the said
improvements had not been made; (3) An account of interest at the rate of
five per cent. per annum on the value of the said improvements made by the
third defendant such account to be taken by apportioning the total value of the
said improvements as certified under the inquiry numbered (2) rateably between
each of the said improvements according to the cost thereof to the third defendant E
and by taking interest on the amount so apportioned to each such improvement
from the date when the same was completed until the date appointed for the
resale; (4) An account of what sum would be payable by the defendant if he
were charged an occupation rent in respect of the said properties at the rate of
£754 per annum from June 5, 1962, to Sept. 29, 1962, and at the rate of £1,457 per
annum from Sept. 30, 1962, until the date appointed for the resale and (5) An F
inquiry what amounts shall be due in respect of principal interest and cost as at
the date appointed for the resale to any incumbrancers who shall not consent
to the resale.

" AND IT IS ORDERED that the said reserve price shall be the amount by which
the said sum of £32,250 together with the aggregate of the amounts certified
under the accounts numbered (1) and (3) and the inquiry numbered (2) shall G
exceed the aggregate of the amounts certified under the account numbered (4)
and the inquiry numbered (5) AND IT IS ORDERED that if the said reserve price
shall be reached and the said properties shall be resold accordingly the third
defendant shall be paid out of the money to arise from the resale the amount by
which the said reserve price shall exceed the amount to be paid to any incumbrancers who consent to the resale AND IT IS ORDERED that upon the actual H
completion of the resale the third defendant shall deliver to the purchaser or
purchasers of the said properties all title deeds and other documents relating
thereto which shall be in his possession or power and which ought properly to be
delivered to such purchasers or purchasers AND THIS COURT DOTH ORDER that
the plaintiff do within twelve months from the date of this order deliver up to
the third defendant the possession |of the farmhouse situate on . . . Glebe Farm I
referred to in the counterclaim of the said defendant.

" AND IT IS ORDERED that it be referred to the taxing master to tax the costs
of this action of the first and second defendants and that the plaintiff do pay to
the first and second defendants a sum equal to three-quarters of the amount of
such costs when taxed or such sum as shall be determined by the judge as hereinafter mentioned whichever sum shall be the less AND IT IS ORDERED that it be
referred to the taxing master to tax the costs of the counterclaim of the third
defendant and that the plaintiff do pay to the third defendant the amount of

A such costs when taxed or such sum as shall be determined by the judge as hereinafter mentioned whichever sum shall be the less AND IT IS ORDERED that it be
referred to the taxing master to tax in accordance with the provisions of Sch. 3
to the Legal Aid and Advice Act, 1949, the costs to which that Act applies
incurred on behalf of the plaintiff AND IT IS ORDERED that it be referred to
the judge in person sitting in Chambers to determine in accordance with s. 2

B (2) (*e*) of the Legal Aid and Advice Act, 1949, the amount for which the plaintiff
should be made liable under the foregoing orders for costs against him AND the
costs of and incidental to any resale or attempted resale are reserved.

" AND any person beneficially interested under the said will is to be at liberty
within a reasonable time after the date of this order to apply for an order that
the plaintiff do give security for the costs of any such sale or attempted resale

C AND any party is to be at liberty to apply generally."

Solicitors: *Rowberry, Morris & Co.*, Gloucester (for the plaintiff); *Griffiths &
Lewis*, Cheltenham (for the first and second defendants); *T. Weldon Thomson &
Co.*, Tewkesbury (for the third defendant).

[*Reported by* JACQUELINE METCALFE, *Barrister-at-Law.*]

D

TYNAN *v.* BALMER.

E [QUEEN'S BENCH DIVISION (Lord Parker, C.J., Sachs and Widgery, JJ.), February
8, 1966.]

*Trade Dispute—Picketing—Obstruction of highway—Obstruction of police—
Forty pickets moving in continuous circle on a highway outside main entrance
to factory—Approaching vehicles likely to be caused to halt and pedestrians
likely to be impeded—No breach of peace anticipated—Refusal to comply
F with police instructions to desist—Whether conduct justified by Trade Disputes
Act, 1906 (6 Edw. 7 c. 47), s. 2 (1).*

On Nov. 23, 1964, while an official strike by draftsmen at a factory
was in progress, some forty pickets under the direction of the appellant
began to walk in a circle in a service road which was part of the highway
near the main entrance of the factory. It was inferred that one of the

G objects of the circling manoeuvre was to seal off the area occupied by the
circle and to bring traffic to a standstill. The appellant was arrested,
having declined to tell the pickets to desist when requested by a police
constable to stop them as they were obstructing the highway. On appeal
against conviction of obstructing the constable in the execution of his duty,

Held: the circling manoeuvre, viewed independently of s. 2 of the Trade

H Disputes Act, 1906, obstructed the highway and amounted in law to
a nuisance; since the pickets were not there merely for the purposes of
s. 2 (1)*, but also for the purpose of causing vehicles approaching the factory
premises to stop, what was being done was something beyond what was
authorised by s. 2, and accordingly the conviction would be upheld (see p. 136,
letter F, and p. 137, letters A and D, E, *post*).

I Decision of JUDGE CHAPMAN (sub nom. *Tynan v. Chief Constable of
Liverpool* [1965] 3 All E.R. 99) affirmed.

[As to peaceful picketing, see 38 HALSBURY's LAWS (3rd Edn.) 361, para. 625.
As to intimidation, see ibid., pp. 68, 69, para. 78; and for cases on intimidation
in relation to trade disputes, see 15 DIGEST (Repl.) 917, 918, *8809-8818*.

As to the offence of obstructing the police, see 30 HALSBURY's LAWS (3rd Edn.)
142, para. 231, note (*b*).

------

* Section 2 (1) is printed at p. 136, letter G, *post*.

Dictum of LORD PARKER CJ *at* 137
applied in HUNT v BROOME
2 All ER 1035 [1973]

Applied in BROOME v DPP
1 All ER 314 [1974]

As to the offence of wilfully obstructing free passage along a highway, see A
19 HALSBURY'S LAWS (3rd Edn.) 286, para. 455, note (o); and for cases on the
subject, see 26 DIGEST (Repl.) 468-470, *1569-1586*.

For the Trade Disputes Act, 1906, s. 2, see 25 HALSBURY'S STATUTES (2nd
Edn.) 1267.

For the Highway Act, 1959, s. 121, see 39 HALSBURY'S STATUTES (2nd Edn.)
542.   B

For the Police Act 1964, s. 51, see 44 HALSBURY'S STATUTES (2nd Edn.) 924.]

Case referred to:

Lyons (J.) & Sons v. Wilkins, [1899] 1 Ch. 255; 68 L.J.Ch. 146; 79 L.T. 709;
63 J.P. 339; 36 Digest (Repl.) 271, *238*.

Case Stated.
This was a Case Stated by the Recorder of Liverpool (JUDGE CHAPMAN) in   C
respect of his decision, dated May 7, 1965, and reported [1965] 3 All E.R. 99,
dismissing an appeal by Harold Kenneth Tynan against his conviction by a
magistrates' court on Jan. 8, 1965, on a charge of wilfully obstructing a police
constable in the execution of his duty on Nov. 23, 1964, contrary to the Police
Act 1964, s. 51 (3).

The facts found were as follows.   On Nov. 23, 1964, a strike was in progress at   D
English Electric Co., Ltd.'s, factory on the East Lancashire Road at Liverpool.
The strike concerned the draftsmen of the factory who numbered about three
hundred and the appellant was the leader of the strikers and chairman of the
negotiating committee.   The strike was in operation on Nov. 16, when pickets
were first posted at the gates.   It was a well managed strike entirely lacking   E
in disturbances or bad temper and all strikers were decent, well mannered people
who maintained good friendly relations with the police.

On Nov. 20, the pickets under the appellant's direction were moving in a
circle outside the main entrance to the factory.   The access to this main entrance
to the factory was provided by a private road belonging to the factory; south
of this was a line of guard rails, then there was a service road, used for buses
bringing people to the works, then there was a reservation and then there were   F
the north and south carriageways of the East Lancashire Road.   The service road
was part of the highway.   On Nov. 20 the pickets were walking round in a circle
in the mouth of the main entrance and the circle extended into the service road
which was part of the public highway.   An inspector of police who was there
told the appellant that he was not happy about the circling procedure but did not
press the matter further pending reference to higher authority.   On Monday,   G
Nov. 23, two police constables were on duty outside the factory and they saw the
appellant leading about forty strike pickets in a circular movement.   The police
constable requested the appellant to stop the pickets from circling, expressing the
view that it was an obstruction.   The appellant replied, " No, I am challenging
your authority on this . . .we want to make a test case of it ", and continued with
the circling movement.   At this, the police constable arrested him and charged him   H
with the offence of obstruction.

The recorder having found the primary facts posed and answered five questions*:
—" (Q) Was Police Constable O'Hare a constable? Yes. (Q) Was Police Constable
O'Hare obstructed? Yes. (Q) Was the refusal to comply with the constable's request wilful? Yes. (Q) Was the constable in giving the instructions which he did
acting in the exercise of his duty? Yes. (Q) Was the appellant's conduct justified   I
by the Trade Disputes Act, 1906, s. 2 (1) ? No."

The recorder found that the pickets were not attending merely for the purposes
described in s. 2, but that in part their object was to seal off the highway and
to cause vehicles approaching the premises to stop.   He came to the conclusion
that the Trade Disputes Act, 1906, did not operate to protect the appellant and
that the facts disclosed an offence, and he dismissed the appeal.

---

* See [1965] 3 All E.R. at pp. 105, 106.

A   *P. R. Pain, Q.C.*, and *B. A. Hytner* for the appellant.
     F. J. Nance for the respondent.

WIDGERY, J., delivered the first judgment at the request of LORD PARKER,
C.J., in which he stated the nature of the appeal and the facts and continued:
The recorder dealt with the crucial issue in this case, which is whether the action
of the pickets was authorised by s. 2 of the Trade Disputes Act, 1906, in this way.
B
He said (1):

> " I think the contention of counsel for the appellant goes much too far.
> It is, I think, clear that the main purpose of s. 2 (1) of the Act of 1906 was to
> make lawful what was otherwise expressly forbidden by various anti-Trade
> Union Acts such as the Conspiracy and Protection of Property Act, 1875.
C   > Incidentally it may well have rendered lawful what would otherwise have
> been unlawful at common law. If, for example, a person is found standing
> in a public highway and is instructed by a constable ' move along there,
> please ', it may well be a valid answer to say ' I am attending at a person's
> place of work as a peaceful picket in pursuance to the Trade Disputes
> Act, 1906 '. But that would not mean that if there was a strike at the
D   > Ritz Hotel, all the strikers, numbering perhaps several hundred, could
> gather in a block in Piccadilly and bring the whole of the traffic to a standstill,
> and it would make no difference to my mind if, instead of being stationary,
> they produced the same result by walking round and round in an unbroken
> circle. If the Trade Disputes Act, 1906, confers any right to produce what
> would otherwise be an obstruction in a public highway (and it may be that
E   > it does) it only does so to the extent that attendance at a place for the
> purpose of peacefully obtaining or communicating information or of peace-
> fully persuading people to abstain from working cannot reasonably take place
> at all without producing that result."

The recorder then went on to deal with the question of whether it was reasonably
necessary for the purpose of obtaining or communicating information or of
F   peacefully persuading people not to work, to have forty men at the entrance in
question, and whether it was necessary that they should be kept circling. In
regard to the first of those points he said (2):

> " I can quite see the value, from the point of view of advertising the
> strike and underlining the number of people involved and demonstrating
> their solidarity, of having a substantial number of people near the prestige
G   > entrance, but, from the point of view of the purposes set out in the Trade
> Disputes Act, 1906, forty seem to me to be a number far in excess of what
> was reasonably required. Two or three men would have been sufficient to
> cope with the cars likely to be passing to and fro—the regular attenders in
> cars would, after a week, know all about the strike anyhow—and for foot
> passengers, most of whom would be workers in the factory, quite a few would
H   > similarly suffice."

Then he said in regard to the circling manoeuvre (3):

> " I entirely fail to see how the circling manoeuvre could have any bearing
> on the purposes set out in the Trade Disputes Act, 1906; it would hinder
> rather than facilitate the obtaining or communicating of information (except
I   > in so far as it would ensure that vehicles were brought temporarily to a
> standstill) and its power of persuasion would be nil (except in so far as it
> would have a deterrent effect). The purposes of the Act of 1906 could have
> been achieved just as effectively, indeed more effectively, by a few men
> lined up as a guard of honour on each side of the way in or out, without
> blocking it at all. I feel forced to the conclusion that at any rate one of the

---

(1) [1965] 3 All E.R. 99 at p. 103.   (2) [1965] 3 All E.R. at pp. 103, 104.
                    (3) [1965] 3 All E.R. at p. 104.

objects designed to be achieved by having the men circling was the effective   A
sealing off of the area occupied by the circle so as to secure that traffic,
particularly vehicular, was brought to a standstill. One of course appreciates what was in the mind of the author (who was not disclosed to me)
of the book of instructions which the appellant possessed in recommending
that pickets should be kept moving; if they were on a public highway, it
made it possible at any rate to argue that they were exercising their ordinary   B
common law right of passing and repassing if they were going to and fro.
But I should myself regard that argument as a thin one: if in fact the men
created a complete blockage of the highway, they could not be said to be
exercising their common law rights merely because the blockage took the
form of a revolving circle."

Accordingly, the recorder held (4) that this action was not justified by s. 2 of the   C
Trade Disputes Act, 1906, and dismissed the appeal.

In my judgment, the proper way to approach this question, and it is a way
which may well have commended itself to the recorder also, is to ask whether
the conduct of the pickets would have been a nuisance at common law as an
unreasonable user of the highway. It seems in my judgment that it clearly
would have been so regarded. One leaves aside for the moment any facilities   D
enjoyed by those acting in furtherance of a trade dispute, and if one imagines
these pickets as carrying banners advertising some patent medicine or advocating
some political reform, it seems to me that their conduct in sealing off a part of
the highway by this moving circle would have been an unreasonable user of the
highway.

In so far as it is a question of fact, the learned recorder took the same view,   E
and has, as I read his judgment, found that it was an unreasonable user of the
highway. Indeed, counsel appearing for the appellant today does not seek to
argue the contrary.

In my judgment, therefore, if one ignores s. 2 of the Trade Disputes Act, 1906,
for the moment and considers the position at common law, this action would
have been an unreasonable use of the highway, admittedly a nuisance, and a   F
police officer would be fully entitled to take action to move the pickets on.

If one can start from that foundation, it seems to me that the sole question
in this case is whether the activity was authorised and made legal by s. 2 (1) of
the Act of 1906. I have not read it yet, but I will read it now:

"(1) It shall be lawful for one or more persons, acting on their own behalf   G
or on behalf of a trade union or of an individual employer or firm in contemplation or furtherance of a trade dispute, to attend at or near a house
or place where a person resides or works or carries on business or happens
to be, if they so attend merely for the purpose of peacefully obtaining or
communicating information, or of peacefully persuading any person to work
or abstain from working."

   H

As counsel for the appellant has suggested, it would seem that the genesis of
that section is the decision of the Court of Appeal in *J. Lyons & Sons* v. *Wilkins*
(5). It is not necessary to take time by looking at that report in detail, but it is
of great interest to see that in that case it was accepted as possible at common law
that watching and besetting a man's house would be a nuisance and a wrongful
act, quite apart from any obstruction of the highway thereby caused. One   I
should not, in my judgment, therefore regard s. 2 as being primarily a highway
section, because there may be many other wrongs which could be committed
by citizens which are now authorised by that section. What in my view, however, one must do is to look carefully at s. 2 and see exactly what it authorises.
It authorises in its simplest terms that a person may attend at or near one of
the places described if he does so merely for the purpose of peacefully obtaining

---

(4) [1965] 3 All E.R. at p. 106.   (5) [1899] 1 Ch. 255.

A or communicating information or of peacefully persuading any person to work or abstain from working.

The recorder has found (6) as a fact that the pickets in this case were not attending merely for the purposes described in the section. He has found as a fact that their object at any rate in part was to seal off the highway and to cause vehicles approaching the premises to stop. In my judgment that finding of fact B is quite enough to require the court to say that as a matter of law the recorder's judgment in this case should be upheld.

Counsel for the appellant, however, submits that a somewhat different test must be applied. He says that s. 2 has put beyond doubt that picketing is a lawful user of the highway, and that as a lawful user of the highway it is not the subject of interference by a constable provided the picket has reasonable regard C for the rights of others. In this case, as I understand him, he says that as the pickets did not in fact cause any actual obstruction to any person, the fact that they were circling in the road had not brought them to the point at which it was proper for the police to interfere. In particular, he says that the police might have properly interfered half an hour later when work people were coming out for their lunch and might be obstructed, but had no right to interfere at the time D when Police Constable O'Hare took action in this case.

For my part I cannot accept that this is a proper approach to the problem. Once one accepts that independently of s. 2 this action was unlawful and a nuisance, the only question left is whether s. 2 by its terms authorises it or not. On the learned recorder's finding (7) s. 2 clearly did not authorise this conduct and it therefore seems to me that this appeal should be dismissed.

E
SACHS, J.: I agree.

LORD PARKER, C.J.: I also agree, and I would only add this in deference to counsel for the appellant's argument that despite the finding here that one of the objects was to ensure that vehicles were brought to a stop, even so, that was permitted, if I may use that term, by s. 2 of the Trade Disputes Act, 1906, F because the rights conferred by that section involve, as he would say, the stopping of a vehicle for the purpose, for instance, of communicating information. Counsel conceded that no right was conferred of stopping a pedestrian, apparently on the basis that you could communicate your information by walking alongside him, but he suggested that when you get to a vehicle the section authorised and permitted the stopping of vehicles. I am quite unable to accept that argument, G and on the findings of the recorder in this case I am quite clear that an offence was committed.

Appeal dismissed.

Solicitors: *W. H. Thompson* (for the appellant); *Cree, Godfrey & Wood*, agents for *R. H. Nicholson, Prosecuting Solicitor*, Liverpool (for the respondent).

H
[*Reported by* Kaushalya Purie, *Barrister-at-Law.*]

I

---

(6) [1965] 3 All E.R. at p. 105.   (7) [1965] 3 All E.R. at p. 106.

SWAN v. SALISBURY CONSTRUCTION CO., LTD.   A

[PRIVY COUNCIL (Lord Morris of Borth-y-Gest, Lord Pearce, and Lord Upjohn),
November 23, 24, 25, 1964, February 1, 1965.]

*Privy Council—Bermuda—Negligence—Res ipsa loquitur—Burden of proof
shifted—Pile-driving operations—Collapse of crane—Injury to servant.*

The appellant, a semi-skilled labourer was employed by the respondents.   B
On Sept. 28, 1959, he was one of a crew of four engaged in pile-driving operations for which process a crane was used. The crane was mounted on a
chassis supported by four wheels. Just before the mid-day break it was
moved to a new position in readiness for driving a new group of piles, and one
pile had been placed vertically. Two of the crew failed to re-appear after the
break, and the appellant was asked to climb up the lead of the crane in order   C
to get the one pile into position under the maul. As the pile was being
hoisted, the crane toppled over throwing the appellant to the ground thereby
causing him serious injury. Examination after the accident revealed a
hole in the ground where previously the right front wheel of the crane had
been standing and that all the bolts connecting the right front wheel of the
crane to the axle had been broken or sheared off. The trial judge found as a   D
fact " that the crane toppled over because the ground suddenly gave way
under the right front wheel ". In an action for damages the appellant claimed
that his injuries resulted from the negligence of the respondents in failing
to provide a safe system of work and effective supervision.

Held: the mere fact that the crane fell did not inevitably entitle the
appellant to succeed, for the respondents were liable only if they were   E
negligent; as, however, cranes did not ordinarily collapse, the principle of res
ipsa loquitur applied, with the consequence that the burden was on the
respondents to prove that they had not been negligent; they had satisfied
the trial judge that there was no negligence on their part, and, as his conclusion was not based on any error in law there was no reason to interfere
with his finding (see p. 143, letter F, and p. 144, letter A, post).   F

Dictum of LORD SIMONDS in *Woods* v. *Duncan* ([1946] A.C. at p. 439)
and dicta of LORD PORTER and LORD NORMAND in *Barkway* v. *South Wales
Transport Co., Ltd.* ([1950] 1 All E.R. at pp. 394, 399) applied.

Appeal dismissed.

Cases referred to:
> *Barkway* v. *South Wales Transport Co., Ltd.*, [1950] 1 All E.R. 392; [1950]   G
> A.C. 185; 114 J.P. 172; 36 Digest (Repl.) 144, 764.
> *Woods* v. *Duncan, Duncan* v. *Hambrook, Duncan* v. *Cammell Laird & Co., Ltd.*,
> [1946] 1 All E.R. 420, n.; [1946] A.C. 401; [1947] L.J.R. 120; 174
> L.T. 286; 36 Digest (Repl.) 52, 286.

Appeal.   H
This was an appeal in forma pauperis by special leave from a judgment and
order of the Supreme Court of Bermuda (SMITH, A.J.) dated June 10, 1963, whereby an action brought by the appellant, Sinclair Eugene Swan, against the respondents, Salisbury Construction Co., Ltd., his employers, claiming damages for
breach of contract and negligence arising out of an accident to the appellant on
Sept. 28, 1959, during the course of his employment, was dismissed with costs.   I
The facts are set out in the judgment of the Board.

S. C. Silkin, Q.C., J. A. Baker and *E. Cotran* for the appellant.
Martin Jukes, Q.C., and *A. K. Allen* for the respondents.

LORD MORRIS OF BORTH-Y-GEST: This is an appeal in forma
pauperis, by special leave, from a judgment and order (dated June 10, 1963),
of the Supreme Court of Bermuda (SMITH, A.J.) whereby the claim of the appellant
against the respondents was dismissed. The appellant was employed by the

A respondents and on Sept. 28, 1959, he suffered injuries owing to the collapse of a
crane on which he was working. By a writ issued on Oct. 31, 1962, he brought
an action claiming that his injuries resulted from the negligence of the respondents
in failing to provide a safe system of work and effective supervision.

At the time of the accident the respondent were driving piles for the foundations
of a warehouse on a site in Pembroke. The piles (in groups of three) were to be

B driven into the ground to depths varying from fourteen to twenty-seven feet
and a crane was used for the process. The crane was capable of lifting five tons
with the boom swung out to a radius of ten feet. It was mounted on a chassis
supported by four wheels. Each wheel had double tyres. The boom was about
thirty-five feet long. The lead for driving the piles was about twenty-six feet
long and consisted of a three-sided frame with a heavy maul. The total weight of

C the lead and maul was about three tons. The piles were up to thirty feet long and
weighed approximately three-quarters of a ton.

The method of pile driving was as follows. The crane was moved or manoeuvred
near to the point where a pile was to be driven and the lead (with the maul on it)
was then lifted to a vertical position but with its main weight resting on the
ground. By the use of a second wire which was attached to the upper end of a

D pile the pile was then lifted to a vertical position with its lower (and pointed)
end resting on the ground at the point on the ground into which it was to be driven.
At that stage one man of the crew engaged in the process climbed up the lead.
The lead with the man on it, was then hoisted to such height as would bring the
maul above the top of the pile. The man then manoeuvred the pile into the slot
of the lead after which he inserted bolts across the open side of the lead. So that

E pile driving could thereafter take place he disconnected the wire from the top
of the pile and connected it to the top of the maul. He then made his way down to
the ground. Pile-driving then commenced.

Pile-driving had taken place at the site for some days before the date of the
accident. About twelve piles had been driven during those days. On Sept. 28,
1959, further pile-driving took place. The work in the morning was done by a

F crew consisting of four people. One was the foreman Correia, another was the
crane-driver, Philpott, and the remaining two (of whom the appellant was one)
were labourers. Three piles were driven during the morning. Just before the
mid-day break the crane was moved to a new position in readiness for the driving
of a further group of piles and before work stopped the lead was brought into
position for the first pile of the new group and that pile was lifted up to a vertical

G position with its lower end resting on the ground at the point into which it was to
be driven. When the mid-day break ended and the time came for work to be
resumed the crane-driver (Philpott) and the second labourer did not re-appear.
Only Correia (the foreman) and the appellant were present. Correia was an
experienced and competent crane operator and was recognised by the appellant
to possess skill superior to that of Philpott. As the crane and the lead and the

H one pile had been positioned before the mid-day break in readiness for the driving
of the pile Correia decided that the best plan was that he and the appellant should
proceed to drive that one pile but should not thereafter (in the absence of the other
two) continue with pile-driving operations. Correia took charge of the crane and
he asked the appellant to climb up the lead in order to get the pile into position
under the maul. The appellant had not previously undertaken that part of the

I work involved in the pile-driving process. After the appellant had climbed up
the lead it was hoisted by the crane. After it had been hoisted up some distance
the crane began to " shake " or to " tremble ". It was Correia's opinion that the
boom was then extending to a radius of about ten feet. Correia's evidence was
that the right front wheel sank with a sudden drop into the ground, that the
crane vibrated and that the boom and lead swayed over to the right. He called
out to the appellant to jump. The appellant however did not hear him. Thereafter
the crane veered to the side and toppled over on to the ground. The appellant
who was on the lead was brought to the ground and received injury.

Examination after the accident revealed two important facts. One was that A
at the spot where previously the right front wheel of the crane had been standing
there was after the accident a hole in the ground. It was about eleven inches deep
according to Mr. Diel a director of the respondents who was called to the scene:
according to Correia it was some twelve to eighteen inches deep. The other fact
was that it was found that all the bolts connecting the right front wheel of the
crane to the axle had been broken or sheared off.   B

In his action the appellant's claim for damages was based on allegations that
the respondents (his employers) had in five ways failed to provide a safe system
of work and effective supervision. They may be summarised as follows:

(i) in not ensuring the stability of the crane in relation to the nature of the
operation and of the surface of the ground,

(ii) in not providing a sufficient number of workmen including one to give   C
signals to the crane operator,

(iii) in not providing means to ascertain the degree to which the jib (or
boom) of the crane could be safely extended having regard to the weight being
carried,

(iv) in extending the jib (or boom) excessively, and

(v) in not taking proper precaution for the safety of the appellant.   D

Having in mind some of the submissions advanced on appeal to their lordships'
Board it is necessary to refer briefly to the course of the trial. Apart from evidence
relating to the injuries sustained by the appellant and evidence relating to his
financial loss there was the evidence of the appellant himself and there was the
evidence, called on his behalf, of a linesman named Trott, who was working nearby
and who saw the crane falling, and of a labourer named Fough, whose work was   E
that of digging preparatory holes into which the piles could be inserted and who
also saw the crane falling. The evidence called on behalf of the respondents was
that of Mr. Diel the director (who had twenty-six years' experience in construction
work) and that of Correia. The trial took place in March, 1963. The evidence on
behalf of the appellant was given on Mar. 25 and 26: the evidence on behalf of
the respondents was given on Mar. 26 and 29. The judge gave judgment on   F
June 10, 1963.

Certain defences pleaded in the respondents' defence (that the appellant
voluntarily ran a risk, that the accident was an inevitable one, that the appellant
was negligent in a manner contributing to the accident) were either abandoned
at the trial or were negatived by the judge and need not be further mentioned or
considered. The respondents also pleaded that the cause of the accident was   G
that the ground under one of the wheels of the crane gave way. They averred
that they

" had no reason to suspect that the ground which gave way under the said
wheel would in fact give way and further that normal and reasonable inspection and precautions pertaining to the site of operation of this kind did not
reveal the existing condition of the ground under the said wheel."   H

Their lordships think that it is important to observe that it would appear that
all the available evidence in regard to the occurrence was placed before the court
and all the theories, surmises and suggestions which either party wished to advance
were apparently put forward. In a very careful judgment the judge examined
the evidence in order to arrive at a conclusion as to the cause of the collapse of   I
the crane. Having come to a conclusion on that matter he then proceeded to
consider whether the respondents had been negligent.

In investigating the cause of the collapse of the crane the judge considered a
number of possible causes. The collapse could have resulted from extending the
boom further than it should have been extended having regard to the weight that
was being lifted. On the evidence that he accepted, the judge ruled out that possible cause. Likewise he ruled out as a possible cause that Correia had started the
lift too quickly and had applied a jerking force to the crane. These findings were

A   essentially findings of fact. They were not challenged on appeal. Two other possible causes were examined and having regard to the argument before their lordships it is necessary to state them. One was " that some part of the mounting of the crane was too weak and gave way under the strain of the lift ". The other was " that the ground under the wheels was not sufficiently solid and gave way under the weight of the lift ". The judge ruled out the first of these two. In doing

B   so he referred to the evidence that the bolts securing the wheel to its mounting on the axle had all sheared off. He accepted the view, which Mr. Diel had put forward, that the shearing off of the bolts was caused by the sudden dropping of the wheel into the hole. That view was supported by the fact that the bolts had all been broken off together. He rejected the view that the wheel had been broken off by a twisting force as the crane toppled over: had that been what had happened

C   the expectation would have been that the bolts would have been broken off unevenly. In dealing with this matter the judge said that he had no evidence from any disinterested witness as to the condition of the bolts " to contradict or correct Mr. Diel's evidence, nor was there any evidence suggesting that the bolts had become weakened or loosened by wear or neglect before the accident ". On behalf of the appellant this passage in the judgment was criticised. It was sub-

D   mitted that, as the collapse of a crane is something that should not happen, it was for the respondents to explain the occurrence and to show that the cause of the collapse, if ascertained, did not involve any negligence on their part. It was submitted that the respondents should have called positive evidence to establish that the bolts had been properly maintained and had not, before the accident, been in a weak state and had not been neglected. It was submitted that in the

E   words quoted above the judge was placing an onus on the appellant which properly fell on the respondents. Their lordships consider that when read in their full context the words of the judge do not show error of approach. The respondents were at the trial calling evidence to explain what had happened. Mr. Diel gave his views and they were subject to testing by cross-examination. His view was that the ground under the wheel gave way and that in consequence the wheel suddenly

F   dropped and that as a result the bolts securing the wheel to its mounting on the axle sheared off. It was implicit in his evidence that the sudden dropping of the wheel was the only reason why the bolts sheared off. The judge was saying no more than that there was no evidence which contradicted or corrected the evidence of Mr. Diel. In the result the judge rejected the view " that some part of the mounting of the crane was too weak and gave way under the strain of the lift ",

G   and he came to the conclusion " that the crane toppled over because the ground suddenly gave way under the right front wheel ". It seems clear that he was deciding that that was the cause, and the only cause, of the accident.

That cause being established it was undoubtedly for the respondents to absolve themselves from liability. The crane was under their control and it was their duty to take all reasonable care to ensure the safety of the appellant (whom they re-

H   quired to mount the boom of the crane) and to avoid subjecting him to unnecessary risks. There was clearly a duty in the respondents to take all reasonable care to see that the crane was not positioned on insecure and unstable ground. There was an onus on them at the trial to show that they had taken all such proper and reasonable care. Had the judge been of the opinion that they had not discharged the onus his decision would doubtless have been difficult to attack.

I   There was much evidence on this issue (which their lordships need not fully state) which might have led the judge either to conclude that the respondents had been negligent or to conclude that they had not. The site where the pile-driving was taking place was on the fringes of Pembroke Marsh. Some years previously the site had been filled by the dumping of rubble on it. There was evidence that the place was muddy and marshy. The ground was soft in some places though hard in others. There was water at a depth of about three feet six inches below the surface. The very circumstance that piles were being driven in order to make it possible to erect a building was an indication that the site could not or might

not sustain much weight. All these considerations were present to the mind of the A
judge. There was evidence however that the respondents had given thought to the
question whether the ground was sufficiently solid for the operation of the crane
without having extra supports, such as planks, under the wheels. Before the work
commenced on the site both Mr. Diel and Correia had inspected it. Before
Sept. 28 twelve piles had been driven without incident. During the morning of
Sept. 28 three piles had been driven. The crane had then been moved to a new B
position which was on a roadway which trucks had made across the site. Before
the mid-day break the crane had lifted the lead and pile into position. The judge
said in his judgment

    " in the light of all this was it reasonable to anticipate that there might
    still be some danger of the ground giving way and that extra precautions
    should be taken to guard against it? In my opinion the answer to this ques- C
    tion is no."

Their lordships are not able to say that this conclusion cannot stand. The
respondents had shown to the satisfaction of the judge, or on an examination
of the whole of the evidence he was satisfied, that they had not failed to take
reasonable care.   D
    In the submissions presented to their lordships on behalf of the appellant it
was said that the judge had ignored the principles which are summarised in the
phrase " res ipsa loquitur ". It was urged that in the circumstances of the case
a burden lay on the respondents to show either that they had not in any potentially
relevant way been negligent or that the accident was due to a specific cause which
did not involve negligence. If the view was accepted that the ground gave way E
and that the bolts sheared when the wheel jolted into the bottom of the hole,
even then, so the argument ran, it was for the respondents positively to prove that
the bolts were in good condition and had been well maintained : the bolts may
have been neglected and may have been in bad condition : had they been in good
condition they might not have been sheared off : if they had not been sheared off
the crane might not have collapsed : the respondents had not shown that the F
crane would be liable to topple over simply because one wheel fell into a place
where the ground gave way and had not shown that there would have been a
collapse whether the bolts had been sheared off or not. Hence it was argued that
in the absence of evidence that the bolts had been properly inspected and properly
maintained the respondents had failed to show that the collapse of the crane had
taken place without any failure of due care on their part. Because the appellant G
had specified certain particulars of negligence the judge, so the argument continued, had fallen into the error of failing to require the respondents to show that
they had taken all due care.
    These submissions, skilfully developed and presented, seem to involve a greater
concentration on some parts of the evidence and on some lines of enquiry than was
directed to them by the appellant at the trial. As cranes ought not to collapse, it H
was essential for the respondents to explain why the collapse occurred on Sept. 28
if they were to absolve themselves from those indications of negligence which
could arise from the very fact of the occurrence itself. It was therefore necessary
for the respondents to deal not only with any specific allegations of negligence
which the appellant formulated against them, but also to show that they were not
otherwise at fault. The evidence that they adduced was, however, subject to all I
such testing and probing as the appellant desired. When therefore Mr. Diel
gave evidence to the effect that the front wheel of the crane sank into the ground
and that the bolts broke as a result of the jolt, it was open to the appellant to
suggest that the breaking of the bolts was not solely due to the sudden jolt but
was at least partly due to some poor condition which existed because they had
not been properly looked after. Mr. Diel could have given his views in regard to
the suggestion. It would seem however that the bolts received more attention
in the argument on appeal than at the trial. As their lordships have earlier

A   stated the evidence of Mr. Diel, unless challenged and unless wholly or partly rejected, can fairly be regarded as stating that the sudden dropping of the wheel was the only reason why the bolts sheared off. In the result on evidence which he was entitled to accept the judge decided that the real cause of the accident was that the ground gave way under the right front wheel. As this conclusion was not reached as the result of any wrong approach, their lordships are unable to

B   accept the submissions advanced on behalf of the appellant which they have indicated.

Their lordships have likewise been unable to accept certain additional contentions which were advanced. It was contended that the work ought not to have been continued after the mid-day break on Sept. 28 in the absence of a full crew. A consideration of the evidence shows, however, that having regard to the

C   limited work that was to be undertaken it was legitimate for Correia to proceed as he did. Further it was contended that there should have been a third man on the ground to give to the crane operator early warning of any signs of instability. Their lordships can see no error in that part of the judgment in which the judge gave his reasons for rejecting this contention.

Criticism was made of the following sentences in the judgment:

D   " The onus lies on [the appellant] to establish a balance of probability that he sustained his injuries as a result of some failure of duty by his employer to take proper precautions for his safety. The fact that the crane toppled over speaks for itself up to a point: but this by itself is not sufficient. Taking the evidence as a whole I am not satisfied that [the appellant] has proved that he was injured as the result of any failure in the duty which his employer owed

E   to him and give judgment for [the respondents]."

When read in their context the words of the judge do not reveal error. They occur almost at the end of a long judgment in which the issues had been fully and minutely examined and conclusions clearly expressed. The appellant as plaintiff had to prove his case, but once he had proved that he was injured by the collapse of the crane he was well on the way to proving it. Res ipsa loquitur. The mere

F   fact that the crane fell did not however establish that the case must inevitably succeed for the respondents were only liable if they were negligent. As however cranes do not ordinarily collapse a prima facie case was made out against the respondents and the burden was on them to show that they had not been negligent. As LORD SIMONDS said in Woods v. Duncan (1):

G   " But to apply this principle [of res ipsa loquitur] is to do no more than to shift the burden of proof. A prima facie case is assumed to be made out which throws upon him [that is a defendant] the task of proving that he was not negligent."

So also in Barkway v. South Wales Transport Co., Ltd. (2), LORD PORTER in speaking of the maxim res ipsa loquitur said (3):

H   " The doctrine is dependent on the absence of explanation, and, although it is the duty of the defendants, if they desire to protect themselves, to give an adequate explanation of the cause of the accident, yet, if the facts are sufficiently known, the question ceases to be one where the facts speak for themselves, and the solution is to be found by determining whether, on the facts as established, negligence is to be inferred or not "

I   and LORD NORMAND said (4):

" The maxim is no more than a rule of evidence affecting onus. It is based on commonsense, and its purpose is to enable justice to be done when the facts bearing on causation and on the care exercised by the defendant are at the outset unknown to the plaintiff and are or ought to be within the knowledge of the defendant."

(1) [1946] A.C. 401 at p. 439.   (2) [1950] 1 All E.R. 392; [1950] A.C. 185.
(3) [1950] 1 All E.R. at pp. 394, 395.   (4) [1950] 1 All E.R. at p. 399.

In his judgment the judge recorded a conclusion as to the cause of the collapse A
of the crane, and decided on the evidence that such cause did not connote
negligence on the part of the respondents.

In their lordships' view the main issue which arose in the case was whether
the respondents showed that they had taken all due and reasonable care in the
positioning of the crane. The judge held that they had. His conclusion on this
difficult matter was a conclusion of fact and was not based on any error in law. B
However sympathetic they may be for the appellant their lordships are unable
to interfere with it. Accordingly their lordships will humbly advise Her Majesty
that the appeal should be dismissed.

Appeal dismissed.

Solicitors: *Hatchett Jones & Co.* (for the appellant); *Pothecary & Barratt* (for C
the respondent).

[*Reported by* KATHLEEN J. H. O'BRIEN, *Barrister-at-Law.*]

D

E

PRACTICE NOTE.

*Divorce—Petition—Form of petition—Child of the family—Requirements not
changed by Matrimonial Causes Act 1965—Martimonial Causes Rules, 1957
(S.I. 1957 No. 619, as amended by S.I. 1958 No. 2082 and S.I. 1965 No.* F
2137), r. 4 (1) (c), (cc) and (ccc).

The form of a petition is still governed by the wording of the Matrimonial
Causes Rules, 1957. The phrase " child of the family " is there defined (1) " in
relation to any proceedings " and the requirements of r. 4 (1) (c), r. 4 (1) (cc) and
r. 4 (1) (ccc) remain (2) unchanged by the passing of the Matrimonial Causes
Act 1965. There is no present intention of amending the Rules on this point. G

It is to be observed that the phrase " relevant children " used in the Matrimonial Causes Act 1965 is defined in the Act merely for the purposes of that
Act.

COMPTON MILLER,
Mar. 31, 1966.   Senior Registrar.
                                                                        H

I

---

(1) By r. 1 (3) of the Matrimonial Causes Rules, 1957, as amended by S.I. 1958 No. 2082.
(2) Paragraph (c) of r. 4 (1) and the original para. (cc) were inserted by S.I. 1958
No. 2082. By S.I. 1965 No. 2137, which came into force on Jan. 11, 1966, a new para.
(cc) was inserted after para. (c) and the original para. (cc) became para. (ccc).

A

NOTE.

B. *v.* ATTORNEY-GENERAL (B. AND OTHERS INTERVENING).

[PROBATE, DIVORCE AND ADMIRALTY DIVISION (Ormrod, J.), November 18, 1965.]

B   *Legitimacy—Jurisdiction—Declaration of illegitimacy on cross-prayer—Blood test evidence—Matrimonial Causes Act,* 1950 (14 *Geo.* 6 *c.* 25), *s.* 17.

[**Editorial Note.** Section 17 of the Matrimonial Causes Act, 1950, as amended, is superseded by s. 39 of the Matrimonial Causes Act 1965.

As to decrees on application for declarations of legitimacy, see 3 HALSBURY'S LAWS (3rd Edn.) 103, para. 158; and for cases on the subject, see 3 DIGEST

C   (Repl.) 415-417, *136-158.*

For the Matrimonial Causes Act, 1950, s. 17, see 29 HALSBURY'S STATUTES (2nd Edn.) 403.]

Cases referred to:

FitzWilliam v. *A.-G.,* (1951), " The Times ", Mar. 15.

Starkowski (*otherwise Urbanski*) (*otherwise Juszczkiewicz*) (*by his next friend*)

D   v. *A.-G.* (*Starkowski cited*), [1952] 1 All E.R. 495; [1952] P. 135; *affd.* C.A., [1952] 2 All E.R. 616; [1952] P. 302; *affd.* H.L., [1953] 2 All E.R. 1272; [1954] A.C. 155; [1953] 3 W.L.R. 942; Digest (Cont. Vol. A) 236, *966.*

Petition.

This was a petition by J.L.B. for a declaration of legitimacy. The respondent

E   was the Attorney-General and there were four interveners. The first intervener was N.E.B., who would be the petitioner's father if the petition were to succeed, and the three other interveners were children of N.E.B., all of whom were interested under a settlement under which the petitioner, if he were the legitimate child of N.E.B., would also be entitled to share. The interveners, by their answer, cross-prayed for a declaration that the petitioner was not the legitimate

F   child of N.E.B.

E. R. Moulton-Barrett for the petitioner.

C. J. S. French for the Attorney-General.

R. J. A. Temple, Q.C., and *D. R. Ellison* for the interveners.

Bruce Holroyd Pearce for the trustees.

G   **ORMROD, J.:** The matter is not now contested before me, because as a result of evidence which came to light in July, 1965, the petitioner recognises that he cannot now continue to petition for a declaration that he is the legitimate son of N.E.B. It is, perhaps, a case which illustrates very clearly the extraordinary advantages and immense value of blood tests properly and fully carried out to determine issues of paternity of this kind (1). It is fortunate in this case

H   that the blood groups of N.E.B. and the petitioner are in one respect, into which I need not go into detail, entirely inconsistent, and it is therefore possible for the doctor who ascertained the blood groups to say very positively that the one could not be the son of the other. That brings to an end a mass of litigation and saves the court having to rely on presumptions in order to help out with the evidence which would otherwise be called. The petitioner, in effect, discontinues

I   the suit, although, to put it formally, counsel for the petitioner simply calls no evidence.

In the answer filed on behalf of the interveners there is a cross-prayer for a declaration that the petitioner is not the legitimate child of N.E.B., and it was by the consent of all parties, despite the fact that the petitioner is not proceeding with the allegation of his prayer, that I heard the evidence. I am still doubtful, very doubtful, whether there is jurisdiction in these circumstances to entertain the cross-prayer; I am doubtful, indeed, whether there is jurisdiction

---

(1) Compare [1966] 1 All E.R. 356, letters H and I. See also p. 147, post.

to entertain cross-prayers at all in proceedings for a declaration of legitimacy. **A** I suspect that the correct order in this situation is simply to dismiss the petition. That, in substance, is the order which was made in *Fitzwilliam* v. *A.-G.* (2), at which I have had the advantage of looking because counsel for the petitioner bespoke the file in that case; for my part I think that that is the right order to draw up. I am prepared to say in my judgment that I find as a fact that the petitioner is not the child of N.E.B., and as a judicial determination of fact I **B** trust that that will be good enough, but I am not prepared at present to go further and make a declaration in the terms of the prayer in the interveners' answer. I know that the reports of *Starkowski* (*orse. Urbanski*) (*orse. Juszczkie-wicz*) v. *A.-G.* (*Starkowski cited*) (3) suggests that BARNARD, J., made such an order; but the proper order in this case, in my judgment, is merely to hold that the petitioner has not proved the contents of his petition. My judgment has just **C** the same effect.

[HIS LORDSHIP then turned to the question of costs.]

Petition dismissed.

Solicitors: *Clarke & Mostyn* (for the petitioner); *Treasury Solicitor; Winter & Co.* (for the interveners); *Freshfields* (for the trustees). **D**

[*Reported by* ALICE BLOOMFIELD, *Barrister-at-Law.*]

E

PRACTICE DIRECTION.

F

CHANCERY DIVISION (COMPANIES COURT).

Company—Reduction of Capital—Petition—Evidence—Shares issued for a consideration other than cash.

The evidence in support of a petition to confirm a reduction of capital need not in future show as regards any issue of shares made since 1900 for a considera- **G** tion other than cash that the statutory requirements as to registration were complied with. Henceforth it will be sufficient to state in the petition the extent to which any issued shares (other than shares issued otherwise than for cash before 1901) are or are deemed to be paid up.

The existing practice will remain unaltered in respect of issues of shares otherwise than for cash made before 1901 whilst s. 25 of the Companies Act, 1867, **H** remained in operation.

MAURICE BERKELEY,
Apr. 5, 1966.   Registrar.

I

---

(2) (1951), "The Times", Mar. 15.
(3) [1952] 1 All E.R. 495, see at p. 501, letter B; [1952] P. 135, see at p. 148. The court subsequently checked the file in *Starkowski*, and found that a declaration of illegitimacy was made.

A   *NOTE.*

STOCKER (by his next friend) *v.* STOCKER (otherwise WOODRUFF, by her guardian).

[PROBATE, DIVORCE AND ADMIRALTY DIVISION (Karminski, J.), January 28,
B   1966.]

*Nullity—Pregnancy at date of marriage by person other than petitioner—Blood
tests—Haptoglobin tests.*

[As to marriages voidable for pregnancy at date of marriage by person other
than petitioner, see 12 HALSBURY'S LAWS (3rd Edn.) 225, 226, para. 421, notes
C   (c)-(f); and for cases on the subject, see 27 DIGEST (Repl.) 282, *2265-2267.*]

Petition.

This was a petition by the husband for a decree of nullity on the grounds that
at the time of the marriage the wife (i) was pregnant by some person other than
the husband, and (ii) was subject to recurrent attacks of epilepsy.

The parties met on Apr. 13, 1963, and within a fortnight of meeting were
D having regular sexual intercourse together. The husband took the precaution
of wearing a contraceptive sheath on all occasions. He thought that perhaps
both by what she said and by her own general demeanour to intercourse that he
was not the first man whom she had known carnally, but he was not very critical of
her in that respect. Towards the end of June, 1963, the wife moved to another
part of the country. The parties kept in touch, mostly by letter, and at about
E that time the wife told the husband that she had missed a period and suspected
that she was pregnant. The husband genuinely thought that he was the father
of the expected child, and on that assumption he thought it proper to marry
the wife; but he was anyhow in love with her and would have liked to marry
her in due course. The marriage took place on Aug. 3, 1963. With regard to
the allegation of epilepsy, the trial judge found as a fact that, at the time of the
F marriage the wife was suffering from recurrent attacks of epilepsy, but that
at that time the husband was ignorant of that fact. The report deals only
with the question of pregnancy.

Margaret Puxon for the husband.
The wife did not appear and was not represented.

G   **KARMINSKI, J.,** in the course of his judgment said: The husband undoubtedly had intercourse with the wife for some time before the marriage,
beginning towards the end of April, 1963. Dr. Hope Gill saw the wife, who was
brought by the husband's mother, on Aug. 7, 1963, and on the information
she gave he was in no doubt that she was pregnant. She gave as her last period
Apr. 21, 1963; accepting that date, the doctor decided that her expected time
H of delivery would be towards the end of January, 1964. In September, 1963,
however, he saw the wife again on a number of occasions and on Oct. 2 he
examined the wife for her pregnancy and thought then that she was thirty
weeks pregnant. She had some tests done at the local hospital which confirmed
that view, but the doctor had already communicated his doubts to the husband's
mother with the result that, on Sept. 18, 1963, she went to see the husband's
I present solicitors and the husband himself saw the solicitors on Sept. 28. The
child was born, as we know from the birth certificate which has been proved
as having been signed by the wife, on Dec. 11, 1963, at Hitchin; the child weighed
over seven pounds at birth, and on the evidence of Dr. Hope Gill it is clear that
the child was full time and not premature. I have no doubt at all on the medical
evidence that this child must have been conceived at a time before the husband
and the wife had ever met each other, that is before Apr. 13, 1963. On that
finding, the child cannot have been the child of the husband. That finding was
reinforced, however, by very important evidence by Dr. Grant on the subject of

blood tests.   Dr. Grant is a well known authority in this field, and amongst   A
other qualifications he is a lecturer in forensic serology at Guy's Hospital, and
he has often given evidence on these matters in these courts.   What I may call
the ordinary tests (1), which were performed by taking blood samples from the
husband, the wife and the baby, did not exclude the husband as the father;
nor, as Dr. Grant explained, did it exclude about sixty per cent. of the male
population of these islands; he used a new, or comparatively new, test, which   B
deals with haptoglobin, which in Dr. Grant's view is very nearly infallible.
This is a comparatively recent development in medical science, originating at the
University of Copenhagen.   It seems to have been accepted by the scientific
world and, indeed, by forensic medical science and the courts of Denmark as a
standard test—though I confess that it is new to me.   Dr. Grant established to
my complete satisfaction on the haptoglobin tests that the husband could not   C
have been the father of this child, so that I am satisfied beyond any doubt that,
at the time of the marriage, the wife was pregnant by some person other than
the husband.

I now come to apply the tests demanded by s. 9 (2) of the Matrimonial Causes
Act 1965, (2).   The court has to be satisfied that, at the time of the marriage,
the husband was ignorant of the fact that the wife was pregnant by another man.   D
I am perfectly satisfied that the husband was.   He believed, and reasonably
believed on the facts as he knew them, that he was the father of the child that
was expected, and he believed that because the wife told him so.   He told the
doctor that the child was expected at a time which was consistent with the
intercourse between the husband and the wife before marriage.   So that, as in
the case of the epilepsy, I am satisfied that the husband has established that he   E
was ignorant at the time of the marriage of the facts alleged concerning her
pregnancy.   The proceedings were instituted within a year of the marriage.
The marriage was celebrated on Aug. 3, 1963, and the petition was presented on
Feb. 26, 1964; in other words very well within the twelve months.

I now come to perhaps the more difficult part of s. 9 (2) (c), namely, that marital
intercourse with the consent of the petitioner has not taken place since the   F
petitioner discovered the existence of the grounds for a decree.   The intercourse,
I am satisfied, finished on Sept. 7 or 8, 1963.   By that time the husband began
to have doubts as to the paternity of the child, but the matter was no more than
a vague suspicion indeed until the mother, having obtained some information
from the doctor, saw the solicitors on Sept. 18, 1963, and those doubts were
further consolidated when the husband saw the solicitors on Sept. 28; all doubts   G
were removed by October, when Dr. Hope Gill established that the child was
likely to be born a great deal earlier than had been previously estimated.   I find
as a fact that no intercourse took place after the husband discovered that the
wife was pregnant by a man other than himself; and that, for the purposes of
this case, disposes of the matter.

Decree of nullity.   H

Solicitors: *Lovell, Son & Pitfield*, agents for *Oglethorpe & Anderson*, Petworth
(for the husband).

[*Reported by* ALICE BLOOMFIELD, *Barrister-at-Law.*]

---

(1) Cf., e.g., p. 145, ante.
(2) Section 9, so far as relevant, provides: " (1) In addition to any other grounds
on which a marriage is by law void or voidable, a marriage shall, subject to the next
following subsection, be voidable on the ground . . . (d) that the respondent was at the
time of the marriage pregnant by some person other than the petitioner.   (2) The court
shall not grant a decree of nullity in a case falling within para. . . . (d) of the foregoing
subsection unless it is satisfied that—(a) the petitioner was at the time of the marriage
ignorant of the facts alleged; and (b) proceedings were instituted within a year from the
date of the marriage; and (c) marital intercourse with the consent of the petitioner
has not taken place since the petitioner discovered the existence of the grounds for a
decree.

A

Re KILPATRICK'S POLICIES TRUSTS.
KILPATRICK AND ANOTHER *v.* INLAND REVENUE COMMISSIONERS.

[COURT OF APPEAL (Lord Denning, M.R., Diplock and Russell, L.JJ.), February
B   14, 15, 16, March 16, 1966.]

*Estate Duty—Passing of property—Property deemed to pass—Policies of assurance
—Policies effected for benefit of assured's wife if she should survive him
for more than one month—Single premium policies effected under Married
Women's Property Act, 1882, s. 11—Interests provided by assured—Wife
survived assured by more than one month—Whether beneficial interest in*
C   *policies arose on assured's death—Change from defeasible to indefeasible
interest at end of month—No difference in value of interest before and after
change—Whether interest in expectancy could include an interest, whether
defeasible or not, in possession—Finance Act, 1894 (57 & 58 Vict. c. 30),
s. 2 (1) (d), s. 22 (1) (l)—Finance Act, 1934 (24 & 25 Geo. 5 c. 32), s. 28.*

In 1952 K. effected fourteen single premium policies on his life, each under
D   s. 11 of the Married Women's Property Act, 1882, for the benefit of Mrs. K.
if she should survive him for more than one month. If she did not so survive
him, the policies were to be for the benefit of K.'s two sons in equal shares.
The trusts declared were trusts of the policies, not merely of the moneys to
arise from them. There were powers under which the trustees would not be
obliged to retain the policies in specie, but they might be sold or surrendered
E   or money might be raised on them, with the consequence that the trust fund
might come to consist of income-producing securities. K. died in October,
1961. All the policies were subsisting at his death and an aggregate sum of
£66,638 19s. 2d. became payable thereunder. Mrs. K. was living at the
expiration of one month from his death. The Crown claimed estate duty on
the policies or their proceeds under s. 2 (1) (d)* of the Finance Act, 1894, as
F   affected by s. 28† of the Finance Act, 1934.

Held: no estate duty became payable on the death of K. in respect of the
policy moneys because—
(i) in 1952 Mrs. K. acquired in each policy a vested interest in possession
subject to being divested, with the consequence that no beneficial interest
accrued or arose on K.'s death (see p. 152, letters A and F, p. 154, letters
G   F and H, and p. 156, letter E, post).
Phipps v. *Akers* ((1842), 9 Cl. & Fin. 583) and *Westminster Bank, Ltd.* v.
Inland Revenue Comrs., Wrightson v. *Inland Revenue Comrs.* ([1957] 2 All
E.R. 745) applied.
Re Heath, Public Trustee v. *Heath* ([1935] All E.R. Rep. 677) approved.
(ii) a beneficial interest which was vested but defeasible was not an
H   " interest in expectancy " within s. 28 of the Finance Act, 1934, where that
term bore its ordinary technical meaning, and thus the value of Mrs. K.'s
interest in the policies prior to K.'s death was not required by s. 28 to be
ignored in computing the value of the interest that became indefeasible one
month after his death, viz., at a period ascertainable by reference to K.'s
death within s. 22 (1) (l) of the Act of 1894; accordingly, even if the change
I   from defeasibility to indefeasibility had rendered s. 2 (1) (d) of the Act of
1894 applicable, yet the value of what was deemed to pass would be nil (see
p. 153, letter E, p. 155, letters D and F, and p. 156, letter G, post).
A.-G. v. *Adamson* ([1932] All E.R. Rep. 159) considered.
Decision of CROSS, J. ([1965] 2 All E.R. 673) affirmed.

[As to estate duty on policy moneys and interests arising on death, see 15

---

* Section 2 (1) (d), so far as material, is set out at p. 151, letter B, post.
† Section 28, so far as material, is set out at p. 151, letter D, post.

HALSBURY'S LAWS (3rd Edn.) 25, 26, para. 47; and for cases on the subject, see A
21 DIGEST (Repl.) 13-15, *42-49*; 34-37, *125-138*.
    For the Finance Act, 1894, s. 2 (1) (*d*) and s. 22 (1) (*l*), see 9 HALSBURY'S
STATUTES (2nd Edn.) 350, 383.
    For the Finance Act, 1934, s. 28, see 9 HALSBURY'S STATUTES (2nd Edn.) 453.]
Cases referred to:
    A.-G. v. *Adamson*, [1932] All E.R. Rep. 159; 148 L.T. 365; sub nom. *Adamson* B
        v. *A.-G.*, [1933] A.C. 257; 102 L.J.K.B. 129; 21 Digest (Repl.) 31, *115*.
    Childs Trustee Co. v. *Inland Revenue Comrs.*, [1960] 2 All E.R. 209; [1960]
        Ch. 534; [1960] 2 W.L.R. 903; 21 Digest (Repl.) 37, *137*.
    D'Avigdor-Goldsmid v. *Inland Revenue Comrs.*, [1953] 1 All E.R. 403; [1953]
        A.C. 347; [1953] 2 W.L.R. 372; 21 Digest (Repl.) 14, *45*.
    Heath, Re, Public Trustee v. *Heath*, [1935] All E.R. Rep. 677; [1936] Ch. 259; C
        105 L.J.Ch. 29; 154 L.T. 536; Digest Supp.
    McGredy and McGredy's Trustees v. *Inland Revenue Comrs.*, [1951] N.I. 155;
        32 Tax Cas. 338; 28 Digest (Repl.) 409, **933*.
    Phipps v. *Akers*, (1842), 9 Cl. & Fin. 583; 4 Man. & G. 1107; 134 E.R. 453;
        44 Digest 1044, *8993*.
    Westminster Bank, Ltd. v. *Inland Revenue Comrs., Wrightson* v. *Inland Revenue* D
        Comrs., [1957] 2 All E.R. 745; [1958] A.C. 210; [1957] 3 W.L.R. 427;
        21 Digest (Repl.) 15, *47, 48*.

Appeal.
    This was an appeal by the Crown from an order of CROSS, J., dated May 11,
1965 (reported [1965] 2 All E.R. 673) on an application by the plaintiffs, Stewart E
Kilpatrick and John Bewley Gilbart-Smith, by originating summons dated
Nov. 16, 1964. By the order of May 11, 1965, it was declared that no estate duty
became payable on the death of Stewart Kilpatrick, the first plaintiff's father, in
respect of any of fourteen policies of assurance, either by the effect of s. 2 (1) (*d*)
of the Finance Act, 1894, or by the joint effect of s. 2 (1) (*d*) and s. 22 (1) (*l*) of that
Act.
                                                                                    F
    J. L. Arnold, Q.C., and *J. P. Warner* for the Crown.
    E. I. Goulding, Q.C., and *P. W. E. Taylor* for the trustees.

                                                                    Cur. adv. vult.
    Mar. 16. The following judgments were read.

    LORD DENNING, M.R.: In 1952 Mr. Kilpatrick took out fourteen policies
of assurance on his own life for the benefit of his wife, Mrs. Kilpatrick, and his G
two sons, Stewart and Allen Kilpatrick. These policies were made under the
provisions of s. 11 of the Married Women's Property Act, 1882, and consequently
created a trust for his wife and two sons. They were single premium policies. Mr.
Kilpatrick paid the single premiums in 1952 once and for all. He appointed he
himself and his wife to be trustees of each of the policies and of all moneys
payable thereunder. On each policy there was endorsed this special note: H

    " 1. This policy is effected under the provisions of the Married Women's
    Property Act, 1882, for the benefit of Rochelle Edith Kilpatrick, the wife of
    the assured, if she shall survive the assured for more than one month.
    " 2. If the said Rochelle Edith Kilpatrick shall not survive the assured for
    the period of one month, then this policy shall be for the benefit of the two
    sons of the assured, namely, Stewart Kilpatrick, Junior, and Allen James   I
    Kilpatrick otherwise known as Allan James Kilpatrick in equal shares."

There were also express provisions giving the trustees " power at any time at
their discretion *to borrow* any money required for the purposes of the policy and
the trusts " and also " power at any time *to invest* moneys " with the " absolute
power *of varying such investments* ". Nine years later, on Oct. 20, 1961, Mr.
Kilpatrick died. The trustees never did borrow or invest any moneys during Mr.
Kilpatrick's lifetime. Mrs. Kilpatrick survived her husband. So did their two

A   sons. Mrs. Kilpatrick survived for more than one month. Accordingly, the benefit of all the policy moneys went to her and none to the two sons. The total sum of all fourteen policies came to £66,638 19s. 2d.

The Crown now claim to be entitled to estate duty amounting to £26,000. They can, of course, make no claim under s. 1 of the Act of 1894, because the property in these policies did not pass on Mr. Kilpatrick's death in October, 1961. It
B   passed in 1952 when he created them for the benefit of his wife and two sons. The Revenue say that the property is *deemed* to have passed under s. 2 (1) (d) of the Act of 1894. That subsection says that:

" Property passing on the death of the deceased shall be *deemed* to include . . . (d) any . . . interest purchased or provided by the deceased, . . . to the extent of the beneficial interest accruing or arising by survivorship or
C   otherwise on the death of the deceased."

These policies were clearly an interest provided by the deceased. By s. 22 (1) (l), the phrase " on the death " includes " at a period ascertainable by reference only to the death ". So it includes the period of one month after Mr. Kilpatrick's death mentioned in the policies. Subsection 2 (1) (d) is qualified by s. 28 of the
D   Finance Act, 1934, which says that

". . . where an annuity or other interest has been purchased or provided by the deceased . . . the extent of any beneficial interest therein accruing or arising by survivorship or otherwise on the death of the deceased shall be ascertained, and shall be deemed always to have been ascertainable, without regard to any interest in expectancy the beneficiary may have had therein
E   before the death."

Counsel for the Crown put his arguments under four heads with which I will deal separately.

(i) He said that the beneficial interest of the widow in the policy moneys was a *contingent* interest up to the moment when it vested at the end of a month after her husband's death. At that moment the beneficial interest " arose ", and as it
F   was provided by the deceased, it was chargeable under s. 2 (1) (d) of the Act of 1894. The interest which the widow had before that moment was an expectant interest, being one which existed by reason only of the expectation that the contingency would occur, and accordingly to be ignored under s. 28 of the Act of 1934. If I were untrammelled by authority, I would have accepted this contention. It seems to me obvious that Mrs. Kilpatrick had no beneficial interest
G   until one month after her husband's death, and that then she got the whole £66,638 19s. 2d. So estate duty should be payable; but I am compelled by authority to come to a different conclusion. First, in *D'Avigdor-Goldsmid* v. *Inland Revenue Comrs.* (1), the House of Lords held that the words " beneficial interest " in s. 2 (1) (d) do not mean financial benefit. They mean legal or equitable right. We have to see, therefore, whether Mrs. Kilpatrick, before her
H   husband's death, had a legal or equitable right to the policies, or whether she only acquired a right on his death or a month afterwards. Second, in *Phipps* v. *Ackers* (2), the House of Lords held that when property is given in these terms: to A " if " or " when " or " as soon as " a time is reached, but that if A dies before that time, then the property is to go to B; in such a case A takes, not a contingent interest, but a *vested* interest which passes to him at once as soon as
I   the gift is made, though the interest is liable to be defeated if he dies before the time. *Phipps* v. *Ackers* (2) was decided in regard to real property; but it was assumed by the text book writers to extend also to personalty, and eventually it was decided by the judges to extend to personalty. In particular by Farwell, J., in 1936 in *Re Heath, Public Trustee* v. *Heath* (3), and in 1951 by Black, L.J., in *McGredy and McGredy's Trustees* v. *Inland Revenue Comrs.* (4). I do not think

---

(1) [1953] 1 All E.R. 403; [1953] A.C. 347.   (2) (1842), 9 Cl. & Fin. 583.
(3) [1935] All E.R. Rep. 677; [1936] Ch. 259.   (4) [1951] N.I. 155.

that we can possibly overrule those cases, seeing that so many transactions have A
been effected on the faith of them.

We must take it, therefore, that *as from 1952* when these policies were effected,
Mrs. Kilpatrick had a *vested* interest in these policies, which was liable to be
defeated by her death before her husband or within one month after his death.
She had the legal and equitable right to the policies all the time. That disposes
of counsel's first point.   B

(ii) Counsel for the Crown next said that, even if the interest of the widow was
not contingent until the end of the month but was vested until defeasance, it was
not, until her husband died, an interest *in possession* but it was an interest *in
futuro*, and therefore was an interest in expectancy. When it fell into possession
on the husband's death, it " accrued " or " arose " within the meaning of
s. 2 (1) (*d*).   C

If I were untrammelled by authority, I would have accepted this contention
also. It seems to me plain that no one contemplated that there would be any
income from these policies during the husband's lifetime. The whole object was
to provide capital on the husband's death and not to provide any income beforehand. There was nothing coming into possession during his life, but only on his
death when the policies matured and the moneys became payable. But again I   D
am compelled by authority to come to a different conclusion. In *Westminster
Bank, Ltd.* v. *Inland Revenue Comrs.*, *Wrightson* v. *Inland Revenue Comrs.* (5),
a father assigned policies of assurance on his life to trustees on the terms that
on maturity, i.e., on his death, the moneys were to be divided amongst his sons.
The House of Lords held that the beneficial interest remained unchanged in
character from the date of the settlement. No beneficial interest accrued or arose E
to the sons on the father's death. So estate duty was not payable. In *Childs
Trustee Co.* v. *Inland Revenue Comrs.* (6), CROSS, J., managed to distinguish *Wrightson's* case (5) in some way which is not very clear to me. Suffice it to say that I
cannot distinguish *Wrightson's* case (5) here. Indeed, the present case is stronger
in favour of the taxpayer than *Wrightson's* case (5): because here there was some
possibility of income during Mr. Kilpatrick's life. The trustees had power to F
borrow and to invest. If there had been income during Mr. Kilpatrick's life, it
would seem that Mrs. Kilpatrick ought to receive it. However that may be, this
case is not distinguishable from *Wrightson's* case (5): and I feel bound to hold
that Mrs. Kilpatrick had a vested interest *in possession as from 1952* when the
policies were taken out: that her beneficial interest came into existence then:
and did not accrue or arise on or after her husband's death.   G

(iii) Counsel for the Crown next submitted that, if (i) and (ii) were both wrong,
and the widow had a vested interest in possession all the way through, and
liable to be defeated only by death before maturity, then the widow's entitlement
consisted of two interests: (a) a right to the income until the end of the month
or her earlier death; (b) a right to capital if she should be living at the end of the
month. Right (a) came to an end when right (b) came into existence. Right (b) H
was an interest in expectancy until it came into existence at the end of the month
and then it accrued or arose for the first time as an indefeasible beneficial interest.
I do not think that this submission merits prolonged examination. If the first
two propositions are wrong, then Mrs. Kilpatrick had a vested interest in
possession from 1952 and this did not change in character at any time. She had
the one contractual right all the time—the one entitlement—from which she was I
entitled to receive the income during his life and for one month thereafter, and
the capital moneys one month after his death.

(iv) Counsel for the Crown lastly submitted that the acquisition at the end of
the month of the quality of indefeasibility—standing by itself—constituted the
accrual of a beneficial interest provided by the deceased, and accordingly is
deemed to pass on his death. It does not fall to be reduced in value by reference

(5) [1957] 2 All E.R. 745; [1958] A.C. 210.
(6) [1960] 2 All E.R. 209; [1960] Ch. 534.

A   to the pre-existing defeasible interest which, by reason of its defeasibility, was an " interest in expectancy " within s. 28 of the Act of 1934.

I am prepared to assume that, when the defeasible interest became indefeasible at the end of the month, a beneficial interest " accrued " or " arose "; but I do not think that the pre-existing defeasible interest was an " interest in expectancy ". Counsel urged that s. 28 was passed so as to overrule *A.-G.* v. *Adamson*

B   (7). In *Adamson's* case (7) the House of Lords, as I read their speeches, held that there was a defeasible interest which became indefeasible. It " arose " or " accrued " on the death, but the duty fell to be reduced almost to nothing because the expectant beneficial interest before the death was nearly equal in value to the beneficial interest which accrued on the death. This decision was so unwelcome to the Revenue that Parliament passed the Act of 1934 to contradict

C   it. Counsel urged that, in order to give effect to the intentions of the legislature, we should read the words " interest in expectancy " in s. 28 as meaning, not only an interest in futuro, but also a defeasible interest which becomes indefeasible, such as was in question in *Adamson's* case (7). I think that may well have been the intention of the legislature. There is no reason in this context for distinguishing between an interest in futuro and a defeasible interest which becomes

D   indefeasible; but, for present purposes, there is a statutory definition of " interest in expectancy ". It is contained in s. 22 (1) (*j*) of the principal Act, which says:

" The expression ' interest in expectancy ' includes an estate in remainder or reversion and every other future interest whether vested or contingent, but does not include reversions expectant upon the determination of leases."

E
That definition seems to me to give to the words " interest in expectancy " their technical meaning: and I think that we must go by them. They include a contingent interest or a future interest. They do not include a defeasible interest *vested in possession* which becomes indefeasible. The interest here was, according to *Phipps* v. *Ackers* (8), not a contingent interest, nor a future interest, but a

F   vested interest, though defeasible. It was vested in possession. It cannot, therefore, be disregarded. The taxable subject-matter is, therefore, the difference in value of Mrs. Kilpatrick's interest, as it stood immediately before the month was out, and its value as it stood immediately after the month was out. This difference is admittedly nil.

I reject, therefore, all four heads of counsel for the Crown's argument. I do

G   so because of the decisions of the House of Lords which bind this court. I would dismiss this appeal.

DIPLOCK, L.J.: The argument in this appeal is not about " How many angels can stand on the point of a needle ". It is about £26,000, but it would have had a familiar ring to the schoolmen of the fifteenth century. Perhaps that is why when counsel for the Crown first put his four propositions I thought, and

H   was overheard in doing so, that they were four different ways of putting the same thing. I am afraid that I still think so.

The first and, as I think, the only question in this case is this. Immediately before the expiry of one month after Mr. Kilpatrick's death was his widow entitled to a vested but defeasible beneficial interest in the capital moneys payable under the insurance policies on Mr. Kilpatrick's life or was her beneficial interest in

I   such capital moneys an interest in expectancy contingent on her surviving to the end of the month? The answer depends on the legal nature of the settlements of the policies made by Mr. Kilpatrick and this in turn depends on the words he used to express his intentions.

Phipps v. *Ackers* (8) and *Re Heath, Public Trustee* v. *Heath* (9) were decisions about the meaning of particular words used by settlors to express their intentions.

---

(7) [1932] All E.R. Rep. 159; [1933] A.C. 257.   (8) (1842), 9 Cl. & Fin. 583.
(9) [1935] All E.R. Rep. 677; [1936] Ch. 259.

Whether these decisions were initially right or wrong in 1842 and 1936 respec- A
tively, they have become entries in the legal lexicon used by those who draft and
administer settlements. Once that has happened—and *Re Heath* (10) had stood
unchallenged for sixteen years when Mr. Kilpatrick's advisers drafted his
commendably laconic settlement—a court when confronted with the same words
in a subsequent settlement ought to assume, in the absence of indications to the
contrary in the document itself or in the relevant surrounding circumstances, B
that the settlor intended them to bear the meaning in the legal lexicon. It ought
not to query the accuracy of the original entry. What *Re Heath* (10) decided was
that the rule of construction in *Phipps* v. *Ackers* (11) applied to the construction
of settlements of personal property. Personally I think that the decision was
right in 1936, but even if it were not, the lapse of thirty years has made it right
by now. The rule is that where a settlor makes a gift to A if A fulfils in the future C
some condition, and to B if A does not fulfil that condition, his intention is to
make to A an immediate gift of the property including its income, of which,
however, A is liable to be divested if and when the condition becomes impossible
of fulfilment.

Is there anything in Mr. Kilpatrick's settlements to show that such was not
his intention? All that can be pointed to is the nature of the property settled, D
viz., assurance policies on his life. These, it is argued, are not in their nature
income-producing property. They are like timber which grows and is cut down
on maturity but in the meantime produces no fruit. There is thus no purpose
served by making an immediate instead of a future gift; but there are several
ways in which the policies might produce income during the period before Mrs.
Kilpatrick's interest became indefeasible. Quite apart from a calamity such as E
the liquidation of the insurance companies and ignoring the month after the policies
had matured on Mr. Kilpatrick's death, the trustees from the outset had power to
surrender the policies and to invest the proceeds in income-bearing investments
or to borrow money on the security of the policies and to invest the sums so
borrowed. I find nothing in the settlement to indicate an intention on the part
of the settlor that if either of these powers were exercised, his wife, if still alive, F
should not be entitled to the income.

I agree, therefore, with the learned judge (12) that as from the date of each
settlement, Mrs. Kilpatrick had a vested beneficial interest in possession in the
trust property (which in the result continued to consist of the assurance policies)
of which she was liable to be divested if she should die before one month elapsed
after Mr. Kilpatrick's death. Because of the liability to divestment, although she G
had a right to any income which the trust property might produce in the meantime, she had no right to demand the capital until the date when there ceased to
be any possibility of divestment.

What was the effect on Mrs. Kilpatrick's beneficial interest in possession in the
trust property, first, of her husband's death, and, secondly, of the expiry of one
month thereafter? On her husband's death her beneficial interest became more H
valuable but its legal nature remained unchanged. No beneficial interest in the
trust property accrued or arose on that date (see *D'Avigdor-Goldsmid* v. *Inland
Revenue Comrs.* (13)).

On the expiry of one month after her husband's death Mrs. Kilpatrick's
beneficial interest in possession in the trust property, which theretofore had been
liable to divestment, ceased to be so. She had previously a defeasible interest: she I
had now an indefeasible interest in the same property. Her rights were in consequence altered: whereas previously she could only demand payment of the
income (if any) from the trust property, she could now demand payment of the
capital moneys as well. Did this change in her interest from a defeasible to an
indefeasible interest in the same property amount to a " beneficial interest

(10) [1935] All E.R. Rep. 677; [1936] A.C. 259.   (11) (1842), 9 Cl. & Fin. 583.
(12) [1965] 2 All E.R. 673 at p. 680, letter F.
(13) [1953] 1 All E.R. 403; [1953] A.C. 347.

A accruing or arising " on the date on which the change occurred? I do not pretend to know. And for reasons which appear below, I do not think that it matters in the present case. In *A.-G.* v. *Adamson* (14), the House of Lords appeared to draw no distinction between an interest in expectancy contingent on the occurrence of an event and an interest in possession defeasible on the occurrence of an event. The former is clearly a beneficial interest accruing or arising on the

B occurrence of the event, the change from defeasibility to indefeasibility of an interest in possession is less clearly so. In *Adamson's* case (14), however, the distinction had no practical consequences because the House of Lords went on to hold that s. 2 (1) (d) of the Finance Act, 1894, required the duty to be assessed on the difference in the value of the beneficial interest of the beneficiary in the property immediately before and immediately after the settlor's death, and

C whether the previous beneficial interest were in expectancy or in possession but defeasible the difference in value would be the same and nominal. The distinction does, however, matter today because s. 28 of the Finance Act, 1934, requires " any interest in expectancy the beneficiary may have had [in the property] before his death " to be ignored in assessing the duty. Whether Mrs. Kilpatrick's interest in the trust property before the month had elapsed was " an interest

D in expectancy " therein within the meaning of that section is therefore crucial. If it was not, no estate duty is payable even if the change from a defeasible to an indefeasible interest constitutes an accrual of a beneficial interest.

If " an interest in expectancy " is to be given its correct meaning as a term of art, I am of opinion, for the reasons that I have already given, that Mrs. Kilpatrick's beneficial interest in the trust property before the month had elapsed

E was a vested interest in possession and not " an interest in expectancy ". It is urged on behalf of the Crown that we should assume that s. 28 of the Finance Act, 1934, was intended to reverse the decision of the House of Lords in *Adamson's* case (14) and should construe it accordingly. This involves assuming, however, first that Parliament understood precisely what the House of Lords did decide in a case which has baffled CROSS, J., (15) and at least this member of the

F Court of Appeal, and wanted to reverse the whole of whatever the House of Lords did decide. I do not think that it would be safe to make either of these assumptions. I think that we must adopt the timorous course of construing the term of legal art which Parliament used, an " interest in expectancy ", in its correct, and not in some vague and extended, meaning.

In considering whether Mrs. Kilpatrick's beneficial interest before the month

G had elapsed was an interest in possession or an interest in expectancy, I have spoken so far of her interest in the trust property. It remains to deal with the Crown's contention that Mrs. Kilpatrick's interest should, for the purposes of s. 2 (1) (d) of the Finance Act, 1894, and s. 28 of the Finance Act, 1934, be treated as two separate beneficial interests, an interest in possession in the income of the trust property and an interest in expectancy in the capital of the trust property.

H I think that this is too great a refinement. The right to income does not constitute a separate beneficial interest in the trust property; it is a right which flows from and is ancillary to a defeasible interest in possession in a single trust property, the assurance policies.

I, therefore, agree with the reasoning of the learned judge and would dismiss this appeal.

I As in nearly all appeals about estate duty, I reach my decision without confidence. Were I a betting man I should lay the odds on its being right at 6 to 4 (i.e. 3 to 2) on—or against. If ever a branch of law called for reform in 1966, it is the law relating to estate duty. It ought to be certain: it ought to be sensible—it is neither. One cannot read even the score of cases which have been cited in the present case without realising that it has got into a mess from which I see no hope of the courts' rescuing it without drastic legislative assistance.

(14) [1932] All E.R. Rep. 159; [1933] A.C. 257.
(15) [1965] 2 All E.R. at p. 683, letter A.

RUSSELL, L.J.: I have no doubt that the principle applied in *Phipps* v. **A** *Ackers* (16) applies to this case, notwithstanding that the subject-matter is personalty. If that principle had its origin in an anxiety to preserve contingent remainders, I do not think that that can be regarded as its sole justification. It seems to me to be quite sensible to construe what appear at first sight to be two contingent dispositions as in substance an absolute gift to the first taker defeasible in favour of the substitute takers on a contingency: as it has been put, **B** the intention is then and there to give the whole property to A except to the extent to which it is effectively given to B. I consider that *Re Heath, Public Trustee* v. *Heath* (17) was rightly decided, as was assumed by counsel in *McGredy and McGredy's Trustees* v. *Inland Revenue Comrs.* (18). Accordingly we must treat the present case as if the documents in terms declared an absolute trust in favour of the wife subject to defeasance of her vested interest in the event of **C** her death before the expiration of one month after her husband's, the settlor's, death.

If a person is given a vested beneficial entitlement to property subject to divesting in a certain event, prima facie that person is entitled to receive and retain any income that accrues from the property in respect of the period during which her interest is still vested. It is argued that the nature of the property **D** settled—in each case a paid-up policy on the settlor's life—is sufficient in the present case to demonstrate an intention that should any capital come to the hands of the trustees before its maturity, the wife is not to be then entitled to any income from such capital: either the income must be directly accumulated to await the event or a similar effect produced by acquisition of a substituted policy. I do not accept that argument: indeed the documents by their reference **E** to surrender, investment and borrowing point rather in the other direction. Without expressing an opinion on *Childs Trustee Co.* v. *Inland Revenue Comrs.* (19), it seems to me that the present case is nearer to *Westminster Bank, Ltd.* v. *Inland Revenue Comrs., Wrightson* v. *Inland Revenue Comrs.* (20). Accordingly, it is in my judgment correct to say that the wife had from the outset a vested interest in possession in the property settled, subject to defeasance in a particular **F** event.

It is not necessary to say whether a mere extinction of the possibility of defeasance of a beneficial interest vested in possession can be said to give rise to a beneficial interest. By itself that would not assist the Crown: it is necessary for the Crown also to show that the Act of 1934 applies. I entirely agree with Cross, J., (21) that by no stretch of language can a beneficial interest vested **G** in possession be described as an " interest in expectancy ". It is said that the House of Lords in *A.-G.* v. *Adamson* (22), in effect accepted that it was so describable. *Adamson's* case (22), however, was one in which there was provision for accumulation: though the son had a vested interest liable to be divested, it was not until the death an interest in possession. **H**

Finally, I notice the argument for the Crown that anyway there were here two interests, one in income and the other in capital: that the latter beneficial interest accrued or arose in possession at the end of the month, the previous beneficial interest in capital having been an interest in expectancy only. This argument, if sound, would include a case in which a fund of present investments were settled by A on B absolutely with a provision for defeasance in favour of C should B die **I** before A or within one month after A. I do not accept this argument, which seems to return by a back door to taxation in the event of a financial benefit

(16) (1842), 9 Cl. & Fin. 583.   (17) [1935] All E.R. Rep. 677; [1936] Ch. 259.
(18) [1951] N.I. 155.   (19) [1960] 2 All E.R. 209; [1960] Ch. 534.
(20) [1957] 2 All E.R. 745; [1958] A.C. 210.
(21) [1965] 2 All E.R. at p. 683, letter B.
(22) [1932] All E.R. Rep. 159; [1933] A.C. 257.

A arising and not by reference to a beneficial interest arising. In truth the wife had one beneficial interest only in both tree and fruit.

I agree that this appeal fails.

Appeal dismissed. Leave to appeal to the House of Lords granted.

Solicitors: *Solicitor of Inland Revenue; Fladgate & Co.* (for the plaintiffs).

B   [*Reported by* F. GUTTMAN, ESQ., *Barrister-at-Law.*]

Re T. D. WALTON, LTD.

C [CHANCERY DIVISION (Plowman, J.), March 23, 1966.]

Execution—Company—Winding-up—Creditors' rights—Liquidator's rights—Goods sold under writs of fi. fa.—Notice under s. 293 of the Companies Act, 1948, sent to under-sheriff—Proceeds paid to execution creditors—Whether notice under s. 293 was sufficient notice for purposes of s. 326 (2)—Whether liquidator or execution creditors entitled to proceeds of execution—Companies
D *Act, 1948 (11 & 12 Geo. 6 c. 38), s. 326 (2).*

A private company had two shareholders who were also directors. On Oct. 28, 1961, the under-sheriff sold goods of the company under writs of fi. fa. On Nov. 8, 1961, a letter was sent, together with a notice under s. 293 of the Companies Act, 1948, to convene a meeting for Nov. 22; this letter and notice did not mention s. 326 nor did they intimate that a resolu-
E tion for voluntary winding-up would be proposed. Copies of these were received by the under-sheriff on Nov. 9. On Nov. 11, 1961, the fourteen days period envisaged by s. 326 (2)* expired, and two days later the under-sheriff paid the execution creditors. On Nov. 20, 1961, notice of an extra-ordinary general meeting to pass a resolution for voluntary winding-up was given, a copy being sent to the under-sheriff. The liquidator of the
F company claimed the proceeds of the execution under s. 326 (2).

Held: s. 326 (2), being an enactment which divested rights, must be construed strictly; on the facts a meeting of the company at which a resolution for voluntary winding-up was to be proposed had not been called at the time when the notice of Nov. 8 was given, and accordingly the liquidator's claim failed (see p. 161, letter G, post).
G *Bluston & Bramley, Ltd.* v. *Leigh* ([1950] 2 All E.R. 29) distinguished.

[As to the effect of winding-up on the rights of execution creditors, see 6 HALSBURY'S LAWS (3rd Edn.) 690-692, paras. 1377-1380; and for cases on the subject, see 10 DIGEST (Repl.) 1017-1019, *6999-7013.*

For the Companies Act, 1948, s. 326 (2) and s. 293, see 3 HALSBURY'S STATUTES
H (2nd Edn.) 708, 685.]

Cases referred to:
Bluston & Bramley, Ltd. v. *Leigh (Euler and Another, Third Parties)*, [1950] 2 All E.R. 29; [1950] 2 K.B. 548; 10 Digest (Repl.) 1019, *7013.*
Hockley (William), Ltd., Re, [1962] 2 All E.R. 111; [1962] 1 W.L.R. 555; Digest (Cont. Vol. A) 186, *5720a.*

I **Adjourned Summons.**

This was an application by originating summons dated Feb. 23, 1965, issued by Clifford George Sparrow, the liquidator of T. D. Walton, Ltd. (" the company ") which was in a creditors' voluntary liquidation for the determination by the court of the following questions. 1. Whether the proceeds of the sale on Oct. 28, 1961, by the first respondent as under-sheriff of the county of Durham of the goods of the company in execution of judgments respectively obtained

---

* Section 326 (2) is printed at p. 158, letter H, post.

by the second, third, fourth and fifth respondents or alternatively the money A
paid by the company to avoid a sale should have been retained by him for a
period of fourteen days after Oct. 28, 1961, pursuant to s. 326 (2) of the Companies
Act, 1948. 2. Whether during the said period of fourteen days there was served
on the first respondent as such under-sheriff a notice of a meeting or notices of
meetings at which there was to be proposed a resolution for the winding-up of
the company within the meaning of s. 326 (2). 3. Whether by reason of the B
service of such notice or notices as aforesaid the first respondent was under an
obligation to pay the net proceeds of the said sales, after deducting his costs, to
the applicant as such liquidator as aforesaid, pursuant to the said s. 326 (2).
4. Whether the first respondent on Nov. 13, 1961, having paid away the said
net proceeds of sale or alternatively the money paid by the company to avoid a
sale to the second, third, fourth and fifth respondents respectively to the extent C
of the respective sums set out in the schedule thereto was liable to pay to the
applicant as liquidator as aforesaid the aggregate of the said sums, viz., £1,045
19s. 6d. together with interest thereon at the rate of five per cent. per annum from
the date of the said liquidation, namely Nov. 22, 1961, until payment or judgment. 5. Alternatively whether the second, third, fourth and fifth respondents
were respectively liable to repay to the applicant as such liquidator, together D
with such interest as aforesaid, the sum respectively received by each of them
from the first respondent. 6. Whether there were any grounds for the setting
aside in favour of the second, third, fourth and fifth respondents or any of them,
to any extent or at all, of the applicant's right as such liquidator pursuant to
s. 326 (3) of the Act of 1948. No point was taken on s. 326 (3) at the hearing.
The respondents were (i) Allan Aylmer Luxmoore, the under-sheriff of the county E
of Durham, (ii) Adamson & Co. (Tyne), Ltd., (iii) W. & S. Summerscales, Ltd.,
(iv) Rest Assured, Ltd. and (v) Robert Glew & Co., Ltd., the last four respondents
being execution creditors of the company. The facts and relevant statutory
provision are set out in the judgment.
The cases noted below* were cited during the argument in addition to those
referred to in the judgment.   F

A. L. *Figgis* for the applicant, the liquidator.

G. B. H. *Dillon*, Q.C., for the first respondent, the under-sheriff.

R. A. K. *Wright* for the second, third, fourth and fifth respondents, the
execution creditors of the company.

PLOWMAN, J.: The summons in this case, which is issued by the liquidator G
of T. D. Walton, Ltd., raises the question whether it is the liquidator or certain
execution creditors who are entitled to the proceeds of certain executions. The
respondents to the summons are the under-sheriff for the county of Durham and
the execution creditors in question of whom there are four. The matter which
I have to determine depends on s. 326 (2) of the Companies Act, 1948, which is
in these terms: H

" Subject to the provisions of sub-s. (3) of this section, where under an
execution in respect of a judgment for a sum exceeding £20 the goods of a
company are sold or money is paid in order to avoid sale, the sheriff shall
deduct the costs of the execution from the proceeds of the sale or the money
paid and retain the balance for fourteen days, and if within that time notice
is served on him of a petition for the winding-up of the company having I
been presented or of a meeting having been called at which there is to be
proposed a resolution for the voluntary winding-up of the company and an
order is made or a resolution is passed, as the case may be, for the winding-up
of the company, the sheriff shall pay the balance to the liquidator, who shall
be entitled to retain it as against the execution creditor."

---

* *Re Eros Films, Ltd.*, [1963] 1 All E.R. 383; [1963] Ch. 565; *Re Rainbow Tours, Ltd.*,
[1963] 2 All E.R. 820; [1964] Ch. 66; *Re Caribbean Products (Yam Importers), Ltd.*,
[1966] 1 All E.R. 181.

A Subsection (3) of s. 326 does not enter into this matter.

 The facts on which this matter depends are as follows: before Oct. 28, 1961, there had been a number of seizures by the sheriff of the goods of this company under writs of fi. fa. issued by the creditors. On that date, Oct. 28, 1961, the relevant sale of the goods took place. The next event in chronological order was this, that on Nov. 3, 1961, a resolution was passed at an extraordinary

B general meeting of the members of the company, of whom there were only two, a Mr. Walton and a Miss Dodds, who were also the two directors of the company, that in view of the company's inability to meet its current debts it should go into voluntary liquidation, that a provisional liquidator, Mr. Mitford, should be appointed and that a meeting of the creditors should be called as soon as possible. It is, I think, common ground that the proceedings of that meeting

C had no effect at all, but it is perhaps worth noticing that the meeting decided that a meeting of creditors be called as soon as possible. That would not do for the purposes of s. 293 (1) of the Companies Act, 1948, (1), because the creditors' meeting has to be summoned " for the day, or the day next following the day " on which the meeting of the members resolving on liquidation is held. On Nov. 8, 1961, a notice was sent out to the creditors of the company. The

D notice was a notice of a meeting for Nov. 22, and a copy of that notice was sent to the first respondent, the under-sheriff, with a covering letter. The letter emanates from a firm of chartered accountants, J. C. Gregory, Johnson, Mitford & Co., is addressed to the first respondent, and is in these terms:

 " Dear Sir,

T. D. Walton, Ltd.

E We enclose herewith a formal notice calling a meeting of creditors of the above company to be held on Nov. 22, 1961, at 2.30 p.m. As you will be aware, there are a number of writs outstanding against this company. We shall be glad if you will kindly acknowledge receipt of this notification."

 The notice enclosed with that letter is on a printed form and headed " Notice of Meeting of Creditors, T. D. Walton, Ltd." It states as follows:

F " Notice is hereby given, pursuant to s. 293 of the Companies Act, 1948, that a meeting of the creditors of the above-named company will be held at Bondgate Methodist Church Hall (Primary Room) on Wednesday, Nov. 22, 1961, at 2.30 o'clock in the afternoon for the purpose of having a full statement of the position of the company's affairs, together with a list of the creditors of the company and the estimated amount of their claims

G laid before them, and for the purpose, if thought fit, of nominating a liquidator and of appointing a committee of inspection."

 That, I think, is all of the notice that I need read. That notice was received by the first respondent the following day, namely Nov. 9. On Nov. 11, 1961, the fourteen days referred to in s. 326 (2) of the Companies Act, 1948, expired. Two

H days later, on Nov. 13, the under-sheriff paid out the execution creditors. On Nov. 20, 1961, Messrs. J. C. Gregory, Johnson, Mitford & Co. sent out a notice of an extraordinary general meeting of the company to be held two days later, on Nov. 22. That notice was sent to the under-sheriff with a covering letter in these terms:

 " We enclose herewith formal notice of an extraordinary general meeting

I to be held on Wednesday, Nov. 22, 1961, for the purpose of passing a resolution that the company be wound up voluntarily. We shall be pleased if you kindly acknowledge receipt."

 The notice itself is on a printed form and states that

 " Notice is hereby given that an Extraordinary General Meeting of the members of the above-named company will be held at 77, Bondgate, Darlington, on Wednesday, Nov. 22, 1961, at two o'clock in the afternoon precisely,

---

(1) For s. 293 (1) of the Companies Act, 1948, see 3 Halsbury's Statutes (2nd Edn.), p. 685.

for the purpose of considering, and if thought fit passing as an extraordinary   A
resolution, the resolution set out below."

The resolution set out below is this:

" That it has been proved to the satisfaction of this meeting that the
company cannot, by reason of its liabilities, continue its business, and that
it is advisable to wind up the same, and accordingly that the company be
wound up voluntarily, and that Mr. Peter Vernon Mitford be and is hereby   B
appointed liquidator for the purpose of such winding-up."

The under-sheriff received that notice on Nov. 21. On Nov. 22 the meeting was
held and the resolution was passed in accordance with the terms of the resolution
that I have read out.

The question which I have to decide is whether the notice that was sent out   C
on Nov. 8, 1961, which as I have already said was a notice given pursuant to
s. 293 of the Companies Act, 1948, was a sufficient notice for the purposes of
s. 326 (2), " of a meeting having been called at which there was to be proposed
a resolution for the voluntary winding up of the company ".

It was submitted by counsel on behalf of the liquidator, that what I may call
a s. 293 notice is a sufficient notice for the purposes of s. 326 (2).   He submitted   D
that a notice of a creditors' meeting has been assumed to give notice of a meeting
at which a resolution for voluntary winding up is to be proposed, at any rate for
the purposes (2) of s. 325 (1), which it is said is in pari materia with s. 326 (2).

The only case in which the matter has been argued to which I was referred
was the case of *Bluston & Bramley, Ltd.* v. *Leigh* (3), where it was in fact argued
in relation to s. 326, although part of MORRIS, J.'s judgment dealing with that   E
part is admittedly obiter because the case was decided on s. 325 and not s. 326.
In that case on Aug. 19, 1948, a notice was served on the sheriff of a meeting of
the creditors of the company under s. 293 of the Companies Act, 1948, to be held
on Sept. 17.   That notice was accompanied by a letter addressed to the sheriff's
officer which began thus:

" In reference to s. 326 (2) of the Companies Act, 1948, we enclose notice   F
of meeting of creditors of the above company under s. 293 of the said Act."

So far as is material to the matter with which I am concerned, the passage in
the judgment of MORRIS, J., which relates to the matter is where, after deciding
that s. 325 applied to the case before him, he said (4):

" As I have formed that view, it would be sufficient if I did not consider   G
the other part of the case, namely the arguments presented by [counsel for
the sheriff], but I think it only fair that I should state my views on the three
points that he has submitted.   The first point is whether there was a notice
to the sheriff within the statutory fourteen days of a meeting having been
called at which there was to be proposed a resolution for the voluntary
winding-up of the company.   The letter of Aug. 18 enclosing the notice of the   H
meeting of creditors began by making reference to s. 326 (2) and three other
sections of the Act, s. 293, s. 294 and s. 295 were referred to in that letter
or in the notice."

Then MORRIS, J., referred to s. 293 (1) and went on (5):

" In my judgment, the result of the sheriff having that letter and that
notice was that there was notice served on him of a meeting having been   I
called at which there was to be proposed a resolution for the voluntary
winding-up of the company.   The actual notice served, together with the

---

(2) For s. 325 of the Companies Act, 1948, see 3 HALSBURY'S STATUTES (2nd Edn.),
p. 707.
(3) [1950] 2 All E.R. 29; [1950] 2 K.B. 548.
(4) [1950] 2 K.B. at p. 556; [1950] 2 All E.R. at p. 34.
(5) [1950] 2 K.B. at pp. 556, 557; [1950] 2 All E.R. at p. 34.

A   letter, contained a sufficient notice, in my judgment, of the fact that a meeting
had been convened at which there was to be proposed a resolution for the
voluntary winding-up of the company."

That citation of the case shows, I think, two things. First, that there was an
express reference to s. 326 (2) in the letter enclosing the notice of the s. 293
meeting, and MORRIS, J., held that it was the letter and the notice which amounted
B   to a notice " of a meeting having been called at which there was to be proposed
a resolution for the voluntary winding-up of the company " within s. 326 (2).
Second, it appears that the meeting at which it was proposed that a resolution for the voluntary winding-up of the company should be submitted had
in fact already been called at the time when the s. 293 notice and its accompanying letter were sent out. Counsel for the liquidator also referred me to
C   certain other cases in which he submitted that it had been assumed that a s. 293
notice was sufficient for the purposes of s. 325, but I do not propose to refer to
them otherwise than to notice them in that way in passing, because not only
was there no argument in any of them on the point with which I am concerned,
but also in all of them the notice of the company's meeting had been given at
the time the s. 293 notice was sent out.
D   The vital question, as I see it, in the case with which I am concerned is not
so much whether the notice of Nov. 8 and its accompanying letter were such that
a normally intelligent person reading them would know that a meeting of the
company to consider a resolution for winding-up was likely to be held but whether
they amounted to a notice of a meeting having been called at which a resolution
to wind up the company was to be proposed. Counsel for the liquidator lays
E   stress on the fact which I have already mentioned that there were only two
members of this company, who were also its only two directors, that there was
no necessity for them to give formal notice of a meeting to themselves and submits
that I should infer from the facts that before Nov. 8 they had already decided on a
meeting of the company for Nov. 22 and that that was sufficient notice " of a
meeting having been called " for the purposes of s. 326 (2).
F   Counsel on behalf of the under-sheriff submitted to the contrary. He pointed
out that s. 326 (2) is a subsection which, where it operates, operates to divest
vested rights, and for that proposition he referred me to the decision of PENNY-
CUICK, J., in Re William Hockley, Ltd. (6). Being a section which operates to divest
vested rights, it must, in my judgment, be construed strictly. I find it quite
impossible in the light of the facts, as they appear in the evidence before me, to
G   reach the conclusion that at the time when the notice of Nov. 8, 1961, was given
to the under-sheriff a meeting of the company had in fact been called at which
there was to be proposed a resolution for the voluntary winding-up of the company. As no meeting had in fact been called for that purpose, the notice of
Nov. 8 cannot, in my judgment, operate inferentially as notice of some
non-existing meeting. In those circumstances this claim, in my judgment, fails.
H
Declaration accordingly.

Solicitors: *Butt & Bowyer*, agents for *Latimer, Hinks, Marsham & Little*,
Darlington (for the applicant); *H. A. Crowe & Co.*, agents for *Wilson & Co.*,
Durham (for the first respondent); *Biddle, Thorne, Welsford & Barnes*, agents
for *Hepworth & Chadwick*, Leeds (for all the execution creditor respondents).

I   [*Reported by* JACQUELINE METCALFE, *Barrister-at-Law.*]

---

(6) [1962] 2 All E.R. 111.

COMMISSIONER FOR RAILWAYS v. McDERMOTT.   A

[PRIVY COUNCIL (Lord Gardiner, L.C., Lord Morris of Borth-y-Gest, Lord Guest, Lord Pearce and Lord Pearson), January 11, 12, 13, 17, March 10, 1966.]

Privy Council—Australia—New South Wales—Negligence—Railway—Level crossing—Licensee—Level crossing only access to village—Plaintiff inhabitant of village—Lawfully using crossing—Fell on uneven sleepers and was injured by train—Whether general duty of care on part of corporate body charged with running the railway extended to static conditions of railway track—Whether that duty limited by common law duty owed by the occupier of the land (viz., the railway lines) to the plaintiff as licensee.   B

The appellant was a body corporate which was charged with the duty of administering the railway system of New South Wales, including the running   C of railway traffic carrying passengers and goods thereon, and in which was vested the lands on which its railway tracks were situated. Koolewong, a village on the central coast, had a small unattended railway station. There was a level crossing a little to the north, which was the only way of entering or leaving the village and was used substantially by the inhabitants of the village and their guests. M. had lived in the village for about ten years.   D The crossing was paved with disused sleepers, laid roughly on the ground, and these sometimes moved when stepped on. It was unlit at night. At a little before 6.20 p.m. M. approached the crossing intending to cross on her way home. She fell, the inference being that her fall was due to the state of the sleepers and the darkness. Her feet were over the rails. A train approached round the bend in the line at a speed of about forty miles per   E hour, and, though the fireman saw M. in the light of the engine light, the train could not be pulled up in time and passed over her, amputating her feet. In an action by M. against the appellants her allegations of negligence, as finally settled, were limited to the nature of the crossing and its condition, including the fact that it was unlit, and there was no issue of excessive speed. On appeal on the question whether there was a duty of care under   F which M. could be entitled to recover,

Held: (i) the carrying on of the inherently dangerous activity of running express trains through a level crossing, which was lawfully and necessarily used by local inhabitants, their guests and persons visiting on business, imposed on the appellant a general duty of care toward those who were lawfully on the level crossing; the duty owed by the appellant as occupier to   G M. as licensee existed in addition to this general duty and did not limit the general duty of care (see p. 169, letter G, p. 168, letters C to F, and p. 167, letter I, post).

(ii) the appellant's general duty of care to take all reasonable precautions to ensure the safety of persons lawfully using a level crossing extended not merely to positive operations but also to static conditions, and included an   H obligation to keep the crossing itself in reasonably adequate condition (see p. 170, letters A and B, post).

Comr. for Rys. v. *Quinlan* ([1964] 1 All E.R. 897) distinguished, and dictum of VISCOUNT RADCLIFFE (at p. 911) applied.

Appeal dismissed.

[As to the common law duty of railway undertakers to persons crossing the   I lines, see 31 HALSBURY'S LAWS (3rd Edn.) 598-600, para. 915; and for cases on the subject, see 38 DIGEST (Repl.) 358-361, *387-399.*]

Cases referred to:

Alchin v. *Railways Comr.*, (1935), 35 S.R.N.S.W. 498; 52 N.S.W.W.N. 156; 38 Digest (Repl.) 362, *759.*

Bilbee v. *London, Brighton & South Coast Ry. Co.*, (1865), 18 C.B.N.S. 584; 34 L.J.C.P. 182; 13 L.T. 146; 144 E.R. 571; 38 Digest (Repl.) 357, *382.*

A   *Cliff* v. *Midland Ry. Co.*, (1870), L.R. 5 Q.B. 258; 22 L.T. 382; 34 J.P. 357; 36 Digest (Repl.) 137, *724.*

Comr. for Rys. v. *Dowle*, (1958), 99 C.L.R. 353.

Comr. for Rys. v. *Quinlan*, [1964] 1 All E.R. 897; [1964] A.C. 1054; [1964] 2 W.L.R. 817; [1964-5] N.S.W.R. 157; [1964] A.L.R. 900; 3rd Digest Supp.

B   *Donoghue (or McAlister)* v. *Stevenson*, [1932] All E.R. Rep. 1; [1932] A.C. 562; 101 L.J.P.C. 119; 147 L.T. 281; 36 Digest (Repl.) 85, *458.*

Ellis v. *Great Western Ry. Co.*, [1874-80] All E.R. Rep. 699; (1874), L.R. 9 C.P. 551; 43 L.J.C.P. 304; 30 L.T. 874; 38 Digest (Repl.) 358, *388.*

Gallagher v. *Humphrey*, (1862), 6 L.T. 684; 27 J.P. 5; 36 Digest (Repl.) 66, *357.*

Grant v. *Caledonian Ry. Co.*, (1870), 9 Macph. (Ct. of Sess.) 258; 43 Sc. Jur. 115;
C   38 Digest (Repl.) 362, *783.*

Hendrie v. *Caledonian Ry. Co.*, 1909 S.C. 776; 46 Sc.L.R. 601; [1909] 1 S.L.T. 328; 38 Digest (Repl.) 356, *713.*

Jenner v. *South Eastern Ry. Co.*, (1911), 105 L.T. 131; 75 J.P. 419; 38 Digest (Repl.) 359, *390.*

Liddiatt v. *Great Western Ry. Co.*, [1946] 1 All E.R. 731; [1946] K.B. 545;
D   175 L.T. 224; 38 Digest (Repl.) 365, *404.*

Lipman v. *Clendinnen*, (1932), 46 C.L.R. 550; 6 A.L.J. 150; 31 Digest (Repl.) 100, *835.*

Lloyd's Bank, Ltd. v. *British Transport Commission*, [1956] 3 All E.R. 291; [1956] 1 W.L.R. 1279; 38 Digest (Repl.) 366, *408.*

Lloyds Bank, Ltd. v. *Railway Executive*, [1952] 1 All E.R. 1248; 38 Digest
E   (Repl.) 358, *384.*

Smith v. *London Midland & Scottish Ry. Co.*, 1948 S.C. 125; 38 Digest (Repl.) 362, *756.*

South Australian Ry. Comr. v. *Thomas*, (1951), 84 C.L.R. 84.

Wakelin v. *London & South Western Ry. Co.*, (1886), 12 App. Cas. 41; 56 L.J.Q.B. 229; 55 L.T. 709; 51 J.P. 404; 38 Digest (Repl.) 359, *392.*

F   **Appeal.**

This was an appeal from a judgment of the Supreme Court of New South Wales (MACFARLAN, MOFFITT and TAYLOR, JJ.), dated Dec. 1, 1964, dismissing the appellant's appeal from a judgment of the Supreme Court (CLANCY, J., sitting with a jury) dated Mar. 16, 1964. The respondent had instituted proceedings as plaintiff in the Supreme Court in its common law jurisdiction on Oct. 26, 1959,
G   against the appellant as defendant. The respondent by her declaration claimed damages from the appellant (which was a body corporate charged with the duty of administering the railway system of the State of New South Wales, including the running of railway traffic carrying passengers and goods, and in which was vested the track on which the railway lines were situated) on two counts which were to the following effect. (i) By her first count the respondent
H   sued the appellant in negligence relying on the relationship between the parties as declared in *Donoghue (or McAlister)* v. *Stevenson**, and arising on the facts. (ii) By her second count the respondent sued the defendant for breach of duty in his capacity of occupier of the land on which the railway lines were situated, she being lawfully thereon. The appellant denied negligence and pleaded general issue by statute, thus putting in issue the whole of the respondent's
I   case. There were two trials. The first trial was before WALLACE, J., and a jury, and resulted in a verdict for the respondent in the sum of £14,000. The appellant appealed to the Full Court of the Supreme Court and on Apr. 11, 1963, the appeal was allowed (HERRON, C.J., RICHARDSON and BRERETON, JJ.) and the matter was returned for re-trial. The re-trial took place before CLANCY, J., when the jury returned a verdict for the respondent in the sum of £10,000. The present appeal was against the verdict on that re-trial.

---

* [1932] All E.R. Rep. 1.

II. Jenkins, Q.C., and *A. H. Conlon* (both of the New South Wales Bar) for A
the appellant.

R. Watson, Q.C., and *R. B. Murphy* (both of the New South Wales Bar) for
the respondent.

LORD GARDINER, L.C.: This case arises out of a tragic accident which
befell the respondent on June 10, 1959, at Koolewong in New South Wales. B
She had somehow fallen on to a railway track a few feet from a level crossing.
She was lying there, presumably unconscious or dazed, with the rest of her body
safely within the " four foot " space between the rails, but with her feet over
one of the rails.   In the darkness a train came round a curve in the railway line,
travelling at forty miles an hour or more.   The fireman with the aid of the engine
light saw her lying there, but by that time the train was only about 150 feet C
away from her and could not be pulled up in time.   The train passed over her
amputating her feet.

In October, 1959, she commenced an action in the Supreme Court of New
South Wales against the Commissioner for Railways, claiming damages for
negligence.   There have been two trials and two appeals to the Full Court
with both of the jury verdicts and both of the decisions of the Full Court in D
favour of the plaintiff.   The present appeal is by the Commissioner for Railways
against the decision of the Full Court, given on Dec. 1, 1964, dismissing his appeal
against the verdict of the jury in favour of the respondent on the re-trial.

The main question of law raised in this appeal is, what was the measure of
the duty of care owing by the appellant to the respondent?   The direction given
by the judge to the jury on the re-trial was in these terms: E

" Under those circumstances it is the duty of the railway authorities to
do everything which is reasonably necessary to ensure the safety of those
persons using the crossing, to do everything reasonably necessary to protect
them against foreseeable damage and foreseeable injury."

The duty so measured can conveniently be referred to as " the general duty of F
care ".   The direction given by the learned judge in the re-trial was in conformity with the direction given by another learned judge at the first trial and
with the judgments of the Full Court given on Apr. 11, 1963, in the first appeal,
and it was approved by the Full Court in the second appeal after careful consideration of the effect of the decision of the Judicial Committee in *Comr. for
Rys.* v. *Quinlan* (1) that the general duty of care was not in that case owing G
by the defendant to the plaintiff as the plaintiff was trespassing on the private
level crossing at which he was injured.   Thus *Quinlan's* case (1) was concerned
with a trespasser.   This present case is concerned with a person who was a
licensee, though there were additional circumstances which will be mentioned
as materially affecting her position in relation to the appellant.   The appellant
has contended that the ratio decidendi of *Quinlan's* case (1) applies here, so as H
to exclude the general duty of care and to leave in operation only the special
limited duty of care owing by an occupier to his licensee.   As to the nature
of this special limited duty of care, DIXON, J., said in *Lipman* v. *Clendinnen* (2):

" The result of the authorities appears to be that the obligation of an
occupier towards a licensee is to take reasonable care to prevent harm to
him from a state or condition of the premises known to the occupier, but   I
unknown to the visitor, which the use of reasonable care on his part would
not disclose and which, considering the nature of the premises, the occasion
of the leave and licence, and the circumstances generally, a reasonable
man would be misled into failing to anticipate or suspect."

(1) [1964] 1 All E.R. 897; [1964] A.C. 1054.
(2) (1932), 46 C.L.R. 550 at pp. 569, 570.

A As the respondent had lived in Koolewong for about ten years before the accident, the appellant contends that she must have known very well the state and condition of the level crossing and that, therefore, the conclusion follows that she cannot succeed in her claim if only the special limited duty of care was owing by the defendant to her. That conclusion is disputed by the respondent, but at any rate the determination of the proper measure of the duty of care is the crucial

B point in the case, although there are also some other disputed points which will be mentioned. Some aspects of the facts of the case and of the history of the action are material for the determination of the proper measure of the duty of care and there are some special, rather artificial, problems to be elucidated.

It is convenient to adopt Herron, C.J.'s description of the scene of the accident, and to insert a few additional points from the evidence or from other judgments.

C Koolewong, the scene of the accident, is a small village between Woy Woy and Gosford on the central coast. At that place there is a small unattended railway station with two platforms between which run two sets of rails, one on the western side for north bound trains, the other on the eastern side for south bound trains running towards Sydney. The village is on the western side of the line and in 1959 it contained between thirty and forty houses. On the eastern

D side is Brisbane Water Drive with Brisbane Water beyond it, and there is a shop and a telephone. A little north of the station is a level crossing available to both vehicles and pedestrians. The crossing has large vehicular gates to close the crossing to vehicles and these, so far as relates to the present case, were always in the closed position. They are " penalty gates ", that is to say that a person who opens them to take his vehicle through will be liable to a

E penalty if he does not close them again. There were on the southern side of the crossing wicket gates for pedestrians which were always available for their use, night and day. Residents could enter or leave the village only by crossing the lines. No other mode of ingress or egress was available, as the road through the village, running parallel with the railway line, ended at the north in bushland and at the south came to a dead end, and on the west of this road there was

F impenetrable scrub, heavy bush and a rock escarpment. Furthermore the only means of access to the station was by the use of the crossing and the permanent way. Thus passengers embarking or alighting at this station would have to use the crossing if the relevant platform was not on their side of the line, and therefore they would have a special right (greater than a mere licensee's right) to use the crossing as invitees of the appellant or as persons contracting or

G intending to contract with him.

The crossing had been constructed by the appellant some distance north of the station and was in the centre partly paved with disused sleepers about five feet long (eight feet long according to one witness) placed north and south between and a little beyond the sets of rails. There was evidence that the ground was not level and that the sleepers were roughly laid on the ground in such

H a way that the sleepers were not level with each other or with the rails, and gaps existed not only alongside the rails (where gaps are required to take the flange of a wheel) but also between the sleepers. Also there was evidence that they did not lie firmly: they would " jump " when a vehicle went over them, and might move when stepped on. Evidence was given that persons crossing

I over the sleepers might fall, and instances of actual or near falls were deposed to by witnesses. The evidence may have convinced a jury that a hazard existed for pedestrians, especially at night, as the crossing was in darkness, the nearest light in the station some distance away not illuminating the crossing at all. Furthermore the sleepers made only a narrow bridge, as it were, and were laid in the centre of the crossing, and therefore were to the north of the wicket gates, so that a pedestrian, entering by one of the wicket gates and wishing to cross on the sleepers, could not walk directly to the other wicket gate but would have to walk somewhat diagonally.

It could not be ascertained with certainty what the respondent had been doing   A
immediately before the accident. She herself remembered nothing of what had
happened for a considerable time before the accident. Nobody saw her going
on to the level crossing or on to the track or falling down. There was some evidence as to her movements and condition on that afternoon, but it was not
wholly consistent. It was submitted on behalf of the appellant that the respondent was a trespasser, being on the track and away from the level crossing and   B
so outside the area of the licence, or that at any rate her presence on the track
remained unexplained and she had failed to prove that she was lawfully there or
that the accident was due to any fault on the part of the defendant. *Wakelin* v.
London & South Western Ry. Co. (3) was relied on. It is however possible, on
the basis of the evidence and by drawing inferences from the verdict of the jury
in conjunction with the summing-up, to form a view as to what probably happened   C
to the plaintiff before the accident. The view expressed by HERRON, C.J., on
the first appeal to the Full Court was adopted and repeated by MACFARLAN, J.,
giving the first judgment in the Full Court in the second appeal, the evidence
having been almost identical in the two trials. Their lordships accept this view
of what happened as being the probable version. HERRON, C.J., said:

    " Evidence was given that shortly before 6.20 p.m., the timetable estimate   D
of the passing of the train, the respondent had alighted from a taxicab at the
gates on the eastern side of the crossing. The jury could have inferred that
she intended to cross from east to west to return to her home. Evidence was
given that she was somewhat affected by liquor. This was disputed.
Although it has been described by the appellant's counsel as mere conjecture,
I am of opinion that the jury was entitled to have drawn the inference that,   E
in the darkness, the respondent probably stumbled and fell prostrate on
the city-bound tracks due to the rough and uneven surface of the sleepers.
It could be inferred that on the times deposed to in evidence, she may have
fallen thus only a brief time before the train came upon her. The probabilities favour the inference that the respondent fell due to the state of the sleepers
and the darkness."   F

From the acceptance of this version of the probable events it follows that the
appellant's contentions (a) that the respondent should be inferred to have been
deliberately or negligently trespassing on the track, and alternatively (b) that
her presence on the track was unexplained and her case was not proved, must be
rejected.

  In the first trial of the action the learned judge had in effect directed the   G
jury that the appellant owed to the respondent the general duty of care (" a
general duty to do everything which in all the circumstances was reasonably
necessary to secure the safety of persons using the crossing ") and in the first
appeal that direction was approved by the Full Court. He had however left
to the jury as possible heads of negligence, not only the roughness of the sleeper-
built crossing, but also three other matters namely (i) the lack of a warning   H
system at the crossing; (ii) excessive speed of the train in all the circumstances
and (iii) lack of a gatekeeper. It was held by the Full Court that these matters
should have been withdrawn from the jury, as none of them could reasonably
be regarded as in itself constituting negligence or as a proved cause of the accident.
Therefore a new trial was ordered. The respondent would naturally not rely in the
new trial on any of these three matters as heads of negligence. There was how-   I
ever no intention to restrict the circumstances to be taken into account by the
jury in deciding whether the appellant's failure to provide a smooth and firm
surface for the crossing and his failure to light it constituted negligence. HERRON,
C.J., said:

    " The whole of the appellant's works and operations at the point of the
crossing must be considered together. The state of darkness, the absence

(3) (1886), 12 App. Cas. 41.

A   of lighting, the position and state of the sleepers and of the crossing apart from them, the compulsion for the residents to use the crossing and the knowledge of the appellant that a fast express train would pass the spot according to a known timetable, all were factors to be considered not in isolation but taken together. I may also add the circumstance, even if it is no more than a factual consideration, that there was an absence of warning

B   devices at the crossing and that the small gates were at all times open for pedestrians."

However, as the Full Court had decided that the complaint of excessive speed had been wrongly left to the jury at the first trial, there was inevitably no such complaint at the retrial; and thus the allegations of negligence related only to

C   the nature of the crossing, the manner in which it was constructed, the manner in which it was maintained and the failure to light it at night. That is a feature of the retrial which complicates the argument, because no complaint of any positive activity was made.

Another feature of the retrial is that it was conducted on the basis that the respondent and the other persons using the crossing were licensees of the appellant.

D   The learned judge said in his summing-up:

" It is certainly in contest as to whether [the respondent] was in fact using the crossing, but that this crossing was used by the residents of Koolewong, and those others who had business there, with the permission of the [appellant]—and I invite correction if I am wrong—does not seem to be contested in this case. In other words, it seems to me from the manner in

E   which the case has progressed, it has been fought on the basis of the [respondent] being a licensee of the [appellant]."

That may well have been a sufficient assumption according to the law as it had been previously understood, but it is another feature of the retrial which complicates the argument in the appeal.

F   In the second appeal to the Full Court, and in the present appeal, the appellant has been asking only for a verdict to be entered in his favour and has not been asking for a retrial. Moffitt, J., said in his judgment:

" The appellant abandoned all grounds of appeal which would merely result in a new trial and does not seek to disturb the verdict on the ground of any direction given and has said that, if the respondent can show any

G   basis which would enable her on the evidence adduced to have the matter left to the jury, he does not seek to have the verdict set aside even although the form of pleading and directions given be inappropriate."

The appellant's main argument has been that (i) the respondent was at the time and place of the accident a mere licensee; (ii) at the trial she was complaining

H   only of the static condition of the crossing, and was not complaining of any positive activity carried on by the appellant; (iii) therefore the appellant owed to her only the special limited duty of care which belongs to the relationship of an occupier and his licensee; (iv) there was no breach of that duty, because there was between these parties no concealed danger, the respondent having from some ten years of experience full knowledge of the state of the crossing

I   and the absence of light. Is the appellant entitled to succeed with that argument?

In their lordships' opinion the basic principle for a case such as this is that occupation of premises is a ground of liability and is not a ground of exemption from liability. It is a ground of liability because it gives some control over and knowledge of the state of the premises, and it is natural and right that the occupier should have some degree of responsibility for the safety of persons entering his premises with his permission. In the language of the well-known passage in

LORD ATKIN's speech in *Donoghue* (*or McAlister*) v. *Stevenson* (4) there is a A
" proximity " between the occupier and such persons, and they are his " neighbours ".   Thus arises a duty of care, but the measure of it is not defined by or
derivable from *Donoghue* v. *Stevenson* (5).   At common law the measure of that
duty is a limited one: that has been established by many well-known authorities,
as was stated in the passage in *Lipman* v. *Clendinnen* (6) which has been cited
above.   In Australia there has been no statutory alteration of the common law B
such as has been effected in England and Wales by the Occupiers' Liability Act,
1957, and in Scotland by the Occupiers' Liability (Scotland) Act, 1960.   Therefore whenever there is a relationship of occupier and licensee, the special duty
of care which arises from that relationship exists.   If there is no other relevant
relationship, there is no further or other duty of care; but there is no exemption
from any other duty of care which may arise from other elements in the situation C
creating an additional relationship between the two persons concerned.   Theoreti-
ally in such a situation there are two duties of care existing concurrently, neither
displacing the other.   A plaintiff could successfully sue for breaches of either or
both of the duties if the defendant had committed such breaches, although for
practical purposes the plaintiff could be content with establishing the general
duty and would not gain anything by adding the special and limited duty.   D
    Subject to the two rather artificial problems which have to be considered, it
can be said that there was in this case another relevant relationship, creating a
general duty of care and justifying the direction given by the trial judge to
the jury.   The appellant was carrying on the inherently dangerous activity of
running express trains through a level crossing which was lawfully and necessarily
used by the local inhabitants and their guests and persons visiting them on busi- E
ness.   Such an activity was likely to cause serious accidents, unless it was carried
on with all reasonable care.   Therefore there was a duty for the appellant to
use all reasonable care.   It was open to the jury to find that there was some
negligence on the part of the appellant in respect of the state of the sleepers and
the lack of lighting at night, and that the respondent's accident was caused by
that negligence.   F
    One problem arises from the weakness of the assumed title of the respondent
and others using this level crossing.   It was assumed only that they crossed
with the permission of the appellant.   In most of the cases in which an operator
of railways had been held to owe a general duty of care to persons using a level
crossing there had been a public road or street across the railway or at least a
public right of way.   Australian examples are *Alchin* v. *Railways Comr.* (7), G
South Australian Ry. Comr. v. *Thomas* (8), *Comr. for Rys.* v. *Dowle* (9).   In
principle the liability is not based, however, on matters of title but on the
perilous nature of the operation and the de facto relationship (which after
Donoghue v. *Stevenson* (10) would be called " proximity " or " neighbourly "
relation) between the railway operator and a substantial number of persons
lawfully using the level crossing.   In England and Scotland we have had the H
following cases: *Bilbee* v. *London, Brighton & South Coast Ry. Co.* (11) (where
the road was described as an accommodation road); *Cliff* v. *Midland Ry. Co.* (12)
(where the road was described as an occupation road); *Ellis* v. *Great Western Ry.
Co.* (13) (" The case must be looked at with reference to the great additional
danger to the foot passengers from the velocity of trains, and the fatal consequences of a collision when produced by a train "; per COCKBURN, C.J. (14)); I

(4) [1932] All E.R. Rep. 1 at p. 11; [1932] A.C. 562 at p. 580.
(5) [1932] All E.R. Rep. 1; [1932] A.C. 562.
(6) (1932), 46 C.L.R. at pp. 569, 570; see p. 164, letter I, ante.
(7) (1935), 35 S.R.N.S.W. 498.   (8) (1951), 84 C.L.R. 84.
(9) (1958), 99 C.L.R. 353.   (10) [1932] All E.R. Rep. 1; [1932] A.C. 562.
(11) (1865), 18 C.B.N.S. 584.   (12) (1870), L.R. 5 Q.B. 258.
(13) [1874-80] All E.R. Rep. 699; (1874), L.R. 9 C.P. 551.
(14) [1874-80] All E.R. Rep. at p. 701; (1874), L.R. 9 C.P. at p. 556.

A *Jenner* v. *South Eastern Ry. Co.* (15); *Liddiatt* v. *Great Western Ry. Co.* (16) (citing Mellor, J., and Lush, J., in *Cliff's* case (17)); *Smith* v. *London, Midland & Scottish Ry. Co.* (18); *Lloyd's Bank, Ltd.* v. *Railway Executive* (19); *Lloyd's Bank, Ltd.* v. *British Transport Commission* (20).   In *Smith's* case (21) the Lord President (Lord Cooper) said:

B " I deduce from the decision in *Cliff* v. *Midland Ry. Co.* (22) and from (what is probably more significant for us) a whole series of Scottish decisions, beginning with *Grant* v. *Caledonian Ry. Co.* (23) and going on to *Hendrie* v. *Caledonian Ry. Co.* (24) that the railway company has a duty at every level-crossing where members of the public have a right to be, and where there is reason to expect them to be, to take all reasonable precautions in train operations (and perhaps in other respects) to reduce the danger to a minimum, C the nature of the precautions which are required and the question whether the duty has been fulfilled depending upon the circumstances of each case . . . I do not, therefore, think that in a case of this kind the critical question is whether the crossing is, in the technical sense of the Railway Clauses Act, 1845, an ' accommodation crossing ' or not, but whether it was used legitimately by members of the public, and the nature and volume of such traffic D reasonably to be anticipated.   There is all the difference in the world between an accommodation crossing which carries public vehicular traffic along a made road, and an accommodation crossing which consists of a gate in a railway fence in a remote rural area to enable a farm labourer or a shepherd to pass at rare intervals from one field to another."

E In the present case there is at least a de facto accommodation crossing for the use of the inhabitants of Koolewong and their guests and persons having business with them, and such persons lawfully use the crossing and necessarily use it as there is no other means of access.   Moffitt, J., in the course of his discussion of the possibility that on proper investigation a public right to use this crossing might be found to exist, said:

F " Even when the crossing is not a public road the use of the crossing as a means of access for the public in any practical sense is as if it were pursuant to a public right to cross the railway line.   The reality of the situation appears more to accord with the notion of a general public right to cross than with a miscellany of individual rights classifying the public users into categories according to the occasion of their crossing."

G However that may be, their lordships, accepting the assumed weakness of the title, consider that there was in this case the general duty of care in respect of the level crossing towards those who were lawfully on it.

The other problem arises in respect of the nature of the breaches alleged. In all or most of the decided cases the breaches have been acts or omissions in the actual operation of the trains or the signalling or the giving of warnings, H and not in the condition of the level crossing.   It can be contended that the general duty of care applies only in respect of such positive operations, whereas the limited duty applies to the static condition of the crossing.   This contention however is, on the facts of the present case, too artificial and unrealistic to be acceptable.   The positive operations and the static condition interact, and the grave danger is due to the combination of both.   It is dangerous to drive the I trains, especially at night, round the curve in the line and into the crossing at forty miles per hour, because the state of the crossing is so bad that somebody may fall on it in the path of an oncoming train.   The bad state of the crossing

---

(15) (1911), 105 L.T. 131.
(16) [1946] 1 All E.R. 731 at pp, 734, 735;   [1946] K.B. 545 at pp. 550, 551.
(17) (1870), L.R. 5 Q.B. at pp. 261, 264.   (18) 1948 S.C. 125.
(19) [1952] 1 All E.R. 1248.   (20) [1956] 3 All E.R. 291.
(21) 1948 S.C. at p. 136.   (22) (1870), L.R. 5 Q.B. 258.
(23) (1870), 9 Macph. (Ct. of Sess.) 258.   (24) 1909 S.C. 776.

involves serious danger because there are trains coming fast round the curve in A
the line and into the crossing. The railway operator's general duty of taking
all reasonable precautions to ensure the safety of persons lawfully using a level
crossing must include an obligation to keep the crossing itself in reasonably
adequate condition according to the circumstances. The breaches alleged
were breaches of this obligation.

This case is concerned with a level crossing lawfully and necessarily used B
to a substantial extent by all the inhabitants of a village and their guests and
persons having business with them. No opinion is expressed with regard to
private crossings or crossings only slighly used.

Quinlan's case (25) is readily distinguishable, because the position of a trespasser
is radically different from that of a person lawfully using a crossing. A trespasser
should not be there at all, and it would be unfair to allow him by his wrong-doing C
to interfere seriously with the occupier's freedom of action in making proper use
of the premises. Moreover the interference with the occupier's freedom of
action would be very serious, if a general duty of care were imposed on the
occupier in relation to the trespasser, because it is often not foreseeable when or
where or by what route or for what purpose the trespasser will be entering and
moving about the land. The reductio ad absurdum would be to require trains D
to be limited to a speed of ten miles per hour because there always might be a
trespasser on the line at any place at any time. No duty is owing to a trespasser
until it becomes known either that he is present or that the presence of a
trespasser is extremely likely. The duty, when it arises, is a duty of a very
limited character—not to injure him wilfully, and not to behave with reckless
disregard for his safety. These considerations do not apply in the case of a E
person lawfully using a well-defined level crossing provided by the railway
authority.

There is also in *Quinlan's* case (26) a dictum as to what the position would
have been if the respondent plaintiff had been a licensee instead of a trespasser:

" Whether, even so, such a character would have protected the respondent
in this case, it is not necessary to inquire. Presumably, in accordance with F
the principle laid down by the Court of Queen's Bench in *Gallagher* v.
Humphrey (27), he would have had to take the crossing with its risks as
he found it, but would have been entitled to complain of any positive act
of negligence on the part of the railway staff."

That was of course a summary statement, not going into problems of demarcation
and combination of static condition and positive operations, but recognising G
that the duty arising from the relationship of occupier and licensee did not
exclude any duty which might arise from other features of the situation.

There have been two further contentions on behalf of the respondent. The
first was that the respondent is in this case not prevented by her previous
experience of the crossing from showing a breach by the appellant of the limited
duty which he as occupier owed to her as licensee. It was said that her previous H
experience of the crossing was, according to her own evidence, only in daylight
and so was not sufficient to give her full knowledge of the perils of crossing in
darkness. It was said also that the licensee's knowledge of a peril should not
exempt the occupier from responsibility, if the licensee had no option to avoid
the peril, and in this case the plaintiff could not reach her home without using
the crossing in the darkness. These are interesting points, but could not properly I
be dealt with here as the case was fought on a different basis at the trial and
there were no directions given to the jury with regard to them. Secondly it
was contended that the respondent is entitled to recover for breach of a
" *Donoghue* v. *Stevenson* (28) duty ". But, in this case at any rate, there is no
room for a separate "*Donoghue* v. *Stevenson* (28) duty ". The general principle

---

(25) [1964] 1 All E.R. 897; [1964] A.C. 1054.
(26) [1964] 1 All E.R. at p. 911; [1964] A.C. at pp. 1082, 1083.
(27) (1862), 6 L.T. 684.   (28) [1932] All E.R. Rep. 1; [1932] A.C. 562.

A of " proximity " or " duty to a neighbour " is illustrated in the present case by the two relations which give rise to duties of care owing by the appellant to the respondent (a) as occupier to licensee and (b) as railway operator to lawful user of this level crossing.   There is no other relevant relation.

Their lordships will humbly advise Her Majesty that this appeal should be dismissed.   The appellant must pay the respondent's costs of this appeal.

B   *Appeal dismissed.*

Solicitors: *Light & Fulton* (for the appellant); *Kingsford, Dorman & Co.* (for the respondent).

[*Reported by* Kathleen J. H. O'Brien, *Barrister-at-Law.*]

C

HARRISON v. WELLS.

[Queen's Bench Division (His Honour Percy Lamb, Q.C.) (Official Referee), February 7, 8, 1966.]

D *Landlord and Tenant—Tenancy by estoppel—Repairing covenants by lessee— Lease granted by one of several proving executors without power to demise legal estate—Whether lessee estopped from denying lessor's title after surrendering tenancy—Whether repairing covenants enforceable by lessor's successors in title.*

Mrs. H., who was one of three executors of a deceased freeholder, all of whom had proved his will, granted a lease of premises, a ground floor shop
E and basement, which were part of his estate, to the defendant for seven years at an annual rent.   The lease contained a repairing covenant by the tenant in usual form.   The tenancy continued under s. 24 of the Landlord and Tenant Act, 1954.   In June or July, 1961, the defendant surrendered the tenancy and vacated the premises.   He was in breach of the repairing cove-
F nant.   In December, 1961, Mrs. H. died.   In March, 1962, the plaintiff, who was the executor of Mrs. H., brought an action for damages for breach of the repairing covenant.   In July, 1962, the freehold property was conveyed by trustees of the will of the deceased freeholder to the purchaser.   It was not disputed for present purposes that Mrs. H. had not had power to demise a legal estate by the lease by reason of s. 2* of the Administration of Estates Act, 1925.   By s. 18† of the Landlord and Tenant Act, 1927, damages for
G breach of the repairing covenant could not exceed the amount by which the value of the reversion was diminished.   The cost of performing the repairing covenant was agreed to be £760 10s.

Held: (i) after the surrender of the lease the defendant was no longer estopped from averring that Mrs. H. had no power to demise the premises to him (see p. 180, letter D, post).
H Dictum of Lord Blackburn in *Clark* v. *Adie* (*No. 2*) ((1877), 2 App. Cas. at pp. 435, 436) followed.

(ii) nevertheless the defendant was bound by his covenant with Mrs. H., which was enforceable by the plaintiff; accordingly the plaintiff was entitled to recover £760 10s., that sum not exceeding, if in fact it were necessary so to find, the value of the reversion (see p. 180, letters D and E, post).
I Dictum of Martin, B., in *Cuthbertson* v. *Irving* ((1859), 28 L.J.Ex. at p. 310) applied.

[As to a tenant being estopped from disputing his landlord's title, see 15 Halsbury's Laws (3rd Edn.) 248, 249, para. 457; p. 250, para. 460; and 23 ibid., 409, para. 988; and for cases on the subject, see 30 Digest (Repl.) 367-381, 63-238.

---

* Section 2, so far as material, is set out at p. 174, letter H, post.
† Section 18, so far as material, is set out at p. 175, letter A, post.

Reversed. C.A. [1966] 3 All E.R. 524.

As to covenants running with the land where the landlord's title is by estoppel, A
see 23 HALSBURY'S LAWS (3rd Edn.) 644, para. 1359, note (r).

As to statutory limitation of damages for breach of repairing covenant, see
23 HALSBURY'S LAWS (3rd Edn.) 589, 590, para. 1275.

For the Administration of Estates Act, 1925, s. 2, see 9 HALSBURY'S STATUTES
(2nd Edn.) 721.

For the Landlord and Tenant Act, 1927, s. 18, see 13 HALSBURY'S STATUTES B
(2nd Edn.) 902.]

Cases referred to:

Clark v. Adie (No. 2), (1877), 2 App. Cas. 423; 46 L.J.Ch. 598; 37 L.T. 1;
    30 Digest (Repl.) 368, 90.
Cuthbertson v. Irving, (1859), 4 H. & N. 742; 28 L.J.Ex. 306; 33 L.T.O.S.
    328; affd. Ex.Ch. (1860), 6 H. & N. 135; 29 L.J.Ex. 485; 3 L.T. 335; C
    158 E.R. 56; 21 Digest (Repl.) 347, 956.
Doe d. Higginbotham v. Barton, [1835-42] All E.R. Rep. 546; (1840), 11 Ad. &
    El. 307; 9 L.J.Q.B. 57; 113 E.R. 432; 30 Digest (Repl.) 378, 213.
Doe d. Johnson v. Baytup, (1835), 3 Ad. & El. 188; 4 L.J.K.B. 263; 111 E.R.
    384; 30 Digest (Repl.) 373, 156.
Jacquin v. Holland, [1960] 1 All E.R. 402; [1960] 1 W.L.R. 258; Digest D
    (Cont. Vol. A) 1016, 5050a.
Lloyds Bank, Ltd. v. Lake, [1961] 2 All E.R. 30; [1961] 1 W.L.R. 884; Digest
    (Cont. Vol. A) 1015, 5047b.
Palmer v. Ekins, (1728), 2 Ld. Raym. 1550; 92 E.R. 505; 21 Digest (Repl.)
    326, 804.
Pargeter v. Harris, (1845), 7 Q.B. 708; 15 L.J.Q.B. 113; 5 L.T.O.S. 346; E
    115 E.R. 656; 21 Digest (Repl.) 334, 870.
Sturgeon v. Wingfield, (1846), 15 M. & W. 224; 15 L.J.Ex. 212; 153 E.R. 831;
    21 Digest (Repl.) 360, 1051,
Tadman v. Henman, [1893] 2 Q.B. 168; 57 J.P. 664; 21 Digest (Repl.) 361,
    1055.
Walton v. Waterhouse, (1672), 2 Wms. Saund. 415c. F

Action.

In this action commenced by writ dated Mar. 2, 1962, Charles Benjamin
Harrison, the executor of the estate of Mrs. Blanche Madeline Tulk-Hart, claimed
against the defendant, Bedford Wells, damages for breaches of repairing covenants
contained in a document under seal dated June 16, 1949, described as a lease, G
made between the deceased and the defendant, whereby the deceased purported
to grant to the defendant a tenancy of a ground floor shop and basement known
as no. 18, Beynon Parade, Beynon Road, Carshalton, Surrey, for a term of seven
years from June 24, 1949, at a rent of £125 per annum. After the expiration of the
lease, the term of years continued, by virtue of s. 24 of the Landlord and Tenant
Act, 1954. The defendant vacated the premises (as he alleged) on June 24, 1961, H
or (as the plaintiff alleged) on July 27, 1961. The plaintiff also claimed mesne
profits for the period, June 24 to July 27, 1961. The facts and pleadings are set
out in the judgment.

Christopher Priday for the plaintiff.
Michael Hoare for the defendant.

HIS HONOUR PERCY LAMB, Q.C.: In this action the executor of Mrs.
Blanche Madeline Tulk-Hart, who died on Mar. 16, 1961, claims damages for
breach of covenant to repair premises at no. 18, Beynon Parade, Beynon Road,
Carshalton, Surrey. In order that everybody may appreciate what I am now
going to say, I am going to refer to the abstract of title of those premises before
continuing with my judgment. This was agreed and accepted as accurate.

On Sept. 19, 1906, Dr. Tulk-Hart by his will of this date appointed his wife,
Mrs. Tulk-Hart, and Mr. Hayllar Hayllar executors of his will. On Oct. 3, 1922,

A   Dr. Tulk-Hart appointed Charles Hilary Bryant as an additional executor to his will of Sept. 19, 1906. On June 23, 1927, there was a conveyance of property by W. T. Wheeler to G. A. Smith. On Oct. 8, 1928, there was a conveyance of property by G. A. Smith to Dr. Tulk-Hart. On Mar. 17, 1930, Dr. Tulk-Hart died. On July 8, 1930, all three executors proved the above-mentioned will and codicil thereto in the Lewes District Probate Registry. On June 16, 1949, there

B   was a lease of the premises by Mrs. Tulk-Hart to Mr. Bedford Wells, the defendant. On Apr. 26, 1951, the executors vested property in themselves in fee simple on trust for sale by vesting assent. On Apr. 27, 1951, by deed of appointment of this date made between Mrs. Tulk-Hart and Mr. Hayllar Hayllar of the first part, Charles Hilary Bryant of the second part and Charles Benjamin Harrison of the third part, Mr. Harrison was appointed a trustee of the will and codicil in

C   place of Mr. Bryant. On June 20, 1961, Mr. Hayllar Hayllar died. On Dec. 16, 1961, Mrs. Tulk-Hart died. On Apr. 19, 1962, Mr. Harrison appointed Cyril Keith Cullen as trustee of the will of Dr. Tulk-Hart in place of Mrs. Tulk-Hart, and on July 23, 1962, there was a conveyance of the property by Mr. Harrison and Mr. Cullen to a Mr. Mutch, and I was told (and I find as a fact) that the price paid
•   therefor was £2,250.

D   The covenants of which breach is alleged in this action are the usual repairing covenants which are contained in a document under seal dated June 16, 1949, described as a lease, and made between the deceased lady, Mrs. Tulk-Hart, and the defendant, whereby she purported to grant the tenancy of a ground floor shop and basement, which is at no. 18, Beynon Parade, Carshalton, for a term of seven years at an annual rent of £125.

E   The action was commenced on Mar. 2, 1962, by a writ on which was endorsed the statement of claim. Paragraph 1 recites the lease. Paragraph 2 sets out the relevant covenants which I need not read; they are the usual form of repairing covenants and for yielding up at the determination of the term. Paragraphs 3 to 7 are as follows:

F   "3. After the expiration of the aforesaid lease the aforesaid term of years continued by virtue of s. 24 of the Landlord and Tenant Act, 1954. 4. The aforesaid term of years terminated by the defendant's surrender thereof on June 24, 1961. The defendant vacated the premises on July 27, 1961. Between June 24, 1961, and July 27, 1961, the defendant carried out works on the premises in purported compliance with the aforesaid covenants. 5. In breach of each and all of the aforesaid covenants the defendant has failed to

G   yield up the premises repaired maintained or kept in compliance with the aforesaid covenants . . . Full particulars of the defendant's said breaches are set out in a schedule of dilapidations prepared on May 5, 1961, . . . and served on the defendant before action. 6. The cost of remedying the aforesaid breaches is £1,138 5s. 7d. and the value of the reversion expectant upon the expiration of the said term of years has depreciated by this amount.

H   A reasonable time for carrying out the works necessary to remedy the said breaches is eight weeks. 7. The plaintiff is the executor of the estate of the deceased and as such entitled to the reversion expectant upon the expiration of the said lease and of the freehold of the premises."

It is a strange allegation in a statement of claim when the admitted abstract of

I   title shows that the people entitled to the freehold were the plaintiff and Mr. Cullen because they conveyed it to Mr. Mutch, and the plaintiff claims damages for breaches of covenant and mesne profits.

By his defence dated Sept. 26, 1962, the defendant admits the execution of the lease and the covenant therein and that, having held over at the end of his term until June 24, 1961, he vacated the premises on that date. He goes on to allege that between June 24 and July 27, 1961, he carried out a number of repairs but denies that he was, during this period, in occupation of the premises save for

the purpose of doing such works. He then denies any breach of any of the coven- **A**
ants and denies any damage as alleged or at all.

On Oct. 3, 1963, SIR WALKER CARTER, Q.C., ordered the preparation of an
official referee's schedule. This was done, and as a result the parties have agreed
subject to liability that repairs to the value of £760 10s. were necessary to comply
with the covenant alleged to be broken.

Discovery took place in due course, but due no doubt to an oversight a con- **B**
veyance of the property on July 23, 1962, to which I have already referred, and
made between the plaintiff and Cyril Keith Cullen, the trustees of the will of
Dr. Tulk-Hart deceased, as vendors to a Donald Patrick Mutch as purchaser for
the sum of £2,250, was not disclosed.   The defendant's solicitors pressed for
disclosure and eventually some time before July, 1965, it was disclosed. This led
the defendant's solicitors to write to the plaintiff's solicitors asking them to **C**
agree to an amendment of the defence. That request was not granted, so a summons was issued which led to an order giving leave to amend the defence, as
appears in red in the defence which is filed with the court. It was in these terms:

" 5. Further the defendant will rely upon the facts and documents recited
in a conveyance of the said property no. 18, Beynon Road dated July 23,
1962, and made between the plaintiff and one Cyril Keith Cullen as ' vendors ' **D**
and one Donald Patrick Mutch as ' purchaser ' whereby it appears that the
deceased had not in June, 1949, or at any material time any sufficient title to
the said property entitling her as sole lessor to grant the lease referred to in
the statement of claim."

That led to a reply joining issue. Paragraph 2 of the reply says: **E**

" In answer to the facts and matters alleged in para. 5 of the amended
defence the plaintiff will if necessary contend that the defendant is estopped
from denying the plaintiff's title to the said property or her right to grant
the said lease by reason of the facts admitted in paras. 1 and 2 of the amended
defence and the defendant's acknowledgment of the deceased and after her
death of the plaintiff as his landlord from the commencement of the said **F**
lease until the amendment of the defence in this action."

The cost of that summons was reserved to the trial. I have already decided and
told the parties that in my judgment the request should have been acceded to
and that the costs unnecessarily incurred should be the defendant's in any event
with a certificate for counsel.

Counsel for the plaintiff on those pleadings informed me, and counsel for the **G**
defendant agreed, that the abstract of title to the property, which I have read,
was accurate and complete, and that the will of Dr. Tulk-Hart and the grant of
probate thereof were also admitted and lodged with the court. From this it
followed without any doubt that Mrs. Tulk-Hart was not in a position to grant a
tenancy of these premises which form part of the estate of the deceased Dr.Tulk-
Hart on June 16, 1949, or at any time, and I was referred to the Administration of **H**
Estates Act, 1925, s. 2 (2), which took the place of the Land Transfer Act, 1897,
s. 2 (2) and the Conveyancing Act, 1911, s. 12:

" Where as respects real estate there are two or more personal representatives [as there were in this case] a conveyance of real estate devolving
under this Part of this Act shall not, save as otherwise provided as respects
trust estates including settled land, be made without the concurrence therein **I**
of all such representatives or an order of the court . . .".

That is all that I need read of the section.

Nevertheless counsel for the plaintiff submitted that a landlord's title cannot be
questioned by his tenant so that he becomes a landlord by estoppel, and such a
creature known only to the law also has a reversion by estoppel. At that stage
of the case he was at pains to satisfy me that such a reversion has a value which is
capable of assessment by a court, and this he regarded as a necessary part of his

A case because of the Landlord and Tenant Act, 1927, s. 18. Section 18 (1) reads:

" Damages for a breach of a covenant or agreement to keep or put premises
in repair during the currency of a lease, or to leave or put premises in repair at
the termination of a lease, whether such covenant or agreement is expressed
or implied, and whether general or specific, shall in no case exceed the amount
(if any) by which the value of the reversion (whether immediate or not) in the
B premises is diminished owing to the breach of such covenant or agreement
as aforesaid . . ."

That is all that I need read of that.

Counsel made reference to a case of *Lloyds Bank, Ltd.* v. *Lake* (1), which was
tried by His Honour Sir Brett Cloutman, V.C., Q.C., as an official referee, and
C part of the judgment to which counsel referred was in these terms (2):

" Now I am greatly indebted to counsel for the defendant's careful arguments and industry in the defence of this claim, and I will add that this
reasoning is ingenious and almost attractive; but I have no doubt at all
that it is wrong. As a matter of simple logic it will not do to say that because
the value of property in repair is nil, therefore, the value is still nil if it is out
D of repair due to the breaches of the outgoing tenant. Not at all. The value
is minus £X, which is what the tenant must pay someone to take over, first
the fag end of the lease, and later the last moment of the lease. Certainly,
the reversion on the defendant's lease is only momentary and notional (see
per Devlin, L.J., in *Jacquin* v. *Holland* (3)) but this need not prevent it
from being valued."

E Of course I shall follow that and accept it with gratitude. Counsel next submitted
that the plaintiff had a reversion by estoppel, and he referred to the most interesting case of *Cuthbertson* v. *Irving* (4), and to the judgment of the court which was
delivered by Martin, B. The court consisted of Pollock, C.B., Martin, Bramwell and Watson, BB. Martin, B., said this (5):

F " The second objection is, that the case shows that the lessor had no legal
estate in the premises demised at the time of the lease, and, therefore, had no
estate in reversion to assign, and, consequently, the plaintiff was not an
assignee within the meaning of the statute (6) . . . Upon consideration, we
think that the authorities show that the defendant is estopped from disputing
that the lessor was seised of an estate in reversion, and as there are apt words
G in the assignment to convey a legal estate in fee in reversion to the plaintiff,
the estoppel continues, notwithstanding the assignment to him shows a
want of title. The estate in reversion by estoppel was created before the
assignment was executed, and, in our opinion, was not destroyed by it. It
would have been otherwise if the want of title had appeared on the face of
the lease itself. In that case, the true facts being there disclosed, there
H would have been no estoppel at all—*Pargeter* v. *Harris* (7). There are some
points in the law relating to estoppels which seem clear; first, when a lessor,
without any legal estate or title, demises to another, the parties themselves
are estopped from disputing the validity of the lease on that ground; in
other words, a tenant cannot deny his landlord's title, nor can the lessor
dispute the validity of the lease: secondly, where a lessor, by deed, grants a
I lease without title, and subsequently acquires one, the estoppel is said to be
fed, and the lease and reversion then take effect in interest, and not by
estoppel, and an action will lie by the assignee of the reversion against the
tenant on the covenants in the leases . . .

" A question which further arises is, that in the present case, namely,

---

(1) [1961] 2 All E.R. 30.   (2) [1961] 2 All E.R. at p. 34.
(3) [1960] 1 All E.R. 402 at p. 409.   (4) (1859), 28 L.J.Ex. 306.
(5) (1859), 28 L.J.Ex. at pp. 308, 309.
(6) 32 Hen. 8 c. 34 (1540) (grantees of reversions).   (7) (1845), 7 Q.B. 708.

whether the assignee of a lessor, on a lease by deed, who has no estate in the land, has the reversion by estoppel as against the lessee. This question arises not unfrequently, as in the present instance, where a mortgagor makes a lease by indenture, and afterwards assigns his equity of redemption by a deed that would pass a legal reversion in fee. It seems clearly established that upon a mortgage of lands, whatever the title of the mortgagor may be, his subsequent possession or occupation is at the will of the mortgagee, and he has nothing in the land whereout any interest can pass to a tenant so as to affect the right of the mortgagee, and that in the present instance no further or other interest passed to the defendant than by estoppel. Thus far seems plain, but upon the remaining part of the question the authorities unfortunately are not uniform."

I need not read that part. Later, MARTIN, B., said (8):

" In *Sturgeon* v. *Wingfield* (9) the same view will be found laid down by the same learned judge (10). That was a case where a lease by indenture was originally good only by estoppel, and the supposed reversion was assigned to the defendant, together with a subsequently acquired legal term for years which fed the estoppel. His lordship said, that taking it in point of fact that the lessor had no interest originally, there was an estate by estoppel, and that the estate was prima facie an estate in fee simple. *Palmer* v. *Ekins* (11) was an action, by the assignee of the reversion, against the lessee for non-payment of rent; plea, that the lessor, before making the lease, conveyed his estate to another. It was held, that the plea simply amounted to a special nil habuit in tenementis, and was bad; and LORD RAYMOND, in giving the judgment of the court, expressly says that the assignee shall take advantage of the estoppel. The note of Mr. Serjeant Williams to *Walton* v. *Waterhouse* (12) is: ' Where the grantor or lessor has nothing in the land at the time of the grant or lease, and where no interest passed out of him to the grantee, or also by the grant or lease, and the title begins by the estoppel which the deed creates between the parties [all that, of course, is applicable to the case which I am considering] such estoppel will run with the land ' (and it is presumed with the reversion also) [I do not know whether those are the words of MARTIN, B., or the words of Mr. Serjeant Williams, but that is where it appears in the report] ' into whosesoever hands it comes, whether heir or assignee.' We apprehend this note is the right statement of the law; and on that the following propositions may be laid down: first, if any estate or interest passes from the lessor, or the legal title is shown upon the face of the lease, there is no estoppel at all; secondly, if the lessor have no title, and the lessee be evicted by him who has, the lessee can defeat him, and establish a defence to any action brought against him—*Doe d. Higginbotham* v. *Barton* (13). But, thirdly, so long as the lessee continues in possession under the lease [counsel for the defendant attached great importance to those words when he came to his submissions] the law will not permit him to set up any defence, founded upon the fact that the lessor nil habuit in tenementis, and that upon the execution of the lease the lessor has created, in contemplation of law, a reversion in fee simple, transmissible, by descent, to his heir, and, by purchase, to an assignee or devisee."

MARTIN, B., then said (14):

" This state of the law in reality tends to maintain right and justice and the enforcement of the contracts which men enter into with each other

---

(8) (1859), 28 L.J.Ex. at pp. 309, 310.   (9) (1846), 15 M. & W. 224.
(10) PARKE, B.   (11) (1728), 2 Ld. Raym. 1550.
(12) (1672), 2 Wms. Saund. 415c.
(13) [1835-42] All E.R. Rep. 546; (1840), 11 Ad. & El. 307.
(14) (1859), 28 L.J.Ex. at p. 310.

A (one of the great objects of all law), for so long as the lessee enjoys everything which his lease purports to grant, how does it concern him what the title of the lessor, or who the heir or the assignee of the lessor really is? All that is required of him is, that having the full consideration for the contract he has entered into, he should on his part perform his.''

B That was a very interesting and enlightening judgment, and it has helped me in this case.

  Counsel for the plaintiff suggested that having made those submissions in law it would be convenient not to call any evidence at that stage but to hear what counsel for the defendant had to say about it. Counsel for the defendant did not demur, and I agreed, so no evidence was called and I asked him to make his submissions on behalf of the defendant. He referred again to the Administration C of Estates Act, 1925, s. 2, which I have read, pointing out very forcibly that Mrs. Tulk-Hart had no power to lease the property, and that as a result there never was any lease recognisable by the law. From that submission he went on to contend that there being no lease there was no estoppel, which of course was a very interesting approach to the matter. He said: suppose during the occupation of the premises by his client there was an estoppel (for the sake of argument) and D that he could not be heard to dispute that his landlord was in fact and in law entitled to let the property and to enforce the covenant in the document called a lease when in fact it was not a lease at all, so soon as the defendant vacated the premises he was free to tell the world and this court the true facts. To support that submission he referred me to 15 HALSBURY'S LAWS OF ENGLAND (3rd Edn.), 248, 249, para. 457. Incidentally, he referred me, first of all, to p. 168, para. 334 E (the meaning of estoppel) but I do not think that I need read it. This is what he cited:

    " A tenant is not estopped either before or after the expiration of the term from showing that his lessor's title has determined. If, however, the tenant came into possession under the lessor, the better opinion would seem to be F   that he must surrender possession before he disputes the lessor's title . . .''

  That seems clearly to show that if the tenant has vacated the premises and surrendered his apparent interest therein, he is at liberty to tell the truth to the court about the landlord's position, and counsel went back to Cuthbertson v. Irving (15), and cited again the portion beginning " for so long as the lessee enjoys everything . . .'' which I have read (16), and he said that that necessarily G implies that it only refers to the time when he is in occupation of the premises. To support that he referred me to SPENCER BOWER ON ESTOPPEL at p. 265. Having looked at the book carefully and studied it, I would be very slow—and I think any court would be very slow—not to accept this statement as being good law. This is what it says:

    " A landlord or tenant who is estopped by his acts and conduct from H   disputing the existence of the other's title or right at the date of the demise is nevertheless, if and when that title or right comes to an end, at liberty to say so, because there is obviously no inconsistency here between the two assertions. Accordingly, if and when the landlord's title is determined, either by his death, if he had an estate for life only, or by the death of another, if his estate was pur autre vie, or by the expiration of his term, if he was a termor, I   or by any other means, the tenant, who was theretofore estopped from disputing his landlord's title, becomes (in the language of the old authorities) ' unmuzzled ', and there is nothing to preclude him from setting up such determination against the landlord, or (as the case may be) against any person claiming as his heir, devisee, or assignee, or from showing that such person is not in fact or law the heir or devisee of the original lessor, or the assignee of his reversion; and, conversely, the landlord, under the like

---

(15) (1859), 28 L.J.Ex. at p. 310.   (16) See letter A, supra.

conditions, enjoys a corresponding freedom as against the tenant. The **A**
estoppel, however, continues if there is no strict proof of the determination
of the title from denying which the party was originally precluded, as, for
instance, when it is shown that the title expired before, and not after,
the commencement of the tenancy created by the estoppel, or where the
tenant's evidence in support of a case of expiration of title proves too much,
and shows that the landlord never had any title at all, an assertion which **B**
the tenant is clearly estopped from making. Unless the tenant can establish
the expiration of his landlord's title in any of the ways suggested, he must
himself determine the relation by giving up possession of the demised
premises, if he is to regain his freedom from the estoppel; by this means
alone can he set himself at liberty to take up an independent and adverse
attitude towards his former landlord."   **C**

That seems pretty clear and concise, and if I may respectfully say so to the
learned author, good sense. From there counsel for the defendant went to the
case of *Clark* v. *Adie* (*No. 2*) (17), and he relied on the speech of LORD BLACKBURN
in that case which relates to patents, but nevertheless is very apposite and very
helpful. LORD BLACKBURN, referring to the position of a licensee working under
a licence for a patent right said (18):   **D**

" The position of a licensee who under a licence is working a patent right,
for which another has got a patent, is very analogous indeed to the position
of a tenant of lands who has taken a lease of those lands from another. So
long as the lease remains in force, and the tenant has not been evicted from
the land, he is estopped from denying that his lessor had a title to that land.
When the lease is at an end, the man who was formally the tenant, but has **E**
now ceased to be so, may show that it was altogether a mistake to have taken
that lease, and that the land really belonged to him; but during the continuance of the lease he cannot show anything of the sort: it must be taken as
against him that the lessor had a title to the land. Now a person who takes
a licence from a patentee is bound upon the same principle and in exactly **F**
the same way. The two cases are very closely analogous; in analogies there
are always apt to be some differences, but I know of none in this. The tenant
under a lease is at liberty to show that the parcel of land which he and the
lessor are disputing about was never comprised in the lease at all; he may
show that he took the lease of Blackacre from the person who granted him
the lease, and that the spot of land then in question, Greenacre, we will **G**
suppose, is a piece of land which was never included in the lease at all, and
which belongs to him (the tenant) under some other right. So may a licensee
under a patent show . . ."

That was very conclusive too, but counsel went on to refer me to *Tadman* v.
Henman (19), which was an interesting action tried by CHARLES, J. The headnote
to the report reads (19):   **H**

" Although a tenant who has been let into possession of land by a lessor is
estopped from disputing his lessor's title, third persons, not claiming possession
of the land under the tenant, are not so estopped. A person, therefore, who
lets premises to which he has no title to a tenant, cannot distrain for arrears
of rent due from the tenant the goods of a third person which happen to have
been brought on to the premises by the tenant's licence."   **I**

This was the case of a man who was carrying on the occupation of an undertaker
and had hearses on the land for that purpose. The hearses, however, belonged to
his wife, and when he did not pay his rent the landlord distrained for the rent
and the wife said " You cannot do that; they are mine and you are not the
landlord ". CHARLES, J., supported her defence and he said this (20):

---

(17) (1877), 2 App. Cas. 423.   (18) (1877), 2 App. Cas. at pp. 435, 436.
(19) [1893] 2 Q.B. 168.   (20) [1893] 2 Q.B. at pp. 170, 171.

A   " Now, the land was not the defendant's to let; he had no title to it whatever. The only person who had any title to it was the Bishop of London,
and there is no evidence that the letting by the defendant was authorised or
ratified by the bishop. It is true that, notwithstanding the absence of title
in the defendant, and the consequent invalidity of the agreement of tenancy
[I draw attention to those words " the consequent invalidity of the agreement
B   of tenancy "] the tenant Tadman himself having been let into possession by
the defendant under the agreement, cannot be heard to say that the defendant had no right to make the agreement. He is estopped from disputing
his lessor's title. So far as Tadman is concerned, the rent is payable, and
the ordinary incidents of a valid tenancy are applicable; so that, on non-
payment of rent, Tadman's goods would be liable to be distrained. But the
C   hearse distrained was not Tadman's, but his wife's. Does, then, the estoppel
which binds him extend also to her? It is contended that, as she brought the
article upon the premises by the licence of her husband, she is so bound;
and in support of that contention the case of *Doe d. Johnson* v. *Baytup* (21)
was cited. It was there held that a person who had got into possession of
premises by the licence of the lessor of the plaintiff could not defend an
D   ejectment, but was estopped from disputing the title of the lessor of the
plaintiff . . . [Charles, J., said that that had nothing to do with the case
before him and only decided another matter with which he was not con-
cerned]. That case concedes that a tenant or licensee may always dispute
his lessor's or licensor's title, provided he first gives up possession of the
premises [and that is the phrase and submission on which counsel for the
E   defendant so strongly bases his submissions to this court. Charles J.,
continued (22):] But here Mrs. Tadman had no possession of the premises
to give up."

But she is not the tenant and she can be heard to say that the plaintiff was not the
landlord; therefore he had not a right to distrain.

All those, as I say, were very convincing submissions, and they led counsel to
F   submit first that there was no power in the plaintiff to execute a lease; therefore
there was no lease known to the law. It follows from that that there was no
reversion—there never was—and the next step was that the plaintiff has suffered
no damage. If damage there is, he is the wrong plaintiff, and any rule of law
precluding the defendant from raising these points because a tenant is estopped
from doing so is quite ineffective once the defendant has vacated the premises,
G   and by common acknowledgment of everybody he did vacate them (23) in June,
1961; therefore, he said, the action must fail.

To those submissions counsel for the plaintiff made reply. For the purposes of
his argument he accepted that there was no power in Mrs. Tulk-Hart to execute
a lease because of the provision of s. 2 of the Administration of Estates Act, 1925.
I add that he did that for the purposes of argument; he did not put it forward
H   as part of his case, but for the purposes of his submission in reply he accepted it.
Therefore, he said, if no lease, no reversion, and if there is no reversion s. 18 of the
Landlord and Tenant Act, 1954, does not apply. [The Official Referee read
the terms of s. 18 (1) which are set out at p. 175, letter A, ante, and continued:]
There is nothing there to say that the damages shall be the damage to the reversion; it says that they are not to exceed the damages to the reversion, and counsel
I   for the plaintiff submitted that on counsel for the defendant's own argument the
plaintiff was clearly entitled to succeed because the defendant had covenanted
under a deed to carry out certain repairs to 18, Beynon Parade, and he had on
the evidence which was subsequently called and which satisfied me (and as I
find as a fact) failed to perform the covenant in that document in a number of
ways. Further, said counsel for the plaintiff, the defendant was liable under his

---

(21) (1835), 3 Ad. & El. 188.   (22) [1893] 2 Q.B. at p. 171.
(23) The plaintiff alleged that the defendant vacated the premises on July 27, 1961;
see p. 172, letter H, ante.

contract under seal, for breach of covenant, and matters of interest to lawyers   A
about landlords by estoppel or reversion by estoppel do not arise. Counsel went
back again to MARTIN, B., as I will, where he says this (24):

" This state of the law in reality tends to maintain right and justice and the
enforcement of the contracts which men enter into with each other (one
of the great objects of all law), for so long as the lessee enjoys everything
which his lease purports to grant, how does it concern him what the title of   B
the lessor, or who the heir or the assignee of the lessor really is? All that is
required of him is, that having the full consideration for the contract he has
entered into, he should on his part perform his."

What the plaintiff did with the rent, or rather the deceased lady did with the rent,
or what the true owners have or may do about the wrongful exercise of powers of   C
leasing by the deceased lady, whether or not the occupation by the defendant for
the twelve years was profitable or not, were matters which both counsel agreed
were irrelevant, and I heard no evidence on those matters at all.

With considerable gratitude to both counsel for their help in what might have
been a very difficult question to decide, I have no hesitation now in finding these
facts: (i) that the cost of performing the covenant contained in the deed of   D
June 16, 1949, made between Mrs. Tulk-Hart, whose executor the plaintiff is,
amounts to £760 10s., the figure which the parties have agreed subject to liability;
(ii) that in so far as it is necessary for me so to do, which I very much doubt, I
find that the figure does not exceed the damage to the reversion. With those facts
found, I hold on my understanding of the law that by surrendering and vacating
the premises on June 24, 1961, (25), the defendant was no longer precluded from
averring that the lady who let him into the premises on June 16, 1949, had no   E
power so to do. I further hold that the defendant is bound by the common law
of England to perform his covenant contained in the deed between himself and
that lady which was executed on June 16, 1949, an obligation which he has
failed to observe, and that those covenants are enforceable by the plaintiff as
her executor, and I rely on MARTIN, B.'s speech (26) for that. They are perfectly
clear covenants under seal. The defendant is proved not to have obeyed those   F
covenants and to be in breach of his contract, and I see no reason why he should
not pay the cost of performing them.

The action also includes a claim for mesne profits. I dismiss that part of the
claim because they obviously are only recoverable by the landlord, and this lady
was not the landlord, but I give judgment for the plaintiff for £760 10s.

Order accordingly.   G

Solicitors: *Sharpe, Pritchard & Co.*, agents for *Jolly & Co.*, Brighton (for the
plaintiff); *C. H. Stanley Smith*, Carshalton (for the defendant).

[*Reported by* MARY COLTON, *Barrister-at-Law.*]

H

I

---

(24) (1859), 28 L.J.Ex. at p. 310; see p. 176, letter I, to p. 177, letter A, ante.
(25) See footnote (23), p. 179, ante.   (26) See p. 177, letter A, ante.

A

TAYLOR v. ROVER CO., LTD. AND OTHERS
(RICHARD W. CARR & CO., LTD., Third Party).

[BIRMINGHAM ASSIZES (Baker, J.), December 2, 3, 10, 13, 1965.]

Master and Servant—Liability of master—Accident to servant—Tool bought from reputable manufacturers—Defect in tool due to work done by manufacturers'

B *independent contractors—Previous accident to another servant from same tool of which employers had knowledge—Whether manufacturers were liable to servant.*

Negligence—Causation—Intervening cause—Negligence attributable to employer—Tool bought from reputable manufacturers—Previous accident to another servant due to defect in tool—Tool not withdrawn from use.

C   The plaintiff, in the course of his employment with the first defendants, was injured and subsequently lost an eye when a splinter of steel flew from the top of a chisel which he was hammering and entered his eye. The chisel was fashioned by the second defendants and was made according to a specification and blue print supplied by the first defendants, from alloyed steel purchased from the third party, who also heat-treated it for the second defendants,

D   after it had been fashioned by the second defendants; the chisel, so hardened, was then supplied by the second defendants to the first defendants (the employer). The trial judge held that the plaintiff was entitled to succeed against the first defendants, his employer, because there had previously been an accident caused by the chisel to the plaintiff's leading hand who had failed to withdraw the chisel from circulation and whose knowledge of the danger

E   was that of the first defendants. The trial judge found that the defect in the chisel, i.e., the hardness, was not caused during its use by the first defendants, but that it was caused by neglect in the original heat treatment by the third party*, and that there was no reasonable probability of examination of the chisel by the first defendants before the accident to the leading hand†. The second defendants relied on the third party for hardening and would not have

F   examined the chisel for hardening in the absence of a special condition in the contract to supply the chisel.

Held: the second defendants were not liable to the plaintiff, because—
(i) it was the keeping of the chisel in circulation by the first defendants with the knowledge that it was dangerous that caused the accident, and accordingly the chain of causation by the second defendants was broken (see

G   p. 185, letter G, post); and
(ii) the second defendants, having got a competent hardener (the third party) to do the hardening of the chisel for them, were entitled to assume that the work was properly done, and were under no duty to examine and test the chisel themselves for hardness; thus they were not liable for the faulty hardening by their hardening agent or independent contractor (see p. 186,

H   letter G, post).
Dictum of LORD MORTON OF HENRYTON in *Davie* v. *New Merton Board Mills, Ltd.* ([1959] 1 All E.R. at p. 357) followed.

[As to a master's duty to provide suitable appliances, see 25 HALSBURY'S LAWS (3rd Edn.) 511, para. 978; and for cases on the subject, see 34 DIGEST (Repl.) 251-254, *1812-1842*.]

I Cases referred to:
Buckner v. *Ashby and Horner, Ltd.*, [1941] 1 K.B. 321, 337; 110 L.J.K.B. 460; 105 J.P. 220; 36 Digest (Repl.) 15, *64*.
Davie v. *New Merton Board Mills, Ltd.*, [1959] 1 All E.R. 346; [1959] A.C. 604; [1959] 2 W.L.R. 331; 34 Digest (Repl.) 253, *1836*.
Haseldine v. *Daw & Son, Ltd.*, [1941] 3 All E.R. 156; [1941] 2 K.B. 343; 111 L.J.K.B. 45; 36 Digest (Repl.) 29, *125*.

---

* See p. 185, letter C, post.   † See p. 184, letter D, post.

M'Alister (or Donoghue) v. *Stevenson,* [1932] All E.R. Rep. 1; [1932] A.C. 562;   A
101 L.J.P.C. 119; 147 L.T. 281; 36 Digest (Repl.) 85, *458.*

Mason v. *Williams and Williams, Ltd. and Thomas Turton & Sons, Ltd.,* [1955]
1 All E.R. 808; [1955] 1 W.L.R. 549; 34 Digest (Repl.) 253, *1835.*

Action.

On Oct. 23, 1961, the plaintiff was injured and subsequently lost his left eye
when a splinter of steel flew from the top of a chisel which he was hammering   B
and entered his eye. He was working in the course of his employment with the
first defendants, the Rover Co., Ltd. The first defendants obtained the chisel
from the second defendants. The second defendants, the Speedwell Tool and
Gauge Co., Ltd., were the fashioners of the chisel, which was made according to a
specification and blue print supplied by the first defendants, from alloyed steel
purchased from the third party, Richard W. Carr & Co., Ltd. The third party   C
also heat-treated the chisel after it had been fashioned by the second defendants;
and returned it to the second defendants, who sold and supplied it to the first
defendants. At the time of the accident, the plaintiff was knocking tab washers
over fly wheel retaining bolts on an assembly line, using the chisel which he was
tapping with a hammer. It was estimated that he would tap something like
1,680 times a day on top of the chisel. The plaintiff had been using the chisel,   D
which he had received from his leading hand, Mr. Jones, for approximately
six weeks at the time of the accident and he and Mr. Jones were the only two
people who used it, the latter using it when the plaintiff left for any purpose his
place on the assembly line. Some three or four weeks before the plaintiff's
accident, Mr. Jones had had a slight accident with the chisel, a very small piece
flying off the chisel and cutting his cheek when he was knocking the tab washers   E
by tapping the top of the chisel with a hammer. Beyond telling the surgery that
the cut on his cheek had been caused by the chisel, which was written down, no
other official report was made. The trial judge held that the plaintiff was entitled
to succeed against the first defendants, because there was a failure by Mr. Jones
to withdraw the chisel from circulation, it being his duty as the leading hand to do
so, and his knowledge of the danger was that of the first defendants. The trial   F
judge awarded the plaintiff £2,250 damages.

The first defendants alleged that the accident was caused by the negligence of
the second defendants in that they failed to test the chisel and supplied it with
its head too hard and brittle for safe use and when it was not contemplated that
the first defendants would test the hardness and when the second defendants knew
the particular purpose for which the chisel was required and would be used, and   G
that the hardness defect might endanger a person such as the plaintiff using it.

I. J. Black for the plaintiff.
Piers Ashworth for the first defendants.
S. Brown for the second defendants.
R. H. Tucker for the third party.

Cur. adv. vult.   H

Dec. 13.   **BAKER, J.,** read the following judgment, in which he stated the
facts, held that the plaintiff was entitled to succeed against the first defendants
and that there was no heating or attempted hardening or grinding or any other
such operation on the chisel during its use by the first defendants after it left
the control of the second defendants, and continued: The third main question   I
is whether there was a reasonable probability of independent examination of this
tool after it came into the hands of the employers, the first defendants. Counsel
for the second defendants accepts, and I agree, that, as the law stands, the test is:
" was there a reasonable probability of independent examination? ". If there
was, then the employer and not the supplier—I am using the term " supplier "
in the wide sense for the moment—is responsible. In dealing with this problem,
it has to be remembered that this tool was designed by the employers. The blue
print of the design which is in evidence provides various measurements and that

A the steel was to be " Astra ". That has been deleted in pencil, and I accept that there was an agreement that other steel could be substituted, as appears from the words " Carr's BCC ". That is in fact what was used to make the guilty chisel. Then appear the words " HDN " for " hardened ", and " TEMP " for " tempered ". Dealing with tools for which there is a design, VISCOUNT SIMONDS in his speech in *Davie* v. *New Merton Board Mills, Ltd.* (1) said:

B   " It was said that an employer might, instead of purchasing tools of a standard design either from the manufacturer direct or in the market, order them to be made to his own design. If he did so and if they were defective and an accident resulted, it was clear (so the argument ran) that he would be responsible. I agree that he would, if the fault lay in the design and was due to lack of reasonable care or skill on his part. There is no reason why he should

C   not. A more difficult question would arise if the defect was not due to any fault in design (for which the employer was responsible) but to carelessness in workmanship. But that is a far cry from the present case and, recognising as I do that in this area of the law there is a borderline of difficult cases, I do not propose to say more than I need."

D In so far as the blue print is a matter of design, it does not seem that there was any fault in this chisel. The abbreviation for " hardened " and " tempered " it is said puts the onus on the first defendants to make an examination of the chisel when it came to them, because they were providing that it should be hardened and tempered. But of course the tip of the chisel would be hardened and tempered by the chisel makers, and I do not think that these words really advance

E this matter any further. Next it is said that the chisel should be manufactured in accordance with the British Standards Specifications. I have already outlined what they are, and there is no doubt that it should have been according to British Standards Specifications. I fail to see why that throws on to the employers the duty of inspection.

I find that this guilty chisel was one of a batch of six chisels which came from

F the second defendants some time shortly after July 19, 1961, having been hardened and tempered for them by the third party, as appears on the invoice S.D.9. The order for these six chisels (which is S.D.3) bears in red on it " The above tools must be marked as drawing instructions and will be subject to rigid inspection upon receipt ". Moreover, says counsel for the second defendants, when one looks at the terms and conditions on the back of this document, the first defen-

G dants, although no doubt trying to put themselves in the best possible position, have, in fact, landed themselves in difficulties because they bound themselves to inspect the chisel. What the relevant condition, condition 1, says is:

        " The goods shall conform in every respect to the specifications, drawings, samples, or descriptions, furnished or adopted by us and shall be fit and sufficient for the purposes intended, merchantable and free from defect in

H   material and workmanship and will be subject to inspection on or after delivery at our premises. We reserve the right to reject any raw or finished material which is faulty in quality or construction or which does not come up to the standard specified."

They then go on to say they could keep the goods and so on. Condition 13 is also said to be relevant:

I   " If any claim is made against us in respect of loss, injury or damage of any kind due or alleged to be due to a defect in the goods or their design or workmanship, the supplier will provide all facilities, assistance and advice required by us for the purpose of contesting or dealing with such claim."

At first sight condition 1 is very much against the first defendants, but I think that, when one reads the face of this document, " will be subject to rigid inspection on receipt ", it is clear that what the first defendants were doing in this

(1) [1959] 1 All E.R. 346 at p. 354; [1959] A.C. 604 at p. 626.

particular case was to specify the size of a tool and the design of a tool, and to A
specify that it should be hardened and tempered, and that can relate only to the
tip and not to the top of the chisel. Inspection must relate only to inspection of
the design, and that is all that was ever contemplated. Even if there was a testing
in the sense of an independent examination by using the Vickers scale or some
other scale to test the hardening, it would be a testing of the tip, although I bear
in mind that, in the British Standards Specification, hardness of the head (top) B
is given. In this respect I cannot find any distinction between this case and
Mason v. *Williams and Williams, Ltd. and Thomas Turton & Sons, Ltd.* (2).

Conclusive on this point is the evidence of Mr. Smith, the managing director of
the second defendants. Although he contended strongly that he understood there
would be inspection by the first defendants, including tests for hardness, I do
not think that he believed any such thing. When he was cross-examined by C
the plaintiff he said:

> " I should have known [the first defendants] were not chisel makers. We
> proceeded on the footing with [the first defendants] that the British
> Standards Specification would have been complied with. We ourselves would
> not have inspected for hardness without a special condition. We rely on the
> professional hardeners; we don't do any hardening ourselves." D

I do not accept that he was ever relying on the first defendants or ever thought
that the first defendants would test the top of this chisel for hardness; there was
no reason why the first defendants should do anything of the kind. I find, therefore, that there was no reasonable probability of examination by the first
defendants before Mr. Jones's accident.

That brings me to the fourth and last point which raises the most difficult E
questions of all. In such circumstances are the second defendants also liable to
the plaintiff? In *Mason's* case (3), FINNEMORE, J., said:

> " I appreciate that I am faced with another problem, as was indicated in
> the case of *M'Alister (or Donoghue)* v. *Stevenson* (4), that res ipsa loquitur does
> not apply and that the court has to be satisfied, and therefore the plaintiff F
> has got to prove, that there was negligence on the part of the manufacturers.
> Of course that cannot be proved normally by saying that on such and such a
> date such and such a workman did this, that, or the other. I think that when
> you have eliminated anything happening in the present case at the employers'
> factory, whither, as is undisputed, this chisel came direct from the manu-
> facturers—and when it came from the manufacturers the head was too hard, G
> and that undue hardness could have been produced only while it was being
> manufactured by them, and could have been produced by someone there
> either carelessly or deliberately to make a harder and more durable head—
> that is really as far as any plaintiff can be expected to take his case."

All that applies to this case. FINNEMORE, J., continued (3):

> " What the plaintiff says here is:—' This is your chisel, you made it and H
> I used it as you made it, in the condition in which you made it, in the way
> you intended me to use it, and you never relied on any intermediate examina-
> tion; therefore I have discharged the onus of proof by saying that this trouble
> must have happened through some act in the manufacture of this chisel in
> your factory, and that was either careless or deliberate, and in either event
> it was a breach of duty towards me, a person whom you contemplated would I
> use this article which you made, in the way you intended it to be used.' He
> is entitled to succeed against the manufacturers."

All that applies equally to the present case.

A complicating feature in the present case is that two new chisels which they
received subsequently from the second defendants were produced by the first

(2) [1955] 1 All E.R. 808.   (3) [1955] 1 All E.R. at p. 810.
          (4) [1932] All E.R. Rep. 1; [1932] A.C. 562.

A defendants from store. They are equally dangerous because they have equally hard heads. It so happens that the steel for these chisels was obtained not from the third party but from other steel manufacturers in Sheffield called Cooke. I think that the proper inference, however, is that the hardening of these two chisels must have been done by the third party, because the evidence is that the third party did the hardening for the second defendants, and the third party had

B premises in Birmingham to which it would be much simpler to take chisels, as chisels were taken, for hardening rather than to send them to Sheffield. I find that the other two chisels, F.D.4 and F.D.5, which were just as dangerous as the guilty chisel, were produced and fashioned by the second defendants for the first defendants, and were hardened by the third party who made the tops far too hard and brittle. It is said that I should not pay too much attention to that,

C but I think that it is a matter of some significance. There has, in my view, been negligent heat treatment of the new chisels by the third party, who heat treated them. I have carefully considered the evidence which they have given. Unfortunately, the man who actually carried out the heat treatment of the guilty chisel, or was directly responsible for it, is dead, but it seems to me that everything points to some neglect or some deliberate action in the original heat treatment as

D the only possible cause of the hardness of this guilty chisel.

Two questions now arise. The first I put in this way. Did the action or inaction of Mr. Jones break the chain of causation? Can the second defendants ever remain liable after what Mr. Jones did or did not do? There is a passage in Salmond on Torts (12th Edn.) p. 570, which raises some difficulty. The heading is " Unsuccessful intermediate examination ".

E   " What is the position if an intermediate examination has been carried out, but so carelessly that it fails to reveal the defect? It has been held that the manufacturer is exonerated in such circumstances [*Buckner* v. *Ashby and Horner, Ltd.* (5)], but the better view now is that the manufacturer is not in general excused by the fact that an intermediary has failed to perform his duties properly."

F
If that be a correct statement of the law, and applicable to the present case, it follows that the plaintiff is entitled to succeed also against the second defendants. I do not accept that, in the present circumstances, that can be so. It seems to me, first, that there was actual knowledge here by Mr. Jones. This was not carelessness which failed to reveal the defect, the defect was known. This was

G a dangerous chisel. A piece had flown and cut Mr. Jones's cheek. Secondly, this guilty chisel ought then to have been taken out of circulation; it was the keeping of the chisel in circulation with the knowledge that it was dangerous that caused the accident. It seems to me, therefore, that, in this case, the second defendants cannot be liable to the plaintiff.

There remains the second and final question under the fourth main issue and

H it is: could the second defendants ever be liable in the circumstances of this case, not for something which has been their own act, their own breach of duty or negligence, but for something which is the negligence or breach of duty of the third party? Here one enters a realm of difficult and uncertain law. In *Davie's* case (6), Lord Simonds said:

I   ". . . as I have said, the difficulty arises not on the primary statement of liability but on the question for whom is the employer responsible. Clearly he is responsible for his own acts, and clearly, too, for those of his servants. To them at least the maxims ' respondeat superior ' and ' qui facit per alium facit per se ' will apply. It is the next step that is difficult. The employer is said to be liable for the acts of his ' agents ' and with greater hesitation for the acts of ' independent contractors '. My lords, fortunately we are not troubled here with the word ' agent '."

   (5) [1941] 1 K.B. 321.   (6) [1959] 1 All E.R. at p. 351; [1959] A.C. at p. 620.

Unfortunately I am. There are two other passages in LORD SIMONDS' speech   A
which are relevant in this context. Having dealt with the pleadings, he said (7):

"... secondly, it may mean that the supply of an unsuitable drift was
due to a want of reasonable care on their part."

And (8):

"... much as I distrust analogies, I would add that there is a striking   B
resemblance between the shipowner who is held not to be liable for the
bad workmanship, undiscoverable by him, of the shipbuilder's employees
and the employer who claims not to be liable for the bad workmanship,
equally undiscoverable, of the employees of the manufacturer who supplied
at secondhand the tools with which he has provided his workman."

  C

And LORD MORTON OF HENRYTON (9):

" I would dismiss the appeal, and my conclusion would have been the same
if the first defendants had bought this tool directly from the manufacturers,
the second defendants. In that case, also, there would have been no
delegation of the master's duty to take reasonable care."

  D

It seems to me that the logical conclusion must be that a fashioner or fabricator,
such as the second defendants, who is not proved to have been guilty of any
breach of duty or negligence in the fashioning of a guilty tool, can only be liable
if the maxim respondeat superior applies. Why should his liability, however, be
different from that of the employer who, if one follows LORD MORTON, as I
respectfully do, is clearly not liable for his agent's negligence?   E
A passage has been cited from CHARLESWORTH ON NEGLIGENCE (4th Edn.),
para. 797:

" A manufacturer's duty is not limited to those parts of his product which
he makes himself. It extends to component parts, supplied by his sub-
manufacturers or others, which he uses in the manufacture of his own
products. He must take reasonable care, by inspection or otherwise, to   F
see that those parts can properly be used to put his product in a condition
in which it can be safely used or consumed in the contemplated manner
by the ultimate user or consumer."

I see no reason to disagree in any way with that statement of the law. The
important passage is " He must take reasonable care, by inspection or otherwise,   G
to see that those parts can properly be used . . .".
What, however, is reasonable care? The second defendants were entitled to
assume, in my view, having got competent hardeners to do the hardening of this
guilty chisel for them, that the work was properly done, and it was no part of
their duty in law or in good sense to set about the chisel when they received it
from the hardeners and to examine it and test it by hardness test to see that the   H
top was no more than Vickers 350, and that the tip was Vickers 700. I cannot
think that they are liable for the hardening by their hardening agents or their
independent contractors, or call them what one may. (See also *Haseldine* v.
Daw & Son, Ltd. (10).)
On these findings and conclusions, the plaintiff succeeds against the first
defendants, and the second defendants succeed and are entitled to judgment   I
against the plaintiff.

*Judgment for the plaintiff against the first defendants. Judgment for the second
defendants against the plaintiff.*

---

(7) [1959] 1 All E.R. at p. 349; [1959] A.C. at p. 618.
(8) [1959] 1 All E.R. at p. 353; [1959] A.C. at pp. 623, 624.
(9) [1959] 1 All E.R. at p. 357; [1959] A.C. at p. 629.
(10) [1941] 3 All E.R. 156; [1941] 2 K.B. 343.

A   [Feb. 16. In the third party proceedings in London, BAKER, J., awarded the
first defendants £2 damages against the second defendants who were entitled
to recover the same amount against the third party.]

Solicitors: *F. A. Greenwood & Co.*, Birmingham (for the plaintiff); *T. Haynes
Duffell & Son*, Birmingham (for the first defendants); *Hewitt & Walters*,
Birmingham (for the second defendants); *T. H. Ekins & Son*, Birmingham (for
B   the third party).

[*Reported by* GWYNEDD LEWIS, *Barrister-at-Law.*]

KOPPEL *v.* KOPPEL (WIDE Claimant.)

C
[COURT OF APPEAL (Harman, Diplock and Winn, L.JJ.), March 11, 14, 1966.]

*Bill of Sale—Absolute bill of sale—Apparent possession—Chattel in common
establishment—Contents of house given to housekeeper in consideration of
her agreeing to look after children permanently—Transaction evidenced by
unregistered bill of sale—Whether goods in possession or apparent possession*
D   *of maker of bill—Whether judgment creditor of maker of bill entitled to levy
execution on contents of house—Bills of Sale Act, 1878 (41 & 42 Vict. c. 31),
s. 4, s. 8.*

*Sale of Goods—Passing of property—Bargain to give contents of house in return
for services—Common establishment—Housekeeper undertaking to look after
children permanently—Sale of Goods Act, 1893 (56 & 57 Vict. c. 17), s. 18,*
E   *r. 1.*

In order to persuade a Mrs. W. to return to his home to act as housekeeper,
and particularly to look after his two young children on a permanent basis,
K. agreed that if she would come, having sold so much of her own belongings
in her flat as could not be accommodated in K.'s house, he would make
over to her the contents of his house. This arrangement was affirmed by
F   K. in a letter dated Sept. 29, 1961, as follows: " This is to state that on this
date I transfer the entire contents of this house . . . to [Mrs. W.]. This is
to compensate her, as agreed, for her giving up her own and daughter's home
and for disposing of her furniture . . . in order to look after my children
permanently." There was no registration of the letter as a bill of sale.
Mrs. W. went to live at K.'s house in accordance with the agreement. In
G   1965 a writ of fi. fa. was issued against K. and the sheriff took walking
possession of the contents of the house. Mrs. W. claimed title to the
contents. The sheriff took out interpleader proceedings. On the question
whether, on the basis that the transaction in September, 1961, was a genuine
transaction and that the letter was an absolute bill of sale*, the transaction
was void under s. 8† of the Bills of Sale Act, 1878, on the ground that the
H   goods were still in the possession or apparent possession of K., who was the
person making the bill of sale.

Held: the property in the contents of the house had passed to Mrs. W.
under the transaction in September, 1961, and, as K. and Mrs. W. had set
up a common establishment in which she looked after the house and K.'s
children, possession of the contents was referable to her legal title; the execu-
I   tion creditor, therefore, had not proved that the contents were in the possession or apparent possession of K., who was the person who made the bill of
sale, and the transaction was not rendered void by s. 8 of the Bills of Sale
Act, 1878 (see p. 193, letters D and F, and p. 195, letters D and E, post).

Dicta of SCRUTTON and ATKIN, L.JJ., in *French* v. *Gething* ([1921] All E.R.
Rep. at pp. 419, 420) and *Ramsay* v. *Margrett* ([1891-94] All E.R. Rep. 453)
applied.

---

* See p. 189, letter H, and p. 193, letter H, post.
† The relevant terms of s. 8 are printed at p. 190, letters B and C, post.

Per HARMAN, L.J.: the property in the goods passed under s. 18, r. 1,   A
of the Sale of Goods Act, 1893 (see p. 193, letter E, post).
Appeal allowed.

[As to bills of sale of chattels in common establishment and apparent possession, see 3 HALSBURY's LAWS (3rd Edn.) 270, para. 499, p. 309, para. 577; and for
cases on the subject, see 7 DIGEST (Repl.) 117, 118, 697-702.

As to transactions of barter or exchange, etc., being treated as a sale of goods,   B
see 34 HALSBURY's LAWS (3rd Edn.) 5, 6, para. 1.

For the Bills of Sale Act, 1878, s. 4, s. 8, see 2 HALSBURY's STATUTES (2nd Edn.)
558, 565.

For Sale of Goods Act, 1893, s. 18, r. 1, see 22 HALSBURY's STATUTES (2nd
Edn.) 996.]

Cases referred to: C

Antoniadi v. *Smith* (*Smith claimant*), [1901] 2 K.B. 589; 70 L.J.K.B. 869;
85 L.T. 200; 7 Digest (Repl.) 162, *870.*

Charlesworth v. *Mills*, [1892] A.C. 231; 61 L.J.Q.B. 830; 66 L.T. 690; 7
Digest (Repl.) 4, *7.*

French v. *Gething* (*Gething claimant*), [1921] All E.R. Rep. 415; [1922] 1 K.B.
236; 91 L.J.K.B. 276; 126 L.T. 394; 7 Digest (Repl.) 117, *699.*   D

Ramsay v. *Margrett*, [1891-94] All E.R. Rep. 453; [1894] 2 Q.B. 18; 63
L.J.Q.B. 513; 70 L.T. 788; 7 Digest (Repl.) 117, *697.*

Youngs v. *Youngs* (*Baker claimant*), [1940] 1 All E.R. 349; [1940] 1 K.B. 760;
109 L.J.K.B. 747; 7 Digest (Repl.) 118, *702.*

Appeal.
This was an appeal by the intervener and claimant, Mrs. Anne Vera Wide,   E
by notice dated Feb. 4, 1966, from so much of the order of Mr. Registrar
COMPTON-MILLER dated Jan. 28, 1966, as ordered that the claim of the claimant
to certain goods and chattels seized by the sheriff of Surrey under the writ of fi. fa.
issued in this suit be dismissed; and the claimant sought an order setting
aside the order of Jan. 28, 1966, and the seizure of the goods. The goods and
chattels subject to the writ of fi. fa. were in the house of the petitioner, Ernest   F
Franz Koppel, and included furniture and household equipment which the
claimant claimed to be hers. The facts are set out in the judgment of HARMAN, L.J.

The case noted below* were cited during the argument in addition to the cases
referred to in the judgments.

M. A. Thorpe for the claimant.
A. H. Tibber for the execution creditor.   G

HARMAN, L.J.: In this case in March, 1961, the husband started proceedings for a divorce against his wife on the ground of cruelty. She was then
still living in the house. In June of that year things between them were very bad
and there was one, or it may be two, young children whom the husband thought
to be in need of someone to look after them. According to Mrs. Wide, the   H
intervener-claimant in the case, he telephoned to her in June of that year and
asked her to come over to his house, 31, Broadfields, East Molesey, in order to
look after the children. She agreed to do so and she did. There she stayed
until about September, looking after his children.

In September of that year the husband's mother, who is a German national
living in Germany, came over to see her son; and at that point the claimant   I
decided to go back to her own house. She had a flat of her own which was
completely furnished and had a daughter of her own, not then living there but
whom she was expecting to come back shortly. In September she went back to
her flat in order to look after her belongings. The husband and his mother
could not apparently find anybody to take her place and they urged her, by all
the means in their power, to come back and look after the house and the children.

───

* *Re Cole* (*a Bankrupt*), *Ex p. The Trustee* v. *Cole*, [1963] 3 All E.R. 433; [1964]
Ch. 175.

A   Thereafter some telephoning went on and the claimant agreed to come back; but she did not do so unconditionally.   She made a bargain with him, which was that if she sold up so much of her own belongings as he could not accommodate in his house, he would make over the contents of his house, or such part as belonged to him, to her.   Those were the terms on which she agreed to go back. She has been there ever since.   There have been proceedings between the

B   husband and his wife, as the result of which, after long delay, in April, 1964, a decree nisi of divorce was pronounced in favour of the wife, the claimant having been made intervener in the suit.   That decree has been made absolute and an order for maintenance was made in January, 1965, with which the husband has not   complied.

   In September, 1965, the wife issued a writ of fieri facias for the sum of £114

C   arrears.   The sheriff took what is called walking possession of the contents of the house: the claimant came into the matter to make a claim, and the sheriff took out interpleader proceedings.   It is the appeal from the registrar on those interpleader proceedings with which this court is concerned.   The matter came before Mr. Registrar COMPTON-MILLER.   Before him the question was primarily whether a certain document, which was signed by the husband, was a genuine

D   document made on the date that it purported to bear or whether it had been manufactured for the purpose of defeating the wife's claim.   That document is on printed writing paper headed " Ernest Koppel, 31, Broadfields, East Molesey ", and in type is the word " Agreement ".   It is in these terms:

   " This is to state that on this date, I transfer the entire contents of this

E   house, 31, Broadfields, to Mrs. Anne Vera Wide.   This is to compensate her, as agreed, for giving up her own and daughter's home and for disposing of her furniture, her washing-machine, her refrigerator, her carpets and other household goods, in order to look after my children permanently. Ernest Franz Koppel."

   The registrar having seen the husband and his mother (and I take it the wife also) in the witness box, was impressed with the truth of their testimony and

F   concluded that this document was not a sham and that it did come into existence at the time and for the purpose which is indicated.   He then took the point which had not been taken earlier that it may be the document was a bill of sale and, therefore, was hit by the Bills of Sale Act, 1878.   As to that the registrar concluded (and, I think, concluded quite rightly) that this was a bill of sale.   He further concluded that if that was the case, it was an end of the matter and the

G   transaction was void and did not protect the goods against the execution creditor because they remained the goods of the grantor of the bill.   It is in that state of things that the case comes before us today.

   In fact the point which the registrar had reached was not the end of the case at all, and the real point, as I see it, is this.   Admitting that this document is a bill of sale, does it pass nevertheless the test of s. 8 of the Act of 1878 (to which

H   I will come in a moment) because, if the goods were not in the possession of the grantor of the bill at the time the claim was made, the Bills of Sale Act, 1878, does not invalidate the transaction and they remain the goods of the grantee. For that purpose one must look at the Bills of Sale Act, 1878.   It starts with a definition section, s. 4, under which the expression " bill of sale " is said to include

I   " receipts for purchase moneys of goods, and other assurances of personal chattels . . . and also any agreement, whether intended or not to be followed by the execution of any other instrument, by which a right in equity to any personal chattels . . . shall be conferred . . ."

   I do not think that it very much matters which of those particular words are the ones which catch the document in this case because I think they do catch it, for this reason.   It has been held that a receipt does not come within the definition, provided that it is not a part of the transaction.   If it is merely meant to be evidence of the making of the agreement, then the fact that it is a receipt for

the purchase of goods does not bring it within the section. When one looks at the A
words (this being a written document, one can only go by what is written) I
cannot but think that this document, made at the insistence of the claimant
herself who desired the protection of the document to ensure her future and that
of her daughter, is an essential part of the transaction and is in fact what it
purports to be—a transfer of the entire contents of the house—and therefore it is
a bill of sale within s. 4 and comes within s. 8 which says: B

"Every bill of sale to which this Act applies shall be duly attested and
shall be registered under this Act . . ."

Then there is a good deal about the form in which it ought to be. Then after a
very long and rather confusing paragraph s. 8 says that, if the bill is not registered,
it

"shall be deemed fraudulent and void so far as regards the property in   C
or right to the possession of any chattels comprised in such bill of sale which,
at or after the time of filing the petition . . . or of executing such process
[and here it is execution and not process] . . . are in the possession or apparent
possession of the person making such bill of sale . . ."

What is submitted (and this is the crux of the case) is that this furniture, which D
is comprised in the bill of sale, remains in the possession or the apparent
possession of the grantor, namely, the husband, and is not in the possession of
the claimant. As to that there has been a great deal of, I will not say judicial
manoeuvring, but judicial exegesis. The first case that one must mention is
Ramsay v. *Margrett* (1), a very well known case, in which a wife, who had separate
property, agreed to buy furniture belonging to her husband, which was in the   E
house where they lived together, and she took a receipt. It was held first of all
that the receipt did not form part of the transaction passing the property,
but that the property had passed to her by the prior and independent bargain
and consequently the receipt did not require registration. It was also held that
the wife had a sufficient possession of the goods to take the case out of the Act
of 1878. That is to say, that though he and she continued to live in the house F
and to enjoy as husband and wife the furniture there, that furniture after this
transaction was neither in his possession, not in his apparent possession, because
as between husband and wife there is no saying, since the Married Women's
Property Act, 1882, who is the owner of any furniture in the house, and the fact
that it is in the matrimonial home and is being enjoyed by the husband and wife
as such, is no evidence that it belongs either to the husband or to the wife. So
that one must look for the person to whom title to the property has gone. In that G
case it had gone to the wife and, therefore, it was in her possession and also in
her apparent possession and the Bills of Sale Act, 1878, did not nullify the
transaction.

LORD ESHER, M.R., after remarking that the case could not have arisen before
the Married Women's Property Act, 1882, said this (2):   H

"So in this case the money which the plaintiff had was her money, and
the furniture was her husband's, and she had the right to buy with her
money whatever she chose. When she bought these goods from her husband
and paid him the price, they became her separate property. The goods
were in the house in which the husband and the wife were living together,
and in that state of things you could not say which of them had the actual   I
possession of the goods. What is the rule of law as to possession in such a
case? When the possession is doubtful it is attached by law to the title.
Therefore, under such circumstances, the law considers the goods to be in
the possession of the wife, who has the legal title to them."

LOPES, L.J., agreed (2) and for much the same reasons. He purported to follow
an earlier case of *Charlesworth* v. *Mills* (3), which shows that where it is a case

(1) [1891-94] All E.R. Rep. 453; [1894] 2 Q.B. 18.
(2) [1894] 2 Q.B. at p. 25; [1891-94] All E.R. Rep. at p. 456.   (3) [1892] A.C. 231.

A as between husband and wife, one must look to the legal title when one finds goods in the house, and ownership and also apparent ownership will follow the legal title.

To the same effect as that case is *French* v. *Gething* (*Gething claimant*) (4). There again it was a case of husband and wife, and *Ramsay* v. *Margrett* (5) was followed.   I do not think that I need read from the judgment of Bankes, L.J.

B Scrutton, L.J., as always, hit the nail directly on the head.   He said this (6):

> " But the creditors must go further and prove that the goods remained in the possession or apparent possession of the grantor, the husband.   At the present day, when wives can, and often do, possess as much property as their husbands, it is impossible to say whether the husband or the wife is in possession or apparent possession of the household furniture if nothing
C > more is known than that the parties live together in the house.   But if the furniture is in the apparent possession of both, s. 8 of the Act of 1878 does not apply [that is to say, s. 8 only applies if it is in the apparent possession of one of them alone].   That is the first answer to the creditors on this point.   The second is that, if it is doubtful which of two persons is in posses- sion of property, possession is in that one who has the right and title to
D > possession.   That person in this case was the wife.   Therefore the claim under the Act of 1878 fails."

Atkin, L.J., said this (7):

> " I think that case [he is talking about *Ramsay* v. *Margrett* (5)] implies that ' possession ' and ' apparent possession ' mean sole possession and
E > apparent sole possession just as ' possession ' and ' reputed ownership ' were held to mean sole possession and sole reputed ownership when it was a question whether goods were in the order and disposition clause of the Bankruptcy Act, 1869, s. 15."

He then gives an example of three men in a boat belonging to one of them.   He said (8):

F
> " . . . the boat is in the possession of the owner and not in the possession of the two visitors or either of them; it is in his apparent possession and not in that of them or either of them; and if the owner sells the boat to one of the visitors intending to pass the property in it to him, then possession and apparent possession are in the purchaser and not in the former owner."

G I do not think that I need read the passage where he went further into that matter and said that was clear even before *Ramsay* v. *Margrett* (5).

Of course, that is as between husband and wife.   The answer to the question does not, however, depend on the relationship being that of husband and wife. That was first apparent in the case of *Antoniadi* v. *Smith* (*Smith claimant*) (9). That was the case of a man who lived in the same house as his mother-in-law;
H he was the occupier and he resided there with her.   There was a bill of sale, and it was registered at one time, but the registration lapsed.   It was held nonetheless that the two being co-partners in a joint household, one had to look at the title, and if one found that the chattels were in the hands of the mother-in- law, they were not either in the possession or apparent possession of her son-in- law, she having the title and not he.   That shows that the doctrine is not confined
I to the relationship of husband and wife.

Finally I must mention *Youngs* v. *Youngs* (*Baker claimant*) (10) in 1940, in which *Ramsay* v. *Margrett* (5) was distinguished.   There a man sold

---

(4) [1921] All E.R. Rep. 415; [1922] 1 K.B. 236.
(5) [1891-94] All E.R. Rep. 453; [1894] 2 Q.B. 18.
(6) [1921] All E.R. Rep. at p. 419; [1922] 1 K.B. at p. 245.
(7) [1921] All E.R. Rep. at p. 419; [1922] 1 K.B. at p. 247.
(8) [1921] All E.R. Rep. at p. 420; [1922] 1 K.B. at p. 247.
(9) [1901] 2 K.B. 589.   (10) [1940] 1 All E.R. 349; [1940] 1 K.B. 760.

furniture in his house to a woman who was living in his house as his housekeeper A and he gave a receipt to her with an inventory attached. The county court judge found as a fact on an interpleader issue " that the man had no intention to part with the possession of the furniture to his domestic servant, and that she used the furniture only in so far as she was a member of the man's household; that the receipt with the inventory attached was a bill of sale ". Thus *Ramsay* v. *Margrett* (11) was distinguished on that occasion, but it was distinguished B because of the finding of fact at which the county court judge arrived and at which, as the court held, he was entitled to arrive on the evidence before him. SLESSER, L.J., said this (12):

" He [the county court judge] has found that the furniture which is the subject of these bills of sale, which has never been moved from the house, is still being used by the husband for himself and his daughter, and that the C claimant uses the furniture only in so far as she is in the house as a member of the household. That is to say, being a servant or housekeeper, she does not use the furniture [and then he describes it] as of right, but as a servant. Therefore this is not one of the cases where it is doubtful whether the apparent possession is in A or B . . ."

and he affirmed the county court judge. D
    MACKINNON, L.J., said this (13):

" There is no more apparent possession of the furniture by her [the housekeeper] than there would be apparent possession of furniture in the house by any servant living permanently in the house. Therefore *Ramsay* v. *Margrett* (11) is not a binding authority in this case." E

GODDARD, L.J., went perhaps even further. He said (14) :

". . . as he was selling to his housekeeper, the last thing he would desire would be that the furniture which he was using, although he had been paid for it by her, should be liable to execution, and I have not the least doubt but that he and the claimant intended that there should be a document F which could be shown to the sheriff proving that the property had been transferred to the claimant . . . But it is not because of the existence of a marriage tie that the section does not apply. It is the existence of what I may call a common establishment that is the important factor. This is shown by *Antoniadi* v. *Smith* (15) . . . But the doctrine cannot, in my opinion, apply to a transaction between a man and his domestic servant, even though G he may have misconducted himself with her. In the present case the claimant was in his house for eleven months as a housekeeper, and received wages as such. It is impossible to say that a servant has a common use of the furniture in the house in which she is living with her master in the sense in which that expression is used by DAVEY, L.J., in *Ramsay* v. *Margrett* (11), or that it comes within the class of cases which is contemplated by the H passage in LITTLETON ON TENURES, s. 701. It is perfectly true that my servant has the use of the furniture which I provide for his or her bedroom, or for his or her sitting room, and has the use of the kitchen utensils, and so forth, but he or she has not a common use with me; he or she is using them as my servant. Therefore, it seems to me it would be carrying the doctrine of *Ramsay* v. *Margrett* (11) to an extravagant length to say that I if a man sells his household furniture to his housemaid, or to his butler, and things go on exactly as before, the property ceases to be in the apparent possession of the master merely because the butler or housekeeper or servant

---

(11) [1891-94] All E.R. Rep. 453; [1894] 2 Q.B. 18.
(12) [1940] 1 All E.R. at p. 352; [1940] 1 K.B. at p. 766.
(13) [1940] 1 All E.R. at p. 353; [1940] 1 K.B. at p. 768.
(14) [1940] 1 K.B. at pp. 769, 770; [1940] 1 All E.R. at pp. 354, 355.
(15) [1901] 2 K.B. 589.

A   remains in the house and goes on rendering him services. It is entirely different from the case where a mother-in-law and son-in-law, or a mother and son may be living in the same house, or where two friends may be sharing a common establishment."

That case, therefore, went on the finding of fact by the county court judge.

The question here is on which side of the line does the matter fall. Is it
B plain that the claimant is merely a housekeeper working there for a wage or is she a person who has gone there on a permanent basis to set up a common establishment with the owner of the house, albeit she gets a wage for services which she renders as his housekeeper, looking no doubt after his house but more particularly looking after his children on a permanent basis? The registrar held that the bill of sale was not a sham but was a genuine document and repre-
C sented the real position. I think that we are, therefore, entitled to receive what help we can from the words used by the husband who signed that document. It does seem to show that the footing on which she came into the house was " to look after my children permanently ". It does look also as if there was a genuine parting with some of the contents of the house in order to compensate her for selling her own goods and chattels. In other words, the transaction was not
D in any sense a sham, as it was, I think, in *Youngs* v. *Youngs* (16), where there was a sale but no intention by the vendor to part with possession of the chattels which he was selling. Here, I think, on the documents and on the evidence, such as it is, there was an intention on the part of this man, in order to compensate the woman and induce her to come into the house and perform services which he found urgently necessary, to part with his chattels in her favour so as to leave her
E in a position in which she was to that extent secure as regards the future. I think that the property in the goods, this being a document evidencing a transaction for consideration, passed under s. 18, r. 1, of the Sale of Goods Act, 1893, which provides:

" Where there is an unconditional contract for the sale of specific goods,
F in a deliverable state, the property in the goods passes to the buyer when the contract is made . . ."

The observation by the registrar that there had been no formal delivery is not in point. There is no question of a gift here. It was money or money's worth. That being so, the property passed and I think that she was in such a position in the house that the doctrine of *Ramsay* v. *Margrett* (17) does apply and not the
G exception which GODDARD, L.J., pointed out.

This is a point which was not taken below and never discussed by the registrar. Nevertheless it does seem to me when he got to the point of saying this was a bill of sale, that was not the end, and the end is that which I have been discussing and on which I would allow the appeal.

H   **DIPLOCK, L.J.:** I agree that this appeal should be allowed.

When the interpleader issue first came before the registrar, there was nothing in the wife's case to suggest that any point was being taken under the Bills of Sale Act, 1878, and indeed we are told that the point about the Bills of Sale Act, 1878, was noticed by the registrar himself. He found, as I think rightly, that the document of Sept. 29, 1961, which HARMAN, L.J., has read, was an absolute bill of sale. He also found—this was the main matter of dispute of fact before him
I —that the transaction of which it formed part was a genuine transaction entered into for good consideration by the claimant. The registrar, having taken the point, however, seems to have considered that a finding that the document was an unregistered bill of sale entitled the execution creditor to succeed. Indeed, he went on to say: " I am not concerned to consider questions of apparent possession." For my part I think that it is plain that an execution creditor who

---

(16) [1940] 1 All E.R. 349; [1940] 1 K.B. 760.
(17) [1891-94] All E.R. Rep. 453; [1894] 2 Q.B. 18.

claims to take a person's goods in execution for the debt of another person not **A** only must show that the transfer of the property has taken place under an unregistered bill of sale, but also must show that the goods are at the time of the execution, being more than seven days after the date of the bill of sale, in the possession or apparent possession of the person making such bill of sale, and I have no doubt that the onus of so showing lies on the execution creditor. That is made quite clear by the decision of this court in *Antoniadi* v. *Smith* (18), to **B** which HARMAN, L.J., has referred, and which dealt with a case where a mother-in-law and son-in-law were sharing a house. VAUGHAN WILLIAMS, L.J., said this (19):

" In the first place, in order that the execution creditor may rely on the absence of registration of the bill of sale, he must make out that the circum-stances were such as to render registration necessary [as the wife has done **C** here] and he ought to have obtained a clear finding from the county court judge that the goods were in the apparent possession of the execution debtor. This he has not done."

Now, no doubt it is true that if a simple man, or a simple lawyer, reads s. 4 of the Bills of Sale Act, 1878, without the benefit of the judicial exegesis which it has subsequently received, he might have little doubt that goods are in the apparent **D** possession of the grantor

". . . so long as they remain or are in or upon any house . . . or other premises occupied by him, or are used and enjoyed by him in any place whatsoever . . ."

However, as HARMAN, L.J., has pointed out, at a fairly early stage the courts **E** placed on those words a gloss which, I think, no one sought to relate to the actual words of the section until ATKIN, L.J.'s judgment in 1921 in *French* v. *Gething* (20). In the same case to which I have already referred, however, *Antoniadi* v. *Smith* (21), there are some passages which are not uninteresting in the history of the growth of that gloss. VAUGHAN WILLIAMS, L.J., said (21):

". . . I think that upon the evidence as given there is nothing whatever **F** to displace the actual possession of Mrs. Melland [she was the transferee] which I should infer to have existed, in the absence of evidence to the con-trary, from the fact that she was living all along in the house in which the goods were, though no doubt the execution debtor lived there also."

But, with great respect, what had to be displaced was not the actual possession of the transferree, but the " apparent possession " of the execution creditor **G** resulting from his occupation of the house in which the furniture remained and was there used by him. Then VAUGHAN WILLIAMS, L.J., said (21):

" Moreover, one must not forget that s. 4 of the Bills of Sale Act, 1878, gives a definition of apparent possession; and I think that, having regard to the terms of that definition, it would be a difficult thing to prove apparent **H** possession of the grantor where there is anything in favour of the grantee beyond a mere formal taking of possession by him."

How the definition in its natural meaning could lead to this conclusion VAUGHAN WILLIAMS, L.J., omitted to state.

The rationalisation of the gloss is ultimately to be found by ATKIN, L.J., in his judgment in *French* v. *Gething* (20) where he said: **I**

" I think that case [he is referring to *Ramsay* v. *Margrett* (22)] implies that ' possession ' and ' apparent possession ' mean sole possession and apparent sole possession just as ' possession ' and ' reputed ownership ' were held to mean sole possession and sole reputed ownership when it was a question

(18) [1901] 2 K.B. 589.   (19) [1901] 2 K.B. at p. 593.
(20) [1921] All E.R. Rep at p. 419; [1922] 1 K.B. at p. 247.
(21) [1901] 2 K.B. at p. 594.
(22) [1891-94] All E.R. Rep. 453; [1894] 2 Q.B. 18.

A   whether goods were in the order and disposition clause of the Bankruptcy
     Act, 1869, s. 15.''

     This, I think, leads one to the conclusion that one must read the definition of
     " apparent possession " in s. 4 of the Bills of Sale Act, 1878, as if it read—and
     I read only the relevant words here—

B   " personal chattels shall be deemed to be in the ' apparent possession ' of
         the person making . . . a bill of sale, so long as they remain or are in or upon
         any house . . . or other premises [solely] occupied by him, or are [solely]
         used and enjoyed by him in any place whatsoever."

     In the present case we have to decide (and we have had no assistance from the
     registrar on this point) whether the proper inference from the evidence is that
C   the claimant and the husband, when they entered into the transaction in Septem-
     ber, 1961, did so with the intention of thereafter setting up a common establish-
     ment, or whether they did so merely with the intention of the claimant acting as
     an ordinary paid domestic servant to the husband. As I say, the onus of showing
     that the latter was the true position in my view lies on the execution creditor.
     HARMAN, L.J., has already set out the facts. It seems to me that the irresistible
D   inference from those facts, unless one is going to shut one's eyes to what goes on
     in the world, is that the intention of the claimant and of the husband was that in
     future they should set up a common establishment in the house and that she
     would look after the house and look after the children.

     In those circumstances I think that the execution creditor has failed to show
     that this case falls over the line which lies between such cases as *Antoniadi* v.
E   *Smith* (23) and ATKIN, L.J.'s imaginary three men in a boat (24), on the one side,
     and the case of *Youngs* v. *Youngs* (25) on the other. I too would allow the appeal.

         WINN, L.J.: I agree with both the judgments which my lords have delivered.
     Explicitly I agree with the construction given by DIPLOCK, L.J., to the phrase
     " premises occupied by him " in the last paragraph of s. 4 of the Bills of Sale
F   Act, 1878, at which I had arrived quite independently. To that extent it is clear
     that DIPLOCK, L.J., and I have added something intentionally and expressly to
     what was said by ATKIN, L.J., on the topic of " apparent possession " in *French*
     v. *Gething* (26).

     I agree that this appeal should be allowed.

                    Appeal allowed. Order that the sheriff do withdraw from possession.

G   Solicitors: *Jay, Benning & Co.* (for the claimant); *Rowley, Ashworth & Co.*
     (for the execution creditor).

                              [*Reported by* F. GUTTMAN, ESQ., *Barrister-at-Law.*]

H

I

---

(23) [1901] 2 K.B. 589.
(24) [1921] All E.R. Rep. at p. 420; [1922] 1 K.B. at p. 247.
(25) [1940] 1 All E.R. 349; [1940] 1 K.B. 760.
(26) [1921] All E.R. Rep. at p. 419; [1922] 1 K.B. at p. 247.

A

GREGORY AND ANOTHER v. LONDON BOROUGH
OF CAMDEN.

[QUEEN'S BENCH DIVISION (Paull, J.), December 20, 21, 1965.]

Town and Country Planning—Development—Planning permission—Ultra vires—
Declaration—Applicant must show injuria as well as damnum—No legal   B
right of applicant infringed by development on adjoining land to which
planning permission related—No locus standi to maintain action against
planning authority for declaration that permission ultra vires.

The plaintiffs were the owners and occupiers of two houses at the back of
which was a large open space forming part of the grounds of a convent.
The defendants, the local planning authority, granted planning permission   C
to the trustees of the convent to erect a large new school in the convent
grounds and, later, for a second means of access to it which would probably
affect the amenities of the plaintiffs' houses, as many hundreds of pupils
might well use this access and pass close to them. The plaintiffs brought an
action for a declaration that the grants of planning permission were ultra
vires the defendants. On a preliminary issue whether the plaintiffs had a right   D
to ask for the declarations, assuming that the grants of planning permission
were ultra vires,

Held: the plaintiffs had no status to claim as against the defendants
declarations that the grants of planning permission were ultra vires, because
there was no infringement of any legal right of the plaintiffs; for what was
taking place on the land behind the plaintiffs' houses was something in regard   E
to which, as between the plaintiffs and the trustees of the convent, there
were no legal rights (see p. 203, letters G and H, and p. 204, letter G, post).

R. v. *Hendon Rural District Council, Ex p. Chorley* ([1933] All E.R. Rep.
20) not followed.

Dictum of WIDGERY, J., in *R.* v. *Bradford-on-Avon Urban District Council,*
Ex p. Boulton ([1964] 2 All E.R. at p. 494) applied.   F

[As to the right to challenge orders under the Town and Country Planning
Acts, see 37 HALSBURY'S LAWS (3rd Edn.) 203-205, para. 315; and for cases on
the subject, see 45 DIGEST (Repl.) 340, *53-55.*

As to the rule that declarations must relate to a legal right, see 22 HALSBURY'S
LAWS (3rd Edn.) 748, para. 1610, note (*s*).]
G
Cases referred to:

Barnard v. *National Dock Labour Board,* [1953] 1 All E.R. 1113; [1953]
   2 Q.B. 18; [1953] 2 W.L.R. 995; Digest (Cont. Vol. A) 970, *280a.*

Buxton v. *Minister of Housing and Local Government,* [1960] 3 All E.R. 408;
   [1961] 1 Q.B. 278; [1960] 3 W.L.R. 866; 124 J.P. 489; 45 Digest (Repl.)
   340, *55.*   H

R. v. *Bradford-on-Avon Urban District Council, Ex p. Boulton,* [1964] 2 All
   E.R. 492; [1964] 1 W.L.R. 1136; 128 J.P. 339; 45 Digest (Repl.) 340,
   53.

R. v. *Electricity Comrs., Ex p. London Electricity Joint Committee Co. (1920), Ltd.,*
   [1923] All E.R. Rep. 150; [1924] 1 K.B. 171; 93 L.J.K.B. 390; 130
   L.T. 164; 88 J.P. 13; 20 Digest (Repl.) 202, *3.*   I

R. v. *Hendon Rural District Council, Ex p. Chorley,* [1933] All E.R. Rep. 20;
   [1933] 2 K.B. 696; 102 L.J.K.B. 658; 149 L.T. 535; 97 J.P. 210;
   45 Digest (Repl.) 336, *36.*

R. v. *Surrey Justices,* (1870), L.R. 5 Q.B. 466; 39 L.J.M.C. 145; 34 J.P. 614;
   26 Digest (Repl.) 374, *838.*

R. v. *Woodhouse, Ex p. Ryder,* [1906] 2 K.B. 501; 75 L.J.K.B. 745; 95 L.T.
   367; 70 J.P. 485; *revsd. on other grounds* sub nom. *Leeds Corpn.* v.
   Ryder, [1907] A.C. 420; 16 Digest (Repl.) 443, *2504.*

A   **Preliminary Issue.**

This was a preliminary issue, tried pursuant to an order of Master HARWOOD dated July 20, 1965, in an action by the plaintiffs claiming declarations against the defendants that planning permission granted by the defendants to the trustees of a school situated on land at the back of the plaintiffs' houses was ultra vires the defendants. The facts are set out in the judgment.

B   *D. D. H. Sullivan* for the plaintiffs.

J. D. James for the defendants.

PAULL, J.: I should like to start my judgment by expressing my gratitude to both counsel for the very interesting and detailed arguments which have been placed before me.

C   This matter comes before me under an order, dated July 29, 1965. The order, or the material parts of it, is as follows:

" The points of law raised by para. 18 and para. 19 of the defence be tried upon the amended pleadings by a judge alone in London as a preliminary issue and before the hearing and determination of other issues herein under Ord. 34, r. 2."

D   I am, therefore, in the position of simply having to decide the points of law raised under para. 18 and para. 19 of the defence. I turn at once to those paragraphs. They read:

" 18. Furthermore this action is in the defendants' respectful submission misconceived. It is not brought to enforce or declare any right of the plain-

E   tiffs or either of them in connexion with the matters complained of in the statement of claim, or to secure the performance of any duty owed by the defendants to the plaintiffs or either of them.

" 19. A declaration or declarations against the defendants as claimed would not effectively remedy any grievance or supposed grievance of the plaintiffs against the former defendants or the defendants nor make available

F   to the plaintiffs or either of them any or any additional remedy against the said Westminster Diocese Roman Catholic Trustees or any persons entitled to avail themselves of the benefit of the said planning permissions, or purporting to act thereunder."

In order to explain the words " the former defendants or the defendants ", I should point out that this action was originally brought against the London

G   County Council, but, as the duties of the London County Council have now devolved on the London Borough of Camden, that body has been substituted as defendants. When I use the term " the defendants " in my judgment, I am using that as covering both bodies and making no distinction between them, since the present defendants are the successors in title to the old defendants.

This being a point of law, I must assume that all the facts set out in the state-

H   ment of claim have been proved. In the few minutes which I have had to consider my judgment, I have tried to analyse the facts in the statement of claim fairly shortly. I think that they can be analysed in this way. The plaintiffs are owners and occupiers of Nos. 51 and 55, Croftdown Road, N.W.5, the first plaintiff owning and occupying No. 51 and the second plaintiff No. 55. At all material times before the present matters arose, at the back of these houses was a large

I   open space forming part of the grounds of a convent, and no doubt it was a very great amenity to the houses to be able to look on to that open space rather than on to rows of houses and other buildings. On Aug. 12, 1963, an application for detailed planning permission to erect a school for seven hundred children in the grounds of the convent came before the defendants. This school, if erected, would be the second school in the grounds of the convent. There is already one school there, that forming part of the convent building. This was to be a big new school, and was to be maintained by the defendants. That application was granted, and, being for detailed planning permission of this sort, the plaintiffs had no knowledge

of the granting of that application. On Dec. 1, 1963, a second application was   A
made, which, in effect, merely added a second means of access to that new proposed school. That means of access would run between Nos. 51 and 53, and the
effect, of course, would be that many hundreds of the pupils might well use that
means of access and pass next to or very close to the houses of the plaintiffs.
The whole of the land in question had been allocated under the County of London
Development Plan primarily for residential use, apart from the existing school   B
which was part of the convent building.

The statement of claim alleges that the orders to which I referred were ultra
vires the defendants. As that has to be assumed, I will not spend much time in
considering all the various provisions of the Acts, the statutory instruments, and
the circulars to which my attention has been referred. It is, I think, sufficient
to make the matter clear to say that a direction was given by the Minister of   C
Housing and Local Government, which is headed " H.L.G. 4441 ". Under that
direction, the Minister directed, first of all, that

" A local planning authority is hereby authorised to grant permission for
development of land which does not accord with the provisions of the
development plan in any case where in their opinion the development
authorised by the permission, if carried out in accordance with the con-   D
ditions, if any, to be imposed, would neither involve a substantial departure
from the provisions of the plan nor injuriously affect the amenity of adjoining
land."

The plaintiffs allege that the order made did in fact involve a substantial departure
from the provisions of the Greater London Development Plan, and also injuriously   E
affected the amenity of adjoining land, part of which adjoining land was that
space occupied by the two houses Nos. 51 and 55. The second paragraph of the
direction is as follows:

" In any other case, before granting permission for development which
does not accord with the provisions of the development plan a local planning
authority shall send to the Minister a copy of the application made to them   F
and of any plans and drawings which accompanied it, together with a
statement of the reasons for which they desire to grant the permission and
of the conditions, if any, which they propose to impose, and shall not grant
permission for that development until the expiration of twenty-one days (or
such shorter period as he [that is, the Minister] may in any particular case
appoint) from the date on which such copy is received by the Minister."   G

I must assume—and indeed I think that it is agreed between the parties—that,
there being a substantial departure from the provisions of the plan, no copy
of the application was sent to the Minister, and, indeed, that the provisions of
para. 2 were not complied with. Then comes another paragraph:

" Failing any direction from the Minister within the said period the local
planning authority shall be authorised to grant permission for that develop-   H
ment at the expiration of that period."

In other words, supposing that the defendants had performed their duties under
this circular, then, if the Minister did not communicate with them for twenty-one
days, they were at liberty to make the order which they made. Counsel for the
plaintiffs says: " My complaint is that I lost the opportunity which the Minister   I
might have taken to say: ' Before I will agree to this being done, I will '—and
then make certain conditions, such as ' require you to send notices to the persons
affected ', or ' hold an enquiry ', or ' take some other step '." It is to be noticed
that, if nothing had been done by the Minister, then the plaintiffs would be in
exactly the same position as that in which they now are. There is another fact
which is alleged in the statement of claim—which must be taken to be proved—
and that is that the defendants, when they made the order which they made, knew
that the order would injuriously affect the amenities of the plaintiffs' lands. There

A   is no claim that the effect of the order has been, or might be, to cause the plaintiffs
any monetary loss. At one time I wondered whether that would not be a necessary
allegation in order to establish a legal right. It does not follow by any means that
the building of a school would diminish the value of the land; indeed, it might,
from the point of view of parents wanting to find houses close to a school, increase
the value. I have come to the conclusion, however, that that does not matter,
B   and that the plaintiffs must not be prejudiced, and cannot be prejudiced, by the
fact that there is no such claim in the statement of claim.

It is in those circumstances that I have to determine whether, in law, the
plaintiffs are entitled on those facts to the declaration which they claim in their
statement of claim. The declarations are two, and they are these:

C   " (i) A declaration that the grant by [and I leave out the word " former ";
I only use the word " defendants " all the way through] the defendants of
planning permission on each of the said applications was ultra vires the
defendants. (ii) Alternatively, a declaration that the grant by the defendants
of planning permission on the said second application was ultra vires the
defendants in so far as it related to the formation of an access from the said day
school through No. 53, Croftdown Road, London, N.W.5 to the highway."

D
On the facts, which I have to assume, there can be no doubt that the order was
ultra vires. It is so alleged, and I must assume that that is right. The question
before me is: have the plaintiffs a right to come to court for a declaration that
the orders were ultra vires, or are the defendants right when they say under para.
18 that the action is misconceived? That is the point which I have to determine.
E   Is this action misconceived in that the plaintiffs, even on those facts, have no
right to come to court for a declaration?

That matter has produced most interesting arguments. One starts with this,
that the main case relied on by counsel for the plaintiffs is a case where a writ
of certiorari was sought, and counsel's first argument to me is that if the plaintiffs
had known in time they could have applied for certiorari; that it was not their
F   fault that they did not know in time, and that if they had the right to apply for
certiorari, then they were entitled to the declarations sought, since the courts have
held that the right to a declaration is not destroyed because proceedings for
certiorari could have been brought. In that connexion counsel cited *Barnard* v.
National Dock Labour Board (1). All that I need refer to there is Denning, L.J.'s
judgment where he said (2):

G   " It is axiomatic that when a statutory tribunal sits to administer justice,
it must act in accordance with the law. Parliament clearly so intended. If
the tribunal does not observe the law, what is to be done? The remedy by
certiorari is hedged round by limitations and may not be available. Why,
then, should not the court intervene by declaration and injunction? If it
cannot so intervene, it would mean that the tribunal could disregard the law."

H   At first sight, those appear to be very strong words, and, indeed, they are strong
from the point of view that, if proceedings for certiorari can be brought and are
not taken, that does not necessarily do away with the right to bring proceedings
for a declaration. It is, however, to be noted that in this case there is no claim
for an injunction at all; the plaintiffs do not claim that they are entitled to an
injunction. The only effect of my making a declaration would be, as counsel for
I   the plaintiffs puts it, that it would give the defendants an opportunity of having
second thoughts. The building of this school is still going on and the building is
rapidly being erected, but counsel for the plaintiffs says that, though any declaration will not affect that, yet the building is to be built in two stages, and there is
the question of the second access; so that, if the court makes a declaration, the
defendants may have second thoughts and may not proceed with the second
stage of building, or may not allow the second access. That is vague. This is

(1) [1953] 1 All E.R. 1113; [1953] 2 Q.B. 18.
(2) [1953] 1 All E.R. at p. 1119; [1953] 2 Q.B. at p. 41.

not a case where the court is being asked to stop something. The court is simply A
being asked for a declaration.

In determining whether the plaintiffs are entitled to a declaration, I start by
considering the only case which is on the point of whether a writ of certiorari lay;
R. v. *Hendon Rural District Council, Ex p. Chorley* (3). Before I refer to it, I
should say that that was an application for a writ of certiorari, not under the
modern scheme of town and country planning at all, but under the old scheme B
which came into force under the Town Planning Act, 1925, which one might
almost say has been done away with, first by the Town and Country Planning
Act, 1947, and since then by further acts of Parliament. The whole scheme now
is one quite different from the scheme which was in force when that case was
heard in 1933. That case requires rather careful consideration in several respects.
It was an application for certiorari to quash the decision, so that the decision C
should be treated as null and void. It was a case where the order had been brought
about by malpractice. On the findings of the court a gentleman who was very
much involved in the building of the garage, for which town planning permission
was sought, had himself voted that the order should be passed, and, being
present, other members of the council sat under his eagle eye. When that sort
of matter arises, the court is extremely anxious that such an order should not D
be allowed to stand. That does not mean, of course, that the court will find bad
law, but it does mean that one has to look at that case with that very much in
mind. The facts of that case were these. The application was brought by
Mr. Chorley, who was the owner and occupier of premises known as the Rookery,
Great Stanmore, Middlesex. Almost immediately opposite his house were premises
known as the Old Brewery Stables, and they both came under the town planning E
scheme. The application was made for permission, in effect, to turn the Old
Brewery Stables, which were residential buildings, into a garage, and it was on
that application that the gentleman who was very much involved in the whole of
that scheme attended and voted at the council. The application to turn the Old
Brewery Stables building into a garage was an application by a Mr. Archer.
One of the points was that Mr. Archer had no interest in the land to entitle him F
to make the application. Another point which was taken was that Mr. Chorley
was interested in the matter not only from the point of view of the amenities
of his house, but also from the point of view of being a ratepayer; and one of the
arguments of counsel on Mr. Chorley's behalf was (4) that as adjoining owner
he might be affected by the proposed development as a ratepayer, and he might
be called on in the future to contribute to the compensation which might have to G
be paid. It was in those circumstances that the court gave their decision.
They gave it under the terms of the Town Planning Act, 1925, and I would
just like shortly to see what the basis of that decision was. In the first place,
as counsel for the plaintiffs points out, AVORY, J.'s judgment was based on the
fact that the order would entitle Mr. Archer in certain events to compensation,
and, as the council was, therefore, dealing with a matter which affected the H
rights of an individual, Mr. Archer, the case came within the principles laid down
in *R.* v. *Electricity Comrs., Ex p. London Electricity Joint Committee Co. (1920),
Ltd.* (5). That case was referred to by HUMPHREYS, J., in these words (6):

"With regard to the difficult question, whether the proceedings of this
council on this occasion were proceedings which can be questioned by
certiorari, many observations are to be found in different cases by many I
learned judges who have endeavoured to express the particular circumstances
in which a body admittedly exercising not the jurisdiction of a court, but a
discretion of some sort or other, should be regarded as proceedings which can
be dealt with by this court by a writ of certiorari. The passage which my

(3) [1933] All E.R. Rep. 20; [1933] 2 K.B. 696.
(4) [1933] 2 K.B. at pp. 701, 702.
(5) [1923] All E.R. Rep. 150; [1924] 1 K.B. 171.
(6) [1933] All E.R. Rep. at p. 23; [1933] 2 K.B. at p. 705.

A   lord has read from the judgment of ATKIN, L.J., in R. v. Electricity Comrs. (7), leaves unexplained to some extent the meaning of the words ' to act judicially '. ' Whenever any body of persons having legal authority to determine questions affecting the rights of subjects, and having the duty to act judicially '—says ATKIN, L.J.—' act in excess of their legal authority, they are subject to the controlling influence of the King's Bench Division . . .'.

B   I think some assistance is to be obtained as to the meaning of the word ' acting judicially ' from the judgment of FLETCHER MOULTON, L.J., in the case of R. v. Woodhouse, Ex p. Rider (8), where the learned lord justice said: ' There must be the exercise of some right or duty to decide in order to provide scope for a writ of certiorari at common law '."

C   LORD HEWART, C.J., in his judgment, in quoting another passage from R. v. Electricity Comrs. (7), quotes the following words (9):

    " Whenever any body of persons having legal authority to determine questions affecting the rights of subjects, and having the duty to act judicially, act in excess of their legal authority, they are subject to the controlling jurisdiction of the King's Bench Division, exercised in these writs."

D   The learned lord chief justice goes on (9):

    " I think it is clear from the affidavits that the hearing of this resolution was advertised, objections were invited and objections were considered, and further the decision at which the Hendon Rural District Council arrived was a decision which conferred, contingently at any rate, a legal right, and affected the rights of subjects."

E   That, as far as I know, is the only case under the Act of 1925 which bears on this matter. It bears on this matter only in this way, that, this being an action for a declaration, counsel for the plaintiffs argues that as his clients would have had an action for certiorari, therefore, they have a right to a declaration. I am not quite satisfied that that is quite right. When one is dealing with certiorari, one is quashing. When one is dealing with a declaration, one is not quashing; all that

F   one is doing is to declare the rights of the particular individual who brings the action. One has to look at the matter a little differently, because, in a matter of a declaration, only the rights of the plaintiff and the defendant are involved, and not the rights of all persons who might be governed by the order made.

    Looking at the general position in law in this case, I start with this. Building

G   on the convent land raises the question of a loss of amenity by the plaintiffs, the occupiers of a piece of land, because of acts of an adjoining occupier of the land. I will refer to that adjoining occupier as " the trustees ", because this building was in fact being erected under the aegis of trustees, who in fact are the trustees of the lands of the convent. Apart from having to get permission from the planning authority, the trustees have the absolute right in law

H   to do what they are doing, namely, to build a school on that land and to make the access to the school over those pieces of their land for which permission was given to have access. That might hit the plaintiffs hard, but things done by an occupier may hit hard the occupier of adjoining land. To give two examples: I own a house, and on the next plot to my house, which I thought was going to be part of a large garden, there is erected another house. It is erected within two or three feet of my house, just over the border. The effect

I   of that is to block out the light from my windows. Unless I have the right of ancient lights, no legal right of mine has been affected. It is to be noticed that, all the way through in the case to which I have referred, the words " legal rights " are used. One has to consider the legal rights of someone. Again, next to my land there may be built a school. I may be very much affected by the noise of the

---

(7) [1923] All E.R. Rep. at p. 161; [1924] 1 K.B. at p. 205.
(8) [1906] 2 K.B. 501 at p. 535.
(9) [1933] All E.R. Rep. at p. 22; [1933] 2 K.B. at p. 702.

children coming out to play, by the shouts, by the laughter and everything else; **A**
but unless I can establish that it is a nuisance, I have lost no legal right. I have
lost amenities, but no legal rights. My legal rights are exactly as they were before
the building was built and the noise arose.

In this case, no question of public rights is involved, as where there is interference with the highway. There is a long series of cases on this, and my attention
has been drawn to a number of them, ranging from *R.* v. *Surrey Justices* (10) to **B**
R. v. *Bradford-on-Avon Urban District Council, Ex p. Boulter* (11). All those cases
involve rights over public roadways in one shape or another; in other words,
places where the public have rights. In this case, I have merely to consider the
right of one landowner in relation to the acts of another landowner, and in
relation to the fact that the adjoining landowner is putting up a building to be
used in a certain way.   **C**

The question that I would ask on this matter is: I am concerned with the
rights of adjoining occupiers so far as the building is concerned, and if there
is no cause of action against a neighbour because he is putting up that building,
or because he is proposing to use it for a certain purpose, then is there any right
to step in if the adjoining occupier has to ask a third party for permission before
he can begin?   Let me take the case of contract. I occupy land next door to **D**
B. So far as I am concerned, B. has a perfect right to build right up to my
border; but suppose B. cannot do that because he has a contract with X whereby
he has to get the permission of X to build. B starts to build, not having got
the permission of X. Am I entitled to enjoin him? Or is B entitled to say
that that is nothing to do with me, it is a matter between X and himself? In
my view, quite clearly B is so entitled. I, as occupier, although affected by **E**
what B is doing, must put up with the consequences unless B is in some way
affecting my legal rights, and I have no legal right to object to the building which
he is putting up. Therefore, if this were a case of contract between the defendants
and the trustees, the plaintiffs would have no rights at all.

If that is how the matter stands in contract, does it make any difference that
the matter is not one of contract but of statute? That may well depend on the **F**
purpose for which the statute was passed. There are certain statutes which were
passed to protect a certain class of people; and, if a statute is passed to protect
a class of persons, then anyone in that class who is affected by a breach of the
statute may bring an action for damages in respect thereof. The Town Planning
Acts, however, have been passed to give rights to the public only, and not
to any particular class of the public. On that I am assisted by SALMON, J., in **G**
Buxton v. *Minister of Housing and Local Government* (12). That was a case where
the Minister ordered an inquiry with regard to planning consent being given in
respect of the development of the land by digging chalk. At that planning inquiry
certain occupiers of adjoining land came forward and said that it would be quite
improper to make such an order because their land would be very badly affected,
and the inspector holding the inquiry agreed and recommended to the Minister **H**
that permission should not be given because of the effect that it would have on
the adjoining land and because there was no real necessity for chalk to be dug on
that land; there was plenty of chalk otherwise. The Minister differed from his
inspector, and granted the order. Thereupon the persons concerned brought
proceedings and tried to say that the Minister ought not to have made the order.
For that purpose, of course, they had to come within that class of persons who, **I**
under the statute (13), were called " an aggrieved person "; in other words, somebody who was aggrieved by the order. If I read one paragraph of SALMON, J.'s
judgment, it will make the matter quite clear. He said (14):

" Superficially there is much to be said for the view that the applicants

---

(10) (1870), L.R. 5 Q.B. 466.   (11) [1964] 2 All E.R. 492.
(12) [1960] 3 All E.R. 408; [1961] 1 Q.B. 278.
(13) The Town and Country Planning Act, 1959, s. 31.
(14) [1961] 1 Q.B. at p. 283; [1960] 3 All E.R. at p. 411,

A   are aggrieved by the Minister's action. For example, Mr. Buxton, one of the applicants, as the inspector's report shows, has an estate of about 250 acres adjoining the operators' land. He is interested in landscape gardening and ornithology and has spent large sums of money for these purposes on his land. Moreover, he has a herd of pedigree pigs and some breeding mares very close indeed to the site from which the chalk is to be won. I can well under-

B   stand his annoyance at the Minister's decision to reject recommendations which the Minister's inspector has made after a thorough inspection of the site and the careful investigation of a considerable body of evidence. If I could approach this problem free from authority, without regard to the scheme of the town and country planning legislation and its historical background, the arguments in favour of the applicants on the preliminary

C   point would be most persuasive, if not compelling, for in the widest sense of the word the applicants are undoubtedly aggrieved. In my judgment, however, I am compelled to restrict the meaning of the words ' person aggrieved ' to a person with a legal grievance."

I think that here one must add " that is, that amenities are affected in such a way as to give a legal right ". Then SALMON, J., went on (15):

D
    " Before the town and country planning legislation any landowner was free to develop his land as he liked, provided he did not infringe the common law. No adjoining owner had any right which he could enforce in the courts in respect of such development unless he could show that it constituted a nuisance or trespass or the like. The scheme of the town and country plan-

E   ning legislation, in my judgment, is to restrict development for the benefit of the public at large and not to confer new rights on any individual members of the public, whether they live close to or far from the proposed development."

In this case, as I see it, the plaintiffs are really saying that in effect they have a right which they would not have had but for the passing of the Town and Country

F   Planning Act, viz., a right to look and see if the Minister or the town planning authority has made an order which is not a good order, and, if they find that this is so, then they can take steps whereby this building may possibly be stopped. That is essentially what the plaintiffs are saying for this action is no use to them whatsoever unless in some way it will influence the question whether the trustees can or cannot go on with their building. Looking at it in that rather

G   simple way, it seems to me that the answer to the question which I have to determine is that the plaintiffs have no legal right to step in at all. They may have suffered damnum, that is to say, loss in one way or another, but they have not suffered injuria, that is to say, any legal wrong. There are many acts which cause loss which give no legal rights. Before one can come to a court of law, one must suffer an injuria as well as damnum; one must have suffered a legal

H   wrong as well as an actual loss of money or amenity or something else. What is taking place on this land behind Nos. 51 and 53 is something in respect of which, as between the plaintiffs and the trustees, there are no legal rights what-soever, and the plaintiffs cannot interfere by maintaining that a third party's permission must be got before the building can be built. This may be a simple way of looking at this matter, but it seems to me that that is the way by which

I   one can find the solution which seems to fit in with legal principles and with the purposes for which these Acts have been passed.

There is one case to which I should refer, because stress was laid on it, and that is *R. v. Bradford-on-Avon Urban District Council, Ex p. Boulton* (16). That was an application to quash an order relating to a matter which involved the user of the highway and, therefore, there was a proper foundation for bringing the proceedings. It was queried whether the applicant had sufficient interest

(15) [1961] 1 Q.B. at p. 283; [1960] 3 All E.R. at p. 411,
(16) [1964] 2 All E.R. 492.

in that he lived a long way away, and it was said that the right merely to pass **A** and re-pass on that particular piece of land was not sufficient to found his right to bring proceedings for certiorari to quash the order. In the course of his judgment, WIDGERY, J., said this (17):

" It is obviously open to question, to say the least of it, whether someone who describes himself as the applicant describes himself, really has status to move for certiorari in a case of this kind at all. The matter is not entirely **B** free of authority, and we have been referred to the decision in *R. v. Hendon Rural District Council, Ex p. Chorley* (18). That was a case in which certiorari was granted at the suit of the owner of land adjacent to land which was liable to be affected by a decision of what today we would call a local planning authority. It is to be noted that the applicant in that case **C** was not merely a member of the public living in the locality, but he was the owner of land which was likely to be affected by the decision itself, and it is, perhaps, not altogether surprising that in that case there was held to be sufficient status to apply for certiorari. Here the applicant is the user of the highway, he lives ten miles away, we are told, and, although he uses this road more frequently than many, he has no greater or closer interest in the **D** problem than that. For reasons which will appear in a moment, I for my part do not find it necessary to decide finally whether he has the status to move the court in this way at all. I would leave that matter for consideration if necessary, on another occasion. I will assume for the purposes of the rest of my judgment that he has that status, but I do not decide it, and, indeed, I have grave doubts, speaking for myself, whether he has." **E**

It is to be noted that WIDGERY, J. (who is, of course, a great authority on these matters), was rather careful in the way in which he expressed himself. It will be noticed that he did not say, as he might well have said: " We have authority with regard to this matter; *R. v. Hendon Rural District Council* (18), which decides that a person who is affected in the way that that applicant was affected has a right to bring the proceedings." He was deliberately very careful for **F** two reasons: first, that the *Hendon* case (18) is a case in which there is a good deal to be said, I think, on both sides; and, secondly, that, since that case, there has been a completely changed system of town and country planning, and certainly I do not feel that I am in any way bound by that case, which was decided under the Act of 1925.

My conclusion, therefore, is that, on this point of law, the defendants are right. **G** There is no status for the plaintiffs to claim a declaration, which is what they are doing, not asking that the order should be set aside, but asking that, as between themselves and the defendants, they should have a declaration that the defendants acted ultra vires. I think that they have no standing for that purpose, and, therefore, my decision is in favour of the defendants.

Order accordingly. **H**

Solicitors: *Holt, Beever & Kinsey* (for the plaintiffs); *B. H. Wilson* (for the defendants).

[*Reported by* LAURENCE H. KINGSLEY, ESQ., *Barrister-at-Law.*]

I

---

(17) [1964] 2 All E.R. at p. 494.
(18) [1933] All E.R. Rep. 20; [1933] 2 K.B. 696.

A

CORFIELD *v.* HODGSON.

[QUEEN'S BENCH DIVISION (Lord Parker, C.J., Sachs and Widgery, JJ.), February 22, 1966.]

Affiliation—Evidence—Corroboration—Lie by putative father on whether oppor-
tunity for intercourse alleged by mother occurred—Affiliation Proceedings
B *Act,* 1957 (5 & 6 *Eliz.* 2 *c.* 55), *s.* 4 (2).

The respondent preferred a complaint against the appellant that she had been delivered of a bastard child, of which she alleged that the appellant was the father. In examination-in-chief, the appellant denied that, as was alleged by the respondent, he had ever taken her home from a dance, but in cross-examination he admitted that he had done so on two occasions,
C adding, after a pause, that on each occasion they had been accompanied by his sister. The justices did not believe that his sister had been with him and found that he was the father of the appellant's child, being of the opinion that the respondent's evidence was corroborated in a material particular as required by s. 4 (2) of the Affiliation Proceedings Act, 1957, by his own evidence. On appeal,

D **Held:** a lie told in those circumstances might be of a character which was capable of being corroboration in the sense that it disclosed a guilty mind, and the justices were justified in their conclusion (see p. 207, letters C and H, post).

Appeal dismissed.

E [As to corroboration of the mother's evidence on an application for an affiliation order, see 3 HALSBURY'S LAWS (3rd Edn.) 120, 121, para. 184; and for cases on the subject, see 3 DIGEST (Repl.) 452-454, *412-428.*

For the Affiliation Proceedings Act, 1957, s. 4, see 37 HALSBURY'S STATUTES (2nd Edn.) 40.]

Case Stated.

F This was a Case Stated by justices for the county of Cumberland in respect of their adjudication as a magistrates' court sitting at Keswick on Apr. 2, 1965. On Feb. 17, 1965, the respondent, Jennifer Hodgson, preferred a complaint against the appellant, Kenneth William Corfield, that she was delivered of an illegitimate child at City Maternity Hospital, Carlisle, on Jan. 5, 1965; she alleged that the appellant was the father of such child, and she applied for a
G summons to be served on him to answer such complaint under s. 1 of the Affiliation Proceedings Act, 1957. The following facts were found. The respondent was a single woman within the meaning of s. 1 of the Affiliation Proceedings Act, 1957. She resided at 57, Winderbrowe Avenue, Keswick, with her parents. On Jan. 5, 1965, the respondent gave birth to an illegitimate child, Tracy Jane Hodgson, at Carlisle City Maternity Hospital. The respondent lived in the same street
H as the appellant, and about one hundred yards away, and met the appellant at the appellant's home when she visited his sister, and she had known him for about two years. On every Saturday night the respondent went with the appellant's sister to the Pavilion Dance Hall at Keswick. After New Year, 1964, she met the appellant on several occasions (but not regularly) at the Pavilion Dance Hall, Keswick, and he took her home afterwards. About Mar. 20, 1964,
I the appellant took her home from a dance and on the way she had sexual intercourse with him. On Apr. 11, 1964, the appellant again took her home from a dance and she again had sexual intercourse with him. She only had sexual intercourse with the appellant on these two occasions, and had never had sexual intercourse with any other man. In May, 1964, the respondent had reason to believe that she was pregnant.

It was contended before the justices by the appellant that the evidence of the respondent should not be relied on, that his evidence should be accepted and that the complaint should be dismissed. It was contended before the justices

by the respondent that her evidence should be accepted in preference to that   A
of the appellant.

The facts proved were accepted from the evidence of the respondent. Apart
from the appellant and the respondent, seven other persons testified, but the
justices found that their evidence was not material and were of the opinion that
the respondent's evidence was true and was to be preferred to that of the appellant. The justices were of opinion that the respondent's evidence was corro-   B
borated in a material particular as required by s. 4 (2) of the Affiliation Proceedings Act, 1957, by the appellant's own evidence, in so far as they were of
opinion that he denied that he had ever taken the respondent home from a
dance in his examination-in-chief, but later, under persistent cross-examination,
admitted that he had done so on two occasions, then, after a pause, added that on
each occasion they had been accompanied by his sister. The justices did not   C
believe that his sister had been with him.

The justices adjudged the appellant to be the putative father of the respondent's child, and made an order against him for the payment of £1 10s. a week
to the respondent from the date of birth until the child attained the age of sixteen
years. The appellant now appealed.

The cases noted below* were cited during the argument.   D

G. I. Rich for the appellant.
I. H. M. Jones for the respondent.

LORD PARKER, C.J., having stated the nature of the proceedings and summarised the facts, continued: The justices were of opinion that the respondent's
evidence was true, and was to be preferred to that of the appellant. If one reads   E
the justices' notes of the evidence, it is quite clear that the justices must have
wholly disbelieved the appellant when he attacked the character of the respondent, saying that she was easy prey, that she went with all kinds, and that she
had a reputation in Keswick, whereas he was merely friendly with her and
indeed was not attracted to girls. The question, of course, turns, as always in
these cases, on the question whether there was evidence capable of amounting   F
to corroboration, and, as to that, I will read what the justices say:

" We were of opinion that the respondent's [the mother's] evidence was
corroborated in a material particular as required by s. 4 (2) of the Affiliation
Proceedings Act, 1957, by the appellant's own evidence in so far as we were
of opinion that he denied that he had ever taken the respondent home from
a dance in his examination-in-chief, but later, under persistent cross-   G
examination, admitted that he had done so on two occasions, then, after a
a pause added that on each occasion they had been accompanied by his
sister. We did not believe that his sister had been with him."

Counsel for the appellant takes as his first point that, if one looks at the clerk's
notes, which the justices in the Case say is an accurate transcript, it is quite
impossible to say either that there has been an admission that the appellant   H
took the respondent home alone because the transcript shows that he added that
his sister was there, and also that, if one takes that answer in cross-examination
and compares it with the answer given in chief, there really was no inconsistency
and, accordingly, the appellant told no lie. I quite appreciate the force of
counsel for the appellant's argument, having read the clerk's notes. For my
part, I feel that I am bound to accept the conclusion reached by the justices   I
on hearing that evidence and watching the witnesses. When it is said in the
Case that, after admitting that the appellant had taken the girl home, he added
after a pause that he had been accompanied by his sister, that does not appear
in any way, of course, on the transcript. I feel bound to accept what the justices,
who heard the case and saw the appellant, felt was the true inference. They
were clearly of opinion that, under persistent cross-examination, he had admitted

---

* *Jones* v. *Thomas*, [1934] 1 K.B. 323; *Holland* v. *Roberts*, (1938), 158 L.T. 313.

A that he had taken the girl home on two occasions. If that be so, then it does seem to me that it conflicts with the evidence which he did give in chief, as found by the justices, that he had never taken the girl home from a dance alone. Accepting that, as I think that I am bound to, I am quite satisfied that there was evidence capable of amounting to corroboration. If the admission, as the justices found it was, in cross-examination that he had taken the girl home on

B two occasions alone stood by itself, that would be mere admission of opportunity and would not be enough; equally, if the lie stood alone it would be incapable of amounting to corroboration, because on that basis there would have been no admission by the appellant that he had taken this girl home alone; but, accepting the justices' finding, there is here an admission of opportunity and a prior statement in evidence itself that he had never taken the girl home, which on his later

C admission was a lie.

It seems to me that a lie told in those circumstances may be of a character which is capable of being corroboration in the sense that it discloses a guilty mind. In those circumstances, though the evidence of corroboration was not strong, I am quite satisfied that the justices were justified in coming to the conclusion which they reached. I would dismiss this appeal.

D

SACHS, J.: I agree. Naturally it cannot properly be said in affiliation cases that every lie told by the respondent can in law be held to be capable of being corroboration; and nothing that I am about to say is intended to suggest that there is any general rule as to which specific lie can, and which specific lie cannot, be so held. Nor is anything that I am about to say intended to derogate from the well established rule that evidence of opportunity is not of itself evidence

E that can constitute corroboration.

This particular case, however, is concerned with one type of lie that in sexual cases has frequently had to be considered by this court and by the Court of Criminal Appeal on the issue whether it is capable of constituting corroboration. It is a lie on the issue whether there did occur the particular opportunity for

F sexual intercourse which the respondent in affiliation cases (or the victim of a criminal assault in other cases) says occurred, and further says was the one of which advantage was taken by the putative father (or the accused). That type of lie is one which, in a number of cases before this court and before the Court of Criminal Appeal, has been held to be one which may well in all the circumstances be capable of constituting corroboration as indicative of a man's sense

G of guilt. Indeed, the present case is but one example of several that have been before the courts within this term. The argument that, because independent evidence of opportunity is not of itself corroboration, therefore, a lie about that opportunity cannot be capable of constituting corroboration has each time been unsuccessfully repeated; and for that reason only I have ventured to add these brief observations to emphasise the risks on costs that may be incurred by any further repetition on some future occasion.

H

WIDGERY, J.: I also agree with the order proposed and have nothing to add.

Appeal dismissed.

Solicitors: *Beachcroft & Co.*, agents for *Curwen & Co.*, Workington (for the appellant); *Speechly, Mumford & Soames*, agents for *Saul & Lightfoot*, Carlisle

I (for the respondent).

[*Reported by* LAURENCE H. KINGSLEY, ESQ., *Barrister-at-Law.*]

WESTWOOD v. NATIONAL COAL BOARD.

A

[COURT OF APPEAL (Sellers, Danckwerts and Salmon, L.JJ.), January 12, 13, 14, February 17, 1966.]

Mine—Railway above ground—Material placed less than three feet from track— Loose material on route for shunter going in course of duty from one point to another—Safe route available—Whether shunter " required " in the course of his duty to pass on foot over that material or between it and the line— Whether breach of Coal and Other Mines (Sidings) Order, 1956 (S.I. 1956 No. 1773), Sch., reg. 20.

B

An experienced shunter working with a railway train was killed by the train at a surface siding at the defendants' colliery. Where he was killed the distance between the railway track and the edge of an adjacent colliery dirt-stack was (for some yards) less than three feet so that, as the wagons had an overhang of one foot four inches and the locomotive an overhang of two feet, it was impossible to walk there safely. Some time before the accident a bull-dozer, which had been used investigating the contents of the dirt-stack, had left an uneven but passable track, about five feet wide, on the stack, near its edge, about two feet above the level of and running parallel to the rails, with a bank beneath it sloping towards the rails at an angle of about forty-five degrees. On the occasion of the accident the deceased was last seen walking on the right of the outside right rail of the track on which the train was proceeding. He was some few yards in front of the leading wagon. The train had reversed, and at the moment when the accident must have happened the train was on a curve and the driver's vision was obscured by the wagons that his engine was pushing. The engine was pushing three wagons and the speed of the train was seven or eight m.p.h. In an action by the shunter's widow against the defendant mine owners for damages for personal injuries causing his death, the widow alleged that the mine manager was in breach of his duty under reg. 20* of the Coal and Other Mines (Sidings) Regulations, 1956.

C

D

E

F

Held (DANCKWERTS, L.J., dissenting): reg. 20 had no application because on the evidence the deceased was not required, by the duties which he had to perform or by reg. 9† of the regulations of 1956, to walk within three feet of the outside rail of the track; accordingly breach of statutory duty under reg. 20 on the part of the defendants was not established (see p. 210, letter H, and p. 213, letter H, post).

Per CURIAM: the word " required " in reg. 20 does not involve an order to the employee to pass over the route in question (see p. 210, letter G, p. 211, letter I, to p. 212, letter A, and p. 212, letter F, post).

G

Dictum of LEWIS, J., in *Henaghan* v. *Rederiet Forangirene* ([1936] 2 All E.R. at p. 1433) applied.

Appeal allowed.

H

[As to railway lines above ground at a mine, see 26 HALSBURY'S LAWS (3rd Edn.) 658, para. 1270.

For a summary of the Coal and Other Mines (Sidings) Order, 1956, see 14 HALSBURY'S STATUTORY INSTRUMENTS (1st Re-issue) 89.]

Cases referred to:
Henaghan v. *Rederiet Forangirene*, [1936] 2 All E.R. 1426; 24 Digest (Repl.) 1029, *50*.

I

Wenborn v. *Harland and Wolff, Ltd.*, [1952] 1 Lloyd's Rep. 255.

Appeal.
This was an appeal by the National Coal Board, the defendants, against the

---

* Regulation 20 is printed at p. 210, letter B, post. The regulations are set out in the schedule to the Coal and Other Mines (Sidings) Order, 1956, S.I. 1956 No. 1773.
† The relevant terms of reg. 9 are set out in footnote (1), p. 210, post.

Reversed. H.L. [1967] 2 All E.R. 593.

A   decision of BAKER, J., dated July 12, 1965, at Leeds Assizes awarding the
plaintiff, Kathleen Westwood, widow and administratrix of Frank Westwood,
deceased, damages under the Fatal Accidents Acts, 1846 to 1959, and the Law
Reform (Miscellaneous Provisions) Act, 1934, for personal injuries resulting in
the death of the deceased.   The trial judge found that the defendants were
negligent at common law and were in breach of their statutory duty under the
B   Coal and Other Mines (Sidings) Regulations, 1956, reg. 20. He rejected an allegation of contributory negligence on the part of the deceased and awarded damages
of £5,000 (an agreed amount) in favour of the plaintiff.

The deceased was killed on Apr. 14, 1964, by a colliery train consisting of
three ten-ton wagons and a diesel locomotive weighing forty tons at a surface
siding at Whitwood Colliery, Normanton, Yorkshire. The deceased was employed
C   by the defendants and at the time of the accident was thirty-seven years of age.
He was an experienced shunter. The accident happened at the right rail (looking
east) of track no. 5, which was an outside line.   Track no. 5 was seldom used.
To the south of track no. 5 a dirt-stack, containing shale and other substances,
had been built up.   Some time before the date of the accident samples of shale
had been taken from this dirt-stack. Access for this purpose had been had with
D   a bulldozer to enable estimation to be made whether the shale was fit for use as
ballast. The result of this was that a sort of path about five feet wide at a height
of two feet above the level of the rails had been made; this had a slope of above
forty-five degrees down to the rails. The path on the bank produced in this way
was very uneven and covered with loose stones. The foot of the bank was about
eight feet from the line at the westerly end and veered towards the rail to a
E   distance of about two feet at the easterly end.   At that end some old wood,
about eighteen feet in length, possibly two sleepers end-on, lay between the
bottom of the bank and the rail. They lay adjacent to the rail.

The deceased had come across from track no. 1 to track no. 5 and met the
train. It had probably been his duty to inspect some points in order to see that
they were correctly set.   He met the train near the points.   It had recently
F   reversed. It consisted of three wagons with a diesel locomotive behind them. The
train was moving east on track no. 5. When the train arrived at track no. 5, it
was travelling at seven or eight m.p.h., which was twice the deceased's walking
pace. The driver saw the deceased six or seven yards ahead of the leading wagon
walking along a space on the right-hand side of the track.   This was a usual
practice when, as in this instance, the driver was operating the locomotive from
G   the right-hand side of the cab. Through the window of the cab the driver could
see the track ahead, except that he could not see the track near to the leading
wagon.   He soon lost sight of the deceased because a slight curve caused the
wagons to obscure his view, and the train was bound to overtake the deceased
by reason of its speed. When the driver had reached a point a little beyond where
the track straightened after the curve, he looked to see the deceased's position
H   but did not see him ahead;   accordingly he looked back and saw the deceased
lying across the right-hand rail. The driver stopped the train instantly and went
to the deceased.   The place where the deceased was run over was identified.
Evidence of human blood, etc. on the wheels of the locomotive and the wagon
nearest to it (no. 3 wagon) suggested (per DANCKWERTS, L.J.) that the deceased
was not knocked down by the leading wagon but somehow fell between wagons
I   no. 3 and no. 2.

At the trial it was a substantive contention of the defendants that the deceased
had inserted his shunter's pole into the framework under a wagon and was
" pole-riding " on it.   The evidence accepted by the trial judge left the pole
riding explanation unproved and the defendants did not pursue it on appeal.

J. F. S. Cobb, Q.C., and P. J. M. Kennedy for the defendants.
P. Stanley Price, Q.C., and H. G. Bennett for the plaintiff.

                                                      Cur. adv. vult.
Feb. 17. The following judgments were read.

SELLERS, L.J., having referred to the nature of the accident and to the A
fact that no one saw the accident in which the deceased was killed, said that,
though it was possible to hazard ways in which the accident had happened, yet
he did not find the necessary degree of probability to justify a version of what
actually happened. HIS LORDSHIP reviewed the evidence, concluded that he
would not hold liability at common law established, and continued: The main
case of liability was placed on reg. 20 of the Coal and Other Mines (Sidings) B
Regulations, 1956, which is as follows:

> " The manager of every mine shall make and secure the efficient carrying
> out of arrangements whereby, in every case in which any material is placed
> (otherwise than on ground ordinarily used for the stocking of material) at a
> distance less than three feet from the track of rails of a line and any person
> employed at the mine is required in the course of his duty to pass on foot over C
> that material or between it and the line, that material is so placed in such
> manner that—(a) every such person can so pass without being exposed to
> risk of injury by traffic on that line; and (b) if that material extends (whether
> continuously or not) for a distance exceeding sixty feet measured parallel
> with that line, there are provided at intervals not greater than sixty feet
> adequate spaces or recesses in that material."   D

I find this a difficult regulation to interpret and apply. One thing that it does
not do is to require a clear space of three feet from the track of the rails, for it
recognises that this area may be impeded by material. It seems to recognise
that the space of three feet from the line, so impeded, will not be safe, and para.
(b) requires recesses in the material to provide refuge. The impeding material E
has to be placed in such a manner that under para. (a) every person can so pass
(that is on foot over it) without being exposed to risk of injury by traffic on that
line. Perhaps some trains do not have an overlap, but if there is an overlap, as
here, of two feet I do not see how a person can be safe or without risk of injury
in a three feet space whatever be its nature or the manner in which any material
is placed in the space. The regulation may be directed to the safety of persons F
who have some special duty within that confined space which may require them
to pass over it in order to get away from any approaching train or engine. " In
such a manner " seems to refer to the security of the foothold, for example, so
that a person would not be tripped up, rather than to the provision of adequate
space which it recognises not to exist.

I find difficulty in applying the regulation to this case as it only applies where G
any person employed at the mine is required in the course of his duty to pass on
foot over that material or between it and the line. The word in the regulation
is " required ". It does not say " ordered ". I see no reason to substitute any
other word for the one used. The question of fact is, was the deceased required
to travel within three feet of the off side rail? He was not required to do so in
the fulfilment of his duties under reg. 9 or otherwise (1), and I fail to see how any H
man could think that he was required to do so in order to perform the duties
which the deceased had to perform. He would have been but little safer than
if he had walked on the line itself or between the rails.

I think that the defendants are right when they submit that the regulation
cannot be applied in this case.

If I am wrong in my view that it is not possible to find out what happened I
with sufficient certainty to require an investigation into the incidence of liability,
I would hold on the version reached by the judge and by my brethren in this

---

(1) Regulation 9 provides: " In every case in which any person employed at a mine
is or might be exposed to risk of injury by reason of the movement on a line of two
or more other vehicles pushed by a locomotive, the person in charge of those other
vehicles shall—(a) accompany or precede the leading vehicle, watch the line ahead of it,
and give any warning which may be requisite for the purpose of minimising that risk;
or . . .".

A court that the defendants ought not to be held liable either for breach of the statutory duty alleged or at common law.

I would allow the appeal.

B **DANCKWERTS, L.J.**, having stated the nature of the action, the facts (2) and the conclusions reached by the trial judge, continued: It has been said that it is desirable, first of all, to consider how the accident is likely to have occurred. On this part of the case, in my view, the probabilities point strongly to a certain explanation of the accident. It seems to me to be unthinkable that the deceased would have continued walking close to the rails when the space between the rails and the foot of the bank narrowed to less than three feet. He was a very good and experienced shunter and knew very well that the train was

C coming along behind him. It seems obvious to me that when he got near to this point he must have decided to get up on to the bulldozed track two feet above the level of the rails. The probability is of his having fallen between no. 2 and no. 3 wagons, in getting up on to the bulldozed track. He must have slipped, or tripped (possibly on a loose stone) either on the sloping bank or on the edge of the track and fallen head-foremost between the passing wagons. The slope seems

D to have been about forty-five degrees, and the surfaces of the slope and the track of the bulldozer were very uneven and covered with stones and tufts of grass, as the photographs show. This is, in my view, a most compelling explanation of what occurred. The suggestion of pole-riding (3) seems to me to be most improbable.

I now turn to reg. 20 of the Coal and Other Mines (Sidings) Regulations, 1956.

E It is curiously worded and perhaps even ineptly expressed, though I think that the object of it is clear. [HIS LORDSHIP read the regulation, which is printed at p. 210, letter B, ante, and continued:] The object of the regulation is, of course, to prevent men being knocked down by passing trains. Paragraph (*b*) does not apply in the present case because the relevant portion of the site was much less than sixty feet. Where the material is on ground ordinarily used for the stocking of materials, presumably persons are not supposed to pass beside the rails at all.

F The regulation does not prohibit the placing of materials at a distance less than three feet from the track of rails of a line. It merely requires that where that occurs something is to be done. That is specified in para. (*a*):

"... that material is so placed in such manner that (*a*) every such person can so pass [that is, on foot over that material or between it and the line]

G without being exposed to risk of injury by traffic on that line."

The absurdity of the regulation is that owing to the normal overhang of vehicles, a person cannot pass between the material and the line, if the material encroaches to less than three feet from the line, and if he passes over the material that is less than three feet from the line he will be in danger of being hit by traffic on the line. The only way to construe the regulation so as to make sense of it is to treat

H it as requiring that a space sufficient to give safety shall be provided, not necessarily over the part of the material which is within the distance of three feet from the rails, but over such part of the material as will enable passage over it to be made clear of any danger from passing traffic. This might be done by flattening so much of the material as necessary to provide a safe passage on foot, or by providing a form of bridge over an appropriate part of the material at a safe

I distance from the rails.

The regulation only applies if " any person employed at the mine is required in the course of his duty to pass on foot over that material or between it and the line ". It is reasonably clear that " required " does not necessarily involve an

---

(2) DANCKWERTS, L.J., in summarising the facts stated that the deceased was accompanying the train " as required by reg. 9 ". The relevant terms of reg. 9 are set out in footnote (1), p. 210, ante.

(3) See p. 209, letter I, ante.

order to the employee to pass by that route: see *Henaghan* v. *Rederiet Forangirene,* A per LEWIS, J. (4), a case where the words " may be required to proceed ", used in the Docks Regulations, 1934, were considered.

It was argued on behalf of the defendants that there were other perfectly safe routes which the deceased could have selected, in particular the route over the bulldozed track starting from the points; but I do not think that the phrase means that the employee was under an absolute necessity to go by the route in B question. In my opinion the condition is satisfied if the route selected was incidental to the duty of the employee, in that it was an ordinary and normal way of going to a place where his duty required him to go.

In the present case the duty of the deceased as shunter was to proceed in charge of the train to the point beside the reservoir along the track where the wagons were to be uncoupled. It was shown in evidence that the usual practice C was to proceed on the right of the lines when the driver was using the right-hand controls in the locomotive. In order to keep up with the train so far as he could, it would be natural for the shunter to take the shortest and most direct route, and so it was to be expected that the deceased would go along the space between the rails and the dirt-stack until the narrowing of this space compelled him to mount the bank of the material.   D

Accordingly, in my opinion, the defendants were in breach of the absolute obligation imposed by the regulation, and are liable on this ground. [HIS LORD-SHIP turned to the allegation of common law negligence and, having stated that he agreed with the trial judge's conclusion, continued:] Accordingly, I would dismiss the appeal.

SALMON, L.J.: Was the deceased, the plaintiff's husband, " required in E the course of his duty " to pass over the material which for a distance of only four or five yards lay within three feet of the line or to pass between that material and the line itself? That, in my view, is the crucial question on this appeal. In order to solve this problem, it is necessary first to consider the meaning of the words " required in the course of his duty " as used in reg. 20 of the Coal and Other Mines (Sidings) Regulations, 1956. The meaning given by the courts to the F word " required " in other regulations is by no means conclusive of its meaning in reg. 20; but some help can be found in the authorities. In *Henaghan* v. *Rederiet Forangirene* (5) LEWIS, J., held that the words " required to proceed " in the Docks Regulations, 1934, did not necessarily mean ordered to proceed. I agree with that view and would apply it to reg. 20. In *Wenborn* v. *Harland and Wolff, Ltd.* (6), my brother SELLERS, at first instance, whilst agreeing with the G decision of LEWIS, J., held that a place to which persons were " required to pro-ceed " within the meaning of those words in the Shipbuilding Regulations, 1931, (7), meant a place to which it was necessary for persons to proceed. Whether this construction of the word " required " is to be applied to the present case must, in my view, depend on the meaning given to the word " necessary ". I would not agree that this regulation applies only if there was no way in which the H deceased could have carried out his duty other than by passing over the material or between it and the line. I consider that this would be to give the regulation too narrow a construction. On the other hand the obligation imposed by the regulation would not arise merely because the deceased in the course of his employment passed over the material or between it and the line. One of the dictionary meanings of the word " required " is " called for ". In my view a I person is " required in the course of his duty " if in the course of his duty which he is at the time performing, he reasonably considers that his employers would call for, that is require, him to pass over the material or between it and the line.

What was the duty which the deceased was performing at the time of his death? [HIS LORDSHIP considered the evidence and continued:] There is no direct

(4) [1936] 2 All E.R. 1426 at pp. 1432, 1433.   (5) [1936] 2 All E.R. 1426.
(6) [1952] 1 Lloyd's Rep. 255.   (7) S.R. & O. 1931 No. 133.

A evidence how the accident happened for no one saw it happen, but in my view the established facts show that it is highly likely that the accident occurred in the way described by DANCKWERTS, L.J. (8). I am however unable to accept the conclusion that at the time the deceased was carrying out the duties of a shunter as laid down (9) in reg. 9. Indeed the facts seem to me consistent only with the view that the deceased was merely making his way on foot from the point where

B he had coupled the wagons to the locomotive to the point by the reservoir where he expected to uncouple the wagons from the locomotive. On the way he had probably made a detour and checked the points between no. 4 and no. 5 tracks. Regulation 9 requires a person to accompany or precede the leading vehicle, watch the line and give warning only when any person employed at the mine is or might be exposed to risk of injury by the movement on the line of two or more

C vehicles pushed by a locomotive. The evidence shows that no. 4 and no. 5 tracks were seldom used and were not being used by anyone other than the driver and the deceased on the day of the accident and that at any rate on the reservoir side of the points there was unlikely to be anyone employed in the mine.

In these circumstances, I can see no reason why the deceased should have been carrying out any duties under reg. 9, and indeed the evidence in my view shows

D that he was not doing so. Had he intended to carry out these duties on the way to the reservoir, he would, I think, obviously have looked out for the locomotive and wagons which he must have known were approaching. He would have signalled the driver to slow down to walking pace and then preceded the leading wagon looking out for dangers (which he must have known were unlikely to exist) so that he might give warning to the driver or to the persons endangered. The

E evidence shows that he did nothing of the kind. The fact that he was walking along with his back to the wagons approaching him at about twice his own pace seems to me to show quite clearly that he considered that his only duty at the time was to get to the reservoir and then uncouple the wagons with which he was not concerned until they arrived at their destination. If he was merely walking to the reservoir, as I think that he was, how could he, had he considered

F the question, reasonably have concluded that his employers called for or required him to walk over the material lying within three feet of the line or pass between it and the line? Clearly it seems to me, had he reasonably considered the question, he would have concluded that as far as his employers were concerned he might just as well walk along the track on the top of the bank or along no. 4 track or between it and no. 5 track. No doubt the track on the top of the bank was fairly

G rough but there is nothing to suggest that it was not reasonably passable. To walk over the material within three feet of no. 5 track was hardly any less dangerous than to walk along the track itself. Neither operation could be safely performed without satisfying oneself that nothing was approaching along the track. Both could be carried out safely if nothing was in fact approaching. Accordingly I am driven to the conclusion that the deceased was not " required

H in the course of his duty " to pass over any material within three feet of the line or to pass between any such material and the line itself.

It follows that reg. 20 has no application to this case. In my view the plaintiff would have been no better off if the deceased had been performing the duties of a shunter under reg. 9 at the time of his accident. His duty would have been to look out for any dangers that lay ahead of the train and to take appropriate

I action to avoid them. The train would have been following him and keeping behind him on his direction. The material which had fallen to within three feet of the line for a distance of only four or five yards would have been clearly visible certainly when he was twenty-five yards away. He could not reasonably have supposed that his employers required him to keep straight on, and walk over the loose material—with the obvious risk of falling in front of the train. The tracks and the terrain on the reservoir side of the material were clearly visible.

---

(8) See p. 211, letters B and C, ante.
(9) For the relevant terms of reg. 9, see footnote (1), p. 210, ante.

There were many courses that he could have taken which obviously from the A
point of view of his employers would have discharged his duty to them as well
as, if not better than, walking over the material. He could have walked up the
gentle slope parallel with his course on to the track above the bank and continued
along that track and down the slope on the reservoir side, so that he by-passed
the material lying within three feet of the line. He would thus have had the
driver and the track in view and he would have been in view of the driver all the B
time: alternatively, he could have stopped the train, crossed in front of it and
then called it on and preceded it on no. 4 track or in the space between no. 4
and no. 5 tracks until the obstruction on the right of no. 5 track was passed:
alternatively, before arriving at the obstruction he could have satisfied himself
that no possible danger lay ahead between the train and the reservoir, and then
stood aside and waved the train past him. I do not understand how he could C
reasonably have thought that his employers required him to walk over the
material or pass between it and the line with the train following just behind him.

Having regard to the conclusion at which I have arrived on this part of the
case, it is unnecessary for me to express any concluded view on the obligation
cast by reg. 20 of the Coal and Other Mines (Sidings) Regulations, 1956, on the
mine manager. Out of respect, however, for the arguments addressed to us on D
this topic I will briefly deal with it. The regulation is most obscurely drafted. It
plainly does not prohibit material being placed less than three feet from the
line. It provides only that where material is so placed and any person is required
in the course of his duty to pass on foot over that material or between it and the
line, the manager shall make and secure the efficient carrying out of arrangements
whereby that material   E

   " is so placed in such a manner that—(a) every person can so pass without
   being exposed to risk of injury . . . and (b) if that material extends . . . for
   a distance exceeding sixty feet measured parallel with that line, there are
   provided at intervals not greater than sixty feet adequate spaces or recesses
   in that material."
                                                                              F
The wagons in question overhung the line by one foot, four inches and the locomotive by two feet. There is nothing to suggest that this overhang was in any
way exceptional. In these circumstances I cannot believe that the regulations
contemplated that it could be safe for any man to walk within three feet of the
line at the moment when a train was passing. It seems to me that it may have
been contemplated that a space of three feet was reasonably safe in which to take G
refuge sideways whilst a train was passing. This view gains some support from
the reference to " adequate spaces or recesses " in reg. 20 (b). It could, I think,
have been contemplated that the recesses should be more than three feet deep
since there is nothing in the regulations to prevent the ground up to a point
three feet from the line being filled with materials placed there in any manner.
If this be right, it seems to follow that the obligation on the manager of the mine H
is to see to it that material placed less than three feet from the line is so placed
that persons required to pass over it or between it and the line can take refuge
as safely as if there were an uninterrupted walkway for three feet from the line.
The regulation to my mind contemplates that the persons to whom it refers
shall have an opportunity of taking safe refuge when a train is approaching.
Regulation 10, reg. 11 and reg. 12 deal with the warning to be given by approach- I
ing trains. It is difficult enough to see how a space of three feet could provide safe
refuge for any but the slimmest employees in the mine. It is impossible to see how
any man could walk safely within three feet of the line whilst a train was passing
which overhung the line by not less than one foot, four inches. It seems unlikely
that reg. 20 was attempting to achieve what is manifestly impossible. For these
reasons I incline to the view that the obligation imposed on the mine manager is
such as I have just stated. Since, however, the deceased in my judgment was not
required to pass over the material or between it and the line, and reg. 20 does not

A bite, the question whether or not the mine manager complied with his obligations under the regulation does not arise. [HIS LORDSHIP then considered the allegation of common law negligence, held that it failed, and concluded:] For these reasons I am reluctantly but inexorably driven to the conclusion that this appeal must be allowed.

Appeal allowed. Leave to appeal to the House of Lords granted.

B Solicitors: *D. H. Haslam*, agent for *C. M. H. Glover*, Doncaster (for the defendants); *Corbin, Greener & Cook*, agents for *Raley & Pratt*, Barnsley (for the plaintiff).

[*Reported by* HENRY SUMMERFIELD, ESQ., *Barrister-at-Law.*]

C ————————

R. v. CHURCHILL AND OTHERS (No. 2).

[COURT OF CRIMINAL APPEAL (Hinchcliffe, Thompson and John Stephenson, JJ.), March 15, 16, 17, 18, 21, 1966.]

D *Criminal Law—Conspiracy—Conspiracy to commit absolute statutory offence— Whether mens rea an element of conspiracy—Customs and Excise Act, 1952 (15 & 16 Geo. 6 & 1 Eliz. 2 c. 44), s. 200 (2).*

Criminal Law—Sentence—Fine—Amount of fine should be within offender's capacity to pay.

E A person can be guilty of criminal conspiracy to commit a statutory offence, which is an absolute offence, although he has no knowledge either of the existence of the statutory offence or of any material fact which constituted the offence (see p. 220, letter A, post).

R. v. Sorsky ([1944] 2 All E.R. 333), *R. v. Jacobs* ([1944] 1 All E.R. 485) and *R. v. Clayton* ((1943), 33 Cr. App. Rep. 113) considered.

F The appellant had been convicted of conspiracy to contravene s. 200 (2) of the Customs and Excise Act, 1952, viz., in effect, of agreeing with other defendants to use as fuel for road vehicles heavy oils on which a rebate of duty of 2s. 7d. per gallon had been allowed but in respect of which a sum equivalent to the rebate had not been paid. Such rebated oil ought to have been dyed red and kept for other uses than as fuel for road vehicles. This fuel was rebated but had not been dyed and was re-sold as "Derv" for G use in road vehicles. The verdicts of the jury at the trial showed that they had convicted the appellant on the basis of having acquitted him of dishonest intention but of finding that he had in fact joined in agreeing to the use of the fuel for road vehicles, although he did not know that it had not been fully taxed. He was sentenced to a fine of £2,000, with eight months' imprisonment in default of payment. He was an ill man, a retired postman, H and could not pay a fine of that magnitude. On appeal against conviction and sentence,

Held: (i) mens rea was not a necessary ingredient in the charge of which the appellant had been convicted, viz., of conspiracy to commit an absolute statutory offence, and the conviction should stand (see p. 221, letter B, post).

I *R. v. Sorsky* ([1944] 2 All E.R. 333) applied.

(ii) a fine should be within the offender's capacity to pay, and, in the circumstances of the present case, the appellant's fine would be reduced to £100 (see p. 221, letter D, post).

Appeal against conviction dismissed.

[As to mens rea in common law offences, see 10 HALSBURY'S LAWS (3rd Edn.) 273, para. 507, text and note (*b*), 275, 276, para. 511; and for cases on the subject, see 14 DIGEST (Repl.) 31-33, 33-45.

As to conspiracy, see 10 HALSBURY'S LAWS (3rd Edn.) 310, 311, para. 569; A
and for cases on the subject, see 14 DIGEST (Repl.) 121-125, *851-860, 870*; 128,
891, 892.

For the Customs and Excise Act, 1952, s. 200, see 32 HALSBURY'S STATUTES
(2nd Edn.) 810.]

Cases referred to:

Ackroyds Air Travel, Ltd. v. Director of Public Prosecutions, [1950] 1 All E.R.   B
    933; 114 J.P. 251; 14 Digest (Repl.) 101, *644*.
Gardner v. Akeroyd, [1952] 2 All E.R. 306; [1952] 2 Q.B. 743; 116 J.P. 460;
    25 Digest (Repl.) 159, *674*.
Henshall (John) Quarries, Ltd. v. Harvey, [1965] 1 All E.R. 725; [1965] 2 Q.B.
    233; [1965] 2 W.L.R. 758; 129 J.P. 224.
Johnson v. Youden, [1950] 1 All E.R. 300; [1950] 1 K.B. 544; 114 J.P. 136;   C
    17 Digest (Repl.) 453, *170*.
R. v. Clayton, (1943), 33 Cr. App. Rep. 113; 17 Digest (Repl.) 475, *264*.
R. v. Jacobs, [1944] 1 All E.R. 485; [1944] K.B. 417; 113 L.J.K.B. 433;
    171 L.T. 264; 30 Cr. App. Rep. 1; 17 Digest (Repl.) 472, *248*.
R. v. Lewis, [1965] Crim. L.R. 121.
R. v. Sorsky, [1944] 2 All E.R. 333; 30 Cr. App. Rep. 84; 17 Digest (Repl.)   D
    475, *263*.

Appeal.

This was an appeal by Victor George Churchill, Senior (the father), against
his conviction after trial before THESIGER, J., and a jury on June 3, 1965. The
trial lasted from Apr. 27 to June 3, 1965; it started in the Central Criminal Court,   E
but was later removed to the Royal Courts of Justice, Strand, London. The
appellant was charged with his sons, Victor George Churchill, Junior, John
Henry Churchill and Leslie William Churchill, and with one Alexander James
Lowdell, a driver of a petrol tank lorry, and two companies, Universal Fuel
Oils, Ltd. and Olympic Petroleum Co., Ltd., on two counts. The first count
charged that they between Oct. 1, 1961, and Oct. 9, 1963, conspired together   F
with one Sauter (who fled the country) and other persons unknown to cheat and
defraud the Crown of the rebate duty to be repaid on diesel fuel used in road
vehicles. The second count charged a conspiracy to contravene s. 200 (2) of the
Customs and Excise Act, 1952, giving as particulars that between the same dates
the appellant conspired with the same persons to use in road vehicles, to which
s. 200 applied, heavy oil in respect of which rebate of duty had been allowed   G
but the sum equivalent to the current rebate on such oils had not been paid to
the Commissioners of Customs and Excise. The appellant was acquitted on
count 1. He was convicted on count 2. He appealed against conviction and
sentence. His two sons John and Leslie also appealed. All accused other than
the appellant and Sauter, were convicted on count 1, the jury being discharged
in regard to them from giving a verdict on count 2. Victor George Churchill,   H
Junior, was sentenced to four years' imprisonment and John Henry Churchill
and Leslie William Churchill were sentenced to two and a half years' imprisonment. All the three last-mentioned accused were ordered to pay not more
than £6,000 towards the costs of the prosecution. Lowdell was sentenced to
eighteen months' imprisonment. Universal Fuel Oils, Ltd., was fined £10,000
and was ordered to pay £10,000 costs, and Olympic Petroleum Co., Ltd., was   I
fined £100 and ordered to pay £6,000 costs. Only John Henry Churchill, Leslie
William Churchill and the appellant appealed. The appeal of the appellant,
Victor George Churchill, Senior, is reported on the point of law which he raised
as to the mental element in a charge of criminal conspiracy to commit an absolute
statutory offence.

The circumstances and general nature of the conspiracy and transactions were
as follows. In 1957 Victor George Churchill, Junior, and John Henry Churchill
had set up in business as Churchill Bros., dealing in fuel oils. They made an

A agreement with Petrofina for the purchase and sale of gas oil. The same year
Universal Fuel Oils, Ltd., was incorporated with Victor George Churchill and
John Henry Churchill as directors. The latter was secretary, and Leslie William
Churchill was the door-to-door salesman of paraffin. In 1960 the appellant,
on retirement from the Post Office, where he had worked as a postman, was
taken on as book-keeper. The company had premises at Croydon with storage
B tanks both for gas oil and Derv. The accused, Lowdell, was a driver employed
by a company named Olympic Petroleum Co., Ltd., and was concerned with the
collection and delivery of un-dyed gas oil. In April, 1962, this company,
Olympic Petroleum Co., Ltd.. was formed. Victor George Churchill, Junior, and
John Henry Churchill were directors, and the premises were at Gillingham,
where the depot was managed by Sauter. The company dealt in petrol and gas
C oil.
      Derv was a type of heavy oil which could be used in certain road vehicles.
The same fuel could also be used for stationary plant and installations, when it
was known as gas oil. Derv attracted a duty of 2s. 9d. per gallon. Gas oil
was chemically indistinguishable from Derv, but the duty on it was only 2d. a
gallon. In and after July, 1961, gas oil was distinguished from Derv by the
D addition of a chemical dye which coloured it. If un-dyed gas oil were bought
and sold as Derv, without accounting to the Customs for the amount of the
rebate, the Revenue would lose 2s. 7d. a gallon. Section 200 (2) of the Customs
and Excise Act, 1952, provided that no heavy oils on the delivery of which for
home use rebate had been allowed should be used in vehicles to which s. 200 (2)
applied unless an amount equal to the rebate on like oils had been paid to the
E commissioners. Thus the commissioners should receive 2s. 7d. per gallon on gas
oil used for road vehicles. The oil in this case was obtained from the B.P.
refinery on the Isle of Grain. The wholesaler was a firm called Petrofina. Until
October, 1963, dye was manually added at the refinery by a loader or filler,
either of whom, or, perhaps the tank driver, might be able to be persuaded or
bribed not to put the dye into oil invoiced as gas oil. In this manner both
F Universal Fuel Oils, Ltd. and Olympic Petroleum Co., Ltd. obtained thousands
of gallons of un-dyed gas oil and sold it as Derv. During the period between
January, 1962, and October, 1963, the sales of Derv by these two companies
exceeded their recorded purchases by nearly three hundred thousand gallons.
On Aug. 14, 1963, customs officers stopped a tanker containing un-dyed gas oil,
and enquiries led to these two companies and the Churchill family.
G   On the tenth day of the trial, after evidence had been given by a Petrofina
driver, Victor George Churchill, Junior, changed his plea to one of guilty.
Thereafter the question in regard to John Henry Churchill, Leslie William
Chuchill and the appellant was whether they were parties to the conspiracy.
All three, Victor George Churchill, Senior (the appellant) and his two sons,
John and Leslie, gave evidence, each seeking to depreciate his position, denying
H the existence of a conspiracy and alleging that each merely did as he was told
and that everything was left to Victor George Churchill, Junior. The material
directions of the trial judge (THESIGER, J.) are at p. 218, letters C to F, post. The
appeals of John and Leslie against conviction on count 1 were dismissed. The
trial judge's ruling at an earlier stage of the trial, reported [1965] 2 All E.R. 793,
was considered and approved* in the course of these appeals.

I _____

    * In regard to the ruling given by the trial judge (THESIGER, J.), and reported [1965]
2 All E.R. 793, HINCHCLIFFE, J., in delivering the judgment of the court said this:
" [Count 1] was defective, it is said, because the [trial judge] ought to have ordered
particulars of overt acts. It is said by counsel [for the appellants John and Leslie]
that the subject has a right to know with what offence he is charged; what is the case
that he has to meet, what criminal agreement he has made; what section of the Act
has been broken and what regulation of which statutory instrument has been contravened. So he has. Whether particulars of the overt acts are ordered depends on the
wording of the count and the particular circumstances of the case. Here there was

(*Continued at foot of page 218.*)

The authorities and cases noted below* were cited in argument in addition to **A** those referred to in the judgment.

Leonard Lewis for the appellant, Victor George Churchill, Senior.
J. B. R. Hazan and *A. S. Troup* for the Crown.

HINCHCLIFFE, J., delivered the following judgment of the court in which after stating the nature of the appeals, stating the facts summarised **B** above and dismissing the appeals of John Henry Churchill and Leslie William Churchill, HIS LORDSHIP continued: I now turn to deal with the appeal of Victor George Churchill, Senior, against his conviction on count 2. The offence of which he was convicted was stated in the indictment to be " Conspiracy to contravene s. 200 (2) of the Customs and Excise Act, 1952 ". The particulars of the offence have already been stated. The appellant was acquitted on count 1 **C** and he now appeals against his conviction on count 2 on the ground that the judge's discretion was erroneous in point of law. This is really the only ground argued by counsel on behalf of the appellant. The trial judge directed as follows:

" Secondly, it would be unlawful, and I so direct you, to take part in an arrangement to use unmarked gas oil in road vehicles, when it had not, in fact, borne the fuel tax and was not going to do so. That is the second **D** charge."

Then later the trial judge said:

" The second charge, the less serious charge, accuses the defendants of agreeing together and, again, with Sauter and others unknown, to do an unlawful act, and that act was to use in road vehicles fuel which, in fact, **E** had been allowed the rebate of 2s. 7d. and therefore ought not to have been used in road vehicles, but should have been marked with dye and kept for other uses. The second charge simply involves an agreement to use such fuel in road vehicles as Derv when it had not, in fact, borne the fuel tax. It does not involve any proof of dishonest intent or of knowledge that such use would cheat the revenue out of 2s. 7d. a gallon." **F**

It is plain that in returning a verdict of not guilty on the first charge and convicting on the second charge, the jury were acquitting the appellant of any dishonest intention or knowledge and were convicting him merely as joining in an agreement to do an unlawful act; that is to say, to have fuel used in road vehicles which had not in fact (albeit not to his knowledge) been fully taxed as Derv. This is a sufficient answer to the contention of the Crown in this court **G** that in truth the appellant did know all the material facts and we deal with the appeal on this basis.

We have considered the various grounds of appeal put forward by counsel for the appellant, but the only really substantial ground is his main submission, namely that a charge of criminal conspiracy cannot be sustained without proof

H

(Continued from foot of page 217.)

no problem. One conspiracy was charged and there was in reality only one conspiracy. It had as its object the defrauding of the Revenue. In order to carry out the conspiracy, oil had to be extracted without the dye and distributed, sold and used. This was a very clear case. It cannot seriously be contended that the defence were in any way taken by surprise or that any unfair addition was sprung on them by the Crown; and indeed after the first few days the Crown did prepare and deliver points of evidence. In our **I** judgment there was abundant evidence which the jury must have accepted that this was a family conspiracy; that each member played a different but essential part. Victor organised the obtaining; John and Leslie organised the receipt and the sale and [Victor George Churchill, Senior] did the book-keeping. The trial judge gave a ruling on this matter, which is reported [1965] 2 All E.R. 793, and that ruling, in the opinion of this court, is correct having regard to the circumstances of the case."

* WRIGHT ON THE LAW OF CRIMINAL CONSPIRACIES AND AGREEMENTS (1873), pp. 70-71; ARCHBOLD'S CRIMINAL PLEADING, EVIDENCE AND PRACTICE (35th Edn.), paras. 49, 4051, 4075; *Reynolds* v. *G. H, Austin & Sons, Ltd.*, [1951] 1 All E.R. 606; [1951] 2 K.B. 135.

A of mens rea and that a person cannot agree to commit an absolute offence unless
he knows all the facts material to the commission of that offence. Here it is
urged that the appellant could only be guilty of a conspiracy to contravene
s. 200 (2) if he was found to have known all the material facts, including the fact
that fuel oil which he had agreed should be used in road vehicles was rebated
fuel oil which had not borne tax. If this submission is right then the judge's
B direction was wrong in law and the appellant's conviction on count 2 should be
quashed. It is not suggested by the Crown that the court ought to use the
proviso. Counsel further submits that there is no authority decisive on the
point, and that the three conspiracy cases, *R.* v. *Clayton* (1), *R.* v. *Jacobs* (2)
and *R.* v. *Sorsky* (3) are not binding authorities which compel or justify the
direction of which he complains; and he submits that there are authorities which
C deal with the position of those charged with aiding and abetting the commission
of an absolute statutory offence and he quotes *Johnson* v. *Youden* (4), and with
attempting to commit such an offence or doing an act preparatory to the commission of an offence, and he quotes *Gardner* v. *Akeroyd* (5), which he says point
strongly to the law being what he submits it to be. In these cases the court held
that knowledge of material facts is essential. Counsel for the appellant contends
D that since the crime of conspiracy is an extension of the law relating to attempts,
knowledge of material facts is just as essential in conspiracy cases as in offences
of aiding and abetting and attempting to commit an offence. This is an attractive argument which at first sight would seem to be right.

It is plain that in its inception conspiracy involved a criminal intent. The
court's attention has been drawn to WRIGHT on the LAW OF CRIMINAL CON-
E SPIRACIES AND AGREEMENTS (1873) at p. 6 where he deals with the period 1600-
1800. Until absolute offences were created by statute no difficulty seems to
have arisen. The intention was to violate the law and to do so a conspirator
necessarily had to know what the law was that he was agreeing to break. It is
interesting to note that according to WILLIAMS' CRIMINAL LAW, THE GENERAL
PART (2nd Edn.), pp. 246, 288, it has been held in the United States of America
F that conspiracy is an exception to the rule that ignorance of the law is no excuse,
and that on a charge of conspiracy to do an act that is malum prohibitum the
prosecution must prove on the part of the person agreeing (i) knowledge of the
statutory prohibition and (ii) an intention to do an act in contravention of it.
In this country the law has not developed in this way. It may be for consideration whether that is not the way in which the law should be declared so far as
G conspiracy to commit an absolute statutory offence is concerned, or it may be
that conspiracy should be confined to agreements to commit an intentional
violation of the law.

Counsel for the Crown submits that the judge's direction was right, that the
offence of conspiracy is complete when the agreement to commit an unlawful
act is made, and he further submits that knowledge of the illegality of the object
H of the agreement is unnecessary since ignorance of the law is no excuse. The
Crown relies on the three conspiracy cases which I have mentioned, *R.* v. *Clayton*
(1), *R.* v. *Jacobs* (2) and *R.* v. *Sorsky* (3). Each one of these cases was decided
during the last war, each was concerned with war-time regulations, each of the
regulations created an absolute statutory offence. Counsel for the appellant
seeks to distinguish these cases from the present one on the ground that they
I were concerned only to decide that ignorance of the law or mistake of the law is
no defence to a charge of conspiracy to commit an absolute offence. On the
other hand, counsel for the Crown contends that the judgments go beyond this
and that in plain words the judgments lay down that on a charge of conspiracy
to commit an absolute statutory offence, neither mens rea nor knowledge of
illegality is required. While we think there is great force in counsel for the

(1) (1943), 33 Cr. App. Rep. 113.   (2) [1944] 1 All E.R. 485; [1944] K.B. 417.
(3) [1944] 2 All E.R. 333.   (4) [1950] 1 All E.R. 300; [1950] 1 K.B. 544,
        (5) [1952] 2 All E.R. 306; [1952] 2 Q.B. 743.

appellant's submission, we regret that our understanding of the judgments in A
these cases, and in particular the case of *R.* v. *Sorsky* (6) compels us to reject it
and to uphold the contention of the Crown.   The decisions in *R.* v. *Clayton* (7),
R. v. *Jacobs* (8) and *R.* v. *Sorsky* (6) clearly establish that a person can conspire
to commit a statutory offence which is absolutely prohibited without having
any knowledge of the existence of the statutory prohibition and therefore any
intent to break the law or commit a crime.   We think further that *R.* v. *Sorsky* B
(6) decided what *R.* v. *Clayton* (7) had indicated, that is to say that he could
also be found guilty of conspiring to commit such an absolute offence without
knowing a material fact which constituted the offence so that his mind was
equally innocent of any criminal intent.

In giving the judgment of the court, which consisted of VISCOUNT CALDECOTE,
C.J., who had been a party to the decision in *R.* v. *Clayton* (9) and HUMPHREYS, C
J., who had given the judgment in *Jacob's* case (8), and OLIVER, J., who had
also been a party to the decision in *Clayton's* case (7), HUMPHREYS, J., said (10):

> " Passing next to counts 3 and 4, upon which all three appellants were
> convicted, counsel for Sorsky was bold enough to contend that the person
> supplying in these circumstances could not be convicted of an offence
> against the order unless there was proof of a mens rea on his part and that a D
> charge of conspiracy to supply contrary to the order therefore involved
> knowledge by the accused that the amount of the quota of the supplier had
> been or would be exceeded. The all sufficient answer to that argument is to
> be found in the wording of the orders in question, which makes it abundantly
> plain that the supply of controlled goods contrary to the order is an offence
> irrespective of any knowledge or state of mind of the supplier. If authority E
> is required in support of that proposition it will be found in the judgment of
> this court in *R.* v. *Clayton* (7).   That case is also an authority for the proposi-
> tion that conspiracy to contravene the terms of these orders does not require
> proof of that knowledge on the part of the accused indicated by the
> expression mens rea. To the same effect is *R.* v. *Jacobs* (8), in which case it
> was contended for the appellants (who had been convicted of conspiring to F
> contravene the provisions of the Price of Goods Act, 1939, by selling price
> controlled goods at a price in excess of the permitted price) that the conviction
> was wrong in that there was no evidence that the vendors were aware that
> the permitted price had been exceeded.   That argument was rejected by
> this court, it being pointed out in the judgment that a criminal conspiracy
> consists in the agreement to do an unlawful act without reference to the G
> knowledge on the part of the accused of its illegality."

This court was very clearly deciding that Sorsky's ignorance of a material fact,
namely that the supplies he agreed to exceeded Bresler's quota, was completely
irrelevant to the charge of conspiracy to contravene the order in question. We
think that the court only went on to consider what was the state of Sorsky's H
mind on his own evidence in order to show that his conviction could not be
regarded as unjust even if it were wrong to apply, as the court had, the doctrine
of absolute liability to the offence of conspiracy to commit an absolute statutory
offence.   We can find no material difference between Sorsky's ignorance that
Bresler had exceeded his quota and the appellant's ignorance that the oil used
had evaded the tax. We consider that some of the language used in the judgment I
in *R.* v. *Sorsky* (6) may be unsatisfactory and might well have been different if
the distinction later drawn in *Johnson* v. *Youden* (11) had been brought to the

---

(6) [1944] 2 All E.R. 333.   (7) (1943), 33 Cr. App. Rep. 113.
(8) [1944] 1 All E.R. 485; [1944] K.B. 417.
(9) (1943), 33 Cr. App. Rep. 113, where in the case of *R.* v. *Percy Dalton (London),
Ltd. and Others* the material portion of the judgment in *Clayton* (Feb. 22, 1943, C.C.A.
VISCOUNT CALDECOTE, C.J., ASQUITH and OLIVER, JJ.) is set out at pp. 113-120.
(10) [1944] 2 All E.R. at p. 336.
(11) [1950] 1 All E.R. 300; [1950] 1 K.B. 544.

A attention of the court. Indeed if the law as to those who aided and abetted the commission of acts absolutely prohibited by statutory provisions had in 1944 been clarified as it was in *Johnson's* case (12) and the lengthening line of cases where it has since been restated from *Ackroyds Air Travel, Ltd.* v. *Director of Public Prosecutions* (13) to *John Henshell Quarries, Ltd.* v. *Harvey* (14), we might not be bound by authority to leave those accused of conspiring to commit such
B offences in a worse defensive position than those accused of aiding and abetting their commission. We are, however, bound to hold that mens rea is not a necessary ingredient in a charge of such a conspiracy to commit an absolute offence as that of which the jury convicted the appellant. All the prosecution had to prove on the authorities was that the appellant agreed to do an act which in fact contravened s. 200 (2) of the Act of 1952 regardless of whether he intended to
C contravene it or knew from his acquaintance with the law or the facts that the act to which he agreed would contravene it. We, therefore, are of opinion that the learned judge's direction is right and we dismiss the appeal against conviction.

[HIS LORDSHIP then considered the appeal against sentence and continued:] The appellant was sentenced to a fine of £2,000 with eight months' imprisonment in default. He was acquitted of the more serious charge and he was recommended
D to mercy by the jury. When he gave his evidence he was extremely frank, indeed his evidence almost amounted to a plea of guilty. These matters were known to the judge but it now seems plain that the appellant is an ill man and that he cannot pay a fine of £2,000 and that his sons are unable or unwilling to help him. This court has said in the case of *R.* v. *Lewis* (15), which was decided not very long ago, that a fine, as opposed to costs, should be within an offender's
E capacity. £2,000 is far beyond the capacity of the appellant to pay and we think justice will be met by altering the fine to one of £100. He will be given a week in which to pay and eight months' imprisonment in default.

Appeal dismissed. Sentence varied.

The court certified, under s. 1 of the Administration of Justice Act, 1960, that the
F *following point of law of general public importance arose in this case and was fit for consideration by the House of Lords, viz., " Whether mens rea is an essential ingredient in conspiracy to commit the absolute offence charged in count 2 of the indictment, and if so, what knowledge of the facts and/or law on the part of the defendant must be established to prove the charge ". The court granted leave to appeal and legal aid.*

G Solicitors: *Goodman, Monroe & Co.* (for the appellant); *Solicitor for the Commissioners for Customs and Excise.*

[*Reported by* N. P. METCALFE, ESQ., *Barrister-at-Law.*]

H

I

(12) [1950] 1 All E.R. 300; [1950] 1 K.B. 544. (13) [1950] 1 All E.R. 933.
(14) [1965] 1 All E.R. 725; [1965] 2 Q.B. 233. (15) [1965] Crim. L.R. 121.

BARTON, THOMPSON & CO., LTD. v. STAPLING MACHINES CO.

[CHANCERY DIVISION (Pennycuick, J.), February 11, 17, 1966.]

Equity—Forfeiture—Relief—Hiring of chattels—Machines leased to plaintiff —Plaintiff defaulted in paying rent—Defendant gave notice to determine agreement—Plaintiff issued originating summons claiming to be relieved from forfeiture of its interest in machines—Motion by defendant to strike out summons—Affidavit on behalf of plaintiff showing plaintiff not ready to discharge arrears of rent—Summons struck out—R.S.C., Ord. 18, r. 19.

The plaintiff company and the defendant company were parties to a lease agreement whereby the defendant leased to the plaintiff for a term of twenty-five years certain machines for making wirebound boxes. The agreement provided for rental and other payments. In the case of a breach by the plaintiff of any of the terms of the agreement the defendant was entitled to serve thirty days' notice to remedy the breach and in default to terminate the agreement. The plaintiff defaulted in a number of payments due under the agreement. The defendant sent notice of intention to terminate the agreement, and, after the prescribed thirty days had elapsed, sent notice of immediate determination. The arrears remained unpaid. The plaintiff issued a summons claiming to be relieved from forfeiture of its interest in the machines. On a motion by the defendant to strike out the summons on the ground that it disclosed no reasonable cause of action, the affidavit evidence on behalf of the plaintiff did not show that the plaintiff was ready to discharge the arrears, but its tenor was that the plaintiff was not in a position to do so. A petition had been presented by a creditor for compulsory winding-up of the plaintiff company.

Held: it was an invariable condition of relief from forfeiture for non-payment of rent that the arrears, if not already available to the lessor, should be paid within a time specified by the court and it followed that readiness to pay arrears within the time specified by the court was a necessary condition of a tenant's claim for relief; it might not be necessary for a tenant to aver such readiness specifically in his pleading or affidavit, but where, as in the present case, the plaintiff's (i.e., the tenant's) affidavit showed an absence of readiness the claim for relief from forfeiture was defective and would be struck out under R.S.C., Ord. 18, r. 19* (see p. 225, letters F to I, post).

[As to relief from forfeiture for non-payment of rent, see 23 HALSBURY'S LAWS (3rd Edn.) 681, 682, para. 1409; and for cases on the subject, see 31 DIGEST (Repl.) 535-537, 6592-6612.

As to relief against conditions involving forfeiture, see 14 HALSBURY'S LAWS (3rd Edn.) 622, 623, paras. 1151, 1152; and for cases on the subject, see 20 DIGEST (Repl.) 549, 550, 2566-2579.

For the Common Law Procedure Act, 1852, s. 210, s. 212, see 18 HALSBURY'S STATUTES (2nd Edn.) 412, 416.

For the Supreme Court of Judicature (Consolidation) Act, 1925, s. 46, see ibid., p. 483.]

Cases referred to:

Chandless-Chandless v. *Nicholson*, [1942] 2 All E.R. 315; [1942] 2 K.B. 321; 112 L.J.K.B. 19; 167 L.T. 198; 31 Digest (Repl.) 536, 6608.

---

* R.S.C., Ord 18, r. 19, provides: " (1) The court may at any stage of the proceedings order to be struck out or amended any pleading or the indorsement of any writ in the action, or anything in any pleading or in the indorsement, on the ground that—(*a*) it discloses no reasonable cause of action or defence, as the case may be, or (*b*) it is scandalous, frivolous or vexatious, or (*c*) it may prejudice, embarrass or delay the fair trial of the action, or (*d*) it is otherwise an abuse of the process of the court; and may order the action to be stayed or dismissed or judgment to be entered accordingly, as the case may be. (2) No evidence shall be admissible on an application under para. (1) (*a*). (3) This rule shall, so far as applicable, apply to an originating summons and a petition as if the summons or petition, as the case may be, were a pleading."

A   *Dagenham (Thames) Dock Co., Re, Ex p. Hulse*, (1873), 8 Ch. App. 1022; 43
         L.J.Ch. 261; 38 J.P. 180; 20 Digest (Repl.) 544, *2535*.
    Dixon, Re, Heynes v. *Dixon*, [1900] 2 Ch. 561; 69 L.J.Ch. 609; 83 L.T. 129;
         43 Digest 711, *1499*.
    Hubbuck & Sons, Ltd. v. *Wilkinson, Heywood and Clark, Ltd.*, [1895-99] All
         E.R. Rep. 244; [1899] 1 Q.B. 86; 68 L.J.Q.B. 34; 79 L.T. 429; 32
B   Digest (Repl.) 248, *2765*.
    Tankexpress (A/S) v. *Compagnie Financière Belge des Petroles S.A., The Petrofina*,
         [1948] 2 All E.R. 939; [1949] A.C. 76; [1949] L.J.R. 170; 41 Digest
         (Repl.) 221, *482*.

    Motion.
    The plaintiff, Barton, Thompson & Co., Ltd., claimed by originating summons
C   dated Jan. 13, 1966, that it might be relieved from forfeiture of its interest in
    the machines comprised in and demised by a lease agreement dated July 9,
    1962, and made between the defendant, Stapling Machines Co. of the one part
    and the plaintiff of the other part on such terms as to the court should seem
    just and equitable. By a notice of motion dated Jan. 26, 1966, the defendant
    applied for an order under R.S.C., Ord. 18, r. 19, or under the inherent jurisdiction
D   of the court that the originating summons be struck out on the grounds that it
    disclosed no reasonable cause of action, was scandalous, frivolous and vexatious
    and was otherwise an abuse of the process of the court, and for an order that
    the originating summons be dismissed. The facts are set out in the judgment.
    The cases noted below* were cited during the argument in addition to those
    referred to in the judgment.
E
    G. B. H. Dillon, Q.C., and *M. Miller* for the plaintiff.
    Peter Foster, Q.C., and *A. R. Barrowclough* for the defendant.

                                                        Cur. adv. vult.

    Feb. 17.   **PENNYCUICK, J.:** By this motion the defendant, Stapling
    Machines Co. (an American corporation), seeks an order under R.S.C., Ord. 18,
F   r. 19, that an originating summons dated Jan. 13, 1966, issued by the plaintiff,
    Barton, Thompson & Co., Ltd. may be struck out on the grounds (a) that it
    discloses no reasonable cause of action, and (b) that it is scandalous, frivolous
    and vexatious, and (c) that it is otherwise an abuse of the process of the court.
    The plaintiff and the defendant were parties to a lease agreement dated July 9,
    1962, whereby the defendant leased to the plaintiff for a term of twenty-five
G   years certain machines for making wirebound boxes. The agreement provided
    for rental and other payments, particulars of which I need not specify. In the
    case of a breach by the plaintiff of any of the terms of the agreement the defen-
    dant is entitled to serve thirty days' notice to remedy the breach and in default
    to terminate the agreement. The agreement is to be governed by the law of
    England. It is not in dispute that the agreement is a simple contract of hire
H   and not a contract of hire-purchase.
    The plaintiff defaulted on a number of payments due under the agreement.
    On Nov. 29, 1965, the defendant sent notice of intention to terminate the agree-
    ment. On Jan. 13, 1966, the prescribed thirty days having elapsed the defendant
    sent notice of immediate determination. The arrears remain unpaid. On the
    last named date, namely Jan. 13, 1966, the plaintiff issued the summons now
I   sought to be struck out. This summons claims that the plaintiff may be relieved
    from forfeiture of its interest in the machines comprised in the lease agreement
    on such terms as the court shall think just and equitable. On Jan. 26, 1966, the

---

    * *Popham* v. *Bampfeild*, (1682), 1 Vern. 79; *Grimston* v. *Lord Bruce*, (1701), 1 Salk.
    156; *Hill* v. *Barclay*, (1811), 18 Ves. 56; *Re Blanshard, Ex p. Hattersley*, (1878), 8 Ch.D.
    601; *Howard* v. *Fanshawe*, [1895-99] All E.R. Rep. 855; [1895] 2 Ch. 581; *Dyson* v.
    A.-G., [1911] 1 K.B. 410; *Stockloser* v. *Johnson*, [1954] 1 All E.R. 630; [1954] 1 Q.B. 476;
    Gill v. *Lewis*, [1956] 1 All E.R. 844; [1956] 2 Q.B. 1; *Belgravia Insurance Co., Ltd.* v.
    Meak, [1963] 3 All E.R. 828; [1964] 1 Q.B. 436.

defendant gave notice of the present motion. On the same day it issued a writ **A**
in the Queen's Bench Division claiming payment of the arrears of rent and
delivery up of the machines.

In support of the motion, Mr. Neil, a partner in the firm of solicitors acting
for the defendant swore an affidavit exhibiting the lease agreement and proving
the arrears. In answer, Mr. Maislish, a director of the plaintiff, swore an affidavit,
in which he gives certain information concerning the machines and states that **B**
the company had had to meet expenses of not less than £150,000 to bring them
into production. He does not challenge the allegations in Mr. Neil's affidavit
concerning the default in payment and the giving of notices. He does not
allege any unconscionable behaviour on the part of the defendant. Nor does
he state that the plaintiff is ready to discharge the arrears. On the contrary,
the whole tenor of his affidavit is that the plaintiff is not presently so ready. **C**
There was an affidavit in reply, to which I need not refer except to mention that
on Feb. 4, 1966, a petition was presented by a creditor for the compulsory
winding-up of the plaintiff company, based on a judgment debt of £24,636.
This petition has not yet come on for effective hearing.

I must say at the outset that I am by no means persuaded that it is open to a
tenant to claim relief from forfeiture before the lessor has either commenced **D**
proceedings for possession or taken possession. Relief against forfeiture is an
equitable protection against the enforcement by the lessor of his legal rights.
It is appropriate where the lessor has commenced proceedings for possession.
It is also available within certain limits after the lessor has taken possession;
but it does not appear appropriate in advance of proceedings for possession
or actual possession. Advance relief has no place in the statutory provisions **E**
applicable in the case of land (see s. 210 and s. 212 of the Common Law Procedure
Act, 1852, and s. 46 of the Supreme Court of Judicature (Consolidation) Act,
1925). Nor does there appear to be any reference to advance relief in the text
books (see 23 HALSBURY'S LAWS OF ENGLAND (3rd Edn.), p. 681, para. 1409,
for a convenient statement of the law). Counsel for the plaintiff contended
that a tenant may apply for relief at any time after the lessor has done some **F**
act which shows an unequivocal intention to determine the tenancy. He cites
no authority in support of this proposition. However, counsel for the defendant
did not put this procedural objection in the forefront of his argument and I do
not propose to strike out the summons on this ground.

I turn now to the points of substance which were raised by counsel on either
side. Counsel for the defendant contended that the plaintiff's claim for relief **G**
is misconceived on three grounds: (i) relief against forfeiture is not available
under a contract for hire of chattels except where a party seeking forfeiture has
acted unconscionably; (ii) relief from forfeiture is not available where the
parties themselves have prescribed a thirty-day period in which the breach may
be remedied and that period has elapsed; (iii) it is a condition of relief from
forfeiture for payment of rent that the lessee shall be ready to pay off the arrears. **H**
Counsel for the defendant also relied on the presentation of the petition, but
did not strongly press this contention.

Counsel for the plaintiff stressed that a pleading will only be struck out under
R.S.C., Ord. 18, **r.** 19, in a plain and obvious case where it is apparent that even
if the facts are proved the plaintiff is not entitled to the relief that he seeks
(see *Hubbuck & Sons Ltd.* v. *Wilkinson, Heywood and Clark Ltd.*, per SIR **I**
NATHANIEL LINDLEY, M.R. (1)). That is, of course, so, and I bear it well in
mind. Counsel for the plaintiff then addressed himself to the three particular
grounds relied on by counsel for the defendant.

(i) He contended that while relief against forfeiture is normally granted under
a lease of land and by statute only under a lease of land, the basic principle under
which such relief is afforded is applicable to subject matter other than land.

(1) [1895-99] All E.R. Rep. 244 at p. 247; [1899] 1 Q.B. 86 at p. 91.

A He quoted a number of authorities for the nature of the basic principle.   For a convenient summary, see *Re Dixon, Heynes v. Dixon*, per RIGBY, L.J. (2)

B
" The Court of Chancery gave relief against the strictness of the common law in cases of penalty or forfeiture for non-payment of a fixed sum on a day certain, on the principle that the failure to pay principal on a certain day could be compensated sufficiently by payment of principal and interest with costs at a subsequent day."

For a recent statement on the principle, see *Chandless-Chandless* v. *Nicholson*, per LORD GREENE, M.R. (3):

C
" The court, in exercising its jurisdiction to grant relief in cases of non-payment of rent is, of course, proceeding upon the old principles of the Court of Equity.   The Court of Equity always regarded the condition of re-entry as being merely security for payment of the rent, and, provided the landlord could get his rent, relief was given."

Neither counsel was able to cite a case directly in point one way or the other on a lease of chattels.   Counsel for the defendant relied on *A/S Tankexpress* v. *Compagnie Financière Belge des Petroles S.A.*, *The Petrofina* (4), where the House of
D Lords clearly envisaged that if there was indeed a default in punctual payment there could be no question of relief, but a charterparty is a different kind of contract from an ordinary lease and I do not think this decision is conclusive.   I am not prepared to hold that it is plain and obvious as a matter of law that in the absence of unconscionable behaviour the court has in no circumstances power to relieve against forfeiture under any conceivable lease of a chattel.   This is, I think,
E a point which the plaintiff should be allowed to argue if his case is otherwise maintainable.

(ii) Nor do I think that the presence of the thirty-day period in the lease agreement is conclusive so as to make it clear beyond argument that relief from forfeiture is not available.

(iii) On the third point the plaintiff is in grave difficulty.   It is an invariable
F condition of relief from forfeiture for non-payment of rent that the arrears, if not already available to the lessor, shall be paid within a time specified by the court.   The precise length of time is a matter of discretion and the time may be extended on subsequent application, but the imposition of the condition is not a matter of discretion; it is a requirement of law rooted in the principle on which relief is granted.   It follows that readiness to pay arrears within such time as the
G court shall think fit is a necessary condition of the tenant's claim for relief.   It may not be necessary for the tenant to aver such readiness specifically in his pleading or affidavit (see ANNUAL PRACTICE, 1966, pp. 372-373, note on R.S.C., Ord. 18, r. 7).   Where the pleading or affidavit, however, so far from averring readiness, shows an absence of readiness, the claim is on its face defective by reason of non-fulfilment of a necessary condition.   It must follow that the lessor
H is entitled to have the claim struck out under one or other sub-paragraph of R.S.C., Ord. 18, r. 19 (1).   It is immaterial for this purpose whether the proceeding is commenced by writ or originating summons (see R.S.C., Ord. 18, r. 19, para. (3)).

In the present case Mr. Maislish, in his affidavit, makes no pretence that the plaintiff is ready to pay the arrears either presently or within any ascertainable
I time.   On the contrary, the whole tenor of his affidavit is that the plaintiff is not in a position to do so.   Nor does counsel for the plaintiff suggest that the plaintiff is in any better position today.   It follows, in my judgment, that the originating summons, read in the light of Mr. Maislish's affidavit, shows no ground for the relief claimed.   I think, further, that it is an abuse of the process of the court.

Counsel for the plaintiff seeks to escape from the difficulty by saying that

(2) [1900] 2 Ch.D. 561 at p. 576.
(3) [1942] 2 All E.R. 315 at p. 317; [1942] 2 K.B. 321 at p. 323.
(4) [1948] 2 All E.R. 939; [1949] A.C. 76.

when the summons comes on for hearing the plaintiff may then be ready to **A**
pay the arrears. I do not think, however, that where a plaintiff is unable to
aver a necessary condition of the relief claimed he is entitled to keep his claim on
foot on the ground that there is a possibility that the condition may be fulfilled
before the hearing. Counsel for the plaintiff relied in this connexion on *Re
Dagenham (Thames) Dock Co., Ex p. Hulse* (5), where the liquidator of a purchaser
company obtained relief from forfeiture under a penal stipulation, part of the **B**
purchase price having been already paid, this relief being on the terms that the
liquidator paid the balance of the purchase price. I find nothing in the report
to indicate that the liquidator, when he raised his claim for relief, was not ready
to pay this balance and I do not think this decision helps the plaintiff here.

I conclude that the originating summons should be struck out on that ground.
I do so with the minimum of compunction since, if the plaintiff is at any future **C**
time in a position to comply with the necessary condition for relief, there could
be nothing to prevent him from renewing this claim in the proper place, that is,
in the Queen's Bench action.

Order accordingly.

Solicitors: *Beer & Co.* (for the plaintiff); *Simmons & Simmons* (for the **D**
defendant).

[*Reported by* JENIFER SANDELL, *Barrister-at-Law.*]

NOTE.   **E**

VOSE *v.* BARR.

[LIVERPOOL ASSIZES (Lyell, J.), February 25, 1966.]

*Costs—Discretion—Misconduct or neglect—Medical report—Question of liability
settled—Refusal to disclose plaintiff's medical report until just before trial—* **F**
Supreme Court Costs Rules, 1959, *r.* 7.

[As to the exercise of the court's discretion as to costs, see 30 HALSBURY'S
LAWS (2nd Edn.) 421, para. 795.]

Application.

This was an application by the plaintiff for the costs of an action against the
defendant for damages for personal injuries which had been settled. On Apr. 23, **G**
1964, the plaintiff was a pillion passenger on a motor cycle being driven by one
Crawford which came into collision with a motor car driven by the defendant.
In an action by Crawford against the defendant on May 31, 1965, GLYN-JONES, J.,
held that Crawford was twenty-five per cent. and the defendant seventy-five
per cent. to blame for the accident. On June 17, 1965, having obtained a
medical report dated June 12, 1965, the plaintiff commenced his action against **H**
the defendant. The defendant's solicitors, writing to say that they were prepared
to accept service on his behalf, asked if, having regard to the judgment in the
previous case, the plaintiff was prepared to accept seventy-five per cent. of the
value of his claim which would avoid the necessity of third party proceedings
against Crawford. The plaintiff's solicitors replied that they were prepared to
recommend the plaintiff to agree. On July 2, 1965, the defendant's solicitors **I**
wrote asking for a copy of the plaintiff's medical evidence and particulars of his
special damage so that they could enter into negotiations for a settlement of
his claim. On July 12, 1965, the plaintiff's solicitors replied enclosing the statement of claim and saying that, when the defence was received, they would
consider the request for a copy of the plaintiff's medical report. On July 13,
1965, the defendant's solicitors, acknowledging receipt of the statement of claim

---

(5) (1873), 8 Ch. App. 1022.

A and asking for a copy of any certificate of earnings which had been obtained from the plaintiff's employers, asked why the plaintiff's solicitors were not prepared to supply a copy of their medical report at that stage, there being no issue as to liability, so that a reasonable offer to dispose of the claim could be made. The plaintiff's solicitors replied that they were quite prepared to negotiate a settlement and awaited the defendant's formal pleading without delay; but so

B far as the medical evidence was concerned, they would consider the matter. On July 19, 1965, the defendant's solicitors wrote that they were unable to put forward an offer until a copy of the medical report had been supplied. On July 28, 1965, they again asked for a copy of the medical report and on July 30, the plaintiff's solicitors replied asking for confirmation that no further discovery or a list of documents to be delivered was required. On Aug. 4, 1965, the

C defendant's solicitors wrote saying that they had delivered their defence on July 28, but that they had not yet received a copy of the medical report. On Aug. 12, 1965, the plaintiff's solicitors replied that their client was prepared to accept three-quarters of the value of his claim, but they regretted that they were not prepared to supply a copy of the medical report, though the defendant could have facilities to examine the plaintiff on the usual terms. In fact, the

D medical report was disclosed to the defendant only a few days before the trial of the action and resulted in an immediate settlement of the case.

> *G. P. Crowe** for the plaintiff.
> *T. H. Pigot** for the defendant.

LYELL, J.: In this case, the parties have reached agreement as to liability

E and as to the amount of damages, and the defendant consented to judgment for that amount. The only question which is left before me is as to the application by the plaintiff that he should have the costs of the action down to today's date. Broadly, counsel for the plaintiff puts his application in this way, that he is a successful plaintiff and is accordingly entitled, unless there be good grounds to the contrary, to recover the costs of the action between the two parties. Counsel

F on behalf of the defendant says that the plaintiff ought not to be given the costs of the action because they have been unnecessarily incurred, and he relies on the provisions of r. 7 of the Supreme Court Costs Rules, 1959. The onus is on counsel for the defendant, in my judgment, to establish the matter which would justify me, on the facts of this case, in refusing to grant the plaintiff the normal order that the defendant should pay his costs. Rule 7, so far as relevant, reads

G as follows:

> " (1) Where in any cause or matter anything is done or omission is made improperly or unnecessarily by or on behalf of a party, the court may direct that any costs to that party in respect of it shall not be allowed to him and that any costs occasioned by it to other parties shall be paid by him to them.

H   " (2) Without prejudice to the generality of para. (1) of this rule, the court shall for the purpose of that paragraph have regard in particular to the following matters, that is to say—(a) the omission to do anything the doing of which would have been calculated to save costs . . .''

What counsel for the defendant relies on as the omission to do something which has resulted in costs being incurred which could otherwise have been saved is

I that at a very early stage in this action, the plaintiff refused to allow the defendant's advisers to see a copy of a medical report on the condition of the plaintiff. The decision in this case to which I have come depends entirely on the particular facts of this case, and it is necessary that I should outline the matters which have affected my mind in coming to that conclusion. [His Lordship stated the facts, and continued:] The medical report shows clearly that by June 12, 1965, the plaintiff had wholly recovered, in the view of Dr. Gould, from the injuries

---

* Counsel were duly instructed by solicitors.

which he had sustained in the accident fourteen months earlier. From that A
time onwards any medical examination by the defendant would have produced
precisely nothing except an account by the plaintiff as to his injuries, all of
which is contained in the medical report which was ultimately produced.

There has been a very long delay and a great deal of correspondence. What
counsel for the defendant says is that, if that report had been disclosed when it
was first asked for on July 2, 1965, the overwhelming balance of probabilities B
is that it would have resulted in a settlement of the action at that date, having
regard to the fact that, as soon as it was produced, the defendant made an
estimate of what was a proper figure to offer in the light of that report, and it
was accepted forthwith. He invites me to say that there has been, in the course
of this action, an omission on the part of the plaintiff's solicitors to do a thing,
the doing of which would have been calculated to save costs. I have no doubt C
whatsoever that the delivery of the report to the defendant's solicitors would
have saved costs. I am far from satisfied that, in every case, a refusal to disclose
a medical report would be a matter which could be fairly treated as an omission
which would justify affecting the order as to costs, and I decide this entirely on
the facts of this case. The only right of a party not to disclose a privileged
document is for his protection, and there have been many cases in which it was D
perfectly proper to refuse. What I have to consider in this case is whether
there really could have been any good ground for saying that the plaintiff might
be harmed and/or was risking anything by disclosing this report at that stage.

The situation was this, that the defendant had had no medical examination.
There was no possibility of him challenging what the doctor said unless it was
apparent on the face of it that it was not so—I think that is so remote that I can E
dismiss it. He was genuinely saying " Let me know what the medical evidence
is so that we may assess what the value of the plaintiff's injuries set out in it are,
so that we may know what the extent of the injuries are ", and I regret to have
to say that the impression which I have here is that the plaintiff's solicitor
refused this for reasons quite unconnected with his client's interest, but because
there has been some ill-feeling between him and the defendant's solicitors. F
No possible harm could, in my view, have come to his client. That is borne out
by the facts that no harm did come to his client from the ultimate disclosure
of the report after all these costs had been incurred. In those circumstances,
there was, in my judgment, an omission on the part of the plaintiff's solicitors
within the provisions of r. 7 (2) of the Supreme Court Costs Rules, 1959, to do
something which would have been calculated to save costs and for that reason, G
in my judgment, the defendant ought not to be required to pay any costs beyond
the time when he asked for a medical report and that request was parried with
a truly unnecessary request that a defence should be filed before the request
was considered.

There will be judgment for the plaintiff with costs taxed if not agreed down to
July 12, 1965. Counsel for the defendant has asked me that I should make a H
further order that his client should have his costs after that date. In my discretion, the view which I formed is that it is sufficient to mark the lack of proper
conduct of this action if I deprive the plaintiff of his costs after that date.

Order accordingly.

[*Reported by* K. B. EDWARDS, ESQ., *Barrister-at-Law.*]

A

NEWNHAM *v.* BROWN.

[COURT OF APPEAL (Lord Denning, M.R., Harman and Russell, L.JJ.), March 15, 1966.]

B
Mortgage—Payment—Action to recover principal moneys and interest due under second mortgage—Default of appearance by mortgagor—Mortgaged property sold by first mortgagee before issue of writ—Whether judgment could be entered summarily by plaintiff or whether leave required—Meaning of " mortgagee "—R.S.C., Ord. 13, r. 1; Ord. 55, r. 5A, r. 5C, r. 5E (a).

The plaintiff was a second mortgagee of land. Some £1,630 odd principal, part of the mortgage debt, remained owing together with interest at five per
C cent. The first mortgagee sold the property, and nothing remained out of the proceeds of sale for the second mortgagee. In an action by writ in the Chancery Division by the second mortgagee for payment of the £1,630 odd and arrears of interest the mortgagor did not enter appearance and the plaintiff sought to enter judgment under R.S.C., Ord. 13, r. 1; but his application was refused on the ground that he must obtain the leave of the
D judge under R.S.C., Ord. 55, r. 5E, r. 5A*. On appeal,

Held: since at the time when the writ was issued no money was secured by the second mortgage on the property formerly subject to it, R.S.C., Ord. 55, r. 5E and r. 5A did not apply and the plaintiff was entitled to enter judgment under R.S.C., Ord. 13, r. 1 (see p. 231, letters A, E and I, post).

Per LORD DENNING, M.R., and RUSSELL, L.J.: the action could have been
E brought in the Queen's Bench Division (see p. 231, letters A and I, post).

Decision of CROSS, J., ([1966] 1 All E.R. 281) reversed.

[**Editorial Note.** The relevant provisions of R.S.C., Ord. 55, r. 5E, r. 5A will be superseded on Oct. 1, 1966, by R.S.C., Ord. 88, r. 1 (1) (*a*), r. 7 (1) (2), which are to the same effect.
F
As to procedure to enforce covenants for payment of moneys under a mortgage, see 37 HALSBURY'S LAWS (3rd Edn.) 360, para. 677; and for cases on actions on the covenant for payment in mortgages, see 35 DIGEST (Repl.) 602-604, *2763-2770*, and for cases on the practice, see ibid., 610, *2807-2811.*]

Appeal.

This was an appeal by the plaintiff, Caleb John Newnham, from a decision
G of CROSS, J., dated Dec. 9, 1965, and reported [1966] 1 All E.R. 281, that the plaintiff was not entitled to sign judgment in default of appearance of the defendant, but that, under R.S.C., Ord. 55, r. 5E and r. 5A, leave of the court was required where payment of moneys which were at any time secured by mortgage was sought, and that the plaintiff was bound to take out a summons before a Chancery master. The facts are set out in the judgment of LORD DENNING, M.R.

H   *G. T. Hesketh* for the plaintiff.
The defendant did not appear and was not represented.

LORD DENNING, M.R.: Many years ago the plaintiff, Mr. Newnham, supplied goods to the defendant, Mr. Armstrong Brown, to the amount of £2,000. In August, 1953, by way of security the defendant executed a legal charge over
I some property in favour of the plaintiff for the £2,000. (It was a second charge because the property was already charged to a first chargee.) The legal charge contained a covenant by the defendant to pay the £2,000 on Nov. 4, 1953, with interest from that date at five per cent. For a month or two the defendant managed to make payments which reduced the sum owing to £1,630 19s. 7d. This sum ought to have been paid on Nov. 4, 1953, but it has never been paid. Nor has the defendant paid any interest. In 1957 the first chargee realised his

---
* R.S.C. Ord. 55, r. 5A is printed at p. 230, letter F, post.

security. He sold the property and took the proceeds. There was nothing left **A**
for the second chargee, the plaintiff. So from that date onwards the plaintiff
had no charge on any property. He only had his remedy on the personal covenant.

The period of limitation on the covenant is twelve years. It would expire on
Nov. 4, 1965. Shortly before that time on Aug. 13, 1965, the plaintiff issued a
writ against the defendant claiming the £1,630 19s. 7d. (which fell due on Nov. 4,
1953), together with six years' interest. The writ was issued in the Chancery **B**
Division. No appearance was entered. The plaintiff applied to the Chancery
Registrar's department for judgment to be entered under R.S.C., Ord. 13, r. 1,
in default of appearance. He was told by the Chancery Registrar that this was
not permissible. His proper course, it was said, was to apply to a judge under
R.S.C., Ord. 55, r. 5E for leave to enter judgment: whereupon the judge might
require the application to be supported by affidavit or other evidence, and **C**
notice given to the defendant; and, after all that was done, then if leave was given,
he could enter judgment; but not before. The registrar referred it to the chief
master, who referred it to CROSS, J. (1). He upheld the view of the registrar.
The plaintiff appeals to this court.

The point is a short one. It depends on the Rules of the Supreme Court. R.S.C.,
Ord. 13, r. 1 says that: **D**

" Where a writ is endorsed with a claim against a defendant for a liquidated
demand only, then, if that defendant fails to enter an appearance, the plaintiff
may, after the time limited for appearing, enter final judgment against that
defendant . . ."

Prima facie the plaintiff here brings himself within that rule. R.S.C., Ord. 55,
r. 5E, however, says that: **E**

" In any action in which the plaintiff is claiming any relief of the nature or
kind specified in r. 5A—(a) no judgment shall be entered in default of
appearance or of defence without the leave of the court or a judge . . ."

So that throws us back to r. 5A, which says that:

" Any mortgagee or mortgagor, whether legal or equitable, or any person **F**
entitled to or having property subject to a legal or equitable charge . . .
may take out as of course an originating summons . . . for such relief of the
nature and kind following as may by the summons be specified, and as the
circumstances of the case may require; that is to say—payment of moneys
secured by the mortgage or charge; sale; foreclosure; delivery of possession
. . . to the mortgagee or person entitled to a charge . . . redemption; **G**
reconveyance; delivery of possession by the mortgagee."

The whole question in the case is whether the plaintiff, when in August, 1965, he
claimed by his writ payment of the £1,630 19s. 7d., was claiming " *payment of
moneys secured* by the mortgage or charge ". Counsel for the plaintiff said that
at that date the plaintiff was not claiming any money secured by any mortgage
or charge on any property. The property had been realised by the first chargee **H**
as long ago as 1957. The plaintiff was claiming money which was not secured
on any property at all. CROSS, J., has rejected that view. He said (2) that r. 5A
applied to a claim for the payment of moneys which *at any time have been* secured
by a mortgage or charge. That was the practice of the Chancery Division and it
might lead to unfortunate results were it otherwise.

I think that we should go by the wording of the rule and I do not think it will **I**
lead to any unfortunate results. Rule 5A in this regard means payment of moneys
which, *at the time of the writ or summons, were secured by a mortage or charge*.
The object of R.S.C., Ord. 55, r. 5A, was to ensure that all claims on a mortgage
or charge, where the defendant was in possession, should be brought in the
Chancery Division and be subject to the control of the judges of that division.
The rule has no application, however, when there is no property which is the
subject of a mortgage or charge.

(1) [1966] 1 All E.R. 281.   (2) [1966] 1 All E.R. at p. 284.

A   In this case it is plain from the statement of claim that, at the time of the writ, no moneys were secured by a mortgage or charge. R.S.C., Ord. 55, r. 5A and r. 5E do not apply. Nor does r. 5C. The writ could have been taken out in the Queen's Bench Division: and, on default of appearance, judgment could have been entered automatically in the Central Office. So also, now that it has been taken out in the Chancery Division, judgment should be entered in the Chancery

B   Registrar's department automatically. There is no need to go through the machinery of R.S.C., Ord. 55, r. 5E and obtain the leave of the judge.

As to the costs, I know that the plaintiff has had to come to this court; but the defendant has done nothing wrong. He should pay only the fixed costs payable on default of appearance. He should not have to pay the costs of the application to the judge or to this court. He took the point in a letter to this court

C   and I think that we should give effect to it.

I would allow the appeal accordingly.

HARMAN, L.J.: It is provided by R.S.C., Ord. 55, r. 5E:

" In any action in which the plaintiff is claiming any relief of the nature or kind specified in r. 5A—(*a*) no judgment shall be entered in default of

D   appearance . . . without the leave of the court."

One must, therefore, look back to r. 5A to see whether this is an action in which the plaintiff is claiming any of the relief under that order. When one looks at r. 5A one sees that it reads:

" Any mortgagee . . . or any person entitled to or having property subject

E   to a legal . . . charge . . . or any person having the right to foreclose . . . may take out as of course an originating summons . . ."

None of those things can be said of this plaintiff. He is just an unsecured creditor like any other unsecured creditor, and I am quite unable to see why he should be less able to pursue his remedy under R.S.C., Ord. 13, than if he had never had any security at all. If it had been a loan on a personal I.O.U., he could have proceeded

F   under R.S.C., Ord. 13. He was at one time, perhaps, better off than that. He had a second charge, but that second charge disappeared in 1957 when the first chargee realised the security and there was not anything left after paying the amount due. Therefore, it seems to me it would be adding insult to injury to say to this plaintiff: " Although you are now unsecured, you have not the remedies of an unsecured creditor. You must pretend that you are secured because the courts

G   are so careful of the rights of a mortgagor that anybody who has once been a mortgagor gets privileges which others do not get." That works the other way too. If a man does not choose to enter an appearance, the most merciful thing for the plaintiff to do is to sign judgment without more and to recover the fixed costs.

In my judgment it was not right to press the words, as the judge did (3), so

H   as to mean something which, with all respect to him, they do not say, for an object which I do not see has any practical significance at all. I agree with the order proposed by Lord Denning, M.R., and I would allow the appeal.

RUSSELL, L.J.: I also agree. The question whether leave to sign judgment is required by R.S.C., Ord. 55, r. 5E, depends on whether this is an action in which the plaintiff is claiming relief of the nature or kind specified in r. 5A. That depends

I   on whether the plaintiff is claiming payment of moneys secured by a mortgage or charge. The claim expressly states that since 1957 the covenant or charge has not been secured on any property at all. I agree that " secured " refers to the time when the claim is made, and that therefore no leave to sign judgment was required. Indeed, in such a case r. 5C does not in my view exclude a writ in the Queen's Bench Division; and r. 5A does not permit a proceeding by originating summons.

---

(3) [1966] 1 All E.R. 281.

I draw attention to the fact that for some years now in the ANNUAL PRACTICE (4)   A
in the notes to r. 5A there has appeared a statement on these lines: " Both rules
apply to claims for principal or interest so long as the debt is secured." I find it
not very easy to see how, if the general practice in the Chancery Division has
been to think otherwise, that note has managed to stay for so long in its present
form.

I would only add this. It is possible (though I do not pursue the matter further)   B
that some support for the view which we have formed is to be found in the
language of R.S.C., Ord. 55, r. 5D and r. 9A (1), both of which appear to assume
that property exists on which there is at the relevant time a charge.

Appeal allowed with fixed costs as on a judgment in default of appearance.

Solicitors: *Gamlen, Bowerman & Forward*, agents for *Tomkins & Bowes*, Bexhill,   C
(for the plaintiff).

[*Reported by* F. GUTTMAN, ESQ., *Barrister-at-Law.*]

D

GREEN AND OTHERS *v.* ASHCO HORTICULTURIST, LTD.

[CHANCERY DIVISION (Cross, J.), March 14, 15, 16, 17, 1966.]

Easement—Right of way—Creation—Consensual privilege not capable of being
the subject of a legal grant—Use of back entrance through courtyard by tenant
of greengrocers' shop—Use confined to business hours and subject to exigencies   E
of landlords' business on their adjoining and neighbouring land—New
leases successively granted to tenant whose consensual use of back entrance
continued—Whether tenant obtained a right of way limited to business hours
under Law of Property Act, 1925 (15 & 16 Geo. 5 c. 20), s. 62.

Landlords, who were coal and horticultural merchants, thrice successively
leased premises to G. for a greengrocer's shop. The first lease was in 1931   F
for fourteen years; the second was in 1945 for fourteen years and the third
was in 1959 for twenty-one years. The third lease, and also the earlier
leases, contained a clause (cl. 2 (*p*)*) reserving to the landlords power to deal
as they thought fit with neighbouring lands and to erect buildings on such
lands whether or not diminishing light or air enjoyed by tenants of the
demised premises.   G

A passageway led from the High Street to and past an entrance to a courtyard at the back of the demised premises. The leases did not expressly confer
on G. any right to use this back entrance. There were wooden doors across
the entrance, at any rate until 1960, and these were often kept closed out of
business hours, with the consequence that G. might have to ask an employee
of the landlords to open them. G. made considerable use of the passageway   H
and entrance for getting goods to his shop. The court found that this use was
by consent of the landlords and that this consent was subject to the exigencies
of their own business and to the requirements of tenants of their neighbouring
garages. The landlords sold the freehold of G.'s premises together with
adjoining land to the defendants. G. (and assignees of his lease) claimed a
right of way over the courtyard and through the back entrance to and from   I
the High Street.

Held: (i) the intermittent consensual privilege enjoyed by G. to use the
back entrance was not user that could have been the subject of a grant of
a legal right, and accordingly had not been converted by s. 62† of the Law of
Property Act, 1925, into a legal easement on the occasion of the grant of

---

(4) In the ANNUAL PRACTICE 1966, the note is printed on p. 1487.
* Clause 2 (*p*) is printed at p. 237, letter H, post.
† Section 62, so far as material, is printed at p. 237, letters D to G, post.

A   either the second or the third lease; the plaintiff's claim, therefore, failed (see p. 239, letters C and E, post).

International Tea Stores Co. v. *Hobbs* ([1900-03] All E.R. Rep. 303) distinguished.

Wright v. *Macadam* ([1949] 2 All E.R. 565) applied.

Ward v. *Kirkland* ([1966] 1 All E.R. 609) considered.

B   (ii) cl. 2 (*p*) was confined to easements and quasi-easements of light and air and had no application to the question determined at (i) ante (see p. 238, letter E, post).

Dictum of SARGANT, L.J., in *Gregg* v. *Richards* ([1926] Ch. at p. 534) followed.

[As to creation of easements and the effect of s. 62 of the Law of Property Act,
C   1925, see 12 HALSBURY's LAWS (3rd Edn.) 535, 536, paras. 1161, 1162; and for cases on the subject, see 19 DIGEST (Repl.) 35-40, *182-205.*

For the Law of Property Act, 1925, s. 62, see 20 HALSBURY's STATUTES (2nd Edn.) 559.]

Cases referred to:

Gregg v. *Richards,* [1926] Ch. 521; 95 L.J.Ch. 209; 135 L.T. 75; 70 Sol. Jo.
D   443; 19 Digest (Repl.) 36, *191.*

International Tea Stores Co. v. *Hobbs,* [1900-03] All E.R. Rep. 303; [1903] 2 Ch. 165; 72 L.J.Ch. 543; 19 Digest (Repl.) 38, *198.*

Ward v. *Kirkland,* [1966] 1 All E.R. 609.

Wright v. *Macadam,* [1949] 2 All E.R. 565; [1949] 2 K.B. 744; 19 Digest (Repl.) 39, *203.*

E   **Action.**

This was an action begun by writ, dated Dec. 23, 1963, and issued by the first plaintiff, Gilbert Green, who was then the lessee of a shop and premises, 33, High Street, Wimbledon, under a lease dated May 26, 1959, and made between W. C. Billings & Sons, Ltd. (" Billings ") the landlords, the predecessors in title to the defendants. By assignment dated Dec. 7, 1964, the lease was assigned to
F   Edward Casey and Margaret Brenda Casey and in December, 1964, they were added as plaintiffs. By their statement of claim re-served on July 27, 1965, as amended, the plaintiffs claimed a declaration that the second and third plaintiffs were entitled to a right of way over a passageway and courtyard in the terms set out at p. 236, letter C, post, and ancillary relief. Paragraphs 11 to 14 of the statement of claim are set out at p. 235, letters F to I, post. The defen-
G   dants, by para. 1 of their defence re-delivered on July 30, 1965, as amended, stated that they would rely on cl. 2 (*p*)* of the lease dated May 26, 1959, and of two leases dated Apr. 10, 1931, and Oct. 2, 1945, made between the same parties as the first mentioned lease and relating to the same property, and would contend that the clauses showed a contrary intention within the meaning of s. 62 (4)† of the Law of Property Act, 1925, or alternatively that the plaintiffs' rights (if
H   any) over the passageway and courtyard took effect subject to the provisions of cl. 2 (*p*) of the lease of May 26, 1959. Paragraphs 2 to 5 of the defence were as follows:

" 2. At all times from April, 1931 to 1960 the defendants and their predecessors in title [Billings] maintained across the courtyard . . . a pair of green gates. During the said period the said gates were locked every
I   evening by servants of Billings and the defendants, and when locked as aforesaid all access from the passageway to the [first] plaintiff's premises was obstructed. On numerous occasions during the said period the [first] plaintiff or his servants or agents requested Billings or the defendants or their respective servants or agents to open the said gates.

" 3. On numerous occasions during the said period Billings used the said courtyard for the purpose of unloading vehicles and bringing goods to the

* See footnote *, p. 232, ante.
† See footnote †, p. 232, ante.

adjoining property . . . and for mixing horse fodder. On the said occasions   **A**
. . . access over the said courtyard to the [first] plaintiff's property was
wholly obstructed.

" 4. On numerous occasions during the said period the [first] plaintiff and
his servants orally requested Billings its servants and agents to permit the
[first] plaintiff and his servants to gain access to the [first] plaintiff's property
over the said passageway and courtyard. Billings its servants and agents   **B**
on occasion gave consent to such use but on divers other occasions throughout the said period refused to permit the [first] plaintiff or his servants
access along the said passageway and courtyard . . .

" 5. Any permission given by Billings to the [first] plaintiff to use the
said passageway and courtyard was given to the [first] plaintiff presumably
to use the said passageway and courtyard. Further and in the alternative   **C**
any permission to use the said passageway and courtyard was limited to use
during normal working hours."

By further and better particulars of para. 5 of their defence, the defendants stated
that by the allegation that permission was given to the [first] plaintiff presumably,
they alleged that permission was given to the [first] plaintiff his servants and
agents, but that no permission was given to the [first] plaintiff's successors in   **D**
title.

The cases noted below* were cited during the argument in addition to those
referred to in the judgment.

S. L. Newcombe for the plaintiffs.
N. C. H. Browne-Wilkinson for the defendants.
                                                                                E
   CROSS, J.: On Apr. 10, 1931, W. C. Billings & Sons, Ltd. (" Billings "),
who were coal and horticultural merchants, granted to the first plaintiff, Gilbert
Green, a lease for fourteen years from Mar. 25, 1931, of a shop and premises,
No. 33, on the south side of High Street, Wimbledon, for use as a greengrocers
shop. Mr. Green remained in occupation after that lease expired, and on Oct. 2,
1945, Billings granted another lease of the premises for fourteen years from   **F**
Mar. 25, 1945, to him and a Mrs. Tyler, who was at one time a partner of his in
business. Save as regards rent, the terms of the lease were the same. Mr. Green
remained in occupation again after the end of the second lease, and on May 26,
1959, Billings granted him a third lease for twenty-one years from Mar. 25, 1959.
Again, save as regards rent, the terms were the same.

On Nov. 3, 1959, Billings conveyed to the defendants, Ashco Horticulturist,   **G**
Ltd. (" Ashco "), the freehold of 33, High Street, subject to Mr. Green's lease,
and also the freehold of some adjoining property. In December, 1963, disputes
arose between Mr. Green and Ashco whether there was or was not included in
the third lease by virtue of s. 62 of the Law of Property Act, 1925, a right of way
over part of the adjoining property; and on Dec. 23, 1963, Mr. Green issued the
writ in this action against Ashco to determine that question. In the course of the   **H**
proceedings Green assigned the twenty-one years lease to Edward and Margaret
Brenda Casey, who were added as second and third plaintiffs as being the persons
now entitled to the right of way if it exists.

I must now try and describe the locus in quo. At the back of the shop on the
ground floor of 33, High Street there is a yard, and in the southern wall of the
yard there is a small door suitable for passage on foot. This door leads into a court   **I**
which at all material times was surrounded by properties belonging to Billings.
If one turns to the left, that is, eastwards, on coming out of this door one can pass
(subject to the existence of gates blocking the way, about which I shall have to
say something in a minute) into a passageway which runs southward from the
High Street past the entrance to this court down to a number of garages, also
owned by Billings at all material times and let out on hire. The passageway

---

* *Birmingham, Dudley and District Banking Co.* v. *Ross*, (1888), 38 Ch.D. 295; *Godwin*
v. *Schweppes, Ltd.*, [1902] 1 Ch. 926; *Goldberg* v. *Edwards*, [1950] Ch. 247.

A   opposite the entrance to the court is not broad enough to allow a lorry and a car
to pass one another. The entrance to the court where it adjoins the passageway
is large enough to hold a small van or car being parked there, but not a lorry. No
evidence was given when the doorway in the southern wall of No. 33, High Street
was made or what use of it was made before Apr. 10, 1931, the date of the first
lease. It may be that at one time one could get from the court into the passageway
B   at some other point; but at all material times, so far as the evidence before me
goes, the only way out of the court was the one which I have tried to describe.
     There is no doubt that from before the date of the first lease down to the middle
of 1960 there were green wooden doors across the entrance to the court some ten
feet or so inwards from the passageway. There is also no doubt that Billings kept
these doors shut at night and during the luncheon interval. They were open
C   only in business hours. There is no doubt also that throughout the period from
1931 to 1959 Mr. Green made considerable use of the back entrance to his premises
for the purposes of his business. He would get up early in the morning, go out
into the High Street, pass down the passageway to the garages, in one of which
his lorry was garaged, drive to Covent Garden to get his produce and return
some time between eight and half-past nine with the lorry loaded. More often
D   than not he or his men would unload the lorry in the passageway at the entrance
to the court and convey the goods through the back door into the shop instead
of going into the High Street and using the front door. Again, more often than
not, when goods, and particularly potatoes, were delivered to him during the
day, as they often were, that delivery was effected from the passageway in the
same way, and not from the front entrance in the High Street. Further, there is
E   no doubt that until about 1958 Mr. Green had a small delivery van for delivery
to customers, and that that van was often loaded and unloaded in the passageway
and via the court and back door instead of at the front door.
     At this stage it will be convenient to refer to the plaintiffs' claim. After setting
out the leases and describing the physical layout of the property the statement of
claim continues as follows in paras. 11, 12, 13 and 14:
F
     "11. Ever since April, 1931, when the first plaintiff first went into posses-
sion and occupation of the demised premises until Dec. 15, 1963, the first
plaintiff has enjoyed a right of way or passage (hereinafter called ' the right
of way ') from Wimbledon High Street aforesaid along the passageway
through the courtyard to the rear entrance (hereinafter called ' the rear
entrance ') of the demised premises which rear entrance gives onto the
G   courtyard. 12. The right of way has at all material times been enjoyed and
exercised by the first plaintiff his servants and licensees: (i) openly; (ii)
without the permission of the landlord; (iii) without any protest from the
landlord; (iv) on foot and with lorries motor cars and motor vans laden or
unladen; and (v) in particular for the delivery of goods for the purposes of
the first plaintiff's said business to the rear entrance and for the collection of
H   refuse from the demised premises. 13. In the alternative, if the right of way
was at any time enjoyed and exercised by the first plaintiff by permission of
the landlord (which is denied) the same was at all material times enjoyed
and exercised by the first plaintiff in the manner set out in the preceding
paragraph hereof (save that the same was not being enjoyed or exercised
without the permission of the landlord). 14. In the premises, since the right
I   of way was enjoyed and exercised by the first plaintiff as set out in para. 12
hereof (or para. 13 hereof as the case may be) at the time of the execution of
the present lease (and so far as is relevant, at the time of the execution of the
second lease) the same was or had become at such time or times a right or
privilege appertaining to and enjoyed with the demised premises which said
right or privilege passed with the demised premises under or by virtue of the
present lease (and so far as is relevant, the second lease) to the first plaintiff
as appertaining thereto or being enjoyed therewith."

Pausing there, it will be seen that the plaintiffs were not saying that any right of   A
way was included in the first lease, although the door was there. There is, as I
say, no available evidence as to what, if any, use was made of it by the former
tenants. The case is that Mr. Green was allowed to use the right of way during the
term of the first lease, and on the execution of the second lease, therefore, he
obtained under s. 62 of the Law of Property Act, 1925, a right to use it which
continued after the execution of the present lease.   B
    The statement of claim then sets out certain admitted facts about the transfer
of the freehold reversion and the dispute which arose, and it ends with a claim
in the following terms, so far as relevant:

    " A declaration that the second and third plaintiffs are entitled to a right
    of way for themselves their servants under-tenants and licensees at all times   C
    and for all purposes whether with or without lorries motor cars motor vans
    or any other vehicles laden or unladen or on foot from Wimbledon High Street
    aforesaid along the passageway through the courtyard to the rear entrance."

There are ancillary claims for injunctions and damages. In the course of his
opening, counsel for the plaintiffs admitted that, in view of the fact that the
gates were shut at night-time and during the luncheon interval, he could not   D
contend for a right of way at all times and limited his claim to a right of way
during business hours.
    By way of defence two points are taken. First, Ashco raise a point of construc-
tion on the lease, which I need not set out in detail at this point. Secondly, they
say that, although the first plaintiff and his servants and licensees openly used
the passageway with lorries and vans and thence traversed the courtyard on foot   E
for the purpose of delivery to and removal of goods from No. 33, High Street
through the back entrance, yet this was done by the licence of Billings, and by a
licence of such a character as prevented s. 62 from operating. They do not,
however, dispute that if these two points fail—that is, the question of construction
and the point about the licence—the plaintiffs are entitled to the relief for which
they ask.   F
    Now I must turn to the evidence on the question of licence or consent,
which was conflicting. Mr. Green said that he never found the green doors shut
at any time when he wanted to unload goods from the lorry via the back door.
He said that there was never any trouble between him and Billings and their
employees with regard to the parking of his lorry or the delivery lorries in the
passageway while unloading, and that he was never refused permission to unload   G
in or to take deliveries from the passageway. Ashco's evidence was quite contrary
to this, and I have no hesitation in preferring the evidence of Ashco to that
of Mr. Green. Speaking generally, the evidence of the defendants amounted
to this. First, it was by no means unusual for Mr. Green to find the green doors
still shut when he arrived back from Covent Garden in the morning and for him
to have to ask one of Billings' employees to open them for him. Secondly, there   H
were throughout the period from 1931 to 1959 recurrent troubles over the parking
of Mr. Green's lorry and the delivery lorries in the passageway while loading and
unloading, since they blocked the access to the garages and, therefore, interfered
with the tenants of the garages, and also interfered sometimes with Billings' own
business when they themselves had heavy deliveries either of coal or horticultural
goods. Thirdly, Ashco's evidence showed that on some occasions Mr. Green was   I
told in no uncertain terms that he could not unload or take deliveries in the
passageway on some particular day, because Billings were taking large deliveries
themselves, and that he acquiesced in that position. Indeed, I think it is clear
that Billings regarded themselves as doing an act of friendship to Mr. Green in
allowing him to unload in the passageway from lorries which were blocking it
or liable to block it in the way that they did. The defendants' evidence was partly
the oral evidence of employees of Billings—and I would particularly mention Mr.
Waring and Mrs. Norton—and partly signed statements made by two directors

A of Billings, a Mr. Billings and a Mr. Lavender, at the end of 1963 or the beginning of 1964 when these proceedings were pending. Mr. Lavender is now dead, and Mr. Billings is in such bad health that he could not give evidence. I admitted those statements under the Evidence Act, 1938, because it was clear, and indeed was conceded by counsel for the plaintiffs, that it could not be said that either of those gentlemen were interested within the meaning of s. 1 (3) of the Act of 1938.

B In considering the weight to be given to those statements, however, I have to bear in mind that they are not contemporary statements, but were made some time after Billings ceased to be interested in the property, and that the makers of the statements were old men even then, and that they were not subject to cross-examination. What they say in the statements, however, is completely consistent with the oral evidence given on behalf of Ashco, and although it is

C clean contrary to the evidence of Mr. Green. I should have paid little attention to the evidence of Mr. Green, quite apart from the statements, as I preferred the evidence of Mr. Waring and Mrs. Norton.

I must now turn to s. 62 of the Law of Property Act, 1925, and read sub-ss. (1), (2) and (4):

D " (1) A conveyance of land shall be deemed to include and shall by virtue of this Act operate to convey, with the land, all buildings, erections, fixtures, commons, hedges, ditches, fences, ways, waters, watercourses, liberties, privileges, easements, rights, and advantages whatsoever, appertaining or reputed to appertain to the land, or any part thereof, or, at the time of conveyance, demised, occupied, or enjoyed with or reputed or known as part or parcel of or appurtenant to the land or any part thereof. (2) A conveyance

E of land, having houses or other buildings thereon, shall be deemed to include and shall by virtue of this Act operate to convey, with the land, houses, or other buildings, all outhouses, erections, fixtures, cellars, areas, courts, court-yards, cisterns, sewers, gutters, drains, ways, passages, lights, watercourses, liberties, privileges, easements, rights, and advantages whatsoever, apper-taining or reputed to appertain to the land, houses, or other buildings con-

F veyed, or any of them, or any part thereof, or, at the time of conveyance, demised, occupied or enjoyed with, or reputed or known as part or parcel of or appurtenant to, the land, houses or other buildings conveyed, or any of them, or any part thereof . . . (4) This section applies only if and as far as a contrary intention is not expressed in the conveyance, and has effect subject to the terms of the conveyance and to the provisions therein contained."

G And by definition, in the Act of 1925 the word " conveyance " includes a lease.

The first point taken by Ashco against the plaintiffs is that there is a clause in the present lease—and I think that there was a similar clause in the earlier leases—which either amounts to the expression of an intention that this section should not apply at all or at least makes any rights acquired by the tenant under the section defeasible by the landlord. That clause, which is cl. 2 (p), reads as

H follows:

" That [Billings] shall at all times have power without obtaining any consent from or making compensation to the lessee to deal as [Billings] may think fit with any of the lands and premises adjoining contiguous or opposite or near to the demised premises and to erect or suffer to be erected upon such

I adjoining contiguous opposite or neighbouring lands or premises any buildings whatsoever whether such buildings shall or shall not affect or diminish the light or air which may now or at any time during the term hereby granted be enjoyed by the lessee or other [Billings'] tenants or occupiers of the demised premises or any part thereof."

The way in which one ought to approach this problem is, I think, stated very clearly by SARGANT, L.J., in his judgment in Gregg v. Richards (1):

(1) [1926] Ch. 521 at pp. 534, 535.

" I think it is important to point out that because the words are in the   **A**
statute and do not appear in the conveyance they must not be looked upon
as mere implied words or anything of the sort. LINDLEY, L.J., said in terms
that it must be looked on as being an express grant, though no doubt an
express grant which may fail altogether if an intention is expressed to
exclude it, or may be limited if an intention is shown to limit it. It is a little
difficult to see how that is to be dealt with in practice, but I think perhaps the   **B**
way to regard it may be this, to consider that in such a conveyance there is
added to the parcels a printed form of words such as you find in the common
form printed forms of clause, and that then if the conveyance expresses an
intention to exclude, you may consider that printed form of words struck out
in ink and removed from the conveyance in that way; while, if an intention
is shown to limit or alter the form, the limitation or alteration being intro-   **C**
duced in the particular conveyance would of course prevail, according to the
ordinary rules of construction of such documents, over the common form
which you find in the print. It may be that that would practically give effect
to the provisions of the statute, but it is to be noticed that it is by way of
express grant that it operates and not by way of implied grant, and that it is
for the grantor who seeks to show that that express grant is limited to prove   **D**
affirmatively that there is some limitation of that express grant."

Now to construe cl. 2 (*p*) in the way contended for by Ashco would lead to
very far-reaching results. It would mean, for instance, that Billings could
by operations on their own adjoining land cut through and block up any drains
serving No. 33 which happened to pass under their land. In my judgment,
it would require far clearer words than appear in cl. 2 (*p*) to produce that sort   **E**
of result. It is perfectly true that the opening four lines of the clause are in
very wide terms; but the clause must be read as a whole and not be split into
two parts, and reading it as a whole, I have no doubt that its operation is confined
to easements or quasi-easements of light and air and has no application to this
case at all. So, in my judgment, that point taken by Ashco fails.

On the basis that s. 62 is not excluded the plaintiffs put their case in this way.   **F**
It is said that at the date of the present lease, the third lease, Mr. Green was in
fact using this passageway, the court and the back door for the conveyance of
goods, which were unloaded from his lorry or from the delivery lorries in the
passageway, and that until shortly before the lease he was using also his small
delivery van in the same way. He says that the question whether or not what he
was doing was being done by the express consent of Billings, who were Ashco's   **G**
predecessors, is irrelevant as a matter of law.

Looking at the matter for a moment apart from authority, one might have
thought that in a case of this sort the question whether or not there was an
express licence by the landlord for the doing of the acts in question was a highly
relevant matter. If the owner of two properties, one of which is in lease, allows
the tenant to make use of the adjoining property which the owner has in hand in   **H**
a certain way without protest or the grant of any express consent the tenant may
well be justified in thinking, when his lease is renewed, that he is to have under
the renewed lease an automatic right to do on the adjoining property what the
landlord previously knew he was doing and did not require him to obtain any
express licence to do. On the other hand, if he has had to obtain an express licence
to do the acts in question, one might think that he could hardly expect to get   **I**
a right to go on doing the acts under the new lease without a further express
permission. Be that as it may, however, it is clear that the law is otherwise. In
the case of the *International Tea Stores Co.* v. *Hobbs* (2), the facts of which are
strikingly similar to the facts here, FARWELL, J., decided that for the purpose
of the operation of the section in the Conveyancing Act, 1881, which corresponded
to s. 62 of the Law of Property Act, 1925, it made no difference whatever whether

(2) [1900-03] All E.R. Rep. 303; [1903] 2 Ch. 165.

A the consent of the landlord was tacit or express; and that decision was approved
by the Court of Appeal in the case of *Wright* v. *Macadam* (3). Indeed, in the
recently reported case of *Ward* v. *Kirkland* (4) UNGOED-THOMAS, J., said (I
think by way of dictum, having regard to his findings of fact) that it makes
no difference whether the express consent was given to endure for a period of
time or was asked for and given every time the right was exercised; and given
B the principle laid down in *Hobbs'* case (5), it is difficult to see any logical distinction between an express consent to last over a period and an express consent
to each separate act of user. I share the doubts expressed by TUCKER, L.J.,
in *Wright* v. *Macadam* (6) as to the justice of the law in this regard; but there is
no doubt what the law is.

But as FARWELL, J., pointed out in *Hobbs'* case (7) and JENKINS, L.J.,
C repeated in *Wright* v. *Macadam* (8), there are two sets of circumstances which may
prevent s. 62 from operating. In the first place, the section can operate only if
the kind of user relied on could have been the subject of a grant of a legal right;
and secondly, the section will not operate if at the time of the conveyance or
lease in question it was or should have been apparent to the grantee or lessee that
the enjoyment which he claims to have been converted into a right by the section
D was only temporary. I do not think that the second qualification on the general
rule has any application here. Mr. Green ought perhaps to have realised—perhaps,
indeed, he did—that Billings were consenting to his doing what he was doing
only because of their personal regard for him, and that they would not necessarily be so considerate to a successor in title. He had no reason to think,
however, that so long as he was tenant things would not be allowed to go on as
E before. The first qualification on the general rule appears to me, however, to
place an insuperable obstacle in the plaintiffs' way. On the facts as I find them,
the consent which Billings gave to Mr. Green using the back entrance was always
subject to the exigencies of their own business and the requirements of the
tenants of their garages. They were prepared to let Mr. Green use the back
entrance if and when it was not inconvenient to them and their tenants. If it was
F inconvenient, they told him so; and for the time being he had to desist from
using the back entrance. But a purported grant of a right of way for such periods
as the servient owner may permit one to use it would not confer any legal right at
all. When I asked counsel for the plaintiffs to say how he suggested that an express
grant of the easement which he is claiming for the plaintiffs would be worded, he
said that it would have taken the following form: a right at all times during
G business hours to pass and repass along the passageway and courtyard from
Wimbledon High Street to the back door of No. 33 by himself, his servants or
suppliers for the purpose of delivering and supplying goods either on foot or, to
the extent of the passageway but not the courtyard, with vehicles: provided
that such right be not used or exercised in such manner as to obstruct the
grantors or their successors in title in the carrying on of their business and also
H so as not to obstruct the tenants of the garages at the end of the said passageway.
That, however, would make the question whether or not Billings needed to
prevent Mr. Green from using the right a question for the court and not for
Billings, in default of agreement. Thus Mr. Green would be getting under s. 62
a larger legal easement than the privilege which he was in fact enjoying. There
is nothing in *Hobbs'* case (5) which forces me to arrive at so unjust a result.

I   In the course of his reply counsel for the plaintiffs, who has taken every possible
point on behalf of his clients, submitted that even if the plaintiffs were not
entitled to a right to unload their lorries, which would necessarily block the

---

(3) [1949] 2 All E.R. 565; [1949] 2 K.B. 744.
(4) [1966] 1 All E.R. 609 at p. 620, letter A.
(5) [1900-03] All E.R. Rep. 303; [1903] 2 Ch. 165.
(6) [1949] 2 All E.R. at p. 573; [1949] 2 K.B. at pp. 754, 755.
(7) [1900-03] All E.R. Rep. at p. 306; [1903] 2 Ch. at p. 171.
(8) [1949] 2 All E.R. at pp. 569, 570; [1949] 2 K.B. at p. 749.

passageway, I ought nevertheless to hold that they were entitled to use the back A
entrance for the purpose of bringing in goods which were either (a) unloaded from
a van small enough to be parked in the entrance of the court, where, as the
evidence showed, Mr. Green's van was sometimes parked and where it did not
obstruct the passageway, or (b) brought round in trolleys from the High Street.
In fact, as I have said, Mr. Green disposed of his van in 1958—that is, shortly
before the grant of the present lease—and the only evidence of the trolleying of B
goods to the back entrance from the High Street was on an occasion after the
grant of the present lease when there had been particular trouble between the
defendants and Mr. Green over a large delivery van which damaged the sides of
the passageway. The defendants had then insisted on certain goods being
unloaded in the High Street and trolleyed up the passageway and through
the court. If one looks strictly only at the mode of user obtaining at the time C
of the grant of the present lease, it was only user by means of Mr. Green's lorry
and the large delivery vans, both of which blocked the passageway. Whatever
may be the position, however, with regard to the trolleying, of which there is no
evidence before the present lease, I do not think that it would be right to dismiss
the alternative claim, so far as concerns Mr. Green's small van, simply on the
ground that he had no such van at the date of the grant of the present lease. One D
ought not, I think, in a case like this to confine oneself to a single moment of
time—when possibly there might have been no user at all. One ought to look
at a reasonable period of time before the grant in question in order to see whether
there was anything over that period which could be called a pattern of regular
user in any particular way or ways. Here, if one looks at the evidence over
the whole period from 1931 to 1959, there is no doubt that there was regular E
user by this small delivery van. Although he disposed of this van in 1958,
it was not clear in 1959 that he would never get another one. The difficulty
in the plaintiffs' way, however, in regard to this alternative claim—over and
above the fact that it was never pleaded or, indeed, hinted at until the reply
—is that one cannot know for certain what the reactions of Billings would
have been if the user by Mr. Green had been confined to user by this small F
van and trolleys. It may well be that, as the small van and the trolleys would
not have caused any obstruction of the passageway, they would have
acquiesced in the user and Mr. Green would have obtained a legal right under
s. 62; but there is no certainty about this. The evidence showed that on occasions
Billings mixed horse fodder in the entrance to the courtyard. On such occasions
the van could not have been parked there, nor could Mr. Green's men have G
trolleyed his goods in—though they might, I suppose, have carried goods in by
stepping round or over the fodder. On occasions of this sort there might well
have been trouble, even though Mr. Green never used a large lorry which blocked
the passageway, and the trouble might have led to the same sort of consent as I
find was given in this case,.namely, a consent which reduced the privilege
enjoyed to something which could not be the subject of a legal easement. H

For those reasons, therefore, I hold that the alternative claim also fails, and it
follows that the action must be dismissed.

Action dismissed.

Solicitors: *Greysons* (for the plaintiffs); *S. R. Pinks & Co.* (for the defendants).

[*Reported by* JACQUELINE METCALFE, *Barrister-at-Law.*]

A   THOMAS v. THE TIMES BOOK CO., LTD.

[CHANCERY DIVISION (Plowman, J.), March 8, 9, 10, 11, 18, 1966.]

Gift—Chattels—Delivery—Possession obtained, with the consent of the donor, by finding—Whether delivery.

Gift—Death of donor—Proof of intention—Donee's account of events to be
B   *approached with suspicion—Burden of proof on donee.*

T. delivered a manuscript of a work, which had been commissioned by the B.B.C. nearly ten years previously, to C., a B.B.C. producer, who was in charge of the project for the B.B.C. and whom T. had known for some years in connexion with the preparation of the work. The manuscript was delivered on a Friday in October, 1953, for a stencil to be cut and copies made. T. was
C   to fly to America on the following Monday, where he was to give readings from the manuscript. The manuscript was returned to T. on Saturday, but he lost it. C. took three copies of the script to the air terminal in London and gave them to T. before T. left on the Monday. T. was grateful and told C. that if he could find the manuscript he could keep it. T. told him of places where it might have been left. C. found the manuscript a few days later in
D   one of the places of which T. had told him. T. died in America in November, 1953, without having returned to England. His administratrix sued the defendants for the return of the manuscript, which they had bought from a purchaser from C.

Held: although, in view of T.'s death the burden of proof was on the defendants to establish the gift to C. and the donee's account of events was
E   to be approached with suspicion (*Re Garnett*, (1885), 31 Ch.D. 1, followed), yet on the evidence the defendants had discharged the burden of proof and had established both an intention on T.'s part to make a gift of the manuscript and delivery of it to the donee, C., for the fact that C. had obtained possession of the manuscript with T.'s consent was sufficient delivery to perfect a gift (see p. 244, letter G, and p. 246, letters C and H, post).

F   [As to proof in regard to claims against a deceased, see 16 HALSBURY'S LAWS (3rd Edn.) 446, para. 882: and for cases on the subject, see 24 DIGEST (Repl.) 857, 858, *851*7*-852*5.

As to constructive delivery for the purposes of gift, see 18 HALSBURY'S LAWS (3rd Edn.) 382, 383, para. 729; and for cases on the subject, see 25 DIGEST (Repl.) 557, *64-70*.]
G   Cases referred to:

Cole (a Bankrupt), Re, Ex p. The Trustee v. *Cole*, [1963] 3 All E.R. 433; [1964] Ch. 175; [1963] 3 W.L.R. 621; Digest (Cont. Vol. A) 627, *51a*.

Edginton v. *Clark (Macassey and Others (Trustees of Whitley House Trust) third parties*), [1963] 3 All E.R. 468; [1964] 1 Q.B. 367; [1963] 3 W.L.R. 721; Digest (Cont. Vol. A) 324, *845a*.
H
Garnett, Re, Gandy v. *Macaulay*, (1885), 31 Ch.D. 1; 24 Digest (Repl.) 857, *852*1.

Action.

This was an action begun by writ dated Oct. 26, 1961, by Caitlin Thomas, the plaintiff, against The Times Book Co., Ltd., the defendants. Pursuant
I   to orders of Master PENGELLY, dated June 6 and Oct. 11, 1962, James Stevens Cox was added as third party by a third party notice dated Aug. 13, 1962, and by a fourth party notice dated Oct. 12, 1962, Douglas Cleverdon was added as fourth party. The plaintiff, who sued as administratrix of the estate of Dylan Thomas, deceased, claimed against the defendants a declaration that the original manuscript of the deceased's play " Under Milk Wood " then in the possession of the defendants formed part of his estate, and an order for delivery up of the manuscript to the plaintiff. The defendants, by their defence dated Jan. 31, 1962, alleged that they had acquired the manuscript for £2,000 from the third

Distinguished in JOHNSON V RIBBINS [1977] 1 All ER 806

party at the Antiquarian Book Fair of the National Book League on June 10, A
1961, and that the third party had acquired the manuscript for valuable consideration from the fourth party, to whom it had been given by the deceased.
The plaintiff, by her reply dated May 10, 1962, admitted this allegation except
that she denied that the fourth party was at any time the owner of the manuscript, and pleaded that the defendants could not rely on s. 3 of the Limitation
Act, 1939, since the fourth party had fraudulently concealed the plaintiff's right B
of action.   By their rejoinder, delivered on June 20, 1962, and re-served as
amended on Apr. 20, 1965, the defendants stated that they did not admit the
alleged fraudulent concealment and pleaded that if the fourth party had fraudulently concealed the plaintiff's right of action as alleged they were not a party
to the fraud, did not know of it and did not have reason to believe that it had
been committed.   The defendants claimed against the third party in the event C
of the plaintiff succeeding in her claim repayment of the sum of £2,000 and
an indemnity in respect of any sum and costs that they might be ordered to
pay to the plaintiff.   The third party admitted the defendants' claim, but not
that the plaintiff's claim was well founded, and as against the fourth party,
alleged that he sold the manuscript as agent for the fourth party, and claimed
repayment of £1,620 (the net amount paid by the third party to the fourth party D
on the sale of the manuscript) and indemnification against any sums payable
by the third party to the defendants by way of damages and costs.   The
fourth party by his defence, re-delivered on Nov. 12, 1963, as amended, pleaded
that he did not admit that he or the third party as his agent had no right to
sell the manuscript or that it was at any material time the plaintiff's property
and traversed all allegations of fact in the third party's statement of claim. E
The facts are stated in the judgment.

Charles Sparrow for the plaintiff.
A. J. Balcombe for the defendants.
G. T. Hesketh for the third and fourth parties.

Mar. 11.   **PLOWMAN, J.:** This is an action by Mrs. Caitlin Thomas, who F
is the widow of the late Dylan Thomas, and the sole administratrix of his estate,
to recover from the defendants, The Times Book Co., Ltd., the manuscript of Dylan
Thomas's best known work Under Milk Wood. The defendants claim that Dylan
Thomas made a gift of this manuscript to Douglas Cleverdon, a B.B.C. producer,
and they claim title through him. It is also pleaded by way of defence that
even if the plaintiff ever had a claim to the return of the manuscript it is a stale G
claim and barred by the Limitation Act, 1939.

The primary question with which I am concerned is, therefore, whether Dylan
Thomas made a gift of this manuscript to Mr. Cleverdon. The manuscript in
question consists of two parts. The first part, which is the earlier part of the
play, is a fair copy in Dylan Thomas's own handwriting of some earlier draft, or
drafts, or sketches. The latter part is a typescript not made by Dylan Thomas, H
but made by a copyist of the later part of the play, and it contains emendations
made by Dylan Thomas himself.

Under Milk Wood is a work which was commissioned by the B.B.C. in, I think,
1943 or 1944. In 1946, when Mr. Cleverdon first enters this story, very little had
been done by Dylan Thomas. About this time, that is to say, 1946, Mr. Cleverdon,
who was on the staff of the B.B.C., inherited the Under Milk Wood project from I
another producer, a Mr. Burton, and Mr. Cleverdon, as he says, badgered and
cajoled Dylan Thomas to get on with Under Milk Wood. The work proceeded
slowly. There was a time, apparently, when Dylan Thomas got stuck with it,
and there was an interval before it was restarted. Eventually, on Thursday,
Oct. 15, 1953, Dylan Thomas delivered the manuscript to Mr. Cleverdon at his
office in the B.B.C. In that office there was also present Mr. Cleverdon's secretary,
Miss Fox. Now Dylan Thomas was due to fly to America on the following Monday,
Oct. 19, and he was going there to try to raise some money by giving readings

A of Under Milk Wood. He told Mr. Cleverdon that he wanted his manuscript
back by Monday to take to the United States with him. Mr. Cleverdon told his
secretary, Miss Fox, to cut a stencil of the manuscript as quickly as possible.
She did so, and she gave Dylan Thomas his manuscript back on Saturday, Oct. 17.
She gave it him back on the Saturday morning, and he lost it. He was perturbed
about this loss; he had not any other copy of it, and he was due to fly to America
B on the following Monday, and he needed the manuscript for that trip.

Some time over the weekend Dylan Thomas telephoned Mr. Cleverdon at the
latter's home and told him that he had lost the manuscript. Mr. Cleverdon told
him not to worry about it because the B.B.C. had had this script stencilled, and
he, Mr. Cleverdon, would take three copies of it to the air terminal at Victoria
on Monday and would hand them over before Dylan Thomas left for America.
C On the Monday Mr. Cleverdon told his secretary what had happened; he asked her
to get three copies rushed off, and that was done. Mr. Cleverdon, in the early
evening, took a taxi to the London Air Terminal and there he found Dylan Thomas
in company with his wife and a Mr. and Mrs. Locke. Mr Cleverdon handed over
to him the three copies of the B.B.C. script. I now quote the actual words of
Mr. Cleverdon's evidence, which I read from a press cutting which is substantially
D the same, and is the same in all material respects, as my own note. Mr. Cleverdon
said that the poet was extremely grateful, and then I quote:

> " The only words I can recall him actually saying were that I had saved
> his life. I said it seemed an awful pity that the original had been lost, and
> that it meant an awful lot to me. I had been working on it very closely over
> six or seven years, and it was the culmination of one of the most interesting
E > things I had produced. He said if I could find it I could keep it. He told me
> the names of half a dozen pubs, and said if he had not left it there he might
> have left it in a taxi."

Either later that day or the next day—probably, I think, the next day—Mr.
Cleverdon told his secretary, Miss Fox, what had happened. He told her that
F Dylan Thomas had given him the manuscript, which was still missing, and he
told her that he was going to look for it. Within a day or two he found it; and
he found it in one of the public houses in Soho, the name of which he had been
given by Dylan Thomas. He took possession of it, and he retained it until 1961,
when he sold it to a Mr. Cox, through whom it came to the defendants. Two or
three days after finding it, a friend of Mr. Cleverdon, a Mr. Cranston, who is a
G Reader in Political Science at the London School of Economics, and literary
adviser to Messrs. Methuen's, the publishers, was having lunch with Mr. Cleverdon
at his house. On this occasion, Mr. Cleverdon told him the story of the loss of the
manuscript; he told him how he had delivered copies of it to Dylan Thomas
at the air terminal; he told him that Dylan Thomas had said that if he could find
the original which had been lost he could keep it, and he told him how he had
H found it.

To go back a little way, as I have already said, on Monday, Oct. 19, Dylan
Thomas flew to the United States. About three weeks later, namely, on Nov. 9,
he died in that country. On Dec. 7, 1953, letters of administration were granted
to the plaintiff in this action. On Dec. 28, 1953, the plaintiff, Mrs. Thomas, made
a settlement of the copyrights in Dylan Thomas's works. There were three
I trustees of that settlement: a Mr. Higham, who had been Dylan Thomas's
literary agent; a Dr. Jones, who was an old friend of Dylan Thomas going back
to school days, and who wrote the music for Under Milk Wood, and who edited
the first published edition for Dents, the publishers; and the third trustee was a
Mr. Stuart Thomas, a solicitor. The manuscript of Under Milk Wood, as a chattel,
was not included in that settlement and, therefore, if there was no gift of it, and
if the Limitation Act, 1939, is not a defence to this action, the plaintiff as
administratrix of the estate is entitled to recover this manuscript.

The plaintiff submits that there was no gift of this manuscript to Mr. Cleverdon,

but let me make it quite plain from the start that the onus is not on the plaintiff **A**
to disprove that that was a gift; the onus is on the defendants and is accepted
by their counsel as being on them to prove affirmatively that a gift was made.
Counsel on behalf of the plaintiff submits that there was no gift, and that in order
to establish a gift the defendants have to prove two things. The two things which
counsel says that the defendants have to prove are, first, the relevant animus
donandi or the intention of making a gift and, second, a delivery of the subject **B**
matter of the gift, this manuscript, to the donee. I accept this submission.
Counsel submits that the gift claimed in this action fails on both scores: first,
for the reason that there was no intention to give and, secondly, for the reason that
it is said that there was no sufficient delivery of the subject matter of the gift.

Now let me first of all say something about the question whether the defendants
have succeeded in establishing the necessary intention. It is said, first of all, and **C**
accepted by both sides, that in considering whether the defendants have discharged the onus of proof which is on them, I must approach the claim made by
the defendants that there was a gift with suspicion. Reference was made in this
connexion to the decision of the Court of Appeal in *Re Garnett, Gandy* v. *Macaulay*
(1), where SIR BALIOL BRETT, M.R., said this (2):

" Another point was taken. It was said that this release cannot be **D**
questioned because the person to whom it was given is dead, and also that
it cannot be questioned unless those who object and state certain facts are
corroborated, and it is said that that was a doctrine of the Court of Chancery.
I do not assent to this argument; there is no such law. Are we to be told
that a person whom everybody on earth would believe, who is produced as a
witness before the judge, who gives his evidence in such a way that anybody **E**
would be perfectly senseless who did not believe him, whose evidence the
judge, in fact, believes to be absolutely true, is, according to a doctrine
of the courts of equity, not to be believed by the judge because he is not
corroborated? The proposition seems unreasonable the moment it is stated.
There is no such law. The law is that when an attempt is made to charge a
dead person in a matter, in which if he were alive he might have answered **F**
the charge, the evidence ought to be looked at with great care; the evidence
ought to be thoroughly sifted, and the mind of any judge who hears it
ought to be, first of all, in a state of suspicion; but if in the end the truthfulness of the witnesses is made perfectly clear and apparent, and the tribunal
which has to act on their evidence believes them, the suggested doctrine
becomes absurd. And what is ridiculous and absurd never is, to my mind, **G**
to be adopted either in Law or in Equity."

Therefore, not only in this case is the onus of proof on the defendants, but I am
enjoined by authority to approach their story with suspicion having regard to the
fact that the other actor in this story, the late Dylan Thomas, is dead and cannot
therefore give his own version of what took place.

Then counsel for the plaintiff submits that the story which is put forward **H**
on behalf of the defendants is so improbable as not to be credible. For example,
it is said that the late Dylan Thomas was always hard up, and on the evidence it
appears quite clearly that he was. It is said that he was setting off on this trip
to the United States in order to try to raise some money, and that, no doubt, is
equally true. It is said that this was the major work of a great poet; that he
must have known that the manuscript was of considerable value; that he had **I**
previous experience of using his manuscripts as a form, as it were, of currency;
that he had sold manuscripts of poems previously for an odd pound or two;
that the manuscript was a thing over which he had lavished great care and devo-
tion over a number of years, and that in those circumstances it is really inconceivable that he should have made this present of it to Mr. Cleverdon. In
addition, it is said that when Dylan Thomas got to America he spent a good deal

(1) (1885), 31 Ch.D. 1.   (2) (1885), 31 Ch.D. at pp. 8, 9.

A of time with a close friend of his, Mr. Ruthven Todd—and Mr. Ruthven Todd has given evidence before me. He said that Dylan Thomas used to come and see him at his house in Greenwich Village, and he remembers that Dylan Thomas told him about the loss of the manuscript on his arrival in the United States, and how upset he was. He said " I have done it now ". He said the manuscript contained material to which he wanted to refer. He hoped that the manuscript

B was going to turn up, and that he would hear about it. He said that Douglas— that is to say, Mr. Cleverdon—gave him the scripts he had. He said that Douglas was looking for the other, and that is all he said about it.

It is submitted by counsel for the plaintiff that there, in effect, is Dylan Thomas giving evidence in this court, and that on that evidence, as it were, given by Dylan Thomas, I am bound to deduce that he had not made a gift of the manu-

C script to Mr. Cleverdon, because if he had done so he could not have said what he did to Mr. Todd. Against that, of course, I have to remember this. While I have no doubt that Mr. Todd was telling what he remembered to the best of his ability, what he was deposing to were conversations which took place over twelve years ago. It is hard enough to remember a conversation one had a week ago, let alone twelve years ago; and while those matters are no doubt matters which have

D remained in Mr. Todd's recollection, the fact that these conversations were so long ago is a matter which I am bound to take into account in evaluating the evidence given by Mr. Todd. There is no contemporaneous record of the conversations that Dylan Thomas had with Mr. Todd, in the way in which there is an almost contemporaneous record by Mr. Cleverdon of the conversation which he had with Dylan Thomas, and on which the defendants base their claim that there

E was a gift.

I agree with counsel for the plaintiff that it is right to weigh probabilities in assessing the weight of the affirmative evidence which is given; but I am bound to say that I think that counsel for the defendants was perfectly justified in saying that a great many of these matters which are now being put forward as establishing the inherent improbability of a gift are pure matters of hindsight.

F At the time when the alleged gift was made, that is to say, in October, 1953, Dylan Thomas was a comparatively young man; he was thirty-nine years old, and he was still alive. Under Milk Wood had not then been performed in England. It had its first performance on the B.B.C. in January, 1954. It had not been published in England. It is quite true, as counsel for the plaintiff said, that Dylan Thomas was recognised as a considerable poet, but he was recognised as a

G considerable poet by a comparatively small number of people. It was only after the B.B.C. performance of Under Milk Wood that Dylan Thomas's name became known to the public at large. Although I do not think that the question of the value of the manuscript has really very much to do with this case it was only after the death of Dylan Thomas that this manuscript with which I am concerned became really valuable.

H Another thing that I have to bear in mind in weighing the probabilities of the matter is this. When he made the alleged gift, he had not got the manuscript— it had been lost. Nobody knew whether it would ever turn up again. The character of Dylan Thomas, so far as it is delineated by the evidence that I have heard in this court, shows that he was generous, impulsive, capable of spontaneous gestures. It seems to me quite in keeping with that character—insofar as that

I has emerged in the course of this hearing—that he should have made the gesture of telling Mr. Cleverdon that if he found this manuscript he could keep it. Let me say a word about the word " keep ", because a good many semantic points have been made about the actual word used, whether it was " keep it ", or " have it ", or " welcome to keep it ", or " keep it for yourself ". I shall not attempt to draw any distinction between them. They all seem to me to come to exactly the same thing if Mr. Cleverdon is to be believed, because he was quite clear, and always has been quite clear, that the words used were not words by which Dylan Thomas was enjoining him to do something, but were words of gift.

There is another matter which seems to me to be relevant. Obviously, Dylan **A**
Thomas was very relieved to have these B.B.C. manuscripts. He had even hinted
that there might not be any point in going to America when he lost his own
manuscript, and now it was all right. He was clearly relieved. Mr. Cleverdon was
not a stranger to him who had suddenly come on the scene. They had been working together for the past six or seven years and, for myself, I see no inherent
improbability at all in the story which the defendants put forward in this case **B**
through the mouth of Mr. Cleverdon.

Any question of probability or improbability fades into the background and
disappears once I find myself forced to the conclusion that Mr. Cleverdon was
telling the truth and that I ought to accept his evidence. Having seen him and
listened carefully, and having approached this matter in a proper state of suspicion, I find myself in the end forced to the conclusion that Mr. Cleverdon was **C**
speaking the truth, and I accept his evidence. One of the reasons which certainly
assists me very much in coming to that conclusion is this. I cannot believe
that Mr. Cleverdon would have told Miss Fox and Mr. Cranston that Dylan
Thomas had given him the manuscript if it was not true, because Dylan Thomas,
at the time when he told both those persons, was still alive, and everybody was
expecting him to come back from America within a short time. It would have **D**
been absolutely stupid to have invented a lie in those circumstances, and Mr.
Cleverdon certainly is not a stupid person.

I think that I ought to say a word about the evidence of Dr. Jones. It was he
who edited the first published text of Under Milk Wood in this country. As an
editor, he would naturally be interested in any manuscript material which was
available. As I understand it, the object of introducing his evidence into this case **E**
was to support the suggestion that from the death of Dylan Thomas until the year
1961, when the manuscript was sold, Mr. Cleverdon was concealing the existence
of this manuscript from Dr. Jones. That does not seem to me to make sense. As
early as January, 1954, Mr. Cleverdon was writing to one of Dr. Jones' co-trustees
of the Dylan Thomas copyrights, telling the story of the gift of the manuscript
to him, just as it was told to me. And, incidentally, Mr. Higham, who was the **F**
trustee in question, had no hesitation in accepting that story. From that time on
Mr. Cleverdon told the story of the recovery of the manuscript both in broadcasts
and in press interviews, and I have been shown the reports of three press interviews in the year 1956 in which Mr. Cleverdon was telling the story of the gift,
and how Dylan Thomas told him that if he could find the manuscript he could
keep it, and how he found it. I am unable to find any foundation for the suggestion **G**
that Mr. Cleverdon was concealing this manuscript from anyone.

So much for the question of intention. It is then said on behalf of the plaintiff
that even if Dylan Thomas intended to give this manuscript to Mr. Cleverdon, he
did not succeed in giving effect to that intention because there was no delivery
of the subject matter of it to Mr. Cleverdon by Dylan Thomas. I feel bound to
reject that argument. The fact is that Mr. Cleverdon got possession of this manu- **H**
script from the Soho public house in which it had been left by Dylan Thomas,
and he got that possession with the consent of Dylan Thomas. That, in my
judgment, is sufficient delivery to perfect a gift in Mr. Cleverdon's favour. I
can see nothing in the case of *Re Cole (a Bankrupt), Ex p. The Trustee* v. *Cole* (3),
on which counsel for the plaintiff relied, which precludes me from taking what
appears to me to be the comon sense view of the matter, and concluding that when **I**
Mr. Cleverdon got possession of the manuscript with the consent of Dylan Thomas,
the gift was perfected.

In those circumstances, my conclusion is that the defendants have succeeded
in establishing that Dylan Thomas made a gift of this manuscript to Mr. Cleverdon,
and in those circumstances the plaintiff's action must fail.

Action dismissed.

---

(3) [1963] 3 All E.R. 433; [1964] Ch. 175.

A   [Mar. 18, 1966. HIS LORDSHIP considered the question of the costs of the third
and fourth parties, and, having said that in view of the decision in *Edginton* v.
Clark (4) it was clear that he had complete discretion, concluded that the plaintiff's claim had rendered the third and fourth party proceedings inevitable and
that the fourth party was amply justified in being represented by counsel;
accordingly the plaintiff would be ordered to pay the third and fourth parties'
B   costs.]

Solicitors: *Prothero & Prothero*, agents for *D. O. Thomas & Co.*, Swansea
(for the plaintiff); *Charles Russell & Co.* (for the defendants); *Moon, Gilks &
Moon*, agents for *Kitson & Trotman*, Beaminster (for the third party), and
Stephenson, Harwood & Tatham (for the fourth party).

C   [*Reported by* JACQUELINE METCALFE, *Barrister-at-Law.*]

LIPTROT *v.* BRITISH RAILWAYS BOARD.

[COURT OF APPEAL (Willmer, Danckwerts and Salmon, L.JJ.), February 25, 28,
March 1, 1966.]

Factory—Dangerous machinery—Mobile crane—Failure to fence—Gap between
D   *rotating body and wheel—Injury to workman trapped in gap—Whether mobile*
        crane was machinery within Factories Act, 1961 (9 & 10 Eliz. 2 c. 34), s. 14 (1).

A mobile crane, being a crane mounted on a chassis on wheels, used for
sorting metal on premises that are a factory by virtue of s. 175 (2) (*b*) of the
Factories Act, 1961, is part of the factory equipment and is " machinery "
within s. 14, just as a static crane in a factory is " machinery "; but it
E   does not necessarily follow that every part of the mobile crane is a
" part of machinery " within s. 14 (see per SELLERS and SALMON, L.JJ.,
DANCKWERTS, L.J., dissenting, p. 251, letter G, p. 252, letter A, and p. 256,
letters D and E, post).

Cherry v. *International Alloys, Ltd.* ([1960] 3 All E.R. 264) distinguished.
In a scrap metal yard, which was a factory within s. 175 (2) (*b*) of the
F   Factories Act, 1961, a mobile crane was used for collecting and sorting scrap
metal dumped in the yard and for loading it into wagons. The crane was
mounted on a chassis fitted with four rubber-tyred wheels, and it could
move from place to place under its own power. The body of the crane could
be rotated on the chassis throughout 360 degrees, and its lifting tackle
comprised an electrical magnet for picking up metal. The crane was operated
G   by a driver in a cab in the body, from which he could see only ahead. Sometimes wire would lodge in the gap between the body and the chassis. Then a
slinger operating on the ground would signal to the driver to stop and together
they would clear the wire. Disregarding this procedure, a slinger attempted
to clear a small piece of wire so lodged without warning the driver who,
being unable to see the slinger, rotated the crane and trapped the slinger
H   in a gap between the body and a chassis wheel, and injured him. The gap was
not fenced. In an action by the slinger against his employers for damages for
negligence and breach of statutory duty it was found by the trial judge that
no negligence was attributable to the employers, but that the unfenced gap
between the rotating body of the crane and the wheel constituted a dangerous
part of machinery within s. 14 of the Factories Act, 1961, if the crane
I   was machinery for the purposes of that section.

Held (DANCKWERTS, L.J., dissenting): the crane was machinery within
s. 14 (1)* of the Factories Act, 1961, and it therefore followed from the findings
of the trial judge that the employers were liable to the slinger for damages
for breach of statutory duty under s. 14 (see p. 252, letter B, and p. 256,
letter G, post).

Appeal allowed.

---

(4) [1963] 3 All E.R. 468; [1964] 1 Q.B. 367.
* Section 14 (1) is printed at p. 252, letter I, post.

Affirmed.
1072.

H.L.   [1967] 2 All E.R.

[As to what is machinery for the purposes of the Factories Act, 1961, see 17 **A**
HALSBURY's LAWS (3rd Edn.) 70-76, paras. 122-126; and for cases on the subject,
see DIGEST (Repl.) 1052-1062, *202-254.*
For the Factories Act, 1961, s. 14 (1), see 41 HALSBURY's STATUTES (2nd Edn.)
256.]

Cases referred to:
  Biddle v. *Truvox Engineering Co., Ltd.*, [1951] 2 All E.R. 835; [1952] 1 K.B.   **B**
    101; 24 Digest (Repl.) 1059, *243.*
  Carrington v. *John Summers & Sons, Ltd.*, [1957] 1 All E.R. 457; [1957]
    1 W.L.R. 504; Digest (Cont. Vol. A) 591, *254a.*
  Cherry v. *International Alloys, Ltd.*, [1960] 3 All E.R. 264; [1961] 1 Q.B. 136;
    [1960] 3 W.L.R. 568; Digest (Cont. Vol. A) 586, *205a.*
  Fowler v. *Yorkshire Electric Power Co., Ltd.*, [1939] 1 All E.R. 407; 160 L.T.   **C**
    208; 24 Digest (Repl.) 1049, *184.*
  Parvin v. *Morton Machine Co., Ltd.*, [1952] 1 All E.R. 670; [1952] A.C. 515;
    116 J.P. 211; 24 Digest (Repl.) 1059, *239.*
  Smith v. *Chesterfield & District Co-operative Society, Ltd.*, [1953] 1 All E.R.
    447; [1953] 1 W.L.R. 370; 24 Digest (Repl.) 1051, *193.*
  Summers (John) & Sons, Ltd. v. *Frost*, [1955] 1 All E.R. 870; [1955] A.C. 740;   **D**
    [1955] 2 W.L.R. 825; 24 Digest (Repl.) 1055, *217.*
  Walker v. *Bletchley Flettons, Ltd.*, [1937] 1 All E.R. 170; 24 Digest (Repl.)
    1054, *212.*

Appeal.
The plaintiff appealed to the Court of Appeal against an order of BARRY, J.,   **E**
made on Oct. 11, 1965, dismissing the plaintiff's action for damages for negligence
and breach of statutory duty in failing to fence alleged dangerous machinery in
contravention of s. 14 (1) of the Factories Act, 1961, as a result of which the plaintiff
claimed that he had sustained injuries in the course of his employment as a slinger
at the defendants' locomotive works at Horwich, near Bolton, Lancashire. The
grounds of appeal were (i) that the judge misdirected himself and was wrong in   **F**
law in holding that the mobile crane from which the plaintiff sustained his
injury was not a machine or machinery to which the provisions of the Factories
Act, 1961, and particularly s. 14 (1), applied; and (ii) that the judge ought on
the evidence, and on the facts that he had found, to have held that the mobile
crane was a machine or machinery to which those provisions applied.

  G. Heilpern, Q.C., and *A. M. Prestt* for the plaintiff.   **G**
  Marven Everett, Q.C., and *P. C. Carcoran* for the defendants.

  WILLMER, L.J.: This is an appeal from a judgment of BARRY, J., given at
Manchester Assizes on Oct. 11, 1965, whereby he dismissed a claim by the plaintiff against his employers for personal injuries arising out of an accident at
work. The accident causing the injuries took place on May 24, 1962, and it   **H**
occurred in a scrap metal yard which formed part of the defendants' locomotive
works at Horwich in Lancashire. The scrap metal yard is an open yard where
scrap metal is collected for sorting and subsequent disposal, but it is admitted
on the pleadings that it is a " factory " within the meaning of the Factories Act,
1961.
  The plaintiff was employed as a " slinger ", and his job as such was to work   **I**
in conjunction with the driver of a mobile crane, which was used for the purpose
of collecting the scrap metal dumped in the yard and loading it into wagons for
removal. The crane itself is mounted, by means of a vertical shaft, on a chassis
fitted with four rubber-tyred wheels, on which it is able to move from place to
place under its own power. It is thus at one and the same time a vehicle and also a
piece of mechanism designed for the lifting of weights. The body of the crane is
capable of being rotated on the chassis through 360 degrees. The lifting tackle
may be used either with a hook or, as in the present case, with an electrical magnet

A   for the purpose of picking up the objects to be lifted. The crane is operated by a driver who sits in a cab in the body of the crane, from where he can see ahead (i.e., in the direction in which the jib is pointing) so that he can control the lift; but in his position in the cab the driver is unable to see what goes on behind him.

The objects to be lifted and sorted apparently comprise a wide variety of pieces of scrap metal, or at least they did at the time when the accident happened.

B   This scrap metal may include (and on the occasion of this accident did include) lengths of wire. The evidence showed that sometimes a piece of wire, when put under tension by the lifting operation, may be caused to spring violently towards the body of the crane, and when this occurs the wire may lodge in the gap between the body and the chassis. When this occurs it has to be cleared by hand before the crane can continue to operate. There was apparently a well-recognised procedure

C   which was normally adopted for clearing the wire on occasions such as that. The procedure was that the slinger, the plaintiff in the present case, who would be stationed on the ground, would signal to the crane driver to stop the crane. The crane driver, having stopped the crane, would then dismount, and he and the slinger between them would set about the task of clearing the wire, either by cutting it or by breaking it. On the occasion of this accident a piece of wire did

D   in fact become jammed between the body and the chassis of the crane. The plaintiff was on the point of giving the usual warning to the crane driver to stop, so that the two of them could carry out the normal procedure for freeing the wire; but he then saw that it was only a short length of wire which was caught, and he appears to have thought that he would have time to clear it by himself whilst the crane was stationary, and before the driver could operate the crane for the

E   purpose of picking up the next load of scrap. So, without giving any warning to the driver of what he was doing, he positioned himself between the body of the crane and the nearside wheel of the chassis; and in that position the plaintiff proceeded to try to clear the wire. The crane driver, not knowing that the plaintiff was there, proceeded to rotate the crane for the purpose of picking up another load. The result was that, as the body of the crane rotated, the plaintiff

F   was trapped between it and the top of the wheel of the chassis. In consequence he sustained severe personal injuries through the crushing of his chest, abdomen and pelvis.

The plaintiff brought this action against the defendants alleging that they were guilty both of negligence at common law and of breach of their statutory duty under s. 14 of the Factories Act, 1961, in that they failed to fence the dangerous

G   nip between the body of the crane and the wheel of the chassis. The judge dismissed the action, holding that neither negligence at common law nor breach of statutory duty had been proved against the defendants. At the plaintiff's request, however, he proceeded to assess the damages which he would have awarded, which he fixed at the sum of £2,321 13s. 6d., a sum which included within it an agreed amount of special damage. The judge intimated that, even if he had

H   found some fault on the part of the defendants, he would in any case have held that the plaintiff himself was to blame to the extent of two-thirds. On this appeal it has not been contended that the defendants were guilty of any negligence at common law. The appeal is based solely on the contention that they were in breach of their statutory duty in failing to fence what the judge himself described as a dangerous part of the machinery. The plaintiff accepts the judge's assessment

I   of damages. He also accepts that he was at fault to the extent of two-thirds; but we are invited to find that the defendants were also at fault to the extent of one-third, and in these circumstances to enter judgment for the plaintiff for one-third of the damages found by the judge, viz., £773 17s. 10d.

The question which we have to decide is whether this crane, while in use within an area admitted to be a " factory ", constituted " machinery " within s. 14 of the Act of 1961, so as to require that any dangerous part of it should be securely fenced. The judge, in reaching his conclusion, considered and rejected an argument that s. 14 could not be held applicable having regard to the fact that cranes and lifting machines are specifically dealt with by s. 27 of the Act of 1961. In rejecting **A** that argument he was following the decision of STREATFEILD, J., in *Carrington* v. *John Summers & Sons, Ltd.* (1). The judge took the view (in my view rightly) that the mere fact of cranes being specifically dealt with in s. 24 (7) of the Factories Act, 1937, would not prevent a mobile crane from being held to be subject also to s. 14 if it constituted machinery within that section.

If s. 14 were held to apply to this mobile crane, the judge expressed himself **B** as satisfied that the nip between the rotating body and the wheel of the chassis would constitute a dangerous part so as to call for fencing. In the course of his argument for the defendants, counsel has sought to attack that finding. It was, however, pointed out to him that no respondent's notice had been filed in this case, and in those circumstances, at a very late stage of his argument, he applied for leave even at that stage to file a respondent's notice. We considered that **C** application very carefully, but (as I have already announced) we did not see fit to grant leave at that stage of the appeal to file a respondent's notice. As was pointed out by counsel for the plaintiff, the effect of granting leave at that stage would have been to open up a whole new vista of questions both of fact and of law which had not been dealt with at all in the presentation of the appeal on behalf of the plaintiff. In those circumstances we did not think it right, at this stage in **D** an action of this character, to grant that concession to the defendants.

It follows that the only question left for decision in this appeal is the question which I have already stated, viz., whether this mobile crane did constitute " machinery " within s. 14 of the Factories Act, 1961. The judge quite clearly did not find that an easy question to decide. Indeed, he said so in terms and expressed the view that the case fell very, very near the border line. In the end, **E** however, he came to the conclusion which I have stated, viz., that s. 14 did not apply. What he said in his judgment was this:

" Hundreds, even thousands, of these cranes are in use throughout the country on sites which may or may not be factories within the meaning of the Factories Act, 1961. They are fully mobile. Indeed, as I understand it, sub- ject to adequate licensing they can move along the highway, and on the whole **F** I am satisfied that the dangers which they create are really quite different from those caused by factory machinery. Indeed, it seems to me that one is much more likely to be run over by the wheels of one of these mobile cranes than caught in the very unusual position in which the plaintiff found himself when this accident occurred. It is common knowledge that these machines are often let out on hire, and it seems to me it would be placing an almost **G** intolerable burden on a factory owner if he had to ensure that every mobile crane which was on his premises, even for a short time, complied with all the requirements of the Factories Act. So far as the evidence goes, no one has ever even tried to guard these wheels or the nip in which the plaintiff was unfortunately caught. I think this is somewhat significant if it is to be said these machines were such that all the rigorous requirements as to fencing **H** imposed by the Factories Act were *to be* complied with. These cranes, of course, have lifting equipment and are indeed primarily designed for lifting purposes, but, doing the best that I can, I do not think this distinction really affects the matter. They are self-contained units which can move out of factories, and on the whole I am bound to say, with very considerable hesitation, I have come to the conclusion that this crane was not a piece of **I** factory machinery to which s. 14 (1) of the Act applies."

In reaching his conclusion the judge appears to have taken the view that a good deal of help was to be derived from the decision of this court in *Cherry* v. *Inter- national Alloys, Ltd.* (2). That case concerned a Lister truck, which was used within a factory for the purpose of transporting the materials which had been produced in the factory. The plaintiff in that case, while adjusting the oil-feed

---

(1) [1957] 1 All E.R. 457.   (2) [1960] 3 All E.R. 264; [1961] 1 Q.B. 136.

A of the engine of the truck, had his hand injured by the revolving fan which
was unguarded. He brought an action against his employers in which it was
sought to say that the truck was " machinery " within the Factories Act, 1937,
and that the fan was a dangerous part which should have been securely fenced
in pursuance of s. 14. It was decided, however, by this court that the truck was a
vehicle, and was not " machinery " to which s. 14 applied. As DEVLIN, L.J.,
B said (3), the object of the Factories Act is not to make safety provisions for
vehicles, which may travel inside or outside a factory, but for plant and machinery
inside them.

In my judgment the judge in the present case fell into error in seeking to find
an analogy between the Lister truck in that case and the mobile crane which is in
question in the present case. I venture to think that the members of this court
C who heard the appeal in the *Cherry* case (4) would have been somewhat surprised
to learn that their decision was put forward as a guide to a case such as the present
one. It is, I think, significant that in the course of the *Cherry* case (4) specific
reference was made to the sections of the Act dealing with cranes and lifting equipment. SELLERS, L.J., who delivered the first judgment, having referred to these
sections of the Act, went on (5):

D   " The plant included in these sections serves to remove goods in the course
    of the processes of production, but there is no reference, directly or by
    implication, to a vehicle such as a motor car or a truck. The express pro-
    visions of s. 24 [i.e., s. 24 of the Act of 1937 corresponding to s. 27 of the
    Act of 1961] prevent any analogy between cranes and other lifting machines
    and the mobile truck on the factory floor. The Lister truck under
E   consideration had no lifting power but served only to carry goods."

PEARCE, L.J., said (6):

    " In argument we have discussed such things as travelling cranes and
    mobile drills. But these things do not come within so well-known a class
    with such well-defined attributes as motor vehicles."

F Counsel for the defendants, in the course of his argument this morning, advanced
the proposition that this mobile crane was really nothing more than a vehicle
used for the transport of material from place to place, in much the same way as a
lorry might be used to transport material from place to place. He will, I am sure,
forgive me if I say that I think that argument was rather far-fetched. Coming
back, however, to the question whether *Cherry's* case (4) does afford any guide
G to the solution of the problem in the present case, it seems to me that the two
cases are quite different. In *Cherry's* case (4) the truck with which the court was
concerned was basically a vehicle, and nothing but a vehicle. In the present
case the piece of equipment, to use a neutral phrase, with which we are concerned is basically a crane. The fact that it happens to be fitted with wheels
which make it mobile is merely an irrelevant detail. Had this crane been mounted
H on a fixed pedestal, I do not see how it could be doubted but that it would have
constituted factory machinery, so as to be capable of falling within s. 14 of the
Act of 1961. It appears to me that it can make no difference to the nature of a
piece of machinery that it happens to be mounted on a mobile chassis.

No case has been cited to us in which the exact question before us has been the
subject of specific decision; but three cases have been called to our attention in
I which equipment of a similar character has been held to constitute " machinery "
within s. 14 of the Factories Act apparently without argument to the contrary.
I refer first to the well-known and oft-quoted case of *Walker* v. *Bletchley Flettons,
Ltd.* (7), a case concerning a mechanical excavator; *Fowler* v. *Yorkshire Electric
Power Co., Ltd.* (8), a case concerning a crane which travelled on overhead rails,

(3) [1960] 3 All E.R. at p. 269; [1961] 1 Q.B. at p. 148.
(4) [1960] 3 All E.R. 264; [1961] 1 Q.B. 136.
(5) [1960] 3 All E.R. at p. 266; [1961] 1 Q.B. at p. 143.
(6) [1960] 3 All E.R. at p. 268; [1961] 1 Q.B. at p. 147.
(7) [1937] 1 All E.R. 170.   (8) [1939] 1 All E.R. 407.

and *Biddle* v. *Truvox Engineering Co., Ltd.* (9), a case concerning an electric stack- A
ing truck. It seems to me that the mobile crane with which we are concerned
in the present case is an object bearing certain quite striking similarities with the
objects in those cases to which we have been referred. I can see no real answer to
the contention advanced on behalf of the plaintiff that this crane constitutes
part of the factory machinery, so as to be capable of being caught by s. 14 of the
Act of 1961. If that be right, then on the judge's finding there can, I think, be B
no doubt but that the defendants were in breach of their statutory duty in failing
to fence what he found to be a dangerous part of the machinery. I wish to make
it clear that in a sense that point, in so far as this appeal is concerned, goes by
default. I am not expressing any personal view of my own whether the judge was
right or wrong in coming to the conclusion that the place where this man was
trapped did constitute a dangerous part within the meaning of the Act. For the C
reasons that I have given I do not regard that point as having been before us;
but on the one point that has been argued before us it seems to me that the
plaintiff is entitled to succeed and to have his one-third share of the damages.
It may be said that this result is liable to lead to absurd consequences. Some
of them have been mentioned in argument. The matter which most appeals to me
as a difficulty is that a mobile crane such as this is obviously a piece of mechanism D
which is designed to operate (and no doubt many such cranes do habitually
operate) in places which are not factories. It may well be that when a crane is
operating in other places it is subject to no requirement as to fencing, but that as
soon as it is brought within the confines of a factory it becomes subject to s. 14
as part of the factory machinery. Yet the danger of an accident such as occurred
to this plaintiff is the same wherever the crane may be used. I accept that that E
apparently absurd result may follow from the decision at which I have arrived;
but, if it be so, it appears to me that the remedy lies with the legislature and not
with this court. I cannot think that an argument based on possible absurd
consequences is really a sound argument for saying that, when such a crane as
this is used within what is admittedly a factory, so that it does for the time being
form part of the factory equipment, it is not subject to the relevant provisions F
of the Factories Act, 1961.

For the reasons which I have given, I would allow this appeal and enter
judgment for the plaintiff for the limited sum found by the judge, viz., £773
17s. 10d.

DANCKWERTS, L.J.: I find myself in disagreement. I think that the
judge reached the right result, and I would dismiss the appeal. In this case I G
find myself caught between sympathy for the plaintiff and the injuries which he
received, and exasperation at the artificial results produced by the provisions of
the Factories Act, 1961. In the present case, however, no ordinary person would
call this yard a factory. It is brought in apparently simply by the provisions of
s. 175 (2) (*b*):

> "Any premises in which the business of sorting any articles is carried on
> as a preliminary to the work carried on in any factory or incidentally to the
> purposes of any factory."

The yard here is an open space. It is not a building such as one would suppose a
factory to be. It is by reason of that provision that it has been possible to argue
that this particular piece of equipment, this travelling crane, falls within the I
provisions of s. 14 (1) of the Act of 1961, that subsection providing, and I had
better read it:

> "Every dangerous part of any machinery, other than prime movers and
> transmission machinery, shall be securely fenced unless it is in such a position
> or of such construction as to be as safe to every person employed or working
> on the premises as it would be if securely fenced."

(9) [1951] 2 All E.R. 835; [1952] 1 K.B. 101.

A It is therefore contended on behalf of the plaintiff that this is factory machinery and caught by the provisions of that section.

The first thing is to look at the actual situation. We have some excellent photographs. Photograph No. 3 appears to me to give an utterly misleading picture of the nature of the accident which happened. It shows a man thrusting his hand in between the body of the travelling crane and the base on which it

B revolves, and would suggest it to be one of these familiar cases where a man's arm or hand was caught in machinery used in a factory. Nothing of the sort happened. What happened is shown more clearly by photograph No. 2. It is merely the bulging face of the part of the crane which, when it was turned round by the action of the driver, who could not see the plaintiff, pressed the middle of the plaintiff's body between that bulge and the wheel which is seen on the left-hand

C side of the photograph, and in that way he suffered a very severe injury. The plaintiff, of course, was utterly foolhardy. He knew perfectly well, having been working with this driver on the site for a considerable time, we are told, that it was impossible for the driver to see him at all, his view being only to the front from the offside front of the vehicle. The plaintiff took a chance because he thought that he could pull out some wire before the driver operated the crane, which he

D knew was about to pick up some of the scrap in this yard, and in that way he met with this unfortunate accident.

Lord Morton of Henryton in *John Summers & Sons, Ltd.* v. *Frost* (10), pointed out that in s. 14 of the Factories Act, 1937, the words "dangerous machine" are not used at all, nor are they used in any of the group of sections which include s. 14; and the argument against the application of the section, as I

E understand it, has been based in part on the point that this is not machinery in the natural sense of the term. As Pearce, L.J., pointed out in *Cherry* v. *International Alloys, Ltd.* (11), practically anything can be brought within the term "machinery" in one sense of that word.

In *Cherry's* case (12) a very different kind of vehicle was involved. It was a Lister truck which apparently moved about in the factory, and it had not any

F lifting machinery. I cannot appreciate, however, why the absence of lifting machinery in that case and the presence of lifting machinery in the present case make the two cases in principle distinguishable. Pearce, L.J., said (11):

"It is clear that the provisions of the Act and s. 14 itself are not apt for application to trucks and lead to some unreasonable results; and one may fairly assume that trucks were not in the mind of the draftsman. Trucks are

G self-contained units and the dangers that they create are different dangers from those caused by factory machinery with which the Act was primarily concerned. The danger of being run over or knocked down is wholly different from the dangers that arise in factories from catching, cutting, pinching and crushing. And any dangers that may arise from contact with the internal engines of the trucks are far more frequent in garages (to which the Act does

H not apply) than in factories."

No doubt, of course, in the present case the travelling crane has machinery in which a finger may be caught if there is no guard, in the same way that an accident can occur with an internal combustion engine in a truck. Pearce, L.J., continued (11):

I "Nevertheless, if the Act uses plain language that must embrace the Lister truck, the provisions apply to it when it is on factory premises. The question whether an article is machinery, like the question whether any part of the machinery is dangerous, is a question of fact for the court to determine in each case; but 'the question must . . . be judged by reference to the right

---

(10) [1955] 1 All E.R. 870 at p. 874; [1955] A.C. 740 at p. 754.
(11) [1960] 3 All E.R. at p. 267; [1961] 1 Q.B. at p. 146.
(12) [1960] 3 All E.R. 264; [1961] 1 Q.B. 136.

principle of law ' (see JENKINS, L.J., in *Smith* v. *Chesterfield & District*   A
Co-operative Society, Ltd. (13)).   *Parvin* v. *Morton Machine Co., Ltd.* (14)
shows that the words ' any machinery ' in this Act do not include all machinery of every kind, since they do not include machinery that is manufactured
by the factory. One is thus entitled to apply these ordinary words in the
context of the Act and in the context of a factory."

And DEVLIN, L.J., said (15):   B

  " I have no doubt that a truck is a machine and its engine is machinery,
  but I think the full width of the words ' any machinery ' in s. 14 of the
  Factories Act, 1937, must be controlled by consideration of the scope and
  objects of the Act."

There, I think, DEVLIN, L.J., put his finger on the point. He continued (16):   C

  " The relevant principle of construction is, in my opinion, correctly and
  concisely set out in MAXWELL ON THE INTERPRETATION OF STATUTES (10th
  Edn.) at p. 60. Dealing with the interpretation of general words and phrases,
  the author says: ' While expressing truly enough all that the legislature
  intended, they frequently express more, in their literal meaning and natural
  force; and it is necessary to give them the meaning which best suits the   D
  scope and object of the statute without extending to ground foreign to the
  intention. It is, therefore, a canon of interpretation that all words, if they be
  general and not express and precise, are to be restricted to the fitness of the
  matter '."

There DEVLIN, L.J., quoted with approval a passage from MAXWELL ON THE
INTERPRETATION OF STATUTES, which covered the point which I am trying   E
to make at the present time. It seems to me that one should apply common sense
in these cases and apply a reasonable construction to the words which are found
in the Factories Act, 1961, in such a way that they do not produce an absurd and
entirely unexpected result. The accident in the present case seems to me to be of a
type which is not that which one would ordinarily associate with factory machinery
at all. It was caused by the revolution of part of the main body of the crane so   F
as to produce a space in which the plaintiff happened to be standing which was
not wide enough for his body to be between the body of the crane and the wheel,
and thus caused him to suffer the severe injury which he did. I cannot believe that
this machine, the travelling crane, is properly within the meaning of " factory
machinery " contained in the Factories Act, 1961, and in particular in s. 14,
the section which we have been considering. I think that the judge was right   G
in coming to the conclusion that s. 14 is not dealing at all with this kind of thing,
and that he was right, therefore, in excluding the provisions of s. 14 from applying
to the present case. I would accordingly dismiss the appeal.

  SALMON, L.J.: The point raised on this appeal is evidently by no means
easy of solution, for my lords have disagreed and the judge below expressly   H
stated that this is a very difficult borderline case. I confess that I should otherwise have thought that it was a reasonably clear case.
  The premises at which this accident occurred were an open space, which I
suppose no layman would regard as a factory. In my view, one's approach to
the present problem tends to be bedevilled by that circumstance, for it is difficult
to think of anything in that open space as being factory machinery. Nevertheless,   I
that open space was a factory within the meaning of the Factories Act, 1961,
since it comes within the definition of a " factory " in s. 175 (2) (*b*) of that
Act. The premises were premises in which the business of sorting articles was
carried on as a preliminary to the work carried on in a factory or incidentally

  (13) [1953] 1 All E.R. 447 at p. 450.
  (14) [1952] 1 All E.R. 670; [1952] A.C. 515.
  (15) [1960] 3 All E.R. at pp. 268, 269; [1961] 1 Q.B. at p. 148.
  (16) [1960] 3 All E.R. at p. 269; [1961] 1 Q.B. at p. 148.

A to the purposes of a factory. The contrary has not been argued. The sorting was carried on by means of a mechanically operated mobile crane. The sole question that arises on this appeal is whether a mobile mechanically operated crane used in a factory of this kind is a machine to which the Act of 1961 applies. It is conceded that, if the crane in this factory had been on a fixed platform, it would fall within the Act of 1961. I ask myself the question: Why should it make any

B difference, in considering whether a crane is part of the factory machinery, that it happens to be on wheels and moveable? I confess that I find great difficulty in supplying any sensible answer to that question. In the cases to which WILLMER, L.J., has referred, it seems to have been assumed that mechanical excavators, travelling cranes and electric stacking trucks, if used in a factory, are machines or machinery within the Act. Since the point was not argued, these cases, of

C course, cannot be regarded as decisions in the plaintiff's favour; but it is to be observed that in the first of those cases, *Walker* v. *Bletchley Flettons, Ltd.* (17), DU PARCQ, J., was the trial judge, and SELLERS, K.C., was leading counsel for the defendants. If the pieces of equipment in those cases were rightly assumed to be within the Factories Act, it is difficult to see why mobile cranes in a factory should be excluded.

D   In *Parvin* v. *Morton Machine Co., Ltd.* (18) it was decided that machinery manufactured in a factory was not machinery within the Factories Act, 1937. According to LORD NORMAND (19), the Act of 1937 applied only to " machines or machinery for use in the factory in the processes of manufacture, or as ancillary to those processes ". The factory there being considered was a factory in which processes of manufacture took place. Here it is a factory where processes of

E sorting take place. There can be no doubt that this mobile crane was used in this factory in the processes of sorting. LORD REID (20) considered the machinery could not be within the scope of the Act of 1937 unless it was part of the equipment of the factory. According to LORD ASQUITH OF BISHOPSTONE (21), the Act of 1937 applied only to "machinery used as a productive agent, and does not extend to machinery emerging as a product ". I appreciate that it was not

F laid down by the House of Lords that all machinery that was used in the factory processes or was part of the factory equipment, or used as a productive agent in the factory, was necessarily " machinery " within the meaning of the Factories Act, 1937, but I think that it emerges from the case that, prima facie, at any rate, such machinery is " machinery " within the meaning of the Act of 1937.

G   In *Cherry* v. *International Alloys, Ltd.* (22), the facts were very different from those in the present case. The machine in question there was a petrol-driven Lister truck which was used to carry various manufactured parts from one place to another inside the factory. This court came to the conclusion that a Lister truck was much more akin to an ordinary motor vehicle than it was to what could properly be described as factory machinery, and that, therefore, it

H did not come within the scope of the Act of 1937. SELLERS, L.J., who delivered the leading judgment in that case, drew attention to the fact that the Lister truck under consideration had no lifting power, but served only to carry goods. It seems to me that by necessary implication he was at any rate expressly reserving the position had the vehicle in question had lifting power in addition to its capacity for carrying goods. PEARCE, L.J., said (23):

I   " In argument we have discussed such things as travelling cranes and mobile drills. But these things do not come within so well-known a class with such well-defined attributes as motor vehicles."

---

(17) [1937] 1 All E.R. 170.
(18) [1952] 1 All E.R. 670; [1952] A.C. 515.
(19) [1952] 1 All E.R. at p. 670; [1952] A.C. at p. 520.
(20) [1952] 1 All E.R. at p. 673; [1952] A.C. at p. 523.
(21) [1952] 1 All E.R. at p. 674; [1952] A.C. at pp. 524, 525.
(22) [1960] 3 All E.R. 264; [1961] 1 Q.B. 136.
(23) [1960] 3 All E.R. at p. 268; [1961] 1 Q.B. at p. 147.

I think that it might have surprised those members of this court to be told that **A** their decision would be relied on as an authority for excluding mobile cranes from the ambit of the Factories Acts.

If I approach this problem using my common sense, as I have been invited to do by both counsel, I would have thought that a mobile crane used in a factory is much closer in its character to a piece of factory machinery than it is to a motor vehicle such as a Lister truck. If the argument advanced by the defen- **B** dants is correct, at least as startling results would follow as the results which the defendants contend would flow from this appeal being allowed. Imagine a factory in which there is a crane mounted on a fixed platform; the mechanical parts which operate the crane are unfenced. Some workman inserts some part of his anatomy into those moveable parts and is injured; clearly the occupiers of the factory have contravened the statute and are liable to pay the workman **C** damages. Imagine the same factory and precisely the same type of crane mounted on a mobile chassis. The only function of each crane is to lift. Neither of them has any other function; the only difference between the two is that one is mobile and the other is static. In the second case the workman is injured in precisely the same way as in the first case, yet in the second case (if the argument on behalf of the defendants is sound) the occupiers of the factory escape liability **D** —on no principle that I can imagine save the novel one that mobility spells immunity. *Cherry's* case (24) is certainly no authority for so startling a proposition. In my judgment a crane used for sorting purposes in a factory such as the one under consideration in the present case is part of the factory equipment, and falls within the provisions of the Factories Act, 1961, whether it be mobile or static. That, as I desire to emphasise, is the only point that has been raised **E** on this appeal. I emphasise that point because I do not wish it to be thought that I am deciding that the parts of the crane with which this unfortunate plaintiff came into contact are parts of machinery within the meaning of s. 14. I expressly desire to reserve that point. I have not even formed a provisional view about it. No point has been taken as to whether the wheel or the other part of the crane which came into contact with the plaintiff is a " *part* of any **F** machinery " to which s. 14 of the Factories Act, 1961, applies. No cross-notice was served to raise this point. Counsel for the defendants at first told us that the defendants had decided not to raise it. Just before the conclusion of his speech, however, he asked for leave to serve a cross-notice raising the point. The defendants are, of course, at liberty to change their minds, but we refused leave as we considered that the application had come much too late. Counsel for **G** the plaintiff was not in a position to deal with the point sought to be raised at the eleventh hour. I do not know what conclusion I might have reached on this point had it been raised.

I am clearly of the opinion, however, on the only point which has been argued, that the appeal should be allowed.

Appeal allowed.   Leave to appeal to the House of Lords granted. **H**

Solicitors: *Gibson & Weldon*, agents for *John Whittle, Robinson & Bailey*, Manchester (for the plaintiff); *M. H. B. Gilmour* (for the defendants).

[*Reported by* F. A. AMIES, ESQ., *Barrister-at-Law.*]

I

(24) [1960] 3 All E.R. 264; [1961] 1 Q.B. 136.

A

SHELDON *v.* SHELDON.

[COURT OF APPEAL (Lord Denning, M.R., Davies and Salmon, L.JJ.), November 11, 1965, February 21, March 31, 1966.]

Divorce—Cruelty—Intercourse—Refusal by husband of intercourse for six years after normal intercourse for eight years—Injury to wife's health—Absence of justification—Husband's conduct by such refusal amounting to cruelty.

B

A young couple married and lived together, having normal sexual intercourse. Eight years later the husband's work took him to Scotland for a year. After his return he and his wife again lived together, but he never had sexual intercourse with her, although they slept together and she asked him to, herself wanting a child. In consequence she became ill. He knew

C

that his refusal was affecting her health for this was explained to him by her doctor. He had no infirmity. After six years she left him, and took proceedings for divorce on the ground of cruelty.

Held: the husband's persistent refusal of sexual intercourse over so long a period without excuse, causing grave injury to his wife's health, amounted to cruelty on his part; accordingly she would be granted a decree

D

nisi (see p. 261, letters B and C, p. 263, letters C and D, and p. 265, letter E, post).

Gollins v. *Gollins* ([1963] 2 All E.R. 966) and *Williams* v. *Williams* ([1963] 2 All E.R. 994) applied.

Clark v. *Clark* (1958, " The Times ", June 25) and *Hayes* v. *Hayes* ((1958), unreported) criticised as no longer binding authorities.

E

Per SALMON, L.J.: if the evidence in the present case had been equally consistent with impotence as with wilful refusal, the decree would have been rightly refused, for impotence is not a ground of divorce (see p. 264, letters G and I, post).

P. v. *P.* ([1964] 3 All E.R. 919) and *P. (D.)* v. *P. (J.)* ([1965] 2 All E.R. 456) considered.

F

Appeal allowed.

[As to refusal of sexual intercourse constituting cruelty, see 12 HALSBURY'S LAWS (3rd Edn.) 275, para. 527, notes (k) and (l); and for cases on the subject, see DIGEST (Cont. Vol. A) 286, *2441b-2441d.*]

Cases referred to:

G

B. (L.) v. *B. (R.)*, [1965] 3 All E.R. 263; [1965] 1 W.L.R. 1413.

Baxter v. *Baxter*, [1947] 2 All E.R. 886; [1948] A.C. 274; [1948] L.J.R. 479; 27 Digest (Repl.) 280, *2253.*

Bravery v. *Bravery*, [1954] 3 All E.R. 59; [1954] 1 W.L.R. 1169; Digest (Cont. Vol. A) 710, *2537c.*

Cackett (otherwise Trice) v. *Cackett*, [1950] 1 All E.R. 677; [1950] P. 253; 27

H

Digest (Repl.) 281, *2259.*

Clark v. *Clark*, (1958), " The Times ", June 25; [1958] C.L.Y. 968.

Evans v. *Evans*, [1965] 2 All E.R. 789.

Gollins v. *Gollins*, [1963] 2 All E.R. 966; [1964] A.C. 644; [1963] 3 W.L.R. 176; Digest (Cont. Vol. A) 705, *2416a.*

Hayes v. *Hayes*, (1958), unreported.

I

Kaslefsky v. *Kaslefsky*, [1950] 2 All E.R. 398; [1951] P. 38; 114 J.P. 404; 27 Digest (Repl.) 296, *2413.*

Knott v. *Knott*, [1955] 2 All E.R. 305; [1955] P. 249; [1955] 3 W.L.R. 162; Digest (Cont. Vol. A) 706, *2441a.*

Lawrance v. *Lawrance*, [1950] P. 84; 27 Digest (Repl.) 366, *3031.*

P. v. *P.*, [1964] 3 All E.R. 919; 3rd Digest Supp.

P. (D.) v. *P. (J.)*, [1965] 2 All E.R. 456; [1965] 1 W.L.R. 963.

Walsham v. *Walsham*, [1949] 1 All E.R. 774; [1949] P. 350; [1948] L.J.R. 1476; 27 Digest (Repl.) 299, *2440.*

White (otherwise Berry) v. *White,* [1948] 2 All E.R. 151; [1948] P. 330; [1948] A
    L.J.R. 1476; 27 Digest (Repl.) 281, *2258.*
Williams v. *Williams,* [1963] 2 All E.R. 994; [1964] A.C. 698; [1963] 3 W.L.R.
    215; Digest (Cont. Vol. A) 711, *2537e.*

Appeal.

This was an appeal by the wife petitioner from a judgment of His Honour
JUDGE CARR sitting at Worcester as a special commissioner in divorce, dated B
June 30, 1965, dismissing the undefended petition of the wife on the ground that
mere refusal to have sexual intercourse did not in law amount to cruelty.   When
the appeal came on in November, 1965, the Court of Appeal adjourned the
hearing to enable the Queen's Proctor to instruct counsel to argue the point of
law.   The facts are stated in the judgment of LORD DENNING, M.R.
                                                                      C

K. Bruce Campbell, Q.C., and *R. F. Solman* for the wife.
The husband did not appear and was not represented.
N. H. Curtis-Raleigh for the Queen's Proctor.

                                                   Cur. adv. vult.

Mar. 31, 1966.   The following judgments were read.

                                                                  D

LORD DENNING, M.R.: On July 8, 1950, Richard Sheldon, then aged
twenty-six, married Barbara Sellers, then aged twenty-one.   For the first eight
years they were reasonably happy and had sexual intercourse together in a
normal way.   In 1958 the husband had to go on his work to Scotland for about
a year.   He came home occasionally for weekends; but he never had sexual
intercourse with his wife on these visits.   He returned from Scotland after a E
year and went back home to his wife; but he never had sexual intercourse with
his wife.   They were sleeping together in the same bed.   She asked him to have
intercourse with her.   He refused.   She asked him why.   He would give no
reason.   He just said: " Leave it."   She said that she would like to have a child;
but he would not discuss it.   He would not say anything at all.   In consequence
she became ill.   In 1960 she went to the doctor.   The doctor found that she was F
suffering from depression and sexual frustration due to her unhappy sexual
relationship with her husband.   The doctor treated her with sedative drugs and
reassurance, but he was not successful in alleviating her condition.   The doctor
then spoke to the husband and explained to him that his conduct, in refusing
to allow her to have children and his refusal of sexual intercourse, was affecting
her health.   Still the husband did nothing.   She spoke to him and told him it G
was affecting her health.   His attitude is best shown by the wife's answer to the
judge:

    " (Q)—What did he say when you said it (her illness) was because you
were not having intercourse with him?   (A)—He said he was no longer
physically attracted to me.

    " (Q)—You had no reason to suppose he was associating with another H
woman?   (A)—He was, definitely.

    " (Q)—Did you know that?   (A)—I can't prove it.   I haven't got it in
black and white, but I do know he had various girl friends over the years.

    " (Q)—Did he admit it to you?   (A)—He said they were only friends."

Eventually the wife moved from his bed into another room: and finally in
February, 1964, she left him.   She was in a very bad state of health, owing to his I
conduct.   A year later, on Feb. 20, 1965, she brought this petition for divorce
alleging that her husband had treated her with cruelty.   The petition was heard
by JUDGE CARR at Worcester.   The husband did not defend; but the judge
felt bound to dismiss the petition.   He said:

    " I should have liked to have been able to hold that that amounted to
cruelty . . . but, as I understand it, this case stands or falls on whether the
mere refusal of sexual intercourse amounts to cruelty and on the authorities

A quoted to me, I am afraid I am bound to say—although I have the greatest sympathy with [the wife]—that it does not, and therefore the petition must be dismissed."

When the case came before us, we saw that a point of some importance arose and we adjourned the case so as to obtain the assistance of the Queen's Proctor. We have now had the benefit of it. One thing emerged quite clearly from the

B discussion. Counsel for the Queen's Proctor submitted that this was a case of cruelty or nothing. If the husband's conduct did amount to cruelty, the wife was justified in leaving him and should get a divorce. If it did not amount to cruelty, she was not justified in leaving him. She ought to have stayed there, even though her health was suffering greatly. By leaving him she was guilty of desertion. We can put aside, therefore, the refinements of "just cause" for

C desertion, and of "constructive desertion" and come down to the root question: was the husband guilty of cruelty or the wife guilty of desertion? For it must be one or the other. I should be reluctant on these facts to find this wife guilty of desertion, seeing how her husband treated her. I should prefer to hold him guilty of cruelty. Can it be done?

Before the decisions of the House of Lords in *Gollins* v. *Gollins* (1) and *Williams*

D v. *Williams* (2) many of us would have said, as Hodson, L.J., said in *Clark* v. *Clark* (3)

   " the mere fact that sexual intercourse does not take place between the parties, even if that is because one unjustifiably refuses to have intercourse, if not of itself cruelty."

E We should not have held the refusal to be cruelty unless it was done with an intention to inflict misery. Both Bucknill, L.J., and I said as much in *Kaslefsky* v. *Kaslefsky* (4); but now *Kaslefsky* v. *Kaslefsky* (4) has been overruled. It has been laid down that in cruelty it is not necessary to show an intention to injure or inflict misery. Nor is it necessary to show a guilty mind. One essential element is injury or apprehended injury to health. In *Gollins* v. *Gollins* (5)

F Lord Pearce said:

   " In the light of the vital fact the court has then to decide whether the sum total of the reprehensible conduct was cruel. That depends on whether the cumulative conduct was sufficiently weighty to say that from a reasonable person's point of view, after a consideration of any excuses which the respondent might have in the circumstances, the conduct is such that the

G petitioner ought not to be called on to endure it."

The other essential element is that the conduct must be grave and weighty. In *Williams* v. *Williams* (6) Lord Reid said that

   ". . . after making all allowances for his disabilities and for the temperaments of both parties, it must be held that the character and gravity of his

H acts were such as to amount to cruelty."

The House of Lords did not set any limits to the kind of conduct which may constitute cruelty. The categories of cruelty are not closed. The persistent refusal of sexual intercourse is not excluded. It may amount to cruelty, at any rate when it extends over a long period, and causes grave injury to the health of the other. One must, of course, make allowances for any excuses that may

I account for it, such as ill-health, or time of life, or age, or even psychological infirmity. These excuses may so mitigate the conduct that the other party

---

(1) [1963] 2 All E.R. 966; [1964] A.C. 644.
(2) [1963] 2 All E.R. 994; [1964] A.C. 698.
(3) (1958), " The Times ", June 25. For a summary of this case, see [1964] 3 All E.R. at p. 924, footnote (22).
(4) [1950] 2 All E.R. 398; [1951] P. 38.
(5) [1963] 2 All E.R. at p. 992; [1964] A.C. at p. 695.
(6) [1965] 2 All E.R. at p. 1004; [1964] A.C. at p. 723.

ought to put up with it.   If, after making all allowances, however, the conduct **A**
is such that the other party should not be called on to endure it, then it is cruelty.

It may be helpful if I go through the cases before 1964 to see how far they
stand up to the new tests.   These following would plainly be decided the same
way.   When a husband persistently refused to have intercourse with his wife
and, when she complained, used offensive language to her; see *Lawrance* v.
Lawrance (7).   When a husband persistently refused to have intercourse with **B**
his wife except with contraceptives or by coitus interruptus, thereby depriving
his wife of the chance of having a child; see *White* (*otherwise Berry*) v. *White* (8);
Walsham v. *Walsham* (9); *Cackett* (*otherwise Trice*) v. *Cackett* (10); *Knott* v.
Knott (11).   And when a husband, without his wife's consent, got himself
sterilised so that he could perform the sexual act of intercourse but deprived
his wife of any chance of bearing a child: see *Bravery* v. *Bravery* (12).   I doubt, **C**
however, whether *Hayes* v. *Hayes* (13) and *Clark* v. *Clark* (14) would be decided
the same way now.

Since 1964 the cases stand in this way.   Two wives have been found guilty
of cruelty in refusing sexual intercourse.   Thus when a wife persistently refused
her husband completion of the act of sexual intercourse, she was held guilty of
cruelty, even though it was, in a sense, not her fault but was due to a deep-rooted **D**
fear of bearing a child.   Making all allowances for her psychological infirmity,
it was still cruelty; see *P.* (*D.*) v. *P.* (*J.*) (15).   Also where a wife persistently
refused her husband sexual intercourse, quite inexcusably, she was held guilty
of cruelty; see *Evans* v. *Evans* (16).   Two husbands, however, have been held
not guilty of cruelty.   Where a husband aged thirty-five with a young wife,
after the first year, refused altogether for fifteen years became of an innate **E**
disinclination for sexual intercourse, he was held not guilty of cruelty; see
P. v. *P.* (17).   Again, where a young husband aged twenty-seven was very
undersexed and completely disinclined for sexual intercourse with his young
wife, save at rare intervals; see *B.* (*L.*) v. *B.* (*R.*) (18).   Those were cases where,
on making just allowances, the man was to be excused.   The wife had to put
up with it. **F**

This is a very different case.   There is no suggestion of any infirmity on either
side.   Here we have a young couple who had a normal married life for eight
years.   Then the husband goes off to Scotland for a year: and thenceforward
for six years refuses to have any sexual intercourse with her at all.   He sleeps
in the same bed with her and still refuses.   He knows that it is injuring her
health.   The doctor tells him so.   Still he refuses.   Is there any excuse?   None **G**
that he has put forward save that he says she has ceased to be physically attractive to him.   But why is that?   Not because he is undersexed, or anything of
that sort.   The wife thinks that it is because he is associating with other women.
She may be right about this: because, after all, what young man of normal
instincts, in bed with his wife, will go on refusing for years to have sexual intercourse with her, unless he gets satisfaction elsewhere?   I do not, however, rest **H**
my opinion on any inference that he has committed adultery.   I do not think
that that would be right.   I rest my judgment on the ground that he has persistently, without the least excuse, refused her sexual intercourse for six years.
It has broken down her health.   I do not think that she was called on to endure
it any longer.

It has been said that, if abstinence from intercourse causing ill-health can be **I**

---

(7) [1950] P. 84.   (8) [1948] 2 All E.R. 151; [1948] P. 330.
(9) [1949] 1 All E.R. 774; [1949] P. 350.
(10) [1950] 1 All E.R. 677; [1950] P. 253.
(11) [1955] 2 All E.R. 305; [1955] P. 249.   (12) [1954] 3 All E.R. 59.
(13) (1958), unreported.   For a summary of this case, see [1964] 3 All E.R. at p. 923,
footnote (21).
(14) (1958), " The Times ", June 25.   (15) [1965] 2 All E.R. 456.
(16) [1965] 2 All E.R. 789.   (17) [1964] 3 All E.R. 919.
                    (18) [1965] 3 All E.R. 263.

A held to be cruelty, so should desertion simpliciter leading to the same result (see
P. v. *P.* (19) by Judge Harold Brown, Q.C.); but the two things are different.
It is one thing to live in the same house and sleep in the same bed and refuse
sexual intercourse. It is quite another to leave the house altogether. The real
difficulty that I see is to keep the matter within bounds. It may be said that, if
refusal of sexual intercourse is to be regarded as cruelty, we should be opening
B far too wide a door to divorce; but I do not think so. No spouse would have
any chance of obtaining a divorce on such a ground except after persistent
refusal for a long period; and it would usually need to be corroborated by the
evidence of a medical man who had seen both parties and could speak to the
grave injury to health consequent thereon.

   I come back to the alternative presented to us. Was the husband guilty of
C cruelty? Or the wife guilty of desertion? It is one or the other. On the facts
of this case I would hold that she is not guilty of desertion, and that she was
justified in leaving him because of his cruelty. I would, therefore, pronounce
a decree nisi on the grounds of the husband's cruelty.

   DAVIES, L.J.: On the facts of this case, which have been fully stated by
D Lord Denning, M.R., the learned commissioner would undoubtedly have
granted a decree to the petitioner had he not been of the opinion that on the
authorities a refusal of sexual intercourse, even though resulting in injury to the
health of the other spouse, cannot as a matter of law amount to cruelty. The
question for decision is whether he was correct in so holding.

   In approaching the problem it is perhaps right to emphasise that we are here
E concerned with a complete cessation of sexual intercourse between a comparatively young married couple following on several years of ordinary normal
relations. This is not, therefore, such a case as *B.* (*L.*) v. *B.* (*R.*) (20), where the
petitioner's complaint was that acts of sexual intercourse were not sufficiently
frequent. Nor, on the other hand, is it a case where there has never been any
intercourse at all, a state of affairs which could, of course, result in a decree of
F nullity on the ground of incapacity or of wilful refusal.

   The authorities have been reviewed by Lord Denning and it is not necessary
therefore to go over the same ground. There are undoubtedly dicta in the
cases to the effect that a mere refusal of sexual intercourse cannot amount to
cruelty; see, for example, *Walsham* v. *Walsham* (21), per Wallington, J.,
though that observation was obiter as the case was one of coitus interruptus.
G More important perhaps are the two unreported decisions of this court in 1958,
Hayes v. *Hayes* (22) and *Clark* v. *Clark* (23). In the former case Hodson, L.J.,
said that sexual maladjustment cannot be regarded as cruelty and does not
become cruelty by reason of its consequences. That case, however, was not
one of refusal of intercourse: the trouble there was that the husband was unable
to give sexual satisfaction to the wife; so that it might well be said that the
H effect on the wife's health was not caused by any act on the part of the husband.
Much closer to the present case was *Clark* (23). There the husband after two
years of marriage refused intercourse, and as a result the wife's health was affected.
This court affirmed the decision of the commissioner that the wife had failed to
make out a case of cruelty; and in the course of his judgment Hodson, L.J.,
said:

I   " The mere fact that sexual intercourse does not take place between the
      parties, even if that is because one unjustifiably refuses to have intercourse,
      is not of itself cruelty, and one has to consider each case on its particular
      facts before one can arrive at a just conclusion."
There are, however, two respects in which it may be said that the present case

---

(19) [1964] 3 All E.R. at p. 925.   (20) [1965] 3 All E.R. 263.
(21) [1949] 1 All E.R. at p. 775, letter D; [1949] P. at p. 352.
(22) (1958), unreported.   (23) (1958), " The Times ", June 25.

differs from *Clark* (24). In that case neither the wife nor the doctor whom she **A**
consulted spoke to the husband about the injury to her health which was being
caused by his abstinence. Secondly, and more important, it is reasonably plain
that the decision in *Clark* (24) was largely based on the decision in *Kaslefsky*
v. *Kaslefsky* (25); and *Kaslefsky* (25) has now been disapproved in *Gollins* v.
Gollins (26).

The authorities which tend the other way start with the oft-quoted words **B**
from the speech of LORD JOWITT, L.C., in *Baxter* v. *Baxter* (27). That expression
of opinion did not decide that conduct such as that here in question does
amount to cruelty, but it clearly contemplated that it might do so. Perhaps
the most important case is the decision of the DIVISIONAL COURT in *Lawrance*
v. *Lawrance* (28). It is true that there the wife had other matters of complaint,
such as neglect and obscene language; but LORD MERRIMAN, P., said (29): **C**

" . . . there is no doubt what is the real crux of this case: the fundamental
trouble was sexual . . . The wife's complaint, in effect, is this: the marriage
has been reduced to a shadow, to the mere simulacrum of a marriage, by
neglect and above all, by the refusal of ordinary conjugal rights to a wife
who ardently desired a child."

D

The court accordingly upheld the decision of magistrates who had found the
husband guilty of constructive desertion.

As LORD DENNING has said, however, the whole approach to this problem has
been changed by the decisions of the House of Lords in *Gollins* v. *Gollins* (26)
and *Williams* v. *Williams* (30). LORD DENNING, M.R., has referred to the
words of LORD PEARCE in the former case (31). To supplement that citation I **E**
would quote the words of LORD REID in the latter case (32) referred to by
STIRLING, J., in *P.* (*D.*) v. *P.* (*J.*) (33). LORD REID there said (32).

" Then we come to the really difficult cases if blameworthiness is to be a
test. There are many cases of husbands and wives not insane but either
sick in mind or body or so stupid, selfish or spoilt that they plainly do not
appreciate or foresee the harm which they are doing to the other spouse, **F**
and perhaps they are now so self-centred that nothing would ever get the
truth into their heads. Certainly allowances have to be made, particularly
when their condition is due to misfortune. But I suppose that no one would
now maintain that cruelty cannot be proved against such a person if his
acts are sufficiently grave and really imperil the other spouse.

" It is often untrue that such a man is able to exert his reason so as to **G**
control his acts in the normal way or even that he is capable of forming a
rational decision about them. Yet these are often the cases where the other
spouse is most in need of protection. It is difficult in some of these cases
to attribute more than a speck or scintilla of blame to the respondent in
the sense that he, not the reasonable man, ought to have realised the consequences of what he was doing and could have done otherwise if he had tried. **H**
If we are to make culpability an essential element in cruelty, we can really
only bring in these people by deeming them to have qualities and abilities
which the evidence shows that they do not possess. Surely it is much more
satisfactory to accept the fact that the test of culpability has broken down
and not to treat entirely differently two people one of whom is just short of
and the other just over the invisible line which separates abnormality **I**
from insanity.

---

(24) (1958), " The Times ", June 25.   (25) [1950] 2 All E.R. 398; [1951] P. 38.
(26) [1963] 2 All E.R. 966; [1964] A.C. 644.
(27) [1947] 2 All E.R. 886 at p. 892; [1948] A.C. 274 at p. 290.
(28) [1950] P. 84.   (29) [1950] P. at p. 87.
(30) [1963] 2 All E.R. 994; [1964] A.C. 698.
(31) [1963] 2 All E.R. at p. 992; [1964] A.C. at p. 695.
(32) [1963] 2 All E.R. at p. 1004; [1964] A.C. at pp. 722, 723.
(33) [1965] 2 All E.R. at pp. 462, 463.

A   " In my judgment, a decree should be pronounced against such an abnormal person, not because his conduct was aimed at his wife, nor because a reasonable man would have realised the position, nor because he must be deemed to have foreseen or intended the harm he did, but simply because the facts are such that, after making all allowances for his disabilities and for the temperaments of both parties, it must be held that the character and gravity of his acts

B   were such as to amount to cruelty."

It is, in my judgment, plain beyond argument that that principle applies to such a state of affairs as we find in the instant case. It might indeed well apply to a case in which the abstinence from sexual intercourse was caused by some physical or mental affliction; but it is not necessary for the purposes of the present appeal to pronounce on this point and I would expressly refrain from so doing. For

C   there is nothing here to indicate that the husband was unable to have sexual intercourse. The facts proved were that after eight years of marriage he ceased to have intercourse. That conduct injured his wife's health. She told him so and protested. So did the doctor. Yet the husband persisted in his course of conduct.

Such a case, in my view, falls four square within the principles enunciated by

D   the majority of the House of Lords in *Gollins* (34) and *Williams* (35), and there was accordingly nothing in law to prevent the learned commissioner from pronouncing a decree. On the facts of this case the wife, in my judgment, did establish that the husband had treated her with cruelty, and I would accordingly allow the appeal.

E   **SALMON, L.J.:** At the time of the marriage the husband was twenty-six and his wife twenty-one years of age. For the first eight years of the marriage, regular sexual intercourse took place between them in the normal way. After eight years of married life, the husband was sent to work in Scotland for a year. During that time he occasionally visited his wife at weekends, but he had no sexual intercourse with her on any of these occasions. After a year in Scotland

F   he returned home, but still he had no sexual intercourse with his wife. This, not unnaturally, distressed her and had a serious effect on her health. She told him so and asked him on many occasions why they were leading such an unnatural life. He refused to discuss the subject. When pressed he told her that he no longer found her physically attractive. Because of the effect that her husband's conduct was having on her health, she consulted their family doctor. The

G   doctor talked the matter over with the husband, but the husband gave no explanation at all about his extraordinary conduct. Eventually the wife left the husband in 1965 and brought this petition for divorce on the ground of cruelty. The bare facts that I have recited do in my judgment afford a basis from which cruelty may and should be inferred. It is true that in the unreported cases to which my lords have referred (*Clark* v. *Clark* (36) and *Hayes* v. *Hayes* (37))

H   this court held that an unjustified refusal of sexual intercourse cannot of itself amount to cruelty. This, I think, was because of the decision in *Kaslefsky* v. *Kaslefsky* (38), which held that an act to be cruel had to be aimed at the complaining spouse. Now that the *Kaslefsky* (38) case has been overruled, *Clark* v. *Clark* (36) and *Hayes* v. *Hayes* (37) are in my view no longer binding authorities. In my judgment the facts of the present case establish on a balance of probabilities

I   that this husband had no sexual intercourse with his wife, not because he could not, but because he would not, do so. He moreover persisted in his conduct knowing that it was causing a breakdown in his wife's health.

For my part I am quite satisfied that if the husband's failure to have sexual intercourse had been due to impotence, whether from some psychological or physical cause, this petition would have been hopeless. No doubt the lack of

---

(34) [1963] 3 All E.R. 966; [1964] A.C. 644.
(35) [1963] 2 All E.R. 994; [1964] A.C. 698.   (36) (1958), " The Times ", June 25.
(37) (1958), unreported.   (38) [1950] 2 All E.R. 398; [1951] P. 38.

sexual intercourse might in such a case equally have resulted in a breakdown A
in his wife's health. I would, however, regard the husband's impotence as a
great misfortune which had befallen both of them. I could not accept that, if
words have any meaning, a husband can in such circumstances truly be said to
be treating his wife with cruelty. I do not think that in *P. (D.)* v. *P. (J.)* (39)
STIRLING, J., intended to decide anything to the contrary. In that case the
wife had a psychological or morbid fear of bearing a child, and because of this B
allowed the husband to have sexual intercourse only very infrequently and then
only with contraceptives or practising coitus interruptus. She knew that
this conduct of hers was bringing her husband near to a nervous breakdown
but she persisted in it. Not surprisingly, the learned judge found cruelty against
her. She was quite capable of having sexual intercourse in the normal way but
she refused to do so because of her morbid fear of bearing a child. Nor do I C
consider that *Gollins* v. *Gollins* (40) and *Williams* v. *Williams* (41), would compel
me to hold that true impotence by itself can ever amount to cruelty. As I
understand the speeches in *Gollins* v. *Gollins* (40), conduct to be cruel must still
be inexcusable. It is manifestly impossible to say that a man who is impotent
has no good excuse for not having sexual intercourse with his wife. In *Williams*
v. *Williams* (41) the husband had insane delusions that his wife was consorting D
with other men. He was cruel for he persisted in continually accusing her of
immoral behaviour, although he knew that his accusations were making her ill.
He did what he did of his own volition and with knowledge of its effect on his
wife. His reason or motive for doing it was that he had the insane belief that
what he was saying was true. There are many obiter dicta of persuasive
authority in that case. There is, however, nothing in the actual decision E
which would bind us to hold that impotence which is not the husband's fault
and is necessarily involuntary could be a basis for cruelty.

The law has always recognised that in marriage the parties take each other
"for better for worse, for richer for poorer, in sickness and in health". The
law also recognises that a husband and wife normally enter into a contract of
marriage on the fundamental assumption that they are each capable of con- F
summating the marriage and that it will be consummated. Accordingly, if the
marriage is not consummated, it may be annulled. Once the marriage has been
consummated, the law will grant either party a divorce on any of the following
grounds: (i) Adultery. (ii) Desertion. (iii) Cruelty. (iv) In certain circumstances
incurable insanity. The first three grounds have generally been regarded as
matrimonial offences. The last ground—incurable insanity—is in no sense an G
offence, nor is impotence, both are illnesses. Incurable insanity is the only
illness which Parliament has made a ground for divorce. Whilst it is an important function of our courts to mould and develop the common law to meet the
changing needs of time, the courts have no power to add a ground for divorce
to the Matrimonial Causes Act, 1950. If Parliament had intended to make
impotence as well as incurable insanity a ground for divorce, it would no doubt H
have done so. There are some who believe that a complete breakdown of a
marriage should be a ground for divorce. Whether this should be so is a matter
of public policy, which is of the greatest social importance and is essentially for
Parliament to decide. The courts cannot do so—certainly not by putting on
the meaning of the word "cruelty" a strain which it is wholly unable to bear.

Accordingly, if in the present case the evidence was equally consistent with I
impotence as with a wilful refusal of intercourse, the commissioner would have
been right in refusing a decree. It seems to me, however, that this evidence
establishes wilful refusal. At the time that intercourse ceased the husband was
only about thirty-four years of age and for eight years previously he had had
normal sexual intercourse with his wife. He never at any time suggested that

---

(39) [1965] 2 All E.R. 456.   (40) [1963] 2 All E.R. 996; [1964] A.C. 644.
                    (41) [1963] 2 All E.R. 994; [1964] A.C. 698.

A he was impotent even when he was told by his wife and the family doctor that his conduct was making his wife ill. Of course it is possible that he had become impotent but was ashamed to admit it. It is, however, in my view very much more likely that he was not having intercourse with his wife because he preferred to satisfy his sexual appetite elsewhere. In these circumstances when a man knows that his young wife is being made ill through sexual starvation, it is indeed

B cruel for him wilfully to refuse her sexual intercourse.

We have been referred by counsel for the Queen's Proctor to the judgment of Judge Harold Brown, Q.C., in P. v. P. (42). I am greatly impressed by that judgment but the facts of that case were very different, for there the husband was virtually impotent. I appreciate the difficulties which may arise in cases such as the present. It may be asked what if a wife is made ill not because of

C total abstinence from sexual intercourse, but because after many years of normal sexual relationship, her young husband has sexual intercourse with her only very infrequently—and knows that because of this she is becoming a nervous wreck. His behaviour might be suspicious but it seems to me that in such a case it would usually be very difficult, if not impossible, to draw any inference save that his conduct was due to a natural abatement of his sexual powers. If, of

D course, the evidence became available that the husband's behaviour was in fact due to some other cause, then his conduct might in my judgment amount to cruelty. The question whether or not desertion can ever be a ground of cruelty does not arise in this case, and I prefer to express no view about it; much would necessarily depend on the facts of each particular case. I desire only to emphasise that in the present case there was persistent refusal over a long period

E without any explanation by a young man who had shown himself to be virile, and that there was abundant corroboration that his conduct was, to his knowledge, causing grave injury to his wife's health. Without such a combination of facts, it would not in my view be possible for a wife to obtain a decree for cruelty based on a refusal of sexual intercourse. On the particular facts of this case, however, I consider that the husband's conduct was inexcusable and that the wife is

F entitled to succeed.

I would allow the appeal accordingly.

Appeal allowed. Decree nisi granted and made absolute forthwith.

Solicitors: *Robbins, Olivey & Lake*, agents for *Weston, Fisher & Weston*, Kidderminster (for the wife); *Treasury Solicitor.*

G   [*Reported by* F. Guttman, Esq., *Barrister-at-Law.*]

H

I

---

(42) [1964] **3** All E.R. 919.

A

BECKER *v.* PARTRIDGE.

[COURT OF APPEAL (Lord Denning, M.R., Danckwerts and Salmon, L.JJ.), February 4, 7, 8, 9, March 4, 1966.]

Sale of Land—Title—Leasehold—Disclosure—Contractual provision that vendor's B
title accepted—Vendor's duty to disclose any defect of which he knows or ought
to know—Vendor's sub-underlease granted in breach of covenant in underlease
which was thus liable to forfeiture—Underlease not inspected by vendor's
solicitor on occasion of sub-letting to vendor—Whether purchaser entitled to
rescission.

Sale of Land—Lease—Sub-underlease of flat described by vendor in contract of
sale as " underlease "—Flat comprised in head lease which included other C
flats in same former house—Enforceability of contract of sale.

On assignment of an underlease the assignee, S., covenanted to observe the tenant's covenants in the underlease, which included a covenant not to assign or underlet without the reversioner's consent. The underlease contained a proviso for re-entry on breach of covenant. S. sub-let the second floor flat to P., but the reversioner's consent to the sub-letting was D not obtained. P.'s solicitors did not inspect the underlease and accepted an oral communication by S.'s husband that no consent to the sub-letting was needed; consequently P. had constructive notice, but not actual knowledge, of the requirement of consent and of liability to forfeiture for failure to obtain it. P. agreed to sell his sub-lease of the second floor flat. Clause 3 of the contract provided that the " vendor's title which has been accepted by the E purchaser shall commence with an underlease dated Dec. 28, 1963 [which was the sub-lease to P.] and the purchaser shall raise no requisition or objection thereon ". The purchaser applied to S. for consent to the assignment and S. communicated this to the reversioner, whose solicitors intimated that, as rent was overdue and there were outstanding breaches of covenant, consent could not be given. The purchaser elected to treat the contract as F discharged and brought an action in the county court for rescission. On appeal against dismissal of the claim,

Held: since the vendor, P., had not disclosed the defect in his title which it was his duty to disclose when cl. 3 was included in the contract, the purchaser was not precluded from relying on the defect; accordingly the purchaser was entitled to rescission (see p. 270, letter I, and p. 271, G letters F and G, post).

Re Haedicke and Lipski's Contract ([1901] 2 Ch. 666) and principle stated by LORD ELDON, L.C., in *Jenkins* v. *Hiles* ((1802), 6 Ves. at p. 655) approved.

Quaere whether the description of a sub-underlease as an " underlease " was a sufficient misdescription to give rise to a right of rescission (see p. 270, letter E, post). H

Re Russ and Brown's Contract ([1933] All E.R. Rep. 997) and *Re Beyfus and Masters' Contract* ((1888), 39 Ch.D. 110) considered.

Per CURIAM: the objection, on a sale of leaseholds, that the property sold is included with other property in the headlease (see *Re Lloyds Bank, Ltd. and Lillington's Contract* ([1912] 1 Ch. 601) is weakened if the property is part of a house and so would almost certainly be the subject of a letting of the I whole house (see p. 270, letter H, post).

Appeal allowed.

[As to a vendor of land's duty to disclose defects of title, see 34 HALSBURY'S LAWS (3rd Edn.) 218, 219, para. 362; as to this duty in relation to leasehold land, see ibid., pp. 221, 222, paras. 366, 367; as to stipulations for acceptance of vendor's title, see ibid., p. 239, 240, para. 401, and for cases on these subjects, see 40 DIGEST (Repl.) 143-145, *1093-1114*.]

A　Cases referred to:

　　Beyfus and Masters' Contract, Re, (1888), 39 Ch.D. 110; 59 L.T. 740; 53 J.P.
　　　293; 40 Digest (Repl.) 153, *1174*.

　　Haedicke and Lipski's Contract, Re, [1901] 2 Ch. 666; 70 L.J.Ch. 811; 85 L.T.
　　　402; 40 Digest (Repl.) 145, *1111*.

　　Jenkins v. *Hiles*, (1802), 6 Ves. 646; 31 E.R. 1238; 44 Digest (Repl.) 138, *1142*.

B　*Lloyds Bank, Ltd. and Lillington's Contract, Re*, [1912] 1 Ch. 601; 81 L.J.Ch.
　　　386; 106 L.T. 561; 40 Digest (Repl.) 152, *1165*.

　　Russ and Brown's Contract, Re, [1933] All E.R. Rep. 997; [1934] Ch. 34; 103
　　　L.J.Ch. 12; 150 L.T. 125; 40 Digest (Repl.) 153, *1179*.

Appeal.

C
　　This was an appeal by the plaintiff, Mrs. Becker, the purchaser under a contract
of sale of a leasehold flat, from the refusal of His Honour JUDGE SIR ALUN PUGH,
at Bloomsbury County Court on July 28, 1965, to recall the judgment given by
him on July 20, 1965, dismissing the purchaser's claim for rescission of the contract
and ordering specific performance of it, which had been counterclaimed by the
defendant vendor, Mr. Partridge. The facts are stated in the judgment.

D　　*R. A. Scaramanga* for the purchaser.
　　V. G. Wellings for the vendor.

　　　　　　　　　　　　　　　　　　　　　　　　　　　　Cur. adv. vult.

　　Mar. 4. **DANCKWERTS, L.J.**, read the following judgment of the court:
This is an appeal from a judgment of His Honour JUDGE SIR ALUN PUGH dated
E　July 28, 1965, at Bloomsbury County Court.　　That judgment was in fact a
judgment refusing an application to recall the judgment of the learned county
court judge delivered on July 20, 1965. The action was by a purchaser for rescission of her agreement to purchase the residue of an underlease of a second floor
flat at 27, Devonshire Place, St. Marylebone in the County of London, with a
counterclaim for specific performance by the vendor. By his judgment of July 20,
F　1965, the learned county court judge dismissed the claim for rescission and ordered
specific performance of the agreement on the counterclaim with certain
consequential relief.

　　By the agreement of Oct. 26, 1964 (cl. 1), Mr. Partridge, the defendant vendor,
agreed to sell and Mrs. Becker, the plaintiff purchaser, agreed to purchase the
property described in Sch. 1 and Sch. 3 at the price of £250, which had been
G　placed on deposit at the Westminster Bank, Marylebone, in the joint names of the
vendor's and the purchaser's solicitors. Clause 2 incorporated the Law Society's
Conditions of Sale, 1953 (thereinafter referred to as " the general conditions ")
so far as they were not varied by or inconsistent therewith and were applicable to
a sale by private treaty, and subject also to the special conditions therein
contained. Clause 3 of the contract was in these terms:

H　　　" The vendor's title which has been accepted by the purchaser shall com-
　　mence with an underlease dated Dec. 28, 1963, and the purchaser shall raise
　　no requisition or objection thereon."

　　Clause 4 provided that completion of the sale and purchase would take place on
Dec. 23, 1964, when vacant possession of the property would be given. Clause
I　5 provided that the vendor was selling as beneficial owner. By cl. 7 it was provided
that the property was also sold subject to and with the benefit of the matters
referred to in Sch. 2 thereto and copies of any documents referred to therein
having been produced to the purchaser, she should be deemed to purchase with
full knowledge thereof and should raise no requisition or objection thereto.
Clause 8 provided that the sale included the chattels, fittings and other separate
items specified in Sch. 3 thereto, the proportion of the said purchase price
attributable thereto being £250 (which was in fact the whole price). The
description of the property in Sch. 1 was:

"All that flat comprising three living rooms, hall, kitchen and bathroom   A
situated on the second floor of the building known as 27, Devonshire Place,
St. Marylebone in the County of London together with and subject to the
rights granted and reserved and subject to the covenants and conditions
contained in the underlease referred to in cl. 3 hereof."

Schedule 2 was in these terms:

"Matters referred to in cl. 7. The provisions of the underlease dated   B
Dec. 28, 1963, made between Pauline Mary Smith of the first part and the
vendor of the second part referred to in cl. 3 hereof."

The reason for the payment of the sum of £250 into the Westminster Bank was
that the purchaser entered into possession of the property on Oct. 26, 1964, the
date of the agreement. She thereby became subject to the terms of No. 6 of the   C
general conditions which (amongst other things) required her "to pay all rents,
rates, taxes, costs of insurance and repairs and other outgoings in respect of the
property", and required her also to pay interest on the purchase money. There
was also a provision in the same condition that if the vendor should at any time
in writing so demand or if the contract were rescinded or should become void,
the purchaser should forthwith deliver up possession of the property to the   D
vendor in as good a state of repair and condition as it was at the time of taking
possession.

Owing to the provisions of s. 44 (2) and s. 45 (1) of the Law of Property Act,
1925, the underlease of Dec. 28, 1963, provided for as the commencement of title
in cl. 3 of the agreement, was in fact the same as that provided for by law and the
purchaser's enquiries were restricted accordingly. The assumptions, however,   E
which s. 45 (1) and s. 45 (3) require a purchaser to make are only "unless the contrary appears"; and unless a purchaser is prohibited from raising objection to
the title by a bona fide and clear special condition, a purchaser will not be prevented from objecting to the vendor's title by reason of a defect which the
purchaser discovers by other means.

The authorities in regard to this matter will be discussed later, but meanwhile   F
it is necessary to consider the devolution of this leasehold flat. This starts with a
lease dated Jan. 2, 1957, by Howard de Walden Estates, Ltd. to Miss Margaret
Eileen Alexander of 27, Devonshire Place (the whole house) for the sixteen years
from July 6, 1956 (i.e., to July 5, 1972) at a rent of £500 per annum. There is a
restriction of use to (a) a private dwelling house and (b) self-contained private
residential flats (except the basement, which is only to be used for the service   G
of other parts). There is also a covenant against making alterations without
the lessor's licence in writing; and there is a condition of re-entry on failure to
pay rent or breach of covenant. On July 23, 1959, there was an underlease by
Cily Sophie Behr to Ernest Geoffrey Williams of the second, third and fourth
floors for a term from June 24, 1959, to July 1, 1972, at a rent of £525 per annum
plus fire insurance. There were covenants not to make alterations, to use and   H
to occupy as a private dwellinghouse or as two private residential flats, and not to
assign, underlet, etc., without the landlord's consent in writing (not to be unreasonably withheld); and there was a condition for re-entry.

On Aug. 8, 1961, there was a licence by Howard de Walden Estates, Ltd. to
Mrs. Esther Caseley-Hayford (who apparently had acquired the reversion on the
term granted by Cily Sophie Behr to Ernest Geoffry Willliams) to carry out cer-   I
tain alterations on the fourth floor. A Mr. Sigsworth was to be allowed to occupy
the second and third floors for residential purposes until July 1, 1963, but he was
not to underlet or part with possession of any part of the second and third
floors; and a Mr. Truscott who was to be allowed to occupy the fourth floor till
July 1, 1963, but was not to underlet or part with the possession of any part of
the fourth floor. Howard de Walden Estates, Ltd. were evidently keeping a close
control over the premises. On Mar. 7, 1962, Mrs. Caseley-Hayford licensed Ernest
Geoffrey Williams to underlet the fourth floor to Mr. Truscott and the second and

A third floors to Mr. Bigsworth in each case to July 1, 1963. On Mar. 7, 1962, Mrs. Caseley-Hayford granted a licence to Ernest Geoffrey Williams to assign the second, third and fourth floors to Mrs. Pauline Mary Smith for the residue of his term ending on July 1, 1972, and Mrs. Smith covenanted with Mrs. Caseley-Hayford to pay the rent and perform and observe the tenant's covenants in the lease of July 23, 1959. On Mar. 23, 1962, Ernest Geoffrey Williams in consideration

B of £1,500 assigned his leasehold term to Mrs. Pauline Mary Smith.

By an underlease dated Dec. 28, 1963, Mrs. Pauline Mary Smith sublet the second floor flat to the defendant vendor, Mr. Partridge, for a term from Dec. 25, 1963, to June 2, 1972, at the yearly rent of £520 and by way of additional rent forty per cent. of the insurance premium. There was a covenant not to assign, underlet or part with possession of any part of the premises, but a provision that

C the tenant might assign or underlet the whole of the premises to a person who should be approved by the landlord; and there was the usual condition for re-entry. Apparently Mrs. Pauline Mary Smith did not trouble to obtain or ask for the consent of Mrs. Caseley-Hayford to the underletting by Mrs. Smith to the vendor.

On Dec. 24, 1963, the vendor's solicitors wrote to Mr. Smith (Mrs. Smith's

D husband who apparently managed her business affairs) a letter from which it appears that they had been told over the telephone by Mr. Smith that no consent was required to the underletting and that he was not aware of any reason which would prevent the underlease being granted in the agreed terms—they seem to have accepted Mr. Smith's statement as true and did not ask for inspection of the underlease to Ernest Geoffrey Williams and the licence to assign to Mrs.

E Smith, which would have revealed that the consent of Mrs. Caseley-Hayford, as the reversioner, was required to the underletting by the terms of the lease under which Ernest Geoffrey Williams held and the licence granted by Mrs. Caseley-Hayford to the assignment by him to Mrs. Smith under Mrs. Smith's covenant in the licence. This was a terrible mistake because, unlike the plaintiff purchaser, the vendor was entitled by law to call for the lease out of which the underlease

F by Mrs. Smith to him was to be granted. As a result of this, the vendor was affected by constructive notice of the requirement of consent to the underletting to him and the liability to forfeiture by reason of the breach of covenant against underletting without consent.

On Oct. 14, 1964, the purchaser's solicitors applied for Mrs. Smith's licence to assign and for formal receipts for the last payment of rent. On Oct. 16, 1964,

G Mr. Smith wrote that he had submitted the purchaser's references to Mrs. Smith's superior landlord for approval but that he understood that she was touring abroad. On Oct. 26, 1964, the deeds of assignment were signed by the parties and, as already mentioned, the purchaser entered into possession of the property. On Oct. 28, 1964, a letter of Oct. 27 was received by the purchaser's solicitors from Mrs. Caseley-Hayford's solicitors stating that the rent under Mrs. Smith's lease

H was considerably overdue and that there were also outstanding breaches of covenant with regard to sublettings and unauthorised alterations. The letter added that until such time as the rent should be paid and Mrs. Caseley-Hayford's and the freeholder's requirements in connexion with the other breaches complied with, no licences could be issued. A copy of this letter was sent to the vendor's solicitors on Oct. 28. After further correspondence, the purchaser's solicitors

I wrote on Jan. 8, 1965, to the vendor's solicitors that the purchaser had no alternative but to treat the contract as discharged and requested the vendor's solicitors to treat that letter as formal notification thereto (meaning I suppose " thereof "). The letter added that the purchaser was then making arrangements to vacate the premises without delay.

The points taken on behalf of the purchaser in that letter were (i) that the interest of the vendor was a sub-underlease instead of an underlease as contracted to be sold; (ii) that no consent by the immediate superior landlord to the underletting had been obtained; and (iii) breaches of covenant in respect of the alterations.

On Feb. 1, 1965, the purchaser's solicitors delivered particulars of claim in A
Bloomsbury County Court. In addition to the above-mentioned three points
(which were raised in the particulars of claim) a fourth point was raised on
behalf of the purchaser in her reply and defence to counterclaim, that the property
agreed to be sold was comprised with other property in the head lease and that
this was never disclosed to the plaintiff. As already mentioned, the learned county
court judge gave judgment for the defendant vendor on the claim and gave judg- B
ment for the defendant vendor on the counterclaim for specific performance.
The application on July 28, 1965, for recall of the judgment was dismissed and
so the judgment of July 20, 1965, stands.

One curious feature of the case is that at the date of the hearing before us the
purchaser was still in possession of the property and had paid no rent except by a
sum of £130 which was taken out of the deposit made in respect of the purchase C
money. There was discussion in the arguments on the question whether the purchaser had thereby waived her objections to the title; but we think that this
point cannot be pressed in the circumstances. The point was certainly not taken
expressly in the defence and counterclaim. It seems to have been raised at the
hearing, but the learned county court judge does not seem to have dealt with the
point or to have decided whether leave to amend was necessary. In any case it D
was said on behalf of the purchaser that, if the point had been properly raised, the
circumstances would have shown that the purchaser remained in possession, after
the question of rescission had been raised, by agreement between the parties and
without prejudice to the position. In the circumstances we do not think that it
would be right to decide the case on this point.

As to the alleged misdescription of the vendor's title as not being by underlease, E
there is some authority supporting this kind of point in *Re Russ and Brown's
Contract* (1), and *Re Beyfus and Masters' Contract* (2); but we feel doubt whether
the rule stated in these cases should be applied in the circumstances of the present
case. The document under which the vendor holds was described therein as an
" underlease ", and in some senses it is an underlease. The term " sub-
underlease " is not really a conveyancing expression in established use. F

As to the alleged breach by alterations, it seems possible that these may
have been waived. Presumably they were made when the second floor was made
into a separate flat, and rent may have been accepted with knowledge of the
alterations, but, if this is not so, then of course this may be a ground of forfeiture
in addition to the more serious grounds of underletting without consent and
non-payment of rent. G

The objection that the property sold was included with other property in the
headlease is supported by *Re Lloyds Bank, Ltd. and Lillington's Contract* (3),
the reason being that this fact subjects the purchaser to the risk of forfeiture
owing to the acts of persons over whom he has no control; but this is weakened
in the present case by the fact that the property is part of a house, and it is
practically obvious that it would almost certainly be the subject of a letting of H
the whole house. It was pointed out on behalf of the vendor that no steps had yet
been taken by the superior landlords (including Mrs. Caseley-Hayford) to enforce
the forfeiture of the property under the conditions for re-entry; but the letter
from Mrs. Caseley-Hayford's solicitors of Oct. 27, 1964, clearly indicates that she
is alive to the point, and if an interest in leaseholds is subject to determination
by the exercise of a right of re-entry for breaches of covenant which have already I
been committed, then that is a title which is not a good title, for it is defeasible.

There remains, therefore, the most important point whether the purchaser is
precluded from taking objection by reason of the provisions of cl. 3 of the agreement. It was argued by counsel for the purchaser that the words in the clause
" the vendor's title which has been accepted by the purchaser " were limited in

(1) [1933] All E.R. Rep. 997; [1934] Ch. 34.   (2) (1888), 39 Ch.D. 110.
(3) [1912] 1 Ch. 601.

A meaning to the title which the purchaser by her solicitors had seen, i.e., the document of Dec. 28, 1963, referred to in the schedules to the agreement. We doubt whether, in view of the words " and the purchaser shall raise no requisition or objection thereon " (i.e., on the vendor's title) that argument can prevail. Anyhow, assuming that the clause should be given the wider meaning, that of precluding objection to the vendor's title, there is a further difficulty in the vendor's

B way. The purchaser has discovered by other means a vital defect in the vendor's title which would mean that the purchaser is asked to accept something which may be made worthless. Can the clause prevail?

It is necessary to distinguish the case of a vendor and purchaser summons in which the question for the court is: has the vendor shown a good title in accordance with the contract? There are also cases in which, though the court has

C held the purchaser to be bound by the terms of the contract of sale, because the title is so bad really as not to be " a good holding title " the court refuses to grant specific performance but leaves the purchaser liable to the vendor's remedies at law. We do not propose to go through these numerous cases which were cited to us.

There is no doubt that by a clearly drawn special condition which is put in the

D contract by a vendor who acts in good faith, and which discloses a possible defect in the title, the purchaser may be compelled to accept the title offered by the vendor; but the vendor must have disclosed the defects of which he knew. In this case the vendor did not know of the breaches which would give rise to forfeiture; but he ought to have known that such breaches might exist. His solicitors ought to have insisted on seeing the underlease to Ernest Geoffrey Williams

E (assigned to Mrs. Smith) out of which the further underlease to the vendor was to be created, as they were entitled by law. The vendor's solicitors instead accepted an untrue statement by Mrs. Smith's husband (who was not a lawyer anyhow). The position is covered by the decision of BYRNE, J., in *Re Haedicke and Lipski's Contract* (4). In a reserved judgment BYRNE, J., ordered return of the deposit with interest and the costs of investigation of title on the ground that a purchaser

F has a right to assume when a condition of this kind is inserted that the vendor has disclosed what it is his duty to disclose. That case has stood for over sixty years and, so far as we know, has not been criticised.

In our view the principle was stated by LORD ELDON, L.C., in *Jenkins* v. *Hiles* (5), in a passage quoted by BYRNE, J. (6), namely, that there should be no surprise on the purchaser, and that there has been a full and fair representation as to the

G title on the part of the plaintiff.

In our opinion the vendor cannot rely on the clause in the present case, and the purchaser is entitled to rescission. In the result we must allow the appeal.

Appeal allowed.

Solicitors: *J. J. Saunders & Co.* (for the purchaser); *Harbottle & Lewis* (for the vendor).

H

[*Reported by* HENRY SUMMERFIELD, ESQ., *Barrister-at-Law.*]

I

---

(4) [1901] 2 Ch. 666.   (5) (1802), 6 Ves. 646 at p. 655.
        (6) [1901] 2 Ch. at pp. 669, 670.

Re CLORE'S SETTLEMENT TRUSTS.   A
SAINER AND OTHERS v. CLORE AND OTHERS.

[CHANCERY DIVISION (Pennycuick, J.), March 16, 1966.]

*Trust and Trustee—Powers of trustee—Advancement—Charitable donation—
Benefit of beneficiary—Discharge by wealthy person of moral obligation to
make donation to charity.*   B

A settlor made a settlement in favour of his son and daughter in equal
moieties. The son's share was held on trust for him on attaining thirty years
of age, with a proviso in favour of his children should he die under thirty.
He had attained the age of twenty-one and the trust fund had become of
considerable value. Clause 8 of the settlement provided that the trustees
might raise any part, not exceeding two-thirds, of the share in the trust fund C
of any person who had attained twenty-one years of age under the trusts
thereinbefore declared and might pay or apply it for his advancement or
benefit in such manner as the trustees should in their absolute discretion
think fit. The trustees applied to the court for a declaration that they
were at liberty, in exercise of the power conferred by cl. 8, to raise one-seventh
of the son's share of the trust fund to apply it for his benefit by paying it to D
the trustees of a charity, a foundation established by the settlor, as an
accretion to its funds. Everyone, including the son, concerned was in
favour of the proposal and the trustees considered that it was for the
benefit of the son.

Held: the power of advancement had to be exercised for the benefit, i.e.,
the improvement of the material situation, of the beneficiary, which in the   E
case of a wealthy man included enabling him to discharge obligations that
he recognised as obligations on him to make charitable donations; accordingly it lay within the scope of the power given by cl. 8 for the trustees to
raise capital for the purpose of relieving the beneficiary of the moral
obligation that he recognised to make the proposed donation, and, as one-
seventh of his share was reasonable in amount, the court would declare   F
that the trustees were at liberty to exercise the power of advancement by
making the donation direct to the foundation (see p. 274, letters G and I,
and p. 275, letters E and H, post).

Dictum of VISCOUNT RADCLIFFE in *Pilkington* v. *Inland Revenue Comrs.*
([1962] 3 All E.R. at p. 628) applied.

Dictum of FARWELL, J., in *Re Walker, Walker* v. *Duncombe* ([1901] 1 Ch.   G
at p. 887) applied.

[As to the purpose of an advancement, see 21 HALSBURY'S LAWS (3rd Edn.) 178,
para. 386 and cf. 18 ibid., 704; and for cases on the subject, see 28 DIGEST
(Repl.) 598-601, *1101-1125*, and 43 DIGEST 789, 790, *2279*, *2280*.]

Cases referred to:
Pilkington v. *Inland Revenue Comrs.*, [1962] 3 All E.R. 622; [1964] A.C. 612;   H
        [1962] 3 W.L.R. 1051; Digest (Cont. Vol. A) 922, *1132a*.
Walker, Re, *Walker* v. *Duncombe*, [1901] 1 Ch. 879; 70 L.J.Ch. 417; 84 L.T.
        193; 28 Digest (Repl.) 571, *861*.

Adjourned Summons.

This was an application by originating summons dated Nov. 17, 1965, by the   I
plaintiffs, Leonard Sainer, the Right Hon. Julian Edward Alfred, Baron Melchett,
and Harold Lancelot Roy Mathews for the determination of the following
questions and for the following relief: whether the plaintiffs as trustees of a
settlement dated Dec. 12, 1951, and made between the third defendant, Charles
Clore (the settlor) and two others were at liberty (subject to the written consent
of the settlor) in exercise of the power conferred on them by cl. 8 of the settlement, to raise out of the share of the trust fund defined by the settlement as
Alan's share a specified amount of cash and to apply it for the benefit of the

A defendant Alan Evelyn Clore by (i) paying it to the trustees of the charity at
present known as the Charles Clore Foundation constituted by a trust deed
dated Oct. 12, 1964, and made between the settlor of the one part and the plaintiffs of the other part as an accretion to the funds of the charity or alternatively
(ii) by paying it to the defendant Alan Evelyn Clore to enable him to pay it
to the trustees of the charity as such accretion as aforesaid. The defendants
B were (i) Alan Evelyn Clore, (ii) Vivien Louise Clore and (iii) the settlor. The
facts are set out in the judgment.

The cases noted below* were cited during the argument in addition to those
referred to in the judgment.

J. A. Brightman, Q.C., and Martin Nourse for the plaintiffs.
Robert S. Lazarus, Q.C., and P. A. Goodall for the first defendant.
C Raymond Walton, Q.C., and M. W. Jacomb for the second defendant.
Sir Milner Holland, Q.C., and J. E. Vinelott for the third defendant.

PENNYCUICK, J.: This summons relates to the trusts of a settlement
dated Dec. 12, 1951, made by Mr. Charles Clore. The question raised by the
summons is whether the plaintiffs, who are the trustees of this settlement, are at
D liberty, in exercise of a power conferred on them by the settlement, to pay a
proportion of the trust fund to one of the beneficiaries, the defendant Alan
Evelyn Clore, with a view to his paying the amount so paid to him over to
charity, or, alternatively, whether the trustees can pay that proportion directly
to charity.

The settlement was made between Charles Clore, the settlor, of the one part,
E and two individuals, the trustees, of the other part. The first recital states
that the settlor had two children, namely Alan Evelyn Clore and Vivien Louise
Clore, born on Apr. 28, 1944, and Mar. 26, 1946, respectively. Then it recites
the payment of a sum of money to the trustees. After a definition clause setting
out the constitution of that trust fund, it is provided that

F " The trustees shall stand possessed of the trust fund upon trust to divide
the same into two equal moieties and hold the same upon the trusts
hereinafter declared concerning the same."

Clause 4 (a) provides:

" (1) The trustees shall hold one of the aforesaid moieties (hereinafter
referred to as ' Alan's share ') upon trust to collect the income . . . [and to
accumulate the balance after payment of primary expenses during his
G minority]. (2) Subject as aforesaid to pay the balance of income to Alan until
he attains the age of thirty years. (3) If and when Alan attains the age of
thirty years to hold Alan's share as to both capital and income upon trust
for Alan absolutely."

Then there is a provision in favour of the children of Alan should he die under
H the age of thirty. By cl. 5 the trustees are to hold the other of the moieties on
the like trusts in favour of Vivien. Clause 8 is the provision which has given rise
to the present question. It runs as follows:

" The trustees may at any time after the death of the settlor or during
his life with his written consent (but subject nevertheless to the exercise of
all or any of the powers herein contained or of this present power) raise any
I part or parts not exceeding altogether two-thirds of the then expectant or
presumptive or vested share in the trust fund of any person who shall have
attained twenty-one years of age under the trusts hereinbefore declared
and may pay or apply the same for his or her advancement or benefit in such
manner as the trustees shall in their absolute discretion think fit."

---

* Langton v. Brackenbury, (1846), 10 Jur. 302; Re Kershaw's Trusts, (1868), L.R. 6
Eq. 322; Roper-Curzon v. Roper-Curzon, (1871), L.R. 11 Eq. 452; Gisborne v. Gisborne,
(1877), 2 App. Cas. 300; Re Price, (1887), 34 Ch.D. 603; Re Halsted's Will Trusts,
Halsted v. Halsted, [1937] 2 All E.R. 570.

The son Alan has recently attained the age of twenty-one years. The trust fund A is now of very considerable value. What is sought to be done under cl. 8 is that one-seventh of his share of the trust fund shall be raised and paid over to the trustees of an existing charity known as the Charles Clore Foundation which was established by Mr. Charles Clore. Everyone concerned is in favour of the proposal. The trustees consider that, in all the circumstances, the transaction is for the benefit of Alan. The latter desires it to be effected and so does Mr. Charles B Clore. I understand that Vivien who is under twenty-one is personally in favour of this transaction; but counsel on her behalf contends that it is not within the power conferred by cl. 8.

Counsel who appears for the plaintiffs formulated his argument on cl. 8 in the form of five propositions. The first is that payment or application for the advancement or benefit of a person means " any use of the money which will improve C the material situation of the beneficiary ". That expression is taken from the opinion of VISCOUNT RADCLIFFE in *Pilkington* v. *Inland Revenue Comrs.* (1). The proposition is well established and requires no further elaboration.

The second proposition is that the improvement of the material situation of a beneficiary is not confined to his direct financial advantage. That may be amplified, I think, by saying that it includes the discharge at any rate of certain D moral, or social, obligations on the part of the beneficiary, for example towards dependants. In support of that, counsel for the plaintiffs cites a series of cases in which the court has held that trustees can properly exercise such a power by paying money to the trustees of a settlement for the benefit of the beneficiary and the members of his family. There is no doubt that that is so: *Pilkington* v. *Inland Revenue Comrs.* (2) is an example and there have been many others. In E such a case the interest which the beneficiary would take on attaining the age at which the interest would vest absolutely is reduced from an absolute interest to a more limited interest, normally a life interest, but none the less the court treats the settlement as being for his benefit, that is, as improving his material situation.

The third proposition is the crux of the present application. It is that the court F has always recognised that a wealthy person has a moral obligation to make charitable donations. The court has recognised this in several cases, though generally it has been concerned with relatively small sums of income; see, in particular, *Re Walker, Walker* v. *Duncombe* (3). It seems to me that a beneficiary under a settlement may indeed in many cases be reasonably entitled to regard himself as under a moral obligation to make donations towards charity. G The nature and amount of those donations must depend on all the circumstances including the position in life of the beneficiary, the amount of the fund, and the amount of his other resources. Once that proposition is accepted, it seems to me that it must lie within the scope of a power such as that contained in cl. 8 of this settlement for the trustees to raise capital for the purpose of relieving the beneficiary of his moral obligation towards whatever charity he may have in H mind. If the obligation is not to be met out of the capital of the trust fund he would have to meet it out of his own pocket if at all. Accordingly, the discharge of the obligation out of the capital of the trust fund does improve his material situation. The precise amount which the trustees can in any given case apply for this purpose must depend, I think, on the particular circumstances, and in this respect quantum is a necessary ingredient in the proper I exercise of the power. It is difficult for example to see how the trustees, under a power such as that in cl. 8 could validly pay over the whole authorised two-thirds to charitable purposes. On the other hand, it is certainly not for the court to say precisely where the line is to be drawn. In the present case, having regard to all the circumstances, I think that the proposed proportion of one-seventh can fairly be regarded as on the right side of the line. It appears

(1) [1962] 3 All E.R. 622 at p. 628, letter A; [1964] A.C. 612 at p. 635.
(2) [1962] 3 All E.R. 622; [1964] A.C. 612.   (3) [1901] 1 Ch. 879.

A from the evidence that the son, Alan, recognises that he is under a moral obligation to make payments to charity. He has not yet been subjected to any public
or social pressure in this respect though he believes that may come about in the
future. Once he recognises this obligation, then it seems to me that the trustees
may properly regard it as improving his material situation to discharge the
obligation out of the trust fund, and, as I have said, the proportion they propose
B to apply for this purpose is not excessive.

Counsel for the plaintiffs added in his formulation two further propositions.
The fourth is that a wealthy person can discharge his moral obligation at a less
cost to himself if he makes a charitable settlement and, fifthly, it follows that
any advance of an appropriate sum under the settlement is capable of improving
his material situation by enabling him to discharge his moral obligation without
C undue burden on himself.   It is certainly true that by making a capital settlement, Alan can confer the same benefit on the charity at much less expense to
himself than if he were to make a corresponding payment to the charity
personally out of income, which, at the present rate of income tax, it would be
impossible for him to do. This last consideration emphasises the desirability of
making the proposed advance, but I do not think that it is essential to the power
D of the trustees to make the advance.

Counsel for Vivien, the second defendant, in his argument that it was not
within the power of the trustees to make the proposed advance, cited a number of
authorities and contended that the advance must be for the direct material
advantage of the beneficiary concerned; that requirement may be said to
be satisfied if it be shown that public pressure would be such that it would be
E seriously detrimental to the material position of the beneficiary not to make a
charitable donation; that, however, does not arise in the present case. I think
that that is too narrow a view of what represents a benefit in a material sense to
the beneficiary. It seems to me that, once the beneficiary himself regards the
payment as a moral obligation, then it may be for his benefit to be relieved
of it.

F To avoid misunderstanding, it seems to me that in the case of a moral obligation
it is an essential ingredient of a valid exercise of the power that the beneficiary
himself should recognise the moral obligation. It is not open to trustees to pay
away the beneficiary's prospective capital over his head or against his will in
discharge of what they consider to be his moral obligation.

I have not thought it useful to go at length into the evidence sworn by Alan
G himself, but, taking his present position in life and his social outlook, it must be
said that he does consider it to be his moral obligation to make a contribution
on this scale to this charity.

I propose, accordingly, to answer the question in the summons by declaring
that the plaintiffs as trustees of the settlement of Dec. 12, 1951, with the consent
of Mr. Charles Clore, which consent he is willing to give, are at liberty in exercise
H of the power conferred on them by cl. 8 of the settlement to pay out of the trust
fund a specified amount and to apply the same for the benefit of the defendant
Alan Evelyn Clore by paying the same to the trustees of the charity known as
the Charles Clore Foundation as an accretion to the funds of the said charity. I
do not think that any advantage could be gained by making the payment to the
son, Alan, on the terms that he should pay the sum over to the trustees of the
I Foundation.

Declaration accordingly.

Solicitors: *Titmuss, Sainer & Webb* (for all parties).

[*Reported by* JENIFER SANDELL, *Barrister-at-Law.*]

COZENS v. NORTH DEVON HOSPITAL MANAGEMENT   A
COMMITTEE AND ANOTHER.
HUNTER v. TURNERS (SOHAM), LTD.

[QUEEN'S BENCH DIVISION (Thompson, J.), March 25, 1966.]

Limitation of Action—Extension of time limit—Ex parte order made by judge in   B
chambers granting proposed plaintiff leave to contend in action that the
Limitation Act, 1939, s. 2 (1) should afford no defence—Application to set
aside order on ground that it was wrongly made on material before judge—
Whether defendant had right to apply to judge in chambers to set aside the
order on such a ground—Limitation Act 1963 (c. 47) s. 1, s. 2 (1) (2).

Defendants in an action in which the plaintiff has obtained ex parte*
an order of the judge in chambers granting leave for the purposes of s. 1†   C
of the Limitation Act 1963 (viz., leave to contend at the trial that s. 2 (1)
of the Limitation Act, 1939, should not afford a defence to the claim) have no
right to apply in chambers that the order should be set aside on the ground
that it was wrongly made on the material before the judge who made it
(see p. 279, letter I, to p. 280, letter A, p. 281, letter G, and p. 282, letter E,
post).   D

Re Clark v. *Forbes Stuart (Thames Street), Ltd. (intended action)* ([1964]
2 All E.R. at p. 282) considered.

[As to the extension of the limitation period in certain cases, see SUPPLEMENT
to 24 HALSBURY'S LAWS (3rd Edn.) para. 381; and for cases on process to prevent
statutory bar, see 32 DIGEST (Repl.) 625, *2018-2022*, and 3rd CUM. SUPP.

For the Limitation Act 1963, s. 1, see 43 HALSBURY'S STATUTES (2nd Edn.)   E
614.]

Cases referred to:

Archer (H.M.S.), [1919] P. 1; 88 L.J.P. 3; 42 Digest (Repl.) 929, *7209.*

Boyle v. *Sacker*, (1888), 39 Ch.D. 249; 58 L.J.Ch. 141; 16 Digest (Repl.) 141,
    237.   F

Cartledge v. *E. Jopling & Sons, Ltd.*, [1963] 1 All E.R. 341; [1963] A.C. 758;
    [1963] 2 W.L.R. 210; 32 Digest (Repl.) 401, *259.*

Clarke v. *Forbes Stuart (Thames Street), Ltd. (intended action), Re*, [1964] 2 All
    E.R. 282; [1964] 1 W.L.R. 836; 3rd Digest Supp.

Summonses.

In each of these two actions the defendants applied to the judge in chambers   G
to set aside orders made respectively by NIELD, J., and MOCATTA, J., on ex parte
applications by the plaintiffs made for the purposes of s. 1 of the Limitation
Act 1963 in accordance with R.S.C., Ord. 128, r. 2. Writs had been issued and
served in both actions. The facts are set out in the judgment, which was
given in open court.

J. R. Whitley and *D. O. Thomas* for the plaintiff in the first action.   H

P. D. J. Scott and *P. E. Webster* for the first and second defendants in the first
action.

J. P. M. Phillips for the plaintiff in the second action.

P. H. Otton for the defendants in the second action.

Cur. adv. vult.

    I

Mar. 25. **THOMPSON, J.**, read the following judgment: These two applications came before me in chambers. In each the defendants ask me to set aside
orders made ex parte in chambers by NIELD, J., and by MOCATTA, J., respectively.
By these orders these learned judges granted to Mrs. Cozens in one case and to
Mr. Hunter in the other—they being at the time of their applications proposed

---

* I.e., pursuant to s. 2 (1), (2), of the Limitation Act 1963, for the relevant terms of
which see p. 278, letters D to G, post.

† Section 1, so far as material, is printed at p. 278, letters A to D, post.

Affirmed. C.A. Post, p. 799.

A plaintiffs—leave pursuant to and for the purposes of s. 1 of the Limitation Act 1963. It is now argued in each case that the defendants have the right to come to chambers to apply to set aside the orders and that on the merits the order in each case be set aside.

. A note in the 1966 ANNUAL PRACTICE at p. 1999/209E, under the title " Application to discharge order granting leave ", supports the contention that the defen-

B dants have such a right and refers to two cases. In consequence of that note the matter has arisen previously in chambers, but has not, I am told, hitherto been fully argued, nor has the decision of the judge (adverse to the defendants' claim to be entitled to apply) been given in open court. Accordingly, and since I have had the benefit of full argument, it is desirable that I should give my decision in open court. The note in the ANNUAL PRACTICE is in these terms:

C   " Application to discharge order granting leave. It is a fundamental rule of practice that a party affected by an ex parte order may apply to the court to discharge it, inasmuch as he has not had an opportunity of being heard (see per COTTON, L.J., in *Boyle* v. *Sacker* (1); *H.M.S. Archer* (2); and cf. (n) ' Application to set aside the order or service ' under R.S.C., Ord. 11,

D   r. 4). Accordingly the defendant may, if he wishes, apply to set aside an order obtained ex parte granting leave for the purposes of s. 1 of the Act of 1963 . . . The application is made by summons to the judge in chambers (though strictly it could be made to a master) specifying the grounds and supported by an affidavit stating the facts relied on . . ."

The first observation which I have to make about this note is that in neither

E of the present applications has counsel appearing for the respective defendants felt able to rely on either of the cases cited as supporting the claim to be entitled to apply to set aside the leave here granted.

The Limitation Act 1963, was passed in consequence of a report (Cmnd. 1829) of the Committee on Limitation of Actions in Cases of Personal Injury. That committee was appointed by the Lord Chancellor on Jan. 27, 1961, after the

F case of *Cartledge* v. *E. Jopling & Sons, Ltd.* (3) had been decided adversely to the plaintiffs at first instance and before the Court of Appeal had heard the appeals, which were dismissed. The committee reported in August, 1962, which was before the appeals to the House of Lords came on for hearing.

While maintaining, correctly, that the report of the committee could not be looked at to interpret the Act of 1963, counsel who appeared for the defendants

G in the first of the present applications referred me to certain parts of the report to demonstrate that there was nothing in the recommendations of the committee which was inimical to the present application or which showed that the committee had even considered whether a defendant should, after leave granted by the judge in chambers, have the right to apply to set aside the leave. The submissions of counsel for the defendants were as follows. (i) A party had a right to be heard as to any order affecting him. (ii) This is a fundamental right and is

H the foundation of the rule that every party affected by an order made in his absence may apply to set it aside. (iii) He is not to be deprived of such right unless it can be said that the legislature has intended to deprive him of it. (iv) The Act of 1963 exhibits no such intention and does not so deprive him. Counsel for the defendants submitted that even if the effect of s. 2 (2) of the Act of 1963 was to prevent the defendant from adducing evidence, he should still be entitled

I to argue before the judge in chambers that on the plaintiff's evidence leave should not have been given.

Counsel who appeared for the defendants in the second of the present applications made a short submission in line with the note in the ANNUAL PRACTICE.

The relevant provisions of the Limitation Act 1963 are these. Section 1 (1) reads:

---

(1) (1888), 39 Ch.D. 249 at p. 251.   (2) [1919] P. 1 at p. 4.
          (3) [1963] 1 All E.R. 341; [1963] A.C. 758.

" Section 2 (1) of the Limitation Act, 1939 (which in the case of certain   A
actions, imposes a time-limit of three years for bringing the action) shall not
afford any defence to an action to which this section applies, in so far as the
action relates to any cause of action in respect of which: (a) the court, has,
whether before or after the commencement of the action, granted leave for
the purposes of this section, and (b) the requirements of sub-s. (3) of this
section are fulfilled."   B

Subsection (2) describes the actions to which s. 1 applies and it suffices to say that
both the present actions are such actions. Subsection (3) reads:

" The requirements of this subsection are fulfilled in relation to a cause of
action if it is proved that the material facts relating to that cause of action
were or included facts of a decisive character which were at all times outside   C
the knowledge (actual or constructive) of the plaintiff until a date which—
(a) either was after the end of the three-year period relating to that cause
of action or was not earlier than twelve months before the end of that
period, and (b) in either case, was a date not earlier than twelve months before
the date on which the action was brought."

For present purposes sub-s. (4) of s. 1 is immaterial.   Section 2, however, is   D
important. Subsection (1) of s. 2 reads:

" Any application for the leave of the court for the purposes of the preceding section shall be made ex parte except . . ."

The words following are immaterial, for neither of the present cases is within
the exception. Subsection (2) reads: E

" Where such an application is made before the commencement of any
relevant action, the court shall grant leave in respect of any cause of action
to which the application relates if, but only if, on evidence adduced by or on
behalf of the plaintiff, it appears to the court that, if such an action were
brought forthwith and the like evidence were adduced in that action, that
evidence would, in the absence of any evidence to the contrary, be sufficient—   F
(a) to establish that cause of action, apart from any defence under s. 2 (1) of
the Limitation Act, 1939, and (b) to fulfil the requirements of sub-s. (3) of
the preceding section in relation to that cause of action."

Subsection (3) of s. 2, which deals with applications made after the commencement of a relevant action, is inapplicable to the actions with which I am concerned.
Subsection (4) of s. 2 reads: G

" No appeal shall lie from any decision of the Court of Appeal on an appeal
against a decision on an application under this section."

Subsection (5) reads:

" In this section ' relevant action ', in relation to an application for the
leave of the court, means any action in connexion with which the leave sought   H
by the application is required."

Section 7 is the interpretation section, and sub-ss. (3), (4) and (5) are especially
important for the court to have in mind when considering whether the requirements of sub-s. (3) of s. 1 are fulfilled. However, nothing, in my judgment, in
s. 7 or in any of the sections other than those I have cited bears on the question
whether the defendants have the right to make application to set aside the leave   I
granted to a proposed plaintiff.
    The Rules of the Supreme Court made in relation to the Limitation Act 1963
are contained in Ord. 128. Rule 1, so far as material to the present case, reads:

" (1) . . . the jurisdiction of the High Court to grant leave for the purposes
of s. 1 of the Limitation Act 1963, shall be exercised by a judge in chambers
in person . . . (3) In this order ' relevant action ' has the same meaning as in
s. 2 of the Limitation Act 1963."

A Rule 2, so far as material, reads:

" (1) An application for the grant of leave for the purposes of the said s. 1 made before the trial of the relevant action must be made by ex parte summons which shall, if the application is made before the commencement of the relevant action, be an ex parte originating summons. (2) The summons by which any such application is made must specify the cause of action to

B which the application relates and must be supported by an affidavit to which, in the case of an application made before the commencement of the relevant action, the statement of claim proposed to be served in that action must be exhibited."

Sub-rule (3) is for present purposes immaterial.

C Rule 3 is in these terms:

" Where the judge makes an order granting leave for the purposes of the said s. 1 on an application made before the trial of the relevant action, a copy of the order must be served (*a*) if the application was made before the commencement of that action, with the writ of summons by which that action was begun . . .''

D Since in both of the cases now before me the application for leave was made before the issue of the writ, the rest of r. 3 is inapplicable.

These are the provisions of the Act of 1963 and of the Rules of the Supreme Court relevant to the making of an application for leave for the purposes of s. 1 of the Limitation Act 1963. Procedurally each plaintiff acted in conformity with the requirements applicable in the case of a proposed plaintiff who desires to

E contend that s. 2 (1) of the Limitation Act, 1939, should afford no defence in the proposed action. The submission in each case on behalf of the defendants is, and must be, that the judge in chambers came to a wrong decision in granting leave, and that, since the decision was one given on an ex parte application, the defendants have the right to be heard to argue that the order should be revoked and the leave set aside.

F Before discussing the validity of that submission, it is desirable to mention what appears to be the only reported case on the Limitation Act 1963. It is a decision of the Court of Appeal. Its title is *Re Clark* v. *Forbes Stuart (Thames Street), Ltd.* (*intended action*) (4). It is not a decision on the present point. That matter came before the Court of Appeal because the judge in chambers had refused to grant leave. The proposed plaintiff, pursuant to s. 2 (4) of the Act of

G 1963, had then on appeal applied to the Court of Appeal to grant leave, which that court did. Inevitably in the course of their judgments the members of the Court of Appeal discussed the meaning of provisions in the Act of 1963. While not directly dealing with the point before me, I have found the analysis and interpretation of the scheme of the Act contained in these judgments of great assistance. They appear to me to reinforce the conclusion to which I have come

H on the points that I have to decide.

I would, however, respectfully suggest that LORD DENNING, M.R., in two places in his judgment per incuriam incorrectly described the nature of the leave which the Act of 1963 allows to be granted. LORD DENNING, M.R., said (5):

" The Act enables such a person to get the leave of the court to bring an action, notwithstanding that three years have expired . . . They [the appli-

I cant's solicitors] applied to MOCATTA, J., for leave under that Act to start a new action . . .''

In my respectful judgment, these are not strictly correct descriptions of what the leave, if granted, enables or permits the proposed plaintiff to do. The proposed plaintiff can without leave issue a writ and start an action even if three years have expired, though the action may, of course, meet a summary fate. What the proposed plaintiff cannot, however, do without leave is to contend in the

---

(4) [1964] 2 All E.R. 282.   (5) [1964] 2 All E.R. at p. 283.

action that s. 2 (1) of the Limitation Act, 1939, should afford no defence to his A
claim. The leave for the purposes of the Act of 1963 is, in my judgment, leave to
the plaintiff to advance in the action the contention that he should not be limited
by the Act of 1939 and that his complaint should not be restricted to matters
falling within the three years prior to the issue of the writ. I think that the precise
nature of what the plaintiff is given leave to do if he obtains an order on his
application may be not unimportant in considering the point which I have to B
determine.

It is to be observed that the defendants in the second of the present cases,
Hunter v. *Turners (Soham), Ltd.*, by their summons erroneously describe what the
judge in chambers did as giving leave to the plaintiff to commence this action,
and erroneously ask that the writ and its service should be set aside. That is not
what was asserted or asked on the hearing before me.   C

The combined effect of the Act of 1963 and the rules appears to be that s. 2 (1)
of the Limitation Act, 1939, is not to afford a defence to an action if (a) leave is
granted, (b) the requirements of s. 1 (3) of the Act of 1963 are fulfilled. Whether
they are or are not fulfilled would, of course, be determined in the action. To
get leave, the intended plaintiff must apply by ex parte summons to a judge in
chambers in person, and in cases like the present ones the summons should be an D
ex parte originating one. The summons must specify the cause of action and
must be supported by an affidavit to which in cases where, as here, the applications preceded the issue of the writ the proposed statement of claim must be
exhibited. Having come before the judge in chambers in this way, the grant of
leave is not a matter of discretion. The intended plaintiff is to be given leave if,
but only if, on the evidence produced by or on his behalf it appears to the judge E
in chambers that if his action were brought forthwith and his evidence were the
only evidence before the court hearing the action such evidence would be sufficient
(a) to establish his cause of action apart from any Limitation Act defence, and
(b) to fulfil the requirements of sub-s. (3) of s. 1.

The judge in chambers accordingly is required to form, on the evidence laid
before him on behalf of the plaintiff, a prima facie view as to matters which the F
Act contemplates will be decided (if leave be granted) only in the action itself.
These matters are: (i) has the plaintiff a good cause of action; (ii) does the
plaintiff fulfil the requirements of sub-s. (3) of s. 1? These, as I say, are the
questions at trial. So far as the second matter is concerned, the question as it
arises on the application for leave is this: does it appear to the judge in chambers
that, if the evidence laid before him by the intended plaintiff were uncontradicted G
or unqualified at the trial by any other evidence, it would fulfil the requirements
of sub-s. (3) of s. 1; that is to say, would establish his ignorance of material
facts of a decisive character until such a date as the subsection indicates? It is
clear from s. 7, sub-ss. (3), (4) and (5), which, as I have earlier said, contain
important definitive provisions, that the judge in chambers is required to form a
prima facie view on matters of law as well as of fact as to actual or constructive H
knowledge and as to what facts are material facts and whether they are of a
decisive character. This prima facie decision the judge in chambers is required to
come to on an application which the Act and rules say shall be made to him ex
parte and on material which is laid before him on behalf of the plaintiff. No
provision is made for contrary evidence from the defendant's side.

I have described the decision of the judge in chambers on these matters when I
he grants leave as a prima facie one. That is what it is. It creates no presumption
in the plaintiff's favour. It has resulted in his getting leave—leave to try to
prove in the action, against the opposition on fact and law of the defendant,
that material facts of a decisive character were at the relevant times outside
his knowledge, actual or constructive.

In granting leave in the case of *Clark* (6) the members of the court all made
clear the provisional or prima facie nature of the conclusion which they were

(6) [1964] 2 All E.R. 282.

A reaching in performing by virtue of s. 2 (4) their duty as " the court " for the purpose of s. 2 (3). LORD DENNING, M.R., said (7):

   " On this prima facie case, I think that this court should give leave ex parte; but this is without prejudice to the right of the defendants in the action itself to say that this prima facie view is wrong either on the facts or on the law."

B The whole tenor of the judgment of PEARSON, L.J., is to that effect, and concludes with this sentence (8):

   " But it is not common to have an application made by one side only, and for that reason the matter [whether the requirements of s. 1 (3), a matter about which the court granting leave could form only a prima facie view] should be left entirely open to the judge at the trial who has to decide these matters."

C SALMON, L.J., in his judgment said (9) this, which I have shortened as I read:

   " I agree that, not having heard the arguments that might be advanced on behalf of the defendants, it is possible, as my lords have said, to form only a provisional view. Provisionally I have come to the conclusion that . . .

D Again, I am very conscious of the fact that we have not heard the argument the other way and that the judge at the trial may, as he would be fully entitled to do, come to a different conclusion . . . On the whole I think that there is just enough evidence for the purposes of this ex parte application— again without prejudice to how the matters may be decided at the trial . . ."

E The procedure of requiring leave to be obtained affords the defendant some protection. It does not guarantee that he will be troubled only with actions in which the plaintiff can conclusively prove that he was ignorant of material facts of a decisive character. It contemplates, as the judgments in the Court of Appeal show, that the defendant may have to contest an action in which either on the facts or on the law he may be able successfully to controvert the provisional

F conclusion of the judge in chambers, reached on evidence and argument from one side only.

   What the procedure does do, however, is to deny to a plaintiff the unrestricted right in every case to carry to trial the question of the applicability or in-applicability of the three-year time limit. The need to obtain leave is the restriction on that right. Parliament, in my judgment, intended to go no further than that on behalf of a defendant. It did not, in my judgment, intend that he should

G have the right to call in question the grant of leave by an application to set aside the order granting that leave. On the terms of the Act, as I read them, he could not in any event do so by advancing fresh material not contained in the plaintiff's application. I do not regard Parliament as having intended to allow what in any event would be an unusual and embarrassing proceeding, that is to

H say, the review by the same or another judge in chambers (or, if the note in the ANNUAL PRACTICE is right, by a master) on the same material of a decision which has to be made ex parte and which does not determine the issue between the parties, but merely permits the issue to be debated in the action. It is to be observed that the note in the 1966 ANNUAL PRACTICE, p. 1999/209E, in support of the view there advanced, invites reference to the note to R.S.C., Ord. 11, r. 4,

I under the title " Application to set aside the order or service ". (The subject-matter of R.S.C., Ord. 11 is: " Principal cases in which service of writ out of jurisdiction is permissible ".) That note to r. 4 includes these words (10):

   " An objection to the order or service cannot be made in the defence . . . But, in accordance with general principles of practice, the order, having been obtained by the plaintiff ex parte can be set aside on application by the

---

(7) [1964] 2 All E.R. at p. 284.   (8) [1964] 2 All E.R. at p. 285.
(9) [1964] 2 All E.R. at pp. 285, 286.   (10) ANNUAL PRACTICE, 1966, p. 113.

defendant after service . . .   The application is decided on the affidavit   A
evidence of the parties . . . ''

In the present cases, and indeed it would presumably always be so, the objection
to the grant of leave which the defendants desire to make is that the plaintiff was
not throughout the material time in ignorance of material facts of a decisive
character. That is an objection that can be made in the defence. Indeed, such
ignorance is something which the plaintiff has affirmatively to prove at the trial.   B
That is one distinction between the present cases and ex parte orders under
R.S.C., Ord. 11. Another distinction is that in an application under Ord. 11 the
defendant can adduce evidence on affidavit.

It is further to be observed that in the case of *Boyle* v. *Sacker*, referred to in the
note on p. 1999/209E of the 1966 ANNUAL PRACTICE, COTTON, L.J., used these
words (11):   C

" Order 63, r. 12, only applies to reversing or varying an order made by a
vacation judge; discharging an order is not the same thing as reversing or
varying an order, it does not go on the ground that there has been an erroneous
decision, but on the ground that the opposing party has not had an
opportunity of being heard.''   D

In the present case, Parliament denied him that opportunity in the Act of 1963
and the present applications are put, and can only be put, on the ground that
there has been an erroneous decision. The suggested error in each case is that the
judge in chambers was wrong on the material before him and in his application
thereto of the definitive provisions of s. 7 to conclude that it appeared to him that
the proposed plaintiff was throughout the relevant period ignorant of material   E
facts of a decisive character. I cannot think that it is right that defendants can
come into chambers to say that the judge in chambers came to a wrong conclusion.

In my judgment, for the reasons which I have endeavoured to explain, defendants do not have the right to apply to set aside leave granted ex parte for the
purposes of s. 1 of the Limitation Act 1963.

It was acknowledged by counsel for the defendants in the first action in the   F
course of his argument that if the leave here granted were to be set aside the
plaintiff could not then in the action contend that s. 2 (1) of the Limitation Act,
1939, should not be a defence. The discharge of the leave would be a final determination of that matter and not merely a provisional conclusion on the way to
its consideration in the action. I appreciate that, of course, it can correctly be
said that if leave is not granted at all, then the plaintiff cannot in the action   G
contend that s. 2 (1) of the Act of 1939 affords no defence. Moreover it might be
said—though I do not think that it was said by counsel for the defendants in
the first action—that there is no difference between the refusal of leave and the
setting aside of leave. There may be no difference in the consequential limitation
on the plaintiff's freedom to contend in the action, but there is, I think, the important difference that in one case the intended plaintiff has surmounted, and in the   H
other case has failed at, the fence erected by Parliament.

Having reached the conclusion that I cannot entertain the present applications,
I think that the less I say about the contentions on the merits, the better. I
can, however, I think, say this. For the final determination of the contention
which the plaintiffs have each been given leave to advance I should myself want
further information than there was, or than it was intended that there should be,   I
before the judge in chambers when he was called on to reach his provisional
conclusion leading to his decision to grant leave. I fancy that this would commonly
be the case. I find it difficult to visualise a case in which on such an application
as this a judge in chambers could find himself able to say that the material on
which leave had been granted was so clearly incapable of supporting even a
provisional conclusion favourable to the plaintiff that he would set aside the leave

(11) (1888), 39 Ch.D. at p. 251.

A and so determine the matter adversely and finally. The conclusion is that in each of these applications the defendants' application fails.

Defendants' applications refused.

Solicitors: *Baileys, Shaw & Gillett,* agents for *Tozers,* Dawlish (for the plaintiff in the first action); *Lovell, White & King,* agents for *Bevan, Hancock & Co.,* Bristol (for the first defendants in the first action); *Hempsons* (for the second defendant in the first action); *Pattinson & Brewer* (for the plaintiff in the second action); *Berrymans* (for the defendants in the second action).

[*Reported by* MARY COLTON, *Barrister-at-Law.*]

C

QUINN *v.* BURCH BROTHERS (BUILDERS), LTD.

[COURT OF APPEAL (Sellers, Danckwerts and Salmon, L.JJ.), March 1, 8, 1966.]

Contract—Breach—Damages—Causation—Breach of contract providing oppor-
D *tunity for plaintiff to injure himself—Implied contractual term to supply equipment to independent contractor for building work on site—Negligent use by contractor of substitute for equipment not supplied—Whether action by him for damages for personal injuries, based on breach of contract, failed by reason of his negligence causing his injury—Law Reform (Contributory Negligence) Act, 1945 (8 & 9 Geo. 6 c. 28), s. 1 (1).*

E The plaintiff was engaged in carrying out certain building work as a sub-contractor of the defendants. It was an implied term of the contract between them that the defendants should supply any equipment reasonably necessary for the work within a reasonable time of being requested to do so. The defendants were in breach of that term in that they failed to provide a step-ladder which the plaintiff had requested. To prevent loss of time the plaintiff used a trestle, which he knew to be unsuitable unless it was footed by another
F workman. The trestle was not footed by another workman; it slipped while the plaintiff was on it and he suffered injury.

The defendants' foreman admitted that it was foreseeable that in the absence of a step-ladder the plaintiff might use an unfooted trestle. In an action by the plaintiff for the defendants' breach of contract in failing to supply a step-ladder the plaintiff claimed damages in respect of this injury.
G **Held:** the defendants' breach of contract provided the occasion for the plaintiff to injure himself but was not the cause of his injury, which was caused by his own voluntary act in using the trestle; accordingly the defendants were not liable to pay damages for the plaintiff's injury, for his damage was not a natural and probable consequence of the breach of contract even if, as was in fact doubtful, it was a foreseeable consequence of that
H breach (see p. 286, letters C and H, p. 287, letters F and I, p. 288, letter I, and p. 289, letter G, post).

Decision of PAULL, J. ([1965] 3 All E.R. 801) affirmed, but on rather different reasoning.

[As to the chain of causation in the law of damages, see 11 HALSBURY'S LAWS
I (3rd Edn.) 281, para. 466 (tort), note (d) p. 282 (contracts); and for cases on the subject, see 17 DIGEST (Repl.) 145-147, *470-486.*]

Cases referred to:

Bolton v. *Stone,* [1951] 1 All E.R. 1078; [1951] A.C. 850; 36 Digest (Repl.) 18, *79*

Compania Naviera Maropan S.A. v. *Bowaters Lloyd Pulp and Paper Mills, Ltd.,* [1954] 3 All E.R. 563; [1954] 3 W.L.R. 894; *affd.* C.A., [1955] 2 All E.R. 241; [1955] 2 Q.B. 68; [1955] 2 W.L.R. 998; 41 Digest (Repl.) 189, *259.*

(margin note, right side:) Distinguished in SOLE v HALT [1973] 1 All ER 1032

Thorogood v. *Van Den Berghs and Jurgens, Ltd.*, [1951] 1 All E.R. 682; [1951] **A**
    2 K.B. 537; 24 Digest (Repl.) 1023, *13*.
Victoria Laundry (Windsor), Ltd. v. *Newman Industries, Ltd. (Coulson & Co.,*
    Ltd. (Third Party)), [1949] 1 All E.R. 997; [1949] 2 K.B. 528; 17
    Digest (Repl.) 92, *100*.

Appeal.

This was an appeal by the plaintiff, James Quinn, from the judgment of PAULL, **B**
J., given on Nov. 1, 1965, and reported [1965] 3 All E.R. 801, dismissing his
action for damages for breach of contract against the defendants, Burch Brothers
(Builders), Ltd. The facts are stated in the judgment of SELLERS, L.J.

P. H. *Ripman* for the plaintiff.
F. B. *Purchas*, Q.C., and A. *Bradshaw* for the defendants.
                                                                                  C

SELLERS, L.J.: The plaintiff sought to recover damages for personal
injuries in this action, which came before PAULL, J. (1), on the basis of a liability
on the defendants for breach of contract. The learned judge found for the defendants and in that, having heard the argument on this appeal, I have come to
the conclusion that the learned judge was unquestionably right.

The contract, which was set up and which is alleged to have been broken, was **D**
a contract between the defendants, who were the main contractors, and the
plaintiff and his colleague, Mr. Dunk, who were engaged on building work for the
repairs which were taking place for which the defendants were the main contractors. The contract was with these two, who were acting in partnership, as
sub-contractors. The facts are not really in dispute. No written contract was
produced but it appears that for several years the plaintiff and Mr. Dunk (I **E**
describe them, as the judge did, as the firm) had been doing plastering in
particular and kindred sorts of work for the defendants on their various building
contracts. Some time prior to the accident giving rise to this claim for personal
injuries, work had been done on the Ladywell Institute in Lewisham, the main
work being, as I understand it, the installation of some heating apparatus. The
firm did preliminary work which would assist the main contract and did various **F**
incidental subsequent work, when the installation had been made, in filling up
holes which had been made in the concrete and work of the like character.
When the work commenced I do not know, but it has been accepted that when
it did, the equipment, the plant, and also all the materials required by the firm
were to be supplied by the defendants: that is, the contract was to use the firm's
labour and pay for their work on a basis which was at one time an all-in sum **G**
but which for many years had been at a rate of 6s. an hour each. On occasions
the firm employed someone to assist them.

At the outset of this work there was an arrangement whereby the defendants
were to provide the material and the plant and the firm were to do the work.
The question arose in this action what the precise contract was. I do not find
any very satisfactory evidence of it or how it came about, whether it was expressly **H**
stated orally, or whether it was a bargain which was to be inferred from the
conduct of the parties; but the court is relieved from considering that by what
took place at the trial. It was agreed on behalf of the defendants that there was
an obligation on the defendants to supply the plaintiff and his colleague with
any equipment reasonably necessary for the work within a reasonable time of
any request so to do. In the performance of it, at the outset of the work, some **I**
plant, which was necessary, was supplied. The work had to be done in all sorts
of circumstances. Some would be done from the floor, some had to be done at
ceiling level, and three quite large step-ladders, of dimensions sufficient to
give access to some work which had to be done at a height of ten feet or more,
had been made available. As would naturally happen in the course of work of
this character, there came a stage when the firm could not usefully do any more

---

(1) [1965] 3 All E.R. 801.

A until the main contracting work had proceeded further, and the two of them went off for a time.

On a Friday before the week in which the events happened which are the subject-matter of this case, the firm were asked to go back and conclude their work, filling up the holes that had been made. They returned on the Monday, which was Sept. 17, 1962. When they returned there they could not find any

B of the three ladders which had been there before. The arrangement was that the firm would themselves decide what was the appropriate plant that they required to give access to their work, and would provide themselves with it from any of the plant on the site, which belonged to the defendants, which was available, and if there was none available they would ask for it. It was a somewhat loose arrangement, and the first question is whether in an agreement of that sort there

C was anything sufficiently specific to indicate what was a reasonable time for the defendants to make provision for the plant. That was answered by the learned judge (2) in favour of the plaintiff. He found that in the circumstances there had been sufficient time to enable other step-ladders to be provided, since the time was about to come when the two men would want them.

The question arose on the Monday where the ladders were; and a Mr. Boston,

D the representative of the defendants who was their foreman, said " Well, they are on the site ". It may well be that they were somewhere in the Institute building, because work was being done in other blocks than the one on which these two men had been called back to work on the Monday; but the ladders could not be found. When Mr. Boston was down there on the Monday he took the view that they could be found if they were looked for further, and that there

E was no necessity to provide any more. On the Monday the ladders were not found; but Mr. Dunk, the partner, found a ladder. Quite where he got it from is not very clear. It may be that it belonged to the Institute. At any rate, that was satisfactory for him to work on. The plaintiff was working on the floor of the particular room with which he was concerned and he did not need a ladder. That work continued until some time on the Tuesday. On the Tuesday Mr. Dunk, the

F partner, and a Mr. Kimber (3) went to the office of the defendants to ask about a ladder. There was a little confusion about the evidence but the learned judge (4) took the view that that visit was made. The object of it was to request the defendants to provide at least one other ladder.

In this rather uncertain situation contractually the learned judge has found (2) that there was a breach, because during that morning, when the plaintiff wished to change his activities from the task on which he had been working to

G making some repair or filling up some holes in the ceiling, no ladder had been provided. I doubt whether in all the circumstances I should have thought that that constituted a breach of contract in view of the somewhat vague arrangement. I should have thought that, before it could be said that the defendants were in breach of contract, the circumstances required the plaintiff, when he had

H come to the end of his work, which was on the ground floor, and found that no ladder was there, to make an express request indicating to the defendants the situation in which he found himself; that he was held up. A telephone was at hand, and he could have telephoned them. If he had done so, it is more than likely that the defendants would have provided what was required; but he did not telephone in that way, and the learned judge has held (2) that the circum-

I stances were sufficient to establish the request for further plant, in particular another step-ladder, and as it was not complied with that was a breach of the contract.

If that is a breach of contract, what is the position in law? Damages can be claimed for breach of contract if damage has been caused. In fact no damage was caused to the plaintiff and his partner as it stood, because they were to lose

_____

(2) [1965] 3 All E.R. at p. 805.
(3) A part-time fellow labourer employed by the firm.
(4) [1965] 3 All E.R. at p. 804.

nothing financially by that fact. It would have meant only that the payment to **A**
them of 6s. an hour would have been due from the defendants, but that they
would not have advanced the work for which they were engaged. They would
have made no financial loss. If there had been any prospect of financial loss it
would have been their duty to minimise it. One cannot conjecture what might
have been done. The obvious way to minimise damage for the failure to supply
a ladder would have been to acquire another ladder of like kind. The plaintiff **B**
did not do that and did not seek to charge the defendants with any such loss
which might have occurred by the firm having to acquire plant on their own
instead of having it supplied for them. That would have been clearly an acceptable claim if that had taken place, because their earnings were not based on
having to provide their own material and plant but on its being provided.

It is sought, however, to say in this case—if there is any basis for the case— **C**
that because there was that breach of contract the defendants are liable not on
the basis of damages for breach of contract flowing in the way which I have
indicated, with an obligation on the plaintiff to mitigate them, but on the basis
of what in fact took place subsequently. It is said that it could have been foreseen
that what took place would take place. I should not take the view that it could,
despite the evidence of the foreman; but even if it could, it does not mean that **D**
the defendants are liable for what took place. The breach of contract was not a
cause of the subsequent events which brought about the plaintiff's accident.
What the plaintiff seems to have done is to have looked about—perhaps not
very diligently—for a step-ladder, which the defendants had said was on the site.
He came across a trestle, or one leg of a trestle, somewhere on the site. That is
the well known type of trestle, hinged at the top and with sides which can come **E**
together, but if they are extended they form a step-ladder up each side. That
was not used as a trestle, as one of a pair, with a boarding on top forming a
platform on which the plaintiff could have stood. It was used in a way for which
it is not intended nor designed. The plaintiff put it up against the wall with the
two sides of the trestle together, just like a single ladder, and he failed to secure
the foot either by propping it up in some way on the floor (it was on a wooden **F**
floor) or, better still, by having it footed, which I think, if the matter had been
the subject of the building regulations, would have been an obligation. Why he
did not have it footed was because this small partnership had no other labour on
the site. There had been a Mr. Kimber but, when he left on some work of his
own, no steps were taken to meet the situation that someone would be required
to foot a ladder; and Mr. Kimber was not there. The plaintiff had put the steps **G**
up against the wall unsecured at the bottom—possibly at a reasonable angle—but
the fact is that he had hardly been up more than a moment or two with his
material for performing the task that he had to do in the ceiling when the trestle
collapsed and he unfortunately met with a nasty injury to the os calcis of one of
his heels.

One only has to state the facts in that way to reveal that this cannot be said **H**
to be an accident which was caused by the defendants' breach of contract. No
doubt the circumstance was the occasion which brought about this conduct of the
plaintiff, but it in no way caused it. It was in no way something flowing probably
and naturally from the breach of contract. The situation so depicted is so clear
that the matters which have been argued in this case in so much detail hardly
arise for consideration. It is not surprising that the learned judge speaks about **I**
a paucity of authority (5) to meet a case of this sort. Facts such as these do not
give rise, one would have thought, to any legal issue which could be advanced.
Some of the confusion which has entered into the argument has arisen because
regard was not fully had, first, to this case not being based in tort but in breach
of contract, and, second, to its being a case of an independent contractor or sub-
contractor and a main contractor: it is not a case of master and servant. Neither
is it a case (and this perhaps is the most outstanding difference) where the contract

(5) [1965] 3 All E.R. at p. 805.

A which existed between the parties placed the burden of providing proper equipment at all times (as in the contract between master and servant and as the
obligation would arise if the building regulations applied) on the defendants. The
defendants were not under a duty to see that this work was done by these two
men as independent contractors in the same way as if they were servants. That
is, it was not a case where the defendants had to take reasonable care to see that
B reasonable plant was provided in that sense. Their obligation was purely contractual, to provide a ladder. I do not think that it varies in substance from a
case where a firm has not contracted with the defendants but has contracted with
some shop or some builder's merchant to provide ladders for their job and has
asked for a ladder by mid-day on Tuesday and the builder's merchant fails to
send one along. If that happened, the builder's merchant would indeed be
C surprised if it were said that, because his ladder had not arrived by mid-day, he
was liable for an accident, such as happened here, where the other contracting
party found and used some wholly unsuitable piece of plant for his task. The
accident would have had nothing to do with the default of the contracting party.

That seems to me to be the position here. If the defendants had been under
the obligation to supply a ladder in the sense that they had to comply with the
D duties arising between master and servant, the position would have been different.
It would have been different, too, if they had provided on the site a step-ladder
which was faulty. That would be comparable to the case cited by the learned
judge (6) where he deals with *Compania Naviera Maropan S.A.* v. *Bowaters
Lloyd Pulp and Paper Mills, Ltd.* (7)—the nomination by a shipowner of an unsafe
port. There, the contractual duty of the defendant was to nominate a safe port. To
E nominate an unsafe port is comparable to supplying an unsafe ladder. If the defendants had provided an unsafe ladder, then, the question would have arisen, if an
accident had happened, whether the plaintiff would have been entitled to recover.
On the face of it he would have been able to recover, because it would have been
a breach of duty to provide a ladder which was unsafe, unless the ladder was so
obviously unsuitable for use that he should never have used it and it was his
F own conduct which brought about his damage; but that is not this case. This is a
case where no ladder was supplied at all. There was not a ladder supplied, and the
plaintiff chose to do this work, most unfortunately, and no doubt most conscientiously, from the trestle without using the trestle properly but by propping it up
against the wall unsecured. In those circumstances I think that his accident was
in no way caused by the breach of contract and did not arise in any circumstances
G in which the defendants can be held to blame.

The learned judge was right in dismissing the claim, and I would dismiss the
appeal.

DANCKWERTS, L.J.: I agree. The argument in this case seemed to me
to go round and round; but I can express my judgment in four propositions which
I believe to be established by the facts, and the law relating to the matter. (i)
H Assuming that the defendants were in breach of contract by not providing the
equipment reasonably necessary for the work, there was no obligation on the
plaintiff to do the work without suitable equipment. (ii) The plaintiff voluntarily
and without the defendants' knowledge chose to use the trestle which was
unsuitable and subject to the risk of slipping. (iii) The cause of the plaintiff's
accident was the choice by the plaintiff to use the unsuitable equipment. (iv)
I The failure of the defendants to provide the equipment required may have been
the occasion of the accident, but was not the cause of the accident.

Accordingly, the defendants are not liable; and I would dismiss the appeal.

SALMON, L.J.: The defendants were the main contractors for certain
works to be carried out at Ladywell Lodge, in Lewisham, and the plaintiff
was an independent sub-contractor for the plastering work. The learned

---

(6) [1965] 3 All E.R. st p. 805.   (7) [1954] 3 All E.R. 563; [1955] 2 Q.B. 68.

judge found (8) that it was a term of the contract between the plaintiff and   A
the defendants that the defendants should supply the plaintiff with all equipment which he required for the purpose of carrying out the plastering work
and, moreover, would supply the equipment within a reasonable time of its
being demanded by the plaintiff. The learned judge further found (9) that,
in breach of their contractual obligation, the defendants failed to supply certain
step-ladders, which were reasonably necessary for the plastering work, within   B
a reasonable time of those ladders being demanded by the plaintiff.

To my mind, those findings by the learned judge are unassailable. It is to be
observed that in this contract between the plaintiff and the defendants there is
no term that the defendants shall take reasonable care for the plaintiff's safety.
The contract had nothing to do with topics such as that, although, it is true, no
doubt, that there was an implied term in the contract that any equipment which   C
might be supplied by the defendants should be reasonably safe and suitable for
the purpose for which it was required. The reason for the obligation written into
the contract that the defendants should supply the plaintiff with equipment is
obvious. The plaintiff was a small plastering sub-contractor. He was working
for remuneration at the rate of 6s. per hour. He had not the financial
resources to buy or hire the equipment, and accordingly, the defendants assumed   D
responsibility for supplying it.

When the defendants committed their breach of contract in failing to supply
the step-ladders, the plaintiff, rather than wait for the step-ladders to arrive, or
make any further demand for step-ladders, as he would have been entitled to do,
chose to do something which he was under no obligation to do. Moreover it was
something which the defendants had neither authorised nor requested him to   E
do. He looked around, and found a trestle, and he put the trestle against the
wall with a view to going up the trestle as if it were a ladder and doing the work
from the top of the trestle. He elected to do that of his own volition, and he
elected to do it without getting anyone to foot the trestle. He realised, as he
admitted, that to go up the trestle when it was not footed was dangerous because
there was the risk that the trestle might slip, and he might fall. He realised the   F
risk, but decided to take the chance. He did mount the trestle: it did slip: he
fell, and he was injured. The only question in this case is whether the breach of
contract to which I have referred caused the injuries which the plaintiff suffered.

Now the sheet-anchor of the plaintiff's case is to be found in some answers
which were skilfully elicited from the defendants' foreman by counsel for the
plaintiff in cross-examination. He was asked: G

" Supposing a man did not have a step-ladder to use and he wanted to
work, making good the ceiling, you would not be surprised if the man used
a trestle leaning against the wall, would you? A.—No. Q.—And you would
not be surprised if he did it without somebody footing it? A.—It has been
done before. Q.—The sort of thing one expected to happen if there was not a
step-ladder available? A.—Especially if you get a conscientious man. He is   H
like that. Q.—You are implying that [the plaintiff] was a conscientious man?
A.—Definitely. Q.—The sort of thing you expect to happen if there is not
a step-ladder and the man wants to get on with the job? A.—That is right.
Q.—What I mean is that [the plaintiff] was not the sort of man to say:
' They have not brought us the plant, and we get paid for it. We can play a
game of cards.' That was not his attitude, was it? A.—No, definitely not."   I

So, says counsel for the plaintiff, here you have a plain admission by the defendants' foreman that he reasonably foresaw that, in the absence of a step-ladder,
unfooted trestles might be used by the plaintiff as a result of which he might
suffer injury. Counsel for the plaintiff has argued very attractively that once one
reasonably foresees that damage may follow one's breach of contract, then that
damage is caused by one's breach of contract.

---

(8) [1965] 3 All E.R. at p. 802.   (9) [1965] 3 All E.R. at p. 805.

A   The true nature of causation has long been debated by philosophers and lawyers. I do not think that it is necessary, or desirable, to attempt to add to the anthology of phrases that have been used with a view to describing the true nature of causation. Foreseeability of possible injury is, no doubt, the true criterion where negligence is in issue: *Thorogood* v. *Van den Berghs and Jurgens, Ltd.* (10). Similarly, when the question arises whether damages are too remote—damages,

B   be it observed, which are admitted to have been caused by a breach of contract—the test is whether the damages which were actually sustained were reasonably foreseeable at the time the contract was entered into as likely to result from its breach: *Victoria Laundry (Windsor), Ltd.* v. *Newman Industries, Ltd. (Coulson & Co., Ltd. (Third Party))* (11). Although the foreseeability test is a handmaiden of the law, it is by no means a maid-of-all-work. To my mind, it cannot serve as

C   the true criterion when the question is: how was the damage caused? It may be a useful guide, but it is by no means the true criterion. For example, in *Bolton* v. *Stone* (12), the celebrated case of the cricket ball being hit for six out of the ground and injuring the plaintiff, it was held that the defendant was not negligent because it could not reasonably be foreseen that a cricket ball hit out of the ground was likely to injure a passer-by. So the damage that occurred in that

D   case was not reasonably foreseeable. Yet, quite obviously, the damage was caused by the cricket ball being hit out of the ground.

Conversely, suppose that a garage proprietor enters into a contract to supply A. with a motor car and a chauffeur to take him, say, from London to Birmingham. The garage proprietor, in breach of his contract, fails to supply a motor car or chauffeur. The garage proprietor is then very skilfully cross examined by

E   counsel and he is asked: " Did you know this plaintiff? A.—Yes. Q.—Did you know he was a very careless driver? A.—Well, I did not think much of his driving. Q.—Did you know he had a rather ramshackle motor car of his own? A.—Yes. Q.—Now tell me: do you think it was likely that if you failed to supply him with a car he might go to Birmingham and through carelessly driving his own motor car meet with an accident? A.—Yes, I suppose that could have happened." It

F   seems to me, that, in spite of those answers it would be quite impossible to hold that the breach of contract to supply the motor car and chauffeur was a cause of the accident which occurred to the plaintiff on his way to Birmingham through his own careless driving.

All, I think, that the answers which the counsel for the plaintiff elicited in this case from the defendants' foreman really amount to is that the defendants

G   realised that, if there was a breach of contract on their part to supply the step-ladder, that breach would afford the plaintiff the opportunity of acting negligently, and that he might take it and thereby suffer injury; but it seems to me quite impossible to say that in reality the plaintiff's injury was caused by the breach of contract. The breach of contract merely gave the plaintiff the opportunity to injure himself and was the occasion of the injury. There is always a

H   temptation to fall into the fallacy of post hoc ergo propter hoc; and that is no less a fallacy, even if what happens afterwards could have been foreseen before it occurred.

In my judgment, the learned judge in this case came to the only possible conclusion, and I am quite satisfied that the breach of contract cannot, in the circumstances of this case, be said to have caused the plaintiff's injury. I would dismiss

I   the appeal.

Appeal dismissed.

Solicitors: *Graham Dawson*, Bromley (for the plaintiff); *Hare & Co.* (for the defendants).

[*Reported by* Henry Summerfield, Esq., *Barrister-at-Law.*]

---

(10) [1951] 1 All E.R. 682; [1951] 2 K.B. 537.
(11) [1949] 1 All E.R. 997 at p. 1002; [1949] 2 K.B. 528 at p. 539.
(12) [1951] 1 All E.R. 1078; [1951] A.C. 850.

A

BAKER *v.* BOWKETTS CAKES, LTD.

[COURT OF APPEAL (Lord Denning, M.R., Harman and Winn, L.JJ.), March 16,
1966.]

*Writ—Extension of validity—Cause of action statute barred—Writ issued before
cause of action statute barred, but not served—Application for extension made
within twelve months of issue of writ—Burden on applicant to show good
cause for extension—Defendants registered company—Service by post at
very end of twelve months attempted—Address of registered office of company
given by local director of defendants and not completely correct—Copy
writ returned undelivered—Legal aid needs not a factor in exercise of
discretion to extend validity of writ—R.S.C., Ord. 6, r. 8 (1), (2)—Legal
Aid and Advice Act, 1949 (12 & 13 Geo. 6 c. 51), s. 1 (7) (b).*

B

C

The plaintiff's cause of action in negligence against his employers for a
disease contracted during his employment accrued (if at all) not later than
January, 1962, when he left their employment. The last meeting between his
solicitors and the employers' insurers was in October, 1962; his solicitors then
knew that in order to recover damages he would have to prove negligence. In
1963 application was made for legal aid. On May 11, 1964, legal aid was
granted for counsel's opinion and to issue (but not to serve) a writ. A writ was
issued on behalf of the plaintiff on May 28, 1964. On May 24, 1965, the
plaintiff's solicitors applied to the district registrar to extend the validity of
the writ under R.S.C., Ord. 6, r. 8 (2). On May 25 the registrar adjourned the
application. The plaintiff's solicitors telephoned the local director of the
employers, a company, and asked the address of the company's registered
office. They were told an address which was only partly correct. They sent the
copy writ by post to the address, but the letter was returned marked " not
known ". In August, 1965, the vacation judge granted ex parte an extension
of the writ for four months from May 28, 1965. On Sept. 10, 1965, the writ was
served on the defendants. In February, 1966, the writ was set aside by the
same judge on the defendants' application, after argument, on the ground
that time should not have been extended in August, 1965. On appeal,

D

E

F

Held (WINN, L.J., dissenting): where time had run under the Limitation
Act, 1939, a plaintiff seeking an extension of a writ must show sufficient
reason for it; in the present case it was the plaintiff's solicitors' fault that the
writ had not been served previously and, having left its service so late, it
behoved them to do whatever was needed to ensure that no mistake over its
service was made; accordingly, the decision of the judge on the inter partes
application that, in effect, time should not have been extended was right (see
p. 292, letter G, p. 293, letters A to D and G, H, and p. 294, letter B, post).

G

Dictum of MEGAW, J., in *Heaven* v. *Road and Rail Wagons, Ltd.* ([1965] 2
All E.R. at p. 414) approved.

Per LORD DENNING, M.R.: even if difficulty arose because of the need to
obtain legal aid, that could not affect, by virtue of s. 1 (7) (b) of the Legal Aid
and Advice Act, 1949, the principles on which the discretion of the court to
grant or refuse an extension of a writ was exercised; accordingly, in considering such an extension legal aid must be ignored (see p. 292, letter C,
post).

H

Appeal dismissed.

I

[As to the renewal of a writ of summons, see 24 HALSBURY'S LAWS (3rd Edn.)
199, 200, para. 357, and 30 ibid., 303, para. 558; and for cases on the subject,
see 32 DIGEST (Repl.) 623, 624, *2001-2013*, Digest, title PRACTICE 311, 312,
358-368, and 3rd DIGEST SUPP., title PRACTICE, *358a-368b*.

For the Limitation Act, 1939, s. 2 (1), see 13 HALSBURY'S STATUTES (2nd Edn.)
1160; and for the Law Reform (Limitation of Actions, &c.) Act, 1954, s. 2 (1),
see 34 ibid., p. 464.

A   For the Legal Aid and Advice Act, 1949, s. 1 (7) (*b*), see 18 HALSBURY'S
STATUTES (2nd Edn.) 534.]

Cases referred to:

    Battersby v. *Anglo-American Oil Co., Ltd.*, [1944] 2 All E.R. 387; [1945] K.B.
        23; 114 L.J.K.B. 49; 171 L.T. 300; 2nd Digest Supp.

    Heaven v. *Road and Rail Wagons, Ltd.*, [1965] 2 All E.R. 409; [1965] 2 Q.B.

B   355; [1965] 2 W.L.R. 1249.

Interlocutory Appeal.

This was an appeal by the plaintiff, George Victor Baker, from an order made
by BROWNE, J., in chambers, on Feb. 14, 1966, whereby he set aside on inter
partes application by the defendants, Bowketts Cakes, Ltd., his previous order
dated Aug. 16, 1965, extending the validity of the writ, issued in the Ramsgate
C District Registry, for four months from May 28, 1965, and further ordered that
the service of the writ, which was effected on Sept. 10, 1965, should be set aside.
The facts are set out in the judgment of LORD DENNING, M.R.

The case noted below* was cited during the argument in addition to those
referred to in the judgments.

D   *Michael Lewis* for the plaintiff.
    M. J. Turner for the defendants.

    LORD DENNING, M.R.: Several years ago the plaintiff, Mr. Baker, was
employed as a baker with the defendants, Bowketts Cakes, Ltd. at Broadstairs.
In the course of his employment he contracted dermatitis or eczema. He left
their employment in January, 1962, so that any cause of action must have
E occurred before that time. He received industrial insurance benefit on account of
the dermatitis or eczema. In April, 1962, he went to solicitors who wrote a letter
on his behalf to the defendants, who put them in touch with the insurance company. Two meetings took place. The last meeting was in October, 1962, at which
the insurers pointed out that the plaintiff had no claim against his employers
unless he could prove negligence. The defendants heard nothing more of the case
F for three years, until a writ was served on them on Sept. 10,1965. What we have to
consider today is whether the writ was validly in force so as to be able to be
properly served on that day.

Why did it take so long for the plaintiff's solicitors to issue the writ and serve
it? It seems that in 1963 they applied for legal aid. It was a long time in coming.
Eventually on May 11, 1964, they got leave to seek counsel's opinion and leave
G to issue a writ, but to go no further. They did not get leave to serve the writ.
On May 28, 1964, on behalf of the plaintiff, they issued a writ against the defendants for damages for dermatitis contracted by him owing to negligence on the
part of the defendants in the course of the plaintiff's employment between
August, 1958, and January, 1962. The writ was not served because the legal aid
certificate did not include service. During the next year there were further
H discussions, medical examinations, references to counsel, and so forth; but still
the writ was not served. Eventually the time came in May, 1965, when this writ
was nearly twelve months old. Now a writ is only valid in the first instance for
twelve months. So this writ was only valid from May 28, 1964, until May 28,
1965. Seeing that the twelve months were nearly up, on May 24, 1965, the
plaintiff's solicitors applied to the district registrar to extend the validity of the
I writ for a further period. The district registrar on May 25, thought that it was a
difficult matter. He adjourned it for a time which would go beyond the twelve
months. This roused the plaintiff's solicitors into action. They felt that they must
serve the writ straight away if they could. They telephoned the local director
of the defendants and asked for the registered office of the company. The message
was that it was " at Berkeley House, 40, Berkeley Square, London, W.1 ". So
on May 25, they sent off the copy writ by post to that address; but unfortunately

---

* *The Prins Bernhard*, [1963] 3 All E.R. 735; [1964] P. 117.

it was the wrong address. Berkeley House was not the registered office of this **A** company. Eventually the letter was returned " not known at Berkeley House ". So it was not served within the twelve months.

In this situation the only hope for the plaintiff's solicitors was to obtain an extension of the validity of the writ. The district registrar had adjourned the application. He eventually referred it to the judge. It came before BROWNE, J., as vacation judge in August, 1965. He heard it ex parte and granted an extension **B** for four months from May 28, 1965. The writ was served on Sept. 10, 1965. The defendants entered a conditional appearance and applied to set aside the writ. Eventually in February, 1966, BROWNE, J., again heard the case. He reversed his previous decision which he had made ex parte. After hearing argument he held that as a matter of discretion it was not right to extend the writ. It had expired on May 28, 1965. Not having been served within the twelve months, **C** the action must be dismissed.

Now there is an appeal from his decision to this court. It has been said that the difficulty arose because of the need to get legal aid at various stages; but I do not think that that can affect our decision. Under the Legal Aid and Advice Act, 1949, s. 1 (7) (*b*), the rights conferred on a person receiving legal aid do not affect the principles on which the discretion of this court is exercised. This is only **D** fair to the defendants. The defendants here did not know that the plaintiff was legally aided. They did not know that he had issued a writ. In considering whether to extend the writ, we must ignore legal aid.

The rules governing the extension of time are now contained in R.S.C., Ord. 6, r. 8 (2), which says:

" Where a writ has not been served on a defendant, the court may by order **E** extend the validity of the writ from time to time for such period, not exceeding twelve months at any one time, beginning with the day next following that on which it would otherwise expire, as may be specified in the order, if an application for extension is made to the court before that day or such later day (if any) as the court may allow."

F

In seeing whether the discretion should be exercised under that rule we must remember the Limitation Act, 1939. A plaintiff in an action for personal injuries has three years to issue his writ. If he issues it within those three years, he has another twelve months within which he can serve the writ. If he requires to extend it for a further time before service, he ought to show sufficient reason for an extension of time. That follows from what LORD GODDARD said in *Battersby* v. *Anglo-* **G** *American Oil Co., Ltd.* (1), and from what MEGAW, J., said in *Heaven* v. *Road and Rail Wagons, Ltd.* (2). In particular, when the Limitation Act, 1939, has run or is running in favour of a defendant, as here, the plaintiff who desires a further extension must show sufficient reason for an extension. These cases ought to be brought on for trial as soon as reasonably may be, while the facts are fresh in people's minds and while medical evidence and so forth can be obtained. If the **H** plaintiff delays until the very last minute he has only himself to thank. If it is his solicitors' fault, he can blame them; but he ought not to get an extension, to the prejudice of the defendants, except for good cause. In this case the application was made long after the three years. The cause of action accrued in January, 1962. The three years period of limitation expired in January, 1965. The writ was issued in May, 1964. During the whole of the year from May, 1964, to May, **I** 1965, the solicitors for the plaintiff could and should have got on with the case and done whatever was necessary, for the purposes of legal aid and the writ, to have the writ served within the twelve months. I see no sufficient reason why they should not have got on with the case. They ought to have collected all the medical evidence and done whatever was necessary within the twelve months.

(1) [1944] 2 All E.R. 387 at p. 391; [1945] K.B. 23 at p. 32.
(2) [1965] 2 All E.R. 409; [1965] 2 Q.B. 355.

A They did not do so. It was their fault. Thus far I see no reason for extending the time.

The one point that has troubled me in the case is the last minute effort of the plaintiff's solicitors to serve the defendants. They telephoned and tried to find the address of the registered office and were given the wrong address. By reason of that mistake they failed to serve the writ on the last day or the last day

B but one. If they had been given the right address, they would have served the writ on May 26, 1965, and would have been in time. It seems to me that, if they leave it as late as that, it behoves them to make absolutely sure that they have it properly served. They left it until the very last day, or the last day but one or two, of the twelve months. They should not have relied on the telephone message. They should have instructed London agents, or done whatever was

C necessary, to ensure that no mistake was made. Having failed to have it properly served, they must take the consequences. It seems to me that in fairness to the defendants, who did not hear of this matter from October, 1962, until Sept. 10, 1965, the application to extend the writ beyond the normal twelve months was rightly refused by the judge in his discretion.

I would therefore dismiss the appeal.

D

HARMAN, L.J.: I am of the same opinion. There are really two points in this case. The first of them deals with the long period that elapsed after the end of the plaintiff's negotiations through his solicitors with the insurance company, which was in October, 1962, when he knew he would have to prove negligence on the part of his employers and could get nothing out of them short of that.

E From that date, October, 1962, it took his solicitors until May, 1964, to issue a writ. No doubt the application for legal aid took some time, but legal aid need not take anything like that time. Even when they received from the legal aid committee permission to go as far as issuing (but not serving) the writ, they appear not to have obtained any materials which would enable counsel to advise the legal aid committee that there was a fair prima facie case which justified a

F certificate to go further. What was happening all that time, Heaven knows. The end of May seems to have been the time which roused the plaintiff's solicitors to action. On May 28, 1964, they went as far as issuing the writ and they were galvanised in the last ten days of May, 1965, into making some effort to serve it. They also made an effort to extend the time for service. It is true that at the time when they applied for a renewal of the period over which the writ should

G run, this interest by three or four days had not accrued to the defendants. Nevertheless he who leaves a thing like this until the last possible moment must run the risk that the last possible moment will go by and that he will find that he has not got over the fence.

So here the district registrar did not like the responsibilities involved and after a discreet interval adjourned the matter to the judge. In August, 1965, the

H judge, having heard only one side, allowed the extension. Having at a later date heard both sides, he decided that fairness to defendants, which, after all, is no less necessary than fairness to plaintiffs, required that he should withdraw that extension. Having regard to the delay from 1962 to 1965, I see no reason whatever for interfering with that decision.

The only matter which has given me pause, as it did LORD DENNING, M.R., was

I this matter of trying to serve the defendants by post in the last two days. Now it is true that you may wait until the 364th day of the third year before issuing your writ and until the 364th day of one year more before serving it and you will still be in time. If you choose, however, to wait until the last moment like that, you must be very careful to be right and there is no reason why you should be given any further indulgence. The nearer you are to the last moment, the stricter ought to be the attitude of the court. Here it was possible, even on May 27, to serve the defendants at their registered office with the writ, but it was not done. The information on which the plaintiff's solicitors acted was wrong information.

It may be said that it was given by somebody representing the defendants so that A
it was not their fault. I do not think that that is right. It was given apparently to
the solicitors' clerk by a local director. It is not a local directors' duty to give such
information: nor is it necessary that the local director should know where the
registered office is. He apparently did not know. He gave the wrong information.
The solicitors took a chance. They sent the letter only slightly wrongly addressed,
but still wrongly addressed, and it did not reach its destination in time. I do not B
see that that is a sufficient reason for giving further time to these penultimate
kind of efforts.

On the whole I think that justice is done to the defendants by affirming the
learned judge's decision, and I would dismiss the appeal.

WINN, L.J.: With diffidence, I declare myself unable to concur. Since my C
judgment will have no effect, I will state it succinctly, indicating only one or two
relevant points.

As at present advised, I think that the decision of MEGAW, J., in *Heaven* v.
Road and Rail Wagons, Ltd. (3) is sound in law, though I cannot concur in the
short phrase: " they were surplusage " (4). However, I think the use in the
headnote (5) of the expression " exceptional circumstances ", which has found D
its way into the ANNUAL PRACTICE, 1966, p. 68 under the note headed: " Extend
the validity of the writ ", is not justified by the judge's judgment (6). I think,
like MEGAW, J., that the change in wording of the new R.S.C., Ord. 6, as compared
with the old R.S.C., Ord. 8, is not material and has not changed the old law in
any relevant respect.

Therefore, the test remains whether or not the court or judge is satisfied that E
reasonable efforts have been made to serve the defendant with the writ, the
extension of which is sought by the application, at any rate if that application is
made, as it was here, during the validity of the writ. In my judgment, whilst it
is, of course, essential that the court should always bear in mind the maxim
interest reipublicae ut sit finis litium, that is no justification for reading the word
" prompt " or " energetic " into the words " if satisfied that reasonable efforts F
have been made ". As my lords have said, the conduct of this litigation was
lamentably lethargic. It is not the conduct of the litigation, however, which in
my judgment provides the criterion for the exercise of the discretion of the court;
it is whether or not during the currency of a writ, i.e., whilst it is valid, reasonable
efforts have been made to serve it. I cannot for my part think what effort to
serve a writ could be more reasonable than to adopt the one and only method of G
service on a limited company prescribed by the Companies Act, 1948, namely,
putting it into the post directed to the registered office of the company. It is
true that the address written on the envelope was only in part the true address
of the registered office of the defendants, but since another envelope posted at
the same time and addressed in the same way arrived, the effort to deliver this
one seems to me to have been at least reasonable. It would be most unfortunate
if failure on the part of the Post Office, whether or not that is to be regarded in H
these days as an " exceptional circumstance ", were to deprive this plaintiff of
whatever rights he may have in respect of the litigation which he has tried to
start. I myself would not have dismissed this appeal.

Appeal dismissed. Leave to appeal to the House of Lords refused.

Solicitors: *Payne, Hicks Beach & Co.*, agents for *Weigall & Inch*, Margate I
(for the plaintiff); *E. P. Rugg & Co.* (for the defendants).

[*Reported by* F. GUTTMAN, ESQ., *Barrister-at-Law.*]

---

(3) [1965] 2 All E.R. 409; [1965] 2 Q.B. 355.
(4) [1965] 2 All E.R. at p. 414, letter H; [1965] 2 Q.B. at p. 364, letter A.
(5) [1965] 2 W.L.R. 1249 at p. 1250.
(6) Compare, however, [1965] 2 All E.R. at p. 413, letter C, line 3, p. 416, letter E.

A

COTTRILL *v.* STEYNING AND LITTLEHAMPTON BUILDING SOCIETY.

[QUEEN'S BENCH DIVISION (Elwes, J.), June 25, 26, 27, 28, 29, July 2, 3, 4, 5, 6, 25, 1962.]

B *Sale of Land—Option—Breach—Damages—Measure—Repudiation of option by vendor—Intention of purchaser to develop property—Vendor having knowledge of purchaser's intention—Damages for loss of profits.*

In February, 1957, vendors granted to the plaintiff an option to purchase a house and land for £5,000; the option included a term that he should apply for planning permission and modification of a tree preservation order
C to permit alteration of the house and building on the land. At the time when the option was granted the vendors knew that the purchaser intended to develop the land. The plaintiff promptly took steps towards obtaining planning permission and modification of the tree preservation order. He left England, however, for a month in April, 1957, returning on May 10. The vendors, wrongly as the court found, treated this as repudiation and
D re-sold for £6,250. They were thus in breach of their contract with the plaintiff. The plaintiff, who had developed other properties, effected his developments of land through companies, and he had, on a former occasion, conveyed a neighbouring property for development to one of his companies without taking a profit on the sale. The vendors had no knowledge at the time of the option contract of the method used by plaintiff in developing
E land through companies or of his intentions in that respect.

Held: the plaintiff's damages for breach of contract should be assessed by reference to the profits which both parties contemplated that he would make and which the defendants' breach of contract had prevented him from making; accordingly, the market value of the property should be assessed on the footing that planning permission would be granted and the
F tree-preservation order would be modified within six months of the plaintiff's return on May 10, 1957, and that the building and alteration would have been completed within eighteen months of May 10, 1957, with the consequence that the damages would be the difference between the market value so estimated and the expenses of building together with the agreed price of the land (see p. 298, letters A and F, G, post).

G   Dictum of DEVLIN, J., in *Biggin & Co., Ltd.* v. *Permanite, Ltd.* ([1950] 2 All E.R. at p. 869) applied.

[As to the measure of damages for loss of a bargain, see 34 HALSBURY'S LAWS (3rd Edn.) 336, 337, para. 569; and for cases on the subject, see 40 DIGEST (Repl.) 290, 291, *2430-2439.*

H   As to the exercise of a mortgagee's power of sale, see 27 HALSBURY'S LAWS (3rd Edn.) 302, 303, para. 567; and as to the position of building society mortgages, see 3 ibid., 605, para. 1229.]

Cases referred to:

Biggin & Co., Ltd. v. *Permanite, Ltd., Berry Wiggins & Co., Ltd., Third Parties,* [1950] 2 All E.R. 859; [1951] 1 K.B. 422; *revsd.* C.A., [1951] 2 All E.R.
I   191; [1951] 2 K.B. 314; 17 Digest (Repl.) 130, *377.*

Diamond v. *Campbell-Jones,* [1960] 1 All E.R. 583; [1961] Ch. 22; [1960] 2 W.L.R. 568; Digest (Cont. Vol. A) 1313, *2435a.*

Engell v. *Fitch,* (1868), L.R. 3 Q.B. 314; *affd.* C.A., (1869), L.R. 4 Q.B. 659; 38 L.J.Q.B. 304; 40 Digest (Repl.) 285, *2369.*

Hadley v. *Baxendale,* [1843-60] All E.R. Rep. 461; (1854), 9 Exch. 341; 23 L.J.Ex. 179; 23 L.T.O.S. 69; 17 Digest (Repl.) 91, *99.*

Victoria Laundry (Windsor), Ltd. v. *Newman Industries, Ltd.,* [1949] 1 All E.R. 997; [1949] 2 K.B. 528; 17 Digest (Repl.) 92, *100.*

Wright v. *Dean*, [1948] 2 All E.R. 415; [1948] Ch. 686; [1948] L.J.R. 1571; A
30 Digest (Repl.) 501, *1430*.

Action.

This was an action by the plaintiff against the defendants for damages for
breach of an agreement dated Feb. 25, 1957, granting him an option to purchase
landed property, the Highclyffe Hotel at Seaton, Devonshire, of which the
defendants were mortgagees. In November, 1949, Mr. and Mrs. Lock had bought B
the hotel for £10,000, the defendants lending £6,000 secured on a mortgage
containing no provision for periodical reduction of the capital debt. In September, 1950, the Locks sold the hotel to Mr. and Mrs. Sharpe for £12,000, subject
to the mortgage and a second mortgage for £1,800 to the Locks. Mr. Sharpe
having died, Mrs. Sharpe continued the hotel business until the autumn of 1955
and kept up interest payments to the defendants until March, 1956, whereafter C
she defaulted. By June, 1956, the defendants' mortgage interest was two months
in arrear and their statutory power of sale enured. The property was put up
for sale by auction in April, 1956, but there were no bids. In July, 1956, Mr.
Cox was formally appointed the defendants' agent and he obtained an offer of
£5,000 for the hotel from the plaintiff, who had bought a comparable property
on the other side of the road and intended developing it. The plaintiff's offer D
was subject to four conditions. The trial judge (ELWES, J.) found that, after
lengthy negotiations, the plaintiff and the defendants entered into a binding
agreement granting the plaintiff an option* to purchase the Highclyffe Hotel
property for £5,000, the option to be exercised as soon as reasonably possible
after a successful conclusion of negotiations with the local authority to obtain
planning permission to convert the hotel into self-contained flats and to build E
six dwelling-houses and to obtain a modification of a tree preservation order
(which had been made in October, 1956) to permit the plaintiff's intended development of the land, or after the result of an appeal to the Minister if that proved to be
necessary. This option agreement was reached by correspondence on or about
Feb. 25, 1957. By two letters dated Mar. 2 and 12, 1957, an offer of £4,000 was
made for the property by another purchaser, a Mr. Dodge. On Mar. 6, 1957, there F
was a meeting between the plaintiff and representatives of the planning authority
and other persons concerned. At this meeting the plaintiff in great measure
attained his objectives regarding planning permission and modification of the
tree preservation order. A public local inquiry due to take place on Mar. 20,
1957, was postponed, and this was communicated to Mr. Dodge. On Mar. 23
£6,700 was offered on behalf of Mr. Dodge. On Apr. 5, the planning officer G
confirmed approval of the plaintiff's development even if the property should
be sold to a different purchaser. The plaintiff left England on a month's holiday
from Apr. 8 to May 9, 1957. By letter dated Apr. 27, 1957, the defendants
formally cancelled the plaintiff's option. At the trial there was a question
whether the plaintiff had agreed to its suspension, but this was decided against
the defendants. The plaintiff returned to business on May 10, 1957. The H

---

* The defendants contended that the grant of the option was ultra vires and void,
citing *Oceanic Steam Navigation Co.* v. *Sutherberry* ((1880), 16 Ch.D. 236). They also
contended that it constituted a clog on the equity of redemption and was invalid for
that reason. The trial judge held on the facts that the property had been virtually
not saleable at the time, apart from the plaintiff's offer of which the grant of an option
was a condition, and that in agreeing to that the defendants were endeavouring to sell I
so soon as they could and at the best price. Moreover, for this reason as well as because
the option did not relieve the defendants of any obligation under s. 10 of the Building
Societies Act, 1939 (cf. s. 36 of the Building Societies Act, 1962; 42 HALSBURY'S STATUTES,
2nd Edn., 91), a grant of the option was not invalidated by s. 10. The trial judge held
that if the grant of an option were reasonably necessary to obtain the best price, then,
in the absence of an express prohibition (and the defendants' rules contained no express
prohibition), such a grant was permissible. Accordingly the argument of invalidity on
the ground of ultra vires failed. The alleged clog on the equity of redemption was
rejected on the ground that the projected sale was not in fact by the defendants as
mortgagees but by them as agents for and with the concurrence of the mortgagor.

A defendants contended that the plaintiff's departure abroad on holiday at this time amounted to repudiation. The trial judge (ELWES, J.) held that it did not, but that the defendants were in breach of the option contract. The defendants eventually sold the property to Mr. Dodge for £6,250. The trial judge having held that the agreement to grant the option was not ultra vires the defendants, went on to deal with the issue of damages on which his judgment is reported.

B   *A. E. James*, Q.C., and *J. D. A. Fennell* for the plaintiff.
Nigel Warren, Q.C., and *J. A. R. Finlay* for the defendants.

Cur. adv. vult.

July 25. **ELWES, J.:** I am not asked to assess the damages in terms of money, but to decide the principle on which such an assessment should proceed.
C For the defendants, it is contended that the proper measure of damages is the difference between the contract price of £5,000 and the profit which the plaintiff could have made on a re-sale at the date of the breach. The best evidence of that, say the defendants, is the price actually paid at that time by Mr. Dodge, £6,250, and damages should accordingly be assessed at £1,250. Counsel for the defendants cites *Engell* v. *Fitch* (1). Until that decision it seems to have been widely
D thought that damages for breach of a contract for the sale of land were limited to the return of the deposit and the expenses of investigating the title. *Engell's* case (1) is clear authority for the proposition that, when a vendor's failure to complete is not merely inability to make a good title, but something other (in that case a voluntary decision not to proceed because a suit for ejectment was necessary and would have been too expensive), the measure of damages is the
E profit the purchaser could have made on a re-sale. In that case, the evidence showed that the intending purchaser had agreed to sell at a profit of one hundred guineas, and the court, accordingly, had to decide as between alternative ascertained sums. Counsel for the defendants contends that this decision fixes the measure of damages to the market price at the date of the breach. The principle enunciated, however, is much wider. The disappointed purchaser was held to
F be entitled to the profit which it was shown he could have made on re-sale. In that case, the evidence showed that he intended to sell again at once, and at a price. No other evidence was tendered.
Counsel for the plaintiff relies on some modern cases: first, a decision of WYNN-PARRY, J., in *Wright* v. *Dean* (2). In that case, the learned judge treated the breach of an option to purchase land as a breach of contract to which the
G common law rule as to damages applied. He applied *Hadley* v. *Baxendale* (3), and assessed damages by reference to the value of the property in the open market at the date of the breach. It was not shown in that case that any special ulterior purpose was contemplated by the parties when the contract was made. In *Biggin & Co., Ltd.* v. *Permanite, Ltd., Berry Wiggins & Co., Ltd., Third Parties* (4), DEVLIN, J., made some observations on *Hadley* v. *Baxendale* (3) and *Victoria*
H *Laundry (Windsor), Ltd.* v. *Newman Industries, Ltd.* (5) which I find helpful. He said (6) that the later decision

"makes it clear that there is only one area of indemnity to be explored, and that is what is within the prevision of the defendant as a reasonable man in the light of the knowledge, actual or imputed, which he has at the time of the contract."

I In *Diamond* v. *Campbell-Jones* (7), BUCKLEY, J., had occasion to apply the same principle, and held on the facts of that case that the plaintiff was not entitled to

---

(1) (1868), L.R. 3 Q.B. 314.
(2) [1948] 2 All E.R. 415; [1948] Ch. 686.
(3) [1843-60] All E.R. Rep. 461; (1854), 9 Exch. 341.
(4) [1950] 2 All E.R. 859; [1951] 1 K.B. 422.
(5) [1949] 1 All E.R. 997; [1949] 2 K.B. 528.
(6) [1950] 2 All E.R. at p. 869; [1951] 1 K.B. at p. 436.
(7) [1960] 1 All E.R. 583; [1961] Ch. 22.

damages referable to profits obtainable by developing the property in the absence A of knowledge by the defendant vendor of the purchaser's intention to develop.

It is clear, in my opinion, that, if the defendants are shown to have known that the plaintiff intended to develop the land for profit, the special circumstances are established which entitle the plaintiff to have the damages assessed by reference to the profits which both parties contemplated that he would make. There cannot be the slightest doubt here that the defendants knew what the B plaintiff's intentions were, and knew exactly how he intended to pursue them. Subject to one other matter, I hold that the assessment of damages here should proceed on that basis.

The other matter to which I have alluded is this. The plaintiff conducts the business of a developer of land by means of limited companies which he has formed. In 1957, there were two of these companies, Wichell Park Properties, C Ltd. and Seaton Properties Investment, Ltd., each of which was in substance his alter ego. He seems to have contemplated in a vague kind of way the formation of another company to develop " Highclyffe " in which a friend of his might have taken an interest. I am satisfied that the defendants had no knowledge of this aspect of the plaintiff's methods and intentions, which were, of course, no business of theirs. Counsel for the defendants contends that, since D a limited company is an independent legal persona, any profit made by a company formed by the plaintiff would be too remote to be recoverable. He extracted from the plaintiff an admission that he conveyed Seaforth Estates to one of these companies without taking a profit on the sale, presumably to avoid paying tax on it, assessable no doubt on him in respect of his business as a developer of property. Ought those factors to prevent the court from applying the ordinary common law E principle as to damages? On one view, if pressed, the result will be to restrict the plaintiff to nominal damages only. I cannot think that this is right. The evidence about the plaintiff's companies may make the quantum of damages more difficult to ascertain, but it cannot, in my opinion, save the defendants from their liability to compensate the plaintiff for their breach of contract, and they must pay him such a sum as shall be proved to represent the net prospective F profit which he has been prevented from making.

I accordingly direct, on the basis of reasonable probability, that the damages should be assessed on the footing that planning permission would have been granted six months after May 10, 1957, the date of the plaintiff's return from abroad, and that the required modifications of the tree preservation order would have been made; that the plaintiff would have been able to proceed with his G plan to turn the hotel into flats and build six dwelling-houses, and that such building and alteration would have been completed within eighteen months of May 10, 1957. The market value of the property is to be ascertained, accordingly, and the damages assessed at that figure less the expenses attributable to the building work and all matters ancillary thereto. There will be judgment for the plaintiff with costs.   H

Judgment for the plaintiff.

Solicitors: *Canter & Martin*, agents for *Maurice Putsman & Co.*, Birmingham (for the plaintiff); *Robins, Hay & Waters*, agents for *Raper & Co.*, Chichester (for the defendants).

[*Reported by* K. DIANA PHILLIPS, *Barrister-at-Law.*]

A

COMMISSIONERS OF CUSTOMS AND EXCISE
v. SAVOY HOTEL, LTD.

[QUEEN'S BENCH DIVISION (Sachs, J.), March 4, 10, 1966.]

*Purchase Tax—Chargeable goods—Manufactured beverages—Orange juice freshly
pressed from a single orange—Purchase Tax Act* 1963 *(c.* 9), *s.* 2 (1), (2),
B   *Sch.* 1, *Pt.* 1, *Group* 35 *(a).*

In a group of London hotels guests who ordered orange juice were served
with the juice of an orange, unsweetened, freshly pressed to their order.
On the question whether the orange juice so served was chargeable goods
within Group 35 (*a*) of Sch. 1 to the Purchase Tax Act 1963, as being within
the description "manufactured beverages, including fruit juices" in that
C   group,

Held: a portion of orange juice, so prepared and served, was not a
"manufactured beverage" and the description "including fruit juices"
was to be construed in the context of the words which preceded it; accordingly the orange juice was not chargeable goods within s. 2 (1), (2) of the
Act of 1963 and Group 35 (*a*) of Sch. 1 thereto (see p. 302, letters A and D, post).

D   [As to the charge of purchase tax on chargeable goods, see 33 HALSBURY'S
LAWS (3rd Edn.) 223, para. 382.

As to the meaning of the word "including", see 36 HALSBURY'S LAWS (3rd
Edn.) 385, para. 574, notes (i), (k).

For the Purchase Tax Act 1963, s. 2, s. 40 (1), Sch. 1, Group 35, see 43
HALSBURY'S STATUTES (2nd Edn.) 1016, 1055, 1068.]

E
Cases referred to:

Dilworth v. Comr. of Stamps, [1899] A.C. 99; 79 L.T. 473; sub nom. Dilworth
v. New Zealand Stamps Comrs., 68 L.J.P.C. 1; 19 Digest (Repl.) 659,
348.

Savoy Hotel Co. v. London County Council, [1900] 1 Q.B. 665; 69 L.J.Q.B. 274;
82 L.T. 56; 64 J.P. 262; 24 Digest (Repl.) 1107, 518.

F
Originating Summons.

This was an application by the Commissioners of Customs and Excise by
originating summons to determine whether orange juice as sold by the defendants,
Savoy Hotel, Ltd., at the Savoy, Berkeley and Claridge's Hotels was within
the meaning of chargeable goods in s. 2 of the Purchase Tax Act 1963 and
G   Group 35 of Sch. 1 thereto.

Nigel Bridge for the commissioners.
G. B. Graham, Q.C., and *S. T. Crump* for the defendants.

SACHS, J.: In this case the court is called on to decide the fascinating
and no doubt important problem as to whether the guest who from his bedroom
H   in Claridge's (or for that matter the Savoy or the Berkeley) calls at breakfast
time for his orange juice and a few minutes later receives the juice of a single
orange freshly pressed out for his benefit in its purest form—unsweetened at that
—is provided with a manufactured beverage within the meaning of those words
in Group 35 of Sch. 1 to the Purchase Tax Act 1963. Any tendency to approach
this question with undue levity was checked by the information that in the course
I   of a single year there were served in those three hotels no less than one hundred
thousand of what it is convenient to call "portions" of orange juice, and that
the Commissioners of Customs and Excise were industriously chasing a sum of
the order of £1,500, having previously succeeded in bringing into the purchase
tax net the ices consumed by diners at those institutions.

To establish that items of this type attract purchase tax on delivery to the
bedrooms the commissioners must show, first, that they were then "chargeable
goods" (see s. 2 of the Act of 1963); next, that the sale was by a manufacturer
who was carrying on a business of manufacturing goods (see s. 10 (1) and the

definition of " manufacturor " in s. 40 (1)); and, thirdly, that the manufacturers' A
total business in chargeable goods was of the extent (over £500 per annum) laid
down by s. 4 (2).

The sole issue in the present case was whether the portions of orange juice as
delivered were " chargeable goods ". (No distinction was sought to be drawn
between the way in which the portion was prepared and supplied to bedrooms,
at a bar, or in the restaurants.) That issue depended on whether such a portion B
fell within Group 35 of Pt. 1 (List of Chargeable and Exempt Goods and Rates
of Tax) of Sch. 1 to the Act of 1963. This Group is defined as follows:

" Group 35. (a) Manufactured beverages, including fruit juices and
bottled waters, and syrups, concentrates, essences, powders, crystals or
other products for the preparation of beverages, but not including beverages
or products in the list set out at the end of this Group. (b) Containers of C
gas for the preparation of carbonated beverages."

There follows the list of excluded beverages and products.

It was common ground between the parties that the issue turned entirely on
the interpretation of the relevant words in para. (a) above. In the course of
the submissions by both parties reference has been made, inter alia, to the D
definition of " manufacturer " and " manufacturing process " in s. 40 (1) and
also to s. 40 (2) which defines what treatment of goods shall be deemed to be
the application of a process; but in the end counsel for the commissioners conceded
that the word " manufactured " in " manufactured beverages " must be given
its ordinary meaning without reference to other definitions in the Act of 1963,
and specifically included in that concession that no aid could or should be sought E
from s. 40 (2)—a point which counsel for the defendants had pressed. No
authorities were cited as to that meaning.

Turning then to the relevant words in Group 35, there inevitably occurs, as
counsel for the commissioners readily agreed, a strong first impression that a
portion of fresh natural orange juice pressed from a single orange for a particular
person ordering it cannot in common sense be called a " manufactured beverage ". F
In part that impression is due to mental resistance to applying the words " manufactured beverage" to something like natural juice that is in no way synthetic, and
partly to resistance to the idea that such an extraction of juice specially effected
for a particular person comes within the " factory " concept evoked by the word
" manufactured ". That concept is one which brings to mind elements that include
operations on a scale larger than that employed to produce one portion of orange G
juice for an individual and (even if the juice need not be synthetic) then at least
some intention that the relevant process should form part of a series capable of
leading the product to the equivalent of a shelf in a supermarket. Nevertheless
counsel for the commissioners firmly pressed that, however incongruous it
might appear, yet on the proper construction of the relevant words of sub-para.
(a) taken as a whole, the housewife whenever she in similar fashion provided a H
member of the family with a glass of fresh orange juice, had " manufactured " it
—albeit, of course, not in business even if she so provided one thousand or fifteen
hundred portions a year.

That first impression and initial avulsion from incongruity was formed before
counsel for the commissioners had deployed his arguments. The first of these
was that the word " included " in sub-para. (a) of Group 35 was used in its I
extensory meaning, and not in that more normal meaning of " such as " which
may so often cover matters mentioned ex abundante cautela. He started by
citing that passage of the speech of LORD WATSON in Dilworth v. Comr. of Stamps
(1), where he said:

" The word ' include ' is very generally used in interpretation clauses in
order to enlarge the meaning of words or phrases occurring in the body of

_____

(1) [1899] A.C. 99 at pp. 105, 106.

A   the statute; and when it is so used these words or phrases must be construed as comprehending, not only such things as they signify according to their natural import, but also those things which the interpretation clause declares that they shall include."

To that he added the passage in the judgment of CHANNEL, J., in the next cited case, where it is stated (2) that

B   " the result of an interpretation clause is frequently to bring the most incongruous things within the operation of a statute."

Having thus firmly grasped the incongruity nettle flourishing in the centre of that strong first impression, he then uprooted it by apt reference to the effect of the decision in *Savoy Hotel Co.* v. *London County Council* (3), by which it was

C   held that this very establishment, the Savoy Hotel, was a " shop " for the purpose of the Shop Hours Act, 1892. In this way counsel for the commissioners consigned common sense, for the purposes of the present case, to a casualty clearing station.

It being clear that, for instance, " crystals or other products for the preparation of beverages " are not of themselves " manufactured beverages " and that quoad those items " included " must obviously have an extensory meaning,

D   counsel for the commissioners proceeded as follows. The word " including " being used in its extensory sense it follows that the words " fruit juices " and " bottled waters " must refer to something that would not normally come within the meaning of the words " manufactured beverage ". It followed again that as all fruit juices with additives would automatically be " manufactured beverages " even if not mentioned in the words following " included ", the only

E   thing " fruit juices " could really refer to was pure and natural fruit juice—by whatever method extracted from the fruit, whether by an individual pressing or by some massive mechanical pulping. Moreover, he pointed out, the very use of the word " bottled " in " bottled waters " tended to show that no factory or other bottling was needed to attract natural fruit juice into the realm of chargeable goods. As to " bottled waters " he similarly contended that as

F   soda water, tonic water and the like are clearly manufactured beverages, thus bottled waters could only refer to those that emerge so naturally, so usefully and so profitably from areas such as Malvern and Vichy—though he conceded that in some way there was excluded natural water sold bottled at a garage-or elsewhere for purposes other than that of being drunk.

" Included " is a word to which parliamentary draftsmen seem considerably

G   addicted: one reason for this may be that in law it can have, according to its context, not only one or other of simple but in essence quite differing effects (for instance, in relation to the words that follow it may be found to have been used simply to enlarge, to limit, to define exhaustively or for the avoidance of doubts to repeat the preceding word or phrase), but it may also be used to secure on one and the same occasion more than one of those effects thus putting the

H   draftsman, but not necessarily the court, in a happy position. In the present case it in the end became evident that as regards each and every one of the items mentioned after the word " included " that word must, if the argument for the commissioners was to succeed, have exactly the same simple meaning as " and ": and this counsel for the commissioners readily agreed. When, however, asked why the draftsman (assuming he had not temporarily lost his capacity to

I   spell) did not then use that simple word of three letters, no satisfactory explanation appeared available.

However persuasive may be the exercise in logical approach adopted on behalf of the commissioners, it seems to break down at this point. The approach of the draftsman was probably not after all as limpidly lucid as the submissions of counsel for the commissioners. So one arrives at the not wholly unknown situation that a word (here " included ") has been used by the draftsman in a

---

(2) [1900] 1 Q.B. 665 at p. 669.   (3) [1900] 1 Q.B. 665,

schedule in a somewhat ambivalent way; and that the path yet remains open A for a modicum of common sense to emerge after its battering.

To talk of natural juice extracted by hand from a single orange for the use of the particular person who wishes to have it fresh to drink, as a " manufactured beverage " does not, as I have already indicated, make sense; and there is nothing here in the use of the word " included " that compels the court to say that " fruit juices " must be construed without reference to the two words with B which the sentence begins and which should, where practicable, be given some effect in relation to the words that follow.

Whether pure extracted juice can ever form a manufactured beverage any more than milk extracted from cow or coco-nut (or, if it happened to be drinkable, some natural liquid from the earth) it does not seem necessary to decide. Nothing in the judgment is intended unduly to deter the commissioners from pursuing C the case of someone who uses mass pulping methods and then puts the product in can, bottle, flagon or cask and from attempting in such a case to establish that manufactured beverages can in certain circumstances include liquids that are in no way synthetic—whatever may be the difficulty of persuading a court that a fruit juice which is natural can yet be " manufactured ". Suffice it here to say that " manufactured " is, in any event, a word that embodies some elements D that are wholly absent in what is simply done for the benefit of the individual guest who asks for the fresh juice of a single orange at breakfast time in any place, be it grand or homely. To my mind, neither the Savoy nor the housewife on such occasions provides a manufactured beverage.

Order accordingly.

Solicitors: *D. J. Willson* (for the commissioners); *Simmons & Simmons* (for E the defendants).

[*Reported by* K. DIANA PHILLIPS, *Barrister-at-Law.*]

LUCAS v. RUSHBY.

[QUEEN'S BENCH DIVISION (Lord Parker, C.J., Sachs and Veale, JJ.), March 23, F 1966.]

Weights and Measures—Pre-packed goods—Meat exposed for sale on bit of paper slightly larger than piece of meat—Whether the bit of paper was " packaging "—Whether the meat was pre-packed goods—Weights and Measures Act 1963 (c. 31), s. 22 (1), s. 58 (1), Sch. 4, Pt. 1, para. 2 (a).

Bacon or ham was displayed on a slab in the window of a retail shop, each G piece of meat standing on a bit of paper slightly larger than the base of the piece of meat but not large enough to completely wrap it. Except in two cases, each piece of meat was offered for sale by price and not by weight. On a sale, after being weighed in the presence of the customer, the meat was partially wrapped in its bit of paper before being put in a paper bag. The manager of the shop was charged under s. 27 (4) of the Weights and Measures H Act 1963, with exposing for sale articles of food, which, unless pre-packed, were required to be sold by net weight under Sch. 4, Pt. 1, para. 2*, to the Act of 1963, contrary to s. 22 (1)† of that Act. By s. 58 (1)‡ of the Act of 1963, " pre-packed " meant made up in advance ready for retail sale in or on a container, and " container " included any form of packaging of goods for sale as a single item, whether by way of wholly or partly enclosing the I goods and in particular included a wrapper. On appeal against the dismissal of the charge,

Held: the mere fact that the bit of paper on which each piece of meat stood got ultimately into the bag taken by the customer did not render the bit of

---

* Schedule 4, Pt. I, para. 2 (*a*), is set out at p. 304, letter B, post.
† Section 22 (1), so far as material, is set out at p. 304, letter C, post.
‡ Section 58 (1), so far as material, is set out at p. 304, letters D and E, post.

A   paper part of the packaging of pre-packed goods; accordingly the meat was not " pre-packed " goods and, not being exposed for sale by net weight, s. 22 (1) was contravened (see p. 304, letter H, and p. 305, letter A, post).

[As to pre-packed articles of common consumption including bacon and ham, see 39 HALSBURY'S LAWS (3rd Edn.) 809, 810, paras. 1224, 1225.

For the Weights and Measures Act 1963, s. 22, s. 58, Sch. 4, Pt. 1, see 43

B   HALSBURY'S STATUTES (2nd Edn.) 1396, 1434, 1450.]

Case Stated.

This was a Case Stated by justices for the county of Lincoln (Parts of Lindsey) in respect of their adjudication as a magistrates' court sitting at Scunthorpe on Oct. 28, 1965. On Oct. 28, 1965, an information was preferred by the appellant, Myles Trevor Lucas, a chief inspector of weights and measures, for and on behalf

C   of Scunthorpe Borough Council, that Home and Colonial Stores, Ltd., whose head office was situate at 179/189, City Road, London, E.C.1, on Sept. 17, 1965, exposed for sale non-pre-packed articles of food of one of the kinds set forth in Sch. 4 to the Weights and Measures Act 1963, namely, thirty-five pieces of bacon or ham otherwise than by weight, namely, by marked price, contrary to s. 22 (1) of the Weights and Measures Act 1963. Scunthorpe Borough Council, the weights

D   and measures authority concerned, being reasonably satisfied that the offence was due to the act or default of the respondent, George Raymond Rushby, and that the Home and Colonial Stores, Ltd. could establish a defence under s. 27 (1) of the Weights and Measures Act 1963, the appellant applied that the respondent might be charged with the offence in accordance with s. 27 (4) of the Weights and Measures Act 1963.

E   The following facts were found. Home and Colonial Stores, Ltd. were the occupiers of a shop in High Street, Scunthorpe, of which the respondent was the manager. On Sept. 17, 1965, the appellant in the course of his duty observed the window of the shop and took note that there were approximately thirty-eight pieces of meat, of bacon and ham cuts, exposed in the window. Those pieces of meat were exposed on the window display slab, each piece of meat on a piece of

F   paper approximately eight inches by five inches. Each piece of meat had a ticket stuck into it and it had space for the following: " price per lb., price of joint ", and on the bottom was a statement that read " Re-weighed on sale ". Only two of these tickets had the weight on them. As to the remainder, the only representations were by price on the ticket. Each piece of meat stood on a piece of paper which was larger than the base of the piece of meat. On a sale, the meat

G   was weighed on the scales the readings of which showed on both sides of the scale so as to be visible both to the assistant and the customer, and each piece of meat was partially wrapped in the above-mentioned piece of paper before being put in a paper bag and taken away by the customer. The above-mentioned pieces of paper on which the pieces of meat stood for display were large enough to partially wrap the pieces of meat but were not large enough to completely wrap

H   the pieces of meat. When the pieces of meat were exposed for sale in the shop, they were made up in advance ready for retail sale on a container, and did not require to be cut or have anything further done to them except for the weight to be made known to the customer before delivery to the customer.

It was contended by the respondent that s. 22 (1) of the Weights and Measures Act 1963, had no application to the case in that the subsection only applied to

I   goods which were not pre-packed and that the pieces of meat were pre-packed goods. The respondent referred to the definitions of " pre-packed " and " container " contained in s. 58 of the Act of 1963, and contended that the pieces of meat were made up in advance, ready for retail sale in or on containers, namely, the pieces of paper which partially enclosed the pieces of meat. The appellant submitted that the respondent's contentions were not well founded.

The justices dismissed the information, and the appellant now appealed.

Ian McLean for the appellant.

P. D. J. Scott for the respondent.

LORD PARKER, C.J., stated the facts, and continued: The sole question A
here is whether this meat was pre-packed within the meaning of the Weights and
Measures Act 1963.   It is necessary to look at one or two sections of the Act of
1963; to begin with, s. 21 (1) provides that certain schedules " shall have effect
for the purposes of transactions in the goods therein mentioned ".   Schedule 4,
Pt. 1, deals with the sale of meat and food containing meat.   Paragraph 2 says
that, subject to a later paragraph: B

">. . . any goods to which this Part of this schedule applies which are not
pre-packed shall be sold only—(a) by net weight . . ."

Passing then to s. 22 (1), it is provided that:

" Subject to the provisions of this Part of this Act, in the case of any goods   C
which, when not pre-packed, are required by or under this Act to be sold only
by quantity . . . [in the present case net weight] . . . any person shall be guilty
of an offence who—(a) whether on his own behalf or on behalf of another
person, offers or exposes for sale, sells or agrees to sell, or (b) causes or suffers
any other person to offer or expose for sale, sell or agree to sell on his behalf,
those goods otherwise than by quantity expressed in that manner . . .",
                                                                                D
i.e., net weight.   It is clear, therefore, that an offence was committed unless these
goods were pre-packed goods.   For that one turns to the definition section, s. 58
(1), " ' pre-packed ' means made up in advance ready for retail sale in or on a
container . . .", and

" ' container ' includes any form of packaging of goods for sale as a single   E
item, whether by way of wholly or partly enclosing the goods or by way of
attaching the goods to, or winding the goods round, some other article, and
in particular includes a wrapper or confining band."

For my part, I find it very difficult to say that, when one finds a piece of meat
standing on a bit of greaseproof paper in a shop window, no doubt for hygienic F
purposes to protect the meat from the slab, and when it comes to weighing, to
convey the meat to the weighing machine, that that bit of paper can conceivably
by said to be any form of packaging of goods.   The magistrates were apparently
influenced by the fact that, when the meat was weighed, and weighed of course
on this bit of paper, and was finally wrapped up, the bit of paper on which it
stood did physically remain with the meat and partially wrapped it.   They say: G

" On a sale, the meat was weighed on the scales the readings of which
showed on both sides of the scale so as to be visible both to the assistant
and the customer, and each piece of meat was partially wrapped in the above-
mentioned piece of paper before being put in a paper bag and taken away by
the customer."   H

For my part, I am quite unable to say that such a bit of paper is a form of packaging; the mere fact that it gets into the package eventually because nobody takes
it off the meat or the meat off the paper does not seem to me to make it in any
proper sense part of the packaging of the goods.   That being so, I find it unnecessary to consider further matters, such as when the container must be wholly or   I
partly enclosing the goods; whether it be at the time of exposure or at the time
of sale; whether it has to enclose the goods to some extent at the time, or whether
it is sufficient that it will be used for that purpose in the future.   Solely on the
ground that this bit of paper is quite incapable of being said to form part of the
packaging of goods, I would allow this appeal.   I would only add that the justices
may, of course, think that, as in every case it was intended that the meat should
be weighed in full view of the customer, this was purely a technical offence.

A   **SACHS, J.:** I agree and have nothing to add.

VEALE, J.: I also agree.

Appeal allowed. Case remitted.

Solicitors: *Sharpe, Pritchard & Co.*, agents for *T. M. Lister*, Scunthorpe (for the appellant); *Hett, Davy & Stubbs*, Scunthorpe (for the respondent).

B
[*Reported by* N. P. METCALFE, ESQ., *Barrister-at-Law.*]

WHEELER v. SOMERFIELD AND OTHERS.

C   [COURT OF APPEAL (Lord Denning, M.R., Harman and Winn, L.JJ.), March 22, 1966.]

Costs—Appeal to Court of Appeal—Appeal as to costs without leave of the trial judge—Genuine appeal on several matters including costs—Appeal unsuccessful on all matters except costs—Whether appeal as to costs only within Supreme Court of Judicature (Consolidation) Act, 1925 (15 & 16 Geo. 5 c. 49), s. 31 (1) (h).

D

Libel—Damages—Health—Injury to health—Whether admissible head of damage.

Libel—Innuendo—Article in newspaper—Similar articles about others in same newspaper bearing alleged particular character—Innuendo attributing consequential like character to article in question—Irrelevance of prior articles about others.

E

In an action for libel the plaintiff, by para. 2 of his statement of claim, complained of four passages in one fairly long article in a weekly newspaper. Before trial he amended his statement of claim by leave to add para. 2A, alleging that the entire article meant that he was a dishonest or disreputable person and not a reputable or trustworthy businessman. He gave particulars which stated that on occasions too numerous to specify articles had appeared in the newspaper exposing the malpractice and dishonesty of other people.

F

In support of the innuendo in para. 2A the plaintiff gave a list of nearly one hundred articles that had appeared in the newspaper; none of these articles referred to the plaintiff. At the trial these articles were not admitted. The plaintiff was also refused at the trial leave to amend so as to claim damages for injury to health (aggravation of cataract) which he alleged, but he admitted that his medical evidence might not prove, to be due to the libel. The jury found that two out of the four statements complained of in para. 2 of the statement of claim constituted libels and awarded damages of £1,650.

G

The plaintiff had conducted the action and appeared in person. On the question of costs the trial judge first gave him half of the costs of the action and awarded the defendants no costs. On being informed, however, that the costs of making photostatic copies of the articles referred to in the list delivered for the purposes of para. 2A amounted to £400, the trial judge varied his proposed order as to costs by giving the plaintiff his costs of the action and the defendants the costs of the issue on para. 2A. The plaintiff's costs (out-of-pocket expenses) were taxed at £29 19s.; the defendants' costs on para. 2A were taxed at £391 14s. 8d. After the trial it was found that the costs of the photostats were only £80, as they had been prepared in the offices of the defendant newspaper. On appeal, the plaintiff not having obtained the leave of the trial judge, pursuant to s. 31 (1) (h)* of the Supreme Court of Judicature (Consolidation) Act, 1925, to appeal as to costs,

H

I

Held: (i) although a weekly publication could be so made up that a particular part of it became associated with matter having a particular character so that to include matter there might be to attribute to it that

---

* Section 31 (1) (h) is printed at p. 310, letter E, post.

particular character, with the consequence of making the inclusion libellous   A
if the character were defamatory, yet in the present case there was no
foundation for the drawing of any such inference; accordingly any libel must
be found in the article complained of itself, and the articles sought to be
adduced under para. 2A of the amended statement of claim had been rightly
rejected (see p. 309, letters C and D, p. 311, letter A, and p. 311, letter I,
to p. 312, letter C, post).   B

    Monson v. *Tussauds, Ltd.* ([1894] 1 Q.B. 671) distinguished.

    (ii) damages in a libel action were for the injury to reputation not to
health, and although it was possible that a libel might cause injury to health
and the possibility that damages might be awarded for such injury could not
be wholly excluded, yet a claim had not theretofore, it seemed, been allowed,
and in the present case the plaintiff failed on the facts as his medical evidence   C
might not be such as to prove that the alleged injury to health was
attributable to the libel (see p. 309, letter F, and p. 311, letters A and E,
post).

    (iii) the plaintiff was entitled to appeal as to costs, because there was a
genuine appeal, although in the outcome it was unsuccessful, on other issues,
and in such circumstances s. 31 (1) (*h*) did not preclude appeal as to costs with-   D
out leave of the trial judge; accordingly the plaintiff would be awarded half
his costs of the action (viz., half £29 19s.) and the defendants would have no
costs (see p. 310, letters G and I, and p. 311, letters B and E, post).

    Appeal as to costs allowed.

[Editorial Note. The decision regarding entitlement to appeal on costs is
to the same effect as that of the Court of Appeal in *Crystall* v. *Crystall* ([1963]   E
2 All E.R. 330, holding (ii)).

As to the right of appeal on costs to the Court of Appeal, see 30 HALSBURY'S
LAWS (3rd Edn.) 423, para. 798; and for cases on appeals as to costs only, see
DIGEST (Practice) 924, 925, *4671-4686*; and as to appeal on costs, see DIGEST
SUPP. Pleading and Practice, 36, *4036a*.

As to the need for an innuendo, see 24 HALSBURY'S LAWS (3rd Edn.) 86, para.   F
154; and for cases on the subject, see 32 DIGEST (Repl.) 74, 75, *970-979*; and
as to pleading, ibid., 78-80, *1001-1021*.

For the Supreme Court of Judicature (Consolidation) Act, 1925, s. 31 (1) (*h*),
see 5 HALSBURY'S STATUTES (2nd Edn.) 359.]

Cases referred to:
    Astaire v. *Campling*, [1965] 3 All E.R. 666; [1966] 1 W.L.R. 34.   G
    Monson v. *Tussauds, Ltd.*, [1894] 1 Q.B. 671; rvsd. C.A., [1891-94] All E.R.
        Rep. 1051; [1894] 1 Q.B. at p. 681; 63 L.J.Q.B. 454; 70 L.T. 335;
        58 J.P. 524; 32 Digest (Repl.) 10, *23*.

Appeal.

    This was an appeal by the plaintiff, Gerald Charles David Wheeler, by notice   H
of appeal dated Jan. 4, 1966, from the rulings and judgment of MILMO, J., at the
trial of the action on Oct. 25, 26, 27, 28 and 29, 1965, in so far as it was
adjudged (i) that leave to amend the statement of claim to include damage to
the plaintiff's health discovered shortly before trial be refused; (ii) that para.
2A of the amended statement of claim be withdrawn from the jury both as a
separate cause of action and as a matter affecting damages, and (iii) that the   I
defendants' costs of the issues raised under para. 2A of the amended statement of
claim be paid by the plaintiff. By his statement of claim the plaintiff pleaded
that he was an insurance claims assessor and had for the past three years and
was carrying on business in London, and that the first defendant, Stafford
William Somerfield, was the editor of a weekly journal called " The News of the
World ". The second defendant was The News of the World, Ltd. and the third
defendant was one Ron Mount. By para. 2 of the statement of claim, so far as
relevant to be set out herein, the plaintiff alleged—

A   " 2. In the issue of the said journal for June 28, 1964, the defendant, Ron Mount, falsely and maliciously wrote, and the defendant Stafford William Somerfield falsely and maliciously caused to be printed and published, and the defendants The News of the World, Ltd. falsely and maliciously printed and published of the plaintiff and of him in the way of his said business the words following, that is to say—(a) ' Glib, white-

B   haired Gerald Charles David Wheeler . . .' The said words, in their natural and ordinary meanings, meant and were intended to mean that the plaintiff was more fluent than sincere and had sought to explain his position in an easy and facile manner with no sufficient regard for the truth. (b) . . . (c) . . . (d) ' I was a nightwatchman when I started off in June, 1951, but I preferred to call myself a security guard '. The plaintiff did not utter the said

C   words but words to the reverse effect and the said words, in their natural and ordinary meanings, meant and were intended to mean, that the plaintiff was a false and pretentious person."

The sub-paras. (b) and (c) above set out particular short passages complained of in the article, but are not material to this report. By order dated Aug. 12, 1965, the plaintiff was given leave to amend his statement of claim by adding thereto a

D   paragraph which became para. 2A, and the plaintiff was ordered to serve a list of the specific articles on which he intended to rely as a sample of the publications referred to in the para. 2A of the amended statement of claim. Paragraph 2A was as follows—

E   " 2A. Further, or in the alternative, the entire article complained of meant and was understood to mean that the plaintiff was a dishonest and/or disreputable person and not a reputable or trustworthy businessman.

Particulars pursuant to Ord. 82, *r.* 3 (1)

On occasions too numerous to specify articles written by the third defendant and/or other journalists concerning various forms of business and of obtaining money by business men and other persons have been published

F   in The News of the World. The great majority of such articles have exposed the malpractices and/or dishonesty of their subjects. In the result, by publishing an article of similar kind hostile to the plaintiff's way of business the defendants in this suit have raised a clear inference that the plaintiff belonged to the category of disreputable and/or dishonest businessmen and

G   persons."

The plaintiff claimed damages. By their defence the defendants admitted publication, but denied that any of the words bore the specific natural and ordinary meanings pleaded in para. 2 of the amended statement of claim and that the words bore or were capable of bearing the innuendo meaning pleaded in para. 2A of the amended statement of claim. They also pleaded justification and that the

H   words complained of in para. 2 (*d*) of the amended statement of claim were published with the leave and licence of the plaintiff given orally. On Aug. 18, 1965, the plaintiff delivered a list setting out just under one hundred articles and reports on which he relied to support the innuendo pleaded in para. 2A of the amended statement of claim.

By letter dated Oct. 14, 1965, to the defendants' solicitors the plaintiff gave

I   notice of intention, subject to further medical advice, to ask leave at the commencement of the trial to amend the statement of claim to include injury to his health as damage suffered. The particulars would be that the alleged libel and subsequent conduct of the defendants caused the plaintiff to suffer prolonged mental stress so as to precipitate or aggravate a toxic condition or premature degeneration of the bodily organs. On Oct. 25, 1965, the trial judge (MILMO, J.), rejected the plaintiff's application to amend so as to claim damages for injury to his health.

On Oct. 26, 1965, the trial judge ruled that none of the articles referred to in the

list delivered for the purposes of para. 2A of the amended statement of claim was   A
relevant and that, accordingly, they could not be admitted.

The case noted below† was cited during the argument in addition to those
referred to in the judgments.

The plaintiff appeared in person.

G. R. F. Morris, Q.C., David Hirst, Q.C., and R. L. C. Hartley for the defendants.
                                                                                B

   LORD DENNING, M.R.: The plaintiff, Mr. Wheeler, brought an action
for libel against the defendants, The News of the World, Ltd., the editor, Mr.
Somerfield, and a journalist, Mr. Mount, in respect of an article in the defendant's
newspaper in June, 1964 headed: " Give the claim chasers a rude answer ". It
starts by saying:

> " Glib, white-haired Gerald Charles David Wheeler peeled off his heavy   C
> horn-rimmed spectacles, took a sip at his half pint of bitter and declared:
> ' I am not a vulture '."

It contains four passages of which he complained. The action was tried before
MILMO, J., and a jury. It took five days. The jury awarded the plaintiff £1,500
damages for a passage describing him as " glib " which was alleged to mean that   D
he

> " was more fluent than sincere and had sought to explain his position
> in an easy and facile manner with no sufficient regard for the truth."

In addition the jury awarded the plaintiff £150 damages for a passage in which
it was said that he had told the journalist:
                                                                                E
> " I was a night watchman when I started off in June, 1951 but I preferred
> to call myself a security guard ":

when he said he had not told the journalist any such thing. There were two other
passages of which the plaintiff complained, but on which the jury found against
him.

In the course of the case the plaintiff sought to make an amendment by adding   F
para. 2A of the statement of claim. He sought to say that

> " the entire article complained of meant and was understood to mean that
> the plaintiff was a dishonest and/or disreputable person and not a reputable
> or trustworthy businessman."

I read that paragraph as alleging a strict innuendo. He gave particulars pursuant   G
to the rules saying that on occasions too numerous to specify articles had appeared
in this newspaper exposing the malpractices and dishonesty of other people.
Before the trial BROWNE, J., gave leave to the plaintiff to make that amendment,
but ordered him to give particulars of the articles. The plaintiff gave a list of
one hundred articles spread over a period of eighteen months. At the trial the
defendants objected to evidence being given on the amendment. They said that   H
the plaintiff ought not to be allowed to bring in all these other articles written
in the newspaper about other people over a period of eighteen months. The judge,
after a day's argument, upheld that contention. He rejected para. 2A and did
not allow the plaintiff to complain of the entire articles, but only of the four
specific passages.

The plaintiff appeals to this court. He relied on the authorities which say that   I
when you are seeking to establish a libel, you can bring in evidence of the circumstances in which it is published to show the meaning which an ordinary reader
would put on it. He cited the case of Monson v. Tussauds, Ltd. (1). That was a
case where Mr. Monson's effigy had been put in Madame Tussauds in a room
near to the Chamber of Horrors. The judges thought it was open to a jury to

---

† Camrose v. Action Press, Ltd., (1937), " The Times ", Oct. 14.
(1) [1894] 1 Q.B. 671.

A find a defamatory meaning owing to the situation in which it was placed. MATHEW, J., went on to give this illustration (2):

B "But suppose that for the purposes of a newspaper mainly devoted to chronicling criminal cases it was found worth while to shadow a man who had been acquitted of a crime, to take portraits of him and to publish them, stating that they were the portraits of the man who had been tried in such and such a case, would that be actionable? It is possible that such a newspaper would be a sharp instrument of torture, and an outrage on the man's comfort and peace? That is really analogous to what has been done here."

C I would agree that if this newspaper, the News of the World, week after week on a particular page had, so to speak, its own rogues' gallery, that would be ground from which it could be understood that a plaintiff who appeared on that page was a rogue; but on an analysis of these articles—and the judge went through them all—I am quite satisfied that that was not this case. These articles were about different people on different occasions for all sorts of reasons. No reasonable person could draw any inference from them adverse to the plaintiff. The judge was quite right in ruling that that evidence was irrelevant. I know that

D para. 2 (a) refers to the "entire article". Nevertheless, it was pleaded as a strict innuendo, and treated as such in the defence. The only words properly complained of were the four passages that I have mentioned. The jury could look at the entire article, of course, to see the meaning, but the only passages which were the subject of the action were those four.

E Then the plaintiff had this other point. He wanted to give evidence of his ill-health. He suffers severely from cataract in the eyes. He sought to give evidence of it before the jury. First, on the ground that the cataract was aggravated, if not caused, by the libel. Secondly, that it was relevant on damages to show that he was a man, if ruined by the libel, who could not get work elsewhere. I have never heard of a case (and counsel told us they have not found any) where a man has been allowed to claim damages in a libel action for injury to his

F health. A libel action concerns injury to reputation and not injury to health. I can imagine that there might be cases in which a libel might cause injury to health. I would not exclude the possibility of such an action; but none as yet has ever appeared in the books. And this will not be the first. The plaintiff before us had to admit that his own medical evidence might not have proved that the cataract was due to the libel. So on the facts this point fails.

G Then comes the third point—costs. This is difficult. The plaintiff succeeded before the jury very substantially. He got £1,500 damages on one passage and £150 damages on another. On two passages he failed. He also failed on para. 2A about all these other articles. When it came to costs, after some considerable discussion the judge said this:

H "What I propose to do is not to involve the parties in a difficult and lengthy taxation, separating the issues, but I propose to award [the plaintiff] half his costs of the action and judgment for the two sums which have been awarded by the jury."

That seems to me a definite decision by the judge given in his discretion as to costs. Then counsel for the defendants said: "I am not quite clear. Your lordship is saying half his costs in the action. Is your lordship dealing separately

I with the issues on which he has failed?" The judge said: "No, I am not. I am only just awarding half his costs." So for the second time the judge was saying: "I give [the plaintiff] half his costs: I do not give the newspaper any." Then counsel said:

"A difficulty arises in that I mentioned earlier about the photostating of the articles which was done for [the plaintiff] (he had no facilities) and the cost of those alone was over £400."

(2) [1894] 1 Q.B. at p. 678.

The judge said: " I am sorry; I did not realise it was all that sum." The **A**
disclosure of the costs of £400 seems to have affected his mind greatly. After
some discussion the judge altered the whole form of the order and said:

" [The plaintiff] will have the general costs of the action except for the
costs which are attributable to the amendment of the statement of claim,
para. 2A, which must be paid by him to the defendants."

B

Unfortunately, counsel had not been instructed rightly as to the costs of the
photostats being over £400. It would have cost £400 if an outside firm had been
employed; but this photostating was done in the offices of the News of the World
and the cost in fact was some £80. Counsel, very properly, wrote a letter to the
judge a few days later saying that the defendants had been advised that on
taxation the claim in respect of the photostats should be limited to £80.

C

The costs were taxed and this was the result. The plaintiff was entitled to the
general costs of the action. He had conducted the case throughout in person.
There is no legal aid for libel. He claimed for all the work that he had done in
preparing the case, but it was all disallowed. A litigant in person can get nothing
except his out-of-pockets. His general costs of the action were taxed at £29 14s.
The newspaper, however, had an order for their costs on the issue about para.
2A. On taxation the defendants were awarded £391 14s. 8d. on that issue. So
if the order as to costs stands, it means that the plaintiff, who won the action,
gets £29; and the defendants, who lost, get £391 14s. 8d. That does not seem
right to me.

D

The plaintiff appeals on that question of costs. It was said that he cannot
appeal at all. The Supreme Court of Judicature (Consolidation) Act, 1925, s. 31
says:

E

" (1) No appeal shall lie . . .—(h) without the leave of the court or judge
making the order, from an order of the High Court or any judge thereof
made with the consent of the parties *or as to costs only* which by law are left
to the discretion of the court."

It was said that, seeing that in the result the plaintiff has failed on the substantive **F**
points, this appeal comes down to an appeal as to costs only and, therefore, it is
prohibited without the leave of the trial judge.

I do not agree with that interpretation. As I have always understood this
section of the Act of 1925, it means this: if a person makes no complaint against
the judgment below, except about the order for costs, then he must obtain the
leave of the trial judge before he can come to this court. If he makes a complaint, **G**
however, not only about the costs, but also about other matters, then he can
appeal both on those other matters and also on the costs; and the court has full
jurisdiction to deal with them. Even if he fails on the other matters, this court
has jurisdiction to deal with the costs. His complaint on the other matters must,
of course, be genuine. That is what has happened in this case. The plaintiff has
brought genuine complaints of other matters. He has also complained about the **H**
costs. Although he has lost on the other matters, nevertheless his appeal as to
costs stands. It is within the jurisdiction of the court to consider it.

What ought the court to do? It seems to me quite plain that when the judge
made his first order (giving the plaintiff half his costs of the action) he had
considered all the matters relevant to his discretion and had made up his mind.
He only altered it because of the later misunderstanding. He was not deliberately **I**
misled; but he was under the impression that the cost of these photostats was
£400 when they came to nothing of the kind. I am quite satisfied that the judge's
original order represents the correct order. His discretion was properly exercised
on that footing.

We should allow the appeal by varying the judge's order as to costs. The
plaintiff should have half his costs of the action and judgment for the two sums
awarded by the jury and the defendants should have no costs. I would allow the
appeal accordingly.

A   **HARMAN, L.J.:** I agree. On the libel aspect of the matter I do not propose to venture. As to the costs, I do not think that I was justified in the construction which I suggested to counsel, but I think that the rule is as stated by Lord Denning, M.R. It cannot be right to say that the question of jurisdiction to deal with the costs depends on whether the appellant succeeds on some other issue in the action. Suppose he appeals on six points and he fails on five of them and

B   there remains the sixth point, which is an appeal against the order as to costs. If the points that he has taken are genuine points, he can at the end appeal on the costs issue although his opponent has knocked out his other points one by one. If, of course, his appeal is as to the costs only or if the court should be satisfied that that is all he really intended to appeal about and has put in the other issues as a kind of " smoke screen ", it may be that the court will refuse to entertain

C   the real object of the appeal, which is in truth against the order as to costs only. If there is a genuine appeal of substance, the fact that it fails does not make it impossible for the court to go on and deal with the costs, provided of course that they are discretionary costs. If the costs are, for instance, executor's costs which are not discretionary, then the court does not have to look to see if there was leave below or not. That is the meaning of the words at the end of the rule about

D   costs which are in the discretion of the court.

Therefore, we are entitled to take the course proposed by Lord Denning, which is to restore what was the original order of the judge and the order which he would undoubtedly have made but for these unfortunate instructions given to counsel to inform him, quite wrongly, about the costs of a certain item on an issue on which he had failed. If that had not been done, it seems to me that the matter

E   was closed. The judge had made his order and nobody could say there was anything wrong with it. That is the order which I would propose to restore.

WINN, L.J.: I agree with both the judgments delivered by my lords. I propose to presume to take a few minutes of the time of the court to say a little about this para. 2A of the statement of claim as amended, mainly with the

F   motive, which I hope may be understood by the plaintiff, of endeavouring to explain to him just why in my judgment he failed in that respect. In the first place there was a matter which was possibly of a somewhat technical nature and could have been cured, either at the trial or even in this court, by an amendment, which would however have been an extremely fundamental amendment; the trouble was that the plaintiff's para. 2A did not plead the whole article

G   as a libel. It pleaded the article only in relation to the words which he had pleaded as a libel and only as something giving rise to an innuendo as to the meaning of those words, viz. to the words which he had complained of in para. 2 as the libel. However, supposing hypothetically that in one way or the other, this pleading had been so altered as to read that the action was for a libel contained in and co-extensive with the whole of the article in question, still

H   in my view this part of the case would have been bound to fail. The plaintiff will, I think, understand from what I am endeavouring to say in simple terms, that the learned judge dealt with this question of the earlier articles in two quite separate and logically distinct stages. First of all he ruled, and in my judgment perfectly correctly, that the other articles which it was sought to put in evidence were irrelevant. Secondly he ruled, and again in my judgment perfectly correctly

I   in law, that the pleading made in para. 2A was itself, in law, invalid—that it raised no matter for the consideration of the jury.

It is my opinion, inexperienced relatively as I am in the practice of the law relating to libel, that a libel can be found only in the document or the passage in a document alleged to be libellous. I have said in the course of the hearing of this appeal, I hope not too often, that there could be, as I see it, a situation in which a periodical or a magazine or a newspaper, published daily or weekly, could be so made up in format as to be understood to say by that which any one issue contained—this is an article or a statement of the same character or falling into

the same category as those which we ourselves have made in earlier issues. Any A
such format would depend for its significance on heading and locality in the
periodical, or perhaps on some note on, e.g., the outside of, or on, e.g., the front
page of, the newspaper, emphasising that such article is published in pursuit of a
particular campaign or practice of the publishers. That, or similar circumstances,
could give rise to a situation in which a publication so situated and set out could
itself by its own terms and by force of such matters be deemed to incorporate B
all relevant statements that had appeared before in the same series, so as in effect
to repeat those defamations if they were defamatory, albeit of other persons:
thus on a proper construction the article itself might be taken to be saying very
much the same thing about any man the subject of the particular article. In the
absence of such a foundation, i.e., such circumstances leading to the reading of the
article or publication complained of in that special sense, it is only within the C
confines of the article or other publication *read alone* that the search for the libel
can be legitimately conducted.

In this context it seems to me that the case of *Astaire* v. *Campling* (3) is relevant
and has an interesting comparative application. In that case libels had been
published—I use the hypothesis on which the decision turned—by other people
about the plaintiff in the action. In this case, according to the plaintiff's presenta- D
tion of it, on which I sincerely congratulate him for his acuity and eloquence,
libels had been published about other people by the same defendants. The cases
differ in that respect but they have a common identical and, in my judgment,
essential feature, that in the particular libel complained of, there was no such
reference to the contents of other publications as amounted to a repetition or
adoption of those publications. I think the words of DIPLOCK, L.J., in the *Astaire* E
case (4) are of great importance in this field of the law of libel:

" A statement does not give rise to a cause of action against its publisher
merely because it causes damage to the plaintiff. The statement must be false
and it must also be defamatory of the plaintiff: that is to say, the statement
must *itself* contain, whether expressly or by implication, a statement of fact
or expression of opinion which would lower the plaintiff in the estimation of F
a reasonable reader who had knowledge of such other facts, not contained in
the statement, as the reader might reasonably be expected to possess. I
emphasise this: the statement of fact or expression of opinion relied on as
defamatory must be one which can be reasonably said to be contained in the
statement in respect of which the action is brought and not merely in some
other statement." G

I regret that I should have taken up time in saying this, which after all is only
an expression of agreement with my lords' judgments, but I was anxious that
the plaintiff should be helped, if possible, to understand why it was that he
failed, in my judgment, on para. 2A.

Appeal allowed as to costs. No order as to the costs of the appeal. H

Solicitors: *Theodore Goddard & Co.* (for the defendants).

[*Reported by* F. GUTTMAN, ESQ., *Barrister-at-Law.*]

I

---

(3) [1965] 3 All E.R. 666.   (4) [1965] 3 All E.R. at pp. 668, 669.

A

SIMS v. FOSTER WHEELER, LTD. AND ANOTHER, (PLIBRICO CO., LTD. AND ANOTHER, Third and Fourth Parties).

B

[COURT OF APPEAL (Willmer and Russell, L.JJ., and Scarman, J.), March 2, 3, 4, 1966.]

Building Contract—Breach of contract—Damages—Sub-contract—Implied warranty of fitness of staging for use—Defective staging erected for spraying operation by sub-sub-contractors—Use by contractors for lining operation under liberty reserved in sub-contract—Collapse causing contractors' employee's death—No examination of staging by contractors—Liability of

C

contractors to employee's widow for breach of statutory duty—Twenty-five per cent. responsibility apportioned to contractors for breach of statutory duty to employee—Whether sub-contractors liable, by way of damages for breach of warranty, to indemnify contractors—Law Reform (Married Women and Tortfeasors) Act, 1935 (25 & 26 Geo. 5 c. 30), s. 6.

Contractors (W., Ltd.) constructing reactors for a petroleum concern

D

engaged sub-contractors (P., Ltd.) to carry out certain of the works, including that of spraying the interior walls of the reactors with a special cement. The sub-contractors further sub-contracted with a company (C., Ltd.) to perform the spraying work and for the purpose to prepare the necessary staging. Under a term of their contract with the sub-contractors (P., Ltd.), the contractors (W., Ltd.) were free to use and used the staging for work in connexion

E

with the fitting of a shroud ring round the inside of a reactor about twenty feet up from the floor. They took no steps to satisfy themselves that the staging was safe. Owing to a defect in the staging it collapsed, and one of their employees was killed. In an action brought by his widow, judgment was given against C., Ltd. for breach of their statutory duty to see that every scaffold should be of good construction, of suitable and sound material and

F

adequate stength under reg. 7 of the Building (Safety, Health and Welfare) Regulations, 1948*; and also against the contractors (W., Ltd.) for breach of their statutory duty under reg. 21 to satisfy themselves that the scaffold was stable, its materials were sound and the safeguards required by the regulations were in position. The damages awarded to the widow were apportioned as to seventy-five per cent. against C., Ltd. and as to twenty-

G

five per cent. against the contractors (W., Ltd.). The Court of Appeal found that, on the construction of the contract between the contractors and the sub-contractors (P., Ltd.), there was an obligation on P., Ltd., amounting to a warranty, that the staging would be safe and fit for use for the purposes of the spraying operation† by C., Ltd.; the court further found that there was a breach of that obligation in that the staging was not fit for the purpose,

H

and that the accident happened as a result of that breach. On the question of the measure of liability of the sub-contractors (P., Ltd.) to the contractors (W., Ltd.) for breach of that contractual obligation,

Held: as between the contractors and the sub-contractors (P., Ltd.), the contractors were entitled to rely on the warranty in their contract with P., Ltd. and the contractors rights in respect of the breach of this

I

warranty were not affected or restricted by the contractors' liability to their employee for breach of statutory duty under reg. 21; accordingly the sub-contractors (P., Ltd.) were liable to the contractors for the resulting damage, that is, the damages and costs payable to the plaintiff widow by the

---

* S.I. 1948 No. 1145.

† This was the majority view, see p. 319, letter H, post. WILLMER, L.J., held that the obligation extended to fitness for the shroud ring operation as well as for the spraying operation, and that the staging was not fit for either purpose (see p. 316, letter I, post).

Applied in DRIVER v. WILLETT.
[1969] 1 All E.R. 665.

contractors (W., Ltd.) and the contractors' taxed costs of the action and the   A
appeal (see p. 317, letter B, p. 319, letters C and D, and p. 320, letters B and C,
post).

    Mowbray v. *Merryweather* ([1895-99] All E.R. Rep. 941) applied.

    Appeal allowed.

    [As to relations between the principal contractor and a sub-contractor to a
building contract, see 3 HALSBURY'S LAWS (3rd Edn.) 514, 515, paras. 1023,   B
1024; and for cases on the subject, see 7 DIGEST (Repl.) 439-443, *393-413*.

    For the Law Reform (Married Women and Tortfeasors) Act, 1935, s. 6, see
25 HALSBURY'S STATUTES (2nd Edn.) 359.

    For the Building (Safety, Health and Welfare) Regulations, 1948, reg. 7, reg.
21, see 8 HALSBURY'S STATUTORY INSTRUMENTS (First Re-issue) 190, 195.]

Cases referred to: C

    Kate, The, [1935] All E.R. Rep. 912; [1935] P. 100; 104 L.J.P. 36; 154 L.T.
        432; 42 Digest (Repl.) 1143, *9513*.

    Mowbray v. *Merryweather*, [1895-99] All E.R. Rep. 941; [1895] 2 Q.B. 640;
        65 L.J.Q.B. 50; 73 L.T. 459; 59 J.P. 804; 3 Digest (Repl.) 97, *245*.

Appeal.   D

    The first defendants appealed against an order of PAULL, J., made on the
trial of third and fourth party proceedings in an action on Apr. 9, 1965, dismissing
their claim against the third parties in respect of the proportion of the damages
and costs for which the first defendants had been held liable to the plaintiff in
the action. The grounds of appeal were: (i) that, on the true construction of
cl. 2 (k) of the first defendants' general notes for sub-contractors forming part   E
of the contract between the first defendants and the third parties, the third parties
were obliged to provide scaffolding which was reasonably safe for the purposes
for which they or their agents knew it was to be used whether by themselves
or by the first defendants; (ii) that the judge misdirected himself in holding that
on the true construction of the clause the third parties' obligation was to provide
scaffolding which would be reasonably safe for the purpose of their own or their   F
sub-contractors' work under the contract; (iii) that the judge failed to apply his
findings that the piece of timber which broke and thereby caused the collapse
of the scaffolding ought never to have been used but should have been rejected
when the scaffolding was constructed by the third parties' sub-contractors;
and that in consequence of those findings the scaffolding in fact provided by the
third parties under their contract was not of the standard required according to   G
the construction placed on it by the judge; (iv) that, on the true construction of
the general notes for sub-contractors, the erection and supply of scaffolding and
the removal and replacement of a shroud ring before and after the application
of Gunnite to the inside of the reactor vessel in which the deceased was fatally
injured constituted or arose out of or were connected with the work or works
undertaken by the third parties under the contract; and the collapse of the   H
scaffolding, the death of the deceased and the action arose out of or were connected with such works and the judge misdirected himself in that regard; (v) that
the judge misdirected himself in construing the proviso to cl. 2 (g) (i) of the same
general notes; (vi) that the judge misdirected himself in holding that, by reason
of the apportionment between the first and second defendants of their joint
liability to the plaintiff, the first defendants' claim against the third parties was   I
for an indemnity against the first defendants' share of such joint liability and
for that reason was a claim to be indemnified against damage caused solely by
the first defendants; (vii) that the judge should have held that the third parties
were in breach of their contract with the first defendants and that the first
defendants' liability to the plaintiff was damage flowing from such breach, and
further that the first defendants were entitled to be indemnified against the
plaintiffs' claim by virtue of the provisions of the contract. By their notice of
appeal the first defendants asked that judgment might be entered for them against
the third parties for an indemnity against the plaintiff's claim for damages and

A   costs in the action, or for damages for breach of contract amounting to such an indemnity, and that the third parties might be adjudged to pay to the first defendants their costs of the action and of the appeal to be taxed.

A. T. Davies, Q.C., and *E. D. B. Powell* for the employers, the first defendants.

P. M. O'Connor, Q.C., and *R. A. Gatehouse* for the third parties, the sub-contractors.

B

WILLMER, L.J.: The employers, who are the first defendants in the action, were at the time of the accident (i.e., in May, 1960) engaged in constructing the last of a number of reactors for the Esso Petroleum Co., Ltd.'s works at Milford Haven. The accident which occurred has already resulted in a long history of litigation, in the course of which judgments have been delivered both in this C court and in the court below; and in the course of delivering those judgments various judges have described the nature of the work that was in progress and have set out the facts relating to the accident in some detail. In those circumstances I do not regard it as necessary for me to go over all the details again. I will content myself with a brief summary, sufficient (I hope) to make the rest of what I have to say intelligible.

D   The employers had engaged the third parties as sub-contractors to carry out certain of the work in connexion with the construction of these reactors, and notably the work of spraying the interior walls of the reactors with a kind of cement called Gunnite. The sub-contractors in turn sub-contracted with the fourth parties, Cement Gun Co., who were to perform the actual work of spraying the Gunnite, and were also to prepare the necessary staging for the purpose E of that work. Cement Gun Co. duly erected a circular staging, which consisted of boards bolted to a framework of bearers. This staging was then lowered into the inside of the reactor, where it was suspended from tackle which enabled the platform to be raised or lowered as required for the work.

Cement Gun Co. then proceeded with the work of spraying the Gunnite on the inside of this last of the reactors. I understand that they began at the bottom F and gradually worked upwards until they reached a height of something like twenty feet or rather more. They then had to discontinue the work of spraying the Gunnite in order to give an opportunity to fit a metal ring round the inside of the reactor called a " shroud ring ". That appears to have been effected at a height of something like twenty feet or more above the floor of the reactor. This work of fitting the shroud ring was not sub-contracted, but was carried out by the G employers themselves. For the purpose of doing the work they used the same staging as had been erected and used by Cement Gun Co. Whilst engaged on the task of fitting this shroud ring, the deceased (the plaintiff's husband) and six other men, all of whom I gather were employees of the employers, were working on the staging when it collapsed and fell with all the men to the bottom of the reactor. The plaintiff's husband was killed, and all the other six sustained H injuries.

The plaintiff in due course brought her action against the employers under the Fatal Accidents Acts, alleging both negligence and breach of statutory duty on the ground that the staging on which the deceased man was working was defective. The employers instituted third party proceedings against the sub-contractors, who in turn brought fourth party proceedings against Cement Gun I Co., and in consequence of the defence delivered by the employers, the plaintiff added Cement Gun Co., as second defendants to the action. In due course the action came on for trial before PAULL, J., who by his judgment delivered on Oct. 31, 1963, found in favour of the plaintiff against both defendants and gave judgment for the plaintiff for what I think was an agreed sum of £7,200. The judge then proceeded to consider the matter of apportionment as between the two defendants, and on that he came to the conclusion that Cement Gun Co. were liable for one hundred per cent. He found that the cause of the collapse of this staging was the presence, in one of the main bearers, of what was described

as an " arris knot ", which was a defect of sufficient importance to render that A
particular bearer quite unfit for use.   The judge held that that defect constituted
a breach of reg. 7 of the Building (Safety, Health and Welfare) Regulations, 1948,
which requires every scaffold to be of good construction, of suitable and sound
material and of adequate strength.

Having been found one hundred per cent. liable, Cement Gun Co. then appealed
to this court, and on Apr. 17, 1964, another division of this court allowed their B
appeal, varied the apportionment arrived at by the judge, and held Cement Gun
Co. liable for only seventy-five per cent. of the damage, leaving the employers to
bear the remaining twenty-five per cent.

The ground of that decision of the Court of Appeal was that, in addition to the
breach of reg. 7 to which I have already referred, the employers were themselves
separately and independently guilty of a breach of reg. 21.   Regulation 21 is C
headed: " Scaffolds used by workmen of more than one employer ", and it
provides as follows:

" Where a scaffold or part of a scaffold is to be used by or on behalf of an
employer other than the employer for whose workmen it was first erected,
the first-mentioned employer shall, before such use, and without prejudice D
to any other obligations imposed upon him by these regulations, take
express steps, either personally or by a competent agent, to satisfy himself
that the scaffold or part thereof is stable, that the materials used in its
construction are sound and that the safeguards required by these regulations
are in position."

E

It is admitted that in fact the employers took no express steps to satisfy themselves about the condition of this staging, although it is conceded that they could
have done so, had they so desired, at the time when the staging was first assembled
outside the reactor before it was lowered into the reactor.

The employers, having been found liable for twenty-five per cent. of the
plaintiff's damage, then proceeded to prosecute their third party claim against F
the sub-contractors.   This matter again came before the same judge, PAULL, J.,
and it is his judgment in those proceedings that is the subject of the present
appeal.   The claim against the sub-contractors in the third party proceedings
was put on two grounds.   First, it was alleged that the sub-contractors, as such,
were in breach of an implied term in their sub-contract to the effect that the
staging should be of sound construction and suitable for the purpose for which G
it was to be used.   Secondly, the claim was put on the ground of an express
agreement to indemnify the employers against claims by and liabilities to third
parties in respect of personal injury arising out of or connected with the
execution of the works.   The judge found against the employers on both points,
and accordingly dismissed their claim in the third party proceedings.   It followed
from that that he also had to dismiss the third party's claim against the fourth H
party, Cement Gun Co.

[HIS LORDSHIP examined the terms of the contract between the employers
and the sub-contractors and held that the sub-contractors were in breach of an
obligation amounting in effect to a warranty, that the staging would be safe for the
employers to use it for the work in contemplation, or, if the obligation was limited
to the erection of a scaffolding fit for use for the purpose of spraying the Gunnite, I
were in breach of that obligation, because the scaffolding which they supplied
was not fit for that or for any other purpose.   He continued:] There being
then a breach of the obligation assumed by the sub-contractors, there next comes
the question what damages, if any, flow from the breach.   What has been
argued on behalf of the sub-contractors is that the employers can recover only
such financial loss as is shown to result from the sub-contractors' breach of their
obligation.   Thus it is said that, on the basis of PAULL, J.'s original judgment,
there would have been no financial loss, and consequently no right to recover

A (except possibly nominal damages); for the employers would under that judgment
have got one hundred per cent. indemnity from a solvent sub-contractor.

As a result of the Court of Appeal's decision in the previous proceedings,
however, the employers now show a financial loss which consists, I apprehend, of twenty-five per cent. of the plaintiff's damage claim, plus the
costs payable to the plaintiff, and plus presumably their own costs of the
B trial proceedings; but, argues counsel for the sub-contractors, on the Court of
Appeal decision the employers only came under this liability and suffered this
financial loss because of their own quite separate and independent breach of
reg. 21 of the regulations. Their loss, therefore, does not result from any breach
of contract on the part of the sub-contractors, but is a loss entirely of their own
making. That, as I follow his judgment, represents in substance the view which
C the judge took.

The argument for the employers, on the other side, is that this contention is
quite beside the mark. The employers, as between themselves and the sub-
contractors, are, it is said, entitled to rely on the warranty contained in their
contract. It may very well be that, as between themselves and the plaintiff, they
came under an independent duty to comply with reg. 21 and that they were
D guilty of a civil wrong in failing to comply with that duty. That breach of duty
towards the plaintiff, it is said, however, does nothing to break the chain of
causation resulting from the sub-contractors' breach of warranty. The fact
remains, and has remained throughout, that this staging collapsed because it
was defective staging, and was defective in breach of reg. 7 of the regulations.
For all the damage resulting from that the employers are, it is contended, entitled
E under their contract to look to the sub-contractors. Their right, it is argued,
is a right under their contract, and is not in any way affected by the apportionment of liability in tort which was arrived at in relation to the injured plaintiff.

I hope that I have summarised in an intelligible form the rival contentions put
forward on behalf of the parties. I confess that I have not found this at all an
easy point on which to make up my mind. I have, however, found helpful
F guidance in the decision of this court in *Mowbray* v. *Merryweather* (1), which
was a case very properly brought to our attention by counsel for the sub-contractors in the course of his argument. It seems to me that, unless it can be
said that for one reason or another that case no longer represents the law today,
it does really conclude this particular point in favour of the employers and against
the sub-contractors. In that case the plaintiffs, a firm of stevedores, contracted
G to discharge a cargo from the defendant's ship, the defendant agreeing to supply
all necessary cranes, chains and other gearing reasonably fit for that purpose.
The defendant in breach of his agreement supplied a defective chain, which broke
while being used, and in consequence one of the plaintiff's workmen was injured.
The plaintiffs might have discovered the defect in the chain by the exercise of
reasonable care. The workman brought an action for compensation under the
H Employers' Liability Act, 1880, s. 1 and s. 2, against the plaintiffs, who settled
the action by paying the workman £125, which sum they sought to recover from
the defendant as damages for breach of his contract. It was not disputed that
the settlement of the action brought by the workman was a proper one. It was
held that the plaintiffs' liability to pay compensation to their workman was the
natural consequence of the defendant's breach of contract, and such as might
I reasonably be supposed to have been within the contemplation of the parties
when the contract was entered into; and therefore the damages claimed were
not too remote.

It will be seen that the facts in that case substantially reproduced the same
features as we have in this case. The contract was subject to an implied term
to provide a proper appliance; there was an opportunity on the part of the
party to whom it was applied to carry out an independent examination for

---

(1) [1895-99] All E.R. Rep. 941; [1895] 2 Q.B. 640.

himself, an opportunity that was neglected.   The fact that in those circumstances   A
the plaintiffs became liable to the injured workman because of the breach of duty
which they owed to him was held to go no distance towards preventing them from
recovering from the defendants the damages which they had to pay as damages
for the defendant's breach of contract.   I would refer only to three very short
passages in the judgments of the members of the court, which seem to me to
make the point of the decision quite clear.   LORD ESHER, M.R., said (2):   B

> " The plaintiffs owed no duty to the defendant to examine the chain before
> allowing it to be used by their workman.   The only duty they owed in that
> respect was to the workman."

KAY, J., said (3):

> " The plaintiffs were guilty of no negligence as between themselves and the   C
> defendant, and they are entitled, I think, to say as between themselves and
> the defendant that he gave them a warranty on which they had a right to
> rely.   I think the damages claimed by the plaintiffs must be considered as
> being the natural result of the breach of warranty, and one which must be
> deemed to have been within the contemplation of both parties as likely to
> spring from that breach."   D

Lastly, RIGBY, L.J., having said (4): " It is clear that he [the defendant] used
no care at all ", went on (4):

> " It seems to me that the effect of the warranty is that the defendant
> agrees with the plaintiffs that they may rely on him for the sufficiency of
> the chain as a matter of contract, and as between him and them there was
> no duty whatever on their part to examine the chain to see whether it was   E
> sufficient."

That case has been more than once followed in the years that have elapsed since
1895, notably in *The Kate* (5) to which our attention was directed this morning.
There is no doubt that SIR BOYD MERRIMAN, P., founded his decision in the
latter case on what had been said in the case of *Mowbray* v. *Merryweather* (6).   F
   It is, however, sought on behalf of the sub-contractors to distinguish *Mowbray*
v. *Merryweather* (6) and the line of cases that followed it on the ground that at
the time when they were decided machinery simply did not exist for apportioning
liability between wrongdoers.   What is argued is that the whole situation has
changed since the passing of the Law Reform (Married Women and Tortfeasors)
Act, 1935, which has made it possible to pursue an enquiry which it was not open   G
to the court to pursue in 1895 at the time when *Mowbray* v. *Merryweather* (6)
was decided.   Now, as we all know, it is possible for the court to divide the
liability between the several wrongdoers.   What is said is that, once that has
been done, as it has in the present case, and liability for damages has been
established against the employers in respect of the breach of their own independent duty, as distinct from the duty owed by the sub-contractors, they are no   H
longer in a position to prove that their damages flow from the sub-contractors'
breach of contract.   What is said by way of illustration is that, supposing
Cement Gun, Co. had proved to be insolvent, then the employers would have
had to discharge one hundred per cent. of the damages; but, says counsel for the
sub-contractors, in that case their right of recovery against the sub-contractors
would have been limited to the seventy-five per cent. which they would have
paid in effect on behalf of Cement Gun, Co.   It would not have included the   I
twenty-five per cent. attributable to their own independent wrongdoing.
   That argument, of course, is directly contrary to what had been held in the
older cases, and I hope that I may be forgiven for making this comment.   It is

(2) [1895] 2 Q.B. at p. 644; [1895-99] All E.R. Rep. at p. 943.
(3) [1895] 2 Q.B. at p. 645; [1895-99] All E.R. Rep. at p. 943.
(4) [1895] 2 Q.B. at p. 646; [1895-99] All E.R. Rep. at p. 944.
(5) [1935] All E.R. Rep. 912; [1935] P. 100.
(6) [1895-99] All E.R. Rep. 941; [1895] 2 Q.B. 640.

A now 1966, and over thirty years have elapsed since the Act of 1935 came into force. It is perhaps rather curious, if the argument presented to us is sound, that no authority has been found to support it in the cases which have been tried in the last thirty years. Furthermore, it seems curious, if the argument is sound, that no authority in support of it has been discovered within the Admiralty jurisdiction of the court. I mention that point simply because, as is well known,

B the power of the court to divide responsibility between different wrongdoers has existed in that jurisdiction for many, many years. It might have been expected, therefore, that over the years this problem would have arisen; and, if it be right to say that, where an apportionment of liability in tort has been ascertained, the plaintiff is debarred from obtaining full damages for breach of contract, support might have been expected to be found for that in the records

C of the Admiralty court. However, no such authority has been drawn to our attention.

I am forced to the conclusion that the argument of counsel for the sub-contractors is ill-founded. I think that the fallacy of the argument lies in the fact that it treats the breach of duty owed by the employers to the plaintiff as though it were also a breach of duty to the sub-contractors. As the authorities which

D have been brought to our attention stand, I can see no support for the proposition that the employers' contractual right against the sub-contractors is in any way affected by their own separate liability in tort to the plaintiff. In those circumstances I find myself unable to agree with the conclusion at which the judge arrived. In my judgment the employers have made out their claim based on breach of contract, and are entitled to succeed against the sub-contractors in

E these proceedings in their claim for damages. That conclusion renders it unnecessary to deal, at any rate deal at any length, with the alternative claim based on the alleged indemnity; for so far as the money recoverable is concerned I apprehend that it can add nothing to the right which I have already held the employers have to recover damages for breach of contract.

[HIS LORDSHIP examined the clause in the contract relating to the employer's

F right to indemnity by the sub-contractors against claims by and liabilities to third parties arising out of or in connexion with the execution of the works, held that the employers were not entitled to succeed on that part of their case, and concluded:] But since, for the reasons which I have already given, I am satisfied that they are entitled to succeed on the first part of their argument, viz., on the ground of breach of contract, that question does not arise. In my

G judgment the appeal succeeds and the employers are entitled to relief on the basis of a breach of contract.

RUSSELL, L.J.: I agree that this appeal succeeds, and I need state my reasons only shortly. Under cl. 2 (k) of the general notes for sub-contractors forming part of the contract, one of the things for which the employers were paying was the right to use scaffolding provided by the sub-contractors. There

H is plainly to be implied a warranty by the sub-contractors that the scaffolding should be properly constructed for safe use as scaffolding for the lining operation. I do not find myself able to imply a warranty that it was properly constructed for safe use for the shroud ring operation; but that matters not. Assuming the narrower warranty, there was quite plainly a breach of it; and it is moreover clear that, but for the arris knot defect, the platform would not have given way

I under the additional stresses involved in the shroud ring operation. The accident therefore happened as a result of the breach of the warranty.

I cannot accept the argument which in effect says that the apportionment between the employers and Cement Gun Co. by this court necessarily decides that the accident as to twenty-five per cent. was not caused by the sub-contractors' breach of warranty. It seems to me quite clear from cases such as *Mowbray* v. *Merryweather* (7) that, in determining the extent of damage accruing to the

---

(7) [1895-99] All E.R. Rep. 941; [1895] 2 Q.B. 640.

employers by reason of the breach of warranty, there is no restriction by reason A
of the employers' failure in their duty under reg. 21 of the Building (Safety,
Health and Welfare) Regulations, 1948, a duty owed not to the sub-contractors
but to the employers' own men. The employers were entitled vis-à-vis the sub-
contractors to rely on the warranty. I cannot see why this application of the
law of contract is altered or superseded by the introduction and exercise of the
jurisdiction under the Law Reform (Married Women and Tortfeasors) Act, 1935, B
to apportion the incidence of liability between joint tortfeasors. So I consider
that that part of the judgment in favour of the plaintiff which the employers
cannot pass on to Cement Gun Co., the twenty-five per cent., is recoverable from
the sub-contractors, as damages for breach of the implied warranty.

[HIS LORDSHIP referred to the indemnity clause in the contract, held that the
employers were not entitled to succeed under it, and concluded:] But, as I have C
said, on the first ground I agree that the appeal succeeds.

SCARMAN, J.: I agree that the appeal succeeds, and do so for the reason
given by RUSSELL, L.J.

Appeal allowed. Leave to appeal to the House of Lords refused.

Solicitors: *Theodore Goddard & Co.*, agents for *T. B. Walker-Jones & Gardner*, D
Swansea (for the employers, the first defendants); *Ponsford & Devenish,
Tivendale & Munday* (for the sub-contractors, the third parties).

[*Reported by* F. A. AMIES, ESQ., *Barrister-at-Law.*]

E

F

PRACTICE DIRECTION.

PROBATE, DIVORCE AND ADMIRALTY DIVISION (DIVORCE).

*Divorce—Maintenance—Income tax—Small maintenance payments—Payments
to be made direct to children included—Income Tax Act, 1952 (15 & 16 G
Geo. 6 & 1 Eliz. 2 c. 10), s. 205 (1) (b), as amended by Finance Act, 1960
(8 & 9 Eliz. 2 c. 44), s. 40.*

Hitherto it has been considered that a payment direct to a child was outside
the meaning of s. 205 (1) of the Income Tax Act, 1952, (1), relating to "small
maintenance payments". The Inland Revenue authorities have, upon a
recent reference to them, expressed the view that the language in s. 205 (1) (b) H
is capable of including a payment which is to be made direct to a person, and
that since para. (b) also uses the emphatic expression "to any person", the
preferable construction of para. (b) is to regard it as applicable to payments to
be made direct to children.

COMPTON MILLER,
Apr. 25, 1966.   Senior Registrar.   I

(1) For s. 205, as amended, see HALSBURY'S STATUTES (2nd Edn.), AMENDED TEXTS
to title Income Tax, Vol. 31, para. [207].

A
BOARD OF GOVERNORS OF THE HOSPITAL FOR SICK CHILDREN *v.* WALT DISNEY PRODUCTIONS, INC.

[CHANCERY DIVISION (Buckley, J.), March 7, 8, 9, 10, 1966.]

Cinematograph—Registration of titles—Contract by registered holder of title
B   *including provision not to object to film being produced under that title after*
a period had elapsed and granting licence in respect of rights necessary to give
effect to that provision—What constituted an objection for the purposes of the
contract—Remedies for breach of the provision of the contract.

Copyright — Assignment — Licence — Exclusive licence assignable only with
author's consent—Death of author—Invalidity of purported assignment
C   *without consent.*

Copyright—Licence—Exclusive licence to produce author's literary and dramatic
works in cinematograph or moving picture films—Licence granted in 1919
—Sound track films not then produced commercially—Whether licence
extended to sound motion pictures or only to silent films.

By an agreement dated Aug. 19, 1919 (the " 1919 agreement ") Sir James
D   Barrie granted to a motion picture company, sole and exclusive licence
to produce all his literary and dramatic works for the terms of their copyrights in " cinematograph or moving picture films ". By the agreement
the company was required to announce the films by the name of the work
on which they were based, and it was provided that the benefit of the
agreement should not be assignable without the author's consent. In 1919
E   sound recording for films was unknown as a commercial proposition, the
first commercial use of sound-track film being in 1927 or 1928. By an assignment dated Aug. 14, 1929, Sir James Barrie assigned his copyright in Peter
Pan to the hospital, the predecessor of the plaintiffs, whose rights vested
subsequently in the plaintiffs by virtue of the National Health Service Act,
1946. Sir James Barrie died in 1937. By agreement and assignment dated
F   Oct. 10, 1938 (the " 1938 assignment ") P. (an American motion picture
corporation which had validly acquired the rights of the motion picture
company) granted all its motion picture rights, including sound and talking
motion picture rights, and assigned the benefit of the 1919 agreement, to
the defendant. It was found at the hearing that there was no consent to
this purported assignment*. By cl. 4 of an agreement dated Jan. 11, 1939,
G   the defendant agreed that it would not object to the hospital making an
ordinary sound motion film exclusively with living actors based on Peter
Pan, if it were not publicly exhibited before the expiration of ten years
from the première of the defendant's animated cartoon, and the defendant
thereby granted a licence to the hospital " in respect of such of the rights
acquired [by the defendant from P.] as shall be necessary to give effect "
H   to the provisions of this clause. The defendant, an American corporation,
was a participant in the scheme of registration of titles conducted in the
United States by the Motion Picture Association of America, Inc. On the
release of a film the registrant of its title could claim permanent protection
for that title. The defendant was on the release index in respect of the
title " Peter Pan ", as the defendant had made an animated cartoon film
I   under that name which had its world première in 1953. There was nothing,
however, to compel the defendant to insist on its contractual rights under the
registration scheme. In the summer of 1964 the plaintiffs were negotiating
for the acquisition by a film director and a film producer of the right to
make a sound motion picture based on Peter Pan. By letter dated June 5,
1964, to the director and the producer the defendant indicated that it

---

* The facts in regard to the absence of consent are involved and the position is
explained at p. 331, letters C and F, post.   There was in fact a written consent by the
plaintiffs, but the assignment was not strictly in accordance with it.

M

Affirmed, C.A. [1967] 1 All E.R. 1005.

would oppose a film under the title Peter Pan. The plaintiffs brought an   A
action for a declaration that the defendant had no right to object to the
plaintiffs or their licensees making a sound motion picture by living actors
under the title Peter Pan, for an injunction and for damages.

Held: (i) on the true construction of the 1919 agreement it was effective
to grant rights only as to silent films, for those only could have been in the
contemplation of the parties at its date (see p. 336, letter C, post).   B
Reasoning in *Pathé Pictures, Ltd.* v. *Bancroft* ((1933), MacG. Cop. Cas.
(1928-35) 403) not followed.

(ii) since the 1938 assignment of the rights granted by the 1919 agreement
was made without consent, it was ineffective to pass the rights, with the
consequence that no sound film rights were vested in the defendant; moreover, if it were a fact that the sound film rights were outstanding in a third   C
person, that would not affect the position as between the plaintiffs and the
defendant (see p. 336, letters E and F, post).

(iii) in the circumstances the defendant's protected title to the name
" Peter Pan " was such a right as fell within the closing words, quoted
above, of cl. 4 of the agreement of 1939, and the plaintiffs were thereby
licensed to use it; moreover insistence by the defendant on protecting its   D
registered title against the plaintiffs would amount to derogation from grant
and a breach of contract; with the consequence that the plaintiffs were
entitled to a declaration of their rights and to an injunction (see p. 337, letters
D and E, post).

(iv) the letter of June 5, 1964, was an " objection " within cl. 4 of the
agreement of 1939, and accordingly the defendant was in breach of contract   E
at the time when the writ was issued, and the plaintiffs were entitled to an
inquiry as to damages (see p. 337, letter I, to p. 338, letter A, post).

[As to the effect of an assignment of copyright, see 8 HALSBURY'S LAWS
(3rd Edn.) 415 para. 759; and for cases on the subject see 13 DIGEST (Repl.)
89-93, *314-354*.]   F

Cases referred to:

Cinema Corpn. of America v. *De Mille*, (1933), 267 N.Y.S. 327. The series of
    reports is the NEW YORK SUPPLEMENT.
Kalem Co. v. *Harper Brothers*, (1911), 222 U.S. 55. The series of reports is
    the UNITED STATES REPORTS.
Kirke La Shelle Co. v. *Paul Armstrong Co.*, (1932), 257 N.Y.S. 38; on appeal   G
    (1933), 188 N.E. 163. The first named series of reports is the NEW
    YORK SUPPLEMENT, and the second named series is the NORTH EASTERN
    REPORTER.
Page (L. C.) & Co. v. *Fox Film Corpn.*, (1936), 83 F. (2d) 196. The series
    of reports is the FEDERAL REPORTER, second series.
Pathé Pictures, Ltd. v. *Bancroft*, (1933), MacG. Cop. Cas. (1928-35) 403.   H
Williamson (J. C.), Ltd. v. *Metro-Goldwyn-Mayer Theatres, Ltd.*, [1937] V.L.R.
    67, 140; on appeal, 56 C.L.R. 567; 11 A.L.J. 112; 13 Digest (Repl.)
    96, **88*.

Action.

This was an action by the plaintiffs, the Board of Governors of the Hospital   I
for Sick Children, by writ dated July 10, 1964, claiming (i) a declaration that the
defendant Walt Disney Productions, Inc., of California, U.S.A., by virtue of
an agreement dated Jan. 11, 1939, between the plaintiffs of the one part and
the defendant, or its predecessors, Walt Disney Enterprises, of the other part
(hereinafter called " the 1939 agreement "), had no right to object to the plaintiffs
or their assignees or licensees making or exhibiting an ordinary sound motion
picture exclusively with living actors based on the play " Peter Pan " by Sir
J. M. Barrie, and that the plaintiffs were fully entitled to licence the production

A and release of a film bearing the said title " Peter Pan " starring Miss Audrey
Hepburn directed by George Cukor and produced by Mel Ferrer; (ii) an injunction
to restrain the defendant by itself or by its servants or agents in breach of the 1939
agreement from objecting to the plaintiffs or their assignees or licensees making or
exhibiting a film with living actors based on the play " Peter Pan " by Sir J. M.
Barrie under the title of " Peter Pan " and from threatening Mr. George Cukor
B and Mr. Mel Ferrer or any other person or persons in respect of the production
and release of a film starring Miss Audrey Hepburn or any other well known
actors and entitled " Peter Pan "; (iii) an inquiry as to damages suffered by
the plaintiffs by reason of the breach by the defendant of the 1939 agreement
and payment by the defendant to the plaintiffs of all sums found due on such
inquiry; (iv) an injunction to restrain the defendant by itself, its servants or
C agents from publishing by letter or otherwise any statement to licensees or
proposed licensees of the plaintiffs, or to any other persons, calculated to lead
to the belief that the plaintiffs or their assignees or licensees were not entitled
to make or exhibit ordinary sound motion pictures exclusively with living
actors based on the play " Peter Pan " by Sir J. M. Barrie under the title " Peter
Pan " and from continuing to publish untrue statements or any of them con-
D tained in a letter dated June 5, 1964, addressed by the defendant to Mr. George
Cukor and Mr. Mel Ferrer or any statements to like effect, and (v) an inquiry as to
damages suffered by the plaintiffs by reason of slander of title, and payment
by the defendant to the plaintiffs of all sums found due on such inquiry. The
claim for damages for slander of title was withdrawn before the defence was
delivered, but the claim for damages for breach of contract (the 1939 agreement)
E was pursued.

Sir *Milner Holland, Q.C.* and *A. D. Russell-Clarke* for the plaintiffs.
Frank Whitworth, Q.C. and *E. P. Skone James* for the defendant.

BUCKLEY, J., stated the nature of the action and continued: The nature
of the case cannot be understood without some recital of the history of Sir
F James Barrie's dealings with rights in his works and particularly in " Peter
Pan " and of the dealings between other parties in those rights.

The first document of which I should make mention is an agreement dated
June 28, 1916, by which Sir James granted to an American company, Charles
Frohman, Inc., sole and exclusive rights to produce a number of his plays and
dramatic works, including " Peter Pan ", on the stage in the United States of
G America and the Dominion of Canada during a period which ended on July 1,
1921. That agreement is of no particular significance in this case, except that it
is recited and relied on in an agreement dated Jan. 11, 1939 (which I will call
" the 1939 agreement " (1)). On the same day on which he made that agreement
of June 28, 1916, Sir James executed an agreement supplemental to the first-
mentioned agreement, which I need not describe in any detail. Those two
H agreements I will refer to as " the 1916 agreements ".

On Aug. 19, 1919, Sir James entered into an agreement with an English
company, Famous Players Film Co., Ltd., which recited that he was the author
of and entitled to deal with and dispose of all existing cinematograph rights
in various literary works including " Peter Pan ". By that agreement Sir James
granted to Famous Players Film Co., Ltd., " the sole and exclusive licence to
I produce all his literary and dramatic works existing and future ", subject to
certain specified exceptions which do not include " Peter Pan ", for the terms of
their respective copyrights " in cinematograph or moving picture films " and
to exhibit such films and so on; and he undertook that he would not grant
any authorisations, rights, or licences in respect of cinematograph or moving
picture films in any of his existing or future works to any other person, firm
or company whatsoever. Famous Players Film Co., Ltd., were required by this

---

(1) Referred to at p. 322, letter I, ante; the relevant contents of the 1939 agreement
are stated at p. 326, letters A to I, post.

agreement to announce the films (that is to say, I think, to put the films out to A
the public) by the name of the work of the author on which they were respectively based. I have no doubt Sir James regarded the titles of his works as being
of importance. Clause 8 of the agreement was in these terms:

> " The company shall be entitled to acquire copyright in all countries
> of the world when copyright exists in the said films and moving pictures
> and may use lines or excerpts from the said literary and dramatic com-   B
> positions for the titles and/or sub-titles thereof."

By cl. 11 it was provided that the benefit of the agreement should not be assignable without the written permission of the author. That agreement I will call
" the 1919 agreement ". On Oct. 10, 1919, Sir James consented to Famous
Players Film Co., Ltd., assigning the benefit of the 1919 agreement to Famous C
Players Lasky Corpn., an American company which eventually, after a series of
changes of name, assumed the name of Paramount Pictures, and which it will
be simpler for me to call in the course of this judgment by that name.

On Oct. 27 and Nov. 4, 1921, a number of assignments were made by a firm of
publishers in the United States, Charles Scribner's Sons, to Paramount Pictures
of motion picture rights in certain works of Sir James Barrie, namely, " The Little D
White Bird or Adventures in Kensington Gardens ", " Peter Pan in Kensington
Gardens " and " Peter and Wendy ". Those assignments are not, I think, of
any significance in this case. Again, I mention them only because they are
recited in the 1939 agreement. No evidence has been adduced to show that
Scribner's had any motion picture rights which they could pass by those
assignments to Paramount Pictures.   E

On June 1, 1925, Famous Players Film Co., Ltd., assigned the benefit of the
1919 agreement to Paramount Pictures under their then name of Famous Players
Lasky Corpn. That assignment was, of course, made in pursuance of or under
the authority of the consent which Sir James Barrie had given.

On Aug. 14, 1929, by an assignment made between Sir James Barrie of the
one part and the Hospital for Sick Children Great Ormond Street London, a F
company incorporated in this country (which I will refer to as the " hospital "),
whereby it was recited that Sir James was the author and owner of the copyright in the play " Peter Pan " and other works mentioned in Sch. 1 to this
assignment, Sir James assigned to the hospital all his copyright in those works
throughout the British Dominions together with the benefit of the 1919 agreement, subject to an exception which is irrelevant for the present purposes. The G
works mentioned in the schedule to the agreement are the book " Peter Pan
and Wendy ", the book " Peter Pan in Kensington Gardens " and the book
" The Little White Bird " in various editions and forms, including those stories
retold for boys and girls and for little people. Those works and the play " Peter
Pan " I will compendiously refer to as " the Peter Pan works ", for they all
relate to a character called " Peter Pan " although in some of them that character H
is a baby and in some he is the character well known in Sir James's play. Clause 2
of the assignment declared that the hospital should stand possessed of the
copyright and other rights assigned to them thereby, subject to payment out
of the profits accruing therefrom all administrative costs and expenses, on trust
to apply the profits to and for such of the purposes of the hospital as were
charitable within the legal meaning of that term. Clause 3 provided that the I
hospital should not sell or part with the copyright without the consent of Sir
James during his life or of his personal representatives after his death, but
that subject thereto the hospital should have all the powers of an absolute
owner in respect of the copyright and other rights assigned to it by the assignment, and in particular should be entitled to grant licences and make other
contracts for the exploitation of the works or any of them by reproduction or
performance in any form or by any means whatsoever. Clause 4 of the assignment was in these terms:

A   " If except as hereinbefore provided the hospital shall without the consent in writing of the settlor during his life or after his death without the like consent of his personal representatives do or suffer any act or thing whereby the said copyright or any part thereof would (but for this provision) become vested in or charged in favour of any other person persons or corporation then and in any such case the trusts and powers hereinbefore

B   declared and contained shall forthwith cease and the said copyright and all other such rights as aforesaid together with the benefit of all then existing contracts relating thereto shall be held upon trust for such charitable object or objects as the settlor [that is Sir James] or (if he be dead) his personal representatives shall in writing appoint and shall be assigned or transferred to or in trust for such charitable object or objects in such manner and form

C   in every respect as the settlor or his personal representatives (as the case may be) shall in writing direct."

Then cl. 5 provides for what is to happen if the hospital is wound up for the purpose of reconstruction or amalgamation. I am not concerned with that. This assignment I will refer to as " the 1929 assignment ".

D   On Apr. 21, 1932, Paramount Pictures by their then name Paramount Publix Corpn. reassigned to Sir James Barrie all the right, title and interest of Paramount Pictures in Sir James' literary works except such literary works from or on which motion pictures had then already been made or based by Paramount Pictures or by any person authorised by them. At the date of this reassignment Paramount Pictures had already made, in fact in the year 1925, a silent picture

E   of " Peter Pan " under that title, and accordingly the rights which were at the date of this reassignment vested in Paramount Pictures in " Peter Pan ", and it may be other of the " Peter Pan " works so far as the film was based on any of those works, were not reassigned to Sir James. That document I will call " the 1932 reassignment ".

Sir James Barrie died on June 19, 1937, having made his last will five days

F   earlier on June 14. By cl. 7 of his will he declared as follows:

    " . . . And as to my play ' Peter Pan ' I bequeath to the Hospital for Sick Children Great Ormond Street London all performing rights to which my estate is entitled whether in reversion on the determination of the assignment which I have made during my lifetime or otherwise, and I direct my trustees to execute and do all such instruments acts and things as

G   may be required to make this bequest effective."

By cl. 8 he bequeathed to the hospital all rights and interests whether in the nature of copyright or otherwise which he was competent to dispose of by will in the other works mentioned in Sch. 1 to the 1929 assignment. So that if after the 1929 assignment was made any residual rights in any of the " Peter Pan "

H   works remained in Sir James Barrie or were capable of reverting to him, those rights would pass under his will to the hospital. Sir James' will was in due course proved by the executors appointed by it, and on Jan. 20, 1942, those executors assented to all performing rights and all rights and interests which are in the nature of copyright or otherwise in the play " Peter Pan " and other " Peter Pan " works vesting in the hospital.

I   On Oct. 10, 1938, Paramount Pictures entered into an agreement with the defendant under its then name of Walt Disney Enterprises and by that document Paramount Pictures granted and assigned to the defendant all the right, title and interest which Paramount Pictures might have acquired in and to the motion picture rights, including sound and talking motion picture rights, in " Peter Pan ", " The Little White Bird ", " Peter Pan in Kensington Gardens " and " Peter and Wendy ". On the same day a shorter and formal instrument of transfer of those rights was also executed. That, I understand, was with a view to the shorter and somewhat less explicit document being filed on some

public file. Those documents I will refer to as " the 1938 agreement and A
assignment ".

On Jan. 11, 1939, the hospital and the defendant entered into the 1939 agreement on which the questions which arise in this action really turn. This
agreement, which is by its terms to be construed in accordance with the laws of
England, recited that Sir James Barrie was the author of a play entitled " Peter
Pan " and the other works mentioned in the schedule thereto, which were B
thereinafter called " the literary and dramatic works ". The other works mentioned in the schedule to the 1939 agreement are the other " Peter Pan " works.
The agreement then recited that the defendant claimed that pursuant to various
instruments certain cinematograph and moving picture film rights in the said
literary and dramatic works became vested in Paramount Pictures or its predecessors which rights had since been acquired by the defendant. The instruments C
which are referred to are the 1916 agreement including the supplemental agreement, the 1919 agreement, the 1921 assignments, the 1929 assignment, the 1932
reassignment and the will of Sir James Barrie. By cl. 1 the hospital warranted
that except for such rights as were granted by these instruments, the hospital
had not and to the best of the knowledge of the hospital Sir James had not
granted, licensed or assigned to any person any motion picture rights in the D
literary and dramatic works or any of them which would prevent or restrict
the making or exhibition by the defendant in any part of the world of an animated
sound cartoon based on the literary and dramatic works. By cl. 2, in consideration
of certain payment, the hospital granted to the defendant for the full terms of
the respective copyrights thereof the sole and exclusive licence to exploit in any
part of the world all rights which might be vested in the hospital in the literary E
and dramatic works so far as such rights related to the making, reproduction
and exhibition of animated cartoons with or without sound or dialogue, including
the presentation of television or radio adaptations thereof. By cl. 3 the hospital
agreed that subject to the provisions of cl. 4 it would not at any time exercise,
sell, transfer or part with the motion picture rights in the literary and dramatic
works which might be vested in the hospital. Clause 4, which is of the greatest F
importance in this case was in these terms:

" [The defendant (that is, Walt Disney Productions Inc.)] hereby agrees
that it or its assigns or licensees will not object to the hospital or its assigns
or licensees making and exhibiting an ordinary sound motion picture
exclusively with living actors based on the literary and dramatic works
provided that such ordinary sound motion picture is not exhibited in public   G
in any part of the world prior to the expiration of ten years from the date
of the world première of an animated cartoon made by [the defendant]
hereunder and [the defendant] hereby grants a licence to the hospital in
respect of such of the rights acquired by [the defendant] from Paramount
Pictures Inc. as aforesaid as shall be necessary to give effect to the provision   H
of this clause."

Clause 8 provided that the defendant should be entitled in connexion with any
such animated cartoon to adapt, arrange, change, dramatise, make musical
versions of, interpolate in, transpose, add to and subtract from the literary
and dramatic works or any part of them to such extent as the defendant in its
discretion might desire and to use any title or titles used in connexion with   I
the literary and dramatic works or any part of them.

The plaintiffs plead that it was an express or alternatively an implied term
of the 1939 agreement that the defendant would not, after the expiration of
the period of ten years mentioned in cl. 4, object to the making and exhibition
of a motion picture of the play " Peter Pan " under the title " Peter Pan ".
As the case has proceeded, however, it has become clear that the plaintiffs'
contentions do not really rest on any implied term but depend on the effect

A of the agreement as properly construed.   For they say that on the true construction of the agreement and in the events which have happened the defendant is not entitled to object to a certain course of action which the plaintiffs are desirous of pursuing which would result in the production of a film which the plaintiffs wish to be produced under the title " Peter Pan ".

The defendant by para. 11 of its defence pleads that it objects to and is entitled
B to object to the use as the title for such a film of the name " Peter Pan ".   The defendant in its defence refers to and places reliance on a scheme for the registration of titles which is in operation in the United States under the aegis of a body called the Motion Picture Association of America, Inc.   That is a scheme directed to avoiding undesirable similarities or identity of titles in the motion picture industry and is binding on the members of the Motion Picture Association
C and on non-member participants in the registration of title scheme.

The defendant is a non-member participant in this scheme.   As such, on becoming a non-member participant, it signed an agreement as part of the established procedure governing administration of the scheme.   This, I take it, is an agreement which all non-member participants are required to sign and by that agreement the defendant agreed to comply fully and in all respects with
D all the provisions of the memoranda of the title committee of the association effected on a certain date; that is to say, in effect the defendant agreed to abide by the rules of the registration scheme and further specifically agreed to refrain from using any title which has been refused registration by the association in the exercise of the authority vested in the officers of that association under the scheme.   The scheme is one for the registration of titles proposed to be used
E for intended films, and it enables the registrant of any title while his registration stands to resist the use of an identical title by anyone else thereafter or any title which would be harmfully similar to the title he has registered.   There are provisions which require that in the case of a title submitted for registration which is identical with a title already on the register, the association shall refuse registration and that in the case of a title which though not identical is similar
F to one already on the register, the title shall be registered but notice shall be given to persons registered in respect of similar titles, and there are provisions for disputes between parties as to which shall have the right to use of the title being referred to arbitration, and so on.   As soon as a film is released those provisions of the scheme cease to operate, but if the film is one made from copyrighted material or a play which has been produced in public, within a certain
G definition which is laid down in the rules of the scheme, then on the film being released the title is transferred to an index called the release index and the registrant of the title may claim permanent protection under the registration scheme in respect of that title.   If the picture has not been made from copyrighted material or from a produced play, the title is not entitled to permanent protection, but only to a short-term protection.   This scheme is one which has
H contractual effect between the members of the association and non-member participants in the scheme, and the evidence is that in the United States of America the big film distributors, that is to say, the only distributors who would have facilities for nationwide distribution with a large box office potential, are members of the association and so are most, if not all, of the well known makers of films in the industry in the United States of America.

I As will appear from my further recital of the facts, the defendant is now on the release index in respect of the title " Peter Pan " and it is part of the defendant's case that it would not be a commercial possibility for a film to be made by anyone other than the defendant under the title " Peter Pan " and distributed in the United States of America, because there would be no suitable persons free either to make the film or to distribute it under the title " Peter Pan ". Although the registration scheme, however, confers on anyone who has registered a title or is entitled to protection under the scheme the right to protect the use of that title in the way that the scheme is designed to achieve, it does not compel

them to insist on that right. If it be the fact that the defendant has contracted   A
with the hospital that in respect of a film made under cl. 4 of the 1939 agreement
the defendant will not insist on the protection afforded by the registration scheme,
then the scheme does not present an obstacle in the way of the plaintiffs doing
what they want to do.

Paramount Pictures, having made a film of " Peter Pan " in 1925, registered
that title under the association's registration scheme, and on Dec. 14, 1938,   B
they transferred the benefit of that registration to the defendant. The defendant
is thus entitled as between itself and members of the association and non-member
participants in the title registration scheme to such protection as the scheme
affords, but as I pointed out the defendant is not bound to insist on that protection. The scheme, of course, has no effect at all on the plaintiffs, who are successors
in title to the hospital. The hospital was never a member of the scheme, the   C
plaintiffs are not members or participants in the scheme and the scheme is,
so far as the plaintiffs are concerned, entirely res inter alios acta.

The defendant made an animated cartoon film under the title " Peter Pan "
in exercise of the rights in that behalf conferred on it by the 1939 agreement
which had its world première in January, 1953. The delay in making that film
was no doubt much greater than had been anticipated when the 1939 agreement   D
was entered into, and it was, of course, very largely due to the fact that the
second world war intervened. Accordingly the ten year period referred to in
cl. 4 of the 1939 agreement expired in January, 1963.

I should mention that the defendant in its defence also plead a similar registration scheme which is in operation and has been in operation since about
the year 1942 in this country under the aegis of the British Film Producers   E
Association, but the defendant is not a participant in that scheme, although an
English company which is some part of Mr. Disney's complex of companies is a
member of that scheme. The plaintiffs and the hospital have never been in any
way associated with that scheme, and in the event no reliance has been placed
on the English title registration scheme in the course of the trial of this case.

On July 5, 1948, the vesting provisions of the National Health Service Act,   F
1946, came into operation and the defendant concedes that subject to the effect
(if any) of cl. 4 of the 1929 assignment the effect of the Act of 1946 was to vest
in the plaintiffs all the rights assigned to the hospital or acquired by the hospital
under the 1929 assignment and under the 1939 agreement. It is suggested that
in some way or other the effect of cl. 4 of the 1929 assignment would be to prevent
the vesting provisions of the statute operating to transfer these particular assets   G
from the hospital to the plaintiffs, but that is a suggestion which I feel unable to
accept, for I think that it is clear when one reads cl. 4 of the 1929 assignment
that on the contingency contemplated in that clause, that is to say, in the event
of the hospital suffering any act or thing whereby the copyright assigned by that
agreement would become vested in any other person without the consent of
Sir James or his personal representatives—an event which occurred on July 5,   H
1948—what was to happen was not something which would affect the ownership
of the property at all, but would merely bring one set of charitable trusts to an
end and bring another set of charitable trusts into operation. It might be that
there would be an interval before the second set of charitable trusts would be
identified, but the actual operation of the clause would be to affect equitable
interests applicable to the profits received through the copyright, and it would   I
not in any way affect the ownership and, therefore, would not affect the operation
of the vesting provisions of the Act of 1946. Consequently, I do not pause to
consider precisely which vesting provisions of the Act of 1946 operated in this
case for, as I say, it is conceded by the defendants that the effect of the Act
was to vest these rights, in respect of which the plaintiffs are now suing, in the
plaintiffs.

In the summer of 1964 the plaintiffs were in active negotiation with Mr.
George Cukor, a well known director of films, and Mr. Mel Ferrer, an equally

A   well known film producer, for them to acquire from the hospital the right to make a sound motion picture based on the play " Peter Pan " which they were minded to make with Miss Audrey Hepburn in the title role. When these negotiations were in an advanced stage and indeed, I think, were practically concluded the defendant became aware of them through a press announcement. The defendant then wrote on June 5, 1964, a letter addressed to Mr. Cukor and to Mr. Ferrer

B   in which the defendant said that it had seen the announcements of the negotiations going on between those two gentlemen and the plaintiffs, and the defendant stated in the letter that pursuant to rights acquired some time ago from the hospital the defendant had produced a feature length animated theatrical cartoon entitled " Peter Pan " based on Sir James' work and that the defendant had the title " Peter Pan " permanently protected in the United States under the

C   title registration rules of the Motion Picture Association of America Inc. and in the United Kingdom under comparable title registration rules in effect there. The defendant then said that it followed a pattern of periodic reissues of films of this kind and that there would be a possibility that there might be a coincidence in time between the reissue of the defendant's film and the release of the film which Mr. Cukor was proposing to make. The defendant concluded its letter

D   in these terms:

> " By reason of the very substantial investment we have in our film and its title, and in view of our firm intention to reissue it at an appropriate time, we feel called upon to let you know of these facts at this early stage so that they will not come as a surprise to you later on. In the same vein we must
>
> E   state that should you elect to produce and release a film bearing the same title, or any other title confusingly similar to ' Peter Pan ', we will have no choice but to assert such remedies as may be available to us, including the rights we have established in the title as a permanently protected one and also our rights under principles of unfair competition."

  The letter is a courteous one, but couched in perfectly firm and clear terms

F   indicating that if Mr. Cukor and Mr. Ferrer were to proceed to make a film under the title " Peter Pan " they would be met with the most vigorous opposition of the defendant. Not surprisingly that resulted in some correspondence and discussions between the various parties. On July 1, 1964, the plaintiffs' solicitors wrote to the defendant drawing attention to the terms of cl. 4 of the 1939 agreement and asking for a withdrawal of what had been said in the letter

G   to Mr. Cukor and Mr. Ferrer and an undertaking that in future the defendant would not repeat the statements contained in that letter or any similar statements to Mr. Cukor or Mr. Ferrer, or anyone else. That letter produced a reply from the defendant's solicitors in which they said that they failed to see that any complaint could be made of the letter of June 5, 1964, and that the requirements of cl. 4 of the 1939 agreement that the defendant would not object to the hospital

H   or their assigns or licensees making and exhibiting an ordinary sound motion picture based on the literary and dramatic works did not, in their opinion, involve a need to use the same title. That letter was written before the solicitors had obtained firm instructions from their clients in the United States. By July 9, they had obtained such instructions and they wrote a further letter to the plaintiffs' solicitors in which they said that their clients endorsed the comments made in their letter of July 7, and confirmed that their remarks reflected

I   their own views on the matter.

  On July 10, the writ in this action was issued. In those circumstances the relief which the plaintiffs are claiming is, first, a declaration that the defendant has no right to object to the plaintiffs or their assignees or licensees making or exhibiting an ordinary sound motion picture film exclusively with living actors based on Sir James Barrie's play " Peter Pan " and under that title, a further declaration that the plaintiffs and their licensees are fully entitled to licence the production and release of a film bearing the title " Peter Pan "

starring Miss Audrey Hepburn, directed by Mr. George Cukor and produced   A
by Mr. Mel Ferrer; and an injunction to restrain the defendant by itself, its
servants or agents, in breach of the 1939 agreement, from objecting to the
plaintiffs or their assignees or licensees making or exhibiting a film with live
actors based on the play " Peter Pan " by Sir James Barrie under the title of
" Peter Pan " and from threatening Mr. Cukor or Mr. Ferrer or any other person
or persons in respect of the production or release of a film starring Miss Audrey   B
Hepburn or any other well known actors and entitled " Peter Pan "; and
they also seek an inquiry as to damages suffered by the plaintiffs by reason
of the breach by the defendant of the 1939 agreement and payment by the
defendant of the sum found due.

The plaintiffs say that on the construction of the 1939 agreement, cl. 4, the
right granted to the defendant to make a cartoon film was subject to no restriction   C
as to title, and that the right granted to the plaintiffs to make an ordinary
sound motion picture with living actors is also subject to no restriction as to
title. There is, as counsel for the plaintiffs put it, no silent exception from the
general effect of this clause in respect of title. Therefore each party is entitled
to use any title it chooses, including the title " Peter Pan ", and counsel contends
that the ten year period which is provided for in cl. 4 is designed to avoid con-   D
fusion and competition resulting from identity or similarity of title and supports
the view that each party was entitled to use for its film whatever title it chose.
Therefore, it is contended that the plaintiffs are entitled to licence the making
of a film under the name " Peter Pan " without objection from the defendant and
are licensed to do that by the terms of cl. 4 itself, that is to say, by the latter part
of the clause whereby the defendant licensed the hospital in respect of such of the   E
rights acquired by the defendant from Paramount Pictures as should be necessary
to give effect to the provisions of that clause.

It is also said on behalf of the plaintiffs that the defendant's attempt to
prevent the plaintiffs by their licensees from making a film under the title
" Peter Pan " is a derogation from the grant which is to be found in cl. 4 of the
1939 agreement. It seems to me that the breach of contract argument and the   F
derogation from grant argument are really the same point, or at any rate involve
considering exactly the same considerations, for in each case the plaintiffs'
rights depend on the true nature and extent of the defendant's obligations under
the clause. It may well be that the title " Peter Pan " is the title best calculated
to promote the success of any cinematographic entertainment based on Sir
James' work, and if the defendant is bound not to object to the plaintiffs making   G
or licensing the making of a film under that title by cl. 4, then to make such
an objection would be both a serious breach of the contract and also
commensurately derogation from its grant.

If the defendant has any exclusive right to the use of the title " Peter Pan ",
it acquired this right from Paramount Pictures as ancillary to the 1938 assignment, and accordingly is bound, so it is said, under the closing part of cl. 4 of   H
the 1939 agreement to authorise the plaintiffs to use that title and indeed has
authorised them to use that title, the exclusive right being one of the rights
acquired by the plaintiffs from Paramount Pictures within the meaning of the
clause.

Alternatively it is said on behalf of the plaintiffs that on its true construction
the 1919 agreement granted only silent rights and did not confer any rights to   I
make sound motion pictures, that the 1939 agreement granted only cartoon
rights to the defendant and that, therefore, the defendant is not entitled to
any sound rights at all, but only to rights to make silent films and cartoon films
based on Sir James' work and that the right to make sound films is now vested
in the plaintiffs, who have obtained all the rights in the works except such as
either Sir James or the hospital have granted away at some time. It is said that
therefore the plaintiffs are entitled, having the sound rights vested in them, to
license the making of a sound film, and the defendant has got no locus standi

A from which it can object to such a licence. Once again it is said in this connexion that the defendant is bound to permit or facilitate the use of the title " Peter Pan ", because of the terms of cl. 4 of the 1939 agreement.

Finally, it is said that even if the 1919 agreement included a grant of the right to make sound films, these rights are not now vested in the defendant, because of the terms of cl. 11 of the 1919 agreement which provided (it will be

B remembered) that the benefit of that agreement should not be assigned without the written permission of the author. No permission was ever sought from Sir James during his lifetime, and it might have been contended that the effect of this clause was to make the benefit of this assignment incapable of transfer after Sir James' death, but counsel for the plaintiffs has said that he does not desire to take that point. What happened was this: in September, 1938, the hospital

C was asked by the solicitors acting for the defendant or some part of Mr. Walt Disney's empire to grant a consent to the assignment of the 1919 agreement from Paramount Pictures to Walt Disney Productions, Inc., and on Sept. 13, 1938, the hospital signed such a written consent. Walt Disney Productions Inc. was a company incorporated in the United States, one of the complex of Mr. Disney's companies. On Sept. 29, 1938, Walt Disney Productions, Inc., and two

D other Disney companies were consolidated; that is to say, as I understand the evidence that I have heard, the shareholders or stockholders in those companies surrendered their certificates in respect of their holdings in those companies and were issued with certificates for corresponding holdings of stock in a new corporate body Walt Disney Enterprises, which was the name under which the defendant was first organised, and the assets of the three pre-existing companies,

E including Walt Disney Productions, Inc., were either by operation of law or by some instrument or instruments of transfer, I do not know which, transferred from the pre-existing companies to Walt Disney Enterprises and the three pre-existing companies thereupon ceased to exist, having no members and no assets. On Oct. 10, 1938, the agreement and assignment of that date to which I have referred in the course of my recital of the various relevant documents

F were executed whereby Paramount Pictures purported to assign the benefit of the 1919 agreement to the defendant, and it is said and seems to be impossible of contradiction, that that assignment was not an assignment in accordance with the consent which was given, and that no consent was given by anybody to an assignment from Paramount Pictures to the defendant, and on that ground the plaintiffs contend that the chain of title which the defendant puts forward to

G sound picture rights stemming from the 1919 agreement is broken, and those rights were never successfully vested in the defendant.

The defendant on the other hand contends that on the true construction of the 1939 agreement, the use of the title " Peter Pan " was not necessary for the exercise of the plaintiffs' rights under cl. 4. The defendant points out that that clause is altogether silent on the subject of the titles, that there is a wide choice

H of titles open to the plaintiffs, and that accordingly for the defendant to object to the plaintiffs using the title " Peter Pan " is not in any way in breach of the defendant's obligations under cl. 4 of the 1939 agreement or a derogation from any grant by it to be found in that clause. Secondly, the defendant says that in any case no breach is shown to have occurred, for neither Mr. Cukor nor Mr. Ferrer has ever yet become a licensee of the plaintiffs, they are only

I prospective licensees. Thirdly, as to the defendant's title to the sound rights, it claims that the plaintiffs are estopped from disputing the defendant's title to sound rights in the film by the recitals contained in the 1939 agreement. Perhaps it would be convenient to dispose of that point now, for in my judgment it is not a sound point. The recitals are not recitals that Walt Disney are entitled but that Walt Disney claim to be entitled to certain rights under the recited documents, and the language seems to me to be carefully phrased in such a way as not to give rise to an estoppel on the question of whether that claim is or is not well founded. The defendant asserts that the 1919 agreement was effective to pass the right to make sound films and says that in consequence of the various A assignments of those rights and the devolution of title, it is now entitled to all sound film rights in " Peter Pan " with the exception of whatever they have granted to the plaintiffs by cl. 4 of the 1939 agreement.

In 1919 sound recording as a commercial proposition was still unknown. It seems that as far back as 1896 Mr. Edison had made some experiments with a view to the synchronisation of sound and moving pictures using a disc or some B other form of recording medium of that kind, but by 1919 neither the problem of synchronisation nor the problem of amplification of sound had been solved in such a way as to make the use of sound a commercial proposition. Indeed, it was not until 1923 that the earliest demonstrations took place, not, of course, on a commercial basis at all, but in the scientific world, of the use of a thermionic valve to produce amplification of sound. It was not until 1925 that the first C efforts were made in the commercial field to use synchronised sound produced from a disc, and it was not until about the years 1927 and 1928 that a sound track on films was first used commercially. The contention of the plaintiffs is that in these circumstances when the 1919 agreement was entered into, the making of sound films cannot have been in the contemplation of the parties and that when Sir James granted to Famous Players Film Co., Ltd., the right D to produce his works in cinematograph or moving picture films and to exhibit such films, he could have had only silent films in mind and that as the function of the court in interpreting the contract is to discover what was the intention of the parties, what was in the contemplation of the parties must govern the construction of the language which they have used.

I have been referred to various authorities in this connexion, of which perhaps E I should make some mention. The first to which I will refer is an Australian case, *J. C. Williamson, Ltd.* v. *Metro-Goldwyn-Mayer Theatres, Ltd.* (2). In that case the court was concerned with a grant which was executed in September, 1924, which provided for the grant of the exclusive right to produce and perform a certain musical play, namely, " Rose Marie ", but there was excepted from the grant all motion picture film rights and the question was what was the extent F of that exception. It was held both in the Court of Appeal (2) in the State of Victoria, reversing the chief justice, and in the High Court of Australia (3), having regard to the business of the parties, both of whom were engaged in the motion picture industry, and their knowledge of the state of the art, that sound pictures were within the exception from the grant. It is, I think, clear from the language which is used by the judges both in the Court of Appeal (3) G in the State of Victoria and also in the High Court of Australia (4) that the decision turned on what the court considered to have been in the minds of the parties.

In the High Court of Australia I find this (5):

" The agreement must be construed in the light of the circumstances and conditions attending the matters upon which the agreement was to operate, H and it is conceded that a knowledge of the relevant circumstances and conditions was common to the parties. The combination of sound with the visual exhibition of films was then threatened. Whatever opinions they may have held about the probability or imminence of the development so threatened, the parties to the contract knew that if it took place, it would or might affect the regular business in the production and exhibition of I moving pictures and do so in a very important manner. The simultaneous oral and visual mechanical reproduction of the play by means of films could not be regarded as so entirely different from the exhibition of motion pictures as then commercially practised that it would altogether fall outside the reservation and form part of the general performing right granted to the

_____

(2) [1937] V.L.R. 67, 140; on appeal, 56 C.L.R. 567.   (3) [1937] V.L.R. 67, 140.
(4) (1937), 56 C.L.R. 567.   (5) (1937), 56 C.L.R. at p. 579.

A   appellants. So far as it was visual, such a reproduction would, we think, necessarily involve an exercise of or an infringement of the motion picture film rights reserved or excepted and the parties must be taken to have so understood. Upon the appellants' view the only alternative is that the agreement divides the right to exhibit sound films between the parties to it. That they entertained an actual intention to do so seems to us to
B   be very unlikely."

Then there is this passage (6):

"When the purpose of the reservation and the state of the art are considered, it appears to us that those rights necessarily included the privilege or monopoly of every form of mechanical reproduction or exhibition which
C   developed in the business of entertainment by motion picture films. Sound pictures appear to us not only such a development but one necessarily within the proximate contemplation of the parties."

That case, in my judgment, proceeds on the footing that the interpretation to be placed on the language of parties to a contract must be ascertained in the light of what must be taken to have been in the contemplation of the parties
D   at the time the contract is entered into, but the particular facts of that case led to the conclusion that it was within the contemplation of the parties that the rights contained in the reservation extended to sound rights.

   In the case of *Kirke La Shelle Co.* v. *Paul Armstrong Co.* (7), which is a case in the courts of the State of New York, the defendant contracted in 1921 to pay to the plaintiff one half of the proceeds received from revival productions of a
E   certain play, and agreed that all future contracts " affecting the title to the dramatic rights (exclusive of motion picture rights) " should be subject to the plaintiff's approval. In 1928 the defendant sold the talking moving picture rights without obtaining the plaintiff's approval. The action sought to recover one-half of the proceeds of that sale. The defendant succeeded in the court of first instance but the judgment was reversed on appeal. On appeal this is
F   what was said (8):

"Since ' talkies ' were unknown at the time when the contract was entered into, it cannot be said that ' talkie ' rights were within the contemplation of the parties either as a subject for the transfer of an interest therein to the appellant or as included in the motion picture rights specifically excepted."
G
That decision seems to me to proceed on the same basis as the Australian case, but in different circumstances which led to a different result.

   In *L. C. Page & Co.* v. *Fox Film Corpn.* (9), which was a case heard in the Circuit Court of Appeals, Second Circuit, in the United States of America, the court was concerned with an agreement entered into on Oct. 8, 1923, and with
H   a grant which excluded moving picture rights. The court is reported as saying this (10):

" ' Talkies ' were not commercially known in 1923, but inventors had been experimenting with the idea for some years, and plainly the plaintiff contemplated the possibility of the commercial development of sound with motion pictures, for almost contemporaneously with obtaining the licence from
I   Mrs. Richards, it granted Principal Pictures Corpn. the exclusive right to produce or sell or license motion picture versions of Captain January, with an express reservation of ' the right to use in connection with said motion picture versions any spoken words or words produced by sound of any kind '. It does not appear, however, that Mrs. Richards knew of this

---

(6) (1937), 56 C.L.R. at p. 579.   (7) (1932), 257 N.Y.S. 38.
(8) (1933), 188 N.E. 163 at p. 166.   (9) (1936), 83 F. (2d) 196.
                    (10) (1936), 83 F. (2d) at pp. 198, 199.

reservation or that sound motion pictures were within her contemplation   A
when she executed the 1923 agreement. Nevertheless, we can entertain
no doubt that the words used, ' the exclusive moving picture rights ', were
sufficient to embrace not only motion pictures of the sort then known but
also such technical improvements in motion pictures as might be developed
during the term of the license, namely, the term of the copyright. The
development of mechanism making it possible to accompany the screen   B
picture with the sound of spoken words was but an improvement in the
motion picture art. As the plaintiff well says, ' talkies ' are but a species
of the genus motion pictures; they are employed by the same theatres,
enjoyed by the same audiences, and nothing more than a forward step in
the same art. Essentially the form and area of exploitation were the same.
The mere fact that the species ' talkies ' may have been unknown and not   C
within the contemplation of the parties in their description of the generic
' moving pictures ' does not prevent the latter from comprehending the
former."

Then the court cited a case of *Kalem Co.* v. *Harper Brothers* (11), in which (12):

" it was held that the words, ' exclusive right to dramatize ', in the   D
copyright statute, though used when motion pictures were unknown, included
the right to produce by motion pictures when that mechanism was later
developed; that is to say, the genus embraced the later developed species.
In 1915 when the author and the plaintiff first employed the words ' motion
picture rights ' in the informal agreement evidenced by letters, there can be
no doubt that ' talkies ' were unknown; hence the analogy of the *Kalem*
case (11) is perfect. The fact that there the words of a statute were being   E
construed and here the words of a contract are involved does not make
the case inapposite. The agreement of 1923 was an amendment of the earlier,
less formal agreement and, like it, used the phrase ' moving picture rights '.
Obviously the phrase should have the same meaning in each. Hence we think
it beyond question that the plaintiff was given the exclusive right to sell
or lease talking moving picture rights as well as silent motion picture rights."   F

With the utmost respect to the distinguished judges who decided that case in
the Circuit Court, I do not feel that I am able to concur in their view that the
development of a mechanism making it possible to accompany the screen picture
with sound and spoken words was but an improvement of the motion picture art.
For the introduction of such a mechanism introduced a new medium of com-   G
munication, and the new technique which made that medium possible had nothing
whatever to do with photography, which was the medium employed in making
silent pictures. The medium of a talking picture, it seems to me, was a result of a
marriage of two quite distinct arts and techniques and I should have thought
that a talking picture could no more properly be said to be merely an improvement or development of the technique of making silent films than the motor-car   H
can be said to be an improvement or development of the technique of making
an ordinary horse-drawn waggon. Indeed, I should have thought there was
rather less connexion between the sound film and the silent film than there is
between the two vehicles; but in my view it is really fallacious to say that a
talking picture is solely an improvement or development of the technique of
making silent films. Silent films involved photographic problems and depended   I
for their effect purely on the visual element in the picture. Talking films introduced
an entirely new dramatic technique, different as regards the technique of reproduction, and presenting different problems in presentation and projection to
the audience. For my part, with the utmost respect to the distinguished judges
who decided *L. C. Page & Co.* v. *Fox Film Corpn.* (13) it appears to me that they
proceeded on a misappreciation of the relation of silent films to talking films.

---

(11) (1911), 222 U.S. 55.   (12) (1936), 83 F. (2d) at p. 199.
(13) (1936), 83 F. (2d) 196.

A   Moreover, the case of *Kalem Co. v. Harper Brothers* (14), which is one which concerned the interpretation of a wide term in a statute, seems to me to be very far from being a reliable guide to use in interpreting contracts between parties where, as I have said, what the court is concerned with is merely to discover the intention of the parties at the time that they made their contract. Accordingly, I do not feel able to accept the decision in *L. C. Page & Co.* v. *Fox Film Corpn.* (15)

B   as a satisfactory guide for myself in the consideration of the present case.

The next case to which I might refer is *Cinema Corpn. of America* v. *De Mille* (16). The court in that case was concerned with a grant of all rights in a book, dramatic rights, moving picture rights, royalties on the sale of the book and from serial rights. Not surprisingly, the learned judge came to the conclusion that dramatic rights and moving picture rights taken together were sufficient

C   to extend to sound picture rights, but he did towards the end of his judgment say this (17):

> " However, the talking motion picture combines the pictorial element of the old silent pictures with the new element which was formerly inseparable from dramatic rights, namely, the audible reproduction of words. If the various recognised forms of rights in a story are split up so that one person
D   becomes the owner of the silent motion picture rights and another person becomes the owner of the dramatic rights, a party wishing to make a talking motion picture of that story would have to obtain the permission both of the owner of the silent motion picture rights and the owner of the dramatic rights. Each one controls an element essential to the production of a talking picture."

E   Basing himself on those observations, counsel for the defendant said that, as at any rate the silent picture rights were assigned by the 1919 agreement, the plaintiffs have not got all of the rights which entitle them to make a sound picture because, unless they obtain rights to make the visual part of the picture from the person in whom the silent rights are vested, they are not in a

F   position to make a sound picture, and counsel says that if it be the fact that the sound rights have never successfully devolved on the defendant because of the technical point about lack of consent to an assignment then the sound rights are outstanding in some third party and unless and until the plaintiffs have acquired those rights they are not in a position to make a sound picture at all. I fail myself to understand how the possibility that some rights may be out-

G   standing in a third party can affect the rights and interests of the parties to the proceedings and if what the plaintiffs are desiring to do involves an infringement of some third party's rights that is nothing whatever to do with the defendant. If on the other hand the silent picture rights are in the defendant then the defendant is under an obligation under cl. 4 of the 1939 agreement to license the plaintiffs, so far as may be necessary, to use those rights for the purpose of

H   making their film.

The only other case that I need mention is an English decision of SWIFT, J., given on July 6, 1933, in *Pathé Pictures, Ltd.* v. *Bancroft* (18). That case related to the grant of rights in the play called " The Ware Case ". It was recited that the author was the proprietor of all existing cinematograph rights in a novel and play entitled " The Ware Case ". By the document the author granted to

I   the grantees for a certain period of years " a sole and exclusive licence to produce the said work in moving picture films ". On the construction of this document the learned judge came to the conclusion that the grant of the right to make moving picture films did not confer on the grantee a right to make sound pictures. He arrived at this conclusion because of the distinction in the language used in the two expressions " all existing cinematograph rights " and " moving

(14) (1911), 222 U.S. 55.
(15) (1936), 83 F. (2d) 196.
(16) (1933), 267 N.Y.S. 327.
(17) (1933), 267 N.Y.S. at p. 328.
(18) (1933), MacG. Cop. Cas. (1928-35) 403.

picture films ". He proceeded on the footing that " all existing cinematograph A
rights " must mean something different from " moving picture films " and
therefore he came to the conclusion that the former must have been intended to
extend to sound rights whereas the latter expression was intended to be confined
to silent films.

In my judgment the proper conclusion to reach in the present case as to the
effect of the 1919 agreement does depend on what was then properly to be B
regarded as being in the contemplation of the parties and the fact that the
language used is " in cinematograph or moving picture films ", which might
at first sight suggest the possibility of an argument such as was followed by
SWIFT, J. (19) in the case that I have just mentioned, does not in my judgment
really help at all; for if at the date that this agreement was entered into the
only kind of cinematograph or moving picture films that were known as being C
commercial propositions or likely to become commercial propositions within the
period contemplated by the agreement were silent films it is impossible to conclude that by using the word " cinematograph " the parties intended to refer to
something other than the production of silent films. In my judgment on the
true construction of the 1919 agreement it was effective only to grant silent
film rights.   D

In any case it seems to me that regrettable though it is—and nobody has
stressed his regret about it more than counsel for the plaintiffs—the technical
point about the evolution of the title granted by the 1919 agreement is a valid
point. It is regrettable because I have no doubt that it was merely an error by
those concerned with dealing with these matters at the time, but the fact remains
that the assignment by Paramount Pictures to the defendant of the rights E
granted by the 1919 agreement was made not only without the consent of Sir
James Barrie but without anybody's consent at all and therefore was, in my
judgment, ineffective to pass the rights. Therefore I reach the conclusion that
in fact no sound rights are now vested in the defendant and that the only rights
that they have in these works of Sir James are the rights that they acquired
under the 1939 agreement, that is to say, the right to make a cartoon film. F
If as a result of what I have called the technical point the sound rights are
outstanding in some third party that, as I say, does not affect the position
between the plaintiffs and the defendant in these proceedings.

Whether the defendant has or has not sound rights in these works, is it obliged
to facilitate the use of the title " Peter Pan " by the plaintiffs or their licensees?
That seems to me to be the crucial question in this case, for the defendant is G
not objecting to the plaintiffs or their licensees making a sound film based on
" Peter Pan ". What they are objecting to is the making of such a film under
that particular title. Now there is no reason to suppose that the registration of
title scheme was in any way known to or in the mind of the hospital when the
1939 agreement was entered into. The hospital had nothing to do with the film
industry and no evidence has been led to lead to the conclusion that the hospital H
knew anything about any system of registration of titles. As I have already
pointed out, the plaintiffs contend, as I think with some force, that the presence
of the ten year period in cl. 4 itself tends to negative any idea that the parties
thought that either of them could insist on the exclusive use of a particular title.
It tends to make one think that the parties thought that an interval of time
between the presentation of one film and another was desirable just because I
similarity of the subject matter and similarity of the titles might otherwise result
in unsatisfactory confusion and competition. There is nothing to indicate that
at the time the 1939 agreement was entered into either of the parties had in
contemplation that the defendant would reissue its cartoon film after its first
release.

(19) (1933), MacG. Cop. Cas. (1928-35) 403.

A   Now as against the plaintiffs the defendant has got no title protection, because, as I have pointed out, the plaintiffs are not in any way bound by any title registration scheme. Had it been the intention of the parties that the plaintiffs themselves should be restricted in any way as to the title which they should be at liberty to use, it would have been necessary expressly to provide for this in the 1939 agreement and no such provision was made. If the plaintiffs were through

B   competent agents to make the proposed film themselves and to exhibit it, the defendant could not object, whatever title the plaintiffs chose to use. If, on the true construction of the 1939 agreement, that is the plaintiffs' own right, as it seems to me it clearly is, it must, in my judgment, have been the intention of the parties that this should be the right that the plaintiffs should be able to assign to an assignee or that they should be able to license a licensee to enjoy.

C   If, as the defendant says, a film made under the title " Peter Pan " could not as a commercial matter be satisfactorily exploited because of the rights of protection which the defendant has in the United States enforceable against those who make films and those who distribute films, then the insistence by the defendant on those rights would tend to stultify the plaintiffs' rights and the more so the more advantageous the title might be which the plaintiffs desired to use.

D   It follows, it seems to me, that the defendant's authority for the plaintiffs or their assignees or their licensees to use the protected title " Peter Pan " would be necessary to give effect to the provisions of cl. 4. The defendant's own ability to use the title " Peter Pan " having come to them as an incident of the 1938 assignment to Paramount Pictures is, I think, such a right as is mentioned in the closing words of cl. 4, so that the defendant by that clause has licensed the

E   plaintiffs to use the protected title. Even if this were not so, the defendant's insistence on protecting its registered title as against those who make films or those who distribute films would amount, I think, to a derogation from the right which it agreed by cl. 4 that the plaintiffs should enjoy either by way of grant from the defendant or by way of exception from the provisions of cl. 3 of the 1939 agreement, and such derogation would amount to a breach of contract.

F   For these reasons it seems to me that the plaintiffs are entitled to relief by way of declaration of their rights and a corresponding injunction, but are they presently entitled to damages? This depends on whether the defendant had at the issue of the writ already committed a breach of contract. Now the defendant contends that no breach has yet occurred, because all that had occurred when the writ was issued was that the defendant had warned the potential licensees

G   that they would object if and when the title " Peter Pan " or any other title confusingly similar to it were used. For the plaintiffs it is said that the letter of June 5, 1964, amounted to an objection to the making of the film by Mr. Cukor and Mr. Ferrer under the title intended to be used and that to give the agreement business efficacy cl. 4 must be so construed as to preclude the defendants from frightening off prospective assignees or licensees. It is true that the

H   letter of June 5, 1964, is expressed in warning terms only, courteous (as I have said) but firm, but I think that objection can be taken to something before that thing occurs. If I say I object to anybody leaving this court before I have completed this judgment the fact that everybody is quietly sitting in his seat does not make my remark any less an objection. By the letter of June 5, 1964, the defendant, it seems to me, in the clearest terms indicated that it objected to

I   the plaintiffs licensing Mr. Cukor and Mr. Ferrer to make a film under the title " Peter Pan " and that it objected to these gentlemen, who I agree were not yet licensees, making a film under that title as licensees of the plaintiffs. That objection had the not surprising effect of bringing the negotiations between the plaintiffs and Mr. Cukor and Mr. Ferrer to a halt and for the time being at any rate they are at an end. In my judgment the letter did constitute an objection of the kind which the defendant had bound itself by cl. 4 not to make. Accordingly I am of opinion that when the writ was issued there had already been a

breach of contract in respect of which the plaintiffs are entitled to an inquiry A
as to damages.

Order accordingly.

Solicitors: *Waterhouse & Co.* (for the plaintiffs); *Warren, Munton & Co.*
(for the defendants).

[*Reported by* JENIFER SANDELL, *Barrister-at-Law.*] B

THORNE *v.* UNIVERSITY OF LONDON.

C

[COURT OF APPEAL (Diplock and Salmon, L.JJ.), March 18, 1966.]

University—Examination—Conferring of degrees—Alleged misjudging of degree
candidate's examination papers—Matter one for visitor of university—
Action by candidate for alleged negligence and for mandamus—No jurisdic-
tion in High Court.

The High Court has no jurisdiction to hear complaints by a member of D
London University, or by a person seeking a degree from the university,
against the university about its examinations or conferment of degrees,
because those matters are within the exclusive jurisdiction of the visitor
of the university.

Thomson v. *London University* ((1864), 33 L.J.Ch. 625) and *R.* v. *Duns-*
heath, Ex p. Meredith ([1950] 2 All E.R. 741) approved. E

[As to non-interference by the High Court in matters within the province
of the visitor of a university, see 13 HALSBURY'S LAWS (3rd Edn.) 709, para. 1445,
text and note (*o*); and for cases on the subject, see 11 DIGEST (Repl.) 654, 655,
316-321 and also *Sammy* v. *Birkbeck College,* The Times, May 20, 1965, p. 6.]

Cases referred to: F

R. v. *Dunsheath, Ex p. Meredith,* [1950] 2 All E.R. 741; [1951] 1 K.B. 127;
   8 Digest (Repl.) 504, *2258.*
Thomson v. *London University,* (1864), 33 L.J.Ch. 625; 10 L.T. 403; 8 Digest
   (Repl.) 505, *2265.*

Application for leave to appeal.

This was an application on notice dated Feb. 25, 1966, by Dr. Carl-Theo Thorne, G
the plaintiff in an action against University of London, for leave to appeal out
of time from an order of JOHN STEPHENSON, J., made in chambers on Jan. 26,
1966, dismissing the plaintiff's appeal from an order of Master CLAYTON, dated
Nov. 26, 1965, ordering that the writ and statement of claim be struck out under
R.S.C., Ord. 18, r. 19, and under the inherent jurisdiction of the court on the
ground that they disclosed no reasonable cause of action and were frivolous and H
vexatious and an abuse of the process of the court, and that the plaintiff's action
be dismissed.   The facts are set out in the judgment of DIPLOCK, L.J.

The plaintiff appeared in person.
Brian T. Neill, for the defendant university, was not called on.

   DIPLOCK, L.J.:   This is an application for leave to appeal from an order I
of STEPHENSON, J., striking out the plaintiff's writ and statement of claim and
dismissing the action which he brought against the University of London, the
defendant.   The endorsement on the writ reads as follows:

" The plaintiff's claim is for damages for negligently misjudging the plaintiff's examination papers for the Intermediate and Finals LL.B. and for a
mandamus commanding the defendant to award the plaintiff the grade
at least justified."

A In his statement of claim the plaintiff sets out a good deal of praise of his ability as a lawyer. He goes on to say that he sat for some examinations in the London LL.B. examination, papers in criminal law, the law of trusts and the law of evidence, and that he received notice that he had failed in the papers for trusts and criminal law; and he claims that that was a result of negligence on the part of the examiners.

B   There is clear and recent authority in *R.* v. *Dunsheath, Ex p. Meredith* (1) that actions of this kind relating to domestic disputes between members of London University (as is the case with other universities) are matters which are to be dealt with by the visitor and the court has no jurisdiction to deal with them. In that case, which was a decision of the Divisional Court, LORD GODDARD, C.J., referred with approval to *Thomson* v. *London University* (2), which was decided

C in 1864. That was another case in which a budding lawyer complained about what had happened to him in the examinations held by the university, and there is a passage (3) in the judgment of KINDERSLEY, V.-C., which covers exactly the sort of claim which the plaintiff has put forward in this case. KINDERSLEY, V.-C., said this (3):

D   " The holding of examinations and the conferring of degrees being one, if not the main or only object of this university, all the regulations, that is, the construction of all the regulations and the carrying into effect of all those regulations as among persons who are either actually members of the university or who come in and subject themselves to be at least pro hac vice members of the university—I mean with respect to the degrees which

E   they seek to have conferred upon them—all those are regulations of the domus; they are regulations clearly in my mind coming within the jurisdiction, and the exclusive jurisdiction of the visitor."

Those words, which were approved in *R.* v. *Dunsheath* (1), cover precisely the sort of claim which the plaintiff seeks to bring before the High Court in this action. The High Court does not act as a Court of Appeal from university

F examiners; and, speaking for my own part, I am very glad that it declines this jurisdiction. Clearly it does decline the jurisdiction.

The action was wholly misconceived, and the decision of the learned judge to strike out the endorsement on the writ and the statement of claim and to dismiss the action was clearly right.

G   **SALMON, L.J.:** I agree.

Application dismissed.

Solicitors: *Coward, Chance & Co.* (for the defendant, the university).

[*Reported by* HENRY SUMMERFIELD, ESQ., *Barrister-at-Law.*]

H

I

---

(1) [1950] 2 All E.R. 741; [1951] 1 K.B. 127.   (2) (1864), 33 L.J.Ch. 625.
(3) (1864), 33 L.J.Ch. at p. 634.

SALOMON v. COMMISSIONERS OF CUSTOMS AND EXCISE.   A

[QUEEN'S BENCH DIVISION (Megaw, J.), March 21, 22, 28, 1966.]

*Customs—Duties—Valuation of goods for purposes of duty—Open market price
—Importation of new camera by private traveller—Whether duty should be
based on open market retail price prevailing in the United Kingdom for
new cameras of that type less purchase tax and duty—Customs and Excise* B
Act, 1952 (15 & 16 Geo. 6 & 1 Eliz. 2 c. 44), s. 258 (1), (2), Sch. 6, paras. 1, 2.

By s. 258 and paras. 1, 2* of Sch. 6 to the Customs and Excise Act, 1952,
where customs duty is chargeable on goods by reference to their value, that
value is to be the normal price, namely, the price which they would fetch
on a sale in the open market between buyer and seller independent of
each other, pre-supposing price to be the sole consideration.   C

S., a private traveller returning to the United Kingdom from a visit to
the United States, brought with him a new American camera, still in its
wrappings with the seal unbroken, which had been given to him in the
United States. The American manufacturers of the camera had sole concessionaries in the United Kingdom. There was a market for cameras of
that type in the United Kingdom. The retail price of such a camera in   D
the United States, and the price paid by a dealer in the United Kingdom
buying such a camera from a private owner, were both substantially less
than the retail price of such cameras new in the United Kingdom. The
Commissioners of Customs and Excise assessed the value of the camera for
customs duty at the retail price in the United Kingdom market less the
tax element, viz., the price which the camera would have fetched on the   E
date of importation on a sale in the United Kingdom by a retailer to a
consumer, excluding purchase tax and customs duty.

Held: the Commissioners' basis of assessment was right, because on the
true construction of Sch. 6, paras. 1 and 2, the open market was a market
in the United Kingdom, buyer and seller were notional persons neither of
whom was related to the person importing the goods, and the notional   F
seller must be deemed to have a desire and a full facility to sell the camera
on the relevant date in the open market at the highest price then obtainable, that price being the retailer's price less purchase tax and customs duty
(see p. 344, letter C, and p. 345, letters E, H and I, post).

Rolex Watch Co., Ltd. v. Comrs. of Customs and Excise ([1956] 2 All E.R.
589), distinguished.   G

[As to the evaluation of imported goods for the purpose of customs duty, see
33 HALSBURY'S LAWS (3rd Edn.) 147-149, paras. 252, 253.

As to international agreements as aids to the construction of statutes, see
36 HALSBURY'S LAWS (3rd Edn.) 411, para. 623.

For the Customs and Excise Act, 1952, s. 258 and Sch. 6, paras. 1, 2, see
32 HASLBURY'S STATUTES (2nd Edn.) 855, 909.]   H

Cases referred to:
Ellerman Lines, Ltd. v. *Murray. White Star Line of Royal and United States
Mail Steamers Oceanic Steam Navigation Co., Ltd.* v. *Comerford,* [1930]
All E.R. Rep. 503; [1931] A.C. 126; sub nom. *The Croxteth Hall, The
Celtic,* 100 L.J.P. 25; 144 L.T. 441; 44 Digest (Repl.) 228, *462.*
Rolex Watch Co., Ltd. v. *Comrs. of Customs and Excise,* [1956] 2 All E.R. 589;   I
[1956] 1 W.L.R. 612; 39 Digest (Repl.) 250, *77.*

Case Stated.
The complainant, Mr. Walter H. Salomon, was a private traveller who, returning to the United Kingdom after a visit to the U.S.A., arrived at London Airport
on Nov. 16, 1963, with a new Polaroid Automatic 100 Camera which had been

_____
* Section 258 and Sch. 6 are set out, so far as material, at p. 342, letter F, to p. 343,
letter D, post.

Reversed. C.A. [1966] 3 All E.R. 871.

A given to him in the U.S.A. and was still in its original wrappings with the seal unbroken. The Commissioners of Customs and Excise (" the Commissioners ") assessed the value of the camera and case for customs duty and for purchase tax. Mr. Salomon disputed the assessments and gave notice requiring reference to arbitration under the Customs and Excise Act, 1952. The referee appointed for the purpose, Mr. A. W. ROSKILL, Q.C., upheld the contentions of

B the Commissioners as to the value of the camera for customs duty under the Customs and Excise Act, 1952, s. 258 and Sch. 6, and at the request of both parties made his award, so far as concerned the customs duty dispute, in the form of a Special Case. The question of law for the decision of the court was whether, under the material statutory provisions and on the facts found, the value for customs duty on Nov. 16, 1963, of the camera and the case was: (i) the value

C for customs duty of such camera and case, of the same type as the camera and the case, imported into the United Kingdom by the sole concessionaries, Polaroid (U.K.), Ltd., namely £31 6s. 10d. for the camera and £2 13s. for the case; or (ii) the price paid in the United States by travellers not trading in such goods for cameras and cases of the same type as the camera and the case (with the addition of 5s. to the price paid for each camera and of 2s. 4d.

D to the price paid for each case), namely £30 10s. 8d. for the camera and £2 7s. 2d. for the case; or (iii) the price which the camera and the case would have fetched (less purchase tax) on a sale by the individual bringing the camera into the country to a dealer in such goods in the United Kingdom, namely £65 (including a nominal sum for the case) less £17 8s. 4d. purchase tax, resulting in a value for customs duty of the camera and the case of £47 11s. 8d.; or (iv)

E the price which the camera and the case would have fetched on a sale in the United Kingdom by a retailer to a consumer, that is to say the list price of the camera and of the case (excluding purchase tax) less customs duty, resulting in a value for duty of £70 8s. 7d. for the camera and £7 2s. 8d. for the case. Sub-paragraph (iv) represented the contention of the Commissioners.

F *M. Waters* for the complainant, Mr. Salomon.

    J. J. Finney for the Commissioners of Customs and Excise.

Cur. adv. vult.

    Mar. 28. **MEGAW, J.,** read the following judgment. The complainant, Mr. Walter H. Salomon, in the course of a visit to the United States of America, was given a Polaroid Automatic 100 camera in a leather case. I shall refer to the

G camera and case collectively as " the camera " except where camera and case have to be distinguished. It was manufacturered in the United States and there cost $92.10, the equivalent of £30 10s. 8d. Mr. Salomon returned to the United Kingdom by air, landing at London Airport on Nov. 16, 1963. He brought with him the camera, still in its original wrappings, with the seal unbroken, new and unused.

H   The Commissioners of Customs and Excise (to whom I shall refer as " the Commissioners ") assessed the value of the camera on Nov. 16, 1963, for customs duty at £77 11s. 3d., being £70 8s. 7d. for the camera itself and £7 2s. 8d. for the case. On the basis of that assessment, they claimed that the customs duty on the camera was £29 11s. 11d. being forty per cent. of the assessed value of the camera and twenty per cent. of the assessed value of the case. They also made

I assessments for purchase tax, but these are no longer in dispute. Mr. Salomon disputed the assessments and gave notice requiring reference to arbitration under the Customs and Excise Act, 1952. The dispute was referred to the arbitration of Mr. A. W. ROSKILL, Q.C., the referee appointed for the purpose. The referee made his award on Nov. 5, 1965, on the basis of pleadings, evidence and the submission of counsel. So far as concerns the customs duty dispute, he made his award in the form of a Special Case at the request of both parties. By para. 7 of the award, he upheld the contentions of the Commissioners, and, subject to the decision of the court, awarded that the value of the camera for

customs duty on Nov. 16, 1963, was £77 11s. 3d. (£70 8s. 7d. for the camera **A**
itself and £7 2s. 8d. for the case). The referee then made provision as to the
costs, and in para. 10 set out alternative awards, should the question of law be
answered differently by the court.

For the understanding of the questions of law posed for the decision of the
court, it is necessary to refer to certain facts found in the award. Mr. Salomon
was not at any time engaged in the business of buying and selling cameras. **B**
Duty was chargeable on the camera at the rate of forty per cent. of its value,
and in respect of the case, at twenty per cent. At all material times the vast
majority of such cameras imported into the United Kingdom were imported by
Polaroid (U.K.), Ltd., who were the sole concessionaries in the United Kingdom
of the American manufacturers. A few of such cameras were imported individually by travellers such as Mr. Salomon. The retail list price in the United Kingdom **C**
on Nov. 16, 1963, was £107 3s. 2d., being £98 12s. for the camera itself and
£8 11s. 2d. for the case, in each instance before purchase tax. As regards imports
into the United Kingdom of such cameras by the sole concessionaries, the sum
of 7s. 4d. was added to the concessionaries' buying price f.o.b. Cambridge,
Massachusetts, to represent the cost of the freight, etc., in order to satisfy the
presuppositions of para. 2 of Sch. 6 to the Customs and Excise Act, 1952 (" the **D**
Act of 1952 "). On the relevant date, the value for customs duty of cameras
of this type, imported by the sole concessionaries, was £33 19s. 10d. The price
which the camera would have fetched on a sale in the United States of America,
on the relevant date, to Mr. Salomon or some other traveller, not being a dealer
in such goods, would not have exceeded £32 17s. 10d. On the relevant date,
the price which the camera would have fetched on a sale by Mr. Salomon to a **E**
dealer in such goods in the United Kingdom, namely the second-hand value of
the camera, would not have exceeded £65, which amount includes £17 8s. 4d.
purchase tax. On the relevant date, new cameras of this type were freely on
sale in the United Kingdom and could have been purchased there at the retail
price of £107 3s. 2d., excluding purchase tax, but including customs duty of
£29 11s. 11d., which is the sum claimed by the commissioners. **F**

I shall now refer to the relevant statutory provisions of the Customs and
Excise Act, 1952. Section 258 says so far as material:

" (1) For the purposes of any enactment for the time being in force
whereunder a duty of customs is chargeable on goods by reference to their
value, the value of any imported goods shall be taken to be that laid down **G**
by Sch. 6 to this Act, and duty shall be paid on that value:

" Provided that, in the case of goods imported under a contract of sale
and entered for home use, duty shall be deemed to have been paid on
that value if, before the goods are delivered for home use, duty is tendered
and accepted on a declared value based on the contract price.

" (2) For the purpose of the proviso to the foregoing subsection—(*a*) the **H**
declared value of any goods is their value as declared by or on behalf of
the importer in making entry of the goods for home use; (*b*) that value
shall be deemed to be based on the contract price if, but only if, it represents that price properly adjusted to take account of circumstances
differentiating the contract from such a contract of sale as is contemplated
by Sch. 6 to this Act; (*c*) the rate of exchange to be used for determining **I**
the equivalent in sterling of any foreign currency shall be the current
selling rate in the United Kingdom as last notified before the time when
the goods are entered for home use."

Paragraph 1 of Sch. 6 is as follows:

" (1) The value of any imported goods shall be taken to be the normal
price, that is to say the price which they would fetch, at the time when
they are entered for home use (or, if they are not so entered, the time of

A importation), on a sale in the open market between buyer and seller independent of each other;

   " (2) The normal price of any imported goods shall be determined on the following assumptions:—(a) that the goods are treated as having been delivered to the buyer at the port or place of importation; and (b) that the seller will bear freight, insurance, commission and all the other costs,
B charges and expenses incidental to the sale and the delivery of the goods at that port or place; but (c) that the buyer will bear any duty or tax chargeable in the United Kingdom."

Paragraph 2 says:

   " A sale in the open market between buyer and seller independent of
C each other pre-supposes (a) that the price is the sole consideration; and (b) that the price made is not influenced by any commercial, financial or other relationship, whether by contract or otherwise, between the seller or any person associated in business with him and the buyer or any person associated in business with him (other than the relationship created by the sale of the goods in question); and (c) that no part of the proceeds of the
D subsequent re-sale, use or disposal of the goods will accrue either directly or indirectly to the seller or any person associated in business with him."

   The award summarises the arguments on behalf of Mr. Salomon and the Commissioners. I need not read them. In para. 6, the question of law is stated as follows:

   " The question of law for the decision of the court is whether, under the
E material statutory provisions and upon the facts found, the value for customs duty on Nov. 16, 1963, of the camera and the case is: (i) the value for customs duty of such camera and case, of the same type as the camera and the case, imported into the United Kingdom by the sole concessionaires, Polaroid (U.K.), Ltd., namely, £31 6s. 10d. for the camera and £2 13s. for the case; or (ii) the price paid in the United States of America by
F travellers not trading in such goods for cameras and cases of the same type as the camera and the case (with the addition of 5s. to the price paid for each camera and of 2s. 4d. to the price paid for each case) namely £30 10s. 8d. for the camera and £2 7s. 2d. for the case; or (iii) the price which the camera and the case would have fetched (less purchase tax) on a sale by the complainant to a dealer in such goods in the United Kingdom,
G namely, £65 (including a nominal sum for the case) less £17 8s. 4d. purchase tax, resulting in a value for customs duty of the camera and the case of £47 11s. 8d.; or (iv) the price which the camera and the case would have fetched on a sale in the United Kingdom by a retailer to a consumer, that is to say the list price of the camera and of the case (excluding purchase tax) less customs duty, resulting in a value for duty of £70 8s. 7d. for the
H camera and £7 2s. 8d. for the case."

   Sub-paragraphs (i), (ii) and (iii) represent Mr. Salomon's three alternative contentions. Sub-paragraph (iv) is the Commissioners' contention. In my judgment, the referee's conclusion upholding the Commissioners' contention on the question of law is right.

I Mr. Salomon's proposition of law as set out in sub-para. (ii) of para. 6 of the award is that on which he primarily relies. As I understand the argument, it involves two propositions in relation to para. 1 of Sch. 6 to the Act of 1952. First, it is contended that, in the notional bargain in the open market between buyer and seller independent of each other, the importer is to be considered as being the buyer. Mr. Salomon has to be treated as the buyer. He himself has to be treated as notionally buying such a camera from a notional seller. Secondly, the market to be considered is not, or at least is not necessarily limited to, a market in the United Kingdom. By putting these two propositions together,

the conclusion is reached that, in assessing the value of the camera, one is   A
entitled, and indeed bound, to look at any market for such cameras in any part
of the world, so long as it can be regarded as having been available to Mr.
Salomon; and, in particular, to look at the market in Cambridge, Massachusetts,
or in the United States of America as a whole; since it was there presumably
that the camera in question was bought by someone who presented it to Mr.
Salomon. The price at which such a camera could have been bought in that   B
market having been ascertained, that price determines the value for customs
duty. The camera could have been bought there on the relevant date for
£32 17s. 10d., when the dollar price is converted into sterling.

I do not propose to go in detail into the arguments put forward by counsel
for Mr. Salomon in support of these propositions. In my judgment, they are
wrong. " Buyer and seller " in Sch. 6 are notional persons. Neither of them is   C
related to, or bears the particular characteristics of, the person importing the
goods, here, Mr. Salomon. The open market contemplated by Sch. 6 is a
market within the United Kingdom. It is not open to either the Commissioners
or the importer to seek to enhance or reduce the value of the goods imported
for customs duty purposes (after all, it is the United Kingdom customs duty)
by reference to places elsewhere in the world where similar goods may be   D
available for purchase and may have a different value.

Counsel for Mr. Salomon sought to rely on the Convention on the Valuation
of Goods for Customs Purposes made at Brussels on Dec. 15, 1950 (1). The
United Kingdom ratified that Convention on Sept. 27, 1952, after the Act of
1952 had received the royal assent. The convention is nowhere mentioned in
the Act of 1952. At best, the convention could only be referred to if there were   E
an ambiguity in the Act of 1952, and, as I understand the decision of the House
of Lords in *Ellerman Lines, Ltd.* v. *Murray* (2), only then, if the Convention
had been expressly referred to in, or scheduled to, the Act of 1952. I did, however, look at the convention, de bene esse, and heard counsel's submissions
thereon. I can see nothing in the convention which would assist the submission
of counsel for Mr. Salomon. It is then said that, even if the " open market " in   F
para. 1 of Sch. 6 includes the United Kingdom, it is not confined to the United
Kingdom; or, alternatively, that, because of modern means of communication,
a market in the United Kingdom includes the possibility of making purchases
and sales overseas; for example, in the United States; and that therefore prices
and values in such places are relevant in assessing the value of goods for United
Kingdom customs duty. Of course, in many cases the price which has been   G
paid by the importer to a foreign seller for goods sold by him for import into
the United Kingdom may be relevant and helpful in assessing the value of
imported goods for the purpose of s. 258 and Sch. 6 to the Act of 1952. The
proviso in s. 258 (1) itself contemplates that such use may be made of the contract
price at the discretion of the Commissioners (3).

Mr. Salomon's proposition of law in sub-para. (i) of para. 6 of the award—   H
that the value for customs duty of Mr. Salomon's camera was the value for
customs duty of the cameras imported by the sole concessionaires—is said to be
founded on the decision of the Court of Appeal in *Rolex Watch Co., Ltd.* v.
Comrs. of Customs and Excise (4). It is said that it was held in that case that
there was no open market, because there were sole concessionaires, and that
therefore one must ascertain the proper customs duty by looking at the price   I
paid by the importer to his foreign seller, with any necessary adjustments. The
importer here did not buy from any foreign seller. In any event, for the reasons
put forward by counsel for the Commissioners, I do not think that the *Rolex*
case (4) is relevant. There the question was as to the goods imported by the
sole concessionaires, there being no question of any import into this country

(1) Cmd. 9233 (Treaty Series No. 49 (1954)).
(2) [1930] All E.R. Rep. 503; [1931] A.C. 126.
(3) The proviso is set out at p. 342, letter G, ante.   (4) [1956] 2 All E.R. 589.

A by any other person. Here, the question relates to an import by someone other than the sole concesssionaires, and completely different considerations apply. Moreover, different considerations, no doubt, apply as between the assessment of customs duty on Mr. Salomon's camera and the assessment in respect of the cameras imported by the sole concessionaires.

I reject the submissions on behalf of Mr. Salomon that the importer of goods

B must be treated as the notional buyer referred to in Sch. 6 to the Act of 1952; that the relevant market for the purpose of that schedule is, or may be, a market outside the United Kingdom (5); and that there can in the present case be no open market because the American manufacturer has a sole concessionaire in the United Kingdom.

There remains the third alternative put forward on behalf of Mr. Salomon,

C in sub-para. (iii) of para. 6 of the award. That is, that the price which the camera would have fetched on a sale by Mr. Salomon to a dealer in the United Kingdom would have been £65, less £17 8s. 4d. purchase tax; that is, a customs duty value of £47 11s. 8d. There is, it is said, a market in the United Kingdom for cameras such as this; in that market the buyer is a dealer in cameras. The dealer, of course, pays less than the ordinary retail price, because he takes the

D goods into stock in the hope of a sale, and on that sale, if and when it comes, he will wish to make a profit. Therefore, if this camera, though entering the United Kingdom new and unused, had been sold to a dealer, the price would have been substantially less than the United Kingdom retail price, as shown by the figures in the award which I have just cited. Therefore, it is said, that should be the value for customs duty.

E In my view, the notional seller in para. 1 of Sch. 6 is, as is contended on behalf of the Commissioners, a seller whose object is to get the highest available price. " Available ", of course, connotes that there are buyers in the market prepared to pay that price. The notional seller must be treated as one who has access to the market—whatever available market there may be. If there is a retail market, he must be treated as free and able to deal in that market. The

F personal attributes of the individual importer do not enter into the question at all. It does not matter that the individual importer, Mr. Salomon, is not a trader in cameras, whether a dealer or a retailer. The notional seller can go into the market, notionally, and can, and must be deemed to, go to that part of the market—to adopt that manner of selling the one, single, new, imported camera —which is most favourable to him in price. He must not be deemed not to be

G able to use the retail market, if that be the most favourable way in which a notional seller, unrestricted by any assumed personal characteristics or limitations on facility of trading, would seek to sell. The criterion laid down by para. 1 (1) of Sch. 6 to the Act of 1952 is the price which the goods in question—the single, new, unopened camera—" would fetch " on a sale in the open market between buyer and seller independent of each other (6). I am not, of course, here concerned with imports in quantity, but with the import of a single article.

H As it was put by counsel for the Commissioners, the notional buyer and seller in Sch. 6 are both " ghosts ". To put it another way, the notional seller is an imaginary person, with no personal characteristics or attributes, positive or negative, except a deemed desire, and a full facility, to take the camera in question into the open market, and there sell it for the highest price obtainable.

I Since the referee has found as a fact that new cameras of this type were freely on sale in the United Kingdom and could have been purchased there, on the relevant date, at a stated retail price, it follows in my judgment that there was a relevant open market for this camera, that the notional seller must be assumed to have access to, and to use, that market, and to obtain that price in that market. Hence the value for customs duty at the relevant date is that price, less the purchase tax element in it. It is on that value that the Commissioners

---

(5) The material part of Sch. 6 is set out at p. 342, letter I, to p. 343, letter D, ante.
(6) Paragraph 1 (1) of Sch. 6 is set out at p. 342, letter I, to p. 343, letter A, ante.

claim. It is that value, and the customs duty referable to it, which the referee **A**
has upheld. Accordingly, I affirm his award as set out in para. 7 of the Special
Case.

Order accordingly.

Solicitors: *Tarlo, Lyons & Aukin* (for the complainant); *Solicitor, Commissioners of Customs and Excise.*

[*Reported by* K. DIANA PHILLIPS, *Barrister-at-Law.*] **B**

R. *v.* JACKSON (alias RINTOUL).

C

[COURT OF CRIMINAL APPEAL (Edmund Davies, Thompson and John Stephenson,
JJ.), February 15, 1966.]

*Criminal Law—Sentence—Youthful offender—Imprisonment—Statement of
reason why no other sentence appropriate—Offender had twice been sentenced
to borstal training—Criminal Justice Act, 1948 (11 & 12 Geo. 6 c. 58), s. 17 (3)
—Criminal Justice Act, 1961 (9 & 10 Eliz. 2 c. 39), s. 3 (3).*

D

The appellant, having pleaded guilty to shopbreaking and larceny, to
possessing housebreaking implements by night and to malicious wounding,
was sentenced to a total of three years' imprisonment. He was nearly
twenty-one years of age and had been sentenced twice to borstal training.
When passing the sentence, the recorder observed that a sentence of borstal
training for the third time would be useless. On appeal against sentence **E**
on the ground that there had been non-compliance with the Criminal Justice
Act, 1948, s. 17 (3), which required the court to state the reason for its
opinion that no other method of dealing with the appellant was appropriate,

Held: the recorder had sufficiently indicated his reason for concluding
that borstal training would be inappropriate for the appellant; even if he
had not done so, the consequence would not have been that his sentence **F**
would not stand, but it would still have been for the Court of Criminal Appeal
to adjudicate on its appropriateness (see p. 348, letter D, post).

[As to the punishment of youthful offenders, see 10 HALSBURY'S LAWS (3rd
Edn.) 514, 515, para. 935; as to borstal training, see ibid., p. 517, para. 943;
and for cases on the subject, see 14 DIGEST (Repl.) 591, *5872-5881.*

For the Criminal Justice Act, 1948, s. 17, see 28 HALSBURY'S STATUTES (2nd **G**
Edn.) 366 and SUPPLEMENT, Amended Texts to Vol. 28, para. [448].

For the Criminal Justice Act, 1961, s. 3, see 41 HALSBURY'S STATUTES (2nd
Edn.) 132.]

Case referred to:

R. v. *Frew,* (1963), unreported. **H**

Appeal.

This was an appeal by Raymond Jackson (alias Rintoul) against a sentence of
three years' imprisonment imposed on him by the recorder at Birmingham
quarter sessions on Dec. 8, 1965, in respect of his conviction for shopbreaking
and larceny, possessing housebreaking implements by night without a lawful
excuse and malicious wounding. He was under twenty-one years of age **I**
and appealed on the ground that there had been non-compliance with the
requirements of s. 17 (3) of the Criminal Justice Act, 1948.

The cases noted below* were cited during the argument in addition to the case
referred to in the judgment of the court.

K. H. Clarke for the appellant.

The Crown was not represented.

---

* *R.* v. *Chambers,* (1952), **36** Cr. App. Rep. 104; *R.* v. *Lowe,* [1964] 2 All E.R. 116.

A   **EDMUND DAVIES, J.,** delivered the following judgment of the court:
On Dec. 8, 1965, when the appellant was about three months short of his twenty-
first birthday, he pleaded guilty at the Birmingham quarter sessions first to
shopbreaking and larceny and then to possessing housebreaking implements by
night without a lawful excuse, and finally to malicious wounding. He was
sentenced in all to three years' imprisonment, that is to say six months and six
B   months concurrent on the shopbreaking and larceny and on possessing shopbreaking implements by night, and to thirty months consecutive on the malicious
wounding count. He now applies by leave of the single judge against his sentence.
       The facts are these. On Oct. 31, 1965, the appellant then being about twenty
and a half years of age, a police officer saw him standing by a broken shop
window. He had under his arm some clothing which he had taken from the
C   shop and was busily engaged in enlarging the hole by removing further pieces of
broken glass from the window. The police officer challenged him and then the
appellant said to the officer, " You've bit off more than you can chew ", and
thrust a piece of glass at the officer's face. The officer warded off the blow with
his hand but he sustained on the hand a four inch cut. There was a violent
struggle, when the appellant again attacked the officer as he tried to telephone
D   for help, and he was restrained only by the assistance of four members of the
public doing their duty. The appellant gave the impression of having taken a
heavy amount of drink and had a hacksaw and bit. He said that he had been
drinking but he had committed the offence with another man, using the implements that belonged to that other man. As to the wounding, he said that he
could not really remember what had happened; but he expressed his regret and
E   said that he had no intention of hurting the officer. He is a married man with
a child. He has had an unfortunate upbringing. At the age of four he was
taken into the care of the local authority and has lived in institutions or with
foster parents. In 1960 he was sent to an approved school and absconded and
was returned after a conviction for malicious wounding. He again absconded
and in the following year, 1961, he was sent to borstal for theft by housebreaking.
F   He was released from borstal on licence in November, 1962, and worked as a
labourer until January, 1964, when he was again sent to borstal for six breaking
offences. He was last released therefrom in December, 1964, and married the
next month and lived with his wife's parents. He (and this is to his credit)
worked consistently and well during 1965 and was latterly earning £25 a week.
He has a summary conviction for being drunk and disorderly. The probation
G   officer reported he was of low intelligence and immature; the poor home conditions led to many difficulties and he had recently been drinking heavily; that
his marriage, so recently entered into, was in jeopardy and his future looked
very doubtful.
       Counsel urged on his behalf his genuine regret for wounding the officer. He
submitted that the appellant had a piece of glass in his hand when challenged;
H   that he was drunk and the wounding was in the nature of an accident; that the
appellant himself had received a broken jaw in the course of the struggle; that
he had tried to go straight despite home difficulties but had fallen into bad
company. The learned recorder, who has great experience in these matters,
said:

I   " You come before this court being nearly twenty-one and having twice
       been sent to Borstal already, and I am quite satisfied that in this case it
       would be wrong, it would be useless, to send you back to Borstal again,"

and he thereupon proceeded to pass the sentences which have been already
indicated. He said that he could not accept that the wounding was accidental.
       It is now said by counsel on behalf of the appellant that there was non-com-
pliance by the learned recorder with s. 17 (3) of the Criminal Justice Act, 1948,
which requires that where quarter sessions imposes imprisonment on a person
under twenty-one, "... the court shall state the reason for its opinion that no

other method of dealing with him is appropriate ".   Counsel for the appellant **A**
says that that requirement is not complied with and that, as a legal consequence
of that omission, the sentences of imprisonment cannot in law stand, and that
there must now be substituted a sentence that he undergoes borstal training.
That is not, with respect to counsel, the law as laid down by this court.   In
the unreported case of *R.* v. *Frew* (1), decided by this court on Dec. 20, 1963,
STREATFEILD, J., having dealt with the merits of the case generally, said: **B**

" The only matter which does call for comment is that the court of quarter
sessions, in passing sentence, did not, as required by the Criminal Justice
Act, 1948, s. 17 (2) and (3), state their reasons for sending him to prison.
This court only wishes to state that it is desirable that courts of quarter
sessions, when they are taking the course of sending someone under the
age of twenty-one to prison, should state in open court, so that it is recorded   **C**
on the shorthand note, the reasons for which they have decided to pass a
sentence of imprisonment instead of Borstal.   It is to be hoped that in future
that requirement will not again be overlooked."

It was, in the judgment of this court, not overlooked by the learned recorder
in the present case.   By expressing himself as he did he indicated his reasons   **D**
for coming to the conclusion that a sentence of borstal training would be inappropriate in the case of the appellant.   Even if he had not done so, the consequences
would not have been that the sentence of imprisonment could not stand.   It
would be still for this court to adjudicate on its appropriateness.

Counsel for the appellant has finally drawn the court's attention to the fact
that by virtue of s. 3 (3) of the Criminal Justice Act, 1961, the learned recorder   **E**
in the circumstances of this case, the appellant having previously been to borstal,
did not have to impose sentences of three years' imprisonment but could have
imposed a sentence of eighteen months and upwards.   We have no doubt that
the learned recorder, again in the light of his experience, was perfectly familiar
with that statutory provision, but, bearing it in mind, nevertheless came to the
conclusion that in this case sentences totalling three years were called for.   Indeed,   **F**
that he did have s. 3 (3) in mind is manifested by the fact that in respect of the
malicious wounding count he imposed a sentence of thirty months' imprisonment.
[HIS LORDSHIP referred to a letter from the Home Office concerning the appellant
in Borstal and continued:] Keeping all those matters in mind, this court is
forced to the conclusion that these sentences not only are not wrong in principle
but that they were merited by the circumstances of this case.   It follows, therefore,   **G**
that this appeal against sentence fails.

Appeal dismissed.

Solicitors: *Registrar, Court of Criminal Appeal.*

[*Reported by* KAUSHALYA PURIE, *Barrister-at-Law.*]

H

I

---

(1) (1963), unreported.

A
RODRIGUEZ v. PARKER.

[QUEEN's BENCH DIVISION (Nield, J.), April 6, 1966.]

Practice—Parties—Adding or substituting party as defendant—Amendment of writ to substitute for the defendant, R.J.P., his son R.S.P.—Limitation
B *period expired—Action for personal injuries in road accident—Genuine mistake and intended defendant not misled—Whether rule of court permitting amendment ultra vires—Whether leave to amend just in the circumstances—Supreme Court of Judicature (Consolidation) Act, 1925 (15 & 16 Geo. 5, c. 49), s. 99 (1), Sch. 1—R.S.C., Ord. 20, r. 5.*

On Oct. 30, 1961, the plaintiff was injured by a motor van driven by R. S.
C Parker, the son of its owner, R. J. Parker. On June 11, 1964, a writ was issued on the plaintiff's behalf in which the defendant was mistakenly described as R. J. Parker. The claim was for damages for personal injuries. The writ was served on Jan. 4, 1965, by which time the limitation period had expired. In July, 1965, the defence was delivered; it included a denial that the defendant was driving the van. On Jan. 17, 1966, an order was made, under
D R.S.C., Ord. 20*, r. 5 (see particularly para. (2)), for amendment of the writ by substituting R. S. Parker as defendant.

Held: (i) R.S.C., Ord. 20, r. 5 was intra vires (see p. 364, letter D, post).

(ii) leave to substitute R. S. Parker as defendant was properly given because (a) the mistake had been a genuine mistake, (b) it was not mis-leading nor such as to cause any reasonable doubt as to the identity of the
E person intended to be sued and (c) to make the amendment was just (see p. 365, letters D and H, post).

(iii) the validity of the writ should also be extended (see p. 366, letter B, post).

[As to the power to make Rules of the Supreme Court, see 9 HALSBURY's LAWS (3rd Edn.) 422, para. 973.
F As to misjoinder of parties, see 30 HALSBURY's LAWS (3rd Edn.) 394, 395, para. 735; and for cases on the subject, see DIGEST (Practice) 405, 406, *1062-1076*.

As to amendments being refused on the ground that they would defeat the Limitation Acts, see 24 HALSBURY's LAWS (3rd Edn.) 200, 201, para. 358.

For the Supreme Court of Judicature (Consolidation) Act, 1925, s. 99 and Sch. 1, see 18 HALSBURY's STATUTES (2nd Edn.) 511, 518.]

G Cases referred to:

Battersby v. *Anglo-American Oil Co., Ltd.,* [1944] 2 All E.R. 387; [1945] K.B. 23; 114 L.J.K.B. 49; 171 L.T. 300; 2nd Digest Supp.

Clark v. *Forbes Stuart (Thames Street), Ltd. (intended action), Re,* [1964] 2 All E.R. 282; [1964] 1 W.L.R. 836; 3rd Digest Supp.

Davies v. *Elsby Bros., Ltd.,* [1960] 3 All E.R. 672; [1961] 1 W.L.R. 170;
H 32 Digest (Repl.) 617, *1961.*

Don v. *Lippmann,* (1837), 5 Cl. & Fin. 1; 7 L.T. 102; 7 E.R. 303; 6 Digest (Repl.) 409, *2903.*

Dornan v. *Ellis (J. W.) & Co., Ltd.,* [1962] 1 All E.R. 303; [1962] 1 Q.B. 583; [1962] 2 W.L.R. 250; 32 Digest (Repl.) 621, *1992.*

Doyle v. *Kaufman,* (1877), 3 Q.B.D. 7, 340; 47 L.J.Q.B. 26; Digest (Practice)
I 845, *3924.*

Harris v. *Quine,* (1869), L.R. 4 Q.B.D. 653; 38 L.J.Q.B. 331; 20 L.T. 947; 32 Digest (Repl.) 399, *244.*

Holmes Road, Kentish Town, Re Nos. 55 & 57, [1958] 2 All E.R. 311; [1959] Ch. 298; [1958] 2 W.L.R. 975; Digest (Cont. Vol. A) 1060, *7417sa.*

Huber v. *Steiner,* [1835-42] All E.R. Rep. 159; (1835), 2 Bing. N.C. 202; 132 E.R. 80; 6 Digest (Repl.) 409, *2902.*

---

* R.S.C., Ord. 20, r. 5, is set out at p. 356, letter I, post.

Mabro v. *Eagle, Star and British Dominions Insurance Co., Ltd.*, [1932] All E.R. A
Rep. 411; [1932] 1 K.B. 485; 101 L.J.K.B. 205; 146 L.T. 433; 32
Digest (Repl.) 618, *1967.*

Marshall v. *London Passenger Transport Board*, [1936] 3 All E.R. 83; 32 Digest
(Repl.) 620, *1984.*

Pontin v. *Wood*, [1962] 1 All E.R. 294; [1962] 1 Q.B. 594 at p. 601; [1962]
2 W.L.R. 258; 32 Digest (Repl.) 615, *1941.*   B

Smalley v. *Robey & Co., Ltd.*, [1962] 1 All E.R. 133; [1962] 1 Q.B. 577; [1962]
2 W.L.R. 245; 3rd Digest Supp.

Société Anonyme Metallurgique de Prayon, Trooz, Belgium v. *Koppel*, (1933),
77 Sol. Jo. 800; 11 Digest (Repl.) 554, *1604.*

Weldon v. *Neal*, (1887), 19 Q.B.D. 394; 56 L.J.Q.B. 621; 32 Digest (Repl.)
620, *1981.*   C

Whittam v. *Daniel (W. J.) & Co., Ltd.*, [1961] 3 All E.R. 796; [1962] 1 Q.B. 271;
[1961] 3 W.L.R. 1123; 32 Digest (Repl.) 618, *1972.*

Interlocutory Appeal.

This was an appeal to the Judge in Chambers against the decision of Master
CLAYTON on Jan. 17, 1966, ordering that the plaintiff, Frances Joseph Rodriguez,
have leave to amend his writ and all subsequent proceedings by substituting for D
the present named defendant " R. J. Parker (Male) " that defendant's infant
son " R. S. Parker (Male) " and extending the validity of the writ. The writ was
originally issued by the plaintiff on June 11, 1964, and claimed damages for
personal injury and consequential loss arising as a result of an accident which
occurred on Oct. 30, 1961, owing to the alleged negligent driving of the defendant,
described in the writ as R. J. Parker (Male). The driver of the vehicle concerned E
was in fact the defendant's seventeen year old son, Robert Stuart Parker, who
lived at the same address as his father, Robert Job Parker, and was at the time
and place of the accident driving his father's motor van. The facts are set out in
the judgment, which was delivered in open court.

Esyr Lewis for the plaintiff.   F
R. G. Rougier for the defendant.

                                                            Cur. adv. vult.

NIELD, J., read the following judgment. This is an appeal from the decision
of Master CLAYTON given on Jan. 17 this year ordering that on the plaintiff paying
all costs thrown away, he should have leave to amend the writ and all subsequent
proceedings by substituting " R. S. Parker (Male) " as the defendant, and also I G
am told, although it does not appear on the notice of appeal before me, extending
the validity of the writ. The effect of the first part of this decision was to permit
the plaintiff to amend his writ by substituting for the defendant therein named,
R. J. Parker (Male), another person as defendant, namely, R. S. Parker (Male).
I adjourned the matter into court for judgment, since it has raised a question of
general importance.   H

On Oct. 30, 1961, the plaintiff, a pedestrian, was knocked down and injured
by a motor van owned by Robert Job Parker, and at the time driven by his son,
an infant, aged seventeen, Robert Stuart Parker. Father and son both then lived
at Cock Hill Farm, Cragg Vale, near Halifax. On Mar. 8, 1962, R. S. Parker, the
son, was concerned in proceedings as the driver of the van at the time of the
accident, and counsel agreed that this fact should be mentioned. On Apr. 20, I
1962, Messrs. Wilkinson, Woodward & Ludlam, the solicitors then acting for the
plaintiff, wrote a letter addressed to Mr. R. S. Parker, saying:

> " We have been consulted by Mr. F. J. Rodriguez with regard to serious
> personal injuries which he sustained on Monday, Oct. 30 as a result of your
> negligent driving of a motor vehicle on the main highway at Cragg Vale and
> beg to advise that we hold you responsible in damages to our client."

And in the last sentence:

A   " We suggest, however that you pass this letter to your insurers who will no doubt arrange to establish contact with us in early course."

On May 1, 1962, the National Farmers Union Mutual Insurance Co., Ltd., the insurers of R. J. Parker, the father, wrote two letters, the first headed " Without Prejudice ", and further headed, " R. J. Parker ":

B   " Referring to your letter of Apr. 20 addressed to our insured, we have written to you today an open letter containing a formal repudiation of liability. This further communication is addressed to you to indicate that in due course we will arrange for our representative to call and discuss this matter with you."

I need not read the rest of it. The second letter of the same date was also headed
C " R. J. Parker ", and merely repudiated liability.

In the correspondence which followed, the insurance company headed their letters " R. J. Parker ", and the plaintiff's then solicitors headed their letters either " R. J. Parker " or simply " Parker ". Discussions took place between the plaintiff's then solicitors and the insurance company. However, in March, 1963, Messrs. Wilkinson, Woodward & Ludlam ceased to act for the plaintiff.

D   On Aug. 28, 1963, the Amalgamated Engineering Union, of which the plaintiff was a member, wrote to the insurers, and the heading of that letter was " Re: Frank J. Rodriguez, Anna Butt Lee, Cragg Vale, Nr. Halifax. Your Insured— R. S. Parker ", and read:

" The above member has been to see me in connexion with his claim against
E   your company in connexion with an accident sustained on Monday, Oct. 30, 1961. I understand that Mr. H. Ludlam of Halifax has been acting on his behalf until recently when Mr. Rodriguez withdrew his instructions. I have discussed this matter very fully with Mr. Ludlam and he has allowed me to examine his correspondence. I would be grateful if you would note my interest in this matter and if you could arrange an early interview with me, in an effort to obtain a settlement."
F
In November, 1963, the plaintiff instructed his present solicitors, Messrs. Evill & Coleman. After negotiation, the insurance company made an offer in settlement of the plaintiff's claim, and here again counsel agreed that I should refer to it. On Apr. 3, 1964, the plaintiff refused that offer.

The writ in the action was issued on June 11, 1964, and the defendant named in
G   it was " R. J. Parker (Male) ". It was endorsed as follows:

" The plaintiff's claim is for damages for personal injury and consequential loss arising as a result of an accident which occurred on Oct. 30, 1961, at Blackstone Edge Road owing to the negligent driving of the defendant."

On Oct. 29 or 30, 1964, the period of three years following the date on which the
H   cause of action arose expired. On Jan. 4, 1965, the writ was served on R. J. Parker (Male), named in the writ as the defendant. On the same day Messrs. Berrymans, London agents for the defendant's solicitors, entered an unconditional appearance. On Jan. 12, 1965, Messrs. Evill & Coleman wrote to Messrs. Berrymans,

" We thank you for your letter of Jan. 8, enclosing sealed duplicated appearance. Without prejudice: We anticipate that our client will be
I   changing solicitors soon. In the meantime, will you please keep the time for service of the statement of claim open."

On Jan. 18, 1965, Messrs. Berrymans replied:

" Rodriguez v. Parker. We have now obtained our professional clients' instructions on your letter of Jan. 12. They have no objection to extending the time for service of the statement of claim; however, they desire us to point out to you that they are going to say that you have sued the wrong defendant."

In the affidavit of Mr. Raymond George Farr of Messrs. Evill & Coleman it is   A
said that this letter was not received. In March, 1965, Messrs. Evill & Coleman
obtained a police report on the accident. That is before the court and in para. 2,
headed " Vehicles involved ", it says:

> " Commer Cob motor van MCP 37—Owned by Robert Job Parker, Cock-
> hill Farm, Cragg Vale, Halifax, and driven by Robert Stuart Parker of the
> same address. Insurance particulars:—The National Farmers Union Mutual   B
> Insurance Society Ltd., Cert. No. 3B5335."

On June 8, 1965, Messrs. Berrymans wrote to Messrs. Evill & Coleman:

> " Your letter of June 4, together with its enclosures has been received.
> The writer is dealing with your letter in the absence of Mr. York, on holiday,
> and on looking at the papers he finds it difficult to appreciate your letter   C
> and the enclosure, having in mind our letter to you of Jan. 18 last which
> appears to have been the last document on our file. Perhaps you could en-
> lighten us and let us know why you have sent your letter of June 4, to us in
> the circumstances."

There was no reply to that letter, and on June 11, 1965, the period of one year
from the date of the issue of the writ expired.   D
On June 14, 1965, Messrs. Evill & Coleman sent the statement of claim to
Messrs. Berrymans, who accepted it by post. In that statement of claim, it is
said:

> " 2. The defendant was driving a motor van along the said road in the
> same direction as the plaintiff was walking as aforesaid.
> " 3. The said accident was caused by the negligent driving of the defendant.   E
> " Particulars of negligence:
> " The defendant was negligent in that he: (a) drove the said motor
> van too fast when approaching the plaintiff."

And other particulars are given.
It will be remembered that the defendant named in the statement of claim,   F
as in the writ, is " R. J. Parker (Male) ", the father of R. S. Parker (Male),
who was the driver of the van at the time of the accident.
After an extension of time, the defence was delivered on July 1, 1965, and in
para. 2 it is said on behalf of R. J. Parker (Male), described as the defendant
there: " The defendant was not driving any motor vehicle at the time or place
alleged. " According to Mr. Farr, it was at this point that his firm realised that a   G
mistake as to the name of the defendant had been made, and on Aug. 10, 1965,
Messrs. Evill & Coleman wrote to Messrs. Willey Hargrave & Co., the defendant's
solicitors in Leeds, the following letter:

> " We refer to our telephone conversation of today when we informed
> you that due to a typing error the writ in this case had been wrongly issued
> against R. J. Parker rather than R. S. Parker. As you will know, R. J.   H
> Parker was the owner of the car and R. S. Parker the driver. You will know
> yourself that throughout the lengthy correspondence which has been written
> in this case over a period of almost 3½ years reference on both sides has
> been solely to R. J. Parker. The only exception is the letter before action
> dated Apr. 20, 1962, which was addressed to R. S. Parker. Since this date
> without exception the correspondence referred to R. J. Parker."   I

Then at the end of the letter:

> " You will realise the difficulty in which we are placed and we trust that
> you will not oppose an application at this stage to add to the writ as defendant
> R. S. Parker an infant and R. J. Parker as guardian. We would add that
> if Messrs. Berrymans had drawn our attention to the error then the amend-
> ment would immediately have been made."

And they ask for the fullest co-operation. The answer, however, was on Sept. 24,

A 1965: " We would refer to our letter to you of Aug. 10 to which we have received no reply." This is a reminder. The reply came on Sept. 27, 1965, from Messrs. Willey Hargrave & Co.:

" We duly received your letter of Sept. 24. By the same post, we have heard from our clients that they are not prepared to allow the correct defendant to be added to the writ in this case. Our clients have done nothing

B wrong in this case. The wrong defendant has been sued, and this was pointed out to you in Messrs. Berrymans' letter of Jan. 18, 1965." (1)

It is clear that Messrs. Evill & Coleman asked for a copy of the letter of Jan. 18, which they assert they never received, and such a copy was enclosed with a letter of Sept. 28, 1965.

As I have indicated, the parties appeared before the master on Jan. 17, 1966,

C when the plaintiff sought to substitute as defendant " R. S. Parker (Male) ", the driver of the van, for his father " R. J. Parker (Male) ", who had by mistake appeared in the proceedings as the defendant. This application was made at a time when the three years period of limitation had expired, and the plaintiff relied on the provisions of R.S.C., Ord. 20, r. 5, a rule made in 1964 (2) as to proceedings and relaxing the former rule of practice that a new defendant would

D not be substituted if such a course would result in a defendant losing any advantage that he might have by virtue of the Statutes of Limitations. The master allowed the new defendant to be substituted on the terms which I have mentioned (3).

That concludes the history of this case up to the present time, and I turn to consider the submissions made to me and how the issues here raised are to be

E determined. Counsel for the defendant puts forward three points in asking that the master's order should be set aside. He submits (i) that the provisions of R.S.C., Ord. 20, r. 5, are ultra vires. This point was not taken before the master, but it was the central and most important issue in the appeal, and the issue which raises the question of general interest and importance. (ii) that in any event the court's discretion in the circumstances here should not be exercised in favour of

F the plaintiff so as to allow him to substitute a new defendant for the defendant named in the writ. (iii) that the court's discretion should not be exercised in favour of the plaintiff so as to extend the validity of the writ under R.S.C., Ord. 6, r. 8. Although the submission on behalf of the defendant is put in this three-fold way, counsel for both parties agreed that if the court finds on the second point that its discretion should be exercised in favour of the plaintiff, it must

G follow that on the third point it would be right to extend it to the validity of the writ (4).

I think it is useful to look at the decisions before the making of R.S.C., Ord. 20, r. 5, which considered the rule of practice to which I have referred. Some of the judgments contain phrases which might be regarded as throwing light on the question whether it can properly be said that the Statute of Limitations confers

H a right on defendants or merely debars a plaintiff from pursuing his cause of action after the specified period of time and enables a defendant to plead that the plaintiff is so debarred.

In *Weldon* v. *Neal* (5) the plaintiff sought to add fresh causes of action after the limitation period, and LORD ESHER, M.R., said (6):

" If an amendment were allowed setting up a cause of action, which, if

I the writ were issued in respect thereof at the date of the amendment, would be barred by the Statute of Limitations, it would be allowing the plaintiff to take advantage of her former writ to defeat the statute and taking away an existing right from the defendant, a proceeding which, as a general rule, would be, in my opinion, improper and unjust."

(1) The relevant part of the letter of Jan. 18, 1965, is set out at p. 351, letter I, ante.
(2) R.S.C., Ord. 20, r. 5, is set out at p. 356, letter I, post.
(3) See at p. 350, letter F, ante.   (4) R.S.C., Ord. 6, r. 8.
(5) (1887), 19 Q.B.D. 394.   (6) (1887), 19 Q.B.D. at p. 395.

And LOPES, L.J., at the end of his judgment said (7):

A

" The effect of allowing these amendments would be to take away from the defendant the defence under that statute and therefore unjustly to prejudice the defendant."

It is important to notice the words " and taking away an existing right from the defendant ".

In *Mabro* v. *Eagle Star & British Dominions Insurance Co., Ltd.* (8), it was sought to add a plaintiff after the limitation period, and in the judgment of SCRUTTON, L.J., appears this passage (9):

B

" In my experience the court has always refused to allow a party or a cause of action to be added where, if it were allowed, the defence of the Statute of Limitations would be defeated. The court has never treated it as just to deprive a defendant of a legal defence. If the facts show either that the particular plaintiff or the new cause of action sought to be added are barred, I am unable to understand how it is possible for the court to disregard the statute."

C

GREER, L.J., said (10):

" It has been the accepted practice for a long time that amendments which would deprive a party of a vested right ought not to be allowed."

D

Those two expressions are, in the one case the defence provided by the statute, and, in the other, a vested right in the defence.

In *Marshall* v. *London Passenger Transport Board* (11) it was sought to amend the particulars of negligence and to include allegations of breach of statutory duty. I read the relevant part of the headnote (11):

E

" *Held*: (i) the amendment introduced a new case which if set up in an action commenced at the date of the amendment would have been barred by lapse of time, and the amendment must be disallowed."

LORD WRIGHT, M.R., referring to the proposed amendment, said (12):

F

" The question is whether that [the alleged breach of a statutory duty] involves a new cause of action within the meaning of the Public Authorities Protection Act, 1893, within the meaning of the words which I have just read. I think it does, and I think that the learned judge was right in dismissing the application, because it is well settled that an amendment will not be allowed if its introduction would deprive the defendant of a defence under the Statute of Limitations or under the Public Authorities Protection Act, 1893—in other words, if it is something which involves a new departure, a new head of claim, or a new cause of action."

G

Thus LORD WRIGHT referred to the advantage of that to the defendant as a defence.

The case of *Marshall* v. *London Passenger Transport Board* (11), was distinguished in the case of *Dornan* v. *J. W. Ellis & Co., Ltd.* (13). In that case, when the action came on for hearing on Oct. 12, 1961 (more than three years after the accrual of the cause of action in negligence) the plaintiff workman applied for leave to amend his claim by adding to the particulars of negligence allegations which in substance claimed that the accident had been caused by the negligence of the fellow-worker S. or other servants or agents of the defendants, and that the defendants were therefore vicariously liable. The trial judge, WINN, J., refused to allow the amendment on the ground that the amendment sought raised a fresh cause of action which would by that date be statute-barred; and that,

H

I

---

(7) (1887), 19 Q.B.D. at p. 396. (8) [1932] All E.R. Rep. 411; [1932] 1 K.B. 485.
(9) [1932] All E.R. Rep. at p. 412; [1932] 1 K.B. at p. 487.
(10) [1932] All E.R. Rep. at p. 413; [1932] 1 K.B. at p. 489.
(11) [1936] 3 All E.R. 83.   (12) [1936] 3 All E.R. at p. 87,
(13) [1962] 1 All E.R. 303; [1962] 1 Q.B. 583.

A accordingly, the court was precluded from exercising its discretion in favour of the plaintiff. On appeal by the plaintiff, it was held, allowing the appeal, that though the new particulars of negligence were different in quality from the original particulars, they did not raise a new cause of action nor a different case of negligence, but merely invited a different approach to the same facts; and accordingly, although the dilatory conduct of the plaintiff's case was censurable,

B the court was in the circumstances of the case not precluded by any general rule of practice from exercising its discretion to allow the amendment of the particulars after the expiry of the statutory period of limitation.

This in my opinion sufficiently set out that part of the judgment of HOLROYD PEARCE, L.J. (14) to which I would otherwise have referred.

In addition to these cases dealing with the general rule of practice before the

C coming into effect of R.S.C., Ord. 20, r. 5, there arose also the further question whether the proposed amendment would indeed permit a new defendant to be substituted, or would merely allow the correction of a misnomer.

In *Davies* v. *Elsby Bros., Ltd.* (15), the question arose whether the plaintiff was seeking to substitute a new defendant after the period of limitation had passed, or whether it was merely a case of misnomer which could be corrected, if that

D course would be a proper one to take. On Mar. 18, 1959, the plaintiff issued a writ against " Elsby Brothers—a firm ", claiming damages for negligence in respect of injuries sustained while he was an employee of the defendants. The accident giving rise to the cause of action occurred on Mar. 20, 1956, though this date did not appear on the writ. The plaintiff had been employed by the firm of Elsby Brothers until the firm's business was taken over by a limited company,

E Elsby Brothers, Ltd., in 1955, and thereafter the plaintiff continued in the employment of the company. Before the writ had been served it was amended on Mar. 17, 1960, by striking out the words, " a firm " and adding the word " Limited " to " Elsby Brothers ", and the writ as amended was served on the same day. ELWES, J., allowed the defendants' appeal from the registrar's refusal of their application to set aside the writ on the ground that the company were

F substituted as defendants after the claim against them had become barred by the expiration of three years from the date of the accident by virtue of the Limitation Act, 1939, as amended. PEARCE, L.J., said (16):

" In my opinion the addition of a defendant is governed by the same considerations as the addition of a plaintiff. Therefore the principle of *Mabro's case* (17) prevents the amendment in this case if the amendment

G involves the addition of a party and not the mere correction of a misnomer. That principle also applies to the substitution of a party, since substitution involves the addition of a party in replacement of the party that is removed . . . If, however, the addition of the word ' Ltd.' is not the addition or substitution of a party but the mere correction of a misnomer, we can properly allow it, if the merits justify that course. Is this the mere correction

H of a misnomer? Counsel for the plaintiff argues that the real question is: who did the plaintiff intend to sue? There was, he argues, only one party in existence at one time, since the two parties concerned, namely the firm and the company, were mutually exclusive and were consecutively engaged in carrying on the same business; and he relied on the words of HARMAN, J.,

I in *Re Nos. 55 & 57, Holmes Road, Kentish Town* (18): ' It is not as if the other title were that of a non-existent person, or as if the tenants were under any misapprehension '."

DEVLIN, L.J., said (19):

---

(14) [1962] 1 All E.R. at 304 et seq.; [1962] 1 Q.B. at 589 et seq.
(15) [1960] 3 All E.R. 672.   (16) [1960] 3 All E.R. at p. 674.
(17) [1932] All E.R. Rep. 411; [1932] 1 K.B. 485.
(18) [1958] 2 All E.R. 311 at p. 316; [1959] Ch. 298 at p. 304.
(19) [1960] 3 All E.R. at p. 675.

" Counsel for the defendants has argued that, when the distinction is   A
between an entity such as a person or a firm and an entity such as a limited
company, the omission of the word " Ltd. ' is fatal: it ceases to be a mere
matter of description, he says: it is not like a case where one of the Christian
names of the defendant has been got wrong: without the word ' Ltd.' a
company cannot be identified as an entity at all . . ."

Later DEVLIN, L.J., said (20):   B

" The test must be: How would a reasonable person receiving the document take it? If, in all the circumstances of the case and looking at ·the
document as a whole, he would say to himself, ' Of course it must mean
me, but they have got my name wrong ', then there is a case of mere
misnomer. If, on the other hand, he would say: ' I cannot tell from the   C
document itself whether they mean me or not and I shall have to make
inquiries ', then it seems to me that one is getting beyond the realm of
misnomer."

Counsel for the plaintiff submitted that it was to meet the sort of situation which
obtained in the case of *Davies* v. *Elsby Bros., Ltd.* (21) and to meet any possible
consequent injustice which might flow from that situation that the new R.S.C.,   D
Ord. 20, r. 5, was introduced in 1964. He also pointed out that the case of *Davies*
v. *Elsby Bros., Ltd.* (21) was distinguished in the case of *Whittam* v. *W. J.
Daniel & Co., Ltd.* (22). In that case on Sept. 9, 1960, the plaintiff issued a
writ against " W. J. Daniels & Company (a firm) " claiming damages for injuries
sustained by her on Sept. 10, 1957, in the course of her employment by the
defendants. On Oct. 12, 1960, Master CLAYTON allowed the amendment of the   E
writ by substituting as defendants " W. J. Daniel & Co., Ltd.". The defendants
applied to have the writ struck out on the ground that the amendment substituted
a new defendant against whom the plaintiff's claim had been barred by the
Limitation Acts. ELWES, J., allowed the defendants' appeal from the master's
order and ordered that the writ be set aside. It was held that, on the facts, there
was no reasonable doubt as to the identity of the proposed defendants, and this   F
was a case of mere misnomer and not the substitution of a new defendant.
DONOVAN, L.J., quoted the test prescribed by DEVLIN, L.J., in *Davies* v. *Elsby
Bros., Ltd.* (20), and said (23):

" Applying that test, there could have been no doubt in the mind of the
defendants when they got the writ that it was they whom the plaintiff
intended to sue, and that she had simply got the name wrong. But now   G
one has to deal with the much wider point . . . ."

and he goes on to consider another point which is not material to the present
appeal. It is I think proper to refer to a passage in the judgment of DANCKWERTS,
L.J., where he said (24):

" The present case is plainly distinguishable from the decision of this   H
court in *Davies* v. *Elsby Bros., Ltd.* (21), because in the present case there
is no other entity to which the description in the writ could be taken to
refer."

To this issue, whether the situation here is one of mere misnomer as opposed
to substituting a new defendant I shall return later in my judgment.

Let me come, then, to the relevant order, which is R.S.C., Ord. 20, r. 5:   I

" 5 (1) Subject to Ord. 15, rr. 6, 7 and 8 and the following provisions
of this rule, the court may at any stage of the proceedings allow the plaintiff
to amend his writ, or any party to amend his pleading, on such terms as to
costs or otherwise as may be just and in such manner (if any) as it may direct.

(20) [1960] 3 All E.R. at p. 676.   (21) [1960] 3 All E.R. 672.
(22) [1961] 3 All E.R. 796; [1962] 1 Q.B. 271.
(23) [1961] 3 All E.4. at p. 799; [1962] 1 Q.B. at p. 277.
(24) [1961] 3 All E.R. at p. 802; [1962] 1 Q.B. at p. 282.

A   " (2) Where an application to the court for leave to make the amendment mentioned in paras. (3), (4) or (5) is made after any relevant period of limitation current at the date of issue of the writ has expired, the court may nevertheless grant such leave in the circumstances mentioned in that paragraph if it thinks it just to do so.

" (3) An amendment to correct the name of a party may be allowed

B   under para. (2) notwithstanding that it is alleged that the effect of the amendment will be to substitute a new party if the court is satisfied that the mistake sought to be corrected was a genuine mistake and was not misleading or such as to cause any reasonable doubt as to the identity of the person intending to sue or, as the case may be, intended to be sued.

" (4) An amendment to alter the capacity in which a party sues (whether

C   as plaintiff or as defendant by counterclaim) may be allowed under para. (2) if the capacity in which, if the amendment is made, the party will sue is one in which at the date of issue of the writ or the making of the counterclaim, as the case may be, he might have sued.

" (5) An amendment may be allowed under para. (2) notwithstanding that the effect of the amendment will be to add or substitute a new cause

D   of action if the new cause of action arises out of the same facts or substantially the same facts as a cause of action in respect of which relief has already been claimed in the action by the party applying for leave to make the amendment."

It is proper to refer to the relevant notes in the ANNUAL PRACTICE (25), in which the authors seek to give their explanation of the effect of R.S.C., Ord. 20, r. 5:

E   " The provisions of r. 5 empower the court to grant leave to amend the writ or pleading in the particular circumstances mentioned in paras. (3), (4) or (5), even though the application for such amendment is made after the expiry of any relevant period of limitation current at the date of the issue of the writ. These powers in no way affect or prejudice the substantive rights of the parties under any relevant Statute of Limitations; nor do

F   they affect or alter the practice of the court in cases outside the scope of the circumstances mentioned in paras. (3), (4) and (5). On the other hand, in the specified classes of cases mentioned in these paras., r. 5 regulates afresh the practice which the court may follow in exercising its unfettered discretion under r. 8 to amend any document in the proceedings; in these cases r. 5 regularises the practice of the court for curing the specified defects in an

G   action begun after the relevant time limit has expired. The principle underlying the new powers of the court under r. 5 is that if the proceedings had been, from the beginning, properly formulated or constituted in the respects specified in paras. (3), (4) and (5), the defence of the Statute of Limitations would not have been available to the defendant; and accordingly, if in its discretion, the court thinks it just to grant leave to amend

H   defects in the writ or pleading within the scope of the circumstances specified in these paras., so that such defects in the proceedings are treated as having been cured ab initio, the defendant is not being deprived of the benefit of a defence which he would not have had if the proceedings had been so properly formulated or constituted in the first place. To contend in the cases specified in these paras., that the defendant has an existing right which will be preju-

I   diced by the amendment is to argue in a circle, since he only has an existing right if one presupposes that the court will not use its powers to amend under R.S.C., Ord. 20, r. 2, and R.S.C., Ord. 15, rr. 6, 7 and 8."

This brings me to the fundamental point urged by counsel for the defendant, namely, that R.S.C., Ord. 20, r. 5 is ultra vires. I consider the problem under three heads: (i) the source from which the Rules of the Supreme Court derive their authority; (ii) the purpose and effect of the Limitation Acts themselves; and

(25) 1966 Edn. at p. 455.

(iii) whether or no those enactments can properly be regarded as dealing with **A** practice and procedure rather than conferring substantive rights on the subject.

Under the first head, the source from which the Rules of the Supreme Court derive their authority is in the main s. 99 of the Supreme Court of Judicature (Consolidation) Act, 1925. In its material parts that section reads thus:

> " (1) Rules of Court may be made under this Act for the following pur- **B** poses: (a) For regulating and prescribing the procedure (including the method of pleading) and the practice to be followed in the Court of Appeal and the High Court respectively in all causes and matters whatsoever in or with respect to which those courts respectively have for the time being jurisdiction (including the procedure and practice to be followed in the offices of the Supreme Court and in district registries), and any matters incidental **C** to or relating to any such procedure or practice, including (but without prejudice to the generality of the foregoing provision) the manner in which, and the time within which, any applications which under this or any other Act are to be made to the Court of Appeal or to the High Court shall be made; (b) For regulating and prescribing the procedure on appeals from any court or person to the Court of Appeal or the High Court . . . (c) For **D** regulating the sittings of the Court of Appeal . . . [and other courts]; (d) For prescribing what part of the business which may be transacted and of the jurisdiction which may be exercised by judges of the High Court in chambers may be transacted or exercised by matters . . . of the Supreme Court (26); . . . (e) For regulating any matters relating to the costs of proceedings in the Court of Appeal or the High Court. (f) For regulating and prescribing the **E** procedure and practice to be followed in the Court of Appeal or the High Court . . . in cases in which the procedure or practice is regulated by enactments in force immediately before the commencement of this Act or by any provisions of this Act re-enacting any such enactments (including so much of any of the Acts set out in Sch. 1 to this Act as is specified in col. 3 of that Schedule): (g) For repealing any enactments which relate to matters with **F** respect to which rules are made under this section."

I need not I think read further.

It is s. 99 (1) (a) on which counsel for the defendant has principally relied. Schedule 1 is headed: " Section 99. Enactments containing and regulating matters with respect to which Rules of Court may be made." In col. 1 is set out the Statute concerned; in col. 2, its title or short title; and, in col. 3, the sections **G** affected. Counsel for the defendant analysed the enactments referred to in the Schedule, and showed that only four could be said to be in any way concerned with the limitation of actions, and that the sections referred to in col. 3, with one exception, were not concerned with limitation. I refer to each of these enactments which were put before me as having any connexion with matters of limitation. **H** The first was 4 & 5 Anne, c. 16, which (27) is to be found in the Statutes at Large (1764), Vol. XI. Section 12 and s. 13 relate (28) to procedural matters, enabling payment to be pleaded in bar and dealing with the bringing of money into court. Sections, however, which deal with limitation, namely ss. 17 to 19, were repealed by the Limitation Act, 1939. The second of these enactments is an Act of 3 and 4 William 4, c. 42, the Civil Procedure Act, 1833. Section 16 and **I**

---

(26) The whole of para. (d) down to the semi-colon was repealed by the Administration of Justice Act, 1956, s. 57 (2), Sch. 2.

(27) This statute, the Administration of Justice Act, 1705, as named by S.L.R. Act, 1948, Sch. 2, is Cap. 3 in the Statutes of the Realm. It was finally repealed by the Administration of Justice Act 1965, s. 34 and Sch. 2.

(28) For s. 12 and s. 13, see 2 HALSBURY'S STATUTES (2nd Edn.) 593. Section 12 was repealed by S.L.R. Act, 1948.

A s. 18, referred to in col. 3 of the Schedule, were (29) not concerned with limitation. The third statute is 5 & 6 Vict., c. 97, the Limitations of Actions and Costs Act, 1842, and it is s. 4 and s. 5 which are referred to in col. 3. Section 4 lays down (30) that where notice of action is required, for the sake of uniformity this shall be given one month at least before any action shall be commenced. This is clearly a practice point. Section 5, however, was concerned with limitation;
B but this again has been repealed by the Act of 1939; this is the only section appearing in col. 3 of the Schedule which is concerned with limitation, and, as I say, it has been repealed. The last of these statutes is 36 & 37 Vict., c. 66, the Supreme Court of Judicature Act, 1873. The material sections (31) are s. 46, s. 64 and s. 66. Section 46 enables a judge to reserve a point to the Divisional Court. Section 64 dealt with proceedings which could be taken in
C the district registry; and s. 66 allows accounts and inquiries to be referred to district registrars.

It will be observed that the principal Limitation Act current in 1925, namely, the Limitation Act, 1623, is not included in Sch. 1 to the Act of 1925; and it is also pointed out that the Act of 1623 is also not included in the ANNUAL PRACTICE, 1966, at p. cciii, which is headed: " Table 1: Revocations. Section 1. Rules
D of the Supreme Court, 1883, wholly revoked "; and then below under s. 2: " Statutes Repealed "; and as I say, the Limitation Act, 1623, is not mentioned in any way. I think further that s. 99 of the Supreme Court of Judicature (Consolidation) Act, 1925, was in the main the source of the authority for this. I have to make this qualification because s. 15 of the Administration of Justice Act, 1956, also enables rules of the Supreme Court to be made, but the provisions
E of that statute are not material for the purposes of the present appeal.

Having considered, then, the source from which the rules of the Supreme Court derive their authority, I turn to the second head, the purpose and effect of the Limitation Acts themselves. The first principal Act, that of 1623, is to be found in the Statutes at Large for 1697. It is s. 3 which is material:

F " And be it further enacted that all actions . . . upon the case shall be commenced and sued within the time and limitation hereafter expressed, and not after (that is to say) the said actions upon the case . . . within three years next after the end of this present session of Parliament or within six years next after the cause of such actions or suit, and not after."

It seems to me that s. 3 had (32) as its purpose and effect the barring of the plain-
G tiff's action after the specified time; and as a matter of interest one observes that nearly 350 years ago by s. 7 there was a saving of those actions.

The next enactment is the Limitation Act, 1939, (33). Section 2 (1) in its material part reads thus:

" The following actions shall not be brought after the expiration of six years from the date on which the cause of action accrued, that is to say:—(a) actions
H founded on simple contract or on tort;"

and in the note on this section this statement appears (34): " In general, if it is intended to rely upon this section as a defence, it must be specially pleaded."

Section 22 of this statute (35), provides for an extension of time in cases of disability, and is, therefore, the successor to s. 7 of the Act of 1623. The section
I in its earlier part reads:

---

(29) Section 16 and s. 18; 18 HALSBURY'S STATUTES (2nd Edn.) 364; were repealed by R.S.C. (1883), Ord. 53G, r. 1 (1), which was added by S.I. 1957 No. 1178 and revoked by R.S.C. (Revision) 1962, S.I. 1962 No. 2145.
(30) For s. 4, see 18 HALSBURY'S STATUTES (2nd Edn.) 368.
(31) For s. 46, s. 64 and s. 66, see 18 HALSBURY'S STATUTES (2nd Edn.) 468, 469. Section 64 was repealed by R.S.C. (Revision) 1962, S.I. 1962 No. 2145.
(32) Section 3 was repealed by the Limitation Act, 1939.
(33) For the Limitation Act, 1939, see 13 HALSBURY'S STATUTES (2nd Edn.) p. 1160.
(34) Ibid., at p. 1161.   (35) Ibid., at p. 1183.

" If on the date when any right of action accrued for which a period   A
of limitation is prescribed by this Act, the person to whom it accrued was
under a disability, the action may be brought at any time before the expiration of six years . . . one year from the date when the person ceased to be
under a disability . . ."

And then there is a proviso which I need not read.

I refer also to the recent Act, the Limitation Act 1963, (36). The first part of   B
s. 1 reads thus:

" (1) Section 2 (1) of the Limitation Act, 1939 (which, in the case of certain
actions, imposes a time-limit of three years for bringing the action) shall not
afford any defence to an action to which this section applies . . ."

The Act of 1963 permits the extension of the time for bringing an action in certain   C
circumstances if material decisive facts were outside the knowledge of the plaintiffs at the time mentioned. It is to be observed in this regard that the amendment
of the law so as to extend the time appears to have been considered to be achieved
by an Act of Parliament and not by rule of the court; but it does seem to me
that the power to extend the time is much more fundamental than a power to
amend the writ, as is sought to be permitted in R.S.C., Ord. 20, r. 5. In the Act   D
of 1963, s. 1 postulates that s. 2 of the Act of 1939 " affords a defence ", and this
is to be contrasted with the words appearing in s. 2 of the Act of 1939, as follows:
" the following actions shall not be brought after the expiration of six years
. . .". The former words afford a defence but might indicate that a right was
conferred on the defendant. The latter, " the following actions shall not be
brought ", might indicate that only the plaintiff's remedy was barred.

Having, then, considered the Limitation Acts themselves, I turn to the third   E
head in order to consider whether the various statutes, the Limitation Acts, can
properly be regarded as dealing with practice and procedure rather than conferring substantive rights. A number of textbooks has been quoted, and in particular,
some passages concerned with private international law. Weight was sought to
be attached to these writings, and I therefore quote from them. In PRESTON   F
AND NEWSOM ON LIMITATION OF ACTIONS (1st Edn., 1940), p. 16, the authors
wrote (36a) under the heading " Private International Law ":

" The English Courts have adopted a very simple method of dealing
with the rules of limitation in private international law. It is common ground
between all systems of private international law that matters of procedure
are to be determined by the lex fori. In so far as the Statutes of Limitation   G
prescribe periods within which actions may be brought, they are in English
courts classified as methods of procedure."

Then at p. 17 of the 1st Edn., after referring to the case of *Don* v. *Lippmann*
(37) to which I shall myself refer later, the authors wrote:

" But a foreign rule of limitation is not classified as a matter of procedure
in an English court if it extinguishes the right as well as the remedy. The   H
fact that on the expiration of the foreign period the plaintiff's right will be
extinguished does not help a plaintiff who fails to sue in England within the
English period, but the defendant may rely on the extinguishment of the
right by the foreign period, irrespective of whether the English period has
elapsed . . ."

Again in CHESHIRE ON PRIVATE INTERNATIONAL LAW (7th Edn.), p. 585, the   I
heading is " Matters Appertaining to Procedure ".

" (1) The time within which an action must be brought. English law is
unfortunately committed to the view that statutes of limitation, if they
merely specify a certain time after which rights cannot be enforced by action,
affect procedure, not substance. They concern, it is said, not the merits of the
cause, but the manner in which the remedy must be pursued. They ordain

(36) For the Limitation Act 1963, see 43 HALSBURY'S STATUTES (2nd Edn.) p. 613.
(36a) Cf. 3rd Edn., 1953, pp. 15, 16.   (37) (1837), 5 Cl. & Fin. 1.

A   that procedure is available only when set in motion within a certain fixed
time after the cause of action arose. In the result, therefore, any relevant
statute of limitation that obtains in the lex fori may be pleaded, while a
statute of some foreign law, even though it belongs to the proper law of the
transaction, must be disregarded . . . The rules of English private international law upon this matter, however, pay little attention to the proper
B   law of the transaction that is in issue."

Thus the author there recognises, without very much commendation, what he
regards as an unfortunate principle, namely that a limitation provision affects
procedure, not substance.

Then in CHESHIRE AND FIFOOT ON LAW OF CONTRACT (6th Edn.) pp. 541, 542,
we find this:

C   "If the statutory period expires before action brought, the plaintiff's
right is not extinguished. He is merely deprived of his two remedies of action
and set-off. The statute is procedural not substantive. A statute barred
debt is still payable despite the fact that its payment cannot be enforced
by action, and if there is any other method by which the creditor can obtain
satisfaction it is at his disposal. Thus if a debtor pays money on account of
D   debts, some of which are statute-barred and some not, and does not expressly
indicate that the payment is made in respect of those which are still actionable, the creditor may appropriate the money to those that are statute-
barred. Again if a party is entitled to a lien on goods for a general balance,
and he gets possession of the goods of his debtor, he may hold them until his
whole demand is satisfied notwithstanding that it is barred by the Limitation
E   Act."

That is a very unequivocal statement as to the nature and purpose of the
Limitation Act.

As I have already pointed out, one must add to these views of writers those
which are clearly to be inferred to be held by the author of the notes in the
F   ANNUAL PRACTICE and by the author of R.S.C., Ord. 20, r. 5, himself (38). The
textbooks, as I say, recognise that the Limitation Acts are matters of practice
and procedure, and I have been referred to three decisions supporting this view
in the particular circumstances of those cases.

In the case of *Harris* v. *Quine* (39), the plaintiffs, attorneys in the Isle of Man,
were retained by the defendant, in 1858, to conduct a suit in one of the Manx
G   courts in which he was defendant. The suit was dismissed in April, 1861; in
September, 1861, the plaintiff in the suit appealed to a superior court, and
the plaintiffs continued to act for the defendant and conducted the appeal on his
behalf up to Oct. 1, 1862. By the Manx statute law an action on simple contract
brought in the temporal courts of the island must be commenced within three
years of the cause of action. The plaintiffs brought an action in one of the Manx
H   courts more than three years after October, 1862, and the court decided that the
action was barred by the statute. The plaintiffs commenced an action in this
country in January, 1868, to which the defendant pleaded—1. The judgment of
the Manx court. 2. The English Statute of Limitations. It was held (i) that, as
the Manx statute barred the remedy only and did not extinguish the debt, the
judgment of the Manx court was no bar; (ii) that, under the circumstances, there
was a continuous employment of the plaintiffs; and that therefore none of the
I   items were barred by the Statute of Limitations. SIR ALEXANDER COCKBURN,
C.J., in the course of his judgment referred to the earlier case of *Huber* v. *Steiner*
(40), and he said (41):

"On the question as to whether the judgment on the plea in the Manx
court is a bar to bringing an action in the courts of this country, I think we

---

(38) See the 1966 Edn. at pp. 452, 455.   (39) (1869), L.R. 4 Q.B.D. 653.
(40) [1835-42] All E.R. Rep. 159; (1835), 2 Bing. N.C. 202.
(41) (1869), L.R. 4 Q.B.D. at p. 657.

are bound by authority that it is not; *Huber* v. *Steiner* (42), and other cases,   A
having decided that such a statute of limitations as the present simply applies
to matter of procedure, and not to the substance of the contract."

LUSH, J., referred to the Manx statute and said (43):

" But the Manx law is like our Statute of Limitations, and bars the
remedy only; and all that was decided in the Manx court was, that the   B
action could not be maintained there."

Then much more recently there was decided a case called the *Société Anonyme
Metallurgique de Prayon, Trooz, Belgium* v. *Koppel* (44). In that action the
plaintiffs, a company carrying on business in Belgium, claimed from the defendant
Koppel a sum of more than £300 due under a bill of exchange. The defendant
alleged that even if the plaintiffs were the holders for value as alleged, they had   C
no claim whatever against him, because under the provisions of the German law
the claims of a holder against a drawer and endorsee of a bill of exchange lapsed in
three months from the date of protest being made, and that inasmuch as the
bill was protested on Mar. 5, 1932, the plaintiff's claim, if any, lapsed on June 5,
1932.

ROCHE, J., said that it was contended that by German law the rights of the   D
plaintiffs against the defendant terminated within three months of the date of
protest. The main question in controversy was whether the German law of limitation applicable extinguished the rights of the party suing, or whether it merely
barred or interfered with his remedy. He (His Lordship) had arrived at a clear
opinion, on the weight of authority, that the present effect of German law was
that under a document such as the one in issue the rights of the party were not   E
extinguished, but the remedy was barred. What, then, was the result of that
finding in English law? In that matter his decision was fixed by two old authorities: *Huber* v. *Steiner* (42) and *Harris* v. *Quine* (45). It was clear from those
authorities that English law regarded the law of limitation as a matter of procedure, and the English courts were unable to apply any law of procedure other
than the law of England. It was clear that by the law of England there was no   F
statute of limitation in operation against the plaintiffs, and there was nothing to
prevent them from recovering.

I must also refer to a very much earlier case which in my judgment is of very
great weight as clarifying the true position here. It is the case of *Don* v. *Lippmann*
(46). It was said that the law of a country, where a contract is to be enforced,
must govern the enforcement of such contract. Where, therefore, bills were drawn   G
and accepted, and became due in France, but the acceptor, a Scotsman, before
such bills became due, returned to Scotland, and there continued till his death,
it was held by the Lords (reversing the decision of the Court of Session) that
more than six years having elapsed between the time of the bills becoming due
and the action being brought, the Scottish law of prescription applied, and that its
effect was not prevented by the fact that the payee had taken legal proceedings   H
in France during the absence of the debtor, and had obtained judgment against
him. LORD BROUGHAM, in the course of his speech, referred to *Huber* v. *Steiner*
(42), and said (47):

" The contract being silent as to the law by which it is to be governed,
nothing is more likely than that the lex loci contractus should be considered
at the time the rule, for the parties would not suppose that the contract might   I
afterwards come before the tribunals of a foreign country. But it is otherwise
when the remedy actually comes to be enforced. The parties do not necessarily
look to the remedy when they make the contract . . . Not only the principles
of the law, but the known course of the courts renders it necessary that the

---

(42) [1835-42] All E.R. Rep. 159; (1835), 2 Bing. N.C. 202.
(43) (1869), L.R. 4 Q.B.D. at p. 658.
(44) (1933), 77 Sol. Jo. 800.
(45) (1869), L.R. 4 Q.B.D. 653.
(46) (1837), 5 Cl. & Fin. 1.
(47) (1837), 5 Cl. & Fin. at pp. 13, 14.

A   rules of precedent should be adopted, and that the parties should take
the law as they find it, when they come to enforce their contract. It is true
that there may be no difficulty in knowing the law of the place of the contract,
while there may be a great difficulty in knowing that of the place of the
remedy. But that is no answer to the rule. The distinction which exists
as to the principle of applying the remedy, exists with even greater force
B   as to the practice of the courts where the remedy is to be enforced.''

Later LORD BROUGHAM said (48):

" First, it is said that the party is bound for a given time, and for a given
time only: that is a strained construction of the obligation. The party does
not bind himself for a particular period at all, but merely to do something on a
C   certain day, or on one or other of certain days. In the case at the bar the
obligation is to pay a sum certain at a certain day, but the law does not
suppose that he is at the moment of making the contract contemplating
the period at which he may be freed by lapse of time from performing it.
The argument that the limitation is of the nature of the contract, supposes
that the parties look only to the breach of the agreement. Nothing is more
D   contrary to good faith than such a supposition. If the law of the country
proceeds on the supposition that the contracting parties look only to the
period at which the Statute of Limitations will begin to run, it will sanction
a wrong course of conduct, and will turn a protection against laches into a
premium for evasiveness. Then it is said, that by the law of Scotland not
the remedy alone is taken away, but that the debt itself is extinguished, and
E   thus a distinction is relied on as taken by the law between an absolute
prescription and the limitation provided by the statute. But it seems to
me that there is no good ground for supposing such a distinction. I do not
read the statute in that manner. The Act of 1772 [a Scottish Act] is an
Act for the limitation of the enforcement of titles to bills and notes, and the
enactments of it are strong with respect to the remedy to be enforced.
F   The debt, however, is still supposed to be existing and owing.''

Having considered all these matters, I form my own opinion on this point, which
must be formed, of course, in the light of the authorities, that the Limitation Acts
are procedural. I base this opinion principally on the words of the Act of 1939
itself, s. 2 (1), which I have quoted, namely: " The following actions shall not be
brought after the expiration of six years. '' The Act of 1939 does not provide
G   that after such period the plaintiff's remedy shall be extinguished or even wholly
cease to be enforceable, and indeed the remedy is not extinguished, nor does it
wholly cease to be enforceable; for if a defendant elects not to plead the Statute
of Limitations, the remedy may be pursued after the period of limitation.

Further than that, the benefit which a defendant derives from the Statute of
Limitations is not I think properly described as a substantive benefit but really
H   merely as a right to plead a defence if he chooses to, so that the plaintiff is barred
from prosecuting his claim. I am fortified in this opinion by one short sentence, in
addition to the other matters to which I have referred, in the case of *Battersby*
v. *Anglo-American Oil Co., Ltd.* (49). LORD GODDARD said (50):

" As we have just said, there is a consistent line of authority that the
I   court will not extend the time in such cases, so as to deprive the defendant
of the benefit of the statute.''

I pause there to say that I have used in lieu of the words " the benefit " the
phrase " any advantage " (51), and LORD GODDARD is there again using a neutral
word, " benefit ". LORD GODDARD continued (50):

---

(48) (1837), 5 Cl. & Fin. at pp. 15, 16.   (49) [1944] 2 All E.R. 387; [1945] K.B. 23.
(50) [1944] 2 All E.R. at p. 389; [1945] K.B. at p. 29.
(51) See at p. 353, letter D, ante.

" The first case is *Doyle* v. *Kaufman* (52).   In the Divisional Court,   A
Cockburn, C.J., with whom Lush, J., concurred, said (53): ' The power to
enlarge the time given by R.S.C., Ord. 57, r. 6 [now R.S.C., Ord. 3, r. 5]
cannot apply to the renewal of the writ when, by virtue of a statute, the cause
of action is gone.' Perhaps it might have been more accurate to say ' when
the remedy is barred ', but the effect is the same."

In my view, it would of course not be right to deal with this matter merely on the   B
question of choice of language.   One must construe the true position, and my view
is that Cockburn, C.J., was wrong, if I may respectfully say so, in saying that by
virtue of the Statute of Limitation the cause of action had gone, and Lord
Goddard was right when he suggested that the proper way of putting it was that
the remedy was barred.

To complete this part of my judgment, which I fear is of very great length,   C
and to deal with counsel for the defendant's last point on this part of the appeal,
I would add that in my judgment R.S.C., Ord. 20, r. 5, falls within s. 99 (1) (*a*)
of the Supreme Court of Judicature (Consolidation) Act, 1925, (54) as being a
rule for regulating and prescribing the procedure and practice to be followed in
the High Court in a matter in which the High Court has jurisdiction.   Thus,
on the fundamental plea, I find that R.S.C., Ord. 20, r. 5, is intra vires.   D

Let me now turn to consider the second point advanced on behalf of the
defendant, namely, that in the circumstances here the court's discretion should
not be exercised in favour of the plaintiff so as to allow him to substitute a new
defendant for the defendant whom he named in the writ.   On this part of the case
three points are particularly urged.   The first, which is advanced by counsel for
the plaintiff, is that the court should treat this matter as the equivalent of a mere   E
misnomer.   The second point which is advanced by counsel for the defendant,
is that this is not a case of a defect in the pleadings which can be cured in the way
proposed by the plaintiff.   The third point, which is advanced by counsel for the
plaintiff, is that when the provisions or the terms of R.S.C., Ord. 20, r. 5 (3)
are applied to the facts of the present case, it appears that the court's discretion
should be exercised in favour of the plaintiff.   F

On the first of these points, namely, that this should be treated as a case of a
misnomer.   I have already referred to the cases of *Davies* v. *Elsby Bros., Ltd.*
(55), and *Whittam* v. *W. J. Daniel & Co., Ltd.* (56), and I would say further that
the point is touched on in the case of *Re Clark* v. *Forbes Stuart (Thames Street),
Ltd. (Intended action)* (57).   Considering these decisions, I am much in doubt
whether this could be regarded as a case of mere misnomer; but I prefer to rest   G
my judgment on other grounds.

On the second of these points, that this is not a case of curable defect, counsel
for the defendant called attention to a trilogy of cases reported in 1962.

In *Smalley* v. *Robey & Co., Ltd.* (58) the places in the writ where the Division
of the High Court and the district registry should have been named were left
blank.   A notice of change of solicitors, however, provided the missing informa-   H
tion, and so it was held that the defect could be cured.   I have already dealt
with the case of *Dornan* v. *J. W. Ellis & Co., Ltd.* (59).   In *Pontin* v. *Wood* (60)
the writ was defective in that it claimed damages for personal injuries without
alleging any negligence.   It was held, however, not to be a nullity and the
defence could be cured by a proper statement of claim, even if delivered after
the period of limitation.   In this case it seems to me right to refer to some   I
observations of Holroyd Pearce, L.J., since it is relevant on the general question

---

(52) (1877), 3 Q.B.D. 7, 340.   (53) (1877), 3 Q.B.D. at p. 8.
    (54) R.S.C., Ord. 20, r. 5, is set out at p. 356, letter I, ante; s. 99 (1) (*a*) is set out
at p. 358, letter B, ante.   (55) [1960] 3 All E.R. 672, see at p. 355, letters C to F, ante.
    (56) [1961] 3 All E.R. 796; [1962] 1 Q.B. 271, see at p. 356, letters D to E, ante.
    (57) [1964] 2 All E.R. 282.   (58) [1962] 1 All E.R. 133; [1962] 1 Q.B. 577.
    (59) [1962] 1 All E.R. 303; [1962] 1 Q.B. 583; see at p. 354, letter H, to p. 355,
letter B, ante.
    (60) [1962] 1 All E.R. 294; [1962] 1 Q.B. 594.

A of the exercise of the court's discretion. Holroyd Pearce, L.J., said (61):

"The two preceding cases (62) in our list also dealt with difficulties in which plaintiffs found themselves through delay in issuing and serving their writs. There was no reason why they should not have issued and served the writs in good time and then continued to negotiate at leisure, if they so desired, on a firmer footing free from danger. Quite apart from the
B fact that every judge rightly looks askance at a stale claim, the plaintiff jeopardises the very existence of his action by such unjustifiable delay. Process put together hurriedly in the dark eleventh hour is prone to error; and on such occasions the defendant's pardonable enthusiasm subjects the plaintiff's proceedings to a microscopic and pedantic scrutiny. This trilogy
C of cases may serve as a warning to dilatory plaintiffs that such delay is likely to lead them into serious trouble and expense, if not to complete disaster."

Unhappily this warning did not reach the plaintiff's advisers in this present case. On the third of these points I am of opinion that the ultimate outcome of this appeal depends on a consideration of the provisions of R.S.C., Ord. 20, r. 5 (3),
D in the light of the present facts (63). In my judgment before the court will grant leave to amend as proposed here the court must be satisfied of three things: first, that the mistake sought to be corrected was a genuine mistake; secondly, that the mistake was not misleading nor such as to cause any reasonable doubt as to the identity of the person intended to be sued; thirdly, that it is just to make the amendment.

E It is admitted that the mistake made by the plaintiff's solicitors when they named " R. J. Parker (Male) " as defendant in the writ was a genuine mistake. Was it then misleading or such as to cause any reasonable doubt as to the identity of the person intended to be sued? In my judgment it was not, for the following reasons: (i) The letter before action written on Apr. 20, 1962, was addressed to Mr. R. S. Parker and said that the plaintiff's solicitors had been consulted
F with regard to the personal injuries sustained by the plaintiff " as the result of your driving of a motor vehicle ", that is to say, R. S. Parker's driving. (ii) Again, in their letter of May 1, 1962, the insurance company, although heading the letter " R. J. Parker ", began " Referring to your letter of Apr. 20 addressed to our insured ". (iii) Again, on Aug. 28, 1963, the plaintiff's union wrote to the insurance company heading their letter " Your insured, R. S. Parker ".
G (iv) Again, the plaintiff's claim as endorsed on the writ was for damages for personal injuries arising as a result of an accident " owing to the negligent driving of the defendant ". (v) Again, the statement of claim further made it clear that the person being sued, or intended to be sued was the person who had been driving at the time of the accident. I am wholly satisfied that R. J. Parker —and I infer his son R. S. Parker too—and their legal advisers and their insurers
H knew full well that the person intended to be sued was the driver of the motor van at the time of the accident. The driver at the time was R. S. Parker.

The final question in this appeal is: am I justified in saying it would be just to allow the amendment? Having regard to all the circumstances, I am satisfied that it would. Counsel for the defendant submits that there was much delay in issuing the writ, and calls attention to the words of Holroyd Pearce, L.J.,
I which I have quoted from Pontin's case (64). It is, however, the case here that a claim by the plaintiff was intimated within six months of the accident, and the intended defendant had ample time and opportunity to prepare his

---

(61) [1962] 1 All E.R. at pp. 300, 301; [1962] 1 Q.B. at p. 614.
(62) Namely, Smalley v. Robey & Co., Ltd., and Dornan v. Ellis (J. W.) & Co., Ltd., just cited, footnotes (58), (59).
(63) R.S.C., Ord. 20, r. 5 (3), is set out at p. 357, letter B, ante.
(64) [1962] 1 All E.R. at pp. 300, 301; [1962] 1 Q.B. at p. 614; see at letter A, supra.

case, and in my view cannot have been misled in any way and cannot have been A
prejudiced.

As I have said, it is agreed that if I exercise my discretion in favour of the
plaintiff in allowing the amendment of the writ, it must follow that I should
also exercise my discretion so as to extend the validity of the writ. Therefore,
I have not thought it necessary to refer to the authorities put before the court
on that subject; I merely say that I am satisfied that it is just that I should B
extend the validity of the writ.

The appeal is therefore dismissed, and it remains only for me to express the
court's gratitude to learned counsel for their erudite arguments on the hearing
of the appeal.

Appeal dismissed.   Order accordingly.

Solicitors: *Evill & Coleman* (for the plaintiff); *Berrymans*, agents for *Willey*, C
Hargrave & Co., Leeds (for the defendant).

[*Reported by* K. DIANA PHILLIPS, *Barrister-at-Law.*]

D

ROYAL v. PRESCOTT-CLARKE AND ANOTHER.

[QUEEN'S BENCH DIVISION (Lord Parker, C.J., Winn, L.J., and Sachs, J).
January 21, 1966.]

*Magistrates—Procedure—Adjournment—Application by prosecution for adjourn-
ment during submission of No Case—Discretion—Adjournment to permit* E
*evidence on formal requirement—Special road—Failure by prosecution to
prove notices and regulations—Whether magistrates justified in refusing
application—Road Traffic Act,* 1960 (8 & 9 *Eliz.* 2 *c.* 16), *s.* 20 (5), *s.* 37 (5)—
Special Roads (Notice of Opening) Regulations, 1962 (*S.I.* 1962 *No.* 1320),
reg. 1.

Informations were preferred against the respondents, a learner driver and F
her driving instructor, charging the former with driving along a portion of a
special road (a motorway) on which a learner driver was not permitted to
drive, contrary to reg. 11 of the Motorways Traffic Regulations, 1959, and
the latter with aiding and abetting her, contrary to s. 35 of the Magistrates'
Courts Act, 1952. No evidence was given at the trial that any notice of the
opening of the road as a special road had been published as required by G
reg. 1 of the Special Roads (Notice of Opening) Regulations, 1962, made
under s. 20 (5) of the Road Traffic Act, 1960, despite the fact that counsel for
the respondents had intimated to the prosecutor that he would require proof
of the regulations and notices. Section 37 (5) of the Act of 1960 provided that
the restrictive provisions contemplated by the section and to be enacted by
regulation should not apply to any part of a special road until the require- H
ments of s. 20 (5) of the Act had been complied with. At the conclusion of
the case, the justices accepted a submission by counsel for the respondents
that the prosecution had failed to prove the notices. In the course of counsel's
submission the prosecution applied for an adjournment to enable the regulations and notices in question to be proved. On appeal against the refusal of
the application, and the dismissal of the informations, I

Held: it was a matter for the justices' discretion, as in any other case
where the circumstances were not very peculiar and special, whether or not to
grant the application; but, as the adjournment applied for was to establish
by production of further evidence something which was only a formal
requirement which had to be satisfied, the discretion had been wrongly
exercised and the case must be remitted for further consideration (see p. 369,
letters B, E and G, post).

Appeal allowed.

A   [As to magistrates' powers of adjournment, see 25 HALSBURY'S LAWS (3rd Edn.) 198, 199, para. 360; and for cases on the subject, see 33 DIGEST (Repl.) 230, *626, 627*.

As to regulations applying to special roads, see 19 HALSBURY'S LAWS (3rd Edn.) 395, para. 641.

For the Road Traffic Act, 1960, s. 20, s. 37, see 40 HALSBURY'S STATUTES B (2nd Edn.) 726, 743.]

Case referred to:

> *Duffin* v. *Markham*, (1918), 88 L.J.K.B. 581; 119 L.T. 148; 82 J.P. 281; 33 Digest (Repl.) 230, *626*.

Case Stated.

C   This was a Case Stated by justices for the county of Middlesex in respect of their adjudication as a magistrates' court sitting at Brentford on June 17, 1965. On Apr. 5, 1965, the appellant, Frank Anthony Royal, preferred informations against the respondents, Patricia Norreys Prescott-Clarke and Patrick John Bane, charging that, on Feb. 27, 1965, they unlawfully drove a motor vehicle on the M.4 motorway, the first respondent being the holder of a provisional licence, D contrary to reg. 11 of the Motorways Traffic Regulations, 1959, and that the second respondent, on the same day, aided, abetted, counselled and procured the first respondent to commit the said offence, contrary to s. 35 of the Magistrates' Courts Act, 1952. The following facts were found. The appellant, a police constable of the Metropolitan Police, was on motor-cycle duty on Feb. 27, 1965. The first respondent was driving a school of motoring car, displaying L plates, E and the second respondent was sitting beside her as her instructor. The first respondent, on the instructions of the second respondent, and because of quite heavy traffic which was then on the A.4 road, drove from that road in an easterly direction, up an approach road to the east of Clayponds Avenue, Brentford, and on to a section of the M.4 motorway. In following this route, the respondents passed signs which purported to declare the section to be a motorway and to F prohibit, amongst other things, its use by learner drivers. The appellant followed the car and stopped it at the end of the section, near to a point at which the motorway crosses Oxford Road. The first respondent was the holder of a provisional driving licence. The second respondent said to the appellant " I was definitely told that the regulations did not apply until the whole of the motorway was opened ". The section of the M.4 motorway which stretched in a westerly G direction from the point at which the car entered the motorway was not yet opened on Feb. 27, 1965. The section of the road over which the first respondent had driven the car had been open to, and used by, traffic for about three months prior to Feb. 27, 1965. When that section of road was first opened to, and used by, traffic, some of the signs purporting to declare the section to be a motorway and to prohibit, amongst other things, its use by learner drivers had not been H erected and some were covered up by sacking until a date prior to Feb. 27, 1965, but by the latter date all the usual signs in relation to the section of the road had been erected and were uncovered and clearly visible to traffic.

It was contended on behalf of the respondents that (a) the appellant was required as a matter of law to prove by proper production the notices which he alleged had been published as required by the Special Road (Notice of Opening) I Regulations, 1962, in relation to the section of motorway; (b) alternatively, if the appellant was not required as a matter of law to prove the notices as above submitted: (i) there was no evidence before the magistrates that the provisions of the Special Roads (Notice of Opening) Regulations, 1962, had been complied with; and (ii) the appellant had failed to satisfy them that the notices had been published. It was contended on behalf of the appellant that he should be allowed an adjournment in order to prove publication of the notices as required by the Special Roads (Notice of Opening) Regulations, 1962. The justices dismissed the

informations and awarded £10 10s. costs to each of the respondents. The A
appellant now appealed.

The case noted below* was cited during the argument in addition to the case
referred to in the judgments.

Paul Wrightson, Q.C., and *P. B. Greenwood* for the appellant.

R. J. Ellis for the respondents.

                                                                    B
WINN, L.J., delivered the first judgment at the request of LORD PARKER,
C.J.: This is an appeal by way of Case Stated from a decision of justices for the
county of Middlesex acting in and for the petty sessional division of Brentford,
and sitting at Brentford. It really is not necessary to go in any detail into the
circumstances which led to a charge being made against the respondents, a
learner-driver and the motoring tutor who was sitting beside her while she was C
driving a motor car along a portion of the special road or motorway known as
M.4. There is a regulation which prohibits such a driver from driving on special
roads. I do not propose to read it in full; it is contained in the (1) Motorways
Traffic Regulations, 1959, reg. 11. Although that regulation was made in
1959, its validity was extended by the provisions of para. 1 of Sch. 19 to the
Road Traffic Act, 1960, so as to give it the equivalent effect in law as though it D
had been made by the Minister in exercise of powers given to him by s. 37 (2) of
the Road Traffic Act, 1960. There is no doubt that, if this road was a special
road to which the respective provisions applied at the time when the first
respondent was allegedly driving on it, these informations were properly laid.

Section 37 (5) of the Road Traffic Act, 1960, provides that the restrictive
provisions contemplated by the section and to be enacted by regulation are not to E
apply to any part of a special road until such date as may be declared by a notice
published by the highway authority in manner prescribed for the publication of
notices in s. 20 (5) of the Road Traffic Act, 1960. The Minister did make regulations, the Special Roads (Notice of Opening) Regulations, 1962, (2), which, by
the preamble, he purported to make in exercise of his powers under s. 20 (5) of
the Road Traffic Act, 1960. I think for myself that it would have been a little F
clearer what these regulations set out to enact if there had been a reference in the
preamble to s. 37 (5) of the Act of 1960 as well as to s. 20 (5). Regulation 1 of
these regulations provides that notice of the opening of any road as a special
road should be published declaring the date on which the road is open for use as
a special road not less than seven days before that date in at least one newspaper
circulating in the area in which the special road or part of the road is situated G
and in the " London Gazette ". When the justices heard this case, no evidence was
tendered that any such notice or notices had been published in any newspaper or
in the " London Gazette ". The court has been informed by counsel who appeared
for the respondents on this appeal that, before the case came on for hearing, he
told the police constable, who was there to give evidence against the respondents,
that he was appearing for both of them, that he would require proof of the H
regulations and of notices under the regulations, and he said that the constable
could have communicated that warning to a senior officer, either an inspector or a
superintendent, who, we are told, was at the court; whether he did so, the court
does not know. When the case had been concluded and counsel for the respondents was addressing the justices, he for the first time submitted to them, and
his submission was upheld by advice that the clerk to the justices gave them, I
that the prosecution was bound to fail because there was no evidence before the
justices that the provisions to which I have referred in respect of notices had been
complied with; put slightly differently, that the prosecution had failed to satisfy
the justices that any such notice had been published. The justices accepted those
submissions, and they have stated in their Case Stated that they thought it was
incumbent on the prosecution as a matter of law to prove affirmatively that the

_____
* *Middleton* v. *Rowlett*, [1954] 2 All E.R. 277.   (1) S.I. 1959 No. 1147.
                        (2) S.I. 1962 No. 1320.

A   notices had been published. That is perfectly right, it was. It was part of the case for the prosecution, and a necessary part of it, and the justices thought that, since the appellant had failed to satisfy them that any such notices had been given, the prosecution had equally failed to satisfy them that the regulations applied to the relevant portion of the road. The prosecution, as counsel for the respondents told the court, asked for an adjournment in the middle of his speech

B   to the justices, and that application was refused by the justices.

In my opinion, it was a matter for the discretion of the justices in this case, as in any other case where the circumstances are not very peculiar and special, whether or not to grant such an application for an adjournment. Here the application for the adjournment was made in order to establish by production of further evidence something which was only a formal requirement which had to be

C   satisfied. Counsel for the appellant has submitted to the court that, in every case where such a situation arises before justices, they are bound as a matter of law to grant the adjournment, and he has relied for that submission on the decision of *Duffin* v. *Markham* (3). I think that that is putting the matter too high and that counsel's submission is too strong and in that form I do not accept it. In any such case as this one where there is no question of the prosecution being

D   given a further opportunity to go out and scout about for evidence to strengthen their case, but it is merely a matter of their going to look in a newspaper, and if they find there what they need, bringing the newspaper to the court, in all ordinary circumstances and in the absence of any conduct on the part of the prosecution which might be properly described as misconduct or election not to call other evidence and in the absence of any grave potential prejudice to

E   the accused, there is only one way in which the discretion can properly be exercised. In this particular case, the justices wrongly exercised the discretion which was entrusted to them; they should, in my view, in law, have granted the adjournment in the particular circumstances of this case. It, therefore, seems to me that this case ought to go back for further consideration by the justices. The prosecution may then produce these notices, if indeed they

F   were ever published. There may very well be an order which the justices will think it right to make with regard to the costs of, and occasioned by, the adjournment, those being reserved for the justices to deal with. I would allow this appeal to that extent.

SACHS, J.: I agree.

G   **LORD PARKER, C.J.:** I also agree.

Appeal allowed; case remitted.

Solicitors: *Solicitor, Metropolitan Police* (for the appellant); *S. Rutter & Co.* (for the respondents).

[*Reported by* N. P. METCALFE, ESQ., *Barrister-at-Law.*]

H

I   ——————

————————————————————————————————

(3) (1918), 82 J.P. 281.

Re CLAYTON (deceased). CLAYTON v. HOWELL AND OTHERS.   A

[CHANCERY DIVISION (Ungoed-Thomas, J.), March, 15, 16, 1966.]

Family Provision—Provision for husband—Small estate—Husband crippled
but able to maintain himself—Prospect of substantial reduction of his means if
he ceased to be employed—No provision made for him by testatrix—Her estate
consisting in large part of proceeds of sale of house that had been her own—   B
Married to husband in later life—Whether unreasonable to make no provision
for him—Inheritance (Family Provision) Act, 1938 (1 & 2 Geo. 6 c. 45),
s. 1, as amended by Intestates' Estates Act, 1952 (15 & 16 Geo. 6 & 1 Eliz. 2
c. 64), s. 7, Sch. 3.

The claimant husband, who was crippled in both legs, married the
testatrix in 1950 when he was forty-one years of age and she was fifty-one.   C
In December, 1960, she went to stay with her sister for a week, and whilst
there, made a will by which, after leaving £10 to the second defendant,
Mrs. W., she gave the residue of her estate subject to the payment of her
funeral and testamentary expenses and debts, to her sister and the latter's
son in equal shares absolutely. She died in February, 1963. The estate
was very small, with a distributable amount of £1,271, of which a large   D
part represented the proceeds of sale of the house that the testatrix had had
before she married the claimant. The claimant's earnings were about £10
a week net, with an annual bonus of £100, and he had capital of £900; thus
he appeared to be able to maintain himself at present, but there was prospect
of substantial diminution in his income in the event of his ceasing to be
employed. He applied for maintenance out of the testatrix' estate. It   E
was not disputed that, if provision for him were ordered, it should be by
lump sum payment.

Held: on claims under the Inheritance (Family Provision) Act, 1938,
as amended, there was not a greater onus of proof on a surviving husband
than there was on a surviving wife; in the present case it was unreasonable
for the testatrix not to have made some provision for the claimant and,   F
in the circumstances, a reasonable provision would be that the executors
should pay him £400 (see p. 372, letter D, p. 373, letter H, and p. 374, letter
B, post).

[As to family provision, see 16 HALSBURY'S LAWS (3rd Edn.) 455-465, paras.
911-930; and for cases on the subject, see 24 DIGEST (Repl.) 967-984, *9753-9810;*
and especially as to provision made for a husband, see ibid., p. 976, *9775-9777.*   G
For the Inheritance (Family Provision) Act, 1938, as amended, s. 1, see 32
HALSBURY'S STATUTES (2nd Edn.) 139.]

Cases referred to:
E. (deceased), Re, E. v. E., ante p. 44.
Watkins (deceased), Re, Hayward v. Chatterton, [1949] 1 All E.R. 695; 24
Digest (Repl.) 968, *9758.*   H

Adjourned Summons.

This was an application by originating summons dated Oct. 7, 1963, by the
claimant, Frank Thomas Clayton, the widower of Veronica Bridgid Clayton,
deceased (the testatrix), and a dependant within the meaning of the Inheritance
(Family Provision) Act, 1938, as amended, for an order under that Act that   I
such reasonable provision as the court might think fit might be made out of the
net estate of the testatrix for the maintenance of the claimant. The testatrix
died on Feb. 7, 1963, having by her will dated Dec. 28, 1960, made no provision
for the plaintiff.

The defendants were (i) Mary Elizabeth Howell, the testatrix' sister, and (ii) Betty
Doreen Williams, the executrices of the testatrix' will, and (iii) Michael Edward
Richard Ward, one of the residuary legatees under the said will and the son of
the first defendant by a previous marriage.

A   *E. R. Moulton-Barrett* for the plaintiff.
    A. J. Balcombe for the defendants.

    UNGOED-THOMAS, J.: This is a widower's application under the Inheritance (Family Provision) Act, 1938, for maintenance out of his wife's estate. It is a very small estate, with a distributable amount of £1,271. The

B   plaintiff himself is completely crippled in both legs, and he is earning, and has earned for a considerable time, £10 a week net.

    The plaintiff married the deceased on Nov. 5, 1950, when he was forty-one years of age and she was fifty-one; and this was the first marriage for each of them. In December, 1960, the deceased went to her sister, Mrs. Howell, in Newport to stay for a week and there made her last will on Dec. 28. By that

C   will she left £10 to a Mrs. Williams, and she left the residue equally between her sister, Mrs. Howell, and her sister's son, Michael Ward—Michael Ward being Mrs. Howell's son by a previous marriage. Just over two years later, on Feb. 7, 1963, the deceased died; and in due course probate was granted to Mrs. Howell and Mrs. Williams, and these proceedings were brought.

    Under the Act of 1938 it is perfectly clear, and has been repeatedly emphasised

D   in these courts, that it is not enough for the judge to think that some provision, or a larger provision, should in his view have been made for the plaintiff; he has to go much further than that. The overall governing consideration is that the court has to find that it was unreasonable on the part of the deceased, in all the circumstances, to have made no provision, or not to have made a larger provision for the claimant.

E   This case has features which have been subject to observations in this and in other cases: first, the smallness of the estate; and, secondly, that the application is by a surviving husband, and not by a surviving wife, child or other dependant of the deceased.

    The Act of 1938 places no bottom limit to the value of the estate in respect of which an application can be made. Dependants of a dead person, including the

F   husband, have the right to make a claim against that person's estate, however small it may be. Small sums matter to very many people, and an order under the Act of 1938 for payment of £1 a week or less might in certain circumstances make all the difference to a claimant. However small the estate, all the relevant circumstances have to be considered before the court's decision is made. The smallness of the estate neither excludes jurisdiction nor full consideration.

G   Smallness of the estate, however, is significant in relation to (i) the availability of state aid for the claimant; (ii) the extent to which the estate can effectively contribute to the claimant's maintenance, and (iii) the costs which are necessarily involved in the application. I will comment on these three matters in turn. As to (i), as emphasised by STAMP, J., in *Re E.* (*decd.*), *E.* v. *E.* (1) in considering *Re Watkins* (*decd.*), *Hayward* v. *Chatterton* (2), the circumstances that have to be considered include the size of the estate and the means of the claimant, so that—

H   and now I quote his observations (3):

> ". . . where the deceased's estate is so small, and the means of the claimant so exiguous, that the only effect of making provision for the claimant will be pro tanto to relieve the national assistance fund it would not be unreasonable for the deceased to take the view that there was no point in making provision
> I   for the claimant, and that it would be reasonable not to do so."

As to (ii), the purpose of the Act of 1938 is not just to give a windfall legacy but to provide maintenance for a dependant who needs maintenance, and the smallness of the estate, taken in conjunction with the claimant's means and standard of living, may be such as to make provision from the estate so comparatively negligible as to make it not unreasonable for the deceased to have made no provision for the claimant. Then, as to (iii), claims in cases where the costs of

---

(1) Ante at p. 44.   (2) [1949] 1 All E.R. 695.   (3) Ante at p. 48.

establishing the claims leave virtually nothing significant for the claimant, **A**
deprive the claim of substance, and are to be discouraged; and there will always
be such cases, despite any reduction in costs that may be effected.

This brings me to a matter on which it might be desirable to comment. At
present, all these applications have to be made in the High Court. This was
obviously a sensible arrangement when this novel and difficult jurisdiction was
introduced; but it may well be that this arrangement has outlasted this particular **B**
justification for it. In the case now before me, witnesses have had to come up
from the country, some from Wales, to litigate in the High Court, obviously at
substantial expense. The costs involved in such a case as this might well be
out of all proportion to the size of the estate, and yet not such as necessarily to
deprive the claim of all substance. It might perhaps now be considered whether
all these cases, however small the estate, should necessarily in all circumstances **C**
be brought only in the High Court.

I come now to the position of a husband in making a claim. The Act of 1938
expressly provides that a surviving husband may be a dependant entitled to claim
for maintenance from his wife's estate. The difference in capacity for self-
maintenance of a woman on the one hand, and of a man on the other hand, is
becoming increasingly less; and the historical prima facie inclination in favour **D**
of a maintenance order for a widow as contrasted with a widower will doubtless
become, as it appears to have become even in very recent years, correspondingly
less, too. I certainly do not see in the Act of 1938 a greater onus of proof on the
surviving husband than on the surviving wife. It is simply a question in each
case, be the claimant husband or wife, whether in all the circumstances as established in evidence, the deceased's failure to make any, or enough, provision for **E**
the surviving spouse is unreasonable; and I, for my part, find no material
assistance nowadays from contemplating the sex of the claimant, or considering
it as a circumstance on its own when all the material circumstances have to be
considered. [HIS LORDSHIP then dealt with the facts, as distinct from the
financial part, of the case and concluded that the relationship of the claimant
husband and his wife, the deceased, before her death were not such as to make **F**
his omission from her will, and from any participation in her estate, reasonable.
HIS LORDSHIP continued:] Now I come to the financial aspect of this case.
It raises the question whether the financial circumstances that I have to consider
are such as to make the exclusion of the husband from the will unreasonable, and,
if so, what reasonable provision should be made for him.

First, this estate, which has a distributable amount of £1,271, was an estate **G**
of £1,402 gross; and of the £1,402, £975 were the net proceeds of the sale by
the deceased of her own house which she had before she married the plaintiff.
Of that £975 she invested £500 in national savings certificates, which now stand
at £706; and the balance of the £975, amounting to £475, was put by her in the
Post Office Savings Bank, and the amount standing to her credit at her death,
doubtless with accumulated interest, was £654. So it is evident that the great **H**
bulk of her estate came from moneys of her own independently of her husband,
and that any sums which came from him and are included as part of her estate
at her death, were comparatively small amounts. Thus this is not a case in
which it can be said for the husband that these were moneys derived substantially
from him.

The second matter which has to be borne in mind is that in this case the **I**
husband is a cripple and, although earning £10 a week, he is naturally handicapped
both in his earning capacity and in looking after himself, as compared with
others not suffering as he does. Thirdly, in this case there is no suggestion that
the beneficiaries under the will are not fully and amply provided for apart
entirely from the estate of the deceased. So that in this case there is no question,
as so often happens, of balancing conflicting needs. Therefore, the case turns
principally financially on the husband's means, his need for maintenance, and
how far this small estate should help in providing it, if in all the circumstances

A   it is unreasonable that provision for his maintenance out of it should not be made.

I come now to the figures. The claimant husband has this net clear payment in his present occupation of £10 1s. 7d. per week. He has, in addition, a bonus at Christmas which varies, depending on the amount of trade and the success of the business, but can be taken generally at about £100; so that the weekly

B   payments and the bonus together come to about £620 a year. In addition to that, he has capital of £900. There is £300 in the savings bank, and when he made his affidavit a couple of years or so ago, he had £185 in a building society, and that has been increased to £600, which is an increase of some £415 in two years. So it looks as if he is in a position to look after himself at present, and to make some savings out of what he is earning. Indeed, as I understand it, it is

C   not suggested that he cannot at present maintain himself. I have no evidence about his expenses, apart from his occupying a house owned by his employer, for which he pays £1 12s. 11d. a week rent. It would be quite impossible for me, on this information, to conclude that he needs maintenance to maintain him as long as he is in his present occupation, and has his present resources and lives as he does now.

D   What has caused me concern in this case is, whether provision should be made for the eventualities which might, and which in the course of nature would be expected to arise. What would be the position if he, for one reason or another found his circumstances to be changed—perhaps because of ill-health, perhaps because of the change in ownership, owing to death or other causes, of the business in which he at present works? It appears that his present employer has intimated

E   that he would pay the claimant, on retirement, a pension and allow him to live rent free in the house which he now occupies. There appears, however, to be no binding obligation; there is no indication of the amount of any pension; and, of course, this intention might, for one reason or another, have to yield to other considerations. What the claimant has here in the way of pension and a rent-free house is not a right, but it is a prospect; and it is a prospect which,

F   from a business and commonsense point of view in deciding what is reasonable, should be taken into consideration together with the risks of non-fulfilment which that prospect inevitably involves. When the husband retires he will presumably have State aid. What the precise amount of that will be, I am not in a position to say. It would appear to be perfectly evident, however, that there would be a very substantial diminution in his income, and in the event of his present employ-

G   ment terminating, from whatever cause, it is to be borne in mind that he is a person under a very serious disability—a disability both in obtaining employment and a disability in looking after himself. These are important factors in deciding reasonableness and unreasonableness in relation to provision for him. There is no indication in the evidence before me that any provision made out of the estate for him would be correspondingly or substantially, or indeed at all, offset

H   by any reduction in State assistance which he might otherwise have; so that element again is not present in this case.

So it becomes simply a question of whether, having regard to the husband's condition and his prospects, it is unreasonable not to have made some provision towards his future maintenance. In my view, it is unreasonable; and the question is, what provision should reasonably be made for him? This again

I   is a difficult question. I am helped to this extent, that the parties before me are agreed that if any provision should be made, then the convenient course would be to order a lump sum payment now in accordance with the power which is given to the court to do so in the case of such small estates as this (4). With a person handicapped as the claimant is, on the small income which he has, out of which he can at present apparently make some savings, but with the prospect of its substantial reduction in the event of his ceasing to be employed as he is at

(4) See s. 1 (4) of the Act of 1938, as amended; 32 HALSBURY'S STATUTES (2nd Edn.) 140.

present—and he is no longer a young man—then even a small provision out of **A** this estate would, on the evidence before me, be a provision that would be likely to help materially in his maintenance within the contemplation of the Act of 1938.

It becomes then a question of what amount should, in all the circumstances, be made by way of lump sum payment at the present time.   This again is a difficult question, on which different minds may come to different conclusions; **B** and nobody can pretend that there is a conclusive and completely satisfying and provable answer in specifying the sum.   Doing the best that I can on all the evidence before me, it seems to me that in all the circumstances a reasonable provision would be the payment of £400.

Order accordingly; costs of the plaintiff, and of the executors, on a common fund basis, out of the testatrix' estate.   **C**

Solicitors: *Sharpe, Pritchard & Co.*, agents for *Farrington & Whiting*, Brighton (for the plaintiff); *Church, Adams, Tatham & Co.*, agents for *Dolman & Sons*, Newport, Mon. (for the defendants).

[*Reported by* JACQUELINE METCALFE, *Barrister-at-Law.*]

D

Re DUCKSBURY (*deceased*).
DUCKSBURY v. DUCKSBURY AND ANOTHER.
[CHANCERY DIVISION (Buckley, J.), February 25, 28, 1966.]   **E**

Family Provision—Daughter—Unmarried daughter of testator's first marriage— Capable of earning livelihood—No provision made for her by testator's will owing to bitter relations between testator and first wife—Custody of daughter given to first wife on divorce—Daughter some years later wrote letter at mother's dictation wounding testator's feelings—Subsequent attempt by daughter **F** *to achieve reconciliation unsuccessful—Daughter's choice of way of life led to her earning little—Whether testator under moral obligation to provide for daughter—Inheritance (Family Provision) Act, 1938 (1 & 2 Geo. 6 c. 45), s. 1 as amended by Intestates' Estates Act, 1952 (15 & 16 Geo. 6 & 1 Eliz. 2 c. 64), s. 7, Sch. 3.*

The testator married twice.   There were two daughters of the first marriage.   **G** This marriage ended by divorce in 1945 in circumstances of great bitterness. The first wife had custody of the daughters, of whom the elder, the plaintiff, was born in 1932.   The testator re-married in 1950.   At his death in October, 1961, he left his whole estate to his second wife, the first defendant, whose health was such that she was unable to earn.   By his will he declared that he made no provision for his daughters as he had already sufficiently provided **H** for them.

In July, 1945, the testator had made a settlement in favour of his two daughters for their maintenance and benefit.   Some £6,000 had been applied out of the trust fund between 1945-46 and 1954-55, but there was question whether his first wife, who was adjudicated bankrupt in 1948, had had the payments or some of them and had not applied them, or not applied them **I** wholly, for the daughters.   In 1955, when the settlement was wound up, the plaintiff (then twenty-two years of age) received £677 on final distribution. In 1959 the testator, who was an hotelier, sold the shares in the hotel company for £30,000.   In his lifetime he made over a half-share (worth £6,000 at his death) in his house to his second wife, and he also transferred to her invest- ments or money amounting to £6,000 and upwards.   His net estate was a little under £16,000.   He had made no provision, other than the settlement of 1945, for his daughters.

A   The plaintiff, after the divorce, lived with her mother. In 1950 she wrote at her mother's dictation a letter to the testator which was intended to and did wound him. Thereafter she never met him, though she made efforts to be reconciled, to which he did not respond, when her mother's influence waned. The plaintiff was able to earn her living as a secretary, but she preferred to work part-time and to pursue part-time studies of art, with the

B   consequence that her earnings were small. She was unmarried. On an application by her for reasonable provision out of the deceased's estate, pursuant to s. 1 (1)* of the Inheritance (Family Provision) Act, 1938,

    Held: the true reason for the testator's not having provided for the plaintiff by his will was the bitterness of relations between him and his first wife and the fact that the plaintiff was " in the camp " of the latter,

C   but the testator had not been justified in allowing this bitterness to come between him and his daughter or in failing to respond to her attempts to achieve reconciliation after her letter of 1950; the testator had moral obligation to make some provision for the plaintiff but, having by his will made no provision for her, had failed thereby to make reasonable provision for her maintenance, and in the circumstances, although she could earn a

D   living and her choice of way of living did not increase her moral claim on the testator, there would be an order in her favour for payment of £2 weekly from the testator's estate (see p. 379, letters A and C, and p. 380, letters B and E, post).

    [As to reasonable provision for a dependant, see 16 HALSBURY'S LAWS (3rd Edn.) 460, 461, para. 920; and for cases on the subject, see 24 DIGEST (Repl.)

E   967-973, *9753-9771*.

    For the Inheritance (Family Provision) Act, 1938, s. 1, as amended, see 32 HALSBURY'S STATUTES (2nd Edn.) 139.]

    Adjourned Summons.

    This was an application by originating summons dated July 5, 1962, by the plaintiff, April Mary Ducksbury, under the Inheritance (Family Provision)

F   Act, 1938, s. 1, as amended, that such reasonable provision as the court should think fit should be made for her maintenance out of the estate of the testator (her father). The plaintiff was a spinster and the elder daughter of the testator by his first marriage. The first defendant, Brenda Ducksbury, was the testator's widow, his second wife. The first and second defendants were the executors of the testator's will. The facts are set out in the judgment.

G   *Charles Sparrow* for the plaintiff.

    A. Heyman for the defendants.

    BUCKLEY, J.: This is an application under the Inheritance (Family Provision) Act, 1938, as amended, which is made by a spinster daughter of a testator who died on Oct. 3, 1961. The testator was a hotelier by profession

H   and he was, until 1955, the owner of the majority of the shares in a company which owned and operated an hotel in Huddersfield called the George Hotel which seems to be, or at any rate, seems to have been at that time, the principal hotel in Huddersfield with a good and flourishing business.

    The testator was married twice, and by his first marriage he had two daughters, of whom the plaintiff is the elder. She was born on Apr. 12, 1932, and is now

I   approaching the age of thirty-four. She has never married. Her sister has married. The first marriage of the testator came to disaster and was dissolved in the year 1945 by divorce in circumstances which seem to have created a great deal of bitterness between the parties. The custody of the children, the elder of whom was then about thirteen, was given to their mother.

    In July, 1945, the testator made a settlement of certain securities including 1,414 ordinary shares in George Hotel (Huddersfield), Ltd., the company owning the hotel, which provided that until the younger daughter should attain the age

---

* The terms of s. 1 (1), so far as relevant, are set out at p. 378, letter A, post.

of twenty-one years, the trustees should apply the capital and income of the trust A
fund comprised in the settlement towards the maintenance, education and
otherwise for the benefit of those two daughters, and authorised payments by
the trustees by instalments not exceeding £267 each to their mother for that
purpose, being three times a year. It is said that their mother behaved improperly
with regard to this settlement in that she induced the trustees to pay over moneys
to her which were not applied for the benefit of the two girls. It appears that B
between the years 1945-46 to 1954-55 inclusive sums amounting to over
£6,000 were paid to their mother for the benefit of the girls, but the suggestion that
is put forward is that a substantial part of that money was not in fact applied for
their benefit but was expended by their mother for her own benefit. In 1948, the
first Mrs. Ducksbury was adjudicated a bankrupt, but even thereafter it is said
that the trustees paid money to her which she did not apply properly for the C
benefit of her daughters.

On Mar. 25, 1950, the testator remarried; his second wife was the first defendant, Mrs. Brenda Ducksbury who has survived him, but who is unfortunately
disabled by ill health from earning her living in any way. She is now aged about
forty-eight years.

In 1951, proceedings were instituted in the Chancery Division of the High Court D
relating to the settlement and in those proceedings a consent order was made on
Jan. 26, 1953, under which the testator was to pay to the trustees of the settlement £600, and to make further payments to the trustees of £2 a week, less tax,
for four years from Jan. 26, 1953. It directed

> " that the trustees shall henceforth administer the trusts of the settlement
> as if cl. 5 thereof had not contained the part beginning with the words ' And E
> may pay the same by instalments not exceeding £267 ' "

and the testator was granted an option to buy back 1,414 ordinary shares of the
hotel company exercisable not later than Jan. 26, 1957. The option was to
be at a price agreed between the trustees and the testator or, in default of agreement, within fourteen days of the exercise of the option, it was to be fixed by F
chartered accountants and agreed by the trustees and the testator, or, in default
of agreement, fixed by such chartered accountant as should be nominated by the
President of the Law Society. In 1955, the testator exercised that option and
bought back the 1,414 shares of the hotel company at par. Those shares represented one-third of the issued share capital of the company. Some four years
later, in 1959, the testator sold the whole of the share capital in that company G
to Trust Houses, Ltd., for a price which seems to have been substantially in
excess of £30,000—although I am not quite clear precisely what the price was.

When the option was exercised in 1955, the settlement was wound up and the
plaintiff, who was then twenty-two years of age, received a sum of £677 in the
final distribution of the trust fund; this, as I understand, was the only sum which
she received under the trust paid directly to herself, for all earlier amounts H
had been applied either by the trustees or her mother for her benefit, or had
been paid to her mother to be so applied and misappropriated in the way which
I have mentioned. Apart from these benefits under the settlement, the plaintiff
received no property from the testator during his lifetime. By his will which
was made on Mar. 18, 1958, the testator appointed the defendants executors,
and he gave all his property of every kind to the first defendant absolutely. He I
declared in his will that he had made no provision thereby for his two daughters,
as he had already adequately otherwise provided for them. There is I think
nothing to which that can refer except the settlement.

In his lifetime, the testator had made over to the first defendant a half-interest
in a property which he owned at Penmon in the county of Anglesey where a house
was in the course of being built at his death. That property was valued for estate
duty purposes at his death at £12,000. The half-share which he gave to the first
defendant accordingly can be taken at about £6,000. He also transferred to her, or

A   paid over to her, securities or sums of money, of a value of £6,000 or possibly
more during his lifetime. It may have been as much as between £9,000 and
£10,000. The net estate at his death, for the purposes of the Inheritance (Family
Provision) Act, 1938, is of a value of a little under £16,000—£15,900 or thereabouts, possibly a little less after provision has been made for the costs of these
proceedings.

B   The plaintiff continued to live with her mother during her childhood after the
divorce, and for some time spent half the holidays with each of her parents, but
she did not see her father after the summer of 1949, when she was about seventeen-
and-a-half years of age, and not long after that it seems that he insisted on her
going to a secretarial school to learn what it is necessary to learn to become a
secretary, which was very much against the wishes of the plaintiff. Egged on,
C   it may be, by her mother, who was apparently very much embittered against
the testator, the plaintiff wrote a letter to the testator, her father, some time
about the middle of 1950, in which she said something very derogatory about the
first defendant: whether she actually used the term mentioned in the evidence it
is really unnecessary for me to determine. She now says that she does not think
that she did, but undoubtedly that was a letter which was calculated to wound,
D   and was intended by her to wound, the testator. She really admitted that in
the witness box and the letter, she said, was dictated by her mother. This
caused a breach between the testator and the plaintiff and, as I say, from the
summer of 1949 to the time of his death they never met, but she did later, when she
was less dominated by her mother, write a letter to the testator apologising for
what she had done and indicating that she would like to make it up with him.
E   Unhappily she received no reply to that letter. She also wrote to the testator on a
few occasions, but not on very many occasions, in connexion with other matters.
As time went by, she did become genuinely anxious to be reconciled to the
testator but, as she never received from him any reply to any communication that
she made to him, she did nothing further and she never went to visit him or do
anything else of a more positive nature with a view to a reconciliation. Perhaps
F   it was not until he died that she really became aware of how disappointed she
was not ever to have made it up with the testator.

        After the plaintiff had completed her course at the secretarial college she took
various appointments as a secretary at what seems to have been a comparatively
modest wage. When she received the sum of money that I mentioned, in 1955,
she gave up that sort of employment and studied languages for a short time. She
G   went for a little while to work with a family at Marseilles au pair. She then took
some further jobs as a typist. In about 1958, when she was really not at all happy
with this sort of life, she started to attend an art school and decided that what
she really wanted to do was to become an artist. By this time she was about
twenty-five years of age. That is what she has continued to pursue ever since,
but having no income of any kind she has been, perforce, obliged to seek employ-
H   ment part-time, and to pursue her studies part-time. She is still in that position.
The fact is that, although she is a woman of robust health and quite able to
earn her living, she has chosen to pursue this course which has resulted in her
earning only a very meagre living.

        The first defendant, as I say, is prevented by the state of her health from
earning anything although, during the testator's lifetime until towards the end
I   of his life, she had worked during her marriage in the hotel business as the head
housekeeper of the hotel. The house which she and the testator were engaged in
building at Penmon at the time of his death has since been completed and she is
living there, but it is a large house for her needs and has cost a good deal of
money. She has no property or means of her own, apart from what she has
derived from the testator, either by way of gifts during his lifetime or under his
will, and comparatively small invested funds which represent her own savings.
She is in receipt of sickness benefit payment under the National Insurance Act
1965, at the rate of £4 a week.

The Inheritance (Family Provision) Act, 1938, s. 1, as amended, provides·   **A**

"(1) Where ... a person dies domiciled in England leaving— ... (b) a daughter who has not been married ... then, if the court on an application by any such ... daughter ... is of opinion that the disposition of the deceased's estate effected by his will ... is not such as to make reasonable provision for the maintenance of that [daughter], the court may order that such reasonable provision as the court thinks fit shall, subject to such conditions or restrictions, if any, as the court may impose, be made out of the deceased's net estate for the maintenance of that [daughter] ..."   **B**

It is under that provision that I am asked to make an order for the benefit of the plaintiff.

Counsel on behalf of the plaintiff has submitted that each of the various classes   **C**
of dependants who are indicated in paras. (a), (b), (c) and (d) of s. 1 (1) of the Act of 1938 has a prima facie right to be maintained or to be provided for under the will of a testator, and that the burden is thrown on the defendant in such a case to show that in fact it was reasonable for the testator to make no more provision for the plaintiff than in fact he has made. I do not feel at all able to accept that view. It seems to me that the subsection does not put the burden of proof one way   **D**
or another. It is for the court to decide on such evidence as it has before it whether or not the testator has made reasonable provision for the maintenance of the applicant, and I do not think that the court should start with a leaning one way or another either in favour of the view or against the view that the testator owed some sort of moral duty to provide for any particular applicant.

In the present case it is submitted on behalf of the defendants that the plaintiff,   **E**
being hale and hearty and in the prime of life and quite able to earn her own living, really requires no provision to be made for her benefit by her father. On the other hand, it is said that the testator left an estate of some size; that the plaintiff was a daughter who, as indeed seems to be the case, had not been brought up with the idea that she would earn her own living, and who was left without any financial backing at all, with no margin or cushion of any   **F**
kind, dependent on only her own efforts, and that the testator did indeed owe a moral duty to make some provisions for this daughter, who has no husband to make provision for her and who has no property and no expectations from any sources. It is of course suggested that the plaintiff, by her own conduct, justified the testator in treating her as having forfeited such moral claims as she might otherwise have had on his bounty, particularly by her conduct in the dispute   **G**
between her mother and the testator, the letter to which I have referred, and the fact that for a good many years before his death she never went near him or saw anything of him at all. There is also the declaration in the testator's will that his reason for not making provision for the plaintiff and his other daughter was that he had already adequately provided for them.

Now in my view the settlement which the testator made in 1945 was clearly   **H**
not intended to be a permanent provision for his daughters, but a provision for their maintenance and education mainly during the period of their minority. The money was mainly spent during their minority. I make no finding of fact whether any of it was or was not wrongly appropriated by their mother, for that is not the issue in this case, but the fact is that the girls themselves received little benefit from the settlement except in the form of maintenance and educa-   **I**
tion during their minority. They did each receive—at least I assume that each received the same amount—a little over £600 on the ultimate distribution of the fund, but for a man in the position of the testator to represent that settlement as being an adequate provision for his daughters in the sense that this testator does in his will is, I think, an abuse of language.

The first defendant in her evidence said that the deceased was very embittered against his first wife, and was very embittered against his daughters while they were with or under the influence of his first wife. She said that he would have

A nothing to do with the plaintiff because she clung to her mother too much, and because the money which he had provided through the settlement had not been used for the proper purpose. She said that that fact had very greatly embittered him against his first wife, and that he would never do anything for his daughters while he knew that they were, as one might say, in the " camp " of his first wife. That is really the explanation why the testator made no provision

B for either of his daughters, and what I have to consider is whether in the circumstances of this case, taking them all into consideration, it was reasonable for the testator to make no provision for his daughters and particularly for the plaintiff.

It seems to me that the testator might well have been excused for not regarding favourably the conduct of the plaintiff in 1950 when the letter to which

C I have referred was written, which was intended both by the testator's first wife and by the plaintiff herself to wound the testator, but he was not justified in entirely ignoring the efforts made by the plaintiff, his daughter, at a later stage to apologise for that conduct and to re-open some sort of relationship with him. It seems to me on the evidence that I have heard that the fault with regard to the lack of contact between the testator and the plaintiff from the

D year 1949 onwards must at any rate, after the letter of apology, rest with the testator rather than with the plaintiff.

It does not seem to me that the testator was justified in allowing his bitterness against his first wife to get between him and what would otherwise, I think, have been his natural affection for his daughters. That he had an affection for his daughters in spite of what had happened does emerge from the

E evidence of his sister-in-law, the sister of the children's mother, a Mrs. Bell. It is true that it would appear from the evidence that I have heard that Mrs. Bell is mistaken in one part of her evidence; that is to say, she must be mistaken in saying that a particular conversation with the testator to which she deposes took place about Christmas 1959, for she says that it took place in Yorkshire and at that time the testator was not in Yorkshire but was already living in

F Anglesey. That fact does not lead me to suppose, however, that the substance of the rest of Mrs. Bell's account of the conversation in question is inaccurate, and that account does indicate that the testator did feel affection for his daughters. Nevertheless, it may have been an affection which could not override the hostility which he felt towards his first wife, and it seems to me that to that hostility, the lack of contact between the plaintiff and the testator is to

G be attributed.

Counsel for the defendants has submitted that, if in this case the court were to make an order in favour of the plaintiff, this would amount to a departure from precedent; he says that no case is to be found in the books in which a court has made an order in favour of an unmarried daughter capable of earning her own living, and therefore, as I think counsel suggests, requiring no

H provision to be made for her maintenance. Whether or not any such case is to be found in the books, to make such an order would not be a departure from the principle on which other cases have been decided. A daughter who has not married but who is not suffering from any kind of mental or physical disability is clearly a dependant in whose favour the court has power to make an order under s. 1 (1) of the Act of 1938; what has to be considered is whether,

I having regard to all the circumstances of the case, the testator has failed to make reasonable provision for the maintenance of such a daughter, and what would be reasonable in any particular case must depend on the circumstances of the daughter, the circumstances of the testator, the amount of his estate, the claims of others on his bounty and all the surrounding circumstances—including, of course, the conduct of the applicant herself.

In the present case, having regard to the frailty of the first defendant's health, I think that the testator was quite right in thinking that he owed a primary duty to provide for her, who was his wife for the last eleven years of his life,

but, his estate being such as it was, I do not think that that obligation was such   A
as to exclude from his proper consideration his obligation to his unmarried
daughter. The fact that she has chosen to pursue a course which has resulted
in her not earning a very enviable living is one which no doubt has some bearing
on the amount of provision that it would be reasonable for the testator to have
made for her. If a young woman who is able to earn her own living, as the
plaintiff is, chooses to follow a course which results in her earning only a meagre   B
living, that will not increase her moral claims on her parents, but I think that
this testator did have some moral obligation to make some provision for his
daughter. What most people might have expected him to do would have been
to make some provision for her after the death of the first defendant, but that
is not a thing which I am able to do by an order under the Act of 1938. Because
I cannot do that, however, it does not follow that I should not direct that some   C
provision should be made for her, so that she may be helped, however little
it may be, to provide for her future needs when she is no longer able to earn
her living.

This is not a case in which it would be proper for me to make a large provision
for the benefit of the plaintiff; it is not for me to try to effect the sort of testamentary dispositions which I think that a testator should have made or would   D
have made had his mind not been affected, as I think that it was, by his matrimonial disputes with his first wife. It is not for me to say what he ought to have
done if he had been generously disposed towards the plaintiff. I have to consider
what it is reasonable in the circumstances of this case to order that she should
receive, having first of all satisfied myself that the testator had failed to make
reasonable provision for her. He has in fact made no provision for her, and for   E
the reasons that I have indicated I think that he was under a moral obligation
to make some provision for her. I am, therefore, satisfied that he has failed
to make reasonable provision for her.

In the circumstances I think that justice will be done if I direct that she
shall receive during her life (1), until she marries, a sum of £2 a week from the
estate.   F
[After discussion His Lordship directed that the weekly payment should
run from the date of the testator's death.]

Order accordingly.

Solicitors: *P. R. Kimber* (for the plaintiff); *Durant, Cooper & Hambling*,
agents for *Ware, Warner, Knowles*, York (for the defendant).

[*Reported by* JENIFER SANDELL, *Barrister-at-Law.*]   G

H

I

_____

(1) By s. 1 (2) of the Act of 1938, as amended, an order for periodical payments to
an unmarried daughter must provide for their termination not later than her marriage.

A   RONSON PRODUCTS, LTD. *v.* RONSON FURNITURE, LTD.

[CHANCERY DIVISION (Stamp, J.), March 1, 4, 15, 1966.]

Contempt of Court—Committal—Breach of undertaking—Order of court incorporating undertaking by company not to do specified acts—Order not served on director of company—Breach of undertaking by company constituting
B   *contempt—Director aware of undertaking and its breach—Whether director liable for contempt of court.*

On motion for judgment in a passing-off action in May, 1954, a limited company gave undertakings not to do certain specified acts whether by their servants or agents. These undertakings were embodied in the order made on the motion. The order was not served on the directors of the company
C   who were also shareholders in the company, which was a private company. In 1966 on motion by the plaintiffs for liberty to sue out a writ of sequestration against the company for contempt of court by breach of the undertakings or for the imposing of a fine on the company, the plaintiffs sought also an order, among other orders, to commit the respondent director to prison for the contempt. The director admitted knowledge*.

D   **Held:** as the undertakings by the company were negative in character, being undertakings not to do certain acts by agents or otherwise, the fact that the order containing the undertakings was not served on the director did not bar proceedings against him for contempt by breach of the undertaking; accordingly, since he knew of the breaches of the undertakings, he was liable in proceedings for contempt but, in all the circumstances, the
E   court would order only that he should pay the plaintiffs' costs on a common fund basis (see p. 386, letters E and G, post).

Dictum of JENKINS, J., in *Redwing, Ltd.* v. *Redwing Forest Products, Ltd.* ((1947), 177 L.T. at p. 388) not followed.

[As to the enforcement of undertakings given to the court, see 8 HALSBURY'S LAWS (3rd Edn.) 29, 30, para. 54; and for cases on the subject, see 16 DIGEST
F   (Repl.) 56, 57, *520-535.*]

Cases referred to:
  A.-G. v. *Wheatley & Co., Ltd.*, (1903), 48 Sol. Jo. 116; 16 Digest (Repl.) 57, *539.*
  D. v. *A. & Co.*, [1900] 1 Ch. 484; 69 L.J.Ch. 382; 82 L.T. 47; 16 Digest (Repl.) 59, *548.*
  Iberian Trust, Ltd. v. *Founders Trust and Investment Co., Ltd.*, [1932] All E.R.
G   Rep. 176; [1932] 2 K.B. 87; 101 L.J.K.B. 701; 147 L.T. 399; 16 Digest (Repl.) 61, *579.*
  McKeown v. *Joint Stock Institute, Ltd.*, [1899] 1 Ch. 671; 68 L.J.Ch. 390; 80 L.T. 641; 16 Digest (Repl.) 64, *616.*
  Redwing, Ltd. v. *Redwing Forest Products, Ltd.*, (1947), 177 L.T. 387; 16 Digest (Repl.) 64, 617.
H   *Tuck, Re, Murch* v. *Loosemore*, [1906] 1 Ch. 692; 75 L.J.Ch. 497; 94 L.T. 597; 16 Digest (Repl.) 62, *586.*
  United Telephone Co. v. *Dale*, (1884), 25 Ch.D. 778; 53 L.J.Ch. 295; 50 L.T. 85; 16 Digest (Repl.) 65, *631.*

Motion.
I   This was a motion on notice dated Feb. 2, 1966, by the plaintiffs, Ronson Products, Ltd., in a passing-off action begun by writ dated Sept. 15, 1953, for leave to sue out a writ of sequestration against the defendant company, Ronson Furniture, Ltd., for contempt of court committed by the defendant company in (a) using the word " Ronson " as part of a trade mark, (b) offering furniture for sale under the trade mark " Ronson " and (c) using after July 23, 1954, the word " Ronson " otherwise than as part of the name Ronson Furniture, Ltd., in breach of undertakings contained in an order made in the action on May 18, 1954,

* See p. 386, letter E, post.

alternatively for an order that the defendant company should bo fined for the A
contempt. The plaintiffs by their motion sought also liberty to issue writs of
attachment against Gerald Ronson and Anne Ronson, his wife, directors of the
defendant company, for breaking the undertakings; alternatively orders
committing them to prison for contempt, and alternatively leave to sue out
writs of sequestration against them. The material terms of the undertakings
are set out at p. 383, letter A, post.   B

Notwithstanding the undertaking, the defendant company had used on writing
paper the word " Ronson " as part of a trade mark (viz., a little carpenter bearing
a banner with the words " Furniture by Ronson ") and had used on that writing
paper the word " Ronson " otherwise than as part of the name Ronson Furniture,
Ltd. This breach, the court accepted, was accidental. There was also a bronze
plate on the wall by the doorway of " Dwell House ", the defendant company's C
place of business, bearing on it the trade mark depicting a carpenter bearing a
banner on which were the words " Furniture by Ronson ". Under this plate
in very much larger letters were the words " Ronson Furniture, Ltd." and
underneath were the words " Dwell Works ". Below that were the words
" General office and showroom entrance ", etc. The word " Ronson " on the
bronze plate stood out on photographs of the wall which were in evidence. D
This bronze plate was not removed when, following the order of the court in
1954, the address of the works was altered from Ronson Works to Dwell Works,
though a metal bar was placed over the words " Ronson Works ". This breach,
so the court found, was neither casual, accidental nor unintentional. Since
May 18, 1954, nineteen companies had been either incorporated or taken over
by Mr. and Mrs. Ronson or by Mr. Ronson and his son. Mr. Ronson was a E
director of sixteen of the companies, which were family companies. Two of
the companies, which were incorporated in 1965 had the word " Ronson " as
part of their names, e.g., Ronson Investments, Ltd. One company had subsequently changed its name so that " Ronson " formed part of it. Mr. Ronson
deposed that he had become interested in 1959 in property development and had
formed companies for each new development; and that in about 1963 a practice F
had grown up amongst the companies of referring to themselves as " The Ronson
Group of Companies ". Prior to 1964 the defendant company's name appeared
in the telephone directory. After 1963 it did not appear, but there was an entry
" Ronson Group of Companies " with the same telephone number. At the date
of the entry in the telephone book no company in the group had " Ronson " as
part of its name except the defendant company, and the court concluded that G
when the defendant company had the old entry deleted it had the new entry put
in thereby using the word " Ronson " otherwise than as part of the name Ronson
Furniture, Ltd. The court (STAMP, J.) found that this breach of the undertaking
was neither casual, accidental nor unintentional.

The cases noted below* were cited during the argument in addition to those
referred to in the judgment.   H

Sir Andrew Clark, Q.C., and *V. G. H. Hallett* for the plaintiffs.
Robert S. Lazarus, Q.C., and *T. L. Dewhurst* for the defendant company and
the respondents, Mr. and Mrs. Ronson.

Cur. adv. vult.

Mar. 15.   **STAMP, J.,** read the following judgment: An action was com- I
menced in 1953 by the plaintiffs, Ronson Products, Ltd., against a company
called Ronson Furniture, Ltd. By an order made in this action by consent on
May 18, 1954, the defendant company by counsel gave certain undertakings.

---

* *Lewis* v. *Pontypridd, Caerphilly and Newport Ry. Co.*, (1895), 11 T.L.R. 203; *Milburn*
v. *Newton Colliery, Ltd.*, (1908), 52 Sol. Jo. 317; *Gordon* v. *Gordon*, [1946] 1 All E.R. 247;
[1946] P. 99; *Edward Grey, Ltd.* v. *Greys (Midlands), Ltd.*, (1952), 70 R.P.C. 25; *Phono-
graphic Performance, Ltd.* v. *Amusement Caterers (Peckham), Ltd.*, [1963] 3 All E.R. 493;
[1964] Ch. 195.

A   There were in fact four undertakings, of which I need refer only to two. One was in these terms, not to

"(a) use the word ' Ronson ' or any word so nearly resembling it as to be calculated to be confused therewith as or as part of a trade mark,"

and the other was not to

B   "(c) use after July 23, 1954, the word ' Ronson ' except as part of the name Ronson Furniture, Ltd. and in such case not in larger letters or more distinctively than the rest of that name."

The plaintiffs now apply by motion against the defendant company and against two of its directors, Mr. Gerald Ronson and Mrs. Anne Ronson, to whom I will refer as Mr. and Mrs. Ronson, for certain relief as follows. The plaintiffs ask for

C   "leave to sue out a writ of sequestration directed to commissioners to be therein named to sequester the goods, chattels and personal estate and the rents, issues and profits of the real estate of the defendants for contempt of this court committed by the defendants in (a) using the word ' Ronson ' as part of a trade mark and (b) offering furniture for sale under the trade mark ' Ronson ' [that is not now persisted in] and (c) using after July 23,

D   1954, the word ' Ronson ' otherwise than as part of the name Ronson Furniture, Ltd. in breach of the undertakings . . .."

of May 18, 1954. Alternatively, the plaintiffs ask for an order that the defendant company be fined by this court for the said contempt, and an order that the plaintiffs may be at liberty to issue a writ or writs of attachment against Mr. and

E   Mrs. Ronson, the directors of the defendant company, for their contempt in breaking the undertakings; alternatively, for an order that Mr. and Mrs. Ronson do stand committed to Brixton Prison for that contempt, and alternatively, for leave to sue out a writ or writs of sequestration in respect of the goods, chattels and personal estate and the rents, issues and profits of the real estate of Mr. and Mrs. Ronson.

F   It is common ground that proceedings to enforce this order can only be brought against Mr. and Mrs. Ronson as directors of the defendant company if the defendant company has itself been guilty of a punishable contempt. The plaintiffs allege that the defendant company has been guilty of several breaches of the undertaking. [His Lordship having reviewed the evidence and made the findings which are summarised at p. 382, letter B, ante, et seq., concluding that

G   the breach (that is, the breach by entering " Ronson Group of Companies " in the telephone directory) was neither casual nor unintentional, continued:] On the other hand, the breach derives its gravity from the fact that it is associated with acts, which were in no way a breach of the undertaking, namely, the formation of other companies carrying on business as members of the Ronson Group of Companies, in the way that I have outlined. The case is not so serious,

H   in my judgment, that I ought to deal with it by sequestration of the company's assets or anything more than a fine, which, taking into account the retention of the bronze plate, which I regard as the more serious breach of the undertaking, I fix at £250.

I have now to consider the position of the individual respondents, Mr. and Mrs. Ronson. At a not very early stage of the hearing of the motion the claim

I   for relief against Mrs. Ronson except as to costs was abandoned. She claims to have played no active part in the affairs of the defendant company and apologises for any breach of the undertaking. I accept that position and will make no order of a penal nature against her. Mr. Ronson is in quite a different position.

On behalf of the two directors, counsel for the defendants took two preliminary points. He submitted as a matter of law that the directors of a corporation can never be made liable for proceedings for committal or attachment in respect of a breach of an order against, or an undertaking by, a company contained in the order unless they were served with the order. Mr. and Mrs. Ronson were not so

served. He also submitted as a matter of law that, whether or not his first proposi-   A
tion was well founded, directors could never be so proceeded against in respect
of an undertaking by, as distinct from an order against, a corporation.

Several authorities were relied on as supporting the first proposition, and one
was relied on in support of the second proposition; but, with one exception to
which I will refer, they are all authorities on the position where there has been
an order or undertaking to do a positive act and not where an order or under-   B
taking has been of a prohibitive nature. The distinction in law between an order
to do an act and one which prohibits an act being done is not, in my judgment, a
merely historical or technical distinction. It depends on practical considerations.
If a man be ordered to do an act, so that his failure to do it may lead him to
prison, justice requires that he know precisely what he has to do and by what
time he is to do it, and this consideration finds its expression in R.S.C., Ord. 41,   C
r. 5, which provides as follows:

> " Every judgment or order made in any cause or matter requiring any
> person to do an act thereby ordered shall state the time, or the time after
> service of the judgment, or order, within which the act is to be done, and
> upon the copy of the judgment or order which shall unless R.S.C., Ord. 24,
> r. 17 (3) or R.S.C., Ord. 26, r. 6 (3) applies or the court or a judge otherwise   D
> orders, be served personally upon the person required to obey the same
> there shall be endorsed a memorandum in the words or to the effect
> following . . ."

and there then follow the well known penal words.

The operation of the rule is exemplified in one of the cases which was relied
on by counsel for the defendants, A.-G. v. Wheatley & Co., Ltd. (1). In that   E
case the order containing the undertaking by the company did not specify the
time within which the act had to be done and there had been no order against
its directors to do it. It followed that the order could not be enforced against
the company, which was not in contempt, and, because directors as such can
only be proceeded against for a contempt if the company itself is in contempt,
there could at that stage be no relief against the company's directors. It is   F
convenient that I should say at once that A.-G. v. Wheatley & Co., Ltd. (1), on
which much reliance was placed on behalf of Mr. and Mrs. Ronson, is referred
to in textbooks as authority for the general proposition that an undertaking by
a company cannot be enforced against its directors; but it relates only to an
undertaking to do a positive act and is neither authority for that general proposition nor for the proposition that an undertaking by a company contained in an   G
order of the court, can in no case be enforced against a director unless the order
has been served on him.

The practical difference between an order under which a positive act is to be
done and one where an act is prohibited must lead to the conclusion that the
former class of order ought not to be enforced against a director unless he has
been served with it, so that he, like the company, knows precisely what is to be   H
done and the period during which it has to be done. See, for example, McKeown
v. Joint Stock Institute, Ltd. (2) where a supplemental order requiring an officer
of the company to do the act had to be obtained. It would be an injustice to
make a director liable for a failure of a company to do the required act within
twenty-one days of service of the order on the company if the director became
aware of the order only on the eighteenth day.   I

Different considerations apply where the undertaking or the order to be
enforced is of a negative character. An undertaking not to do an act need not
be personally served on him who gave the undertaking, for he must be aware
of its contents (see D. v. A. & Co. (3), and, although it is no doubt convenient that
an order restraining a party from doing a particular act should be served on him,
for if this is not done it may be difficult for the party seeking to enforce the order

---

(1) (1903), 48 Sol. Jo. 116.   (2) [1899] 1 Ch. 671.   (3) [1900] 1 Ch. 484.

A to satisfy the court that it was brought to the party's notice, the contention
that there is a rule that such an order must be served before it can be enforced
was decisively rejected in *United Telephone Co.* v. *Dale* (4); see also *Re Tuck,
Murch* v. *Loosemore* (5), where the distinction between an order to do and an
order not to do an act was emphasised by the Court of Appeal.

I refer at more length to the judgment of Pearson, J., in *United Telephone
B Co.* v. *Dale* (4) because, although it is concerned with the enforcement of an
order prohibiting an act against the party against whom the order was made
and is not addressed to such a case as the present, where it is sought to enforce
an order against a director containing an undertaking by a company not to do
specified acts, what was said by Pearson, J., in that case, based as it was on
reason and good sense, ought, in my judgment, subject to any authority pointing
C in the opposite direction, to be applied as well to the latter as to the former
type of case. There, the order being of a prohibitive character, the point was
taken that it could not be enforced by the committors because it had not been
served, and what Pearson, J., said on that element was this (6):

> " But I do not believe the rule to be, and I shall not act upon the rule
> as it has been stated to me, that in no case will the court enforce obedience
D > to its injunction by means of a committal to prison, simply upon the ground
> that the order has not been served, when it appears beyond all doubt or
> dispute that the defendant is aware that the injunction has been granted,
> and that it is the intention of the plaintiff to enforce it."

Then further on in his judgment he said (7):

E > " The court would be to a great extent incapable of doing its duty to
> itself, as well as to Her Majesty's subjects, if it were to say that, with
> perfectly accurate knowledge of the order of the court, a defendant is at
> liberty to defy the court's authority, and then come to the court and say,
> ' You cannot visit me for that breach of your order, because the order has
> not been served upon me '. What is the necessity for serving an order upon
F > a defendant if he knows perfectly well without that service what it is which
> he is bound to obey? "

It is difficult to discern any good reason why the views expressed by Pearson, J.,
are not applicable in the case of a director who has not been served with the
order on, or undertaking by, his company not to do an act, but who, being
fully aware of the terms of the order, procures the company to do the prohibited
G act. Where the undertaking or order is of a perpetual character, the practical
difficulty of serving the order on a director need not be emphasised.

The only authority relied on on behalf of Mr. Ronson indicating that an
order on or undertaking by a company not to do a particular act cannot be
enforced against a director who has not been served with the order was a
judgment of Jenkins, J., in *Redwing, Ltd.* v. *Redwing Forest Products, Ltd.* (8).
H The passage relied on by counsel for the defendants is this (9):

> " Counsel, who appears for the defendant company and for its directors,
> points out that these proceedings so far as the directors are concerned are
> fatally defective in that the order on which the motion is founded was not
> personally served on the directors, and he refers me to two authorities,
> *McKeown* v. *Joint Stock Institute, Ltd.* (10), and *Iberian Trust, Ltd.* v.
I > *Founders Trust and Investment Co., Ltd.* (11) on which he relies as authorities
> for that proposition. Counsel for the plaintiff company, when this point
> was taken, frankly admitted that on the authorities he could not contend
> that this motion as a motion for the attachment of the directors was

---

(4) (1884), 25 Ch.D. 778.   (5) [1906] 1 Ch. 692.
(6) (1884), 25 Ch.D. at pp. 786, 787.   (7) (1884), 25 Ch.D. at p. 787.
(8) (1947), 177 L.T. 387.   (9) (1947), 177 L.T. at p. 388.
(10) [1899] 1 Ch. 671.   (11) [1932] All E.R. Rep. 176; [1932] 2 K.B. 87.

properly constituted or could be entertained without personal service. It A
is, therefore, clear that the motion so far as the directors are concerned
fails in limine and must be dismissed as against them."

The two cases relied on on behalf of the defendants and referred to by the learned
judge were both cases where the order was one requiring a positive act to be
done, subject to this, that in *Iberian Trust, Ltd.* v. *Founders Trust and Investment
Co., Ltd.* (12) LUXMOORE, J., assumed for the purpose of the relevant part of his B
judgment that this was the position. As I have indicated, different considerations,
in my judgment, apply to orders and undertakings to do positive acts from those
pertaining where a prohibited act is in question. Counsel for the defendants
while conceding that the passage in the judgment of JENKINS, J., was founded
on a concession, which in turn rested on authorities relating to positive and not
negative orders or undertakings, urged on me the persuasive nature of that C
dictum. Whilst I have the greatest aversion, however, to disregarding any dictum
which fell from the lips of that learned judge, if ever Homer can be excused for
a momentary nod, it is in a passage in an extemporary judgment founded on a
concession made by counsel as to the existence of a principle which was in turn
founded on authorities which laid down or established a different or more limited
principle. D

The undertaking in the present case being a negative undertaking and there
being no authority other than *Redwing, Ltd.* v. *Redwing Forest Products, Ltd.* (13)
to constrain me to take another view, I hold in principle that the failure to
serve Mr. Ronson with that order containing the undertaking is not a bar to
proceedings against Mr. Ronson for its breach. Similarly, there being no
authority, in my judgment, that a negative undertaking by a company cannot E
be enforced against a director who, knowing of the undertaking, procures its
breach, I hold in principle that Mr. Ronson, who admitted that he was fully
aware of it, has made himself liable in proceedings for contempt.

In considering what the court ought to do in relation to Mr. Ronson, I have to
bear in mind the same considerations as those to which I have already referred
in relation to the defendant company. The gravity of the offence of which the F
plaintiffs principally complain—the use of the description " The Ronson Group
of Companies " in the telephone directory—derives not from the fact that the
defendant company is one of those companies but from the existence of the other
nineteen companies to which the description likewise applies, and I must treat
this aspect of the matter as one which ought not to be taken into account in
judging the gravity of the contempt. Having regard to the fact that I propose G
to fine the company £250 and that the company is one in which Mr. and Mrs.
Ronson are directors, and also shareholders, I have come to the conclusion—
but not without considerable hesitation—that I should take a merciful view of
Mr. Ronson's acts in relation to the company, but mark the court's disapproval
not only of those acts but also of his evidence by ordering him to pay the
plaintiffs' costs on a common fund basis. H

[Order that the plaintiffs' costs be taxed on a common fund basis and paid by
Mr. Ronson, and, if and in so far as they are not recoverable from him, paid by
the defendant company.]

Order accordingly.

Solicitors: *Lawrence Jones & Co.* (for the plaintiffs); *S. A. Bailey & Co.* I
(for the defendants).

[*Reported by* JENIFER SANDELL, *Barrister-at-Law.*]

---

(12) [1932] All E.R. Rep. 176; [1932] 2 K.B. 87.   (13) (1947), 177 L.T. 387.

A   **STEINER PRODUCTS, LTD. *v.* WILLY STEINER, LTD.**

[CHANCERY DIVISION (Stamp, J.), March 22, 24, 1966.]

Contempt of Court—Sequestration—Breach of undertaking by company—Dis-
regard of undertaking that was not casual, accidental or unintentional—
Conduct amounting to contumacious disregard and wilful disobedience of
B   *order of court embodying undertaking—Breaches remedied before hearing—*
Defendant company fined and ordered to pay plaintiffs' costs on a common
fund basis—R.S.C., Ord. 42, r. 31.

By a consent order dated Apr. 30, 1965, the defendant company gave an
undertaking not to carry on business as ladies' hairdressers under the
name " Steiner " other than under the name Willy Steiner, Ltd.   They
C   undertook not to represent the name " Steiner " in script similar to the
distinctive script of the plaintiffs and/or when associated with any decoration
of their premises that consisted of pink and white stripes; and they undertook not to use, whether by agents or otherwise, the name " Steiner " solely
in describing their business but to use the words Willy Steiner, Ltd.   They
were, however, entitled to use the name " Willy Steiner " on existing
D   premises for a period that could not exceed six months.   The plaintiffs
sought leave to sue out a writ of sequestration against the defendants
for contempt of court by committing breaches of the undertakings in that
they had, since Oct. 30, 1965, carried on business as ladies' hairdressers
under a name other than Willy Steiner, Ltd. at six premises, that they
had used the name Steiner in a script similar to the distinctive script of
E   the plaintiffs at three premises and that they had described their business
otherwise than as Willy Steiner, Ltd. in answer to telephone calls.   The
name " Willy Steiner ", without the word " Limited ", had, for example,
remained on the glass panel of the door of the ground floor entrance to
certain of the defendant company's premises until at any rate about Christmas, 1965.   The court found that the defendant company had committed
F   breaches of the undertakings, and that the breaches were not casual, accidental or unintentional.   They had been remedied before the hearing.

Held: disregard of an undertaking given to the court, which was not
casual, accidental or unintentional, constituted contumacious disregard of
the undertaking and was wilful disobedience for the purposes of R.S.C., Ord.
42, r. 31*; in all the circumstances, however, liberty to sue out a writ of
G   sequestration would not be granted but the defendant company would be
fined and ordered to pay the plaintiffs' costs on a common fund basis (see
p. 390, letter B, and p. 391, letter A, post).

Fairclough & Sons v. *Manchester Ship Canal Co. (No. 2)* ([1897] W.N. 7)
applied.

[As to leave to issue a writ of sequestration, see 16 HALSBURY'S LAWS (3rd
H   Edn.) 69, 70, para. 106; and for cases on the subject, see 21 DIGEST (Repl.)
686, 687, *1812-1816.*]

Cases referred to:

A.-G. v. *Walthamstow Urban District Council*;   *Walthamstow Sewage Question,*
(1895), 11 T.L.R. 533; 21 Digest (Repl.) 688, *1837.*
Fairclough & Sons v. *Manchester Ship Canal Co. (No. 2)*, [1897] W.N. 7;
I   21 Digest (Repl.) 686, *1813.*
Stancomb v. *Trowbridge Urban District Council*, [1910] 2 Ch. 190;   79 L.J.Ch.
519; 102 L.T. 697; 74 J.P. 210; 21 Digest (Repl.) 686, *1815.*
Worthington v. *Ad-Lib Club, Ltd.*, [1964] 3 All E.R. 674; [1965] Ch. 236;
[1964] 3 W.L.R. 1099; 3rd Digest Supp.

---

* R.S.C., Ord. 42, r. 31, provides: " Any judgment or order against a corporation
wilfully disobeyed may, by leave of the court or a judge, be enforced by sequestration
against the corporate property, or by attachment against the directors or other officers
thereof, or by writ of sequestration against their property."

Motion.   A

The plaintiffs, Steiner Products, Ltd., brought two actions against the defendants, Willy Steiner, Ltd., which were consolidated by order dated July 22, 1964. By a consent order, dated Apr. 30, 1965, and made in the consolidated action, the defendants undertook, inter alia, (a) not to carry on business as ladies' hairdressers under any name or style that consisted of or comprised the name " Steiner " other than under the name Willy Steiner, Ltd., subject however to   B the right of the defendants to use the name " Willy Steiner " on its existing premises until such time as they were renovated but in any event not later than six months; (b) not to use in connexion with their business as ladies' hairdressers the name " Steiner " when represented in script similar to the distinctive script of the plaintiffs; and (c) not to use, whether by their servants or agents or otherwise, the name " Steiner " solely in describing their business but should C at all times use the words " Willy Steiner, Ltd." except as otherwise provided by (a) above. The plaintiffs moved for an order that they might be at liberty to sue out a writ of sequestration to sequestrate the goods, chattels and personal estate, and the rents, issues and profits of the real estate of the defendant company for contempt of court committed by the defendants in wilfully disobeying the order of Apr. 30, 1965. The facts are stated in the judgment.   D

P. J. Stuart Bevan for the plaintiffs.
E. P. Skone James for the defendants.

STAMP, J.: By a consent order made in this consolidated action dated Apr. 30, 1965, the defendants gave an undertaking which was contained in the Schedule to the order, that (amongst other things)   E

> " (3) The defendants shall not carry on business as ladies' hairdressers under any name or style that consists of or comprises the name ' Steiner ' other than under the name Willy Steiner, Ltd., subject however to the right of the defendants to use the name of ' Willy Steiner ' on its existing premises until such times as the said premises are renovated but in any event not later   F than six months."

I pause to observe that the six months period expired on Oct. 30, 1965.

> " (4) The defendants shall not use in connexion with their business as ladies' hairdressers the name ' Steiner ' when represented in script similar to the distinctive script of the plaintiffs and/or when associated with any decoration of their premises that consists of pink and white stripes.   G
>
> " (5) The defendants shall not whether by their servants or agents or any of them or otherwise howsoever use the name ' Steiner ' solely in describing their business but shall at all times use the words ' Willy Steiner, Ltd.' except as otherwise provided by cl. 3."

The plaintiffs now move for an order for sequestration against the defendants in H respect of the alleged breaches of the undertakings. It is alleged that the defendants have, since Oct. 30, 1965, first, carried on business as ladies' hairdressers under a name other than " Willy Steiner, Ltd.", namely, " Willy Steiner " or " Willy Steiner Salon " at the following premises which are tabulated in the notice of motion: (a) 4a, High Street, Newport, Monmouthshire; (b) 6a, Duke Street, Arcade, Cardiff; (c) 30, Wellfield Road, Cardiff; (d) Fowlers Departmental I Store, Pontypool, Monmouthshire; (e) Manor House, Bank Square, Chepstow; (f) East Gate Street, The Cross, Gloucester. Secondly that they have used in connexion with their business as ladies' hairdressers the name " Steiner " represented in script similar to the distinctive script of the plaintiffs: (a) on the door at, and on appointment cards issued from, their premises at 4a, High Street, Newport, Monmouthshire; (b) on the door at their premises at East Gate Street, The Cross, Gloucester; and (c) on appointment cards issued from their premises at Fowlers Departmental Store, Pontypool, Monmouthshire.

A   Thirdly, it is alleged that they have described the defendants' business otherwise than as " Willy Steiner, Ltd." in answer to telephone calls made at certain dates in December, 1965, January and February, 1966. It is convenient that I should say at once that, although it is admitted by the defendants that they have so described their business in answer to telephone calls in the way alleged, they did so apparently following advice which they had received as to the effect of the

B order. Counsel who appears for the plaintiffs does not press these breaches because, as I think, the breaches in that respect were not wilful or, if you will, contumacious.

   A Mrs. Truscott and her husband made what appears to have been a tour of some of the defendants' premises on Dec. 23, 1965. Her evidence, so far as is relevant for the purposes of this motion, is not really controverted. She first

C of all visited the premises of the defendants in High Street, Newport. She found on the ground floor entrance a glass panelled door, and on the glass panel was the name " Willy Steiner " in italic or script handwriting. She then went into those business premises and she made an appointment for her hair to be dressed. When she asked for an appointment card, she was given an appointment card which also had on it in script writing " Willy Steiner " and which had not got

D on it the word " Limited ".

   Mrs. Truscott then drove to 6a, Duke Street, Arcade, Cardiff, where a somewhat similar state of affairs existed. There was on the glass panel of the door in script the words " Willy Steiner ". When she got her appointment card, she found that it was in the same form as that to which I have already referred. At the Pontypool branch she found at the foot of the stairs a card which said, " To Willy

E Steiner Salon " and the word " Limited " was not on that. The salon was on the first floor. She went in and she got an appointment card which had the words " Willy Steiner " on it in script writing. At the Manor House premises in Chepstow there was a name plate outside the premises, not this time in script, but in block letters, with the words " Willy Steiner " without the word " Limited " after them. She was given an appointment card there which had the words

F " Willy Steiner " not in script, but in block capitals without the word " Limited " on it. Mrs. Truscott then went to the premises at East Gate Street, Gloucester. There she got an appointment card which was in block capitals without the word " Limited " on it.

   Her evidence is virtually uncontroverted and except that there is no evidence of any breach of the undertakings in respect of the premises at 30, Wellfield Road,

G Cardiff, I find that the allegations are proved and that the defendant has committed those breaches of the undertaking.

   It was said on behalf of the defendants regarding these matters that the managing director, Mr. Wilhelm Steiner, gave instructions to a firm called Advertising & Design, Ltd., in which a Mr. Doody appears to be the moving spirit, to take the necessary steps to comply with the undertaking regarding not only the

H nameplates on the premises but also the cards. Mr. Doody, in turn, says that he gave instructions to the employees of Advertising & Design, Ltd. to take the necessary steps, and that these steps were not taken. He says that Mr. Wilhelm Steiner, the managing director of the defendants, from time to time spoke to him, complaining that the notices on the doors had not been put into the correct form, and he, Mr. Doody, appears to have been extremely inactive, at least so

I far as the premises to which I have referred are concerned. He says that one of the difficulties was that of finding signwriters to make the alterations to the signs on the doors. I can only say this: that when the notice of motion in the present proceedings was served on the defendants, the instructions which were given for the removal of the offending signs were promptly carried out and cards with unoffending descriptions of the defendant company were put out in place of the previous cards. That of course, where necessary, ought to have been done within the six months period limit in the order and there was not the slightest difficulty in doing it. If it was impossible to get a signwriter to put

up another sign in place of the signs which it was necessary to remove, that was **A**
just unfortunate from the point of view of the defendants, but it in no way
justified a failure to comply with the undertaking which the defendants had
given. The truth is that Mr. Wilhelm Steiner quite failed to see, as it was his
duty to see, that his orders had been carried out and that the undertaking had
been complied with.

This is not a case where the complaints are complaints of conduct which can **B**
properly or fairly be described as casual or accidental, because these offending
signs were on the doors of the defendants' premises for many weeks, for all to
see and for all employees of the defendant company to see. It seems to me that
the undertaking has, within the meaning of R.S.C., Ord. 42, r. 31, been wilfully
disobeyed.

Counsel, on behalf of the defendants, apologised fully and freely for what the **C**
defendants have done or left undone, but he submitted that the conduct of the
defendants had not been wilful or " contumacious ", which, as I understand it,
he equated with the word " wilful " or " wilfully " in R.S.C., Ord. 42, r. 31.
As I have indicated I take another view.

Counsel for the defendants relied extensively on a recent judgment of STIRLING,
J., in *Worthington* v. *Ad-Lib Club, Ltd.* (1). He asked me to say that the effect **D**
of that decision was that nothing short of stubborn opposition to the terms of an
order or undertaking amounted to wilful disobedience so as to be punishable by
proceedings for attachment. I do not think that STIRLING, J., so held, but, if
contrary to my view, he did so hold, then I prefer to follow the remarks of the
Court of Appeal in *Fairclough & Sons* v. *Manchester Ship Canal Co. (No. 2)* (2),
were it was said: **E**

" The principles on which the court acts when it is asked to sequestrate
the property of a company upon the ground of disobedience to one of its
orders are the same as those applicable where it is sought to commit a private
individual to prison for contempt. In these cases, casual, or accidental
and unintentional disobedience to an order of the court is not enough to
justify either sequestration or committal; the court must be satisfied that **F**
a contempt of court has been committed—in other words, that its order
has been contumaciously disregarded."

I do not think that the Court of Appeal intended to use the word " contumaciously " as meaning something different from " wilfully ", for to do so would
be to put a gloss on the words of the order, which they will not, in my judgment, **G**
tolerate. CHITTY, J., took the view that disobedience which was worse than
casual, accidental or unintentional must be regarded as wilful, in *A.-G.* v.
Walthamstow Urban District Council; Walthamstow Sewage Question (3) and
WARRINGTON, J., in *Stancomb* v. *Trowbridge Urban District Council* (4), took a
similar view.

It does not seem to me that the failure of the defendants in the present case **H**
can possibly be regarded as accidental or as anything other than wilful. The
objectionable notices appeared on the doors for all to see for many weeks, and
I cannot hold that Mr. Steiner, the managing director of the defendant company,
was not fully aware of that fact, or that they could not have been removed in a
few moments. On the other hand, the case is not one which it is possible to
regard as an obstinate disregard of the terms of the undertaking. It was simply **I**
a case of a failure of the company, for no excuse whatever, to carry out the terms
of its undertaking. I do not think that I ought to make an order for sequestration which would affect, no doubt, the livelihood of persons who are wholly
innocent in this matter. Furthermore, the contempt has, to this extent, been
remedied, in that, as I understand it, there is now no further cause for complaint.

(1) [1964] 3 All E.R. 674; [1965] Ch. 236.   (2) [1897] W.N. 7.
(3) (1895), 11 T.L.R. 533.   (4) [1910] 2 Ch. 190.

A   The defendants will be sufficiently punished if 1 impose a fine of £150 and order them to pay the costs of the plaintiffs on a common fund basis.

Order accordingly.

Solicitors: *Kenneth Brown, Baker, Baker* (for the plaintiffs); *Nash, Field & Co.*, agents for *Jacklyn, Dawson & Meyrick Williams*, Newport, Monmouthshire (for the defendants).

B

[*Reported by* Jenifer Sandell, *Barrister-at-Law.*]

C   ## MANSELL v. MANSELL.

[Probate, Divorce and Admiralty Division (Cumming-Bruce, J.), March 8, 10, 1966.]

Divorce—Foreign decree—Recognition by English court—Domicil—Change of domicil of husband during foreign proceedings—Husband domiciled in
D   *Denmark at date of wife's application for divorce—Husband resumed domicil of origin in England before date of Danish royal decree of dissolution— Whether Danish decree recognised as valid.*

Domicil at the date of institution of proceedings for dissolution of marriage is not only necessary but also sufficient to found jurisdiction at date of decree (see p. 395, letter G, post).

E   Dictum of Brett, L.J., in *Niboyet* v. *Niboyet* ((1878), 4 P.D. at pp. 13, 14) applied.

Dictum of Edwards, J., in *Kerrison* v. *Kerrison* ((1952), 69 W.N. (N.S.W.) at p. 308) not applied.

The husband's domicil of origin was English. In 1960, he married the wife who was domiciled in Denmark and, by forming a settled intention
F   to make Denmark his permanent home, became domiciled in Denmark. In March, 1961, the parties entered into a separation agreement and in May, 1961, a separation grant was filed in the Danish court records. The husband temporarily returned to England and in October, 1962, he signed an application for divorce, initiated by his wife in Denmark. In December, 1962, or early January, 1963, a consensual application for divorce was
G   made to the Danish court. Sometime after Feb. 1, 1963, but before Feb. 15, 1963, the husband resumed his domicil of origin. On Feb. 15, 1963, a royal decree was issued in Denmark which, by Danish law, dissolved the marriage. The husband sought a declaration that the Danish decree of dissolution of the marriage was valid.

Held: the husband was entitled to the declaration for which he asked
H   for the reasons set out at letter D, above; moreover the husband should not be taken to have dissociated himself from the determination of his status by the Danish court, in which the reference to which he was party was proceeding, merely because he changed his domicil during pendency of the proceedings (see p. 395, letter D, post).

[As to recognition by English courts of foreign decrees of divorce, see 7 Hals-
I   bury's Laws (3rd Edn.) 112, 113, para. 200; and for cases on the subject, see 11 Digest (Repl.) 481-483, *1079-1097.*]

Cases referred to:

Balfour v. *Balfour*, [1922] W.L.D. 133.
Brownrigg v. *Brownrigg*, (1963), 107 Sol. Jo. 176.
Gane v. *Gane*, (1941), 58 W.N. (N.S.W.) 83; 11 Digest (Repl.) 466, *505.*
Garrow v. *Garrow*, (1965), " The Times ", June 30.
Goulder v. *Goulder*, [1892] P. 240; 61 L.J.P. 117; 11 Digest (Repl.) 337, *89.*

Dictum of Cumming-Bruce, J., at p. 395 *applied in* Leon v. Leon. [1966] 3 All E.R. 820.

Flakemore v. *Flakemore*, [1942] V.L.R. 156.   A
Henderson v. *Henderson*, [1965] 1 All E.R. 179; [1965] 2 W.L.R. 218.
Kerrison v. *Kerrison*, (1952), 69 W.N. (N.S.W.) 305.
Le Mesurier v. *Le Mesurier*, [1895-99] All E.R. Rep. 836; [1895] A.C. 517;
    64 L.J.P.C. 97; 72 L.T. 873; 11 Digest (Repl.) 468, *1011*.
Niboyet v. *Niboyet*, (1878), 4 P.D. 1; 48 L.J.P. 1; 39 L.T. 486; 43 J.P. 140;
    11 Digest (Repl.) 469, *1021*.   B
Pearson v. *Pearson and Menard*, [1951] 2 D.L.R. 851; [1951] O.L.R. 344;
    [1951] O.W.N. 353; 11 Digest (Repl.) 470, *527*.
Shaw v. *Gould*, (1868), L.R. 3 H.L. 55; 37 L.J.Ch. 433; 18 L.T. 833; 11
    Digest (Repl.) 481, *1081*.
Silver v. *Silver*, (1962), 106 Sol. Jo. 1012.
Wilson v. *Wilson*, (1872), L.R. 2 P. & D. 435; 41 L.J.P. & M. 74; 27 L.T. 351; C
    11 Digest (Repl.) 468, *1010*.

Petition.

This was a petition by the husband for a declaration that a decree of dissolution
of marriage made by royal decree of the Kingdom of Denmark on Feb. 15, 1963,
was valid. The facts are set out in the judgment.
                                                                                D
D. E. Roberts for the husband.
The wife did not appear and was not represented.

                                                               Cur adv. vult.

    Mar. 10. **CUMMING-BRUCE, J.:** This case raises for decision the
question whether the courts of England will recognise as valid the decree of a
foreign court granted at a time when the husband had abandoned the domicil E
which gave the foreign court jurisdiction at the time when those proceedings
were commenced.

    The facts are as follows. The husband was born in England in 1936. He was
brought up in England, and his domicil of origin was indisputably English.
In 1959, he visited Denmark on holiday. There he met Karen Margrethe
Kirchoff Hensen, a lady domiciled in Denmark. They agreed to marry. He F
was greatly taken with Denmark, and she was reluctant to leave Denmark.
He arranged to enter employment with a company which carried on business
in Denmark as well as England, and, after discussion with Miss Hensen, decided
to live permanently in Denmark. On June 25, 1960, they married in Denmark,
and thereafter cohabited in Copenhagen in an apartment which they rented
and furnished as the matrimonial home. Although he contemplated a future G
period of technical training in England, I am perfectly satisfied on the evidence
that he had then formed a settled intention to make Denmark his permanent
home, and became domiciled in Denmark. The marriage was not a success.
After a few months the wife consulted lawyers. In February, 1961, she left
and returned to her parents' home. On Mar. 15, 1961, the parties entered into
a separation agreement. In accordance with Danish law, which was the proper H
law, consent to the separation was given by the municipality of Copenhagen
on May 13, 1961, and the separation grant, to which was annexed the separation
agreement, was duly filed in the Danish court records. In August, 1961, the
husband's employers in Denmark posted the husband to England on a course
of training lasting eighteen months. They paid his expenses and salary, and
the common intention of the husband and his employers at that time was that I
he should return to Denmark when his training course was completed. His
intention was to resume his profession in Copenhagen as a resident engineer.
During his course of training in England he was twice paid supervisory visits
by senior executives of the Copenhagen department of the firm, and he retained
during this period his Danish domicil of choice.

    The court received, and accepted, evidence as to Danish matrimonial law
from an expert qualified in Danish law. By s. 52 of the Danish Marriage Act,
1922, spouses are enabled to obtain a legal separation by agreement if they are

A   unable, owing to irreconcilable differences, to cohabit. Section 54 provides
that, where spouses have been thus separated for one year and six months
without having resumed cohabitation, a divorce by royal decree shall be granted
to such spouses if they both want a decree.   The Danish court assumes jurisdiction to dissolve the marriage where, at the time of the grant of the separation,
both spouses were resident in Denmark, but the concept of residence is indis-
B   tinguishable, I am told, from the concept of domicil as recognised in these courts.
In October, 1962, the husband was still temporarily resident in England but
domiciled in Denmark.   He then received from the wife's Danish lawyer a
letter enclosing an application for divorce, initiated by the wife, which required
his signature.   He signed the application before the Danish consul as a person
wanting a decree, and returned the document to the wife's lawyer in Denmark
C   with the intention that it should be transmitted to the Danish court.   This
consensual application for divorce was duly made to the Danish court in December, 1962, or early January, 1963.   On Feb. 15, 1963, a royal decree was issued
in Denmark dissolving the marriage.   By Danish law the marriage was thereby
dissolved.   On Dec. 24, 1962, the husband had met a girl in England.   In
January, 1963, they were contemplating marriage as soon as he was free.   They
D   discussed their future together and decided to set up home together in England.
     The husband has given his evidence with the utmost candour, and, though it
was against his interest, has satisfied me that, by early February, 1963, but
before Feb. 15, 1963, he had finally decided to stay in England, sever his connexion with his Danish employers and thereafter make England his home.
From that moment his residence in England ceased to be merely a temporary
E   residence explained by his technical training in aid of Danish employment;
it was impressed with the permanent characteristic arising from his recent but
settled intention to make England his home.   He implemented this intention
by giving notice to his employers on Mar. 1, 1963, and left their employment at
the end of that month.   Since then he has lived in England.   Thanks to the
candour of the husband, I must find as a fact that he resumed his domicil of
F   origin after Feb. 1, 1963, and before Feb. 15, 1963.   So by his petition filed on
May 27, 1964, he alleges correctly that he is domiciled in England.   He also
alleges that the wife is domiciled in Denmark.   That is correct if by English
law the Danish decree of divorce is recognised as valid.   Provided that the
requirement of Danish domicil at the relevant time is satisfied, it is clear that
this court will accept the validity of the decree of dissolution issued by the Danish
G   court though the ground thereof was consensual separation.   This is now so
well established that it is unnecessary to cite authority.   So at the date of the
institution of the Danish proceedings for divorce the husband was still domiciled
in Denmark; by the date of the decree he was domiciled in England.   On these
facts it is necessary to decide whether the English courts should refuse to recognise the validity of the Danish Royal decree because the husband resumed his
H   English domicil during the brief interval which elapsed between the date of
institution of the proceedings and the date of the issue of the decree.
     There is no doubt that domicil in the country of the forum at the date of the
institution of proceedings is regarded by English law as necessary to found
jurisdiction but is it also sufficient to continue jurisdiction until termination
of the proceedings?   The editors of the eighth and ninth editions of RAYDEN ON
I   DIVORCE (1) submit that the critical date is date of decree, thereby joining issue
with PROFESSOR CHESHIRE, who robustly propounds the opposite view in his
treatise on PRIVATE INTERNATIONAL LAW (2).   In modern times there have
been a series of unequivocal judicial pronouncements that the conditions for
jurisdiction are satisfied by domicil at the date of institution of proceedings; see,
for example, *Silver* v. *Silver* (3), *Brownrigg* v. *Brownrigg* (4), in which SCARMAN,

---

(1) See 8th Edn., pp. 30, 811; 9th Edn., pp. 31, 858.   (2) See 7th Edn., p. 332.
(3) (1962), 106 Sol. Jo. 1012.   (4) (1963), 107 Sol. Jo. 176.

J., expressly stated that the critical time for the purpose was the date of in A
stitution of proceedings, and not the date of the foreign decree, *Henderson*
v. *Henderson* (5), *Garrow* v. *Garrow* (6), in the Court of Appeal.

These observations are consistent with the observations in the older cases.
In *Shaw* v. *Gould* (7), the headnote to which is misleading, LORD WESTBURY
stated that jurisdiction was founded on domicil before and at the time of the
suit.   In *Wilson* v. *Wilson* (8), LORD PENZANCE said: B

" Now, it is not disputed that if the petitioner was domiciled in England at
the time the suit was commenced this court has jurisdiction . . . It is the
strong inclination of my own opinion that the only fair and satisfactory
rule to adopt on this matter of jurisdiction is to insist upon the parties in
all cases referring their matrimonial differences to the courts of the country
in which they are domiciled.   Different communities have different views   C
and laws respecting matrimonial obligations, and a different estimate of the
causes which should justify divorce.   It is both just and reasonable, therefore, that the differences of married people should be adjusted in accordance
with the laws of the community to which they belong, and dealt with by
the tribunals which alone can administer those laws."

In 1878, there was *Niboyet* v. *Niboyet* (9), to which I advert below.   In 1892, D
in *Goulder* v. *Goulder* (10), LOPES, L.J., accepted the requirement of domicil
at the commencement of proceedings.   In *Le Mesurier* v. *Le Mesurier* (11), the
Judicial Committee concurred without reservation with the statement of LORD
PENZANCE that I have quoted from *Wilson* v. *Wilson* (12).

In none of these cases, however, was the court considering a change of domicil E
after institution of suit.   The problem has, however, frequently arisen for
decision elsewhere in the Commonwealth.   In South Africa there is *Balfour* v.
Balfour (13).   There the court held that proceedings instituted in the forum
of domicil at the time may be continued although there has been a subsequent
change of domicil.   The learned judge held that, once domicil at the initiation
of the proceedings was established, the court has jurisdiction to deal with the F
matter until the final end thereof.   In Canada, in *Pearson* v. *Pearson and Menard*
(14), the Ontario High Court took the same view where the husband had changed
his domicil between the decree nisi and the decree absolute.   In Australia there
have been a number of cases.   In *Gane* v. *Gane* (15) the learned judge accepted
the view taken in South Africa and Canada, but apparently he was not followed
on appeal by the Full Court of Victoria; see *Flakemore* v. *Flakemore* (16).

A formidable criticism of these decisions has been given in the decision of G
EDWARDS, J., in *Kerrison* v. *Kerrison* (17).   After reviewing a number of cases,
including many of those which I have cited, and in particular the decision in
Gane v. *Gane* (15), the judge stated:

" In my opinion it is quite clear in principle that wherever possible courts
should attempt to give effect to the doctrine that the court of the domicil H
shall be the one and only court with power to dissolve a marriage and should
narrowly construe statutory modifications of this principle which has been
recognised by the common law and international law alike.   In such a case
there can be no doubt that the court of jurisdiction is the court of the domicil
at the time of the decree affecting the status, not of any court of some past
and abandoned domicil.   If a change of domicil is to have any meaning it   I

(5) [1965] 1 All E.R. 179.   (6) (1965), " The Times ", June 30.
(7) (1868), L.R. 3 H.L. 55 at p. 85.
(8) (1872), L.R. 2 P. & D. 435 at pp. 441, 442.   (9) (1878), 4 P.D. 1.
(10) [1892] P. 240 at p. 243.
(11) [1895-99] All E.R. Rep. 836 at p. 847; [1895] A.C. 517 at p. 540.
(12) (1872), L.R. 2 P. & D. at p. 442.
(13) [1922] W.L.D. 133.   (14) [1951] 2 D.L.R. 851.
(15) (1941), 58 W.N. (N.S.W.) 83.   (16) [1942] V.L.R. 156.
(17) (1952), 69 W.N. (N.S.W.) 305 at p. 308.

A   must mean that the person concerned has become subject to the laws and institutions of his new domicil and entitled to its privileges; conversely he must be taken to have dissociated himself from his previous domicil and his obligations and privileges thereunder. To hold that a man may retain the privileges of both his past and present domicil is to destroy the meaning and effects of the legal doctrine of domicil."

B   I respectfully recognise the persuasive force of this reasoning, but I do not accept its application to the case before me for the following reasons. I have been impressed by the approach of BRETT, L.J., in *Niboyet* v. *Niboyet* (18), and in particular by observations in his judgment (19), which I find it unnecessary to quote verbatim. He expressed his conclusions in these words (20):

C   " From all these considerations it seems that the only court, which on principle ought to entertain the question of altering the relation in any respect between parties admitted to be married . . . is a court of the country in which they are domiciled at the time of the institution of the suit."

Though this was a dissenting judgment, the view of the majority was disapproved by the Privy Council in *Le Mesurier* v. *Le Mesurier* (21) and BRETT, L.J.'s

D   views are consistent with the advice of the Privy Council in that case.

One of the features of the instant case is that the husband was himself a party to the reference of his status to the Danish court. I am unable to see why he should be taken to have dissociated himself from the determination of his status by the very court in which he was still proceeding merely because, during the pendency of that suit, he changed his domicil. On that narrow

E   ground I could rest my decision in this case; but the concept of domicil has been made the test of jurisdiction as a matter of convenience and comity. Where the matrimonial status has been referred to the court of domicil at the date of institution of proceedings, I can see no ground, in convenience or comity, in raising, or applying, a presumption that, by subsequent change of domicil, either party had dissociated himself from the final determination of those

F   proceedings and the result thereof. In my respectful opinion, EDWARDS, J. (22), was led by the logic which explains the selection of domicil as the test of jurisdiction to a conclusion which (a) gives rise to a serious inconvenience in the administration of private international law, and (b) is liable to lead to injustice, as BRETT, L.J., indicated in his judgment in *Niboyet* v. *Niboyet* (23).

For these reasons, I hold that domicil at the date of institution of proceedings

G   is not only necessary but also sufficient to found jurisdiction at date of decree, and the husband is entitled to the declaration for which he asks.

Declaration accordingly.

Solicitors: *Sydney Mitchell & Co.*, Birmingham (for the husband).

[*Reported by* ALICE BLOOMFIELD, *Barrister-at-Law.*]

H

I

---

(18) (1878), 4 P.D. 1.   (19) (1878), 4 P.D. at pp. 13, 14, 15.
(20) (1878), 4 P.D. at pp. 13, 14.
(21) [1895-99] All E.R. Rep. at p. 842; [1895] A.C. at p. 531.
(22) (1952), 69 W.N. (N.S.W.) at p. 308.   (23) (1878), 4 P.D. at p. 14.

SANSOM *v.* SANSOM.   A

[PROBATE, DIVORCE AND ADMIRALTY DIVISION (Sir Jocelyn Simon, P.), March 25,
1966.]

*Divorce — Judicial separation — Permanent alimony — Variation — Appeal —
Onus—Factors—Whether past domestic infelicity may be taken into account
as precluding wife sharing in subsequent increase in earnings—Whether* B
*wife's extravagance or thrift a factor—Whether registrar entitled to take into
consideration as against wife that she had taken proceedings for judicial
separation rather than divorce.*

In so far as questions of onus of proof arise on an appeal against an order
of the registrar granting permanent alimony to the wife after judicial
separation, the onus lies on the appellant to show that the registrar was   C
wrong (see p. 398, letter F, post).

Stibbe v. *Stibbe* ([1931] P. 105) applied.

On a claim by the wife for permanent alimony after judicial separation, the
fact that the wife has taken proceedings for judicial separation rather than
divorce should not be taken into consideration against her (see p. 400,
letter C, post).   D

Dictum of HODSON, L.J., in *Pigott* v. *Pigott* (Oct. 17, 1957, unreported
on this point) followed.

The parties were married in 1936, and separated in 1945 or 1946. The
wife then started proceedings for divorce on the ground of the husband's
adultery but finally changed her petition to one for judicial separation,
and a decree of judicial separation was granted to her in 1947. The husband   E
did not defend the proceedings in any way. The wife then applied for
permanent alimony. In 1947 the husband was earning £900 a year. A
series of consent orders was made which reflected the husband's increase in
emoluments over the years. In 1961, an agreed order was made that the
husband should pay the wife permanent alimony at the rate of £1,150 a
year. The registrar varied that order in 1966 to £1,900 a year. The wife   F
had an income from investments of £53, and a figure of £100 was ascribed
as a notional figure in respect of her accommodation. The husband's income
averaged £7,155 gross* over three years. He had an annual surtax liability
of £250 and a " Tophat " insurance policy for £3,000 payable at age sixty-five,
for which £250 a year was deducted from his gross salary and he paid £150
annually by way of superannuation contribution. He had prospective   G
school fees of £250. On appeal by the husband, he contended, inter alia,
that it would be inequitable for the wife to get the benefit of the increase
in emoluments which he had enjoyed since the marriage broke up and that,
irrespective of figures, as the wife not only had managed to live on £1,150
a year but also had been able to make savings on it, she had no need of any
increase.   H

Held: the court would not interfere with the registrar's order, both for
the reasons set out at letters B and C, supra, and because—

(i) no relevant inference could be drawn from the fact that the large
increase in the husband's income came after he left his wife, though, if
it were proved that a husband's increase in emoluments was due to the
domestic, social or business gifts of his mistress, that might be a matter   I
to be taken into account (see p. 400, letters E and G, post);

(ii) it was no concern of the court or of the husband how the wife laid out
her money; and, just as a wife's extravagance in living beyond her allotment
could not be a reason for increasing it, so also her thrift in living within
it was no ground for limiting her allotment (see p. 400, letter I, to p. 401,
letter A, post).

---

* The deductions allowed by the court are summarised at p. 402, letter I, to p. 403,
letter A, post; they result in a net figure of £6,255 p.a.

A   *Dean* v. *Dean* ([1923] P. 172) and *Pigott* v. *Pigott* (Oct. 18, 1957, unreported on this point), followed.

Appeal dismissed.

[As to the proportion allotted on grant of permanent alimony, see 12 Hals-bury's Laws (3rd Edn.) 429, 430, para. 963; and for cases on the subject, see 27 Digest (Repl.) 604-606, *5648-5679*.]

B
Cooper v. *Cooper*, [1936] 2 All E.R. 542; 27 Digest (Repl.) 540, *4886*.

Dean v. *Dean*, [1923] P. 172; 92 L.J.P. 109; 129 L.T. 704; 27 Digest (Repl.) 603, *5639*.

Evans v. *Bartlam*, [1937] 2 All E.R. 646; [1937] A.C. 473; 106 L.J.K.B. 568; sub nom. *Bartlam* v. *Evans*, 157 L.T. 311; Digest Supp.

C
Kershaw v. *Kershaw*, [1964] 3 All E.R. 635; [1964] 3 W.L.R. 1143; 128 J.P. 589; 3rd Digest Supp.

Leslie v. *Leslie*, [1911] P. 203; 80 L.J.P. 139; sub nom. *L.* v. *L.*, 104 L.T. 462; 27 Digest (Repl.) 603, *5646*.

Otway v. *Otway*, (1813), 2 Phillim. 109; 161 E.R. 1092; 27 Digest (Repl.) 604, *5648*.

D
Pigott v. *Pigott*, [1957] 3 All E.R. 432; [1958] P. 1; [1957] 3 W.L.R. 781; " The Times ", Oct. 17, 18, 1957; Digest (Cont. Vol. A) 677, *636o*.

Stibbe v. *Stibbe*, [1931] P. 105; 100 L.J.P. 82; 144 L.T. 742; 27 Digest (Repl.) 623, *5820*.

Appeal.

This was an appeal by the husband from an order of Mr. Registrar Caird, E   dated Feb. 22, 1966, varying a previous order for permanent alimony, and ordering the husband to pay to the wife the sum of £1,900 a year, as from Jan. 1, 1966. The facts are stated in the judgment, which was delivered in open court.

J. P. Harris for the husband.
M. H. Potter for the wife.

Cur. adv. vult.

F
Mar. 25.   **SIR JOCELYN SIMON, P.,** read the following judgment: This is an appeal from an order of Mr. Registrar Caird, dated Feb. 22, 1966, in which he varied a previous order for permanent alimony, now ordering the husband to pay to the wife £1,900 a year by way of permanent alimony as from Jan. 1, 1966. The appeal has been well argued in chambers; but I have adjourned G   it into open court for judgment, as it raises some issues on which there is little guidance from authority.

An outline of the history of the matter is as follows. The marriage was in 1936. There is one child of the marriage, a daughter, who married in 1962 at the age of eighteen: the husband has paid nothing in respect of her since then, but she and her husband live with the petitioner, her mother. The parties separated in H   1945 or 1946; and the wife then started proceedings for divorce on the ground of the husband's adultery. The husband says that the marriage was never happy and that at one time he contemplated divorce proceedings against his wife on the ground of cruelty; but he never initiated any such proceedings nor raised any allegations and, indeed, he provided the evidence that he was living with the woman named on which the wife could obtain relief. The wife finally changed her I   petition to one for judicial separation; the husband says that this was at the hearing itself; the wife denies that and says (though this is not on affidavit) that the husband was notified well before the trial that such was her intention. In my view, it is immaterial, even were it desirable, to attempt to resolve this difference after the long lapse of time. In any event, the upshot was that the wife, on June 19, 1947, obtained a judicial separation on the ground of the husband's adultery. The husband did not defend the proceedings in any way. The wife then made application for permanent alimony. She seems to have acquired shares in the company (formerly private, now public) by which the

husband was and is employed and of which he is now a director. I was told that **A**
she attended company meetings and obtained information as to her husband's
emoluments; the husband was inclined to make a grievance of this, but I cannot
see it as such—at any rate as a matter which ought in any way to influence the
outcome of this appeal. In the event, a series of consent orders for alimony were
carried in to the registrar which reflected the husband's increase in emoluments
over the years. The last such was on Jan. 4, 1961, when an agreed order was made **B**
that the husband should pay the wife permanent alimony at the rate of £1,150
a year. This was the order which the learned registrar varied in the way which
I have described.

Before I come to examine the figures in detail there are five preliminary
matters with which I ought to deal. (i) What weight should the decision of the
registrar have with me; and on whom, in consequence, does the onus of proof **C**
rest on this appeal? In *Cooper* v. *Cooper* (1) and *Evans* v. *Bartlam* (2), it was laid
down that, where a jurisdiction is given to the court or a judge, the discretion is
that of the judge in chambers, the decision being no more than initially delegated
to master or registrar. By the Matrimonial Causes Act 1965, s. 20 (1) (replacing
the Matrimonial Causes Act, 1950, s. 20 (2)),

" On granting a decree of judicial separation or at any time thereafter **D**
the court may make such order as it thinks just for the payment of alimony ..."

(my emphasis). On this basis it was argued on behalf of the husband that the
onus rested on the wife as applicant. The Matrimonial Causes Rules, 1957,
r. 45, r. 47 and r. 51, provide, however, for the preliminary investigation by the
registrar of applications for permanent alimony or for variation of an existing
order, and r. 61 provides for appeals on such matters to the judge in chambers. **E**
(These rules replace the Matrimonial Causes Rules, 1924: see *Stibbe* v. *Stibbe* (3).)
In that case, the Court of Appeal laid down that, if the judge on the hearing of an
appeal comes to the conclusion that the direction of the registrar was wrong and
ought not to have been made, he can recall the order issued in pursuance of such
direction and make such order as in his judgment he deems just, though he should
give due weight to the decision of the registrar and be slow to disturb that **F**
decision on a mere question of quantum. That was a decision on maintenance
after divorce; but, in my judgment, it is equally applicable to permanent alimony
after judicial separation. It follows, in my view, that, in so far as questions of
onus arise in such proceedings (and they might here, in view of some lacunae in the
evidence), the onus lies on the appellant to show that the registrar was wrong.
One reason for giving weight to the decision of the registrar, and particular weight **G**
on matters merely of quantum, is that the registrars see many more of these
cases than do the judges, and no doubt tend to develop a sort of sixth sense in
dealing with them. Moreover, any other rule would be to invite invariable appeals
from the registrars' decisions, very frequently at public expense.

(ii) How far is the so-called " one-third rule " applicable? It was the general **H**
practice of the ecclesiastical courts in assessing alimony after a divorce a mensa et
thoro to award the wife one-third of the husband's income. But this was not an
absolute rule: see for example *Otway* v. *Otway* (4); *Leslie* v. *Leslie* (5); *Dean* v.
Dean (6); the considerations laid down in s. 32 of the Matrimonial Causes Act,
1857, in relation to maintenance after divorce were, in my view, declaratory of
the practice of the ecclesiastical courts in their jurisdiction in alimony as to what **I**
was a reasonable amount, having regard to the ability of the husband and the conduct of the parties. In *Kershaw* v. *Kershaw* (7), I tried to state the underlying
principles, which, in my view, are applicable to permanent alimony as well as to
maintenance under the Matrimonial Proceedings (Magistrates' Courts) Act, 1960.
In *Stibbe* v. *Stibbe* (8), LORD HANWORTH, M.R., described the " rule of one-third "

(1) [1936] 3 All E.R. 542.   (2) [1937] 2 All E.R. 646; [1937] A.C. 473.
(3) [1931] P. 105.   (4) (1813), 2 Phillim. 109.
(5) [1911] P. 203.   (6) [1923] P. 172.
(7) [1964] 3 All E.R. 635, at pp. 636, 637.   (8) [1931] P. at p. 110.

A as " a sound working rule . . ., yet . . . not an absolute rule ", and again as " a guide ". The reason why the " rule of one-third " so often worked out soundly and fairly was because in a typical case the court was concerned with three groups of needs—those of the wife, those of the husband and those of children for whose support the husband was liable; again, after divorce a respondent husband will sometimes have remarried and thus have undertaken obligations to another

B woman and possibly their children (though I am not intending to say that the claims of this group are in all circumstances entitled to rank with, much less before, the claims of a wife petitioner for divorce and the children of the marriage). In the present case, counsel are agreed, the registrar, although making a calculation on the one-third basis, did not apply it strictly, but in fact awarded the wife somewhat less than that calculation indicated. I do not think that the learned

C registrar can be in any way criticised in his approach on this matter.

(iii) Next, it is claimed by counsel on behalf of the husband that the wife, in procuring a judicial separation from her husband rather than a divorce, had acted maliciously and has forced him, contrary to his inclination, to live in adultery with the woman named for twenty years and to father an illegitimate child by her. The court is bound to consider the conduct of the wife no less than that of the

D husband (see *Leslie* v. *Leslie* (9); *Dean* v. *Dean* (10)); and the foregoing was said to be misconduct on the part of the wife which should be taken into account against her and be reflected in a diminution of the alimony to which she might otherwise have been entitled. I cannot accede to that argument. In the first place, by a re-enactment as recently as 1965 (see s. 12 of the Matrimonial Causes Act 1965), Parliament has left it entirely open to a wronged wife to seek either

E a judicial separation or a divorce; she will suffer some financial detriment by choosing a judicial separation, in that she cannot get maintenance secured for her whole life, as she can after divorce under s. 16 (1) (*a*) of the Matrimonial Causes Act 1965; but, in my view, it is not for the courts to impose further financial penalties if a wife chooses one course rather than the other. Secondly, although it does not appear from the evidence that the wife has any religious objection to

F divorce, there are other reasons beside spite which might have impelled her to prefer a judicial separation—she had a young child and was possibly hoping that, if the husband were not tied to the woman named, he might in time tire of the latter and return to his original family. Thirdly, it is, in my view, Humpty-Dumpty language to speak of the wife having " forced " the husband to live in adultery. Fourthly, there is, in any event, authority which precludes me from

G acceding to the husband's argument. In *Pigott* v. *Pigott* (11), heard by the Court of Appeal on Oct. 16, 17, 1957, the parties had lived apart for some seventeen years. The husband had deserted the wife and had in addition committed adultery; but the wife, a Roman Catholic, had refused to divorce him and instead instituted proceedings for maintenance. The learned commissioner who tried the case criticised the wife's conduct, and made a small order only in her favour, which

H was moreover unsecured. He said (12):

"It does not seem to me to be right in the circumstances where quite clearly the marriage has broken down, that a situation should be kept in fact so that children who will be born will be illegitimate."

" But what business is that of the court? " asked Hodson, L.J. (12). According

I to the transcript of his judgment of Oct. 17, 1957, Hodson, L.J., said that, although the sum to be awarded by way of maintenance was a matter at the discretion of the commissioner, the latter had allowed himself to be influenced by matters which ought not to have affected his mind:

"The wife had not taken advantage either of the husband's desertion of her or of the adultery of her husband when it became known to her in

---

(9) [1911] P. at p. 206.   (10) [1923] P. at p. 179.
(11) [1957] 3 All E.R. 432; [1958] P. 1.   (12) (1957), " The Times ", Oct. 17.

1955. It was not a relevant consideration in deciding the amount of   A maintenance to be allotted to her."

MORRIS, L.J., said:

" The wife could have adopted a different course altogether and could, had she been so minded, have taken proceedings to obtain a divorce . . . The consideration . . . was not one which should have affected the mind of the   B court."

SELLERS, L.J., agreed. (I have quoted from the transcript of the judgments, which differs, though immaterially, from the report in " The Times " newspaper of Oct. 18, 1957; the case is reported (13) elsewhere on another point.) These observations are as relevant to alimony after judicial separation, as to maintenance after wilful neglect to maintain.   C

In view of the foregoing, I think that the registrar in this case was quite right to refuse to take into consideration as against the wife the fact that she had taken proceedings for judicial separation rather than divorce.

(iv) Next, it was argued on behalf of the husband by way of preliminary point that it would be inequitable to allow the wife to get the benefit of the increase in emoluments which the husband has enjoyed since the marriage broke up; at   D that time he was a mere buyer for his firm, earning (his counsel told me) some £900 a year, and he would be unlikely to have achieved his present lucrative post of executive director, the fees of which together with salary and commission amount to over £7,000 a year, if he had continued in the unhappy domestic atmosphere of his life with the petitioner. " Had I continued to live with the [wife] ", he avers, " my income would have been very much less than I earn today. "   E As to this, however, first, I do not think that any relevant inference can be drawn from the fact that the large increase in the husband's income came after he left his wife; quite apart from the general contemporary increase in salaries, it was at that age and point in career that I should have expected a breakthrough, if one was to come at all. Secondly, the husband did not raise until these proceedings (over twenty years after the events) any allegation against his wife;   F and now—not surprisingly—he puts forward the merest generalities. Even if the marriage was unhappy, it would be most unjust to penalise the wife without any misconduct being proved against her to which the unhappiness could be ascribed. Thirdly, I am far from persuaded that domestic infelicity necessarily precludes worldly success—it may even rather stimulate it; after all, Socrates achieved considerable influence, Xanthippe notwithstanding; Louis VII of France and   G Henry II of England each made a mark on their age, though they were married in succession to Eleanor of Aquitaine; the turmoil of Lord Coke's second marriage was a public scandal; and Doctor Proudie achieved the bishopric of Barchester. But it is unnecessary to multiply instances. If it were clearly proved that a husband's increase in emolument was due to the domestic, social or business gifts of his mistress or second wife, that might well be a matter to be taken into   H account; but I am certainly not prepared to accept the interested ipse dixit of the husband in this case, unsupported as it is even by any evidence from his employers.

(v) The husband finally argues, on the case generally irrespective of figures of income, that the wife has not only managed to live on the £1,150 a year which she has been enjoying by way of permanent alimony, but has actually been able to   I make savings from it reflected in the purchase of a car and some securities. This shows, it is argued, that she does not need an increase in permanent alimony: why then should she be awarded it at the expense of her husband, who does need the money? Here again, both principle and authority are against the husband's contention. First, it is no business of the court or the husband (now that cohabitation has been disrupted through his own misconduct) how the wife lays out

(13) [1957] 3 All E.R. 432; [1958] P. 1.

A   her money, and in particular what proportions she devotes to current consumption and provision for the future respectively. Secondly, a wife's extravagance in living beyond her allotment could hardly be a reason for increasing her alimony; why, then, should her thrift in living within her allotment be a ground for limiting it? Thirdly, in any event, a similar argument was addressed to the Court of Appeal in *Dean* v. *Dean* (14) and *Pigott* v. *Pigott* (15) and there rejected.

B   I, therefore, cannot find any particular circumstances in this case which should have the effect of reducing as against the wife the amount of alimony which is otherwise suggested as just and fair in all the circumstances having regard to the ability of the husband.

I turn then to consider the detailed figures of income and the adjustments that have been claimed on either side should be made to them. The wife has an
C   income from investments of £53 a year. The husband is paid a salary, commission and director's fees by the company by which he is employed. Together, these have averaged at £7,155 a year over the last three years. However, the income has been a rising one, amounting to £7,728 in 1965; but the husband claims in his affidavit that his income in the current year will be some £500 to £750 less. I, therefore, think that the fair figure to assess as his gross income for alimony
D   purposes is the average which I have taken, namely £7,155.

It is, however, claimed that these figures require adjustment in a number of respects; and I now turn to consider these arguments: (a) *Accommodation*. The wife lives in a house at Headington, Oxford, the freehold of which she owns. She values it at £3,000. The husband bought the house in which he lives in Southgate in 1954; he does not say how much he gave for it, though there is still £3,450
E   outstanding on the mortgage. In 1961 he transferred the house to the woman named by way of gift, subject to the mortgage, the payments on which the husband continues to discharge. He lives there rent-free, of course. He avers that the maintenance of the house and the mortgage payments and the interest on the mortgage loan amount to £370 a year. His house is rated at £98, as against the wife's at £55. The husband claims that it is unreasonable for the wife to allow her
F   daughter and son-in-law to live rent free in her house; she should either let the accommodation to someone who can pay her rent or should at least charge her son-in-law rent. The husband claims that, taking this factor into account, the wife's occupation of her house should be ascribed a notional value of £500 a year; whereas to his own accommodation should be ascribed only £250 a year. Counsel tell me that the registrar so far acceded to this argument as to ascribe to the
G   wife £100 a year notional income, otherwise disregarding the accommodation on each side. If anything, this is, in my view, unduly favourable to the husband. If the marriage had subsisted, it would not be unreasonable to have expected the husband and wife to allow their daughter and her newly married husband to live rent-free in their house for a few years after the marriage; nor would they, in the husband's present circumstances, have contemplated taking lodgers.
H   Moreover, the fact remains that the husband is living in more expensive accommodation than the wife; and, though it can be said that he has the moral obligation to discharge the outgoings on that house in order to provide accommodation for the woman named and their child, to take that into account *before* performing a one-third computation would be in effect compelling the wife to contribute out of her alimony towards the accommodation of the woman named and her
I   child.

(b) *The Car*. The husband receives an allowance of £78 a year from his employers towards the cost of running a motor car; but, he says, "this by no means covers the expenses which I have to incur in running a car". He claims to deduct from his income before it is assessed for alimony purposes an additional £477 a year, including £300 depreciation. He produces no income tax assessments to show how the Inland Revenue treat the car expenses. It is true that the test which the

---

(14) [1923] P. 172.   (15) (Oct. 17, 1957), unreported on this point.

Inland Revenue would impose on the husband is not the same as of the Divorce   A
Court—the Inland Revenue would have to be satisfied that he was necessarily
obliged to incur the amount of car expenses he claimed in travelling in the
performance of his duties (see Income Tax Act, 1952, Sch. 9, r. 7; see also s. 160
and s. 161), whereas the Divorce Court asks whether the expenses were reasonably
incurred for such purpose.   I would certainly not be prepared to act on the
husband's unsupported statement; but, in any case, he makes no claim as to what,   B
if any, part of the expenses of running the car over and above the £78 allowed by
his company is incurred for business purposes, in contradistinction to personal
pleasure.   In the absence of such information, I do not think that any part of this
sum is properly deductible.

(c) *Surtax.*   The husband claims that there is a contingent liability to the Inland
Revenue for surtax amounting approximately to £2,000.   On the other hand, he   C
has some £8,500 invested with building societies, £500 on deposit at the bank,
nearly £400 on current account and 470 National Savings Certificates, to none
of which he ascribes any income.   In these circumstances, the surtax liability
of £2,000 can be left out of account.   On the other hand, I am told that he has an
annual surtax liability of some £250 a year; and, in my view, this is properly
deductible before assessing alimony.   D

(d) *Insurances.*   The husband has a " Tophat " policy for £3,000 payable at
sixty-five, and £250 a year is deducted from his gross salary in respect of this.
This is conceded by the wife as an allowable deduction.   If it had been contested,
some difficult questions might arise to determine how far is it to be considered as
enuring in any way to the benefit of the wife, so that she is to be compelled in
effect to contribute towards it out of her alimony.   The wife's rights under the   E
Inheritance (Family Provision) Act, 1938, would have to be considered, on the
one hand; and, on the other, the likelihood of this sum passing at all into the
husband's estate.   However, the wife's concession relieves me of the necessity of
trying to weigh these imponderables.   In addition, the husband pays £150 annually
by way of superannuation contribution.   This is clearly deductible before any
alimony computation, since the wife will be entitled, by way of alimony, to   F
share in any superannuation benefit.

(e) *Covenant in favour of woman named.*   In 1961, the husband covenanted by
deed to provide the woman named with a tax free sum of £500 a year for eight
years.   I am told that this corresponds to a sum £670 a year gross, at the current
rate of tax to which the husband is subject; though there are no doubt some tax
advantages in this arrangement.   If a one-third computation is to be made as a   G
" sound working basis ", none of these sums is deductible; otherwise it would
be, in effect, requiring the wife to contribute out of her alimony towards the
covenant in favour of the woman named.

(f) *School Fees.*   The husband is at present paying school fees for his daughter
by the woman named at the rate of £120 a year; but she is shortly going to
change her school and he estimates that the cost will then be £250 a year   H
for " school fees, lunches and other extras ".   Again some difficult questions
might arise were this deduction to be contested, but it is conceded; though I am
asked to bear in mind that this is a man who requires an expensive private
education for his daughter and to aliment the wife accordingly.

The husband also sets out expenses by way of clothing and holidays.   Although
the court must always consider whether sufficient is left to a husband for necessary   I
or reasonable expenses, I do not think that, in the present case, these matters
fall for assessment at this stage.

My final computation is, therefore, as follows: Wife's income from investments £53; benefit of superior accommodation as allowed by registrar, but
query, £100: giving her an income at most of £153.   Husband's income: gross
average over three years £7,155, less surtax annually £250, tophat insurances
and superannuation £250 and £150, prospective school fees, etc., £250, giving

A   a reduction of £900 in all. This leaves a sum of £6,255 as the husband's income for alimony purposes.

    In these circumstances, I can see no reason to disagree with the order of the registrar and I dismiss the appeal.

Appeal dismissed.

B   Solicitors: *R. C. Bartlett & Co.* (for the husband); *Trower, Still & Keeling*, agents for *Thomas Mallam, Grimsdale & Co.*, Oxford (for the wife).

[*Reported by* Alice Bloomfield, *Barrister-at-Law.*]

C

Re ST. JOHN'S CHURCH, BISHOP'S HATFIELD.

[St. Alban's Consistory Court (Chancellor G. H. Newsom, Q.C.), May 24, June 24, 1965.]

Ecclesiastical Law—Faculty—Jurisdiction—" Curtilage "—Unconsecrated yard
D   *surrounding church—Whether curtilage of church—Whether faculty for use as a youth centre, a non-ecclesiastical purpose, would be granted—Appropriate form of relief and time for application—Faculty Jurisdiction Measure 1964 (No. 5), s. 7.*

  For land to be curtilage of a church, both the land and the church must be occupied together, must belong together in a physical sense and their titles must not be such as to conflict with their belonging together (see
E   p. 406, letter A, post).

  Pilbrow v. *St. Leonard, Shoreditch, Vestry* ([1895] 1 Q.B. 433), and *Harris* v. *Scurfield* ((1904), 91 L.T. 536) considered.

  By a conveyance dated Mar. 24, 1960, land comprising a church building with a surrounding yard was conveyed to the Church Commissioners to be devoted when consecrated to ecclesiastical purposes for ever. On Mar. 26,
F   1960, the church was consecrated, whereupon it and the yard became vested in the incumbent. A faculty was sought by the incumbent and the church-wardens for a building to be erected, joined to the church, and used for ecclesiastical purposes only, which building would link with another also to be erected on the yard for use as an interdenominational youth centre, which centre would be leased to special trustees for at least twenty-eight
G   years and would be used for non-ecclesiastical purposes. The " link " building and the youth centre were to be vested in the Diocesan Board of Finance on trust for the parochial church council. The erecting of the buildings had been approved by interlocutory direction.

  Held: the unconsecrated yard was curtilage of the church, since it was within the requirements stated at letter D, supra, and thus was within the
H   jurisdiction of the court by virtue of s. 7* of the Faculty Jurisdiction Measure 1964; and on the facts a confirmatory faculty approving the erection of the buildings would be granted (see p. 406, letters B and F, post).

  Observations on the form of petition where buildings on land within the jurisdiction of the court and conveyance of the land with the consequence of terminating the jurisdiction of the court is sought (see p. 406, letter I,
I   to p. 407, letter A, post).

  [As to the meaning of curtilage, see 10 Halsbury's Laws (3rd Edn.) 805, para. 1558, note (g); and for cases on the subject, see 41 Digest (Repl.) 3, 7, 12, *83*, *84*.

---

  * Section 7, so far as material, provides: " (1) For the avoidance of doubt it is hereby declared that where unconsecrated land forms, or is part of, the curtilage of a church within the jurisdiction of a court that court has the same jurisdiction over such land as over the church."

Considered in Re St Peter's [1971] 2 All ER 704

Followed in Re Christ Church [1974] 1 All ER 146

Doubted in Re St George's Church, Oakdale [1975] 2 All ER 870

As to petitions for a faculty, see 13 HALSBURY'S LAWS (3rd Edn.) 515, 516, **A**
para. 1107.

For the New Parishes Measure, 1943, s. 17, as originally passed, see 7 HALS-
BURY'S STATUTES (2nd Edn.) 168, and as substituted by the Church Property
(Miscellaneous Provisions) Measure, 1960, s. 6, see 40 ibid., p. 274.

For the Parochial Church Councils (Powers) Measure, 1956, s. 5, see 36 HALS-
BURY'S STATUTES (2nd Edn.) 312; and for the Faculty Jurisdiction Measure 1964, **B**
s. 7, see 44 ibid., p. 231.]

Cases referred to:

Harris v. Scurfield, (1904), 91 L.T. 536; 68 J.P. 516; 41 Digest (Repl.) 3, 7.
Pilbrow v. St. Leonard, Shoreditch, Vestry, [1895] 1 Q.B. 433; 64 L.J.M.C. 130;
    72 L.T. 135; 59 J.P. 68; 41 Digest (Repl.) 12, 83.
Plumstead District Board of Works v. Ecclesiastical Comrs. for England, [1891] **C**
    2 Q.B. 361; 64 L.T. 830; 55 J.P. 791; 26 Digest (Repl.) 557, 2258.

Petition for faculty.

On Mar. 24, 1960, an area of land in Hatfield was conveyed by the St. Albans
Diocesan Board of Finance to the Church Commissioners for England as the
site for the Church of St. John, South Hatfield, " with the surrounding yard **D**
and enclosure thereto to be devoted when consecrated to ecclesiastical purposes
for ever ". At the date of the conveyance there was on the land a church
building completed but not yet consecrated. On Mar. 26, 1960, the church
was consecrated by the Bishop of St. Albans, and thereupon it, and the yard,
which remained unconsecrated, vested in the incumbent.

Hatfield, which before the war was a relatively small country town, had since **E**
become the centre of a new town and its population, in particular children and
young persons, was increasing fast. In these circumstances great problems
faced the Hatfield church authorities, and in 1964 or 1965 the parochial church
council decided that there ought to be a youth centre for South Hatfield and
that the most practical and economical place for it would be the yard. Plans
were prepared by the architect in charge of the building of the church for the **F**
erection on the yard of a youth centre and a " link " to the church. The link
was to be a building physically joining the church to the youth centre and consisting of rooms to be used by the incumbent and the parochial church council
for purely ecclesiastical purposes.

In order that those responsible for the youth centre might obtain grants
from the department of Education and Science under the Physical Training and **G**
Recreation Act, 1937, and from other public bodies, it was necessary that the
youth centre should be vested for a term of at least twenty-eight years in special
trustees who would ensure that during that term the department's requirements
were provided for. Since the department required that the youth centre should
be interdenominational, the trusts on which the trustees were to hold it could
not be the existing ecclesiastical trusts. Accordingly, the incumbent intended, **H**
under the authority of the New Parishes Measures Act, 1943, s. 17, as substituted,
to convey the site of the proposed youth centre back to the St. Albans Diocesan
Board of Finance on trust for the parochial church council. The board, with the
council's approval, would in due course grant a lease, under the authority of the
Parochial Church Councils (Powers) Measure, 1956, s. 5, for twenty-eight years at
a nominal rent to a body of special trustees who would hold on trusts acceptable **I**
to the department. The incumbent intended to convey the link, under the
authority of s. 17 of the Act of 1943, to the board to hold on trust for the council.
The link would in effect be land of the council which was in hand.

By a petition dated June 7, 1964, the incumbent and churchwardens sought
authority for the appropriation of part of the yard to the board to hold in trust
for the council " for a church youth centre with a link to the church " and for
the holding of such land for the purposes of the youth centre and link and for
the centre to be leased to the proposed body of trustees. At the hearing the

A petition was amended, with leave, so as to seek a faculty and a confirmatory faculty for the building works and approval for the proposed lease of the youth centre. The petition was unopposed.

W. S. Wigglesworth for the petitioners.

Cur. adv. vult.

B June 24. **THE CHANCELLOR:** On Mar. 24, 1960, an area of land at Hatfield was conveyed by the St. Albans Diocesan Board of Finance to the Church Commissioners for England

" as the site of and for a church to be called the Church of St. John, South Hatfield . . . with the surrounding yard and enclosure thereto to be devoted when consecrated to ecclesiastical purposes for ever."

C At the date of this conveyance there was on the premises a church building, completed but not yet consecrated. " The surrounding yard and enclosure " (to which I shall refer as the yard) has not been consecrated. On Mar. 26, 1960, the Bishop of St. Albans consecrated the church, which thereupon vested in the incumbent under s. 17 (*a*) of the New Parishes Measure, 1943 (in the form in which it then existed). The yard was not consecrated, but it too vested in the incumbent on the consecration of the church; see *Plumstead District Board of Works* v. *Ecclesiastical Comrs. for England* (1). Thus, on Mar. 26, 1960, both the church and the yard became vested in the incumbent, and they are still so vested. On consecration the church building became subject to the jurisdiction of the consistory court. Whether the yard also became subject to the jurisdiction depends on whether, once the church was consecrated, it was curtilage of the church. The jurisdiction is primarily over consecrated land and buildings, but by the Faculty Jurisdiction Measure 1964, s. 7, it is declared that the unconsecrated curtilage of a church is subject to the jurisdiction of the consistory court. This section has not been considered in any reported case. " Curtilage " is a familiar term in the common law and statutes. It has been the subject of a number of definitions in the law dictionaries and decisions of the secular courts. A homely instance of its use is in the Gun Licence Act, 1870, where s. 7 allows one to carry a shot-gun without a licence within the curtilage of a dwelling. The word also appears in the Larceny Act, 1916, where s. 26 makes it an offence to break and enter " any dwellinghouse or any building within the curtilage thereof and occupied therewith " and to commit a felony therein.

G At the hearing, counsel for the petitioners referred me for a discussion of " curtilage " to *Pilbrow* v. *St. Leonard, Shoreditch, Vestry* (2). I have also consulted Termes de la Ley (1671 Edn.) and Burn's Law Dictionary (1792). The former defines " curtilage " as " A garden, yard, field or piece of void ground lying near and belonging to the messuage ", a definition which is adopted by Stroud's Judicial Dictionary (3rd Edn.), quoting Sheppard's Touchstone (7th Edn.) to the same effect. Burn gives the following: " A courtyard, backside, or piece of ground lying near and belonging to an house." These definitions show that curtilage must be near a house and must " belong " to it. They must be occupied together: see *Harris* v. *Scurfield* (3). In my opinion " belong " in this context means that the curtilage and the house must belong, or go, together in a physical sense. They will clearly be unable to do that if their titles are such that their connexion is fortuitous and temporary, but I do not think that they must necessarily be vested in the same person for the same legal estate. In my judgment all that is required of their titles is that they shall not conflict with the conclusion that house and curtilage belong together in the sense which I have mentioned. Although the dictionary definitions refer to curtilage as being an open space, it is clear from the provision of the Larceny Act, 1916, quoted above, that it can also mean an enclosure with buildings within the enclosure.

---

(1) [1891] 2 Q.B. 361.   (2) [1895] 1 Q.B. 433.   (3) (1904), 91 L.T. 536.

The concept of belonging together must apply equally to a church and its A
curtilage. Church and curtilage must be occupied together, they must belong
together in a physical sense, and their titles must not be such as to conflict with
their belonging together. The whole area comprised in the conveyance of
Mar. 24, 1960, clearly fulfilled these requirements on that day. It follows that,
two days later, at the moment when the church building became a church by
consecration, the rest of the area became curtilage of the church and so within B
the jurisdiction of the consistory court. This state of affairs was continuing on
June 7, 1964, the date of the first petition in these proceedings. Although this
was a plain and simple case, the legal titles being identical and the yard being
an open space, I am of opinion that it would not have mattered if the yard had
been vested in a different estate owner (for example, the diocesan board of
finance) on the relevant trust for ecclesiastical purposes, or if there had been a C
building on the yard (for example, a vestry block). These last propositions will
become directly relevant at a later stage of this judgment. [The Chancellor
stated the facts as to the need for a youth centre and its proposed form (see p. 404,
letter E, ante) and continued:] After hearing the evidence, I am satisfied that
the building as a whole, youth centre and " link " alike, is needed and that the
plans for its erection are in themselves fit to be sanctioned by faculty. The D
question is whether I can and should grant a faculty approving the proposed
legal transactions. [The Chancellor stated the proposed legal transactions
which are set out at p. 404, letter G, ante, and continued:] These proceedings
were initiated by a petition of June 7, 1964, the incumbent and churchwardens
of Hatfield being petitioners, seeking authority for the " appropriation " of
part of the yard to the diocesan board of finance to hold in trust for the parochial E
church council " for a church youth centre with a link to the church " and for the
holding of such land for the purposes of that youth centre and link and for the
centre to be leased to the proposed body of trustees. On July 28, 1964, I decreed
a citation which in due course was returned unopposed. On Nov. 3, 1964, being
by then satisfied with the plans as such, I directed the registrar to inform the
incumbent that the building works might proceed; in fact they have proceeded F
on the provisional authority of this interlocutory direction. I now propose to
make a final decree authorising the erection of the building in accordance with
the plans and confirming what has already been done under the interlocutory
direction.
    I further instructed the registrar to acquaint the petitioners with the fact
that I felt considerable doubts whether the relief which they sought was correct G
in form. In consequence, they and the diocesan board of finance lodged a
further petition on Feb. 22, 1965. I decreed further citation on Apr. 8, 1965;
it too has been returned unopposed. The second petition goes further than the
first in that it seeks a faculty and a confirmatory faculty for the building works
and also approval for the proposed lease of the youth centre. At the hearing,
I granted leave to amend the first petition by adding to it paragraphs corres- H
ponding with the additional paragraphs in the second petition. Thus the whole
matter is now before me on the first petition, as so amended. The second petition
becomes superfluous and I give leave to withdraw it. At the date of the first
petition, there were no buildings on the yard and it was held for ecclesiastical
purposes. The matter was res integra. In my opinion the correct form of
relief which should then have been asked for, and could have been granted if I
judgment had been given before anything else was done, was a faculty authorising
(a) the erection of the proposed buildings and (b) the conveyance of the site of
the centre to the diocesan board of finance for the broader purposes that were
contemplated. Authority to build on land within the jurisdiction is always
necessary, and authority to convey the legal estate so as to terminate the court's
jurisdiction is in my opinion, equally necessary. In future cases of a similar
sort the petition should be framed in the form which I have indicated and should
be accompanied by such plans as are lodged in ordinary building cases and by a

A draft conveyance.   The petition should be presented early enough to enable the court to dispose of it before any building work is started.   Such is in my judgment the correct practice.   That practice has not been followed here, and it is therefore necessary to deal specially with the particular facts of this case.

There now is a building, the construction of which was provisionally authorised by my interlocutory direction.   I am about to grant a confirmatory faculty B finally legalising its presence and completion.   Part of this building is the " link " which is to continue to be held for ecclesiastical purposes and to belong to the church.   It is to be conveyed to the diocesan board of finance on trust for the parochial church council, under s. 17 of the New Parishes Measure, 1943 (in its present form).   It will continue to be curtilage of the church and so subject to the jurisdiction of the court and I therefore need make no order about C the proposed conveyance of it.   The rest of the building is designed to be occupied as a youth centre, a purpose which is not an ecclesiastical purpose at all and one that is separate from the church.   If the presence on the yard of such a building is definitively legalised by faculty, that building and its site will in my judgment cease to belong to the church.   Thus they will cease to be curtilage of the church, and the court's jurisdiction will cease, unless or until developments occur which D make them curtilage of the church once more.

I am asked (among other things) to grant a faculty which will finally legalise the presence and completion of the building, with the legal consequences described above.   Obviously it is my duty to consider, before granting the final faculty to authorise building, the general nature of the scheme which is proposed, including the proposed conveyancing documents which will come after that faculty.   I E must be satisfied that due provision is made for securing their propriety.   Since in this case, however, the building is already on the site, and the physical separation has occurred, I shall cease to have jurisdiction once I have granted the confirmatory faculty authorising its presence.   In these particular circumstances, no authority to execute the conveyance is necessary or possible;   for by the time it is executed the centre will have ceased to be curtilage.

F At the hearing, counsel for the petitioners explained the proposed documents to me and I made certain observations on them.   In particular I stated that it was desirable that the lease should contain a covenant forbidding the trustees to use the youth centre, or permit or suffer it to be used, for any purpose which is, in the opinion of the minister of the parish in which the centre is from time to time situated, a nuisance or annoyance to such minister or to those who G worship in St. John's Church.   The petitioners undertook, through their counsel, that the documents would be executed in a form settled by him so as to give effect to the points discussed at the hearing.   This undertaking I accept as securing the propriety of these documents and satisfying me that the scheme as a whole is one which the court ought to facilitate.

A faculty will therefore pass the seal on the first petition, as amended.   It will H recite the petitioner's undertaking, it will confirm the building works already effected, and it will authorise the completion of the building works as shown by the plans which were made exhibits at the hearing.   There will be general liberty to apply.

Order accordingly.

Solicitors: *Lee, Bolton & Lee* (for the petitioners).
I

[*Reported by* F. GUTTMAN, ESQ., *Barrister-at-Law.*]

Re ST. MARY'S, GILSTON.   A

[ST. ALBAN'S CONSISTORY COURT (Chancellor G. H. Newsom, Q.C.), November 29,
December 9, 1965.]

*Ecclesiastical Law—Faculty—Jurisdiction—Sale of chattel—Communion vessel
—Whether jurisdiction to authorise sale on open market.*

A silver flagon made in 1639, which belonged to a church and for a time,   B
ending probably in the nineteenth century, had been in regular use as a
communion vessel, had since at least 1941 been kept unused at the bank.
There was no prospect of its being used again, and it was superfluous to the
needs of the parish, which was amply supplied with other vessels. On
an unopposed petition by the incumbent and churchwardens for a faculty
authorising the sale of the flagon on the open market to provide funds for   C
repairs to the church,

Held: the petitioners having established by reference to the finances
and needs of the church and the usefulness and value of the flagon a proper
case for allowing the disposal of the flagon, a faculty for the sale of the flagon
on the open market would be granted, subject to certain conditions (see
p. 409, letter A, p. 412, letter E, and p. 413, letter C, post).   D

Dictum of Chancellor KEMPE, in *St. Mary, Northolt (Vicar and Church-
wardens) v. St. Mary, Northolt (Parishioners)* and *St. George-in-the-East
(Rector and Churchwardens) v. St. George-in-the-East (Parishioners)* ([1920]
P. at pp. 99, 100) not followed.

[As to the granting of faculties, see 13 HALSBURY'S LAWS (3rd Edn.) 414-418,
paras. 921-924; and for cases on purposes for which faculties may be granted,   E
see 19 DIGEST (Repl.) 377, 378, *1752-1766*.]

Cases referred to:

Sacombe Church, Re, (1964), unreported.
St. Mary, Northolt (Vicar and Churchwardens) v. St. Mary, Northolt (Parishioners)
and *St. George-in-the-East (Rector and Churchwardens) v. St. George-   F
in-the-East (Parishioners)*, [1920] P. 97; 19 Digest (Repl.) 536, *3717*;
543, *3805*.

Petition for faculty.

This was a petition by the incumbent and churchwardens of the united parish
of Eastwick with Gilston for a faculty authorising the sale on the open market
of a silver flagon made in 1639, which had long been the property of the church   G
at Gilston and was thought to be likely to fetch about £2,000. The grounds for
the application were that the flagon had not been in use for many years and there
was no prospect of its being used, that there were other adequate communion
vessels and that the parochial church council was faced with very heavy liabilities,
totalling over £3,000 in the near future, and more in prospect, for repairing the
church at Gilston. No appearance had been entered in opposition and the   H
council supported the petition by a majority of eight to one. The facts are
stated in the judgment.

B. T. Buckle for the petitioners.

Cur. adv. vult.

Dec. 9. **THE CHANCELLOR,** stated the object and grounds of the applica-   I
tion (see letter G, supra) and continued: The petitioners agree that, if the
faculty is granted, part only of the proceeds of the sale of the flagon shall be
spent on the repairs to the church, the rest being retained and the income
therefrom accumulated so as to replace what is used, with liberty to apply.

It is clear that a chattel belonging to a church cannot lawfully be sold without
the authority of the consistory court conferred by faculty. It is equally clear
that this jurisdiction must be exercised with great care in regard to church
treasures. It would not do for the court to allow the wholesale dispersal of

A them. In each case the burden of satisfying the court that a sale of the church treasure should be allowed lies on the petitioners. To discharge this burden they must show, by reference to the finances and needs of their church and the usefulness and value of the object concerned, that there is a proper case for allowing the treasure to be disposed of. If they wish to use any of the proceeds (which are in the nature of capital) otherwise than by way of re-investment

B in securities producing income, the burden is also on them to establish this further point. Besides all this, which applies to church treasures of all kinds, it was said in evidence by Mr. Croome, the vice-chairman of the Central Council for the Care of Churches, that communion vessels ought never to be sold on the open market, which involves their secularisation, and that only as " the very last resort " should they be sold at all, and then to a museum if no sale to another

C church can be arranged. By " communion vessels " in this context is meant vessels which have been regularly used for holding the consecrated elements.

The parishes of Eastwick and Gilston were united in the year 1954. Mr. Tyndale-Biscoe is the incumbent; he came in 1960. The parish church is at Eastwick; Gilston church is a chapel of ease (1). The adult population of Eastwick is about 240 and that of Gilston is about 160. The parish is near

D Harlow, but it is in the green belt and there is no prospect of a large influx of population. The income and expenditure accounts of the parochial church council show about £300 a year of receipts from collections and donations, out of which the council pays its way and has, over the last four years, built up a reserve fund, amounting at the time of the hearing to £450, for the preservation of the buildings. Special collections, apart from the Easter offering, were

E £13 6s. 6d. in 1963 and £13 10s. 8d. in 1964. The parish has hitherto made a gift of £10 a year to the church overseas, which it has now undertaken to raise to £20 a year. Gilston church was inspected under the diocesan scheme in 1963 and Eastwick church in 1964. Very considerable repairs are needed at Gilston. Mr. Bingham Harris, the architect in charge, gave evidence about them. The first phase is now in progress under an archdeacon's certificate of July 29, 1965.

F Under it some urgent repairs to the south aisle, costing about £150, are in progress. Some urgent repairs to the tower are almost finished : they will cost about £900. Urgent work to the west window will complete this phase; it is estimated to cost £500. So the total cost of the first phase will be about £1,550. The petitioners are faced with a serious question : how is this £1,550 to be provided? They have the reserve fund of some £450. They have a further sum of £180 in the diocesan

G savings scheme, and they have received a grant of £150 from the Hertfordshire historic churches trust. These items total £780. They have also £96 on current account at the bank, which they wish to keep for current contingencies : I agree that this is reasonable. With £780 available, there is £770 to find. The diocese offers a loan of £500 for five years; but that is merely to anticipate current savings and can usefully be kept in reserve in case other repairs become urgent.

H After the first phase, there is a second one to come which the architect expects to cost a further £1,500; but this phase is not, he said, very urgent and could be carried out in 1966 or later. The church at Eastwick is not an old one and is in a much better state, but the architect said that, when funds permit, one could usefully spend £500 on it.

The two churches are amply supplied with silver vessels. There are a sixteenth

I century chalice, chalice cover, and paten, belonging to Gilston, now in use for both parishes, and in a safe, though not in use, there is a full set of eighteenth century vessels belonging to Eastwick. In the bank, where it has been since at least as long ago as 1941, is the flagon, the subject matter of these proceedings. Its hall-marks show that it was made in 1639. The church records show that it was in the possession of the church in 1853, but its earlier history is unknown. It bears no symbols or inscriptions of any sort except the word " Gilston "

_____

(1) As to a chapel of ease, see 13 Halsbury's Laws (3rd Edn.) 469, 470, paras. 1013, text and note (e), 1014.

which is engraved on it.   Mr. Grimwade of Messrs. Christies told me in evidence   A
that the word was probably inscribed when the flagon was new.   On these
facts, I am of the opinion that the flagon is superfluous to the needs of the parish.
Mr. Croome suggested that it might usefully be put on the altar as an ornament
at great festivals or that it could be used in procession at the offertory at the
parish communion; but the incumbent saw no prospect of the latter use and
said that he would think it wrong to place £2,000 worth of ornament on his   B
altar when money is so badly needed for other church purposes, here and overseas.
Mr. Grimwade told me that if the flagon is sold at auction it should fetch towards
£2,000.   This would, of course, be a sale to a collector and not to another church
or to a museum.   On the other hand, a collector who has paid this kind of sum
for it is hardly likely to treat the flagon as a plaything.   If I feel able to authorise
the sale and to allow part of the proceeds to be applied in paying for repairs   C
to the church, there is no doubt that the serious financial situation of the parochial
church council will be much alleviated.   If the flagon were a mere ornament,
for example a porringer, as is sometimes found belonging to a church, I should
have no hesitation in allowing the sale.   For there is ample evidence of the
need for money and of the fact that the flagon has long been unused and unseen,
and that there is no foreseeable prospect of it being put to any use.   Mr. Croome,   D
however, said in evidence that the flagon almost certainly was a communion
vessel.   For this proposition he made out a formidable and documented case
Put shortly, it is this.   Communion in one kind having been the practice for
centuries, the cup was again allowed to the laity after the Reformation.   It
was sparingly used at first and the normal Elizabethan type of chalice was
probably adequate.   By the end of the sixteenth century, however, the new   E
practice was in full use and very large quantities of wine were consumed at the
communion service, which took place infrequently and was fully attended.
Larger vessels were therefore introduced in which the larger amounts of wine
were consecrated, and were poured into the chalice for administration.   The
rubric of 1662 which requires the priest to lay his hand on every vessel (be it
chalice or flagon) in which there is any wine to be consecrated is not in the earlier   F
prayer books and is likely to have been introduced in consequence of the change
in practice.   Having regard to the full evidence on this point, which was not
available to me when I heard *Re Sacombe Church* (2), eighteen months ago, I
am satisfied on the balance of probability that this flagon was for some considerable time used regularly as a communion vessel.   The practice as to the quantities
of wine used appears to have changed during the nineteenth century, and probably   G
it was then that this flagon was put away.

I turn now to the submission of the Central Council, put forward by Mr.
Croome, that no communion vessel ought ever to be sold except as a last resort,
and then not on the open market.   He said that such a sale would be an impropriety in itself, that the sale of pious gifts would discourage other pious gifts,
that the time might come when the flagon could be used as an ornament or at   H
the offertory and that there was a reasonable chance that the money could be
raised somehow else—he mentioned the Incorporated Church Building Society
and the Historic Churches Preservation Trust, in which he is himself chairman
of the grants committee.   He added that something which is of historic interest
is lost if a church treasure is separated from the church to which it has belonged.
With all these opinions I sympathise, but sympathy is no sure guide in exercising   I
a judicial discretion.   I asked Mr. Croome how far the Central Council was
prepared to press its submission.   If the argument is valid for communion
vessels, why not also for the altar on which they stand, its frontals, coverings
and ornaments?   Indeed why not the church itself, which contains all these
things?   The witness told me that the council's objections are confined to
chalice, paten and flagon; but I am not at all satisfied of the logic of this limitation.

What is the law?   Counsel for the petitioners referred me to a decision of the

(2) (1964), unreported.

A London Consistory Court in the cases *St. Mary, Northolt (Vicar and Church-wardens)* v. *St. Mary, Northolt (Parishioners)*; and *St. George-in-the-East (Rector and Churchwardens)* v. *St. George-in-the-East (Parishioners)* (3) which seems to be the only relevant and available decision. This is a judgment of Chancellor KEMPE given in 1920. Though it is not binding on me, it is entitled to great respect. There were two separate cases but only one judgment. In both

B cases the vessels concerned included undoubted communion vessels. In one case the chancellor refused a faculty; in the other he granted it (4) " subject to the destination of the plate being specified and approved by the chancellor of the diocese before the plate is actually sold ". The sale was evidently not to be on the open market. For the present purpose the important passage in the judgment is as follows (5):

C   " In the first place the court should be satisfied that if the sale takes place the sacred vessels will be protected from profane or secular use. The principle that ornaments of the church devoted to sacred uses should not be applied to other purposes is stated in a Constitution of Archbishop Edmund Rich, made in the year 1236, which is to be found in Lyndwood's Provinciale at pp. 33, 34: ' Panni Chrysmales non nisi in usum ornamentorum Ecclesiae

D   convertantur: similiter alia ornamenta ecclesiae quae pontificalem accipiunt benedictionem nullo modo in prophanos usus depulentur '; which is thus translated in Johnson's Ecclesiastical Laws: ' Let the Chrysoms be made use of, for the ornaments of the church only; let the other ornaments of the church which have been blest by the Bishop be applied to no common use '."

E I pause here to say that this passage, as set out in the Law Reports (5), contains one misprint and one clear mistranslation. In the Latin version, the last word is not in fact " depulentur ", but " deputentur ". In the English version " Panni Chrysmales " should be " Cloths for the Chrysoms ", i.e., fabrics, and not " Chrysoms ", i.e., vessels. Chancellor KEMPE continued (6):

F   " Modern religious feeling does not sanction a departure from this principle. The vessels which have been made use of for the administration of the Holy Communion should not be sold so that, for instance, they may become merely the ornament of a rich man's side-board or table; and I am, as at present advised, unable to see any circumstances under which the court would be justified in permitting the sale of such vessels without restriction

G   and could allow them to pass into the hands of a dealer for resale to an unknown purchaser."

The learned chancellor evidently contemplated that the proposition which he stated at the conclusion of this passage was not necessarily valid as a matter of law for all time. He was interpreting and applying what he described as " modern religious feeling ", a criterion capable of change. Many years have passed since

H his decision, and the present climate of opinion in the Church of England has greatly changed. In particular, and especially since the recent deliberations at Toronto, churchmen are much more conscious of the need to make full and deliberate use of the resources of the church for the benefit of the church as a whole. Further, the St. Albans diocesan congress, held in May, 1965, concluded inter alia that " We must take care not to let ourselvses be bled to death by our

I own buildings ", and " We have been reminded once more that the church is more a living body than a stone building ". These expressions of opinion appear to me relevant to the question what " modern religious feeling " would now sanction. A vessel which has long been kept in a bank and is likely to stay there does not contribute at all to the work of the church. A building which needs great sums spent on it is a burden to the life of the parish. The proceeds

---

(3) [1920] P. 97.
(5) [1920] P. at pp. 99, 100.

(4) [1920] P. at p. 102.
(6) [1920] P. at p. 100.

of the useless vessel, if spent on such a building, will at least release the energies A
of the parishioners for other tasks more useful than that of raising money to
repair the building. If I am not precluded by authority from allowing the
sale of a communion vessel on the open market, my duty is to consider whether
the best use is at present being made of the capital which it represents, and
whether a better use can be made of the proceeds of sale.

Am I, then, precluded by authority? The researches of counsel have not B
brought to light any other authority than Chancellor KEMPE's decision (7),
which rests, in point of law, only on the passage from Archbishop Edmund Rich.
Counsel for the petitioner referred me to the passage in the original Latin, with
the results noted above. Further, the passage is headed " Archidiaconus, ne
res sacra in prophanum usum cedat, observet et caveat ", and it concludes:
" et archidiaconus in sua visitatione ad hoc observetur, diligenter inquirat ". C
This, in my opinion, is an instruction to archdeacons to see that proper use is
made of things belonging to the church while they belong to the church. It is
not a statement of what the bishop, or the consistory court exercising his jurisdiction, may allow to be done with objects which the church is proved no longer
to need. It is, further, confined to objects which have received " pontifical
blessing ": Lyndwood, in a gloss, says that this phrase means the bishop's D
blessing (of which there is no evidence in the present case) and not a blessing
given " a simplici sacerdote ". Further, a gloss by Gibson defines " alia ornamenta ecclesiae " by a list of vestments and other objects, all of which are of
cloth or like fabric and not of metal at all. It is at this point that the mistranslation of " Panni Chrysmales " is material, since it colours the whole passage.
I therefore decline to follow Chancellor KEMPE in his application of Archbishop E
Rich's constitution, which in my opinion he misinterpreted. In the absence of
other authority, I hold that I am entitled to exercise my discretion to allow the
sale of a communion vessel on the open market. It goes without saying that this
power is one to be exercised most sparingly. But I accept the submission of
counsel for the petitioners that there is a parallel to be drawn between such a
sale and the deconsecration of a church. A church, though consecrated " for F
ever ", can be deconsecrated under lawful authority, in this country that of
Parliament; if such authority is given, the bishop, or someone acting under
his commission, may make a declaration at the last service that the building has
been " surrendered by due process of law to secular uses " and that accordingly

" We do now declare that this building shall not longer be set apart for
the ministrations of the church but shall henceforward be employed for   G
such purposes or in such manner as the law may enjoin or allow; which
declaration all Christian people shall with quiet minds receive and obey."

The form of service was issued in 1947 by the authority of the Archbishops of
Canterbury and York. The consecrated elements are contained within the
vessels and the vessels are contained within the church. If, then, the church H
can be surrendered to secular uses by lawful authority, I see no reason why the
vessels should not be capable of a similar surrender. The only difference is
that in this country the lawful authority to authorise deconsecration of the church
is that of Parliament, while the lawful authority to authorise sale of the vessels
is that of the consistory court. If, following a faculty conditionally authorising
a sale, the bishop sees fit to make a declaration that this flagon is surrendered I
to secular uses, it is my opinion that the transaction would be no more objectionable than the demolition of the church and the sale of its materials and contents.
Nor do I think that it would be useful to attempt to control the destination of a
vessel. The burden of a restrictive covenant cannot be made to run with a
chattel, and as the only practicable means of effecting such control would be to

(7) [1920] P. 97.

A forbid a sale except to a buyer in whose hands the vessel would still be subject
to the control of this, or some other, consistory court.   Such a sale might well
be the best use of the asset in some cases, but in this case, according to the
evidence, it would be very difficult, if not impossible, to arrange, and the price
would of course be far below the market price.   To insist on it in the present
circumstances would not, in my opinion, be requiring the asset to be put to the
B most beneficial use.

Obviously, orders for the sale of church treasures must never be made lightly.
Moreover, for the present at least, I do not propose to grant faculties authorising
the sale of communion vessels except after a full oral hearing and consideration
of all the relevant circumstances.   In the present case, however, I am satisfied
that it would be proper to grant a faculty.   I have consulted the bishop of the
C diocese, who has expressed his concurrence in the main provisions of the order
which I now propose to make.   The faculty will authorise the sale of the flagon
subject to certain conditions.   The sale is not to take place unless and until,
at a service conducted by the bishop himself or the archdeacon of St. Albans
acting under the bishop's commission, a declaration is made that the flagon shall
no longer be set apart for the ministrations of the church but shall henceforth
D be employed for such purposes as the law may enjoin or allow.   The form of
service is to follow, mutatis mutandis, the form for declaring that a church
has been delivered over to secular uses; the exact form of declaration is to be
approved by the bishop in person.   The written certificate of the person offici-
ating is to be conclusive evidence for all purposes that this condition has been
fulfilled.   Subject as aforesaid, the flagon may be sold on the open market.
E The auction particulars and the terms and conditions, including the reserve
price, are to be approved by the registrar.   The proceeds of sale are to be paid
to the St. Albans diocesan board of finance.   The petitioners are to give an
undertaking to the court, recited in the faculty, that the sale shall be in strict
accordance with the approved conditions, and for due payment to the board of
the whole of the proceeds.

F   Subject as aforesaid, the proceeds of sale are to be dealt with as follows:
(i) The costs of the petitioners of these proceedings (to which are to be added
all court fees and the expenses of the hearing, including those of the judge's
witness) are to be taxed by the registrar and paid thereout together with the
expenses of the sale and the auctioneer's commission; (ii) A sum of £750, or a
sum equal to half the residue after making the foregoing payments (whichever
G is less), shall be set aside and shall be applied as and when required to defray
in whole or in part the contractors' bills in respect of the works authorised by
the archdeacon's certificate of July 29, 1965.   If any of this sum remains unused
on Dec. 31, 1966, it shall be dealt with under the next following provision;
(iii) Subject as aforesaid, the fund is to be invested by the board and the income
H accumulated and invested for a period of fourteen years, which will be about
sufficient to restore the fund to its original value; (iv) Subject as aforesaid, the
income is to be paid to the parochial church council for its general purposes.

The parochial church council and the diocesan board of finance are to be
joined as respondents, since both are interested in the working out of this order.
Both these bodies, and the petitioners and their respective successors in office,
I are to have liberty to apply in the proceedings at any time, both generally and
for the purpose of varying my present directions as to the use of the capital and
income of the fund.   I do not by making this provision imply that I shall necessarily allow any part of the fund to be used for financing any repairs to either
church beyond those authorised by the current archdeacon's certificate.   The
architect said in evidence that nothing except the first phase was particularly
urgent.   The Archdeacon of St. Albans and his successors in office are to have
liberty to apply at any time to be joined as parties, so that they can ensure the

due execution of the order. Finally, I direct that minutes of order shall be drawn A
up and settled by counsel for the petitioners, the costs thereof to be part of the
costs of the petitioners in the proceedings.

Decree accordingly.

Solicitors: *Penningtons and Lewis & Lewis* (for the petitioners).

[*Reported by* F. GUTTMAN, ESQ., *Barrister-at-Law.*] B

Dictum of WINN LJ at 427 applied in
BELVOIR FINANCE v STAPLETON
1970] 3 All ER 664

KINGSLEY v. STERLING INDUSTRIAL SECURITIES, LTD.

[COURT OF APPEAL (Sellers, Harman and Winn, L.JJ.), February 15, 16, 17, 18, C
March 31, 1966.]

*Hire-Purchase—Re-financing arrangements—Loan desired by borrower on
security of own car—Payment of amount of first deposit by cancellation of
indebtedness—Borrower sold car to A., Ltd., which re-sold it to finance company, which let the car on hire-purchase to borrower—First deposit met by
set-off allowed by A., Ltd., of its amount from price paid to borrower and* D
*by finance company deducting amount from price paid to A., Ltd.—Whether
hire-purchase agreement void as unregistered bill of sale—Whether there was
actual payment of the amount of the first deposit before entering into the
hire-purchase agreement—Whether title would pass notwithstanding illegality
—Money borrowed or otherwise " acquired "—Hire-Purchase and Credit
Sale Agreements (Control) Order, 1960 (S.I. 1960 No. 762), art. 1 (1),* E
Sch. 2, Pt. 1, para. 3, Pt. 2.

K. owned a car that he had bought for £2,112 in October, 1963. He
wished to raise money on it. He was told on behalf of S., Ltd., who were
motor dealers, that they could not effect the transaction by lending money,
but that S., Ltd., would buy the car and would sell it to a finance company,
who would let it back to K. on hire-purchase. The terms of the documents F
did not in certain respects fit the proposed " re-financing " transaction,
but on Feb. 13, 1965, K. signed (i) an agreement with S., Ltd. for S., Ltd.
to buy the car for £1,848, authorising S., Ltd. to set-off moneys due from K.
against the purchase price, (ii) an agreement requesting S., Ltd. to sell the
car to the finance company if they were willing to let it to K. for a cash
price of £1,850 on usual hire-purchase terms, and (iii) an hire-purchase G
agreement with the finance company (subsequently signed on behalf of
the finance company on Feb. 17, 1965) in which the cash price was stated
as £1,850. The price (£1,848) at which K. sold the car to S., Ltd., was, on
the evidence, a fair and reasonable value for the car at the time of the sale.
The hire-purchase agreement provided for a first deposit of £600 being made.
K. handed over the log book of the car, but retained possession of the car. H
On Feb. 14, 1965, S., Ltd. gave K. their cheque for £1,248 (i.e., £1,848 less
the £600). The finance company paid S., Ltd. £1,250, being the cash price
(£1,850) less the amount (£600) of the deposit. In April, 1965, the finance
company took possession of the car on the ground of default in payment
of hire-purchase instalments. On appeal in an action by K. to recover
possession of the car, I

Held: (i) although K.'s purpose was to raise money on the car, yet the
intention of the parties to the re-financing transaction was that it should
have the effect of divesting K. of ownership of the car and of vesting it
first in S., Ltd., and then in the finance company; accordingly the hire-
purchase transaction was not a sham and the hire-purchase agreement
was not void as being an unregistered bill of sale by way of security (see
p. 417, letter G, p. 421, letter D, and p. 426, letter G, post).

Stoneleigh Finance, Ltd. v. *Phillips* ([1965] 1 All E.R. 513) distinguished.

A (ii) (per SELLERS and WINN, L.JJ.) the transaction was not illegal as infringing the Hire-Purchase and Credit Sale Agreements (Control) Order, 1960, for the following reasons—

 (a) the retaining by S., Ltd. of £600 on purchasing from K. the car, whose value was £1,848, and the cancellation of S., Ltd.'s indebtedness to K. in that sum on effecting the hire-purchase transaction, whereby K. obtained

B £1,248 only from the finance company, amounted to payment of £600 by K., and amounted, for the purpose of para. 3* of Pt. 1 of Sch. 2 to the Order of 1960, to " actual " payment of a sum exceeding the deposit required by that Order (see p. 418, letter D, p. 419, letters A and F, p. 420, letter D, and p. 428, letters G and H, post).

 (b) it was irrelevant to consider whether there had been payment or actual

C payment to the finance company (see p. 420, letter E, and p. 428, letter C, post).

 (iii) (HARMAN, L.J., concurring) the ownership of the car passed on sale to the finance company and K.'s claim that they had wrongfully taken possession of it failed (see p. 420, letter I, p. 423, letter E, and p. 429, letter C, post), and (HARMAN, L.J., dissenting; see p. 423, letter F, post) the

D finance company's counter-claim succeeded for the reason stated at (ii) above.

 Per WINN, L.J.: (a) even if the hire-purchase transaction had infringed the Order of 1960, by reason of there having been failure to make actual payment of the deposit, it would not have followed that the property in the car had not passed under the hire-purchase transaction (see p. 426, letter H, post).

E *Sajan Singh* v. *Sardara Ali* ([1960] 1 All E.R. 269) applied.

 (b) the word " acquired " in Pt. 2 of Sch. 2 to the Order of 1960† meant " obtained otherwise than by exchange or provision of commensurate value "; and the word generally connotes getting something for nothing or getting something without giving for it any barter or services constituting a comparable return (see p. 429, letter B, post; cf. p. 420, letter E, post).

F Decision of McNAIR, J. ([1966] 1 All E.R. 37) affirmed on (i) and reversed on (ii) above.

 [**Editorial Note.** The current order at the date of this report is the Hire-Purchase and Credit Sale Agreements (Control) Order 1964, S.I. 1964 No. 942, as amended by S.I. 1965 No. 1471 and 1966 No. 113. Paragraph 3 of Pt. 1, and Pt. 2, of Sch. 2 to the Order of 1964 are similar to the corresponding para. 3

G and Pt. 2 of the Order of 1960.

 As to the statutory control of hire-purchase agreements under emergency legislation, see 19 HALSBURY'S LAWS (3rd Edn.) 518, 519, para. 834; and for cases on the subject, see 26 DIGEST (Repl.) 663, *20, 21.*

 As to distinction between hire-purchase transactions and bills of sale, see 19 HALSBURY'S LAWS (3rd Edn.) 512, 513, para. 827; and for cases on the subject,

H see 7 DIGEST (Repl.) 16-19, *71-86.*]

Cases referred to:

 Eastern Distributors, Ltd. v. *Goldring (Murphy, Third Party),* [1957] 2 All E.R. 525; [1957] 2 Q.B. 600; [1957] 3 W.L.R. 237; 26 Digest (Repl.) 675, *77.*

I * Paragraph 3, so far as material, is printed at p. 419, letters E and G, post.

 † Part 2 of Sch. 2 provided that " The requirement specified in para. 3 of Pt. 1 of this Schedule shall be deemed not to be complied with in relation to a hire-purchase . . . agreement if, for the purpose of enabling the payment mentioned in that paragraph or any part of that payment to be made, money had been borrowed or otherwise acquired (whether by the person making the payment or by some other person) under or as a result of an agreement or arrangement to which one or more of the following persons are parties, that is to say—(*a*) the person disposing of the goods under the hire-purchase agreement . . .; (*b*) a person who has supplied or is to supply those goods to another person with a view to their being disposed of thereunder; (*c*) the manufacturer of the goods to be disposed of thereunder."

Sajan Singh v. *Sardara Ali,* [1960] 1 All E.R. 269; [1960] A.C. 167; [1960] A
    2 W.L.R. 180; 39 Digest (Repl.) 597, *1146.*
Stoneleigh Finance, Ltd. v. *Phillips,* [1965] 1 All E.R. 513; [1965] 2 Q.B. 537;
    [1965] 2 W.L.R. 508.
Yorkshire Railway Wagon Co. v. *Maclure,* (1882), 21 Ch.D. 309; 51 L.J.Ch.
    857; 47 L.T. 290; 26 Digest (Repl.) 17, *55.*

Appeal.   B

This was an appeal by the defendant finance company from the decision of
McNAIR, J., dated Nov. 2, 1965, and reported [1966] 1 All E.R. 37, ordering the
finance company to hand over a Rover motor car, Index No. 52 GXX, to the
plaintiff customer, Percival Kingsley (from whom the finance company had
retaken possession of the car), declaring that the car was the plaintiff customer's
property, referring the assessment of damages for the defendant finance com-   C
pany's detention of the car to a Master, and dismissing the finance company's
counterclaim for £174 6s. 8d. arrears of rentals under a hire-purchase agreement
dated Feb. 17, 1964, by which they had let the car to the plaintiff customer.
By a cross notice of appeal the plaintiff customer sought to uphold the decision
of McNAIR, J., on the additional ground (on which McNAIR, J., had found in
the finance company's favour) that the hire-purchase agreement was void as an D
unregistered bill of sale. The facts are stated in the judgment of WINN, L.J.
(post p. 423, letter G, to p. 424, letter G.)

A. D. Rawley for the plaintiff customer.
S. Terrell, Q.C., and *P. B. Creightmore* for the defendant finance company.

                                                                      Cur. adv. vult. E
Mar. 31.   The following judgments were read.

    SELLERS, L.J.:   The defendants, who appeal to this court, are a hire-
purchase finance company. They are in close business relationship with A.
Saxon, Ltd., who carry on business as the Saxon Finance Agency and whose
trade is that of financing transactions for customers. They do not hold a stock F
of motor vehicles for sale. In this—in so far as it relates to transactions on motor
vehicles—their trade differs from the ordinary trade of motor dealers who hold
a stock of vehicles which they offer for sale and who frequently take a motor
vehicle belonging to a customer in part-exchange for a newly acquired vehicle.
If hire-purchase terms are desired by the customer, the dealer sells the selected
vehicle to a hire-purchase company who hire it out to the customer. Such a   G
transaction has to comply with the Hire-Purchase Acts and in particular requires
a minimum deposit against the agreed price. This deposit or initial payment is
customarily made to the dealer either by a cash payment or by a credit for a
vehicle taken in part-exchange and it is the balance of the agreed purchase price
plus the hire-purchase charges which the customer has to pay to the hire-purchase
company. In this way the customer provides the deposit. The statutory deposit H
material to the present case was a minimum of twenty per cent. of the price.
    There are two other types of transactions in motor vehicles, perhaps less common
than those through a motor dealer holding stock for sale. In these two types
Saxon are interested. What have been described as " private transactions "
arise where an owner, A, of a motor vehicle finds a private buyer, B, who wishes
to acquire A.'s car but wishes to pay by instalments by a hire-purchase agreement. I
Saxon would finance such a transaction by buying the car from A and selling it to
the defendants, who would hire it out to B on hire-purchase terms, and provision
would be made for at least the minimum statutory deposit to be made by B.
In such a case B would acquire possession of a car which was not previously
his and the transaction in that respect resembles the ordinary transaction.
    The third type, described as " refinancing transactions ", arises where A
wishes to raise money on his own motor vehicle but wishes at the same time
to retain possession of it and make use of it. The present case falls into that

A category. If the vehicle owner retains possession of the vehicle and raises money on it by a document transferring the ownership of the vehicle as security for a loan, the transaction would have to be in a prescribed form and registered under the Bills of Sale Acts in order to be effective. It is one of the pitfalls which confront parties to " refinancing transactions ". So as to avoid evasion of the Bills of Sale Acts the court looks behind the apparent bargain to ascertain what the B parties truly intended in their transaction.

In *Stoneleigh Finance, Ltd.* v. *Phillips* (1) such an investigation took place in a " refinancing transaction ". The documents were inappropriate to the transaction and produced, as all the court held, inaccuracies and artificial statements, but the majority of the Court of Appeal upheld them as being a genuine and not a fictitious or sham presentation of the bargain there involved. If parties use C documents which are inappropriate to the transaction in hand and involve statements which are inaccurate, the court may rightly be suspicious that the parties are trying to make the transaction appear to be something other than it really is. McNair, J., took the view in the *Stoneleigh* case (1) that the documents did not reflect the true transactions but in the present case, no doubt influenced by the majority view in *Stoneleigh* (1), the same learned judge has taken the D contrary view (2). I think that must be accepted. We had much argument from the Bar, not surprisingly distinguishing or applying *Stoneleigh* (1) as it suited the party, but I do not find the comparisons profitable. *Stoneleigh* (1) is an illustration of how far the court will go in overlooking inconsistencies and inaccuracies in documents in relation to the bargain which they are relied on to establish. The present case has to be looked at on its own facts and on the E court's view of them. The detailed facts of this case are carefully found by the learned judge (3) and fully stated in the judgment of Winn, L.J., and I do not restate them.

It appears that, although Mr. Dobney of Saxon was far from revealing any exact knowledge of the law, he at least knew of the pitfalls in a " refinancing transaction ". When Mr. Kingsley, the plaintiff customer, approached him in F order to raise as much money as he could by borrowing it on the car's security and not selling it outright, Mr. Dobney explained that they were not money-lenders and could not arrange it that way. He explained that Saxon could purchase the vehicle and then sell the vehicle to a finance company (they had the defendants in mind) who would hire it back to the customer and that if he entered into the transaction he would lose the title to the vehicle, he would G part with it to Saxon and Saxon in turn would sell it to the hire-purchase company. Once that conversation was accepted, as it was by the learned judge, that threw light on the nature of the transaction and, I think, distinguishes *Stoneleigh* (1).

There followed an agreement in writing dated Feb. 13, 1964, by which the customer sold to Saxon his Rover 3-litre coupé at a price of £1,848. On the back of the same form the customer signed a printed form requesting Saxon as owners H of the Rover 3-litre coupe to arrange to sell the vehicle to Sterling (the defendant finance-company) on hire-purchase terms for a cash price of £1,850 with their usual charges payable by a first deposit of £600 and by thirty-six monthly instalments of £43 11s. 8d. That document was dated Feb. 14, 1964, although the evidence was that it was signed on Feb. 13, at the same time as the contract of sale. Clause 4 of the request states that " the hirer [the customer] declares I that he has inspected, tried and approved the vehicle ", a declaration hardly appropriate to the circumstances, as its implication is that he is taking over a vehicle with which he was previously unfamiliar.

After that the plaintiff customer and Mr. Dobney went to the car and there was some " by-play ", as the judgment describes it, which was to effect a delivery of the car by the customer to Saxon and a re-delivery by Saxon in anticipation

---

(1) [1965] 1 All E.R. 513; [1965] 2 Q.B. 537.   (2) [1966] 1 All E.R. 37 at p. 40.
(3) See [1966] 1 All E.R. at pp. 38-40.

of the hire-purchase arrangement which was in contemplation. As soon as the A
finance company had agreed to the transaction Saxon sent to the customer a
cheque for £1,248, which was the purchase price less £600 which was the amount
of the " first deposit " which the request document required and which was
agreed when both the customer and Saxon signed it. On Feb. 14, 1964, Saxon
sold the Rover car to the defendant finance company for £1,850 as " cash price
of goods " and the invoice evidencing the sale showed an initial payment of £600 B
and a balance due of £1,250. This sum of £1,250 the finance company duly paid
to Saxon.

Once it was accepted—as I think on the whole rightly accepted—that there
had been a genuine sale to Saxon, their position became similar to that of the
motor dealer in the ordinary transaction. Saxon owned the car, the plaintiff
customer desired to buy it back on hire-purchase terms; this involved an initial C
payment or a deposit. Saxon, the dealers, required £600 (which was in excess of
the statutory minimum of £370) and this Saxon retained and obtained the
balance from the defendants, the hire-purchase company. Saxon retained the
customer's deposit against the price and obtained the hire-purchase terms for the
customer for the balance only. The £2 difference does not affect the nature of
the transactions. If the transactions had gone through precisely to their tenor D
Saxon would have paid the customer £1,848 and the customer would immediately
have paid back £600 in compliance with the request for hire-purchase. The
fact that those motions were not actually gone through can make no difference
to the transaction. As I see it the deposit became a real or actual payment. It
was a credit by Saxon to the customer which went to extinguish the like indebtedness of the customer to Saxon. It might have been unreal or fictitious if the E
price of the car, fixed at £1,848, had been much greater than its value. On the
evidence, however, £1,848 was a fair and reasonable value and the customer
had to forgo or put up £600 of the £1,848 in order to buy his car back. The £600
was a real loss to the customer because he had paid some £2,100 for the car
three months earlier and the car was worth the £1,848. He had the money, in
the value of the car and the transaction was in no sense one where a man acquired F
a car when he had nothing with which to acquire it and was unable to find the
deposit.

On Feb. 17, 1964, the customer and the finance company entered into the hire-
purchase agreement in a common form on the terms which had been stated in
the customer's request to Saxon. It showed the £600 " initial payment paid
before signing agreement " (which Saxon had retained and therefore reduced G
the balance of the purchase price of £1,850 due from the finance company to
Saxon to £1,250). Saxon received from the finance company £1,250 and that sum,
together with charges of £319, a total of £1,569, had to be repaid by the customer.
Again a common form for " ordinary transactions " was used and it contained
statements which were inappropriate and inaccurate. In particular the customer
appended his signature to a certificate that " he had never had prior title to the H
goods ". He had in fact owned the car for some three months.

I think that the courts which have the task of ensuring that the requirements
of the Bills of Sale Acts and the Hire-Purchase Acts are complied with might
with strictness require the parties to transactions of this character to use documents which unequivocally depict the intended transaction and which are wholly
suited to the purpose. Endless time was taken up in the Stoneleigh case (4) and I
in this case in both courts in an endeavour to discover the true nature of the
arrangement. In Stoneleigh (4), of the four judges who heard the case there was an
equal division of opinion and in the present case the position is the same on one
issue. If the transactions are genuine and within the law I can see no reason
why there should be use of documents which give rise to suspicion and permit
allegations that they are sham or fictitious or a " charade ". However, I

(4) [1965] 1 All E.R. 513; [1965] 2 Q.B. 537.

A take less exception in this case than I did to the documents in the *Stoneleigh* case (5), where the views of the trial judge and mine did not prevail.

There was a second point on which the customer relied and this found favour with the trial judge (6). It was that there had been no actual payment of the deposit. If the transactions, found to be genuine, are rightly to be viewed in the way that I have stated above I hardly think that the second point can be main-

B tained. The customer was foregoing £600 in money's worth in his car and only obtaining £1,248 of its worth or price in order to obtain hire-purchase.

There came into operation after the transactions the subject of the *Stoneleigh* case (5) the Hire-Purchase and Credit Sale Agreements (Control) Order, 1960, (7). Article 1 of that Order provided:

C " A person shall not dispose of any goods to which this Order applies in pursuance of a hire-purchase or credit sale agreement entered into after Apr. 28, 1960 . . . unless the requirements specified in Pt. 1 of Sch. 2 hereto are or have been complied with in relation to that agreement."

Part 1 of Sch. 2 is as follows, as far as is material for the purposes of this judgment:

D " 1. The agreement is in writing. 2. The agreement contains in respect of each description of goods a statement of the cash price of the goods of that description comprised in the agreement and of any amount payable by instalments under the agreement for the installation or maintenance of those goods."

E Those two provisions have clearly been complied with.

" 3. Before the agreement was entered into actual payment was made in respect of each description of goods comprised in the agreement of not less than an amount equal to the percentage specified in column 2 of Pt. 1 of Sch. 1 hereto in relation to that description of goods . . ."

As I have already said, the appropriate percentage here was twenty per cent.

F The £600 is greatly in excess of twenty per cent. of £1,850, but it was found by the judge (6) and it has been submitted on behalf of the plaintiff customer before us that it was not in the circumstances an actual payment. That it was not handed over in cash or paid by cheque is clear, but if the dealer (Saxon) allocated a credit which the customer (the plaintiff) had with him I feel no doubt that in a commercial transaction that is real and genuine payment and

G equivalent to cash or cheque and would comply with the requirements of the Order. The Order expressly provided, by para. 3 of Pt. 1 of Sch. 2,

" In computing . . . the total amount to be paid before any agreement is entered into account may be taken of any allowance for any goods taken in part exchange for goods comprised in that agreement, being an allowance which is reasonable in relation to the value of the goods so taken in part

H exchange."

McNair, J., stated (8):

" That is the only exception from the requirement of actual payment, and it makes this plain to my mind, that the exception being one relating to a part exchange allowance, it relates to an allowance granted by the hire-purchase company itself and not to an allowance which may have been

I given by a motor dealer, nor to anything of that kind."

With respect, I think not, in the way I understand it to be put by the judge.

In practice over many years it has been the motor dealer who has made the allowance to the customer for the car taken in exchange and the customer has placed the allowance so made towards the deposit or initial payment required

---

(5) [1965] 1 All E.R. 513; [1965] 2 Q.B. 537.   (6) [1966] 1 All E.R. at pp. 41, 42.
(7) S.I. 1960 No. 762.   This order was revoked and repealed by S.I. 1964 No. 942.
(8) [1966] 1 All E.R. at p. 42.

by law and by the hire-purchase company and the customer has only received A
the hire-purchase finance in respect of the balance of the price. This practice
has long been recognised in the administration of the law relating to hire-purchase
and the Order of 1960 did not intend a departure from it. As Mr. Smith of the
finance company said: " I agree we never looked to receiving the deposit. No
hire-purchase company ever does." By the credit for the car in part exchange
the dealer receives a part payment from the customer and the hire-purchase B
company pays him, the dealer, the balance only and gives to the customer hire-
purchase terms for the balance only. That is, the customer pays the deposit or
" initial payment ".

It is true that para. 3 is the only exception in Pt. 1 of Sch. 2 to the Order.
It may be because it recognises the practice and it became necessary to stipulate
that the allowance should be at a reasonable value. If the exchange vehicle C
were worth £100 and the allowance shown in the document was £300, being the
required deposit, the customer would clearly not have complied with the Order.
but if the dealer already owed the customer £300 due from some wholly distinct
transaction and he extinguished the indebtedness by crediting the £300 to the
deposit required from the customer, I cannot think that the Order requires the
£300 to be paid in cash or by cheque and forthwith to be returned by the customer D
to the dealer. The debit to the customer against his credit would be actual
payment. It is real and of equal substance and it is not the manner of payment
which the regulation effects but its reality.

I am in agreement with what WINN, L.J., has said more fully on this topic
in his judgment. I cannot see that Pt. 2 of Sch. 2 has any bearing on this case,
when the plaintiff customer owned at the outset the car in question worth £1,848. E
He had no need to borrow or acquire funds for a deposit. He had them in the
car and realised them.

HARMAN, L.J., views the matter differently and would support the judge in
finding that there was no actual payment of a deposit. I differ from them with
deference. HARMAN, L.J., regards the £600 as a mere fiction and would prefer
to draw the inference that there was a sale of the car by the plaintiff customer F
to Saxon for £1,248 cash plus a promise of a hire-purchase agreement. Whatever
sympathy one may have for that view, it runs counter to the three documents
involved in the transactions, which have been accepted as genuine. It is said
that Saxon never had the £600 and were never richer by that sum; but Saxon
acquired the car worth £1,848 for a cash payment of £1,248 and whilst Saxon
held the car as owners they were richer by that precise sum. The customer was G
poorer by the same sum because he had parted with an article worth £1,848
and only received £1,248 for it. Likewise the finance company obtained from
Saxon the car worth £1,850 and only paid £1,250 for it, because Saxon, the
vendors, already had £600. That is not inequitable because the customer, having
paid £600, the deposit, only had to pay the balance plus charges for the financial
facilities in order to receive it back again. The factor of progressive depreciation H
on the car's value would have arisen whether the car had belonged throughout
to the customer or, as here, where the ownership changed to the finance company
through Saxon.

I would hold that the ownership of the car passed to the finance company
and that the hire-purchase agreement was valid and that the finance company
were entitled to seize the car by reason of the customer's default under the I
hire-purchase agreement, and therefore the plaintiff customer's claim in the
action that the defendant finance company wrongfully seized and detained his
car fails. The hire-purchase agreement entitled the defendant finance company
to the amount claimed for arrears of hire by their counterclaim.

I would allow the appeal accordingly.

HARMAN, L.J.: This action started by specially endorsed writ as a claim
by the plaintiff customer in detinue in respect of his motor car said to have been

A wrongfully seized by the defendant finance company. The defence was that the finance company were the true owners of the car and had hired it to the customer in pursuance of a hire-purchase agreement on which the customer had made default thus entitling the finance company to retake possession, as they had done. There was a counterclaim for the balance of instalments due up to the date of possession. The main issue in the case was raised by the reply,

B which alleged that the so-called hire-purchase agreement was a mere sham and a cloak for the loan made by the finance company to the customer, the true transaction consisting of a loan by the finance company to the customer on the security of his car and void under the Bills of Sale Acts because not registered. Alternatively it was said that the hire-purchase agreement was void and unen- forceable because of the absence of payment of a twenty per cent. deposit under

C the statutory regulation in that behalf.

   The judge, having seen the witnesses, came to the conclusion (9) that the hire-purchase agreement and the accompanying documents were not a sham but must be taken as they stand. This conclusion was, it is true, an inference drawn by the judge from the primary facts and could therefore be a proper subject of attack in this court but I do not feel that we ought to reverse the judge

D on this point. It is clear enough that the customer, although his object was to raise a loan on the security of his motor car, thought he was doing it in some way which he did not trouble to understand, through the medium of a hire-purchase agreement. It seems to me also clear that the finance company had no reason to suppose that this was not a hire-purchase transaction. I am therefore of opinion that the attack on the validity of the document alleging it to be void as an

E unregistered bill of sale must fail.

   The judge decided (10) the question on the alternative point, and as I see it the question in this case is whether, before the hire-purchase agreement was made between the finance company and the customer, there was an " actual payment " by the customer of not less than twenty per cent. of the purchase price as a deposit. It is admitted by the finance company that they never received

F such a sum. According to them the finance company never does, and that is perhaps true. The ordinary hire-purchase agreement is made on the basis that the dealer has received at least the required sum as a deposit by the customer and that is what in fact happens. The customer wishing to acquire a car from a dealer on hire-purchase terms pays the dealer the agreed deposit (which must at present be at least twenty per cent. of the cash price) and requests the dealer

G to arrange hire-purchase terms for the balance. This the dealer does by selling the car to the finance company, which pays him the price of the car less the deposit which he has already received. The finance company then hires the car to the customer at a price representing the excess of the purchase price over the sum paid to the dealer plus interest charges based on the deferred terms. So here the hire-purchase figure, plus interest charges, was £1,569 and that was

H what the finance company would have received if the transaction had gone to its expected conclusion. The dealer would thus be satisfied by receiving the whole agreed price made up of the deposit paid by the customer plus the balance paid by the finance company, which was here £1,250.

   In fact that was not the transaction here: it was what is apparently termed a " refinancing " transaction. This happens when the customer instead of buying

I the car starts by being its owner. He wants to raise money on it without parting with its possession and without executing a bill of sale. I do not see why this may not be done by a genuine sale by the owner to the finance house and a hiring back of the car to him on deferred terms; these, having regard to the regulations, must begin with a twenty per cent. deposit. Thus here the customer could have sold the car to the finance company for £1,848 and they could have hired it back to him for £1,848 plus interest on payments spaced over three years. That

---

(9) [1966] 1 All E.R. at pp. 40, 41.   (10) [1966] 1 All E.R. at pp. 41, 42.

howover was not this transaction. This hire-purchase agreement was based on a **A**
sum of only £1,250. Here, to go by the documents, the customer sold his car to
an intermediary (Saxon) for £1,848, of which he received £1,248, thus on the
face of it leaving £600 still due to him. Saxon then represented to the finance
company that Saxon had received the £600 and invoiced the car to the finance
company on that footing. The finance company without any enquiry accepted
that situation and hired the car to the customer for a sum based on the balance **B**
of £1,250, that is to say £1,569.

In these circumstances the question is whether the £600 was ever actually
paid. It is said that Saxon, owing this sum to the customer, " applied it " in
paying the like sum as a deposit. To whom? To the finance company? Admittedly
not. To themselves? Again admittedly not. They were never £600 the richer
by the transaction. If you looked in Saxon's books you would nowhere find this **C**
£600 as a credit to them. Their profit was £2 plus a commission on the hire-
purchase charge amounting to £319. Nor was the customer £600 the poorer.
He never paid that or any other like sum. It is said that he allowed Saxon to
retain it out of the £1,848 being the price at which he sold the car to them of
which he only received £1,248. This cannot be right: if it were, Saxon would
either owe him £600 or be that much the richer, which no one suggests they were. **D**
The truth is that the £600 was a mere fiction. The only reason why that sum was
arrived at seems to be that £1,248 was all the customer could induce the finance
company to lend him on a car which Saxon valued at £1,848—that is to say
two thirds of its cash price.

If I had been trying the case I think that I should have drawn from the facts
the inference that there was a sale by the customer to Saxon for a consideration **E**
of £1,248 cash plus a promise of a hire-purchase agreement whereby some finance
company would relet it to the customer on deferred terms based on that sum.
There is no sign in the oral evidence that £600 was ever agreed as a deposit
between the customer and Saxon. It might so far as I can see have been any
other sum as long as it exceeded the fraction required to satisfy the Hire-Purchase
and Credit Sale Agreements (Control) Order, 1960.   **F**

Was there then an " actual " payment? In my view no.

The judge found that the hire-purchase transaction was not a sham. In a
sense this is right because the customer thought that he was entering into a
hire-purchase transaction. He only wanted to raise the wind on the security of
his car and he did not care how that result was brought about. He knew nothing
about the Bills of Sale Acts or the Order of 1960 requiring the actual payment **G**
of a twenty per cent. deposit. He was emphatic that he paid none and this did
strike him as making this transaction different from hire-purchase agreements
with which he was familiar; but he did think that he was getting the money
on some hire-purchase terms: by this he meant that he could continue in possession of the car if he made the monthly payments which the agreement required.
Accepting the judge's view (11) that we must take the documents as we find them, **H**
the first shows an agreement by the customer to sell his car to Saxon for £1,848
payable on delivery. The second (on the back of the first) shows Saxon as the
owner and a request to them by the customer to arrange a hiring by the finance
company at a cash price of £1,850 together with hire-purchase charges. The
third invoices the car to the finance company at that sum " less initial payment
£600 ". It is here that fiction creeps in. There was no such payment, and Saxon **I**
knew it. Last comes the hire-purchase agreement, whereby the finance company
hire the car to the customer for £1,250 plus charges, that sum being stated to
be the cash price of £1,850 " less initial payment paid before signing agreement ".

It is said that this payment was credit given to Saxon by the customer
representing the £600 owed to the customer by Saxon on the original sale by the
customer to Saxon. Saxon's representative appears to have thought that the true

(11) [1966] 1 All E.R. at p. 41.

A transaction was that there was a sale by the customer to Saxon for £1,848 and a
resale by Saxon to the customer for £1,850, a profit to Saxon of £2, the £600 being
the deposit constituted by a cross-credit. Everyone agrees that this was a mistake.
Saxon in fact sold to the finance company, but for £1,250, and that company
hired the car to the customer at a price based on that figure. The so-called deposit
was a fiction brought into being because the Order of 1960 made a deposit
B necessary. I cannot agree that this was in any sense an " actual " payment.

The matter may perhaps be tested by seeing what would have happened if the
whole transaction had run its appointed course. In that event the customer
would have remained the owner of his car, having received £1,248 and having
paid £1,569 for the accommodation; the finance company would have received
the £1,569; while Saxon would have received the so-called " profit " of £2, the
C difference between what they paid the customer and what they received from the
finance company plus commission on the £319 hire purchase charges. No one
paid nor received £600. There was nothing dishonest about it, but it was contrary
to the Order of 1960, which requires a twenty per cent. deposit actually to be paid.

It was insisted by counsel for the finance company that this was contrary to
the *Stoneleigh Finance, Ltd.* v. *Phillips* (12) decision of this court, but I do not
D agree, for that case preceded the Order of 1960 which requires an " actual "
deposit. " Actual " here must mean " real ", and is in contrast to what DAVIES,
L.J., in that case called (13) a " notional " deposit.

What is the result of that view of the facts? Taking the documents at their
face value they show a sale to Saxon and title passing to Saxon, and a further
sale by Saxon to the finance company also passing title. Thus the finance
E company became the owners of the car and could rightly repossess it as such when
the customer made default in the hiring terms. The claim therefore fails and the
action should be dismissed: but when I turn to the counterclaim I find that the
finance company, having neglected to see that a proper deposit had been paid,
cannot enforce the hire-purchase agreement any further because the Order of
1960 has invalidated it. They cannot therefore enforce it further and their
F counterclaim fails. I do not agree with the submission of counsel for the customer
that the Order of 1960 has a retroactive effect invalidating what has already been
done: if that were right the customer would have to repay the £1,248 which he
has had. The law in my judgment leaves things to stand as they fall and forbids
further performance; and the counterclaim should be dismissed.

G WINN, L.J.: In October, 1963, the plaintiff customer bought a new 3-litre
Rover coupé and paid for it, including certain accessories, £2,112, taking delivery
on Nov. 6, 1963. Between that date and the beginning of February, 1964, he
made very little use of the car, partly because he made a trip to the West Indies.
The value stated in the January issue of Glass's Guide for such a car in a new
state was a little over £1,900: it follows that a figure of £1,850, i.e., £262 less than
had been paid some three months before—a figure which is of significance in the
H circumstances of the present case—does not on the face of the matter appear to
be unreal or an unduly inflated estimate of its value. In my judgment this fact
is of great significance and a dominant feature of this case.

On Feb. 13, 1964, the plaintiff customer went with his car to see a Mr. Dobney,
the manager of A. Saxon, Ltd. (" Saxon "), who traded as Saxon Finance Agency,
and told him that he wished to raise as much money as possible " by financing
I the car ". The customer said expressly in evidence that what he wanted to do
was to borrow money on the security of his car. The learned judge found (14) as
a fact that Mr. Dobney told the customer " we are not moneylenders and it
cannot be arranged that way ", and that Mr. Dobney explained to the customer
that what he could do was to buy the car and sell it to a finance company who
would hire it back on hire-purchase to the customer. The judge accepted (14), on

(12) [1965] 1 All E.R. 513; [1965] 2 Q.B. 537.
(13) [1965] 1 All E.R. at p. 523; [1965] 2 Q.B. at p. 570.
(14) [1966] 1 All E.R. at pp. 40, 41.

the evidence of Mr. Dobney and of the customer, that in substance Mr. Dobney   **A**
made it clear that if he entered into such a transaction the customer would part
with the ownership of the car, but would be able to recover this by completing
the hire-purchase of it from the finance company. Mr. Dobney also said in
evidence that he told the customer that he was prepared to buy the car at
" round about Glass's Guide figure " and gave an approximate value subject to
inspection of the car of £1,800 to £1,850. The learned judge did not find specifically   **B**
whether or not these two statements were made. Manifestly Mr. Dobney and his
firm were minded to buy the customer's car only if it could be sold on at once to
the finance company with which they did all their business, the defendants in
the action. Although certain documents were filled in whilst the customer was
with Mr. Dobney and signed by the customer, and thereafter Mr. Dobney visually
inspected the car and, having been shown the key by the customer, took posses-   **C**
sion of the log book, the transaction was not then completed; the customer drove
away in his car and continued to keep it in his possession, as it was intended that
he should, whatever dealings took place with respect to the ownership of it.

The same afternoon Mr. Dobney telephoned to a Mr. Smith, the general
manager of the defendant finance company, and told him that the customer,
whose employment status he described, wished to hire-purchase the Rover from   **D**
the finance company. Mr. Dobney said in evidence, and the judge accepted, that
he did not disclose to Mr. Smith that the real nature of the transaction was that
the customer was selling his own car and then seeking to re-purchase it from the
finance company. It seems to me that the learned judge accurately described
Mr. Smith's attitude when he said (15):

> ". . . he did not know that this particular transaction which had been put   **E**
> before him was in fact a re-financing operation, and, indeed, he did not care
> provided that the terms of the hire-purchase agreement were satisfactory in
> other respects . . ."

Mr. Smith told Mr. Dobney to go ahead; the same afternoon Mr. Dobney telephoned to the customer and told him that the matter could go ahead and he was   **F**
putting a cheque in the post for him straight away. All these matters took place
on Feb. 13 though one of the two documents signed by the customer on that day,
which appears on the back of the other of those documents, is dated Feb. 14. The
cheque mentioned was dated Feb. 13 and was for the sum of £1,248, drawn to
" bearer "; on the back of it was a receipt form signed by the customer, dated
Feb. 14.   **G**

The two documents signed by the customer on Feb. 13 consisted of forms
appropriate for the conduct of a transaction between a customer and a motor car
dealer whereby the customer sells a car to the dealer, or barters it in part exchange,
and the dealer supplies to the customer a different car, taking from him either
part of the agreed purchase price of the second car or the value of the customer's
former car by way of part exchange, and arranges for the balance of the purchase   **H**
price to be obtained by hire-purchase of the second car from a hire-purchase
finance company, to whom the dealer will sell that car for the outstanding balance
of the purchase price agreed between him and the customer. Naturally if forms
designed to effect such a transaction are used to carry out a refinancing transaction in which the customer sells his own car with a view to re-acquiring it by
hire-purchase, they will ill fit the real terms of such a transaction.

In my judgment the time of this court in hearing this appeal has been largely   **I**
consumed to no good purpose in meticulous semantic discussions of the verbal
peculiarities of the documents in question, the only relevance of which—and it is
a remote one—would depend on their being shown to be evidentiary of an intent
of the parties to the transaction differing in substance from the record thereof
which the documents purport to provide. I do not propose to embark on any
discussion of such matters.

(15) [1966] 1 All E.R. at p. 40.

A   The judge declared his view (16) that although Mr. Dobney may well have been confused about the meaning of the documents and, indeed, of the true legal analysis of the deal he made with the customer, he, the judge, was (16) " not prepared to hold that this was a sham. I think that one has to give effect to the documents as they stand ". For myself I regard that decision of the judge as one of fact; I am unable to accept the submission that it is a ruling of law founded,

B   inter alia, on the construction of the documents or a mere inference from primary facts. Even if this view be not correct it is nevertheless clear that this court would still be bound to give weight to the judge's ruling or inference: on either footing I am myself of the opinion that the judge's view was sound and I would uphold it.

It is, I think, reasonably clear, though not specifically so stated by the judge,

C   that he intended no less to give effect " as it stood " to another document of which mention has not yet been made. This is a document described as " hire-purchase agreement made between Sterling Industrial Securities, Ltd." (the finance company) and the customer in which the finance company are referred to as " the owner " and the customer as " the hirer ". This document was signed by the customer on Feb. 13 and witnessed by Mr. Dobney, and by Mr. Smith on

D   behalf of the finance company on Feb. 17. In form this agreement was the same as that of any usual hire-purchase agreement used in transactions where a customer is acquiring a car from a dealer by paying part of its purchase price to the dealer and, after a sale of the car by the dealer to a hire-purchase finance company, undertaking to pay the balance of the purchase price plus interest by instalments to the hire-purchase finance company. I see no indication in the

E   judge's judgment that he drew any distinction between this " hire-purchase agreement " and the other two documents already mentioned in this judgment in respect of the effect which he thought it right to give respectively to them. The judge clearly appreciated, as one would expect of a judge of his great experience and familiarity with commercial affairs, what was the essential question or issue for him to determine for the purposes of the present action with regard to the two

F   transactions, intimately interconnected, which were entered into between the customer and Saxon, and between Saxon and the finance company. He stated it, in my view correctly, as follows (17): " The material question which may be a matter of difficulty to decide is what was the common intention of the parties." He stated (17) (as I think, after hearing the arguments in this court, correctly) that this became a question of fact. He proceeded to make what in my view are

G   essential findings of primary facts by saying (17):

" I, having heard the evidence here, am quite certain of one thing: that the only thing which matters to the [customer] was to get the money, and he did not concern himself at all whether he got it as a straight loan or by some other means. I am also satisfied that when he signed these documents,

H   although he did not read them, he thought that they were, as he said, ordinary hire-purchase documents: I am also satisfied that Mr. Dobney . . . did in fact go through the process . . . of explaining what the documents meant . . ."

The main attack made by the customer in this court on the transactions and the several documents brought into existence to give effect to them or provide

I   evidence of their terms, was on the ground that, as the customer by the most able submission of his counsel, contended, they amounted to bills of sale. It would not have availed the customer to establish that they were, or that either of them amounted to an absolute bill of sale, since notwithstanding any technical objection partially invalidating them or it, such a bill of sale would have remained binding on the customer vis-à-vis the other party to it. Accordingly, the contention necessarily concentrated on establishing a bill of sale by way of security,

---

void if not in accordance with the statutory form; none of these documents was, **A** of course, in accordance with that form.

In my definite view the sole or entirely dominant question on that part of the appeal to which I have so far adverted is whether in reality and on a true analysis of the transactions and each of them, and having regard in particular to the intention of the parties, they constituted loans or sales. It is clear on the authorities that if a transaction is in reality a loan of money intended to be **B** secured by, for example, a sale and hiring agreement, the document or documents embodying the arrangement will be within the Bills of Sale Acts: it is equally clear that each case must be determined according to the proper inference to be drawn from the facts and whatever form the transaction may take the court will decide according to its real substance.

I find a clear and helpful exposition of the matter in two passages in the judg- **C** ments of this court in *Stoneleigh Finance, Ltd.* v. *Phillips* (18). One, where DAVIES, L.J., said (19):

" A sale of goods by A to B followed by a hiring back of the goods by B to A is not, if the parties genuinely intend the transactions to be effective, a bill of sale or otherwise invalid (see *Yorkshire Railway Wagon Co.* v. *Maclure* (20); *Eastern Distributors, Ltd.* v. *Goldring* (*Murphy, Third Party*) (21)). **D** Still less it is so if the transaction takes the form of a sale by A to B, a sale by B to C and a subsequent hiring by C to A."

RUSSELL, L.J., also said (22):

" It was pointed out by SIR GEORGE JESSEL, M.R., in *Yorkshire Railway Wagon Co.* v. *Maclure* (23), that both parties to the transaction must intend **E** to mask a mere loan. He there said ' But even if the wagon company understood it as a loan, in order to set aside the deed, that is to treat it as a nullity, you must show that the railway company were parties to the understanding '."

RUSSELL, L.J., for himself said (24):

F

" The statutory disability in this case can attach if it is shown that the transaction is on both sides, contrary to the tenor of the documents, intended to create only the relationship of secured creditor and debtor."

In the light of the evidence in this action which I have set out and of the findings of the judge, it is impossible for this court to hold that the customer at the time when he signed the documents intended only to borrow money, or to hold that **G** all the parties to the transaction did not intend that they should have in reality the effect of divesting the customer of ownership of his car and vesting it in Saxon and through Saxon in the finance company. This seems to me to be the end of any discussion of the effect in law of the transactions on the ownership of or title to the customer's car.

It was contended for the customer that apart altogether from the provisions **H** of the Bills of Sale Acts the transactions were rendered illegal by the provisions of a statutory Order to which I am about to turn my attention; but it does not seem to me to follow, from a finding that any particular contract of sale by which the parties intended—as they clearly did in the present case on the findings of the learned judge—to pass property in the article sold by force of the contract itself was illegal, that the property in the article did not pass from vendor to **I** purchaser. In the course of the argument I myself referred to the opinion of the Privy Council in *Sajan Singh* v. *Sardara Ali* (25), and I am bound to say that I

(18) [1965] 1 All E.R. 513; [1965] 2 Q.B. 537.
(19) [1965] 1 All E.R. at p. 522; [1965] 2 Q.B. at pp. 569, 570.
(20) (1882), 21 Ch.D. 309.   (21) [1957] 2 All E.R. 525; [1957] 2 Q.B. 600.
(22) [1965] 1 All E.R. at p. 528; [1965] 2 Q.B. at p. 579.
(23) (1882), 21 Ch.D. at p. 314.
(24) [1965] 1 All E.R. at p. 529; [1965] 2 Q.B. at p. 580.
(25) [1960] 1 All E.R. 269; [1960] A.C. 167.

A do not think that that case was satisfactorily distinguished from the present case: although it is true to say that there were two grounds for it, the second of which would have been sufficient alone to sustain it, it is the first ground which is relevant in the circumstances of the case now before this court. In my opinion that does not make the first ground a mere obiter dictum and I think that this court must give due weight to it. In *Singh's* case (26) the Privy Council was

B concerned with regulations made in Malaya at the end of the last war, which provided inter alia that no one could lawfully sell any motor vehicle for the carriage of goods without a haulage permit. The plaintiff in the action bought from the defendant one of six motor vehicles which the defendant had·acquired from the British Military Disposals Board. Although the plaintiff acquired " ownership " of the lorry from the defendant and operated it for the carriage

C of goods on his own account, the defendant obtained and held the only haulage permit for that lorry, thereby deceiving the public administration of Malaya and doing so pursuant to an agreement with the plaintiff, to whom no haulage permit would have been issued. Subsequently the defendant took the lorry from the plaintiff and refused to return it. The Privy Council held that notwithstanding that the contract for the sale of the lorry was unlawful, yet when in pursuance of

D the contract the lorry was sold and delivered to the plaintiff the property in it passed to him and he was entitled to sue the defendant in detinue. I have not, of course, overlooked the fact that in the present case there was no real delivery of the car by the customer to either Saxon or the finance company, but in my opinion it is clear that the parties intended property to pass without delivery, and it is clear from the Sale of Goods Act, 1893, that delivery is not an essential

E condition of the passing of property unless the parties intend that it should be such a condition.

The ground on which the interrelated transactions to which I have referred are said to have been illegal is that, as it was contended for the customer, they contravened the provisions of the Hire-Purchase and Credit Sale Agreements (Control) Order, 1960. By art. 1 (1) and art. 2 (*b*) respectively of that Order it

F was enacted that it should be unlawful for any person (a) to dispose of any article by hire-purchase or credit sale, (b) to be in possession of any article by virtue of a hire-purchase or credit sale agreement, unless the requirements set out in a schedule had been complied with. So far as relevant it was thus required (27) that:

G "Before the agreement was entered into actual payment was made in respect of each description of goods comprised in the agreement of not less than an amount . . ."

which in the instant case would have been twenty per cent. of the aggregate of the cash price. The cash price stated in the hire-purchase agreement of Feb. 17 was £1,850: twenty per cent. thereof would be £370. The hire-purchase agreement

H purported to show that before it was signed an initial payment had been made of £600.

As I have already said, the judge, if, as I think, I have rightly understood his judgment in this respect, held that " one has got to give effect to " this recital in the agreement as well as to the statement to be found in an invoice of Feb. 14 sent by Saxon to the finance company in respect of the car which set out its

I cash price payable by the finance company to Saxon as £1,850 less "initial payment £600 ", and thus showed a balance due of £1,250. Equally, in the view of the judge (28), and in my own view, effect must be given to the two agreements made on Feb. 13, on the front and back respectively of the same piece of paper, reciting that Saxon agreed to pay to the customer for his car £1,848 and that Saxon were to endeavour to arrange to sell the car to the finance company

(26) [1960] 1 All E.R. 269; [1960] A.C. 167.
(27) By Sch. 2, Pt. 1, para. 3: see p. 419, letter G, ante.
(28) [1966] 1 All E.R. at p. 41.

and arrange for the finance company to hire-purchase it to the customer for A £1,850 payable by a first deposit of £600 and as to the balance by thirty-six instalments, and to the receipt on the back of the cheque for £1,248 received by the customer from Saxon reciting that that sum was the balance of the purchase price of the car. The relevant effects are, first, that Saxon retained £600 which as purchaser of the customer's car at the price of £1,848 the dealer owed to the customer; second, that Saxon stated to the finance company that the value of B the car to Saxon was £1,850 but that Saxon, having received £600 part thereof, required only £1,250 from the finance company for the purchase of the car by the finance company from Saxon. The finance company did pay £1,250 to Saxon as one of the items to which a cheque dated Feb. 17 for £2,430 related.

Two questions then arise: (a) was there payment of £600 by the customer to Saxon; (b) was such payment " actual payment " within the meaning of the C Order of 1960?

I do not myself think it relevant to consider whether there was either payment or actual payment of £600 to the finance company, despite the contrary view expressed by McNAIR, J., (29) from which I differ with deference.

In my view money may be paid, and in everyday usage constantly is paid, without any currency passing. An obvious instance is where A, being indebted D to B in the sum of, say, £10, offers 10 £1-notes to B, who, being himself indebted to the extent of £5 to C, requests A to retain £5 of the notes and hand them to C in discharge of B's indebtedness to C. If this is done B has paid his debt to C though no currency has passed from B to C. In practice in the modern commercial world the mechanism more usually adopted is that of account entries; and I think it is equally true that where X, being a customer of the Y E bank with a credit balance on his account, draws a cheque in favour of Z which on presentation to the Y bank is met, and there results a debit entry in X's account, X thereby pays the amount of that debit entry to his bank, the Y bank, in reimbursement of the Y bank for the payment by them of the same amount to Z. Incidentally, if Z also happens to be a customer of the Y bank, payment to him will have been effected by a credit entry in his account with that bank. F

It seems to me quite clear that when Saxon, with the consent of the customer, retained £600 part of the £1,848, which Saxon agreed to pay the customer for his car, Saxon thereafter held that sum at the customer's disposal; and that on acceptance by the finance company of the proposal put to them, Saxon applied the £600 on the customer's behalf as part-payment to Saxon of the price of the car, by then Saxon's property, which Saxon were selling to the finance Company: G it does not seem to me to be material whether, on a true analysis, Saxon are to be regarded as crediting the finance company with that amount or as taking it for themselves.

The question remains whether the £600 referred to was actually paid, i.e. whether within the terms of the Order of 1960 " actual payment " was made to the extent of that sum in respect of the car to Saxon and/or the finance company H before the hire-purchase agreement was entered into. In my opinion that question should be answered in the affirmative, since I do not think that the Order of 1960 requires payment to be made in currency. Its purpose, in my judgment, is to restrain the mischief of inflating credit by means of what has been called in this appeal " a charade " of payment, and to prohibit bogus pretences of payment designed to present a false picture of the price element of the purchase, in order I to conceal the fact that no payment, or no such payment as the Order of 1960 requires, has been made by the customer to the dealer or the finance company before the signing of the agreement. The final sentence (30) of para. 3 of Pt. 1 of Sch. 2 to the Order of 1960 recognises that the giving of value may constitute payment within the meaning of the Order and fortifies my view that the provisions of Pt. 2 of that schedule have no impact on the facts of the present case.

---

(29) [1966] 1 All E.R. at pp. 41, 42.   (30) See p. 419, letter G, ante.

A   In my judgment the operative word in those provisions is the word " acquired ". This word, used there in association with the word " borrowed " and in relation to the three several situations referred to under (a), (b) and (c) of the Order of 1960, (31), does not seem to me capable, on the proper construction of criminal provisions imposing sanctions, of so wide a connotation as such a general word as for example " received " or " obtained ". In my view its proper meaning for

B   the purposes of those provisions is synonymous with: obtained otherwise than by exchange or provision of commensurate value. By way of comment I would add that to my mind, apart from any rule of construction which requires any ambiguity in a criminal provision to be resolved in favour of the subject, the word " acquired " generally connotes: getting something for nothing or getting something without giving for it any barter or services constituting a comparable

C   return.

For the reasons which I have endeavoured to express I would allow this appeal both as to the plaintiff customer's claim for the return of the car and as to the defendant finance company's counterclaim.

Appeal allowed on the counterclaim, judgment for the defendant finance company for £174 6s. 8d., cross-appeal by the plaintiff customer dismissed. Leave to appeal
D   *to the House of Lords refused.*

Solicitors: *Victor Mishcon & Co.* (for the defendant finance company); *Malcolm Fraser & Co.* (for the plaintiff customer).

[*Reported by* HENRY SUMMERFIELD, ESQ., *Barrister-at-Law.*]

E   TOOHEY v. WOOLWICH JUSTICES AND ANOTHER.

[HOUSE OF LORDS (Lord Reid, Lord MacDermott, Lord Hodson, Lord Pearce and Lord Pearson), March 24, 28, May 18, 1966.]

Magistrates—Summary trial—Election of trial by jury—Assault on police constable in execution of his duty—Whether accused entitled to claim trial by
F   *jury—Magistrates' Courts Act, 1952 (15 & 16 Geo. 6 & 1 Eliz. 2 c. 55), s. 25 (1), as amended—Police Act 1964 (c. 48), s. 51 (1).*

The word " assault " is apt to include any form of aggravated assault whether on a young male or a female (under s. 43* of the Offences Against the Person Act, 1861) or on a police officer in the execution of his duty (under s. 51 (1)† of the Police Act 1964), and the exception for the offence of
G   " an assault " to the right to trial by jury provided by s. 25 (1)‡ of the Magistrates' Courts Act, 1952, is equally applicable to both aggravated assaults and common assault (see p. 432, letter F, p. 430, letter E, p. 430, letter I, to p. 431, letter A, and p. 432, letter H, post).

Decision of the DIVISIONAL COURT (sub nom. *R. v. Woolwich Justices, Ex p. Toohey* [1965] 3 All E.R. 825) affirmed.

H   [As to the offence of assaulting a police officer, see 10 HALSBURY'S LAWS (3rd Edn.) 634, 635, para. 1207; and for cases on the subject, see 15 DIGEST (Repl.) 852, *8194-8203.*

As to the meaning of assault, see 10 HALSBURY'S LAWS (3rd Edn.) 740, para. 1423; 38 ibid., 761, 762, paras. 1255, 1256.

As to claim to trial by jury by person charged with summary offence, see
I   25 HALSBURY'S LAWS (3rd Edn.) 179-181, para. 330; and for cases on the subject, see 33 DIGEST (Repl.) 192-194, *365-380.*

For the Offences against the Person Act, 1861, s. 43, see 5 HALSBURY'S STATUTES (2nd Edn.) 803.

---

(31) The terms of Part 2 of Sch. 2 to the Order of 1960, which are those referred to, are set out in footnote † at p. 415, ante.
  * Section 43, so far as material, is set out at p. 432, letter D, post.
  † Section 51 (1), so far as material, is set out at p. 431, letter B, post.
  ‡ Section 25 (1) is set out at p. 431, letter E, post.

For the Magistrates' Courts Act, 1952, s. 25, see 32 HALSBURY'S STATUTES A
(2nd Edn.) 443.

For the Police Act 1964, s. 51, see 44 HALSBURY'S STATUTES (2nd Edn.) 924.]

Appeal.

This was an appeal by the appellant, Brian Anthony Toohey, from an order
of the Divisional Court (LORD PARKER, C.J., ASHWORTH and WIDGERY, JJ.),
dated Nov. 4, 1965, and reported sub nom. *R.* v. *Woolwich Justices, Ex p.* B
Toohey, [1965] 3 All E.R. 825, dismissing the appellant's motions for orders of
prohibition and mandamus directed to the first respondents, the justices for
the petty sessional division of Woolwich, to prohibit them from hearing summarily a charge brought against him under s. 51 (1) of the Police Act 1964, and
to allow him to go forward to be tried by a jury for that offence, viz., assaulting
a police constable in the execution of his duty. The Divisional Court certified C
that a point of law of general public importance was involved, viz., " Whether
an offence against s. 51 (1) (*a*) of the Police Act 1964, is an assault within the
meaning of s. 25 (1) of the Magistrates' Courts Act, 1952, as amended by the
Sexual Offences Act, 1956 ". The second respondent was the Commissioner
of Police for the Metropolis.

E. Terrell, Q.C., and *H. M. Self* for the appellant.   D
J. H. Buzzard for the respondents.

Their lordships took time for consideration.

May 18. The following opinions were delivered.

LORD REID: My Lords, I agree with the reasons given by my noble and
learned friends, and I shall, therefore, move that this appeal be dismissed.   E

LORD MACDERMOTT: My Lords, the appellant having been charged
under s. 51 (1) of the Police Act 1964, with assaulting a police constable while
in the execution of his duty—a charge which made him liable on a first summary
conviction to imprisonment for a term not exceeding six months—applied under
s. 25 (1) of the Magistrates' Courts Act, 1952, (1) to be tried by a jury. That F
subsection provides that a person over fourteen years of age who is charged
before a magistrates' court with a summary offence punishable by imprisonment
for a term exceeding three months may " claim to be tried by a jury, unless the
offence is an assault . . ." The justices refused the appellant's application on the
ground that the offence charged was " an assault " within the meaning of this
provision. The Divisional Court (2) affirmed this ruling, and the sole question G
for your Lordships' determination, therefore, is whether the offence alleged
against the appellant is " an assault " on the true construction of that expression
as used in s. 25 (1) of the Act of 1952.

These words cannot, of course, include every offence involving an assault,
if only because the subsection is concerned with summary offences alone. That,
however, is far from saying, as counsel for the appellant contended, that they H
must be confined to common or ordinary assaults. No doubt the offence charged
against the appellant would not be properly spoken of as a common assault.
It is an assault of an aggravated kind; but, according to their common usage,
the words " an assault " are apt to describe such an assault as well as a common
assault, and I can find nothing in their context or in the policy of the relevant
legislation to give them a narrower import. There is certainly no constitutional I
issue worthy of the name to justify a departure from the natural meaning; and,
in my opinion, the history of the material enactments affords cogent support
for the adoption of the natural meaning as the true meaning. That history is
set out so clearly in the judgment of LORD PARKER, C.J., (3), in the Divisional
Court that I do not propose to detail it again. I would only add that I fully
agree with the reasoning of LORD PARKER, and also with that of my noble and

_____

(1) As amended by the Sexual Offences Act, 1956, s. 48 and Sch. 3.
(2) [1965] 3 All E.R. 825.   (3) [1965] 3 All E.R. at pp. 826, 827.

A learned friend, Lord Hodson, whose opinion in this case I have had the advantage
of reading.

I would, therefore, dismiss the appeal.

LORD HODSON: My Lords, this appeal raises the question whether an
offence against s. 51 (1) of the Police Act 1964, is " an assault " within the meaning
of s. 25 (1) of the Magistrates' Courts Act, 1952, as amended by the Sexual Offences
B Act, 1956. The former section provides:

" Any person who assaults a constable in the execution of his duty, or a
person assisting a constable in the execution of his duty, shall be guilty of an
offence and liable—(*a*) on summary conviction to imprisonment for a term
not exceeding six months or in the case of a second or subsequent offence
nine months, or a fine not exceeding £100, or to both; (*b*) on conviction on
C indictment to imprisonment for a term not exceeding two years . . ."

The appellant was arrested on May 13, 1965, and charged with an offence contrary to the section, namely,

" Wilfully assaulting Dennis Watson a constable of the metropolitan
police force when in the execution of his duty at Woolwich New Road,
D S.E.18 on May 13, 1965."

The charge came up for hearing on May 31, 1965, before the justices sitting in the
petty sessional division of Woolwich, whereupon the prosecution applied to the
justices to hear the case summarily under s. 51 (1) (*a*) of the Police Act 1964.
The appellant through his counsel then submitted that, under s. 25 (1) of the
Magistrates' Courts Act, 1952, he had a right to elect to be tried by jury. This
E subsection, which superseded and substantially re-enacted s. 17 of the Summary
Jurisdiction Act, 1879, provides, as amended:

" Where a person who has attained the age of fourteen is charged before a
magistrates' court with a summary offence for which he is liable, or would
if he were adult, be liable, to be sentenced by the court to imprisonment for
a term exceeding three months, he may, subject to the provisions of this
F section, claim to be tried by a jury, unless the offence is an assault or an
offence under s. 30, s. 31 or s. 32 of the Sexual Offences Act, 1956."

The material words are " unless the offence is an assault ", and the question is:
are these words of a width sufficient to include an assault of a particular aggravated
nature, that is to say, an assault on a constable in the execution of his duty?

The justices ultimately adjourned the hearing in order that application might
G be made to the Divisional Court for mandamus and prohibition. The application
to the Divisional Court (4) failed, and from the refusal this appeal has been
brought. As pointed out by Lord Parker, C.J., (5) the exception " unless the
offence is an assault " comes forward from s. 17 (1) of the Summary Jurisdiction
Act, 1879, when, for the first time, similar words appeared. These words (6) are:

" A person when charged before a court of summary jurisdiction with an
H offence, in respect of the commission of which an offender is liable on summary
conviction to be imprisoned for a term exceeding three months, and which
is not an assault, may, on appearing before the court and before the charge
is gone into, but not afterwards, claim to be tried by a jury ... ."

The position prior to 1879 was regulated as to summary trial of persons charged
with assaults on constables by the Prevention of Crimes Act, 1871, which pro-
I vided, by s. 12, (7):

---

(4) [1965] 3 All E.R. 825.   (5) [1965] 3 All E.R. at p. 826, letter G.

(6) The text is of the enactment as originally enacted. By the Criminal Justice
Act, 1948, s. 79 and Sch. 9, for the words from " on appearing " to " gone into " there
were substituted the words " if he appears in person to answer the charge and before
he pleads to the charge ".

(7) Section 12 was extended to all cases of resisting and wilfully obstructing any
constable or peace officer by the Prevention of Crime Amendment Act, 1885, s. 2
(repealed); the words " with or without hard labour " ceased to have effect by operation
of the Criminal Justice Act, 1948, s. 1 (2); and the section was repealed by the Police
Act 1964, s. 64 (3) and Sch. 10, and replaced by s. 51 (1) of that Act.

" Where any person is convicted of an assault on any constable when in   A
the execution of his duty, such person shall be guilty of an offence against
this Act, and shall, in the discretion of the court, be liable either to pay a
penalty not exceeding £20, and in default of payment to be imprisoned, with
or without hard labour, for a term not exeeding six months . . ."

Section 17 of the Act of 1871 provided: " Any offence against this Act may be
prosecuted before a court of summary jurisdiction . . ." The offence created by   B
the Act of 1871 (s. 12) was substantially the same as that created by the Act of
1964 (s. 51 (1)), and it is to be observed that, from 1871 until 1879, the offence was
to be dealt with summarily and there was no right to claim trial by jury. Since
the Act of 1879 came into operation, it has been the accepted view that the right
to claim trial by jury under s. 17 of the Act did not apply to assaults on any
constable: see STONES' JUSTICES MANUAL (20th Edn. 1880), at p. 41, and the   C
28th Edn., 1895, at p. 164. The same view was taken of another kind of aggravated
assault (see p. 32 of the 20th Edn. of STONE), namely, that covered by s. 43 of
the Offences Against the Person Act, 1861, which provided:

" When any person shall be charged . . . with an assault or battery upon
any male child whose age shall not in the opinion of such justices exceed
fourteen years, or upon any female, either upon the complaint of the party   D
aggrieved or otherwise, the said justices, if the assault or battery is of such
an aggravated nature that it cannot in their opinion be sufficiently punished
under the provisions hereinbefore contained as to common assaults and
batteries, may proceed to hear and determine the same in a summary way . . ."

Punishment on conviction was by imprisonment with or without hard labour   E
for not exceeding six months. The provisions hereinbefore contained are those
in s. 42 of the same Act dealing with common assaults and imposing a punishment not exceeding two months, and in s. 43 Parliament was clearly considering
something different from a common assault.

The word " assault " is apt to include any form of aggravated assault whether
on a young male or a female (under s. 43 of the Act of 1861) or on a police officer   F
in the execution of his duty (under s. 12 of the Act of 1871 or s. 51 (1) of the
Police Act 1964), and the exception to the right to trial by jury contained in the
Act of 1879 and in the Magistrates' Courts Act, 1952, is, on its face, equally applicable to both. The appellant has contended that the exception only applies to
what he describes as domestic assaults, of which those referred to in s. 43 are
only an aggravated form of those assaults which are dealt with by s. 42, and that   G
the assault on a constable is in an entirely different category and not covered by
the language used " unless it is an assault ". I am unable to accept this contention
and, on the contrary, am clearly of the opinion that the two kinds of aggravated
assault to which I have referred are in each case something more than a common
assault but not for that reason to be disregarded as assaults for the purpose of the
exception, which is expressed in clear language.   H

I would dismiss the appeal.

LORD PEARCE: My Lords, for the reasons set out in the opinions of my
noble and learned friends, LORD MACDERMOTT and LORD HODSON, I would
dismiss this appeal.

LORD PEARSON: My Lords, I concur.   I

Appeal dismissed.

Solicitors: *H. Ragol-Levy* (for the appellant); *Solicitor, Metropolitan Police*
(for the respondents).

[*Reported by* KATHLEEN J. H. O'BRIEN, *Barrister-at-Law.*]

A

CENTRAL AND DISTRICT PROPERTIES, LTD.
v. INLAND REVENUE COMMISSIONERS.

[HOUSE OF LORDS (Lord Reid, Lord MacDermott, Lord Hodson, Lord Pearce
and Lord Pearson), March 28, 29, 30, May 18, 1966.]

B *Stamp Duty—Reconstruction or amalgamation of companies—Relief from duty—*
Acquisition by one company of another's shares—Relief where ninety per
cent. of consideration in shares—Subsidiary company acquiring parent
company's shares—Intermediate acquisition of subsidiary company's
ordinary shares by a third company—Third company's offer of low priced
option over subsidiary company's ordinary shares as inducement to preference
C *shareholders of parent company to exchange their shares—Whether offer so*
made by third company was part of the consideration for the acquisition of
the parent company's preference shares within Finance Act, 1927 (17 & 18
Geo. 5 *c.* 10), *s. 55* (1).

The appellant company was a subsidiary of U., Ltd., ninety-eight per
cent. of whose ordinary share capital was held by two directors. The appellant
D company had a stock exchange quotation, but the parent company, U., Ltd.,
whose shares were very valuable, had not. In order to render U., Ltd.'s
shares more marketable the two directors took steps to enable the whole of
the shares of U., Ltd. to be acquired by the appellant company, of which
they were also directors but of which they had not shareholding control,
with a view to " merger " of the companies. Ordinary shares of the appellant
E company were accordingly sold by U., Ltd. to L., Ltd., an issuing house
unconnected by shareholding with either U., Ltd. or the appellant company,
so that the appellant company would cease to be a subsidiary of U., Ltd.
(a subsidiary company being debarred by s. 27 of the Companies Act, 1948,
from acquiring shares in its parent company). In order to induce ninety
per cent. of the preference shareholders of U., Ltd. to exchange their preference
F shares for preference shares of the appellant company, U., Ltd.'s preference
shareholders were offered, in the event of the exchange offer becoming
unconditional, transferable low priced options over certain ordinary shares
of the appellant company. These ordinary shares were provided in part
by U., Ltd. selling to L., Ltd. more shares of the appellant company, and as
to the rest were to be provided by the two directors transferring shares to
G L., Ltd. Under s. 55 (1) (c) of the Finance Act, 1927, there would be exemption from ad valorem stamp duty on the transfers of shares involved in the
" merger " if the " consideration for the acquisition " consisted as to not less
than ninety per cent. thereof in the issue of shares by way of exchange. If
the value of the option rights previously mentioned was part of the consideration, then less than ninety per cent. of the consideration would consist in the
H issue of shares by way of exchange, and the ad valorem stamp duty exemption
would not apply. The inducement put forward to preference shareholders
of U., Ltd. was in a circular accompanying an elaborate document entitled
" merger proposals " (both documents being dated July 25, 1958) and
addressed by the boards of U., Ltd. and the appellant company to the
shareholders of both companies. The circular stated that if the offers became
I unconditional L., Ltd. would in due course offer stock units of the appellant
company to the preference shareholders of U., Ltd. by way of negotiable
letters of entitlement, and that the rights under these could be sold.
Accompanying the merger proposals were also the formal offers and other
documents. In due course the offers became unconditional. The Commissioners of Inland Revenue assessed ad valorem stamp duty of £109,098
7s. 6d. on the transaction on the basis that the condition of exemption
provided by s. 55 (1) (c) of the Finance Act, 1927, was not satisfied.

Held: taking the transaction as a whole, the appellant company had made

itself legally responsible for (or had warranted*) L., Ltd.'s carrying out the **A**
options offer; accordingly the value of the options was part of the consideration for the acquisition of the preference shares in U., Ltd., the condition
of para. (c) of s. 55 (1) of the Finance Act, 1927 was not satisfied, and
exemption from ad valorem stamp duty under s. 55 (1) was not established
(see p. 438, letter G, p. 442, letter D, p. 443, letters F and G, and p. 444,
letters C and I, post). **B**

SEMBLE: in s. 55 (1)† of the Finance Act, 1927, which provides exemption
from ad valorem stamp duty on certain conveyances or transfers on sale in
connexion with the reconstruction or amalgamation of companies, the
natural meaning of the words " consideration for the acquisition " by the
transferee company of the undertaking or of ninety per cent. of the issued
share capital of the existing company is the quid pro quo provided by, or **C**
moving from, the acquiring company (see p. 437, letter A, p. 441, letter H,
and p. 444, letter C, post); consequently a truly independent additional
inducement from an independent source, at any rate if not devised as part
of the scheme of reconstruction or amalgamation, will not be part of the
" consideration for the acquisition " within s. 55 (1) (c) (see p. 441, letter I,
to p. 442, letter A, and p. 444, letter A, post). **D**

Appeal dismissed.

[As to relief from stamp duty on conveyances or transfers in connexion
with amalgamations of companies, see 33 HALSBURY'S LAWS (3rd Edn.) 318,
319, para. 556; and for cases on the subject, see 9 DIGEST (Repl.) 420, 2718-2720,
39 DIGEST (Repl.) 325, 326, 686-688.

For the Finance Act, 1927, s. 55 (1) see 21 HALSBURY'S STATUTES (2nd Edn.) **E**
935.]

Appeal.

This was an appeal from an order, dated Feb. 26, 1965, of the Court of Appeal
(WILLMER, HARMAN and SALMON, L.JJ.), allowing an appeal by the respondents,
the Commissioners of Inland Revenue, from an order dated July 31, 1964, of
the Chancery Division of the High Court of Justice (UNGOED-THOMAS, J.) in **F**
favour of the appellant company, Central and District Properties, Ltd., on a
Case Stated under s. 13 of the Stamp Act, 1891, for the opinion of the court
as to the stamp duty chargeable on certain instruments, which were described
as forms of acceptance and transfer, and on three forms of transfer executed
pursuant to s. 209 (3) of the Companies Act, 1948. These instruments were
executed for the purpose of transferring to the appellant company the shares in **G**
Unicos Property Corporation, Ltd. (hereinafter called " Unicos "). The question
at issue was whether, as the appellant company contended, the instruments,
which had been adjudicated, were exempt from stamp duty under the heading
" Conveyance or Transfer on Sale " in Sch. 1 of the Stamp Act, 1891, by virtue
of s. 55 (1) of the Finance Act, 1927, or, as the commissioners contended, the
exemption conferred by that subsection was inapplicable in the circumstances **H**
of the case. It was not in dispute that if the exemption applied the instruments
were not liable to stamp duty but that, if it did not apply, they were liable to
the duty that the commissioners had assessed, amounting in the aggregate to
£109,098 7s. 6d.

The facts are summarised in the opinion of LORD REID and are more fully
stated in the judgment of WILLMER, L.J., at p. 445, letter H, et seq., post. **I**

Sir Andrew Clark, Q.C., *G. B. Graham*, Q.C., and *S. T. Crump* for the appellant
company.

Michael Wheeler, Q.C., and *J. P. Warner* for the Crown.

Their lordships took time for consideration.

May 18. The following opinions were delivered.

---

* See p. 444, letter G, post.
† Section 55, so far as material, is set out at p. 435, letter H, to p. 436, letter D, post.

A   **LORD REID:** My Lords, the question in this case is whether the respondent commissioners were right in deciding that a number of transfers of shares were chargeable to stamp duty. The appellant company maintains that by reason of the provisions of s. 55 (1) of the Finance Act, 1927, no stamp duty was exigible, and therefore seeks repayment of £109,098 which has already been paid. It is admitted that if the appeal succeeds no duty is payable.

B   It will, I think, make for clarity if I first describe the position in 1958 before the events which have given rise to this case. The appellant company was a subsidiary of another company which I shall refer to as Unicos. The latter had a capital of £1,500,000, all in cumulative preference shares except one million ordinary shares of 1s. each. Ninety-eight per cent. of these ordinary shares were owned by Mr. Rubens and Mr. Shine, who were two of the four directors. The

C appellant company had an authorised capital of £600,000, the issued capital being 183,428 cumulative preference shares of £1 each and 1,343,000 ordinary stock units of 4s. each: Mr. Rubens and Mr. Shine were directors, but they did not have sufficient shares to control this company. Unicos had prospered exceedingly, the value of each 1s. share being about £3 10s.; but these shares were not quoted on any stock exchange whereas the appellant company's shares

D were. So, in order to make their holdings more marketable Mr. Rubens and Mr. Shine took steps to enable the appellant company to acquire the whole share capital of Unicos in exchange for shares of the appellant company.

The first step was to cause the appellant company to cease to be a subsidiary of Unicos. On July 2, 1958, Unicos sold 255,000 ordinary stock units of the appellant company at 9s. 3d. each to Leadenhall Investments and Finance, Ltd. (" Leaden-

E hall "). Leadenhall had no connexion with Unicos or the appellant company beyond the chairman of Leadenhall being a director of the appellant company. Then it was necessary to induce ninety per cent. of the owners of the preference shares of Unicos to agree to accept preference shares of the appellant company in exchange, and apparently it was thought well to make this offer more attractive by adding to it an offer that if ninety per cent. of these shareholders, who were

F numerous, agreed to the exchange they would receive transferable options to purchase ordinary stock units of the appellant company at a low price: the market price of these units was about 14s. and it was proposed to offer one unit per preference share at 9s. 9d.; but the offer of these units was to be made not by the appellant company but by Leadenhall. Leadenhall already held 255,000 of these units but this offer required that Leadenhall should have 1,443,588

G units available. The rest were provided first by Unicos selling to Leadenhall 658,687 units which they still held and secondly by Mr. Rubens and Mr. Shine agreeing to transfer to Leadenhall 529,901 out of the units which they would receive if the proposed merger was completed. In each case Leadenhall paid 9s. 3d. per unit and undertook to sell the units to the preference shareholders of Unicos or their nominees at 9s. 9d.

H   It is fairly obvious that the details of this scheme were devised with the object of avoiding stamp duty by bringing the scheme within the scope of s. 55 of the Finance Act, 1927. The relevant parts of that section are as follows:

" (1) If in connexion with a scheme for the reconstruction of any company or companies or the amalgamation of any companies it is shown to the satisfaction of the Commissioners of Inland Revenue that there exist the
I   following conditions, that is to say—

   (*a*) that a company with limited liability is to be registered, or that since the commencement of this Act a company has been incorporated by letters patent or Act of Parliament, or the nominal share capital of a company has been increased;

   (*b*) that the company (in this section referred to as ' the transferee company ') is to be registered or has been incorporated or has increased its capital with a view to the acquisition either of the undertaking of,

or of not less than ninety per cent. of the issued share capital of, any   A
particular existing company;

  (c) that the consideration for the acquisition (except such part thereof
       as consists in the transfer to or discharge by the transferee company
       of liabilities of the existing company) consists as to not less than
       ninety per cent. thereof—

         (i) . . .   B
        (ii) where shares are to be acquired, in the issue of shares in the
           transferee company to the holders of shares in the existing
           company in exchange for the shares held by them in the existing
           company;

     then, subject to the provisions of this section,

        (A)   C
        (B) stamp duty under the heading ' Conveyance or Transfer on
           Sale ' in Sch. 1 to the Stamp Act, 1891, shall not be chargeable
           on any instrument made for the purposes of or in connexion
           with the transfer of the . . . shares . . ."

The commissioners were satisfied that conditions (a) and (b) existed in this case.   D
They decided that stamp duty was payable because they held that condition (c)
was not satisfied. The case turns on whether the value of the option given to
each Unicos shareholder to purchase one ordinary stock unit of the appellant
company per share held by him was or was not part of " the consideration for
the acquisition " of his shares. If it was not, then the shares in the appellant
company to be given in exchange for the Unicos shares formed more than ninety   E
per cent. of the consideration for their acquisition. If, however, the agreed value
of the option—4s. 3d. per share—was part of the consideration, then the proportion of the consideration attributable to the shares of the appellant company
given in exchange was reduced to less than ninety per cent., so that s. 55 would
not apply and stamp duty would be payable.

The proposals were duly submitted to the Unicos preference shareholders   F
and accepted by the owners of more than ninety per cent. of these shares. Each
of these shareholders in fact received for each of his shares not only a preference
share of the appellant company but also the option to buy an ordinary stock
unit at the price of 9s. 9d.; but the appellant company contends that this option
was not part of the consideration for the acquisition of the Unicos shares.
Consideration for the acquisition must mean consideration for the acquisition   G
by the appellant company, and therefore it can include only what was provided
directly or indirectly by the appellant company. It is said that the appellant
company had nothing to do with the offer of the option. That offer was not
made by the appellant company or on its behalf. It was made by Leadenhall
who held the units offered and who were making the offer because they had
undertaken to do so to Mr. Ruben and Mr. Shine, or to Unicos, which was con-   H
trolled by Mr. Rubens and Mr. Shine, who had their own reasons for causing the
offer to be made.

The Crown maintain that, even if that were the true view of the facts, the
offer of the units must nevertheless be held to be part of the consideration for
the acquisition. They point to the initial words of the subsection—" If in connexion with a scheme "—and say that any valuable consideration put to the   I
transferor shareholders as part of a scheme and in fact received by them must be
regarded as part of the consideration for the acquisition. The Crown have to
admit, however, that not every valuable advantage received by transferor shareholders can be regarded as part of the consideration for the acquisition. Suppose
that Mr. Rubens and Mr. Shine had gone direct to the transferor shareholders
behind the back of the appellant company, and told them that if they would
agree to accept the appellant company's offer they would receive this option
as an inducement provided by Mr. Rubens and Mr. Shine, then the Crown admit

A that the value of the option could not be regarded as part of the consideration for the acquisition.

I find some difficulty in accepting the Crown's argument in this matter. I think that the natural meaning of " consideration for the acquisition " is the quid pro quo provided by or moving from the acquiring company. No doubt this phrase is capable of a wider meaning if the context in which it is used so requires;

B but, even if the apparent general intention of the section could be held to justify a wider meaning, I would not find it easy to define just what that wider meaning should be. So I am inclined to agree with the tentative views expressed by HARMAN and SALMON, L.JJ., (1). Like them, however, I do not find it necessary to reach a final conclusion because I think that, even if the appellant company is right on this matter, the appeal fails for other reasons.

C I must now consider whether the offer of the option was really made by Leadenhall quite independently of the appellant company. On July 25, 1958, Leadenhall sent to each Unicos shareholder a letter accompanied by an elaborate document, " Merger Proposals ", addressed by the boards of directors of both Unicos and the appellant company to the shareholders of both companies. In that letter Leadenhall first referred to the merger proposals enclosed and said:

D " Accordingly, on behalf of [the appellant company] we hereby offer to purchase your shares in Unicos on the basis that for each share sold as set out in col. 1 below you will receive in exchange the consideration set out in col. 2 . . ."

Then after sundry explanations they said in the last paragraph—

E " You will see from para. 12 of the merger proposals that if the offers become unconditional Leadenhall will in due course offer 1,443,588 ordinary stock units of [the appellant company] to the preference shareholders of Unicos by way of negotiable letter of entitlement. If you do not wish to purchase stock units when the offer is made, you should be able to sell the right to do so to a third party. Leadenhall will not make the offer for sale

F to Unicos preference shareholders unless the offers on behalf of [the appellant company] to acquire the share capital of Unicos become unconditional."

Stopping there I doubt whether the casual reader would realise (or was meant to realise) that Leadenhall were acting in two quite different capacities: first as agents for the appellant company in offering the exchange of shares, and secondly as principals in offering the ordinary stock units. The careful reader would,

G however, notice the different phraseology in the last paragraph and he would turn to the merger proposals for an explanation. There he would first find para. 6 in these terms:

" 6. It is proposed that the merger will be effected by the acquisition by [the appellant company] of all the shares of Unicos in exchange for shares in [the appellant company] together with certain cash adjustments as set

H out below in para. 7. Accordingly the shareholders of Unicos will find enclosed with these merger proposals the formal offers from Leadenhall Investments & Finance, Ltd. (' Leadenhall ') on behalf of [the appellant company] to the holders of the various classes of preference shares and of the ordinary shares of Unicos. In addition, if the merger is successfully accomplished, the present Unicos preference shareholders will be able to

I purchase [the appellant company's] ordinary stock from Leadenhall as set out in Part 3 below."

There the only reference to the option is that he " will be able to purchase " the units from Leadenhall as set out in Part 3. Again there is certainly no clear indication that Leadenhall were acting independently of the appellant company.

Next the reader would have to turn to Part 3 of the merger proposals. There he would find para. 11 and para. 12 as follows:

(1) See p. 451, letter F, and p. 451, letter I, to p. 452, letter A, post.

" 11. Under the terms of contracts numbered (i), (ii) and (iii), referred   A
to in appendix D to this document, Leadenhall has either acquired or agreed
to acquire 1,443,588 ordinary stock units of 4s. each and 56,678 preference
shares of £1 each in [the appellant company].

" 12. If the offers referred to in para. 7 become unconditional Leadenhall
will offer all the ordinary stock of [the appellant company] referred to in
para. 11, totalling 1,443,588 units, to the Unicos preference shareholders.   B
Within fourteen days after the offers become unconditional Leadenhall will
post to the Unicos preference shareholders on the register as at July 15,
1958, negotiable letters of entitlement whereby they may purchase from
Leadenhall these ordinary stock units at 9s. 9d. per unit (free of stamp duty,
commission and fee) in the proportion of one stock unit for each £1 of Unicos
preference capital held.   This offer for sale by Leadenhall is independent   C
of the offers referred to in para. 7.

" Any Unicos preference shareholder who does not himself wish to buy the
stock units will be able to sell the right to do so to a third party."

There he would see that the offer of the units is independent of the earlier offer:
but that need mean no more than that this offer will only arise if and after the
earlier offer has been accepted by a sufficient number of the shareholders.   D

Finally the reader must go to appendix D.   There he would find an explanation
of why Leadenhall were offering these units at a cheap price from reading
particulars (i), (ii) and (iii).   And he would also read (iv):

" July 21, 1958, [contract] between (a) [the appellant company] and its
directors, (b) Messrs. J. B. Rubens and B. Shine, (c) Unicos and its directors,
and (d) Leadenhall.   Under this agreement [the appellant company] agreed   E
to make the offers contemplated by para. 7 of the merger proposals and
Leadenhall agreed to make the offer for sale contemplated by para. 12 of
the said proposals."

There is certainly no indication here that Leadenhall were acting independently
of the appellant company.   On the contrary it is stated that in this quadripartite
contract to which the appellant company was a party Leadenhall agreed to   F
make the offer.   It was argued that if one turns to the contract itself one sees
that Leadenhall made no contract with the appellant company.   That is a possible
interpretation of the contract, which is ambiguous, but more important is the
clear representation here made to the shareholders.

On the whole matter I think that these documents though far from clear do
point to there being an agreement between the appellant company and Leadenhall   G
regarding this offer.   It appears to me that they indicate that the appellant
company was adopting Leadenhall's offer as an inducement to the shareholders
to agree to the whole scheme, and making itself responsible so that if Leadenhall
had defaulted the appellant company would have had to make good the default
or be liable in damages.   The documents which were tendered to the shareholders
by or on behalf of the appellant company must be construed contra proferentem,   H
and that is what in my view a careful and well informed shareholder would have
understood from them.   If that is right then counsel for the appellant company
rightly admitted that the appeal could not succeed.

Finally I would adopt the concluding part of the judgment of SALMON, L.J.:

" No doubt the merger proposals were carefully drafted with a view   I
to taking advantage of the stamp duty exemption in s. 55 if possible, but
also with commercial considerations well in mind.   Had it not been for
the latter, the task of the draftsmen would have been much easier.   Plain
words could have been used to make it clear that the statements by [the
appellant company] in relation to the negotiable letters of entitlement were
not intended as a promise by [the appellant company] nor as imposing any
legal liability on them in the event of these letters not being forthcoming.
This would have made it plain that no consideration moved from [the

A   appellant company], save that set out in para. 7 of the merger proposals, but it might not have inspired confidence in the Unicos preference shareholders and indeed might have killed the merger."

I shall therefore move that this appeal be dismissed with costs.

LORD MACDERMOTT: My Lords, the claim for stamp duty which is the
B   subject of this appeal arises from an amalgamation between Central and District Properties, Ltd. (hereafter called the " appellant company ") and Unicos Property Corpn., Ltd. (hereafter called " Unicos ") as the result of which the appellant company acquired the issued preference and ordinary shares of Unicos from the shareholders of that company.

This amalgamation was accomplished by the operation of a scheme whose
C   leading promoters included the appellant company, Unicos, a finance company named Leadenhall Investments and Finance, Ltd. (hereafter called " Leadenhall ") and Mr. J. B. Rubens and Mr. B. Shine who were directors of both Unicos and the appellant company and the owners of large and controlling shareholdings in Unicos. This scheme envisaged a complex series of steps for its completion in the course of which—(*a*) the appellant company ceased to be a subsidiary of
D   Unicos and Unicos became a subsidiary of the appellant company; (*b*) Leadenhall not only acted as agent for the appellant company but acquired or agreed to acquire, for the purposes of the scheme, its ordinary shareholding which consisted of ordinary stock units of 4s. each; and (*c*) detailed provision was made as to what the shareholders of Unicos would get on the transfer of their shares to the appellant company.

E   My lords, the nature of the present dispute does not call for a full description of this scheme or of what was done to implement it. The transfer of shares which it brought about involved the execution of numerous instruments which were assessed to stamp duty by the Commissioners of Inland Revenue in sums amounting in the aggregate to £109,098 7s. 6d. This figure is not in question. What is in issue is whether the exemption from stamp duty provided for by s. 55
F   of the Finance Act, 1927, applies. If it does, no part of this assessment is exigible. If it does not, the entire assessment must stand affirmed.

Section 55 (1) of this statute enacts that " If in connexion with a scheme for the . . . amalgamation of any companies . . ." certain conditions are shown to exist, then stamp duty on the instruments for transferring the shares shall not be chargeable. It is admitted that these conditions have been satisfied in this
G   case with the exception of that contained in para. (*c*) of s. 55 (1). As applied to this particular amalgamation, this condition (hereafter called " condition (*c*) ") required that " the consideration for the acquisition " by the appellant company of the issued shares of Unicos should consist, as to not less than ninety per cent. thereof, in the issue of shares in the appellant company to the holders of shares in Unicos in exchange for their shares in that company.

H   Now, it was part of the scheme that the shareholders of Unicos should, on transferring their holdings to the appellant company, be given shares in it of a corresponding class with, in some cases, a cash payment by way of adjustment as well. I shall refer to this quid pro quo hereafter as the " share consideration " and to the offer to give it as the " share consideration offer ". If the transaction had ended with this offer and its acceptance, condition (*c*) would have been
I   satisfied, and no stamp duty would have been payable, because the consideration consisting in the issue of shares in the appellant company would have been not less than ninety per cent. of the total consideration for the acquisition. The preference shareholders in Unicos in fact, however, obtained more than the share consideration on the transfer of their shares to the appellant company. They were offered in addition, and eventually got, a negotiable option to take up the ordinary stock units of the appellant company at a price which was about 4s. 3d. per unit below market value. I shall call this offer the " option offer ". When it became effective it conferred a freely realisable right of value, and the question which

now arises is this—did it form part of " the consideration for the acquisition " **A**
by the appellant company of the Unicos shares? That is the kernel of this
appeal, for if the consideration included this additional element it is clear on the
arithmetic of the scheme that condition (c) has not been satisfied and that there
is no exemption. The answer to this question invites two enquiries. The first
relates to the true nature of the transaction whereby the preference shareholdings
in Unicos were acquired by the appellant company; and the second is concerned **B**
with the true meaning of condition (c).

My lords, the first of these enquiries is in large degree a question of fact and
construction. Before your lordships it involved a close scrutiny of the findings
and numerous exhibited documents which together depict the general character
and the main features of the scheme for amalgamation. I do not think that it
would serve any useful purpose to review these exhibits at length, and I propose **C**
instead to refer to several salient aspects of the scheme and to follow that reference
with a statement of conclusions based on those aspects and supported, as I think,
by the rest of the voluminous material that was canvassed during the debate.

The holding in the appellant company which Leadenhall had acquired for the
purposes of the scheme was 1,443,588 ordinary stock units, and the main object
of this acquisition was, beyond question, to provide a means of making to the **D**
preference shareholders of Unicos the crucial, additional, offer which I have called
the option offer. This was not an independent project by Leadenhall. In my
view, there can be no doubt that it was an integral part of the scheme for
amalgamation, and that Unicos, the appellant company, Leadenhall and Mr.
Rubens and Mr. Shine were all acting in concert respecting the purposes,
formulation and execution of that scheme. **E**

The most important documents in connexion with this first enquiry are those
which conveyed this option offer to the preference shareholders of Unicos. In
an elaborate document entitled " Merger Proposals " and dated July 25, 1958,
Unicos, the appellant company, and their respective directors informed the
membership of both companies as to the proposals for their merger. Part 2
of this document is headed " Merger Terms ". Paragraph 6 thereof refers to **F**
what I have called the share consideration for the acquisition of the Unicos
shareholdings, and ends by saying:

" In addition, if the merger is successfully accomplished, the present
Unicos preference shareholders will be able to purchase [the appellant
company's] stock from Leadenhall as set out in Part 3 below."

G

Paragraph 7 details the share consideration offers. Then, in Part 3, para. 12 begins
with this sentence:

" If the offers referred to in para. 7 become unconditional Leadenhall
will offer all the ordinary stock of [the appellant company] . . . totalling
1,443,588 units, to the Unicos preference shareholders."

After this follow details as to price and distribution of the option offer, and the **H**
paragraph continues—" This offer for sale by Leadenhall is independent of the
offers referred to in para. 7 ". That, as a statement of fact, was accurate in the
sense that the option offer, as I have called it, only came into force if and when
the share consideration offer had been sufficiently accepted to become unconditional. Whether it had any further effect on the nature of the transaction
remains to be seen. **I**

The merger proposals were sent out with a circular letter of the same date
to the preference and ordinary shareholders of Unicos. This circular letter was
signed by Leadenhall acting on behalf of the appellant company. It refers to the
merger proposals and describes the share consideration offer in detail. Then, at
the end, it adds this in leaded type:

" You will see from para. 12 of the merger proposals that if the offers
become unconditional Leadenhall will in due course offer 1,443,588 ordinary

A stock units of [the appellant company] to the preference shareholders of Unicos by way of negotiable letter of entitlement. If you do not wish to purchase stock units when the offer is made you should be able to sell the right to do so to a third party. Leadenhall will not make the offer for sale to Unicos preference shareholders unless the offers on behalf of [the appellant company] to acquire the share capital of Unicos become unconditional."

B The share consideration offer having been accepted sufficiently to become unconditional, Leadenhall sent a further circular letter, dated Aug. 18, 1958, to the preference shareholders of Unicos advising them to this effect and stating that, in accordance with para. 12 of the merger proposals,

C " Leadenhall is now offering 1,443,588 Ordinary Stock Units of 4s. each of [the appellant company] to the preference shareholders of Unicos on the register on July 15, 1958. The stock units are quoted on the London Stock Exchange."

A negotiable letter of entitlement was enclosed and the preference shareholders of Unicos can have had no doubt on receiving this circular that, whether they took up the option or not, they had a disposable right of value in their hands.

D My lords, the conclusions which I reach on this first enquiry—that relating to the true nature of the transaction whereby the preference shares in Unicos were acquired by the appellant company—are: (i) That the consideration moving to the Unicos preference shareholders—the quid pro quo for their shares—consisted of the option offer as well as the share consideration. The option offer has been described as an inducement to accept the share consideration offer,

E and so it was; but it was before the preference shareholders from the beginning as an offer of value and cannot well be left out of account in describing the bargain as they saw and were meant to see it. (ii) That the option offer moved directly from Leadenhall since it made the offer, issued the negotiable letters of entitlement and could make title to the shares offered. (iii) That the appellant company's offer, as contained in the circular letter of July 25, 1958, included not only the

F share consideration offer but a promise that, if that offer became unconditional, Leadenhall would make the option offer. The words " Leadenhall will in due course offer . . ." are words of promise and must, in my opinion, have been used by the appellant company as such and with the intention of creating a contractual obligation. (iv) Leadenhall, in making the option offer, was not acting outside the scheme, but within it and for its purposes. That offer finds a place in the

G merger proposals and, however independent of the share consideration offer it may have been in point of fact, I think that the reasonable and only inference is that both offers were mentioned in the merger proposals because the promoters of the scheme intended and had agreed that both should play a part in bringing the desired amalgamation about.

I now turn to the second enquiry—that as to the true meaning of condition (c).

H The words in this condition " the consideration for the acquisition " must, having regard to the terms of condition (b), refer to what is acquired by the transferee company—in this case the appellant company. And it is common ground that they must, at any rate, include what would be consideration in the contractual sense, that is to say consideration moving from the transferee company. That, in the submission of counsel for the appellant company was the only meaning of

I the words in this context. Counsel for the Crown, however, contended for a wider meaning by which the words in question would include everything which *under the relevant scheme* was offered to the holders of shares in the " existing company " as an inducement to them to part with their shares. It is possible that inducements to secure the participation of such shareholders in an amalgamation of companies may move from some person or body other than the transferee company. Indeed, it is not difficult to imagine an inducement of this sort which takes the shape of an offer from someone who has an interest in promoting the acquisition but is outside the scheme and has nothing to do with those who are acting under it. It

has not been suggested that a truly independent inducement like this would **A**
be consideration within the meaning of s. 55 (1) (c), and it is hard to see any ground
on which such an extended interpretation could be justified notwithstanding the
width of the words " If in connexion with a scheme . . ." with which that subsection begins. The Crown, however, stopped well short of that interpretation
by limiting their submission, as has been seen, to offers made *under the relevant
scheme*; and they contended that if, in the present case, the option offer did not **B**
move from the appellant company, it was nevertheless enough for them to show
that it moved from Leadenhall in accordance with the scheme as revealed in
the exhibited documents, including the merger proposals. This seems to me an
arguable proposition and one which is not without its attractions. While it denies
the word " consideration " a constant contractual flavour, it may be said that
s. 55 (1) is not concerned with the formation of contractual obligations, and that **C**
the intention of Parliament in providing an exemption from stamp duty seems,
on the whole, rather better served by the wider interpretation.

I need not, however, reach a conclusion on this interesting point, and would
prefer to leave it until it can be investigated more fully in the light of the facts
of some case which necessitates its determination. I find this course open because,
on the accepted contractual meaning of " consideration ", I am of opinion that **D**
the appeal is bound to fail. That follows on the views that I have expressed earlier.
The option offer did not move directly from the appellant company, but it
nevertheless moved from it, if indirectly, because the appellant company promised,
and promised contractually, that that offer would be made in the events which
happened. That promise being part of the consideration moving from the appellant
company, the option offer has to be taken into account in applying condition (c), **E**
and that means that that condition has not been satisfied and that there is no
exemption.

For these reasons I would dismiss the appeal.

LORD HODSON: My Lords, the appellant is a company called Central and
District Properties, Ltd. which appeals against a charge of stamp duty in a total
sum of £109,098 7s. 6d. The duty was charged on a number of instruments being **F**
forms of acceptance and transfer and three forms of transfer executed pursuant to
s. 209 (3) of the Companies Act, 1948. These documents were executed to give
effect to the acquisition by the appellant company of the whole of the issued
shares of a company called Unicos Property Corpn., Ltd.

They are to be stamped unless the transactions fall within the exemption
contained in s. 55 (1) of the Finance Act, 1927, which so far as material provides: **G**

" 55.—(1) If in connexion with a scheme for the . . . amalgamation of any
companies it is shown to the satisfaction of the Commissioners of Inland
Revenue that there exist the following conditions, that is to say—
(a) that . . . the nominal share capital of a company has been increased;
(b) that the company (in this section referred to as ' the transferee **H**
company ') . . . has increased its capital with a view to the acquisition
. . . of not less than ninety per cent. of the issued share capital of any
particular existing company;
(c) that the consideration for the acquisition . . . consists as to not less
than ninety per cent. thereof—
(i) . . .   **I**
(ii) where shares are to be acquired, in the issue of shares in the
transferee company to the holders of shares in the existing
company in exchange for the shares held by them in the
existing company;
then, subject to the provisions of this section,—
(A) . . .
(B) Stamp duty under the heading ' Conveyance or Transfer on
Sale ' in Sch. 1 to the Stamp Act, 1891, shall not be chargeable

A
on any instrument made for the purposes of or in connexion
with the transfer of the . . . shares . . ."

The conditions prescribed by para. (*a*) and para. (*b*) of the subsection admittedly
existed. The sole question is whether the requirements of para. (*c*) were also
satisfied, that is to say whether the consideration for the acquisition by the
appellant company of the Unicos shares consists as to not less than ninety per
B cent. thereof in the issue of shares in the appellant (transferee) company to the
holders of shares in Unicos in exchange for the shares held in Unicos.

The question turns on whether or not certain negotiable letters of entitlement
which were offered to and received by the preference shareholders of Unicos fall
to be included as part of " the consideration for the acquisition " within the meaning of para. (*c*). There is no dispute as to figures and the assessment for stamp
C duty made by the Commissioners of Inland Revenue must be discharged if, as
UNGOED-THOMAS, J., thought on the Case being submitted for the opinion of the
court, the conditions of exemption contained in s. 55 (1) (*c*) of the Finance Act,
1927, are satisfied. The Court of Appeal were of the contrary opinion and restored
the assessment of the commissioners. From that decision this appeal is brought.

A mass of detail was necessarily investigated in order to ascertain precisely
D how the takeover of Unicos by the appellant company was effected. This is
fully set out in the Case Stated and in the judgment of WILLMER, L.J., in the
Court of Appeal (2) and has been already summarised by my noble and learned
friend, LORD REID. The appellant company has always contended—(i) that in
the context of s. 55 of the Finance Act, 1927, the expression " consideration for
the acquisition " is confined in its meaning to consideration moving from the
E acquirer, and (ii) that the negotiable letters of entitlement did not so move.
UNGOED-THOMAS, J., accepted the appellant company's contention as to the
meaning of " consideration " and held that the letters of entitlement were offered
by a finance company described as Leadenhall to the Unicos shareholders
not on behalf of the appellant company but independently. He held that there
was no promise made by the appellant company that Leadenhall should make
F such an offer and that, therefore, relief from stamp duty was available in respect
of the acquisition.

I understand that all your lordships are in agreement with the Court of Appeal,
as I am, in holding that on the footing that the consideration for the acquisition
is confined in its meaning yet there is no question but that, on the construction
of the circular letter of July 25, 1958, containing the offer to the Unicos share-
G holders and of the merger proposals themselves which were enclosed in and referred
to in the circular letter, the appellant company warranted to the Unicos preference
shareholders that they would receive the negotiable letters of entitlement, if
ninety per cent. of each class of them should accept the offer for their shares made
on behalf of the appellant company by Leadenhall in the latter's circular. Here
was consideration moving from the appellant company which with the other
H consideration mentioned in the circular would have exceeded ten per cent. of
the total consideration. The merger proposals made the position perfectly clear
to the Unicos shareholders as appears from Part 3, para. 12, which has already
been quoted.

The Crown has, however, taken up the stand that even if the Leadenhall offer
was independent in the sense that it was not warranted or backed in any way
I by a promise of the appellant company to the Unicos shareholders yet the offer
was within the language of the section in that it was made " in connexion with a
scheme for the . . . amalgamation of any companies ". These introductory words
were said to give a wider meaning to the phrase " consideration for the acquisition " than would naturally suggest itself. The natural meaning is surely
" consideration given by or moving from the acquiring company ", not everything which is offered by anyone else. Even if the word " scheme " assists towards

---

(2) See pp. 445, letter H, et seq., post.

the wider construction, I find it difficult to appreciate how these matters can be   **A**
tested in any individual case for, as I understand it, the Crown do not seek to
include a wholly independent offer such as one made by an altruistic benefactor
but only an offer which comes within the scheme, that is to say within the plan
of action devised in order to obtain the end desired, the end being the amalgamation of the companies. No doubt the offer by Leadenhall comes within the scheme
in this sense, but if it is a truly independent offer unbacked by any warranty of   **B**
the appellant (the acquiring company) it is hard to see how the question of
consideration can arise.

It is, of course, unnecessary to express a final opinion on this point, since
the appellant company has not succeeded in escaping from its difficulty even on
the construction of the section on which it relies, but for my part I would be
disposed to agree with the opinion tentatively expressed by the Court of Appeal   **C**
that the appellant company's contention was right on this matter.

I would, however, dismiss the appeal for the reasons I have indicated which are
substantially those given by the Court of Appeal.

LORD PEARCE: My Lords, I agree with the opinion of my noble and
learned friend, LORD REID, and I would therefore dismiss this appeal.   **D**

LORD PEARSON: My Lords, the question arising under s. 55 of the
Finance Act, 1927, is whether the consideration for the acquisition of the Unicos
shares consisted as to not less than ninety per cent. thereof in the issue of shares
in the appellant company to the holders of shares in Unicos in exchange for the
shares held by them in Unicos. The answer to the question depends on whether
the value of the offer by Leadenhall of 1,443,588 ordinary stock units of the   **E**
appellant company to the preference shareholders of Unicos should in some way
be taken into account as part of the consideration for the acquisition of the
Unicos shares by the appellant company. Leadenhall offered the ordinary stock
units of the appellant company at 9s. 9d. per unit; the market price of such
units was about 14s. per unit: therefore, it is assumed that the value of the offer
was about 4s. 3d. per unit. If the value of 1,443,588 units at about 4s. 3d. per   **F**
unit form part of the consideration and has to be added to the cash part of the
consideration, the two taken together are more than ten per cent. of the consideration, and it follows that the issued shares are less than ninety per cent. of
the consideration and so the requirements of s. 55 are not fulfilled.

The Court of Appeal have said that on the true construction of the documents
there was a warranty by the appellant company that Leadenhall would make   **G**
their offer of the stock units (3), and the warranty was part of the consideration
for the acquisition, even if (as the Court of Appeal were inclined to think) the
consideration must be something moving from the acquirer, i.e., the appellant
company. SALMON, L.J., explained what was meant by " warranty "; he said:
" A warranty may be defined as a collateral promise intended and understood
to be legally binding ". It is not necessary to consider whether this contractual   **H**
promise amounted to a condition (breach of which would entitle the shareholders
in some circumstances to rescind their acceptances) or a mere warranty (breach
of which would entitle them only to sue for damages). I agree with the Court of
Appeal that there was a contractual promise by the appellant company that
Leadenhall would make the offer of the stock units. Accordingly the value of
Leadenhall's offer was to be taken into account as part of the consideration for   **I**
the acquisition, and the effect was that the requirements of s. 55 were not fulfilled
and there was no exemption from stamp duty.

There is also a second argument that on the facts of this case a similar conclusion
can be reached without deciding whether there was any such contractual promise.
There was a scheme, to which several companies and persons were parties, viz.,
the appellant company, Unicos, Leadenhall, Mr. Rubens and Mr. Shine. They

---

(3) See p. 450, letter D, p. 451, letter I, and p. 452, letter F, post.

A were all in different ways going to benefit from the scheme if it were carried out. They were acting together and had agreed on the steps to be taken by each of them in furtherance of the common purpose. The main common purpose was that the appellant company should take over the Unicos shares, but there were also subsidiary common purposes, e.g., that Leadenhall should make a profit by buying stock units at 9s. 3d. and selling them at 9s. 9d. per unit. All these com-

B panies and persons associated in the scheme intended and arranged, as part of the scheme, that the consideration to the Unicos shareholders for the takeover trans-action should consist of three elements, viz. (a) the issue of shares in the appellant company by the appellant company; (b) payments of cash by the appellant company; (c) the offer of stock units in the appellant company at a favourable price by Leadenhall. It can be argued therefore that, on the assumption that the

C "consideration for the acquisition" must be moving from the acquirer, i.e., in this case the appellant company, that requirement was satisfied in this case because all the three elements of the consideration were provided by the associates in the scheme acting together, and the associates in the scheme included the appellant company. No part of the consideration was provided by anyone acting inde-pendently. I find this second argument attractive, but there is no need to come to

D a firm conclusion on it and I prefer to keep it open.

I would dismiss the appeal.

Appeal dismissed.

Solicitors: *Paisner & Co.* (for the appellant company); *Solicitor of Inland Revenue.*

[*Reported by* KATHLEEN J. H. O'BRIEN, *Barrister at Law.*]

E

NOTE.

F In view of the references to the judgments in the Court of Appeal which are made in speeches in the House of Lords, the judgments of the Court of Appeal (WILLMER, HARMAN and SALMON, L.JJ.) are set out in this note. They were reserved judgments. In this report of them the appellant company in the appeal to the House of Lords was respondent and is referred to as " Central ".

Feb. 26. The following judgments were read (4). WILLMER, L.J., having stated the question raised on the appeal and having read s. 55 (1) of the Finance Act, 1927 (4a) so far as relevant, continued: There can be no doubt that s. 55 of the Finance Act, 1927,

G affords a very considerable concession in cases to which it applies. We were informed, and I am prepared to accept, that the object of the section was to remove liability for stamp duty on transfers in cases of genuine amalgamations or reconstructions, where the shareholders remain substantially the same and there has been no real change of ownership. This is the effect of the decisions in *Oswald Tillotson, Ltd.* v. *Inland Revenue Comrs.* (5) and *Lever Bros.* v. *Inland Revenue Comrs.* (6), and I would refer especially to the test posed by LORD HANWORTH, M.R., in the former case, viz., whether there is substantial identity of the new corporators with the old (7).

H The issued share capital of Unicos [viz., Unicos Property Corpn., Ltd.] consisted of three classes of preference shares amounting in total to £1,443,588 and one million ordinary shares of 1s. each. The issued share capital of Central consisted of 183,428 preference shares of £1 each and 1,343,000 ordinary stock units of 4s. each. Of the capital of Central, however, 56,678 preference shares and 913,687 ordinary stock units were held by Unicos which was a sufficient holding to give Unicos control over Central. The two companies were closely associated, both being engaged in the business of

I (4) Cases referred to:
Lever Brothers, Ltd. v. *Inland Revenue Comrs.*, [1938] 2 All E.R. 808; [1938] 2 K.B. 518; 107 L.J.K.B. 669; 159 L.T. 136; 9 Digest (Repl.) 420, 2720.
Tillotson (Oswald), Ltd. v. *Inland Revenue Comrs.*, [1932] All E.R. Rep. 965; [1933] 1 K.B. 134; 101 L.J.K.B. 737; 147 L.T. 481; 9 Digest (Repl.) 420, *2719.*
Yeovil Glove Co., Ltd., Re, [1964] 2 All E.R. 849; [1965] Ch.148; [1964] 3 W.L.R. 406; 3rd Digest Supp.
(4a) See p. 442, letters G to I, ante.
(5) [1932] All E.R. Rep. 965; [1933] 1 K.B. 134.
(6) [1938] 2 All E.R. 808; [1938] 2 K.B. 518.
(7) [1932] All E.R. Rep. at pp. 969, 970; [1933] 2 K.B. at pp. 155, 156.

property investment, they had a common address and (with one exception) common   A
directors. Approximately ninety-eight per cent. of the, ordinary shares in Unicos were
held by two individuals, Mr. Rubens and Mr. Shine, who were directors of both companies. The shares of Central were quoted on the Stock Exchange, but those of Unicos
were not.

Negotiations between the two companies took place during the spring and summer
of 1958. In order to make it possible for the amalgamation to be effected by an exchange
of shares, it was necessary to take steps to increase substantially both the preference
and the ordinary capital of Central. The necessary resolutions to effect this were duly   B
prepared for submission to an extraordinary general meeting of Central and in due
course were passed. It was also necessary for Unicos to get rid of its controlling interest
in Central, for otherwise it would have been illegal under s. 27 of the Companies Act,
1948, for Central as a subsidiary to acquire shares in its parent company, Unicos. This
leads me to introduce on the scene a third company, Leadenhall Investments and
Finance, Ltd., ("Leadenhall") for it is on the part played by this company that the
question now at issue largely depends. By a contract of July 2, 1958, to which I will   C
have to refer again hereafter, Unicos in fact sold to Leadenhall a sufficient number of
ordinary shares in Central to divest itself of the control of Central.

Leadenhall is what is described as an issuing house, and does not appear to have
been associated with either of the other companies, except that its chairman, Mr.
Tillett, was also a director of Central. It was, however, by Leadenhall that the offer
was made to the shareholders of Unicos on behalf of Central. That offer was contained
in a letter of July 25, 1958, which was sent to every shareholder of Unicos together
with (i) a copy of the merger proposals, (ii) a notice of a special meeting to approve   D
the merger proposals, and (iii) a form of acceptance and transfer.

The letter of July 25, which was addressed to the preference and ordinary shareholders of Unicos provided as follows:

" Dear Sir/or Madam,
    You will see from the enclosed merger proposals which set out details of the
proposed merger of your company with [Central] that [Leadenhall] are to make
offers to acquire the preference and ordinary capital of [Unicos]. This letter is sent   E
to you in accordance with para. 6 of that document and contains the formal offer(s)
to acquire your holding(s) of Unicos shares. Accordingly, on behalf of Central we
hereby offer to purchase your shares in Unicos on the basis that for each share
sold as set out in col. 1 below you will receive in exchange the consideration set
out in col. 2 (all shares in col. 2 to be issued credited as fully paid) viz:

Col. 1	Col. 2
For each 6½% cum. ' A ' pref. share of £1 in Unicos	One 6½% cum. pref. share of £1 in Central plus 9d. in cash.
For each 6¼% cum. ' B ' pref. share of £10 in Unicos	Ten 6½% cum. pref. shares of £1 each in Central plus 4s. in cash.
For each 5% cum. ' C ' pref. share of £1 in Unicos	One 6½% cum. pref. share of £1 in Central.
For each 1s. ordinary share in Unicos	Two 4s. ordinary shares and three 4s. ' D ' ordinary shares in Central plus 8s. in cash.

The offers are made upon the terms and subject to the conditions set out in paras.
7 to 9 of the merger proposals."

I pause there to remark that paras. 7 to 9 of the merger proposals made provision for:
(a) the exchange of shares and payments in cash as contained in the letter; (b) tran-
sitional arrangements with regard to dividends; and (c) the terms and conditions on   H
which the offers were made, which included (i) acceptance by the holders of ninety
per cent. of the respective classes of Unicos shareholders, (ii) resolutions being duly
passed by the meetings of shareholders of the respective companies, and (iii) permission
being obtained from the Stock Exchange to deal in the new shares of Central which
were to be issued. If the respective conditions were satisfied the offer was to become
unconditional on Aug. 18, 1958.

If the matter stopped there, it is common ground that the transaction would fall
within s. 55 of the Act of 1927. For the cash element contained in the offer was con-   I
siderably less than ten per cent. of the whole of the consideration. It is necessary, however, to refer back now to para. 6 of the merger proposals, to which reference had
been made in the opening paragraph of the letter of July 25. Paragraph 6 of the
merger proposals provided as follows:

" It is proposed that the merger will be effected by the acquisition by [Central]
of all the shares of Unicos in exchange for shares in [Central] together with certain
cash adjustments as set out below in para. 7. Accordingly the shareholders of
Unicos will find enclosed with these merger proposals the formal offers from
Leadenhall on behalf of [Central] to the holders of the various classes of preference

A shares and of the ordinary shares of Unicos. In addition, if the merger is successfully accomplished, the present Unicos preference shareholders will be able to
purchase [Central] ordinary stock from Leadenhall as set out in Pt. 3 below."

In accordance with this latter proposal the letter of July 25 concluded with the following
paragraph:

" You will see from para. 12 of the merger proposals that if the offers become
unconditional Leadenhall will in due course offer 1,443,588 ordinary stock units
B of [Central] to the preference shareholders of Unicos by way of negotiable letter of
entitlement. If you do not wish to purchase stock units when the offer is made
you should be able to sell the right to do so to a third party. Leadenhall will not
make the offer for sale to Unicos preference shareholders unless the offers on behalf
of [Central] to acquire the share capital of Unicos become unconditional."

This must be read in conjunction with Pt. 3 of the merger proposals which provided as
follows:

C " (11) Under the terms of contracts numbered (i), (ii) and (iii), referred to in
appendix D to this document, Leadenhall has either acquired or agreed to acquire
1,443,588 ordinary stock units of 4s. each and 56,678 preference shares of £1 each
in [Central].
" (12) If the offers referred to in para. 7 become unconditional Leadenhall will
offer all the ordinary stock of [Central] referred to in para. 11, totalling 1,443,588
units, to the Unicos preference shareholders. Within fourteen days after the offers
D become unconditional Leadenhall will post to the Unicos preference shareholders
on the register as at July 15, 1958, negotiable letters of entitlement whereby they
may purchase from Leadenhall these ordinary stock units at 9s. 9d. per unit
(free of stamp duty, commission and fee) in the proportion of one stock unit for
each £1 of Unicos preference capital held. This offer for sale by Leadenhall is
independent of the offers referred to in para. 7. Any Unicos preference shareholder
who does not himself wish to buy the stock units will be able to sell the right to do
so to a third party."

E It was found by the commissioners that the ordinary stock units of Central were
readily marketable at a price of 14s. each. Seeing that these were offered to the preference shareholders of the Unicos company at 9s. 9d. each, the contention of the commissioners is that this represented in effect the equivalent of a cash offer of 4s. 3d. per
share as part of the consideration. If that were so, then the cash element of the consideration would substantially exceed ten per cent. of the total consideration, so that the
relief from stamp duty provided by s. 55 of the Act of 1927 would be excluded. Thus
F the question which has to be decided is whether the value of this 4s. 3d. is or is not to
be included in calculating the consideration for the acquisition by Central of the Unicos
shares.

Contracts (i), (ii) and (iii) referred to in para. 11 of the merger proposals are described
in appendix D thereof under the heading " Statement of directors' interests and relevant
contracts." It is necessary to refer briefly to these contracts in order to explain how
Leadenhall came to be in a position to offer 1,443,588 ordinary stock units in Central
to the preference shareholders of Unicos. These three contracts are described in appendix
G D of the merger proposals as follows:

" (i) July 2, 1958, between Unicos and Leadenhall whereby Unicos sold to
Leadenhall 255,000 ordinary stock units of 4s. each in the capital of [Central] at the
price of 9s. 3d. per stock unit. This purchase has been completed. This agreement
provides also for the resale of the said stock units to Unicos at the same price in
the event of the offers not becoming unconditional."

H This was the contract to which I have already referred, whereby Unicos parted with
sufficient shares to divest itself of the control of Central.

" (ii) July 21, 1958, between Unicos and Leadenhall whereby Unicos (subject to
the offers becoming unconditional) have agreed to sell to [the Leadenhall company]
56,678 five per cent. preference shares of £1 each and 658,687 ordinary stock units of
4s. each in the capital of [Central] at the price of 15s. per preference share and
9s. 3d. per ordinary stock unit."

I (Note: The average cost to Unicos of the preference shares and ordinary stock acquired
or to be acquired under this contract and contract (i) above was approximately 15s.
per preference share and approximately 10s. 10¾d. per ordinary stock unit.)

" (iii) July 21, 1958, between Messrs. J. B. Rubens and B. Shine and Leadenhall
whereby Messrs. Rubens and Shine have agreed to sell to Leadenhall 529,901
of the ordinary stock units of 4s. each in the capital of [Central] which they will
receive in the event of the offers becoming unconditional, at the price of 9s. 3d.
per ordinary stock unit."

It will be seen that the ordinary stock units to be acquired by Leadenhall under these
three contracts were sufficient to enable that company to offer them to the Unicos

preference shareholders at the rate of one ordinary stock unit per preference share. A
In due course the offer made on behalf of Central became unconditional, and Leadenhall
duly made their offer to the Unicos preference shareholders by way of negotiable letters
of entitlement. It is the case for the commissioners that their act in doing so was all
part of the consideration furnished by Central for the acquisition of the Unicos shares.
In support of this contention reliance is placed on yet another document, to which I
have not so far referred, and which is described as contract (iv) in appendix D of the
merger proposals. This is a letter of July 21, 1958, addressed by Central to the directors
of Unicos, signed on behalf of both companies, and countersigned by Leadenhall as B
well as by Mr. Rubens and Mr. Shine personally.
    The letter starts by saying:

    " We confirm the arrangements which have been made between us as a result of
    our recent negotiations."

It then goes on by para. 1 to set out the offer to be made by Central through Leadenhall
for the acquisition of the whole of the share capital of Unicos. Paragraph 3 provides: C

    " The offers are to be communicated to your shareholders under cover of a
    circular from Leadenhall . . ."

Paragraphs 4, 5 and 6 are of no relevance to the present dispute, but considerable
reliance was placed on para. 7, which is in the following terms:

    " As stated in both the said ' merger proposals ' and the said circular Leadenhall
    are to offer for sale by way of negotiable letters of entitlement 1,443,588 ordinary
    stock units of 4s. each in the capital of this company on the terms set out in para. 12 D
    of the said ' merger proposals '. This arrangement is an integral part of the agree-
    ment between our two companies and therefore at our request Leadenhall have
    also signed this letter to testify to their agreement to make the before mentioned
    offer of sale to the Unicos preference shareholders on the terms as set out in the
    said para. 12 of the ' merger proposals '."

The terms of this letter were never specifically brought to the attention of the shareholders in Unicos, though the letter is briefly referred to in appendix D of the merger E
proposals. It is, however, relevant as showing what was in fact the true position of
Leadenhall vis-à-vis Central, and is relied on as showing that Leadenhall was contractually bound to Central to offer to the Unicos preference shareholders ordinary
stock units in Central at a price of 9s. 9d.
    The case for Central, which found favour with the judge, was that Leadenhall's
offer of these 1,443,588 ordinary stock units was an entirely separate transaction
between that company and the Unicos preference shareholders, and that it did not in F
any way represent consideration given by Central. As I read his judgment, the judge
was particularly influenced by two considerations in coming to this conclusion. First,
he drew attention to the way in which the respective offers were expressed in the
circular of July 25, 1958. Whereas the offer to purchase the Unicos shares was expressed
to be made by Leadenhall on behalf of Central, the offer of ordinary stock units to
the preference shareholders of Unicos as contained in the last paragraph of the circular
appears to be made by Leadenhall on its own behalf. Secondly, the judge placed G
reliance on the statement in para. 12 of the merger proposals that " this offer for sale
by Leadenhall is independent of the offers referred to in para. 7."
    It was observed by the judge, and during the argument before us appeared to be
accepted by both sides, that the question to be decided depends (a) on the true construction of s. 55 (1) (c) of the Act of 1927, and (b) on the application of that section as
so construed to the facts of the particular case. The judge appears to have proceeded
on the basis that the word " consideration " in the context of this section bears its
technical meaning as in the law of contract, so that the relevant inquiry is to ascertain
what was the consideration moving from the promisee (that is, in this case Central), H
and whether that consideration contained a cash element above the permitted limit of
ten per cent. Counsel for Central in the course of his argument before us emphasised
the fact that the section speaks of " consideration for the acquisition " and not " consideration for the transfer ". He argued that consideration for the acquisition can only
mean consideration actually given by the transferee company, which may or may not
be the same as that which is to be received by the shareholders of the existing company.
On the other side, counsel for the Crown contended that in this context there is no I
reason to give the word " consideration " any technical meaning. He suggested that
the word means no more than the inducement or quid pro quo offered to the shareholders of the existing company in order to persuade them to part with their shares.
In this connexion reference was made during the argument to the recent case of Re
Yeovil Glove Co., Ltd. (8), where this court, in another context and in relation to a
different statute, did give a much wider meaning to the word " consideration ".
Counsel for the Crown, however, contended in the alternative that, even assuming the
word " consideration " to be used in s. 55 in the strict sense contended for, nevertheless

_____

(8) [1964] 2 All E.R. 849; [1965] Ch. 148.

A on the facts of this case the offer made by Leadenhall to the preference shareholders of Unicos of the chance to purchase ordinary stock units of Central on such favourable terms did in fact constitute consideration given by Central.

For the reasons which follow I have come to the conclusion that the commissioners are entitled to succeed on this alternative ground. I do not therefore find it necessary to decide what is the true construction of the words " the consideration for the acquisition " as used in s. 55 (1) of the Act. I am prepared to assume, without deciding, that counsel for Central is right in saying that this means no more than consideration actually given by the transferee company, i.e., Central. The relevant inquiry therefore is to ascertain what was the consideration actually given by Central, i.e., what was contractually promised by Central to the Unicos shareholders in return for the transfer of their shares. But I preface this by remarking that the section requires it to be " shown to the satisfaction of the Commissioners of Inland Revenue " that the conditions specified exist. For the purposes of an appeal to this court, that means, I apprehend, that it must be shown to the satisfaction of this court that the specified conditions exist.

C In the case of the Unicos preference shareholders, what they were offered consisted of (a) preference shares in Central, (b) a cash allowance (in the case of two classes of preference shareholders) and (c) the opportunity to purchase ordinary stock units of Central at 4s. 3d. less than the market value. I accept, of course, that if the offer of the opportunity to purchase ordinary stock units came to them from Leadenhall as a completely independent third party, and without reference to the offer of preference shares and cash made on behalf of Central, it would be impossible to say that this represented consideration given by or on behalf of Central. That is the view of the facts on which the judge appears to have proceeded. He appears to have arrived at it by first construing the terms of the circular in isolation, and he expressed his conclusion on this as follows:

D

" It seems to me perfectly clear, as far as the circular goes, without reference to the merger proposals, that the offer of the one million odd stock units is not being made on behalf of or promised by the company at all."

E Having thus disposed of the circular the judge then proceeded to examine paras. 11 and 12 of the merger proposals, treating these also in isolation, and reached the same conclusion which he expressed as follows:

" Thus the heading, the statement in para. 11 that ' Leadenhall has either acquired or agreed to acquire ' the million odd units, and the statement in para. 12, ' This offer for sale by Leadenhall is independent of the offers referred to in para. 7 ' (though contingent, of course, upon those offers becoming unconditional) emphasise the distinction between the exchange offer by Leadenhall on behalf of Central and the offer of the million odd units by Leadenhall being units which it itself had acquired."

F

The judge then considered the form of acceptance which was enclosed with the documents sent to the Unicos company shareholders, and expressed his conclusion with regard to that as follows:

" The acceptance is therefore of the offer in the circular in the terms of the offer by the circular without incorporating any provisions mentioned in the merger proposals other than those mentioned in the circular. So that, with regard to the offer itself to the Unicos company shareholders, there is in my opinion no promise by [Central] to the Unicos shareholders that Leadenhall will make them the offer of the 1,443,588 ordinary stock units."

G

Finally the judge turned to consider whether his conclusion was in any way affected by the terms of the contract, i.e., contract (iv) referred to in appendix D of the merger proposals. He expressed his conclusion on this point as follows:

H

" There appears to be no agreement between [Central] and Leadenhall or anyone else by which [Central] was obliged to secure or secured Leadenhall's offer to the Unicos shareholders, and no consideration was specified in contract (iv) as consideration from [Central] to Leadenhall for making that offer. Paragraph 7 of this letter does not persuade me to a different conclusion. It does not appear to me that Leadenhall was making the offer of the one million odd stock units to the Unicos shareholders on behalf of [Central] as a disclosed or undisclosed principal, or was being held out as making the offer on behalf of [Central]; or that the company was making any promise to the Unicos shareholders that Leadenhall would make the offer to them."

I

With all respect to the judge, it seems to me that this is a wholly unrealistic conclusion. Apart from all else it would mean that Leadenhall, for no reason of advantage to itself, was offering to sell shares worth 14s. for 9s. 9d. I find it quite impossible to disregard the light which the letter throws on the realities of the case. I can only construe this document as meaning that Central bound itself contractually to Unicos as an integral part of the agreement between the two companies, that Leadenhall would make the offer to sell the ordinary stock units in Central to the Unicos preference shareholders, and further that Leadenhall by countersigning the document bound itself to both A companies to do so. This to my mind represents the reality of the transaction. It does not, of course, of itself decide the question which arises for determination here. It remains to consider what was in truth promised to the recipients of the circular and the other documents enclosed with it. As to this I agree with the submission put forward on behalf of the commissioners that the judge fell into error in seeking to construe the circular in isolation. The circular itself directed the recipient's attention to the merger proposals, which he was advised to consider carefully. The effect of that was in my B judgment to incorporate the terms of the merger proposals into the offer contained in the circular. The circular itself by its very first paragraph refers specifically to para. 6 of the merger proposals, which contained this statement,

" If the merger is succesfully accomplished, the present Unicos preference share-holders will be able to purchase [Central] ordinary stock from Leadenhall as set out in Pt. 3 below."

I can only construe that sentence as a promise made on behalf of Central that Leaden- C hall will make the offer set out in Pt. 3 of the merger proposals. Similarly the statement in para. 12 of the merger proposals, which again is specifically referred to in the circular, constitutes in my judgment a promise made on behalf of Central to the Unicos prefer-ence shareholders that Leadenhall will offer to the preference shareholders the ordinary stock units there referred to.

I think it is impossible to ignore the language in which these promises are framed. The draftsman of the circular and of the merger proposals could have used much more guarded language. He could for instance have said " It is understood that Leadenhall D intends to make an offer " and so forth. He chose, however, to make the definite promise that Leadenhall would make the offer, and I can only construe that promise as a promise made on behalf of Central. In my judgment this was intended to be con-tractually binding, so as to amount to a warranty. If, as happened, nine-tenths of the preference shareholders accepted the offer made by Central, and if, as happened, the other conditions were satisfied so that the offer became unconditional, and if then Leadenhall failed to implement its promise to offer the ordinary stock units in Central E to the Unicos preference shareholders, I can see no reason why those shareholders should not have an enforceable right against Central. Whether or not Central would in turn have a right over Leadenhall does not matter for this purpose, though for myself I should have thought that it would.

For these reasons the true view, as it seems to me, is that, as part of the consideration for the acquisition of the Unicos preference shares, Central warranted that Leadenhall would make the offer set out in para. 12 of the merger proposals. That offer was worth, as the commissioners found, 4s. 3d. per share, and that, if added to the cash allowance, F admittedly brings the consideration for the acquisition of the shares well above the permitted ten per cent. limit.

It remains only to deal with the argument put forward that this conclusion leads to absurd results. The point was forcibly made by counsel for Central that the shares which Leadenhall was offering were derived in part from Unicos itself and in part were shares to be issued to Mr. Rubens and Mr. Shine in their capacity as ordinary share-holders in Unicos. It was suggested that at least with regard to the latter it would G be absurd if the self-same shares, already issued by Central to Mr. Rubens and Mr. Shine as part of the consideration for the acquisition of their shares in Unicos, could be counted a second time as constituting further consideration when offered by Leaden-hall to the preference shareholders. It seems to me, however, that this argument is open to two answers. First, we are not concerned with the shares themselves as considera-tion, but with the cash value (viz., 4s. 3d.) to be attributed to the negotiable letters of entitlement. For this purpose it does not seem to me to matter where the shares came from. Secondly, even if the shares derived from Mr. Rubens and Mr. Shine are left out H of consideration, the permitted proportion of ten per cent. is still exceeded. I do not therefore accept that the conclusion at which I have arrived does lead to the absurd results contended for.

In my judgment it has not been shown that the conditions specified in s. 55 of the Finance Act, 1927, did exist in the present case so as to exempt the company from the incidence of stamp duty. I would accordingly allow the appeal and restore the assessment of the commissioners.   I

HARMAN, L.J., having referred to the statement of fact made by WILLMER, L.J., continued: There were two persons primarily interested in the amalgamation which really made no very great difference to anyone else. These were Mr. Rubens and Mr. Shine, who held between them practically all the ordinary shares in Unicos which in its turn held a controlling interest in Central. It was they who would profit by the successful outcome of the transaction, because they would have in their hands market-able shares. The only considerable outside element consisted of the preference share-holders in Unicos whose assent was essential. The two amalgamating companies could speak with but one voice having a common board with the exception of Mr. Tillett, who himself was chairman of Leadenhall, the third and an essential unit in the plan.

A The help of Leadenhall was essential for two purposes, first to hold the shares in Central of which it was necessary for Unicos to rid itself in order that Central cease to be its subsidiary. For so long as that state of affairs existed, Central could not, having regard to s. 27 of the Companies Act, 1948, acquire shares in its parent.

The first stage of the plan, therefore, was to unload enough shares on Leadenhall to break the control of Unicos. This was brought about by contract no. (i), referred to in appendix D to the merger proposals. This was an out-and-out sale, that being essential
B to its object, but it is noteworthy that it could be undone by a resale if the response to the merger proposal were insufficient. This shows the contract to be part of the plan. It was, however, a further part of the plan that Leadenhall should acquire enough ordinary stock of Central to enable it to bait the hook to attract the Unicos preference shareholders by offering them an additional inducement. Therefore by contract (ii) the remainder of the ordinary stock held by Unicos in Central was conditionally sold to Leadenhall. Even so that would not provide Leadenhall with enough units, and the deficiency was made good by contract (iii), whereby Messrs. Rubens and Shine made
C a conditional sale of ordinary stock units in Central. These were part of the units which they would acquire by issue if the merger went through.

Thus all these three transactions could be undone if the main deal did not go through, the first by a resale, and the second and third by non-fulfilment of the condition of sale. Leadenhall was thus being provided with means to make the extra offer to the Unicos preference shareholders which it was hoped would make the exchange of their shares attractive. It is to be observed, moreover, that the price in each case was considerably
D below the market value of Central's units. It is obvious that the only reason for this is to provide Leadenhall with something with which to tempt the Unicos preference shareholders. No other reason exists why Leadenhall should acquire the units at an under-value. It can only be explained if Leadenhall was not entitled to retain them but was bound to make the proposed offer.

The ground having been thus prepared, the main offer is put forward. There was, of course, no doubt about the ordinary shares, which were all in the control of Mr. Rubens and Mr. Shine, but the preference shares were apparently fairly widely distributed
E among members of the public and it was necessary to make the offer sufficiently attractive to them to acquire ninety per cent. of their holdings. The attraction held out was the right which Unicos preference shareholders would acquire of purchasing Central's stock units from Leadenhall at over 4s. under their value in the market. It appears that this attraction was enough, and, if it be the true view of it that the cash value so offered to the Unicos preference shareholders ought to be treated as part of the consideration for the acquisition of their shares, then the commissioners are right and the
F stamp duty is payable. If on the other hand Leadenhall's offer was an independent one, then in my opinion the judge was right. He treated the two transactions as separate. I on the whole incline to the view that the consideration here in question must be consideration moving from the transferee company. If therefore the offer was not brought about by Central it did not provide the consideration and it was not within the words of the Act the consideration for the acquisition.

Now there is a statement in the documents, viz., para. 12 of the merger proposals, making this very statement, that Leadenhall's offer of the additional stock units is
G " independent of " the exchange offer made by Leadenhall as agent for Central. It is independent in the sense that the exchange offer is made by Leadenhall as agent for Central while the sale offer is made by Leadenhall as principal. It is, I suppose, also conceivable that the exchange offer might have failed to become unconditional and yet some preference shareholders in Unicos might have had a claim. It seems to me, however, that to accept the view that the offer was truly independent argues a degree of innocence to which I find myself quite unable to attain. There are two direct state-
H ments by or on behalf of Central which seem to me flatly to contradict this view. The first is in the " merger terms " at para. 6 of the merger proposals to the effect that " in addition " preference shareholders " will be able " to acquire the shares from Leadenhall. This amounts as it seems to me to a promise made by Central to the preference shareholders that this will be part of the bargain. There is a further statement that " it is an integral part " of the scheme that Leadenhall should make this offer. It is clear enough from contract no. (iv) in appendix D to the merger proposals that in fact Leadenhall was bound to Central to make the offer, but it is said that this document
I was not disclosed to the Unicos preference shareholders and therefore could not have influenced them and I am willing to leave it out of account. Even without it, however, I am clearly of opinion that there was a promise or warranty by Central to the Unicos preference shareholders that if they would accept the exchange they would reap this additional advantage. This in my judgment was clearly part of the consideration, even on the strictest view of that word, for which Central induced the preference shareholders to accept the exchange and that is an end of the case.

SALMON, L.J. (whose judgment was read by WILLMER, L.J.): I agree with my lords. I am greatly attracted to the argument put forward on behalf of Central on the point of construction. It seems to me that the words " the consideration for the

acquisition " in s. 55 (1) of the Finance Act, 1927, are especially apt to connote some- A
thing passing from the acquirer. This is not because in construing this section I would
apply the artificial doctrine of the law of contract that no consideration can be effective
unless it moves from the promisee. This doctrine is in my view irrelevant to the present
case. I think, however, that, if the legislature was concerned with what the transferor
got rather than what the transferee gave, a more natural form of words would have
been " the consideration for the transfer " rather than " for the acquisition ". The
form of words is of course not conclusive, but if the construction put forward on behalf B
of Central is wrong, some strange results would follow. Suppose that Central gave no
cash and issued only shares in return for the shares in Unicos. Suppose that the ordinary
shareholders in Unicos in order to persuade the Unicos preference shareholders to agree
to Central's terms had independently offered to transfer to those preference shareholders
say thirty per cent. of the Central shares to be issued to them (the Unicos ordinary
shareholders), then, unless the submission of counsel for Central is right, it seems that
no exemption from stamp duty would be conferred by the section. Yet Central would
have given no consideration but shares and the Unicos shareholders would have received C
no money—nothing but shares in Central. Since, however, the extra shares forming
part of the consideration received by the Unicos preference shareholders would not
have been issued to them, but would have been transferred to them by the Unicos
ordinary shareholders, the condition for exemption laid down in s. 55 (1) (c) (ii) would
not have been complied with, for this subsection provides that in order for the exemption
from stamp duty to operate,

> " the consideration for the acquisition [must consist] . . . as to not less than   D
> ninety per cent. thereof . . . in the issue of shares in the transferee company
> [Central] to the holders of shares in the existing company [Unicos] in exchange for
> the shares held by them in the existing company."

The result in the case postulated which would appear to follow from the Commissioners
of Inland Revenue's construction of the section seems so strange and unjust that it
suggests that this construction cannot be right. It is however unnecessary to express,
and I do not express, any concluded opinion on this point since in my judgment the   E
appeal must succeed even on the assumption that Central's submissions on the construction
point are correct.

It has been rightly conceded by counsel for Central that Central must fail if Central
warranted to the Unicos preference shareholders that those shareholders would receive
the negotiable letters of entitlement should ninety per cent. of each class of them
accept the offer for their shares made on behalf of Central by Leadenhall in the circular
of July 25, 1958. In these circumstances the warranty would be consideration moving
from Central in addition to the consideration mentioned in the circular to which I have   F
referred and would have exceeded ten per cent. of the total consideration. Was there
such a warranty? To my mind the answer to this question is clearly Yes. A warranty
may be defined as a collateral promise intended and understood to be legally binding.
When the Unicos preference shareholders opened their post on the morning of July 26,
1958, and found the merger proposals, the circular of July 25, 1958, and the other
documents, they would not in my view have looked at any of the documents in isolation
as the judge appears to have done. Would they as reasonable people have believed   G
and were they intended by Central to believe that Central was making them a legally
enforceable promise that they would receive the negotiable letters of entitlement from
Leadenhall if the merger went through? It is important to note that the merger
proposals were signed by Central and by Unicos but not by Leadenhall which in any
event may well have been quite unknown to the preference shareholders.

Central, one of the signatories to the merger proposals, wanted to acquire the Unicos
shares. The whole purpose of sending out the documents on July 25 was in order to
enable them to do so. The persons to whom the documents were addressed were the   H
shareholders in Unicos. We have been told that Mr. Rubens and Mr. Shine who held
ninety-eight per cent. of the equity in Unicos were the originators of the merger scheme.
This scheme in addition to being in the interests of both companies had great advantages
for them. It would convert their holding of unquoted shares into a holding worth
nearly £5 million (at then current prices) freely marketable on the Stock Exchange.
Presumably the ordinary shareholders needed little persuasion about the benefits which
the merger would confer on them. The preference shareholders, however, might need   I
convincing. One of the obvious attractions for them was the promise of the negotiable
letters of entitlement which in effect gave them about an extra 4s. 1½d. net for each
of their shares. And here was Central telling them to my mind in the plainest terms
in paras. 6 and 12 of the merger proposals that, if the merger went through, i.e., if
ninety per cent. of them would transfer their shares, this is what they would get for
them. That was told them in a commercial document designed (perfectly properly) to
persuade them to part with their shares. It is now said that this was not intended or
understood to be a binding promise. I must confess that but for the finding of the judge
and the force and persuasiveness of counsel for Central's submissions I should have
thought that Central's case on this point was almost unarguable.

A   No doubt the merger proposals were carefully drafted with a view to taking advantage of the stamp duty exemption in s. 55 if possible, but also with commercial considerations well in mind. Had it not been for the latter, the task of the draftsmen would have been much easier. Plain words could have been used to make it clear that the statements by Central in relation to the negotiable letters of entitlement were not intended as a promise by Central nor as imposing any legal liability on them in the event of these letters not being forthcoming. This would have made it plain that no consideration moved from Central save that set out in para. 7 of the merger proposals, but it might

B   not have inspired confidence in the Unicos preference shareholders and indeed might have killed the merger. Central, no doubt for very sound reasons, chose to make what to my mind was a categorical and binding promise in respect of the negotiable letters of entitlement. I have no doubt that it helped the merger to go through and equally little doubt that it is fatal to their case for exemption from stamp duty. I would allow the appeal.

C

NOTE.

R. *v.* AITKEN.

[Court of Criminal Appeal (Lord Parker, C.J., Marshall and James, JJ.),

D   April 25, 1966.]

Criminal Law—Sentence—Murder—Recommendation of minimum period to be served under sentence of life imprisonment—Whether appeal lies—Murder (Abolition of Death Penalty) Act 1965 (c. 71), s. 1 (2).

Appeal and Application.

The appellant, Peter Kenneth Aitken, had been convicted at the Central

E   Criminal Court on Nov. 26, 1965, before Roskill, J., and a jury on a count of murder and on a count of being in illegal possession of firearms in a public place. He was sentenced to life imprisonment and the trial judge made a recommendation* that the sentence to be served should not be less than fifteen years. He appealed against conviction and applied for leave to appeal against the recommendation. The case is reported here only in regard to the appeal

F   against the recommendation, on which counsel for the appellant conceded that there was no ground for appeal.

   J. N. Hutchinson, Q.C., and *Patrick Pakenham* for the appellant.
   M. Corkrey for the Crown.

   MARSHALL, J., in the course of delivering the judgment of the court, said:

G   No ground of appeal against sentence was set out, but this court understands that the ground of appeal in respect of the sentence arose out of the trial judge's recommendation, and it is sufficient to say that under the Murder (Abolition of Death Penalty) Act 1965, s. 1 (2), no right of appeal arises against any such recommendation, and any representation, if made, should be made to the Home Secretary.

H   *Appeal against recommendation not a matter for the court. Appeal against conviction dismissed.*

   Solicitors: *Abbott, Baldwin & Co.* (for the appellant); *Director of Public Prosecutions* (for the Crown).

[*Reported by* N. P. Metcalfe, Esq., *Barrister-at-Law.*]

I

   * Section 1 (2) of the Murder (Abolition of Death Penalty) Act 1965, so far as relevant, provides: " On sentencing any person convicted of murder to imprisonment for life the court may at the same time declare the period which it recommends to the Secretary of State as the minimum period which in its view should elapse before the Secretary of State orders the release of that person on licence under s. 27 of the Prison Act, 1952 . . ."
   Section 2, so far as relevant, provides: " No person convicted of murder shall be released by the Secretary of State on licence under s. 27 of the Prison Act, 1952 . . . unless the Secretary of State has prior to such release consulted the Lord Chief Justice of England . . . together with the trial judge if available."

REGENT OIL CO., LTD. v. J. T. LEAVESLEY (LICHFIELD), LTD.   A

[Chancery Division (Stamp, J.), March 29, April 4, 5, 1966.]

Trade—Restraint of trade—Agreement—Petrol filling station—Solus agreement between owner of garage and motor fuel supplier for purchase and resale exclusively of supplier's products—Obligation to be undertaken by successor— Duration of agreement seven and a half years—Injunction by consent until trial restraining garage owner from purchasing motor fuel from other suppliers— Subsequent decisions of Court of Appeal that doctrine of restraint of trade applied to such agreements—Motion to discharge injunction on ground that agreement was in restraint of trade.

B

The defendants were proprietors of a garage. On Dec. 12, 1960, they entered into a solus agreement with the plaintiff, a supplier of motor fuel. The plaintiff had no interest in the land on which the garage stood. The agreement restricted the defendants during a period of eight and a half years from Feb. 1, 1960, to purchasing the defendants' total requirements of motor fuels and other light petroleum products from the plaintiff. By the agreement the defendants acknowledged receipt of an advance of £2,213 10s. 10d. repayable out of their entitlement under the agreement to a rebate to be allowed on motor fuel sold at the garage. The agreement did not prevent the defendants closing the garage down if business proved unprofitable. There was a continuity clause under which the defendants, if they sold the garage, were to secure that their successors would be bound by the solus agreement. Before the decisions in the Court of Appeal cited below, the plaintiff had obtained ex parte an interlocutory injunction, which was continued later by consent, against contravention of the restriction in the solus agreement. There was no evidence that a restriction for seven and a half years was no longer than was reasonably necessary to protect the plaintiff's interests. On motion to discharge the injunction in view of the subsequent decisions of the Court of Appeal,

C

D

E

Held: after the two decisions of the Court of Appeal the interlocutory injunction would not have been granted because, in the absence of evidence indicating that restriction for a period of seven and a half years was reasonably necessary to protect the plaintiff's legitimate interests, that period was too long, with the consequence that the plaintiff had not made out a prima facie case that the restriction was enforceable as not being in unreasonable restraint of trade; accordingly the interlocutory injunction would be discharged (see p. 458, letters A, H and I, post).

F

G

Petrofina (Gt. Britain), Ltd. v. *Martin* ([1966] 1 All E.R. 126) and *Esso Petroleum Co., Ltd.* v. *Harper's Garage (Stourport), Ltd.* ([1966] 1 All E.R. 725) applied.

[As to agreements in restraint of trade, see 38 Halsbury's Laws (3rd Edn.) 20, para. 13; and for cases on the subject, see 45 Digest (Repl.) 443-449, 271-297.]

H

Cases referred to:

Esso Petroleum Co., Ltd. v. *Harper's Garage (Stourport), Ltd.*, [1965] 2 All E.R. 933; [1965] 3 W.L.R. 469; *rvsd.* C.A., [1966] 1 All E.R. 725.

Petrofina (Gt. Britain), Ltd. v. *Martin*, [1965] 2 All E.R. 176; [1965] Ch. 1073; [1965] 2 W.L.R. 1299; *affd.* C.A.; [1966] 1 All E.R. 126; [1966] 2 W.L.R. 318.

I

Action.

An action was begun by writ dated Oct. 28, 1965, by the plaintiff, Regent Oil Co., Ltd. claiming—(i) an injunction restraining the defendants, J. T. Leavesley (Lichfield), Ltd. (by their directors, servants, agents, workmen or otherwise) from causing or permitting or suffering the sale at or advertising for sale from the defendants' premises at Beacon Street, Lichfield, Staffordshire, of motor fuels or other light petroleum products, transmission oils and lubricating greases other

A than any such articles supplied by the plaintiff; (ii) a mandatory injunction requiring the defendants, and all other persons on their behalf to permit the plaintiff to display its advertising globes on all motor fuels and other light petroleum products' pumps situate on the premises; (iii) an injunction restraining the defendants and others on their behalf from interfering with, disconnecting, removing or obscuring any such advertising globes or the locks,

B seals or pipe-fittings connecting any such pumps to the tanks installed at the premises. The plaintiff obtained an interlocutory injunction on an ex parte application on Nov. 9, 1965. On Nov. 19 injunctions were granted by Cross, J., by consent until the trial in the terms of (i) and (iii) above. This was a motion on notice dated Mar. 1, 1966, by the defendants to discharge those injunctions. The facts are set out in the judgment.

C *P. R. Oliver*, Q.C., and *Jeremiah Harman* for the plaintiff.

S. W. Templeman, Q.C., and *E. W. H. Christie* for the defendants.

STAMP, J.: This action relates to an agreement made on Dec. 12, 1960, between the defendants, J. T. Leavesley (Lichfield), Ltd., of the one part, and the plaintiff, Regent Oil Co., Ltd., of the other. Under that agreement the

D defendants, who have a garage at Beacon Street, Lichfield, in Staffordshire, agreed with the plaintiff, the well known supplier of motor fuel, to purchase the defendants' total requirements of motor fuel and other products for re-sale at their garage premises from the plaintiff and not to sell at the same premises any such products supplied by any other supplier. I will refer to that provision— although it is not a covenant—as " the restrictive covenant ". The agreement

E was what is known in the trade, and has been referred to in several recent decisions, as a solus agreement.

Then, towards the end of September, 1965, when the agreement still had some three years to run, the defendants repented of their bargain and began to obtain and sell motor fuel from another supplier, in contravention of the terms of the restrictive covenant. The plaintiff issued a writ and moved for an interlocutory

F injunction, which it obtained on an ex parte application on Nov. 9, 1965.

Then, on Nov. 19, when the matter ceased to be ex parte and came before the judge then dealing with motions, an injunction was granted by consent until the trial, in effect restraining the defendants from contravening the terms of the covenant. At that date it had been decided, at first instance, in *Esso Petroleum Co., Ltd.* v. *Harper's Garage (Stourport), Ltd.* (1), that the doctrine of restraint of

G trade had no place in commercial agreements which limited the restraint to a particular property. Since then, the law has been illuminated by two decisions of the Court of Appeal: *Petrofina (Gt. Britain), Ltd.* v. *Martin* (2), decided on Dec. 17, 1965; and the *Harper's Garage* case (3), decided on Feb. 23, 1966. In the light of those judgments, the defendants now move to have the injunction discharged, contending that the covenant is a covenant in restraint of trade and

H that the plaintiff has not made out a prima facie case for the continuance of the injunction. In my view, I have now to decide whether, in the light of those two authorities, there ought or ought not to be, until trial of the action, or until further order, an injunction to restrain the continuing breach of the terms of the restrictive covenant. In so doing, I ought not to be inhibited by the fact that before these two cases were decided by the Court of Appeal the existing injunction

I was granted, but, in accordance with the usual practice of this court, I must decide whether the plaintiff has made out a prima facie case having regard to the facts alleged in the evidence and the law as now interpreted by the Court of Appeal.

It is convenient to mention that in this case the plaintiff had no interest as owner, mortgagee or lessor of the land on which the garage and petrol filling

---

(1) [1965] 2 All E.R. 933.   (2) [1966] 1 All E.R. 126.

(3) [1966] 1 All E.R. 725.

station stands. The contract between the plaintiff and the defendants is simply A
a contract regulating their commercial or trading relations.

In my judgment, the two cases establish the law to be as follows. The doctrine
against restraint of trade applies to such an agreement as is here in question, and
indeed this is common ground. Such a covenant must, therefore, if it is not to be
held unenforceable, pass the test of reasonableness and it is for the party seeking
to enforce it to establish that it passes the test. It is also established that though B
a trader in the position of the plaintiff in this case is not entitled to protection
against competition per se, it has an interest in selling as large a quantity of its
goods (in this case motor fuel) as it can, and as profitably as it can. These are
interests which it is legitimate to protect. It has an interest in achieving
continuity of output, which it is also legitimate for it to protect. Counsel on
behalf of the plaintiff, submits that there may—and for the purposes of this C
motion I accept that submission—be other interests which can be proved at the
trial, to be interests which the plaintiff is entitled to protect. It follows that not
all solus agreements are unenforceable, but the cases also establish that unless
the plaintiff is able to show that the restraint is no more than reasonably necessary
to protect the legitimate interests of the plaintiff seeking to enforce the restraint,
whatever those legitimate interests may be, the plaintiff will fail in its action. D

With these general considerations in mind, I turn to consider the terms of the
agreement in this case. It was made on Dec. 12, 1960, between the defendants of
the one part and the plaintiff of the other part. Clause 1 provides that the
plaintiff shall allow the defendants a rebate of 1¼d. a gallon, which was subsequently raised to 1½d., on all motor fuel purchased by the defendants, under the
agreement, such rebate to be paid or credited in arrears as soon as reasonably E
possible after the end of each—then follows a blank and the words, in parenthesis,
" (calculated from the date shown in cl. 2 hereof) " during the currency of the
agreement in respect of the motor fuel purchased by the defendants from the
plaintiff during that year for re-sale at the defendants' premises at Beacon Street,
Lichfield. The defendants acknowledged receipt of the sum of £2,213 10s. 10d.
representing an advance repayable against the defendants' entitlement to rebate F
as set out above. Clause 2 provides that, for the purposes of the agreement, the
expression " currency of this agreement " shall mean the period of eight and a
half years from Feb. 1, 1960, that is to say, a period of approximately seven and
a half years from the actual date of the agreement, or until such time as the
defendants have purchased from the plaintiff, under the agreement, 425,000
gallons of motor fuel, whichever was the longer. Then there is a provision that G
on the termination of the agreement, or in the event of any breach by the
defendants of any of its terms, the defendants shall, on demand, refund to the
plaintiff the total sums advanced, paid or credited to the defendants under the
agreed rebate, less the sum of 1¼d., which was subsequently raised to 1½d., for
every gallon of motor fuel actually purchased by the defendants from the
plaintiff. H

Then follows the restrictive covenant, which is in the following terms:

" The buyers [that is, the defendants] agree, during the currency of this
agreement, that they shall purchase on [the plaintiff's] standard terms from
time to time shown on its sales tickets their total requirements of motor fuels,
other light petroleum products, transmission oils and lubricating greases
(hereinafter known as ' the products ') from [the plaintiff] for resale at the I
said premises and that they shall not sell nor advertise for sale nor permit to
be sold or advertised for sale at the said premises any of such products
supplied by any other supplier."

Then there is the provision regarding lubricating oils, on which neither party
places any great reliance and to which I need not refer.

Clause 4 of the agreement provides that the prices to be paid by the defendants
shall be the plaintiff's standard wholesale zonal prices to dealers ruling on the

A date of delivery. Clause 5 states that the prices to be charged for retail sales of motor fuel and other light petroleum products by the defendants shall be the plaintiff's standard retail prices ruling at the date of each sale and applicable to the product concerned. At the date of the agreement there was nothing void or illegal about such a provision for fixing retail prices, and it does not seem to me that, in deciding the validity or otherwise of the restraint of trade, what B subsequently happened is really relevant.

There follow, in cl. 6, provisions regulating delivery and other matters. In cl. 7, there are provisions as to advertising. Then there is included a provision, in cl. 8, whereby, in effect, if the plaintiff reduced the defendants' profit margin from that ruling at the date of the agreement and other specified leading motor fuel suppliers had not made a corresponding reduction, the defendants might C terminate the agreement. There was a provision, in cl. 11, which was referred to in the *Harper's Garage* case (4) as a continuity provision, and to which I will similarly refer, under which, in the event of the buyers contemplating the sale, or assignment of, or any diminution of, their interest in the garage premises or of the business carried on there, the defendants should give the plaintiff notice in writing and the defendants should be bound to secure that their successors bound themselves to D the plaintiff in the same terms as the defendants themselves were bound.

I accept, for the purposes of this application, the submission of counsel for the plaintiff that the agreement is in some respects less onerous and perhaps a good deal less onerous on the defendants than the agreements in the two cases which fell to be considered by the Court of Appeal. There is a noteworthy distinction in that in both those cases there was an obligation on the defendants to continue E to trade during the currency of the agreement. Here, on the other hand, the defendants can, if business with the plaintiff proves to be unprofitable, close down the business and abandon it and they can, subject to obtaining whatever planning permission may be necessary, carry on some other business on the premises or dispose of the premises to a person who proposes to carry on some different business.

F Another notable difference between this and the *Harper's Garage* case (4) is that in this case the plaintiff could not squeeze the defendants' profit margin except in collaboration with the other principal suppliers of motor fuel as it could at least in the *Harper's Garage* case (4). I must also accept the submission of counsel for the defendants that it is, in another respect, more onerous than the less onerous of the cases dealt with in the Court of Appeal, in that the period of the restriction G in this case is as long as seven and a half years, whereas, for example, in the *Harper's Garage* case (4) a period of four and a half years was held, on the facts of that case, to be too long. I also accept that the Court of Appeal, in both cases, looked at all the clauses of the service agreements there under consideration and put them all together, judging their cumulative effect in coming to their conclusion whether the particular covenant was or was not an unlawful restraint to trade.

H If, however, the agreement in this case is less onerous on a covenantor in as many respects as you please, than the service agreements in the *Petrofina* (5) and *Harper's Garage* (4) cases, there is still here a restrictive covenant for a period of seven and a half years, tying the defendants to the plaintiff, coupled with the continuity clause, which is, I think, a necessary corollary of the restrictive covenant, and in order to succeed in this action the plaintiff would have to I establish that the restrictive covenant, for that period, was no more than reasonably necessary to protect its legitimate interests.

In the *Harper's Garage* case (4), the plaintiff failed to discharge that onus in relation to a different solus agreement and on facts, which, for all I know, may be quite different from the facts which the plaintiff in this case will establish at the trial. There is, however, at present no evidence whatever of any facts to indicate that a restrictive covenant for the period of seven and a half years in

(4) [1966] 1 All E.R. 725.   (5) [1966] 1 All E.R. 126.

the terms which I have read was reasonably necessary in order to protect those **A**
interests. There is, to quote the remarks of DIPLOCK, L.J., in the *Harper's
Garage* case (6), at present no evidence how long a covenant would be needed for
the purposes of protecting the plaintiff's legitimate trading interests, nor is there
any suggestion that the tying covenant which the plaintiff extracted from any
of its filling station operators was fixed with this consideration in mind: a fact
which DIPLOCK, L.J., treated as fatal to the plaintiff's claim in the *Harper's* **B**
Garage case (7). The plaintiff may be able to establish at the trial that the period
of seven and a half years was fixed with an eye to reasonableness, but according
to the defendants' evidence, which is not in this respect disputed, the period fixed
was the residue unexpired of the period of twelve years during which the garage
was tied under a former agreement. This is, in my judgment, a fact from which,
in the absence of evidence to the contrary, one may draw the inference that the **C**
period was not fixed with a reasonable contemplation of the interests of the parties,
a circumstance which HARMAN, L.J., also thought fatal to the plaintiff's claim
in the *Harper's Garage* case (8). In its evidence on this motion, all the plaintiff
says on this aspect of the case is that it will attempt to justify this agreement at
the trial, if that be necessary in law, and in particular will lead evidence to establish that the period covered by the agreement was fair and no more than adequate **D**
to give reasonable protection to the plaintiff. The plaintiff may be able to do so,
but I am quite unable to hold that it has, on the facts now before me, established
a prima facie case for regarding the restraint as an enforceable one. The evidence
simply is not there.

Counsel urged that the plaintiff's interest in the sum of £2,213, which was
advanced on account of rebate, was one which it was entitled to protect by **E**
the restrictive covenant and since on the facts that sum could not be expected
to be earned by the defendants until about the end of the seven and a half year
period, it was no more than reasonably necessary to protect that interest to impose
the restriction for that period. But, in my view, the sum so advanced cannot be
regarded otherwise than as part and parcel of the restrictive agreement and, in **F**
my judgment, there is no more reason to regard the period as fixed by reference
to the fact that it was the period during which an arbitrary sum of £2,213 on
account of rebate would be earned, than there is to regard the sum of £2,213 on
account of rebate as having been fixed at that amount because it was the sum
which might be expected to be earned during an arbitrary period of seven and a
half years. There is no evidence why £2,213 was fixed or why seven and a half **G**
years was fixed; there is no evidence that the period in fact was fixed to protect
the plaintiff's interest in the sum advanced. Again, the plaintiff may be able to
establish at the trial that the period of seven and a half years was fixed in order
to protect its interest in the £2,213, but there is no evidence to suggest that it
will be able to do so and, again, I am unable to hold that it has made out a prima
facie case for its contention that the covenant was no more than reasonably **H**
necessary for that purpose or was fixed with that in view.

For the reasons which I have given, if the plaintiff were today applying for
interlocutory relief, I should be constrained reluctantly to refuse it, reluctantly
because this court is reluctant, on an interlocutory application, not to hold a
party bound to the very words of his covenant and I would have to hold that **I**
there ought not to be an injunction from today until the trial. Taking the view
that I do that the plaintiff has no built-in right to the continuance of the injunction which it has obtained after it has become apparent that it was founded on a
decision which was wrong in law, I ought, in my view, to discharge the injunction,
and this I do.

(6) [1966] 1 All E.R. at p. 736.   (7) [1966] 1 All E.R. at p. 739.
(8) [1966] 1 All E.R. at p. 731.

A
Order accordingly.

Solicitors: *Sharpe, Pritchard & Co.*, agents for *Thomas Cooksey & Co.*, Old Hill, Staffs. (for the plaintiff); *Ford, Michelmore, Rose & Binning*, agents for *Goodger, Lowe & Co.*, Burton-on-Trent (for the defendants).

[*Reported by* JENIFER SANDELL, *Barrister-at-Law.*]

B

OLIVIER AND ANOTHER *v.* BUTTIGIEG.

C
[PRIVY COUNCIL (Lord Morris of Borth-y-Gest, Lord Pearce and Lord Pearson), February 21, 22, 23, 24, April 19, 1966.]

Privy Council—Malta—Constitutional law—Fundamental democratic freedoms— Freedom of expression—Church condemnation of certain newspapers— Government circular prohibiting entry of condemned newspapers to hospitals and health department branches—Whether issue of circular an interference with constitutional rights—Malta (Constitution) Order in Council, 1961, Constitution, s. 13, s. 14.

D
In May, 1961, the ecclesiastical authorities in Malta condemned certain newspapers, including a labour party newspaper called the " Voice of Malta ", of which the respondent was editor. The respondent was the President of the Malta labour party, which was in opposition. The appellants, who were the Minister of Health and the Chief Government Medical Officer in Malta, issued a circular in April, 1962, which, in reference to political discussions by government employees during working hours, prohibited in regard to employees " the entry in the various hospitals and branches of the department of newspapers which are condemned by " the ecclesiastical authorities. The employees concerned numbered 2,660 persons. The respondent claimed that this circular, in so far as it affected the " Voice of Malta ", was a breach of s. 13 and s. 14* of the Malta (Constitution) Order in Council, 1961, and claimed the appropriate remedy in accordance with the provisions of that order in council.

E

F

Held: (i) the prohibition went beyond reasonable orders regulating the conduct of employees during working hours, and constituted a hindrance of the respondent in the enjoyment of his freedom of expression, viz., to impart information and ideas without interference, thereby contravening the respondent's constitutional rights under s. 14 (2) of the Constitution of Malta, although the hindrance was small (see p. 466, letters E and I, and p. 468, letters F and H, post).

G

(ii) the appellants were not protected under s. 14 (2), since publication of the newspaper did not contravene any law providing for public safety, public order or public morality nor was the circular issued under the authority of a law imposing restrictions on public officers, nor could it be considered to be reasonably justifiable in a democratic society (see p. .467, letter E, and p. 468, letter C, post).

H

Per CURIAM: such interference as there was with the respondent's freedom neither amounted, for the purposes of s. 13 (1), to a deprivation of his full liberty of conscience nor, for the purposes of s. 13 (2), to a denial of free exercise of any mode of religious worship (see p. 468, letter I, and p. 469, letter B, post); moreover, although the circular sponsored an ecclesiastical condemnation and thus had in some sense a religious origin, the respondent was not thereby subjected to " disability . . . by reason of his religious profession " within the meaning of s. 13 (2) (see p. 469, letters E and G, post).

I

Appeal dismissed.

---

* The relevant terms of s. 13 and s. 14 are set out at p. 462, letters D to H, post.

Distinguished in SOCIETE UNITED DOCKS v GOVERNMENT OF MAURITIUS [1985] 1 All ER 864

[Editorial Note. The Malta (Constitution) Order in Council, 1961, dated Oct. **A** 24, 1961, was revoked as from Sept. 21, 1964, by the Malta Independence Order 1964, S.I. 1964 No. 1398, ss. 2, 3, made under the Malta Independence Act 1964, s. 1. Protection for freedom of conscience and freedom of expression are now provided by s. 41 and s. 42 of the Constitution contained in the Schedule to the Order of 1964.

As to the right to freedom of speech, see 7 HALSBURY'S LAWS (3rd Edn.) 197, **B** para. 418 (3).]

Cases referred to:

Martin v. *City of Struthers*, (1942), 319 U.S. 141; 87 L.ed. 1313.

Romesh Thappar v. *State of Madras, Re*, (1950), 37 A.I.R. (S.C.R.) 124.

Thomas v. *Collins*, (1944), 323 U.S. 516; 89 L.ed. 430.

C

Appeal.

This was an appeal from a judgment of the Court of Appeal of Malta (MAMO, C.J., GOUDER and CAMILLERI, JJ.) dated Jan. 10, 1964, dismissing the appellants appeal against a judgment of the First Hall, Civil Court (XUEREB, J.) dated Mar. 11, 1963, whereby the respondent, the Hon. Dr. Anton Buttigieg, was granted a declaration that a circular issued on behalf of the appellants had infringed his constitutional rights. By the same judgment the declaration **D** was ordered to be brought, by means of a new circular, to the cognizance of the people to whom the preceding circular was directed and the appellants were ordered to pay the respondent's costs. The first appellant, the Hon. Dr. Paul Borg Olivier, was Minister of Health and the second appellant, Dr. Carmelo Colevio, was Chief Government Medical Officer; but on or after June 15, 1965, he was replaced in the post of chief government medical officer by Dr. John **E** Ottard who became acting chief government medical officer.

J. G. Le Quesne, Q.C., and *Mervyn Heald* for the appellants.

W. T. Williams, Q.C., and *J. W. Priest* for the respondent.

LORD MORRIS OF BORTH-Y-GEST: This is an appeal (by leave of the Court of Appeal of Malta dated Nov. 20, 1964) from a judgment of that **F** court (MAMO, C.J., GOUDER and CAMILLERI, JJ.) dated Jan. 10, 1964, dismissing with costs the appellants' appeal against the judgment and order of the First Hall, Civil Court, Malta (XUEREB, J.) dated Mar. 11, 1963, whereby the respondent was granted a declaration that a circular issued on behalf of the appellants had contravened his constitutional rights. By the judgment and order of Mar. 11, 1963, it was ordered that the declaration be brought, by means of a new circular, **G** to the cognizance of the people to whom the preceding circular was directed and also that the respondent's costs be borne by the appellants.

The case raises important questions whether there were contraventions of the provisions of the Malta (Constitution) Order in Council, 1961, and in particular whether the respondent's rights under s. 13 or under s. 14 or under both those sections were infringed. Section 16 provided for the enforcement of the pro- **H** visions which gave certain fundamental rights and freedoms to individuals. Section 16 (1), (2) and (3) were in the following terms:

" (1) Any person who alleges that any of the provisions of this Part of this Order has been, is being, or is likely to be, contravened in relation to him, or such other person as the Civil Court, First Hall, in Malta may appoint at the instance of any person who so alleges, may, without prejudice **I** to any other action with respect to the same matter that is lawfully available, apply to the Civil Court, First Hall, for redress.

" (2) The Civil Court, First Hall, shall have original jurisdiction to hear and determine any application made in pursuance of the preceding sub-section, and may make such orders, issue such writs and give such directions as it may consider appropriate for the purpose of enforcing, or securing the enforcement of, any rights to which any person concerned may be entitled under this Part of this Order.

A
" Provided that the court may, if it considers it desirable so to do, decline to exercise its powers under this subsection in any case where it is satisfied that adequate means of redress for the contravention alleged are or have been available to the person concerned under any other law.

" (3) Where any question as to the interpretation of any of the provisions of this Part of this Order arises in any proceedings in any court other than
B
the Civil Court, First Hall, or the Court of Appeal in Malta, the person presiding in that court shall refer the question to the Civil Court, First Hall, unless, in his opinion, the raising of the question is merely frivolous or vexatious; and that court shall give its decision on any question referred to it under this subsection and, subject to the next following subsection, the court in which the question arose shall dispose of the question in
C
accordance with that decision."

It is to be observed that an application may be made by a person who alleges that any of the provisions referred to " has been, is being, or is likely to be contravened in relation to him ". The respondent so alleged. He alleged that the provisions of s. 13 and s. 14 had been and were being contravened and that they were so contravened " in relation to him ". He therefore invoked the
D
enforcement procedure laid down in s. 16. In the Civil Court and in the Court of Appeal the appellants raised the issue whether the circular in question was cognisable by the courts of Malta. It was contended that the issue of the circular was " a pure administrative act " and as such was not cognizable in the courts. The courts held that it was cognizable. No contention to the contrary was advanced in the submissions before their lordships' board.
E
For the appreciation of the questions which arise it is necessary to refer to certain sections of the 1961 Constitution and to recount the main facts. Part 2 of the Constitution is headed " Protection of Fundamental Rights and Freedoms of the Individual ". Section 5 is as follows:

" 5.	Whereas every person in Malta is entitled to the fundamental rights
F
and freedoms of the individual, that is to say, has the right, whatever his race, place of origin, political opinions, colour, creed, or sex, but subject to respect for the rights and freedoms of others and for the public interest, to each and all of the following namely—
" (a) life, liberty, security of the person and the protection of the law;
" (b) freedom of conscience, of expression and of assembly and association; and
G
" (c) protection for the privacy of his home and other property and from deprivation of property without compensation,
the provisions of this Part of this Order shall have effect for the purpose of affording protection to the said rights and freedoms subject to such limitations of that protection as are contained in those provisions, being limitations designed to ensure that the enjoyment of the said rights and
H
freedoms by any individual does not prejudice the rights and freedoms of others or the public interest."

It is to be noted that the section begins with the word " Whereas ". Though the section must be given such declaratory force as it independently possesses, it would appear in the main to be of the nature of a preamble. It is an intro-
I
duction to and in a sense a prefatory or explanatory note in regard to the sections which are to follow. It is a declaration of entitlement—coupled however with a declaration that though " every person in Malta " is entitled to the " fundamental rights and freedoms of the individual " as specified, yet such entitlement is " subject to respect for the rights and freedoms of others and for the public interest ". The section appears to proceed by way of explanation of the scheme of the succeeding sections. The provisions of Part 2 are to have effect for the purpose of protecting the fundamental rights and freedoms, but the section proceeds to explain that, since even those rights and freedoms must be subject

to the rights and freedoms of others and to the public interest, it will be found **A**
that in the particular succeeding sections which give protection for the fundamental rights and freedoms there will be " such limitations of that protection
as are contained in those provisions ". Further words, which again are explanatory, are added. It is explained what the nature of the limitations will be found
to be. They will be limitations

" designed to ensure that the enjoyment of the said rights and freedoms **B**
by any individual does not prejudice the rights and freedoms of others or the
public interest."

The succeeding sections show that the promised scheme was followed.   The
respective succeeding sections proceed in the first place to give protection for one
of the fundamental rights and freedoms (e.g., the right to life, the right to personal **C**
liberty) and then proceed in the second place to set out certain limitations—i.e.,
the limitations designed to ensure that neither the rights and freedoms of others
nor the public interest are prejudiced. A persual of s. 6, s. 7, s. 8, s. 9, s. 10, s. 11
and s. 12 (which sections need not for present purposes be set out) illustrates how
the scheme and the scope of Part 2 were unfolded.

Section 13 and s. 14 which are of prime importance must be set out. They are as **D**
follows:

" 13. (1) All persons in Malta shall have full liberty of conscience and
enjoy the free exercise of their respective modes of religious worship.

" (2) No person shall be subject to any disability or be excluded from
holding any office by reason of his religious profession.

" 14. (1) Except with his own consent, no person shall be hindered in the **E**
enjoyment of his freedom of expression, that is to say, freedom to hold
opinions and to receive and impart ideas and information without interference, and freedom from interference with his correspondence.

" (2) Nothing contained in or done under the authority of any law shall be
held to be inconsistent with or in contravention of this section to the extent
that the law in question makes provision— **F**

" (a) that is reasonably required—(i) in the interests of defence, public
safety, public order, public morality or public health; or (ii) for the purpose
of protecting the reputations, rights and freedoms of other persons or the
private lives of persons concerned in legal proceedings, preventing the
disclosure of information received in confidence, maintaining the authority
and independence of the courts, or regulating telephony, telegraphy, posts, **G**
wireless broadcasting, television, public exhibitions or public entertainments;
or

" (b) that imposes restrictions upon public officers,
and except so far as that provision or, as the case may be, the thing done
under the authority thereof is shown not to be reasonably justifiable in a
democratic society." **H**

The main facts giving rise to the case have not been in dispute. At all relevant
times the respondent was the editor of a newspaper called the " Voice of Malta ".
It is a newspaper of, and it is published by, the Malta labour party. It is duly
registered according to law. It is a weekly paper and is published late on Saturday
evenings. It is put on sale by newsagents and newsboys willing to take part in
its distribution. It is also put on sale in labour party clubs. Being a weekly **I**
publication it can be bought throughout the week and particularly on Sundays
which are public holidays. The respondent was President of the Malta labour
party. He was also a member of the Legislative Assembly of Malta. His party
was in opposition. The first appellant was Minister of Health. The second appellant was Chief Government medical officer. As such he was the chief adviser to
the government on medical and health matters. Various hospital establishments
and services in Malta and in Gozo formed part of the medical and health
department.

A   Some years before the events which more particularly gave rise to the present proceedings a circular had been sent from the office of the Prime Minister which referred to political discussions by government employees during working hours. That was in 1955. The circular was in these terms:

"OPM Circular No. 34/55.

Office of the Prime Minister,
B   Valletta, August 22, 1955.

"To Ministers.

"Political Discussions during working hours.

"Reports are continually being received to the effect that government employees of various categories, particularly manual workers, indulge in political discussions during working hours. Such behaviour betrays a serious
C   lack of discipline among the employees concerned and reflects no credit either on them or on the supervisory staff.

"2. I am informed that this may account in part for the poor output still being given by certain employees.

"3. Please therefore instruct all heads of departments in your ministry to warn all employees that these discussions at work are strictly prohibited.
D   Stern disciplinary measures, involving if necessary immediate discharge, will be taken against irresponsible individuals transgressing these instructions.

DOM. MINTOFF,
Prime Minister."

E   No criticism of that circular was made. The propriety of its contents was not questioned. It was not suggested that it was other than appropriate to enforce reasonable discipline among government employees during working hours.

On May 26, 1961, His Grace the Archbishop in a Circular (No. 229) issued over the signature of His Lordship Bishop Galea, Vicar General and Monsignor Canon Mifsud, Chancellor of the Archiepiscopal Curia and addressed to the very reverend archpriests, chaplains, vicar-curates, rectors of churches and superiors
F   of religious orders condemned the respondent's newspaper—the "Voice of Malta". The main parts of the circular were as follows:

"His Grace the Archbishop cannot but feel pain at the conflict which has arisen in Malta as regards religious sentiments. He desires that unity which is desired by Our Lord, Jesus Christ. And since the Church cannot
G   come to an agreement with those who refuse to be guided by the teachings of God, as authoritatively expounded by the Church, the Archbishop has felt it his duty to show what should be at least avoided by those who wish to remain in unity with the Church. His Grace the Archbishop therefore notifies that, in present day circumstances, the following are most strongly to be condemned: (a) the grave insults by word, in writing or by deed
H   against the Archbishop or against the clergy; (b) the support for the leaders of the Malta Labour Party so long as they remain at war with the Church and maintain contacts with Socialists, Communists and the A.A.P.S.O.

"Besides the above, this very day there appeared in 'Il-Helsien' 'An Invitation to the Bishops' issued by the executive of the Malta labour party. This invitation is the most grievous insult that could be levelled
I   at the ecclesiastical authority. And this insult, following the admonition which the ecclesiastical authority had already given to 'Il-Helsien' and to the 'Voice of Malta' is also a challenge. Therefore His Grace the Archbishop condemns the 'Voice of Malta', 'Il-Helsien' and 'The Whip' as dependents of the executive, author of this invitation. This means that no one, without committing a mortal sin, can print, write, sell, buy, distribute or read these newspapers. His Grace the Archbishop reminds parents of the heavy responsibility they assume before God when they allow their children to frequent the M.L.P. Brigade where they learn disrespect towards the

authority of the Church and towards the Church's heavy penalties, besides   A
other things contrary to the teachings of the Church. Since it appears that
there are persons who frequently receive Communion, and do confess sins
such as these, confessors, as in duty bound, must, abiding by the rules of
prudence, put the necessary questions to their penitents.

" It is to be remembered that in the Church, all power resides in her
leaders, chosen by God and not by the people, and that therefore when   B
the Church, within her province issues any directives, no son of hers has the
right to criticise, still less, as has been said on occasions, to condemn her."

The M.L.P. Brigade is the Malta Labour Party Brigade: the A.A.P.S.O. is
the Afro Asian Peoples Solidarity Organisation.

The circular which gives rise to present proceedings was a medical and health
department circular issued by the second appellant on Apr. 25, 1962. It was in   C
the following terms:

" MH. Circular No. 42/62.

Medical and Health Department,
15, Merchants Street,
Valletta.
Apr. 25, 1962.   D

Chairman,
St. Luke's Hospital,
Management Committee,
Medical Superintendents,
Heads of Branches.
                                                                          E
" Political Discussions during working hours.

" The attention of all employees is again drawn to the instructions contained in OPM circular No. 34 of Aug. 22, 1955, which is again being subjoined
herewith for ease of reference.

" The entry in the various hospitals and branches of the department
of newspapers, which are condemned by the church authorities, and the   F
wearing of badges of political parties are strictly forbidden.

" You are requested to ensure that the directions contained in the above-
mentioned OPM circular and in para. 2 above are strictly observed by all the
employees of the department.

C. COLEIRO,
Chief Government Medical Officer."   G

No criticism was made of the first paragraph of the letter. In regard to the second
paragraph inasmuch as the " Voice of Malta " was condemned by the church
authorities, there was a definite prohibition of its entry into the various hospitals
and branches of the department. It is to be observed that employees were not
prohibited from taking newspapers as such into hospitals and branches of the
department. Nor were they prohibited from taking political newspapers. They   H
were prohibited from taking the " Voice of Malta " and two other newspapers.

Certain matters of fact here call for mention concerning (a) the way in which
the circular came to be issued and (b) the numbers to whom it was directed.
Regarding (a) it was common ground that it was the appellants who issued the
circular. Information was received by the first appellant (Dr. P. Borg Olivier)
that some party political activity was being carried on at St. Luke's Hospital.   I
It was thereupon decided to issue a circular calling attention to the earlier
circular relating to political activities during working hours. The way in which
the second paragraph of the circular (the part to which exception is taken)
came to be inserted was explained by the first appellant. He gave evidence at
his own request. That paragraph, he said, " crossed my mind as an afterthought
and this because it came to my knowledge that another circular contemplating
the same subject had already been issued by another department, namely, the
education department ". He said also that his feelings about the matter were

A " on account of the prohibition imposed by the Church ". He made it clear that the prohibition that he imposed was not of political newspapers as such. Newspapers which were not condemned by the church authorities could be freely taken by employees both into hospitals and departmental buildings. Such newspapers could there be read during leisure times though not during working hours. Newspapers that were condemned by the church authorities could not be taken at all
B into hospitals or departmental buildings: it followed that such newspapers could not be read even during leisure hours anywhere within such premises. To the extent to which the ban was imposed it was absolute.

Regarding (b) it was declared at the trial on behalf of the appellants that when the circular in question was issued it was intended to apply only to the employees of and not to patients in or doctors in the medical and health department. At
C the trial it had been contended on behalf of the respondent that the prohibition imposed by the circular was intended to apply to patients and doctors in hospitals as well as to all the employees of the department. That contention was not accepted and their lordships need not further refer to it. The hearing in the Court of Appeal proceeded on the assumption that the circular was only intended to govern the activities of the employees of the State of Malta in the medical and
D health department. The employees in the various offices, stores and branches of the department numbered 1,046: the number of employees in the hospitals of the department was 1,614. The prohibition imposed by the circular was therefore directly imposed on 2,660 persons.

On these facts it may be convenient to consider in the first place whether the provisions of s. 14 of the Constitution were contravened in relation to the respon-
E dent. Was he hindered in the enjoyment of his freedom of expression? If he was there was no suggestion that the hindrance was with his consent. Section 14 (1) states that " freedom of expression " covers freedom to hold opinions and to receive and impart ideas and information without interference. Was the respondent hindered in the enjoyment of his freedom to impart ideas and information without interference? The steps taken by an editor of a newspaper to impart
F ideas and information include the expression of ideas and information in words followed by the printing of such words in the paper followed by publishing the paper and followed by circulating it.

A measure of interference with the free handling of the newspaper and its free circulation was involved in the prohibition which the circular imposed. It was said in an Indian case (*Re Romesh Thappar* v. *State of Madras* (1)):

G   " There can be no doubt that freedom of speech and expression includes freedom of propagation of ideas and that freedom is secured by freedom of circulation. ' Liberty of circulation is as essential to that freedom as the liberty of publication. Indeed without circulation the publication would be of little value '."

H Similar thoughts were expressed by BLACK, J., in his judgment in *Martin* v. *City of Struthers* (2) when he said:

    " Freedom to distribute information to every citizen wherever he desires to receive it is so clearly vital to the preservation of a free society that, putting aside reasonable police and health regulations of time and manner of distribution, it must be fully preserved."

I Though the " Voice of Malta " had been in disfavour with the church authorities there was no suggestion that its publication offended against the provisions of any law. Its publication was permissible and legitimate. The public were free to buy it. Yet the employees of the medical and health department were strictly enjoined that they must not have a copy of it in their possession while on government premises. They could bring any newspapers other than the condemned ones. In their leisure time while on government premises they could read such

---

(1) (1950), 37 A.I.R. (S.C.R.) 124 at p. 127.   (2) (1942), 319 U.S. 141 at p. 146.

other newspapers but not the condemned ones. If it seems surprising that a   A
government Minister should direct State employees that they must not have an
opposition newspaper in their possession while on government premises, it is fair
to remember that the reason which inspired the prohibition was not that the
prohibited newspapers supported the opposition party but rather that they had
been condemned by the church authorities. That condemnation however as the
Church's circular showed was in part attributed to the political complexion of the   B
newspapers.

In their lordships' view the strict prohibition imposed by the circular now being
considered amounted to a hindrance of the respondent in the enjoyment of his
freedom to impart ideas and information without interference. Indeed it seems
difficult to avoid the conclusion that the very purpose and intention of the
prohibition was to hinder such imparting. The prohibition was imposed in order to   C
aid the condemnation of the church authorities. In submissions to their lordships
it was contended that the prohibition did not prevent government employees
from buying and possessing and reading the " Voice of Malta " at all such times as
would not involve their having a copy in their possession while on government
premises. Nor did it. But that is merely to say that the most that the Minister
thought that he could do was not effective to prevent government employees from   D
reading the " Voice of Malta ", if any of them were determined to do so. In this
connexion it is to be observed that s. 14 (1) does not refer to the *prevention* of
freedom of expression: it enacts that no person is to be " hindered " in the enjoyment of his freedom of expression. His freedom of expression includes a freedom
to impart ideas and information " without interference ". Though the respondent was not prevented from imparting ideas and information the inevitable   E
consequence of what was done was that he was " hindered " and that there was
" interference " with his freedom.

It was submitted that the measure of any resulting hindrance was slight
and that it could in the contemplation of the law be ignored as being de minimis.
This submission found favour in the First Hall of Her Majesty's Civil Court
but not in the Court of Appeal. Nor does it find favour with their lordships. The   F
plea that what was done was not very far reaching comes ill from those who
reached as far as they could. The submission fails for two reasons. In the first
place the hindrance cannot, on the facts of the case, be classed as minimal. The
Court of Appeal in accepting that the circular must be considered as limiting the
prohibition therein contained to employees held that, considering the size of the
population and of the country, it affected " a relatively considerable number of   G
people and a number of institutions and places spread all over the two islands ".
Their lordships agree. It is undeniable that the prohibition was imposed on
2,660 civil servants. In this connexion it was contended that there was no
evidence that the circulation of the newspaper, the "Voice of Malta",had declined
by reason of the prohibition. While that was so and while it is therefore unknown
whether the circulation was or was not adversely affected, it is to be remembered   H
that the right given by s. 14 is a right not to be "hindered " in freedom to impart
ideas and information without interference. It is of course not known how many
of the 2,660 civil servants were interested in or were readers of the " Voice of
Malta ". If it had been thought that the numbers were negligible, it would have
been pointless to impose so specific a prohibition in a ministerial circular. The
conclusion appears to their lordships to be irresistible that there was hindrance   I
in the enjoyment by the respondent of his freedom to impart ideas and information without interference. Such hindrance and interference formed the very purpose which inspired and motivated the discriminatory prohibition which was
imposed.

In the second place their lordships consider that, where " fundamental rights
and freedoms of the individual " are being considered, a court should be cautious
before accepting the view that some particular disregard of them is of minimal
account. This is not to say that a court is required to spend its time on matters

A which may be " merely frivolous or vexatious " (compare s. 16 (3)). The present
is no such case but rather one where an important question of principle is involved.
Their lordships note that the Court of Appeal, while not taking the matter into
consideration for the purposes of this case, agreed with the submission that " if
it were to be held that the present appellants had the right to issue the circular in
question naturally the same right would appertain to each and every other minister
B and head of department in respect of the department under his charge, in such a
way that the interference with the circulation and reading of his newspaper would
be vastly widened and extended with impunity ". Here was a reflection of the
words of Portia—" Twill be recorded for a precedent, and many an error by the
same example will rush into the State ". In this connexion their lordships were
referred to an American case, i.e., *Thomas* v. *Collins* (3): in one of the judgments
C it was said (4):

> " The restraint is not small when it is considered what was restrained.
> The right is a national right, federally guaranteed. There is some modicum
> of freedom of thought, speech and assembly which all citizens of the republic
> may exercise throughout its length and breadth, which no State, nor all
> together, not the nation itself, can prohibit, restrain or impede. If the
D restraint were smaller than it is, it is from petty tyrannies that large ones
> take root and grow. This fact can be no more plain than when they are
> imposed on the most basic rights of all. Seedlings planted in that soil grow
> great and, growing, break down the foundations of liberty."

It is next necessary to consider whether the appellants are in any way protected
E by an application of the provisions (5) contained either in s. 14 (2) (*a*) or in
sub-s. (2) (*b*). As regards (*a*) it was not suggested that the " condemned " newspapers were being published in disregard of any provision of any law. Public
safety as provided for by any law was not in question: nor was public order:
nor was public morality. The publication of the newspapers in question did not
contravene any law of the state making provision in respect of any of the matters
F referred to in (*a*). Indeed publication did not contravene any law. As regards (*b*)
it was not shown that the prohibition imposed by the circular was warranted by
any law that imposed " restrictions upon public officers ". In agreement with the
Court of Appeal their lordships consider that the " law " which is referred to in
s. 14 (2) is a law which itself makes provision that (as in (*b*)) "imposes restrictions
upon public officers ". Reliance was placed on the provisions of s. 42 of the 1961
G Constitution which read:

> " (1) Subject to the provisions of this Order, where responsibility for
> the administration of a department of government has been assigned to
> any Minister he shall exercise general direction and control over that depart-
> ment; and, subject as aforesaid and to such direction and control, the
> department shall be under the supervision of a permanent secretary appointed
H in accordance with the provisions of s. 85 of this Order.
> " (2) A Permanent Secretary may be responsible for the supervision of
> more than one department of government.
> " (3) The Prime Minister shall be responsible for assigning departments
> of government to Permanent Secretaries.
> " (4) The references to Permanent Secretaries in this section shall be con-
I strued as if they included references to the Attorney-General."

That provision which in general terms gives power to a Minister to exercise
direction and control over a department and gives power to a Permanent Secretary to exercise supervision is not such a law as is contemplated in s. 14 (2) (*b*).
It would naturally be expected that Ministers and public officers would have
zealous regard for the provisions of the Constitution and any law by the terms of

---

(3) (1944), 323 U.S. 516.   (4) (1944), 323 U.S. st p. 543.
 (5) The provisions of s. 14 (2) are set out at p. 462, letters F and G, ante.

which restrictions could be imposed on public officers, i.e., the holders of offices A of emolument in the public service (6) would need to be specific.

Reference was also made to the Medical and Health Department (Constitution) Ordinance and in particular to s. 17 which gives power to the Governor to make regulations in respect of (inter alia) the management and administration of any of the establishments or services forming part of the department and the maintenance of good order in the establishments and services. It was not shown B that any such regulations had been made.

If it could have been shown that the circular was issued under the authority of a law imposing restrictions on public officers the final words of s. 14 would have called for consideration. The respondent could still have succeeded if the issue of the circular was shown " not to be reasonably justifiable in a democratic society ". Both courts in Malta were prepared to hold that the issue of the C circular could not be considered to be reasonably justifiable in a democratic society. Their lordships see no reason to disagree with that view.

Mention must be made of another submission which was advanced on behalf of the appellants. It was said that the provisions of the Constitution must neither be enforced too literally nor be enforced in disregard of the reasonable rights of others. In this connexion reference was made to s. 11 (1) which provides that : D

" Except with his own consent, no person shall be subjected to the search of his person or his property or the entry by others on his premises."

So it was urged that the respondent had no right of entry for his newspaper to departmental premises : and further that an employer should not be denied his right to control what goes on in his own premises. In regard to these contentions E it is to be observed that the respondent claimed no right of entry into any premises. His case was that the natural consequence of prohibiting those who, for their part, might wish to have his newspaper in their possession, from so having it, was that his freedom of expression was being hindered. His case involves no challenge to the reasonable rights of control of an employer or to the reasonable rights of control of an occupier of premises. F

The reality of the circumstances surrounding the issue of the circular must not be clouded. The appellants were undoubtedly entitled to issue reasonable orders to regulate the conduct of government employees during their working hours. The prohibition that they imposed went far beyond the scope of any such reasonable orders. It was discriminatory. It imposed a partial ban on the possession of certain newspapers only. Furthermore the departmental premises G of the medical and health department were not to be regarded as the private premises of some private employer, and it was specially incumbent on the appellants, having regard to their public positions and responsibilities, to honour the spirit of the Constitution. If s. 5 of the Constitution be regarded as possibly giving a blessing to such interpretations of the later sections in Part 2 as will not allow literalism to run riot but will give common sense its due, their lordships consider H that on the basis of such interpretations and on a rational and restrained view the provisions of s. 14 were contravened in relation to the respondent.

As they take this view of the matter their lordships could be absolved from considering s. 13, but, as the judgment of Her Majesty's Civil Court, First Hall was mainly based on the view that the provisions of that section (7) had been contravened and as the Court of Appeal also considered that s. 13 had been I contravened, their lordships deem it desirable to express certain conclusions. In regard to s. 13 (1) their lordships do not consider that the respondent was deprived of his " full liberty of conscience ". It was submitted that the phrase " liberty of conscience " comprised more than liberty of thought or liberty to hold a faith or belief : it was said that the phrase extended to cover liberty to

---

(6) See definitions of " public office " and " public officer " in s. 3 (1) of the Constitution.

(7) The provisions of s. 13 (1), (2) are set out at p. 462, letter D, ante.

A express beliefs and other similar liberties to make manifest such thoughts, faiths and beliefs as might be held. While there may well be some measure of overlap between the sections in Part 2 with the result that two sections might be contravened by one and the same act, it is to be remembered that s. 14 is a section that is specially related to freedom of expression. It is also to be remembered that s. 14 (2) contains certain limitations whereas there are no words of limitation in

B s. 13. In their lordships' view the respondent was not deprived of his liberty of conscience. Nor do their lordships consider that he was denied a free exercise of any mode of religious worship. The words " religious worship " are words that are readily understood. Such interference as there was with the respondent's freedom did not extend to affect his freedom concerning any mode of religious worship.

C In regard to s. 13 (2) it was not contended that the respondent was or had been " excluded from holding any office ", but it was contended that the issue of the circular subjected him to a " disability " and that he was so subjected " by reason of his religious profession ". The words " religious profession " are again words that are readily understood. The facts of the case do not in their lordships' view support the contention that the circular was issued by reason of any " religious

D profession " of the respondent. It is true that the newspaper came in for the condemnation of the church authorities and that the circular issued by the appellants followed on such condemnation. The respondent was affected by reason of the disfavour of the church authorities, who condemned the buying or the distributing or the reading of his newspaper as being a mortal sin. When the appellants issued the circular they were sponsoring the church authorities'

E condemnation and in one rather limited sense they were therefore introducing a religious element or a religious reason. It can perhaps be said that the circular had an origin of a religious nature. The enquiry must, however, concern itself first with the question whether the respondent was subjected to any " disability " and, if he was, then secondly with the question whether that was " by reason of his religious profession ". In the context of the Constitution a person's " religious

F profession " must be regarded as something apart from and different from a person's political views and faith. The evidence was meagre in regard to the respondent's " religious profession ". Their lordships do not find it necessary to seek to define the word " disability " in s. 13 (2). They incline to the view that it denotes deprivations of kinds other than a deprivation of freedom of expression. Even if, however, it could be said that by issuing their circular the

G appellants had subjected the respondent to a " disability " their lordships are not persuaded that within the meaning of the words in s. 13 (2) he was so subjected " by reason of his religious profession ".

For the reasons earlier stated in this judgment their lordships are of the opinion that the respondent was entitled to the relief which he claimed and which was granted. Their lordships will therefore humbly advise Her Majesty

H that the appeal be dismissed. The appellants must pay the respondent's costs.

Appeal dismissed.

Solicitors: *Charles Russell & Co.* (for the appellants); *Antony Steel* (for the respondent).

[*Reported by* KATHLEEN J. H. O'BRIEN, *Barrister-at-Law.*]

R. v. EWENS.

[COURT OF CRIMINAL APPEAL (Melford Stevenson, Phillimore and Thompson, JJ.)
March 31, 1966.]

*Drugs — Misuse — Unauthorised possession — Burden of proof of exception
from offence—Burden on accused to show that he came within exception
when once his possession of the drug was shown—Drugs (Prevention of
Misuse) Act 1964 (c. 64), s. 1 (1) (a).*

On a charge of being in unauthorised possession of a scheduled substance,
contrary to s. 1 (1)* of the Drugs (Prevention of Misuse) Act 1964, the
burden of proof that an accused is within the exemption enacted in para.
(a) of s. 1 (1) is on him, and accordingly it is for the accused to show, e.g.,
that the substance is in his possession by virtue of the issue of a prescription
by a duly qualified medical practitioner for its administration by way of
treatment to him (see p. 472, letter E, and p. 473, letter I, post).

R. v. Oliver ([1943] 2 All E. R. 800), applied.

Dictum of HUMPHREYS, J., in *R. v. Putland and Sorrell* ([1946] 1 All E.R.
85) considered.

Appeal dismissed.

[As to facts peculiarly within knowledge of accused, see 10 HALSBURY'S
LAWS (3rd Edn.) 437, para. 811; and for cases on the subject, see 14 DIGEST
(Repl.) 494, 495, *4781-4784.*

As to unauthorised possession of scheduled substances and misuse of drugs,
see SUPPLEMENT to 26 HALSBURY'S LAWS (3rd Edn.) para. 491A.

For the Drugs (Prevention of Misuse) Act 1964, s. 1, see 44 HALSBURY'S
STATUTES (2nd Edn.) 734.]

Cases referred to:

R. v. *Oliver*, [1943] 2 All E.R. 800; [1944] K.B. 68; 113 L.J.K.B. 119; 170
    L.T. 110; 108 J.P. 30; 29 Cr. App. Rep. 137; 17 Digest (Repl.) 475,
    265.

R. v. *Putland and Sorrell*, [1946] 1 All E.R. 85; 110 J.P. 115; 31 Cr. App.
    Rep. 27; sub nom. R. v. *Sorrell and Putland,* 174 L.T. 148; 17 Digest
    (Repl.) 473, *254.*

R. v. *Scott*, (1921), 86 J.P. 69; 14 Digest (Repl.) 495, *4784.*

R. v. *Spurge*, [1961] 2 All E.R. 688; [1961] 2 Q.B. 205; [1961] 3 W.L.R. 23;
    125 J.P. 502; 45 Cr. App. Rep. 191; 45 Digest (Repl.) 87, *291.*

Woolmington v. *Director of Public Prosecutions*, [1935] All E.R. Rep. 1; [1935]
    A.C. 462; 104 L.J.K.B. 433; 153 L.T. 232; 25 Cr. App. Rep. 72;
    14 Digest (Repl.) 493, *4768.*

Appeal

This was an appeal by Keith Anderson Ewens against his conviction at South
East London Quarter Sessions on Jan. 14, 1966, before the chairman (T. R.
FITZWALTER BUTLER, Esq.) and a jury of being in unauthorised possession of
a scheduled substance, Drinnamyl, contrary to s. 1 (1) of the Drugs (Prevention
of Misuse) Act 1964. It was accepted at the trial that the substance (which
in the indictment was charged, in count 2, as "five tablets containing amphetamine sulphate ") was within the schedule to the Act of 1964. The appeal
was pursuant to a certificate granted by the chairman under s. 3 (b) of the
Criminal Appeal Act, 1907, the question being whether the chairman correctly
directed the jury on the burden of proof on a count under s. 1 (1) of the Act
of 1964.

---

* Section 1 (1), so far as material, is set out at p. 471, letter I, post.

A   The enactments and cases noted below* were cited during the argument in addition to those referred to in the judgment.

B. A. Anns for the appellant.
C. J. Crespi for the Crown.

MELFORD STEVENSON, J., delivered the following judgment of the
B   court: The appellant was convicted in January, 1966, at the South East London Quarter Sessions of being in unauthorised possession of a scheduled substance, Drinnamyl, contrary to s. 1 (1) of the Drugs (Prevention of Misuse) Act 1964, and against that conviction he now appeals. He was also convicted of the offence of being in charge of a motor car when unfit to drive through drink or drugs, but against that conviction there is no appeal.

C   This appeal comes to this court on a certificate signed by the learned chairman of South East London Quarter Sessions, which raises the question, and I quote the learned chairman's words,

"Whether I gave the jury a correct direction on burden of proof on a count under s. 1 (1) of the Drugs (Prevention of Misuse) Act 1964."

In the course of the argument on this case, counsel for the appellant, to whom
D   we are indebted for a careful and interesting argument on this matter, obtained the leave of the court to add as a ground of appeal that the chairman was wrong in not withdrawing the case on count 2, that is the drugs charge, from the jury at the end of the Crown's case. It is not necessary to deal in any detail with the facts which were that, on Oct. 16, 1965, while the appellant was being examined by a doctor at the Belvedere Police Station, a bottle containing five
E   drinnamyl tablets fell from his pocket and, according to the doctor, the appellant said that he had originally bought that bottle containing fifty tablets that evening at the cost of a shilling per tablet and that he kept several tablets loose in his pocket and took them to calm his nerves. The appellant in his evidence admitted that the bottle was in his possession. He said that he did not remember how he actually got the tablets, and that he had been collecting tablets of that
F   kind over a number of years. He said that he had not bought any tablets that evening and he denied having told Dr. Price that he had. He said that he suffered from mental depression and doctors had prescribed different drugs for him, and when he got a bottle he did not always finish with it and did not usually throw the bottle away but kept it. He said that the drugs found in the bottle, which were in his possession, came from some prescription from some doctor at
G   some time, but he could not say from whom or when.

It was submitted by counsel for the appellant in the court below that the prosecution had to prove three things; first, possession of the drugs, secondly, that the drug was within the Schedule which is part of the Act of 1964, and, thirdly, that the appellant was in possession without being authorised so to be. On these points the first two were, as I have said, not in dispute. On the third
H   point it was submitted by counsel that in all statutes similar to the Drugs (Prevention of Misuse) Act 1964, where the burden of proof was in fact on the defendant, the Act was careful so to state, whereas it was argued in this Act that it was not so stated. Let me at once refer to the actual language of the statute on which the second count of this indictment was based. Section 1 (1), so far as material, is in these terms:

I   "Subject to any exemptions for which provision may be made by regulations made by the Secretary of State and to the following provisions of this section, it shall not be lawful for a person to have in his possession a substance for the time being specified in the Schedule to this Act unless [it is the first of the excepted classes with which we are concerned in this case]

---

* Summary Jurisdiction Act, 1848, s. 14; Summary Jurisdiction Act, 1879, s. 39 (2); Magistrates' Courts Act, 1952, s. 81; *R. v. Turner*, (1816), 5 M. & S. 206; *Mancini* v. *Director of Public Prosecutions*, [1941] 3 All E.R. 272; [1942] A.C. 1; *John* v. *Humphreys*, [1955] 1 All E.R. 793.

(*a*) it is in his possession by virtue of the issue of a prescription by a duly   A
qualified medical practitioner or a registered dental practitioner for its
administration by way of treatment to him, or to a person under his
care; . . ."

Then there is the second class of exception which relates to a prescription by
a registered veterinary surgeon for an animal and there is a third class which
contemplates the possibility of the defendant in such a case being registered   B
in a register kept for the purposes of that paragraph by the appropriate authorities. That, I think, is as much of the section as I need for the moment refer
to. At the conclusion of the prosecution's case, a submission was made by counsel
for the appellant that there was no case for the appellant to answer on the ground
that the prosecution had not established or offered any evidence to the effect that
these drugs were not in the appellant's possession as a consequence of, or in   C
pursuance of, a prescription issued by a medical practitioner under the first
exception which I read from s. 1 (1) (*a*). The learned chairman dealt carefully
and in detail with a number of authorities in which questions similar to that
which is now before the court were examined and in particular he referred to
and relied on *R.* v. *Oliver* (1), to which I will refer more fully later; and the
learned chairman expressed his conclusion on the submission in these terms: D

"I think the principle in the case of *R.* v. *Oliver* (1) applies to the present
case, and I hold that the prosecution are not bound to give prima facie evidence that the [appellant] is not found in any of the excepted categories,
and it is for the defendant to establish the reverse, remembering that where
any burden is laid on the defence the standard of proof is much less onerous
than that on the prosecution; the [appellant] has merely to establish the   E
facts on the balance of probability."

It is to the statement "that the prosecution are not bound to give prima facie
evidence that the [appellant] is not found in any excepted categories" that
exception is taken on this appeal and that is what we have to determine. The
arguments in the court below and, indeed, the decision of the learned chairman   F
took into account the important judgment of this court in *R.* v. *Spurge* (2).
That was the decision of a court of five judges. It was a case of dangerous driving
and the headnote asserts (3):

"A mechanical defect in a motor vehicle may be a defence to a charge
of dangerous driving under s. 11 of the Road Traffic Act, 1930, if it causes
a sudden total loss of control and is in no way due to any fault on the part   G
of the driver, but such defence has no application where the defect is known
to the driver or should have been discovered by him had he exercised
reasonable prudence. The onus of establishing such a defence does not
rest on the accused; it will not be considered by the court unless raised
by the accused, but once raised, it must be considered with the rest of the
evidence and the onus of proof still remains on the prosecution."   H

It is to be observed that that case was concerned solely with the question of
fact whether the accident which gave rise to the prosecution of the appellant
was caused by some mechanical defect of the car of which he did not know
and had no reason to anticipate. The judgment of the court was delivered by
SALMON, J., and reference was made to the well-known case of *Woolmington*
v. *Director of Public Prosecutions* (4), to which our attention has been called   I
in the argument in this case, and SALMON, J., after referring to *Woolmington's*
case (4), then said this (5):

"There is no rule of law that where the facts are peculiarly within the

(1) [1943] 2 All E.R. 800; [1944] K.B. 68.
(2) [1961] 2 All E.R. 688; [1961] 2 Q.B. 205.   (3) [1961] 2 Q.B. 205.
(4) [1935] All E.R. Rep. 1; [1935] A.C. 462.
(5) [1961] 2 All E.R. at p. 692; [1961] 2 Q.B. at pp. 212, 213.

A knowledge of the accused, the burden of establishing any defence based on these facts shifts to the accused. No doubt there is a number of statutes where the onus of establishing a statutory defence is placed on the accused because the facts relating to it are peculiarly within his knowledge. But we are not considering any statutory defence. It is most important that the summing-up should contain a careful direction as to the onus of proof.

B It is equally important that the jury should be clearly told the narrow limits, laid down in this judgment, within which a defence based on sudden mechanical defect can operate."

It is to be observed that the learned judge, having asserted the general principle which he derived from *Woolmington* v. *Director of Public Prosecutions* (6) and, indeed, a number of other authorities, is careful to point out that there is a

C number of statutes where the onus of establishing a statutory defence is placed on the accused because the facts relating to it are peculiarly within his knowledge. This is a statutory offence. It is an offence described in the language which I have already read which declares that

" it shall not be lawful for a person to have in his possession a substance

D for the time being specified in the Schedule to this Act unless . . ."

and then there follow the exceptions to which I have already drawn attention. Without trespassing in the least on the generality of the proposition laid down by the court in *Spurge's* case (7), we desire to make it quite clear that, where it is necessary to consider the impact of the burden of proof in relation to a statutory offence and any statutory exceptions from liability for that offence,

E it is essential to construe the language of the enactment which creates that offence.

It is quite true that there are statutes, of which the Prevention of Crime Act, 1953, and the Firearms Act 1965, are examples, where the Act, in expressing the exception, uses words to the effect that the burden of establishing that exception shall be on the defendant. Where those words are used, it is plain that the kind of question which arises in this case cannot cause any difficulty, but

F we are here faced with a section which contains no such words. Section 1 of the Drugs (Prevention of Misuse) Act 1964 does set out, however, a number of exceptions qualifying or admitting an escape from the generality of the proposition first laid down in s. 1 (1), and we have to determine the true construction of the subsection. There are several authorities in which reference has been made to the importance of the consideration that the facts which bring a defen-

G dant within the ambit of a particular exception, if they are peculiarly or exclusively within the knowledge of the defendant, should be regarded as matters which it is for him to establish and that is not a mere matter of convenience. It is tolerably plain that there must be many statutory prohibitions which would become incapable of enforcement if the prosecution had to embark on inquiries necessary to exclude the possibility of a defendant falling within a

H class of persons excepted by the section when the defendant himself knows perfectly well whether he falls within that class and has, or should have readily available to him, the means by which he could establish whether or not he is within the excepted class. That consideration has proved a powerful one in enabling courts in the past to construe enactments such as the section now before us, and we think that it is of the utmost persuasive importance in relation

I to this section, and we take the view that the burden did lie on the appellant to show that he fell within the excepted class of a person who has possession of this scheduled drug by virtue of the issue of a prescription by a duly qualified medical practitioner. That being so, we take the view that the learned chairman was correct in the view of the section which he expressed at the end of the submission of no case on behalf of the appellant.

It would not be right, I think, to leave the matter by expressing that view

(6) [1935] All E.R. Rep. 1; [1935] A.C. 462.
(7) [1961] 2 All E.R. 688; [1961] 2 Q.B. 205.

by itself. It is important to draw attention to *R.* v. *Oliver* (8), which arose A
out of a conviction on an indictment charging the appellant as a wholesaler
with supplying sugar on various dates otherwise than under the terms of a
licence granted by the then Minister of Food. That was an offence under the
Defence (General) Regulations, and there the contention was advanced that
the burden laid on the prosecution to establish that there was no licence granted
to the appellant to permit him to acquire sugar. The learned deputy chairman B
of the Middlesex Quarter Sessions told the jury in the summing-up that the onus
of proving that the appellant had a licence was on the appellant and that they
must accept his direction that the appellant had no licence in view of his silence.
That was a passage in the summing-up on which the appeal was founded.
VISCOUNT CALDECOTE, C.J., referred to *R.* v. *Scott* (9), in which a similar
question arose under an order made under the Dangerous Drugs Act, 1920, C
which provided that no person should supply any of the specified drugs unless
he was licensed by the Secretary of State to supply the drug. The point was
taken at the close of the case for the prosecution that there was no evidence
that the defendant was an unauthorised person. SWIFT, J. held that, if the
defendant were licensed, it was a fact which was peculiarly within his own
knowledge and there was no hardship on him to prove it. He said (10) that D

" it might be very difficult or impossible for the prosecution satisfactorily to prove that he did not possess any one or other of the qualifications which might entitle him to deal with the drug, but the defendant could
prove without the least difficulty that he had authority to do it."

Having referred to those words of SWIFT, J., LORD CALDECOTE, C.J., in giving E
the judgment of this court said (11):

" Unless we are satisfied that this decision is clearly wrong, we should
think it our duty to follow the decision of SWIFT, J."

A number of authorities were then canvassed, and LORD CALDECOTE continued
(12):
                                                                          F
" In the circumstances of the present case, we are of opinion that the
prosecution was under no necessity of giving prima facie evidence of the
non-existence of a licence."

That authority appears to us to support and completely justify the view taken
by the learned chairman in the present case. It is necessary, however, also to
refer to *R.* v. *Putland and Sorrell* (13), where two persons were charged with G
having conspired to acquire, and having acquired, rationed goods without surrendering the appropriate number of coupons, in contravention of the Consumer
Rationing (Consolidation) Order, 1944. It was submitted on their behalf that
there was no case to go to the jury because there was no evidence in regard
to the non-surrender of coupons. In his summing-up, the trial judge directed
the jury that, in a case of this kind, a defendant alone might know whether H
coupons had been surrendered or not, and, therefore, if the prosecution had
proved the whole case to the satisfaction of the jury, it was not necessary to
prove that no coupons had been given in order to establish a case requiring
an answer from a defendant. The judgment of this court was delivered by
HUMPHREYS, J., who made this reference to *R.* v. *Oliver* (14). He said (15):

" We were referred in regard to that matter to *R.* v. *Oliver* (14), which I
is binding on us so far as it is relevant to the present case."

He then referred to the fact that the order being considered in that case was

---

(8) [1943] 2 All E.R. 800; [1944] K.B. 68.   (9) (1921), 86 J.P. 69.
(10) (1921), 86 J.P. at p. 70.
(11) [1943] 2 All E.R. at p. 802; [1944] K.B. at p. 72.
(12) [1943] 2 All E.R. at p. 803; [1944] K.B. at p. 75.   (13) [1946] 1 All E.R. 85.
(14) [1943] 2 All E.R. 800; [1944] K.B. 68.   (15) [1946] 1 All E.R. at p. 86.

A the Sugar (Control) Order, 1940, which made it an offence for any wholesaler
by way of trade to supply any sugar, and continued (16):

" it is an absolute prohibition, subject to this, that he may do so ' in accordance with the terms of a licence, permit or other authority granted by . . .
the Minister '. So that no person may do the act—no person may deal in
sugar at all—unless he has a licence. The court held, upon the terms of
B that order, that the onus was on the defendant to prove that he had a
licence, that being a fact peculiarly within his own knowledge, and the
prosecution was therefore under no necessity of giving prima facie evidence
of the non-existence of a licence. There is, in our opinion, a very broad
distinction which must be observed between that case and the present.
In that case the prohibition against doing the thing was absolute, and it was
C for the defendant, if he wanted to show that he might do it lawfully, to
provide some excuse such as a licence or other authority from the Minister."

Having formed the view which I have expressed as to the true construction
of s. 1 of the Drugs (Prevention of Misuse) Act 1964, one arrives as I have said,
at the view that the learned chairman's ruling on the submission of no case was
D correct, but it is necessary also to look at the learned chairman's direction to
the jury in the course of his summing-up, where—I am passing to the second
count in the indictment—he said this:

" Here the position is a little different; the prosecution must prove
first of all that this drug does come within the Schedule to the Act. Tablets
which are commonly called drinnamyl and contain amphetamine sulphate
E do come within the Schedule to the Act. It is quite clearly established
that the [appellant] was in possession, exercising control over them; he
has told you that he was; therefore the question is was that possession an
unlawful one? Once the prosecution, as I understand it, proves those
matters then it is for the [appellant] to raise some prima facie evidence
fit for the jury to consider that possession was a lawful one, that he comes
F within one of the privileged categories, but I direct you as a matter of
law that he has raised such prima facie evidence, because his case is that
he obtained these tablets at some uncertain time but as the result of the
prescription of a duly qualified medical practitioner. The position then is
this; if such prima facie evidence has been adduced by the [appellant], if
a jury thinks either that that evidence is true or may reasonably be true,
G then the [appellant] is entitled to be acquitted, but if the jury refuse to
accept the account the [appellant] has given as to how he came into possession, if you came to the conclusion that he came into possession by some
other means, then the possession becomes unlawful and the [appellant]
must be convicted."

The contention advanced on behalf of the appellant is that that direction is
H wrong because the learned chairman, it is said, ought to have told the jury
that they should not convict unless the Crown had satisfied them so that they
felt sure that these drugs were not in the possession of the appellant in pursuance
of the prescription of a qualified medical practitioner. Having arrived at the
view of this section which I have already dealt with, and having applied to the
language of this section the reasoning of the court in *Oliver's* case (17), to which
I I have already referred, we think that, in these words the learned chairman
was giving to this jury a direction which might be regarded as more favourable
to the defence than was in fact justified, more favourable than the view which he
had found acceptable in deciding the submission of no case. However, in
spite of the direction that the appellant had in fact raised such prima facie
evidence, the jury convicted him, and we cannot see that any complaint can be
made of the propriety of that conviction or the way that it was arrived at.

(16) [1946] 1 All E.R. at p. 87.   (17) [1943] 2 All E.R. 800; [1944] K.B. 68.

I ought, perhaps, to mention there was an appeal against sentence, that is A
to say, against a fine of £10 which was imposed on the appellant, but that appeal
has been abandoned.

In the circumstances, this appeal must be dismissed.

Appeal dismissed.

Solicitors; *Registrar, Court of Criminal Appeal* (for the appellant); *Solicitor,*
Metropolitan Police (for the Crown).   B

[*Reported by* N. P. METCALFE, ESQ., *Barrister-at-Law.*]

GIBSON v. SKIBS A/S MARINA AND ORKLA GROBE A/B
AND SMITH COGGINS, LTD.   C

[LIVERPOOL ASSIZES (Cantley, J.), February 4, 7, 8, 9, 1966.]

Dock—Loading and unloading—Lifting gear—Use by stevedores of ship's
derrick and hook and shackle to unload cargo—Fracture of shackle causing
load to fall and kill workman—Inspection of shackle within previous three
months—" Inspection "—" Competent person "—Liability of shipowners   D
and stevedores—Docks Regulations, 1934 (S.R. & O. 1934 No. 279), reg.
19 (a), (c).

A cargo of copper anodes in loads weighing nearly four tons each was
being unloaded at Liverpool from a hold of the first defendants' motor
vessel by stevedores, the second defendants, using the ship's own gear.
While a load was being hoisted on Nov. 6, 1961, steel arms of the shackle   E
supporting the hook fractured; the load fell and the deceased, who was
an employee of the second defendants, was killed. The fracture of the
shackle was found to have resulted from the spreading of a hairline crack
in the shackle. On Feb. 14, 1961, nine months before the accident, the
shackle had been tested and thoroughly examined in the dockyard at
Sandefjord in discharge of the first defendants' obligation under para. (a)*   F
of reg. 19 of the Docks Regulations, 1934. The vessel's gear was stripped
and inspected by able-bodied seamen under the supervision of the bosun
on the voyage to Liverpool before unloading. No defect was discovered
on either occasion.

Held: there was no breach of reg. 19 (c)† by the first defendants for such
an inspection as was thereby required had been made, the bosun and the   G
able-bodied seamen being competent persons for the purposes of reg. 19 (c);
nor was there negligence on the part of the first defendants since the common
law duty to take reasonable care, in so far as it involved examination of the
shackle, did not extend in the absence of special circumstances beyond
careful compliance with the requirements of reg. 19 (a) and (c), and, as
regards examination pursuant to para. (a) of reg. 19, the first defendants   H
were protected by s. 2 (4) (b)‡ of the Occupiers Liability Act, 1957 (see
p. 478, letters E, F and I, post).

---

* Regulation 19 (a) provides: " No chain, rule, hook, shackle, swivel or pulley
block shall be used in hoisting or lowering unless it has been tested and examined by
a competent person in the manner set out in the schedule to these regulations."

† The terms of reg. 19 (c) are printed at p. 477, letter I, to p. 478, letter A, post.   I

‡ Section 2 (4) (b) of the Occupiers' Liability Act, 1957, provides: " In determining
whether the occupier of premises has discharged the common duty of care to a visitor,
regard is to be had to all the circumstances, so that (for example)— . . . (b) where
damage is caused to a visitor by a danger due to the faulty execution of any work of
construction, maintenance or repair by an independent contractor employed by the
occupier, the occupier is not to be treated without more as answerable for the danger
if in all the circumstances he had acted reasonably in entrusting the work to an independent contractor and had taken such steps (if any) as he reasonably ought in order to
satisfy himself that the contractor was competent and that the work had been properly
done."

A   [As to the docks regulations, see 17 HALSBURY'S LAWS (3rd Edn.) 128-130, para. 207.

For the Docks Regulations, 1934, reg. 19, see 8 HALSBURY'S STATUTORY INSTRUMENTS (1st Re-issue) 165.]

Action.

B   This was an action by the plaintiff, Eleanor Gibson, the widow and administratrix of Frederick Gibson, deceased, against the first defendants, Skibs A/S Marina and Orkla Grobe A/B, owners of the motor vessel " Fernpoint " and the second defendants, Smith Coggins, Ltd., stevedores, claiming damages in respect of the death of her husband whilst in the employment of the second defendants on Nov. 6, 1961.

C   The second defendants were engaged in discharging the cargo of the Fernpoint at Liverpool.   The cargo consisted of copper anodes and for the purpose of unloading it the second defendants were using the ship's derrick and a hook and shackle supplied by the ship.   The safe working load of the gear, and in particular of the hook and shackle, was five tons. A considerable number of loads of copper anodes, many of them weighing over four tons but none weighing more than four tons thirteen hundredweight, had been hoisted out of the ship's hold. While

D   a load consisting of twelve anodes and weighing just under four tons was being hoisted, the two arms of the steel shackle supporting the hook fractured and the load fell, killing the deceased.   The trial judge found that there had been a hairline crack on the inner side of the bend of the shackle on each arm, due in some way to metal fatigue, and that those cracks had spread from the exterior inwards until they extended into half the thickness of one arm and four-fifths

E   of the thickness of the other.   Thus weakened, the arms of the shackle had snapped in use.   According to Mr. Merry, a metallurgist, whose evidence the trial judge preferred to that of Mr. Anderson, a consulting engineer and naval architect, the cracking had existed and progressed over a period of at least a month and probably several months.   Such a crack would have been visible. On Feb. 14, 1961, the shackle had been tested and thoroughly examined by a

F   competent person in the dockyard at Sandefjord, in discharge of the first defendants' duty under reg. 19 (*a*) of the Docks Regulations, 1934, and the terms of the certificate* of examination No. 1 issued under those regulations.   No defect was found during that examination.   In addition, the evidence showed that all the gear was stripped, cleaned and inspected during the voyage of the vessel from America to South Africa and from South Africa to Avonmouth prior to its

G   proceeding to Liverpool.   The cleaning and inspection was done by able-bodied seamen under the immediate supervision of the bosun Dinsen and under the general supervision of the chief mate.   Further, the bosun said that he thought that at Avonmouth he personally went over every crane hook himself and that he would be looking for cracks and particularly at any bend.   No defect was discovered during the voyage or at Avonmouth or at any time prior to the

H   accident.

J. E. Jones for the plaintiff.
Andrew Rankin for the first defendants.
R. H. Forrest, Q.C., and *A. M. Maguire* for the second defendants.

CANTLEY, J., stated the facts, and continued: Against the first defendants,
I   this raises two questions.   First, it is alleged that there was a breach by the first defendants of their statutory obligation under reg. 19 (*c*) of the Docks Regulations, 1934 (1).   That paragraph provides that

" All chains, other than bridle chains attached to derricks or masts, and all rings, hooks, shackles, swivels and pulley blocks shall be inspected

---

* The form of certificate and particulars to be given of tests and examinations made under reg. 19 (*a*) are now prescribed by the Docks Certificate Order 1964 (S.I. 1964 No. 532).   (1) S.R. & O. 1934 No. 279.

by a competent person immediately before each occasion on which they   **A**
are used in hoisting or lowering, unless they have been inspected within
the preceding three months."

It will be observed that para. (c) of the regulation uses the word " inspected ";
para. (a) of the regulation uses the word " examined "; and reg. 18 uses the
phrase " thorough examination " and defines that particular phrase. There   **B**
is clearly a difference between a " thorough examination " as contemplated by
the regulations and an " examination " as contemplated by the regulations. Is
there also a difference between " examination " and " inspection " as contemplated by the regulations? Prima facie one would expect that when two different
words, although practically synonymous in ordinary use, are employed in different
parts of the same regulation dealing with the same kind of topic, they are intended   **C**
to have some different meaning.

It seems to me, when I look at the pattern of reg. 18, reg. 19 and reg. 21, that
" examination " in those regulations is a more thorough and scientific process
than " inspection " under those regulations. Indeed, " examination ", like
" testing " and " annealing ", may require technical qualifications, as reg. 21
recognises. Although something less than " examination ", " inspection "   **D**
is something more than a mere casual glance; I think that it involves looking
carefully and critically at the gear with the naked eye, but no more than that.
Who is " a competent person " for the purpose of such an inspection? This
phrase is not defined. I think that it is obviously to be taken to have its ordinary
meaning of a person who is competent for the task. I think that a competent
person for this task is a person who is a practical and reasonable man, who   **E**
knows what to look for and knows how to recognise it when he sees it. I consider
that the bosun was a competent person for the purpose of this regulation. I
also consider on the evidence of Captain Poust that the able-bodied seamen on
this vessel were competent persons for this purpose.

Was there a breach of reg. 19 (c)? The evidence as to inspection of this
particular shackle within the three months preceding the accident lacks precision   **F**
but, on the balance of probabilities, I think that the requisite inspection was made.
It seems to me that I could not possibly find on the evidence in this case that
there had been a breach of reg. 19 (c).

The second question in relation to the first defendants is: was there negligence
on their part? Their duty was to take reasonable care for the safety of persons
using this gear, both generally and in particular when inspecting it. As to the   **G**
general situation and the dangers to be apprehended in connexion with this
particular part of the gear, it may be significant that the event which caused this
tragic accident seems virtually to have been unknown previously. Of those
who gave evidence in the course of this action, Captain Poust, Captain Worrall,
Mr. Anderson and the bosun Dinsen with forty-five years' experience at sea,
all said that they had never previously heard of such an occurrence, and they   **H**
said this although hooks and shackles are in common use.

The more particular question is whether the defect ought to have been discovered during examination or inspection. The common law duty in some
cases may be greater than the statutory duty, but, although that may be the
situation in some matters, in this matter I do not think that, in the absence of
special circumstances, such as known damage to the shackle, the common law   **I**
duty as to examination and inspection should be held to extend beyond careful
compliance with the requirements of reg. 19. So far as reg. 19 (a) is concerned,
I have no reason to suppose that there was a detectable defect in this shackle
when it was examined at Sandefjord in February, 1961, but, in any event, the
first defendants would be protected so far as that examination is concerned by
the provisions of s. 2 (4) (b) of the Occupiers' Liability Act, 1957.

So far as reg. 19 (c) is concerned, it is necessary to look at the evidence. The
witness Mr. Merry described the crack on more than one occasion as " a hairline

A crack ", and it seemed to me in the course of his evidence that he visualised a very fine crack indeed. He said in examination-in-chief that, in his opinion, the crack would be visible in the later stages, but he added that it would be visible for a minimum of one month, probably longer. In cross-examination, he said that the hairline crack would have been visible during the thorough examination contemplated by (as he put it) the Factories Acts, but he said that

B examination on ship by the able-bodied seamen as described in the evidence he had heard could quite well miss the hairline crack even though those inspecting the tackle were doing their job conscientiously. In re-examination, he said that he considered this crack would have been visible on thorough cleaning and careful inspection a day or so before the accident. The evidence of Mr. Merry left me with the clear impression that persons carrying out an inspection under

C reg. 19 (c) could, without negligence, fail to notice the hairline crack on the inner side of the exterior of the arms of the shackle, even assuming that it was in fact present at the time of such inspection, which is not beyond doubt.

I do not, therefore, feel justified in condemning any servants or agents of the first defendants in negligence in the course of the inspections and examinations which were carried out, nor have I seen any reason from the evidence to suppose

D that any examinations or inspections in addition to those to which I have referred ought to have been carried out.

I proceed to consider the situation of the second defendants; they were stevedores. In the statement of claim, a breach of reg. 19 of the Docks Regulations, 1934, (2), was alleged against the second defendants, but the duty of complying with that regulation is not, by the regulations, imposed on the second

E defendants and counsel for the plaintiff did not seek to pursue any contention that the second defendants were under any such statutory duty.

The case ultimately against the second defendants was that they had been guilty of a failure to take reasonable care for the safety of their workmen. It is said that they ought to have made a sufficiently detailed examination which would have discovered the existence of the hairline crack to which I have referred.

F [HIS LORDSHIP reviewed the evidence, considered the legal obligation on the second defendants, and concluded:] I am unable to find that there was any failure by the second defendants to do what a reasonable employer would do, nor do I think that they omitted any precaution which would have occurred to a reasonable stevedore in the circumstances. So far as they are concerned, also, I find myself unable to condemn them in any negligence.

G For these reasons, I consider the action against each of the defendants must fail.

Judgment for the defendants.

Solicitors: *John A. Beyn, Twyford & Co.*, Liverpool (for the plaintiff); *Hill, Dickinson & Co.*, Liverpool (for the first defendants); *Weightman, Pedder & Co.*, Liverpool (for the second defendants).

H
[*Reported by* K. B. EDWARDS, ESQ., *Barrister-at-Law.*]

I

(2) S.R. & O. 1934 No. 279.

NOTE.   A

Re KNOWLES (*deceased*).
KNOWLES *v.* BIRTWELL AND OTHERS.

[CHANCERY DIVISION (Stamp, J.), March 28, April 6, 1966.]

Family Provision—Compromise—Jurisdiction—Application by widow for   B
reasonable provision to be made for her out of estate of £16,700—Court had
no jurisdiction to make lump sum order because of size of estate—Numerous
pecuniary legacies, and nothing would remain for residuary legatees—Order
giving pecuniary legatee authority to defend proceedings on behalf of numerous
other pecuniary legatees not parties to proceedings—Sanction sought for   C
compromise under which £2,000 would be paid to widow and legacies would
abate—No jurisdiction to bind person sui juris not party to proceedings—
Inheritance (Family Provision) Act, 1938 (1 & 2 Geo. 6 c. 45), *s.* 1 (1), (4),
as amended by Intestates' Estates Act, 1952 (15 & 16 Geo. 6 & 1 Eliz. 2 c. 64),
s. 7, Sch. 3—*R.S.C., Ord.* 104, *r.* 6, *Ord.* 15, *r.* 13 (1) (*a*).

[As to parties to applications for family provision see 16 HALSBURY's LAWS   D
(3rd Edn.) 457, para. 915; and for cases on the practice on such applications,
see 24 DIGEST (Repl.) 983, 984, *9800-9810*.

As to the court's power to sanction compromises on behalf of absent parties,
see 30 HALSBURY's LAWS (3rd Edn.) 404, para. 759.

For the Inheritance (Family Provision) Act, 1938, as amended by the
Intestates' Estates Act, 1952, see 32 HALSBURY's STATUTES (2nd Edn.) 139.]   E

Adjourned Summons

By his will Herbert Knowles, deceased, appointed the first defendant to be one
of his executors. The other executor, the second defendant, died after the issue
of the summons. The testator made no provision for his widow in his will.
He bequeathed numerous pecuniary legacies amounting to £16,000. He died on
June 21, 1962, and his net estate amounted to approximately £16,755 7s. 9d.   F
The testator's widow applied by originating summons dated Jan. 9, 1963, for an
order that such reasonable provision might be paid for her out of the testator's
estate as to the court might seem proper. An order was made on Jan. 30, 1964,
by UNGOED-THOMAS, J., authorising the fourth defendant, a residuary legatee, to
defend the proceedings on behalf of the other residuary legatees and authorising the
third defendant, a pecuniary legatee, to defend the proceedings on behalf of the   G
other pecuniary legatees. It was apparent that the amount of the costs of the
proceedings would cause the pecuniary legacies to abate and that the residuary
legatees would receive nothing. Accordingly, the residuary legatees were not
represented. The matter came before STAMP, J., in chambers to sanction on
behalf of the pecuniary legatees a proposed compromise of the plaintiff's claim.
The terms of the compromise were that subject to the due completion of the   H
administration of the estate the executor should raise out of the estate and pay
to the plaintiff the sum of £2,000, the legacies should abate pro tanto and the
plaintiff would release the estate from all further claims. HIS LORDSHIP gave
judgment in open court.

D. H. McMullen for the plaintiff.
M. Nesbitt for the first defendant.   I
J. R. Cherryman for the third defendant.

Cur. adv. vult.

Apr. 6. **STAMP, J.,** read the following judgment: The position of the
estate is such that there must in any event be an abatement of the pecuniary
legacies given by the will of the deceased. The matter came before me in chambers
to sanction a compromise of the claim under the Inheritance (Family Provision)

A Act, 1938, the basis of the compromise being that the applicant should receive a
lump sum payment in satisfaction of her claim. Although there is nothing for
the residuary legatees the net estate of the testator is for the purposes of the
Act approximately £16,755 7s. 9d., so that I cannot make an order under the
Act of 1938 awarding a lump sum payment. An order had been made under
R.S.C., Ord. 104 which deals with the procedure on applications to the High
B Court under the Inheritance (Family Provision) Act, 1938, and more particularly under r. 6 of that order (1), authorising one of the pecuniary legatees, who
are numerous, to defend the action on behalf of, or for the benefit of, all persons
having the same interest, and I am invited to sanction the compromise on behalf
of all those persons. They are, of course, absent pecuniary legatees who are not
parties, but it is submitted that r. 6 enables the court to bind their interests to
C the compromise. In my judgment this submission is not well founded. No doubt
if the court made an order within its jurisdiction under the Inheritance (Family
Provision) Act, 1938, the order would bind these absent pecuniary legatees;
but for the reason that I have given the court, on the facts of this case, has no
jurisdiction under that Act of 1938 to direct a lump sum payment to be made
D to the applicant.

The court has inherent jurisdiction to sanction on behalf of an infant a compromise of proceedings which, but for his infancy, he himself could make, but it
has no such inherent jurisdiction in relation to a party sui juris who is not before
the court, and some provision having the force of statute must be found before
the court can bind such a party to a compromise. Faced with this difficulty
E counsel asked for an order under R.S.C., Ord. 15, r. 13, which enables the court,
subject to certain conditions, to sanction a compromise on behalf of absent parties.
I quote R.S.C., Ord. 15, r. 13, which applies only

"(1) In any proceedings concerning—(a) the administration of the estate
of a deceased person, or (b) property subject to a trust, or (c) the construction
F of a written instrument . . . "

Reliance is placed on para. (a). In my judgment, however, an application that
reasonable provision may be ordered to be made out of the net estate of a deceased person is not a proceeding " concerning the administration of " his estate
within the meaning of the rule. Had the relevant words been " in any proceeding
concerning the estate " the contrary would have been, no doubt, arguable.
G I am indebted to counsel for calling my attention to the difference in language
between the existing R.S.C., Ord. 15, r. 13 (1) (a) and the former R.S.C., Ord. 16,
r. 9A which enabled the court in any proceedings concerning the estate of a
deceased person—note the absence of the words " administration of "—to,
sanction a compromise on behalf of absent parties not only where a person had
H been appointed to represent them under the former R.S.C., Ord. 16, r. 32 (para.
(ii) of the former R.S.C., Ord. 16, r. 9A) but also where there was some person in
the same interest who was before the court and assented to the compromise
(para. (i) of the former R.S.C., Ord. 16, r. 9A). It may be that an application
under the Inheritance (Family Provision) Act, 1938, fell within the former
R.S.C., Ord. 16, r. 9A as an application concerning the estate of a deceased person—
I I say nothing about that—but it does not in my judgment fall within the wording
of the present R.S.C., Ord. 15, r. 13 (1) (a).

---

(1) R.S.C., Ord. 104, r. 6 provides that in applications under the Inheritance (Family
Provision) Act, 1938, " where a defendant has been added and there are other persons
having the same or a similar interest the court or a judge may order that such defendant
be authorised to defend on behalf of or for the benefit of all persons so interested and
that all persons so interested shall be bound by any order made in the proceedings.
An order binding interests under this rule need not be made by the judge in person ".

I regret, therefore, that I am unable to make the order which I am asked to   A
make.

                                              Application dismissed.

    Solicitors: *Denton, Hall & Burgin* agents for *Chas. G. Lester & Russell,*
Bournemouth (for the plaintiff); *Bentleys, Stokes & Lowless,* agents for *Birtwells,*
Burnley (for the defendants).   B
                          [*Reported by* JENIFER SANDELL, *Barrister-at-Law.*]

_____

                    Re JOEL'S WILL TRUSTS.
          ROGERSON AND OTHERS *v.* BRUDENELL-BRUCE   C
                         AND OTHERS.

[CHANCERY DIVISION (Goff, J.), February 23, 24, 25, 1966.]

Accumulation—Income of fund held on trust for grandchildren at twenty-one—
    Statutory power of maintenance—Accumulation of surplus income—Destina-
    tion of accumulations—Trustee Act, 1925 (15 & 16 Geo. 5 c. 19), s. 31 (2).   D
Apportionment—Income—Apportionment in respect of time—Class gift—Trust
    for grandchildren contingent on attaining twenty-one—Whether income of
    trust fund to be apportioned on birth of additional grandchild—Application
    of accumulations of income to which grandchild contingently entitled but
    dying without obtaining vested interest—Apportionment Act, 1870 (33 & 34
    Vict. c. 35), s. 2.   E

    Under a will, an order of court, and a deed of appointment dated in and
between the years 1930 and 1959, a fund was held in trust for a class of
grandchildren of the testator contingently on their attaining twenty-one
years of age. The interest was in possession and carried the intermediate
income. Section 31 of the Trustee Act, 1925, was applicable. Five grandchildren were living at the date of the deed of appointment in 1959 and   F
three were born subsequently.

    Held: (i) when a member of the class of grandchildren died under twenty-
one or another potential member of the class was born there was a change
of interest of the other members of the class to which the Apportionment
Act, 1870, s. 2, applied, with the consequence that the income of the trust
ought to be apportioned so that each member enjoyed only that portion   G
attributable to the time when he was alive; and outgoings ought likewise
to be apportioned equitably (see p. 485, letter I, p. 487, letter C, and p. 490,
letter F, post).

    Donaldson v. *Donaldson* ((1870), L.R. 10 Eq. 635) applied; *Clive* v. *Clive*
((1872), 7 Ch. App. 433) considered.   H
    Re Gourju's Will Trusts ([1942] 2 All E.R. 605) distinguished.
    Bishop of Rochester v. *Le Fanu* ([1906] 2 Ch. 513) followed.
    (ii) the investments representing accumulations of income belonging con-
tingently to a grandchild dying before attaining a vested interest ought
to be added to and thereafter dealt with as part of the entire capital of the
trust fund (see p. 491, letter A, p. 495, letters E and G, and p. 496, letter G,
post).   I
    Re King, Public Trustee v. *Aldridge* ([1927] All E.R. Rep. 214) not followed.

    [As to apportionment in respect of time, see 32 HALSBURY'S LAWS (3rd Edn.)
567, 568, paras. 973, 974. As to gifts carrying intermediate income to a class,
see 39 ibid., p. 1042, para. 1563; and for cases on the subject, see 44 DIGEST
786-788, *6428-6447.*
    For the Apportionment Act, 1870, s. 2, s. 7, see 13 HALSBURY'S STATUTES
(2nd Edn.) 867, 869.]

A Cases referred to:

Clive v. Clive, (1872), 7 Ch. App. 433; 41 L.J.Ch. 386; 26 L.T. 409; 20 Digest (Repl.) 302, *442*.

Donaldson v. Donaldson, (1870), L.R. 10 Eq. 635; 40 L.J.Ch. 64; 23 L.T. 550; 31 Digest (Repl.) 283, *4180*.

Gourju's Will Trusts, Re, Starling v. Custodian of Enemy Property, [1942]
B   2 All E.R. 605; [1943] Ch. 24; 112 L.J.Ch. 75; 168 L.T. 1; 2 Digest (Repl.) 239, *418*.

Holford, Re, Holford v. Holford, [1894] 3 Ch. 30; 63 L.J.Ch. 637; 70 L.T. 777; 23 Digest (Repl.) 469, *5411*.

Howell, Re, Ex p. Mandleberg & Co., [1895] 1 Q.B. 844; 64 L.J.Q.B. 454; 72 L.T. 472; 5 Digest (Repl.) 1030, *8337*.

C Jeffrey, Re, Burt v. Arnold, [1891] 1 Ch. 671; 60 L.J.Ch. 470; 64 L.T. 622; 23 Digest (Repl.) 469, *5409*.

King, Re, Public Trustee v. Aldridge, [1927] All E.R. Rep. 214; [1928] Ch. 330; 97 L.J.Ch. 172; 138 L.T. 641; 40 Digest (Repl.) 618, *1129*.

Lysaght, Re, Lysaght v. Lysaght, [1898] 1 Ch. 115; 67 L.J.Ch. 65; 77 L.T. 637; 9 Digest (Repl.) 634, *4227*.

D Mills v. Norris, (1800), 5 Ves. 335; 31 E.R. 617; 44 Digest 774, *6318*.

Rochester (Bishop of) v. Le Fanu, [1906] 2 Ch. 513; 75 L.J.Ch. 743; 95 L.T. 602; 19 Digest (Repl.) 553, *3947*.

Scott v. Earl of Scarborough, (1838), 1 Beav. 154; 8 L.J.Ch. 65; 48 E.R. 898; 44 Digest 786, *6430*.

Shipperdson v. Tower, (1844), 3 L.T.O.S. 199; 8 Jur. 485; 20 Digest (Repl.)
E   299, *415*.

Swansea Bank v. Thomas, (1879), 4 Ex.D. 94; 48 L.J.Q.B. 344; 40 L.T. 558; 43 J.P. 494; 5 Digest (Repl.) 1022, *8263*.

Tyrrell v. Clark, (1854), 2 Drew. 86; 23 L.J.Ch. 283; 22 L.T.O.S. 313; 61 E.R. 651; 20 Digest (Repl.) 300, *423*.

Wilson, Re, Ex p. Hastings (Lord), (1893), 62 L.J.Q.B. 628; 10 Morr. 219;
F   4 Digest (Repl.) 428, *3800*.

Adjourned summons.

This was an application by the plaintiffs, Frank Leslie John Rogerson, Robert Montgomery and Charles Gordon Johnston, the existing trustees of the trusts constituted by the will, dated Oct. 22, 1930, of Solomon Barnato Joel, deceased,
G who died on May 22, 1931, an order dated Dec. 18, 1958, under the Variation of Trusts Act, 1958, approving an arrangement to vary the trusts of the will, and an appointment dated Mar. 28, 1959, by Stanhope Henry Joel, made in exercise of a power of appointment given to him by the will and the arrangement. The plaintiffs sought the determination of the following questions, among others:

1. Whether in their accounts of the grandchildren's fund representing the
H sum of £420,000 appointed by the above-mentioned appointment dated Mar. 28, 1959, the plaintiffs ought to keep a separate account of the income of the contingent share of each grandchild of Stanhope Henry Joel (hereinafter called " Mr. Joel ") who is from time to time living showing how much income is applied for the maintenance education or benefit of such grandchild or accumulated as an addition to the capital of such share and to prepare such accounts
I with rests at:—(a) the birth of each further grandchild of Mr. Joel born after Mar. 28, 1959, and (b) the death of each grandchild of Mr. Joel who dies.

2. Whether for the purpose of adjusting the said accounts on the birth of each grandchild beyond those living at the date of the said appointment the plaintiffs ought:—(a) to apportion in accordance with the provisions of the Apportionment Act, 1870, all income received and all outgoings paid thereout (whether before or after the birth of that grandchild as the case may be) in respect of the grandchildren's fund or (b) to allocate to the older grandchildren (excluding the newly born grandchild) all income actually received and all

outgoings actually paid or provided for thereout before the birth of such grand A child and to allocate to such newly born grandchild equally with the older grandchildren all income actually received and all outgoings actually paid or provided for after the birth of such grandchild without regard to the period in respect of which such income accrued or such liabilities arose.

4. Whether the plaintiffs ought for the purpose of enabling accumulations of income to be re-allocated on the death of a grandchild before attaining a B vested interest to segregate on the birth of each additional grandchild of Mr. Joel the fund of investments representing the accumulations of income of the share of each older grandchild made since the birth of the last to be born of the older grandchildren then living.

5. If question 4 is answered in the affirmative whether the income arising from each such segregated fund ought to be accumulated as an addition to that C fund or dealt with as income of the original share of the grandchild to whom it contingently belongs.

6. If question 4 is answered in the affirmative whether on the death of a grandchild of Mr. Joel before attaining a vested interest the accumulations of income belonging contingently to such grandchild ought to be re-allocated to the accumulation accounts of the other grandchildren who are then living or D have previously died after attaining a vested interest by dividing each fund of investments segregated in respect of the period immediately preceding any rest in the plaintiffs' accounts equally between the other funds segregated in respect of the same period for the benefit of such other children or in some other and if so what manner.

7. If question 4 is answered in the negative whether on the death of a E grandchild of Mr. Joel before attaining a vested interest the investments representing accumulations of income belonging contingently to such grandchild ought to be re-allocated to the accumulation accounts of the other grandchildren who are then living or have previously died after attaining a vested interest by:—
(a) ascertaining the respective amounts credited to the accumulations account of the deceased child in each period between two rests in the plaintiffs' accounts; F (b) dividing the said investments into separate funds proportionate in value to the amounts so ascertained and (c) dividing each such separate fund equally between the respective accumulation accounts for the same period of the other grandchildren who were living during that period and have survived the deceased grandchild or predeceased him after attaining a vested interest; or in some other and if so what manner. G

By amendment made, by leave, on the hearing, a further question was raised: whether on the death of a grandchild of Mr. Joel before obtaining a vested interest the investments representing accumulations of income applying contingently to such grandchild ought to be added to and thereafter dealt with as part of the entire capital of the grandchildren's fund (see p. 491, letter A, post).

The defendants, each of whom was an infant and a grandchild of Mr. Joel H and had a contingent interest in the capital and income of the grandchildren's fund, were (i) Andrew Robert Joel Brudenell-Bruce; (ii) Diana Elizabeth Solna Thomson Jones; (iii) Christopher Thomson Jones; (iv) Joanna Dana Brudenell-Bruce; (v) Timothy Thomson Jones; (vi) Sara Vivien Brudenell-Bruce; (vii) Nicholas William Joel Jones; and (viii) Patrick Walter Joel Jones. The first five defendants were born before Mar. 28, 1959 (the date of the appointment). I

E. W. Griffith for the plaintiffs, the trustees.
E. F. R. Whitehead for the first five defendants.
J. W. Brunyate for the sixth, seventh and eighth defendants.

GOFF, J.: This summons raises a number of somewhat complicated questions concerning the duty of trustees in administration and rights of the beneficiaries where there is a gift to a class, the shares being contingent and the class being capable of increase by the birth of further members, or of decrease

A   by the death of a potential member without obtaining a vested interest. By
the joint effect of the will dated Oct. 22, 1930, of Solomon Barnato Joel, who died
on May 22, 1931, an arrangement under the Variation of Trusts Act, 1958,
sanctioned by this court, by an order dated Dec. 18, 1958, and an appointment
dated Mar. 28, 1959, by Mr. Stanhope Henry Joel, in exercise of a power of
appointment given to him by the will and the arrangement, a fund is held by
B   trustees in trust for a class of grandchildren contingently on their attaining
twenty-one years of age. The interest is in possession and carries the intermediate income. There are five grandchildren who were in esse at the date of
the appointment, and three grandchildren born subsequently, namely, the sixth,
seventh and eighth defendants. The summons asks that these defendants may
be appointed to represent all unborn grandchildren who may become entitled
C   to beneficial interests in the fund. For the purposes of this hearing, at all
events, their interests are identical.

The first question which is raised on the summons is whether the Apportionment Act, 1870, applies, and, in my judgment, it does, for the following reasons.
The first of those reasons is that, as counsel on behalf of the first five defendants
says, the words of the Act of 1870 are general and unqualified and the cases
D   show that the Act of 1870 is only to be excluded by express words or necessary
implication, not by any general inference. The words of the important section,
s. 2, are:

"... all rents, annuities, dividends, and other periodical payments in the
nature of income (whether reserved or made payable under an instrument
in writing or otherwise) shall, like interest on money lent, be considered as
E   accruing from day to day, and shall be apportionable in respect of time
accordingly."

Section 7 provides:

" The provisions of this Act shall not extend to any case in which it is
or shall be expressly stipulated that no apportionment shall take place."

F   It was held, in *Tyrrell* v. *Clark* (1), under the earlier Act (2), and by the Court
of Appeal in *Re Lysaght*, *Lysaght* v. *Lysaght* (3), in effect that that section meant
what it said, and that the Act of 1870 could be excluded only by words expressly
so stating, or requiring that conclusion by necessary implication.

The second reason for the conclusion which I have reached is that even the
former Act, which referred to death or other termination of interest, was held
G   to apply to a change in interest. I refer to *Donaldson* v. *Donaldson* (4), where
BACON, V.-C., said (5):

" In substance the decision came to this: that wherever a person is in
receipt of rents and profits, and any change takes place whereby that
person's interest ceases or is altered, and another interest begins, or a change
of interest takes place, then an apportionment must be made."
H
Now it is true that if the class changes by a person dropping out through failure
to obtain a vested interest, or by some other person being born, the other members
of the class still take under the same title, but, in my judgment, there is a change
of interest, because they take a different presumptive share of capital. A larger
or smaller share is then available, held in trust for them contingently and,
I   of course they become entitled, subject to the provisions of s. 31 of the Trustee
Act, 1925, to a different share of income. In my judgment, when a person dies
or another potential member is born, there is inevitably a change of interest of
the other members or potential members of the class and, accordingly, on the
principle there stated, the Act of 1870 should apply.

---

(1) (1854), 2 Drew. 86.
(2) The Apportionment Act, 1834; see s. 3 thereof, 13 HALSBURY'S STATUTES (2nd
Edn.) 855.   (3) [1898] 1 Ch. 115.
(4) (1870), L.R. 10 Eq. 635.   (5) (1870), L.R. 10 Eq. at p. 639.

I also derive some support for this conclusion from the case of *Clive* v. *Clive* (6). **A** The headnote reads as follows:

"A testator gave his residuary personal estate, with the accumulations thereof, to his trustees in trust for his two granddaughters C. and P., as tenants in common, their shares to be vested at twenty-one or marriage, the income to be applied for their benefit during minority, and the surplus accumulated. And the testator directed that in case either granddaughter **B** married under twenty-one the trustees should settle her share for her life for her separate use, with remainder to her children. Both the granddaughters married under twenty-one, C. in 1867, and P. in 1870, which was after the passing of the Apportionment Act . . . Held, that in both cases the income of the granddaughter's share was apportionable up to the time of her marriage . . ." **C**

The judgment of JAMES, L.J., is quite short. His Lordship said (7):

"We think that it is too late to raise the question as to apportionment after the cases which have been decided in this court. One of them— *Shipperdson* v. *Tower* (8)—was decided as long ago as 1844, and no attempt has been made to shake or question it. We must, therefore, take it to be the **D** cursus curiae, and also the settled understanding of conveyancers, that the Apportionment Act did apply to cases of this kind. The new Act (9) of 33 & 34 Vict. c. 35, extended the principle of the Act (10) of 4 & 5 Will. 4, c. 22, in the same direction, so as to make it applicable to every form of reservation of income, which was in all cases to be treated as if it were interest accruing de die in diem, so that there might be no more questions on this **E** subject. Therefore the authorities dispose of the question as regards Mrs. Clive's settlement, and the recent Act disposes of the question as regards Lady Peyton's settlement. There must be an apportionment of the income in each case up to the date of the lady's marriage."

Counsel for the sixth, seventh and eighth defendants has argued that the case is distinguishable because there was a change of interest in as much as until **F** twenty-one the relevant trust was to apply income to maintenance and accumulate surplus and on marriage under twenty-one a new trust arose, namely, a trust to settle the share on the granddaughter for life, with remainders over. It may be that that is a stronger case, but it seems to me to be very much akin to the problem which I have to consider, because here one does have a change in the nature of the relevant trust occurring in the event of a death or birth which **G** affects the composition of the class. Counsel has argued that this conclusion is not right because the members of the class and potential members for the time being are not really entitled to the income at all. It should be accumulated for the benefit of the class when ascertained. Only the statute allows application for maintenance, and expressly provides for the destination of the accumulations, and it is only a rule of convenience to ignore the possibility of future **H** children and to divide the income from time to time between the children for the time being existing and, of course, the legal representatives of those dying after obtaining a vested interest. Therefore, he said, if another child is born during any year that child has as much right to income received in that year as the older ones. That seems to me to be inconsistent with the terms of s. 31 itself and with the decision in *Re Holford, Holford* v. *Holford* (11), where it was **I** clearly decided that the possible future rights of persons not yet born are not existing rights. LINDLEY, L.J., said (12):

"There is good sense in saying that the income of property given contingently to a class of persons belongs to its members for the time being, as

(6) (1872), 7 Ch. App. 433.   (7) (1872), 7 Ch. App. at p. 437.
(8) (1844), 3 L.T.O.S. 199.   (9) The Apportionment Act, 1870.
(10) The Apportionment Act, 1834.   (11) [1894] 3 Ch. 30.
                    (12) [1894] 3 Ch. at p. 46.

A against persons who are only entitled if and when the class ceases to exist; but there is no sense in saying that one of a class takes the whole income, in which other persons belonging to the same class have already a contingent interest which may become absolute. In *Mills* v. *Norris* (13) and *Scott* v.

B *Earl of Scarborough* (14), the question for decision was whether some members of a class were entitled to the income of property given to them and others of the same class who were not yet born, and the answer was ' Yes '. The decision was obviously reasonable and just. To treat the future possible rights of unborn persons as existing rights, even if only contingent, would have been to depart from sound principles with no sufficient justification."

C Therefore, a child, until he is born, cannot, in my judgment, have any right to or interest in the accruing income and on principle it ought to be apportioned so that he participates in the portion attributable to the time when he is alive and not to the time when he was not yet born. LINDLEY, L.J., also said (15):

> " I come, therefore, to the conclusion that the infant children are contingently entitled to five-sixths of the residue with which we have to deal, and that neither the whole capital nor the whole income of such residue is
> D during their minority vested in or payable to the child who has attained twenty-one. If this be so, it is plain that the Conveyancing Act, 1881 (44 & 45 Vict. c. 41), s. 43, authorises the trustees to apply the infants' contingent shares of income towards their maintenance."

Later LINDLEY, L.J., said (15):

> E " So although if those children who are still under age should die under twenty-one, the child who has attained twenty-one will take their shares, still the Act authorises the application for their maintenance of the income of their contingent shares, for that income contingently belongs to them."

It seems to me that one has to approach this on the footing that one is dealing with income of the contingent shares and that income can only belong to a

F person who is living at the time when it accrues, which necessarily, in my judgment, lets in the Apportionment Act, 1870.

Again, s. 31 of the Trustee Act, 1925, which is the Act which applies to the present case, says:

> " (1) Where any property is held by trustees in trust for any person for any interest whatsoever, whether vested or contingent . . . (i) during the
> G infancy of any such person, if his interest so long continues, the trustees may, at their sole discretion, pay to his parent or guardian, if any, or otherwise apply for or towards his maintenance, education, or benefit, the whole or such part, if any, of the income of that property as may, in all the circumstances, be reasonable . . ."

H Then there are provisions about what one does with the income of that property when the child attains twenty-one and with the accumulations if the child either does or does not acquire a vested interest in the capital. It is more directly relevant to the later question, but there again what the statute is dealing with is the income of the share. It is a fluctuating share and the income which it carries at any given time may be in greater or less proportion than the share which is ultimately taken, but one is dealing with the income of the share, and

I I can see no real reason why, when the change occurs which entitles the child to a larger share of income, or deprives him of part of the share and reduces it to a smaller one, there should not be an apportionment.

Counsel for the sixth, seventh and eighth defendants has instanced the hardship if a child attains twenty-one and has not then a vested interest, because if the income is apportioned, then he loses the part attributed to the period

---

(13) (1800), 5 Ves. 335.   (14) (1838), 1 Beav. 154.

(15) [1894] 3 Ch. at p. 47.

before he attained twenty-one, because it is then too late for the trustees to A
exercise their power of maintenance, which is only given to them during his
infancy.   Of course, in the case of *Clive* v. *Clive* (16), the same hardship presented
itself, because the income prior to the period of the daughter marrying was
added to capital instead of being paid to her as income under her settlement.
Certainly, in my judgment, any such considerations of hardship are not sufficient
to amount to an express exclusion or an exclusion by necessary implication. B
When I asked counsel to formulate exactly how he submitted the Act of 1870
was excluded, he said that his main argument was that the Act of 1870 does not
apply because s. 31 is a rule for allocating trust income, and the proper rule for
that purpose is to deal with income received and not income accruing and, if
necessary, as an alternative, that s. 31 of the Act of 1925 cannot have intended
that the Act of 1870 should apply.   Indeed, counsel said that really the section C
could not be made to fit.   If a child attains twenty-one during the year, one
cannot apply the part of the income apportioned to the time before he attained
twenty-one for maintenance because the power has expired and one cannot
accumulate it in the terms of the section because the trust to accumulate the
balance is again during the infancy of any such person.   That is s. 31 (2) of
the Act of 1925:   D

" During the infancy of any such person, if his interest so long continues,
the trustees shall accumulate all the residue of that income . . ."

One can, however, add the balance attributed to the time before the child attained
twenty-one to capital.   That is simple accumulation; it is in respect of the
period of infancy; it is not very far removed from the precise wording of the E
section.   Indeed, it is the inevitable consequence of not being able to exercise
the power of maintenance.   Any consideration of that sort, again, in my judgment, cannot be regarded as an express provision excluding the Apportionment
Act, 1870, which would otherwise apply, and I do not accept the proposition
that this is merely allocating trust income.   In my judgment, it is ascertaining
what is the income of the property which is held on trust for the infant.   He is F
entitled to have income applied for his maintenance (otherwise accumulated)
because the section applies where property, which includes his contingent share,
is held in trust for a person, whether his interest be vested or contingent.
Therefore, what one has to do is not to allocate but to ascertain what is truly
the income of that share.   Therefore, I do not accept either the main way of
putting it or the alternative. I have also been referred to the case of *Re Gourju's* G
Will Trusts, Starling v. *Custodian of Enemy Property* (17).   That was a case of a
forfeiture clause and it was held that where income was accruing at the time of
the forfeiture there was no apportionment and the whole of the income when
it became due passed under the trusts taking effect after forfeiture and was not
payable to the person who would have taken but for the forfeiture.   In my
judgment that is a very different type of case.   The decision followed older H
cases, where the trust was to pay the income to a certain person if no event
causing forfeiture had happened.   The words of s. 33 of the Trustee Act, 1925,
are not quite as strong as that because they are to hold it on trust for the principal
beneficiary, but it was held that the same principle applied, and made the
moment of time when the instalment of income reached the trustees' hands or
became payable the relevant time at which to apply the forfeiture clause.   I
It was a decision of SIMONDS, J., who said (18):

" The effect of the clause, I think, is to prevent the destination of the
income being finally determined until the time it has actually accrued due,
or, in other words, become payable, and to direct the trustees, when dealing
with the income, to fix their attention upon the moment of time when the

---

(16) (1872), 7 Ch. App. 433.   (17) [1942] 2 All E.R. 605; [1943] Ch. 24.
  (18) [1942] 2 All E.R. at p. 609; [1943] Ch. at p. 33.   The passage is a citation from
the judgment of SARGANT, J., in *Re Jenkins*, [1915] 1 Ch. at p. 51.

A   instalment of income has either reached their hands or become payable.
I do not think that an instalment or a sum which, if the Apportionment
Act, 1870 had been applied, would have been ultimately payable to the
tenant for life is an instalment or a payment of income to which the terms
of this clause apply."

B   That, in my judgment, is entirely different from the problem which arises where
income is payable to a class of beneficiaries which changes its character during
the year in which the income is accruing.   There is nothing there to direct one's
mind to the moment when the income has accrued as being the relevent time for
determining anything.   In my judgment, it is entirely different from a forfeiture
clause and does not exclude the Act of 1870.

C   I should add that, in my judgment, apportionment is not of the trust income
as a whole, but of the items of which it consists.   There may, of course, be non-
apportionable income.   I should also like to deal with another submission
by counsel for the first five defendants where he said that there were really
two stages.   There is apportionment under the Act to ascertain what the
income is, and then one deals with the income.   Therefore, he said, one could
deal with the whole income which is finally attributable to any given share

D   according to the position which obtains when the income in fact becomes payable.
So if by then a beneficiary is twenty-one one can pay the whole income to him
including income which is attributed to his share by virtue of apportionment
in respect of the period before he was twenty-one.   I think that one cannot
have it both ways.   When the income has been apportioned, one must deal
with the apportioned part according to the state of affairs which obtained

E   during the period in respect of which the income has been apportioned.   If
that be the period of infancy, it follows that the income cannot be applied for
maintenance, because the trustees cannot exercise their discretion in advance
so as to affect the income when it is received, and they cannot apply it in arrear,
because the infancy will have ceased.   That is, to a small extent, perhaps an
unfortunate result of applying the Act, but, in my judgment, it is the right

F   conclusion and certainly does not exclude the Act of 1870.   In my judgment,
therefore, for these reasons the Act of 1870 in its nature applies and there is
nothing to exclude it.

There is the further question what, in those circumstances, is to be done with
outgoings.   It is to be observed that the Apportionment Act, 1870, does not,
in terms, speak of outgoings except in one section and in a somewhat parenthetical

G   way, where, in s. 4, giving remedies, it is provided:

" All persons and their respective heirs, executors, administrators, and
assigns, and also the executors, administrators and assigns respectively of
persons whose interests determine with their own deaths, shall have such
or the same remedies at law and in equity for recovering such apportioned

H   parts as aforesaid when payable (allowing proportionate parts of all just
allowances) . . ."

There is that parenthetical reference.   Otherwise, the Act of 1870 does not, in
terms, speak of outgoings.   The words of s. 2, as I have said, are

". . . all rents, annuities, dividends, and other periodical payments in
the nature of income (whether reserved or made payable under an instrument

I   in writing or otherwise) shall, like interest on money lent, be considered
as accruing from day to day."

In *Bishop of Rochester* v. *Le Fanu* (19), however, to which counsel for the plaintiffs
drew my attention, it was held that the Act of 1870 did apply to outgoings.
The headnote is (19):

" The Apportionment Act, 1870, apportions liabilities as well as rights . . .
The annual sums payable by a bishop in commutation of first fruits and tenths

(19) [1906] 2 Ch. 513.

are ' periodical payments in the nature of income ' within s. 2, and therefore   A
apportionable between successive bishops inter se; but, though now collected
and administered by the Governors of Queen Anne's Bounty, they are still
in fact Crown debts . . ."

The headnote then went on to another point.   The relevant part of the judgment,
which was the judgment of SWINFEN EADY, J., was as follows (20):
                                                                                 B
   " But it was contended that the Apportionment Act, 1870, was only
intended to affect the rights of the persons entitled to receive the income, and
not to apportion, in respect of time, any liability to pay it.   There are,
however, four decisions to the contrary upon the interpretation of the
Act."

Then his lordship reviewed these, and said (21):   C

   " Again, in *Re Howell, Ex p. Mandleberg & Co.* (22) it was held that by
virtue of the Apportionment Act rent for the first two months of a quarter
' accrued due ' from day to day, although not payable until the end of a
quarter.   VAUGHAN WILLIAMS, J., said (23): ' This was the view which I took
in *Re Wilson, Ex p. Lord Hastings* (24), where I held, following the decision of
the Exchequer Division in *Swansea Bank* v. *Thomas* (25), that the Apportion-   D
ment Act was intended not merely to affect the rights of the recipients of the
rent inter se, but also to apportion the liability to pay the rent between the
different occupiers of the premises during the currency of the quarter '.
Although dicta may be found in other cases at variance with these decisions,
there is not any direct authority of the Court of Appeal the other way, and,
in accordance with these cases, I decide that, as against the defendant the   E
Right Rev. Edward Stuart Talbot, as the late Bishop of Rochester, the
annual payments are to be treated as accruing due from day to day, and are
apportionable between the incoming and the outgoing bishop, and that the
said defendant, as the late Bishop of Rochester, is liable for so much of
the sums falling due on Dec. 25, 1905, as accrued due during his tenancy of the
said see, that is to say, the period between Dec. 25, 1904, and May 24, 1905."   F

Even apart from that, in my judgment, if income be apportioned the trustees
must have the right and duty to make all proper apportionments on an equitable
basis with regard to the outgoings in respect of that income.
   On the second half of the summons, as postulated, there are a number of questions designed to give effect to the decision in *Re King, Public Trustee* v. *Aldridge* G
(26), a decision of ROMER, J.   It was felt that there was a difficulty because in that
decision ROMER, J., said that if a person failed to attain a vested interest, then
the accounts had to be re-opened and the income from past years had to be
re-distributed as if that person had never existed although originally it had been
apportioned on the footing that a vested interest would be attained.   It was
appreciated that there were practical difficulties in the way of giving effect to   H
that, apart from complications of accounts, because it did not remain simply
income, which, as it were, could be taken out of a pocket and handed to somebody
else; it would have been invested and accumulated.   The accumulations might
have appreciated or depreciated in value and there might have been bonus issues;
therefore, if that principle were the right one, it was felt that there was difficulty
in knowing exactly how to give effect to it.   Accordingly the plaintiffs made a   I
number of suggestions, and finished, not unnaturally, by asking whether the
accumulations should be divided in some other, and if so, what, manner.
   Counsel for the sixth, seventh and eighth defendants has challenged the whole
basis of that and has sought to simplify the matter by saying that *Re King* (26)

(20) [1906] 2 Ch. at p. 521.   (21) [1906] 2 Ch. at p. 522.
(22) [1895] 1 Q.B. 844.   (23) [1895] 1 Q.B. at p. 847.
(24) (1893), 62 L.J.Q.B. 628.   (25) (1879), 4 Ex.D. 94.
           (26) [1927] All E.R. Rep. 214; [1928] Ch. 330.

A   was wrongly decided and that I ought not to follow it. Counsel submits that the
accumulations of income of the infants who fail to obtain a vested interest should
be added to capital. In view of that I allowed the summons to be amended by
raising a new question, whether on the death of a grandchild of the testator
before attaining a vested interest the investments representing accumulations of
income applying contingently to such grandchild ought to be added to and

B   thereafter dealt with as part of the entire capital of the grandchildren's fund.
As the other questions will not arise if that be right, that question has been
separately argued and I have now to decide it.

I hesitate to differ from ROMER, J.; and I hesitate to reach a different conclusion in respect of a case which was decided as long ago as 1927, that being
a case where a child had died and therefore the express point was argued, but it

C   was not a decision on s. 31 of the Trustee Act, 1925. It was a decision on s. 43
of the Conveyancing Act, 1881, and there are some differences in the form of
s. 31, and, indeed, in the precise language which deals with these particular
accumulations. Section 43 (2) provided:

" The trustees shall accumulate all the residue of that income in the
way of compound interest, by investing the same and the resulting income

D   thereof from time to time on securities on which they are by the settlement,
if any, or by law, authorised to invest trust money, and shall hold those
accumulations for the benefit of the person who ultimately becomes entitled
to the property from which the same arise; but so that the trustees may at
any time, if they think fit, apply those accumulations, or any part thereof,
as if the same were income arising in the then current year."

E
Section 31 of the Trustee Act, 1925, on the other hand, says this:

" (2) During the infancy of any such person, if his interest so long continues,
the trustees shall accumulate all the residue of that income in the way of
compound interest by investing the same and the resulting income thereof
from time to time in authorised investments, and shall hold those accumula-

F   tions as follows: (i) If any such person—(a) attains the age of twenty-one
years, or marries under that age, and his interest in such income during his
infancy or until his marriage is a vested interest; or (b) on attaining the
age of twenty-one years or on marriage under that age becomes entitled to
the property from which such income arose in fee simple, absolute or
determinable, or absolutely, or for an entailed interest; the trustees shall

G   hold the accumulations in trust for such person absolutely . . .; and (ii) In
any other case [which raises the present case] the trustees shall, notwithstanding that such person had a vested interest in such income, hold the
accumulations as an accretion to the capital of the property from which
such accumulations arose, and as one fund with such capital for all purposes
. . ."

H   The section is necessarily different because s. 31 of the Act of 1925 widened the
ambit of s. 43 of the Act of 1881 and applied it not only where the contingency
was infancy but to other contingencies and, therefore, it was necessary to make
express provision what was to happen if the beneficiary attained twenty-one
but his interest did not vest until some time subsequently. That accounts largely,
if not entirely, for the addition of the express provisions that the person

I   concerned shall take the accumulations in certain events specified in sub-s. (2) (i),
(a) and (b), but it does not account for the change in language in para. (ii), where
the subsection no longer says " for the benefit of the person who ultimately
becomes entitled to the property ". It uses stronger language

". . . hold the accumulations as an accretion to the capital of the property
from which such accumulations arose and as one fund with such capital
for all purposes."

Counsel for the sixth, seventh and eighth defendants has pointed out that the

principle of re-allocation adopted in *Re King* (27) could not be applied after the A
beneficiary had attained twenty-one if his interest had not then vested and,
therefore, it would be hard if it applied during the earlier part of the contingency
short of his attaining twenty-one. It may be that *Re King* (27) can be distinguished
and supported as an authority on s. 43, but if it applies to s. 31, in my respectful
judgment, it was wrongly decided, and I think that arose from the fact that two
problems were considered at the same time and the learned judge, having decided B
the first, slipped into the second which he said logically followed, whereas, in my
respectful judgment, it did not logically follow, because the problem was a
problem of a different character. The first problem which was being canvassed,
the decision on which took up the greater part of the judgment, was this: could
a person who had obtained a vested share maintain that he was for the time
being the only member of this class and, therefore, was entitled to the whole C
income until somebody else got a vested interest, notwithstanding that there were
other potential beneficiaries in being, or were those potential beneficiaries entitled
to a share? It was held that one had to allocate the income to all persons who had a
vested interest and all potential members, according to the number for the time
being in existence. Then ROMER, J., dealt with the income, in the case of the
person who had obtained a vested interest, obviously by having it paid to him, D
and, in the case of a person who had not, the statute came into operation and
the income could be applied under the statute for the maintenance of such
person and, if not so applied, it would have to be accumulated. ROMER, J.,
said (28):

"It has long since been laid down by the Court of Appeal, differing from a
view which NORTH, J., had expressed in the case of *Re Jeffery, Burt* v.   E
Arnold (29), that, in a case of that sort, each member of the class as he
attains twenty-one is entitled to receive such part of the income as he would
be entitled to receive if the class were then closed, that is to say, supposing
at the time the eldest of the class attains the age of twenty-one there are only
six members of that class in existence, as from the time he attains twenty-one
he is entitled to receive one-sixth of the income notwithstanding that the class   F
is capable of increase. Should the class increase later by the birth of a
seventh member, as from that time the member of the class who has attained
twenty-one would only receive one-seventh of the income assuming that the
other members of the class are still in existence. That is very well settled
as regards the income of members of the class who have attained the age of
twenty-one years. Now what about the members of the class who have not   G
attained, for the time being, the age of twenty-one years? I think it is equally
well settled that the same thing is done provisionally, that is to say, if there
are six members of the class, of whom one only has attained twenty-one,
one-sixth of the income ought to be provisionally allocated to each of the other
five members. If and when another member comes into existence so that
there are seven members of the class there will thenceforth be allocated   H
to each of the six minors a seventh share of the income."

Counsel for the sixth, seventh and eighth defendants has pointed out that it is
not clear in precisely what sense ROMER, J., used the word "provisionally",
whether he meant provisionally merely because the beneficiary might ultimately
not get a share of income or because at a later stage he would get a larger or   I
smaller share of the income. It does not really touch the problem if he meant
provisionally in the sense that one could allocate, and then have to see later on
whether the allocation was right or wrong, for then it would be impossible to
operate the section because the trustees could not apply under their maintenance
powers income which at the time they did not know for certain was the income

(27) [1927] All E.R. Rep. 214; [1928] Ch. 330.
(28) [1927] All E.R. Rep. at pp. 216, 217; [1928] Ch. at pp. 335, 336.
(29) [1891] 1 Ch. 671.

A of the infant. Counsel forcibly illustrated that by saying that if the trustees recovered, as I believe has happened in this case, some American tax, they might provisionally allocate that as income of a given year, but they could not then distribute it or apply it so long as it was merely a provisional allocation. They would have to hold it in suspense until they knew what the position really was. Then ROMER, J., continued (30):

B   " What is to happen to the income so provisionally assigned to an infant member of a class? In general, that, I think would be governed by s. 31 of the Trustee Act, 1925, replacing s. 43 of the Conveyancing Act, 1881 . . ."

Of course, that was obiter, because in his own case it would be governed by s. 43 of the Conveyancing Act, 1881. ROMER, J., continued (30):

C   ". . . and under that section the trustees would, in my opinion, be justified in treating the income so provisionally assigned to the infant member of the class as the income produced by property to which that infant was contingently entitled and would be justified in applying that income for the maintenance, education and benefit of the infant. So far as not so applied the balance of the income would have to be accumulated under sub-s. (2) of
D   the section. Now as a matter of fact this is exactly what is expressly provided for by cl. 13 of the settlement . . ."

That clause is then set out. It ends with these words (31):

". . . ' and shall pay or apply or deal with the income of the share of the settled fund to which any grandchild who is for the time being living and has not attained a vested interest is for the time being contingently and pre-
E   sumptively entitled as aforesaid in the same manner as it is by s. 43 of the Conveyancing Act, 1881, directed that the trustees shall pay or apply or deal with income to which that section relates '."

ROMER, J., then continued (32): " So far there does not seem much difficulty about the matter." That clause referred back to the section and the case cannot have gone off on any consideration that there was some different provision in the
F   settlement from that which obtained under the relevant statutory provision. Then his lordship said (32):

" But what are the trustees to do with the accumulations of the income provisionally allotted to the members of the class who have not attained twenty-one, that is, that part of the income which has not been applied in maintenance and education of the infant? Let me again take the case of there
G   being six members of the class in existence, five of whom are infants. The trustees provisionally allocate to each of the five infants a sixth part of the income. So far as that sixth part of the income is not applied in maintaining the particular infant for whose benefit it has been provisionally apportioned, it will have to be accumulated."

H I ask myself why? I answer that question this way. It will have to be accumulated because that is what the section says. Having got this share of income dealt with by the section, one has got the power of maintenance. If one does not exercise it, the section directs one to accumulate. ROMER, J., continued (33):

" But supposing by the time the infant attains the age of twenty-one years the class has increased to seven, what is to be done with the accumulations made at a time when the class only consisted of six members? In other words,
I   what is the property from which those accumulations arose, for according to the Act the accumulations only go to the infant on attaining twenty-one if he becomes entitled to that property. In my opinion the property from which the accumulated income arose is the share to which the infant becomes

(30) [1927] All E.R. Rep. at p. 217; [1928] Ch. at p. 336.
(31) [1927] All E.R. Rep. at p. 215, letter H; [1928] Ch. at p. 337.
(32) [1927] All E.R. Rep. at p. 217; [1928] Ch. at p. 337.
(33) [1927] All E.R. Rep. at p. 217; [1928] Ch. at pp. 337, 338.

ultimately entitled, even though that share may be considerably smaller   A
than a sixth by reason of other members of the class coming into existence.
For it appears to me that in each year in which there are only six members of
the class the income of the ultimate share of each member of that class,
whatever it may be, is one-sixth of the income of the trust fund, in other
words, that, during the time that there are only six members of the class,
the ultimate share of each member is earning income and the ultimate shares   B
of persons who are not at that time members of the class are not earning
income. The result of that will be that, as each member of the class attains
twenty-one he will be entitled to be paid all accumulations of income provisionally assigned to him in the way that I have mentioned before, because
that income so provisionally assigned to him is to be regarded as the income
of the property to which he ultimately becomes entitled."   C

So in the case of the child attaining a vested interest, what ROMER, J., is saying
is that the property for the purposes of s. 43 of the Act of 1881 (and I think that
it must be the same under s. 31 of the Act of 1925), the property held by trustees
for the infant which is producing income, is the share to which the infant ultimately
becomes entitled. It produces income so long as the infant is there, but it does
not necessarily produce a share of income which is the same size as the share of   D
capital to which the infant ultimately becomes entitled. According to events
the shares may at the time be carrying a larger share of income than the shares
ultimately would of themselves warrant, and it may carry a smaller share, but the
infant is entitled to property, namely his presumptive share which is producing
income, and then he takes the income of that share notwithstanding, as I have
said, that it may be larger or smaller than the same proportion of income as the   E
capital share.

Then ROMER, J., had to turn to a different problem. In the first place, he had
got an infant who ultimately took a share and all that he was doing was marrying
up with that share the income which it produced. Next he had to deal with an
infant who did not in the end get a share at all. HIS LORDSHIP said (34):

" What is to be done supposing, as has happened in this case, one of the   F
members of the class to whom a share has been provisionally assigned dies
under the age of twenty-one years? It seems to me that logically the trustee
ought to treat the share so provisionally assigned, so far as, of course, it is
not applied in maintenance of the child, as not having been properly assigned,
and then to reassign the income accruing while that infant was a member
of the class amongst the others who were at that time members of the   G
class."

With the greatest respect, I cannot see that it logically follows that because in
the end the infant does not get a share of capital income having been treated as
the income of that share while he had a contingent interest in it which income
falls to be dealt with by the statute as to its whole life because the statute deals   H
with maintenance and accumulation and what has to happen to the accumulations,
one ought to come back and say that it was originally wrong to have treated that
income as income of that share. ROMER, J., was bound to except, and did except,
income which has been applied for the maintenance of the child, but if in truth
one had to go back and say, " Well, in the end we find the apportionment was
wrong, because we thought there were five children but it turned out there were   I
only four ", moneys applied for maintenance would have been wrongly applied,
because the power was to apply the income of that share for the maintenance of
the infant. If one ultimately decides that there was not any such income, one
could not properly have applied it for maintenance. ROMER, J., then continued
(35):

" While there are six members, for instance, the income will be divided

(34) [1927] All E.R. Rep. at pp. 217, 218; [1928] Ch. at p. 338.
(35) [1927] All E.R. Rep. at p. 218; [1928] Ch. at p. 338.

A   into six parts: those who are adults will receive their sixth; for those who are
    minors there will be provisionally allotted their sixth.   When another
    member of the class comes into existence the income will be divided and
    provisionally alloted into sevenths. [I do not quarrel with that.] Supposing
    before another member of the class comes into existence one of the seven dies
    an infant, then it appears to me that the trustee must go back and, if that
B   infant was one of those originally entitled to one-sixth, he must, during
    the period that he was dividing and provisionally assigning the income in
    sixths, divide and provisionally assign it in fifths and as from the time
    that the seventh grandchild was born, instead of dividing and provisionally
    assigning it in sevenths he must divide and provisionally assign it into sixths.
    This is a mere matter of book-keeping and should not be difficult to apply in
C   practice.''

    With respect, I do not see why the trustee should go back. It seems to me that
    he ought to go forward, through the provisions of the section. Having started
    with the premise that the contingent interest of the infant is property and that
    that property produces income while the infant is in existence, he gets income of
    that property. Having got it, it can be applied under the power of maintenance.
D   If that is not done, the trustee is bound to accumulate and then what he has got
    is a fund of accumulations properly made, not, in my respectful judgment, a
    fund representing some income improperly or provisionally apportioned. Then
    when some event happens to the infant, he looks at the section to see what he has
    got to do with the accumulations and sub-s. (2) tells him in all circumstances.
    If the infant attains twenty-one or marries and he had a vested interest in the
E   income during his infancy or until marriage, then the trustee holds the accumula-
    tions for that infant.   Alternatively, if the infant attains twenty-one or marries
    under that age, and he becomes, in effect, absolutely entitled to the property,
    then also he holds the accumulations for that infant.   In any other case, which
    includes the case of the infant failing to attain twenty-one at all and also attaining
    twenty-one but not having had a vested interest during his infancy and not
F   acquiring a vested interest at twenty-one, the trustees shall notwithstanding that
    such person had a vested interest in such income hold the accumulations as an
    accretion to the capital of the property from which such accumulations arose.
       The question then is: what was the property from which the accumulations
    arose? Surely, just as in the case of an infant who gets an interest in capital,
    it is the share that he ultimately obtains, so here the income arose from the
G   share to which the infant was contingently entitled and none the less so because
    in the event the infant did not take it at all. That share goes to the other shares
    because the infant falls out of the class and it goes with the accumulations which
    are added to it. It seems to me by a logical train of reasoning from the premise
    from which ROMER, J., started, the logical conclusion is that accumulations go
    back into a common fund of capital. The same result I think is achieved if one
H   says that the property from which it arose was the whole capital of the trust fund.
    In my judgment, however, the true position is that each infant in existence must
    be treated as having, according to the circumstances, either a vested or contingent
    share of capital. That share, whether it be vested or contingent, carries income and
    the income of that share goes in the way prescribed by the statute. The infant
    may ultimately have no share of capital in which case the income is not, in my
I   judgment, re-allocated as having been wrongly allocated, but goes under s. 31
    (2), (ii), which appears to me to cover the case exactly.
       It was argued by counsel for the first five defendants that such a conclusion
    would fly in the teeth of a well known settled rule of law, that the rights of persons
    not yet born cannot be treated as existing rights, which was laid down or referred
    to in the case of *Re Holford* (36), which I have already mentioned. In my judg-
    ment, however, there is nothing in this conclusion which flies in the teeth of that

    (36) [1894] 3 Ch. 30.

decision at all. So long as an infant has not been born he has not got a share which A
is carrying any income at all and, therefore, the income goes to the other members
of the class, and a person unborn gets no share of that income at all. If and insofar, however, as the income is accumulated and added to capital pursuant to
the Act of 1925, and, the unborn infant having come into existence, in fact
acquires an interest in the capital, there is no reason at all why he should not take
his share of the accretion to capital due to income which arose before he was B
born. It is not that his share has produced income when he was not alive. It is
not that he has received income accruing while he was not alive, but, by virtue
of the statute, income which accrued while he was not alive has become capital,
and there are indeed many cases of accumulations, either express or implied,
whereby income is added to capital and the capital ultimately vests in a person
who was not living when the income accrued. In my judgment, there is nothing C
in that argument.

Various calculations have been laid before me in an attempt to show that one
conclusion may be more fair than another. I think that it is reasonably certain
that in most cases there will not be absolute equality. It is based on a number of
factors, such as the time when children are born and what the trustees apply for
maintenance; but I do not think that I can really adopt considerations of that D
sort. I can proceed only on the basis of the relevant statutory provisions, and I see
nothing unfair in principle in a person who ultimately takes a vested interest
participating in income which arose before he was born. After all, he takes the
share in capital and prima facie ought to have the income which is added to it,
and if in the result, because it has not been applied for maintenance of some
other infant but has been accumulated and added to capital, it comes back to E
him, I see nothing unfair. I do not think that one can weigh considerations
of that sort. One cannot be certain how it will work out. I simply construe the
Act of 1925 and it appears to me to be reasonably plain that the presumptive
share of the infant carries a proper share of income which if not applied for
maintenance is accumulated and if he dies under twenty-one is then part of the
general capital. If I turn to *Re King* (37), the premise on which it proceeds F
produces the same result because ROMER, J., accepts that one has to look to the
presumptive share of the infant as the property, and that that property while he
is alive produces income, and that that has to be dealt with under the section
and only at the final stage does His Lordship depart from my conclusion by
coming back to re-opening all that was done. In my respectful judgment, I
cannot agree with that. In my view, it does not logically follow. On the contrary, G
the opposite logically follows. ROMER, J., should in my view have carried his
argument to its logical conclusion and arrived at the result at which I have
arrived. Therefore, in my judgment, with the very greatest respect to ROMER, J.,
I think that that was wrongly decided. I shall, accordingly, not follow it and I
answer question 4 in the sense proposed by counsel for the sixth, seventh and
eighth defendants. H

Declarations accordingly.

Solicitors: *Ashurst, Morris, Crisp & Co.* (for all parties).

[*Reported by* JENIFER SANDELL, *Barrister-at-Law.*]

I

---

(37) [1927] All E.R. Rep. 214; [1928] Ch. 330.

A
Re GUINNESS'S SETTLEMENT.

GUINNESS AND ANOTHER v. S. G. WARBURG (EXECUTOR AND TRUSTEE), LTD. AND OTHERS.

[CHANCERY DIVISION (Goff, J.), April 5, 6, 1966.]

B
Will—Apportionment—Income of unconverted property in residuary estate given to tenant for life—Discretion whether to convert not exercised by trustees —Apportionment under rule in Re Earl of Chesterfield's Trusts not excluded while discretion not exercised.

Will—Capital or income—Income of settled funds under resulting trust during life of settlor's wife—Income becoming subject to settlor's will after release of life interest—Whether capital or income of settlor's residuary estate.

C
By a settlement made on Aug. 14, 1935, after reciting that the settlor had transferred investments into the joint names of the trustees and after declaring administrative trusts for conversion and investment, it was declared that the trust fund should be held on trust during the joint lives of the settlor's wife, J., and two children to apply two equal third parts of the annual income for the maintenance education and benefit of the two children. Subject to this trust the trustees of the settlement were, by

D
cl. 4, to pay the annual income of the trust fund to J. during her life, and by cl. 6 there was a special power of appointment in favour of the issue of the settlor and J. The marriage was dissolved by a decree made absolute on July 27, 1936. The settlor died on Apr. 10, 1937, having by his will and four codicils given a protected life interest in his residuary estate to J.

E
The definition of the settlor's residuary estate included "investments for the time being remaining unconverted pursuant to " a power therein contained; and the tenant for life under the will and codicils was given the whole income of unconverted property in the residuary estate. By deed of release dated Dec. 31, 1937, J. released to the trustees all her estate and interest in the income of the trust fund to become payable thereafter during

F
her life and all her right title claim and demand to and in the same " to the intent that the settlement may henceforth be read and construed as if cl. 4 thereof . . . were deleted ". The trustees of the settlor's will had not hitherto exercised any discretion, under the power to retain investments unconverted, in regard to the income from the settled trust fund, since it had not been appreciated that their discretion under the will was applicable,

G
and income of the settled trust fund had been held in suspense pending the determination of questions of entitlement to it.

Held: (i) on the true construction of the deed of release and in the events which had happened there was a resulting trust in favour of the settlor's estate in respect of the income released by the deed, which income therefore became subject to the will and codicils of the settlor (see p. 504,

H
letters C and E, post).

(ii) the released income should be treated as capital of the settlor's residuary estate, because it was not produced by a fund forming part of his estate but was the income of the trust fund under the settlement of 1935 (see p. 505, letters B and F, post).

Re Hey's Settlement Trusts ([1945] 1 All E.R. 618) followed.

I
Re O'Hagan ([1932] W.N. 188) not followed.

(iii) the definition in the settlor's will of his residuary estate did not exclude the application of the rule of apportionment in *Re Earl of Chesterfield's Trusts** at a time when the will trustees had not yet exercised any discretion; and, accordingly, income which accrued before the trustees exercised their discretion whether to postpone conversion was subject to apportionment in accordance with the rule, but once the discretion was

---

* [1881-85] All E.R. Rep. 737.

s

oxorcised the rule would thereby be excluded thereafter (see p. 507, letters   A
D and F, post).

Rowlls v. *Bebb* ([1900-03] All E.R. Rep. 756) applied.

Re Earl of Chesterfield's Trusts ([1881-85] All E.R. Rep. 737) considered.

[As to resulting trusts where declared trusts are not exhaustive, see 38
HALSBURY'S LAWS (3rd Edn.) 862, 863, para. 1453.   B
As to whether annuities forming part of residuary estate bequeathed in trust
are capital or income, see 38 HALSBURY'S LAWS (3rd Edn.) 881, para. 1487,
text and note (*d*), and cf. 29 ibid., p. 350, para. 704, note (*q*); and for cases on
the subject, see 40 DIGEST (Repl.) 711, 2058-2060 and 37 DIGEST (Repl.) 159, 764.
As to exclusion of the rule in *Howe* v. *Dartmouth*, see 16 HALSBURY'S LAWS
(3rd Edn.) 381-383, paras. 744-746; and for cases on the subject, see 44 DIGEST   C
200-210, *297-382*.]

Cases referred to:

Chesterfield's (Earl) Trusts, Re, [1881-85] All E.R. Rep. 737; (1883), 24 Ch.D.
    643; 52 L.J.Ch. 958; 49 L.T. 261; 20 Digest (Repl.) 389, *1110*.
Crawley v. *Crawley*, (1835), 7 Sim. 427; 4 L.J.Ch. 265; 58 E.R. 901; 40
    Digest (Repl.) 711, *2059*.   D
Fisher, Re, Harris v. *Fisher*, [1943] 2 All E.R. 615; [1943] Ch. 377; 113 L.J.Ch.
    17; 169 L.T. 289; 24 Digest (Repl.) 964, *9738*.
Grey v. *Pearson*, [1843-60] All E.R. Rep. 21; (1857), 6 H.L. Cas. 61; 26 L.J.Ch.
    473; 29 L.T.O.S. 67; 10 E.R. 1216; 44 Digest (Repl.) 214, *286*.
Hey's Settlement Trusts and Will Trusts, Re, Hey v. *Nickell-Lean*, [1945] 1 All
    E.R. 618; [1945] Ch. 294; 114 L.J.Ch. 278; 172 L.T. 396; 2nd   E
    Digest Supp.
Howe v. *Dartmouth (Earl), Howe* v. *Aylesbury (Countess)*, (1802), 7 Ves. 137;
    32 E.R. 56; 43 Digest 869, *3142*.
Key v. *Key*, (1853), 4 De G.M. & G. 73; 22 L.J.Ch. 641; 22 L.T.O.S. 67;
    43 E.R. 435; 44 Digest 580, *3999*.
Neville v. *Fortescue*, (1848), 16 Sim. 333; 60 E.R. 902; 44 Digest 206, *347*.   F
O'Hagan, Re, O'Hagan v. *Lloyds Bank, Ltd.*, [1932] W.N. 188; 37 Digest
    (Repl.) 159, *764*.
Payne (decd.), Re, Westminster Bank, Ltd. v. *Payne*, [1943] 2 All E.R. 675;
    113 L.J.Ch. 46; 169 L.T. 365; 23 Digest (Repl.) 295, *3614*.
Rowlls v. *Bebb. Re Rowlls, Walters* v. *Treasury Solicitor*, [1900-03] All E.R.
    Rep. 756; [1900] 2 Ch. 107; 69 L.J.Ch. 562; 82 L.T. 633; 43 Digest   G
    618, *589*.
Sherry, Re, Sherry v. *Sherry*, [1913] 2 Ch. 508; 83 L.J.Ch. 126; 109 L.T. 474;
    40 Digest (Repl.) 747, *2336*.
Whitehead, Re, Peacock v. *Lucas*, [1891-94] All E.R. Rep. 636; [1894] 1 Ch.
    678; 63 L.J.Ch. 229; 70 L.T. 122; 40 Digest (Repl.) 711, *2058*.
                                                                                    H
Adjourned Summons.

This was an application by originating summons dated Apr. 23, 1965, by the
plaintiffs, Sir Kenelm Ernest Lee Guinness and Geraldine St. Lawrence Lee
Essayan, for the following relief: (i) the determination by the court of the
question whether on the true construction of the settlement dated Aug. 14, 1935,
and a deed of release dated Dec. 31, 1937, and in the events which had happened,   I
the income disposed of by that deed ought (a) to be held on the trusts applicable
under the settlement to income arising after the death of the defendant Josephine
Guinness; or (b) to be applied as an addition to the income disposed of by cl. 5
of the settlement; or (c) to be paid to the personal representatives of Kenelm
Edward Lee Guinness, deceased, as being undisposed of by the settlement; or
(d) to be dealt with in some other and what manner. (ii) if the income were held
to be payable to the personal representatives of Kenelm Edward Lee Guinness,
the determination of the question whether on the true construction of his will

A and the four codicils thereto and in the events which had happened the same
ought to be treated as capital or as income, or to be apportioned in some and
what manner between capital and income, of his residuary estate. (iii) generally
that the rights and interests of the parties thereto in respect of the income might
be determined. The defendants were (i) S. G. Warburg (Executor and Trustee),
Ltd. and (ii) Alfred Henry Willetts who were the present trustees of the settle-
B ment; (iii) Josephine Guinness who was the sole surviving executrix and one of the
trustees of the will and four codicils thereto of Kenelm Edward Lee Guinness,
deceased, who claimed to be beneficially interested under the trusts of the above-
mentioned instruments or some of them; (iv) Kenneth Jackson who with the
third defendant was the other trustee of the will and codicils; (v) Kenelm
Ernest Lee Guinness; (vi) Joanna Consuelo Essayan; (vii) Martin Sarkis
C Essayan, and (viii) Nigel Digby Lee Guinness, all of whom claimed to be beneficially interested under the trusts. Both the plaintiffs also claimed to be
beneficially interested under the trusts. The settlor Kenelm Edward Lee
Guinness made his will on Dec. 16, 1934. Clause 11 thereof provided as follows:

" I devise and bequeath all the residue of my real and personal estate
wheresoever and whatsoever not hereby or by any codicil hereto otherwise
D disposed of to my trustees upon trust to sell call in and convert into money
such part thereof as shall not consist of money (with power to postpone
such sale calling-in and conversion for such period as my trustees may in
their absolute discretion think fit) and to hold the proceeds of such sale
calling-in and conversion and my ready money (subject to the payment
thereout of my funeral and testamentary expenses and debts and the legacy
E duty on any legacies and annuities hereby or by any codicil hereto bequeathed
free of duty) upon trust to invest the same in any of the investments hereby
authorised and to hold such investments and the investments for the time
being representing the same and any investments for the time being
remaining unconverted pursuant to the power in that behalf hereinbefore
contained (hereinafter collectively called ' my residuary estate ') upon the
F trusts and with and subject to the powers and provisions hereinafter
declared and contained concerning the same."

The settlor made four codicils to his will but they are not material to this report.
The facts are set out in the judgment.
The authority and cases noted below* were cited during the argument in
G addition to the cases referred to in the judgment.

H. E. Francis, Q.C., and J. M. E. Byng for the plaintiffs (the settlor's son
and daughter).
W. T. Elverston for the first and second defendants (the trustees of the
settlement).
E. I. Goulding, Q.C., and E. G. Nugee for the third and fourth defendants
H (the will trustees).
N. C. H. Browne-Wilkinson for the fifth to the eighth defendants.

Apr. 5. GOFF, J.: This is a question of construction which arises on a
deed of release having regard to the terms of the settlement to which it related.
That is a settlement dated Aug. 14, 1935, and made between Kenelm Edward
Lee Guinness as settlor of the one part and certain trustees of the other part.
I It was a settlement of the life interest of the settlor under his marriage settlement
and of a contingent reversionary life interest under the same settlement and of
certain investments which were also brought into the settlement.
I am not really concerned with the fact that the settlement included the life
interest and reversionary life interest because the settlor is long since dead and

* JARMAN ON WILLS (8th Edn.) 1288; Mackie v. Mackie, (1845), 5 Hare 70; Re
Shuckburgh's Settlement, [1900-03] All E.R. Rep. 101; [1901] 2 Ch. 794; Re Blake,
Berry v. Geen, [1938] 2 All E.R. 362; [1938] A.C. 575; Re Wragg (decd.), [1959] 2 All
E.R. 717.

he predeceased the deed of release. I am concerned, however, with the property   A
now representing the investments which were brought into the settlement.
The settlement in question, after reciting the marriage settlement and that
there had been issue of the marriage two children, namely Kenelm Ernest Lee
Guinness, born on Dec. 13, 1928, and Geraldine St. Lawrence Lee Guinness,
born on Sept. 24, 1930, who are the plaintiffs, and reciting that the settlor was
desirous of making further provision for his wife and the issue of the marriage,   B
proceeded in the operative part with an assignment of the life interest and
reversionary life interest on the trusts thereinafter declared concerning the same
and included a provision that the trustees should stand possessed of the investments mentioned in the schedule thereto, being the property to which I have
already referred, on trust at their discretion to permit the same to remain as
invested or to sell the same. Clause 4 commenced the beneficial trusts. It was   C
there provided that:

"Subject to the provisions of cl. 5 hereof the trustees shall pay the
annual income of the trust fund and the dividends interest and income
hereinbefore assigned as and when received to [his wife] during her life
without power of anticipation during any coverture."
                                                                                     D
The wife is, in fact, the third defendant, Josephine Guinness. The restraint on
anticipation is not material because at all material times she was a feme sole.
Then cl. 5 says:

"During the joint lives of the wife and the two children hereinbefore named
and the survivor of such children the trustees shall apply for the maintenance education and benefit of the said two children so long as they shall   E
both be living two equal third parts of the annual income of the trust fund
and of the dividends interest and income hereinbefore assigned as and
when received but in the event of the death of one of the said two children
then the sum to be applied by the trustees for the maintenance education
and benefit of the survivor of the said two children shall be one moiety of
the annual income of the trust fund and of the dividends interest and income   F
hereinbefore assigned."

The rest of that clause is administrative and I need not read it. Clause 6 declared
the trusts to take effect after the death of the wife. It provided:

"After the death of the wife the capital and income of the trust fund
and the dividends interest and income hereinbefore assigned shall be held   G
in trust . . ."

and then followed a special power of appointment in favour of issue of the
marriage as the settlor and the wife should by deed jointly appoint and in
default of, and subject to, any such joint appointment, then as the survivor of
them should by deed or by will or codicil appoint. No appointment has as
yet been made. Then, in cl. 7, were declared trusts in default of appointment   H
which are complicated and in so far as they have taken effect or take effect
might give rise to questions of construction, because they appear not to deal
with the position during the infancy of the plaintiffs but to take the matter up
at twenty-one, and to deal primarily with the period between twenty-one and
twenty-six. The clause provides as follows:
                                                                                     I
"In default of and until and subject to any such appointment as aforesaid the trustees shall after the death of the wife hold the capital and income
of the trust fund and the dividends interest and income hereinbefore assigned
upon trust out of income to hold on protective trusts for the benefit of the
said Kenelm Ernest Lee Guinness in every year from and after his attaining the age of twenty-one years and until he shall attain the age of twenty-
six years such sum or sums as the wife shall from time to time by writing
under her hand or by will have directed to be so held for his benefit and in

A   default of such direction or in addition to the sum or sums so directed to be held for his benefit to pay to him during the like period such sum or sums (if any) as the trustees may in their absolute discretion think desirable in his interests . . .''

Then there is a precisely similar provision concerning the other plaintiff and the clause proceeds with these words:

B   " . . . and subject to the preceding provisions of this clause and to any and every exercise by the trustees of their statutory powers and of the power of advancement hereinafter contained shall pay the income (other than the income of any share of capital already vested) with the approval of the trustees to such person or persons and if more than one in such shares as the wife shall from time to time by writing under her hand or by
C   will have directed (but so that no such direction shall be made in favour of the settlor) until the younger or the survivor of the said two children shall attain the age of twenty-six years or until the death of such survivor whichever event shall first happen to the intent (but without imposing any trust or obligation whatsoever) that the same shall be applied by such person or persons for the maintenance and benefit of the said two children or the
D   survivor of them and upon trust as to capital for the said two children in equal shares or the survivor of them as and when they he or she shall attain the age of twenty-six years.''

The marriage between the settlor and the third defendant was dissolved by decree absolute dated June 27, 1936. The settlor died on Apr. 10, 1937, having
E   by his will and four codicils made various dispositions of his residuary estate under which the wife took a protected life interest.

Then one comes to the deed of release of Dec. 31, 1937, on which the question directly depends. That was made between the wife then described as feme sole of the one part and the trustees of the other part. It recites the settlement. Counsel for the plaintiffs has relied on the precise terms of this recital and I
F   must therefore refer to it. It recites that by a settlement thereinafter called " the settlement ", dated Aug. 14, 1935, and made between, Kenelm Edward Lee Guinness and the trustees, after reciting inter alia that the settlor had transferred the investments mentioned in the schedule thereto into the joint names of the trustees:

    " . . . it was declared that the trustees should stand possessed of such
G   investments upon trust either to permit the same to remain as then invested or to sell and convert the same and invest the proceeds of such sale and conversion in any of the investments thereinafter authorised and should stand possessed of the investments mentioned in the schedule thereto and the investments for the time being representing the same (thereinafter collectively called ' the trust fund ') upon trust during the joint lives of
H   Mrs. Guinness and Kenelm Ernest Lee Guinness and Geraldine St. Lawrence Lee Guinness (the two children of the marriage of the settlor and Mrs. Guinness) to apply for the maintenance education and benefit of the said two children so long as they should both be living two equal third parts of the annual income of the trust fund but that in the event of the death of one of the said two children the sum to be applied by the trustees for the
I   maintenance education and benefit of the survivor of the said two children should be one moiety of the annual income of the trust fund and that it was declared by cl. 4 of the settlement that subject [to the provisions of cl. 5 thereof] the trustees should pay the annual income of the trust fund to Mrs. Guinness during her life without power of anticipation during any coverture and it was further declared by the settlement that after the death of Mrs. Guinness the capital and income of the trust fund should be held in trust for the issue of the marriage of the settlor and Mrs. Guinness as therein mentioned.''

Counsel for the plaintiffs relied on the fact that this recital refers not only to **A**
cl. 4 of the settlement creating the life interest of Mrs. Guinness but goes on to
say that it was further declared by the settlement that after her death the
capital and income of the trust fund should be held in trust for the issue of the
marriage as therein mentioned. Then the deed of release recites the divorce and
that Mrs. Guinness is desirous of releasing her life interest in the trust fund.
Counsel for the plaintiffs also relies on that recital. Then follows the operative **B**
part which is quite short and in these terms:

" This deed . . . witnesseth that Mrs. Guinness as beneficial owner
hereby releases unto the trustees all that the estate and interest of Mrs.
Guinness in all income of the trust fund to become payable hereafter during
the life of Mrs. Guinness and all her right title claim and demand to and in   **C**
the same to the intent that the settlement may henceforth be read and
construed as if cl. 4 thereof aforesaid were deleted."

Following that release the whole income of the trust fund was, in fact, paid to
Mrs. Guinness for the benefit of the plaintiffs down to a date in 1960 or 1961
when, on the appointment of the first defendant to be trustee, doubts were
entertained and advice of counsel was taken and as a result, after six more **D**
years, during which I understand there were negotiations and discussions with
a view to a settlement and during which time the whole of the income was held
in suspense pending the determination of the question, the problem has now
been brought before the court by the plaintiffs in an originating summons which
asks whether on the true construction of the settlement and the deed of release
and in the events which have happened, the income disposed of by the deed **E**
ought (a), to be held on the trusts applicable under the settlement to income
arising after the death of the defendant, Josephine Guinness, which is the construction for which counsel for the plaintiffs has contended, or (b), to be applied
as an addition to the income disposed of by cl. 5 of the settlement; no argument
has been adduced in support of that view; or (c), to be paid to the personal
representative of Kenelm Edward Lee Guinness, deceased, as being undisposed **F**
of by the settlement, which is the contention which has been advanced before
me by counsel on behalf of the third and fourth defendants as trustees of the
will of the testator. If it should be held that it ought to be so paid there is a
further question which has not yet been argued: how the income so falling
back into the settlor's estate ought to be dealt with as between capital and
income. **G**

It is conceded by counsel for the plaintiffs that if cl. 4 had never been in the
settlement at all there would have been a resulting trust because the subsequent
provisions are expressed to be after the death of the wife and there is no context
which would enable one to read those words as meaning merely " subject as
aforesaid " and there would be a hiatus. He has submitted, however, that
notwithstanding the words in the deed of release " as if cl. 4 thereof aforesaid **H**
were deleted " I can and ought to spell out of the deed as a matter of construction
in the light of the surrounding circumstances an intention to bring into operation
so far as concerns the released income the trusts declared by the settlement to
take effect after the death of the wife. In support of that he relied first on the
fact that it is a release of the income (which would otherwise be payable under
cl. 4) to the trustees of the settlement. It is submitted that Mrs. Guinness must **I**
have intended the trustees to deal with it in accordance with the trusts of the
settlement. If she had intended to dispose of it for the benefit of the settlor's
estate he submits that she would have done so directly. That, in my judgment,
does not really assist because it is rarely, if ever, that anyone intends to create
a resulting trust. They do so in law because they fail effectively to declare
complete trusts and when I find in this deed of release a release to the trustees,
it is clear that they cannot take beneficial rights, and there must be a resulting

A trust, unless one can discover on what trusts the trustees were to hold the income released.

Secondly, counsel for the plaintiffs relied on the third recital, a bald statement of Mrs. Guinness's object as a desire to release her life interest in the trust fund. He submits that that connotes an intention to bring into force the trusts to arise on determination of the life interest, but I cannot spell out of that recital

B anything more than the intention to put an end to her life interest. If I am to find what is to happen in consequence of the release it must, in my judgment, be found somewhere other than in that recital which counsel for the plaintiffs has correctly characterised as a bald statement of intention.

Thirdly, counsel for the plaintiffs relies on the point to which I have already adverted in reading the first recital; that it mentions not only cl. 4 of the settle-

C ment but refers to some extent to what is to happen after the death of Mrs. Guinness. The words, it will be remembered, are,

" and it was further declared . . . that after the death of Mrs. Guinness the capital and income of the trust fund should be held in trust for the issue of the marriage of the settlor and Mrs. Guinness as therein mentioned."

D It is submitted that the fact that the recital goes beyond mentioning that Mrs. Guinness takes a life interest under cl. 4 and states that something is to happen after her death assists in showing an intention to bring into operation the trusts declared to take effect after her death. Counsel for the third and fourth defendants (the " will trustees "), on the other hand, stressed the fact that that is a very brief statement indeed. It says no more than " on the trusts therein

E mentioned ", and he argues that if that was put in to show an intention to bring the ultimate trusts into operation, one would have expected to find those trusts set out in much greater detail.

I find that the reference to what is to happen after the death of Mrs. Guinness is very unconvincing. The words are really simply rounding-off the recital and I agree that, if it had been intended to show a specific intention, something more

F express would have appeared than a brief statement using the words " as therein mentioned ".

The fourth point of counsel for the plaintiffs, and in my view his strongest point, was that there was an apparent absurdity in the light of the surrounding circumstances in Mrs. Guinness destroying her life interest under the settlement only to leave the income to fall back into the settlor's estate so that either it

G would all be payable to her as income of his estate or, more probably, would be apportioned between capital and income or possibly all be capital in which case even she would derive some income from the investments of the released income. It is clear from the passages referred to in HAWKINS ON WILLS (3rd Edn.), proposition 4 at p. 6, and in the cases there cited of *Key* v. *Key* (1) on p. 7 and *Grey* v. *Pearson* (2) on p. 8, that the court is entitled to go behind the express

H words of the will, if it can gather from the context that those words do not give effect to the intention and in order to carry out what it is satisfied the testator or settlor, as the case may be, really did intend. In my judgment, however, both the passage there cited from the decision of KNIGHT BRUCE, L.J., in *Key* v. *Key* (1) and the passage from the speech of LORD ST. LEONARDS in *Grey* v. *Pearson* (2) show that one has got to find quite clearly what the

I intention really was.

Here I am left in an area of speculation. It may be that Mrs. Guinness intended simply to bring into operation the trusts declared in cl. 6 and cl. 7 of the settlement, although they are not entirely easy to fit in, and if that had been the intention one would have expected words saving her power of appointment under cl. 6 and her powers of direction under cl. 7. She may have intended, as is suggested in the summons, though no-one has been found to support this in

(1) (1853), 4 De G.M. & G. 73.
(2) [1843-60] All E.R. Rep. 21; (1857), 6 H.L. Cas. 61.

argument, that the two children should have their two-thirds or half share A enlarged to the whole. Counsel for the will trustees has suggested a third possibility, that she may have intended a trust for accumulation; and a fourth, to put the matter back into the settlor's estate merely disclaiming her interest, not technically disclaiming it because she had already begun to enjoy it, but giving up the interest for life given to her under the settlement and leaving it to follow its fate under the will. B

I am not satisfied that I can find in this deed of release even in the light of the surrounding circumstances anything which would enable me safely to depart from the words of cl. 4 which are not ambiguous and not in any way inconsistent. There is a complete and accurate statement throughout. A release to the trustees, which is the proper technical form, of the life interest, followed by an expression of intention " to the intent that the settlement may henceforth be read and C construed as if cl. 4 thereof aforesaid were deleted " which are words that do on their literal construction create a hiatus giving rise to a resulting trust. I find the only safe course here is to stand on the words which the draftsman, and Mrs. Guinness by executing the deed, have chosen to use and I therefore answer question (i) of the summons in the sense of para. (c) [which is at p. 498, letter I, ante]. D

*   *   *   *

Apr. 6. **GOFF, J.**: I decided yesterday that the effect of the deed of release was to create a resulting trust in respect of the released income which therefore falls to be dealt with under the will of the settlor and that gives rise to further questions, first, whether the released income is capital or income in E the residuary estate of the settlor under his will, and, secondly, as to the application of the equitable rules of apportionment known as the rules in *Howe* v. *Earl of Dartmouth*, *Howe* v. *Countess of Aylesbury* (3) and *Re Earl of Chesterfield's Trusts* (4).

Counsel for the will trustees has argued that it ought to be treated as income in the settlor's residuary estate and has relied on *Re O'Hagan, O'Hagan* v. F *Lloyds Bank, Ltd.* (5). He has also presented the matter as one of principle.

On this point there has been a considerable conflict of judicial opinion. In *Crawley* v. *Crawley* (6), it was held that a determinable annuity is capital, though no reasons were given for the decision, and this was followed in *Re Whitehead, Peacock* v. *Lucas* (7), which had to deal with the income of a fund set aside under G the will of a previous testator to answer a legacy which was vested but not presently payable and which did not carry the intermediate income. That case is interesting because a distinction was drawn there between that income which was held to be capital in the second testator's estate and the surplus income of a fund set aside in the first testator's estate to answer a discretionary annuity which was held to be income of the second testator's estate. In the one case the second testator had nothing but the right to the income for a limited period, H and in the other he had the capital which produced the income. Per contra are *Neville* v. *Fortescue* (8), which however turned on a special context, *Re Sherry, Sherry* v. *Sherry* (9) which is not satisfactory because the particular point was not argued, and *Re O'Hagan* (5). There the point was argued, and decided in favour of the contention advanced by counsel for the will trustees. The report of that case, however, is brief and not entirely satisfactory because the decision is I based as reported on the premise that it was well settled that a determinable annuity is income notwithstanding that *Crawley* v. *Crawley* (6) and *Re Whitehead* (7) had been cited to the judge in that case.

---

(3) (1802), 7 Ves. 137.   (4) [1881-85] All E.R. Rep. 737; (1883), 24 Ch.D. 643.
(5) [1932] W.N. 188.   (6) (1835), 7 Sim. 427.
(7) [1891-94] All E.R. Rep. 636; [1894] 1 Ch. 678.   (8) (1848), 16 Sim. 333.
(9) [1913] 2 Ch. 508.

A   In *Re Payne* (decd.), *Westminster Bank, Ltd* v. *Payne* (10), UTHWATT, J.,
suggested a possible explanation of *Re O'Hagan* (11) namely, that "income of
my estate" might mean "income which happens to be part of my estate".
I doubt whether that is open on the wording of this particular will. Be that as
it may, in *Re Hey's Settlement Trusts and Will Trusts, Hey* v. *Nickell-Lean* (12),
COHEN, J., declined to accept that explanation and accepted the view that
B   *Re O'Hagan* (11) is irreconcilable with *Crawley* v. *Crawley* (13) and in *Re Whitehead* (14) and preferred to follow *Crawley* v. *Crawley* (13) in preference to *Re
O'Hagan* (11). The basis of the decision in *Re Hey's Settlement Trusts* (12) is
that the income is not income in the testator's estate, because it is not produced
by any fund forming part of the testator's estate. In the present case the relevant
income is income of the trust fund but that is the settlement trustees' fund. It
C   is not income of any property to be found in the settlor's residuary estate subject
to his will. The principle of *Re O'Hagan* (11), on the contrary, is that there is
property in the testator's estate which produces the income, namely, the testator's
estate pur autre vie in the other fund.

Counsel for the will trustees has argued that if one accepts the decision in
Re Hey's Settlement Trusts (12), rather than *Re O'Hagan* (11), one produces nice
D   and almost capricious distinctions in that the income under a lease or a royalty
arising from minerals owned by a testator apart from the land would be treated
as income of the testator's estate and so would income arising from an estate
pur autre vie in land, as counsel for the will trustees submits, and there is no
real distinction between that interest and an interest pur autre vie in personalty.
I feel the force of such submissions but I cannot say that *Re Hey's Settlement
E   Trusts* (12) was necessarily wrong or contrary to authority or principle and as
this is a matter of administration I think that it would be wrong for me to
import fresh confusion by resurrecting *Re O'Hagan* (11). I propose, therefore,
simply to follow the decision in *Re Hey's Settlement Trusts* (12) and, if that be
wrong, it will be for the Court of Appeal hereafter and not for me to say so.
Therefore, following *Re Hey's Settlement Trusts* (12), I hold that the resulting
F   income in this case is not income in the settlor's residuary estate under his will
but capital. Prima facie, however, the equitable rule of apportionment in *Re
Earl of Chesterfield's Trusts* (15) must be applied to it, but the question then is
how far that is excluded by the provisions of cl. 11 of the will which include in
the definition of residuary estate "investments for the time being remaining
unconverted pursuant to the power in that behalf hereinbefore contained" and,
G   therefore, give the tenant for life the whole income of such unconverted property.

Now, it is established, subject to the question which I must consider in a
moment of the exercise of the trustees' discretion, that where there is a clause
such as that, giving the tenant for life the whole income and therefore excluding
Howe v. *Earl of Dartmouth* (16) in favour of the tenant for life, there must also
be excluded the corollary or, converse, application of the principle, the rule in
H   *Re Earl of Chesterfield's Trusts* (15). It was held, however, in *Rowlls* v. *Bebb,
Re Rowlls, Walters* v. *Treasury Solicitor* (17), that notwithstanding such a clause
the equitable rule of apportionment still applies if the trustees have not, in
fact, exercised any discretion in the matter at all. In that case they had failed
to do so because, although they knew perfectly well that they had the asset,
they did not appreciate that the point arose for their consideration. Counsel
I   for the plaintiffs has sought to distinguish that case on the ground that in the
case before me the position is different in as much as until I decided the first
question yesterday, the will trustees did not know that they had the asset at
all and, therefore, there could be no question of them being required to exercise

(10) [1943] 2 All E.R. 675 at p. 677.   (11) [1932] W.N. 188.
(12) [1945] 1 All E.R. 618; [1945] Ch. 294.   (13) (1835), 7 Sim. 427.
(14) [1891-94] All E.R. Rep. 636; [1894] 1 Ch. 678.
(15) [1881-85] All E.R. Rep. 737; (1883), 24 Ch.D. 643.
(16) (1802), 7 Ves. 137.   (17) [1900-03] All E.R. Rep. 756; [1900] 2 Ch. 107.

any discretion. That, in my judgment, is not a valid distinction. The point, as   A
I see it, was that the interest had been retained without any conscious decision
by the trustees whether they ought to sell it or keep it, and that being so the
court said that it could not allow the equitable rule to be excluded. In my
judgment, it is an a fortiori case if the trustees do not even know that they have
got the interest. Clearly in such circumstances they cannot exercise any discretion in regard to it. Moreover, as far as one can gather what the questions were   B
in *Re Hey's Settlement Trusts* (18), the problem would appear to have arisen
in the same sort of circumstances as those with which I am dealing because in
the course of his judgment COHEN, J., said (19):

> " The last question on this summons is as to the income of the fund
> subject to the donation of trust (which I shall hereinafter refer to as ' the
> settled fund '), which on the basis of my answer to question 2, results, by   C
> way of resulting trust, to the estate of the testator . . ."

So that it would seem there, as here, that it was only on the determination of a
prior question that it appeared that there was in truth a resulting trust.

The second ground of distinction urged before me was, as indeed the position
appears to have been, that in *Rowlls* v. *Bebb* (20) the Court of Appeal held not   D
only that the trustees had not exercised a discretion but that if they had appreciated the position and thought about it, it clearly would have been their duty to
sell. It may be that that is the position in which the will trustees find themselves
but I am not in a position to reach a conclusion on that point because I would
need to have detailed information as to the nature of the property comprising
the testator's estate, but in my judgment that is not a sufficient ground for   E
distinguishing *Rowlls* v. *Bebb* (20) from the present case, and in his judgment
in *Re Hey's Settlement* (21), COHEN, J., plainly put it on the non-exercise of the
power and did not consider whether or not the trustees ought to decide in the
exercise of their discretion to sell. I refer to this passage in his judgment:

> " But it is established by authority that where there is in a will power
> to postpone the sale of assets, followed by a clause excluding the operation   F
> of the rule in *Howe* v. *Earl of Dartmouth* (22), such clause only operates if
> the executors, in proper exercise of the power, determine to postpone sale
> of the asset: (see *Rowlls* v. *Bebb* (20)). See also *Re Fisher*, *Harris* v. *Fisher*
> (23), where BENNETT, J., reached a similar conclusion on the construction
> or effect of the Administration of Estates Act, 1925, s. 33. I, therefore,
> propose to declare that if the testator's executors determine to exercise the   G
> power conferred on them by his will to postpone the sale of the right to
> receive the resulting income, the same should, as and when received, be
> treated as corpus and invested accordingly, the tenant for life receiving
> the income of such investments, but that any such income received or to be
> received before the testator's executors so determine should be apportioned
> between capital and income in accordance with the principle of *Re Earl*   H
> of *Chesterfield's Trusts* (24)."

So that it was quite clear in that case that it was open how the trustees might,
in fact, exercise their discretion.

The third point which counsel for the plaintiffs urged was this. Founding
himself on the form of the proposed declaration which I have just read and the
fact that as yet the will trustees have not received any of this income at all,   I
part of it having been applied by the settlement trustees and part of it having
been retained in a suspense account, he submits that any exercise by the will

---

(18) [1945] 1 All E.R. 618; [1945] Ch. 294.
(19) [1945] Ch. at p. 308; [1945] 1 All E.R. at p. 624.
(20) [1900-03] All E.R. Rep. 756; [1900] 2 Ch. 107.
(21) [1945] 1 All E.R. at p. 627; [1945] Ch. at p. 315.   (22) (1802), 7 Ves. 137.
(23) [1943] 2 All E.R. 615 at pp. 619, 620; [1943] Ch. 377 at p. 385.
(24) [1881-85] All E.R. Rep. 737; (1883), 24 Ch.D. 643.

A trustees of their discretion should exclude apportionment, not only for the
future but for the past, because the declaration says that any such income
received or to be received before the testator's executors so determine should
be apportioned between capital and income. It says that if the executors exercise
their power to postpone sale the income should, as and when received, be treated
as capital and invested accordingly but any such income received or to be
B received before the testator's executors so determine should be apportioned,
making apparently the date of receipt the crucial date for this purpose. But, as
I said in the course of the argument, and as I think counsel for the plaintiffs
was really constrained to admit, the rights of the parties cannot be made to
depend on anything so casual as the actual date of receipt, and I instanced in
this case the possibility that the will trustees might decide to have a meeting
C after Easter to consider the exercise of their discretion and the settlement
trustees might on the one hand pay over the money immediately before such
meeting, or, alternatively, might not be quite so quick and might pay after
the meeting.

In my judgment the rights of the parties could not be different in the one
case from what they would be in the other. It seems to me, and I so hold, that
D the crucial date is the date when the will trustees do, in fact, exercise their
discretion. Income which has accrued in respect of the period down to that
date accrued when the discretion had not been exercised and when therefore
there was nothing to exclude the equitable rule of apportionment in *Re Earl of
Chesterfield's Trusts* (25). Once they have exercised their discretion, if they do
retain this interest, then the curtain has dropped and there is a change from the
E one state of affairs to the other and thereafter the equitable rule of apportionment
is excluded. I think that that is particularly so on the terms of this will where
the relevant clause (26) relied on to exclude the rule of apportionment specifically
refers to investments for the time being remaining unconverted pursuant to the
power in that behalf thereinbefore contained.

In my judgment, therefore, the resulting money is capital in the settlor's
F residuary estate subject to his will but is liable to be apportioned in accordance
with *Re Earl of Chesterfield's Trusts* (25) unless and until the will trustees in the
exercise of their discretion consciously decide to retain this investment of their
testator, the settlor; and whilst now that they know they have got it, it is their
duty to direct their minds to this question and consider it, nothing which I
have said ought to be taken as indicating one way or the other how they ought
G to decide. That is a matter for their discretion. Even if I had the information,
it would not be for me to tell them how to do it.

Order accordingly.

Solicitors: *Coward, Chance & Co.* (for the plaintiffs and the fifth to the
eighth defendants); *William Charles Crocker* (for the first and second defendants);
Slaughter & May (for the third and fourth defendants).
H
[*Reported by* JENIFER SANDELL, *Barrister-at-Law.*]

I   _____

(25) [1881-85] All E.R. Rep. 737; (1883), 24 Ch.D. 643.
(26) See p. 499, letter E, ante.

TUCKER v. FARM AND GENERAL INVESTMENT TRUST, LTD.

[COURT OF APPEAL (Lord Denning, M.R., Harman and Diplock, L.JJ.), March 30, 1966.]

Hire-Purchase—Livestock—Ewes—Lambs born during hiring—Whether property of hirer or of finance company.

In August, 1963, P., a farmer, entered into an hire-purchase agreement with the defendant finance company relating to eighty-four ewes. The total hire-purchase price was £647, the initial payment was £120 and the balance was payable in two instalments of £263 10s. on June 28 and Aug. 28, 1964. The ewes were served and lambs were born. In April, 1964, P. sold the ewes and the lambs to the plaintiff, who was unaware of the hire-purchase agreement. The finance company seized the ewes and the lambs and sold them. In an action by the plaintiff against the finance company for conversion of the lambs,

Held: on a lease of livestock the progeny belonged to the lessee, unless the lease provided to the contrary, and the position was the same where the transaction was one of hire-purchase; accordingly the lambs belonged to the plaintiff and the plaintiff was entitled to damages for conversion of the lambs (see p. 510, letter A, to p. 511, letter B, p. 511, letters F and H, and p. 512, letter F, post).

Wood v. *Ash and Foster* ((1586), Owen 139) followed.

Appeal allowed.

[As to property in the young of domestic animals, see 1 HALSBURY'S LAWS (3rd Edn.) 655, 656, para. 1251, subject to the observation at p. 509, letter G, post; for the nature of hire-purchase agreements, see 19 HALSBURY'S LAWS (3rd Edn.) 510, 511, para. 823; and for cases on the leasing and right to increase of livestock, see 2 DIGEST (Repl.) 29, 30, *133-138*, 299, 300, *80-85*.]

Cases referred to:

Case of Swans, (1592), 7 Co. Rep. 15 b; 77 E.R. 435; 2 Digest (Repl.) 293, *18*.

Morkel v. *Malan*, (1933), C.P.D. 370. The series of reports is Cape Provincial Division Reports of South Africa.

Wood v. *Ash and Foster*, (1586), Owen 139; 74 E.R. 39; 2 Digest (Repl.) 29, *133*.

Appeal.

This was an appeal on notice dated Jan. 18, 1966, by Edwin Frank Tucker, the plaintiff, from a judgment of His Honour JUDGE PRATT given on Dec. 9, 1965, at Tiverton County Court, dismissing the plaintiff's action for damages for conversion of eighty-three lambs, alleged to be his property. The lambs were the progeny of ewes that were the subject of a hire-purchase agreement dated Aug. 28, 1963, and made between Mervin Thomas Petty (the lessee) and the defendant finance company, and the lambs had been born during the subsistence of the hire-purchase agreement. Under the agreement the ewes belonged to the defendant finance company, but there was no express provision therein regarding the property in the lambs. It was not in issue that the finance company was entitled to the ewes. The finance company had seized and sold both the ewes and the lambs. The plaintiff claimed damages for conversion of the lambs.

The case and the authorities noted below* were cited during the argument in addition to those referred to in the judgments.

H. E. L. McCreery, Q.C., and *M. Hutchison* for the plaintiff.

P. L. W. Owen, Q.C., and *S. B. Thomas* for the defendant finance company.

LORD DENNING, M.R.: In August, 1963, Mr. Perry, who was a farmer at Hockworthy near Wellington, Somerset, acquired eighty-four Kerry

* A. G. GUEST ON HIRE-PURCHASE: ACCESSION AND CONFUSION, MODERN LAW REVIEW, Vol. 27, pp. 506, 507; GOODE ON HIRE-PURCHASE LAW AND PRACTICE (2nd Edn.), p. 10; *Westropp* v. *Elligott*, (1884), 9 App. Cas. 815.

A Hill cross ewes, on hire-purchase, The finance company was the defendant, the Farm and General Investment Trust, Ltd. Mr. Perry paid £120 down. The total hire-purchase price was £647. It is significant that having made the initial payment of £120, there were only two instalments payable many months later. The first instalment was payable ten months thereafter on June 28, 1964, the sum of £263 10s. The next one on Aug. 28, 1964, of another

B sum of £263 10s. The reason, no doubt, was to give time for the ewes to have lambs. Then, as is usual under a hire-purchase agreement, at the end of the hiring, if the hirer had paid those instalments, by paying an extra £1 as the option to purchase, he could buy the ewes. It is quite a simple straightforward hire-purchase agreement for livestock.

In September Mr. Perry had those ewes served. They had their lambs at the end

C of February and the beginning of March. Then on Apr. 2, 1964, Mr. Perry apparently being in financial difficulties, sold the ewes and the lambs—I think seventy-three ewes and eighty-three lambs—to the plaintiff, Mr. Tucker, who was also a farmer. Mr. Perry had no right whatever to sell the ewes as they were the property of the finance company; but the plaintiff did not know this. He bought the ewes and lambs in good faith. The plaintiff had not got room for

D the ewes and lambs on his farm, so he asked Mr. Perry to keep them for a bit. Mr. Perry a week later sold them again. He had no right to do so. He sold them to a Mr. Punchard who took them off. Mr. Punchard, however, soon found that there was something wrong about the deal and he called it off. He stopped his cheque. The finance company got to know about it. The finance company on Apr. 22, said: " These ewes and lambs are ours ", and they took possession of

E the ewes and lambs. So the plaintiff, who, as I have said, on Apr. 2 had bought the ewes and lambs and paid for them, found himself without any. He had to admit that the ewes belonged to the finance company, but he said that the lambs were his. He said that they belonged to Mr. Perry at the time when Mr. Perry sold them to him; and Mr. Perry had a right to sell the lambs and so the lambs were his. The county court judge did not accede to the plaintiff's claim.

F He said that there was a principle of English law that, when a person owns livestock, the progeny always belongs to the owner. The property in the young of domestic animals is in the owner of the mother. It says so in 1 HALSBURY'S LAWS (3rd Edn.), p. 656, para. 1251, note (f). The judge said that, as in this case the finance company were the owners of the ewes when the lambs were born, they were the owners of the lambs too and were owners of them on Apr. 2

G and indeed all the time. There was no implication in the contract, said the judge, that they should belong to Mr. Perry.

We have had the benefit before us of many more authorities than the judge had, and I think that I must say that the principle stated in HALSBURY'S LAWS is far too wide. It is based on SIR WILLIAM BLACKSTONE, COMMENTARIES (8th Edn.) Vol. 2, pp. 390, 391, but if you go back to BLACKSTONE you will see that

H BLACKSTONE is considering only a case where the male is owned by one person and the female by another. He is not dealing with lessor or lessee at all. BLACKSTONE says:

"Of all tame and domestic animals, the brood belongs to the owner of the dam or mother; the English law agreeing with the civil that ' partus sequitur ventrem ' in the brute creation, though for the most part in the

I human species it disallows that maxim. And therefore in the laws of England, as well as Rome [then I will translate the Latin into English] ' if your stallion makes my mare become pregnant, then the foal belongs not to you but to me who am the owner of the mare '. And for this PUFFENDORF gives a sensible reason: not only because the male is frequently unknown; but also because the dam, during the time of her pregnancy, is almost useless to the proprietor, and must be maintained with greater expense and care: wherefore as her owner is the loser by her pregnancy, he ought to be the gainer by her brood."

He goes on to give the exception of swans which was mentioned by LORD COKE A as long ago as 1592 in the *Case of Swans* (1). BLACKSTONE says:

" An exception to this rule is in the case of young cygnets; which belong equally to the owner of the cock and hen, and shall be divided between them. But here the reasons of the general rule cease, and ' cessante ratione 'cessat et ipsa lex '; for the male is well known, by his constant association with the female; and for the same reason the owner of the one doth not suffer more disadvantage, during the time of pregnancy and nurture, than the owner of the other."

Swans, as we all know, are faithful unto death and beyond. If the owner of the cock is different from the owner of the hen, they share the cygnets between them.

Turning to cases between lessor and lessee, we have been referred to passages C in the Roman law from JUSTINIAN and THE DIGEST. Also to a helpful case, *Morkel* v. *Malan* (2); in the Cape Province Supreme Court. It is clear that in Roman law, and in Roman Dutch law, the usufructuary—that is the person who is entitled to the enjoyment of the use of the animal—becomes entitled not only to the jus utendi, the right of using it, but also the jus fruendi, the right of having the fruit or progeny of it. I would be quite prepared, if there were no D English authority, to follow that rule of the civil law and apply it to lessor and lessee.

Counsel for the finance company, however, has very properly referred us to an English authority which makes it unnecessary for us to go back into the Roman law. It was decided as long ago as 1586, the case of *Wood* v. *Ash and Foster* (3). A lessor had let land for twenty years with a stock of sheep. The question arose E whether the young of the sheep belonged to the lessor or to the lessee. It was argued there by counsel:

" Although the first stock was changed, yet the new stock does supply, and is in place thereof, and shall be in the same condition as the other stock is, and therefore the lessor shall have property in it."

Then the reporter goes on to give the decision: F

" But the whole court was against him: for they said that the increase of the stock of sheep should be to the lessee, and the lessor shall never have them at the end of the term: but they agreed that if the lease were of the stock with lambs, calves and piggs [that is to say, if the lease expressly provided that it was a lease of the stock together with any lambs, calves and piglets that might be born] there the increase belongs to the lessor."   G

The court went on to make a distinction between dead stock and live stock:

" And all the court took this difference, sc. when a lease is made of dead goods, and when of living; for when the lease is of dead goods, and any thing is added to them for reparations or otherwise, the lessor shall have this addition at the end of the terme, because it belongs to the principle   H [that is, it is added to the principal thing that is leased] but in case of a stock of cattle, which hath an increase, as calves and lambs, there these things are severed from the principle [that is, are severed from the principal animals] and lessor shall never have them, for then [that is, were it otherwise] the lessor shall [would] have the rent, and the lessee shall [would] have no profit."   I

In other words, if the progeny did not belong to the lessee, it would mean that the lessor would have the rent and the lessee would have no profit—which would be absurd.

That seems to me to be a direct authority, now standing for nearly four hundred years, which shows that in the case of a lease of livestock, if during the course of the lease the livestock has progeny, that progeny belongs to the lessee. If

---

(1) (1592), 7 Co. Rep. 15b.   (2) (1933), C.P.D. 370.   (3) (1586), Owen 139.

A   the lessor desires to claim them and to retain the property in them, he must expressly stipulate for it in the lease by saying that the lease is of the livestock together with the progeny that may thereafter be born.

Counsel for the finance company recognised the force of that authority, but he sought to distinguish the case, saying that a hire-purchase agreement was different from a lease. I see no distinction whatever between a lease and a hire-

B   purchase agreement; because after all a hire-purchase agreement is a lease. It is a hiring in point of law, simply with an option to purchase added. I hold that on this hire-purchase agreement, nothing being said about progeny, any progeny that arose during the hiring belonged to the hirer.

The parties must have intended this in this very agreement, for why otherwise was it necessary to put off the instalment for ten months, the first one being on

C   June 28, 1964? The reason no doubt was that the sheep would be served and have their lambs in February or March. The lambs would be ready for sale, separate from their mothers, at the end of May or the beginning of June. Then the farmer, on selling the lambs, could pay the instalments which were then to become due in June or August. The whole of this agreement coincides with the law as I have stated it.

D   We were told that nowadays there are many more hire-purchase agreements of livestock than there were. The finance companies issue advertisements to induce farmers to take cows on hire-purchase, saying—" pay as you milk ". That is obviously on the basis that, when the farmer milks the cows, the milk becomes his, so that he can sell it and with the proceeds pay the instalments. So with sheep. It is—" pay as you sell the lambs ". The farmer was to have

E   the lambs. They were to be his to sell so that he could pay the instalments with the proceeds. The same when he comes to shear and has the wool from the fleeces. He can sell the wool. The law on this matter coincides with what must have been the intention of the parties. The lambs which are bred by the hirer during the currency of the agreement belong to the hirer.

So they were Mr. Perry's lambs when he sold them on Apr. 2, to the plaintiff.

F   He could give a good title to the plaintiff as he did. The plaintiff has a good action in conversion against the finance company when they took them on Apr. 22, wrongly. The value of the lambs is now agreed to be £207 10s.

I would, therefore, allow the appeal and order judgment to be entered for the plaintiff for the sum of £207 10s.

G   **HARMAN, L.J.:** If I were the owner of an apple orchard and let it at a rent to John Doe for a term of five years, nobody would doubt that John Doe, as the apples ripened, could pick and sell them and that the price which he received was his. That is a familiar transaction in England and has been for centuries. It was a surprise to me that livestock were also the subject of lettings, but it evidently has been so for centuries now.

H   There is, as LORD DENNING, M.R., has said, in the case of *Wood* v. *Ash and Foster* (4) a direct authority on the subject. The fact that this is not only a letting but a purchase, that is to say a hire-purchase agreement, in my view makes not the least difference. It is merely a letting with an option to purchase at the end of the term, like thousands of agreements in the past where the lessee has had such an option. Therefore, the case becomes a tolerably simple one.

I   It is merely a case of the lessee taking the fruit which falls from the subject matter of the demise during the term of years created by that document. This includes in this case the fleeces and the lambs, and those went to the lessee because there was nothing expressed to prevent them.

The law seems to me to be tolerably plain. I need not I think go back into the Roman law or bother about Roman Dutch law or authorities from Cape Province. There is a perfectly good English authority, and the analogy with an ordinary letting of farmland is quite clear. In the court below the matter was

---

(4) (1586), Owen 139.

bedevilled by the fact that it was taken that there was a presumption in English **A**
law that the offspring of an animal belonged to the owner of its dam, and that
no doubt is true (except for swans) as between the owner of the dam and the
owner of the sire; but that has nothing to do with the law between landlord
and tenant. Starting from that embroglio, the county court judge was asked
by both sides to read implied terms into this agreement. He I think did so,
although he declined to say what term it was that he read in. All he would say **B**
was that he would not imply the term which he was asked by the applicant to
imply. He said he would read in a term which resulted as he supposed the law
to be. If I were asked to imply a term here, I would not imply one. There is
no need to talk of implied terms. It is a question of a certain number of ewes
demised, and the produce of the ewes during the term of the hiring passed to
the lessee of the ewes. **C**

The appeal must be allowed accordingly.

DIPLOCK, L.J.: I agree. This appeal turns I think on the simple
question: when there is a letting of livestock at common law, does the progeny
and produce of the livestock during the course of the letting belong to the lessee,
who has the actual possession of the beasts, or does it belong to the owner who **D**
has the property? In the county court, and indeed here up to a certain stage,
in this case it was assumed that there was a rule of English common law that
the progeny belonged to the owner of the dam. That clearly was based on the
passage in BLACKSTONE'S COMMENTARIES (8th Edn.) Vol. 2, pp. 390, 391, in
which he is dealing with property in things personal and says:

" In the laws of England as well as in Rome, for here English law follows **E**
the civil law, the property of the progeny is in the owner of the dam."

What does not seem to have been appreciated is that in that passage BLACKSTONE
was dealing with property in possession absolute. He was dealing only with a
case where the owner had the possession, and it is not until a later stage (see
p. 396) that he deals with anything other than property in possession absolute.
So that where he is stating the rule about the progeny belonging to the owner **F**
of the dam, he is dealing only with the case where property and possession are
undivided.

When you come to a case like this, where there is a lease of livestock and where
accordingly property and possession are divided, the English rule and the rule in
the civil law is that the progeny and the produce of the livestock belong to the
person entitled to the possession; that is to say the lessee in English law; the **G**
usufructuary in civil law. The case of *Wood* v. *Ash and Foster* (5) makes that
clear in English law, and the extracts from JUSTINIAN, which are cited in
Morkel v. *Malan* (6), make it clear that in this respect, as in the earliest respect,
the common law and the civil law as to the ownership of the progeny of domestic
animals are the same.

I agree that this appeal should be allowed. **H**

Appeal allowed.

Solicitors: *Robbins, Olivey & Lake*, agents for *Gilbert H. Stephens & Sons*,
Exeter (for the plaintiff); *Foot & Bowden*, Plymouth (for the defendant finance
company).

[*Reported by* F. GUTTMAN, ESQ., *Barrister-at-Law.*] **I**

---

(5) (1586), Owen 139.   (6) (1933), C.P.D. 370.

A   DILCON, LTD. *v.* FEGMAY INVESTMENTS, LTD.

[Queen's Bench Division (Nield, J.), April 6, 1966.]

Arbitration—Costs—Security for costs—Claimants an insolvent company—
Application by respondents for security for costs—Jurisdiction of the court
to order security—Arbitration Act, 1950 (14 Geo. 6 c. 27), s. 12 (6) (a)—
B   *Companies Act, 1948 (11 & 12 Geo. 6 c. 38), s. 447—R.S.C., Ord. 23, r. 1,*
r. 3.

In an arbitration between claimant building contractors and respondent
building owners on a claim arising out of a building contract the claim was
for over £15,000 pursuant to an architect's certificate for building work done,
and for other relief; the defence was that the work had not been properly
C   done and that the certificate was not validly issued, and the respondents
counter-claimed for over £20,000 alleged to have been over-paid to the
claimants. The respondents sought an order for security for costs on the
ground that the claimants, who were a limited company, were insolvent.
There was affidavit evidence that the claimants had liabilities of £45,000
and that their principal asset was a book debt of £43,745, which was the
D   amount of their claim against the respondents, which the respondents
repudiated.

Held: (i) under s. 12 (6) (a)* of the Arbitration Act, 1950, and R.S.C.,
Ord. 23, r. 1† the court had discretion, if it thought it just so to do, to
order claimants to give security for respondents' costs in an arbitration,
and, where claimants were a limited company, the discretionary power
E   so conferred was extended, in view of r. 3† of Ord. 23, by s. 447‡ of the
Companies Act, 1948, to a case where it appeared by credible testimony (as it
did in the present case) that there was reason to believe that the claimant
company was insolvent (see p. 516, letter B, and p. 517, letters D and F, post).

(ii) in the circumstances of the present case it was just to order the
claimants to give security for the respondents' costs, and security in the
F   sum of £1,500 would be ordered (see p. 518, letter A, post).

[As to when security for costs may be ordered in the High Court, see 30
Halsbury's Laws (3rd Edn.) 378-380, para. 706; and for cases on the subject,
see Digest (Practice) 903-907, *4428-4479.*

As to the interlocutory powers of the High Court in relation to a reference to
arbitration, see 2 Halsbury's Laws (3rd Edn.) 38, para. 86.

G   As to security for costs being ordered when a limited company is plaintiff,
see 6 Halsbury's Laws (3rd Edn.) 451-453, para. 875; and for cases on the
subject, see 9 Digest (Repl.) 729-732, *4847-4864.*

For the Companies Act, 1948, s. 447, see 3 Halsbury's Statutes (2nd Edn.)
784.

For the Arbitration Act, 1950, s. 12, see 29 Halsbury's Statutes (2nd Edn.)
H   100.]

Cases referred to:

Cowell v. *Taylor,* (1885), 31 Ch.D. 34; 55 L.J.Ch. 92; 53 L.T. 483; 5 Digest
(Repl.) 1061, *8567.*

Dartmouth Harbour Comrs. v. *Dartmouth Hardness Corpn.,* (1886), 55 L.J.Q.B.
483; 13 Digest (Repl.) 349, *1574.*

I   *Hudson Strumpffabrik G.m.b.H.* v. *Bentley Engineering Co., Ltd.,* [1962] 3 All
E.R. 460; [1962] 2 Q.B. 587; [1962] 3 W.L.R. 758; Digest (Cont. Vol.
A) 45, *2423a.*

Shaw and Ronaldson, Re, [1892] 1 Q.B. 91; 61 L.J.Q.B. 114; 2 Digest (Repl.)
554, *891.*

---

* Section 12 (6) (a) is set out at p. 516, letter A, post.

† The material part of r. 1 of R.S.C., Ord. 23 is set out at p. 514, letter I, to p. 515,
letter C, post; r. 3 of the same order is set out at p. 515, letter G, post.

‡ Section 447 is set out at p. 517, letter E, post.

Interlocutory appeal.

A

This was an appeal to the judge in chambers from an order of Master RITCHIE, dated Jan. 27, 1966, dismissing an application made under s. 12 (6) (a) of the Arbitration Act, 1950, by Fegmay Investments, Ltd., the respondents in a reference to arbitration arising out of a building contract, that the claimants, Bilcon, Ltd., be ordered to give security for the respondents' costs on the ground that the claimants were insolvent. The facts are set out in the judgment of B NIELD, J., which was delivered in open court.

D. H. Gardam and *H. J. Lloyd* for Fegmay Investments, Ltd.

J. C. A. Burke-Gaffney for the claimants.

Cur. adv. vult.

Apr. 6. **NIELD, J.**, read the following judgment: This is an appeal by the C respondents in an arbitration from a decision of Master RITCHIE given on Jan. 27, 1966, ordering that the respondents' application that the claimants give security for the respondents' costs in the arbitration be dismissed. The respondents ask that the order of the master be rescinded and that the claimants be ordered to give security for costs on the ground that the claimants are insolvent.

The claim and counterclaim in the arbitration arise out of a building contract D dated May 4, 1962, by which the claimants, a limited company, agreed with the respondents, also a limited company, to carry out building work at Old Mill Lane, Bray in Berkshire. Before this agreement was reached the claimants had entered on a project for very substantial building development at Bray which entailed the demolition of an existing hotel and other buildings, and the building of a large number of flats and houses, the total capital outlay proposed E being in excess of £350,000. In the arbitration the points of claim delivered on Aug. 12, 1963, claimed a sum of over £15,000 on the architects' certificate of Feb. 27, 1963, and other relief. In their points of defence the respondents admitted the contract and the certificate of Feb. 27, 1963, but contended that the works had not been properly executed and that the certificate was not validly issued. The respondents also put forward a counterclaim saying that F they had over-paid the claimants to the extent of over £20,000, and claiming damages for defective work and for the claimants, as the respondents asserted, wrongly determining their employment. It should be observed further that the respondents are the plaintiffs in an action in the Queen's Bench Division against the architect and quantity surveyor employed in the building work at Bray, claiming damages for negligence.

Two issues arise in this appeal. The first is whether the court has jurisdiction G to make an order for security for costs. It seems to me, looking at the material notes in the ANNUAL PRACTICE, that it has been assumed that the court has such jurisdiction. There is no reported decision on the point, and I am told that only two decisions have been reached on it: the decision of Master RITCHIE in the present case that the court has no jurisdiction, and the decision of another master earlier that the court had such jurisdiction. I am able, therefore, to bring a H fresh mind to the problem. The second issue is whether, if it is decided that the court has jurisdiction, its discretion should be so exercised as to order security for costs, and, if so, in what sum.

I deal first with the question of the court's jurisdiction. The two special circumstances which together produce the problem in this regard are that the proceedings here are an arbitration under the Arbitration Act, 1950, and that I the claimants are a limited company with a special position under s. 447 of the Companies Act, 1948.

It is I think convenient now to look at the rules which govern the question of security for costs. They are to be found in R.S.C., Ord. 23, which was revised in 1962; and the first part of that order reads thus:

" 1. (1) Where, on the application of a defendant to an action or other proceeding in the High Court, it appears to the court—

A   (*a*) that the plaintiff is ordinarily resident out of the jurisdiction, or
(*b*) that the plaintiff (not being a plaintiff who is suing in a representative
capacity) is a nominal plaintiff who is suing for the benefit of some other
person and that there is reason to believe that he will be unable to pay
the costs of the defendant if ordered to do so, or (*c*) subject to para. (2),
that the plaintiff's address is not stated in the writ or other originating
B   process or is incorrectly stated therein, or (*d*) that the plaintiff has
changed his address during the course of the proceedings with a view
to evading the consequences of the litigation,
then if, having regard to all the circumstances of the case, the court thinks
it just to do so, it may order the plaintiff to give such security for the defendant's costs of the action or other proceeding as it thinks just."

C   In the ANNUAL PRACTICE, 1966, p. 505, there is a note headed " Insolvency or
poverty no ground for security ", and the case of *Cowell* v. *Taylor* (1) is cited,
the principle being thus stated:

" The insolvency or poverty of a plaintiff is no ground for requiring him
to give security for costs."

D   I was referred by counsel for the claimants to the case of *Dartmouth Harbour
Comrs.* v. *Dartmouth Hardness Corpn.* (2).   That was an appeal from an order
of the judge in chambers that the plaintiffs should give security for costs.   The
plaintiffs were harbour commissioners, and had agreed with the defendants
to execute certain works at a cost of not less than £10,000 nor more than £13,000,
the amount to be ascertained by arbitration on the completion of the works.
E   The works had been completed, and an award for £13,000 had been made in the
plaintiffs' favour, on which the present action was brought.   Owing to the
misadventure of a ship in their harbour, the plaintiffs were utterly without
funds, and their property, which consisted of harbour tolls worth some £1,900
a year, was in the hands of the receiver.   On these grounds the defendants
applied to a judge in chambers that the plaintiffs should give security for costs,
F   and obtained an order to that effect.   FIELD, J., gave a short judgment, and to
one or two passages of that judgment I think it right to refer.   He said (3):

" This appeal must be allowed.   From what we have had brought before
us to-day, it seems to me that there is no authority enabling us to order
the plaintiffs to give security for costs . . . The general rule is that any man,
however poor, is entitled to bring his action—and a very proper and reason-
G   able rule it is . . ."
Returning to R.S.C., Ord. 23, I read r. 3:

" This order is without prejudice to the provisions of any enactment
which empowers the court to require security to be given for the costs of any
proceedings."

H The note immediately below r. 3 is as follows (4):

" This order replaces the former R.S.C., Ord. 65, rr. 6, 6A, 6B and 7, and
embodies the previous case law dealing with the power of the court to order
security for costs.   It must be read subject to the powers of the court to
order security for costs conferred by any enactment ";

I   the Acts referred to by this rule are the County Courts Act, 1959, s. 46; the
Companies Act, 1948, s. 447; and the Arbitration Act, 1950, s. 12 (6) (*a*).   There
is a further note in the ANNUAL PRACTICE, 1966, p. 506, dealing with the position
of a plaintiff who is a limited company and quoting s. 447 of the Companies Act,
1948, with which I must deal a little later.   Further than that, at p. 508, a note
deals with arbitration proceedings.
It is necessary now to consider what the powers of the High Court are where

(1) (1885), 31 Ch.D. 34.   (2) (1886), 55 L.J.Q.B. 483.
(3) (1886), 55 L.J.Q.B. at p. 484.   (4) ANNUAL PRACTICE, 1966, at p. 501.

the proceedings are an arbitration. Such powers derive from s. 12 (6) of the **A**
Arbitration Act, 1950, and in the material parts that subsection reads:

" The High Court shall have, for the purpose of and in relation to a reference
the same power of making orders in respect of—(a) security for costs . . .
as it has for the purpose of and in relation to an action or matter in the
High Court."

It seems to me clear that this subsection specifically empowers the High Court   **B**
to exercise in relation to an arbitration those powers which the High Court already
has in relation to actions or other proceedings in the High Court to make an
order for security for costs, and such powers are set out in R.S.C., Ord. 23, r. 1.

I was referred in this connexion, although on a different point, to the judgment
of MOCATTA, J., in the case of *Hudson Strumpffabrik G.m.b.H.* v. *Bentley Engin-*   **C**
eering Co., Ltd. (5). I say that it was on a different point for the reason that the
case was dealing with a party outside the jurisdiction. The headnote (6) is
sufficient for the purpose of my judgment:

" Where claimants in a reference under an arbitration agreement are a
foreign corporation without assets within the jurisdiction, the court, in
considering an application by a respondent English company for an order   **D**
for security for costs, pursuant to s. 12 (6) (a) of the Arbitration Act, 1950,
will act on the same principle as it does when a defendant in an action
applies for security for costs against a plaintiff resident abroad without
assets which can be reached within the jurisdiction; on such an application
it has long been regarded as an inflexible rule of practice, under R.S.C.,
Ord. 65, r. 6, (7), that (apart from the particular exceptions created by   **E**
r. 6B), provided the defendant makes timeous application, the court will
exercise its discretion in favour of an order requiring the plaintiff to give
security for costs."

It was contended by counsel for the claimants that they were assisted by the
decision in the case of *Re Shaw and Ronaldson* (8). The headnote reads:

" Where parties agree to refer their disputes to arbitration, no action   **F**
having been brought in respect of those disputes, the court or a judge has no
power under R.S.C., Ord. 37, r. 5, to order the issue of a commission for the
examination of witnesses in the matter referred to arbitration."

MATHEW, J., in the course of his judgment said (9):

" I am of opinion that this appeal should be dismissed. COLLINS, J.,   **G**
at chambers was of opinion that he had no power to make an order for the
issue of a commission in this case, and I am clearly of opinion that he was
right. It was contended on behalf of Shaw that the power was given by
R.S.C., Ord. 37, r. 5, which provides that ' the court or a judge may, in any
cause or matter where it shall appear necessary for the purposes of justice ',
make an order for the examination upon oath of any witness or person   **H**
before the court or judge, or any officer of the court, or any other person,
and at any place. It is conceded that the proceeding in question here is
not a ' cause ', but it is contended that it is a ' matter ' within the meaning
of the rule. By the Supreme Court of Judicature Act, 1873, s. 100, ' matter '
shall include ' every proceeding in the court not in a cause '. Is this arbitration a ' proceeding in the court ' within the meaning of that section? It is   **I**
most clearly a proceeding not in the court. The very purpose of the submission to arbitration is to take the matter away from the jurisdiction of the
court."

At the end of his judgment MATHEW, J., said (10):

---

(5) [1962] 3 All E.R. 460; [1962] 2 Q.B. 587.   (6) [1962] 3 All E.R. 460.
(7) Now re-enacted in different form in R.S.C., Ord. 23.
(8) [1892] 1 Q.B. 91.   (9) [1892] 1 Q.B. at pp. 92, 93.
          (10) [1892] 1 Q.B. at p. 93.

A   " I am of opinion that this clearly was not a ' matter ' within R.S.C., Ord. 37, r. 5, and s. 100 of the Supreme Court of Judicature Act, 1873, and the judge at chambers had, therefore, no power to order the issue of a commission in it."

COLLINS, J., who had sat in chambers and then sat on the Divisional Court, agreed (11) with MATHEW, J.

B   I have reached the conclusion that this decision does not affect the present case. The obstacle in the way of the court in *Shaw's* case (12) ordering evidence to be taken on commission, was removed by s. 12 (6) (*d*) of the Arbitration Act, 1950, and another enactment to which I have not so far referred. That part of s. 12 (6) which is material on the point there decided reads thus:

C   " The High Court shall have, for the purpose of and in relation to a reference, the same power of making orders in respect of—. . . (*d*) examination on oath of any witness before an officer of the High Court or any other person, and the issue of a commission or request for the examination of a witness out of the jurisdiction, . . . as it has for the purpose of and in relation to an action or matter in the High Court."

D   Thus and so far I find that the High Court has power to order security for costs in relation to an arbitration, such power being that contained in R.S.C., Ord. 23, r. 1. It follows from what I have said, however, that if the matter ended there, the court would not make such an order, since the ground for asking for it is that the respondents are insolvent.

Thus I turn to consider s. 447 of the Companies Act, 1948, and that section

E   reads:

    " Where a limited company is plaintiff or pursuer in any action or other legal proceeding, any judge having jurisdiction in the matter may, if it appears by credible testimony that there is reason to believe that the company will be unable to pay the costs of the defendant if successful in his defence, require sufficient security to be given for those costs, and may stay all

F   proceedings until the security is given."

In my opinion the effect of this section is that since a judge of the High Court may by virtue of s. 12 (6) (*a*) of the Arbitration Act, 1950, order security for costs in an arbitration, he is empowered by s. 447 of the Companies Act, 1948, to go outside the conditions laid down by R.S.C., Ord. 23, r. 1, and exercise his

G   discretion to make an order in the circumstances set forth in s. 447, namely, where a limited company is insolvent.

Having decided on the first issue that the court has jurisdiction to make an order for security, I come to the second issue, whether it is right for the court in the exercise of its discretion to do so.

The initial question is whether it appears, in the words of s. 447, " by credible

H   testimony that there is reason to believe that the company will be unable to pay the costs of the " respondents if successful in their defence. The gist of the evidence, which I regard as credible, is contained in para. 3, sub-para. (4) of the affidavit of Mr. Jonas Lyons. That sub-paragraph reads:

    " On or about Apr. 22, 1963, there was a meeting of the creditors of Bilcon, Ltd., at the offices of Messrs. Bernard Phillips and Co., Accountants,

I   at 76, New Cavendish Street, W.1. This followed very shortly after the removal of the said company from its former building activities at the site at Bray, and according to the said accountants the company's liabilities amounted to approximately £45,000 and its principal asset as appears from the accountants' report was a book debt of £43,745 and which was the amount of its claim against the respondent company and which the respondent company repudiated."

---

(11) [1892] 1 Q.B. at p. 93.   (12) [1892] 1 Q.B. 91.

I conclude in all these circumstances that it is " just "—and I use the word **A** appearing in R.S.C., Ord. 23, r. 1—to order that the claimants give security for the respondents' costs; and, having heard argument on the question of amount, I further consider it just that such security should be in the sum of £1,500. The appeal, therefore, is allowed and the order which I have indicated must be substituted for that of the master.

Appeal allowed. **B**

Solicitors: *Gershon, Young & Co.* (for the claimants); *Tarlo, Lyons & Aukin* (for the respondents).

[*Reported by* K. DIANA PHILLIPS, *Barrister-at-Law.*]

C

_____

WRIGHT v. FORD MOTOR CO., LTD.

[QUEEN'S BENCH DIVISION (Lord Parker, C.J., Marshall and James, JJ.), April 28, 1966.]

Factory—Dangerous machinery—Duty to fence—Interference with fence by un- **D** *known employee—Thrust stop in transfer machine forming part of moving platform and fixed structure in juxtaposition—Machine securely fenced except for control panel which controlled by key which opened gate admitting persons to machine — Unknown employee forced lock in gate —Another employee injured by machine—Whether occupiers of factory liable—Factories Act, 1961 (9 & 10 Eliz. 2 c. 34), s. 14 (1), s. 143 (1), s. 155 (1), (2).* **E**

Factory—Offence—Employee's contravention of Factories Act, 1961, by interference with fence of machine—Another employee injured by reason of contravention— Not shown that occupier of factory had failed to take all reasonable steps to prevent contravention—Whether occupier liable—Factories Act, 1961 (9 & 10 Eliz. 2 c. 34), s. 14 (1), s. 143 (1), s. 155 (1), (2).

In a factory of which the respondents were the occupiers there was a **F** large transfer machine which contained a dangerous part, namely, a thrust stop forming part of a moving platform and a fixed structure which in juxtaposition created a dangerous nip. Except for the control panel, the machine was completely fenced in with a fence four feet high with a gate in it. The key which opened the gate was the key which controlled the power in the panel and could not be taken out of the panel for use in the gate **G** without turning off the power. R., an employee of the respondents, finding the gate open, passed through it and went on to the machine. While he was on the machine, the machinery moved and his foot was caught in the danger-ous nip. In fact, the gate was open because an unknown employee of the respondents had forced the lock on the gate and, when R. gained access to the machine, the key was in the control panel and the power was not cut off **H** from the machine. An information against the respondents for contravention of s. 14 (1)* of the Factories Act, 1961, was dismissed by the justices, who were of the opinion that, although s. 14 (1) constituted an absolute offence, the respondents had a defence by reason of the combined effect of s. 143 (1)† of the Act, which put an obligation on employees, and s. 155 (2)‡ which excused from liability an occupier of factory premises who had taken all **I** reasonable steps to prevent the contravention of, inter alia, s. 143 (1). It was not shown that the respondents had failed to take all reasonable steps

_____

* Section 14 (1) provides: " Every dangerous part of any machinery, other than prime movers and transmission machinery, shall be securely fenced unless it is in such a position or of such construction as to be as safe to every person employed or working on the premises as it would be if securely fenced."

† Section 143 (1), so far as material, is set out at p. 520, letter H, post.

‡ Section 155 (2), so far as material, is set out at p. 521, letters A and B, post.

A   to prevent the contravention of s. 143 (1) by the unknown employee. On appeal,

Held: the prosecution not having shown that the respondents had failed to take reasonable steps to prevent the contravention, the information had been rightly dismissed because—

(i) on the true construction of s. 155 (1)* of the Factories Act, 1961, an

B   employer was not thereby made liable, as occupier of a factory, in respect of contravention of provisions of the Act of 1961 for the performance of which the sole obligation was imposed on his employee, and s. 143 (1) of the Act of 1961, was one such provision (see p. 521, letter I, and p. 522, letter F, post); and

(ii) even if the occupier were liable under s. 155 (1) in respect of an

C   employee's contravention of s. 143 (1), yet the words " an offence " in s. 155 (2) were perfectly general and would exempt the occupier not only from liability in respect of the s. 143 (1) offence but also from liability in respect of, e.g., any s. 14 (1) offence (see p. 522, letters B and F, post).

[As to general liability of occupiers of factory premises, see 17 HALSBURY'S LAWS (3rd Edn.) 59, 60, para. 103; and for cases on the subject, see 24 DIGEST

D   (Repl.) 1043, *150, 151,* 1093, *430.*

For the Factories Act, 1961, s. 14, s. 143, s. 155, see 41 HALSBURY'S STATUTES (2nd Edn.) 256, 380, 389.]

Case referred to:

Carr v. Decca Gramophone Co., Ltd., [1947] 2 All E.R. 20; [1947] K.B. 728;

E   [1948] L.J.R. 81; 177 L.T. 402; 111 J.P. 352; 24 Digest (Repl.) 1093, *430.*

Case Stated.

This was a Case Stated by justices for the North East London Commission Area in respect of their adjudication as a magistrates' court sitting at Barking on Oct. 19, 1965. On Sept. 20, 1965, the appellant, William George Wright,

F   one of Her Majesty's inspectors of factories, preferred an information against the respondents, The Ford Motor Co., Ltd., charging that, on Apr. 26, 1965, at Kent Avenue in the London Borough of Barking, being the occupiers of a certain factory within the meaning of the Factories Act, 1961, they contravened the provisions of s. 14 (1) of the Act in that a certain dangerous part of machinery in the factory, to wit, a thrust stop forming part of a moving platform on which

G   one Thomas Edward Reilly was working and a fixed structure of a " Heller " transfer line was not securely fenced, whereby the respondents were guilty of an offence under s. 155 (1) of the Act. The following facts were found. On Apr. 26, 1965, the respondents were, within the meaning of the Factories Act, 1961, occupiers of a factory at Kent Avenue in the London Borough of Barking. At that factory there was a large piece of machinery called a " Heller" transfer machine,

H   which contained a dangerous part, namely, a thrust stop forming part of a moving platform and a fixed structure which in juxtaposition created a dangerous nip. The machine, but for its control panel, was enclosed within a fence four feet high. A gate in the fence gave access to the machine. The gate could be locked by means of a key which was common to, and used in conjunction with, the control panel of the machine; that is to say, the key was kept in the control panel from

I   which it could not be removed unless the power to the machine was cut off, and, if the lock on the gate was in working order, once the key had opened the gate it could not be removed from the lock until the gate had been locked shut. Thus, if the lock was in working order the machine could not be made to function unless the gate were locked. Anyone who had no reason to suppose that the lock was not in working order could reasonably assume that the power to the machine was cut off if the gate was open. On Apr. 26, 1965, Thomas Edward Reilly, an

---

* Section 155 (1), so far as material, is set out at p. 521, letter G, post.

employee of the respondents, found the gate open, assumed that the power of the   A
machine was cut off, passed through the gate and went on to the machine. While
he was on the machine, the machinery moved and his foot was caught in the
dangerous nip between the thrust stop and the fixed structure. In fact, the gate
was open because some person who must have been an employee of the respondents had forced the lock and, when Reilly passed through the fence by means
of the gate and gained access to the machine, the key was in the control panel   B
and power was not cut off from the machine. It was extremely difficult to devise
a lock which was unbreakable. The respondents employed a safety engineer
and safety inspectors whose task was to look after the safety of the respondents'
employees. The machine was inspected every two or three days and, in addition
the supervisory staff were instructed to report any defects or damage which
they observed in the machine. In ordinary use, no one would need to enter the   C
machine and the gate would only need to be opened when maintenance work was
to be carried out on the machine. The respondents were unaware before the
accident to Reilly that the lock on the gate had been forced.

It was contended on behalf of the appellant that s. 14 (1) of the Act of 1961
imposed an absolute obligation on the occupier of a factory to keep every dangerous part of any machinery securely fenced and that, on the facts, the respondents   D
had contravened the provisions of that section and that they were accordingly
guilty of an offence under s. 155 (1) of the Act. It was contended on behalf of
the respondents that the contravention of the provisions of s. 14 (1) of the Act
of 1961 requiring every dangerous part of any machinery to be securely fenced
occurred because a person employed in the factory had wilfully interfered with
the lock of the gate in contravention of s. 143 (1) of the Act, that it had not been   E
proved that the respondents had failed to take all reasonable steps to prevent the
contravention of s. 143 (1) and that, accordingly, by virtue of the provisions of
s. 155 (2) of the Act, the respondents were not guilty of any offence. The respondents also relied on the appellant's concession, which he made in his evidence
before the justices, that, had it been possible to identify the person responsible
for forcing the lock on the gate, he would have prosecuted that person.   F

The justices dismissed the information, and the appellant now appealed.

The authority and case noted below* were cited during the argument in
addition to the case referred to in the judgments.

P. E. Webster for the appellant.
P. Bennett for the respondents.   G

LORD PARKER, C.J., having stated the facts, continued: The justices
came to the conclusion that, although s. 14 (1) of the Factories Act, 1961, constitutes, as is well-known, an absolute offence, yet the respondents did have a
defence by reason of the combined effect of s. 143 (1), which puts an obligation
on employees, and s. 155 (2) dealing with offences under the Act of 1961. Turning
to the Act itself, it is quite unnecessary to read s. 14 (1), but s. 143 (1), which   H
appears in Part 10 of the Act, specifically puts a duty on persons employed, and
it says, so far as is material here:

" No person employed in a factory or in any other place to which any
provisions of this Act apply shall wilfully interfere with or misuse any means,
appliance, convenience or other thing provided in pursuance of this Act for   I
securing the health, safety or welfare of the persons employed in the
factory . . ."

There is no doubt, pausing there, as the justices find, that X, the unknown man,
clearly contravened s. 143 (1). One then turns to s. 155 creating offences. Subsection (2), so far as it is material, provides:

---

* REDGRAVE'S FACTORIES ACTS (20th Edn.) 1962, pp. 361-364, 377-379; *Ginty* v.
Belmont Building Supplies, Ltd., [1959] 1 All E.R. 414.

A   " In the event of a contravention by an employed person of the provisions
of Part 10 of this Act with respect to duties of persons employed . . . [pausing
there, that is saying that, in the event of contravention of s. 143 (1), by Mr.
X, he] shall be guilty of an offence . . ."

The subsection then goes on to provide that the occupier

B   ". . . shall not be guilty of an offence, by reason only of the contravention
of the said provisions of Part 10 of this Act . . . unless it is proved that he
failed to take all reasonable steps to prevent the contravention; but this
subsection shall not be taken as affecting any liability of the occupier or
owner in respect of the same matters by virtue of some provision other
than the provisions or provision aforesaid."

C   The point at issue that arises in this case is what is the offence referred to
when it is said that the occupier shall not be guilty of an offence by reason
only of the employee's contravention. I confess that, when I read this at first, I
thought that the appeal here was really quite hopeless; commonsense seemed
to demand that this was giving the respondents a defence, and was in effect
saying: if the absence of the guard, in this case caused by the unlocking of the
D   gate and, therefore, the offence of the occupier, occurred solely by reason of
Mr. X's contravention of s. 143 (1), then the respondents were not guilty of an
offence against s. 14 (1) unless it was shown by the prosecution that they had
failed to take all reasonable steps to prevent the employee's contravention. In
other words, the offence there of which the employer is not to be guilty is, to
take the present case, the absolute liability under s. 14 (1). The argument which
E   counsel for the appellant has raised in this appeal—a novel argument I confess to
me, but others have greater experience—is that that is a wrong construction,
and that the offence referred to, of which the employer is not guilty, is, to take this
case, not the offence for which he was prosecuted, a breach of s. 14 (1), but is,
it is said, an offence which he, apart from these words, commits whenever a
servant of his wilfully interferes with an appliance, contrary to s. 143 (1). In
F   other words, the conception here is one which is not only novel in practice, but
novel in terms of an employer being criminally vicariously liable for an employee
in regard to an offence for which the employee, on the face of s. 143 (1), is alone
made liable; in other words, it is surprising if the construction which the
magistrates put on this is not right.

Counsel for the appellant's argument is really based entirely on the meaning
G   of s. 155 (1). I think that he would agree that, if his construction of s. 155 (1)
is wrong, his argument on sub-s. (2) fails. Subsection (1) is in these terms:

" In the event of any contravention in or in connexion with or in relation
to a factory of the provisions of this Act . . . the occupier, or (if the contravention is one in respect of which the owner is by or under this Act made responsible), the owner, of the factory shall, subject to the following provisions of
H   this Part of this Act, be guilty of an offence."

Counsel says, what is quite true, that this is prima facie referring to any contravention under the Act, and he would say any contravention by whomsoever
committed, and that, under these wide words, the employer is liable for the offence
committed by the employee. To take the present case, he says that, when one
I   applies sub-s. (1), prima facie the respondents here are guilty of two offences,
one offence against s. 14 (1) and, secondly, an offence against s. 143 (1), although,
as I have said, the obligations or the duties imposed under s. 143 (1) are entirely
those of the servant. For my part, I agree that those are very wide words, but I
feel constrained in the circumstances of the case to interpret them in a way which
will only make the employer liable for all contraventions under the Act other
than those in respect of which the sole obligation to perform is imposed on the
employee. To give it the other meaning seems to me to outrage one's sense of the
criminal law in regard to vicarious liability of a master for crimes of his servant.

If that construction is right, then counsel for the appellant, I think, would agree   A
that, when one gets to s. 155 (2), there is no ground for reading an offence of which
the employer is not to be guilty as an offence other than the offence charged under
s. 14 (1). For my part, I also see a further difficulty in counsel for the appellant's
way, because, even accepting his argument under s. 155 (1), I see no reason for
reading the words " an offence " in sub-s. (2) of s. 155 as meaning that offence,
but rather that the words mean any offence; therefore, even if it is necessary to   B
exempt the employer from a s. 143 (1) offence on the basis that he has been made
liable under s. 155 (1), yet when one reaches s. 155 (2), the words " an offence "
in sub-s. (2) are perfectly general and are capable of meaning not merely the
s. 143 (1) offence but also the s. 14 (1) offence. That being the view which I take
of this, and the prosecution having failed to show that the respondents failed
to take reasonable steps to prevent contravention by Mr. X, I would uphold   C
these magistrates' opinion and dismiss the appeal.

I would only add this, and I find it unnecessary to go through it in any detail,
that there is no doubt that sometime ago now, in 1947, there was a decision of
the Court of Appeal in *Carr* v. *Decca Gramophone Co., Ltd.* (1), which, in the
result, took much the same view that I have taken today, but on a different set
of words. It is also right to say that the undoubted inference is that, as a result   D
of that decision, the Act then in force (2) was amended, and was amended in a
way that is now reflected in s. 155 (2) of the Act of 1961. It may be, to put it
loosely, that Parliament's intention was as counsel for the appellant has interpreted the section in his argument; but what this court is concerned with is
the intention of Parliament as evinced by the words used. In my judgment,
whatever their motive was, they have failed to use words to express an intention   E
which would lead to this appeal being allowed. Accordingly, I would dismiss
this appeal.

MARSHALL, J.: I agree and for the same reasons, and I do so the more
gladly because the interpretation of the relevant section which LORD PARKER,
C.J., has indicated, and with which I agree, is reinforced by the claims of good   F
sense and of justice.

JAMES, J.: I also agree.

*Appeal dismissed. Leave to appeal to the House of Lords refused, but the court
certified under s. 1 of the Administration of Justice Act, 1960, that a point of law of
general public importance was involved, viz., as to the true meaning of the words*
" an offence " in s. 155 (1) of the Factories Act, 1961, (3).   G

Solicitors: *Solicitor, Ministry of Labour* (for the appellant); *A. E. Wyeth & Co.*
(for the respondents).

[*Reported by* N. P. METCALFE, ESQ., *Barrister-at-Law.*]

H

I

---

(1) [1947] 2 All E.R. 20; [1947] K.B. 728.
(2) The Factories Act, 1937; see s. 130 (2) thereof, as amended by s. 10 (1) of the
Factories Act, 1948, 9 HALSBURY'S STATUTES (2nd Edn.) 1104.
(3) On May 25, 1966, leave to appeal was refused by the Appeal Committee of the
House of Lords.

A   LEACH v. STANDARD TELEPHONES & CABLES, LTD.

[QUEEN'S BENCH DIVISION (Browne, J.), March 23, 24, 25, 28, April 20, 1966.]

*Factory—Dangerous machinery—Duty to fence—Contributory negligence—
Plaintiff cutting metal on a machine that he was not authorised to use for that
purpose—Guard not properly adjusted and, even if correctly adjusted, leaving*
B   *gap as metal passed through—Plaintiff injured—Whether faults by plaintiff
and his employers coterminous and co-extensive—Factories Act, 1961 (9 & 10
Eliz. 2 c. 34), s. 14 (1), s. 16.*

The plaintiff, who was employed by the defendants as a Universal miller,
was instructed to do the work specified in a lay-out. This stated that the
work of cutting metal should be done on the plaintiff's Universal milling
C   machine. The plaintiff did the work on a Danckaerts saw. He had not
previously used the saw for cutting metal. The plaintiff was not authorised
to use the saw for cutting metal, and he knew that he had no business to do
so. He was also incompetent to work the saw for that purpose. The fence
of the saw was not adjusted close enough to the metal being cut while the
plaintiff was working on it, there being a gap of about 1½ inches between the
D   top of the metal being cut and the guard on the saw. Even if the guard had
been properly adjusted, it would not have afforded complete protection as
there would have been a gap below the guard through which a finger or
thumb could pass when the material being cut passed through the gap and
off the machine. In the course of cutting metal by the saw the plaintiff's
thumb was cut at a time when he was operating the machine incorrectly.
E   The risk of accident had been greatly increased by the plaintiff's failure to
adjust the guard close to the material being cut.

Held: (i) the defendants were in breach of their statutory duty under
the Factories Act, 1961, s. 14 and s. 16* in that (a) they had not kept the saw
securely fenced nor the fence in position, though it had been also the duty
of the plaintiff to keep the fence in position, and also in that (b) the saw was
F   not securely fenced when there was no material under the guard; the fault
of the defendants went beyond the fault of the plaintiff, and accordingly
the breach of statutory duty was not solely the plaintiff's, nor was the
accident entirely caused by his own fault (see p. 529, letter I, to p. 530,
letter A, and p. 530, letters E and I, post).

Ross v. *Associated Portland Cement Manufacturers, Ltd.* ([1964] 2 All E.R.
G   452) and *Stapley* v. *Gypsum Mines, Ltd.* ([1953] 2 All E.R. 478) applied.

Ginty v. *Belmont Building Supplies, Ltd.* ([1959] 1 All E.R. 414)
distinguished.

(ii) the blame for the accident should be apportioned and in the circumstances the plaintiff's share in the responsibility for the damage was three-
quarters (see p. 531, letter E, post).

H   [As to the duty to fence machinery, see 17 HALSBURY's LAWS (3rd Edn.) 70,
71, para. 122; and for cases on the effect of contributory negligence by an
employee in relation to the duty to fence dangerous machinery, see 24 DIGEST
(Repl.) 1057, 225, et seq.

For the Factories Act, 1961, s. 14 and s. 16, see 41 HALSBURY's STATUTES
(2nd Edn.) 256, 259.]

I   Cases referred to:

Allen v. *Aeroplane and Motor Aluminium Castings, Ltd.*, [1965] 3 All E.R. 377;
[1965] 1 W.L.R. 1244.

Ginty v. *Belmont Building Supplies, Ltd.*, [1959] 1 All E.R. 414; Digest (Cont.
Vol. A) 597, *333a*.

Grant v. *Sun Shipping Co., Ltd.*, [1948] 2 All E.R. 238; [1948] A.C. 549;
[1949] L.J.R. 727; 24 Digest (Repl.) 1082, *371*.

---

* Section 14 (1) and s. 16, so far as material, are set out at p. 527, letter B, post

Horne v. *Lec Refrigeration, Ltd.*, [1965] 2 All E.R. 898.   A
McMath v. *Rimmer Brothers (Liverpool), Ltd.*, [1961] 3 All E.R. 1154; [1962]
    1 W.L.R. 1; Digest (Cont. Vol. A) 598, *337a.*
Manwaring v. *Billington*, [1952] 2 All E.R. 747; 24 Digest (Repl.) 1077, *335.*
Ross v. *Associated Portland Cement Manufacturers, Ltd.*, [1964] 2 All E.R. 452;
    [1964] 1 W.L.R. 768; 3rd Digest Supp.
Rushton v. *Turner Brothers Asbestos Co., Ltd.*, [1959] 3 All E.R. 517; [1960]   B
    1 W.L.R. 96; Digest (Cont. Vol. A) 588, *231a.*
Smith v. *Morris Motors, Ltd. and Harris*, [1949] 2 All E.R. 715; [1950] 1 K.B.
    194; 113 J.P. 521; 24 Digest (Repl.) 1052, *201.*
Stapley v. *Gypsum Mines, Ltd.*, [1953] 2 All E.R. 478; [1953] A.C. 663; [1953]
    3 W.L.R. 279; Digest (Cont. Vol. A) 1147, *157.*
Uddin v. *Associated Portland Cement Manufacturers, Ltd.*, [1965] 1 All E.R.   C
    347; [1965] 2 Q.B. 15; [1965] 2 W.L.R. 327; *affd.* C.A., [1965] 2 All
    E.R. 213; [1965] 2 Q.B. 582; [1965] 2 W.L.R. 1183.

Action.

This was an action for damages for personal injuries brought on the grounds
of alleged negligence and breach of statutory duty under s. 14 (1) and s. 16 of
the Factories Act, 1961. The facts are set out in the judgment.   D

P. R. Pain, Q.C., for the plaintiff.
R. I. Kidwell for the defendants.

Cur. adv. vult.

Apr. 20.   **BROWNE, J.**, read the following judgment: In this case the
plaintiff, Mr. Charles Leach, sues his employers, Standard Telephones & Cables,   E
Ltd., for damages for personal injuries which he sustained on May 6, 1963,
when he was working for them at their factory at New Southgate. On that day,
the plaintiff cut off the top joint of his left thumb while trying to cut a bar of
aluminium lengthwise on a circular saw.
The plaintiff has been employed by the defendants for twenty-five years, and
at the time of the accident he was employed as a miller working on a Universal   F
milling machine. Besides the plaintiff himself, I heard five witnesses who, at
and before the time of the accident, were working in the same part of the defendants' factory as the plaintiff. Mr. Bluffield, who was called on behalf of the
plaintiff, has been employed by the defendants for thirty years, and at the
relevant times was employed as a Universal miller in the same shop as the
plaintiff. The witnesses called on behalf of the defendants, and their positions   G
in the defendants' service at the time of the accident, were Mr. Brim, the foreman
of the machine shop, which included the milling section and other sections;
Mr. Favell, the assistant foreman of this machine shop; Mr. Seach, the charge-
hand of the milling and drilling section; and Mr. Elkington, a setter in the
milling section who acted as charge-hand when Mr. Seach was away.
The milling shop contained sixteen Universal milling machines, and was   H
about forty feet by thirty feet in size. At one end of the shop was a partitioned-
off area about sixteen feet by forty feet, divided from the milling machines by
a partition which at the time of the accident ran continuously up to the ceiling,
and was made of metal for the first two or three feet from the floor and above
that of glass. In this partitioned-off space were several machines of various
kinds, including the saw on which this accident happened, but not any Universal   I
milling machines. Somewhere at the far end of the milling shop was a band
saw, and in or about the shop were one or two small portable power saws.
The circular saw on which the accident happened is known as a Danckaerts saw.
It had been installed about nine months or a year before the accident. It was
primarily intended to cut soft material, which was generally described in the
evidence as fibrous material, and of which two examples were put in evidence
as exhibits. This material was used for what are called packing pieces, which
were used for holding steady in the various machines the metal on which work

A   was being done in the factory.   When the saw was first installed it was fitted
with a seven inch diameter blade, which was made an exhibit and which was
only suitable for cutting fibrous materials and would not cut metal.   This blade
was fitted to the saw during practically all working hours up to the accident.
The seven inch blade was ample for normal work on fibrous materials, but it was
decided to purchase another blade for cutting thick fibrous material and accord-
B   ingly a larger Winet-tip saw was bought.   This was the blade which was operating
at the time of the accident, and it was made an exhibit in the case.   Mr. Brim
said that when the defendants bought the Winet-tip saw it was stated in the
catalogue that it would cut aluminium without any difficulty whatsoever, and
Mr. Brim started to experiment with the cutting of aluminium with that blade.
There had, however, been no production cutting on this saw of anything except
C   fibre before the accident.   At about ten o'clock on the morning of the accident
Mr. Brim had been on this saw experimenting with the cutting of metal in the
form of what are called extrusions.   At about three o'clock that afternoon
Mr. Elkington was using the saw (with the authority of Mr. Brim, as will appear
later) for the purpose of cutting lengths off an aluminium bar, and for the
purpose of this work he set the guard about 1/16th of an inch to 3/32nds of an
D   inch above the material on which he was working.   The accident took place
at 3.55 p.m., and the two photographs of the machine, which are exhibited, were
taken about half an hour after the accident.   The guard over the saw-blade,
which can be seen in the photographs, was found to be $1\frac{7}{8}$th of an inch above
the table.   Mr. Elkington said that the guard as shown in the photographs was
approximately in the position in which it was when he was working, the plaintiff
E   said that he did not touch the guard before he started working, although he was
familiar with guards on his own machine, and Mr. Brim said that the position
of the guard was not changed after the accident.   I am satisfied that at the
time of the accident the guard was in the position shown in the photographs.
On May 6 the plaintiff had received instructions from Mr. Elkington to do
the work set out in what is known as a master process lay-out dated May 2, 1963.
F   That document was accompanied by a drawing which has now, I was told, been
destroyed, but according to the evidence the material to which the instructions
related was thirteen bars of aluminium, each twenty inches long by two inches
wide by three-eighths of an inch thick.   The work which the plaintiff was to do
was that described as operation 2 in the lay-out,

G   " Slit from end to end along the two inch width (equals two piece parts)
and mill complete to drawing including two rebates."

The first part of the operation was therefore to slit each piece of aluminium
lengthwise so as to produce twenty-six pieces from the thirteen, and this is the
explanation of the phrase " twenty-six off " which appears at the top of the
document.   In the column of the lay-out headed Machine & Machine Group
H   appears the figure 106, and it was not disputed that this figure designates the
Universal milling machines.   The piece-work rate applicable to this job also
appears on the lay-out as four hundred pence.   On the document are stamped
the words " Urgent action change ", and the plaintiff said that Mr. Elkington
orally instructed him to do this job first as it was urgent.
The plaintiff agreed that as the master process lay-out specified machine
I   group 106, which was the number of his own milling machine group, it " asked "
(as he put it) for a milling machine, but he said " You sometimes take no notice
and do it the best way you can ".   He said that " When you do a job you take
right over and do it the best and quickest way you can ", and finally that " You
use your own savvy—you look for a quicker and easier way ".   He said that he
decided not to split the aluminium bars by means of his milling machine but to
use the Danckaerts saw instead, because he thought it was the easiest and
quickest way.   I do not propose to go into the details of the plaintiff's piece-
work method of payment, but the plaintiff said that it would have taken $3\frac{1}{4}$ hours

to do the splitting on his own machine, half an hour if he had done it on the A band saw and about ten minutes on the Danckaerts saw if all had gone well. There was therefore a very obvious financial advantage to the plaintiff in using this saw instead of his own machine.

The plaintiff said that it was not his intention at first to use the Danckaerts saw. He had wanted to use the band saw, but it was in use, so he used the circular saw. He was not very familiar with this saw and this was the first time B he had ever used it to cut metal, although he had used it before to cut fibrous material; he made no adjustment to the guard before he started using it in spite of his knowledge of guards on his own machine. [HIS LORDSHIP then reviewed the plaintiff's evidence as to the way in which he was operating the saw, that he was pushing the work through with the right hand, that he did not use a push stick, that after he had split nine pieces of aluminium the next was C jamming and vibrating, and that the plaintiff according to his evidence " just pushed through with my right and left hand and took my thumb off when it vibrated ". The plaintiff had said that he had never used the saw for metal before the day of the accident, and admitted that he knew very little about the machine, and HIS LORDSHIP found that the plaintiff was quite incompetent to work it for cutting metal. HIS LORDSHIP then turned to the evidence concerning D authorisation to use the saw and of the general practice in the factory regarding the use of machines. The saw had previously been used almost always for cutting fibrous material and its use for metal had been only experimental shortly before the time of the accident, when a new and larger blade had been bought and had been fitted to the machine, but this blade was intended for use in cutting fibrous material. HIS LORDSHIP referred to Mr. Brim as an impressive witness, E whose evidence he accepted. In the course of his evidence Mr. Brim testified that if the group figure " 106 " appeared on a lay-out then the workman was expected to use a machine designated by that number, in this instance a Universal milling machine. HIS LORDSHIP continued:] My findings on this part of the case are as follows:—(i) The defendants did not know at the time of the accident that any miller (except Mr. Elkington and possibly one other) had used the F Danckaerts saw for cutting metal, and there is no evidence that any other miller had in fact so used it before the accident. (ii) The defendants ought not reasonably to have foreseen that any other miller (including the plaintiff) would or might use the Danckaerts saw for cutting metal. (iii) I am not satisfied that the plaintiff had been expressly forbidden to use the Danckaerts saw for cutting metal, but I am satisfied that he knew he had no business to use the saw for that G purpose. In my judgment, the truth of this matter is summarised by the conversation which Mr. Brim said that he had with the plaintiff during the latter's convalescence, and as to which I accept Mr. Brim's evidence. According to Mr. Brim, he said to the plaintiff, " You was a bloody fool, Charlie ", and the plaintiff replied " Yes, I know I had no right to be on there ".

As PEARSON, J., said in *Ginty* v. *Belmont Building Supplies, Ltd.* (1), to which H I shall have to refer later, " What is the upshot of all that? ". The plaintiff puts his claim both on breach of statutory duty under the Factories Act, 1961, and on negligence at common law. His claim at common law is pleaded in para. 3 (b) and (c) of the statement of claim and the further and better particulars thereunder. Counsel for the plaintiff did not in his final speech formally abandon this claim, but he said that he did not propose to address me about it separately. I think I that it is enough to say that on my findings of fact this claim must in my judgment clearly fail.

The plaintiff's claim for breach of statutory duty is stated as follows in para. 3 (a) of the statement of claim:

" The defendants, their servants or agents, negligently and/or in breach of s. 14 and/or s. 16 of the Factories Act, 1961, failed securely to fence the

(1) [1959] 1 All E.R. 414 at p. 423.

A   teeth of the saw-blade, being dangerous parts of machinery, with fencing of substantial construction and/or constantly to maintain the same and/or keep the same in position when the said saw was in motion or in use."

The relevant provisions of s. 14 (1) and s. 16 of the Factories Act, 1961, are as follows:

B   " 14—(1) Every dangerous part of any machinery . . . shall be securely fenced unless it is in such a position or of such construction as to be as safe to every person employed or working on the premises as it would be if securely fenced.

" 16. All fencing or other safeguards provided in pursuance of the foregoing provisions of this Part of this Act shall be of substantial construction, and constantly maintained and kept in position while the parts required to be fenced or safeguarded are in motion or use . . ."

C

subject to an exception which is not here material.

The first question is whether this circular saw-blade, which revolved at about seven to eight hundred revolutions per minute, was a dangerous part of any machinery. It is enough to say that it quite obviously was.

D   The part being dangerous, the next question is whether there was a breach by the defendants of their obligations under s. 14 (1) and s. 16 to fence. It is common ground that s. 14 (1) and s. 16 must be read together, and that a breach of duty, or an offence in failing to fence, only arises when the part required to be fenced " is in motion or use ". It is also common ground—(i) that the material time at which one must ascertain whether or not the part is securely fenced is

E   the moment of the accident, and (ii) that if a machine is dangerous because a workman has failed to adjust a guard which would make the machine safe if properly adjusted there is a breach of the statutory duty by the employer (see on both points *Smith* v. *Morris Motors, Ltd. and Harris* (2)). In the present case it is in my judgment clear that this saw-blade was not securely fenced at the moment of the plaintiff's accident and that the fencing was not then kept

F   in position. The guard was 1⅞ths of an inch above the table and the material on which the plaintiff was working was only ⅜ths of an inch thick, so that there was a gap of 1½ inches between the top of the material and the guard even when the material was in position. When the cut was finished the gap was, of course, the whole 1⅞ths of an inch. I therefore find that there was a breach by the defendants of their duties under s. 14 (1) and s. 16 of the Act of 1961.

G   I now come to what I think is the really difficult question in this case, which is—did this breach of duty on the part of the defendants cause the injury suffered by the plaintiff? The injury may have been solely caused by the defendants' breach of duty, or it may have been solely caused by the plaintiff himself, or it may have been caused partly by the one and partly by the other. I take as my guide on this point the following passages from two speeches by

H   Lord Reid. The first is from *Ross* v. *Associated Portland Cement Manufacturers, Ltd.* (3):

" The respondents' case is that they were not at all to blame because they were entitled to leave it to Ross to decide what to do and to come to their chief engineer if he wanted further help or equipment. They say that the cause, and the sole cause, of the breach and resulting accident was

I   Ross's mistaken decision, or negligence, in using the ladder when he ought to have seen that it was unsafe. This defence was accepted by the learned trial judge and by the Court of Appeal, but it seems to me quite unrealistic, and in accepting it I think that the learned judges misdirected themselves in law in founding on what is called ' coterminous ' fault.

" The occupier of a factory cannot delegate his duty to carry out the

(2) [1949] 2 All E.R. 715; [1950] 1 K.B. 194.
(3) [1964] 2 All E.R. 452 at pp. 455, 456.

statutory requirements. He can exempt himself from criminal liability   A
under s. 161 of the Act of 1961 if he proves that he has used all due diligence
and that the actual offender committed the offence without his consent,
connivance or wilful default; and he can avoid civil liability to the actual
offender if he can show that the conduct of this offender was the sole cause
of the breach and resulting injury to him. There are several cases to that
effect. *Manwaring* v. *Billington* (4) was a case where the employer gave   B
proper instructions to the plaintiff but the plaintiff deliberately disobeyed
them and did the work in a way which created a breach of a statutory
regulation. MORRIS, L.J., said (5) ' I would deem it incongruous and
irrational if, on the facts as found by the judge, the plaintiff could in effect
successfully say to his employer: " Because of my disregard of your reasonable instructions I have brought about the position that you are in breach   C
of your statutory obligations, and so I claim damages from you because of
such breach ".' Another typical case of avoiding civil liability was *Ginty*
v. *Belmont Building Supplies, Ltd.* (6). There the plaintiff had been instructed
not to work on asbestos roofs without using boards, and he knew that this
was the subject of statutory regulations and that this particular roof was
unsafe. Boards were available but he did not use them, with the result that   D
he fell through the roof. The terms of the regulation were such that his
failure to use the boards constituted offences both by him and by his
employers. PEARSON, J., held that he was not entitled to recover damages.
He discussed a number of theories which had been elaborated to explain
why damages are not payable in such circumstances, including delegation,
and inference from the principle that a person cannot derive advantage   E
from his own wrong, and the need for avoiding circuity of action. He said (7):
' In my view, the important and fundamental question in a case like this is
not whether there was a delegation, but simply the usual question—
whose fault was it? '

" If the question is put in that way one must remember that fault is
not necessarily equivalent in this context to blameworthiness. The question   F
really is whose conduct caused the accident, because it is now well established
that a breach of statutory duty does not give rise to civil liability unless
there is proved a causal connexion between the breach and the plaintiff's
injury. With regard to what is to be regarded as a causal connexion I
may be permitted to repeat by reference my observations in *Stapley* v.
Gypsum Mines, Ltd. (8). That approach appears to me to avoid the   G
difficulty which has sometimes been felt in explaining why an employer,
put in breach of a statute by the disobedience of his servant, can escape
liability to that servant for injuries caused by the breach. If the employer
exercised all due diligence, and the breach and resultant injuries were
solely caused by the servant's conduct, the employer is liable vicariously
for injuries sustained by a third party just as he would be for injuries   H
caused solely by his servant's common law negligence: but he can say to
the disobedient servant that his conduct in no way caused or contributed
to that servant's injuries.

" If the present case is approached in that way I have no doubt that
the respondents cannot wholly escape liability."

The second passage is from *Stapley* v. *Gypsum Mines, Ltd.* (9):   I

" In these circumstances it is necessary to determine what caused the
death of Stapley. If it was caused solely by his own fault, then the appellant
cannot succeed But if it was caused partly by his own fault and partly by

(4) [1952] 2 All E.R. 747.   (5) [1952] 2 All E.R. at p. 750.
(6) [1959] 1 All E.R. 414.   (7) [1959] 1 All E.R. at pp. 423, 424.
(8) [1953] 2 All E.R. 478 at p. 485; [1953] A.C. 663 at p. 681.
(9) [1953] 2 All E.R. at pp. 485, 486; [1953] A.C. at p. 681.

A the fault of Dale, then the appellant can rely on the Law Reform (Contributory Negligence) Act, 1945. To determine what caused an accident from the point of view of legal liability is a most difficult task. If there is any valid logical or scientific theory of causation, it is quite irrelevant in this connexion. In a court of law, this question must be decided as a properly instructed and reasonable jury would decide it. As LORD DU PARCQ said in

B *Grant* v. *Sun Shipping Co., Ltd.* (10): ' A jury would not have profited by a direction couched in the language of logicians, and expounding theories of causation, with or without the aid of Latin maxims.' The question must be determined by applying common sense to the facts of each particular case. One may find that, as a matter of history, several people have been at fault and that if any one of them had acted properly the accident would not have happened, but that does not mean that the accident must

C be regarded as having been caused by the faults of all of them. One must discriminate between those faults which must be discarded as being too remote and those which must not. Sometimes it is proper to discard all but one and to regard that one as the sole cause, but in other cases it is proper to regard two or more as having jointly caused the accident. I

D doubt whether any test can be applied generally."

Counsel for the defendants first submits that I should hold in this case that the injury to the plaintiff was solely caused by the plaintiff's own fault, relying on *Ginty* v. *Belmont Building Supplies, Ltd.* (11), the principle of which has been approved in later cases though the result of some of these cases has been different because they were distinguishable on the facts. The facts in *Ginty's* case (11)

E have been sufficiently stated in the passage from the speech of LORD REID in *Ross's* case (12) which I have already read. In *Ginty's* case (11) the only breach of statutory duty (in that case under the Building (Safety, Health and Welfare) Regulations, 1948) on the part of the employer was a failure to *use* boards on the roof, and this failure was entirely created by the plaintiff himself, who had failed (in breach of his own statutory duty under the regulations and of his

F instructions) to use the boards provided by the defendants. The defendants had been put in breach of their statutory duty solely by the omission of the plaintiff himself, and in these circumstances the breach of statutory duty by the plaintiff and the defendants was entirely " coterminous and co-extensive ". Where there is some fault, however, on the part of the employer outside and beyond the breach of duty created by the plaintiff himself the principle of

G *Ginty* (11) does not apply—see (for example) *Ross* v. *Associated Portland Cement Manufacturers, Ltd.* (13) and *McMath* v. *Rimmer Brothers (Liverpool), Ltd.* (14).

Counsel for the defendants submits that the present case is within the principle of *Ginty's* case (11). He says that there was no breach of the defendant's duty under s. 14 and s. 16 until the saw was set in motion, and that it was the plaintiff himself who set it in motion (knowing, as I have found, that he had

H no business to do so); the defendants were therefore put in breach of duty only by the plaintiff himself, and their fault is coterminous and co-extensive with his. I cannot accept this argument. Even though there may be no breach of duty by the employer until the machine is set in motion, the breach of duty is not the setting of the machine in motion but the failure to fence. The duty under s. 14 and s. 16 is a duty to fence securely, and this is a duty which the

I employer must discharge personally. These defendants, being a corporation, must, of course, discharge the duty through some agent, but it is not a duty which they can *only* vicariously discharge through the plaintiff himself, as with the use of the boards in *Ginty's* case (11). It was the duty of the defendants to fence securely and to keep the fence in position, and although I think that it

(10) [1948] 2 All E.R. 238 at p. 246; [1948] A.C. 549 at p. 564.
(11) [1959] 1 All E.R. 414.   (12) [1964] 2 All E.R. at pp. 455, 456.
(13) [1964] 2 All E.R. 452.   (14) [1961] 3 All E.R. 1154.

was also the duty of the plaintiff to keep the fence in position (both in his exer- A
cise of reasonable care for his own safety and under s. 143 of the Factories Act,
1961) I cannot regard the two breaches as coterminous and co-extensive. I
think that this view must be implicit in the decision of CANTLEY, J., in *Horne*
v. *Lec Refrigeration, Ltd.* (15). Further, I have come to the conclusion (on the
balance of probabilities) that this saw-blade would not have been securely fenced
when the plaintiff was working on it even if the guard had been properly adjusted. B
Counsel for the defendants submits that if the plaintiff had adjusted the guard
properly the accident would not have happened. I agree that if the guard had
been properly adjusted down to a height of only 1/16th of an inch above the
material which the plaintiff was cutting there would have been no danger of
the plaintiff's thumb getting on to the blade while the material was going through.
Mr. Brim was clear on this point, and the plaintiff himself agreed that with the C
guard adjusted right down it would be very difficult to get one's thumb in.
Nevertheless (as counsel for the defendants agreed) one must also consider the
position when there was no material under the guard, and in particular, I think,
the moment immediately after the cut has been completed. As I understood
Mr. Brim, he was dealing in the evidence to which I have referred with the
position when the material was still under the guard. When the material which D
the plaintiff was cutting was not under the guard, the space between the table
and the guard would have been 7/16ths of an inch if the guard had been properly
adjusted (that is, ⅜ths for the thickness of the material plus another 1/16th of
an inch up to the guard). Mr. Brim agreed in cross-examination that if an
operator followed straight through with his hand on the work-piece there was a
risk of taking off his thumb (or I suppose his finger if operating the machine as E
Mr. Brim said it should be operated), though he said that the operator ought to
take his hand off when the saw was two-thirds of the way through its cut. In
my judgment, this saw was not securely fenced when there was no material
under the guard, although the plaintiff's failure to adjust the guard greatly
increased the risk, and accordingly there was fault on the part of the defendants
which " went beyond " the fault of the plaintiff. I therefore hold that the F
principle of *Ginty* (16) does not apply to this case.

Counsel for the defendants, submits, however, that even if the principle of
Ginty's case (16) does not apply I should still hold that the plaintiff's injury was
solely caused by his own fault. He says that even if the *breach of duty* was not
caused solely by the plaintiff's own fault (as in *Ginty* (16)) the *accident* was caused
entirely by the plaintiff's own fault. In my view there may be cases in which G
an injury suffered by a plaintiff may be held to have been entirely caused by his
own fault although there has been a breach of statutory duty on the part of his
employer, and although the *Ginty* (16) situation of coterminous and co-extensive
fault does not exist—see for example *Rushton* v. *Turner Brothers Asbestos Co.,
Ltd.* (17) and *Horne* v. *Lec Refrigeration, Ltd.* (15). As ASHWORTH, J., said,
however, in *Rushton's* case (18), which was also a breach of the duty to fence H
under the Factories Act:

" I fully appreciate that the occasions on which the court is able to
permit defendants to escape in a case of this sort must be rare. Generally
when they have been in breach of the Factories Act, 1937, they must be
expected to bear some portion of the responsibility and to pay some
proportion of compensation. . . ."   I

See also the speech of LORD UPJOHN in *Ross's* case (19). In the present case
I do not feel able to hold that the accident was solely caused by the plaintiff's
own fault, and the problem therefore becomes one of apportionment of the
damages in respect of the injury which he suffered.

---

(15) [1965] 2 All E.R. 898.   (16) [1959] 1 All E.R. 414.
(17) [1959] 3 All E.R. 517.   (18) [1959] 3 All E.R. at p. 521.
                    (19) [1964] 2 All E.R. at pp. 460, 461.

A   Before going on to consider this problem I should refer to two matters which were pleaded by way of defence—that the plaintiff was not acting in the course of his employment and that he was a trespasser on the machine (see para. 3 of the defence). In view of the recent decisions of the Court of Appeal in *Uddin* v. *Associated Portland Cement Manufacturers, Ltd.* (20) and *Allen* v. *Aeroplane and Motor Aluminium Castings, Ltd.* (21), I am clearly of opinion that these

B   matters do not constitute any defence to this claim, and in the end I think counsel for the defendants relied on them as factors supporting his submission that the accident was caused solely by the plaintiff's own fault rather than as matters strictly of defence.

I must approach the problem of apportionment on the basis that there was more than one cause of this accident, and try to give the proper weight to each

C   cause. The defendants were in breach of their duties under s. 14 (1) and s. 16 of the Act of 1961, and I must remember that the Factories Acts are intended not only for the protection of careful, intelligent and obedient workmen but also of those who are stupid, careless, unreasonable or disobedient. If the duty had been fulfilled the accident could not have happened. I think therefore that I must attribute to the defendants some substantial share of the responsibility

D   for the injury suffered by the plaintiff. On the other hand, the plaintiff was doing something which he knew that he had no business to do and which he ought to have known was dangerous, and (no doubt owing to his ignorance of the machine) he operated the saw in an incompetent and incorrect way which in my judgment increased the risks of what he was doing. The problem of apportionment is always very difficult, but I am satisfied that the major part of

E   the responsibility for this accident must be attributed to the plaintiff himself. Doing my best to approach the problem as " a properly instructed and reasonable jury ", I have come to the conclusion that this accident was caused as to three-quarters by the fault of the plaintiff himself and as to one-quarter by the fault of the defendants.

The plaintiff is now aged fifty-nine and is a right-handed man. As a result

F   of the accident he lost the top $1\frac{3}{8}$ths of an inch of his left thumb, suffered shock and was away from work for five months. It is obvious that he had a very nasty experience and must have suffered considerable pain. He has made a gallant, determined and to a considerable extent successful attempt to overcome his disability, but he said that his thumb still sometimes throbs and is sore if you tap it. He is still employed by the defendants, and so far as can be foreseen there

G   is no danger of his losing his job. If he did lose his job, however, his ability to find other work would be impaired, although in view of his age he might well decide to retire before very long. He suffered no special damage, his loss of wages being extinguished by the national insurance benefits received. Nor is there now, or so long as he keeps his present job, any loss of earnings. I have come to the conclusion that if no reduction had to be made in the plaintiff's

H   damages I should award him the sum of £600, but as I have found that the accident was caused as to three-quarters by his own fault the sum for which I shall give judgment is one-quarter of £600, that is £150.

Judgment for the plaintiff for £150.

Solicitors: *W. H. Thompson* (for the plaintiff); *Herbert Smith & Co.* (for the
I   defendants).

[*Reported by* MARY COLTON, *Barrister-at-Law.*]

---

(20) [1965] 2 All E.R. 213; [1965] 2 Q.B. 582.   (21) [1965] 3 All E.R. 377.

A

BAMBURY AND OTHERS *v.* LONDON BOROUGH OF HOUNSLOW AND ANOTHER.

[QUEEN'S BENCH DIVISION (Lord Parker, C.J., Marshall and James, JJ.), April 29, 1966.]

Town and Country Planning—Enforcement notice—Validity—Owner and   B
occupier notices coming into effect at different dates—Notices served on
owner and occupiers, being different persons, on different dates—Each notice
to come into effect twenty-eight days after service—Appeal by occupiers to
Minister—Consequently notices could not take effect until final determination
of appeal, and would then take effect at the same time—Whether notices valid—
Town and Country Planning Act, 1962 (10 & 11 Eliz. 2 c. 38), s. 45 (3) (a),   C
s. 46 (1), (3), (4).

Enforcement notices in proper form were served on three occupiers of land on Aug. 22, 1964. The substance of the notices, viz., the development complained of, the time (namely twenty-eight days after service) when the notices would come into effect and the time when the occupiers had to discontinue, all were the same. The occupiers were not the owners. In   D purported pursuance of s. 45 (3) (a)* of the Town and Country Planning Act, 1962, a further enforcement notice was served on the owners of the land which was in the same terms as the notices served on the occupiers (including the coming into effect twenty-eight days after service), but that notice was not served until Sept. 8, 1964. The occupiers appealed under s. 46 (1)† to the Minister of Housing and Local Government against the enforcement   E notices. On further appeal to the High Court under s. 180 on a point of law from the decision of the Minister upholding the enforcement notices,

Held: the enforcement notices served on the occupiers would be quashed, because the result of notices being served on the occupiers and owners respectively at different times was that the notices came into effect at different times, which was a fatal defect that was not cured by the fact that   F the occupiers had appealed to the Minister with the consequence (by virtue of s. 46 (3)‡ of the Act of 1962) that all the notices could not take effect until final determination of the appeal, nor could the Minister cure the defect under s. 46 (4)§ since the materiality of the defect was not to be judged at the moment of appeal but at the outset (see p. 535, letters B, F and G, and p. 536, letter A, post).   G

Appeal allowed.

[As to the validity of enforcement notices, see 37 HALSBURY'S LAWS (3rd Edn.) 344, 345, paras. 447, 448, 351, para. 453; and for cases on the subject, see 45 DIGEST (Repl.) 350-354, *91-101*.

For the Town and Country Planning Act, 1962, s. 45, s. 46, see 42 HALSBURY'S STATUTES (2nd Edn.) 1015, 1017.]   H

Case referred to:
Miller-Mead v. *Minister of Housing and Local Government, Same* v. *Same,*
[1963] 1 All E.R. 459; [1963] 2 Q.B. 196; [1963] 2 W.L.R. 225; 127
J.P. 122; 45 Digest (Repl.) 352, *100*.

Motion.   I
This was an appeal by way of motion under s. 180 of the Town and Country Planning Act, 1962, by the appellants, Roy Bambury, John Simon Ross and David Walker, from a decision of the second respondent, the Minister of Housing and Local Government, expressed in a letter of decision dated Dec. 6,

---

* Section 45 (3)-(5), so far as material, is set out at p. 534, letters A to C, post.
† Section 46 (1), so far as relevant, is set out at p. 533, letter H, post.
‡ Section 46 (3) is set out at p. 534, letter E, post.
§ Section 46 (4) is set out at p. 534, letter F, post.

A 1965, whereby he upheld three enforcement notices served on each of the appellants (the occupiers) and Ashley Lass Properties, Ltd. (the owners, who did not appeal) by the first respondents, Heston and Isleworth Borough Council (now the council of the London Borough of Hounslow) on behalf of Middlesex County Council relating to the display and sale of motor vehicles on land formerly the sites of 61 and 63, Staines Road, Hounslow. The facts are set out in the judgment B of LORD PARKER, C.J.

The cases noted below* were cited during the argument in addition to the case referred to in the judgments.

A. B. Dawson for the appellants.

Nigel Bridge for the second respondent, the Minister of Housing and Local Government.

C The first respondents did not appear and were not represented.

LORD PARKER, C.J.: This is an appeal under s. 180 of the Town and Country Planning Act, 1962, from a decision of the Minister of Housing and Local Government expressed in a letter of decision dated Dec. 6, 1965, whereby he upheld three enforcement notices served by Heston and Isleworth Borough D Council on the three appellants, who are the occupiers of the appeal site. Having regard to the sole issues raised in this appeal, it is quite unnecessary to describe the site or to go into the planning history, or to consider the report of the inspector on appeal to the Minister. The enforcement notices were in a common form, addressed severally to the three occupiers. They recited that the addressee in each case was the occupier of the appeal site, and went on to recite that it E appeared to the council that development within the meaning of the Act was carried out by the change of use of the premises to the display and sale of motor vehicles after Feb. 1, 1964. The notices then went on to this effect:

> " Now therefore the council on behalf of the county council of the administrative council of Middlesex as local planning authority . . . hereby give you notice to discontinue the use of the premises for the display and sale of F motor vehicles within twenty-eight days of the date on which this notice takes effect. This notice shall subject to the provisions of the said Act take effect on the expiration of twenty-eight clear days after the service thereof upon you."

Those three enforcement notices were dated Aug. 21, 1964, and were in fact G served the next day. There was an appeal to the Minister on a number of the grounds set out in s. 46 (1) of the Act of 1962, namely, grounds (*a*), (*c*), (*d*) and (*f*). By a letter written before the inquiry, the appellants asked to raise ground (*e*), and at the inquiry itself withdrew the grounds (*c*) and (*d*). The inspector and the Minister both felt that this was a case in which they should accede to the request to consider ground (*e*), and whether ground (*e*) is a ground H on which the Minister ought to quash the notice is the sole issue in this appeal. Ground (*e*) provides

> " that the enforcement notice was not served on the owner or occupier of the land within the relevant period of four years specified in sub-s. (2) of the last preceding section."

Before dealing with the details of the case, I think that it would be right to I refer to the relevant provisions of the Act of 1962. Section 45 provides for the power of a local planning authority to serve enforcement notices. Its provisions are well known, and I will only refer to those that are relevant in these proceedings:

---

* *Burgess* v. *Jarvis*, [1952] 1 All E.R. 592; [1952] 2 Q.B. 41; *Mead* v. *Plumtree*, [1952] 2 All E.R. 723; [1953] 1 Q.B. 32; *Swallow and Pearson* v. *Middlesex County Council*, [1953] 1 All E.R. 580; *Godstone Rural District Council* v. *Brazil*, [1953] 2 All E.R. 763; *East Riding County Council* v. *Park Estate (Bridlington), Ltd.*, [1956] 2 All E.R. 669; [1957] A.C. 223.

" (3) Where the local planning authority serve an enforcement notice,   A
the notice (a) shall be served on the owner and occupier of the land to which
it relates . . .

" (4) An enforcement notice—(a) shall specify the development which is
alleged to have been carried out without the grant of planning permission
as mentioned in para. (a) of sub-s. (1) of this section or, as the case may be,
the matters in respect of which it is alleged that any such conditions or   B
limitations as are mentioned in para. (b) of that subsection have not been
complied with, and (b) may require such steps as may be specified in the
notice to be taken, within such period as may be so specified, for the purpose
of restoring the land to its condition before the development took place . . ."

" (5) Subject to the following provisions of this Part of this Act, an
enforcement notice shall take effect at the end of such period (not being less   C
than twenty-eight days after the service thereof) as may be specified in the
notice."

Pausing there, it is quite clear that there is to be only one enforcement notice,
and that that notice is to be served, in the case of land which is in separate
occupation from that of the owner, both on the owner and on the occupier.
It is also clear that that notice must specify two periods, first, the period at the end   D
of which the enforcement notice is to take effect, which cannot be of a shorter
period than that laid down in s. 45 (5), and, secondly, the period during which
the person on whom the notice is served must restore the land to its condition
before development, which is a period of course which would run only from the
time when the notice takes effect.   Section 46 (1) sets out the grounds on which
a person may appeal, and, by sub-s. (3):   E

" Where an appeal is brought under this section, the enforcement notice
shall be of no effect pending the final determination or withdrawal of the
appeal."

By sub-s. (4):

" On an appeal under this section the Minister may correct any infor-   F
mality, defect or error in the enforcement notice if he is satisfied that the
informality, defect or error is not a material one."

Finally, in passing, it is to be observed that, by s. 177 (1), the validity of an
enforcement notice which has been served shall not, except by way of appeal
to the Minister, be questioned in any proceedings whatsoever on any of the   G
grounds specified in paras. (b) to (e) of s. 46 (1) of the Act of 1962.

Bearing those provisions in mind, it is clear that these three enforcement
notices served on these three occupiers were, on the face of them at any rate,
perfectly valid.   The enforcement notices were all in exactly the same terms.
The development complained of was the same; the date when they would
come into effect was the same in each case, namely, twenty-eight clear days   H
after service, and in each case once the notice came into effect the occupiers
had to discontinue within a further twenty-eight days.   These three occupiers,
however, were not owner occupiers, and, pursuant to the provisions, or in
purported pursuance of the provisions, of the Act of 1962, a further enforcement
notice was served on the owners.   That again recited the same development;
that again used the same formula to describe when the enforcement notice   I
would come into effect, namely, twenty-eight clear days after service, and finally
it also provided that, after the notice came into effect, the owner was to restore
the land within twenty-eight days.   Pausing there, it would look as if the validity
of the enforcement notices served on the occupiers could not be in any way
questioned.   However, the notices on the occupiers were served on Aug. 22, 1964,
and that on the owners was not served until Sept. 8, 1964.   It is in those circumstances that counsel for the appellants argues to this effect.   He says that there
cannot be two dates for the coming into force of an enforcement notice; that,

A if there are two separate dates, then there are in effect two notices differing in an essential part; and, if that be so, then no valid notice has been served on the appellants; and, finally, that they can bring themselves within ground (*e*) in that no valid enforcement notice has been served on them within the four years period (1).

I confess that, at first sight, this seemed to me a highly technical point and
B completely devoid of merit; so far as this case is concerned, I am still of that opinion, but it may, nevertheless, be a good point. Although these two bits of paper served on these two dates were identical, the result of service on different dates was that they purported to take effect at different times, and to that extent they were two separate notices, arising, of course, solely from the fact that they were served at different times. Counsel for the Minister frankly
C concedes the position so far. He agrees that an enforcement notice can have only one effective date, and he goes further and says that, if the appellants had done nothing by way of appeal and had been prosecuted, then, despite s. 177 (1), they would have a valid defence since they would be able to say that no notice had been validly served on them. What counsel says in his ingenious argument, and I do not object to his raising any degree of ingenuity to defeat this point,
D is in effect: that may well be so, but the appellants did appeal, and the effect of their appealing by reason of s. 46 (3) is that these two notices which heretofore had not got a common effective date, now have such a date because in both cases the notices cannot take effect until the final determination of the appeal. In other words, the fact that they have appealed he says has cured the defects. He supports that contention by referring to the Minister's powers of correction
E in s. 46 (4). He says that it was possible for the Minister to correct the defect, in other words, to make the day when the order became effective the same as with regard to the owners and occupiers, but that in fact it is quite academic and unnecessary for him to take that step.

For my part, I am reluctantly forced to the conclusion that really this was a fatal defect. I cannot myself see that the mere fact that the appellants appealed
F can cure that defect. Nor do I think—it is a good way to test it—that the Minister could have exercised his powers under s. 46 (4) to cure the defect. That subsection is designed to give the Minister power to correct defects and errors which are not material ones. No doubt the Minister can say that, at the time when it comes before him on appeal, the question of what is the effective date is not material because it cannot be material until the appeal is determined.
G In my judgment, however, the materiality of the defect is not to be judged at that moment but at the outset, and, looked at in that way, it does not seem to me that those powers are in any way applicable. In saying that, I hope that I have not overlooked, although I do not propose to refer to it, the well-known case of *Miller-Mead* v. *Minister of Housing and Local Government* (2), and to all that was said by Lord Denning, M.R., in that case (3). I am satisfied that the date
H when the enforcement notice took effect is an essential matter to the validity of an enforcement notice. That, indeed, can be seen from the number of cases which have been cited, to which again I find it unnecessary to refer, emphasising the necessity of an enforcement notice setting out clearly the two periods to which I have referred, and in particular the period which is taken last in the section but is logically first in point of time, namely, the period at the end of which the
I enforcement notice takes effect.

I would allow this appeal.

---

(1) The period is provided by s. 45 (2), which so far as relevant is as follows: " The period for the service of an enforcement notice—(a) where the notice relates to the carrying out of development, is the period of four years from the carrying out of that development . . .''
(2) [1963] 1 All E.R. 459; [1963] 2 Q.B. 196.
(3) [1963] 1 All E.R. at pp. 466, 467; [1963] 2 Q.B. at pp. 219-221.

MARSHALL, J.: I agree. A

JAMES, J.: I also agree for the reasons given by LORD PARKER, C.J.

Appeal allowed. Leave to appeal to the Court of Appeal.

Solicitors: *Lucien Fior* (for the appellants); *Solicitor, Ministry of Housing and Local Government.*

[*Reported by* N. P. METCALFE, ESQ., *Barrister-at-Law.*] B

CARL-ZEISS-STIFTUNG v. RAYNER AND KEELER, LTD. AND OTHERS (No. 2).

[HOUSE OF LORDS (Lord Reid, Lord Hodson, Lord Guest, Lord Upjohn and Lord Wilberforce), December 1, 2, 6, 7, 8, 9, 13, 14, 15, 16, 1965; January 31, February 1, 2, 3, 7, 8, 9, 10, 14, 15, 16, May 18, 1966.] C

Conflict of Laws—Foreign law—Recognition—Law as declared by courts of foreign country—Zonal government in Germany—German Democratic Republic not recognised by United Kingdom government as independent sovereign state, but U.S.S.R. recognised as having de jure sovereignty in Eastern Zone of Germany—Council of Gera, created by laws of German Democratic Republic, exercised authority in the district of the Eastern Zone that included Jena—Council entitled according to law of Eastern Zone to act as the special board (the governing authority) of Carl-Zeiss-Stiftung, a corporation domiciled at Jena in Eastern Zone—Council authorised the bringing of an action in England in the name of the foundation—Whether action brought without authority. D

Estoppel—Estoppel by record—Issue estoppel—Foreign judgment—Issue of want of authority to institute action—Judgment in foreign proceedings that Council of Gera, the effective plaintiff, was not entitled to represent foreign corporation—Council of Gera authorised issue of writ to bring passing-off action in England in name of foreign corporation—Defendants in English action applied for stay of proceedings on ground of want of authority to issue writ—Whether defendants entitled to succeed on this application on ground that English solicitors estopped by foreign judgment from maintaining that they were duly authorised. E F

Solicitor—Costs—Payment by solicitor personally—Want of authority to institute action—Action in name of foreign corporation—Corporation domiciled in Eastern Zone of Germany—Law applicable to determine authority to sue. G

In 1896 the Carl-Zeiss-Stiftung, a charitable foundation, was incorporated under articles of constitution at Jena, which was in the district of East Germany that was then the Grand Duchy of Saxe-Weimar. The foundation was administered by a " special board " and the two businesses which it owned—one an optical works (founded in 1846 by Carl Zeiss) and the other a glass works—were run each by a separate board of management. The rights and duties of the special board were (by r. 5 of the constitution) to pertain to " that department of the State Service of the Grand Duchy of Saxe-Weimar under which the affairs of the University of Jena were for the time being placed ". Rule 113 of the constitution provided that if political changes were made the rule regarding representation of the foundation untenable, the rights and duties of the foundation were to be made over to that department of state which occupied with regard to the University of Jena the place of the state department of the Grand Duchy acting as the special board, provided it had its seat in Thüringia, otherwise to the " highest administrative authorities in Thüringia ". In 1918 under the Weimar Republic, the Grand Duchy of Saxe-Weimar was abolished and a new state of Thüringia was set up under which the Minister of Education became the special board. After 1935 under the National Socialist régime, a Reich-Stathalter became the special board in place of the Minister of Education. In 1945 when Thüringia was occupied by American forces, a new provisional H I

Dicta of LORD REID, LORD UPJOHN and of LORD WILBERFORCE at 550, 573, 586 applied in McILKENNY v CHIEF CONSTABLE [1980] 2 All ER 227

Dicta of LORD REID and LORD UPJOHN at 555-556, 574 followed in WESTFAL-LARSEN & CO v IKERIGI COMPANIA [1983] 1 All ER 382

Applied in GUR CORP v TRUST BANK OF AFRICA [1986] 3 All ER 449

A   government of Thüringia was set up and its Minister of Education became the
special board. In July, 1945, by agreement between the allied powers, East
Germany, including Thüringia, was taken over by the Russians. When the
Americans left in 1945 the members of the boards of management, and a
number of scientists and executives went with them to West Germany, where
they developed interests that the Stiftung and the firm of Carl Zeiss had there.

B   In 1945, as a result of Russian confiscatory decrees, assets of the two firms
were confiscated. In 1948 by further decrees of the Russian authorities both
businesses became nationalised industries, referred to as V.e.Bs. In 1949 the
U.S.S.R. set up the German Democratic Republic to govern that part of Germany occupied by Russia and purported to make it an independent sovereign
state. The Minister of Education continued to be allowed to act as the special

C   board. In 1952 the German Democratic Republic abolished the state of
Thüringia and divided the territory of East Germany into districts. Jena was
in the district of Gera and the Council of Gera assumed the position corresponding to the Minister and acted as the special board. In proceedings
brought by the appellant in Eastern Germany to restrain the firm of Carl
Zeiss of West Germany from using the name " Carl Zeiss " in Eastern Ger-

D   many the Supreme Court in East Germany reached, in and before 1961, the
conclusions that the Carl-Zeiss-Stiftung continued to exist as a legal entity
and that the Council of Gera was its special board. The writ in the present
action, dated Oct. 20, 1955, which was a passing-off action for an injunction
to restrain the respondent from using the word " Zeiss " and from selling
optical or glass instruments under that name unless the goods were those

E   of the appellant, was issued in the name of Carl-Zeiss-Stiftung as plaintiff
on instructions on behalf of the foundation (and the V.e.B.) given by a Dr. S.
under his authority as mandatory derived from the Council of Gera.   Thus
the authority of the English solicitors to issue the writ in the name of the
present appellant depended on the authority of the council to act as the
special board of Carl-Zeiss-Stiftung, the appellant. On Nov. 15, 1960,

F   the Federal High Court in West Germany upheld a preliminary objection
that the foundation was not properly before the German court as the Council
of Gera had no authority to represent the foundation. In those proceedings
the effective plaintiff was the Council of Gera, and the third defendant in
the present action (the West German firm of Carl Zeiss of Heidenheim) was
defendant. In February, 1956, the respondents to this appeal applied in

G   the English action that all further proceedings should be stayed on the
ground that the action was brought and was being maintained without the
authority of the foundation.   On Nov. 6, 1964, Her Majesty's Secretary of
State gave a certificate which certified, among other matters, " that Her
Majesty's government has not recognised either de jure or de facto any
other authority," viz., in the context any other authority than the govern-

H   ment of the U.S.S.R., " purporting to exercise governing authority in or in
respect of the [Eastern Zone of Germany]. Her Majesty's government,
however, regards the aforementioned governments as retaining rights and
responsibilities in respect of Germany as a whole ".   The governments last
referred to were those of the French Republic, the United Kingdom, the
United States of America and the Union of Soviet Socialist Republics.

I   **Held:** (i) as the Council of Gera had authorised this action being brought
in the name of the appellant, the respondents had not established want of
authority on the part of the appellant's solicitors to issue the writ, for the
following reasons—

(a) as the court was bound to accept the information afforded by Her
Majesty's government as conclusive concerning the sovereignty of a foreign
state, the East German Democratic Republic set up by the U.S.S.R. in East
Germany must be regarded, in accordance with the Foreign Office certificate
of Nov. 6, 1964, as a subordinate organisation whose acts, being done with
the consent of the government of the U.S.S.R., derived authority from the

sovereignty of the U.S.S.R. in East Germany and could not be regarded   A
by the English court as nullities (see p. 547, letter G, p. 548, letter D,
p. 559, letter G, p. 564, letter F, p. 569, letter E, p. 580, letter B, and
p. 581, letter A, post).

(b) since a foreign corporation was governed by the law of its domicil,
and the appellant's domicil was in East Germany, the capacity of the
appellant was governed by East German law, which should be taken to be the   B
law declared by the East German courts (not by the West German courts)
as Germany was for the time being divided; and by German law the appellant remained in existence and the Council of Gera was entitled to act as the
special board of the appellant (see p. 556, letter D, p. 558, letter G, p. 562,
letter H, p. 568, letters A and H, p. 574, letter H, p. 582, letter A, and
p. 589, letters A, E and I, post).   C

Lazard Bros. & Co. v. *Midland Bank, Ltd.* ([1932] All E.R. Rep. 571)
followed.

(ii) the decision of the Federal High Court in West Germany that the
Council of Gera had no authority to represent the appellant in the proceedings there did not give rise to an estoppel per rem judicatam entitling
the respondents to succeed without further inquiry on their application   D
for a stay of proceedings in the present action on the ground of want of
authority of the appellant's solicitors to issue the writ for the following
reasons—

(a) (LORD WILBERFORCE dissenting as to identity of parties) there was not
identity of parties or privity of interest for the purposes of issue estoppel,
since the Council of Gera was the effective plaintiff* in the West German   E
proceedings, the English solicitors for the appellant were not parties to
those proceedings and there was no privity as regards the English solicitors
(see p. 550, letters B and G, p. 551, letter A, p. 556, letter C, p. 561, letter I,
p. 566, letter G, p. 567, letter C, and p. 572, letters C and D; cf. p. 586, letters
D and I, post).

(b) the question of res judicata in the present case was one of issue estoppel   F
as distinct from cause of action estoppel and, although issue estoppel
could be based on a foreign judgment†, the burden of establishing that the
judgment of the court in West Germany was a final and conclusive judgment,
such as was required to raise estoppel, was on the respondents and (LORD
HODSON, dissenting, see p. 560, letter I, to p. 561, letter A, post) they had
not adduced evidence to satisfy the court of that (see p. 556, letter A, p. 566,   G
letter D, p. 574, letter E, and p. 588, letter A, post); moreover (per LORD
UPJOHN) the question of the solicitors' want of authority could never be an
issue in the action and issue estoppel should not apply (see p. 573, letter E,
and p. 574, letter C, post).

Godard v. *Gray* ((1870), L.R. 6 Q.B. 139) and *Nouvion* v. *Freeman* ((1889),
15 App. Cas. 1) considered.   H

Simpson v. *Fogo* ((1863), 1 Hem. & M. 195) criticised.

Decision of the COURT OF APPEAL ([1965] 1 All E.R. 300) reversed.

[As to the court's taking judicial notice of the status of a foreign state, see
7 HALSBURY'S LAWS (3rd Edn.) 265, 266, para. 569, 15 HALSBURY'S LAWS
(3rd Edn.) 336, 337, para. 612; and for cases on the subject, see 22 DIGEST
(Repl.) 142-144, *1290-1303*.   I

As to the proper law for determining the powers of a foreign corporation,
see 7 HALSBURY'S LAWS (3rd Edn.) 12, para. 21.

As to the essentials of estoppel per rem judicatam, see 15 HALSBURY'S LAWS
(3rd Edn.) 185, para. 358; and p. 182, para. 355; and for cases on the need for
identity of parties or privity, see 21 DIGEST (Repl.) 256-261, *367-409*.

As to the liability of a plaintiff's solicitor for costs where he institutes an

* As to the council being the effective plaintiff, see p. 583, letters A to D, post.
† See p. 555, letter D, p. 560, letters B and C, and p. 585, letters A and H; cf. p. 574,
letter C, post; LORD GUEST not concurring as to that, see p. 567, letter G, post.

A action without authority, see 36 HALSBURY'S LAWS (3rd Edn.) 76, 77, para. 107;
and for cases on the subject, see 43 DIGEST (Repl.) 370-372, *3924-3952,* 374,
3971-3975.]

Cases referred to:

Aksionairnoye Obschestvo A. M. Luther v. *Sagor (James) & Co.,* [1921] 1 K.B.
456; *rvsd.* C.A., [1921] All E.R. Rep. 138; [1921] 3 K.B. 532; 90
B   L.J.K.B. 1202; 125 L.T. 705; 22 Digest (Repl.) 143, *1296.*

Banco de Bilbao v. *Sancha, Banco de Bilbao* v. *Rey,* [1938] 2 All E.R. 253;
[1938] 2 K.B. 176; 107 L.J.K.B. 681; 159 L.T. 369; 11 Digest (Repl.)
612, *420.*

Bankers and Shippers Insurance Co. of New York v. *Liverpool Marine and
General Insurance Co.,* (1925), 21 Lloyd L.R. 86; *rvsd.,* H.L., (1926),
C   24 Lloyd L.R. 85.

Behrens v. *Sieveking,* (1837), 2 My. & Cr. 602; 40 E.R. 769; 21 Digest (Repl.)
274, *483.*

Berne (City of) v. *Bank of England,* (1804), 9 Ves. 347; 32 E.R. 636; 22 Digest
(Repl.) 142, *1290.*

Brunsden v. *Humphrey,* [1881-85] All E.R. Rep. 357; (1884), 14 Q.B.D. 141;
D   53 L.J.Q.B. 476; 51 L.T. 529; 49 J.P. 4; 21 Digest (Repl.) 281, *526.*

Buerger v. *New York Life Assurance Co.,* [1927] All E.R. Rep. 342; 43 T.L.R.
601; 35 Digest (Repl.) 202, *97.*

Bullard & Co. v. *Grace & Co.,* (1925), 1285 N.Y. 388.

Callandar v. *Dittrich,* (1842), 1 Man. & G. 68; 134 E.R. 29; 11 Digest (Repl.)
529, *1417.*
E
Duff Development Co., Ltd. v. *Kelantan Government,* [1924] All E.R. Rep. 1;
[1924] A.C. 797; 93 L.J.Ch. 343; 131 L.T. 676; 22 Digest (Repl.)
143, *1293.*

Fidelitas Shipping Co., Ltd. v. *V/O. Exportchleb,* [1965] 2 All E.R. 4; [1965]
2 W.L.R. 1059.

Flitters v. *Allfrey,* (1874), L.R. 10 C.P. 29; 44 L.J.C.P. 73; 31 L.T. 878; 21
F   Digest (Repl.) 232, *253.*

Godard v. *Gray,* (1870), L.R. 6 Q.B. 139; 40 L.J.Q.B. 62; 24 L.T. 89; 11
Digest (Repl.) 522, *1360.*

Guaranty Trust Co. of New York v. *Hannay & Co.,* [1918-19] All E.R. Rep. 151;
[1918] 2 K.B. 623; 87 L.J.K.B. 1223; 119 L.T. 321; 6 Digest (Repl.)
152, *1091.*
G
Hancock v. *Welsh and Cooper,* (1816), 1 Stark. 347; 30 Digest (Repl.) 377, *196.*

Henderson v. *Henderson,* [1843-60] All E.R. Rep. 378; (1843), 3 Hare, 100;
1 L.T.O.S. 410; 67 E.R. 313; 21 Digest (Repl.) 244, *306.*

Houlditch v. *Donegal (Marquess),* (1834), 8 Bli. N.S. 301; 2 Cl. & Fin. 470;
5 E.R. 955; 11 Digest (Repl.) 502, **720.*

Hoystead v. *Taxation Comr.,* (1921), 29 C.L.R. 537; *rvsd.* P.C., [1925] All E.R.
H   Rep. 56; [1926] A.C. 155; 95 L.J.P.C. 79; 134 L.T. 354; 21 Digest
(Repl.) 249, *330.*

Jones v. *Garcia del Rio,* (1823), 1 Turn. & R. 297; 37 E.R. 1113.

King v. *Hoare,* (1844), 13 M. & W. 494; 14 L.J.Ex. 29; 4 L.T.O.S. 174; 153
E.R. 206; 21 Digest (Repl.) 293, *591.*

Kingston's (Duchess) Case, (1776), 1 East, P.C. 468; 20 State Tr. 355; 21
I   Digest (Repl.) 225, *225.*

Kinnersley v. *Orpe,* (1780), 2 Doug. K.B. 517; 99 E.R. 330; 21 Digest (Repl.)
265, *428.*

Laidlaw v. *Blackwood,* (1843), 15 Sc. Jur. 484; 21 Digest (Repl.) 259, **309.*

Lazard Brothers & Co. v. *Midland Bank, Ltd.,* [1932] All E.R. Rep. 571;
[1933] A.C. 289; 102 L.J.K.B. 191; 148 L.T. 242; *affg.* sub nom.
Lazard Brothers & Co. v. *Banque Industrielle de Moscou,* [1932] 1 K.B.
617; 22 Digest (Repl.) 613, *7070.*

Lockyer v. *Ferryman*, (1877), 2 App. Cas. 519; 21 Digest (Repl.) 272, *178*.   A

Marginson v. *Blackburn Borough Council*, [1939] 1 All E.R. 273; [1939] 2 K.B. 426; 108 L.J.K.B. 563; 160 L.T. 234; 21 Digest (Repl.) 235, *276*.

Mercantile Investment and General Trust Co. v. *River Plate Trust, Loan and Agency Co.*, [1894] 1 Ch. 578; 63 L.J.Ch. 366; 70 L.T. 131; 11 Digest (Repl.) 523, *1367*.   B

Myers v. *Elman*, [1939] 4 All E.R. 484; [1940] A.C. 282; 109 L.J.K.B. 105; 162 L.T. 113; 43 Digest (Repl.) 375, *3981*.

New Brunswick Ry. Co. v. *British and French Trust Corpn., Ltd.*, [1938] 4 All E.R. 747; [1939] A.C. 1; 108 L.J.K.B. 115; 160 L.T. 137; 21 Digest (Repl.) 231, *247*.

Nouvion v. *Freeman*, (1887), 37 Ch.D. 244; *affd.* H.L., (1889), 15 App. Cas. 1; 59 L.J.Ch. 337; 62 L.T. 189; 11 Digest (Repl.) 513, *1282*.   C

Outram v. *Morewood*, (1803), 3 East, 346; 102 E.R. 630; 21 Digest (Repl.) 256, *372*.

Petrogradsky Mejdunarodny Kommerchesky Bank v. *National City Bank*, (1930), 253 N.Y. 23; 170 N.E. 479.   D

Preston (orse. Putynski) v. *Preston (orse. Putynska) (orse. Basinska)*, [1962] 3 All E.R. 928; [1963] P. 141; [1962] 3 W.L.R. 1401; *affd.* C.A., [1963] 2 All E.R. 405; [1963] P. 411; [1963] 2 W.L.R. 1435; Digest (Cont. Vol. A) 238, *966f*.

Queensland Mercantile & Agency Co., Ltd., Re, Ex p. Australasian Investment Co., Ex p. Union Bank of Australia, [1892] 1 Ch. 219; 61 L.J.Ch. 145; 66 L.T. 433; 8 Digest (Repl.) 607, *498*.   E

R. v. *Bottrill, Ex p. Kuechenmeister*, [1946] 2 All E.R. 434; [1947] K.B. 41; 175 L.T. 232; sub nom. *R.* v. *Kuechenmeister, Ex p. Bottrill*, 115 L.J.K.B. 500; 22 Digest (Repl.) 311, *3238*.

R. v. *Hartingdon Middle Quarter (Inhabitants)*, (1855), 4 E. & B. 780; 24 L.J.M.C. 98; 24 L.T.O.S. 327; 19 J.P. 150; 119 E.R. 288; 21 Digest   F (Repl.) 203, *51*.

Ricardo v. *Garcias*, (1845), 12 Cl. & F. 368; 8 E.R. 1450; 11 Digest (Repl.) 530, *1422*.

Richmond v. *Branson & Son*, [1914] 1 Ch. 968; 83 L.J.Ch. 749; 110 L.T. 763; 33 Digest (Repl.) 695, *1491*.

Russian Commercial and Industrial Bank v. *Le Comptoir d'Escompte de Mul-*   G *house*, [1924] All E.R. Rep. 381; [1925] A.C. 112; 93 L.J.K.B. 1098; 132 L.T. 99; 21 Digest (Repl.) 199, *10*.

Simpson v. *Fogo*, (1863), 1 Hem. & M. 195; 32 L.J.Ch. 249; 8 L.T. 61; 71 E.R. 85; 11 Digest (Repl.) 380, *426*.

Society of Medical Officers of Health v. *Hope (Valuation Officer)*, [1960] 1 All E.R.   H 317; [1960] A.C. 551; [1960] 2 W.L.R. 404; 124 J.P. 128; 21 Digest (Repl.) 249, *333*.

Sokoloff v. *National City Bank of New York*, (1924), 239 N.Y. 158; 145 N.E. 917; *on appeal*, (1929), 250 N.Y. 69; 163 N.E. 745.

Taylor v. *Barclay*, (1828), 2 Sim. 213; 7 L.J.O.S. Ch. 65; 57 E.R. 769; 22 Digest (Repl.) 142, *1291*.   I

Thoday v. *Thoday*, [1964] 1 All E.R. 341; [1964] P. 181; [1964] 1 W.L.R. 371; 3rd Digest Supp.

Thompson v. *Powles*, (1828), 2 Sim. 194; 57 E.R. 761; 11 Digest (Repl.) 448, *872*.

U.S. v. *Home Insurance Co.*, *U.S.* v. *Southern Insurance & Trust Co.*, (1874), 89 U.S. 99; 22 Law Ed. 816.

Upright v. *Mercury Business*, (1961), 13 A.D. (2nd) 361.

A   *White, Child & Beney, Ltd.* v. *Simmons*; *White, Child & Beney, Ltd.* v. *Eagle Star & British Dominions Insurance Co.*, [1922] All E.R. Rep. 482; (1922), 127 L.T. 571; 22 Digest (Repl.) 143, *1297*.

  Yonge v. *Toynbee*, [1908-10] All E.R. Rep. 204; [1910] 1 K.B. 215; 79 L.J.K.B. 208; 102 L.T. 57; 43 Digest (Repl.) 56, 441.

B   **Appeal.**

This was an appeal and a cross-appeal. The appeal was by the appellant, Carl-Zeiss-Stiftung, and the cross-appeal was by the respondents, the defendants hereinafter mentioned, from an order of the Court of Appeal (HARMAN, DANCKWERTS and DIPLOCK, L.JJ.) dated Dec. 17, 1964, and reported [1965] 1 All E.R. 300, reversing so much of the order of CROSS, J., dated Mar. 6, 1964, as dismissed the application of the respondents by summons dated Feb. 7, 1956. The sum-
C mons was for an order that all further proceedings in the action by the appellant should be stayed and that the action should be dismissed on the ground that it was begun and maintained without the appellant's authority. The Court of Appeal ordered that the writ and all subsequent proceedings should be set aside, that the respondents should bear their own costs of the action and of applications
D to the Court of Appeal and that the solicitors for the appellant (Carl-Zeiss-Stiftung) should pay to the respondents the costs occasioned by the appeal, such costs to be taxed on the common fund basis. On Mar. 17, 1965, the respondents presented a petition of appeal to the House of Lords naming as sole respondents to the cross-appeal so instituted the partners in the firm of solicitors acting on behalf of Carl-Zeiss-Stiftung, the petition being for an order for the
E payment of costs of the action and other costs.

The action was commenced by writ dated Oct. 20, 1955. In it the appellant claimed an injunction to restrain the respondents and each of them from advertising, offering for sale or selling any optical instruments or any articles containing or consisting of glass under or by reference to the name " Carl-Zeiss " or any name containing " Zeiss ", unless such goods should be those of the appellant or an
F organisation associated with the appellant, and generally from passing off any business or goods as and for those of the appellant or an organisation associated with the appellant. The appellant claimed also an injunction to restrain the third defendants from using the name " Carl-Zeiss-Stiftung " or " Carl-Zeiss " or any name containing " Zeiss " in relation to their business or goods. The plaintiff in the action, Carl-Zeiss-Stiftung, was a German foundation founded,
G so it was alleged, in 1889 and having its registered office at Jena in that part of Germany now constituting the German Democratic Republic. The defendants were Rayner and Keeler, Ltd., Degenhardt & Co., Ltd., and Carl-Zeiss-Stiftung. The first two defendants were retailers of optical instruments, who did not deal in the defendant's goods. The third defendant was, so it was alleged, a German organisation with its registered office at Heidenheim in the Western zone of
H Germany. Originally the third defendant's name on the record was " Carl-Zeiss ". On service of notice of a concurrent writ on the third defendant at Heidenheim, the third defendant entered appearance as Carl-Zeiss-Stiftung trading as " Carl-Zeiss ". Thereafter the writ was amended to describe the third defendant as " Carl-Zeiss-Stiftung ". The appellant's statement of claim was amended and redelivered. By para. 3 of the amended statement of claim the appellant
I pleaded that in pursuance of r. 113 of certain articles of constitution drawn up by one Dr. Ernest Abbé in 1896, the administration of the appellant (viz., Carl-Zeiss-Stiftung domiciled at Jena) had been transferred to the Council of the District of Gera, in which district of the Eastern Zone Jena was then situated. It was alleged that the third respondents to the present appeal had used without the appellant's consent the names " Carl-Zeiss-Stiftung " and " Carl-Zeiss " in relation to their business and goods, such use being calculated to lead to their business and goods being thought to be the business and goods of the appellant. The appellant also alleged that for very many years and at all material times

the name "Carl Zeiss" and any name including "Zeiss" had indicated, when **A** used in relation to a business concerning glass or optical instruments the appellant's goods, and that for very many years the name "Carl-Zeiss-Stiftung" had indicated the appellant exclusively. The appellant then alleged that the respondents and each of them with full knowledge had passed off the third respondent's business and goods as and for the business and goods of the appellant or an organisation associated with the appellant, whereby the appellant had **B** suffered damage.

On the application of the respondents‡, the Court of Appeal (LORD DENNING, M.R., PEARSON and SALMON, L.JJ.) made an order dated July 27, 1964, that a letter be sent to the Secretary of State for a certificate relating to recognition by Her Majesty's government of the German Democratic Republic or its government. By certificate dated Sept. 16, 1964, the Secretary of State replied that **C** Her Majesty's government had not granted any recognition de jure or de facto to the German Democratic Republic or its government. By supplemental notice of appeal dated Sept. 28, 1964, the respondents gave notice that they would rely, inter alia, on the following grounds of appeal—(i) that CROSS, J., erred in recognising the existence of the Council of Gera, which was established by a law of the German Democratic Republic or was an organ thereof, notwithstanding **D** that Her Majesty's government did not recognise the German Democratic Republic as a state or its authorities as a government; (ii) that CROSS, J., erred in paying attention to the decisions of courts which were established by the law of the German Democratic Republic, and (iii) that the action was an attempt to enforce extra-territorially the prerogative or other public laws of the German Democratic Republic. On Oct. 29, 1964, the Court of Appeal (HARMAN, DANCK- **E** WERTS and SALMON, L.JJ.) on the application of the appellants, ordered that a further letter be written to the Secretary of State requesting him to certify to the court the answer to the following questions, among others—

"What (a) states or (b) governments or (c) authorities (if any) had since July 1, 1945, up to the present date been recognised by Her Majesty's government as entitled to exercise or exercising government authority in **F** the area of Germany outside the zones allocated to the governments of the United Kingdom, the United States of America and the French Republic by the Protocol of Sept. 12, 1944, and the agreement of July 26, 1945, concluded between the governments of the said states and the Union of Soviet Socialist Republics. Has such recognition been de jure or de facto?"

In reply to that request Her Majesty's Secretary of State gave the answer dated **G** Nov. 6, 1964, which is set out at p. 545, letters D to H, post, to the effect that Her Majesty's government had recognised the U.S.S.R. as de jure entitled to exercise governing authority in respect of that zone.

The facts and the relevant rules of the articles of constitution of Carl-Zeiss-Stiftung appear in the opinion of LORD REID.

H

G. T. Aldous, Q.C., E. Lauterpacht and *D. W. Falconer* for the appellant.
Mark Littman, Q.C., T. M. Shelford and *Philip Lewis* for the respondents.

Their lordships took time for consideration.

May 18. The following opinions were delivered.

LORD REID: My Lords, in this action the appellant, Carl-Zeiss-Stiftung, **I** is seeking an injunction against the respondents to restrain them from selling optical instruments under the name Carl Zeiss and for other relief. The present appeal arises out of a summons taken out by the respondents on Feb. 7, 1956, for an order for a stay of proceedings and dismissal of the action on the ground that it was commenced and is being maintained without the appellant's authority. At various dates thereafter lengthy affidavits were filed and after long cross-examination CROSS, J., on Mar. 6, 1964, refused to stay the proceedings, having

‡ Reported [1964] 3 All E.R. 326.

A decided against the respondents on the three grounds then put forward by them. The respondents appealed and, having received new advice, put forward a new and quite different ground based on the non-recognition by Her Majesty's government of the German Democratic Republic. The Court of Appeal (1) on Dec. 17, 1964, allowed the respondents' appeal on this new ground and so found it unnecessary to reach any decision on the grounds maintained before
B CROSS, J.

I think that it will be convenient first to deal with the new point raised for the first time in the Court of Appeal (1) and then to deal separately with the other grounds. The issues raised are complex and difficult and your lordships are confronted with some 1,500 pages of affidavits, cross-examination and documents. I shall therefore try to restrict my narrative to those matters
C which are directly relevant to the issues to be decided.

It is necessary to have the appellant's history in mind. About 1846 Carl Zeiss founded an optical business in Jena. He later assumed as a partner Ernst Abbé of Jena University. Then they and Otto Schott founded a glass works. By 1891 Abbé was the owner of the whole (subject to Schott's interest) and he decided to set up a Stiftung or charitable foundation to own and carry
D on the two businesses under the name of the Carl-Zeiss-Stiftung. The main objects were to promote " precise technical industry " (which may not be an adequate translation) and to benefit the employees and the working population of Jena.

The constitution of the Stiftung was elaborately set out. First there was to be a special board for the administration of its estate and the supreme direction of
E its affairs and the rights and duties of the special board were to pertain to " that Department of the State Service of the Grand Duchy of Saxe-Weimar under which the affairs of the University of Jena are for the time being placed ". Then " for directing the industrial operations of the Stiftung " there were to be " boards of management of the various establishments of the Stiftung for the time being " and a permanent official, the deputy (Stiftungs Kommissar) was to be
F appointed to represent the special board on the boards of management, and finally r. 113 provided:

> " Should, in consequence of political changes in the state, the provision according to r. 5 of this statute with reference to the representation of the Stiftung become untenable, this representation including the appointment of the deputy of the Stiftung within the meaning of r. 5 and the statutory
G administration of the Carl-Zeiss-Stiftung shall be made over to that department of state, which with regard to the university of Jena occupies the place of the State Department of the Grand Duchy of Saxe-Weimar acting as special board, provided that its seat is in Thüringia, otherwise to the highest administrative authorities in Thüringia."

H In 1918 under the Weimar Republic the Grand Duchy was abolished and a new State of Thüringia was set up; thereupon the Minister of Education of that state became the special board. Then after 1935 under the National Socialist régime his place was taken by a Reichs-Stathalter; and when Thüringia was occupied by American forces in 1945 a new provisional government of Thüringia was set up by them and its Ministry of Education became the Special Board.
I On July 1, 1945, by agreement between the allied powers Thuringia came under Russian occupation and the present controversy turns on what happened thereafter.

We do not have precise evidence about this, but it is said that in 1949 the U.S.S.R. set up the German Democratic Republic to govern that part of Germany then occupied by Russia, and purported to make it an independent state. Moreover it is further said that thereafter the German Democratic Republic purported to act as an independent state in legislating for and administering the Russian

(1) [1965] 1 All E.R. 300; [1965] Ch. 596.

zone of Germany. That there is a body calling itself the German Democratic   A
Republic and that it does operate in that zone is, I think, common knowledge.
I do not think that common knowledge goes further than that, but for the
purposes of this appeal I am prepared to assume that the U.S.S.R. did purport
to confer independence on the Democratic Republic and that that body does
purport to act as if it were an independent state.

Shortly stated, the respondents' case is that we are bound to have regard to   B
the basis on which the German Democratic Republic purports to act, and that,
as Her Majesty's government has never granted recognition de jure or de facto
to that republic or its government, we must refuse to recognise as effective all
legislation emanating from it, and all acts done under such legislation. For
reasons which I shall give later I do not think that that is right but, first I shall
explain why, if it were right, it would be decisive of the point with which I am   C
now dealing.

In 1952 the German Democratic Republic passed legislation re-organising local
government in its " territory ", and in fact this legislation was put into effect.
The old state or land of Thüringia was abolished and in its place districts were
created each with a Diet and a Council or Rat. Jena fell within the District
of Gera and the Council of Gera did in fact operate as the special board of the   D
appellant, and did in fact authorise the raising of the present action. If the
respondents' argument based on non-recognition is well founded then it must
follow that British courts cannot recognise either the existence of the Council of
Gera or the validity of anything done by it, and in particular cannot recognise
any authority given by it for the raising of the present action. So I must now
examine the principles on which this argument is founded.   E

In the normal case a law is made either by the sovereign directly or by some
body entitled under the constitution of the country to make it or by some person
or body to which the sovereign has delegated authority to make it. On the
other hand there are many cases where laws have been made against the will of
the sovereign by persons engaged in a rebellion or revolution: then until such
persons or the government which they set up have been granted de facto recogni-   F
tion by the government of this country, their laws cannot be recognised by the
courts of this country, but after de facto recognition such laws will be recognised.
So far there is no difficulty. The present case, however, does not fit neatly into
any of these categories. We are considering whether the law of 1952 under
which the Council of Gera was set up can be recognised by our courts and therefore we must ascertain what was the situation in East Germany in 1952. It is   G
a firmly established principle that the question whether a foreign state ruler or
government is or is not sovereign is one on which our courts accept as conclusive
information provided by Her Majesty's government: no evidence is admissible
to contradict that information.

> " It has for some time been the practice of our courts . . . to take judicial
> notice of the sovereignty of a state and for that purpose (in any case of   H
> uncertainty) to seek information from a Secretary of State: and when
> information is so obtained the court does not permit it to be questioned by the
> parties "

(per VISCOUNT CAVE in *Duff Development Co., Ltd.* v. *Kelantan Government* (2)).

> " Such information is not in the nature of evidence: it is a statement   I
> by the sovereign of this country through one of his ministers upon a matter
> which is peculiarly within his cognizance "

(per VISCOUNT FINLAY (3). In the present case the Court of Appeal twice
received such information from the Foreign Secretary. First on Sept. 16, 1964,
it was stated: " Her Majesty's government has not granted any recognition

---

(2) [1924] All E.R. Rep. 1 at pp. 4, 5; [1924] A.C. 797 at p. 805.
(3) [1924] All E.R. Rep. at p. 8; [1924] A.C. at p. 813.

A de jure or de facto to (a) the ' German Democratic Republic ' or (b) its ' government ' '', and secondly on Nov. 6, 1964, a further answer was given to questions
which had been asked on Oct. 29.

In my opinion this latter answer is decisive on the question which I am now
considering and I must therefore quote the relevant question and the relevant
parts of the answer or certificate given by the Foreign Secretary. The question
B was:

" What (a) states or (b) governments or (c) authorities (if any) have since
July 1, 1945, up to the present date been recognised by Her Majesty's govern-
ment as (a) entitled to exercise or (b) exercising governing authority in the
area of Germany outside the zones allocated to the governments of the
United Kingdom, the United States of America and the French Republic
C by the Protocol of Sept. 12, 1944, and the agreement of July 26, 1945,
concluded between the governments of the said states and the Union of
Soviet Socialist Republics. Has such recognition been de jure or de facto? "

The relevant parts of the certificate are as follows:

" The area of Germany to which the question is understood to refer
D comprises (a) the zone of occupation allocated to the Union of Soviet Socialist
Republics under the Protocol of Sept. 12, 1944, and the agreement of July 26,
1945, as modified by the protocol of the proceedings of the Berlin Conference
of Aug. 2, 1945, and (b) the ' Greater Berlin ' area. The question is understood not to relate to the areas of Germany placed under Soviet or Polish
administration in pursuance of the aforesaid protocol of Aug. 2, 1945.

E " (a) From the zone allocated to the Union of Soviet Socialist Republics
Allied forces, under the Supreme Allied Commander, General Eisenhower,
withdrew at or about the end of June, 1945. Since that time and up to the
present date Her Majesty's Government have recognised the state and
government of the Union of Soviet Socialist Republics as de jure entitled to
exercise governing authority in respect of that zone. In matters affecting
F Germany as a whole, the states and governments of the French Republic,
the United Kingdom of Great Britain and Northern Ireland, the United
States of America and the Union of Soviet Socialist Republics were jointly
entitled to exercise governing authority. In the period from Aug. 30, 1945,
to Mar. 20, 1948, they did exercise such joint authority through the Control
Council for Germany. Apart from the states, governments and control
G council aforementioned, Her Majesty's government [has] not recognised
either de jure or de facto any other authority purporting to exercise governing
authority in or in respect of the zone. Her Majesty's government, however, regards the aforementioned governments as retaining rights and
responsibilities in respect of Germany as a whole.''

It was not argued that the matter which I am now considering is one affecting
H Germany as whole; so the rights of the other three allied governments do not
affect this question, and I need only consider what the certificate says with
regard to the U.S.S.R. and the inferences which must be drawn from it.

The purpose of a certificate is to provide information about the status of foreign
governments and states and, therefore, the statement that since June, 1945,

I " Her Majesty's government [has] recognised the state and government
of the Union of Soviet Socialist Republics as de jure entitled to exercise
governing authority in respect of that zone "

cannot merely mean that H.M. government has granted this recognition so as
to leave the courts of this country free to receive evidence whether in fact the
U.S.S.R. are still entitled to exercise governing authority there. The courts
of this country are no more entitled to hold that a sovereign, still recognised by
our government, has ceased in fact to be sovereign de jure, than they are entitled
to hold that a government not yet recognised has acquired sovereign status. So

this certificate requires that we must take it as a fact that the U.S.S.R. have been A
since 1945 and still are de jure entitled to exercise that governing authority.
The certificate makes no distinction between the period before and the period
after the German Democratic Republic was set up. So we are bound to hold
that the setting up of that republic made no difference in the right of the U.S.S.R.
to exercise governing authority in the zone; and it must follow from that that
the U.S.S.R. could at any time lawfully bring to an end the German Democratic B
Republic and its government and could then resume direct rule of the zone.
That is quite inconsistent, however, with there having in fact been any abdication
by the U.S.S.R. of its rights when the German Democratic Republic was set
up.

The judgment of the Court of Appeal (4) appears to me to be based on the
view that the courts of this country can and must accept the position that the C
U.S.S.R. have recognised the German Democratic Republic as an independent
sovereign state. HARMAN, L.J., said (5):

" It is in fact notorious that the U.S.S.R. has recognised the German
Democratic Republic as a sovereign state and treats its law making capacity
accordingly "

and DIPLOCK, L.J., says (6)
                                                                              D

" All that I am prepared to assume—and I think it is a matter of which
I can take judicial notice—is that the government of the U.S.S.R. recognises
the ' government of the German Democratic Republic ' as the independent
sovereign government of an independent sovereign state for whose territory
the government of the U.S.S.R. claims no power to make laws."
                                                                              E
The learned judges of the Court of Appeal, however, do not appear to have had
their attention directed to the true import of the certificate of the Secretary of
State. The U.S.S.R. may have purported to confer independence or sovereignty
on the German Democratic Republic, but in my judgment that certificate clearly
requires us to hold that, whatever the U.S.S.R. may have purported to do, they
did not in fact set up the German Democratic Republic as a sovereign or indepen- F
dent state. If they retained their right to govern its territory they could not
possibly have done so; and the certificate requires us to hold that they did
retain that right.

If we are bound to hold that the German Democratic Republic was not in
fact set up as a sovereign independent state, the only other possibility is that it
was set up as a dependent or subordinate organisation through which the U.S.S.R. G
is entitled to exercise indirect rule. I do not think that we are concerned to
enquire or to know to what extent the U.S.S.R. in fact exercise their right of
control. At a late stage in the argument before your lordships counsel for the
respondents made an application that further questions should be addressed to
Her Majesty's government. That would be a perfectly proper thing to do if
your lordships were of opinion that the existing certificate is ambiguous or H
insufficient; but I can see no ambiguity or insufficiency in this certificate, and
therefore I agree that this application was properly refused.

It was argued that the present case is analogous to cases where subjects of an
existing sovereign have rebelled and have succeeded in gaining control of a
part of the old sovereign's dominions. When they set up a new government in
opposition to the de jure sovereign that new government does not and cannot I
derive any authority or right from the de jure sovereign, and our courts must
regard its acts and the acts of its organs or officers as nullities until it has established and consolidated its position to such an extent as to warrant our government according de facto recognition of it. The case of *Banco de Bilbao* v.
Sancha (7) affords a fairly recent example of this: there General Franco's

(4) [1965] 1 All E.R. 300; [1965] Ch. 596.
(5) [1965] 1 All E.R. at p. 315, letter G; [1965] Ch. at p. 651.
(6) [1965] 1 All E.R. at p. 323, letter E; [1965] Ch. at p. 664.
(7) [1938] 2 All E.R. 253; [1938] 2 K.B. 176.

A adherents had succeeded in gaining control of a large part of Spain and the government which they set up in opposition to the republican government was recognised de facto by the British government. Giving the judgment of the Court of Appeal CLAUSON, L.J., said (8):

B
> " this court is bound to treat the acts of the government which His Majesty's government recognise as the de facto government of the area in question as acts which cannot be impugned as the acts of an usurping government and conversely the court must be bound to treat the acts of a rival government claiming jurisdiction over the same area, even if the latter government be recognised by His Majesty's government as the de jure government of the area, as a mere nullity, and as matters which cannot be taken into account in any way in any of His Majesty's courts."

C
Aksionairnoye Obschestvo A. M. Luther v. *James Sagor & Co.* (9) is another good example. The case turned on whether the courts of this country could recognise a decree made in 1918 by officers of the U.S.S.R. which had by revolutionary means assumed power in Russia. At the time when the case came before ROCHE, J., His Majesty's government had not recognised the U.S.S.R., and therefore

D ROCHE, J., (10) properly held that he could not give effect to that decree; but before the case was decided by the Court of Appeal (9) the court were informed by the Secretary of State that His Majesty's government recognised the Soviet government as the de facto government of Russia. Accordingly the Court of Appeal were able to give effect to the decree (9).

The present case is, however, essentially different. The German Democratic

E Republic was set up by the U.S.S.R. and it derived its authority and status from the government of the U.S.S.R. So the only question could be whether or not it was set up as a sovereign state; but the certificate of our government requires us to hold that it was not set up as a sovereign state because it requires us to hold that the U.S.S.R. remained de jure sovereign and therefore did not voluntarily transfer its sovereignty to the German Democratic Republic. More-

F over, if the German Democratic Republic did not become a sovereign state at its inception, there is no suggestion that it has at any subsequent time attempted to deprive the U.S.S.R. of rights which were not granted to it at its inception. The courts of this country must disregard any declarations of the government of the U.S.S.R. in so far as they conflict with the certificate of Her Majesty's Secretary of State, and we must therefore hold that the U.S.S.R. set up the

G German Democratic Republic not as a sovereign state, but as an organisation subordinate to the U.S.S.R. If that is so, then mere declarations by the government of the German Democratic Republic that it is acting as the government of an independent state cannot be regarded as proof that its initial status has been altered, and we must regard the acts of the German Democratic Republic, its government organs and officers as acts done with the consent of the government

H of the U.S.S.R. as the government entitled to exercise governing authority.

It appears to me to be impossible for any de jure sovereign governing authority to disclaim responsibility for acts done by subordinate bodies which it has set up and which have not attempted to usurp its sovereignty. So in my opinion the courts of this country cannot treat as nullities acts done by or on behalf of the German Democratic Republic. De facto recognition is appropriate—and in

I my view is only appropriate—where the new government have usurped power against the will of the de jure sovereign. I would think that where a sovereign has granted independence to a dependency any recognition of the new state would be a recognition de jure. The general practice of the British government was stated in Parliament on Mar. 21, 1951, by the Secretary of State for Foreign Affairs (HANSARD, Vol. 485, col. 2410) as follows:

---

(8) [1938] 2 All E.R. at p. 260; [1938] 2 K.B. at pp. 195, 196.
(9) [1921] All E.R. Rep. 138; [1921] 3 K.B. 532.   (10) [1921] 1 K.B. 456.

" . . . it is internal law which defines the conditions under which a govern   A
ment should be recognised de jure or de facto, and it is a matter of judgment
in each particular case whether a régime fulfils the conditions.   The
conditions under international law for the recognition of a new régime as
the de facto government of a state are that the new régime has in fact
effective control over most of the state's territory and that this control seems
likely to continue.   The conditions for the recognition of a new régime as   B
the de jure government of a state are that the new régime should not merely
have effective control over most of the state's territory, but that it should,
in fact, be firmly established.   His Majesty's government [considers] that
recognition should be accorded when the conditions specified by international
law are, in fact, fulfilled and that recognition should not be given when
these conditions are not fulfilled.   The recognition of a government de jure   C
or de facto should not depend on whether the character of the régime is
such as to command His Majesty's government's approval."

Recognition implies independence and refusal to recognise the German Democratic
Republic or its government is entirely consistent with that statement if independence was never in fact granted by the U.S.S.R., for no one suggests that the
German Democratic Republic has or could have seized independence in defiance   D
of the U.S.S.R.   So there can in my view be no question of awaiting de facto
recognition before we can recognise as lawful the acts of the German Democratic
Republic.   We recognise them not because they are acts of a sovereign state
but because they are acts done by a subordinate body which the U.S.S.R. set
up to act on its behalf.

I am reinforced in my opinion by a consideration of the consequences which   E
would follow if the view taken by the Court of Appeal (11) were correct.   Counsel
for the respondents did not dispute that in that case we must not only disregard
all new laws and decrees made by the German Democratic Republic or its
government, but we must also disregard all executive and judicial acts done by
persons appointed by that government because we must regard their appoint-   F
ments as invalid.   The result of that would be far reaching.   Trade with the
Eastern zone of Germany is not discouraged; but the incorporation of every
company in East Germany under any new law made by the German Democratic
Republic or by the official act of any official appointed by its government would
have to be regarded as a nullity so that any such company could neither sue nor
be sued in this country.   Any civil marriage under any such new law or owing its   G
validity to the act of any such official would also have to be treated as a nullity
so that we should have to regard the children as illegitimate; and the same
would apply to divorces and all manner of judicial decisions whether in family or
commercial questions.   That would affect not only status of persons formerly
domiciled in East Germany but also property in this country the devolution
of which depended on East German law.

It was suggested that these consequences might be mitigated if the courts   H
of this country could adopt doctrines which have found some support in the
United States of America.   Difficult questions arose there with regard to acts
of administration in the Confederate States during the civil war and again out
of the delay in recognition of the U.S.S.R.   A solution of the earlier difficulty
was found by the Supreme Court in *U.S.* v. *Home Insurance Co.* (12), and other
similar cases; and for the latter difficulty solutions were suggested, particularly   I
by CARDOZO, C.J. in such cases as *Sokoloff* v. *National City Bank of New York* (13)
and *Petrogradsky Mejdunarodny Kommerchesky Bank* v. *National City Bank* (14).
In the view which I take of the present case it is unnecessary to express any
opinion whether it would be possible to adopt any similar solutions in this country
if the need should ever arise.

(11) [1965] 1 All E.R. 300;   [1965] Ch. 596.   (12) (1874), 89 U.S. 99.
(13) (1924), 239 N.Y. 158.   (14) (1930), 170 N.E. 479.

A Finally on this branch of the case I must deal briefly with three grounds on which the appellant argued that the raising of this action should be held to have been properly authorised even if the actions of the Council of Gera must be disregarded. These grounds involved the interpretation and effect of a power of attorney granted to Dr. Schrade in 1951 and questions as to his powers by virtue of appointments in the Stiftung which he then held. These matters involve

B German law. They only became important after the respondents put forward their new case in the court of Appeal (15), so they were only dealt with cursorily, if at all, in the affidavits and in the evidence led before CROSS, J. The Court of Appeal (15) found it possible to decide these questions without receiving further evidence of German law which the appellants wished to adduce. In my opinion these questions could not properly be decided on the evidence as it stands, and,

C if they should ever arise in any other litigation, the judgment of the Court of Appeal (15) cannot be regarded as res judicata or as having binding effect.

The next question for consideration is whether by reason of a decision of the Federal Supreme Court of West Germany the subject-matter of the issue now before this House is res judicata so that the respondents must succeed without further inquiry. I can deal briefly with the events which led up to that decision.

D When the American forces left Jena in 1945 a number of officers of the Stiftung and of the firm Carl Zeiss went with them to West Germany. The Stiftung and the firm already had interests there and these were developed in particular by three of these officers. After a time relations between them and Jena became strained and legal proceedings of various kinds were begun. Decrees were obtained in West Germany to the effect that the domicil of the Stiftung was removed

E from Jena to Heidenheim in Würthemberg, and goods were manufactured and sold under the name Carl Zeiss. Then the West German firm Carl Zeiss sought to prevent the sale in West Germany of the products made in Jena, and in 1953 an action was commenced at Stuttgart by " the Carl-Zeiss-Stiftung of Jena represented by the Council of the District of Gera " against the firm Carl Zeiss of Heidenheim and the three individuals who were directing it. The main purpose

F of this action was to restrain these defendants from using the name Carl Zeiss. Those defendants at once raised the preliminary objection that the Stiftung was not properly before the court as the Council of Gera was not the legal representative of the Stiftung. The proceedings on this objection were elaborate and prolonged, but ultimately on Nov. 15, 1960, it was sustained by the Federal Supreme Court. I do not attempt at this point even to summarise the reasons:

G the various judgments given in this action occupy over two hundred closely typed pages of which the final judgment occupies more than thirty.

The respondents maintain that this decision must be held decisive of the question now before this House because the issue in this appeal is the same as that which was decided by the Federal Supreme Court. So in the first place it is necessary to make clear what is the question now before this House. On Feb. 7,

H 1956, the respondents took out a summons for an order that all further proceedings in this action be stayed and that the action be dismissed on the ground that the same was commenced and was being maintained without the appellant's authority and that Messrs. Courts & Co. the solicitors purporting to act for the appellant herein do pay to the respondents the costs of this action to be taxed as between solicitor and client. This question, whether these solicitors are maintaining this

I action without the authority of the Stiftung is the sole question which your lordships now have to determine.

There is a vast amount of authority on estoppel per rem judicatam.

" The object of the rule of res judicata is always put upon two grounds—the one public policy, that it is in the interest of the state that there should be an end to litigation, and the other, the hardship on the individual, that he should be vexed twice for the same cause "

(15) [1965] 1 All E.R. 300; [1965] Ch. 596.

(per LORD BLACKBURN in *Lockyer* v. *Ferryman* (16)). The general principle is **A**
clear that the earlier judgment relied on must have been a final judgment, and
that there must be identity of parties and of subject-matter in the former and in
the present litigation; but each of these three requirements can give rise—and
in the present case does give rise—to difficult questions.

Let me take first identity of parties. In this preliminary or interlocutory
matter the issue is whether the nominal plaintiff is before the court at all. If it is **B**
decided in favour of the defendant, that establishes that the nominal plaintiff
never was before the court. So I do not see how the nominal plaintiff, here the
Stiftung, can be a party to that issue; and it is admitted that the Stiftung was
not a party to the German proceedings. The respondents are of course parties
for they raise the issue; but who is their opponent? We are not told the precise
implications of the requirement of German procedure as to " representation ", **C**
but I am content to assume that the Council of Gera was a party to the German
proceedings: that council was ordered to pay the costs; but who is the appellant
in this House? Again, I think, not the Stiftung. The issue is whether the solicitors
are maintaining the action without authority and surely they must be parties—
how else could they be made personally liable to the respondents in costs? I
can see no other party—no other appellant. It was argued that the Council of **D**
Gera can be regarded as a party, but I can see no ground for that. There may be
a question when I come to deal with privity; but the Council of Gera has never
sought to be a party and no one has sought to make them a party.

Again there is no doubt that the requirement of identity of parties is satisfied
if there is privity between a party to the former litigation and a party to the
present litigation. The only way in which that could be satisfied in this case would **E**
be if there were privity between the Council of Gera and the solicitors. We have
a letter from the Council of Gera in its capacity of special board of the Stiftung
authorising the raising of this action, but we do not know whether that council
has taken any further part, whether it has given any further instructions, or
whether it is using the funds of the Stiftung to finance this litigation. The most
that can be said is that the council is the " client " instructing the solicitors, **F**
though I doubt whether that is proved; the real question may be whether there
is a " client " at all. Does this make it a privy? It has always been said that
there must be privity of blood, title or interest: here it would have to be privity
of interest. That can arise in many ways, but it seems to me to be essential that
the person now to be estopped from defending himself must have had some kind
of interest in the previous litigation or its subject-matter. I have found no English **G**
case to the contrary. If that is right, then there can be no privity here, because
these solicitors had no connexion with and certainly no interest in the German
litigation.

There does, however, seem to me to be a possible extension of the doctrine of
privity as commonly understood. A party against whom a previous decision was
pronounced may employ a servant or engage a third party to do something which **H**
infringes the right established in the earlier litigation, and so may raise the whole
matter again in his interest. Then, if the other party to the earlier litigation
brings an action against the servant or agent, the real defendant could be said to
be the employer, who alone has the real interest, and it might well be thought
unjust if he could vex his opponent by re-litigating the original question by
means of the device of putting forward his servant. But this is not a case of that **I**
character. The Council of Gera has no substantial interest in this litigation. If
the plaintiff succeeds, the only persons who can benefit are the Stiftung or the
two nationalised firms in Jena to which I shall refer later. The Council of Gera is
merely a local public authority like a county council on which there has been
imposed the duty of acting as the special board of the Stiftung and there is
nothing to show that the Council or any of its members will gain anything if the
plaintiff wins, or lose anything if the plaintiff loses this case. Further, here the

(16) (1877), 2 App. Cas. 519 at p. 530.

A respondents are seeking to make these solicitors personally liable to them in solicitor and client costs—in effect seeking damages against them for breach of warranty of authority. In my view the solicitors cannot properly be held to be estopped from defending themselves, and showing that they have authority to act, by a judgment which had nothing to do with them.

There is little authority bearing on a question of this kind. The only modern
B English case cited was *Mercantile Investment and General Trust Co. v. River Plate Trust, Loan and Agency Co.* (17). The facts were complicated, but it is sufficient for present purposes to say that the plaintiffs in this action had obtained a judgment against another company (" the American company ") and they maintained this as an estoppel against the defendants in this action (" the English company ") on the ground that, by reason of an indemnity given by the
C English company, the English company had assisted the American company in the previous action and had paid their costs, so that they were virtually parties to the previous action. ROMER, J., dealt with this point very briefly (18) and held that there was no estoppel.

I should also refer to *Kinnersley* v. *Orpe* (19), which was cited as relevant on privity. There Dr. Cotton claimed a right to fish and sent a servant, Orpe, to
D assert it. Kinnersley brought an action of trespass and succeeded. Then Dr. Cotton sent another servant, also called Orpe, to fish and this action was brought against him. The plaintiff simply produced the record in the former case and PERRYN, B., (20) held this evidence conclusive " both the Orpes having acted under the authority of Cotton who was the real defendant in both causes ". On a rule (20) " The court also thought that the record in the former cause, though
E admissible evidence, was not conclusive ". With regard to this case LORD ELLENBOROUGH, C.J., said in *Outram* v. *Morewood* (21):

" as to the case of *Kinnersley* v. *Orpe* (19) it is extraordinary that it should ever have been for a moment supposed that there could be an estoppel in such a case. It was not pleaded as such: neither were the parties in the second suit the same with those in the first."

F And a little later (22) he referred to " the defendant who was no party to the former action ". One should not attach too much weight to this because it was a very minor point in LORD ELLENBOROUGH'S elaborate and learned judgment. But at least it never occurred to him that the doctrine of privity could be stretched to affect a defendant from whom a penalty was claimed and who had no connexion with the previous case, merely because his employer had been
G concerned with it.

The respondents sought to rely on American authorities. Their effect is summarised in the American RESTATEMENT OF THE LAW OF JUDGMENTS, Ch. 4. The only section which seemed to me to come near to applying to the appellant solicitors is para. 85 (2):

H   " Where a person is bound by or entitled to the benefits of the rules of res judicata because of a judgment for or against him with reference to a particular subject-matter, such rules apply in a subsequent action brought or defended by another on his account."

With that I would agree; and if these solicitors were bringing this action on account of or for the benefit of the Council of Gera, I would hold that res judicata
I could be pleaded against them. I have already stated my view that this action is not brought on account of or for the benefit of the Council of Gera and, in particular, these solicitors are not contesting the issue now before your lordships for the benefit of that Council. In so far as they are not acting to protect their own interests they are seeking to act for the benefit of the Stiftung, and it is not alleged that the plea of res judicata would be good against the Stiftung.

(17) [1894] 1 Ch. 578.   (18) [1894] 1 Ch. at p. 596.
(19) (1780), 2 Doug. K.B. 517.   (20) (1780), 2 Doug. K.B. at p. 518.
(21) (1803), 3 East 346 at p. 366.   (22) (1803), 3 East, at p. 366.

The second requirement for res judicata is identity of subject matter. As to A
this, it has become common to distinguish between cause of action estoppel and
issue estoppel. There is certainly no cause of action estoppel here. The question
before the German court was whether the Council of Gera was the legal representative of the Stiftung at one date. The question here is whether at a different date
the solicitors had the authority of the Stiftung to raise this action. An answer,
yes or no, to the first question does not necessarily imply a similar answer to the B
second. What the respondents maintain is that the grounds on which the German
court in fact decided the first question are such that we cannot decide this case in
favour of the solicitors without disagreeing with at least some of the findings on
which the German court based their decision. I think that that is true and the
question is whether we are entitled to do that.

Issue estoppel may be a comparatively new phrase but I think that the law of C
England—unlike the law of some other countries—has always recognised that
estoppel per rem judicatam includes more than merely cause of action estoppel.
The earliest case commonly referred to on res judicata is the *Duchess of Kingston's
Case* (23). The Duchess of Kingston was prosecuted for bigamy in this House.
She put forward in defence a decision of an ecclesiastical court that her first
marriage was invalid. The first question put to the judges who were in attendance D
was whether a sentence of the spiritual court against the marriage was conclusive
evidence. The unanimous opinion of the judges was given by DE GREY, C.J.,
and in the course of it he said (24):

" From the variety of cases relative to judgments being given in evidence
in civil suits these two deductions seem to follow as generally true: first that
the judgment of a court of concurrent jurisdiction directly upon the point, is E
as a plea a bar, or as evidence conclusive, between the same parties upon the
same matter directly in question in another court: secondly that the judgment of a court of exclusive jurisdiction directly upon the point is, in like
manner, conclusive upon the same matter, between the same parties, coming
incidentally in question in another court for a different purpose. But neither
the judgment of a concurrent or exclusive jurisdiction is evidence of any F
matter which comes collaterally in question, though within their jurisdiction;
nor of any matter incidentally cognizable; nor of any matter to be inferred
by argument from the judgment."

In referring to a judgment being conclusive on the same matter " coming
incidentally in question in another court for a different purpose " (24) the judges
were clearly going beyond cause of action estoppel, but I need not attempt to G
discover just how far they meant to go because this has been developed in many
later decisions.

In *R.* v. *Inhabitants of the Township of Hartington Middle Quarter* (25) it
appeared that in a previous litigation it had been decided that two young children
had a settlement in the defendants' township. The question at issue in this case
was the settlement of their mother and it was held that the defendants were H
estopped from denying that she had the same settlement. The cause of action
was obviously not the same. COLERIDGE, J., in delivering the judgment of the
court, said (26):

" The question then is, whether the [former] judgment concludes, not
merely as to the point actually decided, but as to a matter which it was I
necessary to decide, and which was actually decided, as the groundwork of the
decision itself, though not then directly the point at issue. And we think it
does conclude to that extent . . . Now it cannot be said that the facts we are
considering were merely collateral to the decision in the former case. The
question then was where two unemancipated children were settled: and it

(23) (1776), 1 East, P.C. 468; 20 State Tr. 355.
(24) (1776), 20 State Tr. at p. 538.   (25) (1855), 4 E. & B. 780.
                    (26) (1855), 4 E. & B. at p. 794.

A   was answered by showing that they were the legitimate issue of William and Esther, that is that these two were lawfully married, and the children born after and that William was settled with the now appellants. Strike either of these facts out, and there is no ground for the decision: these facts were therefore necessarily and directly matter of inquiry. The question now is, where is Esther settled: and this is answered by showing the same two facts,

B   the marriage of Esther and William and the settlement of William, the two facts already decided. The judgments in the two cases therefore rest on the same foundation; which, having been settled in the first, cannot be, as between the same parties, unsettled in the latter."

In *Flitters* v. *Allfrey* (27) a landlord alleging a weekly tenancy obtained a warrant for the eviction of the tenant and then sued him in the county court for 29 weeks'

C   rent. He failed in this action because the judge held that there was a yearly tenancy. Then the tenant sued for damages for eviction. LORD COLERIDGE, C.J., said (28):

"The now plaintiff succeeded upon the trial of a plaint in the county court which involved the same question of fact as that which was in issue in this

D   case, viz. whether the tenancy under the defendant was a weekly or a yearly tenancy. The defendant thought the decision of the county court wrong. Upon the trial of this cause the jury thought so too; and I agreed with them: but the plaintiff, against the right, succeeded upon an estoppel."

Counsel had pointed out that failure to succeed in the action for rent did not on the face of it or necessarily involve any decision that the tenancy was yearly and

E   not weekly: but that was in fact the ground on which the county court judge decided the case and the landlord was not allowed to relitigate that issue in the tenant's subsequent action for damages.

These two cases appear to me to be authorities directly in favour of issue estoppel, but the complications in each were such that it is easy to miss the point, and little attention seems to have been paid to this form of estoppel until

F   comparatively recently.

A case which has given rise to some difficulties is *Hoystead* v. *Taxation Comr.* (29). There an appeal with regard to income tax for an earlier year had been decided on an assumption that certain beneficiaries under a will were joint owners. Then in a case as to liability to tax in a later year the commissioner tried to maintain that that assumption had been wrong but he was held to be estopped.

G   LORD SHAW in delivering the judgment of the Board, after citing numerous authorities including the judgment of LORD ELLENBOROUGH in *Outram* v. *Morewood* (30), said (31):

"It is seen from this citation of authority that if in any court of competent jurisdiction a decision is reached, a party is estopped from questioning it in a new legal proceeding. But the principle also extends to any point, whether

H   of assumption or admission, which was in substance the ratio of and fundamental to the decision."

Comments were made on that passage in *New Brunswick Ry. Co.* v. *British and French Trust Corpn., Ltd.* (32) by LORD RUSSELL OF KILLOWEN (33) and LORD ROMER (34) and in *Society of Medical Officers of Health* v. *Hope* (*Valuation Officer*) (35) by LORD RADCLIFFE. There may well be a difference between a case

I   where an issue was in fact decided in the earlier case, and a case where it was not in fact decided because the earlier judgment went by default or was founded

---

(27) (1874), L.R. 10 C.P. 29.   (28) (1874), L.R. 10 C.P. at p. 43.
(29) [1925] All E.R. Rep. 56; [1926] A.C. 155.   (30) (1803), 3 East, 346.
(31) [1925] All E.R. Rep. at p. 64; [1926] A.C. at p. 170.
(32) [1938] 4 All E.R. 747; [1939] A.C. 1.
(33) [1938] 4 All E.R. at p. 760; [1939] A.C. at p. 28.
(34) [1938] 4 All E.R. at p. 769; [1939] A.C. at p. 42.
(35) [1960] 1 All E.R. 317 at p. 323; [1960] A.C. 551 at p. 566.

on an assumption. Indeed I think that some confusion has been introduced by **A** applying to issue estoppel without modification rules which have been evolved to deal with cause of action estoppel, such as the oft-quoted passage from the judgment of WIGRAM, V.-C., in *Henderson* v. *Henderson* (36). It is unnecessary, however, to pursue that matter, because in the present case the issues with regard to which the respondents plead estoppel were fully litigated in the West German court.   **B**

In *Marginson* v. *Blackburn Borough Council* (37) both the parties had been defendants in a county court action in which a plaintiff claimed damages for negligence and they had been held both to blame. This was held to estop the plaintiff in this action from maintaining (in his personal capacity) that he was not to blame.

" In such a case the question arises, what was the question of law or fact   **C** which was decided [in the earlier case]? And for this purpose, it may be vital in many cases to consider the actual history of the proceedings "

(per SLESSER, L.J., (38) delivering the judgment of the court).

Thoday v. *Thoday* (39) is the most recent of a series of matrimonial cases raising this question. There are special considerations in this field, so WILLMER, L.J.,   **D** only said (40):

" There may be cases in which a party may be held to be estopped from raising particular issues, if those issues are precisely the same as issues which have been previously raised and have been the subject of adjudication."

DIPLOCK, L.J., (41) dealt with the matter on more general lines, however, and what he said is further explained in *Fidelitas Shipping Co.* v. *V/O. Exportchleb*   **E** (42). He drew (43) a distinction between issue estoppel and fact estoppel which I find difficult to understand. Suppose that as an essential step towards the judgment in an earlier case it was decided (a) that on a particular date A. owed B. £100 or (b) that on that date A. was alive. The first is, or at least probably is, a question of law, the second is a pure question of fact. Are these findings to be treated differently when issue estoppel is pleaded in a later case? Or take   **F** marriage—an issue in the earlier case may have been whether there ever was a ceremony (a pure question of fact) or it may have been whether the ceremony created a marriage (a question of law). I cannot think that this would make any difference if in a later case about quite different subject-matter the earlier finding for or against marriage was pleaded as creating issue estoppel.

The difficulty which I see about issue estoppel is a practical one. Suppose the   **G** first case is one of trifling importance but it involves for one party proof of facts which would be expensive and troublesome; and that party can see the possibility that the same point may arise if his opponent later raises a much more important claim. What is he to do? The second case may never be brought. Must he go to great trouble and expense to forestall a possible plea of issue estoppel if the second case is brought? This does not arise in cause of action estoppel: if the cause of   **H** action is important, he will incur the expense; if it is not, he will take the chance of winning on some other point. It seems to me that there is room for a good deal more thought before we settle the limits of issue estoppel; but I have no doubt that issue estoppel does exist in the law of England, and if it does it would apply in the present case if the earlier judgment had been a final judgment of an English court.   **I**

Next I must consider whether it makes any difference that the former judgment

(36) [1843-60] All E.R. Rep. 378 at p. 381; (1843), 3 Hare, 100 at p. 114.
(37) [1939] 1 All E.R. 273; [1939] 2 K.B. 426.
(38) [1939] 1 All E.R. at pp. 277, 278; [1939] 2 K.B. at p. 437.
(39) [1964] 1 All E.R. 341; [1964] P. 181.
(40) [1964] 1 All E.R. at p. 348; [1964] P. at p. 191.
(41) [1964] 1 All E.R. at p. 351; [1964] P. at p. 197.   (42) [1965] 2 All E.R. 4.
        (43) [1964] 1 All E.R. at p. 352; [1964] P. at p. 198.

A was the judgment of a foreign court. At one time foreign judgments were regarded as being only evidence and not conclusive; but at least since the decision in *Godard* v. *Gray* (44) they have been regarded as equally conclusive with English judgments (subject to any difference there may be resulting from there being no merger of a cause of action in a foreign judgment). The same pleas, e.g., fraud or lack of jurisdiction are good against both. It would seem that the only plea

B which may be available against foreign judgments alone is perversity, if *Simpson* v. *Fogo* (45) was rightly decided. In that case SIR WILLIAM PAGE WOOD, V.-C., (46) refused to give effect to a judgment of the Supreme Court of Louisiana. There was no question of perversity in the ordinary sense of obstinately or dishonestly shutting one's eyes to what one knows to be right. The Supreme Court had applied what they believed to be their common law, but it was at variance

C with a generally accepted rule of private international law, which required foreign (in this case, English) law to be applied in the circumstances of that case. SIR WILLIAM PAGE WOOD, V.-C., (47) called this " a perverse and deliberate refusal to recognise the law of the country by which title has been validly conferred ". I shall have to return to this case later.

  I can see no reason in principle why we should deny the possibility of issue

D estoppel based on a foreign judgment, but there appear to me to be at least three reasons for being cautious in any particular case. In the first place, we are not familiar with modes of procedure in many foreign countries, and it may not be easy to be sure that a particular issue has been decided or that its decision was a basis of the foreign judgment and not merely collateral or obiter. Secondly, I have already alluded to the practical difficulties of a defendant in deciding whether

E even in this country he should incur the trouble and expense of deploying his full case in a trivial case: it might be most unjust to hold that a litigant here should be estopped from putting forward his case because it was impracticable for him to do so in an earlier case of a trivial character abroad with the result that the decision in that case went against him. These two reasons do not apply in the present case. The case for the Stiftung, or on this issue those who purported to

F represent it, was fought as tenaciously in West Germany as this case has been fought here, and it is not difficult to see what were the grounds on which the West German judgment was based. The third reason for caution, however, does raise a difficult problem with which I must now deal.

  It is clear that there can be no estoppel of this character unless the former judgment was a final judgment on the merits. But what does that mean in

G connexion with issue estopped? When we are dealing with cause of action estoppel it means that the merits of the cause of action must be finally disposed of so that the matter cannot be raised again in the foreign country. In this connexion the case of *Nouvion* v. *Freeman* (48) is important. There had been in Spain a final judgment in a summary form of procedure; but that was not necessarily the end of the matter because it was possible to reopen the whole question by commencing

H a different kind of action, so the summary judgment was not res judicata in Spain. I do not find it surprising that the House unanimously refused to give effect in England to that summary judgment.

  When we come to issue estoppel, I think that by parity of reasoning we should have to be satisfied that the issues in question cannot be relitigated in the foreign country. In other words it would have to be proved in this case that the courts of

I the German Federal Republic would not allow the re-opening in any new case between the same parties of the issues decided by the Supreme Court in 1960, which are now said to found an estoppel here. There would seem to be no authority of any kind on this matter, but it seems to me to verge on absurdity that we should regard as conclusive something in a German judgment which the German courts themselves would not regard as conclusive. It is quite true that estoppel

(44) (1870), L.R. 6 Q.B. 139.   (45) (1863), 1 Hem. & M. 195.
(46) (1863), 1 Hem. & M. at p. 246.   (47) (1863), 1 Hem. & M. at p. 247.
                        (48) (1889), 15 App. Cas. 1.

is a matter for the lex fori, but the lex fori ought to be developed in a manner **A** consistent with good sense.

The need to prove whether West German law would permit these issues to be re-opened there appears to have escaped the notice of the appellant's advisers, and your lordships are left in considerable difficulty. On the one hand, there is always a presumption that the foreign law on any particular question is the same as English law, unless the contrary is proved. On the other hand, it would be **B** remarkable if German law had reached precisely the same stage of development on issue estoppel as the law of England has, and there are some indications in the German judgments that it has not. I have had an opportunity of reading the views of my noble and learned friend LORD WILBERFORCE on this matter. I do not dissent from them. I must, however, rest my judgment that there is here no res judicata or estoppel on there being no sufficient identity of parties in the **C** West German proceedings and in the matter now before your lordships.

As I am of opinion that the respondents do not succeed on these preliminary pleas I must now turn to the substantial question in this appeal—have the respondents proved that the appellant's solicitors have commenced and are maintaining this action without the appellant's authority? The appellant is a foreign corporation, and it is not maintained that it has ceased to exist. Further, **D** it is not disputed that the capacity of a foreign corporation and the functions and powers of its organs or officers are matters for the law of its domicil. So the first question is—what is the legal domicil of the Stiftung? Its constitution provides in r. 3 " The legal domicil of the Stiftung shall be Jena ". I have mentioned West German decrees to the effect that the domicil shall be Heiden-heim, but counsel for the respondents stated that he did not rely on these decrees **E** in the present appeal. He did however argue that according to German law its domicil is in Germany as a whole; but Germany is, for the time being at least, divided, the Federal Republic being sovereign in West Germany, and the U.S.S.R. having sovereign authority in the Eastern Zone, and the law in those two parts of Germany may now not be the same.

The respondents submitted in argument that we must regard the law of West **F** Germany as paramount. They relied on the language of the second Foreign Office certificate given on Nov. 6, 1964. This contained an extract from a Foreign Minister's communiqué which stated:

" Pending the unification of Germany, the three governments consider the government of the Federal German Republic as the only German government freely and legitimately constituted and therefore entitled to speak for **G** Germany as the representative of the German people in international affairs."

This is followed in the certificate by the following words: " This statement does not constitute recognition of the government of the Federal Republic of Germany as the de jure government of all Germany." It was argued that the determination **H** of the status of and the right to represent a body incorporated under the law of the State of Germany prior to 1945 are matters which affect Germany as a whole and which, if arising outside Germany, are within the scope of the Foreign Office communique; but for the reason given by my noble and learned friend LORD HODSON I cannot accept this argument.

What then is the law of the Eastern Zone with regard to these matters? It is **I** well settled that one does not take the code or statutes or other sources of law and construe them according to English ideas. Foreign law is a question of fact to be decided by evidence.

" The evidence it is clear must be that of qualified experts in the foreign law. If the law is contained in a code or written form, the question is not as to the language of the written law but what the law is as shown by its exposition, interpretation and adjudication: "

A (per LORD WRIGHT in *Lazard Brothers & Co.* v. *Midland Bank, Ltd.* (49)). On
several occasions it has been necessary to decide in a case here what is the law of
a foreign country on a point which has already been the subject of a decision by a
court of that country. A good example is *Bankers and Shippers Insurance Co. of
New York* v. *Liverpool Marine and General Insurance Co.* (50). In that case the
question was whether according to the law of New York State it was necessary to
B the validity of an award that an order of court should have been obtained.
The Court of Appeal (51) in England held that it was not. Then in another case,
Bullard & Co. v. *Grace & Co.* (52) the Court of Appeal of New York decided that it
was necessary. Then this House reversed the decision of the Court of Appeal and
followed the American decision. LORD BUCKMASTER said (53): "Unaided by
that authority your lordships would I think have supported the judgment
C appealed from." LORD SUMNER said (54):

"Evidence of the opinion of the highest court of the foreign State whose
law happens to form the subject matter of proof in this country is obviously
for an English court the best available evidence upon the question, and is
such that, if it is clearly directed to the point in dispute and is insusceptible of
any but one interpretation, other evidence of that law could hardly be set
D against it."

There is a quotation with approval of what SCRUTTON, L.J., had said in the
Court of Appeal (55):

"I agree with the view of PICKFORD, L.J., in *Guaranty Trust Co. of New
York* v. *Hannay & Co.* (56) that, while it is almost certain that an English
E court would not differ from a decision of the supreme court of the state or
the law of that state, a decision of a subordinate court is only an opinion of an
expert on the fact to be treated with respect but not necessarily conclusive."

In the present case we have not only two judgments of the Supreme Court of
the Eastern Zone but also uncontradicted evidence of skilled witnesses that every
court in the Eastern Zone would hold that the Council of Gera is entitled to act
F as the special board of the Stiftung; and we have evidence that the Stiftung has
brought a number of actions in recent years in East Germany and has obtained
judgments in its favour. How then did the West German courts come to decide
as they did?

CROSS, J., was inclined to hold that the West German courts were acting
perversely in disregarding the judgments of the Eastern courts. I do not take
G that view. I am certainly not prepared to hold that the West German courts
gave judgments which they knew to be wrong. They may have erred, but honest
error is a very different thing from perversity. Counsel for the appellants argued
that this case fell within the ratio of *Simpson* v. *Fogo* (57), to which I have already
referred. That case was cited more than once with approval in the nineteenth
century, but in *Luther* v. *Sagor* (58) SCRUTTON, L.J., said that it had been the
H subject of considerable adverse comment. In my view if *Simpson* v. *Fogo* (57)
can stand at all it must be limited to cases where the law of the foreign country
applied in the foreign judgment is at variance with generally accepted doctrines
of private international law. Then one must bear in mind what was said by
LINDLEY, L.J., in *Re Queensland Mercantile and Agency Co., Ex p. Australasian
Investment Co., Ex p. Union Bank of Australia* (59) about different countries
I taking different views on international law; and SIR WILLIAM PAGE WOOD, V.-C.,
(60) himself indicates that there might be a difference if the foreign judgment

(49) [1932] All E.R. Rep. 571 at pp. 576, 577; [1933] A.C. 289 at p. 298.
(50) (1926), 24 Lloyd L.R. 85.   (51) (1925), 21 Lloyd L.R. 86.
(52) (1925), 1285 N.Y. 388.   (53) (1926), 24 Lloyd L.R. at p. 88.
(54) (1926), 24 Lloyd L.R. at p. 94.   (55) (1925), 21 Lloyd. L.R. at p. 91.
(56) [1918-19] All E.R. Rep. 151; [1918] 2 K.B. 623.
(57) (1863), 1 Hem. & M. 195.
(58) [1921] All E.R. Rep. at p. 151; [1921] 3 K.B. at p. 558.
(59) (1892), 1 Ch. at p. 226.   (60) (1863) 1 Hem. & M. at p. 234.

were founded on a statute or on mistake (61)   distinctions which I have difficulty A
in appreciating. To distinguish *Simpson* v. *Fogo* (62) it is sufficient to say that the
West German courts did not refuse to apply the law of East Germany: they
applied what they thought was the law of East Germany.

It is not easy to summarise the long judgment of the Federal Supreme Court,
but it appears to me to be based on the view that Germany is still one country
and that the law of Germany applies equally in the East as in the West subject B
only to new local enactments of which there are none relevant to this case. On
that view the West German courts hold themselves entitled to override the
decisions of the East German courts if they regard those decisions as wrong in
law.

The main question which has given rise to this conflict in the present case is the
effect of confiscatory decrees of the Russian military administration. It is not C
disputed that as a result there was confiscation of the assets of the two firms
Carl Zeiss and Schott & Co., and these two businesses were then carried on as
nationalised industries—Volks Eigene Betriebe, referred to as VEBs. But it is
not clear how far this affected other assets of the Stiftung, and it is proved that in
recent years the Stiftung has been treated by the East German authorities as
owning a large amount of property; it has an annual revenue of some £180,000 D
and employs a staff of about 170.   The Council of Gera has in fact acted as
the special board and in particular has authorised the raising of various legal
proceedings in the Eastern zone.

The main ground of the West German judgment is that, after the businesses
of these two firms were separated from the Stiftung by confiscation, it became
legally impossible under its constitution for the Stiftung to carry on any activities. E
The only lawful course was to wind up the Stiftung as provided in its constitution,
and neither the Stiftung nor any of its organs has any power to carry on any
other activity; so the Council of Gera could not authorise the proceedings in
West Germany, which were brought to an end by the judgment of the Supreme
Court. That court was aware that the East German Supreme Court had reached
a decision to the contrary, but in effect it held that the East German court had F
wrongly applied the law of Germany.

I am not impressed by the reasoning in this judgment but, even if it were
convincing, I cannot see how it would be relevant. The West German courts have
no jurisdiction over East Germany. The two parts of Germany are at present
under different sovereignties: they have separate legal systems and are separate
jurisdictions.   According to the commonly accepted doctrine of private inter- G
national law the courts of one state or jurisdiction cannot of their own knowledge
determine what is the law in a different state or jurisdiction. That has to be proved
by evidence and, if it is clear as in this case it was and is, that all courts in one
state or jurisdiction have decided and will decide a particular question in one
way, the courts of another state or jurisdiction have no right to decide that that
question ought to be have been decided in a different way.   H

Let me take an analogy. Many countries formerly under the British Crown
still follow the common law. Suppose that this House were to reach a decision
on a point of common law which did not meet with general acceptance. All
courts in this country must follow that decision, but courts in other common
law jurisdictions are free to decide otherwise. Suppose however that in one of
those other countries a question arose as to what is the law of England on that I
point: the principles of private international law would require the courts of
that other country to decide that the law of England is what the House of Lords
has said it is, and they could not say that the House of Lords had reached a
wrong decision on this point of common law, however much they might disagree
with it. If they did substitute their own view for that of the supreme authority in
England, they would then be deciding what they thought the law of England

---

(61) (1863), 1 Hem. & M. at p. 242.   (62) (1863), 1 Hem. & M. 195.

A ought to be and not what it in fact is. It appears to me that the only legitimate ground for rejecting a decision of a foreign court as to its own law is an expectation that, if the point arose again in the foreign country and were carried to the Supreme Court, it would be decided differently. The West German courts appear to take a different view of the principles of private international law. The German Federal Republic is a sovereign state and its courts are entitled to their own view.
B But so are we; and I would not accept their view.

Then it is said that the courts of East Germany are influenced by political considerations. It is true that when one examines the judgments of the East German Supreme Court—and particularly the second of them—one finds them plentifully sprinkled with communist clichés. No doubt professing communists find it necessary to adopt this form of embellishment; but going behind this
C ornamentation I find a judicial approach and a reasonable result. Further, even if political considerations were apparent, it would remain true that what the courts have decided is in fact the law which is being enforced in the foreign country.

Finally it is said that, because the members of the Council of Gera are communists and bound to act as communist theory and government directions require,
D therefore they cannot act as the special board in the interests of the Stiftung as the constitution of the Stiftung requires. This may be common knowledge in West Germany, but I cannot agree that it is common knowledge here. On the contrary it is common knowledge here that individuals often fail to live up to— or live down to—their principles. This is an action to vindicate the right of the Stiftung to its own property: this communist body has authorised it, whatever
E view communist theory might take about it.

That brings me to an important question which was raised in the West German case and before CROSS, J. The respondents found on the principle that English courts will not assist the enforcement of foreign confiscatory laws, and argue that therefore the appellant cannot be given the relief which it seeks in this case. Your lordships did not permit that matter to be argued in this appeal
F because it is not relevant on the only question now before this House—the authority of the solicitors to act for the Stiftung. The respondents will be free to raise that issue in their pleadings and at the trial of this action, and nothing that CROSS, J. may have said on this matter can hamper or limit the power of the trial judge to deal with it.

On the whole matter I would allow this appeal and restore the order of CROSS, J.

G
LORD HODSON: My Lords, on the first part of the case I agree entirely with the opinion which has been given by my noble and learned friend, LORD REID. In my view, the Foreign Office certificate was conclusive against the view taken by the Court of Appeal (63). The U.S.S.R. having the de jure sovereignty over the so-called German Democratic Republic there is no room for any other de facto recognition, and the courts of this country must hold that the U.S.S.R. is
H still entitled to exercise authority over the territory and to bring to an end the German Democratic Republic which only exists on sufferance. This effect of the certificate holds good so far as this country is concerned and is not affected by any pronouncement of the U.S.S.R. itself as to whether or not it recognises the German Democratic Republic as a sovereign state.

I
On the second part of the case, the respondents have argued that the solicitors, Messrs. Courts & Co., who have the conduct of these proceedings on behalf of the appellant have no authority to do so, since they are estopped by the judgment of the Supreme Court of the Federal Republic of Germany in an action brought in the name of the appellant as plaintiff against the respondents in this action. This is a formidable argument and involves a consideration of the operation and effect of foreign judgments.

(63) [1965] 1 All E.R. 300; [1965] Ch. 596.

The courts have moved a long way since the opinion was expressed by LORD A
BROUGHAM, L.C., in the Irish appeal of *Houlditch* v. *Marquess of Donegal* (64)
that the judgment of a foreign court in courts of this country is only prima
facie evidence if liable to be averred against and not conclusive. The modern
doctrine accepted since the decision of *Godard* v. *Gray* (65) is that a foreign
judgment may be pleaded and is conclusive. If this is so, I see no reason why the
rule of estoppel per rem judicatam should not be applied, subject to the caution B
contained in LORD BROUGHAM'S observations in the *Houlditch* v. *Donegal* case
(64) as to the difficulties which arise from the differences in the course of procedure
between one jurisdiction and another.

Although estoppel operates most commonly in those cases which cover " cause
of action " the English rule has always been wide enough to cover " issue
estoppel "—see the *Duchess of Kingston's Case* (66), a passage from which has C
been quoted by my noble and learned friend, LORD REID and *R.* v. *Inhabitants of
Hartington Middle Quarter*, (67), likewise quoted by my noble and learned friend.
The estoppel here, if any, must be issue estoppel, the issue being that of want of
authority to bring an action. On this the respondents succeeded in the West
German action in which judgment was delivered by the Federal Supreme Court
on Nov. 15, 1960. On principle the judgment should be binding on the parties D
and their privies, to whom I will later refer. There may be difficulties in applying
the principle through the necessity of following the course of procedure when
pleadings and evidence have to be examined to ascertain what issues have been
determined. There may be cases of manifest injustice, i.e., in a case, perhaps,
where a defendant having a minimal interest in a matter allows a case to go by
default exposing himself to the risk of being bound by the judgment when the E
issue turns out to be more serious for him. None of these difficulties appears to
exist in this case. The West German judgment is detailed and elaborate and
leaves no doubt as to the precise issue about which the parties were contending,
an issue which was regarded as of prime importance by both sides.

In order to comply with r. 183 stated in DICEY'S CONFLICT OF LAWS (7th Edn.),
p. 982, the judgment must be conclusive in order to create an estoppel. In the F
Foreign Judgments (Reciprocal Enforcement) Act, 1933, the expression " final and
conclusive " is to be found, but these words are repetitive and " conclusive " in
the sense of the rule must mean that the judgment cannot, although it may
be subject to appeal, be varied by the court which made it, as can for example,
some maintenance or alimony orders. *Nouvion* v. *Freeman* (68) is an example of an
action which had been tried in Spain under a summary form of procedure leading G
to a " remate " judgment, which was held by this House not to amount to res
judicata since it was possible to reopen the matter which had been tried and to
obtain a "plenary " judgment rendering the " remate " judgment inoperative.
One asks, about what is the judgment to be final and conclusive? The answer is
that it must be on the merits and not only as to some interlocutory matter not
affecting the merits. The question here may, I think, properly be described as H
" on the merits ", the issue being whether or not there was authority to proceed in
an action representing the foundation. On this point I would respectfully dissent
from the opinion expressed by CROSS, J., although I do not disagree with his
main conclusion which distinguishes this action from that commenced by the
foundation suing by the Council of Gera. There was, in my opinion, a decision
against the Council of Gera on the merits of its claim to represent the foundation. I

There is admittedly a gap in the evidence whether the judgment was final and
conclusive. It is for the defendants to show the estoppel and, to prove it, they must
establish as a matter of German law that the judgment is final and conclusive.
This they have failed to do by express evidence and, as my noble and learned
friend LORD WILBERFORCE points out in his opinion, there are passages in the

---

(64) (1834), 8 Bli. N.S. 301.   (65) (1870), L.R. 6 Q.B. 139.
(66) (1776), 20 State Tr. 355.   (67) (1855), 4 E. & B. at p. 794.
               (68) (1889), 15 App. Cas. 1.

A   evidence which at least suggest the possibility of want of authority being re-litigated in the German courts. For my part, I think that it would be legitimate to rely on the assumption commonly made in English courts that in the absence of evidence of foreign law it is taken to be the same as English law and to hold that the judgment relied on for the estoppel is final and conclusive.

Another argument against the estoppel was put forward by the appellant,
B   which I do not find it possible to accept. It was based on the rule which still subsists in English law, notwithstanding animadversions which have been passed on it, that the cause of action in a foreign case does not merge in the judgment but remains available to be sued on, the foreign judgment being only evidence of the cause of action not, as in this country, that in which the cause of action has merged. It seems to me that this argument does not logically
C   involve that there can be no estoppel in the case of a foreign judgment. Indeed, the cases are consistent in admitting that there may be an estoppel notwith-standing the absence of merger. If the fact that the cause of action does not merge prevents the estoppel where issue estoppel is concerned it must similarly, one would suppose, do so were cause of action estoppel is in question. No one has suggested that the latter contention is sound.

D   There was a further contention, accepted by the learned judge, that there could be no estoppel because the judgment of the West German court was perverse in that they knowingly and wilfully declined to give effect to the relevant law, that of East Germany. Like others of your lordships, I find this conclusion too difficult to sustain, although in fairness to the learned judge it should be said that there was strong support for this conclusion in the case of *Simpson* v.
E   *Fogo* (69), on which reliance was placed on behalf of the appellant. "Perverse" is a strong word in this context, meaning, I would say, "obstinate in error" and inappropriate to describe the reasoning of the West German court.

There remains only the question of privity. On this I am in agreement with the learned judge. There was here no privity in estate. The only privity could be privity in interest. The action in West Germany was begun by the Council of
F   Gera claiming to represent the foundation and, on the issue of the right to repre-sent, judgment was given against the Council of Gera, which was ordered to pay the costs. The Council of Gera itself never had any interest in the subject-matter of the action. It was only required to act in order that the foundation might seek to enforce its rights, that is to say, the rights of the foundation itself.

This action is in truth an action by the foundation suing by Messrs. Courts and
G   Co., a firm of solicitors, who again have themselves no interest in the subject-matter of the action. The Council of Gera is not itself before the court. The way in which the respondents seek to put the matter of privity is founded on an ex-tended view of privity taken in America, where authorities show a broader concept of the privity necessary to establish estoppel. This is to be found in the American Restatement, s. 85 (2) which reads:

H   " When a person is bound by or entitled to the benefit of the rules of res judicata . . . such rules apply in a subsequent action brought or defended by another on his account."

The argument is that the solicitors are bringing this action on account of the Council of Gera, but this is not my view of the case. They are acting on behalf of
I   the foundation, and the judgment given in the West German court against the Council of Gera on their claim to represent the foundation does not raise an estoppel against the solicitors acting in this action.

It is on this last ground, namely, absence of privity, that I would hold that there is no estoppel against the solicitors preventing them from representing the foundation in this action.

If there is no estoppel, there remains to be considered whether the effect of the confiscation of the foundation's business was to make it legally impossible

(69) (1863), 1 Hem. & M. 195.

to carry on under its constitution. On this question I am in entire agreement **A**
with the learned judge, and would accept his finding that the foundation still
maintained its existence so as to enable it to give authority to the solicitors to
sue on its behalf. This is partly a question of law and partly one of fact. If it is right
to apply the law of the domicil of the foundation—Jena is in East Germany and
the law applicable is that administered in the court of that part of Germany.
The repondents argued that the law applicable to the matters in dispute between **B**
the parties should, in any event, be the law of the Federal German Republic. They
relied on the language of the second Foreign Office certificate given on Nov. 5,
1964. This contained an extract from a Foreign Ministers' communiqué which
stated:

> " Pending the unification of Germany the three governments consider
> the government of the Federal German Republic as the only German govern- **C**
> ment freely and legitimately constituted and, therefore entitled to speak
> for Germany as the representative of the German people in international
> affiairs."

This is followed in the certificate by the following words—

> " This statement does not constitute recognition of the Government of **D**
> the Federal Republic of Germany as the de jure government of all Germany."

It was argued that the determination of the status of and the right to represent
a body incorporated under the law of the State of Germany prior to 1945 and
now having its " sitz " in the territory of the zone allocated to the U.S.S.R.
are matters which affect Germany as a whole and, if arising outside Germany, **E**
are within the scope of the Foreign Office communiqué.

It is true that the judicial system is an organ of the sovereign power, but the
explanatory footnote to the communiqué indicates the limits to be put on the
Foreign Office certificate and does not support the contention that the West German courts, as courts of the Federal German Republic are entitled to speak for
Germany as a whole. That the communiqué is directed to political representation
only is, I think, clear from the language of the certificate, which makes clear **F**
that the government of the Federal Republic is not thereby to be regarded as
being recognised as the de jure government of all Germany. There are in the
two parts of Germany two separate legal systems operating independently
of one another, the East German courts deriving their authority from the sovereignty of the U.S.S.R. and the West German courts from the sovereignty which
lies in the Federal Republic of Germany as at present constituted. I do not think **G**
that there is any justification for the view that the law common to the whole of
Germany as distinguished from zonal law should be applied on the ground that
the Carl-Zeiss-Stiftung came into existence many years ago before Germany
was divided and that this case concerns operations and issues outside Germany as a
whole, namely, in England and not in the Soviet zone itself. The law in the two
parts of Germany not being the same we must apply the law of the Eastern **H**
zone.

The facts as to the activities of the foundation are not in dispute, and if the
law in operation in the Eastern zone is applied to those facts the appellant
must succeed on this issue.

I would allow the appeal.

I

LORD GUEST: My Lords, the somewhat complicated facts out of which
this appeal arises have been so fully rehearsed in the courts below that I find it
necessary only to state them in broad outline in order to decide the various points
at present in issue between the parties.

The history of Carl-Zeiss-Stiftung begins in 1846, when optical works at
Jena were founded by Carl Zeiss. Thereafter, glass works were founded and
Zeiss was joined by Ernst Abbé and Otto Schott. In 1891 a " Stiftung " or
foundation was formed which was administered by a special board, the optical

A   business and the glass business being run by two separate boards of management. The articles of the Stiftung and constitution have been set out in the courts below, and it is only necessary now to state that the legal domicil of the Stiftung was Jena (r. 3) and that the organisation of the Stiftung was to be, by r. 4, by a special board for representing the Stiftung as an incorporated body, for the administration of its estate and effects and for the supreme direction of its
B   affairs. Rule 113 is in the following terms:

"Should, in consequence of political changes in the state, the provision according to r. 5 of this statute with reference to the representation of the Stiftung become untenable, this representation including the appointment of the deputy of the Stiftung within the meaning of r. 5 and the statutory
C   administration of the Carl-Zeiss-Stiftung shall be made over to that department of state, which with regard to the university of Jena occupies the place of the state department of the Grand Duchy of Saxe-Weimar acting as the Special Board, providing that its seat is in Thüringia, otherwise to the highest administrative authorities in Thüringia."

The business owned by the Stiftung prospered and their products have become
D   world famous. Besides the business the Stiftung owned a large amount of property and substantial capital investments.

In terms of r. 113, owing to the changing political situation in Germany, certain changes in the constitution of the special board took place. Upon the amalgamation in 1918 of certain states in Germany, including the Grand Duchy of Saxe-Weimar Eisenach, in which Jena was situated, into the state of Thüringia,
E   the Thüringian Minister of Education became the special board. In 1935, when the Weimar Republic was replaced by the Third Reich, the "Reichs-Stathalter," as the highest administrative authority in Thüringia, became the special board of the Stiftung.

In April, 1945, when the Hitler régime collapsed the office of Reichs-Stathalter was abolished. Jena was first occupied by American troops, but shortly after
F   it became part of the Russian Zone of occupation and on July 1, 1945, it was occupied by the Soviet forces. When the Americans left they took with them all the members of the boards of management, a number of leading scientists, engineers and senior executives and a large amount of material.

On Oct. 30, 1945, Marshal Zhukov, head of the Russian Military Administration, made an order, "SMAD 124", providing for the sequestration of certain types
G   of property within the Russian zone which included the foundation. Russian officers were stationed in the works until March, 1947, and nearly all the machinery and plant was taken to Russia by way of reparations together with a number of workpeople. At the same time great efforts were made on the German side to get the works running again, and by the beginning of 1948 the works at Jena had been re-equipped.

H   In January, 1948, a central body known as the German Economic Council was set up with legislative authority in East Germany subject to the overriding power of the Russian Military Administration. Between April and June, 1948, orders were made by the Russian authorities confiscating the optical and glass business of the Stiftung. The confiscated business became the "People's Owned Enterprises"—"Volks eigene Betriebe" (VeBs)—and became known as
I   VeB Carl-Zeiss Jena and VeB Schott Jena respectively.

It is now possible to pass over a great amount of history recited in the opinion of Cross J. and to come to 1949. In that year the German Democratic Republic came into being. As a result of an East German law dated July 23, 1952, and an order made under it, the province of Thüringia was divided into three districts and the governmental functions of the province were transferred to the administrative organs of the respective districts. The district in which Jena is situated is the District of Gera, and the body, which stands in the same relation to the University of Jena as the State Department of the Grand Duchy stood to it in

the old days, is the Council (Rat) of Gera. It is common ground that, as a matter A
of political geography, the Council of Gera would be the special board within the
meaning of r. 113.

This action, which is an action for passing off, was commenced on Oct. 20,
1955, by the appellant. On Feb. 7, 1956, the respondents issued a summons
against the appellant asking that all further proceedings in the action be stayed
and the action dismissed on the ground that it had been commenced and was B
being maintained without the appellant's authority. Affidavits were lodged by
both parties and the application to stay was heard by CROSS, J., with cross-
examination during November and December, 1963, and January, 1964. The
judge gave judgment on Mar. 6, 1964, dismissing the summons. When the case
came before the Court of Appeal (70) the respondents applied for an order that a
letter be addressed to Her Majesty's Secretary of State for Foreign Affairs C
concerning the recognition of the German Democratic Republic, a point which had
not been taken in the court below, and had been expressly disclaimed before
CROSS, J. The Court of Appeal (70) accepted the respondents' arguments based on
the non-recognition by Her Majesty's government of the German Democratic
Republic and ordered that the writ and all subsequent proceedings be set aside
on the grounds that the action was instituted and all subsequent proceedings D
on behalf of the appellant had been taken without the authority of the appellant.

The position, accordingly, is that the special board of the Stiftung is now, as
a matter of geography, the Council of Gera established by the law passed on
July 23, 1952, by the German Democratic Republic. The decision of the Court of
Appeal was that as the Council of Gera was set up by the German Democratic
Republic, a government not recognised by Her Majesty's government, the E
special board has no locus to commence proceedings in the English courts, and
the action accordingly was commenced without authority.

Several arguments not including the non-recognition point were taken before
CROSS, J., and decided adversely to the respondents. The Court of Appeal (70),
in view of their decision on the non-recognition point, did not deal with these other
points. F

I have had the advantage of reading in advance the speech prepared by my
noble and learned friend, LORD REID, on the question of the recognition by the
English courts of the Council of Gera as authorising the present action. I agree
with his opinion, and I have nothing to add.

The first question, which arises on what may conveniently be described as
the second stage of the case, is whether the appellant is estopped per rem judica- G
tam by the judgment of the West German court from arguing, in answer to the
respondents' summons to stay the proceedings, that the appellant has authority
to raise this action in the name of the Carl-Zeiss-Stiftung. A considrable part
of the argument was devoted to this question which is not without difficulty and
raises a number of complicated issues.

The doctrine of estoppel per rem judicatam is reflected in two Latin maxims, (i) H
interest rei publicae ut sit finis litium and, (ii) nemo debet bis vexare pro una et
eadem causa. The former is public policy and the latter is private justice. The
rule of estoppel by res judicata, which is a rule of evidence, is that where a final
decision has been pronounced by a judicial tribunal of competent jurisdiction
over the parties to and the subject-matter of the litigation, any party or privy
to such litigation as against any other party or privy is estopped in any subse- I
quent litigation from disputing or questioning such decision on the merits
(SPENCER BOWER ON RES JUDICATA, p. 3).

As originally categorised, res judicata was known as " estoppel by record ".
But as it is now quite immaterial whether the judicial decision is pronounced
by a tribunal which is required to keep a written record of its decisions, this
nomenclature has disappeared and it may be convenient to describe res judicata

---

(70) [1965] 1 All E.R. 300; [1965] Ch. 596.

A in its true and original form as " cause of action estoppel ". This has long been recognised as operating as a complete bar if the necessary conditions are present. Within recent years the principle has developed so as to extend to what is now described as " issue estoppel ", that is to say where in a judicial decision between the same parties some issue which was in controversy between the parties and was incidental to the main decision has been decided, then that may create an

B estoppel per rem judicatam.   The issue arising on the summons to stay the proceedings is whether Messrs. Courts & Co., purporting to act for the plaintiffs, the Carl-Zeiss-Stiftung, have the necessary authority to raise the action in name of the Carl-Zeiss-Stiftung.   The estoppel which is alleged to have been created is by the decision of the West German courts where in an action between the Carl-Zeiss-Stiftung of Jena, represented by the Council of the District of Gera

C and the Carl-Zeiss-Stiftung Heidenheim Brenz, the present respondents, to restrain the defendants from inter alia using the name of Zeiss or Carl Zeiss and from using certain trade marks, it was held that the action was inadmissible on the ground that the constitution of the Stiftung is no longer effective, so that the legal basis for administration of the Stiftung in accordance with the article (71) has been removed and that the Council of Gera has no authority to represent

D the Carl-Zeiss-Stiftung before the court.   The English action is of a different character, namely, a summons to stay proceedings on the ground of lack of authority. It is, therefore, plain that there is no cause of action estoppel because the cause of action in each case is different.   Accordingly, if there is estoppel it must be " issue estoppel ".

The law on the matter is not altogether clear, but I am prepared to assume

E that at any rate in relation to estoppel founded on an English judgment there may be issue estoppel. This was referred to as early as 1776 in the *Duchess of Kingston's Case* (72) as interpreted in *R.* v. *Inhabitants of Hartington Middle Quarter* (73).   It has been approved recently by LORD DENNING, M.R., and DIPLOCK, L.J., in *Fidelitas Shipping Co.* v. *V/O Exportcheb* (74) (see also *Thoday* v. *Thoday* (75), per DIPLOCK, L.J.).   Although not described as " issue estoppel "

F it is inferentially approved in the most recent text book on res judicata by SPENCER BOWER at p. 9, where he speaks of a judicial decision which " involved a determination of the same question as that subject to be contraverted in the litigation in which the estoppel is raised ".   The doctrine of issue estoppel has also been accepted as good law by the courts in Australia for a number of years.

The requirements of issue estoppel still remain (i) that the same question

G has been decided; (ii) that the judicial decision which is said to create the estoppel was final, and (iii) that the parties to the judicial decision or their privies were the same persons as the parties to the proceedings in which the estoppel is raised or their privies. I have for the moment postponed the question whether issue estoppel, if valid in relation to an English judgment, applies to a foreign judgment. There is little doubt that the same question was incidentally

H decided in the West German action as arises in the present summons, namely, whether the Council of Gera have authority to raise the action in name of the Carl-Zeiss-Stiftung.

I turn, therefore, at once to the question of finality. This is understood to mean " final and conclusive on the merits of the cause " (DICEY'S CONFLICT OF LAWS (1st Edn.), r. 196, p. 1052). The decision on which the issue estoppel arises must

I itself be final in this sense.   In other words, the cause of action must be extinguished by the decision which is said to create the estoppel (see per LORD HERSCHELL in *Nouvion* v. *Freeman* (76))—" It puts an end to and absolutely concludes

---

(71) See r. 113 set out at p. 543, letter F, ante; the translation described the provisions of the " articles "   as " rules "—compare [1965] 1 All E.R. at p. 308.
(72) (1776), 20 State Tr. 355.   (73) (1855), 4 E. & B. 780.
(74) [1965] 2 All E.R. at pp. 9, 10.
(75) [1964] 1 All E.R. at pp. 351, 352; [1964] P. at pp. 197, 198.
(76) (1889), 15 App. Cas. at p. 9.

that particular action ", The West German judgment was not a judgment on **A**
the merits, but on a preliminary point relating to the capacity of the Carl-
Zeiss-Stiftung to sue, and it was there held that the Council of Gera had no
authority to raise the action in name of the Carl-Zeiss-Stiftung. I have difficulty
in seeing how a decision on capacity to sue can ever be final or conclusive. The
West German judgment related to the position in 1960 when it was pronounced,
but non constat the position is the same when the English action is tried.   The **B**
appellant would clearly be entitled to show that a change of circumstances had
occurred to affect its capacity to sue. If this is so, it would defeat the whole
purpose of estoppel which is to preclude the appellant from leading evidence to
that effect. I can best illustrate the position by reference to what would happen
if the decision in West Germany had been given by the Scottish courts. The
decision would have been to sustain the plea of " no title to sue ", but this would **C**
not have been final and conclusive as the interlocutor sustaining the plea would
have been one of dismissal. A subsequent action would not be barred per rem
judicatam.

Another aspect of finality relates to the requirement that the decision relied
on as estoppel must itself be res judicata in the country in which it is made.
This is made clear in *Nouvion* v. *Freeman* (77), per LORD HERSCHELL (see also **D**
CHESHIRE'S PRIVATE INTERNATIONAL LAW (7th Edn.), p. 562; DICEY'S CONFLICT
OF LAWS (1st Edn.), p. 1036). It would, indeed, be illogical if the decision were to
be res judicata in England, if it were not also res judicata in the foreign jurisdiction. I am not satisfied that the respondents have discharged the burden of proof
on them of establishing that the West German judgment is res judicata in West
Germany. I would, accordingly, hold that the West German judgment is not final **E**
and conclusive and for these reasons does not create an estoppel.

The next requirement is that the judgment should have been between the same
parties or their privies. The parties to the West German judgment, it is conceded,
were the Council of Gera, on the one hand, and the respondents on the other hand.
The parties to the present proceedings are the respondents and the Carl-Zeiss-
Stiftung. As the question is whether the Carl-Zeiss-Stiftung is properly a party **F**
to the proceedings, the Stiftung is plainly not the other party for the purposes of
res judicata, notwithstanding Mr. Aldous's ingenious argument that the only
party for whom he appears is the Stiftung. Who are the other parties? I am
unable to agree that the Council of Gera is a party. The Council does not appear
on the proceedings as a party, it is not represented, and no order for costs could
be made against it. It has no interest in the subject-matter of these proceedings. **G**
It only comes into the picture as the body who, according to r. 4 of the constitution, is entitled to represent the Carl-Zeiss-Stiftung. In these circumstances, the
only other possible parties to the proceedings are the solicitors, Messrs. Courts &
Co., to whom the summons is directed. As they were not parties to the West
German proceedings, they would only be obnoxious to the plea of res judicata if
they were the privies of the Council of Gera. There is a dearth of authority in **H**
England on the question of privies. The two cases of *Kinnersley* v. *Orpe* (78) and
Hancock v. *Welsh and Cooper* (79), referred to by the respondents are, in my
opinion, of no assistance. " Privies " have been described as those who are " privy
to the party in estate or interest " (SPENCER BOWER, p. 130). Before a person can
be privy to a party there must be community or privity of interest between them.
Messrs. Courts & Co. have no interest in the merits of this action. Their interest is **I**
merely to defend themselves against the claim made against them for costs by the
respondents which is on the basis of breach of warranty of authority (see *Yonge*
v. *Toynbee* (80)). In this matter the Council of Gera has no interest. It is only, as I
understand, by the form of procedure chosen by the respondents that Messrs.
Courts & Co. have been made parties to these proceedings. Assuming that the
summons had not been directed to them, but that the respondents had been

(77) (1889). 15 App. Cas. at p. 9.   (78) (1780), 2 Doug. K.B. 517.
(79) (1816), 1 Stark. 347.   (80) [1908-10] All E.R. Rep. 204; [1910] 1 K.B. 215.

A successful in the West German proceedings and in this summons, the latter would then have been entitled on the authorities to raise an action against the solicitors for breach of warranty of authority claiming the costs in the action. Could it possibly have been said in these circumstances that the solicitors were estopped by the West German judgment, of which they had no knowledge, from arguing that they had authority to raise the present action? I apprehend not, and this must be

B on the basis that they are not privies to the Council of Gera. It was argued for the respondents, although without clear authority in this country, that " privy " covers a person who is in control of the proceedings. Reference was made to the American RESTATEMENT OF THE LAW OF JUDGMENTS, ch. 4, para. 84, where it is said that a person who is not a party, but who controls an action, is bound by the judgment as if he were a party if he has a proprietary or financial interest in the

C judgment as a privy. But this cannot apply to the solicitors who are not in control of the proceedings and have no proprietary or financial interest in the judgment. They are instructed by the Carl-Zeiss-Stiftung who on its side controls the proceedings. No case has been referred to in England in which a solicitor has been held privy to the party instructing him. In Scotland an attempt to make a solicitor a party for the purpose of res judicata failed (*Laidlaw* v. *Blackwood* (81)). We

D were referred to a number of American cases dealing with privies. I am not prepared in this country to extend the doctrine to the extent which it apparently has reached in that country.

I now pass to the question reserved in an earlier part of my speech, namely, whether issue estoppel can ever be operated by a foreign judgment. This was doubted by CROSS, J. It is clear that a foreign judgment can operate as res

E judicata in a cause of action estoppel properly so called (DICEY'S CONFLICT OF LAWS (1st Edn.), rr. 182, 183, pp. 981, 992); but different considerations may, I apprehend, apply to issue estoppel. The first matter to be observed is that a foreign judgment does not have the same finality and conclusiveness as an English judgment. In the case of the latter the cause of action is merged with the judgment, so that action can only be brought to enforce the judgment. Not so in the

F case of foreign judgments. Sub-rule 183 of DICEY, p. 996, states: " A foreign judgment does not of itself extinguish the cause of action in respect of which judgment is given." The plaintiff, therefore, has the option either of suing on the judgment or on the original cause of action. The doctrine of non-merger stated in *Nouvion* v. *Freeman* (82) is still, as I understand it, good law, notwithstanding the animadversions of PROFESSOR READ in his book RECOGNITION AND ENFORCEMENT OF FOREIGN JUDGMENTS (1938) pp. 120, 121, and the doubt

G expressed in DICEY'S CONFLICT OF LAWS (1st Edn.), at p. 997. If this be sound, it means that the unsuccessful litigant can, if he is defendant, table fresh defences to the original cause of action. From this it follows that " issue estoppel " could never operate to shut out the defendant from litigating issues which may have incidentally been determined in the foreign suit.

H There are, in my view, moreover, considerations of policy and expediency which make it undesirable that the doctrine of issue estoppel should be introduced in the case of foreign judgments. There has been no case in which it has been applied in England and while, perhaps, not all estoppels are odious, considerable caution, in my view, should be exercised before the principle is extended any further. In operating issue estoppel it may be necessary, in order to ascertain

I what issues have been inferentially or incidentally decided, to look, not only at the judgment, but also at the pleadings and, it may be, at the evidence. We are not familiar in this country with the practice and procedure in foreign countries, and it may be a matter of considerable nicety in certain cases to find out what issues were determined and whether they were incidental or collateral to the main decision.

For all these reasons I would concur with CROSS, J., in holding that the plea of res judicata is not open to the respondents.

---

(81) (1843), 15 Sc. Jur. 484.   (82) (1889), 15 App. Cas. 1.

If the appellant is not estopped per rem judicatam by the West German   A
judgment from arguing that the Council of Gera is entitled to represent the Carl-
Zeiss-Stiftung, then the matter is at large for the decision of this House. Whether
this action is properly authorised by the Carl-Zeiss-Stiftung is a question of
foreign law to be decided as a question of fact. The law to be applied is the law
of the domicil of the Stiftung, which is in Jena, and the law is that of East
Germany as shown by "its exposition, interpretation and adjudication"   B
(*Lazard Brothers & Co.* v. *Midland Bank, Ltd.* (83)). It must be the law as in
practice interpreted and enforced by the courts of law of the foreign country. A
considerable volume of expert evidence on both sides was devoted to the question;
but in this case one starts with the judgment of the East German courts that the
Carl-Zeiss-Stiftung still exists as a juristic person, notwithstanding the confiscation of its assets in East Germany by the Soviet authorities. This judgment is   C
embodied in the opinion of the Supreme Court of the German Democratic
Republic, dated Apr. 6, 1954, as confirmed by the judgment of the German Democratic Republic Supreme Court, dated Mar. 23, 1961, affirming the judgment of
the District Court of Leipzig. Technically, no foreign judgment would bind the
courts of this country, but prima facie a judgment would be accepted by the
English courts as representing the law. "The comity of international affairs   D
would require special and unusual circumstances to lead this House away from
the clear decision of a final court " (*Bankers and Shippers Insurance Co. of New
York* v. *Liverpool Marine and General Insurance Co., Ltd.*, per LORD BUCKMASTER
(84)):

> " Evidence of the opinion of the highest court of the foreign State whose
> law happens to form the subject-matter of proof in this country is obviously   E
> for an English court the best available evidence upon the question, and is
> such that if it is clearly directed to the point in dispute and is insusceptible of
> any but one interpretation, other evidence of that law could hardly be set
> against it."

(see per LORD SUMNER (85).) The experts on foreign law from both sides were
unanimous that all East German courts would follow the decision of a supreme   F
court of the German Democratic Republic that the Carl-Zeiss-Stiftung still exists
as a juristic person with its domicil at Jena, and that the Carl-Zeiss-Stiftung
had the capacity to sue for the protection of its name, trade-marks and goodwill.
The only criticism which is made by the West German lawyers of the East
German judgment is that there are no free judges in East Germany and that no
East German court would dare to come to a contrary conclusion; but this is only   G
the opinion of the West German lawyers, and there is not a shred of evidence to
support it. On the question of fact as to what the East German law is, the
evidence is really all the one way, consisting of the judgment of the highest court
in East Germany and the opinion of the East and West German lawyers who gave
evidence.

In this state of evidence there is no need to examine further the decisions of the   H
West German courts or the East German courts. Indeed, in this state of affairs
the English courts would not be entitled, in my view, to express their views as to
the soundness or otherwise of either decision (see *Buerger* v. *New York Life
Assurance Co.* (86)). The English courts must accept the East German decision
as being the law of East Germany.

On the whole matter, I would allow the appeal and restore the judgment of   I
CROSS, J.

LORD UPJOHN: My Lords, the issues between the parties in this singularly
complicated appeal fall into two watertight compartments. Into the first compartment falls an issue which has been described in argument as the "non-
recognition" point. It has been admirably and elaborately argued before your

---

(83) [1932] All E.R. Rep. 571 at p. 576; [1933] A.C. 289 at p. 298.
(84) (1926), 24 Lloyd. L.R. at p. 87.   (85) (1926), 24 Lloyd. L.R. at p. 94.
(86) [1927] All E.R. Rep. 342.

A lordships, but in the end the point may shortly be stated: whether the English courts will recognise the legislative and other acts of the German Democratic Republic which operates in the Russian zone of Germany having regard to the fact that Her Majesty's government has not granted any de jure or de facto recognition to that republic or its government. This issue was raised for the first time in the Court of Appeal (87) who held that, as it was common knowledge

B that the U.S.S.R. had recognised the German Democratic Republic as an independent sovereign state but Her Majesty's government had not done so, the courts of this country would not recognise any acts done by that government or by any person appointed by it. This conclusion necessarily led to the result on the facts of this case, to which I shall refer later, that the action was not properly authorised and that the solicitors who issued the writ were acting without

C authority to do so. The result of the decision of the Court of Appeal (87) is, of course, to deny in the courts of this country to the inhabitants, organisations and institutions of East Germany any lawful origin to any acts or events based on any executive, judicial or legislative acts or directions of the government of the German Democratic Republic since it was set up by the U.S.S.R.: a most deplorable result in respect of any highly civilised community, with which we

D have substantial trading relationships I believe, which should be avoided unless our law compels that conclusion.

My lords, my noble and learned friend, Lord Reid, whose opinion I have had an opportunity of reading, has advanced very powerful reasons for preferring the view that the answers of Her Majesty's Secretary of State for Foreign Affairs to the requests for information submitted to him by the Court of Appeal, in accord-

E ance with the well-settled practice, must lead to the conclusion that, so far as the courts of this country are concerned, we ought to assume that, whatever may be thought to be common knowledge on this point, the German Democratic Republic is a subordinate body set up by the U.S.S.R. as the de jure government of East Germany to act on its behalf, and that its legislative executive and judicial acts must receive recognition. I agree entirely with the reasons and conclusions of my

F noble and learned friend, and I cannot usefully add anything on this issue.

It, therefore, becomes necessary to examine the second compartment with which the Court of Appeal quite reasonably did not deal, having regard to their decision on the non-recognition point (87). The issues here are even more complex, and are threefold. Taking them in the order which I think is most convenient, they may be described (as in the arguments addressed to your

G lordships) as (i) the confiscation point, (ii) the estoppel point and (iii) the supreme court point.

The confiscation point depends on proof of the fact that the commercial assets of the Stiftung abroad have been confiscated by legislation in East Germany, and on the respondents' argument that in such event the English courts would not assist the enforcement of expropriatory or penal legislation outside the

H territorial jurisdiction of that country. That plainly is an issue in the action itself, it is a matter for allegation in the pleadings and goes to the question of the relief (if any) that should be granted. It is not a matter which can be dealt with on this appeal, which is concerned solely with the authority of Messrs. Courts & Co. to issue a writ in the courts of this country on behalf of the Stiftung, which has nothing to do with the issues in the action, a matter that I shall develop later.

I Apart from this, I should be very reluctant to deal with this matter, even if it were open to your lordships to do so, on the materials at present available. Plainly there is much scope for further exploration of the relevant facts before this issue in the action can be satisfactorily decided. When (if pleaded) the matter comes on for trial the learned trial judge must not consider himself hampered by any findings or observations of Cross, J., on this matter.

I turn, then, to the estoppel point. This raises a matter of some general

---

(87) [1965] 1 All E.R. 300; [1965] Ch. 596.

importance. This is an appeal based on a summons dated Feb. 7, 1950, whereby   A
the respondents claimed against the solicitors, Messrs. Courts & Co. (respondents
to the summons), that they issued a writ in the name of the Stiftung as plaintiff
without authority to do so and that the action should be stayed and Messrs.
Courts & Co. ordered to pay the respondents' costs on a common fund basis.
This form of summons is well-known and is based not on any misconduct on the
part of the solicitor, as was at one time thought to be necessary to empower the   B
court to exercise its summary jurisdiction over a solicitor, but, as was pointed out
by LORD PORTER in *Myers* v. *Elman* (88), is based on the proposition that

" the solicitor is not party to the action but the court exercises its
summary powers over the solicitor who by issuing a writ warrants his
authority to do so ",
                                                                                     C

and so, if he has no authority, may I add, commits a tort against the so-called
defendants; and therefore has to pay them damages by indemnifying them
against the expenses to which they have been put by paying costs taxed on the
common fund basis rather than on a party and party basis.

It is alleged by the respondents that on this summons Courts & Co. cannot
contest this issue, for it has already been tried conclusively between the parties   D
or their privies in earlier proceedings in the West German Federal Court so that
they are estopped per rem judicatam, or more shortly this matter is res judicata.
It is clear that a party relying on such a plea must at least prove that the earlier
proceedings were determinative of the issues arising in the second proceedings;
that the same parties or their privies are common to both proceedings and that
the earlier proceedings were within the jurisdiction of the court and were final   E
and conclusive of the relevant issues.

This makes it necessary to answer a number of questions: 1. Are the issues in
the former proceedings the same as in the latter? 2. Who are the parties to the
earlier proceedings? 3. Who are the parties to these subsequent proceedings?
4. If there is no complete identity of parties in 2 and 3 above, are the different
parties properly described as in privity one with another for the purpose of the   F
doctrine? 5. Even if the answer to question 1 is " Yes ", is the matter of the lis
between the parties such as to give rise to res judicata? 6. Does the doctrine if
applicable between two sets of English proceedings apply where the former proceedings were in a foreign court? 7. If so (89), were these proceedings final and
conclusive between the parties?

To answer these questions some facts must necessarily be set out, but I shall   G
be as brief as I can. For this purpose it may be taken as common ground that a
local government body acting in that part of Eastern Germany known as
Thüringia and called the Council of Gera (to which I will refer as " the council ")
is the special board within the meaning of r. 113 of the Articles of Association
of the Stiftung (90) and, as such (as provided by r. 4) entitled to represent the
Stiftung in the supreme direction of its affairs including, of course, the power and   H
right to instruct its legal advisers to bring or defend actions on its behalf. However, in proceedings culminating in the Supreme Court of the Federal Republic of
West Germany it was held that the council had no right to instruct anyone to act
for the Stiftung in proceedings in those courts because, since the confiscation of
its industrial assets by certain decrees of the Russian occupying forces in 1948, the
Stiftung, though continuing as a legal entity, became an empty shell incapable of   I
giving any instructions and the council was in effect divested of its powers to act
on its behalf. Whether this is a correct conclusion is the Supreme Court point which
I shall examine later, though with extreme brevity.

---

(88) [1939] 4 All E.R. 484 at pp. 520, 521; [1940] A.C. 282 at p. 336.
(89) Viz., if the answer to question 6 is " Yes ".
(90) These were translated from the German: they were the articles of constitution
of the Stiftung and their provisions were described in the Court of Appeal as " rules ",
which description is retained in the present report (see [1965] 1 All E.R. 308).

A   It must be noted that in contrast to our procedure it appears that in the West German courts the person giving the instructions on the part of a purely juridical person appears on the record; at all events, in the West German proceedings in the Supreme Court the plaintiff is described as " the Carl Zeiss Foundation of Jena represented by the Council of the District of Gera plaintiff and appellant ". In the proceedings before your lordships Messrs. Courts & Co. at once concede

B   that they have received instructions to issue the writ in the name of the Stiftung from the council.

That is a sufficient statement of the facts to answer the first two questions: 1. The issue whether the council had authority to give instructions to begin proceedings in the name of the Stiftung in this country depends on precisely the same facts, circumstances and arguments as were advanced before the West

C   German courts and decided against them. It is not suggested that there has been any relevant change in those facts or circumstances since 1960, when judgment was delivered in the Supreme Court.   2. The parties to the West German proceedings I am prepared to assume are (a) the council, and (b) the third respondents.

The third question has given rise to much argument and some difference of

D   opinion among your lordships. Counsel for the appellant has argued that the Stiftung is a party to the summons; a somewhat dangerous argument, I would have thought, for it seems to presuppose that regardless of authority the Stiftung is a party and so the same argument must apply to the West German proceedings and, if so, identity of parties seems to be established. However, I reject the argument. If the summons succeeds it does so on the footing that the Stiftung

E   is not a party to the writ or the summons and for that reason the action is stayed and the solicitors made personally liable for breach of warranty of authority. Under our procedure in such circumstances no order of any kind, even for costs, can be made against the Stiftung.

Secondly, it seems to me clear that the council is not, under our procedure, a party to the writ or the summons. It can make no difference that in this case in

F   some earlier proceedings in another country the Stiftung is named in the record of those proceedings.   The solicitors are in a special position, for, in respect of a purely juridical person, only a solicitor can issue a writ. He does not thereby become a party to the proceedings but, for the reasons already mentioned, as an officer of the court, he can be made a respondent to a summons to strike out the writ. His liability depends not on agency, for if the summons succeeds

G   he has no principal; it depends solely on his position as a solicitor issuing a writ and thereby warranting his authority to do so to the defendants named in the writ. I am quite unable to understand the argument that those de facto instructing him become parties to the writ or to the summons seeking to strike out the writ. It may be that such body of persons may be liable to the solicitor for breach of warranty of authority, if they have no principal, but that does not

H   make them party to the proceedings nor liable for breach of warranty to the defendants for they, unlike the solicitor who has issued the writ, have warranted nothing to them. To hold the contrary would make all those along the line who may have given instructions to the solicitors to issue a writ from a junior clerk of the instructing body upwards liable as parties to the defendants; but this has never been the law of our country.

I   So I answer this question by saying that the parties to the summons under appeal are (a) Messrs. Courts & Co., (b) the third respondents.

As to question 4, the third respondents are parties to both proceedings, but there is no identity between the council and Messrs. Courts & Co.; so the next question is whether they are in privity one with another for the purpose of the doctrine. The position of the solicitor in proceedings such as these is clear-cut; as I have already pointed out, he is no party to the proceedings; the sole question is as to his authority to initiate proceedings. It is not an issue in the action at all, and that is why it cannot be taken as a plea in defence in contrast to the

confiscation point. This House in *Russian Commercial and Industrial Bank* v. **A**
Le Comptoir D'Escompte de Mulhouse (91) approved the decision of WARRINGTON,
J., in *Richmond* v. *Branson & Son* (92) where he said (93);

> " But the real question is the authority of the solicitor. Is that a question
> which can be raised as a relevant issue in the action and at the trial? . . .
> it is impossible, according to the ordinary practice and procedure of the
> court, to justify that proposition."   **B**

The solicitor has no interest in the action as such, nor under our system (unlike that pertaining for example in the U.S.A.) is he permitted even to participate
in the proceeds of a successful judgment. His duty is to render his services to
his client in the litigation to the best of his skill and ability and his sole reward
is the costs which by law he may charge. I can see nothing in a solicitor's **C**
relationship with his client which renders them privy to one another in the
ordinary sense in which privy or privity is used for the purposes of the doctrine.
As has been said in 15 HALSBURY'S LAWS OF ENGLAND (3rd Edn.), para. 372, privies
are of three classes: (i) privies in blood, (ii) privies in law and (iii) privies in
estate, but they all have an interest in the subject-matter of the action. Though
your lordships have been referred to a number of authorities in other courts **D**
which may expand the meaning of privy, none touch on the question before your
lordships, where the lis has nothing to do with the substance of the action itself.
In my opinion, Messrs. Courts & Co. cannot be described as privy to the council
so as to preclude it from trying to establish its authority to issue the writ, unless,
by reason of some requirement of the law to meet new conditions, a meaning
greatly extended beyond anything the word has borne is to be given to it.

I turn to the fifth question which I have posed. Res judicata may be divided **E**
into a number of classes or branches. The most ancient is estoppel by record
strictly so called. It still exists, though is usually overtaken by the broader
principles that I shall next discuss. In such a case a defendant who has failed
even to enter an appearance and who has taken no part in the earlier litigation
may be estopped if his defence in the second action was necessarily and with **F**
complete precision decided by the previous judgment (see per LORD MAUGHAM,
L.C., in *New Brunswick Ry. Co.* v. *British and French Trust Corpn., Ltd.* (94)).
How narrow is the estoppel in such a case is shown by the actual decision there.
This narrow concept of estoppel has no application to the present case, for the
questions are different; this first is as to the authority of the council to initiate
proceedings on behalf of the Stiftung in West Germany, and the second as to **G**
the authority to initiate proceedings in these courts. Nor is the judgment of the
foreign court one of record.

The broader principle of res judicata is founded on the twin principles so frequently expressed in Latin that they should be at an end to litigation and justice
demands that the same party shall not be harassed twice for the same cause.
It goes beyond the mere record; it is part of the law of evidence for, to see **H**
whether it applies, the facts and reasons given by the judge, his judgement, the
pleadings, the evidence and even the history of the matter may be taken into
account (see *Marginson* v. *Blackburn Borough Council* (95)). Res judicata
itself has two branches:

> (a) Cause of action estoppel—that is where the cause of action in the
> second case has already been determined in the first. To such a case the **I**
> observations of WIGRAM, V.-C., in *Henderson* v. *Henderson* (96) apply
> in their full rigour. These observations have been so often approved in your
> lordships' House that I will not repeat them. I need not pursue this matter

(91) [1924] All E.R. Rep. 381; [1925] A.C. 112.   (92) [1914] 1 Ch. 968.
(93) [1914] 1 Ch. at p. 974.
(94) [1938] 4 All E.R. at p. 755; [1939] A.C. at p. 21.
(95) [1939] 1 All E.R. 273; [1939] 2 K.B. 426.
(96) [1843-60] All E.R. Rep. at p. 381; (1843), 3 Hare at p. 115.

A   further for the alleged res judicata with which your lordships are concerned certainly has nothing to do with any cause of action in the proceedings.

(b) Issue estoppel—a convenient phrase first coined apparently by HIGGINS, J., in the High Court of Australia in *Hoystead* v. *Taxation Comrs.* (97) whose dissenting judgment was upheld by the Privy Council (98); but issue estoppel has been recognised ever since the *Duchess of Kingston's*

B   *Case* (99), and there are many quite early examples of it (see e.g. *R.* v. *Inhabitants of Hartington Middle Quarter* (100) and many others).

Recently in *Thoday* v. *Thoday* (101) and in *Fidelitas Shipping Co.* v. *V/O Exportchleb* (102) the Court of Appeal applied to issue estoppel the full breadth of the observations of WIGRAM, V.-C. in the *Henderson* case (103).   While in this case it is not necessary to decide whether that is right, because for the reasons

C   given in the answer to the first question that I posed for myself it does not arise, I should be reluctant to support that view. As my noble and learned friend, LORD REID, has already pointed out there may be many reasons why a litigant in the earlier litigation has not pressed or may even for good reasons have abandoned a particular issue. It may be most unjust to hold him precluded from raising that issue in subsequent litigation (and see LORD MAUGHAM, L.C.'s observations in the

D   *New Brunswick* case (104)). All estoppels are not odious but must be applied so as to work justice and not injustice, and I think that the principle of issue estoppel must be applied to the circumstances of the subsequent case with this overriding consideration in mind. My lords, I desire to add only one observation on those cases; once it is clear that the principle of res judicata is part of the law of evidence I find it difficult to understand the distinction drawn by DIPLOCK,

E   L.J., in *Thoday* (105) between issue estoppel and fact estoppel, but that does not call for further consideration here.

So if Messrs. Courts & Co. are debarred from arguing their authority to issue the writ, it is because of an issue estoppel. I have already shown, however, that this lis is not and cannot be an issue in the action at all. It is a matter which would seem, to paraphrase the words of DE GREY, C.J., in the *Duchess of Kingston's*

F   *Case* (106) quoted by LORD REID, to be a matter collateral or incidentally cognisable and therefore not the subject of estoppel. No authority has been cited to your lordships which bears any resemblance to the present case. All the authorities which we have examined on issue estoppel have been cases where the earlier action dealt with issues or points which, however inferentially or incidentally, arose in the course of trying the substance of the issues between the

G   parties to the action; not with a lis having nothing to do with those issues, which arises only between the defendant and the solicitor issuing the writ.

Ought the principle of issue estoppel to be extended to a case such as this? I can see no reason for doing so. Under our system the respondent to the summons is necessarily a solicitor, an officer of the court. It would require strong reasons to preclude him from defending his issue of a writ by reason of

H   some decision to which he was no party and of which he may be in complete ignorance. Justice does not require the invocation of the doctrine to protect the defendant from being doubly harassed, for if an officer of the court with full knowledge of some earlier proceedings in these courts which covers exactly and precisely the question of his authority issues a writ, the arm of the court is long enough and strong enough to prevent an abuse of its process without resort

I   to the doctrine. The application of the doctrine may, on the other hand, lead to much injustice. Such summons are normally heard at a very early stage of the

(97) (1921), 29 C.L.R. 537 at p. 561.
(98) [1925] All E.R. Rep. 56; [1926] A.C. 155.   (99) (1776), 20 State Tr. 355.
(100) (1855), 4 E. & B. 780.   (101) [1964] 1 All E.R. 341; [1964] P. 181.
(102) [1965] 2 All E.R. 4.
(103) [1843-60] All E.R. Rep. at p. 381; (1843), 3 Hare at p. 115.
(104) [1938] 4 All E.R. at p. 755; [1939] A.C. at p. 21.
(105) [1964] 1 All E.R. at p. 351; [1964] P. at p. 197.
(106) (1776), 20 State Tr. at p. 538.

proceedings on evidence frequently hurriedly prepared (in marked contrast **A** to this most exceptional case) and some point may be overlooked or misunderstood in the earlier proceedings.

I would deny to these purely incidental proceedings in the action the doctrine of issue estoppel and for the same reasons I would refuse to extend the meaning of the word privy to cover the case of two successive solicitors (for that is what it amounts to) who have issued writs in the name of a common principal; the only **B** so called privity between them is that they have successively issued writs upon the instructions of some persons purporting to act for the principal but that person cannot himself or itself be a party to any proceedings. So I would regard the doctrine as entirely inappropriate to this form of proceedings.

My lords, in these circumstances I can answer the remaining questions 6 and 7 very shortly.
                                                                            C
I accept at once that for the purpose of the doctrine of res judicata in general a prior foreign judgment may be just as effective as an English one. But even if I had come to the conclusion that the doctrine applied to successive summonses the first of which was decided in our courts, raising the question of authority to issue a writ, I would deny the benefit of the doctrine to a prior foreign judgment for the simple reason that I do not think it is necessary in the interests of justice **D** to do so and it may easily be productive of grave injustice. Questions of authority and, indeed, the very concept of authority for this purpose depend so much on matters of procedure in each court and on the precise rules governing the issue of writs therein by persons other than the parties themselves that it is difficult to apply a judgment in the one case to another under a different jurisprudence. This case provides a good example; under our system the council could never be **E** a party to the writ or the summons.

Finally with regard to question 7 the respondents have failed to prove that the proceedings in West Germany were final and conclusive as must necessarily be proved for an estoppel to be successfully established (see *Nouvion* v. *Freeman* (107)).

In conclusion on the estoppel point, even if I had reached a contrary conclusion as between the third respondents and Messrs. Courts & Co., I should require **F** much persuasion that the first and second respondents, who are alleged to be passing off the goods of the third respondents as and for the goods of the Stiftung and thus committing independent torts in this country, are entitled to the benefit of the alleged estoppel, but the point is not an important one.

So it is necessary to turn to the Supreme Court point. I have already set out very briefly the grounds on which the West German Federal Court held that the **G** council had not authority to act for the Stiftung, and the real issue is whether that decision is right or whether on the same facts the decision of the Supreme Court of the East German Republic deciding that the council had authority to issue a writ is to be preferred. This is a question of foreign law which by the law of this country is essentially a matter of fact. It has been discussed very fully by my noble and learned friend, LORD REID, in his opinion and by CROSS, J., **H** in the court of first instance. I agree entirely with what my noble and learned friend has said and also with what CROSS, J., said, though I think that he went too far in describing the judgment of the West German Supreme Court as perverse. As a piece of legal reasoning the decision of the West German court seems to me quite unconvincing, and for my part I can see no ground for holding that the council ceased to have any authority to act on behalf of the Stiftung or that the Stiftung **I** itself was but an empty shell, in existence but incapable of acting, when all the known facts indicate the contrary. I only desire to add that the respondents, in inviting us to prefer the decision of the West German Federal Supreme Court, advanced an argument based on the certificate dated Nov. 6, 1964, given by Her Majesty's Secretary of State for foreign affairs when in answer to question (2) submitted to him he quoted a communiqué dated Sept. 9, 1950, where it

---

(107) (1889), 15 App. Cas. 1.

A was stated that " pending the unification of Germany the three governments consider the government of the Federal Republic as the only German government freely and legitimately constituted and therefore entitled to speak for Germany as the representative of the German people, in international affairs ". It was said that this statement authorised the West German government to speak in the name of the whole German people and this gave a superior sanctity to the decision

B of the West German Supreme Court over the decision of the East German Supreme Court. The argument seems to me to be fallacious. If has never been the practice of Her Majesty's Secretaries of State to express any views on the law. While they constantly express views on recognition in answer to questions submitted to them by the courts, the legal consequences that flow from recognition are matters which are always left to these courts.

C   My lords, for these reasons I would allow this appeal and restore the order of CROSS, J.

   LORD WILBERFORCE: My Lords, the substantive issue in this litigation is whether the right to use in this country the name of Carl-Zeiss or Zeiss, in relation to certain glass or optical goods, and to profit from the goodwill attached to those names, belongs to a body of persons in the West German Federal Repub-

D lic, or to a body of persons in that part of Germany which is outside of, and to the east of, the Republic, which I will call for convenience " East Germany ". The rights in question are claimed by both sides to belong to a corporate entity called Carl-Zeiss-Stiftung (the word " Stiftung " denotes approximately a foundation with corporate status), the contest being as to which body of persons is entitled to

E control that corporate entity. The writ in the action was issued in the name of the Stiftung through English solicitors on the authority of Dr. Schrade, who in turn claimed to act on the authority of the Council of Gera (alleged to be the " special board " of the Stiftung), and also in other capacities, and in accordance with accepted procedure, the issue must be tested in limine, whether the Stiftung is legally before the court. This procedure has some inconveniences, both be-

F cause it normally (and here) takes the form of an application against the solicitors (the difficulty as to which will hereafter appear) and also in that it is traditionally carried out by a motion or summons, supported by affidavit evidence, but without pleadings defining the precise matters in dispute. In a case such as the present, where important and difficult questions of law, including foreign law, arise this may result in some confusion, and I think that it would be advantageous if some method could be found in such cases of defining the issues to be presented

G to the court.

   The issues as to the right or otherwise of Dr. Schrade to authorise the proceedings on behalf of the Carl-Zeiss-Stiftung, as these were debated before CROSS, J., in the Chancery Division, and to which the evidence was directed, were issues, under several headings, of German law and no question arose as to status, inter-

H nationally, of East Germany or of the " government " which claims authority in Eastern Germany. The affidavits on either side were drafted on the basis that, for the purpose of the summons to stay the proceedings, no challenge was made to the validity of East German legislation, and before the court leading counsel for the defendants (the respondents in this appeal) disclaimed any intention to question the status of that government, or to inquire whether it was

I recognised by Her Majesty's government. The facts with regard to, or bearing on recognition, were therefore not examined at that stage; but in the Court of Appeal (108) the respondents sought to base their case on non-recognition of the " government " in East Germany and that court, inevitably as I think because of the public interest involved, allowed them to take the point. Inquiry was made in the usual manner of the Secretary of State and, certificates given by him having shown that Her Majesty's government does not recognise the " government " of East Germany either de jure or de facto, the respondents argued, and

   (108) [1965] 1 All E.R. 300; [1965] Ch. 596.

the Court of Appeal (109) accepted, that the ground on which CROSS, J., held A
the action to be validly commenced no longer existed. The Court of Appeal (109)
also decided against various alternative claims by the appellant as to the authorisation of the proceedings, which CROSS, J., had not found it necessary to consider.
Correspondingly, the Court of Appeal (109) did not find it necessary to deal with
some difficult issues decided in the appellant's favour by CROSS, J. I leave all
these aside for the moment in order to concentrate on that contention which is B
affected by the non-recognition argument.

First, I must explain how the right of Dr. Schrade to authorise the proceedings
is connected with the question of non-recognition. I can do this quite summarily
since the history and the constitution of the Carl-Zeiss-Stiftung have already
been fully explained.

Since the establishment of the Carl-Zeiss-Stiftung in 1891 at Jena as a charita- C
ble foundation, it has by its constitution been linked with the public administration of that district in Germany in which Jena lies. This was at that time the
Grand Duchy of Saxe-Weimar. The " special board " of the foundation, which
is the organ of the Stiftung which (under the issue that I am now considering)
authorised the present action to be brought, was then the department responsible
for the University of Jena. Later, under the Weimar Republic, the appropriate D
district was the State of Thüringia and the authority its Minister of Education.
There was a displacement during the National Socialist régime but in 1945,
when American forces occupied this part of Germany, Thüringia was
restored as a province or Land and its Minister again became the special
board. It is interesting, and relevant to a later argument, to note that this re-
constitution of the regional administration in this part of Germany was apparently E
accomplished without any formality; it simply took place under the authority of
the occupant and, as one of the expert witnesses said, I think correctly, the fact
that the occupation authorities allowed the Ministry of Education to operate
endowed the acts of that Ministry with legal validity. This factual state of affairs
seems to have continued without change when in July, 1945, East Germany,
including Thüringia, was taken over by the forces of the U.S.S.R. The local F
administration continued: the Minister continued to act as the special board
and, as regards this period which lasted until 1952, no challenge has been made
to the validity of that board or to action taken by it. Its legal life-blood can only
have been derived from the Minister of Thüringia, who in turn derived authority
either from the U.S.S.R. as the holder of sovereign power (I shall explain this
later) or possibly from the previous authority of the U.S.A.   G

It is on events occurring in 1952 that the respondents rely for their contention
that the special board which authorised this action had, so far as the courts of
this country are concerned, no legal existence. On July 23, 1952, under a " law "
passed by the " government " of the German Democratic Republic (as East
Germany is called by those in control of it) and an order made on the following
day under that law, the Province or Land of Thüringia was divided into three H
districts and its functions were transferred to the administrative organs of the
respective districts. The district in which Jena is situated is that of Gera and the
body which (admittedly) assumed the position corresponding to the former
Minister of Thüringia was the Council of Gera.

On these facts, the respondents contend that, since the Council of Gera depends
for its creation on a legislative act of the " government of the German Demo- I
cratic Republic " and as no such government is recognised in this country, there
is no legal basis for the Council of Gera as the special board, so that the purported
authority is simply a nullity.

It is as well, before considering the legal consequences of non-recognition, to
appreciate what the respondents' contention involves. The Stiftung is a corporate
body established for industrial and trading purposes under the law of Germany;

---

(109) [1965] 1 All E.R. 300; [1965] Ch. 596.

A one of whose constitutional organs—the special body—is an administrative authority exercising power at the place of the body's operations. As a fact, there is no doubt that at the relevant date this authority was there, that it was exercising its functions, that it was operating as the special board, that (this is proved by the evidence) it would be recognised by the local courts as so doing. Yet, so it is said, because the law and the order which set it up are derived from a body not

B recognised as a lawful government, this authority, qua organ of the Stiftung, has no legal existence: all its transactions in private law are void, as are presumably all other transactions carried out under its authority or by persons who derive their authority from it. By logical extension it seems to follow, and counsel for the respondents accepted, that there is, for many years has been and, until the attitude of Her Majesty's government changes, will be, in East Germany a legal

C vacuum; subject only, it may be, to the qualification that pre-existing German law, so far as it can continue to be operated or have effect, may continue in force. Whether in fact it can continue to be operated to any great extent if its operation depends on administrative or judicial authorities set up by the non-existent " government " must be doubtful. But the respondents, so far from shrinking from these consequences, insist on them as the necessary and, as they say,

D intended consequences of non-recognition. Correspondingly, they argue that if recognition were to be given by the courts to legislative acts of the non-recognised " government " that would be tantamount to recognition of that government, and so in conflict with the policy of the executive.

    My lords, if the consequences of non-recognition of the East German " government " were to bring in question the validity of its legislative acts, I should wish

E seriously to consider whether the invalidity so brought about is total, or whether some mitigation of the severity of this result can be found. As Locke said: " A government without laws is, I suppose, a mystery in politics, inconceivable to human capacity and inconsistent with human society " and this must be true of a society—at least a civilised and organised society—such as we know to exist in East Germany. In the United States some glimmerings can be found of the idea

F that non-recognition cannot be pressed to its ultimate logical limit, and that where private rights, or acts of every-day occurrence, or perfunctory acts of administration are concerned (the scope of these exceptions has never been precisely defined) the courts may, in the interest of justice and commonsense, where no consideration of public policy to the contrary has to prevail, give recognition to the actual facts or realities found to exist in the territory in

G question. These ideas began to take shape on the termination of the Civil War (see *U.S.* v. *Home Insurance Co.* (110)), and have been developed and reformulated, admittedly as no more than dicta, but dicta by judges of high authority, in later cases. I mention two of these: *Sokoloff* v. *National City Bank of New York* (111) and *Upright* v. *Mercury Business* (112), a case which was concerned with a corporate body under East German law. Other references can be found conveniently

H assembled in Professor O'Connell's International Law (1965) pp. 189 ff. No trace of any such doctrine is yet to be found in English law, but equally, in my opinion, there is nothing in those English decisions, in which recognition has been refused to particular acts of non-recognised governments, which would prevent its acceptance or which prescribes the absolute and total validity of all laws and acts flowing from unrecognised governments. In view of the conclusion

I which I have reached on the effect to be attributed to non-recognition in this case, it is not necessary here to resort to this doctrine but, for my part, I should wish to regard it as an open question, in English law, in any future case whether and to what extent it can be invoked.

    I return now to consideration of the effect of the refusal to recognise the " government " of East Germany. The respondents, claiming that non-recognition of a government entails automatically non-recognition of all laws

---

(110) (1874), 89 U.S. 99.   (111) (1924), 239 N.Y. 158.

(112) (1961), 13 A.D. (2nd) 361.

enacted by that government, rely on the well-known line of cases following on **A**
Aksionairnoye Obschestvo A. M. Luther v. *James Sagor & Co.* (113), where non-
recognition had these consequences. Before their argument can be made good,
however, they must show that the present refusal of recognition is given in a
situation comparable with that which is found in the cases. This is the critical
issue here and it is on this that the respondents' argument, in my opinion, breaks
down. For the present situation, as regards sovereignty in Germany, is incom-   **B**
parable with any that has previously come before our courts and, as I shall hope
to show, gives rise to different consequences.

The classic cases of non-recognition of governments arise in two types of
situation. First, where some new state comes into existence, as by separation
from another state or states (in such a case there may be a question of non-
recognition of the state itself as well as of the government); instances of this are   **C**
cases concerned with breakaway Spanish Colonies—*Jones* v. *Garcia del Rio* (114)
(Peru); *Thompson* v. *Powles* (115) (Guatemala); *Taylor* v. *Barclay* (116)
(Colombia). Secondly, where a new government claims authority over an existing
state, or part of it; instances of this are *The City of Berne* v. *Bank of England*
(117); *Luther* v. *Sagor* (118) (U.S.S.R.); *White Child & Beney, Ltd.* v. *Simmons*;
White Child & Beney, Ltd. v. *Eagle Star & British Dominions Insurance Co.* (119)   **D**
(U.S.S.R.) and numerous cases relating to Russian banks. Neither of these is the
situation in East Germany. When Germany surrendered unconditionally to the
allied powers in 1945, instead of proceeding to the traditional status of belligerent
occupancy, they brought a novel legal situation into being. The State of Germany
remained (and remains) in existence: governing authority or supreme authority in
respect of Germany as a whole was reserved to the four allied powers acting   **E**
jointly, and governing authority in respect of each zone was left to be exercisable
by that one of the allied powers to which the zone was allocated; in the Eastern
part of Germany in which Jena is situated by the U.S.S.R. There is no controversy
about this: the facts were so stated by the executive and accepted by the courts
in the cases of *R.* v. *Bottrill, Ex p. Kuechenmeister* (120) and *Preston* v. *Preston* (121).
It is against this background that the certificates of the Secretary of State were   **F**
given in these proceedings in September and November, 1964. The certificate of
Nov. 6 and the questions to which it was directed have been set out in the opinion
of my noble and learned friend, LORD REID, and I shall not repeat them here.
The following are, in my opinion, the conclusions to be drawn from the certificate
—(i) the governments of the four allied powers retain rights and responsibilities
in respect of Germany as a whole; (ii) in respect of the Eastern zone—called   **G**
" the zone of occupation allocated to the U.S.S.R." in which Jena is—the state
and government of the U.S.S.R. are recognised as de jure entitled to exercise
governing authority; (iii) this recognition is stated to extend to the period since
" at or about the end of June, 1945 " to the " present date ", i.e., Nov. 6, 1964;
(iv) apart from the four allied states and their governments and the control
council for Germany (an organ of the four allied governments) Her Majesty's   **H**
government has not recognised de jure or de facto any other authority purporting
to exercise governing authority in or in respect of the Eastern zone.

There should be added to these facts that stated by the earlier certificate dated
Sept. 6, 1964, that (v) Her Majesty's government has not granted any recognition
de jure or de facto to the " German Democratic Republic " or its " government "
—the inverted commas are as in the certificate itself.   **I**

The first question for a court when presented with this certificate (for convenience I treat the two as a single statement) is to consider whether it completely

---

(113) [1921] 1 K.B. 456; on appeal, [1921] All E.R. Rep. 138; [1921] 3 K.B. 532.
(114) (1823), 1 Turn. & R. 297.   (115) (1828), 2 Sim. 194.
(116) (1828), 2 Sim. 213.   (117) (1804), 9 Ves. 347.
(118) [1921] All E.R. Rep. 138; [1921] 3 K.B. 532.
(119) [1922] All E.R. Rep. 482.   (120) [1946] 2 All E.R. 434; [1947] K.B. 41.
(121) [1962] 3 All E.R. 928; [1963] P. 141.

A states the facts and whether there is any ambiguity in it. If so, it may be appropriate to ask the Secretary of State for a supplementary statement. There are only two questions which might arise in relation to the Eastern zone. The first is whether it is admissible in the courts of this country to take account of the fact (if such be the case, as to which I shall make some observation later) that the U.S.S.R. itself considers that there is in existence in the Eastern zone a

B government independent of the U.S.S.R., viz., the "government" of the "German Democratic Republic". In my opinion, the answer to this must be negative: to make any such assertion would be in direct contradiction to the certificate which states without qualification that the U.S.S.R. and its government is entitled de jure to exercise governing authority there and that nobody else is, either de jure or de facto. What view another State may take as to the legal or

C factual situation in any territory is irrelevant to the recognising (or non-recognising) state and, after the latter has defined its own attitude, is inadmissible in its courts. As a well known international law authority puts it—" The recognising State is not concerned with the question whether the state of things which it is recognising "—and I add " or not recognising "—" is legal by the national law of another state " (THE LAW OF NATIONS (1963) BRIERLY/WALDOCK,

D p. 147). The second question is whether consistently with the certificate it is possible to assert that the U.S.S.R. is not de facto exercising governing authority or control in the Eastern zone. It was, indeed, suggested by the respondents that there was a deliberate and significant abstention in the certificate from any positive assertion to this effect, two points being particularly relied on. First it was said that although the question was put what state or governments

E have been recognised as " exercising governing authority " in the Eastern zone, no answer to this was specifically given. Secondly, although in relation to Germany as a whole it was said that until Mar. 20, 1948, the four allied powers " did exercise . . . joint authority through the control council for Germany " no comparable statement was made concerning the Eastern zone. Either, therefore, the inference should be drawn that Her Majesty's government did

F not regard the U.S.S.R. as " exercising governing authority " in the Eastern zone, or at least the certificates were ambiguous and further inquiry ought to be made.

I have no temptation, in a matter of this kind, to speculate or to read into the certificate anything which is not there, but I cannot find that the certificate is either incomplete or ambiguous. In stating that the U.S.S.R. is exercising de

G jure governing authority and that no other body is exercising de facto authority, the two certificates to my mind say all that need or can be said. De jure recognition in all cases but one is the fullest recognition which can be given: the one exception is the case where there is concurrently some other body de facto exercising a rival authority to that of the " de jure " sovereign (as in the case of *Banco de Bilbao* v. *Sancha* (122)); but any such possibility as this is excluded

H by the terms of the certificates. Moreover, some enlightenment (if any be needed) as to what is meant by de jure recognition may be drawn from the official statement made by Mr. Secretary Morrison on Mar. 21, 1951 (quoted in full by my noble and learned friend, LORD REID) in which he said:

> " the conditions for the recognition of a new régime as the de jure govern-
I ment of a state are that the new régime should not merely have effective control over most of the state territory, but that it should, in fact, be firmly established "

—a statement which is not necessarily binding on successor Secretaries of State but which is reproduced, as still effective, in the 1963 edition of BRIERLY'S LAWS OF NATIONS (p. 148). This shows that, if nothing more is said, de jure recognition presupposes effective control in fact. It is consistent with this

---

(122) [1938] 2 All E.R. 253; [1938] 2 K.B. 176.

approach that Mr Secretary Gordon Walker, when asked what states or governments are recognised as (a) entitled to exercise or (b) exercising governing authority, answered only the first question: after doing so there was no occasion to go further. That in doing so there was no intention to deny effective control in fact to the de jure sovereign is shown by the fact that the reply relates, without distinction, to the whole period from 1945-1964. For at any rate some years after 1945, it would not be possible to dispute that the U.S.S.R. was directly governing the Eastern zone, which must dispose of any conjecture that in the words he has used for the period as a whole the Secretary of State is distinguishing between what could be done and the actuality of the situation. The certificates, therefore, in my opinion, establish the U.S.S.R. as de jure entitled to exercise governing authority and in full control of the area of the Eastern zone.

This makes possible a determination of what is the legal character of enactments by the " German Democratic Republic ". To say that this is an unrecognised government, though in a sense correct, may be misleading: it is so in a sense quite different from the sense in which the expression was used of, for example, the Russian revolutionary government prior to (de facto) recognition in 1921, whose status and the validity of whose legislation was considered in *Luther* v. *Sagor* (123). If that government was not recognised, there was nothing which could give international validity to its laws; but the " German Democratic Republic " is making laws in and as to a territory where a recognised " sovereign " exists. Is there, then, any reason for denying validity to its acts? The respondents say that there is: that no documentary authority has been proved to show that the " German Democratic Republic " had power, under the U.S.S.R., to make the law in question, or any law; that there must be either a constitution, or some enabling provision, or some express authority from the " sovereign " or proof positive of some other connexion with the government, to avoid the consequence that the law is simply a nullity, and that none such has been proved.

This argument, in my opinion, is unduly formalistic. The U.S.S.R. and the other allied powers assumed power in Germany after a military collapse followed by a declaration that they had done so : an exceptional, if not unprecedented step which, and the consequences of which, however, we are bound to recognise. Thereafter, for a period, they exercised their power directly through their military commander-in-chief. After a time they set up or allowed to be set up zonal or regional authorities to carry out tasks of government or administration. The United States military authorities, as we know, set up or allowed a " government " in the Land of Thüringia, which was continued by the U.S.S.R. when they took over. It is unnecessary in circumstances such as these to seek for a formal constitutional chain of power. Given the continuance of de jure authority and complete control, it follows that acts done by what are (as we are bound to hold) necessarily subordinate bodies are done under the governing authority of the occupying power. The argument to the contrary becomes all the more unrealistic when it is seen that the respondents themselves, in the evidence filed in these proceedings, have gone to considerable pains to demonstrate the subservient or puppet character of the " German Democratic Republic " and its government. Thus Dr. Walter David, after stating that the Eastern section of Germany (including Jena) remains under the occupation of a foreign power, Russia, continues that the intentions of Dr. Abbé, the founder of the Carl-Zeiss-Stiftung " cannot be implemented if the Council of Gera (*or indeed any authority under Russian or communist control*) were the special board ": and Dr. Richard Moser von Filseck says:

" In East Germany a centralised régime *has been set up by the Soviet Union to which it is subservient* . . . The Council of Gera is, therefore, the *representative of that political power* which carried out the expropriation of the assets of the foundation enterprises."

(123) [1921] All E.R. Rep. 138; [1921] 3 K.B. 532.

A The latter power was the U.S.S.R. Other passages are to a similar effect. Together with the certificate they present a consistent picture of subordinate central and local authorities exercising authority under the sovereignty or control of the U.S.S.R. as occupying power.

I must notice here two arguments: (i) In the Court of Appeal (124), it was assumed, as a matter of which judicial notice should be taken, that the " German

B Democratic Republic " was independent of the U.S.S.R., the conclusion from this being that its acts could not be derived from or attributed to the authority of the latter. Thus HARMAN, L.J., said (125):

" It is in fact notorious that the U.S.S.R. has recognised the German Democratic Republic as a sovereign state and treats its law-making capacity accordingly."

C DIPLOCK, L.J. (126), thought that he could take judicial notice that

" the government of the U.S.S.R. recognises the ' government of the German Democratic Republic ' as the independent sovereign government of an independent sovereign state for whose territory the government of the U.S.S.R. claims no power to make laws."

D I have already stated my opinion that, in the face of the Foreign Office certificate, recognition (if given) by the U.S.S.R. of the German Democratic Republic is something of which the courts of this country cannot take account. But, in addition, as to judicial knowledge, or notoriety, it is not shown, at any rate to my satisfaction, that *in 1952* when the critical " law " was enacted even the U.S.S.R. was claiming that the German Democratic Republic was independent

E of it or was disclaiming its own authority. Without elaboration, it is sufficient to say from official documents to be found in Cmnd. 1552, which the respondents made available to us, the contrary is seen to be clearly the case, and such is also the effect of the respondents' evidence. There is only one piece of evidence to the contrary, a single answer given by Professor von Moser in cross-examination to the effect that sovereignty was transferred to the German Democratic Republic

F in 1949. But this was not directed to the issue now being considered (which had not at that time been raised) and its true meaning was not explored; its apparent meaning seems to be contradicted both by the facts and by the considered evidence on affidavit of the same witness to which I have referred. The Court of Appeal (124), did not rely on it and it should be disregarded.

(ii) It was said by the respondents that to recognise the law setting up the

G Council of Gera of July 23, 1952, would in effect be to recognise the government of East Germany and to create a conflict with the views of the executive. The principle is well established that the courts of Her Majesty do not speak with a different voice from that of Her Majesty's executive government (it was stated as early as *Taylor* v. *Barclay* (127) and has been accepted ever since) but we are not here under the risk of committing the courts to action of this kind.

H Merely because in the class of case, of which *Luther* v. *Sagor* (128) is an example, non-recognition of a " government " entails non-recognition of its laws, or some of them, it does not follow that in a different situation this is so, nor that recognition of a law entails recognition of the law-maker as a government with sovereign power. The primary effect and intention of non-recognition by the executive is that the non-recognised " government " has no standing to represent the state

I concerned whether in public or in private matters. Whether this entails non-recognition of its so-called laws, or acts, is a matter for the courts to pronounce on, having due regard to the situation as regards sovereignty in the territory where the "laws " are enacted and, no doubt, to any relevant consideration of public policy. I can see no inconsistency in (a) accepting the view of the

(124) [1965] 1 All E.R. 300; [1965] Ch. 596.
(125) [1965] 1 All E.R. at p. 315, letter G; [1965] Ch. at p. 651.
(126) [1965] 1 All E.R. at p. 323; letter F; [1965] Ch. at p. 664.
(127) (1828), 2 Sim. 213.　　(128) [1921] All E.R. Rep. 138; [1921] 3 K.B. 532.

executive that there is no recognised (i.e. independent) government in the A
Eastern zone apart from the de jure governing authority of the U.S.S.R. and
(b) attributing legal validity, if no other legal obstacle exists, to a " law "
or act of that " government " as a subordinate or dependent body.

On consideration, therefore, of the whole of the situation in the Eastern
zone of Germany I reach the conclusion that the challenge to the validity of
the law of July 23, 1952, setting up the Council of Gera fails.   I should add that B
even if there was a change in the situation in the Eastern zone between 1952
and the issue of the writ in 1955 (in the direction of a discontinuance of Russian
control) it has not been suggested that this would have invalidated a law already
passed.

I must next mention the alternative contentions of the appellant with regard
to the right to institute the present proceedings.   These are three, namely, that C
Dr. Schrade (who instructed solicitors on behalf of the appellant) had authority
so to do (i) under a power of attorney granted on June 29, 1951, by the then
special board, namely, the Ministry of Education of the Land of Thüringia,
(ii) as mandatory or proxy mandatory under r. 9 of the constitution, (iii) as
the (i.e. the sole member of the) board of management of the optical works,
entitled to act, under r. 114, in the absence of a special board.   These alternative D
contentions were not dealt with by CROSS, J., because he held that the action
was validly authorised by the Council of Gera as the special board so that the
alternatives did not arise.   They were considered by the Court of Appeal (129)
and rejected there after careful examination by both HARMAN, L.J., and DIPLOCK,
L.J.   It was complained by counsel for the appellant that the learned lords
justices, on certain points, came to conclusions on what were essentially matters E
of German law without sufficient evidence, and your lordships were invited to
receive fresh affidavits as to these matters.   In my opinion, the expert evidence
filed at the trial by either side was on some points incomplete and obscure, and,
if these three points had to be decided, it would be unsafe to agree or disagree
with the conclusions of the Court of Appeal (129) on the existing material.

If, however, the appellant is entitled to succeed on the other points raised in F
this appeal, it would be unnecessary for it to rely on these alternatives or to
call any further evidence, and they could be left undetermined, as they were left
by CROSS, J.   I proceed, therefore, to consider the issues which CROSS, J.,
decided in favour of the appellant, and which the respondents now contest.
These are: (i) whether the appellant is estopped from contending that the
Council of Gera had authority to commence this action on behalf of the Stiftung G
by certain judgments given in the Federal Republic of Germany; (ii) whether,
if there is no estoppel, it has been established on the evidence that the Council
of Gera had such authority; (iii) whether the appellant is entitled to bring the
present proceedings in view of the confiscation in East Germany of the optical
business.

The third question was dealt with briefly by CROSS, J., but he expressed some H
doubt whether it was not more properly one which should be left for decision
at the trial rather than decided at the present preliminary stage.   In my opinion,
this doubt was justified and the issue, which may be a substantial and difficult
one, cannot properly be decided on this appeal.   It should be left to the trial as
an open issue on which the parties can put their case unfettered by the tentative
conclusions of CROSS, J.   The remaining two questions require decision.   I

(i) *Estoppel*.   The judgment mainly relied on by way of estoppel is the judgment in West Germany of the Federal High Court (I take the translation which
was used before CROSS, J.) of Nov. 15, 1960.   There are other decisions, but they
carry the matter no further.   This judgment was given in proceedings commenced in the provincial court (Landgericht) at Stuttgart on Apr. 28, 1954, the
parties to which were the Carl-Zeiss-Stiftung represented by the Council of Gera

(129) [1965] 1 All E.R. 300; [1965] Ch. 596.

A as plaintiff and three individuals (Bauersfeld, Heinrichs and Kuppenbender) and the firm Carl Zeiss of Heidenheim as defendants. As regards these parties it is not disputed (a) that the Carl-Zeiss-Stiftung named as plaintiff is the same as the body named as plaintiff in this action, (b) that the firm Carl Zeiss of Heidenheim named as defendants is the same body as that named as the third defendant to this action. It was also accepted that the effective plaintiff in those

B proceedings was the Council of Gera and that the substantive claim sought to be brought for trial related to the use of the names Zeiss or Carl Zeiss and of certain trade marks in the Federal Republic of Germany, so differing from the substantive claim in the present action, which relates to similar matters in this country. Objection was taken, before the West German action could be tried on the merits, to the right of the Council of Gera to represent the Stiftung and

C proceedings on this preliminary issue went through a number of stages and appeals. Finally, the Federal High Court, by its judgment of Nov. 15, 1960, held that the action was inadmissible, on the ground that the Council of Gera had no authority to represent the Carl-Zeiss-Stiftung. The action was, therefore, dismissed and the Council of Gera was ordered to pay the costs.

Several questions, some of difficulty, arise in considering whether the respon-

D dents in the present action can rely on the judgment of the Federal High Court by way of estoppel or as res judicata. The first question arises from the fact that what is relied on here is not the mere fact of a judgment and not a decision on the substantive " cause of action " or claim which the Carl-Zeiss-Stiftung was trying to make good, but only a decision on a particular issue: in other words, what has come to be called an " issue estoppel ". I must begin by

E ascertaining what is meant by " issue estoppel " in English law and then consider how far this kind of estoppel, or something analogous to it, may be applied to judgments of foreign courts.

A convenient starting point, as regards the English doctrine, is to be found in the judgments of the Court of Appeal in *Fidelitas Shipping Co., Ltd.* v. *V/O Exportchleb* (130). The case was concerned with an interim award made in

F a commercial dispute embodied in a Special Case on which the court had given a decision and it was held that an issue raised by the special case so determined was the subject of " issue estoppel " so that it could not be raised again. LORD DENNING, M.R., said this (131):

" The law, as I understand it, is this: if one party brings an action against another for a particular cause and judgment is given on it, there is a strict

G rule of law that he cannot bring another action against the same party for the same cause. Transit in rem judicatam; see *King* v. *Hoare* (132). But within one cause of action, there may be several issues raised which are necessary for the determination of the whole case. The rule then is that, once an issue has been raised and distinctly determined between the parties, then, as a general rule, neither party can be allowed to fight that issue all

H over again . . ."

He goes on to deal with " points " within issues, including those which though not actually raised could have been raised, an argument which is not material here, and which I prefer to leave open. Similarly in the judgment of DIPLOCK, L.J., there is a useful passage which contains these words (133):

I " The final resolution of a dispute between parties as to their respective legal rights or duties may involve the determination of a number of different ' issues ', that is to say, a number of decisions as to the legal consequences of particular facts, each of which decisions constitutes a necessary step in determining what are the legal rights and duties of the parties resulting from the totality of the facts . . ."

(130) [1965] 2 All E.R. 4. (131) [1965] 2 All E.R. at pp. 8, 9.
(132) (1844), 13 M. & W. 494 at p. 504. (133) [1965] 2 All E.R. at p. 9, letter H.

He continues by making a distinction between issue estoppel and fact estoppel **A** which may deserve some further exploration, but it does not arise here.

The doctrine of issue estoppel generally is not a new one. It can certainly be found in the opinion of the judges delivered by DE GREY, L.C.J., in the *Duchess of Kingston's Case* (134), a passage from whic hhas been quoted by my noble and learned friend, LORD REID, and an accepted re-statement of it was given by COLERIDGE, J., in *R.* v. *Inhabitants of Hartington Middle Quarter* (135), **B** which is also quoted by my noble and learned friend. MR. SPENCER BOWER, in his work on RES JUDICATA states (at p. 9) the principle as being " that the judicial decision *was or involved* a determination of the same question as that sought to be controverted in the litigation in which the estoppel is raised "—a formulation which invites the inquiry how what is " involved " in a decision is to be ascertained. One way of answering this is to say that any determination is involved **C** in a decision if it is a " necessary step " to the decision or a " matter which it was necessary to decide and which was actually " decided as the groundwork of the decision " (*R.* v. *Inhabitants of Hartington Middle Quarter* (135)). From this it follows that it is permissible to look not merely at the record of the judgment relied on, but at the reasons for it, the pleadings, the evidence (*Brunsden* v *Humphrey* (136)) and if necessary other material to show what was the issue **D** decided (*Flitters* v. *Allfrey* (137)). The fact that the pleadings and the evidence may be referred to, suggests that the task of the court in the subsequent proceeding must include that of satisfying itself that the party against whom the estoppel is set up did actually raise the critical issue, or possibly, though I do not think that this point has yet been decided, that he had a fair opportunity, or that he ought, to have raised it. **E**

This being the position as regards English judgments, one must next inquire whether a similar principle should apply as regards foreign judgments. It has taken some time before the recognition of foreign judgments by English courts was placed on a logical footing. Unlike English judgments, they were not considered to be judgments of a court of record so that the simplest form of estoppel—by record—could not be applied to them. They were, in the early **F** stages of private international law, considered only to be prima facie evidence of the rights of the parties and were examinable on the merits. This attitude can be found as late as 1834 in the Irish appeal of *Houlditch* v. *Marquess of Donegal* (138) where LORD BROUGHAM, L.C., expressed his disagreement with the opinion of the Lord Chancellor of Ireland that an English Chancery decree was conclusive, in strong terms. He said (139): **G**

" The leaning of my opinion is so strong that I can hardly call it the inclination of an opinion; and we know it is the general sense of lawyers in Westminster Hall (notwithstanding dicta of considerable weight coming from very learned judges' obiter dicta to the contrary) that the judgment of a foreign court in courts of this country is only prima facie evidence—is liable to be averred against and not conclusive. One argument **H** is clear—that the law in the course of procedure abroad sometimes differs so mainly from ours in the principles upon which it is bottomed, that it would seem a strong thing to hold that our courts were bound conclusively to give execution to the sentence of foreign courts . . ."

But the LORD CHANCELLOR's remarks showed that the tide was running in the direction of recognition and in *Ricardo* v. *Garcias* (140) this House assented to **I** the view that when a foreign judgment " comes in collaterally, or the defendant relies upon it under the exceptio rei judicatae, it is then received as conclusive " and LORD BROUGHAM's earlier remarks (139) came to be explained as referring

---

(134) (1776), 20 State Tr. at p. 358.   (135) (1855), 4 E. & B. at p. 794.
(136) [1881-85] All E.R. Rep. 357; (1884), 14 Q.B.D. 141.
(137) (1874), L.R. 10 C.P. 29.   (138) (1834), 8 Bli. N.S. 301.
(139) (1834), 8 Bli. N.S. at p. 338.   (140) (1845), 12 Cl. & Fin. 368.

A only to the limited grounds on which foreign judgments may be examined such as fraud, public policy or want of jurisdiction (see Spencer Bower on Estoppel, p. 38). In this respect, foreign judgments retain their distinction from English judgments. But, these limitations apart, the modern doctrine (usually derived from *Godard* v. *Gray* (141)) is that a foreign judgment may be pleaded and is conclusive.

B Is, then, what may be pleaded in defence to a claim limited to what may be called " cause of action " estoppel, i.e., a judgment which negatives the plaintiff's cause of action, or does it extend to any matter raised between the parties necessary to the decision and actually decided? There is no clear authority on the point. *Henderson* v. *Henderson* (142), in any event a decision of a colonial court, was a simple example of cause of action estoppel, and the same appears

C to be true of the more complicated case of *Callandar* v. *Dittrich* (143).

The appellant, arguing against issue estoppel in the case of foreign judgments, invokes a rule by which it appears that a plaintiff who has obtained a foreign judgment may sue here either on that judgment or on his original cause of action, a rule vouched by a number of decided cases, which maintains a precarious foothold as a sub-rule in Dicey's Conflict of Laws (8th Edn.) p. 996. But

D this rule, which if surviving at all is an illogical survival, affords no sound basis for denying a defendant the benefit of a decision on an issue; if it proves anything it proves too much and would deny both parties to a foreign proceeding the benefit of any estoppel at all.

As a matter of principle (and we are really thrown back on principle), whether the recognition of judgments is based on a recognition of vested rights, or on

E considerations of public interest in limiting relitigation, there seems to be no acceptable reason why the recognition of foreign judgments should not extend to the recognition of issue decisions. From the nature of things (and here it is right to recall Lord Brougham's warning (144)) this, in the case of foreign judgments, may involve difficulties and necessitate caution. The right to ascertain the precise issue decided, by examination of the court's judgment, of the

F pleadings and possibly of the evidence, may well, in the case of courts whose procedure, decision-making technique and substantive law is not the same as our own, make it difficult or even impossible to establish the identity of the issue there decided with that attempted here to be raised, or its necessity for the foreign decision. And I think that it would be right for a court in this country, when faced with a claim of issue estoppel arising out of foreign pro-

G ceedings, to receive the claim with caution in circumstances where the party against whom the estoppel is raised might not have had occasion to raise the particular issue. The fact that the court can (as I have stated) examine the pleadings, evidence and other material, seems fully consistent with its right to take a broad view of the result of the foreign decision. But with these reservations, where after careful examination there appears to have been a full contesta-

H tion and a clear decision on an issue, it would in my opinion be unfortunate to exclude estoppel by issue decision from the sphere of recognition. If that is so, in this case where an explicit statement is available of the decision of the Federal High Court, of the reasons for it, and of the issue as defined between the parties to it, and where the English court has the assistance of expert witnesses to explain the foreign decision, the difficulty should not be too great in ascertaining

I whether the same issues as were there decided are involved in the present action.

The appellant, indeed, says that the issue is not the same: that in the German proceedings it was whether the Council of Gera representing the Carl-Zeiss-Stiftung could sue in respect of certain matters in Germany and that here the issue is whether this can be done in respect of matters arising here. That is to argue for " cause of action " estoppel only. If issue estoppel exists, the issue

---

(141) (1870), L.R. 6 Q.B. 139.
(142) [1843-60] All E.R. Rep. 378; (1843), 3 Hare 100.
(143) (1842), 4 Man. & G. 68.   (144) (1834), 8 Bli. N.S. at p. 338.

is whether (briefly) the Carl-Zeiss-Stiftung has become paralysed or its organs A rendered ineffective so that it cannot act in the manner in which it is purporting to act. Identity of issue is, to my mind, clearly shown.

Next as to identity of parties. Normally to establish this should be the simplest part of the case. But there is a peculiar difficulty here because of the way in which the present issue arises. The proceedings profess to be brought by the Carl-Zeiss-Stiftung, but since it is a legal person there must be some B actual person, or persons, to bring it before the court, who has or have power to do so. The Council of Gera claims to be the relevant organ for this purpose; and it is clear that it is on the council's authority that the action was started. The question to be decided is whether the Carl-Zeiss-Stiftung is before the court or whether it is not; so according to the eventual decision the plaintiff may or may not be the Carl-Zeiss-Stiftung. Obviously in these circumstances the test of identity of C parties cannot be the formal test of identity on the record, so what is it to be? Cross, J., decided that there was not identity of parties and I understand that the majority of your lordships agree with him. I regret that I cannot share this view. The point no doubt merits longer argument, but in view of the numerous points discussed in this appeal I shall abstain from giving at any length the reasons why I think that identity of parties exists. Briefly, in my opinion, one D must look to see who in reality is behind the action: and the reality is that a body of persons, namely, the Council of Gera, is seeking in these proceedings, precisely as in Germany it sought, to set the Carl-Zeiss-Stiftung as plaintiff in motion before the court. One may consider the simpler case of a limited company. If certain persons, claiming to be its directors, start an action in the company's name, the defendant may seek and may obtain a decision that the E company is not properly before the court because the persons concerned had no right to commit the company to the action. As a result the action is struck out. Can it be that those same persons may start another action in the company's name against the same defendant making the same claim? According to the appellant's argument the relevant party as regards the application to strike out the action is the solicitors, so that if the directors started their second action F through the same firm there would be an estoppel; but if they employed a second or a third firm there would not be. I can hardly think so bizarre an argument can be correct. There must surely be an estoppel in the second action for the reason that the effective party to the decided issue (not to the action) is the same in each case—namely, the directors. Admittedly, as I mentioned at the start of this opinion, the involvement of the solicitors in the pro- G ceedings, according to our practice, introduces a complication. This does not, however, to my mind, prevent the party to the proceedings (who is behind the solicitors as we know) being the Council of Gera. To treat the solicitors as the parties to these proceedings seems to me, with respect to the argument, both lacking in reality and unduly technical. There is naturally no authority which deals with such a situation as this, but I find of assistance a passage from the H American RESTATEMENT OF THE LAW OF JUDGMENTS, Ch. 4, para. 85 (2), which reads:

" Where a person is bound by or entitled to the benefits of the rules of res judicata . . . such rules apply in a subsequent action brought or defended by another on his account."
I
We were also referred to passages from 50 CORPUS JURIS SECUNDUM Judgments, paras. 756 et seq., and to American authorities there cited which show that United States courts take a flexible view of the requirements of these estoppel rules. The present case seems to me one which does not require much, if any, adjustment, to fit into the rules as to parties. If the Council of Gera is not itself the party, then the case seems to fall within the " Restatement " rule. So I do not think that the estoppel fails on this ground.

To my mind, a more serious obstacle to the efficacy of the estoppel is to be

A found in the requirement that the foreign judgment should be final and conclusive or, as it is sometimes put, conclusive on the merits. I have no difficulty
as to the latter element, for I cannot accept the argument that, for this purpose,
the merits means the merits of the action as stated in the plaintiff's claim. The
defendants' contention that the Stiftung's ability to act has been fatally impaired
is just as much an argument on the merits: indeed, the issue which group of

B persons is entitled to control the Stiftung is at the root of the present dispute;
but the remaining requirement is more difficult.

The text books are in agreement in stating that for a foreign judgment to be
set up as a bar in this country it must be res judicata in the country in which it
is given (see DICEY'S CONFLICT OF LAWS (7th Edn.), p. 1036; CHESHIRE'S PRIVATE
INTERNATIONAL LAW (7th Edn.), p. 562). The chief authority cited for this is

C *Nouvion* v. *Freeman* (145) in which both LINDLEY, L.J., in the Court of Appeal
(146) and LORD HERSCHELL in this House (147) expressed themselves strongly
in this sense. No doubt that was rather a special case since the remate judgment
was no more than provisional, but, generally, it would seem unacceptable to give
to a foreign judgment a more conclusive force in this country than it has where
it was given. In relation to the present case I think that " conclusive " must be

D taken in the sense that if the Stiftung represented by the Council of Gera were
to attempt to commence another action in West Germany against the same
defendants as were parties to the previous action they would, by the force of
the previous judgment, be prevented from proceeding with it. Moreover, I
think that it is for the defendant, who sets up the bar, to establish the conclusive
character of the judgment. This must be so on principle and there is support

E for it in *Behrens* v. *Sieveking* (148). Unfortunately there is no clear evidence
whether the judgment of the Federal High Court is res judicata (in the sense
which I have mentioned) in Germany or not. The respondents rely on the
accepted presumption that the foreign law is the same as English law, but this
presumption, never more than a fragile support, is less than ever reliable here
when the question is what is the effect of a particular judgment which has no

F exact parallel in English law. There are in fact indications in the evidence to
the contrary.

In 1957 an action, commenced in Dusseldorf in West Germany, came on appeal
before the Federal High Court. The parties to the action were " the firms
Carl Zeiss of Heidenheim, represented by Dr. Bauersfeld " as plaintiff and
(inter alios) V.e.B. Carl Zeiss Jena as defendants. The defendants took the point

G that the plaintiff lacked capacity to sue and was not properly represented, alleging
that Dr. Bauersfeld had resigned from the board of management of the Stiftung.
The Federal High Court in its decision of July 24, 1957, rejected this objection on
the ground that it was not satisfied that Dr. Bauersfeld had resigned.

In 1959 another action, also commenced in Dusseldorf in West Germany, came
on appeal before the Federal High Court with the same plaintiff and (inter alios)

H the same defendant as in the 1957 appeal. The defendants again took the point
that the plaintiff had not the capacity to sue and was not properly represented
because Dr. Bauersfeld had resigned from the board of management of the Stiftung. The Federal High Court again rejected the objection and in doing so used
these words:

I " It had already negatived the question by its judgment dated July 24,
1957 with detailed reasons. This must stand even after repeated examination and assessment of the objections raised against it by the appeal ";

and later: " The court maintains its view even after a re-examination." The
significance of these two judgments in relation to the conclusive effect, in a
subsequent action, of a decision, by way of objection, that a plaintiff was not

(145) (1887), 37 Ch.D. 244; (1889), 15 App. Cas. 1.
(146) (1887), 37 Ch.D. at p. 253.   (147) (1889), 15 App. Cas. at p. 6.
(148) (1837), 2 My. & Cr. 602.

properly represented in an earlier proceeding between the same parties, was not
explored at the trial.   But, if the fate of the estoppel turned on this point (as
it would on my view as to identity of parties) I should be strongly inclined to
hold that the defendants (the present respondents) had not established to the
satisfaction of the court that the judgment of Nov. 15, 1960, was conclusive in
West Germany as regards other proceedings, even between the same parties,
and that consequently it could not be conclusive as regards other proceedings
here.   The estoppel fails, in any event, in view of the conclusion reached by
your lordships as to identity of parties. This being so, it is not necessary to
consider whether the appellants, for their part, could set up the judgments given
in East Germany as a counter-estoppel, or to decide on the effect of an estoppel
as regards the first and second respondents to the present action.

(ii) *Whether Council of Gera had authority in the absence of estoppel* (149). I
now consider, free from any estoppel, whether the Council of Gera had authority
to commence these proceedings on behalf of the Stiftung. The evidence before
the learned judge consisted in the main of decisions of courts in both East and
West Germany.   There were also affidavits by experts on each side, on which
extensive cross-examination took place.   On the appellant's side most reliance
was placed on two judgments of the Supreme Court in East Germany, an
advisory opinion given on Apr. 6, 1954, and a judgment on appeal from the
District Court of Leipzig dated Mar. 23, 1961.   This judgment was given in
proceedings brought by the Stiftung (represented by the Council of Gera as the
special board and by its mandatory, Dr. Schrade) and V.e.B. Carl Zeiss (the
public body which had taken over the optical works in 1948) against " the firm
Carl Zeiss of Oberkochen " (a description intended to apply to the present
third respondents) to restrain them from using the name Carl-Zeiss in the German
Democratic Republic.   Notice of these proceedings was apparently given to
the defendants but they did not appear nor take any part in the action.   These
two decisions, which enter in great detail into both the facts and the law, state
as the conclusions of the Supreme Court (a) that the Stiftung continued to
exist as a legal entity, (b) that the Council of Gera was the special board of the
Stiftung, (c) that r. 116, which provided for liquidation of the Stiftung, had not
come into play.

On the side of the respondents, reliance was in the main placed on the judgment of the Federal High Court of West Germany of Nov. 15, 1960, coupled with
that of the Provincial Court of Appeal of Stuttgart dated Oct. 29, 1958, the
reasoning of which was approved by the Federal High Court. The effect of
these judgments was that, under East German law, the articles of the Stiftung
had been inoperable since and by reason of the confiscations of the undertakings
of the Stiftung in 1948 and that in any event the Council of Gera was not capable
of exercising the functions of the special board by reason (inter alia) of the
political and economic conditions in the " German Democratic Republic ".

There is thus a direct conflict between the views of the two highest courts.
The expert evidence divides itself similarly into two sides supporting the one
or the other set of judgments. The existence of the Stiftung as a legal entity,
though at one time disputed, is now accepted by both sides and the essential
questions which have to be decided may be summarised as being (i) whether
the Stiftung, from 1948 onwards, was incapable of acting and its articles were
inoperative and (ii) whether the Council of Gera was capable or incapable of
fulfilling the functions conferred by the articles on the special board.

Each of these questions may be " classified " as questions relating to the
constitution of a foreign corporation, and so, according to English private
international law, to be decided according to the law prevailing at the place
where the Stiftung was incorporated (see DICEY'S CONFLICT OF LAWS (7th Edn.)
r. 78 (2)).   So far as German private international law is concerned, it appears
that account is taken of the law prevailing at the place of the " domicil " of

(149) For the three issues of which this is the second, see p. 582, letter G, ante.

A the corporation. There is no dispute that the place of incorporation was Jena, and, although an attempt has been made to transfer the domicil or seat of the Stiftung to West Germany, the courts of West Germany have been prepared to assume for the purpose of their decisions (rightly in my opinion) that this remains in Jena. The question, then, on either approach, is, what is the relevant applicable law prevailing at Jena? The expert evidence establishes, in my opinion,

B that the law applicable to Stiftungen in Germany rests on the triple foundation of (a) the German civil code (BGB) of 1900 and in particular arts. 80-88; (b) the legal code of the Land of Thüringia of 1923, and (iii) the articles. From this it would seem to follow that the relevant law should be that stated by the courts having jurisdiction in Thüringia, or whatever geographical area corresponds to Thüringia, viz., the Provisional Court at Leipzig and on appeal the Supreme

C Court in East Germany.

In general, it may be taken to be the case that the best evidence as to the law of a foreign country is the law as stated by its court of last resort. All five speeches in this House in *Bankers and Shippers Insurance Co. of New York* v. *Liverpool Marine & General Insurance Co., Ltd.* (150) accepted this. LORD BUCKMASTER (151) pointed out that, while no foreign judgment is technically

D binding, yet it would require " special and unusual circumstances " to lead the House away from a clear decision of a final court. His opinion was expressed in relation to a matter of construction of a statute, but the principle must apply equally to other matters of foreign law. I need not quote from the other speeches which were, if anything, expressed in still stronger terms. Similarly in *Lazard Brothers & Co.* v. *Midland Bank, Ltd.* (152) LORD WRIGHT said that the question

E is what the foreign law is shown to be by its exposition, interpretation and adjudication. So it would seem that there are strong reasons—if not quite conclusive—why courts in this country should accept the East German judgments as stating the relevant law.

The respondents contest this conclusion on several grounds. They submit that the questions of law as to the constitution of the Stiftung should properly

F be considered to be questions not of East German law but of German law. The questions relate, they say, to the issue how the Stiftung may be represented in Germany as a whole and internationally and how, if at all, it may protect assets outside the Eastern zone. Formally, the questions of law concern the interpretation or application of the German civil code, under which the Stiftung was formed, not of any zonal law. As to such a legal question the decisions of courts

G of the Federal Republic of Germany have a superior or (alternatively) an equal right to international recognition as compared with those of East German courts.

The claim for superior status was based principally on the terms of the certificate of the Secretary of State given on Nov. 6, 1964, already considered in another context and set out in the opinion of my noble and learned friend, LORD REID.

H This certificate makes it clear, so it is said, that the rights of the U.S.S.R. as de jure " sovereign " in the Eastern zone are confined to that zone and explicitly recognises (following a communiqué of the Western allies on Sept. 19, 1950), the government of the Federal Republic as " entitled to speak for Germany as the representative of the German people in international affairs ". So it is argued, in what is essentially an international matter, the courts of the Federal Republic

I should be accepted as the proper organ to declare what the law of Germany is.

I recognise the ingenuity of this argument, but I am not convinced by it. Read as a whole, the certificate gives recognition to the U.S.S.R. as de jure entitled to exercise governing authority in respect of the Eastern zone; and (negatively) the certificate also states, after the passage on which the respondents rely, that the communiqué of 1950 does not constitute recognition of the

---

(150) (1926), 24 Lloyd L.R. 85.   (151) (1926), 24 Lloyd L.R. at p. 87.
(152) [1932] All E.R. Rep. at p. 577; [1933] A.C. at p. 298.

government of the Federal Republic as the de jure government of all Germany. **A**
The right to exercise governing authority includes, in my opinion, the right to
set up or maintain courts and the recognition of the one carries with it the recognition, as a source of law, of the decisions of the courts. The right to " speak
for Germany as the representative of the German people in international affairs "
is a right of diplomatic representation, which is not coincident with, and does not
impinge on, the right of the governing authority in each part of Germany to **B**
make and state the law in the part over which it has power. Furthermore, it by
no means follows from the fact that the present claim of the Stiftung extends
beyond the frontiers of East Germany that the legal question which we are
considering is one of international or interzonal concern. The legal question
relates to the constitution of the Stiftung, which depends on the law of the place
where it is localised. Your lordships were invited by the respondents to consult **C**
the Secretary of State on the matters discussed above, and to seek a further
certificate as to the proper authority to determine the status of and right to
represent the Stiftung. This course, in my opinion, should not be followed.
The questions, which it was suggested should be asked, were questions of law
which it is the function of the courts to determine and which they are in a position
to determine on the basis of the certificate previously given, the terms of which **D**
are sufficiently clear.

The argument therefore that superior recognition should be given to the
West German judgments in my opinion should not be accepted. But there
remains the further submission that the West German judgments should at
least be considered side by side with those of the East German courts—as rival
pieces of evidence entitled to equal weight—and a decision reached on their **E**
respective merits. The arguments for this are that the circumstances prevailing
in Germany are unusual, that the legal questions involved are common to both
parts of divided Germany, that the East German judgments consist of an advisory
opinion and a default judgment, whereas those of West Germany were given
in contested proceedings brought at the present appellant's choice in the courts
of West Germany, and (ultimately if the comparison is admissible) that the West **F**
German judgments are superior in legal reasoning.

These are difficult questions indeed. I am prepared to go so far with the
respondents as to agree that it may be right in the present circumstances to
look beyond the decisions of the East German courts and to consider, and at
least to test them by, the rival decisions in West Germany. But, in making
this comparison, there are two points to bear in mind. First: the question to **G**
be resolved is not merely one of interpretation of a common code—the Civil
Code of 1900—(I pass over for this purpose the Thüringian Law of 1923 whose
provisions are of a general character with no direct bearing on the issues). It is
a question of the application of the somewhat general provisions of the civil
code to a factual situation peculiar to the Eastern zone, the answer to which, by
agreement of both sets of courts, depends upon a consideration of the effect **H**
of the 1948 (Eastern zone) decrees on the actual business undertaking in Jena
of the Stiftung. Both sets of courts in fact give considerable attention to the
factual situation prevailing in Jena since 1948. On such matters, prima facie,
preference should be given to the East German courts, as the appropriate tribunal to deal with the impact of East German legislation on an organisation in
their zone. Secondly: in so far as the questions for decision are general questions **I**
of law rather than questions depending on local considerations, there is no reason
why, given a separation of de jure sovereignty between the two parts of Germany,
there should not be differences of interpretation and application of rules of law
formerly common to the whole of Germany. The respondents' experts, indeed,
asserted that there were such differences; their contentions were that decisions
in East Germany were those appropriate to a centralised socialist state whose
courts were guided by considerations of policy. If this argument could have
been carried to the point of showing that the courts of East Germany are not

A courts of law at all or that their decisions were corrupt or perverse, that might (I do not say would) be a ground for disregarding them in favour of decisions of other courts shown to act more judicially. But the evidence did not, in my opinion, approach this point, and a mere difference in philosophy, or even of method, so far from entitling us to prefer the West German approach, on the contrary gives support to those who argue that the East German variety of B German law should be taken as being the law in East Germany. With these considerations in mind, I consider the two sets of judgments. They have been analysed in detail by Cross, J., and (subject to the one point to which I return later) I am satisfied to accept his analysis. I only make some observations of my own in recognition of their careful re-examination by counsel in the present appeal and because these issues have not been considered by the Court of Appeal C (153).

The East German Supreme Court bases its decisions on the following main points: (i) the confiscations which took place in 1948 were not of the whole business of the Stiftung but were separate acts of confiscation of the assets of the two individual businesses—the optical works and the glass works; (ii) the Stiftung as such retains considerable assets: these produce an income of some D £180,000 per annum. It is able with these assets to fulfil many of the charitable functions for which it was created. The Supreme Court refers to establishments for the development and training of optical personnel, for the promotion of studies, research and training in natural sciences and mathematics, as well as for social and health care of the employees of the plants of the foundation, e.g., schools for opticians, libraries, clinics, recreation and rest homes, and their findings as E to these matters were supported by evidence before Cross, J. There was also evidence as to the ownership of trade marks and other industrial property and as to assets of the Stiftung outside East Germany, but this was perhaps controversial and it is safer to leave these matters out of account; (iii) the Stiftung employs over 400 persons and there are about 4,000 pensioners who are paid according to the pensions statute of the Stiftung. There remain also other F beneficiaries within the purposes of the Stiftung; (iv) the Stiftung is in a position to take and does take legal action for the protection of its assets; (v) the resolution of the German Economic Commission of June 16, 1948, contemplated that the Stiftung should remain in existence and that its constitution should be amended to reflect its changed position. This was not done, but it is consistent with the resolution to hold that the original articles continue in effect.

G The principal reasons for the judgment of the West German Supreme Court are (a) that the articles became unworkable after 1948 because they were dependent for their working on the continued ownership of some business by the Stiftung. After 1948 the foundation ceased to have any interest in its former businesses which became nationalised undertakings. According to the " Soviet zone view ", as interpreted by the Federal High Court, this interfered with the H organisation of the Stiftung to such a far reaching effect that in the Eastern zone the Stiftung no longer had capacity to act as a juristic person; (b) that the centre of gravity of the Stiftung's organisation lay in the industrial enterprises and the removal of these destroyed the balance on which the organisation of the governing bodies of the Stiftung depended; (c) that the Council of Gera, because of its political complexion cannot act as a special board or represent I the interests of the Stiftung or carry on the affairs of the Stiftung consistently with the intentions of the founder, Dr. Abbé.

As between these opinions, and taking also into account the expert evidence on them, much of which was not challenged, and certain supplementary evidence (particularly of Dr. Schrade) regarding the factual position at Jena, I think that the learned judge was fully justified in coming to the conclusion that the East German decisions should be preferred. The decisions of the West German courts

---

(153) [1965] 1 All E.R. 300; [1965] Ch. 596.

carry less conviction, on points (a) and (b) because they were less fully informed **A** than the East German courts as to the existing activity and assets of the Stiftung and because they based their decisions on a view as to the law in the Eastern zone which is not in agreement with that law as declared by the Supreme Court in that zone; on point (c) because it is really impossible to say that, and if so when, the authority designated as the special board diverged from the intentions of the founder so radically that it ceased to be capable of acting. In fact both **B** Supreme Courts claimed that the intentions of the founder were reflected in the very different philosophies prevailing in their respective zones so that, as CROSS, J., observed, the only safe course is to keep to the natural sense of the articles which base the constitution of the special board on considerations of administrative geography.

I must add one point as to the respective merits of the judgments. CROSS, **C** J., in that part of his judgment dealing with res judicata, after a careful analysis of the West German judgments, expressed the view that these were perverse, and so in any case ought to be disregarded. He, of course, had the advantage of hearing the expert witnesses which we have not, but even allowing for this, I do not think that a finding of perversity ought to stand. In my opinion, the case amounts to this: (1) that the law prevailing in East Germany should be **D** taken to be that declared by the East German courts; (2) that the West German decisions proceeded on a view as to the law in East Germany which, for reasons which I have given, ought not to be accepted in preference to the view of the East German courts themselves. Further than this I do not think that the evidence requires or indeed entitles us to go. For my part, I accept the West German decisions as judicial in the fullest sense which could readily be accepted if they **E** stood alone. This being so, I do not consider it necessary (as on some future occasion it may be) to examine the limits in law of the doctrine of perversity, some of the authorities on which (for example *Simpson* v. *Fogo* (154)) seem to me to present difficulties.

My lords, in this long and involved case we have heard many arguments from counsel on either side and many authorities have been referred to. It involves I **F** hope no disrespect to those arguments not to examine them all. In the end, and on the whole of the case, the conclusion emerges that the respondents' preliminary attack on the validity of the action fails: I would allow the appeal and restore the judgment of CROSS, J.

Appeal allowed.

G

Solicitors: *Courts & Co.* (for the appellant); *Herbert Smith & Co.* (for the respondents).

[*Reported by* KATHLEEN J. H. O'BRIEN, *Barrister-at-Law.*]

H

I

---

(154) (1863), 1 Hem. & M. 195.

A

THE HERON II.

C. CZARNIKOW, LTD. *v.* KOUFOS.

[COURT OF APPEAL (Sellers, Diplock and Salmon, L.JJ.), March 15, 16, 17, 21,
April 5, 1966.]

B *Shipping—Carriage by sea—Breach of contract—Damages—Measure—Late
delivery of goods due to deliberate breach of charterparty by deviation—
Charterparty containing no liberty to deviate—Duration of voyage predictable
—Fall in market price of cargo between date ship should have arrived and
date of actual arrival.*

Where a shipper and a shipowner enter into a contract for carriage of goods
C by sea which the shipowner knows, or can be reasonably assumed by the
shipper to know, are marketable goods, and such goods are consigned to a
destination at which, as the shipowner knows or can be reasonably assumed
by the shipper to know, there exists a market for goods of that kind, and
where the voyage is one whose duration in the absence of excepted perils is
reasonably predictable, the measure of damages for breach of contract by
D the shipowner by late delivery, if the market price at the destination has
fallen between the date at which the goods should have arrived and the
date when they in fact arrived, is prima facie the difference in market price
(see p. 606, letter F, p. 610, letter F, and p. 612, letter G, post).

By a charterparty dated Oct. 15, 1960, a ship, which was then in dry
dock at Piraeus " expected ready to load about 25th-27th inst., all going
E well ", was to proceed with all convenient speed to Constanza " lay days for
loading not to count before Oct. 27, 1960, and if ship not ready to load by
Nov. 10, 1960, charterers have the option to cancel this charterparty ",
with an option to the charterers to discharge at Jeddah instead of Basrah
" such option to be declared not later than five days prior to commencement
of loading ". When loaded with a cargo of sugar the ship was to proceed
F with all convenient speed to Basrah, if the Jeddah option had not been
exercised. The charterparty contained no liberty to deviate. The ship
arrived at Constanza on Oct. 27, was loaded (as was expected) within four
days, and sailed on Nov. 1. The charterers did not opt for Jeddah. The
voyage from Constanza to Basrah could be predicted with reasonable
accuracy as taking twenty days, or perhaps a day or two more or less, but
G in deliberate breach of the charterparty the ship deviated by calling at
Berbera, Bahrein and Abadan for purposes of the owner and so as to make
more money, thus prolonging the voyage by ten days, so that the ship
arrived at Basrah on Dec. 2. The existence of a market for sugar in Basrah
was known at all material times to the shipowner. Had the ship arrived
on the date when she should have arrived, if the shipowner had not broken
H the charterparty by deviating, the market value of the sugar at Basrah
would have been £32 10s. per ton, but on Dec. 2 it was only £31 2s. 9d. per
ton. The charterers having sustained for this reason a loss in price of
£1 7s. 3d. per ton, claimed their loss (£4,183 16s. 8d.) as damages for late
delivery.

Held (SELLERS, L.J., dissenting): the measure of damages for breach of
I the charterparty by deviation resulting in late delivery of the sugar was the
difference in market price between the price at the date when the sugar should
have arrived at Basrah and that at the date when it in fact arrived, and the
charterers were entitled to recover damages at the rate of £1 7s. 3d. per ton
of the cargo accordingly (see p. 606, letter H, p. 607, letters B and H, p. 610,
letter H, p. 612, letters A and D, and p. 613, letter E, post).

Victoria Laundry (Windsor), Ltd. v. *Newman Industries, Ltd.* ([1949] 1
All E.R. 997) and *Dunn* v. *Bucknall Bros.* ([1900-03] All E.R. Rep. 131)
applied.

Affirmed H.L. [1967] 3 All E.R. 686.

The Parana ((1877), 2 P.D. 118) not followed.   A

Per SALMON, L.J.: I can see no reason for applying the old practice of
the Court of Admiralty, stemming from the days of sail, which disallowed
such damages as those claimed in the present case, save in those rare cases,
if any such still exist, where no reasonably accurate prediction of the length
of voyage can be made (see p. 611, letter I, post).

Appeal allowed.   B

[As to the measure of damages in contract, see 11 HALSBURY'S LAWS (3rd
Edn.) 241-243, paras. 409, 410; and for cases on the subject, see 17 DIGEST
(Repl.) 91-99, *99-154*; as to the measure of damages for delay in delivery of
goods by a carrier, see 4 HALSBURY'S LAWS (3rd Edn.) 151-154, paras. 400-406;
and for cases on the subject, see 8 DIGEST (Repl.) 150-158, *947-1012*.

As to the measure of damages for delay on voyage of goods carried by sea,   C
see 35 HALSBURY'S LAWS (3rd Edn.) 475, 476, para. 677; and for cases on the
subject, see 41 DIGEST (Repl.) 459-461, *2384-2399*.]

Cases referred to:

Ardennes (Owner of Cargo), The v. *The Ardennes (Owners)*, [1950] 2 All E.R.
 517; [1951] 1 K.B. 55; 41 Digest (Repl.) 241, *623*.   D

British Columbia and Vancouver's Island Spar, Lumber and Saw Mill Co.,
 Ltd. v. *Nettleship*, [1861-73] All E.R. Rep. 339; (1868), L.R. 3 C.P.
 499; 37 L.J.C.P. 235; 18 L.T. 604; 8 Digest (Repl.) 150, *951*.

Collard v. *South Eastern Ry. Co..* [1861-73] All E.R. Rep. 851; (1861), 7 H. & N.
 79; 30 L.J.Ex. 393; 4 L.T. 410; 158 E.R. 400; 17 Digest (Repl.)
 60, *674*.   E

Connolly Shaw, Ltd. v. *Nordenfjeldske Steamship Co.*, (1934),. 49 Lloyd L.R.
 183; 41 Digest (Repl.) 382, *1719*.

Cory v. *Thames Ironworks Co.*, [1861-73] All E.R. Rep. 597; (1868), L.R. 3
 Q.B. 181; 37 L.J.Q.B. 68; 17 L.T. 495; 17 Digest (Repl.) 117, *287*.

Donoghue v. *Stevenson*, [1932] All E.R. Rep. 1; [1932] A.C. 562; 101 L.J.P.C.
 119; 147 L.T. 281; 36 Digest (Repl.) 85, *458*.   F

Dunn v. *Bucknall Bros.*, [1900-03] All E.R. Rep. 131; [1902] 2 K.B. 614;
 71 L.J.K.B. 963; 87 L.T. 497; 9 Asp. M.L.C. 336; 8 Digest (Repl.)
 26, *160*.

Fibrosa Spolka Akcyjna v. *Fairbairn Lawson Combe Barbour, Ltd.*, [1942]
 2 All E.R. 122; [1943] A.C. 32; 111 L.K.J.B. 433; 167 L.T. 101;
 12 Digest (Repl.) 448, *3383*.   G

Gee v. *Lancashire and Yorkshire Ry. Co.*, [1843-60] All E.R. Rep. 131; (1860),
 6 H. & N. 211; 30 L.J.Ex. 11; 3 L.T. 328; 158 E.R. 87; 8 Digest
 (Repl.) 152, *960*.

Hadley v. *Baxendale*, [1843-60] All E.R. Rep. 461; (1854), 9 Exch. 341; 23
 L.J.Ex. 179; 23 L.T.O.S. 69; 156 E.R. 145; 8 Digest (Repl.) 151,
 956.   H

Horne v. *Midland Ry. Co.*, (1873), L.R. 8 C.P. 131; 42 L.J.C.P. 59; 28 L.T.
 312; 8 Digest (Repl.) 153, *964*.

Iossifoglu, The, (1929), 32 Fed. Rep. (2nd) 928.

Montevideo Gas and Dry Dock Co., Ltd. v. *Clan Line Steamers, Ltd.*, (1921),
 37 T.L.R. 866; 8 Digest (Repl.) 151, *953*.

Notting Hill, The, (1884), 9 P.D. 105; 53 L.J.P. 56; 51 L.T. 66; 5 Asp. M.L.C.   I
 241; 41 Digest (Repl.) 388, *1753*.

Parana, The, (1876), 1 P.D. 452; *on appeal* C.A., (1877), 2 P.D. 118; 36 L.T.
 388; 5 Asp. M.L.C. 399; 8 Digest (Repl.) 154, *970*.

Sargant & Sons v. *East Asiatic Co., Ltd.*, (1915), 21 Com. Cas. 344; 85 L.J.K.B.
 277; 41 Digest (Repl.) 388, *1749*.

Smith, Edwards & Co. v. *Tregarthen*, (1887), 57 L.T. 58; 56 L.J.Q.B. 437;
 6 Asp. M.L.C. 137; 8 Digest (Repl.) 154, *976*.

United States v. *Middleton*, (1924), 3 Fed. Rep. (2nd) 384.

A   *Victoria Laundry (Windsor), Ltd.* v. *Newman Industries, Ltd.*, [1949] 1 All E.R.
997; [1949] 2 K.B. 528; 17 Digest (Repl.) 92, *100.*

Appeal.

This was an appeal by C. Czarnikow, Ltd., the charterers of the Heron II from
Nicolas Demetris Koufos, the owner of the ship, under a charterparty dated
Oct. 15, 1960, from the judgment of McNAIR, J., dated Dec. 2, 1965, on a Special
B   Case stated by the umpire, on a claim by the charterers against the shipowner
for damages for breach of the charterparty, causing late arrival of the ship at
Basrah, the port where the cargo, to carry which the ship had been chartered,
was delivered. The umpire had awarded the charterers £4,183 16s. 8d., the
amount by which the market price of the cargo at Basrah had fallen between
the date the ship should have arrived and the actual date of arrival, but
C   McNAIR, J., held that the charterers were only entitled to interest on the value
of the cargo for the period between those dates. The facts are set out in the
judgment of SELLERS, L.J.

A. J. L. Lloyd for the charterers.
M. J. Mustill for the shipowner.

D   *Cur. adv. vult.*
Apr. 5. The following judgments were read.

SELLERS, L.J.: This is an appeal relating to damages only in a claim
by the charterers against the owner of the chartered ship. The umpire who stated
the Special Case on which the dispute has been brought before the courts would
have found in favour of the charterers, but McNAIR, J., applied what he regarded
E   as the law and the established practice and found for the shipowner.
The question is whether in the circumstances of the present case as found by
the award the charterers are entitled to recover as damages for delay the
difference in the market value of a cargo of Hungarian sugar between the day
when it might have arrived if the shipowner had completed the voyage without
deliberate interruption and the day when the cargo in fact arrived after the delay
F   occasioned by the breach of the charterparty. I have used the words " might
have arrived " because the period of a voyage from Constanza in the Black Sea
to Basrah at the head of the Persian Gulf, a distance of 4,370 sea miles, might be
said to be a voyage of twenty days as a fair prediction, but such a voyage might
vary between a day or two more or less. Sea and weather, tide and wind, have not
yet been conquered, although the hazards of sail-power have been greatly con-
G   trolled. Also, even without the shipowner's default, engines and the shafts and
mechanisms which take their driving power do not perform with complete
consistency.
In the course of the voyage and in breach of the charterparty the ship called
at Berbera and took on an additional cargo which she delivered at Bahrein.
She also called at Abadan for bunkers. These diversions occasioned a delay of
H   nine days (inadvertently stated as ten days in the Case) in arriving at Basrah.
During those nine days the value of sugar in the Basrah market declined and this
decline was perhaps accentuated, if not wholly caused, by a shipment of about
eight thousand tons of Formosan sugar (a more normal source of supply for
Basrah) by the s.s. Youmnly, which arrived at Basrah within the nine days
period. The cargo of three thousand metric tons of Hungarian sugar on the
I   contractual voyage was an experimental or pioneering cargo, the first, it appears,
to be put on the Basrah market. The Special Case finds (para. 20 (B)) that

" one of the factors which would normally affect prices is the arrival of a
steamer carrying a cargo of sugar to be sold on or through the market."

After referring to the decision of *The Parana* (1) and reading the most relevant
extract from the judgment of the Court of Appeal (JAMES and MELLISH, L.JJ.,
and BAGGALLAY, J.A.), delivered by MELLISH, L.J., McNAIR, J. (than whom

(1) (1877), 2 P.D. 118.

no one has had greater legal experience of commerce transacted by means of **A** charterparty) said this:

> " In my judgment, ever since that date it has been the general rule of practice, not a rule of law but a general rule of practice, that damages in the case of a breach of contract for carriage by sea, the breach involving delay, do not ordinarily give rise to this measure of damages for the reason which I think is plain in this judgment: nobody can know with any certainty how **B** long a sea voyage would take, still less may they say what the market will be when the ship does ultimately reach that port."

The decision in *The Parana* (2) was reached in these circumstances. The claim of the charterers against the shipowners for damages for loss of market had originated before the registrar in Admiralty after the shipowners had admitted **C** default and liability. Mr. H. C. ROTHERY, the registrar, had had twenty-three years' experience in that office. His reasoned judgment in which he reviewed the authorities up to that date is reported fully (3) in the course of reporting the appeal to PHILLIMORE, J., from the registrar's report. The registrar had concluded his report with these words (4):

> ". . . the practice of the Court of Admiralty, in refusing to entertain any **D** claim for loss of market in such cases, is in accordance with that of the courts of common law . . . I may add that the merchants by whom I am assisted entirely concur with me in the conclusion to which I have come."

PHILLIMORE, J., on appeal in a reserved judgment (5) reversed the finding of the registrar and said that he ought to have included in the damages the difference **E** between the market price of the cargo at the time when it was delivered and at the time when it ought to have been delivered. It was in those circumstances that the matter came before the Court of Appeal (2) in March, 1877. This court in those early days of its existence in a reserved judgment reversed the judgment of PHILLIMORE, J., and held that the consignee could not recover damages for loss of market where, on account of defects of the ship (establishing default and breach of contract by the shipowners) the voyage had been protracted and in the **F** meantime the market price of the goods shipped had fallen.

That case has been distinguished in cases since that date but the decision has been accepted and unchallenged in the courts. It fits this case entirely. The decision has been accepted in the formulation of the law in the leading text books, in SCRUTTON ON CHARTERPARTIES, and in particular in the last edition by SCRUTTON, L.J., himself (6), and in CARVER ON CARRIAGE OF GOODS BY SEA (7). **G** The rule has been questioned in a recent edition by the learned author of MAYNE ON DAMAGES (8). In the United States of America, at least in some States, the rule seems to be contrary to that of *The Parana* (2) and to give the charterer the benefit of the rule which prevails in respect of carriage by land. It is, I would agree, desirable that great trading communities engaged in international trade **H** should agree and not conflict in their interpretation of obligations and liabilities under trading contracts of somewhat similar character, but the divergence of such contrary judicial opinion as may be found in the United States of America has existed over forty years and may be attributed to a different approach.

The questionings give rise to a reconsideration of the practice and the rule in this country, but even if this court were free to take a different view (which I cannot see that it is) we should not readily overrule that which has stood for so **I** long, some ninety years, which has been clearly enough stated to be understood by those whose trade it governs and which, as the learned judge points out, has been the basis on which shipowners and charterers alike have traded over the

---

(2) (1877), 2 P.D. 118.   (3) (1876), 1 P.D. 452 at p. 453.
(4) (1876), 1 P.D. at pp. 460, 461.   (5) (1876), 1 P.D. at p. 465.
(6) The 11th Edn.; see the 17th Edn. at pp. 388, 389.
(7) See 11th Edn. at pp. 1191-1193.   (8) 12th Edn., 1961, at pp. 500-503.

A   years. In my opinion, with deference to my brethren who think otherwise, the decision was good law and good sense in 1877 and it is equally so now.

The Heron II, the chartered ship in question, was no greyhound of the seas. She was a tramp steamer of mediocre capacity and I doubt if she would far excel the achievements of many of the steamships plying the seas in 1877. It is true that sailing ships had not by then ceased to trade, but the steam-

B   ship was well known and active. The Parana herself was a steamship. The uncertainty of the duration of the voyage was no doubt a factor behind the judgment in *The Parana* (9), but it was not stated as the sole basis of the judgment or perhaps as the most vital matter. The judgment showed foresight in contemplating the voyage by sea which might be carried out according to what is sometimes referred to as a " tight schedule ", and gave complete recognition to

C   circumstances which might permit damages for delay to be recovered. An illustration can be extracted from the present case. If the contract had been made on the basis, express or implied, that the ship was required to deliver her cargo of Hungarian sugar before the anticipated arrival of the Youmnly, which in fact spoilt the market, I do not doubt that the charterers would have succeeded. It would fall into line with established authorities where the carrier has been held

D   liable for the loss of a market which he had contracted to reach by a given time.

The judgment in *The Parana* (9) might well be cited in full for it contains matter relevant to, and perhaps decisive of, most of the points here arising, but for brevity I will cite some, though no doubt rather lengthy, extracts. Mellish, L.J., commences the judgment in this way (9):

E
> " The question we have to decide is whether, if there is undue delay in the carriage of goods on a long voyage by sea, it follows as a matter of course that, if between the time when the goods ought to have arrived and the time when they did arrive, there has been a fall in the price of such goods, damages can be recovered by the consignee of the goods."

The important words in that sentence are, " it follows as a matter of course ".

F   The judgment continues (9):

> " Now there is really no difficulty as to the general principles upon which the courts assess the damages. They are accurately stated in the judgment of Phillimore, J. (10): ' The principle is now settled that whenever either the object of the sender is specially brought to the notice of the carrier, or circumstances are known to the carrier from which the object ought in
G   reason to be inferred, so that the object may be taken to have been within the contemplation of both parties, damages may be recovered for the natural consequences of the failure of that object.' He also cites the judgment of Kelly, C.B., in *Horne* v. *Midland Ry. Co.* (11), to the effect that ' Damages for a breach of contract must be such as may fairly and reasonably be considered as arising naturally, i.e., according to the usual course of things,
H   from such breach of contract itself, or such as may be reasonably supposed to have been in the contemplation of both parties at the time they made the contract . . .'."

Then again (12):

> " There is no case, I believe, in which it has ever been held that damages
I   can be recovered for delay in the carriage of goods on a long voyage by sea, where there has been what may be called a merely accidental fall in price between the time when the goods ought to have arrived and the time when they did arrive—no case that I can discover where such damages have been recovered; and the question is, whether we ought to hold that they ought

---

(9) (1877), 2 P.D. at p. 120.
(10) (1876), 1 P.D. at p. 463, citing *Simpson* v. *London & North Western Ry. Co.*, (1876), 1 Q.B.D. 274 at p. 277.
(11) (1873), L.R. 8 C.P. 131 at p. 137.   (12) (1877), 2 P.D. at p. 121.

to bo rocovered. If goods are sent by a carrier to be sold at a particular   A
market; if, for instance, beasts are sent by railway to be sold at Smithfield,
or fish is sent to be sold at Billingsgate, and, by reason of delay on the part
of the carrier, they have not arrived in time for the market, no doubt
damages for the loss of market may be recovered. So, if goods are sent for
the purpose of being sold in a particular season when they are sold at a
higher price than they are at other times, and if, by reason of breach of   B
contract, they do not arrive in time, damages for loss of market may be
recovered. Or if it is known to both parties that the goods will sell at a
better price if they arrive at one time than if they arrive at a later time,
that may be a ground for giving damages for their arriving too late and
selling for a lower sum. But there is in this case no evidence of anything
of that kind. As far as I can discover, it is merely said that when the goods   C
arrived in November they were likely to sell for less than if they had arrived
in October, for the market was lower."

It was contended in that case, as here, that there can be no difference between
the carriage of goods by railway and the carriage of goods by sea. MELLISH, L.J.,
continued (13):

"... it appears to me there may be a very material difference between the   D
two cases. When goods are conveyed by railway, if they are conveyed
for the purpose of sale, it is usually for the purpose of immediate sale; and
if the cases are examined, I think it will be found that the courts treated
them as if the goods were consigned for the purpose of immediate sale. No
doubt if goods are consigned to a railway company under such circumstances,
the railway company may be reasonably supposed to know that they are   E
consigned for the purpose of immediate sale, and if by breach of contract
on the part of the company they do not arrive in time to be sold when the
owner intends them to be sold, that may possibly be a ground for giving
damages for what is called ' loss of market '."

And, in the last vital passage (14), which the judge cited,   F

" The difference between cases of that kind and cases of the carriage of
goods for a long distance by sea seems to me to be very obvious. In order
that damages may be recovered, we must come to two conclusions—first,
that it was reasonably certain that the goods would not be sold until they did
arrive; and, secondly, that it was reasonably certain that they would be
sold immediately after they arrived, and that that was known to the carrier   G
at the time when the bills of lading were signed. It appears to me that
nothing could be more uncertain than either of those two assumptions
in this case. Goods imported by sea may be, and are every day, sold whilst
they are at sea. If the man who is importing the goods finds the market
high, and is afraid that the price may fall, he is not usually prevented from
selling his goods because they are at sea. The sale of goods to arrive, the sale   H
of goods on transfer of bill of lading, with cost bills and insurances, is a common mercantile contract made every day. It may be that from not having
samples of the goods, or from not knowing what is the particular quality
of his goods, the consignee may have a difficulty in selling them until they
arrive, but that would not affect the question. Nor would it signify that the
goods no longer belonged to the original consignee, but to a man who had   I
acquired them by the assignment of the bill of lading whilst the goods were
at sea. We were told that in this case the plaintiff was a person who had
advanced money on the security of the bills of lading. That possibly may be
the case; but whether he has done that, or is the purchaser, would make no
difference. It was said that the goods were sold, and that if the person who
sells them does not suffer the damage, then the purchaser would suffer the

(13) (1877), 2 P.D. at pp. 121, 122.   (14) (1877), 2 P.D. at pp. 123, 124.

A   damage. But that is pure speculation. If a man purchases goods while they are at sea, no person can say for what purpose he purchases them. He may purchase them because he thinks that if he keeps them for six months they will sell for a better sum, or he may want to use them in his trade. It is pure speculation to enter into the question for what purpose he purchases them."

B   Before this court the rule or, as the decision is variously regarded, the two rules, of *Hadley* v. *Baxendale* (15) has or have been discussed and sought to be applied. The more recent decision of this court, *Victoria Laundry (Windsor), Ltd.* v. *Newman Industries, Ltd.* (16), was cited and it was said by counsel for the charterers that it made a material alteration to the decision in *Hadley* v. *Baxendale* (15). The judgment of the court in *Victoria Laundry (Windsor), Ltd.*

C   v. *Newman Industries, Ltd.*, delivered by ASQUITH, L.J., purported expressly (17) to state the propositions relevant to the case in hand which emerge from the three authorities which he had reviewed, *Hadley* v. *Baxendale* (15), *British Columbia and Vancouver's Island Spar, Lumber and Saw Mill Co., Ltd.* v. *Nettleship* (18) and *Cory* v. *Thames Ironworks Co.* (19):

D   " These three cases have on many occasions been approved by the House of Lords without any material qualification."

The " proper rule " in the case of damages for breach of contract stated in *Hadley* v. *Baxendale* (20), stated as its second limb of damages which the other party ought to receive

E   " or such as may reasonably be supposed to have been in the contemplation of both parties at the time they made the contract as the probable result of the breach of it."

ASQUITH, L.J., in the *Victoria Laundry* case says (21):

        " Nor . . . need it be proved that on a given state of knowledge the defendant could, as a reasonable man, foresee that a breach must necessarily result

F   in that loss. It is enough if he could foresee it was likely so to result."

The probable result is the likely result. On the whole I think that " probable " is at least as good as " likely " and somewhat superior to " on the cards ", but there is no real difference in the sense. What is in the contemplation of the parties, or would be in their contemplation if they gave it a thought when making a contract, is the loss which would arise naturally, that is to say according to the

G   usual course of things from the contemplated breach of contract unless there were special, particular or unusual circumstances in their knowledge which would point to some greater or different probable loss.

The phrases and words of *Hadley* v. *Baxendale* (20) have been hallowed by long-user and gain little advantage from paraphrases or substitutes. The ideas and factors conveyed by the words are clear enough. It has often been said, as it was

H   in *The Parana* (22), that the difficulty arises in the application of the well-established principles. As was pointed out in the *Victoria Laundry* decision (23), what is reasonably foreseeable depends on knowledge possessed at the outset by the parties, or at all events by the party who later commits the breach, and further that knowledge may be actual or imputed. It is interesting to observe this extract from the judgment of ASQUITH, L.J., in that case (24):

I
___

(15) [1843-60] All E.R. Rep. 461; (1854), 9 Exch. 341.
(16) [1949] 1 All E.R. 997; [1949] 2 K.B. 528.
(17) [1949] 1 All E.R. at p. 1002; [1949] 2 K.B. at p. 539.
(18) [1861-73] All E.R. Rep. 339; (1868), L.R. 3 C.P. 499.
(19) [1861-73] All E.R. Rep. 597; (1868), L.R. 3 Q.B. 181.
(20) [1843-60] All E.R. Rep. at p. 465; (1854), 9 Exch. at p. 354.
(21) [1949] 1 All E.R. at p. 1003; [1949] 2 K.B. at p. 540.
(22) (1877), 2 P.D. 118.   (23) [1949] 1 All E.R. 997; [1949] 2 K.B. 528.
      (24) [1949] 1 All E.R. at p. 1001; [1949] 2 K.B. at p. 536.

A

" At the other end of the scale are cases where the defendant is not a vendor of the goods, but a carrier: see, for instance, *Hadley* v. *Baxendale* (25) and *Gee* v. *Lancashire and Yorkshire Ry. Co.* (26). In such cases the courts have been slow to allow loss of profit as an item of damage. This was not, it would seem, because a different principle applies in such cases, but because the application of the same principle leads to different results. A carrier commonly knows less than a seller about the purposes for which the buyer or consignee needs the goods, or about other ' special circumstances ' which may cause exceptional loss if due delivery is withheld."

B

In *Dunn* v. *Bucknall Bros.* (27) it was known to the shipowner that the object of the plaintiffs' shipment was the supply of British troops in South Africa, during the South African War, and that the goods would sell at a much higher price if delivered in due course than if delivered at a later date when a large importation of similar goods would have forced prices down. That is a good illustration of " special circumstances " where the knowledge was either actual or imputed. *The Ardennes (Owner of Cargo)* v. *The Ardennes (Owners)* (28), falls into the same category. In *The Parana* (29) the Court of Appeal sought to apply the principles of *Hadley* v. *Baxendale* (25) and to state their effect in relation to that charterparty and the views of the court seem to me to be as relevant today as they were then.

C

D

It is desirable in establishing a basis for damages to avoid fortuitous elements unless the parties have clearly contracted that the chance change of market price should fall on the shipowner if it happened to be less and not equal to or more than the price which could have been obtained without a breach of contract. A shipowner may know that there is a market at the port of destination for the goods in his ship but in a normal charterparty he gets no benefit if by favourable winds and good seamanship his vessel arrives a day or two earlier than expected and meets the market at its peak. Nor indeed does he benefit if the vessel is delayed with or without breach and the consignee, who would have sold on an earlier arrival, has the good fortune to find that the delayed arrival has coincided with an upward jump of the market. These fluctuations are the fortune for good or ill of the importer and seem to have no basis as a standard to apply in a normal carriage by sea where a blameworthy late delivery chances to coincide with a fall in price of the cargo. It is not difficult to contract in " special circumstances " so as to make the loss of a particular market recoverable. A market which has its periods of ups and downs and perhaps steadiness does not serve to indicate, in the ordinary course of things, that loss is liable to result from a breach of contract in delay in delivery, unless the contract falls to be performed on a fixed day as in a normal case of carriage by land where the nature of the contract, making time the essence, may indicate the importance of the receipt of the goods on a particular day with a contemplation that a market on that day may be missed by delay.

E

F

G

How different are so many cases in carriage by sea. There is no contemplation by either party that the requirements of the consignee are that the goods should be delivered on a fixed specified date for sale or resale. *The Parana* (29) recognised that goods in sea transit may be and frequently are sold whilst they are at sea. They may or may not be sold immediately on arrival. Many consignees store goods if it suits their purposes and perhaps especially when uncertain date of arrival does not permit of a precise date of resale. To my mind a no less important factor is that the transaction between the parties, viewed at its inception, normally would give no indication that the goods will arrive at any particular date but only, if all goes well, over a range of dates which in a fluctuating market means that the ship and its cargo may in proper fulfilment of the charterparty arrive on a day when the market is either high, steady or low. A specific time in order to

H

I

(25) [1843-60] All E.R. Rep. 461; (1854), 9 Exch. 341.
(26) [1843-60] All E.R. Rep. 131; (1860), 6 H & N. 211.
(27) [1900-03] All E.R. Rep. 131; [1902] 2 K.B. 614.
(28) [1950] 2 All E.R. 517; [1951] 1 K.B. 55.   (29) (1877), 2 P.D. 118.

A obtain a specific price in the sense of the price on an agreed delivery date is in no way the essence of the contract.

In the present case the charterparty gave the charterers an option of discharging the cargo at Jeddah instead of Basrah " such option to be declared not later than five days prior to commencement of loading ". No inference could be drawn by the shipowner that importance was attached to a specific date of arrival

B at either Basrah or Jeddah. At the date of the charterparty, Oct. 15, 1960, the s.s. Heron II was in dry-dock at Piraeus " expected ready to load about 25th/27th inst., all going well ". Anyone acquainted with dry-docking and surveys and repairs of a ship would not conclude that her date of exit from the dry-dock and her undertaking of the voyage would be certain. All frequently does not go well. The charterers did not wish the ship to arrive at Constanza

C before Oct. 27 and made this provision in the charterparty

" lay days for loading not to count before Oct. 27, 1960, and if ship not ready to load by Nov. 10, 1960, charterers have the option to cancel this charterparty."

If events had so justified it, without breach the ship could have presented herself for loading at Constanza up to Nov. 10, 1960. The charterparty provided that

D the ship should proceed with all convenient speed to Constanza and similarly when loaded from there to Basrah if it remained the port of destination.

These provisions have only to be stated, as it seems to me, to demonstrate how different is a sea voyage under such a charterparty from those cases of carriage by land where a fixed date, or time even within a day, for delivery has been agreed either expressly or impliedly. At the time of the making of this

E contract if the charterers had been asked when, or even where, the goods would arrive they could have only replied that they did not know or vaguely suggested a range of dates according to whether Jeddah or Basrah was to be the port of delivery.

I cannot find in the award evidence sufficient to establish any knowledge or imputed knowledge of the shipowner of a probability of any financial loss to the

F charterers to be occasioned by delayed delivery of the cargo, except of course the loss of interest on their money occasioned by a delayed realisation of their goods. This sum McNAIR, J., has awarded them. In my judgment the judge answered correctly the question put for his consideration in the Special Case and I would dismiss the appeal.

G   **DIPLOCK, L.J.:** Does the judgment of the Court of Appeal in *The Parana* (30) compel this Court of Appeal eighty-nine years later to apply to the assessment of damages for wrongful delay in the delivery of goods under a contract of carriage by sea a special rule as to the measure of damages which was evolved in the days when sailing ships still carried the commerce of the world? That is what this appeal is about.

H In 1853, when Mr. ROTHERY became Registrar of the High Court of Admiralty, it was the practice of the registrar and merchants to award as damages for late delivery of goods carried by sea interest on the value of the goods, but not the difference between their value at destination at the time at which they should have arrived and the time at which they did arrive. This practice made good sense then. Within wide limits the duration of ocean voyages was unpredictable.

I If the cargo consisted of goods for which there was a market at their destination which fluctuated according to supply and demand, neither shipper nor carrier could foresee when they entered into the contract of affreightment whether the ship's voyage would be slow or fast or whether her arrival at her destination would coincide with a superfluity or dearth of similar goods on the market there. The contract was not entered into on the basis that the vessel would arrive at a particular date to coincide with a favourable market for the goods. That delay,

(30) (1877), 2 P.D. 118.

whether caused by wind and weather or by breach of contract by the carrier, **A**
was likely to result in the loss of a favourable market for the goods was not
in the ordinary course of things contemplated by the parties to the contract at
the time they entered into it.

In the twenty-four years of Mr. ROTHERY's tenure of his office which had
elapsed before *The Parana* (31) came before the Court of Appeal things were
happening on the ocean and in Westminster Hall. On the ocean sail was giving **B**
way to steam; in Westminster Hall the measure of damages for breach of contract
had been rationalised in *Hadley* v. *Baxendale* (32); but, as Mr. ROTHERY's
report (33) discloses, no account was taken of these changes in the Admiralty
registry. In *The Parana* (31), in 1877, the Court of Appeal, reversing the decision
of PHILLIMORE, J. (34) and restoring that of Mr. Registrar ROTHERY (33), followed
the traditional practice of not awarding to an assignee of bills of lading damages **C**
for loss of market due to delay in arrival of the vessel in breach of the contract
of carriage where the carriage was by steamship on a voyage from the Phillippines
to London. It is worthy of note that even at that date there was a wide margin
between the various estimates of the time the voyage would have taken but for
the vessel's unseaworthiness, and the unpredictability of the time of arrival of a
vessel on a long ocean voyage was the explanation of the decision of *The Parana* **D**
(31) given by a later Court of Appeal in *Dunn* v. *Bucknall Bros.* (35) although
this reason finds no place among those appearing in the judgment of the Court of
Appeal in *The Parana* (31) itself. The actual grounds on which damages based
on the fall in market price of the goods at their destination between the estimated
date at which the vessel should have arrived and the actual date on which she did
arrive were disallowed, were that it was not known to the carrier, at the time **E**
at which the bills of lading were signed, to be " reasonably certain " first that the
goods would not be sold until they did arrive and secondly that they would be
sold immediately after they did arrive. The plaintiff had, in fact, kept the goods
after their arrival hoping for a rise in market price which did not occur. MELLISH,
L.J., said (36):

> ". . . how can we tell that he would not have done exactly the same thing **F**
> if the goods had arrived in time? Therefore, it seems to me, that to give these
> damages would be to give speculative damages—to give damages when we
> cannot be certain that the plaintiff would not have suffered just as much if
> the goods had arrived in time."

In 1884 *The Parana* (31) was followed with manifest reluctance by SIR JAMES **G**
HANNEN, P., and more willingly by the Court of Appeal in *The Notting Hill* (37),
which was an action in tort; but in 1902 the Court of Appeal in *Dunn* v. *Bucknall
Bros.* (38), to which I have already referred, expressed the view that *The Parana*
(31) laid down

> " no absolute peremptory rule taking voyages by sea out of the principles
> which regulate the measure of damages on breach of other contracts . . . It **H**
> is certainly not a rule of law; . . . it is only an inference of fact that from
> the circumstances of the case no reasonable assumption as to the state of the
> market at the time of arrival could have been a factor in the contract between
> the parties."

In the light of this judgment I think that this court is entitled to treat *The
Parana* (31) as depending on an inference which the Court of Appeal drew from **I**
the particular facts of that case in the circumstances in which trans-ocean trade
was carried on in 1877. If it purported to lay down a rule of law it conflicts

---

(31) (1877), 2 P.D. 118.
(32) [1843-60] All E.R. Rep. 461; (1854), 9 Exch. 341.
(33) (1876), 1 P.D. at p. 457.   (34) (1876), 1 P.D. 452.
(35) [1900-03] All E.R. Rep. 131; [1902] 2 K.B. 614.
(36) (1877), 2 P.D. at p. 124.   (37) (1884), 9 P.D. 105.
(38) [1900-03] All E.R. Rep. at p. 134; [1902] 2 K.B. at pp. 622, 623.

A with *Dunn* v. *Bucknall Bros.* (39) and I would myself follow the law as stated in the later case.

In *Dunn* v. *Bucknall Bros.* (39) damages based on the fall in market price between the time at which the vessel would have arrived but for the breach of the contract of carriage and the time at which she actually arrived were awarded against the carrier; but at that date, and until *Victoria Laundry (Windsor), Ltd.* v.
B *Newman Industries, Ltd.* (40), *Hadley* v. *Baxendale* (41) was generally regarded as laying down two rules as to the measure of damages for breach of contract. The first was a general rule which did not depend on any knowledge actually possessed by the contract-breaker at the time when he entered into the contract. Under it the injured party was entitled to recover only the loss to him arising naturally according to the usual course of things from the breach. The second
C rule, which was regarded as an exception to the first, entitled an injured party who owing to circumstances peculiar to himself had sustained as a result of the breach a greater loss than would arise naturally according to the usual course of things from the breach, to recover such loss, but only if the contract-breaker at the time at which he entered into the contract knew that a breach on his part would lead to an exceptional loss of the kind in fact sustained and entered into the
D contract in such circumstances as would induce the other party to believe that in the event of breach he would accept liability for such exceptional loss. The latter part of the second rule, which requires, in addition to knowledge, an acceptance of contractual liability for exceptional loss, was laid down in *British Columbia and Vancouver's Island Spar, Lumber and Saw Mill Co., Ltd.* v. *Nettleship* (42); but except in the case of a person, like a common carrier, who has no right to
E decline to enter into a contract, it has little application in practice, for it requires no more than that the nature of the exceptional loss should be communicated by the party who will sustain it to the other party in the course of the negotiations for the contract. If the other party then enters into the contract without disclaiming his responsibility for the exceptional loss he will be liable for such loss if it occurs as a result of his breach. *Dunn* v. *Bucknall Bros.* (43) was an example
F of the application of the so-called second rule.

So long as *Hadley* v. *Baxendale* (41) was regarded as laying down two rules, one independent of the knowledge of the contract-breaker and the other dependent on the state of his actual knowledge, there might be room under the first rule for applying to contracts of carriage by sea a different measure of damages for breach of contract by delay in delivery from that applicable to contracts of carriage by
G land or for sale of goods under a contract of sale involving shipment overseas, although as early as 1902 we have the authority of *Dunn* v. *Bucknall Bros.* (43) that there is no such special measure.

In no reported case since *The Notting Hill* (44) has the measure of damages laid down in *The Parana* (45) been followed for goods for which there is a market, even in cases of contracts for carriage of goods by sea. The judgment in *The*
H *Parana* (45) has been referred to without express disapproval in a number of subsequent cases and has been treated in successive editions of such standard text books as Scrutton on Charterparties and Carver on Carriage of Goods by Sea as laying down what is at least a prima facie rule as to the measure of damages for late delivery under a contract of carriage of goods by sea, but in reported cases, at any rate where the length of the voyage was predictable within
I reasonable limits, it has been distinguished on the same lines as it was in *Dunn* v. *Bucknall Bros.* (43) (see for instance per Lord Goddard, C.J., in *The Ardennes (Owners of Cargo)* v. *The Ardennes (Owners)* (46), or treated as inapplicable, as in

(39) [1900-03] All E.R. Rep. 134; [1902] 2 K.B. 614.
(40) [1949] 1 All E.R. 997; [1949] 2 K.B. 528.
(41) [1843-60] All E.R. Rep. 461; (1854), 9 Exch. 341.
(42) [1861-73] All E.R. Rep. 339; (1868), L.R. 3 C.P. 499.
(43) [1900-03] All E.R. Rep. 131; [1902] 2 K.B. 614.
(44) (1884), 9 P.D. 105.   (45) (1877), 2 P.D. 118.
        (46) [1950] 2 All E.R. at p. 520; [1951] 1 K.B. at p. 60.

Smith, Edwards & Co. v. *Tregarthen* (47) and in *Sargant & Sons* v. *East Asiatic* A
Co., Ltd. (48). The latter case is instructive, for the delay there was due to over-
carriage of the goods and their return to the contractual destination. This was
treated as a case of non-delivery for which the ordinary measure of damages has
always been the market price of the goods at their destination at the time at
which they should have been delivered, and the acceptance of the goods on
subsequent delivery when the price was lower was treated as mitigating the B
damages for non-delivery. In the result the plaintiff recovered as damages the
difference in the market prices at the two dates.

The rule in *The Parana* (49) has never been applied to breach of contract for
carriage of goods by land or to damages for late delivery of goods under contracts
for the sale of goods.

In 1924 the United States Court of Appeals for the Fourth Circuit refused to C
treat the decision in *The Parana* (49) as authoritative as to the measure of damages
for late delivery under modern conditions of sea transport (*United States* v.
Middleton (50)). The United States Court accepted the explanation of *The
Parana* (49) given in *Dunn* v. *Bucknall Bros.* (51) and in the light of that explanation treated it as obsolete: but no court in England has yet had occasion to face
the question whether it is not obsolete under modern conditions in England too. D
We have occasion to now; and we do so in the added light of the clear and
comprehensive statement of the modern principles governing the measure of
damages for breach of contract contained in *Victoria Laundry (Windsor), Ltd.*
v. *Newman Industries, Ltd.* (52). This judgment, of ASQUITH, L.J., which owes
much to the revolution in legal thinking initiated by *Donoghue* v. *Stevenson* (53),
made it clear: E

(i) that there are not two rules formulated in *Hadley* v. *Baxendale* (54) but two
different instances of the application of a single rule;

(ii) that the rule as to the measure of damages for breach of contract applies
to all kinds of breaches of all kinds of contracts;

(iii) that the aggrieved party is entitled to recover such part of the loss actually
resulting to him as was at the time of the contract reasonably foreseeable *by* F
the party who broke it as liable to result from the breach.

I have added to the ipsissima verba of ASQUITH, L.J. (55) the words italicised—
" by the party who broke it "—to identify the foreseer. These added words and
the two expressions " reasonably foreseeable " and " liable to result from the
breach " call for further analysis.

What is " foreseeable " depends on the knowledge of the foreseer: what is G
" reasonably foreseeable " depends on the knowledge which a reasonable person
entering into the contract in question might reasonably be expected to possess
as well as any additional information communicated to him by the other party
to the contract. The obligation to pay damages for breach of contract is a consensual obligation. When a party enters into a contract with another party the
obligations towards the other party which he thereby undertakes to fulfil and H
the rights against the other party to which he is entitled are those and only
those which by his words and conduct at the time of the contract he has reasonably
induced the other party to believe that he is accepting a legal obligation to fulfil
or asserting a legal right to claim. This is so not only in respect of what may for
convenience be called the primary obligations and rights created by the contract,
that is, those which are discharged by performance of the contract, but also in I
respect of the secondary obligations and rights which arise on non-performance
of his primary obligations by one of the parties to the contract. Of these the most

(47) (1887), 57 L.T. 58.   (48) (1915), 21 Com. Cas. 344.
(49) (1877), 2 P.D. 118.   (50) (1924), 3 Fed. Rep. (2nd) 384 at p. 393.
(51) [1900-03] All E.R. Rep. 131; [1902] 2 K.B. 614.
(52) [1949] 1 All E.R. 997; [1949] 2 K.B. 528.
(53) [1932] All E.R. Rep. 1; [1932] A.C. 562.
(54) [1843-60] All E.R. Rep. 461; (1854), 9 Exch. 341.
(55) [1949] 1 All E.R. at p. 1002; [1949] 2 K.B. at p. 539.

A important is the obligation of the non-performer to make to the other party, and the corresponding right of the other party to claim from the non-performer, reparation in money for any loss sustained by the other party which results from the failure of the non-performer to perform his primary obligation.

The non-performer may, of course, have expressly stipulated what monetary reparation he will make (by a liquidated damage clause) or excluded his liability
B to make reparation (by an exemption clause) for breach of a particular primary obligation; but if he has not, his conduct in entering into the contract is in itself sufficient to induce the other party to believe that he, the non-performer, undertakes, in the event of non-performance of that primary obligation, a secondary obligation to make monetary reparation for any loss sustained by the other party of a kind which the non-performer has reasonable grounds for assum-
C ing that the non-performer knows is liable to result from the breach. The other party is entitled to assume that the non-performer knows of the kinds of loss which are liable to result from the breach in the usual course of things, for instance that in the case of non-delivery of goods he will have lost the value of the goods at the date at which they should have been delivered; but he is not entitled to assume, unless at the time of the contract he has communicated the information
D to the non-performer, that the non-performer knows of an exceptional kind of loss which is only liable to result because of the existence of special circumstances peculiar to the other party which are outside the usual course of things. For by his own conduct in entering into the contract without communicating such special circumstances to the non-performer the other party reasonably induces the non-performer to believe that he, the other party, is not asserting any legal right
E to claim reparation for any exceptional kind of loss resulting from non-performance of a primary obligation.

In explaining what was meant by " liable to result from the breach ", ASQUITH, L.J. (56) gave effect to the development which had taken place in the common law during the preceding century particularly in the role of " foreseeability " in man's duty towards his neighbour. In both *Hadley* v. *Baxendale* (57) and
F *Horne* v. *Midland Ry. Co.* (58) the phrase " the probable result of the breach " had been used without further exegesis. " Probable " no doubt connotes a greater likelihood than " possible " but it is not restricted to an odds-on chance and, unlike McNAIR, J., in his judgment from which this appeal is brought, I see no conflict between the use of the single adjective " probable " in the earlier cases and ASQUITH, L.J.'s explanation (56) of the degree of probability required
G to make a particular kind of loss recoverable as being a " serious possibility " or a " real danger " or, more colloquially, " on the cards ". This is very different from the " reasonable certainty " treated as the required standard of foreseeability by MELLISH, L.J., in *The Parana* (59). The need for so high a degree of likelihood of loss is not supported by any other leading case before or afterwards and, in this respect at any rate, *The Parana* (60) must in my view be
H regarded as wrong.

When a contract, whether of sale or carriage, is entered into under which a party undertakes a primary obligation to deliver marketable goods at a particular time at a destination where a market for them exists, that party may be assumed to know, in the absence of any information to the contrary communicated to him by the other party, (i) that if he fails to perform this obligation timeously
I the other party will be deprived of any opportunity which he might otherwise have of realising the goods on the market at their destination on the date at which they should have arrived, (ii) that if the other party is still owner of the goods on arrival at their destination he will have an opportunity of selling them on the market but only at the later date at which they actually arrive, and (iii) that there is a serious possibility that the market price will be lower at the later date.

---

(56) [1949] 1 All E.R. at p. 1003; [1949] 2 K.B. at p. 540.
(57) [1843-60] All E.R. Rep. 461; (1854), 9 Exch. 341.
(58) (1873), L.R. 8 C.P. 131.   (59) (1877), 2 P.D. at pp. 123, 124.
(60) (1877), 2 P.D. 118.

A charterparty for the carriage of goods by sea normally provides for the issue **A**
of bills of lading signed on behalf of the shipowner when the goods are received
on board and contemplates that the charterer may sell the goods before arrival
and transfer the bill of lading to the buyer of the goods. If he does so the charterer
assigns to the buyer the benefit of the contract of carriage with the shipowner
and the right to claim performance not only of any primary obligation to be
performed by the shipowner after the goods have been loaded but also of the **B**
secondary obligation to make monetary compensation for any loss to the owner
of the goods which there is a serious possibility may result from non-performance
of a primary obligation if such loss is in fact sustained by the transferee. The
measure of damages is therefore unaffected by a sale of the goods by the charterer
to a buyer before arrival of the goods, for the person entitled to claim performance
of the shipowner's primary obligation to deliver the goods timeously will always **C**
be the owner of the goods at the time of their actual arrival.

If, in the event as in the present case, the charterer does not sell the goods
before arrival, it will be he who will have lost, as a result of the breach, the
opportunity of selling them at their destination at the market price at the date at
which they should have arrived and will have obtained in substitution the
opportunity of selling them at the market price at the date at which they actually **D**
arrived. Whether he would have sold them immediately on arrival had the
contract been performed matters not: nor does it matter whether he in fact sold
them immediately on arrival at the later date when they actually arrived. This
does not affect his loss. If he intended to keep them or to use them in his trade on
arrival his opportunity of doing so has been deferred to a date when he could have
acquired on the market at a lesser price similar goods to keep or use. Or put more **E**
briefly, he was entitled to have delivered to him goods worth £X at their destin-
tion: he has had delivered to him goods worth £X-£Y: the loss he has sustained
is £Y.

In my opinion, today, when a shipper and a shipowner enter into a contract
of carriage by sea of goods, (i) which the shipowner knows or can be reasonably
assumed by the shipper to know are marketable goods, and (ii) such goods are **F**
consigned to a destination at which the shipowner knows or can be reasonably
assumed by the shipper to know that there exists a market for goods of that kind,
(iii) on a voyage the duration of which, in the absence of excepted perils, is
reasonably predictable, the measure of damages for breach of contract by the
shipowner for late delivery, if the market price at the destination has fallen
between the date at which the goods should have arrived and the date at which **G**
they in fact arrived, is prima facie such difference in market price.

The shipowner's actual or imputed knowledge that the goods are marketable
goods may be derived from their mere description. In the present case the
description " white sugar " was in my view sufficient to inform him that the goods
to be shipped were marketable goods. Where the shipowner has no actual
knowledge of the existence of a market at the port of destination for goods of the **H**
kind shipped, the imputation of such knowledge on his part will depend on the
general notoriety in commercial circles of the existence of such a market; but
in the present case there is a finding that the shipowner had actual knowledge of
the existence of such a market at the port of destination, Basrah. It does not, in
my view, matter whether the market is susceptible to regular seasonal trends
or whether such trends, if they exist, are known to the shipowner. The very **I**
existence of a " market " for a commodity implies that prices fluctuate and that
accordingly there is a serious possibility that if there is delay the market price
may fall. If it rises or remains steady the shipper will suffer no loss and can recover
no damages, but the likelihood of its falling is reasonably foreseeable by the
shipowner.

In modern times the duration of any voyage, in the absence of excepted perils,
is reasonably predictable unless the contract of carriage provides for liberty to
deviate. Such a provision would displace the prima facie measure of damages for

A delay in delivery, for the conduct of the shipper in agreeing to the shipowner's liberty to deviate would reasonably induce the shipowner to believe that the shipper was indifferent to the date of arrival within such limits as might result from permitted deviations and did not intend to claim a right to have delivery of the goods on any particular and predictable date (cf. *Connolly Shaw, Ltd.* v. *Nordenfjeldske Steamship Co.* (61)). In the present case the charterparty contained

B no liberty to deviate. There was an option for the shipper to require discharge of the whole of the cargo at Jeddah, such option to be exercised not later than five days prior to commencement of loading; but this does not seem to me to give rise to any inference that the shipper was indifferent to the date of arrival at Basrah if the option to discharge at Jeddah was not exercised.

The difference between the market price of the goods at their destination at the

C date at which they should have arrived and the date at which they in fact arrived is recoverable by the shipper only if he has sustained a loss of at least this amount —for damages are monetary reparation for loss actually sustained. As mentioned above, if he has in fact sold the goods before arrival he may have sustained no loss but his buyer, the transferee of the bill of lading, will have done so. Thus, where the goods are marketable and the market for them at their destination is

D one on which a similar quantity of goods could be bought as well as sold it will, for the reasons already discussed, be rarely that the actual damages for late delivery recoverable against the shipowner will be other than the difference in market price if the market price has in fact fallen.

In the present case the umpire found inter alia the following facts: (A) There was at all material times a market for sugar in Basrah in the sense that sugar

E was regularly bought and sold in large quantities at prices that were published. (B) The existence of the Basrah sugar market was known to the shipowner and his brokers at and before the date of the charterparty and thereafter. (C) The carriage of sugar from the Black Sea to Iraqi ports, including Basrah, is a recognised trade. (D) At the date of the charterparty and at the time when the vessel sailed from Constanza a reasonably accurate prediction of the length

F of the voyage to Basrah was twenty days. (E) The shipowner would have no knowledge in the ordinary course of business whether or not the cargo would be sold by the shippers before arrival at Basrah but, from the presence in the charterparty of the option to discharge at Jeddah he would assume that the cargo had not been sold at the date of the charterparty. (F) The shippers did not sell the cargo before arrival at Basrah. (G) Owing to wrongful deviation by the

G shipowner in breach of the charterparty, the arrival of the vessel in Basrah was delayed by ten days. (H) Had the vessel arrived at the date at which she should have arrived if the shipowner had not broken his contract by deviating, the market value of the sugar at Basrah would have been £32 10s. per ton (cash against documents). The market value of the sugar at Basrah at the date at which the vessel actually arrived was £31 2s. 9d. per ton (cash against documents),

H that is £1 7s. 3d. per ton less.

On these facts the shippers are in my judgment entitled to recover as damages for late delivery of the sound sugar delivered the difference in market price, namely £1 7s. 3d. per ton.

It remains to mention the argument for the shipowner based on the provisions of the charterparty relating to readiness to load and cancelling date. When

I chartered the vessel was undergoing dry-docking in Piraeus and was stated in the charterparty to be " expected ready to load about 25th/27th inst., all going well ". A later clause provided that lay-days for loading should not count until Oct. 27, 1960. The cancelling date was not until Nov. 10, 1960; and it was argued that by assenting to this interval of fourteen days before the option to cancel arose the shippers induced the shipowner to believe that they were indifferent to the late arrival of the vessel in Basrah within a margin of fourteen days. The fallacy in this contention is that cancellation and damages are different

(61) (1934), Lloyd L.R. 183.

and cumulative rights. The first is a primary right conferred on the shipowner A
by the contract and exercisable on the occurrence of a particular event, the non-
arrival of the vessel at Constanza by Nov. 10, irrespective of whether or not that
event was the result of non-performance by the shipowner of a primary obligation on his part. The second is a secondary right of the shippers to claim
performance by the shipowner of his secondary obligation to make reparation
for any monetary loss sustained by the shippers if the failure to arrive at Constanza B
by Oct. 27 is the result of the shipowner's non-performance of his primary obligation to use his best endeavours to bring the vessel to Constanza by that date.
The fixing of a cancellation date in a charterparty merely gives warning to the
shipowner that non-arrival by the cancelling date may go to the root of the
contract so as to entitle the shippers to rescind. It does not relieve the shipowner
of his primary obligation to proceed with all convenient speed to the loading-port C
or of his secondary obligation in the event of non-performance of that primary
obligation, to make reparation in money to the shippers for any loss sustained by
them as a result of such non-performance.

The only consideration which has really given me pause is that referred to by
McNair, J., in the last part of his judgment: that is, that in view of the statements based on the decision in *The Parana* (62) which have appeared in successive D
editions of SCRUTTON ON CHARTERPARTIES and of CARVER ON CARRIAGE OF
GOODS BY SEA as to the measure of damages for late delivery under a contract
for carriage of goods by sea and McNair, J.'s own experience of its frequent
adoption by the courts in cases which, so far as counsel's researches go, have
not attracted the eyes of the reporters even of Lloyd's List Reports, the shippers
and the shipowners who are parties to the charterparty in this case must be taken E
to have contracted on the basis that the secondary obligation of the shipowners
which would arise on non-performance of their primary obligation to deliver the
goods at Basrah timeously would be not to make reparation to the shippers for
the loss sustained by them as a result of the breach of that primary obligation
but to pay them a conventional sum equal to the interest on the value of the goods
for the time for which their delivery was delayed. Such a case was not however F
sought to be made by the shipowner, nor was there any evidence to sustain it.
It may be, as Serjeant Sullivan once informed a lord chief justice, that in the
little village in county Cork where he was born the children talked of little else
but " volenti non fit injuria "; but there is no evidence in the present case that
the judgment in *The Parana* (62) has any decisive influence on the contractual
intentions of the shipowner, and in the absence of such evidence I do not think G
that we are justified in applying to the present case a measure of damages which
takes no account of ninety years' development in ocean transport and in the
common law.

For my part I would allow the appeal.

SALMON, L.J.: The charterers are well-known sugar merchants. On
Oct. 15, 1960, they entered into a charterparty with the owner of Heron II H
which was then in dry-dock at Piraeus. The charter provided that this ship should
proceed with all convenient speed to Constanza where, all going well, it was
expected to be ready to load on or about Oct. 25/27. The load was to be three
thousand metric tons of sugar and the loading was expected to take some four days.
The owner requested that the lay-days should not start until Oct. 27. The ship
in fact arrived at Constanza on Oct. 27 and was loaded by Nov. 1. The charter I
provided that, when loaded, the ship should proceed with all convenient speed to
Basrah. The charterers had an option which they did not exercise to discharge
the cargo at Jeddah. On Nov. 1 the ship sailed for Basrah. A reasonably accurate
prediction of the length of the voyage from Constanza to Basrah was twenty days.
The owner, however, without the knowledge of the charterers wrongfully
deviated from the voyage for his own purposes by calling at Berbera, Bahrein

(62) (1877), 2 P.D. 118.

A and Abadan. By reason of these breaches, the voyage to Basrah was prolonged by nine or ten days. The ship arrived there on Dec. 2. The owner knew
that the charterers were sugar merchants, that there was a sugar market in
Basrah and that the sugar had not been sold prior to the date of the charter.
The questions whether there was a sugar market in Jeddah and as to the reasonably predictable duration of a voyage from Constanza to Jeddah were not
B investigated, presumably because the charterers did not exercise the option to
which I have referred. Between the date when the vessel should have arrived at
Basrah and the date when she did arrive there the price of sugar fell on the
Basrah market. In the ordinary course the prices tended to fall on that market
during October and November to a low point in December. The market was of
course also affected by supply and demand and the fall was partly caused by the
C arrival of a cargo of sugar in the s.s. Youmnly on Nov. 29. Because of the
delay in the arrival of the Heron II until after the fall in the market the
charterers lost £4,183 16s. 8d. There can be no doubt but that they suffered this
damage as a result of the owner's breach of contract. The only question that
arises on this appeal is—are these damages too remote to be recoverable?
    The principles to be applied in solving such questions were stated by this
D court in *Victoria Laundry (Windsor), Ltd.* v. *Newman Industries, Ltd.* (63).
Indeed that case and *Hadley* v. *Baxendale* (64), decided some ninety-five years
previously, are landmarks in our law. Both clarified and developed the law relating to damages. There are difficulties, however, in adjusting thought to change—
difficulties which are not invariably surmounted with success. Although the
judgment in *Hadley* v. *Baxendale* (64) has now long been regarded almost as holy
E writ, there were eminent judges who expressed considerable doubt about it for
some years after it was pronounced; see for example the observations of Wilde,
B., in *Gee* v. *Lancashire and Yorkshire Ry. Co.* (65) and of Sir Baliol Brett,
M.R., in *The Notting Hill* (66). And so today evidently the learned trial judge,
a most eminent commercial lawyer, has not yet become fully reconciled to
the judgment in the *Victoria Laundry* case (63). This case shows that in reality
F *Hadley* v. *Baxendale* (64) did not lay down two different rules, as had been supposed, but only one rule with two different facets. The rule is that any damage
actually caused by a breach of any kind of contract is recoverable providing
that when the contract was made such damage was reasonably foreseeable as
liable to result from its breach. Foreseeability may be established by showing
that on facts presumably within the knowledge of the parties at the date of the
G contract, such damage was, in the ordinary course of things, liable to occur as a
result of the breach. That is one facet of the rule. Foreseeability may also be
established by showing that special facts which would not be presumed to be
within the knowledge of the parties were in fact drawn to the attention of the
contract-breaker when the contract was made from which it could reasonably be
foreseen that such damage was liable to occur as a result of the breach. That is
H the other facet of the rule. In all cases within the rule, the law will presume (in
the absence of any contrary intention expressed in the contract) that both
parties entered into the contract on the basis that he who broke it should be
liable for the damage which he could reasonably foresee was liable to occur as a
result of his breach—*British Columbia and Vancouver's Island Spar, Lumber and
Saw Mill Co., Ltd.* v. *Nettleship* (67). This is entirely appropriate, for the risk
I or loss caused by a breach of contract should not fall on the shoulders of the
innocent party but on those of the party whose breach caused the loss and who
could reasonably foresee that a serious risk of that loss would be incurred by
his breach. This is particularly true where, as in this case, the party in breach

(63) [1949] 1 All E.R. 997; [1949] 2 K.B. 528.
(64) [1843-60] All E.R. Rep. 461; (1854) 9 Exch. 341.
(65) [1843-60] All E.R. Rep. at p. 135; (1860), 6 H. & N. at p. 221.
(66) (1884), 9 P.D. at p. 113.
(67) [1861-73] All E.R. Rep. 339; (1868), L.R. 3 C.P. 499.

deliberately chose to break the contract and run the risk in order to make money   A
In *Hadley* v. *Baxendale* (68) ALDERSON, B., spoke of the damages which

"may reasonably be supposed to have been in the contemplation of both
parties at the time they made the contract as the probable result of the
breach of it."

He did not explain the sense in which he was using the word " probable ". There
are many degrees of probability. I entirely agree with DIPLOCK, L.J., that the   B
word " probable " does not necessarily connote an odds-on chance. In the
Victoria Laundry case (69) ASQUITH, L.J., who delivered the judgment of this
court, clarified the meaning of the word " probable " in its context in ALDERSON,
B.'s judgment. ASQUITH, L.J., said (69) that it need not be

"proved that on a given state of knowledge the defendant could, as a   C
reasonable man, foresee that a breach must necessarily result in loss. It
is enough if he could foresee it was likely so to result. It is enough . . . if
the loss (or some factor without which it would not have occurred) is a
' serious possibility ' or a ' real danger '. For short, we have used the word
' liable ' to result."

I have used the words " liable to result " in the same sense in this judgment.   D
I do not agree with the trial judge that there is anything in ASQUITH, L.J.'s
judgment which is inconsistent with what was said in *Hadley* v. *Baxendale* (70).
As I have already indicated, I regard the *Victoria Laundry* case (71) as a clarifica-
tion of the law. It is thus that the common law develops. It is not static and
inert but a living and growing thing, ready to meet and adapt itself to the changing
needs of time.   E

Applying the principles laid down in the *Victoria Laundry* case (71) to the facts
of the instant case, it seems plain to me that at the time the charterparty was
signed, the owner must be presumed to have known that sugar markets, like all
other commodity markets, are liable to fluctuation. Accordingly, as a reasonable man, he must have foreseen that if he broke his contract and thereby delayed
delivery there was a serious possibility or a real danger that the market might   F
fall and that the charterers would suffer a loss. The loss would be the difference
between the price at the time of delivery and the price at the time when delivery
would have been effected but for the breach. What he must have foreseen is
exactly what in fact happened, and the umpire has awarded the charterers
damages on the basis of the loss to which I have referred. Clearly he was right
unless the principles enunciated in the *Victoria Laundry* case (71) have no applica-   G
tion or only a restricted application to contracts of carriage of goods by sea.

These principles clearly apply with full force to the carriage of goods by land.
If, in such a case, a carrier in breach of contract delays delivery of marketable
goods and the market falls, he must ordinarily pay his customer by way of damages
the difference between the market price on the day of delivery and the market
price on the day on which delivery should have been effected; see *Collard* v. *South*   H
Eastern Ry. Co. (72); *Horne* v. *Midland Ry. Co.* (73). I can see no reason why,
in 1966, when steamships are hardly the comparatively modern innovation that
they were in 1877, the legal principles relating to remoteness of damage applicable
to the carriage of goods by land should not apply with equal force to the carriage
of goods by sea. It is said, however, that the decision of this court in 1877 in
The Parana (74) compels us to find otherwise. That authority purported to decide   I
that in the case of long voyages by sea, if the arrival of goods was delayed by
breach of the charter, the charterers could not recover from the owners any
damages based on a fall in the market between the date on which the goods ought

(68) [1843-60] All E.R. Rep. at p. 465; (1854), 9 Exch. at p. 354.
(69) [1949] 1 All E.R. at p. 1003; [1949] 2 K.B. at p. 540.
(70) [1843-60] All E.R. Rep. 461; (1854), 9 Exch. 341.
(71) [1949] 1 All E.R. 997; [1949] 2 K.B. 528.
(72) [1861-73] All E.R. Rep. 851; (1861), 7 H. & N. 79.
(73) (1873), L.R. 8 C.P. 131.   (74) (1877), 2 P.D. 118.

A to have arrived and the date when they did arrive at their destination. That case
was followed in this court seven years later in *The Notting Hill* (75), in which, as
I have already pointed out, an attempt was made to cast doubt on part of the
judgment in *Hadley* v. *Baxendale* (76). *The Parana* (77) was apparently never
followed again until the trial judge followed it in the present case and in doing so
refused to accept part of the judgment in the *Victoria Laundry* case (78). *The*

B *Parana* (77) has often been distinguished (see for example *The Ardennes (Owners
of Cargo)* v. *The Ardennes (Owners)* (79); *Smith, Edwards & Co.* v. *Tregarthen* (80));
sometimes doubted (see for example *Sargant & Sons* v. *East Asiatic Co., Ltd.* (81));
but never overruled. Its force and effect, however, were much weakened by the
decision of this court in *Dunn* v. *Bucknall Bros.* (82). In that case Sir Richard
Henn Collins, M.R., who delivered the judgment of the court, in referring to

C *The Parana* (77), said (83):

> " It is only because the possible length of voyages and the consequent
> uncertainty as to the times of arrival may in many cases eliminate the
> supposition of any reasonable expectation as to the state of the market
> at the time of arrival that, as a general rule, damages for loss of market by
> late delivery are not recoverable from the carrier by sea. It is certainly
D > not a rule of law; it is only an inference of fact that from the circumstances
> of the case no reasonable assumption as to the state of the market at
> the time of arrival could have been a factor in the contract between the
> parties."

He went on to point out that as the means of sea transport improved, voyages
of three and four weeks' duration may be and were even in 1902 accomplished
E with almost absolute certainty.

Montevideo Gas and Dry Dock Co., Ltd. v. *Clan Line Steamers, Ltd.* (84) is
another case in which it was pointed out by this court that *The Parana* (77) and
The Notting Hill (75) laid down no rule of law but were only examples of cases in
which

F > " the damages claimed could not be said to be within the contemplation
> of the parties . . ., because the uncertainties of the voyage were so great that
> the parties could not be said to have contracted on the footing that the
> goods would arrive at any particular moment."

This, no doubt, was the true basis on which *The Parana* (77) was decided, but
oddly enough no reference was made to it by Mellish, L.J., who delivered the
G judgment of the court. It is important to notice from the report of *The Parana* (85)
at first instance that the voyage took 127 days. The charterers contended
that it ought to have been performed in sixty-five or at the most seventy days.
We do not know what was the owners' estimate, but presumably it was somewhat
greater than ninety days—the time within which Mr. Registrar Rothery
found that the voyage ought to have been completed. Thus the estimates varied
H by upwards of twenty-five days. It will therefore be seen that in that case no
reasonably accurate prediction of the length of the voyage could have been made.
Indeed the vessel's expected time of arrival was practically as uncertain as if
she had been a sailing ship. There was accordingly much to be said for the view
that the old practice of the Court of Admiralty stemming from the days of sail,
which disallowed such damages as those claimed in the present case, should
I be applied in 1876; but I can see no reason for applying it in 1966 save in those
rare cases, if any such still exist, where no reasonably accurate prediction of the
length of the voyage can be made. Except in such a limited class of case, of which

---

(75) (1884), 9 P.D. 105.   (76) [1843-60] All E.R. Rep. 461; (1854), 9 Exch. 341.
(77) (1877), 2 P.D. 118.   (78) [1949] 1 All E.R. 997; [1949] 2 K.B. 528.
(79) [1950] 2 All E.R. 517; [1951] 1 K.B. 55.   (80) (1887), 57 L.T. 58.
(81) (1915), 21 Com. Cas. at p. 348.
(82) [1900-03] All E.R. Rep. 131; [1902] 2 K.B. 614.
(83) [1900-03] All E.R. Rep. at p. 134; [1902] 2 K.B. at pp. 622, 623.
(84) (1921), 37 T.L.R. 866 at p. 867.   (85) (1876), 1 P.D. 452.

tho present is not an example, the so-called rule in *The Parana* (86) has no appli- A
cation in modern conditions and should now be regarded as obsolete. It is said
that the voyage of the Heron II might have been delayed otherwise than by
breach of contract—for example by accident or by some quite exceptional
weather conditions.   But this would be equally true of carriage by rail and
carriage by air respectively.   For all commercial purposes, it was reasonably
predictable that the Heron II would arrive at Constanza on Oct. 27, 1960, B
and would sail loaded with sugar for the Basrah sugar market on Nov. 1, arriving
at her destination some twenty days later.   By his breaches of contract, the
owner prolonged the voyage by nearly fifty per cent. of its reasonably predictable
duration. These are very different facts from those in *The Parana* (86). Nor can I
see that the fact that the charterparty gave the charterers the right to cancel the
charter if the vessel did not arrive at Constanza by Nov. 10 is in any way material. C
She was expected to arrive by Oct. 27.   If she failed to do so because of some
breach by the owner, the owner would be liable in damages.   The charterers
no doubt appreciated that there might be delay through breach or possibly from
other causes. No doubt, within limits, they preferred that the sugar should reach
Basrah late rather than not at all, for damages would afford adequate compensation in most cases.   Unless, however, the vessel arrived at Constanza by Nov. 10 D
it might not be worth sending the sugar to Basrah.   Therefore it was provided
in the charter that if the vessel failed to arrive by Nov. 10, from whatever cause,
the charter might be cancelled.   This does not seem to me to affect the fact that
the parties contracted on the basis that the vessel would in all probability arrive
at Constanza for loading on Oct. 27, take four days for loading, and arrive at
Basrah some twenty days later.   E
    It appears from what was said by MELLISH, L.J., in *The Parana* (87) that that
decision, in addition to the matters alluded to in *Dunn* v. *Bucknall Bros.* (88),
was also based on the proposition that before damages can be recoverable it is
necessary that the parties should have foreseen that it was reasonably certain
that the damages would occur as a result of the breach.   There is nothing to
support this view in *Hadley* v. *Baxendale* (89), and it is wholly contrary to what F
was said by this court in the *Victoria Laundry* case (90). If I had to choose between
The Parana (86) and that case, I would unhesitatingly accept the judgment in the
latter case.
    In *The Parana* (86) it was said that it could not be known with any degree
of reasonable certainty at the date of the contract whether the charterers intended
to sell the goods immediately on arrival or to keep them and sell them sub- G
sequently; nor whether the market would be steady or rise or fall between the
date when the goods ought to have arrived and the date when they did arrive.
This is, no doubt, true.   It is equally true in the case of carriage of goods by land.
In such cases, however, it is well settled that the contract-breaker bears the risk
of the market falling because he must reasonably have foreseen that there was a
real danger that it might do so.   It was also pointed out in *The Parana* (86) H
that one of the differences between carriage of goods by sea and carriage of goods
by land was that in the former case the goods are frequently sold in transit.
This, no doubt, is also true, but it is immaterial. If the goods are sold in transit,
the bill of lading is transferred to the buyer. He stands in the shoes of the original
shipper. He suffers the same damage and is entitled to the same rights of recovery
as the original shipper.   I
    In *The Parana* (86) it was recognised and in *Dunn* v. *Bucknall Bros.* (88)
it was decided that what was then regarded as the second rule in *Hadley* v.
Baxendale (89) applied to carriage of goods by sea equally as it applied to carriage
of goods by land.   Once it is appreciated that there is only one rule depending

---

(86) (1877), 2 P.D. 118.   (87) (1877), 2 P.D. at p. 123.
(88) [1900-03] All E.R. Rep. 131; [1902] 2 K.B. 614.
(89) [1843-60] All E.R. Rep. 461; (1854), 9 Exch. 341.
(90) [1949] 1 All E.R. 997; [1949] 2 K.B. 528.

A on the reasonable foreseeability of a serious possibility or real risk of damage, it seems to me to be wholly illogical to make the liability depend on whether such foreseeability derives from facts presumed by the law to be within the knowledge of the parties or facts to which the parties' attention was expressly drawn when the contract was made.

B Like DIPLOCK, L.J., I was at first attracted by the argument that, since in successive editions of SCRUTTON ON CHARTERPARTIES and CARVER ON CARRIAGE OF GOODS BY SEA, *The Parana* (91) has been accepted as still governing the damages recoverable for delay caused by breach of contract of carriage of goods by sea, owners and charterers must be presumed to have contracted on that basis. On reflection, however, I think that this argument does not survive analysis. The argument comes to this—that owners and charterers must be

C presumed to have entered into contracts on the basis that owners may safely break those contracts without bearing any liability for the loss which they foresee may well result from their breach. In short, they may choose to break the contract and throw the risk of damage, which they have deliberately incurred, on to the shoulders of the innocent charterers. I cannot accept this argument; nor is there any evidence to support it. I do not believe that it would be sensible

D to assume that any ordinary business men would enter into contracts on any such remarkable basis. The same kind of argument, mutatis mutandis, could have been advanced with much more reason in *Fibrosa Spolka Akcyjna* v. *Fairbairn Lawson Combe Barbour, Ltd.* (92), but it did not there prevail.

This is the first time in this century that the courts of this country have had to consider whether in modern conditions *The Parana* (91) is still ordinarily applic-

E able. I confess that I am glad to have come to the conclusion that it is not. This conclusion has been reached on a consideration of the English authorities alone. It accords, however, with the conclusion which has already been reached in the courts of the U.S.A.: see *United States* v. *Middleton* (93) and *The Iossifoglu* (94). It is now undoubtedly the settled law of the United States that (95):

F " in the ordinary case of deviation and delay, the measure of damages is the difference in the market value of the goods at the time when actually delivered and when they should have been delivered."

In my judgment it is now high time that this should be recognised to be the law in this country also. It is, moreover, of great importance that the law merchant should, so far as possible, be uniform in all the great trading nations of the world—

G not least in England and the United States. It would indeed be ridiculous if the question as to whether or not damages for breach of a charterparty are recoverable should depend upon whether that question is decided in the courts of this country or in those of the United States.

I agree with DIPLOCK, L.J., that the award of the umpire, Mr. ANTHONY EVANS, should be restored and that the appeal should be allowed accordingly.

H *Appeal allowed; award of umpire restored. Leave to appeal to the House of Lords granted.*

Solicitors: *William A. Crump & Son* (for the charterers); *Ince & Co.* (for the shipowner).

[*Reported by* HENRY SUMMERFIELD, ESQ., *Barrister-at-Law.*]

I

---

(91) (1877), 2 P.D. 118.   (92) [1942] 2 All E.R. 122; [1943] A.C. 32.
(93) (1924), 3 Fed. Rep. (2nd) 384.   (94) (1929), 32 Fed. Rep. (2nd) 928.
(95) CORPUS JURIS SECUNDUM, Vol. 80, p. 124.

WILLIAMS *v.* WILLIAMS AND HARRIS.   A

[COURT OF APPEAL (Willmer, Davies and Russell, L.JJ.), March 18, April 5, 1966.]

Divorce—Discretion—Candour and truthfulness of party seeking decree—Court not satisfied that full and frank disclosure of adultery made by petitioner— No finding of undisclosed adultery—Factors in exercise of discretion— Petitioner's promiscuity—Deception and attitude towards adultery and B *marriage—Matrimonial Causes Act, 1950 (14 Geo. 6 c. 25), s. 4 (2).*

The parties were married in 1949 and had two children who since 1959 had been brought up by their maternal grandmother. In 1954 the wife ran away with another man and during her two years' absence the husband committed adultery with about six different women, only one of whom he was able to identify by her surname. About 1957 or 1958 the wife was away again   C for about a year, during which period, the husband said, he could not remember whether he committed adultery. In March, 1960, the husband left the wife on account of her association with another man and, during his employment at an hotel between then and September, 1961, he committed adultery with two women, one many times, the other a few times. Late in 1961 he met a Miss K. with whom he frequently committed adultery at her   D father's home over the next four years. Without disclosing his marriage, he obtained a promise of marriage from her, and it was only after banns had been called and the wedding had been fixed that he told her the true facts, thereby causing her to cancel the wedding, though she still wished to marry him if he was free to marry her. He brought a petition for divorce on the ground of the adultery of the wife, who had had an illegitimate child   E by the co-respondent. In regard to discretion the commissioner took into account the interests of the children of the marriage, the interests of Miss K. with special regard to the possibility of marriage, the absence of any likelihood of reconciliation with the wife, the interest of the husband in relation to the possibility of remarriage and the interest of the wife's illegitimate child by the co-respondent, all telling in favour of dissolution. The commis-   F sioner refused, however, to exercise his discretion in favour of the husband because (a) the commissioner was not satisfied that the husband had told the full truth as to his adultery and (b) the commissioner took the view that the over-riding consideration was the husband's utter disregard for the sanctity of marriage as evidenced by his promiscuous adultery and by his behaviour towards Miss K. On appeal,   G

Held: the commissioner's decision would be upheld because—

(i) (RUSSELL, L.J., dissenting) failure on the part of the husband to satisfy the court that he had made full and frank disclosure of his adultery was a relevant matter which might properly be taken into consideration by the court in deciding how discretion should be exercised, even though the evidence was not such as to justify the court in finding that undisclosed   H adultery had been committed (see p. 618, letter G, p. 619, letter C, and p. 620, letter I, post); moreover the court was not bound to refer the matter to the Queen's Proctor for investigation, particularly in such circumstances as those of the present case (see p. 618, letter I, and p. 620, letter I, post).

Goldsmith v. *Goldsmith* (1962), ([1964] 3 All E.R. 321) applied.

Coleman v. *Coleman* ([1955] 3 All E.R. 617), *Sharma* v. *Sharma and Davis*   I ([1959] 3 All E.R. 321) and *Joyce* v. *Joyce* ([1966] 1 All E.R. 905) distinguished.

(ii) (per WILLMER and DAVIES, L.JJ.) the commissioner was entitled to have regard to the husband's promiscuous adultery over the years and more particularly to his deception of Miss K. (see p. 620, letter I, and p. 622, letter D, post); and (per RUSSELL, L.J.) in all the circumstances of the case the commissioner could properly refuse a decree on the general ground of the whole attitude of the husband towards marriage and adultery (see p. 625, letter G, post).

A   Appeal dismissed.

[As to the principles on which the court exercises its discretion in respect of a petitioner's adultery, see 12 Halsbury's Laws (3rd Edn.) 311-313, para. 623; and for cases on the subject, see 27 Digest (Repl.) 427-432, *3582-3613.*

For the Matrimonial Causes Act, 1950, s. 4 (2), see 29 Halsbury's Statutes (2nd Edn.) 394; and for the Matrimonial Causes Act 1965, s. 5, see 45 ibid., 451.]

B   Cases referred to:

   Blunt v. *Blunt*, [1943] 2 All E.R. 76; [1943] A.C. 517; 112 L.J.P. 58; 169
         L.T. 33; 27 Digest (Repl.) 429, *3589.*

   Coleman v. *Coleman*, [1955] 3 All E.R. 617; [1955] 1 W.L.R. 1235; Digest
         (Cont. Vol. A) 752, *3604c.*

C   *Goldsmith* v. *Goldsmith*, (1962), [1964] 3 All E.R. 321; [1965] P. 188; [1964]
         3 W.L.R. 953, n.; 3rd Digest Supp.

   Hanslip v. *Hanslip*, (1953), unreported.

   Joyce v. *Joyce*, [1966] 1 All E.R. 905; [1966] 2 W.L.R. 660.

   Rowley v. *Rowley and Austin and French (Cooper intervening)*, [1964] 3 All E.R.
         314; [1965] P. 178; [1964] 3 W.L.R. 946; 3rd Digest Supp.

D   *Rudman* v. *Rudman and Lee (Queen's Proctor showing Cause)*, [1964] 2 All E.R.
         102; [1964] 1 W.L.R. 598; 3rd Digest Supp.

   Sharma v. *Sharma and Davis*, [1959] 3 All E.R. 321; [1959] 1 W.L.R. 1035;
         Digest (Cont. Vol. A) 752, *3591b.*

   Appeal.

   This was an appeal by the husband from a judgment of Mr. Commissioner
E   Syms, Q.C., sitting as a special commissioner in divorce, given on July 30, 1965,
   dismissing the husband's suit for dissolution of his marriage, the commissioner
   having refused to exercise the discretion conferred on the court by s. 4 of the
   Matrimonial Causes Act, 1950. The grounds of appeal were:—1. That the
   commissioner misdirected himself in finding that the husband had not made a
   full and frank disclosure in his evidence of the adultery committed by the husband
F   during his marriage in that (a) there was no evidence that the husband had
   committed adultery other than the adultery confessed by the husband in
   evidence; (b) alternatively, the matters on which the commissioner relied in
   support of his finding that the husband had not told the truth concerning his
   adultery were insufficient to support such a finding. 2. That the commissioner
   misdirected himself in holding that the circumstances of the case were such that
G   the court ought not to exercise the discretion conferred on the court by s. 4 of
   the Matrimonial Causes Act, 1950, to grant the husband a decree notwithstanding
   the husband's adultery in that (a) the commissioner gave weight to irrelevant
   matters (viz., his findings that (i) the husband had deceived Miss K. as to his status;
   (ii) the husband and Miss K. had committed adultery in Miss K.'s father's house,
   and (iii) the marriage might be dissolved by the wife's presenting a petition for
H   dissolution of marriage), (b) the commissioner exercised the discretion of the
   court on wrong principles in that he held that, notwithstanding that there was
   no prospect of a reconciliation between the parties and that it would be in the
   interests of the children of the marriage, Miss K. (the party whom the husband
   wished to marry), the husband, the wife and the co-respondent and their child
   that the marriage should be dissolved, nevertheless the " interests of the com-
I   munity " were such that " in order to make people respect the sanctity of
   marriage, there must be cases in which it is wrong for the court to exercise its
   discretion in favour of a particular petitioner . . . and that this is one of those
   cases ".

   J. E. Previté for the husband.

   The wife and the co-respondent did not defend the suit and did not appear
   and were not represented on the appeal.

                                                    Cur. adv. vult.

      Apr. 5. The following judgments were read:

WILLMER, L.J.: By his petition in this case the husband prayed for a **A**
decree of divorce on the ground of his wife's adultery.   The suit was undefended,
and the wife's adultery was duly proved.   The husband, however, had himself
been guilty of adultery, and Mr. Commissioner SYMS, Q.C., who heard the case,
declined in the exercise of his discretion to grant relief and dismissed the petition.
The husband now appeals to this court, complaining that the commissioner fell
into error and that he ought to have exercised his discretion in favour of **B**
granting relief.

The relevant facts can be shortly stated.   The parties were married on
Mar. 26, 1949, and cohabited at various addresses in Llanelly, south Wales.
There are two children of the marriage born respectively in December, 1949,
and July, 1953.   The two children have been brought up by their maternal
grandmother since 1959.   The commissioner expressed himself as satisfied with **C**
the arrangements made for the children, and no question arises in relation to
them.   In 1954 the wife ran away with another man and lived apart from the
husband for about two years.   During this period the husband admits that he
committed adultery with about six different women, only one of whom he was
able to identify by her surname.   In 1956 the parties resumed cohabitation,
apparently without asking any questions as to what they had respectively been **D**
doing, and lived together for a year or so.   About 1957 or 1958 the wife
again went away, and was away for about a year.   The husband's discretion
statement is silent as to any adultery committed during this period; but when
he was asked in the course of his evidence whether he had again committed
adultery he said that he could not remember .   The parties again cohabited from
about March, 1959, to March, 1960, when the husband left the wife on learning **E**
that she was again associating with another man.   Since that date there has
been no cohabitation.   It was proved that since early in 1961 the wife has been
living in adultery with the co-respondent, as a result of which she gave birth
to a male child about October, 1961.

When the husband left the wife in 1960, he took employment at the Tattenham
Corner House Hotel, Epsom, Surrey, where he resided until about September, **F**
1961.   During this period he admits that he committed adultery with two
women whom he identified only by their Christian names.   He said that he
committed adultery with one of them " many times ", and with the other
" a few times ".   About the end of 1961 the husband met another lady, to whom
I will refer as Miss K., and with whom he admits that he frequently committed
adultery over a period of about four years.   The adultery was committed at **G**
Miss K.'s home, where she resided with her father.   Without disclosing to Miss K.
that he was a married man, the husband obtained a promise from her that she
would marry him.   Miss K. is a Roman Catholic, and banns were actually called
in a Roman Catholic church in Croydon, the " wedding " being fixed to take
place on Jan. 11, 1964.   It was only a few days before that date that the husband
belatedly disclosed the true facts to Miss K., and caused her to cancel the wedding **H**
arrangements.   To her credit, Miss K. has stood by the husband, even after
she learned the full story of his prior adultery.   She gave evidence at the trial,
and informed the commissioner that she was still willing to marry the husband,
and indeed that she wanted that more than anything.

It will be seen that over the last ten years or so the husband has committed
adultery with at least nine different women, with some of them only once, but **I**
with others on a number of occasions.   In addition he has grossly deceived Miss
K., and only at the last moment restrained himself from adding the criminal
offence of bigamy to his other misconduct.   He claims that since he met Miss K.
he has given up his previous habit of promiscuity and has remained faithful to
her.   Even so, it would be difficult to imagine a more disreputable case or one
more deserving of the censure of the court.

The commissioner delivered a detailed judgment, in the course of which he
gave two reasons for refusing to exercise his discretion in favour of granting relief.

A In the first place he said that he was not satisfied, after hearing evidence from the husband at length, that he had been told the full truth about the husband's adultery. Secondly, he expressed the view that, even on the assumption that a full disclosure had been made, this husband had shown over the years such a complete disregard for the sanctity of marriage that it would be wrong for the court to exercise its discretion in his favour. On this appeal both the reasons

B which the commissioner gave have been attacked by counsel for the husband, who has submitted that neither of them is such as to afford sufficient ground for refusing to exercise discretion in favour of the husband.

Before proceeding to examine the argument put forward on behalf of the husband, it is desirable to refer to the proviso to s. 4 (2) of the Matrimonial Causes Act, 1950, whereby it is enacted

C "... that the court shall not be bound to pronounce a decree of divorce and may dismiss the petition if it finds that the petitioner has during the marriage been guilty of adultery ..."

The first of the two grounds stated by the commissioner for dismissing the petition depends very much on the view which is taken of the facts; but it has also been the subject of a submission in law put forward by counsel on behalf

D of the husband. So far as the facts are concerned, the commissioner made it clear, both by his remarks during the hearing of the evidence, and by what he said in the course of his judgment, that he thought there were significant discrepancies between what the husband had said in his discretion statement and what he said on oath in the course of giving his evidence. It has been

E suggested that there was in fact no substantial discrepancy between the two accounts which the husband gave. If we were confined to a strict analysis of the written word as it appears in the transcript, it may well be that there might be something to be said for the view that the commissioner was unduly severe in his comments.

The matter does not, however, depend only on comparison of the accounts given by the husband in the documents that are before us, for the commissioner

F made it clear that he formed an adverse view of the husband's demeanour in the witness box. He said:

"A much more serious matter to my mind is, I think, a matter to which I cannot find an answer which is satisfactory to [the husband], and that is the impression he created in my mind, by which I mean his general de-

G meanour in the witness box. That is a fact, unfortunately, that, coupled to his demeanour over some further answers that he gave, led me to the view that I was not satisfied that he was telling me the truth."

This expression of view by the commissioner, who had the advantage of seeing the husband and hearing his evidence at considerable length, is something that we in this court are bound to respect. I regard it as quite impossible for this

H court to say that the commissioner fell into error in disbelieving the husband's evidence, or that he ought to have been satisfied that a full and frank disclosure had been made.

Assuming, however, that the commissioner was justified in his suspicion that he had not been told the whole truth, it has been submitted that as a matter of law this was an insufficient ground for refusing to exercise his discretion in favour

I of the husband. The proper course, it has been suggested, would have been to pronounce a decree nisi, but to send the papers to the Queen's Proctor for investigation of the circumstances which gave rise to suspicion in the mind of the commissioner. It is contended that on its true construction the proviso to s. 4 (2) of the Act of 1950 does not justify the court in withholding relief on the ground of mere suspicion; it is entitled to withhold relief only on the basis of adultery which it "finds" was committed by the petitioner. Here there was not, and could not be, any finding that the husband was in fact guilty of adultery beyond that which he had disclosed and admitted. In support of his proposition

counsel for the husband relied on the decisions of this court in *Coleman* v. *Coleman* **A**
(1) and *Sharma* v. *Sharma and Davis* (2). On the other hand we have also
been referred to another decision of this court in *Goldsmith* v. *Goldsmith* (3). In
that case substantially the same argument was put forward as has been put
forward in the present case, but oddly enough the attention of the court does not
seem to have been called to the earlier decisions in *Coleman* v. *Coleman* (1) and
Sharma v. *Sharma and Davis* (2). It was held, however. that if the court is not **B**
satisfied that there has been a full and frank disclosure of adultery, that is a
relevant matter to be taken into consideration in exercising discretion. I am
reported as having said (4):

> " It appears to me that, once the exercise of the court's discretion is called
> for, then all relevant circumstances in relation both to the married life and
> to the conduct of the proceedings in the court can be, and should be, taken **C**
> into consideration in deciding whether the discretion should be exercised in
> one way or the other. Over and over again (and I do not need to cite any
> specific authority for this proposition) it has been emphasised that any
> petitioner who prays for the exercise of the court's discretion in his favour
> must be prepared to make a full, frank and candid disclosure of the conduct
> calling for the exercise of that discretion. It seems to me that, if the court **D**
> is left in a state that it is not satisfied there has been such a full and frank
> disclosure, that is eminently a matter which can be, and should be, taken
> into consideration when the discretion is exercised. It seems to me that in
> the public interest it is vitally important to preserve the principle that the
> utmost frankness must be shown to the court by those who seek relief in
> matrimonial causes where there has been any sort of misconduct." **E**

This is substantially in accordance with an earlier unreported decision of this
court in *Hanslip* v. *Hanslip* (5), heard on Oct. 23, 1953. It is also in accordance
with the statement of principle contained in RAYDEN ON DIVORCE (9th Edn.)
at p. 281, as follows:

> " Complete frankness in the disclosure of the petitioner's adultery is a **F**
> paramount condition of the exercise in the petitioner's favour of the court's
> discretion . . . .",

in support of which proposition a considerable body of authority is cited.

In the light of *Coleman* v. *Coleman* (1) and *Sharma* v. *Sharma and Davis* (2)
are we bound to say that the commissioner fell into an error of principle in refusing
to exercise his discretion in favour of a petitioner by whom he was not satisfied **G**
that a full and frank disclosure had been made? I think not. I reach this
conclusion for two reasons. In the first place, I do not think that either of the
cases cited in this court is to be taken as laying down any general principle.
Rather I think that the decision in each of those cases is to be taken as one based
on the special facts of the particular case. In both of them the information
which gave rise to suspicion in the mind of the trial judge came from an extraneous **H**
source. In one case it was derived from an unsworn statement made by the
wife, who did not, however, give evidence at the trial. In the other case it
was derived from evidence which had been given at a previous trial between the
same parties, as to which the previous trial judge had made certain adverse
comments. In such a context it was an obviously sensible course to direct an
investigation by the Queen's Proctor into the source of the information which **I**
had been placed before the court, rather than reject the petition out of hand. I
do not think, however, that in either case the court is to be taken as laying it down
as a matter of law that, in all cases where the trial judge is not satisfied as to the
candour of the petitioner's disclosure, this is the only course which can properly
be taken.

(1) [1955] 3 All E.R. 617.   (2) [1959] 3 All E.R. 321.
(3) (1962), [1964] 3 All E.R. 321; [1965] P. 188.
(4) [1964] 3 All E.R. at p. 323; [1965] P. at p. 190.   (5) (1953), unreported.

A   Secondly, however, the question to be decided in a case where the petitioner has been guilty of adultery is one which by statute is left to the discretion of the trial judge. It would be wrong to attempt to fetter the exercise of that discretion by laying down any hard and fast rules, and the court has never sought to do so. Each case must be dealt with in the light of its own special circumstances. One of the special circumstances of this case which impresses me is

B the utter futility of taking the course suggested, i.e., sending the papers to the Queen's Proctor for investigation. In the circumstances of this case how could the Queen's Proctor be expected to conduct any useful investigation into acts of adultery committed ten years ago with a number of unidentified women in Llanelly, or even into the more recent adultery committed with the unidentified women encountered at the Tattenham Corner House Hotel? In a case like this

C the only course open to the commissioner was to make up his own mind as to the quality of the husband's behaviour in the light of the information which was before him, and to grant or withhold relief accordingly. If, after hearing the evidence, he was not satisfied that he had been told the truth, this was in my judgment a relevant matter properly to be taken into consideration, and I do not think that it is possible for this court to say that he exercised his discretion

D wrongly by withholding relief.

    Since preparing this part of my judgment I have had the advantage of considering the decision of another division of this court in the recent case of *Joyce* v. *Joyce* (6). In that case SIR JOCELYN SIMON, P., having found the husband guilty of cruelty and the wife guilty of adultery as disclosed in her discretion statement, had declined to exercise his discretion in favour of either

E party, but had rejected the prayers in both petition and answer. On appeal this court thought that discretion should be exercised in favour of both parties, and accordingly pronounced mutual decrees. Most of the matters which were considered in that case were of no relevance to the question raised by this appeal; but on one matter it may well be thought that the decision is directly in point. In addition to the adultery disclosed in the wife's discretion statement (as to

F which there was no issue), the husband had also charged the wife with adultery with a named party cited. SIR JOCELYN SIMON dismissed this charge, saying that he was " not sure " that there had been adultery between them; but in spite of the dismissal of the charge, he remained suspicious. In those circumstances, when he came to consider the exercise of his discretion, he said that he was far from sure that the wife had made a full and frank disclosure in her

G discretion statement, and gave this as a reason for refusing to exercise discretion in her favour. It was held by this court that, having acquitted the wife of the charge of adultery with the party cited, SIR JOCELYN SIMON should not have taken this against her when exercising his discretion, notwithstanding that he remained suspicious. LORD DENNING, M.R., repeated what he had said in *Coleman* v. *Coleman* (7), and both he and SALMON, L.J., expressed the view that

H mere suspicion that a discretion statement is not full and frank is not a sufficient ground for refusing relief. DANCKWERTS, L.J., appears to have based his decision on the particular facts of the case before him. He said (8):

    " On the evidence in this case I should not have come to the conclusion that the wife had committed adultery with the party cited. The evidence seems to me to be weak. There was not much opportunity and no evidence

I   of affection or familiarity. Certainly in my view it was not a case in which suspicion should have influenced the exercise of the court's discretion to the detriment of the wife."

It appears that *Goldsmith* v. *Goldsmith* (9) was brought to the attention of the court, but LORD DENNING, M.R., sought to distinguish that case on the ground (which with all respect I venture to think is not warranted by the report of the

---

(6) [1966] 1 All E.R. 905.   (7) [1955] 3 All E.R. 617.
(8) [1966] 1 All E.R. at p. 909.   (9) (1962), [1964] 3 All E.R. 321; [1965] P. 188.

case) that the court in that case thought the evidence sufficiently strong to   **A**
justify a finding of adultery.   No doubt was cast on the principle which I
endeavoured to state in that part of my own judgment which I have already
quoted.   In these circumstances I do not think that *Joyce* v. *Joyce* (10) is to
be taken as authority against the proposition that, where the court is not satisfied
that there has been a full and frank disclosure, that is a matter which can be,
and should be, taken into consideration when the discretion is exercised.   In my   **B**
view *Joyce* v. *Joyce* (10) like *Coleman* v. *Coleman* (11), is more properly to be
regarded as a decision which turned on its own special, and rather unusual,
facts.   On the whole, therefore, I do not find any reason to alter the view which
I have already expressed.

I can deal quite shortly with the second ground on which the commissioner
based his judgment.   Even assuming in favour of the husband that what he   **C**
disclosed to the court represented the whole truth as to his adulterous behaviour,
I cannot regard this as anything other than a rather shocking case.   The commissioner was well entitled to have regard not only to the husband's promiscuity
over the years, but also and more particularly to the disgraceful manner in which
he deceived Miss K., almost to the point of involving her in a bigamous marriage.
He rightly directed himself in accordance with the principles stated by VISCOUNT   **D**
SIMON, L.C., in *Blunt* v. *Blunt* (12).   He duly considered the interests of the
children of the marriage, the interests of Miss K. with special regard to the
possibility of marriage, the absence of any likelihood of reconciliation with the
wife, the interest of the husband himself in relation to the possibility of re-
marriage, and the interest of the wife's illegitimate child by the co-respondent.
All these considerations, as the commissioner rightly recognised, told in favour   **E**
of dissolving the marriage.   He then had to go on to consider, however, in the
words of VISCOUNT SIMON, L.C. (13),

" the interest of the community at large, to be judged by maintaining a
true balance between the respect for binding sanctity of marriage and the
social considerations which make it contrary to public policy to insist on
the maintenance of a union which has utterly broken down."   **F**

In striking this balance the commissioner took the view that the over-riding
consideration, was the husband's apparent disregard for the sanctity of marriage,
as evidenced both by his promiscuous adultery and by his behaviour towards
Miss K.   I find it quite impossible to say that it was not open to him to take this
view and, in his discretion, to give effect to it.   On the contrary, I think that   **G**
he was plainly right.

It has been argued that the husband's deception of Miss K. was an irrelevant
consideration, as was also the fact that he chose to commit adultery with her
under her father's roof, thereby deceiving him as well.   It has also been suggested
that the commissioner was wrong to take into consideration the fact that, even
though this petition fails, the way may still be open to dissolve the marriage   **H**
on a petition brought by the wife.   I can only say that I do not at all agree that
these are irrelevant considerations.

In my judgment, for the reasons which I have given, the commissioner reached
a conclusion with which it is impossible for this court to interfere, and I would
accordingly dismiss the appeal.

DAVIES, L.J.:   I have had the advantage of reading in advance the judg-   **I**
ment which has just been delivered by WILLMER, L.J.   I agree with it in every
respect.   His observations about the cases of *Coleman* v. *Coleman* (11) and
Sharma v. *Sharma and Davis* (14), which were so strongly relied on by counsel
for the husband, demonstrate in my view that neither of these decisions can be

(10) [1966] 1 All E.R. 905.   (11) [1955] 3 All E.R. 617.
(12) [1943] 2 All E.R. 76;   [1943] A.C. 517.
(13) [1943] 2 All E.R. at p. 78;   [1943] A.C. at p. 525.   (14) [1959] 3 All E.R. 321.

A   taken as in any way altering the view which the court has consistently taken as to the necessity for complete frankness on the part of a person who is asking for a decree of divorce in the exercise of the court's discretion. The practice of the court in that respect is, if I may respectfully venture to say so, correctly set out in the judgment of WILLMER, L.J., in *Goldsmith* v. *Goldsmith* (15), which has already been read and with which I entirely agree.

B   In the circumstances it would be otiose to discuss over again the points dealt with by WILLMER, L.J., and I shall confine myself to a citation from the unreported case of *Hanslip* v. *Hanslip* (16), decided by this court on Oct. 23, 1953. It so happens that that was an appeal from a decision of my own, and I refer to the case not for the purpose of suggesting that any observations of mine were authoritative, but in order to show that this court there approved of the prin-

C ciples on which I approached the facts of the case. It will be observed incidentally that HODSON, L.J., who was a party to the decisions in *Coleman* v. *Coleman* (17) and *Sharma* v. *Sharma and Davis* (18), gave the leading judgment in *Hanslip* v. *Hanslip* (16), and that that decision was two years before *Coleman* v. *Coleman* (17) and six before *Sharma* v. *Sharma and Davis* (18).

  In the course of his judgment HODSON, L.J., said:

D

> " What the learned judge said in his judgment as regards the name of Warrener is this: ' It appears she moved away from these parts and went to live at any rate in Croydon, where for some not very clear reason she is living under the name of " Warrener ". She says, and I do not believe it, that she has changed her name to Warrener because she was frightened of

E   her husband. Now counsel for the wife says however badly she has behaved her adultery was condoned by the husband.' Then appears this significant phrase: ' The only adultery of which I have any knowledge was condoned by the husband; that is perfectly true, and condonation is, of course, a powerful factor in assisting the court on the problem as to whether or not it should exercise its discretion in favour of the party seeking the exercise

F   of that discretion; but on all the facts of this case I have come to the conclusion that the wife's evidence is so unreliable, so untrustworthy, that despite the undoubted condonation of the adultery prior to October, 1945, [then note these words] in the light of her own conduct I feel that I am unable to grant her a decree.' Nothing seems to be plainer than that the learned judge was utterly dissatisfied with the petitioner's evidence, and in considering her evidence he was considering in particular whether he could

G   feel sure that she had made a proper disclosure. I am not for a moment seeking to say that disclosure is the only matter which has to be considered by a judge, but that it is one of the matters is, I think, clear from the speech of LORD SIMON in the case of *Blunt* v. *Blunt* (19), when he referred to the question of disclosure, and in dealing with the trial judge's decision used these

H   words: ' It seems to me clear that the learned judge took into consideration the petitioner's conduct in relation to the court ', and no criticism of that matter appears in LORD SIMON's speech.

  So there was a case, in essence similar to the present one, in which on the case presented by the wife, who had admittedly committed adultery which had been condoned and so ordinarily would have been overlooked, the court was not

I satisfied that it had been told the full story, and on that ground refused to grant a decree. In my view that case is ample authority for the course taken by the learned commissioner in the present one.

  The observations of LORD DENNING, M.R., and SALMON, L.J., in the recent case of *Joyce* v. *Joyce* (20), do at first sight appear to present some difficulty.

---

(15) (1962), [1964] 3 All E.R. 321; [1965] P. 188.   (16) (1953), unreported.
(17) [1955] 3 All E.R. 617.   (18) [1959] 3 All E.R. 321.
(19) [1943] 2 All E.R. at p. 80; [1943] A.C. at p. 529.   (20) [1966] 1 All E.R. 905.

They apparently took the view that SIR JOCELYN SIMON, P., was wrong in refusing   A
a decree to the wife on the ground merely that he was suspicious that she had
committed adultery with the party cited; but the view taken by this court in
that case was, if I may respectfully say so, quite understandable. SIR JOCELYN
SIMON had rejected the charge of adultery made by the husband against the
wife and the party cited; he was not satisfied that it had been made out. It would
seem very odd in those circumstances to refuse a decree on the ground, in effect,   B
that the court was not satisfied that the same adultery had not been committed.
In my judgment, that decision on the particular and unusual facts ought not to
be taken as having been intended to alter what I conceive to be the regular and
well established approach to the exercise of discretion as set out in the judgment
of WILLMER, L.J., in *Goldsmith* v. *Goldsmith* (21).

I would add that, in my view, when a judge refuses to grant a decree on the   C
ground that a petitioner has not made a full and frank disclosure and has not told
him the whole truth, he is not necessarily and inevitably suggesting that more
adultery has taken place than has been admitted. As I understand the law and the
practice, a judge in such cases is bound to examine with care the question of
the credibility and trustworthiness of the petitioner on all material matters on the
case as a whole; and, if he is dissatisfied in that regard, he is entitled to refuse a   D
decree. For the rest, I would only add that, in my view, so far from this case
being one in which it would be right for this court to interfere with the exercise
by the commissioner of his discretion, his decison was on the facts correct.

RUSSELL, L.J.: There were two grounds on each of which the commissioner
declined to make a decree in the exercise of the statutory discretion that exists
where adultery is found, or (as here) admitted to have been committed by the   E
husband during the marriage. The first was that he was not satisfied that in
evidence in the witness box the husband gave a full and frank disclosure in
relation to his adultery. On this aspect he first referred to para. 2 of the discretion
statement, in which the husband referred to a two-year period ten to eight years
earlier when he was apart from his wife.
                                                                                              F
" From about March, 1954, to about March, 1956, the [wife] was living
apart from me at an address in London. During those two years I was
working at a public house in Llanelly and I had sexual intercourse with
about six different women whose names I cannot now remember except
that one was called Mrs. P. [naming her] and the first names of two were
Gwyneth and Maureen. I committed adultery with the said Mrs. P. at her   G
home in Llanelly, the address of which I cannot now remember. The sexual
intercourse with the other women generally took place out of doors."

The husband's oral evidence in respect of this period was that his wife ran away
to London with another man; that he did not commit adultery with any of the
" about six " women referred to until ten or twelve months after she left; that
he committed adultery only once with each of them, and that with all except   H
Mrs. P. it took place out of doors. The commissioner construed para. 2, because
of the word " generally ", as saying that he had committed adultery with one
or more of the women other than Mrs. P. more than once. It is true that that is
one interpretation, but it seems to me that it can also quite fairly be used to mean
that in the case of most of the other women the adultery took place out of doors,
which involves no quantitative discrepancy between the statement and his   I
evidence at all; the only contradiction is on the question whether any adultery
took place indoors; and the commissioner rather severely said that made nonsense
of the statement. I cannot think that the commissioner's construction of para. 2
on this point is a sound basis on which to incline to the view that his " once
only " evidence was untrue. Moreover, what on earth would be the purpose of
contradicting his statement if he thought that he had already admitted to more?

(21) (1962), [1964] 3 All E.R. 321; [1965] P. 188.

A He had no hesitation in the witness box in saying that at a later period he committed adultery many times with the two girls in the Epsom district when his statement left it open to him to say once only.

On the same paragraph the commissioner indicated that he found a discrepancy between its contents and the evidence under another head. He read the paragraph as indicating that the adultery admitted was, so to speak, spread over the whole

B period of two years, and therefore the evidence that it did not start for ten or twelve months was suspect. Again I think that that construction is by no means necessarily the correct one. The two-year period was introduced as the period of the wife's absence and not necessarily for the purpose of defining approximately the period between the first and last act of adultery. It seems to me quite wrong to say that there is a discrepancy between statement and evidence here; the

C adultery described in the witness box *did* take place during the wife's two-year absence. Again I ask why, if the husband *thought* that he had described a full two-year spread, should he contradict it in the witness box? The commissioner's view of the meaning of para. 2 on this point also seems to me an unsound basis on which to incline to the view that the husband's evidence was untrue.

In the forefront of the commissioner's expressed doubts as to the veracity of

D the husband was the answer to a question by counsel. The question was based on the assumption that the discretion statement said that in the period 1954-56 adultery had been committed with six women. The answer was: " It could be." The commissioner said that from then on he felt distinctly uneasy, meaning about the veracity of the husband; but this was, against the discretion statement which referred to " *about* six women ", surely a perfectly honest answer. It could be six

E women, but that was not necessarily the correct number. I think that the commissioner overlooked that the question did not accurately represent the discretion statement and therefore took the answer as shifty or evasive; he said expressly that he thought it " a very surprising answer ". I should have thought the answer no more indicative of evasion than when the commissioner asked: " Are you saying that although you committed adultery with six women

F you only committed adultery altogether on six occasions? ", and the husband answered: " That's about it, before my wife came back to me." The other piece of evidence particularly referred to by the commissioner under this heading was that the husband would not say definitely that he had not committed adultery in the second separation period, though his statement did not disclose any such adultery; but, if he wished to deceive the court, would he not have said No?

G If he was trying to be frank, but could not be sure, would he not have given the answers that he did give? It is, of course, true that the commissioner was unfavourably impressed by the demeanour of the husband in the witness-box; he referred to the " considerable impression " (in an adverse sense) made on him by the husband. The commissioner stated, however, that it was the husband's demeanour, coupled with his answers to certain questions (mentioned above)

H that led him not to be satisfied that the husband was telling the truth.

If the question of full and frank disclosure were the only point in the case, I would not on the facts be happy to leave the case as it stands; but there is also for consideration the question whether in law the commissioner was entitled to have any regard to his suspicion of a failure to make full disclosure of the extent of the husband's adultery. Section 4 of the Matrimonial Causes Act, 1950, requires

I that a petition be dismissed if the court is not satisfied (in an adultery case) that the petition has been proved, and that the petitioner has not been accessory to or condoned or connived at the adultery, or (in a cruelty case) that the petitioner has not condoned the cruelty. The discretion proviso enacts that the court is not bound to pronounce a decree and may dismiss a petition which has passed those tests if it *finds* that the petition is presented in collusion, or *finds* that the petitioner has been guilty of adultery, or if in the opinion of the court the petitioner has been guilty of unreasonable delay, or cruelty, or desertion or wilful separation without reasonable excuse before the adultery or cruelty of the respondent, or of

such wilful neglect or misconduct as has conduced to the adultery or unsoundness A
of mind or desertion on which the petition is grounded.   The Matrimonial
Causes Act 1963, s. 4, (22), moved collusion from the earlier part of the subsection
to the proviso, so that a failure to satisfy the court of the absence of collusion
ceased to be an absolute bar, and a positive finding of collusion was required to
constitute a discretionary bar (the whole matter is now to be found in s. 5 of the
Matrimonial Causes Act 1965).   B

Apart from authority it would seem to me that the subsection does not permit
adultery to be considered as relevant to the exercise of discretion unless it
be adultery *found* (or admitted) to have taken place.   It is true that one act of
adultery found or admitted opens the gate to the exercise of discretion by way
of refusal of a decree; but in exercising that discretion is it right to take into
account *suspicion* that other adultery has been committed?   In effect this is to C
import from the earlier part of the section the notion that difficulty may lie in
the path of a petitioner if he does not satisfy the court that something has not
happened.   If a petitioner puts in no discretion statement, it is clear that the
court has no right to refuse a decree unless it actually finds the petitioner guilty
of adultery.   No amount of suspicion or feeling of dissatisfaction entitles a
decree to be refused; there must be a finding.   It would be curious, to say the D
least, if one admitted act of adultery should put the petitioner at risk of failing
in his petition merely because the judge was not satisfied that there had not been
more adultery, or was suspicious that there had been, while unable to assert by
a finding that that was so.   It seems to me that a possible outcome of that would
be that a petitioner, perhaps one unlikely to make a good witness, who had
committed only one act of adultery, but who had had opportunities for further E
adultery in circumstances which might seem suspicious, might think it politic
either to suppress the one adultery (hoping to depart from the court with an
aura of mere suspicion, but nevertheless a decree) or to invent adultery on the
suspicious occasions so as to avoid losing his decree for lack of frankness.

On this question there seems some conflict of authority.   As I read the case
of *Coleman* v. *Coleman* (23) in this court, it was clearly held that, in exercising F
his discretion where one instance of adultery was admitted, the commissioner
was not entitled to take into account the fact that he was not satisfied that there
was not other adultery, and suspected that there was and that therefore the
petitioner was not being frank with the court.   In effect it was said that one
cannot say that a person has not been frank about the number of times adultery
has been committed unless extra adultery has either been subsequently admitted G
or found to have been committed.   *Coleman* v. *Coleman* (23) was referred to
in this court in *Sharma* v. *Sharma and Davis* (24), though not on this precise
point, without criticism.   In *Rudman* v. *Rudman and Lee* (*Queen's Proctor
showing Cause*) (25) SIR JOCELYN SIMON, P., declined to take into account a
strong suspicion that the petitioner might have committed more adultery than
he ultimately (after perjury) admitted, in deciding whether to exercise his dis- H
cretion in favour of the petitioner, saying that had the further adultery been
proved he would not have done so.   This seems to be in line with *Coleman* v.
Coleman (23), though the case was not referred to.

Then comes *Goldsmith* v. *Goldsmith* (26) in this court in which *Coleman* v.
Coleman (23) was not cited.   CAIRNS, J., had refused to exercise his discretion
in favour of either husband or wife, both of whom had filed discretion statements, I
on the ground that he was not satisfied in either case that their disclosure was
complete, though without finding that any further adultery had been committed.
This court upheld him.   I cannot avoid the conclusion that there is complete
incompatability between the views of the law expressed in that case and in
Coleman v. *Coleman* (23).   The argument of counsel which was flatly rejected

A   might well have been lifted straight from the judgment of Denning, L.J., in *Coleman* v. *Coleman* (27). In *Rowley* v. *Rowley and Austin and French (Cooper intervening)* (28) Cairns, J., followed *Goldsmith* v. *Goldsmith* (29) on the point on which it was relevant to the case, taking into consideration on the question of discretion, inter alia, the fact that he was unconvinced that the husband had made a clean breast of his adultery and strongly suspected from his demeanour that

B   he had committed further adultery. Again the case of *Coleman* v. *Coleman* (27) was not noticed.

Finally comes *Joyce* v. *Joyce* (30) in this court. The wife filed a discretion statement admitting one act of adultery. She denied adultery with the party cited. Sir Jocelyn Simon, P., found the charge not established, but (following *Goldsmith* v. *Goldsmith* (29)) refused to exercise discretion in her favour because

C   he was far from satisfied that her discretion statement contained a full and frank disclosure; indeed, he said that, had the matter depended on balance of probabilities, he would have *found* adultery with the party cited. This was reversed on the grounds stated in *Coleman* v. *Coleman* (27), Lord Denning, M.R., delivering the leading judgment. Danckwerts, L.J., used one phrase which is capable of meaning that in some cases suspicion might influence the exercise of the

D   discretion. However, Salmon, L.J., in terms said (31) that mere suspicion that the discretion statement is not full and frank is not a sufficient ground for refusing a decree. I add that the unreported case of *Hanslip* v. *Hanslip* (32) in 1953 in this court appears to favour the *Goldsmith* v. *Goldsmith* (29) view, though it would seem that the court *found* that on matters other than adultery the petitioner had lied in the witness box.

E   I consider that in that state of authority I am entitled to adhere to the view to which (apart from authority) I would have come: in my judgment, in order that adultery should enter into consideration in the exercise of discretion, it must be adultery found or admitted. A petitioner cannot be accused of a failure to treat the court with frankness about the number of times he has committed adultery unless the court is prepared to find that he has committed it more

F   frequently than he admits and is lying.

The commissioner, however, independently of this question of full disclosure, refused to exercise his discretion in favour of the husband on a more general ground, that of the whole attitude of the husband towards marriage and adultery; and under this head the uncertainty of the husband, assuming it to be honest, is indicative. The commissioner considered with care the points set out in *Blunt*

G   v. *Blunt* (33), and under the fifth of those points decided in his discretion not to grant a decree. This is not an appeal from his discretion to our discretion, and I cannot say that he could not in the circumstances of this case properly refuse a decree. I am inclined to think that I might have exercised discretion in favour of the husband, since both he and Miss K. are anxious to marry, and have apparently remained devoted to each other for several years now, and the husband's

H   wife is anxious to marry the man whose child she has borne, who would thus be legitimated. As I have said, however, the discretion is not mine. I agree that the appeal fails.

Appeal dismissed.   Leave to appeal to the House of Lords refused.

Solicitors: *Baker, Freeman & Co.*, Croydon and Mitcham (for the husband).

I   [*Reported by* F. A. Amies, Esq., *Barrister-at-Law.*]

---

(27) [1955] 3 All E.R. 617.   (28) [1964] 3 All E.R. 314; [1965] P. 178.
(29) (1962), [1964] 3 All E.R. 321; [1965] P. 188.   (30) [1966] 1 All E.R. 905.
(31) [1966] 1 All E.R. at p. 910, letter H.   (32) (1953), unreported.
          (33) [1943] 2 All E.R. 76; [1943] A.C. 517.

NATICNAL AND GRINDLAYS BANK, LTD.   A
v. DHARAMSHI VALLABHJI AND OTHERS.

[PRIVY COUNCIL (Lord Morris of Borth-y-Gest, Lord Pearce and Lord Pearson),
February 14, 15, 16, 17, May 10, 1966.]

*Privy Council—Kenya—Hypothecation—Bank overdraft secured by letter of
hypothecation over stock-in-trade and other articles—Letter of hypothecation   B
unattested and unregistered—Cheques drawn in excess of extended overdraft
—Seizure of stock-in-trade—Letter authorising seizure as overdraft could
not be reduced—Whether unattested letter of hypothecation valid as between
parties thereto—Chattels Transfer Ordinance (No. 24), 1930, s. 15.*

The respondents carried on business in Nairobi and on Apr. 4, 1960, opened
a banking account with the appellant bank which provided overdraft facilities   C
to the amount of Shs. 140,000/- subject to conditions. The conditions were
that the amount was repayable on demand, that the account was to be
conducted to the satisfaction of the appellant bank and that the agreement
be reviewed at the end of April, 1961. As security the respondents gave the
bank a signed letter of hypothecation over their stock-in-trade and certain
other articles. The letter was neither attested nor registered. On several   D
occasions the respondents exceeded the limit of the overdraft facilities and on
Sept. 29, 1960, the appellant bank extended the limit by Shs. 10,000/- until
Oct. 3, 1960. The respondents failed to sign or return documents handed
to them for signature in consideration of the extended overdraft facilities.
On Oct. 6, 1960, the respondents signed fresh documents including an
extension of the letter of hypothecation and a new guarantee. On the same   E
day two of the respondents showed a bank official a draft letter setting out
that the respondents were unable to pay their creditors whereupon the
respondents were asked to reduce their overdraft to the original limit of
Shs. 140,000/-. On the respondents stating they were unable to do so, the
appellant bank, without formal notice, caused the respondents' stock-in-trade
and other articles to be seized under a power contained in the letter of   F
hypothecation. During the seizure on Oct. 6, 1960, two of the respondents
voluntarily signed a letter referring to the letter of hypothecation and
authorising the seizure as the overdraft could not be reduced. In an action
for damages for trespass allegedly committed by the appellant bank in seizing
the respondents' stock-in-trade, it was conceded that if the letter of hypothecation were valid as between the parties the seizure was justified.   G

Held (LORD MORRIS OF BORTH-Y-GEST dissenting*): in the absence of any
express provision in s. 15 of the Chattels Transfer Ordinance, 1930† as to
the consequence of non-attestation, the natural implication from the provisions of s. 15 and its context and the scheme of the Ordinance was that an
unattested instrument was valid between the parties but incapable of
registration and so was ineffective against other persons; accordingly the letter   H
of hypothecation was valid as between the appellant bank and the respondents and the acts of the appellant bank were justified (see p. 633, letter C,
p. 636, letter E, and p. 633, letter E, post).

Davis v. *Goodman* ([1874-80] All E.R. Rep. 996) approved.

Dicta of CONNOLLY, J., in *R.* v. *Dibb Ido* ((1897), 15 N.Z.L.R. at p. 595)
and of DENNISTON, J., in *Lee* v. *Parke's Official Assignee in Bankruptcy* ((1903),   I
22 N.Z.L.R. at p. 750) applied.

Appeal allowed.

---

* By the Judicial Committee (Dissenting Opinions) Order-in-Council dated Mar. 4,
1966, it is provided that any member of the Judicial Committee of the Privy Council
present at the hearing of any appeal, cause or matter who shall dissent from the opinion
of the majority of the members as to the nature of the report or recommendation to
be made to Her Majesty thereon shall be at liberty to publish his dissent in open court
together with his reasons.

† Section 15 is printed at p. 630, letter I, post.

A   [As to attestation of deeds and other instruments, see 11 HALSBURY'S LAWS (3rd Edn.) 345-348, paras. 556-558; and for cases on the subject, see 17 DIGEST (Repl.) 220, *187-199*.]

Cases referred to:

B   *Davis* v. *Goodman*, [1874-80] All E.R. Rep. 996; (1880), 5 C.P.D. 128; 49 L.J.Q.B. 344; 42 L.T. 288; 7 Digest (Repl.) 85, *490*.

D'Emden v. *Pedder*, (1904), 1 C.L.R. 91; 39 Digest (Repl.) 344, *462*.

Dodhia v. *National and Grindlays Bank, Ltd.*, (1962), unreported.

Kavanagh v. *Gudge*, (1844), 7 Man. & G. 316; 13 L.J.C.P. 99; 2 L.T.O.S. 497; 135 E.R. 132; 31 Digest (Repl.) 532, *6567*.

Lee v. *Parke's Official Assignee in Bankruptcy*, (1903), 22 N.Z.L.R. 747; 5 Digest
C   (Repl.) 966, *4256*.

Liverpool Borough Bank v. *Turner*, (1860), 1 John. & H. 159; 29 L.J.Ch. 827; 3 L.T. 84; 70 E.R. 703; *affd.* L.C., 2 De G.F. & J. 502; 45 E.R. 715; 5 Digest (Repl.) 832, *7032*.

Marshall v. *Green*, (1875), 1 C.P.D. 35; 45 L.J.Q.B. 153; 33 L.T. 404; 39 Digest (Repl.) 466, *181*.
D   *R.* v. *Dibb Ido*, (1897), 15 N.Z.L.R. 591; 7 Digest (Repl.) 5, *25*.

Te Aro Loan Co. v. *Cameron*, (1895), 14 N.Z.L.R. 411; 7 Digest (Repl.) 96, *628*.

Webb v. *Outrim*, [1907] A.C. 81; 76 L.J.P.C. 25; 95 L.T. 850; 8 Digest (Repl.) 830, *833*.

E   **Appeal.**

This was an appeal by National and Grindlays Bank, Ltd. by leave of the Court of Appeal for Eastern Africa (SIR TREVOR GOULD, V.P., NEWBOLD and DUFFUS, JJ.A.) from a judgment and order of that court dated Sept. 2, 1964, allowing the appeal of the respondents (Dharamshi Vallabhji and four others trading as " Dharamshi Vallabhji and Bros.") from a judgment of the Supreme
F   Court of Kenya (WICKS, J.), dated May 31, 1963, whereby an action instituted by the respondents against the appellant bank for, inter alia, damages for trespass committed by the appellant bank in seizing the respondents' stock-in-trade which, as security for the respondents' overdraft with the appellant bank, was the subject of a letter of hypothecation given by the plaintiffs to the bank, was dismissed.

G   The letter of hypothecation, by which the respondents hypothecated to the appellant bank as continuing security for payment of the amount owing on overdraft the respondents' goods subsequently described, was dated May 9, 1960, and included among other undertakings the following—

" (9) the [appellant] bank or any person authorised by the [appellant] bank
H   may at any time or times, and whether the power of sale hereinafter contained shall have become exercisable or not, enter the [respondents'] shop and godown or any place where the same may be and take and retain possession of the goods hereby hypothecated or any of them . . .

" (10) if we [the respondents] shall fail to pay on demand the balance for the time being owing on the [overdraft] account or any interest thereon or
I   if there shall be a breach of any of the agreements on our part herein contained [the appellant bank] may at any time thereafter sell or realise in such manner as [the appellant bank] may think fit and without responsibility for any loss in connexion therewith, the goods hereby hypothecated . . . and no previous notice to us of any such sale or realisation shall be necessary . . ."

The description of the goods was as follows—the entire stock-in-trade consisting of piece-goods, ready-made clothes, fancy goods, tailoring materials, sewing machines and their spare parts, trade fittings and fixtures and goods of similar

nature that form part of the respondents' stock while stored or lying in shops   A
and godowns situate at plot no. 467, India Bazaar, Nairobi, and elsewhere.

B. O'Donovan, Q.C. (of the East African Bar) and E. G. Nugee for the appellant
bank.

E. F. N. Gratiaen, Q.C., and R. K. Handoo for the respondents.

LORD PEARSON delivered the following majority judgment: This is an   B
appeal by the appellant bank, by leave of the Court of Appeal for Eastern Africa,
from a judgment of that court given at Nairobi on Sept. 2, 1964, allowing the
respondents' appeal from a judgment of the Supreme Court of Kenya (WICKS, J.)
given on May 31, 1963. The action is for damages for a trespass alleged to have
been committed by the appellant bank on Oct. 6, 1960, in taking possession of
and removing the respondents' stock-in-trade under a letter of hypothecation,   C
which had been given to the appellant bank by the respondents as security for
their overdraft. The trial proceeded on the basis that only the issue of liability
was to be determined initially. WICKS, J., decided in favour of the appellant
bank, holding that, although the letter of hypothecation was wholly void for
lack of attestation of the grantors' signatures, nevertheless no trespass had
been committed, because the respondents had on Oct. 6, 1960, given a consent to   D
the acts of the appellant bank in taking possession of and removing the respondents' stock-in-trade. The Court of Appeal, while agreeing with him that the
letter of hypothecation was wholly void, reversed his decision on the ground
that no fresh consent, independent of the letter of hypothecation, had been given
on Oct. 6, 1960.

In this appeal it has been conceded that, if the letter of hypothecation was   E
valid as between the parties, the acts of the appellant bank were justified
under a clause in the letter of hypothecation. The only issues in this appeal
are (i) whether the letter of hypothecation was valid as between the parties,
and (ii) if not, whether some fresh consent, independent of the letter of
hypothecation, was given by the respondents on Oct. 6, 1960.

There is not now any dispute as to the facts found by WICKS, J., which were   F
summarised in the judgment of NEWBOLD, J.A., in the Court of Appeal as follows:

" On Apr. 4, 1960, the [respondents] opened a banking account with
[the appellant bank] and [the appellant bank] undertook to provide overdraft
facilities to the [respondents]. The limit of the overdraft facilities then
agreed was Shs. 140,000/- and the conditions attached thereto were that the   G
amount was repayable on demand, that the account had to be conducted to
the satisfaction of [the appellant bank] and that the agreement was to
come up for review on Apr. 30, 1961. As security for such overdraft facilities
the [respondents] gave to [the appellant bank], inter alia, a letter of
hypothecation over their stock-in-trade and certain other articles specified in
the letter. This letter of hypothecation was signed by the [respondents] on   H
Apr. 4, 1960, after the printed form had been duly filled in, though it was
dated May 8, 1960. The letter of hypothecation was neither attested nor
registered. Subsequently, on May 13, 1960, [the appellant bank] wrote to
the [respondents] confirming the overdraft facilities. On a number of
occasions the [respondents] exceeded the limits of the overdraft facilities
and on Sept. 29, 1960, [the appellant bank] extended the limit of the overdraft   I
facilities by Shs. 10,000/- to Shs. 150,000/-, but this extension was for a
period only until Oct. 3, 1960. In consideration of this extension certain
documents, including an extension of the limit set out in the letter of
hypothecation, were handed to the [respondents] for signature on the
understanding that they would be returned to [the appellant bank]. These
documents were not returned and cheques were drawn in excess of the
additional limit. On the morning of Oct. 6, 1960, an official of [the appellant
bank] went to the premises of the [respondents] with fresh documents and

A with instructions either to have the original documents, if signed, returned to [the appellant bank] or to obtain the signature of the [respondents] to these fresh documents. That morning the [respondents] signed the fresh documents, which included an extension of the letter of hypothecation and a new guarantee. Later that morning two of the [respondents] went to [the appellant bank] and showed to an official of [the appellant bank] a draft letter setting

B out that the [respondents] were unable to pay their creditors, whereupon the [respondents] were asked to reduce their overdraft to the agreed limit of Shs. 140,000/- and stated that they were unable to do so. Following upon, and consequent upon, this [the appellant bank], without any formal notice, caused the stock-in-trade and other articles of the [respondents] to be seized under a power contained in the letter of hypothecation on the afternoon of

C Oct. 6, and during the course of the seizure two of the [respondents] voluntarily and with knowledge of its contents signed a letter, dated Oct. 6, referring to the letter of hypothecation and authorising the seizure as the overdraft could not be reduced as promised."

The letter of Oct. 6, 1960, as set out in the record, was as follows:

D " The Manager,
    National and Grindlays Bank, Ltd.
      Nairobi.
  Dear Sir,
    With reference to the letter of hypothecation executed by us on May 9, 1960, we hereby authorise you to take over our stocks sowing machines &

E spares as we regret we are not in a position to reduce our overdraft as promised.

Yours faithfully,
Dharamshi Valabhji & Bros.
(Sgd.) K. D. Vaghela
(Sgd.) Dharamshi Vallabhji
(in Gujerati)."

F The second issue can be quickly disposed of. Their lordships agree with NEWBOLD, J.A., that " as [the appellant bank] has seized the goods of the [respondents] then [the appellant bank] is liable in trespass unless it can justify the seizure ". It is clear from BULLEN AND LEAKE'S PRECEDENTS OF PLEADING (3rd Edn.) pp. 414, 415 and p. 740 and (11th Edn.) pp. 637-639, 1046, 1119-1120, that it is

G not for the respondents to prove that the seizure was against their will: they prove the seizure, and it is for the appellant bank to show that the seizure was by leave and licence of the respondents. *Kavanagh* v. *Gudge* (1) illustrates the sequence of pleadings under the old system. If the letters of hypothecation were wholly void they conferred no effective leave or licence; see *Marshall* v. *Green* (2), per LORD COLERIDGE, C.J. Their lordships further agree with NEWBOLD, J.A.,

H that the letter of Oct. 6, 1960

> " does not seek to create any new rights but merely to confirm a position which created rights under the letter of hypothecation. This being so, if no rights existed under the letter of hypothecation, then no rights are created by this letter."

I The sole remaining issue is as to the validity as between the parties of the letter of hypothecation, which had no attestation of the signatures of the respondents as grantors. The respondents contend that by reason of the absence of attestation the letter of hypothecation was wholly void under s. 15 of the Chattels Transfer Ordinance, 1930, cap. 281 of the Laws of Kenya (which may conveniently be called " the Kenya Act "). The appellant bank contends that, though the letter of hypothecation may have been invalid for the purposes of registration under the Kenya Act, it was valid as between the parties.

The choice between these two rival contentions depends on the construction **A** of the latter part of s. 15 of the Kenya Act. The express provisions of the section, its context and the scheme of the Act have to be considered. Decisions of New Zealand courts on similar provisions in a New Zealand Act have to be taken into account (3). Also the English and New Zealand Acts relating to bills of sale may have some relevance as precursors of the Kenya Act (3). The context of s. 15 is important and it is necessary to set out the principal provisions. **B**

" Registration

" 4. All persons shall be deemed to have notice of an instrument and of the contents thereof when and so soon as such instrument has been registered as provided by this Ordinance: . . .

" 5. Registration of an instrument shall be effected by filing the same . . . and an affidavit in the form numbered (1) in Sch. 1 hereto or to the like **C** effect, in the office of the registrar.

" 6. (1) The period within which an instrument may be registered is twenty-one days from the day on which it was executed . . .

Effect of Non-Registration

" 13. (1) Every instrument, unless registered in the manner hereinbefore **D** provided, shall upon the expiration of the time for registration, or if the time for registration is extended by the Supreme Court, then upon the expiration of such extended time, be deemed fraudulent and void as against—

- (a) the official receiver or trustee in bankruptcy of the estate of the person whose chattels or any of them are comprised in any such instrument;
- (b) the assignee or trustee acting under any assignment for the benefit **E** of the creditors of such person;
- (c) any person seizing the chattels or any part thereof comprised in any such instrument, in execution of the process of any court authorising the seizure of the chattels of the person by whom or concerning whose chattels such instrument was made, and against every person **F** on whose behalf such process was issued;

so far as regards the property in or right to the possession of any chattels comprised in or affected by the instrument which, at or after the time of such bankruptcy, or of the execution by the grantor of such assignment for the benefit of his creditors, or of the execution of such process (as the case may be), and after the expiration of the period within which the instrument is **G** required to be registered, are in the possession or apparent possession of the person making or giving the instrument, or of any person against whom the process was issued under or in the execution of which the instrument was made or given, as the case may be . . .

" 14. No unregistered instrument comprising any chattels whatsoever shall, without express notice, be valid and effectual as against any bona fide purchaser or mortgagee for valuable consideration, or as against any person **H** bona fide selling or dealing with such chattels as auctioneer or dealer or agent in the ordinary course of his business.

As to Instruments Generally

" 15. Sealing shall not be essential to the validity of any instrument; but every execution of an instrument shall be attested by at least one **I** witness, who shall add to his signature his residence and occupation.

" 16. Every instrument shall be deemed to be made on the day on which it is executed, and shall take effect from the time of its registration.

" 17. Every instrument shall contain or shall have endorsed thereon or annexed thereto a schedule of the chattels comprised therein, and, save as is otherwise expressly provided by this Ordinance, shall give a good

---

(3) See, generally, pp. 633-635, post.

A   title only to the chattels described in the said schedule, and shall be void as against the persons mentioned in s. 13 and s. 14 of this Ordinance in respect of any chattels not so described.

    " 18. Save as is otherwise expressly provided by this Ordinance, an instrument shall be void as against the persons mentioned in s. 13 and s. 14 of this Ordinance in respect of any chattels which the grantor acquires or becomes

B   entitled to after the time of the execution of the instrument.

    " 21. Nothing in this Ordinance shall be deemed to affect any law for the time being in force—

       (*a*) prescribing any formalities to be observed on or about the execution of instruments within the meaning of this Ordinance; or

       (*b*) conferring or securing any rights or claims under or in respect of any

C   such instrument

Chattels

    " 23. Where an instrument is executed after the execution of a prior instrument which has never been registered, and comprises all or any of the chattels comprised in such prior instrument, then if such subsequent instrument is given as a security for the same debt as is secured by the

D   prior instrument, or for any part of such debt, it shall, to the extent to which it is a security for the same debt or part thereof, and so far as respects the chattels comprised in the prior instrument, be void as against the persons mentioned in s. 13 and s. 14 hereof, unless it is proved to the court having cognizance of the case that the subsequent instrument was bona fide given for the purpose of correcting some material error in the prior instrument,

E   and not for the purpose of evading this Ordinance.

Entry of Satisfaction

    " 34. (1) In the case of an instrument, upon the production to the registrar of a memorandum of satisfaction in the form numbered (5) in Sch. 1 hereto or to the like effect, signed by the grantee thereof or his attorney, discharging the chattels comprised in such instrument or any specified part thereof from

F   the moneys secured thereby or any specified part thereof, or from the performance of the obligation thereby secured or any specified part thereof, and on production of such instrument and payment of a fee of five shillings, the registrar shall file such memorandum and make an entry thereof in the register book on the page where the instrument is registered.

    " (2) The execution of such memorandum shall be attested by at least one

G   witness, who shall add to his signature his residence and occupation and shall be verified by the affidavit of that witness."

Section 15 of the Kenya Act imposes a requirement that every execution of an instrument shall be attested. It can be called a " mandatory " provision because it imperatively requires that something shall be done; but the section does not

H   say what the consequence is to be if the thing is not done. It does not say what purposes will fail to be achieved if there is no attestation. Thus the consequence of non-attestation has to be ascertained by implication from the context and the scheme of the Act.

In the immediate context, the wording of the first part of the section and the word " but " introducing the second part suggest that the consequence of non-

I   attestation is invalidity, but the invalidity may be a total invalidity for all purposes or a limited invalidity for some special purposes only.

Section 21 is important, because it tends to show that neither part of s. 15 is to be understood in an unrestricted sense. The first part, providing that " sealing shall not be essential to the validity of any instrument ", only means that no requirement of sealing is imposed for the purposes of this Act: it does not exempt an instrument from any requirement of sealing which may be imposed by any other law for the time being in force. That seems to be the effect of s. 21 (*a*) in its impact on the first part of s. 15. The second part of s. 15 does not mean by implication that an unattested instrument is invalid for all purposes: some **A** other law for the time being in force may confer or secure rights or claims under or in respect of it. That seems to be the effect of s. 21 (*b*) in its impact on the second part of s. 15. There is a probable conclusion that for an unattested instrument the invalidity which is to be implied from s. 15 is not a total invalidity for all purposes but a limited invalidity for some special purposes only. The nature of the special purposes must be gathered from the context and the scheme of the **B** Act.

It was contended on behalf of the respondents that s. 21 should not be taken into account in the construction of s. 15, because s. 21 (though it is said to have been referred to in the argument of a previous case, *Dodhia* v. *National and Grindlays Bank, Ltd.* (4)) was not specifically relied on or referred to in the present case in the argument before WICKS, J., and the Court of Appeal or in **C** their judgments or in the appellants' case in this appeal. Certainly it would have been most helpful to have the assistance of WICKS, J., and the Court of Appeal in considering the bearing of s. 21. It would, however, be too artificial, in considering the context of s. 15, to ignore s. 21 as though it did not form part of the relevant context, which it plainly does, being in the same group of sections. The relevance of s. 21 for purposes of construction does not depend on the existence or **D** nature or contents of any particular " law for the time being in force " of a description referred to in para. (*a*) or para. (*b*) of the section. The elucidation of such matters would require detailed knowledge of the laws of Kenya. The relevance of the section for purposes of construction depends solely on the saving for any such law that there may be, and this saving is plain on the face of the section and could not properly be ignored when the context of s. 15 is being taken into account **E** for purposes of construction. There are, of course, other relevant parts of the context in addition to s. 21.

Section 5 provides that registration of an instrument is to be effected by filing it together with an affidavit in the form numbered (1) in Sch. 1. That form of affidavit contains para. 5:

" The name subscribed in the said instrument as that of the witness attest- **F** ing the due execution thereof by the said [name of grantor] is in the proper hand writing of me this deponent."

Thus it is necessary for the scheme of registration that there shall be an attesting witness. That could be left to inference, but it is more natural to have an express provision in the Act, and such express provision is to be found in the second part **G** of s. 15, which thus completes the scheme of registration. That is a sufficient explanation of the second part of s. 15: an instrument has to be attested as otherwise it cannot be registered. No wider consequence of non-attestation needs to be implied.

Registration is needed in order to make the instrument effective against persons who are not parties to it, but without registration it can be effective as between **H** the parties to it. That appears by necessary implication from s. 13 and s. 14. Then the provision of s. 16 that " every instrument . . . shall take effect from the time of its registration " must be given a limited meaning, i.e., that the instrument takes effect as a registered instrument, good as against persons who are not parties to it, from the time of its registration. That is in harmony with the limited meaning which may be ascribed to s. 15. More generally it can be said that s. 15 **I** is surrounded by s. 13, s. 14, s. 16, s. 17, s. 18 and s. 19, and all of these are concerned with registration and show that the absence of registration affects only relations with persons who are not parties to the instrument and does not affect the relations between the parties to the instrument. It is natural to attribute to s. 15 an effect which is connected and in harmony with the surrounding sections. If the implied invalidity of an unattested instrument is limited to purposes of registration, this result is achieved. The argument that there is a contrast

(4) Civil case No. 914 of 1962, unreported.

A between the limited invalidity imposed by the surrounding sections and a supposed total invalidity imposed by s. 15 breaks down because it involves a petitio principii. Section 15 does not by its express terms impose any invalidity. The invalidity is only implied, and the extent of it has to be inferred from (inter alia) the surrounding sections, and the natural inference from them is that the invalidity is limited.

B Section 23 also provides for limited invalidity. Section 34 to s. 37 are part of the scheme of registration, providing for the termination of the rights conferred by registration. Under s. 34 (2) the memorandum of satisfaction, which is to be filed and entered in the register, is required to be attested, and the wording of the requirement is the same as that used in the second part of s. 15. Both provisions seem to belong to the scheme of registration.

C In the absence of any express provision in s. 15 as to the consequence of non-attestation of an instrument, the natural implication from the provisions of s. 15 and its context and the scheme of the Kenya Act is that an unattested instrument is valid between the parties but incapable of registration and so ineffective against other persons.

This construction of the Kenya Act is supported by cases decided in New

D Zealand. Owing to the statutory history these cases are relevant to the construction of the Kenya Act and may reasonably be regarded as having considerable persuasive authority for that purpose. In New Zealand the bills of sale legislation began in 1856 with an " Act for preventing frauds upon creditors by secret bills of sale of personal chattels ", modelled on the English Bills of Sale Act, 1854, (5) with the same title. There were numerous later Acts in both countries. Under

E the English Bills of Sale Act, 1878, it was held that on the true construction of s. 8 and s. 10 an unattested instrument was not invalid as between the parties (*Davis* v. *Goodman* (6)). The English Act of 1882, (7) contained in s. 8 and s. 9 new provisions whereby non-compliance with certain requirements rendered a bill of sale given by way of security invalid even as between the parties. These new provisions were not adopted in New Zealand. There was in

F New Zealand an Act of 1889 called the Chattels Transfer Act, 1899—" An Act to consolidate and simplify the law relating to transfer of chattels ". Section 49 of that Act provided that

" Sealing shall not be essential to the validity of any instrument: but every execution of an instrument or memorandum of satisfaction shall be attested by one witness, to whose signature shall be added the residence

G and occupation of such witness."

Three cases were decided in New Zealand under that s. 49 of the Chattels Transfer Act, 1889.

The first was *Te Aro Loan Co.* v. *Cameron* (8). The particulars of claim alleged that by instrument by way of security from the defendants to the plaintiff company, and by virtue of the covenants implied therein by the Chattels Transfer

H Act, 1889, the defendants covenanted to pay to the plaintiff company a certain sum and interest. The witness who attested the defendants' signatures to the instrument described himself as " J. Brown, law clerk, Wellington ". The magistrate non-suited the plaintiff company on the ground that the occupation and address of the attesting witness were not sufficiently set out to comply with s. 49

I of the Act of 1889; that the document was therefore not a valid instrument under that Act, and no covenants were therefore implied in it by virtue of the Act; and that the plaintiff company could not, therefore, sustain the action. The plaintiff company appealed to the Supreme Court. WILLIAMS, J. (9) allowed

---

(5) 17 & 18 Vict. c. 36, which was repealed by the Bill of Sale Act, 1878.
(6) [1874-80] All E.R. Rep. 996; (1880), 5 C.P.D. 128.
(7) Bills of Sale (1878) Amendment Act, 1882; 2 HALSBURY'S STATUTES (2nd Edn.) 574.
(8) (1895), 14 N.Z.L.R. 411.   (9) (1895), 14 N.Z.L.R. at p. 416.

the appeal on the ground that the occupation and address of the attesting witness A
were sufficiently set out. Therefore it was not necessary for him to decide, and
he did not decide, what the position would have been if the attestation had been
defective. He made these observations, after holding that the attestation was
sufficient (10):

> " If this were not so, still, the evidence showed that the defendant was B
> indebted to the plaintiff company in the amount claimed, though possibly
> not in covenant. It may be that this s. 98 of the Magistrates' Courts Act,
> 1893 [which gave a limited power of amendment] would prevent the
> magistrate from giving judgment if a simple contract debt only were proved.
> If that is so, it would be a great misfortune; but I am certainly not prepared
> to decide that such is the law."   C

The second New Zealand case was *R.* v. *Dibb Ido* (11). It was a criminal appeal
by way of Case Stated. The prisoner had bought and taken delivery of a bicycle
on Dec. 24, 1896, at a price of £22 10s., giving a bill of sale for £17 10s. and
promising to pay £5 on Dec. 28. The bill of sale was not attested. The prisoner
made no payment, and on Dec. 30 he pledged the bicycle with a pawnbroker for
£8 10s., having stated in answer to a question from the pawnbroker that the D
bicycle was his. He was prosecuted and convicted on two counts (i) for having
fraudulently obtained the sum of £8 10s. by false pretences (ii) under s. 52 of
the Act of 1889 for having, as grantor of an instrument by way of security,
defrauded the grantee. In the appeal counsel for the prisoner contended that as
the bill of sale had not been attested it was not an " instrument by way of
security " within the meaning of the Act of 1889, and so no offence had been E
committed under s. 52. He also contended that, as the document was not an
instrument by way of security, the bicycle was the prisoner's and he made no
false pretence. In the course of the argument EDWARDS, J., said (12):

> " There cannot be any doubt that at common law this document would
> have passed the property back to the vendors. The whole question is, as I F
> understand it, whether this Chattels Transfer Act, 1889, takes away the
> rights which these parties would have had at common law."

A little later WILLIAMS, J., who presided, said (12): " We are satisfied as far as
the first count is concerned ", and the argument proceeded only on the second
count. The judgment of the court (consisting of WILLIAMS, DENNISTON, CONOLLY
and EDWARDS, JJ.) was delivered by CONOLLY, J., who said (13):   G

> " The 52nd clause of the Chattels Transfer Act, 1889, being a penal clause,
> must be read strictly and its provisions should not be held to extend to
> instruments which are not clearly within its scope. In our opinion it only
> applies to valid instruments by way of security under the Act. The document
> given by the prisoner is not such an instrument, since s. 49, which is impera-
> tive, has not been complied with. The conviction under the second count of H
> the indictment was therefore bad. But, as we intimated on the hearing, the
> conviction under the first count of the indictment was good; and the
> conviction is therefore affirmed."

Thus the reasoning of the appeal court for upholding the conviction on the first
count was not fully set out, but it can be inferred to have been that, although I
the bill of sale was not a valid instrument for the purposes of the Act, it was
nevertheless valid as between the parties and had the effect of re-vesting the
ownership of the bicycle in the sellers. That interpretation of the decision in the
Dibb Ido case (11) is confirmed by the headnote in that case and also by
the judgment of DENNISTON, J. (who had been a member of the appeal court in

---

(10) (1895), 14 N.Z.L.R. at p. 417.   (11) (1897), 15 N.Z.L.R. 591.
(12) (1897), 15 N.Z.L.R. at p. 594.   (13) (1897), 15 N.Z.L.R. at p. 595.

A *Dibb Ido* (14)) given in the third New Zealand case, *Lee* v. *Parke's Official Assignee in Bankruptcy* (15). There were several points in issue between the assignee in bankruptcy and the holder of a bill of sale granted by the bankrupt. It will be sufficient for the present purpose to set out extracts from the first paragraph of the judgment (16).

B " In my opinion non-compliance with . . . the provision in s. 49 requiring every instrument to be attested by one witness in the manner therein provided, does not invalidate such instrument as between the parties. There is nothing in the Act which declares that such non-compliance shall . . . have such effect. The result of such non-compliance would seem only to make the instrument incapable of registration under the Act, or, if registered, to deprive the grantee of the benefit of such registration. Under the English Act of

C 1882 the consequence of non-registration is to avoid the instrument even between grantor and grantee: there is no such provision in the New Zealand Act. In *Davis* v. *Goodman* (17) it was held that non-compliance with the provision which required attestation by a solicitor did not render the instrument void as between grantor and grantee. In *R.* v. *Dibb Ido* (14) the Court of Appeal held that an unattested instrument given by way of security

D was effectual as between the parties to transfer the property to the grantee. And see *Te Aro Loan Co.* v. *Cameron* (18)."

That is a clear statement of the ratio decidendi of the Court of Appeal of New Zealand in the *Dibb Ido* case (14). Apparently there has not been any later case in New Zealand on this point after the judgment in *Lee's* case (19), which may

E thus be said to have held the field for more than sixty years.

The New Zealand Act of 1889 and certain other Acts were consolidated by the Chattels Transfer Act, 1908. Section 49 of the Act of 1889 was replaced by two provisions in the Act of 1908. Section 17 provided that

" Sealing shall not be essential to the validity of any instrument; but every execution of an instrument shall be attested by at least one witness, who

F shall add to his signature his residence and occupation."

Section 37 (2), referring to a memorandum of satisfaction, provided that

" The execution of such memorandum shall be attested by at least one witness, who shall add to his signature his residence and occupation, and shall be verified by the affidavit of that witness."

G Those provisions were repeated verbatim in s. 20 and s. 42 (2) of the Chattels Transfer Act, 1924 (another consolidating Act) of New Zealand and in s. 15 and s. 34 (2) of the Kenya Act under which the question at issue in this appeal arises. It is not disputed that the Kenya Act was modelled on the New Zealand Act of 1924. It seems clear that the decisions in the New Zealand cases of *Dibb Ido* (14) and *Lee* (19) to which reference has been made must apply to s. 20 of

H the New Zealand Act of 1924 and so be relevant authorities for the construction of s. 15 of the Kenya Act, and may properly be considered important authorities for that purpose.

Counsel for the appellant bank sought to attribute a greater effect to the New Zealand decisions. Reference was made to passages in CRAIES ON STATUTE LAW (6th Edn.) pp. 139, 141, 172. At p. 139 there is a citation from an Australian

I case *D'Emden* v. *Pedder* (20) cited in *Webb* v. *Outrim* (21):

" When a particular form of legislative enactment, which has received authoritative interpretation, whether by judicial decision or by a long course of practice, is adopted in the framing of a later statute, it is a sound rule of

---

(14) (1897), 15 N.Z.L.R. 591. (15) (1903), 22 N.Z.L.R. 747 at p. 750.
(16) (1903), 22 N.Z.L.R. at p. 750.
(17) [1874-80] All E.R. Rep. 996; (1880), 5 C.P.D. 128.
(18) (1895), 14 N.Z.L.R. 411. (19) (1903), 22 N.Z.L.R. 747.
(20) (1904), 1 C.L.R. 91 at p. 110. (21) [1907] A.C. 81 at p. 89.

construction to hold that the words so adopted were intended by the   A
legislature to bear the meaning which has been so put upon them."

As there are other grounds for the decision of this appeal, it is not necessary to go
into this point at length. It is enough to say that prima facie it seems unsafe
to assume that, when the Kenya Act of 1930 was originally made as an ordinance
modelled on the New Zealand Act of 1924, the ordinance-making authority
must necessarily be supposed to have intended to import into Kenya the case-law   B
of New Zealand decided under a previous New Zealand Act. NEWBOLD, J.A.,
said in the course of his judgment:

> " I accept that when Kenya adopts the legislation of a Commonwealth
> country with a similar system of law, then, in construing the provisions of
> the adopted legislation, regard should be had to the judicial decisions of
> the Commonwealth country on the meaning of the equivalent section. I   C
> accept that proposition subject to two qualifications: first that any such
> decision is not absolutely binding and may be disregarded if in the view
> of the East African court the decision is clearly wrong; and, secondly, that
> such decisions disclose a consistent interpretation of the section in question
> and are not at variance one with another."
>   D

No fault is to be found in this statement of principle, but in the view of the
majority of their lordships it was not correctly applied in the present case, because
examination of the New Zealand decisions shows that there was no inconsistency
or variance in them and their construction of the relevant provisions was correct.

For the reasons which have been given the appeal will be allowed and the case
will be remitted to the High Court of Kenya for judgment to be entered in   E
favour of the appellant bank. The respondents must pay to the appellant bank
its costs of the action and of the appeal and cross-appeal to the Court of Appeal
for Eastern Africa and of this appeal.

LORD MORRIS OF BORTH-Y-GEST: I have the misfortune to differ
in my conclusion from that which has been reached by the majority of the
Board. With diffidence I feel that I must express my view though I can do so   F
quite shortly.

It seems clear that the seizure by the appellant bank of the respondent's goods
would constitute trespass unless the appellant bank were permitted and entitled
to act as they did. In agreement with the majority of the Board and in agreement
with all the members of the Court of Appeal I consider that the events which took
place in the month of October, 1960, did not by themselves give such entitlement.   G

On the basis of that view the only asserted justification of the seizure was
that cl. 9 of the letter of hypothecation gave a right to seize. The appellant bank
relied therefore on the letter of hypothecation. Without it they had no answer
to a claim in trespass. Within the definition contained in s. 2 of the Chattels
Transfer Ordinance (22) the letter of hypothecation was unquestionably an
" instrument ". It gave a licence to take possession of chattels as security for   H
any debt. It was precisely that licence which the bank exercised. It was vital
therefore for the bank to have a valid instrument.

In a section (s. 15) of the Ordinance which was the first section in a group of
sections under the heading " As to instruments generally " it was provided that

> " Sealing shall not be essential to the validity of any instrument; but   I
> every execution of an instrument shall be attested by at least one witness,
> who shall add to his signature his residence and occupation."

That section deals with validity. In my view it lays down that though sealing is
not essential to validity attestation is. The word " but " points to that conclusion.
So in my view does the word " shall ". That word is imperative. There is a
mandatory requirement that an instrument must be attested. There must be

_____

(22) Dated June 13, 1930, and hereinbefore called " the Kenya Act ".

A   at least one witness. Furthermore there is a mandatory requirement that a witness must add his signature and also his residence and also his occupation. In contrast to something that is not " essential " those mandatory requirements are essential. Even if the word " essential " did not by itself convey its own meaning it is made plain that the word is used in the sense of being essential to validity. An unattested instrument is therefore not a valid instrument. Though the

B   Ordinance contains provisions for registration (and prescribes the effect of non-registration) the path to registration does not and cannot begin until there is a valid instrument. Whether in the present case if the appellant bank had secured a valid instrument they would or would not have had an instrument that could take some effect before registration (see s. 16) and whether registration would in this particular case, having regard to the terms of the instrument and to the

C   provisions of s. 18, have been of much or only of limited advantage, are questions which in my view need not now be considered.

    The Chattels Transfer Ordinance, which was dated June 13, 1930, was " An Ordinance to make Provision Relating to Chattel Securities and the Transfer of Chattels ". It is clear that it was modelled on New Zealand legislation which in turn was considerably derived from English legislation. Section 15 of the

D   Ordinance may be seen to correspond to certain sections in the New Zealand Acts of 1924 and of 1908 which in turn derive from s. 49 of an earlier New Zealand Act of 1889. That section however had no ancestry in the English Acts.

    Though it is interesting and valuable to study the legislation which was undoubtedly used as a guide and basis by those who drafted the Kenya Ordinance the problem which now arises is essentially one of interpreting the Kenya

E   Ordinance as enacted. I do not think that it should be assumed that the Ordinance was enacted on the basis that there was full knowledge of and full acceptance of any decisions in the courts of the country whose legislation was being used as a guide and basis in drafting. When problems of construction arise any such decisions will however naturally be studied in a search for guidance and will be considered with special respect. I have endeavoured so to consider the New

F   Zealand cases cited to the Board.

    The present case depends in my view on the construction of the words in s. 15. I do not find any assistance from a consideration of s. 21 (the effect of which section does not appear to have been canvassed in the Court of Appeal). That section is a saving clause. There is a saving of the effect of " any law for the time being in force " prescribing formalities concerning the execution of instruments or

G   securing rights under them. It was not suggested that there was any such law that called for consideration.

    In my view the words in s. 15 are mandatory and obligatory. The section enacts that every execution of an instrument " shall be attested " in a particular way. It so enacts in the context of " validity ". I do not think that it would be reasonable to read into the section some words to the effect that in certain circum-

H   stances an instrument that has not been attested as directed (and which therefore lacks validity) may nevertheless (e.g., as between the parties) be regarded as only partially invalid. There are no such words. Nor are there any words to the effect that the section is only to apply to instruments which it is proposed to register. In *Liverpool Borough Bank* v. *Turner* (23), SIR WILLIAM PAGE WOOD, V.C., said :

I   ". . . if the legislature enacts that a transaction must be carried out in a particular way, the words that otherwise it shall be invalid at law and in equity are mere surplusage."

On appeal LORD CAMPBELL, L.C., in approving the judgment of the Vice-Chancellor said (24):

---

(23) (1860), 1 John & H. 159 at p. 169.
(24) (1860), 2 De G.F. & J. 502 at pp. 507, 508.

" No universal rule can be laid down for the construction of statutes as **A** to whether mandatory enactments shall be considered directory only or obligatory with an implied nullification for disobedience. It is the duty of courts of justice to try to get at the real intention of the legislature by carefully attending to the whole scope of the statute to be construed."

In regard to s. 15 where there is a mandatory direction in a section dealing with the validity of instruments I consider that the provision as to attestation **B** is a positive and obligatory one: failing obedience to it an instrument is not a valid instrument. That being so it seems to me that in failing to have the instrument attested the bank failed to secure a valid instrument. When the time came that they wished to depend on a clause in an instrument in order to protect themselves from an act that, if done without permission, would be trespass they only had an instrument which by reason of non-compliance with the law was an **C** invalid instrument. The courts ought not in my view in defiance of the law to give recognition to it. I agree therefore with the judgment of WICKS, J., in regard to this point and on this and on all other points with the three judgments in the Court of Appeal.

Appeal allowed.

 D

Solicitors: *Sanderson, Lee, Morgan, Price & Co.* (for the appellant); *Merriman, White & Co.* (for the respondents).

[*Reported by* KATHLEEN J. H. O'BRIEN, *Barrister-at-Law.*]

 E

PRACTICE DIRECTION.

PROBATE, DIVORCE AND ADMIRALTY DIVISION (DIVORCE). **F**

Divorce — Practice — Ancillary relief—Discovery — Application for monetary provision—Procedure where discovery or disclosure inadequate.

In any proceedings comprising an application for a monetary provision where, before the appointment for hearing, a party is advised that discovery or disclosure is inadequate, the solicitors should write to the other side asking for a supple- **G** mentary list of documents (or affidavit if necessary) dealing specifically with alleged lacunae in any earlier one; or, if the alleged lacunae appear in the evidence filed, they should submit a questionnaire to be answered by letter (or on oath if that course is necessary).

If this procedure is not followed, or if the party called on thus to supplement the disclosure has unreasonably failed to do so, these matters may be taken into **H** account by the registrar or judge in dealing with the costs of any adjournment thereby rendered necessary, or otherwise when costs fall to be dealt with.

COMPTON MILLER,

May 12, 1966. Senior Registrar.

A

KURSAAL CASINO, LTD. *v.* CRICKITT.

[QUEEN'S BENCH DIVISION (Lord Parker, C.J., Sachs and Veale, JJ.), March 23, 24, 1966.]

Gaming—Lawful and unlawful gaming—Clubs—Roulette—Odds favoured bank—
Players given option of taking bank provided they could meet commitments
if bank lost—Stakes on single spin of the wheel might amount to £500—
Whether gaming so conducted that chances equally favourable to all players—
Betting, Gaming and Lotteries Act 1963 (c. 2), *s.* 32 (1) (*a*) (ii).

B

C

D

The appellants owned a proprietary club at which on six separate dates in March and April, 1965, the game of roulette was played. The game was played by a number of persons ranging from three to fifty, who sat or stood round roulette tables. The values of chips staked varied but occasionally amounted to as much as £500 in respect of all the players staking on a single spin. A croupier was in attendance at each table for periods of half an hour each, and before commencing his first spin he would announce that the bank was up for option. Any member of the assembled players could thereupon take the bank, if he could show that he was able to meet the financial commitments involved if the bank should lose whilst he was in possession of it, i.e., there was a means test before anyone could take the bank. The players all knew of this requirement. Only once in eighteen months had a player taken the bank, and on all other occasions the bank had been held by a croupier on behalf of the appellants. The odds varied in favour of the bank from three to eleven per cent. The appellants were charged with unlawful gaming contrary to s. 32 (4) of the Betting, Gaming and Lotteries Act 1963. The gaming would be lawful only if within s. 32 (1) (*a*) (ii)*, that is, if so conducted that the chances therein were equally favourable to all players. The magistrates found that the offer of the bank to the assembled players did not mean that the gaming was so conducted that the chances therein were equally favourable to all the players because an offer could only be deemed to be genuine if it was capable of acceptance, and there was no evidence that the financial status of most of the members of the club would make it possible for them to be able to accept the offer under any circumstances. On appeal against conviction,

E

F

Held: it was a question of fact and degree whether an offer to take the bank at roulette was genuine in the sense that it was so capable of attracting and likely to attract acceptance as to cause the gaming to be " so conducted that the chances were equally favourable to all players " within s. 32 (1) (*a*) (ii) of the Act of 1963; on the evidence there was ample material on which the magistrates could reach their finding that the option in the present case was not genuine in the sense previously stated, and accordingly the conviction should stand (see p. 642, letter G, and p. 643, letter C, post).

G

Casino Club (Bolton), Ltd. v. *Parr* ((1966), 64 L.G.R. 155) considered.

H

[As to lawful and unlawful gaming, see SUPPLEMENT to 18 HALSBURY'S LAWS (3rd Edn.) title, Gaming and Wagering, para. 369A, 3; and for cases on unlawful games, see 25 DIGEST (Repl.) 448-450, *292-302.*

For the Betting, Gaming and Lotteries Act 1963, s. 32, see 43 HALSBURY'S STATUTES (2nd Edn.) 343.]

I Case referred to:
Casino Club (Bolton), Ltd. v. *Parr*, (1966), 64 L.G.R. 155.

Case Stated.

This was a Case Stated by the justices for the county borough of Southend-on-Sea in respect of their adjudication as a magistrates' court on Sept. 17, 1965. The appellants, Kursaal Casino, Ltd., were convicted on informations laid by the respondent of being concerned in the management of unlawful gaming contrary

---

* Section 32 (1), so far as material, is set out at p. 641, letter C, post.

to s. 32 (4) of the Betting, Gaming and Lotteries Act 1963. The facts found in A
the Case Stated are summarised in the judgment of SACHS, J.

The cases noted below* were cited during the argument in addition to the case
referred to in the judgment of SACHS, J.

Sebag Shaw, Q.C. and *William Denny* for the appellants.
M. D. L. Worsley for the respondent.

B

SACHS, J., delivered the first judgment at the request of LORD PARKER,
C.J.: The appellants, who are the owners of the Kursaal Casino Club, were
convicted of being concerned in the management of unlawful gaming, that is to
say, of roulette which took place on the relevant premises contrary to s. 32 (4)
of the Betting, Gaming and Lotteries Act 1963.

The convictions related to gaming that had taken place on Mar. 4, 5 and 6, and C
on Apr. 17, 20 and 14, 1965. That gaming was roulette played according to what
appear to be standard casino rules, and the essential facts as found by the magistrates, were as follows. The club occupied premises on the Eastern Esplanade;
it was a proprietary club owned by the appellants; the gaming took place on
the club premises as an activity of the club on each of the relevant dates; the
club was in charge of and responsible for the gaming; the club was so constituted D
as not to be of a merely temporary character; and the club was conducted in a
perfectly proper manner. The roulette in question was played by a number of
persons ranging from three to fifty, who sat or stood around roulette tables;
and the value of the chips staked on any one spin of the wheel naturally varied,
but occasionally amounted to as much as £500 in respect of all the players staking
on a single spin.

E

Then the findings deal with the actual method of play in relation to the
holding of the bank. Each croupier was in attendance at the roulette table
for periods of half an hour, those periods apparently being arranged so that the
croupiers could have reasonable relief; the croupier before commencing his first
spin announced that " The bank is up for option ", and in this way gave any one
of those present an opportunity to act as banker; the same procedure was adopted F
by each croupier as he took over his period at the table; and moreover at any time
after any spin any member of the assembled players could take the bank if he
so desired, and if—and this may be important—he could also show that he
was able to meet the financial commitments should the bank lose whilst he was
in possession. (In other words there was a means test before anybody could take
the bank.) It is also found as a fact that members were aware of this procedure, G
and there is also a finding, from which I in no way desire to differ, in effect that if
there happened to be a member who was both willing and able to take the offer
of the bank and who could pass the means test, then he would in fact be allowed
to take the bank. Further findings of fact show that if none of the players present
wished to take over the bank, it would in fact be taken by a croupier on behalf
of the appellants, and that indeed during a period of eighteen months there was H
only one evening when a person other than a croupier acting on behalf of the
appellants had taken the bank.

The Case then deals with the question of the odds, and as in all this type of
gaming, the odds are in favour of the banker. Zero being as usual one of the
numbers to which the spin might direct the ball, it is stated that the odds in
favour of the bank ranged from three per cent. to eleven per cent. according I
to the combination of numbers on which a player had staked. It is thus to
be noted that if, as would appear, that means that were there was an average
of seven per cent. in favour of the bank, the odds resulted in a sizeable advantage which can perhaps be envisaged in relation to what would happen if there
was £500 worth of chips on a single spin. It is also as well to state the obvious—
that in the main the advantages of a roulette banker derive under standard

---

* *Rogers* v. *Cowley*, [1962] 2 All E.R. 683, *Mills* v. *MacKinnon*, [1964] 1 All E.R. 155;
Vellard v. *Raymond*, [1964] 1 All E.R. 564; [1964] 2 Q.B. 108.

A casino rules from what happens if zero turns up. Those rules can of course be modified so as substantially to nullify that particular advantage, but no such modification had apparently been made here.

Those being the main facts, one turns to s. 32 of the Betting, Gaming and Lotteries Act 1963. Of that section it is only necessary to mention that this was a case in which by sub-s. (2)

B "... it shall be held that the gaming was unlawful gaming unless it is proved that the gaming was conducted in accordance with the conditions set out in sub-s. (1) of this section."

Then sub-s. (1) in so far as relevant reads:

C "... any gaming shall be lawful if, but only if, it is conducted in accordance with the following conditions, that is to say—(*a*) that either (i) the chances in the game are equally favourable to all the players; or (ii) the gaming is so conducted that the chances therein are equally favourable to all the players ..."

It was naturally conceded on behalf of the appellants that roulette could not be brought within sub-s. (1) (*a*) (i), and their case turned in substance on whether

D it could be brought within sub-s. (1) (*a*) (ii), because of the option announced to and known to the players, as already stated.

In this behalf, the appellants relied on the decision in the case of *Casino Club (Bolton), Ltd.* v. *Parr* (1). That case too was concerned inter alia with roulette played on similar rules. There the appellant and his brother, the sole directors and shareholders of the proprietary club, almost invariably held the bank, either

E individually or jointly, although the bank was offered regularly to other players on a limited basis. The essence of the matter which was the subject of decision in that case can be taken from the following passages in the judgment of WINN, L.J., who gave the first judgment. He refers to the finding in the Case Stated that (2):

F " The whole session of two hours was never available to any player other than the second named appellant and/or his brother, ... [and then, later, he puts the case thus] Put perhaps more directly to the point, the chances of any player other than Mr. Atherton Howcroft [Mr. Atherton Howcroft was the brother who was one of the appellants] in the relevant session, of enjoying the advantages of being banker were not equally favourable with the chances

G of Mr. Atherton Howcroft in respect of being banker. That which they had respectively a chance of acquiring was not the same thing; respectively they had a chance of acquiring different things, the one being more valuable than the other, a two hour bank or a forty minute bank."

It is also to be noted that the position of a banker player was dealt with by WINN, L.J., as follows (3):

H " I am further constrained to say that ... a person can be a player in the capacity of banker even though he does not participate in any way in the playing of the game, and even though he be absent at all times when the bank is being managed by a croupier on his behalf."

I mention that point because there is thus disposed of one of the issues raised in the present case.

I The *Bolton* case (1) was decided on the assumption that the offers to players in relation to the bank were made genuinely in the requisite sense discussed later in this judgment: and the decision there was that even if those offers were thus genuine, they were not such as to bring the appellants within the protection of sub-s. (1) (*a*) (ii) which has been quoted. It is perhaps relevant to note that I myself said in that case (4):

---

(1) (1966), 64 L.G.R. 155.   (2) (1966), 64 L.G.R. at p. 164.

(3) (1966) 64 L.G.R. at p. 166.   (4) (1966), 64 L.G.R. at p. 167.

"I would only emphasise that in this case there has not been explored,   A
nor has there been a need to explore, the question at what stage and in what
circumstances the fact that the proprietors of a club (or some person with the
approval of the proprietors) so consistently hold the bank for such a high
proportion of the gaming sessions over a sufficient period might cause the
court to hold that on the realities of the case the conduct of the gaming
on that ground alone falls within the mischief of one or other of the pro-   B
visions of s. 32. That is a matter which may well fall for consideration on
some future occasion."

In other words, in the *Bolton* case (5) it was assumed that the theoretical position
—perhaps paper position is a convenient phrase—so corresponded with the
realities that the gaming was so conducted that the chances therein could in truth
be calculated simply by reference to what was announced. In cases such as the   C
present, however, it may be that though on paper persons other than the proprietors of the club appear to have an equal chance with those proprietors of
having a share in the running of the bank, yet there may be a question of fact
whether, having regard to the particular circumstances over the relevant period,
those paper facilities coincide with the realities. In that connexion, it is to
my mind permissible to enquire into a number of factors. Those can include the   D
type of person who normally frequented the club, the upper limit of the stakes,
the sum that might be reasonably expected to be at risk during the period while
a player held the bank, and last but not least what in fact happened over a
considerable number of sessions of gaming. The factors might also include an
examination of the relation of the number of people playing at any one time to
the number of occasions on which the option could be exercised. Just as an exorbi-   E
tant demand of say £1,000 as a fee or even as deposit for taking the bank could
on the realities ensure that in substance the proprietors held the bank continuously and that the other players as a whole did not have an equal or indeed
any material opportunity of holding it, so other factors could produce the same
result.

In the course of argument counsel for the appellants conceded, as indeed in   F
logic he had to, that if his submissions were accepted then no matter how high the
limit of the stakes, and no matter how low the financial status of ninety-nine per
cent. of the players over a long period, yet the case would fall within the protection of sub-s. (1) (a) (ii) providing the club was prepared to allow an exceptional man with sufficient money to take the bank. If so, of course, the door is
wide open for the establishment of casinos where the roulette is consistently   G
in the hands of some banker to such an extent that it would defeat the object
of the limitation provided by that subsection. Whether an offer of the bank is
such that it is genuine in the sense that in relation to those normally playing it is
so capable of attracting acceptances and so likely to attract them as to cause the
gaming to be " so conducted that the chances therein are equally favourable to
all players ", (I would emphasise the words " all players "), is to my mind a   H
question of fact and of degree.

I now turn back to the findings in relation to this particular case. When one
comes to the views expressed by the magistrates one finds at para. 6 the following:

" We were of the opinion that the gaming was not lawful for the following
reasons:—(a) that the offer of the bank to the assembled players did not
mean that the gaming was so conducted that the chances therein were   I
equally favourable to all the players because . . . [I pass over sub-paras.
(i) and (ii) that follow ' because ' and come to the one that has been the
main subject of discussion before this court, that is to say sub-para. (iii)] an
offer could only be deemed to be genuine if it was capable of acceptance and
there was no evidence that the financial status of most of the members of the
club would make it possible for them to be able to accept the offer under any
circumstances."

(5) (1966), 64 L.G.R. 155.

A It appears to me that the magistrates were correctly directing their minds on the relevant point, and that here is a finding of fact that the option offered was not a genuine one within the meaning of that word as above indicated. That can be a valid finding, however true it may have been, that if some exceptional player had come along who could have passed the means test, he would have been allowed to accept the offer and take his turn at the bank. When one observes

B that during a period of as long as eighteen months the bank was held by a player other than the proprietary club on one single occasion only, that the stakes could run to £500 on a single spin of the wheel, that there was a means test before one could take the bank, and that the only indication with regard to the nature of the membership of the club given in the Case Stated was that the membership included members of the borough police force, there was ample evidence on which

C the magistrates could come to the above conclusion as to the option not being genuine in that sense, whether regarded from the angle of onus of proof or whether regarded as an inference from the other facts found. Indeed, there was ample material on which an inference could be drawn that for a considerable period the appellants had been deliberately carrying on the gaming on the profitable basis that no one but the proprietors of the club was as a rule to have any share in the

D bank: and where standard casino rules are in operation such a method of gaming is something very different from gaming where all players have a chance equally favourable with that of a player banker.

In coming to the above conclusions, it will be noted that it has been assumed, without however deciding the point, that the offer of the " option " would, but for the factors above set out, have brought the appellants within the pro-

E tection of sub-s. (1) (*a*) (ii). This is, however, not a matter for which on my part any opinion is expressed. Moreover, it is right to note that counsel for the respondent in that behalf reserved his position to make certain submissions. These included first a submission that the only effect of the offer of the bank was that, if accepted, the chances of the person who accepted it might well be altered, and that such an effect was something which did not sufficiently

F carry the appellants within the protection of the above subsection. Secondly, he desired to call attention to the fact that in both (i) and (ii) of sub-s. (1) (*a*) of s. 32 the word used was " are " and not " might be "; and he desired to found an argument directed to the position of players who in fact do not adopt a course different from that which they in fact did adopt, and that course was not contrary to any rules of the game. Those points I imply note. Moreover,

G I should mention that there are other issues raised in the Case Stated, some of which have already been dealt with in the course of this judgment, and others need not in my view be further discussed. It is sufficient to my mind to say that on the grounds already stated, I would dismiss this appeal.

VEALE, J.: I agree, and there is nothing which I can usefully add.

H   LORD PARKER, C.J.: I also agree.

Appeal dismissed with costs. The court certified under s. 1 of the Administration of Justice Act, 1960, that a point of law of public general importance was involved, viz.: " In a game of chance, such as roulette, in which there is a bank, and which is played according to rules under which the chances are more favourable to the bank than to the other players, does the standing offer of the bank to any player who wishes

I *to take it, of itself, and irrespective of the circumstances in which it is made, render the chances in the gaming equally favourable to all the players therein in compliance with s. 32 (1) (a) (ii) of the Betting, Gaming and Lotteries Act 1963?". The court refused leave to appeal to the House of Lords.*

Solicitors: *Nelson Mitchell & Williams*, Southend-on-Sea (for the appellants); *Prosecuting Solicitor*, Southend-on-Sea (for the respondent).

[*Reported by* N. P. METCALFE, ESQ., *Barrister-at-Law.*]

R. v. ANDERSON AND MORRIS.   A

[COURT OF CRIMINAL APPEAL (Lord Parker, C.J., Edmund Davies, Marshall, Roskill and James, JJ.), May 2, 1966.]

Criminal Law—Concerted action—Joint enterprise—Death following act of one joint adventurer going beyond tacit agreement—Whether co-adventurer who took no part in killing guilty of manslaughter.   B

Where two person embark on a joint enterprise, each is liable criminally for acts done in pursuance of the joint enterprise, including unusual consequences arising from the execution of the joint enterprise; but if one of them goes beyond what has been tacitly agreed as part of the joint enterprise, the other is not liable for the consequences of the unauthorised act (*see* p. 647, letters D to G, *post*).   C

> *R. v. Smith* ([1963] 3 All E.R. 597) applied.
> *R. v. Salisbury* ((1553), 1 Plowd. 100) not followed.
> *R. v. Betty* ((1963), 48 Cr. App. Rep. 6) commented on.

M., having been engaged in a fight in a street with one W., accompanied A. later on the same day to a different street, where A. attacked W., stabbing him with a knife so that he died. M. denied that he knew A. had a knife   D and that he joined in this fatal attack on W. A. said that he called on M. to assist him, but that the latter refused to do so. The jury were directed that if they thought that there was a common design by A. and M. to attack W. but that it was not proved that M. had any intention to kill W., or to cause him grievous bodily harm, and that the act was outside the common design to which M. had been a party, then they could find A.   E guilty of murder and M. of manslaughter, provided the latter took part in the attack or fight with W. A. was convicted of non-capital murder and M. was convicted of manslaughter. On appeal,

Held: the direction to the jury was a misdirection, the law being as stated at letter B above, and M.'s conviction would be quashed (*see* p. 648, letters F and G, *post*).   F

[As to common design involving homicide, see 10 HALSBURY'S LAWS (3rd Edn.) 715, para. 1370; and for cases on the subject, see 14 DIGEST (Repl.) 91-93, *533, 536, 538-540, 551-561.*]

Cases referred to:

R. v. Betty, [1963] 3 All E.R. 602, n.; 48 Cr. App. Rep. 6; Digest (Cont. Vol. A) 335, *558a.*   G

R. v. Salisbury, (1553), 1 Plowd. 100; 75 E.R. 158; 15 Digest (Repl.) 950, *9174.*

R. v. Smith (Wesley) (1961), [1963] 3 All E.R. 597; [1963] 1 W.L.R. 1200; 128 J.P. 13; Digest (Cont. Vol. A) 335, *542a.*

Applications.

These were applications by Lascelles Fitzalbert Anderson and Emmanuel Morris for leave to appeal against their convictions at Nottingham Assizes   H on July 28, 1965, before HOWARD, J., and a jury. The applicant Anderson was convicted of murder and the applicant Morris of manslaughter, for which the applicant Anderson was sentenced to imprisonment for life and the applicant Morris to three years' imprisonment. The applications first came before the court (MELFORD STEVENSON, PHILLIMORE and THOMPSON, JJ.) on Apr. 6, 1966, when they were adjourned for a court of five judges.   I

The authorities and cases noted below* were cited during the argument in addition to the cases referred to in the judgment.

---

* 1 HALE'S PLEAS OF THE CROWN (1736 Edn.) 446; KENNY'S OUTLINES OF CRIMINAL LAW (15th Edn., 1936), p. 162, footnote 1; *Thody's Case,* (1673), 1 Freem. K.B. 514; *R. v. Edmeads,* (1828), 3 C. & P. 390; *Duffy's Case,* (1830), 1 Lew. C.C. 60; *R. v. Macklin,* (1838), 2 Lew. C.C. 225; *R. v. Price,* (1858), 8 Cox, C.C. 96; *R. v. Luck,* (1862), 3 F. & F. 483; *R. v. Skeet,* (1866), 4 F. & F. 931; *R. v. Caton,* (1874), 12 Cox, C.C. 624; *Kwaku Mensah* v. *Regem,* [1946] A.C. 83.

A   *Geoffrey Lane, Q.C.*, and *John Machin* for the applicant Morris.
H. A. Skinner, Q.C., and *P. J. Walmsley* for the applicant Anderson.
Bernard Caulfield, Q.C., and *C. J. S. French, Q.C.*, for the Crown.

LORD PARKER, C.J., delivered the following judgment of the court:
The two applicants were indicted at Nottingham Assizes in July, 1965, with the
B   murder of a man called Welch. In the result the applicant Anderson was
convicted of what was then non-capital murder, and the applicant Morris of
manslaughter. The applicant Anderson was imprisoned for life, and the applicant Morris was sentenced to a term of three years' imprisonment. They now
each apply for leave to appeal against their convictions.

The facts must be stated in a little detail. The prosecution case in effect was
C   that on May 24, 1965, this man Welch met the applicant Anderson's wife. She
was a white person and a convicted prostitute. The applicant Anderson and
the applicant Morris are both coloured. She apparently took Welch back to
her flat where, so it was said, he tried to strangle her. She ran into the street
pursued by Welch, met the applicant Morris, told him what had happened, and
the applicant Morris and Welch fought. A time came when, so the prosecution
D   said, the applicant Anderson arrived on the scene, learned from his wife what
had happened, got a knife in the applicant Morris' presence, and went off with
the applicant Morris and his wife in a car to find Welch. When Welch was found,
it was said there was a fight as a result of which the applicant Anderson stabbed
Welch to death. That was the prosecution case and it was supported by the
evidence of Mrs. Anderson, and particularly of a man called Christopher. Mr.
E   Christopher described how he had found the applicant Morris and Welch fighting,
that he pretended to be a police officer, separated them and in fact went back
with them to Mrs. Anderson's flat. On the way Mrs. Anderson told them what
had happened and how he, Welch, had tried to strangle her. He also described
the applicant Anderson's arrival on the scene, his anger when he was told by his
wife what had happened, and then proceeded to give this evidence which clearly
F   affected both of the applicants. According to Mr. Christopher, the applicant
Anderson, in the presence of the applicant Morris and himself, went into the
kitchen and armed himself with a knife before they set off to find Welch. A
little later, they apparently arrived at the Granby Hotel, which was an address
which Mrs. Anderson had given them, where she understood Welch was to be
found. The evidence of the wife of the licensee was that after closing time the
G   door bell rang, and when she went down, she found the two applicants there
asking for a man who was said to be of the name of Wisbey or Wesbey. It
so happened, according to the wife of the licensee, Mrs. Binless, that about that
moment a man came along, and that the applicant Morris had said: " Here he
comes now." She then described the incident in which undoubtedly Welch
was stabbed. According to her, the taller of the coloured men, undoubtedly
H   the applicant Anderson, was punching Welch and the applicant Morris was
standing at his back apparently not taking any definite part in the fight. She
went on to describe how the time came when Welch seemed to be trying to push
past the applicant Anderson, and she got hold of Welch's coat and tugged him.
What happened then was that Welch appeared to dive, as she put it, quickly into
the door of the public house, and collapsed and died. In fact he was stabbed in
I   three places, one 3½ inches deep and into the heart. The police proceeded to
question the two applicants. When the applicant Anderson was asked if he
knew anything about this man who had died, he replied—" No, God Almighty,
no ". Later he said—" It was all over in two minutes. I do not know what
really happened ". He then proceeded to make a statement under caution,
the gist of which was that Welch had attacked him, held him and struck him,
and went on: " I maybe had my knife in my pocket and I took it out. It
wasn't even two minutes. I don't know what happened to the knife." In fact
a bloodstained knife was found in an alley way outside the hotel. The applicant

Morris when questioned at first told a lie. He said that he had not been in **A**
Station Street where this incident took place; he said that he had been in his
room from half past five to quarter past eleven and had not been near the scene
of the incident.   Later he confessed that that was a lie, and according to the
police said this:

> " I will give you the truth.   I fight with this man but I not use knife.
> I do not know about the knife being used.   I will give you a statement   **B**
> about it."

In evidence he said that what he was there referring to in fighting Welch was
not the incident when Welch got stabbed but the incident earlier in Cranmer
Street when Mrs. Anderson had come up to him followed by Welch, and in
a statement given afterwards he stated the same, in other words that he had had   **C**
no part in the fighting in Station Street, but had undoubtedly fought Welch at
an earlier stage.   He also denied that the applicant Anderson had armed himself
with a knife in his presence, and denied that he had any idea that a knife was
going to be used. He also denied taking any part in the fight during which
Welch was stabbed.   In passing, it is to be observed that the applicant Anderson's
evidence to a large extent was to the same effect.   He did say that he had a   **D**
knife with him, that he had used it having lost control of himself, but he denied
that the applicant Morris had helped in any way.   Indeed, he went further,
and said that he called on the applicant Morris to help him and that the applicant
Morris refused to do so.   So far as the applicant Anderson is concerned, there
was clearly evidence on which the jury could arrive at their verdict, the verdict
of murder, and in fact before us no suggestion has been made that there was   **E**
any misdirection in regard to the applicant Anderson in the summing-up.   So
far as the applicant Morris is concerned, there was indeed very little evidence
that he had taken any part in the fight in Station Street.   Indeed almost the
only evidence was this statement of his in which he admitted fighting a man which,
as he alleged, although the jury must have found to the contrary, was referring
to the earlier incident in Cranmer Street.   **F**

The position today is that evidence has been produced which throws, to say
the least, a doubt as to how far the jury were entitled to accept the evidence of
Mr. Christopher as accurate.   I say no more about what has been discovered
with regard to Mr. Christopher, because counsel for the prosecution has very
frankly and properly admitted, without the evidence having to be called before
us, that it is fresh evidence and is evidence of a character which would justify   **G**
this court in exercising their powers under the Criminal Appeal Act 1964 to
grant a new trial.   Bearing in mind the importance which the judge undoubtedly
attached to Mr. Christopher's evidence, it would be certainly proper in the
case of the applicant Anderson that a new trial should be granted, and counsel
for the Crown has gone further and has said that he thinks it would be proper
for there to be a new trial also in the case of the applicant Morris.   **H**

Counsel for the applicant Morris, however, while appreciating that if necessary
there should be a new trial in regard to his client, has said that he is entitled to
ask this court to quash the conviction on the basis that on the evidence before
the jury, and without going further into Mr. Christopher's evidence, there was a
clear misdirection.   What is complained of is a passage in the summing-up.
It is unnecessary to read the direction on law in full.   The material direction is   **I**
where the judge said:

> " If you think there was a common design to attack [the applicant
> Welch] but it is not proved, in the case of [the applicant Morris], that he had
> any intention to kill or cause grievous bodily harm but that [the applicant
> Anderson], without the knowledge of [the applicant Morris], had a knife,
> took it from the flat and at some time formed the intention to kill or cause
> grievous bodily harm to Welch and did kill him—an act outside the common
> design to which [the applicant Morris] is proved to have been a party—

A   then you would or could on the evidence find it proved that [the applicant Anderson] committed murder and [the applicant Morris] would be liable to be convicted of manslaughter provided you are satisfied that he took part in the attack or fight with Welch."

B   In passing, I should say that this court has very grave doubts whether the judge really intended to say what he did, and for this reason, that as I have already said, he attached very great importance to the evidence of Mr. Christopher, and indeed had in a later passage gone so far as to say that unless the jury felt sure that they could accept Mr. Christopher's evidence they were to acquit the applicant Morris altogether. Bearing that in mind, one would expect the judge to be giving a direction on the basis that Mr. Christopher's evidence was accepted, and that the jury were satisfied that the applicant Morris knew that

C   the applicant Anderson had this knife and had in a moment of anger armed himself with it. However, whatever we think, the judge on the transcript had told the jury that they could convict or indeed should convict the applicant Morris even though he had no idea that the applicant Anderson had armed himself with a knife. In other words, this court must approach the case on the basis that the jury fully understood that that was being put before them as a

D   direction in law.

Counsel for the applicant Morris submits that that was a clear misdirection. He would put the principle of law to be invoked in this form: that where two persons embark on a joint enterprise, each is liable for the acts done in pursuance of that joint enterprise, that that includes liability for unusual consequences if

E   they arise from the execution of the agreed joint enterprise but (and this is the crux of the matter) that if one of the adventurers goes beyond what has been tacitly agreed as part of the common enterprise, his co-adventurer is not liable for the consequences of that unauthorised act. Finally, he says it is for the jury in every case to decide whether what was done was part of the joint enterprise, or went beyond it and was in fact an act unauthorised by that joint

F   enterprise. In support of that, he refers to a number of authorities to which this court finds it unnecessary to refer in detail, but which in the opinion of this court shows that at any rate for the last 130 or 140 years that has been the true position. This matter was in fact considered in some detail in *R. v. Smith* (1), which was heard by a court of five judges presided over by Hilbery, J., on Nov. 6, 1961, a case in which Slade, J., gave the judgment of the court. That case was referred to at some length in the later decision in this court of *R. v.*

G   *Betty* (2). It is unnecessary to go into that case in any detail. It followed the judgment of Slade, J., in *R. v. Smith* (1), and it did show the limits of the general principle which counsel for the applicant Morris invokes in the present case. In *R. v. Smith* (1) the co-adventurer who in fact killed was known by the accused to have a knife, and it was clear on the facts of that case that the common design involved an attack on a man, in that case a barman, in which the use of a knife

H   would not be outside the scope of the concerted action. Reference was there made to the fact that the case might have been different if in fact the man using the knife had used a revolver, a weapon which he had, unknown to Smith. The court in *R. v. Betty* (2) approved entirely of what had been said in *R. v. Smith* (1), and in fact added to it. In passing, it is to be observed that, as counsel for the applicant Morris has pointed out, the headnote to *R. v. Betty* (3)

I   may go somewhat further and may have led the judge in the present case to think that there were no such limits to the principle. Counsel for the Crown, on the other hand, while recognising that he cannot go beyond this long string of decided cases, has said that they are really all part and parcel of a much wider principle which he would put in this form, that if two or more persons engage

---

(1) (1961), [1963] 3 All E.R. 597.   (2) [1963] 3 All E.R. 602, n.; 48 Cr. App. Rep. 6.
(3) (1963), 48 Cr. App. Rep. 6.

in an unlawful act and one suddenly develops an intention to kill whereby death A
results, not only is he guilty of murder, but all those who have engaged in the
unlawful act are guilty of manslaughter.   He recognises that the present trend
of authority is against that proposition, but he goes back to *R.* v. *Salisbury* (4)
in 1553.   In that case a master had lain in wait to attack a man, and his servants
who had no idea of what his, the master's, idea was, joined in the attack, whereby
the man was killed.   It was held there that those servants were themselves B
guilty of manslaughter.   The court is by no means clear on the facts as reported
that that case is really on all fours, but it is in the opinion of the court quite
clear that that principle is wholly out of touch with the position today.   It seems
to this court that to say that adventurers are guilty of manslaughter when one
of them has departed completely from the concerted action of the common
design and has suddenly formed an intent to kill and has used a weapon and C
acted in a way which no party to that common design could suspect is something
which would revolt the conscience of people today.   Counsel for the Crown in his
attractive argument points to the fact that it would seem to be illogical that, whereas
if two people had formed a common design to do an unlawful act and death
resulted by an unforeseen consequence, they should be held, as they would
undoubtedly be held, guilty of manslaughter; yet if one of them in those circum- D
stances had in a moment of passion decided to kill, the other would be acquitted
altogether.   The law, of course, is not completely logical, but there is nothing
really illogical in such a result, in that it could well be said as a matter
of common-sense that in the latter circumstances the death resulted or was
caused by the sudden action of the adventurer who decided to kill and killed.
Considered as a matter of causation, there may well be an overwhelming super- E
vening event which is of such a character that it will relegate into history matters
which would otherwise be looked on as causative factors.   Looked at in that way,
there is really nothing illogical in the result to which counsel for the Crown
points.   Be that as it may, this court is quite satisfied that they should follow
the long line of cases to which I have referred, and it follows accordingly that,
whether intended or not, the jury were misdirected in the present case, and F
misdirected in a manner which really compels this court to quash the conviction
of the applicant Morris.   In the result leave to appeal will be granted to both
the applicants; this will be treated as the hearing of the appeal and in the case
of the applicant Anderson, instead of quashing the conviction, the court will
direct a new trial under s. 1 of the Criminal Appeal Act 1964.   In the case of the
applicant Morris, they will allow the appeal and quash the conviction.   G

  *Applications granted and treated as appeals.   New trial ordered in respect of
the applicant Anderson, conviction quashed in respect of the applicant Morris.*

  Solicitors: *Claytons,* Nottingham (for the applicant Anderson); *Registrar,
Court of Criminal Appeal* (for the applicant Morris); *Director of Public
Prosecutions* (for the Crown).
                      H

      [*Reported by* N. P. METCALFE, ESQ., *Barrister-at-Law.*]

                          I

---

(4) (1553), 1 Plowd. 100.

A

RICE v. CONNOLLY.

[QUEEN'S BENCH DIVISION (Lord Parker, C.J., Marshall and James, JJ.), May 3, 1966.]

Criminal Law—Obstructing constable when in the execution of his duty—Refusal to answer questions—Whether wilful obstruction—Police Act 1964 (c. 48),

B   *s. 51 (3).*

The appellant was seen by police officers in the early hours of the morning behaving suspiciously in an area where on the same night breaking offences had taken place. On being questioned he refused to say where he was going or where he had come from. He refused to give his full name and address, though he did give a name and the name of a road, which were not

C   untrue. He refused to accompany the police to a police box for identification purposes, saying, "If you want me, you will have to arrest me". He was arrested and charged with wilfully obstructing the police contrary to s. 51 (3)* of the Act of 1964. On appeal it was conceded that " wilfully " imported something done without lawful excuse.

Held: although every citizen had a moral or social duty to assist the

D   police, there was no relevant legal duty to that effect in the circumstances of the present case, and the appellant had been entitled to decline to answer the questions put to him and (prior to his arrest) to accompany the police officer on request to the police box to establish identity; accordingly, in the circumstances, " wilful obstruction " by the appellant was not established, although he had been obstructive, because no obstruction without lawful

E   excuse had been established (see p. 652, letters D and I, post).

Meaning of " obstruction " stated in *Hinchcliffe* v. *Sheldon* ([1955] 3 All E.R. at p. 408, letter F) applied.

Per JAMES, J.: I would not go so far as to say that there may not be circumstances in which the manner of a person together with his silence could amount to an obstruction of the police within s. 51 (3) of the Police Act 1964

F   (see p. 652, letter I, to p. 653, letter A, post).

Appeal allowed.

[Editorial Note. There is real distinction between a case where there is merely a refusal to answer questions and a case where false information is given (see p. 652, letters B and C, post).

As to obstructing the police in the execution of their duty, see 10 HALSBURY'S

G   LAWS (3rd Edn.) 634, para. 1207; and for cases on the subject, see 15 DIGEST (Repl.) 853, 854, *8213-8219.*

As to a constable's right to assistance from private persons, see 30 HALSBURY'S LAWS (3rd Edn.) 142, 143, para. 231.

For the Police Act 1964, s. 51, see 44 HALSBURY'S STATUTES (2nd Edn.) 924.]

H   Case referred to:

Hinchcliffe v. *Sheldon,* [1955] 3 All E.R. 406; [1955] 1 W.L.R. 1017; 120 J.P. 13; 15 Digest (Repl.) 854, *8217.*

Case Stated.

This was a Case Stated by W. A. SIME, ESQ., Q.C., in respect of his adjudication as Recorder of Grimsby Borough Quarter Sessions sitting at Grimsby on

I   May 20, 1965. On that day the appellant, Leonard Rice, appeared before the recorder on appeal against a certain conviction at the Grimsby Borough Magistrates' Court on an information laid by the respondent, Thomas Connolly, an inspector of police, for having on Mar. 8, 1965, in Victor Street in the county borough of Grimsby wilfully obstructed Oliver Baillie a constable of the Grimsby Borough Police Force in the due execution of his duty, contrary to s. 51 (3) of the Police Act 1964. The conduct alleged to amount to obstruction included refusing

* Section 51 (3), so far as material, provides: " Any person who . . . wilfully obstructs a constable in the execution of his duty . . . shall be guilty of an offence . . ."

Explained and distinguished in
INGLETON v DIBBLE [1972] 1 All ER
275

Dictum of LORD PARKER CJ at
651 applied in WILLMOTT v ATACK
3 All ER 794 [1976]

to accompany the constable to a police box for identification. The recorder **A** dismissed the appeal and the appellant being dissatisfied with the said determination of his appeal as being erroneous in point of law requested the recorder to state a Case for the opinion of the High Court. The facts are summarised in the judgment of LORD PARKER, C.J.

The contentions before the recorder were as follows. For the appellant it was contended that although a police officer acting in the execution of his duty **B** was entitled to ask a citizen questions, including questions as to his name and address, there was no legal duty on the citizen, in the absence of some obligation imposed by statute (and there was no such statute applicable in the present case) to answer such questions, nor in the absence of some statutory duty (and there was none in the present case) was there any duty on a citizen to accompany a police officer anywhere in order that his identity might be investigated; the **C** citizen had a right to refuse to answer the questions put to him by the constable and to refuse to accompany him to the police box; it followed, so it was contended, that the constable could not lawfully require answers to his questions and could not lawfully require the appellant to accompany him to the police box and that the appellant's conduct had not amounted to an obstruction of the constable in the execution of his duty. For the respondent it was contended **D** that at common law the citizen had a duty to assist the police in the investigation of crime and that there was therefore a legal duty on the appellant to answer the constable's questions and to accompany him to the police box for the purpose stated, that the appellant had not discharged that legal duty and that he had, therefore, obstructed the constable in the execution of his duty.

The recorder's opinion is set out at p. 651, letter D, post. The question of law **E** for the opinion of the High Court was whether the recorder was right in finding that the conduct of the appellant amounted to a wilful obstruction of the constable in the due execution of his duty.

The cases noted below* were cited during the argument in addition to the case referred to in the judgment.

Geoffrey Lane, Q.C., and *E. F. Jowitt* for the appellant.   **F**
H. A. Skinner, Q.C., and *David Barker* for the respondent.

LORD PARKER, C.J.: In the early hours of the morning (1) of Mar. 8, 1965, Police Constable Baillie was out on patrol duty on his pedal cycle in and around Oxford Street, Grimsby. A number of breaking offences had been committed that night, and the officer was looking out to see if he could see **G** anyone behaving suspiciously. One indeed of these breakings had been committed quite close to where he was, within the previous forty-five minutes. He saw a man who turned out to be the appellant behaving suspiciously, looking into shop windows, looking round, seeing the constable and moving up a side street, coming back later from the side street and going along looking at further shops, and keeping a wary eye on the constable. A time came when Police **H** Constable Baillie, who had by then been joined by another police constable, went up and stopped the appellant. Police Constable Baillie asked where he was going, and the appellant ignored the inquiry, though he heard it. The police constable again asked him where he was going and where he had come from and for his name and address, whereupon the appellant replied: " Give me a good reason why I should ". In due course the appellant was allowed to walk **I** away, and when he had got a little distance away he stopped to light his pipe; the police officers then saw that he had got a cut on his finger. They went up to him again, and again Police Constable Baillie asked for his name and address. After again being asked a second time, he merely replied: " Rice, Convamore Road ". That incidentally was true as far as it went. The police constable

---

* *Bastable* v. *Little*, [1907] 1 K.B. 59; *Thomas* v. *Sawkins*, [1935] All E.R. Rep. 655; [1935] 2 K.B. 249; *R.* v. *Waterfield, R.* v. *Lynn*, [1963] 3 All E.R. 659.
(1) The time was about 12.45 a.m.

Dictum of LORD PARKER CJ at 651-652
explained in HILLS v ELLIS [1983]
1 All ER 667

A said that he wanted his full name and address, and the appellant refused to give it. Finally the police constable asked the appellant to accompany him to a police box to confirm his identity, whereupon the appellant replied: " Look, son, I am not moving from this spot. If you want me you will have to arrest me "; thereupon the police constable arrested him and gave as the ground for arrest that he had obstructed him in the execution of his duty in that he refused to say where he was going, where he had come from and had refused to give his full

B name and address, and had refused to accompany him to the police box. Those were the facts as found by the recorder, with these additions, that throughout the appellant's manner had been sarcastic and awkward, that when, long after the arrest, he was seen by an inspector, the appellant said:

C " I have been arrested. You cannot de-arrest me. It might be worth a bob or two to me. I've done nothing wrong. I am arrested, what are you going to do? "

Lastly it is found that in fact the appellant never was charged with any of the breaking offences in the neighbourhood, nor were there ever any grounds for suspecting that he was guilty of any of them. It was in those circumstances

D that the recorder expressed his decision in these terms:

" I was of the opinion that on the facts as stated above and having regard to those set out in para. [5] (vii) [i.e., the remarks made after arrest to the inspector] the appellant had deliberately intended to distract Police Constable Baillie from his duties and had thereby wilfully obstructed Police Constable Baillie in the due execution of his duty and was guilty of the offence

E charged. I therefore dismiss the appeal."

The question left for the opinion of the court is whether the recorder was right in finding that the conduct of the appellant on the facts stated amounted to a wilful obstruction of the police constable in the due execution of his duty.

The statute creating the alleged offence in this case is s. 51 (3) of the Police Act 1964, which increases the penalties for assaults on police constables and

F obstruction of them in the execution of their duty, but otherwise preserves largely as offences those which appeared in earlier legislation (2). What the prosecution have to prove is that there was an obstructing of a constable, that the constable was at the time acting in the execution of his duty, and that the person obstructing did so wilfully. To carry the matter a little further, it is in my view clear that to " obstruct " in s. 51 (3) is to do any act which makes it more

G difficult for the police to carry out their duty. That description of obstructing I take from the case of *Hinchcliffe* v. *Sheldon* (3). It is also in my judgment clear that it is part of the obligations and duties of a police constable to take all steps which appear to him necessary for keeping the peace, for preventing crime or for protecting property from criminal injury. There is no exhaustive definition of the powers and obligations of the police, but they are at least those, and they

H would further include the duty to detect crime and to bring an offender to justice.

It is quite clear that the appellant was making it more difficult for the police to carry out their duties, and that the police at the time and throughout were acting in accordance with their duties. The only remaining element of the alleged offence, and the one on which in my judgment this case depends, is whether the obstructing of which the appellant was guilty was a wilful obstruction. " Wilful "

I in this context in my judgment means not only " intentional " but also connotes something which is done without lawful excuse, and that indeed is conceded by

(2) See s. 12 of the Prevention of Crime Act, 1871, as amended by s. 2 of the Prevention of Crimes Amendment Act, 1885; 5 Halsbury's Statutes (2nd Edn.) 873, 915. Both s. 12 and the Act of 1885 are repealed by s. 64 (3) of, and Sch. 10 to, the Police Act 1964. Assaults on constables are rendered offences by s. 51 of the Act of 1964. The extension of the offence of assault, enacted in s. 12 of the Act of 1871, to wilfully obstructing a constable in the execution of his duty (which extension was enacted by s. 2 of the Act of 1885) is re-enacted in s. 51 (3) of the Act of 1964.

(3) [1955] 3 All E.R. 406 at p. 408, letter F, per Lord Goddard, C.J.

counsel who appears for the prosecution in this case   Accordingly, the sole A
question here is whether the appellant had a lawful excuse for refusing to answer
the questions put to him.   In my judgment he had.   It seems to me quite clear
that though every citizen has a moral duty or, if you like, a social duty to assist
the police, there is no legal duty to that effect, and indeed the whole basis of the
common law is that right of the individual to refuse to answer questions put to
him by persons in authority, and a refusal to accompany those in authority to B
any particular place, short, of course, of arrest.   Counsel for the respondent
has pointed out that it is undoubtedly an obstruction, and has been so held,
for a person questioned by the police to tell a " cock-and-bull " story, to put the
police off by giving them false information, and I think he would say: well,
what is the real distinction, it is very little away from giving false information
to giving no information at all; if that does in fact make it more difficult for the C
police to carry out their duties then there is a wilful obstruction.   In my judgment there is all the difference in the world between deliberately telling a false
story, something which on no view a citizen has a right to do, and preserving
silence or refusing to answer, something which he has every right to do.   Accordingly, in my judgment, looked on in that perfectly general way, it was not shown
that the refusal of the appellant to answer the questions or to accompany the D
police officer in the first instance to the police box was an obstruction without
lawful excuse.

I would add this, that for my part I have very grave doubt whether the recorder
was approaching the case on that basis.   I think that the recorder had in mind
that though the appellant had a perfect right to refuse to answer questions, his
whole conduct in this instance and the answers he did give were such as to be E
a deliberate obstruction to the police.   I say that for this reason, that he went
out of his way to find that the appellant's manner throughout was sarcastic
and awkward.   He went on to recite that extraordinary attitude taken up by the
appellant after arrest, in the conversation with the police inspector, and finally
he said in his opinion that the appellant had deliberately intended to distract
Police Constable Baillie from his duties.   I cannot help feeling that the recorder F
here was giving full effect to the law as I understand it to be, but also was saying
that the appellant's whole attitude and behaviour amounted to a distracting of
the police constable from his duties.   However, there are certain difficulties in this
in that neither counsel before us today has suggested that that is the true view
of the recorder's decision in this case, and indeed counsel for the respondent has
invited us to deal with the matter on the more general basis.   Finally, I do see G
myself difficulties in upholding the recorder's decision on that ground, if that
be the true ground of his decision.   In the first place it would require conduct
going further than what happened in this case to establish an obstruction, and
secondly one of the matters, and apparently an important matter in the recorder's
view, was the appellant's behaviour after his arrest, in front of the inspector;
this was something long after the event, which could not be evidence of the H
awkward behaviour, if it was awkward, of the appellant at the time of the
incident itself.   In these circumstances I have come to the conclusion that this
appeal succeeds.

MARSHALL, J.: I agree.   In order to uphold this conviction it appears
to me that one has to assent to the proposition that where a citizen is acting
merely within his legal rights, he is thereby committing a criminal offence. I
I cannot see that the manner in which he does it can make any difference
whatsoever, and for the reasons given by LORD PARKER, C.J., I agree that this
appeal should be allowed.

JAMES, J.: For the reasons given by LORD PARKER, C.J., I also agree that
this appeal should be allowed.   For my own part I would only add this, that I
would not go so far as to say that there may not be circumstances in which the
manner of a person together with his silence could amount to an obstruction

A within the section, whether they do remains to be decided in any case that happens hereafter, not in this case, in which it has not been argued.

Appeal allowed.   Conviction quashed.

Solicitors: *Middleton, Lewis & Co.*, agents for *H. K. & H. S. Bloomer & Co.*, Great Grimsby (for the appellant); *Sharpe, Pritchard & Co.*, agents for *Town Clerk*, Great Grimsby (for the respondent).

B

[*Reported by* N. P. METCALFE, ESQ., *Barrister-at-Law.*]

LOCKYER v. GIBB.

C [QUEEN'S BENCH DIVISION (Lord Parker, C.J., Marshall and James, JJ.), May 3, 1966.]

Drugs — Dangerous drugs — Possession — Unauthorised possession — Absolute offence—Dangerous Drugs Act 1965 (c. 15), s. 13 (a)—Dangerous Drugs (No. 2) Regulations 1964 (S.I. 1964 No. 1811), reg. 9.

D The appellant was stopped by the police, and in a hold-all which she was carrying was found a small brown bottle containing tablets. The appellant said that she did not know what the tablets were and that a friend had given them to her to look after for him. When asked for his name, she gave a different explanation saying that she was in a café with him and some other people when the police came in, and he must have dumped them on her. On analysis the tablets were found to contain morphine sulphate, a

E scheduled substance specified in Pt. 1 of the Schedule to the Dangerous Drugs Act 1965. The appellant was charged with possessing the tablets without being duly authorised, contrary to reg. 9* of the Dangerous Drugs (No. 2) Regulations 1964, and s. 13† of the Dangerous Drugs Act 1965. The magistrate convicted the appellant being of the opinion that the offence was sufficiently constituted by her being in unauthorised possession of a bottle

F containing morphine sulphate, notwithstanding she did not know the contents of the bottle and that her contention that mens rea was an essential ingredient of the charge was not well founded. On appeal,

Held: the appellant had been rightly convicted, because reg. 9 of the Dangerous Drugs (No. 2) Regulations 1964, on the face of it imposed an absolute liability subject to licence and authorisation, and, while it was

G necessary to show (as had been shown) that the appellant knew that she had the article which turned out to be a drug, it was not necessary that she should know that in fact it was a drug of a particular character (see p. 656, letters B, E and H, post).

R. v. Hallam ([1957] 1 All E.R. 665) distinguished.

Beaver v. R. ([1957] S.C.R. 531) not followed.

H Appeal dismissed.

[As to mens rea in statutory offences, see 10 HALSBURY'S LAWS (3rd Edn.) 273, 274, para. 508; and for cases on the subject, see 14 DIGEST (Repl.) 35-39, 48-95.

As to offences under the Dangerous Drugs Acts, see 26 HALSBURY'S LAWS (3rd Edn.) 215, para. 487.

I For the Dangerous Drugs Act 1965, s. 13, see 45 HALSBURY'S STATUTES (3rd Edn.) 900.]

Cases referred to:

Beaver v. R., [1957] S.C.R. 531; 33 Digest (Repl.) 557, *353.

R. v. Hallam, [1957] 1 All E.R. 665; [1957] 1 Q.B. 569; [1957] 3 W.L.R. 521; 121 J.P. 254; 41 Cr. App. Rep. 111; Digest (Cont. Vol. A) 450, 12,403a.

---

* Regulation 9, so far as material, is set out at p. 655, letter B, post.

† Section 13, so far as material, is set out at p. 655, letter D, post.

Applied in R. v. WARNER. [1967] 3 All E.R. 93.

Dictum of LORD PARKER, C.J., at pp. 655, 656, considered in WARNER v. MET. POLICE COMR. [1968] 2 All E.R. 356.

Distinguished in R v BUSWELL [1972] 1 All ER 75

R. v. *Langa,* [1936] S.A.L.R. (O.P. Div.) 158.   A

Yeandel v. *Fisher,* [1965] 3 All E.R. 158; [1965] 3 W.L.R. 1002.

Case Stated.

This was a Case Stated by J. H. A. Aubrey-Fletcher, Esq., in respect of
his adjudication as a Metropolitan stipendiary magistrate sitting at Marlborough
Street in the county of London on Oct. 8 and Oct. 22, 1965. On Oct. 1, 1965, B
the respondent, Sheila Gibb, preferred an information against the appellant,
Norma Ann Lockyer, charging that, on Sept. 6, 1965, at Old Compton Street, W.1,
she had in her possession eighty-three tablets of morphine sulphate without
being duly authorised, contrary to reg. 9 of the Dangerous Drugs (No. 2) Regulations 1964, and s. 13 of the Dangerous Drugs Act 1965. The following facts
were found. On Sept. 6, 1965, the appellant was stopped in Old Compton C
Street, W.1, by the respondent, who was a woman police constable of the Metropolitan Police, and another woman police constable. The appellant was carrying
a raffia hold-all containing many items, which was searched. At the bottom
of the hold-all was a " Boots " paper bag containing a number of sanitary towels
and a brown glass bottle. The bottle was not wrapped and a number of small
round tablets were visible within it. The woman police constable asked the D
appellant " What are those tablets? " and she replied " I don't know ". The
woman police constable asked where she got them from and the appellant
replied " A friend from the Huntsman gave them to me this morning to look
after for him ". When asked for his name the appellant replied " He did not
give them to me. I was in a café with him and some other people and the
police came in. He must have dumped them on me ". The tablets were found E
on analysis to contain morphine sulphate, a substance for the time being specified
in Pt. 1 of the schedule to the Dangerous Drugs Act 1965. The appellant was
aware when stopped by the respondent that she was in possession of the bottle
and was aware that the bottle contained tablets, but there was a possibility
that the appellant did not know that the tablets contained morphine sulphate
or any substance specified as above. The magistrate was of the opinion that F
it was not proved by the prosecution that the appellant knew the nature and
substance of the tablets, or that such substance was specified as above. He,
therefore, granted the appellant a legal aid certificate and adjourned the case
for both parties to be represented. On Oct. 22, 1965, no further evidence was
given before him but he heard submissions from counsel for both parties. G

It was contended for the appellant that guilty knowledge was an essential
ingredient in an offence unless a statute clearly or by implication ruled out
the requirement of guilty knowledge. On the construction of the words of s. 13 (*a*)
of the Dangerous Drugs Act 1965, together with the words of reg. 9 of the Dangerous Drugs (No. 2) Regulations 1964, which by s. 27 (2) of the Act of 1965 were
continued in force, guilty knowledge was an essential ingredient to constitute H
the offence and otherwise the words in s. 13 (*a*) would have provided for the
offence to be constituted where the person was in contravention of the regulation
and ruling out the requirement of knowledge. The same principle applied in this
case as in a case where drugs were planted on a person. It was contended for the
respondent that s. 13 of the Act of 1965 together with reg. 9, imposed an absolute I
prohibition and that unauthorised possession without guilty knowledge was
sufficient to constitute the offence. The object of the regulations and Act of
Parliament was to punish the carrying of certain dangerous substances and
that it could not be intended that the prosecution must prove knowledge on the
part of the carrier of the nature of the substance.

The magistrate convicted the appellant and fined her £10, and the appellant
now appealed.

A   The cases noted below* were cited during the argument in addition to the case referred to in the judgment of LORD PARKER, C.J.

Deborah Rowland for the appellant.

D. H. W. Vowden for the respondent.

LORD PARKER, C.J.: It is convenient to look at once at the statute and
B   regulations. The regulations, which were made under the regulation making power of the statute (1), provide by reg. 9 that:

" A person shall not be in possession of a drug . . . unless he is generally so authorised or under this regulation so licensed or authorised . . ."

Regulation 19 defines a drug as meaning, and this is the only part that is relevant here, a drug to which Pt. 1 of these regulations applies. Regulation 20 defines
C   " possession " by saying:

" For the purposes of these regulations a person shall be deemed to be in possession of a drug if it is in his actual custody or is held by some other person subject to his control or for him and on his behalf."

Section 13 of the Act of 1965 itself provides:

D   " A person—(a) who acts in contravention of . . . a regulation made under this Act . . . shall be guilty of an offence against this Act."

[HIS LORDSHIP stated the facts, and continued:] In the end the magistrate in convicting the appellant said this:

" I was of the opinion that the offence was sufficiently constituted by the appellant being in unauthorised possession of a bottle containing morphine
E   sulphate notwithstanding that she did not know the contents of the bottle and that the contention of the appellant that mens rea or guilty knowledge was an essential ingredient of the charge was not well founded."

In my judgment, before one comes to a consideration of a necessity for mens rea or, as it is sometimes said, a consideration of whether the regulation imposed an
F   absolute liability, it is of course necessary to consider possession itself. In my judgment, it is quite clear that a person cannot be said to be in possession of some article which he or she does not realise is, or may be, in her handbag, in her room, or in some other place over which she has control. That, I should have thought, is elementary; if something were tipped into one's basket and one had not the vaguest notion it was there at all, one could not possibly be said to be in
G   possession of it.

What counsel for the appellant contends in the present case, however, goes further. Counsel contends that, while this is not a case of something having been slipped into the appellant's hold-all without her knowledge, she cannot be convicted here unless it is proved that she was knowingly in possession of drugs. She does not say that the prosecution must prove that she knew that it was a
H   particular drug, or even a dangerous drug, but at least that it must be proved that she knew that it was a drug. That question is, as it seems to me, linked up with this question of whether the regulation imposed an absolute liability. As is well known, this is a question which is arising constantly and, indeed, in connexion with another provision (2) dealing with drugs the matter has been before this court recently in *Yeandel* v. *Fisher* (3).   No question of possession was

I   * *R.* v. *Somers, Ex p. General Estates Co.*, [1906] 1 K.B. 326; 70 J.P. 37; *Sambasivan* v. *Public Prosecutor, Federation of Malaya*, [1950] A.C. 458; *Tinsley* v. *Dudley*, [1951] 1 All E.R. 252; [1951] 2 K.B. 18; *Reynolds* v. *G. H. Austin & Sons, Ltd.*, [1951] 1 All E.R. 606; [1951] 2 K.B. 135; *Taylors Central Garages (Exeter), Ltd.* v. *Roper*, [1951] W.N. 383; *Russell* v. *Smith*, [1957] 2 All E.R. 796; [1958] 1 Q.B. 27; *R.* v. *Carpenter*, [1960] Crim. L.R. 633.
(1) I.e., under s. 3 (1) of the Dangerous Drugs Act, 1951, and continued in force by s. 27 (2) of the Dangerous Drugs Act 1965.
(2) The Dangerous Drugs Act 1964, s. 9 (1) (*b*), now s. 5 (*b*) of the Dangerous Drugs Act 1965.
3) [1965] 3 All E.R. 158.

involved in that case, but in giving judgment I did refer (4) to the now familiar A
tests which one applies in these cases: one looks at the mischief aimed at by the
Act, one looks at the sort of provision that is involved, in particular whether it is a
public welfare provision, and one also looks at the exact language used. In that
case, I had no doubt that drugs were a matter of grave concern today to everyone,
that it was the intention of Parliament as evinced by the legislation to tighten up
more and more the control of drugs, and that, if one considered the mischief aimed B
at alone, there was every reason for treating a provision such as this as a provision
i mposing absolute liability.

Having said that, one looks at the language of reg. 9 itself, which is on the face
of it an absolute prohibition, subject to licence and authorisation, and for my
part I cannot, though it is not conclusive, omit from consideration the fact that
the word " knowingly " does not appear before " possession ". This sort of point C
arose in R. v. Hallam (5), a case under s. 4 (1) of the Explosive Substances Act,
1883. It was held there that, in order to establish that a man was in possession of
explosives for the purposes of s. 4 (1), he must at least know that he has the article
which later turns out to be an explosive, which in that case was in his car; it
must not have been slipped in without his knowledge. That much is true, but the
court held that, having regard to the fact that, in addition to that general con- D
sideration, the word " knowingly " was used, the prosecution must prove not only
that he knew that he had an article which turned out to be an explosive, but also
that he knew that that article was an explosive. That consideration, imported
by the word " knowingly " in Hallam's case (5), is wholly absent here, and, in
my judgment, under this provision, while it is necessary to show that the appellant
knew that she had the articles which turned out to be a drug, it is not necessary E
that she should know that in fact it was a drug and a drug of a particular character.
In other words, I have come to the conclusion that the learned magistrate was
right, and I would dismiss this appeal.

I should say that I regret that, in doing so, I find myself unable to follow the
persuasive authority that counsel for the appellant has drawn to our attention
of Beaver v. R. (6), heard on appeal from the Court of Appeal of Ontario. It was F
there held that one who had physical possession of a package which he believed
to contain a harmless substance and which in fact contained a narcotic drug
could not be convicted of being in possession of the drug under a certain provision
of the Opium and Narcotic Drug Act, (7), and that provision said:

" Every person who has in his possession any drug save and except under
authority or licence from a Minister . . . is guilty of an offence."   G

It was a court of five judges; three of them, the majority, in a single judgment
held that the prosecution failed if it might be that the appellant thought that the
substance that she had was a harmless substance. It is to be observed that two
judges of the court gave a strong dissenting judgment, I confess that I prefer the
dissenting judgment and feel unable to follow the decision of the majority. H
There was another case from South Africa which was really to the same effect,
R. v. Langa (8).

MARSHALL, J.: I agree.

JAMES, J.: I also agree.

Appeal dismissed.

Solicitors: *Baines & Baines* (for the appellant); *Solicitor, Metropolitan Police* I
(for the respondent).

[*Reported by* N. P. METCALFE, ESQ., *Barrister-at-Law.*]

---

(4) [1965] 3 All E.R. at p. 161.   (5) [1957] 1 All E.R. 665; [1957] 1 Q.B. 569.
(6) [1957] S.C.R. 531.   (7) R.S.C., 1952, c. 201, s. 4 (1).
                    (8) [1936] S.A.L.R. (C.P. Div.) 158.

WITCHELL v. ABBOTT AND ANOTHER.

[QUEEN'S BENCH DIVISION (Lord Parker, C.J., Sachs and Widgery, JJ.), February 24, 1966.]

Road Traffic—Goods vehicle—" A " licence—Employee driver—Limitation of permitted hours of work—Records—Whether time spent on journey home by private car provided by employer constitutes hours for rest—Road Traffic Act, 1960 (8 & 9 Eliz. 2 c. 16), s. 73 (1), (4)—Goods Vehicles (Keeping of Records) Regulations, 1935 (S.R. & O. 1935 No. 314), reg. 6 (1).

The first respondent was an employee driver of a goods vehicle belonging to the second respondents who were the holders of a public carriers' licence. On several occasions the first respondent finished his work in a town other than where his home was. He would then hand over his vehicle to a relief driver. On such occasions he had the option, either of spending his hours of rest in that town at a subsistence allowance of £1 a night or of returning to his home town by the relief car provided by the employer and being paid at the hourly rate for the time occupied in travelling. On several occasions he returned to his home town by the relief car travelling sometimes as a passenger and sometimes as a driver. If the time spent in travelling home in this way was time during which the first respondent was bound by the terms of his employment to obey the directions of his employer, it was not, by virtue of s. 73 (4)* of the Road Traffic Act, 1960, time for rest, and there would have been contravention of the provisions of the Goods Vehicles (Keeping of Records) Regulations, 1935, reg. 6 (1)† and the Road Traffic Act, 1960, s. 73 (1) (c)‡.

Held: as there was a true option for the driver to decide what he preferred to do, whether to stay at the away town on a subsistence allowance or return to his own home by employer's car, the period of travel was not excluded by s. 73 (4) of the Road Traffic Act, 1860, from being time for rest and there had not been contravention of s. 73 (1) (c) of the Act of 1960 or of reg. 6 (1) of the regulations of 1935 (see p. 659, letter I, p. 660, letters C and H, I, and p. 661, letter B, post).

Appeal dismissed.

[As to restrictions on drivers' hours of work and as to records, see 33 HALSBURY'S LAWS (3rd Edn.) 717, 718, para. 1222, and ibid., pp. 770, 771, para. 1323; and for cases on the subject, see 45 DIGEST (Repl.) 136, 137, *500-506.*

For the Road Traffic Act, 1960, s. 73, s. 186, see 40 HALSBURY'S STATUTES (2nd Edn.) 773, 874.]

Case Stated.

This was an appeal by way of Case Stated from the justices for the County of Cumberland acting in and for the petty sessional division of Penrith in respect of their adjudication on Sept. 28, 1965, whereby they dismissed twenty-three informations against the first respondent, Lawrence Abbott, and twenty-three informations against the respondents, J. H. Henderson and Son, Ltd., preferred by the appellant, George Hunter Witchell. The informations related to alleged offences in February and March, 1965. The second respondents were carriers of goods and owners of a motor vehicle constructed to carry goods other than the effects of passengers; they were holders of a public " A " carriers' licence. The first respondent was the driver employed by them. The informations regarding both respondents fell into two groups. There were fourteen informations against the first respondent, the driver, charging that, when he was the driver of a certain authorised vehicle, he failed to keep a current record of hours of work contrary to reg. 6 of the Goods Vehicles (Keeping of Records) Regulations, 1935, and s. 186 of the Road Traffic Act, 1960. There were nine

---

* Section 73 (4), so far as material, is printed at p. 659, letter B, post.

† Regulation 6 (1), so far as material, is printed at p. 659, letter G, post.

‡ Section 73 (1) (c), so far as material, is printed at p. 658, letter I, to p. 659, letter A, post.

further informations against the first respondent charging that on nine days he   **A**
had not had at least ten consecutive hours for rest in a period of twenty-four
hours calculated from the commencement of the period of driving, contrary to
s. 73 of the Road Traffic Act, 1960. There were fourteen informations against
the second respondents for permitting the first respondent to offend against
reg. 6 of the Regulations of 1935, and nine informations against the second
respondents for permitting the first respondent to commit the alleged offences   **B**
against s. 73 of the Act of 1960.

    Nigel Bridge for the appellant.
    R. M. Yorke for the respondents.

    LORD PARKER, C.J., after summarising the substance of the informations
as previously stated, continued: The first respondent lived near Penrith and
was employed as a driver at a basic wage plus overtime. On each of the dates   **C**
referred to in the informations the first respondent drove the vehicle in the
course of his employment from Penrith finishing at some other town. At the
other town the first respondent then handed over the vehicle that he had been
driving to a relief driver sent for the purpose by the second respondents, the
relief driver then driving the goods vehicle back to Penrith. On each occasion   **D**
the first respondent, after handing the vehicle over to the relief driver, returned
to Penrith in a private car provided by the second respondents. On some
occasions he actually drove that private car; on other occasions he was merely
carried as a passenger in that private car back to his home in Penrith.

    The difficulty that arises in this case is that the first respondent was in fact
paid at the appropriate rate for the time spent in returning in the private car   **E**
to Penrith. There is set out in the Case a table of, I think, all except one of the
dates referred to in the informations, showing the sort of thing that happened.
Thus, on Feb. 22, 1965, it is recorded that he left Penrith at 3.30 a.m., that he
handed over the vehicle to the relief driver in Glasgow at 5.30 p.m., and was then
brought back in the car to Penrith, where he arrived at 7.30 p.m. and for those two
hours spent in returning to Penrith he was paid at the hourly rate.

    The records in the Case give the first respondent's time of ceasing work as the   **F**
time when he handed over the vehicle to the relief driver at the destination, in
the case I have referred to, Glasgow, and if that is the true view, that he ceased
work then, there was no offence whatever, whether against the Road Traffic Act,
1960, or against the Goods Vehicles (Keeping of Records) Regulations, 1935, (1).
On the other hand, if the proper view is that he did not cease work till 7.30 p.m. on
his return to Penrith, then an offence was committed by him both against the   **G**
Act of 1960 and the regulations of 1935, and since the second respondents were
clearly parties to the whole matter, they would equally be guilty of permitting
the first respondent to commit those offences.

    There is a finding in the Case that this method of operation arose in these
circumstances: most drivers employed by the second respondents, including
the first respondent, did not like spending the night away from home. There-   **H**
fore, when a driver exhausted his permitted hours of driving at a place away
from his home, the second respondents arranged to provide a relief driver for
the authorised vehicle and a private car to take the original driver to his home
town. The first respondent had been free on each occasion, had he wished to
do so, to stay overnight at the away town. The second respondents would then
have paid him £1 a night subsistence allowance.   **I**

    Having stated the facts, it is necessary to look at the legislation, and I look,
first, at the Road Traffic Act, 1960, s. 73 which provides, so far as is material to
these proceedings, that:

    " (1) With a view to protecting the public against the risks which arise
in cases where the drivers of motor vehicles are suffering from excessive
fatigue, it is hereby enacted that it shall not be lawful in the case of:— . . .

_____

(1) S.R. & O. 1935 No. 314.

A (c) a motor vehicle constructed to carry goods other than the effects of passengers, for a person to drive or cause or permit a person employed by him or subject to his orders to drive . . . (iii) so that the driver has not at least ten consecutive hours for rest in any period of twenty-four hours calculated from the commencement of any period of driving.

" (4) For the purposes of this section . . . and for the purposes of the
B provisions of this section which relate to the number of consecutive hours for rest which a driver is to have in a specified period, time during which the driver is bound by the terms of his employment to obey the directions of his employer, or to remain on or near the vehicle, or during which the vehicle is at a place where no reasonable facilities exist for the driver to rest away from the vehicle, shall be deemed not to be time which the driver has for
C rest."

Before leaving that, it is clear that the point in these proceedings is whether in this case the driver was provided with ten consecutive hours for rest in each period of twenty-four hours.

The regulations, which are the Goods Vehicles (Keeping of Records) Regulations, 1935, (2), are clearly designed to enable it to be seen in any case
D whether the provisions of s. 73 of the Act of 1960, to which I have been referred, have been carried out. I need refer only to but little of the regulations. By reg. 5 it is provided:

" ' Driver ' means a person employed by the holder of a licence as driver of an authorised vehicle or as driver and on work in connexion with the vehicle or its load and includes the holder of a licence when acting as such a
E driver . . .

" ' Full-time driver ' means a person who is employed solely in driving an authorised vehicle. ' Part-time driver ' means a person who is employed partly in driving an authorised vehicle and partly on other work not connected with a vehicle or its load. ' Statutory attendant ' means a person employed in pursuance of [s. 72 of the Road Traffic Act, 1960,] in attending a
F locomotive or attending to a trailer. ' Work ' includes work of any description performed by a driver or statutory attendant under the terms of his employment whether in connexion with a vehicle or its load or otherwise."

Regulation 6 (1) then goes on to provide that:

" . . . every holder of a licence shall cause to be kept a current record
G divided into periods of twenty-four consecutive hours which shall give in respect of each such period during which or during any part of which the driver was employed in driving the information prescribed . . ."

in certain forms set out in the Schedule. It is unnecessary to refer to those forms in any detail; it is sufficient to say that they are designed in such a way that it can be seen from them, amongst other things, whether the driver, in any particular
H case, has been provided with ten consecutive hours for rest.

The issue, here, is really in a very narrow compass, namely, whether, so far as the regulations of 1935 are concerned, the time occupied by the first respondent in going back to Penrith was a time of work, and whether, so far as the Act of 1960 is concerned, it was a time during which he was bound by the terms of his employment to obey the directions of his employer so as not to count
I as a period for rest.

It is in my judgment, quite clear that, as found by the Case, there was a true option for the driver, the first respondent, to decide what he preferred to do on these occasions, either to stay at the away town and to receive £1 a night subsistence allowance, or to avail himself of the offer of the employers to come back and spend the night in his own home, being provided with transport for that purpose,

---

(2) These regulations were made under s. 16 and s. 25 of the Road and Rail Traffic Act, 1933, and have effect pursuant to s. 186 and s. 190 of the Road Traffic Act, 1960.

and being paid at the hourly rate for the time occupied. I emphasise that at the **A**
outset because I can well understand that there might be cases where the option
was in effect a mere sham and that the employers were really insisting that the
men should come back to base every night, and were providing, as it were, a
sham option rather than ordering them to come back, in which case in my judgment the hours occupied in obeying those orders would clearly not be rest hours
but would be work hours. That is not this case. **B**

Accordingly, one starts with this, that prima facie the employers, the second
respondents, were providing the first respondent with at least ten consecutive
hours for rest which was their only obligation. It has been emphasised more
than once in the cases that the obligation is not to provide hours of rest, but hours
for rest. There is nothing to prevent an employee from doing anything that
he likes during his rest hours, indeed he could take another part-time job, he **C**
could go to a dance hall, he could stay up all night, he could do anything and
no offence would be committed, provided he has ten consecutive hours during
which he can rest if he so desires. What is said, however, in the present case
is that if he does exercise the option to come back to Penrith, then during the
time that he is occupied in coming back to Penrith, he is, under the terms of his
employment, bound to obey the directions of his employer, and therefore that **D**
time does not count as rest time under s. 73 (4).

In my judgment the justices came to a correct decision in the present case in
refusing to convict the respondents. I confess, however, that I do not understand
the reasons which they give in para. 9 of the Case. I do not propose to refer
to them because on other grounds I think that their decision was right. If
one treats this, as I do, as a genuine option, then it seems to me that there is **E**
really no difference between saying: if you like to come back, I will pay your
train fare; or, if you like to come back I will give you not your train fare, but
X shillings or X pounds in lieu, or, indeed, that I will pay you travelling time in
doing so. In any of those cases, the driver is not, as it seems to me, bound
during that period by the terms of his employment to obey the directions of the
employer. He is merely being paid some money in lieu of the subsistence **F**
allowance which would, otherwise, be paid if he had exercised the option in the
other way, and it can make no difference that the sum paid was a sum calculated
in accordance with the hours of travel. I agree, of course, that in the present
case it is the employer's car which is provided, and it could therefore, I suppose,
be said that, it being the employers' car, the employee was clearly under a duty
to obey any orders which might be given in relation to the driving of that car, **G**
orders such as: " This car is being run in, you must not go more than thirty
miles an hour." For my part, however, I cannot think that that sort of obligation to obey the employers' orders or an obligation once the option was exercised
in fact to return to Penrith in the car, can in any way be said to be an obligation
arising out of the terms of his employment. It seems to me that the obligation
which arises in those circumstances arises, if I may put it this way, outside the **H**
terms of his employment, and by reason of the facilities provided by the employers
of which the employee has chosen to avail himself. The justices came to a
correct conclusion, and I would dismiss this appeal.

SACHS, J.: I entirely agree, and only wish to advert to one fallacy that
seemed to my mind to underlie a considerable part of the submissions made by
counsel for the appellant. **I**

In relation to the words " time to work " he pressed that the journeys back to
Penrith were in fact journeys to get to work, and so part of the work of the
employee. Whilst, however, there are many occasions when the actual work
of an employee may involve the making of a journey as part of his or her work,
on the other hand the obligation to present himself for work at a given time
must in many other cases be carefully distinguished from the obligation to work
after arrival. It is a fallacy to say that the period of the journey to work must

A necessarily be one when the employee is at work, nor in many cases does it
necessarily carry the matter any further to ascertain, as regards the financing
of that journey, whether the employer provided the fare or provided free transport, or whether he chose to pay to the man a lump sum or some sum calculated
on a different basis. This distinction, once appreciated, provides one more
step on the way to concluding that in this particular case the period of travel
B was, for the reasons stated by LORD PARKER, C.J., not one which fell within a
period of " time of work " nor was part of the employment of the first respondent.

WIDGERY, J.: I agree that this appeal should be dismissed, and have
nothing to add.

Appeal dismissed.

C Solicitors: *Treasury Solicitor*; *Doyle, Devonshire & Co.*, agents for *T. H.
Wardlaw*, Newcastle-upon-Tyne (for the respondents).

[*Reported by* KAUSHALYA PURIE, *Barrister-at-Law.*]

Re HOLMDEN'S SETTLEMENT TRUSTS.
D HOLMDEN AND OTHERS v. INLAND REVENUE
COMMISSIONERS.

[COURT OF APPEAL (Lord Denning, M.R., Harman and Russell, L.JJ.), March 23
24, May 12, 1966.]

Estate Duty   Determination of life interest—Discretionary trust for class limited
E   *to cease on death of widow—Variation by order of court extending period of
trust until death of widow or twenty-one years from date of order, whichever
was longer—Death of widow within three years after order—Whether order
operated to determine interest of class—Whether estate duty chargeable on trust
fund on death of widow—Whether a collective class under a discretionary trust
can have an interest in possession for estate duty purposes—Finance Act,*
F   *1940 (3 & 4 Geo. 6 c. 29), s. 43 (1), as amended by Finance Act, 1950 (14
Geo. 6 c. 15), s. 43, Sch. 7, Pt. 1.*
*Judgment—Judicial decision as authority—Ratio decidendi—House of Lords
decisions—Two reasons given—Whether both binding if the House of Lords
should subsequently find one to be wrong.*

By cl. 2 (a) of a settlement dated Dec. 28, 1927, the income of the trust
G fund thereby established was directed to be held during the joint lives of the
settlor and his wife and the life of the survivor of them on discretionary
trusts for a specific class consisting of his wife, his children and their issue.
The settlor died on Apr. 16, 1945. By an order dated Jan. 12, 1960, made
on an application under the Variation of Trusts Act, 1958, to which the
trustees and the existing objects of the discretionary trusts were parties,
H an arrangement was approved by which the settlement was to have effect
from Jan. 12, 1960, as varied by the order, and by which the discretionary
trusts of income declared by cl. 2 (a) should have effect during the life
of the settlor's widow or the period of twenty-one years from Jan. 12, 1960,
whichever should be the longer. She died on Dec. 22, 1962. The Crown
claimed that estate duty was payable on the death of the settlor's widow
I on the whole of the trust fund under s. 43 (1)* of the Finance Act, 1940, on

---

* Section 43 (1), as amended, of the Finance Act, 1940, so far as is relevant is as follows:
" Subject to the provisions of this section, where an interest limited to cease on a
death has been disposed of or has determined, whether by surrender, assurance, divesting,
forfeiture or in any other manner (except by the expiration of a fixed period at the
expiration of which the interest was limited to cease), whether wholly or partly, and
whether for value or not, after becoming an interest in possession . . . —(a) if . . . the
property in which the interest subsisted would have passed on the death under s. 1 of
the Finance Act, 1894, that property shall be deemed by virtue of this section to be
included as to the whole thereof in the property passing on the death . . ."

Affirmed, H.L. [1968] 1 All E.R. 148.

the ground that the interest of the specific class under cl. 2 (*a*) was an   A
interest in possession and that the order of the court operated to determine
that interest.

Held (LORD DENNING, M.R., dissenting): estate duty was not exigible
on the death of the settlor's widow for the following reasons—

(i) in regard to the construction and effect of the variation of the discretionary trust—   B

(a) (per HARMAN, L.J.) by virtue of the court's approval of the arrangement
varying the period of the discretionary trust of income the variation must
be read into the settlement with the consequence that, since no duty would
have been payable on the death of the settlor's widow if the settlement had
originally provided that the discretionary trust of income should last for
twenty-one years from Jan. 12, 1960, no duty became leviable on her death   C
in 1962, her death being merely the dropping of the life of a member of a
discretionary class and thus not causing any notional passing of the trust
property under s. 2 (1) (*b*) of the Finance Act, 1894 (see p. 668, letter I,
to p. 669, letter B, post).

(b) (per RUSSELL, L.J.) the effect of the court's approval of the arrangement
was to supersede the discretionary trust under the settlement by a different   D
discretionary trust starting on Jan. 12, 1960 (see p. 670, letter I, post).

(ii) section 43 of the Finance Act, 1950, was inapplicable because—

(a) section 43 did not apply to a determination which did not result in any
change of persons beneficially interested in the relevant life period or change
in their beneficial interests (see p. 671, letter C, and p. 669, letter G, post).   E

Dicta of LORD UPJOHN and LORD DONOVAN, LORD GUEST and LORD
MORTON OF HENRYTON concurring, in *Ralli Brothers, Ltd.* v. *Inland Revenue
Comrs.* ([1966] 1 All E.R. at pp. 72, 67) applied.

(b) (per HARMAN, L.J.) the court's order of Jan. 12, 1960, enlarged rather
than disposed of or determined the discretionary life interest (see p. 669,
letter E, post).   F

Per LORD DENNING, M.R. and HARMAN, L.J.: we agree with the view
expressed by PENNYCUICK, J., that a class of person entitled under a discretionary trust of income can have an interest in possession for the purpose
of s. 43 of the Finance Act, 1940 (see p. 666, letter D, and p. 669, letter H,
post; cf. [1965] 1 All E.R. at p. 752).

Per LORD DENNING, M.R.: if two reasons for decision have been given   G
in the House of Lords, and the House afterwards find that one reason was
right and the other was wrong, they are not bound by the reason that they
find to be wrong (see p. 667, letter A, post).

Decision of PENNYCUICK, J. ([1965] 1 All E.R. 744) affirmed.

[As to the determination of life interests leading to estate duty becoming   H
chargeable, see 15 HALSBURY'S LAWS (3rd Edn.) 15, para. 25; and for cases on
interests in property limited to cease on death, see 21 DIGEST (Repl.) 17-22, *57-77*.

As to the binding effect of reasons for decisions of courts, see 22 HALSBURY'S
LAWS (3rd Edn.) 797, para. *1682.*

For the Finance Act, 1894, s. 1, s. 2, s. 22, see 9 HALSBURY'S STATUTES (2nd
Edn.) 348, 350, 382.   I

For the Finance Act, 1940, s. 43 (1), as amended, see 29 HALSBURY'S STATUTES
(2nd Edn.) 183.]

Cases referred to:

Behrens v. *Bertram Mills, Ltd.*, [1957] 1 All E.R. 583; [1957] 2 Q.B. 1; [1957]
    2 W.L.R. 404; Digest (Cont. Vol. A) 467, *339a.*

Close v. *Steel Co. of Wales, Ltd.*, [1961] 2 All E.R. 953; [1962] A.C. 367; [1961
    3 W.L.R. 319; Digest (Cont. Vol. A) 585, *201c.*

A   *Downshire's Settled Estates, Re, Downshire (Marquis)* v. *Royal Bank of Scotland,*
        Re Chapman's Settlement Trusts, Chapman v. *Chapman, Re Blackwell's*
        Settlement Trusts, Blackwell v. *Blackwell*, [1953] 1 All E.R. 103; [1953]
        Ch. 218; [1953] 2 W.L.R. 94; *affd.* H.L., sub nom. *Chapman* v. *Chapman,*
        [1954] 1 All E.R. 798; [1954] A.C. 429; [1954] 2 W.L.R. 723; 3rd
        Digest Supp.

B   *Jacobs* v. *London County Council*, [1950] 1 All E.R. 737; [1950] A.C. 361;
        114 J.P. 204; 30 Digest (Repl.) 212, *545.*

    Morgan v. *Inland Revenue Comrs.*, [1963] All 1 E.R. 481; [1963] Ch. 438;
        [1963] 2 W.L.R. 416; Digest (Cont. Vol. A) 510, *138a.*

    Public Trustee v. *Inland Revenue Comrs.*, [1964] 1 All E.R. 519; sub nom. *Re*
        Kirkwood, Public Trustee v. *Inland Revenue Comrs.*, [1964] Ch. 527;
C   [1964] 2 W.L.R. 680; *rvsd.* C.A., [1964] 3 All E.R. 780; sub nom. *Re*
        Kirkwood, Public Trustee v. *Inland Revenue Comrs.*, [1965] Ch. 286;
        [1964] 3 W.L.R. 1240; *affd.* H.L., [1966] 1 All E.R. 76; sub nom. *Re*
        Kirkwood, Public Trustee v. *Inland Revenue Comrs.*, [1966] 2 W.L.R.
        136.

D   *Ralli's Settlement, Re, Ralli Brothers, Ltd.* v. *Inland Revenue Comrs.*, [1964] 1
        All E.R. 962; [1965] Ch. 265; [1964] 2 W.L.R. 1351; *rvsd.* C.A.,
        [1964] 3 All E.R. 780; [1965] Ch. 286; [1964] 3 W.L.R. 1240; *affd.*
        H.L. sub nom. *Ralli Brothers, Ltd.* v. *Inland Revenue Comrs.*, [1966]
        1 All E.R. 65; [1966] 2 W.L.R. 119.

Appeal.

E   This was an appeal by the Inland Revenue Commissioners from a determination of PENNYCUICK, J., dated June 15, 1964, reported [1965] 1 All E.R. 744,
declaring, on application to him by originating summons, dated Apr. 23, 1964,
that on the true construction of a settlement dated Dec. 28, 1927, made between
Sir Osborn George Holmden, Dame Mary Mildred Holmden and another, and
an order dated Jan. 12, 1960, made by DANCKWERTS, J., entitled " In the matter
F of the trusts for settlement dated Dec. 28, 1927, and made between Sir Osborn
George Holmden and others and in the matter of the Variation of Trusts Act,
1958 (1959 H.2593) ", the trust fund vested in the respondents to this appeal
as trustees of the settlement did not become liable to estate duty on the death
of Dame Mary Mildred Holmden on Dec. 22, 1962.

    By the settlement Sir Osborn George Holmden (the settlor), after reciting his
G desire to make provision for his wife, Dame Mary Mildred Holmden (" Lady
Holmden "), his son George Alexander Holmden and his daughter Mary Holmden
and their issue, constituted a trust fund, the operative trusts of cl. 2 of which
were as follows—

    " (a) Upon trust during the lives of the settlor and [Lady Holmden] and the
H   life of the survivor to pay or apply the whole or such part of the income of the
    trust fund as [the trustees] shall in their uncontrolled discretion think fit for or
    towards the maintenance education or benefit of all or any one or more to
    the exclusion of the others or other of them [Lady Holmden, and the settlor's
    son and daughter and their issue] for the time being in existence in such
    proportions and manner as the trustees shall in their uncontrolled discretion
    from time to time think fit . . .
I   " (b) Upon trust after the death of the survivor of the settlor and [Lady
    Holmden] as to the capital of the trust fund . . . for such of them [the settlor's
    said children and their issue] . . . in such manner as [Lady Holmden] shall by
    will or codicil appoint and in default of and subject to any such appointment
    upon trust to pay the income from one moiety of the trust fund to [the
    settlor's son] during his life and after his death to pay or transfer the said
    moiety to [his] children or child [on attaining twenty-one etc.] . . . and to pay
    the income from the other moiety of the trust fund to [the daughter] during

her life . . . and after her death to pay or transfer the said moiety to her   A
children or child [on attaining twenty-one etc.] . . ."

The settlor died on Apr. 16, 1945. Lady Holmden survived him. On Jan. 12, 1960,
an order was made under the Variation of Trusts Act, 1958, varying the trusts
of the settlement, the application being made by Lady Holmden who was then
eighty-four.   The respondents included all the then living beneficiaries and the
trustees of the settlement. The terms of the relevant paragraphs of the arrange-   B
ment which the court approved are set out at p. 665, letter E, post. Lady Holmden died on Dec. 22, 1962. The Crown claimed that the trust fund subject to the
settlement became chargeable to estate duty on her death. This claim was put
under three heads—(i) that the trust fund passed under s. 1 of the Finance Act,
1894, unaided by s. 2 (1) (b), but with the assistance of s. 22 (1) (l); (ii) that the
trust fund passed under s. 1 aided by s. 2 (1) (b), again with the assistance of   C
s. 22 (1) (l); and (iii) that the trust fund was deemed to have passed on the
death of Lady Holmden under s. 43 of the Finance Act, 1940. At the hearing
before PENNYCUICK, J. the third contention alone was argued, the Crown desiring
to keep open the first two contentions for argument in a higher court.

    Arthur Bagnall, Q.C., and *J. P. Warner* for the Crown.   D
    J. A. Brightman, Q.C., and *S. W. Templeman, Q.C.*, for the trustees.

                                                Cur. adv. vult.

May 12.   The following judgments were read.

    LORD DENNING, M.R.: On Dec. 28, 1927, Sir George Holmden made a
settlement for his wife, Lady Holmden, and his son George and daughter Mary.
I will call it the settlement.   By it he transferred a large number of shares to   E
trustees on these trusts; cl. 2 (a) contained discretionary *trusts of income*. During
the lives of Sir George and Lady Holmden and the life of the survivor, the trustees
were to pay *the income*, as in their uncontrolled discretion they thought fit,
for this class of person: Lady Holmden, George, Mary, and the issue of George
and of Mary. Clause 2 (b) contained *trusts of capital*. These were trusts as to the
capital, after the death of the survivor, in favour of George and of Mary and   F
of their issue. On Apr. 16, 1945, Sir George died. Lady Holmden survived him.
In 1960 she was aged eighty-four. Her son George had married twice and had
three daughters. Her daughter Mary had married twice and had two daughters.
One of these daughters had married and was expecting her first child (who was
to be the first great-grandchild of Lady Holmden). She has since had two other
children.   In 1960 it was obvious that, if nothing was done, when old Lady   G
Holmden died, estate duty would be payable on her death under s. 2 (1) (b)
of the Finance Act, 1894, because the interest of the beneficiaries under the
discretionary trust was an interest which would cease on Lady Holmden's death,
and a benefit would accrue by reason of the cesser of that interest, and the
value of it would be the value of the shares coming to George and Mary.
    In order to avoid this imminent liability to estate duty, steps were taken to   H
vary the trusts of the settlement. There is nothing wrong about this. We discussed it in *Chapman* v. *Chapman* (1). I said then that (2):

    " Just as people of full age and understanding are entitled so to arrange
their affairs as to reduce the incidence of death duties on their successors,
so also the court will permit the receiver of a lunatic to do it . . . If the court   I
goes thus far, there is no reason why it should not give its consent to a
scheme on behalf of infants for the like purpose."

The House of Lords, in its judicial capacity, thought otherwise. LORD MORTON
OF HENRYTON said that (3)

    (1) [1953] 1 All E.R. 103; [1953] Ch. 218; *on appeal*, [1954] 1 All E.R. 798; [1954]
A.C. 429.
    (2) [1953] 1 All E.R. at p. 136; [1953] A.C. at p. 276.
    (3) [1954] 1 All E.R. at p. 818; [1954] A.C. at p. 468.

A   ". . . If the court had power to approve, and did approve, schemes such
as the present scheme, the way would be open for a most undignified game
of chess between the Chancery Division and the Legislature."

Despite these forebodings, however, Parliament a few years later did give the
court power to vary or revoke trusts, even though the avowed purpose was to
avoid death duties; see the Variation of Trusts Act, 1958. Ever since the Act
B   of 1958 was passed, the Chancery courts have spent much of their time sanctioning
the variation of trusts, the principal object of which is to avoid death duties.
The lawyers have become magicians who perform conjuring tricks. Sometimes
they succeed, as in *Morgan* v. *Inland Revenue Comrs.* (4), and *Ralli Brothers,
Ltd.* v. *Inland Revenue Comrs.* (5). At other times they fail, as in *Re Kirkwood,
Public Trustee* v. *Inland Revenue Comrs.* (6). It has become indeed a game of
C   chess, played by each side with a subtlety and skill worthy of the schoolmen; but
in the long run the legislature is bound to win. It can offset all these devices.
It can call off the game.

This case is an illustration of one of the more recent inventions of Lincoln's
Inn. It is the " grafting operation ". You take an interest which is going to come
to an end when an old lady dies. You treat it like the branch of a tree. You
D   graft on to it an off-shoot which will continue after her death. By this means
you avoid s. 2 (1) (*b*) of the Act of 1894; but it needs great skill to perform this
operation successfully. You must be careful not to cut off the branch itself.
For if you do, you may find that the interest has been determined; and estate
duty will be payable under s. 43 of the Finance Act, 1940.

In an endeavour to avoid estate duty, this settlement was varied by means
E   of an arrangement sanctioned by an order of DANCKWERTS, J., on Jan. 12, 1960.
I will call it the arrangement. The material terms of the arrangement were these:

" 2. As from the operative date [Jan. 12, 1960] the settlement shall have
effect subject to the variations which are hereinafter set forth.
" 3. The discretionary trusts declared by cl. 2 (a) of the settlement shall
F   have effect during the life of Lady Holmden or the period of twenty-one
years from the operative date [Jan. 12, 1960], whichever shall be the longer."

Clause 5 contained new trusts of the capital in place of the trusts in cl. 2 (b).

Lady Holmden died on Dec. 22, 1962. The trustees before her death paid the
income to her and the grandchildren: and after her death to her daughter Mary,
to her grandchildren and great-grandchildren. Now the question is whether
G   estate duty is payable on the death of Lady Holmden: or whether it has been
successfully averted by reason of the arrangement made under the order of
court.

Finance Act, 1894, s. 2 (1) (b):

If the old discretionary trust in the *settlement* continued until the death of
Lady Holmden; and then came to an end; and was succeeded by a new dis-
H   cretionary trust under the *arrangement* for the period until Jan. 12, 1981, then
estate duty would be payable under s. 2 (1) (*b*). The case would be governed
by *Public Trustee* v. *Inland Revenue Comrs.* (7). If, however, the interest under
the discretionary trust in the settlement was extended by a grafting operation
so as to become a single discretionary trust for a period from Jan. 12, 1960,
during the life of Lady Holmden, or until Jan. 12, 1981, whichever was the
I   longer, then estate duty would not be payable under s. 2 (1) (*b*): because the
falling of one life under a single discretionary trust does not give rise to a
claim under s. 2 (1) (*b*), seeing that, being discretionary, the interest is of no
ascertainable value under s. 7 (7).

The choice being these two alternatives is a matter of construction of the
arrangement. I am much impressed by the clear words in cl. 2 and cl. 3 that the

(4) [1963] 1 All E.R. 481; [1963] Ch. 438.   (5) [1966] 1 All E.R. 65.
(6) [1966] 1 All E.R. 76.
(7) [1964] 3 All E.R. 780; [1965] Ch. 286; *on appeal* [1966] 1 All E.R. 76.

settlement and the old discretionary trusts " shall have effect " as from Jan. 12, A
1960. These words " shall have effect " seem to me to make the settlement
itself continue until the death of Lady Holmden: in which case it must be
succeeded on her death by a new discretionary trust under the arrangement.
On that construction the case is covered by *Re Kirkwood, Public Trustee* v.
Inland Revenue Comrs. (8).

If I am wrong about this, then the only alternative is that, by reason of the B
arrangement, there was a new discretionary trust as from Jan. 12, 1960: in
which case I turn to consider s. 43.

Finance Act, 1940, s. 43:

If there was a new discretionary trust for a period starting from Jan. 12,
1960, I think that it follows that the old discretionary trusts determined on
Jan. 12, 1960. You could not have the two—the new and the old—running at C
the same time. This determination of the old trust seems to me to come directly
within the words of s. 43 (1) of the Act of 1940, which says that

" where an interest limited to cease on death has been disposed of or has
determined, whether by surrender, assurance, divesting, forfeiture or in any
other manner . . . after becoming an interest in possession ",
                                                                                      D
the property in which the interest subsisted is (to put it shortly) deemed to
pass on the death.

The interest of the discretionary class under the old settlement was, I think,
clearly an interest in possession limited to cease on the death of Lady Holmden.
I agree with PENNYCUICK, J. (9) on this point. That interest was " determined "
on Jan. 12, 1960, when the new trust took effect. It was determined " in any E
other manner ". So it comes within the words of the charging sub-s. (1) and
estate duty is payable.

It is said, however, that we cannot come to this conclusion. We are prevented,
it is said, by *Ralli's* case (10), recently decided by the House of Lords. When
that case was in this court, RUSSELL, L.J., said (11) that s. 43 applies only when
the transaction   F

" operates wholly or partially to confer a benefit on another or others
at the expense of the life tenant."

When that case reached the House of Lords, this statement won the approval
of LORD DONOVAN (12); and LORD UPJOHN said in terms (13) that

". . . there must be a determination or disposal in favour of some other
party for the section to have any effect . . ."   G

This was agreed to by LORD GUEST (14) and LORD MORTON OF HENRYTON (14).

It was argued before us that the statement of LORD UPJOHN was one of the
reasons for the decision of the House and is binding on this court. I do not agree.
As I read his speech, the reason for the decision was simply that, as a matter
of construction, the life interest of Mrs. Ralli was never determined or disposed H
of. The statement which I have quoted was unnecessary for the purpose in hand.
It was an obiter dictum.

I must, however, consider the statement of LORD UPJOHN on the footing that
it is one of two reasons which he gave for his decision. It is said that both reasons
are binding on all courts in the land, including the House of Lords itself. That
proposition is said to rest on *Jacobs* v. *London County Council* (15) (see also I
Behrens v. *Bertram Mills, Ltd.* (16)). I do not think, however, that those cases
warrant so wide a proposition. It seems to me that, if the House of Lords give

(8) [1964] 3 All E.R. 780; [1965] Ch. 286; *on appeal* [1966] 1 All E.R. 76.
(9) [1965] 1 All E.R. at p. 752.   (10) [1966] 1 All E.R. 65.
(11) [1964] 3 All E.R. at p. 795; [1965] Ch. at p. 353.
(12) [1966] 1 All E.R. at p. 72.   (13) [1966] 1 All E.R. at p. 69.
(14) [1966] 1 All E.R. at p. 67.
(15) [1950] 1 All E.R. 737; [1950] A.C. 361.
(16) [1957] 1 All E.R. 583 at pp. 593, 594; [1957] 2 Q.B. 1 at p. 24.

A two reasons for their decision and afterwards find that one of the reasons was right and the other was wrong, then they are entitled to accept the right reason and reject the wrong. The decision is not authority " for nothing ". It is authority for the right reason, but not for the wrong. I can see no justification whatever for saying that they are bound by the wrong reason. Surely the House are not bound to perpetuate error. Nor is this court. I would repeat the wise words of

B SIR FREDERICK POLLOCK (17), which I quoted in *Close* v. *Steel Company of Wales, Ltd.* (18):

" Judicial authority belongs not to the exact words used in this or that judgment, nor even to all the reasons given, but only to the principles accepted and applied as necessary grounds of the decision."

C In the *Ralli* case (19) it was quite unnecessary for LORD UPJOHN to make the statement that a determination must be " in favour of some other party " for s. 43 to have any effect. The statement is not, in my opinion, binding on this court.

I feel at liberty to inquire into the matter afresh. Subsection (1) is the charging section. It contains no words which expressly or impliedly require the disposal or

D determination to be in favour of " some other party ". Such an implication is somehow said to be recognised by the Inland Revenue because in the past they have made a concession that, if a life tenant acquires a reversion expectant on his life tenancy, estate duty is not payable on his death. That concession can only be supported, it is said, on the ground that the life tenancy in such a case is determined in favour of the deceased and not in favour of some other party. I

E do not think that any such inference is justifiable. LORD UPJOHN himself described it (20) as a " curious " concession. It may well be that the Revenue do not consider that in such a case the life tenancy is determined; but, whatever the origin of the concession, it is, I think, quite illegitimate to construe sub-s. (1) by reference to it.

Subsection (2) is an exception enactment. In order to come within the exception the person who had the interest beforehand must be " entirely excluded ". So

F it is obvious that someone else must take his interest: with the result that there must be " some other party " who fulfils the description of being " the person becoming entitled ". The words of LORD UPJOHN fit the *exception* enactment; but they do not fit the charging subsection. Subsection (1) is the charging subsection.

Take a case where the person who had the interest beforehand is not " entirely

G excluded " but himself retains the beneficial enjoyment. He falls within the *charging* subsection: and he is not within the *exception* subsection. You would not expect that his estate could get out of death duties. If he retains *part* of the beneficial enjoyment himself after the determintion, and " some other party " gets *part*, his estate is admittedly chargeable. I cannot for the life of me see why, if he retains the whole—so there is no other party who enjoys it—his estate

H should not be chargeable at all.

My conclusion is that it is not right to read into sub-s. (1) the words " in favour of some other party ". If the interest which is limited to cease on death has been disposed of or determined in such a way that the person interested still retains the benefit of it, in whole or in part, then his estate is chargeable on his death under sub-s. (1): it does not come within the exception in sub-s. (2) for the simple

I reason that he has not been entirely excluded from it.

I come back to the construction of the arrangement of Jan. 12, 1960, and I think that it presents the taxpayer with a true dilemma. It is another Morton's Fork. If the existing discretionary trust continued in existence during the lifetime of Lady Holmden and was then succeeded by a new trust until Jan. 12, 1981, then

---

(17) See CONTINENTAL LAW IN THE NINETEENTH CENTURY (Continental Legal History Series) XLIV.
(18) [1961] 2 All E.R. 953 at p. 960; [1962] A.C. 367 at p. 388.
(19) [1966] 1 All E.R. at p. 69.   (20) [1966] 1 All E.R. at p. 68, letter A.

the interest of the class under the existing discretionary trust was an interest **A**
which ceased on her death, and estate duty is payable under *Re Kirkwood, Public
Trustee* v. *Inland Revenue Comrs.* (21).   If, however, the existing discretionary
trust was replaced on Jan. 12, 1960, by a new discretionary trust for a new trust
period, then the existing discretionary trust was on that date disposed of or
determined within s. 43 of the Finance Act, 1940; estate duty is payable under
sub-s. (1); and there is no exception available under sub-s. (2).   **B**
  I would allow the appeal accordingly.

  HARMAN, L.J.: This appeal is another chapter in that fascinating serial,
the authors of which are known in the profession as " the grafters ".   These are
people who make grafts by inserting a young shoot into a moribund stock thus
seeking to give it a new lease of life.   Sometimes the graft strikes and produces   **C**
new healthy growth.   A graft failed to strike in *Re Kirkwood, Public Trustee* v.
Inland Revenue Comrs. (21), but succeeded in *Ralli Brothers* v. *Inland Revenue
Comrs.* (22).   In the former case there was a discretionary trust of income during
the life of Mrs. Pattisson (the moribund stock) for her and others with an absolute
interest in remainder.   The remainderman assigned his reversion for a limited
period to the trustees of the settlement on trusts for a class expressed to be the   **D**
same as the then still existing class, but in fact differing from it in that it did not
arise until after the death of Mrs. Pattisson.   WILBERFORCE, J. (23) held that this
document created a single " running " trust and that no interest passed on Mrs.
Pattisson's death, but this view received no approval in the higher courts.   The
vice of the expedient was, of course, that the remainderman had no power to
affect, and did not seek to affect, the interest of Mrs. Pattisson during her lifetime,   **E**
and as a result there was a change of interest at her death in favour of the new
class and the case could not be regarded as one where a single discretionary class
is interested and the dropping of one life gives no claim to duty.   In *Ralli's* case
(22), on the other hand, the graft succeeded because there Mrs. Ralli had a life
interest in the fund which was enlarged by gift of the remaindermen for a period
ending at the end of 1965.   Taking Mrs. Ralli and her estate as one, that interest   **F**
was equivalent to an estate pur autre vie and was not terminated by Mrs. Ralli's
death but remained in force until the end of 1965.   Nothing, therefore, passed
on her death except the interest of which she was competent to dispose, namely,
her interest until the end of that period.
  In the present case the settlor had created an interest in a discretionary class
consisting after his death in 1945 of his wife, children and issue and enduring   **G**
during the life of his wife.   She died in 1962 and the question is whether the fund
passed on her death.   In this case the parties had the happy notion of enlisting
the aid of the Chancery court under the Variation of Trusts Act, 1958.   Lady
Holmden, the wife, was herself the applicant with the result that all possible
interests under the settlement including unborn persons were represented and
the order shows the arrangement made.   This was an arrangement varying the   **H**
settlement, and, as I understand the effect of the Act of 1958, the court's approval
on behalf of infants and unborn persons of an arrangement arrived at by all the
adult beneficiaries has the result of re-writing the settlement from the date of
the order in the terms there proposed.   So here the order dated Jan. 12, 1960,
provides that as from that date the settlement shall have effect as varied by the
order.   The result is to write the variations into the settlement, and cl. 2 (*a*) of the   **I**
settlement, which sets up the discretionary trust, must be read as being effective
not only during the life of Lady Holmden (as the survivor of herself and her
husband) but for twenty-one years from the date of the order if that should exceed
Lady Holmden's lifetime, as it did for she died in 1962.   Now it seems to me clear
that if the settlement as originally drawn had provided that the discretionary
trusts of income should last for twenty-one years from Jan. 12, 1960, no duty

---

(21) [1966] 1 All E.R. 76.   (22) [1966] 1 All E.R. 65.
    (23) [1964] 1 All E.R. 519 at p. 524; [1964] Ch. 527 at p. 537.

A could have been payable on the death of Lady Holmden in 1962. This graft in effect has surmounted the difficulty which was fatal in *Re Kirkwood, Public Trustee* v. *Inland Revenue Comrs.* (24) in that Mrs. Kirkwood's own interest was not embraced in the discretionary trust there set up. Here Lady Holmden assents to the arrangement and brings her own interest into the pool, thus creating a new trust operative from Jan. 12, 1960, for twenty-one years whether she lives or

B dies, and there can, I think, be no passing within s. 2 (1) (*b*) of the Finance Act, 1894, in these circumstances. Lady Holmden's death was merely the dropping of one of the lives comprised in the discretionary class.

On this footing the Crown claims that there was a new trust set up and that the old trust must have disappeared and that duty is payable under s. 43 of the Finance Act, 1940. The argument runs as follows. The collective interest of the

C group of persons interested under the old discretionary trust was an interest limited to cease on the death of Lady Holmden. That interest " has been disposed of or has determined " after becoming an interest in possession and the section applies, with the result that the interest, that is to say the whole fund which would have passed on Lady Holmden's death, must be deemed by virtue of that section to be included in the property passing on her death. The answer of the

D taxpayer is threefold. First, that there has been no " disposition " or " determination " of any discretionary interest; secondly, if there has, it was not a determination in favour of other persons and, therefore, was not within the section, and, thirdly, that the section does not apply to the ending of a discretionary trust because no member of the class has an " interest " within the meaning of the section.

E As to the first point, I do not for myself feel that the effect of the order was to " dispose " of the discretionary trust, still less to " determine " it; it would in my judgment be more accurate to say that the order " enlarged " the discretionary trust. Any member of the class could postulate after the order that he had an interest lasting at least for twenty-one years which in the nature of things and in fact was much longer than an interest during the life of Lady Holmden then

F over eighty-four. The class interested was the same class, but the interest of each member of it was enlarged. On the dropping of any life of a member of the class, duty was not exigible on well known principles because such an interest could not be quantified in money and Lady Holmden was such a member.

If this be right, s. 43 is out of the picture. It if be wrong, there arises the second point, a view favoured by RUSSELL, L.J., in *Ralli's* case (25) and approved by

G LORD UPJOHN and LORD DONOVAN expressly in the House of Lords (26). These views may have been obiter but they are of very great persuasive authority; they do or would in some circumstances produce very odd results, as the judgment just delivered by the Master of the Rolls shows, yet I should not propose to quarrel with them but to follow them.

As to the third point, I do not accept that the aggregate rights of the members

H of a discretionary class do not together amount to an interest within s. 43. On this point I agree with the views expressed by PENNYCUICK, J., in his judgment in this case (27). Though in the issue I agree with the result arrived at by the judge, a good deal of water has flowed under the bridges since he gave judgment and the reason by which he supported it, based as it was on the view of WILBERFORCE, J., in *Re Kirkwood, Public Trustee* v. *Inland Revenue Comrs.* (28), is not now tenable

I on that ground. I would nonetheless dismiss the appeal on the first two points stated above.

RUSSELL, L.J.: The first problem is this. Did the arrangement contained in the order made on Jan. 12, 1960, under the Variation of Trusts Act, 1958, on its true construction create a discretionary trust starting with the date of the

(24) [1966] 1 All E.R. 76.
(25) [1964] 3 All E.R. at pp. 794, 795; [1965] Ch. at pp. 332, 333.
(26) [1966] 1 All E.R. at pp. 69, 72.   (27) [1965] 1 All E.R. at p. 752.
(28) [1964] 1 All E.R. 519; [1964] Ch. 527.

order (" the operative date ") and ending on Jan. 12, 1981, or the later death **A**
of Lady Holmden, in substitution (as from the operative date) for the discretionary
trust in favour of the same class during a period ending on that death? Or did
the arrangement on its true construction merely create (if Lady Holmden should
die before Jan. 12, 1981) a discretionary trust in favour of the same class (*other
than* Lady Holmden) to commence on her death and end on Jan. 12, 1981? If
the latter is the true view, it is accepted by the taxpayer that the case of *Re* **B**
Kirkwood, Public Trustee v. *Inland Revenue Comrs.* (29) applies and duty became
payable on Lady Holmden's death: the reason for this is that a *method* has been
adopted by which the interest of a class consisting of A, B, C, etc., and Lady
Holmden ceased on her death, and a separate and new interest in favour of a
different class consisting of only A, B, C, etc. arose on her death.

I have said that this problem depends for its solution on the true construction **C**
of the arrangement. This is common ground between the parties. The Crown does
not contend that one can regard broadly the substance of the matter and say that
since any mere replacement of the original discretionary trust would (apart from
estate duty legislation) be an idle and fruitless and meaningless frolic, effecting
no change whatever in the beneficial interests of those participating (either
personally or through the court) in the arrangements, such mere replacement can **D**
be ignored for estate duty purposes as having no operation. The Crown admits
that in a case such as this, the result envisaged in my first question could have
been attained by an appropriate choice of language, but contends that the
language chosen is not appropriate for that purpose.

What then of the true construction? In my judgment the arrangement displaces (with effect from the operative date) the original discretionary trust and **E**
sets in train a substituted discretionary trust. The whole matter lay in the hands
of the totality of beneficiaries, some through, so to speak, the agency of the court.
Clause 2 is in the following terms:

" As from the operative date the settlement shall have effect subject to
the variations which are hereinafter set forth."
F

This I take to mean no more than that the variations to the settlement shall have
effect from the operative date; it does not needlessly invigorate the settlement.
It is true that not everything that follows is a variation of the settlement. For
example, cl. 10 expressly states that certain provisions of the settlement shall
continue to apply; but the mind is alerted to look for variations. Turning to cl. 3
of the arrangement, I find this:
G

" The discretionary trusts of income declared by cl. 2 (a) of the settlement
shall have effect during the life of Lady Holmden or the period of twenty-one
years from the operative date whichever shall be the longer (hereinafter
called ' the trust period ')."

The contention of the Crown is that this clause does nothing but to declare a set
of trusts to take effect *after* Lady Holmden's death in a certain event, i.e., is **H**
only a variation of cl. 2 (*b*). I must say that the clause is most peculiarly worded
if that is the achievement for which it is designed. To hold this to be the correct
view would mean that the arrangement provides that a discretionary trust shall
arise in favour of a class *including* Lady Holmden at the precise moment when the
death of Lady Holmden *excludes* her as a possible object of the trustees' discretion.
I am persuaded by this absurdity to the view that the method adopted by the **I**
beneficiaries (some through the agency of the court) has been to supersede (with
effect from the operative date) the discretionary trust under the settlement by a
different discretionary trust starting then and with a terminal occasion other
(or potentially or indeed probably other) than the original terminal occasion.
The same effect is to be attributed to cl. 2 and cl. 3 of the arrangement in this way:
" the discretionary trusts of income declared by cl. 2 (*a*) of the settlement "

(29) [1966] 1 All E.R. 76.

A referred to in cl. 3 of the arrangement mean those trusts unrelated to any period·
the effect of the arrangement is that *as from* the operative date cl. 2 (*a*) of the
settlement is to be read and acted on by the trustees as though the words " during
the lives of the settlor and the said Mary Mildred Holmden and the life of the
survivor " were deleted and for them were substituted the words " during the
life of Lady Holmden or the period of twenty-one years from the operative
B date whichever shall be the longer ".   Accordingly, in my judgment this case
is not covered by *Re Kirkwood, Public Trustee* v. *Inland Revenue Comrs.* (30).

What is the outcome of this?   The Crown argues that the necessary result is
that the original interest under the settlement trusts of the discretionary class
during the life of Lady Holmden, having been superseded on the operative date by
the then substitution of a new trust for a different period, was then " determined "
C and that therefore s. 43 applies.   This question was fully argued in this court in
Ralli Brothers, Ltd. v. *Inland Revenue Comrs.* (31).   My brethren expressed no
concluded view on the point.   I came to the conclusion that s. 43 was not applicable, for two reasons, the second of which is here relevant, viz., that s. 43 did
not apply to a determination which resulted in no change in the persons beneficially
interested in the relevant life period or in their beneficial interests.   In the House
D of Lords LORD UPJOHN (32) expressed the same view: LORD GUEST (33) and
LORD MORTON OF HENRYTON (33) agreed with the whole of his views; and
LORD DONOVAN (34) expressly agreed with the reasons which I had given.   It is
argued before us that these views were obiter dicta without full argument and
wrong.   I think that I am entitled in the circumstances to say simply that I
adhere to my former view (which was not *based* on the commissioners'
E " concession ") and am content to leave the matter to the House of Lords.

The trustees also argued, though ultimately I thought faintly, that though
the original *trust* was determined by supersession, s. 43 speaks of the determination
of *beneficial interests*, and the beneficial interest of the class during the life of Lady
Holmden had not been affected.   A beneficial interest, however, is the creature of
and dependent on a trust: destroy the mother and the foetus must die.

F The trustees further made a submission to the effect, as I understand it, that
s. 43 cannot apply to a discretionary trust either because it involves no interest
in possession or because the group cannot dispose of the interest.   There was no
argument on this.   The trustees said that they wished to reserve the point.
I am not quite sure what was meant by that.   But without argument I do not
propose to express any opinion on the point.   I would dismiss the appeal.

G   *Appeal dismissed.   Leave to appeal to the House of Lords granted.*

Solicitors: *Solicitor of Inland Revenue*; *Macfarlanes* (for the trustees).

[*Reported by* F. GUTTMAN, ESQ., *Barrister-at-Law.*]

H

I

---

(30) [1966] 1 All E.R. 76.   (31) [1964] 3 All E.R. 780; [1965] Ch. 286.
(32) [1966] 1 All E.R. at p. 69.   (33) [1966] 1 All E.R. at p. 67.
(34) [1966] 1 All E.R. at p. 72.

HALE v. VICTORIA PLUMBING CO., LTD.
AND EN-TOUT-CAS CO., LTD.

[COURT OF APPEAL (Danckwerts and Winn, L.JJ.), April 22, 1966.]

*Execution—Garnishee order—Set-off—Judgment debtor employed by garnishee
as sub-contractor on building work—Cross-claims between garnishee and
judgment debtor, the former alleging work badly done—Claim by garnishee
likely to extinguish judgment debtor's claim of indebtedness to him.*

A judgment creditor had a claim against E., Ltd. for work done. The
judgment creditor obtained a garnishee order absolute against E., Ltd., but
the evidence did not establish the nature of E., Ltd.'s debt to the judgment
debtor. On behalf of E., Ltd. it was deposed that E., Ltd. had claims against
the judgment debtor for breaches of contract (apparently for bad work as
sub-contractor under a building contract) exceeding in amount the sum
claimed from E., Ltd. by the judgment debtor.

Held: on the facts disclosed E., Ltd. had an equitable right of set-off for
its claims against the judgment debtor's claim (*Morgan & Sons, Ltd. v. S.
Martin Johnson & Co., Ltd.*, [1948] 2 All E.R. 196, applied), and, as this
set-off seemed likely either to extinguish the judgment debtor's claim or to
leave only a small balance due to the judgment debtor, the garnishee order
would be set aside (see p. 673, letter H, post).

Stumore v. *Campbell & Co.* ([1891-94] All E.R. Rep. 785) explained and
distinguished.

[As to what debts are attachable, see 16 HALSBURY'S LAWS (3rd Edn.) 80, 81,
para. 121; and for cases on the subject, see 21 DIGEST (Repl.) 719-729, *2187-2239.*

As to set-off in proceedings between employer and independent contractor, see
34 HALSBURY'S LAWS (3rd Edn.) 408, para. 709; and for cases on the subject,
see 40 DIGEST (Repl.) 442, *400-303.*

For the Supreme Court of Judicature (Consolidation) Act, 1925, s. 38 to s. 40,
see 18 HALSBURY'S STATUTES (2nd Edn.) 475-477.]

Cases referred to:

Morgan & Sons, Ltd. v. *S. Martin Johnson & Co., Ltd.*, [1948] 2 All E.R. 196;
    [1949] 1 K.B. 107; [1948] L.J.R. 1530; 2nd Digest Supp.
Stumore v. *Campbell & Co.*, [1891-94] All E.R. Rep. 785; [1892] 1 Q.B. 314;
    61 L.J.Q.B. 463; 66 L.T. 218; 40 Digest (Repl.) 444, *319.*

Interlocutory appeal.

This was an appeal by En-Tout-Cas Co., Ltd., the garnishee, against a garnishee
order made on Mar. 28, 1966, in the Leicester County Court, by Mr. Registrar
EVANS, on the application of Charles William Hale, the judgment creditor, in
respect of money alleged to be due from the garnishee to the judgment
debtor, Victoria Plumbing Co., Ltd. The facts are set out in the judgment of
DANCKWERTS, L.J.

J. G. Jones for the garnishee.
M. B. Smith for the judgment creditor.
The judgment debtor did not appear and was not represented.

DANCKWERTS, L.J.: In this case the judgment creditor has obtained a
garnishee order against the garnishee, En-Tout-Cas Co., Ltd., a company which,
we are told, not only makes the well-known hard tennis courts for which it has a
reputation but is also a builder and contractor. The deponent of the affidavit on
behalf of the judgment creditor, after stating the amount of the total sum due
from the judgment debtor as being £256 13s. 10d., says:

" I am informed and verily believe that En-Tout-Cas Co., Ltd. of Syston
aforesaid is indebted to the judgment debtor my grounds of information and
belief being given to me by Mr. R. G. Williams a director of Victoria Plumbing
Co., Ltd."

A   preliminary issue that such a contract, if it had been made which they denied, would have been ultra vires the plaintiff company and void.

Held: the contract was intra vires the plaintiff company for the following reasons—

(i) provided that the directors of the plaintiff company honestly formed the view that particular business could be carried on advantageously in

B   connexion with or as ancillary to the plaintiff company's main business, that additional business was within the plaintiff company's powers by virtue of cl. 3 (c) of the memorandum of association, and for this purpose (as was conceded) the opinion of B. was sufficient as the powers of the board had been delegated to him (see p. 681, letter A, p. 686, letter E, p. 689, letters A and B, and p. 690, letter G, post).

C   *Karen Kayemeth Le Jisroel, Ltd.* v. *Inland Revenue Comrs.* ([1932] All E.R. Rep. 971); *Oxford Group* v. *Inland Revenue Comrs.* ([1949] 2 All E.R. 537), and *Associated Artists, Ltd.* v. *Inland Revenue Comrs.* ([1956] 2 All E.R. 583) applied.

(ii) the contract regarding the procuration fee was a turning to account of an asset of the plaintiff company, viz., B.'s knowledge of a source of finance,

D   and thus was authorised by cl. 3 (q) of the memorandum of association (see p. 690, letter A, post; cf., p. 686, letter H, and p. 690, letter A, post).

(iii) (per SALMON, L.J.) the making of the contract regarding the procuration fee was in fact, as well as in B.'s opinion, incidental and conducive to the plaintiff company's objects of carrying on land development and was authorised under cl. 3 (ii) of the memorandum of association (see p. 689,

E   letter E, post; cf., p. 686, letter H, and p. 690, letter G, post).

Decision of MOCATTA, J. ([1965] 3 All E.R. 427)) reversed.

[**Editorial Note.** The court expressly refrained from expressing any opinion on the " interesting, important and difficult question " which would arise if the contract were ultra vires, viz., whether the plaintiff company having fully

F   performed its part under the contract and the defendants having obtained all benefit under the contract, the defendants could successfully take the point that the contract was ultra vires (see p. 690, letters B and G, and p. 686, letter H, post).

As to acts ultra vires the objects clause of a company's memorandum of association, see 6 HALSBURY'S LAWS (3rd Edn.) 414-418, paras. 802-805, 807-809;

G   and for cases on the subject, see 9 DIGEST (Repl.) 648-657, *4307-4356*.]

Cases referred to:

Ashbury Railway Carriage & Iron Co. v. *Riche*, (1875), L.R. 7 H.L. 653; 44 L.J.Ex. 185; 33 L.T. 450; 9 Digest (Repl.) 648, *4309*.

Associated Artists, Ltd. v. *Inland Revenue Comrs.*, [1956] 2 All E.R. 583; [1956] 1 W.L.R. 752; 36 Tax Cas. 49; 28 Digest (Repl.) 319, *1405*.

H   *A.-G.* v. *Manchester Corpn.*, [1906] 1 Ch. 643; 75 L.J.Ch. 330; 70 J.P. 201; 13 Digest (Repl.) 278, *1001*.

Barned's Banking Co., Re, Ex p. Contract Corpn., (1867), 3 Ch. App. 105; 37 L.J.Ch. 81; 17 L.T. 267; 13 Digest (Repl.) 200, *192*.

Cotman v. *Brougham*, [1918-19] All E.R. Rep. 265; [1918] A.C. 514; 87 L.J.Ch. 379; 119 L.T. 162; 9 Digest (Repl.) 647, *4305*.

I   *Crown Bank, Re*, (1890), 44 Ch.D. 634; 59 L.J.Ch. 739; 62 L.T. 823; 9 Digest (Repl.) 81, *344*.

Crystal Palace Trustees v. *Ministry of Town and Country Planning*, [1950] 2 All E.R. 857 n.; [1951] Ch. 132; 114 J.P. 553; 45 Digest (Repl.) 373, *187*.

Dunne v. *Byrne*, [1911-13] All E.R. Rep. 1105; [1912] A.C. 407; 81 L.J.P.C. 202; 106 L.T. 394; 8 Digest (Repl.) 392, *858*.

German Date Coffee Co., Re, [1881-85] All E.R. Rep. 372; (1882), 20 Ch.D. 169; 51 L.J.Ch. 564; 46 L.T. 327; 9 Digest (Repl.) 81, *342*.

Joint Stock Discount Co. v. *Brown*, (1866), L.R. 3 Eq 139; 15 L.T. 174; 9   A
  Digest (Repl.) 707, *4695*.
Keren Kayemeth Le Jisroel, Ltd. v. *Inland Revenue Comrs.*, [1931] 2 K.B.
  465; 100 L.J.K.B. 596; 145 L.T. 320; *affd.* H.L., [1932] All E.R. Rep.
  971; [1932] A.C. 650; 101 L.J.K.B. 459; 147 L.T. 161; 17 Tax Cas. 27;
  28 Digest (Repl.) 317, *1395*.
London County Council v. *A.-G.*, [1901] 1 Ch. 781; 70 L.J.Ch. 367; 84 L.T.   B
  245; *affd.* H.L., [1902] A.C. 165; 71 L.J.Ch. 268; 86 L.T. 161; 66
  J.P. 340; 13 Digest (Repl.) 282, *1026*.
London Financial Association v. *Kelk*, (1884), 26 Ch.D. 107; 53 L.J.Ch. 1025;
  50 L.T. 492; 3 Digest (Repl.) 289, *873*.
Oxford Group v. *Inland Revenue Comrs.*, [1949] 2 All E.R. 537; 31 Tax Cas. 221;
  28 Digest (Repl.) 316, *1386*.   C

Appeal.
This was an appeal by the plaintiff company, Bell Houses, Ltd., against the
judgment of MOCATTA, J., dated July 5, 1965, and reported [1965] 3 All E.R. 427,
deciding a preliminary issue in favour of, and accordingly giving judgment for,
the defendants, City Wall Properties, Ltd. The facts are set out in the judgment
of DANCKWERTS, L.J.   D

  J. G. Strangman, Q.C., and *Paul Sieghart* for the plaintiff company.
  S. W. Templeman, Q.C., and *J. Milnes Holden* for the defendants.

                                                            Cur. adv. vult.

  Apr. 1. The following judgments were read.

  DANCKWERTS, L.J., read the first judgment at the invitation of   E
SELLERS, L.J.: This is an appeal from a decision of MOCATTA, J. (1) dated
July 5, 1965, in an action brought by the plaintiff company, Bell Houses, Ltd.,
against the defendants, City Wall Properties, Ltd., to recover a commission or
procuration fee of £20,000 under an agreement alleged to have been made between
the parties between Feb. 5 and Mar. 9, 1962.
  The plaintiff company is a private company limited by shares and its principal   F
business in fact is the development of housing estates. The chairman of the
directors, Mr. Randal Mulcaster Bell, controls the company and its administration.
The other directors were his wife and a brother of Mr. Bell, but the brother has
left the company now. All effective dealings of the company were really done by
Mr. Bell, and this was officially authorised by a resolution passed on June 10,
1955, at a meeting of the board of directors whereby it was resolved that the   G
administration of the company generally and with regard to sales be left for the
chairman to deal with together with his principal sales agent. The directors had
power to delegate in this way by virtue of art. 102 of Table A in Sch. 1 to the
Companies Act, 1948, which was incorporated in the company's articles. The
method by which the business of the company was transacted was described
by Mr. Bell in evidence as being the acquisition of vacant sites for which no   H
planning consent had been obtained, because the land is thus obtained at a
cheaper price. The contract of purchase was made subject to planning consent,
and the company then obtained outline planning consent and proceeded with
the development of the site as a housing estate. The practice of the company
was to have the sites conveyed to subsidiary companies controlled by Mr. Bell,
apparently purely as a matter of convenience. Finance had, of course, to be   I
obtained, and so advances on mortgages were obtained for these companies
from some "financier". A noteworthy feature is that the advances to these
companies might exceed the purchase price of the sites, but this was due to the
value provided by the plaintiff company's possession of planning consent and the
enhanced values which would be produced by the development on the sites of
housing estates. For this purpose building leases of the sites were granted to

---

(1) [1965] 3 All E.R. 427; [1966] 1 Q.B. 207.

A the plaintiff company, and this was a condition of the advances made to the companies. The sums advanced were repaid when the purchasers of the houses paid for them by means of loans from building societies obtained in the ordinary way.

It is obvious that in order to finance these transactions Mr. Bell and his company, the plaintiff company, had to know of persons who were willing to

B provide the finance, and knowledge of such sources was a matter of value. Four of such transactions took place with a financing company called Nestlé's Pension Trust, Ltd. (hereinafter called " the Trust "), two of the transactions being with a company called Maes-y-Tannau Estates, Ltd., and the others being with companies called Pont Faen Investments, Ltd. and Golden Court (Richmond), Investments, Ltd. An argument was put forward on behalf of the

C defendants (City Wall Properties, Ltd.) that these were transactions between the trust and these three companies and not the plaintiff company. This argument seems to me to ignore the reality that these properties were conveyed to and the advances by the trust made to these companies merely as the nominees of the plaintiff company and for the convenience of the business of the plaintiff company. It is true that the plaintiff company held no shares in these com-

D panies, but they were controlled by Mr. Bell, the chairman of the plaintiff company and were therefore not independent in fact. The reality is that this was all machinery to effect the plaintiff company's operations. In my opinion there is no substance in this point.

The way in which the defendants came into the matter was as follows. The plaintiff company had been approached by financiers, including apparently

E some Swiss financiers, with a view to the plaintiff company being financed in their business transactions from such sources. The plaintiff company had at the moment no development scheme for which the company could use the money, but in the course of a lunchtime meeting between Mr. Skeggs, who is a solicitor but was acting as the agent of the defendants in financial matters, and Mr. Bell it emerged that the defendants required finance to the extent of £1 million for the

F purpose of their current schemes—what was called " bridging finance ". Mr. Skeggs said that this variety of bridging finance was extremely difficult to obtain. Mr. Bell intimated that he knew of sources from which such finance could be obtained. After a few abortive attempts to obtain it from other sources, eventually the money required was to be provided by the trust.

It is claimed by the plaintiff company that for this service the defendants

G agreed to pay a commission of £20,000 to Bell Houses. The introduction was effected, but the defendants refuse to pay to the plaintiff company the amount in question. In this action the plaintiff company claim payment of this sum as due from the defendants under the alleged agreement. Alternatively, the plaintiff company claims £20,000 damages on an implied term that the defendants would not prevent the plaintiff company earning the commission. The contract is

H denied in the defence, though (i) a letter of Mar. 2, 1962, from Mr. Skeggs to Mr. Bell, (ii) a letter of Mar. 5, 1962, from Mr. Bell to the surveyor of the trust, (iii) his reply to Mr. Bell of Mar. 6, 1962, (iv) a letter of Mar. 9, 1962, from Mr. Bell to Mr. Oppenheim, the chairman of the defendant company, and (v) a letter of Mar. 13, 1962, from Mr. Oppenheim to Mr. Bell, suggest the existence of a contract of the kind alleged; but this issue is not before us because a new point

I was taken by the defendants at the last moment.

The action came on for trial before MOCATTA, J., (2) on Monday, June 28, 1965. On the previous Friday counsel for the defendants informed counsel for the plaintiff company that he had been instructed to take the point that the alleged contract was void as ultra vires the plaintiff company since it was not authorised by the objects clause in the plaintiff company's memorandum of association.

---

(2) [1965] 3 All E.R. 427; [1966] 1 Q.B. 207.

The learned judge (3) allowed the defence to be amended by adding the following A
paragraph:

"The defendants will say that the agreement or agreements herein alleged
by [the plaintiff company] were at all material times ultra vires [the plaintiff
company] and void in that [the plaintiff company] under their memorandum
of association had no power to enter into such agreement or agreements."
                                                                         B
The result of this was that the action took a different turn: the matter raised by
the amendment was heard and decided as a preliminary point.

The learned judge states in his judgment (4) three separate points as arising
for decision. (i) Can a defendant when sued on a contract by a company take the
point that that contract is ultra vires the company? (ii) If he can do so when the
contract is executory, can he do so or is the point relevant when the contract C
has been executed so far as the company's obligations are concerned? (iii) Assuming that the answers to the first two questions are in the affirmative, was the
contract ultra vires the plaintiff company? The learned judge did not deal with
the three points in that order; and, indeed, it is clear that if the answer on the
third of the points is that the contract is not ultra vires the plaintiff company,
the other two points do not arise. The learned judge decided (4) the third point D
in the defendants' favour and dismissed the action. We, also, have heard the
third point argued first, and in the result we have not found it necessary to hear
argument on the other two points.

One point was raised and discussed in argument which is not really involved
in the question of ultra vires, but which I suppose went to the basis of the contract
alleged by the plaintiff company. It was argued on behalf of the defendants that E
the dealings with the defendants were conducted by Mr. Bell on his own behalf
and not on behalf of the plaintiff company, so that the plaintiff company had no
interest in the matter. This argument seems to me to be completely untenable.
There is no evidence that Mr. Bell ever claimed the benefit of the £20,000 for
himself. As has already been mentioned, Mr. Bell controlled the plaintiff company
and administered it completely, and it is evident that he used the company for F
the purposes of the business. He was authorised by the resolution of the board of
directors to conduct the administration of the company's business on behalf of
the board, and it is impossible to suppose that he was distinguishing business
negotiations carried out by him from the business of the company. Letters written
by him in the course of this transaction were always written on the plaintiff
company's notepaper, and though most of his letters were signed by his Christian G
name, that was in accordance with the terms on which these business men were,
and some of the letters, and in particular the letter of Mar. 9, 1962, to Mr. Oppenheim (the chairman of the defendants) were signed by Mr. Bell as "Chairman".
Finally the action has been brought in the name of the plaintiff company. There
is no doubt that if there was a contract to pay commission, the contract was made
with the plaintiff company, through Mr. Bell.   H

Before I consider the provisions of the company's memorandum of association,
there is a point which I wish to make that affects the approach to this matter in
regard to the plaintiff company's objects as stated in the memorandum. In
order to give a more convincing air to their arguments, counsel for the defendants
have treated the transaction which is under discussion as though it was a deliberate embarking by the plaintiff company on a serious new business of what counsel I
called "mortgage broking". In my opinion this is a false approach. From the
plaintiff company's point of view it was not the opening of a new class of business
intended to be carried on by the company on any serious scale. It was simply
an isolated transaction which was intended to assist the defendants (since for the
time being the plaintiff company could not avail itself of the financial opportunity

(3) [1965] 3 All E.R. at p. 430.
(4) [1965] 3 All E.R. at p. 430; [1966] 1 Q.B. at p. 217.
(5) [1965] 3 All E.R. at p. 440; [1966] 1 Q.B. at p. 232.

A because it had at the moment no site for development), and to gain goodwill with not only the defendants but also with the trust, who were thereby to be enabled to carry out a profitable financial transaction. Besides these advantages to the plaintiff company, there was their own interest in getting to know a financial source, since these development companies can only carry on their development business with the aid of borrowed money or temporary " bridging finance ",
B or whatever they choose to call it. Surprisingly little money capital of their own is used in their operations, though, no doubt, plant and such like assets of their own are used by them. The transaction between the plaintiff company and the defendants is, of course, none the less a business transaction, even though larded with lunches and Christian names.

Clause 3 of the plaintiff company's memorandum of association contains the
C usual large number of sub-clauses, identified by the letters (a) to (u). It does not contain the provision sometimes inserted that all the sub-clauses are independent objects, or words to that effect. The following sub-clauses must be referred to :

> " (a) To carry on the trade or business of general, civil and engineering contractors and in particular but without prejudice to the generality of the
D foregoing to construct, alter, enlarge, erect and maintain either by [the plaintiff company] or other parties, sewers, roads, streets, railways, sidings, tramways, electricity works, gas works, bridges, shops, reservoirs, factories, water-works, brick kilns and brick or tile works, timber yards, buildings, houses, offices and all other works, erections, plant, machinery and things of any description whatsoever either upon land acquired by [the plaintiff
E company] or upon other land and generally.

> " (b) To acquire by purchase, exchange or otherwise either for an estate in fee simple or for any interest or estate in land, whether in possession or in reversion and whether vested or contingent, any lands, tenements and premises of any tenure, whether subject or not to any charges or incumbrances and any easements or other rights in or over land and any concessions,
F patents, patent rights, licences, copyright, secret processes, machinery, plant, stock-in-trade and any other real or personal property and to hold or to sell, develop, let on rent, mortgage, charge or otherwise deal with all or any of such lands, tenements or premises and buildings erected thereon and all other such real and personal property.

> " (c) To carry on any other trade or business whatsoever which can, in
G the opinion of the board of directors, be advantageously carried on by [the plaintiff company] in connexion with or as ancillary to any of the above businesses or the general business of [the plaintiff company].

> " (m) To accept payment for any property or rights sold or otherwise disposed of or dealt with by [the plaintiff company].

> " (q) To sell, improve, manage, develop, turn to account, exchange,
H let on rent, royalty, share of profits or otherwise, grant licences, easements and other rights in or over, and in any other manner deal with or dispose of the undertaking and all or any of the property and assets for the time being of the company for such consideration as [the plaintiff company] may think fit.

> " (u) To do all such other things as are incidental or conducive to the
I above objects or any of them."

Paragraph (m) was referred to but does not add anything material for present purposes. By cl. 5 the share capital of the plaintiff company is £2,100, of which £2,000 consists of preference shares, which makes it obvious that the operations of the company must be financed by borrowing.

Mocatta, J., was referred (6) for the purposes of a summary of the law to the passage in Buckley on the Companies Act (13th Edn.) p. 23:

---

(6) [1965] 3 All E.R. at p. 438; [1960] 1 Q.B. at p. 228.

" The doctrine that any act not authorised by the memorandum is ultra   A
vires is to be applied reasonably. Anything fairly incidental to the company's
objects as defined is not (unless expressly prohibited) to be held to be ultra
vires. The question is not, however, whether the act or business not expressly
authorised by the memorandum can conveniently or advantageously be
done or carried on in conjunction with acts or business which are so authorised,
but whether it is reasonably incidental or accessory thereto. Thus it is   B
ultra vires for a company formed to work tramways to carry on either the
business of an omnibus company or a general parcels collection and delivery
business, however conveniently or advantageously such business can be
combined with the tramways business."

Accepting this paragraph as substantially correct, the example given may be
somewhat misleading.   C

The authorities cited for the example given are *London County Council* v.
A.-G. (7) and *A.-G.* v. *Manchester Corpn.* (8). As regards the first of these cases,
the powers of the London County Council were statutory, being derived entirely
under the London County Tramways Act, 1896, under which the council had been
authorised to purchase the tramways undertaking (9). The decision of the
House of Lords was simply that running omnibuses was not incidental to running   D
tramways. In the *Manchester* case (8), the corporation were empowered by
provisional orders and private Acts of Parliament to construct and maintain
tramways, and there was a provision that " the tramways may be used for the
purpose of conveying passengers, animals, goods, minerals, and parcels ". The
corporation proposed to carry on a general parcels delivery business both within
and beyond the area covered by their tramways, not confined to parcels and goods   E
carried on their tramways. This business was held by FARWELL, J., to be beyond
their powers.

These two cases of statutory powers seem to me to be not directly relevant
to a company formed under the Companies Acts the powers of which are established by the memorandum of association of the company with extensive detailed
powers therein contained which have to be construed. For instance, in the present   F
case, cl. 3 (c) of the plaintiff company's memorandum provided (among the
company's objects) express power

" to carry on any other trade or business *whatsoever* which can, *in the
opinion of the board of directors*, be *advantageously* carried on by the company
in connexion with or as ancillary to any of the above businesses or the general
business of the company."   G

This is the clause (amongst others) which has to be construed by the court in
the present case, and I propose to construe the clause in the first place according
to the words used in it, and to consider the authorities subsequently in order to
see whether those words compel us in any way to give a different meaning to the
expressions in this memorandum.   H

For the moment I do not propose to consider the effect produced by the words
" in the opinion of the board of directors ", though an important point is the
effect of these words. In the first place, I would repeat the observation which I
made earlier in this judgment: this is not a case where the company is deliberately
launching out into a completely new field of business, as in the *London County
Council* case (7), or the *Manchester Corpn.* case (8). There is no intention shown   I
on the part of the company to indulge in a general mortgage broking business,
though some alternate openings for the application of the moneys of the trust
were discussed while the negotiations with the defendants were proceeding and,
at the end, a polite hope to do other business was mentioned.

It appears that the opportunity to do a good turn to the defendants and also
to gain the goodwill of the trust arose practically by accident. The features

(7) [1902] A.C. 165.   (8) [1906] 1 Ch. 643.
          (9) See [1901] 1 Ch. 781 at pp. 784, 785.

A mentioned above were plainly advantageous to the plaintiff company, as well as the prospective receipt of a sum of £20,000. In my view, this piece of business arose " in connexion with " the general business of the company and " as ancillary " to the general business of the company, which appears to be as described in sub-cl. (a) and sub-cl. (b) of cl. 3 of the memorandum. In the course of the administration by Mr. Bell of the plaintiff company and its business or

B businesses, Mr. Bell had to find suitable sites for the development of housing estates and sources from which advances could be obtained for the purpose of financing the plaintiff company's operations. The knowledge thus acquired by Mr. Bell was a valuable asset and was not Mr. Bell's personal property but was the property of the company.

In my opinion the provisions of cl. 3 (q) are also applicable. This sub-clause

C empowers the plaintiff company (amongst other things) to " turn to account ", and to " deal with or dispose of ", " all or any of the property and assets for the time being of [the plaintiff company] for such consideration as [the plaintiff company] may think fit ". It seems to me that in communicating to the defendants information as to sources of finance, Mr. Bell, in the administration of the company, was turning to account, dealing with and disposing of an asset of the

D company as authorised by this sub-clause.

Finally, there is the general provision in cl. 3 (u) of the plaintiff company's memorandum, but it does not seem to be necessary for the plaintiff company to rely on this sub-clause in the present case.

I now turn to the authorities. *Ashbury Railway Carriage and Iron Company* v. *Riche* (10) is, of course, the leading authority on the relation of companies formed

E under the Companies Acts to ultra vires. That case established that a company formed under the Companies Acts is not thereby created a corporation with inherent common law powers. It established that the powers of such a company are limited to the objects stated in the company's memorandum of association. Any contract made outside these powers is not necessarily illegal, but it is void and is not binding on the company. It cannot be ratified by the united desire of

F all the shareholders. As LORD CAIRNS, L.C., said so forcibly (11):

" Now, I am clearly of opinion that this contract was entirely, as I have said, beyond the objects in the memorandum of association . . . If so, my lords, it is not a question whether the contract ever was ratified or was not ratified. It was a contract void at its beginning, it was void because the company could not make the contract. If every shareholder of the company had been

G in the room, and every shareholder had said, ' That is a contract which we desire to make, which we authorise the directors to make, to which we sanction the placing of the seal of the company ', the case would not have stood in any different position from that in which it stands now. The shareholders would thereby, by unanimous consent, have been attempting to do the very thing which, by Act of Parliament, they were prohibited from doing."

H That is the approach which must be made to the problem in the present case; but if in the present case we find that the contract was within the powers conferred by the plaintiff company's memorandum of association on its proper construction, then the contract is one which the plaintiff company can make, and objection falls to the ground.

The cases on which counsel for the defendants particularly relied as showing

I that the objects in the company's memorandum of association did not cover the contract alleged in the present case, were early cases in the history of company law and were decided soon after the passing of the Companies Act, 1862. They are not necessarily bad law for that reason, but it seems to me that they were somewhat special cases, in which a complete departure from the real objects of the company had been attempted. In *Joint Stock Discount Co.* v. *Brown* (12), the objects for which the company was established were stated (13) to be

---

(10) (1875), L.R. 7 H.L. 653.   (11) (1875), L.R. 7 H.L. at p. 672.
(12) (1866), L.R. 3 Eq. 139.   (13) (1866), L.R. 3 Eq. at p. 140.

" the carrying on the business of a bill-broker and scrivener; the drawing, A
accepting, endorsing, discounting, and rediscounting bills of exchange and
promissory notes; the making advances and procuring loans on, and the
investing in, securities; the borrowing and lending of money; the guaranteeing payment of bills of exchange, promissory notes, and advances; and
the doing of all such things as the directors shall consider incidental or
conducive to the attainment of the above objects."   B

Shares in a banking company called Barned's Banking Co., Ltd. were paid for
out of the company's money and transferred into the names of some of the
directors as nominees of the company, pursuant to a resolution of the board of
directors (14):

" That as the board consider that the formation of a limited joint stock   C
bank on the basis of the absorption of the old firm of Messrs. J. Barned & Co.,
of Liverpool, will be most conducive to the interests of the company by
increasing its connexions, the company, or its nominees, assist the same by
applying for ten thousand shares in the proposed bank on the terms above
stated."

Orders were subsequently made for the winding-up of both the company and D
Barned's Bank and a bill was presented by the liquidator of the company on
its behalf alleging that the acquisition of the shares was ultra vires. One of the
directors demurred to the bill. SIR WILLIAM PAGE WOOD, V.C., overruled the
demurrer and directed that the charges in the bill must be answered. The Vice-
Chancellor made observations (15) to the effect that in his view the suggestion
that if shares were bought in the bank there would be some control over the E
business of the discounting was wholly unwarranted by the plainest rules of
construction which, he said, " must limit the company's powers to those transactions which are naturally conducive to the objects specified ". It is easy to
see why counsel for the defendants relied on this case; but in fact the decision
merely was that the allegations in the bill must be answered. The objection
that one limited company could not take shares in another limited company F
though authorised by its memorandum, was disposed of by Re Barned's Banking
Co., Ex p. Contract Corpn. (16), and in fact Joint Stock Discount Co. v. Brown (17)
was a simple case of fraud. (See the observations of SIR JAMES BACON, V.-C., in
London Financial Association v. Kelk (18).)

The other case most strongly relied on by counsel for the defendants was
Re German Date Coffee Co. (19). The company was formed to work a German G
patent for manufacturing coffee from dates, and the memorandum contained
powers to acquire other inventions for similar purposes and to import and export
all descriptions of produce for the purposes of food. The intended German patent
was never granted, but the company purchased a Swedish patent and established
works in Hamburg where it made and sold coffee made from dates without a
patent. A petition was presented by two shareholders for the winding-up of the H
company and it was held by KAY, J., and by the Court of Appeal that the substratum of the company had failed, and it was impossible to carry out the objects
for which it was formed, and therefore it was just and equitable that the company
should be wound up. LINDLEY, L.J., said (20):

" The first question we have to consider is: What is the fair construction
of the memorandum of association? It is required by the Companies Act, I
1862, that the memorandum shall state what the objects of the company
are (21). In construing this memorandum of association, or any other

---

(14) (1866), L.R. 3 Eq. at p. 141.   (15) (1866), L.R. 3 Eq. at p. 150.
(16) (1867), 3 Ch. App. 105.   (17) (1866), L.R. 3 Eq. 139.
(18) (1884), 26 Ch.D. 107 at p. 144.
(19) [1881-85] All E.R. Rep. 372; (1882), 20 Ch.D. 169.
(20) [1881-85] All E.R. Rep. at p. 375; (1882), 20 Ch.D. at p. 188.
(21) See now Companies Act, 1948, s. 2 (1) (c).

A   memorandum of association in which there are general words, care must be taken to construe those general words so as not to make them a trap for unwary people. General words construed literally may mean anything . . .; but they must be taken in connexion with that shown by the context to be the dominant or main object or objects of the company. It will not do, under general words, to turn a company for manufacturing one thing into a

B   company for importing something else, however general the words are. Taking that as the governing principle, it appears to me to be plain, beyond all reasonable dispute, that the real object of this company, which is called ' The German Date Coffee Co., Ltd.', was to manufacture a substitute for coffee in Germany under a patent which is valid according to German law. All the rest is subordinate to that main object, and that is what the people

C   subscribe their money for, although the words are general."

Of course, as SALMON, L.J., observed in the course of the argument, if the company's main business is given up, something else cannot be ancillary to it. There is no suggestion that the plaintiff company has given up or is going to give up its main business of developing housing estates. That is sufficient to distinguish *Re German Date Coffee Co.* (22) from the present case.

D   As I have mentioned, it is also necessary to consider the effect of the words in cl. 3 (c) of the memorandum, " in the opinion of the board of directors ". I think that it is plain that these words qualify the whole of that sub-clause. Counsel for the defendants contended that the opinion of the directors must not only be bona fide but also objective. MOCATTA, J., even went so far as to say (23) that

E   " the mere fact that the board of directors of a company may be of opinion that an activity can be advantageously carried on by the company, even if the opinion be well-founded, will not per se make that activity intra vires."

With all respect to the judge, if he is meaning to refer to the opinion required by the sub-clause, he is not quoting it correctly. The requirement of the sub-clause is that in the opinion of the board of directors the other trade or business can

F   be advantageously carried on by the company in connexion with or as ancillary to any of the above businesses or the general business of the company. If the judge means that the opinion of the directors has no effect at all, then I am afraid that I cannot agree with him. On the balance of the authorities it would appear that the opinion of the directors if bona fide can dispose of the matter; and why should it not decide the matter? The shareholders subscribe their money on

G   the basis of the memorandum of association and if that confers the power on directors to decide whether in their opinion it is proper to undertake particular business in the circumstances specified, why should not their decision be binding? The shareholders by taking shares on the terms of the memorandum have agreed to it. It is a matter of internal management principally. Persons dealing with the plaintiff company in the course of trade or business are helped rather

H   than hindered by a provision of this sort. In the result the judge appears to have completely disregarded this provision and to have dealt with the case on the basis that there was no real difference between sub-cl. (c) and sub-cl. (u).

In *London Financial Association* v. *Kelk* (24) the objects clause ended with the words " and the doing of all matters and things which may appear to the company to be incident or conducive to the objects aforesaid or any of them ".

I   SIR JAMES BACON, V.C., in the course of a long judgment discussed (25) the effect of the words, and seems to have thought that they had some purpose and effect but they had to be limited by reference to the objects of the company. This is no doubt so, but in any case SIR JAMES BACON, V.C., held that the transaction, which was connected with the unfortunate Alexandra Palace which

---

(22) [1881-85] All E.R. Rep. 372; (1882), 20 Ch.D. 169.
(23) [1965] 3 All E.R. at p. 438; [1966] 1 Q.B. at p. 229.
(24) (1884), 26 Ch.D. 107.   (25) (1884), 26 Ch.D. at p. 138.

was burnt down on June 2, 1873, almost immediately after completion, was   A
within the company's powers, distinguishing the *Ashbury* case (26).

In *Re Crown Bank* (27) the company had been formed primarily for carrying
on the business of banking, as a country bank, with an office in London. After
a time it gave up its country office, ceased to do banking business and carried
on in London land speculation, promoting a company in a foreign country and
the business of investing in shares and securities. The objects of the company   B
were expressed in very wide terms—NORTH, J., said (28) that they were

" So wide that it might be said to warrant the company in giving up
banking business and embarking in a business with the object of establishing
a line of balloons between the earth and moon."

NORTH, J., on the petition of a shareholder made an order for the winding-up of   C
the company. This was plainly a case where the company had abandoned
its main objects and was attempting to carry on quite a different business.

In *Cotman* v. *Brougham* (29) a company called the Essequibo Rubber &
Tobacco Estates, Ltd. agreed to sub-underwrite twenty thousand shares in another
company and 17,200 of those shares were allotted to it, on which there remained
due and owing the sum of £14,456 for unpaid calls. These shares were transferred   D
to a third company. All three companies were in liquidation, and the liquidator
of the second company settled the transferee company on the A list of contri-
butories and the Essequibo Co. on the B list in respect of the shares. The
liquidator of the Essequibo Co. applied to have that company's name struck
out of the B list, on the ground that the underwriting was ultra vires of the
company. The company's memorandum had thirty clauses enabling the com-   E
pany to carry on almost any kind of business, and the objects clause concluded
with a declaration that every sub-clause should be construed as a substantive
clause and not limited or restricted by reference to any other sub-clause or by
the name of the company and that none of such sub-clauses or the objects specified
therein should be deemed subsidiary or auxiliary merely to the objects mentioned
in the first sub-clause. It was held that the memorandum must be construed   F
according to its literal meaning, and that the underwriting was intra vires.
Both LORD PARKER OF WADDINGTON and LORD WRENBURY criticised the long-
standing practice of elaborating the objects of the company in a long series of
sub-clauses containing, as LORD WRENBURY said (30),

" paragraph after paragraph not specifying or delimiting the proposed
trade or purpose, but confusing power with purpose and indicating every   G
class of act which the corporation is to have power to do."

This practice continues and I have heard it defended by eminent company
lawyers on the ground that it satisfies nervous company directors that they have
the ordinary powers which management of a company requires. I do not
believe that anyone else, including those who have to deal with the company,
usually pays much attention to the matter, unless someone wishes to wriggle   H
out of some obligation. In any case, as LORD PARKER OF WADDINGTON pointed
out (31), s. 17 of the Companies (Consolidation) Act, 1908 (now s. 15 of the
Companies Act, 1948) made the certificate of incorporation conclusive evidence
that (inter alia) the provisions of the Act as to stating the objects of the company
in its memorandum of association have been duly complied with. LORD PARKER
OF WADDINGTON said (32):   I

" The truth is that the statement of a company's objects in its memorandum is intended to serve a double purpose. In the first place, it gives

---

(26) (1875), L.R. 7 H.L. 653.   (27) (1890), 44 Ch.D. 634.
(28) (1890), 44 Ch.D. at p. 641; see also at pp. 644, 645.
(29) [1918-19] All E.R. Rep. 265; [1918] A.C. 514.
(30) [1918-19] All E.R. Rep. at p. 270; [1918] A.C. at p. 523.
(31) [1918-19] All E.R. Rep. at p. 268; [1918] A.C. at p. 519.
(32) [1918-19] All E.R. Rep. at pp. 268, 269; [1918] A.C. at p. 520.

A   protection to subscribers, who learn from it the purposes to which their
money can be applied.   In the second place, it gives protection to persons
who deal with the company, and who can infer from it the extent of the
company's powers.   The narrower the objects expressed in the memorandum
the less is the subscribers' risk, but the wider such objects the greater is the
security of those who transact business with the company.   Moreover,
B   experience soon showed that persons who transact business with companies
do not like having to depend on inference when the validity of a proposed
transaction is in question.   Even a power to borrow money could not always
be safely inferred, much less such a power as that of underwriting shares in
another company.   Thus arose the practice of specifying powers as objects,
a practice rendered possible by the fact that there is no statutory limit on
C   the number of objects which may be specified.   But even thus, a person
proposing to deal with a company could not be absolutely safe, for powers
specified as objects might be read as ancillary to and exercisable only for
the purpose of attaining what might be held to be the company's main or
paramount object, and on this construction no one could be quite certain
whether the court would not hold any proposed transaction to be ultra vires."

D   Except for the valuable general statements contained in it, I do not think that
this case is very relevant to the point which has to be decided in the present
case.

Counsel for the plaintiff company relied on some cases which counsel for the
defendants complained were not cited in the books on company law for the
propositions which counsel for the plaintiff company sought to found on them.
E   In *Keren Kayemeth Le Jisroel, Ltd.* v. *Inland Revenue Comrs.* (33), an association
incorporated as a company limited by guarantee was held in the Court of Appeal
to be a company formed for widely philanthropic objects, but not for charitable
purposes only so as to qualify for exemptions under the Income Tax Act, 1918.
In the memorandum all the twenty-one objects or powers were stated to be
subject to a proviso that they were to be exercised only in such a way as shall
F   in the opinion of the association be conducive to the attainment of the primary
object.   SLESSER, L.J., said (34):

" Secondly, it must be noted that the association itself is made by the
memorandum the judge whether the general powers are or are not exercised
only in such a way as shall be conducive to the attainment of the primary
G   object.   Thus, if the association were to be reasonably of opinion that the
exercise of any of the powers was conducive to the attainment of the primary
object, it would scarcely be possible to say that such an exercise was ultra
vires."

The point in the case—whether the objects were charitable—was decided against
the association.   The decision of the Court of Appeal was affirmed in the House
H   of Lords (35).

The next case is the *Oxford Group* v. *Inland Revenue Comrs.* (36).   The objects
of this company may be summarised as: (A) the advancement of the Christian
religion, (B) the maintenance of the Oxford Group Movement, (C) (9) to establish
and support any charitable or benevolent associations or institutions, and
(10) " To do all such other things as are incidental, or the association may think
I   conducive, to the attainment of the above objects or any of them ".   It was
held that the objects of the company extended beyond purely religious activities
and so the company could not gain exemption from income tax.   The relevance
of that case is that COHEN, L.J., said (37):

" Then, again, under para. (10) of sub-cl. (C), the association is empowered
to do, not merely things which are incidental or conducive to the attainment

(33) [1931] 2 K.B. 465.   (34) [1931] 2 K.B. at p. 489.
(35) [1932] All E.R. Rep. 971; [1932] A.C. 650.   (36) [1949] 2 All E.R. 537.
(37) [1949] 2 All E.R. at pp. 544, 545.

of the main object, but also such things as the association may think con-   **A**
ducive to it. In other words, the question which the court would have to
decide, if any activity of the association was being challenged as being
ultra vires, would be not whether, in the opinion of the court, the activity
was conducive to the main object, but whether the association, in undertaking it, had thought it conducive."

COHEN, L.J., then quoted (38) with approval the views of LAWRENCE, L.J.,   **B**
in the *Keren Kayemeth* case (39) and referred to the Privy Council case of *Dunne*
v. *Byrne* (40).

We were also referred to my decision in *Crystal Palace Trustees* v. *Minister
of Town and Country Planning* (41), which I do not regard as having so much
relevance as the other cases cited because in that case the position was regulated
by a statute, the Crystal Palace Act, 1914.   **C**

In *Associated Artists, Ltd.* v. *Inland Revenue Comrs.* (42) the first object in the
memorandum of a company limited by guarantee was (a) to present classical,
artistic, cultural and educational dramatic works, etc., and, after a number of
sub-clauses, there was sub-cl. (1) " To do all such other things as are incidental
or which [the taxpayer] may think conducive to the attainment of any of the
above objects."   It was held by UPJOHN, J. (43) that the association was not a   **D**
body established exclusively for charitable purposes. UPJOHN, J., held that the
powers in sub-cl. (1) were independent of and not ancillary to the other objects,
and that that clause was of itself sufficient to render the objects of the association
not charitable, since the court in deciding whether any activity of the association
was ultra vires would have to decide whether the association thought that it
was conducive to the attainment of any of the objects of the association and   **E**
what the association might think conducive would not necessarily be so.

The result of these authorities, in my opinion, is to establish that a clause on
the lines of sub-cl. (c) in the present case is able to make the bona fide opinion
of the directors sufficient to decide whether an activity of the plaintiff company
is intra vires.   There was, in the present case, no resolution of the board of
directors expressing the opinion of the board; but I do not think that such a   **F**
resolution was necessary and I do not understand that it was contended that a
resolution was necessary.   In fact Mr. Bell managed the operation of the plaintiff
company and exercised by delegation the functions of the board of directors,
as he was entitled to do, by virtue of the resolution of the board of directors of
June 10, 1955.   It was Mr. Bell's opinion which decided whether certain business
activities should be carried out on behalf of the plaintiff company.   Mr. Bell's   **G**
opinion is evident from what he did and from his evidence.   Further, the facts
support his opinion.   For the reasons which I have mentioned earlier in this
judgment, this transaction was justified and was within the powers of the plaintiff
company under the terms of cl. 3 (c).   The position is also assisted by the terms
of sub-cl. (q) and sub-cl. (u).   I feel no doubt that the transaction with the
defendants was within the powers of the company and was not ultra vires.   **H**

The result is that the question whether a defence of ultra vires could be raised
by the defendants does not arise and we have not thought it necessary to have
it argued.

In my opinion the appeal should be allowed, and the preliminary point decided
in the plaintiff company's favour.
                                                                           I
   SALMON, L.J.: In this action the plaintiff company claimed £20,000
under a contract which it alleged it had made with the defendants in 1962—
Mr. Bell acting for the plaintiff company and Mr. Skeggs acting for the defendants. Broadly, the plaintiff company alleged that under this contract the

---

(38) [1949] 2 All E.R. at p. 545.   (39) [1931] 2 K.B. at p. 482.
(40) [1911-13] All E.R. Rep. 1105; [1912] A.C. 407.
(41) [1950] 2 All E.R. 857n; [1951] Ch. 132.   (42) [1956] 2 All E.R. 583.
              (43) [1956] 2 All E.R. at pp. 587, 588.

A defendants had promised to pay it a commission of £20,000 in the event of it introducing a financier to the defendants who was ready, able and willing to provide the defendants, on certain terms, with bridging finance to the extent of £1 million. The plaintiff company alleged that it introduced such a financier to the defendants, namely the Nestlé's Pension Trust, Ltd., but that the defendants have refused to pay it the commission due under the contract. By their amended

B defence, the defendants denied the contract and alleged that if Mr. Skeggs purported to enter into such a contract on their behalf, he had no authority from them to do so; the defendants also denied that the plaintiff company had performed its part under the contract. The issues raised by this defence were simple and straightforward, but the documents at present before us suggest that they may have presented certain difficulties for the defendants. In any

C event the defendants have shown no enthusiasm for having these issues decided, for at the trial on Monday, June 28, 1965, they asked for leave to re-amend their defence in order to take a highly technical point. Notice that they were proposing to ask for this re-amendment had been given to the plaintiff company only on the previous Friday, June 25. The amended defence had been delivered more than eighteen months previously and no doubt heavy costs had been incurred

D in preparing for trial on the substantive issues. The parties were ready for trial. In these circumstances, most surprisingly, in my view, the application to re-amend the defence was allowed and was allowed without any stringent or indeed any terms as to costs. The re-amended pleading set up the defence that the contract on which the defendants were sued was ultra vires the plaintiff company. In short, the defendants said that even if Mr. Skeggs had acted

E with their authority and they had entered into the contract with the plaintiff company and the plaintiff company had performed its part under the contract so that, under the terms of the contract, £20,000 would be due by them to the plaintiff company, still they were entitled to defeat the plaintiff company's claim because the plaintiff company had had no power under its memorandum of association to enter into the contract in the first place. This point was tried as a

F preliminary issue, decided in favour of the defendants, and the claim was dismissed. The point is conspicuously lacking in merit of any kind. The defendants are of course entitled to take the point and to succeed on it if they can make it good—just as, in other circumstances, a defendant would be entitled to plead the Gaming Act. In my judgment, however, the point is hopelessly bad. It depends primarily on cl. 3 (the objects clause) of the plaintiff company's

G memorandum of association. I need not repeat sub-cl. (a) or sub-cl. (b) of that clause, which in effect respectively provide that carrying on the business of building and land development are among the plaintiffs' objects. Sub-clause (c) is of great importance and reads as follows:

H "To carry on any other trade or business whatsoever which can, in the opinion of the board of directors, be advantageously carried on by [the plaintiff company] in connexion with or as ancillary to ... the general business of [the plaintiff company]."

As a matter of pure construction, the meaning of these words seems to me to be obvious. An object of the plaintiff company is to carry on any business which the directors genuinely believe can be carried on advantageously in

I connexion with or as ancillary to the general business of the company. It may be that the directors take the wrong view and in fact the business in question cannot be carried on as the directors believe; but it matters not how mistaken the directors may be. Providing they form their view honestly, the business is within the plaintiff company's objects and powers. This is so plainly the natural and ordinary meaning of the language of sub-cl. (c) that I would refuse to construe it differently unless compelled to do so by the clearest authority; and there is no such authority. Indeed the authorities establish that the obvious meaning to which I have referred is in law the true meaning of the words. The

Oxford Group is a company limited by guarantee.   Paragraph 10 of sub-cl. (C) **A**
of cl. 3 of its memorandum of association reads as follows: " To do all such
things as are incidental and as the association may think conducive to the
attainment of the above objects or any of them."   The company sought exemption from income tax on the ground that it was established for charitable purposes
only.   That great master of company law, COHEN, L.J., held that its purposes
were not solely charitable because, amongst other things, the words which I have **B**
quoted would give it power to do acts which were in no way conducive to charitable purposes, provided that the company believed that they were.   In this
TUCKER, L.J., and apparently SINGLETON, L.J., agreed (*Oxford Group* v. *Inland
Revenue Comrs.* (44)).   That case followed *Karen Kayemeth Le Jisroel* v. *Inland
Revenue Comrs.* (45) and was followed by UPJOHN, J., in *Associated Artists, Ltd.*
v. *Inland Revenue Comrs.* (46).   It has never been doubted.   It is indistinguish- **C**
able for all material purposes from the present case and binding on us.   Unfortunately this line of authority was not cited to the learned judge.   It is fair to
say that neither leading counsel appearing in this court appeared below, and that
having regard to the extremely late hour at which the defendants sought leave
to re-amend their defence there was scant time to make the necessary researches
into all the relevant authorities.   The judge was persuaded, on the strength of **D**
a passage in NORTH, J.'s judgment in *Re Crown Bank* (47), to hold (48) that the
words in cl. 3 (c), " in the opinion of the directors ", could be ignored.   NORTH, J.,
had expressed the view that a clause containing similar words would not be a
statement of the objects of the company as required by the Act of Parliament
and could be disregarded by the courts.   In this NORTH, J., was mistaken,
for the statute makes the registration of the memorandum of association con- **E**
clusive evidence that it complies with the Act, and thereafter the courts are
confined to the construction of the document.   (See *Cotman* v. *Brougham* (49),
per LORD WRENBURY).   Moreover, in *Re Crown Bank* (47) the court decided only
that the substratum of the company had gone and that it was accordingly just
and equitable that the company should be wound up.   The shareholders had
subscribed on the faith of a prospectus asking for money for a banking business. **F**
When the company ceased to carry on a banking business the shareholders
successfully objected to their money being used for entirely different purposes.
Counsel for the defendants, who has made a valiant and skilful attempt to
make bricks without straw, also relied on *Re German Date Coffee Co.* (50).   This
was another substratum case.   As pointed out by LINDLEY, L.J. (51), the
shareholders had subscribed their money to exploit a German patent for making **G**
coffee out of dates.   The patent was never granted and the courts held that
the company should be wound up; its substratum having gone, it would be
unjust and inequitable for the objecting shareholders' money to be used for any
purpose save the real purpose for which it was subscribed.   The substratum
cases seem to me to be quite irrelevant to the present appeal.   None of the same
questions were there being considered from this point of view.   Moreover it is **H**
quite plain that the present plaintiff company's substratum has not disappeared.
They are still successfully carrying on their main business.

Counsel for the defendants also relied on *Joint Stock Discount Co.* v. *Brown* (52);
but this really is an authority only for the fairly obvious proposition that a
memorandum of association which gives the directors power to do all such things
as they consider incidental or conducive to the company's objects cannot be **I**
construed as a charter for the directors to defraud the company.

---

(44) [1949] 2 All E.R. 537.   (45) [1931] 2 K.B. 465.
(46) [1956] 2 All E.R. 583.   (47) (1890), 44 Ch.D. at p. 644.
(48) [1965] 3 All E.R. at p. 438; [1966] 1 Q.B. at pp. 230, 231.
(49) [1918-19] All E.R. Rep. at p. 270; [1918] A.C. at p. 523.
(50) [1881-85] All E.R. Rep. 372; (1884), 20 Ch.D. 169.
(51) [1881-85] All E.R. Rep. at p. 375; (1884), 20 Ch.D. at p. 188.
(52) (1866), L.R. 3 Eq. 139.

A   Accordingly I come to the conclusion, both on what appears to be the clear meaning of the words and on authority, that under cl. 3 (c) the contract here sued on was intra vires if it constituted carrying on business which in the opinion of the plaintiff company's board of directors could be advantageously carried on by the plaintiff company in connexion with or as ancillary to their general business. It was conceded by the defendants that entering into the contract

B   did constitute carrying on business within the meaning of sub-cl. (c) and also that it would be sufficient for the purposes of sub-cl. (c) if Mr. Bell alone had formed the opinion there referred to, since the powers of the board had been properly delegated to him. Counsel for the defendants did however argue, though faintly, that there was nothing to show that Mr. Bell had formed such an opinion and that this court should therefore come to the conclusion that he had

C   not. I cannot accept this argument. There was ample evidence that Mr. Bell had formed the necessary opinion. Moreover the onus is on the defendants to make out their defence that the contract was ultra vires the plaintiff company. It was for the defendants to prove that Mr. Bell had not formed the necessary opinion, but when Mr. Bell gave evidence at the trial, it was not even suggested to him in cross-examination by counsel then appearing for the defendants that

D   he had not genuinely formed the opinion that the contract sued on was business which could be advantageously carried on by the plaintiff company in connexion with or as ancillary to its general business. It follows that in my view the contract was clearly intra vires cl. 3 (c) of the memorandum of association.

Moreover in my judgment the plaintiff company is also entitled to succeed under cl. 3 (u), for the making of the contract was in fact as well as in Mr. Bell's

E   opinion " incidental and conducive " to the plaintiff company's objects of carrying on the business of building and land development. Finance for the acquisition of land was vital to the plaintiff company. It is true that the mechanics of the plaintiff company's operations involved the land being bought by investment companies owned by Mr. Bell with money borrowed for this purpose by the investment companies. The evidence shows however that the money

F   would not have been advanced unless in the first place the plaintiff company had entered into building leases with the investment companies and had obtained the necessary planning permission. Unless the investment companies were able to obtain finance, the plaintiff company could not have carried on business. Accordingly it was clearly incidental and conducive to the plaintiff company's business to do what it could to help the investment companies to obtain such

G   finance. The Nestlé's Pension Trust, Ltd. was a source of such finance which had proved most useful in the past. I am not impressed by the point referred to by the judge (53), that this trust was not named in the contract between the plaintiff company and the defendants. One could hardly expect it to be. By introducing that trust to the defendants at a time when the trust was looking for an outlet for £1 million by way of a development project, the plaintiff company

H   was cementing its good relations with the trust and thereby increasing the prospect of the trust advancing money in the future for the purpose of the plaintiff company's development projects. After all as a result of the plaintiff company's introduction, the trust stood to make about £50,000 without any real risk and might in the future therefore find it difficult or unwise to refuse the comparatively modest loans required by the plaintiff company's operations.

I   I think that the contract was also intra vires sub-cl. (q) of cl. 3 of the memorandum of association, which so far as material reads as follows: " To . . . turn to account . . . any assets . . . of the company." Knowledge of sources of finance such as the Nestlé's Pension Trust was a most valuable asset of the plaintiff company. Even if the knowledge was originally an asset of Mr. Bell and not of the plaintiff, he was fully entitled to transfer this asset to the plaintiff company and allow it to turn it to their own account. It seems clear to me that the

---

(53) [1965] 3 Q.B. at p. 439; [1966] 1 Q.B. at p. 231.

plaintiff company was turning this asset to account:—and to very good account, **A**
for by comparatively little effort and expense it was putting itself in a position
to gain £20,000. For these reasons I have come to the conclusion that the
contract is clearly covered by sub-clauses (c), (q) and (u) of the memorandum
and is accordingly intra vires.

Having regard to the view which I have formed on this part of the case, it
is unnecessary to consider the interesting, important and difficult question which **B**
would arise were the contract ultra vires, namely whether, the plaintiff company
having fully performed its part under the contract and the defendants having
obtained all the benefit under the contract, the defendants could successfully
take the point that the contract was ultra vires the plaintiff company and so
avoid payment. It seems strange that third parties could take advantage of a
doctrine, manifestly for the protection of the shareholders, in order to deprive **C**
the company of money which in justice should be paid to it by the third parties.
In *Cotman* v. *Brougham* LORD PARKER OF WADDINGTON said (54),

"... the statement of the company's objects in its memorandum is
intended to serve a double purpose. In the first place, it gives protection
to subscribers, who learn from it the purposes to which their money can be
applied. In the second place, it gives protection to persons who deal with **D**
the company, and who can infer from it the extent of the company's powers.
The narrower the objects expressed in the memorandum the less is the
subscriber's risk, but the wider such objects the greater is the security of
those who transact business with the company."

What LORD PARKER OF WADDINGTON was contemplating was that third parties **E**
proposing to deal with the company could, by looking at the memorandum, have
the security of knowing whether they could compel performance by the company
of the contract in contemplation. I hardly think that he had in mind that
third parties by looking at the memorandum should have the security of knowing
that they might safely enter into a contract and promise to pay the company
for services without any obligation to honour their contractual promise after **F**
they had received the services. The judge in effect came to the conclusion
that the reasoning in *Ashbury Railway Carriage and Iron Company* v. *Riche* (55)
led to this strange result. I express no opinion on this point and leave it to be
decided when it arises, for we have heard no argument on it.

I agree that this appeal should be allowed.

SELLERS, L.J. (whose judgment was read by DANCKWERTS, J.): Before **G**
I had prepared a judgment I had the opportunity and the advantage of reading
the judgment of DANCKWERTS, L.J., which deals completely with all the issues
raised in this appeal. I agree with the judgment entirely and have nothing
which I wish to add to it.

Appeal allowed; judgment for the defendants set aside; judgment for the plaintiff
company on the preliminary issue. **H**

Solicitors: *Theodore Goddard & Co.* (for the plaintiff company); *E. Edwards,*
Son & Noice (for the defendants).

[*Reported by* HENRY SUMMERFIELD, ESQ., *Barrister-at-Law.*]

I

---

(54) [1918-19] All E.R. Rep. at p. 268; [1918] A.C. at p. 520.
(55) (1875), L.R. 7 H.L. 653.

A	## WOLMER SECURITIES, LTD. v. CORNE.

[COURT OF APPEAL (Willmer, Davies and Russell, L.JJ.), April 5, 1966.]

Rent Restriction—Possession—Arrears of rent—Landlord's right to forfeiture for non-payment of rent—Reasonableness of order for possession—Arrears due to illness—Form of order—County Courts Act, 1959 (7 & 8 Eliz. 2 c. 22), s. 191 (1) (a)—Rent and Mortgage Interest Restrictions (Amendment) Act, 1933 (23

B	*& 24 Geo. 5 c. 32), s. 3—Rent Act 1965 (c. 75), s. 32.*

The tenant of a residential flat let to him for a term of three years at a rent of £26 a month under a tenancy which was a regulated tenancy under the Rent Act 1965, failed to pay rent due in three successive months totalling £78. In an action by the landlords in the county court for arrears of rent and for possession under a term of the agreement providing for re-entry and

C	forfeiture, the tenant pleaded illness requiring treatment at a hospital as the cause of non-payment. The county court judge treated the defence as a claim for relief from forfeiture and, while making an order for arrears of rent, held that it was not reasonable to order possession and in his order adjudged " that no order for possession in forfeiture be made ". The landlords claimed that the court had ignored s. 191* of the County Courts Act, 1959, requiring

D	an order for possession in not less than four weeks to be made where a right thereto existed, unless the arrears of rent and costs were paid.

Held: the court should have provided in its order for forfeiture and determination of the contractual tenancy if the terms of relief were not complied with, but the forfeiture or determination of the contractual tenancy operated only for the purposes of s. 191 of the County Courts Act, 1959, so that

E	further application to the court would be necessary before possession were obtained where the Rent Act 1965 was applicable (see p. 693, letters B and C, post).

[**Editorial Note.** This decision was approved in *Peachey Property Corpn.* v. *Robinson* (C.A., May 24, 1966, post).

F	As to recovery of possession of premises subject to the Rent Acts on the ground of non-payment of rent, see 23 HALSBURY'S LAWS (3rd Edn.) 818, para. 1595; and for cases on the subject, see 31 DIGEST 699, 700, 7897-7901.

For the Rent and Mortgage Interest Restrictions (Amendment) Act, 1933, s. 3, see 13 HALSBURY'S STATUTES (2nd Edn.) 1048.

For the County Courts Act, 1959, s. 191 (1), see 39 HALSBURY'S STATUTES (2nd Edn.) 230.

G	For the Rent Act 1965, s. 32, see 45 HALSBURY'S STATUTES (2nd Edn.) 846.]

Appeal.

The landlords appealed to the Court of Appeal against an order of His Honour DEPUTY JUDGE FIFE made in Lambeth County Court on Dec. 15, 1965, for the payment of £78 arrears of rent and costs in respect of the tenant's tenancy of a residential flat at Camberwell, but adjudging that no order for possession in

H	forfeiture be made. The grounds of appeal were: (i) that the deputy judge was wrong in law in holding that he had discretion to give relief against forfeiture although the tenant had not complied with s. 191 (1) (a) of the County Courts Act, 1959, and although the deputy judge made no order in accordance with s. 191 (1) (b); (ii) that there was no evidence before the court on which the deputy judge could exercise his discretion to refuse possession or on which he could

I	decide (if such was his decision) that the landlords had not satisfied him that they were entitled to enforce the right of re-entry or forfeiture; the tenant gave no evidence and did not address the court and he did not therefore dispute, nor did the deputy judge of his own motion dispute, the landlords' prima facie right established by the evidence of the landlords' representative, a Mr. Geoffrey Gilmore, that the landlords had the right of re-entry and forfeiture; (iii) that the deputy judge did not decide whether the tenant's lease was forfeited or not; (iv) that by reason of the landlords' representative's uncontradicted evidence that the tenant was in arrear with his rent to the sum of £78, that the defendant had

_____
* Section 191, so far as material, is printed at p. 692, letters G to I, post.

Approved in PEACHEY PROPERTY CORPN. v. ROBINSON. [1966] 2 All E.R. 981.

not paid the arrears despite repeated demands by the landlords, and that the **A** lease contained a term for re-entry in the event of non-payment of rent, the landlords were entitled to an order for forfeiture.

P. Sheridan for the landlords.
The tenant did not appear and was not represented.

RUSSELL, L.J., delivered the following judgment of the court: By a written **B** agreement dated July 7, 1964, the landlords let to the tenant a residential flat in Camberwell for three years from June 1, 1964, at an exclusive rent of £26 a month payable in advance. There was a proviso in common form for re-entry and forfeiture if the rent should be in arrear for twenty-one days. The tenant failed to pay rent due on Sept. 1, Oct. 1 and Nov. 1, 1965, a total of £78. On Nov. 3, 1965, the landlords issued a plaint in the county court summarising the terms of the **C** agreement and the proviso for re-entry and forfeiture, and claiming possession and £78 rent arrears. The tenant did not deny the facts, but explained in his defence that he had been unable to work through illness, for which he was under treatment as an out-patient at the Maudsley Hospital, and therefore he was behind in paying his rent.

The case was heard on Dec. 15, 1965, and we gather that the tenant was present, **D** though not taking part, and a cousin spoke up for him on the lines of the written defence. The landlords' case was established in evidence. The county court judge treated the defence as if it were a claim for relief from forfeiture; but his order was only for £78 arrears of rent and costs. He said that, having regard to the tenant's situation, it was not reasonable to order possession, and the order as drawn up adjudged " that no order for possession in forfeiture be made ". The **E** landlords admitted and admit that, by virtue of s. 1 of the Rent Act 1965, this is a regulated tenancy, and that therefore s. 3 of the Rent and Mortgage Interest Restrictions (Amendment) Act, 1933, applies. Thereunder no order for the recovery of possession or of ejectment may be made unless the court considers it reasonable to make such an order, and either Sch. 1 applies (as it does to cases of rent in arrear) or alternative accommodation is available. **F**

The county court judge appears to have gone direct to that provision in refusing to order possession; but the landlords say that he has omitted an intermediate step, in that he ignored s. 191 of the County Courts Act, 1959. That section, so far as now material, provides:

" (1) Where a lessor is proceeding by action in a county court (being an action in which a county court has jurisdiction) to enforce against a lessee a **G** right of re-entry or forfeiture in respect of any land for non-payment of rent, the following provisions shall have effect:—(*a*) if the lessee pays into court not less than five clear days before the return day all the rent in arrear and the costs of the action, the action shall cease, and the lessee shall hold the land according to the lease without any new lease; (*b*) if the action does not cease as aforesaid and the court at the trial is satisfied that the lessor is **H** entitled to enforce the right of re-entry or forfeiture, the court shall order possession of the land to be given to the lessor at the expiration of such period, not being less than four weeks from the date of the order, as the court thinks fit, unless within that period the lessee pays into court all the rent in arrear and the costs of the action; (*c*) if, within the period specified in the order, the lessee pays into court all the rent in arrear and the costs of the **I** action, he shall hold the land according to the lease without any new lease, but if the lessee does not, within the said period, pay into court all the rent in arrear and the costs of the action, the order shall be enforced in the prescribed manner, and so long as the order remains unreversed the lessee shall be barred from all relief."

By not regarding the Act of 1959 the county court judge has, it is said, left in the air the question whether the three years' tenancy has, subject to possible relief

A from forfeiture, been determined. It is said that he should have expressed himself as satisfied on the facts required to establish forfeiture, and to have provided for effective forfeiture and determination of the tenancy if the terms of relief were not complied with.

In this we consider that the landlords are right. It is, however, to be observed that s. 191, in so to speak closing the door to relief from forfeiture, does it by

B means of an order that possession shall be given to the lessor by a certain date unless payment of arrears is made, and that, if that payment is not made, " the order shall be enforced in the prescribed manner ", which I take to mean by issue of a warrant. This must be read, however, subject to the fact that further restrictions are imposed on the actual attainment of possession, once the con-tractual tenancy has gone, in the case of regulated tenancies by s. 3 of the Rent

C and Mortgage Interest Restrictions (Amendment) Act, 1933, and it would seem in the case of other terminated tenancies by s. 32 of the Rent Act, 1965. In all such cases further application must be made to the court; the original order for possession, when it operates, cannot be regarded as more than forfeiture or determination absolute of the contractual tenancy, and in its ordinary form (see county court form 136) is misleading.

D We think it desirable that in these cases the order for possession should make it plain that it operates for the purposes of s. 191 of the County Courts Act, 1959, only. The form that we propose to substitute for that of the county court judge is, therefore, as follows:

" It is adjudged that the plaintiffs are entitled (for the purposes of s. 191 of the County Courts Act, 1959, only) to recover against the defendant posses-

E sion of the land mentioned in the particulars of claim (that is to say, ' first floor flat together with the ground floor living room, kitchen and garden at 218, Ivydale Road, Camberwell in Greater London ') the rent of the said land amounting to £78 being in arrear and the plaintiffs having a right of re-entry or forfeiture in respect thereof And it is adjudged that the plaintiffs do recover against the defendant the sum of £78 for the arrears of rent aforesaid

F and their costs to be taxed on scale 3 And it is ordered that the defendant shall pay to the registrar of this court the sum above mentioned on or before May 4, 1966, and do pay the amount of the costs when taxed on or before that day or if costs have not been taxed before the expiration of that day within three days of taxation And it is ordered (for the purposes of s. 191 of the County Courts Act, 1959, only) that the defendant do give the plaintiffs

G possession of the said land on May 5, 1966, unless on or before May 4, 1966, the defendant has paid into court the said sum of £78."

We have given a bare four weeks because of the further protection available thereafter to the tenant. We observe that the Administration of Justice Act 1965, by s. 23 enables (1) extension of that period to be later ordered.

H   *Appeal allowed. Order below set aside and order in terms stated substituted.*

Solicitors: *Fremont & Co.* (for the landlords).

[*Reported by* F. A. AMIES, ESQ., *Barrister-at-Law.*]

I

---

(1) For s. 23, see 45 HALSBURY'S STATUTES (2nd Edn.) 189.

FEARON v. SYDNEY.   A

[QUEEN'S BENCH DIVISION (Lord Parker, C.J., Marshall and James, JJ.), May 4, 1966.]

*Road Traffic—Disqualification for holding licence—Two previous convictions
endorsed on licence within previous three years—Mitigating ground—
Disqualification imposed on third offence—Whether the fact that the two*   B
*previous convictions had been taken into consideration on disqualification
for the third offence could be a mitigating ground on fourth offence—Road
Traffic Act, 1962 (10 & 11 Eliz. 2 c. 59), s. 5 (3).*

The respondent pleaded guilty to driving a motor vehicle on a restricted
road at a speed exceeding thirty miles per hour. He had been convicted
of driving offences and his driving licence had been endorsed on two occasions   C
in 1964, and on a third occasion in 1965, on which latter occasion he had
been disqualified for three months, the two previous convictions making
s. 5 (3)* of the Road Traffic Act, 1962, applicable on the third conviction.
The justices decided that, since the previous convictions in 1964 must have
been taken into account on the disqualification in 1965, it would be wrong
to take them into account under s. 5 (3) again on the fourth offence.   D

Held: the ground taken by the justices for mitigating the normal consequences of the fourth conviction was incapable of constituting a mitigating
ground for the purposes of s. 5 (3) of the Road Traffic Act, 1962, and the
matter would be remitted to the justices with a direction to impose, in
accordance with s. 5 (3), a period of disqualification of at least six months
(see p. 695, letter I, to p. 696, letter B, post).   E

Appeal allowed.

[As to the power of ordering disqualification for motoring offences, see 33
HALSBURY'S LAWS (3rd Edn.) 638, 639, para. 1080.

For the Road Traffic Act, 1962, s. 5, see 42 HALSBURY'S STATUTES (2nd Edn.)
891.]   F

Case Stated.

This was a Case Stated by justices for the county of Bedford, in respect of
their adjudication as a magistrates' court sitting at Ampthill, on Nov. 11, 1965.
On Sept. 24, 1965, the appellant, Edward Fearon, preferred an information
against the respondent, Brian Sydney, charging that, on Sept. 10, 1965, at
Westoning in the county of Bedford, he unlawfully drove a motor vehicle on a   G
restricted road there at a speed exceeding thirty miles per hour, contrary to
s. 4 and s. 19 of the Road Traffic Act, 1960. The respondent appeared in person
and pleaded guilty and, without hearing any evidence, the justices convicted
him and imposed a fine of £5 and ordered that his driving licence be endorsed.
No contentions were put forward by the appellant or by the respondent. The
respondent produced his driving licence, and the following was a copy of the   H
endorsements which appeared thereon:

" Kingston-on-Thames 8/3/62. No insurance 23/9/61 £3. Licence endorsed.
Bedford 16/1/64 due care 4/12/63 £10. Costs 3s. 4d. L.E. Hatfield 13/4/64
Speeding on 26/2/64 £3. Licence endorsed. Huntingdon Borough and
Leightonstone P.S.D. 17/3/65. Speed (van) 9/2/63. £3. Licence endorsed.
Huntingdon Borough and Leightonstone P.S.D. having three endorse-   I
ments for convictions on separate occasions since 29th of May 1963 dis-
qualified three months."

The justices decided, having regard to all the circumstances, that there were
grounds for mitigating the normal consequences of the conviction by them,
in that, if they had ordered disqualification under the provisions of the subsection (s. 5 (3) of the Road Traffic Act, 1962), they would thereby have taken

---

* Section 5 (3) is printed at p. 695, letter D, post.

A into account the convictions on Jan. 16, 1964, and Apr. 13, 1964, which had already been taken into account when the respondent was disqualified on Mar. 17, 1965. They stated the grounds for their decision as follows, viz.—" Having already been disqualified is to start a clean sheet. Not to be disqualified again this time ". The appellant now appealed.

D. A. Barker for the appellant.

B E. F. Jowitt for the respondent.

LORD PARKER, C.J.: This is an appeal by way of Case Stated from a decision of justices for the county of Bedford sitting at Ampthill who, on a conviction of the respondent for driving a motor vehicle on a restricted road at a speed exceeding thirty miles an hour, found that there were mitigating circum-
C stances as a result of which they need not disqualify the respondent under s. 5 (3) of the Road Traffic Act, 1962. That subsection provides that:

" Where a person convicted of an offence specified in the said Part 1 or the said Part 2 has within the three years immediately preceding the commission of the offence and since the commencement of this Act been convicted on not less than two occasions of an offence specified in those Parts
D and particulars of the convictions have been ordered to be endorsed in accordance with s. 7 of this Act, the court shall order him to be disqualified for such period not less than six months as the court thinks fit, unless the court is satisfied, having regard to all the circumstances, that there are grounds for mitigating the normal consequences of the conviction and thinks fit to order him to be disqualified for a shorter period or not to order him to
E be disqualified."

The justices, when the respondent's driving licence was produced, found that, on Jan. 16, 1964, he had been convicted of driving without due care and his licence had been endorsed; secondly, that, on Apr. 13, 1964, for speeding his licence had been endorsed; and, finally, that, on Mar. 17, 1965, for speeding his licence had been endorsed and a disqualification of three months imposed
F under s. 5 (3). That disqualification was clearly imposed on the basis that there had been two previous qualifying convictions whereby s. 5 (3) came into operation, but the justices must have found then some grounds for mitigating the consequences of the conviction because six months was not imposed but three months.

In these circumstances, the justices considered whether, there being three
G qualifying convictions then before them, there were any grounds for mitigating the normal consequences of the conviction and imposing a disqualification of less than six months or no disqualification at all. They say this:

" We decided, having regard to all the circumstances, that there were grounds for mitigating the normal consequences of the conviction by us, in that, if we had ordered disqualification under the provisions of the sub-
H section, we should thereby have taken into account the convictions on Jan. 16, 1964, and on Apr. 13, 1964, which had already been taken into account when the respondent was disqualified on Mar. 17, 1965. We stated the grounds for our decision as follows, namely:—' Having already been disqualified is to start a clean sheet. Not to be disqualified again this time '."
I
In my judgment, what the justices sought to rely on as grounds for mitigating the normal consequences of the conviction then before them were incapable of amounting to grounds for mitigating. They seem to have thought that, because on the third occasion there had been a disqualification under s. 5 (3) as a result of the two earlier offences, therefore, it was in some way right for them not to take these two earlier offences into consideration again. For my part, I cannot understand that. The reason that there was a disqualification in March, 1965, a disqualification for the offence then before the justices, was because it was

the third offence; there had been two others. On the present occasion, the **A**
justices were faced not with a third but a fourth offence, and, so far from the
two earlier convictions as it were passing out of the picture, they remained
firmly there as an aggravating feature. The justices' reasoning would apparently
mean that the more a man committed offences, the more grounds there were for
mitigation.

In my judgment, the justices were clearly wrong. There were no grounds for **B**
mitigating the normal consequences of the conviction, and the Case should go
back with a direction to impose a period of disqualification of at least six months.

MARSHALL, J.: I agree.

JAMES, J.: I also agree.

Appeal allowed.   Case remitted. **C**

Solicitors: *Marcan & Dean*, agents for *E. T. Ray & Co.*, Leighton Buzzard
(for the appellant); *C. C. Bell & Son*, Bedford (for the respondent).

[*Reported by* LAURENCE H. KINGSLEY, ESQ., *Barrister-at-Law.*]

D

MOODY v. GODSTONE RURAL DISTRICT COUNCIL.

[QUEEN'S BENCH DIVISION (Lord Parker, C.J., Marshall and James, JJ.),
May 5, 1966.]

E

*Town and Country Planning—Enforcement notice—Service—Posting by prepaid
registered post addressed to owner of caravan site—Certificate of delivery
produced purporting to be signed by owner—Denial of receipt by owner not
challenged in cross-examination—Whether service proved—Interpretation
Act, 1889 (52 & 53 Vict. c. 63), s. 26—Town and Country Planning Act, 1962
(10 & 11 Eliz. 2 c. 38), s. 214 (1) (c).*

F

The appellant, the owner of a caravan site, was convicted of failing
to comply with an enforcement notice. The notice had been sent to him
by the respondent district council by A.R. registered post. There was
evidence on which the justices found as a fact that the notice had been posted
on June 1, 1965, to the appellant by A.R. registered post as evidenced by a
certificate of delivery purporting to be signed by the appellant. The appellant,
however, had denied on oath that it had been served, saying that he had **G**
not been in the country at the time, and he had not been cross-examined on
his denial. On appeal against conviction,

Held: the adducing of evidence of the posting of the notice by prepaid
registered post as shown by the certificate of delivery produced in evidence
was sufficient, by virtue of s. 214 (1) (c)* of the Town and Country Planning
Act, 1962, and s. 26† of the Interpretation Act, 1889, to prove service of **H**
the enforcement notice on the appellant, who accordingly had been rightly
convicted (see p. 701, letter G, and p. 702, letter A, post).

*R. v. Appeal Committee of County of London Quarter Sessions, Ex p.
Rossi* ([1956] 1 All E.R. 670), *Beer v. Davies* ([1958] 2 All E.R. 255), *Layton
v. Shires* ([1959] 3 All E.R. 587) and *Hosier v. Goodall* ([1962] 1 All E.R. 30) **I**
distinguished.

Appeal dismissed.

[As to service of notices under the Town and Country Planning Acts, see 37
HALSBURY'S LAWS (3rd Edn.) 232-234, para. 341.

For the Interpretation Act, 1889, s. 26, see 24 HALSBURY'S STATUTES (2nd
Edn.) 224.

---

* Section 214 (1), so far as material, is set out at p. 698, letter H, post.
† Section 26 is set out at p. 698, letter I, post.

A   For the Town and Country Planning Act, 1962, s. 214, see 42 HALSBURY'S
STATUTES (2nd Edn.) 1175.]

Cases referred to:

   Beer v. Davies, [1958] 2 All E.R. 255; [1958] 2 Q.B. 187; [1958] 2 W.L.R. 920;
      122 J.P. 344; 42 Cr. App. Rep. 198; 45 Digest (Repl.) 112, *379*.

B   Hosier v. Goodall, [1962] 1 All E.R. 30; [1962] 2 Q.B. 401; [1962] 2 W.L.R.
      157; 126 J.P. 52; 45 Digest (Repl.) 110, *364*.

   Layton v. Shires, [1959] 3 All E.R. 587; [1960] 2 Q.B. 294; [1959] 3 W.L.R.
      949; 124 J.P. 46; 44 Cr. App. Rep. 18; 45 Digest (Repl.) 113, *381*.

   Munnich v. Godstone R.D.C., [1966] 1 All E.R. 930; [1966] 1 W.L.R. 427.

   R. v. Appeal Committee of County of London Quarter Sessions, Ex p. Rossi,
C   [1956] 1 All E.R. 670; [1956] 1 Q.B. 682; [1956] 2 W.L.R. 800; 120
      J.P. 239; 33 Digest (Repl.) 302, *1280*.

Case Stated.

   This was a Case Stated by justices for the county of Surrey in respect of their
adjudication as a magistrates' court sitting at Dorking, on Nov. 3, 1965. On
Oct. 11, 1965, an information was preferred by one Maurice Haworth on behalf
D of the respondent, the Godstone Rural District Council, against the appellant,
Leonard Jack Moody, charging that he had failed to comply with an enforcement
notice served under s. 45 of the Town and Country Planning Act, 1962. The
following facts were found. The appellant owned and occupied land situate
at Burstow Lodge Farm, Burstow, Surrey. There had been stationed on that
land caravans used for human habitation during the period Feb. 24, 1965, to
E October, 1965. No permission had ever been granted for such stationing under
Part 3 of the Town and Country Planning Act, 1962. On June 1, 1965, an enforcement notice dated June 1, 1965, was sent to the appellant by A.R. registered post.
The notice took effect on July 1, 1965. The appellant failed to comply with the
terms of the notice by removing the caravans by the time specified in the notice,
that is to say, twenty-eight days after the notice took effect, being July 28, 1965.
F The following is a short statement of the evidence. Arthur Tatham Hatton, the
chief planning assistant to the respondent district council, identified the site and
said that he personally had posted the original enforcement notice, a copy of
which he produced, by prepaid A.R. registered post on June 1, 1965, and that
the certificate of delivery, which he produced purported to be signed by the
appellant. He said that there were two caravans on the site when he inspected it
G on Feb. 24, 1965, nine caravans when he inspected it on Apr. 7, 1965, nine caravans when he inspected it on May 6, 1965, and eight caravans when he inspected
it on Oct. 7, 1965. He said that the use of the site for the stationing of caravans
was made without planning permission.   When asked to cross-examine the
witness the appellant said that he did not have the enforcement notice served on
him, that the A.R. registered letter was not served on him and that he was not
H in the country at that time. In evidence on oath, the appellant said that the
people in the caravans were not served with an enforcement notice nor was he
served. He said that he owned the land but did not occupy it, and that he did
not use the land at all; that each of the people in the caravans lived in his or her
caravan which was stationed on a particular plot of land; that they controlled
the land; that each had a rent book and that each paid rent. He said that the
I people in the caravans would not be entitled to allow any other caravans on their
particular plots without his permission.

   It was contended by the appellant, who was not legally represented before the
justices, (a) that he had not received the enforcement notice, that the A.R.
registered letter was not served on him or acknowledged or signed by him, that
there was no evidence that he had signed it or that it had been served on his
agent and that there was, consequently, no service of the notice on him; (b) that,
on the evidence, the caravan dwellers were occupiers of the land who had not

been served with the enforcement notice as required by the Town and Country   A
Planning Act, 1962, s. 45 (3) (a); and (c) that, by reason of (a) and/or (b) above,
the information should be dismissed. It was contended before the justices by
the respondent that, by reason of s. 214 (1) (c) of the Town and Country Planning
Act, 1962, once the notice was posted in a prepaid registered letter or by the
recorded delivery service addressed to the appellant at his usual abode or an
address for service, that of itself constituted good service; that the caravan   B
dwellers were merely temporary licensees and not occupiers, and that, in any
event, they were not in control of either their individual plots or of the site as
a whole.

The justices found as a fact that the enforcement notice was posted by prepaid
A.R. registered post on June 1, 1965, properly addressed to the appellant as
evidenced by the Post Office delivery receipt, and were, therefore, of opinion that   C
service of the enforcement notice was effected in accordance with s. 214 (1) (c)
of the Act of 1962 and that service on the caravan dwellers was unnecessary
and, accordingly, found the case proved and fined the appellant £50. The appellant
now appealed.

L. Joseph for the appellant.
G. C. Ryan for the respondent district council.   D

JAMES, J., delivered the first judgment, at the invitation of LORD PARKER,
C.J.: This is an appeal by way of Case Stated by the appellant from the
adjudication by the justices of the petty sessional division of Dorking on Nov. 3,
1965, that an enforcement notice under s. 45 of the Town and Country Planning
Act, 1962, had been served on the appellant by the respondent, the Godstone   E
Rural District Council, that it was not necessary for the enforcement notice
to be served on certain caravan dwellers who, so the appellant contended, were
occupiers within the meaning of the Town and Country Planning Act, 1962,
and that the appellant had failed to comply with the enforcement notice. The
justices stated the Case for the opinion of this court in the form of two questions:
first, whether they were right in law and on the evidence in holding that the   F
enforcement notice had been duly served; and, second, whether they were right
to disregard the fact that the caravan dwellers had not been served with the
notice. Only one question now remains, of those two, for counsel for the appellant
does not seek in this court to contend that the caravan dwellers were occupiers
and, therefore, should have been served. The contention had been put forward
to the justices by the appellant, where he was not legally represented, and con-   G
ducted his own case; and, having regard to the judgments of the Court of
Appeal in Munnich v. Godstone Rural District Council (1), the contention was
seen to be erroneous and has now been abandoned. [HIS LORDSHIP stated the
facts, and continued:] Section 214 of the Town and Country Planning Act,
1962, so far as relevant, provides:

" (1) Subject to the provisions of this section, any notice or other docu-   H
ment required or authorised to be served or given under this Act may be
served or given either . . . (c) by sending it in a prepaid registered letter
or by the recorded delivery service addressed to that person at his usual or
last known place of abode, or, in a case where an address for service has
been given by that person, at that address . . ."
                                                                                       I
That being a provision which authorises the service of a document by post, it
brings into operation s. 26 of the Interpretation Act, 1889, which provides that:

" Where an Act passed after the commencement of this Act authorises
or requires any document to be served by post, whether the expression
' serve ', or the expression ' give ' or ' send ', or any other expression is used,
then, unless the contrary intention appears, the service shall be deemed to

(1) [1966] 1 All E.R. 930.

A   be effected by properly addressing, prepaying, and posting a letter containing the document, and unless the contrary is proved to have been effected at the time at which the letter would be delivered in the ordinary course of post."

There is, of course, in s. 214 (1) (c) of the Town and Country Planning Act, 1962, no expression of intention contrary to s. 26 of the Interpretation Act, 1889. Counsel for the appellant's argument before this court can, I think, be fairly put

B   as follows in brief form: the purported service of this enforcement notice was effected by a method prescribed by s. 214 (1) (c) of the Town and Country Planning Act, 1962; because that was an Act of Parliament authorising or requiring a document to be served by post, the provisions of s. 26 of the Interpretation Act, 1889, apply; there was here no evidence of receipt of the notice; there was unchallenged evidence of it not being received; the time of service of this notice

C   was a vital matter to be ascertained, because, under the terms of the notice, the appellant had fifty-six days from the date of service in which to comply with its requirements and, if the information which was laid alleged a failure to comply at a date prior to the expiration of that period, it would be a bad information and must fail. This, says counsel for the appellant, is one of that class of case in which the document has to be received by a certain time in order to support the proceed-

D   ings taken for non-compliance. He contends that, by the evidence in this case, it was shown by the appellant that he had not received that notice at all; that he had thereby discharged the onus of proving the contrary of delivery in the ordinary course of post which would otherwise be deemed the time of receipt pursuant to the Interpretation Act, 1889, s. 26. Thus, says counsel, there was a flaw in the prosecution's case, and the information should have been dismissed.

E   Counsel for the respondent district council asserted that the area of dispute between the respondent district council and the appellant on this question was small. His contention for the respondent district council is that the appellant is wrong in arguing that this is one of that class of case in which a notice has to be served at or by a particular time. Counsel says that an enforcement notice under s. 45 of the Town and Country Planning Act, 1962, does not have to be served

F   by or at a certain time; it is different from that type of notice which is sometimes given under an Act of Parliament or other regulation which is intended to give a person notice of a forthcoming event so that he might prepare himself for it, e.g., notice of fixing a time for a hearing, as was one of the cases to which I will later refer. Counsel says that, provided the service is in conformity with the provisions of s. 214 (1) (c) of the Act of 1962, and provided that there is proof of its posting,

G   prepayment and proper addressing to the addressee, and provided a reasonable time is given before proceedings are taken (that is, a reasonable time between the sending of the notice and after the end of the period in which to comply with the terms of the notice is allowed), then that is sufficient, and the notice is then properly proved to have been served in accordance with the statute. A reasonable time, says counsel for the respondent district council, must of course be a period

H   of time which exceeds the period expressed as the time by which the requirement of the notice must be complied with.

Both counsel refer us to *R.* v. *Appeal Committee of County of London Quarter Sessions, Ex p. Rossi* (2) to support that contention. That case concerned the sending of a notice by the clerk of the peace under s. 3 (1) of the Summary Jurisdiction (Appeals) Act, 1933, the notice being of the date, time and place fixed

I   for the hearing of a bastardy appeal. A number of points arose in the case; it is sufficient for the purpose of this case to set out the second finding and to quote certain extracts from the judgments. It was held that in the context of legislation designed to give parties to an appeal time and opportunity to prepare for and appear at proceedings which were in substance a re-hearing of the original matter, the primary obligation under s. 3 (1) to " give notice in due course " had not been satisfied by adopting the permissive method of sending the notice by post in a

(2) [1956] 1 All E.R. 670; [1956] 1 Q.B. 682.

letter which was proved never to have been received by the party interested. A
The words imported the requirement that the notice given should be received by
the party interested within a reasonable time; and, interpreted in the light of
s. 26 of the Interpretation Act, 1889, the service of that notice could not be
" deemed to be effected " in the ordinary course of post, because it was proved
never to have been effected in time or at all. Accordingly, there had been a
defect in procedure and an order of certiorari should be granted to quash the B
proceedings. DENNING, L.J., said (3):

> " In the present case, therefore, when the case was called on for hearing
> on Sept. 28, 1954, and Mr. Rossi did not appear, it was essential for counsel
> for Mrs. Minors to prove service of the notice in accordance with s. 3 (1) of
> the Act of 1933. He had to prove that the clerk of the peace had in due course
> given Mr. Rossi notice of the date, time and place of the hearing. This   C
> could be done by proof that a notice had been sent to him in good time by
> post in a registered letter which had not been returned, for it could then be
> assumed that it had been delivered in the ordinary course of post: see the
> Interpretation Act, 1889, s. 26. When, however, it had appeared that the
> letter had been returned undelivered, then it was quite plain that Mr. Rossi
> had not been given notice at all of the date, time and place of the hearing.   D
> In short, service had not been effected; and the court should not have
> entered on the hearing at all."

DENNING, L.J., was there expressing his view in terms wider than the views expressed in the two other judgments of MORRIS, L.J., and PARKER, L.J., who were
the other members of that court, and with great respect to DENNING, L.J.,   E
it would appear that he was there stating it somewhat wider than the case
essentially required. MORRIS, L.J., said (4):

> " The Act of 1933 clearly permits or authorises the giving of a notice as to a
> hearing by sending a document by registered post. But if the primary
> obligation of giving notice means in this context the giving of some form of
> notice which reaches the party interested so that he may be present or   F
> represented at a hearing . . . Then by the concluding words of s. 26, the
> sending of the notice was deemed, unless the contrary was proved, to have
> been effected at the time at which the letter would have been delivered in
> the ordinary course of post. Here, however, the contrary was proved. It
> was proved, not merely that the letter was not delivered in the ordinary
> course of post but that the letter was not delivered at all. Service cannot in G
> this case be deemed ' to have been effected ' at some particular time, i.e.,
> in the ordinary course of post: service was proved not to have been effected
> at all. When considering the giving of a notice of a hearing of an appeal
> the element of time is clearly of importance; the notice must be given at
> such time as will enable a party to be present at a hearing. Here it was not."
                                                                                H
Then PARKER, L.J., having referred to the other points in the case, said (5):

> " The matter does not, however, end there, since the clerk of the peace
> in fact sent by registered letter to Mr. Rossi at his last place of abode a
> notice of the hearing for Sept. 28, mentioning the time and place. Though the
> posting of the letter was not strictly proved, it was produced to the chairman
> of the appeal committee having been returned undelivered to the clerk of the   I
> peace. It was produced to us. It was apparently sent on Sept. 21, and was
> returned marked ' no response ' as on Sept. 22. Whether the dispatch of
> this letter, though undelivered, constituted the giving of a notice depends

---

(3) [1956] 1 All E.R. at p. 675; [1956] 1 Q.B. at p. 692.
(4) [1956] 1 All E.R. at pp. 678, 679; [1956] 1 Q.B. at pp. 697, 698.
(5) [1956] 1 All E.R. at pp. 680, 681; [1956] 1 Q.B. at p. 700.

A   on the true construction of s. 3 (1) of the Summary Jurisdiction (Appeals) Act, 1933, read with the Interpretation Act, 1889, s. 26. The latter section—to which the Divisional Court were not referred—is in these terms [after reading the section, His Lordship continued]: The section, it will be seen, is in two parts. The first part provides that the dispatch of a notice or other document in the manner laid down, shall be deemed to be of service thereof.

B   The second part provides that, unless the contrary is proved, that service is effected on the day when in the ordinary course of post the document would be delivered. This second part, therefore, dealing as it does with delivery, comes into play, and only comes into play, in a case where under the legislation to which the section is being applied the document has to be received by a certain time. If in such a case ' the contrary is proved ', i.e., that the

C   document was not received by that time or at all, then the position appears to be that, though under the first part of the section the document is deemed to have been served, it has been proved that it was not served in time."

This court was also referred to *Beer* v. *Davies* (6), where the last-mentioned case was followed, and also *Layton* v. *Shires* (7). Both these cases were cases

D   concerning notices of intended prosecution under s. 21 of the Road Traffic Act, 1930. The other case to which we were referred of *Hosier* v. *Goodall* (8), was under similar provisions of the Road Traffic Act, 1960. All were cases where clearly the purpose of the notice was to bring to the attention of the person being served the matter of intended prosecution at a point of time proximate to the alleged offence, very similar considerations to that applicable in the *Rossi* case (9).

E   Receipt by such a person in that type of case is an essential element. For my part, I do not consider that the same feature is present in this case, and I think, with great respect to counsel for the appellant's careful argument, that there is this flaw in it. I do not consider that one is entitled to look, as his argument would have one look, to a step some distance ahead, namely, the time at which the information is laid, or perhaps more accurately the time at which the offence is

F   alleged to have been committed, and, working backwards from there, to say that on that basis that time is an essential element where notice is served under s. 45 of the Town and Country Planning Act, 1962. I think that one has to look at the event of the serving of the enforcement notice and at that point of time. At that point of time there is no vital element that the enforcement notice has to be served by or at a particular date in question, and it would not matter whether this

G   notice had been served on the first day of the month in which it was dated, or had been left in the office and served a week later or ten days later; any point of time would have done. Thus this type of case is distinguishable. The second limb of s. 26 of the Interpretation Act, 1889, therefore, cannot be invoked in this case, and, in my judgment, the adducing of evidence of the posting of this notice by prepaid registered post addressed to the appellant at Burstow Lodge Farm,

H   Burstow, Surrey, as shown by the document produced in evidence was sufficient to prove, by virtue of s. 214 (1) (c) of the Town and Country Planning Act, 1962, service of the enforcement notice on the appellant.

I would only add that the argument addressed to this court was not addressed to the justices. Their attention was not drawn, it would appear, to the provisions of the Interpretation Act, 1889, and to that extent it can be said that they did not

I   apply their minds to the same particular problem as that to which this court has applied its mind on the argument presented here. It is no criticism or reflection on the justices. In my view, they arrived at the right decision and for my part I would dismiss this appeal.

(6) [1958] 2 All E.R. 255; [1958] 2 Q.B. 187.
(7) [1959] 3 All E.R. 587; [1960] 2 Q.B. 294.
(8) [1962] 1 All E.R. 30; [1962] 2 Q.B. 401.
(9) [1956] 1 All E.R. 670; [1956] 1 Q.B. 682.

MARSHALL, J.: I agree.   A

LORD PARKER, C.J.: I also agree.

Appeal dismissed.

Solicitors: *Ross & Son*, Horley (for the appellant); *Solicitor to Godstone Rural District Council* (for the respondent district council).

[*Reported by* N. P. METCALFE, ESQ., *Barrister-at-Law*.]   B

Re C. W. & A. L. HUGHES, LTD.

[CHANCERY DIVISION (Plowman, J.), April 27, 28, 29, May 11, 1966.]   C

Company—Winding-up—Voluntary winding-up—Creditors' voluntary winding-up—Preferential payments—" Labour only " sub-contractors—Company had from time to time employed gangs of men under a gang-leader on a " labour only " basis to carry out part of its work as building contractors—Payments made to gang-leader only—No deductions made for P.A.Y.E. nor insurance contributions—Control by company over gang very limited—Whether money advanced to company to meet payments to gang leaders entitled to priority in winding-up—Companies Act, 1948 (11 & 12 Geo. 6 *c.* 38), *s.* 319 (4).

D

H., Ltd., building contractors, engaged " labour only " sub-contractors to carry out parts of building work undertaken by H., Ltd., the materials for this work being supplied by H., Ltd. The company would decide what work it wanted to carry out on a " labour only " basis and would fix the price that it was prepared to pay for that work. The contract would then be offered to a gang leader at that price and he could accept or reject it. The members of the gang would be recruited by the gang leader and the size of the gang might vary. The distribution of the work contracted for among the members of the gang was purely a matter for the gang leader. Payment for the work was made by the company to the gang leader alone, and division of the money was a matter for him. The company paid the gang leader weekly sums on account, after inspection of the work in order to ascertain the proper sum to be paid. No payment was made in respect of bad work or for time lost by bad weather. By common consent, no deduction was made by the company from the payments to the gang leader in respect of P.A.Y.E., nor did the company concern itself with the men's national insurance contributions. It made no contribution in respect of the gangs to the holiday scheme it operated for the benefit of its own employees. The control exercised by H., Ltd. over the gangs was very limited; it did not exercise the same control over the hours of work of the gangs as it did over its own employees. On Nov. 28, 1960, H., Ltd. passed a resolution for voluntary winding-up, a creditor's winding-up, and a liquidator was appointed. At the date of the winding-up an overdraft was outstanding on wages account with H., Ltd.'s bank, and £3,843 6s. 10d., part of the overdraft, represented money advanced to pay the gangs in respect of services rendered within four months next before Nov. 28, 1960. The guarantors of the overdraft applied by summons asking to be subrogated to priority rights alleged to be the bank's under s. 319 (4)* of the Companies Act, 1948, in respect of the £3,843 6s. 10d., the liquidator having refused to treat that sum as paid " on account of wages or salary ".

E

F

G

H

I

Held: the gang leaders and the members of the gangs were not in the employment of H., Ltd. and the relationship of master and servant did not subsist between H., Ltd. and them; accordingly the £3,843 6s. 10d. advanced

---

* Section 319, so far as material, is printed at p. 703, letter H, to p. 704, letter E, post.

A   was not given priority by s. 319 (4) of the Companies Act, 1948 (see p. 706, letter B, and p. 708, letter H, post).

   Emerald Construction Co., Ltd. v. *Lowthian* ([1966] 1 All E.R. 1013) applied.

   [As to preference in winding-up for money advanced for wages or salary of a clerk or servant, see 6 HALSBURY'S LAWS (3rd Edn.) 666, 667, para. 1316; as to
B   subrogation of a guarantor, see ibid., p. 667, para. 1317; and for cases on the subject of the wages of clerks and servants, see 10 DIGEST (Repl.) 994-996, *6836-6851.*

   For the Companies Act, 1948, s. 319 (4), see 3 HALSBURY'S STATUTES (2nd Edn.) 700.]

   Cases referred to:
C   *Emerald Construction Co., Ltd.* v. *Lowthian,* [1966] 1 All E.R. 1013; [1966] 1 W.L.R. 691.

   Winter German Opera Ltd., Re, (1907), 23 T.L.R. 662; 10 Digest (Repl.) 995, *6843.*

   Adjourned Summons.

D   This was an application by originating summons dated Aug. 16, 1965, by Charles William Hughes and Albert Leonard Hughes, guarantors of an overdraft granted by Midland Bank, Ltd. to C. W. & A. L. Hughes, Ltd., for an order that Ralph Aylwin Haigh, the respondent, in his capacity of liquidator of C. W. & A. L. Hughes, Ltd. (" the company ") should treat certain payments, made by the company in respect of services rendered to the company during four months
E   next before the date of the passing of the resolution for voluntary winding-up of the company and amounting to a total of £3,843 6s. 10d., as payments falling within the provisions of s. 319 (4) of the Companies Act, 1948. The facts and relevant statutory provisions are set out in the judgment.

   The cases noted below* were cited during the argument in addition to those referred to in the judgment.

F   *J. W. M. Turner* for the applicants.
   F. M. Ferris for the liquidator.

                                                        Cur. adv. vult.

   May 11. **PLOWMAN, J.,** read the following judgment: C. W. & A. L. Hughes, Ltd. (which I will call " the company ") was incorporated in 1953, and on Nov. 28, 1960, it passed a resolution for winding-up. That winding-up is
G   a creditors' voluntary winding-up and the respondent to this summons, Mr. R. A. Haigh, is the liquidator.

   The summons before me is a summons by two of the directors, Mr. C. W. Hughes and Mr. A. L. Hughes, asking, in effect, that, as guarantors of the company's overdraft, they may be subrogated to the rights of Midland Bank, Ltd., under s. 319 (4) of the Companies Act, 1948. The material parts of s. 319 are
H   as follows:

      " (1) In a winding-up there shall be paid in priority to all other debts—

-----

* *Re Byrom, Ex p. Ball,* (1853), 3 De G.M. & G. 155; *Re Disney, Ex p. Allsop,* (1875), 32 L.T. 433; *Graham* v. *Edge,* (1888), 20 Q.B.D. 538; *Re G. H. Morison & Co., Ltd.,* (1912), 106 L.T. 731; *Re Ashley & Smith, Ltd.,* [1918-19] All E.R. Rep. 753; [1918]
I   2 Ch. 378; *Performing Right Society, Ltd.* v. *Mitchell and Booker (Palais de Danse), Ltd.,* [1924] 1 K.B. 762; *Re General Radio Co., Ltd.,* [1929] W.N. 172; *Anderson* v. *James Sutherland (Peterhead), Ltd.,* 1941 S.C. 203; *Century Insurance Co., Ltd.* v. *Northern Ireland Road Transport Board,* [1942] A.C. 509; *Greig or Robertson* v. *Secretary of State for Scotland,* 1943 S.C. 188; *Short* v. *J. & W. Henderson, Ltd.,* 1946 S.C. 24; *Trussed Steel Concrete Co., Ltd.* v. *Green,* [1946] Ch. 115; *Re Benalpha Products, Ltd.,* (1946), 115 L.J.Ch. 193; *Mersey Docks & Harbour Board* v. *Coggins & Griffith (Liverpool), Ltd.,* [1946] 2 All E.R. 345; [1947] A.C. 1; *Stagecraft, Ltd.* v. *Minister of National Insurance,* 1952 S.C. 288; *Pauley* v. *Kenaldo, Ltd.,* [1953] 1 All E.R. 226; *Re Baker,* [1954] 2 All E.R. 790; *Lee* v. *Lee's Air Farming, Ltd.,* [1960] 3 All E.R. 420; [1961] A.C. 12; *Morren* v. *Swinton and Pendlebury Borough Council,* [1965] 2 All E.R. 349.

. . . (*b*) all wages or salary (whether or not earned wholly or in part by way   A
of commission) of any clerk or servant in respect of services rendered to the
company during four months next before the relevant date and all wages
(whether payable for time or for piece work) of any workman or labourer
in respect of services so rendered.

"(2) Notwithstanding anything in paras. (*b*) and (*c*) of the foregoing
subsection, the sum to which priority is to be given under those paragraphs   B
respectively shall not, in the case of any one claimant, exceed £200.

"(4) Where any payment has been made—(*a*) to any clerk, servant,
workman or labourer in the employment of a company, on account of wages
or salary; or (*b*) to any such clerk, servant, workman or labourer or, in the
case of his death, to any other person in his right, on account of accrued
holiday remuneration; out of money advanced by some person for that   C
purpose, the person by whom the money was advanced shall in a winding-up
have a right of priority in respect of the money so advanced and paid up to
the amount by which the sum in respect of which the clerk, servant, workman
or labourer, or other person in his right, would have been entitled to priority
in the winding-up has been diminished by reason of the payment having
been made.   D

"(8) For the purposes of this section— . . . (*d*) the expression ' the relevant
date ' means—(i) in the case of a company ordered to be wound up com-
pulsorily . . . (ii) in any case where the foregoing sub-paragraph does not
apply, means the date of the passing of the resolution for the winding-up of
the company."

The sum in dispute is the sum of £3,843 6s. 10d., part of the company's overdraft,   E
which was disallowed by the liquidator on the ground that it is not within s. 319 (4)
for the reason that it was not, in the liquidator's submission, wages or salary
paid to any person " in the employment " of the company. The money represents the aggregate of payments made by the company to persons engaged by
the company on " labour only " contracts, and the question which I have to
consider is whether such persons were in the employment of the company.   F

The company carried on business as building contractors, and a great deal of
its work consisted of building houses for the Leicester Corporation. From time
to time, the company, as main contractors, employed small gangs of men, under
a gang leader, as sub-contractors on a " labour only " basis to carry out parts of
the work, the materials for this work being supplied by the company. I am
told that these labour only sub-contractors are commonly known as " subbers "   G
in the building trade. Mr. Bennett, a cost accountant with seventeen years'
experience in the building industry, who was formerly in the employment of the
company, latterly as its secretary, says in his affidavit:

"The system of companies employing labour gangs by sub-contractors
has extensively developed in the building industry since the last war.   H
With the expansion of the building programme throughout the country and
the ever increasing cost of labour, all firms found their overheads increasing
year by year. The existence of full employment made it more difficult
to obtain and keep skilled labour and the old loyalty between employer and
employee tended to disappear. This led to difficulty in submitting tenders
and entering into competitive contracts where the margins were so narrow   I
that substantial losses could easily arise. If a firm endeavoured to employ
and maintain a substantial labour force, particularly if it had limited cash
resources as was the case with the company, it soon became financially
embarrassed, especially with local authority contracts where substantial
retention money was often held long after the contract work had been
completed. In order to stabilize this situation, firms endeavoured to keep
their own labour force to a minimum and to reduce their liability to pay
minimum wages between jobs and during inclement weather and to reduce

A   the very heavy burden of overtime payments by making use of sub-contractors to supply labour only. For their part, the workmen readily recognised
the advantage of setting up as sub-contractors for labour only, either by
means of an informal partnership or by means of gangs with a leader as the
sub-contractor. By this method, they obtained a higher rate of return for
their labour so long as the overall shortage of labour in the building industry
B   continued."

In relation to this company, the gang system is incapable of precise definition
since the relevant contracts were never in writing, but the system, as emerged
in the viva voce evidence, appears to have operated as follows. The company
would decide on what work it wanted to carry out on a "labour only" basis
and would fix the price it was prepared to pay for that work. For example,
C   in the case of bricklaying this might be either so much per job—that is to say,
for all the brickwork—or so much per thousand bricks. The contract would
then be offered to a gang leader at this price and he could accept or reject it.
The members of the gang would be recruited by the gang leader and the size
of the gang might vary. Indeed, a "labour only" contract might be carried
out by a single person. The gang leader could, if he chose, increase or reduce
D   the size of his gang during the course of the job without reference to the company,
although he would be expected to keep to the target date for completion of the
job. The distribution of the work contracted for among the members of the
gang was purely a matter for the gang leader. Payment for the work would be
made by the company to the gang leader alone, and division of the money
between the gang leader and the members of the gang was a matter for him and
E   not the concern of the company. The company paid the gang leader weekly
sums on account after inspection of the work in order to ascertain the proper
sum to be paid. A receipt over a 2d. stamp was taken from the gang leader
on each occasion. The law does not require a stamp on receipts given by an
employee for wages, but the object in taking and giving stamped receipts was
to satisfy the revenue and other authorities that the payment had not been
F   made to an employee as such.

Unlike the case of ordinary employees, no extra payment was made for
overtime, no payment was made for time lost by bad weather, and no expenses—
for example, travelling—were paid by the company. If a gang did work badly
and it had to be done all over again no payment was made in respect of the bad
work. By common consent, no deduction was made by the company from the
G   payments to the gang leader in respect of P.A.Y.E.; nor did the company
concern itself with the men's national insurance contributions. It made no
contribution in respect of the gangs to the holiday scheme which was operated
for the benefit of its own employees. The control exercised by the company
over the gangs was very limited. The determination of the amount of the weekly
payment to the gang leader naturally involved an inspection of the gang's work,
H   as did the need to see that their work was up to the standard required of the
company by the main contractor. If it was not, the procedure would be for
the company to discuss the matter with the gang leader. The recruitment and the
dismissal of individual members of the gang was a matter for the gang leader.
The only instance of the dismissal of a member of a gang by the company over
the head of the gang leader was when a man arrived on the site drunk, and this
I   instance is, I think, attributable to the company's right, as the occupier of the
site, to turn off undesirable persons, rather than to any rights as an employer.
The company did not exercise the same control over the hours of work of the
gangs as it did over those of its own employees. It usually tried to arrange with
the gang leader for his men to work the same hours as the company's own
employees, but the gang was allowed latitude in this respect not accorded to
other employees. If it rained, the gang could leave the site with the consent of
the gang leader but without the consent of the company's foreman. Other
workmen could not.

Such being the general picture of how the system of " labour only " contracts A
operated, the question is whether, in those circumstances, the gang leaders and
the members of the gangs were in the employment of the company.   It has not
been suggested that any distinction ought to be drawn between the gang leaders,
on the one hand, and the members of his gang on the other.   This question, in
my judgment, can only be answered in the affirmative if the evidence establishes
that there was a contract of employment between the company, on the one B
hand, and the men on the other so as to create the relationship of master and
servant.   In my judgment no such contract existed in the present case.   I was
referred to a considerable number of authorities on the question of the distinction
between contracts of service and contracts for services, on the criteria for determining whether a man is an employee or an independent contractor, on the
question of control and so on, but I do not propose to review those cases, for C
two reasons.

In the first place, I do not think that the principles applicable are seriously
in doubt; the problem is to determine on which side of the line the present case
falls.   Secondly, the Court of Appeal has very recently expressed what is at any
rate a prima facie view as to the nature of the sort of contract with which I am
here concerned, and I see no reason, on the facts of this case, for reaching a D
different conclusion from the prima facie view of the Court of Appeal, to which
I will refer again in a moment.

So far as the first matter is concerned the principles are, I think, sufficiently
set out in SALMOND ON TORTS (1).   The following passage occurs (2) under
the heading " Servant distinguished from independent contractor ".

" What, then, is the test of this distinction between a servant and an E
independent contractor?   The test is the existence of a right of control
over the agent in respect of the manner in which his work is to be done.
A servant is an agent who works under the supervision and direction of his
employer; an independent contractor is one who is his own master.   A
servant is a person engaged to obey his employer's orders from time to time;
an independent contractor is a person engaged to do certain work, but to F
exercise his own discretion as to the mode and time of doing it—he is bound
by his contract, but not by his employer's orders.   Thus my chauffeur
is my servant; and if by negligent driving he runs over someone in the
street, I am responsible.   But the cabman whom I engage for a particular
journey is not my servant; he is not under my orders; he has made a
contract with me, not that he will obey my directions, but that he will G
drive me to a certain place; if an accident happens by his negligence, he is
responsible, and not I.   So I am responsible for the domestic servants in
my house, but I am not responsible for a skilled man whom I engage to do
a certain job in my house—for example, to paint it, or to mend a window.
(Nor, as we shall see, am I responsible to him for the safety of my premises
to the same degree as I am to a servant.)   H

" This may be put in another way by drawing a distinction between one
employed under a contract of service (a servant) and one employed under a
contract for services (an independent contractor). ' The distinction between
a contract for services and a contract of service can be summarised in this
way : In the one case the master can order or require what is to be done,
while in the other case he can not only order or require what is to be done I
but how itself it shall be done.'   This right of control has always been
accepted since the time of BRAMWELL, B., as the essential mark of a contract of service.   Other marks of a contract of service are (i) the master's
power of selection of his servant, (ii) the payment of wages or other remuneration, (iii) the master's right of suspension or dismissal.   On the servant's side
there is an obligation to present himself for work at the agreed time, to obey
all reasonable directions, to continue to work for the agreed period, and

(1) (14th Edn.) p. 648, para. 192.   (2) At pp. 649, 650.

A   also to indemnify his master against liability to third parties. Yet it cannot
be doubted that a contract of service may exist although one or more of
these elements is absent altogether or present only in an unusual form.
The House of Lords has reserved the right to restate the elements of a
contract of service in the light of modern industrial conditions, for the
powers of the Minister of Labour to control or direct entry into employment
B   and the restrictive practices of trade associations and trade unions may
affect materially the position of an employer as it was formerly understood.
    " The right of control. One criticism of this distinction between a con-
tract of service and a contract for services is that there are many contracts
which are undoubtedly contracts of service but in which the master does
not or cannot control the way in which the work is done . . ."

C   Then there is instanced the captain of a ship or a house surgeon, and I do not
think that I need read any more of that passage.
    Those, then, are the principles, and on the facts of this case I conclude that
the contracts with which I am concerned here were contracts between employer
and sub-contractor—that is to say, gang leader—and not contracts between
master and servant. The degree of control exercised by the company is not
D   such, in my opinion, as to bring them into the latter category.
    This conclusion is, I think, supported by the decision of the Court of Appeal
in the recent case of *Emerald Construction Co., Ltd.* v. *Lowthian* (3). The material
part of the headnote to that case is as follows (3):

      " Main building contractors sub-contracted with the plaintiff for the
E   supply only of labour for work on a building site. The defendants were
officers of a trade union of bricklayers. They knew of the existence of the
sub-contract but did not know, until after the action had started, what its
precise terms were. The union made demands to the main contractors that
the sub-contract should be terminated and endeavoured by industrial
action to bring pressure to bear on the main contractors to get the labour
only sub-contract terminated. They continued such endeavours after they
F   knew of the precise terms of the sub-contract, under which the main con-
contractors had the right to terminate it if the plaintiff did not maintain
reasonable progress. In an action by the plaintiff against the defendants
the plaintiff sought an interlocutory injunction to stop the defendants doing
anything to procure termination by the main contractors of the sub-contract.
On appeal,
G   " HELD: an interlocutory injunction should be granted because—
(i) ignorance of the precise terms of the sub-contract was not enough to
show absence of intent to procure its breach, and on the facts the inference
was that the defendants intended to get the sub-contract terminated if
they could, regardless of whether that would be done in breach of contract
or not;
H   " (ii) the sub-contract was not a ' contract of employment ' within s. 3
of the Trade Disputes Act, 1906, or s. 1 of the Trade Disputes Act 1965,
as it was not a contract between employer and workmen, and accordingly
there was not immunity under those enactments for action to procure its
breach."

I   Holding (ii) was the vital holding. LORD DENNING, M.R., opened his judgment in
this way (4):
      " A great power station is being built at Fiddlers Ferry near Warrington.
It is intended to supply power to new factories in the Liverpool area. The
main contractors for the superstructure are Higgs & Hill, Ltd. They have
engaged a sub-contractor, who is the plaintiff, Emerald Construction Co.,
Ltd. (which I will call ' Emerald '), to erect the brickwork. This sub-
contract is on a ' labour only ' basis. That is to say, Emerald supplies only

_____
(3) [1966] 1 All E.R. 1013.   (4) [1966] 1 All E.R. at p. 1015.

the labour for the work. Higgs & Hill, Ltd. supply the bricks, materials   A
and plant.

"This system of 'labour only' sub-contracting has come under much
discussion lately. It suits the main contractors, because they do not have
to recruit the labour force for the work. They can leave that troublesome
task to the sub-contractors. It suits the sub-contractors, because they
make a profit out of it. They pay their workmen at rates of pay which are   B
certainly no less than union rates, and themselves are remunerated by the
main contractors by contract prices for work done."

Then LORD DENNING, M.R., said this (5):

"The Trade Disputes Acts, 1906 and 1965, do not avail the defendants:
for although this may have been a 'trade dispute', nevertheless this
'labour only' sub-contract is not, as it appears to me at present, a 'con-   C
tract of employment' within s. 3 of the Trade Disputes Act, 1906, or s. 1 of
the Trade Disputes Act 1965. The words 'contract of employment' in this
context seem to me prima facie to denote a contract between employer and
workman; and not a contract between an employer and a sub-contractor,
even though he be a sub-contractor for labour only."

DIPLOCK, L.J., in the course of his judgment, said this (6):   D

"Some arguments, with which I need not deal in detail, were advanced
by the defendants on the construction of the labour only sub-contract. The
first was that on its true construction it was a 'contract of employment'
within the meaning of the Trade Disputes Act 1965 and that to procure
its breach was not actionable; the second was that it did not oblige the   E
main contractors to allocate any work to Emerald; the third was that
Emerald was already in default under the sub-contract, and that the main
contractors have for this reason been entitled at all relevant times lawfully
to terminate it. I am not satisfied that there is sufficient substance in any
of these contentions to overcome the prima facie case of unlawful procure-
ment of a breach of contract made out by Emerald; but more evidence   F
may be forthcoming at the trial about the terms of the contract and of
surrounding circumstances relevant to its construction, and these contentions
will still be open to the defendants at the trial."

And RUSSELL, L.J., added this (6):

"Nor am I persuaded by the arguments advanced that the sub-contract
(a) is a contract of employment, or (b) permitted or now permits Higgs &   G
Hill, Ltd., to terminate it or ignore it without breach."

Counsel for the applicants, citing WARRINGTON, J., in *Re Winter German Opera,
Ltd.* (7), said that cases based on different statutes were of little assistance, and
no doubt this is often true, but the expression " a contract of employment "
in the Trade Disputes Act, 1906, and in the Trade Disputes Act 1965, which the
Court of Appeal was considering in the *Emerald* case (8), seems to me to be H
used in the most general sense, and if a " labour only " contract is not a contract
of employment for the purposes of the Trade Disputes Acts I see no reason for
concluding that it is such a contract for the purposes of s. 319 (4) of the Companies Act, 1948. To hold otherwise would, I think, produce artificial and
unnecessary refinements in the law.

In those circumstances I must dismiss the summons.   I

Summons dismissed.

Solicitors: *Wilberforce, Allen & Bryant,* agents for *Arthur H. Headley & Co.,*
Leicester (for the applicants); *Collyer-Bristow & Co.,* agents for *Ingram & Co.,*
Leicester (for the respondent).

[*Reported by* JACQUELINE METCALFE, *Barrister-at-Law.*]

---

(5) [1966] 1 All E.R. at p. 1018.   (6) [1966] 1 All E.R. at p. 1020.
(7) (1907), 23 T.L.R. 662.   (8) [1966] 1 All E.R. 1013.

A

THE WAGON MOUND (No. 2).

Overseas Tankship (U.K.), Ltd. v. The Miller Steamship Co. Pty. Ltd. and Another.

[Privy Council (Lord Reid, Lord Morris of Borth-y-Gest, Lord Pearce, Lord Wilberforce and Lord Pearson), February 28, March 2, 3, 7, 8, 10, 14, 15,

B   16, 17, May 25, 1966.]

Negligence—Cause of action—Foreseeability—Exceptionally only that risk would become actuality—Whether damage too remote—Criterion of liability.

Nuisance—Damage—Foreseeability—Distinction between measure of damage in all actions in nuisance and special damage required to render public nuisance actionable at suit of member of public—On measure of damages

C   *the criterion of foreseeability arises as in negligence actions.*

Privy Council—Australia—New South Wales—Negligence—Nuisance—Foreseeability—Vessels damaged by fire caused through carelessness of demise charterer's servants in allowing bunkering oil to spill from ship into water— Whether foreseeability essential in determining liability on issue of nuisance.

Foreseeability of the injury is a necessary element in the measure of

D   damages recoverable in cases of nuisance, and it is not sufficient that the injury suffered was the direct result of the nuisance, if that injury was in the relevant sense unforeseeable (see p. 717, letter A, post).

Farrell v. *John Mowlem & Co., Ltd.* ([1954] 1 Lloyd's Rep. 437) not followed.

On Oct. 30, 1951, two of the respondents' vessels were undergoing repairs

E   at Sheerlegs Wharf, Morts Bay in Sydney Harbour. On the same day the vessel Wagon Mound on charter by demise to the appellant, was taking in bunkering oil from Caltex Wharf when, due to the carelessness of the appellant's engineers a large quantity of furnace oil overflowed on to the surface of the water and drifted to Sheerlegs Wharf, where it subsequently caught fire causing extensive damage to the respondents' vessels. In an

F   action by the respondents for damages based on nuisance and on negligence, the trial judge found that the officers of the Wagon Mound would regard furnace oil as being very difficult to ignite on water, but their experience would have been that this had very rarely happened, and that they would have regarded it as a " possibility but one which would become an actuality only in very exceptional circumstances ". He thus found that the damage to

G   the respondents' vessels was not reasonably foreseeable by those for whose acts the appellant was responsible, and he gave judgment, in regard to the issue of negligence, against the respondents. In regard to the issue of nuisance he found that liability did not depend on foreseeability and gave judgment for the respondents on that issue. On appeal and cross-appeal,

Held: on the evidence in the present case (which was different from

H   that in the *Wagon Mound (No. 1)*) there would have been present to the mind of a reasonable man in the position of the engineer of the appellant that there was a real risk of fire, through a continuing discharge of furnace oil on the water, and his knowledge that oil so spread was difficult to ignite and that that would occur only very exceptionally would not, in the circumstances of this discharge, make such a reasonable man think it justifiable

I   to neglect to take steps to eliminate the risk; accordingly negligence, for which the appellant was vicariously responsible, was established, the damages were not too remote and the respondents were entitled to recover on the issue of negligence (see p. 718, letters H and I, and p. 719, letters D, G and I, post).

Bolton v. *Stone* ([1951] 1 All E.R. 1078) explained and distinguished.

Wagon Mound (No. 1) ([1961] 1 All E.R. 404) distinguished on the facts.

Semble: when the word " direct " is used in determining whether damage caused to a member of the public was different from that caused to the rest

Dicta of Lord Reid, at p. 714, *applied in* Tremain *v.* Pike. [1969] 3 All E.R. 1303

Dictum of Lord Reid at 714 considered in Draper v Hodder [1972] 2 All ER 210

ot the public, so as to constitute special damage entitling the particular   A
member of the public to sue in tort for a public nuisance, the meaning of
the word is narrower than when it is used in determining whether damage is
too remote (see p. 714, letter C, post).

Appeal and cross-appeal allowed.

[**Editorial Note.** The difference in the findings of fact on which the different
result reached in the present case to that reached in *Wagon Mound* (*No. 1*) is   B
based is analysed at p. 717, letters G and H, post. It is also pointed out that law in
regard to contributory negligence in New South Wales at the time of the first
trial may have had bearing on what evidence was then tendered (see p. 717,
letter E, post).

As to effective cause, see 28 HALSBURY'S LAWS (3rd Edn.) 27, para. 25; and
for cases on the subject, see 36 DIGEST (Repl.) 34-38, *158-185.*   C

As to the measure of damages in nuisance, see 28 HALSBURY'S LAWS (3rd Edn.)
164, para. 234; as to a private right of action being based on a public nuisance,
see ibid., 159, para. 226.

As to remoteness of damage in negligence, see 11 HALSBURY'S LAWS (3rd Edn.)
278, para. 459.]

Cases referred to: D

Argentino, The, (1888), 13 P.D. 191; 58 L.J.P. 1; 59 L.T. 914; 6 Asp. M.L.C.
    348; 17 Digest (Repl.) 80, *27.*

Benjamin v. *Storr,* (1874), L.R. 9 C.P. 400; 43 L.J.C.P. 162; 30 L.T. 362;
    36 Digest (Repl.) 312, *598.*

Bolton v. *Stone,* [1951] 1 All E.R. 1078; [1951] A.C. 850; 36 Digest (Repl.)   E
    281, *322.*

Clark v. *Chambers,* (1878), 3 Q.B.D. 327; 47 L.J.Q.B. 427; 38 L.T. 454;
    42 J.P. 438; 36 Digest (Repl.) 31, *135.*

Dollman v. *Hillman, Ltd.,* [1941] 1 All E.R. 355; 36 Digest (Repl.) 281, *321.*

Fardon v. *Harcourt-Rivington,* [1932] All E.R. Rep. 81; 146 L.T. 391; 2
    Digest (Repl.) 379, *542.*   F

Farrell v. *John Mowlem & Co., Ltd.,* [1954] 1 Lloyd's Rep. 437.

Hadley v. *Baxendale,* [1843-60] All E.R. Rep. 461; (1854), 9 Exch. 341;
    23 L.J.Ex. 179; 23 L.T.O.S. 69; 156 E.R. 145; 17 Digest (Repl.) 91, *99.*

Harrold v. *Watney,* [1895-99] All E.R. Rep. 276; [1898] 2 Q.B. 320; 67
    L.J.Q.B. 771; 78 L.T. 788; 36 Digest (Repl.) 115, *577.*

Hughes v. *Lord Advocate,* [1963] 1 All E.R. 705; [1963] A.C. 837; [1963]   G
    2 W.L.R. 779; Digest (Cont. Vol. A) 1143, *89a.*

Morton v. *Wheeler,* (1956), unreported.

Notting Hill, The, (1884), 9 P.D. 105; 53 L.J.P. 56; 51 L.T. 66; 5 Asp. M.L.C.
    241; 17 Digest (Repl.) 114, *272.*

Overseas Tankship (*U.K.*), *Ltd.* v. *Morts Dock & Engineering Co., Ltd., Wagon
    Mound* (*No. 1*), [1961] 1 All E.R. 404; [1961] A.C. 388; [1961] 2 W.L.R.   H
    126; [1961] 1 Lloyd's Rep. 1; [1961] A.L.R. 569; Digest (Cont. Vol. A)
    1148, *185a.*

Pearson v. *Cox,* [1874-80] All E.R. Rep. 1164; (1877), 2 C.P.D. 369; 36 L.T.
    495; 42 J.P. 117; 36 Digest (Repl.) 30, *131.*

Sedleigh-Denfield v. *O'Callaghan,* [1940] 3 All E.R. 349; [1940] A.C. 880;
    164 L.T. 72; sub nom. *Sedleigh-Denfield* v. *St. Joseph's Society for
    Foreign Missions,* 109 L.J.K.B. 893; 36 Digest (Repl.) 316, *629.*   I

Sharp v. *Powell,* (1872), L.R. 7 C.P. 253; 41 L.J.C.P. 95; 26 L.T. 436; 36
    Digest (Repl.) 36, *173.*

Wringe v. *Cohen,* [1939] 4 All E.R. 241; [1940] 1 K.B. 229; 109 L.J.K.B. 227;
    161 L.T. 366; 31 Digest (Repl.) 383, *5108.*

Appeal.

This was an appeal by Overseas Tankship (U.K.), Ltd. (" the appellant ") and
a cross-appeal by The Miller Steamship Co., Pty., Ltd., and R. W. Miller & Co.,

A Pty., Ltd., by leave of the Supreme Court of New South Wales granted on Dec. 12, 1963, from the judgment of WALSH, J., in the Supreme Court of New South Wales in commercial causes dated Oct. 10, 1963, wherein judgment was entered against the appellant in favour of The Miller Steamship Co., Pty., Ltd. and R. W. Miller & Co., Pty., Ltd., for the sums of £80,000 and £1,000 respectively.   The circumstances which gave rise to the present actions were the same as those which

B gave rise to proceedings which came before the Judicial Committeee on an earlier occasion (*Overseas Tankship (U.K.), Ltd.* v. *Morts Dock & Engineering Co., Ltd.* [1961] 1 All E.R. 404, called the " *Wagon Mound (No. 1)* "), which concerned damage caused by a spillage of bunkering oil from the s.s. Wagon Mound which caught fire on the waters of Mort's Bay, Sydney Harbour, on Nov. 1, 1951. The plaintiffs in *Wagon Mound (No. 1)* were the owners of a wooden wharf

C known as Sheerlegs Wharf, which was damaged by the fire.   Each of the plaintiffs in the present action, being the respondents on this appeal, was the owner of a ship which at the material time was lying at Sheerlegs Wharf and was damaged by the fire.

   Mark Littman, Q.C., and *Brian Davenport* for the appellant.
   Desmond Ackner, Q.C., W. P. Ash, Q.C., (of the New South Wales Bar) and

D *R. B. Gibson* for the respondents.

   LORD REID: This is an appeal from a judgment of WALSH, J. (1), dated Oct. 10, 1963, in the Supreme Court of New South Wales (Commercial Causes) by which he awarded to the respondents sums of £80,000 and £1,000 in respect of damage from fire sustained by their vessels, Corrimal and Audrey D, on

E Nov. 1, 1951.   These vessels were then at Sheerlegs Wharf, Morts Bay, in Sydney Harbour undergoing repairs.   The appellant was charterer by demise of a vessel, the Wagon Mound, which in the early hours of Oct. 30, 1951, had been taking in bunkering oil from Caltex Wharf not far from Sheerlegs Wharf. By reason of carelessness of the Wagon Mound engineers a large quantity of this oil overflowed from the Wagon Mound on to the surface of the water. Some hours later much of the oil had drifted to and accumulated round Sheerlegs

F Wharf and the respondents' vessels.   About 2 p.m. on Nov. 1 this oil was set alight: the fire spread rapidly and caused extensive damage to the wharf and to the respondents' vessels.

   An action was raised against the present appellant by the owners of Sheerlegs Wharf on the ground of negligence.   On appeal to the Board it was held that the plaintiffs were not entitled to recover on the ground that it was not foreseeable

G that such oil on the surface of the water could be set alight (*Overseas Tankship (U.K.), Ltd.* v. *Morts Dock and Engineering Co., Ltd.* (2)).   Their lordships will refer to this case as the *Wagon Mound (No. 1)*.   The issue of nuisance was also raised but their lordships did not deal with it: they remitted this issue to the Supreme Court and their lordships now understand that the matter was not pursued there in that case.

H In the present case the respondents sue alternatively in nuisance and in negligence.   WALSH, J. (1) had found in their favour in nuisance but against them in negligence.   Before their lordships the appellant appeals against his decision on nuisance and the respondents appeal against his decision on negligence. Their lordships are indebted to that learned judge for the full and careful survey of the evidence which is set out in his judgment (3).   Few of his findings of fact

I have been attacked, and thir lordships do not find it necessary to set out or deal with the evidence at any length; but it is desirable to give some explanation of how the fire started before setting out the learned judge's findings.

   In the course of repairing the respondents' vessels the Morts Dock Co., the owners of Sheerlegs Wharf, were carrying out oxy-acetylene welding and cutting. This work was apt to cause pieces or drops of hot metal to fly off and fall in the

---

(1) [1963] 1 Lloyd's Rep. 402.   (2) [1961] 1 All E.R. 404; [1961] A.C. 388.
(3) [1963] 1 Lloyd's Rep. at pp. 406-408.

ees. So when their manager arrived on the morning of Oct. 30 and saw the A
thick scum of oil round the Wharf, he was apprehensive of fire danger and he
stopped the work while he took advice. He consulted the manager of Caltex
Wharf and, after some further consultation, he was assured that he was safe to
proceed: so he did so, and the repair work was carried on normally until the
fire broke out on Nov. 1. Oil of this character with a flash point of 170°F.
is extremely difficult to ignite in the open; but we now know that that is not B
impossible. There is no certainty about how this oil was set alight, but the most
probable explanation, accepted by WALSH, J., is that there was floating in the
oil-covered water some object supporting a piece of inflammable material, and
that a hot piece of metal fell on it when it burned for a sufficient time to ignite
the surrounding oil.

The findings of the learned trial judge are as follows (4):   C

" (i) Reasonable people in the position of the officers of the Wagon
Mound would regard furnace oil as very difficult to ignite on water.

" (ii) Their personal experience would probably have been that this had
very rarely happened. ·

" (iii) If they had given attention to the risk of fire from the spillage,
they would have regarded it as a possibility, but one which could become D
an actuality only in very exceptional circumstances.

" (iv) They would have considered the chances of the required exceptional
circumstances happening whilst the oil remained spread on the harbour
waters, as being remote.

" (v) I find that the occurrence of damage to [the respondents'] property
as a result of the spillage, was not reasonably foreseeable by those for whose E
acts [the appellant] would be responsible.

" (vi) I find that the spillage of oil was brought about by the careless conduct of persons for whose acts [the appellant] would be responsible.

" (vii) I find that the spillage of oil was a cause of damage to the property
of each of [the respondents].

" (viii) Having regard to those findings, and because of finding (v), I hold F
that the claim of each of [the respondents] framed in negligence fails."

Having made these findings WALSH, J. (4) went on to consider the case in nuisance.
There is no doubt that the carelessness of the appellant's servants in letting
this oil overflow did create a public nuisance by polluting the waters of Sydney
Harbour. Also there can be no doubt that anyone who suffered special damage G
from that pollution would have had an action against the appellants; but the
special damage sustained by the respondents was caused not by pollution but
by fire. So, having held in finding (v) that risk of fire was not reasonably foreseeable, WALSH, J., had to consider whether foreseeability has any place in
the determination of liability for damage caused by nuisance. He made an
extensive survey of the case law and said that the principles which he found H
there (5)

" suggest that a plaintiff may set up a case depending on the following
steps. The defendant has committed a ' wrongful ' act in that it has
created a public nuisance by polluting the harbour waters with oil. As a
result of the presence of that ' nuisance ' (i.e., of the oil) the plaintiff has
suffered damage over and above that suffered by others. This gives the I
plaintiff an action, subject only to proof that there is the requisite relationship between the presence of that nuisance and the injury, so that it can be
said that the injury suffered was direct. It matters not that the injury was
different in kind from a fouling of the ship by the polluted waters."

Then, coming to the words used by the judges in numerous cases of nuisance,
he said that (5)

(4) [1963] 1 Lloyd's Rep. at p. 426.   (5) [1963] 1 Lloyd's Rep at p. 432.

A   ". . . by and large, the judgments are not expressed in terms of the concept
of foreseeability. The term used again and again is 'direct'. It is true
that other expressions are also used, but one does not find in express terms
any testing of the matter by what the defendant might have contemplated
or might have foreseen."

B   And later he added (6)

" I do not find in the case law on nuisance until the time of the [*Wagon
Mound (No. 1)*] decision (7), any authority for the view that liability depends
on foreseeability."

Their lordships must now make their own examination of the case law. They
find the most striking feature to be the variety of words used: and that is not
C   very surprising because in the great majority of cases the facts were such that
it made no difference whether the damage was said to be the direct or the natural
or probable or foreseeable result of the nuisance. The word " natural " is found
very often, and it is peculiarly ambiguous. It can and often does mean a result
which one would naturally expect, i.e., which would not be surprising: or it can
mean the result at the end of a chain of causation unbroken by any conscious
D   act, the result produced by so-called natural laws however surprising or even
unforeseeable in the particular case. Another word frequently used is "probable".
It is used with various shades of meaning. Sometimes it appears to mean more
probable than not, sometimes it appears to include events likely but not very
likely to occur, sometimes it has a still wider meaning and refers to events the
chance of which is anything more than a bare possibility, and sometimes, when
E   used in conjunction with other adjectives, it appears to serve no purpose beyond
rounding off a phrase.

Their lordships must first refer to a number of cases on which WALSH, J., relied
because they require that the damage suffered by the plaintiff must be the direct
or immediate result of the nuisance (generally obstruction of a highway), and
they make no reference to foreseeability or probability. But that is because
F   they were dealing with quite a different matter from measure of damages.

". . . by the common law of England, a person guilty of a public nuisance
might be indicted; but, if injury resulted to a private individual, other and
greater than that which was common to all the Queen's subjects, the person
injured has his remedy by action "

G   (per BRETT, J., in *Benjamin* v. *Storr* (8)). So the first step is to decide whether
the plaintiff has suffered what may for brevity be called special damage. The
authorities on this matter are numerous and exceedingly difficult to reconcile;
but one thing is clear. There have been excluded from the category of special
damage many cases where the damage suffered by the plaintiff was clearly caused
by the nuisance; it was not only foreseeable but probable, and was indeed the
inevitable result of the nuisance—the obstruction by the defendant of a highway
H   giving access to the plaintiffs' premises. The words direct and immediate have
often been used in determining whether the damage caused by the nuisance is
special damage. *Benjamin* v. *Storr* (9) affords a good example. The defendants'
vans were constantly standing in the street outside the plaintiff's coffee house.
They intercepted the light to his windows so that he had to burn gas nearly all
day; they obstructed access by his customers, and the stench from the horses
I   was highly objectionable. The damage caused to the plaintiff by this obstruction
of the highway was obvious, but that was not enough. BRETT, J., said (10):
" It is not enough for him to show that he suffers the same inconvenience in the
use of the highway as other people do . . ." Then he cited two cases (11) in

(6) [1963] 1 Lloyd's Rep. at p. 433.   (7) [1961] 1 All E.R. 404; [1961] A.C. 388.
(8) (1874), L.R. 9 C.P. 400 at p. 406.   (9) (1874), L.R. 9 C.P. 400.
(10) (1874), L.R. 9 C.P. at p. 406.
(11) I.e., *Hubert* v. *Groves*, (1794), 1 Esp. 147 and *Winterbottom* v. *Lord Derby*, (1867),
L.R. 2 Ex. 316.

which the plaintiffs, who had clearly suffered damage as a result of obstruction, A failed because they were unable to show that they had suffered any injury other and different from that which was common to all the rest of the public. And then he said (12)

" Other cases show that the injury to the individual must be direct, and not a mere consequential injury; as where one way is obstructed, but another (though possibly a less convenient one) is left open; in such a case B the private and particular injury has been held not to be sufficiently direct to give a cause of action ".

But he held that in the case before him there was " a particular, a direct, and a substantial damage ."

Such cases have nothing to do with measure of damages: they are dealing C with the entirely different question whether the damage caused to the plaintiff by the nuisance was other and different from the damage caused by the nuisance to the rest of the public. When the word direct is used in determining that question, its meaning or connotation appears to be narrower than when it is used in determining whether damage is too remote, so their lordships do not propose to deal further with cases determining what is and what is not special D damage. No one denies that the respondents have suffered special damage in this case within the meaning of these authorities. The question is whether they can recover notwithstanding the finding that it was not foreseeable.

Of the large number of cases cited in argument there were few in which there was separate consideration of the proper measure of damages for nuisance. Many of the cases cited deal with the measure of damages for breach of contract, E and their lordships will later explain why they do not propose to examine these cases. Moreover a larger number were cases based purely on negligence in which there was no element of nuisance. Their lordships do not intend to examine these cases in detail. It has now been established by the *Wagon Mound* (*No. 1*) (13) and by *Hughes* v. *Lord Advocate* (14) that in such cases damages can only be recovered if the injury complained of not only was caused by the alleged F negligence but also was an injury of a class or character foreseeable as a possible result of it. So it would serve no useful purpose in this case to examine the grounds of judgment in earlier cases of negligence. In so far as they are ambiguous they must now be interpreted in light of these two cases: in so far as they exclude foreseeability they must be taken to be disapproved: and in so far as they take account of foreseeability they do no more than amplify the grounds G of judgment in these two cases. The respondents can only succeed on this branch of the case by distinguishing nuisance from negligence, either because the authorities indicate that foreseeability is irrelevant in nuisance or because on principle it ought to be held to be irrelevant.

In *Sharp* v. *Powell* (15) the defendant's servant washed his van in a public street which was an offence. Owing to a severe frost and a block in a drain the H water did not get away but spread over the street some distance away and became a sheet of ice on which the plaintiff's horse slipped and was injured. The case was laid in nuisance. BOVILL, C.J., decided against the plaintiff because (16)

" the defendant could not reasonably be expected to foresee that the water would accumulate and freeze at the spot where the accident happened." I

KEATING, J., said (17)

" The damage in question, not being one which the defendant could fairly be expected to anticipate as likely to ensue from his act, is in my judgment too remote."

---

(12) (1874), L.R. 9 C.P. at p. 407.   (13) [1961] 1 All E.R. 404; [1961] A.C. 388.
(14) [1963] 1 All E.R. 705; [1963] A.C. 837.   (15) (1872), L.R. 7 C.P. 253.
(16) (1872), L.R. 7 C.P. at p. 259.   (17) (1872), L.R. 7 C.P. at p. 261.

A And the judgment of GROVE, J. (18) was to the same effect. It may be that today the defendant's servant would be expected to be more wide awake and observant, but, given the finding of fact regarding foreseeability, the rest followed. Counsel for the appellant argued that this was really a case of negligence. The relevance of the case to the present issue is that no one concerned thought that there was any difference in this respect between nuisance and negligence.

B The close relation between nuisance and negligence is shown by *Pearson* v. *Cox* (19). Workmen were working in a house. A " straightedge " was balanced on a plank: one of the men shook it and the tool fell on the plaintiff who was passing along the street. The case was laid in negligence but BRAMWELL, B., (20) dealt with it as a case of nuisance. The ground of judgment was expressed by BRETT, J. (21): " The accident was highly improbable and a man need not

C guard against highly improbable accidents." Again it may be that a higher standard of care is required today.

In *Clark* v. *Chambers* (22) an adjoining occupier placed chevaux de frise in the street to restrict passage. Someone moved one of these barriers on to the pavement and at night a foot passenger came in contact with it and was injured. Obstructing the street was clearly a nuisance. The main controversy was

D whether the intervention of the stranger moving the barrier was novus actus interveniens but the plaintiff succeeded. Again there was no suggestion of any difference between negligence and nuisance. SIR ALEXANDER COCKBURN, C.J., (23) doubted whether foreseeability came in at all but held that, if it did, this was foreseeable.

In *Harrold* v. *Watney* (24) a child climbed on to a defective fence beside a

E road. It gave way and the child was injured. The fence was held to be a nuisance and the action succeeded. VAUGHAN WILLIAMS, L.J., said (25):

". . . when asking oneself if the nuisance was the cause of the accident one gets a test in this way: ought what the child did to have been present to the mind of the person who created the nuisance as a probable result of his act? "

F The only case cited where there is an express statement that liability does not depend on foreseeability is *Farrell* v. *John Mowlem & Co., Ltd.* (26) where the defendant had without justification laid a pipe across a pavement and the plaintiff tripped over it and was injured. DEVLIN, J., held this to be a nuisance. He said (27):

G " I think the law still is that any person who actually creates a nuisance is liable for it and for the consequences which flow from it, whether he is negligent or not."

That is quite true, but then he added (27):

" It is no answer to say ' I laid the pipe across the pavement but I did it quite carefully and I did not foresee and perhaps a reasonable man would

H not have foreseen that anybody would be likely to trip over it '."

That case was before the *Wagon Mound (No. 1)* (28) and it may be that DEVLIN, J., thought that the rule was the same in negligence: or it may be that he thought that there was a different rule for nuisance. He cites no authority.

In their lordships' judgment the cases point strongly to there being no difference as to the measure of damages between nuisance and negligence, but they are not

I conclusive. So it is desirable to consider the question of principle.

---

(18) (1872), L.R. 7 C.P. at p. 259.
(19) [1874-80] All E.R. Rep. 1160; (1877), 2 C.P.D. 369.
(20) [1874-80] All E.R. Rep. at p. 1161; (1877), 2 C.P.D. at p. 371.
(21) (1877), 2 C.P.D. at p. 373; [1874-80] All E.R. Rep. at p. 1162.
(22) (1878), 3 Q.B.D. 327.   (23) (1878), 3 Q.B.D. at p. 338.
(24) [1895-99] All E.R. Rep. 276; [1898] 2 Q.B. 320.
(25) [1898] 2 Q.B. at p. 325; [1895-99] All E.R. Rep. at p. 279.
(26) [1954] 1 Lloyd's Rep. 437.   (27) [1954] 1 Lloyd's Rep. at p. 440.
(28) [1961] 1 All E.R. 404; [1961] A.C. 388.

The appellant's first argument was that damages depend on the same principles   A
throughout the law of tort and contract. This was stated emphatically by
SIR BALIOL BRETT, M.R., in *The Notting Hill* (29) and by LORD ESHER, M.R. in *The
Argentino* (30), and it has often been repeated. But the matter has not been
fully investigated recently. There has in recent times been much development
of the law of torts, and developments in the law of contract may not have proceeded on parallel lines. To give but one example, it is not obvious that the   B
grounds of decision of the House of Lords in *Hughes* v. *Lord Advocate* (31) are
consistent with the first rule in *Hadley* v. *Baxendale* (32) as that rule is commonly
interpreted. It is unnecessary, however, to pursue this question in this case,
and therefore their lordships do not intend to examine cases arising out of breach
of contract.

The next argument was that at all events the measure of damages is the same   C
throughout the law of tort; but there are many special features in various kinds
of tort, and again their lordships do not find it necessary to make the extensive
investigations which would be required before reaching a conclusion on this
matter.

Comparing nuisance with negligence the main argument for the respondent
was that in negligence foreseeability is an essential element in determining   D
liability, and therefore it is logical that foreseeability should also be an essential
element in determining the amount of damages: but negligence is not an essential
element in determining liability for nuisance, and therefore it is illogical to
bring in foreseeability when determining the amount of damages. It is quite
true that negligence is not an essential element in nuisance. Nuisance is a term
used to cover a wide variety of tortious acts or omissions, and in many negligence   E
in the narrow sense is not essential. An occupier may incur liability for the
emission of noxious fumes or noise, although he has used the utmost care in
building and using his premises. The amount of fumes or noise which he can
lawfully emit is a question of degree, and he or his advisers may have miscalcu-
lated what can be justified. Or he may deliberately obstruct the highway
adjoining his premises to a greater degree than is permissible hoping that no one   F
will object. On the other hand the emission of fumes or noise or the obstruction
of the adjoining highway may often be the result of pure negligence on his part:
there are many cases (e.g., *Dollman* v. *Hillman* (33)) where precisely the same
facts will establish liability both in nuisance and in negligence. And although
negligence may not be necessary, fault of some kind is almost always necessary
and fault generally involves foreseeability, e.g., in cases like *Sedleigh-Denfield* v.   G
O'Callaghan (34) the fault is in failing to abate a nuisance of the existence of
which the defender is or ought to be aware as likely to cause damage to his neighbour. (Their lordships express no opinion about cases like *Wringe* v. *Cohen* (35)
on which neither counsel relied.) The present case is one of creating a danger
to persons or property in navigable waters (equivalent to a highway) and
there it is admitted that fault is essential—in this case the negligent discharge of   H
the oil.

" But how are we to determine whether a state of affairs in or near a
highway is in danger? This depends, I think, on whether injury may
reasonably be foreseen. If you take all the cases in the books you will find
that if the state of affairs is such that injury may reasonably be anticipated
to persons using the highway it is a public nuisance "   I

(per DENNING, L.J., in *Morton* v. *Wheeler* (36)). So in the class of nuisance
which includes this case foreseeability is an essential element in determining
liability.

(29) (1884), 9 P.D. 105 at p. 113.   (30) (1888), 13 P.D. 191 at p. 197.
(31) [1963] 1 All E.R. 705; [1963] A.C. 837.
(32) [1843-60] All E.R. Rep. 461; (1854), 9 Exch. 341.
(33) [1941] 1 All E.R. 355.   (34) [1940] 3 All E.R. 349; [1940] A.C. 880.
(35) [1939] 4 All E.R. 241; [1940] 1 K.B. 229.   (36) (1956), unreported.

A   It could not be right to discriminate between different cases of nuisance so as to make foreseeability a necessary element in determining damages in those cases where it is a necessary element in determining liability, but not in others. So the choice is between it being a necessary element in all cases of nuisance or in none. In their lordships' judgment the similarities between nuisance and other forms of tort to which the *Wagon Mound* (*No. 1*) (37) applies

B far outweigh any differences, and they must therefore hold that the judgment appealed from is wrong on this branch of the case. It is not sufficient that the injury suffered by the respondents' vessels was the direct result of the nuisance, if that injury was in the relevant sense unforeseeable.

    It is now necessary to turn to the respondents' submission that the trial judge was wrong in holding that damage from fire was not reasonably foreseeable.

C In *Wagon Mound* (*No. 1*) (38) the finding on which the Board proceeded was that of the trial judge:

> "... [the appellants] did not know and could not reasonably be expected to have known that [the oil] was capable of being set afire when spread on water."

D In the present case the evidence led was substantially different from the evidence led in *Wagon Mound* (*No. 1*) (37) and the findings of Walsh, J., (39) are significantly different. That is not due to there having been any failure by the plaintiffs in *Wagon Mound* (*No. 1*) (37) in preparing and presenting their case. The plaintiffs there were no doubt embarrassed by a difficulty which does not affect the present plaintiffs. The outbreak of the fire was consequent on the act of the manager of the plaintiffs in *Wagon Mound* (*No. 1*) (37) in resuming oxy acetylene

E welding and cutting while the wharf was surrounded by this oil. So if the plaintiffs in the former case had set out to prove that it was foreseeable by the engineers of the Wagon Mound that this oil could be set alight, they might have had difficulty in parrying the reply that then this must also have been foreseeable by their manager. Then there would have been contributory negligence and at that time contributory negligence was a complete defence

F in New South Wales.

    The crucial finding of Walsh, J., (40) in this case is in finding (v): that the damage was " not reasonably foreseeable by those for whose acts the defendant would be responsible ". That is not a primary finding of fact but an inference from the other findings, and it is clear from the learned judge's judgment that in drawing this inference he was to a large extent influenced by his view of the

G law. The vital parts of the findings of fact which have already been set out in full are (i) that the officers of the Wagon Mound " would regard furnace oil as very difficult to ignite on water "—not that they would regard this as impossible: (ii) that their experience would probably have been " that this had very rarely happened "—not that they would never have heard of a case where it had happened, and (iii) that they would have regarded it as a " possibility, but

H one which could become an actuality only in very exceptional circumstances "— not, as in *Wagon Mound* (*No. 1*) (37), that they could not reasonably be expected to have known that this oil was capable of being set afire when spread on water. The question which must now be determined is whether these differences between the findings in the two cases do or do not lead to different results in law.

I   In *Wagon Mound* (*No. 1*) (37) the Board were not concerned with degrees of foreseeability because the finding was that the fire was not foreseeable at all. So Viscount Simonds (41) had no cause to amplify the statement that the " essential factor in determining liability is whether the damage is of such a kind as the reasonable man should have foreseen ". Here the findings show,

---

(37) [1961] 1 All E.R. 404; [1961] A.C. 388.
(38) [1961] 1 All E.R. at p. 407; [1961] A.C. at p. 413.
(39) [1963] 1 Lloyd's Rep. 402.   (40) [1963] 1 Lloyd's Rep. at p. 426.
(41) [1961] 1 All E.R. at p. 415; [1961] A.C. at p. 426.

however, that some risk of fire would have been present to the mind of a reason- A
able man in the shoes of the ship's chief engineer.   So the first question must be
what is the precise meaning to be attached in this context to the words
" foreseeable " and " reasonably foreseeable ".

Before *Bolton* v. *Stone* (42) the cases had fallen into two, classes: (i) those
where, before the event, the risk of its happening would have been regarded
as unreal either because the event would have been thought to be physically B
impossible or because the possibility of its happening would have been regarded
as so fantastic or far-fetched that no reasonable man would have paid any
attention to it—" a mere possibility which would never occur to the mind of a
reasonable man" (per LORD DUNEDIN in *Fardon* v. *Harcourt-Rivington* (43))—or
(ii) those where there was a real and substantial risk or chance that something
like the event which happens might occur and then the reasonable man would C
have taken the steps necessary to eliminate the risk.

Bolton v. *Stone* (42) posed a new problem.   There a member of a visiting team
drove a cricket ball out of the ground on to an unfrequented adjacent public
road and it struck and severely injured a lady who happened to be standing in
the road.   That it might happen that a ball would be driven on to this road
could not have been said to be a fantastic or far-fetched possibility: according D
to the evidence it had happened about six times in twenty-eight years.   Moreover
it could not have been said to be a far-fetched or fantastic possibility that such
a ball would strike someone in the road: people did pass along the road from
time to time.   So it could not have been said that, on any ordinary meaning of
the words, the fact that a ball might strike a person in the road was not foreseeable
or reasonably foreseeable.   It was plainly foreseeable; but the chance of its E
happening in the foreseeable future was infinitesimal.   A mathematician given
the data could have worked out that it was only likely to happen once in so many
thousand years.   The House of Lords held that the risk was so small that in the
circumstances a reasonable man would have been justified in disregarding it and
taking no steps to eliminate it.

It does not follow that, no matter what the circumstances may be, it is justifi- F
able to neglect a risk of such a small magnitude.   A reasonable man would only
neglect such a risk if he had some valid reason for doing so: e.g., that it would
involve considerable expense to eliminate the risk.   He would weigh the risk
against the difficulty of eliminating it.   If the activity which caused the injury
to Miss Stone had been an unlawful activity there can be little doubt but that
Bolton v. *Stone* (42) would have been decided differently.   In their lordships' G
judgment *Bolton* v. *Stone* (42) did not alter the general principle that a person
must be regarded as negligent if he does not take steps to eliminate a risk which
he knows or ought to know is a real risk and not a mere possibility which would
never influence the mind of a reasonable man.   What that decision did was to
recognise and give effect to the qualification that it is justifiable not to take steps
to eliminate a real risk if it is small and if the circumstances are such that a H
reasonable man, careful of the safety of his neighbour, would think it right to
neglect it.

In the present case there was no justification whatever for discharging the oil
into Sydney Harbour.   Not only was it an offence to do so, but also it involved
considerable loss financially.   If the ship's engineer had thought about the matter
there could have been no question of balancing the advantages and disadvantages. I
From every point of view it was both his duty and his interest to stop the
discharge immediately.

It follows that in their lordships' view the only question is whether a reasonable
man having the knowledge and experience to be expected of the chief engineer
of the Wagon Mound would have known that there was a real risk of the oil on

---

(42) [1951] 1 All E.R. 1078; [1951] A.C. 850.
(43) [1932] All E.R. Rep. 81 at p. 83.

A the water catching fire in some way: if it did, serious damage to ships or other property was not only foreseeable but very likely.   Their lordships do not dissent from the view of the trial judge that the possibilities of damage (44) " must be significant enough in a practical sense to require a reasonable man to guard against them ", but they think that he may have misdirected himself in saying (45)

B   " there does seem to be a real practical difficulty, assuming that some risk of fire damage was foreseeable, but not a high one, in making a factual judgment as to whether this risk was sufficient to attract liability if damage should occur."

In this difficult chapter of the law decisions are not infrequently taken to apply to circumstances far removed from the facts which give rise to them, and it C would seem that here too much reliance has been placed on some observations in *Bolton* v. *Stone* (46) and similar observations in other cases.

In their lordships' view a properly qualified and alert chief engineer would have realised there was a real risk here, and they do not understand WALSH, J., to deny that; but he appears to have held that, if a real risk can properly be described as remote, it must then be held to be not reasonably foreseeable.   That is a D possible interpretation of some of the authorities; but this is still an open question and on principle their lordships cannot accept this view.   If a real risk is one which would occur to the mind of a reasonable man in the position of the defendant's servant and which he would not brush aside as far-fetched, and if the criterion is to be what that reasonable man would have done in the circumstances, then surely he would not neglect such a risk if action to eliminate it presented E no difficulty, involved no disadvantage and required no expense.

In the present case the evidence shows that the discharge of so much oil on to the water must have taken a considerable time, and a vigilant ship's engineer would have noticed the discharge at an early stage.   The findings show that he ought to have known that it is possible to ignite this kind of oil on water, and F that the ship's engineer probably ought to have known that this had in fact happened before.   The most that can be said to justify inaction is that he would have known that this could only happen in very exceptional circumstances; but that does not mean that a reasonable man would dismiss such risk from his mind and do nothing when it was so easy to prevent it.   If it is clear that the reasonable man would have realised or foreseen and prevented the risk, then it G must follow that the appellants are liable in damages.   The learned judge found this a difficult case: he said that this matter is (47) "one on which different minds would come to different conclusions ".   Taking a rather different view of the law from that of the learned judge, their lordships must hold that the respondents are entitled to succeed on this issue.

The judgment appealed from is in the form of a verdict in favour of the res-
H pondents on the claim based on nuisance, a verdict in favour of the appellant on the claim based on negligence, and a direction that judgment be entered for the respondents in the sums of £80,000 and £1,000 respectively.   The result of their lordships' findings is that the direction that judgment be entered for the respondents must stand, but that the appeal against the verdict in favour of the respondents and the cross-appeal against the verdict in favour of the appellant
I must both be allowed.

Accordingly their lordships will humbly advise Her Majesty that the appeal and the cross-appeal should be allowed and that the judgment for the respondents

---

(44) [1963] 1 Lloyd's Rep. at p. 411.
(45) [1963] 1 Lloyd's Rep. at p. 413.
(46) [1951] 1 All E.R. 1078; [1951] A.C. 850.
(47) [1963] 1 Lloyd's Rep. at p. 424.

in the sums of £80,000 and £1,000 should be affirmed.   The appellant must pay **A**
two-thirds of the respondents' costs in the appeal and cross-appeal.

Appeal and cross-appeal allowed.

Solicitors: *William A. Crump & Son* (for the appellant); *Lovell, White & King*
(for the respondents).

[*Reported by* KATHLEEN J. H. O'BRIEN, *Barrister-at-Law.*] **B**

PRACTICE DIRECTION.

C

*Practice—Trial—Lists—Short causes—Applications in regard to proceedings in
short cause list—Chancery Division.*
*Practice—Trial—Lists—Witness list—Applications in regard to actions in the
witness list Parts 1, 2—Chancery Division.*

On Mar. 9, 1966, **Cross, J.,** gave the following directions amplified from a **D**
statement HIS LORDSHIP made in open court (1).

There are three lists of Chancery causes and matters for hearing in court, viz.,
(i) the Adjourned Summons and Non-Witness List; (ii) the Witness List, Part 1;
(iii) the Witness List, Part 2.

1. *Non-Witness List.*

Applications in regard to a proceeding in this list should be made to the senior **E**
of the judges in group " A ".

Motions, short causes, petitions, procedure summonses and further considerations will be taken by the judge taking the non-witness list who belongs to the
group to which the proceeding is assigned, unless otherwise announced in the
daily cause list.

2. *Witness List, Part 1.* **F**

This consists of actions to be tried on a fixed date.   Actions will appear in this
list twenty-three days after being set down but will not be heard earlier than
twenty-one days from the date on which they first appear.   The date fixed by the
court for the trial of each such case, and the length of time allotted to it, will be
indicated in the list.   A party intending to apply for an alteration of the date fixed
for the trial of any such case must comply with para. 7 of the Practice Direction **G**
dated Apr. 2, 1954 (2).

3. *Witness List, Part 2.*

This consists of those actions estimated to last not more than two days for
which no date has been fixed.   Actions in this part of the witness list will be
liable to appear in the " warned list " at any time after twenty-eight days from **H**
being set down.   When it has been in the " warned list " for seven days an action is
liable to be in the list for hearing on one clear day's notice.

All applications with regard to the hearing of cases appearing in the witness list
must be made to the judge notified in the daily cause list as the judge in charge
of that list.

If a case is settled, or if circumstances affecting its probable length arise, notice **I**
of the fact, and where appropriate, a revised estimate in writing of the length of
the hearing must be left promptly with the cause clerk (room 136), who will note
it and transmit it to the clerk to the judge in charge of the list.

---

(1) [1966] 1 All E.R. 916.   (2) [1954] 1 All E.R. 946.

A

ANDREWS *v.* FREEBOROUGH.

[COURT OF APPEAL (Willmer, Davies and Winn, L.JJ.), March 30, 31, May 9, 1966.]

B *Negligence—Damages—Personal injury—Measure of damages—Loss of amenities of life—Loss of expectation of life—Girl aged eight rendered immediately unconscious as result of injury—Died nearly a year later without regaining consciousness—Action brought by her father as administrator—Law Reform (Miscellaneous Provisions) Act, 1934 (24 & 25 Geo. 5 c. 41), s. 1.*

C A girl aged eight, was injured in a motor accident. From the time of her being injured until her death nearly a year later she was unconscious and without pain and without appreciation of what had happened to her. There was no contributory negligence on her part. In an action by her father as administrator of her estate general damages of £2,500 were awarded against the defendant driver of the car for negligence. Of these £500 was awarded for loss of expectation of life and £2,000 for loss of faculty. On appeal and cross-appeal as to quantum,

D **Held:** (i) (WINN, L.J., dissenting) notwithstanding that the child remained unconscious she would have been entitled, if she had lived, to recover, in addition to damages for loss of expectation of life, substantial damages in respect of the injuries sustained which resulted in the loss of her faculties for nearly a year, and her rights in this respect passed on her death to her personal representative for the benefit of her estate by virtue of s. 1 of the

E Law Reform (Miscellaneous Provisions) Act, 1934; accordingly, there being no sufficient reason to interfere with the award of £2,000 in respect of the loss of faculties, this award should stand (see p. 723, letter E, p. 724, letter I, p. 726, letter F, p. 728, letters F and G, and p. 729, letter D, post).

 Wise v. *Kaye* ([1962] 1 All E.R. 257) and *H. West & Son, Ltd.* v. *Shephard*

F ([1963] 2 All E.R. 625) followed.

 Dictum of HOLROYD PEARCE, L.J., in *Oliver* v. *Ashman* ([1961] 3 All E.R. 323 at p. 332) considered.

 (ii) the award of £500 as damages for loss of expectation of life would not be increased (see p. 727, letter B, and p. 729, letters D and H, post).

 Per WINN, L.J.: it remains, I think, true that it is a somewhat strange

G form of compensation which is neither received by the person entitled to be compensated nor even awarded to him or her in his or her own right (see p. 734, letter C, post).

 Appeal and cross-appeal dismissed.

 [As to measure of damages for personal injury, see 11 HALSBURY'S LAWS (3rd

H Edn.) 255, para. 427; as to damages under the Law Reform (Miscellaneous Provisions) Act, 1934, s. 1, see ibid., pp. 256, 257, para. 428; and for cases on the measure of damages for personal injury, see 36 DIGEST (Repl.) 200, *1053-1057*.

 For the Law Reform (Miscellaneous Provisions) Act, 1934, s. 1, see 9 HALSBURY'S STATUTES (2nd Edn.) 792.]

Cases referred to:

I *Admiralty Comrs.* v. *S.S. Susquehanna (Owners), The Susquehanna,* [1926] All E.R. Rep. 124; [1926] A.C. 55; 95 L.J.P. 128; 135 L.T. 456; 42 Digest (Repl.) 936, *7285.*

 Benham v. *Gambling,* [1941] 1 All E.R. 7; [1941] A.C. 157; 110 L.J.K.B. 49; 164 L.T. 290; 36 Digest (Repl.) 231, *1227.*

 Oliver v. *Ashman,* [1960] 3 All E.R. 677; [1961] 1 Q.B. 337; [1960] 3 W.L.R. 924; *affd.* C.A., [1961] 3 All E.R. 323; [1962] 2 Q.B. 210; [1961] 3 W.L.R. 669; Digest (Cont. Vol. A) 1190, *1053a.*

Phillips v. *South Western Ry. Co.*, (1879), 4 Q.B.D. 406; *affd.* C.A., sub nom. A
    Phillips v. *London & South Western Ry. Co.*, (1879), 5 Q.B.D. 78; 41
    L.T. 121; 43 J.P. 749; *subsequent proceedings*, [1874-80] All E.R. Rep.
    1176; (1879), 5 C.P.D. 280; 49 L.J.Q.B. 223; 42 L.T. 6; 44 J.P. 217;
    17 Digest (Repl.) 190, *860.*
Rose v. *Ford*, [1937] 3 All E.R. 359; [1937] A.C. 826; 106 L.J.K.B. 576; 157
    L.T. 174; 36 Digest (Repl.) 229, *1210.*   B
Skelton v. *Collins*, (1966), 39 A.L.J. 480.
Swift v. *Proud*, (1964), unreported.
West (H.) & Son, Ltd. v. *Shephard*, [1963] 2 All E.R. 625; [1964] A.C. 326;
    [1963] 2 W.L.R. 1359; Digest (Cont. Vol. A) 1191, *1053c.*
Wise v. *Kaye*, [1962] 1 All E.R. 257; [1962] 1 Q.B. 638; [1962] 2 W.L.R. 96;
    Digest (Cont. Vol. A) 1191, *1053b.*   C

Appeal.

This was an appeal by the defendant, Lavinia Freeborough, from a judgment
of LLOYD-JONES, J., dated Nov. 8, 1965, in favour of the plaintiff, Stanley
Andrews, as administrator of his infant daughter, who was killed by the negligent
driving of the defendant. The accident happened about 1.15 p.m. on Feb. 5, 1962,
in Oakhill Road, Liverpool. The deceased child was a girl who was nearly eight D
years old at the time of the accident. She was on her way to school with her
brother. The defendant was travelling at only 15 to 20 m.p.h. in her car, which
was a Morris 1000, and because of the presence of a taxicab was keeping close
to the kerb. No witness saw exactly what happened. The child, however, was
struck by the defendant's car. The child's head came somehow into contact
with and shattered the windscreen of the car. The child sustained severe brain E
injury and lost consciousness at once. She remained in hospital until Jan. 29,
1963, when she died without ever having recovered consciousness.

C. M. Clothier, Q.C., and *N. W. M. Sellers* for the defendant.
F. J. Chance for the plaintiff.

Cur. adv. vult. F
May 9. The following judgments were read.

WILLMER, L.J.: The plaintiff, who was the father of a deceased child,
brought this action as adminstrator of the child's estate under the provisions of
the Law Reform (Miscellaneous Provisions) Act, 1934. He claimed damages
for personal injuries, which resulted in the death of the child, and which were G
sustained in consequence of her being struck by the defendant's motor car.

The action was tried by LLOYD-JONES, J., who by his judgment of Nov. 8,
1965, found in favour of the plaintiff's claim. He found that the accident was
caused by the negligence of the defendant, and that there was no contributory
negligence on the part of the deceased child. He assessed the damages at
£2,531 1s. 3d., of which £31 1s. 3d. represented agreed special damage. The general H
damages of £2,500 were made up of £500 in respect of loss of expectation of life
and £2,000 in respect of the actual injuries and the consequent loss of amenities.
The defendant now appeals both against the finding of liability and against the
assessment of damages. There is a cross-appeal by the plaintiff against the award
of damages. It will be convenient to deal first with the issue of liability. Let me
say at once that the finding of negligence against the defendant is not now I
challenged. What has been contended is that the deceased child should have
been found guilty of contributory negligence and that the damages recoverable
should have been proportionately reduced. [HIS LORDSHIP reviewed the evidence
and found that contributory negligence on the part of the child was not established. He continued:] I turn now to consider the difficult questions which have
been raised with regard to the quantum of damages recoverable. No question
arises as to the special damage of £31 1s. 3d. For the defendant, however, it has
been contended that the award of £2,000 in respect of the injuries sustained and

A the consequent loss of amenities was too high having regard to the fact that the deceased child was completely unconscious from the time of the accident until her death. On behalf of the plaintiff, on the other hand, it has been sought to support the damages awarded under this head; but it has been contended, by way of cross-appeal, that in all the circumstances the award of £500 for loss of expectation of life was insufficient.

B As to the facts, there is no doubt that the child was immediately rendered unconscious, and so remained until her death. In the agreed medical report it is stated:

> " It was agreed that there was severe brain stem damage. She remained deeply unconscious, fed via a gastric tube and with an in-dwelling catheter in place."

C The conclusion expressed in the report is as follows:

> " As far as it is possible to make a statement, it is probably correct to say that this child did not suffer at all; she never reached a stage of consciousness in which pain could be appreciated."

D The action is brought in pursuance of the Law Reform (Miscellaneous Provisions) Act, 1934, which by s. 1 provided that

> " on the death of any person . . . all causes of action subsisting against or vested in him shall survive against or, as the case may be, for the benefit of, his estate."

E There can be no doubt that a cause of action was vested in the child during her life and that it survived for the benefit of her estate. The plaintiff is entitled to recover such damages as the child herself could have recovered had an action been commenced at the moment immediately preceding her death. There is no relevant distinction between an action brought by the injured person during his or her lifetime and an action brought after death by the personal representative for the benefit of the estate except that in the latter case the date of death is an F ascertained fact, so that the court is spared the difficult problem of estimating the probable duration of life.

Since the deceased child was immediately rendered unconscious and so remained throughout the rest of her life, there is clearly in this case no element of pain and suffering to be considered. It might well be said that for all practical purposes the child was in the same position as if she had been killed instan-G taneously. Had she been killed outright I apprehend that no general damages could be awarded except such as would be appropriate to compensate for the loss of expectation of life within the doctrine of *Benham* v. *Gambling* (1). At first sight it would seem tempting to regard this case in the same light; but the authorities which have been cited to us make it abundantly clear that this attractively easy course is not open to us.

H In *Wise* v. *Kaye* (2) this court approved an award of £15,000 general damages to a young woman of twenty who had sustained serious brain injuries rendering her completely helpless and unconscious beyond hope of recovery. It was held that the fact of the plaintiff being ignorant of the loss suffered was irrelevant, except as an element in the assessment of damages for pain and suffering. Sellers, L.J., (3) said:

I > " The first element or ingredient of damages is the physical injury itself, which gives rise to all the consequential claims which may arise from the injury, and the physical injury itself has always, in my opinion, been a head of claim which has justified and required in law an award of damages according to the extent, gravity and duration of the injury."

---

(1) [1941] 1 All E.R. 7; [1941] A.C. 157.
(2) [1962] 1 All E.R. 257; [1962] 1 Q.B. 638.
(3) [1962] 1 All E.R. at p. 263; [1962] 1 Q.B. at p. 651.

Later he said (4):   A

  " It was further submitted that, because the plaintiff has been throughout
unconscious and has so far no knowledge of her condition and, as far as can
be foreseen, never will have any knowledge of the wreck that she is, no
damages or very limited damages, should be awarded. In these circumstances,
there is no room for an award for pain and suffering, but otherwise I regard
it as an untenable submission. The court is, in effect, asked to treat the   B
injured party as if she were dead, and to award compensation for loss of
expectation of life and nothing else by way of general damages. I refuse so
to do. I am not apprised of any branch of our law which permits a person who
is known or believed to be alive to be treated as if he or she were dead."

UPJOHN, L.J., delivered a judgment to the same effect, and said in terms (5):   C

  ". . . ignorance of the injury or of the damage thereby suffered is no ground
for reducing damages . . ."

The decision in that case was subsequently approved by a majority in the House
of Lords in *H. West & Son, Ltd.* v. *Shephard* (6) where they affirmed an award of
£17,500 in favour of a married woman of forty-one who had sustained similar
injuries. In that case there was evidence to the effect that the plaintiff's expecta-   D
tion of life was not likely to extend beyond seven years from the date of the
injury; but there was also some evidence to show that the plaintiff was to a
very limited degree conscious of her predicament. LORD MORRIS OF BORTH-Y-
GEST (with whose opinion LORD TUCKER and LORD PEARCE agreed) accepted that
where there is complete unconsciousness, no damages can be awarded for pain
and suffering; but he went on to hold that even an unconscious plaintiff is   E
entitled to substantial damages in respect of his or her physical injuries and the
resulting loss of amenities of life. He said (7):

  " An unconscious person will be spared pain and suffering and will not
experience the mental anguish which may result from knowledge of what has
in life been lost or from knowledge that life has been shortened. The fact of
unconsciousness is therefore relevant in respect of, and will eliminate, those   F
heads or elements of damage which can only exist by being felt or thought or
experienced. The fact of unconsciousness does not, however, eliminate the
actuality of the deprivations of the ordinary experiences and amenities of life
which may be the inevitable result of some physical injury."

I should also refer to the decision of this court in *Oliver* v. *Ashman* (8), approving   G
an award of £11,000 in favour of a twenty months old boy who had sustained a
serious brain injury reducing him to the condition of a low grade mental defective.
There is a passage in the judgment of PEARSON, L.J., which should, I think, be
quoted. He said (9):

  ". . . there is, so far as can be determined, the absence of any substantial
pain or suffering, physical or mental. In particular, the infant plaintiff seems   H
to have little if any realisation of his own disability and deprivation of the
opportunity of leading and enjoying a normal and full life. The fact of such
disability and deprivation is a major element in the assessment and requires
a large figure for compensation, but it is not in this case accompanied and
aggravated by the presence of pain and suffering to any substantial extent."

In face of these authorities we are bound to hold that this child, notwithstanding   I
that she remained unconscious, would have been entitled, had she lived (and the
plaintiff as her personal representative is now entitled) to recover, in addition to

---

(4) [1962] 1 All E.R. at p. 265; [1962] 1 Q.B. at p. 654.
(5) [1962] 1 All E.R. at p. 268; [1962] 1 Q.B. at p. 661.
(6) [1963] 2 All E.R. 625; [1964] A.C. 326.
(7) [1963] 2 All E.R. at p. 633; [1964] A.C. at p. 349.
(8) [1961] 3 All E.R. 323; [1962] 2 Q.B. 210.
(9) [1961] 3 All E.R. at p. 339; [1962] 2 Q.B. at p. 242.

A damages for loss of expectation of life, substantial damages in respect of the injuries sustained, resulting as they did in the total loss of all amenities of life during the period of a year while the child remained alive.

Since I prepared this part of my judgment my attention has been drawn to the recent decision of the High Court of Australia given on Mar. 7, 1966 in *Skelton* v. *Collins* (10). In that case the plaintiff, who was a youth of nineteen, suffered
B severe brain damage which rendered him unconscious. He remained unconscious, and the evidence showed that he was likely so to remain for the rest of his life, which was not, however, expected to last longer than six months after the trial at first instance. The trial judge awarded £1,500 by way of general damages to cover both the loss of expectation of life and the loss of enjoyment of life during the plaintiff's continuing existence; but he intimated that if he had felt bound
C to follow *Wise* v. *Kaye* (11) he would have awarded £7,000 by way of general damages. The High Court of Australia, by a majority of four to one, upheld the judge's judgment on this point, and made it clear that in their view *Wise* v. *Kaye* (11) and *West* v. *Shephard* (12) were wrongly decided and should not be followed. While making it clear that a decision of the House of Lords should ordinarily be followed by Australian courts, they nevertheless held themselves
D free to take this course for constitutional reasons fully set out in the judgment of OWEN, J., into which I need not enter here.

Any views expressed by the High Court of Australia must clearly be treated with the utmost respect. If the matter were res integra I should, for my part, have felt very much tempted to follow the views expressed by the majority of the court in *Skelton* v. *Collins* (10). I fully appreciate the force of their reasoning
E and of their grounds of criticism of *West* v. *Shephard* (12) and *Wise* v. *Kaye* (11). It must be remembered, however, that the course taken by the High Court of Australia in *Skelton* v. *Collins* (10) is not one that it is open to this court to take. On us in this court the decision of the House of Lords in *West* v. *Shephard* (12) is indubitably binding, and this in my judgment precludes us from saying that for the mere physical injury anything less than substantial damages can afford
F adequate compensation, even in a case where the victim remains wholly unconscious.

How then are such damages to be quantified? It seems to me that in a case such as this the question of damages is even more than usually at large. It is not easy to find in the decided cases any pattern into which an award of damages can readily be fitted as can sometimes be found in the case of simpler injuries, such as
G damage to, or loss of, a limb. We have been referred to an unreported decision of this court in *Swift* v. *Prout* (13), where damages of £6,000 were awarded to a youth of seventeen who, by reason of brain injuries, had lived unconscious for about three years but was not expected to live much longer. It has been suggested that from that case, and from *Wise* v. *Kaye* (11) and *West* v. *Shephard* (12), some sort of pattern emerges, whereby damages can be quantified by reference to the
H length of time, actual or expected, during which the victim survives. It has been submitted that these cases reveal a pattern of about £2,000 a year, and it has been suggested on behalf of the plaintiff that the judge's award in the present case can be justified on this basis.

I do not accept, however, that in this type of case damages can properly be quantified by reference to any such artithmetical calculation. Such a calculation
I could well lead to quite absurd results in some cases where, for instance, the victim is expected to live for a considerable number of years. Thus in *Oliver* v. *Ashman* (14) the infant plaintiff was only twenty months old at the time of the injury, but his expectation of life was said to be thirty years. Yet this court approved

---

(10) (1966), 39 A.L.J. 480.   (11) [1962] 1 All E.R. 257; [1962] 1 Q.B. 638.
(12) [1963] 2 All E.R. 625; [1964] A.C. 326.   (13) (1964), unreported.
(14) [1960] 3 All E.R. 677; [1961] 1 Q.B. 337; *on appeal*, [1961] 3 All E.R. 323; [1962] 2 Q.B. 210.

LORD PARKER, C.J.'s award of £11,000. As appears from the report, HOLROYD **A**
PEARCE, L.J., (15) thought that the award was perhaps on the low side. PEARSON,
L.J., said (16) that he regarded the sum as " sufficient, but not excessive ". I
do not appear from the report to have expressed any view; but all the members
of the court agreed that it was impossible to say that the sum awarded amounted
to a wholly erroneous estimate. I think it is useful to quote the words in which
HOLROYD PEARCE, L.J., expressed his conclusion. He said (17):   **B**

" Any compensation for the child's painless loss of humanity must be
artificial. No sum can compensate or make an appreciable difference. But
one must award such a sum as represents artificially the gravity of the loss.
It is hard to give cogent reasons for this figure or for that. One can merely
assert. I myself would feel inclined towards a larger figure, but LORD PARKER,
C.J., and my brethren all think otherwise. I can give no adequate reason to   **C**
support a higher figure or to show that one figure is more right than the
other. There is no norm by which one can say that this figure is right and the
other wrong."

It has been submitted by counsel for the defendant that in the present case, if
the child had remained conscious for twelve months during which she was endur-   **D**
ing all the pain and discomfort of hospital treatment, an award of £2,000 might
well have been appropriate, but such an award would have included a substantial
element of compensation for conscious pain and suffering. If that be right, then
it is argued that in the absence of consciousness, something much less should
have been awarded. This seems at first sight a formidable argument; but two
things, I think, are to be remembered. First, with the aid of modern medical   **E**
skill and drugs it would no doubt have been possible to reduce the pain and
suffering to a very considerable extent. Secondly, having regard to this child's
tender age, she could not be expected to feel anything like the same degree of
mental anguish through knowledge of her condition as would have been probable
in the case of an adult. I do not think, therefore, that in the circumstances of this
case the child's absence of consciousness is of such vital significance as has been   **F**
suggested.

In all the circumstances I have come to the conclusion that no sufficient
reason has been shown for saying that £2,000 amounts to a wholly erroneous
estimate. In my judgment we should not be justified in interfering.

It remains to deal with the cross-appeal against the award of £500 as compensation for loss of expectation of life. It is recognised that since the decision of the   **G**
House of Lords in *Benham* v. *Gambling* (18) any compensation to be awarded
under this head can only be an artificial sum designed to represent the balance
of probable happiness that remains after life's pains and sorrows have been
subtracted from its joys and pleasures. It has been argued, however, that the
conventional sum generally awarded under this head should now be proportionately increased to compensate for the fall in value of money that has taken place   **H**
during the quarter of a century which has elapsed since *Benham* v. *Gambling* (18)
was decided. In support of this submission reliance has been placed on the views
expressed by DIPLOCK, L.J., in his dissenting judgment in *Wise* v. *Kaye* (19). In
the result, it has been contended, a sum considerably in excess of £500 would
now be justified.

It is to be observed that the sum of £500 awarded in the present case is con-   **I**
siderably larger than that which was thought proper by the members of the
House of Lords in *Benham* v. *Gambling* (18). There can be no doubt that it
already contains a substantial allowance for the fall in the value of money since
that date. It is indeed substantially in line with what is commonly awarded under

(15) [1961] 3 All E.R. at p. 333; [1962] 2 Q.B. 232.
(16) [1961] 3 All E.R. at p. 340, letter B; [1962] 2 Q.B. at p. 243.
(17) [1961] 3 All E.R. at p. 333; [1962] 2 Q.B. at p. 232.
(18) [1941] 1 All E.R. 7; [1941] A.C. 157.
(19) [1962] 1 All E.R. at p. 270; [1962] 1 Q.B. at p. 663.

A this head in other cases at the present day. I observe that in *Benham* v. *Gambling* VISCOUNT SIMON, L.C., (20) expressed the view that the figure for damages under this head should be reduced in the case of a young child because

> " there is necessarily so much uncertainty about the child's future that no confident estimate of prospective happiness can be made."

B His conclusion (21) was that

> " in assessing damages under this head, whether in the case of a child or an adult, very moderate figures should be chosen."

I take this to have been intended as a warning to be heeded in all subsequent cases. In the light of these considerations I do not think that any case has been made out for increasing the sum of £500 awarded as compensation for this child's

C loss of expectation of life.

It follows that in my judgment both appeal and cross-appeal should be dismissed.

DAVIES, L.J., having found that contributory negligence on the part of the child was not established, continued:] The questions of law which have been

D argued in this case may, it would seem, be concisely stated. To what extent may or should damages for personal injuries be awarded in respect of a period of complete unconsciousness? Is or should the award of such damages or their amount be affected by the fact that the injured person is at the date of the award no longer alive, so that the damages will benefit not the injured person but someone else?

E These questions have given rise to a considerable conflict of judicial opinion, as is shown by the dissenting judgment of DIPLOCK, L.J., in *Wise* v. *Kaye* (22), and the dissenting opinions of LORD REID and LORD DEVLIN in *H. West & Son, Ltd.* v. *Shephard* (23). The law is now settled, however, as is clear from the authorities cited by WILLMER, L.J., in his judgment, with which I agree. I shall forbear to repeat the citations made by him but would respectfully seek to

F reinforce the views which he has expressed by some other quotations from the same authorities. In *Wise* v. *Kaye* (24) SELLERS, L.J., said:

> " There remain for consideration two general submissions which were made on behalf of the defendant, which it was argued should greatly modify the award. In the sad circumstances of this case, it would seem that any award of damages will not be personally enjoyed by the plaintiff. They are

G > unlikely to be used to maintain her. She is powerless to dispose of them. But these, in my opinion, are not relevant considerations in the assessment of damages for personal injuries. It has never been so held as was contended, and I can see no good reason for introducing it as a factor for consideration."

In the same case UPJOHN, L.J., said (25):

H > " It seems to me that, on the principle that once the loss is proved and quantified at the proper figure that sum of money becomes the absolute property of the plaintiff, and it matters not that the plaintiff is incapable of personal enjoyment of the money in the very vague and, as I think, indefinable sense of spending it on herself. That has never been the test, and I think it would be a mistake to introduce it now. Indeed, it would, I think, be

I > inconsistent with *Benham* v. *Gambling* (26). In that case, and the earlier case of *Rose* v. *Ford* (27) the short answer would have been: the plaintiff is

---

(20) [1941] 1 All E.R. at p. 13; [1941] A.C. at p. 167.
(21) [1941] 1 All E.R. at p. 13; [1941] A.C. at p. 168.
(22) [1962] 1 All E.R. at p. 270; [1962] 1 Q.B. at p. 663.
(23) [1963] 2 All E.R. at pp. 628, 636; [1964] A.C. at pp. 340, 353.
(24) [1962] 1 All E.R. at p. 264; [1962] 1 Q.B. at p. 653.
(25) [1962] 1 All E.R. at p. 267; [1962] 1 Q.B. at p. 658.
(26) [1941] 1 All E.R. 7; [1941] A.C. 157.
(27) [1937] 3 All E.R. 359; [1937] A.C. 826.

dead; he cannot enjoy the money personally, it will only go to his creditors,   A
his legatees or his next of kin; therefore he has suffered no loss."

And it is indeed true, as the learned lord justice pointed out in the next paragraph
of his judgment, that the opposite conclusion would lead to remarkable results.
UPJOHN, L.J., went on to consider the effect, if any, on the award of damages for
physical injury (what one might call objective physical injury) of the fact of the   B
injured plaintiff's ignorance of that injury. He concluded, as WILLMER, L.J., has
said, that such ignorance was no ground for any reduction in the damages. I
respectfully agree with that view. If the plaintiff loses an arm or a leg owing to
the defendant's negligence, he is entitled to damages. If in addition, however, to
the arm injury or the leg injury his brain is so severely damaged that he is
unconscious and ignorant of his injury, and indeed quite unable to use his arm or   C
leg even if he had not lost it, is it to be said that he is to get for the loss of the
limb no damages, or less damages, than he would otherwise have received?
Surely he ought to be entitled to damages for the injury to his brain over and
above those for the loss of the limb.

Wise v. Kaye (28) was, of course, approved in West v. Shephard (29) and I
would only add from that latter case two quotations from the speech of LORD   D
PEARCE. He said (30):

"... it is argued that such damages are given as compensation or consolation, and therefore, when the respondent's condition is so bad that they
cannot be used by her to compensate or console, they should either be greatly
reduced or should not be awarded at all. No authority is cited in favour of
such a proposition, nor can I see any principle of common law that supports   E
it."

Then LORD PEARCE said (31) after referring to the " conventional sum " awarded
for loss of expectation of life under the principle laid down in Benham v.
Gambling (32):

"... I would not extend that artificial limitation to any claims for loss of   F
some or even all of the amenities of living during a plaintiff's life, however
low that life may have been brought."

In my view, therefore, the position in law in this case is clearly established by the
authorities. (i) The plaintiff is entitled to recover damages for the loss of faculty
suffered by his little daughter during the twelve months for which she survived
after the accident. I have used the word " faculty " rather than " amenity "   G
since the latter word might be thought to involve some subjective element; and
the damages must, of course, not include anything in respect of pain, suffering or
mental anguish, since nothing of that kind was present. (ii) The damages should
be substantial and not merely nominal. (iii) The fact that the damages can be of
no benefit to the deceased child but will go to her next of kin is irrelevant.

Despite this, however, I am bound to say that I have great sympathy with the   H
views to be expressed by WINN, L.J., in his judgment and with the powerful
considerations advanced by the High Court of Australia in the recent case of
Skelton v. Collins (33). Were it open to us to do so, there is obviously a great deal
to be said in favour of coming to the same conclusion as did the Australian court;
but in my judgment it is not so open since we are bound by West v. Shephard
(29) and Wise v. Kaye (28).   I

It was strenuously argued, however, on behalf of the defendant that, even if
this be so, the sum of £2,000 for general damages was wholly excessive. On this
point there is little that I can add to what has been said by WILLMER, L.J. As

---

(28) [1962] 1 All E.R. 257; [1962] 1 Q.B. 638.
(29) [1963] 2 All E.R. 625; [1964] A.C. 326.
(30) [1963] 2 All E.R. at p. 642; [1964] A.C. at p. 364.
(31) [1963] 2 All E.R. at pp. 645, 646; [1964] A.C. at p. 368.
(32) [1941] 1 All E.R. 7; [1941] A.C. 157.   (33) (1966), 39 A.L.J. 480.

A was said by HOLROYD PEARCE in *Oliver* v. *Ashman* (34), in such cases as the present there is no norm. The damages are more than usually at large. Little if any assistance is to be derived from the awards in comparable cases such as *Oliver* v. *Ashman* (35), *Wise* v. *Kaye* (36), *West* v. *Shephard* (37) and *Swift* v. *Prout* (38). It seems to me that mathematical computations or comparisons cannot in such a case as the present assist either the plaintiff or the defendant. It was suggested

B for the defendant that, as in *Swift* v. *Prout* (38), an award of £6,000 to cover a period of three years' unconscious survival for a young man of seventeen was not thought inappropriate, a sum of £2,000 for a girl of eight was too much since, it was submitted, the amenities or faculties of life are more valuable at seventeen than they are at eight; but we just cannot know. Such a comparison is impossible; I can see no more force in that contention than in the opposite argument

C that the cases have fixed a scale of something in the region of £2,000 per annum for such plaintiffs. It is, in my judgment, quite impossible for anyone to lay down any rule or standard as to what the damages should be in such rare and unusual cases.

In these circumstances there is no possible ground on which this court could interfere with the award made by the judge. As to the £500 for loss of expectation

D of life, I have nothing to add to what has been said by WILLMER, L.J. I would accordingly dismiss the appeal and the cross-appeal.

WINN, L.J.: I agree with my lords that this court should not disturb the finding of the learned judge that the tragic accident which gave rise to this action was solely caused by the negligence of the defendant since I am of the

E opinion that on the evidence, and his assessment of its cogency, this was a conclusion to which he was entitled to come.

The issue as to the quantum of damage is far more difficult, and I regret to have to say that I find myself unable to take the same view on it as my lords have expressed. Had this child died at the moment of, or within a minute or two after, this accident it cannot be doubted, and is indeed common ground, that the

F damages recoverable by her estate would have been limited to some £500, being what is often described as a conventional sum for loss of life. As was said by LORD PEARCE in *H. West & Son, Ltd.* v. *Shephard* (39):

"*Benham* v. *Gambling* (40) artificially and drastically limited the liability of defendants in respect of loss of expectation of life."

LORD REID in his dissenting speech put the matter thus (41):

G
"It is now a rule of law that, if a man is cut off in the prime of life, then no matter how bright his prospects only a conventional sum of £500 or so can be awarded in respect of his lost years."

While I personally consider that £500 is a large sum to award under this head for the death of a child of eight since no more would, according to present practice,

H be awarded for the premature termination of the life of an exceptionally happy and healthy adult, I would not seek to disturb that part of the judge's award either by decreasing it or increasing it.

The problem presented by this appeal is whether the award of a further £2,000 in respect of the period of survival of the child between the date of the accident and her death slightly less than twelve months later should be reduced.

I The speeches of the majority of their lordships in *West* v. *Shephard* (37) not only explain but afford substantial support for the reasoning which I think clearly must have led the judge to make this award. To my mind the question

(34) [1961] 3 All E.R. at p. 332, letter I; [1962] 2 Q.B. at p. 231.
(35) [1961] 3 All E.R. 323; [1962] 2 Q.B. 210.
(36) [1962] 1 All E.R. 257; [1962] 1 Q.B. 638.
(37) [1963] 2 All E.R. 625; [1964] A.C. 326.   (38) (1964), unreported.
(39) [1963] 2 All E.R. at p. 645; [1964] A.C. at p. 369.
(40) [1941] 1 All E.R. 7; [1941] A.C. 157.
(41) [1963] 2 All E.R. at p. 629, letter H; [1964] A.C. at p. 343.

which this court must answer is whether those speeches, or the judgments of the **A**
Court of Appeal in *Wise* v. *Kaye* (42), require approval of the award.

I think it right to state frankly that I have myself approached a renewed and
close consideration of all that was said authoritatively in those two cases of *West*
v. *Shephard* (43) and *Wise* v. *Kaye* (42) with a determination to decide whether,
and to what extent, loyal observance of such directions in law as they afford
requires me to reject as erroneous my personal instinctive reaction that the award **B**
is manifestly excessive and out of pattern. I do not think that they require me
to do this. That " instinctive reaction " I now feel even more strongly since
reading the very cogent judgments of the High Court of Australia in the case
(44) mentioned by WILLMER, L.J.   A priori my view would have been exactly
that expressed by LORD DEVLIN (45) that in such a case as the present there is
only one death and one deprivation. As has already been made amply clear, this **C**
poor child was only in a technical sense alive during the twelve months or so
which followed the accident; she had no appreciation of what had happened to
her or of the deprivations to which she had been subjected; she had no pain or
discomfort; it was a period of living death. When death came, little life was lost;
but logically the fact that what was then lost was of minimal value is irrelevant
to any head of damage other than the damages for loss of expectation of life, and **D**
I am not attracted by the idea that this head of damage could in the present case
be accordingly reduced. What is material and indeed essential is to consider the
period between the accident and the death. During that period the child was
deprived of all bodily capacity, a concept which I regard as far more relevant
than that of deprivation of amenities. Amenities are subjects of enjoyment,
visual, auditory or otherwise sensual, and do not seem to me to be separate **E**
relevant factors in a case where all the senses have been destroyed. Before she
was disabled the child had, presumably, such freedom of mobility and other
bodily function as would be normal in a child of that age. She could run about,
play, skip, read, chatter to her friends and parents, and watch television and
other spectacles in the exercise of her bodily capacity. In all those respects her
capacity was destroyed and she was deprived of it for a year. What she was **F**
deprived of in these respects seems to my own mind to be limited in scope, in
kind and in quality compared with the deprivation of bodily capacity suffered by
an adult in the full vigour of youth or the prime of middle age who has developed,
by use and performance, the capacity of his body and limbs, the use of his eyes
and other senses, and all his or her intellectual powers. I cannot help but think
that this consideration must find expression in assessments of damages for **G**
deprivation of bodily capacity.

I think that a similar thought may have been in the mind of SELLERS, L.J.,
when in his judgment in *Wise* v. *Kaye* (42), which was accepted as a correct
analysis of the relevant considerations by the majority of their lordships in *West*
v. *Shephard* (43), he said (46):

" The plaintiff in this case had lived long enough to have been aware of **H**
living her life with all its vicissitudes . . . All that life had to offer, which the
plaintiff would not have relinquished for any money, has been taken from her
completely and irrevocably."

The lord justice also said (46):

" Can it be said that a man who has lost a leg above the knee is any less
happy than if he had lost it only below the knee? I do not think it follows at **I**
all, but he might well be awarded more for the physical injury because he
would be more handicapped in all probability in doing all that he could have
done before."

(42) [1962] 1 All E.R. 257; [1962] 1 Q.B. 638.
(43) [1963] 2 All E.R. 625; [1964] A.C. 326.
(44) I.e., *Skelton* v. *Collins*, (1966), 39 A.L.J. 480.
(45) [1963] 2 All E.R. at p. 639; [1964] at pp. 362, 363.
(46) [1962] 1 All E.R. at p. 264; [1962] 1 Q.B. at p. 653.

A Both those passages appear to me to state a comparison between the bodily capacity and scope of life of the victim of tortious injury before and after the infliction of that injury.

LORD MORRIS OF BORTH-Y-GEST in *Shephard's* case (47) stated a like comparison, saying:

B " At the age of forty-one everything that life held for her was taken away from her. For a period of about seven years instead of having life's activities and amenities she will have mere existence . . . All these matters constitute grave and sombre deprivations . . ."

It was made plain by the majority judgment of the Court of Appeal in *Wise* v. *Kaye* (48), expressly approved by the House of Lords in *West* v. *Shephard* (49),
C that apart altogether from pain and suffering and consciousness of destruction or impairment of physical capacity, damages are properly to be awarded for injury *per se*, that is to say damage to the body of the victim such, for example, as amputation or fracture of a limb or partial destruction of the organic function of the brain. It is immaterial to speculate whether the foundation for this doctrine is some concept of proprietary right in respect of one's body or that of a natural
D right of human beings to immunity from physical harm or impairment, or whether there is some quasi metaphysical idea of a duty to maintain the integrity of the body through this transient life on earth.

The fact is that ever since 1879 the law in this respect has been as stated by COCKBURN, C.J., in *Phillips* v. *South Western Ry. Co.* (50):

E ". . . a jury cannot be said to take a reasonable view of the case unless they consider and take into account all the heads of damage in respect of which a plaintiff, complaining of personal injury, is entitled to compensation. These are the bodily injury sustained; the pain undergone; the effect on the health of the sufferer, according to its degree and its probable duration as likely to be temporary or permanent; the expenses incidental to attempts to effect a cure, or to lessen the amount of injury; the pecuniary loss."

F This passage was cited with approval both by SELLERS, L.J., in *Wise* v. *Kaye* (51) and by LORD PEARCE in *West* v. *Shephard* (52). Commenting on it SELLERS, L.J., said (51): " I know of no authority which excludes damages for an injury in itself " and LORD PEARCE said (52):

" The practice of the courts hitherto has been to treat bodily injury as a deprivation which in itself entitled a plaintiff to substantial damages
G according to its gravity."

LORD PEARCE also said (52) after quoting LORD ROCHE as having said in *Rose* v. *Ford* (53):

" ' I regard impaired health and vitality not merely as a cause of pain and suffering but as a loss of a good thing in itself.' If a plaintiff has lost a leg
H the court approaches the matter on the basis that he has suffered a serious physical deprivation no matter what his condition or temperament or state of mind may be."

It seems to my own mind necessary for the proper application to any given case of this rule of law that regard should be had, in order to assess the deprivation of physical faculty which has occurred, to the extent of such capacity and its
I character possessed by and enjoyed by the victim immediately before the disabling event. If a person who has been tortiously injured was a cripple,

---

(47) [1963] 2 All E.R. at p. 634; [1964] A.C. at p. 351.
(48) [1962] 1 All E.R. 257; [1962] 1 Q.B. 638.
(49) [1963] 2 All E.R. 625; [1964] A.C. 326.
(50) (1879), 4 Q.B.D. 406 at p. 407.
(51) [1962] 1 All E.R. at p. 263; [1962] 1 Q.B. at p. 652.
(52) [1963] 2 All E.R. at p. 643; [1964] A.C. at p. 365.
(53) [1937] 3 All E.R. at p. 379; [1937] A.C. at p. 859.

perhaps a spastic, or paralytic, before he suffered the relevant injury, I cannot   A
think that such a person has been deprived of so much in terms of physical
capacity and bodily function as a vigorous, athletic, healthy man or woman in
the prime of life. In terms of happiness and enjoyment of life he may lose no less
if such functions as he formerly possessed are destroyed; but if it be right, as I
think the court must accept, that there is a particular head of damage which
relates to destruction or impairment of bodily capacity, I feel that such con-   B
siderations must be highly relevant in considering how much should be awarded
under that head. Similarly it seems to me that the value to an individual of a
body or mind, the capacity of which has been impaired by advanced age or
disease, must on a rational assessment be less than the value of the body and
mind in a state approximating to their potential optimum. It is such considerations as these which lead me to express the view that the bodily and physical   C
capacity (I would say the realised life potential) of a child of eight are not
comparable in kind with those of a fully developed adult.

It is plain, and I wholly accept it, that it is not open now to this or any court
to say that the reasoning of VISCOUNT SIMON, L.C., in *Benham* v. *Gambling* (54)
which led to the conclusion that damages for loss of expectation of life should be
restricted to a moderate sum, has any application to cases where the victim of a   D
disabling injury is still alive. VISCOUNT SIMON himself said (55): " Damages
which would be proper for a disabling injury may well be much greater than for
deprivation of life."

LORD MORRIS OF BORTH-Y-GEST in *Shephard's* case (56), having noted that
theoretically it might be argued that the same reasoning should be applied when
bodily deprivations are to be assessed, said:
                                                                                   E

" The guidance given in *Benham* v. *Gambling* (54) was, I consider, solely
designed and intended to apply to the assessment of damages in respect of
the rather special ' head ' of damages for loss of expectation of life."

It is therefore clear that not merely nominal but real damages are attracted by
bodily deprivations; compare per SELLERS, L.J., in *Wise* v. *Kaye* (57):
                                                                                   F
". . . what has been called loss of amenities. This is separate and distinct
from pain and suffering, and in my opinion, means something different from
loss of happiness or even enjoyment. Physical incapacity may restrict
activity in one form or another or alter the conduct of life, the manner or the
extent of living. The inquiry may be taken as far as that, to ascertain the
limitations and variations which a physical injury has imposed, or may   G
impose, so as to compensate for that, but I see no reason for inquiring further
how, in any given case, it has affected the happiness of the victim."

A little later SELLERS, L.J., said (58):

" The circumstances are unprecedented. The only factor that I can see
which would operate to modify the sum awarded is that the plaintiff may not
live very much longer; but, on the other hand, she may."   H

Nor is it open to me since the decision of this court in *Oliver* v. *Ashman* (59) to
take the view which was expressly submitted in that case by counsel that,
although the Law Reform (Miscellaneous Provisions) Act, 1934, enabled executors
or administrators to enforce a cause of action vested in the deceased at the
moment of death, what was thereby caused to survive was only a cause of action   I
and not a measure of damages. HOLROYD PEARCE, L.J., there said (60) that
there was no warrant for drawing a distinction between the assessment of

(54) [1941] 1 All E.R. 7; [1941] A.C. 157.
(55) [1941] 1 All E.R. at p. 13; [1941] A.C. at p. 168.
(56) [1963] 2 All E.R. at p. 632; [1964] A.C. at p. 348.
(57) [1962] 1 All E.R. at p. 264; [1962] 1 Q.B. at p. 652.
(58) [1962] 1 All E.R. at p. 264; [1962] 1 Q.B. at p. 653.
(59) [1961] 3 All E.R. 323; [1962] 2 Q.B. 210.
(60) [1961] 3 All E.R. at p. 332; [1962] 2 Q.B. at p. 230.

A damages in the case of a living plaintiff and a dead man's estate, nor could it be
accepted that *Benham* v. *Gambling* (61) was binding only in the case of a claim by
the estate. What HOLROYD PEARCE, L.J., was there concerned to reject was an
argument that a living plaintiff could recover only such a restricted measure of
damages as was contemplated by the decision in *Benham* v. *Gambling* (61).
Whether or not he would equally have ruled that the damages recoverable by the
B estate of a deceased are to be as ample as those which the deceased could have
recovered in his or her lifetime is less clear to me since, when adverting to a point
which arose in the *Ashman* case (62) about loss of earnings which would have
accrued after the date of the death had it not been brought about, and to the
pre-existing difference of judicial opinion on this point, HOLROYD PEARCE, L.J.,
said (63):

C   ". . . SLADE, J., (64) held that no damages can be recovered in respect of
lost earnings during the period in which the plaintiff would have lived had it
not been for the defendant's negligence. STREATFEILD, J., (65) however, held
that such damages could be recovered. Both judges answered differently the
question to which there is no wholly satisfactory solution. Each view can
produce in certain circumstances common-sense results and each can produce
D   apparent injustices. That of STREATFEILD, J., would seem, perhaps, more
apt for the case of a living plaintiff, that of SLADE, J., for an action by
executors."

HOLROYD PEARCE, L.J., further said (66) that there was no room for distinguishing between a claim brought by a living plaintiff and a claim brought on behalf
of a dead plaintiff in respect of the loss of earnings during the years of which he
E has been deprived, and I quote (66):

     " This is perhaps unfortunate, since otherwise there would be much to be
said for applying the reasoning of [STREATFEILD, J., (65)] to a living plaintiff
and that of [SLADE, J., (64)] to the executors who bring an action for the
estate of a deceased man."

F I recognise that by force of the Act of 1934 any cause of action of the relevant
kind which could have been enforced by a deceased person immediately before
his or her death passes to the executor or administrator, and that this statutory
provision may well as a matter of construction be taken to confer on the
representatives of the estate a right to recover the same amount of damages
that the deceased would have recovered in such a hypothetical action brought
G before the death. None the less, I am oppressed with serious doubt whether such
an effect is required by the statute having regard to two basic principles of law,
(a) that damages are intended to be a compensation so far as money can compensate for injury (compare *Admiralty Comrs.* v. *S.S. Susquehanna (Owners)*,
The Susquehanna (67) per VISCOUNT DUNEDIN), (b) that the death of a human
being should not be a source of profit or advantage to any other person.

H   With regard to the first of these principles, I am fully aware that it has been
said authoritatively in *Wise* v. *Kaye* (68), and by LORD MORRIS OF BORTH-Y-
GEST in *Shephard's* case (69) that it is no concern of the court to consider any
question as to the use that will in fact be made of the money awarded. I accept
this ruling as wholly appropriate in any case where the money is awarded to a
living plaintiff, and further agree that it is irrelevant whether in a given case it is

I
_____

(61) [1941] 1 All E.R. 7; [1941] A.C. 157.
(62) [1961] 3 All E.R. 323; [1962] 2 Q.B. 210.
(63) [1961] 3 All E.R. at p. 328; [1962] 2 Q.B. at p. 225.
(64) In *Harris* v. *Bright's Asphalt Contractors, Ltd.*, [1953] 1 All E.R. 395; [1953] 1
Q.B. 617.
(65) In *Pope* v. *D. Murphy & Son, Ltd.*, [1960] 2 All E.R. 873; [1961] 1 Q.B. 222.
(66) [1961] 3 All E.R. at p. 330; [1962] 2 Q.B. at p. 228.
(67) [1926] All E.R. Rep. 124 at p. 127; [1926] A.C. 655 at p. 661.
(68) [1962] 1 All E.R. 257; [1962] 1 Q.B. 638.
(69) [1963] 2 All E.R. 625; [1964] A.C. 326.

likely that the living plaintiff will be unable to spend or derive any benefit from **A**
the money during his or her surviving lifetime, in which case it or a substantial
part of it may well go to relatives or often to strangers. The fact remains that it
is given to the plaintiff who is entitled to compensation and that, even if he or
she is not sufficiently compos mentis to spend or direct the spending of any of it,
responsible parents or other relatives may well lay out the money to the advantage
of the plaintiff, or it may be practicable for the Court of Protection or a com- **B**
mittee to take charge of the moneys, expend part of them, and secure that they
are ultimately received by a person or persons whom the plaintiff would desire
to benefit. To my own mind a judge or jury may properly have regard to the
contrast between such a situation and the situation where other persons, not
necessarily the parents or others who have suffered distress and grief, receive a
windfall which might well exceed any reasonable solatium. I am not suggesting **C**
that it would be proper for a judge to direct a jury, or himself, to have such a
thought in mind. The view of PEARSON, L.J., expressed in the *Ashman* case (70)
that this might be a proper consideration has been rejected. It remains, I think,
true that it is a somewhat strange form of compensation which is neither received
by the person entitled to be compensated nor even awarded to him or her in his
or her own right. Money can do little to ease the path of a departed soul. **D**
Administrators on an intestacy or beneficiaries under a will may or may not be
persons whom it would seem morally right that the relevant death should benefit;
if they are not dependants of the deceased there may be a duplication or
aggregation of damages payable by the defendant responsible for the death.

The policy of the Fatal Accidents Acts and of the Scots law which provides
for solatium do not support any idea that it is desirable as a matter of public **E**
policy that any individual should benefit from the death of another caused by a
tort, which originally would have been regarded as very much in the nature of
a felony. It is not altogether fanciful to have in mind the possibility that sooner or
later, if substantial damages are to be obtainable in such cases as the present, a
helpless victim incapable of benefiting from hospital care might be released into
the control of someone who, if in a position to benefit on his death, might also be **F**
aware of the maxim " Thou shall not kill but need'st not strive officiously to keep
alive ".

For myself I would have been glad to have been able with some effect to say
that the measure of damages recoverable by the estate of a deceased for the bodily
deprivations or pain and suffering or loss of amenities or fear and misery suffered
in the lifetime of the deceased should be assessed on a more moderate scale than **G**
would be appropriate on a claim under the same heads during the lifetime of the
deceased.

I am further oppressed by the consideration that if £2,000 be an appropriate
sum to award in repect of the bodily deprivations during a period of eleven or
twelve months of this unconscious child, the sum appropriate to compensate her,
had she brought an action to trial during her lifetime and been able to show that **H**
she had suffered a great deal of pain and misery through an appreciation of how
gravely she had been injured and all the happiness and enjoyment of life of which
she had been deprived, must have been very substantially greater perhaps by the
order of at least a multiplier of two or three. Furthermore, had this child in such
an action brought by her during her lifetime satisfied the court that she had an
expectation of life of, say, thirty let alone sixty years, an award of an order **I**
represented by multiplying £2,000 by thirty or sixty, even with appropriate
discounts, would have produced an astronomic figure. Such figures as I have
hypothetically contemplated would, in my judgment, lie outside any pattern of
damages which the courts award even in the gravest cases, including those of
virtually complete paralysis plus grave impairments of mental faculties, and
would, I think, distort that pattern and lead, indirectly if not directly, to wholly

---

(70) [1961] 3 All E.R. at p. 340; [1962] 2 Q.B. at p. 243.

A new assessments in many other classes of case which, I think, would not be consistent with policy nor rebound to the general public good.

I cannot subscribe to a view that any recognisable pattern of awards emerges from the cases of *Wise* v. *Kaye* (71), *West* v. *Shephard* (72) or *Swift* v. *Prout* (73) in the latter of which no contention was raised that the damages were too high. I think it is no more than coincidence that in *West* v. *Shephard* (72) and *Swift* v.

B *Prout* (73) the expectation of life on medical prognosis multiplied by £2,000 per annum of that expectation amounted, as in the present case, to approximately the sum awarded for general damages. In *Wise* v. *Kaye* (71) there was no such estimate of expectation of life; in the other cases the court must have been far less certain how long the victim would survive than in the present case where the period is ascertained.

C Apart from that consideration, however, there have been as yet too few cases of the very special kind where the victim survives unconscious to establish a norm of damages, still less a norm for cases where there is no uncertainty as to the period of survival, no chance of returning or increasing consciousness, and no possibility that any use can ever be made for the benefit of the victim of the damages which must be once and for all assessed.

D For the reasons which I have endeavoured, albeit fruitlessly, to express, I am of the opinion that for the real deprivation of bodily capacity and function which this child suffered for a brief period, painlessly and without knowledge of what she had lost, a moderate award of damages would be appropriate. It is, I think, most noteworthy that so far as the researches of counsel have revealed, this is the first case since that of *Rose* v. *Ford* (74) in which damages have been awarded

E to the estate of a deceased for bodily injury as distinct from loss of expectation of life. I regard that decision as of unimpaired authority in a case where the recipient of the damages to be awarded is not alive to receive them. The deceased in that case was a girl of twenty-three who was seriously injured in a motor car accident on Aug. 4, 1934 when her right leg was seriously injured. Two days later on Aug. 6 it was amputated. On Aug. 8 she died. The learned trial judge, HUM-

F PHREYS, J., awarded the girl's father as her administrator £500 for her pain and suffering and the loss of the right leg. In the Court of Appeal all the judges were agreed that there should be no damages for loss of the leg other than for its loss during the four days that the girl survived, and that the damages for pain and suffering and loss of the leg should be reduced to £22, of which £2 was attributed to the loss of the leg. I do not regard that award as a nominal forty shillings award

G but as an assessment on a moderate basis of the amount which it was right and proper that a tortfeasor should pay to the estate of a deceased person for deprivation during a brief period, not wholly a period of unconsciousness and freedom from pain, of the ownership or capacity of a leg. In the present case the period of survival was considerably longer; the deprivation of bodily capacity was considerably greater, indeed it was complete; but on a like basis of assessment I

H would regard as a proper amount to be awarded, in addition to the damages for loss of expectation of life, the sum of £500.

Appeal and cross-appeal dismissed. Leave to appeal to the House of Lords granted.

Solicitors: *Sharpe, Pritchard & Co.*, agents for *Rutherfords*, Liverpool (for the defendant); *Pritchard, Englefield & Co.*, agents for *Lamb, Goldsmith & Howard*, Liverpool (for the plaintiff).

I

[*Reported by* F. GUTTMAN, ESQ., *Barrister-at-Law.*]

---

(71) [1962] 1 All E.R. 257; [1962] 1 Q.B. 638.
(72) [1963] 2 All E.R. 625; [1964] A.C. 326.   (73) (1964), unreported.
(74) [1937] 3 All E.R. 359; [1937] A.C. 826.

CAMPBELL AND ANOTHER
(TRUSTEES OF DAVIES'S EDUCATIONAL TRUST)
v. INLAND REVENUE COMMISSIONERS.

[CHANCERY DIVISION (Buckley, J.), March 23, 24, 25, April 6, 1966.]

Income Tax—Annual payment—Covenanted payments to charity—Covenantor obtaining benefit of counter-obligations by charity—Obligations not importing absence of bounty—Payments not income in the hands of charity trustees— Educational trust intended to provide means of purchasing goodwill of covenantor's tutorial business—Application of moneys received by trustees on application for charitable purposes, but no tax relief as covenanted sums not annual payments—Income Tax Act, 1952 (15 & 16 Geo. 6 & 1 Eliz. 2 c. 10), s. 169, s. 447 (1) (b).

In order to ensure that a tutorial business carried on by a limited company (called " Tutors ") for many years should continue on an established and permanent basis, a director and the secretary of the company in 1961 executed a declaration of trust, the purpose of which was to establish an educational trust, the " Davies's Educational Trust ", of which they were to be the first trustees. The trustees were to hold the trust fund on charitable trusts for the promotion and furtherance of education and subsequent provisions in the deed were to take effect subject to and only so far as ancillary to, consistent with and in furtherance of that primary charitable trust. The trustees were empowered to purchase and carry on schools and tutorial establishments and to purchase buildings, lands and chattels for that purpose. The following day Tutors and the trustees executed a deed of covenant under which Tutors covenanted to pay annually for seven years out of its taxed income a sum equal to eighty per cent. of its profits in the previous year to the trustees to hold on the trusts. It was understood that the sums, together with income tax recoverable thereon, would be used to purchase Tutors' tutorial business. The following year a new company (D., Ltd.) was incorporated to carry on educational work of every description, the shares in which were held on behalf of the trustees, and the directors of which were the directors of Tutors. The two companies executed a deed of partnership for ten years under which D., Ltd. was to purchase one-fifth of the goodwill of Tutors' business (value £50,000) forthwith and the remainder subsequently, and the two companies were to share the profits of the business in proportion to their respective ownerships of the goodwill. By a supplemental term of the partnership agreed for tax purposes the partnership was to purchase from Tutors for a price to be loaned by that company its trade fixtures and equipment. Tutors paid a sum of £25,527, the aggregate of two years' sums due to the trustees under the deed of covenant, and in 1963 £10,456, in each case less tax at standard rate, the net amounts totalling over £21,900. The trustees advanced £21,900 to D., Ltd., which it used as to £10,000 to purchase the one-fifth share in the goodwill of Tutors' business and as to £11,900 to purchase the trade fixtures, etc. It was conceded by the Crown* that the advance was an application of the income of the trust fund for 1960-61 and 1961-62 for charitable purposes under s. 447 (1) (b)† of the Income Tax Act, 1952. The trustees claimed exemption from tax for 1960-61 and 1961-62 on the payments received by them under the deed of covenant as annual payments under the same enactment and sought recovery of the tax deducted from such payments.

Held: (i) the covenanted payments by Tutors were not " annual payments " for the purposes of s. 169 and s. 447 (1) (b) of the Income Tax Act,

---

* For the limits of this concession, see p. 747, letter B, post.
† Section 447 (1), so far as material, is printed at p. 741, letter G, post.

A 1952, although they had the character of bounty (see (ii) below), and accordingly income tax was not recoverable for the following reasons—

(a) in the circumstances the trustees became bound contractually on the execution of the deed of covenant to apply all sums received from Tutors under the covenant towards purchase of Tutors' business or, if the trustees were not so bound contractually, they received each payment subject to an

B earmark by Tutors for its application exclusively towards the purchase of Tutors' business (see p. 745, letter A, post).

(b) in view of (a) the covenanted payments were not income in the hands of the trustees and thus were not "annual payments" (see p. 746, letters H and I, post).

Dictum of LORD NORMAND in *Inland Revenue Comrs.* v. *City of London*

C *Corpn.* (*as the Conservators of Epping Forest*) ([1953] 1 All E.R. at p. 1085) distinguished.

(ii) the trustees' legal obligation to apply the covenanted payments towards the purchase of Tutors' business did not deprive the payments of the character of being bounty, which was one of the attributes required by law of a payment if it were to be an " annual payment " in the technical sense of that

D term in s. 169 (see p. 746, letter D, post).

Inland Revenue Comrs. v. *National Book League* ([1957] 2 All E.R. 644) explained and distinguished.

(iii) if the sums had been annual payments within s. 169 and s. 447 (1) (*b*), the trustees would have been exempt from tax in respect of them, because the requirements of s. 447 (1) (*b*) were satisfied where it was shown (a) that

E the claimant for relief was established for charitable purposes only and (b) that the sum in respect of which relief was claimed was applied wholly to charitable purposes; and in the present case (a) was conceded and (b) was established, for in determining (b) it was the character of the application that was to be regarded, not the motive for the payment (see p. 747, letters G and H, post).

F *Barclays Bank, Ltd.* v. *Naylor* ([1960] 3 All E.R. 173) applied.

Appeal dismissed.

[As to what are annual payments for income tax purposes, see 20 HALSBURY'S LAWS (3rd Edn.) 362-364, para. 666; and for cases on the subject, see 28 DIGEST (Repl.) 169-176, *678-709.*

For the Income Tax Act, 1952, s. 447 (1), see 31 HALSBURY'S STATUTES (2nd

G Edn.) 427.]

Cases referred to:

Barclays Bank, Ltd. v. *Naylor (Inspector of Taxes)*, [1960] 3 All E.R. 173; [1961] Ch. 7; [1960] 3 W.L.R. 678; 39 Tax Cas. 256; Digest (Cont. Vol. A) 881, *691a.*

H *British Commonwealth International Newsfilm Agency, Ltd.* v. *Mahany (Inspector of Taxes)*, [1963] 1 All E.R. 88; [1963] 1 W.L.R. 69; 40 Tax Cas. 550; Digest (Cont. Vol. A) 848, *173k.*

Hanbury (decd.), Re, Comiskey v. *Hanbury*, (1939), 38 Tax Cas. 588.

Howe (Earl) v. *Inland Revenue Comrs.*, [1918-19] All E.R. Rep. 1088; [1919] 2 K.B. 336; 88 L.J.K.B. 821; 121 L.T. 161; 7 Tax Cas. 289; 28 Digest

I (Repl.) 351, *1549.*

Inland Revenue Comrs. v. *City of London Corpn.* (*as the Conservators of Epping Forest*), [1953] 1 All E.R. 1075; [1953] 1 W.L.R. 652; 117 J.P. 28; 34 Tax Cas. 293; 28 Digest (Repl.) 171, *690.*

Inland Revenue Comrs. v. *National Book League*, [1957] 2 All E.R. 644; [1957] Ch. 488; [1957] 3 W.L.R. 222; 137 Tax Cas. 455; 28 Digest (Repl.) 175, 708.

Inland Revenue Comrs. v. *Ramsey*, [1935] All E.R. Rep. 847; 154 L.T. 141; 20 Tax Cas. 79; 28 Digest (Repl.) 347, *1534.*

Inland Revenue Comrs. v. *Westminster* (*Duke*), [1935] All E.R. Rep. 259; A
[1936] A.C. 1; 104 L.J.K.B. 383; 153 L.T. 223; 19 Tax Cas. 490; 28
Digest (Repl.) 339, *1505.*

Whitworth Park Coal Co., Ltd. v. *Inland Revenue Comrs., Ramshaw Coal Co.,*
Ltd. v. *Same, Brancepeth Coal Co., Ltd.* v. *Same,* [1958] 2 All E.R. 91;
[1958] Ch. 792; [1958] 2 W.L.R. 815; *affd.* H.L., [1959] 3 All E.R. 703;
[1961] A.C. 31; [1959] 3 W.L.R. 842; 38 Tax Cas. 531; Digest (Cont. B
Vol. A) 882, *709.*

Case Stated.

The taxpayers appealed to the Special Commissioners of Income Tax against
the refusal by the Commissioners of Inland Revenue of claims made by the
taxpayers under s. 447 (1) (*b*) of the Income Tax Act, 1952, for exemption from
income tax chargeable for 1960-61 and 1961-62 on payments received by the C
taxpayers under a deed of covenant dated Mar. 30, 1961. The questions for the
commissioners' decision were: (i) whether payments made under the deed of
covenant were annual payments within the meaning of s. 447 (1) (*b*); and (ii)
if so, whether those payments had been applied to charitable purposes only within
the meaning of the subsection. The taxpayers contended that the payments
were annual payments forming part of the income of a trust established for D
charitable purposes only, that the income was applied to charitable purposes only
and that the taxpayers were therefore entitled to exemption. The Crown contended: (a) that the disputed payments were not paid by the paying company,
Davies's (Tutors), Ltd. (" Tutors ") without conditions or counter-stipulations
and were not " pure income profit " in the hands of the taxpayers; (b) that they
were received by the taxpayers subject to an obligation, legal or practical, to use E
them for the benefit of Tutors; (c) that accordingly they were not annual payments within s. 447 (1) (*b*); (d) that they were not applied to charitable purposes
only within s. 447 (1) (*b*), being applied inter alia for the benefit of Tutors by
securing the sale of assets and goodwill of their business; and (e) that the exemption claimed had been properly refused. The commissioners found that the deed
of covenant under which the payments were made was entered into on a clear F
understanding both by Tutors and the shareholders of Tutors and by the taxpayers that the payments would be used to buy Tutors' business. They held
therefore that the understanding was a condition or counter-stipulation attached
to the deed of covenant not falling within the class of incidental privileges which
might be enjoyed by a donor to a charity, and that the disputed payments were
not annual payments. G

Desmond C. Miller, Q.C., and *S. I. Simon* for the taxpayers.
E. I. Goulding, Q.C., *J. R. Phillips* and *J. P. Warner* for the Crown.

Cur. adv. vult.

Apr. 6. **BUCKLEY, J.:** On May 6, 1946, a company was incorporated H
by the name of Davies's (Tutors), Ltd., for the purpose of acquiring as a going
concern the well known tutorial business of Davies's, which had been founded
by Mr. Vernon Davies in 1927. That company at the material time had seven
shareholders only, of whom three, Mr. Campbell, Mr. McBride and Mr. Hall,
were the majority shareholders and they were the three directors of that company, to which I will refer as " Tutors ". The secretary of the company was I
Mr. Fairfax-Jones. The directors and shareholders of Tutors were anxious
that the business, Davies's, should continue on an established and permanent
basis. They were aware that it would be difficult, if not impossible, to find
individuals who were both qualified to run the business and possessed of sufficient
capital to purchase it as a going concern, and they conceived the idea that a
charitable trust should be set up to acquire the business.

On Mar. 29, 1961, the taxpayers, that is to say Mr. Campbell, a director of the
company, and Mr. Fairfax-Jones, the secretary, executed a declaration of trust,

A   the purpose of which was to establish an educational trust to be known as " the Davies's Educational Trust ", of which they would be the first trustees. The declaration of trust declared that

" ' the Trust Fund ' shall mean and include all moneys and other property which may hereafter from time to time be received accepted or held by the trustees on the trusts "

B

of the declaration of trust. Clause 3 of the deed provided that the trustees should hold the trust fund and the income thereof on charitable trusts for the promotion and furtherance of education and that the subsequent provisions of the deed should take effect subject to and only so far as ancillary to, consistent with and in furtherance of, that primary charitable trust. It was expressly provided in the

C   declaration of trust that the trustees should have power, inter alia, to purchase or otherwise acquire or found and to carry on schools and tutorial establishments, and to purchase, take on lease, hire, acquire by gift or on loan or otherwise any buildings and lands and chattels for the carrying on of any school or tutorial establishment and to use the same accordingly.

On the following day, Mar. 30, 1961, Tutors executed a deed of covenant to

D   which Tutors were the parties of the first part and the taxpayers as trustees of the declaration of trust were the parties of the other part, whereby Tutors covenanted with the trustees that they would out of the general fund of taxed income of Tutors annually on Apr. 5 in every year for seven years commencing on Apr. 5, 1961, pay to the trustees to hold on the trusts of the declaration of trust such a sum as would amount to eighty per cent. of the profits or gains accruing to

E   the company from any trade carried on by the company in the accounting year immediately preceding such Apr. 5. The figure of eighty per cent. of the net profits was chosen because the payments to be made to the trustees would not be deductible in computing the profits of Tutors for profits tax purposes. The twenty per cent. of net profits was therefore retained to meet profits tax and the trustees in effect were to get the whole of the net profits of Tutors after meeting

F   profits tax.

The declaration of trust and the deed of covenant were entered into, as the commissioners found, on the clear understanding by the directors and shareholders of Tutors and the trustees that the net sums payable under the deed of covenant, together with the income tax thereon which it was thought would be recoverable under s. 447 (1) (b) of the Income Tax Act, 1952, would be used by the trustees

G   to purchase the business of Davies's. There was no doubt, the commissioners found, in the minds of any of the parties that the trustees would use these moneys to acquire Davies's business. Mr. Barber, who had acted as accountant to Mr. Vernon Davies and as auditor to Tutors, had the full confidence of all the parties concerned, and it was left to him to work out the detailed implementation of the plan for the trust to acquire the business of Tutors by means of the covenanted

H   payments. The intention of all the parties to these arrangements, the commissioners found, was that the future of Davies's should be secured in the hands of an educational trust and that the profits of Davies's should be used to obtain for the shareholders of Tutors a fair and reasonable price for their interests in that company.

The next stage in the working out of this scheme was not reached until Apr. 4,

I   1962, when a company by the name of Davies's Educational Developments, Ltd., was incorporated. I will refer to that company as " Developments ". Developments was incorporated to promote, carry on, further and encourage educational work of every description. Its authorised share capital was £100 divided into one hundred shares of £1 each, but only two shares were issued, one to Mr. Campbell and the other to Mr. Hall. Both those shares were held by the registered holders on behalf of the trustees of the trust. The directors of Developments were Mr. Campbell, Mr. McBride and Mr. Hall, the three gentlemen who were directors of Tutors.

On the following day, Apr. 5, 1962, Tutors entered into a partnership with **A** Developments. Under the terms of the deed of partnership, the value of the good-will of the business, Davies's, was agreed at £50,000. The partnership deed provided that immediately after the execution thereof Developments should purchase from Tutors a one-fifth share of the goodwill of Davies's at a price of £10,000. The deed further provided that Developments

B

" may in any subsequent year calculated from Apr. 6, 1962, purchase from Tutors either the whole of the residue of the goodwill then vested in Tutors or shares or proportions thereof in units of £10,000."

It further provided that as from Apr. 6, 1962, the profits of Davies's should be divided in accordance with the shares or proportions of the goodwill owned by Tutors and Developments from time to time, and that the deed should remain in **C** force for a period of ten years unless sooner determined by, inter alia, Develop-ments acquiring the whole of the goodwill from Tutors. Provision was made in the deed for the partnership to rent from Tutors the premises on which Davies's was carried on, and the trade fixtures, fittings, furniture, books and equipment in those premises, and also for Developments to buy at a fair price the premises, fixtures, etc., in the event of the partnership being determined by Developments **D** acquiring the whole of the goodwill of the business.

After the execution of the partnership deed it was discovered that the pro-visions of that deed relating to trade fixtures and so forth would create difficulties in obtaining capital allowances for income tax purposes in respect of those fittings, and accordingly a supplemental term of the partnership was agreed in the following terms: **E**

" Notwithstanding anything contained in cl. (h) (i) or elsewhere in the within agreement [i.e., the partnership agreement] it is agreed that the partnership will purchase from Davies's (Tutors), Ltd., the trade fixtures fittings furniture books and equipment in or about the respective premises specified in the Schedule to the within agreement at a price to be certified by Messrs. Barber & Co. . . . . as at Apr. 6, 1962, but Davies's (Tutors), Ltd., will **F** leave the whole of the purchase price so certified as a loan to the partnership for the duration of the partnership such price to be paid by the partners or their successors to the business of Davies's within twenty-eight days of the termination of the partnership from whatever cause."

Then there is a provision for interest to be paid on the loan and a proviso that the **G** partnership might at any time make payments on account of or in settlement of the said purchase price and in that case the said share of the profits should be abated pro rata.

On Mar. 31, 1962—i.e., before the partnership deed was entered into—Mr. Barber had informed the directors of Tutors that the value of the goodwill of Davies's in his opinion on the basis of a sale at arm's length between a willing **H** seller and purchaser was not less than £50,000. That figure was adopted as the value of the goodwill for the purposes of the partnership deed accordingly. Mr. Barber's view was that the goodwill was worth between £50,000 and £57,000. Although it was improbable that a private individual or a group of private individuals could have been found with sufficient capital to purchase Davies's, it would have been possible to sell the business to an established large tutorial **I** establishment.

On Apr. 5, 1961, and Apr. 5, 1962, Tutors became indebted under the deed of covenant to the trustees in sums aggregating £25,527 and that amount was paid by Tutors to the trustees subject to deduction of tax at the standard rate. On Apr. 5, 1963, Tutors became indebted to the trustees under the deed of covenant in a further sum of £10,456, which was also paid by Tutors to the trustees subject to deduction of tax at the standard rate. The net amounts so received by the trustees amounted in the aggregate to something in excess of £21,900. During

A the year ended Apr. 5, 1963, the trustees of the trust advanced a sum of £21,900 to Developments which Developments used as to £10,000 to purchase a one-fifth share in the goodwill of Tutors in accordance with the terms of the partnership deed and as to £11,900 to purchase the trade fixtures and so forth of Tutors in accordance with the added term of the partnership deed.

It was admitted for the purposes of the hearing before the commissioners that B that advance of £21,900 by the trustees to Developments was an application for the purpose of s. 447 (1) (*b*) of the Income Tax Act, 1952, of the income of the trust for the two years ended Apr. 5, 1962. Developments have been treated throughout, both before the commissioners and in this court, as an emanation of the trustees and as no more than the machinery by which the trustees were to acquire the business of Davies's and carry it on. Accordingly no point is taken on C the separate existence of Developments as distinct from the trustees. Messrs. Campbell, McBride and Hall had had service agreements with Tutors for many years. These provided, inter alia, that in addition to salaries these three gentlemen should each have a share of the profits of Tutors. On the formation of the partnership between Tutors and Developments, new service agreements were entered into which provided for fixed salaries and no sharing of profits. Up to 1962 Tutors D had paid dividends of eight hundred per cent. on their ordinary shares as well as the preference dividends. Since then no dividends have been paid on the ordinary shares. That, of course, is because the profits of Tutors have been applied in accordance with the provisions of the deed of covenant.

The trustees claimed exemption from income tax chargeable for the years 1960-61 and 1961-62 on the payments so received by them under the deed of E covenant under s. 447 (1) (*b*) of the Act of 1952. The Commissioners of Inland Revenue rejected these claims. The trustees appealed to the Special Commissioners who dismissed the appeal and the trustees now appeal to this court.

The relevant sections of the statutes are these. The charge to tax under Sch. D is to be found in s. 122 and s. 123 of the Income Tax Act, 1952, and the relevant Case for the present purpose is Case III, under which tax is charged in respect of F any interest of money, whether yearly or otherwise, or any annuity, or other annual payment. Section 169 provides:

" (1) Where any yearly interest of money, annuity or other annual payment is payable wholly out of profits or gains brought into charge to tax "

no assessment, putting it shortly, shall be made on the recipient, but the whole shall be assessed on the person liable to make the payment, and the person liable G to make the payment is authorised on making that payment to deduct and retain out of it a sum representing the amount of tax on it at the standard rate for the year in which the payment becomes due. Section 447 (1) provides as follows:

" Exemption shall be granted . . . (*b*) from tax chargeable . . . under Sch. D in respect of any yearly interest or other annual payment, forming part of H the income of any body of persons or trust established for charitable purposes only . . . and so far as the same are applied to charitable purposes only . . ."

The right of Tutors to deduct tax from payments under the deed of covenant depends on those payments being " annual payments " within the meaning of s. 169. If they are not such annual payments Tutors are liable to make them without deduction and there will be no occasion for any claim to exemption by I the trustees under s. 447 (1) (*b*). If, on the other hand, they are such annual payments, the trustees can claim exemption from income tax if, and only if and to the extent that, the amounts received by them from Tutors under the deed of covenant have been applied to charitable purposes only. It is conceded that the trustees are trustees of a trust established for charitable purposes only.

I will consider first whether the payments made by Tutors under the deed of covenant are annual payments within the meaning of s. 169. The Act of 1952 contains no definition of the meaning of " annual payment ", but there is some judicial authority on the interpretation of this expression. The conundrum

" When is an annual payment not an annual payment? " admits of several **A**
answers: when it is an instalment of a capital sum (*Inland Revenue Comrs.* v.
Ramsay (1)); when it is a trading receipt of the recipient against which outgoings
of his trade must be taken into account in order to discover the amount of his
taxable profits (*Earl Howe* v. *Inland Revenue Comrs.* (2), per SCRUTTON, L.J.;
Inland Revenue Comrs. v. *City of London Corpn.* (*as the Conservators of Epping
Forest*) (3), per LORD NORMAND and LORD REID); when it is a payment made to **B**
a trading company to supplement its trading receipts (*British Commonwealth
International Newsfilm Agency, Ltd.* v. *Mahany* (*Inspector of Taxes*) (4)); when it
is a subscription to a charitable body as a consequence of which the subscriber
enjoys certain privileges or amenities provided for subscribers by that body
(*Inland Revenue Comrs.* v. *National Book League* (5)). This catalogue is no doubt
not exhaustive.   **C**

In *Re Hanbury* (*decd.*), *Comiskey* v. *Hanbury* (6), SIR WILFRID GREENE, M.R.,
stated the matter in this way:

" There are two classes of annual payments which fall to be considered for
income tax purposes. There is, first of all, that class of annual payment which
the Acts regard and treat as being pure income profit of the recipient un-
diminished by any deduction. Payments of interest, payments of annuities, **D**
to take the ordinary simple case, are payments which are regarded as part
of the income of the recipient, and the payer is entitled in estimating his total
income to treat those payments as payments which go out of his income altogether. The class of annual payment which falls within that category is
quite a limited one. In the other class there stand a number of payments,
none the less annual, the very quality and nature of which make it impossible **E**
to treat them as part of the pure profit income of the recipient, the proper way
of treating them being to treat them as an element to be taken into account
in discovering what the profits of the recipient are. This matter was dealt
with in a very well known passage in the judgment of SCRUTTON, L.J., in
Earl Howe v. *Inland Revenue Comrs.* (7), which, if I may say so, I have always
found particularly illuminating on questions of this kind. The type of example **F**
he gives is that of a yearly payment made, for instance, to the proprietor of
a garage for the hire of a motor car. Nobody would suggest that on making
that payment the hirer would be entitled to deduct tax, and yet it is annual
payment, the reason being that the very nature of that payment itself, having
regard to the circumstances in which it is made, necessarily makes the sums
paid in the hands of a recipient an element only in the ascertainment of his **G**
profits."

To the question " When *is* an annual payment an annual payment? " in the
sense in which the term is used in these sections of the Income Tax Act, 1952,
the authorities suggest three possible answers: when it is ejusdem generis with
interest of money and annuities (*Earl Howe* v. *Inland Revenue Comrs.* (7), per **H**
SCRUTTON, L.J.; *Whitworth Park Coal Co., Ltd.* v. *Inland Revenue Comrs.* (8));
when the payment is such as to have the character of taxable income of the
recipient (*Earl Howe* v. *Inland Revenue Comrs.* (9), per WARRINGTON, L.J.,
and SCRUTTON, L.J.; *Inland Revenue Comrs.* v. *Duke of Westminster* (10), per
LORD TOMLIN); when it is " pure income profit " or " pure profit income " of

I

(1) [1935] All E.R. Rep. 847; 20 Tax Cas. 79.
(2) [1918-19] All E.R. Rep. 1088 at p. 1098; 7 Tax Cas. 289 at p. 303.
(3) [1953] 1 All E.R. 1075 at pp. 1081, 1086; 34 Tax Cas. 293 at pp. 320, 326.
(4) [1963] 1 All E.R. 881; 40 Tax Cas. 550.
(5) [1957] 2 All E.R. 644; 37 Tax Cas. 455.
(6) (1939), 38 Tax. Cas. 588 at pp. 590, 591.
(7) [1918-19] All E.R. Rep. at p. 1098; 7 Tax Cas. at p. 303.
(8) [1958] 2 All E.R. 91 at p. 102; 38 Tax Cas. 531 at p. 548.
(9) [1918-19] All E.R. Rep. at pp. 1094, 1098; 7 Tax Cas. at pp. 299, 303.
(10) [1935] All E.R. Rep. 259 at p. 266; 19 Tax Cas. 490 at p. 518.

A the recipient (*Re Hanbury* (*decd.*), *Comiskey* v. *Hanbury* (11), per SIR WILFRID GREENE, M.R., in the passage cited). The last two answers may be no more than different ways of saying the same thing. The payment cannot attract income tax unless it can properly be described as income. The payment as a whole cannot be income if any outgoing has to be taken into account against it to discover how much of the payment is profit; i.e., it cannot as a whole be income unless

B as a whole it is clear profit to the recipient. It must not only be income in the recipient's hands: it must all be income in his hands. This was, I think, what LORD NORMAND had in mind when in *Inland Revenue Comrs.* v. *City of London Corpn.* (*as the Conservators of Epping Forest*) (12) he said that SIR WILFRID GREENE's formula would perhaps lose nothing by the omission of the words " pure profit ".

C   That the payments made and to be made by Tutors under the deed of covenant are annual payments in the literal sense of that term cannot be denied. The taxpayers claim that they should properly be described as income of their trust and that they are consequently properly paid by Tutors subject to deduction of tax under s. 169 as " annual payments " within the meaning of that section, and that they are also " annual payments " within the meaning of s. 447 (1) (*b*).

D The Crown contend that the payments are not " annual payments " within s. 169 or s. 447 because, as counsel says, they are not pure bounty.

In *Inland Revenue Comrs.* v. *City of London Corpn.* (*as the Conservators of Epping Forest*) (13) a question arose whether payments made by the Corporation of London under the Epping Forest Act, 1878, to the corporation itself but in its other capacity as the Conservators of Epping Forest were annual payments

E within Case III of Sch. D. It was accepted that the corporation as conservators was a separate legal person from the corporation in its normal capacity and that the conservators were a body established for charitable purposes only. By the Act of 1878 the corporation was required to contribute to the income of the conservators to make up any deficiency in their income to meet their outgoings. These contributions by the corporation were made annually and wholly out of

F profits or gains on which the corporation had paid tax. The case turned on whether the payments were income in the hands of the conservators. The Crown contended that the payments were made in return for services or advantages to the corporation. This contention was rejected by the House of Lords, as also was the suggestion that the payments had the character of trade receipts. LORD NORMAND said (14):

G   " The sum, in my opinion, is in no different position from a sum (having the requisite quality of recurrence) paid without conditions or counter stipulations out of taxed income under a covenant by a private individual to any charitable body."

LORD REID said (15):

H   " But, in my judgment, the payments in this case are not trading receipts in the hands of the conservators even if they are carrying on a trade or something in the nature of a trade. Trading receipts are generally received in return for something done or provided by the recipient for the payer, but, as I have said, that does not appear to me to be the case here. So if the appellants are to succeed it must be because the payments in this case fall within some other class of annual payments which, as well as annual payments

I received as trading receipts in return for something done or provided or to be done or provided, must for some reason be held to be excepted from the scope of Case III. But before considering this difficult question I think it well to consider certain annual payments, not related to any benefit to the payer,

(11) (1939), 38 Tax Cas. at p. 590.
(12) [1953] 1 All E.R. at p. 1081; 34 Tax Cas. at p. 320.
(13) [1953] 1 All E.R. 1075; 34 Tax Cas. 293.
(14) [1953] 1 All E.R. at p. 1085; 34 Tax Cas. at p. 324.
(15) [1953] 1 All E.R. at p. 1087; 34 Tax Cas. at p. 327.

which in my opinion are clearly within the scope of Case III. That most rele-   A
vant to the present case is an annual subscription under covenant to a charity
by a donor who gets no advantage to himself in return for it."

The sum there in question, being one of the annual payments made by the
corporation under the Act of 1878, was held to have been properly treated as an
" annual payment " within the statutory provisions then in force and now
replaced by s. 123 (1) Case III, s. 169 and s. 447 (1) (b).   B

On the other hand, in *Inland Revenue Comrs.* v. *National Book League* (16),
covenanted payments by contributors to the National Book League, a charitable
body, were held not to come within Case III because their payment was not free
from conditions or counter-stipulations. The league offered certain privileges
and amenities to its contributors or members. Until December, 1951, the minimum annual subscription payable by individual members was one guinea for   C
London members and half a guinea for country members. It was then resolved
to increase these subscriptions to £1 10s. and 15s. respectively, except in the
case of members who should covenant to remain members at the existing rates
for at least seven years. In a circular letter the chairman, urging members to
execute covenants, mentioned that the incidental benefits of membership were
considerable. Under the rules of the league the managing committee could have   D
discontinued any of the members' privileges or amenities at any time, but
members who executed covenants were clearly entitled to remain members during
the currency of their covenants at the existing rate of subscription and, as
members, to enjoy such privileges and amenities as the committee of management
elected to make available to members from time to time. On these facts LORD
EVERSHED, M.R., said (17):   E

" As I see it, therefore, the question turns first on this: looking at the
substance and reality of the matter, did those who entered into these covenants pay the sums covenanted without conditions or counter stipulations?
On the whole I have come to the conclusion that they did not."

Later he went on (18):   F

" If, as I think, the test is whether in all the circumstances, and looking
at the substance and reality of the matter, these covenantors can be treated
as donors of the covenanted sums to the charity, I have come to the conclusion that the answer must be in the negative, subject to the point to which
I will now come as to the extent of the conditions or counter-stipulations."

His lordship went on to hold that the benefits conferred by the conditions or   G
counter-stipulations could not be disregarded on the principle that de minimis
non curat lex. MORRIS, L.J., said (19):

" The question arises whether the payments can be said to be pure gifts to
the charity. In the terms of a phrase which has been used, can the payments
be said to be pure income profit in the hands of the charity? If the payments   H
were made in such circumstances that the league was obliged to afford to the
covenantors such amenities and such benefits of membership as would at
any particular time be offered to all members, and if those amenities and benefits were appreciable and not negligible, then I do not think that the payments
were pure income profit in the hands of the charity "

and he went on to decide that the payments were so made and that the benefits   I
were not negligible.

This decision, I think, clearly proceeded on the view that the covenanted
subscriptions were not " annual payments " in the technical sense, because they

(16) [1957] 2 All E.R. 644; 37 Tax Cas. 455.
(17) [1957] 2 All E.R. at p. 650; 37 Tax Cas. at p. 473.
(18) [1957] 2 All E.R. at p. 650; 37 Tax Cas. at p. 474.
(19) [1957] 2 All E.R. at p. 652; 37 Tax. Cas. at p. 475.

A were not clear profit to the National Book League. The observations of LORD NORMAND and LORD REID in the *Epping Forest* case (20) which I have read, show, I think, that they had the same consideration in mind. Payments to a charitable body on terms that the payer shall receive something in return are in fact analogous to payments to a tradesman in consideration of his supplying goods or services. They are not pure profit to the recipient but only a factor in calculating

B the recipient's profit. Basing his argument mainly on *Inland Revenue Comrs.* v. *National Book League* (21), counsel for the Crown contends that the payments made by Tutors under the deed of covenant were not annual payments in the technical sense because they were not pure bounty on account of the fact, as he submits, that the trustees of the trust are obliged to apply all sums so received by them towards buying the business of Davies's from Tutors. Counsel for the

C taxpayers on the other hand contends that the trustees were in fact under no binding obligation in this respect, and further that, to come within the principle of *Inland Revenue Comrs.* v. *National Book League* (21), the condition subject to which payment is made must be for a continuing consideration involving the recipient in expenditure on the supply of goods or services.

I have already read from the Case Stated the commissioners' finding of fact

D about the understanding on which the deed of covenant was entered into, and their finding about the intention of all parties that the profits of Davies's (i.e., as I read the Case, that part of them paid to the trustees under the deed of covenant) should be used to obtain for the shareholders of Tutors a fair and reasonable price for their interests in that company. In this connexion the commissioners in their decision at para. 3 found as follows:

E
"The evidence adduced before us established quite clearly that when Tutors entered into the deed of covenant on Mar. 30, 1961, an understanding had been reached between the three directors of (and main shareholders in) Tutors, the rest of the shareholders in Tutors and the trustees of the trust (who were a director and secretary to Tutors) that the covenanted payments

F would be used by the trustees to buy the business of Tutors as a going concern. The intention of all these parties was that Davies's, in its present form, should be perpetuated in the hands of an educational trust and that the equity shareholders of Tutors should in due course receive a fair but not excessive price for the assets of Tutors. The implementation of these intentions was left to Mr. Barber who had the full confidence of all the parties."

G In my judgment, in the light of these findings the commissioners were fully justified in holding further, as they did, that this use of the covenanted payments was an essential part of the fulfilment of the intentions of all the parties and that the deed of covenant was entered into on the clear understanding by both Tutors and their shareholders on the one hand and by the trustees on the other that the payments thereunder would be used to buy Tutors' business.

H In these circumstances the trustees, in my judgment, on the execution of the deed of covenant, became contractually bound to Tutors to apply all sums received by them under the covenant towards the purchase of the business of Davies's as a going concern, such obligation arising on a collateral contract by conduct. If the trustees were not so bound contractually, I think that the trustees must be regarded as receiving each payment under the deed subject to an earmark

I by Tutors for its application exclusively towards purchase of the business so as to clothe each payment with a trust for that purpose. Accordingly, I reject the taxpayers' submission that the trustees were under no legally binding obligation in this respect.

The commissioners, treating this understanding that the covenanted payments

---

(20) [1953] 1 All E.R. at pp. 1085, 1087; 34 Tax Cas. at pp. 324, 327.
(21) [1957] 2 All E.R. 644; 37 Tax Cas. 455.

would be so used as a condition or counter-stipulation analogous to those con- A
sidered in *Inland Revenue Comrs.* v. *National Book League* (22), held that they
were not " annual payments " in the relevant sense. The obligation to apply the
payments in the purchase of the business extends to the whole of each payment
and differs in that respect from the provision of privileges and amenities as in
Inland Revenue Comrs. v. *National Book League* (22), the cost of which would
have been merely a factor in discovering how far the contributions of members B
to the league constituted clear profit in its hands. Not every condition or stipulation attached to a series of periodical payments to a charity will, I think, be
such as to deprive those payments of the character of " annual payments " in
the special sense. For instance, if a charity were to conduct two schools, one for
boys and one for girls, out of a common fund, and an annual contributor were to
stipulate that his contributions should be used exclusively for the girls' school, C
this would not, as it seems to me, be such a stipulation as to deprive his contributions of the character of annual payments in that sense. A condition or stipulation to have that effect must, I think, be such as to deprive the periodical
payments as a whole of the character of income in the recipient charity's hands.

The fact that the trustees are bound to repay every covenanted sum to Tutors
in the form of purchase money does not seem to me essentially to deprive the D
covenanted payments of the character of bounty. They are at least steps in a
process of pure bounty. If any question of recovery of tax by the trustees be for
a moment put aside, the substance of the arrangement is that Tutors make
gratuitous transfers to the trustees of shares in the business at a rate geared to
the proportion which eighty per cent. of Tutors' profits from the business bears
to £50,000, the value put on the goodwill, and the cost of any other assets. The E
payments under the deed merely pass from Tutors to the trustees and back again
as machinery for determining how quickly and by what stages the business shall
be transferred. The business costs the trustees nothing. They acquire the business
as a pure act of bounty from Tutors. Nor, again ignoring the possibility of the
trustees' recovering any tax, do Tutors secure any advantage from the payments
apart from the implementation of their desire to effect a voluntary transfer of the F
business by stages to the trustees. If the trustees are in fact entitled to recover
tax and to use any amounts recovered as well as the covenanted payments to pay
the agreed purchase price, this will speed the transfer. It will not result in
Tutors' receiving any larger price than otherwise, but will result in their receiving
the whole amount more quickly. This would benefit the trust, which would the
more rapidly become entitled to a larger interest in, and ultimately the whole of, G
the business, and would also to some extent benefit Tutors by making cash
available for distribution amongst their members more rapidly. None of this
would be at the expense of the trust or make the covenanted payments to the
trustees any the less pure profit or bounty. I feel difficulty, therefore, in accepting
the submission of counsel for the Crown that the covenanted payments are not
annual payments in the technical sense because they are not pure bounty. H

Nevertheless they are not, in my judgment, annual payments within the
meaning of the sections to which I have referred, because they are not, in my
judgment, income in the hands of the trustees. Each payment is received by the
trustees committed to its being applied in its entirety to the purchase of a capital
asset which, as the Case Stated makes clear, it was the intention of all parties that
the trustees should retain and maintain as a going concern. Indeed, the preserva- I
tion of the business was the basic objective of the whole transaction. The
covenanted payments, if, as I am prepared to assume, they ought to be regarded
as belonging to the trustees in a real sense at all, in my judgment, were contributions or accretions to the capital stock or endowment of the trust and were just
as truly receipts on capital account and not on account of income as instalments
of the proceeds of sale of a capital asset would be. As such they were not, in my
opinion, ejusdem generis with interest on money and annuities belonging to the

(22) [1957] 2 All E.R. 644; 37 Tax Cas. 455.

A   trustees. I do not forget that in the *Epping Forest* case (23) LORD NORMAND said that one cannot determine the nature of a payment by enquiring what becomes of it or even what must become of it after the payee has received it, but his lordship was not there saying, as I understand him, that one should disregard the nature of the receipt in the recipient's hands.

B   I do not think that the admission recorded in para. 5 (h) of the Case, to which I have referred, precludes me from deciding the case on the ground that the covenanted payments are not income in the hands of the trustees. What the Crown admitted, as I read this paragraph, was that the advance of £21,900 by the trustees to Developments was an " application " of that amount for the purposes of s. 447 (1) (b). Having regard to the Crown's contentions as also recorded in the Case, the Crown cannot, I think, be understood to have admitted that the

C   covenanted payments were income of the trust. Accordingly I reach the conclusion that the covenanted payments, not being income in the trustees' hands, are not annual payments within the special meaning to be attributed to that expression as used in s. 169 and s. 447 of the Income Tax Act, 1952.

If I am wrong in this view, it is necessary to consider whether the trust was established for charitable purposes only and whether the sum of £21,900 has been

D   applied for charitable purposes only. That the trust was established for charitable purposes only is admitted. Nevertheless, it is said that the expenditure of the £21,900, as to £10,000 towards paying the purchase price of the goodwill of Davies's, and as to the balance in paying the price of fixtures and so forth used in connexion with the business, was made for a dual purpose, i.e., first in pursuance of the charitable trusts declared by the declaration of trust, and secondly in

E   pursuance of the obligation of the trustees to Tutors to use the money in this manner. It is of course the character of the application of the moneys by the trustees that must be considered in this connexion, and not the character or motive of the payment by Tutors to the trustees. The purchase of schools and tutorial establishments is a form of expenditure expressly authorised by the declaration of trust so far as ancillary to, consistent with and in furtherance of

F   the primary charitable purpose of promoting education. The purchase by the trustees of the business of Davies's is charitable. The whole of the £21,900 has been applied for that charitable purpose. There is no suggestion that this involved any impropriety on the part of the trustees as trustees of a charitable trust. The whole amount has been applied, and properly applied, to charitable purposes. It is not, in my judgment, necessary or permissible to consider what reason or motive

G   the trustees may have had for their method of applying the money, or whether they were under any obligation to adopt that method, or whether it may have conferred some incidental benefit on someone else—in this case, on Tutors. (See in this connexion *Barclays Bank, Ltd.* v. *Naylor* (*Inspector of Taxes*) (24).) The requirements of s. 447 (1) (b) are in my judgment satisfied so soon as it is shown that the body claiming relief from tax is established for charitable purposes only

H   and that the sum in respect of which relief is claimed has been wholly applied to charitable purposes. In the present case the first of these matters is conceded and the second is established. Accordingly, had I reached a different conclusion on the first question I should have allowed this appeal but on account of my conclusion on the first question I must dismiss it.

Appeal dismissed.

I
Solicitors: *J. S. Fairfax-Jones* (for the taxpayers); *Solicitor of Inland Revenue.*

[*Reported by* F. A. AMIES, ESQ., *Barrister-at-Law.*]

---

(23) [1953] 1 All E.R. at p. 1085; 34 Tax Cas. at p. 324.
(24) [1960] 3 All E.R. 173; 39 Tax Cas. 256.

ASTELL v. LONDON TRANSPORT BOARD.   A

[COURT OF APPEAL (Willmer, Davies and Salmon, L.JJ.), April 21, 22, May 10, 1966.]

Building—Building regulations—Guard-rail—Stairs from which workman liable to fall more than six feet six inches—One guard-rail three feet above stairs provided—Workman falling from stairs under guard-rail—Whether more than one guard-rail necessary—Building (Safety, Health and Welfare) Regulations, 1948 (S.I. 1948 No. 1145), reg. 27 (2) (a).   B

The plaintiff, who was employed by the defendants as an electrician's mate, was engaged in work that was proceeding on the first floor of a building in course of erection. Access to the first floor was obtained by means of an outside staircase, built of concrete, which led to a temporary platform, consisting of scaffolding boards, and leading at right-angles to the staircase to a door in the side of the building. The staircase consisted of two flights, each of nine stairs, divided by a short half-landing. On each side of the staircase was a single guard-rail consisting of a scaffolding pole. The height of the guard-rail above the stairs was roughly three feet. The plaintiff, who was left-handed, was carrying two conduit pipes, each about fifteen feet long, in his left hand up the stairs. When he was just below the landing he crouched down and endeavoured to manoeuvre the conduit pipes through the doorway. While crouching down he was below the level of the guard-rail and he either stepped backward or slipped in such a way that he fell over the side of the staircase, a distance of more than six feet six inches. By reg. 27 (2) (a)* of the Building (Safety, Health and Welfare) Regulations, 1948, stairs from which a person was liable to fall a distance of more than six feet six inches must be provided with suitable guard-rails to a height of at least three feet above the stair.   C   D   E

Held: reg. 27 (2) (a) of the Building (Safety, Health and Welfare) Regulations, 1948 required the defendants to provide such guard-rails as were suitable to form an effective physical barrier against risk of the plaintiff's falling over the side; in the absence of a second or lower guard-rail to the staircase there was no such barrier, and the defendants were in breach of duty under reg. 27 (2) (a) (see p. 752, letter G, p. 753, letter C, p. 754, letter A, and p. 749, letter A, post).   F

Dictum of WILLMER, L.J., in *Corn* v. *Weir's Glass (Hanley), Ltd.* ([1960] 2 All E.R. at p. 303) considered.   G

Appeal allowed.

[As to the Building Regulations, see 17 HALSBURY'S LAWS (3rd Edn.) 125, 126, para. 206.

For the Building (Safety, Health and Welfare) Regulations, 1948, reg. 27, see 8 HALSBURY'S STATUTORY INSTRUMENTS (First Re-Issue) 199.]   H

Cases referred to:

Corn v. *Weir's Glass (Hanley), Ltd.,* [1960] 2 All E.R. 300; [1960] 1 W.L.R. 577; Digest (Cont. Vol. A) 600, *340d.*

Summers (John) & Sons, Ltd. v. *Frost,* [1955] 1 All E.R. 870; [1955] A.C. 740; [1955] 2 W.L.R. 825; 24 Digest (Repl.) 1055, *217.*

Walker v. *Bletchley Flettons, Ltd.,* [1937] 1 All E.R. 170; 24 Digest (Repl.) 1054, *212.*   I

Appeal.

This was an appeal by the plaintiff from a judgment of PAULL, J., dated Dec. 2, 1965, dismissing his action against the defendants for damages for personal injuries sustained in the course of his employment with the defendants on June 25, 1962. The facts are set out in the judgment of WILLMER, L.J.

---

* Regulation 27, so far as material, is set out at p. 750, letter B, post.

A   *D. G. A. Lowe*, Q.C., and *N. F. Irvine* for the plaintiff.
      John D. Stocker, Q.C., and *D. P. O'Brien* for the defendants.

Cur. adv. vult.

May 10.   **WILLMER, L.J.**, read the following judgment: SALMON, L.J.,
who is unable to be present today, authorises me to say that he is in agreement
B with the judgment which I am about to deliver.

This is an appeal from a judgment of PAULL, J., given on Dec. 2, 1965, whereby
he dismissed a claim brought by a workman against his employers for damages
for personal injuries sustained in consequence of an accident in the course of his
employment.   The accident happened on June 25, 1962, when the plaintiff had
the misfortune to fall over the side of an outside staircase erected in connexion
C with building operations on the defendants' building site at Lillie Bridge Depot.
He fell a distance of about ten feet, in consequence of which he sustained an
injury to his back, from which he has now largely recovered.   The plaintiff was
employed as an electrician's mate, and at the time of the accident was engaged
in work that was proceeding on the first floor of a building in course of erection.
Access to the first floor was obtained by means of an outside staircase, built of
D concrete, which at the time of the accident led to a temporary platform, consisting of scaffolding boards, and leading at right-angles to the staircase to a door
in the side of the building.   The building itself was encased in scaffolding, on
which another platform was laid at a level about half-way up the entrance door,
and to that extent obstructing the entrance.   The staircase, and its relation to the
building which was under construction, are well illustrated by the very clear
E photographs that have been placed before us.   The staircase consisted of two
flights, each of nine stairs, divided by a short half-landing.   On each side of the
staircase was a single guard-rail consisting of a scaffolding pole.   The height of the
guard-rail above the stairs was roughly three feet, but varied slightly due to
the fact that the guard-rail was straight, whereas the stairs were divided by
the half-landing.

F   At the time of the accident, the plaintiff had been sent to fetch two conduit
pipes for housing electric cables.   These were quite light, weighing only some
five lbs., but being about fifteen feet long were somewhat difficult to handle in the
forest of scaffolding surrounding the building.   The plaintiff, being left-handed,
carried the pipes in his left hand, holding them at the point of balance, and thus
equipped proceeded to mount the stairs.   According to his own evidence, he
G actually reached the platform, and then proceeded to manoeuvre the pipes
which he was carrying through a turn of ninety degrees to the right for the purpose
of pushing them through the entrance doorway.   This, however, was not accepted
by the learned judge, who preferred the evidence given by witnesses for the
defendants.   They said, and the judge found, that the plaintiff got no further
than a position with one foot on the second, and the other foot on the third, step
H below the landing.   In this position the plaintiff crouched down near the right-
hand edge of the staircase, and endeavoured to manoeuvre the conduit pipes
through the entrance doorway.   While crouching down the plaintiff was below
the level of the guard-rail.   In that position he either stepped backwards or
slipped in such a way that he fell over the side of the staircase.   The plaintiff
complains that his fall was due to the absence of a second guard-rail between the
I existing guard-rail and the stairs.   It has been submitted that the defendants'
failure to fit such a second guard-rail constituted a breach of statutory duty and
also amounted to negligence on their part.   The claim in negligence at common
law has not been seriously pressed, nor do I think that it really adds anything
to the case.   If the defendants were guilty of a breach of their statutory duty, that
is enough for the plaintiff.   If they were not, I think that it would be difficult to
say that the defendants were guilty of common law negligence in the circumstances
of this case in failing to provide a protective device which they were under no
statutory duty to provide.

What is relied on by the plaintiff is reg. 27 of the Building (Safety, Health and   A
Welfare) Regulations, 1948, made in pursuance of the powers conferred by the
Factories Act, 1937, and preservd in operation by s. 183 (1) of, and para. 2 of
Sch. 6 to, the Factories Act, 1961. This regulation provides:

" Guard-rails, toe-boards, hand-rails, etc., for gangways, runs and
stairs.—(1) Stairs shall be provided throughout their length with hand-rails   B
or other efficient means to prevent the fall of persons except for the time and
to the extent necessary for the access of persons or the movement of materials.
If necessary to prevent danger to any person the hand-rails shall be continued
beyond the ends of the stairs. (2) All gangways, runs and stairs from which
a person is liable to fall a distance of more than six feet six inches shall be
provided with—(a) suitable guard-rails of adequate strength to a height of at
least three feet above the gangway, run or stair; (b) except in the case of   C
stairs, toe-boards up to a sufficient height being in no case less than eight
inches and so placed as to prevent so far as possible the fall of persons,
materials and tools. The space between any such toe-board and the lowest
guard-rail above it shall not exceed twenty-seven inches . . ."

That is followed by a proviso which is not relevant to the circumstances of the   D
present case.

It has been contended for the plaintiff that this regulation in terms requires
the provision of a plurality of guard-rails up to a height of three feet in all cases
where, as here, a person is liable to fall a distance of more than six feet six inches.
Reliance is placed both on the use of the plural in sub-para. (a) and on the
reference in sub-para. (b) to " the lowest guard-rail ". In support of this con-   E
tention we have been referred to the decision of this court in *Corn* v. *Weir's Glass
(Hanley), Ltd.* (1). In that case, the plaintiff had fallen from a point on a staircase
less than six feet six inches above the floor, and the actual question for decision
was whether that fall was caused by a breach of his employers' duty to provide a
hand-rail as provided by para. (1) of reg. 27. Opportunity was taken, however,
to draw a distinction between hand-rails, as required by para. (1), and guard-rails   F
as required by para. (2). It fell to my lot to deliver the leading judgment, with
which HODSON, L.J., expressed his concurrence, and with which DEVLIN, L.J.,
did not disagree. I am reported as saying (2):

" I think it is clear, from the fact that different words are used, that a
distinction is to be drawn between a ' hand-rail ', as prescribed by reg. 27 (1),
and ' guard-rails ' which are the subject of reg. 27 (2). There can be no doubt   G
that down to a height of six feet six inches above the floor of the hall guard-
rails ought to have been provided on the open side of the stairs in accordance
with reg. 27 (2). I think that in this context guard-rails must be construed
as rails of such a character as will provide a physical barrier against the
possibility of falling over the side. That this must be so is, I think, borne
out by the provision that such guard-rails must be of ' adequate strength '.   H
Moreover, it seems to me clear from its wording that reg. 27 (2) contemplates
the provision of a plurality of guard-rails. This, I think, is clear enough from
the wording of sub-para. (a), but it is placed beyond doubt by the reference
to ' the lowest guard-rail ' in sub-para. (b). All this goes to emphasise what I
have already said, namely, that the guard-rail contemplated by reg. 27 (2)
must be intended as a physical barrier."   I

Later I said (3):

" A hand-rail may in certain circumstances be required to fulfil the same
function as a guard-rail—that is to say, in some cases a hand-rail may be
required to be fitted in such a way that it serves also as a guard-rail. Equally,

(1) [1960] 2 All E.R. 300.   (2) [1960] 2 All E.R. at p. 303.
                    (3) [1960] 2 All E.R. at p. 304.

A   as it seems to me, a guard-rail may in certain circumstances serve also as a hand-rail. Thus, it is doubtless permissible, where guard-rails are required to be fitted, as for instance under reg. 27 (2), to allow the top guard-rail on the open side to serve as a hand-rail, without the necessity of fitting a separate hand-rail to comply with reg. 27 (1)."

B   It is to be observed that everything which was said in those two passages was obiter, being in no way necessary to the decision of the case then under consideration. Indeed, it is not relied on by counsel for the plaintiff as other than persuasive authority in support of his contention that reg. 27 (2) requires the provision of a plurality of guard-rails so as to furnish an effective physical barrier against falling over the side of the staircase. The learned judge in the present case carefully considered the views which I had expressed in the passages which I have

C quoted. He accepted without question (and it has been accepted before us by counsel for the defendants) that guard-rails, where they are required, are intended to serve as a physical barrier. The learned judge, however, felt unable to accept the proposition that, on its true construction, reg. 27 (2) necessarily requires the provision of a plurality of guard-rails. He was not, of course, bound by anything which I had said so to hold. Moreover, I would point out that, in the passages

D cited, I did not in fact go so far as to say that reg. 27 (2) *requires* a plurality of guard-rails. What I said was that it " *contemplates* the provision of a plurality of guard-rails ", which it plainly does.

   The argument for the defendants which prevailed before the learned judge, and which has been repeated before us, may be summarised as follows. The

E requirement that all gangways, runs and stairs shall be provided with suitable guard-rails means no more, as a matter of English, than that every gangway, every run, and every stair or stairway shall be provided with a suitable guard-rail or guard-rails. This construction would bring reg. 27 (2) into line with the specific requirements of reg. 24 (1) relating to guard-rails at working places. The question whether one or more than one guard-rail should be provided depends on what is

F suitable to the circumstances of the particular gangway, run or stairs in question. In the case of gangways and runs, reg. 27 (2) (*b*) specifically permits a gap of twenty-seven inches between the top of the toe-board which has to be provided and any guard-rail. Allowing for the thickness of the guard-rails, this alone is sufficient to achieve the required height of at least three feet. To insist on the provision of a second and lower guard-rail would render nugatory the permissive

G right to have a gap of twenty-seven inches above the toe-board. It is, therefore, possible, in the case of gangways and runs, to comply strictly with the requirements of sub-para. (*b*) by the provision of a single guard-rail. If that be so, sub-para. (*a*) cannot be construed as requiring the provision of a second guard-rail below a height of three feet in the case of gangways and runs. If that is true of gangways and runs, the same must be true of stairs, which are classed with

H gangways and runs for the purposes of sub-para. (*a*). The only question, therefore, is whether the presence of the word " suitable " may require the provision of an additional guard-rail or guard-rails in the particular circumstances of a particular case. As to that, it would be for the plaintiff in any given case to call evidence as to the particular circumstances calling for the provision of additional guard-rails. This the plaintiff in the present case conspicuously failed to do.

I   On the other hand, counsel for the plaintiff called our attention to s. 28 (3) of the Factories Act, 1961. This provides as follows:

   " (3) Any open side of a staircase shall also be guarded by the provision and maintenance of a lower rail or other effective means."

   It was argued that, if such a degree of protection is thought to be required in the case of a completed factory, all the more is it necessary in the case of an incomplete building where constructional work is actually in progress, and that reg. 27 (2) should be construed accordingly. We were also referred to reg. 9 of the

Docks Regulations, 1934, (4) and reg. 7, reg. 8 and reg. 9 of the Shipbuilding and A
Ship-repairing Regulations, 1960, (5).   Regulation 9 of the Docks Regulations,
1934, provides as follows:

" If a ship is lying at a wharf or quay for the purpose of loading or
unloading or coaling, there shall be safe means of access for the use of
persons employed at such times as they have to pass from the ship to the
shore or from the shore to the ship as follows:—(a) Where reasonably   B
practicable the ship's accommodation ladder or a gangway or a similar construction not less than twenty-two inches wide, properly secured, and
fenced throughout on each side to a clear height of two feet nine inches by
means of upper and lower rails, taut ropes or chains or by other equally safe
means . . ."

C

I do not think that I need actually quote the Shipbuilding and Ship-repairing
Regulations, 1960, to which reference was made.   It is sufficient to say that, in
each case, the means of access are required to be guarded at the side by the
provision of upper and lower rails.   From all this it is argued that the policy
underlying the Act and the regulations made under it is to require that, where
guard-rails are prescribed, more than one should be provided so as to afford an D
effective physical barrier against persons falling.

In my judgment, the argument founded on the provisions of s. 28 (3) of the
Act of 1961 and on the regulations relating to docks and shipbuilding which I
have quoted cuts both ways.   In favour of the defendants it can be said that, in
as much as this section and these regulations make specific provision for a second
and lower guard-rail, reg. 27 (2), which makes no such specific provision, should E
not be construed as requiring a second and lower guard-rail in all cases.   Had this
been the intention, it would have been the simplest possible thing for the draftsman to say so in express terms, as he has in the case of s. 28 (3) of the Act of 1961
and the respective regulations to which I have referred.   I can see no answer to
this argument, and, if it be thought that the dicta in *Corn's* case (6) point to a
contrary conclusion (which for myself I do not think that they necessarily do), F
I would accept that they went further than was required, and should not be
followed.   On the other hand, in considering what is meant by the requirement
in reg. 27 (2) (a) of " suitable " guard-rails, I am of opinion that the provisions
of s. 28 (3) of the Factories Act, 1961, and of the regulations to which I have
referred afford the strongest possible support to the argument for the plaintiff.
To my mind they show that the policy of the Factories Act and of the regulations G
made under it is to ensure that, in cases where guard-rails are called for, these
will be such as will in fact form an effective physical barrier against the risk of
persons falling over the side.   If in any given case it can be shown that, in the
absence of a second guard-rail, there is in fact no effective physical barrier, I
do not see how it could be said that the employer has provided " suitable "
guard-rails within reg. 27 (2) (a).   The word " suitable " no doubt imports an H
element of degree, and must be considered in relation to the purpose intended
to be achieved.   In the case of guard-rails, the purpose to be achieved is the
provision of an effective physical barrier.

I agree with counsel for the defendants that, in considering what is " suitable ",
regard must be had to the circumstances of the particular case.   In the present
case, we are concerned with a staircase, and one which was provided for the use I
of workmen going to and from their place of work, sometimes no doubt carrying
burdens which might, or might not, be awkward and difficult to handle.   In the
case of a staircase, reg. 27 (2) (b) does not apply, so that there is no requirement
that toe-boards be provided.   If there is nothing but a single guard-rail at a
height of three feet or thereabouts, there is no effective physical barrier to prevent
any person who slips and falls from going over the side underneath the guard-rail.

(4) S.R. & O. 1934 No. 279.   (5) S.I. 1960 No. 1932.
(6) [1960] 2 All E.R. at pp. 303, 304.

A In the present case, the plaintiff was engaged in doing what counsel for the defendants himself described as a sensible thing to do and, as found by the learned judge, was using the staircase in a way which was not necessarily unreasonable. This means, I think, that he was acting in a way in which a human being might be reasonably expected to act in circumstances which might be reasonably likely to occur, to adopt the test put by DU PARCQ, J., in *Walker* v.

B *Bletchley Flettons, Ltd.* (7), as qualified by LORD REID in *John Summers & Sons, Ltd.* v. *Frost* (8). In such circumstances, I am of the opinion that reg. 27 (2) (*a*) required the defendants to provide such guard-rails as would be suitable to form an effective physical barrier against the risk of his falling over the side. The learned judge clearly felt considerable doubt about the matter, but, in the end, he came to the conclusion that the single guard-rail provided was a suitable

C guard-rail so as to comply with the requirements of reg. 27 (2) (*a*). With all respect to the view of the learned judge, I do not feel able to agree. In my judgment, having regard to the particular circumstances of this case, the absence of a second and lower guard-rail meant that there was no effective physical barrier to prevent the plaintiff from falling over the side. I cannot, therefore, accept the view that suitable guard-rails were provided, and I would hold that the defendants

D were in breach of their duty under reg. 27 (2) (*a*).

That, however, does not conclude the case, for, by their cross-notice, the defendants invite us to conclude that, even assuming a breach of duty on their part, the plaintiff's accident was wholly caused, or was at least contributed to, by the plaintiff's own negligence. Having regard to the learned judge's finding that the plaintiff was using the staircase in a way which was not necessarily

E unreasonable, I think that it would be difficult to say that he was negligent in choosing this method of carrying out the work which he had to do. On the contrary, I would agree with the view that he was going about his task in a sensible way. But the method which he adopted did involve his crouching down near the edge of the staircase. In this position, the whole of his body must have been below the level of the single guard-rail, and, if he was taking any care for his

F own safety, he must have realised that this was so. He must equally have realised that there was no lower guard-rail and, therefore, nothing to prevent his falling over the edge unless he was careful. The job on which he was engaged was a perfectly simple one and not such as to involve any serious risk if carried out with care. Yet, somehow, he managed to fall over the edge. According to his own account, this was because he stepped backwards, and, if that be true, I can

G only say that he was taking an extremely foolish risk. The evidence of Mr. Collins was rather more favourable to the plaintiff, for this witness said that the plaintiff appeared to slip. But on either view I can only infer that the plaintiff was not taking that degree of care for his own safety that he ought to have taken. In my judgment, his fall was contributed to by his own negligence.

It remains only to apportion the degrees of fault as between the two parties.

H In my judgment, the degree of fault attributable to the plaintiff was a relatively minor one. Both from the point of view of culpability and from the point of view of causative potency, the defendants' fault in failing to provide suitable guard-rails was by far the greater contributing factor. I would apportion three-quarters of the fault to the defendants and only one-quarter to the plaintiff. It follows

I that, in my judgment, the plaintiff is entitled to recover three-quarters of the damages which he can prove. This is as far as the matter can be carried at the moment, since the damages have not so far been assessed. If it is not possible to agree them, it will be necessary for the parties to invite our directions as to how they shall be assessed. In the meantime, however, the appeal should, in my judgment, be allowed to the extent that I have indicated.

(7) [1937] 1 All E.R. 170 at p. 175.
(8) [1955] 1 All E.R. 870 at p. 883; [1955] A.C. 740 at p. 765.

DAVIES, L.J.: I agree and have nothing to add.   A

Appeal allowed.

Solicitors: *Pattinson & Brewer* (for the plaintiff); *Stephen G. Jones* (for the defendants).

[*Reported by* F. GUTTMAN, ESQ., *Barrister-at-Law.*]

B

CALLER *v.* CALLER (by her Guardian).

[PROBATE, DIVORCE AND ADMIRALTY DIVISION (Karminski and Latey, JJ.), April 1, 1966.]

C

Magistrates—Husband and wife—Maintenance—Wilful neglect to maintain child—Child en ventre de sa mère at time of marriage—Child not husband's child—Acceptance of child by husband before marriage as child of the family —Liability of putative father—No proceedings taken by wife against putative father—Effect as regards maintenance order against husband—Matrimonial Proceedings (Magistrates' Courts) Act, 1960 (8 & 9 Eliz. 2 c. 48), s. 2 (1) (h), D *(5), s. 16 (1).*

The husband and wife had known each other since childhood, but had not met for some time. In 1965, the husband, knowing that the wife had become pregnant by another man, decided that he would marry her and agreed to take the child into the family as his own. The husband and wife were married on Aug. 7, 1965. The husband deserted the wife on Sept. 16, E 1965. The child was born on Oct. 6, 1965. The wife took no proceedings against the natural father of her child. On appeal from an order obtained by the wife against the husband for him to pay maintenance of £2 weekly for the child,

Held: (i) a child en ventre de sa mère can be a " child of the family " within s. 16 (1) of the Matrimonial Proceedings (Magistrates' Courts) Act, F 1960, and in the present case the husband, by agreeing immediately before and at the time of marriage to accept the child as a child of the family, had so accepted the child for the purposes of s. 2 (1) (h) of that Act (see p. 756, letter H, p. 757, letter B, and p. 758, letter D, post).

(ii) in view of the court's duty to have regard to the liability of any person other than a party to the marriage to maintain the child, the possibility G of recovering maintenance from the natural father of the child ought to be examined, and accordingly the case would be remitted to the justices on quantum to be reconsidered after the wife had had opportunity to bring affiliation proceedings (see p. 757, letter I, and p. 758, letters E and F, post).

[As to maintenance of children in matrimonial proceedings, see 12 HALBURY'S LAWS (3rd Edn.) 488, para. 1087; and for cases on the subject, see 27 DIGEST H (Repl.) 708, 709, *6756-6762*; DIGEST (Cont. Vol. A) 806, *6341a*, 825, *6757b*, *6757d*.

For the Matrimonial Proceedings (Magistrates' Courts) Act, 1960, s. 2, s. 16, see 40 HALSBURY'S STATUTES (2nd Edn.) 399, 419.]

Case referred to:

Bowlas v. *Bowlas*, [1965] 1 All E.R. 803; [1965] P. 440; [1965] 2 W.L.R. I 1133; *rvsd.* C.A., [1965] 3 All E.R. 40; [1965] P. 450; [1965] 3 W.L.R. 593.

Appeal.

This was an appeal by the husband, P. J. Caller, from an order of the justices of the petty sessional division of North Aylesford, Kent, that he should pay the sum of £2 weekly for the maintenance of the wife's child. The husband had left the wife finally about six weeks after marriage, and the justices found that

A   he had deserted her, and found also wilful neglect to maintain on his part; there was no appeal against these findings. The child was not the husband's, and was conceived before marriage but born after the desertion. The husband agreed to accept the child into the family before, and at the time of, marrying the wife. She had taken no proceedings against the putative father.

B   *R. M. N. Band* for the husband.
A. B. Ewbank for the wife.

KARMINSKI, J.: This is an appeal by a husband from a decision of the justices of the petty sessional division of North Aylesford, Kent, made on Dec. 9, 1965, whereby they decided that a child born to the respondent wife was a child of the family of the husband and the wife. They made an order that the

C   husband should pay £2 a week for the maintenance of the child. They also found against the husband desertion and wilful neglect to maintain on his part, and against that finding there is no appeal. Indeed, it may be said at once that that part of the decision was quite unappealable and it is not for a moment contended otherwise. The husband says first of all, however, that the justices were wrong in law in holding that the child was a child of the family and also

D   that they were wrong in law in ordering him to pay £2 a week for the maintenance of the child.

The facts are simple enough. The husband and wife have known each other since they were children, but apparently had not seen each other for some time. In the early part of 1965 the wife, who is now only aged about seventeen, and is still an infant, became pregnant as a result of intercourse with a man, not the husband.

E   While she was apparently looking for the natural father of the child, she re-met the husband. They went out together and the husband, knowing of the wife's condition, namely that she was expecting a child in the autumn, decided that he would marry her, and told her that he would take the child into the family as his own; indeed he went so far as to tell his friends that the child was his, that is, conceived as a result of pre-marital intercourse by him with the wife. The

F   husband and wife married on Aug. 7, 1965. The marriage never looked like being a success. The husband left after a short time: after a week or two he came back, but on Sept. 16, 1965, he left for good: and he left in such terms that the justices decided that he had deserted the wife. The child was born on Oct. 6, 1965, almost three weeks after the husband deserted the wife, so that it is clear that the child did not and could not have lived as a member of the family

G   of which the husband and wife formed the major part. Counsel on behalf of the husband, has raised the question whether a child unborn can, as such, be accepted as a child of the family. He says that there must be a family into which a child can be accepted, and that that can only be done if the child is a living child. The interpretation section, s. 16 of the Matrimonial Proceedings (Magistrates' Courts) Act, 1960, defines " child of the family ", and it says,

H   inter alia, this:

" ' a child of the family ', in relation to the parties to the marriage, means —(*a*) any child of both parties, (*b*) any other child of either party who has been accepted as one of the family by the other party."

In regard to para. (*a*) above it is common ground that this child, born in October,

I   was not a child of the husband and the wife. Counsel for the husband's argument was that this was not a child but was, as he put it, " an embryo "—though I am inclined to think, on the arithmetic, that this child was in all probability viable at the time of the marriage. Counsel said that a man could change his mind up to the time of the birth of the child, but there has to be real acceptance by the father, in this case, of the child as a child which has been born living. He based his argument largely on a decision of the Court of Appeal, *Bowlas* v. *Bowlas* (1). The facts in that case were very different from the present. There

---

(1) [1965] 3 All E.R. 40; [1965] P. 450.

the wife had been married before to an American in the United States of America   A
There were two children of that marriage, and that marriage had been dissolved
in the United States (in what particular jurisdiction or state is not reported (2))
and she had also there a maintenance order for the two children of that marriage:
and the question to be decided was whether or not in all the circumstances of that
case the two children of the wife by her earlier marriage had, in fact, been accepted
as children of the family.   The appeal really turned on the question of fact and   B
WILLMER, J., who gave the first judgment, dealt with it largely in that way.
Dealing with the judgment of SCARMAN, J., in the Divisional Court (3), to which
I shall refer in more detail in due course, he said this (4):

> ". . . in the remaining part of the passage which I have read the judge
> seems to express the view that, in the circumstances of this case, the mere
> fact of the husband having gone through the ceremony of marriage was   C
> sufficient to prove that he had unconditionally assumed responsibility
> for the maintenance of these two children.   In my judgment the evidence
> which was given before the justices . . . was insufficient to justify that
> conclusion without further inquiry.   I do not say that it may not in the end
> prove to be the right conclusion, but I do not think that without further
> inquiry the evidence before the justices was sufficient to justify it."   D

With that the other two lord justices agreed, and SALMON, L.J., said this (5):

> " If [the justices] had had that question under consideration, they would
> have had to ask themselves: did this man, immediately before or at the
> time of the marriage (and I stress those words), accept the children as
> members of the family and marry the wife on that basis? "   E

Here the justices found, and I think that they were fully entitled to find it on
the facts, that the marriage was on the clear basis that the husband intended
to accept the child, when born, into his family, although he was not the father;
and they stressed the fact that he wanted to take over the responsibility for the
child, married on that basis, and informed his friends that the child was in fact
his.   They state in their last paragraph   F

> ". . . there was a living child which the husband from the beginning of
> things meant to accept as his own, and we made our order of custody of such
> child to the wife with maintenance accordingly."

Clearly a man might say months or even years before marriage, " I will accept
the child, or children, as children of the family ", and then change his mind.   G
If, as here, however, he goes through the ceremony of marriage having said,
as he did immediately before the marriage, that he was going to accept the
child, then asking the question asked by SALMON, L.J. (5):

> " Did this man, immediately before or at the time of the marriage . . .
> accept the [child] as [a member] of the family and marry the wife on that
> basis? "   H

I have to ask myself further in this case whether the word " child " is applicable
to a child not yet born.   I am myself of the opinion that a child can exist en
ventre sa mère: just as much as a child who has in fact been delivered.

Counsel for the wife, argued that here there was not merely an intention, but
an acceptance of the child as a specific term of the marriage, born or unborn,
and he called our attention to certain observations of SCARMAN, J., in *Bowlas* v.   I
Bowlas (6) in this court.   The gist of SCARMAN, J.'s observations is this.   Acceptance need not necessarily be subsequent to marriage;   it may very well be

---

(2) The evidence did not disclose this; see per WILLMER, L.J., [1965] 3 All E.R. at
p. 41, letter I.
(3) [1965] 1 All E.R. 803; [1965] P. 440.
(4) [1965] 3 All E.R. at p. 44; [1965] P. at p. 457.
(5) [1965] 3 All E.R. at p. 46; [1965] P. at p. 461.
(6) [1965] 1 All E.R. at p. 806; [1965] P. at p. 447.

A　accorded to the child on the marriage itself and by reason of it.　If there is an ante-nuptial agreement or promise to accept the child, there is no difficulty in the terms being performed by the marriage ceremony itself, which brings into existence the family contemplated by such agreement or promise.

　　I have come to the clear conclusion that the family was called into its brief existence when the husband and wife married on Aug. 7, 1965.　The fact that
B　the child was not born until almost exactly two months later is relevant, but is relatively unimportant.　The husband accepted the child waiting to be born as a child of the family, as the justices found, just as much as if he had waited and put off the marriage ceremony until after the child was born.　In my view, so far as that part of the case is concerned, this appeal fails.

　　There is left, however, a second limb which is important and possibly more
C　difficult.　It arises in this way.　The husband was ordered to pay £2 a week for the maintenance of the child.　It appears that no proceedings were taken by the wife against the natural father, though she is not yet time-barred from bringing those proceedings, which can be brought within one year of the birth of the child. The duty of a court under the Matrimonial Proceedings (Magistrates' Courts) Act, 1960, s. 2, as to the amount of the order, is set out in s. 2 (5) in these terms:

D
　　　" In considering whether any, and if so what, provision should be included in a matrimonial order by virtue of para. (*h*) of sub-s. (1) of this section for payments by one of the parties in respect of a child who is not a child of that party, the court shall have regard to the extent, if any, to which that party had, on or after the acceptance of the child as one of the family, assumed responsibility for the child's maintenance, and to the liability of any person
E　other than a party to the marriage to maintain the child."

　　It does not appear, perhaps because the matter was not raised by the husband's solicitor, that the justices here considered the possible liability of any person other than the husband.　There is clearly under the section which I have just read, a statutory duty on the court to have regard to such a liability.　It is
F　true that they may have thought that, as the wife had not taken such proceedings, they were not practicable, but there is no evidence of that.　All we know is that no proceedings have been taken, and I think that before the question of quantum can be dealt with there should be at least an opportunity for the wife to try to find and to bring proceedings against the putative father of this child, so that he can if necessary be ordered to pay part or the whole of the
G　maintenance of the child which she says is his.　I have used those words deliberately because I know nothing of the possible merits of her claim against a man whose name we do not even know; but for myself I think it is only fair, in the circumstances of this case, that at least the possibility of claiming maintenance from the real father should be examined before the whole burden is cast on the husband.　Whatever blame may properly be put on him for deserting the wife
H　after the briefest possible period of cohabitation, it is, I think, right to have in mind that at the time when he married the wife he was prepared in a sense to shoulder another man's financial burden in respect of this child, and I think an opportunity of examining that matter should be given to the wife.

　　That results in this.　That on the first part of the appeal the appeal fails, but that on the second part, the question of quantum, there should be an adjourn-
I　ment and the matter should be dealt with as we have indicated on the wife's side, by her seeking out the natural father and bringing proceedings.　The time of the adjournment can, I think, be safely left to the justices and I myself see no reason why it should be remitted to a fresh panel, but it may be convenient and indeed just that the same panel should deal with the matter.

　　LATEY, J.:　I agree.　It is quite plain from the facts, as outlined by KARMINSKI, J., that the husband not only agreed with the wife to take over the responsibility for the unborn child before the marriage and at the time of the

marriage; but indeed, as I think on the evidence and having looked at the letter   A
which he wrote to the wife, was anxious to treat the child entirely as though the
child were his own.

Now the first question, therefore, which was argued by counsel for the husband
is not that there is any doubt that in the husband's mind the matter was agreed,
but whether an unborn child can be accepted as a child of the family: his argument came in the end to be an argument that a child unborn is not a child. I   B
should take a lot of persuading that when Parliament chooses the simple words
" a child ", it intends any special meaning. I do not think that the words are
intended to be used in any way other than the natural way according to the
common use of language. I should have thought for myself that in the ordinary
English language pregnancy means " having a child ", or " having a baby ",
but counsel contends that what should be said is, " I am having an embryo "   C
or " I am having a foetus ", or words to that effect. I am unable to accept that
argument and in my view a man can accept as a child of the family his wife's
unborn child just as readily as he can accept her born child: and that is what
happened in this case.

Therefore I wholly agree that on the first point the appeal fails, and I also entirely agree that on the question of quantum, s. 2 (5) of the Matrimonial Proceedings   D
(Magistrates' Courts) Act, 1960, is quite clear that it is the duty of the court
to have regard, amongst other things, to the liability of any person other than
a party to the marriage to maintain the child. It is plain from the reasons given by
the justices that they did not, or did not at any rate apparently, have regard to
the liability of the natural father of this child, and it may well be that the matter
was overlooked by the justices because it was not brought to their attention.   E
Whatever the reason may be, the Act of 1960 is quite clear about it, and, therefore, I agree that the case should be sent back so that the matter can be looked
into and that the wife should be given a reasonable period of time to take proceedings against the natural father. The justices should be able to judge what
is a reasonable period of time in which to take, or try to take, the proceedings.

F

KARMINSKI, J.: Then there will be an order accordingly. The appeal
on quantum will be remitted to the justices and then be reconsidered after the
wife has had a reasonable opportunity to bring affiliation proceedings against
the putative father. I had better add, to try and help the justices, that the
length of the adjournment is to be in their hands. I think that there should be
an interim order in this case. We have stopped the order in the sense that we   G
have remitted the matter for a re-hearing on the question of quantum: it will
obviously take some time and the child has to be supported in the next months.
I think that the interim order should be £2 a week, but we want to make it clear
we are not saying that £2 on quantum is necessarily wrong because we are making
it an interim order. The interim order will date from today and we set aside the
existing order. An interim order under the summary jurisdiction runs only three   H
months (7), but if by some chance the matter cannot come on again in three
months, a fresh order can be obtained from the justices.

Order accordingly.

Solicitors: *Church, Bruce, Hawkes & Brassington* (for the husband); *Cunliffe
& Mossman*, agents for *Martin, Son & Allen*, Gravesend (for the wife).

[*Reported by* ALICE BLOOMFIELD, *Barrister-at-Law.*]   I

---

(7) See s. 6 (3) (*b*) of the Matrimonial Proceedings (Magistrates' Courts) Act, 1960.

A   R. *v.* SPECIAL COMMISSIONERS OF INCOME TAX,
Ex parte NATIONAL UNION OF RAILWAYMEN.

[QUEEN'S BENCH DIVISION (Lord Parker, C.J., Marshall and James, JJ.), May 18, 19, 1966.]

B   *Income Tax—Exemption—Trade union—Provident benefits—Payments by way of legal assistance—Exemption under Sch. C and Sch. D—Sums paid out of general fund, not special fund, of union—Whether provision of legal assistance a provident benefit within Income Tax Act, 1952 (15 & 16 Geo. 6 & 1 Eliz. 2 c. 10), s. 440 (2).*

C   The N.U.R., a registered trade union, claimed exemption from income tax for sums paid in the years of assessment 1959-60 and 1960-61 by way of legal assistance, as being provident benefits within s. 440 (2)* of the Income Tax Act, 1952. The sums so paid included (a) the cost of prosecuting actions by members for damages for personal injuries suffered in the course of work (£29,000 and £37,000), (b) the cost of inquiries and arbitrations of general concern to the union (£14 and £760) and (c) the cost of the union's legal department (£18,700 and £19,000). By r. 12† of the Rules of the N.U.R. sums
D   paid under head (a) were to be paid out of the union's general fund, and by para. (5) of that rule the costs of all legal proceedings in which the N.U.R. were concerned were to come out of their general fund. On application by the N.U.R. for mandamus to compel allowance of their claim to exemption from income tax,

E   **Held**: the tax exemption conferred by s. 440 (2) of the Income Tax Act, 1952, which should be construed in the light of the Trade Union (Provident Funds) Act, 1893, from which it was derived, was conferred on income from special funds into which money applicable for provident benefits had been paid, and money paid into a general fund did not become applicable (for the purposes of s. 440 (2)) for paying such benefits until it had been transferred to a special fund; accordingly, as payments by way of legal assistance were
F   payable, by virtue of r. 12, out of the N.U.R.'s general fund, sums so paid were not within the exemption conferred by s. 440 (2) (see p. 764, letter H, and p. 765, letter E, post).

Quaere whether payments under heads (b) and (c) above could possibly be provident benefits (see p. 765, letter D, post).

G   [As to trade unions and income tax exemption, see 20 HALSBURY'S LAWS (3rd Edn.) 389, 390, para. 709; 595, para. 1166 (5), note (*m*).

For the Income Tax Act, 1952, s. 440, see 31 HALSBURY'S STATUTES (2nd Edn.) 420.]

Cases referred to:
   Dilworth v. *Stamps Comrs.*, *Dilworth* v. *Land and Income Tax Comrs.*, [1899]
H   A.C. 99; 79 L.T. 473; sub nom. *Dilworth* v. *New Zealand Stamp Comrs.*, 68 L.J.P.C. 1; 19 Digest (Repl.) 659, *348.*
   Gilbert v. *Gilbert and Boucher*, [1928] P. 1; 96 L.J.P. 137; 137 L.T. 619; 27 Digest (Repl.) 641, *6040.*
   Grey v. *Inland Revenue Comrs.*, [1959] 3 All E.R. 603; [1960] A.C. 1; [1959] 3 W.L.R. 759; 39 Digest (Repl.) 333, *723.*

I   **Motion for mandamus.**

This was an application by way of motion by the National Union of Railwaymen (the " N.U.R.") for an order of mandamus " that the Commissioners for the Special Purposes of the Income Tax Acts should allow the claim preferred by the applicants in respect of the years of assessment 1959-60 and 1960-61 for exemption from and repayment of income tax in respect of the sum of

---

* Section 440 (2) is set out at p. 760, letters E and F, post.
† Rule 12, so far as material, is set out at p. 761, letters B to E, post.

£48,095 13s. 2d. expended by the N.U.R. in the year 1959-60, and the sum of A
£57,397 17s. 4d. expended by the N.U.R. in the year 1960-61 as legal assistance
benefits out of taxed interest and dividends received by the N.U.R." The facts
are set out in the judgment of LORD PARKER, C.J.

The cases noted below* were cited during the argument in addition to those
referred to in the judgment of LORD PARKER, C.J.

R. E. *Borneman*, Q.C., and P. W. I. *Rees* for the applicants, the N.U.R.   B

B. L. *Bathurst*, Q.C., and J. R. *Phillips* for the Crown.

LORD PARKER, C.J.: In these proceedings counsel moves on behalf of
the applicants, the National Union of Railwaymen, for an order of mandamus
directed to the Commissioners for the Special Purposes of the Income Tax Acts,
to compel them to allow the claim made by the applicants for the exemption from C
income tax and repayment of the amount paid during two years, 1959-60 and
1960-61, in the form of " legal assistance "—a general phrase which I shall
explain in a moment—which it is said amounts to provident benefits within
s. 440 (2) of the Income Tax Act, 1952. Before dealing with the facts, it is convenient to refer to that subsection. It appears in s. 440, which is dealing with
exemptions, not only for certain trade unions, but for certain friendly societies, D
and the whole section comes within Part 21 dealing with special provisions as to
savings banks, industrial and provident societies, friendly societies and trade
unions and building societies. The subsection provides as follows:

" A registered trade union which is precluded, by Act of Parliament or by
its rules, from assuring to any person a sum exceeding £500 by way of gross
sum or £104 a year by way of annuity, shall be entitled to exemption from E
tax under Sch. C and Sch. D in respect of its interest and dividends which are
applicable and applied solely for the purpose of provident benefits."

The subsection then goes on to add an interpretation clause in these terms:

" In this subsection, ' provident benefits ' includes any payment, expressly
authorised by the registered rules of the trade union, which is made to a F
member during sickness or incapacity from personal injury or while out of
work, or to an aged member by way of superannuation, or to a member who
has met with an accident, or has lost his tools by fire or theft, and includes a
payment in discharge or aid of funeral expenses on the death of a member or
the wife of a member or as provision for the children of a deceased member."

Before leaving the statute, it is convenient to refer to s. 441 which shows the G
procedure for making claims before the Special Commissioners. Subsection (1)
provides that:

" Any claim under the two last preceding sections shall be made to the
Special Commissioners in writing in such form as may be prescribed by the
Commissioners of Inland Revenue, and the Special Commissioners, on proof
of the facts to their satisfaction, shall allow the claim accordingly."   H

Subsection (2) provides that the claim shall be verified by affidavit, and sub-s. (3)

" Where the Special Commissioners allow a claim, they shall issue an order
for repayment."

In passing, it is to be observed that no provision is made for oral argument or oral
hearing or indeed specifically for contentions to be made by the Crown against I
the claim put forward. The matter is dealt with only on an affidavit of facts.

Now the applicants are an old trade union, registered on Mar. 29, 1913, and
r. 1, para. 4, line 29 of the printed rules includes as one of the objects

" to provide legal or other assistance when necessary in matters pertaining

---

* *R.* v. *Hermann*, (1879), 4 Q.B.D. 284; *Bradlaugh* v. *Clark*, (1883), 8 App. Cas. 354;
Mellows v. *Low*, [1923] All E.R. Rep. 537; [1923] 1 K.B. 522; *Barentz* v. *Whiting*,
[1965] 1 All E.R. 685.

A   to the employment of members, or for securing damages or compensation for
members who suffer injury by accidents in their employment, or when
travelling to or from work; also to use every effort to provide for the safety
of its members whilst at work and of the travelling public."

Rule 12 provides for the grant of legal assistance in these terms—and I am reading
para. 1:

B

" Should any member who has been a member six calendar months and
paid twenty-six weeks' contributions be prosecuted or taken into custody
for an offence or offences alleged to have been committed by him in the
execution of his duty, or be unjustly dismissed from his employment with or
without forfeiture of wages, or be in any manner illegally dealt with by his

C   employers or their agents in connexion with the carrying out of his duties,
or have withheld from him by his employers any moneys to which he is
entitled, or if in any way it is necessary for his protection or for the obtaining
of any just claim from his employers, or for the establishment or defence of
his reputation and character in matters connected with his employment, or
for [and these are the important words] obtaining damages or compensation

D   for personal injuries sustained by him, legal proceedings may be instituted
on such member's behalf."

By para. 5 it is provided that:

" The cost of all legal proceedings authorised by or on behalf of the union,
or in which the union is concerned, and whether under this rule or otherwise,
shall be paid from the general fund."

E   It is quite clear therefore that payments by way of legal assistance are expressly
authorised by the registered rules of the trade union.

The claim in the present case in regard to legal assistance comes under three
heads. The first, which I will call head A, is dealing with the institution and
prosecution of legal processes directed towards obtaining damages and compensation for personal injuries sustained by a member of the union in the course of his

F   work. The payments made by the union under that head for the years 1959-60
and 1960-61 were respectively some £29,000 and some £37,000. In addition, the
applicants' claim for relief was based on a second head, head B, which was in
these terms, amounts paid in connexion with enquiries, arbitrations and other
proceedings in respect of matters of general concern to the union and its members,
that is wage rates, conditions of work and redundancy, and the amounts paid

G   under head B in those two years were respectively £14 and some £760.   In
addition, the claim is made up of another head, head C, which is in these terms,
costs of the legal department of the union, and the details of that are made up of
the costs of the staff salaries and superannuation payments of that legal department and an apportionment of rates and taxes, and an apportionment of the cost
of office furnishing, repairs, etc., and the figures claimed in regard to those years

H   were respectively some £18,700 and some £19,000. The total claims under heads
A, B and C, for the two years in question, amounted to £48,095 and £57,397. It is
the amounts paid under those three heads which are treated as coming under the
term " legal assistance ", and it is in respect of the total of those sums that the
applicants claim they are entitled to relief under the subsection.

In due course a claim was put in under s. 441 of the Act of 1952, and in a

I   reasoned decision dated Dec. 1, 1964, the Special Commissioners refused the
claim. After referring to the claims put in and to the statute, the Special
Commissioners say this:

" We are primarily concerned with the content of the word ' includes '
in the first place where it appears. In our opinion, the word ' includes ' in
this context can only bear one or other of the following meanings:—(*a*) it
may be intended to enlarge the natural meaning of the expression ' provident benefits ' in order to comprehend things which otherwise would be left

out. This, we think, is the sense in which the word is most commonly used   A
in interpretation clauses. (b) It may be intended as definitive, i.e., as
indicating that the expression includes, and includes only, the things
mentioned. In our opinion it is clear from *Dilworth* v. *Stamps Comrs., Dilworth* v. *Income Tax Comrs.* (1) that the word, in a given context, is capable
of bearing this meaning. (c) It might be intended as exemplary, i.e., as
indicating the sort of things the expression includes, the list of things set   B
out being not intended as exhaustive. We have been unable to call to mind
any example in the statutes where the word is used in this sense in an interpretation clause, but we do not think we should exclude from our minds the
possibility of this construction. In our opinion the word is here used in a
definitive sense, and the interpretation clause provides a definition of
' provident benefits '; the legal assistance benefits which are the subject of   C
the present claim are not within that definition. We do not leave the matter
there, however, because in case we should be wrong in that we think that the
present claim would not succeed even if we were to adopt either of the other
two possible constructions indicated in (a) and (c) above. If we were to adopt
the construction indicated in (a) above, we would have to regard the natural
meaning of the expression ' provident benefits ' as requiring enlargement in   D
order to include the payments to members which are described. If its natural
meaning is not sufficiently comprehensive to include, for example, a payment
made to a member under the rules during sickness, it cannot be sufficiently
comprehensive to include the legal assistance benefits in issue, and it is not
expressly enlarged so as to include them."

Finally, they say: E

" Assuming the payments described to be a non-exhaustive list provided
as examples, there would be room for including any payments analogous to
them. Legal assistance benefits do not seem to us to be analogous to any
particular one, i.e., in the sense that loss of tools in a flood disaster might be
analogous to loss by fire or theft. Nor do we think it analogous to the   F
conception indicated by the totality. The common thread running through
them all is that they are all authorised payments, the first or main category
being all payments to members, and the second or subsidiary category being
payments consequent on the death of a member or his wife; to our minds the
legal assistance benefits are not sufficiently analogous to either category. For
the above reasons our decision is that the claim fails."   G

In this court, counsel for the applicants urges that that decision was wrong. His
submissions can be summarised very shortly in the form that the moneys
expended by way of legal assistance are applied, to take the words of the Act of
1952, " for the purpose of provident benefits ", and secondly, that the interpretation clause does not provide an exhaustive definition. The word " includes " in
its context is designed merely to give examples but does not exhaust them. In my   H
judgment, the Special Commissioners came to the correct conclusion, though, as
I will explain in a moment, I am not deciding the case on the same grounds as
those on which they decided it.

It seems to me that the first question here, and on one view the determining
question, is as to the meaning of the phrase " provident benefits ", before one
ever gets to the interpretation clause, and has to decide whether it is enlarging,
whether it is definitive or whether it is exemplary. If, as counsel for the applicants   I
contends, the words in their natural meaning are wide enough to cover the payment of legal assistance, there is much to be said, as I will indicate in a moment,
for construing the interpretation clause as giving examples of the benefits
envisaged. If, on the other hand, the words are not wide enough, taken by
themselves, in their context, to cover payments by way of legal assistance, then

(1) [1899] A.C. 99.

A even if the words in the interpretation clause are read as enlarging, he cannot succeed because the words that follow do not embrace legal assistance. The first limb of counsel's argument is to the effect, as I have already said, that those words " provident benefits " are wide enough in their natural and ordinary meaning to comprise these payments by way of legal assistance. He refers, and I think that it is right to refer, to the dictionary meaning of " provident ". In

B the SHORTER OXFORD DICTIONARY the meanings are " foreseeing ", " that has foresight of ", and " provides for the future or for some future event " and there follows underneath, " provident society, equals friendly society ". That is merely an example. Accordingly, at any rate so far as the first head, head A, is concerned, counsel for the applicants says that such payments made to support an action to recover damages for personal injury suffered by a member can

C properly be said to be providing for that member's future and are, therefore, according to its ordinary meaning, provident benefits. He recognises that it is more difficult to bring heads B and C within that phrase, but he would do so by taking a broad view and saying that they can properly be said to be all " for the purpose of " legal assistance and are, therefore, themselves provident benefits, provided of course payments by way of legal assistance are provident benefits.

D However, in this court we are not concerned with analysing the different heads. We are faced with the broad question whether the total of heads A, B and C, treated generally as payments by way of legal assistance, come within the term " provident benefits ". In my judgment there are grave practical difficulties in the way of counsel for the applicants' contentions. If he is right, as it seems to me, it will mean that in every case payments made to support an action will have to be

E analysed and it will have to be seen whether they were hopeless actions or not, because I see very great difficulty in seeing how costs paid out to the successful defendant as a result of a hopeless action could on any view be said to be sums paid for providing for that man's future. Quite apart, however, from the practical difficulties which would ensue, it seems to me that the real answer is that there is no natural and ordinary meaning which can be given to that phrase " provident

F benefits ". It is a phrase which has to be construed, as I think both counsel agreed, in the context of the Act of 1952, and in those circumstances and, particularly because the Act of 1952 is a consolidating Act, it seems to me that one is fully justified and indeed bound to go back to the earlier legislation. Now sub-s. (2) of s. 440 in the Act of 1952 is itself lifted verbatim from s. 39 of the Income Tax Act, 1918, an Act which was itself a consolidating Act. Section 39 itself found its

G origin in the Trade Union (Provident Funds) Act, 1893, an Act which was—I think I am right—repealed by the Income Tax Act of 1918. The short title of that Act, as I have already said, is the Trade Union (Provident Funds) Act, 1893. The long title is

> " An Act to exempt from income tax the invested funds of trade unions applied in payment of provident benefits."

H Section 1 provided that:

> " A trade union duly registered under the Trade Union Acts, 1871 and 1876, shall be entitled to exemption from income tax chargeable under Sch. A, Sch. C and Sch. D, of any Acts for granting duties of income tax in respect of the interest and dividends of the trade union applicable and applied

I solely for the purpose of provident benefits. Provided always that the exemption shall not extend to any trade union by the rules of which the amount assured to any member, or person nominated by or claiming under him, shall exceed the total sum of £200, or the amount of any gratuity granted to any member, or person nominated by him, shall exceed the sum of £30 per annum."

Section 3 provided an interpretation clause in these terms:

> " In this Act the expression ' provident benefits ' means and includes any

payment made to a member during sickness or incapacity from personal   A
injury, or while out of work; or to an aged member by way of superannuation,
or to a member who has met with an accident or has lost his tools by fire or
theft, or a payment in discharge or aid of funeral expenses on the death of a
member or the wife of a member, or as provision for the children of the
deceased member, where the payment in respect whereof exemption is claimed
is a payment expressly authorised by the registered rules of the trade union   B
claiming the exemption."

It will be seen immediately that sub-s. (2) of s. 440 of the Act of 1952 reflects and
indeed repeats, subject to slight reconstruction of the layout, the words of the
Act of 1893, the only real exceptions being an alteration in the sums assured to a
person by way of lump sum or annuity which would exclude the trade union
from payment of tax and the fact that instead of " includes " which appears in   C
the interpretation clause in the Act of 1952, the words in the Act of 1893 were
" means and includes ".

Now looking at that Act, it does seem to me that " provident benefits "
there means moneys paid out of the income and dividends of special funds into
which money is paid which is applicable to provident benefits. No doubt in the   D
majority of cases those funds will be contributory funds, but in my judgment in
order to constitute provident benefits it is not necessary that the fund from which
they are paid should be a contributory fund. It seems to me that the words used
in the Act of 1893, not merely its short title, and the fact that the proviso to
s. 1 speaks about rules which assure to any member a sum, show that what is
being considered is not a general fund, but an investment fund, the income and   E
dividends of which are applicable and set aside for the purpose. Accordingly, one
would in those circumstances expect in the absence of clear change of language
that they should bear the same meaning in the Act of 1952. On this point—
because this is a point which comes for consideration prior to the consideration
of the meaning of the word " includes "—the Act of 1952 repeats those very
words on which, as I think, reliance can be placed. Subsection (2) begins by   F
referring to the trade union that can claim the relief as a trade union which is
precluded by its rules from assuring to any person a sum—the same words as in
the Act of 1893—and it goes on to provide in respect of its interest and dividends
which are applicable, again conveying, as it seems to me, exactly the same
meaning as in the Act of 1893. Counsel for the applicants has dealt with the
possible argument based on the word " applicable " by referring to the rules which   G
show clearly in r. 8, by para. 28, that any deficiency in a special fund—what I
may call a provident fund—can be made up from the general fund, and accordingly he would say that it is perfectly apt to speak of the general fund itself as
being applicable for the purpose of paying provident benefit. In my judgment,
that argument fails. It seems to me that on a proper view any money in the
general fund never becomes applicable for the purpose of paying benefits out of   H
provident and special funds until the money is transferred and is in, by the direction of the executive committee, the special fund in question. Now if the position
is right so far, it is quite clear that under s. 12 any sums by way of assistance do
not come out of a special fund, they come out of a general fund. It is also clear,
if one looks at the rules, that there is a number of special funds, true provident
funds, set up under the rules of the trade union. In particular, they are to be   I
found in r. 14, r. 15, r. 16 and r. 17. Moreover, I see this difficulty, that if it can be
said that payments made by way of legal assistance are truly provident benefits,
then when one looks at r. 12, which is the only rule expressly authorising payment
for that purpose, the union is not there precluded from the union assuring to any
person a sum exceeding £500 by way of gross sum or £104 a year by way of
annuity.

That being the position as I see it, it is unnecessary to go on to consider counsel
for the applicants' further argument as to the meaning of the word " includes ".

A Were it necessary to do so, it would, as I see it, involve a very difficult question, having regard to the change in words between 1893 and 1952. Counsel has a forceful argument on the fact that almost certainly, as I see it, " means and includes " is purely definitive, and here one gets a deliberate change of language to a form of language which in its natural meaning at any rate is not definitive. It is true that Lord Watson in *Dilworth's* case (2), referred to by the Special

B Commissioners, envisaged that there might be cases where notwithstanding the word " includes " the words that follow were definitive and purely definitive, but if there is such a case it is but very rare, and one would find it difficult to believe that any draftsman deleting the words " means and " would rely on that very rare interpretation. Based on that argument, counsel for the applicants would then seek to get round the presumption that a consolidating Act is not changing the

C law and he would invoke what Scrutton, L.J., said in *Gilbert* v. *Gilbert and Boucher* (3), a dictum which was affirmed by Viscount Simmonds and Lord Radcliffe specifically in the case of *Grey* v. *Inland Revenue Comrs.* (4). As I have said, however, I find it unnecessary to attempt to resolve those difficulties. Finally, I would add only that, had I felt able to accede to counsel for the applicants' argument, I would have felt constrained to take some steps by way of

D referring the matter back to the Special Commissioners in order that they should analyse in more detail the payments made under the various heads, and to consider in particular whether head C could possibly be said to be provident benefits, and, I think, also head B. Again I find it unnecessary to deal further with that matter.

In the result, I think the Special Commissioners came to the correct conclusion
E and I would dismiss this application.

MARSHALL, J.: For the same reasons, I agree.

JAMES, J.: I agree also.

Application refused.

F Solicitors: *Pattinson & Brewer* (for the applicants); *Solicitor of Inland Revenue.*

[*Reported by* N. P. Metcalfe, Esq., *Barrister-at-Law.*]

G

H ———

I

---

(2) [1899] A.C. at pp. 105, 106. (3) [1928] P. 1 at pp. 8, 9.
  (4) [1959] 3 All E.R. 603 at pp. 606, 608; [1960] A.C. 1 at pp. 13, 17.

PEATE v. COMMISSIONER OF TAXATION OF THE

A

COMMONWEALTH OF AUSTRALIA.

[PRIVY COUNCIL (Viscount Dilhorne, Lord Morris of Borth-y-Gest, Lord Pearce, Lord Donovan and Lord Pearson), January 24, 26, 27, May 17, 1966.]

Privy Council—Australia—Income Tax—Avoidance—Contract, agreement or arrangement having the purpose and effect of avoiding liability—Partnership   B
of medical practitioners dissolved—Formation of group company and sub-sidiary family companies—Agreement to serve family company as medical practitioner at a salary—Agreement to serve group company—Validity of assessment—Income Tax and Social Services Contribution Assessment Act, 1936-1960, s. 6, s. 260.

Since a date in 1954, the appellant, a qualified medical practitioner of New   C
South Wales, practised in partnership with other doctors. In 1956 he was entitled to fourteen per cent. of the partnership profits after deduction of certain expenses. On June 29, 1956, the partners formed a company, W., Ltd. and on Aug. 18, 1956, each partner was appointed a director. The partnership, which then included eight doctors, was dissolved on Aug. 31, 1956 and on that same day eight companies were formed, one in respect of   D
each of the former partners, each of whom subsequently became the governing director of his company. The shares of the appellant's company, R., Ltd. were allotted to trustees for his infant children. One of the objects of R., Ltd. was to carry on the business of providers of medical services. On Sept. 1, 1956, the appellant sold his practice, plant and equipment, to R., Ltd. and entered into a service agreement to serve R., Ltd. as medical practitioner at a   E
salary. R., Ltd. also paid the appellant's wife a salary for secretarial services. On the same day an agreement was made between the appellant, R., Ltd. and W., Ltd., that R., Ltd. would for a fee arrange for the appellant to serve W., Ltd. as a medical practitioner and that the fee would be fourteen per cent. of the balance of the gross income of W., Ltd. after deduction of certain expenses. Similar agreements were made between the other former partners,   F
their respective family companies and W., Ltd. The fees paid by W., Ltd. to the family companies for the services of each doctor were the same percentage of the profits that each doctor had received from the partnership and the shares in W., Ltd. were allotted to each family company in similar proportion. In 1959, one of the eight doctors withdrew from the scheme. In consequence the percentage of gross income of W., Ltd. payable to   G
R., Ltd. increased. There was a further increase in 1960. The appellant in his return of income in 1958 stated that his only professional income was the salary of £1,560 paid to him by R., Ltd. The respondent assessed his taxable income for that year at £4,298. Similar returns were made by the appellant for the years 1959 and 1960 and the respondent made similar assessments for those years. These assessments were made on the basis that the contracts   H
etc. had been rendered void as against the respondent by s. 260* of the Income Tax and Social Services Contribution Assessment Act, 1936-1960, and that the appellant had derived as income from the practice a share of the gross fees returned to tax as income by W., Ltd., less certain expenses incurred by W., Ltd. On appeal from a decision upholding this basis of assessment, subject to certain adjustments.

Held (LORD DONOVAN dissenting, except as to (i) and (ii) (a) below): the   I
assessment was rightly upheld for the following reasons—

(i) the contracts, agreements and arrangements made in 1956 had the purpose and effect of avoiding a liability otherwise imposed on each doctor by the Income Tax and Social Services Contribution Assessment Act, 1936-1960; accordingly they were rendered void as against the respondent by s. 260 of that Act (see p. 770, letter A, post).

---

* Section 260 is printed at p. 769, letter G, post.

A   (ii) (a) as a consequence of (i) the respondent was entitled to assess the appellant on the income that he would have received in each of the three years if the contracts, agreements and arrangements made in 1956 had not been made (see p. 770, letter G, post); (b) accordingly the respondent was entitled to treat the former partnership as continuing, until it would have been dissolved in 1959 by operation of law on the withdrawal of one partner

B   (see p. 771, letter A, post).

(iii) thereafter an association of persons in receipt of income jointly would have been in existence on the footing (required by s. 260) that the formation and existence of W., Ltd. be disregarded, and (in view of s. 6 of the Act of 1936-1960) the respondent was entitled to treat the income of W., Ltd. as the income of a partnership, being the association of persons; accordingly

C   the respondent was entitled to treat as income of the appellant the proportion paid in fact to R., Ltd. from time to time, as this proportion must be regarded as paid with the consent of the association of persons (see p. 771, letters C and D, post).

(iv) in so far as patients did contract to pay W., Ltd. for the treatment that they received, the sums received by W., Ltd. were, if W., Ltd. was

D   disregarded, part of the income of the doctors, no notional substitution of contracts being involved in reaching this conclusion (see p. 771, letter G, post).

Appeal dismissed.

[**Editorial Note.** The enactment under consideration in the present case lacks the power to make adjustment to counteract the tax advantages otherwise

E   gained which is to be found in the comparable English enactment, see p. 770, letter F, post.

As to provisions in United Kingdom legislation to counter tax avoidance, see SUPPLEMENT to 20 HALSBURY'S LAWS (3rd Edn.) para. 276A.

For s. 28 of the Finance Act, 1960, see 40 HALSBURY'S STATUTES (2nd Edn.)

F   447-451.]

Appeal.

This was an appeal by special leave from a judgment and order of the Full Court of the High Court of Australia (MCTIERNAN, KITTO, TAYLOR, WINDEYER and OWEN, JJ.), dated Aug. 12, 1964 dismissing the appeal of the appellant, Desmond Lees Peate, from a judgment and order of MENZIES, J., dated Dec. 3,

G   1962, whereby the appellant's appeal against the respondent's disallowance of his objection in respect of an assessment to income tax and social services contribution by reason of the application of s. 260 of the Income Tax and Social Services Contribution Assessment Act, 1936-1960, in respect of income for the years ending June 30, 1958, June 30, 1959 and June 30, 1960 respectively, was dismissed. The relevant facts are set out in the opinion of VISCOUNT DILHORNE.

H   *Hermann Jenkins, Q.C.,* and *R. B. Murphy* (both of the New South Wales Bar) for the appellant.

M. H. Byes, Q.C., and *J. R. Gilson* (both of the New South Wales Bar) for the respondent.

VISCOUNT DILHORNE delivered the following majority opinion: The

I   appellant, Dr. Peate, was for a time employed by a number of doctors in partnership at Cessnock in New South Wales. He received a salary and any fees he earned through the practice of his profession were handed over to the partnership. In 1954 he became a partner and in 1956 he was entitled to fourteen per cent. of the profits of the partnership after the deduction of expenses.

On June 29, 1956, a company called Westbank, Ltd. (" Westbank ") was formed and on Aug. 18, 1956, the eight doctors who were then in partnership were appointed directors of the company. Two days later the appellant was appointed chairman. One of the objects of the company was to carry on

"the business of chemists, druggists and providers of medicinal [sic]   A
surgical and hospital facilities of all kinds whether alone or in conjunction
with any other person, firm or corporation."

On Aug. 28 it was agreed that the partnership should be dissolved and on Aug. 31,
1956, it was dissolved.   The same day eight companies were formed, each of
which was conveniently described by MENZIES, J., as the "family" company
of one of the eight doctors.   The "family" company of the appellant was called   B
Raleigh, Ltd. ("Raleigh").   Two solicitors who were members of the firm
advising the doctors were the original directors.   One of the objects of this
company was "to carry on the business of . . . providers of medical surgical and
hospital services and facilities of all kinds ". The next day, Sept. 1, this company
purchased the appellant's practice, his library, plant, motor cars, etc. for a sum
which was eventually fixed at £9,542 and entered into a service agreement with   C
him.

By this agreement the appellant agreed to serve the company "as medical
practitioner in the business carried on by the company" at a salary.   He
covenanted that he would act as agent for the company or its nominee to ensure
that any person whom he treated, contracted with the company or its nominee
that payment for the treatment "is due to the company or its nominee directly   D
and even although the account for such services may be rendered by the company
or its nominee in the name of the doctor ". He also by his agreement authorised
the company or its nominee to render in his name accounts for all treatment
given by him and he undertook when required by the board of directors to serve
any company carrying on a similar business to the company as a medical practitioner.   Each of the other seven doctors who had been members of the   E
partnership entered into a similar agreement with his "family" company.

At a second meeting of the directors of Raleigh on Sept. 1, 1956, the appellant
and his wife were appointed directors in place of the original directors.   The same
day Westbank entered into separate agreements with each of the "family"
companies and each of the eight doctors.   By the agreement with Raleigh and   F
the appellant it was agreed that Raleigh would for a fee arrange for the appellant
to serve Westbank as a medical practitioner and that the fee would be fourteen
per cent. of the balance of the gross income of Westbank after deduction of the
expenses of that company including the salaries of doctors who were not directors
of the company but employed by it.

The other agreements with the "family" companies and the other former   G
partners were of a similar character.   In 1959 consequent on the withdrawal of
one of the eight doctors, his "family" company received only 4.235 per cent.
instead of 12.5 per cent. of the profits of Westbank with the result that Raleigh's
share was increased to 14.993 per cent.   In 1960 in consequence of other changes
it was increased to 15.815 per cent.   Not only were the fees paid for the services
of each doctor by Westbank to each "family" company the same percentage   H
of the profits that each doctor in the partnership had been receiving, but also
the shares in Westbank were allotted to each of the "family" companies in
similar proportion.   Raleigh held twenty-eight out of the two hundred shares.

As these arrangements meant that all the net profits of Westbank would be
distributed to the "family" companies in service fees and that no dividends
would be paid by that company, it was later agreed that Westbank should each   I
year keep £5,000 for the payment of taxes and dividends and that the service
fees would be paid out of the balance remaining after the deduction of this sum
and the expenses of the company.   The shares in Raleigh were held by the trustees
of settlements for the children of the appellant and his wife.

The result of this somewhat complicated series of transactions can be summed
up as follows: Westbank replaced the partnership.   The doctors who had been
partners became directors of that company.   The fees earned as a result of their
carrying on the practice of medicine were to be paid into that company's account

A instead of into the partnership account; and after deduction of expenses, including the cost of employment of the other doctors and the £5,000 referred to, were to be paid to each of the " family " companies as service fees. Each " family " company would get the same percentage of the net income less £5,000 of Westbank as each doctor got of the profits of the partnership. Each " family " company would get the same percentage share of any dividends declared by
B Westbank out of the £5,000 retained; and each of the eight doctors would get a salary from his family company.

Raleigh in addition to paying the appellant his salary under the agreement between the company and him, also paid his wife a salary of £1,200 later increased to £1,300 per annum for her services as secretary of the company. Dividends declared by Raleigh went to the trustees of the two settlements for the benefit
C of their children.

The appellant stated in evidence that there were a number of reasons for the replacement of the partnership by Westbank and the creation of the " family " companies. He said that he knew that there were certain tax benefits which could be gained. In 1958 in his return of income the appellant stated that his only professional income was the salary of £1,560 paid to him by Raleigh. This
D was not accepted by the respondent who assessed his taxable income for this year at £4,298. This sum was arrived at in the following way. The net income of Westbank in that year as returned by that company was £5,013. To that the respondent added the service fees paid by the company of £41,574 and superannuation payments of £1,200, making a total of £47,787. He then treated fourteen per cent. of this sum, namely £6,690 as the appellant's income and
E treated some of the expenses claimed as deductions by Westbank and Raleigh as allowable deductions from the appellant's income. He disregarded the salary paid to the appellant by Raleigh entirely. Similar returns were made by the appellant for the years 1959 and 1960 and similar assessments by the respondent for those years. In 1959 his taxable income was assessed at £3,243 and he had returned his income as £1,399 and in 1960 he was assessed at £3,574 when his
F income as returned was £1,731.

In justification of his assessments, the respondent relied on s. 260 of the Income Tax and Social Services Contribution Assessment Act, 1936-1960 which, so far as material, reads as follows:

" Every contract, agreement or arrangement made or entered into, orally or in writing, . . . shall, so far as it has or purports to have the purpose or
G effect of in any way, directly or indirectly

(a) altering the incidence of any income tax

(b) relieving any person from liability to pay any income tax or make any return

(c) defeating evading or avoiding any duty or liability imposed on any person by this Act: or
H (d) preventing the operation of this Act in any respect

be absolutely void as against the [respondent] or in regard to any proceeding under this Act, but without prejudice to such validity as it may have in any other respect or for any other purpose."

The first question therefore to be determined is whether the contracts, agreements
I and arrangements made in 1956 or any part of them had one of the purposes or effects stated in this section.

In the opinion of their lordships the answer is in the affirmative. Before these arrangements were made in 1956 the appellant received fourteen per cent. of the net profits of the partnership and was assessed accordingly. After they were made, the doctors who had been partners treated patients in the same way as they had before but as a result of these arrangements, their incomes from the practice of their profession were reduced to the salaries received from the " family " companies, which received either by way of service fees or dividends

the same percentage of the net profits of Westbank as the doctors had been A
entitled to under the partnership agreement. In their lordships' opinion these
arrangements have the purpose and effect of avoiding a liability imposed on
each doctor by the Income Tax and Social Services Contribution Assessment
Act, 1936-1960. It follows from this conclusion that the respondent was right
to treat as void as against him or in regard to any proceedings under the Act the
whole or any part of any contract, agreement or arrangement which directly or B
indirectly had this effect.

Section 166 of the Act places on the respondent the duty of assessing the
taxable income of the taxpayer. Section 17 provides that income tax shall be
levied on the taxable income derived during the financial year by the taxpayer
and s. 19 provides that the income shall be deemed to have been derived by a
person although it is not actually paid over to him but is reinvested, accumulated, C
capitalised, carried to any reserve, sinking fund or insurance fund however
designated or otherwise dealt with on his behalf or as he directs.

What then was the taxable income of the appellant in each of the three years
in question? The arrangements made in 1956 divested him of income which he
would have received if they had not been made. Tax was avoided on the difference
between the salary that he and his wife as directors of Raleigh agreed that he D
should receive and the amount received each year by Raleigh, from Westbank,
in service fees and dividends. Now, as KITTO, J., said in the course of his judgment in this case, s. 260 " operates only to destroy: it supplies nothing ". It
only operates notionally to destroy, for the validity of the transactions is only
affected so far as the respondent and proceedings under the Act are concerned.
He cannot treat some of the arrangements which come within s. 260 as void and E
others not. He is given no option.

The difficulty in this case lies in determining the taxable income derived by
the appellant or deemed by virtue of s. 19 to have been derived by him with such
of the contracts, agreements and arrangements as come within s. 260 being
treated as void. If the Act provided that the respondent had power to make an
assessment to counteract the tax advantage sought to be obtained by the arrange- F
ments coming within s. 260 this difficulty would not arise. Such a provision is
contained in s. 28 (3) of the Finance Act, 1960 of the United Kingdom.

Section 260 has to be construed with s. 17 and s. 19. It can only have practical
effect in preventing tax avoidance if the respondent is entitled to make an assessment on the basis that the contracts, agreements and arrangements rendered void
by it, had never been made. This necessarily involves treating the taxpayer as G
having derived income in excess of that derived by him pursuant to the arrangements. In their lordships' opinion, reading these three sections together, the
respondent was entitled to assess the appellant on the income he would have
received in each of the three years if the arrangements coming within s. 260 had
not been made in 1956.

The agreement to dissolve the partnership, its dissolution, the formation of the H
two companies, Westbank and Raleigh, and the agreements between the appellant
and Raleigh and between the appellant, Raleigh and Westbank were all part of
the scheme and directly or indirectly had the purpose and effect of avoiding
liability to tax and so come within s. 260. The respondent was therefore entitled
to proceed on the basis that these arrangements had not been made. He was
therefore entitled to treat the partnership as continuing until, if in fact it had I
been in existence, it would have been dissolved by operation of law. Until then
he was entitled to treat the income in fact received by Westbank as if it had been
received by the partnership, and to treat as the appellant's share the same
percentage of the net income of that company as he was entitled to of the income
of the partnership; that is, the same percentage as that provided in the service
agreement between the appellant, Raleigh and Westbank.

In 1959 one of the doctors who had been partners withdrew. He ceased to be
a director of Westbank, and such fees as he earned ceased to be received by the

A company. If in fact the partnership had continued until his withdrawal, it would then have ceased by operation of law. The respondent cannot therefore treat the original partnership as existing after that date. To do so would be not to destroy but to supply.

Section 6 of the Act defines a partnership for the purposes of the Act as inter alia " an association of persons . . . in receipt of income jointly ". Disregarding,

B as the respondent was required by s. 260 to do, the formation and so the existence of Westbank, for its formation was part of the arrangement to avoid tax, there was after the withdrawal of this doctor an association of persons in receipt of income jointly; and so, for the purposes of the Act the respondent was entitled to treat the income received by Westbank as the income of a partnership. Following on this withdrawal, the proportion of the net income of Westbank paid to

C Raleigh was increased to 14.993 per cent. although the agreement between the appellant, Raleigh and Westbank only provided for payment of fourteen per cent. The doctors must have agreed to this increase and the respondent is entitled to treat the appellant's income during the period when Raleigh was paid 14.993 per cent. as that percentage of the net income of Westbank.

Further changes were made in 1960 as a result of which Raleigh's share increased

D to 15.815 per cent. After these changes and disregarding the existence of Westbank, there was still an association of persons in receipt of income jointly and similarly the respondent is entitled to treat the appellant's income as 15.815 per cent. of the net income of Westbank for the period during which that percentage was paid to Raleigh.

On behalf of the appellant it was argued that the contracts made by the

E patients with Westbank to pay Westbank for the treatment which they received from the doctors could not be regarded as replaced by contracts with the doctors either jointly or individually. That, it was argued rightly, would not be just to treat the original contracts as void but to substitute others in their place and s. 260 gives no power to do that.

Whether patients in fact contracted to any substantial extent with Westbank

F is open to doubt. TAYLOR, J., in his judgment in this case pointed out that

> " the evidence disclosed ' that all governmental and institutional fees were paid by cheques payable to the doctors concerned and that most of the private fees that were paid by cheque were paid by cheques in which the doctor and not the company (Westbank) was named as the payee ' and that
> where necessary the doctors endorsed cheques to enable them to be paid into
G > Westbank's bank account."

In these circumstances the bulk of the income earned found its way in the first instance into the hands of one or other of the doctors concerned. In so far as patients did in fact contract to pay Westbank for the treatment they received, treating the income of Westbank as that of the doctors does not in their lordships'

H opinion require any substitution of any contract for that made by the patient. The sums received by Westbank from such patients were, as were the fees earned by the doctors employed by Westbank at a salary, part of the income of the doctors who were, if the existence of Westbank is disregarded, in receipt of income jointly.

In their lordships' opinion the conclusion arrived at by the High Court of

I Australia and by MENZIES, J., was correct and for the reasons stated their lordships will humbly advise Her Majesty that the appeal should be dismissed.

The appellant must pay the costs of the appeal.

LORD DONOVAN: Immediately before Aug. 31, 1956, Dr. Peate, the appellant, was practising his profession as a doctor in New South Wales in partnership with seven other doctors. Their relations were governed by a partnership deed under which their respective shares in the capital and in the profits were defined. The appellant's share was fourteen per cent. On Aug. 31, 1956, this

partnership was by agreement dissolved. The dissolution was consequent on the A
decision of the partners to re-arrange their affairs so that, among other things, a
lighter burden of income tax would be attracted.

In broad outline the plan adopted achieved these results: (i) fees received from
patients no longer belonged to the doctors themselves but to a limited company;
(ii) the limited company after paying certain expenses made payments to its
shareholders; (iii) these shareholders were other limited companies—eight in all, B
one for each doctor; (iv) each of these eight companies used its receipts, partly
to pay a salary for his medical services to the doctor concerned, and partly to
make provision for his family; (v) each doctor then returned for income tax
purposes as professional earnings only his salary. This was considerably less
than his previous share of the partnership profits.

Naturally enough, this result was not welcome to the respondent, the Common- C
wealth Commissioner of Taxation. Nevertheless for the first fiscal year in which
it took effect, he accepted it. This was the year ended June 30, 1957. In that
year, from July 1, 1956, up to Aug. 31, 1956, the appellant had been a member
of the partnership. This having been dissolved on Aug. 31, 1956, he was, for
the rest of the year, a salaried employee of the company. He included in his tax
return for the year his share of partnership profits up to Aug. 31, and his salary D
thereafter. The income tax assessment was computed on the income so returned.

For the following fiscal year, i.e., the year ending June 30, 1958, the respondent
took a different view. He treated the appellant as still carrying on a medical
practice in partnership with his former colleagues and still entitled directly to a
share of the income so produced. The fact that this income had gone to a limited
company in pursuance of the new arrangements mattered not. In the deputy E
commissioner's words:

". . . it is considered that the gross income shown in the company's return
was, in fact and in law, derived by the partnership. Correspondingly, the
expenditure claimed in the company's returns . . . is considered to have been
incurred by the partnership and you through the agency of the companies."
                                                                          F
The basis for this view was that medical services had been personally rendered
to the patients by the appellant and his colleagues, and that the receipt of fees
by the company was simply an application of income after it had been earned by
the doctors. The view was buttressed by a reference to the New South Wales
Medical Practitioners Act, 1938 providing, inter alia, that only a registered
medical practitioner can treat certain diseases, and sue for fees. The limited G
companies were not registered medical practitioners and could not therefore
legally derive the income in question. For the following two fiscal years, namely
the year ending June 30, 1959, and June 30, 1960, the respondent repeated these
views and assessed the appellant in accordance with them.

The appellant having appealed against the foregoing three assessments, the
matter eventually came before the High Court of Australia in September, 1962, H
and was heard by MENZIES, J. Before him, the respondent, while apparently
maintaining the argument that what the patients paid was the doctors' income
supported the assessment on a new ground which he put in the forefront of his case.
This was that the assessments were justified by s. 260 of the Income Tax and
Social Services Contribution Assessment Act, 1936-1960. This claim was upheld
by MENZIES, J., and subsequently, on appeal, by the Full Court; and it is this I
claim on which your lordships have now to pronounce.

I do not find it surprising that a contention which so far has commanded universal
judicial assent was not put forward by the respondent when he made the assessments. Section 260 is limited in its scope, for while it operates to destroy a taxpayer's defences in certain cases, it authorises no new construction in their place.
In particular it does not deem some situation to exist which will support assessments to income tax designed to counter the avoidance. Those assessments must
still be based on facts, namely the facts remaining after s. 260 has done its work.

A This limitation of the section's scope may produce much difficulty in particular cases. In order to ascertain its precise effect in the present case, it is necessary now to describe in a little more detail how the appellant and his colleagues re-arranged their affairs.

The partnership had commenced on Oct. 1, 1954, and was regulated by a deed dated Nov. 30, 1954. Originally it consisted of nine doctors, one of whom retired B on July 1, 1956. In the new partnership which resulted from this retirement, and which consisted of the remaining eight doctors, the appellant's share in the capital, profits and losses was fourteen per cent.

As a result of discussion with their legal and their accountancy advisers, the partners caused the following steps to be taken: Westbank, Ltd. (whom I will call " Westbank ") was incorporated under the Companies Act of New South Wales C on June 29, 1956. One of its objects was to carry on the business of providing medicinal and surgical services. Its nominal capital was £25,000 divided into twenty-five thousand shares of £1 each. By September, 1956, two hundred of these shares had been issued, twenty-eight of them to a company called Raleigh, Ltd. (whom I will call " Raleigh "). The appellant and his seven partners were appointed the directors of Westbank.

D Raleigh was incorporated under the Companies Act of New South Wales on Aug. 31, 1956, as a proprietary company. One of its objects was to purchase the business of any person or partnership, and another was to carry on the business of providing medical services. Its nominal capital was £25,000 divided into twenty-five thousand shares of £1 each. These were divided into various classes. A number of " C " class shares were held in trust for the appellant's infant son E John: and a number of " D " class shares were held in trust for the appellant's infant daughter Carolyn. The appellant and his wife were directors of Raleigh and the appellant was the governing director. It was, in fact, his " family company ". On Aug. 31, 1956, the partnership between the eight doctors was dissolved.

On Sept. 1, 1956, Raleigh agreed to purchase the goodwill and assets of the F appellant's practice, for a price which was settled at £9,542, of which goodwill accounted for £7,500. On the same day the appellant agreed to serve Raleigh as a medical practitioner at a salary of £1,000 per annum, or such other sum as might be agreed from time to time. He further agreed to serve any other company carrying on a similar business to that of Raleigh, if the directors of Raleigh should so direct.

G On the same day another agreement was entered into between Westbank, Raleigh and the appellant. Under this agreement: (i) Raleigh arranged for the appellant to serve Westbank as a medical practitioner; (ii) In consideration, Westbank was to pay Raleigh fourteen per cent. of the net income of Westbank; (iii) The appellant agreed that all fees due from patients whom he treated were to be due to, and belong to, Westbank and authorised Westbank to render H accounts for such services in his name.

On Sept. 3, 1956 the appellant rented to Raleigh the surgery at 230, Main Street, Cessnock, New South Wales (which had apparently been one of the surgeries used by the recent partnership) with the right to sub-let the same. On the same day the appellant's wife was appointed secretary of Raleigh.

Each of the other doctors, the former partners of the appellant, made similar I arrangements. In particular, each had his own family company corresponding to Raleigh holding shares in Westbank, and each doctor agreed to serve his family company, or its nominee, as a medical practitioner in return for a salary. Each doctor was asked by his family company so to serve Westbank and each agreed.

The practice carried on by the partnership up to Aug. 31, 1956, was, pursuant to the foregoing arrangements, carried on thereafter as follows. The same surgeries were used, and the eight doctors rendered medical services there in the same manner as before. Notices were, however, exhibited at the appellant's surgery indicating that the doctors were the employees of Westbank to whom fees were

due. Most of the patients, however, perhaps not unnaturally, paid their accounts A
by cheques payable to the doctor personally. All fees were duly accounted for to
Westbank and Westbank paid all necessary outgoings, save some which were
paid by Raleigh.

The first fiscal year during which these arrangements were effective, i.e., the
year ending June 30, 1957, passed, as I have said, without challenge from the
respondent. For the next year, however, he raised the contention already B
indicated that the income remained that of the doctors and that Westbank paid
the expenses as their agent. So far as the appellant was concerned the respondent
worked out that on this basis his assessable income for the year ended June 30,
1958, was £4,298 as opposed to the £1,232 which the doctor had returned.

It is important, having regard to the present reliance of the respondent on
s. 260, which, so he says, requires him to pay no regard to the formation of C
Westbank and the various agreements which followed, to see exactly how the
respondent arrived at the figure of £4,298. He began with the profit and loss
account of Westbank for the year ended June 30, 1958. From that he discovered
that the gross fees paid or payable to Westbank in respect of the medical services
it had caused to be rendered through the medium of the doctors was £56,245 (I
ignore shillings and pence throughout). Westbank's total expenditure for the year D
was £51,245. The net profit was thus £5,000. The expenses of £51,245 included
service fees payable to Raleigh and the other family companies pursuant to the
agreements whereby these companies made the services of the doctors available
to Westbank. The total sum so paid to the family companies by Westbank in
this year was £41,574. In the case of Raleigh the fee so paid for the appellant's
services was £5,820, i.e., fourteen per cent. of £41,574. E

The respondent proceeded to re-calculate Westbank's income. In its return
that company had shown a taxable income of £5,013. The respondent added to
it the foregoing service fees totalling £41,574, plus a disbursement of £1,200 for
superannuation contributions which he regarded as an inadmissible deduction.
He thus arrived at a net income for Westbank of £47,787. He took fourteen per
cent. of this as the income of the appellant, the fourteen per cent. being the F
appellant's share of the profits of the previous partnership, dissolved in August,
1956. This gave a figure of £6,690.

From this figure the respondent then allowed certain deductions. The salary
of the appellant from Raleigh was, consistently with the respondent's contentions,
one of them. This amounted to £1,560. The expenditure incurred by Raleigh G
during the year, namely £4,767, was also allowed, less however the salary of
£1,560 and less certain other expenses deemed to be inadmissible in whole or in
part. The net amount of Raleigh's expenditure then allowed to the appellant was
£2,066. This, plus the salary of £1,560, now to be excluded from the appellant's
income, gives a total deduction of £3,626.

The appellant had returned as his taxable income the sum of £1,232. The H
respondent added to this the above sum of £6,690, plus a £2 subscription
regarded by him as an inadmissible deduction. This gave a total of £7,924. The
respondent then deducted the foregoing £3,626, leaving a net income for the
appellant on this basis of £4,298.

The calculation is perfectly intelligible on the hypothesis, for which the
respondent was contending at the time, that Westbank and Raleigh were simply I
the appellant's agents. The calculation remained unchanged when the prime
contention was altered on reliance on s. 260. How it squares with that contention,
which requires the respondent to proceed on the basis that Westbank and
Raleigh are to be disregarded, is one of the serious difficulties of the case. For
the succeeding two fiscal years the appellant's income was computed on similar
lines.

I now turn to s. 260. It appears in Pt. 8 of the Act, headed " Miscellaneous "
and so far as it is necessary to quote it in this case, it reads:

A " Every contract, agreement or arrangement made or entered into, orally or in writing, whether before or after the commencement of this Act, shall so far as it has or purports to have the purpose or effect of in any way, directly or indirectly,

(*a*) altering the incidence of any income tax;

(*b*) relieving any person from liability to pay any income tax . . .;

B (*c*) defeating, evading or avoiding any duty or liability imposed on any person by this Act; or

(*d*) . . .;

be absolutely void, as against the [respondent], or in regard to any proceeding under this Act, but without prejudice to such validity as it may have in any other respect, or for any other purpose."

C In regard to any proceeding under the Income Tax and Social Services Contribution Assessment Act, therefore, the section thus sweeps away contracts, agreements or arrangements of the kind described. The respondents must proceed as though they did not exist. Clearly, however, the section does not authorise the respondent to put something new and fictitious in their place. When KITTO, J., said in the present case that the section " operates only to destroy: it supplies D nothing " he was repeating in effect what has been said judicially many times.

There is no doubt, in my mind, that the conditions precedent prescribed in s. 260 exist in the appellant's case. The whole arrangement was designed to relieve him of some liability to tax, and it was, in fact successful in doing so in the first year of its existence. One need hardly consider therefore the remaining content of s. 260, though I should have thought it could also rightly be said that E the arrangement had the object of altering the incidence of income tax on what would ordinarily have been the doctor's professional earnings.

If then the purpose of each of the contracts, agreements or arrangements was to secure relief from income tax, they are wholly void as against the respondent, or in regard to any proceeding under the Act. The respondent in his Case submits F that this involves treating as void—(i) the separate corporate existence of Westbank; (ii) the agreement between the appellant and Raleigh; (iii) the agreement between Westbank, Raleigh and the appellant; and (iv) the agreements (if any) made between Westbank, the patients and the appellant, in so far as they provided that the fees should be the property of Westbank.

With this I agree. I would add, however, that it involves also disregarding G the existence of Raleigh, the formation of which was also part of the plan for tax avoidance. The liability of the appellant now depends on the facts left after the foregoing transactions are treated as void and are therefore disregarded.

What is so left as regards the appellant? The situation, in my opinion, is this: 1. He is found giving medical services to patients. 2. In return the patients pay him money. 3. He cannot, for present purposes, be treated as accountable to H Westbank for this money. Thus he is accountable to no one for it, and it may, again for present purposes, be treated as his own. 4. This money therefore represents the gross, or " assessable " income which he derives from treating patients; but the Act does not tax gross income but " taxable income " which means that all allowable deductions must be made. 5. The allowable deductions are defined by s. 51. They are " all losses and outgoings to the extent to which I they are incurred in gaining or producing the assessable income . . ." 6. The section does not in terms require that it must be the taxpayer himself who disburses the outgoings, though ordinarily, of course, this will be the fact. The deductions which have been allowed to the appellant in the present case were made by Westbank and Raleigh and the amounts have been extracted by the respondent from their accounts. How, one may ask, does this square with s. 260 which requires the respondent to ignore the existence of those companies? Once s. 260 is invoked he is not entitled to recognise these companies for some purposes and disregard them for others. In so far as the formation of these companies were part of the

arrangement which had the purpose of relieving the appellant and others from A
liability to pay income tax, that formation is absolutely void as against the
respondent " or in regard to any proceeding under this Act ". They are, to use
his own expression, " annihilated ". How, in the face of this, the companies are
nevertheless brought to life again for the purposes of seeing what expenses they
incurred and then allowing those expenses to the appellant, I do not understand.
7. What then follows? Is the appellant to be taxed as though his assessable B
income is the same as his taxable income? Or is some liberty to be taken with
the words of s. 260, so as to accord him the benefit of expenditure by the two
companies? Or is the truth that s. 260 is inadequate to deal with this sort of case,
particularly when one still has to face the problem—What part of the expenditure
in question related to the appellant's own activities? 8. I return to this aspect of
the matter presently; but assuming for the moment that the difficulties about C
allowing deductions are surmountable, then s. 260 permits the taxation of the
appellant on what he received for treating the patients he himself attended less
his necessary outgoings. The facts which are left after s. 260 has done its work
entail nothing less and nothing more. It means further, in my opinion, that he
must be assessed on a cash basis, for the facts which remain do not include any
debt to him from patients for unpaid fees.   D

I come now to consider the very different basis of liability which has been
upheld. The respondent, as has been seen, began with the net income of Westbank as disclosed by its accounts, made a number of additions to it, and attributed
a particular portion to the appellant. From this he allowed certain expenses
incurred by Raleigh. This was consistent with the respondent's original contention that the appellant himself owned the fees paid for medical services which E
he rendered; and that in paying expenses Westbank and Raleigh were simply
his agents. But it is wholly, and obviously, inconsistent with s. 260 which treats
the arrangement which brought these companies into being as wholly void against
the respondent or in regard to any proceeding under the Act. To persist in this
basis of assessment as the respondent did when relying on s. 260 is not to
apply that section but to contradict it.   F

What has to be discovered is what is left after s. 260 has done its work, and
what liability to tax is thereby supported. By way of introduction to this
problem, MENZIES, J., in the High Court said this:

"The next question is how much of the arrangement and what was done
to carry it out is void against [the respondent] in assessing [the appellant]
and in these proceedings. It seems to me that it was the making of the   G
agreements with Westbank and the making of [the appellant's] agreement
with Raleigh which effectuated the tax avoiding purpose with regard to
[the appellant]. These agreements must, therefore, be disregarded."

Here, it will be seen, the arrangement is dissected and the two agreements
mentioned are isolated as the matters on which alone s. 260 operates, since they
" effectuated " the tax avoiding purpose.   H

I have the misfortune to disagree with this analysis. In the first place the two
agreements would not have effected the tax avoiding purposes without the
existence of Westbank and Raleigh. In the second place the test prescribed by
s. 260 is not merely whether some contract agreement or arrangement " effectu-
ates " such a purpose, but whether the contract agreement or arrangement " has
or purports to have the *purpose or effect* . . . in any way, directly or indirectly ". I
In the face of this language, I do not understand how the formation of Westbank
can be treated as being outside it; and I agree with the respondent who, in his
case, adopts as his main contention that the existence of Westbank is also to be
disregarded. I would repeat that in my opinion the same must be said of the
formation of Raleigh.

The treatment of the formation of Westbank as being unaffected by s. 260
facilitates, however, the conclusion of the judge, which he proceeds to express
as follows:

A "What then is left of a group of doctors practising together but without any formal agreement of partnership using Westbank to receive all fees paid, to provide services for the group, to pay group expenses, and to make distributions of what remained in agreed proportions, and using their family companies to receive those distributions and to pay the individual expenses of practice. On this basis the assessable income of the doctors as a group was
B the total of gross fees earned."

For me, at least, this reasoning is vitiated by its reliance on the existence and the actions of Westbank and Raleigh notwithstanding s. 260. In this context it is not without significance that the respondent and his advisers take a different view of "what was left". They say it was (a) the appellant practising as before;
C (b) income being produced by that practice; (c) that income being paid with other income into a bank account; (d) the payment thereout of the cost of production of the entire income; (e) the dealing with part of that income (after such payment) in accordance with the appellant's directions. I respectfully think that this analysis though not perfect is, at any rate, more in accordance with the effect of s. 260.

D Other questions are provoked by the passage that I have quoted from the judgment of MENZIES, J., which was substantially adopted by the Full Court. First, what is the significance of the reference to "a group of doctors practising together but without any formal agreement of partnership"? The pre-existing partnership between the doctors was dissolved on Aug. 31, 1956. It was clearly part of the entire tax avoiding arrangement. The respondent is at liberty there-
E fore to treat the agreement for dissolution as void as against him, or in relation to any proceeding under the Act; but what does this involve? In your lordships' view the consequence is that the respondent was entitled "to treat the partnership as continuing until, if in fact it had been in existence, it would have been dissolved by operation of law".

I regret that I am unable to share in this conclusion which admittedly substi-
F tutes fiction for fact, and is thus in conflict with repeated judicial pronouncements that s. 260 does not permit such inventions. If your lordships' view is correct, it would surely have been shared and applied both by the respondent and by the six judges in Australia who have considered this case. It would also have made all the elaborate arguments to which both they and your lordships have listened largely unnecessary. Moreover the respondent would presumably have called for
G a return of the partnership income pursuant to s. 91 of the Act which he has not done.

It may well be asked, "What is the point of declaring the deed of dissolution void, unless the result be to keep the partnership alive"? The answer is, I think, simply this: that in considering what liability flows from the facts which are left after s. 260 has done its work, the respondent is not to be affected by the
H circumstance that the doctors formally dissolved partnership on Aug. 31, 1956. He is to consider the facts which remain after that date untrammelled by that fact. This is what the respondent and the High Court proceeded to do, and in my respectful view, this was the right approach. It is noteworthy, moreover, how partnership, as a conclusion from the facts surviving the application of s. 260, is carefully avoided. The respondent speaks of "the appellant carrying on his
I practice in association with a group of other medical practitioners"; and MENZIES, J. (see above) speaks of "a group of doctors practising together without any formal agreement of partnership etc.".

In my opinion the "facts exposed" do not themselves support the conclusion of partnership. The sharing of gross returns, if Australian law be the same as English law in this respect, would be no evidence of partnership. The sharing of net profits, on the contrary, is prima facie evidence of partnership. The crucial point, however, is whether these eight medical practices were carried on *in common* pursuant to some agreement to that effect, express or implied. The facts

which remain include the fact that this is the one thing the doctors intended A
should *not* happen after Aug. 31, 1956, which seems to be highly relevant, though
by itself not conclusive.   Moreover I can find a sharing of net profits only by
tracing the gross receipts through Westbank and Raleigh taking into account
the payment of expenses by those companies, and attributing to the appellant
moneys which he did not receive.   The doctors, it is true, used the same surgeries
as before, and may be said to have practised as a " group ", both of which features B
carry one hardly any distance along the road to partnership.   What really stands
out in this context is the absence of evidence which points unequivocally to the
conclusion that despite the doctors' intention to practise otherwise than in
partnership, they nevertheless in fact continued to do so.

Section 6 of the Act, however, contains an extended definition of partnership.
It is " an association of persons carrying on business as partners or in receipt of C
income jointly . . ."   As regards these last words the appellant received no
moneys " jointly ".   What was paid to him for his services was received by him
alone, not by the other doctors as well.   Nor did he receive, jointly with them, the
fees they received for services which they rendered.   This result is not reversed
by the fact that all the money was paid into one account not in the doctors' names.
If no partnership is exposed when s. 260 has done its work, I do not know what D
significance, in relation to the appellant's income tax liability, is to be attached
to the reference to " a group of persons practising together etc."   The doctor
and his colleagues seem to have used the same surgeries as before, and no doubt
this had its conveniences, one doctor coming to the help of another in times of
difficulty.   In this sense they can be said to be practising together as a group, as
doctors do in some of our own towns.   Short of partnership, however, the E
circumstance is, in relation to tax liability, irrelevant.

Next, in the passage which I am considering from the judgment of MENZIES, J.,
comes the reference to the doctors

" using Westbank to receive all fees paid, to provide services for the
group, to pay group expenses and to make distributions of what remained
in agreed proportions, and using their family companies to receive those   F
distributions and pay the individual expenses of practice."

I repeat that, after s. 260 has directed that the whole tax avoiding arrangement
be regarded for present purposes as absolutely void, this resurrection of the
companies which were an essential part of that arrangement, for the purpose of
fixing liability on the taxpayer, is, in my opinion, wholly inadmissible.   G

The argument before your lordships did not seek to support the opposite
proposition.   On the contrary it was said, inter alia, that the formation of Westbank was avoided.   It was added that so far as Raleigh was concerned it was
unnecessary to contend that its formation was also avoided.   I can understand
this view; but whether the contention were necessary or not, the formation of
Raleigh clearly fell within the scope and effect of s. 260.   H

The respondent, for his part, contends that the application of s. 260 exposes
the appellant carrying on practice, receiving moneys, paying those moneys into
a bank account, and the other doctors doing the same. Then part of that income,
after payment of the expenses, is dealt with in accordance with the appellant's
directions, and thus liability to tax on that part is brought home to him.

This, if I may say so, is the most attractive way in which the case for the   I
respondent can be put; but on analysis this, too, is found to be contravening
s. 260. Thus the justification for the expression " after payment of the expenses "
is that Westbank paid them.   If, for example, the respondent challenged the
admissibility of any of the expenses, it is the accounts of Westbank which would
have to be produced in support of the deduction sought, and evidence from
Westbank which would have to be produced if the purpose of any particular
disbursement were challenged.   Then as regards the " application of part of
that income in accordance with the appellant's directions ", the appellant

A himself gave no personal directions on this matter. He joined in the collective decision of the board of directors of Westbank. If Westbank is to disappear pursuant to s. 260, the board and its actions disappear with it. In its place there is not left a decision by individuals acting on their own, and to proceed on the basis that such a decision is one of the facts " which are left " is again to employ a fiction.

B Before stating my conclusions I should perhaps say a word about s. 19 of the Act which enacts that

" income shall be deemed to have been derived by a person although it is not actually paid over to him but is re-invested, accumulated, capitalized . . . or otherwise dealt with on his behalf or as he directs."

C This section is not one which imposes liability in the present case independently of s. 260. It does not apply, for example, to make Westbank's income the income of the appellant and his colleagues whether s. 260 applies or not. Section 19 is not intended to override contracts which make a particular piece of income legally and beneficially the income of someone else. Otherwise the income of a limited company might be treated as the income of the board of directors who could direct how it should be dealt with. The section deals with, and defeats, any

D possible argument of a taxpayer that income which would otherwise be " derived " by him is not to be so treated because it has been accumulated re-invested or capitalized etc. It comes into play in the present case if s. 260 has the effect of making the fees received by the appellant from the patients whom he treated his own income. Then, whatever other answer he might have to s. 260, he could not

E be heard to say that in any event he had diverted most of that income elsewhere.

In the end I reach these conclusions:

1. The purpose of the whole arrangement was relief in some measure from income tax.

2. The application of s. 260 would involve treating the fees paid to the appellant for the services he rendered to patients as his gross or " assessable " income.

F 3. The deduction of expenses to arrive at his net or " taxable " income involves looking at the accounts of Westbank and Raleigh; and in as much as the formation of these two companies is, under s. 260, to be regarded as absolutely void " in regard to any proceedings under this Act " this procedure is not permissible. The result is not to make the appellant taxable on his gross or " assessable " income, for this would be contrary to the Act. It is, on the contrary, to raise

G serious doubt as to the applicability of s. 260 to such a case as the present.

4. This doubt is increased when the amount of net income to be attributed to the appellant can be determined only by attributing to him and his colleagues a decision which they never took except as directors of Westbank.

5. Section 260 does not, in truth, meet such a case as the present with which its terms are inadequate to cope. It is a section which dates back, it is said, to

H 1915 when tax avoidance schemes were less sophisticated and complex. If a charge is created on income so as to lessen the tax; or property is transferred for that purpose; then s. 260 will work. The charge and the transfer can be ignored as void, leaving the income as it was; but when a taxpayer puts an end to one source of income and creates another in its stead, the section does no more than destroy the new arrangements so far as the respondent and the Act are concerned. This is not enough. The old order is not revived by thus annihi-

I lating the new. What is needed is authority for the respondent to make such assessments to tax as in his view are required to prevent the avoidance of tax which would otherwise occur. Section 260 contains no such authority; and without it, the attempt to impose liability in accordance with " the facts that remain " leads to difficulty and frustration. The section is obeyed at one time and disobeyed at another. The respondent was quite right in my opinion in his initial disregard of the section and on better ground in his attempt to establish liability by contending that Westbank and Raleigh were mere agents of the

doctors, and that the doctors themselves owned the income that their efforts A
procured. This does not mean that I think the contention right, for it involves
treating the agreements between the doctors and Westbank, and between themselves and their family companies, as shams. On the evidence I do not at present
see how this contention can be sustained; but if it fails then, unless and until
the legislature adds further and suitable provisions to s. 260, the respondent
must take the facts as he finds them, and assess the appellant on the basis of B
the doctor's own return.

I therefore respectfully dissent from your lordships' conclusion, and would
humbly advise Her Majesty that the appeal should be allowed.

Appeal dismissed.

Solicitors: *Light & Fulton* (for the appellant); *Coward, Chance & Co.* (for the C
respondent).

[*Reported by* KATHLEEN J. H. O'BRIEN, *Barrister-at-Law.*]

————

D

S. J. & M. M. PRICE, LTD. *v.* MILNER.

[QUEEN'S BENCH DIVISION (Edmund Davies, J.), May 5, 11, 1966.]

*Arbitration—Special Case—Setting aside—Jurisdiction—Discretion—Power of
court to remit award of its own volition—Delay by arbitrator exceeding four* E
*years in stating award—Sums of money involved small—Justice best served
by remitting award for reconsideration by same arbitrator—Matters for
reconsideration to be agreed by parties and submitted in writing to arbitrator.*

A dispute having arisen between builders and the building owner, with
whom the builders had contracted to build a bungalow, the parties resorted to
arbitration before a duly appointed architect arbitrator in June, 1960. The F
builders claimed £839 19s. 4d. for work done and materials supplied; the
owner counter-claimed £109 12s. for failure by the builders to execute the
work in a good and workmanlike manner. On Jan. 1, 1965, the arbitrator
purported to make his award in the form of a Special Case Stated, as
requested by the owner. The award was in form defective, in that, inter alia,
it insufficiently narrated the events and documents which led to the G
arbitrator's findings of fact, and, instead of posing the questions of law on
which the court was to adjudicate, it stated the issues which in the arbitrator's opinion arose and then gave his conclusions thereon. In making his
award, which was substantially in favour of the builders, the arbitrator
directed that if his findings were not set down for hearing by either party on
a point of law within six weeks of his award being taken up then judgment H
" would be at first instant " (sic). On Apr. 22, 1965, the builders took up the
award; on May 28, 1965, the owner set down the award as being a Special
Case for hearing, and on May 31, 1965, he gave notice of motion to set aside
the award on the grounds that the arbitrator had misconducted himself and
that, on the face of it, the award was bad in law. On the hearing of the
motion to set aside the award on Mar. 7, 1966, the court at the instance of the I
parties restricted itself to determining the motion and did not consider the
Special Case. The motion, being out of time under R.S.C., Ord. 88, r. 5 (1)*,
was barred by that rule. No explanation of the delay was given, no application to extend time was made, and the motion was dismissed. The owner
did not appeal from the dismissal of the motion. At the hearing of the

———

* R.S.C., Ord. 88, r. 5 (1) requires that an application to remit or set aside an award
be made " within six weeks after the award has been made and published to the
parties ".

A   Special Case, the court found that, despite its manifest defects, the award must be regarded as having been stated in the form of a Special Case. On application by the owner at the hearing to have the award set aside or remitted on the ground of defects in form and inconsistencies in findings of fact therein,

      Held: the owner, not having appealed from the court's decision refusing
B his motion to set aside the award, could not seek to evade that decision by making application to set aside the award on the hearing of the Special Case; moreover, even assuming that the court could of its own volition now set aside the award, the court in its discretion would not take that course but would, in the exceptional circumstances of the present case, remit the award to the arbitrator on matters to be agreed by counsel for submission to
C him (see p. 782, letter I, and p. 784, letters A, B and D, post).

      Per CURIAM: I am not satisfied that the court has any power, of its own volition and in the absence of any duly instituted application by either party to that end, to set aside an award in the form of a Special Case (see p. 783, letter G, post).

      [As to the mode in which an arbitrator should state a Special Case for the
D opinion of the court, see 2 HALSBURY'S LAWS (3rd Edn.) 39, 40, para. 90; and for cases on the subject, see 2 DIGEST (Repl.) 580, *1120, 1121.*

      As to the power of the court to remit or set aside an arbitrator's award, see 2 HALSBURY'S LAWS (3rd Edn.) 55-61, paras. 119-127; and for cases on the grounds for setting aside and remitting awards, see 2 DIGEST (Repl.) 678-685, *1929-1987,* 694-697, *2078-2102*; for cases on the subject of applications to set aside and/or
E remit awards, see ibid., pp. 686-693, *1988-2077,* 698, 699, *2103-2119.*

      For the Arbitration Act, 1950, s. 21-s. 23, see 29 HALSBURY'S STATUTES (2nd Edn.) 106-109.]

Cases referred to:

   Dexters, Ltd. v. *Hill Crest Oil Co. (Bradford), Ltd.*, [1925] All E.R. Rep. 273;
F   [1926] 1 K.B. 348; 95 L.J.K.B. 386; 134 L.T. 494; 2 Digest (Repl.) 587, *1175.*

   Universal Cargo Carriers Corpn. v. *Citati*, [1957] 3 All E.R. 234; [1957] 1   W.L.R. 979; [1957] 2 Lloyd's Rep. 191; Digest (Cont. Vol. A) 41, *1956a.*

Special Case.

   The respondents at the hearing of the Special Case, S. J. & M. M. Price, Ltd.,
G were builders and decorators at Worthing, Sussex, who by a contract in writing made on June 16, 1958, had agreed with the applicant at the hearing of the Special Case, Ebenezer Lyle Milner, to build him a bungalow in accordance with plans and a specification annexed to the contract for the sum of £4,000, and to complete the said bungalow by Nov. 15, 1958. Differences having arisen between the parties, they resorted to arbitration, which took place before a duly appointed
H architect arbitrator in June, 1960. The builders (as applicants in the arbitration) claimed £839 19s. 4d. for work done and materials supplied, and the bungalow owner (as respondent in the arbitration) counter-claimed £109 12s. for failure by the builders to execute the work in a good and workmanlike manner. The arbitrator made his award, purportedly in the form of a Case Stated, on Jan. 1, 1965. The award was substantially in favour of the builders. On May 28, 1965, the
I owner set down the award as a Special Case for hearing, and on May 31, 1965, he gave notice of motion to set aside the award. The relevant facts in respect of that motion, which was dismissed by MEGAW, J., on Mar. 7, 1966, are set out at p. 782, letters F to I, post. The Special Case having come on before the court for hearing, counsel for the owner applied to have the Special Case set aside or remitted for defect in form and inconsistency in findings of fact.

   D. H. Gardam for the applicant owner.

   A. J. D. McCowan for the respondent builders.

EDMUND DAVIES, J.: These disastrous proceedings arise out of a contract A
in writing entered into on June 16, 1958, whereby S. J. & M. M. Price, Ltd.
agreed to build a bungalow at Worthing for Mr. Milner, in accordance with the
annexed plans and specifications, for the sum of £4,000, practical completion to
be effected by the following November. Completion was not so effected and,
differences having arisen between the parties, they resorted to arbitration. This
took place as long ago as June, 1960, but, despite the entreaties and expostulations B
of both parties, the arbitrator did not make his award until Jan. 1, 1965. The
builders were claiming in the proceedings £839 19s. 4d. for work done and
materials supplied, the building owner counter-claiming £109 12s. for failure by
the builders to execute the work in a good and workmanlike manner. The
money claims were therefore distinctly moderate, the issues raised such as are
commonly met with in disputes over building contracts, and the delay of nearly C
five years before making an award is as remarkable as it is regrettable.

Although counsel for the builders denied before me that it was so, I have no
doubt both that the arbitrator was clearly requested by counsel appearing for
the owner to make his award in the form of a Special Case and that that is what
the arbitrator set out to do. The transcript of counsel's final address, the opening
words of the award itself—" I . . . make my award in the form of a Case Stated " D
—and a joint letter of protest over the delay sent on behalf of both parties on
Apr. 14, 1961, make this perfectly clear. The award itself, however, which was
in a most unusual form, purported to award the builders the sum of £580 plus
interest and ordered that the owner was, in addition, to pay both the costs of the
arbitration and the fees of the arbitrator. The arbitrator further directed

". . . that if my findings are not set down for hearing by either party on a E
point of law within six weeks of my award being taken up then judgment
shall be at first instant (sic) and my award shall be as follows."

This he did at the express request of counsel appearing for the owner, the present
applicant.

Neither party proceeded to take up the award of Jan. 1, 1965, until Apr. 22, F
when the builders took it up. On May 28, i.e., within the six weeks prescribed by
the arbitrator, the owner set down the award as being a Special Case for hearing,
and on May 31, he gave notice of motion to set aside the award on the grounds
(i) that the arbitrator had misconducted himself and (ii) that, on the face of it,
the award was bad in law. Both the argument on the Special Case and the
motion to set aside could, of course, and indeed should, have been considered G
together by the single judge, but when the matter came before MEGAW, J., on
Mar. 7, 1966, he was told in terms that he had to consider only the motion to set
aside and he accordingly restricted himself to that matter only. In respect of
that motion, he held that the owner was barred by R.S.C., Ord. 88, r. 5 (1), which
requires that an application to remit or set aside an award must be made " within
six weeks after the award has been made and published to the parties ", for H
while the award had been published on Jan. 1, 1965, the application to set aside
or remit was not made until May 28, and no explanation for this delay was
offered or any application to extend the time made to the court. If I may
respectfully say so, MEGAW, J., was perfectly right in so holding, and no criticism
has been levelled at that decision.

In these unfortunate circumstances, the only duty facing me should now be that I
of answering the questions of law which are required to be stated in the Special
Case. But counsel for the owner has not contented himself with arguing what those
answers should be. Instead, he now, in effect, applies primarily to have the
Special Case set aside, alternatively to have it remitted, on the grounds (a) that
it is defective in form and (b) that the findings of fact contained in the award are
grotesquely inconsistent with each other. In my judgment, he cannot do so. Not
having appealed the decision of MEGAW, J., he is now seeking to evade its effect
by a rearguard action, and that tactic is, in the existing circumstances, not open

A to him. Counsel for the builders, on the other hand, contends that this award is not stated as a Special Case. In support of this contention, he seeks to rely on that part of MEGAW, J.'s judgment which held that:

> " So far as the arbitrator is concerned, whether the award was good or bad, in substance or in form, he had adjudicated . . . finally."

B By so holding, however, the learned judge did not, in my judgment, purport to decide whether this award was, or was not, in the form or purported form of a Special Case, for, as PARKER, L.J., said in *Universal Cargo Carriers Corpn.* v. *Citati* (1):

> ". . . an award in the form of a Special Case is intended to be and should be regarded as final subject only to the point of law raised. So far as the
C facts are concerned, it should be regarded as entirely final."

The question whether this award has been stated as a Special Case was, accordingly, not disposed of by anything that MEGAW, J., said and remains at large for me to consider. That it was most unusual in form has already been remarked on. It consists very largely of lengthy extracts from legal text-books, it insufficiently narrates the events and documents which led to the findings of fact, and (instead
D of posing those questions of law on which the court is to be called on to adjudicate) the arbitrator states the three issues which, in his judgment, arise and then proceeds to give his conclusions thereon. He might, with advantage, have looked at and been guided in his task of framing his award by many of the decided cases, of which *Dexters, Ltd.* v. *Hill Crest Oil Co. (Bradford), Ltd.* (2) is one, and by Form 36 in RUSSELL ON ARBITRATION (17th Edn.) at p. 429. Nevertheless, despite all
E these criticisms, I have come to the conclusion that this award must be regarded, despite its manifest defects, as having been stated in the form of a Special Case.

However, because of its defects in form and (so it is alleged) inconsistent findings of fact, counsel for the owner persists in asking this court to set it aside or remit it. Confronted by the obstacle presented to him by the judgment of MEGAW, J., he submits that this court can, of its own volition, set aside or remit.
F Counsel for the builders concedes that, in the light of the decision in the *Universal Cargo* case (3), in very special cases, the court may *remit* for further consideration an award in the form of a Special Case, but denies that there is any power in the court of its own volition to set it aside, and asserts that the present circumstances are not such as to justify the court in remitting. He submits that, be it a Special Case or an ordinary final award, it is valid and enforceable by his clients. In the
G alternative, he understandably urges that if this court is to interfere with the award in any way, it should be by way of remitter, rather than by setting it aside.

I am not satisfied that the court has any power, of its own volition and in the absence of any duly instituted application by either party to that end, to set aside an award in the form of a Special Case. Even if such a power exists, however, its exercise must be a matter for the court's discretion and one to be determined by
H consideration of what is best calculated to do justice between the parties. Owing to the gross delay in making this award, it would have been open to either or both of them to apply for the removal of the arbitrator, but the owner declined the invitation of the builders to join them in making such an application (4). Having regard to the smallness of the claim and counter-claim, it would, as it seems to me, be deplorable if this dispute had to begin all over again before a fresh arbitrator.
I No kind of attack has been made on the bona fides of the present arbitrator and, notwithstanding his extreme dilatoriness, he is (or should be) seised of all the facts and, properly guided, should now be capable of presenting his award as a Special Case properly stated. Accordingly, even assuming that in the present

---

(1) [1957] 3 All E.R. 234 at p. 237, letter I.
(2) [1925] All E.R. Rep. 273; [1926] 1 K.B. 348.
(3) [1957] 3 All E.R. 234.
(4) An application for the removal of an arbitrator may be made to the High Court under s. 13 (3) of the Arbitration Act, 1950.

circumstances this court could now of its own volition set aside this award, I should not be prepared so to exercise my discretion. Instead, I think that the better course for the parties in the sorry plight in which they now find themselves is that I should remit the award to the same arbitrator for further consideration. It may be that the builders, in whose favour an award for £580 has been made, do not regard themselves as being in any sorry plight. However, it is at least open to argument what benefit (if any) enures to them from this award which the arbitrator has directed is to be regarded as a " judgment . . . at first instant " *provided* that his findings were " *not* set down for hearing by either party on a point of law within six weeks " of its being taken up, whereas the award was so set down within the stipulated time. Be that as it may, in the fortunately exceptional circumstances of this case and notwithstanding its unfortunate background, it seems to me that justice is more likely to be served by my remitting this award to the arbitrator generally for reconsideration.

In the usual run of cases, the court would at this juncture indicate to the arbitrator the further findings of fact at which he should arrive or the points of law which appear to be involved. I have, indeed, been asked by counsel for the owner to make such indications in the present case, for he seeks no less than five further findings of fact and he points out that the Special Case by no means raises all seven of the questions of law which, in his final address, he requested the arbitrator to put to the court. I have, however, decided on what may be an unusual course in the circumstances of this unusual case, for I think that it might prove an embarrassment, rather than a help, were I to proceed to indicate the matters of fact or of law which should be found in or raised by the Special Case when it comes to be amended or re-drafted. Instead, I think that the better course would be for counsel to agree among themselves as to these matters, put them in writing jointly, and for them then to be submitted to the arbitrator. If, unhappily, counsel cannot agree on these points, the arbitrator is free to enlist their assistance at a further hearing, but it is to be hoped that it will not be necessary to re-open any other matters in this small case, in the hearing of which four days were expended so many years ago. It is certainly not this court's intention that the arbitrator should re-hear the whole case submitted to him and (while we give no direction on this point) it ought not to be necessary for him to hear any further evidence. That the arbitrator should show celerity is manifest, and his attention is drawn to s. 22 (2) of the Arbitration Act, 1950, which requires him to make his new award within three months after the date of this court's order to remit. Power is given by the Act to the court to direct otherwise, but in view of the nature of the case and the inordinate delay which has already occurred, I am certainly not disposed to allow the arbitrator longer than the statutory three months to complete his task.

Special Case remitted, reserving costs of this application and further argument to the arbitrator.

Solicitors: *Bowles & Stevens*, Worthing (for the applicant owner); *Malcolm, Wilson & Cobby*, Worthing (for the respondent builders).

[*Reported by* K. DIANA PHILLIPS, *Barrister-at-Law.*]

A

INLAND REVENUE COMMISSIONERS
v. PARK INVESTMENTS, LTD.

Applied in WILLINGALE v ISLINGTON
GREEN CO [1972] 1 All ER 199

[COURT OF APPEAL (Sellers, Danckwerts and Winn, L.JJ.), April 19, 20, 21, 1966.]

B *Surtax—Investment company—Directions and apportionments—Company under control of not more than five persons—" Public "—Exclusion of relatives, nominees, etc., of persons having control, when determining whether public substantially interested—Choice of shareholdings by Revenue—Settlements— Relatives—Whether trustees or executors, being shareholders, were persons interested in shares—Income Tax Act, 1952 (15 & 16 Geo. 6 & 1 Eliz. 2*

C *c. 10), s. 256 (1), (3), (5).*

The shares of a limited company were quoted on The Stock Exchange, London, and each carried one vote. For the purposes of s. 245 of the Income Tax Act, 1952 (that is, for the purposes of surtax directions) the company was controlled by not more than five persons. Some 54.21 per cent. of the shares was held by three brothers and four sisters (treated as one for those

D purposes by virtue of s. 256 (3)*); 11.89 per cent. were held by their spouses and 31.73 per cent. by a bank nominee for the trustees of five family settlements made by two of the brothers, the three brothers being, in various groups of two, together the trustees of all the settlements and thus the registered holders of the shares. The Special Commissioners of Income Tax made surtax directions under s. 245 of the Income Tax Act, 1952, that the income

E of the company for four successive years ending in 1959 be deemed to be the income of its members for those years.

Held: the surtax directions were properly made, as the company was one to which s. 245 of the Income Tax Act, 1952, applied by virtue of s. 256, for the following reasons—

(i) a person who, as a relative or nominee etc., was by s. 256 (3) to be

F treated as one with another person when determining the number of persons by whom a company was controlled could not also be a member of " the public " for the purposes of s. 256 (1), (5); and, since sub-s. (5) predicated twenty-five per cent. voting power as constituting a substantial interest for the public (whereas on the facts, if relatives, etc., were excluded, only 2.15 per cent. voting power or at any rate less than twenty-five per cent. would

G remain available to be held by members of the public) the taxpayer company was not one in which the public was substantially interested, with the consequence that s. 245 applied to it (see p. 793, letter H, to p. 794, letter A, p. 794, letters B and I, p. 795, letters F and H, and p. 797, letter I, post).

Tatem Steam Navigation Co., Ltd. v. *Inland Revenue Comrs.* ([1941] 2 All E.R. 616) considered.

H *Morrisons Holdings, Ltd.* v. *Inland Revenue Comrs.* ([1966] 1 All E.R. 789) applied.

(ii) the Crown was not limited to the 54.21 per cent. shareholding but might add the other group of 31.73 per cent. which would leave less than twenty-five per cent. voting power available to be held by members of the public (see p. 794, letters D and I, p. 795, letters D and H, and p. 798,

I letter D, post).

Inland Revenue Comrs. v. *J. Bibby & Sons, Ltd.* ([1945] 1 All E.R. 667) applied.

(iii) (per DANCKWERTS and WINN, L.JJ.) " persons interested in any shares " in s. 256 (3) include trustees and executors (see p. 795, letter C, and p. 797, letter C, post).

Decision of BUCKLEY, J. ([1966] 1 All E.R. 803) affirmed.

---

* Section 256, so far as material, is printed at p. 789, letter H, to p. 790, letter D, post.

[**Editorial Note.** BUCKLEY, J., decided that s. 256 (1), (5) could be applied A
in alternative ways by taking alternative groupings of shareholders of the taxpayer company; the Court of Appeal do not dissent from that (see p. 794,
letter D, post), but found their decision on one conjunction of groups, viz.,
the 54.21 per cent. and the 31.73 per cent., making together 85.94 per cent.,
which would leave less than twenty-five per cent. available to constitute the
interest of the public, and thus would leave too little to satisfy the amount or B
percentage required to constitute substantial interest within sub-s. (5) of s. 256.

As to the control of companies and companies in which the public are substantially interested for surtax direction purposes, see 20 HALSBURY'S LAWS
(3rd Edn.) 548-550, paras. 1066, 1069;   and for cases on the subject, see 28
DIGEST (Repl.) 369-374, *1614-1632*.

For the Income Tax Act, 1952, s. 245 and s. 256, see 31 HALSBURY'S STATUTES C
(2nd Edn.) 232, 244.]

Cases referred to:

Income Tax Comr. v. *Bjordal*, [1955] 1 All E.R. 401;   [1955] A.C. 309;   [1955]
2 W.L.R. 342;   28 Digest (Repl.) 359, *1585.*

Inland Revenue Comrs. v. *J. Bibby & Sons, Ltd.*, [1944] 1 All E.R. 548;   170 D
L.T. 370;   *affd.* H.L., [1945] 1 All E.R. 667;   114 L.J.K.B. 353;   173
L.T. 17;   29 Tax Cas. 167;   28 Digest (Repl.) 429, *1884.*

Morrisons Holdings, Ltd. v. *Inland Revenue Comrs.*, [1966] 1 All E.R. 789;
[1966] 1 W.L.R. 553.

Tatem Steam Navigation Co., Ltd. v. *Inland Revenue Comrs.*, [1941] 2 All E.R.
111;   [1941] 2 K.B. 194;   *affd.* C.A., [1941] 2 All E.R. 616;   [1941] 2 E
K.B. 194;   111 L.J.K.B. 17;   165 L.T. 182;   24 Tax Cas. 57;   28 Digest
(Repl.) 359, *1584.*

Appeal.

The taxpayer company appealed from an order of BUCKLEY, J., made on
Dec. 16, 1964, and reported [1966] 1 All E.R. 803, allowing the appeal of the
Crown by way of Case Stated from a decision of the Commissioners for the F
Special Purposes of the Income Tax Acts in their judicial capacity discharging
directions made by the Special Commissioners under s. 245 and s. 262 (1) of the
Income Tax Act, 1952, by which the income of the taxpayer company for the
years ending July 31, 1955, 1956, 1957, 1958 and 1959 was to be deemed to be
the income of its members for the respective years. The question for determination on the appeals was whether the taxpayer company was one in which the G
public at all material times was substantially interested within the meaning of
s. 256 of the Act of 1952, so as to exclude it from surtax directions under s. 245.

The taxpayer company was incorporated on Dec. 10, 1919, under the Companies Acts, 1908 to 1917, with a nominal capital of £50,000 divided into fifty
thousand shares of £1 each which were later subdivided into two hundred
thousand shares of 5s. each.   Ten thousand £1 shares were offered for public H
subscription at once to obtain working capital. At that time and at all material
times the name of the taxpayer company was Maroc, Ltd.   It was changed to
Park Investments, Ltd., on Dec. 4, 1959. The taxpayer company was formed to
carry on business as a prospecting and development company with a view, in
particular, to prospecting in Morocco and other parts of Africa. The memorandum
of association contained all the powers required for that purpose. By the middle I
of 1952 the taxpayer company had become dormant and a resolution for a
members' voluntary winding-up was due to be submitted to a meeting called
for Nov. 19, 1952. The meeting was, however, adjourned for consideration of
an offer to purchase all the taxpayer company's shares which had been received
from Wood Hall Trust, Ltd.   In May and June, 1953, the following events
occurred.   (i) The majority of the taxpayer company's issued share capital, which
then consisted of 137,514 shares of 5s. each, was bought by two brothers, Arnold
and Ralph Silverstone and their families and relations.   (ii) The former directors

A of the taxpayer company resigned and thereafter, throughout the period under
consideration, the board of directors consisted of Arnold Silverstone (chairman),
Ralph Silverstone and Cedric A. Smith (also secretary from Nov. 30, 1953). By
a special resolution passed on Dec. 30, 1953, the memorandum of association was
altered so as to show as the company's principal object the investment of funds
in the acquisition of land and other property. In accordance with that declared
B object the taxpayer company's business was throughout the period relevant to
the appeal that of a property investment company, the properties being held for
investment purposes by a number of subsidiary companies. Arnold Silverstone
and Ralph Silverstone were the sole shareholders of eleven companies holding
freehold and leasehold properties (" the property investment companies "), and
it was proposed that the taxpayer company should acquire the entire issued
C share capitals of the property investment companies. Arnold and Ralph Silverstone thought it an opportune moment to settle funds for the benefit of their
families and other relations, and shares in certain of the property investment
companies were first so settled by deeds of settlement dated Mar. 17, 1955. The
various steps, not material to this report, were carried out for the purpose of the
proposed acquisition by the taxpayer company of the shares of the property
D investment companies from Arnold and Ralph Silverstone and by the trustees of
the settlements. On Apr. 4, 1955, the share capital of the taxpayer company
was increased to £234,400 by the creation of 737,600 shares of 5s. each. On
Apr. 4, 1955, eight hundred thousand shares in the taxpayer company were
issued and allotted as follows: to Trexco, Ltd., 216,076, to Trucidator Nominees,
Ltd., 216,076, and to Trexco, Ltd., and Trucidator Nominees, Ltd., 367,848
E shares. Those companies were both owned by the taxpayer company's solicitors
and the shares were held by them for a short period while formalities were being
completed. They were later transferred as follows: to Arnold Silverstone,
250,000, to Mrs. Lillian Silverstone (wife of Arnold), 57,500, to Ralph Silverstone,
195,000 and to Barclays Nominees (Branches), Ltd., 297,500, making a total of
eight hundred thousand shares. The shares held by Barclays Nominees (Branches),
F Ltd., were held as nominee for the trustees of the five settlements made on Mar. 17,
1955, by Arnold and Ralph Silverstone.

The following is a brief summary of the settlements:

Trust No. 1.—Settlor, Arnold Silverstone; trustees, Ralph Silverstone and
J. E. Stone, shares 102,500. Trusts—on trust for such of the settlor's nephews
or nieces (being children or adopted children of J. E. Stone, Myra Lucas, Ethel
G Solomons, Winifred Lewis and Freda Silver) as attained twenty-one, if more than
one in equal shares, on protected life interests and after their death on trust for
their children or remoter issue. If all foregoing trusts failed, on trust for the
settlor's wife absolutely.

Trust No. 2.—Settlor, Ralph Silverstone; trustees, Arnold Silverstone and
J. E. Stone; shares 58,500. Trusts—on trust for the settlor's wife for life and
H after her death to the trustees of trust No. 5 to hold on the trusts thereof.

Trust No. 3.—Settlor, Ralph Silverstone; trustees, Arnold Silverstone and
J. E. Stone; shares 19,500. Trusts—on trust for the settlor's wife for life and
subject thereto for such of the settlor's children as should be living on the
perpetuity day or attain the age of thirty before that day; if these trusts should
fail, then to the trustees of trust No. 5 to hold on the trusts thereof.
I
Trust No. 4.—Settlor, Ralph Silverstone; trustees, Arnold Silverstone and
J. E. Stone; shares thirty-nine thousand. Trusts—on trust for such of the
settlor's children as should be living on the perpetuity day or attain the age of
thirty before that day; if all previous trusts failed, on trust for the settlor's wife
absolutely.

Trust No. 5.—Settlor, Ralph Silverstone; trustees, Arnold Silverstone and
J. E. Stone; shares seventy-eight thousand. Trusts, on trust for such of the
settlor's nephews, and nieces (being children or adopted children of J. E. Stone,

Myra Lucas Ethel Solomons, Winifred Lewis and Freda Silver) as should attain   **A**
twenty-one, if more than one in equal shares, on protected life interests and after
their death on trust for their children or remoter issue; on failure of all the
foregoing, for the trustees of trust No. 3 to hold on the trusts thereof.

The total number of shares of the taxpayer company comprised in all five
settlements was 297,500.

From Apr. 4, 1955, to the end of the period relevant to the appeal, the issued   **B**
share capital of the taxpayer company was 937,514 shares of 5s. each. For the
purposes of the appeal by Case Stated the shareholders at Apr. 5 and at July 31
(the end of the taxpayer company's accounting period) in each of the years 1956,
1957, 1958 and 1959 were grouped under four headings.

A. (Arnold and Ralph Silverstone, their brother and sisters)   **C**

Name	No. of shares
Arnold Silverstone	270,031
Ralph Silverstone	215,000
Freda Silver	6,757
Ethel Solomons	5,977
Joseph E. Stone	2,500
Winifred Lewis	5,000
Myra Lucas	3,000

D

508,265   (54.21 per cent.)

B. (Wives and husbands of the persons in heading A)   **E**

Lillian Silverstone	72,500
Joy S. Silverstone	15,000
George Silver	8,000
Samuel Solomons	5,000
Beryl F. E. Stone	1,000
Harry Lewis	5,000
Gershon M. Lucas	5,000

F

111,500   (11.89 per cent.)

C. (Nominees)

Barclays Nominees (Branches), Ltd. as nominee
    for the settlement trustees   297,500   (31.73 per cent.)   **G**

D. (Others)

Forty-six other shareholdings   20,249   (2.15 per cent.)

Aggregate   937,514   (99.98 per cent.)   **H**

The shareholdings at Apr. 5 and at July 31, 1955, differed from those set out
above only in that the eight hundred thousand newly-issued shares were held by
Trexco, Ltd., and Trucidator Nominees, Ltd. at those dates before being transferred to their intended holders. The taxpayer company's shares were at all
material times quoted in the official list of The Stock Exchange, London, and in   **I**
each of the years to which the appeals related were the subject of dealings on that
Stock Exchange. There was only one class of share in the taxpayer company and
each of its shares carried one vote. No conditions were attached to the allotment
or acquisition of the 297,500 shares held by Barclays Nominees (Branches), Ltd.
as nominees for the trustees of the settlements, shown under C above.

The Special Commissioners gave their decision in writing on July 24, 1963.
They held that the taxpayer company was at all relevant times an investment
company under the control of not more than five persons, and was not a subsidiary

A company. They held further that the taxpayer company was controlled by the "single person" in heading A, p. 788, letters C and D, ante, but that the shares held by all the other groups were held by the public. They therefore allowed the appeal, and discharged the surtax directions and apportionments. On Dec. 16, 1964, Buckley, J., allowed the Crown's appeal against that decision. The taxpayer company appealed to the Court of Appeal.

B   The cases noted below* were cited during the argument in addition to those referred to in the judgments.

Heyworth Talbot, Q.C., G. B. Graham, Q.C., and *S. T. Crump* for the taxpayer company.

Arthur Bagnall, Q.C., J. R. Phillips and *J. P. Warner* for the Crown.

C   **SELLERS, L.J.:** This case has been subject to some vicissitudes of fortune. The taxpayer company, an investment company, was thought by those responsible for taxing them to fall under s. 245 of the Income Tax Act, 1952, and it was accordingly treated in accordance with those provisions. It was held that it had failed to distribute a reasonable proportion of its income for the relevant years, which started in 1954-55 and ran up to 1958-59. The income was apportioned

D (as is required by the relevant sections of that Act) between the members. It was deemed to be the members' income and consequently would be subject to surtax, if that were payable. An appeal was taken to the Special Commissioners in their judicial capacity and they allowed the appeal and held that the taxpayer company was not a company to which s. 245 applied. A Case was stated, and the decision of Buckley, J., (1) before whom the appeal came, restored the directions

E and the findings of the original commissioners.

Section 245 is familiar and I need not further refer to it. The issue which arises in this case is whether the taxpayer company is a company to which that section applies. That involves a consideration of s. 256—indeed only part of that section in the circumstances of this case becomes relevant. Subsection (1) is as follows:

F   " (1) Section 245 of this Act shall apply to any company which is under the control of not more than five persons and which is not a subsidiary company or a company in which the public are substantially interested."

In this case it has been accepted, and indeed it is clearly established, that the company is under the control of not more than five persons. It is accepted also that it is not a subsidiary company, and the whole question is whether it is, on

G the right interpretation of the law, a company in which the public are substantially interested.

I need not read (although it is not without its importance) sub-s. (2); but sub-s. (3) of s. 256 is as follows:

" (3) In determining for the purposes of this section [it says, ' of this

H *section* '] whether a company is or is not under the control of not more than five persons, persons who are relatives of one another, persons who are nominees of any other person together with that other person, persons in partnership and persons interested in any shares or obligations of the company which are subject to any trust or are part of the estate of a deceased person shall respectively be treated as a single person. For the purposes of

I this subsection—(*a*) ' relative ' means husband, wife, ancestor, lineal descendant, brother or sister; and (*b*) a person shall be deemed to be a nominee of another person if, whether directly or indirectly, he possesses on behalf of that other person, or may be required to exercise on the direction of or on

---

* *Speyer Brothers* v. *Inland Revenue Comrs.*, [1908-10] All E.R. Rep. 474; [1908] A.C. 92; *Liverpool and London and Globe Insurance Co., Ltd.* v. *Bennett,* [1913] A.C. 610; *Re Butt* (decd.), *Butt* v. *Kelsen,* [1952] 1 All E.R. 167; [1952] Ch. 197; *Inland Revenue Comrs.* v. *Harton Coal Co., Ltd.* (*in liquidation*), [1960] 3 All E.R. 48; [1960] Ch. 563.
(1) [1966] 1 All E.R. 803.

behalf of that other person, any right or power which, by virtue of any of the   **A**
provisions of this section, is material in determining whether a company is
or is not to be deemed to be under the control of not more than five persons."
Subsection (4) I need not read: that deals with a subsidiary company. Subsection
(5) is the most important subsection:

" (5) For the purposes of this section, a company shall be deemed to be a   **B**
company in which the public are substantially interested if shares of the
company (not being shares entitled to a fixed rate of dividend, whether with
or without a further right to participate in profits) carrying not less than
twenty-five per cent. of the voting power have been allotted unconditionally
to, or acquired unconditionally by, and are at the end of the year or other
period mentioned in s. 245 of this Act for which the accounts of the company   **C**
have been made up beneficially held by, the public (not including a company
to which the said s. 245 applies) and any such shares have in the course of
such year or other period been the subject of dealings on a stock exchange
in the United Kingdom and the shares have been quoted in the official list of
such a stock exchange."

Under that subsection it has been accepted that the shares of the company have   **D**
been quoted in the official lists of a stock exchange and there have been dealings
in the company's shares on a stock exchange. The question for consideration is
relative to the twenty-five per cent.—the more than twenty-five per cent.—
voting power which, so it is said by the taxpayer company, has been allocated to
the public. There is no definition of " the public " and the court has to construe
this matter as best it can—in this case not free from some control in the construc-   **E**
tion and application of this section, because there was in 1941 a case under the
predecessor of this section in another Act (2) in somewhat similar terms, the
decision of *Tatem Steam Navigation Co., Ltd.* v. *Inland Revenue Comrs.* (3), which
has to be regarded, and the court is called on to interpret and apply the provisions
and the decision.

For myself, although we have heard no argument on the other side, if one were   **F**
free to do so one would feel inclined to give weight to the submission, which was
merely indicated by counsel for the Crown, that " the public " here could be
regarded in a very general and acceptable way by relating the twenty-five per
cent. of the shares of a company which would otherwise be within the Act of
1952 to an unconditional offer by the company of at least twenty-five per cent.
of the shares as an allocation to the public which had been taken up—i.e., taken   **G**
up by the public at large—or to the circumstances where members of the family
or within the group had sold shares up to twenty-five per cent. at least so that
the public had acquired them. Having regard to the *Tatem* case (2), however, it
was submitted by the Crown, I think rightly, that that argument was not open
to them here, and therefore we have to decide this case on some narrower ground
and in the light of such guidance as this court has.   **H**

Before coming to the *Tatem* case (2) it is unnecessary, I think, to set out the
facts in detail. They appear in the Case Stated and they are stated clearly in the
judgment of the judge (4). It is important to consider, however, how this company
does fall within these provisions, at any rate in so far as the control is said to be
a control of not more than five persons. When one looks at the whole of the
members, apart from a small percentage, two per cent., who do not come into   **I**
consideration at all, they are all members of a family in their different relationships. They are set out in the Case Stated and are referred to in the judgment (5).
The Crown has grouped together, or there had been grouped together, various
people having regard to the provisions of s. 256 (3), showing that with regard to

---

(2) Finance Act, 1922, s. 21 (6) as substituted and amended by the Finance Act, 1927,
and the Finance Act, 1936; see 12 HALSBURY'S STATUTES (2nd Edn.) 239.
(3) [1941] 2 All E.R. 616; 24 Tax Cas. 57.
(4) [1966] 1 All E.R. at pp. 804-808.   (5) [1966] 1 All E.R. at pp. 806, 810.

A   this Silverstone family (one of the brothers, who is I think a doctor, has altered his name from Silverstone to Joseph Stone) the grouping which has taken place is of Mr. Arnold Silverstone and Mr. Ralph Silverstone, who are brothers, and then Mr. Joseph Stone, who is the brother who is a doctor, and four sisters. The relationship was that of brothers and sisters. They are grouped together and their total holdings come to some 508,265 shares. At the material time the issued

B   shares of this company were 937,514 shares, fifty per cent. of which would be 468,757 shares and twenty-five per cent. of which would be 234,379 shares. So that that grouping of those brothers and sisters did give them fifty-four per cent. of the shares and therefore control. There was another grouping of the wives and the husbands, the spouses, of those seven persons enumerated under heading "A", and they each had various holdings amounting in total to over 111,000

C   shares, or something over eleven per cent. of the holding of the company. There was another grouping of shares which were held on trust: they were in the name of a nominee—Barclays Nominees (Branches), Ltd.—but that is of no moment having regard to the provisions of s. 256 (3). They were in fact held by two of the three brothers in various associations, some five trusts in all, and were for the benefit again of members of the family within the class of relatives specified in

D   sub-s. (3). Those trust holdings amounted to 297,500, or 31.73 per cent. of the total shares of the company, leaving only that small balance of 2.15 per cent. which can undoubtedly be regarded as in the hands of the public.

    The question in this case is whether it is established for the purposes of s. 256 (5), approaching the question directly from the point of view of s. 256 (5), that not less than twenty five per cent. of the voting power of the shares has

E   been allotted unconditionally to or acquired unconditionally by, and is beneficially held by, the public. "The public" is not defined, but, in circumstances such as these, and having regard to the provisions of the Act of 1952, one would not expect "the public" to include members of a family; it is said, however, that, in the light of a decision of this court, that is not the right interpretation. It is said by the taxpayer company that the case requires strict application of the

F   authorities and, however unreasonable it appears, the taxpayer company is entitled to have the benefit of the decision in its favour.

    The *Tatem* case (6) arose in the course of the last war, in June, 1941, and was considered by SCOTT, L.J., with whom the other two lords justices, CLAUSON, L.J., and GODDARD, L.J., agreed. The question arose under s. 21 (6) of the Finance Act, 1922, as amended by the Finance Act, 1927, s. 31 (3). The question was

G   whether some twenty thousand shares, or at any rate sixteen thousand of them more specifically, which had been transferred by Lord Glanely to his niece— a niece not within the relatives specified in s. 22 (6) of the Act of 1922—were to be regarded as held by a member of the public. This court held that that was so. The basis of the judgment, as I read it, is to be found in this passage from SCOTT, L.J.'s judgment (7):

H   "The scheme of the subsection undoubtedly was that, where the control of a company is in fact held by not more than five persons, and the company is not one in which the public are substantially interested in the manner indicated by the proviso, the persons controlling the company should be treated as running it in their own interests, and, therefore, in a position which, from the public point of view, ought to make them liable to pay sur-tax just

I   as if the company had been a firm and they had drawn their share of profits direct from the business. However, a limitation was imposed on that general principle, not only by limiting it to a case of not more than five persons having control and by excluding the case of a subsidiary company, but also by the provision that, if the public held shares to the extent of twenty-five per cent., that would take the company wholly outside the section. I can see no reason

---

(6) [1941] 2 All E.R. 616; 24 Tax Cas. 57.
(7) [1941] 2 All E.R. at pp. 618, 619; 24 Tax Cas. at p. 67.

whatever for introducing any other notions of control than those plainly **A**
indicated in the section as constituting the de facto control which is what the
section primarily contemplates. There is no suggestion of that in this case.
There is no suggestion, there is no evidence, and there is no finding that Lord
Glanely had in fact any control over his niece. Nor is there any suggestion
that his niece was a nominee of his, or of any of the other persons within the
limited category of five. Nor is there any suggestion that he even had any **B**
influence over her. An implication of control is raised by the statutory
presumption in the case of husband and wife, ancestor, lineal descendant,
brother and sister, but in the case of no others. Consequently, we must regard
a person in the position of a niece as being treated by the statute as a member
of the public. The statute contains no prohibition against avuncular
generosity, any more than against generosity to a person between whom **C**
and the donor there is no consanguinity or relationship at all."

That is the basis of the decision, the judgment previously having analysed the
reasons given by the Special Commissioners (which were dealt with by LAWRENCE,
J., (8) who tried the case at first instance), the lord justice disagreeing with all
the reasons which had been given by them.

Now the effect of that case has been sought to be interpreted. It was said by **D**
BUCKLEY, J., in his judgment (9), and I think not challenged by the Crown and
it was certainly accepted by the taxpayer company, that that judgment of this
court drew a dividing line, and that those who were in control of the company
were on one side of the line and that anyone else, the classes being mutually
exclusive, was to be regarded as the public. I am not sure that I myself would
have considered that that was clearly so. It may be that that is the implication. **E**
It is not said in terms by LAWRENCE, J., (8) or by the Court of Appeal (10). The
decision really turns on the passage which I have read—that this lady, the niece,
was not in the category of what SCOTT, L.J., speaks of as under " an implication
of control ". The taxpayer company's case, as I understood it, put most forcibly
in this court, was that this is quite a simple matter of construction; that, applying
authority established already in this court, one has the position that the control **F**
here is established in one single person; that under the provisions which I have
read one does not count heads, but groups people together in order to put together
those who can properly be put into the category of an artificial or statutory
single person; and that, when they are put together and one has the grouping
of the brothers and sisters making a total shareholding of over five hundred
thousand shares, fifty-four per cent., there one has the control established, **G**
fifty-four per cent. as the controlling factor, and all the remainder become
members of the public, and the twenty-five per cent. is well exceeded.

I would reject that argument. It seems to me that it ignores many of the factors
and considerations which arise under this particular set of provisions. The
contention before the judge on behalf of the Crown when the Crown was appellant
was also put in a simple and direct way, and it is stated in the judgment of **H**
BUCKLEY, J., as the first submission made on behalf of the Crown. It is convenient
to keep it in the form in which it is there stated. It is to be found in the report
(11). It was similarly advanced before this court. Counsel for the Crown advanced
several alternative arguments, and indeed the phraseology of these relevant
sections, particularly s. 256, permits of many forensic presentations and a variety
of arguments one way or the other. First, he accepted that group A holds a **I**
controlling interest; then he pointed out that in that group there are the three
brothers who are the trustees of five separate trusts which come under heading
C, the shares being in the names of a nominee—in fact the trustees are two of
each of the three in each of the trusts, but not always the same two. Counsel
pointed out further that they, as controllers of the company, not only are the

---

(8) [1941] 2 All E.R. 111; 24 Tax Cas. 57. (9) [1966] 1 All E.R. at p. 811, letter E.
(10) [1941] 2 All E.R. 616; 24 Tax Cas. 57. (11) [1966] 1 All E.R. at p. 810.

A registered holders of the shares which are entered under heading A against their names but also are the registered holders of the shares of the trusts which total 297,500, and that that 31.73 per cent. added on to the 54.21 per cent. of heading A, the personal group which is in control of the company, gives those shareholders, those controllers, the control of some eighty-five per cent.

B The judge set that out in his judgment (11a), but he does not seem to have accepted it as the basis on which he decided in favour of the Crown. It seems to me that it is a sufficient presentation of the case to establish the Crown's point. It leaves at best only fourteen per cent. of the shares available to the public. Whether on the facts of this case that fourteen per cent. could properly be said to be held by the public I am not sure, but that is not important, if one gets the position established that eighty-six per cent. are held by those in control. It may

C well be that on a true construction of this provision the spouses, the wives and husbands of those named, and their holdings could also be taken into consideration, which would account for practically the whole of the shares in the company. The identification of these persons, whether they be the trustees or the beneficiaries, is to be made with those who come under heading "A" in control of the company, in my view, and this is probably a very clear case where a company

D falls under the provisions of s. 245 so that surtax directions can properly be made.

Reliance is placed on the three brothers as being in control of the company and including in their holding the shares of the trust by the use of the decision in *Inland Revenue Comrs.* v. *J. Bibby & Sons, Ltd.* (12), which came before the House of Lords in somewhat different circumstances in 1944. There the question was who had the controlling interest. It was held by the Court of Appeal (13)

E and affirmed by the House of Lords (12) that shares owned by the directors as trustees should be taken into account in ascertaining whether the directors of the company had a controlling interest therein. It is said, and in my view rightly said, that that can be applied to the present case, and that the shares which the directors and the major shareholders held on trust can be taken into account so as to give them that preponderance of control in the company. Taken more

F generally, however, I think that it can be said, as an outcome of what was said in the *Tatem* case (14), that, if the niece in that particular case had not been a niece but had fallen into the category of " relatives " as defined in the Act (15), the decision would have been the other way.

This is put quite neatly in a decision of PENNYCUICK, J., in a case which followed somewhat shortly after the matter now under appeal. He had to consider kindred

G questions in *Morrisons Holdings, Ltd.* v. *Inland Revenue Comrs.* (16). After considering the authorities he took the view that the effect of the decision in the *Tatem* case (14) was as follows. He said (17):

" As I read the passages which I have quoted, LAWRENCE, J., (18) and SCOTT, L.J., (19) contrast the class of ' relatives ' within the statutory definition and the ' public '. This is made particularly clear by the use of

H the word ' consequently ' in SCOTT, L.J.'s judgment. It is because no implication of control is raised in the case of a niece that she must be regarded as a member of the public. The corollary is, I should have thought, that, where the implication of control is present, the relative is not a member of the public. The effect of the judgment as I read it is to draw a sharp line of demarcation round the control group including relatives (and presumably

I also partners) and to hold that everyone outside that line is a member of the public."

(11a) [1966] 1 All E.R. at p. 810.   (12) [1945] 1 All E.R. 667; 29 Tax Cas. 167.
(13) [1944] 1 All E.R. 548; 29 Tax Cas. 167.
(14) [1941] 2 All E.R. 616; 24 Tax Cas. 57.
(15) Finance Act, 1922, s. 21 (6), as amended by Finance Act, 1927, s. 31 (3).
(16) [1966] 1 All E.R. 789.   (17) [1966] 1 All E.R. at p. 799.
(18) [1941] 2 All E.R. at p. 114; 24 Tax Cas. at p. 64.
(19) [1941] 2 All E.R. at pp. 618, 619; 24 Tax Cas. at p. 67.

I would express complete approval of that and would apply it to this case. It **A** was challenged by counsel for the taxpayer company, but it seems to me that that is the effect of the judgment of this court in the *Tatem* case (20), and that one has for the purposes of this subsection (21) to look at the statutory identification (22) or the identification which one would take apart from the statute that a relative is not a member of the public. Common sense seems to establish that, and I think that this statute follows it. No one can be a member of the public **B** if he is at the same time identified with or in fact a person who has control. The line of demarcation is there drawn, and if it is, then this case falls clearly on the side of the Crown's contentions and the necessary twenty-five per cent. interest of the public is not established.

A great deal of argument has taken place and I do not intend to refer to the various submissions which have been made. It seems to me, as I say, that this **C** sort of legislation permits of a vast amount of forensic argument, but the application of those two cases, the decision in *Tatem's* case (20) as I would apply it and the decision in *Bibby's* case (23), seems to me to be an answer to this appeal and to establish that the decision of the judge (24) was right. He did not decide the case quite on those grounds, but I have no quarrel with the alternative way in which he put it. He looked at it first from the point of view of the second sub- **D** mission of counsel for the Crown and, as I understand it, he accepted that. That was to the effect that, accepting class A, as is specified in the Case, fifty-four per cent. control, one can add to that. That only made one person in control: there may be five persons in control—not more than five—and another four can be obtained from the five trusts. Any four can be taken. The judge gives (25) the figures. He added those to the half-million shares under heading A and they **E** bring the matter up to a figure which does not leave a balance of twenty-five per cent.

I have not made reference to the case in the Privy Council of *Income Tax Comrs.* v. *Bjordal* (26) because it seems to me that that case is not helpful. It was decided on a different ordinance which has different provisions and indeed it might tend to be a little misleading rather than helpful. In so far as it says **F** that more than fifty per cent. gives control of a business I think that that can be accepted.

The judge took another point (27), with which I agree. It is that if one looks at the matter from the point of view of the beneficiaries under the five trusts, then in so far as they have an interest—and it is an interest which is referred to in s. 256 (3); an interest in the trusts seems to me to involve both the trustees and **G** the beneficiaries—if one seeks to look to the beneficiaries and applies the requirements of the statute to them, they (in the words of the judge (27)) are not beneficiaries who have acquired the shares. Although they may be beneficially owned by the beneficiaries, the judge says (27), it is the trustees who have acquired the shares, whether conditionally or unconditionally; the shares have not been acquired by the beneficiaries. Therefore, on that ground also—but mainly on the **H** ground that they are identified with the control of the company—I think that the beneficiaries cannot be regarded as part of the public.

There may be other grounds and perhaps better grounds to defeat this appeal but in my view it ought to fail and I would dismiss the appeal.

DANCKWERTS, L.J.: I agree with the judgment of SELLERS, L.J. The **I** position, as I see it, is as follows. The whole object of s. 256 of the Income Tax Act, 1952, is to make sure that the persons who control the company should not be able artificially to create a control in more than five persons by handing over

(20) [1941] 2 All E.R. 616; 24 Tax Cas. 57.
(21) See s. 256 (5) of the Income Tax Act, 1952.
(22) See s. 256 (3) of the Income Tax Act, 1952.
(23) [1945] 1 All E.R. 667; 29 Tax Cas. 167.   (24) [1966] 1 All E.R. 803.
(25) [1966] 1 All E.R. at p. 810.   (26) [1955] 1 All E.R. 401; [1955] A.C. 309.
(27) [1966] 1 All E.R. at p. 813.

A shares to various relatives or other persons with whom they are in collaboration, or by creating trusts. So most artificial provisions are inserted in sub-s. (3) in order to restrict the number of persons holding the controlling shares to a small number, or even to one person, by amalgamating in one artificial person a number of separate individuals. This is the object of sub-s. (3), which is concerned with the number of persons in control, and with reducing their number. The language

B which is used is quite different from that of sub-s. (5), which is no doubt concerned with persons having beneficial interests. The obscurities of the section are infuriating, but we have to do the best we can and give the section an intelligible meaning, if that is possible.

I do not accept the argument that " persons interested in any shares . . . which are subject to any trust " (28) does not include trustees. The words, in my opinion,

C are exactly applicable to the position of a trustee who holds shares subject to a trust, and a trustee has an interest in such shares—a legal interest. Further, I do not accept the argument that, once the figure of fifty-four per cent. is reached, which, of course, confers a controlling interest, the matter then comes to a stop. In my opinion, s. 256 (3) is still operative, with the result that the shares held by the brothers as trustees for the beneficiaries under the five settlements are to be

D added to the holdings of the brothers in their own right for the purposes of control. I think that *Inland Revenue Comrs.* v. *J. Bibby & Sons, Ltd.* (29), a decision of the House of Lords, requires us to reach this result. I also think that the shares of husbands and wives have to be added. The phrase " persons who are relatives of one another " in sub-s. (3), in my view, is satisfied by relationship to one other relevant person, and does not require relationship to all the others.

E The result is that a far greater number of controlling shares emerges. If fifty-four per cent. gives control, a fortiori eighty-six per cent., or a higher figure, gives the holders of the shares control. This, of course, renders it impossible to produce members of " the public " holding twenty-five per cent.

I also am of opinion that " the public " does not include any of the persons who are mentioned in sub-s. (3). I do not accept the argument for the taxpayer com-

F pany that once fifty-four per cent. has been ascertained as held by less than five persons, all others are members of the public. That would make nonsense of the section.

It is unfortunate that no definition or guide is given in sub-s. (5) of what is meant by " the public ". I think that I know what a public-house is, or what a public meeting is, or what a public procession is. I do not know, however,

G what exactly is meant by " the public " in sub-s. (5). At any rate, I am sure that it does not mean the family of those in control of the company as defined in sub-s. (3). No one would regard a party to which only relatives of the giver of the party were invited as a " public " party. I think that in *Morrisons Holdings, Ltd.* v. *Inland Revenue Comrs.* (30) PENNYCUICK, J., drew the right conclusion as to the effect of what SCOTT, L.J., said in *Tatem Steam Navigation Co., Ltd.* v. *Inland*

H *Revenue Comrs.* (31). For these reasons I would dismiss the appeal.

WINN, L.J.: I agree with the judgments delivered by my lords. In one or two minor and unimportant respects I may express some slightly different views, but in substance I agree with each of the judgments already delivered that this appeal should be dismissed. This court is bound by the ratio decidendi of *Tatem Steam Navigation Co., Ltd.* v. *Inland Revenue Comrs.* (32) to dismiss this

I appeal. In particular, I think that that conclusion must be reached on that passage in the judgment of SCOTT, L.J., (33), to which I am about to refer. Had it not been for that decision I, too, no less than SELLERS, L.J., would have found very attractive the argument adumbrated, though not developed because

(28) See s. 256 (3) of the Income Tax Act, 1952.
(29) [1945] 1 All E.R. 667; 29 Tax Cas. 167.   (30) [1966] 1 All E.R. at p. 799.
(31) [1941] 2 All E.R. at pp. 618, 619; 24 Tax Cas. at p. 67.
(32) [1941] 2 All E.R. 616; 24 Tax Cas. 57.
(33) [1941] 2 All E.R. at p. 619; 24 Tax Cas. at p. 67.

of the controlling effect of *Tatem's* case (34) by counsel for the Crown.   In my **A** case, though not of course in his, the attractiveness of that argument may be inherent in what counsel for the taxpayer company has called its immaturity, or its attractiveness to immature minds.

What puzzled me more than anything about the *Tatem* case (34) (until about fifteen minutes ago) was how to analyse the reasoning lying behind what I am sure was the deliberate choice on the part of SCOTT, L.J., (35) of the use of the **B** words " An implication of control is raised by the statutory presumption ". That same phrase has been adopted and applied by PENNYCUICK, J., in a recent decision in *Morrisons Holdings, Ltd.* v. *Inland Revenue Comrs.* (36).   I think that the explanation for the use of that phrase (which is not, in my own view, at all appropriate when considering the proper construction of the Income Tax Act, 1952, s. 256) is that the wording to which SCOTT, L.J., was applying himself **C** was, as I have just discovered, quite different in important respects: it is to be found set out in the report (37).   The earlier section of which SELLERS, L.J., has made mention, s. 21 of the Finance Act, 1922, did in most respects conform in its language almost exactly and on all important points with the language of the Act of 1952, s. 256.   The Act of 1922, s. 21 (6), however, gave this definition of a " company " to which the power to give directions applied: **D**

> " A company shall be deemed to be under the control of any persons where the majority of the voting power or shares is in the hands of those persons or relatives or nominees of those persons . . . The expression ' relative ' means . . ."

and there is a definition which is narrower than the definition (38) in s. 256 (3) **E** of the Act of 1952.   Therefore it was natural that SCOTT, L.J., should be talking of an implication of control in relatives, because that is just what the provision refers to—the control shall be deemed to be in the persons who have the majority voting power or their relatives.   Here, however, as SELLERS, L.J., has already said and as I think that I put during the argument, what matters is identification —not implication of control but identification of persons; and, if I may say so, **F** with respect to counsel for the taxpayer company's fascinating final submission, that seems to me to be destructive of his submission whereas different wording might not have been so destructive.

I shall have to come back for another purpose to that particular page in the report of the *Tatem* case (39).   Meanwhile I proceed to say this, that what is provided by s. 256 (3) of the Income Tax Act, 1952, is a statutory notional **G** identification of human beings who in reality are not the same persons.   I think that the proper meaning of sub-s. (3) is better seen if (and this is entirely in accordance with what has fallen from each of my lords) one puts the whole provision into a negative form and appreciates that its object is to prevent those who de facto control the affairs of a company by voting power from putting shares into the hands and names of others in order to be able to say: " Well, **H** these shares which control the company and which must be aggregated together in order to give over fifty per cent. of the voting power are not found in the hands of five or fewer people but more than five in fact hold them ".   I do not propose to take up time in developing this point fully, but I would read sub-s. (3) as being equivalent to saying that persons who are relatives of one another (etc.)

I

(34) [1941] 2 All E.R. 616;   24 Tax Cas. 57.
(35) [1941] 2 All E.R. at p. 619;   24 Tax Cas. at p. 67.
(36) [1966] 1 All E.R. at p. 799.
(37) [1941] 2 All E.R. at p. 618;   24 Tax Cas. at p. 66.
(38) The words of s. 256 (3) of the Income Tax Act, 1952, derive from s. 19 (2) of the Finance Act, 1936;   see 12 HALSBURY'S STATUTES (2nd Edn.) 357.   The words from s. 21 (6) of the Finance Act, 1922, quoted above, were repealed by the Finance Act, 1936, s. 35 and Sch. 4.
(39) [1941] 2 All E.R. at p. 618;   24 Tax Cas. at p. 66.

A shall not be deemed to be different persons from one of the persons looked at to see whether control resides in that person and not more than four others.

Whilst on this matter of the construction of the wording of that section, I would say (as Danckwerts, L.J., has said) that I regard " relatives " as meaning and being satisfied by any such relationship as is referred to in the definitions. The wording is " relatives of one another ", not " relatives each of all the others ".

B I would also say, in so far as it has any relevance, that it seems to me that the phrase " persons in partnership " must mean persons in partnership in relation to the holding of shares in the company, and must further mean persons in partnership in relation to the holding of shares in the company who do not include any person in whom the control of the company resides; and I think for myself that the expression in the rest of the subsection, " persons interested in any

C shares ", etc., does include trustees, does include executors, but is in the sub-section for the sole purpose of preventing the addition of one or more persons as holders of shares by putting the shares into the hands of two or three or four trustees instead of one trustee, and also in contemplation of a case where there is more than one executor or administrator of an estate—all aimed against the arithmetical aggregation of or expansion of the number of people holding the

D shares giving control of the company.

I think it is perhaps worth saying that in my opinion sub-s. (3) presents difficulties of construction which have to be resolved in order to give sense to the section as a whole, and on these difficulties my own mind fluctuated during the hearing of this appeal. As at present advised, I am of the opinion that the proper construction of the words " For the purposes of this subsection ", which intro-

E duce the definitions under (*a*) and (*b*), is that these definitions are to be read into sub-s. (3) as though therein contained in place of the respective words to which they relate, with the result that the subsection is to be read as though it were correspondingly expanded.

The introductory words of sub-s. (3) are, " In determining for the purposes of this section ", viz., s. 256 of the Act, and must I think be equivalent to: any

F purpose of s. 256. These words are not, I think, equivalent in meaning to: for the purposes of s. 256 (1) of the Act of 1956; they have a wider effect. It follows, in my opinion, that the words in sub-s. (3) " In determining . . . whether a company is or is not under the control of not more than five persons " are to be applied wherever, for any purpose of any subsection of s. 256, one is concerned to look and see where the control of the company resides, and who are identified

G as the persons, real, i.e., human, or fictitious by force of statute, in whom the control of the company resides. Moreover the force, in my judgment, of the identificatory provisions in sub-s. (3) is that any person who is a relative within the meaning of the definition (or a nominee, a fortiori) cannot for any purpose of s. 256 be treated as a person different from, additional to, distinguishable from, the person with whom he or she, or they, have been thereby identified.

H Since, then, not only by force of the *Tatem* decision (40) but by compulsion of common sense (as has been delightfully illustrated in the judgment of Danck-werts, L.J.), one is compelled to postulate that no person who is not separate from a person in whom the control of the company resides can be a member of the public, it follows, in my judgment, as night follows the day, that none of these shareholdings, other than the 2.15 per cent. outside shareholdings, can be regarded

I as shares which, within the meaning of sub-s. (5), have been allotted to or acquired by a member of the public or are held by a member of the public beneficially.

I quite agree that counsel for the taxpayer company is clearly right in saying that what must be concentrated on for the purposes of s. 256 (5) of the Income Tax Act, 1952, is ownership of shares. It is allotment—or acquisition—plus beneficial ownership, of shares carrying not less than twenty-five per cent. of the voting power. That does not, however, in the least detract from the essential

_____

(40) [1941] 2 All E.R. 616; 24 Tax Cas. 57.

requirement that, in order to take this company—any company—out of the **A** operation of s. 245 of the Act of 1952 it must be shown that shares carrying not less than twenty-five per cent. of the voting power are in the hands of persons who are members of the public, or may be members of the public, since they are not identified with—not the same persons as—those in whom control of the company resides.

Before I leave the identification point it is necessary, logically, for me to refer **B** to a passage in the judgment of BUCKLEY, J., (41) which has already been mentioned dealing with the first submission of counsel for the Crown to that judge. The judge said (41):

"... the three brothers and four sisters are by the terms of s. 256 (3) to be treated as one person. They hold beneficially 54.21 per cent. of the issued share capital; but not only that, they also hold among them, that is to say, **C** members of that class of brothers and sisters also hold, the 31.73 per cent. of the shares in the taxpayer company which are the subject-matter of the settlements . . ."

I agree with the view that the judge is there expressing, but for quite a different reason. I would myself have put it this way—as is clear from what I have said. **D** I would have said: (not only that) but members of the class of brothers and sisters also hold 31.73 per cent. of the shares as trustees under the settlements and by force of the subsection they are identified with and cannot be regarded as persons different from those already referred to as holding fifty-four per cent. of the shares in the company.

Returning to the *Tatem* case (42), it no longer is necessary for me to venture **E** even to suggest that SCOTT, L.J., should have taken identification as a more accurate criterion than implication of control, because he was considering a different statutory provision. It is equally unnecessary (and so I only mention it for the sake of completeness) to draw attention to the fact that, with all respect to the lord justice, he has in five consecutive sentences on that same page (41) used the word " control " in two independent, irreconcilable and **F** fluctuating senses, which tends just slightly to obscure the meaning of what he was there expressing: all that is relevant is voting control of the company.

The other point (it is the last one, and I apologise for speaking at such length at this stage) is that I think myself that in sub-s. (5) of s. 256 of the Act of 1952, on its proper construction, the phrase " any such shares have . . . been the subject of dealings on a stock exchange " (etc.) must mean shares which have been allotted **G** unconditionally to, or acquired unconditionally by, and are at the relevant date beneficially held by, the public. Not only does grammar point to that construction, but I think it is impossible to give that expression any other meaning when it is immediately followed by " and the shares have been quoted in the official list . . ." Had the meaning been different, it would have been quite unnecessary to include the words " the shares " in the final line of the subsection: **H** it would have read " any such shares have been the subject of dealings and have been quoted on the stock exchange ". That is of no direct relevance in this case but it was discussed.

I agree that this appeal should be dismissed.

Appeal dismissed. Leave to appeal to the House of Lords granted.

Solicitors: *Slaughter & May* (for the taxpayer company); *Solicitor of Inland* **I** *Revenue.*

[*Reported by* F. A. AMIES, ESQ., *Barrister-at-Law.*]

---

(41) [1966] 1 All E.R. at p. 810.
(42) [1941] 2 All E.R. at p. 619; 24 Tax Cas. at p. 67.

A   COZENS *v.* NORTH DEVON HOSPITAL MANAGEMENT
COMMITTEE AND ANOTHER.

[COURT OF APPEAL (Lord Denning, M.R., Danckwerts and Salmon, L.JJ.),
May 2, 3, 24, 1966.]

Limitation of Action—Extension of time limit—Ex parte order granting proposed
B   *plaintiff leave to contend in action that Limitation Act, 1939, s.* 2 (1) *should*
afford no defence—Writ issued—Application by defendants to set aside ex
parte order—Whether defendants had right to make such application—Whether
appeal to House of Lords excluded—Limitation Act 1963 (c. 47), s. 1 (1) (*a*),
s. 2 (1), (2), (4).

C   In April, 1957, the second defendant performed on the plaintiff an operation in a hospital under the management of the first defendants. A gauze
swab was left in the plaintiff's body. Three months later this was discovered
and was removed. In 1958 another operation was performed to cure the ill
effects, but it did not do so. The plaintiff was advised that yet another
operation was necessary; she postponed having it until October, 1964. This,
too, was unsuccessful and the plaintiff was told that no more could be done for
D   her. On Sept. 28, 1965, on an ex parte application the plaintiff was granted
leave under s. 1 (1)* of the Limitation Act 1963 to contend that s. 2 (1) of
the Limitation Act, 1939, should not afford a defence in a proposed action
against the first defendants and the surgeon who performed the original
operation. On the next day the plaintiff issued a writ for damages for
personal injuries. The defendants applied to set aside the ex parte order
E   granting leave. On appeal from refusal of the application,

Held (SALMON, L.J., dissenting): (i) although it was a general principle in
regard to ex parte orders that the party affected by the order could apply
for it to be discharged, yet it would be contrary to the intention of the
Limitation Act 1963 to allow a defendant to apply, before the trial of the
action, to set aside an ex parte order obtained under s. 2 (1) giving leave for
F   the purposes of s. 1 (1) (*a*) (see p. 801, letter G, and p. 804, letter F, post).

(ii) s. 2 (4) of the Limitation Act 1963 excluded an appeal to the House of
Lords from a decision of the Court of Appeal concerning an application to
set aside an ex parte order granting leave under s. 2 (1) (see p. 808, letter B,
post).

Decision of THOMPSON, J., (ante, p. 276) affirmed.

G   [As to the extension of the limitation period in certain cases, see SUPPLEMENT
to 24 HALSBURY's LAWS (3rd Edn.) para. 381; and for cases on process to prevent
statutory bar, see 32 DIGEST (Repl.) 625, *2018-2022*, and 3rd CUM. SUPP.

For the Limitation Act 1963, s. 1, s. 2, see 43 HALSBURY's STATUTES (2nd Edn.)
614, 615.]

H   Cases referred to:
Bidder v. *Bridges,* (1884), 26 Ch.D. 1; 53 L.J.Ch. 479; 50 L.T. 287; 22 Digest
(Repl.) 542, *6101.*
Cartledge v. *E. Jopling & Sons, Ltd.,* [1961] 3 All E.R. 482; [1962] 1 Q.B. 189;
[1961] 3 W.L.R. 838; *affd.* H.L., [1963] 1 All E.R. 341; [1963] A.C.
758; [1963] 2 W.L.R. 210; 32 Digest (Repl.) 401, *259.*
I   *Clarke* v. *Forbes Stuart (Thames Street), Ltd. (intended action), Re,* [1964] 2
All E.R. 282; [1964] 1 W.L.R. 836; 3rd Digest Supp.
R. v. *Morley (Valuation Officer), Ex p. Peachey Property Corpn., Ltd.,* (Jan. 25,
1966), unreported.

Appeal.
This was an appeal by the defendants from an order of THOMPSON, J., dated
Mar. 25, 1966 and reported [1966] 2 All E.R. 276, refusing to set aside an ex parte

---

* Section 1 (1), so far as material, is set out at p. 802, letter E, post.

order made in chambers by NIELD, J , granting leave to the plaintiff for the **A** purposes of s. 1 (1) (*a*) of the Limitation Act 1963.

P. E. Webster and *D. Henry* for the defendants.
D. C. Calcutt for the plaintiff.

Cur. adv. vult.

May 24. The following judgments were read.

B

LORD DENNING, M.R.: In April, 1957, the plaintiff Mrs. Cozens went into the North Devon Infirmary in Barnstaple. The surgeon, Mr. Brook, the second defendant, together with the staff, carried out an operation for a hysterectomy. Unfortunately by some mistake a swab was left in her body. Three months later this was discovered. The swab was removed; but it left ill effects on her. In an attempt to correct the damage in April, 1958, she went into the **C** hospital again. Another operation was performed; but without success. The ill effects continued. The second defendant advised a further operation, but she did not have it for a long time. The reason was because her son was young and she would not leave him. In October, 1964, she did have the further operation at the same hospital. It was performed by a different surgeon. This too was not successful. The surgeon told her on this occasion that a similar operation was **D** virtually impossible and that no more could be done for her. She says that it was not till this time, October, 1964, that she realised that her condition was so serious. She went to solicitors and, on their advice, wishes to bring an action for damages.

Prima facie any action is statute barred. The period of limitation in cases of this kind is three years—and three years have long since passed since the swab **E** was left in her body. The plaintiff will be barred by the lapse of time unless she can take advantage of the new Limitation Act 1963. That Act was passed especially to enable a plaintiff to overcome the time bar in cases of personal injury where he or she did not know material facts until too late. Shortly stated, it is this: if he brings the action within twelve months of discovering material facts (being facts which are of a decisive character) he is not to be barred; see s. 1 (3) **F** of the Act of 1963. In this case the plaintiff would have to prove that she did not know the extent of her injuries until the last twelve months and, furthermore, that this lack of knowledge was of a decisive character. She would have to show that until the last twelve months a reasonable person in her place would not have regarded the injuries as so serious as to make it reasonable for her to bring an action. She says she can prove it: because it was only in October, 1964, **G** that she discovered her injuries serious enough to warrant an action.

The plaintiff has to get over a preliminary hurdle, however, before she can embark on proof of these facts. Parliament has set up a hurdle so as to protect defendants from being harassed by actions when there is no reasonable ground for lifting the time bar. The hurdle is this. Every plaintiff who seeks to take advantage of the Act of 1963 must get the leave of the court for the purpose. Section **H** 2 (1) provides that:

" Any application for the leave of the court for the purposes of the preceding section shall be made ex parte . . ."

He or she must apply ex parte to a judge in chambers and produce evidence to show that he has a good cause of action and also that he did not know the decisive **I** facts until the last twelve months. In short, the plaintiff must satisfy the judge that the plaintiff has a prima facie case. If the judge is satisfied that the plaintiff's evidence, if believed, is sufficient to overcome the time bar, then he must grant him leave: but otherwise he must refuse. The plaintiff got over that preliminary hurdle successfully. On Sept. 28, 1965, her counsel went ex parte before NIELD, J., in chambers and produced affidavits by the plaintiff and her general practitioner. She gave the history which I have recounted. Her general practitioner said that her condition is " probably irremediable and [the plaintiff]

A   has only now become aware of this, after the unsuccessful operation of October, 1964 ". On reading the affidavits, the judge gave her leave for the purposes of s. 1 of the Limitation Act 1963. The defendants, of course, were not heard. It was ex parte and they knew nothing of the application.

Now the defendants apply to set aside that leave. They say that even on those affidavits, the judge ought not to have given leave. They say that it is a

B   fundamental rule of practice that a party affected by an ex parte order may apply to the court to discharge it inasmuch as he has not had an opportunity of being heard. The defendants recognise that, owing to the very words of s. 2 (2), they cannot give evidence to contradict the plaintiff's evidence. They must accept the plaintiff's evidence as correct; but they wish to argue that, even on that footing, leave ought not to have been given. The judge, they say, went wrong in law.

C   Now I quite agree that in general a party affected by an ex parte order can apply to discharge it. We applied this rule as of course in *R.* v. *Morley* (*Valuation Officer*), *Ex p. Peachey Property Corpn., Ltd.* (1) recently; but the procedure under the Limitation Act 1963 is altogether exceptional. It says in terms that an application *shall* be made ex parte. This is a strong indication that the judge is to decide the application on hearing one side only. No provision is made for

D   the defendant being heard; and I do not think that we should allow it to be done at this stage. It must be remembered that, even when the judge grants leave, there is nothing final about it. It is merely provisional. The defendant will have every opportunity of challenging the facts and the law afterwards at the trial. The judge who tries the case is the one who must rule finally whether the plaintiff has satisfied the conditions for overcoming the time bar. He is not in the least

E   bound by the provisional view expressed by the judge in chambers who gave leave; see *Re Clark* v. *Forbes Stuart* (*Thames Street*), *Ltd.* (*intended action*), (2).

Suppose we were to allow the defendant to challenge the ex parte order at this stage, we should be putting up an additional hurdle which the legislature have not put up; and I do not think that we should do it. We should be requiring the plaintiff to get the view of another judge in her favour in this way—first, there

F   would be the judge who grants leave ex parte; second, the judge who reviews it on hearing the defendant's application to set aside. I do not think that this second judge should be interposed. If he refused leave, the plaintiff would be out of court. She would be barred, save for an appeal to this court. If he granted leave, it might embarrass the judge at the trial, because he would be faced with a prior decision by a judge, made after argument, on the very point

G   of issue.

In my opinion, therefore, the defendants have no right to apply at this stage to set aside the leave which was given ex parte. The defendants must go on to trial where everything will be open to them. The note in the ANNUAL PRACTICE 1966, p. 1999/209E is wrong.

On this ground I would dismiss the appeal. We heard argument on the merits.

H   All I would say is that, even if it were open to us (which it is not), I would not have disturbed the leave granted by NIELD, J. There was, I think, a sufficient prima facie case to warrant the grant of leave.

DANCKWERTS, L.J.: The occasion which gave rise to the proceedings in this case was the leaving of a gauze swab when an operation was performed on

I   the unfortunate lady concerned in the case. After the subsequent discovery that the swab had been left behind, a series of operations was performed with the object of putting right the after effects of this mishap. The patient delayed taking proceedings because she disliked the idea of taking proceedings against the hospital and hoped that the subsequent operations would rectify the situation. In this way she let the normal period of the Limitation Act, 1939, pass by, and she had to seek the relief provided by the Limitation Act 1963.

The original operation when the swab was overlooked was in April, 1957. In

---

(1) (Jan. 25, 1966), unreported.   (2) [1964] 2 All E.R. 282.

July, 1957, the matter became apparent to the patient. By October, 1904, it A
became apparent to the patient that her condition was not going to be put right.
On Sept. 28, 1965 on an application made to NIELD, J., under the Act of 1963,
ex parte as thereby required, an order was made by that learned judge under s. 1
of the Act of 1963 giving leave to bring the action against the North Devon
Hospital Management Committee and the surgeon who did the original operation.
The writ was issued on Sept. 29, 1965.   B

The present application was made to THOMPSON, J., (3) to set aside the order
of NIELD, J., under the fundamental rule of practice that any party affected by
an ex parte order may apply to discharge the order on the ground that he has not
had an opportunity of being heard. THOMPSON, J., however, held that by reason
of the terms of the Limitation Act 1963 he had no jurisdiction to interfere with
the order of NIELD, J., and on Mar. 25, 1966, he refused to set aside the orders of C
NIELD, J. There were in fact two applications and two orders, but they both
involve the same point of law.

It is necessary, therefore, to examine the provisions of the Limitation Act
1963. The point is whether, having regard to the terms of that Act, the general
rule as to ex parte orders is inapplicable in the present case. Section 1 of the Act
of 1963 applies in respect of the period of three years which applies to certain D
actions mentioned in s. 1 (2) of the Limitation Act, 1963. The present case is one
of those actions.

Section 1 (1) provides that s. 2 (1) of the Limitation Act, 1939

". . . shall not afford any defence to an action to which this section applies,
in so far as the action relates to any cause of action in respect of which: (a)
the court, has, whether before or after the commencement of the action,   E
granted leave for the purpose of this section, and (b) the requirements of
sub-s. (3) of this section are fulfilled."

Section 1 (3) provides that

" the requirements of this subsection are fulfilled in relation to a cause of
action if it is proved that the material facts relating to that cause of action   F
were or included facts of a decisive character which were at all times outside
the knowledge (actual or constructive) of the plaintiff until a date which—
(a) either was after the end of the three-year period relating to that cause of
action or was not earlier than twelve months before the end of that period,
and (b) in either case, was a date not earlier than twelve months before the
date on which the action was brought."   G

These provisions are explained in s. 7 (the interpretation section) which provides:

" (3) In this Part of this Act any reference to the material facts relating
to a cause of action is a reference to anyone or more of the following, that is to
say—(a) the fact that personal injuries resulted from the negligence, nuisance
or breach of duty constituting that cause of action; (b) the nature or extent   H
of the personal injuries resulting from that negligence, nuisance or breach of
duty; (c) the fact that the personal injuries so resulting were attributable
to that negligence, nuisance or breach of duty, or the extent to which any of
those personal injuries were so attributable.

" (4) For the purposes of this Part of this Act any of the material facts
relating to a cause of action shall be taken, at any particular time, to have
been facts of a decisive character if they were facts which a reasonable   I
person, knowing those facts and having obtained appropriate advice with
respect to them, would have regarded at that time as determining, in relation
to that cause of action, that (apart from any defence under s. 2 (1) of the
Limitation Act, 1939) an action would have a reasonable prospect of succeeding and of resulting in the award of damages sufficient to justify the bringing
of the action.

_____

(3) Ante, p. 276.

A   " (5) Subject to the next following subsection, for the purposes of this Part of this Act a fact shall, at any time, be taken to have been outside the knowledge (actual or constructive) of a person if, but only if—(*a*) he did not then know that fact; (*b*) in so far as that fact was capable of being ascertained by him, he had taken all such action (if any) as it was reasonable for him to have taken before that time for the purpose of ascertaining it; and (*c*) in so

B   far as there existed, and were known to him, circumstances from which, with appropriate advice, that fact might have been ascertained or inferred, he had taken all such action (if any) as it was reasonable for him to have taken before that time for the purpose of obtaining appropriate advice with respect to those circumstances."

C   The following subsection deals with persons under disability and is not material to this case. If the applicant's application is not maintainable having regard to the provisions of the Act of 1963, it is unnecessary to consider whether NIELD, J., was justified in giving leave for proceedings to be taken. I will merely say that leaving a swab in the body of a patient must raise a prima facie case of negligence, and the fact that the patient did not realise until after the final operation in October, 1964 that the injury caused by the original mistake could not be put

D   right might, on the evidence before NIELD, J., well justify leave being given.
       The matter of jurisdiction in respect of the present application depends on the provisions of s. 2 of the Act of 1963. That section provides as follows:

       " (1) Any application for the leave of the court for the purposes of the preceding section shall be made ex parte, except in so far as rules of court

E   may otherwise provide in relation to applications which are made after the commencement of a relevant action.
       " (2) Where such an application is made before the commencement of any relevant action, the court shall grant leave in respect of any cause of action to which the application relates if, but only if, on evidence adduced by or on behalf of the plaintiff, it appears to the court that, if such an action were

F   brought forthwith and the like evidence were adduced in that action, that evidence would, in the absence of any evidence to the contrary, be sufficient —(*a*) to establish that cause of action, apart from any defence under s. 2 (1) of the Limitation Act, 1939, and (*b*) to fulfil the requirements of sub-s. (3) of the preceding section in relation to that cause of action.
       " (3) Where such an application is made after the commencement of a

G   relevant action, the court shall grant leave in respect of any cause of action to which the application relates if, but only if, on evidence adduced by or on behalf of the plaintiff, it appears to the court that, if the like evidence were adduced in that action, that evidence would, in the absence of any evidence to the contrary, be sufficient—(*a*) to establish that cause of action, apart from any defence under s. 2 (1) of the Limitation Act, 1939, and (*b*) to fulfil

H   the requirements of sub-s. (3) of the preceding section in relation to that cause of action, and it also appears to the court that, until after the commencement of that action, it was outside the knowledge (actual or constructive) of the plaintiff that the matters constituting that cause of action had occurred on such a date as (apart from the preceding section) to afford a defence under s. 2 (1) of the Limitation Act, 1939."

I   Rules of Court have in fact been made, as contemplated by sub-s. (1), in R.S.C., Ord. 128, r. 2, which is as follows:

       " (1) An application for the grant of leave for the purposes of the said s. 1 made before the trial of the relevant action must be made by ex parte summons which shall, if the application is made before the commencement of the relevant action, be an ex parte originating summons. (2) The summons by which any such application is made must specify the cause of action to which the application relates and must be supported by an affidavit to which,

in tho caso of an application made before the commencement of the relevant   A
action, the statement of claim proposed to be served in that action must be
exhibited. (3) The requirement in s. 2 (1) of the Limitation Act, 1963, that
an application for the leave of the court for the purposes of s. 1 thereof shall
be made ex parte shall not apply if the application is made during the trial
of the relevant action."

When the matter was first stated to us, I was impressed by the general principle   B
that ex parte orders are always open to revision or reconsideration at the instance
of the party affected. This is a principle of natural justice which is required for
the protection of a party from the effects of an order made when he had no
opportunity of being heard. On further consideration, however, reasons appear
which can justify the effective granting of leave which will exclude the normal
operation of the limitation period on an ex parte application which will not be   C
subject to challenge.

It would appear that the reason for the application for leave being made ex
parte is to prevent the application for leave becoming a substantive hearing of
the issues in the action. On the hearing of the action, apparently the whole
position on the facts then proved will be open to the decision of the court. The
applicant for leave has on his ex parte application to make out a prima facie case,   D
and by his evidence will have to show sufficient ground for invoking the assistance
of the statute. Subsection (1) of s. 2 requires the application to be made ex parte;
and in sub-s. (2), in the case of an application before action, and in sub-s. (3),
after the commencement of an action, there is repeated insistence on the matter
being decided on the evidence adduced by or on behalf of the plaintiff. Any attack
by the defendant or other party affected by the ex parte order by means of an   E
application like the present would, it seems, be restricted to the evidence adduced
on the part of the plaintiff. It is only when the case is brought to trial that
evidence to the contrary is admissible.

It appears to me that it would be contrary to the clear intention of the Act
of 1963 if, once an ex parte order has been made, an application to set that order
aside could be made before the trial of the action. In the result the general   F
principle in regard to ex parte orders has, in my opinion, been excluded. I
think that THOMPSON, J. (4), reached the right conclusion and I would dismiss
the appeal.

SALMON, L.J.: I have the misfortune to differ from my lords and the
learned judge (4). The Limitation Act 1963 was passed to remedy the injustice   G
caused by s. 2 (1) of the Limitation Act, 1939—the case of Cartledge v. E. Jopling
& Sons, Ltd. (5), having brought this injustice into the limelight. Under the
Act of 1939 once the period of three years had elapsed from the date when the
cause of action arose, in cases such as the present, there was a complete defence
to the action. This was so even if the plaintiff's failure to bring the action
earlier was due solely to ignorance of the material facts for which he was in no   H
way to blame. This injustice could have been cured by a short and simple
amendment of s. 26 of the Act of 1939. It is perhaps a pity that this method
was not adopted. Instead machinery that to my mind is unnecessarily cumber-
some and complicated was set up by the Act of 1963. That Act lays down
circumstances in which s. 2 (1) of the Act of 1939 shall no longer afford a defence.
The onus is on the plaintiff to establish those circumstances. Before, however,   I
the plaintiff may avail himself of the protection of the Act of 1963, he has to
fulfil certain conditions. He must either before or after the commencement of
the action obtain the leave of the court (s. 1 (1) (a)). If he applies for leave
before issuing his writ, he must apply ex parte. The application will be granted
if, on evidence adduced on the plaintiff's behalf, it appears to the court that in
the absence of any evidence to the contrary he will be able to establish at the
trial that he has a good cause of action, and that the material and decisive facts

_____
(4) Ante, p. 276.   (5) [1961] 3 All E.R. 482; [1962] 1 Q.B. 189.

A relating to it were unknown to him until after or not earlier than twelve months before the end of the three year period of limitation, and that he brought his action within twelve months of these facts coming to his knowledge (s. 1 (3)). What are material and decisive facts is defined by s. 7. to which I shall presently refer. The Act of 1963 does not expressly state what leave is granted for. It certainly is not granted for bringing the action. This the plaintiff may do

B without leave, but he will then be defeated by the Act of 1939 if the defendant relies on it and the three years period of limitation has expired before the plaintiff issued his writ. The leave, in my judgment, is leave to set up facts in the action which, if established, will by virtue of the Act of 1963 knock the defence under s. 2 (1) of the Act of 1939 (which would otherwise be available) from under the defendant's feet.

C Evidently the legislature intended that this leave should normally be obtained before the writ was issued. It is true that there is a provision for an application for leave being made after the issue of the writ, but this is only when the plaintiff does not discover until then that his action is barred by the Act of 1939; see s. 2 (3) of the Act of 1963. The statute lays down that applications for leave after the issue of the writ shall be ex parte unless the rules of court otherwise

D provide (s. 2 (1)). Clearly, therefore, the statute envisages circumstances in which applications for leave need not be made ex parte. It seems to me that the legislature provided for the applications normally to be made ex parte in order to save unnecessary costs. If defendants or proposed defendants had to be made parties to the application, the costs relating to applications would be greatly increased. The normal case is unlikely to present any difficulty. The

E evidence adduced by the plaintiff will make it obvious either that the application for leave should be granted or that it should be refused. In the one case the defendant will not consider it worth while challenging the decision: in the other case he will not wish to do so; but what of the case in which leave is given and it is arguable or the defendant believes that it is arguable that it should have been refused? Does the fact that the Act of 1963 provides that the application

F shall be made ex parte in certain cases deprive the defendant of the right to be heard should he wish to ask for the order obtained ex parte to be set aside? In considering this problem, I start from the point that the general rule of law is that the courts will not make orders in legal proceedings affecting a party's rights without giving that party an opportunity of being heard. Leave, e.g., may be given ex parte to apply for certiorari or mandamus. The party against

G whom it is made can, however, always apply to discharge it; see R. v. Morley (Valuation Officer), Ex p. Peachey Property Corpn., Ltd. (6). As a rule, the party applying to discharge the ex parte order may file affidavit evidence. It is clear that, on an application under the Act of 1963, the only evidence to be considered is that adduced on behalf of the plaintiff. Does it follow from this that Parliament intended to deprive defendants of the right to apply to discharge the order?

H I think not. To my mind very clear words would be required to take away fundamental rights which are ordinarily accorded by the law and indeed by natural justice. In interlocutory matters parties exercising their normal rights to be heard often argue successfully on the other party's evidence alone that no order should be made in favour of that other party. Sometimes an application is successfully made to discharge an ex parte order without any further evidence

I being filed (Bidder v. Bridges (7)). The fact that the legislature takes away the right to file evidence in reply does not in my view raise any presumption that it intended also to take away the right to be heard. Indeed, the very fact that the legislature states that only the evidence of the plaintiff is to be considered on an application under the Act of 1963 suggests that the legislature envisaged that the defendants may apply to discharge the order, but that if they do, they must argue the case on the basis that the plaintiff's evidence is accurate

---

(6) (Jan. 25 1966), unreported.   (7) (1884), 26 Ch.D. 1.

and no other evidence is to be considered. This might well be considered appro- A
priate because the only issue is whether or not the plaintiff has made out a
prima facie case of lack of knowledge of the matters referred to in the statute.

The argument has been put forward on behalf of the plaintiff that the defendants cannot be prejudiced by leave being given to the plaintiff, since this is not
a final determination of the issues under the statute; these remain to be decided
in the action, and indeed the onus will remain on the plaintiff of establishing the B
facts necessary for these issues to be decided in his favour. I cannot accept
this argument. No doubt it is true that the issues remain to be decided in the
action with the onus left on the plaintiff, but the granting of leave under
the statute takes away from the defendant a most valuable right. But for the
leave obtained by the plaintiff, the defendants would have an unassailable
defence under the Limitation Act, 1939. Accordingly, it is unlikely that a C
plaintiff would issue a writ without first obtaining leave. If he did, the defendants could take the appropriate and inexpensive steps to have the action
dismissed in limine. This is a most valuable right, particularly when the claim
is a very stale one and the defendant no longer has his witnesses available. In
any event when leave is granted and only because leave has been granted, the
defendant is faced with fighting what may be expensive and complicated issues D
under the Act of 1963 and probably with the expense of preparing to fight all the
issues in the action. Although, as I have already said, it will usually be obvious
whether or not leave should be granted, there are cases, and this in my judgment
is one of them, in which applications for leave raise difficult points for consideration. A judge might well decide such an application one way without having
had the advantage of hearing any arguments on the defendant's behalf, and the E
other way having heard those arguments. In my judgment, there is nothing in
the Act of 1963 which takes away the defendant's right to adduce arguments in
favour of rescinding the order granting leave should he wish to advance them.
It is plain, as I have already pointed out, that the Act of 1963 envisages that
after the issue of the writ, there may be circumstances in which the application
for leave should be made on notice to the defendant (s. 2 (1)). In such a case, F
although the only evidence to be considered is that adduced on behalf of the
plaintiff, the defendants can of course argue that leave should not be granted
because the requirements of s. 1 (3) of the Act of 1963 have not been satisfied.
It would be odd that, because the application before the issue of the writ must
be made ex parte, the defendant can in such a case never be heard to ask for the
order made in his absence to be set aside. The order will in every case, whether G
made before or after the issue of the writ, deprive the defendant of the important
rights and advantages to which I have already referred. I cannot, with respect,
agree that if the defendant is heard and the judge in chambers refuses to discharge the order granting leave, this would cause any embarrassment for the
judge who decides the issue at the trial. He will be in quite a different position
from the judge in chambers. The judge in chambers only decides on the basis H
that the plaintiff's evidence is accurate. On the other hand, the judge at the
trial decides after hearing the plaintiff cross-examined and after the defendant's
evidence has been called.

I will now consider whether or not the order for leave should stand. The
facts are fairly plain. Much, however, turns on the true construction of sub-s. (3)
and sub-s. (4) of s. 7 of the Act of 1963, which define what are " material " and I
" decisive " facts for the purpose of s. 1 (3). These subsections seem to me to
be most complicated and obscure. I agree, however, with LORD DENNING, M.R.,
that they probably mean that in order to obtain leave this plaintiff would have
to show that until the last twelve months a reasonable person in her place would
not have regarded her injuries as so serious as to make it reasonable for her to
bring an action or (as it might equally well be put) would not have thought
that there was a reasonable prospect of an action resulting in an award of damages
sufficient to justify bringing it. For my part I cannot find that she has succeeded

A in this task.   She underwent a hysterectomy operation and Manchester repair in April, 1957.   For thirteen or fourteen weeks afterwards she had great difficulty in passing water.   She then discovered that a gauze swab had been left in her body after the operation.   A further operation was performed for the purpose of removing the gauze swab from her urethera.   At this stage she clearly knew that there had been negligence during the first operation and that as a result of

B it she had suffered about three months' inconvenience and pain and had to endure a second operation.   I can, however, well understand that a reasonable person might, and probably would, have thought that as her troubles were then over, it would be unreasonable to sue the defendants.   It soon became apparent, however, that her troubles were not over, for after the second operation she became incontinent, a distressing complaint from which she had never

C previously suffered.   The second defendant advised physiotherapy to try and cure her incontinence.   Accordingly she had a course of physiotherapy for six months; but it did her no good.   She was then advised by the second defendant that she had to have another operation.   This she underwent in April, 1958, and remained in hospital for three weeks.   She was not, however, cured and in August, 1958, she was advised by the second defendant that she would have to

D undergo yet another operation to cure the result of the original negligence.   It seems to me that by this time any reasonable person would have rightly regarded the consequences of the defendants' negligence as very serious and would have certainly considered that there was a reasonable prospect of an action resulting in an award of damages sufficient to justify bringing it.   The plaintiff, however, did nothing for years.   In fact it was inconvenient for her to have the third

E remedial operation when it was advised and she postponed it for over six years.   All this time she suffered from incontinence.   In October, 1964, another operation was performed in an unsuccessful attempt to cure her.   She then learnt that her condition was probably incurable.   If the complaint is incurable only because she delayed having the final operation, the fact that it is incurable is not the result of the original negligence.   Her position would now be no different vis-à-vis

F the defendants than it was in August, 1958.   No allegation is made against the second defendant that he was negligent in the advice he gave or did not give in August, 1958.   If, however, as I think, it must be assumed in her favour for present purposes that the complaint was already irremediable in August, 1958, this would have come to light had she, at that time, had the operation then advised.   On the facts as at present known, it would seem that there must have

G been negligence at the original operation and inordinate and inexcusable delay by the plaintiff in bringing this action.   No doubt it would be regrettable if these defendants should escape paying for their negligence even nine years after it occurred.   It may be that in the circumstances of this case they are not prejudiced by the delay.   There are, however, many cases in which the defendants would be prejudiced by what, to my mind, is such inordinate and inexcusable

H delay on the part of a plaintiff.   I do not think that the Act of 1963 was intended to protect, nor does it protect, a plaintiff who forbears for years from bringing an action after she knows that it will probably succeed and result in an award of very substantial damages—not even when years later she discovers that her damages might be even greater than she may originally have supposed.   For these reasons I would allow the appeal.

Appeal dismissed.

I

D. Henry: The defendants ask for leave to appeal to the House of Lords.   I submit that s. 2 (4) of the Limitation Act 1963 does not preclude such an appeal.   It provides:

" No appeal shall lie from any decision of the Court of Appeal on an appeal against the decision on an application under this section."

The decision of THOMPSON, J., (8) refusing the defendants' application to set aside

(8) Ante, p. 276.

the ex parte order was not a " decision on an application under this section " A within s. 2 (4).

D. C. *Calcutt*: Leave to appeal to the House of Lords should not be granted as this matter is interlocutory, and there should be finality; further, s. 2 (4) shows intention that appeal to the Court of Appeal shall be the end of the matter. If, however, your lordships should be minded to give leave, I should ask that terms as to costs should be imposed. B

LORD DENNING, M.R.: We think that this application must end here. The appeal was against a " decision on an application " under s. 2. So leave is not granted.

Leave to appeal to the House of Lords refused.

Solicitors: *Lovell, White & King*, agents for *Bevan, Hancock & Co.*, Bristol C (for the first defendant); *Hempsons* (for the second defendant); *Baileys, Shaw & Gillett*, agents for *Tozers*, Dawlish (for the plaintiff).

[*Reported by* F. GUTTMAN, ESQ., *Barrister-at-Law.*]

D

VERRALL v. FARNES.

[CHANCERY DIVISION (Cross, J.), April 21, 22, 25, 26, 28, May 19, 1966.]

Agriculture—Agricultural holding—Tenancy—Arrangement whereby defendant went into possession of plaintiff's farm for a trial period of a year without paying rent and on footing that he was to be entitled to any profits—Legally E *enforceable contract—Whether land let to defendant during continuance of an appointment under the plaintiff—Whether arrangement should take effect as creating tenancy from year to year—Agricultural Holdings Act, 1948 (11 & 12 Geo. 6 c. 63), s. 1 (1), s. 2 (1).*

The defendant, who had worked as a cowman, wanted a farm of his own. The plaintiff, wishing to help him, bought a farm at Horsham, comprising F some eighty-eight acres for £11,000 odd in January, 1963. The plaintiff arranged with the defendant that he should farm seventy-five acres for a year, as a trial period, without paying rent and on the footing that the defendant was to be entitled to any profits. It was expected by both parties that the defendant would remain in possession after the end of the year, paying an appropriate rent as from the expiry of the year. Friendly relations between G the parties deteriorated within the year. The defendant felt insecure and sought a written document evidencing that he was tenant. Eventually, on May 13, 1964, the plaintiff issued a writ against the defendant claiming a mandatory injunction that he should leave the farmhouse of which he was in possession and the stock of the farm. The defendant counterclaimed that he was entitled to retain possession by virtue of s. 2 (1)* of the Agricultural H Holdings Act, 1948.

Held: (i) there was not an " appointment " of the defendant under the plaintiff which would exclude the land from being an agricultural holding by virtue of the exception in s. 1 (1) of the Agricultural Holdings Act, 1948 (see p. 813, letter G, post).

(ii) the arrangement between the plaintiff and the defendant was a legally I enforceable contract (see p. 814, letter C, post), and took effect by virtue of s. 2 (1) of the Agricultural Holdings Act, 1948, as a tenancy from year to year, with the consequence that the defendant was entitled to retain possession of the land (see p. 815, letter H, post).

Goldsack v. *Shore* ([1950] 1 All E.R. 276) distinguished.

Harrison-Broadley v. *Smith* ([1964] 1 All E.R. 867) considered and explained.

---

* Section 2, so far as material, is printed at p. 812, letters E to H, post.

A   [As to licences to occupy agricultural land creating a tenancy, see 1 HALSBURY'S
LAWS (3rd Edn.) 256, para. 556, and notes (i) to (k); and for cases on s. 2 (1) of
the Agricultural Holdings Act, 1948, see 2 DIGEST (Repl.) 7, 12-14.
     For the Agricultural Holdings Act, 1948, s. 2 (1), see 28 HALSBURY'S STATUTES
(2nd Edn.) 29.]

B   Cases referred to:
     Goldsack v. Shore, [1950] 1 All E.R. 276; [1950] 1 K.B. 708; 2 Digest (Repl.)
        7, 12.
     Harrison-Broadley v. Smith, [1964] 1 All E.R. 867; [1964] 1 W.L.R. 456;
        3rd Digest Supp.

     Action.

C   This was an action brought by the plaintiff, Hector Jack Verrall, by writ
issued on May 13, 1964, against the defendant, William Patrick Farnes, claiming
a mandatory injunction ordering the defendant to leave the farmhouse of Lower
Perrylands Farm, Horsham, and the stock of the farm, and damages. The
following statement of facts is summarised from the judgment of CROSS, J.
     In 1958 the plaintiff and his wife came to live at Haywards Heath.
D   The defendant's wife came into their employ as daily help. The defendant
then worked as a cowman for a Mr. Wise. In 1961 he gave up that employment and worked on various other jobs. It was his ambition to save
enough money to have a small farm of his own. Mrs. Verrall told this to the
plaintiff, who told the defendant that he might be able to help him by purchasing
a suitable farm of which the defendant might become tenant. On Jan. 12, 1963,
E   the plaintiff bought Lower Perrylands Farm for £11,000 odd together with
livestock, consisting of forty-three cows and seven hundred chickens, and certain
machinery, implements and other dead stock at a valuation of £3,758. He
reserved thirteen acres for his own use, on which he intended to build a bungalow,
but left the defendant with possession of the farmhouse and the rest of the farm
and all the stock. The terms on which the defendant went into possession were
F   the outcome of various oral discussions, but were not reduced into writing. The
defendant was to farm seventy-five acres for a year without paying any rent and
on the footing that he was to be entitled to any profits; he was to be free to sell
any of the live or dead stock which he did not want, paying over the proceeds of
sale to the plaintiff. At the end of the year the plaintiff's accountant was to
examine the books to see how the defendant had been doing. It was the expecta-
G   tion of both parties that the defendant would remain in possession after the end
of the year, paying an appropriate rent as from the expiry of the year, and paying
the plaintiff for the live and dead stock of which he had not disposed during the
year by instalments which were suitable to his capacity to pay. The difference
between the plaintiff and defendant in regard to the terms agreed was this. The
plaintiff said that the defendant was " on trial " for the twelve months, so that
H   the plaintiff was to be at liberty to refuse to allow him to become tenant or to
purchase the stock. The defendant said that he became tenant at once and owner
of the stock at once, though he was not liable to pay any rent or anything for the
stock (save in so far as he might dispose of it) during the first twelve months.
The defendant sold some of the cattle and duly paid over the proceeds of sale
to the plaintiff. Until about September relations between the parties were fairly
I   good, but they then deteriorated as a result of two incidents with the consequence
that the defendant felt that his position was insecure. He was confident, despite
the worsening of their relations, that the plaintiff would not let him down; he
approached the plaintiff sometime in the autumn of 1963 and said that he wanted
security. There was a conflict of evidence on what passed at that interview but
there was no doubt that the plaintiff in fact got a Mr. Williams, who was the
manager of a company of which he was chairman, to work out the sum which
the defendant would have to pay at the end of the year for a tenancy in order to
reimburse the plaintiff for what he was out-of-pocket. After giving credit for

what the defendant had already paid to the plaintiff in respect of stock sold or   **A**
otherwise disposed of, some £3,200 was owing on the valuation, to which Mr.
Williams added interest at six per cent. on the sum that the plaintiff had paid
for the land and stock, which he had in fact borrowed from the bank, making a
total of just over £4,000. On Dec. 15, the plaintiff took Mr. Williams with him to
see the defendant, and they had a discussion in the car. The defendant did not
dispute that he was told that to obtain his tenancy he would have to produce the   **B**
sum of £4,000 odd by the beginning of January, 1964. On Jan. 1, 1964, Mr.
Williams wrote to the defendant as follows:

" I am sorry you have been unable to take up [the plaintiff's] offer to sell
the live and dead stock, at Dec. 31, 1963, for the sum of £4,076. As you know,
[the plaintiff] is out of the country at present and will be so until the middle
of February, if not later, and as I am unable to contact him, in the circum-   **C**
stances I must formally confirm that you have no tenancy of the farm, and
it could well be that [the plaintiff] on his return, may have to seriously
consider disposing of both the live and dead stock and the farm, although
this would seem a pity after all the efforts he has made on your behalf. In
view of the opportunity [the plaintiff] has offered you, I am sure that you will
continue to look after his interests."   **D**

The defendant handed the letter to his solicitors, who answered it at once as
follows:

" Your letter of the 1st instant addressed to [the defendant] has been
handed to us. We wish to emphasise that [the defendant] is not refusing [the
plaintiff's] offer and is, indeed, anxious to take it up and he is making   **E**
arrangements to obtain the necessary moneys and trust, therefore, that you
will keep the offer open for a short time. With regard to the second paragraph
of your letter, your statement that [the defendant] has no tenancy is denied
and he will rely upon the Agriculture Act if need be. The local agricultural
committee have been consulted and they are most satisfied with the way in
which [the defendant] has conducted the farm."   **F**

Mr. Williams, on his side, instructed solicitors. Correspondence between the two
firms of solicitors ensued. The plaintiff returned from abroad in February, 1964,
and after an interview with the defendant, he instructed T. Bannister & Co.,
a local firm of estate agents, to fix the rent for a tenancy. They fixed it at £375,
and on Mar. 5, 1964, wrote to the defendant's solicitors as follows:

" [The plaintiff] has been to see us again and states that he is still prepared   **G**
to grant [the defendant] a tenancy of the farm extending to approximately
seventy-five acres at a rental of £375 per annum, from the date when the live
and dead stock are paid for. [The plaintiff] is still agreeable to sell the live
and dead stock to [the defendant] at a figure equivalent to £4,075, plus an
addition equivalent to six per cent. per annum calculated on the amount
which [the plaintiff] has invested in the freehold and the live and dead stock   **H**
from Dec. 31 last to the date of the transfer. We are instructed to say that
unless this offer is accepted and paid for on or before the 25th instant, that is
Lady Day, 1964, the offer of the tenancy and of the live and dead stock will
be withdrawn and the live and dead stock will be sold."

The defendant then changed his solicitors, and his new advisers raised the   **I**
contention that there was a binding agreement for a tenancy and a sale of the
stock to the defendant when he took possession. On May 13, 1964, the plaintiff
issued a writ against the defendant, endorsed with a statement of claim. The
defendant delivered a defence and counterclaim, paras. 13 to 16 of which were as
follows:

" 13. The defendant says that by virtue of the said oral agreement there
was a binding contract for the sale to the defendant of the said live and dead
stock at a price of £3,758 and for the grant to the defendant of a tenancy of

A   the said farm buildings and seventy-five acres at a rent to be fixed by the plaintiff's valuers or accountants (which rent was on or about Feb. 21, 1964 fixed by the plaintiff's valuers at £375 per annum). The defendant further says that it was an implied term of the said agreement that in default of agreement as to the period of payment the said live and dead stock should be paid for by reasonable instalments and reasonable instalments would be

B   £676 per annum. 14. The defendant took possession of and worked the said land in performance of the said agreement and is and has at all material times been ready and willing to perform his obligations thereunder. 15. Alternatively, if (which is denied) the said oral agreement did not constitute a binding contract for the grant to the defendant of a tenancy of the said land the defendant was a tenant at will or licensee for value thereof and

C   claims to retain possession thereof pursuant to s. 2 (1) of the Agricultural Holdings Act, 1948. 16. In the further alternative if (which is denied) the said oral agreement did not constitute a binding contract for the purchase by the defendant from the plaintiff of the said live and dead stock and the grant to the defendant of such tenancy as aforesaid the defendant has paid to the plaintiff under the said agreement and for no consideration a sum of

D   £160 3s. 6d. (being the amount by which the said sums of £530 9s. 9d. and £65 16s. mentioned in para. 8 of the defence herein exceeded the amount of the proceeds of sale of such items of live and dead stock as were sold by the defendant) and has devoted the whole of his time to the management of the said land and stock and is entitled to reasonable remuneration therefor. A reasonable remuneration for the year to Dec. 31, 1963, would be £2,000."

E   The defendant counterclaimed for a declaration that under the oral agreement there was a binding contract; for specific performance of the agreement; or, alternatively, a declaration that he is entitled to retain possession of the land pursuant to s. 2 (1) of the Agricultural Holdings Act, 1948; for repayment to the defendant of the sum of £160 3s. 6d., mentioned in para. 16, and for £2,000 or such other sum as the court should think fit as quantum meruit for services

F   rendered by him. The plaintiff joined issue.

     The case noted below* was cited during the argument in addition to those referred to in the judgment.

     L. A. Blundell, Q.C., and *K. R. Bagnall* for the plaintiff.
     D. M. Burton for the defendant.

G
                                                      Cur. adv. vult.

     May 19. **CROSS, J.**, read the following judgment in which, after reviewing the facts, and referring to the correspondence and the pleadings he continued: I now turn to consider whose version of the arrangement under which the defendant took possession of the farm and stock is to be preferred so far as they differ. On that point, I have no hesitation in preferring that of the plaintiff. It

H   may well be that, looking back now, he thinks that he laid more emphasis than he in fact did on the fact that the twelve months was a trial period. Both parties were confident that the matter would go through, and neither directed his mind to the legal position or what would happen if the arrangement fell through. I am satisfied, however, that the plaintiff never intended to grant the defendant an immediate tenancy or to make him owner of the stock at once; and I am

I   equally certain that the defendant did not think at the time that he had obtained an immediate tenancy or that the stock had become his. He was quite prepared to trust the plaintiff.

     Further, I prefer the plaintiff's account of the interview in the autumn to that given of it by the defendant, which is really quite inconsistent with his attitude at the meeting on Dec. 15. I would add in this part of the case, that even if I thought that the parties intended an immediate tenancy and an immediate sale of

---

     * *Martineau* v. *Kitching*, (1872), L.R. 7 Q.B. 436.

the stock, I should have great difficulty in seeing how legal effect could be given A
to that intention, since their verbal arrangement did not include any method of
fixing the rent or for determining the amount and number of the instalments by
which the stock was to be bought.

It follows, therefore, that the defendant has been detaining this stock unlawfully and that the plaintiff is entitled to an order for its return or for damages in
lieu of its return, and for payment in respect of its use, subject always to any B
adjustment necessary to give effect to the point raised in para. 16 of the defence.
It also follows that the defendant is not entitled to any remuneration for the
first twelve months in which, as I have said, he was entitled to the profits of the
farm. Further, if there were no Agricultural Holdings Act, 1948, the plaintiff
would also be entitled to an order for possession of the farm with mesne profits
since January, 1964.   C

I must now, however, turn to consider the contention that though the plaintiff
never agreed to grant him a tenancy, the defendant nevertheless became an
agricultural tenant on taking possession by the operation of the Agricultural
Holdings Act, 1948. The relevant sections of the Act of 1948 are these. Section 1.

" Meaning of ' agricultural holding '.—(1) In this Act the expression
' agricultural holding ' means the aggregate of the agricultural land com- D
prised in a contract of tenancy, not being a contract under which the said
land is let to the tenant during his continuance in any office, appointment
or employment held under the landlord."

" Contract of tenancy " is defined in s. 94 (1), as follows:

" ' Contract of tenancy ' means a letting of land, or agreement for letting
land, for a term of years or from year to year . . ."   E

Then one comes to s. 2, which is the vital section here:

" (1) Subject to the provisions of this section, where under an agreement
made on or after the first day of March, 1948, any land is let to a person for
use as agricultural land for an interest less than a tenancy from year to year,
or a person is granted a licence to occupy land for use as agricultural land, F
and the circumstances are such that if his interest were a tenancy from year
to year he would in respect of that land be the tenant of an agricultural
holding, then, unless the letting or grant was approved by the Minister
before the agreement was entered into, the agreement shall take effect, with
the necessary modifications, as if it were an agreement for the letting of the
land for a tenancy from year to year."   G

Then there is a proviso which I need not read. Then, sub-s. (2) reads:

" Any dispute arising as to the operation of the foregoing subsection in
relation to any agreement shall be determined by arbitration under this
Act."

Then, s. 5 reads: H

" (1) Where there is not in force in respect of a tenancy of an agricultural
holding, whether created before or after the commencement of this Act, an
agreement in writing embodying the terms of the tenancy, or there is such an
agreement in force but it contains no provision for one or more of the matters
specified in Sch. 1 to this Act, the landlord or the tenant of the holding may, if
he has requested his tenant or landlord to enter into such an agreement contain- I
ing provision for all of the said matters but no such agreement has been
concluded, refer the terms of the tenancy to arbitration under this Act. (2)
On any such reference the arbitrator shall by his award specify the existing
terms of the tenancy, subject to any variations thereof agreed between the
landlord and the tenant, and, in so far as those terms as so varied make no
provision therefor and do not make provision inconsistent therewith, make
provision for all the matters specified in Sch. 1 to this Act having such effect
as may be agreed between the landlord and the tenant, or, in default of

A agreement, as appears to the arbitrator to be reasonable and just between the landlord and the tenant. (3). On any such arbitration the arbitrator may include in his award any further provisions relating to the tenancy which may be agreed between the landlord and the tenant."

Schedule 1 contains the " Matters for which provision is to be made in written tenancy agreements "; and it includes:

B   " 1. The names of the parties. 2. Particulars of the holding . . . 3. The term or terms for which the holding or different parts thereof is or are agreed to be let. 4. The rent reserved and the dates on which it is payable."

There are various other matters in 5, 6, 7, 8 and 9, to which I do not think that I need refer.

C Then, finally, s. 8 is to this effect:

  " (1) Subject to the provisions of this section, the landlord or the tenant of an agricultural holding may, whether the tenancy was created before or after the commencement of this Act, by notice in writing served on his tenant or landlord demand a reference to arbitration under this Act of the question what rent should be payable in respect of the holding as from the

D   next ensuing day on which the tenancy could have been determined by notice to quit given at the date of demanding the reference, and on a reference under this subsection the arbitrator shall determine what rent should be properly payable in respect of the holding at the date of the reference and accordingly shall, as from the day aforesaid, increase or reduce the rent previously payable or direct that it continue unchanged."

E Counsel for the defendant submitted that the arrangement under which the defendant took possession of the farm in January, 1963, was an agreement under which he was granted a licence by the plaintiff to occupy land for use as agricultural land, and that the circumstances were such that if his interest had been a tenancy from year to year he would be the tenant of an agricultural holding. Accordingly, counsel said that the agreement to grant the defendant a

F licence to occupy took effect as if it were an agreement for the letting of the land for a tenancy from year to year.

  In answer to this claim counsel for the plaintiff first submitted—though without much enthusiasm—that the circumstances were not such that if the defendant had been granted a tenancy from year to year he would have been tenant of an agricultural holding. The argument was that the defendant's relation to the

G plaintiff under the arrangement into which they had entered constituted an " appointment " under him, with the result that the land comprised in the assumed contract of tenancy would by virtue of the exception in s. 1 (1) not be an agricultural holding to which s. 2 (1) could apply. I reject that submission. The defendant's position with regard to the land and stock during the twelve months' probationary period cannot, in my judgment, be described as an appointment

H under the plaintiff.

  The next submission for the plaintiff was based on the decision of the Court of Appeal in *Goldsack* v. *Shore* (1) in which it was held that the word " agreement " in s. 2 (1) meant an enforceable contract and did not include a gratuitous licence to occupy under which the licensee had no legal rights whatever, except the right to be given reasonable notice to give up occupation.

I   It could not, of course, be argued that the defendant's position—once he had gone into occupation—was that of a mere gratuitous licensee whose licence could be terminated at any time on reasonable notice. The plaintiff was plainly obliged to allow him to remain on the land for the twelve months' probationary period. Nevertheless, it was argued that there was not really any enforceable contract between them such as would take this case out of the scope of the *Goldsack* decision (1), since the defendant was under no obligation to the plaintiff to remain

---

(1) [1950] 1 All E.R. 276; [1950] 1 K.B. 708.

on the land. The position was that the plaintiff having represented to the defen- **A** dant that if he went into occupation he would be allowed to remain in occupation rent free for twelve months in order to prove his capacity, would be estopped from going back on his word once the defendant had taken him at his word by going into occupation; but it would be wrong, so the argument runs, to say that there was any enforceable contract between them. Even if that were a correct analysis of the position, I am by no means sure that the defendant would not be **B** in occupation under an agreement within the meaning of s. 2 (1) of the Act of 1948; but in fact I do not think that the arrangement was as one-sided as the argument suggests. Once the defendant accepted the plaintiff's offer of a free trial period of twelve months with the right to take any profits he could not abandon the farm and the stock as and when he chose. At the very least he would have to give the plaintiff reasonable notice of his intention to go out of occupation. **C** In my judgment, the arrangement under which the defendant was allowed to go into occupation was a legally enforceable contract.

Then it was submitted that to allow s. 2 (1) to operate on the agreement made in this case would result in its being transformed into something totally different in character. The defendant was allowed to occupy rent free because his rent free occupation was only to be for a trial period of twelve months; at the end **D** of that period he would either go out of occupation or be granted a tenancy at a rent. If, however, his licence to occupy rent free for twelve months was converted into a tenancy from year to year it would become a tenancy from year to year free of rent. The Act of 1948, it was submitted, should not be construed so as to produce such a fantastic result.

In support of this argument reliance was placed on the judgment of PEARSON, **E** L.J., in the case of *Harrison-Broadley* v. *Smith* (2). There a landowner had entered into an agreement for the farming of her land in partnership with the defendant. She gave notice to dissolve the partnership and in answer to a claim for possession the defendant argued that the partnership agreement gave the partnership a licence to occupy the land to be farmed which was converted by s. 2 (1) of the Act of 1948 into a tenancy from year to year at no rent. The court **F** rejected that contention on the ground that the plaintiff landowner did not need to grant herself any licence to occupy her own land, and that the only licence to be implied in the partnership agreement was a licence to the defendant to occupy for the purpose of the business jointly with the plaintiff land of which the plaintiff was already in occupation. The Act of 1948 could not convert that licence into a tenancy in favour of the defendant alone since he was not in sole occupation **G** under the agreement, and it could not convert it into a tenancy in favour of the partnership because the licence was not to the partnership but only to the defendant.

In rejecting the defendant's contention, however, PEARSON, L.J., used language on which the plaintiff relies in this case, when he said (3):

    " It is to be observed that ' the agreement ' under which a person is granted **H** a licence to occupy land for use as agricultural land is to ' take effect, with the necessary modifications, as if it were an agreement for the letting of the land, for a tenancy from year to year '. That which is to take effect is the original agreement, with the necessary modifications. It is not permissible to substitute for the original agreement a radically different agreement and make that **I** take effect instead of the original agreement. In my view that is the principle which SIR RAYMOND EVERSHED, M.R., had in mind in *Goldsack* v. *Shore* (4) when he said: ' It is to be observed that the subsection goes on to say that the transaction which has been previously described must be such that, if the interest given were capable of being translated into a tenancy from year to year, then it shall take effect as such with the necessary modifications. It

---

(2) [1964] 1 All E.R. 867.   (3) [1964] 1 All E.R. at p. 874.
    (4) [1950] 1 All E.R. at p. 278; [1950] 1 K.B. at p. 713.

A   follows, therefore, that, if the subsection applies to it, it must be capable of
being so modified (and that must mean modified consistently with its own
terms) as to become enlarged into a tenancy from year to year.' Any modification of an agreement must be in a sense inconsistent with its own terms;
but I understand that passage to mean that the agreement must remain
recognisably the same agreement after the necessary modifications have been
B   made. This section is not applicable to an agreement which is not capable
of taking effect, with the necessary modifications, as an agreement for the
letting of the land for a tenancy from year to year. The necessary modifications have to be distinguished from a transformation of the agreement into
something radically different."

C   If the section applies here, the agreement between the parties will, it is said,
have been transformed into something radically different. What can be more
radical than a change from a rent free trial run of twelve months to a rent free
tenancy from year to year which means, for practical purposes, a tenancy for as
long as the defendant wishes to remain tenant? Pearson, L.J.'s words must be
read, however, in the context in which he used them. His language (5) shows
that the " radical difference " which he had in mind was the difference between
D   the party to whom the licence to occupy was given and the parties who would
become tenants of the land under the tenancy into which the agreement was said
to have been converted. He did not allude in any way to the fact that the tenancy
from year to year which was contended for would be free of rent, and I cannot
read his words as meaning that the court has a general discretion to exclude from
the operation of the section cases where the application of its produces surprising
E   results which Parliament may not have contemplated.

If one has an enforceable contract between A and B under which B, not
being an employee of A, is given a licence to occupy the land and farm it, then,
as I read the section, B gets a tenancy from year to year even though no rent is
payable under the agreement, and so no rent will be payable under the yearly
tenancy unless and until the tenant offers to pay a rent or the landlord succeeds
F   in getting a rent fixed by arbitration under one or other of the several sections
which provide for arbitration. After all, one of the objects of the Agricultural
Holdings Act, 1948, as I understand the matter, was to give security of tenure to
those actually farming the land, so that they should not be tempted to take the
last halfpenny of profit out of it during the period for which they had a contractual
right to remain in occupation, without regard to its future welfare after the date
G   when they were liable to be turned out. If one views the matter in this way it is
not perhaps altogether unreasonable that if a landowner wishes to " try out " a
possible future tenant in the way in which the plaintiff wished to try out the
defendant he should either employ him as bailiff or, if he wishes him to take the
profits and bear the losses during the trial period, seek the approval of the
Minister to the agreement.

H   For these reasons I feel obliged, though with some reluctance having regard to
the relations between the parties, to refuse the plaintiff any relief in relation to
the land as opposed to the stock, and to make the appropriate declaration with
regard to the land on the counterclaim.

Judgment for the plaintiff as regards the stock. Declaration on counterclaim as
I   *regards the land.*

Solicitors: *Vizard, Oldham, Crowder & Cash*, agents for *Bennett & Gawthrop*,
Hassocks, Sussex (for the plaintiff); *Churchill, Clapham & Co.*, agents for *Wannop
& Falconer*, Chichester (for the defendant).

[*Reported by* Jacqueline Metcalfe, *Barrister-at-Law.*]

---

(5) [1964] 1 All E.R. at p. 875.

A

GRANDI AND OTHERS v. MILBURN.

[QUEEN'S BENCH DIVISION (Lord Parker, C.J., Marshall and James, JJ.), May 19, 1966.]

Petroleum—Petrol tanker—Petrol sold direct from tanker into car tanks in café forecourt—Whether owner of forecourt occupier of premises on which petrol "kept" without licence—Whether owners of tanker occupiers of "premises", viz., petrol tanker, for keeping petrol without licence—Whether owners of tanker conveying petrol—Petroleum (Consolidation) Act, 1928 (18 & 19 Geo. 5 c. 32), s. 1 (1), (2), s. 6 (2)—Petroleum-Spirit (Conveyance by Road) Regulations, 1957 (S.I. 1957 No. 191), reg. 9.

B

The first appellant occupied premises consisting of a shop where a café business was carried on and a forecourt, not forming part of the highway, for access of vehicles to and from the highway. A petrol tanker with a capacity for 2,500 gallons of petroleum-spirit, owned and operated by the second appellants, drove on to the forecourt and remained there for some four hours. The tanker was equipped with hand operated pumps. Signs advertising the sale of petrol were erected, and petrol was sold by uniformed attendants direct from the tanker into the petrol tanks of cars belonging to members of the public, including the respondent, who drove their cars onto the forecourt. The first appellant took no part himself in the selling of the petrol and exercised no control over the tanker, but the tanker was there with his knowledge and consent for the purpose of selling petrol. On appeal by the first appellant against a conviction of keeping petroleum-spirit on his premises without there being in force a licence under s. 1 (1)* of the Petroleum (Consolidation) Act, 1928, and by the second appellants of (a) aiding and abetting the first appellant in the commission of the offence of which he was convicted, (b) being the occupier of premises, viz., the petrol tanker, in which petroleum-spirit was kept without there being a licence in force under s. 1 (1) of the Act of 1928, and (c) contravening (contrary to s. 6 (2) of the Act of 1928) reg. 9† of the Petroleum-Spirit (Conveyance by Road) Regulations, 1957, in that they replenished the fuel tank of a mechanically propelled vehicle with petroleum-spirit direct from the petrol tanker in such circumstances that the regulations applied to the tanker, as a conveyance of petroleum-spirit by road was taking place.

C

D

E

F

Held: (i) the first appellant had been rightly convicted under s. 1 (1), (2), of the Petroleum (Consolidation) Act, 1928, of keeping petroleum-spirit on his premises without a licence under that Act, because there was the element that the petroleum-spirit was "kept" (by reason of its quantity, the duration of four hours on the forecourt, and the purpose of trading), and the first appellant was the occupier of the premises on which the tanker was and it was common ground that there was no licence in force; accordingly, the second appellants had been rightly convicted of aiding and abetting him (see p. 820, letter H, to p. 821, letter A, and p. 821, letter H, post).

G

H

Dictum of LORD MACNAGHTEN in *Thompson* v. *Equity Fire Insurance Co.* ([1910] A.C. at p. 596) applied.

(ii) the second appellants had been wrongly convicted of being the occupiers of premises, viz., the petrol tanker, as there was no basis for extending the meaning of the word "premises" beyond its ordinary and natural meaning, which connoted land or buildings on land (see p. 821, letters B and H, post).

I

Coleman v. *Goldsmith* ((1879), 43 J.P. 718) distinguished.

(iii) the second appellants had been rightly convicted of contravening reg. 9

---

* Section 1 (1) is set out at p. 819, letter C, post.
† Regulation 9 is set out at p. 819, letter H, post.

A   of the Petroleum-Spirit (Conveyance by Road) Regulations, 1957, because, although by reg. 1 (1) the regulations of 1957 were applied to the conveyance of petroleum-spirit by road, yet in the present case there had been such conveyance and there could at one and the same time be both a " keeping " of petroleum-spirit contrary to s. 1 of the Act of 1928 and a conveyance of it by road, and in the present case the petrol had in the course of such
B   conveyance been supplied direct into the tanks of other motor vehicles (see p. 821, letters E, F and H, post).

     Appeal allowed in part.

     [As to petroleum-spirit licences, see 31 HALSBURY's LAWS (3rd Edn.) 408, para. 593; and as to the conveyance of petroleum-spirit, see ibid., pp. 398-400,
C para. 583.

     For the Petroleum (Consolidation) Act, 1928, s. 1, s. 6, see 19 HALSBURY's STATUTES (2nd Edn.) 270, 273.

     For the Petroleum-Spirit (Conveyance by Road) Regulations, 1957, reg. 1, reg. 9, see 17 HALSBURY's STATUTORY INSTRUMENTS (1st Re-Issue) 77, 79.]

     Cases referred to:
D   *Coleman* v. *Goldsmith*, (1879), 43 J.P. 718; 33 Digest (Repl.) 498, *544.*
     Pasky v. *Crafter*, [1941] S.A.S.R. 132.
     Thompson v. *Equity Fire Insurance Co.*, [1910] A.C. 592; 80 L.J.P.C. 13; 103 L.T. 153; 29 Digest (Repl.) 460, *3354.*

Case Stated.

E   This was a Case Stated by justices for the petty sessional division of Dartford in the county of Kent in respect of their adjudication as a magistrates' court sitting at Dartford on Nov. 8 and Dec. 2, 1965. On Oct. 21, 1965, the respondent, James Henry Milburn, preferred informations, (i) against the first appellant, Ralph John Grandi charging that on Aug. 30, 1965, at St. Bernard's Stores, Main Road, West Kingsdown, in the county of Kent, he, being the occupier
F   of the premises, kept petroleum-spirit there without there being in force under the Petroleum (Consolidation) Act, 1928, a petroleum-spirit licence authorising the keeping thereof, contrary to s. 1 of the Petroleum (Consolidation) Act, 1928; (ii) against the second appellants, European Petroleum Distributors, Ltd., charging that on Aug. 30, 1965, at St. Bernard's Stores, Main Road, West Kingsdown, in the county of Kent, they aided and abetted the first appellant in the
G   commission of the following offence, namely, that, on that day, he was the occupier of the premises in which petroleum-spirit was kept without there being in force under the Petroleum (Consolidation) Act, 1928, a petroleum-spirit licence authorising the keeping thereof, contrary to s. 1 of the Act of 1928; (iii) against the second appellants, charging that on Aug. 30, 1965, at St. Bernard's Stores, Main Road, West Kingsdown, in the county of Kent, they were the
H   occupiers of premises, namely, a petrol tanker in which petroleum-spirit was kept without there being in force under the Petroleum (Consolidation) Act, 1928, a petroleum-spirit licence authorising the keeping thereof, contrary to s. 1 of the Act of 1928; (iv) against the second appellants charging that on Aug. 30, 1965, at St. Bernard's Stores, Main Road, West Kingsdown, in the county of Kent, they contravened reg. 9 of the Petroleum-Spirit (Conveyance by Road)
I   Regulations, 1957, duly made by the Secretary of State on Feb. 7, 1957, under s. 6 of the Petroleum (Consolidation) Act, 1928, in that on that date and at that place, they replenished the fuel tank of a mechanically propelled vehicle, namely, a Ford car registered number 2588D, with petroleum-spirit direct from a vehicle, namely, a petrol tanker, conveying petroleum-spirit in such circumstances that the regulation applied to that conveyance, which regulation was at the date of the commission of the offence, and is still, in force, contrary to s. 6 of the Act of 1928. The following facts were found. The first appellant was the occupier of St. Bernard's Stores, Main Road, West Kingsdown, within the area of the

Dartford Rural District Council, his premises consisting of a shop with a fore- **A**
court with an exit for vehicles on to the main road, the forecourt not being part
of the public highway. On Aug. 30, 1965, a 2,500 gallon tanker, owned and
operated by the second appellants, drove on to the forecourt of St. Bernard's
Stores and remained there for approximately four hours. It had carried and
contained petroleum-spirit. There were two removable hand-operated petrol
pumps mounted on the tanker at the rear. Signs advertising the sale of petrol **B**
were put up and cars drew into the forecourt and were supplied with petrol by
uniformed attendants, the method of supply being by a pipe, leading direct from
the pump on the tanker, which was inserted into the fuel tanks of the cars, just
as if a car were being driven up to an ordinary petrol pump in a filling station
and supplied from an ordinary pump there. Amongst those who purchased
petrol was the respondent. He purchased three gallons for his car, paid for it **C**
and was given a receipt. He watched several other cars being filled with petrol
and saw money being paid for it. At no time was the first appellant seen to
intervene, and it was assumed, therefore, that the tanker was there with the
consent of the first appellant, but that he was in no way in charge of or exercising
any control over the tanker.

It was contended before the justices on behalf of the respondent that: (a) on **D**
a true construction of the Act and regulations, from the moment when petroleum-
spirit came on to any premises until the moment when it was taken away or
consumed, it must be either being " kept " or being " conveyed "; it was possible
that, at one time, it should be both being "kept" and being "conveyed", but
it was not possible that it should be neither " kept " nor " conveyed "; (b) in
deciding whether petroleum-spirit was being " kept " on any premises, the **E**
court should consider not only the length of time that it was on the premises
but the purpose for which it was there, and in this case the petroleum-spirit
was on the premises for the purpose of sale; (v) the word " premises " could
include and did include, the petrol tanker; the " conveyance " of the petroleum-
spirit still continued during the time that the tanker was stationary on the
forecourt. It was contended before the justices on behalf of the appellants **F**
(a) as to informations (i) and (ii), that the word "keep" implied some degree
of permanence, and the fact that petrol was in a tanker which was parked on
a forecourt for four hours did not mean that petrol was " kept " on the forecourt;
(b) as to information No. (iii), that a petrol tanker was not "premises", but a
vehicle; if a tanker was premises, where was the line to be drawn? Was a hearse, **G**
a pram, a bicycle (which had been held to be a vehicle) premises? No. The
definitions in several other statutes had persuasive authority, e.g., the Food and
Drugs Act, 1955, s. 135 (1): " a building or part of a building ", etc.; the Public
Health Act, 1936, s. 343 (1): ". . . include messuages buildings lands easements
and hereditaments." As these enactments tended to confirm, premises meant
buildings or land, and, as far as land was concerned, usually the land attached to **H**
buildings. A vehicle moved; premises, by their very nature, were immovable;
(c) as to information No. (iv): that reg. 9 applied only " in such circumstances
that these regulations apply to that conveyance ". The regulations did not
apply, because reg. 1 provided

" these regulations shall apply to the conveyance of petroleum-spirit by **I**
road . . . conveyance means such conveyance as aforesaid."

When the tanker had been on the road it was conveying but not dispensing;
but it was no longer conveying and it was not on a road; it was stationary and
had completed its journey and arrived at its destination for which the journey
had been made.

The justices convicted the appellants on all the four informations, and the
appellants now appealed.

A   The cases noted below* were cited during the argument in addition to those
referred to in the judgment of James, J.

    S. A. Morton for the appellants.
    Alan Fletcher for the respondent.

    JAMES, J., delivered the first judgment at the invitation of Lord Parker,
B C.J., in which after stating the facts, he continued: It is convenient to refer
at this stage to the provisions of the Petroleum (Consolidation) Act, 1928, and
the Petroleum-Spirit (Conveyance by Road) Regulations, 1957. Section 1 (1)
of the Petroleum (Consolidation) Act, 1928, provides:

    " Subject to the provisions of this Act, petroleum-spirit shall not be
    kept unless a petroleum-spirit licence is in force under this Act authorising
C   the keeping thereof and the petroleum-spirit is kept in accordance with such
    conditions, if any, as may be attached to the licence . . ."

The court has been invited to consider in the course of argument the terms of
s. 2 (3) of the Act. Section 2 provides the powers that local authorities can
exercise in respect of the granting of petroleum-spirit licences, and sub-s. (3)
D thereof provides:

    " A local authority may attach to any petroleum-spirit licence such
    conditions as they think expedient, as to the mode of storage, the nature
    and situation of the premises in which, and the nature of the goods with
    which petroleum-spirit is to be stored, the facilities for the testing of
    petroleum-spirit from time to time, and generally as to the safe-keeping of
E   petroleum-spirit."

By s. 6 (1) of the Act:

    " The Secretary of State may make regulations as to the conveyance of
    petroleum-spirit by road and for protecting persons or property from
    danger in connexion with such conveyance, and in particular . . . (d) for
    prescribing the precautions to be observed in the conveyance of petroleum-
F   spirit by road, and in loading and unloading vehicles used in such con-
    veyance and the time during which the petroleum-spirit may be kept during
    such conveyance, loading, and unloading as aforesaid."

Regulations were made by virtue of that statutory provision, and are the
Petroleum-Spirit (Conveyance by Road) Regulations, 1957. Regulation 1 (1)
G provides:

    " Subject as provided in this regulation, these regulations shall apply in
    relation to the conveyance of petroleum-spirit by road, and hereafter in
    these regulations the expression ' conveyance ' means such conveyance as
    aforesaid."

    Regulation 9, which is the particular one referred to as being infringed by the
H terms of the fourth information, reads:

    " The fuel tank of a mechanically propelled vehicle shall not be filled or
    replenished with petroleum-spirit direct from a vehicle conveying petroleum-
    spirit in such circumstances that these regulations apply to that conveyance."

    Three questions really arise in this appeal, and they are respectively as to the
I meaning to be given to the word " kept " where it appears in s. 1 (1) of the Act
of 1928, as to the meaning of the word " premises "—and in particular the
question arises can a petrol tanker be premises within the meaning of that term

---

* *Appleyard* v. *Bangham*, [1914] 1 K.B. 258; *Whitley* v. *Stumbles*, [1930] A.C. 544;
Blue v. *Pearl Assurance Co., Ltd.*, [1940] 3 W.W.R. 13; *West Mersea Urban District
Council* v. *Fraser*, [1950] 1 All E.R. 990; [1950] 2 K.B. 119; *Gardiner* v. *Sevenoaks
Rural District Council*, [1950] 2 All E.R. 84; *R.* v. *Smith*, [1962] Q.S.R. 226; *Cowlairs
Co-operative Society, Ltd.* v. *Glasgow Corpn.*, [1957] S.L.T. 288; *Stone* v. *Boreham*, [1958]
2 All E.R. 715; [1959] 1 Q.B. 1; *Kahn* v. *Newberry*, [1959] 2 All E.R. 202; [1959]
2 Q.B. 1.

as used in this legislation and the meaning of the word " conveyance ", A
where it appears in the regulations made under the Act of 1928. Counsel for
the appellants has favoured the court with an extensive review of all the authorities which he could find that might assist the court. In particular, he had, in
connexion with his submissions that the circumstances here did not amount to a
keeping of petroleum-spirit at these premises, referred us to the meaning to be
given to the word " keep ", and the word " kept ", as shown in the SHORTER B
OXFORD ENGLISH DICTIONARY (2nd Edn., pp. 1079, 1081) from which he culls
this element, namely, that " to keep " involves some degree of permanence, an
element of time, duration. He also urges in respect of the meaning to be given
to the word " kept " that, by virtue of the terms of s. 2 (3) of the Act of 1928,
it is kept with a degree of permanence in or on particular premises. He has
cited cases where the word " kept " or " keeping " have been used, words used C
in different statutes dealing with different subject-matters. I hope counsel will
acquit me of any discourtesy towards his arguments if I do not review the
authorities which he has cited in any detail. As I ventured to suggest in the
course of argument, I think that there is a real danger to be met when one seeks
to construe a word in one statute by reference to the construction given to the
same word in a different statute dealing with a wholly different subject-matter. D
I would refer straight away to the case which I, for my part, found most helpful
and that was *Thompson* v. *Equity Fire Insurance Co.* (1), and in particular to
the passage in LORD MACNAGHTEN'S judgment which was the judgment of their
lordships in that case, where he was dealing with the meaning to be attributed
to the words " stored or kept ". He said (2):

" What is the meaning of the words ' stored or kept ' in collocation and in E
the connexion in which they are found? They are common English words
with no very precise or exact signification. They have a somewhat kindred
meaning and cover very much the same ground. The expression as used
in the statutory condition seems to point to the presence of a quantity not
inconsiderable, or at any rate not trifling in amount and to import a notion
of warehousing or depositing for safe custody or keeping in stock for trading F
purposes. It is difficult, if not impossible, to give an accurate definition of
the meaning, but if one takes a concrete case it is not very difficult to say
whether a particular thing is ' stored or kept ' within the meaning of the
condition."

That observation has been referred to and relied on in subsequent cases in this G
country and also in the Commonwealth. For my part I think that it is unnecessary to seek to define what is the meaning of " kept " in the Petroleum (Consolidation) Act, 1928. Apart from being unnecessary, I think that it would be
highly inexpedient to seek to do so. I bear in mind the words of RICHARDS, J.,
in *Parkyn* v. *Crafter* (3), where he said:

". . . it might be dangerous to commit oneself to a pronouncement intended H
to meet every case that may arise."

For my part, looking at the facts of this case as found by the justices, there is
present the element of considerable quantity, a tanker with a capacity of 2,500
gallons of petroleum-spirit, there is the element of duration—true only a matter
of about four hours, but certainly not a fleeting passing call—there is also the
element of being there for the purpose of trade, namely, selling, and, by reason I
of the presence of those elements, I should say that there is no doubt that this
was a case in which the first appellant was the occupier of premises on which on
this occasion petroleum-spirit was " kept ". It is common ground that there
was no licence in force and, therefore, for my part, I consider that the justices
came to a right conclusion in respect of that information.

---

(1) [1910] A.C. 592.   (2) [1910] A.C. at p. 596.
                    (3) [1941] S.A.S.R. 132 at p. 138.

A   As to the second information (4), aiding and abetting, it is, I think, conceded that the result in respect of information No. (i) really governs information No. (ii), and that there is an aiding and abetting of petroleum-spirit being "kept", if in fact it was kept as I find that it was.

As to the third information, the question arises whether the petrol tanker can properly be termed " premises " within the meaning of that word as used in this **B**   legislation. In the context of this legislation, I see no basis whatsoever for extending the meaning of the word " premises " beyond its ordinary and natural meaning, namely, that it connotes land or buildings on land and, for my part, in the absence of any indication at all that that meaning should have been extended, I think that the justices fell into error in holding that this petrol tanker was " premises " and that, therefore, the second appellants were occupiers **C**   of the premises, namely, a petrol tanker.   In view of that the conviction on that information was wrong.

As to the last information, which alleged contravention of reg. 9 of the regulations of 1957, there is no authority covering this situation which has been cited and is directly in point, but one really does not need authority, for, in my judgment, the words are quite plain, and where the facts are that petroleum-spirit **D**   is loaded into a petrol tanker so that that petrol tanker can carry that spirit by road, then the conveyance of petroleum-spirit by road takes place from then on until the petrol tanker is emptied of its load.   In my judgment, there can be at one and the same time a conveyance of petroleum-spirit by road taking place and that petroleum-spirit being kept on the premises occupied by some person. On the facts here it is quite clear that, if one looked at the matter differently **E**   and said that conveyance by road came to an end when this petrol tanker stopped and became stationary for four hours on this forecourt, then all the provisions of the regulations designed to secure safety for the public and those persons who are attending the vehicle would not apply at all, and all those safety provisions could be disregarded.   That would make a nonsense of the situation, and, in my judgment, the facts here quite clearly show that there was indeed a con-**F**   veyance of petroleum-spirit by road, that, in the course of that conveyance, the petroleum-spirit from the tanker was supplied direct into the tanks of other motor vehicles, and, therefore, that there was in fact a contravention of reg. 9, and in that respect the justices arrived at a correct conclusion.

In my judgment, this appeal should be allowed to this extent only, that the conviction on the third information against the second appellants of being **G**   occupiers of premises, namely, a petrol tanker in which petroleum-spirit was kept, should be quashed.   For the rest, I would say that the appeal should be dismissed.

MARSHALL, J.:   I agree.

LORD PARKER, C.J.:   I agree, and I would only add my thanks to **H**   counsel for the appellants for his careful argument, and my congratulations to the justices who dealt so carefully with a situation that was not altogether an easy one.   Although we are quashing the third information, no blame in any way attaches to the justices who quite clearly relied on and, in my judgment were misled by, *Coleman* v. *Goldsmith* (5).   In my judgment, that case is distinguishable on the ground that the keeping there was a keeping—if there was a keeping—in " a place " and not on " premises ".   In my judgment, " place " **I**   is a much wider term, and on that basis *Coleman* v. *Goldsmith* (4) could be justified, but not a conviction in the present case.

Appeal allowed in part.

Solicitors: *Wood & Sons* (for the appellants); *Hewitt & Co.* (for the respondent).

[*Reported by* N. P. METCALFE, ESQ., *Barrister-at-Law.*]

---

(4) The informations are set out at p. 817, letters F to I, ante.
(5) (1879), 43 J.P. 718.

DONAGHEY v. P. O'BRIEN & CO., AND ANOTHER.   A

[COURT OF APPEAL (Willmer, Davies and Russell, L.JJ.), May 3, 4, 5, 25, 1966.]

Building—Building regulations—Roof—Roof work—Sloping surface—Protection against falling down and off roof but not against falling through hole in roof under construction—Liability of contractors to servants of sub-contractors— Employee of sub-contractors falling through gap between purlins of roof— Crawling boards provided but not used—Foreman of sub-contractors present but did not ensure that crawling boards used—Whether accident solely caused by employee in relation to contractors' liability—Building (Safety, Health and Welfare) Regulations, 1948 (S.I. 1948 No. 1145), reg. 4, reg. 31 (1), (3).

Court of Appeal—Ground of appeal—Contention not pressed in court of first instance—Inapplicability of building regulations—All necessary facts found at trial—Whether contention should be allowed to be argued on appeal.   C

The plaintiff was employed as a steel erector by the first defendants, who were sub-contractors of the second defendants and were engaged to lay asbestos sheets on the roof of a hangar. The roof consisted of a number of bays, the height to the apex of each bay being sixty-two feet from the ground and that to the gutters between the bays being about fifty feet. The slope of   D the roof was twenty-two degrees. The asbestos sheets were being laid transversely on angle-iron purlins running longitudinally. While the plaintiff and another workman were trying to replace a sheet which was out of position, the plaintiff overbalanced and fell through an aperture where there was no sheeting. He was severely injured. There was no evidence that the nature of the surface of the roof was slippery or of the state of the weather. The   E foreman of the first defendants was present, but did not insist on crawling boards being used. Crawling boards had been provided by the second defendants and were available on the floor of the hangar. It was for the plaintiff to put them in position, but he did not use them. In an action by the plaintiff for damages for personal injuries, the second defendants were found to have been in breach of statutory duty under reg. 31 (1)* of the   F Building (Safety, Health and Welfare) Regulations, 1948. The second defendants did not expressly abandon at the trial any contention that reg. 31 (1) had no application, but it was not pursued on their behalf. On appeal on the ground (among other contentions) that reg. 31 (1) did not apply,

Held: (i) all relevant evidence as to facts on which the court would   G have decided whether reg. 31 (1) applied had been given, and the material facts were not in dispute; in such circumstances the Court of Appeal would allow the question whether reg. 31 (1) applied to be argued on the appeal although it had not been argued at the trial (see p. 829, letters B and C, p. 824, letter B, and p. 831, letter B, post).

Principle stated by LORD WATSON *in* Connecticut Fire Insurance Co. v.   H
Kavanagh *([1892] A.C. at p. 480) applied.*

(ii) reg. 31 (1) of the Building (Safety, Health and Welfare) Regulations, 1948, did not apply because it was directed to precautions against falling down and off a roof but not against falling through an opening or hole in it (see p. 830, letter B, p. 824, letter B, and p. 831, letter I, post).

(iii) moreover there was no breach of reg. 31 (3) (see p. 830, letter F, p. 824,   I letter B, and p. 831, letter C, post).

(iv) if, however, reg. 31 (1) were applicable, then there was a breach of it for which the second defendants were liable by virtue of reg. 4 (ii), and this liability was not vicarious; further, a defence that the plaintiff was the sole cause of the breach by reason of his failure to use crawling boards would not be maintainable, because the failure of the first defendants' foreman to

---

* Regulation 31 (1) is printed at p. 826, letter D, post.

H.L. [1967] 2 All E.R.

Reversed.
1014.

A   ensure that crawling boards were used was also a cause of the breach, and
       this factor could not be disregarded merely because the first defendants'
       foreman was not the servant of the second defendants (see p. 827, letters
       B, H and I, p. 824, letter B, and p. 831, letter C, post).
           Ginty v. *Belmont Building Supplies, Ltd.* ([1959] 1 All E.R. 414)
       distinguished.
B   Appeal allowed.

       [**Editorial Note.** Openings in a roof are the subject of reg. 30 of the Building
       (Safety, Health and Welfare) Regulations, 1948, but reg. 30 did not impose a duty
       on the second defendants in the circumstances of the present case as the plaintiff
       was not in their employment (see reg. 4 (i); and p. 829, letter I, post).
           As to safety provisions for roof work under building regulations, see 17 HALS-
C   BURY'S Laws (3rd Edn.) 127, para. 206 notes (*k*) (*l*); and for cases on the subject,
       see 24 DIGEST (Repl.) 1075, *327*; 1077, *333, 334*; 1081, *361-363*.
           For the Building (Safety, Health and Welfare) Regulations, 1948, reg. 4,
       reg. 31, see 8 HALSBURY'S STATUTORY INSTRUMENTS (1st Re-issue) 189, 202.]

       Cases referred to:
D   *British Fame (S.S. or Vessel) (Owners)* v. *S.S. or Vessel Macgregor (Owners)*,
           [1943] 1 All E.R. 33; [1943] A.C. 197; 112 L.J.P. 6; 168 L.T. 193;
           42 Digest (Repl.) 913, *7085*.
       Connecticut Fire Insurance Co. v. *Kavanagh*, [1892] A.C. 473; 61 L.J.P.C. 50;
           67 L.T. 508; 57 J.P. 21; 29 Digest (Repl.) 488, *3489*.
       Ginty v. *Belmont Building Supplies, Ltd.*, [1959] 1 All E.R. 414; Digest (Cont.
E   Vol. A) 597, *333a*.
       Grant v. *National Coal Board*, [1956] 1 All E.R. 682; [1956] A.C. 649; [1956]
           2 W.L.R. 725; 33 Digest (Repl.) 901, *1332*.
       Jenner v. *Allen West & Co., Ltd.*, [1959] 2 All E.R. 115; [1959] 1 W.L.R. 554;
           Digest (Cont. Vol. A) 599, *340c*.
       Moorcraft v. *Thomas Powles & Sons, Ltd.*, [1962] 3 All E.R. 741; [1962] 1
F   W.L.R. 1447; Digest (Cont. Vol. A) 598, *333b*.
       Mulready v. *J. H. & W. Bell, Ltd.*, [1953] 2 All E.R. 215; [1953] 2 Q.B. 117;
           24 Digest (Repl.) 1075, *327*.
       Phillips v. *Robertson Thain, Ltd.*, [1962] 1 All E.R. 527; [1962] 1 W.L.R. 227;
           Digest (Cont. Vol. A) 606, *364f*.
       Ross v. *Associated Portland Cement Manufacturers, Ltd.*, [1964] 2 All E.R. 452;
G   [1964] 1 W.L.R. 768; 3rd Digest Supp.
       Smith v. *Cammell Laird & Co., Ltd.*, [1938] 3 All E.R. 52; [1938] 2 K.B. 700;
           107 L.J.K.B. 529; 139 L.T. 25; *rvsd.* H.L., [1939] 4 All E.R. 381;
           [1946] A.C. 242; 109 L.J.K.B. 134; 163 L.T. 9; 104 J.P. 51; 24 Digest
           (Repl.) 1087, *396*.
       Tasmania (Owners) & Freight Owners v. *Smith, City of Corinth (Owners)*,
H   *The Tasmania*, (1890), 15 App. Cas. 223; 63 L.T. 1; 6 Asp. M.L.C.
           517; 42 Digest (Repl.) 813, *5883*.
       Warehousing & Forwarding Co. of East Africa, Ltd. v. *Jafferali & Sons, Ltd.*,
           [1963] 3 All E.R. 571; [1964] A.C. 1; [1963] 3 W.L.R. 489; Digest
           (Cont. Vol. A) 150, *558b*.

I   **Appeal.**
       This was an appeal by the second defendants, Boulton & Paul, Ltd., from a
       judgment of JAMES, J., given at the Bedford Assizes on Feb. 3, 1966, awarding
       the plaintiff against both the first defendants and the second defendants
       £13,873 1s. 2d. damages for personal injuries, the cause of action as against the
       second defendants being breach of statutory duty under reg. 31 (1) of the Building
       (Safety, Health and Welfare) Regulations, 1948. Contributory negligence
       on the part of the plaintiff was established, he being held to be twenty-five per
       cent. at fault. The second defendants appealed. The plaintiff served a cross-notice

that the judgment should be affirmed on the alternative ground that the second A
defendants were in breach of reg. 31 (3) of the regulations of 1948.

J. D. May, Q.C., and *F. M. Drake* for the second defendants.
R. E. G. Howe, Q.C., and *M. Walker* for the plaintiff.
The first defendants did not appear and were not represented.

Cur. adv. vult.

May 25. The following judgments were read.   B

WILLMER, L.J.: RUSSELL, L.J., who is unfortunately not able to be present
today, authorises me to say that he agrees with the judgment which I am about
to deliver.

This is an appeal by the second defendants against a judgment of JAMES, J.,
given at Bedford Assizes on Feb. 3, 1966, in an action brought by the plaintiff C
against two defendants claiming damages for personal injuries sustained in
the course of his work. The judge found both defendants at fault, but he also
found that the plaintiff himself was at fault to the extent of twenty-five per cent.
He assessed the plaintiff's damages at £18,497 8s. 2d. and gave judgment against
both defendants for three-quarters of that sum, namely, £13,873 1s. 2d. He also
held that the second defendants were entitled to a hundred per cent. indemnity D
against the first defendants. On this appeal we have been concerned only with
the liability of the second defendants. The first defendants are said to be without
financial means and, although they delivered a defence, they took no part in the
trial of the action, but allowed the claim against them to go by default; nor
have they taken any part in this appeal.

The contentions put forward on behalf of the second defendants are (i) that the E
judge was wrong in finding them responsible in any degree for the plaintiff's injuries, and (ii) in the alternative that the plaintiff's share of the responsibility
ought to have been assessed at something more than twenty-five per cent.
The plaintiff filed a cross-notice contending that the second defendants should
have been found to be wholly at fault, but this contention was abandoned
during the course of the argument, and it is not now in issue that the plaintiff F
was at fault in some degree. By the cross-notice it was also sought to support the
judge's conclusion on grounds other than those on which he based his judgment.
No question as to the quantum of the damages assessed by the judge has been
raised on either side.

The plaintiff's claim arose out of an accident which occurred on Feb. 3, 1962,
in the course of the construction of a hangar at Luton Airport. The plaintiff G
was a steel erector employed by the first defendants, who were sub-contractors
to the second defendants, being themselves sub-contractors to the main contractors. The work which the first defendants were engaged to carry out was that
of laying asbestos sheets on the roof of the hangar. The roof of the hangar
consisted of a number of bays, the height to the apex of each bay being sixty-two
feet from the ground, and that to the gutters between the bays about fifty feet. H
The asbestos sheets were laid transversely on angle-iron purlins which ran
longitudinally along the bays. The slope of the roof in each bay from apex to
gutter was said to be twenty-two degrees.

The plaintiff was working in company with a man called Crean under the
supervision of the first defendants' foreman, Mr. Boyle. The second defendants
were not immediately concerned with the laying of the asbestos sheets, for which I
they had contracted with the first defendants; but they had a foreman, Mr.
Gregory, in charge of their own men on the site, and he was exercising some degree
of general supervision over the progress of the work as a whole. In particular
it was his responsibility to arrange for the provision of safety appliances, where
these were required, both for the second defendants' own men and for their various
sub-contractors. On the day of the accident the plaintiff and Mr. Crean were
engaged in relaying certain asbestos sheets which had been displaced by a gale.
In the course of this work the foreman, Mr. Boyle, observed that one of these

A sheets had been relaid out of line, and he instructed the men to adjust it. Having done this, the plaintiff and Mr. Crean were standing on the outside of the roof endeavouring to shift the sheet which was out of place. They had to stand on opposite sides of the sheet. Mr. Crean was able to stand on one of the asbestos sheets in the next adjacent tier; but on the plaintiff's side there was no sheeting, and he had to stand with his right foot on the sheet next below in the same tier,

B and with his left foot on one of the longitudinal purlins. Standing thus, the plaintiff and Mr. Crean proceeded to tug at the sheet which was out of place. It suddenly came free, with the result that the plaintiff over-balanced backwards and fell through the aperture where there was no sheeting to the ground some fifty or sixty feet below. In consequence the plaintiff sustained serious injuries which have not been the subject of any controversy in this court. The plaintiff

C alleged that the accident was due to the failure of both defendants to provide any protective appliances to prevent his fall. He based his claim against both defendants on negligence at common law and on breach of statutory duty. As against the first defendants, his own employers, he alleged breach of several of the Building (Safety, Health and Welfare) Regulations, 1948, but as against the second defendants he alleged only breach of reg. 31 of the regulations of 1948. His case was

D that roof ladders or crawling boards should have been provided so as to enable the work on the outside of the roof to be carried on in safety.

The second defendants alleged, and the judge found, that a suitable supply of crawling boards had been provided by them, and that these were readily available on the floor of the hangar. The plaintiff and Mr. Crean, however, did not see fit to use them, and the foreman, Mr. Boyle, who was watching their operations, did

E not insist on their doing so. It is common ground that no crawling boards or other safety appliances were in fact used. Mr. Rimmer, an architect and surveyor called on behalf of the plaintiff, gave evidence which the judge accepted, that having regard to the pitch of the roof, the fragile nature of the materials and the height above the ground, some safety equipment in the nature of roof ladders or crawling boards ought to have been provided and used. The judge found,

F however, that it would be the workmen's job (in this case the plaintiff's) to place such equipment in the position where it was required for use, and that he could not expect anyone else to do it for him.

In these circumstances the judge had no difficulty in finding that the first defendants were guilty of negligence at common law. He expressed the view that there was the grossest lack of care on the part of Mr. Boyle, the foreman, in

G allowing work to be done on the roof without any roof ladder or crawling board. He also found the first defendants to be in breach of their statutory duty under reg. 24 and reg. 31 (1). As to the second defendants, the judge acquitted them of the charge of negligence at common law. They were not the employers of the plaintiff, and accordingly were not under the duty owed by a master to his servant. Having employed a competent firm, experienced in roofing work, and

H having themselves provided an adequate supply of safety appliances, they were, in the judge's view, justified in leaving the details of the safety of their subcontractors' men to the sub-contractors' own organisation, and owed no further duty at common law. This conclusion has not been challenged before us.

The learned judge, however, while acquitting the second defendants and their foreman, Mr. Gregory, of any moral blame, held that they were in breach, equally

I with the first defendants, of their statutory duty under reg. 31 (1). Following the decision of this court in *Mulready* v. *J. H. & W. Bell, Ltd.* (1), he held that the second defendants, as sub-contractors responsible for the construction of the roof, were under a duty to comply with that regulation and that they could not avoid responsibility for the performance of that duty by delegating the work to their own sub-contractors. Since, in the judge's view, the statutory duty was not in fact performed, the second defendants, equally with the first defendants, must

---

(1) 1953] 2 All E.R. 215; [1953] 2 Q.B. 117.

accept responsibility for its non-performance. A further charge against the A
second defendants of breach of reg. 31 (3) was dismissed by the judge, who
expressed the view that this paragraph of the regulation had no application to the
circumstances of the present case. Having found the second defendants guilty of a
breach of their statutory duty, the judge went on to find that the plaintiff, having
failed to use the safety appliances which were in fact provided, was himself in
breach of his duty under reg. 4 to co-operate in carrying out the requirements of B
reg. 31 (1). He considered, but rejected, a contention put forward on behalf of
the second defendants, based on *Ginty* v. *Belmont Building Supplies, Ltd.* (2), that
the plaintiff's breach in this respect was co-terminous and co-incident with the
only breach found against the second defendants, and was therefore to be regarded
as the sole cause of the accident. The judge declined to accept this contention
having regard to the presence of the foreman, Mr. Boyle, and to the failure of the C
latter to see that the provisions of the regulations were carried out. In the
event he concluded that the plaintiff's breach contributed only to the extent of
twenty-five per cent., and on this basis he gave judgment in favour of the plaintiff
for three-quarters of the damages assessed.

It will be desirable at this stage to refer to the relevant regulations. Regulation
31 is headed " Roof work ", and the relevant parts of it provide as follows: D

" (1) Where work is done on the sloping surface of a roof and, taking into
account the pitch, the nature of the surface, and the state of the weather,
a person employed is likely to slip down or off the roof, then unless he has
adequate hand-hold or foothold or is not liable to fall a distance of more than
six feet six inches from the edge of the roof, suitable precautions shall be
taken to prevent his so falling . . . (3) Where work is being done on or near E
roofs or ceilings covered with fragile materials through which a person is
liable to fall a distance of more than ten feet—(*a*) where workmen have to
pass over or work above such fragile materials, suitable and sufficient
ladders, duck ladders or crawling boards, which shall be securely supported,
shall be provided and used . . .''

Reference must also be made to reg. 4, the relevant provisions of which are as F
follows:

" It shall be the duty of every contractor and employer of workmen who is
undertaking any of the operations to which these regulations apply (i) to
comply with such of the requirements of regs. 5-30 . . . 80-84 . . . as
affect any workman employed by him . . . (ii) to comply with such of the G
requirements of regs. 31-33 . . . as relate to any work, act or operation
performed or about to be performed by such contractor or employer of
workmen; . . . It shall be the duty of every person employed to comply
with the requirements of such regulations as relate to the performance of an
act by him and to co-operate in carrying out Parts 2 to 7 of these regulations
. . .''   H

Before the judge the argument proceeded on the basis that reg. 31 (1) applied
without question to the operation which was in progress. Although there was no
express abandonment of the point, counsel for the second defendants never argued
that this regulation had no application. On the footing that the regulation applied
the judge held that the taking of suitable precautions involved that roof ladders
or crawling boards should not only be provided but should also be used. In the I
present case, though crawling boards were provided, none was in fact used.
Having regard to the answers given by Mr. Rimmer in his evidence, I think that
the judge was well justified in his conclusion that the provision and use of roof
ladders or crawling boards would have been a proper precaution to prevent workmen from slipping or falling on this roof. Since no crawling board was used, it
would follow that, if reg. 31 (1) applied, the second defendants as contractors,

(2) [1959] 1 All E.R. 414.

A equally with the first defendants as employers, were in breach of their obligation to comply with it, as required by reg. 4 (ii).

In this court we are bound, as was the judge, to hold, following the decision in *Mulready* v. *J. H. & W. Bell, Ltd.* (3), that the second defendants cannot escape liability for this breach by delegating the performance of their obligation to their sub-contractors. Counsel for the second defendants has intimated to us that, in

B the event of this case going further, he desires to keep open a submission that *Mulready* v. *J. H. & W. Bell, Ltd.* (3) was wrongly decided; but that is not a submission that we in this court can entertain. It follows that in my judgment, if reg. 31 (1) applied, the judge was right in his conclusion that the second defendants were in breach of it.

The next point argued on behalf of the second defendants was that, assuming

C the non-use of a crawling board to constitute a breach of the regulation on their part, that breach was solely due to the plaintiff's own failure, in breach of his duty under reg. 4, to use any of the crawling boards provided. The plaintiff's breach was accordingly precisely co-terminous and co-incident with the only breach of which the second defendants were guilty within the principle applied by PEARSON, J., in *Ginty* v. *Belmont Building Supplies, Ltd.* (4). Later cases have shown that the

D application of that principle is to be confined within very narrow limits. In the latest case, that of *Ross* v. *Associated Portland Cement Manufacturers, Ltd.* (5), LORD REID neatly stated the principle as it applies to the occupier of a factory in the following terms:

"... he can avoid civil liability to the actual offender if he can show that the conduct of this offender was the sole cause of the breach and resulting

E injury to him."

Much to the same effect were the words of PEARCE, L.J., in *Jenner* v. *Allen West & Co., Ltd.* (6):

"An employer can defeat such a claim if he can say: ' I am in breach of the regulations because of, and only because of, your default '."

F It is argued in the present case that the second defendants show precisely that, namely, that their only breach (the non-use of crawling boards) was solely caused by the plaintiff's own breach of his duty to use one. The fact that the first defendants' foreman, Mr. Boyle, was also a party to the breach is, it is said, of no relevance, for the second defendants were not the employers of Mr. Boyle and were under no liability for any failure on his part. In this connexion it is emphasised

G that any liability incurred by the second defendants under the principle of *Mulready* v. *J. H. & W. Bell, Ltd.* (3) was a primary liability, and in no sense a vicarious liability for the faults or omissions of their sub-contractor. I do not dissent from this proposition, but in spite of the ingenious argument presented by counsel for the second defendants, I remain quite unable to see how it is relevant to the circumstances of the present case. Here there was a breach of the

H regulation for which the second defendants must assume responsibility, and I accept that that is a primary, and not a vicarious, responsibility. Yet the breach, consisting in the non-use of the crawling boards provided, was brought about partly by the plaintiff's own failure to use them, and partly by the failure of Mr. Boyle to insist on their use. I do not see in those circumstances how it is possible for the second defendants to say, in the words of LORD REID, that the conduct

I of the plaintiff " was the sole cause of the breach ". In my judgment the judge was plainly right in holding that the complicity of Mr. Boyle would render it impossible for the second defendants to escape liability on the principle of *Ginty's* case (4).

The last point taken on behalf of the second defendants, on the assumption that there has been a breach of reg. 31 (1), was that the judge fell into error in

---

(3) [1953] 2 All E.R. 215; [1953] 2 Q.B. 117.   (4) [1959] 1 All E.R. 414.
(5) [1964] 2 All E.R. 452 at p. 455.   (6) [1959] 2 All E.R. 115 at p. 120.

apportioning only twenty-five per cent. of the responsibility to the plaintiff. I **A**
am satisfied that there is no merit in this point. It is not necessary to express any
concluded view on the question whether the decision of the House of Lords in
Owners of S.S. or Vessel British Fame v. *Owners of S.S. or Vessel Macgregor* (7)
is strictly applicable to questions of apportionment under the Law Reform
(Contributory Negligence) Act, 1945, though for my part I incline to the opinion
that the words of LORD WRIGHT (8) were intended to be of general application. **B**
I conceive it to be well established as a matter of general principle that this court
will be slow to interfere with the apportionment of responsibility arrived at by a
judge who has seen and heard the witnesses, unless satisfied that he has fallen
into some error of law or has taken a wholly wrong view of the relevant facts.
Nothing of the sort can be contended in the present case. On the contrary,
bearing in mind that the plaintiff was working under the direct supervision of his **C**
own foreman, Mr. Boyle, I would regard the judge's apportionment of responsibility
as eminently fair and just.

So far, therefore, I reach the conclusions that, assuming reg. 31 (1) to be applicable, (i) there has been a breach of that regulation in respect of which the second
defendants cannot evade responsibility; (ii) the judge was right in holding
that the second defendants were not entitled to invoke the principle of *Ginty's* **D**
case (9) to defeat the plaintiff's claim entirely; but (iii) the case is one calling
for contribution as to which no criticism can properly be brought against the
learned judge's apportionment.

I come then to consider what I regard as the most difficult question in the case,
namely, whether reg. 31 (1) applied at all to the circumstances in which the
plaintiff's accident occurred. The first difficulty which presents itself is whether **E**
we ought to allow the point to be taken in this court having regard to the fact
that it was not argued below. On this point we have been referred by counsel
for the second defendants to the most recent decision on the subject, namely,
that of the Privy Council in *Warehousing & Forwarding Co. of East Africa, Ltd.*
v. *Jafferali & Sons, Ltd.* (10). In that case LORD GUEST, in delivering the judgment of the Privy Council, quoted and adopted the words of LORD WATSON in **F**
Connecticut Fire Insurance Co. v. *Kavanagh* (11), as follows (12):

> " When a question of law is raised for the first time in a court of last resort,
> on the construction of a document, or on facts either admitted or proved
> beyond controversy, it is not only competent but expedient, in the interests
> of justice, to entertain the plea. The expediency of adopting that course may
> be doubted, when the plea cannot be disposed of without deciding nice **G**
> questions of fact, in considering which the court of ultimate review is placed
> in a much less advantageous position than the courts below. But their
> lordships have no hesitation in holding that the course ought not, in any
> case, to be followed unless the court is satisfied that the evidence upon which
> they are asked to decide establishes beyond doubt that the facts, if fully
> investigated, would have supported the new plea." **H**

On the other side we were referred to the judgment of GREER, L.J., in *Smith*
v. *Cammell, Laird & Co., Ltd.* (13) in which he quoted LORD HERSCHELL'S
statement of the principle in *Owners and Freight Owners of the Tasmania* v.
Smith, Owners of the City of Corinth, The Tasmania (14), as follows:

> " A point . . . not taken at the trial, and presented for the first time in the **I**
> Court of Appeal, ought to be most jealously scrutinised . . . A Court of Appeal
> ought only to decide in favour of an appellant on a ground there put forward

(7) [1943] 1 All E.R. 33; [1943] A.C. 197.
(8) [1943] 1 All E.R. at p. 35; [1943] A.C. at p. 200.
(9) [1959] 1 All E.R. 414.   (10) [1963] 3 All E.R. 571; [1964] A.C. 1.
(11) [1892] A.C. 473 at p. 480.
(12) [1963] 3 All E.R. at p. 576; [1964] A.C. at pp. 10, 11.
(13) [1938] 3 All E.R. 52 at p. 55; [1938] 2 K.B. 700 at p. 717.
(14) (1890), 15 App. Cas. 223 at p. 225.

A for the first time if it is satisfied beyond doubt first, that it has before it all the facts bearing upon the new contention . . . as would have been the case if the controversy had arisen at the trial, and next, that no satisfactory explanation could have been offered by those whose conduct is impugned if an opportunity for explanation had been afforded them when in the witness-box."

B In the present case the question whether reg. 31 (1) applied depends, as I see it, entirely on the construction of the regulation itself as applied to facts which are in no way in controversy. No evidence which might have been, but which was not, adduced could possibly have made any difference. Indeed, the question whether the regulation applied could arise only after the evidence had been given and all the facts, as we now know them, had been elicited. We in this court are in as good a position to form our own conclusion as the judge would have been had the question been argued before him. In these circumstances I am of the opinion that it would be wrong to exclude the second defendants from taking the point in this court. I would hold the point to be open for our consideration.

C The second difficulty which I feel arises from the fact that neither the experienced counsel who appeared for the second defendants nor the judge himself, whose experience in relation to the building regulations is almost unrivalled, appears to have thought that the question whether reg. 31 (1) applied to the circumstances of this case was really worthy of serious consideration. It is only after much consideration and with considerable hesitation that I feel impelled to take a different view. I comfort myself, however, with the reflection that sometimes even Homer nods. In the event I find myself very far from being satisfied that reg. 31 (1) had any application, or that the second defendants were in breach of it. I have reached that conclusion for two reasons. First, I do not think that there was sufficient proof of the existence of the conditions required to bring the regulation into operation. It must be shown in the first place that

F ". . . taking into account the pitch, the nature of the surface, and the state of the weather, a person employed is likely to slip down or off the roof . . ."

Here there was no evidence whatsoever as to the state of the weather, nor was there evidence to show that the asbestos surface of the roof was such as to make a person likely to slip. As to the pitch of the roof, the only evidence of any danger of slipping from that cause was contained in a single answer given by Mr. Rimmer in his evidence. I cannot regard that as sufficient. Furthermore, reg. 31 (1) does not apply where the person is not liable to fall a distance of more than six feet six inches from the edge of the roof. Construing the words " the edge of the roof " in their ordinary sense, I think it is obvious that a person slipping on this roof could not by any possibility fall six feet six inches from the edge thereof; he would merely end up in the gutter at the bottom of the bay. It is said, however, on behalf of the plaintiff that where, as in the present case, there is a hole in the roof, due to the absence of asbestos sheeting, that introduces a new " edge " to the roof, so that if a person is liable to fall through a hole, he can properly be said to be liable to fall from the edge of the roof. I find myself quite unable to accept this submission, which seems to me to do violence to the plain meaning of the words used. Openings or holes in roofs are the subject of a separate regulation, namely, reg. 30, but that regulation, it is accepted, would not apply to persons in the position of the second defendants.

Secondly, it seems to me that the accident which befell the plaintiff was not an accident against which reg. 31 (1) was designed to protect him. The precautions to be taken under the regulation are such as to prevent the person " so falling ", that is, falling a distance of more than six feet six inches from the edge of the roof. The provision of crawling boards, such as the judge thought would be a suitable precaution, would not (save in so far as they might diminish the risk of slipping) be otherwise effective to obviate the danger against which this regulation is

designed to afford protection. What I think is envisaged as amounting to " suit- **A**
able precautions " to obviate this risk is something of the nature prescribed by
reg. 31 (2) (c), that is, some form of physical barrier to prevent a person from
going over the edge of the roof. It is obvious, however, that the provision of any
such barrier would not have been in any way effective to prevent the plaintiff's
fall through the hole in the roof. In *Grant* v. *National Coal Board* (15), it was
pointed out by VISCOUNT SIMONDS that where damages are claimed for breach **B**
of statutory duty, the plaintiff must prove that his injury was one against which
the legislation was designed to protect him. For the reasons which I have given
I do not think that reg. 31 (1) was designed to protect the plaintiff from falling
through a hole in the roof. I cannot, therefore, accept that this accident was
caused by any breach of reg. 31 (1), and I am of opinion that the judge fell into
error in holding the second defendants liable on that ground.   **C**

It remains only to consider the point raised by the plaintiff's cross-notice,
namely, that the judge's decision should be affirmed on the ground that the second
defendants were in breach of reg. 31 (3). The judge dismissed this contention in a
very summary manner, holding that reg. 31 (3) had not anything to do with this
accident. In my judgment the judge was plainly right, and I hope that I may be
forgiven if I too deal with this point very shortly. I do not doubt that asbestos **D**
sheeting is a fragile material, and it is perfectly true that the plaintiff's work
necessitated his passing over it and working above it. I think that it is plain,
however, that the mischief against which reg. 31 (1) is directed is the risk
of a collapse of the fragile material causing the workman to fall through it. There
is no evidence in the present case of any collapse of the asbestos sheeting, nor did
the plaintiff fall through it. He fell through a hole where there was in fact no **E**
asbestos sheeting. Counsel for the plaintiff put his contention in the only possible
way in which it could be put. He argued that in the present case the fragility
of the material was a factor contributing to the plaintiff's fall, because the plaintiff only placed his foot on the purlin (thereby exposing hiself to the risk of falling
through the open hole) in order to avoid standing with all his weight on the fragile
material. In my judgment this contention is much too far-fetched. I cannot **F**
regard the plaintiff's accident as in any sense due to failure on the part of the
second defendants to protect him against the risk of working on or above fragile
material, and I am of the opinion that the judge rightly dismissed the charge of
breach of reg. 31 (3).

While there is much in the judge's judgment with which I whole-heartedly
agree, I am of the opinion that he fell into error in holding the second defendants **G**
to be in breach of reg. 31 (1). In my judgment the second defendants were not
shown to be guilty of any of the breaches of statutory duty alleged.

The appeal should accordingly be allowed, the cross-appeal dismissed, and
judgment entered for the second defendants. I cannot refrain from expressing
my sympathy with the plaintiff, who established a clear case of common law
negligence against the first defendants, but now finds that the judgment which he **H**
obtained against them is unlikely to be satisfied.

DAVIES, L.J.: There are unfortunate features about this case. The
plaintiff suffered very serious injuries. He has been awarded a large sum of
damages, £13,873 1s. 2d., against both defendants. That award is not challenged
by the first defendants, but they are without means and, it would appear, not **I**
insured. So the judgment against them is worthless. If, therefore, contrary to
the view of the judge, the plaintiff is not entitled to recover against the second
defendants, he will recover nothing. Another awkward point is the fact that what,
in my judgment, is the most powerful argument for the second defendants on this
appeal, viz., that reg. 31 (1) of the Building (Safety, Health and Welfare) Regulations, 1948, had no application to the circumstances of this case was, though not

---

(15) [1956] 1 All E.R. 682 at p. 684; [1956] A.C. 649 at p. 655.

A   abandoned, not seriously pressed in the court below. From this it resulted that
the judge, who while at the Bar was pre-eminently expert in this branch of the
law, did not find it necessary to deal with the point at all in his judgment. Despite
this, however, I have reluctantly come to the conclusion that the point is open to
the second defendants in this court. For unless the point was expressly abandoned
below, it is difficult to see how we can support a judgment which is based solely on
B   a breach of reg. 31 (1) if, in our view, that regulation did not apply. All the
relevant evidence as to the facts which might decide whether or not reg. 31 (1)
applied had already been given—indeed, the facts were not very much in dispute—
when, as we were informed, counsel for the second defendants in his closing speech
informed the judge that he was not pursuing the point that reg. 31 (1) did not
apply. I, therefore, with reluctance, agree with what has been said on this matter
C   by WILLMER, L.J., and consider that we ought to allow the second defendants to
advance this argument in this court.

On the various questions which arise for consideration in the case, I am in
entire agreement with what has been said by WILLMER, L.J., and I do not propose
to add anything except to make a few observations as to the application of reg.
31 (1). Before so doing, however, it is in my view right to comment on the wording
D   of these regulations. There have been several cases in this court recently in which
attention has been called to their unsatisfactory drafting. It is not perhaps
necessary to give examples. One finds frequently that different words are used to
mean apparently the same thing, and conversely that one and the same phrase
has been used to mean apparently two different things. This makes it very
difficult to apply the ordinary rules of construction; and I cannot help feeling
E   that clarity and precision might well be improved if a thorough revision were
undertaken by the appropriate authority.

To turn now to reg. 31 (1) and to apply it to the facts of the present case. The
regulation has already been quoted. Work was being done on a sloping surface
of a roof. The pitch of the roof was very shallow, namely, twenty-two degrees.
There was no evidence that there was anything slippery or otherwise wrong in the
F   surface of the roof. There was no evidence as to the state of the weather, or that
it introduced any special hazard. There was in the circumstances, as I think,
no evidence that the plaintiff, owing to these matters or otherwise, was likely
to slip down the roof. Neither do I think that there was evidence that he was likely
to slip off the roof. For reg. 31 (1) seems to contemplate a situation in which a
man is likely to slip off the roof at the end of a downward slip. Here the
G   plaintiff did not slip downward; if anything, he slipped upwards. Moreover,
I cannot see that in the position where the plaintiff was working he was liable to
fall from the edge of the roof. If he slipped down, he would land in the gutter.
The edge of the roof cannot, in my judgment, in ordinary English, mean an edge
in the roof created by the removal of some of the roofing material.

Openings in roofs are dealt with by reg. 30, to which, as WILLMER, L.J., has
H   pointed out, the second defendants were not subject. Moreover even under that
regulation a hole or gap, such as that through which the plaintiff fell, might well
not be held to be an opening in a roof; see Phillips v. Robertson Thain, Ltd. (16)
and Moorcraft v. Thomas Powles & Sons, Ltd. (17). If this be right, then there was
under reg. 31 (1) no obligation to take suitable precautions to prevent a man from
falling through such a gap. It seems to follow, therefore, that even though the
I   provision and use of crawling boards and roof ladders might have prevented the
plaintiff's accident, their absence or non-use did not constitute a breach of the
second defendant's obligations under reg. 31 (1) and reg. 4 (ii).

As to the rest of the case, I have nothing to add to what has been said by
WILLMER, L.J. As I said at the beginning of this judgment, the result is most
unfortunate; but I agree that the appeal should be allowed.

---

(16) [1962] 1 All E.R. 527.   (17) [1962] 3 All E.R. 741.

Appeal allowed. Respondent's notice dismissed. Leave to appeal to House of A
Lords granted.

Solicitors: *Denis Hayes,* agent for *John G. Clayton & Co.,* Luton (for the second defendants); *T. D. Jones & Co.,* agents for *Tearle & Herbert Jones,* Luton (for the plaintiff).

[*Reported by* F. GUTTMAN, ESQ., *Barrister-at-Law.*] B

PRINCES INVESTMENTS, LTD. AND OTHERS v. INLAND REVENUE COMMISSIONERS. CLORE v. INLAND REVENUE COMMISSIONERS. C

[CHANCERY DIVISION (Buckley, J.), April 1, 4, 5, 1966.]

Surtax—Undistributed income—Direction and apportionment—Apportionment of actual income of relevant year—Actual income was income actually received, although subsequent income was included in profit and loss account D *—Application of actual income toward reducing debit balance—Dividend declared—Chain of companies—Sub-apportionment of excess over amount received by second company from actual income of first company—Dividend of first company not paid out of actual income of first company—Whether dividend deductible on sub-apportionment—Income Tax Act, 1952 (15 & 16 Geo. 6 & 1 Eliz. 2 c. 10), s. 245, s. 254 (1).* E

Surtax—Investment company—Apportionments and sub-apportionments—Notice of sub-apportionments—Failure to give notice of sub-apportionments to company subject of the surtax direction—Effect—Income Tax Act, 1952 (15 & 16 Geo. 6 & 1 Eliz. 2 c. 10), s. 248 (1), (2), (3), s. 254 (3), (4), (5).

All the ordinary share capital of company A in a group of associated companies was owned by company B and virtually all the share capital of F company B by company C. On Oct. 19, 1956, company A declared a dividend (the " 1956 dividend ") on its ordinary shares of £15,771, and on Mar. 24, 1957, it paid the dividend to company B. Company B brought the £15,771 dividend into its profit and loss account for the accounting year ended on Mar. 31, 1956, i.e., before the dividend was declared or paid, reducing (after deduction of outgoings) an existing debit balance to G £1,256 14s. 11d. It was found that to formulate a profit and loss account by bringing into account as receipts dividends not declared or received until after the period of the account ended was in accordance with good accountancy practice*. On Dec. 31, 1957, company A declared and on Feb. 10, 1958, it paid a further dividend of £15,771 (the " 1957 dividend "), H which company B credited to its profits and loss account for the accounting year ending on Mar. 31, 1957, i.e., again for an accounting year that had ended before the dividend was declared or paid. The net profit of company B was transferred to an appropriation account, in which, taken with other items, the total to be appropriated was £18,963 5s. 7d. On Mar. 28, 1957, company B declared, and on Mar. 31 it paid, out of that sum an interim dividend for the year ending Mar. 31, 1957, the gross amount of the divi- I dend being £14,000 and the net amount being £8,050. The Special Commissioners of Income Tax made a surtax direction that the actual income of company B for the year ending on Mar. 31, 1957, should be deemed to be the income of its members and apportioned the whole of company B's actual income for that year (which was computed in accordance with the Income Tax Act, 1952, at £14,290) among its members. The

* See p. 836, letter H, post.

Affirmed. C.A. [1967] 2 All E.R. 238.

A   members were, virtually, company C. The Special Commissioners then
made sub-apportionments, sub-apportioning through a chain of two companies to an individual shareholder, to whom £14,283 10s. 6d. was sub-
apportioned. No notice of these sub-apportionments was given to company
B. No deduction of the dividend of £8,050 net, which had been declared and
paid by company B in March, 1957, was made on sub-apportionment to
B   members of company C. Under s. 254 (1) of the Income Tax Act, 1952, it
was only the excess of any amount apportioned to company C over any
amount received by company C out of the " income as aforesaid " of company
B that was to be sub-apportioned to members of company C, so that the
question arose whether there should have been deduction of the £8,050
dividend when making the sub-apportionment.

C   **Held:** the apportionment, and the sub-apportionment without deduction
for the £8,050 dividend, were correct in principle for the following reasons—
     (i) in computing the actual income of company B for the year ending
Mar. 31, 1957, the income to be taken into account was income received
in that year, which accordingly included the 1956 dividend, which
had been paid in March, 1957, although the profit and loss account of
D   company B for the year ending Mar. 31, 1957, included the 1957 dividend
which was not paid until February, 1958 (see p. 839, letters E and H, post).
     (ii) the amount which by s. 254 (1) of the Income Tax Act, 1952, was to
be sub-apportioned to members of a second company (in this case the
members of company C) was the excess of the amount apportioned to
the second company over "the amount, if any, which has been received by the
E   second company out of the income as aforesaid of the first company ",
and in that context the words " income as aforesaid " referred to the actual
income of the first company, viz., in the present case the actual income of
company B for the year ending Mar. 31, 1957 (see p. 840, letter C, post).
     (iii) so much of the actual income of company B for the year ending
Mar. 31, 1957, as consisted of the 1956 dividend had been used for a purpose
F   other than paying the £8,050 dividend, having been appropriated in the
profit and loss account of company B to reducing a debit balance, and that
that application of the 1956 dividend was the result of a definite decision
from which it was not open to company B to depart; accordingly, on the
facts, the £8,050 dividend paid by company B had been met from sources
other than the actual income of company B which was the subject of appor-
G   tionment, and s. 254 (1) did not allow deduction of the £8,050 on sub-
apportionment to members of company C (see p. 841, letters D and E, post).
     (iv) notice of the apportionment and sub-apportionments was required
by s. 248 (1), (2) and (3)* and s. 254 (3), (4), (5)† of the Income Tax Act, 1952,
to be given to company B as the company whose undistributed income was
the subject-matter of the surtax direction, but such notice was not a condition
H   precedent to a valid and effective apportionment, and the effect of failure
to give it was merely to extend the time within which an appeal could be
made against the sub-apportionments (see p. 843, letters B and C, post).
       Appeal dismissed.

     [As to computation of actual income for the purposes of a surtax direction,
     see 20 HALSBURY'S LAWS 556-558, paras. 1082-1084; and for cases on the subject,
I   see 28 DIGEST (Repl.) 358-368, *1580-1613.*
       For the Income Tax Act, 1952, s. 245, s. 248, s. 249, s. 254 and s. 255, see
     31 HALSBURY'S STATUTES (2nd Edn.) 232, 235, 236, 242, 243.]

     Cases referred to:
       Chancery Lane Safe Deposit & Offices Co., Ltd. v. *Inland Revenue Comrs.,*
           [1966] 1 All E.R. 1; [1966] 2 W.L.R. 256.

     ---
     * Section 248, so far as material, is set out at p. 841, letters G to I, post.
     † Section 254, so far as material, is set out at p. 838, letters C to I, post.

Nobes (B. W.) & Co., Ltd. v. *Inland Revenue Comrs.*, [1966] 1 All E.R. 30; **A**
[1966] 1 W.L.R. 111.

Case Stated.

The first, second and third taxpayer companies (respectively Princes Investments, Ltd.*, Princes Realisations, Ltd., and Envoy Investments, Ltd.) appealed
to the Special Commissioners of Income Tax against three notices of sub-apportionments of the actual income from all sources of New Century Finance Co., Ltd., **B**
(the "New Century Co.") made by the Special Commissioners of Income
Tax on June 29, 1962, under s. 254 of the Income Tax Act, 1952, for the year of
assessment 1956-57. The grounds of appeal in each case were that the amounts
sub-apportioned were excessive in so far as no allowance had been made under
s. 254 in respect of income received by the first taxpayer company out of the
actual income from all sources of the New Century Co. in that year, and received **C**
also by the second and third taxpayer companies, from the first and second taxpayer companies respectively. The taxpayer companies contended: (i) that the
dividend amounting to £14,000 gross (£8,050 net) paid by the New Century Co. to
the first taxpayer company during the year of assessment 1956-57 was an amount
received by the first taxpayer company out of the income of the New Century Co.
as shown by its profit and loss account for the year ended Mar. 31, 1957; (ii) **D**
alternatively that that dividend of £14,000 gross (£8,050 net) was an amount
received by the first taxpayer company out of the £14,290 statutory income of the
New Century Co. for the year of assessment 1956-57; and (iii) that in either event
in sub-apportioning for the purpose of s. 254 (1) the actual income from all sources
of the New Century Co. through the first taxpayer company to the second taxpayer company and Checkendon Investments, Ltd., and through the second **E**
taxpayer company to the third taxpayer company and Checkendon Investments,
Ltd., and through the third taxpayer company to the fourth taxpayer (Mr.
Charles Clore) and to Checkendon Investments, Ltd., only the excess of the
actual income of the New Century Co. over the amount of the dividend of £14,000
gross (£8,050 net) fell to be sub-apportioned.

The Crown contended: (i) that the dividend of £14,000 gross (£8,050 net) **F**
paid by the New Century Co. to the first taxpayer company during the year of
assessment 1956-57 was not an amount received by the first taxpayer company
out of the actual income from all sources of the New Century Co. in such manner
as would in the case of an individual render the amount so received liable to be
included in the statement of his total income for the purposes of surtax within
the meaning of s. 254 (1) of the Act of 1952; (ii) that the circumstance that the **G**
statutory income of the New Century Co. for the year of assessment 1956-57
was greater in amount than the dividend of £14,000 gross (£8,050 net) paid by
the New Century Co. to the first taxpayer company was immaterial; and (iii)
that in sub-apportioning for the purposes of s. 254 (1) the actual income from all
sources of the New Century Co. from the first taxpayer company to the second
taxpayer company and Checkendon Investments, Ltd.; from the second taxpayer **H**
company to the third taxpayer company and Checkendon Investments, Ltd.;
and from the third taxpayer company to the fourth taxpayer and Checkendon
Investments, Ltd., no deduction fell to be made in respect of that dividend.
The commissioners held that the dividend received by the first taxpayer company
in March 1957 was not income paid out of the statutory income of the New
Century Co., which was the income referred to in s. 254 of the Income Tax Act, **I**
1952, in a surtaxable form for 1956-57 within the meaning of s. 254 (1). They
therefore dismissed the appeals and confirmed the sub-apportionments. The
taxpayer companies appealed by way of Case Stated to the High Court.

The fourth taxpayer appealed against a notice of sub-apportionment of the
income of the New Century Co. as sub-apportioned to the third taxpayer company

---

* Princes Investments, Ltd. is company C in the headnote; company A being Investment Registry, Ltd., and company B being New Century Finance Co., Ltd.

A for the year of assessment for 1956-57 to him and to Checkendon Investments, Ltd., on similar grounds. He also appealed on the ground that notices of the sub-apportionments were not served in accordance with s. 248 (2) of the Act of 1952. The commissioners dismissed his appeal, and he appealed by way of Case Stated to the High Court.

The cases noted below* were cited during the argument in addition to those
B referred to in the judgment.

C. N. Beattie, Q.C., and *J. E. H. Pearce* for the taxpayers.
Arthur Bagnall, Q.C., *J. R. Phillips* and *J. P. Warner* for the Crown.

BUCKLEY, J.: These two appeals arise out of a surtax direction made in respect of the undistributed profits of New Century Finance Co., Ltd. (the " New
C Century Co.") for the year of assessment 1956-57. The New Century Co. was the holder or beneficial owner of all the ordinary share capital in Investment Registry, Ltd. (the " Registry Co."). The share capital of the New Century Co. consisted of thirty thousand shares, of which 29,999 were held and beneficially owned by the first taxpayer company, Princes Investments, Ltd., and one share was held by Checkendon Investments, Ltd. (the " Checkendon Co."). The share
D capital of the first taxpayer company consisted of fifty thousand shares, of which 49,999 were held and beneficially owned by the second taxpayer company. Princes Realisations, Ltd., and one was held by the Checkendon Co. The share capital of the second taxpayer company consisted of five thousand shares, of which 4,999 were held and beneficially owned by the third taxpayer company, Envoy Investments, Ltd., and one was held by the Checkendon Co. The share
E capital of the third taxpayer company consisted of five thousand shares, of which 4,999 were held and beneficially owned by Mr. Charles Clore, the fourth taxpayer, and one was held by the Checkendon Co.

The shares of those various companies held by the Checkendon Co. were beneficially owned by the Checkendon Co., which was an investment company within the meaning of s. 257 of the Income Tax Act, 1952, having an issued share
F capital of 720 shares, 718 of which were held by the fourth taxpayer and the other two by two other gentlemen. Those 718 shares were beneficially owned by the fourth taxpayer. The New Century Co. was at all times a company to which s. 245 of the Income Tax Act, 1952, was applicable.

The issued share capital of the Registry Co. consisted of preference shares and ordinary shares. The dividend on the preference shares was payable half-yearly.
G On Oct. 19, 1956, the Registry Co. declared a dividend on its ordinary shares, which was paid on Mar. 24, 1957. The gross amount of that dividend was £15,771. That dividend was received by the New Century Co. on Mar. 24, 1957. The accounting year for the New Century Co. ended on Mar. 31 in each year, and that dividend was brought into the accounts of the New Century Co. for the year ended Mar. 31, 1956.
H The dividend that I have just mentioned, declared in October, 1956, but not paid until Mar. 24, 1957, was brought into the profit and loss account of the New Century Co. for the accounting year ending Mar. 31, 1956. That profit and loss account shows, on its right-hand side, " Dividends (gross) " receivable on shares in the Registry Co., £19,355. That was made up as to £3,585 of preference dividends received during the accounting year in question, and as to £15,771
I of ordinary dividend. The ordinary dividend in question, which was not declared until Oct. 19, 1956—i.e., after the end of the accounting year to which the profit and loss account to which I am now referring relates—was not paid until Mar. 24, 1957, still later after the end of the accounting year in question. After charging against those gross dividends certain outgoings—i.e., loan interest, secretarial

---

* *Thomas Fattorini (Lancashire), Ltd.* v. *Inland Revenue Comrs.*, [1942] 1 All E.R. 619; [1942] A.C. 643; *Allchin* v. *Coulthard*, [1943] 2 All E.R. 352; [1943] A.C. 607; *Inland Revenue Comrs.* v. *Hudspeth*, [1959] 2 All E.R. 752.

charges and disbursements, bank charges, audit and accountancy charges and **A**
income tax—a net profit is shown in the profit and loss account of £8,321 18s. 6d.
In the balance sheet of the New Century Co. at Mar. 31, 1956, that last-
mentioned figure is brought in as a deduction from an existing debit balance on
profit and loss account, leaving the profit and loss account of the company still in
debit to the extent of £1,256 14s. 11d. The whole of the net profit shown on
the profit and loss account was accordingly treated as absorbed in that way, in **B**
reducing the debit balance theretofore existing on the profit and loss account
of the New Century Co. On Mar. 28, 1957, the New Century Co. declared an
interim dividend of 9s. 4d. per share in respect of the year ending Mar. 31, 1957,
and that dividend was paid on that date. The total gross amount of that
dividend was £14,000, and the net amount was £8,050.

On Dec. 31, 1957, the Registry Co. declared a further dividend on its ordinary **C**
shares, which was paid to the New Century Co. on Feb. 10, 1958. The amount
of that dividend was again £15,771. In the profit and loss account of the New
Century Co. for the accounting year ended Mar. 31, 1957, there is shown on the
right-hand side, " Dividends (gross) " receivable, £19,574 8s. 5d. That figure is
made up as to £3,803 of dividends on the preference shares of the Registry Co.,
which were received during the accounting year in question by the New Century **D**
Co., and the last-mentioned dividend on the ordinary shares of the Registry Co.,
i.e., the dividend which was not declared until Dec. 31, 1957, and not received
until Feb. 10, 1958, both dates being after the end of the accounting year to which
this profit and loss account relates. In the profit and loss account of the New
Century Co. interest and various expenses are brought in, and the tax based on
the profit for the year, leaving a net profit for the year of £8,280 7s. 11d. That **E**
is carried down to an appropriation account. There is added to it a loan of
£10,000, waived by the first taxpayer company, and certain interest at £682
17s. 8d., which the first taxpayer company also waived the right to receive;
making a total to be appropriated of £18,963 5s. 7d. Out of that sum, the net
interim dividend of £8,050 is provided for. Provision is also made for a further
dividend on the shares of the New Century Co., which was declared on Feb. 28, **F**
1958, and paid on that date, the net amount of which was £9,200. Taking those
two figures into account and the debit balance of £1,256 14s. 11d. carried forward
from the previous year, that appropriation account left a credit balance on
profit and loss account of £456 10s. 8d., which is carried forward.

Now it seems strange to the uninstructed mind that there should be brought
into these accounts in the two accounting years with which I have dealt, as **G**
receipts or profits of the New Century Co., dividends which were not declared
by the Registry Co. until after the ends of the respective financial years and which
were not received until a considerable time after the ends of those respective
financial years; but the commissioners, in their Case Stated, find that to formulate the accounts in this way is in accordance with good accountancy practice,
and I accept that that is so. It is, as I understand it, a consequence of the **H**
necessity, where one has a chain of holding companies, such as one has in this
case, to produce group accounts. In order to produce group accounts, the
accounts of the various companies must be consistent inter se, for which purpose
it may be necessary to anticipate, so I understand, in the accounts of the companies, the probable receipts from other companies in the group although those
receipts are not yet the subject-matter of declarations of dividend. **I**

On June 29, 1962, a surtax direction under s. 245 of the Income Tax Act,
1952, was made in respect of the undistributed profits of the New Century Co.
for 1956-57. The actual income of the New Century Co. for that accounting
year—for the purposes of this judgment, I treat the fiscal year and the accounting
year as coinciding, although there are in fact a few days of variation between
the two; but no point has been taken about the need to make any apportionment
in that respect—is set out in para. 3 (13) of the Case. It comprised preference
dividends received from the Registry Co. during that year amounting to £3,803,

A and the ordinary dividend declared by the Registry Co. which was received, as I have said, on Mar. 24, 1957; i.e., the dividend which had been declared on Oct. 19, 1956, and which for the sake of clarity I will call " the 1956 dividend ".

When loan interest and expenses of management had been deducted from the aggregate of those amounts of dividend received, the actual income of the New Century Co. for that year, 1956-57, computed in accordance with the provisions

B of the Income Tax Act, 1952, amounted to £14,290, and that was the sum which was treated as apportioned amongst the members of the New Century Co. in consequence of the surtax direction.   Of the sum which, as a result of that surtax direction, was apportioned to the first taxpayer company, £14,289 4s. 10d. was, on a sub-apportionment, apportioned to the second taxpayer company; on a further sub-apportionment, £14,286 7s. 8d. was apportioned to the third taxpayer

C company; and on a still further sub-apportionment, £14,283 10s. 6d. was apportioned to the fourth taxpayer. The other small sums which, on each apportionment or sub-apportionment, did not find their way down to the fourth taxpayer, went, of course, to the Checkendon Co. and through the Checkendon Co., no doubt, to the fourth taxpayer and the other two shareholders.

The taxpayers appeal against these apportionments and sub-apportionments

D on the ground that they were excessive because no allowance had been made under s. 254 of the Act of 1952 in respect of the dividend declared by the New Century Co. on Mar. 28, 1957; and the question for determination on this appeal is whether or not some abatement of the amount of assessment to surtax as a result of the surtax direction ought to be made in respect of that dividend. The Special Commissioners before whom the appeal against the apportionments came

E in the first instance rejected that suggestion and held that the undistributed income of the New Century Co. for the year 1956-57 had been duly apportioned and sub-apportioned in the way that I have described, and that nothing fell to be taken into account as a reduction of the amount of undistributed income to be so apportioned and sub-apportioned by reason of the dividend in question; and against that decision the taxpayer companies now appeal to this court.

F The section of the Act under which the direction is given is s. 245.   I will not pause to read that, but I would draw attention to this fact: that that section clearly directs attention to the actual income position of the company which is the subject of the direction in respect of the year which is the subject-matter of the direction.   The provisions of the section are expressed to be for the purpose of " preventing the avoidance of the payment of surtax through the withholding

G from distribution of income ", and one cannot withhold distribution of income which has not yet been received.   It is a reasonable part of the actual income from all sources for the year in question that the commissioners have to take into consideration, and it is that income—i.e., the actual income from all sources of the company for the year in question—that is to be deemed to be the income of the members and apportioned amongst them.   Section 249 deals with the

H consequences of apportionment of the income of a company, and provides:

> " (1) Where an apportionment has been made . . . surtax shall be assessed and charged . . . in respect of the sum so apportioned after deducting in the case of each member any amount which has been distributed to him by the company in respect of the year or period in question in such manner that the amount distributed falls to be included in the statement of total income

I to be made by that member for the purposes of surtax.
>
> " (2) The income apportioned to a member of a company so far as assessable and chargeable to surtax under this Chapter—(a) shall be deemed for the purposes of surtax to represent income from his interest in the company for the year or other period in question . . ."

Once again, attention is directed to the particular year or period in question. Then, under para. (c) of sub-s. (2), it is provided that the income apportioned to a member

" shall be deemed . . . to have been received by him on the date to which   **A**
the accounts of the company for the year or period were made up . . ."

So it becomes his income for that year, or it is to be treated as his income for
that year, for tax purposes. Subsection (3) of that section provides that the
surtax chargeable in respect of the income apportioned to any member " shall be
assessed upon that member in the name of the company ".

That is the consequence where there are no complications arising from the   **B**
fact that a member of the company on whom the direction is made is itself
another company to which s. 245 applies. Where that is the state of affairs,
s. 254 applies, sub-s. (1) of which is in these terms:

" Where a member of a company (in this section referred to as ' the first
company ') the income of which for any year or period has been deemed to   **C**
be the income of its members and has been the subject of an apportionment
(in this section referred to as the ' original apportionment ') under the
provisions of this Chapter is itself a company (in this section referred to as
' the second company ') to which s. 245 of this Act applies, the excess of the
amount so apportioned to the second company over the amount, if any,
which has been received by the second company out of the income as afore-   **D**
said of the first company in such manner as would, in the case of an individual
render the amount so received liable to be included in the statement of his
total income for the purposes of surtax, shall, for the purposes of this Chapter,
be deemed to be income of the members of the second company and shall be
apportioned among them in accordance with their respective interests in
that company, and the provisions of this Chapter shall, with any necessary   **E**
modifications, apply accordingly."

Under sub-s. (2), the income apportioned under sub-s. (1) to the members of the
second company is, for the purposes of surtax, to be deemed

"to have been received by those members on the date on which the
income apportioned . . . to the members of the first company is deemed to
have been received by them."   **F**

Under sub-s. (3), the tax is to be assessed on the members of the second company
in the name of the first company,

" and the provisions of this Chapter as to the assessment, collection and
recovery of surtax chargeable in respect of the income of a company
apportioned to any member thereof "   **G**

are, with any necessary modifications, to apply accordingly.

Where a member of the second company is also a company to which s. 245
applies, then, under s. 254 (4) there is a further sub-apportionment in the same
sort of way as there has already been an apportionment among the members of
the second company, and once again the provisions of this Act are to apply,
with any necessary modifications, to such successive apportionments and any   **H**
further sub-apportionments,

" and to the furnishing of statements and to the assessment, collection and
recovery of surtax in respect of income apportioned thereunder, and, in
particular, the date on which any such income is to be deemed to have been
received by the member to whom it is apportioned shall be the date
mentioned in sub-s. (2) "   **I**

of s. 254; and the individual to whom the income is eventually apportioned as a
result of these successive apportionments or sub-apportionments—i.e., any
person who is not a company to which s. 245 applies—is to be assessed in the
name of the first company.

Section 254 (5) is in these terms:

" (5) In this Chapter—' original apportionment ' has the same meaning
as in this section; and ' sub-apportionment ' means such an apportionment

A   of income as is provided for by the preceding provisions of this section, and, subject to any express provision of this Act, any reference in any enactment (whether contained in this or in any other Act) to apportioning income under or for the purposes of the provisions, or any specified provisions, of this Chapter shall be construed as a reference not only to apportioning by means of an original apportionment but also to apportioning by means of an
B   original apportionment together with one or more sub-apportionments or series of sub-apportionments."

Section 255 (3) provides:

" In computing, for the purposes of this Chapter, the actual income from all sources of a company for any year or period, the income from any source shall be estimated in accordance with the provisions of this Act relating to
C   the computation of income from that source, except that the income shall be computed by reference to the income for such year or period as aforesaid and not by reference to any other year or period."

Once again, attention is directed perfectly clearly to what actually occurs in the relevant year or period . It is the income for that year or that period which
D   is to be computed—i.e., the actual income of the company for that year or period—and it is to be computed by reference to the income of that year or period, and not by reference to any other measure. I think that those are all the sections of the Act to which I need refer.

The result, I think, may be summarised as follows. If a company has not, within a reasonable time after the end of the accounting period in question,
E   distributed a reasonable part of its actual income for that period—i.e., in my judgment, the income which it has received during that period—the actual income for that period is to be deemed to be the income of the members and apportioned, and if necessary sub-apportioned until one reaches persons who are not companies to which s. 245 applies. For discovering the amount to be so apportioned, the amount of the actual income for the period in question must be
F   computed in accordance with the provisions of the Act of 1952, but by reference to the income actually received during the period in question and not by reference to any other measurement.

Now, the actual income of the New Century Co. for the year 1956-57 was that which is to be found set out in para. 3 (13) of the Case Stated, and it was the sum of £14,290, or thereabouts, made up in the way set out in that paragraph
G   of the Case. That is not the same as the profit of the company shown in its profit and loss account for the year ended Mar. 31, 1957, for, although the gross receipts amount in each case to £19,574, the ingredients of that figure in the computation of the actual income of the company and in the figure shown in the profit and loss account are different, in that the actual income included the 1956 dividend, whereas the profit and loss account figure includes the 1957
H   dividend declared on Dec. 31, 1957.

The question to which the Special Commissioners who made the direction had to address their minds was this. Had the New Century Co., within a reasonable time after Mar. 31, 1957, distributed a reasonable part of its actual income for that year? They thought that it had not, and they made the direction accordingly; and no complaint is made about that. Therefore, that actual
I   income falls to be dealt with in accordance with the provisions of s. 254 of the Act of 1952. The only question to be considered is whether, having regard to the provisions of s. 254 (1), anything has to be taken into account in deciding what should be apportioned and sub-apportioned in respect of the dividend declared by the New Century Co. on Mar. 28, 1957, for under that subsection it is only the excess of the amount apportioned to the second company over the amount, if any, which has been received by the second company out of the income of the first company that is to be sub-apportioned.

The question, therefore, is—Did the first taxpayer company receive any

amount out of what, in s. 254 (1), is called " the income as aforesaid ", of the **A**
New Century Co.?   Now those words, " the income as aforesaid ", are not perhaps
very graceful words in the context in which they are found.   They must, I
think, mean " the aforesaid income " or " such income as aforesaid ".   That
must relate back to the words,

> " Where a member of a company . . . the income of which for any year
> or period has been deemed to be the income of its members . . ."   **B**

That takes one back to s. 245, to discover what income of the New Century Co.
was to be deemed to be the income of its members as a result of the surtax
direction; and the income which was to be deemed to be the income of the
members of the New Century Co. was the actual income from all sources of
the New Century Co. for 1956-57.   The first taxpayer company received from the **C**
New Century Co. a net dividend of £8,050 in respect of the year ended Mar. 31,
1957, and the question is whether that dividend was received out of the actual
income of the New Century Co. for that period.   Of that actual income amounting
to £14,290, the £15,771 representing the 1956 dividend declared by the Registry
Co. had been appropriated in the balance sheet of the New Century Co. as at
Mar. 31, 1956, to reduction of the adverse balance on profit and loss account, **D**
and the whole of that dividend had been absorbed in that way.   Accordingly,
it is contended that that part of the actual income of the New Century Co. for
1956-57 was not available to meet the dividend declared by the New Century
Co., and that consequently no part of that dividend has been paid out of the
actual income of the New Century Co. for the year in question.

The taxpayers submit that, to determine whether the dividend has been paid **E**
out of income, one should look at the accounts of the company and see if the
commercial profit of the company—i.e., the profit as shown by the profit and
loss account of the company for the relevant period—is sufficient to cover the
dividend or not.   That, in my judgment, is an erroneous approach, because the
profit and loss account of a company is not directed to showing what its income
is for tax purposes: it is directed to showing a fair appreciation of the financial **F**
position of the company with regard to its profits and losses; and in the present
case I have explained that the profit and loss account of this company took into
account prospective receipts which were not yet even debts due to the company.
It does not relate to the actual income received by the company during the
accounting year in question, which is the matter with which I am concerned.
Therefore, I think that it is a fallacious approach to say that it is necessary **G**
to consider the commercial profit of the company in that sense.

Alternatively, it is said on behalf of the taxpayers that all that they have to
show is that the statutory income of the company—i.e., the income of the company, as I understand it, calculated for tax purposes—was sufficient to cover
the dividend in question.   The statutory income is what I have called the
actual income calculated in accordance with the methods of computation **H**
provided by the Income Tax Acts; and counsel for the taxpayers said that I
should look at that income without regard to the way in which it has been dealt
with by the company, or the way in which any part of it has been dealt with,
in its accounts.   That, again, seems to me to be an erroneous approach, for,
if the company has in some way or other appropriated or used some part of that
actual income for some purpose other than providing for the dividend which is in **I**
question, then it seems to me to be clear that it is impossible to say that the
dividend is paid out of that part of the actual income of the company.

In the present case the actual income of the company for the year 1956-57 was,
as I have said, to the extent that it consisted of an ordinary dividend received by
the New Century Co. in that accounting year but brought into its own profit and
loss account in the preceding accounting year, entirely exhausted by the application of the net profit of the company for the preceding accounting year (i.e., the
accounting year ended Mar. 31, 1956) to the reduction of the then existing

A adverse balance on the company's profit and loss account. That was an appropriation of that part of the prospective receipts of the New Century Co. which the directors decided to make. It was a definite decision, and it produced practical results in this sense: that the company presented its position on its profit and loss account in a more favourable light to the world in general and to its own members than it would have done had that sum not been used to reduce
B the adverse balance on the profit and loss account, and the directors may well have thought that that would be a matter which might have some effect on the likelihood or otherwise of a surtax direction being made in respect of that year, or some other year, of the company's trading. It has not been suggested in the course of the argument that the company could re-write that part of its accounts and treat that profit as being otherwise appropriated or otherwise used, and I
C do not think, having regard to what was said in the House of Lords in two cases to which I was referred, *Chancery Lane Safe Deposit & Offices Co., Ltd.* v. *Inland Revenue Comrs.* (1), and *B. W. Nobes & Co., Ltd.* v. *Inland Revenue Comrs.* (2), that it would be open to the company to seek to re-write that part of its accounts.

Accordingly, I must proceed on the basis that, of the actual income of the company for the accounting year 1956-57, so much of it as consisted of the 1956
D dividend from the Registry Co. had been already used for another purpose. That leaves by way of receipt only the preference dividends received during that year amounting to £3,803, which are insufficient to counterbalance the loan interest charges and expenses which are to be taken into account in computing the income of the company for that year, with the result that no income for that year is left available to meet the dividend, which must therefore have been
E met from other sources. For these reasons, it seems to me that the conclusion at which the Special Commissioners arrived was the correct conclusion, and that the apportionments and sub-apportionments resulting from the surtax direction which was made in this case fall to take effect without any deduction in respect of the dividend declared by the New Century Co. That disposes of the appeals of the three taxpayer companies.

F The other appeal before me is an appeal by the fourth taxpayer, Mr. Charles Clore himself, which raises the same questions with which I have been dealing with regard to the companies but which raises another point as well. So far as the points raised on the fourth taxpayer's appeal are the same as those involved in the companies' appeals, I need not say anything more about them. The other point raised by the fourth taxpayer is that proper notices of the sub-
G apportionments were not served in accordance with the requirements of s. 248 (2) of the Act of 1952. Section 248 provides:

" (1) Where a direction has been given under s. 245 of this Act with respect to a company, the apportionment of the actual income from all sources of the company shall be made by the Special Commissioners in accordance with the respective interests of the members.

H " (2) Notice of any such apportionment shall be given by serving on the company a statement showing the amount of the actual income from all sources adopted by the Special Commissioners for the purposes of the said s. 245 and either the amount apportioned to each member or the amount apportioned to each class of shares, as the commissioners think fit.

I " (3) A company which is aggrieved by any such notice of apportionment shall be entitled to appeal to the Special Commissioners on giving notice to an officer of the Commissioners of Inland Revenue within thirty days after the date of the notice."

I have read those subsections in the form in which they have now been amended (3).

---

(1) [1966] 1 All E.R. 1.   (2) [1966] 1 All E.R. 30.
(3) By the Finance Act, 1958, s. 23, Sch. 6, Pt. 2, para. 5 and the Income Tax Management Act 1964, s. 17 (3), Sch. 4.

It is said that notice of the sub-apportionments ought to have been given to A the New Century Co., and that no such notice was given. Section 248, of course, makes no reference to sub-apportionments, but to discover how the thing would work where there were sub-apportionments one has to go to s. 254, sub-s. (3) of which says:

> " Any surtax chargeable by reference to the provisions of this Chapter in B respect of the amount of the income of the first company apportioned to any member of the second company shall be assessed upon that member in the name of the first company, and shall, subject to the provisions of this Chapter as to payment by the member, be payable by the first company, and the provisions of this Chapter as to the assessment, collection and recovery of surtax chargeable in respect of the income of a company apportioned to any C member thereof shall, with any necessary modifications, apply accordingly."

I would draw attention to the fact that what is referred to there is " the provisions of this Chapter " of the Act " as to the assessment, collection and recovery . . .". In the same way, in sub-s. (4), which deals with further sub-apportionments, it is provided that

> ". . . the provisions of this Chapter shall, with any necessary modifications, D apply to such successive apportionments, and to the furnishing of statements and to the assessment, collection and recovery of surtax in respect of income apportioned thereunder . . ."

I think that it is relevant in this connexion to remember that sub-s. (5), which I E read earlier, provides that any reference to apportioning income

> " shall be construed as a reference not only to apportioning by means of an original apportionment but also to apportioning by means of an original apportionment together with one or more sub-apportionments or series of sub-apportionments."

It seems to me that the references in sub-s. (3) and sub-s. (4) of s. 254 to " the F provisions of this Chapter ", which are to apply " with any necessary modifications ", do not bear on the question of what notices should be given under s. 248, which is not a provision that relates to assessment, collection or recovery of surtax; but I have to consider how s. 248 should be operated in the light of sub-s. (5). Now, if one were to read s. 248 (1) in the light of s. 254 (5), it would read G somewhat like this: " Where a direction has been given under s. 245 of this Act with respect to a company, the apportionment and any one or more sub-apportionments of the actual income from all sources shall be made by the Special Commissioners in accordance with the respective interests of ", and then one gets into difficulties because the words " the members ", which under s. 248 (1), read in its normal form, clearly refer to members of the company which is H the subject-matter of the surtax direction, are inappropriate or difficult to apply when one is dealing with a succession of companies through whom sub-apportionments are made. I think one would have to read it as, " in accordance with the respective interests of the persons ultimately entitled ", or something of that kind.

Then, sub-s. (2) would read somewhat like this: " Notice of any such appor- I tionment and of any one or more sub-apportionments shall be given by serving on the company a statement showing the amount of the actual income from all sources adopted by the Special Commissioners for the purposes of s. 245 ", and so on. It does not seem to me that there is any necessity, in applying s. 248 (2), in a case where there are sub-apportionments, to read the words " the company " there as extending to anything more than the company whose profits are the subject-matter of a surtax direction; for that is the company which is referred to in sub-s. (1), and it must be, I think, the same company that is referred to in

A sub-s. (2). As counsel for the taxpayers has pointed out, that is the company which will be assessed to surtax whether the case is one in which there are sub-apportionments or not; and that is the company which is concerned with the question of whether the right amount has been inserted as being the actual income from all sources for the relevant period.

It seems to me, although the point is not a very easy one, that, in a case where
B there are sub-apportionments, still the notice of the apportionment and of those sub-apportionments is to be given to the company whose undistributed income is the subject-matter of the surtax direction. I think that, reading s. 248 (2) in the light of s. 254 (5), the notice must be not only notice of apportionment but also notice of any one or more sub-apportionments which result from the surtax direction. Accordingly, I think notice of the sub-apportionments should have
C been given in the present case to the New Century Co. Such notice was not given, but it does not seem to me that, from that, it follows that there is anything wrong with the apportionments. Failure to give the notice would have the effect of extending the time within which an appeal could be made against the sub-apportionments; but, unless such an appeal, when brought, were to succeed, there would be nothing wrong with the apportionments. In my judgment, the
D giving of the notice is not a condition precedent to a valid and effective apportionment.

Accordingly, it seems to me that really the question whether or not notice of these sub-apportionments was given to the New Century Co. is not a matter of any significance now, for the fourth taxpayer has brought his appeal, and there can be no question of his being out of time. The matter has been ventilated and
E dealt with, both by the Special Commissioners and now by this court; and there seems to me to be nothing in the circumstances which in any way invalidates the apportionments or makes the tax such that it is not properly exigible by the Inland Revenue. On these grounds, I do not think that there is any substance in that point which is taken on the fourth taxpayer's appeal. Accordingly, on these grounds, I think that both appeals should be dismissed.
F
Appeals dismissed.

Solicitors: *Titmuss, Sainer & Webb* (for the taxpayers); *Solicitor of Inland Revenue.*

[*Reported by* F. A. AMIES, ESQ., *Barrister-at-Law.*]

A

NOTE.

Re DREWE'S SETTLEMENT.
DREWE AND OTHERS *v.* WESTMINSTER BANK, LTD.
AND ANOTHER.

B

[CHANCERY DIVISION (Stamp, J.), May 4, 5, 1966.]

Trust and Trustee—Variation of trusts by the court—Release of life interest—
Application to approve transaction on behalf of tenant for life's future
children—Special power of appointment exercisable by deed or will vested in
tenant for life—Provision in proposed arrangement to extinguish testamentary C
element in power of appointment—Power to appoint by deed left untouched—
Clause to be included in arrangement precluding power from being exercised
until estate duty implications have been the subject of proper professional advice
—Variation of Trusts Act, 1958 (6 & 7 Eliz. 2 c. 53), s. 1.

[As to the jurisdiction under the Act of 1958 to vary trusts, see 38 HALSBURY'S
LAWS (3rd Edn.) 1029, 1030, para. 1772; and for cases on the subject, see 3rd D
DIGEST SUPP., title TRUSTS AND TRUSTEES, *2859g et seq.*

As to the release of powers, see 30 HALSBURY'S LAWS (3rd Edn.) 284, para. 535;
and for cases on the subject, see 37 DIGEST (Repl.) 401, *1303-1308.*

For the Variation of Trusts Act, 1958, s. 1, see 38 HALSBURY'S STATUTES
(2nd Edn.) 1130.]

E

Adjourned Summons.

This was an application by originating summons dated Dec. 9, 1965, by the
plaintiffs, who were Basil Drewe, who had a protected life interest in a one-fourth
share of the funds subject to the trusts of a settlement dated Mar. 25, 1929,
and Anthony Drewe, John Drewe and Rosemary Gilchrist, who had beneficial
interests in that share in reversion expectant on the death of their father (the F
plaintiff, Basil Drewe), for an order pursuant to s. 1 of the Variation of Trusts
Act, 1958, approving an arrangement in the terms set out in the summons
(or on such other terms as the court might think fit and the plaintiffs assented
to) on behalf of (a) all persons unborn who might become entitled to beneficial
interests in the settled share of the plaintiff, Basil Drewe under the trusts of the
settlement and (b) all persons other than the plaintiffs who might be objects of G
the discretionary trust which would arise if the plaintiff, Basil Drewe, incurred a
forfeiture of his protected life interest in such share. The defendants were
Westminster Bank, Ltd., and Sir Cedric Drewe who were the trustees of the
settlement. The facts are set out in the judgment.

E. W. Griffith for the plaintiffs.
D. K. Rattee for the defendants.

H

Cur. adv. vult.

May 5. **STAMP, J.,** read the following judgment: This application raises a
point which has from time to time occasioned me some anxiety. The application
is one under the Variation of Trusts Act, 1958. Its purpose is described—and
this is an accurate description, although, perhaps, unfortunate because it may I
give rise to misapprehension in the minds of the uninitiated—to avoid estate
duty on death of a tenant for life. The basis and policy of the law of estate duty
is to charge with the duty property which passes on a death. There is no legal
or moral duty not to part with your property during your lifetime. In order to
protect the Exchequer it is, however, provided that if you give away property
towards the end of your life—the period was originally, I think, three months,
but has been extended by successive Parliaments, so that it is now five years—
it shall be as if you had retained the property until you died, but if you make

A the gift more than five years before your death and retain no interest in it, it has not been the policy of Parliament to exact estate duty on that property on your subsequent death.

In the present case a life tenant having a life interest in property forming part of a trust fund proposes, in effect, to release that life interest in return for the release by those who come after him of their interest in another part. Such a

B transaction, which is, I think, typical of the majority—perhaps the vast majority —of applications which come before this court under the Variation of Trusts Act, 1958, in no way takes advantage of a loophole in the law: for the property which the tenant for life gives up will be subject to estate duty if he dies within the five year period and as regards the property which will come into his own hands it will, as regards estate duty, be in the same position as any other property

C of his. Moreover, if those who may become interested in the fund on the death of the tenant for life were all adult persons, they could carry out the transaction themselves and an application to this court would be unnecessary.

In the present case there are, however, included among those persons future children of the tenant for life and the court is asked, in effect, to approve the transaction on their behalf, subject to one point, which has now been covered.

D I had no hesitation in doing so, but because the point arises in many cases I thought it desirable that I should deliver a formal judgment on it.

The life tenant, in addition to the life interest in the property which he proposes to give up, has also a power of appointment over it, which he may exercise by deed or will in favour of his children and remoter issue. Subject to any exercise of that power the property will go to his children equally. From what I may

E describe as the family point of view it is desirable that this power of appointment should not be extinguished, but should remain exercisable. The retention of the power is dangerous, however, and if it were exercised by will, and Mr. Drewe, the present tenant for life, died, having so exercised it, even twenty years hence— twenty years after he had given up all interest in the fund—a new liability for estate duty would almost certainly be attracted on his death, and a transaction

F which would otherwise have been fair and beneficial to the children would in the event have been disastrous. To obviate this danger those who negotiated this transaction very properly provided that the testamentary power should be extinguished. The power to appoint by deed was, however, left untouched, the position being that the mere exercise of the power by deed, where the person making the appointment did not provide the property, would not attract a

G liability for estate duty on his death. Nevertheless, and this is what gives rise to anxiety, the power, even though it is only exercisable by deed, which, if exercisable at all, will of necessity be exercised during Mr. Drewe's lifetime, might be exercised incautiously in such a way that there was, on his death, some such change in the interests of the beneficiaries as would result in a passing, or notional passing, giving rise to liability to estate duty. Although the risk of

H this happening in any particular case is not considerable, it ought, I think, to be guarded against. What is required is a provision precluding the power from being exercised until the possible estate duty implications of the proposed appointment have been the subject of proper professional consideration and advice.

In order to meet the point, which has been raised and similarly met in a number

I of cases, counsel in a recent case drew a clause, a copy of which he has been good enough to furnish for the assistance of the court. With the inclusion of that clause, which is accepted by the other parties, I have approved the arrangement on behalf of the persons on whose behalf the court is asked to approve it. The clause provides that the power

"... shall not be exercisable without the consent of the trustees which consent the trustees shall not withhold if advised by counsel of not less than ten years standing [at the Bar] that any proposed appointment will not

under the law in force for the time being give rise to any claim for estate   **A**
duty on the reversioners' fund or any part thereof on the death of Mr.
Drewe."

Order accordingly.

Solicitors: *Linklaters & Paines* (for the plaintiffs); *Slaughter & May* (for the
defendants).

[*Reported by* JENIFER SANDELL, *Barrister-at-Law.*]   **B**

R. *v.* HOARE.

C
[COURT OF CRIMINAL APPEAL (Lord Parker, C.J., Sachs and Browne, JJ.),
March 17, 1966.]

*Criminal Law—Trial—Jury—Direction to jury—Alibi—Comment on defence
not being disclosed before trial.*

The appellant was charged, inter alia, with robbery with violence. From
the outset he maintained that he had nothing to do with the robbery.   **D**
It was not, however, until the trial that he disclosed for the first time that
his defence was an alibi.   In summing-up to the jury the trial judge adverted
to the fact that that defence had only been produced at the trial and in two
passages clearly conveyed to the jury the inconceivability of an innocent
man not giving the details of his alibi at once to the police if it were a true one.
He did not tell them that an accused was entitled to stand on his rights and   **E**
say nothing and that he was entitled to keep back the nature and details
of his defence for reasons which he might think good.   On appeal against
conviction,

Held: the conviction must be quashed.

R. v. *Davis* ((1959), 43 Cr. App. Rep. 215) followed.

Appeal allowed.   **F**

[As to commenting on the failure of accused to disclose his defence before
trial, see 10 HALSBURY'S LAWS (3rd Edn.) 424, 425, para. 780; and for cases on
the subject, see 14 DIGEST (Repl.) 656, 657, *6668-6674.*]

Cases referred to:

R. v. *Davis*, (1959), 123 J.P. 645; 43 Cr. App. Rep. 215.
R. v. *Gerrard*, [1948] 1 All E.R. 205; 112 J.P. 164; 32 Cr. App. Rep. 132;   **G**
14 Digest (Repl.) 657, *6674.*

Appeal.

This was an appeal by leave of the Court of Criminal Appeal by the appellant,
Anthony James Hoare, against his conviction before the commissioner (JUDGE
BAILEY) and a jury at Liverpool Crown Court on Apr. 12, 1965, of robbery with   **H**
violence, receiving a Jaguar motor car and receiving an excise licence off another
car, for which he was sentenced in all to six years' imprisonment.   He pleaded
guilty to four other offences, for which he was sentenced to a further two years'
imprisonment.   He was indicted with one Henry Wren, who was convicted of
the robbery with violence, and of receiving a motor car, but did not appeal.

The cases noted below* were cited during the argument in addition to those   **I**
referred to in the judgment of the court.

Rose Heilbron, Q.C., and *Sylvia Corkhill* for the appellant.
J. K. Gore for the Crown.

LORD PARKER, C.J., delivered the following judgment of the court:
The appellant was convicted at Liverpool Crown Court of three offences, first,

---

* *R.* v. *Naylor*, [1932] All E.R. Rep. 152; [1933] 1 K.B. 685; *R.* v. *Leckey*, [1943] 2
All E.R. 665; [1944] K.B. 80.

A robbery with violence, secondly, receiving a Jaguar motor car, and thirdly, receiving an excise licence which had come off another car, and was in fact found on the Jaguar car. He pleaded guilty to certain other offences, and he received sentences which in the aggregate total eight years' imprisonment. Now, by leave of the court, he appeals against his three convictions. Two points were taken both in his grounds of appeal and by counsel on his behalf; first,

B that the learned judge ought to have acceded to a submission of no case in that, at the end of the prosecution case, there was insufficient evidence to go to the jury, and secondly, that certain comments made by the judge as to the failure of the appellant to disclose his alibi at an early stage amounted to misdirection. Having regard to the view that the court has taken on the second point, misdirection, it is really unnecessary to go into the facts here in any detail.

C It is sufficient to say that the robbery was a well-planned robbery, that a number of men must have been involved in it, that three different cars were used, and that an unfortunate Mr. Pickett was robbed of some £1,156, punched and kicked, and the money was taken.

The appellant from the very outset maintained that he had nothing to do with the robbery at all. He was first interviewed on Sept. 24, 1964, the robbery

D having occurred on Aug. 4, 1964. At the trial, for the first time, he disclosed that his defence was that, on Aug. 4, he had been staying with his parents at Luton. In summing-up to the jury, the learned commissioner adverted in three places to the fact that this alibi had only been produced at the trial. In reminding the jury of what the prosecution's case against the appellant and his co accused Wren was, one of the points which the learned commissioner put

E forward as part of the prosecution's case was this:

"... perhaps you may think one of their strongest points—it is entirely for you—on which they attach great importance, was the failure by [the appellant] to mention ever before until last Friday that he was on holiday with his parents at Luton at the time of the commission of the crime."

F A little later he went on:

" The prosecution invite you to say that those are matters which transcend all commonsense as matters which would be overlooked or forgotten."

Then the matter is put a little stronger against the appellant; the learned commissioner said:

G " The prosecution say that [the appellant] must have known full well, if he is telling the truth when he gives evidence before you, that he had been nowhere near Liverpool on that day, but had been at his parents' home at Luton. They say it is inconceivable that an innocent man could forget that fact,"

and finally, the learned commissioner said:

H " Ask yourselves, members of the jury, what would you have done if you were an innocent man and the police had been alleging that you on a certain day at a certain place had committed a serious offence like robbery with violence, with others, and you knew that at the time you were nowhere near the scene of the crime. What would you think it best to do—to say nothing, or to say: ' This is a ghastly mistake, go and check with my mother

I and father, they will tell you where I was '? It is a matter entirely for you."

What counsel on behalf of the appellant says in regard to those passages is really this, that, whatever comment is justified in the particular circumstances on the fact that a man does not give an explanation, or a full explanation, or disclose a defence, when he is cautioned or when he is arrested and charged, at any rate what was said by the learned commissioner went beyond what could possibly be justified as comment. This matter has come before the courts on a great number of occasions; it is unnecessary to go through all the cases, many A of which, if my recollection is right, cannot be completely reconciled the one with the other. The court thinks that it is unnecessary to do more than refer to the last reported case on the matter, *R. v. Davis* (1). That again was a case where, after caution, the accused did not put forward the explanation which he put forward at the trial, which was not an alibi defence, but the court can see no reason to distinguish an alibi defence from any other. In that case, the deputy B chairman had said (2):

" Members of the jury, a man is not obliged to say anything, but you are entitled to use your common sense. If Davis was in the position that he now would have you believe he was in . . . would he say to the police ' I am saying nothing '? . . . Can you imagine an innocent man who had behaved like that not saying something to the police about this in the course of the C evening or the next day, or even a little time afterwards. He said nothing."

In those circumstances, this court felt bound to quash the conviction. A number of cases had been cited, and the court in its judgment (3) referred to the well-known passages of HUMPHREYS, J., in *R. v. Gerard* (4), where he said:

" It can only be a misdirection if it was an invitation to the jury to form D an adverse opinion against the applicant because he did not then give an explanation . . ."

The court then went on (5):

" We have been referred to a number of cases, some of which fall on one side of the line and some on the other, but here in this case the court feels E that undoubtedly this was making a comment about the prisoner which was inconsistent with his innocence. The expression ' Can you imagine an innocent man doing this? ' is not a mere comment on the fact that perhaps it was unfortunate he did not give an answer, but is really saying ' Do you as a jury of people of common sense really think that a man can be innocent if he makes no reply in those circumstances? ' "   F

In the judgment of this court, the present case really falls fairly and squarely within what was said in *R. v. Davis* (1). Indeed, it is a stronger case in that, in *R. v. Davis* (1), the deputy chairman had reminded the jury of the caution, and had gone on to explain that, in the light of that caution, the prisoner was not obliged to say anything. In the present case, though no doubt the jury had the words of the caution in their mind, they were never expressly told that G a man was entitled to stand on his rights and say nothing, that he was entitled to keep back for reasons which he might think good the nature and details of his defence. Nothing of that was explained to the jury, and on top of that come the passages to which I have referred, the last two of which would clearly convey to the jury the inconceivability of an innocent man not giving the details of his alibi at once to the police if it were a true one.   H

In these circumstances, as in *R. v. Davis* (1), this court has no option but to quash these convictions.

Appeal allowed.

Solicitors: *Registrar, Court of Criminal Appeal* (for the appellant); *Cree, Godfrey & Wood*, agents for *T. Alker*, Liverpool (for the Crown).

[*Reported by* KAUSHALYA PURIE, *Barrister-at-Law.*]   I

(1) (1959), 43 Cr. App. Rep. 215.   (2) (1959), 43 Cr. App. Rep. at p. 217.
(3) (1959), 43 Cr. App. Rep. at pp. 217, 218.
(4) [1948] 1 All E.R. 205 at p. 206; 32 Cr. App. Rep. 132 at p. 134.
(5) (1959), 43 Cr. App. Rep. at p. 218.

A   Re AGREEMENT OF THE MILEAGE CONFERENCE GROUP
OF THE TYRE MANUFACTURERS' CONFERENCE, LTD.

[RESTRICTIVE PRACTICES COURT (Megaw, P., McVeigh, L.J., Mr. W. L. Heywood,
Mr. D. V. House and Maj.-Gen. W. E. V. Abraham), May 9, 10, 11, 12, 13,
16, 17, 18, June 17, 1966.]

B   *Contempt of Court—Mitigation—Legal advice that a course of conduct would not
amount to breach of undertakings given to court—Acts in fact done constituting
contempt—Whether acts must be contumacious to constitute contempt of
court by breach of undertaking—Whether legal advice mitigated contempt.*

*Restrictive Trade Practices—Court—Contempt of court—Undertakings to court
not to enter into any arrangement to the like effect as former agreement*

C   *in respect of restrictions rendered void on reference to court—Former agreement superseded by new rate notification scheme, which was in part permissive
—No agreement amongst member companies that they would all operate the
new scheme, but each soon aware that others were doing so—Whether an
" arrangement "—Whether to " the like effect " as original agreement—
Whether contempt of court—Legal advice as mitigation of contempt.*

D   Eight tyre-manufacturing companies, being members of the Mileage
Conference Group of the Tyre Manufacturers' Conference, Ltd., were engaged
in mileage contracts by which they undertook to keep fleets of motor vehicles
equipped with tyres in return for payments related to the miles run by each
vehicle. By the original agreement entered into by the group, members
agreed to observe certain restrictions, one of which was not to tender at

E   mileage rates lower than the lowest price (i.e., mileage rate) insisted on by
any member at a meeting held in accordance with a specified procedure
without first notifying the other members. During the operation of this
agreement departures from level tendering were rare. In 1961 the group
decided to terminate the agreement, which had already been referred to the
court by the registrar. The court made an unopposed order declaring the

F   restrictions contrary to the public interest and accepted the group's undertakings not to give effect to the agreement in respect of specified restrictions
(including the one exemplified above) nor to enter into nor make any agreement or arrangement to the like effect to which Part 1 of the Restrictive
Trade Practices Act, 1956, applied.*

While the reference of the original agreement was pending a new " rate

G   notification scheme " was devised and this was set out in a document. The
scheme consisted of a compulsory part, by which a member notified the
secretary and he notified other members of any rate which the member had
already quoted, and a permissive part, by which, as understood by the
members of the group, they could also notify the secretary of rates which they
were minded to quote to operators and any changes in them, and the secretary

H   would then notify these to other members. It was not suggested that the
compulsory part of the scheme was a breach of the undertakings. With rare
exceptions, which were concealed from other members of the group, all
members in fact notified all intended quotations between the inception of
the rate notification scheme in 1961 and its abandonment in 1965. Level
tendering continued throughout this period, although other factors might

I   have contributed to this.

The draft of the rate notification scheme had been discussed and orally
approved at a consultation with leading and junior counsel, who had received
no written instructions and gave no written opinion. It was understood
by the solicitor for the group, and explained to member companies, that the

---

* See s. 6 (3) of the Act of 1956 whereby " agreement " in Part 1 of the Act of 1956
includes any agreement or arrangement, whether or not it is or it is intended to be
enforceable by legal proceedings. By s. 6 (3) also " restriction " includes any negative
obligation whether express or implied and whether absolute or not.

scheme could operate in the way stated above, by permitting notification   A
of provisional intentions as to rates which members were going to
quote. On a natural construction of the words of the scheme, however,
it meant that a member company should be free to notify a rate which it
had finally decided to offer or had quoted, not merely a provisional intention,
and notification of a rate quoted would not have been a breach of the
undertakings. Before the scheme was adopted members of the group   B
were told that they must neither agree with each other that they would
all operate the permissive part of the scheme, nor discuss with each other
any proposed rates. In fact they never informed each other in advance
of their intentions to make use of the permissive part of the scheme, but it
necessarily involved mutuality and observance by members independently,
and it must have become apparent to each member soon afterwards that   C
all other members were using the scheme. Notifications under the permissive part of the scheme in respect of tenders called for by local authority
operators were given on two occasions in the autumn of 1961, and those
notifications were circulated. In 1963 the decision in *Re British Basic Slag,
Ltd.'s Agreements* ([1963] 2 All E.R. 807) indicated the wide meaning which
could be attached to the word " arrangement ". In 1964 the Birmingham   D
Corpn. protested strongly against the submission of level tenders and alleged
the existence of a price ring. On neither of these occasions (referred to in
holding (ii) post as the " later events ") was further advice sought from
counsel, nor was there any evidence that the legality of the position was
seriously re-considered by the higher management of the member companies.

On a motion by the Registrar of Restrictive Trading Agreements for seques-   E
tration of the assets of the companies belonging to the group, on the grounds
that they had broken their undertakings to the court,

Held: (i) the members were in breach of their undertakings to the court
and the breaches were contempts of court because

(a) although when members separately and individually decided to try to
operate the permissive part of the rate notification scheme, there might not   F
then be an " arrangement ", yet when it became clear to all of them by
reason of the acts of others that all of them had decided to operate the
permissive part of the scheme, there was then an "arrangement" to which
Part 1 of the Restrictive Trade Practices Act, 1956, applied and which
involved a restriction within s. 6 (1), (3) of that Act (see p. 859, letters E and
F, p. 860, letters B and I, and p. 861, letter A, post).   G

Re British Basic Slag, Ltd.'s Agreements ([1963] 2 All E.R. 807) applied.

(b) the restrictions under the rate notification scheme were to the like
effect as those under the former agreement, for the purposes of the permissive
part of the scheme and of the former agreement were the same and, although
the machinery employed was different, the differences were not such as to
make the restrictions of different effect (see p. 861, letter G, post).   H

Re Black Bolt and Nut Association of Great Britain's Agreement (No. 2)
([1962] 1 All E.R. 139) considered.

(c) the acts of the members being in breach of their undertakings to the
court, it was no answer to the present proceedings for contempt to maintain
that the breaches were not contumacious, for the breaches of the undertakings would have constituted contempts even though the acts were things   I
done reasonably after all due care and attention and in the belief, based on
legal advice, that they were not breaches of the undertakings (see p. 862,
letter C, post).

Dictum of WARRINGTON, J., in *Stancomb v. Trowbridge Urban District
Council* ([1910] 2 Ch. at p. 194) applied.

(ii) the conception involved in the rate notification scheme, viz., of obtaining the same results thereby as those obtained under the former agreement,
was no novel conception, and reliance on legal advice could not be a complete

A mitigation, as a matter of course (see p. 863, letter D, post); further, although members of the group might initially have believed reasonably, in reliance on counsel's advice as explained to them, that the permissive part of the rate notification scheme would not involve breach of the undertakings, ·yet after the later events (cf. p. 850, letter D, ante) the managements of the member companies had shown reckless disregard of their duty to the court

B by their inaction in failing to have the legality of the scheme reviewed and by their delegation, complete and without supervision, of observance of the undertakings to subordinate employees, no evidence being before the court of any adequate instructions to employees having been given (see p. 866, letters G to I, and letter C, post).

Dicta of DIPLOCK, J., in *Re Agreement between Newspaper Proprietors'*

C *Association, Ltd. and National Federation of Retail Newsagents, Booksellers and Stationers* ([1961] 3 All E.R. 428) applied.

Fairclough v. *Manchester Ship Canal Co.* ([1897] W.N. 7; 41 Sol. Jo. 225) and *Worthington* v. *Ad Lib Club, Ltd.* ([1964] 3 All E.R. 674) considered.

[As to contempt of the Restrictive Practices Court, see 38 HALSBURY'S LAWS

D (3rd Edn.) 112, para. 147; and for the jurisdiction to impose fines for contempt of court, see 8 HALSBURY'S LAWS (3rd Edn.) 3, para. 3.]

Cases referred to:

Associated Newspapers, Ltd. v. *Registrar of Restrictive Trading Agreements,* [1964] 1 All E.R. 55; sub nom. *Re Newspaper Proprietors' Agreement,* (1964), L.R. 4 R.P. 361; [1964] 1 W.L.R. 31; 45 Digest (Repl.) 430,

E *230.*

Black Bolt and Nut Association of Great Britain's Agreement, Re, (No. 2), [1961] 3 All E.R. 316; (1961) L.R. 2 R.P. 433; [1961] 1 W.L.R. 1139, *affd.* C.A., [1962] 1 All E.R. 139; (1962), L.R. 3 R.P. 43; [1962] 1 W.L.R. 75; 45 Digest (Repl.) 412, *171.*

British Basic Slag, Ltd.'s Agreements (or Appln.), Re, [1963] 2 All E.R. 807;

F (1963), L.R. 4 R.P. 116; [1963] 1 W.L.R. 727; 45 Digest (Repl.) 405, *161.*

Fairclough v. *Manchester Ship Canal Co.,* [1897] W.N. 7; 41 Sol. Jo. 225; 16 Digest (Repl.) 52, *483.*

Galvanized Tank Manufacturers' Association's Agreement, Re, [1965] 2 All E.R. 1003; (1965), L.R. 5 R.P. 315; [1965] 1 W.L.R. 1074.

G *National Federated Electrical Association's Agreement, Re,* (1961), L.R. 2 R.P. 447; 45 Digest (Repl.) 438, *227.*

Newspaper Proprietors' Association, Ltd., and National Federation of Retail Newsagents, Booksellers & Stationers, Agreement between, Re, [1961] 3 All E.R. 428; (1961), L.R. 2 R.P. 453; [1961] 1 W.L.R. 1149; 45 Digest (Repl.) 431, *195.*

H *Stancomb* v. *Trowbridge Urban District Council,* [1910] 2 Ch. 190; 79 L.J.Ch. 519; 102 L.T. 647; 74 J.P. 210; 16 Digest (Repl.) 52, *484.*

Worthington v. *Ad Lib. Club, Ltd.,* [1964] 3 All E.R. 674; [1965] Ch. 236; [1964] 3 W.L.R. 1094; 3rd Digest Supp.

Motion.

I This was a motion on notice dated Mar. 7, 1966 by the Registrar of Restrictive Trading Agreements for writs of sequestration against the respondent companies for contempt of court in wilfully disobeying an order of the court made in the matter of an *Agreement between the Members of the Mileage Conference Group of the Tyre Manufacturers' Conference, Ltd.* on Oct. 9, 1961, in that the respondent companies and each of them in breach of undertakings given to the court on their behalf that without leave of the court they (a) would not nor would any of them whether by themselves or by their respective servants, agents or otherwise give effect to or enforce or purport to enforce the said agreement in respect of

any of the restrictions declared by the court to be contrary to public interest, **A**
and further (b) would not nor would any of them whether by themselves or by
their respective servants, agents or otherwise enter into or make any other
agreement or arrangement to which Part 1 of the Restrictive Trade Practices
Act, 1956, applies, to the like effect to the said agreement in respect of the said
restrictions or any of them, did, without leave of the court, enter into or make
another agreement or arrangement or other agreements or arrangements to the **B**
like effect in respect of the restrictions numbered 2, 3, 4 and 6 in Sch. 3 to the
said order of the court.   The facts are set out in the judgment of the court.

  J. F. Donaldson, Q.C., R. A. Barr and *P. F. Macrory* for the registrar.
  R. I. Threlfall, Q.C., and *R. O. Havery* for the respondents.

Cur. adv. vult.
C

  June 17.   **MEGAW, P.,** read the following judgment of the court: By this
motion the Registrar of Restrictive Trading Agreements applies for an order
for the sequestration of the assets of eight tyre-manufacturing companies, members of the Mileage Conference Group of the Tyre Manufacturers' Conference,
Ltd., on the ground that each of these companies has broken undertakings given
to this court on their behalf on Oct. 9, 1961.   The respondent companies are **D**
The Avon Rubber Co., Ltd., The Dunlop Rubber Co., Ltd., Firestone Tyre &
Rubber Co., Ltd., The Goodyear Tyre & Rubber Co. (Great Britain), Ltd., India
Tyres, Ltd., Michelin Tyre Co., Ltd., Uniroyal, Ltd., and Pirelli, Ltd.

  The relevant business of each of these companies, so far as concerns this
motion, is mileage contracts.   A mileage contract is an agreement between a
tyre manufacturer and an owner of a fleet of motor vehicles, normally passenger **E**
transport vehicles.   The owner of the fleet is described as an " operator ".   By
the agreement the manufacturer undertakes to keep the operator's vehicles, or
some proportion of them, adequately equipped with tyres throughout the period
of the agreement.   In return the operator pays to the manufacturer a rate of so
much per mile run by the vehicles.   This is known as " the mileage rate ".   We
shall refer to it as " the rate ".   Since it is, in effect, a payment for the hire of the **F**
tyres, and not for their sale, the word " rate ", meaning rate per mile, is more
appropriate than the word " price ".   Not infrequently operators prefer to
make mileage contracts with two or more manufacturers, dividing up the fleet
of vehicles among them, usually on a percentage basis.

  The Mileage Conference Group, of which each of the respondent companies
is a member, is an organisation within the Tyre Manufacturers' Conference, Ltd. **G**
We shall call it " the group ".   It, and its members, are concerned with mileage
contracts.   Up to July, 1961, it provided machinery for collaboration among
its members by means of an agreement to which they were all parties.   The
agreement was, after the passing of the Restrictive Trade Practices Act, 1956,
duly registered with the registrar as registered agreement No. 964.   We shall call
it " the former agreement ".   **H**

  The former agreement dealt in particular with four aspects of the mileage
contract business.   First, there was new business, where an operator who had
previously bought tyres for his vehicles changed over to mileage contracts for
the first time.   Second, it covered " re-tenders ", which arose when an existing
mileage contract had been terminated by the operator and the operator called
for fresh tenders for a new contract.   Third, it dealt with " rate reviews ".   These **I**
arose because the standard form of contract, which existed during the period
of the former agreement and continued to be used in substantially the same form
after the former agreement had been terminated, permitted revision of the agreed
rate on the manufacturer giving one month's notice.   In practice, during the
period with which we are concerned, reviews were made by the manufacturers
every six months, covering the periods beginning on Jan. 1 and July 1 in each
year.   In the rate reviews, the rates affecting each existing mileage contract of
each operator were reviewed, and as a result the rates for the next period of six

A months might remain the same, or they might be altered upward or downward.
We do not propose to trouble about the fourth facet, known as " tyre
allowances ".

The former agreement contained restrictions in respect, inter alia, of each of
these facets of the business. For simplicity, it will be sufficient for the purpose
of this judgment to refer to one of those restrictions, and to set it out in the form
B in which it appears in the schedule of restrictions annexed to, and forming part
of, the undertakings which were given to the court by the respondents. It was:

" Not to offer or supply tyres on a mileage basis at a price lower than the
lowest price insisted on by any manufacturer at a meeting held in accordance
with the procedure set out in [and then certain passages in certain registered
documents are referred to] without notifying the other parties."

C

The word " price " means what we have called " rate ". It was used in the order
of the court because s. 6 (1) (a) of the Act of 1956 uses the word " price "; but
by s. 36 (1) it is defined as including " a charge of any description ". It is not
necessary to set out in any detail the procedure specified in the registered documents. It involved in certain cases the calculation by the secretary of the
D conference (who also acted as secretary of the group) of a weighted average of
rates supplied to him by interested members as being their desired future rates.
This, with other information, was circulated to manufacturer members. A
meeting of members then took place. At the meeting there emerged " the lowest
rate which is insisted upon by a manufacturer ". The lowest rate thus emerging
was circulated to all members, and, in the words of the registered document,
E " there is an arrangement that no manufacturer will quote " (which means, of
course, quote to the operator as the offered future contractual rate) " lower
than that rate without notifying the other members ".

The meaning and purpose of the restriction is clear. Each manufacturer,
before he committed himself by making a quotation to the operator, either on a
rate review or a tender or a re-tender, should have the opportunity to know and
F consider the lowest rate which any of his competitors was going to quote. One
economic effect of this restriction is also clear, and we cannot doubt that it was
realised and intended by the manufacturers concerned: that is, that no manufacturer need have been haunted by the thought that the rate which he was first
minded to quote might be higher than that of one or more of his competitors
and that, as a result, he might find himself undercut when the quotations were
G put in to the operator: for he knew that he would have the opportunity to
revise his original intention, if he thought it necessary in the light of any lower
quotation by a competitor. Not surprisingly, under the former agreement there
was a very large measure of level tendering, both on tenders and re-tenders
and on rate reviews. So far as the evidence shows, departures from level tendering
were rare. There are, undoubtedly, a number of features in this trade which would
H tend to produce level rates apart from such an agreement; but there is equally
no doubt that the former agreement was a very powerful factor in ensuring that
level tendering was almost universal.

The former agreement was referred to the court by the registrar. On May 24,
1961, the group passed a resolution to terminate it as from July 31, 1961. Other
things then happened to which we shall refer later. The former agreement
I came before this court on Oct. 9, 1961. No evidence was offered on behalf of the
respondents. The court made an order declaring the restrictions in the former
agreement to be contrary to the public interest. Undertakings were offered to
the court on behalf of each of the respondents; accordingly, the court did not
issue injunctions. The undertakings were that the respondents would not give
effect to the former agreement in respect of any of the restrictions set out in the
schedule to the court's order, and that they would not enter into or make any
other agreement or arrangement to which Part 1 of the Act of 1956 applied to
the like effect to the former agreement in respect of any of those restrictions.

The registrar contends that the respondents have broken those undertakings A in that each of them has entered into or made an arrangement or arrangements, within Part 1 of the Act, to the like effect to the former agreement, in respect of four of its restrictions. We have already set out, as being sufficient for our decision in this case, the wording of one of those four restrictions as contained in the schedule.

It is now necessary to go back in time to a period six months before the court B condemned the former agreement. By April, 1961, a new scheme had been devised by lawyers in consultation with the secretary of the conference, as a possible replacement of the former agreement, the termination of which was then in active contemplation. We shall have to consider later the question of the legal advice given in respect of that scheme; but that question is not relevant to the first issue which we have to decide: that is, whether the undertakings were C broken.

The respondents say that there was no such breach. They say, first, that no arrangement was entered into; second, that, if there was an arrangement, it contained no registrable restriction; and, third, that if there was a registrable restriction, it was not " to the like effect " to any restriction comprised in the undertakings.   D

The new scheme was known as " the rate notification scheme ". It was contained in a document of which we shall have more to say hereafter. The scheme has been treated in argument as being divided into two parts. One part has been called " the compulsory part ", since it contained provisions which, if the scheme were adopted, as it was adopted, would have to be complied with by any party to it. The other part has been called " the permissive part ", since, it is said, a E party who adopted the scheme was not thereby obliged to carry out or adhere to the provisions of that part, whatever they may have been. He could do so, but he need not. Broadly, the compulsory part was intended to provide the members of the group with information as to the rates which their competitors *had quoted* to operators. The permissive part, according to the respondents' interpretation of it, was intended, if it were operated, to provide members with information F as to the rates which their competitors were from time to time *minded to quote* to operators.

The terms of the compulsory part are clear enough. Inquiries by an operator, or applications to vary an existing contract, had to be reported to the secretary by members who received them within forty-eight hours of receipt. The secretary had to record such information on a master card, on which he would subsequently G collate all information received in respect of that inquiry or application. The information on the master card was to be available to any member on request. When any member submitted an offer to an operator, he was obliged to send details to the secretary at the same time as he submitted his offer. The secretary was required to circulate to members (presumably whether or not they had specifically asked for such information, or generally for all information on the H card) " the rate quoted and any discount allowed ". If a member varied his offer (that is, a quotation which had already been made to the operator) he was obliged, at the same time as he submitted his revised offer, to send details to the secretary who had to notify all the members. The registrar does not suggest in these proceedings that the agreement so far as concerns the compulsory part of the scheme constituted a breach of the undertakings. Presumably this is I because it may be the true view that an agreement by persons to inform one another of prices which they have quoted, after they have committed themselves by actually putting in the quotation, does not involve a restriction within s. 6 (1) of the Act of 1956, on the basis that it is not a restriction in respect of prices *to be* quoted. We do not have to consider the compulsory part of the scheme, except to note that it was abandoned in July, 1965, along with the permissive part of the scheme.

A   The permissive part of the scheme is much more obscure as a matter of proper construction of the document setting out the rate notification scheme. We shall have to return to that later, when we consider the question and effect of the legal advice given to the members. For present purposes we are concerned primarily with what the respondents did. As interpreted by the respondents, the permissive part of the scheme allowed each of them, if he wished, to notify the secretary

B   of the rate which it was in his mind to quote thereafter to the operator, without the member in question being in any way committed not to change his mind or not to put in a different quotation from that which he had notified. Still as interpreted by the respondents, the secretary was obliged to circulate such notifications to the other members. Then any member, having received information as to what his competitors were proposing to quote, was entirely free to

C   revise his originally notified intention as to the rate to be quoted. If he thereupon notified the secretary of his revised intended quotation, the secretary would be bound to circulate to the other members the revised rate so notified. There might then again be further thoughts by any of the members in the light of that information, and if any of them again changed his proposed rate and chose to notify the secretary, he would again be bound to circulate such proposed changed rate

D   to all concerned.

     One thing is abundantly clear on the evidence, and we have no doubt that it was realised by every one of the members from the time when they first considered the permissive part of the scheme: namely, that it would not work—could not work—unless all or substantially all the members were prepared to participate in it. No member was going to supply information to his competitors as to the rate

E   which he intended to quote, unless he was confident that all his competitors would do the same for him. If all the members operated the permissive part of the scheme, it would be to the commercial advantage of each of them, just as the abandoned and condemned former agreement had been to the commercial advantage of each of them. But if any substantial part of the membership, for any substantial period, did not operate the permissive part of the scheme—if

F   they failed to do substantially everything under it which they were, according to the respondents, entitled to do—the scheme would be useless and would promptly break down. If any member, for example, having received notification from other members of their intentions, refrained from making a further notification to them, through the secretary, of his revised intention to quote a rate lower than the lowest of their rates, the permissive part of the scheme would have

G   broken down within a very short time. None of them would be prepared to continue to supply information on such a basis. It is therefore not surprising to find that during the period when all the manufacturers were in fact operating the permissive part of the scheme, between the latter part of 1961 and July, 1965, each of them operated it, with very few exceptions, in precisely that way. Where they were interested in a rate revision or a tender or re-tender for a mileage

H   contract in respect of any operator, they sent their notifications of intended rates; and if, having received notification of the rates of other members, any member decided to reduce his own rate below the lowest rate of which he had received information, he in his turn notified the other members, through the secretary, of his revised intention.

     There were a few exceptions, where certain members in one way or another

I   sought to offer an advantage to the operator: some collateral advantage, not directly reflected in the rate notified to his competitors and quoted to the operator. These exceptions were rare, however, and were concealed. In general, and to all appearances on the surface, each member during more than three and a half years was supplying to his competitors all relevant notifications permitted by the scheme, in respect of any transaction in which he was interested. This, we have no doubt, was because each member realised that any other course would involve the breakdown of a method of carrying on their business which was regarded by all of them as advantageous so long as it was adhered to by all of them. We have no doubt also, despite the exceptional cases, that each member A would have regarded it as a reciprocal moral obligation—an obligation binding on the honour of the companies concerned, as it would have been in personal honour—not to take advantage of information which he was receiving from his competitors on the understanding that it was given on the basis of reciprocity, without himself showing full reciprocity.   In particular, it would have been, and would have been recognised as, a breach of moral obligation, each one B having held himself out as a giver and receiver of information, to have refrained from giving information when he was going to quote to an operator a rate below that which was the lowest rate of which he and his fellow members had been informed under the mutual exchange of information which was the essence of the scheme.   The fact that on a few occasions certain members found means of secretly evading their obligations does not show that the obligation did not exist. C Indeed, the concealment, or attempted concealment, confirms that it did exist.

It is not surprising to find that, almost without exception, there was level tendering in rate reviews and tenders and re-tenders for the mileage contracts throughout the whole period, just as there had been during the operation of the former agreement.   The evidence before us relates to part only of the mileage contract business done by these respondents.   It relates to the contracts of the D public transport undertakings of sixteen local authorities.   An analysis of the unchallenged evidence given on behalf of those sixteen local authorities shows that, between Oct. 9, 1961, the date of the court's order on the former agreement, and July, 1965, when the scheme was terminated by resolution of the group, there were eighteen instances of tenders, which produced 117 separate quotations by the respondent companies, for new contracts, or re-tenders where there had E previously been a contract.   In fourteen of the eighteen, all quotations were identical.   In the remaining four tenders, where there was not complete unanimity, there was a common view among several of the respondents as to the lowest tender: the divergence was at the higher end of the scale.   As regards rate reviews, there was a total of 294 quotations during this period.   Of the 294, only two were not fully identical, and in one of the two the difference was minimal. F

As we have already said, and as counsel for the respondents stressed, there are other factors which tend to lead frequently to level tendering in this business. One factor is that where a contract is shared, the operator may find means to persuade a manufacturer who has put in a higher quotation to reduce it to the rate quoted by the contractor with the major share of the business.   Another factor is that a manufacturer seeking new business may be reluctant to quote G below the previous going rate because of the possibility of a loss.   This factor is important because, as it would appear, the general profits of this business are not high, and in some cases losses occur.   We certainly would not draw any inference that the undertakings were broken merely because there was much level tendering under the former agreement, and much level tendering after the undertakings had been given.   But it has to be recorded as a fact—or as a necessary inference H from the facts proved—that the permissive part of the rate notification scheme was an important factor in producing level tenders.

The London Transport Board, we ought to mention, at all times carried out its mileage contract operations in such a way that it was not affected by the former agreement, and the manufacturers tacitly treated that agreement as not applying to the board; nor was it affected by, or treated as coming within the I operation of, the rate notification scheme.

So much for the way in which this business has in fact been operated by the respondents since the adoption of the rate notification scheme.   We now have to come back to the circumstances of its adoption.   This is relevant because the respondents say that they never agreed with one another—they never by word or writing told one another—that they were going to make use of the permissive part of the scheme.   Therefore, it is said, there cannot have been any arrangement

A in respect of it or incorporating it, and therefore there cannot have been any
breach of the undertaking.

This issue is, of course, of great importance to the respondents themselves
because they are answering a serious allegation of contempt of court and if they
are right on this proposition there can be no contempt. It is also of general
importance in relation to the meaning and effect of the Act. For both reasons it
B is necessary for us to deal with this question at some length; though we think
that, on the facts and inevitable inferences, the answer in relation to the present
case is beyond doubt. There was an arrangement.

On Apr. 13, 1961, the secretary, Mr. Byford, and three representatives of the
group who have not given evidence, attended a consultation with leading and
junior counsel and a solicitor, Mr. W. J. Brown, at which the draft of the rate
C notification scheme, substantially in its ultimate wording, was discussed and
approved orally by counsel. Counsel received no written instructions and no
written opinion was given. On Apr. 14, 1961, there was a meeting of the group,
when the members were informed that counsel had advised that the former
agreement would be most unlikely to be upheld by the court; and the suggested
rate notification scheme was circulated with an intimation that it had been
D approved by counsel. At another meeting on May, 24 1961, it is recorded that
further consideration was given to the draft scheme and, to quote the minutes,

" after considering the subject at length, it was decided to discuss the
subject at a further meeting to be called in the near future with the object of
formally adopting the new scheme."

E The evidence which we have heard indicates a lack of recollection of any discussion of the scheme by members at this, or any other, meeting of the group;
the recollection of witnesses is that it was explained at length by a legal adviser,
but was not discussed by the members. Mr. Brown does not appear to have been
present at the meeting of May 24, 1961, and we have not had the advantage of
hearing evidence from whatever legal representative was present. However,
the evidence suggests that the gist of the legal adviser's advice, on this and
F perhaps other occasions, was again to tell the members that the rate notification
scheme had been approved by counsel; that they would, by adopting it, bind
themselves as to the compulsory part; but that, if and in so far as they chose
to operate the permissive part and to interchange information thereunder, " that
must and could only be permissive ". (We quote the last words from Mr. Brown's
evidence.) It would seem also from Mr. Brown's evidence that he must have
G discussed the scheme on other occasions. For example, he says that he told the
members, to the best of his ability, what was meant by concluding an arrangement. He says:

" An arrangement, one told them, was the same thing for this purpose as
an agreement. They must not come to any agreement between themselves;
they must not make any looser form of agreement, which they would probably
H understand as an arrangement, between themselves that they would operate
the permissive part of the scheme. That was repeated, how many times I
do not know."

Mr. Brown, or other representatives of his firm, also made it clear to the members
that they must never talk to one another about any proposed rate, much less
I agree with one another on it. To ensure compliance, a legal adviser, sometimes
Mr. Brown, was always present at meetings of the group, with the function of
immediately stopping members if they appeared to be treading on dangerous
ground in their discussions. On some occasions the legal adviser for this purpose
was Mr. Rissik, a gentleman with legal qualifications in the employment of The
Dunlop Rubber Co., Ltd., who was apparently treated at these meetings as
being an independent legal adviser. We have not had the advantage of his
evidence. We accept, as was stated by every witness called for the respondents,
that none of them ever did orally discuss or agree rates or any similar matter,

whether at or outside meetings of the group; though occasionally, according to A
Mr. Byford, they had to be restrained at the meetings.

So far as the evidence goes, the further meeting which was to be held " in the
near future " under the decision of the meeting of May 24, 1961, was not held
until Aug. 3, 1961. No doubt meanwhile the members had been brooding on
the rate notification scheme. At that meeting, it was resolved that the rate
notification scheme should be adopted. According to the evidence, no member B
then indicated to the others any decision or view of his company as to the use by
that company of the permissive part of the rate notification scheme, and some
witnesses have said in evidence that they, or their companies, had not yet made
up their minds. One witness has said: " It is common sense the thing would be
adopted ". We think that sums up the position. Certainly it did not take them
long to make up their minds. The former agreement, as we have said, had been C
abandoned with effect from July 31, 1961. Mr. Byford does not remember
whether he asked members if they wished to be supplied with information as to
members' notifications; but each member within a very short time after the
meeting of Aug. 3, 1961, wrote to him and asked him to supply them with all
information that might become available. One of these letters, from the Dunlop
Rubber Co., is actually dated Aug. 2, but we accept that this must be a mis- D
dating and that it was sent, not before, but after the meeting. The other seven
respondents sent very similar letters on Aug. 4, 8, 9, 10 and 14, three such letters
being sent on Aug. 10. The effect of these letters is, necessarily, that each company
had then decided to put itself in a position to operate the permissive part of the
scheme, at least initially. Otherwise they would not have asked to receive
information that might be supplied by others. As we have said before, it was E
clearly in the individual interest of each to operate that part of the scheme to the
full, if the others were prepared to do likewise. Indeed there can be little doubt
that it was the permissive part of the scheme which primarily and principally
made the scheme attractive to each of them.

It has been said in evidence by each of the witnesses for the respondent companies that he arrived at his decision to use the permissive part of the scheme, F
if the others also did so, quite independently. There was, it is said, no discussion
among them and no indication by any one to any other or others that he had
reached that decision. They each hoped, and, we believe, fully expected, that
the others would do so, but they did not give any verbal or written intimation
to one another of their respective intentions or decisions. We accept that no
such actual intimation was given. It is accepted by counsel for the respondents G
that, had there been such mutual intimations at that stage, that would have
given rise to an arrangement. We do not propose to stay to consider whether the
absence of an express intimation at that stage, having regard to the special
and peculiar circumstances, would be sufficient to prevent that which would
otherwise have been an arrangement from being an arrangement. It is unnecessary to consider the matter, because we are satisfied that, assuming in the H
respondents' favour that there was at that stage no arrangement, an arrangement
in respect of the permissive part of the scheme undoubtedly came into existence
not very long thereafter.

The first occasion which occurred for the use of the permissive part of the
scheme, so far as concerns the operators about whom we have evidence, the
sixteen local authorities, was at the end of September, 1961, Birmingham Corpn. I
having called for tenders for a mileage contract by Oct. 2, 1961. The second
occasion was when the Bournemouth Corpn. had called for tenders with a closing
date of Oct. 9, 1961. We need not go into the details; but on each occasion all, or
substantially all, the respondents gave notifications under the permissive part
of the scheme, and these were circulated. The notifications and quotations
in each case were identical. Then in November, 1961, there was the usual comprehensive half-yearly rate review for the six months from Jan. 1, 1962. On
Nov. 16, 1961, the secretary circulated a comprehensive schedule, showing, though

A not, of course, with the names of the manufacturers concerned, all the notified rates. A revised edition of the schedule was circulated on Nov. 22, showing alterations downwards in certain instances as a result of second thoughts. A second revised edition was circulated on Nov. 27, showing a number of third thoughts. All this, of course, was in good time for any manufacturer, if he so desired, to take account of indicated intentions of his competitors before he

B committed himself by actually quoting to the operators concerned. When the operators made their decisions on this rate review and these became known to the manufacturers interested, it cannot but have been clear to all the respondents, if it was not clear before, that the permissive part of the scheme was working, and it was working because all the members of the group had decided to work it, and were in fact so doing. So it went on, smoothly and efficiently, for some three

C and a half years thereafter, until July, 1965; and members of the group cannot have been, and were not, left in any doubt what the others were doing as regards the permissive part of the scheme. The knowledge was derived from the conduct of each, in that he was in fact doing all that the permissive part of the scheme, on the respondents' interpretation of it, contemplated that he could do.

Counsel for the respondents, as we have said, accepts that, if there had been an

D express intimation in August, 1961, by each member to each of the others of his intention to try to operate the permissive part of the scheme if the others did likewise, there would have been an arrangement. But, he contends, there cannot be an arrangement on the facts of this case because an arrangement necessarily pre-supposes a promissory representation, and here there was no representation. An arrangement, he submits, cannot arise out of observed conduct. Observed

E conduct, he submits, can only be evidence of a pre-existing, express, common assent; and if there was no such express assent, conduct cannot take its place.

We do not accept that argument. When all that has happened is that a number of people, separately and individually, have decided to try to operate a scheme which involves mutuality, it may well be that at that stage there is no arrangement. Nevertheless when thereafter, as happened here, it became clear to each

F of them by the acts of all of them, that all had decided to operate the scheme, and were in fact operating it, and the essence of its operation—the only basis on which it could operate—rested in the acceptance of mutual obligations by all the participants towards each other, the scheme thereon, if not before, became an arrangement. It makes no difference to the result that any one of them is entirely free to cease to operate it at any time, subject to the fulfilment of the

G moral obligations relating to a particular transaction in respect of which he has already given or received information under the scheme. An agreement is still an agreement, so long as it is operated, even though it is terminable at will. So is an arrangement.

There is nothing, we think, technical or recondite in the conception that there is here an arrangement. It would be particularly odd if it were otherwise,

H where, as here, the members all deliberately abstained in August, 1961, from informing their fellow members of their individual decisions to try to operate the scheme or from asking their fellow-members as to their decisions, despite the fact that the practical effect of the decision of each was dependent on the decisions of the others. The only reason which we can infer to have existed for that abstention at that stage—in the absence of which abstention an arrangement

I would admittedly have come into existence in August, 1961—was the conception that such abstention would prevent the coming into being of an arrangement. The law is not so subtle or unrealistic as to involve the conclusion that, while an arrangement can come into being as a result of information as to one another's intentions supplied in words or writing or by a nod or a wink, it cannot come into being as a result of information as to one another's intentions derived from their actual and continuing conduct towards one another.

There is no doubt that there was here a scheme. It was so described. It was operated. It is not without interest that the primary definition of " scheme "

in the Concise Oxford Dictionary is " systematic arrangement, proposed or A
in operation ".

There can be no doubt, for reasons which we have already given, that the operation of the permissive part of the scheme involved mutual obligations, not binding
in law, but moral obligations binding in honour, as well as according with the
individual interest of each member, because the continuance of the scheme
depended on their general observance.   B

The mutual representations, by conduct, and the resulting mutual moral
obligations make the permissive part of the scheme an arrangement, consistent
with the ordinary use of language and with the expositions of the meaning of the
word " arrangement " in the Act of 1956, to be found in the judgments of
WILLMER, L.J., and DIPLOCK, L.J., in Re British Basic Slag, Ltd.'s Agreements (1).
In this context, we would quote, and respectfully adopt, the words of LORD C
PEARCE in his speech in the House of Lords in relation to a different part of the
Act of 1956, in Associated Newspapers, Ltd. v. Registrar of Restrictive Trading
Agreements (2):

> " That result is supported by practical considerations, since it is not
> likely that Parliament was intending to create for the enforcement of its
> purpose a jurisdiction that could so easily be evaded."   D

What the respondents are suggesting here is, in effect, that the parties can give
to the court an undertaking not to make an arrangement, and can themselves
prevent what would otherwise be an arrangement from being such by the simple
device of taking care not to tell one another what they are going to do before
they start to do it; even though over a period of years thereafter they each carry E
out a course of conduct involving the acceptance of mutual obligations, which
are implicit if their conduct is to achieve its only point and purpose; and they
carry it out in the knowledge, and because of the knowledge, that the others are
all doing likewise and can be expected to continue so to do. In such circumstances
there is an arrangement, just as much as if they had each said to the other in
advance: " We shall do this, if you also do this ". It is unnecessary in the F
circumstances to consider whether there were also separate arrangements arising
in each transaction in respect of which members sent in notifications, knowing
that all the others would receive them and rely on them as being given in pursuance
of the permissive part of the scheme.

The respondents take two other points, with which we can deal more shortly,
in support of their contention that no breach of the undertakings was committed, G
even if there was an arrangement.

The first of these points is that the arrangement did not involve any restriction
which would be registrable under s. 6 (1) of the Act of 1956. If that were right,
the entering into the arrangement would not be a breach of the undertakings.
The argument is put thus. The only relevant part of s. 6 (1) is that which makes
registrable an agreement containing restrictions in respect of the prices to be H
quoted for goods supplied. The mere obligation to notify prices, or rates, in
advance does not, it is said, involve any restriction in respect of the prices to
be quoted. The respondents were free to quote whatever rates they wished, subject to notification. The only obligation is to notify before they quote; that is
not " in respect of the prices ". In our view the argument is not sustainable. A
restriction is described in s. 6 (3) of the Act of 1956 as including any negative
obligation, whether absolute or not. It therefore includes a qualified negative I
obligation. Plainly, we think, there is such an obligation here. The restriction
involved in the arrangement is:

> " I will not quote to the operator a price which is lower than the lowest
> price which has been notified by anyone, unless, before quoting, I have
> notified my competitors."

---

(1) [1963] 2 All E.R. 807; (1963), L.R. 4 R.P. 116.
(2) [1964] 1 All E.R. 55 at p. 64; (1964), L.R. 4 R.P. 361 at p. 398.

A   We find it difficult to see how that is anything other than a negative obligation, albeit a qualified negative obligation, in respect of the prices to be quoted. The member is precluded from quoting rates below a certain figure unless he has first done certain things.

The second point is that the respondents say that, assuming there was an arrangement and it is within Part 1 of the Act, nevertheless the restriction or

B   restrictions contained in it is or are not " to the like effect " to the restrictions under the former agreement in respect of which they gave their undertakings.

We have carefully considered the passages cited to us by counsel from the judgments of DIPLOCK, J., and the Court of Appeal in *Re Black Bolt and Nut Association of Great Britain's Agreement (No. 2),* (3). In the present case, in contrast with that case, we have to compare, not an agreement with an agreement,

C   but an arrangement with an agreement—or rather the relevant restrictions in an arrangement with the relevant restrictions in an agreement.

What we have to compare is the restriction in the schedule to the court's order on the former agreement, which we have previously quoted, with the restriction which was actually involved in the arrangement. The former precluded the respondents from quoting a rate below the lowest rate insisted on at a meeting,

D   at which a weighted average was available, without first informing the other respondents. The latter precluded the respondents from quoting a rate below the lowest rate notified in writing through the secretary, without first informing the other respondents. The purpose of the two restrictions was the same. The machinery to achieve it was somewhat different. There were three differences. Under the arrangement, correspondence took the place of a face-to-face meeting;

E   the members did not know which other member had notified which particular rate; and there was no weighted average. On the evidence the weighted average does not appear to have had any substantial significance under the former agreement. In these circumstances, we think that the question of " like effect " is one of degree and of fact: of the application of common-sense, having regard, of course, to the evidence offered as to the differences. We have well in mind

F   here, as throughout this judgment, the point stressed by counsel for the respondents: namely, that this is a motion for contempt of court; that the onus is on the registrar on the question whether there was a contempt, and that it is a heavy onus. Bearing this in mind, we are left in no doubt that the degree of difference in the machinery to be used under the respective restrictions is not such that they are to a different effect. They are to the like effect, the one to

G   the other.

The respondents have broken their undertakings; but the respondents say that even so, as a matter of law, they are not in contempt of court. They rely on the decision of STIRLING, J., in *Worthington* v. *Ad Lib Club, Ltd.* (4), in which, regarding himself as bound by a decision of the Court of Appeal, he declined to follow a decision of WARRINGTON, J., in *Stancomb* v. *Trowbridge Urban District*

H   *Council* (5). STIRLING, J., held that, even where a breach of an injunction was proved, it was not contempt of court unless the breach of the injunction was " contumacious ".

It is unfortunate that the only report which was cited to STIRLING, J., of the decision of the Court of Appeal in *Fairclough* v. *Manchester Ship Canal Co.* (6) was the abbreviated eight-line report in [1897] W.N. 7, and not the fuller and

I   better report in 41 Sol. J. 225. The latter report shows, as the report which was before the learned judge does not, that the remarks of the court as to the requirements and remedies for contempt of court were obiter dicta. Moreover, the Court of Appeal was dealing with the question whether the particular penalties of imprisonment or sequestration were appropriate where there was no deliberate

---

(3) [1961] 3 All E.R. 316; (1961), L.R. 2 R.P. 433; [1962] 1 All E.R. 139; (1962), L.R. 3 R.P. 43.

(4) [1964] 3 All E.R. 674; [1965] Ch. 236.   (5) [1910] 2 Ch. 190.

(6) [1897] W.N. 7; 41 Sol. Jo. 225.

defiance. The court expressly recognised that, even though the breach was not A
" contumacious " or reckless, the person in breach might be ordered to pay
damages, as well as costs. We accept the view of the law expressed by WARRING-
TON, J., in *Stancomb* v. *Trowbridge Urban Council* (7):

> ". . . if a person or corporation is restrained by injunction from doing a
> particular act, that person or corporation commits a breach of the injunction,
> and is liable for process for contempt, if he or it in fact does the act, and it is   B
> no answer to say that the act was not contumacious in the sense that, in
> doing it, there was no direct intention to disobey the order."

We conclude, therefore, that the breaches of undertaking here were contempts
of court, even though it were to be shown that they were things done, reasonably
and despite all due care and attention, in the belief, based on legal advice, that C
they were not breaches.

We are also of opinion that, just as the court can require, at least, payment
of damages, where there has been a breach of an injunction by a party to litigation between two individual citizens, so also where the injunction or undertaking
is given in litigation between the registrar, as representing the public interest, and
an individual or a company, the court, in imposing a financial penalty, may take D
into account, in addition to other factors, the injury to the public which must
be deemed to be involved in the breach.

Questions as to the bona fides of the persons who are in contempt, and their
reasons, motives and understandings in doing the acts which constitute the
contempt of court may be highly relevant in mitigation of the contempt. Bona
fide reliance on legal advice, even though the advice turns out to have been E
wrong, may be relevant, and sometimes very important, as mitigation. The
extent of such mitigation must, however, depend on the circumstances of the
particular case, and the evidence adduced.

At the initiation of the rate notification scheme, the persons who were allowed
to act on behalf of the companies concerned realised that the permissive part of
the scheme amounted to an attempt, by a somewhat technical device, to achieve F
lawfully (that is, without breach of the anticipated undertakings) substantially
the same object as had been achieved by the restrictions which were about to be
condemned as being contrary to the public interest. They realised at the outset
that, if the permissive part of the scheme worked at all, it would achieve that
result; and they realised, when it became effective, that it was achieving that
result. To what extent the companies themselves, the boards of directors and the G
higher managements, realised these facts and their implications, we cannot say,
because the evidence adduced in mitigation has provided scarcely any indication.
That they ought to have so realised is, however, clear. The technical device was,
in substance, the deliberate refraining by all companies from giving to one
another express intimation of their individual decisions to operate the permissive
part of the scheme in accordance with its supposed terms, even though " it was H
common sense that the thing would be adopted " by each of them. If the advice
was correct, so that the device was not merely subtle, but successful, the respondents were lawfully entitled to do what they did. If it was wrong, it would be a
breach of undertakings in a matter affecting the public interest. In such circumstances, parties, even though acting on legal advice, are playing with fire, and they
ought to realise that they are playing with fire; and all the more so when it is I
the public interest which is involved. That is no novel conception. It was clearly
expressed by this court, in a judgment delivered by DIPLOCK, J., on July 28,
1961. In *Re National Federated Electrical Association's Agreement* (8), these
words were used:

> " As it appears from the evidence that the association has been considering
> ways of obtaining precisely the same results as those obtained under the

---

(7) [1910] 2 Ch. at p. 194.   (8) (1961), L.R. 2 R.P. 447 at p. 452.

A   agreement, it is desirable to say that the effect of a breach of an undertaking
is as serious as a breach of an injunction. If persons try to get round the
provisions of the Restrictive Trade Practices Act, 1956, they must understand that they are playing with fire, and, if they are unsuccessful, the
results can be serious."

In *Re Agreement between Newspaper Proprietors' Association, Ltd., and National*
B   *Federation of Retail Newsagents, Booksellers and Stationers* (9), the court, in a
judgment which was also delivered by DIPLOCK, J., went further. In relation
to the special facts of that case, the court said:

"... I also desire to make it crystal clear, since the object is plain, that the
court will not regard as a mitigating circumstance the fact that any such
person has acted on the advice of lawyers, solicitors or counsel, and that,
C   if the advice which they have received is wrong and they are in fact in breach
of the injunction, the fact that they were wrongly advised that their attempt
to evade the provisions of the Act was lawful will not be regarded as a
mitigating circumstance ..."

While this statement does not, of course, mean that bona fide legal advice can
D   never be a mitigating circumstance, it lends force to the view which we hold
that reliance on legal advice certainly cannot be relied on, as a matter of course,
as complete mitigation.

Supposing, then, that the respondents had acted throughout the period of the
rate notification agreement in the reasonable, though mistaken, belief, because
of the legal advice which they had received and the absence of changed advice,
E   that no breach of their undertakings was involved, that fact would not amount to
full mitigation of their contempt. It might be a mitigating factor, but no more
than that.

We still have to consider, therefore, to what extent the respondents' reliance
on the advice was reasonable throughout this period, as bearing on mitigation.

The initial advice on the scheme was given by Mr. Brown, after consultation
F   with leading and junior counsel, one of whom is now a judge of the High Court.
We accept, from Mr. Brown's evidence, that he fully believed that counsel had
orally approved the rate notification scheme in the way in which Mr. Brown
understood that it could operate: that is, permitting notifications of members'
provisional intentions as to the rates which they were going to quote, with
compulsory notification by the secretary to all members interested, of such
G   intended offers; and the right of all members to change their minds with consequential further notifications and circulation thereof. We find it difficult,
however, to accept that that was what the wording of the scheme meant, in its
natural and ordinary construction. The natural meaning of the words used, read
as a whole, is that a member should be free to notify a rate which he had decided
to offer: " decided " in the sense of final decision, not a provisional intention.
H   There is no express provision, in the words used, that the secretary should
circulate such decisions or provisional intentions. There is express provision that
the secretary shall circulate " the rate quoted ". In the ordinary use of language,
that would mean the rate which had actually been quoted to the operator: it
would thus, by implication, exclude rates provisionally intended, which might or
might not subsequently be quoted to the operator. On the natural construction
of the words, we can understand advice by counsel that the scheme would not
I   involve a registrable arrangement. Such advice would not have involved approval
of the scheme as it was in fact operated. Counsel do not appear to have been
consulted in relation to the scheme or its operation at any time thereafter.
Since Mr. Brown, or some colleague of his, genuinely so believing, whether mistakenly or otherwise, told the members of the group that counsel had approved
the scheme in the way in which he understood and explained it, we do not think
that the representatives of the respondent companies who heard his exposition

_____
(9) [1961] 3 All E.R. 428 at p. 445; (1961), L.R. 2 R.P. 453 at pp. 499, 500.

woro unreasonable at that stage in believing that no breach of their anticipated A
undertakings would be involved.

There were two later events, during the period with which we are concerned,
which have to be considered from the point of view of deciding whether and to
what extent a careful and sensible person, who understood the seriousness of an
undertaking to the court, would have, at least, been put on inquiry as to the
propriety of what was being done in relation to the undertakings which were in B
force. The first of these events was the judgment of the Court of Appeal in
Re British Basic Slag, Ltd.'s Agreement (10), delivered on May 27, 1963. From
then on, it should have been apparent to anyone who had the duty to advise on
this branch of the law, that the word " arrangement " was wide in its meaning,
and that any earlier narrower conceptions which might have been held would
have to be carefully reviewed and revised; not least in relation to circumstances, C
and past advice, such as here existed. Mr. Brown read, and carefully considered,
that judgment. He did not, as he first thought when he gave evidence, send a
copy of it to the secrtary, Mr. Byford. He sent a copy of it to Mr. Rissik, the
assistant secretary of Dunlops, a legally qualified gentleman. He discussed the
judgment with Mr. Rissik. What Mr. Rissik did, we have not been told. Mr.
Brown, unfortunately we think, did not feel it necessary to alter the advice which D
he had given earlier in relation to the rate notification scheme or to suggest that
counsel should be consulted afresh in respect of it. Apart from his discussions
with Mr. Rissik, he did not think it necessary to inform the secretary or any
representative of any other company in the group about the decision, or any
possible bearing of it on their undertakings. Some of the witnesses for the companies heard of the decision, and one of them at least, as will appear, at a later E
stage knew sufficient of it to be exercised in his mind about its implications in
relation to what was being done under the rate notification scheme. We do not
think, however, that it would be fair, in the circumstances, to attach personal
blame to any of those witnesses, in relation to the contempt, for their individual
failures to ensure that action was taken by their companies to review the propriety
of their actions urgently in the light of that decision.   F

The second event was in the autumn of 1964. The Birmingham Corpn.'s
transport committee gave notice of determination of its existing mileage contracts and called for tenders returnable on Sept. 14. The permissive part of the
scheme was operated by all the main manufacturers in its normal way, the first
notification being by Dunlops who held the major share of the contract. The
tenders, as usual, were level. The transport committee on this occasion reacted G
vigorously, and wide publicity was given to the strong views expressed by the
chairman of the committee as to the level tendering and the existence of a
" price ring ". It was indicated that action was going to be taken to procure
investigation. The group met on Nov. 13, 1964. The only lawyer present on that
occasion was Mr. Rissik. We have not heard an account from him of what took
place, or what, if anything, he advised, or what, if anything, he did in alerting H
Dunlops, if their higher management, indeed, needed alerting by him. The
relevant minute of the group meeting is as follows:

" It was reported that the operator had not yet made a decision in regard
to a mileage contract for a period of three years commencing Jan. 1, 1965.
Reference was made to the press and television publicity in regard to the
contract. It was reported that it was understood that a complaint was being I
lodged with the Registrar of Restrictive Trading Agreements and an outline
was given of the courses which the registrar could adopt upon receipt of such
a complaint. The secretary, in consultation with legal advisers, was
authorised to take such steps as were considered necessary."

The representatives of the respondent companies who attended that meeting
unfortunately have little recollection of any particular discussion. Mr. Byford

(10) [1963] 2 All E.R. 807; (1963), L.R. 4 R.P. 116.

A says that no doubts were voiced about the legality of the scheme. He was authorised, in consultation with his legal advisers, to take whatever steps were considered necessary. So far as the evidence shows, no step was considered necessary by them.

The Birmingham Corpn. called for fresh tenders. The same rate notification scheme procedure was followed. The same identical quotations were put in,
B by all except Pirelli who did not tender again on this second occasion; and the operation of the scheme continued as before for another six months, until July, 1965. The Birmingham incident caused considerable anxiety to three of the witnesses who appeared before us; and that anxiety must have been related to the legal position in respect of the rate notification scheme. Mr. Godwin, the mileage contracts manager of Michelin, on Nov. 20, 1964, sent a memorandum to his
C superior, the general sales manager, and to the company secretary. In it he wrote:

" Our ' voluntary information scheme ' [in quotation marks] was approved by counsel, but in consequence of a decision taken in the *Basic Slag* case (11) it may be necessary to take his advice again."

D In relation also to possible repercussions from the Birmingham incident, he wrote:

" In the event the registrar was still not satisfied the worst that could happen would be for an injunction to be made ordering us to stop the practice. A further breach would of course have severe penalties."

We are driven to wonder whether the reference to the *Basic Slag* case (11) and
E the supposed legal position were not reflections of things discussed at the meeting of Nov. 13. No evidence has been offered by the higher management, or any director, of Michelin as to their action or reaction on receipt of this memorandum. We must assume, since no evidence to the contrary has been put forward by way of mitigation, that the company was content that things should go on as before, possibly because they were content to believe that " the worst that could happen "
F was not very serious.

Mr. Hill, sales manager, Passenger Transport Division of Dunlop, was also perturbed by the Birmingham incident. He has told us that he prepared a note on the subject for his general manager, who is a member of the board, and that the latter submitted it to the managing director. He received some advice, presumably in a memorandum. We have not seen any documents. Mr. Norbury,
G sales manager of the Tyre Contracts Division of Pirelli, Ltd., discussed the Birmingham incident with his executive directors. They all thought it was, to quote Mr. Norbury, " a very unsavoury matter ". Pirelli, alone of the respondents, did not quote when the Birmingham Corpn. called for further tenders; but they did not cease to operate the scheme until July, 1965.

So far we have been considering the reasonableness of the attitude of the
H particular employees of the respondent companies who were concerned with the operation of the rate notification scheme. They are the eight gentlemen who have given evidence before us on behalf of their respective companies. They were all, in description or effect, sales managers, dealing either exclusively or as a major part of their duties with the mileage contract part of their companies' businesses. They are all truthful persons, and, we have no doubt, fully competent in carrying
I out mileage contract business. But none of them was a director, nor could he appropriately be described as being of the higher management of his company; nor should he have been left to cope, without clear and specific guidance and instructions, with the task of ensuring compliance with the obligations undertaken by his company to the court. This court was not laying down any novel principle when it said, in *Re Galvanized Tank Manufacturers' Association's Agreement* (12):

---

(11) [1963] 2 All E.R. 807; (1963), L.R. 4 R.P. 116.
(12) [1965] 2 All E.R. 1003 at p. 1109; (1965), L.R. 5 R.P. 315 at p. 348.

"We would, however, emphasize that a company which has given an **A** undertaking to the court must be treated as having failed lamentably and inexcusably in its elementary duty if it fails to take adequate and continuing steps to ensure, through its responsible officers, that these officers themselves, and anyone to whom they may delegate the handling of matters which fall within the scope of the undertaking, do not forget or misunderstand or overlook the obligations imposed by such undertaking." **B**

We have looked in vain for evidence to show that any of the companies properly realised, or took adequate steps to carry out, that duty. It would be no answer to say: "These undertakings related only to a small part of our total business".

There was some evidence, which we have carefully considered, that the proposed rate notification scheme, and in some instances the legal advice which had been given, was discussed by the witnesses with their superiors, who in some cases **C** were directors of their companies. That evidence, not coming from anyone in the higher management, is, at the best vague and unsatisfactory. We have had no evidence of any adequate instructions on behalf of any of the companies to their employees who had the responsibility of dealing with the mileage contract business as to the necessity of ensuring that the undertakings were not infringed, nor as to the duty of reporting to anyone at a higher level if doubts or questions should **D** arise affecting the undertakings. We have had no sufficient evidence of any continuing supervision, or, indeed, of any realisation that such supervision was required. No single document has been produced by any of the respondents to show that they ever considered, at board or higher managerial level, the obligations involved in their undertakings, or the possible dangers of the rate notification scheme, or even the obvious questions about compliance with the undertakings **E** which were thrown up, at least, by the Birmingham incident. It may be that, if they had duly appreciated and carried out their duty, most, if not all, of the respondent companies would, up to the time of the Birmingham incident in the autumn of 1964, have taken the same view as was taken by their respective employees who were actively concerned with the mileage contract business: that is, that they had legal advice from experts, and, subject to any knowledge **F** which they may or should have had of the *Basic Slag* case (13), that nothing had occurred to require reconsideration of the manner in which their undertakings to the court were being performed.

The higher management of each of the companies must have known of the Birmingham incident in the autumn of 1964. If any of them did not, they certainly should have done, had they given adequate instructions to their sub- **G** ordinates to whom they left the operation of the business to which the undertakings applied. With that knowledge, and against the background of the awareness which they assuredly ought to have had that the rate notification scheme as operated involved at least playing with fire, they evinced a reckless lack of regard for, or understanding of, their duty to the court in not considering the question promptly and seriously, and in not taking at least the action which Mr. **H** Godwin suggested to his superiors: that is, to cause the question of the legality of the scheme to be re-examined. If they had done so, they ought to have been advised, and probably would have been advised, that the operation of the scheme involved, at the least, grave danger of constituting a breach of their undertakings.

Even if the true view were that the apparent total inaction of the higher management of the companies in relation to the Birmingham incident was **I** reasonable and understandable, we should still have taken the view that the apparently complete and substantially unsupervised delegation, to subordinate employees, of the discharge of the companies' obligations towards the court could not be overlooked. It is not enough for a company, when breaches of its undertaking to the court have taken place, to say: "If we had ourselves considered the matter, we should have done the same as the subordinates who acted on our behalf". In the present case, however, not even that position can be maintained.

(13) [1963] 2 All E.R. 807; (1963), L.R. 4 R.P. 116.

A　In these circumstances, the contempts which have been committed cannot be passed over by a mere order for payment of costs. We see no ground for distinguishing in respect of penalty between one company and another. Each of them will pay £10,000 for their contempt of court. We would emphasise that these amounts are small, indeed, in relation to the amounts which would have been imposed if it had not appeared that the companies had taken expert legal opinion

B　in 1961; and that for some years they either believed, or might have believed, if they had given the requisite high-level attention to their obligations towards the court, that they were acting within, even if just within, their undertakings. We have taken into account also the belated, but complete, abandonment of the scheme in July, 1965.

　　The decision of the court in this case should be taken as a warning to others,

C　if such there be, who, after giving an undertaking to this court, have sought to achieve similar results to those arising from a condemned agreement by replacing it with a scheme which to any reasonable minded person must appear to be dangerously near to the line dividing what is legal and permissible from what is not: a warning, that is, as to the consequences, if it should turn out that the dividing line had in fact been crossed. Those consequences might be much more

D　severe, because, in the light of the lessons of this case, a contention that the dangers of playing with fire were not realised might not fall on sympathetic ears.

　　The respondent companies will pay the registrar's costs on a common fund basis. The undertakings remain in force.

Orders accordingly.

E　Solicitors: *Treasury Solicitor; Bristows, Cooke & Carpmael* (for the respondents).

[*Reported by* MARY COLTON, *Barrister-at-Law.*]

F　Re WILSON (*deceased*). WILSON *v.* MACKAY AND OTHERS.

[CHANCERY DIVISION (Pennycuick, J.), April 26, 27, 1966.]

Administration of Estates—Order of application of assets—Administration expenses—Debts—Pecuniary legacies—Solvent estate—Will—Estate insufficient to meet pecuniary legacies—Gift of " all my real estate " was

G　*residuary gift, although testatrix had only one property, her dwelling-house, which was real estate—Pecuniary legacies to be paid out of personal estate—Debts and administration expenses to be paid out of real estate—Administration of Estates Act, 1925 (15 & 16 Geo. 5 c. 23), s. 34 (3), Sch. 1, Pt. 2, para. 2.*

　　By her will, dated May 31, 1962, a testatrix bequeathed pecuniary legacies amounting in the aggregate to over £27,000 and concluded " I

H　devise and bequeath all my real estate and the residue of my personal estate to my daughter absolutely ". She died on Feb. 1, 1964. Her estate comprised gross personalty of £20,877 13s. and gross realty, consisting of her dwelling-house, of £8,250. The estate duty on personalty was £3,757 11s. and on realty £1,485. The debts and funeral expenses amounted to £293 8s. The specific bequests were of a value of £551 5s. and the executors incurred

I　expenses of about £560 relating to the testatrix' house. Accordingly the estate was insufficient, after payment of outgoings, to pay the pecuniary legacies in full. The questions arose out of what fund the legacies were to be paid and out of what fund the debts and administration expenses were to be paid and in what order.

　　Held: (i) on the true construction of the testatrix' will, having regard to the contrast between the devise of " all my real estate " and " the residue of my personal estate " in the gift quoted above, the legacies were intended to be paid exclusively out of the testatrix' personal estate, and this was a

provision of the will subject to which, by virtue of s. 34 (3)* of the Administra-   A
tion of Estates Act, 1925, Pt. 2 of Sch. 1 to that Act took effect (see p. 871,
letter B, post).

(ii) the devise of " all my real estate " was a residuary gift for the purpose
of Pt. 2 of Sch. 1 to that Act, although there was no prior or other devise of
realty (see p. 873, letters B and D, post).

Re Rowe ([1941] 2 All E.R. 330) distinguished.   B
Re Ridley ([1950] 2 All E.R. 1) considered.

(iii) the proper course was to retain the whole of the personal property as
the fund prescribed by para. 2† of Pt. 2 of Sch. 1 to the Act of 1925 to bear
the pecuniary legacies, which would be applied rateably towards paying them
in so far as it was sufficient, leaving the real property as the asset out of which
the debts and administration expenses were to be paid (see p. 873, letter G,   C
post).

Dictum of UTHWATT, J., in *Re Anstead* ([1943] 1 All E.R. at p. 524)
applied.

[As to the order of application of assets of solvent estates, see 16 HALSBURY'S
LAWS (3rd Edn.) 344, 345, paras. 666-668; and for cases on the subject, see 23
DIGEST (Repl.) 480-484, *5476-5519*; 504-506, *5683-5702*.   D

For the Administration of Estates Act, 1925, s. 34 (3) and Sch. 1, Pt. 2, see 9
HALSBURY'S STATUTES (2nd Edn.) 737, 767.]

Cases referred to:

Anstead, Re, Gurney v. *Anstead*, [1943] 1 All E.R. 522; [1943] Ch. 161; 168
    L.T. 309; sub nom. *Re Anstead, Anstead* v. *Gurney*, 112 L.J.Ch. 161;   E
    23 Digest (Repl.) 541, *6054*.

Berrey's Will Trusts, Re, Greening v. *Warner*, [1959] 1 All E.R. 15; [1959] 1
    W.L.R. 30; Digest (Cont. Vol. A) 561, *6051a*.

Gillett's Will Trusts, Re, Barclays Bank, Ltd. v. *Gillett*, [1949] 2 All E.R. 893;
    [1950] Ch. 102; 23 Digest (Repl.) 417, *4871*.

Hensman v. *Fryer*, (1867), 3 Ch. App. 420; 37 L.J.Ch. 97; 17 L.T. 394; 23   F
    Digest (Repl.) 391, *4621*.

Lancefield v. *Iggulden*, [1874-80] All E.R. Rep. 910; (1874), 10 Ch. App. 136;
    44 L.J.Ch. 203; 31 L.T. 813; 23 Digest (Repl.) 531, *5972*.

Martin (decd.), Re, Midland Bank Executor and Trustee Co., Ltd. v. *Marfleet*,
    [1955] 1 All E.R. 865; [1955] Ch. 898; [1955] 2 W.L.R. 1029; 23
    Digest (Repl.) 541, *6053*.   G

Ridley (decd.), Re, Nicholson v. *Nicholson*, [1950] 2 All E.R. 1; [1950] Ch. 415;
    23 Digest (Repl.) 544, *6072*.

Rooke (decd.), Re, Jeans v. *Gatehouse*, [1933] All E.R. Rep. 978; [1933] Ch. 970;
    102 L.J.Ch. 371; 149 L.T. 445; 23 Digest (Repl.) 543, *6064*.

Rowe, Re, Bennetts v. *Eddy*, [1941] 2 All E.R. 330; [1941] Ch. 343; 110
    L.J.Ch. 145; 165 L.T. 76; 23 Digest (Repl.) 541, *6055*.   H

Thompson, Re, Public Trustee v. *Husband*, [1936] 2 All E.R. 141; [1936] Ch.
    676; 105 L.J.Ch. 289; 155 L.T. 474; 23 Digest (Repl.) 541, *6056*.

Worthington, Re, Nichols v. *Hart*, [1933] All E.R. Rep. 189; [1933] Ch. 771;
    102 L.J.Ch. 273; 149 L.T. 296; 23 Digest (Repl.) 540, *6049*.

Adjourned Summons.

This was an application by originating summons dated Jan. 3, 1966, by the   I
plaintiff, Charles Trevor Bowman Wilson, who was an executor and a pecuniary
legatee under the will dated May 31, 1962, and the codicil thereto dated June 1,
1962, of Eleanor Wilson (" the testatrix "), who died on Feb. 1, 1964. The
plaintiff asked whether all or any and if so, which of the undermentioned payments which fell to be made in the course of the administration of the testatrix'
estate, that is to say payments in respect of (i) her funeral, testamentary and

---

* Section 34 (3) is set out at p. 870, letter E, post.
† Schedule 1, Pt. 2, para. 2 is set out at p. 870, letter F, post.

A   administration expenses (other than estate duty) and debts; (ii) the pecuniary
    legacies; (iii) the estate duty payable in respect of personal estate; (iv) the
    estate duty payable in respect of real estate; and (v) expenses and outgoings
    incurred in the upkeep, preservation and sale of the real estate, ought to be paid
    (a) exclusively out of the testatrix' personal estate; or (b) exclusively out of her
    real estate; or (c) out of both the real and personal estate of the testatrix, and,
B   if so, in what proportions or shares, or amounts. The plaintiff asked, secondly,
    that for the purposes of the application the first defendant, Brenda Hamilton
    Mackay might be appointed to represent all the pecuniary legatees in the will
    and codicil other than such of them as were parties to the action, namely the
    second and third defendants who were Maud Wrigley and Melissa Mary Cox.
    The fourth defendant was Brenda Miller Lambert who claimed under the will
C   and codicil to be the devisee of the testatrix' real estate and the legatee of the
    residue of her personal estate as well as being a pecuniary legatee and an
    executrix. The only realty comprised in the testatrix' estate was her dwelling-
    house, " The Beeches ", which was sold for £8,250 on Nov. 30, 1964. The facts
    are set out in the judgment.
        The cases noted below* were cited during the argument in addition to those
D   referred to in the judgment.

        D. H. Mervyn Davies for the plaintiff.
        G. C. Rafferty for the first, second and third defendants.
        J. F. Mummery for the fourth defendant.

        PENNYCUICK, J.: This summons raises certain questions as to the
E   incidence of first, the debts and testamentary expenses and secondly, legacies in
    the estate of Eleanor Wilson, to whom I will refer as the testatrix.
        The testatrix made her will on May 31, 1962. The will runs as follows:
        " I hereby revoke all my former wills and codicils. I appoint my daughter
        Brenda Miller Lambert and my son Charles Trevor Wilson to be the executors
        of this my will."

F   Then come two specific bequests, one to her daughter and one to her son. Then
    comes a bequest of a very large number of pecuniary legacies which amount in all
    to £27,550. The will then concludes:
        " I devise and bequeath all my real estate and the residue of my personal
        estate to my said daughter Brenda Miller Lambert absolutely."

    The testatrix made a codicil on June 1, 1962, whereby she bequeathed certain
G   additional pecuniary legacies amounting to £350. So the total amount of the
    pecuniary legacies is £27,900. The testatrix died on Feb. 1, 1964. The will was duly
    proved by her son and daughter. The estate included gross personalty of
    £20,877 13s. and gross realty of £8,250. The debts and funeral expenses amounted
    to £293 8s. The estate duty on personalty was £3,757 11s., including interest.
    The estate duty on realty amounted to £1,485. The items specifically bequeathed
H   were of the value of £551 5s. In the course of the administration of the estate the
    executors incurred certain expenses relating particularly to the realty, that
    realty consisting of a freehold house in which the testatrix resided; the house
    is known as " The Beeches ". The expenses consisted of £164 2s. 6d. in
    maintenance and £397 4s. 8d. for the costs of sale.
        It will be seen that the estate is less than sufficient, after the payment of out-
I   goings, to meet in full the pecuniary legacies. Still more is the personalty
    insufficient to meet them. The question which has arisen is out of what fund are

    * Roberts v. Walker, (1830), 1 Russ. & M. 752; Greville v. Brown, [1843-60] All E.R.
    Rep. 888; (1859), L.R. 7 H.L. Cas. 689; Bathamley v. Sherson, (1875), L.R. 20 Eq. 304;
    Sharp v. Lusk, (1879), 10 Ch.D. 968; Wells v. Row, (1879), 48 L.J.Ch. 476; James v.
    Jones, (1882), 9 L.R. Ir. 489; Re Salt, [1893] 2 Ch. 203; Mason v. Ogden, [1903] A.C. 1;
    Re Pearse's Settlement, [1909] 1 Ch. 304; Re Littlewood, [1930] All E.R. Rep. 151;
    [1931] 1 Ch. 443; Re Beaumont's Will Trusts, [1950] 1 All E.R. 802; [1950] Ch. 462;
    Re Timson (decd.), [1953] 2 All E.R. 252; Re Midgley, [1955] 2 All E.R. 625; [1955]
    Ch. 576.

the legacies to be paid, and out of what fund are the debts and administration   A
expenses to be paid, and in what order. The present summons was taken out by
one of the executors, Mr. Wilson. The first three defendants are three pecuniary
legatees. The fourth defendant, Mrs. Lambert is the other executor and also
the beneficiary to whom the testatrix devises and bequeaths all her real estate
and the residue of her personal estate.

[HIS LORDSHIP read the question asked by the originating summons, which is   B
printed at p. 868, letter I to p. 869, letter B, ante.] I will mention first the items
for estate duty, expenses and outgoings, in order to get them out of the way. It is
not in dispute that the estate duty in respect of personal estate is a testamentary
expense and falls to be dealt with as such. Nor is it in dispute that the incidence
of the estate duty payable in respect of the real estate is on the real estate. It is
further not seriously challenged on behalf of Mrs. Lambert that the expenses and   C
outgoings incurred in the up-keep, preservation and sale of the real estate ought to
be borne by her. I say it is not seriously challenged because there was one
authority to the contrary cited. However, the trend of modern authorities is
to the contrary. The latest is *Re Rooke (decd.), Jeans* v. *Gatehouse* (1).

I now turn to the main question, namely how the legacies, debts and administration expenses are to be dealt with. Before going further I will read s. 34 (3)   D
of the Administration of Estates Act, 1925, and certain provisions from Pt. 2
of Sch. 1 to that Act. Section 34 (3) reads:

" Where the estate of a deceased person is solvent his real and personal
estate shall, subject to rules of court and the provisions hereinafter contained as to charges on property of the deceased, and to the provisions, if
any, contained in his will, be applicable towards the discharge of the funeral,   E
testamentary and administration expenses, debts and liabilities payable
thereout in the order mentioned in Pt. 2 of Sch. 1 to this Act."

Part 2 of Sch. 1, which is headed " Order of application of assets where the estate
is solvent ", says:

" 1. Property of the deceased undisposed of by will, subject to the retention   F
thereout of a fund sufficient to meet any pecuniary legacies. 2. Property of
the deceased not specifically devised or bequeathed but included (either by a
specific or general description) in a residuary gift, subject to the retention
out of such property of a fund sufficient to meet any pecuniary legacies, so
far as not provided for as aforesaid. 3. Property of the deceased specifically
appropriated or devised or bequeathed (either by a specific or general descrip-   G
tion) for the payment of debts. 4. Property of the deceased charged with, or
devised or bequeathed (either by a specific or general description) subject
to a charge for the payment of debts. 5. The fund, if any, retained to meet
pecuniary legacies. 6. Property specifically devised or bequeathed, rateably
according to value. 7. Property appointed by will under a general power,
including the statutory power to dispose of entailed interests, rateably   H
according to value. 8. The following provisions shall also apply—(a) The
order of application may be varied by the will of the deceased. (b) This part
of this Schedule does not affect the liability of land to answer the death duty
imposed thereon in exoneration of other assets."

I will consider first the position of the pecuniary legacies. As regards these, it
seems to me that the terms of the will itself are quite unequivocal. It will be   I
borne in mind that the will contains no express directions as to the payment
of debts or administration expenses. After the appointment of executors it
starts straight away with specific and pecuniary bequests. It then concludes
with the words which I have already read, but which I will read again:

" I devise and bequeath all my real estate and the residue of my personal
estate to my said daughter Brenda Miller Lambert absolutely."

_____

(1) [1933] All E.R. Rep. 978; [1933] Ch. 970.

A It seems to me that in that context the word " residue " can only mean that part of her personal estate which remains after the discharge thereout of the legacies, that is the specific and pecuniary legacies. To that in sharp contrast comes the expression " all my real estate ", those words indicating that the daughter is to take the real estate intact. It seems to me clear that on those words the legacies are made payable exclusively out of the personal estate and are not charged on

B the real estate at all. That is a provision contained in the will of the testatrix within the meaning of s. 34 (3), and all the provisions of Pt. 2 of Sch. 1 must take effect subject to that provision in the will. The same result is reached under para. 8 (*a*) of Sch. 1 itself. The result then—leaving aside altogether for the moment the matter of debts and administration expenses—is simply that the whole of the legacies come out of the personal estate so far as that is sufficient.

C The legacies are not charged on the real estate, and that goes intact to Mrs. Lambert.

It may well be that if the incidence of legacies were not covered by express provision in the will the result would be the same under para. 2 of Pt. 2 of Sch. 1. I was referred on this point to a number of cases, in particular to *Re Thompson, Public Trustee* v. *Husband* (2), *Re Rowe, Bennetts* v. *Eddy* (3) and *Re Anstead,*

D *Gurney* v. *Anstead* (4). However, it seems unnecessary to pursue those cases on this point because the incidence of the legacies is determined, as it seems to me, quite unequivocally by the terms of the will itself. I was also referred to a line of cases under para. 1 of Pt. 2, that being the paragraph which relates to property undisposed of by the will, those cases beginning with *Re Worthington, Nichols* v. *Hart* (5) in the Court of Appeal, and including *Re Gillett's Will Trusts, Barclays*

E *Bank, Ltd.* v. *Gillett* (6), *Re Martin (decd.), Midland Bank Executor and Trustee Co.* v. *Marfleet* (7) and *Re Berrey's Will Trusts, Greening* v. *Warner* (8). It is not necessary to refer further to those cases which, having regard to the express terms of the will, throw no light on the points in question.

The real difficulty in this case arises, so it seems to me, in regard to the debts and expenses of administration. As to these the will contains no provision at all.

F Therefore one must go to Pt. 2 of Sch. 1 in order to ascertain how the debts and expenses are to be borne. The relevant paragraph is para. 2:

" Property of the deceased not specifically devised or bequeathed but included (either by a specific or general description) in a residuary gift, subject to the retention out of such property of a fund sufficient to meet any pecuniary legacies, so far as not provided for as aforesaid."

G It will be observed that in this paragraph, as in the other paragraphs of Pt. 2, all property passing under a will is treated as falling under one or other of two mutually exclusive heads, namely, (i) property specifically devised or bequeathed and (ii) property not specifically devised or bequeathed but included in a residuary gift. There is no intermediate head into which any property could be thrust. It will further be observed that para. 2 unequivocally contemplates that there may

H be real property which is not specifically given but which is included in a residuary gift. This is apparent from the use of the expression " devised or bequeathed ".

Apart from authority, the natural view, so it seems to me, is that where a testator makes a general or universal gift of his real estate, that is " all my property ", the subject-matter of that gift falls under the second head, that is as being property not specifically devised but included in a residuary gift. A gift

I in this form does not indicate any particular item of property but covers all items of real property to which the testator may be entitled at his death. In ordinary language today lawyers would, I think, not inaptly describe such a gift as a residuary devise. They would certainly not describe it as a specific devise.

(2) [1936] 2 All E.R. 141; [1936] Ch. 676.   (3) [1941] 2 All E.R. 330; [1941] Ch. 343.
(4) [1943] 1 All E.R. 522; [1943] Ch. 161.
(5) [1933] All E.R. Rep. 189; [1933] Ch. 771.
(6) [1949] 2 All E.R. 893; [1950] Ch. 102.
(7) [1955] 1 All E.R. 865; [1955] Ch. 698.   (8) [1959] 1 All E.R. 15.

Counsel for Mrs. Lambert advanced certain arguments to the contrary. His **A** first argument was that all devises are from their nature specific. It seems that this was indeed so, at any rate until 1925; see in particular *Hensman* v. *Fryer* (9) and *Lancefield* v. *Iggulden* (10).

On the other hand, as I have said, it is clear that Pt. 2 of Sch. 1 contemplates that real property may be capable of being comprised in a residuary gift. I do not think that in the context of Sch. 1 to the Act of 1925 one should put such a **B** construction on the words " specifically devised " and " residuary gift ", as would in effect deprive the class of residuary gifts of realty of any possible content at all.

Counsel for Mrs. Lambert referred me to dicta in two post-1925 cases in support of his argument on this point. In *Re Rowe, Bennetts* v. *Eddy* (11) the relevant words of the will were: **C**

" I devise all my real estate and bequeath all the residue of my personal estate . . ."

to certain persons. FARWELL, J., after deciding the question on a different ground, added (12):

". . . for according to the construction which I place upon this particular **D** will the real estate is devised, not as part of the residue, but as a specific devise to the named persons, the residue which is given being the residue of the personal estate."

In *Re Ridley (decd.)*, *Nicholson* v. *Nicholson* (13) the relevant words in cl. 6 of the will were:

" I give free of all death duties all my real estate which includes Manmead, **E** Covert and Maperton and my advowsons to the said [G.] absolutely ",

and in cl. 8 of the will the testatrix gave

" the residue of my property including property over which I have a general power of appointment to the said [G.]."

HARMAN, J., pointed out (14) that although by cl. 6 the testatrix gives all her **F** real estate, by cl. 8 she gives the residue of her property, and that he describes as a " true residuary clause ". After referring to *Hensman* v. *Fryer* (9) and *Lancefield* v. *Iggulden* (15), he said (16):

" In my judgment, cl. 6 of this will, although it contains a general devise of realty, is not a residuary gift. I cannot think that a clause placed as this one is, even though it might have a certain sweeping-up effect by virtue of **G** s. 24 of the Wills Act, 1837, is a residuary gift within the meaning of the Act of 1925. I am supported in that view by a dictum of FARWELL, J., in *Re Rowe* (17)."

HARMAN, J., then referred to that case. He concluded (18):

" If that be right, it is clear that the present case is a stronger one, and **H** although I am not bound by that decision because it was not necessary for the conclusion at which he arrived, it is none the less a decision of that learned judge, and I should be very sorry to differ from it. I agree with the reasoning: I cannot think that cl. 6 was what is meant in this Schedule as being a residuary gift, and if necessary I should be prepared so to hold; . . ."

I

(9) (1867), 3 Ch. App. 420.
(10) [1874-80] All E.R. Rep. 910; (1874), 10 Ch. App. 136.
(11) [1941] 2 All E.R. 330; [1941] Ch. 343.
(12) [1941] Ch. at p. 348; [1941] 2 All E.R. at p. 334.
(13) [1950] 2 All E.R. 1; [1950] Ch. 415.
(14) [1950] 2 All E.R. at pp. 2, 3; [1950] Ch. at pp. 418, 419.
(15) [1874-80] All E.R. Rep. 910; (1874), 10 Ch. App. 136.
(16) [1950] 2 All E.R. at p. 5; [1950] Ch. at p. 421.
(17) [1941] 2 All E.R. at p. 334; [1941] Ch. at p. 348.
(18) [1950] 2 All E.R. at p. 5; [1950] Ch. at p. 422.

A   I must, of course, pay great respect to those two dicta, but it is important to observe that HARMAN, J., considered that it was cl. 8 and not cl. 6 which was the true residuary gift. On the best consideration that I can give it I do not think that it would be right for me to hold that for the purpose of para. 2 in Pt. 2 of Sch. 1 there is no such thing as a residuary gift of realty and that all realty must be treated as specifically devised.

B   Counsel for Mrs. Lambert's second point was that a devise is residuary only if there has been a previous devise, so that the residuary devise operates on what remains after the previous devise has taken effect. That is grammatically a good point. On the other hand, the expression " residuary gift " is habitually used to denote a general or universal gift and, as I have said, it seems to me natural so to treat the words " residuary gift " here.

C   The only alternative in the context of para. 2 is to treat a general or universal gift as a specific gift, and that I should have thought certainly it was not. This construction would produce a wholly illogical result as regards payment of debts. On the one hand a residuary devise following a specific devise would be a residuary gift for the purpose of para. 2. On the other hand, a general or universal devise would be a specific devise and would fall not within para. 2 but para. 6. I

D   cannot think that that is right. I conclude therefore that the devise of " all my real estate " to Mrs. Lambert in this will is a residuary gift for the purpose of para. 2 of Pt. 2 of Sch. 1 to the Administration of Estates Act, 1925.

What then is the result? In the first place it is necessary under para. 2 to retain out of the property included in the residuary gift a fund sufficient to meet any pecuniary legacies. There is no doubt that those words apply as regards the

E   personal estate. The pecuniary legacies in fact exceed in the aggregate the amount of the personal estate. Therefore the whole of the personal estate must go into that fund. On the other hand, I find great difficulty in seeing how it can be right to bring into that fund any part of the real estate. It does not appear reasonable to bring into a fund sufficient to meet pecuniary legacies items of property on which the pecuniary legacies are not charged. In this connexion it is

F   worthwhile to bear in mind that under para. 1 of Pt. 2 it has been held that the fund sufficient to meet pecuniary legacies, which has to be retained, must in due course be used in paying those legacies. It would be entirely remarkable if that was the position under para. 1 and not under para. 2. I think, therefore, that the proper course is to take the whole of the personal property and retain that as the fund prescribed by para. 2 of Pt. 2 of Sch. 1 to the Administration of Estates Act,

G   1925. If one does that the effect is that the real property remains, and it seems to me that the real property must then be the asset out of which the debts and expenses of administration are to be paid. They are sufficient for the purpose and there will remain a small balance available for Mrs. Lambert. The fund retained will be applied rateably towards the payment of the pecuniary legacies.

The conclusion which I have expressed is, I think, in accordance with the

H   decision of UTHWATT, J., in *Re Anstead, Gurney* v. *Anstead*. I will not read the headnote (19) which is in one respect inaccurate. I will read one paragraph (20):

" It follows that the first thing to be done in administering a solvent estate is to set aside out of the residue a fund to satisfy the pecuniary legacies. That is the first charge, and it is a charge primarily upon residuary

I   personalty rather than on the residuary real estate: *Re Thompson* (21). The result is notionally to divide the residue into two separate funds, the first to meet pecuniary legacies (and for the purposes of this fund personal estate is the primary fund and only in so far as it is insufficient is there to be any resort to realty) and a second fund consisting of the balance of the residue, including residuary real estate. In meeting debts and testamentary expenses

_____

(19) [1943] Ch. 161; [1943] 1 All E.R. 522.
(20) [1943] 1 All E.R. at p. 524; [1943] Ch. at p. 164.
(21) [1936] 2 All E.R. 141; [1936] Ch. 676.

the second fund must be exhausted before the first is touched. It follows   A
that in the present case the whole of the residuary personalty, other than the
part thereof directed to be appropriated to meet the annuity payable to the
wife, is to be made available to satisfy the pecuniary legacies, and estate duty
will only be chargeable on such legacies if and so far as such personalty is
insufficient to meet them, and they are satisfied out of real estate."

It will be seen that in that passage UTHWATT, J., considered that the retained   B
fund is to be constituted in the first place out of the personalty and as to any
balance, if necessary, out of realty. That may well be explained by the fact that
in the will with which he was concerned the pecuniary legacies were charged in
the first place on personalty, but were also charged in the second place on realty.
That is not the position here. I cannot, as I have said, myself see any logical
ground for including in the retained fund any part of the real estate. If one did   C
so include part of the real estate, that is to say so much of the real estate as was
sufficient with the personal estate to make up the amount of the pecuniary
legacies, that would not help Mrs. Lambert. It would mean that in the first
place there would be a very small balance of real estate available under para. 2
for payment of debts and administration expenses; but then the balance of the
debts and administration expenses would fall on the retained fund under para. 5   D
and the rest of that would, so far as I can see, be applied in the discharge of the
pecuniary legacies. That would leave Mrs. Lambert worse off than she is after
what seems to me to be the correct method of applying para. 2.

Counsel for Mrs. Lambert says that the proper course is first to set aside the
whole of the personalty and so much of the realty in the retained fund as is
necessary to meet the pecuniary legacies. Then, keeping the two components of   E
that fund, the personalty and realty, separate the debts should be paid out of that
part of the retained fund which consists of personalty, the balance of so much of
the fund as consists of personalty should be divided between the pecuniary
legacies, and, finally, so much of the fund as consists of realty should be restored
to Mrs. Lambert as the devisee of realty, leaving her in exactly the same position
as if no part of her realty had ever been put into the fund at all. That is an   F
ingenious argument, but I can see nothing in the terms of para. 2 which would
justify such a procedure.

I would only make one further point on this: in WOLSTENHOLME AND CHERRY'S
CONVEYANCING STATUTES, Vol. 2, p. 1,524 in the note under para. 5 there occurs
this sentence: "The legatees of pecuniary legacies have now the right to marshal
against the residuary legatees and devisees." I do not propose to analyse that   G
statement, but it does appear to conform to the view which I take in the
circumstances of this case.

Order accordingly.

Solicitors: *Harold Benjamin & Collins*, agents for *Lambert, Hanna & Lambert*,
Sunderland (for all parties).   H

[*Reported by* JENIFER SANDELL, *Barrister-at-Law.*]

A

GRIST *v.* BAILEY.

[CHANCERY DIVISION (Goff, J.), April 19, 20, 21, May 17, 1966.]

*Mistake—Mistake of fact—Common mistake—Sale of freehold property for £850
subject to existing tenancy—Mistake as to existence of statutory tenancy—
Vendor believed property to be in occupation of statutory tenant—Market
value of property with vacant possession would have been approximately
£2,250—Original tenant might be wife or husband, but both of them had died
—Their son was in occupation but did not claim protection under Rent Acts
—Whether vendor entitled to rescission of agreement.*

B

The plaintiff brought an action for specific performance of an agreement
in writing dated Sept. 11, 1964, whereby the defendant agreed to sell to the
plaintiff a freehold house for the sum of £850, cl. 7 of the agreement providing
that the property was sold " subject to the existing tenancy thereof ". The
defendant alleged that the agreement had been entered into by her under
mistake of fact, viz., in the belief that the property was in the occupation of
a statutory tenant, a Mrs. B., and her husband, whereas the fact was that
Mrs. B. died in 1961 and her husband died in June, 1964. The value of the
property on the basis that it was in the occupation of a statutory tenant
was then about £850, but its value with vacant possession would have then
been about £2,250. In fact Mrs. B. and her husband had died at the dates
mentioned, and their son continued in occupation after his father's death,
paying the rent, until he finally left in January, 1965, without having claimed
to have a statutory tenancy under s. 12 (1) (*g*) of the Increase of Rent and
Mortgage Interest (Restrictions) Act, 1920. Rent had throughout been
paid at the office of solicitors, being received by a junior boy or girl, who took
the book in from the outer office to be signed. The court found that there
was a common mistake of fact between the plaintiff and the defendant
that there was in existence a protected tenancy of the house in favour of
Mrs. B. or her husband*. It was not established whether Mrs. B. or her
husband, who had together occupied the property since 1946, was originally
contractual tenant of it, and it was therefore uncertain whether the son
had a right to continue as statutory tenant after his father's death. The
defendant counterclaimed for rescission of the sale agreement.

Held: there was equitable jurisdiction to set aside the sale agreement
for common mistake of fact and the sale agreement would be set aside
because the mistake was fundamental, even on the footing that it had been
open to the son in September, 1964, to maintain a claim to protection as a
statutory tenant, and any fault of the defendant vendor in not knowing who
her tenant was was not sufficient to disentitle her to relief, the defendant
offering to submit to a condition that she would enter into a fresh contract
to sell the property to the plaintiff at a proper vacant possession price (see
p. 880, letters A and H, and p. 881, letters A and C, post).

Dictum of DENNING, L.J., in *Solle* v. *Butcher* ([1949] 2 All E.R. at p. 1120)
applied.

Bell v. *Lever Bros., Ltd.* ([1931] All E.R. Rep. 1) distinguished.

[As to the circumstances in which relief on the ground of mistake of private
right may be granted, see 26 HALSBURY'S LAWS (3rd Edn.) 895, 896, para. 1656;
and for cases on the subject, see 35 DIGEST (Repl.) 95-103, *9-68.*

As to mistake as a defence to an action for specific performance, see 26 HALS-
BURY'S LAWS (3rd Edn.) 894, 895, para. 1653; and for cases on the subject, see
44 DIGEST (Repl.) 64-66, *498-515.*

For s. 12 of the Increase of Rent and Mortgage Interest (Restrictions) Act, 1920,
see 13 HALSBURY'S STATUTES (2nd Edn.) 998.]

_____

* See p. 879, letter I, post.

Applied in LAURENCE v LEXCOURT
HOLDINGS [1978] 2 All ER 810

Cases referred to: A
Beauchamp (Earl) v. *Winn*, (1873), L.R. 6 H.L. 223; 35 Digest (Repl.) 102, *61*.
Bell v. *Lever Bros., Ltd.*, [1931] All E.R. Rep. 1; [1932] A.C. 161; 101 L.J.K.B.
    129 ; 146 L.T. 258; 35 Digest (Repl.) 102, *63*.
Cooper v. *Phibbs*, (1867), L.R. 2 H.L. 149; 16 L.T. 678; 35 Digest (Repl.)
    98, *28*.
Huddersfield Banking Co., Ltd. v. *Henry Lister & Son, Ltd.*, [1895-99] All E.R.   B
    Rep. 868; [1895] 2 Ch. 273; 64 L.J.Ch. 523; 72 L.T. 703; 35 Digest
    (Repl.) 365, *673*.
Leaf v. *International Galleries*, [1950] 1 All E.R. 693; [1950] 2 K.B. 86; 35
    Digest (Repl.) 72, *659*.
Oscar Chess, Ltd. v. *Williams*, [1957] 1 All E.R. 325; [1957] 1 W.L.R. 370;
    39 Digest (Repl.) 514, *559*.   C
Rose (Frederick E.) (London), Ltd. v. *Wm. H. Pim, Junr. & Co., Ltd.*, [1953]
    2 All E.R. 739; [1953] 2 Q.B. 450; [1953] 3 W.L.R. 497; 35 Digest
    (Repl.) 147, *369*.
Solle v. *Butcher*, [1949] 2 All E.R. 1107; [1950] 1 K.B. 671; 31 Digest (Repl.)
    674, *7699*.
Summers v. *Donohue*, [1945] 1 All E.R. 599; [1945] K.B. 376; 114 L.J.K.B.   D
    401; 172 L.T. 310; 31 Digest (Repl.) 665, *7646*.

Action.
This was an action brought by writ issued on Mar. 2, 1965, by the plaintiff,
Frank Grist, against the defendant, Mrs. Minnie Bailey, for specific performance
of an agreement in writing dated Sept. 11, 1964, whereby the defendant agreed
to sell, and the plaintiff agreed to purchase, for £850 the freehold dwelling house   E
with yard, garden and other land belonging thereto known as No. 248, Rainsford
Road, Chelmsford, in the county of Essex.   The defendant admitted the sale
agreement and that she would not complete the sale, but averred that at the
date of the agreement she believed the property sold to be in the occupation of a
Mrs. Brewer as statutory tenant, whereas the true facts were that Mrs. Brewer
died in August, 1961, and her husband died in June, 1964, which facts were   F
unknown to the defendant.   The defendant counterclaimed for rescission,
alleging that, if it should be found that the plaintiff's agent believed the property
to be in the occupation of a statutory tenant, then the sale agreement was void,
or should be set aside in equity, for fundamental mistake of fact.   The facts are
set out in the judgment.
The case noted below* was cited during the argument in addition to those   G
referred to in the judgment.
A. A. Baden Fuller for the plaintiff.
G. M. Godfrey for the defendant.

Cur. adv. vult.

May 17.   **GOFF, J.**, read the following judgment: This is an action for   H
specific performance of an agreement dated Sept. 11, 1964, for the sale by the
defendant to the plaintiff of a freehold house known as No. 248, Rainsford Road,
Chelmsford, for the sum of £850.   The only term in that agreement to which
I need refer is cl. 7, which provides that " the property is sold subject to the
existing tenancy thereof ".   The defence raised a number of alternatives depending on how the facts might turn out concerning the state of knowledge about   I
the tenancy of the plaintiff's agent, a certain Mr. Rider, who gave evidence
before me.   In the end, the defence maintained was that the agreement had
been entered into under a common mistake of fact, and there was a counterclaim
on the same grounds to have the agreement rescinded or set aside.
The facts giving rise to the dispute are as follows: The defendant who used
to live in Chelmsford, purchased the property in 1946; it was then in the occupation of a Mr. and Mrs. Brewer, both since deceased.   Mrs. Brewer died on Aug. 18,

---

* *Salter* v. *Lask*, [1925] 1 K.B. 584.

A   1961, survived by Mr. Brewer, who died on June 6, 1964. This left their son, Mr. Terry Brewer, the sole occupant of the premises. He carried on living there until November, and as the only rent book produced in evidence shows, he continued to pay rent in advance down to Sept. 10, 1964, that payment covering a period up to Oct. 12, 1964. He left certain furniture and other things on the premises until January, 1965, when he finally left of his own accord and paid

B   rent down to that date in one lump sum.

The defendant moved from Chelmsford in 1956 and left the management of the property to a firm of solicitors, Messrs. Stamp, Wortley & Co. The rent was paid by attendance at Messrs. Stamp, Wortley & Co.'s office. It was received by a junior boy or girl who used to take the book in to be signed.

A proposal to buy the property was first made by Mr. Rider as agent for the

C   plaintiff to Messrs. Stamp, Wortley & Co. by a letter dated Feb. 13, 1963, and on Mar. 30, 1963, he offered £600, which he later increased to £800. This was not accepted and on July 19, 1963, he withdrew his offer. There the matter rested for over a year until it was taken up again on Aug. 6, 1964, by Messrs. Stamp, Wortley & Co. who made an offer to sell for £850 subject to contract, which was accepted and after usual conveyancing business resulted in the agreement of

D   Sept. 11, 1964. The matter proceeded nearly to completion and in fact on Oct. 14, 1964, Messrs. Stamp, Wortley & Co. actually delivered a completion statement and asked for an appointment to complete, but on Nov. 9, 1964, they wrote to the plaintiff's solicitors claiming that the contract was entered into on the basis that the property was subject to a Rent Act protected tenancy, but that it had since the date of the contract been ascertained that the original protected

E   tenant and her husband were both dead at the date of the contract, and that there was resident in the property a son of the former tenant who had no protection under the Rent Acts, and on that ground contending that the contract was unenforceable and refusing to complete.

In these circumstances, the first question which arises is one of law, namely, what is the effect of common mistake? The leading case on this subject is

F   *Bell* v. *Lever Bros., Ltd.* (1). This, of course, is binding on me and if exhaustive is really fatal to the defendant, since it lays down very narrow limits in which mistake operates to avoid a contract. It was there held that mistake as to the quality of the subject-matter of the contract must be such as to make the actual subject-matter something essentially different from what it was supposed to be— see per LORD ATKIN (2). In that case the plaintiffs sought to recover large

G   sums which they had paid by way of compensation for the determination of certain contracts of service, which, though they did not know it, they were entitled to rescind. The case as pleaded was not one of mutual mistake, and LORD BLANESBURGH held it was too late to amend, and LORD ATKIN doubted whether amendment was permissible but on the assumption that the pleadings were amended to raise this issue they and LORD THANKERTON all agreed that the

H   case must fail. I should have thought that this was more fundamental than any mistake made in the present case, and moreover the examples of the horse, picture, and garage, given by LORD ATKIN in his speech (3) would, in my judgment, apply to prevent any mistake as to the nature of the tenancy affecting the property being sufficient to avoid the present agreement.

Counsel for the defendant has argued, however, that there is a wider principle

I   in equity in support of which he quotes CHESHIRE AND FIFOOT ON LAW OF CONTRACT (5th Edn.), p. 184, *Solle* v. *Butcher* (4), particularly the judgment of DENNING, L.J., and *Huddersfield Banking Co., Ltd.* v. *Henry Lister & Son, Ltd.* (5), and see also CHITTY ON CONTRACTS, Vol. 1, p. 90, para. 191, and p. 115, para. 254.

(1) [1931] All E.R. Rep. 1; [1932] A.C. 161.
(2) [1931] All E.R. Rep. at p. 28; [1932] A.C. at p. 218.
(3) [1931] All E.R. Rep. at pp. 30, 31; [1932] A.C. at p. 224.
(4) [1949] 2 All E.R. 1107; [1950] 1 K.B. 671.
(5) [1895-99] All E.R. Rep. 868; [1895] 2 Ch. 273.

In *Solle's* case (6), as it seems to me, DENNING, L.J., clearly drew a distinction **A**
between the effect of mistake at law, which, where effective at all, makes the
contract void, and in equity where it is a common ground for rescission or for
refusing specific performance; and, as it further seems to me, he clearly thought
that this was wider than the jurisdiction at law. DENNING, L.J., said (7):

" The principle so established by *Cooper* v. *Phibbs* (8) has been repeatedly
acted on; see for instance *Earl Beauchamp* v. *Winn* (9) and *Huddersfield*   **B**
Banking Co., Ltd. v. *Henry Lister & Son, Ltd.* (10). It is in no way impaired
by *Bell* v. *Lever Bros., Ltd.* (11) which was treated in the House of Lords as a
case at law depending on whether the contract was a nullity or not. If it
had been considered on equitable grounds the result might have been
different."

DENNING, L.J., laid down the equitable rule in these terms (12):   **C**

" A contract is also liable in equity to be set aside if the parties were
under a common misapprehension either as to facts, or as to their relative
and respective rights, provided that the misapprehension was fundamental
and that the party seeking to set it aside was not himself at fault."

BUCKNILL, L.J., did not specifically refer to *Bell* v. *Lever Bros., Ltd.* (11), but he   **D**
laid down the principle in similar terms (13):

". . . there was a mutual mistake of fact on a matter of fundamental
importance, namely, as to the identity of the flat with the dwelling-house
previously let at a standard rent of £140 a year, and that the principle laid
down in *Cooper* v. *Phibbs* (8) applies."

Counsel for the plaintiff has submitted that there is no difference between law   **E**
and equity and no case which suggests that *Bell* v. *Lever Bros* (11) does not cover
the whole field save what he describes as one casual remark of DENNING, L.J.,
in *Solle's* case (6); and he says, moreover, that DENNING, L.J., himself resiled
from his earlier view in the later case of *Leaf* v. *International Galleries* (14).

I cannot accept this interpretation of DENNING, L.J.'s judgment, or indeed of
Solle's case (6) as a whole. It was a carefully considered view of the relevant   **F**
law and equity, and I do not think that DENNING, L.J., resiled from it in any way
in the later case. As counsel for the defendant has pointed out, relief in equity
was not possible in *Leaf's* case because it was too late (15); and DENNING, L.J.,
again accepted the equitable view in *Frederick E. Rose (London), Ltd.* v. *Wm. H.*
Pim Junr. & Co., Ltd. (16), where he said:

" At the present day, since the fusion of law and equity, the position   **G**
appears to be that, when the parties to a contract are to all outward appearances in full and certain agreement, neither of them can set up his own
mistake, or the mistake of both of them, so as to make the contract a nullity
from the beginning. Even a common mistake as to the subject-matter
does not make it a nullity. Once the contract is outwardly complete, the
contract is good unless and until it is set aside for failure of some condition   **H**
on which the existence of the contract depends, or for fraud, or on some
equitable ground: see *Solle* v. *Butcher* (6). Could this contract, then, have
been set aside? I think it could, if the parties had acted in time."

Again, in *Oscar Chess, Ltd.* v. *Williams* (17), DENNING, L.J., said:

(6) [1949] 2 All E.R. 1107; [1950] 1 K.B. 671.   **I**
(7) [1949] 2 All E.R. at p. 1120; [1950] 1 K.B. at p. 694.
(8) (1867), L.R. 2 H.L. 149.   (9) (1873), L.R. 6 H.L. 223.
(10) [1895-99] All E.R. Rep. 868; [1895] 2 Ch. 273.
(11) [1931] All E.R. Rep. 1; [1932] A.C. 161.
(12) [1949] 2 All E.R. at p. 1120; [1950] 1 K.B. at p. 693.
(13) [1949] 2 All E.R. at p. 1116; [1950] 1 K.B. at p. 686.
(14) [1950] 1 All E.R. 693; [1950] 2 K.B. 86.
(15) [1950] 1 All E.R. at p. 695; [1950] 2 K.B. at p. 91.
(16) [1953] 2 All E.R. 739 at p. 747; [1953] 2 Q.B. 450 at p. 460.
(17) [1957] 1 All E.R. 325 at p. 327.

A   " They both believed that the car was a 1948 model, whereas it was only
a 1939 one.   They were both mistaken and their mistake was of fundamental
importance.   The effect of such a mistake is this: it does not make the
contract a nullity from the beginning, but it does in some circumstances
enable the contract to be set aside in equity.   If the buyer had come
promptly, he might have succeeded in getting the whole transaction set aside
B   in equity on the grounds of this mistake (see *Solle* v. *Butcher* (18)); but he
did not do so, and it is now too late for him to do it; see *Leaf* v. *International
Galleries* (19)."

Be that as it may, I cannot dismiss what DENNING, L.J., said in *Solle's* case (20)
as a mere dictum.   It was in my judgment the basis of the decision and is binding
on me; and, as I have said, I think BUCKNILL, L.J., took the same view.   Whether
C   the mistake in the *Huddersfield Banking* case (21) would have been sufficient at
law, KAY, J.'s statement (22) is, I think, further support for the view that there
is this equitable jurisdiction.

Then I have to decide first—Was there a common mistake in this case?
Secondly—Was it fundamental?   Thirdly, perhaps—Was the defendant at
fault?

D   The first question presents some difficulty because there was, I think, some
divergence between the views of Mr. Rider and the defendant.   The former
clearly thought that the tenant was Mr. Brewer, and indeed he was at the time
when Mr. Rider began the negotiations, since if Mr. Brewer was not the original
contractual tenant, he clearly became a statutory tenant, after his wife's death.
The defendant, however, gave evidence that Mrs. Brewer was the tenant, although
E   in cross-examination she said she could not say whether Mrs. Brewer was
the tenant when she, the defendant, purchased the property.   There is a letter
dated Jan. 31, 1964, from Messrs. Stamp, Wortley & Co. to Mr. Rider on another
matter, in which they refer to " our client's tenant, Mrs. Brewer "; but the
partner, a Mr. Bailey, who attended to this property on behalf of the defendant,
was not called to give evidence, so I have no direct evidence what the defendant's
F   agents thought.   Mr. Ginn, a legal executive employed by Messrs. Stamp,
Wortley & Co., who took over the conveyancing on their behalf after the subject
to contract agreement of August, 1964, in reply to No. 37 of the plaintiff's
solicitors' preliminary inquiries, said " Tenant Mr. E. F. Brewer ", and he said
that he got the answer from records in the office.   It is clearly established,
however, that the defendant did not know that either Mr. or Mrs. Brewer had
G   died.   Even if Mr. Bailey knew that Mrs. Brewer was dead, as to which I have no
evidence, I am bound to infer that he did not know that Mr. Brewer was also
dead.   Mr. Ginn did not know that either was dead, and Mr. Rider said that he
first learned that Mr. Brewer was dead after the date of the agreement, and that
he then learned that Mr. Terry Brewer was in occupation.   Mr. Rider further
gave evidence that so far as investment was concerned his mind went no further
H   than that the sort of prices they were discussing were prices relevant to a tenant
remaining there, and that he assumed all along there was a protected tenant and
when completed they would have a protected tenant, and again that he would
never have expected to get this property for anything like £850 with vacant
possession.   He said that he made his offer on the basis that there was a protected
tenant and that he would stay there.

I   Such being the state of the evidence, in my judgment there was a common
mistake—namely, that there was still subsisting a protected tenancy in favour
of Mr. or Mrs. Brewer; and it is to be remembered that the language of cl. 7
of the agreement is " subject to the existing tenancy thereof ".   In my view,

(18) [1949] 2 All E.R. 1107; [1950] 1 K.B. 671.
(19) [1950] 1 All E.R. 693; [1950] 2 K.B. 86.
(20) [1949] 2 All E.R. at p. 1120; [1950] 1 K.B. at p. 693.
(21) [1895-99] All E.R. Rep. 868; [1895] 2 Ch. 273.
(22) [1895-99] All E.R. Rep. at p. 873; [1895] 2 Ch. at p. 284.

this was nonetheless a common mistake, though the parties may have differed A
in their belief as to who the tenant was, whether Mrs. or Mr. Brewer, although
that may have a bearing on materiality.

Then, was it fundamental? In view of Mr. Rider's own evidence to which I
have referred, and the evidence of Mr. Cooper Hurst, a surveyor called on behalf
of the defendant, that in his opinion the vacant possession value as at August,
1964, was £2,250, in my judgment it must have been if Mr. Terry Brewer had no B
rights under the Rent Acts.

This was the case pleaded in para. 3 of the defence and counterclaim, but it
depends on showing that Mrs. Brewer was the contractual tenant, since then her
husband became statutory tenant, and the effect of s. 12 (1) (g) of the Increase
of Rent and Mortgage Interest (Restrictions) Act, 1920, was spent leaving no
protection for Mr. Terry Brewer; see *Summers* v. *Donohue* (23).   The onus of C
proving the premise on which that way of presenting her case depends is on the
defendant, and in my opinion she has failed to discharge it. The defendant herself
was uncertain, and Mr. Bailey was not called. There was evidence that during
her life Mrs. Brewer's was the hand by which payment was made, but that is by
no means inconsistent with her husband having been the tenant, and the conveyance to the defendant which was produced stated that the property was then D
in the occupation of Mr. Brewer. The only rent book in evidence is in the name
of Mrs. Brewer, but that was clearly inaccurate as it starts some years after her
death; nor can I infer that the earlier ones were also all in that name which had
merely been perpetuated after her death, since though counsel for the defendant
was unable to prove and therefore unable to put in any earlier ones, he very
properly disclosed to me that they were not consistent, being sometimes in Mrs. E
Brewer's name, but sometimes in that of Mr. Brewer.

In my view, however, that is not the end of the matter. It is still necessary in
my judgment to consider whether, even so, the true facts were not materially
different from those supposed. I thought at one time they were not, since just as
a statutory tenant is a person who is free to leave but cannot be dispossessed
against his will, save on certain limited grounds, so Mr. Terry Brewer could F
either leave as he did, or claim a statutory tenancy under s. 12 (1) (g) of the Act
of 1920, with the like protection. In truth, however, in my view the two positions
are not the same, but are, on the contrary, materially different. One is a status
quo which one has no reason to believe will not continue indefinitely. The other
is a state of flux. I am satisfied, and I draw the inference, that had they known
the true state of affairs, the defendant's agents would never have offered, nor G
would she have agreed to sell, the property at a price anything like as small as
£850 without first making inquiries as to Mr. Terry Brewer's intentions. Moreover,
at the date of the agreement he had not claimed protection under the Act of 1920,
and he never did; and in my judgment, those are facts which I am entitled to
take into account in considering whether the mistake was material.

His right to claim to be a tenant under the Act of 1920, which he never H
exercised, was not in my judgment an existing tenancy within the meaning of the
agreement, and not what either Mr. Rider or the defendant contemplated. It was
argued for the plaintiff that Mr. Terry Brewer was a tenant of some kind; but I
think not, because the periodic payments of rent which he made were before
Messrs. Stamp, Wortley & Co. knew of his father's death, whilst the final payment was on quitting the premises, and receipt of that sum could not recognise I
him as a tenant. If he ever were tenant, it was certainly not the existing tenancy
contemplated by the parties.

There remains one other point, and that is the condition laid down by
DENNING, L.J., (24) that the party seeking to take advantage of the mistake
must not be at fault. DENNING, L.J., did not develop that at all, and it is not,
I think with respect, absolutely clear what it comprehends. Clearly, there must

(23) [1945] 1 All E.R. 599; [1945] K.B. 376.
(24) In *Solle* v. *Butcher*, [1949] 2 All E.R. at p. 1120; [1950] 1 K.B. at p. 693,

A be some degree of blameworthiness beyond the mere fault of having made a mistake; but the question is, how much or in what way? Each case must depend on its own facts, and I do not consider that the defendant or her agents were at fault so as to disentitle them to relief.

It was argued that the vendor should know who her tenants are, but this was a case of a long-standing and informal tenancy, the rent under which was paid
B simply by attendance in the outer office, where it was received by some junior boy or girl, and Mr. Brewer had but recently died.

The result, in my judgment, is that the defendant is entitled to relief in equity, and I do not feel that this is a case for simply refusing specific performance. Accordingly, the action fails, and on the counterclaim I order rescission. It is clear that this being equitable relief may be granted unconditionally or on terms, and
C counsel on behalf of the defendant, has offered to submit to a condition that the relief I have ordered should be on condition that the defendant is to enter into a fresh contract at a proper vacant possession price, and if required by the plaintiff, I will impose that term.

Action dismissed. Order for rescission on counterclaim.

D Solicitors: *Candler, Stannard & Co.*, agents for *Leonard Gray & Co.*, Chelmsford (for the plaintiff); *Jaques & Co.*, agents for *Smith, Morton & Long*, Halstead, Essex (for the defendant).

[*Reported by* JACQUELINE METCALFE, *Barrister-at-Law.*]

E

R. v. ASSIM.

[COURT OF CRIMINAL APPEAL (Lord Parker, C.J., Sachs, Edmund Davies,
F Thompson and Browne, JJ.), March 29, 30, May 9, 1966.]

Criminal Law—Indictment—Joinder—Joinder of offenders—When several offenders charged with committing individual offences may be tried together.
Criminal Law—Indictment—Joinder of counts—Whether r. 3 confined to joinder of charges against one accused—Indictments Act, 1915 (5 & 6 Geo. 5 c. 90), Sch. 1, r. 3.

G Questions of joinder, be they of offences or of offenders, are matters of practice on which the court has, unless restrained by statute, inherent power both to formulate its own rules and to vary them in the light of current experience and the needs of justice (see p. 886, letter D, post); and there is no rule of law that the court has not jurisdiction to try two defendants together on an indictment containing only two separate counts, each being
H a count against one defendant alone (see p. 887, letter C, and p. 883, letter G, post).

As a general rule, it is no more proper to have tried by the same jury several offenders on charges of committing individual offences that have nothing to do with each other, than it is to try before the same jury offences committed by the same person that have nothing to do with each other. Where,
I however, the matters which constitute the individual offences of the several offenders are on the available evidence so related, whether in time or by other factors, that the interests of justice are best served by their being tried together, then they can properly be the subject of counts in one indictment and can, subject always to the discretion of the court, be tried together. Such a rule includes cases where there is evidence that several offenders acted in concert but is not limited to such cases (see p. 887, letters H and I, post).

R. v. Leigh and Harrison ([1966] 1 All E.R. 687) overruled.

Per CURIAM: there seems to be no reason for departing from the view

GG

that r. 3* of Sch. 1 to the Indictment Act, 1915, is confined to joinder of A
offences (see p. 888, letter E, post).

Dictum in *R.* v. *Tizard* ([1962] 1 All E.R. 209 at p. 211) considered.

[As to the joinder of offences and offenders, see 10 HALSBURY'S LAWS (3rd
Edn.) 391, 392, paras. 708, 710; and for cases on the subject, see 14 DIGEST
(Repl.) 253, 254, *2189-2212*; 256, 257, *2228-2244*.

For the Indictments Act, 1915, Sch. 1, r. 3, see 5 HALSBURY'S STATUTES (2nd B
Edn.) 998.]

Cases referred to:

Crane v. *Director of Public Prosecutions*, [1921] All E.R. Rep. 19; sub nom.
  Crane v. *Public Prosecutor*, [1921] 2 A.C. 299; 90 L.J.K.B. 1160; 125
  L.T. 642; 82 J.P. 245; 15 Cr. App. Rep. 183; 14 Digest (Repl.) 661, C
  6700.

R. v. *Adler*, [1958] Crim. L.R. 539.

R. v. *Atkinson*, (1706), 11 Mod. Rep. 79; 1 Salk. 382; 88 E.R. 906; 14
  Digest (Repl.) 253, *2193*.

R. v. *Baker*, (1909), 2 Cr. App. Rep. 249; 14 Digest (Repl.) 254, *2212*.

R. v. *Barber*, (1844), 1 Car. & Kir. 434; 8 J.P. 644; 174 E.R. 880; sub nom. D
  R. v. *Richards, Barber, Fletcher and Dovey*, 3 L.T.O.S. 142; 14 Digest
  (Repl.) 316, *3021*.

R. v. *Bingham*, [1964] Crim. L.R. 327.

R. v. *Cox*, [1895-99] All E.R. Rep. 1285; [1898] 1 Q.B. 179; 67 L.J.Q.B.
  293; 77 L.T. 534; 18 Cox, C.C. 672; 14 Digest (Repl.) 253, *2197*.

R. v. *Kingston*, (1806), 8 East 41; 103 E.R. 259; 14 Digest (Repl.) 254, *2205*. E

R. v. *Lee*, [1958] Crim. L.R. 247.

R. v. *Leigh and Harrison*, [1966] 1 All E.R. 687.

R. v. *Lockett, Grizzard, Gutwirth and Silverman*, [1914] 2 K.B. 720; 83 L.J.K.B.
  1193; 110 L.T. 398; 78 J.P. 196; 9 Cr. App. Rep. 268; 14 Digest (Repl.)
  258, *2248*.

R. v. *Messingham and Messingham*, (1830), 1 Moo. C.C. 252; 168 E.R. 1263; F
  15 Digest (Repl.) 1140, *11,484*.

R. v. *Muir*, [1938] 2 All E.R. 516; 26 Cr. App. Rep. 164; 14 Digest (Repl.)
  260, *2267*.

R. v. *Philips*, (1713), 2 Stra. 921; 93 E.R. 943; 14 Digest (Repl.) 254, *2209*.

R. v. *Scaramanga*, [1963] 2 All E.R. 852; [1963] 2 Q.B. 807; [1963] 3 W.L.R.
  320; 127 J.P. 476; 47 Cr. App. Rep. 23; Digest (Cont. Vol. A) 399, G
  6653a.

R. v. *Smith* (*No. 2*), [1960] Crim. L.R. 267.

R. v. *Thompson*, [1914] 2 K.B. 99; 83 L.J.K.B. 643; 110 L.T. 272; 78 J.P.
  212; 9 Cr. App. Rep. 282; 14 Digest (Repl.) 251, *2168*.

R. v. *Tizard* (*or Tizzard*), *R.* v. *Ruxton*, [1962] 1 All E.R. 209; [1962] 2 Q.B.
  608; [1962] 2 W.L.R. 652; 126 J.P. 137; 46 Cr. App. Rep. 82; Digest H
  (Cont. Vol. A) 337, *774a*.

R. v. *Trafford*, (1831), 1 B. & Ad. 874; 109 E.R. 1011; *on appeal* Ex. Ch.
  sub nom. *Trafford* v. *R.*, (1832), 8 Bing. 204; 14 Digest (Repl.) 253, *2194*.

R. v. *Weston*, (1725), Sess. Cas. K.B. 188; 1 Stra. 623; 93 E.R. 190; 14
  Digest (Repl.) 254, *2203*.

Appeal. I

This was an appeal by the appellant, Ismet Assim, against his conviction on
Jan. 5, 1966, at Inner London Quarter Sessions before the deputy chairman
(P. H. LAYTON, ESQ.) and a jury on one count of maliciously wounding one
Wilkinson. He was sentenced to nine months' imprisonment. He had been
indicted with one Cemal, who was convicted on a separate count of assaulting

---

* Rule 3 provides: " Charges for any offences, whether felonies or misdemeanours,
may be joined in the same indictment if those charges are founded on the same facts, or
from or are a part of a series of offences of the same or a similar character."

A one Longton, thereby occasioning him actual bodily harm. The appellant's ground of appeal was " that the court had no power in law to try two defendants on an indictment containing only two counts, one being against the appellant alone for maliciously wounding Wilkinson, and the second count being against his co-defendant alone for assaulting Longton ". On Mar. 3, 1966, the court (Hinchcliffe, Nield and Widgery, JJ.) adjourned the appeal for considera-

B tion before a court of five judges. The facts are set out in the judgment of the court.

The authorities and cases noted below* were cited during the argument in addition to those referred to in the judgment of the court.

Paul Wrightson, Q.C., B. T. Wigoder, Q.C., and *A. T. Glass* for the appellant.
Sebag Shaw, Q.C., W. M. F. Hudson and *J. G. Leach* for the Crown.

C
Cur. adv. vult.

May 9. **SACHS, J.**, read the following judgment of the court at the invitation of Lord Parker, C.J.: At the Inner London Sessions in January, 1966, the appellant was charged and tried together with his co-accused Cemal on an indictment containing two counts. Count 1 was against the appellant alone, and

D charged him with maliciously wounding Wilkinson on Oct. 29, 1965. Count 2 charged Cemal alone that on the same date he assaulted Longton and so occasioned him actual bodily harm. At the outset of the trial the deputy chairman asked the two defending counsel whether they had any objection to the counts being tried together and each gave a negative reply (1). The case for the Crown was that Wilkinson, Longton and two other men went to a club where

E the appellant was employed as a receptionist and Cemal as a doorman. After they had consumed champagne and beer, they were presented with a bill for £28, which they protested was excessive. They paid £20 and then started to leave, but after Longton and one other of the quartet had gone outside, the glass door was shut behind them. According to Wilkinson, both the accused then approached him and the appellant said, " You pay now or I'll mark you for life ",

F and shortly thereafter he slashed Wilkinson's face with a knife. Seeing this incident through the glass door, Longton tried to re-enter the club to assist his friend and there ensued a struggle in the course of which Cemal assaulted him. The deputy chairman having directed the jury that the case in relation to each accused must be looked at " independently of the other charge against the other accused ", they convicted both accused. Cemal was fined and the appellant

G received a sentence of nine months' imprisonment. The sole ground of the appellant's appeal against that conviction is thus stated:

" That the court had no power in law to try together two defendants on an indictment containing only two counts, one count being against this appellant alone for maliciously wounding one Wilkinson, and the second count being against his co-defendant alone for assaulting one Longton."

H
It is submitted that, in consequence of this alleged misjoinder, the whole trial was a nullity, that there was, accordingly, a fundamental defect which cannot be cured by applying the proviso to s. 4 (1) of the Criminal Appeal Act, 1907, and that venire de novo does not lie in the circumstances.

I * Archbold's Criminal Pleading and Practice (1st Edn. 1822), p. 29; 5 Halsbury's Statutes (2nd Edn.) 725, 726, 994, 995, 998, 1036, 1039; Archbold's Criminal Pleading, Evidence and Practice (35th Edn.) paras. 127, 130, 137, 138, 172; *R. v. Benfield and Saunders,* (1760), 2 Burr. 980; *R. v. Tucker,* (1767), 4 Burr. 2046; *R. v. Hurse and Dunn,* (1841), 2 Mood. & R. 360; *R. v. Dovey and Gray,* (1851), 4 Cox, C.C. 428; *R. v. Jones,* [1896] 1 Q.B. 4; *R. v. Harris,* (1910), 5 Cr. App. Rep. 285; *R. v. Baker,* (1912), 7 Cr. App. Rep. 217; *R. v. Edwards,* [1913] 1 K.B. 287; *R. v. Hooley,* (1922), 27 Cox, C.C. 248; *R. v. Wilmot,* [1933] All E.R. Rep. 628; 49 T.L.R. 427; *R. v. Gee, R. v. Bibby, R. v. Dunscombe,* [1936] 2 All E.R. 89; [1936] 2 K.B. 442; *R. v. Sims,* [1946] 1 All E.R. 697; [1946] K.B. 531; *R. v. Hudson and Hagan,* [1952] W.N. 284; 36 Cr. App. Rep. 94; *R. v. McVitie,* [1960] 2 All E.R. 498; [1960] 2 Q.B. 483.

(1) Counsel for the appellant in the court below did not appear for him on the appeal.

Counsel for the appellant's submissions, which were developed in an elaborate   A
argument for which the court is indebted, may be summarised in this way.
At common law, there could be a joinder of offenders in the same indictment
only if (a) they had joined in committing the offence charged (*R.* v. *Atkinson* (2);
R. v. *Weston* (3)); or (b) they were principals and accessories (2 HALE'S PLEAS
OF THE CROWN, p. 173; 2 HAWKINS' PLEAS OF THE CROWN (1824 Edn.), p. 831);
or (c) a public nuisance was the result of the separate acts of several defendants   B
(*R.* v. *Kingston* (4); *R.* v. *Trafford* (5)). It was said to be significant that it required
statutory authority to enable separate receivers to be tried in the same indictment, and this was provided by the Criminal Procedure Act, 1851, s. 14 (now
replaced by s. 44 (5) of the Larceny Act, 1916), and the Accessories and Abettors
Act, 1861, s. 6 and s. 8. The Indictments Act, 1915, and the appended rules
made no provision, it was submitted, for the joinder of offenders, s. 4 and s. 5   C
relating solely to the joinder of offences against the same accused, and r. 3
having the same limited scope (*R.* v. *Tizard* (6)). It was said that the inclusion
in the present indictment of these two offenders is not permitted by common
law or authorised by statute and that there was here, accordingly, a fatal
misjoinder.

This court has already intimated its rejection of this appeal against conviction   D
and now proceeds to give its reasons therefor. At the outset it seems desirable,
however, to emphasise that, when reference is had to the old authorities on
joinder, care is needed in ascertaining whether the point at issue was the joinder
of separate offenders in the same count or their inclusion in separate counts in
the same indictment. A classical instance of this source of confusion is *R.* v.
Philips (7), which is commonly cited as authority for the proposition that two   E
perjurers cannot be charged in separate counts in the same indictment (see,
e.g., *R.* v. *Leigh and Harrison* (8)). The report itself, however, is not explicit,
and it has been pointed out (JOURNAL OF CRIMINAL LAW (1938), Vol. 2, pp. 240,
241) that STARKIE in his CRIMINAL PLEADING (2nd Edn., 1822), Vol. 1, p. 36,
discusses *R.* v. *Philips* (7) on the basis that what was there condemned was not
the inclusion in the indictment of separate counts for perjury against several   F
accused, but their inclusion in one count. It is distinctly germane to the present
appeal to observe that, when dealing in a later passage with the charging of
different offences against several persons in separate counts, STARKIE wrote
at p. 43:

" But though an indictment would be vicious which alleged that several
persons, jointly, committed an offence, which from its nature must have been   G
the several offence of each; yet if, in the same indictment, as found by the
grand jury, several offences be alleged to have been committed by several
persons, no advantage it seems can be taken, either upon demurrer or in
arrest of judgment, though the court will, in its discretion, either quash
the indictment altogether, or use such measures as shall obviate any inconvenience to the defendants which might otherwise arise. For the charging   H
of the offences to have been committed severally makes each charge a
separate indictment."

Contrary to what we understand to be counsel for the appellant's submission,
the Criminal Procedure Act, 1851, s. 14, had nothing to do with authorising the
joinder of receivers in the same indictment, but (like s. 44 (5) of the Larceny
Act, 1916) with the conviction of those jointly charged in the same count when   I
it has been shown that, though the property was all stolen at the same time,
the receivings themselves occurred separately at different times. As was pointed
out in *R.* v. *Scaramanga* (9), it was probably enacted to overcome the sort of

---

(2) (1706), 1 Salk. 382.   (3) (1725), Sess. Cas. K.B. 188.
(4) (1806), 8 East. 41.   (5) (1831), 1 B. & Ad. 874.
(6) [1962] 1 All E.R. 209; [1962] 2 Q.B. 608.   (7) (1731), 2 Stra. 921.
(8) [1966] 1 All E.R. 687.   (9) [1963] 2 All E.R. 852; [1963] 2 Q.B. 807.

A difficulty which had arisen in such cases as *R.* v. *Messingham and Messingham* (10). Again, while the Accessories and Abettors Act, 1861, s. 6, made provision for including in the same indictment accessories at different times to the same felony and offenders who had at different times received stolen property where the only nexus was that the property had all been stolen at one time, it by no means follows from this that, if there was some other and closer link between receivers

B or other types of offenders, they could not at common law have been individually charged in separate counts in the same indictment. On the contrary, nearly twenty years earlier it had been held proper in *R.* v. *Barber* (11) to charge several accused persons even in the same count with feloniously inciting another to forge a will, notwithstanding that only separate and independent acts done at separate and distinct times were alleged. Moreover, in the present century, in

C *R.* v. *Baker* (12), where two men were charged with rape and tried together and one of them was convicted, the objection that they should not have been tried together was overruled, LORD ALVERSTONE, C.J., saying that (13):

"... there was no ground for such objection. Many of the acts which constituted the crime happened when both ... were together upon the scene."

D
Moreover, in 1778 and 1800 it was stated by HALE that it was then common practice for twenty persons to be charged in one indictment for keeping bawdy houses, provided that the word " separaliter " was used in relation to each case (HALE'S PLEAS OF THE CROWN, 1778 (New Edn.) p. 174 (1800 Edn.) p. 173): and a similar indictment of several offenders for several offences is mentioned

E in MINCHIN AND HERBERT'S CROWN CIRCUIT COMPANION (9th Edn., 1820) (the predecessor of ARCHBOLD's work).

Turning next to a joint count against two defendants followed in the same indictment by a separate count or counts against one or more of the accused even in relation to a distinct matter (*R.* v. *Cox* (14)) counsel for the appellant conceded that no objection could successfully be taken to such an indictment,

F as indeed he had to in the face of well established practice. He further conceded in the present case that, had both accused been jointly charged in the first count with wounding Wilkinson and Cemal alone charged in the second count with assaulting Longton, the indictment would have been unobjectionable and the trial valid even had the Crown failed as against Cemal on a submission of no case on the first count. Counsel for the appellant was quite unable to indicate

G any principle of law or reason in practice why the absence of such a joint count should in the present case render the joint trial of the two accused a nullity. While certain definite principles as to joinder have been established—as, for example, that there can be no joint trial of separate indictments (*Crane* v. *Director of Public Prosecutions* (15)), and that wholly disconnected and dissimilar offences ought not to be joined in the same indictment even against the same accused

H (*R.* v. *Muir* (16))—it is noteworthy that no decision directly or clearly in support of the present submission advanced on the appellant's behalf was cited to the court. In *R.* v. *Lee* (17), however, STREATFEILD, J., held that separate counts in the same indictment against three accused men, and in *R.* v. *Adler* (18), the indicting of three defendants in three separate counts for contravention of the Betting Houses Act, 1853, was upheld, it being there held that " the common factor

I of the premises provided a sufficient nexus ". Moreover, in *R.* v. *Bingham* (19), MOCATTA, J., clearly expressed the view that the joinder of defendants is essentially one for the discretion of the trial judge. On the other hand, SALMON, J.,

(10) (1830), 1 Moo. C.C. 257.   (11) (1844), 1 Car. & Kir. 434.
(12) (1909), 2 Cr. App. Rep. 249.   (13) (1909), 2 Cr. App. Rep. at p. 256.
(14) [1895-99] All E.R. Rep. 1285; [1898] 1 Q.B. 179.
(15) [1921] All E.R. Rep. 19; [1921] 2 A.C. 299.
(16) [1938] 2 All E.R. 516.   (17) [1958] Crim. L.R. 247.
(18) [1958] Crim. L.R. 539.   (19) [1964] Crim. L.R. 327.

quashed the indictment in *R.* v. *Smith (No. 2)* (20), where three men were separately A
charged in the same indictment with independent acts of incest, but the ratio
decidendi there appears to have been that such joinder of offenders was not
permitted by r. 3 of Sch. 1 to the Indictments Act, 1915, and no broader justification for their joinder was presented for the court's consideration. As regards
R. v. *Scaramanga* (21), it is to be noted that this is a special case which deals only
with the effect of a verdict exonerating one of two persons charged on a joint B
count when there are not further counts charging each separately.

Having summarised the submissions made and the principal authorities cited,
it is convenient first to consider the position quite apart from the provisions
of the Indictments Act, 1915, in general and of r. 3 of the dependent rules in
particular. It is at the outset to be noted that, if r. 3 does cover joinder of
offenders, then it is conceded that there is no misjoinder in the present case; C
if, however, r. 3 does not deal with joinder of offenders, but only with the joinder
of offences, then the joinder in the present case is not dealt with in any other
of the rules, nor has any statute passed since 1915 affected the pre-existing
powers of the court either to permit or to refuse to permit such joinders. The
first point that becomes quite clear on an examination of the authorities is that
questions of joinder, be they of offences or of offenders, are matters of practice D
on which the court has, unless restrained by statute, inherent power both to
formulate its own rules and to vary them in the light of current experience and
the needs of justice. Thus, in *Tizard's* case (22), it was specifically stated that
the relative principles have been evolved as rules of practice, and attention
was drawn to the fact that the court need not be astute so to define the rules as
to preclude joinders in view of the overall discretion of the judge to order separate E
trials where the interests of justice so require. Moreover, in *R.* v. *Lockett, Grizzard,
Gutwirth and Silverman* (23), where the position as regards joinder of offences
was fully reviewed shortly before the passing of the Indictments Act, 1915,
it was stated by SIR RUFUS ISAACS, C.J. (sitting with BRAY, J., a master of
procedural questions, and LUSH, J.) that:

". . . in dealing with these and similar questions which arise upon indict- F
ments we are only dealing with matters of practice and procedure devised by
the judges who have presided in the past at criminal trials, for the purpose of
protecting prisoners from oppression, and that they are not laid down as,
and are not, rules of law, but are guides to the course which will and can in
such circumstances be adopted by judges, which will entitle them, if as a
matter of prudence and discretion they think it right, either to quash the G
indictment or to call upon the prosecution to make its election."

Secondly, it is also clear that, joinder of counts being a matter of practice,
any error in the application of relevant rules would normally amount to an irregu-
larity and would not result in the trial court having no jurisdiction. Moreover,
this court is not generally disposed to quash a conviction on account of such H
irregularities unless objection is taken before plea at the trial itself (cf., *R.* v.
Thompson (24)) though there is no hard and fast rule on this point. Further,
in relation to such matters an essential issue to be considered is whether any
real injustice has been done to the applicant as otherwise the proviso to s. 4 (1)
of the Criminal Appeal Act, 1907, can be applied.

Thirdly, on an examination of the authorities, this court considers that there I
never has been a clear, settled and general practice based on principle as to the
occasions when joinder of offenders is in practice correct; moreover, there may
well have been wide fluctuations as to what might be called the terminal limits
at any one time of the application of the practice then in force. Indeed, as regards

(20) [1960] Crim. L.R. 267.
(21) [1963] 2 All E.R. 852; [1963] 2 Q.B. 807.
(22) [1962] 1 All E.R. at pp. 210, 211; [1962] 2 Q.B. at pp. 611, 612.
(23) [1914] 2 K.B. 720 at p. 731.   (24) [1914] 2 K.B. 99.

A past centuries, this absence of settled practice is reflected in the variations of views between eminent writers, as for instance those expressed in the 1778 and 1800 editions of 2 HALE'S PLEAS OF THE CROWN at p. 174 and p. 175, respectively; and the 1824 Edn. of 2 HAWKINS' PLEAS OF THE CROWN at pp. 331, 332. In that latter volume, it is indeed stated at p. 332: ". . . I do not find it settled in what cases several offences of several persons may be joined in one indictment ".

B To this day the authorities give instances of how courts dealt with individual situations but provide no general guide as to the principles to be applied. Whether, however, one looks at the older cases such as that of *R. v. Trafford* (25) or more modern ones such as *R. v. Baker* (26), or at the older text books or the more modern ones, it is in the view of this court plain that there never has existed the general rule of the type propounded by counsel for the appellant. The court also

C rejects the submission that, when examining the question whether a joinder is or is not proper, the court can look only at what appears on the face of the indictment and is debarred from looking at the substance of the case as disclosed in the depositions.

Once the position is reached that the matter of joinder is one of practice and that there is no such general rule such as counsel for the appellant propounded,

D there remains the question whether, in the light of the varying practices now known to exist, any general rule of practice can be formulated and in particular how it applies to the present case. The present case is one in which it would, on the facts in evidence, clearly have been open to the Crown to insert in the indictment a count for one offence charging both accused of acting in concert; and it is thus particularly a case which demonstrates how artificial it would be to say

E that the joinder would have been proper if the Crown had added such a count but was improper because that had not been done. This court has said more than once that counts simply charging the several accused individually with particular offences committed are often to be preferred to counts, such as conspiracy, which involve the establishment of some additional element of acting in concert; but that was largely with a view to simplifying the issues to be placed before the jury,

F and there is no warrant for an accused saying that that practice rule results in it being wrong that, in the absence of such a count, he should be tried with the other persons involved in the same series of incidents. The present case is thus, indeed, one which inevitably falls within the four corners of any rule of practice, however narrowly it might be formulated, permitting the joinder of several offences. Whilst, however, it is of course not practicable for this court to attempt to lay

G down exhaustive rules dealing specifically with every type of case after hearing submissions many of which were directed in the main to facts under consideration in this particular case, yet equally it is desirable to come to some general conclusions as to what would nowadays be in general an appropriate rule of practice on the basis that none of the rules of 1915 deal with the joinder of offenders.

As a general rule it is, of course, no more proper to have tried by the same jury

H several offenders on charges of committing individual offences that have nothing to do with each other, than it is to try before the same jury offences committed by the same persom that have nothing to do with each other. Where, however, the matters which constitute the individual offences of the several offenders are on the available evidence so related, whether in time or by other factors, that the interests of justice are best served by their being tried together, then they can

I properly be the subject of counts in one indictment and can, subject always to the discretion of the court, be tried together. Such a rule, of course, includes cases where there is evidence that several offenders acted in concert but is not limited to such cases. Again, while the court has in mind the classes of case that have been particularly the subject of discussion before it, such as incidents which, irrespective of there appearing a joint charge in the indictment, are contemporaneous (as where there has been something in the nature of an affray), or

---

(25) (1831), 1 B. & Ad. 874. (26) (1909), 2 Cr. App. Rep. 249.

successive (as in protection racket cases), or linked in a similar manner as where **A**
two persons individually in the course of the same trial commit perjury as regards
the same or a closely connected fact, the court does not intend the operation of
the rule to be restricted so as to apply only to such cases as have been discussed
before it. If examples are needed, it is sufficient to say that, whilst it would be
obviously irregular to charge two men in separate counts of the same indictment
with burglary simply and solely because they had purely by coincidence **B**
separately broken into the same house at different times on the same night, this
court sees nothing in the facts in *R*. v. *Leigh & Harrison* (27) which in principle
prevented the joint trial of such closely related counts for perjury as were there
separately laid against the two accused. The last named decision is overruled;
whilst it accorded with the two cases (28) that appear in the books of 1731 and
which have since been consistently cited in ARCHBOLD, it was, of course, reached **C**
without the trial judge having the benefit of that considerable review of authorities which is so often impracticable on circuit. Save for that case, however, the
court has not deemed it necessary as regards each of the many authorities cited
to state seriatim whether it does or does not accord with the rules of practice as
above formulated.

The court has already emphasised, and desires to repeat, that it is the interests **D**
of justice as a whole that must be the governing factor and that, amongst those
interests, are those of the accused. It is essentially a matter for the discretion of
the court whether several offenders can properly be tried together at the same
time, and it is necessary for the trial judge to scrutinize matters closely with the
same degree of care that is applied in dealing with the question whether a single
person can be charged with several offences before the same jury. Counsel for **E**
the Crown urged that r. 3 of Sch. 1 to the Indictments Act, 1915, was not confined
to a joinder of offences, but this court sees no reason, as at present advised, to
depart from the contrary view expressed in *R*. v. *Tizard* (29). Be that as it may,
for the reasons we have given, no occasion to involve r. 3 arises in the present
case.

It remains to be stated that there is no vestige of merit in the appeal. The **F**
evidence against the appellant was cogent; the suggestion that the verdict was
not in accordance with the weight of evidence has been abandoned; the appellant
by his counsel specifically refrained from requesting that there be separate trials
of himself and his co-accused, despite having had his attention directed to the
point by the deputy chairman; he was, contrary to counsel's submission, in no
way improperly prejudiced in his defence by the procedure to which his counsel **G**
had assented; there is no suggestion that there was any misdirection of the jury;
and, having slashed a customer in the face with a knife after saying that he
intended to mark that customer for life, he has been given the quite astonishingly
light sentence of nine months' imprisonment.

The appeal is, accordingly, dismissed.

Appeal dismissed. **H**

Solicitors: *Peter Sabel & Co.* (for the appellant); *Solicitor, Metropolitan Police*
(for the Crown).

[*Reported by* N. P. METCALFE, ESQ., *Barrister-at-Law.*]

I

---

(27) [1966] 1 All E.R. 687.
(28) I.e., *R*. v. *Philips*, (1731), 2 Stra. 921; *R*. v. *Harvey*, (1731), Sess. Cas. K.B. 122.
(29) [1962] 1 All E.R. 209; [1962] 2 Q.B. 608.

A

W. *v.* W.

[PROBATE, DIVORCE AND ADMIRALTY DIVISION (Sir Jocelyn Simon, P.), May 26, 1966.]

Divorce—Petition—Petition within three years of marriage—Approach of court to determining whether to grant leave—Exceptional hardship—Past conduct and future hardship if leave not granted—Whether inability to marry father of child conceived extramaritally constitutes exceptional hardship—Matrimonial Causes Act 1965 (c. 72), s. 2 (2).

B

The wife applied for leave, under s. 2 (2)* of the Matrimonial Causes Act 1965, to present a petition for divorce within three years of marriage, on the ground that the case was one of exceptional hardship suffered by her or of exceptional depravity on the husband's part. The parties were married on Dec. 24, 1963, the wife being then twenty-four and the husband, whose previous marriage had been dissolved, being thirty-eight years of age. The wife left the husband on Aug. 6, 1964. The ground of her proposed petition for divorce was cruelty, the allegations being of the husband's shouting at her, following her in silence and staring, of his excessive sexual demands, his refusal to give her a house-keeping allowance, his living on credit and spending on drink, and his beating down the door of a separate bedroom and causing her fear; by reason of this conduct she had suffered, so she alleged, injury to her health. In her affidavit supporting the application for leave the wife alleged that the husband had told her before marriage that he had had a child by another woman, not his first wife, that this woman got in touch with him after his marriage to the wife and that in the summer of 1965 he was living with her and in February, 1966, had a child by her. The wife herself was expecting a child in September, 1966, by another man whom she wished to marry.

C

D

E

Held: (i) on such applications the court's approach was to examine critically the affidavit allegations, which the court was not bound to accept, and from them to reach conclusions whether, if the allegations were true and if account were taken of improbabilities and inconsistencies, the matters alleged would amount to exceptional hardship or exceptional depravity, but the court would not at that stage determine such issues as at a trial (see p. 892, letters F to H, post).

F

Winter v. *Winter* ([1944] P. 72) and *Owen* v. *Owen* ([1964] 2 All E.R. 58) applied.

(ii) leave to present the petition within the three years would be refused in the circumstances of the present case for the following reasons—

G

(a) the conduct alleged was not of exceptional depravity (see p. 892, letter I, post).

(b) though, in regard to exceptional hardship, s. 2 (2) was primarily directed to past suffering, yet the court would also take into account whether an applicant would suffer exceptional hardship if the remedy of divorce were postponed until the three years had elapsed; on the evidence the wife had not suffered exceptional hardship, and her present pregnancy would not make the case one of exceptional hardship if she were not enabled to petition until after the three years, particularly as her child might subsequently be legitimated by the marriage of the child's parents (see p. 893, letters B, C, F and G, post).

H

I

Hillier v. *Hillier and Latham* ([1958] 2 All E.R. 261) and *Brewer* v. *Brewer* ([1964] 1 All E.R. 539) considered.

[As to applications for leave to present petitions for divorce within three years of marriage, see 12 HALSBURY'S LAWS (3rd Edn.), 234, 235, paras. 441, 442; and for cases on the subject, see DIGEST (Cont. Vol. A) 737, 738, *3079a-3081b.*

For the Matrimonial Causes Act 1965, s. 2, s. 5, see 45 HALSBURY'S STATUTES (2nd Edn.) 449, 451.

---

* Section 2 (1), (2) is printed at p. 890, letters G and H, post.

For the Legitimacy Act, 1959, s. 1, see 39 HALSBURY'S STATUTES (2nd Edn.) 31. A
For the Matrimonial Causes Rules, 1957, r. 36, see 10 HALSBURY'S STATUTORY
INSTRUMENTS (First Re-issue) 237.]

Cases referred to:

Bowman v. Bowman, [1949] 2 All E.R. 127; [1949] P. 353; [1949] L.J.R. 1416;
   27 Digest (Repl.) 373, 3081.
Brewer v. Brewer, [1964] 1 All E.R. 539; [1964] 1 W.L.R. 403; 3rd Digest B
   Supp.
Fisher v. Fisher, [1948] P. 263; 27 Digest (Repl.) 373, 3080.
Hillier v. Hillier and Latham, [1958] 2 All E.R. 261; [1958] P. 186; [1958] 2
   W.L.R. 937; Digest (Cont. Vol. A) 737, 3081b.
Owen v. Owen, [1964] 2 All E.R. 58; [1964] P. 277; [1964] 2 W.L.R. 654; 3rd
   Digest Supp.   C
Stollery, Re, Weir v. Treasury Solicitor, [1926] All E.R. Rep. 67; [1926] Ch.
   284; 95 L.J.Ch. 259; 134 L.T. 430; 90 J.P. 90; 22 Digest (Repl.)
   315, 3279.
Winter v. Winter, [1944] P. 72; 113 L.J.P. 49; 171 L.T. 111; 27 Digest (Repl.)
   373, 3077.   D

Application.

This was an application by the wife for leave, under s. 2 (2) of the Matrimonial
Causes Act 1965, to present a petition for divorce, notwithstanding that three
years had not elapsed since the date of the marriage. The facts are set out in the
judgment.

The application was heard in chambers and judgment given in open court. E

A. B. Hollis for the wife.
The husband appeared in chambers.

                                                        Cur. adv. vult.

May 26. **SIR JOCELYN SIMON, P.**, read the following judgment: This
is an application by the wife for leave, under s. 2 (2) of the Matrimonial Causes F
Act 1965 to present a petition for divorce from the husband notwithstanding
that three years have not elapsed since the date of the marriage. The husband
does not oppose the application, although he does not admit the charges made
against him. The marriage was on Dec. 24, 1963. The wife was a spinster aged
twenty-four. The husband is described in the certificate of marriage as " an
artist ", aged thirty-eight years, his previous marriage having been dissolved. G
Section 2 of the Matrimonial Causes Act 1965 reads as follows:

" (1) Subject to the next following subsection, no petition for divorce shall
be presented to the court before the expiration of the period of three years
from the date of the marriage (hereafter in this section referred to as ' the
specified period ').

" (2) A judge of the court may, on an application made to him, allow the H
presentation of a petition for divorce within the specified period on the ground
that the case is one of exceptional hardship suffered by the petitioner or of
exceptional depravity on the part of the respondent; but in determining
the application the judge shall have regard to the interests of any relevant
child and to the question whether there is reasonable probability of a
reconciliation between the parties during the specified period." I

These provisions in effect re-enact s. 2 (1) and (2) of the Matrimonial Causes Act,
1950, which in turn re-enacted s. 1 (1) and (2) of the Matrimonial Causes Act,
1937. According to BUCKNILL, L.J., in Fisher v. Fisher (1), these enactments were

" not only to deter people from rushing into ill-advised marriages, but also
to prevent them from rushing out of marriage so soon as they discovered
that their marriage was not what they expected."

(1) [1948] P. 263 at p. 264.

A Nevertheless, a considerable number of these applications succeed: for example, between Jan. 11 and May 16 this year, forty-seven summonses under s. 2 of the Act of 1965 were heard; one was dismissed, three adjourned, and in forty-three leave to proceed was granted.   But the fact that a high proportion of these applications are acceded to should not be a matter of surprise: marriages do generally survive at least three years in the face of ordinary depravity or hardship;

B moreover, the very existence of the section no doubt acts as a deterrent to premature access to the court for divorce.

It is now clear on the authorities that the first question that arises is one of fact and degree: is this a case of exceptional hardship suffered by the petitioner or of exceptional depravity on the part of the respondent? It is only if the case falls within one or both of these categories that the court has any discretion to

C allow the petition to be presented; and it is at this latter discretionary stage that prospects of reconciliation stand to be weighed. See *Fisher* v. *Fisher* (2), per Bucknill, L.J., and Hodson, J., and *Brewer* v. *Brewer* (3); what Denning, L.J., said in *Bowman* v. *Bowman* (4) must, in my view, be read subject to these judgments. I have, therefore, first to consider whether the wife has established a case of exceptional depravity on the part of the husband or exceptional hardship

D suffered by her. She puts her case on both grounds.

In her proposed petition the wife charges her husband with cruelty and adultery. The particulars of cruelty read as follows:

" 9. That [the husband] frequently shouted at [the wife] and on other frequent occasions followed [the wife] about the house in silence and stared at her in a frightening manner, causing her distress.

E " 10. That [the husband] persistently made excessive sexual demands upon [the wife] and often woke her up on several occasions throughout the night, and habitually sulked if [the wife] sought to refuse any of his said demands, causing her distress.

" 11. That [the husband] refused to give [the wife] a house-keeping allowance, persistently lived on credit, and spent an undue proportion of

F his money on drink, causing [the wife] worry and distress.

" 12. That on an occasion in July, 1964, when [the wife] had locked herself in a separate bedroom in order to avoid [the husband], he attempted to break down the door of the said room, causing [the wife] fear.

" 13. That on Aug. 4, 1964 [the wife] again attempted to beat down [the wife's] bedroom door, and when she came out shouted at her, threw her

G to the ground, dragged her along and threw her bodily onto a sofa, causing her fear.

" 14. That by reason of [the husband's] conduct as aforesaid [the wife] suffered injury and apprehension of further injury to her health."

In her affidavit in support of the present application the wife states that her

H marriage was most unhappy by reason of the husband's cruelty to her: since she exhibits her petition to the affidavit, I think that she may fairly be taken to be verifying and relying in support of this application on the foregoing charges. Moreover, her affidavit carries the matter this much further: she alleges as follows:

" 6. Before I married [the husband] he told me that he had had an affair

I with a woman named [J. G.] and had had a child by her. After the marriage J. G. frequently got in touch with [the husband] and this was an additional distressing factor in my marriage. In about the summer of 1965 I heard that [the husband] was again living with J. G. at Ruston, Cape Cornwall, but it was only recently that I was able to prove that he had committed adultery with her. There is now produced, shown to me and exhibited to this my

---

(2) [1948] P. at pp. 264, 267.   (3) [1964] 1 All E.R. 539.
(4) [1949] 2 All E.R. 127 at p. 129; [1949] P. 343 at p. 357.

affidavit a certified copy of an entry of birth which purports to show that J. G. on Feb. 3, 1966, gave birth to a child of whom [the husband] is the father."

The wife avers that she was forced to leave her husband on Aug. 6, 1964, and has never lived with him since. Marital cohabitation therefore lasted just over seven months.

As I have said, the wife also proposes to charge her husband with adultery and in her affidavit she swears:

" In about the summer of 1965 I heard that [the husband] was again living with [J. G.] at Ruston, Cape Cornwall, but it was only recently that I was able to prove that he had committed adultery with her."

The proposed petition charges adultery in May, 1965, at a place unknown to the proposed petitioner, " as a result of which adultery the said J. G. gave birth to a child on Feb. 3, 1966 ". The wife's affidavit exhibits the birth certificate of that child, which purports to show that the father was [a man of the same name as the husband], an artist, and that he was one of the informants of the birth of the child. The synonymity is sufficient at this stage to implicate the husband as the father of the child; see Re Stollery, Weir v. Treasury Solicitor (5).

Some time after leaving the husband the wife herself committed adultery with a single man and she is now expecting his child to be born on Sept. 3, 1966: she exhibits a medical certificate to this effect. She avers that she and the father of the child intend to marry one another as soon as her marriage is dissolved and that they are extremely anxious to marry before the birth of the child. She finally swears that there is no chance of a reconciliation between the husband and herself. In view of the fact that both the wife and the husband have become, or are shortly to become, parent of a child extra-maritally conceived, I think myself that there is indeed no reasonable probability of a reconciliation; though, as I have said, I do not consider that this question arises at the present stage.

On what material should the court form a judgment whether the case is one of exceptional hardship or exceptional depravity? I think that the approach of the court here is similar to that of the Divisional Court in applications under r. 36 of the Matrimonial Causes Rules, 1959, (6). In other words, the court cannot at this stage try whether the case is one of exceptional hardship or exceptional depravity, since this would involve deciding whether the allegations in the proposed petition are true: all that the court can do is come to a conclusion that the allegations made in the affidavits filed on the application are such that, if true, they would amount to exceptional hardship or depravity; see GODDARD, L.J., in Winter v. Winter (7). Nevertheless the court is not bound to accept such evidence uncritically: it can consider it against the general background of the marriage as disclosed at this stage, and against any evidence filed in opposition. The court can also take into account, if such be the case, that the charges are inherently improbable, or that conduct complained of seems to have been provoked, or that there is a self-inconsistency in the evidence filed (cf., Owen v. Owen (8)). As in the r. 36 applications, the court can, if necessary, order a deponent to be cross-examined on his affidavit: see SCOTT, L.J., in Winter v. Winter (9): though this will be done only in exceptional circumstances.

If leave is given under sub-s. (2) of s. 2 and if it should turn out at the trial that the allegations made at the stage of application are exaggerated, there is power in the court to postpone the operation of any decree of divorce (see the Matrimonial Causes Act 1965, s. 5 (5)).

I am satisfied that the conduct of the husband, as averred by the wife, cannot properly be stigmatised as exceptional depravity. The question, therefore, is whether the case is one of exceptional hardship suffered by the wife.

---

(5) [1926] All E.R. Rep. 67; [1926] Ch. 284.   (6) S.I. 1957 No. 619.
(7) [1944] P. 72 at p. 75.   (8) [1964] 2 All E.R. 58 at p. 64; [1964] P. 277 at p. 285.
(9) [1944] P. at p. 74.

A   There has been a difference of opinion by members of the Court of Appeal whether " exceptional hardship " relates, or relates primarily, to past, present or future suffering; see *Hillier* v. *Hillier and Latham* (10) and *Brewer* v. *Brewer* (11). In my view the facts that the word " suffered " is in the past tense and that the depravity of the husband must necessarily be in the past suggest that the legislature had in mind primarily the past suffering of the applicant (see

B   Pearson, L.J., in *Brewer* v. *Brewer* (12)); but there is ample authority that the words are apt to extend to present and future suffering. In particular, the court may be concerned with whether the applicant will suffer exceptional hardship if the remedy in divorce is postponed until three years have elapsed from the marriage: see Bucknill, L.J., in *Bowman* v. *Bowman* (13); Romer, L.J., in *Hillier* v. *Hillier and Latham* (14) and Willmer, L.J., in *Brewer* v. *Brewer* (15).

C   I do not think that what the wife alleges that she has suffered by reason of the conduct of the husband can properly be described as " exceptional hardship ". Nevertheless she relies also on the impending birth to her of a child whom she has conceived by some other man than her husband: she argues that it will be exceptional hardship if she is not enabled to marry the father of the child before the child's birth. The child was conceived as a result of an action in which she

D   was a willing participant; but I do not think that this factor necessarily precludes her from relying on the impending birth as exceptional hardship. I must consider the impact on the wife subjectively (*Hillier* v. *Hillier and Latham* (16)). I must take her as she is, subject to ordinary human frailty and not the less disposed to rail against her fate by reason of the fact that she has been partly instrumental in bringing it about. For example, if the worry of her situation had brought the

E   wife to the edge of a serious nervous breakdown, the fact that it was partly or even principally of her own making would not necessarily preclude it from being considered a case of exceptional hardship suffered by her. Nevertheless, in common sense and short of such extreme situations, a state of affairs which a party brings on him or herself, is likely to have less impact by way of hardship than a wholly undeserved stroke of fate or gratuitous misconduct by some other

F   person.

    In considering whether this is a case of exceptional hardship suffered by the wife I also have in mind s. 1 of the Legitimacy Act, 1959, whereby the Legitimacy Act, 1926, was amended, so that a child may now be legitimated by the subsequent marriage of its parents, notwithstanding that they were not free to marry each other at the time of its birth.

G   Taking all these matters into consideration, I do not think that the wife's pregnancy constitutes this a case of exceptional hardship suffered by her, either intrinsically or cumulatively with the matters she alleges by way of misconduct on the part of the husband.

    I therefore dismiss the application.

Application dismissed.

H
    Solicitors: *Blacket Gill & Small* (for the wife).

[*Reported by* Alice Bloomfield, *Barrister-at-Law.*]

I

---

(10) [1958] 2 All E.R. 261; [1958] P. 186.   (11) [1964] 1 All E.R. 539.
(12) [1964] 1 All E.R. at pp. 542, 543.
(13) [1949] 2 All E.R. at p. 128; [1949] P. at p. 355.
(14) [1958] 2 All E.R. at pp. 263, 264; [1958] P. at p. 191.
(15) [1964] 1 All E.R. at pp. 541, 542.
(16) [1958] 2 All E.R. 261; [1958] P. 186.

J. H. MILNER & SON *v.* PERCY BILTON, LTD.

[QUEEN'S BENCH DIVISION (Fenton-Atkinson, J.), May 17, 18, 1966.]

Contract—Enforceability—" Understanding "—No binding legal contract created—Solicitors stating in correspondence their " understanding " that they would be employed for all legal work on development of a building site.

Solicitor—Retainer—Termination of retainer—Non-contentious business—Legal work in connexion with a property development and likely to extend over years—Whether entire contract—Whether retainer terminable by client on notice.

Negotiations being in progress between the defendants and others with a view to developing a London building site through the medium of a building agreement and subsequent lease, a partner in a firm of solicitors concerned, who had long acted for B., one of the parties to the negotiations, wrote to the defendants on Mar. 11, 1959, a letter confirming the basis of agreement between the defendants and B. The letter included the following paragraph—" May we please take this opportunity of placing on record the understanding that all the legal work of and incidental to the completion of the development and the grant of the leases shall be carried out by us ". A letter of Mar. 12, 1959, written in reply on behalf of the defendants, included the following—" I see that you have tied up the legal work and, of course, it has never been agreed and I do not like tying it up unless it has been agreed. I am quite prepared, however, to accept it in relation to this particular property ". At the time of the letter of Mar. 11, 1959, there was no existing agreement, so the court found, between the solicitors and the prospective client (the defendants) for employment in legal business. The solicitors in fact transacted some legal work in connexion with the development and with fringe properties. In 1962 the solicitors enquired of the defendants whether they should call for a lease in pursuance of the building agreement and as to the method of disposing of flats built on the site, and the defendants replied that they had by then their own legal department and were unable to instruct the solicitors. By further letter of Nov. 5, 1962, the defendants wrote to the solicitors saying that they had acquired B.'s interests in 1959 and had established their own legal department, and that it was desirable that their legal work should be carried out by their own solicitor. The solicitors brought an action against the defendants claiming damages for breach of contract to employ them.

Held: the claim for damages failed because—

(i) the letters of March, 1959, did not amount to a binding legal contract, but at most produced confirmation on behalf of the defendants of a present intention to instruct the solicitors to do legal work as and when it arose (see p. 898, letter I to p. 899, letter A, post).

(ii) even if, however, there were a binding contract of retainer, it was a retainer for non-contentious business and was not an entire contract; the defendants were entitled to terminate the retainer at any time on giving notice to the solicitors, and had terminated it by their letters in 1962 (see p. 900, letter F, post).

[As to the duration of a solicitor's retainer, the ways in which it may be terminated, and the position on termination, see 36 HALSBURY'S LAWS (3rd Edn.) 67-73, paras. 98, 100-102; and for cases, see 43 DIGEST (Repl.) 53-55, *415-435.*

As to the distinction between entire and divisible contracts, see 8 HALSBURY'S LAWS (3rd Edn.) 166, 167, para. 284.]

Cases referred to:

Hall and Barker, Re, (1878), 9 Ch. 538 ; 47 L.J.Ch. 621; 43 Digest (Repl.) 53, *417.*

A *Trollope (George) & Sons* v. *Martyn Brothers*, [1934] 2 K.B. 436; 103 L.J.K.B. 634; 152 L.T. 88; 30 Digest (Repl.) 236, *841.*

Action.

The plaintiffs in this action, J. H. Milner & Son, were a firm of solicitors in practice in Norfolk Street, London, W.C.2. The defendants, Percy Bilton, Ltd., were a company engaged in property development. By their statement of
B claim dated Sept. 13, 1963, as amended, the plaintiffs claimed damages totalling £10,812 10s. for alleged breach of contract by the defendants' failure to employ the plaintiffs as their solicitors in connexion with the legal work involved in the selling or letting of flats in a newly erected block known as Bilton Towers (near Marble Arch, London, W.1) and other work incidental to the completion of the development of this property by the defendants. The defendants by their
C defence, as amended and re-amended, denied that there was any agreement with the plaintiffs as alleged, and pleaded alternatively that if there were any such agreement it was an implied term thereof that the agreement could be determined by notice, and that the agreement, if any, was so determined by notice in writing.

The cases noted below* were cited during the argument in addition to those
D referred to in the judgment.

C. F. Dehn for the plaintiffs.

D. J. Turner-Samuels for the defendants.

FENTON ATKINSON, J.: The plaintiffs in this action are a firm of solicitors carrying on practice in Norfolk Street, Strand, and in 1958 they had
E seven partners, or it may be eight. There were certainly Lord Milner and the Honourable Michael Milner, a Mr. Fitzgerald, a Mr. Hodge, a Mr. Jones, a Mr. Nutt and a Mr. Lyon. In addition to the London office there was also a Leeds office, and Mr. Nutt was permanently at Leeds. He had no connexion whatever with the work done in the London office. Lord Milner himself moved between the two offices. At the end of 1962, Lord Milner and Mr. Nutt retired
F and were later, at some uncertain date, replaced by a new partner who was taken in; but from first to last neither Lord Milner himself nor Mr. Nutt had any direct contact with the defendants and in no way handled any of the matters arising in this case; and from first to last it was Mr. Lyon and Mr. Lyon alone who dealt with the defendants and the matters with which we are here concerned.

The defendants, Percy Bilton, Ltd., are a company of property developers.
G From 1946, or thereabouts, Mr. Lyon had been acting for a Mr. and Mrs. Bomberg who were in the same line of business as the defendants. The Bombergs were thus old clients of the plaintiffs, and in October, 1958, the Bombergs had become interested in a particular site which, for convenience, we will call the Great Cumberland Place site, the site near Marble Arch where the freeholders, Portman Estates (who had leased the site to Seymour Properties, Ltd.), and
H the Bombergs and the defendants, were together in negotiation with Seymour Properties, Ltd. The state of those negotiations, as at Oct. 28, 1958, is indicated by a letter of that date from some estate agents, Edward Erdman & Co., addressed to Mr. Bomberg, and I need not refer to that further in this judgment. At the same time negotiations were going on between the Bombergs and the defendants, and the position between them at Oct. 30, 1958, is summarised in a letter of
I that date. They were intending to form a company called Glenhazel House, Ltd., broadly speaking to take over and develop this particular Great Cumberland

---

* *Emmens* v. *Elderton*, (1853), 4 H.L.Cas. 624; *Hawkes* v. *Cottrell*, (1858), 3 H. & N. 243; *Rees* v. *Williams*, (1875), L.R. 10 Exch. 200; *Re Galland*, (1885), 31 Ch.D. 296; *Court* v. *Berlin*, [1897] 2 Q.B. 396; *Underwood, Son & Piper* v. *Lewis*, [1891-94] All E.R. Rep. 1203; [1894] 2 Q.B. 306; *Re Wingfield and Blew*, [1904-07] All E.R. Rep. 667; [1904] 2 Ch. 665; *Watts* v. *Official Solicitor*, [1936] 1 All E.R. 249; *Warmingtons* v. *McMurray*, [1936] 2 All E.R. 745; [1937] 1 All E.R. 562; *Thomas* v. *Hammersmith Borough Council*, [1938] 3 All E.R. 203; *Francis* v. *Municipal Councillors of Kuala Lumpur*, [1962] 3 All E.R. 633.

Place site. The first direct contact between the plaintiffs and the defendants **A** comes in a letter of Oct. 30, 1958, from the defendants to the plaintiffs saying:

" In association with Mr. J. Bomberg we have been negotiating the lease for property as mentioned above near Marble Arch."

They enclose copies of the letter from the estate agents of Oct. 28 and of their confirmation of Oct. 30, and say:
B
" When you receive the necessary documents, we shall be glad if you will confer with our Mr. Bond at this office along with Mr. Bomberg, if there are any observations requiring elucidation."

Then, so far as the correspondence is concerned, there is something of a lull and we pass to Mar. 5, 1959. On Mar. 5, 1959, there was a meeting between Mr. Lyon, of the plaintiffs' firm, the Bombergs, and Mr. Bilton and Mr. Bond repre- **C** senting the defendants, and there was a long discussion as to the share the Bombergs should have in that proposed venture. It appears from Mr. Lyon's attendance note, dated Mar. 5, 1959, setting out the substance of the discussion, that the Bombergs were anxious to retain a substantial share of the venture, whereas Mr. Bilton and Mr. Bond were rather trying to keep their participation to a minimum, but it was certainly contemplated that Glenhazel House, Ltd., **D** would erect some seventy-four flats on this site for letting, and the other matters discussed are set out in that attendance note of Mar. 5. One thing is quite clear, that nothing whatever was said at that interview between Mr. Lyon and the defendants as to the plaintiffs' being given any legal work in connexion with the development or the subsequent leases, and so far as the defendants were concerned there was no sort of agreement or understanding between them **E** and Mr. Lyon in that connexion.

Then comes a letter of Mar. 11, 1959, from the plaintiffs to the defendants, written by Mr. Lyon. It begins:

" With reference to our interview on the fifth instant with Mr. Percy Bilton, we are writing to confirm the basis of the agreement between you and Mr. and Mrs. Bomberg." **F**

He then sets out a number of points, which it is not necessary here to recite, and then this paragraph:

" May we please take this opportunity of placing on record the under-standing that all the legal work of and incidental to the completion of the development and the grant of the leases, shall be carried out by us. We **G** shall be glad if you will acknowledge receipt of this letter, as we feel sure that the position can be satisfactorily dealt with by correspondence rather than formal agreement."

On Mar. 12, 1959, there is an answer to Mr. Lyon from Mr. Bilton, writing as chairman of Percy Bilton, Ltd., and he agrees the items concerning the Bombergs **H** with one slight alteration to item 6, and then goes on in this way:

" I see that you have tied up the legal work and, of course, it has never been agreed and I do not like tying it up unless it has been agreed. I am quite prepared, however, to accept it in relation to this particular property."

The next letter, twelve days later, is dated Mar. 24, from Mr. Lyon to Mr. Bilton. He deals first with the amendment to item 6 of the Bomberg agreement and **I** then adds:

" I note what you say with regard to the legal work. Mr. and Mrs. Bomberg gave me to understand that this was verbally agreed at the outset, and I thought it opportune to refer to it in my letter. We are pleased to note that you accept it in relation to this particular property."

It is contended that, by those letters, or by their letter of Mar. 12, the defendants bound themselves, by contract, to employ the plaintiffs for all the legal work

A of and incidental to the completion of the development and the grant of the leases, work which might well be spread over a period of some years, and that, thereafter, they would have no right to dispense with the plaintiffs' services, even if they wished to do so.   Thereafter, the plaintiffs in fact did certain work. They dealt with items (i) and (ii) in the Schedule exhibited, and there was some further legal work in connexion with some fringe properties, as they have been

B called, some properties closely surrounding the relevant site.   For all those items separate bills were rendered and those were paid at the time.   Then we move on to a letter from the plaintiffs to the defendants, dated Aug. 28, 1962, nearly three and a half years having passed since the agreement,

C " Our Mr. Lyon was passing Bilton Towers over the week-end and noted the progress that had been made.   We understand from the agents that it is hoped to have the first flats ready by the end of the year.   Has the stage yet been reached when we should call for the lease pursuant to cl. 2 of the building agreement?   We would appreciate your observations and instructions.   We presume that you have considered the precise method of disposing of the several flats and we shall be glad to discuss this with you also.

D We did, of course, give preliminary consideration to this in November, 1958, and we have referred to the memorandum prepared at the time dated Nov. 17, 1958."

The answer to that, dated Aug. 31, 1962, signed by Mr. Bond on behalf of the defendants reads :

E " As you already know we have our own legal department now and they are dealing with all matters in connexion with the sale of these flats.   I regret, therefore, we are unable to instruct you to act on this development."

Subsequent correspondence followed : there was a letter dated Sept. 3, 1962, written I think by Mr. Fitzgerald, from the plaintiffs to the defendants :

F " In the absence from the office of my partner, Mr. Lyon, my attention has been drawn to his letter to your company dated the 28th ultimo and your company's reply of the 31st ultimo.   I feel sure that when your company wrote their letter to my firm on the 31st ultimo they overlooked the agreement made between your company and my firm which agreement is contained in letters passing between us dated Mar. 11, 1959, and Mar. 12, 1959,"

G and asking the defendants to look into the matter.   Then there was some confusion because it appears that, at the same time as the letters were written in March, 1959, concerning the Great Cumberland Place site, there were other letters passing between the parties about some Bayswater Road site, where the defendants had made it entirely clear that they were not binding themselves to employ the plaintiffs for the legal work concerned and there was some con-

H fusion, apparently, on the defendants' side at first about those two quite separate transactions ; but of course the defendants were reminded of the letters, reminded that the originals were in the plaintiffs' possession, and could be produced.

Finally comes the letter of Nov. 5, 1962, from the defendants, signed by Mr. Percy Bilton, to Mr. Fitzgerald,

I " Thank you for the copy letters, these now clear the confusion that had arisen, due to the duplication of correspondence between us on the same dates but relating to different matters.   Originally, when Mr. and Mrs. Bomberg had an interest in the above development, as you were at that time acting on their behalf, we instructed you so far as the legal work was concerned in connexion with this development.   Since then (1959), however, two events have occurred, namely, Mr. and Mrs. Bomberg's interest has been acquired by one of our companies and, in addition, we have established our own legal department.   I am sure you will agree that the changes in circumstances mentioned above are such that it is now desirable for the legal work

relating to the leasing of flats in Bilton Towers to be carried out by our own   A
company solicitor. I am sorry we did not write to you specifically on this
change but I rather presumed that you would have realised the changed
position having had contact with our legal department on various matters."
I do not think that the subsequent correspondence really helps. There is the
usual argument proceeding on both sides. There was a suggestion by the
defendants that the matter might be referred to the Law Society, but the plain-   B
tiffs did not accept that and in due course a writ was issued and statement of
claim delivered in which the plaintiffs claimed damages of £10,312 10s., damages
for breach of contract to employ them in connexion with this legal work and, by
a subsequent amendment, not content with £10,312 10s., an additional claim
was added for a further £500. The master's order is that liability shall be
determined first, so that I am not concerned directly with damages and that   C
has not been argued, and so I refrain from comment, however tempting, on the
size of this claim.

Various points arise. The two I propose specifically to deal with are these:
Was there a legally enforceable agreement contained in the letters of Mar. 11
and 12, 1959, with the possible addition of the letter of Mar. 24? Secondly, if
there was, had the defendants the right to terminate the retainer of the solicitors,   D
as they purported to do, without committing any breach of contract? Counsel
for the plaintiffs argued that in contentious business a client has long had
the right to terminate his solicitor's retainer at any time and now has a statutory
right to do so, but that a client has no similar right in the case of non-contentious
business, or certainly not in such non-contentious business as we are concerned
with in this case.   E

So I return to the letter of Mar. 11, 1959. This is a letter being written by a
solicitor to a layman, a prospective client, at a time when there is no existing
agreement whatever between them for employment in legal business nor any
understanding whatever between them to that effect; but the solicitor is clearly
seeing the chance of some very profitable legal business for his firm and is anxious
to obtain it. So Mr. Lyon writes: F

" May we please take this opportunity of placing on record the understanding that all the legal work of and incidental to the completion of the
development and the grant of the leases, shall be carried out by us."

Well, of course, he is placing on record an understanding. It did not in fact
exist at all. If he had said in that letter, " We offer to enter into a binding legal   G
contract and do all the legal work of and incidental to the completion of the
development and the grant of the leases and furthermore you will appreciate
that it will be a term of that contract that you cannot thereafter dispense with
our services until all the work is completed, however long that may take ",
I should have thought that it was quite plain that the defendants would not have
agreed and equally plain that Mr. Lyon knew this, or at least had a very shrewd   H
suspicion to that effect, and it appears to me that he quite deliberately used this
somewhat vague and equivocal language in his letter and that he did this on
the basis—that if it should be accepted by Mr. Bilton without demur, he, Mr.
Lyon, reckoned that he would then have an agreement in his pocket. I must
say I should be sorry if I felt bound to hold that he had succeeded in his desire.
If, instead of using the vague word " understanding ", he had said, " we under-   I
stand that it is your present intention to instruct us as and when matters arise ",
and Mr. Bilton had accepted that, then clearly a legal claim would not have
arisen when the defendants decided to make other arrangements, and in my
judgment that was in truth the result of these letters. Mr. Lyon deliberately
uses the word " understanding ", which, whatever it may mean, means something quite different from a binding legal contract and I think that, at the most,
these letters achieved something in the nature of a gentleman's agreement,
or extracted from Mr. Bilton confirmation of a present intention on his part

A to instruct Mr. Lyon to do this legal work as and when it arose. To seek to hold the defendants to more than that is, in my view, not legally sound, and it is quite unnecessary to consider whether it would be ethically laudable or desirable to do so.

I then pass on to the second point, in case I am wrong on the first. If there was a contract, was there a right here to terminate? In contentious business it has

B long been held that the client has the right to terminate a solicitor's retainer at any time and there are statutory provisions to that effect in the Solicitors' Act, 1957 (1). I have heard in this case an elaborate and sustained argument from counsel for the plaintiffs accompanied by citations of all the authorities that great industry could discover, and I am very grateful to him for his submissions and most able argument. He says that the same principle does not

C apply to non-contentious business of this description and he says that his clients are in just the same position as an estate agent employed to sell a particular house, or an architect employed to produce the plans for a new town hall or something of that sort, and if, before the work is done, the client chooses to vary his instructions then the solicitor, of course, cannot claim to do the work against the client's will but he is entitled forthwith to claim damages.

D In this context, in my view, it is necessary first to distinguish between an entire contract and a non-entire contract. For a definition of an entire contract I have turned to CORDERY ON SOLICITORS, (5th Edn.), p. 94, and that is under the heading " Termination of Retainer ". The paragraph begins in this way:

E " Before considering the ways in which a retainer may be terminated it is necessary to consider whether the retainer amounts to an ' entire contract ', i.e., one to complete the work for which the retainer was given and therefore one which cannot be terminated before completion. A retainer may be said to be an ' entire contract ' where the client cannot receive the benefit of the consideration until the contract is completed. Thus, under a retainer to sue for damages for breach of contract the client cannot get any benefit

F until judgment has been obtained so that the solicitor should not be entitled to tax his costs until he has either obtained the judgment or lost the suit, for ' if a shoemaker agrees to make a pair of shoes he cannot offer you one shoe and ask you to pay half the price ' (2). And again, on the sale of a house the client does not get any benefit (normally) until the sale is completed and the completion of the sale is a condition precedent to the solicitor becoming

G entitled to the scale fee on the purchase price."

It may well be the law that, if the client retains a solicitor to act for him on the sale of a particular house, or, as in one of the authorities, a gas works, and later seeks to terminate that retainer, before the work has been completed, the solicitor can sue for damages, just as an estate agent, who has been employed to sell a particular house, can sue for damages if his authority is withdrawn; or an

H architect, engaged to produce plans for the town hall, can sue for damages if his instructions are cancelled before the work is completed. None of those instances, however, seem to me to cover this case.

In my judgment, if this was an agreement at all, it was not an entire contract. It was an agreement to employ the solicitors in work of a certain class, which

I might extend over a period of years and involve legal work of various kinds, but it was a clear contemplation on both sides that bills would be rendered and paid as the matters proceeded; there would be no question of the solicitors having to wait for payment until they completed the whole of the lettings of these flats; and of course the client would be getting benefit as matters proceeded. So, what is the position as to the termination of retainer where there

---

(1) See s. 62 (2); 37 HALSBURY'S STATUTES (2nd Edn.) 1105.
(2) This quotation is from the judgment of SIR GEORGE JESSEL, M.R., in *Re Hall and Barker*, (1878), 9 Ch.D. 538 at p. 545.

is no entire contract? The view expressed in CORDERY ON SOLICITORS (5th A
Edn.), at p. 96, is that in such a case one of the ways in which a retainer may be
determined, without giving rise to a breach of contract, is " by discharge by the
client in the absence of any agreement to the contrary ".   That of course,
among other things, would cover the case where, for example, a solicitor had
been employed to act in certain matters for some particular fixed period of time,
I refer to SIR THOMAS LUND's article on solicitors in 36 HALSBURY's LAWS OF B
ENGLAND (3rd Edn.), p. 69, para. 98, where he is considering the period of
retainer and the view expressed is

". . . that a term will also be implied enabling the client to withdraw the
retainer at any time."

Authorities are quoted in a note, all of which, I think, have been referred to by C
counsel. In note (k) this appears:

" If a contract is entire then, unless a term is implied enabling a party to
terminate it, termination thereof by a party before the time for performance
is completed or has arrived gives the other party a right of action; "

and there is a reference there to a well-known case on estate agents' commission—
George Trollope & Sons v. *Martyn Brothers* (3). The note goes on: D

" This principle is applicable to a contract of retainer as to other contracts,
but there is not, it is believed, any reported instance of a claim for damages
having been advanced upon the withdrawal by the client of an indefinite
retainer . . ."

I understand the reference there to " indefinite retainer " to cover the case E
where there is a retainer but there is not an entire contract. I agree with those
passages from CORDERY ON SOLICITORS and from HALSBURY's LAWS.

In my judgment, this not being an entire contract, the clients were entitled
to terminate the retainer at any time on giving notice to that effect to the plaintiffs. I do not think that any question on length of notice arises. They were
entitled at any time to write and say, " We have changed our minds, we have F
got our own legal department and we will not require your services any further ",
which is what in fact they did. Thus if I am wrong on the first point, if there
was a contract, I think that the defendants had a right to terminate it, as they
did by their letter of Aug. 31, 1962; alternatively by their letter of Nov. 5,
1962.

The views which I have expressed on those two points make it unnecessary G
to consider counsel for the defendants' further point as to the effect, if any, on
this contract of the retirement of Lord Milner and Mr. Nutt. I confess that at
first blush I found his submissions startling, but at least if counsel for the
plaintiffs, at some future date, can satisfy the Court of Appeal that I am wrong,
on either or both of the two points on which I have decided this case, counsel for
the defendants will have an opportunity to argue that matter and may receive H
a much more sympathetic response than he did here. We have not had it argued
at any length here, although both counsel, as one would expect, were armed
with all the authorities.

For the reasons which I have given this claim fails and the defendants are
entitled to judgment.

Judgment for the defendants. I

Solicitors: *Milners, Curry & Gaskell* (for the plaintiffs); *B. Turner-Samuels*
(for the defendants).

[*Reported by* K. DIANA PHILLIPS, *Barrister-at-Law.*]

---

(3) [1934] 2 K.B. 436.

A **HANCOCK AND OTHERS *v.* B. W. BRAZIER (ANERLEY), LTD.**

[COURT OF APPEAL (Lord Denning, M.R., Danckwerts and Salmon, L.JJ.), May 5, 1966.]

Sale of Land—Warranty—House—Sale by builder of house in course of erection—
B *Express term for completing house in proper manner—Whether warranty of*
fitness of materials should also be implied—Whether defective work done
before contract of sale was within clause for properly completing house—
Defects clause not taking away rights under warranty clause—National
Conditions of Sale (16th Edn.) condition 12 (3).

A builder sold a house, which he was then erecting, to a purchaser under
C a contract which provided by cl. 9 that the builder would " prior to completion . . . in a proper and workmanlike manner erect build and complete
. . . a dwelling-house in accordance with the plan and specification ". The
plan showed the foundations of the ground floor as " four inch site concrete
on hardcore ". The contract further provided, by cl. 11, that " if the
purchaser shall discover any structural defects in the said house and works
D within six months from the date of completion and shall notify the [builder]
thereof in writing the [builder] shall forthwith make good such structural
defects without expense to the purchaser ". The sale was, by cl. 12, made
" subject to . . . the National Conditions of Sale (16th Edn.) so far as the
same are applicable to a sale by private treaty and are not inconsistent with
the aforesaid conditions ". By condition 12 (3) of the National Conditions
E " the purchaser shall be deemed to buy with full notice in all respects of the
actual state and condition of the property and shall take the property as
it is ".

Before the contract was made the builder had already completed laying
the foundations and the ground floors, and had used as the hardcore, underneath the four inches of concrete, material which contained sodium sulphate,
F and so was wholly unsuitable for use as hardcore beneath concrete. It would
not have been apparent to the builder, on reasonable examination, that this
material was unsuitable for this use, nor was the danger of sodium sulphate
in the hardcore generally recognised at the time, so that the builder was
not negligent in failing to appreciate either the presence or the danger of the
sodium sulphate. More than two years after the sale had been completed
G and the purchaser had moved in, the sodium sulphate, by absorbing moisture
and swelling caused the floors to crack, causing substantial damage to the
house.

Held: the purchaser was entitled to damages for breach by the builder
of implied warranty in the contract of sale for the following reasons:

(i) where a purchaser bought a house from a builder who contracted to
H build it, a threefold warranty was implied (a) that the builder would do
his work in a good and workmanlike manner; (b) that he would supply
good and proper materials, and (c) that the house would be reasonably fit
for human habitation (see p. 903, letter H, post); and warranty (b) extended
to materials used before the contract was signed (see p. 904, letter D, post).
Lawrence v. *Cassel* ([1930] All E.R. Rep. 733) followed.

I (ii) clause 9 of the contract dealt only with workmanship, not with fitness
of materials, and, though it was the only clause expressed in the contract
regarding the builder's obligation, it did not have the consequence of excluding the implied warranty regarding fitness of materials (see p. 903, letters F
and I, post).

(iii) condition 12 (3) of the National Conditions of Sale applied to the
contract only in regard to the obligation as to conveyance of the land, not to
the obligation as to building work (see p. 904, letter E, post).
Jennings v. *Tavener* ([1955] 2 All E.R. 769) approved.

(iv) the contract to build did not merge in the conveyance (see p. 904,   A
letter B, post).

(v) clause 11 did not take away the right to sue in respect of structural
defects which were not discoverable within six months, and, even with respect
to those discovered within six months, did not exclude the builder's liability
in damages (see p. 904, letters H and I, post).

Decision of DIPLOCK, L.J. (ante, p. 1) affirmed.   B

[As to the implied warranty given by a builder who sells a house in course of
erection, see 34 HALSBURY'S LAWS (3rd Edn.) 213, 214, para. 356, text and notes
(b), (c); as to the right of a purchaser to recover damages after conveyance
in respect of breach of a collateral stipulation, see 34 HALSBURY'S LAWS (3rd
Edn.) 379, para. 662, text and note (m); and for cases on remedies after completion, see 40 DIGEST (Repl.) 379-387, 3044-3059.]   C

Cases referred to:
Jennings v. Tavener, [1955] 2 All E.R. 769; [1955] 1 W.L.R. 932; 7 Digest
    (Repl.) 347, 43.
Kent v. Saltdean Estates Co., Ltd. (1964), 114 L.Jo. 555.
Lawrence v. Cassel, [1930] All E.R. Rep. 733; [1930] 2 K.B. 83; 99 L.J.K.B.   D
    525; 143 L.T. 291; 40 Digest (Repl.) 380, 3052.
Lynch v. Thorne, [1956] 1 All E.R. 744; [1956] 1 W.L.R. 303; 7 Digest (Repl.)
    347, 44.
Marsden Urban District Council v. Sharp, (1930), 47 T.L.R. 549; on appeal,
    C.A., (1931), 48 T.L.R. 23; 7 Digest (Repl.) 402, 254.
Miller v. Cannon Hill Estates, Ltd., [1931] All E.R. Rep. 93; [1931] 2 K.B. 113; E
    100 L.J.K.B. 740; 144 L.T. 567; 7 Digest (Repl.) 346, 39.

Appeal.

This was an appeal by the defendants, the builders, from a decision of DIPLOCK,
L.J., sitting as an additional judge of the Queen's Bench Division, given on
Feb. 2, 1966, and reported ante, p. 1. The plaintiffs, who were purchasers
from the defendants of houses in the course of erection by the defendants, each   F
sued for damages for breach of contract to erect and complete the house purchased
in a proper and workmanlike manner in accordance with the plan and specification applicable to the house. DIPLOCK, L.J., found that the defendants were
in breach of implied warranties in the contracts of sale, and gave judgment for
the plaintiffs, the damages, if not agreed, to be referred for assessment to an
official referee. The facts are set out in the judgment of DIPLOCK, L.J., at   G
pp. 3-5, ante.

Ian Percival, Q.C., and J. G. K. Sheldon for the builders.
H. E. L. McCreery, Q.C., and E. H. Laughton-Scott for the first purchaser.
E. H. Laughton-Scott for the second and third purchasers.

LORD DENNING, M.R.: In the autumn of 1958 the builders, B. W. Brazier
(Anerley) Ltd. were proposing to develop an estate of some forty houses known as   H
the Haven Close Estate in Swanley. They laid it out in plots. Each prospective
purchaser could choose his own plot. The three plaintiffs did so. Each of them
selected a plot and paid a sum down to get it allotted to him; but no contract
was made at that time for the erection of the houses. In the next three months,
between October, 1958, and January, 1959, the defendants did a good deal of
work on the foundations. They put in some hardcore and then put a layer of   I
four inch concrete above it. They started to build the houses. All this before
any contracts were signed. After the work had been done written contracts
were entered into by the purchasers with the builders. By cl. 1 the purchaser
contracted to buy the house for £2,750. Clause 9 said:

"The vendor [Braziers] will prior to completion at its own cost and
charge and in a proper and workmanlike manner erect build and complete
on the above freehold land a messuage or dwelling-house in accordance

A   with the plan and specification supplied to the purchaser subject only to such variations as may be ordered by the purchaser."

The plan and specification were in the ordinary form providing for the brickwork, the rooms, and so forth. There was nothing in the specification about the foundations, except that the site concrete was to be four inches thick and laid to required levels. On the plan there was this: " four-inch site concrete on B hardcore ".

The builders went on with their work. By May, 1959, the houses were substantially finished. Completion took place on May 20. The purchasers went into occupation. All appeared well; but two years later there was trouble in one house. Three or four years later in another house. Then in other houses. The trouble was this: the floors were cracking and breaking up. It was investi- C gated. The cause was found in the hardcore which had been put into the foundations. It was not just the ordinary kind of hardcore which comes out of demolished buildings, such as bricks, flints, chalk and earth. There was quite a lot of sodium sulphate in this hardcore. We have been shown some of this sodium sulphate. The blocks of it look very much like flints or chalk. Anyone might easily mistake it for ordinary hardcore. Somebody must have got it D from some old dump from a factory, must have thought it was stones and must have used it for hardcore. Yet it turns out to be a dangerous substance to use as hardcore. I say it is a " dangerous substance " because, when it is dry, it soaks up water whenever it gets the chance, and then it expands with almost irresistible force. If it is already damp, it will soak up more water and expand. If it gets into contact with concrete, it brings about a chemical reaction which may cause the E concrete to disintegrate. Hence the damage caused to these houses. It was the sodium sulphate in the hardcore that caused the floors to break up. The purchasers have been put to much expense to get it put right.

Let me say at once that all this trouble was in no way the fault of the builders. They had no reason to suspect the hardcore. They bought it in good faith. The defects were not apparent. No one could tell by looking at this hardcore F that it had sodium sulphate mixed in with it. The builders used all reasonable care, skill and judgment. Counsel for the builders says that in these circumstances they were not guilty of any breach of contract. The entire obligation of the builders, was contained in cl. 9 of the contract. That was a clause whereby they had to use only all reasonable care and skill and judgment in their work. It did not mean that they warranted the suitability of the materials which G they used. He relies on the principle that where a matter is covered by express provision in a contract, it is not for the courts to make an implication on the same matter.

It is quite clear from *Lawrence v. Cassel* (1) and *Miller v. Cannon Hill Estates, Ltd.* (2), that when a purchaser buys a house from a builder who contracts to build it, there is a threefold implication: that the builder will do his work in a H good and workmanlike manner; that he will supply good and proper materials; and that it will be reasonably fit for human habitation. Sometimes this implication, or some part of it, may be excluded by an express provision, as for instance in *Lynch v. Thorne* (3). The specification there expressly provided that the walls were to be nine-inch brick walls. The work was done with good materials and workmanship and exactly in accordance with the specification; but the walls I did not keep out the driving rain. The builder was held not liable. The question in this case is whether the threefold implication is excluded by cl. 9. I think that it is not, for this simple reason: cl. 9 deals only with workmanship. It does not deal with materials. The quality of the materials is left to be implied; and the necessary implication is that they should be good and suitable for the work. I am quite clear that it is implied in the contract that the hardcore must be good

---

(1) [1930] All E.R. Rep. 733; [1930] 2 K.B. 83.
(2) [1931] All E.R. Rep. 93; [1931] 2 K.B. 113.   (3) [1956] 1 All E.R. 744.

and proper hardcore, in the same way as the bricks must be good and proper   A
bricks. I know that the builders were not at fault themselves. Nevertheless
this is a contract: it was their responsibility to see that good and proper hardcore
was put in. As it was not put in, they are in breach of their contract. If it is
any consolation to them, they can try and get hold of their suppliers and sue
them if they can prove it against them; but they have to take responsibility so
far as the purchasers are concerned.   B

Counsel for the builders next relied on the doctrine of merger. He said that
the contract to build the houses was merged in the conveyance and did not
continue afterwards. He urged that it was all a matter of the intention of the
parties, and the intention here was that the contract should be replaced by the
completed conveyance. I cannot accept this view. The case is governed by the
decision of this court in *Lawrence* v. *Cassel* (4). The contract continued, even   C
after the conveyance.

Counsel for the builders then said that this defective hardcore was put into
the foundations before the contract was signed: and that on that account the
builders were not liable. But this will not do. The implication is that all the
materials, both those already included, and those afterwards to be included, in
the work should be good and proper.   D

Counsel also drew attention to condition 12 (3) of the National Conditions of
Sale (16th Edn.), which (5) says:

" The purchaser shall be deemed to buy with full notice in all respects
of the actual state and condition of the property and shall take the property
as it is."

                                                                                E
That condition applies merely to the contract for conveyance, not to the contract
to erect the building. It does not apply to the building work. It does not
derogate from the implied term that the builder will do his work well and with
proper materials and that the house will be fit for human habitation. I agree
with AUSTIN JONES, J., in *Jennings* v. *Tavener* (6).

The final point which council for the builders took is a matter of some   F
interest. It relates to cl. 11, which is the defects liability clause:

" If the purchaser shall discover any structural defects in the said house
and works within six months from the date of completion and shall notify
the vendor thereof in writing the vendor shall forthwith make good such
structural defects without expense to the purchaser."

It was said that when you have a clause which says expressly what defects are   G
to be made good by the vendor, it covers the whole ground and there is no room
for the purchaser to complain of other defects. The case of *Marsden Urban
District Council* v. *Sharp* (7), at first sight seemed to bear out that contention. So,
too, does the decision of His Honour NORMAN RICHARDS, Q.C., on Apr. 24, 1964,
in *Kent* v. *Saltdean Estate Co., Ltd.* (8). I think that it must depend in every case,
however, on the true construction of the contract. Moreover, if a builder has   H
done his work badly, and defects afterwards appear, then he is not to be excused
from liability except by clear words. I am of opinion that cl. 11 is no defence to
the builders here. It applies only to defects which the purchaser discovers within
six months, not to those which he discovers afterwards. Even with regard to
those discovered within six months, it only compels the vendor to make them
good. It does not excuse him from liability in damages. There is nothing in   I
cl. 11 to take away the right of a man to sue in respect of structural defects
which were not discoverable within six months. It does not, therefore, take away
the rights of the purchasers here.

_____

(4) [1930] All E.R. Rep. 733; [1930] 2 K.B. 83.
(5) The National Conditions were incorporated in the contract by cl. 12; see ante, at
p. 5, letter D.
(6) [1955] 2 All E.R. 769.   (7) (1931), 48 T.L.R. 23.
                         (8) (1964), 114 L.Jo. 555.

A   I have now gone through all the points which counsel for the builders has raised before us.   I find myself in agreement with the judgment of DIPLOCK, L.J. (9), and I would dismiss this appeal.

DANCKWERTS, L.J.: I agree. I also am satisfied that DIPLOCK, L.J. (9), reached the right conclusion and I also would dismiss the appeal.

B   **SALMON, L.J.:** I agree.

Appeal dismissed.

Solicitors: *Bower, Cotton & Bower,* agents for *R. E. Bishop & Co.,* Swanley (for the builders); *Warren & Warren,* agents for *Chancellor & Ridley,* Dartford, Kent (for the purchasers).

C   [*Reported by* F. GUTTMAN, ESQ., *Barrister-at-Law.*]

D   ## *PRACTICE NOTE.*

[COURT OF CRIMINAL APPEAL (Lord Parker, C.J., Fenton Atkinson and James, JJ.)
June 21, 1966.]

Criminal Law—Sentence—Corrective training—Notice of previous convictions—
E   *Cases where notices need not be served under Criminal Justice Act,* 1948 (11 & 12
Geo. 6 c. 58), s. 23.
Criminal Law—Sentence—Preventive detention—Notice of previous convictions—
Cases where notices need not be served under Criminal Justice Act, 1948
(11 & 12 *Geo.* 6 *c.* 58), *s.* 23.

[As to notices to be served on accused with a view to corrective training or
F preventive detention, see 10 HALSBURY'S LAWS (3rd Edn.) 511, para. 928, 513, para. 932; and for cases on the subject, see 14 DIGEST (Repl.) 584, *5817, 5818.*
For the Criminal Justice Act, 1948, s. 23, see 28 HALSBURY'S STATUTES (2nd Edn.) 374.]

LORD PARKER, C.J., at the sitting of the court said: In the light of the
Practice Direction of Feb. 26, 1962, (1) and recent decisions of the Court of
G Criminal Appeal, the occasions when a sentence of corrective training or preventive detention can properly be imposed are comparatively rare.   In the result much time is wasted by the police in serving notices under s. 23 of the Criminal Justice Act, 1948, (2) on those defendants who, while eligible, will not receive such sentences.   Accordingly chief officers of police are being informed that such notices need not be served (a) in the case of defendants eligible for corrective
H training who either have already served a period of borstal training or are over thirty years of age; (b) in the case of defendants eligible for preventive detention who are under forty years of age.

[*Reported by* N. P. METCALFE, ESQ., *Barrister-at-Law.*]

I

---

(9) Ante, p. 1.
(1) See [1962] 1 All E.R. 671.
(2) Section 23 (1) provides: " For the purpose of determining whether an offender
is liable to be sentenced to corrective training or preventive detention or to be ordered
to be subject to the provisions of the last foregoing section, no account shall be taken
of any previous conviction or sentence unless notice has been given to the offender
and to the proper officer of the court at least three days before the trial that it is intended
to prove the conviction or sentence; ... "

A

BOSTON v. W. S. BAGSHAW & SONS AND OTHERS.

[COURT OF APPEAL (Lord Denning, M.R., Harman and Diplock, L.JJ.), April 26, 27, 1966.]

Libel—Privilege—Qualified privilege—Broadcast—Circular letter by auctioneers to other auctioneers—Theft of pigs at auction—Television flash arranged B *through chief officer of police containing offer of reward by auctioneers— Whether matter of public concern and for public benefit—Defamation Act, 1952 (15 & 16 Geo. 6 & 1 Eliz. 2 c. 66), s. 7, s. 9, Sch., para. 12.*

Libel—Privilege—Qualified privilege—Malice—Summing-up.

On Sept. 20, 1962, at a sale of livestock held by the defendant auctioneers three pedigree pigs were knocked down to a bidder who gave his name as C Boston of Rugeley. That name was false. He stole the pigs, taking them without paying the price. On the next day the defendants sent a circular letter to other auctioneers informing them of the theft, giving them a description of the thief and mentioning that he gave as his name Boston of Rugeley. There were several persons of this name living at Rugeley. The plaintiff, who was a well-known farmer there, was one. The defendants also D reported the matter to the police and suggested that a police notice should appear on television, saying that they would offer a reward of £25. The defendants made it clear that they knew that the plaintiff had not stolen the pigs, and that a man who gave a false name and address had done so. On Sept. 28, 1962, a notice mentioning the name of Boston of Rugeley was broadcast. The plaintiff brought an action for defamation against the E auctioneers and the television authority. The trial judge ruled that both the letter and the broadcast were published on occasions that were privileged. In summing-up on the question of malice the judge dealt only with matters that he considered of importance. The jury found that the publications were defamatory of the plaintiff but negatived malice. On appeal the Court of Appeal, having found that the auctioneers' letter was published F on an occasion that was clearly privileged,

Held: (i) the occasion of publication of the broadcast was privileged by virtue of s. 9 (2) of the Defamation Act, 1952, applying s. 7 (1) and para. 12 of the schedule to that Act, because, although the theft was a small crime, it was proper for the police to take steps by means of newspaper announce- ments or broadcasts to give information to the public so as to try to find G the criminal, and the matter was not excepted under s. 7 (3) as something which was not of public concern (see p. 910, letters F and H, and p. 912, letters A and F, post).

(ii) it had not been necessary for the judge in summing-up to put each piece of evidence of malice to the jury, and he was entitled to leave the question of malice at large to them; malice had not been established and H the plaintiff's claim failed (see p. 911, letter D, and p. 912, letters D and F, post).

Dictum of LORD PORTER in *Turner (otherwise Robertson)* v. *Metro-Goldwyn-Mayer Pictures, Ltd.* ([1950] 1 All E.R. at p. 455) considered and not applied.

Appeal dismissed. I

[As to defamation by broadcasting, see 24 HALSBURY'S LAWS (3rd Edn.) 41, para. 71; as to the qualified privilege of newspapers or broadcasts, see ibid., p. 68, para. 120; as to common interest creating a privileged occasion, see ibid., p. 57, para. 101, and as to proof of malice, see ibid., pp. 79, 80, para. 140; and for cases on the subject, see 32 DIGEST (Repl.) 155, 156, *1719-1727*, 186-188, *1988-2010*, 193, 194, *2065-2074*.

For the Defamation Act, 1952, s. 7, s. 9 and Sch. para. 12, see 32 HALSBURY'S STATUTES (2nd Edn.) 403, 404, 405, 409.]

A Cases referred to:

Chapman v. *Ellesmere (Lord)*, [1932] All E.R. Rep. 221; [1932] 2 K.B. 431; 101 L.J.K.B. 376; 146 L.T. 538; 32 Digest (Repl.) 30, *185*.

Turner (orse. Robertson) v. *Metro-Goldwyn-Mayer Pictures, Ltd.*, [1950] 1 All E.R. 449; 32 Digest (Repl.) 31, *186*.

B **Appeal.**

This was an appeal by the plaintiff, Alfred Robert Boston, from a judgment for the first defendants entered pursuant to the order of MILMO, J., dated Nov. 26, 1965, at the trial of a libel action before him with a jury, in which the plaintiff claimed damages against the first defendants, W. S. Bagshaw & Sons, a firm of auctioneers, for alleged libel in a circular letter dated Sept. 21, 1962,

C published by the first defendants to livestock auctioneers in the Midlands, and against the second defendant, Associated Television, Ltd., for libel published by them in a television programme entitled " Police 5 " on Sept. 28, 1962, damages for this alleged libel being also claimed against the first defendants. The jury found the following answers—A. *Circular letter* (i) Is it defamatory of the plaintiff? (A) Yes; (ii) Were the defendants actuated by malice? (A.) No;

D (iii) If the answer to (i) is " Yes " what damages? (A.) £5,500. B. *Broadcast* (i) Is it defamatory of the plaintiff? (A.) Yes; (ii) If so, did the defendants authorise the inclusion in the broadcast of the matter defamatory of the plaintiff? (A.) Yes; (iii) Did the defendants prior to the broadcast inform the police authorities that they were satisfied that the plaintiff had not stolen the pigs? (A.) Yes; (iv) Was the draft script [of the relevant broadcast] issued by or on behalf of the Chief Officer of Police? (A.) Yes; (v) Were the defendants actuated

E by malice? (A.) No; (vi) If the answers to B (i) and B (ii) are " Yes " what damages? (A.) £5,500. C. (i) Did the man who successfully bid for the pigs steal them? (A.) Yes; (ii) Were the pigs removed from the sale unaccounted for and not returned? (A.) Yes; (iii) Were the pigs taken away in a trailer drawn by a Hillman or Singer motor car? (A.) No; (iv) Did the defendants honestly

F believe the pigs were stolen by the man who made the successful bid or his accomplices? (A.) Yes.

Terms of settlement were agreed between the plaintiff and the second defendants and a statement was read in open court. At the close of the evidence the trial judge was asked to rule on the question whether publication was on a privileged occasion. He was also asked to rule whether there was evidence to

G establish that the defendants could be held responsible in law for any matter defamatory of the plaintiff which might have been contained in the broadcast. The trial judge ruled that the occasion of the publication of the letter dated Sept. 21, 1962, was privileged and further that the broadcast on Sept. 28, 1962, was also privileged under s. 7 (1) of the Defamation Act, 1952. He found that the first defendants had made it clear that they knew from the start that the

H plaintiff had not stolen the pigs and that it was a man who had given a false name and address who had done so.

It having been agreed that all issues of fact should be dealt with by the jury at one time and that the trial judge should rule on the law in the light of these findings, the trial judge (MILMO, J.) then ruled that as the publication of the circular letter to other firms of auctioneers was clearly privileged and the jury

I had negatived malice on the part of the first defendants, the cause of action alleged to arise out of that circular must necessarily fail. His Lordship stated that the draft script for the broadcast, which was sent to the Chief Constable of the City of Birmingham Police had been found by the jury to have been issued by or on behalf of a chief officer of police; and that the actual script which was broadcast, although different in its language from the draft script so submitted, was nevertheless a script by or on behalf of the Chief Constable of the Birmingham City Police. In his judgment it was also a summary of the draft, which was in itself a notice supplied by or on behalf of the Chief Constable of the Staffordshire Constabulary. Therefore it came within para. 12* of the A schedule to the Defamation Act, 1952. His Lordship said that he was unable to hold that the publication of this matter was not of public concern or that its publication was not for the public benefit, and that in those circumstances he held that the broadcast was protected by the privilege conferred by the Defamation Act, 1952, s. 7 (1), s. 9 (2) and Schedule, para. 12. Again, in view of the finding of the jury that the first defendants were not actuated by malice B the claim for libel against them based on the broadcast failed. On the further question His Lordship found that having regard to the jury's answer to question B (iii) there was no material on which they could find that the first defendants authorised the inclusion in the broadcast of matter defamatory to the plaintiff. The actual script of the broadcast had never been seen or approved by the first defendants at any time, nor were they in direct communication with the broad- C casting authorities. The jury having found that the defendants had made known to the police in Staffordshire that the plaintiff was not concerned with the theft and that he was not the man, it could not be said that what was broadcast " adhered to the sense and substance ", to use the words of MONTAGUE SMITH, J., in *Parkes* v. *Prescott*† of what the first defendants had communicated. His Lordship held, as an additional ground, that for that reason the defendants could D not be found to be in law responsible for the broadcast.

David Hirst, Q.C., and *D. Hancock* for the plaintiff.
Quintin Hogg, Q.C., and *F. M. Drake* for the first defendants.

LORD DENNING, M.R.: On Thursday, Sept. 20, 1962, a firm of auctioneers called Bagshaw & Sons, were holding a sale of livestock at Rolleston E Grange, Tutbury in Staffordshire. The auctioneer, Mr. Naylor, put up for sale three lots of pedigree Wessex Saddleback Gilts, each earmarked. Amongst the bidders there was a man of about thirty to thirty-five years of age, wearing a brown smock. His bids were the highest. The three pigs were knocked down to him. The price was £103 19s. He gave his name as " Boston of Rugeley ". He ought of course to have paid for the pigs before he took them away; but he F somehow managed to get hold of them without paying for them. He was seen to go off with them in a trailer. He was never seen again. When the auctioneers found it out they tried to trace the man. There are three or four people named Boston who live at Rugeley. All of them said that they had not been at the sale that day. It was clear that the man who bid for the pigs was a fraud. He gave a false name. He never had any intention of paying for the pigs. He had stolen G them. The jury so found.

The auctioneers took steps to catch the culprit. They reported the matter to the local police. The police took statements from Mr. Naylor, the auctioneer, and his assistant, Mr. Marshall. The auctioneers also warned other auctioneers in the Midlands. On Sept. 21, 1962, they wrote this letter to thirty-four or thirty-five auctioneers: H

" Dear Sirs, Yesterday, Sept. 20, we held an auction sale at Rolleston Grange, Tutbury, where a person purchased three pedigree Wessex Saddle-back Gilts and gave the name ' Boston ' of Rugeley when these pigs were ' knocked down ' to him. Subsequent to the sale this person did not pay and at the time of writing this letter we have been unable to trace this purchaser." I

They went on to say the pigs were loaded in a trailer, and they said:

---

* Paragraph 12 of the schedule to the Defamation Act, 1952, provides: " A copy or fair and accurate report or summary of any notice or other matter issued for the informa-tion of the public by or on behalf of any government department, officer of state, local authority or chief officer of police." By s. 7 (1) qualified privilege is extended to the reports or other matters mentioned in the schedule, and by s. 9 (2) the privilege conferred by s. 7 (1) is extended to broadcasts.
† (1869), L.R. 4 Exch. 169 at p. 179; 32 Digest (Repl.) 97, *1194*.

A   " If at any of your subsequent auction sales a person offers for sale pedigree Wessex Saddleback pigs which you think may answer the description of these pigs, then we would be obliged if you would contact the police."

Then they gave the full description of the pigs, the earmarks and the lot numbers which were painted on their backs.

B   Mr. Naylor also telephoned to the chief constable of Staffordshire, Mr. Peck. He told him that he was ready to give £25 reward if the pigs could be recovered and inquired whether it would be possible to get the matter put out on television. Now it so happened that about that time the television people, A.T.V., had started a programme which they called " Police Five ". They devoted five minutes to information from the police seeking the help of the public, such as

C   information about criminals who had escaped or people who were wanted for offences. Mr. Naylor told Mr. Peck: " If a ' flash ' could be put on the A.T.V. ' Police Five ' programme on Friday next, it might lead to their recovery." He confirmed that conversation by a letter on Sept. 23, 1965. The chief constable of Staffordshire took action accordingly. He got in touch with the police at Birmingham who arranged these broadcasts with the television people. He sent

D   them a script about the missing pigs and the £25 reward. The Birmingham police discussed the programme with the television producer, with the result that on Sept. 28, this item was included in the " Police Five " programme:

" Finally, an opprtunity for you to earn a £25 reward. A number of little piggies went to market at Rolleston Grange, Tutbury, on Thursday, Sept. 20. Three little piggies, Wessex Saddleback Gilts, to be precise, left

E   the market on a trailer [then they had a little picture of a trailer with three little pigs in] towed by either a green Hillman or Singer car, in the care of a gentleman who said his name was Boston and he came from Rugeley. He is about thirty-five, tall, mousey-haired, and was wearing a brown smock. The auctioneers cannot trace Mr. Boston, so if you know of anyone of that description who has just acquired three pedigree Wessex Saddleback Gilts

F   —the £25 reward could be yours, or at least bacon for breakfast. Goodnight."

Now there is a real Mr. Boston of Rugeley, who is quite unconnected with the rogue. He is Mr. Alfred Robert Boston who is a farmer in Rugeley. He sues Bagshaw & Sons for libel. He complains that the letter of Sept. 21, to the auctioneers and the broadcast of Sept. 28 were libels on him: because, so he

G   says, people understood them to refer to him. No evidence was called in confirmation of this.

I can well understand how annoying it must have been for the plaintiff to have the name " Boston of Rugeley " used in this way by a rogue and for it to have been broadcast as it was; but it does not follow that he has any cause of action. He must first show that the letter and the broadcast were defamatory

H   of him. I doubt myself whether they were reasonably capable of being understood to refer to him. I should have thought that any ordinary person reading the letter or hearing the broadcast would have realised that some rogue must have given a fictitious or fraudulent name. No reasonable person would think it referred to the plaintiff, a well known farmer, for there could be no difficulty in tracing him. Nevertheless the judge must have thought it was just capable of

I   being understood to refer to the plaintiff, for he left to the jury the question, both in regard to the letter and to the broadcast: Was it defamatory of the plaintiff? To each they answered: Yes. I am ready to assume for the purposes of this judgment that that answer was correct and cannot be disturbed.

The next question is, however, whether the words were published on occasions that were privileged. As to the letter to the auctioneers, I am clearly of opinion that the occasion was privileged. The rogue who stole the pigs would try and dispose of them as soon as he could. He would not wish to be caught with them in his possession. He would probably take them off to some other market and

sell them. It was, I should have thought, the public duty of Mr. Naylor to warn A
other auctioneers of the position so that they should not be induced to handle
the pigs. It might indeed help catch the thief. At any rate it was a matter in
which the auctioneers had a common interest fit to be protected.

As to the television broadcast, there might have been some difficulty at
common law in holding that the occasion was privileged. The case of *Chapman*
v. *Lord Ellesmere* (1), made it very difficult for a newspaper to claim privilege. B
Likewise with a television broadcast. But the common law position has been
altered very much by the Defamation Act, 1952. Section 7 (1) and s. 9 (2) of
the Act of 1952 give a privilege to newspapers and to broadcasts for many
matters of public concern. In particular para. 12 in the Schedule gives a qualified
privilege to

> " A copy or fair and accurate report or summary of any notice or other   C
> matter issued for the information of the public by or on behalf of any
> government department, officer of state, local authority or chief officer of
> police."

Counsel for the plaintiff argued that the notice in this case was issued not on
behalf of the chief officer of police but on behalf of the auctioneers. It was done, D
he said, so as to give publicity to their offer of a reward of £25; and he relied
for this argument on some answers given by Mr. Peck, the chief constable of
Staffordshire. Reading the evidence as a whole, however, I have no doubt the
notice was issued on behalf of the police in the course of their duty to try and
find a criminal. The announcement of a reward (even though it was a reward
offered by the auctioneers) was a reasonable incident in the course of their duty.

Next counsel for the plaintiff argued that this case was excepted from the E
privilege because of s. 7 (3) of the Act of 1952, which excepts a matter " which
is not of public concern and the publication of which is not for the public benefit ".
Counsel agreed that the great train robbery or the theft of the world cup might
be of public concern and the publication would be for the public benefit; but
he said that a small crime like this would not be. I cannot agree with counsel
for the plaintiff's suggestion at all. It seems to me that, in regard to most crimes, F
if not all crimes, and certainly such a crime as this, it is perfectly proper for the
police to take steps by means of newspaper announcements or broadcasts to give
information to the public so as to try and find the criminal: and, as such, publication is privileged by reason of the Act of Parliament. It is no doubt possible that
on some occasions innocent people may be affected by it, especially when there
are two people of the same name or a rogue gives a false name; but that is a G
misfortune which an innocent person must endure for the sake of the public
good. He can immediately ask for an explanation to be given and the position
made clear, see s. 7 (2) of the Act of 1952; but that is all. Save for that protection,
the occasion is privileged. The publication is only a libel if it is actuated by
malice.

I hold, therefore, in agreement with the judge, that both these occasions were H
privileged. That leaves the issue whether the defendants were actuated by
malice or not.

On this point I must point out that the plaintiff himself made a most unfounded
charge of malice against the auctioneers. He went so far as to say that the
auctioneers fabricated the whole story about the man " Boston " of Rugeley.
They made it up, he said, so as to injure him, the real Mr. Boston of Rugeley,   I
because he had ceased to deal with them and had taken his custom elsewhere.
Counsel for the defendants castigated that suggestion as a " monstrous " suggestion. It was said that counsel's conduct was itself evidence of malice. I do
not think so at all. I think his conduct was perfectly justifiable. It was indeed
a monstrous suggestion for the plaintiff to make. No such suggestion was made
in the pleadings and there was not a shred of evidence to warrant it. On the

---

(1) [1932] All E.R. Rep. 221; [1932] 2 K.B. 431.

A contrary there was positive evidence that the defendants had no wish to injure the plaintiff at all. There was overwhelming evidence to show that these auctioneers, when they reported the matter to the police, told them: " The man who bid for the pigs gave his name as Boston of Rugeley, but it was not Bob Boston of Rugeley, that is, it was not the plaintiff. He is a very well known farmer and we know it was not him." This very point was put to the jury.

B They were asked:

> " Did the defendants prior to the broadcast inform the police that they were satisfied that the plaintiff had not stolen the pigs."

They answered: " Yes." In the face of that finding it is very difficult to see that the defendants were actuated by malice. By making that statement to the

C police, they made it clear that the plaintiff was in no way implicated.

Counsel for the plaintiff said that there was evidence of malice in a few incidents which he drew to our attention. He complained that the judge had not put certain points to the jury and had misdirected them on other matters. He also suggested that the judge ought to have followed a dictum of Lord Porter in *Turner* v. *Metro-Goldwyn-Mayer Pictures, Ltd.* (2). The judge, he said, ought to

D have put each piece of evidence of malice to the jury: and told them that they could act on it, even though there was very strong evidence to negative malice. I do not think that it was necessary for the judge to direct the jury in that way. He was entitled to leave the question of malice at large to them. And as to the suggested omissions and misdirections, I reject them altogether. It is wrong to go through a summing-up in minute detail and subject it to a lot of verbal

E criticisms. A judge need not draw the attention of the jury to every incident that has been mentioned by counsel. The judge here opened his summing-up by telling the jury that he would deal only with the matters which he thought important and that they were at liberty to look at other matters if they so wished which had been explored by counsel. I see no justification whatever for the suggestion that the summing-up was unbalanced or unfair.

F That is the end of the case. The occasions being privileged and there being no malice, the plaintiff must fail. The jury, of course, did not know that the occasions were privileged. They did not realise that if they found no malice, the plaintiff would lose. They no doubt hoped he would win. They assessed damages in all of £11,000 in case he should succeed. When they found that he lost and got nothing, they sought to go back on their finding of no malice. It

G was then too late. Their finding of " no malice " was a true finding in accordance with the evidence: and on it the law is clear. The plaintiff fails.

In the circumstances there is no need for me to go into a further point on which the judge decided in favour of the defendants. Seeing that the defendants told the police that the plaintiff was not implicated, it follows that they did not authorise the police or the broadcasting people to impute that the plaintiff was

H implicated. On this point I would agree with the judge. The defendants did not authorise any broadcast which defamed the plaintiff.

In my opinion the judgment which the judge gave at the conclusion of the case was perfectly correct and I would dismiss the appeal.

HARMAN, L.J.: I agree. Notwithstanding the strenuous advocacy of counsel for the plaintiff I think that this is an unarguable case. The words

I complained of were, no doubt, defamatory words in themselves, but that they were defamatory of the plaintiff I cannot see. I think that that should not have been left to the jury, but the question was left, and the jury being, I daresay, rather simple-minded people, thinking they were defamatory words, might omit the particulars at the end, namely, " of the plaintiff ". However that may be, they found that the words were defamatory of the plaintiff.

The judge then found on the facts (and I think he was entitled so to find)

---

(2) [1950] 1 All E.R. 449 at p. 455.

that these wore occasions which were privileged. They were first privileged **A** under common law in the case of the letter because the persons to whom the letter was written had an interest to receive it. As to the second, I agree with LORD DENNING, M.R., that they fit exactly into the Defamation Act, 1952, and the Schedule, having been issued on behalf of a chief officer of police. The argument that it was not issued by the police, but by the defendants seems to me to fail absolutely.   **B**

The occasions being, therefore, privileged, and the jury having negatived malice, that is the end of the case, but I should not like to leave it without saying that I view with distaste and disapproval the extraordinary attack developed on the defendants in the course of the case. It did not arise out of anything in the pleadings at all, but out of suggestions that they had fabricated the entire story from beginning to end with a view to sharpening the teeth of **C** their malice against the plaintiff. There was no justification whatever for those sort of allegations which should never have been made and I think it was a great pity that they were allowed to be made and persisted in.

However that may be, the judge, in a very long and careful summing-up, which only erred, if at all, on the ground of prolixity, put everything that he should have put before the jury, and the criticism that he did not dot the i's **D** and cross the t's in a few places is quite by the way in a case of this length. In my opinion the plaintiff had every patience expended on him, perhaps more than he deserved. He deserved to fail and the appeal ought to be dismissed.

DIPLOCK, L.J.: This is an ordinary simple case of libel. It took fifteen days to try: the summing-up lasted for a day: the jury returned thirteen **E** special verdicts. The notice of appeal sets out seven separate grounds why the appeal should be allowed and ten more why a new trial should be granted, the latter being split up into over forty sub-grounds. The respondents' notice contained fifteen separate grounds. The costs must be enormous. Lawyers should be ashamed that they have allowed the law of defamation to have become bogged down in such a mass of technicalities that this should be possible. **F**

I agree with my lords that this was a simple case. The issues were simple and I do not find it necessary to add anything to what has been said by LORD DENNING, M.R., except particularly to echo his expression of his view as to the submission that what LORD PORTER in *Turner* v. *Metro-Goldwyn-Mayer Pictures, Ltd.* (3) described as the principle to be applied when the House of Lords was seeing whether there was any evidence fit to be left to a jury on an issue of **G** malice should form a part of every summing-up to a jury on this issue. If that were done, the jury would be even more bemused than they usually are by the summing-up.

I think that the judge's summing-up was perfectly right and none of the criticisms directed against it is valid.

Appeal dismissed. **H**

Solicitors: *Gregory, Rowcliffe & Co.*, agents for *F. S. Hawthorn & Son*, Uttoxeter (for the plaintiff); *Collyer-Bristow & Co.*, agents for *Wilkins & Thompson*, Uttoxeter (for the defendants).

[*Reported by* F. GUTTMAN, ESQ., *Barrister-at-Law.*]

I

---

(3) [1950] 1 All E.R. at p. 455.

A   COBB & CO., LTD. AND OTHERS *v.* KROPP.
COBB & CO., LTD. AND OTHERS *v.* HILEY AND ANOTHER.

[PRIVY COUNCIL (Lord Morris of Borth-y-Gest, Lord Guest, Lord Devlin, Lord
Upjohn and Lord Wilberforce), March 28, 29, 30, May 24, 1966.]

B   *Privy Council—Australia—Queensland—Statute—Powers of legislature—Acts
conferring authority on Commissioner for Transport to license road services
and to fix and exact licence fees—Validity—Whether legislature thereby
purported to delegate sovereign powers, i.e., of taxation, to commissioner—
State Transport Facilities Acts, 1946-1959—State Transport Act of 1960.*

In April, 1964, the six appellant companies sued the respondent, as nominal
defendant for the government of Queensland, for the return of moneys levied
C   as fees for licences and permits purported to have been issued to the appellants
under the State Transport Facilities Acts, 1946 to 1959. These Acts conferred powers on the Commissioner for Transport, whose decisions were
subject to confirmation by the Minister of Transport; and among the
powers was that of deciding as to licensing road services for the carriage of
persons and goods, as to the terms of licences and the amount of licence fees.
D   Fees collected were paid into the consolidated revenue fund. The appellants
claimed that the Acts had not at any time been valid or in lawful operation.
The respondent demurred that the claim was bad in law. A similar issue was
raised by five of the appellants in relation to the State Transport Act of 1960.
It was contended* that the statutes unlawfully and unconstitutionally
delegated to the Commissioner for Transport sovereign powers of the legis-
E   lature of Queensland to impose and levy taxes, or transferred or abdicated
such power in favour of the commissioner; it was also further contended
that the Transport Acts had not been enacted in accordance with s. 3† of the
Constitution Act Amendment Act, 1934, in that the commissioner was
another legislative body, and had been purportedly set up without the
referendum required by s. 3.
F   **Held:** the legislature of Queensland were entitled to use any subordinate
agency or machinery that they considered appropriate for carrying out
objects and purposes that they designated and, in using the Commissioner
for Transport as their instrument to fix and recover the licence and permit
fees, they were not abrogating their power to levy taxes nor transferring it
to the commissioner, nor had they, by the Transport Acts, given away or
G   relinquished their taxing powers, but they retained their capacity and
control in that they could at any time repeal the legislation; accordingly,
and also despite the contention raised on s. 3 of the Act of 1934, the Transport
Acts were not invalid (see p. 920, letter I, and p. 921, letters D, E and G, post).

R. v. Burah ((1878), 3 App. Cas. 889) considered.

Dictum of SIR BARNES PEACOCK in *Hodge* v. *R.* ((1883), 9 App. Cas. at
H   p. 132) applied.

Per CURIAM: the phrase " peace, welfare and good government " is one
which is habitually employed to denote the plenitude of sovereign legislative
power (see *McCawley* v. *R.* [1920] A.C. 691, at p. 714), and within certain
limits the power to legislate for the peace, welfare and good government of
the State of Queensland (originally conferred by cl. 2 of an Order in Council
I   of June 6, 1859) is full and plenary (see p. 919, letters C and D, post).

Appeal dismissed.

[**Editorial Note.** In regard to the phrase " peace, welfare and good government, see *The Bribery Comr.* v. *Ranasinghe* ([1964] 2 All E.R. 786, at p. 791,
letter G). The present decision should be considered with *Western Transport
Pty., Ltd.* v. *Kropp* ([1964] 3 All E.R. 722).

* See p. 915, letter I, to p. 916, letter E, post, where these contentions are fully stated.
† See p. 917, letters B to D, post.

As to the application of the doctrine of repugnancy to the legislation of A
Australian States, see 5 HALSBURY'S LAWS (3rd Edn.) 474, para. 1051; as to
the establishment of responsible government in the State of Queensland, see
ibid., pp. 505, 506, para. 1108.]

Cases referred to:

Baxter v. Taxation Comrs., (1907), 4 C.L.R. 1087; 8 Digest (Repl.) 833, *1466.
Hodge v. R., (1883), 9 App. Cas. 117; 53 L.J.P.C. 1; 50 L.T. 301; 8 Digest   B
   (Repl.) 703, 113.
Initiative and Referendum Act, Re, [1919] A.C. 935; 88 L.J.P.C. 143; sub
   nom., Re Manitoba Initiative and Referendum Act, 121 L.T. 651; 8
   Digest (Repl.) 733, 271.
McCawley v. R., [1920] A.C. 691; 89 L.J.P.C. 130; 123 L.T. 177; 8 Digest   C
   (Repl.) 760, 310.
Powell v. Apollo Candle Co., Ltd., (1885), 10 App. Cas. 282; 54 L.J.P.C. 7;
   53 L.T. 638; 8 Digest (Repl.) 699, 87.
R. v. Burah, (1878), 3 App. Cas. 889; 8 Digest (Repl.) 764, 317.
Western Transport Pty., Ltd. v. Kropp, Marenoa Transport Pty., Ltd. v. Kropp,
   [1964] 3 All E.R. 722; [1965] A.C. 914; [1964] 3 W.L.R. 1082; Digest   D
   Supp.

Appeal.

These were consolidated appeals from judgments of the Full Court of the
Supreme Court of Queensland (STABLE, GIBBS and HART, JJ.) dated Apr. 14,
1965, and June 18, 1965, respectively allowing the demurrer of the respondent
(in the second case, of the respondents) against the appellants' claim for repay- E
ment of moneys levied by the respondent, Norman Eggert Kropp, under the
State Transport Facilities Acts, 1946 to 1959, and the State Transport Act
of 1960 (hereinafter referred to as " the Transport Acts ") in respect of the
carriage of goods and passengers on motor vehicles operated by the appellants
in the State of Queensland, and dismissing the respective appellants' actions
with costs. In the first action, the six appellant companies, Cobb & Co., Ltd., F
Downs Transport Pty., Ltd., South Queensland Transport Pty., Ltd., Northern
Downs Transport Pty., Ltd., Northern Transport Pty., Ltd., and Cobb & Co.
Coaches Pty., Ltd. sued the respondent Norman Eggert Kropp as nominal
defendant for the government of Queensland appointed pursuant to the Claims
Against Government Act of 1866, and as holder of the office of Commissioner for
Transport pursuant to the State Transport Act of 1960. In the second action the G
first five named appellants sued the first respondent the Hon. Thomas Alfred
Hiley as nominal defendant for the government of Queensland and the second
respondent Norman Eggert Kropp as Commissioner for Transport. The appellants'
statements of claim alleged that moneys paid to the respective respondents had
been levied in the guise of licensing or permit fees under the provisions of the
Transport Acts in respect of the carriage of goods and passengers on motor   H
vehicles operated by the appellants in the State of Queensland. The respondents
demurred to the whole of the claim on the ground that there was no cause of
action since the Transport Acts had at all material times been good and valid
law within the competence of the legislature of Queensland. By orders dated
May 11 and June 18, 1965, the Full Court of the Supreme Court of Queensland I
granted the appellants leave to appeal to Her Majesty in Council from the
judgments of the Full Court allowing the demurrers. The statements of claim,
the demurrers thereto and the relevant facts and statutes are referred to in the
judgment of the Board.

J. G. Le Quesne, Q.C., and Mervyn Heald for the appellants.
A. L. Bennett, Q.C., (of the New South Wales Bar) and R. A. Gatehouse for the
respondents.

A   **LORD MORRIS OF BORTH-Y-GEST:** These two appeals, which were consolidated pursuant to an order of the Judicial Committee dated Nov. 29, 1965, are from two judgments of the Supreme Court of Queensland respectively dated Apr. 14, 1965, and June 18, 1965, in two actions which were brought for the repayment and recovery of licence and permit fees.

B   The first action was commenced by writ of summons with statement of claim endorsed thereon dated Apr. 28, 1964. The six appellant companies joined as plaintiffs and brought their claims against the respondent, Mr. Kropp, as nominal defendant for the government of Queensland appointed pursuant to " The Claims against Government Act " of 1866 and as the Commissioner for Transport. The claims were for the repayment of various amounts, which the respective appellant companies had paid to the respondent and which had been levied by

C   him " in the guise of licensing or permit fees under the provisions of ' The State Transport Facilities Acts, 1946 to 1955 ' and ' The State Transport Facilities Acts, 1946 to 1959 ', in respect of the carriage of goods and passengers on motor vehicles operated by [the appellants] in the State of Queensland ". Shortly stated the basis of the claims (which were claims for money had and received to the use of the appellants) was that the amounts had been demanded by the respondent

D   unlawfully under colour of office of " The Commissioner for Transport in that the Transport Acts referred to ' had not at any time valid or lawful operation ' ".

The respondent on May 25, 1964, demurred to the statement of claim on the grounds that it was bad in law and did not show any cause of action. It is sufficient for present purposes to refer to one of the grounds of the demurrer. It was that the State Transport Facilities Acts, 1946 to 1959, were, or alternatively so far as

E   material were, at all material times good and valid law and were at all material times in operation. It should however be mentioned that another ground was that The State Transport Facilities Acts, 1946 to 1959, were as at all material times validated and made operative other than s. 49, s. 50, s. 51 and, so far as it relates to carriage by water, s. 55, by the Transport Laws Validation Act of 1962. The demurrer was heard and argued on June 18, 1964, and on Feb. 23

F   and 24, 1965, before the Full Court of the Supreme Court of Queensland (STABLE, GIBBS and HART, JJ.). By their judgment on Apr. 14, 1965, the demurrer was allowed and the respondent was awarded his costs of the demurrer and of the action. By their order dated May 11, leave to appeal to Her Majesty in Council was granted.

The second action, brought by five of the appellant companies as plaintiffs,

G   was commenced, by writ of summons (with statement of claim specially indorsed) dated Feb. 8, 1965. The first respondent [The Hon. Thomas Alfred Hiley] was sued as the nominal defendant for the government of Queensland and the respondent, Mr. Kropp, was sued as the holder of the office of The Commissioner for Transport under the provisions of " The State Transport Act of 1960 ". The basis of the claims which were made (being claims for fees paid)

H   was similar to that in the first action, save that the impugned legislation, which was said not to be a valid and effective statute within the competence of the legislature of Queensland, was " The State Transport Act of 1960 ".

Particulars were given of the grounds of the allegation that the Act of 1960 was not valid or effective. As these grounds (so far as now relevant) summarise the main submissions which have been presented by the appellants in these

I   appeals it will be convenient to refer to them. They were:

" The said statute, if valid:
(1) would unlawfully and unconstitutionally delegate to the Commissioner for Transport the sovereign powers of the legislature of Queensland—
   (a) to impose and levy taxes (in the guise of license and permit fees) in his virtually unrestricted and unfettered discretion and in so doing would violate the principle that no tax may be imposed save with the full assent of Parliament and the assent of the Crown.

    (b) to repeal, alter and amend the taxes imposed by him and to sub-   **A**
        stitute other taxes therefor.

    (c) to enact or determine as a self-contained legislative body or organ
        matters of substantive law as between the citizen and the State
        in his unrestricted and unfettered discretion without the sanction
        or supervision of Parliament or the Governor-in-Council or the
        courts of justice of the State contrary to law and in particular   **B**
        contrary to the provisions of s. 3 of ' The Constitution Act Amend-
        ment Act of 1934 '.

(2) would constitute an unlawful and unconstitutional transfer of sovereign
    power of the legislature to the said commissioner or an abdication of
    such power in his favour.

(3) would confer on the said commissioner a power of dispensing individuals   **C**
    from compliance with or observance of the law conditionally or un-
    conditionally in his discretion and a power to differentiate between
    individuals.

(4) would give to each determination of the said commissioner and of the
    Governor-in-Council of a monetary nature the legal effect of a ' Money
    Bill ' duly passed and assented to without compliance with the require-   **D**
    ments of law and of parliamentary usage in respect of such bills and
    without the royal assent.

(5) would confer on the said commissioner a power of regulating ' supply ',
    which is an exclusive power of Parliament and in dispensing with pay-
    ment of fees a power of appropriating public moneys.

(6) would confer on the Governor-in-Council and the Commissioner for   **E**
    Transport indirect power of repeal of the Act or some of the provisions
    thereof."

The respondents demurred to the statement of claim on the grounds that it was
bad in law and did not show any cause of action for the reason that The State
Transport Act of 1960 was a good and valid and effective law within the com-   **F**
petence of the legislature of Queensland. The demurrer came on for hearing
before the Full Court of the Supreme Court of Queensland (HANGER, GIBBS
and HART, JJ.) on June 18, 1965. In view of the decision in the first action the
appellants did not and did not wish to submit further arguments to the court.
No separate or further judgment dealing with the Act of 1960 was sought. The
demurrer was allowed with costs and leave to appeal to Her Majesty in Council   **G**
was granted.

It will be seen that the first action relates to The State Transport Facilities
Act, 1946 (the amendments made in later acts from time to time up to 1959
do not call for special notice) while the second action relates to The State Transport Act of 1960. There are differences between the two Acts, which were the
subject of careful detailed analysis in the argument presented to their lordships'   **H**
Board. In particular it was submitted that under the Act of 1960 the Commissioner is subject to less control than under the earlier Act. The main question
of principle that is raised is however common to the two actions. It was submitted
by the appellants that both the Act of 1946 and the Act of 1960 were invalid
and void for the reason that the Queensland legislature had no power to legislate
as they did.   **I**

It was submitted that the various Acts were invalid because they set up the
Commissioner for Transport as a new legislative power with wide or sovereign
authority to make decisions concerning the imposition of taxes (in the form of
fees) and to make decisions as to the range and incidence of such taxes: and that
the various Acts were invalid, because they sought to impose taxes and levy them
without parliamentary sanction and in so doing violated a long-established
principle that no tax may be imposed save with the full assent of Parliament and
of the Crown, and that the Transport Laws Validation Act, 1962, could not cure so

A   fundamental an invalidity. In particular it was urged that the legislature is
     endowed constitutionally with an exclusive power of taxation, and that by the
     Acts in question the legislature had purported to abrogate its power. As a variant
     or possibly as an extension of the main argument it was submitted that The Facili-
     ties Acts (meaning thereby The State Transport Facilities Acts, 1946 to 1959)
     and the Act of 1960 had not been enacted in accordance with s. 3 of The Constitu-
B   tion Act Amendment Act, 1934. Since the year 1922 the Parliament or legislature
     of Queensland has been constituted by Her Majesty and the legislative assembly of
     Queensland in Parliament assembled. Prior to that time there had also been a
     legislative council. The Act of 1934 was an Act to amend the constitution of
     Queensland by providing (inter alia) that a legislative council or other similar
     legislative body should not be restored or constituted or established unless or
C   until a referendum of the electors should so approve. Section 3 (1) of the Act
     provided that the Parliament (or legislature) of Queensland should not be altered

> " in the direction of providing for the restoration and/or constitution and/
> or establishment of another legislative body (whether called the ' Legislative
> Council ' or by any other name or designation in addition to the Legislative
D   Assembly) except in the manner "

     which was provided for—which was by referendum. It was contended that the
     setting up of a Commissioner for Transport constituted the establishment of
     " another legislative body ".
          The State Transport Facilities Act, 1946, was an Act to provide for the
     improvement and extension of transport facilities within the state. As already
E   mentioned there were various amending Acts. The State Transport Act of 1960
     was an Act to consolidate and amend the law relating to transport. It repealed
     The State Transport Facilities Acts, 1946 to 1959. Following on certain litigation
     the Transport Laws Validation Act was passed in 1962. The course of proceedings
     and of events concerning this latter Act was referred to in the judgment of their
     lordships' Board in *Western Transport Pty., Ltd.* v. *Kropp* (1).
F   It was provided by the Act of 1946 that the Act was to be administered by
     the Minister (usually the Minister for Transport) and subject to the Minister by
     the Commissioner for Transport (see s. 8). The latter was to be appointed from
     time to time by the Governor in Council (see s. 9). A determination or decision
     of the commissioner was to be submitted to the Minister for his confirmation
     (see s. 16 (2)). As STABLE, J., expressed it the commissioner had " a parliamentary
G   hand on his shoulder ". The commissioner had the duty of regulating and
     controlling carriage within the state with a view to ensuring that such transport
     facilities would be available as were reasonably adequate to meet the convenience
     and requirements of the public for the carriage of persons and goods (see s. 18).
     He had certain powers to license services for the carriage of passengers and goods
     (see s. 19 and s. 27) and certain protection from proceedings in respect of his
H   decisions concerning licences (see s. 20). Section 24 laid down conditions under
     which it was lawful to use vehicles on roads. Under this section the commissioner
     had certain powers of decision and was entrusted with the exercise of discretion
     (see s. 3, s. 4, s. 9, s. 21, s. 23). Section 31 and s. 32 gave the commissioner powers
     to decide as to the duration and the terms and conditions of licences. A licensing
     fee of the amount or at the rate determined by the commissioner was payable by
I   every licensee (see s. 35 (1)). Other subsections of s. 35 gave powers of determina-
     tion to the commissioner (see s. 2, s. 3, s. 4, s. 5). Other sections (such as s. 36,
     s. 37, s. 44, s. 56, s. 58) endowed the commissioner with varying powers of decision.
          Revenues (fees and moneys collected) derived under the Act were to be paid
     into and to form part of the consolidated revenue fund and administration costs
     and expenses were to be paid out of moneys appropriated by Parliament from
     time to time (see s. 22). Under s. 70 the commissioner was required to present an

---

(1) [1964] 3 All E.R. 722; [1965] A.C. 914.

annual report setting out particulars of action taken under the Act and any general   A
information regarding matters relating to state transport as he should think
desirable.

It has been necessary to refer in general to the provisions of the Act of 1946
for the purpose of giving consideration to the contentions of the appellants.
There is no doubt that the fees imposed under the Act of 1946 (and under the
Act of 1960) are to be regarded as constituting taxation. Accordingly it was   B
submitted by the appellants that in legislating in the terms of the Act of 1946
the Queensland legislature had abrogated its exclusive power of levying taxation.
The circumstance that within the terms of the Act of 1946 the commissioner had
a discretion which enabled him to decide which transport operators would pay
fees and which would not, and the circumstance that the commissioner could
under certain conditions fix fees at rates which varied as between one operator   C
and another, showed, it was submitted, that the legislature had abrogated a
function which was exclusively its own. Additionally it was submitted that the
provisions of s. 70 would not enable the legislature to possess such adequate
information as would or could result in the exercise of effective control by the
legislature.

The argument submitted by the appellants recognised that under the Act of   D
1946 (and the State Transport Facilities Acts, 1946 to 1959) a determination or
decision of the commissioner had to be submitted to the Minister for his confirmation. It was contended however that an examination of The State Transport
Act of 1960 (the Act of 1960) showed t' at the commissioner was subject to less
control than under the earlier Acts and in particular that the Act of 1960 contained no provision corresponding to s. 16 (2) of the Act of 1946. The sections   E
in the Act of 1960, under which there was a " permit " system, were examined in
detail in the arguments submitted by the appellants with a view to showing
that the commissioner was given power to decide whether charges should be
imposed or not, and power to decide the amounts of charges imposed, and power
to decide as to which operators should pay and which should not and power to
fix the rates which individual operators should pay. It was further contended   F
that an examination of the provisions of the Act (the Act of 1960) showed that
no effective day-to-day control of the commissioner could be exercised either by
the Minister or by the legislature. For those reasons, if they were established, it
was contended that the legislature had abrogated and indeed had transferred
powers which were exclusive to itself and that legislation purporting so to do
was void.   G

These contentions make it necessary for their lordships to refer to the powers
of the Queensland legislature. As has already been mentioned prior to 1922 there
was a legislative council as well as a legislative assembly. By cl. 2 of the Order in
Council of June 6, 1859 (made pursuant to the Act 18 and 19 Vict. c. 54 (2))
it was provided that:

" within the said colony of Queensland Her Majesty shall have power by   H
and with the advice and consent of the said council and assembly to make
laws for the peace, welfare and good government of the colony in all cases
whatsoever."

There was however a proviso to the clause that

" all Bills for appropriating any part of the public revenue for imposing   I
any new rate tax or impost subject always to the limitations hereinafter
provided "

should originate in the legislative assembly. Section 2 of the Constitution
Act, 1867, was in similar terms to s. 2 of the Order in Council. By the Constitution Act Amendment Act of 1922 the legislative council of Queensland was
abolished and the Parliament of Queensland (or as sometimes called the legislature

(2) The New South Wales Constitution Act, 1855.

A of Queensland) was constituted " by His Majesty the King and the legislative assembly of Queensland in Parliament assembled ". The controversy which arose in 1885 concerning the question whether the legislative council had power to amend money bills is of historical interest, but has no substantial bearing on the questions raised in these appeals. As related by SIR SAMUEL GRIFFITH, C.J., in his judgment in *Baxter* v. *Taxation Comrs.* (3), an address was presented to

B Her Majesty praying that certain questions might be submitted for the opinion of the Privy Council. There was a report to Her Majesty which upheld the supremacy of the legislative assembly as regards bills of aid and supply. The report negatived the claim of the legislative council to amend such bills.

Inasmuch as Her Majesty has power by and with the advice and consent of the legislative assembly of Queensland to make laws for the peace welfare and

C good government of the State of Queensland it would seem surprising if the enactment of the various Transport Acts now being considered was not within such power. The phrase " peace, welfare and good government " is one that is

" habitually employed to denote the plenitude of sovereign legislative power, even though that power be confined to certain subjects or within certain reservations "

D (see *McCawley* v. *R.* (4)). Within certain limits, which do not here call for full mention or consideration, the power to legislate for the peace, welfare and good government of the State of Queensland is full and plenary. As already stated the basis of the argument on behalf of the appellants was that the effect of the Acts was to create a new legislative authority and that this could not constitu-

E tionally be achieved.

In their lordships' opinion the argument wholly fails. It cannot rationally be said that there was any abandonment or abdication of power in favour of a newly created legislative authority. In *R.* v. *Burah* (5) a question arose as to the powers of the Indian Legislature. In delivering the judgment of the Board LORD SELBORNE said (6):

F   " The Indian Legislature has powers expressly limited by the Act of the Imperial Parliament which created it, and it can, of course, do nothing beyond the limits which circumscribe these powers. But, when acting within those limits, it is not in any sense an agent or delegate of the Imperial Parliament, but has, and was intended to have, plenary powers of legislation, as large, and of the same nature, as those of Parliament itself."

G LORD SELBORNE further said (7):

" Their lordships agree that the Governor-General in Council could not, by any form of enactment, create in India, and arm with general legislative authority a new legislative power, not created or authorised by the Councils' Act."

H In their lordships' view nothing comparable with " a new legislative power " armed with " general legislative authority " has been created by the passing by the Queensland legislature of the various Transport Acts. The circumstance that the commissioner was endowed with certain powers of decision and measures of discretion does not in any realistic sense support the contention that the Queensland legislature exceeded its plenary and ample powers. It was pointed

I out in the judgment of the Board in *Hodge* v. *R.* (8) that, when the British North America Act enacted that there should be a legislature for Ontario and that its legislative assembly should have exclusive authority to make laws for the province and for provincial purposes in relation to enumerated matters, it conferred powers not in any sense to be exercised by delegation from or as agents of the Imperial Parliament but authority " as plenary and as ample " within the

(3) (1907), 4 C.L.R. 1087 at pp. 1106, 1107.   (4) [1920] A.C. 691.
(5) (1878), 3 App. Cas. 889.   (6) (1878), 3 App. Cas. at p. 904.
(7) (1878), 3 App. Cas. at p. 905.   (8) (1883), 9 App. Cas. 117.

prescribed limits as the Imperial Parliament in the plenitude of its power possessed A
and could bestow.   Within those limits there was full authority

> " to confide to a municipal institution or body of its own creation authority
> to make by-laws or resolutions as to subjects specified in the enactment
> and with the object of carrying the enactment into operation and effect."

In the judgment of the Board it was said (9):   B

> " It is obvious that such an authority is ancillary to legislation, and without
> it an attempt to provide for varying details and machinery to carry them
> out might become oppressive, or absolutely fail.   The very full and very
> elaborate judgment of the Court of Appeal contains abundance of precedents
> for this legislation, entrusting a limited discretionary authority to others,
> and has many illustrations of its necessity and convenience.   It was argued   C
> at the bar that a legislature committing important regulations to agents or
> delegates effaces itself.   That is not so.   It retains its powers intact, and
> can, whenever it pleases, destroy the agency it has created and set up
> another, or take the matter directly into his own hands.   How far it shall
> seek the aid of subordinate agencies, and how long it shall continue them,
> are matters for each legislature, and not for courts of law, to decide."   D

In *Powell* v. *Apollo Candle Co., Ltd.* (10) questions were considered comparable
to those raised in the present case.   By a section of the New South Wales Customs
Regulation Act, 1879, it was provided that if in the opinion of the collector an
article possessed properties which could be used for a purpose similar to that of a
dutiable article the governor was authorised in a manner prescribed to direct a
levy of duty upon the article at a rate to be fixed in proportion to the degree in   E
which the article approximated in its qualities or uses to such dutiable article.
In pursuance of the section an Order in Council was issued imposing a duty on
the importation of a certain article and the collector of customs required duty
to be paid.   It was contended that the section was invalid on the ground that
the legislature had exceeded its powers in enacting it.   It was argued that the
power given to the legislature to impose duties was to be executed by themselves   F
alone and could not be entrusted by them wholly or in part to the governor or
any other person or body.   The contention failed.   The cases of *R.* v. *Burah* (11)
and *Hodge* v. *R.* (12) were referred to in the judgment of the Board where it
was said (13):

> " These two cases have put an end to a doctrine which appears at one time
> to have had some currency, that a colonial legislature is a delegate of the   G
> imperial legislature.   It is a legislature restricted in the area of its powers,
> but within that area unrestricted and not acting as an agent or a delegate."

In the course of the judgment of their lordships' Board it was further said (14):

> " It is argued that the tax in question has been imposed by the governor,
> and not by the legislature, who alone had power to impose it.   But the   H
> duties levied under the Order in Council are really levied by the authority
> of the Act under which the order is issued.   The legislature has not parted
> with its perfect control over the governor, and has the power, of course, at
> any moment, of withdrawing or altering the power which they have entrusted
> to him."

In their lordships' view the Queensland legislature were fully warranted in   I
legislating in the terms of the Transport Acts now being considered.   They
preserved their own capacity intact and they retained perfect control over the
Commissioner for Transport inasmuch as they could at any time repeal the
legislation and withdraw such authority and discretion as they had vested in

---

(9) (1883), 9 App. Cas. at p. 132.   (10) (1885), 10 App. Cas. 282.
(11) (1878), 3 App. Cas. 889.   (12) (1883), 9 App. Cas. 117.
(13) (1885), 10 App. Cas. at p. 290.   (14) (1885), 10 App. Cas. at p. 291.

A him. It cannot be asserted that there was a levying of money by pretence of prerogative without grant of Parliament or without parliamentary warrant. As STABLE, J., said in his judgment in the first action:

B " Obviously Parliament cannot directly concern itself with all the multitudinous matters and considerations which necessarily arise for daily and hourly determination within the ramifications of a vast transport system in a great area in the fixing of and collection of licensing fees. So, as I see it on the face of the legislation, Parliament has lengthened its own arm by appointing a commissioner to attend to all these matters, including the fixing and gathering of the taxes which Parliament itself has seen fit to impose . . . The commissioner has not been given any power to act outside the law as laid down by Parliament. Parliament has not abdicated from any of its

C own power. It has laid down a framework, a set of bounds, within which the person holding the office created by Parliament may grant, or refrain from granting licences, and fix, assess, collect or refrain from collecting fees which are taxes."

D The legislature were entitled to use any agent or any subordinate agency or any machinery that they considered appropriate for carrying out the objects and purposes that they had in mind and which they designated. They were entitled to use the Commissioner of Transport as their instrument to fix and recover the licence and permit fees. They were not abrogating their power to levy taxes and were not transferring that power to the commissioner. What they created by the passing of the Transport Acts could not reasonably be described

E as a new legislative power or separate legislative body armed with general legislative authority (see *R.* v. *Burah* (15)). Nor did the Queensland legislature " create and endow with its own capacity a new legislative power not created by the Act to which it owes its own existence " (see *Re Initiative and Referendum Act* (16)). In no sense did the Queensland legislature assign or transfer or abrogate their powers or renounce or abdicate their responsibilities. They did not

F give away or relinquish their taxing powers. All that was done was done under and by reason of their authority. It was by virtue of their will that licence and permit fees became payable. Nor was there any alteration of the legislature " in the direction of providing for the restoration and/or constitution and/or establishment of another legislative body (whether called ' the legislative council ' or by any other name or designation in addition to the legislative assembly) "

G (see s. 3 of the Constitution Act Amendment Act of 1934).

Without referring further to " The Transport Laws Validation Act of 1962 " their lordships consider that the attack on the validity of the Transport Acts fails. Their lordships are in agreement with the decisions of the Supreme Court and accordingly they will humbly advise Her Majesty that the appeals should be dismissed. The appellants must pay the respondents' costs.

H   *Appeal dismissed.*

Solicitors: *Blyth, Dutton, Wright & Bennett* (for the appellants); *Freshfields* (for the respondents).

[*Reported by* KATHLEEN J. H. O'BRIEN, *Barrister-at-Law.*]

I

---

(15) (1878), 3 App. Cas. 889.   (16) [1919] A.C. 935 at p. 945.

PAUL & FRANK, LTD. AND ANOTHER v. DISCOUNT   A
BANK (OVERSEAS), LTD. AND ANOTHER.

[CHANCERY DIVISION (Pennycuick, J.), May 12, 13, 16, 17, 1966.]

Company—Charge—Registration—Charge on book debts—Letter of authority
authorising moneys payable under exports guarantee policy to be paid to bank
—Foreign buyers unable to meet bill of exchange discounted by bank—Amount   B
of bill of exchange was price payable by foreign buyers on export sale within
policy—Liquidation of vendor company—Whether letter of authority was a
charge on vendor company's book debts so as to be void as against liquidator
for want of registration—Companies Act, 1948 (11 & 12 Geo. 6 c. 38), s. 59 (1),
(2) (e).

In January, 1961 the plaintiff company completed a letter of authority   C
to the second defendant, the Board of Trade Export Credits Guarantee
Dept. (" E.C.G.") in the standard E.C.G. form authorising E.C.G. to pay
direct to the first defendant Discount Bank (Overseas), Ltd. (" Discount ")
any moneys which might become payable under a policy then in preparation
for insurance of the liabilities of foreign customers of the plaintiff company.
Particulars of this letter, as creating a charge on book debts within s. 95 (2) (e)*   D
of the Companies Act, 1948, were not registered. On Jan. 27, 1961, Discount
discounted a bill of exchange accepted by foreign purchasers of goods from
the plaintiff company and paid to the plaintiff company £4,212 2s. 10d.
The E.C.G. policy was completed on Mar. 8, 1961. By it the guarantors,
in consideration of a premium, agreed to pay to the plaintiff company sixty
per cent. of the amount of any loss sustained in connexion with export   E
transactions including this sale of goods. The bill of exchange was not met
on presentment in May, 1961. In July, 1961, a petition for compulsory
winding-up of the plaintiff company was presented and a winding-up
order was made. In April, 1962, payment was made to Discount under the
policy, the foreign purchasers having become bankrupt. The plaintiff
company and the liquidator brought an action against Discount claiming   F
a declaration that the letter of authority created a charge on book debts
within s. 95 (2) (e) and that the charge was rendered void against the
liquidator by s. 95 (1). At the hearing, evidence of accountancy practice was
given, on which (a) it was common ground that the E.C.G. policy would
not be entered as a book debt in company accounts at the date of the letter
of authority, (b) the court found that the policy would not in practice be   G
entered as a book debt before the admission of liability and ascertainment
of amount, and (c) that the policy would not, in practice, be entered as a
book debt even after the admission of liability and ascertainment of amount.

Held: (i) in determining whether any charge was a charge on book debts
within s. 95 (2) (e) regard must be had to the items of property forming
the subject matter of the charge at the date of its creation, and, where the   H
item of property at that time was the benefit of a contract which did not
then comprehend a book debt, the contract could not be brought within
s. 95 merely because it might ultimately result in a book debt; in the present
case the E.C.G. policy did not comprehend any book debt at the date of
the letter of authority, and accordingly the charge created by the letter of
January, 1961, was not rendered void by s. 95 (1) for want of registration   I
(see p. 927, letters A and B, post).

Dictum of BYLES, J., in *Shipley* v. *Marshall* ((1863), 14 C.B.N.S. at p. 573)
as to the meaning of " book debt " applied.

Dictum of BUCKLEY, J., in *Independent Automatic Sales, Ltd.* v. *Knowles*
& Foster ([1962] 3 All E.R. at p. 36) distinguished.

(ii) even if the test whether there was a charge on book debts were the

---

* Section 95, so far as material, is set out at p. 925, letters E and F, post.

A   character of the obligation under the policy when liability was admitted and its amount was ascertained, yet the action would fail on the accountancy evidence (see p. 927, letter I, post.)

[As to the types of charges created by companies in relation to which registration is required, see 6 HALSBURY'S LAWS (3rd Edn.) 493, 494, para. 953; and for cases on the subject, see 10 DIGEST (Repl.) 813-815, 5272-5287.

B   For the Companies Act, 1948, s. 95, s. 96, see 3 HALSBURY'S STATUTES (2nd Edn.) 533, 536.]

Cases referred to:

Independent Automatic Sales, Ltd. v. *Knowles & Foster*, [1962] 3 All E.R. 27; [1962] 1 W.L..R 974; Digest (Cont. Vol. A) 181, *5287b*.

C   *Shipley* v. *Marshall*, (1863), 14 C.B.N.S. 566; 32 L.J.C.P. 258; 8 L.T. 430; 143 E.R. 567; 5 Digest (Repl.) 1038, *8386*.

Tailby v. *Official Receiver*, [1886-90] All E.R. Rep. 486; (1888), 13 App. Cas. 523; 58 L.J.Q.B. 75; 60 L.T. 162; 5 Digest (Repl.) 751, *6463*.

Action.

This was an action begun by writ dated Nov. 7, 1963, by the plaintiffs, Paul
D   & Frank, Ltd. and their liquidator, Kenneth Russell Cork, against both defendants, Discount Bank (Overseas), Ltd. and the Board of Trade for a declaration that the letter of authority (individual transactions) no. 282387 on form E.C.G. 85 (a) dated Jan. 23, 1961, constituted a charge on the book debts of Paul & Frank, Ltd., and a declaration that the said charge on book debts was void against the plaintiffs. There had not been registration of particulars of the charge, created
E   by the letter of authority, for the purposes of s. 95 of the Companies Act, 1948. The plaintiffs claimed secondly against the second defendants, the Board of Trade, payment to the plaintiff Kenneth Russell Cork of the sum of £2,573 15s. 6d. or in the alternative damages in the same amount. The facts are set out in the judgment.

The cases noted below* were cited during the argument in addition to those
F   referred to in the judgment.

E. D. Sutcliffe, Q.C., and *Allan Heyman* for the plaintiffs.
Michael Wheeler, Q.C., and *M. J. Mustill* for the first defendants.
A. J. Bateson for the second defendants.

PENNYCUICK, J.: By this action Paul & Frank, Ltd. (to which I will
G   refer as " the company ") and Mr. Kenneth Russell Cork, its liquidator, as plaintiffs, seek as against Discount Bank (Overseas), Ltd. (to which I will refer as " Discount ") and the Board of Trade as defendants, a declaration that a certain letter of authority dated Jan. 23, 1961, constituted a charge on the book debts of the company and, as such, is void against the plaintiffs under s. 95 of the Companies Act, 1948.

H   The course of events is not in dispute and may be shortly stated as follows. In September, 1960, the company submitted to the Board of Trade certain proposals for insurance by the Export Credits Guarantee Department (which I will refer to as " E.C.G.") of the liabilities of foreign customers of the company. On Dec. 15, 1960, the company entered into a contract with a Belgian firm known as E. T. S. Jean Robinet (to which I will refer as " Robinet ") for the
I   sale of 1,080 raw black broadtail lamb skins at the price of £4,289 12s. 6d. In payment for those goods the company sent a bill of exchange to Robinet, which Robinet accepted and returned on Dec. 22, 1960. That was a bill of exchange for £4,289 12s. 6d. maturing on May 4, 1961. The goods were in due course delivered by the company to Robinet. On Jan. 23, 1961, the company completed a letter of authority in the standard E.C.G. form, with variations, under which the company authorised E.C.G. to pay direct to Discount any moneys

* *Tuck & Sons* v. *Priester*, (1887), 19 Q.B.D. 629; *Saunderson & Co.* v. *Clark*, (1913), 29 T.L.R. 579; *Re Kent and Sussex Sawmills, Ltd.*, [1946] 2 All E.R. 638; [1947] Ch. 177.

which might become payable under a policy then in preparation. On Jan. 27   **A**
Discount discounted the bill of exchange drawn by the company and accepted
by Robinet, and paid to the company the sum of £4,212 2s. 10d. The E.C.G.
policy was finally completed on Mar. 8, 1961. Paragraph 1 of the policy runs as
follows:

> " The guarantors, in consideration of the premium paid and to be paid   **B**
> by the exporter as specified in para. 18 hereof agree, subject to the terms
> hereof, to pay to the exporter a percentage of the amount of any loss as
> hereinafter defined which he may sustain in connection with the export
> from the United Kingdom between Oct. 1, 1960, and Sept. 30, 1961, of any
> goods under a contract to which this guarantee applies by reason of the
> occurrence after the export of such goods of any of the following causes: **C**
> (i) the insolvency of the buyer as hereinafter defined, or (ii) the failure
> of the buyer to pay to the exporter within six months after due date of
> payment the gross invoice value of goods delivered to and accepted by the
> buyer . . ."

The specified percentage is sixty per cent., and the goods cover those comprised
in the sale to Robinet. Nothing has turned on the fact that the letter of authority   **D**
was signed before the execution of the policy.

Robinet was unable to meet the bill at the due date. The company made
requests to Discount for an extension of time, but Discount refused. The bill
was presented on May 4 and not met, and was protested on May 8. On July 6,
1961, a petition was presented for the compulsory winding-up of the company.
The winding-up order was made on July 24, and the second plaintiff, Mr. Cork,   **E**
was appointed liquidator on Dec. 1. The firm of Robinet became bankrupt
on Oct. 9. In April, 1962, the Board of Trade or E.C.G. made a payment to
Discount of the sum of £2,753 15s. 6d., representing the percentage of sixty
per cent. of the sum of £4,289 12s. 6d., that sum being paid against an
undertaking by Discount to which I need not refer further.

On the hearing of the action evidence was given as to accountancy practice.   **F**
No other evidence was given. The witnesses were Mr. Weiss on behalf of the
plaintiffs, Mr. Ray Smith on behalf of the first defendants, and Mr. Russell
and Mr. Gidley-Kitchin on behalf of the second defendants. All these four
gentlemen are chartered accountants of standing. The effect of their evidence
may be summarised as follows. Mr. Weiss had himself no personal experience
of E.C.G. policies, but gave evidence as to matters of accountancy principle.   **G**
The other three accountants had personal experience of E.C.G. policies and also
gave evidence as to matters of principle. All four agreed that at the date of the
letter of authority the E.C.G. policy ought not, in accordance with accountancy
principle, to be entered in the books of the company as a book debt. When I say
" in accordance with accountancy principle ", I mean in accordance with the
ordinary double-entry system adopted by accountants. The three witnesses   **H**
for the defendants also agreed that in practice such a policy never would be
entered in the books of the company. I accept that evidence.

Then as to the next stage—that is to say, after the contingency under the
policy had happened, and before the liability was accepted by E.C.G. and the
amount ascertained—Mr. Weiss deposed that, in his view, the policy ought to
have been entered in the books of the company in accordance with accountancy   **I**
principle. On the other hand, the three accountants called by the defendants
deposed that at that stage it would not be in accordance with accountancy
principle to enter the policy in the books of the company; and further, that
at that stage such a policy never is, in practice, entered in the books of a company.
I accept on this point the evidence of the accountants called for the defendants.

Then comes the final stage at which the liability under the policy has been
accepted by E.C.G. and the amount has been ascertained. Mr. Weiss considers
that as a matter of accountancy principle the policy should already have been

A entered in the books of the company: a fortiori it should be so at this stage. Mr. Ray Smith said that as a matter of principle an entry as a debt could be made, but it would be unusual.   Mr. Russell said that it could be entered as a book debt. Mr. Gidley-Kitchin said that it would be wrong to enter until the amount was agreed. All three accountants called by the defendants agreed that even at that stage it is not the practice to enter the liability of E.C.G. as a debt.   On

B that evidence I find, first, that as regards accountancy principle it would not be contrary to principle either to enter the liability of E.C.G. as a debt or not to enter it as a debt—that is to say, that, as a matter of principle, either course would be legitimate; and secondly, that as a matter of practice, the liability of E.C.G. even at that stage is not entered as a book debt by companies concerned with E.C.G. policies.   To avoid misunderstanding, I should add that all the

C accountants, either in terms or impliedly, agreed that some form of record or memorandum of the E.C.G. policy would have to be kept by the company concerned; and further, that if it so happened that a balance sheet date occurred, at any rate between the date when the liability was accepted and the amount ascertained and the actual payment by E.C.G., the rights of the company under the policy would have to be reflected in whatever is the appropriate way in the

D balance sheet in order to show the true position of the company.

I turn now to s. 95 of the Companies Act, 1948.   That section, so far as now material, runs as follows:

> " (1) Subject to the provisions of this Part of this Act, every charge created after the fixed date by a company registered in England and being a charge to which this section applies shall, so far as any security on the

E company's property or undertaking is conferred thereby, be void against the liquidator and any creditor of the company, unless the prescribed particulars of the charge together with the instrument, if any, by which the charge is created or evidenced, are delivered to or received by the registrar of companies for registration in manner required by this Act within twenty-one days after the date of its creation, but without prejudice to any contract or

F obligation for repayment of the money thereby secured, and when a charge becomes void under this section the money secured thereby shall immediately become payable. (2) This section applies to the following charges— . . . (e) a charge on book debts of the company . . . "

It is not suggested that any of the other paragraphs in sub-s. (2) are material.

G Looking at that matter for a moment apart from authority, I do not think that in ordinary speech one would describe as a book debt the right under a contingency contract as that right stands before the contingency happens. By " contingency contract " in this connexion I mean contracts of insurance, guarantee, indemnity and the like. However, this point is not free from authority and I have been referred to two cases as to what is meant by a " book debt ".

H The first case is that of Shipley v. Marshall (1).   In that case the four members of the Common Pleas Divisional Court gave judgments as to the meaning of the word " book debt ", and I will quote a few sentences from those judgments. ERLE, C.J., said (2):

> " By ' book debts ', the legislature doubtless intended to describe debts in some way connected with the trade of the bankrupt; and I am inclined

I to give the term a wider range. But it is enough to say that this was a debt connected with and growing out of the plaintiff's trade."

He finally said (3):

> " To constitute the debt a ' book debt ', it cannot to my mind be necessary that the transaction should be entered in a book."

WILLIAMS, J., said (4):

(1) (1863), 14 C.B.N.S. 566.   (2) (1863), 14 C.B.N.S. at p. 570.
(3) (1863), 14 C.B.N.S. at p. 571.   (4) (1863), 14 C.B.N.S. at pp. 571, 572.

" This, it is said, can only mean debts which are actually entered in   A
some book kept by the bankrupt in the course of his trade. I cannot,
however, accede to that construction. I think the meaning of the statute is,
that the assignees shall dispose of all debts due to the bankrupt in respect
of which entries could be made in the ordinary course of his business:
otherwise, a debt by accident omitted to be entered would not pass by the
assignment. But the difficulty which I feel in this case is to arrive at   B
the conclusion that this is a debt arising out of a transaction which in the
ordinary course of the bankrupt's business would find its way as an entry
into any of the trade-books."

WILLES, J., stated (5): " I entirely agree with my lord . . ." BYLES, J., said (6):
" I agree with WILLIAMS, J., that they must be such debts as are commonly
entered in books."   C

The other case is that of *Independent Automatic Sales, Ltd.* v. *Knowles &*
Foster (7). In that case BUCKLEY, J., had to deal with a deposit on certain
hire-purchase agreements. He said (8):

" So far as I am aware, no more precise definition of the meaning of the
term ' book debts ' has ever been attempted judicially and I shall not attempt   D
one. *Shipley* v. *Marshall* (9), I think, establishes that, if it can be said of a
debt arising in the course of a business and due or growing due to the
proprietor of that business that such a debt would or could in the ordinary
course of such a business be entered in well-kept books relating to that
business, that debt can properly be called a book debt whether it is in fact
entered in the books of the business or not."   E

There are small verbal differences in the way in which this definition is expressed
by the various judges. I do not, however, read BUCKLEY, J., as intending either
to differ from the members of the Common Pleas Divisional Court or as regarding
them as having put different definitions on the expression. A certain difficulty
is caused by the use of the words " would or could ". It will be remembered that
WILLIAMS, J., uses both; BYLES, J., uses " such debts as are commonly entered   F
in books "; and BUCKLEY, J., says " would or could . . . be entered in well-
kept books ". I think, however, that, bearing in mind the context and the use
of the following words, " in the ordinary course of such a business ", and the
reference to " well-kept books ", BUCKLEY, J., is intending to apply what may
be called a practical rather than a theoretical test, the test being whether it is
the practice in well-kept books to enter, in the ordinary course of business,   G
the debt in question. If there is any difference between the way in which it
is put by the various judges, I would myself adopt the way in which BYLES, J.,
put it, that " they must be such debts as are commonly entered in books ".
I will refer again to the judgment of BUCKLEY, J., on another point.

I return now to the present case. On the accountancy evidence, it is common
ground that the E.C.G. policy would not be entered as a book debt at the date   H
of the letter of authority. I have found that the E.C.G. policy would not, in
practice, be entered as a book debt before the admission of liability and the
ascertainment of the amount; and I have further found that it would not,
in practice, be entered as a book debt even after the admission of liability and
the ascertainment of the amount.

Counsel on both sides have addressed their arguments in great part to   I
the nature of the company's right at the date when the contingency under the
policy occurred, or alternatively the date when the liability of E.C.G. was
accepted and the amount ascertained. Even if this is the true test, the finding
on accountancy practice which I have made would conclude the case in favour
of the defendants; but I do not think that this is the true test. Section 95 of

---

(5) (1863), 14 C.B.N.S. at p. 572.   (6) (1863), 14 C.B.N.S. at p. 573.
(7) [1962] 3 All E.R. 27.   (8) [1962] 3 All E.R. at p. 34.
         (9) (1863), 14 C.B.N.S. 566.

A   the Companies Act, 1948, requires registration of a charge on book debts within twenty-one days of creation. It seems to me that, in order to ascertain whether any particular charge is a charge on book debts within the meaning of the section, one must look at the items of property which form the subject-matter of the charge at the date of its creation and consider whether any of those items is a book debt. In the case of an existing item of property, this question can only

B   be answered by reference to its character at the date of creation. Where the item of property is the benefit of a contract and at the date of the charge the benefit of the contract does not comprehend any book debt, I do not see how that contract can be brought within the section as being a book debt merely by reason that the contract may ultimately result in a book debt. Here the E.C.G. policy admittedly did not comprehend any book debt at the date of the

C   letter of authority, and that seems to me to be an end of the matter.

Counsel for the plaintiffs, contended that a contract requires registration under para. (e) if at any time it may result in a book debt. If this were right, the section would be of wide scope and would cover a charge on any possible contract which might produce a money obligation unless it could be shown that the obligation, even when admitted and quantified, was such as is not

D   commonly entered in the books of a company.

Counsel for the plaintiffs relied on another principle laid down by BUCKLEY, J., in *Independent Automatic Sales, Ltd.* v. *Knowles & Foster* (10), where, after holding that on the true interpretation of the hire-purchase agreement he said:

E   " the hirer became liable immediately on the agreement coming into operation to the extent of his minimum liability under it notwithstanding that some part of that liability was to be discharged by future payments . . ."

The judge then went on as follows (10):

" Secondly, in my judgment, a charge on future book debts of a company is registrable under s. 95. It is not disputed that it is competent for anyone to whom book debts may accrue in the future to create an equitable charge

F   on those book debts which will attach to them as soon as they come into existence. (See *Tailby* v. *Official Receiver* (11).) That such a charge can accurately be described as a charge on book debts does not appear to me to be open to question. Such a charge would not, of course, be effective until a book debt came into existence on which it could operate. Nevertheless, I think that it would be accurate to speak of the charge being created

G   at the date of the instrument, deposit or other act giving rise to it, for no further action on the part of the grantor would be required to bring the charge to life."

Counsel for the first defendant, and counsel for the second defendant, unless I misunderstood them, found it difficult to resist the contention of counsel for the plaintiffs on this point except by saying that the second proposition

H   of BUCKLEY, J., was wrong. I confess that I do not share that difficulty. If a charge, on its proper construction, covers future debts, in the sense of debts under a future contract which when that contract comes to be made will constitute book debts, I see no reason why s. 95 (2) (e) should not be applicable to the charge; and that, I think, is all that BUCKLEY, J., said. It by no means follows, it seems to me, that para. (e) applies to an existing contract

I   which does not comprehend a book debt merely by reason that that contract may result in a book debt in the future. Nor did BUCKLEY, J., say so.

I prefer to rest my decision on the ground which I have indicated. But, as I have said, if indeed the test were the character of E.C.G.'s obligation when liability is admitted and the amount ascertained, then the plaintiffs' claim would fail on the facts, namely, the evidence of accountancy practice.

---

(10) [1962] 3 All E.R. at p. 36.
(11) [1886-90] All E.R. Rep. 486; (1888), 13 App. Cas. 523.

I should mention that the defendants place some reliance on the penal provi- **A** sions of s. 96 of the Companies Act, 1948. I have arrived at my conclusion on the construction of s. 95, and I do not think that it is necessary to rely on s. 96. That conclusion disposes of the action, but I will mention shortly one further issue which arose. It was contended by the defendants that on its true construction the letter of authority represented not an assignment by way of charge, but an absolute assignment, and that s. 95 did not apply to it on that ground. Having **B** decided that the charge is not a charge on book debts, it is not necessary for me to give a decision on this second issue, but as I have heard argument on it, I will say simply this: that the letter of authority beyond question represented an assignment by way of charge. I propose, therefore, to dismiss this action.

Action dismissed. **C**

Solicitors: *Sole, Sawbridge & Co.* (for the plaintiffs); *Denton, Hall & Burgin* (for the first defendants); *Solicitor, Board of Trade.*

[*Reported by* JENIFER SANDELL, *Barrister-at-Law.*]

D

PRACTICE DIRECTION.

E

HOUSE OF LORDS.

*House of Lords—Appeal to—Time—Presentation of appeal out of time—Leave
—Consideration of petition for leave in private where founded on
misunderstanding or technicality and with respondent's consent.*

F

The Lord Chancellor announces a change of practice in cases where an appeal is offered for presentation to the House of Lords outside the time limit laid down by Standing Order No. 1.

In cases where an appeal is offered for presentation outside the time limit (1) imposed by Standing Order No. 1, owing to a misunderstanding or a technicality, provided that the consent of the respondent is obtained to the presentation of **G** the appeal out of time, the petition for leave to present an appeal out of time will be considered in private by three Lords of Appeal. Their Lordships' decision will be conveyed to the parties by the Clerk of the Parliaments.

This practice, which will take effect as from July 1, 1966, will replace the old practice whereby agents for the parties were required to attend and to be heard by the appeal committee. **H**

DAVID STEPHENS,
June 28. 1966.   Clerk of the Parliaments.

I

(1) See 9 HALSBURY'S LAWS (3rd Edn.) 369, 370, para. 861.

A

PRACTICE DIRECTION.

[Court of Criminal Appeal (Lord Parker, C.J., Fenton Atkinson and James, JJ.), June 21, 1966.]

B

Criminal Law—Practice—Previous convictions—Particulars of previous convictions must be supplied by police to defending solicitor or counsel on request—Proof of police evidence as to history of accused, including summary of previous convictions, to be given to counsel for prosecution either with brief or at outset of case—Copy of proof of this evidence to be supplied to counsel for prisoner, or the prisoner, in case of plea of guilty or when jury retire—Copy to be given to shorthand writer when officer called to prove contents.

C

[As to the statement of a prisoner's previous convictions after his conviction of a further offence, see 10 Halsbury's Laws (3rd Edn.) 432, 433, para. 799; p. 489, para. 891; as to shorthand notes concerning the prisoner's record, see ibid., p. 529, para. 972, note (*i*); and for cases on these subjects, see 14 Digest (Repl.) 373, *3638-3643*, 618, *6176*.]

D

LORD PARKER, C.J., at the sitting of the court, read the following statement: The judges of the Queen's Bench Division have reconsidered the Practice Direction of Jan. 31, 1955 (1), in regard to the disclosure to the defence of antecedents (as opposed to convictions) in cases tried on indictment. They are of opinion that provision should be made for the disclosure of such antecedents at an earlier stage than that set out in that Practice Direction. They

E

have resolved that para. (3) of the direction should be amended and that the direction in its amended form should be re-issued. It now will read as follows:

(1) Details of previous convictions must always be supplied by the police to the defending solicitor, or if no solicitor is instructed to defending counsel, on request. The judges are of opinion that there is no obligation on a police officer to satisfy himself that the prisoner has authorised a statement of previous

F

convictions to be given as it is clearly within the ordinary authority of solicitor and counsel to obtain this information. In order that the defence may be properly conducted, the prisoner's advisers must know whether they can safely put the prisoner's character in issue.

(2) There is no need for police officers to supply a list of previous convictions to the court before conviction, because the prisoner's previous convictions are

G

always set out in the confidential calendar with which the judge is supplied by the governor of the gaol, whose duty it is to supply it. The police will, of course, give any information to the governor that he may require to enable him to perform his duty.

(3) A proof of evidence should be prepared by a police officer containing particulars of the prisoner's age, education and employment, the date of arrest,

H

whether the prisoner has been on bail, and a statement summarising any previous convictions and any previous findings of guilt (including findings of guilt excluded from the details of previous convictions by reason of (2) the Children and Young Persons Act 1963, s. 16 (2)). It should also set out the date (if known) of the last discharge from prison or other place of custody. It may also contain a short and concise statement as to the prisoner's domestic and family circum-

I

stances, his general reputation and associates. Attached to the proof of evidence should be a factual statement of any convictions and of any previous findings

---

(1) See [1955] 1 All E.R. 386.

(2) Section 16 (2) provides: " In any proceedings for an offence committed or alleged to have been committed by a person of or over the age of twenty-one, any offence of which he was found guilty while under the age of fourteen shall be disregarded for the purposes of any evidence relating to his previous convictions; and he shall not be asked, and if asked shall not be required to answer, any question relating to such an offence, notwithstanding that the question would otherwise be admissible under s. 1 of the Criminal Evidence Act, 1898."

of guilt, which should be supplied in accordance with para. (1) above (except **A**
those excluded by operation of the Children and Young Persons Act 1963,
s. 16 (2)).

This proof, other than the attachment, should be given either with his brief
or at the outset of the case to counsel for the prosecution. Subject in any
particular case to a direction by the presiding judge to the contrary, counsel for
the prisoner (or the prisoner if not legally represented) should be entitled to be **B**
supplied with a copy of such proof of evidence as relates to his client (or himself
if not represented): (a) in the case of a plea of not guilty as soon as the jury
retire to consider their verdict, (b) in the case of a plea of guilty as soon as the
plea is entered.

A copy of the proof of evidence shall be given to the shorthand writer when
the officer is called to prove the contents. He may use it to check his note, **C**
but must only transcribe so much as is given in evidence.

[*Reported by* N. P. METCALFE, ESQ., *Barrister-at-Law.*]

DAVIES (Inspector of Taxes) *v.* DAVIES JENKINS & CO., LTD. **D**

[COURT OF APPEAL (Harman, Diplock and Winn, L.JJ.), May 5, 6, 1966.]

*Income Tax—Deductions in computing profits—Subvention payments—Payments
to meet deficits of associated company—Associated company no longer
trading—Not trading expenses—Finance Act, 1952 (1 & 2 Eliz. 2 c. 34),
s. 20 (1), (9), (10).* **E**

The taxpayer company had an associated company which was found to
have been a company resident in the United Kingdom and carrying on a
trade there within the meaning of the Finance Act, 1953, s. 20 (9)*, up to
Dec. 21, 1959. On that date the associated company ceased trading and
subsequently it received subvention payments from the taxpayer company
in respect of deficits which it had incurred in its accounting years 1958-59 **F**
and 1959-60. The subvention payments were made in pursuance of a subvention agreement made between the companies in March, 1955. The taxpayer company sought to deduct the payments as trading expenses in
computing its profits for income tax purposes under s. 20 (1)* of the Act of
1953.

Held (HARMAN, L.J., dissenting): the payments were not deductible in **G**
computing the taxpayer company's profits because s. 20 (1), construed with
s. 20 (9) and (10), authorised such deduction only where the recipient company was carrying on a trade and was an associated company at the time of
the receipt of the payment as well as during the accounting period in which
the deficit was incurred (see p. 934, letters D and F, post).

Decision of STAMP, J., ([1966] 1 All E.R. 716) affirmed. **H**

[As to payments between associated companies in respect of losses for income
tax purposes, see 20 HALSBURY'S LAWS (3rd Edn.) 154, 155, para. 270.

For the Finance Act, 1953, s. 20, see 33 HALSBURY'S STATUTES (2nd Edn.)
121.]

Appeal. **I**

The taxpayer company appealed to the Special Commissioners of Income Tax
against assessments to income tax made on it under Case 1 of Sch. D to the
Income Tax Act, 1952, for 1959-60 and 1960-61 in the sums of £5,000 and £20,000
respectively. The sole question for decision which ultimately remained in issue
was whether certain payments made by the taxpayer company under a subvention
agreement were allowable deductions under s. 20 of the Finance Act, 1953, in

---

* Section 20, so far as material, is printed at p. 932, letter I, to p. 933, letter C, and p.
933, letter I, post.

A   computing its profits for the purposes of Case 1 of Sch. D for 1959-60 and 1960-61, the payments having been made after the payee company had ceased trading. The subvention agreement was entered into on Mar. 17, 1955, between Wood Brothers (Glossop) Holdings, Ltd., Wood Brothers (Glossop), Ltd., the taxpayer company (Davies Jenkins & Co., Ltd.), Thomas Nuttall & Sons (Bolton), Ltd., Thomas Nuttall & Sons (Oak Mill), Ltd., and Wood Bros. (Men's Wear), Ltd. Two

B   payments under the agreement were made by the taxpayer company to Wood Brothers (Glossop), Ltd., the first of £13,327 on Feb. 24, 1960, in respect of the accounting period Apr. 1, 1958, to Mar. 31, 1959, and the second of £12,395 on Mar. 28, 1961, in respect of the accounting period Apr. 1, 1959, to Mar. 31, 1960. From Apr. 1, 1958, to Apr. 28, 1961, all the ordinary shares of Wood Brothers (Glossop), Ltd., were held by Wood Brothers (Glossop) Holdings, Ltd., and all the

C   taxpayer company's shares were held by Wood Brothers (Glossop), Ltd. The taxpayer company had surpluses under s. 20 (5) of the Finance Act, 1953, in the two accounting periods ending Mar. 31, 1959, and Mar. 31, 1960, sufficient to justify the payments made. Wood Brothers (Glossop), Ltd. had deficits under s. 20 (5) during the first of the accounting periods sufficient to absorb the payment from the taxpayer company, and during the second of the accounting periods sufficient

D   to absorb £6,669 of the taxpayer company's payment.

    On Dec. 17, 1965, as reported at [1966] 1 All E.R. 716, STAMP, J., allowed the Crown's appeal by way of Case Stated against the commissioners' decision. He held that the subvention payments were not deductible as expenses in computing the taxpayer company's profits because s. 20 (1), construed with s. 20 (9) and (10), authorised the deduction only where the recipient company had at the time of

E   receipt the qualifications of trading in the United Kingdom and being an associated company, which it would not have if it were not then trading. He referred to the Crown's contentions and said*:

    " Even if the reference to a company in sub-s. (10) [of s. 20 of the Finance Act, 1953] is not to be construed as a reference to a company having the sub-s. (9) qualification, one is still left with a situation in which the two

F   subsections have to be applied to sub-s. (1) independently. Subsection (1) is the enacting part of s. 20 and, applying to the reference to a company in the opening words of sub-s. (1) the qualification or description that sub-s. (9) requires one to apply, one finds that it is where a company trading in the United Kingdom has a deficit in any accounting period and receives a subvention payment in respect of that period that the payment is to

G   receive the treatment required by the section. Moreover it is to be noted that it is the word ' payment ' which is grammatically the subject of the sentence which one finds in sub-s. (1) and it is the payment which is to receive the treatment prescribed; and, if the question be asked, at what moment of time is the company which receives the payment to have the qualification required by sub-s. (9), I would, in the absence of something indicating the

H   contrary, conclude that it was at the time of the payment which brings sub-s. (1) into operation.

    " There is another approach which leads to the same conclusion. Subsection (9) requires one to ' take ' (note the words ' shall be taken ') the reference to a company in sub-s. (1) as applying only to a company (note the present tense) ' resident in the United Kingdom and carrying on ' (note

I   again the present tense) a trade there; and before sub-s. (1) can apply, one must find the case to be one where, reading sub-s. (9) into sub-s. (1) ' a company resident in the United Kingdom ' and carrying on a trade there, has such a deficit as is there described and receives a subvention payment. In this case no such company did receive a subvention payment. Similarly, in the absence of some contrary indication, I would conclude that the paying company must have the qualification of being an associated company at the

---

* [1966] 1 All E.R. at p. 721, letter D.

moment of receipt and payment. Subsection (10), however, requires that   A
qualification to subsist as well over the whole period between the beginning
of the payee's accounting year and the payment.''

The taxpayer company appealed to the Court of Appeal.

The cases noted below* were cited during the argument.

Heyworth Talbot, Q.C., and *P. W. I. Rees* for the taxpayer company.   B
Sir George Honeyman, Q.C., *J. R. Phillips* and *J. P. Warner* for the Crown.

HARMAN, L.J.: This is a short point but none the easier for that. The
taxpayer company, Davies Jenkins & Co., Ltd., is a subsidiary of another company called Wood Brothers (Glossop), Ltd., which in its turn is a subsidiary
of Wood Brothers (Holdings), Ltd. They are a series of interlocked companies
having something to do with the textile trade. It was for long a grievance in   C
cases of companies which worked on this system of interlocked subsidiaries
that the profits of one could not be set off against losses of another. The Finance
Act, 1953, proposed to remedy this defect. It is said that the provisions of
s. 20 of that Act do not apply to the circumstances of this case—that, although
the taxpayer company is a company which is in this interlocked position and
although its subsidiary did make a loss, or rather have a deficit as it is called, it   D
is not possible to allow to the taxpayer company the amount which it paid to its
subsidiary to make good that loss, because at the date when the payment was
made the subsidiary had ceased to carry on trade. The trading ceased on
Dec. 21, 1959. Two payments were in respect of the periods first to March,
1959, and second to March, 1960. The payments were made first in February,
1960, and secondly in March, 1961, and on those last dates the subsidiary was   E
not carrying on a trade. It was not wound up, but it had ceased to do any
business. It is said, therefore, that the section does not apply. The Special
Commissioners held that it did apply, but their decision was reversed by the
judge (1), who, in a very careful judgment, explained why, although he thought
it anomalous, he did not see how on the wording of the Finance Act, 1953, it
was possible to avoid the result which the Crown claimed.   F

Now that is admittedly an anomaly, and in my judgment it is a hardship.
The Crown says that it can be mitigated by some forecasting by one or other of
the two companies in question, and the fact that they do not get it quite right
does not very much matter between companies which are as closely interlocked
as these companies are. I do not think that that is a very satisfactory way of
managing legislation, but there it is. Otherwise the result of the Crown's   G
argument is that, for the last trading year of any subsidiary which makes a
deficit, it can never receive a subvention payment. I ought perhaps to say
that a subvention payment is a payment under an agreement between companies
in an interlocked position such as there is here. In this case the agreement
was made in 1955, and it provided that, if any one of the group made a loss, one
or other of the remaining members of the group should make it good. It was   H
decided by the holding company (which had the decisive voice in the matter,
as I understand) that the taxpayer company which had trading surpluses in
the accounting years in question, should be the member of the group to make
good these deficits. That it has done, and it claims to be allowed that in its
accounts under s. 20. That has been denied to it by the judge (1): hence this
appeal.   I

Section 20 of the Finance Act, 1953, is a comparatively long and involved
section. One should start at the back end of it and look at sub-s. (9), which (in
rather odd language) provides that

" For the purposes of this section . . . references to a company shall be

---

* *Astor* v. *Perry (Inspector of Taxes)*, [1935] All E.R. Rep. 713; [1935] A.C. 398; *Inland
Revenue Comrs.* v. *Clifforia Investments, Ltd.*, [1963] 1 All E.R. 159.

(1) [1966] 1 All E.R. 716.

A   taken to apply only to a company resident in the United Kingdom and carrying on a trade wholly or partly in the United Kingdom . . ."

So in reading sub-s. (1), references to a company are references to what I may call an English trading concern. So you begin like this:

B   " Subject to the provisions of this section, where [an English trading concern] has a deficit for tax purpose during any accounting period of [that concern], and receives a subvention payment in respect of that period from an associated company [trading in England] having a surplus for tax purposes in the corresponding period, then in computing for the purposes of income tax the profits or gains or losses of those companies the payment shall be treated as a trading receipt receivable by the one company on the

C   last day of the accounting period during which it has the deficit, and shall be allowed as a deduction to the other company as if it were a trading expense incurred on that day."

Therefore one has to have a company trading in England and incurring a deficit over one of its accounting periods. The company to which the payment was

D   made here was trading in England when it made the deficit first in question, and it did receive a subvention payment in respect of that period from another company, the taxpayer company, which was also a company trading in England over the same period—or rather the corresponding period: it is not necessary that it be the same but it must be a corresponding period—and the taxpayer company had a surplus for that time. If that is so, I do not for myself quite

E   see why the subvention payment made under the subvention agreement for that period should not rank within sub-s. (1), because it is to be treated as receivable by the one company on the last day of the accounting period during which it had a deficit and is to be allowed to the other as if it were a trading expense incurred on that day. So that of the two companies one puts it down as a debt incurred in the accounting period and the other puts it down as a credit receivable

F   during the same period. The section does not say that the subvention payment has to be received in that period.

What happened here was that the losses of one, and the profits of the other, company were not ascertained until a later period so that each payment was not made till that later period. In the books of both companies, however, the entries are taken to be made in respect of the period during which each of these

G   companies was trading and it does not seem to me that the fact that the company had ceased to trade makes any difference. What is said is that the company must be trading in England when it receives the payment and if it is not trading in England at the date of receipt it cannot qualify. With all respect I think, however, that " receives " there means nothing in respect of time: it is not the present tense in the temporal sense at all. One might as well say " it has

H   received "; or one might easily say " it shall receive ". It is " *whenever* it receives "—" where " means " whenever ". Thus where a company has plied its trade in England, has made its deficit during a given accounting period and has a parent or an associated company which has a surplus over the corresponding period and there is a subvention agreement between them, I cannot see why that subvention should not rank as s. 20 (1) says that it does.

I   It is said, however, as I understand it, that s. 20 (10) makes that impossible. That reads:

" For the purposes of this section [that, I suppose, is s. 20 and not the subsection], a company making a subvention payment to another shall be treated as the other's associated company if, but only if, at all times between the beginning of the payee company's accounting period in respect of which the payment is made and the making of the payment one of them is a subsidiary of the other . . ."

In this case with regard to those two companies one remained a subsidiary of **A**
the other during the whole period and both of them in fact (as the definition
goes on) were subsidiaries of the holding company, and I do not see why that
particular definition destroys what I would otherwise call the proper meaning
of sub-s. (1) because of the reference to the making of the payment. One does
not cease to be a subsidiary of the other simply because one of them or the other
of them ceases to trade. " Subsidiary " company has nothing to do with trading. **B**
A company is subsidiary if all its shares, or seventy-five per cent. of them, are
held by the parent.

If it lay with me I should allow this appeal; but I understand that my lords
are of another opinion.

DIPLOCK, L.J.: If I thought that the words of s. 20 of the Finance Act, **C**
1953, were equivocal, I should be the first to adopt an interpretation which would
avoid what, as is common ground between the taxpayer and the Crown, is an
anomaly where a subsidiary company has given up trading before it receives
the subvention payment under s. 20 (1).

It is always invidious, when HARMAN, L.J., and STAMP, J. (2), have taken
different views as to the construction of the section to say that there is only one **D**
possible meaning to be ascribed to the words. For my part, however, I think
that the words are too plain and that, to qualify for the relief afforded by s. 20 (1),
the recipient must be a company carrying on a trade wholly or partly in the
United Kingdom at the time of the receipt of the payment, as well as during the
accounting period in which the deficit is incurred. STAMP, J., in his judgment (2)
sets out the reasons for arriving at this view in terms much more felicitous than **E**
I could achieve and lengthier than I need attempt on Friday afternoon. I
would dismiss the appeal for the reasons which STAMP, J. (2), gave.

WINN, L.J.: I agree explicitly with the judgment delivered by DIPLOCK,
L.J. It seems to me that there is only one answer to the question whether,
when this payment was received by the recipient company and paid by the
taxpayer company, the recipient company was a resident trading company **F**
and was, within the limited meaning of the word " company " prescribed by
s. 20 (9), an associated company of the payor company. That answer is " No ".
I regret this decision, but for my own part I can see no way of avoiding it. Neither
the delightful advocacy of counsel for the taxpayer company, nor (still less) any
of the suggestions I myself threw out in a futile attempt to help his case in this
court have, in my view, any real validity. I, too, think that this appeal must be **G**
dismissed.

Appeal dismissed. Leave to appeal to the House of Lords granted.

Solicitors: *Coward, Chance & Co.* (for the taxpayer company); *Solicitor of
Inland Revenue.*

[*Reported by* F. A. AMIES, ESQ., *Barrister-at-Law.*] **H**

 I

---

(2) [1966] 1 All E.R. 716.

A

ELLIS (Inspector of Taxes) *v.* LUCAS.

[CHANCERY DIVISION (Ungoed-Thomas, J.), March 8, 22, 1966.]

Income Tax—Income—Payment of lump sum—Compensation for loss of office—
B *Accountant—Auditor to group of companies—Fees taxed under Sch. E—*
Payment on relinquishing office—Office as an asset of accountant's business
and a subject of taxation under Sch. D—Inconsistency of findings of Special
Commissioners with view that the auditorships were such an asset—No ground
for holding findings unreasonable—No factual basis in findings for establishing
that auditorships were such an asset—Finance Act, 1960 (8 & 9 Eliz. 2 c. 44),
s. 38 (3).

C
    The taxpayer practised as a qualified accountant. He was appointed
auditor to a company in 1952, and auditor to associated companies from 1954
to 1960. He was remunerated as auditor by fees, which covered some
accountancy work done in connexion with the audit, and he also received
fees from the companies for some ordinary accountancy work. Following a
dispute with the person controlling the companies, the taxpayer agreed to
D relinquish his auditorships at the end of their financial years falling within
the fiscal year 1961-62 in return for a payment of £1,500, described in documents relating to the agreement as " compensation for loss of office ". The
auditorships represented about seventeen per cent. of the taxpayer's fees.
He was assessed to income tax on the £1,500 on the basis that the sum was not
compensation for loss of office, or alternatively that, even if it were, it fell to
E be treated as part of the income receipts of his profession on the ground that
the auditorships (though their emoluments were taxed under Sch. E) constituted an asset of his profession. On appeal the Special Commissioners
of Income Tax found in effect that £1,125, part of the £1,500, was compensation for loss of office and that the £1,125 fell to be assessed under Sch. E
to the Income Tax Act, 1952, but was exempted from income tax by s. 38 (3)
F of the Finance Act, 1960.

    Held: (i) an office, the emoluments of which were taxable under Sch. E,
could be an asset of a trade subject to taxation under Sch. D, so as to make
compensation for loss of that asset assessable to tax under Sch. D (see p. 942,
letter E, post).

G
    Blackburn v. *Close Brothers, Ltd.* ((1960), 39 Tax Cas. 164) applied.

    (ii) the decision of the commissioners that the apportioned part of the
compensation (the £1,125) fell to be assessed under Sch. E was, however, a
finding contrary to the contention of the Crown that the office of auditor was
such an asset in the present case; and, as the facts found afforded no basis
for establishing the Crown's contention on appeal, nor for upsetting as
unreasonable any decision of the commissioners that the office was not such an
H asset, the apportioned sum was exempted from tax by s. 38 (3) of the Act of
1960 (see p. 942, letter H, to p. 943, letter B, post).

    Semble: the payment of £1,500 was not compensation for damage to the
whole structure of the taxpayer's profession (see p. 943, letter C, post).

    Appeal dismissed.

I
    [As to income tax in respect of compensation for loss of office, see 20 HALS-
BURY'S LAWS (3rd Edn.) 324, 325, paras. 593, 594; and for cases on the subject,
see 28 DIGEST (Repl.) 225-237, *971-1039.*

    As to income tax in respect of other compensation payments, see 20 HALS-
BURY'S LAWS (3rd Edn.) 150, 151, para. 264, and for cases on the subject, see 28
DIGEST (Repl.) 115-124, *431-480.*

    For the Finance Act, 1960, s. 38 (3), see 40 HALSBURY'S STATUTES (2nd Edn.)
460.]

Cases referred to:

A

Blackburn (Inspector of Taxes) v. Close Brothers, Ltd., (1960), 39 Tax Cas. 164;
     Digest (Cont. Vol. A) 848, 173h.

Fry v. Salisbury House Estate, Ltd., [1930] All E.R. Rep. 538; [1930] A.C.
     432; 99 L.J.K.B. 403; 143 L.T. 77; 15 Tax Cas. 266; 28 Digest (Repl.)
     33, 148.

Hughes (Inspector of Taxes) v. Bank of New Zealand, [1936] 3 All E.R. 975; **B**
     [1937] 1 K.B. 419; 156 L.T. 153; affd. H.L., [1938] 1 All E.R. 778;
     [1938] A.C. 366; 107 L.J.K.B. 306; 158 L.T. 463; 21 Tax Cas. 472;
     28 Digest (Repl.) 264, 1174.

Mitchell (Inspector of Taxes) v. Ross. Mitchell (Inspector of Taxes) v. Hirtenstein.
     Mitchell (Inspector of Taxes) v. Marshall. Taylor-Gooby (Inspector of
     Taxes) v. Tarnesby. Taylor-Gooby (Inspector of Taxes) v. Drew, [1959]   **C**
     3 All E.R. 341; [1960] Ch. 145; [1959] 3 W.L.R. 550; affd., C.A.,
     [1960] 2 All E.R. 218; [1960] Ch. 498; [1960] 2 W.L.R. 766; rvsd.,
     H.L. [1961] 3 All E.R. 49; [1962] A.C. 813; [1961] 3 W.L.R. 411; 40
     Tax Cas. 11; Digest (Cont. Vol. A) 888, 962a.

Case Stated.

D

The taxpayer appealed to the Special Commissioners of Income Tax against
an assessment to income tax made on him under Sch. D to the Income Tax Act,
1952, in respect of his profits as an accountant for the year of assessment 1962-63
in the sum of £5,118. His grounds of appeal were that, in computing his profits
or gains for the accounting period relevant to the assessment, the sum of £1,500
received by him from a company called Books for Pleasure, Ltd., fell to be
excluded as being compensation for loss of office exempted from income tax under   **E**
the provisions of s. 38 (3) of the Finance Act, 1960, by reason of its amount, or
alternatively as being a capital receipt of his profession. The taxpayer contended
as follows: (i) that the sum of £1,500 received by him from the company was a
sum received as compensation for loss of the office of auditor to the company
and its associates, which fell to be assessed if at all under the provisions of
Sch. E to the Act of 1952, but by virtue of s. 38 (3) of the Act of 1960 was exempted   **F**
from income tax. (ii) alternatively that the sum of £1,500 received by the taxpayer
from the company was a capital sum received as compensation for damage to
the whole structure of his profit-making capacity and fell to be excluded in
computing the taxpayer's profits or gains for the accounting period relevant to
the assessment under appeal.

G

The Crown contended as follows: (a) that the sum of £1,500 was attributable
not only to the loss of the post of auditor but also to the loss of general accountancy work; (b) that in so far as the sum was attributable to the loss of general
accountancy work it constituted a receipt of the taxpayer's profession and fell
to be assessed under the provisions of Case II of Sch. D to the Act of 1952; (c) that
in so far as the sum was attributable to the loss of the position of auditor it fell   **H**
to be assessed under the provisions of Case II of Sch. D; (d) that the £1,500 was
not a capital sum received by the taxpayer as compensation for damage to the
whole structure of his profit-making capacity; and (e) that in computing the
taxpayer's profits or gains for the accounting periods relative to the assessment
under appeal the £1,500 fell to be included.

The commissioners decided as follows: (i) that the sum of £1,500 was not   **I**
compensation for damage to the whole structure of the taxpayer's profession;
(ii) that the sum related to the whole of the taxpayer's professional work undertaken for the company and its associates and the best estimate they could make
of its apportionment was £1,125 to be attributable to auditing and £375 to general
accountancy work; (iii) that the apportioned sum of £1,125 fell to be assessed
under the provisions of Sch. E to the Act of 1952, but by reason of the express
provisions of s. 38 (3) of the Act of 1960 was exempted from income tax; and
(iv) that of the sum of £1,500 received by the taxpayer only the sum of £375 so

A apportioned fell to be included in computing the profits or gains of the taxpayer's profession for the relevant accounting period. They therefore determined the appeal by reducing the assessment to £3,993. The Crown appealed by way of Case Stated to the High Court.

J. R. Phillips for the Crown.

The taxpayer appeared in person.

B

Cur. adv. vult.

Mar. 22. **UNGOED-THOMAS, J.:** This is an appeal by the Crown from a decision of the Special Commissioners of Income Tax with regard to an assessment under Sch. D on the taxpayer in respect of profits as an accountant for the year 1962-63. The question raised is whether £1,125, part of £1,500 paid to the

C taxpayer on the occasion of the termination of his engagements by certain companies, should be included in computing such profits. The taxpayer's main contention is that the £1,125 was received as compensation for loss of office as auditor. The Crown's counter-contention is that it was not so received, but that, even if it were so received, it fell to be treated as part of income receipts of his profession of accountant on the ground that the auditorships (even though the

D emoluments were taxable under Sch. E) constituted an asset of the profession. The Crown concedes that, if the taxpayer's contention is correct and its counter-contention is not correct, then under s. 38 (3) of the Finance Act, 1960, the £1,125 is exempt from tax.

Section 37 (1) and (2) of the Finance Act, 1960, reads as follows:

E " (1) Subject to the provisions of this and the next following section, income tax shall be charged under Sch. E in respect of any payment to which this section applies which is made to the holder or past holder of any office or employment, or to his executors or administrators, whether made by the person under whom he holds or held the office or employment or by any other person.

F " (2) This section applies to any payment (not otherwise chargeable to income tax) which is made, whether in pursuance of any legal obligation or not, either directly or indirectly in consideration or in consequence of, or otherwise in connection with, the termination of the holding of the office or employment or any change in its functions or emoluments, including any payment in commutation of annual or periodical payments (whether chargeable to tax or not) which would otherwise have been made as

G aforesaid."

If, as the Crown contends, the £1,125 falls to be treated as part of income receipts of the profession of accountant, then it would be otherwise chargeable to income tax under Sch. D and not subject to charge under Sch. E, s. 37. Section 38 (3) provides that tax shall not be chargeable under s. 37 " in respect of a payment of

H an amount not exceeding £5,000 ", and it is under this provision that the £1,125 is exempted from taxation if it falls within s. 37.

The taxpayer practised as a qualified accountant under the firm name of Henry Lucas & Co. In September, 1952, he was appointed auditor of a company called Books for Pleasure, Ltd., which is referred to in the Case Stated as " the principal company ". From 1954 to 1960 he was appointed auditor of companies associated

I with the principal company. He was remunerated as auditor by payment of fees, but his work for the companies also included some accountancy work in connexion with the audit, payment for which was covered by the fees paid to him as auditor. He also did some ordinary accountancy work for the companies, for which he was paid separate fees.

In 1961 a dispute arose between the taxpayer and a Mr. Hamlyn, who controlled the companies. As a result of this, the taxpayer eventually agreed to relinquish the auditorships of the companies at the end of their respective financial years falling within the fiscal year 1961-62, and to co-operate with the new accountants;

and he was to receive, in addition to his fees as auditor, £1,500. That is the   A
£1,500 to which I have referred, and it was, in fact, paid to him in February, 1962.
It appears from the Case Stated that on June 2, 1961, Mr. Hamlyn wrote to the
taxpayer a letter, in the course of which he, as he described it, " reassessed the
situation ". In the course of reassessing the situation, he stated as follows:

> " You have expressed the wish to resign from your appointment to all the
> Books for Pleasure group companies if I will agree to pay a cash sum as   B
> ' compensation for loss of office '. You mentioned the figure of £2,500.
> (iii) You have stated that only if such compensation were paid would you
> relinquish your association with my companies and co-operate in the handing
> over of all essential information and documents to Jenks, Percival and Co.,"

the new auditors. Then Mr. Hamlyn set out what had been his proposals, which   C
included an alternative, which the taxpayer was to have the choice of accepting,
in these terms:

> " To relinquish your appointment to *all* companies at their respective
> year end, and having fully co-operated with Jenks, Percival and Co. in the
> meantime, receive—in addition to your usual fee—a sum of £1,500 in
> recognition of your past services to Books for Pleasure, Ltd."   D

Mr. Hamlyn, in the same letter, then submitted what he referred to as his " final
proposal ", which included the proposal

> " that you relinquish your appointment to all companies on the completion
> of their present annual accounts and accept, in addition to fees, a sum of
> £1,500."   E

On Aug. 4 the taxpayer replied to Mr. Hamlyn saying that he accepted the terms
set out in Mr. Hamlyn's letter. He said that he accepted the position of Jenks,
Percival & Co., that he would co-operate with Mr. Barnard and that he would
" relinquish " his

> " appointment to all companies on the completion of their present annual
> accounts and accept in addition to fees a sum of £1,500."   F

On Feb. 5, 1962, on completion of the current work, the taxpayer handed to Mr.
Hamlyn a statement of account, which is set out in the Case Stated. It is dated
Feb. 5, 1962, and is addressed to the principal company. It then states: " To
compensation for loss of office as auditors to your company, as agreed between
Mr. Hamlyn and Mr. Lucas £1,500." The Case Stated adds: " A cheque for   G
£1,500 was handed to the [taxpayer] and this invoice was receipted on the spot
without comment."

So the £1,500 is described as " compensation for loss of office " in both Mr.
Hamlyn's first letter and in the final document described in the Case Stated as
" a statement of account "—i.e., the document which was handed by the taxpayer to Mr. Hamlyn—but in between times the £1,500 was described either   H
ambiguously or on one occasion by Mr. Hamlyn as " in recognition of your past
services ". After this review of the communications between Mr. Hamlyn and the
taxpayer, the Special Commissioners added:

> " There was no agreement between Mr. Hamlyn and the [taxpayer] that
> the sum of £1,500 was solely for ' compensation for loss of office as auditors '."

Then, in para. 6 of the Case Stated, the commissioners said that they   I

> " upon consideration of the evidence adduced and the arguments addressed
> to us by the parties and the cases cited to us . . . decided "

and their decision included, under sub-para. (ii),

> " that the aforementioned sum of £1,500 related to the whole of the
> [taxpayer's] professional work undertaken for the principal company and its
> associates and the best estimate we could make of its apportionment was
> £1,125 to be attributable to auditing and £375 to general accountancy work,"

A and, under sub-para. (iii),

"that the said apportioned sum of £1,125 fell to be assessed under the provisions of Sch. E, Income Tax Act, 1952, but by reason of the express provisions of s. 38 (3), Finance Act, 1960, was exempted from income tax."

B The inevitable inference, to my mind, from sub-paras. (ii) and (iii) of the decision in the context of the Case Stated was that the Special Commissioners held that the £1,125 was compensation for loss of office—and this inference is conceded by the Crown. There is, so it appears to me, ample evidence to justify the conclusion that the £1,125 was compensation for loss of office. Indeed, on the evidence before me it would appear to me to be more doubtful whether the £375 should be attributable to general accountancy work. The Special Commissioners, C however, heard evidence which was not referred to before me—and doubtless it was unnecessary so to refer to it because there was no appeal by the taxpayer in respect of the £375. With regard to the £1,125, I for my part, on such evidence as is before me, would come to the same conclusion as the Special Commissioners, viz., that it was compensation for loss of office.

That, however, does not conclude the case, for the question then arises whether D the £1,125 nevertheless falls to be treated as part of the taxpayer's income and receipts of his profession of accountant on the ground that the auditorship constituted an asset of it. It is clear and not disputed that the taxpayer did not traffic in his offices of auditor so as to make them part of his stock-in-trade, and so as to make compensation for loss of such offices taxable under Sch. D as compensation for loss of stock-in-trade. It is also not disputed by the Crown for E the purposes of this case that auditorship is an office the fees for which are taxable exclusively under Sch. E, and that the taxpayer's income tax liability for fees earned from his offices of auditor falls within Sch. E. What is said for the Crown, however, is that, even though, whilst the office exists, the fees arising from it fall to be treated under Sch. E, in this case the office is nevertheless related to and part of the assets of the taxpayer's professional venture or practice as accountant; that, when that office is lost, those assets are correspondingly diminished; and F that, when compensation is paid for such loss, it is payment in respect of that asset of the taxpayer's accountancy practice and so, it is said, is taxable under Sch. D.

In *Fry* v. *Salisbury House Estate, Ltd.* (1), a company occupying a block of buildings let rooms to tenants, managed the property and provided services. It admitted liability to taxation under Sch. D in respect of profits from those services, but it contended that it was not liable under Sch. D but only under Sch. A in G respect of rents received on its lettings. The company succeeded on the ground, preferred by Lord Atkin, that the income tax schedules were mutually exclusive, and that Sch. D was the residual schedule; and on the ground, preferred by Lord Warrington of Clyffe and Lord Macmillan, that, in respect of the lettings, the company was not carrying on a trade but was acting as landowner, Lord Tomlin based his decision on both grounds.

H In *Hughes (Inspector of Taxes)* v. *Bank of New Zealand* (2), investments which were purchased out of floating capital and were producing income not chargeable to tax were part of the business of the taxpayer's trade and were, in fact, part of his stock-in-trade. It was held that the expenses incurred in obtaining the investments were wholly and exclusively laid out for the purposes of the trade, and were allowable as a deduction in computing the taxpayer's liability to tax I under Sch. D. Although the investments in that case were such that interest on them was exempted from tax by special provisions of the Income Tax Acts applicable to such investments, yet, as was emphasised by Lord Thankerton (3) the investments were part of the business of the taxpayer's trade; and, as was emphasised by Lord Wright, M.R. (4), there was in that case only one indivisible

(1) [1930] All E.R. Rep. 538; 15 Tax Cas. 266.
(2) [1938] 1 All E.R. 778; 21 Tax Cas. 472.
(3) [1938] 1 All E.R. at p. 784; 21 Tax Cas. at p. 524.
(4) [1936] 3 All E.R. 975 at p. 998; 21 Tax Cas. at p. 507.

trade of which the investments formed part, as contrasted with cases such as the A
Salisbury House case (5), where the taxpayer carried on two separate and distinct
functions " and, therefore, the various exemptions or rules which applied to the
one did not apply to the other ". So the expenses incurred in obtaining the investments forming part of the business of the taxpayer's trade were allowable under
Sch. D, although the interest on those investments was exempt from taxation by
special exemption provisions applicable to such interest—but the expenses were B
so allowable only because the investments themselves formed part of a business
the profits of which were liable to taxation under Sch. D.

In *Mitchell* (*Inspector of Taxes*) v. *Ross* (6), it was held by the Court of Appeal
that part-time appointments as consultants under the National Health Service
of specialists who also carried on private practices were offices, and that the
remuneration from them was assessable under Sch. E; and, by the House of C
Lords, that expenses attributable to those offices could only be allowed so far as
they satisfied, not the test applicable to private practice under Sch. D, but
the test laid down in the rules applicable to such offices under Sch. E. UPJOHN, J.,
in a judgment upheld by the House of Lords, said (7):

" The question is a narrow one and without the slightest importance
except for the purpose of income tax. In a general sense, of course, the D
first taxpayer is carrying on the profession of a radiologist whether he is
performing his national health functions or attending to private patients.
It is all part of his vocation as a medical adviser. In my judgment, however,
the argument ought not to succeed. When carrying out his national health
duties, the first taxpayer is performing the duties of an office and he is
taxed under Sch. E. When attending private patients he is exercising his E
profession and is taxed under Sch. D. Each Schedule and the rules thereunder
contain, in the words of LORD ATKIN in *Fry* v. *Salisbury House Estate, Ltd.* (8):
' definite codes applying exclusively to their respective defined subject-
matters '. Once the conclusion is reached that the national health appointment is the holding and exercise of an office (and that is the vital decision),
the expenses attendant thereon must be taxed under the rules applicable to F
Sch. E and in my judgment under no other schedule. The fact that the
exercise of that office may truly be described as an incident of the profession
of radiologist cannot alter that position."

This passage brings out clearly, to my mind, that for tax purposes—and I emphasise that phrase—in so far as Sch. E applies, Sch. D does not apply; that in so G
far as an activity falls within Sch. E, whether it be called an office or profession,
it is not an activity that falls within Sch. D; but that in so far as they fall within
separate schedules they are separate activities and are not one indivisible activity
for tax purposes. LORD RADCLIFFE said (9):

" Generally speaking, the five schedules of taxable categories are distinguished from each other by distinctions as to the nature of the source H
from which the chargeable profit arises. The source may be property in the
ordinary sense such as land, securities, copyright, office, or it may be an
activity sufficiently coherent, trade or profession, for example, to be regarded
as itself the stock on which profits grow. That is not an exhaustive account,
but it is, I think, a sufficient general introduction. Before you can assess a
profit to tax, you must be sure that you have properly identified its source I
or other description according to the correct schedule: but, once you have
done that, it is obligatory that it should be charged, if at all, under the
Schedule and strictly in accordance with the rules that are there laid down

(5) [1930] All E.R. Rep. 538; 15 Tax Cas. 266.
(6) [1961] 3 All E.R. 49; 40 Tax Cas. 11.
(7) [1959] 3 All E.R. 341 at p. 349; 40 Tax Cas. at p. 37.
(8) [1930] All E.R. Rep. at p. 552; 15 Tax Cas. at p. 320.
(9) [1961] 3 All E.R. at pp. 54, 55; 40 Tax Cas. at p. 61.

A for assessments under it. It is a necessary consequence of this conception
that the sources of profit in the different Schedules are mutually exclusive."

Then LORD RADCLIFFE refers to extracts from the speeches of VISCOUNT DUNEDIN
and LORD ATKIN in the *Salisbury House* case (10), and adds (11):

B " I do not see how anyone can doubt these propositions today: but, if they
are accepted, they seem to me to rule out the idea that, though the respondents' appointments were offices and so chargeable under Sch. E, they
could also form a part or a branch of the ' profession ' that is the subject of
charge under Sch. D. And yet that is the whole case. The profession, for
this purpose, is a coherent series of activities of a particular character giving
rise to assessable profits: it is not an abstract description in a dictionary.

C If the activities relating to the employment in the office are excluded, as
they must be because they belong to Sch. E, the profession the profits
of which are assessable under Sch. D must consist only of the remaining
activities. And, if that is so, the rules of Sch. D (see s. 137 (a) of the Income
Tax Act, 1952) prohibit the deduction in that assessment of any expenses
incurred in relation to the activities of the office, since such expenses are not

D ' wholly and exclusively laid out . . . for the purposes of . . . the profession '."

A little later, however, when dealing with the case of *Hughes* v. *Bank of New
Zealand* (12), LORD RADCLIFFE stated (13):

" The deductions that were claimed were not the expenses of obtaining the
tax-free income but the expenses of obtaining the stock-in-trade that went

E into the investments that produced the income; and that is a different
matter."

Here LORD RADCLIFFE apparently contemplates that the expenses of obtaining
what produced the income may fall to be dealt with under a different schedule
from that under which the expenses of obtaining that income fall.

In *Blackburn (Inspector of Taxes)* v. *Close Brothers, Ltd.* (14), the respondent

F company carried on the business of merchant bankers and of a finance and issuing
house, and also entered into agreements to provide managerial and secretarial
services to other companies, for which it received fees and allowances. One
such agreement dated May 3, 1950, was terminated in consideration of a payment
to the company as compensation for loss of such offices. It was clear and conceded
by the Crown that moneys received under the agreement were chargeable under

G Sch. E and not under Sch. D, yet it was held that the compensation was a trading
receipt to be included in the computation of the company's profits under Sch. D.
PENNYCUICK, J., said (15):

" Counsel for the Crown accepts the position that any fee paid under the
agreement dated May 3, 1950, would have been chargeable under Sch. E,
but he points out that a trader, the profits of whose trade are chargeable

H under Case I of Sch. D, may in the course of carrying on that trade acquire
and dispose of assets which are themselves the source of income chargeable
under another schedule—for example, land or government securities—and
that in such circumstances the cost of acquisition of the assets is a deduction
in computing the profit of the trade, and the price upon disposition of the asset
is a receipt in computing the profit of the trade. So here, the company's trade

I is that of merchant bankers and a finance and issuing house. The company
made the agreement in the course of carrying on this trade. If the company
had had to pay a premium to obtain the contract, that premium would have

---

(10) [1930] All E.R. Rep. 538; 15 Tax Cas. 266.
(11) [1961] 3 All E.R. at p. 55; 40 Tax Cas. at p. 61.
(12) [1938] 1 All E.R. 778; 21 Tax Cas. 472.
(13) [1961] 3 All E.R. at p. 56; 40 Tax Cas. at p. 62.
(14) (1960), 39 Tax Cas. 164.   (15) (1960), 39 Tax Cas. at p. 173.

been a deduction in computing the profits of the trade. Equally, in my judg- A
ment, the sum received in consideration of the cancellation of the contract
is a receipt of the trade."

PENNYCUICK, J., appears to have found liability to payment of tax under Sch. E
on emoluments from an office no hindrance to deciding that compensation for loss
of such office (described in the words quoted above from LORD RADCLIFFE'S
speech (16) as " the stock on which profits grow ") should be chargeable to tax B
under Sch. D.

Counsel appearing for the Crown before me was good enough to suggest, against
the Crown's interest and contrary to his own submission, that it might be considered that a distinction should be drawn between land or government securities,
referred to by counsel for the Crown in *Blackburn's* case (17), forming part of
stock-in-trade and a service agreement which formed no part of stock-in-trade. C
PENNYCUICK, J., drew no such distinction, however, for present purposes, and
it seems to me that this view is in accordance with the distinction which LORD
RADCLIFFE drew in the passage which I quoted in *Mitchell* (*Inspector of Taxes*) v.
Ross (18) on which I have already commented.

The taxpayer points out, however, that in *Blackburn* v. *Close Brothers, Ltd.* (17)
the taxpayer was a company and not, as he is, an individual. I appreciate that D
it may be easier, in the case of a company, the objects of which are specified
in its memorandum, to hold that an office is incidental to a trade carried on in
pursuance of those objects, particularly if the office, considered in isolation and
apart from the trade, would not be within the objects. This does not, however,
affect the question whether an office, the emoluments of which are taxable under
Sch. E, is capable of being an asset of a trade subject to taxation under Sch. D E
so as to make compensation for loss of that asset also accountable to tax under
Sch. D. In my view, the answer to that question is " Yes ". It is a question,
depending on the facts in each case, be the taxpayer a company or an individual,
whether the office is an asset of the trade including (as in the case of the taxpayer's
activities) business of an accountant. Thus, in *Blackburn* v. *Close Brothers, Ltd.*
(19), PENNYCUICK, J., said: " The company made the agreement in the course F
of carrying on this trade ", i.e., the taxpayer's trade of merchant bankers and a
finance and issuing house.

In this case, however, there is a difficulty in ascertaining whether or not the
appointments as auditor were made or accepted in the course of the taxpayer's
carrying on of his business as accountant. There is no express finding or decision
on this, but, as appears from para. 5 (iii) of the Case Stated, the Crown contended, G
inter alia,

" that in so far as the said sum of £1,500 was attributable to the loss of the
position of auditor it fell to be assessed under the provisions of Case II of
Sch. D."

This contention would appear to be directed to, and would certainly be wide H
enough to cover, the Crown's contention before me that the auditorships constituted an asset of the taxpayer's business of accountant. It was after setting out
the Crown's contention which I have quoted from the Case Stated that the
Special Commissioners concluded that £1,125 of the £1,500 fell to be assessed
under Sch. E—a conclusion contrary to the contention that the auditorships
constituted an asset of the business of accountant. Either the contention was I
raised before the Special Commissioners under the contention which I have just
quoted, in which case it appears to me that the Special Commissioners decided
that the auditorships were not an asset of the taxpayer's accountancy business,
or it was not so raised, in which case it is a contention raised before me for the

---

(16) [1961] 3 All E.R. at p. 55; 40 Tax Cas. at p. 61.
(17) (1960), 39 Tax Cas. 164.
(18) [1961] 3 All E.R. at p. 56; 40 Tax Cas. at p. 62.
(19) (1960), 39 Tax Cas. at p. 173.

A first time. It appears to me that the facts found by the Special Commissioners do not provide the necessary basis for enabling this contention to be established at this stage of the proceedings, or for upsetting as unreasonable any decision of the Special Commissioners that the auditorships were not an asset of the taxpayer's accountancy business. The result, therefore, is that the appeal fails.

I would add a brief reference to the taxpayer's further contention that the
B payment which he received was " compensation for damage to the whole structure of his profit-making capacity ". The Case Stated shows that the auditorships represented about seventeen per cent. of the taxpayer's fees, and that the decline in his receipts for the year following the termination of the auditorships was about ten per cent. Were it necessary so to decide, I would accept the Special Commissioners' conclusion that the payment of £1,500 " was not compensation
C for damage to the whole structure of the [taxpayer's] profession ".

Appeal dismissed.

Solicitor: *Solicitor of Inland Revenue.*

[*Reported by* F. A. Amies, Esq., *Barrister-at-Law.*]

D

E

F

PRACTICE NOTE.

Affidavit—Filing—Title of affidavit.

Notwithstanding Ord. 41, r. 1 (2) of the R.S.C. (Revision) 1965 (1), it will be convenient and helpful to the Filing Department and will tend to avoid any risk
G of confusion in the indexing of affidavits if practitioners will adopt the following practice which has been approved by the Senior Master and the Chief Master:

If the title of the cause or matter contains the name of a person (including any company or corporate body), with reference to whom or to whose property (including any trust affecting his property) the proceedings are brought, such name should continue to be included in the title of the affidavit. For example,
H such titles as " In the Estate of A. B. deceased " or " In the matter of the Trusts of . . ." etc. (as the case may be) should continue to be used.

B. A. Harwood,
June 30, 1966.   Senior Master.

I

---

(1) R.S.C. 1965 Ord. 41, r. 1 (2) provides: " Where a cause or matter is entitled in more than one matter, it shall be sufficient to state the first matter followed by the words ' and other matters ', and, where a cause or matter is entitled in a matter or matters and between parties, that part of the title which consists of the matter or matters may be omitted."

A

LAWSON (Inspector of Taxes)
v. HOSEMASTER MACHINE CO., LTD.

[COURT OF APPEAL (Sellers, Danckwerts and Winn, L.JJ.), April 26, 27, 28, 29, May 19, 1966.]

Agent—Ratification—Receiver appointed by debenture-holders of first company—
Contract for purchase of shares by another company on behalf of first company   B
without receiver being a party to contract or authorising it—Ratification of
contract some years later by successor to receiver—Validity.

Income Tax—Relief—Losses—Repayment claim—Tax deducted from dividends
on shares—Ownership of shares—Acquisition without receiver's authority—
Ratification by successor receiver—Validity—Income Tax Act, 1952 (15 & 16
Geo. 6 & 1 Eliz. 2 c. 10), s. 341.   C

The taxpayer company* had made losses; it ultimately had discontinued business, and debenture-holders under four debentures had appointed the same individual as receiver and manager, or receiver with like powers, but the taxpayer company was not in liquidation. With a view to making an income tax repayment claim to off-set the losses against dividends available   D
for distribution by another company to be acquired, a finance company purchased the debentures for £127,500, which was more than the value of the taxpayer company's assets (about £100,000). A solicitor of the group of companies which included the finance company, acting without the actual authority of the receiver, viz., of the first receiver appointed by the debenture-holders, but as if he were himself the receiver or had his ostensible authority,   E
arranged for the purchase by the taxpayer company of the shares of a third company which had £472,779 undistributed profits available for distribution as dividend. For financial reasons arising out of the need to borrow the funds necessary for the purchase, the purchase of the third company's shares was carried out by another member of the finance company's group, expressly purporting to act as agent for the taxpayer company (but having no authority   F
at that time to do so) at a fee of £250. The reduced purchase price was £446,556 and the purchase was completed in March, 1956, part of the consideration remaining to be paid later. A few days later in March, 1956, in accordance with the arrangement made with the original debenture-holders, their receiver and manager retired and was replaced by a second receiver and manager appointed by the finance company as the new   G
debenture-holder. In April, 1956, the third company (the company with undistributed profits) paid a net dividend of £225,000, which was credited to the taxpayer company's account, and later it paid further dividends which were similarly dealt with. The taxpayer company paid off the loan raised for the purchase of the third company's shares, being then left with a profit on the transaction amounting to £21,444 less the fee of £250. In 1960   H
the then receiver (who was the third receiver appointed under the debentures) expressly ratified the purchase by the taxpayer company of the third company's shares. In 1963 he sold the shares of the third company (which had been bought by the taxpayer company for £446,556) for £1,200; the whole transaction was thus completed. The taxpayer company meanwhile had claimed repayment of tax deducted from the dividends received (a   I

* In endeavouring to simplify for the purposes of the headnote the statement of essential facts, the names of the companies have not been stated. The " taxpayer company " is the appellant company, Hosemaster Machine Co., Ltd.; the " finance company " is Hallamshire Industrial Finance Trust, Ltd.; the " third company " is F.S. Securities, Ltd., and the other " member of the finance company's group " is Eastlandia, Ltd. The first receiver is Mr. Arthur Eaves, and the third receiver (who ratified the contract) is Mr. Miskin. The second receiver, Mr. Myers, also, so it was alleged, ratified the contract, but Mr. Myers' confirmation was not regarded as amounting to ratification, while Mr. Miskin expressly ratified the contract (see [1965] 3 All E.R., pp. 406, letter E, 407, letter E, and p. 410, letter A).

A   sum of over £240,000), the claim being based on off-setting prior losses in accordance with s. 341 of the Income Tax Act, 1952. On this claim the question* before the court was whether the ratification was effective to vest the dividends on the third company's shares in the taxpayer company at the material dates.

Held: (i) no prior receiver having disclaimed the transaction, the third

B   receiver of the taxpayer company could ratify the transaction as it was done purportedly on behalf of the taxpayer company; on his ratification of it on behalf of the taxpayer company, the title of the taxpayer company to the property acquired (the shares of the third company) related back to the date of the contract to purchase them, and the dividends declared on those shares were property of the taxpayer company at the relevant times, with

C   the consequence that the taxpayer company was entitled to the relief that it claimed under s. 341 of the Income Tax Act, 1952 (see p. 952, letters A and G, post).

(ii) a receiver appointed under the debentures had power to enter into the transaction, and, in view of his primary duty to get in the property charged and for that purpose to carry on and manage the taxpayer company's

D   affairs, he would have failed in his duty in that respect if he had not ratified the transaction in question, which would produce some £240,000 in repayment of tax to add to the taxpayer company's funds available for, among others, the debenture-holders (see p. 950, letter I, and p. 951, letter B, post).

(iii) assuming (as was correct) that the original receiver and manager could not be made personally liable by virtue of s. 369 (2) of the Companies

E   Act, 1948, on the contract to purchase the shares of the third company, as he was never a party to that contract, that did not make any subsequent affirmation of the contract a novation rather than a ratification; moreover, the personal liability of the first receiver on the contract was never a term of the agreement between the vendors and the purchaser of the third company's shares, but such personal liability would have been merely the

F   consequence of s. 369 (2), and its absence (since the first receiver was never a party to the purchase) was no ground for negativing the effectiveness of the subsequent ratification (see p. 950, letters F and H, post).

Decision of CROSS, J., ([1965] 3 All E.R. 401) reversed.

[As to relief from income tax in respect of trading losses, see 20 HALSBURY'S

G   LAWS (3rd Edn.) 465-468, paras. 880-886; and for cases on the subject, see 28 DIGEST (Repl.) 308, *1351, 1352*.

As to who can ratify an agent's acts capable of ratification by his principal, see 1 HALSBURY'S LAWS (3rd Edn.) 177, para. 414; and for cases on the subject, see 1 DIGEST (Repl.) 457-459, *1067-1086*.

As to the position of a receiver and manager for debenture-holders of a com-

H   pany, see 6 HALSBURY'S LAWS (3rd Edn.) 502, 503, paras. 974, 975, and for cases on the subject, see 10 DIGEST (Repl.) 821-823, 5366-5379.]

Cases referred to:

Bird v. *Brown*, (1850), 4 Exch. 786; 19 L.J.Ex. 154; 154 E.R. 1433; 1 Digest (Repl.) 462, *1102*.

Bolton Partners v. *Lambert*, (1889), 41 Ch.D. 295; 58 L.J.Ch. 425; 60 L.T. 687;

I   1 Digest (Repl.) 460, *1088*.

Boston Deep Sea Fishing & Ice Co., Ltd. v. *Farnham (Inspector of Taxes)*, [1957] 3 All E.R. 204; 37 Tax Cas. 505; 28 Digest (Repl.) 268, *1187*.

Gaskell & Grocott v. *Gosling*, [1896] 1 Q.B. 669; 65 L.J.Q.B. 435; 74 L.T. 674; *rvsd.* H.L., sub nom. *Gosling* v. *Gaskell and Grocott*, [1895-99] All E.R. Rep. 300; [1897] A.C. 575; 66 L.J.Q.B. 848; 77 L.T. 314; 10 Digest (Repl.) 822, *5367*.

---

* See p. 950, letter C, post.

Maclean v. *Dunn*, (1828), 4 Bing. 722; 6 L.J.O.S.C.P. 184; 130 E.R. 947; A
1 Digest (Repl.) 476, *1196*.

Meigh v. *Wickenden*, [1942] 2 All E.R. 68; [1942] 2 K.B. 160; 112 L.J.K.B. 76;
167 L.T. 135; 106 J.P. 207; 24 Digest (Repl.) 1043, *151*.

Rochefoucauld v. *Boustead*, [1897] 1 Ch. 196; 66 L.J.Ch. 74; 74 L.T. 502;
12 Digest (Repl.) 190, *1308*.

Spence v. *Inland Revenue Comrs.*, (1941), 24 Tax Cas. 311; 28 Digest (Repl.) B
350, *1548*.

Appeal.

The taxpayer company appealed to the Special Commissioners of Income
Tax against the refusal by the inspector of taxes of its claim made under s. 341
of the Income Tax Act, 1952, for an adjustment of its tax liability under Sch. D
to the Act by reference to losses incurred in 1955-56 and 1956-57. The question C
for decision was whether certain dividends paid by F.S. Securities, Ltd., from
which tax had been deducted were income of the taxpayer company. The
purchase of the shares in F.S. Securities, Ltd., was negotiated wholly or in part by
Mr. Sebag Cohen, one of the solicitors who acted for Hallamshire Industrial
Finance Trust, Ltd., purportedly on behalf of the taxpayer company, the purchase D
being in favour of an associated company as nominee for the taxpayer company.
The taxpayer company contended before the commissioners as follows: (i) Mr.
Cohen had authority, either actual or ostensible, from Mr. Arthur Eaves, as
receiver and manager of the taxpayer company to buy F.S. Securities, Ltd.'s
shares; (ii) if Mr. Cohen had no authority of any kind to buy F.S. Securities,
Ltd.'s shares, their purchase had been ratified by subsequent receivers and E
managers, Mr. Myers and Mr. Miskin, and by the taxpayer company itself;
(iii) if Mr. Cohen had no authority of any kind to buy F.S. Securities, Ltd.'s
shares and their purchase had not been ratified and consequently the dividends
on those shares did not rightly belong to the taxpayer company, nevertheless
the taxpayer company had in fact received the dividends and the taxpayer
company and no other person had suffered tax on them; the taxpayer company F
was therefore entitled to repayment of the tax it had suffered; and (iv) alternatively, if Mr. Cohen had no authority of any kind to buy F.S. Securities, Ltd.'s
shares, nevertheless the dividends on those shares belonged to the taxpayer
company, because all parties concerned in the payment of the dividends agreed
that they should so belong.

The Crown contended before the commissioners as follows: (i) Mr. Cohen had G
no authority of any kind as the taxpayer company's agent to buy F.S. Securities,
Ltd.'s shares; (ii) as regards ratification (a) the only person who could ratify
a contract was the person who, had he been the principal, could have ratified,
(b) a receiver and manager was complete master of the affairs of the company,
having absolute and complete power to manage the property of which he took
possession (*Meigh* v. *Wickenden**), and (c) the only persons, therefore, who could H
have ratified the contract for the purchase of F.S. Securities, Ltd.'s shares
were Mr. Arthur Eaves and Mr. Gilbert Eaves, it did not matter which, and
neither of them had done so; and (iii) there was no valid contract for the purchase
by the taxpayer company of F.S. Securities, Ltd.'s shares, which, therefore, did
not belong to the taxpayer company, with the consequence that, as the taxpayer
company had no title to the dividends in question, it was not entitled under I
s. 341 to repayment of tax deducted from them.

The commissioners found that the determination of the question of entitlement
to the dividends depended on the answers to the following questions. (i) Were
the shares on which the dividends were declared bought by Mr. Cohen as agent
for the taxpayer company with either actual or ostensible authority to buy
them? (ii) If Mr. Cohen had neither type of authority, was the purchase of the
shares ratified by or on behalf of the taxpayer company? (iii) Assuming that the

---

* [1942] 2 All E.R. 68.

A answers to both questions were unfavourable to the taxpayer company, were the dividends nevertheless the income of the taxpayer company for the purposes of the Income Tax Act, 1952? The commissioners found that neither the receiver and manager of the taxpayer company, Mr. Arthur Eaves, nor his brother and partner, Mr. Gilbert Eaves, to whom Mr. Arthur Eaves had delegated much of the conduct of the receivership, had given Mr. Cohen actual authority to buy

B the shares of F.S. Securities, Ltd., as agent of either of them or of the taxpayer company. In so far as it was a question of fact, however, the commissioners found that Mr. Cohen had ostensible authority to buy the shares, and they so held in so far as it was a question of law. If they were wrong in so finding on the evidence, they would have found that there was valid ratification of the purchase. Accordingly the commissioners found that the shares and the relevant dividends thereon

C were the property of the taxpayer company and that the claim succeeded.

On July 22, 1965, as reported at [1965] 3 All E.R. 401, CROSS, J., allowed the Crown's appeal against that decision. The taxpayer company appealed to the Court of Appeal.

The cases noted below* were cited during the argument in addition to those referred to in the judgment of the court.

D J. G. Strangman, Q.C., G. B. H. Dillon, Q.C., and J. L. Creese, for the taxpayer company.

Hubert H. Monroe, Q.C., J. R. Phillips and J. P. Warner for the Crown.

Cur. adv. vult.

May 19. **DANCKWERTS, L.J.**, read the following judgment of the court

E at the invitation of SELLERS, L.J.: This is an appeal from a judgment of CROSS, J. (1) dated July 22, 1965. The case arises out of a claim by the taxpayer company, Hosemaster Machine Co., Ltd., to set off losses incurred by that company in its ordinary trading operations against tax deducted from dividends received from a company called Federated Securities, Ltd., in the years 1955-56 and 1956-57. The matter arises out of the provisions of s. 341 of the Income Tax

F Act, 1952, which enabled companies (and other persons) to claim repayment of tax which had been paid in respect of dividends by setting off trading losses. The Crown have, since the material years, put their finger in the hole in the dyke by subsequent legislation (according to their habit), but at the material time what was carried out by the company which was concerned was lawful if it was successfully carried out, and has been labelled with the opprobrious but possibly not

G inappropriate name of " dividend-stripping ". The Special Commissioners held that the relevant companies had carried out the operation successfully, but CROSS, J. (1) reversed their decision and held that the operation had failed.

---

* Taylor v. Neate, (1888), 39 Ch.D. 538; Lyell v. Kennedy, (1889), 14 App. Cas. 437; Metropolitan Asylums Board (Managers) v. Kingham & Sons, (1890), 6 T.L.R. 217;

H Fleming v. Bank of New Zealand, [1900] A.C. 577; Keighley Maxted & Co. v. Durant, [1900-03] All E.R. Rep. 40; [1901] A.C. 240; Re British Power Traction and Lighting Co., Ltd., Halifax Joint Stock Banking Co., Ltd. v. British Power Traction and Lighting Co., Ltd., [1907] 1 Ch. 528; Aramayo Francke Mines, Ltd. v. Eciott, [1925] A.C. 634; Gough's Garages, Ltd. v. Pugsley, [1930] 1 K.B. 615; Anderton and Halstead, Ltd. v. Birell, [1931] All E.R. Rep. 796; [1932] 1 K.B. 271; Dodworth v. Dale, [1936] 2 All E.R. 440; [1936] 2 K.B. 503; Regal (Hastings), Ltd. v. Gulliver, [1942] 1 All E.R. 378; Re Schebsman, Ex p. Official Receiver, The Trustee v. Cargo Superintendents (London), Ltd.,

I [1943] 2 All E.R. 768; [1944] Ch. 83; Oxford Group v. Inland Revenue Comrs., [1949] 2 All E.R. 537; Solomons v. R. Gertzenstein, Ltd., [1954] 2 All E.R. 625; [1954] 2 Q.B. 243; Re B. Johnson & Co. (Builders), Ltd., [1955] 2 All E.R. 775; [1955] Ch. 634; London County Council v. Farren, [1956] 3 All E.R. 401; Moriarty (Inspector of Taxes) v. Evans Medical Supplies, Ltd., [1957] 3 All E.R. 718; Griffiths (Inspector of Taxes) v. J. P. Harrison (Watford), Ltd., [1962] 1 All E.R. 909; [1963] A.C. 1; Warehousing & Forwarding Co. of East Africa, Ltd. v. Jaffarali & Sons, Ltd., [1963] 3 All E.R. 571; [1964] A.C. 1; Whitehead v. Haines, [1964] 2 All E.R. 530; [1965] 1 Q.B. 200; R. v. Board of Trade, Ex p. St. Martin's Preserving Co., Ltd., [1964] 2 All E.R. 561; [1965] 1 Q.B. 603; Phipps v. Boardman, [1965] 1 All E.R. 849; [1965] Ch. 992.

(1) [1965] 3 All E.R. 401.

In its essence, it was an operation which has been described as " marrying " A
a company which had sustained considerable trading losses to another company
which had considerable moneys in its account representing profits which were
available for distribution as dividends and which would be subject to deduction
of income tax. This marriage of two companies was, of course, a marriage of
convenience which brought a dowry with it, and subsequent events show that
once the object of the union was produced the marriage was speedily dissolved. B
There is no doubt that, if the operation was lawfully carried out, the result would
be that the company with the losses, the taxpayer company, would be entitled
to repayment of sums paid for income tax of over £240,000. The whole point in
the case is whether the operation was effectively and successfully carried out.

The facts are somewhat complicated and involve a lot of technical points, of
which the Crown have sought to take advantage. Some people, on the other C
hand, may be critical of the technicalities and the artificial aspects of the taxpayer company's scheme, which might involve the Crown in a heavy claim.
The old and well-established maxim in regard to taxation (when, indeed, it was
not so penal) was that the taxpayer was fully entitled to arrange his affairs so
as to minimise his liability; but, as has been observed in a previous case, now
the supremacy over the taxpayer has been handed to the taxing authorities. D
However, for the purposes of the present case, we have to decide whether, at
the material date, and on the statutory provisions then existing, the taxpayer
company concerned had carried out a transaction which entitled the company
to repayment of tax. Any other considerations are irrelevant.

The taxpayer company was a company which carried on the business of
manufacturing knitting machines and general engineering. We have not had the E
advantage of seeing the company's memorandum of association, but we think
that it may safely be assumed that it was in the usual elaborate form, covering
most operations and concluding with a final general clause including operations
incidental to and conducing to the company's businesses as previously stated.
At any rate, we understand that the Crown have never contended that the
material transaction was ultra vires in respect of the company. We are told that F
the taxpayer company discontinued the business of manufacturing knitting
machines on July 18, 1956, but what business the company did thereafter we do
not know. At any rate, it is not in liquidation and, therefore, exists as an operating company. Four debentures were issued by the taxpayer company before
June 24, 1955, and were held by (i) Industrial and Commercial Finance Corpn.;
(ii) the Treasury, who held two debentures, and (iii) Lloyds Bank, Ltd. On G
June 24, 1955, Mr. Arthur Eaves was appointed by the finance corporation
to be receiver and manager, and on July 15, 1955, he was appointed receiver by
the Treasury, but, in view of the powers conferred on a receiver appointed under
the finance corporation's debenture, there would be no real difference between a
receiver and a manager so appointed, unless the terms of the other three debentures were different, which is improbable; the other three debentures were H
never put in evidence.

In 1955, Mr. Sandelson, a solicitor, who was a director of Hallamshire Industrial
Finance Trust, Ltd., and was a member of what was called the " Hallamshire
group ", conceived the idea of buying the taxpayer company's debentures and
acquiring a company with dividends available for distribution, against which
the losses could be off-set for the purpose of an income tax repayment claim. I
Accordingly, by an agreement of Dec. 7, 1955, the taxpayer company's debentures
were bought by the Hallamshire company for £127,500. This was a sum greater
than the assets of the taxpayer company in value (which were worth about
£100,000) and it was clear that nothing would be available for the shareholders of
the taxpayer company. The negotiations for this deal were carried out by Messrs.
Coward, Chance & Co., solicitors, who were acting primarily for the finance
corporation, but also for the Treasury and Lloyds Bank, Ltd. (in other words,
for all the debenture-holders), Mr. Sandelson, and a Mr. Sebag Cohen, a solicitor,

A who was acting as one of the Hallamshire company's solicitors. All the debenture-holders including the Treasury obtained the advantage of this price. It was agreed between the parties that Mr. Arthur Eaves, the receiver, should resign from his receivership within twenty-eight days after the transfer of the debentures had taken place. The debenture-holders, who were selling their debentures, were content that any administration of the assets of the taxpayer company should be

B undertaken by the Hallamshire company, as obviously they, the original debenture-holders, would no longer be interested in this after the sale of the debentures.

The next step was that a company with funds available for distribution by way of dividend was found (probably by Mr. Cohen), viz., Federated Securities, Ltd., now called F.S. Securities, Ltd. Money had then to be found for the purchase

C of the shares of F.S. Securities, Ltd., and this had to be financed by borrowing. One of the companies in the Hallamshire group, Eastlandia, Ltd., of which Mr. Sandelson was a director, was used to buy the F.S. Securities, Ltd.'s shares as agent for the taxpayer company. The reason for this was that the money required could be borrowed by the Eastlandia company from the National Bank of Greece at the low rate of interest of one half per cent., because of an arrangement between

D the bank and the Hallamshire group that, as long as the group was in credit, the bank would lend money at that rate. There is not the slightest doubt, however, that everyone concerned knew that Eastlandia, Ltd., was acting in the matter as the agent of the taxpayer company, and on Mar. 20, 1956, a resolution was passed by the directors of Eastlandia, Ltd., authorising Mr. Sandelson to sign the agreement for the purchase of the shares of F.S. Securities, Ltd. (which were

E registered in the names of nominees), and confirming that Eastlandia, Ltd., was entering into this agreement as agent for the taxpayer company at an agreed fee of £250.

Mr. Cohen seems to have been largely concerned with this transaction, acting as if he were the receiver and manager of the taxpayer company or as authorised by Mr. Arthur Eaves to act in this way. The Special Commissioners found that

F neither Mr. Arthur Eaves nor his brother Mr. Gilbert Eaves (who acted for him) had given Mr. Cohen actual authority to buy F.S. Securities, Ltd.'s shares as the agent of them or of the taxpayer company, but they found, so far as it was a question of fact, and held so far as a question of law, that Mr. Cohen had ostensible authority to buy the shares. Eastlandia, Ltd., at the time of the operations mentioned, had no authority to act as the taxpayer company's agent. The

G vendors sold the hundred issued £1 shares of F.S. Securities, Ltd., to Eastlandia, Ltd., for £446,556 by an agreement dated Mar. 20, 1956, and a supplementary agreement dated Mar. 20, 1958. F.S. Securities, Ltd., had undistributed profits of £472,779 available for distribution as dividends. The purchase was to be completed on Mar. 20, 1956, and the consideration was to be paid as to £233,000 on completion and the balance not later than twelve months from the date of the

H agreement.

On Apr. 5, 1956, F.S. Securities, Ltd., paid a dividend of £225,000 by means of a cheque in favour of the National Bank of Greece, which apparently was credited to the account of the taxpayer company. The further dividends of £100,000 on Apr. 2, 1957, and £143,000 on Dec. 16, 1960, were paid direct to the taxpayer company. The loan from the National Bank of Greece was duly repaid, and the

I purchase price for the shares was duly paid to the nominees, who were the registered shareholders of F.S. Securities, Ltd. At some time before the third payment of a dividend, Eastlandia, Ltd., had become the registered owner of the shares. The result of the transaction was that, after reimbursing Eastlandia, Ltd., the price paid for the shares, the taxpayer company received a profit on the transaction of £21,444, less the £250 fee which was paid to Eastlandia, Ltd.

Neither Mr. Arthur Eaves nor Mr. Gilbert Eaves took any part in these trans-actions, though Mr. Gilbert Eaves, who seems to have conducted the receiver's business in respect of the taxpayer company, knew Mr. Cohen well and must

have known what was going on. Mr. Arthur Eaves did not in fact retire from the A
receivership on Jan. 17, 1956, but retired on Mar. 28, 1956, when he was replaced
by Mr. Bernard Myers, who acted as receiver and manager until Sept. 17, 1957,
when Mr. Edgar Miskin was appointed the receiver and manager. On Feb. 14,
1963, Mr. Miskin sold the F.S. Securities, Ltd.'s shares for £1,200, and that sum
was paid by him into the taxpayer company's account, and so the whole transaction was conducted as every person concerned intended.   B

There cannot be any doubt on the facts that the purchase of the F.S. Securities,
Ltd., shares was adopted or ratified in fact on behalf of the taxpayer company,
which acquired the shares beneficially (until they were sold) and received the
three dividends on the shares. The whole point is whether the ratification was
effective to vest the property in the dividends in the taxpayer company at the
material dates so as to enable the company to claim repayment of the tax paid C
in respect of the dividends. The points taken against that result are of the most
technical kind, but, of course, if they are well-founded they must prevail in
favour of the Crown.

The Special Commissioners' finding that Mr. Cohen had ostensible authority
to purchase the F.S. Securities, Ltd., shares was reversed by CROSS, J. (2). Before
us the case really was argued on the question whether there had been an effective D
ratification of the purchase of the F.S. Securities, Ltd., shares by Eastlandia,
Ltd., by the conduct of Mr. Myers. CROSS, J., decided (3) that there had not been
an effective ratification. The judge was principally influenced in this result by
the provisions of s. 369 (2) of the Companies Act, 1948, which put a debenture-
holder's receiver in the same position as a receiver appointed by the court, in
providing that such a receiver is to be personally liable on any contracts entered E
into by him, unless the contrary was provided. The judge was impressed by the
possibility that a ratification by reason of the subsection would place a personal
liability on Mr. Eaves against his will in a transaction in which he had taken no
part.

The argument before us proceeded on a rather different footing. Assuming
(as we think correctly) that Mr. Eaves could not be subjected to personal liability F
on a contract to which he was never a party, it was contended that the vendors
were deprived of a security which the contract with Mr. Eaves (as the receiver
at the material time) would have given, by an attempt to ratify the contract at a
later date and by a different receiver, and, therefore, it was said that this was a
different contract and not a ratification, and could only be effective from the
later date as a novation. This seems to us to be based on a misapprehension of G
the situation. In the first place, the interested parties to the contract, viz., the
vendors of the shares in F.S. Securities, Ltd., never raised any objection as to
any loss of Mr. Eaves' personal liability, and never needed any such liability,
and the contract was completed to everyone's satisfaction and exactly as planned
by the persons financially interested. In the second place, the personal liability
of the original receiver, Mr. Eaves, was not a term of the contract of the parties, H
the vendors and the purchasing company; it would simply be imposed by a
statutory provision contained in s. 369 (2) of the Companies Act, 1948; but as
Mr. Arthur Eaves was never a party to the contract that subsection never took
effect.

It was contended before us that a receiver appointed under the debenture had
no power to enter into this transaction. This contention, in our opinion, fails. I
The powers conferred on such a receiver by cl. 7 of the debenture are extremely
wide. We would refer particularly to paras. (1), (b) and (j). We do not think that
para. (f) is appropriate to the present transaction. The primary duty of a receiver
of this character was to get in the property charged, and to carry on and manage
the businesses of the company in that process. It was his duty to carry out those
duties to the best advantage of the company and, therefore, the debenture-
holders. What could be more advantageous than to carry out a transaction

(2) [1965] 3 All E.R. at p. 409, letter I.   (3) [1965] 3 All E.R. at pp. 409, 410.

A which added to the assets covered by the debentures the sum of over £240,000 by repayment of tax, exactly as foreseen by the shrewd Mr. Sandelson? This involves management of the business of the taxpayer company, and in the course of it the borrowing from the National Bank of Greece, which, therefore, was authorised by para. (b). The whole transaction was so advantageous to the finances of the taxpayer company that the receiver of the taxpayer company

B would have been foolish not to adopt and ratify the operations conducted on behalf of the taxpayer company (though without authority as that company's agent) and, if he had refused to adopt the transaction, he would, in our opinion, have been in default as regards his duty. No reflection is made in regard to Mr. Eaves. He was not directly concerned and his later doubts seem to us to be misplaced.

C That is really the end of this case. There is no doubt that on ratification the title of the ostensible principal dates back to the date of the contract adopted: *Maclean* v. *Dunn* (4); *Bolton Partners* v. *Lambert* (5) (in the Court of Appeal); *Spence* v. *Inland Revenue Comrs.* (6) (Court of Session).

Eastlandia, Ltd., was clearly bound by the resolution of the capacity in which it purported to enter into the contract, i.e., as agent for the taxpayer company.

D It is true that it could not make that resolution evidence in favour of itself. The point is that Eastlandia, Ltd., could not prevent the taxpayer company taking advantage of it, and taking up the contract purported to be made on its behalf and adopting it. Once the taxpayer company had adopted the contract and ratified the agency, it was impossible legally for Eastlandia, Ltd., to refuse to carry out its obligations as agent of the taxpayer company and Eastlandia,

E Ltd., held whatever interest it had in the shares of F.S. Securities, Ltd., whether an equitable interest behind the registration of the nominees, or its legal interest in the shares as the registered proprietors on the companies register, as trustees for the taxpayer company. It was in no different position from the express agents in *Rochefoucauld* v. *Boustead* (7).

This is really all elementary law. We were referred to a large number of

F authorities which the commendable industry of counsel had discovered or their experience and knowledge had provided for them, but nearly all of them had no real relevance to this case: for instance, the peculiar results produced by the Factories Acts in *Meigh* v. *Wickenden* (8) or the eccentric meaning given to the word " owner " in respect of certain special legislation in regard to property.

We think that it is desirable to lay emphasis on the point that at all times

G the taxpayer company was an existing company, not in liquidation, and apparently carrying on business of some sort. It was capable of carrying out any business transaction which was within its powers as contained in its memorandum of association. There has to be some effective agent to operate the company, as there must be always in respect of a corporation. As long as there was some person who was at the material moment able to carry out the operation on behalf

H of the company, there was no bar to the company carrying out the transaction, as there was in *Boston Deep Sea Fishing & Ice Co., Ltd.* v. *Farnham (Inspector of Taxes)* (9), where the status of an enemy alien made the operations of the company wholly unlawful. No reference has been made in the course of this case to the directors of the company and, presumably, after appointment of the receiver, they could not act, or at any rate could only act under the directions

I of the receiver: see the masterly statement in regard to the position of a debenture-holder's receiver by RIGBY, L.J., in *Gaskell & Grocott* v. *Gosling* (10), a case which went to the House of Lords (11).

---

(4) (1828), 4 Bing. 722.　　　　　　　　　　　(5) (1889), 41 Ch.D. 295.
(6) (1941), 24 Tax Cas. 311.　　　　　　　　　(7) [1897] 1 Ch. 196.
(8) [1942] 2 All E.R. 68; [1942] 2 K.B. 160.
(9) [1957] 3 All E.R. 204; 37 Tax Cas. 505.
(10) [1896] 1 Q.B. 669 at pp. 691-693.
(11) [1895-99] All E.R. Rep. 300; [1897] A.C. 575.

With all respect to the judge, we think that he took too narrow a view in regard A
to the powers of a debenture-holder's receiver. We can see no reason why an
act purported to be done by some person as the agent of the taxpayer company,
though without authority, cannot be ratified by a subsequent receiver or any
other person competent to act on behalf of the company, as long as the act had
not been disclaimed by the original receiver. Whatever Mr. Eaves' subsequent
views may have been, there is no evidence that Mr. Eaves ever disclaimed the B
transaction. There is some evidence that he acquiesced in the scheme which was
carried out, and he seems to have agreed readily to retire when the debentures
were purchased (12).

The judge seems to have been mistaken in thinking (13) that the ratification of
the contract by a subsequent receiver could impose, against his will, and in the
absence of any participation by him in the transaction, any personal liability. C
This view influenced his opinion towards a result which was not correct. As we
have pointed out earlier, the true position was that no personal liability ever fell
on Mr. Eaves. The only persons who could claim that they were adversely affected
were the vendors, who never took the point and were never affected in fact by
it, and, as we have explained, it was purely a statutory incident and no part of
the bargain by the parties, and in fact never applied as Mr. Arthur Eaves was D
not a party to the transaction.

Of course, if between the date of the purported contract on behalf of the
taxpayer company and the attempted ratification, the rights of third parties had
attached to the property purported to be dealt with, as in *Bird* v. *Brown* (14),
there might well be difficulties; but we cannot regard the Crown as having any
such rights. They had no interest in the shares of F.S. Securities, Ltd., which E
were purchased, or even in the dividends which were declared, or the funds out
of which these were paid. The only right they had was to tax the company,
F.S. Securities, Ltd., which was always liable to be affected by a situation in which
offset losses might result in a claim for repayment.

In reaching the result which we have reached we have not found it necessary
to rely on the usual formal provision in the debenture by which the receiver F
is to be deemed to be the agent of the company. In our view, the true position
of the receiver is amply sufficient to support the result in view of the powers
conferred on him by the debenture. In the result, we think that the taxpayer
company has made out its case and is entitled to repayment as claimed. The
judgment of CROSS, J. (15), must be reversed and the claim allowed, as decided
by the Special Commissioners, though not for precisely the same reasons. G

Appeal allowed. Leave to appeal to House of Lords refused.

Solicitors: *Beer & Co.* (for the taxpayer company); *Solicitor of Inland Revenue.*

[*Reported by* F. A. AMIES, ESQ., *Barrister-at-Law.*]

H

I

---

(12) I.e., purchased by Hallamshire Industrial Finance Trust, Ltd.
(13) [1965] 3 All E.R. at p. 410.   (14) (1850), 4 Exch. 786
        (15) [1965] 3 All E.R. 401.

A

NOTE.

R. *v.* SCULLY.

B
[Court of Criminal Appeal (Lord Parker, C.J., Marshall and James, JJ.), May 26, 1966.]

Criminal Law—Sentence—Youthful offender—Age within limits of qualification for borstal training—Consecutive sentences of a year or less in the aggregate exceeding three years—Whether such sentences of imprisonment can properly be passed in view of Criminal Justice Act, 1961 (9 & 10 Eliz. 2 c. 39), s. 3 (1), s. 38 (4).

C
[Editorial Note. This case should be considered with *R. v. Lowe*, [1964] 2 All E.R. 116.

As to punishment of youthful offenders, see 10 Halsbury's Laws (3rd Edn.) 514, 515, para. 935.

For the Criminal Justice Act, 1961, s. 3, s. 38, see 41 Halsbury's Statutes (2nd Edn.) 132, 143.]

D
Appeal.

The appellant, Terence Scully, pleaded guilty on Mar. 3, 1966, at Liverpool Crown Court before the recorder (Judge Chapman, Q.C.) to three counts of driving whilst disqualified, asked for seven other offences to be taken into consideration and was sentenced to six months' imprisonment on each count
E
consecutive and disqualified from holding a driving licence for twelve months. He was also sentenced in respect of seven offences to which he had pleaded guilty at Liverpool magistrates' court on Feb. 25, 1966, viz., (1) dangerous driving, (2) driving whilst disqualified, (3) and (6) driving whilst uninsured, (4) larceny of a driving licence, (5) larceny of a car and (7) fraudulent use of the licence. The committals in respect of (1) to (4) and (7) were under s. 28 of the Magistrates'
F
Courts Act, 1952, and that in respect of (5) and (6) under s. 29 of that Act. He was sentenced to twelve months' imprisonment consecutive on (1) and (5); to six months' imprisonment consecutive on (2) and to three months' imprisonment concurrent on each of (3), (4), (6) and (7), making thirty months' imprisonment in all to run consecutively with the sentences imposed by the recorder in respect of the offences to which he pleaded guilty (four years in all). The report of the
G
case is confined to a question of law, viz., the validity of the aggregate sentence of imprisonment in view of s. 3 (1) and s. 38 (4) of the Criminal Justice Act, 1961. It was, however, clear that the sentence on (1) being a sentence of twelve months' imprisonment for dangerous driving imposed on committal under s. 28 of the Act of 1952 could not stand in view of s. 20 of the Criminal Justice Act, 1948, and s. 2 (1) (*b*) of the Road Traffic Act, 1960, but must be reduced to one of
H
four months; and certain orders of disqualification needed variation in view of s. 5 of the Road Traffic Act, 1962. The appellant appealed against sentence.

G. Abrahams for the appellant.
The Crown was not represented.

JAMES, J., delivered the judgment of the court, in which, after stating
I
the offences and sentences and the relevant facts and circumstances and history of the appellant, he said: It is urged on his behalf before this court that both in respect of law and on the merits the sentences imposed were wrong. As to the law, it is urged that, under s. 3 (1) of the Criminal Justice Act, 1961, the power of the recorder in respect of imprisonment was to sentence the appellant, a young man of twenty, to a term not exceeding six months or, where the court had power to pass such a sentence, to a term of not less than three years, and it is argued on his behalf that the provisions of s. 38 (4) of the Act of 1961 do not

_____
* Section 38 (4) is set out at p. 954, letter B, post.

enable the court to pass a sentence for an offence between the period of six   A
months and three years or to aggregate sentences so as to bring them up above
the period of three years.   The terms of s. 38 (4) are:

> " For the purposes of any reference in this Act to a term of imprisonment
> or of detention in a detention centre or to a term of imprisonment or deten-
> tion, consecutive terms and terms which are wholly or partly concurrent   B
> shall be treated as a single term."

Counsel for the appellant argues that the working of the court's mind should be
first to fix a sentence, and that must be done within the strict limits of s. 3 (1)
of the Act of 1961 and must be done independently of s. 38 (4) of that Act.
This court is not of that view and does not accept that contention.   The court
can look to s. 38 (4) and, in the light of the terms of that subsection, the court   C
can impose a sentence which is one of less than six months or one of three years
or more, provided that such a sentence can be properly passed in respect of the
offences the court is dealing with.   The contentions put forward in respect of
the law in this matter are rejected by this court, save and except that the sentence
of twelve months' imprisonment for the dangerous driving offence, for which
the committal order was under s. 28 of the Magistrates' Courts Act, 1952, is   D
bad in law and must be reduced to a sentence of four months' imprisonment
in respect of that charge, and this court varies and substitutes the period of
four months for twelve months in that case.

[HIS LORDSHIP referred to the argument on behalf of the appellant on the
merits and continued:] Having listened to all that has been said on the appel-   E
lant's behalf, the court has reached the very firm conclusion that, both in law
and on the merits, the sentence of three years four months' imprisonment which
will now stand, is richly deserved.   The appeal, therefore, will be allowed to
this extent, and this extent only, that the sentence of four months' imprisonment
will be substituted for the sentence of twelve months' imprisonment in respect
of the dangerous driving charge, and there will be the variation in the orders   F
of disqualification to which I have earlier referred.

Appeal allowed in part.   Sentence varied.

Solicitors: *Registrar, Court of Criminal Appeal* (for the appellant).

[*Reported by* N. P. METCALFE, ESQ., *Barrister-at-Law.*]

A

CURTIS'S FURNISHING STORES, LTD. *v.* FREEDMAN.

[CHANCERY DIVISION (Cross, J.), May 6, 9, 10, 11, 27, 1966.]

Company—Misfeasance—Misfeasance by director—Release of indebtedness of director to company made a term of his selling his controlling shares to individuals—Company subsequently releasing by conduct his indebtedness without consideration for the release—Subsequent liquidation of company— Whether director guilty of misfeasance by entering into the agreement— Companies Act, 1948 (11 & 12 Geo. 6 c. 38), s. 54 (1).

B

Company—Winding-up—Voluntary winding-up—Misfeasance action by company in liquidation against director—Whether liquidator necessary as co-plaintiff.

C

At the beginning of 1959 a private company was controlled by the defendant, who held 29,898 of the 30,000 shares of £1 each forming the capital of the company, his wife holding one share and the remaining 101 shares being held by the executors of his father's will. The defendant and his wife were the sole directors. Both the company and the defendant were in serious financial difficulties. The company's assets, available for unsecured creditors, apart from a debt of £22,548 owed to it by the defendant, were worth some £7,500. Its preferential creditors amounted to £589 and its other unsecured debts to £17,000 odd. The general creditors might expect to receive about 8s. in the £1. The company had " tax losses " of about £25,000. I.F., Ltd. a company controlled by M. and J., the elder brother and nephew of the defendant, agreed to pay off the preferential creditors and to buy the unsecured debts of the company on payment of 12s. in the £1 of their face value. On Mar. 20, 1959, an agreement was entered into between the defendant and his wife of the one part and M. and J. of the other part, whereby the vendors agreed to sell and the purchasers to buy the whole share capital of the company for £1, and the vendors agreed that on completion, which was fixed for the same day, they would retire from office as directors and would procure the appointment of such new directors as the purchasers should require. Clause 6 was as follows—" Upon completion of the sale and purchase of the shares in the company . . . the purchasers shall procure that the company will forthwith without payment release the vendor . . . from his . . . indebtedness to the company as at the completion date ". This agreement was carried out, save that the debt of the defendant was merely treated by the company as extinguished, no deed of release being executed. On May 30, 1962, the company went into a creditors' voluntary liquidation. The liquidator caused the company to bring an action to recover the amount of the debt from the defendant, alleging misfeasance as a director on the defendant's part in bargaining with M. and J. for a gratuitous release of the debt by the company in consideration of his selling his shares in the company to M. and J. and in thereby causing a breach of s. 54 (1)* of the Companies Act, 1948, to be committed. It was accepted that, though no formal release of the debt had been executed, the company in liquidation could not contend that the debt was still an enforceable liability of the defendant's.

D

E

F

G

H

I

Held: (i) in the contract of Mar. 20, 1959, the defendant had merely stipulated as a term of his transferring his shares that he should get an effective release for his debt to the company, and, as there was no reason why M. & J. should not have paid to the company such sum as would justify the company in releasing the debt, no misfeasance nor any infringement of s. 54 (1) of the Companies Act, 1948, was necessarily involved in carrying out the terms of transfer; accordingly the defendant was not party to any misfeasance and the action failed (see p. 961, letters D and F, post).

---

* Section 54 is printed in footnote (1), p. 959, post.

(ii) the action was properly constituted without the liquidator being a   A
party (see p. 961, letter A, post).

Independent Automatic Sales, Ltd. v. *Knowles and Foster* ([1962] 3 All
E.R. 27) distinguished.

Per CURIAM: if a director, who is about to retire and to sell his shares in
the company, makes a bargain with his intended successor and the purchaser
of the shares that, when he controls the company, he will procure it to   B
make a present to him out of its assets, the recipient of the resulting present
is as guilty of misfeasance as the directors who have procured the gift to
be made (see p. 960, letter G, post).

Head v. *Gould* ([1898] 2 Ch. 250) applied.

[As to a company's assisting the purchase of its shares, see 6 HALSBURY'S
LAWS (3rd Edn.) 170, 171, para. 358; and for cases on the subject, see 9 DIGEST   C
(Repl.) 649-652, *4313-4333.*

As to a director's liability for misfeasance, see 6 HALSBURY'S LAWS (3rd Edn.)
623, para. 1227.

For the Companies Act, 1948, s. 54, see 3 HALSBURY'S STATUTES (2nd Edn.)
507.]
                                                                          D
Cases referred to:

Head v. *Gould,* [1898] 2 Ch. 250; 67 L.J.Ch. 480; 78 L.T. 739; **43** Digest
    667, *988.*

Independent Automatic Sales, Ltd. v. *Knowles and Foster,* [1962] 3 All E.R. 27;
    [1962] 1 W.L.R. 974; Digest (Cont. Vol. A) 181, *5287b.*

Steen v. *Law,* [1963] 3 All E.R. 770; [1964] A.C. 287; [1963] 3 W.L.R. 802;   E
    Digest (Cont. Vol. A) 169, *1353b.*

Victor Battery Co., Ltd. v. *Curry's, Ltd.,* [1946] 1 All E.R. 519; [1946] Ch. 242;
    115 L.J.Ch. 148; 174 L.T. 326; 9 Digest (Repl.) 651, *4330.*

Action.

This was an action brought by the plaintiffs, Curtis's Furnishing Stores, Ltd.,
a company in voluntary liquidation, against the defendant, Phineas Louis   F
Freedman, a former director and principal shareholder of the company whereby the
plaintiffs claimed (i) payment of the sum of £22,548 as money owed by the defendant to the plaintiffs, or as money had and received to the use of the plaintiffs, or (ii) that sum by way of damages for misfeasance as a director of the
plaintiffs. The facts are set out in the judgment, the ground of contention
at the hearing being stated at p. 959, letters E and F, post.   G

The cases noted below* were cited during the argument in addition to those
referred to in the judgment.

R. A. K. Wright for the plaintiffs, the company.
Muir Hunter, Q.C., and *E. C. Evans-Lombe* for the defendant.

                                                        Cur. adv. vult.   H

May 27. **CROSS, J.,** read the following judgment: The plaintiffs, Curtis's
Furnishing Stores, Ltd. (which I will call " the company ") is a private company
incorporated in 1917. At the beginning of 1959, it was controlled by Phineas
Louis Freedman, the younger son of its founder. He held 29,898 of the 30,000
shares, his wife held one share and the remaining 101 shares were held by the
executors of his father's will. He and his wife were the sole directors. The   I

* *Re Exchange Banking Co. (Flitcroft's case)* (1882), 21 Ch.D. 519; *Re Lee, Behrens & Co., Ltd.,* [1932] All E.R. Rep. 889; [1932] 2 Ch. 46; *Spink (Bournemouth), Ltd.* v. *Spink,* [1936] 1 All E.R. 597; [1936] Ch. 544; *Crofter Hand Woven Harris Tweed Co., Ltd.* v. *Veitch,* [1942] 1 All E.R. 142; [1942] A.C. 435; *Re V. G. M. Holdings, Ltd.,* [1942] 1 All E.R. 224; [1942] Ch. 235; *Re M. Kushler, Ltd.,* [1943] 2 All E.R. 22; [1943] Ch. 248; *Kiriri Cotton Co., Ltd.* v. *Dewani,* [1960] 1 All E.R. 177; [1960] A.C. 192; *Parke* v. *Daily News, Ltd.,* [1962] 2 All E.R. 929; [1962] Ch. 927; *Mistry Amar Singh* v. *Kulubya,* [1963] 3 All E.R. 499; [1964] A.C. 142; *Ridge Securities, Ltd.* v. *Inland Revenue Comrs.,* [1964] 1 All E.R. 275.

A company at that time was in serious financial difficulties. Its assets, available for unsecured creditors, apart from a debt of £22,548 owing to it by P. L. Freedman, were worth some £7,500. Its preferential creditors amounted to £589 and its other unsecured debts to £17,000 odd. Mr. Freedman was also in serious financial difficulties himself. He owed large sums for tax and the revenue authorities were in fact administering his affairs under an informal

B arrangement with him.

In those circumstances, at the suggestion of Mr. Hirshfield, a member of the firm of Hesketh, Hardy, Hirshfield & Co., the company's accountants, a meeting of the company's creditors was called on Feb. 9, 1959, to discuss the position. At that meeting, a statement of the company's affairs was produced and a committee representing the principal creditors was appointed. The statement

C of affairs showed the debt owing by P. L. Freedman as valueless. The company had " tax " losses of some £25,000 and P. L. Freedman was prepared to sell or procure the sale of the shares to a purchaser for a nominal consideration, provided that he was released from any liability for his debt. If, therefore, they could be assured that the debt was, in fact, irrecoverable at that date, the creditors might prefer not to put the company into liquidation but to assign

D their debts to a purchaser who, in order to acquire the company with its tax losses as a going concern, might be prepared to give them rather more than the value of 8s. in the pound which their debts would seem to be worth.

The minutes of the meetings of the committee of creditors held on Feb. 1 and Feb. 20 were put in evidence and supplemented by the oral evidence of Mr. Hirshfield, of Mr. Pegley, an employee of his firm at that date, and of Mr. Shaw,

E a member of the committee of inspection. What happened was this. Some of the creditors raised the question of the value of Mr. Freedman's debt but Mr. Hirshfield explained to them that if they sought to recover the debt by liquidating the company, the revenue authorities would make Mr. Freedman bankrupt and take all or the bulk of his assets as preferential creditors for tax. Being satisfied that the debt should be treated as having no value to them, the creditors were

F willing to assign their debts to a purchaser and several offers were received. The best proved to be one from Islington Furnishing Co., Ltd., a company which was controlled by Myer Freedman and Joseph Freedman, the elder brother and nephew of P. L. Freedman. This offer was not prompted by family affection for the two brothers were not then on speaking terms, but Mr. Hirshfield had thought that Myer Freedman and Joseph Freedman

G might be interested in acquiring the shares for the sake of the tax losses and so had brought the facts to their notice. Their offer was accepted; they paid off the preferential creditors and the other unsecured creditors of the company assigned their debts to them on payment of 12s. in the pound on their face value.

On Mar. 20, 1959, an agreement was entered into between P. L. Freedman and his wife of the one part and Myer Freedman and Joseph Freedman

H of the other part whereby the vendors agreed to sell and the purchasers agreed to purchase the whole share capital, thirty thousand shares of £1 each in the company for £1, and the vendors agreed that on completion—which was fixed for the same day—they would retire from office as directors and procure the appointment of such new directors as the purchasers should require. Clause 6 was in the following terms:

I " Upon completion of the sale and purchase of the shares in the company as hereinbefore provided the purchasers shall procure that the company will forthwith without payment release the vendors or either of them and one Neil Solomon Freedman the present secretary of the company from his her or their indebtedness to the company as at the completion date."

It does not appear that Mrs. Freedman in fact owed any money to the company and the question of the debt of the secretary, their son, Neil Solomon Freedman, is irrelevant to the present proceedings.

The share transfers were delivered and the directorships were resigned on the   A
same day.   The following correspondence then took place between the solicitors
for the parties.   On Mar. 24, 1959, P. L. Freedman's solicitors wrote to the
solicitors acting for Myer Freedman and Joseph Freedman as follows:

> " We refer to the completion of this matter, which took place on Friday
> last.   We now enclose draft deed of release for approval on behalf of your
> clients, and return to us in the usual way.   We enclose a carbon copy thereof   B
> for your file purposes."

The draft release was between the company of the one part, Myer Freedman
and Joseph Freedman (called Messrs. Freedman) of the second part and
P. L. Freedman and his wife (the debtors) of the third part, and was in the
following terms:
C
> " Whereas Messrs. Freedman have agreed with the debtors to procure
> that the company will forthwith without payment release the debtors and
> each of them from his her or their indebtedness to the company in manner
> hereinafter appearing.   Now this deed witnesseth as follows: 1. In pur-
> suance of the said agreement and at the request of Messrs. Freedman the
> company hereby release and forever discharge the debtors and each of   D
> them their and every of their personal representatives and assigns from all
> debts due from the debtors or any of them to the company and all parts
> thereof and from all interest now due or hereafter to become due thereon
> and from all actions proceedings claims and demands in respect of the said
> debts or any of them and the interest thereon or otherwise in relation to
> the premises.   In Witness, etc., . . ."
E
Then the purchasers' solicitors, Myer Freedman's and Joseph Freedman's
solicitors, wrote on Mar. 25, 1959,

> " We thank you for your letter of yesterday's date and its enclosures
> and are returning the draft deed of release herewith duly approved.   If you
> will kindly let us have the engrossment in due course we will have it duly   F
> executed."

On Mar. 31, the vendors' solicitors sent the engrossment to the purchasers'
solicitors and on Apr. 1 the purchasers' solicitors wrote back saying:

> " We thank you for your letter of yesterday's date enclosing the engross-
> ment of the deed of release for sealing by the company and execution by
> [Myer Freedman and Joseph Freedman].   We have forwarded the deed   G
> to our clients for this purpose and will return it to you duly executed in
> due course."

Then on Apr. 14, the vendors' solicitors asked whether they could have the deed
of release duly executed and returned to them and on Apr. 15, there comes this
letter from the purchasers' solicitors:

> " We thank you for your letter of yesterday's date, but understand from   H
> our clients that after a discussion with P. L. Freedman, it has been
> arranged that the formal deed of release shall not be executed for the time
> being."

I do not know why that deed of release was not executed.   Neither Myer
Freedman nor P. L. Freedman, who both gave evidence, can remember the   I
reason—or indeed anything about the matter.   Joseph Freedman did not give
evidence and it may possibly be that it was he who discussed the question
with his uncle.   But although no document was executed by the company
the debt was treated by it as extinguished.   It had appeared as an asset in
the accounts of 1958 but in the accounts for the year ending Dec. 31, 1959,
it was written off, and those accounts were approved by the shareholders, that
is to say Myer Freedman and Joseph Freedman, at an annual general meeting
held on Apr. 7, 1961.

A   The company, under its new management, issued a number of new shares, took over the Islington Furnishing Co. and presumably reaped some benefit from its past tax losses.   Nevertheless, it once more fell on evil days, as a result, Myer Freedman told me, of the credit squeeze and on May 30, 1962, it went into a creditors' voluntary liquidation.   Many of the creditors, to whom the company owed money in 1959 and who had assigned their debts to Myer

B   Freedman and Joseph Freedman, gave fresh credit to the company after the change of management and are creditors in the present liquidation.

Mr. Hedges, the liquidator, on looking through the company's books, was struck by the fact that a debt of over £22,000 had been written off for no apparent reason and raised the matter with P. L. Freedman.   Having been advised that, notwithstanding what had happened in 1959, the company was still entitled to

C   enforce the debt, he demanded payment of it and, as P. L. Freedman claimed that it had been effectively released, the company started this action against him by specially endorsed writ in the Queen's Bench Division on Feb. 7, 1963. P. L. Freedman obtained leave to defend; the statement of claim was amended and as in its amended form it raised issues of company law the action was, on Feb. 20, 1964, transferred to this division.   There was a good deal of discussion

D   before me as to what points were open to the parties on the amended pleadings, but I do not propose to refer to them in detail.   I shall simply state what was and was not contended before me.   In the first place, it was accepted that though no formal release had been executed, the company, even though now in liquidation, could not contend that this debt was still in being as a liability which the company could enforce against P. L. Freedman in the ordinary way.   I do not suggest

E   that this concession was not rightly made; but it is desirable to record that it was made.   What the company did contend was that P. L. Freedman who was still a director when he entered into the agreement of Mar. 20, 1959, committed a misfeasance in bargaining with Myer Freedman and Joseph Freedman, his successors as directors, that, in consideration of his selling to them his shares, they would use their directors' powers to cause the company to release his debt

F   without consideration and, at the same time, to commit a breach of s. 54 (1) of the Companies Act, 1948 (1), by providing them financial assistance in their purchase of the shares.   For good measure, the company also alleged that by entering into this agreement P. L. Freedman " conspired " with Myer Freedman and Joseph Freedman, to injure the company, but such an allegation was surplusage.   If his entering into the agreement was not a misfeasance, he

G   cannot have taken part in a conspiracy by doing so, and if it was a misfeasance it adds nothing to say that he thereby also entered into some sort of conspiracy.

In answer to those contentions, P. L. Freedman sought to show that the company had received consideration for the release either from the creditors or from Myer Freedman and Joseph Freedman or from all of them.   I could

---

H   (1) Section 54 provides as follows: " (1) Subject as provided in this section, it shall not be lawful for a company to give, whether directly or indirectly, and whether by means of a loan, guarantee, the provision of security or otherwise, any financial assistance for the purpose of or in connexion with a purchase or subscription made or to be made by any person of or for any shares in the company, or, where the company is a subsidiary company, in its holding company: Provided that nothing in this section shall be taken to prohibit—(a) where the lending of money is part of the ordinary business of a com-

I   pany, the lending of money by the company in the ordinary course of its business; (b) the provision by a company, in accordance with any scheme for the time being in force, of money for the purchase of, or subscription for, fully-paid shares in the company or its holding company, being a purchase or subscription by trustees of or for shares to be held by or for the benefit of employees of the company, including any director holding a salaried employment or office in the company; (c) the making by a company of loans to persons, other than directors, bona fide in the employment of the company with a view to enabling those persons to purchase or subscribe for fully-paid shares in the company or its holding company to be held by themselves by way of beneficial ownership. (2) If a company acts in contravention of this section, the company and every officer of the company who is in default shall be liable to a fine not exceeding £100."

not follow this argument. The creditors were not interested in the question A
whether the debt was released. No doubt they knew, or at least those of them
who were represented on the committee knew, that any purchaser of the shares
would be required to procure that the debt was released, but all that was of
interest to them was to be satisfied that the debt had no present value to them.
The arrangement into which they entered was simply between themselves and
Myer Freedman and Joseph Freedman, and what arrangement, if any, Myer B
Freedman and Joseph Freedman made with P. L. Freedman for the release
of the debt was a matter of indifference to them. Nor did Myer Freedman
and Joseph Freedman give any consideration to the company or deal with the
company as a separate entity in any way. They simply bought up the unsecured debts and stepped into the shoes of the creditors. No doubt it can
be said that the company was better off with the debts vested in Myer Freedman C
and Joseph Freedman than it was with the debts vested in the original creditors,
because Myer Freedman and Joseph Freedman were going to acquire the shares
and continue to carry on the business. But the fresh lease of life which the
company gained from the arrangement was not the outcome of any agreement
to which the company was a party and, as I see it, cannot be treated as consideration to the company for the release of P. L. Freedman's debt.   D

As regards s. 54 of the Companies Act, 1948, counsel for P. L. Freedman pointed
out that the infringement occurred, not when the agreement was entered into
but later when the company, under the control of Myer Freedman and Joseph
Freedman, released the debt, as I must take it that it did. It was further
pointed out that the decision of ROXBURGH, J., in *Victor Battery Co., Ltd.* v.
Curry's, Ltd. (2), showed that although the section made the company guilty of E
a criminal offence, it did not invalidate the disposition—in this case the release—
which the company had made. On the other hand, the case of *Steen* v. *Law* (3),
shows that directors who have caused a company to enter into a transaction
which infringes s. 54 are guilty of misfeasances and are liable to recoup to the
company the loss which it has suffered, even though they were themselves
ignorant of the law. It is true that P. L. Freedman was no longer a director F
when the company released, or must be assumed to have released, the debt for
no consideration and infringed s. 54. I see no reason, however, why the well-
known principle of trustee law, referred to in *Head* v. *Gould* (4), should not apply
to misfeasances by directors. If a director, who is about to retire and sell his
shares, makes a bargain with his intended successors and the purchasers of his
shares that when they are in control of the company they will procure it to make a G
present to him out of its assets and this is done, the recipient is in my judgment
as guilty of misfeasance as the directors who actually procure the company to
make the gift.

Another point taken by P. L. Freedman, which I reject, is that the liquidator
should have been a co-plaintiff. This argument was based on the recent
decision in *Independent Automatic Sales, Ltd.* v. *Knowles and Foster* (5); but H
that was an action by a company based on an allegation that a charge created
by it was void because it had not been registered under s. 95 of the Act of 1948.
The judge held that the company, as opposed to the liquidator, could not bring
such an action first because the section in terms only made the charge void as
against the liquidator and creditors and, secondly, because s. 96 imposes a duty
on the company to register the charge and that if it was allowed to allege that I
it was void it would be relying on its own default. Here, however, the company is
not claiming that the release, which I assume that it made, is void by reason of
s. 54. It is claiming against a director for misfeasance in being a party to a
transaction which resulted in the application of its property in a manner not
authorised by the law. I can see no reason why the company should not be able

(2) [1946] 1 All E.R. 519; [1946] Ch. 242.
(3) [1963] 3 All E.R. 770; [1964] A.C. 287.   (4) [1898] 2 Ch. 250.
          (5) [1962] 3 All E.R. 27.

A to bring such an action in its own name or, if it is in liquidation, why the liquidator should not be able to bring it in the name of the company, without suing personally.

Although, however, I am against P. L. Freedman on many of the points which were urged on his behalf, I think, nevertheless, that the plaintiffs fail to establish the misfeasance, on which they have chosen to pin their faith,

B because, as I see it, the purchasers' obligations under cl. 6 of the contract could have been performed without any misfeasance on any one's part. "Without payment" in this clause means without payment by P. L. Freedman, but it does not preclude payment by the purchasers to the company. It is, of course, true that P. L. Freedman's solicitors assumed that cl. 6 would be implemented by a release by the company not supported by any

C consideration moving to it from the purchasers of the shares, and the purchasers' solicitors seem to have agreed, to begin with at any rate, that that would be an acceptable way of carrying out this transaction. In fact, such a release was not executed, and for all that I know the reason why it was not executed was that it had occurred to some one that its execution might infringe some principle of company law. But, in any case, I am satisfied that P. L. Freedman himself

D knew nothing of company law at all. He merely stipulated that, as a term of the transfer of his shares, he should get an effective release of his debt from the company. He was entitled to stipulate that. There was no reason whatever why the purchasers should not have paid the company what was needed—in the circumstances it would not have been much—to justify the company in releasing the debt. Why should I hold P. L. Freedman guilty of misfeasance because the

E release was made without any consideration moving from Myer Freedman and Joseph Freedman to the company? No doubt misfeasances, like breaches of trust, may be innocent; but one ought not to hold any one who is completely free from any moral blame to be guilty of a misfeasance or of a breach of trust, unless there is no other possible construction to be put on what he did. Here the carrying out of cl. 6 of the agreement did not necessarily involve

F any misfeasance or any infringement of s. 54. If the purchasers carried it out, or must be deemed to have carried it out, in a way which amounted to a misfeasance and an infringement of s. 54, that is something for which, no doubt, they were responsible but for which, as I see it, P. L. Freedman was not responsible.

For these reasons, I hold that the action fails. If I had thought that it succeeded, I would have directed an enquiry to ascertain what damage the company had

G suffered by the release. That would depend on P. L. Freedman's financial position at the time when the release must be taken to have been made which, I suppose, was in April, 1961.

Action dismissed.

Solicitors: *Fairchild, Greig & Co.* (for the plaintiffs, the company); *Matthew, Trackman, Lifton & Spry* (for the defendant).

H

[*Reported by* JACQUELINE METCALFE, *Barrister-at-Law.*]

DIETZ v. LENNIG CHEMICALS, LTD.   A

[COURT OF APPEAL (Lord Denning, M.R., Davies and Russell, L.JJ.), May 26, 1966.]

Fatal Accident—Compromise—Infant not bound until settlement approved by court—Consent order not perfected—Misrepresentation—Innocent misrepresentation—Defendants consented to order to pay lump sum for widow and infant child not knowing that widow was re-marrying—Widow re-married before order—Order set aside—R.S.C., Ord. 80, r. 11, r. 12.

The deceased was killed in an accident whilst employed by the defendants. He left a widow and an infant son.   A settlement of the claim of the widow and child was arranged, subject to the approval of the court, before any action was begun.   A summons for approval of the settlement was taken out,   C the widow being plaintiff.   She re-married on Oct. 25, 1965.   On Nov. 12, 1965, at which date her solicitors and the defendants' solicitors did not know of her re-marriage, the settlement was approved by the court.   Before the order was drawn up the plaintiff told her solicitors of her re-marriage, they told the defendants' solicitors, and the order approving the settlement was set aside.   On appeal,   D

Held: the settlement arranged was not binding until approved by the court on behalf of the infant, the altered wording of the new rules, R.S.C., Ord. 80, r. 11, r. 12, making no difference in this respect (*Jeffrey* v. *Kent County Council*, [1958] 3 All E.R. 155, approved); accordingly, as the consent order had not been perfected and as the defendants' consent to it on Nov. 12, 1965, was given under misapprehension that the plaintiff was   E still a widow, it had been rightly set aside (see p. 964, letters B, D and G, and p. 965, letter A, post).

Appeal dismissed.

[As to the compromise of claims by persons under disability, see 30 HALSBURY'S LAWS (3rd Edn.) 404, para. 760; and as to the jurisdiction of the court in regard to approving compromises on behalf of infants generally, see 21 HALS-   F BURY'S LAWS (3rd Edn.) 326, para. 687; and for cases on the subject, see 36 DIGEST (Repl.) 227, *1207, 1208*, and DIGEST (Cont. Vol. A) 1211, *1208c*; and 28 DIGEST (Repl.) 698-702, *2083-2120*.

As to taking into account changes in circumstances when assessing damages under the Fatal Accidents Acts, see 28 HALSBURY'S LAWS (3rd Edn.) 102, para. 111.]   G

Cases referred to:

Harvey v. *Croydon Union Rural Sanitary Authority*, [1881-85] All E.R. Rep. 1031; (1884), 26 Ch.D. 249; 53 L.J.Ch. 707; 50 L.T. 291; 28 Digest (Repl.) 917, *1503*.

Holt v. *Jesse*, (1876), 3 Ch.D. 177; 48 L.J.Ch. 254; 43 Digest (Repl.) 70, *583*.

Jeffrey v. *Kent County Council*, [1958] 3 All E.R. 155; [1958] 1 W.L.R. 927;   H Digest (Cont. Vol. A) 1209, *1200a*.

Taylor (formerly Ryan) v. *Cheltenham and Hereford Breweries, Ltd.*, [1952] 1 All E.R. 1135; [1952] 2 Q.B. 493; 36 Digest (Repl.) 227, *1208*.

Interlocutory Appeal.

This was an appeal by the plaintiff, Doreen Dietz, married woman, formerly   I Doreen Wilson, widow and administratrix of the estate of James Wilson, deceased, from an order of VEALE, J., in chambers, dated Mar. 10, 1966, dismissing her appeal from an order of Master CLAYTON, dated Feb. 9, 1966, setting aside his order of Nov. 12, 1965.   By the order of Nov. 12, 1965, Master CLAYTON approved a settlement between the plaintiff and the defendants of her claim under the Fatal Accidents Acts, 1846 to 1959, and Law Reform (Miscellaneous Provisions) Act, 1934, in respect of the death of her late husband in an accident in the course of his employment by the defendants, the claim being on her own behalf and on

Affirmed. H.L. [1967] 2 All E.R. 282.

A certainly have refused to consent to the order until the financial repercussions of her marriage were ascertained. In those circumstances I think that the defendants were clearly entitled to the order which the master made and which was upheld by the judge. I agree that the appeal should be dismissed.

B RUSSELL, L.J.: I agree. I do not want it to be thought that the plaintiff was in any way to blame. She probably thought that once the £10,000 had been offered and accepted, that was the end of the matter, except for machinery. Indeed, it took a little discussion in this court before we came to the conclusion that it could not be said that there was a binding contract made on Aug. 11.

On the other aspect of the case, the bargain here depended for its effective existence on an order of the court. In this case I should have thought that it C was plainly right that the defendants should be entitled to withdraw their consent, the order of the court not having been perfected. I am not in the least alarmed by the suggestion which was made that any compromise arrived at in any action might be wholly unreliable unless and until an order of the court was perfected because somebody who had misunderstood some factor behind the compromise might then repent of it. First of all, for the reasons which LORD D DENNING, M.R., has given, this is not that sort of case; and, secondly, in most of the cases which were referred to in the argument, the embodiment of an agreement of compromise in an order is not an essential part of the agreement of compromise. It is a useful method of recording what is in fact a perfectly ordinary contract made between two parties. In those cases the fact that the order has not been drawn up is neither here nor there. In those cases it would E be far more difficult for the parties to get out of the actual contract as made, probably through their counsel in the form of terms endorsed on counsel's brief. That is all that I wish to add. I agree that the appeal fails.

LORD DENNING, M.R.: Then the appeal is dismissed with costs.

D. P. Croom-Johnson, Q.C.: I would like to make an application for leave to take this case to the House of Lords. If your lordships would be good enough, in F view of the emphasis placed in the judgments of LORD DENNING, M.R., and DAVIES, L.J., on misrepresentation, to look at the ANNUAL PRACTICE, p. 1950, there is a little passage which I must apologise for not having called to the attention of the court before on re-marriage of widow. That is the decision of this court in *Taylor (formerly Ryan)* v. *Cheltenham and Hereford Breweries, Ltd.* (5):

G " By re-marriage a widow changes her status from widow to married woman, but she remains ' the widow of the person whose death gave rise to the claim ' under the Fatal Accidents Acts . . ."

DAVIES, L.J.: That does not help you in this case, Mr. Croom-Johnson.

Appeal dismissed. Leave to appeal to the House of Lords refused.

H Solicitors: *W. H. Thompson* (for the plaintiff); *Berrymans* (for the defendants).

[*Reported by* F. GUTTMAN, ESQ., *Barrister-at-Law.*]

I

---

(5) [1952] 1 All E.R. 1135; [1952] 2 Q.B. 493.

HOUSLEYS, LTD. *v.* BLOOMER-HOLT, LTD.   A

[COURT OF APPEAL (Sellers, Diplock and Russell, L.JJ.), May 11, 1966.]

Landlord and Tenant—New tenancy—Business premises—Opposition by landlord—Intention to demolish and carry out substantial work of construction —Premises comprised in holding—Wooden garage and a wall covering part only of site—Whole of site to be concreted, but no building to be erected— Notice stating ground of opposition not following wording of s. 30 (1) (f) *of Landlord and Tenant Act, 1954—Sufficiency of notice—Landlord and Tenant Act, 1954 (2 & 3 Eliz. 2 c. 56), s. 30 (1) (f).*

Tenants who used their premises, which consisted of a yard, partly covered with cinders, on which stood only a wooden garage covering about one-third of the site and a brick boundary wall adjacent to the highway, for business purposes, applied for a new tenancy under Part 2 of the Landlord and Tenant Act, 1954. The landlords who had purchased the premises only a few months previously, opposed the application on a ground which they stated in their notice and in their answer to the application as " that on the termination of the current tenancy we intend to demolish or reconstruct the whole or substantial part of the premises or carry out substantial work for reconstruction on the whole or part of the land and that we could not reasonably do so without obtaining possession of the premises ". They intended to demolish the garage and wall (which were the only premises on the holding that could be demolished) and to concrete the site, their reason for this being that they could not obtain planning permission to erect a shed on their own adjacent premises unless they provided within their own curtilage a turning space for lorries.

Held: (i) this notice, although it differed from the wording of s. 30 (1) (f)* of the Act of 1954, sufficiently revealed on which of the grounds set out in s. 30 (1) the landlords were relying, and entitled the landlords to oppose the application on the ground set out in para. (f) (see p. 968, letter F, p. 970, letters A and C, and p. 971, letter D, post).

(ii) the application for a new tenancy must be refused by virtue of s. 30 (1) (f)* of the Act of 1954, because the landlord's intention to demolish the shed and wall, the only buildings on the site, was an intention to demolish the whole of " the premises comprised in " the holding within the meaning of s. 30 (1) (f) as distinct from the whole of " the holding " itself (see p. 969, letter D, p. 970, letter I, and p. 971, letter F, post).

Semble: concreting the site could amount to " substantial work of construction " within the meaning of s. 30 (1) (f) (see p. 969, letter I, post).

[As to statement of grounds of opposition to the grant of a new tenancy in the landlords' notice, see 23 HALSBURY'S LAWS (3rd Edn.) 890, para. 1711, text and note (m); and as to the ground of proposed demolition or reconstruction, see ibid., p. 893, para. 1717.

For the Landlord and Tenant Act, 1954, s. 30, see 34 HALSBURY'S STATUTES (2nd Edn.) 414.]

Cases referred to:

Atkinson v. *Bettison*, [1955] 3 All E.R. 340; [1955] 1 W.L.R. 1127; Digest (Cont. Vol. A) 1051, *7417p.*

Betty's Cafés, Ltd. v. *Phillips Furnishing Stores, Ltd.*, [1958] 1 All E.R. 607; [1959] A.C. 20; [1958] 2 W.L.R. 513; Digest (Cont. Vol. A) 1061, *7417pa.*

Fisher v. *Taylors Furnishing Stores, Ltd.*, [1956] 2 All E.R. 78; [1956] 2 Q.B. 78; [1956] 2 W.L.R. 985; Digest (Cont. Vol. A) 1052, *7417pc.*

Young v. *Bristol Aeroplane Co., Ltd.*, [1946] 1 All E.R. 98; [1946] A.C. 163; 115 L.J.K.B. 63; 174 L.T. 39; 30 Digest (Repl.) 225, *691.*

---

* Section 30 (1), so far as material, is printed at p. 967, letter I, and p. 968, letter B, post.

A   **Appeal.**

In June, 1965, the landlords, Bloomer-Holt, Ltd., purchased a timber yard, on which they carried on their own business, and the adjacent premises, subject to the tenants' yearly tenancy of those adjacent premises, which the tenants occupied for the purposes of their business of motor dealers and repairers   The tenants' premises consisted of a yard on which stood a brick boundary wall,

B   adjacent to the highway, and a wooden garage which occupied about one-third of the area, the remainder of which was bare earth partly surfaced with cinders. The landlords wished to erect an additional shed or sheds in their timber yard, but the local planning authority refused to grant permission for this erection unless the landlords provided turning space for their lorries within their curtilage because, as the trial judge found, the entry and exist of lorries into and from the

C   timber yard created a traffic hazard. On July 22, 1965, the landlords gave the tenants notice to terminate the tenants' tenancy on Jan. 31, 1966. The tenants applied to the Manchester county court for the grant of a new tenancy pursuant to Part 2 of the Landlord and Tenant Act, 1954. In their answer to the tenants' application for a new lease the landlords stated that " we oppose the grant of a new tenancy on the following grounds stated in our notice under s. 25 of the

D   Landlord and Tenant Act, 1954, namely that on the termination of the current tenancy we intend to demolish or reconstruct the whole or substantial part of the premises or carry out substantial work for reconstruction on the whole or part of land and that we could not reasonably do so without obtaining possession of the premises ".

On the hearing of the application on Jan. 12, 1966, at Manchester county court,

E   His Honour JUDGE STEEL found that if the landlords gained possession of the tenants' premises they intended to demolish the garage and the wall, and to concrete the whole site, and to use it for a turning space for their lorries   He granted the tenants a new tenancy because he found that " the real intention of the landlords in this case is their wish to get possession of the tenants' holding so that they may improve their own premises by using it for turning space . . .

F   This resistance by the landlords to the tenants' application for a new tenancy is merely colourable. The landlords propose no reconstruction at all. Laying concrete is not in the contemplation of the Act. There is no demolition of a substantial part of the premises. The landlords do not intend to build on the site ". The landlords appealed.

G   *Raymond Walton*, Q.C., and *G. C. H. Spafford* for the landlords.
C. N. Glidewell for the tenants.

SELLERS, L.J.: The landlords, the respondents in the court below, Bloomer-Holt, Ltd., who are the appellants in this court, acquired some property part of which was the subject of an application before the county court judge in June, 1965. When the landlords acquired the property from the British Trans-

H   port Commission it included the premises occupied by the applicant tenants, Housleys, Ltd., on a lease. Very shortly after that acquisition the tenants were given notice to quit; they served a counter-notice, and the matter called for consideration under the Landlord and Tenant Act, 1954.

I need not go into the routine notices. Everything was in order when the matter came before the county court judge and the only question for his con-

I   sideration was whether the landlords could resist the tenants' application for a new tenancy. The ground of resistance which the landlords had set out in the formal notice and which they repeated in their answer was to be found under s. 30 (1) (*f*) of the Act of 1954, which reads as follows:

" (1) The grounds on which a landlord may oppose an application under sub-s. (1) of s. 24 of this Act are such of the following grounds as may be stated in the landlord's notice under s. 25 of this Act, or, as the case may be, under sub-s. (6) of s. 26 thereof, that is to say:"

The ground stated in para. (*f*) was the only ground on which reliance was placed,   **A**
subject to the comments of counsel as to the adequacy of the notice which was
given and the answer which was subsequently pleaded. Paragraph (*f*) reads
as follows:

> " that on the termination of the current tenancy the landlord intends to
> demolish or reconstruct the premises comprised in the holding or a substantial
> part of those premises or to carry out substantial work of construction on   **B**
> the holding or part thereof and that he could not reasonably do so without
> obtaining possession of the holding."

Although there may have been earlier authorities, yet by the time when the
Court of Appeal had considered *Fisher* v. *Taylors Furnishing Stores, Ltd.* (1)
and the House of Lords had considered *Betty's Cafés, Ltd.* v. *Phillips Furnishing*
Stores, Ltd. (2), where LORD MORTON OF HENRYTON in particular quotes (3) with   **C**
approval what PARKER, L.J., had said in the *Fisher* case (4), it was clear that
each of the several grounds which were available under s. 30 is an entirely
separate and independent ground which, if proved, entitles the landlord to
succeed. The question at this trial was whether the landlords had brought
themselves within one of the provisions of s. 30 (1) (*f*).

A point has been taken in para. (i) of the answer and here that the landlords'   **D**
notice of opposition to the grant of a new tenancy was not a sufficient notice to
cover all the matters relied on by the landlords which have been argued here.
That notice is as follows:

> " We oppose the grant of a new tenancy on the following grounds stated
> in our notice under s. 25 of the Landlord and Tenant Act, 1954, namely   **E**
> that on the termination of the current tenancy we intend to demolish or
> reconstruct the whole or substantial part of the premises or carry out sub-
> stantial work for reconstruction on the whole or part of the land and that we
> could not reasonably do so without obtaining possession of the premises."

It will be seen that that does not follow word for word the provision of s. 30 (1) (*f*)
of the Act of 1954. It is said that under s. 31 and under s. 25 (6) that is not an   **F**
adequate and clear notice. In my view it is a sufficient notice. It reveals,
although not in the precise language, yet sufficiently closely thereto, what are the
matters relied on by the landlords. I am far from saying that it may not be
desirable always to refer to the particular part of s. 30 (1) which is relied on, or
even to set out the words precisely; but the differences, which are several, really
do not amount to substantial difference from the words of the section itself.   **G**

The main argument turned on the use, in the second part of the grounds relied
on, of the words " carry out substantial work for " (it ought to be " of ") " reconstruction ". It is said that that is something different from " construction ".
Of course it is, but in the context, having regard to the previous limb relied on,
the intent to demolish or reconstruct, it is clear that the landlords are relying
on " substantial work of construction ".   **H**

The judge has set out the facts adequately and clearly in his judgment and I
need refer to them but very briefly. It is regrettable that the actual documents
with regard to the planning permission—as to what applications were made and
what answers were given—have not been produced, so that the court should be
able to see precisely what had happened. [HIS LORDSHIP stated the facts
found by the county court judge, and continued:] The learned judge, His Honour   **I**
JUDGE STEEL, who no doubt is very well versed in these matters, took at the
outset the view, which has not arisen on this appeal, that the main intention of
the landlords was to occupy the site for themselves, but that they could not in
the circumstances bring themselves within s. 30 (1) (*g*), which was appropriate,

---

(1) [1956] 2 All E.R. 78; [1956] 2 Q.B. 78.
(2) [1958] 1 All E.R. 607; [1959] A.C. 20.
(3) [1958] 1 All E.R. at p. 619; [1959] A.C. at pp. 44, 45.
(4) [1956] 2 All E.R. at p. 84; [1956] 2 Q.B. at pp. 91, 92.

A because they had only just acquired the premises. The learned judge thought that this was a secondary matter but, having regard to the authorities to which I have just referred that each one of these is a separate and distinct ground on which a landlord can oppose an application for a new tenancy, I think that it called for consideration whether the facts brought the landlords within this particular ground, that in para. (*f*) on which they relied. The judge, after

B dealing with the first question of the purpose for which the landlords wished to have the premises, sums up the matter at the end of his judgment in a very few lines:

" The landlords propose no reconstruction at all. Laying concrete is not in the contemplation of the Act. There is no demolition of a substantial part of the premises. The landlords do not intend to build on the site."

C

I propose to deal here mainly with one of those grounds, because one is quite sufficient. That is, that on the termination of the tenancy the landlords intend to demolish the premises comprised in the holding or a substantial part of those premises. The fact is that what was to be demolished was all that there was to demolish on the site, the garage and the wall, and that seems to be demolishing

D the whole of the premises as far as any structure was to be demolished. It seems to me that that fulfils the requirements sufficiently. I am not concerned at the moment to consider what would be the position if this had been some very small dog-kennel or very small hut on a very large area. It was in fact, quite apart from the wall, a garage occupying one-third of the site. It seems to me that that was to be demolished, and that, construing this as I would construe

E it, is demolishing the premises comprised in the holding.

Counsel for the tenants submitted that that part of this clause or sentence should be construed so as to read " a substantial part of the premises comprised in the holding " as if it was " a substantial part of the holding "; but when one looks at the words " or a substantial part of the premises " it is quite clear that that does not mean " a substantial part of the holding ": it means, demolishing

F the premises comprised in the holding, or a substantial part of any premises. In fact this was a demolition of the whole.

In my view this is not merely a question of fact. It is a question of law on which the judge has gone wrong. He has taken the view that there was to be no demolition of a substantial part of the premises when in fact on the evidence there was an intended demolition of the whole of the premises—of all that were

G on the holding. I would therefore allow this appeal on that ground, although I am far from saying that it could not be dealt with in the same way on the facts as they are before the court on the other ground on which the landlords rely— that substantial work of construction was contemplated. The whole of the area was to be concreted in a sufficiently substantial way to carry this traffic which would come in. While it is not necessary in this case, I should have thought

H that there was only one view to be taken on that—that there was a substantial work of construction which was intended to be carried out. It is true that the judgment does not find that affirmatively, but the judge said, I think erroneously, " laying concrete is not in the contemplation of the Act ", and, " the landlords do not intend to build on the site ". That seems to me unnecessary. One can view " construction " without the building of a structure above the site in that

I way as a building; and the laying of concrete—the laying of a roadway, the laying of a runway, or any other substantial work of concreting—may well be within the contemplation of the Act of 1954 and may well be " substantial work of construction ".

I would allow the appeal in favour of the landlords and refuse the tenants a new tenancy.

DIPLOCK, L.J.: I also agree that the appeal should be allowed; and I need add little to what SELLERS, L.J., has already said.

First, as regards the technical point that the notice by the landlords given A
under s. 25 (6) of the Landlord and Tenant Act, 1954, did not follow precisely
the wording of s. 30 (1) (f) of the Act of 1954.   This is a highly technical point.
It is not, in my view, an attractive one; nor do I find it well-founded.   It is
sufficient if a notice under s. 25 (6) makes it clear to the tenant on which of the
seven separate grounds specified in s. 30 (1) the landlord is relying.   The purpose
of the notice under s. 25 (6) is to let the tenant know on what grounds his request B
for a new tenancy, if made, will be resisted, so that he may make up his mind
whether to exercise his rights and bring the matter eventually before the court
for a decision.   If one reads the grounds put forward in the landlords' notice,
no one could be under any possible misapprehension that they were relying on
s. 30 (1) (f)—or, I would add, could be under any possible misapprehension that
they were also relying on the last part of that paragraph, namely, carrying out C
" substantial work of construction on the holding or part thereof".

With regard to the substance of the appeal, the judge seems, I think, to have
been largely influenced by the short-lived fallacy in the judgment of the Court
of Appeal in *Atkinson* v. *Bettison* (5), which seemed to suggest that one had got
to look and see what the primary intention or purpose or motive of the landlord
was.   I say that because of the judge's references, " Here the landlords' over- D
riding intention is to improve their business ", and then,

> " The real intention of the landlords in this case is their wish to get
> possession of the tenants' holding so that they may improve their own
> premises by using it for turning space.   In my judgment, and I do not say
> this in a sense of criticism, this resistance by the landlords to the tenants'
> application for a new tenancy is merely colourable."   E

I think that that is clearly directed to the fallacy to which I have already referred.
It was a short-lived fallacy, because the year after, in *Fisher* v. *Taylors Furnishing
Stores, Ltd.* (6) the Court of Appeal itself refused to follow that part, the first
part, of its ratio decidendi in *Atkinson* v. *Bettison* (5).   If anyone were in doubt
whether the Court of Appeal was, under the rule in *Young* v. *Bristol Aeroplane* F
Co., Ltd. (7), entitled to reverse its own decision, the matter was put right in
1959, when the House of Lords in *Betty's Cafés, Ltd.* v. *Phillips Furnishing Stores,
Ltd.* (8), made it clear that the first ratio decidendi of the Court of Appeal in
Atkinson v. *Bettison* (5) was ill-founded.

Therefore the only question for the judge to decide was whether or not the
intentions of the landlords, to which SELLERS, L.J., has referred and which were G
found by the county court judge to be

> " to knock down the wall between the tenants' holding and Ashton
> Old Road, knock down the wooden garage, and concrete the whole site ",

did satisfy the requirements of s. 30 (1) (f) of the Act of 1954.   It is to be observed
that the garage and the wall were the only parts of the holding which were
capable of being demolished: the rest of it was ordinary earth, perhaps with H
cinders on it.   It was contended by counsel for the landlords, and in my view
contended rightly, that that intention constituted an intention to demolish
" the premises comprised in the holding ".   It is plain, on the true construction
of para. (f), that " the premises " there referred to must be limited to that part
of the holding which is capable of being demolished and capable of being
reconstructed.   Here, as I have already said, the garage and the wall were the I
only parts of the holding which were capable of being demolished and therefore
were " the premises comprised in the holding ".

In my view, then, on that finding of the county court judge as to their intention,
the landlords had established the necessary requirements under para. (f).

---

(5) [1955] 3 All E.R. 340.   (6) [1956] 2 All E.R. 78; [1956] 2 Q.B. 78.
(7) [1946] 1 All E.R. 98; [1946] A.C. 163.
(8) [1958] 1 All E.R. 607; [1959] A.C. 20.

A   It is, therefore, not necessary for us to decide the other part of the case raised in the notice of appeal, that is to say whether the concreting of the whole of the site of the holding would amount to a " substantial work of construction ". The judge plainly took the view, expressed in the sentence in his judgment

B
" Laying concrete is not in the contemplation of the Act; . . . the landlords do not intend to build on the site ",

that laying concrete over the whole of the site could not in law amount to a " work of construction " at all. Counsel for the tenant concedes that that would not be correct, if that is the view that the learned judge took. He has made no findings whether the intended covering by concrete would amount to a " substantial " work or not; and it may be that if this appeal had not been allowed
C on the earlier point about demolition it would have been necessary to send the matter back to the county court judge to make a finding of fact on that; but in the circumstances, since the landlords have brought themselves within the requirements of the paragraph without the need for going further to show that the concreting would amount to a " substantial work of construction ", I think that this appeal can be allowed without any reference back to the county court.

D   **RUSSELL, L.J.:** I agree that this appeal succeeds.

It seems clear to me that what is proposed is the demolition of the whole premises comprised in the holding. The county court judge said that there was to be " no demolition of a substantial part of the premises ". This seems to me to confuse the premises comprised in the holding with the holding. Counsel for the tenants argues that the section means: " to demolish the premises (being
E premises comprising a substantial part of the holding) or a substantial part of such premises "; but I can see no ground for construing the section thus. There is in this case no doubt of the purposeful intention of the landlords to demolish. The fact that the motive leading to that intention is to improve the use of the other holding is neither here nor there. I would allow the appeal on this one ground. It has escaped the notice of the county court judge that the proposal
F involves demolition not of a part, let alone an insubstantial part, of the premises but of the whole of the premises.

The fact that I confine myself to that point is not to be taken as indicating my opposition to the landlords' other points. I simply need say nothing on them. Therefore the decision should be reversed and the application of the tenants to be granted a new lease should be refused.
G
Appeal allowed. Judgment below set aside. Tenants' application for new lease refused.

Solicitors: *Gregory, Rowcliffe & Co.,* agents for *Brett, Ackerley & Cooke,* Manchester (for the landlords); *A. D. Vandamm & Co.,* agents for *Lingard & Wright,* Manchester (for the tenants).

H   [*Reported by* HENRY SUMMERFIELD, ESQ., *Barrister-at-Law.*]

A

LICKISS v. MILESTONE MOTOR POLICIES AT LLOYDS.

[COURT OF APPEAL (Lord Denning, M.R., Danckwerts and Salmon, L.JJ.),
May 12, 1966.]

*Insurance—Motor insurance—Conditions of policy—Notification to insurers—
Failure of insured to inform insurers of accident and to forward notice of
prosecution and summons—Insurers informed by other persons before hearing
of summons—No prejudice to insurers—Whether condition a bar to recovery
under policy—Waiver of condition.*

B

A motor cyclist was insured under a motor policy against third party
risks. Condition 1 of the policy provided that " the insured shall give full
particulars in writing " to the insurers " as soon as possible after the occurrence of any accident . . . and shall forward immediately any letter, notice
of intended prosecution, writ, summons or process relating thereto ".
That condition was a condition precedent to any liability of the insurers.
On May 17, 1964, the motor cyclist collided with a taxicab, which was
damaged. The motor cyclist received a notice of intended prosecution, and
was served with a summons returnable on July 2, 1964, By letter of June 18,
1964, the police informed the insurers of these proceedings. On June 23,
1964, the insurers wrote to the motor cyclist—" We understand that proceedings are being taken against you on July 2 . . . It would be appreciated
if you would let us know why you have not notified us of these proceedings,
since we will wish to arrange your defence. We await your comments ".
On July 2, 1964, the motor cyclist pleaded guilty by letter and was fined £5.
On Aug. 10, 1964, the insurers repudiated liability. In an action by the taxicab proprietor the motor cyclist was held liable for the damage to the taxicab,
and failed to recover indemnity as against the insurers on the ground of his
breach of condition 1 by not having sent to them the notice of prosecution and
the summons.

C

D

E

Held: the motor cyclist's claim was not barred by condition 1 of the policy,
but he was entitled to recover from the insurers in respect of his liability to
the taxicab proprietor, for the following reasons—

F

(i) the insurers' letter of June 23, 1964, was tantamount to their saying
that they did not want to see the notice of prosecution and the summons,
and the sending of the letter in the circumstances was a waiver of the terms
of condition 1 regarding the notice and summons; accordingly the defence
founded on breach of condition 1 failed, and the motor cyclist was entitled
to recover on the policy in respect of his liability to the taxicab proprietor
(see p. 976, letters A, C and F, post).

G

Plasticmoda Societa per Azioni v. *Davidsons (Manchester), Ltd.,* ([1952]
1 Lloyds' Rep. 527) applied.

(ii) (per LORD DENNING, M.R., and DANCKWERTS, L.J.; SALMON, L.J.,
dissenting) since the insurers had received all the necessary information
about the prosecution from the police, it was unnecessary for the motor
cyclist to give the insurers the same information under condition 1 of the
policy, and the insurers could no longer rely on that condition (see p. 976,
letters B and C, post).

H

Appeal allowed.

I

[**Editorial Note.** On appeal it was not disputed that the policy did not give
the insurers the right to have the motor cyclist defended by a solicitor of their
choice at the hearing before the magistrates, see p. 975, letter E, post.

As to a condition subsequent affecting recovery under a policy of insurance,
see 22 HALSBURY'S LAWS (3rd Edn.) 220, 221, para. 416; as to what constitutes
a waiver, see ibid., at pp. 227, 228, para. 430; see also 8 ibid., 198, note (d);
and for cases on conditions subsequent in liability insurance policies, see 29
DIGEST (Repl.) 509, 510, *3595-3598.*

A   As to the right of insurers to conduct the defence of proceedings, see 22 Halsbury's Laws (3rd Edn.) 338, para. 694.]

Case referred to:

Plasticmoda Societa per Azioni v. Davidsons (Manchester), Ltd., [1952] 1 Lloyd's Rep. 527.

B   **Appeal.**

This was an appeal by Mr. D. Lickiss (" the motor cyclist "), who was the first third party in an action in Blackpool county court brought by Barratt Bros. (Taxis), Ltd., the plaintiff, against Robert Davies. The plaintiff's claim was for money alleged to be due from the defendant in respect of work done to the defendant's taxi, amounting to £137 4s. 3d. By a third party notice dated May 19, C   1965, the defendant claimed against the motor cyclist indemnity in respect of the cost of repairs, alleged to be caused by the negligence of the motor cyclist in driving a motor cycle on May 17, 1964, whereby it collided with the defendant's taxi. The defendant claimed also loss of use of the taxi. By the same notice the defendant claimed against Milestone Motor Policies, as second third party, that the repair work on the taxi had been carried out by the plaintiff on their instructions and indemnity in respect of the cost of the repairs. The second D   third party, Milestone Motor Policies at Lloyds, was a firm, and is referred to in this report as " the insurers ". By order of the county court dated Jan. 24, 1966, it was adjudged that the plaintiff should recover against the defendant £123 for debt and should recover its taxed costs; and that the defendant should recover against the motor cyclist the sum of £168 damages and one half of the costs that the defendant was ordered to pay to the plaintiff in addition to the E   defendant's own costs of the action against the motor cyclist to be taxed; and that judgment should be entered for the insurers with costs to be paid by the defendant. The motor cyclist as appellant gave notice of appeal seeking an order that the judgment of the county court be set aside insofar as it ordered the motor cyclist's claim against the insurers to be dismissed and judgment to be entered for the insurers, and that in lieu thereof, judgment for £168 damages F   should be entered for the motor cyclist against the insurers with costs to be taxed, together with an order that the insurers should pay to the motor cyclist the one half of the costs of the defendant in the action which the defendant was ordered to pay to the plaintiff and which the motor cyclist was ordered to pay to the defendant. The facts are summarised in the judgment of Lord G   Denning, M.R.

The authority and the cases noted below* were cited during the argument in addition to the case referred to in the judgment.

J. D. Walker for the motor cyclist.

J. M. Collins for the insurers.

H   **LORD DENNING, M.R.:** On May 17, 1964, there was an accident between a taxicab and a motor cycle at Blackpool. Both vehicles were damaged. The motor cyclist was prosecuted for careless driving and fined £5. The motor cyclist was insured against third party liability, but not against damage to his own motor cycle. He was insured with Milestone Motor Policies at Lloyds. He seeks to recover the damages which he has to pay to the taxi owner; but Lloyds have rejected his claim on the ground that he did not fulfil the conditions of the I   policy. In particular, because he did not send them the notice of prosecution or the summons. Under the policy Lloyds agreed in s. 1 (a) to indemnify the motor cyclist against damage to property. Section 1 (b) said:

" The underwriters will pay all legal charges and expenses incurred with their written consent in defending any claim under this section and will at

* 22 Halsbury's Laws of England (3rd Edn.) p. 220; Austin v. Zurich General Accident and Liability Insurance Co., Ltd., [1944] 2 All E.R. 243; [1945] 1 All E.R. 316; [1945] K.B. 250.

tho insured's request (or may at their option) arrange for and pay the fee of
a solicitor to represent the insured at any coroner's inquest or fatal enquiry
in respect of any death which may be the subject of indemnity under this
section or for defending in any court of summary jurisdiction any
proceedings."

On the back there were the conditions of the policy. Condition 1 said:

" The insured shall give full particulars in writing to Milestone Motor
Policies, London House . . . as soon as possible after the occurrence of any
accident, loss or damage and shall forward immediately any letter, notice of
intended prosecution, writ, summons or process relating thereto."

Condition 13 said:

" The due observance and fulfilment of the terms, provisions, conditions
and endorsements of this policy in so far as they can apply and the truth
of the statements and answers in the proposal form shall be conditions
precedent to any liability of the underwriters to make any payment under
this policy."

The motor cyclist did not at once tell the insurers about the accident; but the
solicitors for the taxicab driver did so. They got in touch with the motor cyclist's
insurers and told them about the accident. The insurers on May 25, 1964 wrote
to the motor cyclist and said:

" We understand that you were involved in an accident on May 17 and we
now attach hereto a claim form which we would like you to complete and
return to us as soon as possible."

This crossed a letter from the motor cyclist. On May 25 he told the insurers
about the accident. He told them that the motor cycle was in the hands of the
police and he enclosed a letter from the solicitors for the taxicab driver. A few
days later he returned the claim form duly filled in.

It turned out that he also received a notice of intended prosecution from the
police. Later he received a summons returnable on July 2, 1964, at the Blackpool
magistrates' court; but he did not send those forward to the insurers. In those
respects he did not fulfil condition 1. We know, however, that the police told
the insurers. On June 18, 1964, police headquarters at Blackpool wrote to the
claims manager of the insurers and said:

" We would inform you that proceedings are pending against the above
named [that is D. Lickiss the motor cyclist] and the hearing will take place
on July 2, next in the Blackpool magistrates' court."

So although the motor cyclist had not himself told the insurers about the notice
or the summons, the insurers had reliable information from the police themselves.
On June 23 the insurers wrote to the motor cyclist and said:

" We understand that proceedings are being taken against you on July 2,
in Blackpool magistrates' court. It would be appreciated if you would let
us know why you have not notified us of these proceedings, since we will
wish to arrange your defence. We await your comments."

The motor cyclist says that he replied and explained that he had written to the
court saying that he was pleading guilty, but the insurers say that they received
no reply. On July 2, the case came before the magistrates at Blackpool. The
motor cyclist did not appear but wrote a letter pleading guilty. It appears that he
belonged to a trade union which gave him free legal advice, and they, having
considered all the facts, thought it was his own fault. They advised him to plead
guilty. So he wrote a letter to the magistrates' court and pleaded guilty. He was
fined £5. No doubt it was a very wise course for him to take. By pleading guilty
by letter he saved a lot of costs and was not away from his work. He did not,
however, tell the insurers about it at the time. Later on by letter of July 21,
1964, the insurers wrote and said:

A   " We would point out that we cannot deal with the claim which has been submitted by the owner of the taxi until we have from you the full details of the police proceedings."

He replied to that letter. He told them that he had pleaded guilty and was fined £5. Eventually, after a certain amount of correspondence, on Aug. 10, 1964, the insurers repudiated all liability for paying for the damage which he had done

B to the taxicab. They said:

     " We consider that our position with regard to the third party claim has been prejudiced by your action, and we are not prepared to indemnify you for the claims arising out of the accident in which you were involved on May 17, last."

C The matter went to the county court. The taxicab owner claimed against the motor cyclist for damages to the taxicab. The motor cyclist claimed to be indemnified by the insurers. The county court judge held the motor cyclist liable to the taxicab owner, and then had to consider the claim of the motor cyclist against the insurers.

     The insurers took this point before the judge. They said that they were entitled

D to insist on conducting the defence of the motor cyclist at the magistrates' court by their own solicitor. They were entitled to represent him. It was in " their option " under s. 1 (b). The judge rejected that contention. He said it was contrary to public policy. A man who is accused is entitled to have a solicitor of his own choice: or to defend himself if he likes. The insurers cannot compel him to have their own solicitor. I think that that is clearly right. Before us

E counsel for the insurers did not dispute the validity of the judge's ruling. He further doubted whether the clause on its true construction would have given them the right which they claimed to represent him.

     The insurers took this further point. The motor cyclist had not sent to the insurers the notice of prosecution or the summons. On this point the county court judge decided in favour of the insurers. He said:

F   " The motor cyclist did not send on to them the notice of intended prosecution or the summons and they were entitled to rely on that as a condition precedent . . . Insurers are sometimes regarded as hard-hearted men but I cannot say that hard-hearted men are not entitled to rely on their contract."

I take a different view from the county court judge for two reasons. First, it

G was unnecessary for the motor cyclist to send the documents to the insurers. They had all the relevant facts, and that absolved the motor cyclist from doing more. The police headquarters at Blackpool by their letter of June 18, 1964, gave to the insurers all the material information. The insurers would be entitled, if they so wished, to send their own representative to the magistrates' court and watch the proceedings or, indeed, to take such other steps, if any, as they were entitled to take. Seeing that they had received the information from the police,

H it would be a futile thing to require the motor cyclist himself to give them the self-same information. The law never compels a person to do that which is useless and unnecessary.

     Secondly, the letter of June 23, 1964, was a waiver of the condition. The principle of waiver is simply this: that if one party by his conduct leads another

I to believe that the strict rights arising under the contract will not be insisted on, intending that the other should act on that belief, and he does act on it, then the first party will not afterwards be allowed to insist on the strict rights when it would be inequitable for him so to do (see *Plasticmoda Societa per Azioni* v. *Davidsons (Manchester), Ltd.* (1)). When the insurers got the letter from the police on June 18, they could have asked for the notice of prosecution and the summons if they had wanted them. Instead of doing so, they merely wrote to the motor cyclist on June 23 saying: " It would be appreciated if you

(1) [1952] 1 Lloyd's Rep. 527.

would let us know why you have not notified us of these proceedings." By not **A** asking for the documents, they as good as said that they did not want them. So he did not send them. I do not think that they should be allowed now to complain of not receiving them. I think that they waived the condition.

Apart from these two points, I would put the matter more broadly. Condition 1 was inserted in the policy so as to afford a protection to the insurers so that they should know in good time about the accident and any proceedings consequent on **B** it. If they obtain all the material knowledge from another source so that they are not prejudiced at all by the failure of the insured himself to tell them, then they cannot rely on the condition to defeat the claim.

The net result is this, that the motor cyclist, who has been made responsible for the repair of the taxicab is entitled to recover the amount from the insurers with whom he had insured.   **C**

I would allow the appeal accordingly.

DANCKWERTS, L.J.: I agree entirely with the judgment of LORD DENNING, M.R.

SALMON, L.J.: I agree. For my part I would have held that there was a **D** clear breach of condition 1 of the policy. This imposed an absolute obligation on the motor cyclist to forward the summons to the insurers when he received it and also to notify them about the intended prosecution. The observance of that obligation was by condition 13 made a condition precedent to the insurers liability to pay. But for waiver, I should have felt obliged to hold that, although there is absolutely no merit in the defence—indeed, it is somewhat surprising to **E** find insurers of this standing in circumstances such as these taking the point— they were entitled to succeed.

Happily, however, there is the point of waiver. I entirely agree with my lords that the letter of June 23, 1964, is a clear waiver by the insurers. It is conceded that when the motor cyclist received this letter, he would still have been in time to give the notice and forward the summons. In my judgment any reasonable **F** person receiving that letter would have concluded that the insurers, having learnt all about the intended prosecution, no longer required him to notify them of it or send them the summons. All that they wanted was to be told why he had not done so already. I would accordingly allow the appeal.

Appeal allowed.

Solicitors: *Collyer-Bristow & Co.*, agents for *Payne & Payne*, Hull (for the **G** motor cyclist); *A. W. Mawer & Co.*, Manchester (for the insurers).

[*Reported by* F. GUTTMAN, ESQ., *Barrister-at-Law.*]

A

LAXTON *v.* LAXTON AND EAGLAN.

[COURT OF APPEAL (Davies and Winn, L.JJ.), May 13, 1966.]

Divorce—Custody—Children aged six and seven—Wife's misconduct—Husband's exemplary conduct—Both offering good homes—Postponement of order for three months—Children remaining meanwhile with wife—Husband's liberal

B

access—Valid exercise of discretion—Custody to be awarded to husband but not care and control during the three months.

A marriage celebrated in 1958 had been a happy one until the wife began to commit adultery with the co-respondent in July, 1965. When she confessed to her husband in November, he sought a reconciliation, wanted the wife to stay with him and their two children aged six and seven, and offered to accept

C

the child of the co-respondent by whom she was pregnant as a child of the family. Failing in that offer, he filed a divorce petition in January, 1966, and left the house shortly after, taking the two children with him. After the wife had had access to the two children at the matrimonial home a week later, she refused to surrender them, and she subsequently removed them to another house. In April, the husband was granted a decree nisi and the decree absolute was

D

expedited. A week after it the wife married the co-respondent and subsequently she gave birth to his child. With her and the co-respondent was living a daughter of the co-respondent by a previous marriage aged sixteen. The former husband was living with his widowed father. He had engaged a young lady as a nannie and he applied to the court for an order for full custody and care and control of the two children. The divorce commissioner

E

found that there was nothing to choose as between the two houses where the husband and wife were living, but he preferred the evidence of the husband to that of the wife throughout, found that he had behaved in the most exemplary manner and had a good and normal relationship with the children, and he said that, if he had to decide then to which party to give full custody and care and control, he would give it to the husband. In view, however, of

F

the tie that was bound to exist between a mother and a young child he decided to postpone the final decision for three months, the children to remain with the wife, the father to have them each week-end, from Friday night to Sunday evening. On appeal by the husband,

Held: though the course which the commissioner took was an unusual one, there was no misdirection in law nor was his decision plainly wrong, and the

G

court would not interfere, save to direct that custody of the children should be in the husband with no order yet as to care and control but the children should continue to live with the wife, the husband to have access as already directed; the matter must be reconsidered at the end of the three months, when an order should be made for the care and control of the children (see p. 980, letters E to I, *post*).

H

Re L. (Infants) ([1962] 3 All E.R. 1) distinguished.

Appeal dismissed.

[As to the award of custody to the guilty party in a divorce, see 12 HALS-BURY'S LAWS (3rd Edn.) 393, 394, para. 873; and for cases on the subject, see 27 DIGEST (Repl.) 665, 666, *6293-6305*.]

I

Cases referred to:

L. (Infants), Re, [1962] 3 All E.R. 1; [1962] 1 W.L.R. 886; Digest (Cont. Vol. A) 924, *1265a.*

Ward v. James, [1965] 1 All E.R. 563; [1965] 2 W.L.R. 455; 3rd Digest Supp.

Appeal.

The husband appealed to the Court of Appeal against an order of MR. COM-MISSIONER SYMS made on Apr. 20, 1966, on the hearing of cross-applications as to the custody and care and control of the two children of the marriage, Sarah Ann Laxton and Stephen James Albert Laxton. The commissioner ordered that

Dictum of DAVIES, L.J., at p. 980, *considered in* Re M. [1967] 3 All E.R. 1071.

the cross-applications stand adjourned until mid-July, 1966, that the children A
go each week-end on Friday night to the husband and return to the wife in time
for bed on Sunday evening, and that they spend one half of their school holidays
with the husband. The grounds of appeal were: (i) that the commissioner had
no or no sufficient grounds for making the order in the form used and wrongly
exercised his discretion in making it; (ii) that the order was not in the best
interests of the children; (iii) that the order was against the weight of the evidence B
and contrary to and inconsistent with facts as found by the commissioner; (iv)
that the commissioner failed to have or to pay any or any sufficient regard to the
wishes of the husband; (v) that the order was contrary to justice and wrong in
law; (vi) that the commissioner ought to have ordered that the husband have
custody and care and control of the children and that the wife have reasonable
access to them; and (vii) that the commissioner exercised his discretion without C
any or adequate grounds, or alternatively wrongly, in ordering that the cross-
applications stand adjourned until mid-July, 1966.

The cases noted below* were cited during the argument in addition to those
referred to in the judgment of DAVIES, L.J.

N. A. Medawar for the husband.
J. J. Davis for the wife.   D

DAVIES, L.J.: This is an appeal by a petitioning husband from a decision
of MR. COMMISSIONER SYMS given on Apr. 20, 1966, in regard to the two young
children of the marriage. Rather unusually in such cases the commissioner gave
a full and detailed judgment, which we have had the advantage of having read
to us. He had heard oral evidence by the parties and a number of witnesses E
extending over two days. In effect what the commissioner decided, as I will
explain in a moment, was not to make any order as to the custody or care and
control of these children at the moment, but to adjourn and postpone a decision
on the matter until July, i.e., for a period of three months; and he said that he
would then reconsider the matter in the light of what had happened during this
intervening period with the assistance, no doubt, of any further evidence which F
might then be put before him together with a welfare officer's report.

The facts are so fully stated in the commissioner's judgment that I do not
propose to state them in detail, but merely to give the principal dates. The
parties, who were quite young at the time, the husband twenty-seven and the
wife twenty-three years of age, were married in April, 1958, and the two children
with whom we are concerned are a girl born in February, 1959, now aged seven, G
and a boy born in April, 1960, now aged six. The marriage was apparently a
happy one at any rate until 1964, but unfortunately in July, 1965, the wife
commenced to commit adultery with the co-respondent, and she confessed this
to the husband in November of that year. Apparently she had discovered about
that time that she was pregnant, though it was doubtful at that time whether the
baby whom she was carrying would be successfully delivered. However, that H
child has been born recently, in fact since the commissioner's decision. Early in
January, 1966, the husband filed his petition alleging adultery. Apparently after
that the parties continued living in the same house until, on Jan. 22, the husband
left, taking the two children with him. A week later the wife had access to the
children at what had been the matrimonial home. At the end of the period of
access she refused to surrender the children to the husband. She subsequently I
removed them to another house in Croydon. The husband has, since January,
1966, been living with his widowed father at a house owned by his sister in
Wembley.

MR. COMMISSIONER SYMS heard the undefended petition on Apr. 5, 1966,
granted a decree nisi and expedited the decree absolute. A week later the wife

_____

* *Re B. (an Infant)*, [1962] 1 All E.R. 872; *Re O. (Infants)*, [1962] 2 All E.R. 10; *Jeffrey*
v. *Jeffrey*, (1962), 106 Sol. Jo. 686; *M.* v. *M. & G.*, (1962), 106 Sol. Jo. 877; *D.* v. *D.*,
(1965), 109 Sol. Jo. 573.

A married the co-respondent, and since then she has given birth to this child. Also in the house where she is now living with the co-respondent there is a child of the co-respondent by a previous marriage, a girl aged sixteen. The husband's application was for full custody and care and control of the two children of the marriage. He is living with his own father and in the hope that he will be granted care and control of the two children he has engaged a young woman, Miss

B Winstanley, as a nannie, who is there and ready and willing to look after these children.

There is no doubt at all what the commissioner's findings of fact were. He preferred all through the evidence of the husband to that of the wife. He found, and in my view rightly found, that the husband had behaved in the most exemplary manner throughout, so much so indeed that after the husband dis-

C covered that the wife was pregnant by the co-respondent, he wanted a reconciliation, wanted the wife to stay with him and the children, and was prepared to accept as a child of the family the child that the mother was expecting by the co-respondent. He found that there was a good and normal relationship between the children and the husband, and he found that as between the two houses where the husband and wife were living there was really nothing to choose. He found

D also, of course, as is apparent from what I have said, that the wife had behaved extremely badly. Those were the circumstances with which the commissioner was faced. He said explicitly that, if he had to decide then and there to which of the parties he would give the full custody and care and control, he would have decided in favour of the husband; but he said that to take that course might involve a risk. He said:

E   " One can never lose sight of the tie that is bound to exist between a mother and a young child. In my view that is a biological fact."

He went on:

       " The proposal which I should say I have decided to adopt arises because the risk of cutting the cord between this mother and these two children is

F   sufficiently grave to make a controversial proposal worth trying; it is certainly only an experiment for a limited period of time."

And coming back to what I said a moment ago, he said:

       " If faced with only the two alternatives, I think that the risk would have to be taken, and is one which would be justifiably taken."

G In those circumstances what the commissioner decided to do was to postpone the final decision for a period of three months. Until then he decided that the children should remain with the wife, but he also directed that the husband should have very liberal access.

       " It is further ordered that the said children go each week-end on Friday nights to the [husband] and return to the [wife] in time for bed on Sunday

H   evenings."

Counsel for the husband has challenged that order on a number of grounds. He says, first, that this was a completely innocent husband whose conduct was in every respect laudable, who had a very guilty wife, and that in those circumstances the commissioner completely misdirected himself in failing to give any

I weight to that consideration, and so never exercised his discretion at all. As I ventured to say to counsel during the course of the argument, I think that that is a criticism which cannot properly be made of this judgment. One has only to read it in extenso to appreciate how very carefully the commissioner considered all the matters that should be taken into account. The husband's conduct and the wife's misconduct weighed with him very heavily, and he rightly bore in mind the tie between a mother and children. It is plain that he had well in mind that the first and paramount consideration is the welfare of the children. It seems to me that the basis of his decision was that, although, if there had to be a decision forthwith, the children would go to the husband, the commissioner **A** thought in all the circumstances that was too risky. He said to himself: " Let us see how the children will get on and how they will settle down if they stay with the mother for three months and see the father frequently."

Two other criticisms of the course taken by the commissioner were made. First, what is to happen about Miss Winstanley if the husband has to keep her and pay her every week when she is looking after the children for only two days **B** in the week? Possibly she will not stay, and then what is to happen to the children if that happens? Secondly, it is said that it may be very unsettling for the children to have to go every week-end from Croydon to Wembley. Those are obviously matters for consideration. It may be that these parties might perhaps by consent come to some slightly modified arrangements about access; that is a matter for them. What we have to decide is whether or not we should or should not interfere **C** with the decision of the commissioner. I can see no ground here for saying that he erred in principle in any respect or that he failed to exercise his discretion.

The case of *Re L. (Infants)* (1) in this court to which we were referred seems to me to be quite distinguishable. That was a wardship case and not a custody case, and PLOWMAN, J., the judge at first instance, expressly directed himself that he must put out of his mind altogether the misconduct of the guilty wife in that **D** case. The members of this court, in particular HARMAN, L.J., and RUSSELL, L.J., made it quite plain that that was a fundamental misdirection and vitiated the judge's judgment. Here there is no such misdirection. Nor in this case is there any ground on which we could say that the commissioner was plainly wrong, so that on the authorities which have been cited to us, including *Ward* v. *James* (2), we ought to interfere. The commissioner was doing everything that he could to **E** serve the interests of these two young children. The course which he took was admittedly an unusual one, and I suggest that we amend his order in one respect. It is desirable that someone should have the formal custody of the two children, and it would, therefore, be right to direct that the custody be in the husband, and that no order for care and control be made at present. The children should continue to live with their mother, and the directions as to access should remain as **F** indicated by the commissioner.

There is one other matter which I am sure that the commissioner, who was clearly seriously exercised in his mind in this case, would not object to our suggesting, and that is this. I think that at the end of this period of three months the matter should be (I do not like the word, but I will use it) finalised in so far as any such order is ever final. If the commissioner decides that the children **G** should continue to remain with their mother, then he should make an order giving care and control to her. If, on the other hand, in the light of what happens during this intervening period, he decides after all that the children should go to the father, then he must make an order for custody and care and control in favour of the father. Subject to one variation, therefore, I would dismiss the appeal. **H**

WINN, L.J.: I agree in every respect with the judgment delivered by DAVIES, L.J., and desire to add only this. There must be a further hearing of the case in July, 1966, by the commissioner, and nothing should be allowed to prevent an order then being made in respect of care and control.

Appeal dismissed subject to variation directed by the court. Leave to appeal to **I** *the House of Lords refused.*

Solicitors: *Hutton & Co.*, Wallington (for the husband); *Michael R. Pringle*, Croydon (for the wife).

[*Reported by* F. A. AMIES, ESQ., *Barrister-at-Law.*]

---

(1) [1962] 3 All E.R. 1.   (2) [1965] 1 All E.R. 563.

A
PRACTICE DIRECTION.

PROBATE, DIVORCE AND ADMIRALTY DIVISION.

Divorce—Petition—Residence of petitioner—Omission of statement of residence—
Procedure—Matrimonial Causes Rules, 1957 (S.I. 1957 No. 619), r. 4 (1) (d).

Cancelled by PRACTICE DIRECTION.
[1968] 2 All E.R. 88.

B   Where it is sought to obtain a registrar's order, under r. 4 (1) (d)* of the
Matrimonial Causes Rules, 1957, that the residence of the petitioner be omitted
from the petition, the petitioner's solicitor should:
   (i) file the petition, the address having been omitted; (ii) at the same time
file the petitioner's civil aid certificate (if any) together with a copy omitting
the address; (iii) immediately thereafter, and before service of the petition,
C   apply ex parte on an affidavit by the petitioner stating the address and the
grounds of the application. If the application is refused, the registrar will make
an order directing amendment of the petition before it is served.

                                                    COMPTON MILLER
June 30, 1966.   Senior Registrar.

D   ——————

PEACHEY PROPERTY CORPORATION, LTD. *v.* ROBINSON AND ANOTHER.

[COURT OF APPEAL (Sellers, Salmon and Winn, L.JJ.), May 23, 24, 1966.]

E *Rent Restriction—Possession—Procedure—Court—Judgment for possession signed*
   in High Court by landlord in default of appearance—Premises to which
   Rent Acts applied by Rent Act 1965—Invalidity of judgment for recovery
   of possession for want of determination whether reasonable to give judgment
   for possession—Jurisdiction of High Court to determine forfeiture of lease—
   Policy of legislature that proceedings for possession of rent restricted premises
F   *should be brought in county court—Rent and Mortgage Interest Restrictions*
   (Amendment) Act, 1933 (23 & 24 Geo. 5 c. 32), s. 3 (1)—Rent Act 1965
   (c. 75), s. 31, s. 35 (1), (3).

After the Rent Act 1965 came into operation landlords issued a writ to
recover possession of a flat, let to tenants who resided there, for non-payment
of rent. The rateable value of the premises, which were in London, was
G   less than £400 per annum. No appearance was entered and judgment was signed
in default of appearance. On application for leave to issue a writ of possession
leave was refused on the ground that the judgment by default was not
effective for the purpose, owing to want of compliance with s. 3 (1) of the
Rent and Mortgage Interest Restrictions (Amendment) Act, 1933, which
was applied to the premises by s. 1 (1) of the Rent Act 1965, in that there had
H   been no determination by the court that it was reasonable to give judgment
for possession.
   Held: (i) the judgment in default of appearance for recovery of possession
was a nullity, as there had been no determination (as was required by s. 3 (1)
of the Act of 1933) that it was reasonable to give judgment for recovery of
possession (see p. 983, letter D, p. 987, letter C, and p. 988, letter E, post).
I   (ii) although by s. 35 (3) of the Rent Act 1965 the High Court had power
to entertain proceedings for forfeiture of a lease for breach of covenant, yet
the jurisdiction to determine whether it was reasonable to order possession,
in a case where s. 3 (1) of the Act of 1933 applied, and to enforce recovery
of possession was jurisdiction given to the county court by s. 31 and s. 35 (1)
of the Act of 1965, and it was more appropriate that proceedings for recovery
of possession in cases within the limits of the county court jurisdiction

——————

* For r. 4 (1) (d), see 10 HALSBURY'S STATUTORY INSTRUMENTS (1st Re-Issue) 220.

in actions for the recovery of land should be brought in the county court   **A** (see p. 983, letter H, p. 984, letter G, p. 987, letter D, and p. 988, letters D and G, post).

Smith v. *Poulter* ([1947] 1 All E.R. 216) and *Wolmer Securities, Ltd.* v. *Corne* (ante p. 691) approved.

Appeal dismissed.

[**Editorial Note.** The jurisdiction of the county court in actions for the   **B** recovery of land was increased to £400 net annual value for rating by the County Courts (Jurisdiction) Act 1963, s. 1.

As to restrictions on the court's power to make or give an order or judgment for possession of premises to which the Rent Acts apply, see 23 HALSBURY'S LAWS (3rd Edn.) 813, 814, para. 1592; and for cases on the subject, see 31 DIGEST (Repl.) 721, 722, *8045-8057.*   **C**

For the Rent and Mortgage Interest Restrictions (Amendment) Act, 1933, s. 3, see 13 HALSBURY'S STATUTES (2nd Edn.) 1048.

For the Rent Act 1965, s. 1, s. 31, s. 35, see 45 HALSBURY'S STATUTES (2nd Edn.) 822, 846, 849.]

Cases referred to:

> *Russoff* v. *Lipovitch*, [1925] All E.R. Rep. 100; [1925] 1 K.B. 628; 94 L.J.K.B.   **D** 355; 132 L.T. 789; 31 Digest (Repl.) 722, *8054.*
>
> *Smith* v. *Poulter*, [1947] 1 All E.R. 216; [1947] K.B. 339; [1947] L.J.R. 847; 31 Digest (Repl.) 721, *8047.*
>
> *Wolmer Securities, Ltd.* v. *Corne*, ante, p. 691.

Appeal.   **E**

This was an appeal with leave of the judge by the plaintiff landlords, Peachey Property Corpn., Ltd., against the order of CANTLEY, J., made in chambers, upholding the decision of Master ELTON refusing the landlords leave to issue a writ of possession of 147, Chiswick Village, Oxford Road, Hounslow, Greater London, which was a flat of a rateable value of less than £400 per annum let to the defendant tenants, Colin Brian Robinson and his wife Isabel Sheila Robinson,   **F** who resided there. The landlords signed judgment in default of appearance in the High Court on Jan. 26, 1966, against the tenants for possession of the premises and £278 15s. 1d. arrears of rent and service charges on a writ issued on Jan. 17, 1966.

L. A. Blundell, Q.C., and *W. A. Macpherson* for the landlords.

The tenants did not appear and were not represented.   **G**

WINN, L.J., delivered the first judgment at the invitation of SELLERS, L.J.: By a writ dated Jan. 17, 1966 (issued, therefore, after the commencement of the Rent Act 1965) the plaintiff landlords claimed, specially endorsing their claim on the writ, possession of 147, Chiswick Village, Oxford Road (which is in Hounslow, which itself is in Greater London), on which rent reserved under a 7½-year lease containing an express power of re-entry was in arrear to a substantial   **H** extent, totalling, with several service charges, £278 odd, consisting, so far as rent was concerned, of arrears to Dec. 24, 1965, of £119 odd, and a quarter's rent, due in advance on Christmas Day, 1965 of £91. That writ was duly served, according to certificates endorsed on it, on each of the two defendants, the tenants Colin Brian Robinson and Isobel Sheila Robinson (his wife). Neither of them appeared to the writ. On Jan. 26, 1966, judgment was signed in default of   **I** appearance, that judgment being signed as an administrative or ministerial step. The judgment so signed recites:

" It is this day adjudged that [the landlords] recover against [the tenants] possession of [the flat in question] together with arrears of rent and service charges . . ."

The rateable value of this flat was less than £400 a year. It follows that, by s. 1 (1) of the Rent Act 1965, the Rent Acts were applied to it, since that subsection provides that

A   " The Rent Acts shall apply . . . to every tenancy of a dwelling-house the rateable value of which on the appropriate day did not exceed, in Greater London £400 . . ."

The Rent Acts so applied are the Rent and Mortgage Interest Restrictions Acts, 1920 to 1939, or any of those Acts: that appears from a reference to the definition section, s. 47 (1) of the Act of 1965.   Accordingly, the Rent and Mortgage Interest Restrictions (Amendment) Act, 1933, s. 3 (1), was made to apply to these premises, and that subsection provided:

B

" No order or judgment for the recovery of possession of any dwelling-house to which the principal Acts apply or for the ejectment of a tenant therefrom shall be made or given unless the court considers it reasonable to make such an order or give such a judgment, and . . ."

C

—one or other of two additional conditions is satisfied.   It is perfectly plain from what I have said that before the judgment in default of appearance was entered no court had determined whether it was reasonable to make such an order or give such a judgment.   In my view, therefore, by express force of that section the judgment in default of appearance here was a nullity.   It was, according to its terms, a judgment for recovery of possession of these premises, and that is something which the section prohibits unless there has been a prior determination by the court that it was reasonable to give such a judgment.

D

Smith v. *Poulter* (1) was a case which concerned a somewhat similar, though by no means identical, situation.   It was heard by DENNING, J.   The circumstances there were as follows.   The dwelling-house in question was within the Rent Restrictions Acts.   The landlord of it had given the tenant notice to quit, and issued a writ in the High Court claiming possession.   The tenant failed to enter an appearance, and the landlord signed judgment for possession, as well as for arrears of rent and costs.   DENNING, J., held (in my respectful view rightly) that the judgment was bad because, under s. 3 of the Act of 1933 (which I have read), the court had no power to give judgment for possession unless it considered it reasonable to do so and in that case the question whether the conditions of the Act of 1933 were satisfied had not been considered.   It is perhaps as well to use his own words (2).

E

F

" That provision [i.e., s. 3 of the Act of 1933] limits the jurisdiction of the court, with the result that in any case where there is reason to think that the house is within those Acts, it is the duty of the court to see whether the conditions required by the Acts are satisfied, even though not pleaded or raised by the tenant."

G

The judge referred to three previous decisions (3) and went on to say: " That was not done in this case before judgment was signed."

In my view equally it is clear, and indeed irrefutable, that in this present case there was no compliance with the requirement of s. 3 of the Act of 1933 before this judgment in default of appearance was signed.

H

In *Smith* v. *Poulter* (4) DENNING, J., went on to observe—and indeed he gave effect to his view, applying the provisions of s. 17 (2) of the Increase of Rent and Mortgage Interest (Restrictions) Act, 1920, by depriving the plaintiff landlord of his costs—that he thought it more appropriate that such cases as the one with which he was dealing should be brought in the county court.   I share that view.   I note that it was expressed so long ago as 1925 in *Russoff* v. *Lipovitch* (5) where ATKIN, L.J. said:

I

---

(1) [1947] 1 All E.R. 216; [1947] K.B. 339.
(2) [1947] 1 All E.R. at p. 217; [1947] K.B. at pp. 340, 341.
(3) *Barton and Mitchell* v. *Finchan*, [1921] All E.R. Rep. 87; [1921] 2 K.B. 291;
Salter v. *Lask*, [1923] All E.R. Rep. 89; [1924] 1 K.B. 754; and *Davies* v. *Warwick*,
[1943] 1 All E.R. 309; [1943] K.B. 329.
(4) [1947] 1 All E.R. at p. 217; [1947] 1 K.B. at p. 341.
(5) [1925] 1 K.B. 628 at pp. 639, 640; [1925] All E.R. Rep. 100 at pp. 108, 109.

" I think it is fairly plain that in the opinion of the legislature it was   A
advisable that proceedings in respect to small houses, which are generally
let to poor people, should be taken in the county court rather than in the
High Court, especially as there are certain applications which have to be made
in connexion with such proceedings, the sole jurisdiction to deal with which
is given to the county court. And even where the jurisdiction is not exclusively given to the county court, as for instance where the question is whether   B
suitable alternative accommodation is offered by the landlord, the county
court judge, who is presumably familiar with the conditions of the district,
is better able to decide that question than a judge of the High Court.

To my mind it is an a fortiori proposition that the county court judge, familiar
with the locality, is better able to consider and decide such matters than a master
of the Queen's Bench Division of the High Court, sitting in London, who, if the   C
landlords' contention in the present appeal is right, might be called on to deal
from time to time—very often in the absence of the defendant tenants—with
premises situated in remote parts of the United Kingdom, in localities with which
he was unlikely to be personally very familiar.

The same policy is, I think, expressed in the Rent Act 1965, which provides,
by s. 35 (1) that: D

" The court for the purposes of this Part of this Act [that is to say
Part 3 of that Act] shall be . . . (a) in England and Wales, in relation to
premises with respect to which the county court has for the time being
jurisdiction in actions for the recovery of land, the county court . . ."

It goes on to provide that, " in relation to other premises " (that is to say in   E
cases in respect of which the county court has no jurisdiction) it shall be " the
High Court ".

Section 31 of the Rent Act 1965, in Part 3 of the Act, provides that

" Where any premises are let as a dwelling on a lease which is subject to a
right of re-entry or forfeiture [and this was a case where there was a letting
on lease for $7\frac{1}{2}$ years with a right of re-entry and forfeiture (which has been   F
asserted) for non-payment of rent] it shall not be lawful to enforce that
right otherwise than by proceedings in the court while any person is lawfully
residing in the premises or part of them "

—which was the position in the instant case.

I think, therefore (as indeed counsel for the landlords conceded), that it cannot
be doubted that jurisdiction in the present case was given to the county court;   G
but attention was drawn—properly—to the provisions of s. 35 (3) of the Act of
1965, which are as follows:

" Nothing in this Part of this Act [and, therefore, nothing in section
35 (1) (a)] shall affect the jurisdiction of the High Court in proceedings
to enforce a lessor's right of re-entry or forfeiture . . ."
        H
I do not read the rest of the subsection. It is said, therefore, that by those
last-read provisions jurisdiction is to be found in the High Court in the present
case to enforce the landlord's right of forefeiture. I agree that that is so; but
it is not possible, in my view, further to contend that those provisions have any
effect on the overriding control on recovery of possession imposed by s. 3 of the
Act of 1933. Reading the provisions together, it seems to me that clearly Parlia-   I
ment has enacted that there shall still be jurisdiction in the High Court to entertain proceedings in which the landlord claims a right to forfeit a lease for breach
of covenant, inter alia for a breach of covenant duly to pay the rent; but that,
in all other respects, the Rent Acts, which are expressly preserved and applied
by the Act of 1965, will still operate to prevent any judgment being given for
the recovery of possession or for the ejectment of a tenant.

How, then, are the two seemingly contradictory statutory provisions to be
reconciled? In my view, quite simply in this way. Historically, and really

A by nothing but a historical accident, the court procedure for enforcing a forfeiture of a lease for breach of covenant has resulted—by practice and by procedure of the court—in a judgment declaring a right to recover possession, when
all that is meant in reality is that there is a valid right of forfeiture and that the
term created by the lease has been validly and effectively brought to an end so
that the interest in the term re-vests in the landlord. Although the judgment
B recites, as I have said, a right in the plaintiff landlords, by force of the judgment,
to recover possession from the defendant tenants, it is clear from R.S.C., Ord. 42,
r. 5 that that judgment can only be enforced by a writ of possession, and that
application must be made for leave to issue such a writ of possession. It is under
the provisions of R.S.C., Ord. 47, r. 1 and to some extent r. 2 that such an
application must be made.

C A very similar situation exists in the county court, under the provisions of
s. 191 of the County Courts Act, 1959. That section and its effect recently called
for the consideration of another division of this court (6). The judgment of the
court was given by RUSSELL, L.J. It is unnecessary to go fully into the matter,
but the effect of that judgment is this, that where, in comparable circumstances,
a right of forfeiture has arisen and has been enforced by proceedings in the county
D court under s. 191 of the County Courts Act, 1959, the right order for the county
court judge to make is an order so limited that its effect will only be to produce
a forfeiture and not to procure delivery of possession of premises to the plaintiff-
landlord. The court declared (7) that the proper order in such circumstances is
this (so far as material):

E   " It is adjudged that the plaintiffs are entitled (for the purposes of s. 191
of the County Courts Act, 1959, only) to recover against the defendant
possession of the land mentioned in the particulars of claim . . . [reciting
the premises and reciting the arrears of rent and the order for costs]; And it
is ordered (for the purposes of s. 191 of the County Courts Act, 1959, only)
that the defendant do give the plaintiffs possession of the said land on
[a certain date] unless on or before [a certain date] the defendant has paid
F   into court [a certain sum]."

RUSSELL, L.J., in his judgment said (7):

       " In all such cases further application must be made to the court [that
is to say, an application to obtain possession]; the original order for
possession, when it operates, cannot be regarded as more than forfeiture
G   or determination absolute of the contractual tenancy, and in its ordinary
form (see county court Form 136) is misleading."

In my view, equally, the form of judgment which was obtained by the plaintiff
landlords in this case in the High Court is misleading. If it is not misleading,
it seems to me that a dilemma arises. If it is a judgment for the recovery of
possession, it is prohibited by s. 3 of the Act of 1933, and so it is no less a nullity
H than the judgment which was disposed of as a nullity by DENNING, J., in *Smith*
v. *Poulter* (8). If, on the other hand, it is properly to be regarded as understood,
however ostensibly misleading its terms are, as meaning no more than a declaration that the right to forfeiture has accrued, then it is not a judgment for the
recovery of possession which can found an application for the issue of a writ of
possession pursuant to the terms of R.S.C., Ord. 47. These provide (by r. 1 (1))
I that:

       " A judgment or order that a party do recover possession of any land
may by leave obtained on ex parte application to the court or a judge
supported by affidavit, be enforced by writ of possession in manner immediately before Nov. 1, 1875, used in actions of ejectment in the superior
courts of common law."

---

(6) In *Wolmer Securities* v. *Corne*, ante p. 691.   (7) Ante at p. 693.
(8) [1947] 1 All E.R. 216; [1947] K.B. 339.

That order was apparently first made in 1883; and it may be that there again **A**
there is an historical practice which has not been adapted to modern situations.

I desire to make it perfectly clear that in my view the plaintiff landlords in this
action did not behave in any way improperly or seek to take any improper
advantage of their tenants. They filed an affidavit in accordance with the required
form, in R.S.C., Appendix B, No. 40, which set out all the information, correctly
and frankly, which is required to be set out in such an affidavit. It is only by **B**
the alertness of Master ELTON that this matter was (if I may use the expression)
" spotted ". Through his refusal to issue a writ of possession, after reference to
the opinion expressed in *Smith* v. *Poulter* (9) the matter proceeded on appeal
from him to the judge in chambers, who upheld Master ELTON'S decision, and
from the judge in chambers to us. Before the judge and the master it was contended that the Rent Acts did not apply by reason of s. 35 (3) of the Act of 1965: **C**
that was utterly wrong. I say in passing that I cannot understand why there was
any difficulty about bringing on the appeal, since the judge in chambers gave
leave to appeal and it was quite supererogatory to serve a notice of motion,
which is only needed after a judgment at trial.

Therefore one ultimately comes to this. There may be a need, or it may be a
topic worthy of consideration whether there is any need, to amend the existing **D**
procedure and practice of the High Court as it stands at the moment. I cannot
think that it is right that it should be left to an ex parte application made by
depositing in the office of the practice master the judgment obtained in default
of appearance and filing the affidavit required in Form 40 of Appendix B for the
court to determine whether or not it is reasonable to require tenants to give up
possession of the house in which they are living. Nor do I see how defendants who **E**
have not appeared are likely effectively to be able—since really they can only
do it orally—to bring themselves to London and represent to the master that
there are considerations why he should not consider it reasonable to order them
to give up the house in which they are living. In my view, what is contemplated
by the statutes is a decision of a court, not a decision taken on the occasion of an
ancillary step in the process of execution of a judgment so obtained. **F**

For the reasons which I have endeavoured to indicate—basically because I
think that s. 3 of the Act of 1933 prohibits what has been done here—I am of the
opinion that this appeal should be dismissed.

SALMON, L.J.: I entirely agree.

I confess that on the particular facts of this case I have some sympathy with **G**
the plaintiff landlords, who may have been misled by the language of s. 35 (3)
of the Rent Act 1965, and who certainly fully informed the defendant tenants
of every step they were about to take as they took it, giving them every opportunity of putting forward any ground on which it might be held unreasonable
to make the order for which the landlords were asking. The tenants did nothing
at all. Although I do not wish in any sense to prejudge what may happen when **H**
the matter comes before a county court judge, when further evidence may be
adduced on the part of the tenants, on the material at present before us it seems
to me that, if there had been any consideration by the court whether or not it
was reasonable to give the judgment which the landlords have now recovered,
the answer would plainly have been that it was reasonable that they should have
that judgment. **I**

The issues raised in this case, however, are very far-reaching. Wherever the
merits may lie in this particular case, they cannot affect the construction of the
statute. Section 3 (1) of the Rent and Mortgage Interest Restrictions (Amendment) Act, 1933, in so far as it is material, reads as follows:

" No order or judgment for the recovery of possession of any dwelling-
house to which the principal Acts apply or for the ejectment of a tenant

(9) [1947] 1 All E.R. 216; [1947] K.B. 339.

A   therefrom shall be made or given unless the court considers it reasonable to make such an order or give such a judgment . . ."

The judgment on which the landlords rely and which they applied for leave to enforce under R.S.C., Ord. 47, r. 1 and r. 2, is a judgment for the recovery of possession of a dwelling-house to which the principal Acts apply. It is quite plain that when that judgment was given, there was no consideration at all
B   whether or not it was reasonable to give it. This was so for the simple reason that that judgment was obtained in default of appearance and, in such cases, under the Rules of Court judgment is obtained automatically. The fact that it may well have been reasonable is beside the point if the court never considered the question; and here it is conceded that the court did not consider the question.
C   Accordingly that judgment, on the plain wording of s. 3 of the Act of 1933 was a nullity; and plainly the application for leave to enforce it had to be refused.

I would add only this, that under the Rent Acts, 1920 to 1933, the High Court certainly had jurisdiction to entertain the action: nevertheless the policy of the legislature was clearly to discourage actions under these Acts from being
D   brought in the High Court, for it is provided that in such a case no costs should be awarded to the plaintiff: see s. 17 (2) of the Increase of Rent and Mortgage Interest (Restrictions) Act, 1920. This is most understandable, because the county court is essentially the appropriate tribunal in which these matters should be considered. As WINN, L.J., has said, poor tenants have much easier access to the county courts than to the High Court. Besides, county court judges
E   have the widest experience of dealing with cases of this sort whereas judges and masters of the High Court have not.

When s. 35 (3) of the Rent Act 1965 was introduced, this merely preserved the jurisdiction of the High Court in cases to which the Act of 1965 applied, amongst other things in proceedings to enforce a lessor's right of re-entry for forfeiture. Section 35 (3) was written into the Act of 1965 because other sections
F   excluded the High Court jurisdiction in other cases to which I need not refer. The fact that the High Court jurisdiction was preserved to entertain such a case as the present does not mean that there had been any change in policy. The policy of the legislature was no different from what it had been under the other Acts. It left the High Court jurisdiction, but it still discouraged plaintiffs from using it.

G   Counsel for the landlords has advanced a most ingenious argument. He has said that, since the High Court has jurisdiction in the present type of case, if a plaintiff issues his writ in the High Court, as he is entitled to do, the defendant, if he has no answer, may not trouble to appear and judgment will be signed in default of appearance: so, when you are looking at s. 3 of the Act of 1933, you should fit into it a judgment for the recovery of possession obtained in default
H   of appearance because the section must have been intended to cover such a judgment. Counsel has attempted in many ways and with great ingenuity to support this argument, but I cannot accept it. In the end I think he was driven to concede that for the purposes of his argument one would have to read the words " judgment for the recovery of possession of any dwelling-house " as if there were added to them the words " which may be enforced without leave
I   or further order "; but those additional words are not there. I can see no reason for writing them into the section, more particularly as the policy of the legislature, as acknowledged by the courts, is to discourage cases of this sort from being brought in the High Court. If the plaintiff landlord does bring his action in the High Court and the defendant tenant is inconsiderate enough not to enter an appearance, it follows that the plaintiff cannot get the reasonableness of the judgment for which he is asking considered, and, therefore, cannot get it at all.

It is impossible for another reason, in my view, to read the section in the way for which counsel for the landlords contends. Supposing one did write into the **A** statute the words which he suggests, one cannot then find in the statute any corresponding requirement that when one applies for leave to enforce such a judgment the court shall not give leave unless it considers it reasonable to do so. If I may say so with respect, the words on which counsel relies for this part of his argument are wholly inappropriate for any such purpose. The words are " no order for the ejectment of a tenant shall be made or given unless the court **B** considers it reasonable ". The judgment is for recovery of possession: when one seeks leave to enforce it one is not asking for an order for ejectment, but one is asking for leave to enforce the judgment. That is not dealt with anywhere in s. 3. So that if counsel for the landlord's construction were right, there would be this astonishing result, that in a county court case the judgment could not be obtained unless the court considered it reasonable; but in the High Court one **C** could always get judgment without reasonableness being considered, and there would be nothing, so far as the statute is concerned, to prevent a plaintiff landlord in such circumstances from obtaining an order to enforce the judgment without the question of reasonableness being considered. That would be a very remarkable result, particularly when the policy of the legislature is to discourage people from proceeding in the High Court.   **D**

I think, too, that this matter is concluded by the decision of DENNING, J., in *Smith* v. *Poulter* (10), a decision with which I respectfully agree.

I would dismiss the appeal.

SELLERS, L.J.: I agree with the judgment of WINN, L.J.

I am of opinion that it is not possible, for the reasons given, to accede to the **E** argument for the landlords, however reasonable, on the facts of this case at least, it may seem.   Once it is established (as it clearly is) that the premises are within the Rent Acts, then it seems to me that Master ELTON's decision was right. He said:

" While the High Court has jurisdiction to make orders for possession in certain cases in respect of premises to which the Rent Acts apply, the **F** court still has to be satisfied before making an order for possession in such a case that the provisions of s. 3 of the Rent and Mortgage Interest Restrictions (Amendment) Act, 1933, have been complied with. A judgment obtained in default in these circumstances is of no effect ";

and he cited *Smith* v. *Poulter* (10).   I too would respectfully agree that the latter decision was rightly decided and that the principles can properly be applied **G** here.

I think that the appeal should be dismissed.

Appeal dismissed.   Judgment obtained in default of appearance set aside save for money award of £278 15s. 1d.   Leave to appeal to the House of Lords refused.

Solicitor: *G. L. Leigh* (for the landlords).   **H**

[*Reported by* HENRY SUMMERFIELD, ESQ., *Barrister-at-Law.*]

I

---

(10) [1947] 1 All E.R. 216; [1947] K.B. 339.

A   GOLDMAN v. HARGRAVE AND OTHERS.

[PRIVY COUNCIL (Lord Reid, Lord Morris of Borth-y-Gest, Lord Pearce, Lord
Wilberforce and Lord Pearson), April 25, 26, 27, June 13, 1966.]

B
*Negligence—Duty to take care—Arising out of foreseeable risk of injury—Hazard
—Removal of hazard from land—Fire caused by lightning—Steps initially
taken to deal with source of danger—Subsequently fire left to burn itself out—
Negligence in leaving fire to burn itself out—Escape of fire to adjacent premises
—Fire so escaping did not accidentally begin within Fires Prevention
(Metropolis) Act, 1774 (14 Geo. 3 c. 78), s. 86.*

C
*Privy Council—Australia—Western Australia—Negligence—Fire—Tree struck
by lightning—Burning tree felled—Fire left to burn out—Revival—Escape
to adjacent premises—Liability of occupier.*

There is a general duty of care on an occupier of land, on which a hazard
to his neighbour arises, to remove or reduce the hazard, whether it arises by
the act of God, or from natural causes or by human agency; and the standard
of the duty of care is to require the occupier to do what is reasonable having
D   regard to his individual circumstances (see p. 994, letter I, and p. 996,
letter D, post).

Sedleigh-Denfield v. *O'Callaghan* ([1940] 3 All E.R. 349) and *Boatswain* v.
Crawford ([1943] N.Z.L.R. 109) applied.

The appellant was the owner and occupier of land adjacent to that of the
respondents. On Feb. 25, 1961, a tall redgum tree in the centre of the
appellant's land was struck by lightning and began to burn in a fork eighty-
E   four feet from the ground. Early the next morning the appellant telephoned
to the district fire officer and asked for a tree feller to be sent. The tree was
cut down about midday on the same day. Up to this time the appellant's
conduct in relation to the fire was not open to criticism. The appellant,
it was found, could have extinguished the fire by putting water on it that
evening or the following morning, but instead of adopting that method,
F   which was the prudent method, he adopted the method of letting the tree
burn itself out and took no steps to prevent the fire spreading. The method
so adopted by the appellant brought a fresh risk, the risk of revival of the
fire, which was a foreseeable risk by a man in the appellant's position.
On Mar. 1, the wind having freshened, the fire revived and spread
westwards on to the respondents' property causing extensive damage.
G
Held: the appellant was liable in negligence for the damage done by the
fire to the respondents' property because—

(i) the action needed to put out the fire on Feb. 26 or Feb. 27 was within
the capacity and resources of the appellant, and in not taking the prudent
steps to put out the fire by water the appellant had, for the reason stated at
letter C, above, been guilty of negligence notwithstanding that he did
H   not initially cause the fire, and this negligence caused the damage to the
respondent's property (see p. 996, letter G, and p. 997, letter E, post).

(ii) as the fire which caused the damage was that which revived on Mar. 1,
as a result of the appellant's negligence on Feb. 26 or Feb. 27, it did not
" accidentally begin " within the meaning of the Fires Prevention (Metropolis) Act, 1774, which accordingly did not afford a defence (see p. 997, letter
I   D, post).

Musgrove v. *Pandelis* ([1918-19] All E.R. Rep. 589) approved.

Appeal dismissed.

[As to liability of occupier of premises for damage by fire, see 28 HALSBURY'S
LAWS (3rd Edn.) 52, 53, para. 48; and for cases on the subject, see 36 DIGEST
(Repl.) 76, 77, *406-415.*

For the Fires Prevention (Metropolis) Act, 1774, s. 86, see 13 HALSBURY'S
STATUTES (2nd Edn.) 10.]

Applied in LEAKEY v NATIONAL
TRUST [1978] 3 All ER 234

Applied in LEAKEY v NATIONAL
TRUST [1980] 1 All ER 17

Cases referred to: A

Batchelor v. Smith, (1879), 5 V.L.R. (L.) 176; 36 Digest (Repl.) 77, *428.

Boatswain v. Crawford, [1943] N.Z.L.R. 109.

Davey v. Harrow Corpn., [1957] 2 All E.R. 305; [1958] 1 Q.B. 60; [1957]
2 W.L.R. 941; Digest (Cont. Vol. A) 11, 1a.

Eastern Asia Navigation Co., Ltd. v. Fremantle Harbour Trust Comrs. and the
Commonwealth of Australia, (1950), 83 C.L.R. 353.   B

Filliter v. Phippard [1843-60] All E.R. Rep. 879; (1847), 11 Q.B. 347; 17
L.J.Q.B. 89; 10 L.T.O.S. 225; 11 J.P. 903; 116 E.R. 506; 36 Digest
(Repl.) 76, 407.

Giles v. Walker, [1886-90] All E.R. Rep. 501; (1890), 24 Q.B.D. 656; 59
L.J.Q.B. 416; 62 L.T. 933; 54 J.P. 599; 36 Digest (Repl.) 294, 402.

Havelberg v. Brown, [1905] S.A.L.R. 1; 36 Digest (Repl.) 77, *429.   C

Hunter v. Walker, (1898), 6 N.Z.L.R. 690; 36 Digest (Repl.) 77, *434.

Job Edwards, Ltd. v. Birmingham Navigations, [1924] 1 K.B. 341; 93 L.J.K.B.
261; 130 L.T. 522; 36 Digest (Repl.) 316, 628.

Landon v. Rutherford, [1951] N.Z.L.R. 975; 36 Digest (Repl.) 79, *493.

Musgrove v. Pandelis, [1918-19] All E.R. Rep. 589; [1919] 2 K.B. 43; 88
L.J.K.B. 915; 120 L.T. 601; 36 Digest (Repl.) 77, 412.   D

Noble v. Harrison, [1926] All E.R. Rep. 284; [1926] 2 K.B. 332; 95 L.J.K.B.
813; 135 L.T. 325; 90 J.P. 188; 36 Digest (Repl.) 285, 340.

Pontardawe Rural Council v. Moore-Gwyn, [1929] 1 Ch. 656; 98 L.J.Ch. 242;
141 L.T. 23; 93 J.P. 141; 36 Digest (Repl.) 295, 408.

Rylands v. Fletcher, [1861-73] All E.R. Rep. 1; (1868), L.R. 3 H.L. 330; 37
L.J.Ex. 161; 19 L.T. 220; 33 J.P. 70; 36 Digest (Repl.) 282, 334.   E

Sedleigh-Denfield v. O'Callaghan, [1940] 3 All E.R. 349; [1940] A.C. 880;
164 L.T. 72; sub nom. Sedleigh-Denfield v. St. Joseph's Society for
Foreign Missions, 109 L.J.K.B. 893; 36 Digest (Repl.) 316, 629.

Sparke v. Osborne, (1908), 7 C.L.R. 51; 36 Digest (Repl.) 295, *132.

Torette House Proprietary, Ltd. v. Berkman, (1940), 62 C.L.R. 637; 13 A.L.J.
514; 57 W.N. 48; 40 S.R.N.S.W. 8; 36 Digest (Repl.) 76, *426.   F

Wagon Mound, The (No. 2), Overseas Tankship (U.K.), Ltd. v. The Miller
Steamship Co., Pty., Ltd., ante p. 709.

Appeal.

This was an appeal by special leave from a judgment of the High Court of
Australia (TAYLOR, WINDEYER and OWEN, JJ.) dated Nov. 22, 1963, allowing
an appeal from a judgment of JACKSON, J., dated Jan. 9, 1963, in the Supreme   G
Court of Western Australia, dismissing the respondents' claims for damages.
The facts are summarised in the opinion of LORD WILBERFORCE.

P. H. F. Bristow, Q.C., F. T. P. Burt, Q.C. (of the Bar of Western Australia) and
M. E. I. Kempster for the appellant.

Gresley Clarkson, Q.C. (of the Bar of Western Australia) and M. C. Anwyl-   H
Davies for the respondents.

LORD WILBERFORCE: This consolidated appeal from a decision of the
High Court of Australia reversing that of the Supreme Court of Western Australia,
arises out of a bush fire, which developed in the grazing area of Gidgegannup,
Western Australia, and did extensive damage to the respondents' properties. The
High Court decided that the appellant, on whose property the fire started,   I
was liable for the damage, and this decision the appellant now contests.

The circumstances in which the fire started are concisely stated in the judgments
of the High Court, which accepted the findings of the trial judge. There was an
electrical storm on Feb. 25, 1961, and a tall redgum tree, about one hundred feet
in height, in the centre of the appellant's property, was struck by lightning.
This tree was about 250 yards from the western boundary of the appellant's
property (in which direction the respondents' properties lie) and rather less
from the eastern boundary. The redgum caught fire in a fork eighty-four feet

A from the ground, and it was evidently impossible to deal with the blaze while the tree was standing. Early in the morning of Feb. 26, the appellant telephoned the district fire control officer, appointed as such under the Bush Fires Act, 1954-58, and asked for a tree feller to be sent. Pending his arrival the appellant cleared a space round the tree of combustible material and sprayed the surrounding area with water. The tree feller arrived at mid-day on Feb. 26, at which time

B the tree was burning fiercely, and it was cut down. The trial judge found, and the High Court accepted the finding, that up to this point the appellant's conduct in relation to the fire was not open to criticism.

The judge also found, however, that if the appellant had taken reasonable care he could, on the Sunday evening (Feb. 26), or at least early on the next morning, have put out the first by using water on it. The appellant indeed

C claimed that he spent two hours on Monday, Feb. 27, in extinguishing the fire, but his evidence as to this was rejected. The judge referred to evidence which indicated that the appellant's method of extinguishing a fire of this kind was to burn it out. " You burn it out " he was reported as saying " that is the only way I know to put a fire out."

On Tuesday, Feb. 28, the appellant was away from the property for a sub-

D stantial part of the day, and it was found that he did not at any time after Feb. 27 take any steps which could be regarded as reasonable to prevent the fire from spreading. On Wednesday, Mar. 1, there was a change in the weather; the wind, which had previously been light to moderate, freshened to about twenty m.p.h. with stronger gusts. The air temperature rose some $10°$ to $105°F$. The fire revived and spread over the appellant's paddock towards the west and

E on to the respondents' properties: it was not observed by the appellant until about noon on Mar. 1, and by then it could not be stopped. The damage to the respondents' properties followed.

It is important at once to deal with an argument, as to the facts, which was advanced by the respondents at the trial. It was sought to contend that although the fire commenced accidentally, the appellant, whether by heaping combustible

F material on to it, after the tree had been felled, or even by permitting the tree to burn in the way in which it did on the ground, had adopted the fire as his own —as suus ignis—and had made use of it for his own purpose or advantage.

Their lordships (in agreement with the High Court) do not accept this view of the facts. The result of the evidence, in their lordships' opinion, is that the appellant both up to Feb. 26, and thereafter was endeavouring to extinguish

G the fire; that initially he acted with prudence, but that there came a point, about the evening of Feb. 26 or the morning of Feb. 27, when, the prudent and reasonable course being to put the fire out by water, he chose to adopt the method of burning it out. That method was, according to the finding of the trial judge, unreasonable, or negligent in the circumstances: it brought a fresh risk into operation, namely the risk of a revival of the fire, under the influence of changing

H wind and weather, if not carefully watched, and it was from this negligence that the damage arose. That a risk of this character was foreseeable by someone in the appellant's position was not really disputed: in fact danger arising from weather conditions is given official recognition in the Bush Fires Act, 1954-58, which provides for their classification according to the degree of danger arising from them.

I This conclusion has an important bearing on the nature of the legal issue which has to be decided. It makes clear that the case is not one where a person has brought a source of danger on to his land, nor one where an occupier has so used his property as to cause a danger to his neighbour. It is one where an occupier, faced with a hazard accidentally arising on his land, fails to act with reasonable prudence so as to remove the hazard. The issue is therefore whether in such a case the occupier is guilty of legal negligence, which involves the issue whether he is under a duty of care, and if so, what is the scope of that duty. Their lordships propose to deal with these issues as stated, without attempting

to answer the disputable question whether if responsibility is established it should A
be brought under the heading of nuisance or placed in a separate category. As
this Board has recently explained in *The Wagon Mound No. 2, Overseas Tankship
(U.K.), Ltd.* v. *The Miller Steamship Co., Pty., Ltd.* (1), the tort of nuisance, uncertain in its boundary, may comprise a wide variety of situations, in some of
which negligence plays no part, in others of which it is decisive. The present
case is one where liability, if it exists, rests on negligence and nothing else; B
whether it falls within or overlaps the boundaries of nuisance is a question of
classification which need not here be resolved.

What then is the scope of an occupier's duty, with regard to his neighbour,
as to hazards arising on his land? With the possible exception of hazard of fire,
to which their lordships will shortly revert, it is only in comparatively recent
times that the law has recognised an occupier's duty as one of a more positive C
character than merely to abstain from creating, or adding to, a source of danger
or annoyance. It was for long satisfied with the conception of separate or autono-
mous proprietors, each of which was entitled to exploit his territory in a
" natural " manner and none of whom was obliged to restrain or direct the
operations of nature in the interest of avoiding harm to his neighbours.

This approach, or philosophy, found expression in decisions both in England D
and elsewhere. In *Giles* v. *Walker* (2) a claim that an occupier had a duty to
protect his neighbour against the invasion of thistledown was summarily rejected
by the Queen's Bench Division. Moreover, in a similar field, it was held in 1908
by the High Court of Australia (*Sparke* v. *Osborne* (3)) that an occupier was not
under a duty to prevent a noxious weed, prickly pears, from attacking a neighbour's fence. The case was decided on a demurrer to a pleading in which E
negligence was not alleged. In relation to fires, there were similar decisions. In
Australia, in 1879, the Supreme Court of Victoria, decided on a demurrer to a
pleading which alleged negligence, that an occupier of land on which a fire
accidentally occurs is not under any duty to put it out (*Batchelor* v. *Smith* (4)).
In New Zealand, in 1888, the Supreme Court in Banco held that there is no legal
duty cast on the owner of land on which a fire originates to prevent it from F
spreading to the land of another, though he was present immediately after it was
lighted and might have put it out (*Hunter* v. *Walker* (5)). It is interesting to see
(since the present case is concerned with an accidental fire) that RICHMOND, J. (6)
in a learned judgment examines the common law from the YEAR BOOK 2 Hen. 4,
18, and expresses this opinion on the state of the law prior to the statute 6 Anne
c. 31 (7): G

" (The authorities) leave it doubtful what would be the responsiblity of
the owner for damage done by a fire beginning on his property the origin
of which is not known. It seems to have been supposed that at common law
the owner would be answerable for such fires, which may be properly called,
so far as the owner is concerned, accidental "

H

—and in fact his decision, against liability, was based on an exempting statute—
the Fires Prevention (Metropolis) Act, 1774 (replacing the earlier 6 Anne c. 31)
to which reference will later be made.

That, at common law, an occupier of premises from which fire escapes was
liable if either the origin, or the escape, of the fire was due to his negligence seems
also to have been the opinion of SIR JOHN SALMOND—see *Eastern Asia Navigation
Co., Ltd.* v. *Fremantle Harbour Trust Comrs. and the Commonwealth of Australia* (8) I
where FULLAGER, J. in the High Court of Australia left the point open (9).

Lastly in 1905 the Supreme Court of South Australia in *Havelberg* v. *Brown* (10)

(1) Ante p. 709.   (2) [1886-90] All E.R. Rep. 501; (1890), 24 Q.B.D. 656.
(3) (1908), 7 C.L.R. 51.   (4) (1879), 5 V.L.R. (L.) 176.
(5) (1898), 6 N.Z.L.R. 690.   (6) (1898), 6 N.Z.L.R. 690 at p. 692.
(7) (1898), 6 N.Z.L.R. at p. 694.   (8) (1950), 83 C.L.R. 353.
(9) (1950), 83 C.L.R. at p. 393.   (10) [1905] S.A.L.R. 1.

A   held that an occupier who remains passive is under no responsibility, and that if he interferes, he is liable only on proof of negligence. The argument against responsibility is powerfully stated by Way, C.J., where, referring to the occupier's duty, he says (11):

B   " It is one example among many of imperfect obligations, of a moral as opposed to a legal duty, and one can see how difficult it would be to frame a law making an occupier liable for a fire arising upon his premises, annexing to him legal responsibilities, when he was in no way connected with the act. Should such a legal duty apply in all cases, irrespective of age or sex? Should it be made applicable in spite of the absence or illness of the owner, or in the case of a fire out of his sight or without his knowledge? Is it to apply to a man who is weak or unskilful? The slightest reflection must

C   shew any one how difficult it would be to frame a law that would be applicable to all cases, and any one who has seen, as most of us have, the frequent bush fires in the hills adjacent to Adelaide, will understand that there really is no necessity for any such law. People not only extinguish dangerous fires from self-interest, and for the preservation of themselves and their families, but in the summer we see every week the whole countryside turning

D   out and using the utmost endeavours to prevent danger to life and injury to the property of others."

That a person who takes some action (though mistaken) to deal with an accidental fire should not be in a worse position as regards civil liability than one who does nothing is clearly a consideration of importance not to be overlooked when stating a rule as to liability.

E   These three decisions relating to fires were followed by the learned trial judge in the present case.

A decision which, it can now be seen, marked a turning point in the law was that of *Job Edwards, Ltd.* v. *Birmingham Navigations* (12). The hazard in that case was a fire which originated in a refuse dump placed on land by the act of a

F   third party. When the fire threatened to invade the neighbouring land, the owners of the latter, by agreement, entered and extinguished the fire at a cost of some £1,000. The issue in the action was whether the owners of the land, where the fire was, were liable to bear part of the cost. The Court of Appeal (12) by a majority answered this question negatively, but Scrutton, L.J.'s dissenting judgment contained the following passage (13):

G   " There is a great deal to be said for the view that if a man finds a dangerous and artificial thing on his land, which he and those for whom he is responsible did not put there; if he knows that if left alone it will damage other persons; if by reasonable care he can render it harmless, as if by stamping on a fire just beginning from a trespasser's match he can extinguish it; that then if he does nothing, he has ' permitted it to continue ', and becomes respon-

H   sible for it. This would base the liability on negligence, and not on the duty of insuring damage from a dangerous thing under *Rylands* v. *Fletcher* (14). I appreciate that to get negligence you must have a duty to be careful, but I think on principle that a landowner has a duty to take reasonable care not to allow his land to remain a receptacle for a thing which may, if not rendered harmless, cause damage to his neighbours."

I   One may note that this passage is dealing with a different set of facts from that involved in the case then under consideration: the one referring to a fire just beginning which can be extinguished by stamping on it, the other concerned with a smouldering dump to extinguish which involves both effort and expense, so that it is quite possible to approve both of the majority decision and of the passage quoted from the dissenting judgment.

---

(11) [1905] S.A.L.R. at p. 11.   (12) [1924] 1 K.B. 341.
(13) [1924] 1 K.B. at pp. 357, 358.
(14) [1861-73] All E.R. Rep. 1; (1868), L.R. 3 H.L. 330.

This was followed in 1926 by *Noble* v. *Harrison* (15). The damage there was **A**
caused by an overhanging tree with a latent defect and the decision was against
liability. The judgment of ROWLATT, J. in the Divisional Court contains this
passage (16):

". . . a person is liable for a nuisance constituted by the state of his property
(i) if he causes it; (ii) if by neglect of some duty he allows it to arise; and
(iii) if, when it has arisen without his own act or default, he omits to remedy **B**
it within a reasonable time after he did or ought to have become aware of it."

It will be seen that the learned judge in the third category makes no distinction
according to whether the " nuisance " is caused by trespassers or by natural
causes, and that he does not enter into any question as to the limits of the effort
or expenditure required of the occupier. As a general statement of the law it **C**
was cited with apparent approval by DIXON, J., in *Torette House Proprietary, Ltd.*
v. *Berkman* (17).

In 1940 the dictum of SCRUTTON, L.J., (18) passed into the law of England
when it was approved by the House of Lords in *Sedleigh-Denfield* v. *O'Callaghan*
(19). Their lordships need not cite from this case in any detail since it is now
familiar law. It establishes the occupier's liability with regard to a hazard created
on his land by a trespasser, of which he has knowledge, when he fails to take **D**
reasonable steps to remove it. It was clear in that case that the hazard could
have been removed by what VISCOUNT MAUGHAM (20) described as the " very
simple step " of placing a grid in the proper place. The members of the House
approved the passage just cited from SCRUTTON, L.J.'s (18) judgment and
VISCOUNT MAUGHAM (21) and LORD WRIGHT (22) also adopted the statement **E**
of the law in SALMOND's LAW OF TORTS (5th Edn.) (1920) pp. 258-265:

" When a nuisance has been created by the act of a trespasser or otherwise
without the act, authority, or permission of the occupier, the occupier is not
responsible for that nuisance unless, with knowledge or means of knowledge
of its existence, he suffers it to continue without taking reasonably prompt
and efficient means for its abatement." **F**

The appellant, inevitably, accepts the development, or statement, of the law
which the *Sedleigh-Denfield* case (19) contains—as it was accepted by the High
Court of Australia. He seeks to establish, however, a distinction between
the type of hazard which was there involved, namely one brought about by
human agency such as the act of a trespasser, and one arising from natural causes,
or act of God. In relation to hazards of this kind it was submitted that an occupier **G**
is under no duty to remove or to diminish it, and that his liability only commences
if and when by interference with it he negligently increases the risk or danger
to his neighbour's property.

Their lordships would first observe, with regard to the suggested distinction,
that it is well designed to introduce confusion into the law. As regards many
hazardous conditions arising on land, it is impossible to determine how they **H**
arose—particularly is this the case as regards fires. If they are caused by human
agency, the agent, unless detected in flagrante delicto, is hardly likely to confess
his fault. And is the occupier, when faced with the initial stages of a fire, to ask
himself whether the fire is accidental or man-made before he can decide on his
duty? Is the neighbour, whose property is damaged, bound to prove the human
origin of the fire? The proposition involves that if he cannot do so, however **I**
irresponsibly the occupier has acted, he must fail. The distinction is not only
inconvenient, but also it lacks, in their lordships' view, any logical foundation.

(15) [1926] All E.R. Rep. 284; [1926] 2 K.B. 332.
(16) [1926] All E.R. Rep. at p. 287; [1926] 2 K.B. at p. 338.
(17) (1940), 62 C.L.R. 637 at p. 652.   (18) [1924] 1 K.B. at pp. 357, 358.
(19) [1940] 3 All E.R. 349; [1940] A.C. 880.
(20) [1940] 3 All E.R. at p. 359; [1940] A.C. at p. 895.
(21) [1940] 3 All E.R. at p. 357; [1940] A.C. at p. 893.
(22) [1940] 3 All E.R. at p. 369; [1940] A.C. at p. 910.

A   Within the class of situations in which the occupier is himself without responsibility for the origin of the fire, one may ask in vain what relevant difference there is between a fire caused by a human agency such as a trespasser and one caused by Act of God or nature. A difference in degree—as to the potency of the agency—one can see but none that is in principle relevant to the occupier's duty to act. It was suggested as a logical basis for the distinction that in the

B   case of a hazard originating in an act of man, an occupier who fails to deal with it can be said to be using his land in a manner detrimental to his neighbour and so to be within the classified field of responsibility in nuisance, whereas this cannot be said when the hazard originates without human action so long at least as the occupier merely abstains. The fallacy of this argument is that, as already explained, the basis of the occupier's liability lies not in the use of

C   his land: in the absence of " adoption " there is no such use: but in the neglect of action in the face of something which may damage his neighbour. To this, the suggested distinction is irrelevant.

   On principle therefore, their lordships find in the opinions of the House of Lords in Sedleigh-Denfield v. O'Callaghan (23) and in the statements of the law by Scrutton, L.J. (24) and Salmond (25), of which they approve, support for

D   the existence of a general duty on occupiers in relation to hazards occurring on their land, whether natural or man-made. The matter does, however, not rest there. First, the principle has been applied to the specific hazards of fire by the more recent decision of the Supreme Court of New Zealand in Boatswain v. Crawford (26). That was a case of a fire of unknown origin which could easily have been controlled in its initial stages. The court (26) held the defendant liable

E   for breach of duty following expressly Sedleigh-Denfield v. O'Callaghan (23) and applying the passage above quoted from Salmond on Torts. The High Court of Australia, which may be taken to be aware of the present day conditions as regards bush fires, considered that this decision is now to be preferred to the older cases as in accordance with the trend of the law, and their lordships agree with their view. A still later case in New Zealand, Landon v. Rutherford (27),

F   followed Boatswain v. Crawford (26)—though, as was pointed out by Taylor, J., and Owen, J., in their judgment in the High Court of Australia, it placed too heavy an onus of proof on the defendant. Secondly, it appears that the movement of American decisions has been towards the development of a duty of care on the part of occupiers in relation to hazards arising on their land both generally and of fire. Their lordships were referred to three successive series of the American

G   Law Reports Annotated in the years 1926, 1937 and 1951 referring to a number of decided cases in various jurisdictions, all of which, save one, point in the same direction. The cumulative result of these is to establish the occupier's duty of care towards his neighbour to a similar extent as the English and New Zealand cases. Their lordships were also referred to the RESTATEMENT OF THE LAW OF TORTS, the relevant portion of which (Vol. IV, para. 839-40) dates from

H   1939. This makes a distinction between invasions of a neighbour's interest arising from a natural condition of land and other invasions, which is expressed in somewhat general terms and which is of less direct application to such a case as the present than the American decisions.

   Thirdly their lordships have considered the modern text books of authority on the law of torts, CLERK AND LINDSELL (12th Edn.) 1961, SALMOND (13th

I   Edn.) 1961, WINFIELD (7th Edn.) 1963, FLEMING 1965, as well as a formative article by DR. A. L. GOODHART in 4 CAMBRIDGE LAW JOURNAL (1932) p. 13. All of these endorse the development, which their lordships find in the decisions, towards a measured duty of care by occupiers to remove or reduce hazards to their neighbours.

   So far it has been possible to consider the existence of a duty, in general

---

(23) [1940] 3 All E.R. 349; [1940] A.C. 880.   (24) [1924] 1 K.B. at pp. 357, 358.
(25) SALMOND'S LAW OF TORTS (5th Edn.) (1920) pp. 258-265.
(26) [1943] N.Z.L.R. 109.   (27) [1951] N.Z.L.R. 975.

terms; but the matter cannot be left there without some definition of the scope   A
of his duty. How far does it go? What is the standard of the effort required?
What is the position as regards expenditure? It is not enough to say merely that
these must be " reasonable " since what is reasonable to one man may be very
unreasonable, and indeed ruinous, to another: the law must take account of the
fact that the occupier on whom the duty is cast, has, ex hypothesi, had this
hazard thrust on him through no seeking or fault of his own. His interest, and   B
his resources whether physical or material, may be of a very modest character
either in relation to the magnitude of the hazard, or as compared with those of his
threatened neighbour. A rule which required of him in such unsought circumstances in his neighbour's interest a physical effort of which he is not capable,
or an excessive expenditure of money, would be unenforceable or unjust. One
may say in general terms that the existence of a duty must be based on knowledge   C
of the hazard, ability to foresee the consequences of not checking or removing it,
and the ability to abate it. Moreover in many cases, as for example in SCRUTTON,
L.J.'s (28) hypothetical case of stamping out a fire, or the present case, where the
hazard could have been removed with little effort and no expenditure, no problem
arises; but other cases may not be so simple. In such situations the standard
ought to be to require of the occupier what it is reasonable to expect of him in   D
his individual circumstances. Thus, less must be expected of the infirm than of
the able bodied: the owner of a small property where a hazard arises which
threatens a neighbour with substantial interests should not have to do so much
as one with larger interests of his own at stake and greater resources to protect
them: if the small owner does what he can and promptly calls on his neighbour
to provide additional resources, he may be held to have done his duty: he should   E
not be liable unless it is clearly proved that he could, and reasonably in his
individual circumstance should, have done more. This approach to a difficult
matter is in fact that which the courts in their more recent decisions have taken.
It is in accordance with the actual decision in the *Job Edwards* case (29) where to
remove the hazard would have cost the occupier some £1,000—on this basis
the decision itself seems obviously right. It is in accordance with *Pontardawe*   F
Rural Council v. *Moore-Gwyn* (30) where to maintain the rocks in a state
of safety would have cost the occupier some £300; and if some of the situations
such as those in *Giles* v. *Walker* (31) (thistledown) and *Sparke* v. *Osborne* (32)
(prickly pears) were to recur to-day, it is probable that they would not be decided
without a balanced consideration of what could be expected of the particular
occupier as compared with the consequences of inaction. That *Giles* v. *Walker*   G
(31) might now be decided differently was indeed suggested by LORD GODDARD,
C.J., giving the judgment of the English Court of Appeal in *Davey* v. *Harrow*
Corpn. (33). In the present case it has not been argued that the action necessary
to put the fire out on Feb. 26 to 27 was not well within the capacity and resources
of the appellant. Their lordships therefore reach the conclusion that the
respondents' claim for damages, on the basis of negligence, was fully made out.   H
    One final point was raised by the appellant by way of defence to the claim.
This was based on the provisions of the Fires Prevention (Metropolis) Act, 1774,
s. 86 which provides that no action shall lie against any person on whose estate
" any fire shall accidentally begin ". This statute replaces the earlier Act of
Anne (6 Anne c. 31). It is accepted that this statute is part of the law in Western
Australia, and that it applies to such an area as that in which the fire in question   I
arose.
    The words " shall accidentally begin " are simple enough, but the simplicity is
deceptive. Read literally they suggest that account need be taken of nothing

---

(28) [1924] 1 K.B. at p. 357.   (29) [1924] 1 K.B. 341.
(30) [1929] 1 Ch. 656.
(31) [1886-90] All E.R. Rep. 501; (1890), 24 Q.B.D. 656.
(32) (1908), 7 C.L.R. 51.
(33) [1957] 2 All E.R. 305 at p. 310; [1958] 1 Q.B. 60 at p. 72.

A except the origin of the fire and that given an accidental beginning, no supervening negligence or even deliberate act can deprive a defendant of the benefit
of the statute. Further reflection, however, suggests a doubt both because such
a result seems capable of producing absurdity and injustice, and because of the
inherent difficulty of saying what the expression " any fire " is intended to mean.
A fire is an elusive entity: it is not a substance, but a changing state. The words
B " any fire " may refer to the whole continuous process of combustion from birth
to death, in an Olympic sense, or reference may be to a particular stage in that
process—when it passes from controlled combustion to uncontrolled conflagra-
tion. Fortunately, the Act of 1774 has been considered judicially and, as one
would expect, the process of interpretation has taken account of these considerations. In *Filliter* v. *Phippard* (34) Lord Denman, C.J., explained the purpose
C of the earlier Act (6 Anne c. 31 s. 6) as being to remove the supposed common law
liability of a person " in whose house a fire originated which afterwards spread
to his neighbour's property " and held that it did not apply to a fire caused
deliberately or negligently. This was carried further in *Musgrove* v. *Pandelis* (35)
where a fire started accidentally in the carburettor of a car, but spread because
the chauffeur negligently failed to turn off the petrol tap. The Court of Appeal
D held that the Act did not apply. Bankes, L.J. (36) put it that the Act of 1774
relieved an owner for a mere escape of fire from his premises, but did not relieve
him against a claim for damages for negligence. The fire which caused the damage
was, he thought, not the spark which caused the initial ignition, but the raging
fire which arose from the act of negligence. Their lordships accept this interpretation: it makes sense of the statute, it accords with its antecedents, and it makes
E possible a reasonable application of it to the facts of the present case, that is to
say that the fire which damaged the respondents' property was that which arose
on Mar. 1 as the result of the negligence of the appellant. The statutory defence
therefore fails.

   Their lordships will humbly advise Her Majesty that the appeal should be
dismissed. The appellant must pay the costs of the appeal.

F
Appeal dismissed.

   Solicitors: *Ingledew, Brown, Bennison & Garrett* (for the appellant); *Montagu's
and Cox & Cardale* (for the respondents).

[*Reported by* Kathleen J. H. O'Brien, *Barrister-at-Law.*]

G

H

I

(34) [1843-60] All E.R. Rep. 879 at p. 880; (1847), 11 Q.B. 347 at p. 354.
(35) [1918-19] All E.R. Rep. 589; [1919] 2 K.B. 43.
(36) [1918-19] All E.R. Rep. at p. 592; [1919] 2 K.B. at p. 48.

Re DEMETRIOUS.

A

[QUEEN'S BENCH DIVISION (Lord Parker, C.J., Sachs and Veale, JJ.), March 22, 1966.]

Extradition—Fugitive offender—Jurisdiction—Extension of Act of 1881 to foreign country in which Her Majesty had jurisdiction—Consequential reciprocal operation of Act of 1881 between foreign country and United Kingdom—Alleged crime committed in Qatar—Whether Qatar to be treated as a British possession for purposes of Act of 1881—Fugitive Offenders Act, 1881 (44 & 45 Vict. c. 69), s. 2, s. 36—Foreign Jurisdiction Act, 1890 (53 & 54 Vict. c. 37), s. 5—Qatar Order, 1959 (S.I. 1959 No. 1038), art. 12 (b), Sch. 2.

B

The applicant was detained in Brixton Prison pursuant to an order made under s. 5 of the Fugitive Offenders Act, 1881, the order having been made as a result of an endorsed warrant from the State of Qatar alleging two offences by the applicant of obtaining in Qatar money by false pretences. The applicant applied for an order of habeas corpus, contending that the magistrate making the order had no jurisdiction to do so under the Fugitive Offenders Act, 1881. By art. 12 (b)* of the Qatar Order, 1959, Her Majesty's criminal jurisdiction in Qatar was, so far as circumstances admitted, to be exercised on the principles of, and in conformity with the Acts of Parliament and Orders in Council of the United Kingdom set out in Sch. 2 to the order (which included the Fugitive Offenders Act, 1881), subject to the exceptions, adaptations and modifications therein specified. It was conceded that the order did not purport to invoke s. 36† of the Fugitive Offenders Act, 1881, and must have been made under the powers provided in the Foreign Jurisdiction Acts, 1890 and 1913. By s. 5 (1)‡ of the Act of 1890, it was lawful for Her Majesty the Queen in Council to direct that the enactments described in Sch. 1 to that Act (which included the Act of 1881) were to extend to any foreign country in which for the time being Her Majesty had jurisdiction and, by s. 5 (2)‡, thereupon these enactments were, to the extent of that jurisdiction, to operate as if that country were a British possession.

C

D

E

F

Held: on the true construction of s. 5 of the Act of 1890, when once an enactment was extended by virtue of s. 5 (1) to a foreign country in which Her Majesty had jurisdiction, the enactment was to operate (i.e., to operate also in the United Kingdom if it was reciprocal in character) as if the foreign country were a British possession for the purposes of s. 36 of the Act of 1881, though such operation would be subject to any limitation on Her Majesty's jurisdiction in the foreign country; thus the effect of the Qatar Order, 1959, was to create reciprocity when applying the Fugitive Offenders Act, 1881, and to give it reciprocal operation in the United Kingdom, not merely in Qatar, with the consequence that there was jurisdiction to make the extradition order and the application for habeas corpus failed (see p. 1002, letters A, B and F, post).

G

H

[As to the application of fugitive offenders legislation to places outside Her Majesty's dominions, see 16 HALSBURY'S LAWS (3rd Edn.) 584, para. 1213; and for cases on the subject, see 24 DIGEST (Repl.) 1010, 1011, *154-157.*

For the Fugitive Offenders Act, 1881, s. 2, s. 36, see 9 HALSBURY'S STATUTES (2nd Edn.) 897, 910.

I

For the Foreign Jurisdiction Act, 1890, s. 5, see 6 HALSBURY'S STATUTES (2nd Edn.) 555.]

Case referred to:

R. v. *Earl of Crewe, Ex p. Sekgome,* [1910] 2 K.B. 576; 79 L.J.K.B. 574; 102 L.T. 700; 24 Digest (Repl.) 1010, *155.*

---

* Article 12, so far as material, is set out at p. 1000, letter D, post.

† Section 36 is set out at p. 999, letter H, post.

‡ Section 5 is set out at p. 1000, letters G and H, post.

A   **Motion for habeas corpus.**

This was a motion for an order of habeas corpus by the applicant, Demetris Demetrious, who was detained in Brixton Prison pursuant to an order made on Feb. 14, 1966, by the chief magistrate at Bow Street magistrates' court pending his return to Qatar in respect of two offences of obtaining money by false pretences in Qatar on Sept. 5 and Oct. 1, 1963. The applicant had been

B   arrested on a warrant dated Nov. 15, 1964, signed by a judge of Her Majesty's court for Qatar and endorsed by the Bow Street magistrate on Nov. 30, 1964, alleging that he obtained on Sept. 5, 1963, 2,670 rupees, the equivalent of £200 and on Oct. 1, 1963, 10,008 rupees, the equivalent of £748 from a business man of Doha, Qatar, Persian Gulf, in exchange for two cheques which proved to be false, thereby obtaining money by false pretences, contrary to s. 242 of the

C   Qatar Penal Code.

R. D. L. Du Cann for the applicant.

Nigel Bridge for the Secretary of State for Home Affairs and the Governor of Brixton Prison.

J. C. Mathew for the State of Qatar.

D   **LORD PARKER, C.J.:** In these proceedings, counsel moves on behalf of the applicant, one Demetris Demetrious, at present detained in Her Majesty's Prison at Brixton, for an order of habeas corpus. The applicant was detained in Brixton Prison pursuant to an order made on Feb. 14, 1966, by the chief magistrate at Bow Street under s. 5 of the Fugitive Offenders Act, 1881, that order having been made as a result of an endorsed warrant from the State of

E   Qatar. The warrant alleged two offences by the applicant of obtaining in Qatar money by false pretences. No question arises in the present case as to the merits; there is no doubt that the learned magistrate was entitled to find on the depositions a prima facie case for committal. The only question here is whether, as the applicant alleged, the chief magistrate had in fact no jurisdiction under the Act of 1881 to make the order. The Fugitive Offenders Act,

F   1881, s. 2, provides that:

" Where a person accused of having committed an offence . . . in one part of Her Majesty's dominions has left that part, such person . . . if found in another part of Her Majesty's dominions, shall be liable to be apprehended and returned in manner provided by this Act to the part from which he is a fugitive."

G   The words there are " part of Her Majesty's dominions ", and it is clear from the interpretation section, s. 39, that a British possession means any part of Her Majesty's dominions exclusive of the United Kingdom, the Channel Islands and the Isle of Man. The real question here, therefore, is whether the State of Qatar is to be treated as if it was a British possession. Section 36 of the Fugitive

H   Offenders Act, 1881, itself provides that:

" It shall be lawful for Her Majesty from time to time by Order in Council to direct that this Act shall apply as if, subject to the conditions, exceptions, and qualifications (if any) contained in the order, any place out of Her Majesty's dominions in which Her Majesty has jurisdiction, and which is named in the order, were a British possession, and to provide for carrying

I   into effect such application."

There undoubtedly have been cases, so we have been told, in which the powers of s. 36 of the Act of 1881 have been specifically invoked, and in which an Order in Council has been made providing that a place where Her Majesty exercises jurisdiction shall be treated as a British possession. However, in most of the cases, as I understand it, an Order in Council has been made under the Foreign Jurisdiction Acts, 1890 and 1913, applying certain provisions of English law in a foreign country, and amongst others applying or extending, as it is said, the

Fugitive Offenders Act, 1881, to that foreign country (1). In passing, it is to be **A** observed that, since 1953 or thereabouts, there has been a change in wording. In the Qatar Order in Council, 1949 (2), art. 12 (1) provided that:

" The following enactments shall apply to Qatar as if it were a British Colony or possession but subject to the provisions of this order and to the exceptions, adaptations, and modifications specified in para. (2) of this article . . ."   **B**

Amongst the enactments applied was the Fugitive Offenders Act, 1881. Counsel for the applicant has conceded, though it is unnecessary to go into the matter, that that provision in the order of 1949 was apt to make the Fugitive Offenders Act, 1881, reciprocal in its operation as between Qatar and this country. He would, I think, say that that order had been made not only in the exercise of **C** the powers provided by the Foreign Jurisdiction Act, 1890, but under the powers described by the words " or otherwise in His Majesty vested " in the recitals to the order. However that may be, since 1953, and in particular in the relevant Order in Council now in force, namely, the Qatar Order, 1959 (3), the relevant provision is art. 12, and that article provides, so far as it is material that

" Subject to the other provisions of this order, Her Majesty's criminal and **D** civil jurisdiction in Qatar shall, so far as circumstances admit, be exercised on the principles of, and in conformity with . . . (b) The Acts of Parliament and Orders in Council of the United Kingdom set out in Sch. 2 of this order subject to the exceptions, adaptations and modifications therein specified."

In Sch. 2 of the order are set out a number of Acts of Parliament of the United Kingdom, amongst which is to be found the Fugitive Offenders Act, 1881. By **E** para. (2) of that schedule certain modifications are made. It is conceded both by counsel for the Secretary of State and counsel for the State of Qatar that, whether or not there was power for the Order in Council to invoke s. 36 of the Fugitive Offenders Act, 1881, the order certainly did not purport to do so, and must have been made under the powers provided in the Foreign Jurisdiction Acts, 1890 and 1913, themselves.   **F**

Accordingly, one must look at those Acts, and for the present purpose it is unnecessary to go beyond the Foreign Jurisdiction Act, 1890. If there was power to make the Fugitive Offenders Act, 1881, operate reciprocally between the State of Qatar and this country, it is to be found, and to be found only, in s. 5 of the Foreign Jurisdiction Act, 1890, which provides:

" (1) It shall be lawful for Her Majesty the Queen in Council, if she thinks **G** fit, by order to direct that all or any of the enactments described in Sch. 1 to this Act [that Schedule does include the Fugitive Offenders Act, 1881], or any enactments for the time being in force amending or substituted for the same, shall extend, with or without any exceptions, adaptations, or modifications in the order mentioned, to any foreign country in which for the time being Her Majesty has jurisdiction.   **H**

" (2) Thereupon those enactments shall, to the extent of that jurisdiction, operate as if that country were a British possession, and as if Her Majesty in Council were the legislature of that possession."

Pausing there, I would read sub-s. (2) once more with the omission of the words " to the extent of that jurisdiction ". Those words are: " Thereupon "—that **I** is, after Her Majesty has directed that the Fugitive Offenders Act, 1881, shall extend to Qatar—" Thereupon those enactments shall operate as if that country were a British possession . . ." This is a statute of this country, and, if one pauses there, it is plainly saying, as it seems to me, that this country is recognising that, once the Fugitive Offenders Act, 1881, has been extended to Qatar,

---

(1) For the countries to which the Act of 1881 has been extended by Orders in Council, see 6 HALSBURY'S STATUTORY INSTRUMENTS (First Re-Issue) 135.
(2) S.I. 1949 No. 595.   (3) S.I. 1959 No. 1038.

A Qatar shall be deemed to be a British possession, and, if that be the true view
and if one does get to that stage, then clearly there is reciprocity between this
country and Qatar by reason of s. 36 of the Fugitive Offenders Act, 1881, and
this motion must fail.

What, however, counsel for the applicant says in his very careful argument
is that that interpretation is not giving full and proper effect to the words which
B I deliberately omitted, " to the extent of that jurisdiction ". Counsel then goes
back, as I understand it, to the preamble in particular and certain other sections
of the Act of 1890. The preamble provides that:

" Whereas by treaty, capitulation, grant, usage, sufferance, and other
lawful means, Her Majesty the Queen has jurisdiction within divers foreign
countries, and it is expedient to consolidate the Acts relating to the exercise
C of Her Majesty's jurisdiction out of her dominions."

Pausing there, counsel points out that this is dealing with the exercise by Her
Majesty of jurisdiction out of Her dominions, in other words as if she were the
ruler and legislature of the State of Qatar. He says that that qualifies the whole
of the Act of 1890, and that any powers and jurisdiction that she is given by that
D Act are purely and clearly in relation to what is done in Qatar. Accordingly,
he would say that, before there can be reciprocity between this country and
Qatar under the Fugitive Offenders Act, 1881, there would have to be another
Order in Council under the Fugitive Offenders Act, 1881, either under s. 36 or s. 32,
because this legislation which Her Majesty puts into effect under the Foreign
Jurisdiction Act, 1890, is only legislation internal to Qatar. He relies further on
E the general tenor, and I find it unnecessary to read them, of the earlier sections of
the Act of 1890, s. 1, s. 2, s. 3, s. 4, and he also invokes what was said by KENNEDY,
L.J., in R. v. Earl of Crewe, Ex p. Sekgome (4) in 1910, where he said this:

" If this view is correct, the Protectorate of a foreign country in which
His Majesty has and exercises power and jurisdiction as a protecting and
not as a ruling Sovereign, and which he has never annexed to the possession
F of the British Crown, certainly cannot properly be treated as part of His
Majesty's dominions."

Accordingly, so runs the argument, when one comes to s. 5 (2) the limitation there
expressed, namely, " to the extent of that jurisdiction ", is referable, and referable
only, to the extent to which Her Majesty by reason of the Act of 1890 can exercise
jurisdiction, and that is a purely internal jurisdiction.
G Attractive as counsel for the applicant's argument is, it seems to me that
there are many answers to it. In the first place it is wrong to say that the
preamble here is such as to necessitate the restriction of the ambit of the Act of
1890 to matters which Her Majesty can do qua legislature of Qatar. It is not
without interest that the wording of the preamble itself is to consolidate the
Acts relating to the exercise of Her Majesty's jurisdiction. Once one is applying
H or extending the Fugitive Offenders Act, 1881, to Qatar, it is certainly a related
matter that Parliament should say that thereupon as a consequence and as a
result of that extension Qatar shall be treated for that purpose as a British
possession. But, quite apart from that, it seems to me that the natural meaning
of s. 5 in its entirety is against counsel for the applicant's argument. Subsection
(1) is giving Her Majesty power to extend certain enactments into any foreign
I country in which for the time being Her Majesty has jurisdiction; that is purely
internal, if I may so put it, legislation internal to Qatar. Then one looks to
sub-s. (2) to find what the consequences of that are; it seems to me that in its
natural meaning it is saying that, once that is done, then this country will treat
Qatar for the purposes of that legislation as a British possession. The words
" to the extent of that jurisdiction " are clearly necessary because the jurisdiction
is certainly not unlimited; it may be limited in area to certain parts of a foreign

_____
(4) [1910] 2 K.B. 576 at p. 623.

state; it may be of a temporary nature; it may extend only to certain subject- A
matters, property or persons. Therefore, some limitation is clearly necessary.
In my judgment, on its natural meaning those words are going to the limitation
of the jurisdiction in that sense, and are not limited to the internal effect of the
legislation.

Finally on this point though I have tried to follow counsel for the applicant's
argument, I fail to see why, if his argument is right, there was ever any B
necessity to say that those enactments shall operate as if that country were a
British possession, unless it be for the purposes of making the Fugitive Offenders
Act, 1881, in the present case, and other Acts to which I will refer, reciprocal in
their operation. He does suggest that those words were necessary in order to
invoke the provisions of Part 2 of the Fugitive Offenders Act, 1881, a group of
sections under the heading of " Inter-Colonial Backing of Warrants, and C
Offences ". For my part, I find it difficult to see why those words operate for
that purpose and do not operate for the purposes of Part 1 where a British
possession is part of Her Majesty's dominions and where s. 2 would operate.
Perhaps what is conclusive in this case is a reference to the Acts which Parliament
gave power to apply, and which are applied, both under the Foreign Jurisdiction
Act, 1890, and under the Foreign Jurisdiction Act, 1913. I find it unnecessary D
to refer to those Acts save to say this, that many of them are Acts which clearly
can only properly be operated on a reciprocal basis; they are intended to provide
for reciprocity, and yet in many of them, unlike the Fugitive Offenders Act, 1881,
itself, there is, as it were, no built-in provision providing for that reciprocity,
and, accordingly, if counsel for the applicant's argument is right, the effect of
the Foreign Jurisdiction Act, 1890, and the Orders in Council made thereunder E
is to render Acts, though they are clearly designed to operate reciprocally, capable
only of operating one way, namely in the State of Qatar.

It seems to me that that really is conclusive of the case; and that s. 5 (2) is
clearly intended by Parliament to be a provision whereby this country recognises
a foreign country in which Her Majesty has jurisdiction to be a British possession
for the purposes of the enactments which Her Majesty has extended to that F
foreign country. In those circumstances, I have come to the conclusion that
this application fails and should be dismissed.

SACHS, J.: I entirely agree and there is nothing which I wish to add.

VEALE, J.: I agree. The main issue is as to the true construction and
meaning of s. 5 of the Foreign Jurisdiction Act, 1890; the unilateral construction
which has been pressed on us by counsel for the applicant is that the Fugitive G
Offenders Act, 1881, by reason of the Qatar Order, 1959, has become part of the
law of Qatar, but there is no reciprocity because there is no provision anywhere
making Qatar the equivalent of a British possession so far as the Fugitive
Offenders Act, 1881, in this country is concerned. I do not accept this construction. For my part, I take it as clear that Her Majesty's jurisdiction in a foreign
country may be limited in more than one way, by area, by time, or by quo ad H
persons or property. I see no difficulty in reading s. 5 (1) of the Act of 1890 as
empowering the extension of the Acts in Sch. 1 to a foreign country and in reading
sub-s. (2) as limiting the extension to the extent to which the jurisdiction is in
fact limited already by area or otherwise.

In my judgment, the argument that the construction advanced by counsel for
the applicant is not the true construction of the section is strongly reinforced I
when one considers the Acts other than the Fugitive Offenders Act, 1881, set
out in Sch. 1 to the Act of 1890 and the extension thereof by the Foreign
Jurisdiction Act, 1913. I agree that this application should be dismissed.

Application dismissed.

Solicitors: *Kingsley, Napley & Co.* (for the applicant); *Treasury Solicitor;*
Charles Russell & Co. (for the State of Qatar).

[*Reported by* KAUSHALYA PURIE, *Barrister-at-Law.*]

A L. P. ARTHUR (INSURANCE), LTD. *v.* SISSON AND OTHERS.

[CHANCERY DIVISION (Ungoed-Thomas, J.), April 29, 1966.]

Company—Receiver—Appointment by court—Action begun by company in
liquidation against receiver and manager to challenge propriety of payments
made before liquidation—Creditor's voluntary liquidation supervening after
B *appointment of receiver and manager—Receiver and manager appointed*
in an action in which the company was originally plaintiff—Whether a new
action could be brought against the receiver and manager by the company
at the instance of the liquidator.

A receiver and manager of a company's business was appointed by the
court in an action in which the company was plaintiff when the receiver
C was appointed. The company went into a creditors' voluntary liquidation
after the action had begun. The company at the instance of the liquidator
applied for leave to bring an action against the receiver in respect of the
payment of certain insurance premiums which the receiver had paid to
another company on the basis that he had received them as agent for that
company.

D **Held:** by leave of the court an action could be brought against the
receiver appointed by the court by a person at whose instance he had been
appointed, and in the present case leave would be granted to the company
to proceed against the receiver by action to recover the payment in question
(see p. 1005, letter D, post).

Re Potter, Ex p. Day ((1883), 48 L.T. 912) distinguished.

E [As to proceedings against a receiver, see 32 HALSBURY'S LAWS (3rd Edn.)
420, paras. 685, 686; and for cases on the subject, see 4 DIGEST (Repl.) 15, *63-65*.]

Case referred to:
Potter, Re, Ex p. Day, (1883), 48 L.T. 912; 4 Digest (Repl.) 15, *65*.

Motion.

F This was a motion in an action begun by writ issued on Sept. 24, 1963 (" the
present action "). There were four relevant actions. The first was begun by
writ on Aug. 16, 1963 (1963 L. 2141) in the Queen's Bench Division for moneys
allegedly misappropriated by a director. The company (L.P. Arthur (Insurance),
Ltd.), which carried on the business of an insurance broker, was plaintiff. The
present action (1963 A. 2748) was the second action, and was brought in the
G Chancery Division; the same director, Leslie Parkes Arthur (" Mr. Arthur "), and
the company were plaintiffs, but by a consent order dated Mar. 2, 1966, the company was struck out as plaintiff and added as defendant. The action concerned
the constitution of the board of directors of the company. By an order in the
present action made by consent on Oct. 11, 1963, John Hamilton Sisson, the
first respondent to the present motion, was appointed receiver and manager
H of the company's business. The company went into a creditor's voluntary
liquidation in March, 1964; and the applicant on this motion, Edgar Miskin,
was appointed liquidator by resolution dated Mar. 18, 1964. Pursuant to a
resolution of the company's board in January, 1963, a company, A-Plan Protection, Ltd., had been formed whose shares were issued to the directors of the
company, and the undertaking and assets of the company were transferred
I to A-Plan Protection, Ltd. During the period between the receiver's appointment and the company's liquidation certain insurance premiums (amounting
to £7,827 13s. 1d.) were received by the receiver and paid to A-Plan Protection,
Ltd. on the basis that they were received on behalf of A-Plan Protection, Ltd.,
to which the relevant business of the company had been transferred. The
propriety of the payment thus depended on the propriety of the transaction
with A-Plan Protection, Ltd. At a hearing before the master (Master NEAVE)
concerning the course of the present action on June 29, 1965, it was intimated
that the company wished to challenge the propriety of the payment to A-Plan

Protection, Ltd.   This hearing was adjourned to Oct. 7, 1965, the Master indica-   **A**
ting that unless a new writ was issued he would proceed with the taking of the
receiver's accounts, but that if a writ were issued he would stay the taking of the
accounts.   The remaining two of the four actions previously mentioned were
begun by writs issued on Sept. 14, 1965, at the instance of the liquidator of the
company, the company being the plaintiff.   One of these actions (viz., 1965 L.
No. 2730) was a misfeasance action in which Mr. Arthur and other former directors   **B**
of the company were defendants; and the other action (viz., 1965 L. No. 2729)
was against A-Plan Protection, Ltd., and the receiver, and in this action the
claims included payment of the £7,837 13s. 1d. to the liquidator.

By the notice of motion in the present action (1963 A. 2748) the company
at the instance of the liquidator sought, among other relief, leave for the issue
of the writ in the action against A-Plan Protection, Ltd. (1965 L. 2729), and the   **C**
receiver.

P. J. Millett for the company.
T. L. G. Cullen for the respondent receiver.

UNGOED-THOMAS, J.: The question raised by this motion is whether
an action can be brought against a receiver by a party who was an applicant   **D**
to his appointment with the leave of the court, or whether the court invariably
takes the view that no action can be brought, even with leave.

In this case, the company, which is now in liquidation, L.P. Arthur (Insurance),
Ltd., ran an insurance brokers business and in 1963, when it was contemplating
insolvency, the directors passed a resolution to form a new company whose
shares were to be held by the directors and to transfer the whole business and   **E**
assets of the old company, L.P. Arthur (Insurance), Ltd., to the new company.
This was, in fact, done.   The action in which this motion is made is an action for a
declaration to establish who the directors were.

A receiver was appointed in October, 1963, by consent on the motion of the
plaintiffs, which included the old company.   In March, 1964, the company
went into creditor's voluntary liquidation, and between October, 1963, when   **F**
the receiver was appointed, and March, 1964, when the company went into
liquidation, the receiver received £7,800 premiums arising in the old company's
insurance brokers business and paid them into the new company, without the
order of the court, because, as the receiver claims, the new company claimed
that the premiums were part of the business transferred to it by the old company,
and the receiver obviously took the same view.   Thus, the receiver says he   **G**
received the premiums as agent for the new company and not as receiver at all.
He says, in fact, that in relation to these premiums he was not acting as receiver.

There is in existence another action (1) in which the company makes claims
against its directors, and I understand it not to be disputed that the convenient
course for trying this issue which I have indicated between the liquidator and
the receiver with regard to these premiums would be by joining the receiver   **H**
as a party to the action which the company has on foot against the directors.
It is common ground that the facts and the evidence in the company's claims
both against the receiver and against the directors would be largely identical,
although the legal results might not necessarily be the same.   That would be
the convenient course.

A difficulty, however, has arisen, by reason of a statement in KERR ON LAW   **I**
OF RECEIVERS (13th Edn.) p. 162 that an action cannot be brought against a
receiver by a person at whose instance he has been appointed.   The authority
quoted for that proposition is *Re Potter, Ex p. Day* (2).   In that case the action
had been brought by a party on whose application a receiver had been appointed
against that receiver without applying to the court at all.   So it is perfectly clear
that in accordance with well established principle to bring an action against a

_____

(1) 1965 L. No. 2730, the misfeasance action.
(2) (1883), 48 L.T. 912.

A receiver appointed by the court without the leave of the court is a course which is not countenanced by the court. The chief judge in delivering his judgment in *Re Potter, Ex p. Day* (3) said:

B
> " It cannot be endured that an action should be brought against a receiver by a person at whose instance he has been appointed. If the receiver has done anything wrong the party who has suffered the wrong has a right to complain to the court of bankruptcy, which appointed the receiver, and he will get full justice done to him in that court."

It is very understandable how the statement came to be made in Kerr on Law of Receivers, p. 162, in view of these opening remarks by the chief judge.

C Nevertheless, these remarks have got to be considered and construed in the light of the facts of that case, and the facts are as I have stated them, the crucial consideration being that in that case no application had been made to the court for any leave to bring the action at all.

It does not follow from the chief judge's observations that if an application had been made to the court of bankruptcy, or whatever other court appoints a receiver, that that court would be precluded from considering whether, provided

D that leave were asked for, the best course of disposing of an issue involving a receiver would be to have it tried by action. That clearly is the most convenient course here, and I see nothing in *Re Potter, Ex p. Day* (4) which precludes me from giving leave for such a course to be taken. *Re Potter, Ex p. Day* (4), in my view, is no authority for the proposition that an action cannot be brought against a receiver by a person at whose instance he has been appointed, provided,

E of course, that the leave of the court is obtained, and in my view such a proposition does not form part of the law.

I will give leave to the liquidator to join the receiver as a party to the action on foot by the company against the directors (5), on the liquidator's undertaking to use all dispatch in proceeding with that action and bringing it on.

F   *Order accordingly.*

Solicitors: *D. B. Levinson & Co.* (for the applicant); *Clifford-Turner & Co.* (for the first respondent).

[*Reported by* Jacqueline Metcalfe, *Barrister-at-Law.*]

G

H

I

---

(3) (1883), 48 L.T. at p. 912.   (4) (1883), 48 L.T. 912.
(5) 1965 L. No. 2730, the misfeasance action.

Reversed H.L. [1966] 3 All E.R. 177.

Re KWESI ARMAH.   A

[QUEEN'S BENCH DIVISION (Edmund Davies, Fenton Atkinson and Lyell, JJ.), June 7, 8, 10, 1966.]

Extradition—Habeas corpus—Fugitive—Ghana—Constitution of Republic of Ghana suspended—Ghana still recognised as member of Commonwealth— Whether Fugitive Offenders Act, 1881 (44 & 45 Vict. c. 69), applied to   B *government of Ghana in new form.*

Extradition—Habeas corpus—Fugitive—Evidence—" Strong or probable presumption "—Fugitive Offenders Act, 1881 (44 & 45 Vict. c. 69), s. 5.

Extradition—Discharge of fugitive—Discretion—Whether unconditional undertakings as to trial of fugitive should be accepted by English court—Fugitive Offenders Act, 1881 (44 & 45 Vict. c. 69), s. 10.   C

Extradition—Fugitive offender—Evidence—Depositions—Sufficiency—No provision made in Ghana for taking there of depositions by magistrate for purpose of Fugitive Offenders Act, 1881—Depositions authenticated as taken on oath— Admissibility—Fugitive Offenders Act, 1881 (44 & 45 Vict. c. 69), s. 29, s. 39.

On July 1, 1960, Ghana, while remaining by virtue of the Ghana (Conse-   D quential Provisions) Act, 1960, a member of the Commonwealth, became a republic. On Feb. 24, 1966, as a result of a coup d'état, its constitution was suspended. The applicant having been arrested under a provisional warrant under the Fugitive Offenders Act, 1881, a magistrate being satisfied that the Act of 1881 still applied to Ghana and that a prima facie case had been made out against the applicant in respect of two alleged   E contraventions of the Ghana Criminal Code, 1960, by corruption and extortion when he was a public officer, committed the applicant to prison pending his return to Ghana to undergo his trial on those charges. The committal order was made on depositions taken in Accra for the purpose of the Act of 1881, and on certain oral evidence. By the Ghana Corrupt Practices (Prevention) Act, 1964, the President of Ghana was empowered to appoint   F a commission to enquire into (inter alia) allegations of misconduct in the performance of his duties by any person paid out of public funds (which the applicant was). By s. 5 (2)* of that Act the findings of the commission were made prima facie evidence of the facts therein found, and it was for the accused to show cause why he should not be sentenced according to law; and by s. 6†, the accused was denied legal right to cross-examine any   G prosecution witness or even to call any witnesses on his own behalf. In March, 1966, the National Liberation Council of Ghana appointed a one-man commission under the Act of 1964, which proceeded to enquire into complaints (which were the same allegations as those on which the applicant was committed to prison pending his return to Ghana) against the applicant, but the commissioner had not yet rendered his report. By s. 5 of the Act   H of 1881, a magistrate was empowered to make a committal order only if such evidence was produced as according to the law ordinarily administered by him, raised a strong or probable presumption that the fugitive committed the offence mentioned in the warrant. On an application for a writ of habeas corpus or alternatively, for an order under s. 10‡ of the Act of 1881, whereby the applicant's release from detention might be obtained, the   I government of Ghana gave unconditional undertakings that the applicant would not be tried under the Act of 1964 but under the Ghana Criminal Procedure Act, 1960, and that, if acquitted, he would be free to leave Ghana.

Held: (i) habeas corpus must be refused, because, notwithstanding that the form of government had changed, the independent Republic of Ghana

---

* Section 5 is set out at p. 1009, letter G, post.
† Section 6 is set out at p. 1009, letters H and I, post.
‡ Section 10, so far as material, is set out at p. 1012, letter F, post.

A still existed, the Crown had recognised Ghana's continued membership of the Commonwealth and, accordingly, by virtue of the Ghana (Consequential Provision) Act, 1960, s. 1 (1), the Fugitive Offenders Act, 1881, applied to the Republic of Ghana in its new form (see p. 1011, letter B, p. 1013, letter I, and p. 1014, letter C, post);

(ii) relief under s. 10 of the Fugitive Offenders Act, 1881, must be refused,
B because—

(a) the court was bound by authority to treat the words " strong or probable presumption " in s. 5 of the Act of 1881 as requiring no more than that a prima facie case must be established, and it was not possible for the appellate court to interfere where (as here) there was evidence on which the magistrate could rule that a prima facie case had been made out on the
C evidence before him (see p. 1011, letter E, p. 1012, letter D, and p. 1014, letters A and C, post).

Dictum of FIELD, J., in *R.* v. *Maurer* ((1883), 10 Q.B.D. at p. 515) applied.
R. v. *Brixton Prison Governor, Ex p. Bidwell* ([1936] 3 All E.R. 1), dictum of LORD PARKER, C.J., in *Re Shalom Schtraks* ([1962] 3 All E.R. at pp. 185, 186) and *Zacharia* v. *Republic of Cyprus* ([1962] 2 All E.R. 438) followed.

D (b) although it would have been unjust and oppressive within the meaning of s. 10 of the Act of 1881 to return the applicant to Ghana, but for the unconditional undertakings given by the Government of Ghana, yet, accepting these as honourable undertakings, which would be fulfilled, they eliminated this consideration (see p. 1013, letter D, and p. 1014, letters B and I, post).

E (iii) the magistrate was obliged to take the sworn statements from Accra into account in coming to his decision, because, even if there were no provision in the law of Ghana for the taking there of depositions by a magistrate for the purposes of the Act of 1881, the sworn statements satisfied s. 29 and s. 39 of that Act (see p. 1013, letters G and I, and p. 1014, letter C, post).

R. v. *Secretary of State for India, Ex p. Ezekiel* ([1941] 2 All E.R. 546)
F and *R.* v. *Brixton Prison Governor, Ex p. Caldough* ([1961] 1 All E.R. 606) applied.

Application dismissed.

[As to sufficiency of evidence on application for habeas corpus, see 16 HALSBURY'S LAWS (3rd Edn.) 576, 577, para. 1193; and for cases on the subject, see 24 DIGEST (Repl.) 1006, 1007, *130-140.*
G As to evidence and committal in extradition proceedings, see 16 HALSBURY'S LAWS (3rd Edn.) 588, 589, para. 1222; and for cases on the subject, see 24 DIGEST (Repl.) 1012-1015, *162-177.*

As to discharge of fugitive by order of a superior court, see 16 HALSBURY'S LAWS (3rd Edn.) 589, 590, para. 1225; and for cases on the subject, see 24 DIGEST (Repl.) 1014, 1015, *174, 175.*
H For the Indictable Offences Act, 1848, s. 25, see 5 HALSBURY'S STATUTES (2nd Edn.) 681.

For the Fugitive Offenders Act, 1881, s. 2, s. 5, s. 10, s. 29, s. 39, see 9 HALSBURY'S STATUTES (2nd Edn.) 897, 898, 901, 907, 911.]

Cases referred to:
I *Gohoho* v. *Guinea Press, Ltd.,* [1962] 3 All E.R. 785; [1963] 1 Q.B. 948; [1963] 3 W.L.R. 1471; 3rd Digest Supp.

Huguet, Ex p., [1861-73] All E.R. Rep. 770; (1873), 29 L.T. 41; 12 Cox, C.C. 551; 24 Digest (Repl.) 1006, *130.*

Meunier, Re, [1894] 2 Q.B. 415; 63 L.J.M.C. 198; 71 L.T. 403; 18 Cox, C.C. 15; 24 Digest (Repl.) 994, *38.*

Naranjan Singh, Re, [1961] 2 All E.R. 565; sub nom. *R.* v. *Governor of Brixton Prison, Ex p. Naranjan Singh,* [1962] 1 Q.B. 211; [1961] 2 W.L.R. 980; Digest (Cont. Vol. A) 580, *175a.*

R. v. *Brixton Prison Governor, Ex p. Bidwell*, [1936] 3 All E.R. 1; [1937]   A
    1 K.B. 305; 106 L.J.K.B. 599; 155 L.T. 453; 100 J.P. 458; 30 Cox,
    C.C. 462; 24 Digest (Repl.) 1013, *171*.

R. v. *Brixton Prison Governor, Ex p. Caldough*, [1961] 1 All E.R. 606; [1961]
    1 W.L.R. 464; Digest (Cont. Vol. A) 577, *163a*.

R. v. *Holloway Prison Governor, Ex p. Siletti*, [1900-03] All E.R. Rep. 609;
    (1902), 71 L.J.K.B. 935; 87 L.T. 332; 20 Cox, C.C. 353; 67 J.P. 67;   B
    24 Digest (Repl.) 1007, *133*.

R. v. *Maurer*, (1883), 10 Q.B.D. 513; sub nom. *Re Maurer*, 52 L.J.M.C. 104;
    24 Digest (Repl.) 1007, *131*.

R. v. *Secretary of State for Indiz, Ex p. Ezekiel*, [1941] 2 All E.R. 546; [1941]
    2 K.B. 169; 111 L.J.K.B. 237; 24 Digest (Repl.) 1012, *163*.

Shalom Schtraks, Re, [1962] 2 All E.R. 176; 126 J.P. 277; sub nom. *R.* v.   C
    Brixton Prison Governor, Ex p. Schtraks, [1963] 1 Q.B. 55; [1962] 2
    W.L.R. 976; affd., H.L. sub nom. *Schtraks* v. *Government of Israel*,
    [1962] 3 All E.R. 529; [1964] A.C. 556; [1962] 3 W.L.R. 1013; Digest
    (Cont. Vol. A) 575, *4a*.

Zacharia v. *Republic of Cyprus, Arestidou* v. *Same*, [1962] 2 All E.R. 438;
    [1963] A.C. 634; [1962] 2 W.L.R. 1163; Digest (Cont. Vol. A) 579,   D
    174b.

Motion for writ of habeas corpus.

This was an application by way of motion by Kwesi Armah, now detained in
H.M. Prison Brixton, that a writ of habeas corpus be issued directed to the
Ghanian Government representative in London and to the Governor of Brixton   E
Prison to bring the applicant before the Divisional Court of the Queen's Bench
Division; alternatively, for an order under s. 10 of the Fugitive Offenders Act,
1881, whereby his release from detention might be obtained. The facts are set
out in the judgment of EDMUND DAVIES, J.

The authorities and the cases noted below* were cited during the argument in
addition to the cases referred to in the judgment of EDMUND DAVIES, J.   F

T. O. Kellock, Q.C., and *G. L. D. de Silva* for the applicant.
M. Finer, Q.C., and *J. M. Cope* for the Government of Ghana.
J. H. Buzzard for the Governor of Brixton Prison.

Cur. adv. vult.

May 10. **EDMUND DAVIES, J.**, read the following judgment. On July 1,   G
1960, Ghana, while remaining a member of the Commonwealth, became a
republic. On Feb. 24, 1966, as the result of a coup d'état, its constitution
was suspended. On Apr. 27, 1966, the applicant, Mr. Kwesi Armah, was arrested
on a provisional warrant issued by the chief magistrate at Bow Street under the
Fugitive Offenders Act, 1881, and he was then remanded in custody. On May 19,
1966, another magistrate expressed himself as satisfied (i) that the Act of 1881   H
still applied to Ghana, and (ii) that a prima facie case had been made out against
the applicant in respect of two alleged contraventions of s. 239 of the Ghana
Criminal Code, 1960, by corruption and extortion when he was a public officer.
The magistrate accordingly committed the applicant to Brixton prison, pending
his return to Ghana to undergo his trial on these charges. In essence, what is
alleged is that, as Minister of Trade, he attempted in January, 1966, to obtain   I
from a Mr. Fattal a bribe of £40,000, and actually obtained £20,000, for the

---

* 11 HALSBURY's LAWS (3rd Edn.) 33, para. 55; CLARKE ON EXTRADITION (1874
Edn.), pp. 155-156; PHIPSON ON EVIDENCE (10th Edn.) para. 101; *Re Henderson,
Henderson* v. *Secretary of State for Home Affairs*, [1950] 1 All E.R. 283; *Re Government
of India and Mubarak Ali Ahmed*, [1952] 1 All E.R. 1060; *R.* v. *Brixton Prison Governor,
Ex p. Frenette*, (1952), The Times, Mar. 19; *R.* v. *Brixton Prison Governor, Ex p. Penn*,
(1952), 96 Sol. Jo. 696; *R.* v. *Brixton Prison Governor, Ex p. Mourat Mehmet*, [1962]
1 All E.R. 463; [1962] 2 Q.B. 1; *R.* v. *Brixton Prison Governor, Ex p. Sadri*, [1962]
3 All E.R. 747.

A granting of an import licence or licences. After some four years in this country as its High Commissioner, the applicant became Minister of Trade in Ghana in June, 1965, and so remained until, in February, 1966, the Nkrumah Government was overthrown and replaced by the National Liberation Council. At that time the applicant was out of the country, and he made his way to the United Kingdom early in March, 1966. On Feb. 26, 1966, the National Liberation Council

B proclaimed the suspension of " the operation of the Constitution of the Republic of Ghana which came into force on July 1, 1960 ". The proclamation also declared that, by para. 3:

" (1) Until such time as a new constitution is promulgated by the people of Ghana, the National Liberation Council shall have power for such purposes as they may think fit and in the national interest to make and issue decrees

C which shall have the force of law in Ghana. (2) Subject to any decree made under the immediately preceding sub-paragraph, any enactment or rule of law in force in Ghana immediately before Feb. 24, 1966, shall continue in force and any such enactment or rule of law may by decree of the National Liberation Council be revoked, repealed, amended (whether by addition, omission, substitution or otherwise) or suspended. (3) Where any enactment

D or rule of law in force immediately before Feb. 24, 1966, is in conflict with any provision of a decree made by the National Liberation Council the said provision shall prevail over that enactment and to the extent to which the enactment conflicts with the provision of the decree, that enactment shall be deemed to be amended by the decree."

E On Mar. 2, 1966, the council decreed that

" all ministers in the government of Kwame Nkrumah [and] all other members of Parliament [be taken] and kept in protective custody for such period as the National Liberation Council may determine."

At this point, one must look back a few years to the Nkrumah régime. In 1964 the Corrupt Practices (Prevention) Act, 1964, was passed. This empowered

F the President to appoint a commission to enquire into (inter alia) allegations of misconduct in "the performance of his duties by any person paid out of public funds ". The commission was thereafter to prepare a report of its findings, and in appropriate cases the Attorney-General could then institute criminal proceedings against any person against whom adverse findings had been made. As certain sections of the Act of 1964 are important, they must be quoted verbatim:

G " 5 (1) In proceedings under this Act, the accused shall not be asked to plead, and subject to s. 6 of this Act the prosecution shall not be called upon to lead evidence. (2) Notwithstanding the provisions of s. 1 of the Criminal Procedure Code, 1960 (Act 30), the findings of the commission shall be prima facie evidence of the facts found, and the accused shall be called on

H to show cause why he should not be sentenced according to law for the commission of the offence charged.

" 6 (1) Where the accused, in showing cause under s. 5 of this Act, states— (a) that he had no opportunity of cross-examining any of the witnesses referred to in para. (b) of sub-s. (2) of s. 3 of this Act, the court may call such witnesses to be cross-examined by the accused, in which case both the court and the Attorney-General can put further questions to the witness;

I or (b) that the findings of the commission are not supported by the evidence before it, the court or the Attorney-General may in such case call additional witnesses. (2) In addition to any witness or witnesses which the court may call under sub-s. (1) of this section for cross-examination by the accused the court may allow the accused to call any other witness to give evidence on his behalf and the court and the Attorney-General may put questions to the additional witness called for the accused.

" 8. (1) The accused in any proceedings instituted under s. 4 of this Act shall be convicted of the offence charged against him on the basis of the findings of the commission unless he establishes to the satisfaction of the court that the findings of the commission cannot be sustained. (2) Any person convicted under sub-s. (1) of this section shall be liable to a term of imprisonment of not less than three years."

In exercise of the powers conferred on it by this Act, the National Liberation Council by an executive instrument of Mar. 5, 1966, appointed a one-man commission, consisting of Mr. Ollenu, a judge of the Supreme Court, specifically to enquire into

"alleged irregularities and malpractices in connexion with the grant of import licences . . . perpetrated by persons paid out of public funds in the performance of their public duties."

On Mar. 17, 1966, the commissioner proceeded to enquire (inter alia) into the complaint of Mr. Fattal that he had been induced to pay a bribe of £20,000 to the applicant and had agreed to pay a further like sum in return for the applicant, as Minister of Trade, ensuring that he be issued with certain import licences. Mr. Fattal gave evidence before the commissioner, and the applicant (being then out of Ghana) submitted a memorandum giving his version of the matters enquired into and emphatically asserting his innocence of any malpractices. This court has been informed that the commissioner has not yet rendered his report on any of the cases being considered by him. On Mar. 26, 1966, at the district court of Accra, depositions were taken for the purpose of the Fugitive Offenders Act, 1881, in relation to the two charges preferred against the applicant. It was on these depositions and certain oral evidence that the committal order was made by the Bow Street magistrate. His competence to do so is the subject-matter of the present application.

Release from detention is first sought by way of habeas corpus. The submissions on behalf of the applicant may be summarised in this way. His committal to Brixton prison was initiated by a provisional warrant issued under the Act of 1881, and his continued detention was thereafter ordered by the magistrate in purported exercise of his powers under s. 5 thereof. But the Act of 1881 has no application to the present case, for s. 2 limits its operation to circumstances where "a person accused of having committed an offence . . . in one part of her Majesty's dominions has left that part" and is thereafter "found in another part of her Majesty's dominions". When, on July 1, 1960, Ghana became a republic, it ceased to be a part of her Majesty's dominions, notwithstanding that it remained within the Commonwealth. Without more, the present committal into custody would, therefore, have been unlawful. The Ghana (Consequential Provision) Act, 1960, which was enacted on June 2, 1960, in contemplation of Ghana becoming a republic, admittedly perpetuated the application of the Act of 1881 to the republic established in the following month (see *Gohoho* v. *Guinea Press, Ltd.* (1)), but it did nothing of the sort in relation to the new Ghanaian Constitution which came into being in February, 1966, notwithstanding that s. 1 (1) thereof provided that:

"On and after the date on which Ghana becomes a Republic, all existing law, that is to say, all law which, whether being a rule of law or a provision of an Act of Parliament or of any other enactment or instrument whatsoever, is in force on that date or has been passed or made before that date and comes into force thereafter, shall, until provision to the contrary is made by an authority having power to alter that law and subject to the provisions of this Act, have the same operation in relation to Ghana, and to persons and things in any way belonging to or connected with Ghana, as it would have had if Ghana had not become a republic."

For the applicant, it is submitted that this provision contemplated, and had reference to, the 1960 Republic alone and that, when the constitution was

(1) [1962] 3 All E.R. 785; [1963] 1 Q.B. 948.

A suspended earlier this year, the Ghana (Consequential Provision) Act, 1960, became a dead letter. In the result, there has occurred what counsel for the applicant described as " a legal accident arising out of a revolutionary situation ", the effect of which has been to render the Fugitive Offenders Act, 1881, no longer applicable to Ghana. In my judgment, this submission is unsound. Notwithstanding that the form of government has changed, the independent republic

B of Ghana still exists. The court was informed (and it was not challenged) that the Crown has appointed a High Commissioner to the new government and has recognised Ghana's continued membership of the Commonwealth. We are, therefore, not called on to consider what the legal position might be in various hypothetical circumstances which were suggested—as, for example, if Ghana withdrew from the Commonwealth, or established a monarchy, or united with

C another country, as Tanganyika and Zanzibar have done. In my judgment, the Act of 1881 applies to the Republic of Ghana, in its new form, just as it did before the coup d'état of last February took place.

I now turn to consider the relief sought under the Fugitive Offenders Act, 1881. The first point taken in this connexion necessitates consideration of s. 5 thereof, which empowers a magistrate to make a committal order only if

D " . . . such evidence is produced as . . . according to the law ordinarily administered by the magistrate, raises a strong or probable presumption that the fugitive committed the offence mentioned in the warrant . . .''

Were I free to consider the words " a strong or probable presumption " without reference to long-standing decisions, I should have interpreted them as requiring that the evidence must be such as to create a high probability that, were it

E uncontradicted, a conviction would result. But it is settled law that these words require no more than that a prima facie case must be established, and by that is meant only that there must be such evidence that, if it be uncontradicted at the trial, a reasonably minded jury may (not probably will) convict on it; see *R.* v. *Brixton Prison Governor, Ex p. Bidwell* (2), *Re Shalom Schtraks* (3), and *Zacharia* v. *Republic of Cyprus, Arestidou* v. *Same* (4). It is in the light of these

F decisions that I am obliged to approach the question whether the magistrate was entitled to make a committal order in the present case.

It is submitted for the applicant that the case for the prosecution rests solely on the uncorroborated evidence of Mr. Fattal, who on his own showing was an accomplice to the alleged corruption and extortion with which the applicant is charged. It being conceded, however, that this would not of itself be sufficient

G to prevent his evidence from raising a strong or probable presumption of guilt (see *Re Meunier* (5)), counsel for the applicant has analysed that evidence in detail and has thereby sought to show that it is inherently improbable and, therefore, unlikely to be accepted by any resonably minded jury. He makes the strong point that certain answers given on oath by Mr. Fattal in Ghana indicate that he was then alleging that the £20,000 bribe to obtain the licences was paid

H by him at a time when the available documents establish that the licences had in fact already been approved of by the applicant and issued in Mr. Fattal's favour. He has made critical comparisons between the deposition of Mr. Fattal and a statement which he gave to the police. He has submitted other points of a trenchant character and contends that, in the result, so far from this being a " strong or probable " case for the prosecution, it is weak and improbable in the extreme.

I On the other hand, counsel for the Republic of Ghana, while conceding that this is not what he called " an open-and-shut case ", has repudiated these criticisms and has further submitted that there is independent evidence which in some degree supports Mr. Fattal's testimony. I do not deem it necessary to consider further the details of the attack made and the defence advanced in this connexion. It must suffice for me to say that, had the magistrate come to the conclusion that the evidence presented before him did not raise "a strong or probable

(2) [1936] 3 All E.R. 1; [1937] 1 K.B. 305.
(3) [1962] 2 All E.R. 176 at pp. 185, 186; [1963] 1 Q.B. 55 at p. 78.
(4) [1962] 2 All E.R. 438; [1963] A.C. 634.   (5) [1894] 2 Q.B. 415 at p. 418.

presumption " of guilt against the applicant, I, for my part, would certainly A
have been far from surprised; but that is not the test. Nor, as I see it, is it relevant
to consider what course I personally would take at the end of the prosecution
were I sitting with a jury and the evidence for the Crown consisted solely of that
which was here presented to the magistrate, although I feel that I should make
clear that, while leaving the case to the jury, I should have summed-up strongly
in favour of an acquittal. Regard must be had, however, to several decisions B
under the Extradition Act, 1870, which are here apposite. In *R.* v. *Maurer* (6),
FIELD, J., said:

" So long as the magistrate keeps within his jurisdiction, we have no power
to interfere with his decision. It is only when there is no jurisdiction, as
when there is no evidence before the magistrate, that we can interfere. It
seems to me that in *Ex p. Huguet* (7) all the judges intended to decide that   C
it is not for this court to weigh the evidence, if there is any reasonable
evidence for an extradition crime for the magistrate to act upon. If there is
such evidence the magistrate is not going beyond his jurisdiction in committing
the prisoner upon such evidence."

Expressions of a like kind are to be found in *R.* v. *Holloway Prison Governor,
Ex p. Siletti* (8) and *Schtraks* v. *Government of Israel* (9). Applying the test D
thereby laid down, with hesitation I have come to the conclusion that it is
not possible to hold that the magistrate was not entitled to rule that a prima
facie case had been made out on the evidence before him.

I finally turn to consider the points addressed on the applicant's behalf under
s. 10 of the Act of 1881. That section confers on this court wide powers, in
appropriate circumstances, to discharge a fugitive offender; see *Re Naranjan* E
Singh (10). The present case is obviously not of a " trivial nature ", and counsel
for the applicant has not sought to argue that the application for the return of
the applicant is not " made in good faith ". Section 10 goes on, however, to
provide that if, " having regard . . . to all the circumstances of the case ", this
court comes to the conclusion that it would be " unjust or oppressive . . . to
return the fugitive ", we may order his release, and it is in reliance on these F
words that we have been invited to adopt that course in the present case. Such
invitation is based on two grounds: (i) It is said that the Corrupt Practices
(Prevention) Act, 1964, which (although enacted by the Nkrumah Government)
is still the law of Ghana, provides a form of trial which is, or at least may be,
contrary to natural justice. By s. 5 thereof, which has already been quoted
verbatim, the findings of the Ollenu Commission are made prima facie evidence G
of the facts therein found, and it is for the accused to show cause why he should
not be sentenced according to law. But—and this is far more important—under
s. 6 the accused has no legal right to cross-examine any prosecution witness or
even to call any witnesses on his own behalf, for each of these courses depends on
whether or not the court permits him so to do. This is in marked contrast to
the provisions as to trials on indictment contained in s. 265 to s. 276 of the H
Criminal Procedure Act, 1960, which enable an accused person as of right to
cross-examine prosecution witnesses (s. 267) and to call witnesses in his defence
(s. 272). It is submitted that it would, therefore, be both " unjust " and " oppressive " to allow the applicant to be returned to Ghana to face a trial which may be
conducted in the manner provided for by the Act of 1964. (ii) It is said that, even
if the applicant succeeded in showing cause why he should not be sentenced I
according to law—and be it noted that s. 239 of the Criminal Code of 1960
enables sentences of up to twenty-five years to be imposed for the offences here
charged—the decree of Mar. 2, 1966, involves that he nevertheless must be
" kept in protective custody for such period as the National Liberation Council
may determine ". Counsel for the applicant concedes that, at times of consti-

(6) (1883), 10 Q.B.D. 513 at p. 515.   (7) [1861-73] All E.R. Rep. 770.
(8) [1900-03] All E.R. Rep. 609.   (9) [1962] 3 All E.R. 529; [1964] A.C. 556.
(10) [1961] 2 All E.R. 565; [1962] 1 Q.B. 211.

A tutional upheaval, a measure of this kind may be necessary for the public weal, but he nevertheless submits that to return the applicant to Ghana when such a fate awaits him, even were he acquitted on the present charges, would be unjust and oppressive.

For my part, I regard these as most telling points and (but for certain undertakings about to be referred to) I should have held that their combined effect

B (and particularly when considered in conjunction with the thinness of the prosecution case) was such as to render it clearly unjust and oppressive to permit the applicant to be returned to Ghana. On the second day of the hearing, however, the Government of Ghana gave to the court and to the applicant through its learned counsel two unconditional undertakings: (i) that if the applicant be returned to Ghana, he will be tried in accordance with the Criminal Procedure

C Act, 1960, and not under the provisions of the Corrupt Practices (Prevention) Act, 1964, and (ii) that if, on his trial so conducted, the applicant is acquitted of the charges, he will not be taken into protective custody, but will then be entirely free to leave Ghana. I desire to make it clear that these undertakings have operated powerfully and decisively on my mind. Counsel for the applicant, however, whilst in no way impugning the good faith of those giving the under-

D takings, has urged that, being in their nature unenforceable and capable of being frustrated, for example, by further constitutional changes in Ghana, they ought not to influence the decision of this court on the present application. I do not think that that is right. I naturally accept them as honourable undertakings which the Government of Ghana intend to implement fully. That being so, the injustice and oppression which I would otherwise have held to

E exist have, to my way of thinking, been eliminated, as far as this court can foresee.

It remains for me to deal with one last matter. Althouth he candidly indicated that he did not regard it as his strongest point, counsel for the applicant made a further submission that there is a lacuna in the law of Ghana in that no provision is made thereby for the taking there of depositions by a magistrate for the

F purposes of the Fugitive Offenders Act, 1881, and that, accordingly, the Bow Street magistrate was not entitled to have regard to the so-called depositions taken in Ghana in deciding to commit the applicant under s. 5 of the Fugitive Offenders Act, 1881. In my judgment, this point is unsound. By s. 29, "Depositions... may, if duly authenticated, be received in evidence in proceedings under this Act ", and by s. 39 the expression " deposition " is defined as including

G " any affidavit, affirmation or statement made upon oath . . ." The duly authenticated documents emanating from Ghana do record and consist of statements made on oath. Accordingly, and in the light of the decisions in *R.* v. *Secretary of State for India, Ex p. Ezekiel* (11) and *R.* v. *Brixton Prison Governor, Ex p. Caldough* (12), in my judgment, even if the alleged lacuna in Ghanaian law exists, the Bow Street magistrate was entitled (and, indeed, obliged) to take

H these sworn statements into account in coming to his decision.

It follows from what I have already said that, in my judgment, relief by way of habeas corpus must be refused, for the applicant is now in custody under an order for committal which the magistrate, in the exercise of his discretion as he saw fit to exercise it, was entitled to make. Relief under s. 10 of the Fugitive Offenders Act, 1881, must also be refused. I should, accordingly, dismiss this

I application.

FENTON ATKINSON, J.: I agree and wish only to add a few words on two points. If free to interpret the words " a strong or probable presumption that the fugitive committed the offence ", in s. 5 of the Fugitive Offenders Act, 1881, according to the ordinary, natural meaning of those words, I would have said that no reasonable magistrate applying his mind to the question could conceivably have made this committal order. The evidence is far from strong; and, in my view, the case is in fact so weak that the probable result, assuming

(11) [1941] 2 All E.R. 546; [1941] 2 K.B. 169.   (12) [1961] 1 All E.R. 606.

(as I do) a fair and proper trial, is acquittal. But this court is bound by authority **A**
to treat those words " strong or probable presumption " as meaning no more than
a prima facie case; and on that basis, with regret, I feel unable to say that the
magistrate in his discretion could not decide as he did. I say " with regret "
because if I were free, which I am not, to substitute my own discretion for his,
I would have reached the opposite conclusion. I would only add that, like
EDMUND DAVIES, J., and for the reasons which he has given, but for the combined **B**
effect of the two undertakings which were given to the court on the second day
of the hearing I would have considered it both unjust and oppressive to return
the applicant to Ghana.

LYELL, J.: I agree with both the judgments which have been delivered
and wish to add only a few words of my own. I share to the full the regret and
hesitation which have been expressed as to the necessity for finding that the **C**
evidence before the magistrate was sufficient to justify his order. I would also
add that I am in full agreement with the meaning which EDMUND DAVIES, J.,
would, in the absence of authority, put on the phrase " strong or probable
presumption " of guilt in s. 5 of the Fugitive Offenders Act, 1881. That phrase,
as is noted in several of the authorities, goes back at least to s. 25 of the Indictable
Offences Act, 1848. It is perhaps, however, not without interest to note the **D**
context in which it appears. The relevant parts of that section read as follows:

" When all the evidence offered upon the part of the prosecution against
the accused party shall have been heard, if the justice or justices of the
peace then present shall be of opinion that it is not sufficient to put such
accused party upon his trial for any indictable offence, such justice or justices
shall forthwith order such accused party, if in custody, to be discharged as **E**
to the information then under inquiry; but if in the opinion of such justice
or justices such evidence is sufficient to put the accused party upon his trial
for an indictable offence, or if the evidence given raise a strong or probable
presumption of the guilt of such accused party; then such justice or justices
shall, by his or their warrant, commit him to the common gaol . . . or place,
to which by law he may now be committed . . ." **F**

It seems to me strange that Parliament should, by the use of two alternative
expressions, have intended to set up alternative standards for committal for
trial. The word " sufficient " is a more indefinite concept than that, in my
view, expressed by the phrase " strong or probable presumption of guilt ", and
it appears to me that the addition of the second alternative was intended as an
exposition of the first, rather than an alternative standard. However that may be, **G**
I am unable to find—and I say this humbly and only after careful thought, in
view of the long series of authorities that point to the contrary—either in the
Indictable Offences Act, 1848, or in the Fugitive Offenders Act, 1881, any words
which would justify giving to the word " probable " anything less than its natural
and ordinary meaning of " more likely than not ". I feel this especially in view
of the fact that the application of those words must in the context bear strongly **H**
on questions of liberty of the subject. Had I been untrammelled by authority,
I should have held that the evidence presented by the Government of Ghana
failed to satisfy that test. Finally, I wish to say that, had the Government of
Ghana not given, through counsel, the unconditional undertakings which EDMUND
DAVIES, J., has stated fully, I should unhesitatingly have held that it would have
been both unjust and oppressive to have allowed the order of the learned **I**
magistrate to stand.

Application refused. Leave to appeal to the House of Lords granted.

Solicitors: *Hatchett, Jones & Co.* (for the applicant); *Alan, George & Sacker*
(for the Government of Ghana); *Director of Public Prosecutions* (for the Governor
of Brixton Prison).

[*Reported by* N. P. METCALFE, ESQ., *Barrister-at-Law.*]

A   GRIFFITHS v. LIVERPOOL CORPORATION.

[COURT OF APPEAL (Sellers, Diplock and Salmon, L.JJ.), March 23, 24, May 26, 1966.]

Highway—Non-repair—Breach of statutory duty—Defence—Such care as in all the circumstances was reasonably required—Projecting flagstone in pavement—
B   *Pedestrian injured by tripping and falling—No regular inspections of highway—Absolute statutory duty subject to statutory defence—Statutory defence not proved—Liability of highway authority to injured pedestrian—Highways (Miscellaneous Provisions) Act, 1961 (9 & 10 Eliz. 2 c. 63), s. 1.*

Liability for breach of statutory duty by non-repair of a highway, arising in consequence of s. 1 (1)* of the Highways (Miscellaneous Provisions) Act,
C   1961, is absolute, subject to the statutory defence made available by sub-s. (2); the care that a highway authority have to prove that they took in order to make out a defence under sub-s. (2) is such care as in all the circumstances can reasonably be required of them, and accordingly, if they show that through no fault of their own they have been unable to take steps to make the highway safe, they will still succeed in their defence (see p. 1021,
D   letter G, p. 1022, letters C and F, p. 1023, letter B, and p. 1024, letters F and H, post).

A pedestrian slipped and fell and suffered injury when walking on a flagstone in a pavement which was part of the highway. The flagstone rocked on its centre, and it protruded one half inch above the adjacent flagstones. It was found as a fact that the flagstone was dangerous, and there was no
E   appeal against this finding. On the evidence a regular system of inspection of highways was desirable, and labourers could have been obtained to make such inspections, but, if dangers had been discovered, there were not sufficient tradesmen to make them safe; this particular flagstone, however, could have been made safe by a labourer. Further, it was not proved that, if regular inspections had been made, danger from the flagstone would not have been discovered and averted. On appeal in an action by the pedestrian for breach
F   of duty† to maintain the highway causing personal injuries to her,

Held (SELLERS, L.J., dissenting): on the evidence the highway authority had not proved that they had taken such care as in all the circumstances was reasonably required of them to secure that the relevant part of the highway was safe, and thus they had not made out a defence under sub-s. (2)
G   of s. 1 of the Highways (Miscellaneous Provisions) Act, 1961; accordingly they were liable in damages for breach of statutory duty to the plaintiff (see p. 1023, letter C, p. 1025, letters E, G and H, and p. 1021, letter G, post).

Quaere whether, if a highway authority could show that no amount of reasonable care on their part could have prevented the danger, the common law defence of inevitable accident would be available for them (see p. 1024,
H   letter C, post).

Appeal dismissed.

[As to the principle that highway authorities were not liable to individuals for non-repair, see 19 HALSBURY'S LAWS (3rd Edn.) 149, 150, para. 228; and for cases on the subject, see 26 DIGEST (Repl.) 418-422, *1278-1309.*

As to liability at common law for failure to repair a highway lying in nuisance,
I   see 19 HALSBURY'S LAWS (3rd Edn.) 271, 272, para. 435.

For the Highways Act, 1959, s. 44 (1), see 39 HALSBURY'S STATUTES (2nd Edn.) 461.

For the Highways (Miscellaneous Provisions) Act, 1961, s. 1, see 41 HALSBURY'S STATUTES (2nd Edn.) 453.]

---

* Section 1 (1) is printed in footnote (1), p. 1016, post; s. 1 (2) and the relevant part s. 1 (3) are printed at p. 1019, letters E to H, post. There are exceptions from the scope of s. 1, which are in sub-s. (7) and are irrelevant to the present case.

† The action was based, or treated as based, on breach of statutory duty (under s. 44 (1)) of the Highways Act, 1959 (see p. 1024, letter C, post).

Cases referred to: A

Lochgelly Iron and Coal Co., Ltd. v. *M'Mullan*, [1934] A.C. 1; 102 L.J.P.C. 123; 149 L.T. 526; 34 Digest (Repl.) 709, *4852*.

Rudd v. *Elder, Dempster & Co., Ltd.*, [1933] 1 K.B. 566; 102 L.J.K.B. 275; 148 L.T. 337; *on appeal*, H.L., [1934] A.C. 244; 34 Digest (Repl.) 709, *4851*.

Appeal.   B

This was an appeal by the defendant highway authority, the Liverpool Corporation, from the judgment of His Honour JUDGE CUNLIFFE, at Liverpool County Court on Dec. 17, 1965, awarding the plaintiff, Mrs. Edith May Griffiths, £75 damages for injuries that she suffered when she fell on a pavement in Liverpool. The facts are set out in the judgment of SELLERS, L.J.

I. H. M. Jones for the defendant highway authority.   C
H. L. Lachs for the plaintiff.

Cur. adv. vult.

May 26. The following judgments were read.

SELLERS, L.J.: The Highways (Miscellaneous Provisions) Act, 1961, by s. 1 (1) abrogated (1) the rule of law exempting the inhabitants at large and any D other persons as their successors from liability for non-repair of highways. This section became operative in August, 1964, (2). On June 9, 1965, the plaintiff fell on a footpath in Smithdown Road, Liverpool, a busy main thoroughfare, and subsequently she claimed damages against the Liverpool Corporation as the highway authority alleging that owing to their negligence and/or non-feasance and/or misfeasance she had tripped or fallen on a flagstone and suffered personal E injuries. The action was heard before His Honour JUDGE CUNLIFFE in the Liverpool County Court and judgment was given in favour of the plaintiff on Dec. 17, 1965. From that judgment the highway authority appeal. It has been said that the case was possibly the first to be decided since the new law became effective and it seems to be the first time that the Court of Appeal has been called on to consider the Act of 1961.   F

This court is confronted with a judgment which holds the highway authority liable and awards £75 damages to the plaintiff and then concludes with these words of the judge:

"I am conscious of the fact that I am holding the defendants liable in law for something which I have held that it was impossible for them to prevent. Such a result may seem worthy of the late W. S. Gilbert or may G even justify the famous remark of Mr. Bumble, but such thoughts must not divert me from a decision which I find myself unable to avoid on any other ground."

Is this what the common law of England has come to in its most modern presentation? It has long been thought that a highway authority's immunity from liability for non-feasance should be abolished, but if the new legislation requires H a decision which provokes such comment from the judge who pronounced it the pendulum would seem to have swung so far over the other way as to substitute one unfair law for another.

In my judgment it has not done so. At the outset I would, if free and unfettered, take exception to the finding which is the very basis of the claim. As the claim in the action was for damages not exceeding £300 an appeal on fact lies I to this court, and further the judge does not seem to have directed himself correctly or at all on an important requirement of the statute. A witness for the defendant highway authority did say that the unevenness of the flagstone

(1) Section 1 (1) provides: "The rule of law exempting the inhabitants at large and any other persons as their successors from liability for non-repair of highways is hereby abrogated."

(2) By virtue of s. 1 (8), s. 1 came into force on the expiration of three years beginning with the passing of the Act; it, therefore, came into force on Aug. 3, 1964.

A   was dangerous and the judge held it to be a potential danger and held that the plaintiff fell by reason of it.   The fetter on this court is that the defendant highway authority did not challenge the finding of danger on the appeal.

This is an action only between two parties but the standard of construction, maintenance and repair which is to be established is of the utmost importance generally.   The Act of 1961 applies to every area in the country, city, town and

B   village, and in my judgment the finding of fact that such defect as there was in the pavement here was a danger in the sense that it could give rise to liability of a highway authority under the Highways Act, 1959, and the Act of 1961 read together would, if it were accepted and established, create a standard of construction, maintenance and repair which is well-nigh unattainable.   The liability for damages might well become an intolerable burden.   The red carpet will

C   cease to have significance if all within our island are to require and receive the same treatment wherever they may go on a public highway.   If what is required is a highway safe and fit for ordinary traffic or reasonably passable or usable the evidence in this case shows that the pavement in question fulfilled that requirement, for it was in daily use up to the plaintiff's accident and, what is more important, for about a month after her accident, in the same or possibly

D   aggravated condition without any untoward event in a place where " people walk up and down the pavement more or less all day ".   In the course of this appeal, in the mid-day adjournment, on a route which I ought not perhaps to specify, I came across projections and depressions, cracks and chips in paving stones in many places which could all be described as defects and which could have caused a fall such as occurred to the plaintiff.   Since then in wider areas

E   of footpaths and roadways similar conditions have become increasingly apparent. All these areas are walked over by the multitude, who traverse them with safety and without complaint day by day and night by night.   We are all of us accustomed to walk on uneven and irregular surfaces and we can all of us trip on cobblestones, cat's-eyes, studs marking pedestrian crossings, as well as other projections.   If the finding that the half-inch projection of a solitary flagstone

F   in a wide pavement has to be accepted because of the technicalities of this case, as my brethren think, I have perhaps said enough to indicate that it is a standard which in my view should not become a precedent or guide in ordinary circumstances.

On the morning of June 9, 1965, the plaintiff walked along Magdala Street and turned right into Smithdown Road and was walking along the footpath

G   towards a bus stop in order to board a bus to take her to work when she slipped on a paving stone which was raised above the other flags.   She was sixty years of age and was badly shaken by the fall; one knee was scraped and her right thigh muscle was hurt.   She was off work four weeks and it has not been suggested that the damages that the judge awarded were not adequate.   On or about June 22, that is about thirteen days after the accident, a surveyor went with

H   the plaintiff to the site and it was found then that one flagstone in the second row from the kerbstone protruded half-inch above the adjacent flagstone and when trodden on that particular flag rocked on its centre.

On July 7, immediately after a claim had been made against the highway authority on behalf of the plaintiff, about a month that is after her accident and a fortnight after the surveyor's inspection, the highway authority's district

I   highway superintendent went to the site and saw what the plaintiff's surveyor had seen earlier, but had not thought necessary to report at once as a danger which required immediate attention.   The superintendent thought the flagstone unsafe, and he was the highway authority's witness who said so at the trial, and he had it repaired the next day.   For a month at least this " danger " had been walked over by those who used this busy thoroughfare.   The highly qualified surveyor who saw it on June 22 was content to leave it unreported, unguarded and unrepaired, and it was similarly left unguarded and unrepaired from one day until the next by the superintendent and no other accident occurred.

No one could explain what had caused that particular flagstone to project A
and on the probabilities it had not been in that condition long prior to the plaintiff's fall. The plaintiff herself and her friend Mrs. Tootill used to go the same
way to work each day and neither of them had seen anything wrong until after
the plaintiff had fallen. It seems that the flagstone was loose but it does not
appear that any movement of the flag caused the fall. It was the slight projection only, according to the evidence. For some six months prior to June, 1965, B
the demolition and reconstruction of the buildings on the corner site of Smithdown Road and Magdala Street had been taking place. Vehicles had damaged
the footpath in Magdala Street by passing over it in the course of work but
this had not affected the footpath in front of the site in Smithdown Road where
the plaintiff fell. There had been a complete reconstruction of the road in
1954, when the tram tracks were taken up. The footpath was then remade and C
efficiently remade with concrete flags. Their durable life was stated to be thirty
years and they had been down only eleven years. The superintendent said that
he would not expect trouble in this time. There had been no complaint from
the police (a normal and expected source of information of dangers in the highway) or from the public or from any employees of the highway department who
were instructed to keep their eyes open as they moved about and to report D
defects. The superintendent passed regularly down Smithdown Road (it would
seem in a car) but had not noticed anything wrong and could not be expected
to have seen a minor unevenness of this character. As demolition had been
taking place on the adjoining corner, the pavement had been inspected in January
or February, 1965, and no defect was apparently found then. These factors
indicate that reasonable care had been taken of this part of the highway. It E
had not been neglected or ignored and allowed to deteriorate. We know that
the pavement was used normally for a month after the accident and the longer
the damaged condition existed before that the more does it show that the unevenness was a blemish but not a danger in normal ordinary use. The defect may
have developed overnight before the accident.

The case has been built up against the highway authority, as I see it, on a F
remark by the superintendent recorded in the judge's notes: " I would say that
if the staff were available inspection once every three months of classified roads
would be desirable." There are many things in life which might be said to be
desirable if they were attainable, but I do not understand desirability to be a
principle underlying our common law. Such evidence does not establish a
reasonable standard of routine inspection. Reasonableness must have some G
regard to cost and capacity.

Is there, then, such a standard imposed by statute? If it is, then it must be
enforced, but a highway authority's defence is put in general terms (3): " that
the authority had taken such care as in all the circumstances was reasonably
required to secure that the part of the highway to which the action relates
was not dangerous for traffic." It would be surprising if, after abrogating H
the age-long immunity given to highway authorities for non-feasance, it had
been enacted that unless an inspection of each part of a highway in a city were
made every three months the highway authority would automatically be liable
in damages to any user of the highway who fell and was injured; and would
be so liable no matter how trivial might be the defect in the highway—disregarding the relative newness of the offending part of the highway and any I
inspection, say, within the previous six months, disregarding the impracticability
of maintaining such a standard and notwithstanding that a judge could say,
as the judge does here, " I am quite unconvinced that it [that is, a routine
inspection] would have resulted in the repair of the particular defect in question
in this case " [because it would not have been discovered]. There was no
evidence that a routine three-monthly inspection was normal in cities, and in

(3) See s. 1 (2) of the Act of 1961, which is printed at p. 1019, letters E to H, post.

A fact it would appear not to be so and to be wholly impracticable, at least under present labour conditions.

The defendant highway authority, as one would expect, maintain a substantial highways department and its establishment was given in detail. The superintendent of South 1 Area of Liverpool, covering about two hundred miles of roadway, said that he could not get sufficient tradesmen and that if there was

B a regular inspection he would not have enough men to follow up all the faults. The judge has accepted that and held that " tradesmen just could not be found in the vicinity of Liverpool ".

Has, then, the Act of 1961 imposed on highway authorities liability in a case such as the present?

The Highways Act, 1959, s. 44 (1) provides that the highway authority for a

C highway maintainable at the public expense shall be under a duty to maintain the highway. In 1959 a highway authority was not liable for non-feasance in an action for damages at the suit of a person who had suffered injury from a failure to repair a highway, and this exemption was expressly preserved by s. 298 of the Act of 1959. The Act of 1959 was dealing with administration and not with the standard of maintenance. Flagstones are a proper and recognised

D form of footpath and those in Smithdown Road were no doubt brought on to the highway as part of its construction and in performance of the authority's duty and obligation. It is unthinkable that any indictment could have lain against the inhabitants at large or any authority responsible for the maintenance of the highway at any time in this highway's history for such defect as existed at the time of the plaintiff's accident.

E I now turn to the Highways (Miscellaneous Provisions) Act, 1961, s. 1 (2) and (3) which are as follows:

" (2) In an action against a highway authority in respect of damage resulting from their failure to maintain a highway maintainable at the public expense, it shall be a defence (without prejudice to any other defence or the application of the law relating to contributory negligence) to prove

F that the authority had taken such care as in all the circumstances was reasonably required to secure that the part of the highway to which the action relates was not dangerous for traffic.

" (3) For the purposes of a defence under the last foregoing subsection, the court shall in particular have regard to the following matters, that is to say—(*a*) the character of the highway, and the traffic which was reasonably

G to be expected to use it; (*b*) the standard of maintenance appropriate for a highway of that character and used by such traffic; (*c*) the state of repair in which a reasonable person would have expected to find the highway; (*d*) whether the highway authority knew, or could reasonably have been expected to know, that the condition of the part of the highway to which the action relates was likely to cause danger to users of the highway; (*e*)

H where the highway authority could not reasonably have been expected to repair that part of the highway before the cause of action arose, what warning notices of its condition had been displayed . . ."

I need not read the further part of that subsection.

These provisions in my view make negligence the essential and ultimate basis

I of a claim against a highway authority, as it had always been and still is in respect of misfeasance. The facts as to maintenance and repair lie for the most part with the relevant highway authority and not with a party who may sustain damage from a failure to maintain part of a highway, and the proof of reasonable care is placed on the highway authority concerned. If a highway authority when sued does not show that reasonable care had been taken to maintain the part of the highway which caused the damage the plea of contributory negligence is available in defence of the claim.

The construction of sub-s. (2) must, I think, be made with the guidance of

sub-s. (3) and particularly sub-s. (3) (*d*). It is unlikely that the statute would   A
set up an artificial standard which could not be complied with and say that,
unless that unattainable standard had been complied with, the highway authority
had failed in its duty (as I understand the judgment below to hold). It is more
likely that the statute would recognise the different circumstances of highway
authorities throughout the country. I think that it does. Under sub-s. (3)
the court must have regard " in particular " to the character of the highway and   B
its normal user; the standard of maintenance appropriate to the circumstances
and (in this case of especial importance) the state of repair in which a reasonable
person would have expected to find the highway.

It is in this that I think, with respect, the learned judge erred. No reference
is made by him to sub-s. (3) (*c*) and there is no finding of what a reasonable person
would have expected. Having regard to the known user and the fact that the   C
plaintiff is one only of the thousands who had used the pavement in this condition—and many other pavements with comparable defects—without accident,
I apprehend that the reasonable ratepayer would say that the misfortune of one
amongst so many did not show a state of disrepair which called for immediate
action. The reasonable person, I think, would have regard to the cost which he
and his fellow-citizens would be put to if such a standard were to be obligatory.   D
A reasonable time in which to repair must depend on the nature and urgency of
the defect.

Subsection (3) (*d*) clearly requires regard to what the highway authority
" could reasonable have been expected to know ", and that must bring into
consideration their capacity to enquire as well as the steps that they took or
ought to have taken to ascertain whether the condition of the part of the highway   E
to which the action relates was likely to cause danger to its users.

I have already referred to sub-s. (2), which provides generally that a highway
authority should show that they have taken reasonable care if they wish to escape
liability.

The judge came to the conclusion that

> " The case which [the highway authority] must establish, if they are to   F
> succeed in their defence, is not such as was within their power in fact but
> such as satisfied the standard reasonably required of all highway authorities
> and that such a standard requires them to have a practical system for
> acquainting themselves of all defects in their highways within a reasonable
> time of such defects coming into existence."

  G

In the light of the whole section I would not construe the section as setting up
an artificial standard and making it obligatory. " In all the circumstances " must
I think embrace all facts and include the capacity of the highway authority acting
reasonably to remove the danger. The standard of routine inspection in comparable circumstances will be a factor in assessing negligence or lack of care, as
also will the strength and constitution of the maintenance department of a   H
highway authority in common practice. Comparable circumstances and common
standards are a guide in issues of negligence but the conclusion must be reached
on the facts of any particular case.

The defendant highway authority had not found it practical to have a routine
examination. The statute does not say that they must. The statute does not lay
down any period for inspection. The conditions and circumstances are so various   I
that it would be quite impossible to do so. The judgment finds that

> " although a system of inspection could be devised, it would in fact result
> in no practical improvement in the general condition of the roads, but at
> best would only result in an increased labour force, increased expenditure
> and possibly some change in the details of the actual work done but no
> increase in the amount of that work."

The judge accepted the view that there were not sufficient skilled men available.

A   The judgment seems to exonerate the highway authority from negligence yet holds them liable as it were for a breach of an absolute statutory duty, citing an observation of LORD ATKIN in *Lochgelly Iron and Coal Co., Ltd.* v. *M'Mullan* (4). That was a very different case with an absolute obligation to fence dangerous machinery whether reasonable care had been taken or not. The standard was rigid and inflexible. I do not find any such absolute statutory

B   obligation or standard imposed on highway authorities.

Nor does it seem to me that any nuisance had been brought on to or had been created on the highway by the defendant highway authority which would give rise to liability. It was in this case mere nonfeasance. Repair or disrepair cannot be said to be an absolute standard. It is a matter of fact to be assessed by a judge or jury according to what is reasonable and practicable in all the circum-

C   stances. The *Lochgelly* decision (5) is not without its critics in its sphere of the factory legislation. It forestalled—unfortunately as some may think—*Rudd* v. *Elder, Dempster & Co., Ltd.* (6), which was under appeal to the House of Lords. There seems no reason for applying it to the maintenance of highways, if that is what the learned judge felt himself bound to do.

The highway authority's liability arises if they fail to take reasonable care in

D   all the circumstances. The judgment expressly or impliedly holds that in the circumstances reasonable care was taken. It also holds in effect, as is so obvious, that if the standard which has been artificially erected of an inspection every three months had been in operation, for instance if such a routine inspection had occurred in April or May, 1965, or even in the first week of June, it would not have detected this particular defect for on the probabilities it would not have been

E   there. That in my view is sufficient to exonerate the defendant highway authority.

Further, if it had been there and had been detected it is perhaps improbable that with reasonable care it would have been repaired forthwith. The evidence is that there are other defects, more serious defects, possibly, to be remedied and it is a question of priorities.

A threatened action not unnaturally drew attention to and brought about

F   repair of this particular flagstone in its position on the pavement, but that is insufficient evidence to establish that it called for immediate action in priority to hundreds of other defects to be found so universally in places where people walk—and walk freely and without accident—in public thoroughfares as also in private places.

I would allow this appeal and find for the defendant highway authority.

G   **DIPLOCK, L.J.:** I have read the judgment which will shortly be delivered by SALMON, L.J. I agree with it and do not propose to cover the same ground so far as his analysis of the evidence and the conclusions of law which he draws from it are concerned; but as this is the first case in which s. 1 of the Highways (Miscellaneous Provisions) Act, 1961, has come up for consideration I propose to say a few words about its true construction, on which I too differ from the

H   county court judge, and also to make brief comments on two other matters which arise from his judgment.

The duty which at common law rested on the inhabitants at large to maintain the highways in their parish, was long ago transferred to local authorities acting as highway authorities and has become a statutory duty currently imposed by s. 44 (1) of the Highways Act, 1959. The duty at common law to maintain, which

I   includes a duty to repair a highway, was not based in negligence but in nuisance. It was an absolute duty to maintain, not merely a duty to take reasonable care to maintain, and the statutory duty which replaced it was also absolute. At common law the duty, being a duty to the public, was enforceable by indictment, but its rigour was reduced by another rule of common law that a private indi- vidual who suffered damage as a result of a highway's being out of repair could not recover damages in a civil action against the inhabitants at large if the lack

---

(4) [1934] A.C. 1 at p. 9.   (5) [1934] A.C. 1.   (6) [1933] 1 K.B. 566.

of repair was due to mere failure to repair (that is non-feasance), and not to A
acts of repair or other acts in relation to the highway improperly performed
(that is misfeasance). When the common law duty of the inhabitants at large
was converted into a statutory duty of the highway authority the rule excluding
liability for nonfeasance was, by judicial construction, treated as applicable to
the statutory duty as well. And so matters remained until Aug. 3, 1964: the
duty to maintain the highways in their area was an absolute duty of the highway B
authority, but subject to an exemption from liability in a civil action by a private
individual for damages sustained by him as a consequence of mere non-repair.

By s. 1 (1) of the Highways (Miscellaneous Provisions) Act, 1961, this exemption
from liability for non-repair of a highway was abrogated as from Aug. 3, 1964
(see s. 1 (8)). Had sub-s. (1) stood alone the liability of the highway authority
for nonfeasance as well as misfeasance in maintaining the highways in its area C
would have been absolute and a plaintiff who proved in a civil action against a
highway authority the presence of a danger in the highway which caused him to
sustain damage would have been entitled to succeed without proving that the
existence of such danger was due to any lack of care on the part of the highway
authority. Furthermore, although it may be that the highway authority could
have escaped liability by proving that the danger was caused by inevitable acci- D
dent or the malicious act of a stranger, it would have been no defence to them
merely to prove that they had in fact taken all reasonable care to prevent the
existence of the danger. Section 1 (1) of the Act of 1961, however, does not stand
alone. The legal consequences which would otherwise flow from it are qualified
by the provisions of sub-s. (2) and sub-s. (3)—and also by sub-s. (7), which is
not relevant to the present case. Where I differ, with respect, from SELLERS, L.J., E
is in the view which he expresses (7) that sub-s. (2) and sub-s. (3) " make negligence the essential and ultimate basis of a claim against a highway authority ".
As he has already read these two subsections I will not repeat them. Subsection (2)
does not, in my opinion, make proof of lack of reasonable care on the part of a
highway authority a necessary element in the cause of action of a plaintiff who
has been injured by a danger on a highway. What it does is to enable the highway F
authority to rely on the fact that it has taken reasonable care as a defence—the
onus of establishing this resting on it. A convenient way of expressing the effect
of the subsection is that it does not qualify the legal character of the duty imposed
by sub-s. (1), but provides the highway authority with a statutory excuse for
not performing it.

Nevertheless there are two crucial differences between a liability in negligence G
and the statutory liability of a highway authority under the section. To succeed
in an action for negligence the plaintiff must prove inter alia (i) that the defendant
had been guilty of lack of reasonable care, and (ii) that such lack of reasonable
care was the cause of the injury to him. In an action under the statute against
a highway authority for injury sustained from a danger on a highway the plaintiff
need prove neither of these things in order to succeed. Unless the highway H
authority proves that it did take reasonable care the statutory defence under
sub-s. (2) is not available to it at all. Nor is it a defence for the highway authority
to show that even had it taken all reasonable care this might not have prevented
the danger which caused the injury. It may be that if the highway authority
could show that no amount of reasonable care on their part could have prevented
the danger the common law defence of inevitable accident would be available I
to them; but that is not relied on in the present case and it is not necessary to
express a final conclusion on it.

The county court judge was accordingly in my view right in regarding a breach
of the duty imposed by sub-s. (1) as not requiring proof by the plaintiff either of
lack of reasonable care by the highway authority or that such lack of care was
the cause of the injury to him; but JUDGE CUNLIFFE appears to have construed
sub-s. (2) as if the statutory defence which it creates were available to a highway

(7) See p. 1019, letter I, ante.

A authority only on proof that they had in fact done all acts reasonably necessary to secure that the part of the highway to which the action related was not danger-ous to traffic, irrespective of whether or not in the actual circumstances affecting the authority it was impracticable or even impossible for them to do such acts. Here, I think, the judge fell into error. The duty which the highway authority must prove that they have fulfilled is not a duty to secure a certain result but to

B " take care " to do so, and such a duty is fulfilled by the person on whom it is imposed if he has done all that it is reasonably practicable for him to do to secure that result even though, through circumstances which are beyond his control, he does not succeed in achieving it. This view as to the nature of the duty which the highway authority must prove that they have fulfilled is borne out by the provisions of paras. (*d*) and (*e*) of sub-s. (3), which in my view clearly require that

C regard should be had to all the circumstances affecting the particular highway authority against whom the action is brought.

Although I think that the county court judge misconstrued the statute in this respect, I agree that, for the reasons to be given by SALMON, L.J., he nevertheless reached the right result. I would only add that, accepting as I do the county court judge's finding that it was not reasonably practicable for the defendant

D highway authority to obtain more tradesmen and that regular inspection of the highways by labourers, which was practicable, would not have enabled the defen-dant highway authority to repair more speedily dangers, perhaps of a more serious character than that which caused the present accident, which could only be repaired by tradesmen, I do not see how this can justify their failure to make any regular inspection to see whether there were any dangers which could be repaired

E by a labourer (as could the danger which caused the accident in the present case) or, if not immediately repairable by labourers, could be guarded against by the display of warning notices as contemplated by para. (*e*) of sub-s. (3).

I agree, not without regret, that it is not open to us on this appeal to disturb the judge's finding that the paving-stone on which the plaintiff tripped was dangerous to pedestrian traffic. I might not myself have reached the same

F conclusion, but there was evidence on which the judge could do so and—what is decisive—there is no appeal against this finding.

One last matter: the county court judge points out, quite correctly, that had a proper and practicable system of inspection been adopted by the defendant highway authority (for example regular inspection at three-monthly intervals) it is a matter of speculation whether the defect in the paving-stone would have

G been discovered, for it is impossible to tell when it first manifested itself; and he appears to think it odd that the plaintiff should be entitled to recover damages for an accident which might not have been averted even if the defendant highway authority had exercised all reasonable care. It is this to which he is referring in the passage of his judgment that SELLERS, L.J., has cited; but, as I have already said, their statutory defence under sub-s. (2) does necessitate their proving that

H they did exercise all reasonable care in relation to that part of the highway where the accident occurred, and, if they seek to rely on the common law defence of inevitable accident, they must at least prove that even if they had exercised all reasonable care in relation to that part of the highway the accident could not have been averted. If they did not exercise such care and it is left as a matter of speculation whether the accident would or would not have occurred if they had,

I neither defence is made out.

For my part I would dismiss this appeal.

SALMON, L.J.: On June 9, 1965, the plaintiff slipped whilst walking on a flagstone on the pavement in Smithdown Road, Liverpool. As a result she fell and injured herself. Apparently the flagstone rocked when walked on, and when at rest one of its edges protruded by half-inch above the adjacent flagstone. Accord-ing to the evidence given by the surveyor on her behalf and by the district highway

superintendent called on behalf of the defendant highway authority and the find- **A**
ing of the county court judge, this flagstone was in a dangerous condition. That
is the cardinal factor in this case. It seems to me idle to approach this appeal
on any basis save that this flagstone was dangerous. I, of course, appreciate
that in the court below a different view might have been taken. The conclusion
might well have been reached that there was so little wrong with this flagstone
that its condition would generally be regarded as acceptable and could not **B**
properly be stigmatised as dangerous. In these circumstances, the defendant
highway authority would no doubt have won. We, however, are not concerned
with what might have been, nor even with what we may think should have been
the finding of fact. We are concerned only with what was the finding of fact—
and we are bound to accept it. The surveyors on both sides agreed that the flagstone was dangerous; the county court judge found that it was dangerous, and **C**
there is no appeal from this finding.

The Highways Act, 1959, s. 44, imposes a duty on the defendants, who are the
highway authority for the highway in question, to keep it in repair. The plaintiff
brought this action claiming damages from the defendants for breach of that
duty. The particulars of claim do not expressly refer to the Highways Act, 1959,
but the highway authority take no point on this. The learned county court judge **D**
found in the plaintiff's favour and awarded her £75 damages.

The Highways (Miscellaneous Provisions) Act, 1961, s. 1, was in force at the
date of the plaintiff's accident. Prior to the time when that section came into
force, highway authorities could not be made liable for non-repair of a highway.
They were liable only for misfeasance in relation to a highway. Section 1 (1)
of the Act of 1961 provided however as follows: **E**

" The rule of law exempting [highway authorities] from liability for
for non-repair of highways is hereby abrogated."

Prima facie, therefore, since the flagstone was dangerous, the defendants were
liable to the plaintiff—absolutely and irrespective of any negligence on their
part. They however contended that they had a good defence under s. 1 (2) and
(3) of the Act of 1961—which have aleady been read by SELLERS, L.J. The **F**
county court judge held that no defence had been made out under those subsections
and the defendants appeal from that finding.

The question arises as to the true construction of the words

" such care as in all the circumstances was reasonably required to secure
that the part of the highway to which the action relates was not dangerous
for traffic." **G**

Do the words mean " reasonably necessary to secure " or " reasonably required
of the highway authority to secure "? As I read his careful judgment the county
court judge favoured the first meaning. He thought that if the highway was
dangerous, the highway authority would be liable unless they could show that
they had taken such care as was reasonably necessary to make it safe. On this **H**
view the circumstances in which the defendants found themselves, for example
lack of available labour, would be irrelevant. I cannot accept this conclusion.
In my view the care postulated by this subsection is the care which in all the
circumstances could reasonably be required of a highway authority. Accordingly
if a highway authority could prove that it had taken such care as, in all the
circumstances, it reasonably could, but that through no fault of the highway **I**
authority it had been unable to take steps to make the highway safe, it would
escape liability. I find support for this view in paras. (d) and (e) of s. 1 (3).
Whether a highway authority could reasonably have been expected (i) to know
the condition of the highway or (ii) to have it repaired must depend, in my view,
on the labour force which it in fact had available or could reasonably have been
expected to obtain; and sub-s. (3) requires that such matters shall be taken
into consideration in deciding whether a highway authority has established that
it has taken care under sub-s. (2).

A   The district highway superintendent said in evidence that in Liverpool there
are a lot of paving stones in a dangerous condition with nothing being done about
them. This was because of a lack of tradesmen; as far as the majority of dangerous
paving stones were concerned tradesmen would be required to make them safe.
What steps he had taken to find tradesmen, or the amount that the defendants
were prepared to pay in order to obtain their services in competition with other
B   employers, was never canvassed. On the other hand, the district highway
surveyor said that there was no regular system of inspection and that inspection
was desirable every three months. He said categorically that there would have
been no difficulty in obtaining labourers to carry out such inspections. The
only reason that he had not done so was that, even if the dangers were discovered,
no sufficient tradesmen were employed to make them safe; and so presumably
C   there was no point in going to the expense of engaging labourers to carry out
regular inspections. I do not think that this evidence helps the defendants.
As far as the dangerous flagstone in question is concerned, the defendants'
surveyor admitted that, had it been discovered, it could have been repaired and
made safe by a labourer. It follows, therefore, that if an adequate number of
labourers had been employed by the defendants (and this admittedly could have
D   been done) dangers such as the one here in question could have been discovered
and made safe by repair. I am far from saying that in my view every flagstone
which protrudes by half-inch is dangerous. If however flagstones had been
discovered which were in fact dangerous and could not have been repaired
except by tradesmen, they could neverthelesss have been made safe by labourers
putting up warning notices or, better still, by fencing them off. In these circum-
E   stances, it seems to me impossible on the evidence to conclude that the defendants
have proved that they took such care as in all the circumstances was reasonably
required of them to secure that the part of the highway relating to the present
action was safe. This to my mind concludes the appeal in favour of the plaintiff,
for the defendants have not established what s. 1 (2) of the Act of 1961 requires
them to establish in order to avoid the absolute liability imposed on them by s. 44
F   of the Highways Act, 1959, and s. 1 (1) of the Act of 1961. If, contrary to my
present view, it could be a good defence for them to say: although we have in
fact taken no reasonable care, the accident would still have happened even
if we had taken such care, nevertheless on the evidence this would not avail
them. The onus would be on them to establish that defence, and this they have
failed to do. They have not proved that with regular three-monthly inspections
G   this dangerous flagstone would not have been discovered and made safe. Speaking
of these inspections which the highway authority's surveyor admitted should
have taken place, the county court judge said: " It is clearly pure speculation
whether it would or would not have disclosed this defect."

     I have reached a clear conclusion in favour of the plaintiff, albeit for somewhat
different reasons from those relied on by the county court judge, and I would
H   accordingly dismiss the appeal.

Appeal dismissed. Leave to appeal to the House of Lords refused.

Solicitors: *Cree, Godfrey & Wood,* agents for *Town Clerk,* Liverpool (for the
defendant highway authority); *Robbins, Olivey & Lake,* agents for *Ernest B.
Kendall & Rigby,* Liverpool (for the plaintiff).

[*Reported by* Henry Summerfield, Esq., *Barrister-at-Law.*]

THE FAIRPORT.

VOGIATZIS AND OTHERS *v.* OWNERS OF STEAMSHIP FAIRPORT.

[PROBATE, DIVORCE AND ADMIRALTY DIVISION (Cairns, J.), May 10, 12, 1966.]

Admiralty—Practice—Action in rem—Wages—Whether wages of foreign master and crew accruing after issue of writ can be included in judgment and allowed as such out of proceeds of sale of ship.

Shipping—Seamen—Foreign seamen—Contract of service—Wages—Whether contract of service terminated by issue of writ—Whether judgment in action can be given for wages accruing after issue of writ.

The s.s. Fairport was a vessel flying the Panamanian flag, but manned entirely by Greeks. During the year from April, 1964, to March, 1965, her master was supplied by the owners with funds which were insufficient to meet his outgoings. Wages were paid irregularly and, by March, 1965, the master, officers and crew all had substantial wages due to them, which there were no funds to meet. On Mar. 12, 1965, the master and chief officer issued a writ in rem claiming wages and other moneys due to them. On Mar. 15 the vessel was arrested at Dover. On Mar. 26, 1965, the writ was amended to add as plaintiffs the other officers and all the crew members, similarly claiming wages and other moneys due. On May 18, 1965, two officers and ten seamen being still on board, judgment was given by default for the plaintiffs for unpaid wages subject to proof and an order was made for appraisement and sale; it was intimated that officers and crew remaining on board should leave at once. The vessel was sold. On a preliminary point, arising on the reference, viz., whether judgment could be given for payment out of the fund in court of wages accrued after the date* of the issue of the writ,

Held: the plaintiffs were entitled out of the fund in court to wages accruing after (as well as before) the issue of the writ because—

(i) the issue of a writ claiming only wages and other moneys due did not have the effect of putting an end to the contract of service, with the consequence that wages continued to accrue after the issue of the writ (see p. 1034, letter F, post), and

(ii) the rule that claims in an action could be made only in respect of causes of action that had accrued at the commencement of the action was a rule of practice rather than a rule of law, and was subject to exceptions; it was well established that claims for viaticum†, covering expenses incurred after the date of the writ, could be made in actions in rem against a ship by seamen and the same should apply to claims for wages (see p. 1035, letters C and D, post).

The Carolina ((1875), 34 L.T. 399; 3 Asp. M.L.C. 141) overruled.

The Raffaelluccia ((1877), 37 L.T. 365; 3 Asp. M.L.C. 505) and *The Bridgwater* ((1877), 37 L.T. 366; 3 Asp. M.L.C. 506) applied.

Eshelby v. *Federated European Bank, Ltd.* ([1931] All E.R. Rep. 840) distinguished.

[As to when a seaman's right to wages ends, see 35 HALSBURY'S LAWS (3rd Edn.) 168, 169, para. 260; and for cases on the subject, see 42 DIGEST (Repl.) 707, *4593-4594*; 1091, *9037, 9038*; 1105, *9216*.]

Cases referred to:

Arosa Star, The, [1959] 2 Lloyd's Rep. 396.

Beaver, The, (1800), 3 Ch. Rob. 92; 165 E.R. 397; 42 Digest (Repl.) 690, *4409*.

Bridgwater, The, (1877), 37 L.T. 366; 3 Asp. M.L.C. 506; 1 Digest (Repl.) 162, *501*.

---

* In the case of the plaintiffs other than the master and chief officer the relevant date was the date when they were joined as plaintiffs; see p. 1028, letter G, post.

† Viz., travelling-money. As regards repatriation of seamen, and return where service terminates abroad, see 35 HALSBURY'S LAWS (3rd Edn.) 165, 164, paras. 254, 252.

A *British Trade, The*, [1924] All E.R. Rep. 519; [1924] P. 104; 93 L.J.P. 33; 130 L.T. 827; 16 Asp. M.L.C. 296; 42 Digest (Repl.) 1090, *9032*.

Camilla, The, (1858), Sw. 312; 31 L.T.O.S. 282; 166 E.R. 1152; 42 Digest (Repl.) 701, *4526*.

Carolina, The, (1875), 34 L.T. 399; 3 Asp. M.L.C. 141; 42 Digest (Repl.) 707, *4593*.

B *Eliza, The*, (1823), 1 Hag. Adm. 182; 166 E.R. 65; 42 Digest (Repl.) 698, *4493*.

Elizabeth, The, (1819), 2 Dods. 403; 165 E.R. 1527; 42 Digest (Repl.) 722, *4740*.

Ernst Merck, The, (1865), Admiralty Reference Book 234 (No. 2663), Dec. 13, 1865.

Eshelby v. *Federated European Bank, Ltd.*, [1931] All E.R. Rep. 840; [1932]
C 1 K.B. 254; *affd.* C.A., [1931] All E.R. Rep. 845; [1932] 1 K.B. 423; 101 L.J.K.B. 245; 146 L.T. 336; 17 Digest (Repl.) 302, *1090*.

Exeter, The, (1799), 1 Ch. Rob. 173; 165 E.R. 139; 30 Digest (Repl.) 203, *448*.

Gerdmor, The. Larsen v. *Owners of M.V. Gerdmor*, (1950), Oct. 25, unreported.

Great Eastern, The, (1867), L.R. 1 A. & E. 384; 36 L.J.Adm. 15; 17 L.T. 228; 1 Digest (Repl.) 157, *448*.

D *Gustaf, The*, (1862), Lush. 506; 31 L.J.P.M. & A. 207; 6 L.T. 660; 167 E.R. 230; 42 Digest (Repl.) 1088, *9008*.

Immacolata Concezione, The, (1883), 9 P.D. 37; 52 L.J.P. 19; 50 L.T. 539; 5 Asp. M.L.C. 208; 42 Digest (Repl.) 1091, *9039*.

James W. Elwell, The, [1921] P. 351; 90 L.J.P. 355; 125 L.T. 796; 15 Asp. M.L.C. 418; 42 Digest (Repl.) 1096, *9103*.

E *Johnstone* v. *Milling*, (1886), 16 Q.B.D. 460; 55 L.J.Q.B. 162; 54 L.T. 629; 50 J.P. 694; 12 Digest (Repl.) 377, *2961*.

Madonna D'Idra, The, (1811), 1 Dods. 37; 165 E.R. 1224; 42 Digest (Repl.) 1091, *9038*.

National Coal Board v. *Galley*, [1958] 1 All E.R. 91; [1958] 1 W.L.R. 16; Digest (Cont. Vol. A) 463, *89a*.

F *Raffaelluccia, The*, (1877), 37 L.T. 365; 3 Asp. M.L.C. 505; 42 Digest (Repl.) 722, *4742*.

Tagus, The, [1903] P. 44; 72 L.J.P. 4; 87 L.T. 598; 9 Asp. M.L.C. 371; 42 Digest (Repl.) 1090, *9026*.

Tergeste, The, [1903] P. 26; 72 L.J.P. 18; 87 L.T. 567; 9 Asp. M.L.C. 356; 42 Digest (Repl.) 1105, *9216*.

G
Motion in objection to registrar's decision.

This was a motion on behalf of the plaintiffs, the master, officers and crew of the s.s. Fairport, in objection to an interim decision of the Admiralty Registrar dated July 9, 1965, ordering that the wages entitlement of the Fairport's master and chief officer terminated at midnight on Mar. 12, 1965, and that of the other officers and crew terminated on Mar. 26, 1965, the respective dates on which the writ
H was issued and they joined as plaintiffs. The motion came before HEWSON, J., on Jan. 17, 1966, when he adjourned it to enable counsel to be instructed by the Treasury Solicitor. The facts are set out in the judgment.

The authorities and the cases noted below* were cited during the argument in addition to those referred to in the judgment.

I *D. H. Hene* for the plaintiffs.

B. C. Sheen, Q.C., and *A. P. Clarke* as amici curiae.

The defendants, the owners of the s.s. Fairport, did not appear and were not represented.

Cur. adv. vult.

---

* WILLIAMS AND BRUCE: ADMIRALTY PRACTICE (3rd Edn., 1902) p. 203; ROSCOE'S ADMIRALTY LAW AND PRACTICE (4th Edn.) 244, 251; *Ingall* v. *Moran*, [1944] 1 All E.R. 97; [1944] K.B. 160.

May 12. **CAIRNS, J.,** read the following judgment: The question which A I have to decide is whether, in an action in rem for seamen's wages, judgment can be given for wages accruing after the date of the writ.   The s.s. Fairport was a vessel flying the Panamanian flag, but manned entirely by Greeks.   During the year from April, 1964, to March, 1965, her master was supplied by the owners with funds which were insufficient to meet his outgoings.   Wages were paid irregularly and, by March, 1965, the master, officers and crew all had B substantial wages due to them which there were no funds to meet.   In March, 1965, when the Fairport had reached London, the master and chief officer consulted solicitors.   On Mar. 12, 1965, a writ was issued claiming on their behalf wages and other moneys due to them, and on Mar. 15, 1965, the vessel was arrested in Dover harbour.   There was no appearance to the writ and the vessel remained under arrest.   On Mar. 26, 1965, the writ was amended to add as C plaintiffs the other officers and all the crew members, all claiming wages and other moneys due; and on Apr. 14, 1965, it was amended again to add two Greek organisations claiming pension fund contributions and union dues.   I am only concerned with the wages claims.   The statement of claim with a schedule of the claims was filed on May 3, 1965, and on May 18, 1965, the action came before HEWSON, J., on a motion for judgment in default of appearance (1).   By D that time the master, chief officer and two members of the crew had left the ship, but two officers and ten seamen were still on board.   HEWSON, J., made it clear that they should leave at once.   He gave judgment for all the plaintiffs except the two organisations and made an order for appraisement and sale, that order to lie in the office until all on board had left.   In the course of his judgment he said (2):

E

" They are entitled to their unpaid wages at least until the date of issue of the writ, subject to proof.   That is a matter for the reference.   I cannot do it to-day.   It is not the machinery of the court at all.   One thing I can say and that is that if there is anybody left on board twenty-four hours from now he will get nothing thereafter."

On May 26, 1965, HEWSON, J., dealt with the claims of the two organisations, F but added nothing with regard to the wages claims.   Shortly afterwards those still on board left and the vessel was sold.   The proceeds remain in court.   On July 7, 1965, the reference came before the registrar, and he was asked to decide as a preliminary point whether the plaintiffs' entitlement to wages came to an end when the writ was issued (or in the case of all except the master and chief officer when they were joined as plaintiffs), or whether it continued so long as G they continued to serve.   On July 9, 1965, the registrar issued his interim decision to the effect that the entitlement terminated at the earlier dates.   A motion in objection to this decision came before HEWSON, J., on Jan. 17, 1966, and, as only the plaintiffs were represented before him and he considered the point to be one of some difficulty and importance, he adjourned the hearing to enable the Treasury Solicitor to instruct counsel to appear as amicus curiae. H As it was not possible for HEWSON, J., to continue the hearing without inconvenient delay, SIR JOCELYN SIMON, P., under R.S.C., Ord. 4, r. 8 (2), nominated me to continue it.   I heard the arguments of counsel on May 10 and I would like to express my gratitude for the assistance they gave me both to counsel on behalf of the plaintiffs, and to counsel as amici curiae.

The registrar's decision was founded on *The Carolina* (3), decided in 1875. I In that case, PHILLIMORE, J., enunciated the principle that, when a seaman institutes a suit for wages, he ceases to have any claim for subsequent wages on the ship.   Before the registrar, it was sought to distinguish that case on grounds which seem to me to have no substance and which were not persisted in before me.   Counsel for the plaintiffs now contends that *The Carolina* (3)

---

(1) See [1965] 2 Lloyd's Rep. 183.   (2) [1965] 2 Lloyd's Rep. at p. 185.
        (3) (1875), 34 L.T. 399; 3 Asp. M.L.C. 141.

A did not decide what it has since been taken to decide, alternatively, that it was wrongly decided and should not be followed. I can find no basis for the argument that there has been any misinterpretation of Phillimore, J.'s decision. Assuming the report to be accurate, he laid down in clear terms the principle which I have quoted and I can see no room for any misunderstanding. I have, therefore, the invidious task of considering whether a proposition enunciated

B ninety-one years ago by a distinguished Admiralty Judge and since quoted in the text-books without question as to its validity, and acted on in the registry, is right or wrong. I approach this task with the utmost diffidence, with a recognition of the importance of not lightly departing from a rule which has stood for so long, but at the same time with the consciousness that, as a judge of equal status (in a purely technical sense) with Phillimore, J., I am not bound by his

C decision and must hold it to be wrong if I am clearly satisfied that it was wrong.

I may first remark that *The Carolina* (4) is not based on any earlier judicial decisions and has not been expressly followed in any reported case, though it has once or twice been cited in argument. I have been referred to a number of earlier decisions which I will mention only briefly because they seem to me to have little or no bearing on the point. There is, however, one registrar's report

D made in 1865 which the industry of officers in the registry has brought to light, and which indicates the existence of a practice at that time. Having looked at this, I shall examine a registrar's report in *The Carolina* (4) itself as well as the judgment on the motion in objection. I shall then go on to such later cases as there are touching on the matter, including again a document emerging from the registry.

E The first case is *The Exeter* (5), decided in 1799 by Scott, J., who awarded to the master of a ship wages for the time after his discharge on the ground that he had been wrongfully discharged for misconduct. It would appear that the suit was instituted after the period for which the wages were claimed. In *The Beaver* (6), decided in 1800 by the same judge, he awarded wages to a seaman for the period between his unlawful discharge and the ship's return to Liverpool.

F The date of the writ is not mentioned. In *The Madonna D'Idra* (7), in 1811, it was held that mariners were entitled to subsistence till conveyed back to their own country unless some special reason was shown to the contrary, such as desertion or any kind of conduct which would work a forfeiture of wages. It would appear that the seamen had intervened in the suit before returning to their own country, so this case may be some authority for the proposition that a

G claim can be recognised for a period subsequent to such intervention. *The Elizabeth* (8), in 1819, was a similar case to *The Exeter* (5) and *The Beaver* (6). The plaintiff was awarded his wages until his return to England, but there is nothing to indicate that this covered a time after the issue of his writ. *The Eliza* (9), decided in 1823 by Lord Stowell (as Scott, J., had by that time become), was another case of the same kind, except that the plaintiff had volun-

H tarily quitted the ship, having a right to do so. He was awarded only half his wages from the time of his departure, apparently because he was supplied with some money and food on leaving. *The Camilla* (10), in 1858, is again similar to *The Exeter* (5). In *The Gustaf* (11), Dr. Lushington had to consider the competing claims against a ship of the mariners for wages and of a shipwright for repairs. He allowed the mariners' claim in priority up to the time when the

I vessel entered the shipwright's yard. He refused to allow, as against the claim of the shipwright, a lien for later wages. This is merely a case of competing priorities and has nothing to do with the question of when the right to wages came to an end. In *The Great Eastern* (12), in 1867, the plaintiffs had been

---

(4) (1875), 34 L.T. 399; 3 Asp. M.L.C. 141.   (5) (1799), 1 Ch. Rob. 173.
(6) (1800), 3 Ch. Rob. 92.   (7) (1811), 1 Dods. 37.
(8) (1819), 2 Dods. 403.   (9) (1823), 1 Hag. Adm. 182.
(10) (1858), Sw. 312.   (11) (1862), Lush. 506.
(12) (1867), L.R. 1 A. & E. 384.

engaged for a voyage to expire on June 30, 1867, and they were wrongfully **A**
discharged on May 1, 1867. The form of their claim was for damages for wages
from May 1 to June 30. The defendants moved to strike out the suit on the
ground that there was no lien on the ship for damages as distinct from wages.
DR. LUSHINGTON rejected the motion. It is clear that the proceedings were
started well before June 30, 1867, because judgment was actually given on
June 29, 1867. The decision is, however, of no assistance because the considera- **B**
tions applicable to a claim for damages for wrongful dismissal are obviously
different from those applicable to a claim for wages, even though the damages
in the former type of case may be quantified by reference to the contractual
rate of wages.

In none of these cases is there any hint of the principle referred to in *The*
Carolina (13). The conclusion to be drawn from them is, however, negative, **C**
because in none of them, with the possible exception of *The Madonna D'Idra* (14),
is there anything to show that the principle would have been applicable if it
existed. In 1865, however, in a reference to the registrar and merchants in
The Ernst Merck (15), the master, having commenced proceedings for his wages
on Mar. 14, 1865, continued in charge of the ship up to Apr. 19 and claimed
wages up to the latter date. The report states (16) that the registrar and mer- **D**
chants allowed the master's wages up to Mar. 14, 1865, when he commenced the
proceedings and when by so doing he " virtually displaced himself ". This is
the first emergence, so far as I am aware, of the idea that, by bringing an action,
a person in any sense discharges himself from his service. In *The Carolina* (17),
the report in ASPINALL sets out the position as follows:

" This was a motion in objection to the registrar's report made in a cause **E**
of wages instituted on behalf of the first and second mates and a seaman
of the American ship Carolina. The plaintiffs had been engaged to serve
on board the Carolina, on a voyage from Grimsby to Cardiff, and thence to
Buenos Ayres; but whilst the ship was at Cardiff she was arrested in a cause
of necessaries and, no appearance being entered on behalf of her owners
or any other persons, the master dismissed the remainder of the crew, but **F**
retained the plaintiffs on board until he could have an opportunity of
hearing from his owners, and they remained on board until Sept. 2, 1875,
when the master, without dismissing them, told them to board themselves
ashore, as he had no credit, and could not provide them with food. They
did so, remaining, however, on board the ship at other times and in her
service until she was sold after the decree (Nov. 2, 1875). On Sept. 5, 1875, **G**
the plaintiffs instituted a cause of wages against the ship and, no appearance
having been entered, their petition was filed on Oct. 12, and a decree was
obtained on Nov. 2, 1875, pronouncing for the claims. The petition claimed
wages and subsistence money up to the date of the decree, and the whole
question of the amount due was referred to the registrar, who reported that
the plaintiffs were entitled to their wages and subsistence money up to the **H**
date of the commencement of the suit, but disallowed all wages, etc.,
subsequent to that date. To this report the plaintiffs now objected."

I have not seen the registrar's report on the claim of the objectors, but a copy
of his report on the master's claim was shown to me. It contains this passage (18):

" The master's suit was instituted on Sept. 4, 1875, and it was not shown **I**
that he had rendered any service to the ship after that date; the owner had
previously become insolvent, his affairs were in his creditor's hands, and
there was no prospect of a settlement which would release the ship. The

---

(13) (1875), 34 L.T. 399; 3 Asp. M.L.C. 141.   (14) (1811), 1 Dods. 37.
(15) (1865), Admiralty Reference Book 234 (No. 2663).
(16) (1865), Admiralty Reference Book at p. 236.
(17) (1875), 3 Asp. M.L.C. at p. 141.
(18) See (1876-77) Admiralty Reference Book at pp. 84, 85.

A institution, therefore, by the master of a suit to recover his wages and
disbursements was taken to indicate that he considered his connexion with
the ship as captain to be severed and ended. He had given leave to the crew
to sue and had ceased to provide them with provisions, and he was justified in
proceedings against the ship himself, but he should have been prompt in
prosecuting his suit instead of which he was very dilatory, and he finally

B quitted the country without waiting to explain his claim. Under these
circumstances his claim for wages was allowed up to Sept. 12, 1875, instead
of Jan. 3, 1876."

In this report, I note the following points: the disallowance of the master's
wages after Sept. 12, 1875, does not purport to be based on any absolute rule
that no wages can be claimed after the initiation of proceedings; indeed, wages

C were allowed for eight days following the commencement of his suit. Account
was taken of his having rendered no services after Sept. 4 and of his delay in
prosecuting his suit, as if it was a matter of discretion whether the later wages
could be allowed or not. Returning now to ASPINALL's report, the argument of
counsel for the objectors together with the interventions of the registrar and
the judge need to be read. Counsel in support of the objection said (19):

D
" The question is whether wages and subsistence money should be given
up to Nov. 2 or only to Sept. 5. [The registrar:] The claim from Sept. 5 to
Nov. 2 was disallowed, because it has always been the practice in the registry
to give subsistence money and compensation for detention from the date
of the institution of the suit in the way of costs; and because plaintiffs in
wages suits cannot get wages for a period after they have left the service

E of the ship, which they practically do before instituting their suit. [Counsel
continued:] There is no reason why a servant should not continue in a
person's service, and yet sue that person for his wages; the commencement
of the action does not terminate the contract of service. [PHILLIMORE, J.:]
Practically, however, the commencement of an action would operate as the
termination of the contract. [Counsel went on:] Here, however, the

F plaintiffs actually remained on board and in the service of the ship after the
institution of the suit, and did not terminate their contract. They remained
in the service of the ship until she was sold. It is constantly the practice
to allow wages to foreign seamen after the institution of their suit when they
are sent home from this country: WILLIAMS AND BRUCE, ADMIRALTY
PRACTICE (1st Edn.) (1869), p. 165. On taxation of costs the plaintiffs

G would not get the same amount as they would for wages."

Then the short judgment reads as follows (20):

" I should be loth to alter the established practice of the court, which
unquestionably does exist, without some very strong authority being shown
to me. The practice of the registry in this respect is founded upon the

H principle that when a seaman institutes a suit for wages he ceases to have
any claim for subsequent wages upon the ship, and that principle has been
acted upon in a great variety of cases. It is said that there is a great hardship in the mariner being left without any claim for support after he has
left the ship, in the interval between the institution of the suit and the hearing
of the cause. But, substantially, he would receive a sum of money for his

I maintenance and detention when the question of costs came to be decided.
It is said that these men stayed on board after the institution of the suit,
and at the request of the master. Those are circumstances to be brought
before the taxing officer, and I should surmise that the registrar would pay
considerable attention to an affidavit with regard to the employment of
seamen on board the vessel after the institution of the suit. There would
be a ground of appeal if it were not given due weight to, and a

(19) (1875), 3 Asp. M.L.C. at p. 141.
(20) (1875), 34 L.T. at p. 400; 3 Asp. M.L.C. at p. 141.

proper allowance not made to the seamen. I decline to vary the registrar's   A
report, as such a variation as that asked for would be a subversion of the
practice of the court, which has existed for a very long period."

It, therefore, appears that there are two bases for the decision, first, that the
institution of proceedings operated as the virtual termination of the contract
of service, and, secondly, that it was the practice of the registry to allow compensation for detention and subsistence money from the time the proceedings   B
were started by way of costs. Counsel as amicus curiae has not felt able to
support either of these grounds of the decision and, indeed, joined with counsel
for the plaintiffs in inviting me to say that they are both wrong.

As to the first ground, I fail to see how the institution of a claim for wages
can automatically terminate a contract of service. There is nothing inconsistent
with the continuance of service in a claim of this kind. Even if it could be said   C
that the making of such a claim was an act of disloyalty to the employer which
amounted to a repudiation of the contract (a proposition which I should find
it difficult to accept in 1966 even if it could be so regarded in 1875), this would,
at the most, entitle the employer to accept the repudiation and dismiss the servant. If he allows him to continue working, I can see no reason for saying that
the contract is at an end and that wages no longer accrue. Alternatively, if it   D
were suggested that the non-payment of wages was a repudiation of the contract
by the employer, I do not consider that the issue of a writ merely claiming the
wages is an acceptance of such repudiation. It would be a different matter if
the plaintiff by his writ or statement of claim alleged a fundamental breach of
contract and claimed damages on the basis that the contract was at an end.

As to the other grounds of the decision in *The Carolina* (21), that is to say,   E
the registry's practice, it does appear from the report in *The Ernst Merck* (22)
that such a practice existed, but nobody has been able to explain to me how any
remuneration to which a seaman might become entitled could properly be
regarded as part of his costs of action. He has not in this respect put himself to
any expense or undertaken any labours in order to promote his success in the
proceedings; he has simply performed his ordinary duties aboard ship. I can   F
only suppose that because for some reason it was considered that wages were
not payable after the start of proceedings this sum was allowed to be included
in costs out of tenderness for the interests of the seamen, but as a matter of law
and of common sense I fail to see how they can have any connexion with costs.

I turn now to cases since 1875, first noting that, under s. 4 (4) of the Merchant
Seamen's (Payment of Wages and Rating) Act, 1880, later re-enacted (23), a   G
British seaman's wages now continue to run until the time of settlement thereof,
so that after 1880 the problem that I am considering arose only with foreign
seamen. *The Immacolata Concezione* (24) is worth mentioning because it is one
of the very few reported cases in which *The Carolina* (21) has been referred to.
It was referred to in argument, and what its relevance was is not apparent from
the report. The actual decision is of no help, because the writ for wages had   H
been issued after the end of the services for which the wages claimed.
In *The Tergeste* (25), PHILLIMORE, J. (this was not SIR ROBERT PHILLIMORE who
had decided *The Carolina* (21), but SIR WALTER PHILLIMORE, then a judge of the
King's Bench Division, who had had great experience in Admiralty matters),
said (26):

"I do not think that the crew are entitled, at any rate, in priority to the   I
material man, to any allowance for subsistence money, from the time when
they issued their writ to the time when they were provided for by the marshal.
It may be that the registrar will allow some sum in respect of costs according

(21) (1875), 34 L.T. 399; 3 Asp. M.L.C. 141.
(22) (1865), Admiralty Reference Book 234.
(23) In s. 134 (c) of the Merchant Shipping Act, 1894.
(24) (1883), 9 P.D. 37; 5 Asp. M.L.C. 208.   (25) [1903] P. 26; 9 Asp. M.L.C. 356.
        (26) [1903] P. at p. 32; 9 Asp. M.L.C. at p. 357.

A   to whatever is the usual rule in those matters.   That I leave entirely to
him."

The judge was there expressing no firm opinion as to what the rights might be
after the issue of the writ except in relation to priorities.   In *The Tagus* (27),
the same judge gave judgment (28) for seamen's wages up to the date of their
writ and subsistence money thereafter.   So there, although he described it as

B   subsistence money and not as wages, he gave judgment for it as part of the claim
and not as costs.   In *The James W. Elwell* (29), HILL, J., said:

> " Whether the contract of the master comes to an end or not upon his
> arrest of the ship I think it is a rule of law acted upon in this court, that
> the master's right to wages ceases at the date of his writ.   But it has been

C   > the invariable practice of this court so long as the master remains in charge
> of the ship (that is, until he has been discharged or the ship has been sold by
> the marshal) to allow him wages and subsistence money on the basis of his
> previous emoluments and to add them to his claim for wages under the head
> of costs.   However they are described he is entitled to have added to his
> wages and to have covered by his maritime lien his wages and subsistence

D   > money up to the time when in fact his employment as master is determined."

In that passage I note the following points: HILL, J., at least casts doubt on the
proposition that the contract of the master necessarily comes to an end on his
arrest of the ship; secondly, HILL, J., does not say that, from the date of the
proceedings, there is due only something in the nature of a quantum meruit, but
says in terms that, however they are described, the plaintiff is entitled to have

E   his wages.   So, under this view, it appears to be merely a matter of practice
whether the wages should be awarded as part of the substantive claim or as part
of the costs.   I can see no theoretical grounds, and certainly no grounds of
practical convenience, why they should be artifically classed as costs rather than
as part of the substantive claim.

In *The British Trade* (30), one of the issues was whether a certain claim could

F   properly be advanced as wages or as damages for breach of contract.   SIR
HENRY DUKE, P., said (31):

> " The distinction between a claim for wages and a claim for damages
> under a seaman's contract which has been broken depends upon purely
> legal considerations.   The best answer, I think, is that, if there has been

G   > merely a breach of the contract by the employer, the contract subsists and
> can be made the subject of a simple claim for wages, but, on the other hand,
> if the employer has repudiated the contract and the seaman has accepted
> the repudiation the contract is at an end, and any claim to be made by him
> in respect of its stipulations is a claim for damages: see *Johnstone* v. *Milling*
> (32).   It is not clear in the present case that the repudiation of the contracts

H   > in question by the owners was accepted by the plaintiffs before the issue of
> the writ.   On this footing a claim for wages might have subsisted until
> that date."

I do not think that SIR HENRY DUKE is there laying down that wages can never
be claimed after the date of the writ; he is saying that the issue of the writ
claiming damages on the basis of repudiation constituted acceptance of the

I   repudiation and thereby brought the contract of service to an end so that no
wages accrued thereafter.

The last Admiralty case referred to was *The Arosa Star* (33), a decision of the

---

(27) [1903] P. 44; 9 Asp. M.L.C. 371.
(28) [1903] P. at p. 50; 9 Asp. M.L.C. at p. 377.
(29) [1921] P. 351 at p. 357.   (30) [1924] All E.R. Rep. 519; [1924] P. 104.
(31) [1924] All E.R. Rep. at p. 523; [1924] P. at p. 110.
(32) (1886), 16 Q.B.D. 460.   (33) [1959] 2 Lloyd's Rep. 396.

Chief Justice of Bermuda.   As I understand the report, wages were there claimed   A
for a period after the issue of the writ and SIR NEWNHAM WORLEY, C.J., said (34):

> " I do not see how the owners could be heard to say in this court that any
> portion of the sums claimed was not wages due under the contract, and if
> they cannot do so, then, following DR. LUSHINGTON, neither can the mort-
> gagees. To adopt the language, once again, of the President in *The British*
> *Trade* (35), there was merely a breach of the contract by the employer (by
> his default in not paying the wages) and the contract subsisted and could
> be made the subject of a simple claim for wages; there was no repudiation
> of the contract accepted by the seamen which would have put an end to the
> contract and given rise to a claim for damages."

Though this decision is only of persuasive effect in this court, it is based on a   C
close analysis of a number of English authorities and I treat it with respect and
find it helpful.   That the practice of including wage claims in the costs has to
some extent persisted in the registry up to fairly recent times is indicated by a
taxed bill of costs, dated 1950, which was shown to me.   The case was *The*
Gerdmor. Larsen v. *Owners of M.V. Gerdmor* (36), and the plaintiff was the master,
Birger Larsen.   The bill includes the items: " Birger Larsen for wages £70,   D
ditto for subsistence £20 ", and these items were allowed subject to £6 being
taxed off.

The conclusion which I draw from a consideration of these precedents is that
remuneration can be claimed by seamen in respect of a period subsequent to the
issue of their writ, but that there has been some variation in practice as to
whether this remuneration should or should not be described as wages and some   E
variation in practice as to whether it is recoverable as part of the claim or as
part of the costs.

In the absence of any authority which binds me to say that the issue of a
writ puts an end to the contract of service, and being satisfied in principle that
the issue of a writ claiming only wages and other moneys due can have no such
effect, I am of the opinion that the wages continue to accrue after proceedings   F
are commenced.   And, if wages continue to accrue, I think that it must follow
that they are recoverable by action and not merely as part of the costs of an
action.

So far I am acceding to the arguments which both counsel have presented to
me.   But now counsel as amicus curiae raises a formidable point.   He says
that, quite apart from the special Admiralty decisions, there is a well-established   G
rule in litigation generally that a plaintiff can claim only in respect of a cause
of action which already exists when he starts his proceedings.   The principal
authority for this proposition (which is constantly acted on in practice in all
divisions of the High Court and also in the county court) is *Eshelby* v. *Federated*
European Bank, Ltd. (37).   There an official referee had allowed a statement
of claim to be amended so as to claim an instalment of debt which had fallen   H
due since the writ.   The Queen's Bench Divisional Court, consisting of SWIFT
and CHARLES, JJ., allowed an appeal from the official referee and held that the
instalment could not be claimed in the existing action.   I may refer also to the
decision of the Court of Appeal in *National Coal Board* v. *Galley* (38), where the
question was whether damages could be recovered in respect of breaches of
contract after the writ on the ground that the cause of action was a continuing   I
one, and, PEARCE, L.J., delivering the judgment of the court, said (39):

> "Where, however, a contract requires payments to be made on stated dates
> (for example, a contract to pay an annuity of £1,000 per annum in equal

(34) [1959] 2 Lloyd's Rep. at p. 401.
(35) [1924] All E.R. Rep. 519; [1924] P. 104.
(36) (1930), Oct. 25, unreported.
(37) [1931] All E.R. Rep. 840; [1932] 1 K.B. 254.
(38) [1958] 1 All E.R. 91.   (39) [1958] 1 All E.R. at p. 101.

A   monthly instalments on the first day of each calendar month) failure to pay the instalment due on Feb. 1 is not, we should have thought, a continuance of the cause of action constituted by failure to pay the instalment due on Jan. 1, but a distinct cause of action arising for the first time on Feb. 1 and at no earlier date."

B   The inference was that the Court of Appeal considered that the instalment accruing due after the writ could not be recovered in the action commenced by the writ.

Is it, then, necessary for the plaintiffs to issue a further writ and then come back to the court to claim the wages now in question? I am reluctant to reach a conclusion which would cause additional delay and expense and will benefit nobody. The rule that claims in an action can be made only in respect of causes C of action that have accrued at the commencement of the action is, I think, a rule of practice rather than a rule of law. It is subject to exceptions. Mesne profits and interest are two that occur to me. In none of the Admiralty cases to which I have referred is it suggested that this rule is a ground for disallowing a claim for wages and, indeed, it seems to me that the reasoning in *The Carolina* (40) and in *The James W. Elwell* (41) is inconsistent with it. The strongest reason D for considering that the rule is not applicable in connexion with seamen's actions in rem against a ship is that it is well established that claims for viaticum can be made covering expenses incurred after the date of the writ. *The Raffaelluccia* (42) and *The Bridgwater* (43) are two old authorities to this effect, and Hewson, J.'s, judgment in this very case included the expenses of the plaintiffs' repatriation which obviously had not been incurred at the date of the writ.

E   I see no reason why a different rule should apply in relation to the wages. I, therefore, allow the appeal. The registrar was, of course, bound to follow *The Carolina* (40), but I have reached the conclusion that that case was wrongly decided and hold that the entitlement to wages did not terminate on Mar. 12, or Mar. 26, 1965, but continued until the plaintiffs' services came to an end. It would appear from para. 5 of the statement of claim that the date of discharge F of the master was earlier than that of the crew and probably different members of the crew were discharged on different dates, but that is a matter which will be investigated by the registrar on his resumed consideration of the reference. I understand that the chief engineer alone among the plaintiffs did not join in the notice of objection. As, however, the registrar's decision was an interim decision, I think that he is entitled along with the other plaintiffs to have his G claim allowed on what I have held to be the right basis.

Appeal allowed.

Solicitors: *Keene, Marsland & Co.* (for the plaintiffs); *Treasury Solicitor.*

[*Reported by* N. P. Metcalfe, Esq., *Barrister-at-Law.*]

H

I

---

(40) (1875), 34 L.T. 399; 3 Asp. M.L.C. 141.   (41) [1921] P. 351.
(42) (1877), 37 L.T. 365; 3 Asp. M.L.C. 505.
(43) (1877), 37 L.T. 366; 3 Asp. M.L.C. 506.

RYSAK *v.* RYSAK AND BUGAJASKI.   A

[PROBATE, DIVORCE AND ADMIRALTY DIVISION (Park, J.), May 27, 1966.]

Divorce—Damages—Costs—Co-respondent—Death of co-respondent after order
for payment of damages and costs made against him—Whether cause of action
that survived against his estate by virtue of Law Reform (Miscellaneous
Provisions) Act, 1934 (24 & 25 Geo. 5 c. 41), s. 1 (1).   B

The husband was granted a decree nisi on the ground of the wife's adultery
with the co-respondent. The co-respondent was ordered to pay the husband's
costs, and to lodge in court within twenty-eight days from service of the order
on him £1,500 assessed damages. A few hours after the making of the order
the co-respondent died, before the order was served on him. By s. 1 (1)*
of the Law Reform (Miscellaneous Provisions) Act, 1934, on the death of a   C
person all causes of action subsisting against him survived against his
estate; but, by the proviso, that subsection did not apply to a husband's
claim for damages on the ground of adultery with his wife. In an application
by the husband that the damages and costs should be obtained against the
co-respondent's estate,

Held: the husband was entitled, as against the co-respondent's estate,   D
to the damages and costs ordered to be paid by the co-respondent, because—

(i) when the order to lodge the damages in court was made, the right under
it, enforceable by proceedings in the Divorce Court, was not a mere hope or
contingency, and constituted, notwithstanding that the order had not yet
been served and the absence of any further order, a cause of action within
s. 1 (1) of the Act of 1934 which, on the co-respondent's death, survived   E
against his estate (see p. 1039, letters A and B, post);

Dictum of DENNING, L.J., in *Sugden* v. *Sugden* ([1957] 1 All E.R. at p. 302)
applied.

(ii) when once a claim for damages on the ground of a person's adultery
has been heard, and damages had been assessed, awarded and ordered to be
paid into court before that person's death, the claim for damages was satis-   F
fied; accordingly, as the proviso to s. 1 (1) of the Act of 1934 applied only
to the claim, and the claim had ceased to exist, the proviso did not bar
the cause of action constituted by the order, which survived against the
co-respondent's estate (see p. 1039, letter C, post);

(iii) the order for costs having been made against the co-respondent in
his lifetime, there was an enforceable claim against him which was kept   G
alive by s. 1 (1) of the Act of 1934 (see p. 1039, letter G, post).

Richards v. *Richards and Flockton* ([1942] P. 68, n.) followed.

[As to survival of causes of action, see 16 HALSBURY'S LAWS (3rd Edn.)
481, 482, para. 981; and for cases on the subject, see DIGEST (Cont. Vol. A)
565, 7540, 7540a.

As to the effect of death of co-respondent, see 12 HALSBURY'S LAWS (3rd Edn.)   H
381, para. 834.

For the Law Reform (Miscellaneous Provisions) Act, 1934, s. 1, see 9 HALS-
BURY'S STATUTES (2nd Edn.) 792.]

Cases referred to:

Dipple v. *Dipple*, [1942] 1 All E.R. 234; [1942] P. 65; 111 L.J.P. 18; 166
        L.T. 120; 24 Digest (Repl.) 764, 7539.   I

Hyde v. *Hyde*, [1948] 1 All E.R. 362; [1948] P. 198; L.J.R. 641; 27 Digest
        (Repl.) 629, 5898.

Mosey v. *Mosey and Barker*, [1955] 2 All E.R. 391; [1956] P. 26; [1955]
        2 W.L.R. 1118; Digest (Cont. Vol. A) 788, 5730b.

Richards v. *Richards and Flockton*, (1940), [1942] P. 68, n.; 111 L.J.P. 20, n.;
        27 Digest (Repl.) 573, 5291.

---

* Section 1 (1), so far as material, is set out at p. 1037, letter G, post.

A *Sugden* v. *Sugden*, [1957] 1 All E.R. 300; [1957] P. 120; [1957] 2 W.L.R. 210; 121 J.P. 121; Digest (Cont. Vol. A) 565, 7540.

Summons.

This was an application by summons by the husband for an order that the costs and damages ordered to be paid by the co-respondent should be obtained against the co-respondent's estate. The summons was adjourned into open court
B for judgment. The facts are set out in the judgment.

Roger Gray for the husband.
J. D. K. Burton for the wife.
M. R. Hoare for the co-respondent's executors.

PARK, J.: This is an application by the husband petitioner for an order
C that the costs and damages ordered to be paid by the co-respondent should be obtained against the co-respondent's estate. On Feb. 24, 1966, after a trial lasting some eight days, in the course of which the husband, the wife, the co-respondent and other witnesses gave evidence, I held that the husband had proved that the co-respondent had committed adultery with the wife. I granted the husband a decree nisi of dissolution of his marriage to the wife and ordered the co-respon-
D dent to pay costs and damages. By the order for costs, the co-respondent was

" condemned in the costs incurred on behalf of the [husband] in this cause and such further costs to be incurred on behalf of the [husband] as the court shall direct to be costs in the cause, such costs incurred and to be incurred and to be taxed as between party and party, but such costs to exclude those costs occasioned by the [wife's] allegations of cruelty and
E adultery in her said answer."

The order with regard to the payment of damages was in the following terms:

" And it is further ordered that the said co-respondent do within twenty-eight days from service of the order upon him lodge in court the sum of £1,500 assessed by the judge as damages."

F On the day on which these orders were made but some hours after they had been made, the co-respondent died. The net value of his estate is just over £900.

Counsel for the husband submits that, by virtue of the provisions of s. 1 (1) of the Law Reform (Miscellaneous Provisions) Act, 1934, the husband is entitled to enforce both the order for the payment of damages and the order for payment of costs against the estate of the co-respondent. The relevant part of s. 1 (1)
G is as follows:

" Subject to the provisions of this section, on the death of any person after the commencement of this Act, all causes of action subsisting against . . . him shall survive against . . . his estate. Provided that this subsection shall not apply to . . . claims under s. 189 of the Supreme Court of Judicature (Consolidation) Act, 1925, for damages on the ground of adultery."
H
Section 189 of the Supreme Court of Judicature (Consolidation) Act, 1925, is now s. 41 of the Matrimonial Causes Act 1965, sub-s. (1) of which provides as follows:

" A husband may, on a petition for divorce or for judicial separation or for damages only, claim damages from any person on the ground of adultery
I with the wife of the petitioner."

Subsection (3) provides:

" The court may direct in what manner the damages recovered on any such petition are to be paid or applied, and may direct the whole or any part of the damages to be settled for the benefit of the children, if any, of the marriage, or as a provision for the maintenance of the wife."

The first question which I have to decide, therefore, is whether the order to lodge in court the sum of £1,500 within twenty-eight days of the service of that order on the co-respondent is a cause of action within the meaning of s. 1 (1) **A** of the Act of 1934. Counsel for the husband relied on the following observations made by DENNING, L.J., on the meaning of " cause of action " in his judgment in *Sugden* v. *Sugden* (1):

" The subsection only applies to ' causes of action ' which subsist against the deceased at the time of his death.   The legislature had particularly in mind causes of action in tort which used to fall with the death of either **B** party under the old common law maxim actio personalis moritur cum persona. ' Causes of action ' in the subsection means, I think, rights which can be enforced, or liabilities which can be redressed, by legal proceedings in the Queen's courts. These now survive against the estate of the deceased person. ' Causes of action ' are not, however, confined to rights enforceable *by action*, strictly so called—that is, by action at law or in equity.   They **C** extend also to rights enforceable by proceedings in the Divorce Court, provided that they really are rights and not mere hopes or contingencies. They include, for instance, a sum payable for costs under an order of the Divorce Court, or a right to a secured provision under an order already made against a man before his death; see *Hyde* v. *Hyde* (2) and *Mosey* v. *Mosey and Barker* (3). It must be noticed, however, that the subsection **D** only applies to causes of action ' subsisting against ' the deceased on his death.   This means that the right or liability must have accrued due at the time of his death. There is no difficulty in an ordinary action in determining when the right or liability accrued due; but there is more difficulty in proceedings in the Divorce Court. In that court there is no right to maintenance, or to costs, or to a secured provision, or the like, until the court makes an **E** order directing it.   There is, therefore no cause of action for such matters until an order is made. In order that the cause of action should subsist at the death, the right under the order must itself have accrued at the time of death.   Thus a cause of action subsists against a husband for arrears of maintenance due at his death, but not for later payments.   This view of proceedings in the Divorce Court is supported by the decision of HODSON, J., **F** in *Dipple* v. *Dipple* (4), where he pointed out that all that the wife had was the hope that the court would in its discretion order a secured provision. She had no right to it at all until the order was actually made, and hence she had no cause of action at his death . . . The only thing which takes a case out of the Act is the absence of an enforceable right at the time of death." **G**

Counsel for the husband submitted that the order for damages in this case falls fairly and squarely within the meaning of " cause of action " because, first, the order is a right which can be enforced by legal proceedings in the Divorce Court, and, secondly, because the order had been made and the right had in consequence accrued due at the time of the co-respondent's death. On the other hand, counsel for the co-respondent's executors contended that the order **H** is not a cause of action which survives against the co-respondent's estate because it was not served on the co-respondent, with the result that there was no obligation to pay the damages into court, and because the court did not make either an order with regard to the manner in which any damages paid into court pursuant to the order should be applied, or, pursuant to r. 64 (3) of the Matrimonial Causes Rules, 1957, (5) an order varying the existing order by giving directions to the **I** husband as to the payment of the damages. Counsel submitted that, until a final order of this kind were made, there was no debt due from the co-respondent

(1) [1957] 1 All E.R. 300 at p. 302; [1957] P. 120 at pp. 134, 135.
(2) [1948] 1 All E.R. 362; [1948] P. 198.
(3) [1955] 2 All E.R. 391; [1956] P. 26.
(4) [1942] 1 All E.R. 234; [1942] P. 65.
(5) S.I. 1957 No. 619; for r. 64 (3) see 10 HALSBURY'S STATUTORY INSTRUMENTS (1st Re-Issue) 250.

A to the husband and no judgment against the co-respondent and, in the circum stances, that there was no cause of action which survived against the co-respondent's estate. In my judgment, however, when the order to lodge the damages in court was made, it became, and was, in the words of DENNING, L.J., in *Sugden* v. *Sugden* (6), one of those rights enforceable by proceedings in the Divorce Court and not a mere hope or contingency. Accordingly, notwithstanding non-

B compliance with that part of the order relating to service and the absence of any further order, I hold that the order is a cause of action which, on the co-respondent's death, was subsisting against him and which survives against his estate.

Counsel for the co-respondent's executors further submitted that causes of action founded on claims for damages on the ground of adultery were by the

C proviso to s. 1 (1) expressly excluded from the Act of 1934. It is to be observed, however, that the proviso refers to *claims* for damages on the ground of adultery. In my judgment, where a claim for damages on the ground of a person's adultery has been heard, and damages have been assessed, awarded and ordered to be paid into court before that person's death, the proviso does not operate to bar the order because, at the moment when the order is made, the claim for damages

D is satisfied. The claim has in consequence ceased to exist and, in its place, there is an order for the payment of damages which survives as a subsisting cause of action against the adulterer's estate.

Counsel for the co-respondent's executors did not contend that the order for the payment of costs was not a cause of action within the meaning of the Act of 1934. He submitted, however, that the correct procedure for the enforcement

E of that order had not been followed in this case, and that the husband should have sued the co-respondent's executors for the costs. Counsel for the husband, however, relied on *Richards* v. *Richards and Flockton* (7). In that case, HODSON, J., on the application of the husband, made an order for costs to be taxed against the estate of the co-respondent who had died about three weeks after the order for costs had been made against him. In *Dipple* v. *Dipple* (8), HODSON, J.,

F referred to his decision in *Richards* v. *Richards and Flockton* (7) in these words:

" I should add that I have been referred to an order made in chambers in another case [*Richards* v. *Richards and Flockton* (7)] where taxation of costs was allowed to proceed against the personal representative of a co-respondent who had died after decree. The order for costs having been made against the co-respondent in his lifetime, there was an

G enforceable claim against him which was kept alive by the Law Reform (Miscellaneous Provisions) Act, 1934."

Counsel for the co-respondent's executors was not able to support his submission with any authority. I, therefore, propose to follow *Richards* v. *Richards and Flockton* (7).

H In my judgment, for these reasons, this application succeeds and the husband is entitled to the order which he seeks.

Order accordingly.

Solicitors: *Tilbury, Cowles & Co.* (for the husband); *F. W. Hughes & Son* (for the wife); *Marshall, Liddle & Downey* (for the co-respondent's executors).

I [*Reported by* ALICE BLOOMFIELD, *Barrister-at-Law.*]

---

(6) [1957] 1 All E.R. 300; [1957] P. 120.   (7) [1942] P. 68, n.
(8) [1942] 1 All E.R. at pp. 235, 236; [1942] P. at p. 68.

A

PRACTICE DIRECTION.

CHANCERY DIVISION.

Practice—Chambers—Chancery Division—Adjournment to judge—Infants—
Contested applications relating to infants in which witnesses are to be cross-   B
examined—Fixing date for hearing—Counsel's certificate as to estimated
length of hearing—Application to vary date fixed.

1. On the adjournment to the judge in chambers of any contested application
relating to infants in which witnesses are to be cross-examined and the hearing
date remains to be fixed, it shall be the duty of the parties' solicitors to inform
the master of the names of counsel to whom they expect to deliver briefs for the   C
hearing.

2. Forthwith after such adjournment the master's summons clerk shall send
to the clerk to the appropriate judge a notice of such adjournment, specifying
the names of counsel and solicitors for the plaintiff or the applicant for the
adjournment if not the plaintiff.

3. Within fourteen days after such adjournment the solicitor having the   D
carriage of the proceedings shall lodge with the master's summons clerk a certificate, signed by all counsel to appear at the hearing, as to the length of time
which they estimate the hearing will take and the master's clerk shall send
such certificate to the judge's clerk forthwith after recording such estimate.

4. Unless within twenty-one days after such adjournment the clerk of counsel
intended to be briefed by the solicitors having the conduct of the proceedings   E
has attended on the judge's clerk to arrange for a date to be fixed for the hearing,
the judge's clerk shall request counsel's clerk to communicate with him for the
purpose of fixing such a date.

5. Unless within twenty-eight days after such adjournment counsel's clerk
has so attended as aforesaid the judge's clerk shall fix a date for the commencement of the hearing having regard to the said certificate as to the estimated   F
length of hearing or, in its absence, such information as may be available to him
after consultation with the master, and shall notify counsel's clerk of such
hearing date and of the judge by whom such application is to be heard.

6. After the date for commencement of the hearing has been fixed any
application to vary such date shall be made to the designated judge in court.

By direction of CROSS, J.   G

W. F. S. HAWKINS,
Chief Master
June 27, 1966.   Chancery Division.

[END OF VOLUME TWO.]